Environmental Law

Statutory and Case Supplement 2021–2022

Environmental Law

Statutory and Case Supplement 2021–2022

Robert V. Percival
University of Maryland Francis King Carey School of Law

Christopher H. Schroeder
Duke University School of Law

 Wolters Kluwer

Published by Wolters Kluwer in New York.

Wolters Kluwer Legal & Regulatory U.S. serves customers worldwide with CCH, Aspen Publishers, and Kluwer Law International products. (www.WKLegaledu.com)

To contact Customer Service, e-mail customer.service@wolterskluwer.com, call 1-800-234-1660, fax 1-800-901-9075, or mail correspondence to:

> Wolters Kluwer
> Attn: Order Department
> PO Box 990
> Frederick, MD 21705

Printed in the United States of America.

1 2 3 4 5 6 7 8 9 0

ISBN 978-1-5438-4135-0

ISSN 1536-4933

About Wolters Kluwer Legal & Regulatory U.S.

Wolters Kluwer Legal & Regulatory U.S. delivers expert content and solutions in the areas of law, corporate compliance, health compliance, reimbursement, and legal education. Its practical solutions help customers successfully navigate the demands of a changing environment to drive their daily activities, enhance decision quality and inspire confident outcomes.

Serving customers worldwide, its legal and regulatory portfolio includes products under the Aspen Publishers, CCH Incorporated, Kluwer Law International, ftwilliam.com and MediRegs names. They are regarded as exceptional and trusted resources for general legal and practice-specific knowledge, compliance and risk management, dynamic workflow solutions, and expert commentary.

Contents

Contents

Contents Organized by U.S. Code Title and Section Numbers

Introduction

About This Statutory and Case Supplement

While statutory supplements have become an essential tool for students of environmental law, they have not been as useful as they could be in helping students to navigate the complex labyrinth of environmental regulation. This supplement is different. It is designed to make environmental law easier to understand. It includes not only the text of the important statutes but also material to help students understand their most important provisions.

Organizing the statutes by subject matter, rather than their location in the U.S. Code, this supplement introduces the statutes with detailed outlines that highlight their most important provisions. The supplement also includes legislative history timelines that trace the evolution of the statutes by explaining when they were enacted and when their most significant amendments were added.

In recent years, there has been a dramatic increase in the amount of material on environmental regulation available on the internet. Nearly all federal (and most state) environmental agencies have websites that provide information concerning regulatory developments. Studies and reports issued by these agencies and by nongovernmental organizations frequently are available for downloading over the web. The entire Code of Federal Regulation is now available online, making it easy for students to consult regulatory materials when necessary. The rich array of materials now available online can make it much easier for students, professors, and practicing lawyers to do research in environmental law and to stay abreast of the very latest regulatory developments.

This book explains how to access the rich resources available on the internet for obtaining additional information about various aspects of environmental law and policy. For each statute, the book includes a guide to resources available on the internet for obtaining additional information. This should help encourage students to explore the internet to learn more about the issues that most interest them.

Chapter 11 of this supplement also includes excerpts from judicial decisions in important environmental cases that have been decided during the past several years. This feature enables professors to supplement reading assignments from environmental law casebooks without requiring students to purchase a separate case supplement. While this supplement is organized in a manner that tracks the organization of the authors' casebook, it easily can be used with any of the other fine environmental law casebooks on the market.

New editions of this Statutory and Case Supplement are issued annually in time for the start of the next academic year. The authors welcome suggestions for material to put into future editions, including website links that readers find to be particularly useful. The authors may be contacted by email at RPercival@law.umaryland.edu and Schroeder@law.duke.edu. The authors are grateful to Samuel Boden, Madeleine Dwyer, and Zoe Rydzewski for their assistance in preparing this edition.

Environmental Legislation in Historical Perspective

The statutes contained in this book are the foundation of federal regulatory programs to protect the environment mandated by Congress during the 1970s and 1980s. However, the roots of environmental law run much deeper. For centuries common law courts wrestled with conflicts that invariably arise when human activity interferes with the interests of others in the quality of their physical surroundings. Using doctrines of public and private nuisance, courts sought to protect communities and property owners from the most egregious consequences of industrial activity.

Early in the seventeenth century, English courts recognized that even nontresspasory invasions of property could be actionable as nuisances. Courts adopted the Latin maxim sic utere tuo ut alienum non laedas, or "every man must so use his own as not to damnify another." This "sic utere" principle — that no one has the right to use their property in a manner that foreseeably causes substantial harm to the property of others — became a universal tenet of the common law of private nuisance. A separate branch of nuisance law, derived from the common law of crimes, deems actions that cause substantial harm to the commons (property owned by the government) to be public nuisances.

By itself, the sic utere principle is not much help in resolving environmental disputes. It does not specify how substantial harm must be before it is actionable or what remedy courts should impose to rectify it. Courts can issue injunctions requiring abatement of nuisances, but they often are reluctant to enjoin activities that have great economic value. Uncertainty about the fate, transport, and effects of pollutants also makes it difficult for courts to resolve environmental disputes. While the common law can provide redress when a single source of particularly egregious pollution visibly alters the surrounding landscape, it has proven to be a crude vehicle for preventing harm caused by the cumulative impact of more diffuse pollutants. The common law's requirement that plaintiffs prove causal injury is often difficult to satisfy, particularly when there are multiple sources of pollution.

In the early years of the republic, environmental protection was rarely a concern of the federal government. Following the Louisiana Purchase, the United States was thought to possess seemingly limitless natural resources. The focus of federal policy was to encourage resource exploitation by transferring land in the public domain to private parties. When the Department of the Interior was established in 1849, a large part of its initial mission was to help process federal land transfers. The Homestead Act of 1862 and the Mining Act of 1872 allowed private parties to acquire title to federal land and the mineral resources found on it. But the seeds of a new conservation movement had been planted as popular travel literature extolled the virtues of outdoor recreation. As art and literature celebrated the wonders of the American West, the public began to appreciate the natural world as a source of inspiration and spiritual renewal.

After lengthy debate, Congress in 1872 adopted the Yellowstone Park Act, preserving Yellowstone as the first national park. The national park concept — providing permanent protection to certain natural areas — has proven to be one of the most influential innovations of U.S. environmental law, widely emulated around the world. U.S. states also joined in the movement. In 1885, New York State established the Adirondack Forest Preserve and decreed that it be kept "forever wild," protections later embedded in the state constitution. In 1891, Congress established the national forest system by enacting the Forest Reserve Act, which gave the president authority to withdraw forest reserves from the public domain.

As the conservation movement gained momentum, grassroots groups began to organize at the national level, forming organizations that became powerful influences on the development of environmental law. In 1892, the Sierra Club was founded by John Muir and friends. In 1901, the American Scenic and Historic Preservation Society was established from state-level organizations that promoted preservation of nature and culture. The National Association of Audubon Societies for the Protection of Wild Birds and Animals was founded in 1905, uniting numerous state organizations that had been voices for conservation since 1896.

When Theodore Roosevelt assumed the presidency in 1901 upon the death of President McKinley, the conservation movement gained an outspoken presidential champion. Roosevelt convened a national governors' conference on conservation at the White House and he pioneered the use of executive orders to protect federal lands. Beginning with his order creating the Pelican Island bird sanctuary in Florida, Roosevelt issued 53 executive orders establishing national wildlife refuges. In 1906 Congress enacted the Antiquities Act (reproduced in Chapter 10), which authorizes the president to set aside federal lands as national monuments to preserve "features of historic, prehistoric, and scientific interest." Roosevelt used this authority to establish Devil's Tower as the first national monument. He later designated the Grand Canyon as a national monument, the first of many monuments that later became national parks.

Beginning in 1908, the Sierra Club waged an aggressive national campaign opposing construction of a dam in the Hetch Hetchy Valley, a wilderness preserve that was part of Yosemite National Park. This battle exposed sharp differences between preservationists like John Muir who wanted wilderness protected for its own sake and conservationists like Gifford Pinchot who supported conserving public lands to maximize their consumption value. While the preservationists ultimately lost the fight, their campaign gave environmental concerns national visibility. Hetch Hetchy was flooded to provide power to San Francisco, but Congress continued to create national parks and in 1916 it established the National Park Service as part of the Department of the Interior.

Federal responsibility for environmental protection evolved gradually. In 1918 Congress adopted legislation to protect migratory birds to implement a treaty negotiated with Great Britain on behalf of Canada. States challenged this legislation as an infringement of their Tenth Amendment rights, but the Supreme Court upheld the law as a valid exercise of federal authority, citing the supremacy of federal law under the constitution. Missouri v. Holland, 252 U.S. 416 (1920).

In the decades that followed, concern for the impact of environmental conditions on human health spawned efforts to improve sewage disposal and to control smoke pollution in urban areas. Prior to World War II, these concerns were regarded as the responsibility of state and local governments. Congress had adopted legislation regulating waste disposal in navigable waters in the Rivers and Harbors Act of 1899, but this law was designed to prevent obstruction of navigation rather than to protect the national environment. The Federal Insecticide Act of 1910 prohibited the sale of misbranded pesticides to prevent consumer fraud rather than to control environmental risks. When deaths of workers from exposure to toxic substances grabbed national headlines, the Surgeon General convened national conferences of experts to investigate how to improve workplace safety. But it was not until the 1970s that Congress established national regulatory programs to protect public health from environmental risks.

President Franklin Roosevelt's New Deal programs of the 1930s laid the groundwork for the greater federal role in protecting consumer and environmental interests that Congress ultimately assumed in the 1970s. The Civilian Conservation Corps helped to restore public lands and to promote outdoor recreation. The Duck Stamp Act of 1934 provided additional funds for wildlife refuges through a federal licensing fee on hunters.

After World War II, the federal government assumed an active role encouraging states to adopt environmental protection measures. The Federal Water Pollution Control Act of 1948 provided federal funding to assist states in developing pollution control programs. In 1956 Congress overrode President Eisenhower's veto to launch a massive program to fund the construction of municipal sewage treatment plants. During the 1960s, Congress prodded states to adopt air pollution controls in the Clean Air Act of 1963 and to develop programs to handle waste disposal problems in the Solid Waste Disposal Act of 1965.

During the 1960s, the popularity of outdoor recreation and concern over the environmental effects of toxic chemicals helped spawn a powerful national environmental movement. The movement was not alone in agitating for change. The civil rights and consumer protection movements also were important at this time. The crowning achievement of the former was enactment of the Civil Rights Act of 1964, which banned employment discrimination on the basis of race or sex and included the federal prohibition on discrimination in federally funded programs contained in Title VI (reproduced in Chapter 1).

The early legislative triumphs of the environmental movement at the federal level involved measures to improve management of public lands. Shifting its emphasis away from resource extraction on public lands, Congress mandated that public lands be managed to promote "multiple uses" including outdoor recreation and protection of watersheds, fish, and wildlife. This mandate is contained in the Multiple Use Sustained Yield Act (reproduced in Chapter 10), adopted by Congress in 1960. Subsequent legislation enacted during the 1970s, including the Forest and Rangeland Renewable Resources Planning Act and the Federal Land Policy and Management Act (both reproduced in Chapter 10), sought to ensure that comprehensive management plans incorporating these values would govern use of public lands.

Concern over toxic chemicals was spawned by the publication of Rachel Carson's *Silent Spring* in 1962. Carson issued a stern warning about the environmental harm that could occur from a buildup of persistent toxins in the food chain as a result of pesticide use. Her warnings helped mobilize a national environmental movement. Concerned scientists formed the Environmental Defense Fund, which launched a successful campaign to have DDT banned. Another new group, the Natural Resources Defense Council, challenged the refusal of the Federal Power Commission to consider environmental concerns when it licensed environmentally destructive power projects.

Congress responded to the burgeoning environmental movement with a remarkable burst of legislation establishing national regulatory programs. The laws adopted during the 1970s created the federal regulatory infrastructure that remains in place today. Congress first directed all federal agencies to make environmental protection an important part of their mission when it enacted the National Environmental Policy Act (NEPA) (reproduced in Chapter 8). Signed into law by President Nixon on New Year's Day 1970, NEPA requires all agencies to assess the environmental impacts of their actions before making any decisions likely to have a significant effect on the environment.

Later in 1970, Congress enacted the Clean Air Act (reproduced in Chapter 5), which requires EPA to establish uniform national air quality standards to ensure protection of public health. It also mandated that automobile manufacturers dramatically reduce emissions from mobile sources. In 1972, Congress tackled national water pollution problems when it adopted the Federal Water Pollution Control Act, now known as the Clean Water Act (reproduced in Chapter 6). The Act created a national permit program that requires all point sources of water pollution to comply with technology-based regulations for reducing pollution. In 1972, Congress also enacted the Marine Protection, Research, and Sanctuaries Act, known as the Ocean Dumping Act, which requires a permit before materials can be discharged into ocean waters.

In 1973, Congress adopted the Endangered Species Act (reproduced in Chapter 9), which prohibits actions that harm species in danger of extinction. A year later it enacted the Safe Drinking Water Act (reproduced in Chapter 3), which requires EPA to set limits on levels of contaminants in water supplied by public water supply systems. In 1976, Congress adopted the Resource Conservation and Recovery Act (reproduced in Chapter 4), which required EPA to regulate the management of hazardous waste from "cradle to grave." The Toxic Substances Control Act (reproduced in Chapter 3), also enacted in 1976, gives EPA broad authority to ban or regulate any chemical substance found to pose an unreasonable risk to public health or the environment.

These and other federal environmental laws seek to prevent harm before it occurs by regulating pollutants, products, and practices that make environmental damage more likely to occur. Unlike the common law, which requires individual victims to prove what caused their particular harm, the environmental statutes authorize preventive regulation in circumstances where it would not be possible to meet the common law's requirement of individualized proof of causal injury. Except in the case of pesticides, the environmental laws require government regulators to make some threshold showing of potential for harm before substances or activities can be regulated. The Federal Insecticide, Fungicide, and Rodenticide Act (reproduced in Chapter 3), adopted in 1972, places the burden on pesticide manufacturers to convince EPA that their products will not have unreasonable adverse effects before they can be marketed.

The judiciary played a major role in the development of environmental law by opening the courthouse doors to citizens seeking to require agencies to implement the new regulatory programs. In 1972, the Supreme Court ruled that environmental and aesthetic interests were no less deserving of judicial protection than economic interests for purposes of assessing whether plaintiffs had sufficient "injury in fact" to give them standing to sue. Sierra Club v. Morton, 405 U.S. 727 (1972). Because they contained provisions authorizing citizen suits and judicial review, the new environmental laws allowed the public to go to court repeatedly to force reluctant officials to implement the laws. The message that the new regulatory programs were to be taken seriously was delivered by the Supreme Court in 1978 when it halted construction of a nearly-completed dam in order to protect the snail darter, a tiny fish listed as endangered under the new Endangered Species Act. TVA v. Hill, 437 U.S. 153 (1978).

When Congress reauthorized the first generation of federal environmental laws during the 1980s, it strengthened their requirements, set new deadlines for agencies to implement them, and increased penalties for violators. Congress also added some new weapons to the environmental protection arsenal. In 1980, Congress enacted the Comprehensive Environmental Response, Compensation, and Liability Act (reproduced in Chapter 4), which imposes strict, joint, and several liability for cleanup costs on broad classes of parties associated with releases of hazardous substances. In response to the chemical accident in Bhopal, India, that killed thousands, Congress in 1986 adopted the Emergency Planning and Community Right-to-Know Act (EPCRA) (reproduced in Chapter 3), which gives citizens the right to know about toxic chemicals released in their neighborhoods. Outrage over the 1989 Exxon Valdez oil spill helped overcome a lengthy legislative stalemate over oil spill liability legislation, culminating in the enactment of the Oil Pollution Act of 1990 (reproduced in Chapter 6). The 1990 Clean Air Act Amendments mandated sharp reductions in sulfur dioxide emissions from powerplants while creating an emissions trading program that allows companies to reduce compliance costs by buying and selling emissions allowances.

States also have generated important innovations in environmental law. Perhaps the most significant is California's Proposition 65 (reproduced in Chapter 3), which prohibits companies from exposing the public, without warning, to significant quantities of substances that cause cancer or reproductive toxicity. By placing the burden on companies to decide whether to warn or to eliminate the risk, the law avoids the need for government regulators to make difficult judgments about the significance of risks and the best means for controlling them.

The initial generation of federal environmental statutes adopted breathtakingly ambitious goals coupled with seemingly impossible mandates directed primarily at large industries. Despite protestations that what the laws required was technologically impossible, or impossibly costly, they helped spawn the development of new technology that has greatly reduced the costs, while improving the effectiveness, of pollution controls. While these laws generally have succeeded in controlling large point sources of pollution, nonpoint source pollution remains a significant problem. Efforts to enact national land use legislation to combat nonpoint source pollution failed during the early 1970s. However, in 1972, Congress did enact the Coastal Zone Management Act (reproduced in Chapter 7), which created a program of federal financial assistance to coastal states who develop federally approved land management plans. This legislation also requires that federal activities affecting the coastal zone comply with the state coastal management plans.

Vital to the success of the federal environmental laws has been their profound commitment to involving the public in the development, implementation, and enforcement of regulatory policy. NEPA's environmental impact assessment requirement, widely emulated throughout the world, gave the public an important tool for ensuring that agencies considered the environmental consequences of their action. Because Congress incorporated citizen suit and judicial review provisions into virtually all the federal regulatory statutes, the public repeatedly has been able to go to court to ensure that the laws are implemented and enforced.

Congress frequently has sought to enlist the states in cooperative partnerships to achieve environmental goals while respecting federalism concerns. Thus, the federal environmental laws largely eschew federal preemption of state regulation except for pesticide labeling and chemical regulation. The federal statutes seek to ensure a federally defined minimum level of environmental protection while leaving states free to adopt more stringent regulations if they choose. Despite these provisions, environmental regulation remains a subject of considerable friction between federal and state officials.

While the initial generation of environmental laws focused on prescriptive requirements (sometimes referred to as "command and control" regulation), more recent initiatives seek to change behavior through information disclosure and market-based approaches that reduce the cost of emissions reductions. EPCRA's toxics release inventory and right-to-know requirements have created a powerful tool for encouraging emissions reductions, while the Clean Air Act's emissions trading program has demonstrated that substantial emissions reductions can be achieved at moderate cost.

Issues of fairness are at the forefront of many contemporary environmental policy debates. Property rights groups and small business interests argue that environmental regulation frequently imposes disproportionate burdens on their property or enterprises, a factor that led to enactment of the Regulatory Flexibility Act (reproduced in Chapter 2). The environmental justice movement argues that environmental risks are disproportionately concentrated in poor and minority communities. Data show that members of minority groups and the poor have higher levels of lead in their blood than the rest of the population and that hazardous waste dumpsites and incinerators tend to be disproportionately located in poor and minority communities. While some dispute whether undesirable land uses initially are sited in a discriminatory manner, few doubt that minorities and the poor are exposed to greater risks than the rest of the population. Executive Order 12,898 (reproduced in Chapter 1) directs federal agencies to identify and address environmental justice problems. Efforts to address questions of fairness — both in the distribution of environmental risks and in the impact of environmental regulation — will be an important challenge for policymakers in the years to come.

The election of President Donald J. Trump in November 2016 produced some abrupt changes in federal environmental policy. During the first few months of his administration, President Trump signed joint resolutions of disapproval passed by Congress on party line votes pursuant to the Congressional Review Act (reproduced in Chapter 2) to veto regulations issued during the last six months of the Obama administration. President Trump also issued several executive orders directing agencies to reconsider regulations that had been in effect long enough not to be subject to CRA vetoes. These include Executive Order 13,783, Promoting Energy Independence and Economic Growth, rescinding President Obama's Climate Action Plan and directing the EPA Administrator to reconsider its Clean Power Plan and other regulations to control greenhouse gas emissions; Executive Order 13,778, Restoring the Rule of Law, Federalism, and Economic Growth by Reviewing the "Waters of the United States" Rule, directing reconsideration of the definition of waters subject to federal jurisdiction under the Clean Water Act; and Executive Order 13,792, directing the Secretary of Interior to review designations of protected areas under the Antiquities Act, and Executive Order 13,771, Reducing Regulation and Controlling Regulatory Costs, directing all federal agencies to repeal two existing regulations for each new regulation they promulgate. These executive orders were revoked by President Biden shortly after he took office on January 20, 2021. Biden also immediately repealed Executive Order 13,766 on Expediting Environmental Reviews and Approvals for High Priority Infrastructure Projects and Executive Order 13,807 on Establishing Discipline and Accountability in the Environmental Review and Permitting Process for Infrastructure.

During his second year in office, President Trump issued Executive Order 13,840 on Ocean Policy to Advance the Economic, Security, and Environmental Interests of the United States (reproduced in Chapter 6); and Executive Order 13,855 on Promoting Active Management of America's Forests, Rangelands, and Other Federal Lands to Improve Conditions and Reduce Wildfire Risk (reproduced in Chapter 10).

During President Trump's last year in office, the Council on Environmental Quality promulgated new regulations comprehensively revising procedures for implementing the National Environmental Policy Act for the first time since 1978. These regulations, promulgated on July 26, 2020, are reproduced in Chapter 8. Although the regulations have survived an initial legal challenge, the Biden administration has signaled its intent to revise them. Upon taking office President Biden issued Executive Order 13,990 on Protecting Public Health and the Environment and Restoring Science to Tackle the Climate Crisis, and Executive Order 14,008, Tackling the Climate Crisis at Home and Abroad. Both are reproduced in Chapter 1. President Biden also issued Executive Order 13,992, Revocation of Certain Executive Orders Concerning Federal Regulation, which is reproduced in Chapter 2.

Environmental Law

Statutory and Case Supplement 2021–2022

1

ENVIRONMENTAL JUSTICE

The environmental justice movement has become one of the most important currents within the environmental movement. It seeks to connect environmental issues to a larger agenda of social justice by focusing on the connections between discrimination, poverty, and the distribution of environmental risk. The environmental justice movement seeks to redress the disproportionate concentration of risks on poor and minority communities.

EPA defines "environmental justice" as the "fair treatment and meaningful involvement of all people regardless of race, color, national origin, or income with respect to the development, implementation, and enforcement of environmental laws, regulations and policies." By "fair treatment" the agency means "that no group of people, including racial, ethnic, or socioeconomic group should bear a disproportionate share of the negative environmental consequences resulting from industrial, municipal, and commercial operations or the execution of federal, state, local and tribal programs and policies."

While there is a broad consensus concerning the importance of environmental justice, it has been difficult to develop effective legal remedies to combat disproportionate exposure to risk among poor and minority communities. Proof of discriminatory intent is necessary before decisions to site locally undesirable land uses in such communities would give rise to violations of the Constitution's guarantee of equal protection of the laws. Section 601 of Title VI of the Civil Rights Act of 1964 prohibits discrimination on the basis of race, color, or national origin in any program or activity receiving federal funding. However, proof of intentional discrimination is required for a private litigant to establish a violation of Section 601. Section 602 of Title VI authorizes federal agencies to effectuate the provisions of Section 601 by issuing rules, regulations, and orders. In Guardians Association v. Civil Service Commission of the City of New York, 463 U.S. 582 (1983), the U.S. Supreme Court held that claims for violations of regulations issued under Section 602 did not require proof of discriminatory intent, but could be based on evidence of disparate impact. However, in Alexander v. Sandoval, 532 U.S. 275 (2001), the Supreme Court held that the private right of action to enforce Section 601 does not include a private right to enforce these regulations. Thus, while federal agencies can still bring actions to enforce Title VI regulations, citizens seeking to challenge permitting decisions on environmental justice grounds will have to rely on 42 U.S.C. §1983 instead.

A GUIDE TO ENVIRONMENTAL JUSTICE
MATERIALS ON THE INTERNET

The U.S. Environmental Protection Agency maintains information on environmental justice issues on its website located at *http://www.epa.gov/environmentaljustice*.

EPA's Office of Civil Rights maintains a website located at *http://www.epa.gov/ocr*. It includes links to publications and fact sheets on Title VI issues. In February 1998, EPA issued Interim Guidance for Investigating Title VI Administrative Complaints Challenging Permits. In June 2000, EPA issued a revised draft of this guidance, 65 Fed. Reg. 39,650. Annual environmental justice progress reports are available at *https://www.epa.gov/environmentaljustice/annual-environmental-justice-progress-reports*.

ENVIRONMENTAL JUSTICE LEGISLATIVE HISTORY TIMELINE

July 2, 1964: The Civil Rights Act of 1964, Pub. L. 88-352, 78 Stat. 241, is signed into law by President Johnson. Title VI, 78 Stat. 252, prohibits discrimination on the ground of race, color, or national origin in programs or activities receiving federal financial assistance. The original legislation includes §§601 to 605 as they appear today.

November 3, 1966: The Elementary and Secondary Education Amendments of 1966, Pub. L. 89-750, 80 Stat. 1191, add the first sentence of 42 U.S.C. §2000d-5, 80 Stat. 1209. This requires that local educational agencies be given an opportunity for a hearing concerning their compliance with Title VI before action on their applications for federal funds is deferred for more than 60 days.

January 2, 1968: The Elementary and Secondary Education Amendments of 1967, Pub. L. 90-247, 81 Stat. 783, are signed into law. They add a proviso to 42 U.S.C. §2000d-5, 81 Stat. 787, specifying that compliance with a federal desegregation order shall be deemed compliance with Title VI with respect to matters covered by the order.

April 13, 1970: An Act to Extend Programs of Assistance for Elementary and Secondary Education, Pub. L. 91-230, 84 Stat. 72, adds 42 U.S.C. §2000d-6, 84 Stat. 121, declaring that it is federal policy for Title VI's non-discrimination policy to be applied uniformly throughout the United States regardless of the origin or cause of segregation in a particular place.

July 5, 1973: EPA issues its initial Title VI Regulations, 38 Fed. Reg. 17968.

January 12, 1984: EPA issues revised Title VI regulations, 49 Fed. Reg. 1659.

October 21, 1986: The Rehabilitation Act Amendment of 1986, Pub. L. 99-506, 100 Stat. 1807, adds 42 U.S.C. §2000d-7, 100 Stat. 1845, waiving states' Eleventh Amendment immunity from suit for violations of Title VI.

March 22, 1988: The Civil Rights Restoration Act of 1987, Pub. L. 100-259, 102 Stat. 28, adds §606, 102 Stat. 31, to clarify that Title VI bars discrimination in any part of an institution receiving federal funds. The legislation overturns Grove City College v. Bell, 465 U.S. 555 (1984), which had limited the reach of Title VI to the parts of a recipient's programs that directly benefited from federal financial assistance.

February 11, 1994: President Clinton issues Executive Order 12,898, directing federal agencies to make achievement of environmental justice part of their missions by identifying and addressing disproportionately high and adverse human health or environmental effects of their programs on minority and low-income populations.

February 5, 1998: EPA issues "Interim Guidance for Investigating Title VI Administrative Complaints Challenging Permits," which outlines how EPA's Office of Civil Rights (OCR) expects to process and investigate Title VI complaints filed with EPA involving allegations of discriminatory impacts from recipients' permitting decisions. Congress inserts language in EPA's fiscal years 1999 and 2000 appropriations prohibiting EPA from using funds "to implement or administer the interim guidance" for Title VI complaints filed after October 21, 1998.

June 27, 2000: EPA publishes "Draft Revised Guidance for Investigating Title VI Administrative Complaints Challenging Permits" and "Draft Title VI Guidance for EPA Assistance Recipients Administering Environmental Permitting Programs." EPA solicits public comment on these guidance documents, which address approaches and activities for responding to potential Title VI concerns.

August 11, 2000: President Clinton signs Executive Order 13,166, which requires Federal agencies to examine the services they provide, identify any need for services to limited English proficient (LEP) persons, and develop and implement a plan to provide those services so that LEP persons can have meaningful access to them.

August 4, 2011: The heads of 17 federal agencies signed a Memorandum of Understanding (MOU) on Environmental Justice and Executive Order 12,898. The MOU broadens the Environmental Justice Interagency Working Group to include agencies not named in Executive Order 12,898 and requires each agency to issue an annual implementation report.

January 27, 2021: President Biden signs Executive Order 14,008, 86 Fed. Reg. 7619, which directs federal agencies to take an "all of government" approach to environmental justice. The order directs federal agencies to develop programs, policies, and activities to address disproportionate health, environmental, economic, and climate impacts on disadvantaged communities. It establishes a White House Environmental Justice Interagency Council and a White House Environmental Justice Advisory Council to address current and historical environmental injustices. The order establishes a goal of delivering 40 percent of the overall benefits of relevant federal investments to disadvantaged communities and initiates a Climate and Environmental Justice Screening Tool to identify disadvantaged communities and inform equitable decision making across the federal government.

Title VI of the Civil Rights Act of 1964

42 U.S.C. §§2000d to 2000d-7

CHAPTER 21—CIVIL RIGHTS

SUBCHAPTER V—FEDERALLY ASSISTED PROGRAMS

§2000d. Prohibition against exclusion from participation in, denial of benefits of, and discrimination under federally assisted programs on ground of race, color, or national origin

[TITLE VI §601]

No person in the United States shall, on the ground of race, color, or national origin, be excluded from participation in, be denied the benefits of, or be subjected to discrimination under any program or activity receiving Federal financial assistance.

§2000d-1. Federal authority and financial assistance to programs or activities by way of grant, loan, or contract other than contract of insurance or guaranty, rules and regulations; approval by President; compliance with requirements; reports to Congressional committees; effective date of administrative action

[TITLE VI §602]

Each Federal department and agency which is empowered to extend Federal financial assistance to any program or activity, by way of grant, loan, or contract other than a contract of insurance or guaranty, is authorized and directed to effectuate the provisions of section 2000d of this title with respect to such program or activity by issuing rules, regulations, or orders of general applicability which shall be consistent with achievement of the objectives of the statute authorizing the financial assistance in connection with which the action is taken. No such rule, regulation, or order shall become effective unless and until approved by the President. Compliance with any requirement adopted pursuant to this section may be effected (1) by the termination of or refusal to grant or to continue assistance under such program or activity to any recipient as to whom there has been an express finding on the record, after opportunity for hearing, of a failure to comply with such requirement, but such termination or refusal shall be limited to the particular political entity, or part thereof, or other recipient as to whom such a finding has been made and, shall be limited in its effect to the particular program, or part thereof, in which such noncompliance has been so found, or (2) by any other means authorized by law: *Provided, however,* That no such action shall be taken until the department or agency concerned has advised the appropriate person or persons of the failure to comply with the requirement and has determined that compliance cannot be secured by voluntary means. In the case of any action terminating, or refusing to grant or continue, assistance because of failure to comply with a requirement imposed pursuant to this section, the head of the Federal department or agency shall file with the committees of the House and Senate having legislative jurisdiction over the program or activity involved a full written report of the circumstances and the grounds for such action. No such action shall become effective until thirty days have elapsed after the filing of such report.

§2000d-2. Judicial review; administrative procedure provisions
[TITLE VI §603]

Any department or agency action taken pursuant to section 2000d-1 of this title shall be subject to such judicial review as may otherwise be provided by law for similar action taken by such department or agency on other grounds. In the case of action, not otherwise subject to judicial review, terminating or refusing to grant or to continue financial assistance upon a finding of failure to comply with any requirement imposed pursuant to section 2000d-1 of this title, any person aggrieved (including any State or political subdivision thereof and any agency of either) may obtain judicial review of such action in accordance with chapter 7 of Title 5, and such action shall not be deemed committed to unreviewable agency discretion within the meaning of that chapter.

§2000d-3. Construction of provisions not to authorize administrative action with respect to employment practices except where primary objective of federal financial assistance is to provide employment
[TITLE VI §604]

Nothing contained in this subchapter shall be construed to authorize action under this subchapter by any department or agency with respect to any employment practice of any employer, employment agency, or labor organization except where a primary objective of the Federal financial assistance is to provide employment.

§2000d-4. Federal authority and financial assistance to programs or activities by way of contract of insurance or guaranty
[TITLE VI §605]

Nothing in this subchapter shall add to or detract from any existing authority with respect to any program or activity under which Federal financial assistance is extended by way of a contract of insurance or guaranty.

§2000d-4a. "Program or activity" and "program" defined
[TITLE VI §606]

For the purposes of this subchapter, the term "program or activity" and the term "program" mean all of the operations of —

(1) (A) a department, agency, special purpose district, or other instrumentality of a State or of a local government; or

(B) the entity of such State or local government that distributes such assistance and each such department of agency (and each other State or local government entity) to which the assistance is extended, in the case of assistance to a State or local government;

(2) (A) a college, university, or other postsecondary institution, or a public system of higher education; or

(B) a local educational agency (as defined in section 7801 of Title 20), system of vocational education, or other school system;

(3) (A) an entire corporation, partnership, or other private organization, or an entire sole proprietorship—

(i) if assistance is extended to such corporation, partnership, private organization, or sole proprietorship as a whole; or

(ii) which is principally engaged in the business of providing education, health care, housing, social services, or parks and recreation; or

(B) the entire plant or other comparable, geographically separate facility to which Federal financial assistance is extended, in the case of any other corporation, partnership, private organization, or sole proprietorship; or

(4) any other entity which is established by two or more of the entities described in paragraph (1), (2), or (3);

any part of which is extended Federal financial assistance.

§2000d-5. Prohibited deferral of action on applications by local educational agencies seeking federal funds for alleged noncompliance with Civil Rights Act

The Secretary of Education shall not defer action or order action deferred on any application by a local educational agency for funds authorized to be appropriated by this Act, by the Elementary and Secondary Education Act of 1965, by the Act of September 30, 1950, or by the Cooperative Research Act, on the basis of alleged noncompliance with the provisions of this subchapter for more than sixty days after notice is given to such local agency of such deferral unless such local agency is given the opportunity for a hearing as provided in section 2000d-1 of this title, such hearing to be held within sixty days of such notice, unless the time for such hearing is extended by mutual consent of such local agency and the Secretary, and such deferral shall not continue for more than thirty days after the close of any such hearing unless there has been an express finding on the record of such hearing that such local educational agency has failed to comply with the provisions of this subchapter: *Provided*, That, for the purpose of determining whether a local educational agency is in compliance with this subchapter, compliance by such agency with a final order or judgment of a Federal court for the desegregation of the school or school system operated by such agency shall be deemed to be compliance with this subchapter, insofar as the matters covered in the order or judgment are concerned.

§2000d-6. Policy of United States as to application of nondiscrimination provisions in schools of local educational agencies

(a) Declaration of uniform policy—It is the policy of the United States that guidelines and criteria established pursuant to title VI of the Civil Rights Act of 1964 and section 182 of the Elementary and Secondary Education Amendments of 1966 dealing with conditions of segregation by race, whether de jure or de facto, in the schools of the local educational agencies of any State shall be applied uniformly in all regions of the United States whatever the origin or cause of such segregation.

(b) Nature of uniformity — Such uniformity refers to one policy applied uniformly to de jure segregation wherever found and such other policy as may be provided pursuant to law applied uniformly to de facto segregation wherever found.

(c) Prohibition of construction for diminution of obligation for enforcement or compliance with nondiscrimination requirements—Nothing in this section shall be construed to diminish the obligation of responsible officials to enforce or comply with such guidelines and criteria in order to eliminate discrimination in federally assisted programs and activities as required by title VI of the Civil Rights Act of 1964.

(d) Additional funds — It is the sense of the Congress that the Department of Justice and the Secretary of Education should request such additional funds as may be necessary to apply the policy set forth in this section throughout the United States.

§2000d-7. Civil rights remedies equalization

(a) General provision —

(1) A State shall not be immune under the Eleventh Amendment of the Constitution of the United States from suit in Federal court for a violation of section 504 of the Rehabilitation Act of 1973, title IX of the Education Amendments of 1972, the Age Discrimination Act of 1975, title VI of the Civil Rights Act of 1964, or the provisions of any other Federal statute prohibiting discrimination by recipients of Federal financial assistance.

(2) In a suit against a State for a violation of a statute referred to in paragraph (1), remedies (including remedies both at law and in equity) are available for such a violation to the same extent as such remedies are available for such a violation in the suit against any public or private entity other than a State.

(b) Effective date — The provisions of subsection (a) of this section shall take effect with respect to violations that occur in whole or in part after October 21, 1986.

U.S. Environmental Protection Agency
Title VI Regulations
40 C.F.R. §§7.10 to 7.135

SUBPART A — GENERAL

§7.10 Purpose of this part.

This part implements: Title VI of the Civil Rights Act of 1964, as amended; section 504 of the Rehabilitation Act of 1973, as amended; and section 13 of the Federal Water Pollution Control Act Amendments of 1972, Public Law 92-500, (collectively, the Acts).

§7.15 Applicability.

This Part applies to all applicants for, and recipients of, EPA assistance in the operation of programs or activities receiving such assistance beginning February 13, 1984. New construction (§ 7.70) for which design was initiated prior to February 13, 1984, shall comply with the accessibility requirements in the Department of Health, Education and Welfare (now the Department of Health and Human Services) nondiscrimination regulation, 45 CFR 84.23, issued June 3, 1977, or with equivalent standards that ensure the facility is readily accessible to and usable by handicapped persons. Such assistance includes but is not limited to that which is listed in the Catalogue of Federal Domestic Assistance under the 66.000 series. It supersedes the provisions of former 40 CFR Parts 7 and 12.

§7.20 Responsible agency officers.

(a) The EPA Office of Civil Rights (OCR) is responsible for developing and administering EPA's means of assuring compliance under the Acts.

(b) EPA's Project Officers will, to the extent possible, be available to explain to each recipient its obligations under this Part and to provide recipients with technical assistance or guidance upon request.

§7.25 Definitions.

As used in this part:

Action, for purposes of subpart F of this part, means any act, activity, policy, rule, standard, or method of administration; or the use of any policy, rule, standard, or method of administration.

Administrator means the Administrator of EPA. It includes any other agency official authorized to act on his or her behalf, unless explicitly stated otherwise.

Age, for purposes of subpart F of this part, means how old a person is, or the number of elapsed years from the date of a person's birth.

Age distinction, for purposes of subpart F of this part, means any action using age or an age-related term.

Age-related term, for purposes of subpart F of this part, means a word or words which necessarily imply a particular age or range of ages (for example; "children," "adult," "older persons," but not "student" or "grade").

Alcohol abuse means any misuse of alcohol which demonstrably interferes with a person's health, interpersonal relations or working ability.

Applicant means any entity that files an application or unsolicited proposal or otherwise requests EPA assistance (see definition for *EPA assistance*).

Assistant Attorney General is the head of the Civil Rights Division, U.S. Department of Justice.

Award Official means the EPA official with the authority to approve and execute assistance agreements and to take other assistance related actions authorized by this Part and by other EPA regulations or delegation of authority.

Drug abuse means:

(a) The use of any drug or substance listed by the Department of Justice in 21 CFR 1308.11, under authority of the Controlled Substances Act, 21 U.S.C. §801, as a controlled substance unavailable for prescription because:

    (1) The drug or substance has a high potential for abuse,

    (2) The drug or other substance has no currently accepted medical use in treatment in the United States, or

    (3) There is a lack of accepted safety for use of the drug or other substance under medical supervision.

Note: — Examples of drugs under paragraph (a)(1) of this section include certain opiates and opiate derivatives (e.g., heroin) and hallucinogenic substances (e.g., marijuana, mescaline, peyote) and depressants (e.g., methaqualone). Examples of (a)(2) include opium, coca leaves, methadone, amphetamines and barbiturates.

(b) The misuse of any drug or substance listed by the Department of Justice in 21 CFR 1308.12-15 under authority of the Controlled Substances Act as a controlled substance available for prescription.

EPA means the United States Environmental Protection Agency.

EPA assistance means any grant or cooperative agreement, loan, contract (other than a procurement contract or a contract of insurance or guaranty), or any other arrangement by which EPA provides or otherwise makes available assistance in the form of:

    (1) Funds;

    (2) Services of personnel; or

    (3) Real or personal property or any interest in or use of such property, including:

        (i) Transfers or leases of such property for less than fair market value or for reduced consideration; and

        (ii) Proceeds from a subsequent transfer or lease of such property if EPA's share of its fair market value is not returned to EPA.

Facility means all, or any part of, or any interests in structures, equipment, roads, walks, parking lots, or other real or personal property.

Handicapped person:

(a) *Handicapped person* means any person who (1) has a physical or mental impairment which substantially limits one or more major life activities, (2) has a record of such an impairment, or (3) is regarded as having such an impairment. For purposes of employment, the term *handicapped person* does not include any person who is an alcoholic or drug abuser whose current use of alcohol or drugs prevents such individual from performing the duties of the job in question or whose employment, by reason of such current drug or alcohol abuse, would constitute a direct threat to property or the safety of others.

(b) As used in this paragraph, the phrase:

    (1) *Physical or mental impairment* means (i) any physiological disorder or condition, cosmetic disfigurement, or anatomical loss affecting one or more of the following body systems: neurological; musculoskeletal; special sense organs; respiratory, including speech organs; cardiovascular; reproductive; digestive; genito-urinary; hemic and lymphatic; skin; and endocrine; and (ii) any mental or psychological disorder, such as mental retardation, organic brain syndrome, emotional or mental illness, and specific learning disabilities.

    (2) *Major life activities* means functions such as caring for one's self, performing manual tasks, walking, seeing, hearing, speaking, breathing, learning, and working.

    (3) *Has a record of such an impairment* means has a history of, or has been misclassified as having, a mental or physical impairment that substantially limits one or more major life activities.

    (4) *Is regarded as having an impairment* means:

        (i) Has a physical or mental impairment that does not substantially limit major life activities but that is treated by a recipient as constituting such a limitation;

        (ii) Has a physical or mental impairment that substantially limits major life activities only as a result of the attitudes of others toward such impairment; or

        (iii) Has none of the impairments defined above but is treated by a recipient as having such an impairment.

Normal operation, for purposes of subpart F of this part, means the operation of a program or activity without significant changes that would impair its ability to meet its objectives.

Office of Civil Rights or OCR means the Director of the Office of Civil Rights, EPA Headquarters or his/her designated representative.

Program or activity and *program* mean all the operations of any entity described in paragraphs (1) through (4) of this definition, any part of which is extended Federal financial assistance:

(1)(i) A department, agency, special purpose district, or other instrumentality of a State or of a local government; or

(ii) The entity of such State or local government that distributes such assistance and each such department or agency (and each other State or local government entity) to which the assistance is extended, in the case of assistance to a State or local government;

(2)(i) A college, university, or other postsecondary institution, or a public system of higher education; or

(ii) A local educational agency (as defined in 20 U.S.C. 7801), system of vocational education, or other school system;

(3)(i) An entire corporation, partnership, or other private organization, or an entire sole proprietorship—

(A) If assistance is extended to such corporation, partnership, private organization, or sole proprietorship as a whole; or

(B) Which is principally engaged in the business of providing education, health care, housing, social services, or parks and recreation; or

(ii) The entire plant or other comparable, geographically separate facility to which Federal financial assistance is extended, in the case of any other corporation, partnership, private organization, or sole proprietorship; or

(4) Any other entity which is established by two or more of the entities described in paragraph (1), (2), or (3) of this definition.

Project Officer means the EPA official designated in the assistance agreement (as defined in EPA assistance) as EPA's program contact with the recipient; Project Officers are responsible for monitoring the project.

Qualified handicapped person means:

(a) With respect to employment: A handicapped person who, with reasonable accommodation, can perform the essential functions of the job in question.

(b) With respect to services: A handicapped person who meets the essential eligibility requirements for the receipt of such services.

Racial classifications:[1]

(a) *American Indian or Alaskan native.* A person having origins in any of the original peoples of North America, and who maintains cultural identification through tribal affiliation or community recognition.

(b) *Asian or Pacific Islander.* A person having origins in any of the original peoples of the Far East, Southeast Asia, the Indian subcontinent, or the Pacific Islands. This area includes, for example, China, Japan, Korea, the Philippine Islands, and Samoa.

(c) *Black and not of Hispanic origin.* A person having origins in any of the black racial groups of Africa.

(d) *Hispanic.* A person of Mexican, Puerto Rican, Cuban, Central or South American or other Spanish culture or origin, regardless or race.

(e) *White, not of Hispanic origin.* A person having origins in any of the original peoples of Europe, North Africa, or the Middle East.

Recipient means, for the purposes of this regulation, any State or its political subdivision, any instrumentality of a State or its political subdivision, any public or private agency, institution, organization, or other entity, or any person to which Federal financial assistance is extended directly or through another recipient, including any successor, assignee, or transferee of a recipient, but excluding the ultimate beneficiary of the assistance.

Section 13 refers to section 13 of the Federal Water Pollution Control Act Amendments of 1972.

Statutory objective, for purposes of subpart F of this part, means any purpose of a program or activity expressly stated in any Federal statute, State statute, or local statute or ordinance adopted by an elected, general purpose legislative body.

United States includes the states of the United States, the District of Columbia, the Commonwealth of Puerto Rico, the Virgin Islands, American Samoa, Guam, Wake Island, the Canal Zone, and all other territories and possessions of the United States; the term "State" includes any one of the foregoing.

SUBPART B —DISCRIMINATION PROHIBITED ON THE BASIS OF RACE, COLOR, NATIONAL ORIGIN OR SEX

§7.30 General prohibition.

No person shall be excluded from participation in, be denied the benefits of, or be subjected to discrimination under any program or activity receiving EPA assistance on the basis of race, color, national origin, or on the basis of sex in any program or activity receiving EPA assistance under the Federal Water Pollution Control Act, as amended, including the Environmental Financing Act of 1972.

§7.35 Specific prohibitions.

(a) As to any program or activity receiving EPA assistance, a recipient shall not directly or through contractual, licensing, or other arrangements on the basis of race, color, national origin or, if applicable, sex:

(1) Deny a person any service, aid or other benefit of the program or activity;

---

1. Additional subcategories based on national origin or primary language spoken may be used where appropriate on either a national or a regional basis. Subparagraphs (a) through (e) are in conformity with Directive 15 of the Office of Federal Statistical Policy and Standards, whose function is now in the Office of Information and Regulatory Affairs, Office of Management and Budget. Should that office, or any successor office, change or otherwise amend the categories listed in Directive 15, the categories in this paragraph shall be interpreted to conform with any such changes or amendments.

(2) Provide a person any service, aid or other benefit that is different, or is provided differently from that provided to others under the program or activity;

(3) Restrict a person in any way in the enjoyment of any advantage or privilege enjoyed by others receiving any service, aid, or benefit provided by the program or activity;

(4) Subject a person to segregation in any manner or separate treatment in any way related to receiving services or benefits under the program or activity;

(5) Deny a person or any group of persons the opportunity to participate as members of any planning or advisory body which is an integral part of the program or activity, such as a local sanitation board or sewer authority;

(6) Discriminate in employment on the basis of sex in any program or activity subject to section 13, or on the basis of race, color, or national origin in any program whose purpose is to create employment; or, by means of employment discrimination, deny intended beneficiaries the benefits of EPA assistance, or subject the beneficiaries to prohibited discrimination.

(7) In administering a program or activity receiving Federal financial assistance in which the recipient has previously discriminated on the basis of race, color, sex, or national origin, the recipient shall take affirmative action to provide remedies to those who have been injured by the discrimination.

(b) A recipient shall not use criteria or methods of administering its program or activity which have the effect of subjecting individuals to discrimination because of their race, color, national origin, or sex, or have the effect of defeating or substantially impairing accomplishment of the objectives of the program or activity with respect to individuals of a particular race, color, national origin, or sex.

(c) A recipient shall not choose a site or location of a facility that has the purpose or effect of excluding individuals from, denying them the benefits of, or subjecting them to discrimination under any program: or activity to which this part applies on the grounds of race, color, or national origin or sex; or with the purpose or effect of defeating or substantially impairing the accomplishment of the objectives of this subpart.

(d) The specific prohibitions of discrimination enumerated above do not limit the general prohibition of §7.30.

SUBPART C — DISCRIMINATION PROHIBITED ON THE BASIS OF HANDICAP

§7.45 General prohibition.

No qualified handicapped person shall solely on the basis of handicap be excluded from participation in, be denied the benefits of, or otherwise be subjected to discrimination under any program or activity receiving EPA assistance.

§7.50 Specific prohibitions against discrimination.

(a) A recipient, in providing any aid, benefit or service under any program or activity receiving EPA assistance shall not, on the basis of handicap, directly or through contractual, licensing, or other arrangement:

(1) Deny a qualified handicapped person any service, aid or other benefit of a federally assisted program or activity;

(2) Provide different or separate aids, benefits, or services to handicapped persons or to any class of handicapped persons than is provided to others unless the action is necessary to provide qualified handicapped persons with aids, benefits, or services that are as effective as those provided to others;

(3) Aid or perpetuate discrimination against a qualified handicapped person by providing significant assistance to an entity that discriminates on the basis of handicap in providing aids, benefits, or services to beneficiaries of the recipient's program or activity;

(4) Deny a qualified handicapped person the opportunity to participate as a member of planning or advisory boards; or

(5) Limit a qualified handicapped person in any other way in the enjoyment of any right, privilege, advantage, or opportunity enjoyed by others receiving an aid, benefit or service from the program or activity.

(b) A recipient may not, in determining the site or location of a facility, make selections: (1) That have the effect of excluding handicapped persons from, denying them the benefits of, or otherwise subjecting them to discrimination under any program or activity that receives or benefits from EPA assistance or (2) that have the purpose or effect of defeating or substantially impairing the accomplishment of the objectives of the program or activity receiving EPA assistance with respect to handicapped persons.

(c) A recipient shall not use criteria or methods of administering any program or activity receiving EPA assistance which have the effect of subjecting individuals to discrimination because of their handicap, or have the effect of defeating or substantially impairing accomplishment of the objectives of such program or activity with respect to handicapped persons.

(d) Recipients shall take appropriate steps to ensure that communications with their applicants, employees, and beneficiaries are available to persons with impaired vision and hearing.

(e) The exclusion of non-handicapped persons or specified classes of handicapped persons from aid, benefits, or services limited by Federal statute or Executive Order to handicapped persons or a different class of handicapped persons is not prohibited by this subpart.

§7.55 Separate or different aid, benefits, or services.

Recipients shall not deny a qualified handicapped person an opportunity equal to that afforded others to participate in or benefit from the aid, benefit, or service in the program or activity receiving EPA assistance. Recipients shall administer programs or activity in the most integrated setting appropriate to the needs of qualified handicapped persons.

§7.60 Prohibitions and requirements relating to employment.

(a) No qualified handicapped person shall, on the basis of handicap, be subjected to discrimination in employment under any program or activity that receives Federal assistance.

(b) A recipient shall make all decisions concerning employment under any program or activity to which this part applies in a manner which ensures that discrimination on the basis of handicap does not occur, and shall not limit, segregate, or classify applicants or employees in any way that adversely affects their opportunities or status because of handicap.

(c) The prohibition against discrimination in employment applies to the following activities:

(1) Recruitment, advertising, and the processing of applications for employment;

(2) Hiring, upgrading, promotion, award of tenure, demotion, transfer, layoff, termination, right of return from layoff, and rehiring;

(3) Rates of pay or any other form of compensation and changes in compensation;

(4) Job assignments, job classifications, organizational structures, position descriptions, lines of progression, and seniority lists;

(5) Leaves of absence, sick leave, or any other leave;

(6) Fringe benefits available by virtue of employment, whether or not administered by the recipient;

(7) Selection and financial support for training, including apprenticeship, professional meetings, conferences, and other related activities, and selection for leaves of absence to pursue training;

(8) Employer sponsored activities, including those that are social or recreational; or

(9) Any other term, condition, or privilege of employment.

(d) A recipient shall not participate in a contractual or other relationship that has the effect of subjecting qualified handicapped applicants or employees to discrimination prohibited by this subpart. The relationships referred to in this paragraph include relationships with employment and referral agencies, with labor unions, with organizations providing or administering fringe benefits to employees of the recipient, and with organizations providing training and apprenticeships.

(e) A recipient shall make reasonable accommodation to the known physical or mental limitations of an otherwise qualified handicapped applicant or employee unless the recipient can demonstrate that the accommodation would impose an undue hardship on the operation of its program or activity.

(f) A recipient shall not use employment tests or criteria that discriminate against handicapped persons and shall ensure that employment tests are adapted for use by persons who have handicaps that impair sensory, manual, or speaking skills.

(g) A recipient shall not conduct a preemployment medical examination or make a preemployment inquiry as to whether an applicant is a handicapped person or as to the nature or severity of a handicap except as permitted by the Department of Justice in 28 CFR 42.513.

§7.65 Accessibility.

(a) *General.* A recipient shall operate each program or activity receiving EPA assistance so that when each part is viewed in its entirety it is readily accessible to and usable by handicapped persons. This paragraph does not:

(1) Necessarily require a recipient to make each of its existing facilities or every part of an existing facility accessible to and usable by handicapped persons.

(2) Require a recipient to take any action that the recipient can demonstrate would result in a fundamental alteration in the nature of its program or activity or in undue financial and administrative burdens. If an action would result in such an alternation or such financial and administrative burdens, the recipient shall be required to take any other action that would not result in such an alteration or financial and administrative burdens but would nevertheless ensure that handicapped persons receive the benefits and services of the program or activity receiving EPA assistance.

(b) *Methods of ensuring compliance in existing facilities.* A recipient may comply with the accessibility requirements of this section by making structural changes, redesigning equipment, reassigning services to accessible buildings, assigning aides to beneficiaries, or any other means that make its program or activity accessible to handicapped persons. In choosing among alternatives, a recipient must give priority to methods that serve handicapped persons in the most integrated setting appropriate.

(c) *Deadlines.*

(1) Except where structural changes in facilities are necessary, recipients must adhere to the

provisions of this section within 60 days after the effective date of this Part.

(2) Recipients having an existing facility which does require alterations in order to comply with paragraph (a) of this section must prepare a transition plan in accordance with §7.75 within six months from the effective date of this Part. The recipient must complete the changes as soon as possible, but not later than three years from date of award.

(d) *Notice of accessibility.* The recipient must make sure that interested persons, including those with impaired vision or hearing, can find out about the existence and location of the services, activities, and facilities that are accessible to and usable by handicapped persons.

(e) *Structural and financial feasibility.* This section does not require structural alterations to existing facilities if making such alterations would not be structurally or financially feasible. An alteration is not structurally feasible when it has little likelihood of being accomplished without removing or altering a load-bearing structural member. Financial feasibility shall take into account the degree to which the alteration work is to be assisted by EPA assistance, the cost limitations of the program under which such assistance is provided, and the relative cost of accomplishing such alterations in manners consistent and inconsistent with accessibility.

§7.70 New construction.

(a) *General.* New facilities shall be designed and constructed to be readily accessible to and usable by handicapped persons. Alterations to existing facilities shall, to the maximum extent feasible, be designed and constructed to be readily accessible to and usable by handicapped persons.

(b) *Conformance with Uniform Federal Accessibility Standards.*

(1) Effective as of January 18, 1991, design, construction, or alteration of buildings in conformance with sections 3-8 of the Uniform Federal Accessibility Standards (USAF) (Appendix A to 41 CFR Subpart 101-19.6) shall be deemed to comply with the requirements of this section with respect to those buildings. Departures from particular technical and scoping requirements of UFAS by the use of other methods are permitted where substantially equivalent or greater access to and usability of the building is provided.

(2) For purposes of this section, section 4.1.6(1)(g) of UFAS shall be interpreted to exempt from the requirements of UFAS only mechanical rooms and other spaces that, because of their intended use, will not require accessibility to the public or beneficiaries or result in the employment or residence therein of persons with physical handicaps.

(3) This section does not require recipients to make building alterations that have little likelihood of being accomplished without removing or altering a load-bearing structural member.

§7.75 Transition plan.

If structural changes to facilities are necessary to make the program or activity accessible to handicapped persons, a recipient must prepare a transition plan.

(a) *Requirements.* The transition plan must set forth the steps needed to complete the structural changes required and must be developed with the assistance of interested persons, including handicapped persons or organizations representing handicapped persons. At a minimum, the transition plan must:

(1) Identify the physical obstacles in the recipient's facilities that limit handicapped persons' access to its program or activity,

(2) Describe in detail what the recipient will do to make the facilities accessible,

(3) Specify the schedule for the steps needed to achieve full program accessibility under § 7.65(a), and include a year-by-year timetable if the process will take more than one year,

(4) Indicate the person responsible for carrying out the plan.

(b) *Availability.* Recipients shall make available a copy of the transition plan to the OCR upon request and to the public for inspection at either the site of the project or at the recipient's main office.

SUBPART D — REQUIREMENTS FOR APPLICANTS AND RECIPIENTS

§7.80 Applicants.

(a) *Assurances.* —

(1) *General.* Applicants for EPA assistance shall submit an assurance with their applications stating that, with respect to their programs or activities that receive EPA assistance, they will comply with the requirements of this part. Applicants must also submit any other information that the OCR determines is necessary for preaward review. The applicant's acceptance of EPA assistance is an acceptance of the obligation of this assurance and this part.

(2) *Duration of assurance.* —

(i) *Real property.* When EPA awards assistance in the form of real property or assistance to acquire real property, or structures on the property, the assurance will obligate the recipient, or transferee, during the period the real property or structures are used for the purpose for which EPA assistance is extended, or for another purpose in which similar services or benefits are provided. The transfer instrument shall contain a covenant running with the land which assures nondiscrimination. Where applicable, the covenant shall also retain a right of reverter which will permit EPA to recover the property if the covenant is ever broken.

(ii) *Personal property.* When EPA provides assistance in the form of personal property, the assurance will obligate the recipient for so long as it continues to own or possess the property.

(iii) *Other forms of assistance.* In all other cases, the assurance will obligate the recipient for as long as EPA assistance is extended.

(b) *Wastewater treatment project.* EPA Form 4700-4 shall also be submitted with applications for assistance under Title II of the Federal Water Pollution Control Act.

(c) *Compliance information.* Each applicant for EPA assistance shall submit regarding the program or activity that would receive EPA assistance:

(1) Notice of any lawsuit pending against the applicant alleging discrimination on the basis of race, color, sex, age, handicap, or national origin;

(2) A brief description of any applications pending to other Federal agencies for assistance, and of Federal assistance being provided at the time of the application; and

(3) A statement describing any civil rights compliance reviews regarding the applicant conducted during the two-year period before the application, and information concerning the agency or organization performing the reviews.

§7.85 Recipients.

(a) *Compliance information.* Each recipient shall collect, maintain, and on request of the OCR, provide the following information to show compliance with this part:

(1) A brief description of any lawsuits pending against the recipient that allege discrimination which this part prohibits;

(2) Racial/ethnic, national origin, sex and handicap data, or EPA Form 4700-4 information submitted with its application;

(3) A log of discrimination complaints which identifies the complaint, the date it was filed, the date the recipient's investigation was completed, the disposition, and the date of disposition; and

(4) Reports of any compliance reviews conducted by any other agencies.

(b) *Additional compliance information.* If necessary, the OCR may require recipients to submit data and information specific to certain programs to determine compliance where there is reason to believe that discrimination may exist in a program or activity receiving EPA assistance or to investigate a complaint alleging discrimination in a program or activity receiving EPA assistance. Requests shall be limited to data and information which is relevant to determining compliance and shall be accompanied by a written statement summarizing the complaint or setting forth the basis for the belief that discrimination may exist.

(c) *Self-evaluation.*

(1) Each recipient must conduct a self-evaluation of its administrative policies and practices, to consider whether such policies and practices may involve handicap discrimination prohibited by this part. When conducting the self-evaluation, the recipient shall consult with interested and involved persons including handicapped persons or organizations representing handicapped persons. The evaluation shall be completed within 18 months after the effective date of this part.

(2) Each recipient employing the equivalent of 15 or more full time employees may be required to complete a written self-evaluation of its compliance under the Age Discrimination Act as part of a compliance review or complaint investigation. This self-evaluation will pertain to any age distinction imposed in its program or activity receiving Federal assistance from EPA. If required, each recipient's self-evaluation shall identify and justify each age distinction imposed by the recipient and each recipient shall take corrective and remedial action whenever a self-evaluation indicates a violation of the Age Discrimination Act.

(d) *Preparing compliance information.* In preparing compliance information, a recipient must:

(1) [Reserved]

(2) Use the racial classifications set forth in §7.25 in determining categories of race, color or national origin.

(e) *Maintaining compliance information.* Recipients must keep records for paragraphs (a) and (b) of this section for three (3) years after completing the project. When any complaint or other action for alleged failure to comply with this part is brought before the three-year period ends, the recipient shall keep records until the complaint is resolved.

(f) *Accessibility to compliance information.* A recipient shall:

(1) Give the OCR access during normal business hours to its books, records, accounts and other sources of information, including its facilities, as may be pertinent to ascertain compliance with this part;

(2) Make compliance information available to the public upon request; and

(3) Assist in obtaining other required information that is in the possession of other agencies, institutions, or persons not under the recipient's control. If such party refuses to release that information, the recipient shall inform the OCR and explain its efforts to obtain the information.

(g) *Coordination of compliance effort.* If the recipient employs fifteen (15) or more employees, it shall designate at least one person to coordinate its efforts to comply with its obligations under this part.

§7.90 Grievance procedures.

(a) *Requirements.* Each recipient shall adopt grievance procedures that assure the prompt and fair resolution of complaints which allege violation of this Part.

(b) *Exception.* Recipients with fewer than fifteen (15) full-time employees need not comply with this section unless the OCR finds a violation of this Part or determines that creating a grievance procedure will not significantly impair the recipient's ability to provide benefits or services.

§7.95 Notice of nondiscrimination.

(a) *Requirements.* A recipient shall provide initial and continuing notice that it does not discriminate on the basis of race, color, national origin, or handicap in a program or activity receiving EPA assistance or, in programs or activities covered by section 13, on the basis of sex. Methods of notice must accommodate those with impaired vision or hearing. At a minimum, this notice must be posted in a prominent place in the recipient's offices or facilities. Methods of notice may also include publishing in newspapers and magazines, and placing notices in recipient's internal publications or on recipient's printed letterhead. Where appropriate, such notice must be in a language or languages other than English. The notice must identify the responsible employee designated in accordance with § 7.85.

(b) *Deadline.* Recipients of assistance must provide initial notice by thirty (30) calendar days after award and continuing notice for the duration of EPA assistance.

§7.100 Intimidation and retaliation prohibited.

No applicant, recipient, nor other person shall intimidate, threaten, coerce, or discriminate against any individual or group, either:

(a) For the purpose of interfering with any right or privilege guaranteed by the Acts or this Part, or

(b) Because the individual has filed a complaint or has testified, assisted or participated in any way in an investigation, proceeding or hearing under this Part, or has opposed any practice made unlawful by this regulation.

SUBPART E — AGENCY COMPLIANCE PROCEDURES

§7.105 General policy.

EPA's Administrator, Director of the Office of Civil Rights, Project Officers and other responsible officials shall seek the cooperation of applicants and recipients in securing compliance with this Part, and are available to provide help.

§7.110 Preaward compliance.

(a) *Review of compliance information.* Within EPA's application processing period, the OCR will determine whether the applicant is in compliance with this Part and inform the Award Official. This determination will be based on the submissions required by §7.80 and any other information EPA receives during this time (including complaints) or has on file about the applicant. When the OCR cannot make a determination on the basis of this information, additional information will be requested from the applicant, local government officials, or interested persons or organizations, including aged and handicapped persons or organizations representing such persons. The OCR may also conduct an on-site review only when it has reason to believe discrimination may be occurring in a program or activity which is the subject of the application.

(b) *Voluntary compliance.* If the review indicates noncompliance, an applicant may agree in writing to take the steps the OCR recommends to come into compliance with this Part. The OCR must approve the written agreement before any award is made.

(c) *Refusal to comply.* If the applicant refuses to enter into such an agreement, the OCR shall follow the procedure established by paragraph (b) of §7.130.

§7.115 Postaward compliance.

(a) *Periodic review.* The OCR may periodically conduct compliance reviews of any recipient's programs or activities receiving EPA assistance, including the request of data and information, and may conduct on-site reviews when it has reason to believe that discrimination may be occurring in such programs or activities.

(b) *Notice of review.* After selecting a recipient for review or initiating a complaint investigation in accordance with §7.120, the OCR will inform the recipient of:

(1) The nature of and schedule for review, or investigation; and

(2) Its opportunity, before the determination in paragraph (d) of this section is made, to make a written submission responding to, rebutting, or denying the allegations raised in the review or complaint.

(c) *Postreview notice.*

(1) Within 180 calendar days from the start of the compliance review or complaint investigation, the OCR will notify the recipient in writing by certified mail, return receipt requested, of:

(i) Preliminary findings;

(ii) Recommendations, if any, for achieving voluntary compliance; and

(iii) Recipient's right to engage in voluntary compliance negotiations where appropriate.

(2) The OCR will notify the Award Official and the Assistant Attorney General for Civil Rights of the preliminary findings of noncompliance.

(d) *Formal determination of noncompliance.* After receiving the notice of the preliminary finding of noncompliance in paragraph (c) of this section, the recipient may:

(1) Agree to the OCR's recommendations, or

(2) Submit a written response sufficient to demonstrate that the preliminary findings are incorrect, or that compliance may be achieved through steps other than those recommended by OCR.

If the recipient does not take one of these actions within fifty (50) calendar days after receiving this preliminary notice, the OCR shall, within fourteen (14) calendar days, send a formal written determination of noncompliance to the recipient and copies to the Award Official and Assistant Attorney General.

(e) *Voluntary compliance time limits.* The recipient will have ten (10) calendar days from receipt of the formal determination of noncompliance in which to come into voluntary compliance. If the recipient fails to meet this deadline, the OCR must start proceedings under paragraph (b) of §7.130.

(f) *Form of voluntary compliance agreements.* All agreements to come into voluntary compliance must:

(1) Be in writing;

(2) Set forth the specific steps the recipient has agreed to take, and

(3) Be signed by the Director, OCR or his/her designee and an official with authority to legally bind the recipient.

§7.120 Complaint investigations.

The OCR shall promptly investigate all complaints filed under this section unless the complainant and the party complained against agree to a delay pending settlement negotiations.

(a) *Who may file a complaint.* A person who believes that he or she or a specific class of persons has been discriminated against in violation of this part may file a complaint. The complaint may be filed by an authorized representative. A complaint alleging employment discrimination must identify at least one individual aggrieved by such discrimination. Complaints solely alleging employment discrimination against an individual on the basis of race, color, national origin, sex or religion shall be processed under the procedures for complaints of employment discrimination filed against recipients of Federal assistance (see 28 CFR part 42, subpart H and 29 CFR part 1691). Complaints of employment discrimination based on age against an individual by recipients of Federal financial assistance are subject to the Age Discrimination in Employment Act of 1967 and should be filed administratively with the Equal Employment Opportunity Commission (see 29 CFR part 1626). Complainants are encouraged but not required to make use of any grievance procedure established under §7.90 before filing a complaint. Filing a complaint through a grievance procedure does not extend the 180 day calendar requirement of paragraph (b)(2) of this section.

(b) *Where, when and how to file complaint.* The complainant may file a complaint at any EPA office. The complaint may be referred to the region in which the alleged discriminatory acts occurred.

(1) The complaint must be in writing and it must describe the alleged discriminatory acts which violate this part.

(2) The complaint must be filed within 180 calendar days of the alleged discriminatory acts, unless the OCR waives the time limit for good cause. The filing of a grievance with the recipient does not satisfy the requirement that complaints must be filed within 180 days of the alleged discriminatory acts.

(c) *Notification.* The OCR will notify the complainant and the recipient of the agency's receipt of the complaint within five (5) calendar days.

(d) *Complaint processing procedures.* After acknowledging receipt of a complaint, the OCR will immediately initiate complaint processing procedures.

(1) *Preliminary investigation.*

(i) Within twenty (20) calendar days of acknowledgment of the complaint, the OCR will review the complaint for acceptance, rejection, or referral to the appropriate Federal agency.

(ii) If the complaint is accepted, the OCR will notify the complainant and the Award Official. The OCR will also notify the applicant or recipient complained against of the allegations and give the applicant or recipient opportunity to make a written submission responding to, rebutting, or denying the allegations raised in the complaint.

(iii) The party complained against may send the OCR a response to the notice of complaint within thirty (30) calendar days of receiving it.

(iv) Complaints alleging age discrimination under the Age Discrimination Act of 1975 will be referred to a mediation agency in accordance with §7.180.

(2) *Informal resolution.*

(i) OCR shall attempt to resolve complaints informally whenever possible. When a complaint cannot be resolved informally, OCR shall follow the procedures established by paragraphs (c) through (e) of §7.115.

(ii) [Reserved]

(e) *Confidentiality.* EPA agrees to keep the complainant's identity confidential except to the extent necessary to carry out the purposes of this part, including the conduct of any investigation, hearing, or judicial proceeding arising thereunder. Ordinarily in complaints of employment discrimination, the name of the complainant will be given to the recipient with the notice of complaint.

(f) [Reserved]

(g) *Dismissal of complaint.* If OCR's investigation reveals no violation of this part, the Director, OCR, will dismiss the complaint and notify the complainant and recipient.

§7.125 Coordination with other agencies.

If, in the conduct of a compliance review or an investigation, it becomes evident that another agency has jurisdiction over the subject matter, OCR will cooperate with that agency during the continuation of the review of investigation. EPA will:

(a) Coordinate its efforts with the other agency, and

(b) Ensure that one of the agencies is designated the lead agency for this purpose. When an agency other than EPA serves as the lead agency, any action taken, requirement imposed, or determination made by the lead agency, other than a final determination to terminate funds, shall have the same effect as though such action had been taken by EPA.

§7.130 Actions available to EPA to obtain compliance.

(a) *General.* If compliance with this part cannot be assured by informal means, EPA may terminate or refuse to award or to continue assistance. EPA may also use any other means authorized by law to get compliance, including a referral of the matter to the Department of Justice.

(b) *Procedure to deny, annul, suspend or terminate EPA assistance* —

(1) *OCR finding.* If OCR determines that an applicant or recipient is not in compliance with this part, and if compliance cannot be achieved voluntarily, OCR shall make a finding of noncompliance. The OCR will notify the applicant or recipient (by registered mail, return receipt requested) of the finding, the action proposed to be taken, and the opportunity for an evidentiary hearing.

(2) *Hearing.*

(i) Within 30 days of receipt of the above notice, the applicant or recipient shall file a written answer, under oath or affirmation, and may request a hearing.

(ii) The answer and request for a hearing shall be sent by registered mail, return receipt requested, to the Chief Administrative Law Judge (ALJ) (A-110), United States Environmental Protection Agency, 1200 Pennsylvania Ave., N.W., Washington, DC 20460. Upon receipt of a request for a hearing, the ALJ will send the applicant or recipient a copy of the ALJ's procedures. If the recipient does not request a hearing, it shall be deemed to have waived its right to a hearing, and the OCR finding shall be deemed to be the ALJ's determination.

(3) *Final decision and disposition.*

(i) The applicant or recipient may, within 30 days of receipt of the ALJ's determination, file with the Administrator its exceptions to that determination. When such exceptions are filed, the Administrator may, within 45 days after the ALJ's determination, serve to the applicant or recipient, a notice that he/she will review the determination. In the absence of either exceptions or notice of review, the ALJ's determination shall constitute the Administrator's final decision.

(ii) If the Administrator reviews the ALJ's determination, all parties shall be given reasonable opportunity to file written statements. A copy of the Administrator's decision will be sent to the applicant or recipient.

(iii) If the Administrator's decision is to deny an application, or annul, suspend or terminate EPA assistance, that decision becomes effective thirty (30) days from the date on which the Administrator submits a full written report of the circumstances and grounds for such action to the Committees of the House and Senate having legislative jurisdiction over the program or activity involved. The decision of the Administrator shall not be subject to further administrative appeal under EPA's General Regulation for Assistance Programs (40 CFR part 30, subpart L).

(4) *Scope of decision.* The denial, annulment, termination or suspension shall be limited to the particular applicant or recipient who was found to have discriminated, and shall be limited in its effect to the particular program or activity or the part of it in which the discrimination was found.

§7.135 Procedure for regaining eligibility.

(a) *Requirements.* An applicant or recipient whose assistance has been denied, annulled, terminated, or suspended under this Part regains eligibility as soon as it:

(1) Provides reasonable assurance that it is complying and will comply with this part in the future, and

(2) Satisfies the terms and conditions for regaining eligibility that are specified in the denial, annulment, termination or suspension order.

(b) *Procedure.* The applicant or recipient must submit a written request to restore eligibility to the OCR declaring that it has met the requirements set forth in paragraph (a) of this section. Upon determining that these requirements have been met, the OCR must notify the Award Official, and the applicant or recipient that eligibility has been restored.

(c) *Rights on denial of restoration of eligibility.* If the OCR denies a request to restore eligibility, the applicant or recipient may file a written request for a hearing before the EPA Chief Administrative Law Judge in accordance with paragraph (c) §7.130, listing the reasons it believes the OCR was in error.

Federal Actions to Address Environmental Justice in Minority and Low-Income Populations, Executive Order 12,898

59 Fed. Reg. 7629 (1994), as amended by EO 12,948 60 Fed. Reg. 6381 (1995)

By the authority vested in me as President by the Constitution and the laws of the United States of America, it is hereby ordered as follows:

§1-1 Implementation

1-101. *Agency Responsibilities*. To the greatest extent practicable and permitted by law, and consistent with the principles set forth in the report on the National Performance Review, each Federal agency shall make achieving environmental justice part of its mission by identifying and addressing, as appropriate, disproportionately high and adverse human health or environmental effects of its programs, policies, and activities on minority populations and low-income populations in the United States and its territories and possessions, the District of Columbia, the Commonwealth of Puerto Rico, and the Commonwealth of the Mariana Islands.

1-102. *Creation of an Interagency Working Group on Environmental Justice.*

(a) Within 3 months of the date of this order, the Administrator of the Environmental Protection Agency ("Administrator") or the Administrator's designee shall convene an interagency Federal Working Group on Environmental Justice ("Working Group"). The Working Group shall comprise the heads of the following executive agencies and offices, or their designees: (a) Department of Defense; (b) Department of Health and Human Services; (c) Department of Housing and Urban Development; (d) Department of Labor; (e) Department of Agriculture; (f) Department of Transportation; (g) Department of Justice; (h) Department of the Interior; (i) Department of Commerce; (j) Department of Energy; (k) Environmental Protection Agency; (l) Office of Management and Budget; (m) Office of Science and Technology Policy; (n) Office of the Deputy Assistant to the President for Environmental Policy; (o) Office of the Assistant to the President for Domestic Policy; (p) National Economic Council; (q) Council of Economic Advisers; and (r) such other Government officials as the President may designate. The Working Group shall report to the President through the Deputy Assistant to the President for Environmental Policy and the Assistant to the President for Domestic Policy.

(b) The Working Group shall:

(1) provide guidance to Federal agencies on criteria for identifying disproportionately high and adverse human health or environmental effects on minority populations and low-income populations;

(2) coordinate with, provide guidance to, and serve as a clearinghouse for, each Federal agency as it develops an environmental justice strategy as required by section 1-103 of this order, in order to ensure that the administration, interpretation and enforcement of programs, activities and policies are undertaken in a consistent manner;

(3) assist in coordinating research by, and stimulating cooperation among, the Environmental Protection Agency, the Department of Health and Human Services, the Department of Housing and Urban Development, and other agencies conducting research or other activities in accordance with section 3-3 of this order;

(4) assist in coordinating data collection, required by this order;

(5) examine existing data and studies on environmental justice;

(6) hold public meetings as required in section 5-502(d) of this order; and

(7) develop interagency model projects on environmental justice that evidence cooperation among Federal agencies.

1-103. *Development of Agency Strategies.*

(a) Except as provided in section 6-605 of this order, each Federal agency shall develop an agency-wide environmental justice strategy, as set forth in subsections (b)-(e) of this section that identifies and addresses disproportionately high and adverse human health or environmental effects of its programs, policies, and activities on minority populations and low-income populations. The environmental justice strategy shall list programs, policies, planning and public participation processes, enforcement, and/or rulemakings related to human health or the environment that should be revised to, at a minimum: (1) promote enforcement of all health and environmental statutes in areas with minority populations and low-income populations; (2) ensure greater public participation; (3) improve research and data collection relating to the health of and environment of minority populations and low-income populations; and (4) identify differential patterns of consumption of natural resources among minority populations and low-income populations. In addition, the environmental justice strategy shall include, where appropriate, a timetable for undertaking identified revisions and consideration of economic and social implications of the revisions.

(b) Within 4 months of the date of this order, each Federal agency shall identify an internal administrative process for developing its environmental justice strategy, and shall inform the Working Group of the process.

(c) Within 6 months of the date of this order, each Federal agency shall provide the Working Group with an outline of its proposed environmental justice strategy.

(d) Within 10 months of the date of this order, each Federal agency shall provide the Working Group with its proposed environmental justice strategy.

(e) By March 24, 1995, each Federal agency shall finalize its environmental justice strategy and provide a copy and written description of its strategy to the Working Group. From the date of this order through March 24, 1995, each Federal agency, as part of its environmental justice strategy, shall identify several specific projects that can be promptly undertaken to address particular concerns identified during the development of the proposed environmental justice strategy, and a schedule for implementing those projects.

(f) Within 24 months of the date of this order, each Federal agency shall report to the Working Group on its progress in implementing its agency-wide environmental justice strategy.

(g) Federal agencies shall provide additional periodic reports to the Working Group as requested by the Working Group.

1-104. *Reports to the President.* Within 14 months of the date of this order, the Working Group shall submit to the President, through the Office of the Deputy Assistant to the President for Environmental Policy and the Office of the Assistant to the President for Domestic Policy, a report that describes the implementation of this order, and includes the final environmental justice strategies described in section 1-103(e) of this order.

§2-2. Federal Agency Responsibilities for Federal Programs

Each Federal agency shall conduct its programs, policies, and activities that substantially affect human health or the environment, in a manner that ensures that such programs, policies, and activities do not have the effect of excluding persons (including populations) from participation in, denying persons (including populations) the benefits of, or subjecting persons (including populations) to discrimination under, such programs, policies, and activities, because of their race, color, or national origin.

§3-3. Research, Data Collection, and Analysis

3-301. *Human Health and Environmental Research and Analysis.*

(a) Environmental human health research, whenever practicable and appropriate, shall include diverse segments of the population in epidemiological and clinical studies, including segments at high risk from environmental hazards, such as minority populations, low-income populations and workers who may be exposed to substantial environmental hazards.

(b) Environmental human health analyses, whenever practicable and appropriate, shall identify multiple and cumulative exposures.

(c) Federal agencies shall provide minority populations and low-income populations the opportunity to comment on the development and design of research strategies undertaken pursuant to this order.

3-302. *Human Health and Environmental Data Collection and Analysis.* To the extent permitted by existing law, including the Privacy Act, as amended (5 U.S.C. section 552a):

(a) Each Federal agency, whenever practicable and appropriate, shall collect, maintain, and analyze information assessing and comparing environmental and human health risks borne by populations identified by race, national origin, or income. To the extent practical and appropriate, Federal agencies shall use this information to determine whether their programs, policies, and activities have disproportionately high and adverse human health or environmental effects on minority populations and low-income populations;

(b) In connection with the development and implementation of agency strategies in section 1-103 of this order, each Federal agency, whenever practicable and appropriate, shall collect, maintain and analyze information on the race, national origin, income level, and other readily accessible and appropriate information for areas surrounding facilities or sites expected to have a substantial environmental, human health, or economic effect on the surrounding populations, when such facilities or sites become the subject of a substantial Federal environmental administrative or judicial action. Such information shall be made available to the public, unless prohibited by law; and

(c) Each Federal agency, whenever practicable and appropriate, shall collect, maintain, and analyze information on the race, national origin, income level, and other readily accessible and appropriate information for areas surrounding Federal facilities that are: (1) subject to the reporting requirements under the Emergency Planning and Community Right-to-Know Act, 42 U.S.C. section 11001-11050 as mandated in Executive Order No. 12856; and (2) expected to have a substantial environmental, human health, or economic effect on surrounding populations. Such information shall be made available to the public, unless prohibited by law.

(d) In carrying out the responsibilities in this section, each Federal agency, whenever practicable and appropriate, shall share information and eliminate unnecessary duplication of efforts through the use of existing data systems and cooperative agreements among Federal agencies and with State, local, and tribal governments.

§4-4. Subsistence Consumption of Fish and Wildlife

4-401. *Consumption Patterns.* In order to assist in identifying the need for ensuring protection of populations with differential patterns of subsistence consumption of fish and wildlife, Federal agencies, whenever practicable and appropriate, shall collect, maintain, and analyze information on the consumption patterns of populations who principally rely on fish and/or wildlife for subsistence. Federal agencies shall communicate to the public the risks of those consumption patterns.

4-402. *Guidance.* Federal agencies, whenever practicable and appropriate, shall work in a coordinated manner to publish guidance reflecting the latest scientific information available concerning methods for evaluating the human health risks associated with the consumption of pollutant-bearing fish or wildlife. Agencies shall consider such guidance in developing their policies and rules.

§5-5. Public Participation and Access to Information

(a) The public may submit recommendations to Federal agencies relating to the incorporation of environmental justice principles into Federal agency programs or policies. Each Federal agency shall convey such recommendations to the Working Group.

(b) Each Federal agency may, whenever practicable and appropriate, translate crucial public documents, notices, and hearings relating to human health or the environment for limited English speaking populations.

(c) Each Federal agency shall work to ensure that public documents, notices, and hearings relating to human health or the environment are concise, understandable, and readily accessible to the public.

(d) The Working Group shall hold public meetings, as appropriate, for the purpose of fact-finding, receiving public comments, and conducting inquiries concerning environmental justice. The Working Group shall prepare for public review a summary of the comments and recommendations discussed at the public meetings.

§6-6. General Provisions

6-601. *Responsibility for Agency Implementation.* The head of each Federal agency shall be responsible for ensuring compliance with this order. Each Federal agency shall conduct internal reviews and take such other steps as may be necessary to monitor compliance with this order.

6-602. *Executive Order No. 12250.* This Executive order is intended to supplement but not supersede Executive Order No. 12250, which requires consistent and effective implementation of various laws prohibiting discriminatory practices in programs receiving Federal financial assistance. Nothing herein shall limit the effect or mandate of Executive Order No. 12250.

6-603. *Executive Order No. 12875.* This Executive order is not intended to limit the effect or mandate of Executive Order No. 12875.

6-604. *Scope.* For purposes of this order, Federal agency means any agency on the Working Group, and such other agencies as may be designated by the President, that conducts any Federal program or activity that substantially affects human health or the environment. Independent agencies are requested to comply with the provisions of this order.

6-605. *Petitions for Exemptions.* The head of a Federal agency may petition the President for an exemption from the requirements of this order on the grounds that all or some of the petitioning agency's programs or activities should not be subject to the requirements of this order.

6-606. *Native American Programs.* Each Federal agency responsibility set forth under this order shall apply equally to Native American programs. In addition, the Department of the Interior, in coordination with the Working Group, and, after consultation with tribal leaders, shall coordinate steps to be taken pursuant to this order that address Federally-recognized Indian Tribes.

6-607. *Costs.* Unless otherwise provided by law, Federal agencies shall assume the financial costs of complying with this order.

6-608. *General.* Federal agencies shall implement this order consistent with, and to the extent permitted by, existing law.

6-609. *Judicial Review.* This order is intended only to improve the internal management of the executive branch and is not intended to, nor does it create any right, benefit, or trust responsibility, substantive or procedural, enforceable at law or equity by a party against the United States, its agencies, its officers, or any person. This order shall not be construed to create any right to judicial review involving the compliance or noncompliance of the United States, its agencies, its officers, or any other person with this order.

WILLIAM CLINTON
THE WHITE HOUSE
February 11, 1994

Protecting Public Health and the Environment and Restoring Science to Tackle the Climate Crisis, Executive Order 13,990

86 Fed. Reg. 7037 (2021)

By the authority vested in me as President by the Constitution and the laws of the United States of America, it is hereby ordered as follows:

Section 1. *Policy.* Our Nation has an abiding commitment to empower our workers and communities; promote and protect our public health and the environment; and conserve our national treasures and monuments, places that secure our national memory. Where the Federal Government has failed to meet that commitment in the past, it must advance environmental justice. In carrying out this charge, the Federal Government must be guided by the best science and be protected by processes that ensure the integrity of Federal decision-making. It is, therefore, the policy of my Administration to listen to the science; to improve public health and protect our environment; to ensure access to clean air and water; to limit exposure to dangerous chemicals and pesticides; to hold polluters accountable, including those who disproportionately harm communities of color and low-income communities; to reduce greenhouse gas emissions; to bolster resilience to the impacts of climate change; to restore and expand our national treasures and monuments; and to prioritize both environmental justice and the creation of the well-paying union jobs necessary to deliver on these goals.

To that end, this order directs all executive departments and agencies (agencies) to immediately review and, as appropriate and consistent with applicable law, take action to address the promulgation of Federal regulations and other actions during the last 4 years that conflict with these important national objectives, and to immediately commence work to confront the climate crisis.

Sec. 2. *Immediate Review of Agency Actions Taken Between January 20, 2017, and January 20, 2021.* (a) The heads of all agencies shall immediately review all existing regulations, orders, guidance documents, policies, and any other similar agency actions (agency actions) promulgated, issued, or adopted between January 20, 2017, and January 20, 2021, that are or may be inconsistent with, or present obstacles to, the policy set forth in section 1 of this order. For any such actions identified by the agencies, the heads of agencies shall, as appropriate and consistent with applicable law, consider suspending, revising, or rescinding the agency actions. In addition, for the agency actions in the 4 categories set forth in subsections (i) through (iv) of this section, the head of the relevant agency, as appropriate and consistent with applicable law, shall consider publishing for notice and comment a proposed rule suspending, revising, or rescinding the agency action within the time frame specified.

(i) Reducing Methane Emissions in the Oil and Gas Sector: "Oil and Natural Gas Sector: Emission Standards for New, Reconstructed, and Modified Sources Reconsideration," 85 FR 57398 (September 15, 2020), by September 2021.

(ii) Establishing Ambitious, Job-Creating Fuel Economy Standards: "The Safer Affordable Fuel-Efficient (SAFE) Vehicles Rule Part One: One National Program," 84 FR 51310 (September 27, 2019), by April 2021; and "The Safer Affordable Fuel-Efficient (SAFE) Vehicles Rule for Model Years 2021-2026 Passenger Cars and Light Trucks," 85 FR 24174 (April 30, 2020), by July 2021. In considering whether to propose suspending, revising, or rescinding the latter rule, the agency should consider the views of representatives from labor unions, States, and industry.

(iii) Job-Creating Appliance- and Building-Efficiency Standards: "Energy Conservation Program for Appliance Standards: Procedures for Use in New or Revised Energy Conservation Standards and Test Procedures for Consumer Products and Commercial/Industrial Equipment," 85 FR 8626(February 14, 2020), with major revisions proposed by March 2021 and any remaining revisions proposed by June 2021; "Energy Conservation Program for Appliance Standards: Procedures for Evaluating Statutory Factors for Use in New or Revised Energy Conservation Standards," 85 FR 50937(August 19, 2020), with major revisions proposed by March 2021 and any remaining revisions proposed by June 2021; "Final Determination Regarding Energy Efficiency Improvements in the 2018 International Energy Conservation Code (IECC)," 84 FR 67435 (December 10, 2019), by May 2021; "Final Determination Regarding Energy Efficiency Improvements in ANSI/ASHRAE/IES Standard 90.1-2016: Energy Standard for Buildings, Except Low-Rise Residential Buildings," 83 FR 8463 (February 27, 2018), by May 2021.

(iv) Protecting Our Air from Harmful Pollution: "National Emission Standards for Hazardous Air Pollutants: Coal- and Oil-Fired Electric Utility Steam Generating Units—Reconsideration of Supplemental Finding and Residual Risk and Technology Review," 85 FR 31286 (May 22, 2020), by August 2021; "Increasing Consistency and Transparency in Considering Benefits and Costs in the Clean Air Act Rulemaking Process," 85 FR 84130 (December 23, 2020), as soon as possible; "Strengthening Transparency in Pivotal Science Underlying Significant Regulatory Actions and Influential Scientific Information," 86 FR 469 (January 6, 2021), as soon as possible.

(b) Within 30 days of the date of this order, heads of agencies shall submit to the Director of the Office of Management and Budget (OMB) a preliminary list of any actions being considered pursuant to section (2)(a) of this order that would be completed by December 31, 2021, and that would be subject to OMB review. Within 90 days of the date of this order, heads of agencies shall submit to the Director of OMB an updated list of any actions being considered pursuant to section (2)(a) of this order that would be completed by December 31, 2025, and that would be subject to OMB review. At the time of submission to the Director of OMB, heads of agencies shall also send each list to the National Climate Advisor. In addition, and at the same time, heads of agencies shall send to the National Climate Advisor a list of additional actions being considered pursuant to section (2)(a) of this order that would not be subject to OMB review.

(c) Heads of agencies shall, as appropriate and consistent with applicable law, consider whether to take any additional agency actions to fully enforce the policy set forth in section 1 of this order. With respect to the Administrator of the Environmental Protection Agency, the following specific actions should be considered:

(i) proposing new regulations to establish comprehensive standards of performance and emission guidelines for methane and volatile organic compound emissions from existing operations in the oil and gas sector, including the exploration and production, transmission, processing, and storage segments, by September 2021; and

(ii) proposing a Federal Implementation Plan in accordance with the Environmental Protection Agency's "Findings of Failure To Submit State Implementation Plan Revisions in Response to the 2016 Oil and Natural Gas Industry Control Techniques Guidelines for the 2008 Ozone National Ambient Air Quality Standards (NAAQS) and for States in the Ozone Transport Region," 85 FR 72963 (November 16, 2020), for California, Connecticut, New York, Pennsylvania, and Texas by January 2022.

(d) The Attorney General may, as appropriate and consistent with applicable law, provide notice of this order and any actions taken pursuant to section 2(a) of this order to any court with jurisdiction over pending litigation related to those agency actions identified pursuant to section (2)(a) of this order, and may, in his discretion, request that the court stay or otherwise dispose of litigation, or seek other appropriate relief consistent with this order, until the completion of the processes described in this order.

(e) In carrying out the actions directed in this section, heads of agencies shall seek input from the public and stakeholders, including State local, Tribal, and territorial officials, scientists, labor unions, environmental advocates, and environmental justice organizations.

Sec. 3. *Restoring National Monuments.* (a) The Secretary of the Interior, as appropriate and consistent with applicable law, including the Antiquities Act, 54 U.S.C. 320301 *et seq.,* shall, in consultation with the Attorney General, the Secretaries of Agriculture and Commerce, the Chair of the Council on Environmental Quality, and Tribal governments, conduct a review of the monument boundaries and conditions that were established by Proclamation 9681 of December 4, 2017 (Modifying the Bears Ears National Monument); Proclamation 9682 of December 4, 2017 (Modifying the Grand Staircase-Escalante National Monument); and Proclamation 10049 of June 5, 2020 (Modifying the Northeast Canyons and Seamounts Marine National Monument), to determine whether restoration of the monument boundaries and conditions that existed as of January 20, 2017, would be appropriate.

(b) Within 60 days of the date of this order, the Secretary of the Interior shall submit a report to the President summarizing the findings of the review conducted pursuant to subsection (a), which shall include recommendations for such Presidential actions or other actions consistent with law as the Secretary may consider appropriate to carry out the policy set forth in section 1 of this order.

(c) The Attorney General may, as appropriate and consistent with applicable law, provide notice of this order to any court with jurisdiction over pending litigation related to the Grand Staircase-Escalante, Bears Ears, and Northeast Canyons and Seamounts Marine National Monuments, and may, in his discretion, request that the court stay the litigation or otherwise delay further litigation, or seek other appropriate relief consistent with this order, pending the completion of the actions described in subsection (a) of this section.

Sec. 4. *Arctic Refuge.* (a) In light of the alleged legal deficiencies underlying the program, including the inadequacy of the environmental review required by the National Environmental Policy Act, the Secretary of the Interior shall, as appropriate and consistent with applicable law, place a temporary moratorium on all activities of the Federal Government relating to the implementation of the Coastal Plain Oil and Gas Leasing Program, as established by the Record of Decision signed August 17, 2020, in the Arctic National Wildlife Refuge. The Secretary shall review the program and, as appropriate and consistent with applicable law, conduct a new, comprehensive analysis of the potential environmental impacts of the oil and gas program.

(b) In Executive Order 13754 of December 9, 2016 (Northern Bering Sea Climate Resilience), and in the Presidential Memorandum of December 20, 2016 (Withdrawal of Certain Portions of the United States Arctic Outer Continental Shelf From Mineral Leasing), President Obama withdrew areas in Arctic waters and the Bering Sea from oil and gas drilling and established the Northern Bering Sea Climate Resilience Area. Subsequently, the order was revoked and the memorandum was amended in Executive Order 13795 of April 28, 2017 (Implementing an America-First Offshore Energy Strategy). Pursuant to section 12(a) of the Outer Continental Shelf Lands Act, 43 U.S.C. 1341(a), Executive Order 13754 and the Presidential Memorandum of December 20, 2016, are hereby reinstated in their original form, thereby restoring the original withdrawal of certain offshore areas in Arctic waters and the Bering Sea from oil and gas drilling.

(c) The Attorney General may, as appropriate and consistent with applicable law, provide notice of this order to any court with jurisdiction over pending litigation related to the Coastal Plain Oil and Gas Leasing Program in the Arctic National Wildlife Refuge and other related programs, and may, in his discretion, request that the court stay the litigation or otherwise delay further litigation, or seek other appropriate relief consistent with this order, pending the completion of the actions described in subsection (a) of this section.

Sec. 5. *Accounting for the Benefits of Reducing Climate Pollution.* (a) It is essential that agencies capture the full costs of greenhouse gas emissions as accurately as possible, including by taking global damages into account. Doing so facilitates sound decision-making, recognizes the breadth of climate impacts, and supports the international leadership of the United States on climate issues. The "social cost of carbon" (SCC), "social cost of nitrous oxide" (SCN), and "social cost of methane" (SCM) are estimates of the monetized damages associated with incremental increases in greenhouse gas emissions. They are intended to include changes in net agricultural productivity, human health, property damage from increased flood risk, and the value of ecosystem services. An accurate social cost is essential for agencies to accurately determine the social benefits of reducing greenhouse gas emissions when conducting cost-benefit analyses of regulatory and other actions.

(b) There is hereby established an Interagency Working Group on the Social Cost of Greenhouse Gases (the "Working Group"). The Chair of the Council of Economic Advisers, Director of OMB,

and Director of the Office of Science and Technology Policy shall serve as Co-Chairs of the Working Group.

(i) Membership. The Working Group shall also include the following other officers, or their designees: the Secretary of the Treasury; the Secretary of the Interior; the Secretary of Agriculture; the Secretary of Commerce; the Secretary of Health and Human Services; the Secretary of Transportation; the Secretary of Energy; the Chair of the Council on Environmental Quality; the Administrator of the Environmental Protection Agency; the Assistant to the President and National Climate Advisor; and the Assistant to the President for Economic Policy and Director of the National Economic Council.

(ii) Mission and Work. The Working Group shall, as appropriate and consistent with applicable law:

(A) publish an interim SCC, SCN, and SCM within 30 days of the date of this order, which agencies shall use when monetizing the value of changes in greenhouse gas emissions resulting from regulations and other relevant agency actions until final values are published;

(B) publish a final SCC, SCN, and SCM by no later than January 2022;

(C) provide recommendations to the President, by no later than September 1, 2021, regarding areas of decision-making, budgeting, and procurement by the Federal Government where the SCC, SCN, and SCM should be applied;

(D) provide recommendations, by no later than June 1, 2022, regarding a process for reviewing, and, as appropriate, updating, the SCC, SCN, and SCM to ensure that these costs are based on the best available economics and science; and

(E) provide recommendations, to be published with the final SCC, SCN, and SCM under subparagraph (A) if feasible, and in any event by no later than June 1, 2022, to revise methodologies for calculating the SCC, SCN, and SCM, to the extent that current methodologies do not adequately take account of climate risk, environmental justice, and intergenerational equity.

(iii) Methodology. In carrying out its activities, the Working Group shall consider the recommendations of the National Academies of Science, Engineering, and Medicine as reported in Valuing Climate Damages: Updating Estimation of the Social Cost of Carbon Dioxide (2017) and other pertinent scientific literature; solicit public comment; engage with the public and stakeholders; seek the advice of ethics experts; and ensure that the SCC, SCN, and SCM reflect the interests of future generations in avoiding threats posed by climate change.

Sec. 6. *Revoking the March 2019 Permit for the Keystone XL Pipeline.* (a) On March 29, 2019, the

President granted to TransCanada Keystone Pipeline, L.P. a Presidential permit (the "Permit") to construct, connect, operate, and maintain pipeline facilities at the international border of the United States and Canada (the "Keystone XL pipeline"), subject to express conditions and potential revocation in the President's sole discretion. The Permit is hereby revoked in accordance with Article 1(1) of the Permit.

(b) In 2015, following an exhaustive review, the Department of State and the President determined that approving the proposed Keystone XL pipeline would not serve the U.S. national interest. That analysis, in addition to concluding that the significance of the proposed pipeline for our energy security and economy is limited, stressed that the United States must prioritize the development of a clean energy economy, which will in turn create good jobs. The analysis further concluded that approval of the proposed pipeline would undermine U.S. climate leadership by undercutting the credibility and influence of the United States in urging other countries to take ambitious climate action.

(c) Climate change has had a growing effect on the U.S. economy, with climate-related costs increasing over the last 4 years. Extreme weather events and other climate-related effects have harmed the health, safety, and security of the American people and have increased the urgency for combatting climate change and accelerating the transition toward a clean energy economy. The world must be put on a sustainable climate pathway to protect Americans and the domestic economy from harmful climate impacts, and to create well-paying union jobs as part of the climate solution.

(d) The Keystone XL pipeline disserves the U.S. national interest. The United States and the world face a climate crisis. That crisis must be met with action on a scale and at a speed commensurate with the need to avoid setting the world on a dangerous, potentially catastrophic, climate trajectory. At home, we will combat the crisis with an ambitious plan to build back better, designed to both reduce harmful emissions and create good clean-energy jobs. Our domestic efforts must go hand in hand with U.S. diplomatic engagement. Because most greenhouse gas emissions originate beyond our borders, such engagement is more necessary and urgent than ever. The United States must be in a position to exercise vigorous climate leadership in order to achieve a significant increase in global climate action and put the world on a sustainable climate pathway. Leaving the Keystone XL pipeline permit in place would not be consistent with my Administration's economic and climate imperatives.

Sec. 7. *Other Revocations.* (a) Executive Order 13766 of January 24, 2017 (Expediting Environmental Reviews and Approvals For High Priority Infrastructure Projects), Executive Order 13778 of February 28, 2017 (Restoring the Rule of Law, Federalism, and Economic Growth by Reviewing the "Waters of the United States" Rule), Executive Order 13783 of March 28, 2017 (Promoting Energy Independence and Economic Growth), Executive Order 13792 of April 26, 2017 (Review of Designations Under the Antiquities Act), Executive Order 13795 of April 28, 2017 (Implementing an America-First Offshore Energy Strategy), Executive Order 13868 of April 10, 2019 (Promoting Energy Infrastructure and Economic Growth), and Executive Order 13927 of June 4, 2020 (Accelerating the Nation's Economic Recovery from the COVID-19 Emergency by Expediting Infrastructure Investments and Other Activities), are hereby revoked. Executive Order 13834 of May 17, 2018 (Efficient Federal Operations), is hereby revoked except for sections 6, 7, and 11.

(b) Executive Order 13807 of August 15, 2017 (Establishing Discipline and Accountability in the Environmental Review and Permitting Process for Infrastructure Projects), is hereby revoked. The Director of OMB and the Chair of the Council on Environmental Quality shall jointly consider whether to recommend that a replacement order be issued.

(c) Executive Order 13920 of May 1, 2020 (Securing the United States Bulk-Power System), is hereby suspended for 90 days. The Secretary of Energy and the Director of OMB shall jointly consider whether to recommend that a replacement order be issued.

(d) The Presidential Memorandum of April 12, 2018 (Promoting Domestic Manufacturing and Job Creation Policies and Procedures Relating to Implementation of Air Quality Standards), the Presidential Memorandum of October 19, 2018 (Promoting the Reliable Supply and Delivery of Water in the West), and the Presidential Memorandum of February 19, 2020 (Developing and Delivering More Water Supplies in California), are hereby revoked.

(e) The Council on Environmental Quality shall rescind its draft guidance entitled, "Draft National Environmental Policy Act Guidance on Consideration of Greenhouse Gas Emissions," 84 FR 30097 (June 26, 2019). The Council, as appropriate and consistent with applicable law, shall review, revise, and update its final guidance entitled, "Final Guidance for Federal Departments and Agencies on Consideration of Greenhouse Gas Emissions and the Effects of Climate Change in National Environmental Policy Act Reviews," 81 FR 51866 (August 5, 2016).

(f) The Director of OMB and the heads of agencies shall promptly take steps to rescind any orders, rules, regulations, guidelines, or policies, or portions thereof, including, if necessary, by proposing such rescissions through notice-and-comment rulemaking, implementing or enforcing the Executive Orders, Presidential Memoranda, and draft guidance identified in this section, as appropriate and consistent with applicable law.

Sec. 8. *General Provisions.* (a) Nothing in this order shall be construed to impair or otherwise affect:

(i) the authority granted by law to an executive department or agency, or the head thereof; or

(ii) the functions of the Director of the Office of Management and Budget relating to budgetary, administrative, or legislative proposals.

(b) This order shall be implemented in a manner consistent with applicable law and subject to the availability of appropriations.

(c) This order is not intended to, and does not, create any right or benefit, substantive or procedural, enforceable at law or in equity by any party against the United States, its departments, agencies, or entities, its officers, employees, or agents, or any other person.

JOSEPH R. BIDEN, JR.
THE WHITE HOUSE
January 20, 2021

Tackling the Climate Crisis at Home and Abroad, Executive Order 14,008

86 Fed. Reg. 7619 (2021)

The United States and the world face a profound climate crisis. We have a narrow moment to pursue action at home and abroad in order to avoid the most catastrophic impacts of that crisis and to seize the opportunity that tackling climate change presents. Domestic action must go hand in hand with United States international leadership, aimed at significantly enhancing global action. Together, we must listen to science and meet the moment.

By the authority vested in me as President by the Constitution and the laws of the United States of America, it is hereby ordered as follows:

PART I—PUTTING THE CLIMATE CRISIS AT THE CENTER OF UNITED STATES FOREIGN POLICY AND NATIONAL SECURITY

Section 101. *Policy*. United States international engagement to address climate change—which has become a climate crisis—is more necessary and urgent than ever. The scientific community has made clear that the scale and speed of necessary action is greater than previously believed. There is little time left to avoid setting the world on a dangerous, potentially catastrophic, climate trajectory. Responding to the climate crisis will require both significant short-term global reductions in greenhouse gas emissions and net-zero global emissions by mid-century or before.

It is the policy of my Administration that climate considerations shall be an essential element of United States foreign policy and national security. The United States will work with other countries and partners, both bilaterally and multilaterally, to put the world on a sustainable climate pathway. The United States will also move quickly to build resilience, both at home and abroad, against the impacts of climate change that are already manifest and will continue to intensify according to current trajectories.

Sec. 102. *Purpose*. This order builds on and reaffirms actions my Administration has already taken to place the climate crisis at the forefront of this Nation's foreign policy and national security planning, including submitting the United States instrument of acceptance to rejoin the Paris Agreement. In implementing—and building upon—the Paris Agreement's three overarching objectives (a safe global temperature, increased climate resilience, and financial flows aligned with a pathway toward low greenhouse gas emissions and climate-resilient development), the United States will exercise its leadership to promote a significant increase in global climate ambition to meet the climate challenge. In this regard:

(a) I will host an early Leaders' Climate Summit aimed at raising climate ambition and making a positive contribution to the 26th United Nations Climate Change Conference of the Parties (COP26) and beyond.

(b) The United States will reconvene the Major Economies Forum on Energy and Climate, beginning with the Leaders' Climate Summit. In cooperation with the members of that Forum, as well as with other partners as appropriate, the United States will pursue green recovery efforts, initiatives to advance the clean energy transition, sectoral decarbonization, and alignment of financial flows with the objectives of the Paris Agreement, including with respect to coal financing, nature-based solutions, and solutions to other climate-related challenges.

(c) I have created a new Presidentially appointed position, the Special Presidential Envoy for Climate, to elevate the issue of climate change and underscore the commitment my Administration will make toward addressing it.

(d) Recognizing that climate change affects a wide range of subjects, it will be a United States priority to press for enhanced climate ambition and integration of climate considerations across a wide range of international fora, including the Group of Seven (G7), the Group of Twenty (G20), and fora that address clean energy, aviation, shipping, the Arctic, the ocean, sustainable development, migration, and other relevant topics. The Special Presidential Envoy for Climate and others, as appropriate, are encouraged to promote innovative approaches, including international multistakeholder initiatives. In addition, my Administration will work in partnership with States, localities, Tribes, territories, and other United States stakeholders to advance United States climate diplomacy.

(e) The United States will immediately begin the process of developing its nationally determined contribution under the Paris Agreement. The process will include analysis and input from relevant executive departments and agencies (agencies), as well as appropriate outreach to domestic stakeholders. The United States will aim to submit its nationally determined contribution in advance of the Leaders' Climate Summit.

(f) The United States will also immediately begin to develop a climate finance plan, making strategic use of multilateral and bilateral channels and institutions, to assist developing countries in implementing ambitious emissions reduction measures, protecting critical ecosystems, building resilience against the impacts of climate change, and promoting the flow of capital toward climate-aligned investments and away from high-carbon investments. The Secretary of State and the Secretary of the Treasury, in coordination with the Special Presidential Envoy for Climate, shall lead a process to develop this plan, with the participation of the Administrator of the United States Agency for International Development (USAID), the Chief Executive Officer of the United States International Development Finance Corporation (DFC), the Chief Executive Officer of the Millennium Challenge Corporation, the Director of the United States Trade and Development Agency, the Director of the Office of Management and Budget, and the head of any other agency providing foreign assistance and development financing, as appropriate. The Secretary of State and the Secretary of the Treasury shall submit the plan to the President, through the Assistant to the President for National Security Affairs and the Assistant to the President for Economic Policy, within 90 days of the date of this order.

(g) The Secretary of the Treasury shall:

(i) ensure that the United States is present and engaged in relevant international fora and institutions that are working on the management of climate-related financial risks;

(ii) develop a strategy for how the voice and vote of the United States can be used in international financial institutions, including the World Bank Group and the International Monetary Fund, to promote financing programs, economic stimulus packages, and debt relief initiatives that are aligned with and support the goals of the Paris Agreement; and

(iii) develop, in collaboration with the Secretary of State, the Administrator of USAID, and the Chief Executive Officer of the DFC, a plan for promoting the protection of the Amazon rainforest and other critical ecosystems that serve as global carbon sinks, including through market-based mechanisms.

(h) The Secretary of State, the Secretary of the Treasury, and the Secretary of Energy shall work together and with the Export-Import Bank of the United States, the Chief Executive Officer of the DFC, and the heads of other agencies and partners, as appropriate, to identify steps through which the United States can promote ending international financing of carbon-intensive fossil fuel-based energy while simultaneously advancing sustainable development and a green recovery, in consultation with the Assistant to the President for National Security Affairs.

(i) The Secretary of Energy, in cooperation with the Secretary of State and the heads of other agencies, as appropriate, shall identify steps through which the United States can intensify international collaborations to drive innovation and deployment of clean energy technologies, which are critical for climate protection.

(j) The Secretary of State shall prepare, within 60 days of the date of this order, a transmittal package seeking the Senate's advice and consent to ratification of the Kigali Amendment to the Montreal Protocol on Substances that Deplete the Ozone Layer, regarding the phasedown of the production and consumption of hydrofluorocarbons.

Sec. 103. *Prioritizing Climate in Foreign Policy and National Security.* To ensure that climate change considerations are central to United States foreign policy and national security:

(a) Agencies that engage in extensive international work shall develop, in coordination with the Special Presidential Envoy for Climate, and submit to the President, through the Assistant to the President for National Security Affairs, within 90 days of the date of this order, strategies and implementation plans for integrating climate considerations into their international work, as appropriate and consistent with applicable law. These strategies and plans should include an assessment of:

(i) climate impacts relevant to broad agency strategies in particular countries or regions;

(ii) climate impacts on their agency-managed infrastructure abroad (e.g., embassies, military installations), without prejudice to existing requirements regarding assessment of such infrastructure;

(iii) how the agency intends to manage such impacts or incorporate risk mitigation into its installation master plans; and

(iv) how the agency's international work, including partner engagement, can contribute to addressing the climate crisis.

(b) The Director of National Intelligence shall prepare, within 120 days of the date of this order, a National Intelligence Estimate on the national and economic security impacts of climate change.

(c) The Secretary of Defense, in coordination with the Secretary of Commerce, through the Administrator of the National Oceanic and Atmospheric Administration, the Chair of the Council on Environmental Quality, the Administrator of the Environmental Protection Agency, the Director of National Intelligence, the Director of the Office of Science and Technology Policy, the Administrator of the National Aeronautics and Space Administration, and the heads of other agencies as appropriate, shall develop and submit to the President, within 120 days of the date of this order, an analysis of the security implications of climate change (Climate Risk Analysis) that can be incorporated into modeling, simulation, war-gaming, and other analyses.

(d) The Secretary of Defense and the Chairman of the Joint Chiefs of Staff shall consider the security implications of climate change, including any relevant information from the Climate Risk Analysis described in subsection (c) of this section, in developing the National Defense Strategy, Defense Planning Guidance, Chairman's Risk Assessment, and other relevant strategy, planning, and programming documents and processes. Starting in January 2022, the Secretary of Defense and the Chairman of the Joint Chiefs of Staff shall provide an annual update, through the National Security Council, on the progress made in incorporating the security implications of climate change into these documents and processes.

(e) The Secretary of Homeland Security shall consider the implications of climate change in the Arctic, along our Nation's borders, and to National Critical Functions, including any relevant information from the Climate Risk Analysis described in subsection (c) of this section, in developing relevant strategy, planning, and programming documents and processes. Starting in January 2022, the Secretary of Homeland Security shall provide an annual update, through the National Security Council, on the progress made in incorporating the homeland security implications of climate change into these documents and processes.

Sec. 104. *Reinstatement*. The Presidential Memorandum of September 21, 2016 (Climate Change and National Security), is hereby reinstated.

PART II—TAKING A GOVERNMENT-WIDE APPROACH TO THE CLIMATE CRISIS

Sec. 201. *Policy*. Even as our Nation emerges from profound public health and economic crises borne of a pandemic, we face a climate crisis that threatens our people and communities, public health and economy, and, starkly, our ability to live on planet Earth. Despite the peril that is already evident, there is promise in the solutions—opportunities to create well-paying union jobs to build a modern and sustainable infrastructure, deliver an equitable, clean energy future, and put the United States on a path to achieve net-zero emissions, economy-wide, by no later than 2050.

We must listen to science—and act. We must strengthen our clean air and water protections. We must hold polluters accountable for their actions. We must deliver environmental justice in communities all across America. The Federal Government must drive assessment, disclosure, and mitigation of climate pollution and climate-related risks in every sector of our economy, marshaling the creativity, courage, and capital necessary to make our Nation resilient in the face of this threat. Together, we must combat the climate crisis with bold, progressive action that combines the full capacity of the Federal Government with efforts from every corner of our Nation, every level of government, and every sector of our economy.

It is the policy of my Administration to organize and deploy the full capacity of its agencies to combat the climate crisis to implement a Government-wide approach that reduces climate pollution in every sector of the economy; increases resilience to the impacts of climate change; protects public health; conserves our lands, waters, and biodiversity; delivers environmental justice; and spurs well-paying union jobs and economic growth, especially through innovation, commercialization, and deployment of clean energy technologies and infrastructure. Successfully meeting these challenges will require the Federal Government to pursue such a coordinated approach from planning to implementation, coupled with substantive engagement by stakeholders, including State, local, and Tribal governments.

Sec. 202. *White House Office of Domestic Climate Policy*. There is hereby established the White House Office of Domestic Climate Policy (Climate Policy Office) within the Executive Office of the President, which shall coordinate the policy-making process with respect to domestic climate-policy issues; coordinate domestic climate-policy advice to the President; ensure that domestic climate-policy decisions and programs are consistent with the President's stated goals and that those goals are being effectively pursued; and monitor implementation of the President's domestic climate-policy agenda. The Climate Policy Office shall have a staff headed by the Assistant to the President and National Climate Advisor (National Climate Advisor) and shall include the Deputy Assistant to the President and Deputy National Climate Advisor. The Climate Policy Office shall have such staff and other assistance as may be necessary to carry out the provisions of this order, subject to the availability of appropriations, and may work with established or ad hoc committees or interagency groups. All agencies shall cooperate with the Climate Policy Office and provide such information, support, and assistance to the Climate Policy Office as it may request, as appropriate and consistent with applicable law.

Sec. 203. *National Climate Task Force*. There is hereby established a National Climate Task Force (Task Force). The Task Force shall be chaired by the National Climate Advisor.

(a) Membership. The Task Force shall consist of the following additional members:
    (i) the Secretary of the Treasury;
    (ii) the Secretary of Defense;
    (iii) the Attorney General;
    (iv) the Secretary of the Interior;

(v) the Secretary of Agriculture;

(vi) the Secretary of Commerce;

(vii) the Secretary of Labor;

(viii) the Secretary of Health and Human Services;

(ix) the Secretary of Housing and Urban Development;

(x) the Secretary of Transportation;

(xi) the Secretary of Energy;

(xii) the Secretary of Homeland Security;

(xiii) the Administrator of General Services;

(xiv) the Chair of the Council on Environmental Quality;

(xv) the Administrator of the Environmental Protection Agency;

(xvi) the Director of the Office of Management and Budget;

(xvii) the Director of the Office of Science and Technology Policy;

(xviii) the Assistant to the President for Domestic Policy;

(xix) the Assistant to the President for National Security Affairs;

(xx) the Assistant to the President for Homeland Security and Counterterrorism; and

(xxi) the Assistant to the President for Economic Policy.

(b) Mission and Work. The Task Force shall facilitate the organization and deployment of a Government-wide approach to combat the climate crisis. This Task Force shall facilitate planning and implementation of key Federal actions to reduce climate pollution; increase resilience to the impacts of climate change; protect public health; conserve our lands, waters, oceans, and biodiversity; deliver environmental justice; and spur well-paying union jobs and economic growth. As necessary and appropriate, members of the Task Force will engage on these matters with State, local, Tribal, and territorial governments; workers and communities; and leaders across the various sectors of our economy.

(c) Prioritizing Actions. To the extent permitted by law, Task Force members shall prioritize action on climate change in their policy-making and budget processes, in their contracting and procurement, and in their engagement with State, local, Tribal, and territorial governments; workers and communities; and leaders across all the sectors of our economy.

USE OF THE FEDERAL GOVERNMENT'S BUYING POWER AND REAL PROPERTY AND ASSET MANAGEMENT

Sec. 204. *Policy*. It is the policy of my Administration to lead the Nation's effort to combat the climate crisis by example—specifically, by aligning the management of Federal procurement and real property, public lands and waters, and financial programs to support robust climate action. By providing an immediate, clear, and stable source of product demand, increased transparency and data, and robust standards for the market, my Administration will help to catalyze private sector investment into, and accelerate the advancement of America's industrial capacity to supply, domestic clean energy, buildings, vehicles, and other necessary products and materials.

Sec. 205. *Federal Clean Electricity and Vehicle Procurement Strategy*. (a) The Chair of the Council on Environmental Quality, the Administrator of General Services, and the Director of the Office and Management and Budget, in coordination with the Secretary of Commerce, the Secretary of Labor, the Secretary of Energy, and the heads of other relevant agencies, shall assist the National Climate Advisor, through the Task Force established in section 203 of this order, in developing a comprehensive plan to create good jobs and stimulate clean energy industries by revitalizing the Federal Government's sustainability efforts.

(b) The plan shall aim to use, as appropriate and consistent with applicable law, all available procurement authorities to achieve or facilitate:

(i) a carbon pollution-free electricity sector no later than 2035; and

(ii) clean and zero-emission vehicles for Federal, State, local, and Tribal government fleets, including vehicles of the United States Postal Service.

(c) If necessary, the plan shall recommend any additional legislation needed to accomplish these objectives.

(d) The plan shall also aim to ensure that the United States retains the union jobs integral to and involved in running and maintaining clean and zero-emission fleets, while spurring the creation of union jobs in the manufacture of those new vehicles. The plan shall be submitted to the Task Force within 90 days of the date of this order.

Sec. 206. *Procurement Standards*. Consistent with the Executive Order of January 25, 2021, entitled, "Ensuring the Future Is Made in All of America by All of America's Workers," agencies shall adhere to the requirements of the Made in America Laws in making clean energy, energy efficiency, and clean energy procurement decisions. Agencies shall, consistent with applicable law, apply and enforce the Davis-Bacon Act and prevailing wage and benefit requirements. The Secretary of Labor shall take steps to update prevailing wage requirements. The Chair of the Council on Environmental Quality shall consider additional administrative steps and guidance to assist the Federal Acquisition Regulatory Council in developing regulatory amendments to promote increased contractor attention on reduced carbon emission and Federal sustainability.

Sec. 207. *Renewable Energy on Public Lands and in Offshore Waters*. The Secretary of the Interior shall review siting and permitting processes on public lands and in offshore waters to identify to the Task Force steps that can be taken, consistent with applicable law, to increase renewable energy production on those lands and in those waters, with the goal of doubling offshore wind by 2030 while ensuring robust protection for our lands, waters, and biodiversity and creating good jobs. In conducting this review, the Secretary of the Interior shall consult, as appropriate, with the heads of relevant agencies, including the Secretary of Defense, the Secretary of Agriculture, the Secretary of Commerce, through the Administrator of the National Oceanic and Atmospheric Administration, the Secretary of Energy, the Chair of the Council on Environmental Quality, State and Tribal authorities, project developers, and other interested parties. The Secretary of the Interior shall engage with Tribal authorities regarding the development and management of renewable and conventional energy resources on Tribal lands.

Sec. 208. *Oil and Natural Gas Development on Public Lands and in Offshore Waters.* To the extent consistent with applicable law, the Secretary of the Interior shall pause new oil and natural gas leases on public lands or in offshore waters pending completion of a comprehensive review and reconsideration of Federal oil and gas permitting and leasing practices in light of the Secretary of the Interior's broad stewardship responsibilities over the public lands and in offshore waters, including potential climate and other impacts associated with oil and gas activities on public lands or in offshore waters. The Secretary of the Interior shall complete that review in consultation with the Secretary of Agriculture, the Secretary of Commerce, through the National Oceanic and Atmospheric Administration, and the Secretary of Energy. In conducting this analysis, and to the extent consistent with applicable law, the Secretary of the Interior shall consider whether to adjust royalties associated with coal, oil, and gas resources extracted from public lands and offshore waters, or take other appropriate action, to account for corresponding climate costs.

Sec. 209. *Fossil Fuel Subsidies.* The heads of agencies shall identify for the Director of the Office of Management and Budget and the National Climate Advisor any fossil fuel subsidies provided by their respective agencies, and then take steps to ensure that, to the extent consistent with applicable law, Federal funding is not directly subsidizing fossil fuels. The Director of the Office of Management and Budget shall seek, in coordination with the heads of agencies and the National Climate Advisor, to eliminate fossil fuel subsidies from the budget request for Fiscal Year 2022 and thereafter.

Sec. 210. *Clean Energy in Financial Management.* The heads of agencies shall identify opportunities for Federal funding to spur innovation, commercialization, and deployment of clean energy technologies

and infrastructure for the Director of the Office of Management and Budget and the National Climate Advisor, and then take steps to ensure that, to the extent consistent with applicable law, Federal funding is used to spur innovation, commercialization, and deployment of clean energy technologies and infrastructure. The Director of the Office of Management and Budget, in coordination with agency heads and the National Climate Advisor, shall seek to prioritize such investments in the President's budget request for Fiscal Year 2022 and thereafter.

Sec. 211. *Climate Action Plans and Data and Information Products to Improve Adaptation and Increase Resilience.* (a) The head of each agency shall submit a draft action plan to the Task Force and the Federal Chief Sustainability Officer within 120 days of the date of this order that describes steps the agency can take with regard to its facilities and operations to bolster adaptation and increase resilience to the impacts of climate change. Action plans should, among other things, describe the agency's climate vulnerabilities and describe the agency's plan to use the power of procurement to increase the energy and water efficiency of United States Government installations, buildings, and facilities and ensure they are climate-ready. Agencies shall consider the feasibility of using the purchasing power of the Federal Government to drive innovation, and shall seek to increase the Federal Government's resilience against supply chain disruptions. Such disruptions put the Nation's manufacturing sector at risk, as well as consumer access to critical goods and services. Agencies shall make their action plans public, and post them on the agency website, to the extent consistent with applicable law.

(b) Within 30 days of an agency's submission of an action plan, the Federal Chief Sustainability Officer, in coordination with the Director of the Office of Management and Budget, shall review the plan to assess its consistency with the policy set forth in section 204 of this order and the priorities issued by the Office of Management and Budget.

(c) After submitting an initial action plan, the head of each agency shall submit to the Task Force and Federal Chief Sustainability Officer progress reports annually on the status of implementation efforts. Agencies shall make progress reports public and post them on the agency website, to the extent consistent with applicable law. The heads of agencies shall assign their respective agency Chief Sustainability Officer the authority to perform duties relating to implementation of this order within the agency, to the extent consistent with applicable law.

(d) To assist agencies and State, local, Tribal, and territorial governments, communities, and businesses in preparing for and adapting to the impacts of climate change, the Secretary of Commerce, through the Administrator of the National Oceanic and Atmospheric Administration, the Secretary of Homeland Security, through the Administrator of the Federal Emergency Management Agency, and the Director of the Office of Science and Technology Policy, in coordination with the heads of other agencies, as appropriate, shall provide to the Task Force a report on ways to expand and improve climate forecast capabilities and information products for the public. In addition, the Secretary of the Interior and the Deputy Director for Management of the Office of Management and Budget, in their capacities as the Chair and Vice-Chair of the Federal Geographic Data Committee, shall assess and provide to the Task Force a report on the potential development of a consolidated Federal geographic mapping service that can facilitate public access to climate-related information that will assist Federal, State, local, and Tribal governments in climate planning and resilience activities.

EMPOWERING WORKERS THROUGH REBUILDING OUR INFRASTRUCTURE FOR A SUSTAINABLE ECONOMY

Sec. 212. *Policy.* This Nation needs millions of construction, manufacturing, engineering, and skilled-trades workers to build a new American infrastructure and clean energy economy. These jobs will create opportunities for young people and for older workers shifting to new professions, and for people from all backgrounds and communities. Such jobs will bring opportunity to communities too often left behind—places that have suffered as a result of economic shifts and places that have suffered the most from persistent pollution, including low-income rural and urban communities, communities of color, and Native communities.

Sec. 213. *Sustainable Infrastructure.* (a) The Chair of the Council on Environmental Quality and the Director of the Office of Management and Budget shall take steps, consistent with applicable law, to ensure that Federal infrastructure investment reduces climate pollution, and to require that Federal permitting decisions consider the effects of greenhouse gas emissions and climate change. In addition, they shall review, and report to the National Climate Advisor on, siting and permitting processes, including those in progress under the auspices of the Federal Permitting Improvement Steering Council, and identify steps that can be taken, consistent with applicable law, to accelerate the deployment of clean energy and transmission projects in an environmentally stable manner.

(b) Agency heads conducting infrastructure reviews shall, as appropriate, consult from an early stage with State, local, and Tribal officials involved in permitting or authorizing proposed infrastructure projects to develop efficient timelines for decision-making that are appropriate given the complexities of proposed projects.

EMPOWERING WORKERS BY ADVANCING CONSERVATION, AGRICULTURE, AND REFORESTATION

Sec. 214. *Policy.* It is the policy of my Administration to put a new generation of Americans to work conserving our public lands and waters. The Federal Government must protect America's natural treasures, increase reforestation, improve access to recreation, and increase resilience to wildfires and storms, while creating well-paying union jobs for more Americans, including more opportunities for women and people of color in occupations where they are underrepresented. America's farmers, ranchers, and forest landowners have an important role to play in combating the climate crisis and reducing greenhouse gas emissions, by sequestering carbon in soils, grasses, trees, and other vegetation and sourcing sustainable bioproducts and fuels. Coastal communities have an essential role to play in mitigating climate change and strengthening resilience by protecting and restoring coastal ecosystems, such as wetlands, seagrasses, coral and oyster reefs, and mangrove and kelp forests, to protect vulnerable coastlines, sequester carbon, and support biodiversity and fisheries.

Sec. 215. *Civilian Climate Corps.* In furtherance of the policy set forth in section 214 of this order, the Secretary of the Interior, in collaboration with the Secretary of Agriculture and the heads of other relevant agencies, shall submit a strategy to the Task Force within 90 days of the date of this order for creating a Civilian Climate Corps Initiative, within existing appropriations, to mobilize the next generation of conservation and resilience workers and maximize the creation of accessible training opportunities and good jobs. The initiative shall aim to conserve and restore public lands and waters, bolster community resilience, increase reforestation, increase carbon sequestration in the agricultural sector, protect biodiversity, improve access to recreation, and address the changing climate.

Sec. 216. *Conserving Our Nation's Lands and Waters.* (a) The Secretary of the Interior, in consultation with the Secretary of Agriculture, the Secretary of Commerce, the Chair of the Council on Environmental Quality, and the heads of other relevant agencies, shall submit a report to the Task Force within 90 days of the date of this order recommending steps that the United States should take, working with State, local, Tribal, and territorial governments, agricultural and forest landowners, fishermen, and other key stakeholders, to achieve the goal of conserving at least 30 percent of our lands and waters by 2030.

(i) The Secretary of the Interior, the Secretary of Agriculture, the Secretary of Commerce, through the Administrator of the National Oceanic and Atmospheric Administration, and the Chair of the Council on Environmental Quality shall, as appropriate, solicit input from State, local, Tribal, and territorial officials, agricultural and forest landowners, fishermen, and other key stakeholders in identifying strategies that will encourage broad participation in the goal of conserving 30 percent of our lands and waters by 2030.

(ii) The report shall propose guidelines for determining whether lands and waters qualify for conservation, and it also shall establish mechanisms to measure progress toward the 30-percent goal. The Secretary of the Interior shall subsequently submit annual reports to the Task Force to monitor progress.

(b) The Secretary of Agriculture shall:

(i) initiate efforts in the first 60 days from the date of this order to collect input from Tribes, farmers, ranchers, forest owners, conservation groups, firefighters, and other stakeholders on how to best use Department of Agriculture programs, funding and financing capacities, and other authorities, and how to encourage the voluntary adoption of climate-smart agricultural and forestry practices that decrease wildfire risk fueled by climate change and result in additional, measurable, and verifiable carbon reductions and sequestration and that source sustainable bioproducts and fuels; and

(ii) submit to the Task Force within 90 days of the date of this order a report making recommendations for an agricultural and forestry climate strategy.

(c) The Secretary of Commerce, through the Administrator of the National Oceanic and Atmospheric Administration, shall initiate efforts in the first 60 days from the date of this order to collect input from fishermen, regional ocean councils, fishery management councils, scientists, and other stakeholders on how to make fisheries and protected resources more resilient to climate change, including changes in management and conservation measures, and improvements in science, monitoring, and cooperative research.

EMPOWERING WORKERS THROUGH REVITALIZING ENERGY COMMUNITIES

Sec. 217. *Policy.* It is the policy of my Administration to improve air and water quality and to create well-paying union jobs and more opportunities for women and people of color in hard-hit communities, including rural communities, while reducing methane emissions, oil and brine leaks, and other environmental harms from tens of thousands of former mining and well sites. Mining and power plant workers drove the industrial revolution and the economic growth that followed, and have been essential to the growth of the United States. As the Nation shifts to a clean energy economy, Federal leadership is essential to foster economic revitalization of and investment in these communities, ensure the creation of good jobs that provide a choice to join a union, and secure the benefits that have been earned by workers.

Such work should include projects that reduce emissions of toxic substances and greenhouse gases from existing and abandoned infrastructure and that prevent environmental damage that harms communities and poses a risk to public health and safety. Plugging leaks in oil and gas wells and reclaiming abandoned mine land can create well-paying union jobs in coal, oil, and gas communities while restoring natural assets, revitalizing recreation economies, and curbing methane emissions. In addition, such work should include efforts to turn properties idled in these communities, such as brownfields, into new hubs for the growth of our economy. Federal agencies should therefore coordinate investments and other efforts to assist coal, oil and gas, and power plant communities, and achieve substantial reductions of methane emissions from the oil and gas sector as quickly as possible.

Sec. 218. *Interagency Working Group on Coal and Power Plant Communities and Economic Revitalization.* There is hereby established an Interagency Working Group on Coal and Power Plant Communities and Economic Revitalization (Interagency Working Group). The National Climate Advisor and the Assistant to the President for Economic Policy shall serve as Co-Chairs of the Interagency Working Group.

(a) Membership. The Interagency Working Group shall consist of the following additional members:

(i) the Secretary of the Treasury;

(ii) the Secretary of the Interior;

(iii) the Secretary of Agriculture;

(iv) the Secretary of Commerce;

(v) the Secretary of Labor;

(vi) the Secretary of Health and Human Services;

(vii) the Secretary of Transportation;

(viii) the Secretary of Energy;

(ix) the Secretary of Education;

(x) the Administrator of the Environmental Protection Agency;

(xi) the Director of the Office of Management and Budget;

(xii) the Assistant to the President for Domestic Policy and Director of the Domestic Policy Council; and

(xiii) the Federal Co-Chair of the Appalachian Regional Commission.

(b) Mission and Work.

(i) The Interagency Working Group shall coordinate the identification and delivery of Federal resources to revitalize the economies of coal, oil and gas, and power plant communities; develop strategies to implement the policy set forth in section 217 of this order and for economic and social recovery; assess opportunities to ensure benefits and protections for coal and power plant workers; and submit reports to the National Climate Advisor and the Assistant to the President for Economic Policy on a regular basis on the progress of the revitalization effort.

(ii) As part of this effort, within 60 days of the date of this order, the Interagency Working Group shall submit a report to the President describing all mechanisms, consistent with applicable law, to prioritize grantmaking, Federal loan programs, technical assistance, financing, procurement, or other existing programs to support and revitalize the economies of coal and power plant communities, and providing recommendations for action consistent with the goals of the Interagency Working Group.

(c) Consultation. Consistent with the objectives set out in this order and in accordance with applicable law, the Interagency Working Group shall seek the views of State, local, and Tribal officials; unions; environmental justice organizations; community groups; and other persons it identifies who may have perspectives on the mission of the Interagency Working Group.

(d) Administration. The Interagency Working Group shall be housed within the Department of Energy. The Chairs shall convene regular meetings of the Interagency Working Group, determine its agenda, and direct its work. The Secretary of Energy, in consultation with the Chairs, shall designate an Executive Director of the Interagency Working Group, who shall coordinate the work of the Interagency Working Group and head any staff assigned to the Interagency Working Group.

(e) Officers. To facilitate the work of the Interagency Working Group, the head of each agency listed in subsection (a) of this section shall assign a designated official within the agency the authority to represent the agency on the Interagency Working Group and perform such other duties relating to the implementation of this order within the agency as the head of the agency deems appropriate.

SECURING ENVIRONMENTAL JUSTICE AND SPURRING ECONOMIC OPPORTUNITY

Sec. 219. *Policy.* To secure an equitable economic future, the United States must ensure that environmental and economic justice are key considerations in how we govern. That means investing and building a clean energy economy that creates wellpaying union jobs, turning disadvantaged communities — historically marginalized and overburdened — into healthy, thriving communities, and undertaking robust actions to mitigate climate change while preparing for the impacts of climate change across rural, urban, and Tribal areas. Agencies shall make achieving environmental justice part of their missions by developing programs, policies, and activities to address the disproportionately high and adverse human health, environmental, climate-related and other cumulative impacts on disadvantaged communities, as well as the accompanying economic challenges of such impacts. It is therefore the policy of my Administration to secure environmental justice and spur economic opportunity for disadvantaged communities that have been historically marginalized and overburdened by pollution and underinvestment in housing, transportation, water and wastewater infrastructure, and health care.

Sec. 220. *White House Environmental Justice Interagency Council.* (a) Section 1-102 of Executive Order 12898 of February 11, 1994 (Federal Actions to Address Environmental Justice in Minority Populations and Low-Income Populations), is hereby amended to read as follows:

"(a) There is hereby created within the Executive Office of the President a White House Environmental Justice Interagency Council (Interagency Council). The Chair of the Council on Environmental Quality shall serve as Chair of the Interagency Council.

"(b) Membership. The Interagency Council shall consist of the following additional members:

   (i)   the Secretary of Defense;
   (ii)   the Attorney General;
   (iii)   the Secretary of the Interior;
   (iv)   the Secretary of Agriculture;
   (v)   the Secretary of Commerce;
   (vi)   the Secretary of Labor;
   (vii)   the Secretary of Health and Human Services;
   (viii)   the Secretary of Housing and Urban Development;
   (ix)   the Secretary of Transportation;
   (x)   the Secretary of Energy;
   (xi)   the Chair of the Council of Economic Advisers;
   (xii)   the Administrator of the Environmental Protection Agency;
   (xiii)   the Director of the Office of Management and Budget;
   (xiv)   the Executive Director of the Federal Permitting Improvement Steering Council;
   (xv)   the Director of the Office of Science and Technology Policy;
   (xvi)   the National Climate Advisor;
   (xvii)   the Assistant to the President for Domestic Policy; and
   (xviii)   the Assistant to the President for Economic Policy.

"(c) At the direction of the Chair, the Interagency Council may establish subgroups consisting exclusively of Interagency Council members or their designees under this section, as appropriate.

"(d) Mission and Work. The Interagency Council shall develop a strategy to address current and historic environmental injustice by consulting with the White House Environmental Justice Advisory Council and with local environmental justice leaders. The Interagency Council shall also develop clear performance metrics to ensure accountability, and publish an annual public performance scorecard on its implementation.

"(e) Administration. The Office of Administration within the Executive Office of the President shall provide funding and administrative support for the Interagency Council, to the extent permitted by law and within existing appropriations. To the extent permitted by law, including the Economy Act (31 U.S.C. 1535), and subject to the availability of appropriations, the Department of Labor, the Department of Transportation, and the Environmental Protection Agency shall provide administrative support as necessary.

"(f) Meetings and Staff. The Chair shall convene regular meetings of the Council, determine its agenda, and direct its work. The Chair shall designate an Executive Director of the Council, who shall coordinate the work of the Interagency Council and head any staff assigned to the Council.

"(g) Officers. To facilitate the work of the Interagency Council, the head of each agency listed in subsection (b) shall assign a designated official within the agency to be an Environmental Justice Officer, with the authority to represent the agency on the Interagency Council and perform such other duties relating to the implementation of this order within the agency as the head of the agency deems appropriate."

(b) The Interagency Council shall, within 120 days of the date of this order, submit to the President, through the National Climate Advisor, a set of recommendations for further updating Executive Order 12898.

Sec. 221. *White House Environmental Justice Advisory Council.* There is hereby established, within the Environmental Protection Agency, the White House Environmental Justice Advisory Council (Advisory Council), which shall advise the Interagency Council and the Chair of the Council on Environmental Quality.

(a) Membership. Members shall be appointed by the President, shall be drawn from across the political spectrum, and may include those with knowledge about or experience in environmental justice, climate change, disaster preparedness, racial inequity, or any other area determined by the President to be of value to the Advisory Council.

(b) Mission and Work. The Advisory Council shall be solely advisory. It shall provide recommendations to the White House Environmental Justice Interagency Council established in section 220 of this

order on how to increase the Federal Government's efforts to address current and historic environmental injustice, including recommendations for updating Executive Order 12898.

(c) Administration. The Environmental Protection Agency shall provide funding and administrative support for the Advisory Council to the extent permitted by law and within existing appropriations. Members of the Advisory Council shall serve without either compensation or reimbursement of expenses.

(d) Federal Advisory Committee Act. Insofar as the Federal Advisory Committee Act, as amended (5 U.S.C. App.), may apply to the Advisory Council, any functions of the President under the Act, except for those in section 6 of the Act, shall be performed by the Administrator of the Environmental Protection Agency in accordance with the guidelines that have been issued by the Administrator of General Services.

Sec. 222. *Agency Responsibilities.* In furtherance of the policy set forth in section 219:

(a) The Chair of the Council on Environmental Quality shall, within 6 months of the date of this order, create a geospatial Climate and Economic Justice Screening Tool and shall annually publish interactive maps highlighting disadvantaged communities.

(b) The Administrator of the Environmental Protection Agency shall, within existing appropriations and consistent with applicable law:

　(i) strengthen enforcement of environmental violations with disproportionate impact on underserved communities through the Office of Enforcement and Compliance Assurance; and

　(ii) create a community notification program to monitor and provide real-time data to the public on current environmental pollution, including emissions, criteria pollutants, and toxins, in frontline and fenceline communities — places with the most significant exposure to such pollution.

(c) The Attorney General shall, within existing appropriations and consistent with applicable law:

　(i) consider renaming the Environment and Natural Resources Division the Environmental Justice and Natural Resources Division;

　(ii) direct that division to coordinate with the Administrator of the Environmental Protection Agency, through the Office of Enforcement and Compliance Assurance, as well as with other client agencies as appropriate, to develop a comprehensive environmental justice enforcement strategy, which shall seek to provide timely remedies for systemic environmental violations and contaminations, and injury to natural resources; and

　(iii) ensure comprehensive attention to environmental justice throughout the Department of Justice, including by considering creating an Office of Environmental Justice within the Department to coordinate environmental justice activities among

Department of Justice components and United States Attorneys' Offices nationwide.

(d) The Secretary of Health and Human Services shall, consistent with applicable law and within existing appropriations:

(i) establish an Office of Climate Change and Health Equity to address the impact of climate change on the health of the American people; and

(ii) establish an Interagency Working Group to Decrease Risk of Climate Change to Children, the Elderly, People with Disabilities, and the Vulnerable as well as a biennial Health Care System Readiness Advisory Council, both of which shall report their progress and findings regularly to the Task Force.

(e) The Director of the Office of Science and Technology Policy shall, in consultation with the National Climate Advisor, within existing appropriations, and within 100 days of the date of this order, publish a report identifying the climate strategies and technologies that will result in the most air and water quality improvements, which shall be made public to the maximum extent possible and published on the Office's website.

Sec. 223. *Justice40 Initiative.* (a) Within 120 days of the date of this order, the Chair of the Council on Environmental Quality, the Director of the Office of Management and Budget, and the National Climate Advisor, in consultation with the Advisory Council, shall jointly publish recommendations on how certain Federal investments might be made toward a goal that 40 percent of the overall benefits flow to disadvantaged communities. The recommendations shall focus on investments in the areas of clean energy and energy efficiency; clean transit; affordable and sustainable housing; training and workforce development; the remediation and reduction of legacy pollution; and the development of critical clean water infrastructure. The recommendations shall reflect existing authorities the agencies may possess for achieving the 40-percent goal as well as recommendations on any legislation needed to achieve the 40-percent goal.

(b) In developing the recommendations, the Chair of the Council on Environmental Quality, the Director of the Office of Management and Budget, and the National Climate Advisor shall consult with affected disadvantaged communities.

(c) Within 60 days of the recommendations described in subsection (a) of this section, agency heads shall identify applicable program investment funds based on the recommendations and consider interim investment guidance to relevant program staff, as appropriate and consistent with applicable law.

(d) By February 2022, the Director of the Office of Management and Budget, in coordination with the Chair of the Council on Environmental Quality, the Administrator of the United States Digital Service, and other relevant agency heads, shall, to the extent consistent with applicable law, publish on a public website an annual Environmental Justice Scorecard detailing agency environmental justice performance measures.

PART III — GENERAL PROVISIONS

Sec. 301. *General Provisions.* (a) Nothing in this order shall be construed to impair or otherwise affect:

(i) the authority granted by law to an executive department or agency or the head thereof; or

(ii) the functions of the Director of the Office of Management and Budget, relating to budgetary, administrative, or legislative proposals.

(b) This order shall be implemented consistent with applicable law and subject to the availability of appropriations.

(c) This order is not intended to, and does not, create any right or benefit, substantive or procedural, enforceable at law or in equity by any party against the United States, its departments, agencies, or entities, its officers, employees, or agents, or any other person.

> JOSEPH R. BIDEN JR.
> THE WHITE HOUSE
> January 27, 2021

2

THE REGULATORY PROCESS

Environmental law is translated into policy through the regulatory process. Most federal environmental laws delegate responsibility to administrative agencies to promulgate regulations implementing the laws. Federal environmental regulations generally are developed through a process of informal rulemaking. The Administrative Procedure Act (APA) establishes the basic procedural requirements agencies must follow in conducting informal rulemaking. Its basic requirements — that agencies provide public notice and an opportunity to comment prior to promulgating regulations — are implemented through notices published in the Federal Register.

Some environmental statutes supplement the APA by specifying additional procedures agencies must follow before taking certain actions. See, e.g., §6(c) of the Toxic Substances Control Act or §307(d) of the Clean Air Act. The Negotiated Rulemaking Act of 1996 generally codifies agency practices for conducting negotiated rulemaking. The Freedom of Information Act, 5 U.S.C. §552, provides an important tool for obtaining information from agencies. Other statutes require agencies to consider certain factors when undertaking rulemaking. The Regulatory Flexibility Act (RFA), 5 U.S.C. §601, requires agencies to consider the impact of regulations on small businesses, a provision enforceable through judicial review as a result of enactment of the Small Business Regulatory Enforcement Fairness Act. A comprehensive introduction to the regulatory process that highlights important legal and procedural issues is Jeffrey S. Lubbers, A Guide to Federal Agency Rulemaking (6th ed. 2018).

A GUIDE TO MATERIALS AVAILABLE ON THE INTERNET PERTAINING TO THE REGULATORY PROCESS

Regulations.gov is a government-wide, electronic docket that seeks to provide a single Internet access point for all federal regulatory material. It provides access to all open Federal Register notices in searchable format and it allows users to submit comments on them electronically. *RegInfo.gov* allows users to search various agencies' regulatory agendas, as well as information on current and past regulatory reviews conducted by Office of Information and Regulatory Affairs (OIRA).

The National Archives and Records Administration maintains a website that includes a searchable version of the Code of Federal Regulations *(https://www.gpo.gov/fdsys/browse/collectionCfr.action?collectionCode=CFR)*. While the published version of the Code of Federal Regulations (CFR) is updated annually, the website contains an electronic version that is continuously updated. This "e-CFR" can be found at *http://www.ecfr.gov*.

EPA maintains rulemaking dockets that store material considered by the agency during the rulemaking process, including studies relied on by the agency, proposed rules, and comments received from the regulated community, government entities, and the public. Some of the agency's rulemaking dockets make substantial materials accessible to the public online. Information about EPA's dockets, electronic dockets, and information centers is available at *https://www.epa.gov/dockets*.

State officials frequently lobby EPA on regulatory matters. The Environmental Council of the States (ECOS) is a national organization composed of state environmental officials that is active on regulatory issues that raise federalism concerns. It maintains a website located at *http://www.ecos.org*.

The Small Business Administration's Office of Advocacy maintains a website that provides information concerning efforts to make the regulatory process more sensitive to the concerns of small entities. It includes news and publications on regulatory policy developments, a summary of the office's activities *(https://advocacy.sba.gov)*, and a virtual "law library" of information on laws governing the regulatory process *(https://www.sba.gov/category/advocacy-navigation-structure/regulatory-policy_0)*. It also tracks agency compliance with the provisions of the Small Business Regulatory Enforcement Fairness Act (SBREFA) of 1996. The website includes links to downloadable copies of the office's annual reports on implementation of the Regulatory Flexibility Act *(https://www.sba.gov/advocacy/regulatory-flexibility-act-annual-reports)*, and it provides data on the Environmental Protection Agency's use of small business advocacy review panels for various regulatory decisions *(https://www.sba.gov/advocacy/small-business-advocacy-review-panels)*. EPA's Air Program maintains a web page promoting the agency's Technology Transfer Network and Small Business Assistance Program located at *http://www.epa.gov/smallbusiness*.

A variety of organizations are actively involved in debates over regulatory policy issues. The Center for Progressive Reform, a nonprofit organization of university-affiliated academics founded in 2002, has a website at *www.progressivereform.org* that includes valuable research briefs on a wide variety of regulatory policy issues. The Center for Effective Government is an organization that serves as a watchdog over the regulatory review activities of OIRA. The Center for Effective Government maintains a website *(http://www.foreffectivegov.org)* that provides news and reports about regulatory developments and information summarizing the various laws and procedural requirements that govern the regulatory process.

STATUTES AND EXECUTIVE ORDERS GOVERNING THE REGULATORY PROCESS

The materials reproduced below include the Administrative Procedure Act, the Regulatory Flexibility Act, the Information Quality Act, the Congressional Review Act, and Executive Order 12,866, which governs regulatory planning and review. The Administrative Procedure Act (APA) was enacted by Congress in 1946 in response to recommendations from the Attorney General's Committee on Administrative Proceedings. This committee had been established in 1939 and it issued its report and recommendations in 1941. Following enactment of the APA, the Attorney General in 1947 issued a Manual on the Administrative Procedure Act, which clarified some of the terms and procedures in the APA.

The Regulatory Flexibility Act (RFA), Pub. L. 96-354, was adopted by Congress in September 1980 in response to recommendations by the first White House Council on Small Business, which had been convened in April 1980. Although the RFA required agencies to analyze the impact of proposed rules on small businesses and to consider meaningful alternatives to minimize such impacts, it was not until 1996 that agencies began to take these requirements seriously, following enactment of the Small Business Regulatory Enforcement Fairness Act (SBREFA), Pub. L. 104-121, which made compliance with the RFA's provisions subject to judicial review. SBREFA also amended the RFA to require the Environmental Protection Agency and the Occupational Safety and Health Administration (OSHA) to convene small business advocacy review panels when developing regulations likely to have a substantial impact on small entities.

In December 2000, Congress enacted the Information Quality Act (IQA), §515 of Title V of Pub. L. 106-554, 114 Stat. 2763, 2673A-153-154, also commonly known as the Data Quality Act, as part of the FY 2001 Treasury and General Government Appropriations Act. The IQA requires the Office of Management and Budget (OMB) to issue "guidelines ensuring and maximizing the quality, objectivity, utility, and integrity of information (including statistical information) disseminated by Federal agencies." OMB's government-wide guidelines, which were published in final form on February 22, 2002 (67 F.R. 8452), are reproduced below. Federal agencies also were required to publish their own agency-specific guidelines.

The Congressional Review Act, another product of SBREFA, creates a fast track procedure for Congress to use to block regulations from taking effect. It was employed by Congress to veto a regulation for the first time in March 2001 when Congress enacted a resolution disapproving an ergonomics standard promulgated by OSHA during the final days of the Clinton administration. President Bush signed the resolution of disapproval, which repealed the ergonomics regulation and barred OSHA from issuing a new ergonomics rule without congressional approval.

In 2017, with Republicans in control of both Congress and the White House, 14 resolutions of disapproval passed both houses of Congress pursuant to the Congressional Review Act and were signed into law. Three environmental regulations were vetoed by these resolutions. Public Law 115-5 vetoed the Interior Department's "stream protection rule" governing disposal of debris from mountaintop coal removal (Feb. 16, 2017). Public Law 115-12 vetoed a Bureau of Land Management (BLM) rule governing land use plans under the Federal Land Policy and Management Act (March 27, 2017). Public Law 115-20 vetoed Interior Department regulations governing the "Non-Subsistence Take of Wildlife, and Public Participation and Closure Procedures on National Wildlife Refuges in Alaska" (April 3, 2017). After passing the House, a resolution to veto BLM regulations governing methane emissions from oil and gas operations on federal lands surprisingly was defeated in the Senate on May 10, 2017, when three Republican Senators joined all 48 Democrats in voting against the resolution.

In September 1993, President Clinton issued Executive Order 12,866 on Regulatory Planning and Review. This replaced the regulatory review process conducted by OMB's Office of Information and Regulatory Affairs (OIRA) during the Reagan and Bush administrations with a more selective process still managed by OIRA. In January 2007, President Bush issued Executive Order 13,422, which amended EO 12,866 to make it applicable to agency issuance of guidance documents. On January 30, 2009, President Obama revoked EO 13,422 and reinstated EO 12,866 to its original form. On January 18, 2011, President Obama issued EO 13,563, which supplements the regulatory review procedures established by EO 12,866.

On January 30, 2017, President Trump issued Executive Order 13,771, entitled "Reducing Regulation and Controlling Regulatory Costs." The order required federal agencies to repeal two existing regulations for each new regulation they issue. It also purported to create a regulatory budget of zero requiring each agency to offset the cost of new regulations by repealing existing regulations that are at least as costly. The words "cost" or "costs" appeared 18 times in the executive order; entirely missing from it was any discussion of the benefits of regulation. President Biden repealed Executive Order 13,771 by issuing Executive Order 13,992.

Administrative Procedure Act
5 U.S.C. §§551 to 559, 701 to 706

§551. Definitions
[APA §2]

For the purpose of this subchapter —

(1) "agency" means each authority of the Government of the United States, whether or not it is within or subject to review by another agency, but does not include —

(A) the Congress;

(B) the courts of the United States;

(C) the governments of the territories or possessions of the United States;

(D) the government of the District of Columbia; or except as to the requirements of section 552 of this title;

(E) agencies composed of representatives of the parties or of representatives of organizations of the parties to the disputes determined by them;

(F) courts martial and military commissions;

(G) military authority exercised in the field in time of war or in occupied territory; or

(H) functions conferred by sections 1738, 1739, 1743, and 1744 of title 12; chapter 2 of title 41; subchapter II of chapter 471 of title 49; or sections 1884, 1891-1902, and former section 1641(b)(2), of title 50, appendix;

(2) "person" includes an individual, partnership, corporation, association, or public or private organization other than an agency;

(3) "party" includes a person or agency named or admitted as a party, or properly seeking and entitled as of right to be admitted as a party, in an agency proceeding, and a person or agency admitted by an agency as a party for limited purposes;

(4) "rule" means the whole or a part of an agency statement of general or particular applicability and future effect designed to implement, interpret, or prescribe law or policy or describing the organization, procedure, or practice requirements of an agency and includes the approval or prescription for the future of rates, wages, corporate or financial structures or reorganizations thereof, prices, facilities, appliances, services or allowances therefore or of valuations, costs, or accounting, or practices bearing on any of the foregoing;

(5) "rule making" means agency process for formulating, amending, or repealing a rule;

(6) "order" means the whole or a part of a final disposition, whether affirmative, negative, injunctive, or declaratory in form, of an agency in a matter other than rule making but including licensing;

(7) "adjudication" means agency process for the formulation of an order;

(8) "license" includes the whole or a part of an agency permit, certificate, approval, registration, charter, membership, statutory exemption or other form of permission;

(9) "licensing" includes agency process respecting the grant, renewal, denial, revocation, suspension, annulment, withdrawal, limitation, amendment, modification, or conditioning of a license;

(10) "sanction" includes the whole or a part of an agency —

(A) prohibition, requirement, limitation, or other condition affecting the freedom of a person;

(B) withholding of relief;

(C) imposition of penalty or fine;

(D) destruction, taking, seizure, or withholding of property;

(E) assessment of damages, reimbursement, restitution, compensation, costs, charges, or fees;

(F) requirement, revocation, or suspension of a license; or

(G) taking other compulsory or restrictive action;

(11) "relief" includes the whole or a part of an agency —

(A) grant of money, assistance, license, authority, exemption, exception, privilege, or remedy;

(B) recognition of a claim, right, immunity, privilege, exemption, or exception; or

(C) taking of other action on the application or petition of, and beneficial to, a person;

(12) "agency proceeding" means an agency process as defined by paragraphs (5), (7), and (9) of this section;

(13) "agency action" includes the whole or a part of an agency rule, order, license, sanction, relief, or the equivalent or denial thereof, or failure to act; and

(14) "ex parte communication" means an oral or written communication not on the public record with respect to which reasonable prior notice to all parties is not given, but it shall not include requests for status reports on any matter or proceeding covered by this subchapter.

§552. Public information; agency rules, opinions, orders, records, and proceedings
[APA §3]

(a) Each agency shall make available to the public information as follows:

(1) Each agency shall separately state and currently publish in the Federal Register for the guidance of the public —

(A) descriptions of its central and field organization and the established places at which, the employees (and in the case of a uniformed service, the members) from whom, and the methods whereby, the public may obtain information, make submittals or requests, or obtain decisions;

(B) statements of the general course and method by which its functions are channeled and determined, including the nature and requirements of all formal and informal procedures available;

(C) rules of procedure, descriptions of forms available or the places at which forms may be obtained, and instructions as to the scope and contents of all papers, reports, or examinations;

(D) substantive rules of general applicability adopted as authorized by law, and statements of general policy or interpretations of general applicability formulated and adopted by the agency; and

(E) each amendment, revision, or repeal of the foregoing.

Except to the extent that a person has actual and timely notice of the terms thereof, a person may not in any manner be required to resort to, or be adversely affected by, a matter required to be published in the Federal Register and not so published. For the purpose of this paragraph, matter reasonably available to the class of persons affected thereby is deemed published in the Federal Register when incorporated by reference therein with the approval of the Director of the Federal Register.

(2) Each agency, in accordance with published rules, shall make available for public inspection in an electronic format —

(A) final opinions, including concurring and dissenting opinions, as well as orders, made in the adjudication of cases;

(B) those statements of policy and interpretations which have been adopted by the agency and are not published in the Federal Register;

(C) administrative staff manuals and instructions to staff that affect a member of the public;

(D) copies of all records, regardless of form or format—

(i) that have been released to any person under paragraph (3); and

(ii)(I) that because of the nature of their subject matter, the agency determines have become or are likely to become the subject of subsequent requests for substantially the same records; or

(II) that have been requested 3 or more times; and

(E) a general index of the records referred to under subparagraph (D);

unless the materials are promptly published and copies offered for sale. For records created on or after November 1, 1996, within one year after such date, each agency shall make such records available, including by computer telecommunications or, if computer telecommunications means have not been established by the agency, by other electronic means. To the extent required to prevent a clearly unwarranted invasion of personal privacy, an agency may delete identifying details when it makes available or publishes an opinion, statement of policy, interpretation, staff manual, instruction, or copies of records referred to in subparagraph (D). However, in each case the justification for the deletion shall be explained fully in writing, and the extent of such deletion shall be indicated on the portion of the record which is made available or published, unless including that indication would harm an interest protected by the exemption in subsection (b) under which the deletion is made. If technically feasible, the extent of the deletion shall be indicated at the place in the record where the deletion was made. Each agency shall also maintain and make available for public inspection and copying in an electronic format current indexes providing identifying information for the public as to any matter issued, adopted, or promulgated after July 4, 1967, and required by this paragraph to be made available or published. Each agency shall promptly publish, quarterly or more frequently, and distribute (by sale or otherwise) copies of each index or supplements thereto unless it determines by order published in the Federal Register that the publication would be unnecessary and impracticable, in which case the agency shall nonetheless provide copies of such index on request at a cost not to exceed the direct cost of duplication. Each agency shall make the index referred to in subparagraph (E) available by computer telecommunications by December 31, 1999. A final order, opinion, statement of policy, interpretation, or staff manual or instruction that affects a member of the public may be relied on, used, or cited as precedent by an agency against a party other than an agency only if —

    (i) it has been indexed and either made available or published as provided by this paragraph; or

    (ii) the party has actual and timely notice of the terms thereof.

(3)(A) Except with respect to the records made available under paragraphs (1) and (2) of this subsection and except as provided in subparagraph (E), each agency, upon any request for records which (i) reasonably describes such records and (ii) is made in accordance with published rules stating the time, place, fees (if any), and procedures to be followed, shall make the records promptly available to any person.

    (B) In making any record available to a person under this paragraph, an agency shall provide the record in any form or format requested by the person if the record is readily reproducible by the agency in that form or format. Each agency shall make reasonable efforts to maintain its records in forms or formats that are reproducible for purposes of this section.

    (C) In responding under this paragraph to a request for records, an agency shall make reasonable efforts to search for the records in electronic form or format, except when such efforts would significantly interfere with the operation of the agency's automated information system.

    (D) For purposes of this paragraph, the term "search" means to review, manually or by automated means, agency records for the purpose of locating those records which are responsive to a request.

    (E) An agency, or part of an agency, that is an element of the intelligence community (as that term is defined in section 3(4) of the National Security Act of 1947 (50 U.S.C. 401a(4))) shall not make any record available under this paragraph to—

    (i) any government entity, other than a State, territory, commonwealth, or district of the United States, or any subdivision thereof; or

    (ii) a representative of a government entity described in clause (i).

(4)(A)(i) In order to carry out the provisions of this section, each agency shall promulgate regulations, pursuant to notice and receipt of public comment, specifying the schedule of fees applicable to the processing of requests under this section and establishing procedures and guidelines for determining when such fees should be waived or reduced. Such schedule shall conform to the guidelines which shall be promulgated, pursuant to notice and receipt of public comment, by the Director of the Office of Management and Budget and which shall provide for a uniform schedule of fees for all agencies.

    (ii) Such agency regulations shall provide that —

    (I) fees shall be limited to reasonable standard charges for document search, duplication, and review, when records are requested for commercial use;

    (II) fees shall be limited to reasonable standard charges for document duplication when records are not sought for commercial use and the request is made by an educational or noncommercial scientific institution, whose purpose is scholarly or scientific research; or a representative of the news media; and

    (III) for any request not described in (I) or (II), fees shall be limited to reasonable standard charges for document search and duplication.

In this clause, the term "a representative of the news media" means any person or entity that gathers information of potential interest to a segment of the public, uses its editorial skills to turn the raw materials into a distinct work, and distributes that work to an audience. In this clause, the term "news" means information that is about current events or that would be of current interest to the public. Examples of news-media entities are television or radio stations broadcasting to the public at large and publishers of periodicals (but only if such entities qualify as disseminators of "news") who make their products available for purchase by or subscription by or free distribution to the general public. These examples are not all-inclusive. Moreover, as methods of news delivery evolve (for example, the adoption of the electronic dissemination of newspapers through telecommunications services), such alternative media shall be considered to be news-media entities. A freelance journalist shall be regarded as working for a news-media entity if the journalist can demonstrate a solid basis for expecting publication through that entity, whether or not the journalist is actually employed by the entity. A publication contract would present a solid basis for such an expectation; the Government may also consider the past publication record of the requester in making such a determination.

(iii) Documents shall be furnished without any charge or at a charge reduced below the fees established under clause (ii) if disclosure of the information is in the public interest because it is likely to contribute significantly to public understanding of the operations or activities of the government and is not primarily in the commercial interest of the requester.

(iv) Fee schedules shall provide for the recovery of only the direct costs of search, duplication, or review. Review costs shall include only the direct costs incurred during the initial examination of a document for the purposes of determining whether the documents must be disclosed under this section and for the purposes of withholding any portions exempt from disclosure under this section. Review costs may not include any costs incurred in resolving issues of law or policy that may be raised in the course of processing a request under this section. No fee may be charged by any agency under this section —

(I) if the costs of routine collection and processing of the fee are likely to equal or exceed the amount of the fee; or

(II) for any request described in clause (ii)(II) or (III) of this subparagraph for the first two hours of search time or for the first one hundred pages of duplication.

(v) No agency may require advance payment of any fee unless the requester has previously failed to pay fees in a timely fashion, or the agency has determined that the fee will exceed $250.

(vi) Nothing in this subparagraph shall supersede fees chargeable under a statute specifically providing for setting the level of fees for particular types of records.

(vii) In any action by a requester regarding the waiver of fees under this section, the court shall determine the matter de novo: *Provided*, that the court's review of the matter shall be limited to the record before the agency.

(viii)(I) Except as provided in subclause (II), an agency shall not assess any search fees (or in the case of a requester described under clause (ii)(II) of this subparagraph, duplication fees) under this subparagraph if the agency has failed to comply with any time limit under paragraph (6).

(II)(aa) If an agency has determined that unusual circumstances apply (as the term is defined in paragraph (6)(B)) and the agency provided a timely written notice to the requester in accordance with paragraph (6)(B), a failure described in subclause (I) is excused for an additional 10 days. If the agency fails to comply with the extended time limit, the agency may not assess any search fees (or in the case of a requester described under clause (ii)(II) of this subparagraph, duplication fees).

(bb) If an agency has determined that unusual circumstances apply and more than 5,000 pages are necessary to respond to the request, an agency may charge search fees (or in the case of a requester described under clause (ii)(II) of this subparagraph, duplication fees) if the agency has provided a timely written notice to the requester in accordance with paragraph (6)(B) and the agency has discussed with the requester via written mail, electronic mail, or telephone (or made not less than 3 good-faith attempts to do so) how the requester could effectively limit the scope of the request in accordance with paragraph (6)(B)(ii).

(cc) If a court has determined that exceptional circumstances exist (as that term is defined in paragraph (6)(C)), a failure described in subclause (I) shall be excused for the length of time provided by the court order.

(B) On complaint, the district court of the United States in the district in which the complainant resides, or has his principal place of business, or in which the agency records are situated, or in the District of Columbia, has jurisdiction to enjoin the agency from withholding agency records and to order the production of any agency records improperly withheld from the complainant. In such a case the court shall determine the matter de novo, and may examine the contents of such agency records in camera to determine whether such records or any part thereof shall be withheld under any of the exemptions set forth in subsection (b) of this section, and the burden is on the agency to sustain its action. In addition to any other matters to which a court accords substantial weight, a court shall accord substantial weight to an affidavit of an agency concerning the agency's determination as to technical feasibility under paragraph (2)(C) and subsection (b) and reproducibility under paragraph (3)(B).

(C) Notwithstanding any other provision of law, the defendant shall serve an answer or otherwise plead to any complaint made under this subsection within thirty days after service upon the defendant of the pleading in which such complaint is made, unless the court otherwise directs for good cause shown.

[(D) Repealed. Pub. L. 98-620, Title IV, Sec. 402(2), Nov. 8, 1984, 98 Stat. 3357]

(E)(i) The court may assess against the United States reasonable attorney fees and other litigation costs reasonably incurred in any case under this section in which the complainant has substantially prevailed.

(ii) For purposes of this subparagraph, a complainant has substantially prevailed if the complainant has obtained relief through either—

(I) a judicial order, or an enforceable written agreement or consent decree; or

(II) a voluntary or unilateral change in position by the agency, if the complainant's claim is not insubstantial.

(F)(i) Whenever the court orders the production of any agency records improperly withheld from the complainant and assesses against the United States reasonable attorney fees and other litigation costs, and the court additionally issues a written finding that the circumstances surrounding the withholding raise questions whether agency personnel acted arbitrarily or capriciously with respect to the withholding, the Special Counsel shall promptly initiate a proceeding to determine whether disciplinary action is warranted against the officer or employee who was primarily responsible for the withholding. The Special Counsel, after investigation and consideration of the evidence submitted, shall submit his findings and recommendations to the administrative authority of the agency concerned and shall send copies of the findings and recommendations to the officer or employee or his representative. The administrative authority shall take the corrective action that the Special Counsel recommends.

(ii) The Attorney General shall —

(I) notify the Special Counsel of each civil action described under the first sentence of clause (i); and

(II) annually submit a report to Congress on the number of such civil actions in the preceding year.

(iii) The Special Counsel shall annually submit a report to Congress on the actions taken by the Special Counsel under clause (i).

(G) In the event of noncompliance with the order of the court, the district court may punish for contempt the responsible employee, and in the case of a uniformed service, the responsible member.

(5) Each agency having more than one member shall maintain and make available for public inspection a record of the final votes of each member in every agency proceeding.

(6)(A) Each agency, upon any request for records made under paragraph (1), (2), or (3) of this subsection, shall —

(i) determine within 20 days (excepting Saturdays, Sundays, and legal public holidays) after the receipt of any such request whether to comply with such request and shall immediately notify the person making such request of—

(I) such determination and the reasons therefor;

(II) the right of such person to seek assistance from the FOIA Public Liaison of the agency; and

(III) in the case of an adverse determination—

(aa) the right of such person to appeal to the head of the agency, within a period determined by the head of the agency that is not less than 90 days after the date of such adverse determination; and

(bb) the right of such person to seek dispute resolution services from the FOIA Public Liaison of the agency or the Office of Government Information Services; and

(ii) make a determination with respect to any appeal within twenty days (excepting Saturdays, Sundays, and legal public holidays) after the receipt of such appeal. If on appeal the denial of the request for records is in whole or in part upheld, the agency shall notify the person making such request of the provisions for judicial review of that determination under paragraph (4) of this subsection.

The 20-day period under clause (i) shall commence on the date on which the request is first received by the appropriate component of the agency, but in any event not later than ten days after the request is first received by any component of the agency that is designated in the agency's regulations under this section to receive requests under this section. The 20-day period shall not be tolled by the agency except—

    (I) that the agency may make one request to the requester for information and toll the 20-day period while it is awaiting such information that it has reasonably requested from the requester under this section; or

    (II) if necessary to clarify with the requester issues regarding fee assessment. In either case, the agency's receipt of the requester's response to the agency's request for information or clarification ends the tolling period.

(B)(i) In unusual circumstances as specified in this subparagraph, the time limits prescribed in either clause (i) or clause (ii) of subparagraph (A) may be extended by written notice to the person making such request setting forth the unusual circumstances for such extension and the date on which a determination is expected to be dispatched. No such notice shall specify a date that would result in an extension for more than ten working days, except as provided in clause (ii) of this subparagraph.

    (ii) With respect to a request for which a written notice under clause (i) extends the time limits prescribed under clause (i) of subparagraph (A), the agency shall notify the person making the request if the request cannot be processed within the time limit specified in that clause and shall provide the person an opportunity to limit the scope of the request so that it may be processed within that time limit or an opportunity to arrange with the agency an alternative time frame for processing the request or a modified request. To aid the requester, each agency shall make available its FOIA Public Liaison, who shall assist in the resolution of any disputes between the requester and the agency, and notify the requester of the right of the requester to seek dispute resolution services from the Office of Government Information Services. Refusal by the person to reasonably modify the request or arrange such an alternative time frame shall be considered as a factor in determining whether exceptional circumstances exist for purposes of subparagraph (C).

    (iii) As used in this subparagraph, "unusual circumstances" means, but only to the extent reasonably necessary to the proper processing of the particular requests —

    (I) the need to search for and collect the requested records from field facilities or other establishments that are separate from the office processing the request;

    (II) the need to search for, collect, and appropriately examine a voluminous amount of separate and distinct records which are demanded in a single request; or

    (III) the need for consultation, which shall be conducted with all practicable speed, with another agency having a substantial interest in the determination of the request or among two or more components of the agency having substantial subject-matter interest therein.

(iv) Each agency may promulgate regulations, pursuant to notice and receipt of public comment, providing for the aggregation of certain requests by the same requestor, or by a group of requestors acting in concert, if the agency reasonably believes that such requests actually constitute a single request, which would otherwise satisfy the unusual circumstances specified in this subparagraph, and the requests involve clearly related matters. Multiple requests involving unrelated matters shall not be aggregated.

(C)(i) Any person making a request to any agency for records under paragraph (1), (2), or (3) of this subsection shall be deemed to have exhausted his administrative remedies with respect to such request if the agency fails to comply with the applicable time limit provisions of this paragraph. If the Government can show exceptional circumstances exist and that the agency is exercising due diligence in responding to the request, the court may retain jurisdiction and allow the agency additional time to complete its review of the records. Upon any determination by an agency to comply with a request for records, the records shall be made promptly available to such person making such request. Any notification of denial of any request for records under this subsection shall set forth the names and titles or positions of each person responsible for the denial of such request.

    (ii) For purposes of this subparagraph, the term "exceptional circumstances" does not include a delay that results from a predictable agency workload of requests under this section, unless the agency demonstrates reasonable progress in reducing its backlog of pending requests.

    (iii) Refusal by a person to reasonably modify the scope of a request or arrange an alternative time frame for processing a request (or a modified request) under clause (ii) after being given an opportunity to do so by the agency to whom the person made the request shall be considered as a factor in determining whether exceptional circumstances exist for purposes of this subparagraph.

(D)(i) Each agency may promulgate regulations, pursuant to notice and receipt of public comment, providing for multitrack processing of requests for records based on the amount of work or time (or both) involved in processing requests.

(ii) Regulations under this subparagraph may provide a person making a request that does not qualify for the fastest multitrack processing an opportunity to limit the scope of the request in order to qualify for faster processing.

(iii) This subparagraph shall not be considered to affect the requirement under subparagraph (C) to exercise due diligence.

(E)(i) Each agency shall promulgate regulations, pursuant to notice and receipt of public comment, providing for expedited processing of requests for records —

(I) in cases in which the person requesting the records demonstrates a compelling need; and

(II) in other cases determined by the agency.

(ii) Notwithstanding clause (i), regulations under this subparagraph must ensure —

(I) that a determination of whether to provide expedited processing shall be made, and notice of the determination shall be provided to the person making the request, within 10 days after the date of the request; and

(II) expeditious consideration of administrative appeals of such determinations of whether to provide expedited processing.

(iii) An agency shall process as soon as practicable any request for records to which the agency has granted expedited processing under this subparagraph. Agency action to deny or affirm denial of a request for expedited processing pursuant to this subparagraph, and failure by an agency to respond in a timely manner to such a request shall be subject to judicial review under paragraph (4), except that the judicial review shall be based on the record before the agency at the time of the determination.

(iv) A district court of the United States shall not have jurisdiction to review an agency denial of expedited processing of a request for records after the agency has provided a complete response to the request.

(v) For purposes of this subparagraph, the term "compelling need" means —

(I) that a failure to obtain requested records on an expedited basis under this paragraph could reasonably be expected to pose an imminent threat to the life or physical safety of an individual; or

(II) with respect to a request made by a person primarily engaged in disseminating information, urgency to inform the public concerning actual or alleged Federal Government activity.

(vi) A demonstration of a compelling need by a person making a request for expedited processing shall be made by a statement certified by such person to be true and correct to the best of such person's knowledge and belief.

(F) In denying a request for records, in whole or in part, an agency shall make a reasonable effort to estimate the volume of any requested matter the provision of which is denied, and shall provide any such estimate to the person making the request, unless providing such estimate would harm an interest protected by the exemption in subsection (b) pursuant to which the denial is made.

(7) Each agency shall —

(A) establish a system to assign an individualized tracking number for each request received that will take longer than ten days to process and provide to each person making a request the tracking number assigned to the request; and

(B) establish a telephone line or Internet service that provides information about the status of a request to the person making the request using the assigned tracking number, including —

(i) the date on which the agency originally received the request; and

(ii) an estimated date on which the agency will complete action on the request.

(8)(A) An agency shall—

(i) withhold information under this section only if—

(I) the agency reasonably foresees that disclosure would harm an interest protected by an exemption described in subsection (b); or

(II) disclosure is prohibited by law; and

(ii)(I) consider whether partial disclosure of information is possible whenever the agency determines that a full disclosure of a requested record is not possible; and

(II) take reasonable steps necessary to segregate and release nonexempt information; and

(B) Nothing in this paragraph requires disclosure of information that is otherwise prohibited from disclosure by law, or otherwise exempted from disclosure under subsection (b)(3).

(b) This section does not apply to matters that are —

(1)(A) specifically authorized under criteria established by an Executive order to be kept secret in the interest of national defense or foreign policy and (B) are in fact properly classified pursuant to such Executive order;

(2) related solely to the internal personnel rules and practices of an agency;

(3) specifically exempted from disclosure by statute (other than section 552b of this title), if that statute

(A)(i) requires that the matters be withheld from the public in such a manner as to leave no discretion on the issue, or

(ii) establishes particular criteria for withholding or refers to particular types of matters to be withheld; and

(B) if enacted after the date of enactment of the OPEN FOIA Act of 2009, specifically cites to the paragraph.

(4) trade secrets and commercial or financial information obtained from a person and privileged or confidential;

(5) inter-agency or intra-agency memorandums or letters that would not be available by law to a party other than an agency in litigation with the agency, provided that the deliberative process privilege shall not apply to records created 25 years or more before the date on which the records were requested;

(6) personnel and medical files and similar files the disclosure of which would constitute a clearly unwarranted invasion of personal privacy;

(7) records or information compiled for law enforcement purposes, but only to the extent that the production of such law enforcement records or information (A) could reasonably be expected to interfere with enforcement proceedings, (B) would deprive a person of a right to a fair trial or an impartial adjudication, (C) could reasonably be expected to constitute an unwarranted invasion of personal privacy, (D) could reasonably be expected to disclose the identity of a confidential source, including a State, local, or foreign agency or authority or any private institution which furnished information on a confidential basis, and, in the case of a record or information compiled by criminal law enforcement authority in the course of a criminal investigation or by an agency conducting a lawful national security intelligence investigation, information furnished by a confidential source, (E) would disclose techniques and procedures for law enforcement investigations or prosecutions, or would disclose guidelines for law enforcement investigations or prosecutions if such disclosure could reasonably be expected to risk circumvention of the law, or (F) could reasonably be expected to endanger the life or physical safety of any individual;

(8) contained in or related to examination, operating, or condition reports prepared by, on behalf of, or for the use of an agency responsible for the regulation or supervision of financial institutions; or

(9) geological and geophysical information and data, including maps, concerning wells.

Any reasonably segregable portion of a record shall be provided to any person requesting such record after deletion of the portions which are exempt under this subsection. The amount of information deleted, and the exemption under which the deletion is made, shall be indicated on the released portion of the record, unless including that indication would harm an interest protected by the exemption in this subsection under which the deletion is made. If technically feasible, the amount of the information deleted, and the exemption under which the deletion is made, shall be indicated at the place in the record where such deletion is made.

(c)(1) Whenever a request is made which involves access to records described in subsection (b)(7)(A) and —

(A) the investigation or proceeding involves a possible violation of criminal law; and

(B) there is reason to believe that (i) the subject of the investigation or proceeding is not aware of its pendency, and (ii) disclosure of the existence of the records could reasonably be expected to interfere with enforcement proceedings,

the agency may, during only such time as that circumstance continues, treat the records as not subject to the requirements of this section.

(2) Whenever informant records maintained by a criminal law enforcement agency under an informant's name or personal identifier are requested by a third party according to the informant's name or personal identifier, the agency may treat the records as not subject to the requirements of this section unless the informant's status as an informant has been officially confirmed.

(3) Whenever a request is made which involves access to records maintained by the Federal Bureau of Investigation pertaining to foreign intelligence or counterintelligence, or international terrorism, and the existence of the records is classified information as provided in subsection (b)(1), the Bureau may, as long as the existence of the records remains classified information, treat the

45

records as not subject to the requirements of this section.

(d) This section does not authorize withholding of information or limit the availability of records to the public, except as specifically stated in this section. This section is not authority to withhold information from Congress.

(e)(1) On or before February 1 of each year, each agency shall submit to the Attorney General of the United States and to the Director of the Office of Government Information Services a report which shall cover the preceding fiscal year and which shall include —

 (A) the number of determinations made by the agency not to comply with requests for records made to such agency under subsection (a) and the reasons for each such determination;

 (B)(i) the number of appeals made by persons under subsection (a)(6), the result of such appeals, and the reason for the action upon each appeal that results in a denial of information; and

  (ii) a complete list of all statutes that the agency relies upon to authorize the agency to withhold information under subsection (b)(3), the number of occasions on which each statute was relied upon, a description of whether a court has upheld the decision of the agency to withhold information under each such statute, and a concise description of the scope of any information withheld;

 (C) the number of requests for records pending before the agency as of September 30 of the preceding year, and the median and average number of days that such requests had been pending before the agency as of that date;

 (D) the number of requests for records received by the agency and the number of requests which the agency processed;

 (E) the median number of days taken by the agency to process different types of requests, based on the date on which the requests were received by the agency;

 (F) the average number of days for the agency to respond to a request beginning on the date on which the request was received by the agency, the median number of days for the agency to respond to such requests, and the range in number of days for the agency to respond to such requests;

 (G) based on the number of business days that have elapsed since each request was originally received by the agency —

  (i) the number of requests for records to which the agency has responded with a determination within a period up to and including 20 days, and in 20-day increments up to and including 200 days;

  (ii) the number of requests for records to which the agency has responded with a determination within a period greater than 200 days and less than 301 days;

  (iii) the number of requests for records to which the agency has responded with a determination within a period greater than 300 days and less than 401 days; and

  (iv) the number of requests for records to which the agency has responded with a determination within a period greater than 400 days;

 (H) the average number of days for the agency to provide the granted information beginning on the date on which the request was originally filed, the median number of days for the agency to provide the granted information, and the range in number of days for the agency to provide the granted information;

 (I) the median and average number of days for the agency to respond to administrative appeals based on the date on which the appeals originally were received by the agency, the highest number of business days taken by the agency to respond to an administrative appeal, and the lowest number of business days taken by the agency to respond to an administrative appeal;

 (J) data on the 10 active requests with the earliest filing dates pending at each agency, including the amount of time that has elapsed since each request was originally received by the agency;

 (K) data on the 10 active administrative appeals with the earliest filing dates pending before the agency as of September 30 of the preceding year, including the number of business days that have elapsed since the requests were originally received by the agency;

 (L) the number of expedited review requests that are granted and denied, the average and median number of days for adjudicating expedited review requests, and the number adjudicated within the required 10 days;

 (M) the number of fee waiver requests that are granted and denied, and the average and median number of days for adjudicating fee waiver determinations;

 (N) the total amount of fees collected by the agency for processing requests; and

 (O) the number of full-time staff of the agency devoted to processing requests for records under this section, and the total amount expended by the agency for processing such requests.

 (P) the number of times the agency denied a request for records under subsection (c); and

(Q) the number of records that were made available for public inspection in an electronic format under subsection (a)(2).

(2) Information in each report submitted under paragraph (1) shall be expressed in terms of each principal component of the agency and for the agency overall.

(3) Each agency shall make each such report available for public inspection in an electronic format. In addition, each agency shall make the raw statistical data used in each report available in a timely manner for public inspection in an electronic format, which shall be made available—

(A) without charge, license, or registration requirement;

(B) in an aggregated, searchable format; and

(C) in a format that may be downloaded in bulk.

(4) The Attorney General of the United States shall make each report which has been made available by electronic means available at a single electronic access point. The Attorney General of the United States shall notify the Chairman and ranking minority member of the Committee on Oversight and Government Reform of the House of Representatives and the Chairman and ranking minority member of the Committees on Homeland Security and Governmental Affairs and the Judiciary of the Senate, no later than March 1 of the year in which each such report is issued, that such reports are available by electronic means.

(5) The Attorney General of the United States, in consultation with the Director of the Office of Management and Budget, shall develop reporting and performance guidelines in connection with reports required by this subsection by October 1, 1997, and may establish additional requirements for such reports as the Attorney General determines may be useful.

(6)(A) The Attorney General of the United States shall submit to the Committee on Oversight and Government Reform of the House of Representatives, the Committee on the Judiciary of the Senate, and the President a report on or before March 1 of each calendar year, which shall include for the prior calendar year—

(i) a listing of the number of cases arising under this section;

(ii) a listing of—

(I) each subsection, and any exemption, if applicable, involved in each case arising under this section;

(II) the disposition of each case arising under this section; and

(III) the cost, fees, and penalties assessed under subparagraphs (E), (F), and (G) of subsection (a)(4); and

(iii) a description of the efforts undertaken by the Department of Justice to encourage agency compliance with this section.

(B) The Attorney General of the United States shall make—

(i) each report submitted under subparagraph (A) available for public inspection in an electronic format; and

(ii) the raw statistical data used in each report submitted under subparagraph (A) available for public inspection in an electronic format, which shall be made available—

(I) without charge, license, or registration requirement;

(II) in an aggregated, searchable format; and

(III) in a format that may be downloaded in bulk.

(f) For purposes of this section, the term—

(1) "agency" as defined in section 551(1) of this title includes any executive department, military department, Government corporation, Government controlled corporation, or other establishment in the executive branch of the Government (including the Executive Office of the President), or any independent regulatory agency; and

(2) "record" and any other term used in this section in reference to information includes—

(A) any information that would be an agency record subject to the requirements of this section when maintained by an agency in any format, including an electronic format; and

(B) any information described under subparagraph (A) that is maintained for an agency by an entity under Government contract, for the purposes of records management.

(g) The head of each agency shall prepare and make available for public inspection in an electronic format, reference material or a guide for requesting records or information from the agency, subject to the exemptions in subsection (b), including—

(1) an index of all major information systems of the agency;

(2) a description of major information and record locator systems maintained by the agency; and

(3) a handbook for obtaining various types and categories of public information from the agency pursuant to chapter 35 of title 44, and under this section.

(h)(1) There is established the Office of Government Information Services within the National Archives and Records Administration. The head of the Office shall be the Director of the Office of Government Information Services.

(2) The Office of Government Information Services shall—

(A) review policies and procedures of administrative agencies under this section;

(B) review compliance with this section by administrative agencies; and

(C) identify procedures and methods for improving compliance under this section.

(3) The Office of Government Information Services shall offer mediation services to resolve disputes between persons making requests under this section and administrative agencies as a non-exclusive alternative to litigation and may issue advisory opinions at the discretion of the Office or upon request of any party to a dispute.

(4)(A) Not less frequently than annually, the Director of the Office of Government Information Services shall submit to the Committee on Oversight and Government Reform of the House of Representatives, the Committee on the Judiciary of the Senate, and the President—

(i) a report on the findings of the information reviewed and identified under paragraph (2);

(ii) a summary of the activities of the Office of Government Information Services under paragraph (3), including—

(I) any advisory opinions issued; and

(II) the number of times each agency engaged in dispute resolution with the assistance of the Office of Government Information Services or the FOIA Public Liaison; and

(iii) legislative and regulatory recommendations, if any, to improve the administration of this section.

(B) The Director of the Office of Government Information Services shall make each report submitted under subparagraph (A) available for public inspection in an electronic format.

(C) The Director of the Office of Government Information Services shall not be required to obtain the prior approval, comment, or review of any officer or agency of the United States, including the Department of Justice, the Archivist of the United States, or the Office of Management and Budget before submitting to Congress, or any committee or subcommittee thereof, any reports, recommendations, testimony, or comments, if such submissions include a statement indicating that the views expressed therein are those of the Director and do not necessarily represent the views of the President.

(5) The Director of the Office of Government Information Services may directly submit additional information to Congress and the President as the Director determines to be appropriate.

(6) Not less frequently than annually, the Office of Government Information Services shall

conduct a meeting that is open to the public on the review and reports by the Office and shall allow interested persons to appear and present oral or written statements at the meeting.

(i) The Government Accountability Office shall conduct audits of administrative agencies on the implementation of this section and issue reports detailing the results of such audits.

(j)(1) Each agency shall designate a Chief FOIA Officer who shall be a senior official of such agency (at the Assistant Secretary or equivalent level).

(2) The Chief FOIA Officer of each agency shall, subject to the authority of the head of the agency—

(A) have agency-wide responsibility for efficient and appropriate compliance with this section;

(B) monitor implementation of this section throughout the agency and keep the head of the agency, the chief legal officer of the agency, and the Attorney General appropriately informed of the agency's performance in implementing this section;

(C) recommend to the head of the agency such adjustments to agency practices, policies, personnel, and funding as may be necessary to improve its implementation of this section;

(D) review and report to the Attorney General, through the head of the agency, at such times and in such formats as the Attorney General may direct, on the agency's performance in implementing this section;

(E) facilitate public understanding of the purposes of the statutory exemptions of this section by including concise descriptions of the exemptions in both the agency's handbook issued under subsection (g), and the agency's annual report on this section, and by providing an overview, where appropriate, of certain general categories of agency records to which those exemptions apply;

(F) offer training to agency staff regarding their responsibilities under this section;

(G) serve as the primary agency liaison with the Office of Government Information Services and the Office of Information Policy; and

(H) designate 1 or more FOIA Public Liaisons.

(3) The Chief FOIA Officer of each agency shall review, not less frequently than annually, all aspects of the administration of this section by the agency to ensure compliance with the requirements of this section, including—

(A) agency regulations;

(B) disclosure of records required under paragraphs (2) and (8) of subsection (a);

(C) assessment of fees and determination of eligibility for fee waivers;

(D) the timely processing of requests for information under this section;

(E) the use of exemptions under subsection (b); and

(F) dispute resolution services with the assistance of the Office of Government Information Services or the FOIA Public Liaison.

(k)(1) There is established in the executive branch the Chief FOIA Officers Council (referred to in this subsection as the "Council").

(2) The Council shall be comprised of the following members:

(A) The Deputy Director for Management of the Office of Management and Budget.

(B) The Director of the Office of Information Policy at the Department of Justice.

(C) The Director of the Office of Government Information Services.

(D) The Chief FOIA Officer of each agency.

(E) Any other officer or employee of the United States as designated by the Co-Chairs.

(3) The Director of the Office of Information Policy at the Department of Justice and the Director of the Office of Government Information Services shall be the Co-Chairs of the Council.

(4) The Administrator of General Services shall provide administrative and other support for the Council.

(5)(A) The duties of the Council shall include the following:

(i) Develop recommendations for increasing compliance and efficiency under this section.

(ii) Disseminate information about agency experiences, ideas, best practices, and innovative approaches related to this section.

(iii) Identify, develop, and coordinate initiatives to increase transparency and compliance with this section.

(iv) Promote the development and use of common performance measures for agency compliance with this section.

(B) In performing the duties described in subparagraph (A), the Council shall consult on a regular basis with members of the public who make requests under this section.

(6)(A) The Council shall meet regularly and such meetings shall be open to the public unless the Council determines to close the meeting for reasons of national security or to discuss information exempt under subsection (b).

(B) Not less frequently than annually, the Council shall hold a meeting that shall be open to the public and permit interested persons to appear and present oral and written statements to the Council.

(C) Not later than 10 business days before a meeting of the Council, notice of such meeting shall be published in the Federal Register.

(D) Except as provided in subsection (b), the records, reports, transcripts, minutes, appendices, working papers, drafts, studies, agenda, or other documents that were made available to or prepared for or by the Council shall be made publicly available.

(E) Detailed minutes of each meeting of the Council shall be kept and shall contain a record of the persons present, a complete and accurate description of matters discussed and conclusions reached, and copies of all reports received, issued, or approved by the Council. The minutes shall be redacted as necessary and made publicly available.

(l) FOIA Public Liaisons shall report to the agency Chief FOIA Officer and shall serve as supervisory officials to whom a requester under this section can raise concerns about the service the requester has received from the FOIA Requester Center, following an initial response from the FOIA Requester Center Staff. FOIA Public Liaisons shall be responsible for assisting in reducing delays, increasing transparency and understanding of the status of requests, and assisting in the resolution of disputes.

(m)(1) The Director of the Office of Management and Budget, in consultation with the Attorney General, shall ensure the operation of a consolidated online request portal that allows a member of the public to submit a request for records under subsection (a) to any agency from a single website. The portal may include any additional tools the Director of the Office of Management and Budget finds will improve the implementation of this section.

(2) This subsection shall not be construed to alter the power of any other agency to create or maintain an independent online portal for the submission of a request for records under this section. The Director of the Office of Management and Budget shall establish standards for interoperability between the portal required under paragraph (1) and other request processing software used by agencies subject to this section.

§552a. Records maintained on individuals

(a) **Definitions.** — For purposes of this section —

(1) the term "agency" means agency as defined in section 552(e) of this title;

(2) the term "individual" means a citizen of the United States or an alien lawfully admitted for permanent residence;

(3) the term "maintain" includes maintain, collect, use, or disseminate;

(4) the term "record" means any item, collection, or grouping of information about an individual that is maintained by an agency, including, but not limited to, his education, financial transactions, medical history, and criminal or employment history and that contains his name, or the identifying number, symbol,

or other identifying particular assigned to the individual, such as a finger or voice print or a photograph;

(5) the term "system of records" means a group of any records under the control of any agency from which information is retrieved by the name of the individual or by some identifying number, symbol, or other identifying particular assigned to the individual;

(6) the term "statistical record" means a record in a system of records maintained for statistical research or reporting purposes only and not used in whole or in part in making any determination about an identifiable individual, except as provided by section 8 of title 13;

(7) the term "routine use" means, with respect to the disclosure of a record, the use of such record for a purpose which is compatible with the purpose for which it was collected;

(8) the term "matching program" —

(A) means any computerized comparison of —

(i) two or more automated systems of records or a system of records with non-Federal records for the purpose of —

(I) establishing or verifying the eligibility of, or continuing compliance with statutory and regulatory requirements by, applicants for, recipients or beneficiaries of, participants in, or providers of services with respect to, cash or in-kind assistance or payments under Federal benefit programs, or

(II) recouping payments or delinquent debts under such Federal benefit programs, or

(ii) two or more automated Federal personnel or payroll systems of records or a system of Federal personnel or payroll records with non-Federal records,

(B) but does not include —

(i) matches performed to produce aggregate statistical data without any personal identifiers;

(ii) matches performed to support any research or statistical project, the specific data of which may not be used to make decisions concerning the rights, benefits, or privileges of specific individuals;

(iii) matches performed, by an agency (or component thereof) which performs as its principal function any activity pertaining to the enforcement of criminal laws, subsequent to the initiation of a specific criminal or civil law enforcement investigation of a named person or persons for the purpose of gathering evidence against such person or persons;

(iv) matches of tax information (I) pursu-

ant to section 6103(d) of the Internal Revenue Code of 1986, (II) for purposes of tax administration as defined in section 6103(b)(4) of such Code, (III) for the purpose of intercepting a tax refund due an individual under authority granted by section 404(e), 464, or 1137 of the Social Security Act; or (IV) for the purpose of intercepting a tax refund due an individual under any other tax refund intercept program authorized by statute which has been determined by the Director of the Office of Management and Budget to contain verification, notice, and hearing requirements that are substantially similar to the procedures in section 1137 of the Social Security Act;

(v) matches —

(I) using records predominantly relating to Federal personnel, that are performed for routine administrative purposes (subject to guidance provided by the Director of the Office of Management and Budget pursuant to subsection (v)); or

(II) conducted by an agency using only records from systems of records maintained by that agency;

if the purpose of the match is not to take any adverse financial, personnel, disciplinary, or other adverse action against Federal personnel;

(vi) matches performed for foreign counterintelligence purposes or to produce background checks for security clearances of Federal personnel or Federal contractor personnel;

(vii) matches performed incident to a levy described in section 6103(k)(8) of the Internal Revenue Code of 1986;

(viii) matches performed pursuant to section 202(x)(3) or 1611(e)(1) of the Social Security Act (42 U.S.C. 402(x)(3), 1382(e)(1));

(ix) matches performed by the Secretary of Health and Human Services or the Inspector General of the Department of Health and Human Services with respect to potential fraud, waste, and abuse, including matches of a system of records with non-Federal records; or

(x) matches performed pursuant to section 3(d)(4) of the Achieving a Better Life Experience Act of 2014.

(9) the term "recipient agency" means any agency, or contractor thereof, receiving records contained in a system of records from a source agency for use in a matching program;

(10) the term "non-Federal agency" means any State or local government, or agency thereof,

which receives records contained in a system of records from a source agency for use in a matching program;

(11) the term "source agency" means any agency which discloses records contained in a system of records to be used in a matching program, or any State or local government, or agency thereof, which discloses records to be used in a matching program;

(12) the term "Federal benefit program" means any program administered or funded by the Federal Government, or by any agent or State on behalf of the Federal Government, providing cash or in-kind assistance in the form of payments, grants, loans, or loan guarantees to individuals; and

(13) the term "Federal personnel" means officers and employees of the Government of the United States, members of the uniformed services (including members of the Reserve Components), individuals entitled to receive immediate or deferred retirement benefits under any retirement program of the Government of the United States (including survivor benefits).

(b) Conditions of disclosure. — No agency shall disclose any record which is contained in a system of records by any means of communication to any person, or to another agency, except pursuant to a written request by, or with the prior written consent of, the individual to whom the record pertains, unless disclosure of the record would be —

(1) to those officers and employees of the agency which maintains the record who have a need for the record in the performance of their duties;

(2) required under section 552 of this title;

(3) for a routine use as defined in subsection (a)(7) of this section and described under subsection (e)(4)(D) of this section;

(4) to the Bureau of the Census for purposes of planning or carrying out a census or survey or related activity pursuant to the provisions of title 13;

(5) to a recipient who has provided the agency with advance adequate written assurance that the record will be used solely as a statistical research or reporting record, and the record is to be transferred in a form that is not individually identifiable;

(6) to the National Archives and Records Administration as a record which has sufficient historical or other value to warrant its continued preservation by the United States Government, or for evaluation by the Archivist of the United States or the designee of the Archivist to determine whether the record has such value;

(7) to another agency or to an instrumentality of any governmental jurisdiction within or under the control of the United States for a civil or criminal law enforcement activity if the activity is authorized by law, and if the head of the agency or instrumentality has made a written request to the agency which maintains the record specifying the particular portion desired and the law enforcement activity for which the record is sought;

(8) to a person pursuant to a showing of compelling circumstances affecting the health or safety of an individual if upon such disclosure notification is transmitted to the last known address of such individual;

(9) to either House of Congress, or, to the extent of matter within its jurisdiction, any committee or subcommittee thereof, any joint committee of Congress or subcommittee of any such joint committee;

(10) to the Comptroller General, or any of his authorized representatives, in the course of the performance of the duties of the Government Accountability Office;

(11) pursuant to the order of a court of competent jurisdiction; or

(12) to a consumer reporting agency in accordance with section 3711(e) of title 31.

(c) Accounting of certain disclosures. — Each agency, with respect to each system of records under its control, shall —

(1) except for disclosures made under subsections (b)(1) or (b)(2) of this section, keep an accurate accounting of —

(A) the date, nature, and purpose of each disclosure of a record to any person or to another agency made under subsection (b) of this section; and

(B) the name and address of the person or agency to whom the disclosure is made;

(2) retain the accounting made under paragraph (1) of this subsection for at least five years or the life of the record, whichever is longer, after the disclosure for which the accounting is made;

(3) except for disclosures made under subsection (b)(7) of this section, make the accounting made under paragraph (1) of this subsection available to the individual named in the record at his request; and

(4) inform any person or other agency about any correction or notation of dispute made by the agency in accordance with subsection (d) of this section of any record that has been disclosed to the person or agency if an accounting of the disclosure was made.

(d) Access to records. — Each agency that maintains a system of records shall —

(1) upon request by any individual to gain access to his record or to any information pertaining to him which is contained in the system, permit him and upon his request, a person of his own choosing to accompany him, to review the record and have a copy made of all or any portion thereof in a form comprehensible to him, except that the agency may require the individual to furnish a written statement authorizing discussion of that

individual's record in the accompanying person's presence;

(2) permit the individual to request amendment of a record pertaining to him and —

(A) not later than 10 days (excluding Saturdays, Sundays, and legal public holidays) after the date of receipt of such request, acknowledge in writing such receipt; and

(B) promptly, either —

(i) make any correction of any portion thereof which the individual believes is not accurate, relevant, timely, or complete; or

(ii) inform the individual of its refusal to amend the record in accordance with his request, the reason for the refusal, the procedures established by the agency for the individual to request a review of that refusal by the head of the agency or an officer designated by the head of the agency, and the name and business address of that official;

(3) permit the individual who disagrees with the refusal of the agency to amend his record to request a review of such refusal, and not later than 30 days (excluding Saturdays, Sundays, and legal public holidays) from the date on which the individual requests such review, complete such review and make a final determination unless, for good cause shown, the head of the agency extends such 30-day period; and if, after his review, the reviewing official also refuses to amend the record in accordance with the request, permit the individual to file with the agency a concise statement setting forth the reasons for his disagreement with the refusal of the agency, and notify the individual of the provisions for judicial review of the reviewing official's determination under subsection (g)(1)(A) of this section;

(4) in any disclosure, containing information about which the individual has filed a statement of disagreement, occurring after the filing of the statement under paragraph (3) of this subsection, clearly note any portion of the record which is disputed and provide copies of the statement and, if the agency deems it appropriate, copies of a concise statement of the reasons of the agency for not making the amendments requested, to persons or other agencies to whom the disputed record has been disclosed; and

(5) nothing in this section shall allow an individual access to any information compiled in reasonable anticipation of a civil action or proceeding.

(e) **Agency requirements.** — Each agency that maintains a system of records shall—

(1) maintain in its records only such information about an individual as is relevant and necessary to accomplish a purpose of the agency required to be accomplished by statute or by executive order of the President;

(2) collect information to the greatest extent practicable directly from the subject individual when the information may result in adverse determinations about an individual's rights, benefits, and privileges under Federal programs;

(3) inform each individual whom it asks to supply information, on the form which it uses to collect the information or on a separate form that can be retained by the individual —

(A) the authority (whether granted by statute, or by executive order of the President) which authorizes the solicitation of the information and whether disclosure of such information is mandatory or voluntary;

(B) the principal purpose or purposes for which the information is intended to be used;

(C) the routine uses which may be made of the information, as published pursuant to paragraph (4)(D) of this subsection; and

(D) the effects on him, if any, of not providing all or any part of the requested information;

(4) subject to the provisions of paragraph (11) of this subsection, publish in the Federal Register upon establishment or revision a notice of the existence and character of the system of records, which notice shall include —

(A) the name and location of the system;

(B) the categories of individuals on whom records are maintained in the system;

(C) the categories of records maintained in the system;

(D) each routine use of the records contained in the system, including the categories of users and the purpose of such use;

(E) the policies and practices of the agency regarding storage, retrievability, access controls, retention, and disposal of the records;

(F) the title and business address of the agency official who is responsible for the system of records;

(G) the agency procedures whereby an individual can be notified at his request if the system of records contains a record pertaining to him;

(H) the agency procedures whereby an individual can be notified at his request how he can gain access to any record pertaining to him contained in the system of records, and how he can contest its content; and

(I) the categories of sources of records in the system;

(5) maintain all records which are used by the agency in making any determination about any individual with such accuracy, relevance, timeliness, and completeness as is reasonably necessary to assure fairness to the individual in the determination;

(6) prior to disseminating any record about an individual to any person other than an agency, unless the dissemination is made pursuant to subsection (b)(2) of this section, make reasonable efforts to assure that such records are accurate, complete, timely, and relevant for agency purposes;

(7) maintain no record describing how any individual exercises rights guaranteed by the First Amendment unless expressly authorized by statute or by the individual about whom the record is maintained or unless pertinent to and within the scope of an authorized law enforcement activity;

(8) make reasonable efforts to serve notice on an individual when any record on such individual is made available to any person under compulsory legal process when such process becomes a matter of public record;

(9) establish rules of conduct for persons involved in the design, development, operation, or maintenance of any system of records, or in maintaining any record, and instruct each such person with respect to such rules and the requirements of this section, including any other rules and procedures adopted pursuant to this section and the penalties for noncompliance;

(10) establish appropriate administrative, technical, and physical safeguards to insure the security and confidentiality of records and to protect against any anticipated threats or hazards to their security or integrity which could result in substantial harm, embarrassment, inconvenience, or unfairness to any individual on whom information is maintained;

(11) at least 30 days prior to publication of information under paragraph (4)(D) of this subsection, publish in the Federal Register notice of any new use or intended use of the information in the system, and provide an opportunity for interested persons to submit written data, views, or arguments to the agency; and

(12) if such agency is a recipient agency or a source agency in a matching program with a non-Federal agency, with respect to any establishment or revision of a matching program, at least 30 days prior to conducting such program, publish in the Federal Register notice of such establishment or revision.

(f) **Agency rules.** — In order to carry out the provisions of this section, each agency that maintains a system of records shall promulgate rules, in accordance with the requirements (including general notice) of section 553 of this title, which shall —

(1) establish procedures whereby an individual can be notified in response to his request if any system of records named by the individual contains a record pertaining to him;

(2) define reasonable times, places, and requirements for identifying an individual who requests his record or information pertaining to him before the agency shall make the record or information available to the individual;

(3) establish procedures for the disclosure to an individual upon his request of his record or information pertaining to him, including special procedure, if deemed necessary, for the disclosure to an individual of medical records, including psychological records, pertaining to him;

(4) establish procedures for reviewing a request from an individual concerning the amendment of any record or information pertaining to the individual, for making a determination on the request, for an appeal within the agency of an initial adverse agency determination, and for whatever additional means may be necessary for each individual to be able to exercise fully his rights under this section; and

(5) establish fees to be charged, if any, to any individual for making copies of his record, excluding the cost of any search for and review of the record.

The Office of the Federal Register shall biennially compile and publish the rules promulgated under this subsection and agency notices published under subsection (e)(4) of this section in a form available to the public at low cost.

(g)(1) **Civil remedies.** — Whenever any agency

(A) makes a determination under subsection (d)(3) of this section not to amend an individual's record in accordance with his request, or fails to make such review in conformity with that subsection;

(B) refuses to comply with an individual request under subsection (d)(1) of this section;

(C) fails to maintain any record concerning any individual with such accuracy, relevance, timeliness, and completeness as is necessary to assure fairness in any determination relating to the qualifications, character, rights, or opportunities of, or benefits to the individual that may be made on the basis of such record, and consequently a determination is made which is adverse to the individual; or

(D) fails to comply with any other provision of this section, or any rule promulgated thereunder, in such a way as to have an adverse effect on an individual,

the individual may bring a civil action against the agency, and the district courts of the United States shall have jurisdiction in the matters under the provisions of this subsection.

(2)(A) In any suit brought under the provisions of subsection (g)(1)(A) of this section, the court may order the agency to amend the individual's record in accordance with his request or in such other way as the court may direct. In such a case the court shall determine the matter de novo.

(B) The court may assess against the United States reasonable attorney fees and other litigation costs reasonably incurred in any case under this paragraph in which the complainant has substantially prevailed.

(3)(A) In any suit brought under the provisions of subsection (g)(1)(B) of this section, the court may enjoin the agency from withholding the records and order the production to the complainant of any agency records improperly withheld from him. In such a case the court shall determine the matter de novo, and may examine the contents of any agency records in camera to determine whether the records or any portion thereof may be withheld under any of the exemptions set forth in subsection (k) of this section, and the burden is on the agency to sustain its action.

(B) The court may assess against the United States reasonable attorney fees and other litigation costs reasonably incurred in any case under this paragraph in which the complainant has substantially prevailed.

(4) In any suit brought under the provisions of subsection (g)(1)(C) or (D) of this section in which the court determines that the agency acted in a manner which was intentional or willful, the United States shall be liable to the individual in an amount equal to the sum of —

(A) actual damages sustained by the individual as a result of the refusal or failure, but in no case shall a person entitled to recovery receive less than the sum of $1,000; and

(B) the costs of the action together with reasonable attorney fees as determined by the court.

(5) An action to enforce any liability created under this section may be brought in the district court of the United States in the district in which the complainant resides, or has his principal place of business, or in which the agency records are situated, or in the District of Columbia, without regard to the amount in controversy, within two years from the date on which the cause of action arises, except that where an agency has materially and willfully misrepresented any information required under this section to be disclosed to an individual and the information so misrepresented is material to establishment of the liability of the agency to the individual under this section, the action may be brought at any time within two years after discovery by the individual of the misrepresentation. Nothing in this section shall be construed to authorize any civil action by reason of any injury sustained as the result of a disclosure of a record prior to September 27, 1975.

(h) **Rights of legal guardians.** — For the purposes of this section, the parent of any minor, or the legal guardian of any individual who has been declared to be incompetent due to physical or mental incapacity or age by a court of competent jurisdiction, may act on behalf of the individual.

(i)(1) **Criminal penalties.** — Any officer or employee of an agency, who by virtue of his employment or official position, has possession of, or access to, agency records which contain individually identifiable information the disclosure of which is prohibited by this section or by rules or regulations established thereunder, and who knowing that disclosure of the specific material is so prohibited, willfully discloses the material in any manner to any person or agency not entitled to receive it, shall be guilty of a misdemeanor and fined not more than $5,000.

(2) Any officer or employee of any agency who willfully maintains a system of records without meeting the notice requirements of subsection (e)(4) of this section shall be guilty of a misdemeanor and fined not more than $5,000.

(3) Any person who knowingly and willfully requests or obtains any record concerning an individual from an agency under false pretenses shall be guilty of a misdemeanor and fined not more than $5,000.

(j) **General exemptions.** — The head of any agency may promulgate rules, in accordance with the requirements (including general notice) of sections 553(b)(1), (2), and (3), (c), and (e) of this title, to exempt any system of records within the agency from any part of this section except subsections (b), (c)(1) and (2), (e)(4)(A) through (F), (e)(6), (7), (9), (10), and (11), and (i) if the system of records is —

(1) maintained by the Central Intelligence Agency; or

(2) maintained by an agency or component thereof which performs as its principal function any activity pertaining to the enforcement of criminal laws, including police efforts to prevent, control, or reduce crime or to apprehend criminals, and the activities of prosecutors, courts, correctional, probation, pardon, or parole authorities, and which consists of (A) information compiled for the purpose of identifying individual criminal offenders and alleged offenders and consisting only of identifying data and notations of arrests, the nature and disposition of criminal charges, sentencing, confinement, release, and parole and probation status; (B) information compiled for the purpose of a criminal investigation, including reports of informants and investigators, and associated with an identifiable individual; or (C) reports identifiable to an individual compiled at any stage of the process of enforcement of the criminal laws from arrest or indictment through release from supervision.

At the time rules are adopted under this subsection, the agency shall include in the statement required under section 553(c) of this title, the reasons why the system of records is to be exempted from a provision of this section.

(k) Specific exemptions. — The head of any agency may promulgate rules, in accordance with the requirements (including general notice) of sections 553(b)(1), (2), and (3), (c), and (e) of this title, to exempt any system of records within the agency from subsections (c)(3), (d), (e)(1), (e)(4)(G), (H), and (I) and (f) of this section if the system of records is —

(1) subject to the provisions of section 552(b)(1) of this title;

(2) investigatory material compiled for law enforcement purposes, other than material within the scope of subsection (j)(2) of this section: *Provided, however,* That if any individual is denied any right, privilege, or benefit that he would otherwise be entitled by Federal law, or for which he would otherwise be eligible, as a result of the maintenance of such material, such material shall be provided to such individual, except to the extent that the disclosure of such material would reveal the identity of a source who furnished information to the Government under an express promise that the identity of the source would be held in confidence, or, prior to the effective date of this section, under an implied promise that the identity of the source would be held in confidence;

(3) maintained in connection with providing protective services to the President of the United States or other individuals pursuant to section 3056 of title 18;

(4) required by statute to be maintained and used solely as statistical records;

(5) investigatory material compiled solely for the purpose of determining suitability, eligibility, or qualifications for Federal civilian employment, military service, Federal contracts, or access to classified information, but only to the extent that the disclosure of such material would reveal the identity of a source who furnished information to the Government under an express promise that the identity of the source would be held in confidence, or, prior to the effective date of this section, under an implied promise that the identity of the source would be held in confidence;

(6) testing or examination material used solely to determine individual qualifications for appointment or promotion in the Federal service the disclosure of which would compromise the objectivity or fairness of the testing or examination process; or

(7) evaluation material used to determine potential for promotion in the armed services, but only to the extent that the disclosure of such material would reveal the identity of a source who furnished information to the Government under an express promise that the identity of the source would be held in confidence, or, prior to the effective date of this section, under an implied promise

that the identity of the source would be held in confidence.

At the time rules are adopted under this subsection, the agency shall include in the statement required under section 553(c) of this title, the reasons why the system of records is to be exempted from a provision of this section.

(l)(1) Archival records. — Each agency record which is accepted by the Archivist of the United States for storage, processing, and servicing in accordance with section 3103 of title 44 shall, for the purposes of this section, be considered to be maintained by the agency which deposited the record and shall be subject to the provisions of this section. The Archivist of the United States shall not disclose the record except to the agency which maintains the record, or under rules established by that agency which are not inconsistent with the provisions of this section.

(2) Each agency record pertaining to an identifiable individual which was transferred to the National Archives of the United States as a record which has sufficient historical or other value to warrant its continued preservation by the United States Government, prior to the effective date of this section, shall, for the purposes of this section, be considered to be maintained by the National Archives and shall not be subject to the provisions of this section, except that a statement generally describing such records (modeled after the requirements relating to records subject to subsections (e)(4)(A) through (G) of this section) shall be published in the Federal Register.

(3) Each agency record pertaining to an identifiable individual which is transferred to the National Archives of the United States as a record which has sufficient historical or other value to warrant its continued preservation by the United States Government, on or after the effective date of this section, shall, for the purposes of this section, be considered to be maintained by the National Archives and shall be exempt from the requirements of this section except subsections (e)(4)(A) through (G) and (e)(9) of this section.

(m)(1) Government contractors. — When an agency provides by a contract for the operation by or on behalf of the agency of a system of records to accomplish an agency function, the agency shall, consistent with its authority, cause the requirements of this section to be applied to such system. For purposes of subsection (i) of this section any such contractor and any employee of such contractor, if such contract is agreed to on or after the effective date of this section, shall be considered to be an employee of an agency.

(2) A consumer reporting agency to which a record is disclosed under section 3711(e) of title 31 shall not be considered a contractor for the purposes of this section.

(n) Mailing lists. — An individual's name and address may not be sold or rented by an agency unless such action is specifically authorized by law. This provision shall not be construed to require the withholding of names and addresses otherwise permitted to be made public.

(o) Matching agreements. —

(1) No record which is contained in a system of records may be disclosed to a recipient agency or non-Federal agency for use in a computer matching program except pursuant to a written agreement between the source agency and the recipient agency or non-Federal agency specifying —

(A) the purpose and legal authority for conducting the program;

(B) the justification for the program and the anticipated results, including a specific estimate of any savings;

(C) a description of the records that will be matched, including each data element that will be used, the approximate number of records that will be matched, and the projected starting and completion dates of the matching program;

(D) procedures for providing individualized notice at the time of application, and notice periodically thereafter as directed by the Data Integrity Board of such agency (subject to guidance provided by the Director of the Office of Management and Budget pursuant to subsection (v)), to —

(i) applicants for and recipients of financial assistance or payments under Federal benefit programs, and

(ii) applicants for and holders of positions as Federal personnel,

that any information provided by such applicants, recipients, holders, and individuals may be subject to verification through matching programs;

(E) procedures for verifying information produced in such matching program as required by subsection (p);

(F) procedures for the retention and timely destruction of identifiable records created by a recipient agency or non-Federal agency in such matching program;

(G) procedures for ensuring the administrative, technical, and physical security of the records matched and the results of such programs;

(H) prohibitions on duplication and redisclosure of records provided by the source agency within or outside the recipient agency or the non-Federal agency, except where required by law or essential to the conduct of the matching program;

(I) procedures governing the use by a recipient agency or non-Federal agency of records provided in a matching program by a source agency, including procedures governing return of the records to the source agency or destruction of records used in such program;

(J) information on assessments that have been made on the accuracy of the records that will be used in such matching program; and

(K) that the Comptroller General may have access to all records of a recipient agency or a non-Federal agency that the Comptroller General deems necessary in order to monitor or verify compliance with the agreement.

(2)(A) A copy of each agreement entered into pursuant to paragraph (1) shall —

(i) be transmitted to the Committee on Governmental Affairs of the Senate and the Committee on Government Operations of the House of Representatives; and

(ii) be available upon request to the public.

(B) No such agreement shall be effective until 30 days after the date on which such a copy is transmitted pursuant to subparagraph (A)(i).

(C) Such an agreement shall remain in effect only for such period, not to exceed 18 months, as the Data Integrity Board of the agency determines is appropriate in light of the purposes, and length of time necessary for the conduct, of the matching program.

(D) Within 3 months prior to the expiration of such an agreement pursuant to subparagraph (C), the Data Integrity Board of the agency may, without additional review, renew the matching agreement for a current, ongoing matching program for not more than one additional year if —

(i) such program will be conducted without any change; and

(ii) each party to the agreement certifies to the Board in writing that the program has been conducted in compliance with the agreement.

(p) Verification and opportunity to contest findings. —

(1) In order to protect any individual whose records are used in a matching program, no recipient agency, non-Federal agency, or source agency may suspend, terminate, reduce, or make a final denial of any financial assistance or payment under a Federal benefit program to such individual, or take other adverse action against such individual, as a result of information produced by such matching program, until —

(A)(i) the agency has independently verified the information; or

(ii) the Data Integrity Board of the agency, or in the case of a non-Federal agency the Data Integrity Board of the source agency, determines in accordance with guidance issued by the Director of the Office of Management and Budget that —

(I) the information is limited to identification and amount of benefits paid by the source agency under a Federal benefit program; and

(II) there is a high degree of confidence that the information provided to the recipient agency is accurate;

(B) the individual receives a notice from the agency containing a statement of its findings and informing the individual of the opportunity to contest such findings; and

(C)(i) the expiration of any time period established for the program by statute or regulation for the individual to respond to that notice; or

(ii) in the case of a program for which no such period is established, the end of the 30-day period beginning on the date on which notice under subparagraph (B) is mailed or otherwise provided to the individual.

(2) Independent verification referred to in paragraph (1) requires investigation and confirmation of specific information relating to an individual that is used as a basis for an adverse action against the individual, including where applicable investigation and confirmation of —

(A) the amount of any asset or income involved;

(B) whether such individual actually has or had access to such asset or income for such individual's own use; and

(C) the period or periods when the individual actually had such asset or income.

(3) Notwithstanding paragraph (1), an agency may take any appropriate action otherwise prohibited by such paragraph if the agency determines that the public health or public safety may be adversely affected or significantly threatened during any notice period required by such paragraph.

(q) Sanctions. —

(1) Notwithstanding any other provision of law, no source agency may disclose any record which is contained in a system of records to a recipient agency or non-Federal agency for a matching program if such source agency has reason to believe that the requirements of subsection (p), or any matching agreement entered into pursuant to subsection (o), or both, are not being met by such recipient agency.

(2) No source agency may renew a matching agreement unless —

(A) the recipient agency or non-Federal agency has certified that it has complied with the provisions of that agreement; and

(B) the source agency has no reason to believe that the certification is inaccurate.

(r) Report on new systems and matching programs. — Each agency that proposes to establish or make a significant change in a system of records or a matching program shall provide adequate advance notice of any such proposal (in duplicate) to the Committee on Government Operations of the House of Representatives, the Committee on Governmental Affairs of the Senate, and the Office of Management and Budget in order to permit an evaluation of the probable or potential effect of such proposal on the privacy or other rights of individuals.

(s) Biennial report. — The President shall biennially submit to the Speaker of the House of Representatives and the President pro tempore of the Senate a report —

(1) describing the actions of the Director of the Office of Management and Budget pursuant to section 6 of the Privacy Act of 1974 during the preceding 2 years;

(2) describing the exercise of individual rights of access and amendment under this section during such years;

(3) identifying changes in or additions to systems of records;

(4) containing such other information concerning administration of this section as may be necessary or useful to the Congress in reviewing the effectiveness of this section in carrying out the purposes of the Privacy Act of 1974.

(t)(1) Effect of other laws. — No agency shall rely on any exemption contained in section 552 of this title to withhold from an individual any record which is otherwise accessible to such individual under the provisions of this section.

(2) No agency shall rely on any exemption in this section to withhold from an individual any record which is otherwise accessible to such individual under the provisions of section 552 of this title.

(u) Data Integrity Boards. —

(1) Every agency conducting or participating in a matching program shall establish a Data Integrity Board to oversee and coordinate among the various components of such agency the agency's implementation of this section.

(2) Each Data Integrity Board shall consist of senior officials designated by the head of the agency, and shall include any senior official designated by the head of the agency as responsible for implementation of this section, and the inspector general of the agency, if any. The inspector general shall not serve as chairman of the Data Integrity Board.

(3) Each Data Integrity Board —

(A) shall review, approve, and maintain all written agreements for receipt or disclosure of agency records for matching programs to ensure compliance with subsection (o), and all relevant statutes, regulations, and guidelines;

(B) shall review all matching programs in which the agency has participated during the year, either as a source agency or recipient agency, determine compliance with applicable laws, regulations, guidelines, and agency agreements, and assess the costs and benefits of such programs;

(C) shall review all recurring matching programs in which the agency has participated during the year, either as a source agency or recipient agency, for continued justification for such disclosures;

(D) shall compile an annual report, which shall be submitted to the head of the agency and the Office of Management and Budget and made available to the public on request, describing the matching activities of the agency, including —

(i) matching programs in which the agency has participated as a source agency or recipient agency;

(ii) matching agreements proposed under subsection (o) that were disapproved by the Board;

(iii) any changes in membership or structure of the Board in the preceding year;

(iv) the reasons for any waiver of the requirement in paragraph (4) of this section for completion and submission of a cost-benefit analysis prior to the approval of a matching program;

(v) any violations of matching agreements that have been alleged or identified and any corrective action taken; and

(vi) any other information required by the Director of the Office of Management and Budget to be included in such report;

(E) shall serve as a clearinghouse for receiving and providing information on the accuracy, completeness, and reliability of records used in matching programs;

(F) shall provide interpretation and guidance to agency components and personnel on the requirements of this section for matching programs;

(G) shall review agency recordkeeping and disposal policies and practices for matching programs to assure compliance with this section; and

(H) may review and report on any agency matching activities that are not matching programs.

(4)(A) Except as provided in subparagraphs (B) and (C), a Data Integrity Board shall not approve any written agreement for a matching program unless the agency has completed and submitted to such Board a cost-benefit analysis of the proposed program and such analysis demonstrates that the program is likely to be cost effective.

(B) The Board may waive the requirements of subparagraph (A) of this paragraph if it

determines in writing, in accordance with guidelines prescribed by the Director of the Office of Management and Budget, that a cost-benefit analysis is not required.

(C) A cost-benefit analysis shall not be required under subparagraph (A) prior to the initial approval of a written agreement for a matching program that is specifically required by statute. Any subsequent written agreement for such a program shall not be approved by the Data Integrity Board unless the agency has submitted a cost-benefit analysis of the program as conducted under the preceding approval of such agreement.

(5)(A) If a matching agreement is disapproved by a Data Integrity Board, any party to such agreement may appeal the disapproval to the Director of the Office of Management and Budget. Timely notice of the filing of such an appeal shall be provided by the Director of the Office of Management and Budget to the Committee on Governmental Affairs of the Senate and the Committee on Government Operations of the House of Representatives.

(B) The Director of the Office of Management and Budget may approve a matching agreement notwithstanding the disapproval of a Data Integrity Board if the Director determines that —

(i) the matching program will be consistent with all applicable legal, regulatory, and policy requirements;

(ii) there is adequate evidence that the matching agreement will be cost-effective; and

(iii) the matching program is in the public interest.

(C) The decision of the Director to approve a matching agreement shall not take effect until 30 days after it is reported to committees described in subparagraph (A).

(D) If the Data Integrity Board and the Director of the Office of Management and Budget disapprove a matching program proposed by the inspector general of an agency, the inspector general may report the disapproval to the head of the agency and to the Congress.

(6) In the reports required by paragraph (3)(D), agency matching activities that are not matching programs may be reported on an aggregate basis, if and to the extent necessary to protect ongoing law enforcement or counterintelligence investigations.

(v) **Office of Management and Budget responsibilities.** — The Director of the Office of Management and Budget shall —

(1) develop and, after notice and opportunity for public comment, prescribe guidelines and regulations for the use of agencies in implementing the provisions of this section; and

(2) provide continuing assistance to and oversight of the implementation of this section by agencies.

(w) Applicability to Bureau of Consumer Financial Protection. — Except as provided in the Consumer Financial Protection Act of 2010, this section shall apply with respect to the Bureau of Consumer Financial Protection.

§552b. Open meetings

(a) For purposes of this section —

(1) the term "agency" means any agency, as defined in section 552(e) of this title, headed by a collegial body composed of two or more individual members, a majority of whom are appointed to such position by the President with the advice and consent of the Senate, and any subdivision thereof authorized to act on behalf of the agency;

(2) the term "meeting" means the deliberations of at least the number of individual agency members required to take action on behalf of the agency where such deliberations determine or result in the joint conduct or disposition of official agency business, but does not include deliberations required or permitted by subsection (d) or (e); and

(3) the term "member" means an individual who belongs to a collegial body heading an agency.

(b) Members shall not jointly conduct or dispose of agency business other than in accordance with this section. Except as provided in subsection (c), every portion of every meeting of an agency shall be open to public observation.

(c) Except in a case where the agency finds that the public interest requires otherwise, the second sentence of subsection (b) shall not apply to any portion of an agency meeting, and the requirements of subsections (d) and (e) shall not apply to any information pertaining to such meeting otherwise required by this section to be disclosed to the public, where the agency properly determines that such portion or portions of its meeting or the disclosure of such information is likely to —

(1) disclose matters that are (A) specifically authorized under criteria established by an Executive order to be kept secret in the interests of national defense or foreign policy and (B) in fact properly classified pursuant to such Executive order;

(2) relate solely to the internal personnel rules and practices of an agency;

(3) disclose matters specifically exempted from disclosure by statute (other than section 552 of this title), provided that such statute (A) requires that the matters be withheld from the public in such a manner as to leave no discretion on the issue, or (B) establishes particular criteria for withholding or refers to particular types of matters to be withheld;

(4) disclose trade secrets and commercial or financial information obtained from a person and privileged or confidential;

(5) involve accusing any person of a crime, or formally censuring any person;

(6) disclose information of a personal nature where disclosure would constitute a clearly unwarranted invasion of personal privacy;

(7) disclose investigatory records compiled for law enforcement purposes, or information which if written would be contained in such records, but only to the extent that the production of such records or information would (A) interfere with enforcement proceedings, (B) deprive a person of a right to a fair trial or an impartial adjudication, (C) constitute an unwarranted invasion of personal privacy, (D) disclose the identity of a confidential source and, in the case of a record compiled by a criminal law enforcement authority in the course of a criminal investigation, or by an agency conducting a lawful national security intelligence investigation, confidential information furnished only by the confidential source, (E) disclose investigative techniques and procedures, or (F) endanger the life or physical safety of law enforcement personnel;

(8) disclose information contained in or related to examination, operating, or condition reports prepared by, on behalf of, or for the use of an agency responsible for the regulation or supervision of financial institutions;

(9) disclose information the premature disclosure of which would —

(A) in the case of an agency which regulates currencies, securities, commodities, or financial institutions, be likely to (i) lead to significant financial speculation in currencies, securities, or commodities, or (ii) significantly endanger the stability of any financial institution; or

(B) in the case of any agency, be likely to significantly frustrate implementation of a proposed agency action,

except that subparagraph (B) shall not apply in any instance where the agency has already disclosed to the public the content or nature of its proposed action, or where the agency is required by law to make such disclosure on its own initiative prior to taking final agency action on such proposal; or

(10) specifically concern the agency's issuance of a subpena, or the agency's participation in a civil action or proceeding, an action in a foreign court or international tribunal, or an arbitration, or the initiation, conduct, or disposition by the agency of a particular case of formal agency adjudication pursuant to the procedures in section 554 of this title or otherwise involving a determination on the record after opportunity for a hearing.

(d)(1) Action under subsection (c) shall be taken only when a majority of the entire membership of the agency (as defined in subsection (a)(1)) votes to take such action. A separate vote of the agency members shall be taken with respect to each agency meeting a portion or portions of which are proposed to be closed to the public pursuant to subsection (c), or with respect to any information which is proposed to be withheld under subsection (c). A single vote may be taken with respect to a series of meetings, a portion or portions of which are proposed to be closed to the public, or with respect to any information concerning such series of meetings, so long as each meeting in such series involves the same particular matters and is scheduled to be held no more than thirty days after the initial meeting in such series. The vote of each agency member participating in such vote shall be recorded and no proxies shall be allowed.

(2) Whenever any person whose interests may be directly affected by a portion of a meeting requests that the agency close such portion to the public for any of the reasons referred to in paragraph (5), (6), or (7) of subsection (c), the agency, upon request of any one of its members, shall vote by recorded vote whether to close such meeting.

(3) Within one day of any vote taken pursuant to paragraph (1) or (2), the agency shall make publicly available a written copy of such vote reflecting the vote of each member on the question. If a portion of a meeting is to be closed to the public, the agency shall, within one day of the vote taken pursuant to paragraph (1) or (2) of this subsection, make publicly available a full written explanation of its action closing the portion together with a list of all persons expected to attend the meeting and their affiliation.

(4) Any agency, a majority of whose meetings may properly be closed to the public pursuant to paragraph (4), (8), (9)(A), or (10) of subsection (c), or any combination thereof, may provide by regulation for the closing of such meetings or portions thereof in the event that a majority of the members of the agency votes by recorded vote at the beginning of such meeting, or portion thereof, to close the exempt portion or portions of the meeting, and a copy of such vote, reflecting the vote of each member on the question, is made available to the public. The provisions of paragraphs (1), (2), and (3) of this subsection and subsection (e) shall not apply to any portion of a meeting to which such regulations apply: *Provided,* that the agency shall, except to the extent that such information is exempt from disclosure under the provisions of subsection (c), provide the public with public announcement of the time, place, and subject matter of the meeting and of each portion thereof at the earliest practicable time.

(e)(1) In the case of each meeting, the agency shall make public announcement, at least one week before the meeting, of the time, place, and subject matter of the meeting, whether it is to be open or closed to the public, and the name and phone number of the official designated by the agency to respond to requests for information about the meeting. Such announcement shall be made unless a majority of the members of the agency determines by a recorded vote that agency business requires that such meeting be called at an earlier date, in which case the agency shall make public announcement of the time, place, and subject matter of such meeting, and whether open or closed to the public, at the earliest practicable time.

(2) The time or place of a meeting may be changed following the public announcement required by paragraph (1) only if the agency publicly announces such change at the earliest practicable time. The subject matter of a meeting, or the determination of the agency to open or close a meeting, or portion of a meeting, to the public, may be changed following the public announcement required by this subsection only if (A) a majority of the entire membership of the agency determines by a recorded vote that agency business so requires and that no earlier announcement of the change was possible, and (B) the agency publicly announces such change and the vote of each member upon such change at the earliest practicable time.

(3) Immediately following each public announcement required by this subsection, notice of the time, place, and subject matter of a meeting, whether the meeting is open or closed, any change in one of the preceding, and the name and phone number of the official designated by the agency to respond to requests for information about the meeting, shall also be submitted for publication in the Federal Register.

(f)(1) For every meeting closed pursuant to paragraphs (1) through (10) of subsection (c), the General Counsel or chief legal officer of the agency shall publicly certify that, in his or her opinion, the meeting may be closed to the public and shall state each relevant exemptive provision. A copy of such certification, together with a statement from the presiding officer of the meeting setting forth the time and place of the meeting, and the persons present, shall be retained by the agency. The agency shall maintain a complete transcript or electronic recording adequate to record fully the proceedings of each meeting, or portion of a meeting, closed to the public, except that in the case of a meeting, or portion of a meeting, closed to the public pursuant to paragraph (8), (9)(A), or (10) of subsection (c), the agency shall maintain either such a transcript or recording, or a set of minutes. Such minutes shall fully and clearly describe all matters discussed and shall provide a full and accurate summary of any actions taken, and the reasons therefor, including a description of each of the views expressed on any item and the record of any roll-call vote (reflecting the vote of each member on the question). All documents considered in connection with any action shall be identified in such minutes.

(2) The agency shall make promptly available to the public, in a place easily accessible to the public, the transcript, electronic recording, or minutes (as required by paragraph (1)) of the discussion of any item on the agenda, or of any item of the testimony of any witness received at the meeting, except for such item or items of such discussion or testimony as the agency determines to contain information which may be withheld under subsection (c). Copies of such transcript, or minutes, or a transcription of such recording disclosing the identity of each speaker, shall be furnished to any person at the actual cost of duplication or transcription. The agency shall maintain a complete verbatim copy of the transcript, a complete copy of the minutes, or a complete electronic recording of each meeting, or portion of a meeting, closed to the public, for a period of at least two years after such meeting, or until one year after the conclusion of any agency proceeding with respect to which the meeting or portion was held, whichever occurs later.

(g) Each agency subject to the requirements of this section shall, within 180 days after the date of enactment of this section, following consultation with the Office of the Chairman of the Administrative Conference of the United States and published notice in the Federal Register of at least thirty days and opportunity for written comment by any person, promulgate regulations to implement the requirements of subsections (b) through (f) of this section. Any person may bring a proceeding in the United States District Court for the District of Columbia to require an agency to promulgate such regulations if such agency has not promulgated such regulations within the time period specified herein. Subject to any limitations of time provided by law, any person may bring a proceeding in the United States Court of Appeals for the District of Columbia to set aside agency regulations issued pursuant to this subsection that are not in accord with the requirements of subsections (b) through (f) of this section and to require the promulgation of regulations that are in accord with such subsections.

(h)(1) The district courts of the United States shall have jurisdiction to enforce the requirements of subsections (b) through (f) of this section by declaratory judgment, injunctive relief, or other relief as may be appropriate. Such actions may be brought by any person against an agency prior to, or within sixty days after, the meeting out of which the violation of this section arises, except that if public announcement of such meeting is not initially provided by the agency in accordance with the requirements of this section, such action may be instituted pursuant to this section at any time prior to sixty days after any public announcement of such meeting. Such actions may be brought in the district court of the United States for the district in which the agency meeting is held or in which the agency in question has its headquarters, or in the District Court for the District of Columbia. In such actions a defendant shall serve his answer within thirty days after the service of the complaint. The burden is on the defendant to sustain his action. In deciding such cases the court may examine in camera any portion of the transcript, electronic recording, or minutes of a meeting closed to the public, and may take such additional evidence as it deems necessary. The court, having due regard for orderly administration and the public interest, as well as the interests of the parties, may grant such equitable relief as it deems appropriate, including granting an injunction against future violations of this section or ordering the agency to make available to the public such portion of the transcript, recording, or minutes of a meeting as is not authorized to be withheld under subsection (c) of this section.

(2) Any Federal court otherwise authorized by law to review agency action may, at the application of any person properly participating in the proceeding pursuant to other applicable law, inquire into violations by the agency of the requirements of this section and afford such relief as it deems appropriate. Nothing in this section authorizes any Federal court having jurisdiction solely on the basis of paragraph (1) to set aside, enjoin, or invalidate any agency action (other than an action to close a meeting or to withhold information under this section) taken or discussed at any agency meeting out of which the violation of this section arose.

(i) The court may assess against any party reasonable attorney fees and other litigation costs reasonably incurred by any other party who substantially prevails in any action brought in accordance with the provisions of subsection (g) or (h) of this section, except that costs may be assessed against the plaintiff only where the court finds that the suit was initiated by the plaintiff primarily for frivolous or dilatory purposes. In the case of assessment of costs against an agency, the costs may be assessed by the court against the United States.

(j) Each agency subject to the requirements of this section shall annually report to the Congress regarding the following:

(1) The changes in the policies and procedures of the agency under this section that have occurred during the preceding 1-year period.

(2) A tabulation of the number of meetings held, the exemptions applied to close meetings, and the days of public notice provided to close meetings.

(3) A brief description of litigation or formal complaints concerning the implementation of this section by the agency.

(4) A brief explanation of any changes in law that have affected the responsibilities of the agency under this section.

(k) Nothing herein expands or limits the present rights of any person under section 552 of this title, except that the exemptions set forth in subsection (c) of this section shall govern in the case of any request made pursuant to section 552 to copy or inspect the transcripts, recordings, or minutes described in subsection (f) of this section. The requirements of chapter 33 of title 44, United States Code, shall not apply to the transcripts, recordings, and minutes described in subsection (f) of this section.

(l) This section does not constitute authority to withhold any information from Congress, and does not authorize the closing of any agency meeting or portion thereof required by any other provision of law to be open.

(m) Nothing in this section authorizes any agency to withhold from any individual any record, including transcripts, recordings, or minutes required by this section, which is otherwise accessible to such individual under section 552a of this title.

§553. Rule making
[APA §4]

(a) This section applies, according to the provisions thereof, except to the extent that there is involved —

(1) a military or foreign affairs function of the United States; or

(2) a matter relating to agency management or personnel or to public property, loans, grants, benefits, or contracts.

(b) General notice of proposed rule making shall be published in the Federal Register, unless persons subject thereto are named and either personally served or otherwise have actual notice thereof in accordance with law. The notice shall include —

(1) a statement of the time, place, and nature of public rule making proceedings;

(2) reference to the legal authority under which the rule is proposed; and

(3) either the terms or substance of the proposed rule or a description of the subjects and issues involved.

Except when notice or hearing is required by statute, this subsection does not apply —

(A) to interpretative rules, general statements of policy, or rules of agency organization, procedure, or practice; or

(B) when the agency for good cause finds (and incorporates the finding and a brief statement of reasons therefor in the rules issued) that notice and public procedure thereon are impracticable, unnecessary, or contrary to the public interest.

(c) After notice required by this section, the agency shall give interested persons an opportunity to participate in the rule making through submission of written data, views, or arguments with or without opportunity for oral presentation. After consideration of the relevant matter presented, the agency shall incorporate in the rules adopted a concise general statement of their basis and purpose. When rules are required by statute to be made on the record after opportunity for an agency hearing, sections 556 and 557 of this title apply instead of this subsection.

(d) The required publication or service of a substantive rule shall be made not less than 30 days before its effective date, except —

(1) a substantive rule which grants or recognizes an exemption or relieves a restriction;

(2) interpretative rules and statements of policy; or

(3) as otherwise provided by the agency for good cause found and published with the rule.

(e) Each agency shall give an interested person the right to petition for the issuance, amendment, or repeal of a rule.

§554. Adjudications
[APA §5]

(a) This section applies, according to the provisions thereof, in every case of adjudication required by statute to be determined on the record after opportunity for an agency hearing, except to the extent that there is involved —

(1) a matter subject to a subsequent trial of the law and the facts de novo in a court;

(2) the selection or tenure of an employee, except an administrative law judge appointed under section 3105 of this title;

(3) proceedings in which decisions rest solely on inspections, tests, or elections;

(4) the conduct of military or foreign affairs functions;

(5) cases in which an agency is acting as an agent for a court; or

(6) the certification of worker representatives.

(b) Persons entitled to notice of an agency hearing shall be timely informed of —

(1) the time, place, and nature of the hearing;

(2) the legal authority and jurisdiction under which the hearing is to be held; and

(3) the matters of fact and law asserted.

When private persons are the moving parties, other parties to the proceeding shall give prompt notice of issues controverted in fact or law; and in other instances agencies may by rule require responsive pleading. In fixing the time and place for hearings, due regard shall be had for the convenience and necessity of the parties or their representatives.

(c) The agency shall give all interested parties opportunity for —

(1) the submission and consideration of facts, arguments, offers of settlement, or proposals of adjustment when time, the nature of the proceeding, and the public interest permit; and

(2) to the extent that the parties are unable so to determine a controversy by consent, hearing

and decision on notice and in accordance with sections 556 and 557 of this title.

(d) The employee who presides at the reception of evidence pursuant to section 556 of this title shall make the recommended decision or initial decision required by section 557 of this title, unless he becomes unavailable to the agency. Except to the extent required for the disposition of ex parte matters as authorized by law, such an employee may not —

　　(1) consult a person or party on a fact in issue, unless on notice and opportunity for all parties to participate; or

　　(2) be responsible to or subject to the supervision or direction of an employee or agent engaged in the performance of investigative or prosecuting functions for an agency.

An employee or agent engaged in the performance of investigative or prosecuting functions for an agency in a case may not, in that or a factually related case, participate or advise in the decision, recommended decision, or agency review pursuant to section 557 of this title, except as witness or counsel in public proceedings. This subsection does not apply —

　　(A) in determining applications for initial licenses;

　　(B) to proceedings involving the validity or application of rates, facilities, or practices of public utilities or carriers; or

　　(C) to the agency or a member or members of the body comprising the agency.

(e) The agency, with like effect as in the case of other orders, and in its sound discretion, may issue a declaratory order to terminate a controversy or remove uncertainty.

§555. Ancillary matters
[APA §6]

(a) This section applies, according to the provisions thereof, except as otherwise provided by this subchapter.

(b) A person compelled to appear in person before an agency or representative thereof is entitled to be accompanied, represented, and advised by counsel or, if permitted by the agency, by other qualified representative. A party is entitled to appear in person or by or with counsel or other duly qualified representative in an agency proceeding. So far as the orderly conduct of public business permits, an interested person may appear before an agency or its responsible employees for the presentation, adjustment, or determination of an issue, request, or controversy in a proceeding, whether interlocutory, summary, or otherwise, or in connection with an agency function. With due regard for the convenience and necessity of the parties or their representatives and within a reasonable time, each agency shall proceed to conclude a matter presented to it. This subsection does not grant or deny a person who is not a lawyer the right to appear for or represent others before an agency or in an agency proceeding.

(c) Process, requirement of a report, inspection, or other investigative act or demand may not be issued, made, or enforced except as authorized by law. A person compelled to submit data or evidence is entitled to retain or, on payment of lawfully prescribed costs, procure a copy or transcript thereof, except that in a nonpublic investigatory proceeding the witness may for good cause be limited to inspection of the official transcript of his testimony.

(d) Agency subpoenas authorized by law shall be issued to a party on request and, when required by rules of procedure, on a statement or showing of general relevance and reasonable scope of the evidence sought. On contest, the court shall sustain the subpoena or similar process or demand to the extent that it is found to be in accordance with law. In a proceeding for enforcement, the court shall issue an order requiring the appearance of the witness or the production of the evidence or data within a reasonable time under penalty of punishment for contempt in case of contumacious failure to comply.

(e) Prompt notice shall be given of the denial in whole or in part of a written application, petition, or other request of an interested person made in connection with any agency proceeding. Except in affirming a prior denial or when the denial is self-explanatory, the notice shall be accompanied by a brief statement of the grounds for denial.

§556. Hearings; presiding employees; powers and duties; burden of proof; evidence; record as basis of decision
[APA §7]

(a) This section applies, according to the provisions thereof, to hearings required by section 553 or 554 of this title to be conducted in accordance with this section.

(b) There shall preside at the taking of evidence —

　　(1) the agency;

　　(2) one or more members of the body which comprises the agency; or

　　(3) one or more administrative law judges appointed under section 3105 of this title.

This subchapter does not supersede the conduct of specified classes of proceedings, in whole or in part, by or before boards or other employees specially provided for by or designated under statute. The functions of presiding employees and of employees participating in decisions in accordance with section 557 of this title shall be conducted in an impartial manner. A presiding or participating employee may at any time disqualify himself. On the filing in good faith of a timely and sufficient affidavit of personal bias or other disqualification of a presiding or participating employee, the agency shall determine the matter as a part of the record and decision in the case.

(c) Subject to published rules of the agency and within its powers, employees presiding at hearings may —

(1) administer oaths and affirmations;

(2) issue subpenas authorized by law;

(3) rule on offers of proof and receive relevant evidence;

(4) take depositions or have depositions taken when the ends of justice would be served;

(5) regulate the course of the hearing;

(6) hold conferences for the settlement or simplification of the issues by consent of the parties or by the use of alternative means of dispute resolution as provided in subchapter IV of this chapter;

(7) inform the parties as to the availability of one or more alternative means of dispute resolution, and encourage use of such methods;

(8) require the attendance at any conference held pursuant to paragraph (6) of at least one representative of each party who has authority to negotiate concerning resolution of issues in controversy;

(9) dispose of procedural requests or similar matters;

(10) make or recommend decisions in accordance with section 557 of this title; and

(11) take other action authorized by agency rule consistent with this subchapter.

(d) Except as otherwise provided by statute, the proponent of a rule or order has the burden of proof. Any oral or documentary evidence may be received, but the agency as a matter of policy shall provide for the exclusion of irrelevant, immaterial, or unduly repetitious evidence. A sanction may not be imposed or rule or order issued except on consideration of the whole record or those parts thereof cited by a party and supported by and in accordance with the reliable, probative, and substantial evidence. The agency may, to the extent consistent with the interests of justice and the policy of the underlying statutes administered by the agency, consider a violation of section 557(d) of this title sufficient grounds for a decision adverse to a party who has knowingly committed such violation or knowingly caused such violation to occur. A party is entitled to present his case or defense by oral or documentary evidence, to submit rebuttal evidence, and to conduct such cross-examination as may be required for a full and true disclosure of the facts. In rule making or determining claims for money or benefits or applications for initial licenses an agency may, when a party will not be prejudiced thereby, adopt procedures for the submission of all or part of the evidence in written form.

(e) The transcript of testimony and exhibits, together with all papers and requests filed in the proceeding, constitutes the exclusive record for decision in accordance with section 557 of this title and, on payment of lawfully prescribed costs, shall be made available to the parties. When an agency decision rests on official notice of a material fact not appearing in the evidence in the record, a party is entitled, on timely request, to an opportunity to show the contrary.

§557. Initial decisions; conclusiveness; review by agency; submissions by parties; contents of decisions; record

[APA §8]

(a) This section applies, according to the provisions thereof, when a hearing is required to be conducted in accordance with section 556 of this title.

(b) When the agency did not preside at the reception of the evidence, the presiding employee or, in cases not subject to section 554(d) of this title, an employee qualified to preside at hearings pursuant to section 556 of this title, shall initially decide the case unless the agency requires, either in specific cases or by general rule, the entire record to be certified to it for decision. When the presiding employee makes an initial decision, that decision then becomes the decision of the agency without further proceedings unless there is an appeal to, or review on motion of, the agency within time provided by rule. On appeal from or review of the initial decision, the agency has all the powers which it would have in making the initial decision except as it may limit the issues on notice or by rule. When the agency makes the decision without having presided at the reception of the evidence, the presiding employee or an employee qualified to preside at hearings pursuant to section 556 of this title shall first recommend a decision, except that in rule making or determining applications for initial licenses —

(1) instead thereof the agency may issue a tentative decision or one of its responsible employees may recommend a decision; or

(2) this procedure may be omitted in a case in which the agency finds on the record that due and timely execution of its functions imperatively and unavoidably so requires.

(c) Before a recommended, initial, or tentative decision, or a decision on agency review of the decision of subordinate employees, the parties are entitled to a reasonable opportunity to submit for the consideration of the employees participating in the decisions —

(1) proposed findings and conclusions; or

(2) exceptions to the decisions or recommended decisions of subordinate employees or to tentative agency decisions; and

(3) supporting reasons for the exceptions or proposed findings or conclusions.

The record shall show the ruling on each finding, conclusion, or exception presented. All decisions, including initial, recommended, and tentative decisions, are a part of the record and shall include a statement of —

(A) findings and conclusions, and the reasons or basis therefor, on all the material issues of fact, law, or discretion presented on the record; and

(B) the appropriate rule, order, sanction, relief, or denial thereof.

(d)(1) In any agency proceeding which is subject to subsection (a) of this section, except to the extent required for the disposition of ex parte matters as authorized by law —

    (A) no interested person outside the agency shall make or knowingly cause to be made to any member of the body comprising the agency, administrative law judge, or other employee who is or may reasonably be expected to be involved in the decisional process of the proceeding, an ex parte communication relevant to the merits of the proceeding;

    (B) no member of the body comprising the agency, administrative law judge, or other employee who is or may reasonably be expected to be involved in the decisional process of the proceeding, shall make or knowingly cause to be made to any interested person outside the agency an ex parte communication relevant to the merits of the proceeding;

    (C) a member of the body comprising the agency, administrative law judge, or other employee who is or may reasonably be expected to be involved in the decisional process of such proceeding who receives, or who makes or knowingly causes to be made, a communication prohibited by this subsection shall place on the public record of the proceeding:

        (i) all such written communications;

        (ii) memoranda stating the substance of all such oral communications; and

        (iii) all written responses, and memoranda stating the substance of all oral responses, to the materials described in clauses (i) and (ii) of this subparagraph;

    (D) upon receipt of a communication knowingly made or knowingly caused to be made by a party in violation of this subsection, the agency, administrative law judge, or other employee presiding at the hearing may, to the extent consistent with the interests of justice and the policy of the underlying statutes, require the party to show cause why his claim or interest in the proceeding should not be dismissed, denied, disregarded, or otherwise adversely affected on account of such violation; and

    (E) the prohibitions of this subsection shall apply beginning at such time as the agency may designate, but in no case shall they begin to apply later than the time at which a proceeding is noticed for hearing unless the person responsible for the communication has knowledge that it will be noticed, in which case the prohibitions shall apply beginning at the time of his acquisition of such knowledge.

(2) This subsection does not constitute authority to withhold information from Congress.

§558. Imposition of sanctions; determination of applications for licenses; suspension, revocation, and expiration of licenses
[APA §9]

(a) This section applies, according to the provisions thereof, to the exercise of a power or authority.

(b) A sanction may not be imposed or a substantive rule or order issued except within jurisdiction delegated to the agency and as authorized by law.

(c) When application is made for a license required by law, the agency, with due regard for the rights and privileges of all the interested parties or adversely affected persons and within a reasonable time, shall set and complete proceedings required to be conducted in accordance with sections 556 and 557 of this title or other proceedings required by law and shall make its decision. Except in cases of willfulness or those in which public health, interest, or safety requires otherwise, the withdrawal, suspension, revocation, or annulment of a license is lawful only if, before the institution of agency proceedings therefor, the licensee has been given —

    (1) notice by the agency in writing of the facts or conduct which may warrant the action; and

    (2) opportunity to demonstrate or achieve compliance with all lawful requirements.

When the licensee has made timely and sufficient application for a renewal or a new license in accordance with agency rules, a license with reference to an activity of a continuing nature does not expire until the application has been finally determined by the agency.

§559. Effect on other laws; effect of subsequent statute
[APA §12]

This subchapter, chapter 7, and sections 1305, 3105, 3344, 4301(2)(E), 5372, and 7521 of this title, and the provisions of section 5335(a)(B) of this title that relate to administrative law judges, do not limit or repeal additional requirements imposed by statute or otherwise recognized by law. Except as otherwise required by law, requirements or privileges relating to evidence or procedure apply equally to agencies and persons. Each agency is granted the authority necessary to comply with the requirements of this subchapter through the issuance of rules or otherwise. Subsequent statute may not be held to supersede or modify this subchapter, chapter 7, sections 1305, 3105, 3344, 4301(2)(E), 5372, or 7521 of this title, or the provisions of section 5335(a)(B) of this title that relate to administrative law judges, except to the extent that it does so expressly.

§701. Application, definitions
[APA §10]

(a) This chapter applies, according to the provisions thereof, except to the extent that —

(1) statutes preclude judicial review; or

(2) agency action is committed to agency discretion by law.

(b) For the purpose of this chapter —

(1) "agency" means each authority of the Government of the United States, whether or not it is within or subject to review by another agency, but does not include —

    (A) the Congress;

    (B) the courts of the United States;

    (C) the governments of the territories or possessions of the United States;

    (D) the government of the District of Columbia;

    (E) agencies composed of representatives of the parties or of representatives of organizations of the parties to the disputes determined by them;

    (F) courts martial and military commissions;

    (G) military authority exercised in the field in time of war or in occupied territory; or

    (H) functions conferred by sections 1738, 1739, 1743, and 1744 of title 12; chapter 2 of title 41; subchapter II of chapter 471 of title 49; or sections 1884, 1891–1902, and former section 1641(b)(2), of title 50, appendix; and

(2) "person", "rule", "order", "license", "sanction", "relief", and "agency action" have the meanings given them by section 551 of this title.

§702. Right of review
[APA §10(a)]

A person suffering legal wrong because of agency action, or adversely affected or aggrieved by agency action within the meaning of a relevant statute, is entitled to judicial review thereof. An action in a court of the United States seeking relief other than money damages and stating a claim that an agency or an officer or employee thereof acted or failed to act in an official capacity or under color of legal authority shall not be dismissed nor relief therein be denied on the ground that it is against the United States or that the United States is an indispensable party. The United States may be named as a defendant in any such action, and a judgment or decree may be entered against the United States: *Provided*, that any mandatory or injunctive decree shall specify the Federal officer or officers (by name or by title), and their successors in office, personally responsible for compliance. Nothing herein (1) affects other limitations on judicial review or the power or duty of the court to dismiss any action or deny relief on any other appropriate legal or equitable ground; or (2) confers authority to grant relief if any other statute that grants consent to suit expressly or impliedly forbids the relief which is sought.

§703. Form and venue of proceeding
[APA §10(b)]

The form of proceeding for judicial review is the special statutory review proceeding relevant to the subject matter in a court specified by statute or, in the absence or inadequacy thereof, any applicable form of legal action, including actions for declaratory judgments or writs of prohibitory or mandatory injunction or habeas corpus, in a court of competent jurisdiction. If no special statutory review proceeding is applicable, the action for judicial review may be brought against the United States, the agency by its official title, or the appropriate officer. Except to the extent that prior, adequate, and exclusive opportunity for judicial review is provided by law, agency action is subject to judicial review in civil or criminal proceedings for judicial enforcement.

§704. Actions reviewable
[APA §10(c)]

Agency action made reviewable by statute and final agency action for which there is no other adequate remedy in a court are subject to judicial review. A preliminary, procedural, or intermediate agency action or ruling not directly reviewable is subject to review on the review of the final agency action. Except as otherwise expressly required by statute, agency action otherwise final is final for the purposes of this section whether or not there has been presented or determined an application for a declaratory order, for any form of reconsideration, or, unless the agency otherwise requires by rule and provides that the action meanwhile is inoperative, for an appeal to superior agency authority.

§705. Relief pending review
[APA §10(d)]

When an agency finds that justice so requires, it may postpone the effective date of action taken by it, pending judicial review. On such conditions as may be required and to the extent necessary to prevent irreparable injury, the reviewing court, including the court to which a case may be taken on appeal from or on application for certiorari or other writ to a reviewing court, may issue all necessary and appropriate process to postpone the effective date of an agency action or to preserve status or rights pending conclusion of the review proceedings.

§706. Scope of review
[APA §10(e)]

To the extent necessary to decision and when presented, the reviewing court shall decide all relevant questions of law, interpret constitutional and statutory provisions, and determine the meaning or applicability of the terms of an agency action. The reviewing court shall —

    (1) compel agency action unlawfully withheld or unreasonably delayed; and

(2) hold unlawful and set aside agency action, findings, and conclusions found to be —

(A) arbitrary, capricious, an abuse of discretion, or otherwise not in accordance with law;

(B) contrary to constitutional right, power, privilege, or immunity;

(C) in excess of statutory jurisdiction, authority, or limitations, or short of statutory right;

(D) without observance of procedure required by law;

(E) unsupported by substantial evidence in a case subject to sections 556 and 557 of this title or otherwise reviewed on the record of an agency hearing provided by statute; or

(F) unwarranted by the facts to the extent that the facts are subject to trial de novo by the reviewing court.

In making the foregoing determinations, the court shall review the whole record or those parts of it cited by a party, and due account shall be taken of the rule of prejudicial error.

Regulatory Flexibility Act

5 U.S.C. §§601 to 612

§601. Definitions

For purposes of this chapter —

(1) the term "agency" means an agency as defined in section 551(1) of this title;

(2) the term "rule" means any rule for which the agency publishes a general notice of proposed rulemaking pursuant to section 553(b) of this title, or any other law, including any rule of general applicability governing Federal grants to State and local governments for which the agency provides an opportunity for notice and public comment, except that the term "rule" does not include a rule of particular applicability relating to rates, wages, corporate or financial structures or reorganizations thereof, prices, facilities, appliances, services, or allowances therefor or to valuations, costs or accounting, or practices relating to such rates, wages, structures, prices, appliances, services, or allowances;

(3) the term "small business" has the same meaning as the term "small business concern" under section 3 of the Small Business Act, unless an agency, after consultation with the Office of Advocacy of the Small Business Administration and after opportunity for public comment, establishes one or more definitions of such term which are appropriate to the activities of the agency and publishes such definition(s) in the Federal Register;

(4) the term "small organization" means any not-for-profit enterprise which is independently owned and operated and is not dominant in its field, unless an agency establishes, after opportunity for public comment, one or more definitions of such term which are appropriate to the activities of the agency and publishes such definition(s) in the Federal Register;

(5) the term "small governmental jurisdiction" means governments of cities, counties, towns, townships, villages, school districts, or special districts, with a population of less than fifty thousand, unless an agency establishes, after opportunity for public comment, one or more definitions of such term which are appropriate to the activities of the agency and which are based on such factors as location in rural or sparsely populated areas or limited revenues due to the population of such jurisdiction, and publishes such definition(s) in the Federal Register;

(6) the term "small entity" shall have the same meaning as the terms "small business", "small organization" and "small governmental jurisdiction" defined in paragraphs (3), (4) and (5) of this section; and

(7) the term "collection of information" —

(A) means the obtaining, causing to be obtained, soliciting, or requiring the disclosure to third parties or the public, of facts or opinions by or for an agency, regardless of form or format, calling for either —

(i) answers to identical questions posed to, or identical reporting or recordkeeping requirements imposed on, 10 or more persons, other than agencies, instrumentalities, or employees of the United States; or

(ii) answers to questions posed to agencies, instrumentalities, or employees of the United States which are to be used for general statistical purposes; and

(B) shall not include a collection of information described under section 3518(c)(1) of title 44, United States Code.

(8) **Recordkeeping requirement.** — The term "recordkeeping requirement" means a requirement imposed by an agency on persons to maintain specified records.

§602. Regulatory agenda

(a) During the months of October and April of each year, each agency shall publish in the Federal Register a regulatory flexibility agenda which shall contain —

(1) a brief description of the subject area of any rule which the agency expects to propose or promulgate which is likely to have a significant economic impact on a substantial number of small entities;

(2) a summary of the nature of any such rule under consideration for each subject area listed in the agenda pursuant to paragraph (1), the objectives and legal basis for the issuance of the rule, and an approximate schedule for completing action on any rule for which the agency has issued a general notice of proposed rulemaking, and

(3) the name and telephone number of an agency official knowledgeable concerning the items listed in paragraph (1).

(b) Each regulatory flexibility agenda shall be transmitted to the Chief Counsel for Advocacy of the Small Business Administration for comment, if any.

(c) Each agency shall endeavor to provide notice of each regulatory flexibility agenda to small entities or their representatives through direct notification or publication of the agenda in publications likely to be obtained by such small entities and shall invite comments upon each subject area on the agenda.

(d) Nothing in this section precludes an agency from considering or acting on any matter not included in a regulatory flexibility agenda, or requires an agency to consider or act on any matter listed in such agenda.

§603. Initial regulatory flexibility analysis

(a) Whenever an agency is required by section 553 of this title, or any other law, to publish general notice of proposed rulemaking for any proposed rule, or publishes a notice of proposed rulemaking for an interpretative rule involving the internal revenue laws of the United States, the agency shall prepare and make available for public comment an initial regulatory flexibility analysis. Such analysis shall describe the impact of the proposed rule on small entities. The initial regulatory flexibility analysis or a summary shall be published in the Federal Register at the time of the publication of general notice of proposed rulemaking for the rule. The agency shall transmit a copy of the initial regulatory flexibility analysis to the Chief Counsel for Advocacy of the Small Business Administration. In the case of an interpretative rule involving the internal revenue laws of the United States, this chapter applies to interpretative rules published in the Federal Register for codification in the Code of Federal Regulations, but only to the extent that such interpretative rules impose on small entities a collection of information requirement.

(b) Each initial regulatory flexibility analysis required under this section shall contain —

(1) a description of the reasons why action by the agency is being considered;

(2) a succinct statement of the objectives of, and legal basis for, the proposed rule;

(3) a description of and, where feasible, an estimate of the number of small entities to which the proposed rule will apply;

(4) a description of the projected reporting, recordkeeping and other compliance requirements of the proposed rule, including an estimate of the classes of small entities which will be subject to the requirement and the type of professional skills necessary for preparation of the report or record;

(5) an identification, to the extent practicable, of all relevant Federal rules which may duplicate, overlap or conflict with the proposed rule.

(c) Each initial regulatory flexibility analysis shall also contain a description of any significant alternatives to the proposed rule which accomplish the stated objectives of applicable statutes and which minimize any significant economic impact of the proposed rule on small entities. Consistent with the stated objectives of applicable statutes, the analysis shall discuss significant alternatives such as —

(1) the establishment of differing compliance or reporting requirements or timetables that take into account the resources available to small entities;

(2) the clarification, consolidation, or simplification of compliance and reporting requirements under the rule for such small entities;

(3) the use of performance rather than design standards; and

(4) an exemption from coverage of the rule, or any part thereof, for such small entities.

(d)(1) For a covered agency, as defined in section 609(d)(2), each initial regulatory flexibility analysis shall include a description of —

(A) any projected increase in the cost of credit for small entities;

(B) any significant alternatives to the proposed rule which accomplish the stated objectives of applicable statutes and which minimize any increase in the cost of credit for small entities; and

(C) advice and recommendations of representatives of small entities relating to issues described in subparagraphs (A) and (B) and subsection (b).

(2) A covered agency, as defined in section 609(d)(2), shall, for purposes of complying with paragraph (1)(C)—

(A) identify representatives of small entities in consultation with the Chief Counsel for Advocacy of the Small Business Administration; and

(B) collect advice and recommendations from the representatives identified under subparagraph (A) relating to issues described in subparagraphs (A) and (B) of paragraph (1) and subsection (b).

§604. Final regulatory flexibility analysis

(a) When an agency promulgates a final rule under section 553 of this title, after being required by that section or any other law to publish a general notice of proposed rulemaking, or promulgates a final interpretative rule involving the internal revenue laws of the United States as described in section 603(a), the agency shall prepare a final regulatory flexibility analysis. Each final regulatory flexibility analysis shall contain —

(1) a statement of the need for, and objectives of, the rule;

(2) a statement of the significant issues raised by the public comments in response to the initial regulatory flexibility analysis, a statement of the assessment of the agency of such issues, and a statement of any changes made in the proposed rule as a result of such comments;

(3) the response of the agency to any comments filed by the Chief Counsel for Advocacy of the Small Business Administration in response to the proposed rule, and a detailed statement of any change made to the proposed rule in the final rule as a result of the comments;

(4) a description of and an estimate of the number of small entities to which the rule will apply or an explanation of why no such estimate is available;

(5) a description of the projected reporting, recordkeeping and other compliance requirements of the rule, including an estimate of the classes of small entities which will be subject to the requirement and the type of professional skills necessary for preparation of the report or record;

(6) a description of the steps the agency has taken to minimize the significant economic impact on small entities consistent with the stated objectives of applicable statutes, including a statement of the factual, policy, and legal reasons for selecting the alternative adopted in the final rule and why each one of the other significant alternatives to the rule considered by the agency which affect the impact on small entities was rejected; and

(7) for a covered agency, as defined in section 609(d)(2), a description of the steps the agency has taken to minimize any additional cost of credit for small entities.

(b) The agency shall make copies of the final regulatory flexibility analysis available to members of the public and shall publish in the Federal Register such analysis or a summary thereof.

§605. Avoidance of duplicative or unnecessary analyses

(a) Any Federal agency may perform the analyses required by sections 602, 603, and 604 of this title in conjunction with or as a part of any other agenda or analysis required by any other law if such other analysis satisfies the provisions of such sections.

(b) Sections 603 and 604 of this title shall not apply to any proposed or final rule if the head of the agency certifies that the rule will not, if promulgated, have a significant economic impact on a substantial number of small entities. If the head of the agency makes a certification under the preceding sentence, the agency shall publish such certification in the Federal Register at the time of publication of general notice of proposed rulemaking for the rule or at the time of publication of the final rule, along with a statement providing the factual basis for such certification. The agency shall provide such certification and statement to the Chief Counsel for Advocacy of the Small Business Administration.

(c) In order to avoid duplicative action, an agency may consider a series of closely related rules as one rule for the purposes of sections 602, 603, 604 and 610 of this title.

§606. Effect on other law

The requirements of sections 603 and 604 of this title do not alter in any manner standards otherwise applicable by law to agency action.

§607. Preparation of analyses

In complying with the provisions of sections 603 and 604 of this title, an agency may provide either a quantifiable or numerical description of the effects of a proposed rule or alternatives to the proposed rule, or more general descriptive statements if quantification is not practicable or reliable.

§608. Procedure for waiver or delay of completion

(a) An agency head may waive or delay the completion of some or all of the requirements of section 603 of this title by publishing in the Federal Register, not later than the date of publication of the final rule, a written finding, with reasons therefor, that the final rule is being promulgated in response to an emergency that makes compliance or timely compliance with the provisions of section 603 of this title impracticable.

(b) Except as provided in section 605(b), an agency head may not waive the requirements of section 604 of this title. An agency head may delay the completion of the requirements of section 604 of this title for a period of not more than one hundred and eighty days after the date of publication in the Federal Register of a final rule by publishing in the Federal Register, not later than such date of publication, a written finding, with reasons therefor, that the final rule is being promulgated in response to an emergency that makes timely compliance with the provisions of section 604 of this title impracticable. If the agency has not prepared a final regulatory analysis pursuant to section 604 of this title within one hundred and eighty days from the date of publication of the final rule, such rule shall lapse and have no effect. Such rule shall not be repromulgated until a final regulatory flexibility analysis has been completed by the agency.

§609. Procedures for gathering comments

(a) When any rule is promulgated which will have a significant economic impact on a substantial number of small entities, the head of the agency promulgating the rule or the official of the agency with statutory responsibility for the promulgation of the rule shall assure that small entities have been given an opportunity to participate in the rulemaking for the rule through the reasonable use of techniques such as —

(1) the inclusion in an advanced notice of proposed rulemaking, if issued, of a statement that the proposed rule may have a significant economic effect on a substantial number of small entities;

(2) the publication of general notice of proposed rulemaking in publications likely to be obtained by small entities;

(3) the direct notification of interested small entities;

(4) the conduct of open conferences or public hearings concerning the rule for small entities including soliciting and receiving comments over computer networks; and

(5) the adoption or modification of agency procedural rules to reduce the cost or complexity of participation in the rulemaking by small entities.

(b) Prior to publication of an initial regulatory flexibility analysis which a covered agency is required to conduct by this chapter —

(1) a covered agency shall notify the Chief Counsel for Advocacy of the Small Business Administration and provide the Chief Counsel with information on the potential impacts of the proposed rule on small entities and the type of small entities that might be affected;

(2) not later than 15 days after the date of receipt of the materials described in paragraph (1), the Chief Counsel shall identify individuals representative of affected small entities for the purpose of obtaining advice and recommendations from those individuals about the potential impacts of the proposed rule;

(3) the agency shall convene a review panel for such rule consisting wholly of full time Federal employees of the office within the agency responsible for carrying out the proposed rule, the Office of Information and Regulatory Affairs within the Office of Management and Budget, and the Chief Counsel;

(4) the panel shall review any material the agency has prepared in connection with this chapter, including any draft proposed rule, collect advice and recommendations of each individual small entity representative identified by the agency after consultation with the Chief Counsel, on issues related to subsections 603(b), paragraphs (3), (4) and (5) and 603(c);

(5) not later than 60 days after the date a covered agency convenes a review panel pursuant to paragraph (3), the review panel shall report on the comments of the small entity representatives and its findings as to issues related to subsections 603(b), paragraphs (3), (4) and (5) and 603(c), provided that such report shall be made public as part of the rulemaking record; and

(6) where appropriate, the agency shall modify the proposed rule, the initial regulatory flexibility analysis or the decision on whether an initial regulatory flexibility analysis is required.

(c) An agency may in its discretion apply subsection (b) to rules that the agency intends to certify under subsection 605(b), but the agency believes may have a greater than de minimis impact on a substantial number of small entities.

(d) For purposes of this section, the term "covered agency" means —

(1) the Environmental Protection Agency;

(2) the Consumer Financial Protection Bureau of the Federal Reserve System; and

(3) the Occupational Safety and Health Administration of the Department of Labor.

(e) The Chief Counsel for Advocacy, in consultation with the individuals identified in subsection (b)(2), and with the Administrator of the Office of Information and Regulatory Affairs within the Office of Management and Budget, may waive the requirements of subsections (b)(3), (b)(4), and (b)(5) by including in the rulemaking record a written finding, with reasons therefor, that those requirements would not advance the effective participation of small entities in the rulemaking process. For purposes of this subsection, the factors to be considered in making such a finding are as follows:

(1) In developing a proposed rule, the extent to which the covered agency consulted with individuals representative of affected small entities with respect to the potential impacts of the rule and took such concerns into consideration.

(2) Special circumstances requiring prompt issuance of the rule.

(3) Whether the requirements of subsection (b) would provide the individuals identified in subsection (b)(2) with a competitive advantage relative to other small entities.

§610. Periodic review of rules

(a) Within one hundred and eighty days after the effective date of this chapter, each agency shall publish in the Federal Register a plan for the periodic review of the rules issued by the agency which have or will have a significant economic impact upon a substantial number of small entities. Such plan may be amended by the agency at any time by publishing the revision in the Federal Register. The purpose of the review shall be to determine whether such rules should be continued without change, or should be amended or rescinded, consistent with the stated objectives of applicable statutes, to minimize any significant economic impact of the rules upon a substantial number of such small entities. The plan shall provide for the review of all such agency rules existing on the effective date of this chapter within ten years of that date and for the review of such rules adopted after the effective date of this chapter within ten years of the publication of such rules as the final rule. If the head of the agency determines that completion of the review of existing rules is not feasible by the established date, he shall so certify in a statement published in the Federal Register and may extend the completion date by one year at a time for a total of not more than five years.

(b) In reviewing rules to minimize any significant economic impact of the rule on a substantial number of small entities in a manner consistent with the stated objectives of applicable statutes, the agency shall consider the following factors —

(1) the continued need for the rule;

(2) the nature of complaints or comments received concerning the rule from the public;

(3) the complexity of the rule;

(4) the extent to which the rule overlaps, duplicates or conflicts with other Federal rules, and, to the extent feasible, with State and local governmental rules; and

(5) the length of time since the rule has been evaluated or the degree to which technology, economic conditions, or other factors have changed in the area affected by the rule.

(c) Each year, each agency shall publish in the Federal Register a list of the rules which have a significant economic impact on a substantial number of small entities, which are to be reviewed pursuant to this section during the succeeding twelve months. The list shall include a brief description of each rule and the need for and legal basis of such rule and shall invite public comment upon the rule.

§611. Judicial review

(a)(1) For any rule subject to this chapter, a small entity that is adversely affected or aggrieved by final agency action is entitled to judicial review of agency compliance with the requirements of sections 601, 604, 605(b), 608(b), and 610 in accordance with chapter 7. Agency compliance with sections 607 and 609(a) shall be judicially reviewable in connection with judicial review of section 604.

(2) Each court having jurisdiction to review such rule for compliance with section 553, or under any other provision of law, shall have jurisdiction to review any claims of noncompliance with sections 601, 604, 605(b), 608(b), and 610 in accordance with chapter 7. Agency compliance with sections 607 and 609(a) shall be judicially reviewable in connection with judicial review of section 604.

(3)(A) A small entity may seek such review during the period beginning on the date of final agency action and ending one year later, except that where a provision of law requires that an action challenging a final agency action be commenced before the expiration of one year, such lesser period shall apply to an action for judicial review under this section.

(B) In the case where an agency delays the issuance of a final regulatory flexibility analysis pursuant to section 608(b) of this chapter, an action for judicial review under this section shall be filed not later than —

(i) one year after the date the analysis is made available to the public, or

(ii) where a provision of law requires that an action challenging a final agency regulation be commenced before the expiration of the 1-year period, the number of days specified in such provision of law that is after the date the analysis is made available to the public.

(4) In granting any relief in an action under this section, the court shall order the agency to take corrective action consistent with this chapter and chapter 7, including, but not limited to —

(A) remanding the rule to the agency, and

(B) deferring the enforcement of the rule against small entities unless the court finds that continued enforcement of the rule is in the public interest.

(5) Nothing in this subsection shall be construed to limit the authority of any court to stay the effective date of any rule or provision thereof under any other provision of law or to grant any other relief in addition to the requirements of this section.

(b) In an action for the judicial review of a rule, the regulatory flexibility analysis for such rule, including an analysis prepared or corrected pursuant to paragraph (a)(4), shall constitute part of the entire record of agency action in connection with such review.

(c) Compliance or noncompliance by an agency with the provisions of this chapter shall be subject to judicial review only in accordance with this section.

(d) Nothing in this section bars judicial review of any other impact statement or similar analysis required by any other law if judicial review of such statement or analysis is otherwise permitted by law.

§612. Reports and intervention rights

(a) The Chief Counsel for Advocacy of the Small Business Administration shall monitor agency compliance with this chapter and shall report at least annually thereon to the President and to the Committees on the Judiciary and Small Business of the Senate and House of Representatives.

(b) The Chief Counsel for Advocacy of the Small Business Administration is authorized to appear as amicus curiae in any action brought in a court of the United States to review a rule. In any such action, the Chief Counsel is authorized to present his or her views with respect to compliance with this chapter, the adequacy of the rulemaking record with respect to small entities and the effect of the rule on small entities.

(c) A court of the United States shall grant the application of the Chief Counsel for Advocacy of the Small Business Administration to appear in any such action for the purposes described in subsection (b).

Information Quality Act

Sec. 515 of Title V of Treasury and General Government Appropriations Act for FY 2001, Pub. L. 106-554, 44 U.S.C.A. §3516 (note)

(a) In general. —

The Director of the Office of Management and Budget shall, by not later than September 30, 2001, and with public and Federal agency involvement, issue guidelines under sections 3504(d)(1) and 3516 of title 44, United States Code, that provide policy and procedural guidance to Federal agencies for ensuring and maximizing the quality, objectivity, utility, and integrity of information (including statistical information) disseminated by Federal agencies in fulfillment of the purposes and provisions of chapter 35 of title 44, United States Code, commonly referred to as the Paperwork Reduction Act.

(b) Content of Guidelines. — The guidelines under subsection (a) shall —

(1) apply to the sharing by Federal agencies of, and access to, information disseminated by Federal agencies; and

(2) Require that each Federal agency to which the guidelines apply —

(A) issue guidelines ensuring and maximizing the quality, objectivity, utility, and integrity of information (including statistical information) disseminated by the agency, by not later than 1 year after the date of issuance of the guidelines under subsection (a);

(B) establish administrative mechanisms allowing affected persons to seek and obtain correction of information maintained and disseminated by the agency that does not comply with the guidelines issued under subsection (a); and

(C) Report periodically to the director—

(i) the number and nature of complaints received by the agency regarding the accuracy of information disseminated by the agency; and

(ii) how such complaints were handled by the agency.

OMB, Agency Information Quality Guidelines

67 Fed. Reg. 8452 (2002)

Guidelines for Ensuring and Maximizing the Quality, Objectivity, Utility, and Integrity of Information Disseminated by Federal Agencies

I. OMB Responsibilities

Section 515 of the Treasury and General Government Appropriations Act for FY2001 (Public Law 106-554) directs the Office of Management and Budget to issue government-wide guidelines that provide policy and procedural guidance to Federal agencies for ensuring and maximizing the quality, objectivity, utility, and integrity of information, including statistical information, disseminated by Federal agencies.

II. Agency Responsibilities

Section 515 directs agencies subject to the Paperwork Reduction Act (44 U.S.C. 3502(1)) to —

1. Issue their own information quality guidelines ensuring and maximizing the quality, objectivity, utility, and integrity of information, including statistical information, disseminated by the agency no later than one year after the date of issuance of the OMB guidelines;

2. Establish administrative mechanisms allowing affected persons to seek and obtain correction of information maintained and disseminated by the agency that does not comply with these OMB guidelines; and

3. Report to the Director of OMB the number and nature of complaints received by the agency regarding agency compliance with these OMB guidelines concerning the quality, objectivity, utility, and integrity of information and how such complaints were resolved.

III. Guidelines for Ensuring and Maximizing the Quality, Objectivity, Utility, and Integrity of Information Disseminated by Federal Agencies

1. Overall, agencies shall adopt a basic standard of quality (including objectivity, utility, and integrity) as a performance goal and should take appropriate steps to incorporate information quality criteria into agency information dissemination practices. Quality is to be ensured and established at levels appropriate to the nature and timeliness of the information to be disseminated. Agencies shall adopt specific standards of quality that are appropriate for the various categories of information they disseminate.

2. As a matter of good and effective agency information resources management, agencies shall develop a process for reviewing the quality (including the objectivity, utility, and integrity) of information before it is disseminated. Agencies shall treat information quality as integral to every step of an agency's development of information, including creation, collection, maintenance, and dissemination. This process shall enable the agency to substantiate the quality of the information it has disseminated through documentation or other means appropriate to the information.

3. To facilitate public review, agencies shall establish administrative mechanisms allowing affected persons to seek and obtain, where appropriate, timely correction of information maintained and disseminated by the agency that does not comply with OMB or agency guidelines. These administrative mechanisms shall be flexible, appropriate to the nature and timeliness of the disseminated information, and incorporated into agency information resources management and administrative practices.

i. Agencies shall specify appropriate time periods for agency decisions on whether and how to correct the information, and agencies shall notify the affected persons of the corrections made.

ii. If the person who requested the correction does not agree with the agency's decision (including the corrective action, if any), the person may file for reconsideration within the agency. The agency shall establish an administrative appeal process to review the agency's initial decision, and specify appropriate time limits in which to resolve such requests for reconsideration.

4. The agency's pre-dissemination review, under paragraph III.2, shall apply to information that the agency first disseminates on or after October 1, 2002. The agency's administrative mechanisms, under paragraph III.3, shall apply to information that the agency disseminates on or after October 1, 2002, regardless of when the agency first disseminated the information.

IV. Agency Reporting Requirements

1. Agencies must designate the Chief Information Officer or another official to be responsible for agency compliance with these guidelines.

2. The agency shall respond to complaints in a manner appropriate to the nature and extent of the complaint. Examples of appropriate responses include

personal contacts via letter or telephone, form letters, press releases or mass mailings that correct a widely disseminated error or address a frequently raised complaint.

3. Each agency must prepare a draft report, no later than April 1, 2002, providing the agency's information quality guidelines and explaining how such guidelines will ensure and maximize the quality, objectivity, utility, and integrity of information, including statistical information, disseminated by the agency. This report must also detail the administrative mechanisms developed by that agency to allow affected persons to seek and obtain appropriate correction of information maintained and disseminated by the agency that does not comply with the OMB or the agency guidelines.

4. The agency must publish a notice of availability of this draft report in the Federal Register, and post this report on the agency's website, to provide an opportunity for public comment.

5. Upon consideration of public comment and after appropriate revision, the agency must submit this draft report to OMB for review regarding consistency with these OMB guidelines no later than July 1, 2002. Upon completion of that OMB review and completion of this report, agencies must publish notice of the availability of this report in its final form in the Federal Register, and post this report on the agency's website no later than October 1, 2002.

6. On an annual fiscal-year basis, each agency must submit a report to the Director of OMB providing information (both quantitative and qualitative, where appropriate) on the number and nature of complaints received by the agency regarding agency compliance with these OMB guidelines and how such complaints were resolved. Agencies must submit these reports no later than January 1 of each following year, with the first report due January 1, 2004.

V. Definitions

1. "Quality" is an encompassing term comprising utility, objectivity, and integrity. Therefore, the guidelines sometimes refer to these four statutory terms, collectively, as "quality."

2. "Utility" refers to the usefulness of the information to its intended users, including the public. In assessing the usefulness of information that the agency disseminates to the public, the agency needs to consider the uses of the information not only from the perspective of the agency but also from the perspective of the public. As a result, when transparency of information is relevant for assessing the information's usefulness from the public's perspective, the agency must take care to ensure that transparency has been addressed in its review of the information.

3. "Objectivity" involves two distinct elements, presentation and substance.

a. "Objectivity" includes whether disseminated information is being presented in an accurate, clear, complete, and unbiased manner. This involves whether the information is presented within a proper context. Sometimes, in disseminating certain types of information to the public, other information must also be disseminated in order to ensure an accurate, clear, complete, and unbiased presentation. Also, the agency needs to identify the sources of the disseminated information (to the extent possible, consistent with confidentiality protections) and, in a scientific, financial, or statistical context, the supporting data and models, so that the public can assess for itself whether there may be some reason to question the objectivity of the sources. Where appropriate, data should have full, accurate, transparent documentation, and error sources affecting data quality should be identified and disclosed to users.

b. In addition, "objectivity" involves a focus on ensuring accurate, reliable, and unbiased information. In a scientific, financial, or statistical context, the original and supporting data shall be generated, and the analytic results shall be developed, using sound statistical and research methods.

i. If data and analytic results have been subjected to formal, independent, external peer review, the information may generally be presumed to be of acceptable objectivity. However, this presumption is rebuttable based on a persuasive showing by the petitioner in a particular instance. If agency-sponsored peer review is employed to help satisfy the objectivity standard, the review process employed shall meet the general criteria for competent and credible peer review recommended by OMB-OIRA to the President's Management Council (9/20/01) (*https://www.whitehouse.gov/omb/inforeg_oira_review_process*), namely, "that (a) peer reviewers be selected primarily on the basis of necessary technical expertise, (b) peer reviewers be expected to disclose to agencies prior technical/policy positions they may have taken on the issues at hand, (c) peer reviewers be expected to disclose to agencies their sources of personal and institutional funding (private or public sector), and (d) peer reviews be conducted in an open and rigorous manner."

ii. If an agency is responsible for disseminating influential scientific, financial, or statistical information, agency guidelines shall include a high degree of transparency about data and methods to facilitate the reproducibility of such information by qualified third parties.

A. With regard to original and supporting data related thereto, agency guidelines shall not require that all disseminated data be subjected to a reproducibility requirement. Agencies may identify, in consultation with the relevant scientific and technical communities, those particular types of data that can practicable [*sic*] be subjected to a reproducibility requirement, given ethical, feasibility, or confidentiality constraints. It is understood that reproducibility of data is an indication of transparency about research design and methods and thus a replication exercise (i.e., a new experiment, test, or sample) shall not be required prior to each dissemination.

B. With regard to analytic results related thereto, agency guidelines shall generally require sufficient transparency about data and methods that an independent reanalysis could be undertaken by a qualified member of the public. These transparency standards apply to agency analysis of data from a single study as well as to analyses that combine information from multiple studies.

i. Making the data and methods publicly available will assist in determining whether analytic results are reproducible. However, the objectivity standard does not override other compelling interests such as privacy, trade secrets, intellectual property, and other confidentiality protections.

ii. In situations where public access to data and methods will not occur due to other compelling interests, agencies shall apply especially rigorous robustness checks to analytic results and document what checks were undertaken. Agency guidelines shall, however, in all cases, require a disclosure of the specific data sources that have been used and the specific quantitative methods and assumptions that have been employed. Each agency is authorized to define the type of robustness checks, and the level of detail for documentation thereof, in ways appropriate for it given the nature and multiplicity of issues for which the agency is responsible.

C. With regard to analysis of risks to human health, safety and the environment maintained or disseminated by the agencies, agencies shall either adopt or adapt the quality principles applied by Congress to risk information used and disseminated pursuant to the Safe Drinking Water Act Amendments of 1996 (42 U.S.C. 300g-1(b)(3)(A) & (B)). Agencies responsible for dissemination of vital health and medical information shall interpret the reproducibility and peer-review standards in a manner appropriate to assuring the timely flow of vital information from agencies to medical providers, patients, health agencies, and the public. Information quality standards may be waived temporarily by agencies under urgent situations (e.g., imminent threats to public health or homeland security) in accordance with the latitude specified in agency-specific guidelines.

4. "Integrity" refers to the security of information—protection of the information from unauthorized access or revision, to ensure that the information is not compromised through corruption or falsification.

5. "Information" means any communication or representation of knowledge such as facts or data, in any medium or form, including textual, numerical, graphic, cartographic, narrative, or audiovisual forms.

This definition includes information that an agency disseminates from a web page, but does not include the provision of hyperlinks to information that others disseminate. This definition does not include opinions, where the agency's presentation makes it clear that what is being offered is someone's opinion rather than fact or the agency's views.

6. "Government information" means information created, collected, processed, disseminated, or disposed of by or for the Federal Government.

7. "Information dissemination product" means any books, paper, map, machine-readable material, audiovisual production, or other documentary material, regardless of physical form or characteristic, an agency disseminates to the public. This definition includes any electronic document, CD-ROM, or web page.

8. "Dissemination" means agency initiated or sponsored distribution of information to the public (see 5 CFR 1320.3(d) (definition of "Conduct or Sponsor")). Dissemination does not include distribution limited to government employees or agency contractors or grantees; intra- or inter-agency use or sharing of government information; and responses to requests for agency records under the Freedom of Information Act, the Privacy Act, the Federal Advisory Committee Act or other similar law. This definition also does not include distribution limited to correspondence with individuals or persons, press releases, archival records, public filings, subpoenas or adjudicative processes.

9. "Influential", when used in the phrase "influential scientific, financial, or statistical information", means that the agency can reasonably determine that dissemination of the information will have or does have a clear and substantial impact on important public policies or important private sector decisions. Each agency is authorized to define "influential" in ways appropriate for it given the nature and multiplicity of issues for which the agency is responsible.

10. "Reproducibility" means that the information is capable of being substantially reproduced, subject to an acceptable degree of imprecision. For information judged to have more (less) important impacts, the degree of imprecision that is tolerated is reduced (increased). If agencies apply the reproducibility test to specific types of original or supporting data, the associated guidelines shall provide relevant definitions of reproducibility (e.g., standards for replication of laboratory data). With respect to analytic results, "capable of being substantially reproduced" means that independent analysis of the original or supporting data using identical methods would generate similar analytic results, subject to an acceptable degree of imprecision or error.

Congressional Review Act

5 U.S.C. §§801 to 808

§801. Congressional review

(a)(1)(A) Before a rule can take effect, the Federal agency promulgating such rule shall submit to each House of the Congress and to the Comptroller General a report containing —

(i) a copy of the rule;

(ii) a concise general statement relating to the rule, including whether it is a major rule; and

(iii) the proposed effective date of the rule.

(B) On the date of the submission of the report under subparagraph (A), the Federal agency promulgating the rule shall submit to the Comptroller General and make available to each House of Congress —

(i) a complete copy of the cost-benefit analysis of the rule, if any;

(ii) the agency's actions relevant to sections 603, 604, 605, 607, and 609;

(iii) the agency's actions relevant to sections 202, 203, 204, and 205 of the Unfunded Mandates Reform Act of 1995; and

(iv) any other relevant information or requirements under any other Act and any relevant Executive orders.

(C) Upon receipt of a report submitted under subparagraph (A), each House shall provide copies of the report to the chairman and ranking member of each standing committee with jurisdiction under the rules of the House of Representatives or the Senate to report a bill to amend the provision of law under which the rule is issued.

(2)(A) The Comptroller General shall provide a report on each major rule to the committees of jurisdiction in each House of the Congress by the end of 15 calendar days after the submission or publication date as provided in section 802(b)(2). The report of the Comptroller General shall include an assessment of the agency's compliance with procedural steps required by paragraph (1)(B).

(B) Federal agencies shall cooperate with the Comptroller General by providing information relevant to the Comptroller General's report under subparagraph (A).

(3) A major rule relating to a report submitted under paragraph (1) shall take effect on the latest of —

(A) the later of the date occurring 60 days after the date on which —

(i) the Congress receives the report submitted under paragraph (1); or

(ii) the rule is published in the Federal Register, if so published;

(B) if the Congress passes a joint resolution of disapproval described in section 802 relating to the rule, and the President signs a veto of such resolution, the earlier date —

(i) on which either House of Congress votes and fails to override the veto of the President; or

(ii) occurring 30 session days after the date on which the Congress received the veto and objections of the President; or

(C) the date the rule would have otherwise taken effect, if not for this section (unless a joint resolution of disapproval under section 802 is enacted).

(4) Except for a major rule, a rule shall take effect as otherwise provided by law after submission to Congress under paragraph (1).

(5) Notwithstanding paragraph (3), the effective date of a rule shall not be delayed by operation of this chapter beyond the date on which either House of Congress votes to reject a joint resolution of disapproval under section 802.

(b)(1) A rule shall not take effect (or continue), if the Congress enacts a joint resolution of disapproval, described under section 802, of the rule.

(2) A rule that does not take effect (or does not continue) under paragraph (1) may not be reissued in substantially the same form, and a new rule that is substantially the same as such a rule

may not be issued, unless the reissued or new rule is specifically authorized by a law enacted after the date of the joint resolution disapproving the original rule.

(c)(1) Notwithstanding any other provision of this section (except subject to paragraph (3)), a rule that would not take effect by reason of subsection (a)(3) may take effect, if the President makes a determination under paragraph (2) and submits written notice of such determination to the Congress.

(2) Paragraph (1) applies to a determination made by the President by Executive order that the rule should take effect because such rule is —

(A) necessary because of an imminent threat to health or safety or other emergency;

(B) necessary for the enforcement of criminal laws;

(C) necessary for national security; or

(D) issued pursuant to any statute implementing an international trade agreement.

(3) An exercise by the President of the authority under this subsection shall have no effect on the procedures under section 802 or the effect of a joint resolution of disapproval under this section.

(d)(1) In addition to the opportunity for review otherwise provided under this chapter, in the case of any rule for which a report was submitted in accordance with subsection (a)(1)(A) during the period beginning on the date occurring —

(A) in the case of the Senate, 60 session days, or

(B) in the case of the House of Representatives, 60 legislative days,

before the date the Congress adjourns a session of Congress through the date on which the same or succeeding Congress first convenes its next session, section 802 shall apply to such rule in the succeeding session of Congress.

(2)(A) In applying section 802 for purposes of such additional review, a rule described under paragraph (1) shall be treated as though —

(i) such rule were published in the Federal Register (as a rule that shall take effect) on —

(I) in the case of the Senate, the 15th session day, or

(II) in the case of the House of Representatives, the 15th legislative day, after the succeeding session of Congress first convenes; and

(ii) a report on such rule were submitted to Congress under subsection (a)(1) on such date.

(B) Nothing in this paragraph shall be construed to affect the requirement under subsection (a)(1) that a report shall be submitted to Congress before a rule can take effect.

(3) A rule described under paragraph (1) shall take effect as otherwise provided by law (including other subsections of this section).

(e)(1) For purposes of this subsection, section 802 shall also apply to any major rule promulgated between March 1, 1996, and the date of the enactment of this chapter.

(2) In applying section 802 for purposes of Congressional review, a rule described under paragraph (1) shall be treated as though —

(A) such rule were published in the Federal Register on the date of enactment of this chapter; and

(B) a report on such rule were submitted to Congress under subsection (a)(1) on such date.

(3) The effectiveness of a rule described under paragraph (1) shall be as otherwise provided by law, unless the rule is made of no force or effect under section 802.

(f) Any rule that takes effect and later is made of no force or effect by enactment of a joint resolution under section 802 shall be treated as though such rule had never taken effect.

(g) If the Congress does not enact a joint resolution of disapproval under section 802 respecting a rule, no court or agency may infer any intent of the Congress from any action or inaction of the Congress with regard to such rule, related statute, or joint resolution of disapproval.

§802. Congressional disapproval procedure

(a) For purposes of this section, the term "joint resolution" means only a joint resolution introduced in the period beginning on the date on which the report referred to in section 801(a)(1)(A) is received by Congress and ending 60 days thereafter (excluding days either House of Congress is adjourned for more than 3 days during a session of Congress), the matter after the resolving clause of which is as follows: "That Congress disapproves the rule submitted by the _____ relating to _____, and such rule shall have no force or effect." (The blank spaces being appropriately filled in).

(b)(1) A joint resolution described in subsection (a) shall be referred to the committees in each House of Congress with jurisdiction.

(2) For purposes of this section, the term "submission or publication date" means the later of the date on which —

(A) the Congress receives the report submitted under section 801(a)(1); or

(B) the rule is published in the Federal Register, if so published.

(c) In the Senate, if the committee to which is referred a joint resolution described in subsection (a) has not reported such joint resolution (or an identical joint resolution) at the end of 20 calendar days after the submission or publication date defined under subsection (b)(2), such committee may be discharged from further consideration of such joint resolution upon a petition supported in writing by 30 Members of the Senate, and such joint resolution shall be placed on the calendar.

(d)(1) In the Senate, when the committee to which a joint resolution is referred has reported, or when a committee is discharged (under subsection (c)) from further consideration of a joint resolution described in subsection (a), it is at any time thereafter in order (even though a previous motion to the same effect has been disagreed to) for a motion to proceed to the consideration of the joint resolution, and all points of order against the joint resolution (and against consideration of the joint resolution) are waived. The motion is not subject to amendment, or to a motion to postpone, or to a motion to proceed to the consideration of other business. A motion to reconsider the vote by which the motion is agreed to or disagreed to shall not be in order. If a motion to proceed to the consideration of the joint resolution is agreed to, the joint resolution shall remain the unfinished business of the Senate until disposed of.

(2) In the Senate, debate on the joint resolution, and on all debatable motions and appeals in connection therewith, shall be limited to not more than 10 hours, which shall be divided equally between those favoring and those opposing the joint resolution. A motion further to limit debate is in order and not debatable. An amendment to, or a motion to postpone, or a motion to proceed to the consideration of other business, or a motion to recommit the joint resolution is not in order.

(3) In the Senate, immediately following the conclusion of the debate on a joint resolution described in subsection (a), and a single quorum call at the conclusion of the debate if requested in accordance with the rules of the Senate, the vote on final passage of the joint resolution shall occur.

(4) Appeals from the decisions of the Chair relating to the application of the rules of the Senate to the procedure relating to a joint resolution described in subsection (a) shall be decided without debate.

(e) In the Senate the procedure specified in subsection (c) or (d) shall not apply to the consideration of a joint resolution respecting a rule —

(1) after the expiration of the 60 session days beginning with the applicable submission or publication date, or

(2) if the report under section 801(a)(1)(A) was submitted during the period referred to in section 801(d)(1), after the expiration of the 60 session days beginning on the 15th session day after the succeeding session of Congress first convenes.

(f) If, before the passage by one House of a joint resolution of that House described in subsection (a), that House receives from the other House a joint resolution described in subsection (a), then the following procedures shall apply:

(1) The joint resolution of the other House shall not be referred to a committee.

(2) With respect to a joint resolution described in subsection (a) of the House receiving the joint resolution —

(A) the procedure in that House shall be the same as if no joint resolution had been received from the other House; but

(B) the vote on final passage shall be on the joint resolution of the other House.

(g) This section is enacted by Congress —

(1) as an exercise of the rulemaking power of the Senate and House of Representatives, respectively, and as such it is deemed a part of the rules of each House, respectively, but applicable only with respect to the procedure to be followed in that House in the case of a joint resolution described in subsection (a), and it supersedes other rules only to the extent that it is inconsistent with such rules; and

(2) with full recognition of the constitutional right of either House to change the rules (so far as relating to the procedure of that House) at any time, in the same manner, and to the same extent as in the case of any other rule of that House.

§803. Special rule on statutory, regulatory, and judicial deadlines

(a) In the case of any deadline for, relating to, or involving any rule which does not take effect (or the effectiveness of which is terminated) because of enactment of a joint resolution under section 802, that deadline is extended until the date 1 year after the date of enactment of the joint resolution. Nothing in this subsection shall be construed to affect a deadline merely by reason of the postponement of a rule's effective date under section 801(a).

(b) The term "deadline" means any date certain for fulfilling any obligation or exercising any authority established by or under any Federal statute or regulation, or by or under any court order implementing any Federal statute or regulation.

§804. Definitions

For purposes of this chapter —

(1) The term "Federal agency" means any agency as that term is defined in section 551(1).

(2) The term "major rule" means any rule that the Administrator of the Office of Information and Regulatory Affairs of the Office of Management and Budget finds has resulted in or is likely to result in —

(A) an annual effect on the economy of $100,000,000 or more;

(B) a major increase in costs or prices for consumers, individual industries, Federal, State, or local government agencies, or geographic regions; or

(C) significant adverse effects on competition, employment, investment, productivity, innovation, or on the ability of United States-based enterprises to compete with foreign-based enterprises in domestic and export markets.

The term does not include any rule promulgated under the Telecommunications Act of 1996 and the amendments made by that Act.

(3) The term "rule" has the meaning given such term in section 551, except that such term does not include —

(A) any rule of particular applicability, including a rule that approves or prescribes for the future rates, wages, prices, services, or allowances therefor, corporate or financial structures, reorganizations, mergers, or acquisitions thereof, or accounting practices or disclosures bearing on any of the foregoing;

(B) any rule relating to agency management or personnel; or

(C) any rule of agency organization, procedure, or practice that does not substantially affect the rights or obligations of non-agency parties.

§805. Judicial review

No determination, finding, action, or omission under this chapter shall be subject to judicial review.

§806. Applicability; severability

(a) This chapter shall apply notwithstanding any other provision of law.

(b) If any provision of this chapter or the application of any provision of this chapter to any person or circumstance, is held invalid, the application of such provision to other persons or circumstances, and the remainder of this chapter, shall not be affected thereby.

§807. Exemption for monetary policy

Nothing in this chapter shall apply to rules that concern monetary policy proposed or implemented by the Board of Governors of the Federal Reserve System or the Federal Open Market Committee.

§808. Effective date of certain rules

Notwithstanding section 801 —

(1) any rule that establishes, modifies, opens, closes, or conducts a regulatory program for a commercial, recreational, or subsistence activity related to hunting, fishing, or camping, or

(2) any rule which an agency for good cause finds (and incorporates the finding and a brief statement of reasons therefor in the rule issued) that notice and public procedure thereon are impracticable, unnecessary, or contrary to the public interest,

shall take effect at such time as the Federal agency promulgating the rule determines.

Regulatory Planning and Review, Executive Order 12,866

58 Fed. Reg. 51,735 (1993) (EOs 13,258 and 13,422, amending EO 12,866, were revoked by EO 13,497, 74 Fed. Reg. 6113 (2009))

The American people deserve a regulatory system that works for them, not against them: a regulatory system that protects and improves their health, safety, environment, and well-being and improves the performance of the economy without imposing unacceptable or unreasonable costs on society; regulatory policies that recognize that the private sector and private markets are the best engine for economic growth; regulatory approaches that respect the role of State, local, and tribal governments; and regulations that are effective, consistent, sensible, and understandable. We do not have such a regulatory system today.

With this Executive order, the Federal Government begins a program to reform and make more efficient the regulatory process. The objectives of this Executive order are to enhance planning and coordination with respect to both new and existing regulations; to reaffirm the primacy of Federal agencies in the regulatory decision-making process; to restore the integrity and legitimacy of regulatory review and oversight; and to make the process more accessible and open to the public. In pursuing these objectives, the regulatory process shall be conducted so as to meet applicable statutory requirements and with due regard to the discretion that has been entrusted to the Federal agencies.

Accordingly, by the authority vested in me as President by the Constitution and the laws of the United States of America, it is hereby ordered as follows:

§1. Statement of Regulatory Philosophy and Principles.

(a) The Regulatory Philosophy. Federal agencies should promulgate only such regulations as are required by law, are necessary to interpret the law, or are made necessary by compelling public need, such as material failures of private markets to protect or improve the health and safety of the public, the environment, or the well-being of the American people. In deciding whether and how to regulate, agencies should assess all costs and benefits of available regulatory alternatives, including the alternative of not regulating. Costs and benefits shall be understood to include both quantifiable measures (to the fullest extent that these can be usefully estimated) and qualitative measures of costs and benefits that are difficult to quantify, but nevertheless essential to consider. Further, in choosing among alternative regulatory approaches, agencies should select those approaches that maximize net benefits (including potential economic, environmental, public health and safety, and other advantages; distributive impacts; and equity), unless a statute requires another regulatory approach.

(b) The Principles of Regulation. To ensure that the agencies' regulatory programs are consistent with the philosophy set forth above, agencies should adhere to the following principles, to the extent permitted by law and where applicable:

(1) Each agency shall identify the problem that it intends to address (including, where applicable, the failures of private markets or public institutions that warrant new agency action) as well as assess the significance of that problem.

(2) Each agency shall examine whether existing regulations (or other law) have created, or contributed to, the problem that a new regulation is intended to correct and whether those regulations (or other law) should be modified to achieve the intended goal of regulation more effectively.

(3) Each agency shall identify and assess available alternatives to direct regulation, including providing economic incentives to encourage the desired behavior, such as user fees or marketable permits, or providing information upon which choices can be made by the public.

(4) In setting regulatory priorities, each agency shall consider, to the extent reasonable, the degree and nature of the risks posed by various substances or activities within its jurisdiction.

(5) When an agency determines that a regulation is the best available method of achieving the regulatory objective, it shall design its regulations in the most cost-effective manner to achieve the regulatory objective. In doing so, each agency shall consider incentives for innovation, consistency, predictability, the costs of enforcement and compliance (to the government, regulated entities, and the public), flexibility, distributive impacts, and equity.

(6) Each agency shall assess both the costs and the benefits of the intended regulation and, recognizing that some costs and benefits are difficult to quantify, propose or adopt a regulation only upon a reasoned determination that the benefits of the intended regulation justify its costs.

(7) Each agency shall base its decisions on the best reasonably obtainable scientific, technical, economic, and other information concerning the need for, and consequences of, the intended regulation.

(8) Each agency shall identify and assess alternative forms of regulation and shall, to the extent feasible, specify performance objectives, rather than specifying the behavior or manner of compliance that regulated entities must adopt.

(9) Wherever feasible, agencies shall seek views of appropriate State, local, and tribal officials before imposing regulatory requirements that might significantly or uniquely affect those governmental entities. Each agency shall assess the effects of Federal regulations on State, local, and tribal governments, including specifically the availability of resources to carry out those mandates, and seek to minimize those burdens that uniquely or significantly affect such governmental entities, consistent with achieving regulatory objectives. In addition, as appropriate, agencies shall seek to harmonize Federal regulatory actions with related State, local, and tribal regulatory and other governmental functions.

(10) Each agency shall avoid regulations that are inconsistent, incompatible, or duplicative with its other regulations or those of other Federal agencies.

(11) Each agency shall tailor its regulations to impose the least burden on society, including individuals, businesses of differing sizes, and other entities (including small communities and governmental entities), consistent with obtaining the regulatory objectives, taking into account, among other things, and to the extent practicable, the costs of cumulative regulations.

(12) Each agency shall draft its regulations to be simple and easy to understand, with the goal of minimizing the potential for uncertainty and litigation arising from such uncertainty.

§2. Organization.

An efficient regulatory planning and review process is vital to ensure that the Federal Government's regulatory system best serves the American people.

(a) The Agencies. Because Federal agencies are the repositories of significant substantive expertise and experience, they are responsible for developing regulations and assuring that the regulations are consistent with applicable law, the President's priorities, and the principles set forth in this Executive order.

(b) The Office of Management and Budget. Coordinated review of agency rulemaking is necessary to ensure that regulations are consistent with applicable law, the President's priorities, and the principles set forth in this Executive order, and that decisions made by one agency do not conflict with the policies or actions taken or planned by another agency. The Office of Management and Budget (OMB)

shall carry out that review function. Within OMB, the Office of Information and Regulatory Affairs (OIRA) is the repository of expertise concerning regulatory issues, including methodologies and procedures that affect more than one agency, this Executive order, and the President's regulatory policies. To the extent permitted by law, OMB shall provide guidance to agencies and assist the President, the Vice President, and other regulatory policy advisors to the President in regulatory planning and shall be the entity that reviews individual regulations, as provided by this Executive order.

(c) The Vice President. The Vice President is the principal advisor to the President on, and shall coordinate the development and presentation of recommendations concerning, regulatory policy, planning, and review, as set forth in this Executive order. In fulfilling their responsibilities under this Executive order, the President and the Vice President shall be assisted by the regulatory policy advisors within the Executive Office of the President and by such agency officials and personnel as the President and the Vice President may, from time to time, consult.

§3. Definitions

For purposes of this Executive order:

(a) "Advisors" refers to such regulatory policy advisors to the President as the President and Vice President may from time to time consult, including, among others: (1) the Director of OMB; (2) the Chair (or another member) of the Council of Economic Advisers; (3) the Assistant to the President for Economic Policy; (4) the Assistant to the President for Domestic Policy; (5) the Assistant to the President for National Security Affairs; (6) the Assistant to the President for Science and Technology; (7) the Assistant to the President for Intergovernmental Affairs; (8) the Assistant to the President and Staff Secretary; (9) the Assistant to the President and Chief of Staff to the Vice President; (10) the Assistant to the President and Counsel to the President; (11) the Deputy Assistant to the President and Director of the White House Office on Environmental Policy; and (12) the Administrator of OIRA, who also shall coordinate communications relating to this Executive order among the agencies, OMB, the other Advisors, and the Office of the Vice President.

(b) "Agency," unless otherwise indicated, means any authority of the United States that is an "agency" under 44 U.S.C. 3502(1), other than those considered to be independent regulatory agencies, as defined in 44 U.S.C. 3502(10).

(c) "Director" means the Director of OMB.

(d) "Regulation" or "rule" means an agency statement of general applicability and future effect, which the agency intends to have the force and effect of law, that is designed to implement, interpret, or prescribe law or policy or to describe the procedure or practice requirements of an agency. It does not, however, include:

(1) Regulations or rules issued in accordance with the formal rulemaking provisions of 5 U.S.C. 556, 557;

(2) Regulations or rules that pertain to a military or foreign affairs function of the United States, other than procurement regulations and regulations involving the import or export of non-defense articles and services;

(3) Regulations or rules that are limited to agency organization, management, or personnel matters; or

(4) Any other category of regulations exempted by the Administrator of OIRA.

(e) "Regulatory action" means any substantive action by an agency (normally published in the Federal Register) that promulgates or is expected to lead to the promulgation of a final rule or regulation, including notices of inquiry, advance notices of proposed rulemaking, and notices of proposed rulemaking.

(f) "Significant regulatory action" means any regulatory action that is likely to result in a rule that may:

(1) Have an annual effect on the economy of $100 million or more or adversely affect in a material way the economy, a sector of the economy, productivity, competition, jobs, the environment, public health or safety, or State, local, or tribal governments or communities;

(2) Create a serious inconsistency or otherwise interfere with an action taken or planned by another agency;

(3) Materially alter the budgetary impact of entitlements, grants, user fees, or loan programs or the rights and obligations of recipients thereof; or

(4) Raise novel legal or policy issues arising out of legal mandates, the President's priorities, or the principles set forth in this Executive order.

§4. Planning mechanism

In order to have an effective regulatory program, to provide for coordination of regulations, to maximize consultation and the resolution of potential conflicts at an early stage, to involve the public and its State, local, and tribal officials in regulatory planning, and to ensure that new or revised regulations promote the President's priorities and the principles set forth in this Executive order, these procedures shall be followed, to the extent permitted by law:

(a) Agencies' Policy Meeting. Early in each year's planning cycle, the Vice President shall convene a meeting of the Advisors and the heads of agencies to seek a common understanding of priorities and to coordinate regulatory efforts to be accomplished in the upcoming year.

(b) Unified Regulatory Agenda. For purposes of this subsection, the term "agency" or "agencies" shall also include those considered to be independent regulatory agencies, as defined in 44 U.S.C. 3502(10).

Each agency shall prepare an agenda of all regulations under development or review, at a time and in a manner specified by the Administrator of OIRA. The description of each regulatory action shall contain, at a minimum, a regulation identifier number, a brief summary of the action, the legal authority for the action, any legal deadline for the action, and the name and telephone number of a knowledgeable agency official. Agencies may incorporate the information required under 5 U.S.C. 602 and 41 U.S.C. 402 into these agendas.

(c) The Regulatory Plan. For purposes of this subsection, the term "agency" or "agencies" shall also include those considered to be independent regulatory agencies, as defined in 44 U.S.C. 3502(10).

(1) As part of the Unified Regulatory Agenda, beginning in 1994, each agency shall prepare a Regulatory Plan (Plan) of the most important significant regulatory actions that the agency reasonably expects to issue in proposed or final form in that fiscal year or thereafter. The Plan shall be approved personally by the agency head and shall contain at a minimum:

(A) A statement of the agency's regulatory objectives and priorities and how they relate to the President's priorities;

(B) A summary of each planned significant regulatory action including, to the extent possible, alternatives to be considered and preliminary estimates of the anticipated costs and benefits;

(C) A summary of the legal basis for each such action, including whether any aspect of the action is required by statute or court order;

(D) A statement of the need for each such action and, if applicable, how the action will reduce risks to public health, safety, or the environment, as well as how the magnitude of the risk addressed by the action relates to other risks within the jurisdiction of the agency;

(E) The agency's schedule for action, including a statement of any applicable statutory or judicial deadlines; and

(F) The name, address, and telephone number of a person the public may contact for additional information about the planned regulatory action.

(2) Each agency shall forward its Plan to OIRA by June 1st of each year.

(3) Within 10 calendar days after OIRA has received an agency's Plan, OIRA shall circulate it to other affected agencies, the Advisors, and the Vice President.

(4) An agency head who believes that a planned regulatory action of another agency may conflict with its own policy or action taken or planned shall promptly notify, in writing, the Administrator of OIRA, who shall forward that

communication to the issuing agency, the Advisors, and the Vice President.

(5) If the Administrator of OIRA believes that a planned regulatory action of an agency may be inconsistent with the President's priorities or the principles set forth in this Executive order or may be in conflict with any policy or action taken or planned by another agency, the Administrator of OIRA shall promptly notify, in writing, the affected agencies, the Advisors, and the Vice President.

(6) The Vice President, with the Advisors' assistance, may consult with the heads of agencies with respect to their Plans and, in appropriate instances, request further consideration or interagency coordination.

(7) The Plans developed by the issuing agency shall be published annually in the October publication of the Unified Regulatory Agenda. This publication shall be made available to the Congress; State, local, and tribal governments; and the public. Any views on any aspect of any agency Plan, including whether any planned regulatory action might conflict with any other planned or existing regulation, impose any unintended consequences on the public, or confer any unclaimed benefits on the public, should be directed to the issuing agency, with a copy to OIRA.

(d) Regulatory Working Group. Within 30 days of the date of this Executive order, the Administrator of OIRA shall convene a Regulatory Working Group ("Working Group"), which shall consist of representatives of the heads of each agency that the Administrator determines to have significant domestic regulatory responsibility, the Advisors, and the Vice President. The Administrator of OIRA shall chair the Working Group and shall periodically advise the Vice President on the activities of the Working Group. The Working Group shall serve as a forum to assist agencies in identifying and analyzing important regulatory issues (including, among others (1) the development of innovative regulatory techniques, (2) the methods, efficacy, and utility of comparative risk assessment in regulatory decision-making, and (3) the development of short forms and other streamlined regulatory approaches for small businesses and other entities). The Working Group shall meet at least quarterly and may meet as a whole or in subgroups of agencies with an interest in particular issues or subject areas. To inform its discussions, the Working Group may commission analytical studies and reports by OIRA, the Administrative Conference of the United States, or any other agency.

(e) Conferences. The Administrator of OIRA shall meet quarterly with representatives of State, local, and tribal governments to identify both existing and proposed regulations that may uniquely or significantly affect those governmental entities. The Administrator of OIRA shall also convene, from time to time, conferences with representatives of

businesses, nongovernmental organizations, and the public to discuss regulatory issues of common concern.

§5. Existing regulations

In order to reduce the regulatory burden on the American people, their families, their communities, their State, local, and tribal governments, and their industries; to determine whether regulations promulgated by the executive branch of the Federal Government have become unjustified or unnecessary as a result of changed circumstances; to confirm that regulations are both compatible with each other and not duplicative or inappropriately burdensome in the aggregate; to ensure that all regulations are consistent with the President's priorities and the principles set forth in this Executive order, within applicable law; and to otherwise improve the effectiveness of existing regulations:

(a) Within 90 days of the date of this Executive order, each agency shall submit to OIRA a program, consistent with its resources and regulatory priorities, under which the agency will periodically review its existing significant regulations to determine whether any such regulations should be modified or eliminated so as to make the agency's regulatory program more effective in achieving the regulatory objectives, less burdensome, or in greater alignment with the President's priorities and the principles set forth in this Executive order. Any significant regulations selected for review shall be included in the agency's annual Plan. The agency shall also identify any legislative mandates that require the agency to promulgate or continue to impose regulations that the agency believes are unnecessary or outdated by reason of changed circumstances.

(b) The Administrator of OIRA shall work with the Regulatory Working Group and other interested entities to pursue the objectives of this section. State, local, and tribal governments are specifically encouraged to assist in the identification of regulations that impose significant or unique burdens on those governmental entities and that appear to have outlived their justification or be otherwise inconsistent with the public interest.

(c) The Vice President, in consultation with the Advisors, may identify for review by the appropriate agency or agencies other existing regulations of an agency or groups of regulations of more than one agency that affect a particular group, industry, or sector of the economy, or may identify legislative mandates that may be appropriate for reconsideration by the Congress.

§6. Centralized Review of Regulations.

The guidelines set forth below shall apply to all regulatory actions, for both new and existing regulations, by agencies other than those agencies specifically exempted by the Administrator of OIRA:

(a) Agency Responsibilities.

(1) Each agency shall (consistent with its own rules, regulations, or procedures) provide the public with meaningful participation in the regulatory process. In particular, before issuing a notice of proposed rulemaking, each agency should, where appropriate, seek the involvement of those who are intended to benefit from and those expected to be burdened by any regulation (including, specifically, State, local, and tribal officials). In addition, each agency should afford the public a meaningful opportunity to comment on any proposed regulation, which in most cases should include a comment period of not less than 60 days. Each agency also is directed to explore and, where appropriate, use consensual mechanisms for developing regulations, including negotiated rulemaking.

(2) Within 60 days of the date of this Executive order, each agency head shall designate a Regulatory Policy Officer who shall report to the agency head. The Regulatory Policy Officer shall be involved at each stage of the regulatory process to foster the development of effective, innovative, and least burdensome regulations and to further the principles set forth in this Executive order.

(3) In addition to adhering to its own rules and procedures and to the requirements of the Administrative Procedure Act, the Regulatory Flexibility Act, the Paperwork Reduction Act, and other applicable law, each agency shall develop its regulatory actions in a timely fashion and adhere to the following procedures with respect to a regulatory action:

(A) Each agency shall provide OIRA, at such times and in the manner specified by the Administrator of OIRA, with a list of its planned regulatory actions, indicating those which the agency believes are significant regulatory actions within the meaning of this Executive order. Absent a material change in the development of the planned regulatory action, those not designated as significant will not be subject to review under this section unless, within 10 working days of receipt of the list, the Administrator of OIRA notifies the agency that OIRA has determined that a planned regulation is a significant regulatory action within the meaning of this Executive order. The Administrator of OIRA may waive review of any planned regulatory action designated by the agency as significant, in which case the agency need not further comply with subsection (a)(3)(B) or subsection (a)(3)(C) of this section.

(B) For each matter identified as, or determined by the Administrator of OIRA to be, a significant regulatory action, the issuing agency shall provide to OIRA:

(i) The text of the draft regulatory action, together with a reasonably detailed description of the need for the regulatory action and an explanation of how the regulatory action will meet that need; and

(ii) An assessment of the potential costs and benefits of the regulatory action, including an explanation of the manner in which the regulatory action is consistent with a statutory mandate and, to the extent permitted by law, promotes the President's priorities and avoids undue interference with State, local, and tribal governments in the exercise of their governmental functions.

(C) For those matters identified as, or determined by the Administrator of OIRA to be, a significant regulatory action within the scope of section 3(f)(1), the agency shall also provide to OIRA the following additional information developed as part of the agency's decision-making process (unless prohibited by law):

(i) An assessment, including the underlying analysis, of benefits anticipated from the regulatory action (such as, but not limited to, the promotion of the efficient functioning of the economy and private markets, the enhancement of health and safety, the protection of the natural environment, and the elimination or reduction of discrimination or bias) together with, to the extent feasible, a quantification of those benefits;

(ii) An assessment, including the underlying analysis, of costs anticipated from the regulatory action (such as, but not limited to, the direct cost both to the government in administering the regulation and to businesses and others in complying with the regulation, and any adverse effects on the efficient functioning of the economy, private markets (including productivity, employment, and competitiveness), health, safety, and the natural environment), together with, to the extent feasible, a quantification of those costs; and

(iii) An assessment, including the underlying analysis, of costs and benefits of potentially effective and reasonably feasible alternatives to the planned regulation, identified by the agencies or the public (including improving the current regulation and reasonably viable nonregulatory actions), and an explanation why the planned regulatory action is preferable to the identified potential alternatives.

(D) In emergency situations or when an agency is obligated by law to act more quickly than normal review procedures allow, the agency shall notify OIRA as soon as possible and, to the extent practicable, comply with subsections (a)(3)(B) and (C) of this section. For those regulatory actions that are governed by a statutory or court-imposed deadline, the agency shall, to the extent practicable, schedule rulemaking proceedings so as to permit sufficient time for OIRA to conduct its review, as set forth below in subsection (b)(2) through (4) of this section.

(E) After the regulatory action has been published in the Federal Register or otherwise issued to the public, the agency shall:

(i) Make available to the public the information set forth in subsections (a)(3)(B) and (C);

(ii) Identify for the public, in a complete, clear, and simple manner, the substantive changes between the draft submitted to OIRA for review and the action subsequently announced; and

(iii) Identify for the public those changes in the regulatory action that were made at the suggestion or recommendation of OIRA.

(F) All information provided to the public by the agency shall be in plain, understandable language.

(b) OIRA Responsibilities. The Administrator of OIRA shall provide meaningful guidance and oversight so that each agency's regulatory actions are consistent with applicable law, the President's priorities, and the principles set forth in this Executive order and do not conflict with the policies or actions of another agency. OIRA shall, to the extent permitted by law, adhere to the following guidelines:

(1) OIRA may review only actions identified by the agency or by OIRA as significant regulatory actions under subsection (a)(3)(A) of this section.

(2) OIRA shall waive review or notify the agency in writing of the results of its review within the following time periods:

(A) For any notices of inquiry, advance notices of proposed rulemaking, or other preliminary regulatory actions prior to a Notice of Proposed Rulemaking, within 10 working days after the date of submission of the draft action to OIRA;

(B) For all other regulatory actions, within 90 calendar days after the date of submission of the information set forth in subsections (a)(3)(B) and (C) of this section, unless OIRA has previously reviewed this information and, since that review, there has been no material change in the facts and circumstances upon which the regulatory action is based, in which case, OIRA shall complete its review within 45 days; and

(C) The review process may be extended (1) once by no more than 30 calendar days upon the written approval of the Director and (2) at the request of the agency head.

(3) For each regulatory action that the Administrator of OIRA returns to an agency for further consideration of some or all of its provisions, the Administrator of OIRA shall provide the issuing agency a written explanation for such return, setting forth the pertinent provision of this Executive order on which OIRA is relying. If the agency head disagrees with some or all of the bases for the return, the agency head shall so inform the Administrator of OIRA in writing.

(4) Except as otherwise provided by law or required by a Court, in order to ensure greater openness, accessibility, and accountability in the regulatory review process, OIRA shall be governed by the following disclosure requirements:

(A) Only the Administrator of OIRA (or a particular designee) shall receive oral communications initiated by persons not employed by the executive branch of the Federal Government regarding the substance of a regulatory action under OIRA review;

(B) All substantive communications between OIRA personnel and persons not employed by the executive branch of the Federal Government regarding a regulatory action under review shall be governed by the following guidelines:

(i) A representative from the issuing agency shall be invited to any meeting between OIRA personnel and such person(s);

(ii) OIRA shall forward to the issuing agency, within 10 working days of receipt of the communication(s), all written communications, regardless of format, between OIRA personnel and any person who is not employed by the executive branch of the Federal Government, and the dates and names of individuals involved in all substantive oral communications (including meetings to which an agency representative was invited, but did not attend, and telephone conversations between OIRA personnel and any such persons); and

(iii) OIRA shall publicly disclose relevant information about such communication(s), as set forth below in subsection (b)(4)(C) of this section.

(C) OIRA shall maintain a publicly available log that shall contain, at a minimum, the following information pertinent to regulatory actions under review:

(i) The status of all regulatory actions, including if (and if so, when and by whom)

Vice Presidential and Presidential consideration was requested;

    (ii) A notation of all written communications forwarded to an issuing agency under subsection (b)(4)(B)(ii) of this section; and

    (iii) The dates and names of individuals involved in all substantive oral communications, including meetings and telephone conversations, between OIRA personnel and any person not employed by the executive branch of the Federal Government, and the subject matter discussed during such communications.

(D) After the regulatory action has been published in the Federal Register or otherwise issued to the public, or after the agency has announced its decision not to publish or issue the regulatory action, OIRA shall make available to the public all documents exchanged between OIRA and the agency during the review by OIRA under this section.

(5) All information provided to the public by OIRA shall be in plain, understandable language.

§7. Resolution of Conflicts.

To the extent permitted by law, disagreements or conflicts between or among agency heads or between OMB and any agency that cannot be resolved by the Administrator of OIRA shall be resolved by the President, or by the Vice President acting at the request of the President, with the relevant agency head (and, as appropriate, other interested government officials). Vice Presidential and Presidential consideration of such disagreements may be initiated only by the Director, by the head of the issuing agency, or by the head of an agency that has a significant interest in the regulatory action at issue. Such review will not be undertaken at the request of other persons, entities, or their agents.

Resolution of such conflicts shall be informed by recommendations developed by the Vice President, after consultation with the Advisors (and other executive branch officials or personnel whose responsibilities to the President include the subject matter at issue). The development of these recommendations shall be concluded within 60 days after review has been requested.

During the Vice Presidential and Presidential review period, communications with any person not employed by the Federal Government relating to the substance of the regulatory action under review and directed to the Advisors or their staffs or to the staff of the Vice President shall be in writing and shall be forwarded by the recipient to the affected agency(ies) for inclusion in the public docket(s). When the communication is not in writing, such Advisors or staff members shall inform the outside party that the matter is under review and that any comments should be submitted in writing.

At the end of this review process, the President, or the Vice President acting at the request of the President, shall notify the affected agency and the Administrator of OIRA of the President's decision with respect to the matter.

§8. Publication.

Except to the extent required by law, an agency shall not publish in the Federal Register or otherwise issue to the public any regulatory action that is subject to review under section 6 of this Executive order until (1) the Administrator of OIRA notifies the agency that OIRA has waived its review of the action or has completed its review without any requests for further consideration, or (2) the applicable time period in section 6(b)(2) expires without OIRA having notified the agency that it is returning the regulatory action for further consideration under section 6(b)(3), whichever occurs first. If the terms of the preceding sentence have not been satisfied and an agency wants to publish or otherwise issue a regulatory action, the head of that agency may request Presidential consideration through the Vice President, as provided under section 7 of this order. Upon receipt of this request, the Vice President shall notify OIRA and the Advisors. The guidelines and time period set forth in section 7 shall apply to the publication of regulatory actions for which Presidential consideration has been sought.

§9. Agency Authority.

Nothing in this order shall be construed as displacing the agencies' authority or responsibilities, as authorized by law.

§10. Judicial Review.

Nothing in this Executive order shall affect any otherwise available judicial review of agency action. This Executive order is intended only to improve the internal management of the Federal Government and does not create any right or benefit, substantive or procedural, enforceable at law or equity by a party against the United States, its agencies or instrumentalities, its officers or employees, or any other person.

§11. Revocations.

Executive Orders Nos. 12291 and 12498; all amendments to those Executive orders; all guidelines issued under those orders; and any exemptions from those orders heretofore granted for any category of rule are revoked.

Improving Regulation and Regulatory Review, Executive Order 13,563

76 Fed. Reg. 3,821 (2011)

By the authority vested in me as President by the Constitution and the laws of the United States of America, and in order to improve regulation and regulatory review, it is hereby ordered as follows:

§1. General Principles of Regulation. (a) Our regulatory system must protect public health, welfare, safety, and our environment while promoting economic growth, innovation, competitiveness, and job creation. It must be based on the best available science. It must allow for public participation and an open exchange of ideas. It must promote predictability and reduce uncertainty. It must identify and use the best, most innovative, and least burdensome tools for achieving regulatory ends. It must take into account benefits and costs, both quantitative and qualitative. It must ensure that regulations are accessible, consistent, written in plain language, and easy to understand. It must measure, and seek to improve, the actual results of regulatory requirements.

(b) This order is supplemental to and reaffirms the principles, structures, and definitions governing contemporary regulatory review that were established in Executive Order 12866 of September 30, 1993. As stated in that Executive Order and to the extent permitted by law, each agency must, among other things: (1) propose or adopt a regulation only upon a reasoned determination that its benefits justify its costs (recognizing that some benefits and costs are difficult to quantify); (2) tailor its regulations to impose the least burden on society, consistent with obtaining regulatory objectives, taking into account, among other things, and to the extent practicable, the costs of cumulative regulations; (3) select, in choosing among alternative regulatory approaches, those approaches that maximize net benefits (including potential economic, environmental, public health and safety, and other advantages; distributive impacts; and equity); (4) to the extent feasible, specify performance objectives, rather than specifying the behavior or manner of compliance that regulated entities must adopt; and (5) identify and assess available alternatives to direct regulation, including providing economic incentives to encourage the desired behavior, such as user fees or marketable permits, or providing information upon which choices can be made by the public.

(c) In applying these principles, each agency is directed to use the best available techniques to quantify anticipated present and future benefits and costs as accurately as possible. Where appropriate and permitted by law, each agency may consider (and discuss qualitatively) values that are difficult or impossible to quantify, including equity, human dignity, fairness, and distributive impacts.

§2. Public Participation. (a) Regulations shall be adopted through a process that involves public participation. To that end, regulations shall be based, to the extent feasible and consistent with law, on the open exchange of information and perspectives among State, local, and tribal officials, experts in relevant disciplines, affected stakeholders in the private sector, and the public as a whole.

(b) To promote that open exchange, each agency, consistent with Executive Order 12866 and other applicable legal requirements, shall endeavor to provide the public with an opportunity to participate in the regulatory process. To the extent feasible and permitted by law, each agency shall afford the public a meaningful opportunity to comment through the Internet on any proposed regulation, with a comment period that should generally be at least 60 days. To the extent feasible and permitted by law, each agency shall also provide, for both proposed and final rules, timely online access to the rulemaking docket on regulations. gov, including relevant scientific and technical findings, in an open format that can be easily searched and downloaded. For proposed rules, such access shall include, to the extent feasible and permitted by law, an opportunity for public comment on all pertinent parts of the rulemaking docket, including relevant scientific and technical findings.

(c) Before issuing a notice of proposed rulemaking, each agency, where feasible and appropriate, shall seek the views of those who are likely to be affected, including those who are likely to benefit from and those who are potentially subject to such rulemaking.

§3. Integration and Innovation. Some sectors and industries face a significant number of regulatory requirements, some of which may be redundant, inconsistent, or overlapping. Greater coordination across agencies could reduce these requirements, thus reducing costs and simplifying and harmonizing rules. In developing regulatory actions and identifying appropriate approaches, each agency shall attempt to promote such coordination, simplification, and harmonization. Each agency shall also seek to identify, as appropriate, means to achieve regulatory goals that are designed to promote innovation.

§4. Flexible Approaches. Where relevant, feasible, and consistent with regulatory objectives, and to the extent permitted by law, each agency shall identify and consider regulatory approaches that reduce burdens and maintain flexibility and freedom of choice for the public. These approaches include warnings, appropriate default rules, and disclosure requirements as well as provision of information to the public in a form that is clear and intelligible.

§5. Science. Consistent with the President's Memorandum for the Heads of Executive Departments and Agencies, "Scientific Integrity" (March 9, 2009), and its implementing guidance, each agency shall ensure the objectivity of any scientific and technological information and processes used to support the agency's regulatory actions.

§6. Retrospective Analyses of Existing Rules. **(a)** To facilitate the periodic review of existing significant regulations, agencies shall consider how best to promote retrospective analysis of rules that may be outmoded, ineffective, insufficient, or excessively burdensome, and to modify, streamline, expand, or repeal them in accordance with what has been learned. Such retrospective analyses, including supporting data, should be released online whenever possible.

(b) Within 120 days of the date of this order, each agency shall develop and submit to the Office of Information and Regulatory Affairs a preliminary plan, consistent with law and its resources and regulatory priorities, under which the agency will periodically review its existing significant regulations to determine whether any such regulations should be modified, streamlined, expanded, or repealed so as to make the agency's regulatory program more effective or less burdensome in achieving the regulatory objectives.

§7. General Provisions. **(a)** For purposes of this order, "agency" shall have the meaning set forth in section 3(b) of Executive Order 12866.

(b) Nothing in this order shall be construed to impair or otherwise affect:

    (i) authority granted by law to a department or agency, or the head thereof; or

    (ii) functions of the Director of the Office of Management and Budget relating to budgetary, administrative, or legislative proposals.

(c) This order shall be implemented consistent with applicable law and subject to the availability of appropriations.

(d) This order is not intended to, and does not, create any right or benefit, substantive or procedural, enforceable at law or in equity by any party against the United States, its departments, agencies, or entities, its officers, employees, or agents, or any other person.

BARACK OBAMA
THE WHITE HOUSE
January 18, 2011

Regulation and Independent Regulatory Agencies, Executive Order 13,579

76 Fed. Reg. 41,587 (2011)

By the authority vested in me as President by the Constitution and the laws of the United States of America, and in order to improve regulation and regulatory review, it is hereby ordered as follows:

§1. Policy. (a) Wise regulatory decisions depend on public participation and on careful analysis of the likely consequences of regulation. Such decisions are informed and improved by allowing interested members of the public to have a meaningful opportunity to participate in rulemaking. To the extent permitted by law, such decisions should be made only after consideration of their costs and benefits (both quantitative and qualitative).

(b) Executive Order 13563 of January 18, 2011, "Improving Regulation and Regulatory Review," directed to executive agencies, was meant to produce a regulatory system that protects "public health, welfare, safety, and our environment while promoting economic growth, innovation, competitiveness, and job creation." Independent regulatory agencies, no less than executive agencies, should promote that goal.

(c) Executive Order 13563 set out general requirements directed to executive agencies concerning public participation, integration and innovation, flexible approaches, and science. To the extent permitted by law, independent regulatory agencies should comply with these provisions as well.

§ 2. Retrospective Analyses of Existing Rules. (a) To facilitate the periodic review of existing significant regulations, independent regulatory agencies should consider how best to promote retrospective analysis of rules that may be outmoded, ineffective, insufficient, or excessively burdensome, and to modify, streamline, expand, or repeal them in accordance with what has been learned. Such retrospective analyses, including supporting data and evaluations, should be released online whenever possible.

(b) Within 120 days of the date of this order, each independent regulatory agency should develop and release to the public a plan, consistent with law and reflecting its resources and regulatory priorities and processes, under which the agency will periodically review its existing significant regulations to determine whether any such regulations should be modified, streamlined, expanded, or repealed so as to make the agency's regulatory program more effective or less burdensome in achieving the regulatory objectives.

§ 3. General Provisions. (a) For purposes of this order, "executive agency" shall have the meaning set forth for the term "agency" in section 3(b) of Executive Order 12866 of September 30, 1993, and "independent regulatory agency" shall have the meaning set forth in 44 U.S.C. 3502(5).

(b) Nothing in this order shall be construed to impair or otherwise affect:

(i) authority granted by law to a department or agency, or the head thereof;or

(ii) functions of the Director of the Office of Management and Budget relating to budgetary, administrative, or legislative proposals.

(c) This order shall be implemented consistent with applicable law and subject to the availability of appropriations.

(d) This order is not intended to, and does not, create any right or benefit, substantive or procedural, enforceable at law or in equity by any party against the United States, its departments, agencies, or entities, its officers, employees, or agents, or any other person.

BARACK OBAMA
THE WHITE HOUSE
July 11, 2011

Revocation of Certain Executive Orders Concerning Federal Regulation, Executive Order 13,992

86 Fed. Reg. 7049 (2021)

By the authority vested in me as President by the Constitution and the laws of the United States of America, it is hereby ordered that:

Section 1. *Policy.* It is the policy of my Administration to use available tools to confront the urgent challenges facing the Nation, including the coronavirus disease 2019 (COVID-19) pandemic, economic recovery, racial justice, and climate change. To tackle these challenges effectively, executive departments and agencies (agencies) must be equipped with the flexibility to use robust regulatory action to address national priorities. This order revokes harmful policies and directives that threaten to frustrate the Federal Government's ability to confront these problems, and empowers agencies to use appropriate regulatory tools to achieve these goals.

Sec. 2. *Revocation of Orders.* Executive Order 13771 of January 30, 2017 (Reducing Regulation and Controlling Regulatory Costs), Executive Order 13777of February 24, 2017 (Enforcing the Regulatory Reform Agenda), Executive Order 13875 of June 14, 2019 (Evaluating and Improving the Utility of Federal Advisory Committees), Executive Order 13891 of October 9, 2019 (Promoting the Rule of Law Through Improved Agency Guidance Documents), Executive Order 13892 of October 9, 2019 (Promoting the Rule of Law Through Transparency and Fairness in Civil Administrative Enforcement and Adjudication), and Executive Order 13893 of October 10, 2019 (Increasing Government Accountability for Administrative Actions by Reinvigorating Administrative PAYGO), are hereby revoked.

Sec. 3. *Implementation.* The Director of the Office of Management and Budget and the heads of agencies shall promptly take steps to rescind any orders, rules, regulations, guidelines, or policies, or portions thereof, implementing or enforcing the Executive Orders identified in section 2 of this order, as appropriate and consistent with applicable law, including the Administrative Procedure Act, 5 U.S.C. 551 *et seq.* If in any case such rescission cannot be finalized immediately, the Director and the heads of agencies shall promptly take steps to provide all available exemptions authorized by any such orders, rules, regulations, guidelines, or policies, as appropriate and consistent with applicable law. In addition, any personnel positions, committees, task forces, or other entities established pursuant to the Executive Orders identified in section 2 of this order, including the regulatory reform officer positions and regulatory reform task forces established by sections 2 and 3 of Executive Order 13777, shall be abolished, as appropriate and consistent with applicable law.

Sec. 4. *General Provisions.* (a) Nothing in this order shall be construed to impair or otherwise affect:

(i) the authority granted by law to an executive department or agency, or the head thereof; or

(ii) the functions of the Director of the Office of Management and Budget relating to budgetary, administrative, or legislative proposals.

(b) This order shall be implemented in a manner consistent with applicable law and subject to the availability of appropriations.

(c) This order is not intended to, and does not, create any right or benefit, substantive or procedural, enforceable at law or in equity by any party against the United States, its departments, agencies, or entities, its officers, employees, or agents, or any other person.

JOSEPH R. BIDEN, JR.
THE WHITE HOUSE
JANUARY 20, 2021

3

REGULATION OF TOXIC SUBSTANCES

A variety of federal statutes seek to control risks generated by toxic substances. The materials reproduced below include the full texts of the Toxic Substances Control Act (TSCA), the Federal Insecticide, Fungicide, and Rodenticide Act (FIFRA), the Safe Drinking Waste Act (SDWA), the Emergency Planning and Community Right-to-Know Act (EPCRA), and California's Proposition 65 (also known as the Safe Drinking Water and Toxic Enforcement Act).

A. TOXIC SUBSTANCES CONTROL ACT

A GUIDE TO MATERIALS AVAILABLE ON THE INTERNET PERTAINING TO THE TOXIC SUBSTANCES CONTROL ACT

EPA's regulations implementing TSCA are codified at 40 C.F.R. pts. 700-799. These CFR sections are available online through the National Archives and Records Administration's website, which includes a searchable version of the Code of Federal Regulations *(https://www.gpo.gov/fdsys/browse/collectionCfr.action?collectionCode=CFR)* and a continuously updated electronic CFR ("e-CFR") that can be found at *http://www.ecfr.gov.*

EPA's Office of Chemical Safety and Pollution Prevention (OCSPP) is the office responsible for implementing TSCA and FIFRA. The Office of Pollution Prevention and Toxics (OPPT) implements TSCA while the Office of Pesticide Programs (OPP) implements FIFRA. Information about these offices is available at *https://www.epa .gov/aboutepa/about-office-chemical-safety-and-pollution-prevention-ocspp.*

OPPT maintains a database with health and safety information on chemicals that can be accessed at *https:// chemview.epa.gov/chemview.* The database also may be reached by telephone at (202) 566-0556. Chemical databases and software programs produced by or for OPPT can be accessed at *http://www.epa.gov/oppt/tools/ dsalpha.htm.* Searchable databases maintained by OPPT also are accessible here. These include databases of information on chemicals and chemical releases.

Historical documents concerning the history of TSCA are available on a website maintained by EPA's History Office at *http://www2.epa.gov/aboutepa/epa-history-toxic-substances-control-act.*

The TSCA Interagency Testing Committee (ITC), an independent advisory committee consisting of representatives from 15 federal agencies who review priorities for testing chemicals under TSCA, maintains a website at *https://www.epa.gov/chemicals-under-tsca* that explains its work. OPPT's use of TSCA to generate toxicity information on chemicals is summarized at *https://www.epa.gov/chemicals-under-tsca.*

Several webpages discuss EPA's activities to control the risks posed by specific chemicals. EPA's activities to control risks from products containing asbestos are summarized at *http://www2.epa.gov/asbestos.* A "Lead Page" describes OPPT's efforts to control lead exposure at *http://www2.epa.gov/lead.*

A comprehensive practitioner's guide to TSCA is published by the Environmental Law Institute (ELI), E. Brown, et al., TSCA Deskbook (2d ed. 2012) and can be ordered online from ELI at *http://www.eli.org.* EPA maintains a Toxic Substances Control Act Assistance Information Service that can be reached by telephone at (202) 554-1404.

The American Chemistry Council (formerly the Chemical Manufacturers' Association) maintains a website at *http://www.americanchemistry.com.* It provides a daily news digest concerning developments that may affect chemical regulation and links to information about the council's program, including the Responsible Care Program that seeks to eliminate accidents, injuries and harm to the environment from the chemical industry.

TSCA LEGISLATIVE HISTORY TIMELINE

October 11, 1976: The Toxic Substances Control Act (TSCA), Pub. L. 94-469, 90 Stat. 2003, is enacted to provide EPA with comprehensive authority to regulate toxic substances that may pose unreasonable risks to human health or the environment.

October 22, 1986: The Asbestos Hazard Emergency Response Act (AHERA), Pub. L. 99-519, 100 Stat. 2970, is enacted, adding Title II to TSCA. AHERA requires EPA to promulgate regulations requiring inspection of schools for asbestos hazards and defining appropriate response actions.

October 28, 1988: The Indoor Radon Abatement Act of 1988, Pub. L. 100-551, 102 Stat. 2755, amends TSCA by adding Title III, which requires EPA to develop model construction standards for controlling radon levels in new buildings and to provide financial and technical assistance to States for radon control programs.

October 28, 1992: TSCA is amended, Pub. L. 102-550, 106 Stat. 3912, to add Title IV to require EPA to establish a comprehensive program to promote monitoring, detection, and abatement of lead-based paint and other lead exposure hazards and to promulgate regulations identifying lead-based paint hazards and governing the training and accreditation of contractors engaged in abatement of lead hazards.

October 14, 2008: TSCA is amended by enactment of the Mercury Export Ban Act of 2008, Pub. L. 110-414, 122 Stat. 4341, which adds §§6(f) and 12(c) to prohibit the sale, distribution, transfer, and export of elemental mercury.

July 7, 2010: President Obama signs into law the Formaldehyde Standards for Composite Wood Products Act, Pub. L. 111-199, 124 Stat. 1359, which adds §601 to TSCA to require EPA to issue regulations limiting formaldehyde emissions from composite wood products.

June 22, 2016: President Obama signs into law the Frank Lautenberg Chemical Safety for the 21st Century Act, Pub. L. 114-182, 130 Stat. 448, which comprehensively amends the Toxic Substances Control Act to require testing and risk evaluation of chemicals.

OUTLINE OF THE PRINCIPAL PROVISIONS OF THE TOXIC SUBSTANCES CONTROL ACT

TITLE I—CONTROL OF TOXIC SUBSTANCES

§4 (15 U.S.C. §2603) Testing of Chemical Substances and Mixtures: authorizes the EPA Administrator to require testing of any chemical substance or mixture upon finding that such testing is necessary because there is insufficient information from which the chemical's effects can be predicted and the chemical either "may present an unreasonable risk of injury to health or the environment" or the chemical is produced in substantial quantities or may result in substantial human exposure.

§5 (15 U.S.C. §2604) Manufacturing and Process Notices: prohibits any person from manufacturing or processing any new chemical substance or any existing chemical for a significant new use unless the person notifies the EPA Administrator at least 90 days in advance and submits any information that the person believes show that the chemical will not present an unreasonable risk. The Administrator may prohibit or limit the manufacturing, processing, distribution, use, or disposal of any such chemical if he determines that the chemical may present an unreasonable risk or that it may result in significant human exposure and information is insufficient to permit a reasoned evaluation of the effects of the chemical.

§6 (15 U.S.C. §2605) Prioritization, Risk Evaluation, and Regulation of Chemical Substances and Mixtures: authorizes the EPA Administrator, to the extent necessary to protect adequately against such risk using the least burdensome requirements, to prohibit the manufacture, processing, or distribution in commerce of a chemical, to limit the amounts, concentrations, or uses of it, to require labeling or recordkeeping concerning it; or to prohibit or otherwise regulate any manner or method of disposal of it, upon a finding that there is a reasonable basis to conclude that the chemical "presents or will present an unreasonable risk of injury to health or the environment."

§7 (15 U.S.C. §2606) Imminent Hazards: authorizes the EPA Administrator to sue to seize imminently hazardous chemicals or to obtain other relief to protect against them.

§8 (15 U.S.C. §2607) Reporting and Retention of Information: authorizes the EPA Administrator to require recordkeeping or the submission of reports concerning the manufacture or processing of chemicals.

§9 (15 U.S.C. §2608) Relationship to Other Federal Laws: requires the EPA Administrator to refer chemicals to other federal agencies for regulation or to use other laws administered by EPA to regulate the risks they pose if they may be sufficiently prevented or reduced by actions taken under laws other than TSCA.

§15 (15 U.S.C. §2614) Citizens' Civil Actions: authorizes citizen suits against any person alleged to be in violation of TSCA or against the EPA administrator for failure to perform nondiscretionary duties.

§19 (15 U.S.C. §2618) Judicial Review: authorizes judicial review of TSCA regulations issued by EPA.

§21 (15 U.S.C. §2620) Citizens' Petitions: authorizes citizens to petition EPA to commence rulemaking proceedings under TSCA and provides for judicial review of decisions not to commence rulemaking.

TITLE II—ASBESTOS HAZARD EMERGENCY RESPONSE ACT (AHERA)

§§201-216 (15 U.S.C. §§2641-2656) Asbestos Hazard Emergency Response Act: requires EPA to promulgate regulations requiring inspection of schools for asbestos hazards and defining appropriate response actions.

TITLE III—INDOOR RADON ABATEMENT

§§301-311 (15 U.S.C. §§2661-2671) Indoor Radon Abatement: requires EPA to publish "A Citizen's Guide to Radon," to develop model construction standards for controlling radon levels in new buildings, and to provide financial and technical assistance to States for radon control programs.

TITLE IV—LEAD EXPOSURE REDUCTION

§§401-412 (15 U.S.C. §§2681-2692) Lead Exposure Reduction: requires EPA to establish a comprehensive program to promote monitoring, detection and abatement of lead-based paint and other lead exposure hazards and to promulgate regulations identifying lead-based paint hazards and governing the training and accreditation of contractors engaged in abatement of lead hazards.

Toxic Substances Control Act
15 U.S.C. §§2601 TO 2697

SUBCHAPTER VI—FORMALDEHYDE STANDARDS FOR COMPOSITE WOOD PRODUCTS

SUBCHAPTER I — CONTROL OF TOXIC SUBSTANCES

§2601. Findings, policy, and intent
[TSCA §2]
FINDINGS, POLICY, AND INTENT

(a) Findings — The Congress finds that —

(1) human beings and the environment are being exposed each year to a large number of chemical substances and mixtures;

(2) among the many chemical substances and mixtures which are constantly being developed and produced, there are some whose manufacture, processing, distribution in commerce, use, or disposal may present an unreasonable risk of injury to health or the environment; and

(3) the effective regulation of interstate commerce in such chemical substances and mixtures also necessitates the regulation of intrastate commerce in such chemical substances and mixtures.

(b) Policy — It is the policy of the United States that —

(1) adequate information should be developed with respect to the effect of chemical substances and mixtures on health and the environment and that the development of such information should be the responsibility of those who manufacture and those who process such chemical substances and mixtures;

(2) adequate authority should exist to regulate chemical substances and mixtures which present an unreasonable risk of injury to health or the environment, and to take action with respect to chemical substances and mixtures which are imminent hazards; and

(3) authority over chemical substances and mixtures should be exercised in such a manner as not to impede unduly or create unnecessary economic barriers to technological innovation while fulfilling the primary purpose of this chapter to assure that such innovation and commerce in such chemical substances and mixtures do not present an unreasonable risk of injury to health or the environment.

(c) Intent of Congress — It is the intent of Congress that the Administrator shall carry out this chapter in a reasonable and prudent manner, and that the Administrator shall consider the environmental, economic, and social impact of any action the Administrator takes or proposes to as provided under this chapter.

§2602. Definitions
[TSCA §3]
DEFINITIONS

As used in this chapter:

(1) the term "Administrator" means the Administrator of the Environmental Protection Agency.

(2)(A) Except as provided in subparagraph (B), the term "chemical substance" means any organic or inorganic substance of a particular molecular identity, including —

(i) any combination of such substances occurring in whole or in part as a result of a chemical reaction or occurring in nature and

(ii) any element or uncombined radical.

(B) Such term does not include —

(i) any mixture,

(ii) any pesticide (as defined in the Federal Insecticide, Fungicide, and Rodenticide Act [7 U.S.C. §§136 et seq.] when manufactured, processed, or distributed in commerce for use as a pesticide,

(iii) tobacco or any tobacco product,

(iv) any source material, special nuclear material, or byproduct material (as such terms are defined in the Atomic Energy Act of 1954 [42 U.S.C. §§2011 et seq.] and regulations issued under such Act),

(v) any article the sale of which is subject to the tax imposed by section 4181 of the Internal Revenue Code of 1986 [26 U.S.C. §4181] (determined without regard to any exemptions from such tax provided by section 4182 or 4221 or any other provision of such Code) and any component of such an article (limited to shot shells, cartridges, and components of shot shells and cartridges), and

(vi) any food, food additive, drug, cosmetic, or device (as such terms are defined in section 201 of the Federal Food, Drug, and Cosmetic Act [21 U.S.C. §321]) when manufactured, processed, or distributed in commerce for use as a food, food additive, drug, cosmetic, or device.

The term "food" as used in clause (vi) of this subparagraph includes poultry and poultry products (as defined in sections 4(e) and 4(f) of the Poultry Products Inspection Act [21 U.S.C. §453(e) and (f)]), meat and meat food products (as defined in section 1(j) of the Federal Meat Inspection Act [21 U.S.C. §601(j)]), and eggs and egg products (as defined in section 4 of the Egg Products Inspection Act [21 U.S.C. §1033]).

(3) The term "commerce" means trade, traffic, transportation, or other commerce (A) between a place in a State and any place outside of such State, or (B) which affects trade, traffic, transportation, or commerce described in clause (A).

(4) The term "conditions of use" means the circumstances, as determined by the Administrator, under which a chemical substance is intended, known, or reasonably foreseen to be manufactured, processed, distributed in commerce, used, or disposed of.

(5) The terms "distribute in commerce" and "distribution in commerce" when used to describe an action taken with respect to a chemical substance or mixture or article containing a substance or mixture mean to sell, or the sale of, the substance, mixture, or article in commerce; to introduce or deliver for introduction into commerce, or the introduction or delivery for introduction into commerce of, the substance, mixture, or article; or to hold, or the holding of, the substance, mixture, or article after its introduction into commerce.

(6) The term "environment" includes water, air, and land and the interrelationship which exists among and between water, air, and land and all living things.

(7) The term "guidance" means any significant written guidance of general applicability prepared by the Administrator.

(8) The term "health and safety study" means any study of any effect of a chemical substance or mixture on health or the environment or on both, including underlying information and epidemiological studies, studies of occupational exposure to a chemical substance or mixture, toxicological, clinical, and ecological studies of a chemical substance or mixture, and any test performed pursuant to this chapter.

(9) The term "manufacture" means to import into the customs territory of the United States (as defined in general note 2 of the Harmonized Tariff Schedule of the United States), produce, or manufacture.

(10) The term "mixture" means any combination of two or more chemical substances if the combination does not occur in nature and is not, in whole or in part, the result of a chemical reaction; except that such term does include any combination which occurs, in whole or in part, as a result of a chemical reaction if none of the chemical substances comprising the combination is a new chemical substance and if the combination could have been manufactured for commercial purposes without a chemical reaction at the time the chemical substances comprising the combination were combined.

(11) The term "new chemical substance" means any chemical substance which is not included in the chemical substance list compiled and published under section 2607(b) of this title.

(12) The term "potentially exposed or susceptible subpopulation" means a group of individuals within the general population identified by the Administrator who, due to either greater susceptibility or greater exposure, may be at greater risk than the general population of adverse health effects from exposure to a chemical substance or mixture, such as infants, children, pregnant women, workers, or the elderly.

(13) The term "process" means the preparation of a chemical substance or mixture, after its manufacture, for distribution in commerce —

    (A) in the same form or physical state as, or in a different form or physical state from, that in which it was received by the person so preparing such substance or mixture, or

    (B) as part of an article containing the chemical substance or mixture.

(14) The term "processor" means any person who processes a chemical substance or mixture.

(15) The term "protocols and methodologies for the development of information" means a prescription of —

    (A) the —

        (i) health and environmental effects, and

        (ii) information relating to toxicity, persistence, and other characteristics which affect health and the environment,

for which information for a chemical substance or mixture are to be developed and any analysis that is to be performed on such information, and

    (B) to the extent necessary to assure that information respecting such effects and characteristics are reliable and adequate —

        (i) the manner in which such information are to be developed,

        (ii) the specification of any test protocol or methodology to be employed in the development of such information, and

        (iii) such other requirements as are necessary to provide such assurance.

(16) The term "State" means any State of the United States, the District of Columbia, the Commonwealth of Puerto Rico, the Virgin Islands, Guam, the Canal Zone, American Samoa, the Northern Mariana Islands, or any other territory or possession of the United States.

(17) The term "United States", when used in the geographic sense, means all of the States.

§2603. Testing of chemical substances and mixtures

[TSCA §4]
(a) Testing requirements —

    (1) If the Administrator finds that —

(A)(i)(I) the manufacture, distribution in commerce, processing, use, or disposal of a chemical substance or mixture, or that any combination of such activities, may present an unreasonable risk of injury to health or the environment,

(II) there is insufficient information and experience upon which the effects of such manufacture, distribution in commerce, processing, use, or disposal of such substance or mixture or of any combination of such activities on health or the environment can reasonably be determined or predicted, and

(III) testing of such substance or mixture with respect to such effects is necessary to develop such information; or

(ii)(I) a chemical substance or mixture is or will be produced in substantial quantities, and

(aa) it enters or may reasonably be anticipated to enter the environment in substantial quantities or

(bb) there is or may be significant or substantial human exposure to such substance or mixture,

(II) there is insufficient information and experience upon which the effects of the manufacture, distribution in commerce, processing, use, or disposal of such substance or mixture or of any combination of such activities on health or the environment can reasonably be determined or predicted, and

(III) testing of such substance or mixture with respect to such effects is necessary to develop such information; and

(B) in the case of a mixture, the effects which the mixture's manufacture, distribution in commerce, processing, use, or disposal or any combination of such activities may have on health or the environment may not be reasonably and more efficiently determined or predicted by testing the chemical substances which comprise the mixture;

the Administrator shall by rule, or, in the case of a chemical substance or mixture described in subparagraph (A)(i), by rule, order, or consent agreement, require that testing be conducted on such substance or mixture to develop information with respect to the health and environmental effects for which there is an insufficiency of information and experience and which is relevant to a determination that the manufacture, distribution in commerce, processing, use, or disposal of such substance or mixture, or that any combination of such activities, does or does not present an unreasonable risk of injury to health or the environment.

(2) Additional testing authority — In addition to the authority provided under paragraph (1), the Administrator may, by rule, order, or consent agreement —

(A) require the development of new information relating to a chemical substance or mixture if the Administrator determines that the information is necessary —

(i) to review a notice under section 5 or to perform a risk evaluation under section 6(b);

(ii) to implement a requirement imposed in a rule, order, or consent agreement under subsection (e) or (f) of section 5 or in a rule promulgated under section 6(a);

(iii) at the request of a Federal implementing authority under another Federal law, to meet the regulatory testing needs of that authority with regard to toxicity exposure; or

(iv) pursuant to section 12(a)(2); and

(B) require the development of new information for the purposes of prioritizing a chemical substance under section 6(b) only if the Administrator determines that such information is necessary to establish the priority of the substance, subject to the limitations that —

(i) not later than 90 days after the date of receipt of information regarding a chemical substance complying with a rule, order, or consent agreement under this subparagraph, the Administrator shall designate the chemical substance as a high-priority substance or a low-priority substance; and

(ii) information required by the Administrator under this subparagraph shall not be required for the purposes of establishing or implementing a minimum information requirement of broader applicability.

(3) Statement of need — When requiring the development of new information relating to a chemical substance or mixture under paragraph (2), the Administrator shall identify the need for the new information, describe how information reasonably available to the Administrator was used to inform the decision to require new information, explain the basis for any decision to require new information, explain the basis for any decision that requires the use of vertebrate animals, and, as applicable, explain why issuance of an order is warranted instead of promulgating a rule or entering into a consent agreement.

(4) Tiered testing — When requiring the development of new information under this subsection, the Administrator shall employ a tiered screening and testing process, under which the results of screening-level tests or assessments of available information inform the decision as to whether 1 or more additional tests are necessary, unless information available to the administrator justifies more advanced testing of potential health or environmental effects or potential exposure without first conducting screening-level testing.

99

(b) Testing requirement rule, order or consent agreement

(1) A rule under subsection (a) of this section shall include —

(A) identification of the chemical substance or mixture for which testing is required under the rule, order or consent agreement

(B) protocols and methodologies for the development of information for such substance or mixture, and

(C) with respect to chemical substances which are not new chemical substances and to mixtures, a specification of the period (which period may not be of unreasonable duration) within which the persons required to conduct the testing shall submit to the Administrator information developed in accordance with the protocols and methodologies referred to in subparagraph (B).

In determining the protocols and methodologies and period to be included, pursuant to subparagraphs (B) and (C), in a rule, order or consent agreement under subsection (a) of this section, the Administrator's considerations shall include the relative costs of the various test protocols and methodologies which may be required under the rule, order or consent agreement and the reasonably foreseeable availability of the facilities and personnel needed to perform the testing required under the rule, order or consent agreement. Any such rule may require the submission to the Administrator of preliminary information during the period prescribed under subparagraph (C).

(2)(A) The health and environmental effects for which protocols and methodologies for the development of information may be prescribed include carcinogenesis, mutagenesis, teratogenesis, behavioral disorders, cumulative or synergistic effects, and any other effect which may present an unreasonable risk of injury to health or the environment. Protocols and methodologies for the development of information may also be prescribed for the assessment of exposure or exposure potential to humans or the environment. The characteristics of chemical substances and mixtures for which such protocols and methodologies may be prescribed include persistence, acute toxicity, subacute toxicity, chronic toxicity, and any other characteristic which may present such a risk. The methodologies that may be prescribed in such protocols and methodologies include epidemiologic studies, serial or tiered testing, in vitro tests, and whole animal tests, except that before prescribing epidemiologic studies of employees, the Administrator shall consult with the Director of the National Institute for Occupational Safety and Health.

(B) From time to time, but not less than once each 12 months, the Administrator shall review the adequacy of the protocols and methodologies for development of information prescribed in rules, orders, and consent agreements under subsection (a) of this section and shall, if necessary, institute proceedings to make appropriate revisions of such protocols and methodologies.

(3)(A) A rule or order under subsection (a) of this section respecting a chemical substance or mixture shall require the persons described in subparagraph (B) or (C), as applicable to conduct tests and submit information to the Administrator on such substance or mixture, except that the Administrator may permit two or more of such persons to designate one such person or a qualified third party to conduct such tests and submit such information on behalf of the persons making the designation.

(B) The following persons shall be required to conduct tests and submit information on a chemical substance or mixture subject to a rule under subsection (a)(1) of this section:

(i) Each person who manufactures or intends to manufacture such substance or mixture if the Administrator makes a finding described in subsection (a)(1) (A)(i)(II) or (a)(1)(A)(ii)(II) of this section with respect to the manufacture of such substance or mixture.

(ii) Each person who processes or intends to process such substance or mixture if the Administrator makes a finding described in subsection (a)(1)(A)(i)(II) or (a)(1)(A)(ii)(II) of this section with respect to the processing of such substance or mixture.

(iii) Each person who manufactures or processes or intends to manufacture or process such substance or mixture if the Administrator makes a finding described in subsection (a)(1)(A)(i)(II) or (a)(1)(A)(ii)(II) of this section with respect to the distribution in commerce, use, or disposal of such substance or mixture.

(C) A rule or order under paragraph (1) or (2) of subsection (a) may require the development of information by any person who manufactures or processes, or intends to manufacture or process, a chemical substance or mixture subject to the rule or order.

(4) Any rule, order or consent agreement under subsection (a) of this section requiring the testing of and submission of information for a particular chemical substance or mixture shall expire at the end of the reimbursement period (as defined in subsection (c)(3)(B) of this section) which is applicable to information for such substance or mixture unless the Administrator repeals the rule or order or modifies the consent agreement to terminate the requirement before such date; and a rule, order or consent agreement under subsection (a) of this section requiring the testing of and submission of information for a

category of chemical substances or mixtures shall expire with respect to a chemical substance or mixture included in the category at the end of the reimbursement period (as so defined) which is applicable to information for such substance or mixture unless the Administrator before such date repeals or modifies the application of the rule, order, or consent agreement to such substance or mixture or repeals the rule.

(c) Exemption

(1) Any person required by a rule or order under subsection (a) of this section to conduct tests and submit information on a chemical substance or mixture may apply to the Administrator (in such form and manner as the Administrator shall prescribe) for an exemption from such requirement.

(2) If, upon receipt of an application under paragraph (1), the Administrator determines that —

(A) the chemical substance or mixture with respect to which such application was submitted is equivalent to a chemical substance or mixture for which information has been submitted to the Administrator in accordance with a rule, order, or consent agreement under subsection (a) or for which information is being developed pursuant to such a rule, order, or consent agreement.

(B) submission of information by the applicant on such substance or mixture would be duplicative of data which has been submitted to the Administrator in accordance with such rule, order, or consent agreement or which is being developed pursuant to such rule, order, or consent agreement,

the Administrator shall exempt, in accordance with paragraph (3) or (4), the applicant from conducting tests and submitting information on such substance or mixture under the rule or order with respect to which such application was submitted.

(3)(A) If the exemption under paragraph (2) of any person from the requirement to conduct tests and submit information on a chemical substance or mixture is granted on the basis of the existence of previously submitted information and if such exemption is granted during the reimbursement period for such information (as prescribed by subparagraph (B)), then (unless such person and the persons referred to in clauses (i) and (ii) agree on the amount and method of reimbursement) the Administrator shall order the person granted the exemption to provide fair and equitable reimbursement (in an amount determined under rules of the Administrator) —

(i) to the person who previously submitted such information, for a portion of the costs incurred by such person in complying with the requirement to submit such information, and

(ii) to any other person who has been

required under this subparagraph to contribute with respect to such costs, for a portion of the amount such person was required to contribute.

In promulgating rules for the determination of fair and equitable reimbursement to the persons described in clauses (i) and (ii) for costs incurred with respect to a chemical substance or mixture, the Administrator shall, after consultation with the Attorney General and the Federal Trade Commission, consider all relevant factors, including the effect on the competitive position of the person required to provide reimbursement in relation to the person to be reimbursed and the share of the market for such substance or mixture of the person required to provide reimbursement in relation to the share of such market of the persons to be reimbursed. An order under this subparagraph shall, for purposes of judicial review, be considered final agency action.

(B) For purposes of subparagraph (A), the reimbursement period for any information for a chemical substance or mixture is a period —

(i) beginning on the date such information is submitted in accordance with a rule, order, or consent agreement promulgated under subsection (a) of this section, and

(ii) ending —

(I) five years after the date referred to in clause (i), or

(II) at the expiration of a period which begins on the date referred to in clause (i) and which is equal to the period which the Administrator determines was necessary to develop such information, whichever is later.

(4)(A) If the exemption under paragraph (2) of any person from the requirement to conduct tests and submit information on a chemical substance or mixture is granted on the basis of the fact that information is being developed by one or more persons pursuant to a rule, order, or consent agreement under subsection (a) of this section, then (unless such person and the persons referred to in clauses (i) and (ii) agree on the amount and method of reimbursement) the Administrator shall order the person granted the exemption to provide fair and equitable reimbursement (in an amount determined under rules of the Administrator) —

(i) to each such person who is developing such information, for a portion of the costs incurred by each such person in complying with such rule, order, or consent agreement, and

(ii) to any other person who has been required under this subparagraph to contribute with respect to the costs

101

of complying with such rule, order, or consent agreement for a portion of the amount such person was required to contribute.

In promulgating rules for the determination of fair and equitable reimbursement to the persons described in clauses (i) and (ii) for costs incurred with respect to a chemical substance or mixture, the Administrator shall, after consultation with the Attorney General and the Federal Trade Commission, consider the factors described in the second sentence of paragraph (3)(A). An order under this subparagraph shall, for purposes of judicial review, be considered final agency action.

(B) If any exemption is granted under paragraph (2) on the basis of the fact that one or more persons are developing information pursuant to a rule, order, or consent agreement under subsection (a) of this section and if after such exemption is granted the Administrator determines that no such person has complied with such rule, order, or consent agreement, the Administrator shall (i) after providing written notice to the person who holds such exemption and an opportunity for a hearing, by order terminate such exemption, and (ii) notify in writing such person of the requirements of the rule or order with respect to which such exemption was granted.

(d) Notice — Upon the receipt of any information pursuant to a rule, order, or consent agreement under subsection (a) of this section, the Administrator shall publish a notice of the receipt of such information in the Federal Register within 15 days of its receipt. Subject to section 2613 of this title, each such notice shall (1) identify the chemical substance or mixture for which information has been received; (2) list the uses or intended uses of such substance or mixture and the information required by the applicable protocols and methodologies for the development of information; and (3) describe the nature of the information developed. Except as otherwise provided in section 2613 of this title, such information shall be made available by the Administrator for examination by any person.

(e) Priority list

(1)(A) There is established a committee to make recommendations to the Administrator respecting the chemical substances and mixtures to which the Administrator should give priority consideration for the development of information under subsection (a) of this section. In making such a recommendation with respect to any chemical substance or mixture, the committee shall consider all relevant factors, including —

(i) the quantities in which the substance or mixture is or will be manufactured,

(ii) the quantities in which the sub-

stance or mixture enters or will enter the environment,

(iii) the number of individuals who are or will be exposed to the substance or mixture in their places of employment and the duration of such exposure,

(iv) the extent to which human beings are or will be exposed to the substance or mixture,

(v) the extent to which the substance or mixture is closely related to a chemical substance or mixture which is known to present an unreasonable risk of injury to health or the environment,

(vi) the existence of information concerning the effects of the substance or mixture on health or the environment,

(vii) the extent to which testing of the substance or mixture may result in the development of information upon which the effects of the substance or mixture on health or the environment can reasonably be determined or predicted, and

(viii) the reasonably foreseeable availability of facilities and personnel for performing testing on the substance or mixture.

The recommendations of the committee shall be in the form of a list of chemical substances and mixtures which shall be set forth, either by individual substance or mixture or by groups of substances or mixtures, in the order in which the committee determines the Administrator should take action under subsection (a) of this section with respect to the substances and mixtures. In establishing such list, the committee shall give priority attention to those chemical substances and mixtures which are known to cause or contribute to or which are suspected of causing or contributing to cancer, gene mutations, or birth defects. The committee shall designate chemical substances and mixtures on the list with respect to which the committee determines the Administrator should, within 12 months of the date on which such substances and mixtures are first designated, initiate a proceeding under subsection (a) of this section. The total number of chemical substances and mixtures on the list which are designated under the preceding sentence may not, at any time, exceed 50.

(B) As soon as practicable but not later than nine months after January 1, 1977, the committee shall publish in the Federal Register and transmit to the Administrator the list and designations required by subparagraph (A) together with the reasons for the committee's inclusion of each chemical substance or mixture on the list. At least every six months after the date of the transmission to the Administrator of the list pursuant to the preceding sentence, the committee shall make such revisions in the list as it determines to be necessary and shall transmit them to the Administrator together with the committee's reasons for the revisions. Upon receipt of any such revision, the Administrator shall publish in the Federal Register the list with such revision, the reasons for such revision, and the designations made under subparagraph (A). The Administrator shall provide reasonable opportunity to any interested person to file with the Administrator written comments on the committee's list, any revision of such list by the committee, and designations made by the committee, and shall make such comments available to the public. Within the 12-month period beginning on the date of the first inclusion on the list of a chemical substance or mixture designated by the committee under subparagraph (A) the Administrator shall with respect to such chemical substance or mixture issue an order, enter into a a consent agreement, or initiate a rulemaking proceeding under subsection (a), or, if such an order or consent agreement is not issued or such a proceeding is not initiated within such period, publish in the Federal Register the Administrator's reason for not issuing such an order, entering into such a consent agreement, or initiating such a proceeding."

(2)(A) The committee established by paragraph (1)(A) shall consist of ten members as follows:

(i) One member appointed by the Administrator from the Environmental Protection Agency.

(ii) One member appointed by the Secretary of Labor from officers or employees of the Department of Labor engaged in the Secretary's activities under the Occupational Safety and Health Act of 1970 [29 U.S.C. §§651 et seq.].

(iii) One member appointed by the Chairman of the Council on Environmental Quality from the Council or its officers or employees.

(iv) One member appointed by the Director of the National Institute for Occupational Safety and Health from officers or employees of the Institute.

(v) One member appointed by the Director of the National Institute of Environmental Health Sciences from officers or employees of the Institute.

(vi) One member appointed by the Director of the National Cancer Institute from officers or employees of the Institute.

(vii) One member appointed by the Director of the National Science Foundation from officers or employees of the Foundation.

(viii) One member appointed by the Secretary of Commerce from officers or employees of the Department of Commerce.

(ix) One member appointed by the Chairman of the Consumer Product Safety Commission from Commissioners or employees of the Commission.

(x) One member appointed by the Commissioner of Food and Drugs from employees of the Food and Drug Administration.

(B)(i) An appointed member may designate an individual to serve on the committee on the member's behalf. Such a designation may be made only with the approval of the applicable appointing authority and only if the individual is from the entity from which the member was appointed.

(ii) No individual may serve as a member of the committee for more than four years in the aggregate. If any member of the committee leaves the entity from which the member was appointed, such member may not continue as a member of the committee, and the member's position shall be considered to be vacant. A vacancy in the committee shall be filled in the same manner in which the original appointment was made.

(iii) Initial appointments to the committee shall be made not later than the 60th day after January 1, 1977. Not later than the 90th day after such date the members of the committee shall hold a meeting for the selection of a chairperson from among their number.

(C)(i) No member of the committee, or designee of such member, shall accept employment or compensation from any person subject to any requirement of this chapter or of any rule promulgated or order issued thereunder, for a period of at least 12 months after termination of service on the committee.

(ii) No person, while serving as a member of the committee, or designee of such member, may own any stocks or bonds, or have any pecuniary interest, of substantial value in any person engaged in the manufacture, processing, or distribution in commerce of any chemical substance or mixture subject to any requirement of this chapter or of any rule promulgated or order issued thereunder.

(iii) The Administrator, acting through attorneys of the Environmental Protection Agency, or the Attorney General may bring an action in the appropriate district court of the United States to restrain any violation of this subparagraph.

(D) The Administrator shall provide the committee such administrative support services as may be necessary to enable the committee to carry out its function under this subsection.

(f) **Required actions** — Upon the receipt of —

(1) any information required to be submitted under this chapter, or

(2) any other information available to the Administrator,

which indicates to the Administrator that there may be a reasonable basis to conclude that a chemical substance or mixture presents or will present a significant risk of serious or widespread harm to human beings, the Administrator shall, within the 180-day period beginning on the date of the receipt of such information, initiate applicable action under section 2604, 2605, or 2606 of this title to prevent or reduce to a sufficient extent such risk or publish in the Federal Register a finding, made without consideration of costs or other nonrisk factors that such risk is not unreasonable. For good cause shown the Administrator may extend such period for an additional period of not more than 90 days. The Administrator shall publish in the Federal Register notice of any such extension and the reasons therefor. A finding by the Administrator that a risk is not unreasonable shall be considered agency action for purposes of judicial review under chapter 7 of Title 5. This subsection shall not take effect until two years after January 1, 1977.

(g) **Petition for Protocols and Methodologies for the Development of Information** — A person intending to manufacture or process a chemical substance for which notice is required under section 2604(a) of this title and who is not required under a rule, order, or consent agreement under subsection (a) of this section to conduct tests and submit information on such substance may petition the Administrator to prescribe protocols and methodologies for the development of information for such substance. The Administrator shall by order either grant or deny any such petition within 60 days of its receipt. If the petition is granted, the Administrator shall prescribe such protocols and methodologies for such substance within 75 days of the date the petition is granted. If the petition is denied, the Administrator shall publish, subject to section 2613 of this title, in the Federal Register the reasons for such denial.

(h) **Reduction of Testing on Vertebrates** —

(1) **In general** — the Administrator shall reduce and replace, to the extent practicable, scientifically justified, and consistent with the policies of this title, the use of vertebrate animals in the testing of chemicals substances or mixtures under this title by —

(A) prior to making a request or adopting a requirement for testing using vertebrate animals, and in accordance with subsection (a)(3), taking into consideration, as appropriate and to the extent practicable and scientifically justified, reasonably available existing information including —

(i) toxicity information;

(ii) computational toxicology and bioinformatics; and

(iii) high-throughput screening methods and the prediction models of those methods; and

(B) encouraging and facilitating –

(i) the use of scientifically valid test methods and strategies that reduce or replace the use of vertebrate animals while providing information of equivalent or better scientific quality and relevance that will support regulatory decisions under this title;

(ii) the grouping of 2 or more chemical substances into scientifically appropriate categories in cases in which testing of a chemical substance would provide scientifically valid and useful information on other chemical substances in the category; and

(iii) the formation of industry consortia to jointly conduct testing to avoid unnecessary duplication of tests, provided that such consortia make all information from such testing available to the Administrator.

(2) **Implementation of alternative testing methods** — To promote the development and timely incorporation of new scientifically valid test methods and strategies that are not based on vertebrate animals, the Administrator shall —

(A) Not later than June 22, 2016, develop a strategic plan to promote the development and implementation of alternative test methods and strategies to reduce, refine, or replace vertebrate animal testing and provide information of equivalent or better scientific quality and relevance for assessing risks of injury to health or the environment of chemical substances or mixtures through, for example —

(i) computational toxicology and bioinformatics;

(ii) high-throughput screening methods;

(iii) testing of categories of chemical substances;

(iv) tiered testing methods;

(v) in vitro studies;

(vi) systems biology;

(vii) new or revised methods identified by validation bodies such as the Interagency Coordinating Committee on the Validation of Alternative Methods or the Organization for Economic Co-operation and Development; or

(viii) industry consortia that develop information submitted under this title;

(B) as practicable, ensure that the strategic plan developed under subparagraph (A) is reflected in the development of requirements for testing under this section;

(C) include in the strategic plan developed under subparagraph (A) a list, which the Administrator shall update on a regular basis, of particular alternative test methods or strategies the administrator has identified that do not require new vertebrate animal testing and are scientifically reliable, relevant, and capable of providing information of equivalent or better scientific reliability and quality to that which would be obtained from vertebrate animal testing;

(D) provide an opportunity for public notice and comment on the contents of the plan developed under subparagraph (A), including the criteria for considering scientific reliability and relevance of the test methods and strategies that may be identified pursuant to subparagraph (C);

(E) beginning on the date that is 5 years after June 22, 2016, and every 5 years thereafter, submit to Congress a report that describes the progress made in implementing the plan developed under subparagraph (A) and goals for future alternative test methods and strategies implementation; and

(F) prioritize and, to the extent consistent with available resources and the Administrator's other responsibilities under this title, carry out performance assessment, validation, and translational studies to accelerate the development of scientifically valid test methods and strategies that reduce, refine, or replace the use of vertebrate animals, including minimizing the duplication, in any testing under this title.

(3) Voluntary testing —

(A) In general — Any person developing information for submission under this title on a voluntary basis and not pursuant to any request or requirement by the Administrator shall first attempt to develop the information by means of an alternative test method or strategy identified by the Administrator pursuant to paragraph (2)(C), if the Administrator has identified such a test method or strategy for the development of such information, before conducting new vertebrate animal testing.

(B) Effect of paragraph — Nothing in this paragraph shall, under any circumstance, limit or restrict the submission of any existing information to the Administrator.

(C) Relationship to other law — A violation of this paragraph shall not be a prohibited act under section 15.

(D) Review of means — This paragraph authorizes, but does not require, the Administrator to review the means by which a person conducting testing described in subparagraph (A).

§2604. Manufacturing and processing notices [TSCA §5]

(a) In general

(1) (A) Except as provided in subparagraph (B) of this paragraph and subsection (h) of this section, no person may —

(i) manufacture a new chemical substance on or after the 30th day after the date on which the Administrator first publishes the list required by section 2607(b) of this title, or

(ii) manufacture or process any chemical substance for a use which the Administrator has determined, in accordance with paragraph (2), is a significant new use.

(B) A person may take the actions described in subparagraph (A) if —

(i) such person submits to the Administrator, at least 90 days before such manufacture or processing, a notice, in accordance with subsection (d), of such person's intention to manufacture or process such substance and such person complies with any applicable requirement of, or imposed pursuant to, subsection (b), (e), or (f); and

(ii) the Administrator —

(I) conducts a review of the notice; and

(II) makes a determination under subparagraph (A), (B), (C), or (D) of paragraph (3) and takes the actions required in association with that determination under such subparagraph within the applicable review period.

(2) A determination by the Administrator that a use of a chemical substance is a significant new use with respect to which notification is required under paragraph (1) shall be made by a rule promulgated after a consideration of all relevant factors, including —

(A) the projected volume of manufacturing and processing of a chemical substance,

(B) the extent to which a use changes the type or form of exposure of human beings or the environment to a chemical substance,

(C) the extent to which a use increases the magnitude and duration of exposure of human beings or the environment to a chemical substance, and   .

(D) the reasonably anticipated manner and methods of manufacturing, processing, distribution in commerce, and disposal of a chemical substance.

(3) Review and determination — Within the applicable review period, subject to section 18, the Administrator shall review such notice and determine —

(A) that the relevant chemical substance or significant new use presents or will present an unreasonable risk of injury to health or the environment, without consideration of costs or other nonrisk factors, including an unreasonable risk to a potentially exposed or susceptible subpopulation identified as relevant by the Administrator under the conditions of use, in which case the Administrator shall take the actions required under subsection (f);

(B) that —

(i) the information available to the Administrator is insufficient to permit a reasoned evaluation of the health and environmental effects of chemical substance or significant new use; or

(ii)(I) in the absence of sufficient information to permit the Administrator to make such an evaluation, the manufacture, processing, distribution in commerce, use, disposal of such substance, or any combination of such activities, may present an unreasonable risk of injury to health or the environment, without consideration of costs or other nonrisk factors, including an unreasonable risk to a potentially exposed or susceptible subpopulation identified as relevant by the Administrator; or

(II) such substance is or will be produced in substantial quantities, and such substance either enters or may reasonably be anticipated to enter the environment in substantial quantities or there is or may be significant or substantial human exposure to the substance,

in which case the administrator shall take the actions required under subsection (e);

(C) that the relevant chemical substance or significant new use is likely not to present an unreasonable risk of injury to health or the environment, without consideration of costs or other nonrisk factors, including an unreasonable risk to a potentially exposed or susceptible subpopulation identified as relevant by the Administrator under the conditions of use, in which case the submitter of the notice may commence manufacture of the chemical substance or manufacture or processing for a significant new use; or

(D) that the relevant chemical substance is a low-hazard substance, in which case the submitter of the notice may commence manufacture of the chemical substance or manufacture or processing of the chemical substance for a significant new use.

(4) Failure to render determination

(A) Failure to render determination — If the Administrator fails to make a determination on notice under paragraph (3) by the end of the applicable review period

and the notice has not been withdrawn by the submitter, the Administrator shall refund to the submitter all applicable fees charged to the submitter for review of the notice pursuant to section 26(b), and the Administrator shall not be relieved of any requirement to make such determination.

(B) Limitations — (i) A refund of applicable fees under subparagraph (A) shall not be made if the Administrator certifies that the submitter has not provided information required under subsection (b) or has otherwise unduly delayed the process such that the Administrator is unable to render a determination within the applicable review period.

(ii) A failure of the Administrator to render a decision shall not be deemed to constitute a withdrawal of the notice.

(iii) Nothing in this paragraph shall be construed as relieving the Administrator or the submitter of the notice from any requirement of this section.

(5) Article of consideration — The Administrator may require notification under this section for the import or processing of a chemical substance as part of an article or category of articles under paragraph (1)(A)(ii) if the Administrator makes an affirmative finding in a rule under paragraph (2) that the reasonable potential for exposure to the chemical substance through the article or category of articles subject to the rule justifies notification.

(b) Submission of Information

(1)(A) If —

(i) a person is required by subsection (a)(1) of this section to submit a notice to the Administrator before beginning the manufacture or processing of a chemical substance, and (ii) such person is required to submit information for such substance pursuant to a rule, order, or consent agreement under section 2603 of this title before the submission of such notice, such person shall submit to the Administrator such information in accordance with such rule, order, or consent agreement at the time notice is submitted in accordance with subsection (a)(1) of this section.

(B) If —

(i) a person is required by subsection (a)(1) of this section to submit a notice to the Administrator, and

(ii) such person has been granted an exemption under section 2603(c) of this title from the requirements of a rule or order under section 2603 of this title before the submission of such notice,

such person may not, before the expiration of the 90 day period which begins on the date of the submission in accordance with such rule, order, or consent agreement of the information the submission or development of which was the basis for the exemption, manufacture such substance if such person is subject to subsection (a)(1)(A)(i) of this section or manufacture or process such substance for a significant new use if the person is subject to subsection (a)(1)(A)(ii) of this section.

(2)(A) If a person —

(i) is required by subsection (a)(1) of this section to submit a notice to the Administrator before beginning the manufacture or processing of a chemical substance listed under paragraph (4), and

(ii) is not required by a rule, order, or consent agreement under section 2603 of this title before the submission of such notice to submit information for such substance,

such person shall submit to the Administrator information prescribed by subparagraph (B) at the time notice is submitted in accordance with subsection (a)(1) of this section.

(B) Information submitted pursuant to subparagraph (A) shall be information which the person submitting the information believes shows that —

(i) in the case of a substance with respect to which notice is required under subsection (a)(1)(A)(i) of this section, the manufacture, processing, distribution in commerce, use, and disposal of the chemical substance or any combination of such activities will not present an unreasonable risk of injury to health or the environment, or

(ii) in the case of a chemical substance with respect to which notice is required under subsection (a)(1)(A)(ii) of this section, the intended significant new use of the chemical substance will not present an unreasonable risk of injury to health or the environment.

(3) Information submitted under paragraph (1) or (2) of this subsection or under subsection (e) shall be made available, subject to section 2613 of this title, for examination by interested persons.

(4)(A)(i) The Administrator may, by rule, compile and keep current a list of chemical substances with respect to which the Administrator finds that the manufacture, processing, distribution in commerce, use, or disposal, or any combination of such activities, presents or may present an unreasonable risk of injury to health or the environment, without consideration of costs or other nonrisk factors.

(ii) In making a finding under clause (i) that the manufacture, processing,

distribution in commerce, use, or disposal of a chemical substance or any combination of such activities presents or may present an unreasonable risk of injury to health or the environment, the Administrator shall consider all relevant factors, including —

(I) the effects of the chemical substance on health and the magnitude of human exposure to such substance; and

(II) the effects of the chemical substance on the environment and the magnitude of environmental exposure to such substance.

(B) The Administrator shall, in prescribing a rule under subparagraph (A) which lists any chemical substance, identify those uses, if any, which the Administrator determines, by rule under subsection (a)(2) of this section, would constitute a significant new use of such substance.

(C) Any rule under subparagraph (A), and any substantive amendment or repeal of such a rule, shall be promulgated pursuant to the procedures specified in section 553 of Title 5.

(c) Extension of review period — The Administrator may for good cause extend for additional periods (not to exceed in the aggregate 90 days) the period, prescribed by subsection (a) or (b) of this section. Subject to section 2613 of this title, such an extension and the reasons therefor shall be published in the Federal Register and shall constitute a final agency action subject to judicial review.

(d) Content of notice; publications in the Federal Register

(1) The notice required by subsection (a) of this section shall include —

(A) insofar as known to the person submitting the notice or insofar as reasonably ascertainable, the information described in subparagraphs (A), (B), (C), (D), (F), and (G) of section 2607(a)(2) of this title, and

(B) in such form and manner as the Administrator may prescribe, any information in the possession or control of the person giving such notice which are related to the effect of any manufacture, processing, distribution in commerce, use, or disposal of such substance or any article containing such substance, or of any combination of such activities, on health or the environment, and

(C) a description of any other information concerning the environmental and health effects of such substance, insofar as known to the person making the notice or insofar as reasonably ascertainable.

Such a notice shall be made available, subject to section 2613 of this title, for examination by interested persons.

(2) Subject to section 2613 of this title, not later than five days (excluding Saturdays, Sundays and legal holidays) after the date of the receipt of a notice under subsection (a) of this section or of information under subsection (b) of this section, the Administrator shall publish in the Federal Register a notice which —

(A) identifies the chemical substance for which notice or data has been received;

(B) lists the uses of such substance identified in the notice; and

(C) in the case of the receipt of information under subsection (b) of this section, describes the nature of the tests performed on such substance and any information which was developed pursuant to subsection (b) of this section or a rule, order, or consent agreement under section 2603 of this title.

A notice under this paragraph respecting a chemical substance shall identify the chemical substance by generic class unless the Administrator determines that more specific identification is required in the public interest.

(3) At the beginning of each month the Administrator shall publish a list in the Federal Register of (A) each chemical substance for which notice has been received under subsection (a) of this section and for which the applicable review period of this section has not expired, and (B) each chemical substance for which such period has expired since the last publication in the Federal Register of such list.

(e) Regulation pending development of information

(1)(A) If the Administrator determines that —

(i) the information available to the Administrator is insufficient to permit a reasoned evaluation of the health and environmental effects of a chemical substance with respect to which notice is required by subsection (a) of this section; or

(ii)(I) in the absence of sufficient information to permit the Administrator to make such an evaluation, the manufacture, processing, distribution in commerce, use, or disposal of such substance, or any combination of such activities, may present an unreasonable risk of injury to health or the environment without consideration of costs or other nonrisk factors, including an unreasonable risk to potentially exposed subpopulation identified as relevant by the Administrator under the conditions of use, or

(II) such substance is or will be produced in substantial quantities, and such substance either enters or may

reasonably be anticipated to enter the environment in substantial quantities or there is or may be significant or substantial human exposure to the substance,

the Administrator shall issue an order, to take effect on the expiration of the applicable review period of this section, to prohibit or limit the manufacture, processing, distribution in commerce, use, or disposal of such substance or to prohibit or limit any combination of such activities to the extent necessary to protect against any unreasonable risk of injury to health or the environment, without consideration of costs or other nonrisk factors, including an unreasonable risk to a potentially exposed or susceptible subpopulation identified as relevant by the Administrator under the conditions of use, and the submitter of the notice may commence manufacture of the chemical substance, or manufacture or processing of the chemical substance for a significant new use, including while any required information is being developed, only in compliance with the order.

(B) An order may not be issued under subparagraph (A) respecting a chemical substance (i) later than 45 days before the expiration of the applicable review period of this section, and (ii) unless the Administrator has, on or before the issuance of the order, notified, in writing, each manufacturer or processor, as the case may be, of such substance of the determination which underlies such order.

(f) Protection against unreasonable risks

(1) If the Administrator determines that a chemical substance or significant new use with respect to which notice is required by subsection (a) of this section presents or will present an unreasonable risk of injury to health or environment, without consideration of costs or other nonrisk factors, including an unreasonable risk to a potentially exposed subpopulation identified as relevant by the administrator under the conditions of use, the Administrator shall, before the expiration of applicable review period of this section to the manufacturing or processing of such substance, take the action authorized by paragraph (2) or (3) to the extent necessary to protect against such risk.

(2) The Administrator may issue a proposed rule under section 2605(a) of this title to apply to a chemical substance with respect to which a finding was made under paragraph (1) —

(A) a requirement limiting the amount of such substance which may be manufactured, processed, or distributed in commerce,

(B) a requirement described in paragraph (2), (3), (4), (5), (6), or (7) of section 2605(a) of this title, or

(C) any combination of the requirements referred to in subparagraph (B).

Such a proposed rule shall be effective upon its publication in the Federal Register. Section 2605(d)(3)(B) of this title shall apply with respect to such rule.

(3)(A) The Administrator may issue an order to prohibit or limit the manufacture, processing, or distribution in commerce of a substance with respect to which a finding was under paragraph (1). Such order shall take effect on the expiration of the applicable review period.

(B) The provisions of subparagraph (B) of subsection (e)(1) of this section shall apply with respect to an order issued under subparagraph (A).

(4) Treatment of nonconforming uses — Not later than 90 days after taking an action under paragraph (2) or (3) or issuing an order under subsection (e) relating to a chemical substance with respect to which the Administrator has made a determination under subsection (a)(3)(A) or (B), the Administrator shall consider whether to promulgate a rule pursuant to subsection (a)(2) that identifies as a significant new use any manufacturing, processing, use distribution in commerce, or disposal of the chemical substance that does not conform to the restrictions imposed by the action or order, and as applicable, initiate such a rulemaking or publish a statement describing the reasons of the Administrator for not initiating such a rulemaking.

(5) Workplace exposures — To the extent practicable, the Administrator shall consult with the Assistant Secretary of Labor for Occupational Safety and Health prior to adopting any prohibition or other restriction relating to a chemical substance with respect to which the Administrator has made a determination under subsection (a)(3) (A) or (B) to address workplace exposures.

(g) Statement on Administrator Finding — If the Administrator finds in accordance with subsection (a)(3)(C) that a chemical substance or significant new use is likely not to present an unreasonable risk of injury to health or the environment, or in accordance with subsection (a)(3)(D) that the chemical substance is a low-hazard substance, then notwithstanding any remaining portion of the applicable review period, the submitter of the notice may commence manufacture of the chemical substance or manufacture or processing for the significant new use, and the Administrator shall make public a statement of the Administrator's finding. Such a statement shall be submitted for publication in the Federal Register as soon as practicable for the expiration of such period. Publication of such treatment in accordance with the preceding sentence is not a prerequisite to the manufacturing or processing of the substance with respect ot which the stamen is to be published.

(h) Exemptions

(1) The Administrator may, upon application, exempt any person from any requirement of subsection (a) or (b) of this section to permit such person to manufacture or process a chemical substance for test marketing purposes —

(A) upon a showing by such person satisfactory to the Administrator that the manufacture, processing, distribution in commerce, use, and disposal of such substance, and that any combination of such activities, for such purposes will not present any unreasonable risk of injury to health or the environment, including an unreasonable risk to a potentially exposed or susceptible subpopulation identified by the Administrator for the specific conditions of use identified in the application, and

(B) under such restrictions as the Administrator considers appropriate.

(2)(A) The Administrator may, upon application, exempt any person from the requirement of subsection (b)(2) of this section to submit information for a chemical substance. If, upon receipt of an application under the preceding sentence, the Administrator determines that —

(i) the chemical substance with respect to which such application was submitted is equivalent to a chemical substance for which information has been submitted to the Administrator as required by subsection (b)(2) of this section, and

(ii) submission of information by the applicant on such substance would be duplicative of information which has been submitted to the Administrator in accordance with such subsection,

the Administrator shall exempt the applicant from the requirement to submit such information on such substance. No exemption which is granted under this subparagraph with respect to the submission of information for a chemical substance may take effect before the beginning of the reimbursement period applicable to such information.

(B) If the Administrator exempts any person, under subparagraph (A), from submitting data required under subsection (b)(2) of this section for a chemical substance because of the existence of previously submitted data and if such exemption is granted during the reimbursement period for such data, then (unless such person and the persons referred to in clauses (i) and (ii) agree on the amount and method of reimbursement) the Administrator shall order the person granted the exemption to provide fair and equitable reimbursement (in an amount determined under rules of the Administrator) —

(i) to the person who previously submitted the data on which the exemption was based, for a portion of the costs incurred by such person in complying with the requirement under subsection (b)(2) of this section to submit such data, and

(ii) to any other person who has been required under this subparagraph to contribute with respect to such costs, for a portion of the amount such person was required to contribute.

In promulgating rules for the determination of fair and equitable reimbursement to the persons described in clauses (i) and (ii) for costs incurred with respect to a chemical substance, the Administrator shall, after consultation with the Attorney General and the Federal Trade Commission, consider all relevant factors, including the effect on the competitive position of the person required to provide reimbursement in relation to the persons to be reimbursed and the share of the market for such substance of the person required to provide reimbursement in relation to the share of such market of the persons to be reimbursed. For purposes of judicial review, an order under this subparagraph shall be considered final agency action.

(C) For purposes of this paragraph, the reimbursement period for any previously submitted data for a chemical substance is a period —

(i) beginning on the date of the termination of the prohibition, imposed under this section, on the manufacture or processing of such substance by the person who submitted such data to the Administrator, and

(ii) ending —

(I) five years after the date referred to in clause (i), or

(II) at the expiration of a period which begins on the date referred to in clause (i) and is equal to the period which the Administrator determines was necessary to develop such data, whichever is later.

(3) The requirements of subsections (a) and (b) of this section do not apply with respect to the manufacturing or processing of any chemical substance which is manufactured or processed, or proposed to be manufactured or processed, only in small quantities (as defined by the Administrator by rule) solely for purposes of —

(A) scientific experimentation or analysis, or

(B) chemical research on, or analysis of such substance or another substance, including such research or analysis for the development of a product,

if all persons engaged in such experimentation, research, or analysis for a manufacturer or processor are notified (in such form and manner as the Administrator may prescribe) of any risk to health which the manufacturer, processor, or the Administrator has reason to believe may be associated with such chemical substance.

(4) The Administrator may, upon application and by rule, exempt the manufacturer of any new chemical substance from all or part of the requirements of this section if the Administrator determines that the manufacture, processing, distribution in commerce, use, or disposal of such chemical substance, or that any combination of such activities, will not present an unreasonable risk of injury to health or the environment, including an unreasonable risk to a potentially exposed or susceptible subpopulation identified by the Administrator under the conditions of use of this title.

(5) The Administrator may, upon application, make the requirements of subsections (a) and (b) of this section inapplicable with respect to the manufacturing or processing of any chemical substance (A) which exists temporarily as a result of a chemical reaction in the manufacturing or processing of a mixture or another chemical substance, and (B) to which there is no, and will not be, human or environmental exposure.

(6) Immediately upon receipt of an application under paragraph (1) or (5) the Administrator shall publish in the Federal Register notice of the receipt of such application. The Administrator shall give interested persons an opportunity to comment upon any such application and shall, within 45 days of its receipt, either approve or deny the application. The Administrator shall publish in the Federal Register notice of the approval or denial of such an application.

(i) **Definitions** — (1) For purposes of this section, the terms "manufacture" and "process" mean manufacturing or processing for commercial purposes.

(2) For purposes of this Act, the term "requirement" as used in this section shall not displace any statutory or common law.

(3) For purposes of this section, the term "applicable review period" means the period starting on the date the Administrator receives a notice under subsection (a)(1) and ending 90 days after that date, or on such date as is provided for in subsection (b)(1) or (c).

§2605. Prioritization, Risk Evaluation, and Regulation of Chemical Substances and Mixtures

[TSCA §6]

(a) **Scope of regulation** — If the Administrator determines in accordance with subsection (b)(4)(A) that the manufacture, processing, distribution in commerce, use, or disposal of a chemical substance or mixture, or that any combination of such activities, presents or will present an unreasonable risk of injury to health or the environment, the Administrator shall by rule and subject to section 18, and in accordance with subsection (c)(2), apply one or more of the following requirements to such substance or mixture to the extent necessary so that the chemical substance or mixture no longer presents such risk:

(1) A requirement (A) prohibiting or otherwise restricting the manufacturing, processing, or distribution in commerce of such substance or mixture, or (B) limiting the amount of such substance or mixture which may be manufactured, processed, or distributed in commerce.

(2) A requirement —

(A) prohibiting or otherwise restricting the manufacture, processing, or distribution in commerce of such substance or mixture for (i) a particular use or (ii) a particular use in a concentration in excess of a level specified by the Administrator in the rule imposing the requirement, or

(B) limiting the amount of such substance or mixture which may be manufactured, processed, or distributed in commerce for (i) a particular use or (ii) a particular use in a concentration in excess of a level specified by the Administrator in the rule imposing the requirement.

(3) A requirement that such substance or mixture or any article containing such substance or mixture be marked with or accompanied by clear and adequate minimum warnings and instructions with respect to its use, distribution in commerce, or disposal or with respect to any combination of such activities. The form and content of such minimum warnings and instructions shall be prescribed by the Administrator.

(4) A requirement that manufacturers and processors of such substance or mixture make and retain records of the processes used to manufacture or process such substance or mixture or monitor or conduct tests which are reasonable and necessary to assure compliance with the requirements of any rule applicable under this subsection.

(5) A requirement prohibiting or otherwise regulating any manner or method of commercial use of such substance or mixture.

(6)(A) A requirement prohibiting or otherwise regulating any manner or method of disposal of such substance or mixture, or of any article containing such substance or mixture, by its manufacturer or processor or by any other person who uses, or disposes of, it for commercial purposes.

(B) A requirement under subparagraph (A) may not require any person to take any action which would be in violation of any law or requirement of, or in effect for, a State or political subdivision, and shall require each person subject to it to notify each State and political subdivision in which a required disposal may occur of such disposal.

(7) A requirement directing manufacturers or processors of such substance or mixture (A) to give notice of such determination to distributors in commerce of such substance or mixture and, to the extent reasonably ascertainable, to other persons in possession of such substance or mixture or exposed to such substance or mixture, (B) to give public notice such determination, and (C) to replace or repurchase such substance or mixture as elected by the person to which the requirement is directed.

Any requirement (or combination of requirements) imposed under this subsection may be limited in application to specified geographic areas.

(b) Risk Evaluations —

(1) Prioritization for risk evaluations —

(A) Establishment of process — Not later than 1 year after June 22, 2016, the Administrator shall establish, by rule, a risk-based screening process, including criteria for designating chemical substances as high-priority substances for risk evaluations or low-priority substances for which risk evaluations are not warranted at the time. The process to designate the priority of chemical substances shall include a consideration of the hazard and exposure potential of a chemical substance or a category of chemical substances (including consideration of persistence and bioaccumulation, potentially exposed or susceptible subpopulations and storage near significant sources of drinking water), the conditions of use or significant changes in the conditions of use of the chemical substance, and the volume or significant changes in the volume of the chemical substance manufactured or processed.

(B) Identification of priorities for risk evaluation —

(i) High-priority substances — The Administrator shall designate as a high-priority substance a chemical substance that the Administrator concludes, without consideration of costs or other nonrisk factors, may present an unreasonable risk of injury or health or environment because of a potential hazard and a potential route of exposure under the conditions of use, including an unreasonable risk to a potentially exposed or susceptible subpopulation identified as relevant by the Administrator.

(ii) Low-priority substances — Except as provided in clause (iii), the Administrator shall designate a chemical substance as a low-priority substance if the administrator concludes, based on information sufficient to establish without consideration of costs or other nonrisk factors, that such substance does not meet the standard identified in clause (i) for designating a chemical substance a high-priority substance.

(iii) Low-hazard substances — The Administrator may designate a low-priority substance as a low-hazards substance if the Administrator concludes, based on information sufficient to establish, without consideration of costs or other nonrisk factors or exposure, that the chemical substance poses no or low hazard to health or the environment, including any hazard to a potentially exposed or susceptible subpopulation identified as relevant by the administrator.

(C) Information request and review and proposed and final prioritization designation — The rulemaking required in subparagraph (A) shall ensure that the time required to make a priority designation of a chemical substance be no shorter than nine months and no longer than 1 year, and that the process for which such designations includes —

(i) a requirement that the Administrator request interested persons to submit relevant information on a chemical substance that the administrator has initiated the prioritization process on, before proposing a priority designation for the chemical substance, and provide 90 days for such information to be provided;

(ii) a requirement that the Administrator publish each proposed designation of a chemical substance as a high- or low-priority substance, along with an identification of the information, analysis, and basis used to make the proposed designations; and

(iii) a process by which the Administrator may extend the deadline in clause (i) for up to three months in order to receive or evaluate information required to be submitted in accordance with section 4(a)(2)(B), subject to the limitation that if the information available to the Administrator at the end of such an extension remains insufficient to enable the designation of the chemical substance as a low-priority substance, the Administrator shall designate the chemical substance as a high-priority substance.

(2) Initial Risk Evaluations and Subsequent Designations of High-and Low-Priority —

(A) Initial risk evaluations — Not later than 180 days after June 22, 2016, the Administrator shall ensure that risk evaluations are being conducted on at least 10 chemical substances drawn from the 2014 update of the TSCA Work Plan for Chemical Assessments and shall publish the list of such chemical substances during the 180 day period.

(B) Additional risk evaluations — Not later than three and one half years after June 22, 2016, the Administrator shall ensure that risk evaluations are being conducted on at least 20 high-priority substances and that at least 20 chemical substances have been designated as low-priority or low-hazard substances, subject to the limitation that at least 50 percent of all chemical substances on which risk evaluations are being conducted by the Administrator are drawn from the 2014 update of the TSCA Work Plan for Chemical Assessments.

(C) Continuing designations and risk evaluations — The Administrator shall continue to designate priority substances and conduct risk evaluations in accordance with this subsection at a pace consistent with the ability of the Administrator to complete risk evaluations in accordance with the deadlines under paragraph (4)(G).

(D) Preference — In designating high-priority substances, the Administrator shall give preference to —

(i) chemical substances that are listed in the 2014 update of the TSCA Work Plan for Chemical Assessments as having a Persistence and Bioaccumulation Score of 3; and

(ii) chemical substances that are listed in the 2014 update of the TSCA Work Plan for Chemical Assessments that are known human carcinogens and have high acute and chronic toxicity.

(E) Metals and metal compounds — In identifying priorities for risk evaluation and conducting risk evaluations of metals and metal compounds, the Administrator shall use the Framework for Metals Risk Assessment of the Office of the Science Advisor, Risk Assessment Forum, and dated March 2007, or a successor document that addresses metals risk assessment and is peer reviewed by the Science Advisory Board.

(3) Initiation of risk evaluations; designations —

(A) Risk evaluation initiation — Upon designating a chemical substance as a high-priority substance, the Administrator shall initiate a risk evaluation on the substance.

(B) Revision — The Administrator may revise the designation of a low-priority substance or a low- hazard substance based on information made available to the Administrator.

(C) Ongoing designations — The Administrator shall designate at least one high-priority substance upon the completion of each risk evaluation (other than risk evaluations for chemical substances designated under paragraph (4)(C)(ii)).

(4) Risk evaluation process and deadlines —

(A) In general — The Administrator shall conduct risk evaluations pursuant to this paragraph to determine whether a chemical substance presents an unreasonable risk of injury to health or the environment, without consideration of costs or other nonrisk factors, including an unreasonable risk to a potentially exposed or susceptible subpopulation identified as relevant to the risk evaluation by the Administrator under the conditions of use.

(B) Establishment process — Not later than 1 year after June 22, 2016, the Administrator shall establish, by rule, a process to conduct risk evaluations in accordance with subparagraph (A).

(C) Requirement — The Administrator shall conduct and publish risk evaluations, in accordance with the rule promulgated under subparagraph (B), for a chemical substance —

(i) that has been identified under paragraph (2)(A) or designated under paragraph (1)(B)(i); and

(ii) subject to subparagraph (E), that a manufacturer of the chemical substance has requested, in a form and manner and using the criteria prescribed by the Administrator in the rule promulgated under subparagraph (B), be subjected to a risk evaluation.

(D) Scope — The Administrator shall, not later than 6 months after the initiation of a risk evaluation, publish the scope of the risk evaluation to be conducted, including the hazards, exposures, conditions of use, and the potentially exposed or susceptible subpopulations the Administrator expects to consider, and, for each designation of a high-priority substance, ensure not less than 12 months between the initiation of the prioritization process for the chemical substance and the publication of the scope of the risk evaluation for the chemical substance, and for risk evaluations conducted on chemical substances that have been identified under paragraph (2)(A) or selected under subparagraph (E)(iv)(II) of this paragraph, ensure not less than 3 months before the Administrator publishes the scope of the risk evaluation.

(E) Limitation and criteria

(i) Percentage requirements — The Administrator shall ensure that, of the number of chemical substances that undergo a risk evaluation under clause (i) of subparagraph (C), the number of chemical substances undergoing a risk evaluation under clause (ii) of subparagraph (C) is —

(I) not less than 25 percent, if sufficient requests are made under clause (ii) of subparagraph (C); and

(II) not more than 50 percent.

(ii) Requested risk evaluations — Requests for risk evaluations under subparagraph (C)(ii) shall be subject to the payment of fees pursuant to section 26(b), and the Administrator shall not expedite or otherwise provide special treatment to such risk evaluations.

(iii) Preference — In deciding whether to grant requests under subparagraph (C)(ii), the Administrator shall give preference to requests for risk evaluations on on chemical substances for which the Administrator determines that restrictions imposed by 1 or more States have the potential to have a significant impact on interstate commerce or health or the environment.

(iv) Exceptions — (I) Chemical substances for which requests have been granted under subparagraph (C)(ii) and that are not drawn from the 2014 update of the TSCA Work Plan for Chemical Assessments shall not be subject to section 18(b)

(II) Requests for risk evaluations on chemical substances which are made under subparagraph (C)(ii) and that are drawn from the 2014 update of the TSCA Work Plan for Chemical Assessments shall be granted at the discretion of the Administrator and not be subject to clause (i)(II).

(F) Requirements — In conducting a risk evaluation under this subsection, the Administrator shall —

(i) integrate and assess available information on hazards and exposures for the conditions of use of the chemical substance, including information that is relevant to specific risks of injury to health or the environment and information on potentially exposed or susceptible subpopulations identified as relevant by the Administrator;

(ii) describe whether aggregate or sentinel exposures to chemical substance under the conditions of use were considered, and the basis for that consideration;

(iii) not consider costs or other nonrisk factors;

(iv) take into account where relevant, the likely duration, intensity, frequency, and number of exposures under the conditions of use of the chemical substance; and

(v) describe the weight of the scientific evidence for the identified hazard and exposure.

(G) Deadlines — The Administrator —

(i) shall complete a risk evaluation for a chemical substance as soon as practicable, but not later than 3 years after the date on which the Administrator initiates the risk evaluation under subparagraph (C); and

(ii) may extend the deadline for a risk evaluation for not more than 6 months.

(H) Notice and comment — The Administrator shall provide no less than 30 days public notice and an opportunity for comment on a draft risk evaluation prior to publishing a final risk evaluation.

(c) Promulgation of Subsection (a) Rules —

(1) Deadlines — If the Administrator determines that a chemical substance presents an unreasonable risk of injury to health or the environment in accordance with subsection (b)(4)(A), the Administrator —

(A) shall propose in the Federal Register a rule under subsection (a) for the chemical substance not later than 1 year after the date on which the final risk evaluation regarding the chemical substance is published;

(B) shall publish in the Federal Register a final rule not later than 2 years after the date on which the final risk evaluation regarding the chemical substance is published; and

(C) may extend the deadlines under this paragraph for not more than two years subject to the condition that the aggregate length of extensions under this subparagraph and subsection (b)(4)(G)(ii) does not exceed two years, and subject to the limitation that the Administrator may not extend a deadline for the publication of a proposed or final rule regarding a chemical substance drawn from the 2014 update of the TSCA Work Plan for

Chemical Assessments or a chemical substance that, with respect to persistence and bioaccumulation, scores high for 1 and either high or moderate for the other, pursuant to the TSCA Work Plan Chemical Methods Document published by the Administrator in February 2012 (or a successor scoring system), without adequate public justification that demonstrates, following a review of information reasonably available to the Administrator, that the Administrator cannot complete the proposed or final rule without additional information regarding the chemical substance.

(2) Requirements for rule —

(A) Statement of effects — In proposing and promulgating a rule under subsection (a) with respect to a chemical substance or mixture, the Administrator shall consider and publish a statement based on reasonably available information with respect to —

(i) the effects of the chemical substance or mixture on health and the magnitude of the exposure of human beings to the chemical substance or mixture;

(ii) the effects of the chemical substance or mixture on the environment and the magnitude of the exposure of the environment to such substance or mixture;

(iii) the benefits of the chemical substance or mixture for various uses; and

(iv) the reasonably ascertainable economic consequences of the rule, including consideration of —

(I) the likely effect of the rule on the national economy, small business, technological innovation, the environment, and public health;

(II) the costs and benefits of the proposed and final regulatory action and of the 1 or more primary alternative regulatory actions considered by the Administrator; and

(III) the cost effectiveness of the proposed regulatory action and of the 1 or more primary alternative regulatory actions considered by the Administrator.

(B) Selecting requirements — In selecting among prohibitions and other restrictions, the Administrator shall factor in, to the extent practicable, the considerations under subparagraph (A) in accordance with subsection (a).

(C) Consideration of alternatives — Based on the information published under subparagraph (A), in deciding whether to prohibit or restrict in a manner that substantially prevents a specific condition of use of a chemical substance or mixture, and in setting an appropriate transition period for such action, the Administrator shall consider, to the extent practicable, whether technically and economically feasible alternatives that benefit health or the environment, compared to the use so proposed to be prohibited or restricted, will be reasonably available as a substitute when the proposed prohibition or other restriction takes effect.

(D) Replacement parts —

(i) In general — the Administrator shall exempt replacement parts for complex durable goods and complex consumer goods that are designed prior to the date of publication in the Federal Register of the rule under subsection (a), unless the Administrator finds that such replacement parts contribute significantly to the risk, identified in a risk evaluation conducted under subsection (b)(4)(A), to the general population or to an identified potentially exposed or susceptible subpopulation.

(ii) Definitions — In this subparagraph

(I) the term "complex consumer goods" means electronic or mechanical devises composed of multiple manufactured components, with an intended useful life of 3 or more years, where the product is typically not consumed, destroyed, or discarded after a single use, and the components of which would be impracticable to redesign or replace; and

(II) the term "complex durable goods" means manufactured goods composed of 100 or more manufactured components with an intended useful life of 5 or more years, where the product is typically not consumed, destroyed, or discarded after a single use.

(E) Articles — In selecting among prohibitions and other restrictions, the Administrator shall apply such prohibitions or other restrictions to an article or category of articles containing the chemical substance or mixture only to the extent necessary to address he identified risks from exposure to the chemical substance or mixture from the article or category of articles so that the substance or mixture does not present an unreasonable risk of injury to health or the environment identified in the risk evaluation conducted in accordance with subsection (b)(4)(A).

(3) Procedures — when prescribing a rule under subsection (A) the Administrator shall proceed in accordance with section 553 of title 5, United States Code (without regard to any reference in such section to sections 556 and 557 of such title), and shall also —

(A) publish a notice of proposed rulemaking stating with particularity the reason for the proposed rule;

(B) allow interested persons to submit written data, views, and arguments and make all such submissions publicly available;

(C) promulgate a final rule based on the matter in the rulemaking record; and

(D) make an publish with the rule the determination described in subsection (a).

(d) Effective date

(1) In general — In any rule under subsection (a), the Administrator shall —

(A) specify the date on which it shall take effect, which date shall be as soon as practicable;

(B) except as provided in subparagraphs (C) and (D), specify mandatory compliance dates for all the requirements under a rule under subsection (a), which shall be as soon as practicable, but not later than 5 years after the date of promulgation of the rule, except in a case of a use exempted under subsection (g);

(C) specify mandatory compliance dates for the start of ban or phase-out requirements under a rule under subsection (a), which shall be as soon as practicable, but not later than 5 years after the date of promulgation of the rule, except in the case of a use exempted under subsection (g);

(D) specify mandatory compliance dates for full implementation of ban or phase-out requirements under a rule under subsection (a), which shall be as soon as practicable; and

(E) provide for a reasonable transition period.

(2) Variability — as determined by the Administrator, the compliance dates established under paragraph (1) may vary for different affected persons.

(3)(A) The Administrator may declare a proposed rule under subsection (a) of this section to be effective, and compliance with the proposed requirements to be mandatory, upon publication in the Federal Register of the proposed rule and until the compliance dates applicable to such requirements in a final rule promulgated under section 6(a) or until the Administrator revokes such proposed rule, in accordance with subparagraph (B), if —

(i) the Administrator determines that —

(I) the manufacture, processing, distribution in commerce, use, or disposal of the chemical substance or mixture subject to such proposed rule or any combination of such activities is likely to result in an unreasonable

115

risk of serious or widespread injury to health or the environment before such effective date without consideration of costs or other non-risk factors; and

(II) making such proposed rule so effective is necessary to protect the public interest; and

(ii) in the case of a proposed rule to prohibit the manufacture, processing, or distribution of a chemical substance or mixture because of the risk determined under clause (i)(I), a court has in an action under section 2606 of this title granted relief with respect to such risk associated with such substance or mixture.

Such a proposed rule which is made so effective shall not, for purposes of judicial review, be considered final agency action.

(B) If the Administrator makes a proposed rule effective upon its publication in the Federal Register, the Administrator shall, as expeditiously as possible, give interested persons prompt notice of such action in accordance with subsection (c), and either promulgate such rule (as proposed or with modifications) or revoke it.

(e) Polychlorinated biphenyls

(1) Within six months after January 1, 1977, the Administrator shall promulgate rules to —

(A) prescribe methods for the disposal of polychlorinated biphenyls, and

(B) require polychlorinated biphenyls to be marked with clear and adequate warnings, and instructions with respect to their processing, distribution in commerce, use, or disposal or with respect to any combination of such activities.

Requirements prescribed by rules under this paragraph shall be consistent with the requirements of paragraphs (2) and (3).

(2)(A) Except as provided under subparagraph (B), effective one year after January 1, 1977, no person may manufacture, process, or distribute in commerce or use any polychlorinated biphenyl in any manner other than in a totally enclosed manner.

(B) The Administrator may by rule authorize the manufacture, processing, distribution in commerce or use (or any combination of such activities) of any polychlorinated biphenyl in a manner other than in a totally enclosed manner if the Administrator finds that such manufacture, processing, distribution in commerce, or use (or combination of such activities) will not present an unreasonable risk of injury to health or the environment.

(C) For the purposes of this paragraph, the term "totally enclosed manner" means any manner which will ensure that any exposure of human beings or the environment to a polychlorinated biphenyl will be insignificant as determined by the Administrator by rule.

(3)(A) Except as provided in subparagraphs (B), (C), and (D) —

(i) no person may manufacture any polychlorinated biphenyl after two years after January 1, 1977, and

(ii) no person may process or distribute in commerce any polychlorinated biphenyl after two and one-half years after such date.

(B) Any person may petition the Administrator for an exemption from the requirements of subparagraph (A), and the Administrator may grant by rule such an exemption if the Administrator finds that —

(i) an unreasonable risk of injury to health or environment would not result, and

(ii) good faith efforts have been made to develop a chemical substance which does not present an unreasonable risk of injury to health or the environment and which may be substituted for such polychlorinated biphenyl.

An exemption granted under this subparagraph shall be subject to such terms and conditions as the Administrator may prescribe and shall be in effect for such period (but not more than 1 year from the date it is granted except as provided in subparagraph (D)), as the Administrator may prescribe.

(C) Subparagraph (A) shall not apply to the distribution in commerce of any polychlorinated biphenyl if such polychlorinated biphenyl was sold for purposes other than resale before two and one half years after October 11, 1976.

(D) The Administrator may extend an exemption granted pursuant to subparagraph (B) that has not yet expired for a period not to exceed 60 days for the purpose of authorizing the Secretary of Defense and the Secretaries of the military departments to provide for the transportation into the customs territory of the United States of polychlorinated biphenyls generated by or under the control of the Department of Defense for purposes of their disposal, treatment, or storage in the customs territory of the United States if those polychlorinated biphenyls are already in transit from their storage locations but the Administrator determines, in the sole discretion of the Administrator, they would not otherwise arrive in the customs territory of the United States within the period of the original exemption. The Administrator shall promptly publish notice of such extension in the Federal Register.

(4) Any rule under paragraph (1), (2)(B), or (3)(B) shall be promulgated in accordance with paragraph (3) of subsection (c) of this section.

(5) This subsection does not limit the authority of the Administrator, under any other provision of this chapter or any other Federal law, to take action respecting any polychlorinated biphenyl.

(f) Mercury

(1) Prohibition on sale, distribution, or transfer of elemental mercury by federal agencies.

Except as provided in paragraph (2), effective beginning on October 14, 2008, no Federal agency shall convey, sell, or distribute to any other Federal agency, any State or local government agency, or any private individual or entity any elemental mercury under the control or jurisdiction of the Federal agency.

(2) Exceptions.

Paragraph (1) shall not apply to —

(A) a transfer between Federal agencies of elemental mercury for the sole purpose of facilitating storage of mercury to carry out this chapter; or

(B) a conveyance, sale, distribution, or transfer of coal.

(3) Leases of Federal coal.

Nothing in this subsection prohibits the leasing of coal.

(g) Exemptions —

(1) Criteria for exemption — The Administrator may, as part of a rule promulgated under subsection (a), or in a separate rule, grant an exemption from a requirement of a subsection (a) rule for a specific condition of use and a chemical substance or mixture, if the Administrator finds that —

(A) the specific condition of use is a critical or essential use for which no technically and economically feasible safer alternative is available, taking into consideration hazard and exposure;

(B) compliance with the requirement, as applied with respect to he specific condition of use, would significantly disrupt the national economy, national security, or critical infrastructure; or

(C) the specific condition of use of the chemical substance or mixture, as compared to reasonably available alternatives, provides a substantial benefit to health, the environment, or public safety.

(2) Exemption analysis and statement — In proposing an exemption under this subsection, the Administrator shall analyze the need for the exemption, and shall make public the analysis and a statement describing how the analysis was taken into account.

(3) Period of exemption — The Administrator shall establish, as part of a rule under this subsection, a time limit on any exemption for a time to be determined by the Administrator as reasonable on a case-by-case basis, and, by rule, may extend, modify or eliminate an exemption if the Administrator determines, on the basis of reasonably available information and after adequate public justification, the exemption warrants extension or modification or is no longer necessary.

(4) Conditions — As part of a rule promulgated under this subsection, the Administrator shall include conditions, including reasonable record-keeping, monitoring, and reporting requirements, to the extent that the Administrator determines the conditions are necessary to protect health and the environment while achieving the purposes of the exemption.

(h) Chemicals That Are Persistent, Bioaccumulative, and Toxic

(1) Expedited action — Not later than 3 years after June 22, 2016, the Administrator shall propose rules under subsection (a) with respect to chemical substances identified in the 2014 update of the TSCA Work Plan for Chemical Assessments —

(A) that the Administrator has a reasonable basis to conclude are toxic and that with respect to persistence and bioaccumulation score high for one and either high or moderate for the other, pursuant to the TSCA Work Plan Chemicals Methods Document published by the Administrator in February 2012 (or a successor scoring system), and are not a metal or a metal compound, and for which the Administrator has not completed a Work Plan Problem Formulation, initiated a review under section 5, or entered into a consent agreement under section 4, prior to June 22, 2016; and

(B) exposure to which under the conditions of use is likely to the general population or to a potentially exposed or susceptible subpopulation identified by the Administrator, or the environment, on the basis of an exposure and use assessment conducted by the Administrator.

(2) No risk evaluation required — The Administrator shall not be required to conduct risk evaluations on chemical substances that are subject to paragraph (1).

(3) Final rule — Not later than 18 months after proposing a rule pursuant to paragraph (1), the Administrator shall promulgate a final rule under subsection (a).

(4) Selecting restrictions — In selecting among prohibitions and other restrictions promulgated in a rule under subsection (A) pursuant to paragraph (1), the Administrator shall address the risks of injury to health or the environment that the Administrator determines are presented by the chemical substance and shall reduce exposure to the substance to the extent practicable.

(5) Relationship to subsection (b) — If, at any time prior to the date that is 90 days after June 22, 2016, the Administrator makes a designation under subsection (b)(1)(B)(i), or receives a request under subsection (b)(4)(C)(ii) that meets the criteria prescribed by the Administrator in the rule promulgated under subsection (b)(4)(B), such chemical substance shall not be subject this subsection, except that in selecting among prohibitions and other restrictions promulgated in a rule pursuant to subsection (a), the Administrator shall both ensure that the chemical substance meets the rulemaking standard under subsection (a) and reduce exposure to the substance to the extent practicable.

(i) Final Agency Action — Under this section and subject to section 18 —

(1) a determination by the Administrator under subsection (b)(4)(A) that a chemical substance does not present an unreasonable risk of injury or health or the environment shall be issued by order and considered to be a final agency action, effective beginning on the date of issuance of the order; and

(2) a final rule promulgated under subsection (a), including the associated determination by the Administrator under subsection (b)(4)(A) that a chemical substance presents an unreasonable risk of injury to health or the environment, shall be considered to be a final agency action, effective beginning on the date of promulgation of the final rule.

(j) Definition — For the purposes of this Act, the term "requirement" as used in this section shall not displace statutory or common law.

§2606. Imminent hazards
[TSCA §7]
(a) Actions authorized and required

(1) The Administrator may commence a civil action in an appropriate district court of the United States —

(A) for seizure of an imminently hazardous chemical substance or mixture or any article containing such a substance or mixture,

(B) for relief (as authorized by subsection (b) of this section) against any person who manufactures, processes, distributes in commerce, or uses, or disposes of, an imminently hazardous chemical substance or mixture or any article containing such a substance or mixture, or

(C) for both such seizure and relief.

A civil action may be commenced under this paragraph notwithstanding the existence of a determination under section 5 or 6, a

rule under section 4, 5, or 6 or title IV, an order under section 4, 5, or 6 or title IV, or a consent agreement under section 4 of this chapter, and notwithstanding the pendency of any administrative or judicial proceeding under any provision of this chapter.

(2) If the Administrator has not made a rule under section 2605(a) of this title immediately effective (as authorized by section 6(d)(3)(A)(i) of this title) with respect to an imminently hazardous chemical substance or mixture, the Administrator shall commence in a district court of the United States with respect to such substance or mixture or article containing such substance or mixture a civil action described in subparagraph (A), (B), or (C) of paragraph (1).

(b) Relief authorized

(1) The district court of the United States in which an action under subsection (a) of this section is brought shall have jurisdiction to grant such temporary or permanent relief as may be necessary to protect health or the environment from the unreasonable risk (as identified by the Administrator without consideration of tcosts or other nonrisk factors) associated with the chemical substance, mixture, or article involved in such action.

(2) In the case of an action under subsection (a) of this section brought against a person who manufactures, processes, or distributes in commerce a chemical substance or mixture or an article containing a chemical substance or mixture, the relief authorized by paragraph (1) may include the issuance of a mandatory order requiring (A) in the case of purchasers of such substance, mixture, or article known to the defendant, notification to such purchasers of the risk associated with it; (B) public notice of such risk; (C) recall; (D) the replacement or repurchase of such substance, mixture, or article; or (E) any combination of the actions described in the preceding clauses.

(3) In the case of an action under subsection (a) of this section against a chemical substance, mixture, or article, such substance, mixture, or article may be proceeded against by process of libel for its seizure and condemnation. Proceedings in such an action shall conform as nearly as possible to proceedings in rem in admiralty.

(c) Venue and consolidation

(1)(A) An action under subsection (a) of this section against a person who manufactures, processes, or distributes a chemical substance or mixture or an article containing a chemical substance or mixture may be brought in the United States District Court for the District of Columbia, or for any judicial district in which any of the defendants is found, resides, or transacts business; and process in such an action may be served on a defendant in any other district in which such defendant resides or may be found. An action under subsection (a) of this section against a chemical substance, mixture, or article may be brought in any United States district court within the jurisdiction of which the substance, mixture, or article is found.

    (B) In determining the judicial district in which an action may be brought under subsection (a) of this section in instances in which such action may be brought in more than one judicial district, the Administrator shall take into account the convenience of the parties.

    (C) Subpoenas requiring attendance of witnesses in an action brought under subsection (a) of this section may be served in any judicial district.

    (2) Whenever proceedings under subsection (a) of this section involving identical chemical substances, mixtures, or articles are pending in courts in two or more judicial districts, they shall be consolidated for trial by order of any such court upon application reasonably made by any party in interest, upon notice to all parties in interest.

(d) Action under section 2605 — Where appropriate, concurrently with the filing of an action under subsection (a) of this section or as soon thereafter as may be practicable, the Administrator shall initiate a proceeding for the promulgation of a rule under section 2605(a) of this title.

(e) Representation — Notwithstanding any other provision of law, in any action under subsection (a) of this section, the Administrator may direct attorneys of the Environmental Protection Agency to appear and represent the Administrator in such an action.

(f) "Imminently hazardous chemical substance or mixture" defined — For the purposes of subsection (a) of this section, the term "imminently hazardous chemical substance or mixture" means a chemical substance or mixture which presents an imminent and unreasonable risk of serious or widespread injury to health or the environment without consideration of costs or other nonrisk factors. Such a risk to health or the environment shall be considered imminent if it is shown that the manufacture, processing, distribution in commerce, use, or disposal of the chemical substance or mixture, or that any combination of such activities, is likely to result in such injury to health or the environment before a final rule under section 2605 of this title can protect against such risk.

§2607. Reporting and retention of information

[TSCA §8]

(a) Reports

    (1) The Administrator shall promulgate rules under which —

        (A) each person (other than a small manufacturer or processor) who manufactures or processes or proposes to manufacture or process a chemical substance (other than a chemical substance described in subparagraph (B)(ii)) shall maintain such records, and shall submit to the Administrator such reports, as the Administrator may reasonably require, and

    (B) each person (other than a small manufacturer or processor) who manufactures or processes or proposes to manufacture or process —

        (i) a mixture, or

        (ii) a chemical substance in small quantities (as defined by the Administrator by rule) solely for purposes of scientific experimentation or analysis or chemical research on, or analysis of, such substance or another substance, including any such research or analysis for the development of a product,

shall maintain records and submit to the Administrator reports but only to the extent the Administrator determines the maintenance of records or submission of reports, or both, is necessary for the effective enforcement of this chapter.

The Administrator may not require in a rule promulgated under this paragraph the maintenance of records or the submission of reports with respect to changes in the proportions of the components of a mixture unless the Administrator finds that the maintenance of such records or the submission of such reports, or both, is necessary for the effective enforcement of this chapter. For purposes of the compilation of the list of chemical substances required under subsection (b) of this section, the Administrator shall promulgate rules pursuant to this subsection not later than 180 days after January 1, 1977.

    (2) The Administrator may require under paragraph (1) maintenance of records and reporting with respect to the following insofar as known to the person making the report or insofar as reasonably ascertainable:

        (A) The common or trade name, the chemical identity, and the molecular structure of each chemical substance or mixture for which such a report is required.

        (B) The categories or proposed categories of use of each such substance or mixture.

        (C) The total amount of each such substance and mixture manufactured or processed, reasonable estimates of the total amount to be manufactured or processed, the amount manufactured or processed for each of its categories of use, and reasonable estimates of the amount to be manufactured or processed for each of its categories of use or proposed categories of use.

(D) A description of the byproducts resulting from the manufacture, processing, use, or disposal of each such substance or mixture.

(E) All existing information concerning the environmental and health effects of such substance or mixture.

(F) The number of individuals exposed, and reasonable estimates of the number who will be exposed, to such substance or mixture in their places of employment and the duration of such exposure.

(G) In the initial report under paragraph (1) on such substance or mixture, the manner or method of its disposal, and in any subsequent report on such substance or mixture, any change in such manner or method.

(3)(A)(i) The Administrator may by rule require a small manufacturer or processor of a chemical substance to submit to the Administrator such information respecting the chemical substance as the Administrator may require for publication of the first list of chemical substances required by subsection (b) of this section.

(ii) The Administrator may by rule require a small manufacturer or processor of a chemical substance or mixture —

(I) subject to a rule proposed or promulgated under section 2603, 2604(b)(4), or 2605 of this title, an order in effect under section 4 or 5(e), or a consent agreement under section 4 of this title, or

(II) with respect to which relief has been granted pursuant to a civil action brought under section 2604 or 2606 of this title,

to maintain such records on such substance or mixture, and to submit to the Administrator such reports on such substance or mixture, as the Administrator may reasonably require. A rule under this clause requiring reporting may require reporting with respect to the matters referred to in paragraph (2).

(B) The Administrator, after consultation with the Administrator of the Small Business Administration, shall by rule prescribe standards for determining the manufacturers and processors which qualify as small manufacturers and processors for purposes of this paragraph and paragraph (1).

(C) Not later than 180 days after June 22, 2016, and not less frequently than once every 10 years thereafter, the Administrator, after consultation with the Administrator of the Small Business Administration, shall —

(i) review the adequacy of the standards prescribed under subparagraph (B); and

(ii) after providing public notice and opportunity for comment, make a determination as to whether revision of the standards is warranted.

(4) Contents — The rules promulgated pursuant to paragraph (1) —

(A) may impose differing reporting and recordkeeping requirements on manufacturers and processors; and

(B) shall include the level of detail necessary to be reported, including the manner by which use and exposure information may be reported.

(5) Administration — In carrying out this section, the Administrator shall, to the extent feasible —

(A) not require reporting which is unnecessary or duplicative;

(B) minimize the cost of compliance with this section and the rules issued thereunder on small manufacturing and processors; and

(C) apply any reporting obligations to those persons likely to have information relevant to the effective implementation of this title.

(6) Negotiated rulemaking — (A) The Administrator shall enter into a negotiated rulemaking pursuant to subchapter III of chapter 5 of title 5, United States Code, to develop and publish, not later than 3 years after June 22, 2016, a proposed rule providing for limiting the reporting requirements, under this subsection, for manufacturers of any inorganic byproducts, when such byproducts, whether by the byproduct manufacturer or by any other person, are subsequently recycled reused or reprocessed.

(B) Not later than 3 and one-half years after June 22, 2016, the Administrator shall publish a final rule resulting from such negotiated rulemaking.

(7) PFAS data — Not later than January 1, 2023, the Administrator shall promulgate a rule in accordance with this subsection requiring each person who has manufactured a chemical substance that is a perfluoroalkyl or polyfluoroalkyl substance in any year since January 1, 2011, to submit to the Administrator a report that includes, for each year since January 1, 2011, the information described in subparagraphs (a) through (G) of paragraph (2).

(b) Inventory

(1) The Administrator shall compile, keep current, and publish a list of each chemical substance which is manufactured or processed in the United States. Such list shall at least include each chemical substance which any person reports, under section 2604 of this title or subsection (a) of this section, is manufactured or processed in the United States. Such list may not include any chemical substance which was not manufactured or processed in the United States within three years before the effective date of the rules promulgated pursuant to the last sentence of subsection (a)(1) of this section. In the case of a chemical substance for which a notice is submitted in accordance with section 2604 of this title, such chemical substance shall be included in such list as of the earliest date (as determined by the Administrator) on which such substance was manufactured or processed in the United States. The Administrator shall first publish such a list not later than 315 days after January 1, 1977. The Administrator shall not include in such list any chemical substance which is manufactured or processed only in small quantities (as defined by the Administrator by rule) solely for purposes of scientific experimentation or analysis or chemical research on, or analysis of, such substance or another substance, including such research or analysis for the development of a product.

(2) To the extent consistent with the purposes of this chapter, the Administrator may, in lieu of listing, pursuant to paragraph (1), a chemical substance individually, list a category of chemical substances in which such substance is included.

(3) **Nomenclature** —

(A) **In general** — In carrying out all paragraph (1), the Administrator shall —

(i) maintain the use of Class 2 nomenclature in use on June 22, 2016;

(ii) maintain the use of the Soap and Detergent Association Nomenclature System, published in March 1978, by the Administrator in section 1 of addendum III of the document entitled "Candidate List of Chemical Substances", and further described in the appendix A of volume I of the 1985 edition of the Toxic Substances Control Act Substances Inventory (EPA Document No. EPA-560/7-85-002a); and

(iii) treat the individual members of the categories of chemical substances identified by the Administrator as statutory mixtures, as defined in Inventory descriptions established by the Administrator, as being included on the list established under paragraph (1).

(B) **Multiple nomenclature listings** — If a manufacturer or processor demonstrates to the Administrator that a chemical substance appears multiple times on the list published under paragraph (1) under different CAS numbers, the Administrator may recognize multiple listings as a single chemical substance.

(C) **Relationship to section 5** — Nothing in subparagraph (B), nor any action of the Administrator pursuant to subparagraph (B), shall be construed as a basis to conclude that any chemical substance is not a new chemical substance.

(4) **Chemical substances in commerce** —

(A) **Rules** —

(i) **In general** — Not later than 1 year after June 22, 2016, the Administrator, by rule, shall require manufacturers, and may require processors subject to the limitations under subsection (A)(5)(A), to notify the Administrator, by not later than 180 days after the date on which the final rule is published in the Federal Register, of each chemical substance on the list published under paragraph (1) that the manufacturer or processor, as applicable, has manufactured or processed for a non-exempt commercial purpose during the 10-year period ending on the day before June 22, 2016.

(ii) **Active substances** — The Administrator shall designate chemical substances for which notices are received under clause (i) to be active substances on the list under paragraph (1).

(iii) **Inactive substances** — The Administrator shall designate chemical substances for which no notices are received under clause (i) to be inactive substances on the list published under paragraph (1).

(iv) **Limitation** — No chemical substance on the list published under paragraph (1) shall be removed from such list by reason of the implementation of this subparagraph, or be subject to section 5(a)(1)(A)(i) by reason of a change to the active status under paragraph (5)(B).

(B) **Confidential chemical substances** — In promulgating a rule under subparagraph (A), the Administrator shall —

(i) maintain the list under paragraph (1), which shall include a confidential portion and a confidential portion consistent with this section and section 14;

(ii) require any manufacturer or processor of a chemical substance on the confidential portion of the list published under paragraph (1) that seeks to maintain an existing claim for protection against disclosure of the specific chemical identity of the chemical substance as confidential pursuant to section 14 to submit a notice under subparagraph (A) that includes such request;

(iii) require the substantiation of those claims pursuant to section 14 and in accordance with the review plan described in subparagraph (C); and

(iv) move any active chemical substance for which no request was received to maintain an existing claim for protection against disclosure of the specific chemical identity of the chemical substance as confidential from the confidential portion of the list published under paragraph (1) to the nonconfidential portion of that list.

(C) Review plan — Not later than 1 year after the date on which the Administrator compiles the initial list of active substances pursuant to subparagraph (A), the Administrator shall promulgate a rule that establishes a plan to review all claims to protect the specific chemical identities of chemical substances on the confidential portion of the list published under paragraph (1) that are asserted pursuant to subparagraph (B).

(D) Requirements of review plan — In establishing the review plan under subparagraph (C), the Administrator shall —

(i) require, at a time specified by the Administrator, all manufacturers or processors asserting claims under subparagraph (B) to substantiate the claim, in accordance with section 14, unless the manufacturer or processor has substantiated the claim in a submission made to the Administrator during the 5-year period ending on the last day of the time period specified by the Administrator; and

(ii) in accordance with section 14—

(I) review each substantiation —

(aa) submitted pursuant to clause (i) to determine if the claim qualifies for protection from disclosure; and

(bb) submitted previously by a manufacturer or processor and relied in lieu of the substantiation required pursuant to clause (i), if the substantiation has not been previously reviewed by the Administrator, to determine if the claim warrants protection from disclosure;

(II) approve, approve in part and deny in part, or deny each claim; and

(III) except as provided in this section and section 14, protect from the disclosure information for which the Administrator approves such a claim for a period of 10 years, unless, prior to the expiration of the period —

(aa) the person notifies the Administrator that the person is withdrawing the claim, in which case the Administrator shall not protect the information from disclosure; or

(bb) the Administrator otherwise becomes aware that the information does not qualify for protection from disclosure, in which case the Administrator shall take the actions described in section 14(g)(2).

(E) Timeline for completion of reviews —

(i) **In general** — The Administrator shall implement the review plan so as to complete reviews of all claims specified in subparagraph (C) not later than 5 years after the date on which the Administrator compiles the initial list of active substances pursuant to subparagraph (A).

(ii) **Considerations** —

(I) **In general** — The Administrator may extend the deadline for completion of the reviews for not more than 2 additional years, after an adequate public justification, if the Administrator determines that the extension is necessary based on the number of claims needing review and the available resources.

(II) **Annual review goal and results** — At the beginning of each year, the Administrator shall publish an annual goal for reviews and the number of reviews completed in the prior year.

(5) Active and inactive substances —

(A) In general — The Administrator shall keep designations of active substances and inactive substances on the list published under paragraph (1) current.

(B) Change to active status —

(i) **In general** — Any person that intends to manufacture or process for a nonexempt commercial purpose a chemical substance that is designated as an inactive substance shall notify the Administrator before the date on which the inactive substance is manufactured or processed.

(ii) **Confidential chemical identity** — If a person submitting a notice under clause (i) for an inactive substance on the confidential portion of the list published under paragraph (1) seeks to maintain an existing claim for protection against disclosure of the specific chemical identity of the inactive substance as confidential, the person shall, consistent with the requirements of section 14 —

(I) in the notice submitted under clause (i), assert the claim; and

(II) by not later than 30 days after providing the notice under clause (i), substantiate the claim.

(iii) **Active status** — On receiving a notification under clause (i), the Administrator shall —

(I) designate the applicable chemical substance as an active substance;

(II) pursuant to section 14, promptly review any claim and associated substantiation submitted pursuant to clause (ii) for protection against disclosure of the specific chemical identity of the chemical substance and approve, approve in part and deny in part, or deny the claim;

(III) except as provided in this section and section 14, protect from disclosure the specific chemical identity of the chemical substance for which the Administrator approves a claim under subclause (II) for a period of 10 years, unless, prior to the expiration of the period —

(aa) the person notifies the Administrator that the person is withdrawing the claim, in which case the Administrator shall not protect the information from disclosure; or

(bb) the Administrator otherwise becomes aware that the information does not qualify for protection from disclosure, in which case the Administrator shall take the actions described in section 14(g)(2); and

(IV) pursuant to section 6(b), review the priority of the chemical substance as the Administrator determines to be necessary.

(C) **Category status** — The list of inactive substances shall not be considered to be a category for purposes of section 26(c).

(6) **Interim list of active substances** — Prior to the promulgation of the rule required under paragraph (4)(A), the Administrator shall designate the chemical substances reported under part 711 of title 40, code of Federal Regulations (as in effect on June 22, 2016, during the reporting period that most closely preceded June 22, 2016, as the interim list of active substances for the purposes of section 6(b).

(7) **Public information** — Subject to this subsection and section 14, the Administrator shall make available to the public —

(A) each specific chemical identity on the nonconfidential portion of the list published under paragraph (1) along with the Administrator's designation of the chemical substance as an active or inactive substance;

(B) the unique identifier assigned under section 14, accession number, generic name, and, if applicable, premanufacture notice case number for each chemical substance on the confidential portion of the list published under paragraph (1) for which a claim of confidentiality was received; and

(C) the specific chemical identity of any active substance for which —

(i) a claim for protection against disclosure of the specific chemical identity of the active substance was not asserted, as required under this subsection or section 14;

(ii) all claims for protection against disclosure of the specific chemical identity of the active substance have been denied by the Administrator; or

(iii) the time period for protection against disclosure of the specific chemical identity of the active substance has expired.

(8) **Limitation** — No person may assert a new claim under this subsection or section 14 for protection from disclosure of a specific chemical identity of any active or inactive substance for which a notice is received under paragraph (4)(A)(i) or (5)(B)(i) that is not on the confidential portion of the list under paragraph (1).

(9) **Certification** — Under the rules promulgated under this subsection, manufacturers and processors, as applicable, shall be required —

(A) to certify that each notice or substantiation the manufacturer or processor submits complies with the requirements of the rule, and that any confidentiality claims are true and correct; and

(B) to retain a record documenting compliance with the rule and supporting confidentiality claims for a period of 5 years beginning on the last day of the submission period.

(10) **Mercury** —

(A) **Definition of mercury** — In this paragraph, notwithstanding section 3(2)(B), the term "mercury" means —

(i) elemental mercury; and

(ii) a mercury compound.

(B) **Publication** — Not later than April 1, 2017, and every 3 years thereafter, the Administrator shall carry out and publish in the Federal Register an inventory of mercury supply, use, and trade in the United States.

(C) **Process** — In carrying out the inventory under subparagraph (B), the Administrator shall —

(i) identify any manufacturing process or products that intentionally add mercury; and

(ii) recommend actions, including proposed revisions of Federal law or regulations, to achieve further reductions in mercury use.

(D) **Reporting** —

(i) **In general** — To assist in the preparation of the inventory under subparagraph (B), any person who manufactures mercury or mercury-added products or otherwise intentionally uses mercury in a manufacturing process shall make periodic reports to the Administrator, at such time and including such information as the Administrator shall determine by rule promulgated not later than 2 years after the date of enactment of this paragraph.

(ii) Coordination — To avoid duplication, the Administrator shall coordinate the reporting under this subparagraph with the Interstate Mercury Education and Reduction Clearinghouse.

(iii) Exemption — Clause (i) shall not apply to a person engaged in the generation, handling, or management of mercury-containing waste, unless that person manufactures or recovers mercury in the management of that waste.

(c) Records — Any person who manufactures, processes, or distributes in commerce any chemical substance or mixture shall maintain records of significant adverse reactions to health or the environment, as determined by the Administrator by rule, alleged to have been caused by the substance or mixture. Records of such adverse reactions to the health of employees shall be retained for a period of 30 years from the date such reactions were first reported to or known by the person maintaining such records. Any other record of such adverse reactions shall be retained for a period of five years from the date the information contained in the record was first reported to or known by the person maintaining the record. Records required to be maintained under this subsection shall include records of consumer allegations of personal injury or harm to health, reports of occupational disease or injury, and reports or complaints of injury to the environment submitted to the manufacturer, processor, or distributor in commerce from any source. Upon request of any duly designated representative of the Administrator, each person who is required to maintain records under this subsection shall permit the inspection of such records and shall submit copies of such records.

(d) Health and safety studies — The Administrator shall promulgate rules under which the Administrator shall require any person who manufactures, processes, or distributes in commerce or who proposes to manufacture, process, or distribute in commerce any chemical substance or mixture (or with respect to paragraph (2), any person who has possession of a study) to submit to the Administrator —

(1) lists of health and safety studies (A) conducted or initiated by or for such person with respect to such substance or mixture at any time, (B) known to such person, or (C) reasonably ascertainable by such person, except that the Administrator may exclude certain types or categories of studies from the requirements of this subsection if the Administrator finds that submission of lists

of such studies are unnecessary to carry out the purposes of this chapter; and

(2) copies of any study contained on a list submitted pursuant to paragraph (1) or otherwise known by such person.

(e) Notice to Administrator of substantial risks — Any person who manufactures, processes, or distributes in commerce as chemical substance or mixture and who obtains information which reasonably supports the conclusion that such substance or mixture presents a substantial risk of injury to health or the environment shall immediately inform the Administrator of such information unless such person has actual knowledge that the Administrator has been adequately informed of such information.

(f) "Manufacture" and "process" defined — For purposes of this section, the terms "manufacture" and "process" mean manufacture or process for commercial purposes.

§2608. Relationship to other Federal laws [TSCA §9]

(a) Laws not administered by the Administrator

(1) If the Administrator determines that the manufacture, processing, distribution in commerce, use, or disposal of a chemical substance or mixture, or that any combination of such activities, presents or will present an unreasonable risk of injury to health or the environment, without consideration of costs or other nonrisk factors, including an unreasonable risk to a potentially exposed or susceptible subpopulation identified as relevant by the Administrator, under the conditions of use, and determines, in the Administrator's discretion, that such risk may be prevented or reduced to a sufficient extent by action taken under a Federal law not administered by the Administrator, the Administrator shall submit to the agency which administers such law a report which describes such risk and includes in such description a specification of the activity or combination of activities which the Administrator has reason to believe so presents such risk. Such report shall also request such agency —

(A)(i) to determine if the risk described in such report may be prevented or reduced to a sufficient extent by action taken under such law, and

(ii) if the agency determines that such risk may be so prevented or reduced, to issue an order declaring whether or not the activity or combination of activities specified in the description of such risk presents such risk; and

(B) to respond to the Administrator with respect to the matters described in subparagraph (A).

Any report of the Administrator shall include a detailed statement of the information on which it is based and shall be published in the Federal Register. The agency receiving a request under such a report shall make the requested determination, issue the requested order, and make the requested response within such time as the Administrator specifies in the request, but such time specified may not be less than 90 days from the date the request was made. The response of an agency shall be accompanied by a detailed statement of the findings and conclusions of the agency and shall be published in the Federal Register.

(2) If the Administrator makes a report under paragraph (1) with respect to a chemical substance or mixture and the agency to which such report was made either —

(A) issues an order, within the time period specified by the Administrator in the report, declaring that the activity or combination of activities specified in the description of the risk described in the report does not present the risk described in the report, or

(B) responds within the time period specified by the Administrator in the report and initiates, within 90 days of the publication in the Federal Register of the response of the agency under paragraph (1), action under the law (or laws) administered by such agency to protect against such risk associated with such activity or combination of activities,

the Administrator may not take any action under section 6(a) or 7 of this title with respect to such risk.

(3) The Administrator shall take the actions described in paragraph (4) if the Administrator makes a report under paragraph (1) with respect to a chemical substance or mixture and the agency to which the report was made does not —

(A) issue the order described in paragraph (2)(A) within the time period specified by the Administrator in the report; or

(B)(i) respond under paragraph (1) within the timeframe specified by the Administrator in the report; and

(ii) initiate action within 90 days of publication in the Federal Register of the response described in clause (i).

(4) If any agency to which a report is submitted under paragraph (1) does not take the actions described in subparagraph (A) or (B) of paragraph (3), the Administrator shall –

(A) initiate or complete appropriate action under section 6(a); or

(B) take any action authorized or required under section 7 as applicable.

(5) This subsection shall not relieve the Administrator of any obligation to take any appropriate action under section 6(a) or 7 to address risks from the manufacture, processing, distribution in commerce, use, or disposal of a chemical substance or mixture, or any combination of those activities, that are not identified in a report issued by the Administrator under paragraph (1).

(6) If the Administrator has initiated action under section 2605 or 2606 of this title with respect to a risk associated with a chemical substance or mixture which was the subject of a report made to an agency under paragraph (1), such agency shall before taking action under the law (or laws) administered by it to protect against such risk consult with the Administrator for the purpose of avoiding duplication of Federal action against such risk.

(b) Laws administered by the Administrator — (1) The Administrator shall coordinate actions taken under this chapter with actions taken under other Federal laws administered in whole or in part by the Administrator. If the Administrator determines that a risk to health or the environment associated with a chemical substance or mixture could be eliminated or reduced to a sufficient extent by actions taken under the authorities contained in such other Federal laws, the Administrator shall use such authorities to protect against such risk unless the Administrator determines, in the Administrator's discretion, that it is in the public interest to protect against such risk by actions taken under this chapter. This subsection shall not be construed to relieve the Administrator of any requirement imposed on the Administrator by such other Federal laws.

(2) In making a determination under paragraph (1) that it is in the public interest for the Administrator to take an action under this title with respect to a chemical substance or mixture rather than under another law administered in whole or in part by the Administrator, the Administrator shall consider, based on information reasonably available to the Administrator, all relevant aspects of the risk described in paragraph (1) and a comparison of the estimated costs and efficiencies of the action to be taken under this title and an action to be taken under such other law to protect against such risk.

(c) Occupational safety and health — In exercising any authority under this chapter, the Administrator shall not, for purposes of section 653(b)(1) of Title 29, be deemed to be exercising statutory authority to prescribe or enforce standards or regulations affecting occupational safety and health.

(d) Coordination — In administering this chapter, the Administrator shall consult and coordinate with the Secretary of Health and Human Services and the heads of any other appropriate Federal executive department or agency, any relevant independent regulatory agency, and any other appropriate instrumentality of the Federal Government for the purpose of achieving the maximum enforcement of this chapter while imposing the least burdens of duplicative requirements on those subject to the chapter and for other purposes. The Administrator shall, in the report required by section 2629 of this title, report annually to the Congress on actions taken to coordinate with such other Federal departments, agencies, or instrumentalities, and on actions taken to coordinate the authority under this chapter with the authority granted under other Acts referred to in subsection (b) of this section.

(e) Exposure information — In addition to the requirements of subsection (a), if the Administrator obtains information related to exposures or releases of a chemical substance or mixture that may be prevented or reduced under another Federal law, including a law not administered by the Administrator, the Administrator shall make such information available to the relevant Federal agency or office of the Environmental Protection Agency.

§2609. Research, development, collection, dissemination, and utilization of information [TSCA §10]

(a) Authority — The Administrator shall, in consultation and cooperation with the Secretary of Health and Human Services and with other heads of appropriate departments and agencies, conduct such research, development, and monitoring as is necessary to carry out the purposes of this chapter. The Administrator may enter into contracts and may make grants for research, development, and monitoring under this subsection. Contracts may be entered into under this subsection without regard to section 3324(a) and (b) of Title 31 and section 5 of Title 41.

(b) Information systems

(1) The Administrator shall establish, administer, and be responsible for the continuing activities of an interagency committee which shall design, establish, and coordinate an efficient and effective system, within the Environmental Protection Agency, for the collection, dissemination to other Federal departments and agencies, and use of information submitted to the Administrator under this chapter.

(2)(A) The Administrator shall, in consultation and cooperation with the Secretary of Health and Human Services and other heads of appropriate departments and agencies design, establish, and coordinate an efficient and effective system for the retrieval of toxicological and other scientific information which could be useful to the Administrator in carrying out the purposes of this chapter. Systematized retrieval shall be developed for use by all Federal and other departments and agencies with responsibilities in the area of regulation or study of chemical substances and mixtures and their effect on health or the environment.

(B) The Administrator, in consultation and cooperation with the Secretary of Health and Human Services, may make grants and enter into contracts for the development of an information retrieval system described in subparagraph (A). Contracts may be entered into under this subparagraph without regard to section 3324(a) and (b) of Title 31 and section 5 of Title 41.

(c) Screening techniques — The Administrator shall coordinate, with the Assistant Secretary for Health of the Department of Health and Human Services, research undertaken by the Administrator and directed toward the development of rapid, reliable, and economical screening techniques for carcinogenic, mutagenic, teratogenic, and ecological effects of chemical substances and mixtures.

(d) Monitoring — The Administrator shall, in consultation and cooperation with the Secretary of Health and Human Services, establish and be responsible for research aimed at the development, in cooperation with local, State, and Federal agencies, of monitoring techniques and instruments which may be used in the detection of toxic chemical substances and mixtures and which are reliable, economical, and capable of being implemented under a wide variety of conditions.

(e) Basic research — The Administrator shall, in consultation and cooperation with the Secretary of Health and Human Services, establish research programs to develop the fundamental scientific basis of the screening and monitoring techniques described in subsections (c) and (d) of this section, the bounds of the reliability of such techniques, and the opportunities for their improvement.

(f) Training — The Administrator shall establish and promote programs and workshops to train or facilitate the training of Federal laboratory and technical personnel in existing or newly developed screening and monitoring techniques.

(g) Exchange of research and development results — The Administrator shall, in consultation with the Secretary of Health and Human Services and other heads of appropriate departments and agencies, establish and coordinate a system for exchange among Federal, State, and local authorities of research and development results respecting toxic chemical substances and mixtures, including a system to facilitate and promote the development of standard information format and analysis and consistent testing procedures.

§2610. Inspections and subpoenas [TSCA §11]

(a) In general — For purposes of administering this chapter, the Administrator, and any duly designated representative of the Administrator, may inspect any establishment, facility, or other premises in which chemical substances, mixtures, or products subject to subchapter IV of this chapter are manufactured, processed, stored, or held before or after their distribution in commerce and any conveyance being used to transport chemical substances, mixtures, such products, or such articles in connection with distribution in commerce. Such an inspection may only be made upon the presentation of appropriate credentials and of a written notice to the owner, operator, or agent in charge of the premises or conveyance to be inspected. A separate notice shall be given for each such inspection, but a notice shall not be required for each entry made during the period covered by the inspection. Each such inspection shall be commenced and completed with reasonable promptness and shall be conducted at reasonable times, within reasonable limits, and in a reasonable manner.

(b) Scope

(1) Except as provided in paragraph (2), an inspection conducted under subsection (a) of this section shall extend to all things within the premises or conveyance inspected (including records, files, papers, processes, controls, and facilities) bearing on whether the requirements of this chapter applicable to the chemical substances, mixtures, or products subject to subchapter IV of this chapter within such premises or conveyance have been complied with.

(2) No inspection under subsection (a) of this section shall extend to —

(A) financial information,

(B) sales information (other than shipment information),

(C) pricing information,

(D) personnel information, or

(E) research information (other than data required by this chapter or under a rule promulgated, order issued, or consent agreement entered into thereunder),

unless the nature and extent of such data are described with reasonable specificity in the written notice required by subsection (a) of this section for such inspection.

(c) Subpoenas — In carrying out this chapter, the Administrator may by subpoena require the attendance and testimony of witnesses and the production of reports, papers, documents, answers to questions, and other information that the Administrator deems necessary. Witnesses shall be paid the same fees and mileage that are paid witnesses in the courts of the United States. In the event of contumacy, failure, or refusal of any person to obey any such subpoena, any district court of the United States in which venue is proper shall have jurisdiction to order any such person to comply with such subpoena. Any failure to obey such an order of the court is punishable by the court as a contempt thereof.

§2611. Exports
[TSCA §12]
(a) In general

(1) Except as provided in paragraph (2) and subsection (b) of this section, this chapter (other than section 2607 of this title) shall not apply to any chemical substance, mixture, or to an article containing a chemical substance or mixture, if —

(A) it can be shown that such substance, mixture, or article is being manufactured, processed, or distributed in commerce for export from the United States, unless such substance, mixture, or article was, in fact, manufactured, processed, or distributed in commerce, for use in the United States, and

(B) such substance, mixture, or article (when distributed in commerce), or any container in which it is enclosed (when so distributed), bears a stamp or label stating that such substance, mixture, or article is intended for export.

(2) Paragraph (1) shall not apply to any chemical substance, mixture, or article if the Administrator finds that the substance, mixture, or article will present an unreasonable risk of injury to health within the United States or to the environment of the United States. The Administrator may require, under section 2603 of this title, testing of any chemical substance or mixture exempted from this chapter by paragraph (1) for the purpose of determining whether or not such substance or mixture presents an unreasonable risk of injury to health within the United States or to the environment of the United States.

(b) Notice

(1) If any person exports or intends to export to a foreign country a chemical substance or mixture for which the submission of information is required under section 2603 or 2604(b) of this title, such person shall notify the Administrator of such exportation or intent to export and the Administrator shall furnish to the government of such country notice of the availability of the information submitted to the Administrator under such section for such substance or mixture.

(2) If any person exports or intends to export to a foreign country a chemical substance or mixture for which an order has been issued under section 2604 of this title or a rule has been proposed or promulgated under section 2604 or 2605 of this title, or with respect to which an action is pending, or relief has been granted under section 2604 or 2606 of this title, such person shall notify the Administrator of such exportation or intent to export and the Administrator shall furnish to the government of such country notice of such rule, order, action, or relief.

(c) Prohibition on export of elemental mercury and mercury compounds

(1) Prohibition.

Effective January 1, 2013, the export of elemental mercury from the United States is prohibited.

(2) Inapplicability of subsection (a).

Subsection (a) shall not apply to this subsection.

(3) Report to Congress on mercury compounds.

(A) Report.

Not later than one year after October 14, 2008, the Administrator shall publish and submit to Congress a report on mercuric chloride, mercurous chloride or calomel, mercuric oxide, and other mercury compounds, if any, that may currently be used in significant quantities in products or processes. Such report shall include an analysis of —

(i) the sources and amounts of each of the mercury compounds imported into the United States or manufactured in the United States annually;

(ii) the purposes for which each of these compounds are used domestically, the amount of these compounds currently consumed annually for each purpose, and the estimated amounts to be consumed for each purpose in 2010 and beyond;

(iii) the sources and amounts of each mercury compound exported from the United States annually in each of the last three years;

(iv) the potential for these compounds to be processed into elemental mercury after export from the United States; and

(v) other relevant information that Congress should consider in determining whether to extend the export prohibition to include one or more of these mercury compounds.

(B) Procedure.

For the purpose of preparing the report under this paragraph, the Administrator may utilize the information gathering authorities of this title, including sections 2609 and 2610 of this title.

(4) Essential use exemption.

(A) Any person residing in the United States may petition the Administrator for an exemption from the prohibition in paragraph (1), and the Administrator may grant by rule, after notice and opportunity for comment, an exemption for a specified use at an identified foreign facility if the Administrator finds that —

(i) nonmercury alternatives for the specified use are not available in the country where the facility is located;

(ii) there is no other source of elemental mercury available from domestic supplies (not including new mercury mines) in the country where the elemental mercury will be used;

(iii) the country where the elemental mercury will be used certifies its support for the exemption;

(iv) the export will be conducted in such a manner as to ensure the elemental mercury will be used at the identified facility as described in the petition, and not otherwise diverted for other uses for any reason;

(v) the elemental mercury will be used in a manner that will protect human health and the environment, taking into account local, regional, and global human health and environmental impacts;

(vi) the elemental mercury will be handled and managed in a manner that will protect human health and the environment, taking into account local, regional, and global human health and environmental impacts; and

(vii) the export of elemental mercury for the specified use is consistent with international obligations of the United States intended to reduce global mercury supply, use, and pollution.

(B) Each exemption issued by the Administrator pursuant to this paragraph shall contain such terms and conditions as are necessary to minimize the export of elemental mercury and ensure that the conditions for granting the exemption will be fully met, and shall contain such other terms and conditions as the Administrator may prescribe. No exemption granted pursuant to this paragraph shall exceed three years in duration and no such exemption shall exceed 10 metric tons of elemental mercury.

(C) The Administrator may by order suspend or cancel an exemption under this paragraph in the case of a violation described in subparagraph (D).

(D) A violation of this subsection or the terms and conditions of an exemption, or the submission of false information in connection therewith, shall be considered a prohibited act under section 2614 of this title, and shall be subject to penalties under section 2615 of this title, injunctive relief under section 2616 of this title, and citizen suits under section 2619 of this title.

(5) Consistency with trade obligations.

Nothing in this subsection affects, replaces, or amends prior law relating to the need for consistency with international trade obligations.

(6) Export of coal.

Nothing in this subsection shall be construed to prohibit the export of coal.

(7) Prohibition on export of certain mercury compounds —

(A) In general — Effective January 1, 2020, the export of the following mercury compounds is prohibited:

(i) Mercury (I) chloride or calomel.

(ii) Mercury (II) oxide.

(iii) Mercury (II) sulfate.

(iv) Mercury (II) nitrate.

(v) Cinnabar or mercury sulphide.

(vi) Any mercury compound that the Administrator adds to the list published under subparagraph (B) by rule, on determining that exporting that mercury compound for the purpose of regenerating elemental mercury is technically feasible.

(B) Publication — Not later than 90 days after June 22, 2016, and as appropriate thereafter, the Administrator shall publish in the Federal register a list of the mercury compounds that are prohibited from export under this paragraph.

(C) Petition — Any person may petition the Administrator to add a mercury compound to the list published under subparagraph (B).

(D) Environmentally sound disposal — This paragraph does not prohibit the export of mercury compounds on the list published under subparagraph (B) to member countries of the Organization fro Economic Cooperation and Development for environmentally sound disposal, on the condition that no mercury or mercury compounds so exported are to be recovered, recycled, or reclaimed for use, or directly reused, after such export.

(E) Report — Not later than 5 years after June 22, 2016, the Administrator shall evaluate any exports of mercury compounds on the list published under subparagraph (B) for disposal that occurred after such date of enactment and shall submit to Congress a report that —

(i) describes volumes and sources of mercury compounds on the list published under subparagraph (B) exported for disposal;

(ii) identifies receiving countries of such exports;

(iii) describes methods of disposal used after such export;

(iv) identifies issues, if any, presented by the export of mercury compounds on the list published under subparagraph (B);

(v) includes an evaluation of management options in the United States for mercury compounds on the list published under subparagraph (B), if any, that are commercially available and comparable in cost and efficacy to methods being utilized in such receiving countries; and

(vi) makes a recommendation regarding whether Congress should further limit or prohibit the export of mercury compounds on the list published under subparagraph (B) for disposal.

(F) Effect on other law — Nothing in this paragraph shall be construed to affect the authority of the Administrator under the Solid Waste Disposal Act (42 U.S.C. 6901 et seq.).

§2612. Entry into customs territory of the United States
[TSCA §13]

(a) In general

(1) The Secretary of the Treasury shall refuse entry into the customs territory of the United States (as defined in general note 2 of the Harmonized Tariff Schedule of the United States) of any chemical substance, mixture, or article containing a chemical substance or mixture offered for such entry if —

(A) it fails to comply with any rule in effect under this chapter, or

(B) it is offered for entry in violation of section 2604 of this title, 2605 of this title, or subchapter IV of this chapter, a rule or order under section 2604 of this title, 2605 of this title, or subchapter IV of this chapter, or an order issued in a civil action brought under section 2604 of this title, 2606 of this title or subchapter IV of this chapter.

(2) If a chemical substance, mixture, or article is refused entry under paragraph (1), the Secretary of the Treasury shall notify the consignee of such entry refusal, shall not release it to the consignee, and shall cause its disposal or storage (under such rules as the Secretary of the Treasury may prescribe) if it has not been exported by the consignee within 90 days from the date of receipt of notice of such refusal, except that the Secretary of the Treasury may, pending a review by the Administrator of the entry refusal, release to the consignee such substance, mixture, or article on execution of bond for the amount of the full invoice of such substance, mixture, or article (as such value is set forth in the customs entry), together with the duty thereon. On failure to return such substance, mixture, or article for any cause to the custody of the Secretary of the Treasury when demanded, such consignee shall be liable to the United States for liquidated damages equal to the full amount of such bond. All charges for storage, cartage, and labor on and for disposal of substances, mixtures, or articles which are refused entry or release under this section shall be paid by the owner or consignee, and in default of such payment shall constitute a lien against any future entry made by such owner or consignee.

(b) Rules —

The Secretary of the Treasury, after consultation with the Administrator, shall issue rules for the administration of subsection (a) of this section.

§2613. Confidential information
[TSCA §14]

(a) In general — Except as provided in the section, the Administrator shall not disclose information that is exempt from disclosure pursuant to subsection (a) of section 552 of title 5, United States Code, by reason of subsection (b)(4) of that section —

(1) that is reported to, or otherwise obtained by, the Administrator under this Act; and

(2) for which the requirements of subsection (c) are met.

In any proceeding under section 552(a) of title 5, the United States Code, to obtain information the disclosure of which has been denied because of the provisions of this subsection, the Administrator may not rely on section 552(b)(3) of such title to sustain the administrator's action.

(b) Information not protected from disclosure —

(1) Mixed confidential and nonconfidential information — Information that is protected from disclosure under this section, and which is mixed with information that is not protected from disclosure under this section, does not lose its protection from disclosure notwithstanding that it is mixed with information that is not protected from disclosure.

(2) Information from health and safety studies — Subsection (a) does not prohibit the disclosure of —

(A) any health and safety study which is submitted under this Act with respect to —

(i) any chemical substance or mixture which, on the date on which such study is to be disclosed has been offered for commercial distribution; or

(ii) any chemical substance or mixture for which testing is required under section 5; and

(B) any information reported to, or otherwise obtained by, the Administrator from a health and safety study which relates to a chemical substance or mixture described in clause (i) or (ii) of subparagraph (A).

This paragraph does not authorize the disclosure of any information, including formulas (including molecular structures) of a chemical substance or mixture that discloses processes used in the manufacturing or processing of a chemical substance or mixture or, in the case of a mixture, the portion of the mixture comprised by any of the chemical substances in the mixture.

(3) Other information not protected from disclosure — Subsection (a) does not prohibit disclosure of —

(A) any general information describing the manufacturing volumes, expressed as specific aggregate volumes or, if the Administrator determines that disclosure of specific aggregated volumes would reveal confidential information, expressed in ranges; or

(B) a general description of a process used in the manufacture or processing and industrial, commercial, or consumer functions and uses of a chemical substance, mixture or article containing a chemical substance or mixture, including information specific to an industry or industry sector that customarily would be shared with the general public or within an industry or industry sector.

(4) Bans and phase-outs —

(A) In general — If the Administrator promulgates a rule pursuant to section 6(a) that establishes a ban or phase-out of a chemical substance or mixture, the protection from disclosure of any information under this section with respect to the chemical substance or mixture shall be presumed to no longer apply, subject to subsection (g)(1)(E) and subparagraphs (B) and (C) of this paragraph.

(B) Limitations —

(i) Critical use — In the case of a chemical substance or mixture for which a specific condition of use is subject to an exemption pursuant to section 6(g), if the Administrator establishes a ban or phase-out described in subparagraph (A) with respect to the chemical substance or mixture, the presumption against protection under such subparagraph shall only apply to information that relates solely to any conditions of use of the chemical substance or mixture to which the exemption does not apply.

(ii) Export — In the case of a chemical substance or mixture for which there is manufacture, processing, or distribution in commerce that meets the conditions of section 12(a)(1), if the Administrator establishes a ban or phase-out described in subparagraph (A) with respect to the chemical substance or mixture, the presumption against protection under such subparagraph shall only apply to information that relates solely to any other manufacture, processing, or distribution in commerce of the chemical substance or mixture for the conditions of use subject to the ban or phase-out, unless the Administrator makes the determination in section 12(a)(2).

(iii) Specific conditions of use — In the case of a chemical substance or mixture for which the Administrator establishes a ban or phase-out described in subparagraph (A) with respect to a specific condition of use of the chemical substance or mixture, the presumption against protection under such subparagraph shall only apply to information that relates solely to the condition of use of the chemical substance or mixture for which the ban or phase-out is established.

(C) Request for nondisclosure —

(i) In general — A manufacturer or processor of a chemical substance or mixture subject to a ban or phase-out described in this paragraph may submit to the Administrator, within 30 days of receiving a notification under subsection (g)(2)(A), a request, including documentation supporting such request, that some or all of the information to which the notice applies should not be disclosed or that its disclosure should be delayed, and the Administrator shall review the request under subsection (g)(1)(E).

(ii) Effect of no request or denial — If no request for nondisclosure or delay is submitted to the Administrator under this subparagraph, or the Administrator denies such a request under subsection (g)(1)(A), the information shall not be protected from disclosure under this section.

(5) Certain requests — If a request is made to the Administrator under section 552(a) of title 5, United States Code, for information reported or otherwise obtained by the Administrator under this Act that is not protected from disclosure under this subsection, the Administrator may not deny the request on the basis of section 552(b)(4) of title 5, United States Code.

(c) Requirements for confidentiality claims —

(1) Assertion of claims —

(A) In general — A person seeking to protect from disclosure any information that person submits under this Act (including information described in paragraph (2)) shall assert to the Administrator a claim for protection from disclosure concurrent with submission of the information, in accordance with such rules regarding a claim for protection from disclosure as the Administrator has promulgated or may promulgate pursuant to this title.

(B) Inclusion — An assertion of a claim under subparagraph (A) shall include a statement that the person has —

(i) taken reasonable measures to protect the confidentiality of the information;

(ii) determined that the information is not required to be disclosed or otherwise made available to the public under any other Federal law;

(iii) a reasonable basis to conclude that disclosure of the information is likely to cause substantial harm to the competitive position of the person; and

(iv) a reasonable basis to believe that the information is not readily discoverable through reverse engineering.

(C) Additional requirements for claims regarding chemical identity information — In the case of a claim under subparagraph (1) for protection from disclosure of a specific chemical identity, the claim shall include a structurally descriptive generic name for the chemical substance that the Administrator may disclose to the public, subject to the condition that such generic name shall —

(i) Be consistent with guidance developed by the Administrator under paragraph (4)(A); and

(ii) Describe the chemical structure of the chemical substance as specifically as practicable while protecting those features of the chemical structure —

(I) that are claimed as confidential; and

(II) the disclosure of which would be likely to cause substantial harm to the competitive position of the person.

(2) Information generally not subject to substantiation requirements — Subject to subsection (f), the following information shall not be subject to substantiation requirements under paragraph (3):

(A) Specific information describing the processes used in manufacture or processing of a chemical substance, mixture, or article.

(B) Marketing and sales information.

(C) Information identifying a supplier or customer.

(D) In the case of a mixture, details of the full composition of the mixture and the respective percentages of constituents.

(E) Specific information regarding the use, function, or application of a chemical substance or mixture in a process, mixture or article.

(F) Specific production or import volumes of the manufacturer or processor.

(G) Prior to the date on which a chemical substance is first offered for commercial distribution, the specific chemical identity of the chemical substance, including the chemical name, molecular formula, Chemical Abstracts Service number, and other information that would identify the specific chemical substance, if the specific chemical identity was claimed as confidential at the time it was submitted in a notice under section 5.

(3) Substantiation requirements — Except as provided in paragraph (2), a person asserting a claim to protect information from disclosure under this section shall substantiate the claim, in accordance with such rules as the Administrator has promulgated or may promulgate pursuant to this section.

(4) Guidance — The Administrator shall develop guidance regarding —

(A) the determination of structurally descriptive generic names, in the case of claims for the protection from disclosure of specific chemical identity; and

(B) the content and form of the statements of need and agreements required under paragraphs (4), (5), and (6) of subsection (d).

(5) Certification — An authorized official of a person described in paragraph (1)(A) shall certify that the statement required to assert a claim submitted pursuant to paragraph (1)(B), and any information required to substantiate a claim submitted pursuant to paragraph (3), are true and correct.

(d) Exceptions to protection from disclosure — Information described in subsection (a) —

(1) shall be disclosed to an officer or employee of the United States —

(A) in connection with the official duties of that person under any Federal law for the protection of health or the environment; or

(B) for a specific Federal law enforcement purpose;

(2) shall be disclosed to a contractor of the United States and employees of that contractor –

(A) if, in the opinion of the Administrator, the disclosure is necessary for the satisfactory performance by the contractor of a contract with the United States for the performance in connection with this Act; and

(B) subject to such conditions as the Administrator may specify;

(3) shall be disclosed if the Administrator determines that disclosure is necessary to protect health or the environment against an unreasonable risk of injury to health or the environment, without consideration of costs or other nonrisk factors, including an unreasonable risk to a potentially exposed or susceptible subpopulation identified as relevant by the Administrator under the conditions of use;

(4) shall be disclosed to a State, political subdivision of a State, or tribal government, on written request, for the purpose of administration or enforcement of a law, if such entity has 1 or more applicable agreements with the Administrator that are consistent with the guidance developed under subsection (c)(4)(B) and ensure

that the entity will take appropriate measures, and has adequate authority, to maintain with the confidentiality of the information in accordance with the procedures comparable to the procedures used by the Administrator to safeguard the information;

(5) shall be disclosed to a health or environmental professional employed by a Federal or State agency or tribal government or a treating physician or nurse in a nonemergency situation if such person provides a written statement of need and agrees to sign a written confidentiality agreement with the Administrator, subject to the conditions that —

(A) the statement of need and confidentiality agreement are consistent with the guidance developed under subsection (c)(4)(B);

(B) the statement of need shall be a statement that the person has a reasonable basis to suspect that —

(i) the information is necessary for, or will assist in —

(I) the diagnosis or treatment of 1 or more individuals; or

(II) responding to an environmental release or exposure; and

(ii) 1 or more individuals being diagnosed or treated have been exposed to the chemical substance or mixture concerned, or an environmental release of or exposure to the chemical substance or mixture concerned has occurred; and

(C) the person will not use the information for any purpose other than the health or environmental needs asserted in the statement of need, except as otherwise may be authorized by the terms of the agreement or by the person who has a claim under this section with respect to the information, except that nothing in this title prohibits the disclosure of any such information through discovery, subpoena, other court order, or any other judicial process otherwise allowed under applicable Federal or State law;

(6) shall be disclosed in the event of an emergency to a treating or responding physician, nurse, agent of a poison control center, public health or environmental official of a State, political subdivision of State, or tribal government, or first responder (including any individual duly authorized by a Federal agency, State, political subdivision of State, or tribal government who is trained in urgent medical care or other emergency procedures, including a police officer, firefighter, or emergency medical technician) if such person requests the information, subject the conditions that such person shall —

(A) have a reasonable basis to suspect that —

(i) a medical, public health, or environmental emergency exists;

(ii) the information is necessary for, or will assist in, emergency or first aid diagnosis or treatment; or

(iii) 1 or more individuals being diagnosed or treated have likely been exposed to the chemical substance or mixture concerned, or a serious environmental release or exposure to the chemical substance or mixture concerned has occurred; and

(B) if requested by a person who has a claim with respect to the information under this section —

(i) provide a written statement of need and agree to sign a confidentiality agreement, as described in paragraph (5); and

(ii) submit to the Administrator such statement of need and confidentiality agreement as soon as practicable, but not necessarily before the information is disclosed;

(7) may be disclosed if the Administrator determines that disclosure is relevant in a proceeding under this Act, subject to the condition that the disclosure is made in such a manner as to preserve confidentiality to the extent practicable without impairing the proceeding; and

(8) shall be disclosed if the information is requiring to be made public under any other provision of Federal law.

(e) Duration of protection from disclosure —

(1) In general — Subject to paragraph (2), the subsection of (f)(3), and section 8(b), the Administrator shall protect from disclosure information described in subsection (a) —

(A) in the case of information described in subsection (c)(2), until such time as —

(i) the person that asserted the claim notifies the Administrator that the person is withdrawing the claim, in which case the information shall not be protected from disclosure under this section; or

(ii) the Administrator becomes aware that the information does not qualify for protection from disclosure under this section, in which case the Administrator shall take any actions required under subsections (f) and (g); and

(B) in case of information other than information described in subsection (c)(2) —

(i) for a period of 10 years from the date on which the person asserts the claim with respect to the information submitted to the Administrator; or

(ii) if applicable before the expiration of such 10-year period, until such time as —

(I) the person that asserted the claim notifies the Administrator that the person is withdrawing the claim, in which case the information shall not be protected from disclosure under this section; or

(II) the Administrator becomes aware that the information does not qualify for protection from disclosure under this section, in which case the Administrator shall take any actions required under subsections (f) and (g).

(2) Extensions —

(A) In general — In the case of information other than information described in subsection (c)(2), not later than the date that is 60 days before the expiration of the period described in paragraph (1)(B)(i), the Administrator shall provide to to the person that asserted the claim a notice of the impending expiration of the period.

(B) Request —

(i) In general — Not later than the date that is 30 days before the expiration of the period described in paragraph (1)(B)(i), a person reasserting the relevant claim shall submit to the Administrator a request for extension substantiating, in accordance with subsection (c)(3), the need to extend the period.

(ii) Action by Administrator — Not alter than the date of expiration of the period described in paragraph (1)(B)(i), the Administrator shall, in accordance with subsection (g)(1) —

(I) review the request submitted under clause (i);

(II) make a determination regarding whether the claim for which the request was submitted continues to meet the relevant requirements of this section; and

(III) (aa) grant an extension of 10 years; or

(bb) deny the request.

(C) No limit on number of extensions — There shall be no limit on the number of extensions granted under this paragraph, if the Administrator determines that the relevant request under subparagraph (B)(i)—

(i) establishes the need to extend the period; and

(ii) meets the requirements established by the Administrator.

(f) Review and resubstantiation —

(1) Discretion of Administrator — The Administrator may require any person that has claimed protection for information from disclosure under this section, whether before, on, or after June 22, 2016, to reassert and substantiate or resubstantiate the claim in accordance with this section —

(A) after the chemical substance is designated as a high-priority substance under section 6(b);

(B) for any chemical substance designated as an active substance under section 8(b)(5)(B)(iii); or

(C) if the Administrator determines that disclosure of certain information currently protected from disclosure would be important to assist the Administrator in conducting risk evaluations or promulgating rules under section 6.

(2) **Review required** — The Administrator shall review a claim for protection of information from disclosure under this section and require any person that has claimed protection for that information, whether before, on, or after June 22, 2016, to reassert and substantiate or resubstantiate the claim in accordance with this section —

(A) as necessary to determine whether the information qualifies for an exemption from disclosure in connection with a request for information received b the Administrator under section 552 of title 5, United States Code;

(B) if the Administrator has a reasonable basis to believe that the information does not qualify for protection from disclosure under this section; or

(C) for any chemical substance the Administrator determines under section 6(b)(4)(A) presents an unreasonable risk of injury to health or environment.

(3) **Period of protection** — If the Administrator requires a person to reassert and substantiate or resubstantiate a claim under this subsection, and determines that the claim continues to meet the relevant requirements of this section, the Administrator shall protect the information subject to the claim from disclosure for a period of 10 years from the date of such determination, subject to any subsequent requirement by the Administrator under this subsection.

(g) **Duties of Administrator** —

(1) **Determination** —

(A) **In general** — Except regarding information described in subsection (c)(2), the Administrator shall, subject to paragraph (C), not later than 90 days after the receipt of a claim under subsection (c), and not later than 30 days after the receipt of a request for extension of a claim under subsection (e) or a request under subsection (b)(4)(C), review and approve, approve in part and deny in part, or deny the claim or request.

(B) **Reasons for denial** — If the Administrator denies or denies in part a claim or request under subparagraph (A) the Administrator shall provide to the person that asserted the claim or submitted the request a written statement of the reasons for the denial or denial in part of the claim or request.

(C) **Subsets** — The Administrator shall —

(i) except with respect to information described in subsection (c)(2)(G), review all claims or requests under this subsection fro the protection from disclosure of the specific chemical identity of a chemical substance; and

(ii) review a representative subset, comprising at least 25 percent, of all other claims or requests for protection from disclosure under this section.

(D) **Effect of failure to act** — The failure of the Administrator to make a decision regarding a claim or request for protection from disclosure or extension under this section shall not have the effect of denying or eliminating a claim or request for protection from disclosure.

(E) **Determination of requests under subsection (b)(4)(C)** — With respect to a request submitted under subsection (b)(4)(C), the Administrator shall, with the objective of ensuring that information relevant to the protection of health and the environment is disclosed to the extent practicable, determine whether the documentation provided by the person rebuts what shall be the presumption of the Administrator that the public interest in the disclosure of the information outweighs the public or proprietary interest in maintaining the protection for all or a portion of the information that the person has requested not be disclosed or for which disclosure be delayed.

(2) **Notification** —

(A) **In general** — Except as provided in subparagraph (B) and subsections (b), (d), and (e), if the Administrator denies or denies in part a claim or request under paragraph (1), concludes, in accordance with this section, that the information does not qualify for protection from disclosure, intends to disclose information pursuant to subsection (d), or promulgates a rule under section 6(a) establishing a ban or phase-out with respect to a chemical substance or mixture, the Administrator shall notify, in writing, the person that asserted the claim or submitted the request of the intent of the Administrator to disclose the information or not protect the information from disclosure under this section. The notice shall be furnished by certified mail (return receipt requested), by personal delivery, or by other means that allows verification of the fact and date of receipt.

(B) Disclosure of information — Except as provided in subparagraph (C), the Administrator shall not disclose information under this subsection until the date that is 30 days after the date on which the person that asserted the claim or submitted the request receives notification under subparagraph (A).

(C) Exceptions —

(i) Fifteen day notification — For information the Administrator intends to disclose under subsections (d)(3), (d)(4), (d)(5), and (j), the Administrator shall not disclose the information until the date that is 15 days after the date on which the person that asserted the claim or submitted the request receives notification under subparagraph (A), except that, with respect to information to be disclosed under subsection (d)(3), if the Administrator determines that disclosure of the information is necessary to protect against an imminent and substantial harm to health or the environment, no prior notification shall be necessary.

(ii) Notification as soon as practicable — For information the Administrator intends to disclose under paragraph (6) of subsection (d), the Administrator shall notify the person that submitted the information that the information has been disclosed as soon as practicable after disclosure of the information.

(iii) No notification required — Notification shall not be required —

(I) for the disclosure of information under paragraphs (1), (2), (7), or (8) of subsection (d); or

(II) for the disclosure of information for which —

(aa) the Administrator has provided to the person that asserted the claim a notice under subsection (e)(2)(A); and

(bb) such person does not submit to the Administrator a request under subsection (e)(2)(B) on or before the deadline established in subsection (e)(2)(B)(i).

(D) Appeals —

(i) Action to restrain disclosure — If a person receives a notification under this paragraph and believes the information is protected from disclosure under this section, before the date on which the information is to be disclosed pursuant to subparagraph (B) or (C) the person may bring an action to restrain disclosure of the information in —

(I) the United States district court of the district in which the complaint resides or has the principal place of business; or

(II) the United States District Court of the District of Columbia.

(ii) No disclosure —

(I) In general — Subject to subsection (d), the Administrator shall not disclose information that is the subject of an appeal under this paragraph before the date on which the applicable court rules on an action under clause (i).

(II) Exception — Subclause (I) shall not apply to disclosure of information described under subsections (d)(4) and (j).

(3) Request and notification system — The Administrator, in consultation with the Director of the Centers for Disease Control and Prevention, shall develop a request and notification system that, in a format and language that is readily accessible and understandable, allows for expedient and swift access to information disclosed pursuant to paragraphs (5) and (6) of subsection (d).

(4) Unique identifier — The Administrator shall —

(A)(i) Develop a system to assign a unique identifier to each specific chemical identity for which the Administrator approves a request for protection from disclosure, which shall not be either the specific chemical identity or a structurally descriptive generic term; and

(ii) apply that identifier consistently to all information relevant to the applicable chemical substance.

(B) annually publish and update a list of chemical substances, referred to by their unique identifiers, for which claims to protect the specific chemical identity from disclosure have been approved, including the expiration date for each such claim;

(C) ensure that any nonconfidential information received by the Administrator with respect to a chemical substance included on the list published under subparagraph (B) while the specific chemical identity of the chemical substance is protected from disclosure under this section identifies the chemical substance using the unique identifier; and

(D) for each claim for protection of a specific chemical identity that has been denied by the Administrator or expired, or that has been withdrawn by the person who asserted the claim, and for which the Administrator has used a unique identifier assigned under this paragraph to protect the specific chemical identity in information that the Administrator has made public, clearly link the specific chemical identity to the unique identifier in such information to the extent practicable.

(h) Criminal penalty for wrongful disclosure —

(1) Individuals subject to penalty —

(A) In general — Subject to subparagraph (C) and paragraph (2), an individual described n subparagraph (B) shall be fined under title 18, United States Code, or imprisoned for not more than 1 year, or both.

(B) Description — An individual referred to in subparagraph (A) is an individual who —

(i) pursuant to this section, obtained possession of or has access to, information protected from disclosure under this section; and

(ii) knowing that the information is protected from disclosure under this section, willfully discloses the information in any manner to any person not entitled to receive that information.

(C) Exception — this paragraph shall not apply to any medical professional (including an emergency medical technician or other first responder) who discloses any information obtained under paragraph (5) or (6) of subsection (d) to a patient treated by the medical professional, or to a person authorized to make medical or healthcare decisions on behalf of such a patient, as needed for the diagnosis or treatment of the patient.

(2) Other laws — Section 1905 of title 18, United States Code, shall not apply with respect to the publishing, divulging, disclosure or making known of, or making available, information reported to or otherwise obtained by the Administrator under this Act.

(i) Applicability —

(1) In general — Except as otherwise provided in this section, section 8, or any other applicable Federal law, the Administrator shall have no authority —

(A) to require the substantiation or resubstantiation of a claim for the protection from disclosure of information reported or otherwise obtained by the Administrator under this Act prior to June 22, 2016, or

(B) to impose substantiation or resubstantiation requirements, with respect to the protection of information described n subsection (a), under this act that are more extensive than those required under this section.

(2) Actions prior to promulgation of rules — Nothing in this Act prevents the Administrator from reviewing, requiring substantiation or resubstantiation of, or approving, approving in part, or denying any claim for the protection from disclosure of information before the effective date of such rules applicable to those claims as the Administrator may promulgate after June 22, 2016.

(j) Access by Congress — Notwithstanding any limitation contained in this section or any other provision of law, all contained in this section or any other provision of law, all information reported to or otherwise obtained by the Administrator (or any representative of the Administrator) under this Act shall be made available, up on written request of any duly authorized committee of the Congress, to such committee.

§2614. Prohibited acts
[TSCA §15]

It shall be unlawful for any person to —

(1) fail or refuse to comply with any requirement of this title or any rule promulgated, order issued, or consent agreement entered into under this title, or any requirement of subchapter II of this chapter or any rule promulgated or order issued under subchapter II of this chapter;

(2) use for commercial purposes a chemical substance or mixture which such person knew or had reason to know was manufactured, processed, or distributed in commerce in violation of section 2604 or 2605 of this title, a rule or order under section 2604 or 2605 of this title, or an order issued in action brought under section 2604 or 2606 of this title;

(3) fail or refuse to (A) establish or maintain records, (B) submit reports, notices, or other information, or (C) permit access to or copying of records, as required by this chapter or a rule thereunder; or

(4) fail or refuse to permit entry or inspection as required by section 2610 of this title.

§2615. Penalties
[TSCA §16]

(a) Civil

(1) Any person who violates a provision of section 2614 or 2689 of this title shall be liable to the United States for a civil penalty in an amount not to exceed $37,500 for each such violation. Each day such a violation continues shall, for purposes of this subsection, constitute a separate violation of section 2614 or 2689 of this title.

(2)(A) A civil penalty for a violation of section 2614 or 2689 of this title shall be assessed by the Administrator by an order made on the record after opportunity (provided in accordance with this subparagraph) for a hearing in accordance with section 554 of Title 5. Before issuing such an order, the Administrator shall give written notice to the person to be assessed a civil penalty under such order of the Administrator's proposal to issue such order and provide such person an opportunity to request, within 15 days of the date the notice is received by such person, such a hearing on the order.

(B) In determining the amount of a civil penalty, the Administrator shall take into account the nature, circumstances, extent, and gravity of the violation or violations and, with respect to the violator, ability to pay, effect on ability to continue to do business, any history of prior such violations, the degree of culpability, and such other matters as justice may require.

(C) The Administrator may compromise, modify, or remit, with or without conditions, any civil penalty which may be imposed under this subsection. The amount of such penalty, when finally determined, or the amount agreed upon in compromise, may be deducted from any sums owing by the United States to the person charged.

(3) Any person who requested in accordance with paragraph (2)(A) a hearing respecting the assessment of a civil penalty and who is aggrieved by an order assessing a civil penalty may file a petition for judicial review of such order with the United States Court of Appeals for the District of Columbia Circuit or for any other circuit in which such person resides or transacts business. Such a petition may only be filed within the 30-day period beginning on the date the order making such assessment was issued.

(4) If any person fails to pay an assessment of a civil penalty —

(A) after the order making the assessment has become a final order and if such person does not file a petition for judicial review of the order in accordance with paragraph (3), or

(B) after a court in an action brought under paragraph (3) has entered a final judgment in favor of the Administrator,

the Attorney General shall recover the amount assessed (plus interest at currently prevailing rates from the date of the expiration of the 30-day period referred to in paragraph (3) or the date of such final judgment, as the case may be) in an action brought in any appropriate district court of the United States. In such an action, the validity, amount, and appropriateness of such penalty shall not be subject to review.

(b) Criminal

(1) In general — Any person who knowingly or willfully violates any provision of section 2614 or 2689 of this title, shall, in addition to or in lieu of any civil penalty which may be imposed under subsection (a) of this section for

such violation, be subject, upon conviction, to a fine of not more than $50,000 for each day of violation, or to imprisonment for not more than one year, or both.

(2) Imminent danger of death or serious bodily injury —

(A) In general — Any person who knowingly and willfully violates any provision of section 15 or 409, and who knows at the time of the violation that the violation places an individual in imminent danger of death or serious bodily injury, shall be subject on conviction to a fine of not more than $250,000, or imprisonment for not more than 15 years, or both.

(B) Organizations — Notwithstanding the penalties described in subparagraph (A), an organization that commits a knowing violation described in subparagraph (A) shall be subject on conviction to a fine of not more than $1,000,000 for each violation.

(C) Incorporation of corresponding provisions — Subparagraphs (B) through (F) of section 113(c)(5) of the Clean Air Act (42 U.S.C. 7413(c)(5)(B)-(F)) shall apply to the prosecution of a violation under this paragraph.

§2616. Specific enforcement and seizure [TSCA §17]

(a) Specific enforcement

(1) The district courts of the United States shall have jurisdiction over civil actions to —

(A) restrain any violation of section 2614 or 2689 of this title,

(B) restrain any person from taking any action prohibited by section 2604 of this title, 2605 of this title, or subchapter IV of this chapter, or by a rule or order under section 2604 of this title, 2605 of this title, or subchapter IV of this chapter,

(C) compel the taking of any action required by or under this chapter, or

(D) direct any manufacturer or processor of a chemical substance, mixture, or product subject to subchapter IV of this chapter manufactured or processed in violation of section 2604 of this title, 2605 of this title, or subchapter IV of this chapter, or a rule or order under section 2604 of this title, 2605 of this title, or subchapter IV of this chapter, and distributed in commerce, (i) to give notice of such fact to distributors in commerce of such substance, mixture, or product and, to the extent reasonably ascertainable, to other persons in possession of such substance, mixture, or product or exposed to such substance, mixture, or product, (ii) to give public notice of such risk of injury, and (iii) to either replace or repurchase such substance, mixture, or product, whichever the person to which the requirement is directed elects.

(2) A civil action described in paragraph (1) may be brought —

(A) in the case of a civil action described in subparagraph (A) of such paragraph, in the United States district court for the judicial district wherein any act, omission, or transaction constituting a violation of section 2614 of this title occurred or wherein the defendant is found or transacts business, or

(B) in the case of any other civil action described in such paragraph, in the United States district court for the judicial district wherein the defendant is found or transacts business.

In any such civil action process may be served on a defendant in any judicial district in which a defendant resides or may be found. Subpoenas requiring attendance of witnesses in any such action may be served in any judicial district.

(b) Seizure

Any chemical substance, mixture, or product subject to subchapter IV of this chapter which was manufactured, processed, or distributed in commerce in violation of this chapter or any rule promulgated or order issued under this chapter or any article containing such a substance or mixture shall be liable to be proceeded against, by process of libel, for the seizure and condemnation of such substance, mixture, product, or article, in any district court of the United States within the jurisdiction of which such substance, mixture, product, or article is found. Such proceedings shall conform as nearly as possible to proceedings in rem in admiralty.

§2617. Preemption
[TSCA §18]
(a) In General —
(1) Establishment of enforcement — Except as otherwise provided in subsections (c), (d), (e), (f), and (g), and subject to paragraph (2), no State or political subdivision of a State may establish or continue to enforce any of the following:

(A) Development of information — A statute or administrative action to require the development of information about a chemical substance or category of chemical susbtances that is reasonably likely to produce the same information required under section 4, 5, or 6 in —

(i) a rule promulgated by Administrator;
(ii) a consent agreement entered into by the Administrator; or
(iii) an order issued by the Administrator.

(B) Chemical substances found not to present an unreasonable risk or

restricted — A statute, criminal penalty, or administrative action to prohibit or otherwise restrict the manufacture, processing, or distribution in commerce or use of a chemical substance —

(i) for which the determination described in section 6(i)(1) is made, consistent with the scope of the risk evaluation under section (6)(b)(4)(D); or

(ii) for which a final rule is promulgated under section 6(a), after the effective date of the rule issued under section 6(a) for the chemical substance, consistent with the scope of the risk evaluation under section (6)(b)(4)(D).

(C) Significant new use — A statute or administrative action requiring the notification of a use of a chemical substance that the Administrator has specified as a significant new use and for which the Administrator has required notification pursuant to a rule promulgated under section 5.

(2) Effective date of preemption — Under this subsection, Federal preemption of statutes and administrative actions applicable to specific chemical substances shall not occur until the effective date of the applicable action described in paragraph (1) taken by the Administrator.

(b) New Statutes, Criminal Penalties, or Administrative Actions Creating Prohibitions or Other Restrictions —

(1) In general — Except as provided in subsections (c), (d), (e), (f), and (g), beginning on the date on which the Administrator defines the scope of a risk evaluation for a chemical substance under section 6(b)(4)(D) and ending on the date on which the deadline established pursuant to section 6(b)(4)(G) for completion of the risk evaluation expires, or on the date on which the Administrator publishes the risk evaluation under section 6(b)(4)(C), whichever is earlier, no State or political subdivision of a State may establish a statute, criminal penalty, or administrative action prohibiting or otherwise restricting the manufacture, processing, distribution in commerce, or use of such chemical substance that is a high-priority substance designated under 6(b)(1)(B)(i), such chemical substance that has been identified under section 6(b)(2)(A) (except for the first 10 chemical substances so identified), or such chemical substance that has been selected for risk evaluation under section 6(b)(4)(E)(iv)(II).

(2) Effect of subsection — This subsection does not restrict the authority of a State or political subdivision of of a State to continue to enforce any statute enacted, or administrative action taken, prior to the date on which the Administrator defines and publishes the scope of a risk evaluation under section 6(b)(4)(D).

(c) Scope of Preemption — Federal preemption under subsections (a) and (b) of statutes, criminal penalties, and administrative actions applicable to specific chemical substances shall apply only to —

(1) with respect to subsection (a)(1)(A), the chemical substances or category of chemical substances subject to a rule, order, or consent agreement under section 4;

(2) with respect to subsections (a)(1)(B) and (b), the hazards, exposures, risks, and uses or conditions of use of such chemical substances consistent with the scope of the risk evaluation under 6(b)(4)(D); or

(3) with respect to subsection (a)(1)(C), the uses of such chemical substances that the Administrator has specified as significant new uses and for which the Administrator has required notification pursuant to a rule promulgated under section 5.

(d) Exceptions —

(1) No preemption of statutes and administrative actions —

(A) **In general** — Nothing in this Act, nor any amendment made by the Frank R. Lautenberg Chemical Safety for the 21st Century Act, nor any rule, standard of performance, risk evaluation, or scientific assessment implemented pursuant to this Act, shall affect the right of a State or a political subdivision of a State to adopt or enforce any rule, standard of performance, risk evaluation, scientific assessment, or any other protection for public health or the environment that —

(i) is adopted or authorized under the authority of any Federal law or adopted to satisfy or obtain authorization or approval under any other Federal law;

(ii) implements a reporting, monitoring, or other information obligation for the chemical substance not otherwise required by the Administrator under this Act or required under any other Federal law;

(iii) is adopted pursuant to authority under a law of the State or political subdivision of the State related to water quality, air quality, or waste treatment or disposal, except to the extent that the action —

(I) imposes a restriction on the manufacture, processing, distribution in commerce, or use of a chemical substance; and

(II) (aa) addresses the same hazards and exposures, with respect to the same conditions of use as are included in the scope of the risk evaluation published pursuant to section 6(b)(4)(D),

but is inconsistent with the action of the Administrator; or

(bb) would cause a violation of the applicable action by the Administrator under section 5 or 6; or

(iv) subject to subparagraph (B), is identical to a requirement prescribed by the Administrator.

(B) **Identical requirements** —

(i) **In general** — The penalties and other sanctions applicable under a law of a State or political subdivision of a State in the event of noncompliance with the identical requirement shall be no more stringent than the penalties and other sanctions available to the Administrator under section 16 of this act.

(ii) **Penalties** — In the case of an identical requirement —

(I) a State or political subdivision of a State may not assess a penalty for a specific violation for which the Administrator has assessed an adequate penalty under section 16; and

(II) if a State or political subdivision of a State has assessed a penalty for a specific violation, the Administrator may not assess a penalty for that violation in an amount that would cause the total of the penalties assessed for the violation by the State or political subdivision of a State and the Administrator combined to exceed the maximum amount that may be assessed for that violation by the Administrator under section 16.

(2) Applicability to certain rules or orders —

(A) **Prior rules and orders** — Nothing in this section shall be construed as modifying the preemptive effect under this section, as in effect on the day before the effective date of the Frank R. Lautenberg Chemical Safety for the 21st Century Act, of any rule or order promulgated or issued under this Act prior to that effective date.

(B) **Certain chemical substances and mixtures** — With respect to a chemical substance or mixture for which any rule or order was promulgated or issued under section 6 prior to the effective date of the Frank R. Lautenberg Chemical Safety for the 21st Century Act with respect to manufacturing, processing, distribution in commerce, use, or disposal of the chemical substance or mixture, nothing in this section shall be construed as modifying the preemptive effect of this section as in effect prior to the enactment of the Frank

R. Lautenberg Chemical Safety for the 21st Century Act of any rule or order that is promulgated or issued with respect to such chemical substance or mixture under section 6 after that effective date, unless the latter rule or order is with respect to a chemical substance and follows a designation of that chemical substance as a high-priority substance under section 6(b)(1)(B)(i), the identification of that chemical substance under section 6(b)(2)(A), or the selection of that chemical substance for risk evaluation under section 6(b)(4)(E)(iv)(II).

(e) Preservation of Certain Laws —

(1) In general — Nothing in this Act, subject to subsection (g) of this section, shall —

(A) be construed to preempt or otherwise affect the authority of a State or political subdivision of a State or political subdivision of a State to continue to enforce any action taken or requirement imposed or requirement enacted relating to a specific chemical substance before April 22, 2016, under the authority of a law of the State or political subdivision of the State that prohibits or otherwise restricts manufacturing, processing, distribution in commerce, use, or disposal of a chemical substance; or

(B) be construed to preempt or otherwise affect any action taken pursuant to a State law that was in effect on August 31, 2003.

(2) Effect of subsection — This subsection does not affect, modify, or alter the relationship between Federal law and laws of a state or political subdivision of a State pursuant to any other Federal law.

(f) Waivers —

(1) Discretionary exemptions — Upon application of a State or political subdivision of a State, the Administrator may, by rule, exempt from subsection (a), under such conditions as may be prescribed in the rule, a statute, criminal penalty, or administrative action of that State or political subdivision of the State that relates to the effects of exposure to a chemical substance under the conditions of use if the Administrator determines that —

(A) compelling conditions warrant granting the waiver to protect health or the environment;

(B) compliance with the proposed requirement of the State or political subdivision of the State would not unduly burden interstate commerce in the manufacture, processing, distribution in commerce, or use of chemical substance;

(C) compliance with the proposed requirement of the state or political subdivision of the State would not cause a violation of any applicable Federal law, rule, or order; and

(D) in the judgment of the Administrator, the proposed requirement of the State or political subdivision of the State is designed to address a risk of chemical substance, under the conditions of use, that was identified —

(i) consistent with the best available science;

(ii) using supporting studies conducted in accordance with sound and objective scientific practices; and

(iii) based on the weight of the scientific evidence.

(2) Required exemptions — Upon application of a State or political subdivision of a State, the Administrator shall exempt from subsection (b) a statute or administrative action of a State or political subdivision of a State that relates to the effects of exposure to a chemical substance under the conditions of use if the Administrator determines that —

(A)(i) compliance with the proposed requirement of the State or political subdivision of the State would not unduly burden interstate commerce in the manufacture, processing, distribution in commerce, or use of a chemical substance;

(ii) compliance with the proposed requirement of the State shall not cause a violation of any applicable Federal law, rule, or order; and

(iii) the State or political subdivision of the State has a concern about the chemical substance or use of the chemical substance based in peer-reviewed science; or

(B) no later than the date that is 18 months after the date on which the Administrator has initiated the prioritization process for a chemical substance under the rule promulgated pursuant to section 6(b)(1)(A), or the date on which the Administrator published the scope of the risk evaluation for a chemical substance under section 6(b)(4)(D), whichever is sooner, the State or political subdivision of the State has enacted a statute or proposed or finalized an administrative action intended to prohibit or otherwise restrict the manufacture, processing, distribution in commerce, or use of the chemical substance.

(3) Determination of a waiver request — The duty of the Administrator to grant or deny a waiver application shall be nondelegable and shall be exercised —

(A) not later than 180 days after the date on which an application under paragraph (1) is submitted; and

(B) not later than 110 days after the date on which an application under paragraph (2) is submitted.

(4) Failure to make a determination — If the Administrator fails to make a determination under paragraph (3)(B) during the 110-day period beginning on the date on which an application under paragraph (2) is submitted, the statute or administrative action of the State or political subdivision of the State that was the subject of the application shall not be considered to be an existing statute or administrative action for purposes of subsection (b) by reason of the failure of the administrator to make a determination.

(5) Notice and comment — Except in the case of an application approved under paragraph (9), the application of a state or political subdivision of a State under this subsection shall be subject to public notice and comment.

(6) Final agency action — the decision of the Administrator on the application fo a state or political subdivision of a state shall be —

(A) considered to be a final agency action; and

(B) subject to judicial review.

(7) Duration of waivers — A waiver granted under paragraph (2) or approved under paragraph (9) shall remain in effect until such time as the Administrator publishes the risk evaluation under section 6(b).

(8) Judicial review of waivers — Not later than 60 days after the date on which the Administrator makes a determination on an application of a State or political subdivision of a State under paragraph (1) or (2), any person may file a petition for judicial review in the United States Court of Appeals for the District of Columbia Circuit, which shall have exclusive jurisdiction over the determination.

(9) Approval —

(A) **Automatic approval** — If the Administrator fails to meet the deadline established under paragraph (3)(B), the application of a State or political subdivision of a State under paragraph (2) shall be automatically approved, effective on the date that is 10 days after the deadline.

(B) **Requirements** — Notwithstanding paragraph (6), approval of a waiver application under subparagraph (A) for failure to meet the deadline under paragraph (3)(B) shall not be considered final agency action or be subject to judicial review or public notice and comment.

(g) Savings —

(1) No preemption of common law or statutory causes of action for civil relief or criminal conduct —

(A) **In general** — Nothing in this Act, nor any amendment made by the Frank R. Lautenberg Chemical Safety for the 21st Century Act, nor any standard, rule, requirement, standard of performance, risk evaluation, or scientific assessment implemented pursuant to this Act shall be construed to preempt, displace, or supplant any State or Federal common law rights or any State or Federal statute creating a remedy for civil relief, including those for civil damage, or a penalty for a criminal conduct.

(B) **Clarification of no preemption** — Notwithstanding any other provision of this Act, nothing in this Act, nor any amendments made by the Frank R. Lautenberg Chemical Safety for the 21st Century Act, shall preempt or preclude any cause of action for personal injury, wrongful death, property damage, or other injury based on negligence, strict liability, products liability, failure to warn, or any other legal theory of liability under any State law, maritime law, or Federal common law or statutory theory.

(2) No effect on private remedies —

(A) **In general** — nothing in this Act, nor any amendments made by the Frank R. Lautenberg Chemical Safety for the 21st Century Act, nor any rules, regulations, requirements, risk evaluations, risk assessments or orders issued pursuant to this Act shall be interpreted as, in either the plaintiff's or defendant's favor, dispositive in any civil action.

(B) **Authority of courts** — This Act does not affect the authority of any court to make a determination in an adjudicatory proceeding under applicable State or Federal law with respect to the admission into evidence or any other use of this Act or rules, regulations, requirements, standards of performance, risk evaluations, scientific assessments, or orders issued pursuant to this Act.

§2618. Judicial review
[TSCA §19]

(a) In general

(1)(A) Except as otherwise provided in this title, not later than 60 days after the date on which a rule is promulgated under this title, title II or title IV, or the date on which an order is issued under section 4, 5(e), 5(f), or 6(i)(1), of this chapter, any person may file a petition for judicial review of such rule or order with the United States Court of Appeals for the District of Columbia Circuit or for the circuit in which such person resides or in which such person's principal place of business is located. Courts of appeals of the United States shall have exclusive jurisdiction of any action to obtain judicial review (other than in an enforcement proceeding) of such a rule or order if any district court of the United States would have had jurisdiction of such action but for this subparagraph.

(B) Except as otherwise provided in this title, courts of appeals of the United States shall have exclusive jurisdiction of any action to obtain judicial review (other than in an enforcement proceeding) of an order issued under this title, other than an order under section 4, 5(e), 5(f), or 6(i)(1), of this title if any district court of the United States would have had jurisdiction of such action but for this subparagraph.

(C)(i) not later than 60 days after he publication of a designation under 6(b)(1)(B)(ii) or (iii), any person may commence a civil action to challenge the designation.

(ii) The United States Court of Appeals for the District of Columbia Circuit shall have exclusive jurisdiction over a civl action filed under this subparagraph.

(2) Copies of any petition filed under paragraph (1)(A) shall be transmitted forthwith to the Administrator and to the Attorney General by the clerk of the court with which such petition was filed. The provisions of section 2112 of Title 28 shall apply to the filing of the record of proceedings on which the Administrator based the rule or order being reviewed under this section and to the transfer of proceedings between United States courts of appeals.

(b) Additional submissions and presentations; modifications —

If in an action under this section to review a rule, or an order under section 4, 5(e), 5(f), or 6(i)(1), the petitioner or the Administrator applies to the court for leave to make additional oral submissions or written presentations respecting such rule or order and shows to the satisfaction of the court that such submissions and presentations would be material and that there were reasonable grounds for the submissions and failure to make such submissions and presentations in the proceeding before the Administrator, the court may order the Administrator to provide additional opportunity to make such submissions and presentations. The Administrator may modify or set aside the rule or order being reviewed or make a new rule or order by reason of the additional submissions and presentations and shall file such modified or new rule or order with the return of such submissions and presentations. The court shall thereafter review such new or modified rule or order.

(c) Standard of review

(1)(A) Upon the filing of a petition under subsection (a)(1) of this section for judicial review of a rule or order, the court shall have jurisdiction (i) to grant appropriate relief, including interim relief, as provided in chapter 7 of Title 5, and (ii) except as otherwise provided in subparagraph (B), to review such rule or order in accordance with chapter 7 of Title 5.

(B) Section 706 of Title 5 shall apply to review of a rule or order under this section, except that —

(i) in the case of review of —

(I) a rule under section 4(a), 5(b)(4), 6(a) (including review of the associated determination under section 6(b)(4)(A)), or 6(e), the standard for review prescribed by paragraph (2)(E) of such section 706 shall not apply and the court shall hold unlawful and set aside such rule if the court finds that the rule is not supported by substantial evidence in the rulemaking record as a whole; and

(II) an order under section 4, 5(e), 5(f), or 6(i)(1), the standard for review prescribed by paragraph (2)(E) of such section 706 shall not apply and the court shall hold unlawful and set aside such order if the court finds that the order is not supported by substantial evidence in the record taken as a whole; and

(ii) the court may not review the contents and adequacy of any statement of basis and purpose required by section 553(c) of title 5, the United States Code, to be incorporated in the rule or order, except as part of the record, taken as a whole.

(2) The judgment of the court affirming or setting aside, in whole or in part, any rule or order reviewed in accordance with this section shall be final, subject to review by the Supreme Court of the United States upon certiorari or certification, as provided in section 1254 of Title 28.

(d) Fees and costs

The decision of the court in an action commenced under subsection (a) of this section, or of the Supreme Court of the United States on review of such a decision, may include an award of costs of suit and reasonable fees for attorneys and expert witnesses if the court determines that such an award is appropriate.

(e) Other remedies

The remedies as provided in this section shall be in addition to and not in lieu of any other remedies provided by law.

§2619. Citizens' civil actions
[TSCA §20]

(a) In general — Except as provided in subsection (b) of this section, any person may commence a civil action —

(1) against any person (including (A) the United States, and (B) any other governmental instrumentality or agency to the extent permitted by the eleventh amendment to the Constitution)

who is alleged to be in violation of this chapter or any rule promulgated under section 2603, 2604, or 2605 of this title, or subchapter II or IV of this chapter, or order issued under section 4 or 5 of this title or subchapter II or IV of this chapter to restrain such violation, or

(2) against the Administrator to compel the Administrator to perform any act or duty under this chapter which is not discretionary.

Any civil action under paragraph (1) shall be brought in the United States district court for the district in which the alleged violation occurred or in which the defendant resides or in which the defendant's principal place of business is located. Any action brought under paragraph (2) shall be brought in the United States District Court for the District of Columbia, or the United States district court for the judicial district in which the plaintiff is domiciled. The district courts of the United States shall have jurisdiction over suits brought under this section, without regard to the amount in controversy or the citizenship of the parties. In any civil action under this subsection process may be served on a defendant in any judicial district in which the defendant resides or may be found and subpoenas for witnesses may be served in any judicial district.

(b) Limitation

No civil action may be commenced —

(1) under subsection (a)(1) of this section to restrain a violation of this chapter or rule or order under this chapter —

(A) before the expiration of 60 days after the plaintiff has given notice of such violation (i) to the Administrator, and (ii) to the person who is alleged to have committed such violation, or

(B) if the Administrator has commenced and is diligently prosecuting a proceeding for the issuance of an order under section 2615(a)(2) of this title to require compliance with this chapter or with such rule or order or if the Attorney General has commenced and is diligently prosecuting a civil action in a court of the United States to require compliance with this chapter or with such rule or order, but if such proceeding or civil action is commenced after the giving of notice, any person giving such notice may intervene as a matter of right in such proceeding or action;

(2) under subsection (a)(2) of this section before the expiration of 60 days after the plaintiff has given notice to the Administrator of the alleged failure of the Administrator to perform an act or duty which is the basis for such action or, in the case of an action under such subsec-

tion for the failure of the Administrator to file an action under section 2606 of this title, before the expiration of ten days after such notification, except that no prior notification shall be required in the case of a civil action brought to compel a decision by the Administrator pursuant to section 18(f)(3)(B); or

(3) in the case of a civil action brought to compel a decision by the Administrator pursuant to section 18(f)(3)(B), after the date that is 60 days after the deadline specified in section 18(f)(3)(B).

Notice under this subsection shall be given in such manner as the Administrator shall prescribe by rule.

(c) General

(1) In any action under this section, the Administrator, if not a party, may intervene as a matter of right.

(2) The court, in issuing any final order in any action brought pursuant to subsection (a) of this section, may award costs of suit and reasonable fees for attorneys and expert witnesses if the court determines that such an award is appropriate. Any court, in issuing its decision in an action brought to review such an order, may award costs of suit and reasonable fees for attorneys if the court determines that such an award is appropriate.

(3) Nothing in this section shall restrict any right which any person (or class of persons) may have under any statute or common law to seek enforcement of this chapter or any rule or order under this chapter or to seek any other relief.

(d) Consolidation — When two or more civil actions brought under subsection (a) of this section involving the same defendant and the same issues or violations are pending in two or more judicial districts, such pending actions, upon application of such defendants to such actions which is made to a court in which any such action is brought, may, if such court in its discretion so decides, be consolidated for trial by order (issued after giving all parties reasonable notice and opportunity to be heard) of such court and tried in —

(1) any district which is selected by such defendant and in which one of such actions is pending,

(2) a district which is agreed upon by stipulation between all the parties to such actions and in which one of such actions is pending, or

(3) a district which is selected by the court and in which one of such actions is pending.

The court issuing such an order shall give prompt notification of the order to the other courts in which the civil actions consolidated under the order are pending.

§2620. Citizens' petitions
[TSCA §21]

(a) In general — Any person may petition the Administrator to initiate a proceeding for the issuance, amendment, or repeal of a rule under section 2603, 2605, or 2607 of this title or an order under section 4 or 5(e) or (f) of this title.

(b) Procedures

(1) Such petition shall be filed in the principal office of the Administrator and shall set forth the facts which it is claimed establish that it is necessary to issue, amend, or repeal a rule under section 2603, 2605, or 2607 of this title or an order under section 4 or 5(e) or (f) of this title.

(2) The Administrator may hold a public hearing or may conduct such investigation or proceeding as the Administrator deems appropriate in order to determine whether or not such petition should be granted.

(3) Within 90 days after filing of a petition described in paragraph (1), the Administrator shall either grant or deny the petition. If the Administrator grants such petition, the Administrator shall promptly commence an appropriate proceeding in accordance with section 2603, 2604, 2605, or 2607 of this title. If the Administrator denies such petition, the Administrator shall publish in the Federal Register the Administrator's reasons for such denial.

(4)(A) If the Administrator denies a petition filed under this section (or if the Administrator fails to grant or deny such petition within the 90-day period) the petitioner may commence a civil action in a district court of the United States to compel the Administrator to initiate a rulemaking proceeding as requested in the petition. Any such action shall be filed within 60 days after the Administrator's denial of the petition or, if the Administrator fails to grant or deny the petition within 90 days after filing the petition, within 60 days after the expiration of the 90-day period.

(B) In an action under subparagraph (A) respecting a petition to initiate a proceeding to issue a rule under section 2603, 2605, or 2607 of this title or an order under section 4 or 5(e) or (f) of this title, the petitioner shall be provided an opportunity to have such petition considered by the court in a de novo proceeding. If the petitioner demonstrates to the satisfaction of the court by a preponderance of the evidence that —

(i) in the case of a petition to initiate a proceeding for the issuance of a rule under section 2603 of this title or an order under section 4 or 5(e) or (f) of this title —

(I) information available to the Administrator is insufficient to permit a reasoned evaluation of the health and environmental effects of the chemical substance to be subject to such rule or order; and

(II) in the absence of such information, the substance may present an unreasonable risk to health or the environment, or the substance is or will be produced in substantial quantities and it enters or may reasonably be anticipated to enter the environment in substantial quantities or there is or may be significant or substantial human exposure to it; or

(ii) in the case of a petition to initiate a proceeding for the issuance of a rule under section 6(a) or 8 or an order under section 5(f) of this title, there is a reasonable basis to conclude that the issuance of such a rule or order is necessary to protect health or the environment against an unreasonable risk of injury to health or the environment.

the court shall order the Administrator to initiate the action requested by the petitioner. If the court finds that the extent of the risk to health or the environment alleged by the petitioner is less than the extent of risks to health or the environment with respect to which the Administrator is taking action under this chapter and there are insufficient resources available to the Administrator to take the action requested by the petitioner, the court may permit the Administrator to defer initiating the action requested by the petitioner until such time as the court prescribes.

(C) The court in issuing any final order in any action brought pursuant to subparagraph (A) may award costs of suit and reasonable fees for attorneys and expert witnesses if the court determines that such an award is appropriate. Any court, in issuing its decision in an action brought to review such an order, may award costs of suit and reasonable fees for attorneys if the court determines that such an award is appropriate.

(5) The remedies under this section shall be in addition to, and not in lieu of, other remedies provided by law.

§2621. National defense waiver
[TSCA §22]

The Administrator shall waive compliance with any provision of this chapter upon a request and determination by the President that the requested waiver is necessary in the interest of national defense. The Administrator shall maintain a written record of the basis upon which such waiver was granted and make such record available for in camera examination when relevant in a judicial proceeding under this chapter. Upon the issuance of such a waiver, the Administrator shall publish in the Federal Register a notice that the waiver was granted for national defense purposes, unless, upon the request of the President, the Administrator determines to omit such publication because the publication itself would be contrary to the interests of national defense, in which event the Administrator shall submit notice thereof to the Armed Services Committees of the Senate and the House of Representatives.

§2622. Employee protection
[TSCA §23]

(a) In general — No employer may discharge any employee or otherwise discriminate against any employee with respect to the employee's compensation, terms, conditions, or privileges of employment because the employee (or any person acting pursuant to a request of the employee) has —

(1) commenced, caused to be commenced, or is about to commence or cause to be commenced a proceeding under this chapter;

(2) testified or is about to testify in any such proceeding; or

(3) assisted or participated or is about to assist or participate in any manner in such a proceeding or in any other action to carry out the purposes of this chapter.

(b) Remedy

(1) Any employee who believes that the employee has been discharged or otherwise discriminated against by any person in violation of subsection (a) of this section may, within 30 days after such alleged violation occurs, file (or have any person file on the employee's behalf) a complaint with the Secretary of Labor (hereinafter in this section referred to as the "Secretary") alleging such discharge or discrimination. Upon receipt of such a complaint, the Secretary shall notify the person named in the complaint of the filing of the complaint.

(2)(A) Upon receipt of a complaint filed under paragraph (1), the Secretary shall conduct an investigation of the violation alleged in the complaint. Within 30 days of the receipt of such complaint, the Secretary shall complete such investigation and shall notify in writing the complainant (and any person acting on behalf of the complainant) and the person alleged to have committed such violation of the results of the investigation conducted pursuant to this paragraph. Within ninety days of the receipt of such complaint the Secretary shall, unless the proceeding on the complaint is terminated by the Secretary on the basis of a settlement entered into by the Secretary and the person alleged to have committed such violation, issue an order either providing the relief prescribed by subparagraph (B) or denying the complaint. An order of the Secretary shall be made on the record after notice and opportunity for agency hearing. The Secretary may not enter into a settlement terminating a proceeding on a complaint without the participation and consent of the complainant.

(B) If in response to a complaint filed under paragraph (1) the Secretary determines that a violation of subsection (a) of this section has occurred, the Secretary shall order (i) the person who committed such violation to take affirmative action to abate the violation, (ii) such person to reinstate the complainant to the complainant's former position together with the compensation (including back pay), terms, conditions, and privileges of the complainant's employment, (iii) compensatory damages, and (iv) where appropriate, exemplary damages. If such an order issued, the Secretary, at the request of the complainant, shall assess against the person against whom the order is issued a sum equal to the aggregate amount of all costs and expenses (including attorney's fees) reasonably incurred, as determined by the Secretary, by the complainant for, or in connection with, the bringing of the complaint upon which the order was issued.

(c) Review

(1) Any employee or employer adversely affected or aggrieved by an order issued under subsection (b) of this section may obtain review of the order in the United States Court of Appeals for the circuit in which the violation, with respect to which the order was issued, allegedly occurred. The petition for review must be filed within sixty days from the issuance of the Secretary's order. Review shall conform to chapter 7 of Title 5.

(2) An order of the Secretary, with respect to which review could have been obtained under paragraph (1), shall not be subject to judicial review in any criminal or other civil proceeding.

(d) Enforcement — Whenever a person has failed to comply with an order issued under subsection (b)(2) of this section, the Secretary shall file a civil action in the United States district court for the district in which the violation was found to occur to enforce such order. In actions brought under this subsection, the district courts shall have jurisdiction to grant all appropriate relief, including injunctive relief and compensatory and exemplary damages.

(e) Exclusion — Subsection (a) of this section shall not apply with respect to any employee who, acting without direction from the employee's employer (or any agent of the employer), deliberately causes a violation of any requirement of this chapter.

§2623. Employment effects
[TSCA §24]

(a) In general — The Administrator shall evaluate on a continuing basis the potential effects on employment (including reductions in employment or loss of employment from threatened plant closures) of —

(1) the issuance of a rule or order under section 2603, 2604, or 2605 of this title, or

(2) a requirement of section 2604 or 2605 of this title.

(b) Investigations

(1) Any employee (or any representative of an employee) may request the Administrator to make an investigation of —

(A) a discharge or layoff or threatened discharge or layoff of the employee, or

(B) adverse or threatened adverse effects on the employee's employment,

allegedly resulting from a rule or order under section 2603, 2604, or 2605 of this title or a requirement of section 2604 or 2605 of this title. Any such request shall be made in writing, shall set forth with reasonable particularity the grounds for the request, and shall be signed by the employee, or representative of such employee, making the request.

(2)(A) Upon receipt of a request made in accordance with paragraph (1) the Administrator shall (i) conduct the investigation requested, and (ii) if requested by any interested person, hold public hearings on any matter involved in the investigation unless the Administrator, by order issued within 45 days of the date such hearings are requested, denies the request for the hearings because the Administrator determines there are no reasonable grounds for holding such hearings. If the Administrator makes such a determination, the Administrator shall notify in writing the person requesting the hearing of the determination and the reasons therefor and shall publish the determination and the reasons therefor in the Federal Register.

(B) If public hearings are to be held on any matter involved in an investigation conducted under this subsection —

(i) at least five days' notice shall be provided the person making the request for

the investigation and any person identified in such request, and

(ii) each employee who made or for whom was made a request for such hearings and the employer of such employee shall be required to present information respecting the applicable matter referred to in paragraph (1)(A) or (1)(B) together with the basis for such information.

(3) Upon completion of an investigation under paragraph (2), the Administrator shall make findings of fact, shall make such recommendations as the Administrator deems appropriate, and shall make available to the public such findings and recommendations.

(4) This section shall not be construed to require the Administrator to amend or repeal any rule or order in effect under this chapter.

§2624. Studies
[TSCA §25]
Repealed

§2625. Administration
[TSCA §26]

(a) Cooperation of Federal agencies — Upon request by the Administrator, each Federal department and agency is authorized —

(1) to make its services, personnel, and facilities available (with or without reimbursement) to the Administrator to assist the Administrator in the administration of this chapter; and

(2) to furnish to the Administrator such information, data, estimates, and statistics, and to allow the Administrator access to all information in its possession as the Administrator may reasonably determine to be necessary for the administration of this chapter.

(b) Fees

(1) The Administrator may, by rule, require the payment from any person required to submit information under section 4 or a notice or other information to be reviewed by the Administrator under section 5, or who manufactures or processes a chemical substance that is the subject of a risk evaluation under section 6(b), of a fee that is sufficient and not more than reasonably necessary to defray the cost related to such chemical substance of administering sections 4, 5, and 6, and collecting, processing, reviewing and providing access to and protecting from disclosure as appropriate under section 14 information on chemical substances under this title, including contractor costs incurred by the Administrator. In setting a fee under this paragraph, the Administrator shall take into account the ability to pay of the person required to pay such fee and

the cost to the Administrator of carrying out the activities described in this paragraph. Such rules may provide for sharing such a fee in any case in which the expenses of testing are shared under section 2603 or 2604 of this title.

(2) The Administrator, after consultation with the Administrator of the Small Business Administration, shall by rule prescribe standards for determining the persons which qualify as small business concerns for purposes of paragraph (4).

(3) Fund —

(A) Establishment — There is established in the Treasury of the United States a fund, to be known as the TSCA Service Fee Fund (in this paragraph referred to as the 'Fund'), consisting of such amounts as are deposited in the Fund under this paragraph.

(B) Collection and deposit of fees — Subject to the conditions of subparagraph (C), the Administrator shall collect the fees described in this subsection and deposit those fees in the Fund.

(C) Use of funds by Administrator — Fees authorized under this section shall be collected and available for obligation only to the extent and in the amount provided in advance in appropriations Acts, and shall be available without fiscal year limitation for use in defraying the costs of the activities described in paragraph (1).

(D) Accounting and auditing —

(i) Accounting — The Administrator shall biennially prepare and submit to the Committee on Environment and Public Works of the Senate and the Committee on Energy and Commerce of the House of Representatives a report that includes an accounting of the fees paid to the Administrator under this paragraph and amounts disbursed from the Fund for the period recovered by the report, as reflected by financial statements provided in accordance with sections 3515 and 3521 of title 31, United States Code.

(ii) Auditing —

(I) In general — For the purpose of section 3515(c) of title 31, United States Code, the Fund shall be considered a component of a covered executive agency.

(II) Components of audit — The annual audit required in accordance with sections 3515 and 3521 of title 31, United States Code, of the financial statements of activities carried out using amounts form the Fund shall include an analysis of —

(aa) the fees collected and amounts disbursed under this subsection

(bb) the reasonableness of the fees in place as of the date of the audit to meet current and projected costs of administering the provisions of this title for which the fees may be used; and

(cc) the number of requests for a risk evaluation made by manufacturers under section 6(b)(4)(C)(ii).

(III) Federal Responsibility — The inspector General of the Environmental Protection Agency shall conduct the annual audit described in subclause (II) and submit to the Administrator a report that describes the findings and any recommendations of the Inspector General resulting from the audit.

(4) Amount and adjustment of fees; refunds — In setting fees under this section, the Administrator shall —

(A) prescribe lower fees for small business concerns, after consultation with the Administrator of the Small Business Administration;

(B) set the fees established under paragraph (1) at levels such that the fees will, in aggregate, provide a sustainable source of funds to annually defray —

(i) the lower of —

(I) 25 percent of the costs to the Administrator of carrying out sections 4, 5, and 6, and of collecting, processing, reviewing, and providing access to and protecting disclosure as appropriate under section 14 information on chemical substances under this title, other than the costs to conduct and complete risk evaluations under section 6(b); or

(II) $25,000 (subject to adjustment pursuant to subparagraph (F)); and

(ii) the costs of risk evaluations specified in subparagraph (D);

(C) reflect an appropriate balance in the assessment of fees between manufacturers and processors, and allow the payment of fees by consortia of manufacturers or processors;

(D) notwithstanding subparagraph (B)—

(i) except as provided in clause (ii), for chemical substances for which the Administrator has granted a request from a manufacturer pursuant to section 6(b)(4)(C)(ii), establish the full costs to the Administrator of conducting the risk evaluation under section 6(b);

(ii) for chemical substances for which the Administrator has granted a request from a manufacturer pursuant to section 6(b)(4)(C)(ii), and which are included in the 2014 update of the TSCA Work Plan for chemical assessments, establish the fee at a level sufficient to defray 50 percent of the costs to the Administrator of conducting the risk evaluation under section 6(b); and

(iii) apply fees collected pursuant to clauses (i) and (ii) only to defray the cost described in those clauses;

(E) prior to the establishment or amendment of any fees under paragraph (1), consult and meet with parties potentially subject to the fees or their representatives, subject to the condition that no obligation under the Federal Advisory Committee Act (5 U.S.C. App.) or subchapter II of chapter 5 of title 5, United States Code, is applicable with respect to such meetings;

(F) beginning with the fiscal year that is 3 years after the date of enactment of the Frank R. Lautenberg Chemical Safety for the 21st Century Act, and every 3 years thereafter, after consultation with parties potentially subject to the fees and their representatives pursuant to subparagraph (E), increase or decrease the fees established under paragraph (1) as necessary to adjust for inflation and to ensure that funds deposited in the fund are sufficient to defray —

(i) approximately but not more than 25 percent of the costs to the Administrator of carrying out sections 4, 5, and 6, and of collecting, processing, reviewing, and providing access to and protecting from disclosure as appropriate under section 14 information on chemical substances under this title, other than the costs to conduct and complete risk evaluations requested under section 6(b)(4)(C)(ii); and

(ii) the costs of risk evaluations specified in subparagraph (D); and

(G) if a notice submitted under section 5 is not reviewed or such a notice is withdrawn, refund the fee or a portion of the fee if no substantial work was performed on the notice.

(5) Minimum amount of appropriations — Fees may not be assessed for a fiscal year under this section unless the amount of appropriations for the Chemical Risk Review and Reduction program project of the Environmental Protection Agency for the fiscal year (excluding the amount of any fees appropriated for the fiscal year) are equal to or greater than the amount of appropriations for that program project for fiscal year 2014.

(6) Termination — The authority provided by this subsection shall terminate at the conclusion of the fiscal year that is 10 years after June 22, 2016 unless otherwise reauthorized or modified by Congress.

(c) Action with respect to categories

(1) Any action authorized or required to be taken by the Administrator under any provision of this chapter with respect to a chemical substance or mixture may be taken by the Administrator in accordance with that provision with respect to a category of chemical substances or mixtures. Whenever the Administrator takes action under a provision of this chapter with respect to a category of chemical substances or mixtures, any reference in this chapter to a chemical substance or mixture (insofar as it relates to such action) shall be deemed to be a reference to each chemical substance or mixture in such category.

(2) For purposes of paragraph (1):

(A) The term "category of chemical substances" means a group of chemical substances the members of which are similar in molecular structure, in physical, chemical, or biological properties, in use, or in mode of entrance into the human body or into the environment, or the members of which are in some other way suitable for classification as such for purposes of this chapter, except that such term does not mean a group of chemical substances which are grouped together solely on the basis of their being new chemical substances.

(B) The term "category of mixtures" means a group of mixtures the members of which are similar in molecular structure, in physical, chemical, or biological properties, in use, or in the mode of entrance into the human body or into the environment, or the members of which are in some other way suitable for classification as such for purposes of this chapter.

(d) Assistance office — The Administrator shall establish in the Environmental Protection Agency an identifiable office to provide technical and other nonfinancial assistance to manufacturers and processors of chemical substances and mixtures respecting the requirements of this chapter applicable to such manufacturers and processors, the policy of the Agency respecting the application of such requirements to such manufacturers and processors, and the means and methods by which such manufacturers and processors may comply with such requirements.

(e) Financial disclosures

(1) Except as provided under paragraph (3), each officer or employee of the Environmental Protection Agency and the Department of Health and Human Services who —

(A) performs any function or duty under this chapter, and

(B) has any known financial interest (i) in any person subject to this chapter or any rule or order in effect under this chapter, or (ii) in any person who applies for or receives any grant or contract under this chapter,

shall, on February 1, 1978, and on February 1 of each year thereafter, file with the Administrator or the Secretary of Health and Human Services (hereinafter in this subsection referred to as the "Secretary"), as appropriate, a written statement concerning all such interests held by such officer or employee during the preceding calendar year. Such statement shall be made available to the public.

(2) The Administrator and the Secretary shall —

(A) act within 90 days of January 1, 1977 —

(i) to define the term "known financial interests" for purposes of paragraph (1), and

(ii) to establish the methods by which the requirement to file written statements specified in paragraph (1) will be monitored and enforced, including appropriate provisions for review by the Administrator and the Secretary of such statements; and

(B) report to the Congress on June 1, 1978, and on June 1 of each year thereafter with respect to such statements and the actions taken in regard thereto during the preceding calendar year.

(3) The Administrator may by rule identify specific positions with the Environmental Protection Agency, and the Secretary may by rule identify specific positions with the Department of Health and Human Services, which are of a nonregulatory or nonpolicymaking nature, and the Administrator and the Secretary may by rule provide that officers or employees occupying such positions shall be exempt from the requirements of paragraph (1).

(4) This subsection does not supersede any requirement of chapter 11 of Title 18.

(5) Any officer or employee who is subject to, and knowingly violates, this subsection or any rule issued thereunder, shall be fined not more than $2,500 or imprisoned not more than one year, or both.

(f) Statement of basis and purpose — Any final order issued under this chapter shall be accompanied by a statement of its basis and purpose. The contents and adequacy of any such statement shall not be subject to judicial review in any respect.

(g) Assistant Administrator

(1) The President, by and with the advice and consent of the Senate, shall appoint an Assistant Administrator for Toxic Substances of the Environmental Protection Agency. Such Assistant Administrator shall be a qualified individual who is, by reason of background and experience, especially qualified to direct a program concerning the effects of chemicals on human health and the environment. Such Assistant Administrator shall be responsible for (A) the collection of information, (B) the preparation of studies, (C) the making of recommendations to the Administrator for regulatory and other actions to carry out the purposes and to facilitate the administration of this chapter, and (D) such other functions as the Administrator may assign or delegate.

(2) The Assistant Administrator to be appointed under paragraph (1) shall be in addition to the Assistant Administrators of the Environmental Protection Agency authorized by section 1(d) of Reorganization Plan No. 3 of 1970.

(h) Scientific Standards — In carrying out sections 4, 5, and 6, to the extent that the Administrator makes a decision based on science, the Administrator shall use scientific information, technical procedures, measures, methods, protocols, methodologies, or models, employed in a manner consistent with the best available science, and shall consider as applicable —

(1) the extent to which the scientific information, technical procedures, measures, methods, protocols, methodologies, or models employed to generate the information are reasonable for and consistent with the intended use of the information;

(2) the extent to which the information is relevant for the Administrator's use in making a decision about a chemical substance or mixture;

(3) the degree of clarity and completeness with which the data, assumptions, methods, quality assurance, and analyses employed to generate the information are documented;

(4) the extent to which the variability and uncertainty in the information, or in the procedures, measures, methods, protocols, methodologies, or models, are evaluated and characterized; and

(5) the extent of independent verification or peer review of the information or procedures, measures, methods, protocols, methodologies, or models.

(i) Weight of Scientific Evidence — The Administrator shall make decisions under sections 4, 5, and 6 based on the weight of the scientific evidence.

(j) Availability of Information — Subject to section 14, the Administrator shall make available to the public —

(1) all notices, determinations, findings, rules, consent agreements, and orders of the Administrator under this title;

(2) any information required to be provided to the Administrator under section 4;

(3) nontechnical summary of each risk evaluation conducted under section 6(b);

(4) a list of the studies considered by the Administrator in carrying out each such risk evaluation, along with the results of those studies; and

(5) each designation of a chemical substance under section 6(b), along with an identification of the information, analysis, and basis used to make the designations.

(k) Reasonably Available Information — In carrying out sections 4, 5, and 6, the Administrator shall take into consideration information relating to a chemical substance or mixture, including hazard and exposure information, under the conditions of use, that is reasonably available to the Administrator.

(l) Policies, Procedures, and Guidance —

(1) Development — Not later than 2 years after June 22, 2016, the Administrator shall develop any policies, procedures, and guidance the Administrator determines are necessary to carry out the amendments to this Act made by the Frank R. Lautenberg Chemical Safety for the 21st Century Act.

(2) Review — Not later than 5 years after June 22, 2016, and not less frequently than once every 5 years thereafter, the Administrator shall —

(A) review the adequacy of the policies, procedures, and guidance developed under paragraph (1), including with respect to animal, nonanimal, and epidemiological test methods and procedures for assessing and determining risk under this title; and

(B) revise such policies, procedures, and guidance as the Administrator determines necessary to reflect new scientific developments or understandings.

(3) Testing of chemical substances and mixtures — The policies, procedures, and guidance developed under paragraph (1) applicable to testing chemical substances and mixtures shall —

(A) address how and when the exposure level or exposure potential of a chemical substance or mixture would factor into decisions to require new testing, subject to the condition that the Administrator shall not interpret the lack of exposure information as a lack of exposure potential; and

(B) describe the manner in which the Administrator will determine that additional information is necessary to carry out this title, including information relating to potentially exposed or susceptible populations.

(4) Chemical substances with completed risk assessments — With respect to a chemical substance listed in the 2014 update to the TSCA Work Plan for Chemical Assessments for which the Administrator has published a completed risk assessment prior to June 22, 2016, the Administrator may publish proposed and final rules under section 6(a) that are consistent with the scope of the completed risk assessment for the chemical substance and consistent with other applicable requirements of section 6.

(5) Guidance — Not later than 1 year after June 22, 2016, the Administrator shall develop guidance to assist interested persons in developing and submitting draft risk evaluations which shall be considered by the Administrator. The guidance shall, at minimum, address the quality of the information submitted and the process to be followed in developing draft risk evaluations for consideration by the Administrator.

(m) Report to Congress —

(1) Initial report — Not later than 6 months after June 22, 2016, the Administrator shall submit to the Committees on the Energy and Commerce and Appropriations of the House of Representatives and the Committees on Environment and Public Works and Appropriations of the Senate a report containing an estimation of —

(A) the capacity of the Environmental Protection Agency to conduct and publish risk evaluations under section 6(b)(4)(C)(i) and (ii), and the resources necessary to conduct the minimum number of risk evaluations required under section 6(b)(2);

(B) the capacity of the Environmental Protection Agency to conduct and publish risk evaluations under section 6(b)(4)(A)(ii), the likely demand for such risk evaluations, and the anticipated schedule for accommodating that demand;

(C) the capacity of the Environmental Protection Agency to promulgate rules under section 6(a) as required based on risk evaluations conducted and published under section 6(b); and

(D) the actual and anticipated efforts of the Environmental Protection Agency to increase the Agency's capacity to conduct and publish risk evaluations under section 6(b).

(2) Subsequent reports — The Administrator shall update and resubmit the report described in paragraph (1) not less frequently than once every 5 years.

(n) Annual Plan —

(1) In general — The Administrator shall inform the public regarding the schedule and the resources necessary for the completion of each risk evaluation as soon as practicable after initiating the risk evaluation.

(2) Publication of plan — At the beginning of each calendar year, the Administrator shall publish an annual plan that —

(A) identifies the chemical substances for which risk evaluations are expected to be initiated or completed that year and the resources necessary for their completion;

(B) describes the status of each risk evaluation that has been initiated but not yet completed; and

(C) if the schedule for completion of a risk evaluation has changed, includes an updated schedule for that risk evaluation.

(o) Consultation With Science Advisory Committee on Chemicals —

(1) Establishment — Not later than 1 year after June 22, 2016, the Administrator shall establish an advisory committee on Chemicals (referred to in this subsection as the 'Committee').

(2) Purpose — The purpose of the Committee shall be to provide independent advice and expert consultation, at the request of the Administrator, with respect to the scientific and technical aspects of issues relating to the implementation of this title.

(3) Composition — The committee shall be composed of representatives of such science, government, labor, public health, public interest, animal protection, industry, and other groups as the Administrator determines to be advisable, including representatives that have specific scientific expertise in the relationship of chemical exposures to women, children, and other potentially exposed or susceptible subpopulations.

(4) Schedule — The Administrator shall convene the committee in accordance with such schedule as the Administrator determines to be appropriate, but not less frequently than once very 2 years.

(p) Prior actions —

(1) Rules, orders, and exemptions — Nothing in the Frank R. Lautenberg Chemical Safety for the 21st Century Act eliminates, modifies or withdraws any rule promulgated, order issued, or exemption established pursuant to this Act before June 22, 2016.

(2) Prior-initiated evaluations — Nothing in this Act prevents the Administrator from initiating a risk evaluation regarding a chemical substance, or from continuing or completing such risk evaluation, prior to the effective date of the policies, procedures, and guidance required to be developed by the Administrator pursuant to the amendments made by the Frank R. Lautenberg Chemical Safety for the 21st Century Act.

(3) Actions completed prior to completion of policies, procedures, and guidance —

Nothing in this Act requires the Administrator to revise or withdraw a completed risk evaluation, determination, or rule under this Act solely because the action was completed prior to the development of a policy, procedure, or guidance pursuant to the amendments made by the Frank R. Lautenberg Chemical Safety for the 21st Century Act.

§2626. Development and evaluation of test methods
[TSCA §27]

(a) In general — The Secretary of Health and Human Services, in consultation with the Administrator and acting through the Assistant Secretary for Health, may conduct, and make grants to public and nonprofit private entities and enter into contracts with public and private entities for, projects for the development and evaluation of inexpensive and efficient methods (1) for determining and evaluating the health and environmental effects of chemical substances and mixtures, and their toxicity, persistence, and other characteristics which affect health and the environment, and (2) which may be used for the development of information to meet the requirements of rules, orders, or consent agreements under section 2603 of this title. The Administrator shall consider such methods in prescribing under section 2603 of this title protocols and methodologies for the development of information.

(b) Approval by Secretary — No grant may be made or contract entered into under subsection (a) of this section unless an application therefor has been submitted to and approved by the Secretary. Such an application shall be submitted in such form and manner and contain such information as the Secretary may require. The Secretary may apply such conditions to grants and contracts under subsection (a) of this section as the Secretary determines are necessary to carry out the purposes of such subsection. Contracts may be entered into under such subsection without regard to section 3324(a) and (b) of Title 31 and section 5 of Title 41.

(c) Repealed. Pub. L. 104-66, Title I, §1061(a), Dec. 21, 1995, 109 Stat. 719

§2627. State programs
[TSCA §28]

(a) In general — For the purpose of complementing (but not reducing) the authority of, or actions taken by, the Administrator under this chapter, the Administrator may make grants to States for the establishment and operation of programs to prevent or eliminate unreasonable risks within the States to health or the environment which are associated with a chemical substance or mixture and with respect to which the Administrator is unable or is not likely to take action under this chapter for their prevention or elimination. The amount of a grant under this subsection shall be determined by the Administrator, except that no grant for any State program may exceed 75 per centum of the establishment and operation costs (as determined by the Administrator) of such program during the period for which the grant is made.

(b) Approval by Administrator

(1) No grant may be made under subsection (a) of this section unless an application therefor is submitted to and approved by the Administrator. Such an application shall be submitted in such form and manner as the Administrator may require and shall —

(A) set forth the need of the applicant for a grant under subsection (a) of this section,

(B) identify the agency or agencies of the State which shall establish or operate, or both, the program for which the application is submitted,

(C) describe the actions proposed to be taken under such program,

(D) contain or be supported by assurances satisfactory to the Administrator that such program shall, to the extent feasible, be integrated with other programs of the applicant for environmental and public health protection,

(E) provide for the making of such reports and evaluations as the Administrator may require, and

(F) contain such other information as the Administrator may prescribe.

(2) The Administrator may approve an application submitted in accordance with paragraph (1) only if the applicant has established to the satisfaction of the Administrator a priority need, as determined under rules of the Administrator, for the grant for which the application has been submitted. Such rules shall take into consideration the seriousness of the health effects in a State which are associated with chemical substances or mixtures, including cancer, birth defects, and gene mutations, the extent of the exposure in a State of human beings and the environment to chemical substances and mixtures, and the extent to which chemical substances and mixtures are manufactured, processed, used, and disposed of in a State.

§2628. Authorization of appropriations
[TSCA §29]

There are authorized to be appropriated to the Administrator for purposes of carrying out this chapter (other than sections 2626 and 2627 of this title and subsections (a) and (c) through (g) of section 2609 of this title) $58,646,000 for the fiscal year 1982 and $62,000,000 for the fiscal year 1983. No part of the funds appropriated under this section may be used to construct any research laboratories.

§2629. Annual report
[TSCA §30]

The Administrator shall prepare and submit to the President and the Congress on or before January 1, 1978, and on or before January 1 of each succeeding year a comprehensive report on the administration of this chapter during the preceding fiscal year. Such reports shall include —

(1) a list of the testing required under section 2603 of this title during the year for which the report is made and an estimate of the costs incurred during such year by the persons required to perform such tests;

(2) the number of notices received during such year under section 2604 of this title, the number of such notices received during such year under such section for chemical substances subject to a rule, order or consent agreement, and a summary of any action taken during such year under section 2604(g) of this title;

(3) a list of rules issued during such year under section 2605 of this title;

(4) a list, with a brief statement of the issues, of completed or pending judicial actions under this chapter and administrative actions under section 2615 of this title during such year;

(5) a summary of major problems encountered in the administration of this chapter; and

(6) such recommendations for additional legislation as the Administrator deems necessary to carry out the purposes of this chapter.

SUBCHAPTER II — ASBESTOS HAZARD EMERGENCY RESPONSE

§2641. Congressional findings and purpose
[TSCA §201]

(a) Findings — The Congress finds the following:

(1) The Environmental Protection Agency's rule on local educational agency inspection for, and notification of, the presence of friable asbestos-containing material in school buildings includes neither standards for the proper identification of asbestos-containing material and appropriate response actions with respect to friable asbestos-containing material, nor a requirement that response actions with respect to friable asbestos-containing material be carried out in a safe and complete manner once actions are found to be necessary. As a result of the lack of regulatory guidance from the Environmental Protection Agency, some schools have not undertaken response action while many others have undertaken expensive projects without knowing if their action is necessary, adequate, or safe. Thus, the danger of exposure to asbestos continues to exist in schools, and some exposure actually may have increased due to the lack of Federal standards and improper response action.

(2) There is no uniform program for accrediting persons involved in asbestos identification and abatement, nor are local educational agencies required to use accredited contractors for asbestos work.

(3) The guidance provided by the Environmental Protection Agency in its "Guidance for Controlling Asbestos-Containing Material in Buildings" is insufficient in detail to ensure adequate responses. Such guidance is intended to be used only until the regulations required by this subchapter become effective.

(4) Because there are no Federal standards whatsoever regulating daily exposure to asbestos in other public and commercial buildings, persons in addition to those comprising the Nation's school population may be exposed daily to asbestos.

(b) Purpose — The purpose of this subchapter is —

(1) to provide for the establishment of Federal regulations which require inspection for asbestos-containing material and implementation of appropriate response actions with respect to asbestos-containing material in the Nation's schools in a safe and complete manner;

(2) to mandate safe and complete periodic re-inspection of school buildings following response actions, where appropriate; and

(3) to require the Administrator to conduct a study to find out the extent of the danger to human health posed by asbestos in public and commercial buildings and the means to respond to any such danger.

§2642. Definitions
[TSCA §202]

For purposes of this subchapter —

(1) Accredited asbestos contractor — The term "accredited asbestos contractor" means a person accredited pursuant to the provisions of section 2646 of this title.

(2) Administrator — The term "Administrator" means the Administrator of the Environmental Protection Agency.

(3) Asbestos — The term "asbestos" means asbestiform varieties of —

    (A) chrysotile (serpentine),

    (B) crocidolite (riebeckite),

    (C) amosite (cummingtonite-grunerite),

    (D) anthophyllite,

    (E) tremolite, or

    (F) actinolite.

(4) Asbestos-containing material — The term "asbestos-containing material" means any material which contains more than 1 percent asbestos by weight.

(5) EPA guidance document — The term "Guidance for Controlling Asbestos-Containing Material in Buildings", means the Environmental Protection Agency document with such title as in effect on March 31, 1986.

(6) Friable asbestos-containing material — The term "friable asbestos-containing material" means any asbestos-containing material applied on ceilings, walls, structural members, piping, duct work, or any other part of a building which when dry may be crumbled, pulverized, or reduced to powder by hand pressure. The term includes non-friable asbestos-containing material after such previously non-friable material becomes damaged to the extent that when dry it may be crumbled, pulverized, or reduced to powder by hand pressure.

(7) Local educational agency — The term "local educational agency" means —

    (A) any local educational agency as defined in section 7801 of Title 20,

    (B) the owner of any private, nonprofit elementary or secondary school building, and

    (C) the governing authority of any school operated under the defense dependents' education system provided for under the Defense Dependents' Education Act of 1978 (20 U.S.C. §§921 *et seq.*).

(8) Most current guidance document — The term "most current guidance document" means the Environmental Protection Agency's "Guidance for Controlling Asbestos-Containing Material in Buildings" as modified by the Environmental Protection Agency after March 31, 1986.

(9) Non-profit elementary or secondary school — The term "non-profit elementary or secondary school" means any elementary or secondary school (as defined in section 7801 of Title 20) owned and operated by one or more nonprofit corporations or associations no part of the net earnings of which inures, or may lawfully inure, to the benefit of any private shareholder or individual.

(10) Public and commercial building — The term "public and commercial building" means any building which is not a school building, except that the term does not include any residential apartment building of fewer than 10 units.

(11) Response action — The term "response action" means methods that protect human health and the environment from asbestos-containing material. Such methods include methods described in chapters 3 and 5 of the Environmental Protection Agency's "Guidance for Controlling Asbestos-Containing Materials in Buildings".

(12) School — The term "school" means any elementary or secondary school as defined in section 7801 of Title 20.

(13) School building — The term "school building" means —

    (A) any structure suitable for use as a classroom, including a school facility such as a laboratory, library, school eating facility, or facility used for the preparation of food,

    (B) any gymnasium or other facility which is specially designed for athletic or recreational activities for an academic course in physical education,

(C) any other facility used for the instruction of students or for the administration of educational or research programs, and

(D) any maintenance, storage, or utility facility, including any hallway, essential to the operation of any facility described in subparagraphs (A), (B), or (C).

(14) State — The term "State" means a State, the District of Columbia, the Commonwealth of Puerto Rico, Guam, American Samoa, the Northern Marianas, the Trust Territory of the Pacific Islands, and the Virgin Islands.

§2643. EPA regulations
[TSCA §203]

(a) In general — Within 360 days after October 22, 1986, the Administrator shall promulgate regulations as described in subsections (b) through (i) of this section. With respect to regulations described in subsections (b), (c), (d), (e), (f), (g), and (i) of this section, the Administrator shall issue an advanced notice of proposed rulemaking within 60 days after October 22, 1986, and shall propose regulations within 180 days after October 22, 1986. Any regulation promulgated under this section must protect human health and the environment.

(b) Inspection — The Administrator shall promulgate regulations which prescribe procedures, including the use of personnel accredited under section 2646(b) or (c) of this title and laboratories accredited under section 2646(d) of this title, for determining whether asbestos-containing material is present in a school building under the authority of a local educational agency. The regulations shall provide for the exclusion of any school building, or portion of a school building, if (1) an inspection of such school building (or portion) was completed before the effective date of the regulations, and (2) the inspection meets the procedures and other requirements of the regulations under this subchapter or of the "Guidance for Controlling Asbestos-Containing Materials in Buildings" (unless the Administrator determines that an inspection in accordance with the guidance document is inadequate). The regulations shall require inspection of any school building (or portion of a school building) that is not excluded by the preceding sentence.

(c) Circumstances requiring response actions

(1) The Administrator shall promulgate regulations which define the appropriate response action in a school building under the authority of a local educational agency in at least the following circumstances:

(A) Damage — Circumstances in which friable asbestos-containing material or its covering is damaged, deteriorated, or delaminated.

(B) Significant damage — Circumstances in which friable asbestos-containing material or its covering is significantly damaged, deteriorated, or delaminated.

(C) Potential damage — Circumstances in which —

(i) friable asbestos-containing material is in an area regularly used by building occupants, including maintenance personnel, in the course of their normal activities, and

(ii) there is a reasonable likelihood that the material or its covering will become damaged, deteriorated, or delaminated.

(D) Potential significant damage — Circumstances in which —

(i) friable asbestos-containing material is in an area regularly used by building occupants, including maintenance personnel, in the course of their normal activities, and

(ii) there is a reasonable likelihood that the material or its covering will become significantly damaged, deteriorated, or delaminated.

(2) In promulgating such regulations, the Administrator shall consider and assess the value of various technologies intended to improve the decisionmaking process regarding response actions and the quality of any work that is deemed necessary, including air monitoring and chemical encapsulants.

(d) Response actions

(1) In general — The Administrator shall promulgate regulations describing a response action in a school building under the authority of a local educational agency, using the least burdensome methods which protect human health and the environment. In determining the least burdensome methods, the Administrator shall take into account local circumstances, including occupancy and use patterns within the school building and short- and long-term costs.

(2) Response action for damaged asbestos — In the case of a response action for the circumstances described in subsection (c)(1)(A) of this section, methods for responding shall include methods identified in chapters 3 and 5 of the "Guidance for Controlling Asbestos-Containing Material in Buildings".

(3) Response action for significantly damaged asbestos — In the case of a response action for the circumstances described in subsection (c)(1)(B) of this section, methods for responding shall include methods identified in chapter 5 of the "Guidance for Controlling Asbestos-Containing Material in Buildings".

(4) Response action for potentially damaged asbestos — In the case of a response action for the circumstances described in subsection (c)(1)(C) of this section, methods for responding shall include methods identified in chapters 3 and 5 of the

"Guidance for Controlling Asbestos-Containing Material in Buildings", unless preventive measures will eliminate the reasonable likelihood that the asbestos-containing material will become damaged, deteriorated, or delaminated.

(5) Response action for potentially significantly damaged asbestos — In the case of a response action for the circumstances described in subsection (c)(1)(D) of this section, methods for responding shall include methods identified in chapter 5 of the "Guidance for Controlling Asbestos-Containing Material in Buildings", unless preventive measures will eliminate the reasonable likelihood that the asbestos-containing material will become significantly damaged, deteriorated, or delaminated.

(6) "Preventive measures" defined — For purposes of this section, the term "preventive measures" means actions which eliminate the reasonable likelihood of asbestos-containing material becoming damaged, deteriorated, or delaminated, or significantly damaged deteriorated, or delaminated (as the case may be) or which protect human health and the environment.

(7) EPA information or advisory — The Administrator shall, not later than 30 days after November 28, 1990, publish and distribute to all local education agencies and State Governors information or an advisory to —

(A) facilitate public understanding of the comparative risks associated with in-place management of asbestos-containing building materials and removals;

(B) promote the least burdensome response actions necessary to protect human health, safety, and the environment; and

(C) describe the circumstances in which asbestos removal is necessary to protect human health.

Such information or advisory shall be based on the best available scientific evidence and shall be revised, republished, and redistributed as appropriate, to reflect new scientific findings.

(e) **Implementation** — The Administrator shall promulgate regulations requiring the implementation of response actions in school buildings under the authority of a local educational agency and, where appropriate, for the determination of when a response action is completed. Such regulations shall include standards for the education and protection of both workers and building occupants for the following phases of activity:

(1) Inspection.

(2) Response action.

(3) Post-response action, including any periodic reinspection of asbestos-containing material and long-term surveillance activity.

(f) **Operations and maintenance** — The Administrator shall promulgate regulations to require implementation of an operations and maintenance and repair program as described in chapter 3 of the "Guidance for Controlling Asbestos-Containing Materials in Buildings" for all friable asbestos-containing material in a school building under the authority of a local educational agency.

(g) **Periodic surveillance** — The Administrator shall promulgate regulations to require the following:

(1) An identification of the location of friable and non-friable asbestos in a school building under the authority of a local educational agency.

(2) Provisions for surveillance and periodic reinspection of such friable and non-friable asbestos.

(3) Provisions for education of school employees, including school service and maintenance personnel, about the location of and safety procedures with respect to such friable and non-friable asbestos.

(h) **Transportation and disposal** — The Administrator shall promulgate regulations which prescribe standards for transportation and disposal of asbestos-containing waste material to protect human health and the environment. Such regulations shall include such provisions related to the manner in which transportation vehicles are loaded and unloaded as will assure the physical integrity of containers of asbestos-containing waste material.

(i) **Management plans**

(1) In general — The Administrator shall promulgate regulations which require each local educational agency to develop an asbestos management plan for school buildings under its authority, to begin implementation of such plan within 990 days after October 22, 1986, and to complete implementation of such plan in a timely fashion. The regulations shall require that each plan include the following elements, wherever relevant to the school building:

(A) An inspection statement describing inspection and response action activities carried out before October 22, 1986.

(B) A description of the results of the inspection conducted pursuant to regulations under subsection (b) of this section, including a description of the specific areas inspected.

(C) A detailed description of measures to be taken to respond to any friable asbestos-containing material pursuant to the regulations promulgated under subsections (c), (d), and (e) of this section, including the location or locations at which a response action will be taken, the method or methods of response action to be used, and a schedule for beginning and completing response actions.

(D) A detailed description of any asbestos-containing material which remains in the school building once response actions are undertaken pursuant to the regulations promulgated under subsections (c), (d), and (e) of this section.

(E) A plan for periodic reinspection and long-term surveillance activities developed pursuant to regulations promulgated under subsection (g) of this section, and a plan for operations and maintenance activities developed pursuant to regulations promulgated under subsection (f) of this section.

(F) With respect to the person or persons who inspected for asbestos-containing material and who will design or carry out response actions with respect to the friable asbestos-containing material, one of the following statements:

(i) If the State has adopted a contractor accreditation plan under section 2646(b) of this title, a statement that the person (or persons) is accredited under such plan.

(ii) A statement that the local educational agency used (or will use) persons who have been accredited by another State which has adopted a contractor accreditation plan under section 2646(b) of this title or is accredited pursuant to an Administrator-approved course under section 2646(c) of this title.

(G) A list of the laboratories that analyzed any bulk samples of asbestos-containing material found in the school building or air samples taken to detect asbestos in the school building and a statement that each laboratory has been accredited pursuant to the accreditation program under section 2646(d) of this title.

(H) With respect to each consultant who contributed to the management plan, the name of the consultant and one of the following statements:

(i) If the State has adopted a contractor accreditation plan under section 2646(b) of this title, a statement that the consultant is accredited under such plan.

(ii) A statement that the contractor is accredited by another State which has adopted a contractor accreditation plan under section 2646(b) of this title or is accredited pursuant to an Administrator-approved course under section 2646(c) of this title.

(I) An evaluation of resources needed to successfully complete response actions and carry out reinspection, surveillance, and operation and maintenance activities.

(2) Statement by contractor — A local educational agency may require each management plan to contain a statement signed by an accredited asbestos contractor that such contractor has prepared or assisted in the preparation of such plan, or has reviewed such plan, and that such plan is in compliance with the applicable regulations and standards promulgated or adopted pursuant to this section and other applicable provisions of law. Such a statement may not be signed by a contractor who, in addition to preparing or assisting in preparing the management plan, also implements (or will implement) the management plan.

(3) Warning labels

(A) The regulations shall require that each local educational agency which has inspected for and discovered any asbestos-containing material with respect to a school building shall attach a warning label to any asbestos-containing material still in routine maintenance areas (such as boiler rooms) of the school building, including —

(i) friable asbestos-containing material which was responded to by a means other than removal, and

(ii) asbestos-containing material for which no response action was carried out.

(B) The warning label shall read, in print which is readily visible because of large size or bright color, as follows: "CAUTION: ASBESTOS. HAZARDOUS. DO NOT DISTURB WITHOUT PROPER TRAINING AND EQUIPMENT."

(4) Plan may be submitted in stages — A local educational agency may submit a management plan in stages, with each submission of the agency covering only a portion of the school buildings under the agency's authority, if the agency determines that such action would expedite the identification and abatement of hazardous asbestos-containing material in the school buildings under the authority of the agency.

(5) Public availability — A copy of the management plan developed under the regulations shall be available in the administrative offices of the local educational agency for inspection by the public, including teachers, other school personnel, and parents. The local educational agency shall notify parent, teacher, and employee organizations of the availability of such plan.

(6) Submission to State Governor — Each plan developed under this subsection shall be submitted to the State Governor under section 2645 of this title.

(j) **Changes in regulations** — Changes may be made in the regulations promulgated under this section only by rule in accordance with section 553 of Title 5. Any such change must protect human health and the environment.

(k) **Changes in guidance document** — Any change made in the "Guidance for Controlling Asbestos-Containing Material in Buildings" shall be made only by rule in accordance with section 553 of Title 5, unless a regulation described in this section dealing with the same subject matter is in effect. Any such change must protect human health and the environment.

(*l*) **Treatment of Department of Defense schools**

(1) Secretary to act in lieu of Governor — In the administration of this subchapter, any function, duty, or other responsibility imposed on a Governor of a State shall be carried out by the Secretary of Defense with respect to any school operated under the defense dependents' education system provided

for under the Defense Dependents' Education Act of 1978 (20 U.S.C. §§ 921 *et seq.*).

(2) Regulations — The Secretary of Defense, in cooperation with the Administrator, shall, to the extent feasible and consistent with the national security, take such action as may be necessary to provide for the identification, inspection, and management (including abatement) of asbestos in any building used by the Department of Defense as an overseas school for dependents of members of the Armed Forces. Such identification, inspection, and management (including abatement) shall, subject to the preceding sentence, be carried out in a manner comparable to the manner in which a local educational agency is required to carry out such activities with respect to a school building under this subchapter.

(m) Waiver — The Administrator, upon request by a Governor and after notice and comment and opportunity for a public hearing in the affected State, may waive some or all of the requirements of this section and section 2644 of this title with respect to such State if it has established and is implementing a program of asbestos inspection and management that contains requirements that are at least as stringent as the requirements of this section and section 2644 of this title.

§2644. Requirements if EPA fails to promulgate regulations
[TSCA §204]

(a) In general

(1) Failure to promulgate — If the Administrator fails to promulgate within the prescribed period —

(A) regulations described in section 2643(b) of this title (relating to inspection);

(B) regulations described in section 2643(c), (d), (e), (f), (g), and (i) of this title (relating to responding to asbestos); or

(C) regulations described in section 2643(h) of this title (relating to transportation and disposal);

each local educational agency shall carry out the requirements described in this section in subsection (b); subsections (c), (d), and (e); or subsection (f); respectively, in accordance with the Environmental Protection Agency's most current guidance document.

(2) Stay by court — If the Administrator has promulgated regulations described in paragraph (1) (A), (B), or (C) within the prescribed period, but the effective date of such regulations has been stayed by a court for a period of more than 30 days, a local educational agency shall carry out the pertinent requirements described in this subsection in accordance with the Environmental Protection Agency's most current guidance document.

(3) Effective period — The requirements of this section shall be in effect until such time as the Administrator promulgates the pertinent regulations or until the stay is lifted (as the case may be).

(b) Inspection

(1) Except as provided in paragraph (2), the local educational agency, within 540 days after October 22, 1986, shall conduct an inspection for asbestos-containing material, using personnel accredited under section 2646(b) or (c) of this title and laboratories accredited under section 2646(d) of this title, in each school building under its authority.

(2) The local educational agency may exclude from the inspection requirement in paragraph (1) any school building, or portion of a school building, if (A) an inspection of such school building (or portion) was completed before the date on which this section goes into effect, and (B) the inspection meets the inspection requirements of this section.

(c) Operation and maintenance — The local educational agency shall, within 720 days after October 22, 1986, develop and begin implementation of an operation and maintenance plan with respect to friable asbestos-containing material in a school building under its authority. Such plan shall provide for the education of school service and maintenance personnel about safety procedures with respect to asbestos-containing material, including friable asbestos-containing material.

(d) Management plan

(1) In general — The local educational agency shall —

(A) develop a management plan for responding to asbestos containing material in each school building under its authority and submit such plan to the Governor under section 2645 of this title within 810 days after October 22, 1986,

(B) begin implementation of such plan within 990 days after October 22, 1986, and

(C) complete implementation of such plan in a timely fashion.

(2) Plan requirements — The management plan shall —

(A) include the elements listed in section 2643(i)(1) of this title, including an inspection statement as described in paragraph (3) of this section,

(B) provide for the attachment of warning labels as described in section 2643(i)(3) of this title,

(C) be prepared in accordance with the most current guidance document,

(D) meet the standard described in paragraph (4) for actions described in that paragraph, and

(E) be submitted to the State Governor under section 2645 of this title.

(3) Inspection statement — The local educational agency shall complete an inspection statement, covering activities carried out before October 22, 1986, which meets the following requirements:

(A) The statement shall include the following information:

    (i) The dates of inspection.

    (ii) The name, address, and qualifications of each inspector.

    (iii) A description of the specific areas inspected.

    (iv) A list of the laboratories that analyzed any bulk samples of asbestos-containing material or air samples of asbestos found in any school building and a statement describing the qualifications of each laboratory.

    (v) The results of the inspection.

(B) The statement shall state whether any actions were taken with respect to any asbestos-containing material found to be present, including a specific reference to whether any actions were taken in the boiler room of the building. If any such action was taken, the following items of information shall be included in the statement:

    (i) The location or locations at which the action was taken.

    (ii) A description of the method of action.

    (iii) The qualifications of the persons who conducted the action.

(4) Standard — The ambient interior concentration of asbestos after the completion of actions described in the most current guidance document, other than the type of action described in sections 2643(f) of this title and subsection (c) of this section, shall not exceed the ambient exterior concentration, discounting any contribution from any local stationary source. Either a scanning electron microscope or a transmission electron microscope shall be used to determine the ambient interior concentration. In the absence of reliable measurements, the ambient exterior concentration shall be deemed to be —

    (A) less than 0.003 fibers per cubic centimeter if a scanning electron microscope is used, and

    (B) less than 0.005 fibers per cubic centimeter if a transmission electron microscope is used.

(5) Public availability — A copy of the management plan shall be available in the administrative offices of the local educational agency for inspection by the public, including teachers, other school personnel, and parents. The local educational agency shall notify parent, teacher, and employee organizations of the availability of such plan.

(e) Building occupant protection — The local educational agency shall provide for the protection of building occupants during each phase of activity described in this section.

(f) Transportation and disposal — The local educational agency shall provide for the transportation and disposal of asbestos in accordance with the most recent version of the Environmental Protection Agency's "Asbestos Waste Management Guidance" (or any successor to such document).

§2645. Submission to State Governor [TSCA §205]

(a) Submission — Within 720 days after October 22, 1986 (or within 810 days if there are no regulations under section 2643(i) of this title), a local educational agency shall submit a management plan developed pursuant to regulations promulgated under section 2643(i) of this title (or under section 2644(d) of this title if there are no regulations) to the Governor of the State in which the local educational agency is located.

(b) Governor requirements — Within 360 days after October 22, 1986, the Governor of each State —

    (1) shall notify local educational agencies in the State of where to submit their management plans under this section, and

    (2) may establish administrative procedures for reviewing management plans submitted under this section.

If the Governor establishes procedures under paragraph (2), the Governor shall designate to carry out the reviews those State officials who are responsible for implementing environmental protection or other public health programs, or with authority over asbestos programs, in the State.

(c) Management plan review

    (1) Review of plan — The Governor may disapprove a management plan within 90 days after the date of receipt of the plan if the plan —

        (A) does not conform with the regulations under section 2643(i) of this title (or with section 2644(d) of this title if there are no regulations),

        (B) does not assure that contractors who are accredited pursuant to this subchapter will be used to carry out the plan, or

        (C) does not contain a response action schedule which is reasonable and timely, taking into account circumstances relevant to the speed at which the friable asbestos-containing material in the school buildings under the local educational agency's authority should be responded to, including human exposure to the asbestos while the friable asbestos-containing material remains in the school building, and the ability of the local educational agency to continue to provide educational services to the community.

    (2) Revision of plan — If the State Governor disapproves a plan, the State Governor shall explain in writing to the local educational agency the reasons why the plan was disapproved and the changes that need to be made in the plan. Within 30 days after the date on which notice is received of disapproval of its plan, the local educational agency shall revise the plan to conform with the State Governor's suggested changes. The Governor may extend the 30-day period for not more than 90 days.

(d) Deferral of submission

(1) Request for deferral — A local educational agency may request a deferral, to May 9, 1989, of the deadline under subsection (a) of this section. Upon approval of such a request, the deadline under subsection (a) of this section is deferred until May 9, 1989, for the local educational agency which submitted the request. Such a request may cover one or more schools under the authority of the agency and shall include a list of all the schools covered by the request. A local educational agency shall file any such request with the State Governor by October 12, 1988, and shall include with the request either of the following statements:

(A) A statement —

(i) that the State in which the agency is located has requested from the Administrator, before June 1, 1988, a waiver under section 2643(m) of this title; and

(ii) that gives assurance that the local educational agency has carried out the notification and, in the case of a public school, public meeting required by paragraph (2).

(B) A statement, the accuracy of which is sworn to by a responsible official of the agency (by notarization or other means of certification), that includes the following with respect to each school for which a deferral is sought in the request:

(i) A statement that, in spite of the fact that the local educational agency has made a good faith effort to meet the deadline for submission of a management plan under subsection (a) of this section, the agency will not be able to meet the deadline. The statement shall include a brief explanation of the reasons why the deadline cannot be met.

(ii) A statement giving assurance that the local educational agency has made available for inspection by the public, at each school for which a deferral is sought in the request, at least one of the following documents:

(I) A solicitation by the local educational agency to contract with an accredited asbestos contractor for inspection or management plan development.

(II) A letter attesting to the enrollment of school district personnel in an Environmental Protection Agency-accredited training course for inspection and management plan development.

(III) Documentation showing that an analysis of suspected asbestos-containing material from the school is pending at an accredited laboratory.

(IV) Documentation showing that an inspection or management plan has been completed in at least one other school under the local educational agency's authority.

(iii) A statement giving assurance that the local educational agency has carried out the notification and, in the case of a public school, public meeting required by paragraph (2).

(iv) A proposed schedule outlining all significant activities leading up to submission of a management plan by May 9, 1989, including inspection of the school (if not completed at the time of the request) with a deadline of no later than December 22, 1988, for entering into a signed contract with an accredited asbestos contractor for inspection (unless such inspections are to be performed by school personnel), laboratory analysis of material from the school suspected of containing asbestos, and development of the management plan.

(2) Notification and public meeting — Before filing a deferral request under paragraph (1), a local educational agency shall notify affected parent, teacher, and employee organizations of its intent to file such a request. In the case of a deferral request for a public school, the local educational agency shall discuss the request at a public meeting of the school board with jurisdiction over the school, and affected parent, teacher, and employee organizations shall be notified in advance of the time and place of such meeting.

(3) Response by Governor

(A) Not later than 30 days after the date on which a Governor receives a deferral request under paragraph (1) from a local educational agency, the Governor shall respond to the local educational agency in writing by acknowledging whether the request is complete or incomplete. If the request is incomplete, the Governor shall identify in the response the items that are missing from the request.

(B) A local educational agency may correct any deficiencies in an incomplete deferral request and refile the request with the Governor. In any case in which the local educational agency decides to refile the request, the agency shall refile the request, and the Governor shall respond to such refiled request in the manner described in subparagraph (A), no later than 15 days after the local educational agency has received a response from the Governor under subparagraph (A).

(C) Approval of a deferral request under this subsection occurs only upon the receipt by a local educational agency of a written acknowledgment from the Governor that the agency's deferral request is complete.

(4) Submission and review of plan — A local educational agency whose deferral request is approved shall submit a management plan to the Governor not later than May 9, 1989. Such management plan shall include a copy of the deferral request and the statement accompanying such request. Such management plan shall be reviewed in accordance with subsection (c) of this section, except that the Governor may extend the 30-day period for revision of the plan under subsection (c) (2) of this section for only an additional 30 days (for a total of 60 days).

(5) Implementation of plan — The approval of a deferral request from a local educational agency shall not be considered to be a waiver or exemption from the requirement under section 2643(i) of this title for the local educational agency to begin implementation of its management plan by July 9, 1989.

(6) EPA notice

(A) Not later than 15 days after July 18, 1988, the Administrator shall publish in the Federal Register the following:

(i) A notice describing the opportunity to file a request for deferral under this subsection.

(ii) A list of the State offices (including officials (if available) in each State as designated under subsection (b) of this section) with which deferral requests should be filed.

(B) As soon as practicable, but in no event later than 30 days, after July 18, 1988, the Administrator shall mail a notice describing the opportunity to file a request for deferral under this subsection to each local educational agency and to each State office in the list published under subparagraph (A).

(e) Status reports

(1) Not later than December 31, 1988, the Governor of each State shall submit to the Administrator a written statement on the status of management plan submissions and deferral requests by local educational agencies in the State. The statement shall be made available to local educational agencies in the State and shall contain the following:

(A) A list containing each local educational agency that submitted a management plan by October 12, 1988.

(B) A list containing each local educational agency whose deferral request was approved.

(C) A list containing each local educational agency that failed to submit a management plan by October 12, 1988, and whose deferral request was disapproved.

(D) A list containing each local educational agency that failed to submit a management plan by October 12, 1988, and did not submit a deferral request.

(2) Not later than December 31, 1989, the Governor of each State shall submit to the Administrator an updated version of the written statement submitted under paragraph (1). The statement shall be made available to local educational agencies in the State and shall contain the following:

(A) A list containing each local educational agency whose management plan was submitted and not disapproved as of October 9, 1989.

(B) A list containing each local educational agency whose management plan was submitted and disapproved, and which remains disapproved, as of October 9, 1989.

(C) A list containing each local educational agency that submitted a management plan after May 9, 1989, and before October 10, 1989.

(D) A list containing each local educational agency that failed to submit a management plan as of October 9, 1989.

§2646. Contractor and laboratory accreditation [TSCA §206]

(a) Contractor accreditation — A person may not —

(1) inspect for asbestos-containing material in a school building under the authority of a local educational agency or in a public or commercial building,

(2) prepare a management plan for such a school, or

(3) design or conduct response actions, other than the type of action described in sections 2643(f) and 2644(c) of this title, with respect to friable asbestos-containing material in such a school or in a public or commercial building,

unless such person is accredited by a State under subsection (b) of this section or is accredited pursuant to an Administrator-approved course under subsection (c) of this section.

(b) Accreditation by State

(1) Model plan

(A) Persons to be accredited — Within 180 days after October 22, 1986, the Administrator, in consultation with affected organizations, shall develop a model contractor accreditation plan for States to give accreditation to persons in the following categories:

(i) Persons who inspect for asbestos-containing material in school buildings under the authority of a local educational agency or in public or commercial buildings.

(ii) Persons who prepare management plans for such schools.

(iii) Persons who design or carry out response actions, other than the type of action described in sections 2643(f) and 2644(c) of this title, with respect to friable asbestos-containing material in such schools or in public or commercial buildings.

(B) Plan requirements — The plan shall include a requirement that any person in a category listed in paragraph (1) achieve a passing grade on an examination and participate in continuing education to stay informed about current asbestos inspection and response action technology. The examination shall demonstrate the knowledge of the person in areas that the Administrator prescribes as necessary and appropriate in each of the categories. Such examinations may include requirements for knowledge in the following areas:

(i) Recognition of asbestos-containing material and its physical characteristics.

(ii) Health hazards of asbestos and the relationship between asbestos exposure and disease.

(iii) Assessing the risk of asbestos exposure through a knowledge of percentage weight of asbestos-containing material, friability, age, deterioration, location and accessibility of materials, and advantages and disadvantages of dry and wet response action methods.

(iv) Respirators and their use, care, selection, degree of protection afforded, fitting, testing, and maintenance and cleaning procedures.

(v) Appropriate work practices and control methods, including the use of high efficiency particle absolute vacuums, the use of amended water, and principles of negative air pressure equipment use and procedures.

(vi) Preparing a work area for response action work, including isolating work areas to prevent bystander or public exposure to asbestos, decontamination procedures, and procedures for dismantling work areas after completion of work.

(vii) Establishing emergency procedures to respond to sudden releases.

(viii) Air monitoring requirements and procedures.

(ix) Medical surveillance program requirements.

(x) Proper asbestos waste transportation and disposal procedures.

(xi) Housekeeping and personal hygiene practices, including the necessity of showers, and procedures to prevent asbestos exposure to an employee's family.

(2) State adoption of plan — Each State shall adopt a contractor accreditation plan at least as stringent as the model plan developed by the Administrator under paragraph (1), within 180 days after the commencement of the first regular session of the legislature of such State which is convened following the date on which the Administrator completes development of the model plan. In the case of a school operated under the defense dependents' education system provided for under the Defense Dependents' Education Act of 1978

(20 U.S.C. §§921 *et seq.*), the Secretary of Defense shall adopt a contractor accreditation plan at least as stringent as that model.

(c) Accreditation by Administrator-approved course

(1) Course approval — Within 180 days after October 22, 1986, the Administrator shall ensure that any Environmental Protection Agency-approved asbestos training course is consistent with the model plan (including testing requirements) developed under subsection (b) of this section. A contractor may be accredited by taking and passing such a course.

(2) Treatment of persons with previous EPA asbestos training — A person who —

(A) completed an Environmental Protection Agency-approved asbestos training course before October 22, 1986, and

(B) passed (or passes) an asbestos test either before or after October 22, 1986,

may be accredited under paragraph (1) if the Administrator determines that the course and test are equivalent to the requirements of the model plan developed under subsection (b) of this section. If the Administrator so determines, the person shall be considered accredited for the purposes of this subchapter until a date that is one year after the date on which the State in which such person is employed establishes an accreditation program pursuant to subsection (b) of this section.

(3) Lists of courses — The Administrator, in consultation with affected organizations, shall publish (and revise as necessary) —

(A) a list of asbestos courses and tests in effect before October 22, 1986, which qualify for equivalency treatment under paragraph (2), and

(B) a list of asbestos courses and tests which the Administrator determines under paragraph (1) are consistent with the model plan and which will qualify a contractor for accreditation under such paragraph.

(d) Laboratory accreditation

(1) The Administrator shall provide for the development of an accreditation program for laboratories by the National Institute of Standards and Technology in accordance with paragraph (2). The Administrator shall transfer such funds as are necessary to the National Institute of Standards and Technology to carry out such program.

(2) The National Institute of Standards and Technology, upon request by the Administrator, shall, in consultation with affected organizations —

(A) within 360 days after October 22, 1986, develop an accreditation program for laboratories which conduct qualitative and semi-quantitative analyses of bulk samples of asbestos-containing material, and

(B) within 720 days after October 22, 1986, develop an accreditation program for laboratories which conduct analyses of air samples of asbestos from school buildings under the authority of a local educational agency.

(3) A laboratory which plans to carry out any such analysis shall comply with the requirements of the accreditation program.

(e) Financial assistance contingent on use of accredited persons

(1) A school which is an applicant for financial assistance under section 505 of the Asbestos School Hazard Abatement Act of 1984 [20 U.S.C. §4014] is not eligible for such assistance unless the school, in carrying out the requirements of this subchapter —

 (A) uses a person (or persons) —

  (i) who is accredited by a State which has adopted an accreditation plan based on the model plan developed under subsection (b) of this section, or

  (ii) who is accredited pursuant to an Administrator-approved course under subsection (c) of this section, and

 (B) uses a laboratory (or laboratories) which is accredited under the program developed under subsection (d) of this section.

(2) This subsection shall apply to any financial assistance provided under the Asbestos School Hazard Abatement Act of 1984 [20 U.S.C. §§4011 *et seq.*] for activities performed after the following dates:

 (A) In the case of activities performed by persons, after the date which is one year after October 22, 1986.

 (B) In the case of activities performed by laboratories, after the date which is 180 days after the date on which a laboratory accreditation program is completed under subsection (d) of this section.

(f) List of EPA-approved courses — Not later than August 31, 1988, and every three months thereafter until August 31, 1991, the Administrator shall publish in the Federal Register a list of all Environmental Protection Agency-approved asbestos training courses for persons to achieve accreditation in each category described in subsection (b)(1)(A) of this section and for laboratories to achieve accreditation. The Administrator may continue publishing such a list after August 31, 1991, at such times as the Administrator considers it useful. The list shall include the name and address of each approved trainer and, to the extent available, a list of all the geographic sites where training courses will take place. The Administrator shall provide a copy of the list to each State official on the list published by the Administrator under section 2645(d)(6) of this title and to each regional office of the Environmental Protection Agency.

§2647. Enforcement
[TSCA §207]

(a) Penalties — Any local educational agency —

(1) which fails to conduct an inspection pursu-
ant to regulations under section 2643(b) of this title or under section 2644(b) of this title,

(2) which knowingly submits false information to the Governor regarding any inspection pursuant to regulations under section 2643(i) of this title or knowingly includes false information in any inspection statement under section 2644(d)(3) of this title,

(3) which fails to develop a management plan pursuant to regulations under section 2643(i) of this title or under section 2644(d) of this title,

(4) which carries out any activity prohibited by section 2655 of this title, or

(5) which knowingly submits false information to the Governor regarding a deferral request under section 2645(d) of this title

is liable for a civil penalty of not more than $5,000 for each day during which the violation continues. Any civil penalty under this subsection shall be assessed and collected in the same manner, and subject to the same provisions, as in the case of civil penalties assessed and collected under section 2615 of this title. For purposes of this subsection, a "violation" means a failure to comply with respect to a single school building. The court shall order that any civil penalty collected under this subsection be used by the local educational agency for purposes of complying with this subchapter. Any portion of a civil penalty remaining unspent after compliance by a local educational agency is completed shall be deposited into the Asbestos Trust Fund established by section 4022 of Title 20.

(b) Relationship to subchapter I of this chapter — A local educational agency is not liable for any civil penalty under subchapter I of this chapter for failing or refusing to comply with any rule promulgated or order issued under this subchapter.

(c) Enforcement considerations

(1) In determining the amount of a civil penalty to be assessed under subsection (a) of this section against a local educational agency, the Administrator shall consider —

 (A) the significance of the violation;

 (B) the culpability of the violator, including any history of previous violations under this chapter;

 (C) the ability of the violator to pay the penalty; and

 (D) the ability of the violator to continue to provide educational services to the community.

(2) Any action ordered by a court in fashioning relief under section 2619 of this title shall be consistent with regulations promulgated under section 2643 of this title (or with the requirements of section 2644 of this title if there are no regulations).

(d) Citizen complaints — Any person may file a complaint with the Administrator or with the Governor of the State in which the school building is located with respect to asbestos-containing material in a school building. If the Administrator or Governor receives a complaint under this subsection containing allegations which provide a reasonable basis to believe that a violation of this chapter has occurred, the Administrator or Governor shall investigate and respond (including taking enforcement action where appropriate) to the complaint within a reasonable period of time.

(e) Citizen petitions

(1) Any person may petition the Administrator to initiate a proceeding for the issuance, amendment, or repeal of a regulation or order under this subchapter.

(2) Such petition shall be filed in the principal office of the Administrator and shall set forth the facts which it is claimed establish that it is necessary to issue, amend, or repeal a regulation or order under this subchapter.

(3) The Administrator may hold a public hearing or may conduct such investigation or proceeding as the Administrator deems appropriate in order to determine whether or not such petition should be granted.

(4) Within 90 days after filing of a petition described in paragraph (1), the Administrator shall either grant or deny the petition. If the Administrator grants such petition, the Administrator shall promptly commence an appropriate proceeding in accordance with this subchapter. If the Administrator denies such petition, the Administrator shall publish in the Federal Register the Administrator's reasons for such denial. The granting or denial of a petition under this subsection shall not affect any deadline or other requirement of this subchapter.

(f) Citizen civil actions with respect to EPA regulations

(1) Any person may commence a civil action without prior notice against the Administrator to compel the Administrator to meet the deadlines in section 2643 of this title for issuing advanced notices of proposed rulemaking, proposing regulations, and promulgating regulations. Any such action shall be brought in the district court of the United States for the District of Columbia.

(2) In any action brought under paragraph (1) in which the court finds the Administrator to be in violation of any deadline in section 2643 of this title, the court shall set forth a schedule for promulgating the regulations required by section 2643 of this title and shall order the Administrator to comply with such schedule. The court may extend any deadline (which has not already occurred) in section 2644(b), (c), or (d) of this title for a period of not more than 6 months, if the court-ordered schedule will result in final promulgation of the pertinent regulations within the extended period. Such deadline extensions

may not be granted by the court beginning 720 days after October 22, 1986.

(3) Section 2619 of this title shall apply to civil actions described in this subsection, except to the extent inconsistent with this subsection.

(g) Failure to attain accreditation; penalty — Any contractor who —

(1) inspects for asbestos-containing material in a school, public or commercial building;

(2) designs or conducts response actions with respect to friable asbestos-containing material in a school, public or commercial building; or

(3) employs individuals to conduct response actions with respect to friable asbestos-containing material in a school, public or commercial building;

and who fails to obtain the accreditation under section 2646 of this title, or in the case of employees to require or provide for the accreditation required, is liable for a civil penalty of not more than $5,000 for each day during which the violation continues, unless such contractor is a direct employee of the Federal Government.

§2648. Emergency authority
[TSCA §208]

(a) Emergency action

(1) Authority — Whenever —

(A) the presence of airborne asbestos or the condition of friable asbestos-containing material in a school building governed by a local educational agency poses an imminent and substantial endangerment to human health or the environment, and

(B) the local educational agency is not taking sufficient action (as determined by the Administrator or the Governor) to respond to the airborne asbestos or friable asbestos-containing material,

the Administrator or the Governor of a State is authorized to act to protect human health or the environment.

(2) Limitations on Governor's action — The Governor of a State shall notify the Administrator within a reasonable period of time before the Governor plans to take an emergency action under this subsection. After such notification, if the Administrator takes an emergency action with respect to the same hazard, the Governor may not carry out (or continue to carry out, if the action has been started) the emergency action.

(3) Notification — The following notification shall be provided before an emergency action is taken under this subsection:

(A) In the case of a Governor taking the action, the Governor shall notify the local educational agency concerned.

(B) In the case of the Administrator taking the action, the Administrator shall notify both the local educational agency concerned and the Governor of the State in which such agency is located.

(4) Cost recovery — The Administrator or the Governor of a State may seek reimbursement for all costs of an emergency action taken under this subsection in the United States District Court for the District of Columbia or for the district in which the emergency action occurred. In any action seeking reimbursement from a local educational agency, the action shall be brought in the United States District Court for the district in which the local educational agency is located.

(b) Injunctive relief — Upon receipt of evidence that the presence of airborne asbestos or the condition of friable asbestos-containing material in a school building governed by a local educational agency poses an imminent and substantial endangerment to human health or the environment —

(1) the Administrator may request the Attorney General to bring suit, or

(2) the Governor of a State may bring suit, to secure such relief as may be necessary to respond to the hazard. The district court of the United States in the district in which the response will be carried out shall have jurisdiction to grant such relief, including injunctive relief.

§2649. State and Federal law
[TSCA §209]

(a) No preemption — Nothing in this subchapter shall be construed, interpreted, or applied to preempt, displace, or supplant any other State or Federal law, whether statutory or common.

(b) Cost and damage awards — Nothing in this subchapter or any standard, regulation, or requirement promulgated pursuant to this subchapter shall be construed or interpreted to preclude any court from awarding costs and damages associated with the abatement, including the removal, of asbestos-containing material, or a portion of such costs, at any time prior to the actual date on which such material is removed.

(c) State may establish more requirements — Nothing in this subchapter shall be construed or interpreted as preempting a State from establishing any additional liability or more stringent requirements with respect to asbestos in school buildings within such State.

(d) No Federal cause of action — Nothing in this subchapter creates a cause of action or in any other way increases or diminishes the liability of any person under any other law.

(e) Intent of Congress — It is not the intent of Congress that this subchapter or rules, regulations, or orders issued pursuant to this subchapter be interpreted as influencing, in either the plaintiff's or defendant's favor, the disposition of any civil action for damages relating to asbestos. This subsection does not affect the authority of any court to make a determination in an adjudicatory proceeding under applicable State law with respect to the admission into evidence or

any other use of this subchapter or rules, regulations, or orders issued pursuant to this subchapter.

§2650. Asbestos contractors and local educational agencies
[TSCA §210]

(a) Study

(1) General requirement — The Administrator shall conduct a study on the availability of liability insurance and other forms of assurance against financial loss which are available to local educational agencies and asbestos contractors with respect to actions required under this subchapter. Such study shall examine the following:

(A) The extent to which liability insurance and other forms of assurance against financial loss are available to local educational agencies and asbestos contractors.

(B) The extent to which the cost of insurance or other forms of assurance against financial loss has increased and the extent to which coverage has become less complete.

(C) The extent to which any limitation in the availability of insurance or other forms of assurance against financial loss is the result of factors other than standards of liability in applicable law.

(D) The extent to which the existence of the regulations required by subsections (c) and (d) of section 2643 of this title and the accreditation of contractors under section 2646 of this title has affected the availability or cost of insurance or other forms of assurance against financial loss.

(E) The extent to which any limitation on the availability of insurance or other forms of assurance against financial loss is inhibiting inspections for asbestos-containing material or the development or implementation of management plans under this subchapter.

(F) Identification of any other impediments to the timely completion of inspections or the development and implementation of management plans under this subchapter.

(2) Interim report — Not later than April 1, 1988, the Administrator shall submit to the Congress an interim report on the progress of the study required by this subsection, along with preliminary findings based on information collected to that date.

(3) Final report — Not later than October 1, 1990, the Administrator shall submit to the Congress a final report on the study required by this subsection, including final findings based on the information collected.

(b) State action — On the basis of the interim report or the final report of the study required by subsection (a) of this section, a State may enact or amend State law to establish or modify a standard of liability for local educational agencies or asbestos contractors with respect to actions required under this subchapter.

§2651. Public protection
[TSCA §211]

(a) Public protection — No State or local educational agency may discriminate against a person in any way, including firing a person who is an employee, because the person provided information relating to a potential violation of this subchapter to any other person, including a State or the Federal Government.

(b) Labor Department review — Any public or private employee or representative of employees who believes he or she has been fired or otherwise discriminated against in violation of subsection (a) of this section may within 90 days after the alleged violation occurs apply to the Secretary of Labor for a review of the firing or alleged discrimination. The review shall be conducted in accordance with section 660(c) of Title 29.

§2652. Asbestos Ombudsman
[TSCA §212]

(a) Appointment — The Administrator shall appoint an Asbestos Ombudsman, who shall carry out the duties described in subsection (b) of this section.

(b) Duties — The duties of the Asbestos Ombudsman are —

(1) to receive complaints, grievances, and requests for information submitted by any person with respect to any aspect of this subchapter,

(2) to render assistance with respect to the complaints, grievances, and requests received, and

(3) to make such recommendations to the Administrator as the Ombudsman considers appropriate.

§2653. EPA study of asbestos-containing material in public buildings
[TSCA §213]

Within 360 days after October 22, 1986, the Administrator shall conduct and submit to the Congress the results of a study which shall —

(1) assess the extent to which asbestos-containing materials are present in public and commercial buildings;

(2) assess the condition of asbestos-containing material in commercial buildings and the likelihood that persons occupying such buildings, including service and maintenance personnel, are, or may be, exposed to asbestos fibers;

(3) consider and report on whether public and commercial buildings should be subject to the same inspection and response action requirements that apply to school buildings;

(4) assess whether existing Federal regulations adequately protect the general public, particularly abatement personnel, from exposure to asbestos during renovation and demolition of such buildings; and

(5) include recommendations that explicitly address whether there is a need to establish standards for, and regulate asbestos exposure in, public and commercial buildings.

§2654. Transitional rules
[TSCA §214]

Any regulation of the Environmental Protection Agency under subchapter I of this chapter which is inconsistent with this subchapter shall not be in effect after October 22, 1986. Any advanced notice of proposed rulemaking, any proposed rule, and any regulation of the Environmental Protection Agency in effect before October 22, 1986, which is consistent with the regulations required under section 2643 of this title shall remain in effect and may be used to meet the requirements of section 2643 of this title, except that any such regulation shall be enforced under this chapter.

§2655. Worker protection
[TSCA §215]

(a) Prohibition on certain activities — Until the local educational agency with authority over a school has submitted a management plan (for the school) which the State Governor has not disapproved as of the end of the period for review and revision of the plan under section 2645 of this title, the local educational agency may not do either of the following in the school:

(1) Perform, or direct an employee to perform, renovations or removal of building materials, except emergency repairs, in the school, unless —

(A) the school is carrying out work under a grant awarded under section 4014 of Title 20; or

(B) an inspection that complies with the requirements of regulations promulgated under section 2643 of this title has been carried out in the school and the agency complies with the following sections of title 40 of the Code of Federal Regulations:

(i) Paragraphs (g), (h), and (i) of section 763.90 (response actions).

(ii) Appendix D to subpart E of part 763 (transport and disposal of asbestos waste).

(2) Perform, or direct an employee to perform, operations and maintenance activities in the school, unless the agency complies with the following sections of title 40 of the Code of Federal Regulations:

(A) Section 763.91 (operations and maintenance), including appendix B to subpart E of part 763.

(B) Paragraph (a)(2) of section 763.92 (training and periodic surveillance).

(b) Employee training and equipment — Any school employee who is directed to conduct emergency repairs involving any building material containing asbestos or suspected of containing asbestos, or to conduct operations and maintenance activities, in a school —

(1) shall be provided the proper training to safely conduct such work in order to prevent potential exposure to asbestos; and

(2) shall be provided the proper equipment and allowed to follow work practices that are necessary to safely conduct such work in order to prevent potential exposure to asbestos.

(c) "Emergency repair" defined — For purposes of this section, the term "emergency repair" means a repair in a school building that was not planned and was in response to a sudden, unexpected event that threatens either —

(1) the health or safety of building occupants; or

(2) the structural integrity of the building.

§2656. Training grants
[TSCA §216]

(a) Grants — The Administrator is authorized to award grants under this section to nonprofit organizations that demonstrate experience in implementing and operating health and safety asbestos training and education programs for workers who are or will be engaged in asbestos-related activities (including State and local governments, colleges and universities, joint labor-management trust funds, and nonprofit government employee organizations) to establish and, or, operate asbestos training programs on a not-for-profit basis. Applications for grants under this subsection shall be submitted in such form and manner, and contain such information, as the Administrator prescribes.

(b) Authorization — Of such sums as are authorized to be appropriated pursuant to section 4021(a) of Title 20 for the fiscal years 1991, 1992, 1993, 1994, and 1995, not more than $5,000,000 are authorized to be appropriated to carry out this section in each such fiscal year.

SUBCHAPTER III — INDOOR RADON ABATEMENT

§2661. National goal
[TSCA §301]

The national long-term goal of the United States with respect to radon levels in buildings is that the air within buildings in the United States should be as free of radon as the ambient air outside of buildings.

§2662. Definitions
[TSCA §302]

For purposes of this subchapter:

(1) The term "local educational agency" means —

(A) any local educational agency as defined in section 7801 of Title 20;

(B) the owner of any nonprofit elementary or secondary school building; and

(C) the governing authority of any school operated pursuant to section 241 of Title 20, as in effect before enactment of the Improving America's Schools Act of 1994, or successor authority, relating to impact aid for children who reside on Federal property.

(2) The term "nonprofit elementary or secondary school" has the meaning given such term by section 2642(8) of this title.

(3) The term "radon" means the radioactive gaseous element and its short-lived decay products produced by the disintegration of the element radium occurring in air, water, soil, or other media.

(4) The term "school building" has the meaning given such term by section 2642(13) of this title.

§2663. EPA citizen's guide
[TSCA §303]

(a) Publication — In order to make continuous progress toward the long-term goal established in section 2661 of this title, the Administrator of the Environmental Protection Agency shall, not later than June 1, 1989, publish and make available to the public an updated version of its document titled "A Citizen's Guide to Radon". The Administrator shall revise and republish the guide as necessary thereafter.

(b) Information included

(1) Action levels — The updated citizen's guide published as provided in subsection (a) of this section shall include a description of a series of action levels indicating the health risk associated with different levels of radon exposure.

(2) Other information — The updated citizen's guide shall also include information with respect to each of the following:

(A) The increased health risk associated with the exposure of potentially sensitive populations to different levels of radon.

(B) The increased health risk associated with the exposure to radon of persons engaged in potentially risk-increasing behavior.

(C) The cost and technological feasibility of reducing radon concentrations within existing and new buildings.

(D) The relationship between short-term and long-term testing techniques and the relationship between (i) measurements based on both such techniques, and (ii) the actions levels set forth as provided in paragraph (1).

(E) Outdoor radon levels around the country.

§2664. Model construction standards and techniques
[TSCA §304]

The Administrator of the Environmental Protection Agency shall develop model construction standards and techniques for controlling radon levels within new buildings. To the maximum extent possible, these standards and techniques should be developed with the assistance of organizations involved in establishing national building construction standards and techniques. The Administrator shall make a draft of the document containing the model standards and techniques available for public review and comment. The model standards and techniques shall provide for geographic differences in construction types and materials, geology, weather, and other variables that may affect radon levels in new buildings. The Administrator shall make final model standards and techniques available to the public by June 1, 1990. The Administrator shall work to ensure that organizations responsible for developing national model building codes, and authorities which regulate building construction within States or political subdivisions within States, adopt the Agency's model standards and techniques.

§2665. Technical assistance to States for radon programs
[TSCA §305]

(a) Required activities — The Administrator (or another Federal department or agency designated by the Administrator) shall develop and implement activities designed to assist State radon programs. These activities may include, but are not limited to, the following:

(1) Establishment of a clearinghouse of radon related information, including mitigation studies, public information materials, surveys of radon levels, and other relevant information.

(2) Operation of a voluntary proficiency program for rating the effectiveness of radon measurement devices and methods, the effectiveness of radon mitigation devices and methods, and the effectiveness of private firms and individuals offering radon-related architecture, design, engineering, measurement, and mitigation services. The proficiency program under this subparagraph shall be in operation within one year after October 28, 1988.

(3) Design and implementation of training seminars for State and local officials and private and professional firms dealing with radon and addressing topics such as monitoring, analysis, mitigation, health effects, public information, and program design.

(4) Publication of public information materials concerning radon health risks and methods of radon mitigation.

(5) Operation of cooperative projects between the Environmental Protection Agency's Radon Action Program and the State's radon program. Such projects shall include the Home Evaluation Program, in which the Environmental Protection Agency evaluates homes and States demonstrate mitigation methods in these homes. To the maximum extent practicable, consistent with the objectives of the evaluation and demonstration, homes of low-income persons should be selected for evaluation and demonstration.

(6) Demonstration of radon mitigation methods in various types of structures and in various geographic settings and publication of findings. In the case of demonstration of such methods in homes, the Administrator should select homes of low-income persons, to the maximum extent practicable and consistent with the objectives of the demonstration.

(7) Establishment of a national data base with data organized by State concerning the location and amounts of radon.

(8) Development and demonstration of methods of radon measurement and mitigation that take into account unique characteristics, if any, of nonresidential buildings housing child care facilities.

(b) Discretionary assistance — Upon request of a State, the Administrator (or another Federal department or agency designated by the Administrator) may provide technical assistance to such State in development or implementation of programs addressing radon. Such assistance may include, but is not limited to, the following:

(1) Design and implementation of surveys of the location and occurrence of radon within a State.

(2) Design and implementation of public information and education programs.

(3) Design and implementation of State programs to control radon in existing or new structures.

(4) Assessment of mitigation alternatives in unusual or unconventional structures.

(5) Design and implementation of methods for radon measurement and mitigation for non-residential buildings housing child care facilities.

(c) Information provided to professional organizations — The Administrator, or another Federal department or agency designated by the Administrator, shall provide appropriate information concerning technology and methods of radon assessment and mitigation to professional organizations representing private firms involved in building design, engineering, and construction.

(d) Proficiency rating program and training seminar

(1) Authorization — There is authorized to be appropriated not more than $1,500,000 for the purposes of initially establishing the proficiency rating program under subsection (a)(2) of this section and the training seminars under subsection (a)(3) of this section.

(2) Charge imposed — To cover the operating costs of such proficiency rating program and training seminars, the Administrator shall impose on persons applying for a proficiency rating and on private and professional firms participating in training seminars such charges as may be necessary to defray the costs of the program or seminars. No such charge may be imposed on any State or local government.

167

(3) Special account — Funds derived from the charges imposed under paragraph (2) shall be deposited in a special account in the Treasury. Amounts in the special account are authorized to be appropriated only for purposes of administering such proficiency rating program or training seminars or for reimbursement of funds appropriated to the Administrator to initially establish such program or seminars.

(4) Reimbursement of general fund — During the first three years of the program and seminars, the Administrator shall make every effort, consistent with the goals and successful operation of the program and seminars, to set charges imposed under paragraph (2) so that an amount in excess of operation costs is collected. Such excess amount shall be used to reimburse the General Fund of the Treasury for the full amount appropriated to initially establish the program and seminars.

(5) Research — The Administrator shall, in conjunction with other Federal agencies, conduct research to develop, test, and evaluate radon and radon progeny measurement methods and protocols. The purpose of such research shall be to assess the ability of those methods and protocols to accurately assess exposure to radon progeny. Such research shall include —

(A) conducting comparisons among radon and radon progeny measurement techniques;

(B) developing measurement protocols for different building types under varying operating conditions; and

(C) comparing the exposures estimated by stationary monitors and protocols to those measured by personal monitors, and issue guidance documents that —

(i) provide information on the results of research conducted under this paragraph; and

(ii) describe model State radon measurement and mitigation programs.

(6) Mandatory proficiency testing program study

(A) The Administrator shall conduct a study to determine the feasibility of establishing a mandatory proficiency testing program that would require that —

(i) any product offered for sale, or device used in connection with a service offered to the public, for the measurement of radon meets minimum performance criteria; and

(ii) any operator of a device, or person employing a technique, used in connection with a service offered to the public for the measurement of radon meets a minimum level of proficiency.

(B) The study shall also address procedures for —

(i) ordering the recall of any product sold for the measurement of radon which does not meet minimum performance criteria;

(ii) ordering the discontinuance of any service offered to the public for the measurement of radon which does not meet minimum performance criteria; and

(iii) establishing adequate quality assurance requirements for each company offering radon measurement services to the public to follow.

The study shall identify enforcement mechanisms necessary to the success of the program. The Administrator shall report the findings of the study with recommendations to Congress by March 1, 1991.

(7) User fee — In addition to any charge imposed pursuant to paragraph (2), the Administrator shall collect user fees from persons seeking certification under the radon proficiency program in an amount equal to $1,500,000 to cover the Environmental Protection Agency's cost of conducting research pursuant to paragraph (5) for each of the fiscal years 1991, 1992, 1993, 1994, and 1995. Such funds shall be deposited in the account established pursuant to paragraph (3).

(e) Authorization

(1) There is authorized to be appropriated for the purposes of carrying out sections 2663, 2664, and 2665 of this title an amount not to exceed $3,000,000 for each of fiscal years 1989, 1990, and 1991.

(2) No amount appropriated under this subsection may be used by the Environmental Protection Agency to administer the grant program under section 2666 of this title.

(3) No amount appropriated under this subsection may be used to cover the costs of the proficiency rating program under subsection (a) (2) of this section.

§2666. Grant assistance to States for radon programs
[TSCA §306]

(a) In general — For each fiscal year, upon application of the Governor of a State, the Administrator may make a grant, subject to such terms and conditions as the Administrator considers appropriate, under this section to the State for the purpose of assisting the State in the development and implementation of programs for the assessment and mitigation of radon.

(b) Application — An application for a grant under this section in any fiscal year shall contain such information as the Administrator shall require, including each of the following:

(1) A description of the seriousness and extent of radon exposure in the State.

(2) An identification of the State agency which

has the primary responsibility for radon programs and which will receive the grant, a description of the roles and responsibilities of the lead State agency and any other State agencies involved in radon programs, and description of the roles and responsibilities of any municipal, district, or area-wide organization involved in radon programs.

(3) A description of the activities and programs related to radon which the State proposes in such year.

(4) A budget specifying Federal and State funding of each element of activity of the grant application.

(5) A 3-year plan which outlines long range program goals and objectives, tasks necessary to achieve them, and resource requirements for the entire 3-year period, including anticipated State funding levels and desired Federal funding levels. This clause shall apply only for the initial year in which a grant application is made.

(c) Eligible activities

Activities eligible for grant assistance under this section are the following:

(1) Survey of radon levels, including special surveys of geographic areas or classes of buildings (such as, among others, public buildings, school buildings, high-risk residential construction types).

(2) Development of public information and educational materials concerning radon assessment, mitigation, and control programs.

(3) Implementation of programs to control radon in existing and new structures.

(4) Purchase by the State of radon measurement equipment or devices.

(5) Purchase and maintenance of analytical equipment connected to radon measurement and analysis, including costs of calibration of such equipment.

(6) Payment of costs of Environmental Protection Agency-approved training programs related to radon for permanent State or local employees.

(7) Payment of general overhead and program administration costs.

(8) Development of a data storage and management system for information concerning radon occurrence, levels, and programs.

(9) Payment of costs of demonstration of radon mitigation methods and technologies as approved by the Administrator, including State participation in the Environmental Protection Agency Home Evaluation Program.

(10) A toll-free radon hotline to provide information and technical assistance.

(d) Preference to certain States — Beginning

in fiscal year 1991, the Administrator shall give a preference for grant assistance under this section to States that have made reasonable efforts to ensure the adoption, by the authorities which regulate building construction within that State or political subdivisions within States, of the model construction standards and techniques for new buildings developed under section 2664 of this title.

(e) Priority activities and projects — The

Administrator shall support eligible activities contained in State applications with the full amount of available funds. In the event that State applications for funds exceed the total funds available in a fiscal year, the Administrator shall give priority to activities or projects proposed by States based on each of the following criteria:

(1) The seriousness and extent of the radon contamination problem to be addressed.

(2) The potential for the activity or project to bring about reduction in radon levels.

(3) The potential for development of innovative radon assessment techniques, mitigation measures as approved by the Administrator, or program management approaches which may be of use to other States.

(4) Any other uniform criteria that the Administrator deems necessary to promote the goals of the grant program and that the Administrator provides to States before the application process.

(f) Federal share — The Federal share of the cost

of radon program activities implemented with Federal assistance under this section in any fiscal year shall not exceed 75 percent of the costs incurred by the State in implementing such program in the first year of a grant to such State, 60 percent in the second year, and 50 percent in the third year. Federal assistance shall be made on the condition that the non-Federal share is provided from non-Federal funds.

(g) Assistance to local governments — States

may, at the Governor's discretion, use funds from grants under this section to assist local governments in implementation of activities eligible for assistance under paragraphs (2), (3), and (6) of subsection (c) of this section.

(h) Information

(1) The Administrator may request such information, data, and reports developed by the State as he considers necessary to make the determination of continuing eligibility under this section.

(2) Any State receiving funds under this section shall provide to the Administrator all radon-related information generated in its activities, including the results of radon surveys, mitigation demonstration projects, and risk communication studies.

(3) Any State receiving funds under this section shall maintain, and make available to the public, a list of firms and individuals within the State that have received a passing rating under the Environmental Protection Agency proficiency rating program referred to in section 2665(a)(2) of this title. The list shall also include the address

and phone number of such firms and individuals, together with the proficiency rating received by each. The Administrator shall make such list available to the public at appropriate locations in each State which does not receive funds under this section unless the State assumes such responsibility.

(i) Limitations

(1) No grant may be made under this section in any fiscal year to a State which in the preceding fiscal year received a grant under this section unless the Administrator determines that such State satisfactorily implemented the activities funded by the grant in such preceding fiscal year.

(2) The costs of implementing paragraphs (4) and (9) of subsection (c) of this section shall not in the aggregate exceed 50 percent of the amount of any grant awarded under this section to a State in a fiscal year. In implementing such paragraphs, a State should make every effort, consistent with the goals and successful operation of the State radon program, to give a preference to low-income persons.

(3) The costs of general overhead and program administration under subsection (c)(7) of this section shall not exceed 25 percent of the amount of any grant awarded under this section to a State in a fiscal year.

(4) A State may use funds received under this section for financial assistance to persons only to the extent such assistance is related to demonstration projects or the purchase and analysis of radon measurement devices.

(j) Authorization

(1) There is authorized to be appropriated for grant assistance under this section an amount not to exceed $10,000,000 for each of fiscal years 1989, 1990, and 1991.

(2) There is authorized to be appropriated for the purpose of administering the grant program under this section such sums as may be necessary for each of such fiscal years.

(3) Notwithstanding any other provision of this section, not more than 10 percent of the amount appropriated to carry out this section may be used to make grants to any one State.

(4) Funds not obligated to States in the fiscal year for which funds are appropriated under this section shall remain available for obligation during the next fiscal year.

(5) No amount appropriated under this subsection may be used to cover the costs of the proficiency rating program under section 2665(a)(2) of this title.

§2667. Radon in schools
[TSCA §307]
(a) Study of radon in schools

(1) Authority — The Administrator shall conduct a study for the purpose of determining the extent of radon contamination in the Nation's school buildings.

(2) List of high probability areas — In carrying out such study, the Administrator shall identify and compile a list of areas within the United States which the Administrator determines have a high probability of including schools which have elevated levels of radon.

(3) Basis of list — In compiling such list, the Administrator shall make such determinations on the basis of, among other things, each of the following:

(A) Geological data.

(B) Data on high radon levels in homes and other structures nearby any such school.

(C) Physical characteristics of the school buildings.

(4) Survey — In conducting such study the Administrator shall design a survey which when completed allows Congress to characterize the extent of radon contamination in schools in each State. The survey shall include testing from a representative sample of schools in each high-risk area identified in paragraph (1) and shall include additional testing, to the extent resources are available for such testing. The survey also shall include any reliable testing data supplied by States, schools, or other parties.

(5) Assistance

(A) The Administrator shall make available to the appropriate agency of each State, as designated by the Governor of such State, a list of high risk areas within each State, including a delineation of such areas and any other data available to the Administrator for schools in that State. To assist such agencies, the Administrator also shall provide guidance and data detailing the risks associated with high radon levels, technical guidance and related information concerning testing for radon within schools, and methods of reducing radon levels.

(B) In addition to the assistance authorized by subparagraph (A), the Administrator is authorized to make available to the appropriate agency of each State, as designated by the Governor of such State, devices suitable for use by such agencies in conducting tests for radon within the schools under the jurisdiction of any such State agency. The Administrator is authorized to make available to such agencies the use of laboratories of the Environmental Protection Agency, or to recommend laboratories, to evaluate any such devices for the presence of radon levels.

(6) Diagnostic and remedial efforts — The Administrator is authorized to select, from high-risk areas identified in paragraph (2), school buildings for purposes of enabling the Administrator to undertake diagnostic and remedial efforts to reduce the levels of radon in such school buildings. Such diagnostic and remedial efforts shall be carried out with a view to developing technology and expertise for the purpose of making such technology and expertise available to any local educational

agency and the several States.

(7) Status report — On or before October 1, 1989, the Administrator shall submit to the Congress a status report with respect to action taken by the Administrator in conducting the study required by this section, including the results of the Administrator's diagnostic and remedial work. On or before October 1, 1989, the Administrator shall submit a final report setting forth the results of the study conducted pursuant to this section, including the results of the Administrator's diagnostic and remedial work, and the recommendations of the Administrator.

(b) Authorization — For the purpose of carrying out the provisions of paragraph (6) of subsection (a) of this section, there are authorized to be appropriated such sums, not to exceed $500,000, as may be necessary. For the purpose of carrying out the provisions of this section other than such paragraph (6), there are authorized to be appropriated such sums, not to exceed $1,000,000, as may be necessary.

§2668. Regional radon training centers
[TSCA §308]

(a) Funding program — Upon application of colleges, universities, institutions of higher learning, or consortia of such institutions, the Administrator may make a grant or cooperative agreement, subject to such terms and conditions as the Administrator considers appropriate, under this section to the applicant for the purpose of establishing and operating a regional radon training center.

(b) Purpose of centers — The purpose of a regional radon training center is to develop information and provide training to Federal and State officials, professional and private firms, and the public regarding the health risks posed by radon and demonstrated methods of radon measurement and mitigation.

(c) Applications — Any colleges, universities, institutions of higher learning or consortia of such institutions may submit an application for funding under this section. Such applications shall be submitted to the Administrator in such form and containing such information as the Administrator may require.

(d) Selection criteria — The Administrator shall support at least 3 eligible applications with the full amount of available funds. The Administrator shall select recipients of funding under this section to ensure that funds are equitably allocated among regions of the United States, and on the basis of each of the following criteria:

(1) The extent to which the applicant's program will promote the purpose described in subsection (b) of this section.

(2) The demonstrated expertise of the applicant regarding radon measurement and mitigation methods and other radon-related issues.

(3) The demonstrated expertise of the appli-

cant in radon training and in activities relating to information development and dissemination.

(4) The seriousness of the radon problem in the region.

(5) The geographical coverage of the proposed center.

(6) Any other uniform criteria that the Administrator deems necessary to promote the purpose described in subsection (b) of this section and that the Administrator provides to potential applicants prior to the application process.

(e) Termination of funding — No funding may be given under this section in any fiscal year to an applicant which in the preceding fiscal year received funding under this section unless the Administrator determines that the recipient satisfactorily implemented the activities that were funded in the preceding year.

(f) Authorization — There is authorized to be appropriated to carry out the program under this section not to exceed $1,000,000 for each of fiscal years 1989, 1990, and 1991.

§2669. Study of radon in Federal buildings
[TSCA §309]

(a) Study requirement — The head of each Federal department or agency that owns a Federal building shall conduct a study for the purpose of determining the extent of radon contamination in such buildings. Such study shall include, in the case of a Federal building using a nonpublic water source (such as a well or other groundwater), radon contamination of the water.

(b) High-risk Federal buildings

(1) The Administrator shall identify and compile a list of areas within the United States which the Administrator, in consultation with Federal departments and agencies, determines have a high probability of including Federal buildings which have elevated levels of radon.

(2) In compiling such list, the Administrator shall make such determinations on the basis of, among other things, the following:

(A) Geological data.

(B) Data on high radon levels in homes and other structures near any such Federal building.

(C) Physical characteristics of the Federal buildings.

(c) Study designs — Studies required under subsection (a) of this section shall be based on design criteria specified by the Administrator. The head of each Federal department or agency conducting such a study shall submit, not later than July 1, 1989, a study design to the Administrator for approval. The study design shall follow the most recent Environmental Protection Agency guidance documents, including "A Citizen's Guide to Radon"; the "Interim Protocol for Screening and Follow Up: Radon and

Radon Decay Products Measurements"; the "Interim Indoor Radon & Radon Decay Product Measurement Protocol"; and any other recent guidance documents. The study design shall include testing data from a representative sample of Federal buildings in each high-risk area identified in subsection (b) of this section. The study design also shall include additional testing data to the extent resources are available, including any reliable data supplied by Federal agencies, States, or other parties.

(d) Information on risks and testing

(1) The Administrator shall provide to the departments or agencies conducting studies under subsection (a) of this section the following:

(A) Guidance and data detailing the risks associated with high radon levels.

(B) Technical guidance and related information concerning testing for radon within Federal buildings and water supplies.

(C) Technical guidance and related information concerning methods for reducing radon levels.

(2) In addition to the assistance required by paragraph (1), the Administrator is authorized to make available, on a cost reimbursable basis, to the departments or agencies conducting studies under subsection (a) of this section devices suitable for use by such departments or agencies in conducting tests for radon within Federal buildings. For the purpose of assisting such departments or agencies in evaluating any such devices for the presence of radon levels, the Administrator is authorized to recommend laboratories or to make available to such departments or agencies, on a cost reimbursable basis, the use of laboratories of the Environmental Protection Agency.

(e) Study deadline — Not later than June 1, 1990, the head of each Federal department or agency conducting a study under subsection (a) of this section shall complete the study and provide the study to the Administrator.

(f) Report to Congress — Not later than October 1, 1990, the Administrator shall submit a report to the Congress describing the results of the studies conducted pursuant to subsection (a) of this section.

§2670. Regulations
[TSCA §310]

The Administrator is authorized to issue such regulations as may be necessary to carry out the provisions of this subchapter.

§2671. Additional authorizations
[TSCA §311]

Amounts authorized to be appropriated in this subchapter for purposes of carrying out the provisions of this subchapter are in addition to amounts authorized to be appropriated under other provisions of law for radon-related activities.

SUBCHAPTER IV—LEAD EXPOSURE REDUCTION

§2681. Definitions
[TSCA §401]

For the purposes of this subchapter:

(1) Abatement — The term "abatement" means any set of measures designed to permanently eliminate lead-based paint hazards in accordance with standards established by the Administrator under this subchapter. Such term includes —

(A) the removal of lead-based paint and lead-contaminated dust, the permanent containment or encapsulation of lead-based paint, the replacement of lead-painted surfaces or fixtures, and the removal or covering of lead-contaminated soil; and

(B) all preparation, cleanup, disposal, and postabatement clearance testing activities associated with such measures.

(2) Accessible surface — The term "accessible surface" means an interior or exterior surface painted with lead-based paint that is accessible for a young child to mouth or chew.

(3) Deteriorated paint — The term "deteriorated paint" means any interior or exterior paint that is peeling, chipping, chalking or cracking or any paint located on an interior or exterior surface or fixture that is damaged or deteriorated.

(4) Evaluation — The term "evaluation" means risk assessment, inspection, or risk assessment and inspection.

(5) Friction surface — The term "friction surface" means an interior or exterior surface that is subject to abrasion or friction, including certain window, floor, and stair surfaces.

(6) Impact surface — The term "impact surface" means an interior or exterior surface that is subject to damage by repeated impacts, for example, certain parts of door frames.

(7) Inspection — The term "inspection" means (A) a surface-by-surface investigation to determine the presence of lead-based paint, as provided in section 4822(c) of Title 42, and (B) the provision of a report explaining the results of the investigation.

(8) Interim controls — The term "interim controls" means a set of measures designed to reduce temporarily human exposure or likely exposure to lead-based paint hazards, including specialized cleaning, repairs, maintenance, painting, temporary containment, ongoing monitoring of lead-based paint hazards or potential hazards, and the establishment and operation of management and resident education programs.

(9) Lead-based paint — The term "lead-based paint" means paint or other surface coatings that contain lead in excess of 1.0 milligrams per centimeter squared or 0.5 percent by weight or (A) in the case of paint or other surface coatings on target

housing, such lower level as may be established by the Secretary of Housing and Urban Development, as defined in section 4822(c) of Title 42, or (B) in the case of any other paint or surface coatings, such other level as may be established by the Administrator.

(10) Lead-based paint hazard — The term "lead-based paint hazard" means any condition that causes exposure to lead from lead-contaminated dust, lead-contaminated soil, lead-contaminated paint that is deterio-rated or present in accessible surfaces, friction surfaces, or impact surfaces that would result in adverse human health effects as established by the Administrator under this subchapter.

(11) Lead-contaminated dust — The term "lead-contaminated dust" means surface dust in residential dwellings that contains an area or mass concentration of lead in excess of levels determined by the Administrator under this subchapter to pose a threat of adverse health effects in pregnant women or young children.

(12) Lead-contaminated soil — The term "lead-contaminated soil" means bare soil on residential real property that contains lead at or in excess of the levels determined to be hazardous to human health by the Administrator under this subchapter.

(13) Reduction — The term "reduction" means measures designed to reduce or eliminate human exposure to lead-based paint hazards through methods including interim controls and abatement.

(14) Residential dwelling — The term "residential dwelling" means —

(A) a single-family dwelling, including attached structures such as porches and stoops; or

(B) a single-family dwelling unit in a structure that contains more than 1 separate residential dwelling unit, and in which each such unit is used or occupied, or intended to be used or occupied, in whole or in part, as the home or residence of 1 or more persons.

(15) Residential real property — The term "residential real property" means real property on which there is situated 1 or more residential dwellings used or occupied, or intended to be used or occupied, in whole or in part, as the home or residence of 1 or more persons.

(16) Risk assessment — The term "risk assessment" means an on-site investigation to determine and report the existence, nature, severity and location of lead-based paint hazards in residential dwellings, including —

(A) information gathering regarding the age and history of the housing and occupancy by children under age 6;

(B) visual inspection;

(C) limited wipe sampling or other environmental sampling techniques;

(D) other activity as may be appropriate; and

(E) provision of a report explaining the results of the investigation.

(17) Target housing — The term "target housing" means any housing constructed prior to 1978, except housing for the elderly or persons with disabilities (unless any child who is less than 6 years of age resides or is expected to reside in such housing for the elderly or persons with disabilities) or any 0-bedroom dwelling. In the case of jurisdictions which banned the sale or use of lead-based paint prior to 1978, the Secretary of Housing and Urban Development, at the Secretary's discretion, may designate an earlier date.

§2682. Lead-based paint activities training and certification
[TSCA §402]
(a) Regulations

(1) In general — Not later than 18 months after October 28, 1992, the Administrator shall, in consultation with the Secretary of Labor, the Secretary of Housing and Urban Development, and the Secretary of Health and Human Services (acting through the Director of the National Institute for Occupational Safety and Health), promulgate final regulations governing lead-based paint activities to ensure that individuals engaged in such activities are properly trained; that training programs are accredited; and that contractors engaged in such activities are certified. Such regulations shall contain standards for performing lead-based paint activities, taking into account reliability, effectiveness, and safety. Such regulations shall require that all risk assessment, inspection, and abatement activities performed in target housing shall be performed by certified contractors, as such term is defined in section 4851b of Title 42. The provisions of this section shall supersede the provisions set forth under the heading "Lead Abatement Training and Certification" and under the heading "Training Grants" in title III of the Act entitled "An Act making appropriations for the Departments of Veterans Affairs and Housing and Urban Development, and for sundry independent agencies, commissions, corporations, and offices for the fiscal year ending September 30, 1992, and for other purposes", Pub. L. 102-139 [105 Stat. 765, 42 U.S.C. §4822 note], and upon October 28, 1992, the provisions set forth in such public law under such headings shall cease to have any force and effect.

(2) Accreditation of training programs — Final regulations promulgated under paragraph (1) shall contain specific requirements for the accreditation of lead-based paint activities training programs for workers, supervisors, inspectors and planners, and other individuals involved in lead-based paint activities, including, but not limited to, each of the following:

(A) Minimum requirements for the accreditation of training providers.

(B) Minimum training curriculum requirements.

(C) Minimum training hour requirements.

(D) Minimum hands-on training requirements.

(E) Minimum trainee competency and proficiency requirements.

(F) Minimum requirements for training program quality control.

(3) Accreditation and certification fees—

The Administrator (or the State in the case of an authorized State program) shall impose a fee on —

(A) persons operating training programs accredited under this subchapter; and

(B) lead-based paint activities contractors certified in accordance with paragraph (1).

The fees shall be established at such level as is necessary to cover the costs of administering and enforcing the standards and regulations under this section which are applicable to such programs and contractors. The fee shall not be imposed on any State, local government, or nonprofit training program. The Administrator (or the State in the case of an authorized State program) may waive the fee for lead-based paint activities contractors under subparagraph (A) for the purpose of training their own employees.

(b) Lead-based paint activities — For purposes of this subchapter, the term "lead-based paint activities" means —

(1) in the case of target housing, risk assessment, inspection, and abatement; and

(2) in the case of any public building constructed before 1978, commercial building, bridge, or other structure or superstructure, identification of lead-based paint and materials containing lead-based paint, deleading, removal of lead from bridges, and demolition.

For purposes of paragraph (2), the term "deleading" means activities conducted by a person who offers to eliminate lead-based paint or lead-based paint hazards or to plan such activities.

(c) Renovation and remodeling

(1) Guidelines — In order to reduce the risk of exposure to lead in connection with renovation and remodeling of target housing, public buildings constructed before 1978, and commercial buildings, the Administrator shall, within 18 months after October 28, 1992, promulgate guidelines for the conduct of such renovation and remodeling activities which may create a risk of exposure to dangerous levels of lead. The Administrator shall disseminate such guidelines to persons engaged in such renovation and remodeling through hardware and paint stores, employee organizations, trade groups, State and local agencies, and through other appropriate means.

(2) Study of certification — The Administrator shall conduct a study of the extent to which persons engaged in various types of renovation and remodeling activities in target housing, public buildings constructed before 1978, and commercial buildings are exposed to lead in the conduct of such activities or disturb lead and create a lead-based paint hazard on a regular or occasional basis. The Administrator shall complete such study and publish the results thereof within 30 months after October 28, 1992.

(3) Certification determination — Within 4 years after October 28, 1992, the Administrator shall revise the regulations under subsection (a) of this section to apply the regulations to renovation or remodeling activities in target housing, public buildings constructed before 1978, and commercial buildings that create lead-based paint hazards. In determining which contractors are engaged in such activities, the Administrator shall utilize the results of the study under paragraph (2) and consult with the representatives of labor organizations, lead-based paint activities contractors, persons engaged in remodeling and renovation, experts in lead health effects, and others. If the Administrator determines that any category of contractors engaged in renovation or remodeling does not require certification, the Administrator shall publish an explanation of the basis for that determination.

§2683. Identification of dangerous levels of lead

[TSCA §403]

Within 18 months after October 28, 1992, the Administrator shall promulgate regulations which shall identify, for purposes of this subchapter and the Residential Lead-Based Paint Hazard Reduction Act of 1992 [42 U.S.C. §§4851 *et seq.*], lead-based paint hazards, lead-contaminated dust, and lead-contaminated soil.

§2684. Authorized State programs

[TSCA §404]

(a) Approval — Any State which seeks to administer and enforce the standards, regulations, or other requirements established under section 2682 or 2686 of this title, or both, may, after notice and opportunity for public hearing, develop and submit to the Administrator an application, in such form as the Administrator shall require, for authorization of such a State program. Any such State may also certify to the Administrator at the time of submitting such program that the State program meets the requirements of paragraphs (1) and (2) of subsection (b) of this section. Upon submission of such certification, the State program shall be deemed to be authorized under this section, and shall apply in such State in lieu of the corresponding Federal program under section 2682 or 2686 of this title, or both, as the case may be, until such time as the Administrator disapproves the program or withdraws the authorization.

(b) Approval or disapproval — Within 180 days following submission of an application under subsection (a) of this section, the Administrator shall approve or disapprove the application. The Administrator may approve the application only if, after notice and after opportunity for public hearing, the Administrator finds that —

(1) the State program is at least as protective of human health and the environment as the Federal program under section 2682 or 2686 of this title, or both, as the case may be, and

(2) such State program provides adequate enforcement.

Upon authorization of a State program under this section, it shall be unlawful for any person to violate or fail or refuse to comply with any requirement of such program.

(c) Withdrawal of authorization — If a State is not administering and enforcing a program authorized under this section in compliance with standards, regulations, and other requirements of this subchapter, the Administrator shall so notify the State and, if corrective action is not completed within a reasonable time, not to exceed 180 days, the Administrator shall withdraw authorization of such program and establish a Federal program pursuant to this subchapter.

(d) Model State program — Within 18 months after October 28, 1992, the Administrator shall promulgate a model State program which may be adopted by any State which seeks to administer and enforce a State program under this subchapter. Such model program shall, to the extent practicable, encourage States to utilize existing State and local certification and accreditation programs and procedures. Such program shall encourage reciprocity among the States with respect to the certification under section 2682 of this title.

(e) Other State requirements — Nothing in this subchapter shall be construed to prohibit any State or political subdivision thereof from imposing any requirements which are more stringent than those imposed by this subchapter.

(f) State and local certification — The regulations under this subchapter shall, to the extent appropriate, encourage States to seek program authorization and to use existing State and local certification and accreditation procedures, except that a State or local government shall not require more than 1 certification under this section for any lead-based paint activities contractor to carry out lead-based paint activities in the State or political subdivision thereof.

(g) Grants to States — The Administrator is authorized to make grants to States to develop and carry out authorized State programs under this section. The grants shall be subject to such terms and conditions as the Administrator may establish to further the purposes of this subchapter.

(h) Enforcement by Administrator — If a State does not have a State program authorized under this section and in effect by the date which is 2 years after promulgation of the regulations under section 2682 or 2686 of this title, the Administrator shall, by such date, establish a Federal program for section 2682 or 2686 of this title (as the case may be) for such State and administer and enforce such program in such State.

§2685. Lead abatement and measurement [TSCA §405]

(a) Program to promote lead exposure abatement — The Administrator, in cooperation with other appropriate Federal departments and agencies, shall conduct a comprehensive program to promote safe, effective, and affordable monitoring, detection, and abatement of lead-based paint and other lead exposure hazards.

(b) Standards for environmental sampling laboratories

(1) The Administrator shall establish protocols, criteria, and minimum performance standards for laboratory analysis of lead in paint films, soil, and dust. Within 2 years after October 28, 1992, the Administrator, in consultation with the Secretary of Health and Human Services, shall establish a program to certify laboratories as qualified to test substances for lead content unless the Administrator determines, by the date specified in this paragraph, that effective voluntary accreditation programs are in place and operating on a nationwide basis at the time of such determination. To be certified under such program, a laboratory shall, at a minimum, demonstrate an ability to test substances accurately for lead content.

(2) Not later than 24 months after October 28, 1992, and annually thereafter, the Administrator shall publish and make available to the public a list of certified or accredited environmental sampling laboratories.

(3) If the Administrator determines under paragraph (1) that effective voluntary accreditation programs are in place for environmental sampling laboratories, the Administrator shall review the performance and effectiveness of such programs within 3 years after such determination. If, upon such review, the Administrator determines that the voluntary accreditation programs are not effective in assuring the quality and consistency of laboratory analyses, the Administrator shall, not more than 12 months thereafter, establish a certification program that meets the requirements of paragraph (1).

(c) Exposure studies

(1) The Secretary of Health and Human Services (hereafter in this subsection referred to as the "Secretary"), acting through the Director of the Centers for Disease Control, (CDC), and the Director of the National Institute of Environmental

Health Sciences, shall jointly conduct a study of the sources of lead exposure in children who have elevated blood lead levels (or other indicators of elevated lead body burden), as defined by the Director of the Centers for Disease Control.

(2) The Secretary, in consultation with the Director of the National Institute for Occupational Safety and Health, shall conduct a comprehensive study of means to reduce hazardous occupational lead abatement exposures. This study shall include, at a minimum, each of the following —

(A) Surveillance and intervention capability in the States to identify and prevent hazardous exposures to lead abatement workers.

(B) Demonstration of lead abatement control methods and devices and work practices to identify and prevent hazardous lead exposures in the workplace.

(C) Evaluation, in consultation with the National Institute of Environmental Health Sciences, of health effects of low and high levels of occupational lead exposures on reproductive, neurological, renal, and cardiovascular health.

(D) Identification of high risk occupational settings to which prevention activities and resources should be targeted.

(E) A study assessing the potential exposures and risks from lead to janitorial and custodial workers.

(3) The studies described in paragraphs (1) and (2) shall, as appropriate, examine the relative contributions to elevated lead body burden from each of the following:

(A) Drinking water.

(B) Food.

(C) Lead-based paint and dust from lead-based paint.

(D) Exterior sources such as ambient air and lead in soil.

(E) Occupational exposures, and other exposures that the Secretary determines to be appropriate.

(4) Not later than 30 months after October 28, 1992, the Secretary shall submit a report to the Congress concerning the studies described in paragraphs (1) and (2).

(d) Public education

(1) The Administrator, in conjunction with the Secretary of Health and Human Services, acting through the Director of the Agency for Toxic Substances and Disease Registry, and in conjunction with the Secretary of Housing and Urban Development, shall sponsor public education and outreach activities to increase public awareness of —

(A) the scope and severity of lead poisoning from household sources;

(B) potential exposure to sources of lead in schools and childhood day care centers;

(C) the implications of exposures for men and women, particularly those of childbearing age;

(D) the need for careful, quality, abatement and management actions;

(E) the need for universal screening of children;

(F) other components of a lead poisoning prevention program;

(G) the health consequences of lead exposure resulting from lead-based paint hazards;

(H) risk assessment and inspection methods for lead-based paint hazards; and

(I) measures to reduce the risk of lead exposure from lead-based paint.

(2) The activities described in paragraph (1) shall be designed to provide educational services and information to —

(A) health professionals;

(B) the general public, with emphasis on parents of young children;

(C) homeowners, landlords, and tenants;

(D) consumers of home improvement products;

(E) the residential real estate industry; and

(F) the home renovation industry.

(3) In implementing the activities described in paragraph (1), the Administrator shall assure coordination with the President's Commission on Environmental Quality's education and awareness campaign on lead poisoning.

(4) The Administrator, in consultation with the Chairman of the Consumer Product Safety Commission, shall develop information to be distributed by retailers of home improvement products to provide consumers with practical information related to the hazards of renovation and remodeling where lead-based paint may be present.

(e) Technical assistance

(1) Clearinghouse — Not later than 6 months after October 28, 1992, the Administrator shall establish, in consultation with the Secretary of Housing and Urban Development and the Director of the Centers for Disease Control, a National Clearinghouse on Childhood Lead Poisoning (hereinafter in this section referred to as "Clearinghouse"). The Clearinghouse shall —

(A) collect, evaluate, and disseminate current information on the assessment and reduction of lead-based paint hazards, adverse health effects, sources of exposure, detection and risk assessment methods, environmental hazards abatement, and clean-up standards;

(B) maintain a rapid-alert system to inform certified lead-based paint activities contractors of significant developments in research related to lead-based paint hazards; and

(C) perform any other duty that the Administrator determines necessary to achieve the purposes of this chapter.

(2) Hotline — Not later than 6 months after October 28, 1992, the Administrator, in cooperation with other Federal agencies and with State and local governments, shall establish a single lead-based paint hazard hotline to provide the public with answers to questions about lead poisoning prevention and referrals to the Clearinghouse for technical information.

(f) Products for lead-based paint activities — Not later than 30 months after October 28, 1992, the President shall, after notice and opportunity for comment, establish by rule appropriate criteria, testing protocols, and performance characteristics as are necessary to ensure, to the greatest extent possible and consistent with the purposes and policy of this subchapter, that lead-based paint hazard evaluation and reduction products introduced into commerce after a period specified in the rule are effective for the intended use described by the manufacturer. The rule shall identify the types or classes of products that are subject to such rule. The President, in implementation of the rule, shall, to the maximum extent possible, utilize independent testing laboratories, as appropriate, and consult with such entities and others in developing the rules. The President may delegate the authorities under this subsection to the Environmental Protection Agency or the Secretary of Commerce or such other appropriate agency.

§2686. Lead hazard information pamphlet
[TSCA §406]
(a) Lead hazard information pamphlet — Not later than 2 years after October 28, 1992, after notice and opportunity for comment, the Administrator of the Environmental Protection Agency, in consultation with the Secretary of Housing and Urban Development and with the Secretary of Health and Human Services, shall publish, and from time to time revise, a lead hazard information pamphlet to be used in connection with this subchapter and section 4852d of Title 42. The pamphlet shall —

(1) contain information regarding the health risks associated with exposure to lead;

(2) provide information on the presence of lead-based paint hazards in federally assisted, federally owned, and target housing;

(3) describe the risks of lead exposure for children under 6 years of age, pregnant women, women of childbearing age, persons involved in home renovation, and others residing in a dwelling with lead-based paint hazards;

(4) describe the risks of renovation in a dwelling with lead-based paint hazards;

(5) provide information on approved methods for evaluating and reducing lead-based paint hazards and their effectiveness in identifying, reducing, eliminating, or preventing exposure to lead-based paint hazards;

(6) advise persons how to obtain a list of contractors certified pursuant to this subchapter in lead-based paint hazard evaluation and reduction in the area in which the pamphlet is to be used;

(7) state that a risk assessment or inspection for lead-based paint is recommended prior to the purchase, lease, or renovation of target housing;

(8) state that certain State and local laws impose additional requirements related to lead-based paint in housing and provide a listing of Federal, State, and local agencies in each State, including address and telephone number, that can provide information about applicable laws and available governmental and private assistance and financing; and

(9) provide such other information about environmental hazards associated with residential real property as the Administrator deems appropriate.

(b) Renovation of target housing — Within 2 years after October 28, 1992, the Administrator shall promulgate regulations under this subsection to require each person who performs for compensation a renovation of target housing to provide a lead hazard information pamphlet to the owner and occupant of such housing prior to commencing the renovation.

§2687. Regulations
[TSCA §407]
The regulations of the Administrator under this subchapter shall include such recordkeeping and reporting requirements as may be necessary to insure the effective implementation of this subchapter. The regulations may be amended from time to time as necessary.

§2688. Control of lead-based paint hazards at Federal facilities
[TSCA §408]
Each department, agency, and instrumentality of executive, legislative, and judicial branches of the Federal Government (1) having jurisdiction over any property or facility, or (2) engaged in any activity resulting, or which may result, in a lead-based paint hazard, and each officer, agent, or employee thereof, shall be subject to, and comply with, all Federal, State, interstate, and local requirements, both substantive and procedural (including any requirement for certification, licensing, recordkeeping, or reporting or any provisions for injunctive relief and such sanctions as may be imposed by a court to enforce such relief) respecting lead-based paint, lead-based paint activities, and lead-based paint hazards in the same manner, and to the same extent as any nongovernmental entity is subject to such requirements, including the payment of reasonable service charges. The Federal, State, interstate, and local substantive and procedural requirements referred to in this subsection include, but are not limited to, all administrative orders and all civil

and administrative penalties and fines regardless of whether such penalties or fines are punitive or coercive in nature, or whether imposed for isolated, intermittent or continuing violations. The United States hereby expressly waives any immunity otherwise applicable to the United States with respect to any such substantive or procedural requirement (including, but not limited to, any injunctive relief, administrative order, or civil or administrative penalty or fine referred to in the preceding sentence, or reasonable service charge). The reasonable service charges referred to in this section include, but are not limited to, fees or charges assessed for certification and licensing, as well as any other nondiscriminatory charges that are assessed in connection with a Federal, State, interstate, or local lead-based paint, lead-based paint activities, or lead-based paint hazard activities program. No agent, employee, or officer of the United States shall be personally liable for any civil penalty under any Federal, State, interstate, or local law relating to lead-based paint, lead-based paint activities, or lead-based paint hazards with respect to any act or omission within the scope of his official duties.

§2689. Prohibited acts
[TSCA §409]

It shall be unlawful for any person to fail or refuse to comply with a provision of this subchapter or with any rule or order issued under this subchapter.

§2690. Relationship to other Federal law
[TSCA §410]

Nothing in this subchapter shall affect the authority of other appropriate Federal agencies to establish or enforce any requirements which are at least as stringent as those established pursuant to this subchapter.

§2691. General provisions relating to administrative proceedings
[TSCA §411]

(a) Applicability — This section applies to the promulgation or revision of any regulation issued under this subchapter.

(b) Rulemaking docket — Not later than the date of proposal of any action to which this section applies, the Administrator shall establish a rulemaking docket for such action (hereinafter in this subsection referred to as a "rule"). Whenever a rule applies only within a particular State, a second (identical) docket shall be established in the appropriate regional office of the Environmental Protection Agency.

(c) Inspection and copying

(1) The rulemaking docket required under subsection (b) of this section shall be open for inspection by the public at reasonable times specified in the notice of proposed rulemaking. Any person may copy documents contained in the docket. The Administrator shall provide copying facilities which may be used at the expense of the person seeking copies, but the Administrator may waive or reduce such expenses in such instances as the public interest requires. Any person may request copies by mail if the person pays the expenses, including personnel costs to do the copying.

(2)(A) Promptly upon receipt by the agency, all written comments and documentary information on the proposed rule received from any person for inclusion in the docket during the comment period shall be placed in the docket. The transcript of public hearings, if any, on the proposed rule shall also be included in the docket promptly upon receipt from the person who transcribed such hearings. All documents which become available after the proposed rule has been published and which the Administrator determines are of central relevance to the rulemaking shall be placed in the docket as soon as possible after their availability.

(B) The drafts of proposed rules submitted by the Administrator to the Office of Management and Budget for any interagency review process prior to proposal of any such rule, all documents accompanying such drafts, and all written comments thereon by other agencies and all written responses to such written comments by the Administrator shall be placed in the docket no later than the date of proposal of the rule. The drafts of the final rule submitted for such review process prior to promulgation and all such written comments thereon, all documents accompanying such drafts, and written responses thereto shall be placed in the docket no later than the date of promulgation.

(d) Explanation

(1) The promulgated rule shall be accompanied by an explanation of the reasons for any major changes in the promulgated rule from the proposed rule.

(2) The promulgated rule shall also be accompanied by a response to each of the significant comments, criticisms, and new data submitted in written or oral presentations during the comment period.

(3) The promulgated rule may not be based (in part or whole) on any information or data which has not been placed in the docket as of the date of such promulgation.

(e) Judicial review — The material referred to in subsection (c)(2)(B) of this section shall not be included in the record for judicial review.

(f) Effective date — The requirements of this section shall take effect with respect to any rule the proposal of which occurs after 90 days after October 28, 1992.

§2692. Authorization of appropriations
[TSCA §412]

There are authorized to be appropriated to carry out the purposes of this subchapter such sums as may be necessary.

SUBCHAPTER V — HEALTHY HIGH-PERFORMANCE SCHOOLS

§2695. Grants for healthy school environments

(a) In general

The Administrator, in consultation with the Secretary of Education, may provide grants to States for use in —

(1) providing technical assistance for programs of the Environmental Protection Agency (including the Tools for Schools Program and the Healthy School Environmental Assessment Tool) to schools for use in addressing environmental issues; and

(2) development and implementation of State school environmental health programs that include—

(A) standards for school building design, construction, and renovation; and

(B) identification of ongoing school building environmental problems, including contaminants, hazardous substances, and pollutant emissions, in the State and recommended solutions to address those problems, including assessment of information on the exposure of children to environmental hazards in school facilities.

(b) Sunset

The authority of the Administrator to carry out this section shall expire 5 years after December 19, 2007.

§2695a. Model guidelines for siting of school facilities

Not later than 18 months after December 19, 2007, the Administrator, in consultation with the Secretary of Education and the Secretary of Health and Human Services, shall issue voluntary school site selection guidelines that account for —

(1) the special vulnerability of children to hazardous substances or pollution exposures in any case in which the potential for contamination at a potential school site exists;

(2) modes of transportation available to students and staff;

(3) the efficient use of energy; and

(4) the potential use of a school at the site as an emergency shelter.

§2695b. Public outreach

(a) Reports

The Administrator shall publish and submit to Congress an annual report on all activities carried out under this subchapter, until the expiration of authority described in section 2695(b) of this title.

(b) Public outreach

The Federal Director appointed under section 17092(a) of Title 42 (in this subchapter referred to as the "Federal Director") shall ensure, to the maximum extent practicable, that the public clearinghouse established under section 17083(1) of Title 42 receives and makes available information on the exposure of children to environmental hazards in school facilities, as provided by the Administrator.

§2695c. Environmental health program

(a) In general

Not later than 2 years after December 19, 2007, the Administrator, in consultation with the Secretary of Education, the Secretary of Health and Human Services, and other relevant agencies, shall issue voluntary guidelines for use by the State in developing and implementing an environmental health program for schools that —

(1) takes into account the status and findings of Federal initiatives established under this subchapter or subtitle C of title IV of the Energy Independence and Security Act of 2007 and other relevant Federal law with respect to school facilities, including relevant updates on trends in the field, such as the impact of school facility environments on student and staff —

(A) health, safety, and productivity; and

(B) disabilities or special needs;

(2) takes into account studies using relevant tools identified or developed in accordance with section 492 of the Energy Independence and Security Act of 2007;

(3) takes into account, with respect to school facilities, each of —

(A) environmental problems, contaminants, hazardous substances, and pollutant emissions, including —

(i) lead from drinking water;

(ii) lead from materials and products;

(iii) asbestos;

(iv) radon;

(v) the presence of elemental mercury releases from products and containers;

(vi) pollutant emissions from materials and products; and

(vii) any other environmental problem, contaminant, hazardous substance, or pollutant emission that present or may present a risk to the health of occupants of the school facilities or environment;

(B) natural day lighting;

(C) ventilation choices and technologies;

(D) heating and cooling choices and technologies;

(E) moisture control and mold;

(F) maintenance, cleaning, and pest control activities;

(G) acoustics; and

(H) other issues relating to the health, comfort, productivity, and performance of occupants of the school facilities;

(4) provides technical assistance on siting, design, management, and operation of school facilities, including facilities used by students with disabilities or special needs;

(5) collaborates with federally funded pediatric environmental health centers to assist in on-site school environmental investigations;

(6) assists States and the public in better understanding and improving the environmental health of children; and

(7) takes into account the special vulnerability of children in low-income and minority communities to exposures from contaminants, hazardous substances, and pollutant emissions.

(b) Public outreach

The Federal Director and Commercial Director shall ensure, to the maximum extent practicable, that the public clearinghouse established under section 17083 of Title 42 receives and makes available —

(1) information from the Administrator that is contained in the report described in section 2695b(a) of this title; and

(2) information on the exposure of children to environmental hazards in school facilities, as provided by the Administrator.

§2695d. Authorization of appropriations

There are authorized to be appropriated to carry out this subchapter $1,000,000 for fiscal year 2009, and $1,500,000 for each of fiscal years 2010 through 2013, to remain available until expended.

SUBCHAPTER VI – FORMALDEHYDE STANDARDS FOR COMPOSITE WOOD PRODUCTS

§2697. Formaldehyde standards
[TSCA §601]

(a) Definitions

In this section:

(1) Finished good

(A) In general

The term "finished good" means any good or product (other than a panel) containing —

(i) hardwood plywood;

(ii) particleboard; or

(iii) medium-density fiberboard.

(B) Exclusions

The term "finished good" does not include —

(i) any component part or other part used in the assembly of a finished good; or

(ii) any finished good that has previously been sold or supplied to an individual or entity that purchased or acquired the finished good in good faith for purposes other than resale, such as —

(I) an antique; or

(II) secondhand furniture.

(2) Hardboard

The term "hardboard" has such meaning as the Administrator shall establish, by regulation, pursuant to subsection (d).

(3) Hardwood plywood

(A) In general

The term "hardwood plywood" means a hardwood or decorative panel that is —

(i) intended for interior use; and

(ii) composed of (as determined under the standard numbered ANSI/HPVA HP-1-2009) an assembly of layers or plies of veneer, joined by an adhesive with —

(I) lumber core;

(II) particleboard core;

(III) medium-density fiberboard core;

(IV) hardboard core; or

(V) any other special core or special back material.

(B) Exclusions

The term "hardwood plywood" does not include —

(i) military-specified plywood;

(ii) curved plywood; or

(iii) any other product specified in —

(I) The standard entitled "Voluntary Product Standard — Structural Plywood" and numbered PS 1-07; or

(II) The standard entitled "Voluntary Product Standard — Performance Standard for Wood-Based Structural-Use Panels" and numbered PS 2-04.

(C) Laminated products

(i) Rulemaking

(I) In general

The Administrator shall conduct a rulemaking process pursuant to subsection (d) that uses all available and relevant information from State authorities, industry, and other available sources of such information, and analyzes that information to determine, at the discretion of the Administrator, whether the definition of the term "hardwood plywood" should exempt engineered veneer or any laminated product.

(II) Modification

The Administrator may modify any aspect of the definition contained in clause (ii) before including that definition in the regulations promulgated pursuant to subclause (I).

(ii) Laminated product

The term "laminated product" means a product —

(I) in which a wood veneer is affixed to —

(aa) a particleboard platform;

(bb) a medium-density fiberboard platform; or

(cc) a veneer-core platform; and

(II) that is —

(aa) a component part;

(bb) used in the construction or assembly of a finished good; and (cc) produced by the manufacturer or fabricator of the finished good in which the product is incorporated.

(4) Manufactured home

The term "manufactured home" has the meaning given the term in section 3280.2 of title 24, Code of Federal Regulations (as in effect on the date of promulgation of regulations pursuant to subsection (d)).

(5) Medium-density fiberboard

The term "medium-density fiberboard" means a panel composed of cellulosic fibers made by dry forming and pressing a resinated fiber mat (as determined under the standard numbered ANSI A208.2-2009).

(6) Modular home

The term "modular home" means a home that is constructed in a factory in 1 or more modules —

(A) each of which meet applicable State and local building codes of the area in which the home will be located; and

(B) that are transported to the home building site, installed on foundations, and completed.

(7) No-added formaldehyde-based resin

(A) In general

(i) The term "no-added formaldehyde-based resin" means a resin formulated with no added formaldehyde as part of the resin cross-linking structure in a composite wood product that meets the emission standards in subparagraph (C) as measured by —

(I) one test conducted pursuant to test method ASTM E-1333-96 (2002) or, subject to clause (ii), ASTM D-6007-02; and

(II) 3 months of routine quality control tests pursuant to ASTM D-6007-02 or ASTM D-5582 or such other routine quality control test methods as may be established by the Administrator through rulemaking.

(ii) Test results obtained under clause (i)(I) or (II) by any test method other than ASTM E-1333-96 (2002) must include a showing of equivalence by means established by the Administrator through rulemaking.

(B) Inclusions

The term "no-added formaldehyde-based resin" may include any resin made from —

(i) soy;

(ii) polyvinyl acetate; or

(iii) methylene diisocyanate.

(C) Emission standards

The following are the emission standards for composite wood products made with no-added formaldehyde-based resins under this paragraph:

(i) No higher than 0.04 parts per million of formaldehyde for 90 percent of the 3 months of routine quality control testing data required under subparagraph (A)(ii).

(ii) No test result higher than 0.05 parts per million of formaldehyde for hardwood plywood and 0.06 parts per million for particleboard, medium-density fiberboard, and thin medium-density fiberboard.

(8) Particleboard

(A) In general

The term "particleboard" means a panel composed of cellulosic material in the form of discrete particles (as distinguished from fibers, flakes, or strands) that are pressed together with resin (as determined under the standard numbered ANSI A208.1-2009).

(B) Exclusions

The term "particleboard" does not include any product specified in the standard entitled "Voluntary Product Standard — Performance Standard for Wood-Based Structural-Use Panels" and numbered PS 2-04.

(9) Recreational vehicle

The term "recreational vehicle" has the meaning given the term in section 3282.8 of title 24, Code of Federal Regulations (as in effect on the date of promulgation of regulations pursuant to subsection (d)).

(10) Ultra low-emitting formaldehyde resin

(A) In general

(i) The term "ultra low-emitting formaldehyde resin" means a resin in a composite wood product that meets the emission standards in subparagraph (C) as measured by —

(I) 2 quarterly tests conducted pursuant to test method ASTM E-1333-96 (2002) or, subject to clause (ii), ASTM D-6007-02; and

(II) 6 months of routine quality control tests pursuant to ASTM D-6007-02 or ASTM D-5582 or such other routine quality control test methods as may be established by the Administrator through rulemaking.

(ii) Test results obtained under clause (i)(I) or (II) by any test method other than ASTM E-1333-96 (2002) must include a showing of equivalence by means established by the Administrator through rulemaking.

(B) Inclusions

The term "ultra low-emitting formaldehyde resin" may include —

(i) melamine-urea-formaldehyde resin;

(ii) phenol formaldehyde resin; and

(iii) resorcinol formaldehyde resin.

(C) Emission standards

(i) The Administrator may, pursuant to regulations issued under subsection (d), reduce the testing requirements for a manufacturer only if its product made with ultra low-emitting formaldehyde resin meets the following emission standards:

(I) For hardwood plywood, no higher than 0.05 parts per million of formaldehyde.

(II) For medium-density fiberboard —

(aa) no higher than 0.06 parts per million of formaldehyde for 90 percent of 6 months of routine quality control testing data required under subparagraph (A)(ii); and

(bb) no test result higher than 0.09 parts per million of formaldehyde.

(III) For particleboard —

(aa) no higher than 0.05 parts per million of formaldehyde for 90 percent of 6 months of routine quality control testing data required under subparagraph (A)(ii); and

(bb) no test result higher than 0.08 parts per million of formaldehyde.

(IV) For thin medium-density fiberboard —

(aa) no higher than 0.08 parts per million of formaldehyde for 90 percent of 6 months of routine quality control testing data required under subparagraph (A)(ii); and

(bb) no test result higher than 0.11 parts per million of formaldehyde.

(ii) The Administrator may not, pursuant to regulations issued under subsection (d), exempt a manufacturer from third party certification requirements unless its product made with ultra low-emitting formaldehyde resin meets the following emission standards:

(I) No higher than 0.04 parts per million of formaldehyde for 90 percent of 6 months of routine quality control testing data required under subparagraph (A)(ii).

(II) No test result higher than 0.05 parts per million of formaldehyde for hardwood plywood and 0.06 parts per million for particleboard, medium-density fiberboard, and thin medium-density fiberboard.

(b) Requirement

(1) In general

Except as provided in an applicable sell-through regulation promulgated pursuant to subsection (d), effective beginning on the date that is 180 days after the date of promulgation of those regulations, the emission standards described in paragraph (2), shall apply to hardwood plywood, medium-density fiberboard, and particleboard sold, supplied, offered for sale, or manufactured in the United States.

(2) Emission standards

The emission standards referred to in paragraph (1), based on test method ASTM E-1333-96 (2002), are as follows:

(A) For hardwood plywood with a veneer core, 0.05 parts per million of formaldehyde.

(B) For hardwood plywood with a composite core —

(i) 0.08 parts per million of formaldehyde for any period after the effective date described in paragraph (1) and before July 1, 2012; and

(ii) 0.05 parts per million of formaldehyde, effective on the later of the effective date described in paragraph (1) or July 1, 2012.

(C) For medium-density fiberboard —

(i) 0.21 parts per million of formaldehyde for any period after the effective date described in paragraph (1) and before July 1, 2011; and

(ii) 0.11 parts per million of formaldehyde, effective on the later of the effective date described in paragraph (1) or July 1, 2011.

(D) For thin medium-density fiberboard —

(i) 0.21 parts per million of formaldehyde for any period after the effective date described in paragraph (1) and before July 1, 2012; and

(ii) 0.13 parts per million of formaldehyde, effective on the later of the effective date described in paragraph (1) or July 1, 2012.

(E) For particleboard —

(i) 0.18 parts per million of formaldehyde for any period after the effective date described in paragraph (1) and before July 1, 2011; and

(ii) 0.09 parts per million of formaldehyde, effective on the later of the effective date described in paragraph (1) or July 1, 2011.

(3) Compliance with emission standards

(A) Compliance with the emission standards described in paragraph (2) shall be measured by —

(i) quarterly tests shall be conducted pursuant to test method ASTM E-1333-96

(2002) or, subject to subparagraph (B), ASTM D-6007-02; and

(ii) quality control tests shall be conducted pursuant to ASTM D-6007-02, ASTM D-5582, or such other test methods as may be established by the Administrator through rulemaking.

(B) Test results obtained under subparagraph (A)(i) or (ii) by any test method other than ASTM E-1333-96 (2002) must include a showing of equivalence by means established by the Administrator through rulemaking.

(C) Except where otherwise specified, the Administrator shall establish through rulemaking the number and frequency of tests required to demonstrate compliance with the emission standards.

(4) Applicability

The formaldehyde emission standard referred to in paragraph (1) shall apply regardless of whether an applicable hardwood plywood, medium-density fiberboard, or particleboard is —

(A) in the form of an unfinished panel; or

(B) incorporated into a finished good.

(c) Exemptions

The formaldehyde emission standard referred to in subsection (b)(1) shall not apply to —

(1) hardboard;

(2) structural plywood, as specified in the standard entitled "Voluntary Product Standard — Structural Plywood" and numbered PS 1-07;

(3) structural panels, as specified in the standard entitled "Voluntary Product Standard — Performance Standard for Wood-Based Structural-Use Panels" and numbered PS 2-04;

(4) structural composite lumber, as specified in the standard entitled "Standard Specification for Evaluation of Structural Composite Lumber Products" and numbered ASTM D 5456-06;

(5) oriented strand board;

(6) glued laminated lumber, as specified in the standard entitled "Structural Glued Laminated Timber" and numbered ANSI A190.1-2002;

(7) prefabricated wood I-joists, as specified in the standard entitled "Standard Specification for Establishing and Monitoring Structural Capacities of Prefabricated Wood I-Joists" and numbered ASTM D 5055-05;

(8) finger-jointed lumber;

(9) wood packaging (including pallets, crates, spools, and dunnage);

(10) composite wood products used inside a new —

(A) vehicle (other than a recreational vehicle) constructed entirely from new parts that has never been —

(i) the subject of a retail sale; or

(ii) registered with the appropriate State agency or authority responsible for motor vehicles or with any foreign state, province, or country;

(B) rail car;

(C) boat;

(D) aerospace craft; or

(E) aircraft;

(11) windows that contain composite wood products, if the window product contains less than 5 percent by volume of hardwood plywood, particleboard, or medium-density fiberboard, combined, in relation to the total volume of the finished window product; or

(12) exterior doors and garage doors that contain composite wood products, if —

(A) the doors are made from composite wood products manufactured with no-added formaldehyde-based resins or ultra low-emitting formaldehyde resins; or

(B) the doors contain less than 3 percent by volume of hardwood plywood, particleboard, or medium-density fiberboard, combined, in relation to the total volume of the finished exterior door or garage door.

(d) Regulations

(1) In general

Not later than January 1, 2013, the Administrator shall promulgate regulations to implement the standards required under subsection (b) in a manner that ensures compliance with the emission standards described in subsection (b)(2).

(2) Inclusions

The regulations promulgated pursuant to paragraph (1) shall include provisions relating to —

(A) labeling;

(B) chain of custody requirements;

(C) sell-through provisions;

(D) ultra low-emitting formaldehyde resins;

(E) no-added formaldehyde-based resins;

(F) finished goods;

(G) third-party testing and certification;

(H) auditing and reporting of third-party certifiers;

(I) recordkeeping;

(J) enforcement;

(K) laminated products; and

(L) exceptions from the requirements of regulations promulgated pursuant to this subsection for products and components containing de minimis amounts of composite wood products.

The Administrator shall not provide under subparagraph (L) exceptions to the formaldehyde emission standard requirements in subsection (b).

(3) Sell-through provisions

(A) In general

Sell-through provisions established by the

Administrator under this subsection, with respect to composite wood products and finished goods containing regulated composite wood products (including recreational vehicles, manufactured homes, and modular homes), shall —

    (i) be based on a designated date of manufacture (which shall be no earlier than the date 180 days following the promulgation of the regulations pursuant to this subsection) of the composite wood product or finished good, rather than date of sale of the composite wood product or finished good; and

    (ii) provide that any inventory of composite wood products or finished goods containing regulated composite wood products, manufactured before the designated date of manufacture of the composite wood products or finished goods, shall not be subject to the formaldehyde emission standard requirements under subsection (b)(1).

(B) Implementing regulations

The regulations promulgated under this subsection shall —

    (i) prohibit the stockpiling of inventory to be sold after the designated date of manufacture; and

    (ii) not require any labeling or testing of composite wood products or finished goods containing regulated composite wood products manufactured before the designated date of manufacture.

(C) Definition

For purposes of this paragraph, the term "stockpiling" means manufacturing or purchasing a composite wood product or finished good containing a regulated composite wood product between July 7, 2010, and the date 180 days following the promulgation of the regulations pursuant to this subsection at a rate which is significantly greater (as determined by the Administrator) than the rate at which such product or good was manufactured or purchased during a base period (as determined by the Administrator) ending before July 7, 2010.

(4) Import regulations

Not later than July 1, 2013, the Administrator, in coordination with the Commissioner of U.S. Customs and Border Protection and other appropriate Federal departments and agencies, shall revise regulations promulgated pursuant to section 2612 of this title as the Administrator determines to be necessary to ensure compliance with this section.

(5) Successor standards and test methods

The Administrator may, after public notice and opportunity for comment, substitute an industry standard or test method referenced in this section with its successor version.

(e) Prohibited acts

An individual or entity that violates any requirement under this section (including any regulation promulgated pursuant to subsection (d)) shall be considered to have committed a prohibited act under section 2614 of this title.

B. FEDERAL INSECTICIDE, FUNGICIDE, AND RODENTICIDE ACT

A GUIDE TO MATERIALS AVAILABLE ON THE INTERNET PERTAINING TO THE FEDERAL INSECTICIDE, FUNGICIDE, AND RODENTICIDE ACT (FIFRA)

EPA's regulations implementing FIFRA are codified at 40 C.F.R. pts. 150-189. These CFR sections are available online through the National Archives and Records Administration's website, which includes a searchable version of the Code of Federal Regulations *(https://www.gpo.gov/fdsys/browse/collectionCfr.action?collectionCode=CFR)* and an electronic version ("e-CFR") that is continuously updated, which can be found at *http://www.ecfr.gov.*

EPA's Office of Prevention, Pesticides, and Toxic Substances (OPPTS) is the office responsible for implementing FIFRA and TSCA. The Office of Pesticide Programs (OPP) implements FIFRA while the Office of Pollution Prevention and Toxic Substances (OPPT) implements TSCA. OPP's webpage is at *http://www.epa.gov/pesticides*. It contains news updates concerning developments in pesticide regulation, information about registration and pesticide use, labeling, and consumer alerts, and links to sources of pesticide data, scientific information, and laws and regulations.

The National Pesticide Information Center (NPIC) operated by EPA and the Oregon State University Department of Agricultural Chemistry has a webpage at *http://www.npic.orst.edu.*

Documents concerning the history of FIFRA are available on a website maintained by EPA's History Office at *http://www2.epa.gov/aboutepa/epa-history-federal-insecticide-fungicide-and-rodenticide-act*. Information on the Food Quality Protection Act of 1996 is available at *https://www.epa.gov/laws-regulations/summary-food-quality-protection-act.*

An environmental group, Beyond Pesticides (also known as the National Coalition Against the Misuse of Pesticides), has a website located at *http://www.beyondpesticides.org* that provides news, consumer alerts, and access to publications about pesticide safety issues. The principal industry trade group active on pesticide issues is CropLife America, formerly known as the American Crop Protection Association and before that the National Agricultural Chemicals Association. Its website is located at *www.croplifeamerica.org.*

FIFRA LEGISLATIVE HISTORY TIMELINE

June 25, 1947: The Federal Insecticide, Fungicide and Rodenticide Act (FIFRA), Pub. L. 80-104, 61 Stat. 163, is enacted. The Act provides for regulation of the interstate marketing of pesticide products.

October 21, 1972: The Federal Environmental Pesticide Control Act, Pub. L. 92-516, 86 Stat. 973, amends FIFRA to require registration of all pesticide products, even those used wholly intrastate, and to give EPA authority to restrict the use of pesticides and to set packaging standards for them.

October 25, 1988: President Reagan signs the FIFRA Amendments of 1988, Pub. L. 100-532, 102 Stat. 2654. The amendments require a substantial acceleration in the review of the safety of older pesticides by establishing a schedule requiring EPA to complete the reregistration process for 600 older active ingredients of pesticides. The Amendments also require pesticide manufacturers to pay fees to help finance the reregistration process and they require manufacturers to assume responsibility for the storage and disposal of pesticides whose registration is canceled.

August 3, 1996: President Clinton signs the Food Quality Protection Act of 1996, Pub. L. 104-170, 110 Stat. 1489, which amends FIFRA and the Federal Food, Drug, and Cosmetic Act to change the standard used for setting tolerances for pesticide residues on food. The new safety standard directs that tolerance be set to provide a "reasonable certainty of no harm."

January 23, 2004: The Pesticide Registration Improvement Act of 2003, Pub. L. 108-109, 118 Stat. 3, amends FIFRA by adding a provision requiring the EPA Administrator to assess and collect pesticide registration service fees to be used to defray the cost of reviewing pesticide registration applications.

OUTLINE OF THE PRINCIPAL PROVISIONS OF THE FEDERAL INSECTICIDE, FUNGICIDE, AND RODENTICIDE ACT

§3 (7 U.S.C §136a) Registration of Pesticides: prohibits the sale or distribution of any pesticide that is not registered with EPA; directs EPA to register pesticides if applicants demonstrate that they will perform their intended functions without causing "unreasonable adverse effects on the environment"; authorizes EPA to restrict the use of registered pesticides that may cause unreasonable adverse effects if unregulated.

§4 (7 U.S.C. §136a-1) Reregistration of Registered Pesticides: requires EPA to reregister pesticides containing active ingredients first registered before November 1, 1984 and requires pesticide manufacturers to pay fees to help finance the reregistration process.

§5 (7 U.S.C. §136c) Experimental Use Permits: authorizes EPA to issue experimental use permits for pesticides when needed by applicants to accumulate information necessary to register a pesticide under §3.

§6 (7 U.S.C. §136d) Suspension and Cancellation of Registration: authorizes the EPA Administrator to cancel the registration of a pesticide pursuant to §6(b) if the pesticide is found generally to cause "unreasonable adverse effects on the environment." The Administrator normally must conduct adjudicatory hearings before canceling the registration of a pesticide, but §6(c) provides that EPA can suspend a pesticide's registration immediately if she determines that it is "necessary to prevent an imminent hazard" pending completion of the cancellation process.

§16 (7 U.S.C. §136n) Judicial Review: authorizes judicial review in federal district courts of decisions not to cancel or suspend registration of pesticides and authorizes judicial review in the U.S. Courts of Appeals of any orders issued by the EPA Administrator after a public hearing.

§17 (7 U.S.C. §136o) Imports and Exports: authorizes domestic production of unregistered pesticides if produced solely for export to foreign countries whose purchasers have been notified that the pesticide is not registered for use in the United States.

§19 (7 U.S.C. §136q) Storage, Disposal, Transportation and Recall: authorizes the EPA Administrator to recall pesticides whose registration has been suspended or cancelled, provides for reimbursement of end users of such products. and requires manufacturers to assume responsibility for the storage and disposal of such products.

§24 (7 U.S.C. §136v) Preemption: prohibits states from imposing any requirement for labeling or packaging of pesticides that is different from those required by federal regulations.

§26 (7 U.S.C. §136w-1) State Enforcement Responsibility: authorizes the EPA Administrator to delegate primary enforcement responsibility for FIFRA to states that have adequate pesticide-use laws and regulations and adequate procedures for enforcement.

Federal Insecticide, Fungicide, and Rodenticide Act

7 U.S.C. §§136 to 136y

§136. Definitions

[FIFRA §2]

For purposes of this subchapter —

(a) Active ingredient — The term "active ingredient" means —

(1) in the case of a pesticide other than a plant regulator, defoliant, desiccant, or nitrogen stabilizer, an ingredient which will prevent, destroy, repel, or mitigate any pest;

(2) in the case of a plant regulator, an ingredient which, through physiological action, will accelerate or retard the rate of growth or rate of maturation or otherwise alter the behavior of ornamental or crop plants or the product thereof;

(3) in the case of a defoliant, an ingredient which will cause the leaves or foliage to drop from a plant;

(4) in the case of a desiccant, an ingredient which will artificially accelerate the drying of plant tissue; and

(5) in the case of a nitrogen stabilizer, an ingredient which will prevent or hinder the process of nitrification, denitrification, ammonia volatilization, or urease production through action affecting soil bacteria.

(b) Administrator — The term "Administrator" means the Administrator of the Environmental Protection Agency.

(c) Adulterated — The term "adulterated" applies to any pesticide if —

(1) its strength or purity falls below the professed standard of quality as expressed on its labeling under which it is sold;

(2) any substance has been substituted wholly or in part for the pesticide; or

(3) any valuable constituent of the pesticide has been wholly or in part abstracted.

(d) Animal — The term "animal" means all vertebrate and invertebrate species, including but not limited to man and other mammals, birds, fish, and shellfish.

(e) Certified applicator, etc.

(1) Certified applicator — The term "certified applicator" means any individual who is certified under section 136i of this title as authorized to use or supervise the use of any pesticide which is classified for restricted use. Any applicator who holds or applies registered pesticides, or uses dilutions of registered pesticides consistent with subsection (ee) of this section, only to provide a service of controlling pests without delivering any unapplied pesticide to any person so served is not deemed to be a seller or distributor of pesticides under this subchapter.

(2) Private applicator — The term "private applicator" means a certified applicator who uses or supervises the use of any pesticide which is classified for restricted use for purposes of producing any agricultural commodity on property owned or rented by the applicator or the applicator's employer or (if applied without compensation other than trading of personal services between producers of agricultural commodities) on the property of another person.

(3) Commercial applicator — The term "commercial applicator" means an applicator (whether or not the applicator is a private applicator with respect to some uses) who uses or supervises the use of any pesticide which is classified for restricted use for any purpose or on any property other than as provided by paragraph (2).

(4) Under the direct supervision of a certified applicator — Unless otherwise prescribed by its labeling, a pesticide shall be considered to be applied under the direct supervision of a certified applicator if it is applied by a competent person acting under the instructions and control of a certified applicator who is available if and when needed, even though such certified applicator is not physically present at the time and place the pesticide is applied.

(f) Defoliant — The term "defoliant" means any substance of mixture of substances intended for causing the leaves or foliage to drop from a plant, with or without causing abscission.

(g) Desiccant — The term "desiccant" means any substance or mixture of substances intended for artificially accelerating the drying of plant tissue.

(h) Device — The term "device" means any instrument or contrivance (other than a firearm) which is intended for trapping, destroying, repelling, or mitigating any pest or any other form of plant or animal life (other than man and other than bacteria, virus, or other micro-organism on or in living man or other living animals); but not including equipment used for the application of pesticides when sold separately therefrom.

(i) District court — The term "district court" means a United States district court, the District Court of Guam, the District Court of the Virgin Islands, and the highest court of American Samoa.

(j) Environment — The term "environment" includes water, air, land, and all plants and man and other animals living therein, and the interrelationships which exist among these.

(k) Fungus — The term "fungus" means any non-chlorophyll-bearing thallophyte (that is, any non-chlorophyll-bearing plant of a lower order than mosses and liverworts), as for example, rust, smut, mildew, mold, yeast, and bacteria, except those on or in living man or other animals and those on or in processed food, beverages, or pharmaceuticals.

(l) Imminent hazard — The term "imminent hazard" means a situation which exists when the continued use of a pesticide during the time required for cancellation proceeding would be likely to result in unreasonable adverse effects on the environment or will involve unreasonable hazard to the survival of a species declared endangered or threatened by the Secretary pursuant to the Endangered Species Act of 1973 [16 U.S.C. §§1531 *et seq.*].

(m) Inert ingredient — The term "inert ingredient" means an ingredient which is not active.

(n) Ingredient statement — The term "ingredient statement" means a statement which contains —

(1) the name and percentage of each active ingredient, and the total percentage of all inert ingredients, in the pesticide; and

(2) if the pesticide contains arsenic in any form, a statement of the percentages of total and water soluble arsenic, calculated as elementary arsenic.

(o) Insect — The term "insect" means any of the numerous small invertebrate animals generally having the body more or less obviously segmented, for the most part belonging to the class insecta, comprising six-legged, usually winged forms, as for example, beetles, bugs, bees, flies, and to other allied classes of anthropods whose members are wingless and usually have more than six legs, as for example, spiders, mites, ticks, centipedes, and wood lice.

(p) Label and labeling

(1) Label — The term "label" means the written, printed, or graphic matter on, or attached to, the pesticide or device or any of its containers or wrappers.

(2) Labeling — The term "labeling" means all labels and all other written, printed, or graphic matter —

(A) accompanying the pesticide or device at any time; or

(B) to which reference is made on the label or in literature accompanying the pesticide or device, except to current official publications of the Environmental Protection Agency, the United States Departments of Agriculture and Interior, the Department of Health and Human Services, State experiment stations, State agricultural colleges, and other similar Federal or State institutions or agencies authorized by law to conduct research in the field of pesticides.

(q) Misbranded

(1) A pesticide is misbranded if —

(A) its labeling bears any statement, design, or graphic representation relative thereto or to its ingredients which is false or misleading in any particular;

(B) it is contained in a package or other container or wrapping which does not conform to the standards established by the Administrator pursuant to section 136w(c)(3) of this title;

(C) it is an imitation of, or is offered for sale under the name of, another pesticide;

(D) its label does not bear the registration number assigned under section 136e of this title to each establishment in which it was produced;

(E) any word, statement, or other information required by or under authority of this subchapter to appear on the label or labeling is not prominently placed thereon with such conspicuousness (as compared with other words, statements, designs, or graphic matter in the labeling) and in such terms as to render it likely to be read and understood by the ordinary individual under customary conditions of purchase and use;

(F) the labeling accompanying it does not contain directions for use which are necessary for effecting the purpose for which the product is intended and if complied with, together with any requirements imposed under section 136a(d) of this title, are adequate to protect health and the environment;

(G) the label does not contain a warning or caution statement which may be necessary and if complied with, together with any requirements imposed under section 136a(d) of this title, is adequate to protect health and the environment; or

(H) in the case of a pesticide not registered in accordance with section 136a of this title and intended for export, the label does not contain, in words prominently placed thereon with such conspicuousness (as compared with other words, statements, designs, or graphic matter in the labeling) as to render it likely to be noted by the ordinary individual under customary conditions of purchase and use, the following: "Not Registered for Use in the United States of America".

(2) A pesticide is misbranded if —

(A) the label does not bear an ingredient statement on that part of the immediate container (and on the outside container or wrapper of the retail package, if there be one, through which the ingredient statement on the immediate container cannot be clearly read) which is presented or displayed under customary conditions or purchase, except that a pesticide is not misbranded under this subparagraph if —

(i) The size or form of the immediate container, or the outside container or wrapper of the retail package, makes it impracticable to place the ingredient statement on the part which is presented or displayed under customary conditions of purchase; and

(ii) the ingredient statement appears prominently on another part of the immediate container, or outside container or wrapper, permitted by the Administrator;

(B) the labeling does not contain a statement of the use classification under which the product is registered;

(C) there is not affixed to its container, and to the outside container or wrapper of the retail package, if there be one, through which the required information on the immediate container cannot be clearly read, a label bearing —

(i) the name and address of the producer, registrant, or person for whom produced;

(ii) the name, brand, or trademark under which the pesticide is sold;

(iii) the net weight or measure of the content, except that the Administrator may permit reasonable variations; and

(iv) when required by regulation of the Administrator to effectuate the purposes of this subchapter, the registration number assigned to the pesticide under this subchapter, and the use classification; and

(D) the pesticide contains any substance or substances in quantities highly toxic to man, unless the label shall bear, in addition to any other matter required by this subchapter —

(i) the skull and crossbones;

(ii) the word "poison" prominently in red on a background of distinctly contrasting color; and

(iii) a statement of a practical treatment (first aid or otherwise) in case of poisoning by the pesticide.

(r) Nematode — The term "nematode" means invertebrate animals of the phylum nemathelminthes and class nematoda, that is, unsegmented round worms with elongated, fusiform, or saclike bodies covered with cuticle, and inhabiting soil, water, plants, or plant parts; may also be called nemas or eelworms.

(s) Person — The term "person" means any individual, partnership, association, corporation, or any organized group of persons whether incorporated or not.

(t) Pest — The term "pest" means (1) any insect, rodent, nematode, fungus, weed, or (2) any other form of terrestrial or aquatic plant or animal life or virus, bacteria, or other micro-organism (except viruses, bacteria, or other micro-organisms on or in living man or other living animals) which the Administrator declares to be a pest under section 136w(c)(1) of this title.

(u) Pesticide — The term "pesticide" means (1) any substance or mixture of substances intended for preventing, destroying, repelling, or mitigating any pest, (2) any substance or mixture of substances intended for use as a plant regulator, defoliant, or desiccant, and (3) any nitrogen stabilizer, except that the term "pesticide" shall not include any article that is a "new animal drug" within the meaning of section 321(w) of Title 21, that has been determined by the Secretary of Health and Human Services not to be a new animal drug by a regulation establishing conditions of use for the article, or that is an animal feed within the meaning of section 321(x) of Title 21 bearing or containing a new animal drug. The term "pesticide" does not include liquid chemical sterilant products (including any sterilant or subordinate disinfectant claims on such products) for use on a critical or semi-critical device, as defined in section 321 of Title 21. For purposes of the preceding sentence, the term "critical device" includes any device which is introduced directly into the human body, either into or in contact with the bloodstream or normally sterile areas of the body and the term "semi-critical device" includes any device which contacts intact mucous membranes but which does not ordinarily penetrate the blood barrier or otherwise enter normally sterile areas of the body.

(v) Plant regulator — The term "plant regulator" means any substance or mixture of substances intended, through physiological action, for accelerating or retarding the rate of growth or rate of maturation, or for otherwise altering the behavior of plants or the produce thereof, but shall not include substances to the extent that they are intended as plant nutrients, trace elements, nutritional chemicals, plant inoculants, and soil amendments. Also, the term "plant regulator" shall not be required to include any of such of those nutrient mixtures or soil amendments as are commonly known as vitamin-hormone horticultural products, intended for improvement, maintenance, survival, health, and propagation of plants, and as are not for pest destruction and are nontoxic, nonpoisonous in the undiluted packaged concentration.

(w) Producer and produce — The term "producer" means the person who manufactures, prepares, compounds, propagates, or processes any pesticide or device or active ingredient used in producing a pesticide. The term "produce" means to manufacture, prepare, compound, propagate, or process any pesticide or device or active ingredient used in producing a pesticide. The dilution by individuals of formulated pesticides for their own use and according to the directions on registered labels shall not of itself result in such individuals being included in the definition of "producer" for the purposes of this subchapter.

(x) Protect health and the environment — The terms "protect health and the environment" and "protection of health and the environment" mean protection against any unreasonable adverse effects on the environment.

(y) Registrant — The term "registrant" means a person who has registered any pesticide pursuant to the provisions of this subchapter.

(z) Registration — The term "registration" includes reregistration.

(aa) State — The term "State" means a State, the District of Columbia, the Commonwealth of Puerto Rico, the Virgin Islands, Guam, the Trust Territory of the Pacific Islands, and American Samoa.

(bb) Unreasonable adverse effects on the environment — The term "unreasonable adverse effects on the environment" means (1) any unreasonable risk to man or the environment, taking into account the economic, social, and environmental costs and benefits of the use of any pesticide, or (2) a human dietary risk from residues that result from a use of a pesticide in or on any food inconsistent with the standard under section 346a of Title 21. The Administrator shall consider the risks and benefits of public health pesticides separate from the risks and benefits of other pesticides. In weighing any regulatory action concerning a public health pesticide under this subchapter, the Administrator shall weigh any risks of the pesticide against the health risks such as the diseases transmitted by the vector to be controlled by the pesticide.

(cc) Weed — The term "weed" means any plant which grows where not wanted.

(dd) Establishment — The term "establishment" means any place where a pesticide or device or active ingredient used in producing a pesticide is produced, or held, for distribution or sale.

(ee) To use any registered pesticide in a manner inconsistent with its labeling — The term "to use any registered pesticide in a manner inconsistent with its labeling" means to use any registered pesticide in a manner not permitted by the labeling, except that the term shall not include

(1) applying a pesticide at any dosage, concentration, or frequency less than that specified on the labeling unless the labeling specifically prohibits deviation from the specified dosage, concentration, or frequency,

(2) applying a pesticide against any target pest not specified on the labeling if the application is to the crop, animal, or site specified on the labeling, unless the Administrator has required that the labeling specifically state that the pesticide may be used only for the pests specified on the labeling after the Administrator has determined that the use of the pesticide against other pests would cause an unreasonable adverse effect on the environment,

(3) employing any method of application not prohibited by the labeling unless the labeling specifically states that the product may be applied only by the methods specified on the labeling,

(4) mixing a pesticide or pesticides with a fertilizer when such mixture is not prohibited by the labeling,

(5) any use of a pesticide in conformance with section 136c, 136p, or 136v of this title, or

(6) any use of a pesticide in a manner that the Administrator determines to be consistent with the purposes of this subchapter. After March 31, 1979, the term shall not include the use of a pesticide for agricultural or forestry purposes at a dilution less than label dosage unless before or after that date the Administrator issues a regulation or advisory opinion consistent with the study provided for in section 27(b) of the Federal Pesticide Act of 1978, which regulation or advisory opinion specifically requires the use of definite amounts of dilution.

(ff) Outstanding data requirement

(1) In general — The term "outstanding data requirement" means a requirement for any study, information, or data that is necessary to make a determination under section 136a(c)(5) of this title and which study, information, or data —

(A) has not been submitted to the Administrator; or

(B) if submitted to the Administrator, the Administrator has determined must be resubmitted because it is not valid, complete, or adequate to make a determination under section 136a(c)(5) of this title and the regulations and guidelines issued under such section.

(2) Factors — In making a determination under paragraph (1)(B) respecting a study, the Administrator shall examine, at a minimum, relevant protocols, documentation of the conduct and analysis of the study, and the results of the study to determine whether the study and the results of the study fulfill the data requirement for which the study was submitted to the Administrator.

(gg) To distribute or sell — The term "to distribute or sell" means to distribute, sell, offer for sale, hold for distribution, hold for sale, hold for shipment, ship, deliver for shipment, release for shipment, or receive and (having so received) deliver or offer to deliver. The term does not include the holding or application of registered pesticides or use dilutions thereof by any applicator who provides a service of controlling pests without delivering any unapplied pesticide to any person so served.

(hh) Nitrogen stabilizer — The term "nitrogen stabilizer" means any substance or mixture of substances intended for preventing or hindering the process of nitrification, denitrification, ammonia volatilization, or urease production through action upon soil bacteria. Such term shall not include —

(1) dicyandiamide;

(2) ammonium thiosulfate; or

(3) any substance or mixture of substances. —

(A) that was not registered pursuant to section 136a of this title prior to January 1, 1992; and

(B) that was in commercial agronomic use prior to January 1, 1992, with respect to which after January 1, 1992, the distributor or seller of

the substance or mixture has made no specific claim of prevention or hindering of the process of nitrification, denitrification, ammonia volatilization urease production regardless of the actual use or purpose for, or future use or purpose for, the substance or mixture. Statements made in materials required to be submitted to any State legislative or regulatory authority, or required by such authority to be included in the labeling or other literature accompanying any such substance or mixture shall not be deemed a specific claim within the meaning of this subsection.

(jj)[1] Maintenance applicator — The term "maintenance applicator" means any individual who, in the principal course of such individual's employment, uses, or supervises the use of, a pesticide not classified for restricted use (other than a ready to use consumer products pesticide); for the purpose of providing structural pest control or lawn pest control including janitors, general maintenance personnel, sanitation personnel, and grounds maintenance personnel. The term "maintenance applicator" does not include private applicators as defined in subsection 136(e)(2) of this section; individuals who use antimicrobial pesticides, sanitizers or disinfectants; individuals employed by Federal, State, and local governments or any political subdivisions thereof, or individuals who use pesticides not classified for restricted use in or around their homes, boats, sod farms, nurseries, greenhouses, or other noncommercial property.

(kk) Service technician — The term "service technician" means any individual who uses or supervises the use of pesticides (other than a ready to use consumer products pesticide) for the purpose of providing structural pest control or lawn pest control on the property of another for a fee. The term "service technician" does not include individuals who use antimicrobial pesticides, sanitizers or disinfectants; or who otherwise apply ready to use consumer products pesticides.

(ll) Minor use — The term "minor use" means the use of a pesticide on an animal, on a commercial agricultural crop or site, or for the protection of public health where —

(1) the total United States acreage for the crop is less than 300,000 acres, as determined by the Secretary of Agriculture; or

(2) the Administrator, in consultation with the Secretary of Agriculture, determines that, based on information provided by an applicant for registration or a registrant, the use does not provide sufficient economic incentive to support the initial registration or continuing registration of a pesticide for such use and —

(A) there are insufficient efficacious alternative registered pesticides available for the use;

---

1. So in original. No subsec. (ii) has been enacted.

(B) the alternatives to the pesticide use pose greater risks to the environment or human health;

(C) the minor use pesticide plays or will play a significant part in managing pest resistance; or

(D) the minor use pesticide plays or will play a significant part in an integrated pest management program.

The status as a minor use under this subsection shall continue as long as the Administrator has not determined that, based on existing data, such use may cause an unreasonable adverse effect on the environment and the use otherwise qualifies for such status.

(mm)　Antimicrobial pesticide

(1) In general —The term "antimicrobial pesticide" means a pesticide that —

(A) is intended to —

(i) disinfect, sanitize, reduce, or mitigate growth or development of microbiological organisms; or

(ii) protect inanimate objects, industrial processes or systems, surfaces, water, or other chemical substances from contamination, fouling, or deterioration caused by bacteria, viruses, fungi, protozoa, algae, or slime; and

(B) in the intended use is exempt from, or otherwise not subject to, a tolerance under section 346a of Title 21 or a food additive regulation under section 348 of Title 21.

(2) Excluded products — The term "antimicrobial pesticide" does not include —

(A) a wood preservative or antifouling paint product for which a claim of pesticidal activity other than or in addition to an activity described in paragraph (1) is made;

(B) an agricultural fungicide product; or

(C) an aquatic herbicide product.

(3) Included products — The term "antimicrobial pesticide" does include any other chemical sterilant product (other than liquid chemical sterilant products exempt under subsection (u) of this section), any other disinfectant product, any other industrial microbiocide product, and any other preservative product that is not excluded by paragraph (2).

(nn)　Public health pesticide — The term "public health pesticide" means any minor use pesticide product registered for use and used predominantly in public health programs for vector control or for other recognized health protection uses, including the prevention or mitigation of viruses, bacteria, or other microorganisms (other than viruses, bacteria, or other microorganisms on or in living man or other living animal) that pose a threat to public health.

(oo)　Vector — The term "vector" means any organism capable of transmitting the causative agent of human disease or capable of producing human discomfort or injury, including mosquitoes, flies, fleas, cockroaches, or other insects and ticks, mites, or rats.

§136a.　Registration of pesticides
[FIFRA §3]

(a)　Requirement of registration — Except as provided by this subchapter, no person in any State may distribute or sell to any person any pesticide that is not registered under this subchapter. To the extent necessary to prevent unreasonable adverse effects on the environment, the Administrator may by regulation limit the distribution, sale, or use in any State of any pesticide that is not registered under this subchapter and that is not the subject of an experimental use permit under section 136c of this title or an emergency exemption under section 136p of this title.

(b)　Exemptions — A pesticide which is not registered with the Administrator may be transferred if —

(1) the transfer is from one registered establishment to another registered establishment operated by the same producer solely for packaging at the second establishment or for use as a constituent part of another pesticide produced at the second establishment; or

(2) the transfer is pursuant to and in accordance with the requirements of an experimental use permit.

(c)　Procedure for registration

(1) Statement required — Each applicant for registration of a pesticide shall file with the Administrator a statement which includes —

(A) the name and address of the applicant and of any other person whose name will appear on the labeling;

(B) the name of the pesticide;

(C) a complete copy of the labeling of the pesticide, a statement of all claims to be made for it, and any directions for its use;

(D) the complete formula of the pesticide;

(E) a request that the pesticide be classified for general use or for restricted use, or for both; and

(F) except as otherwise provided in paragraph (2)(D), if requested by the Administrator, a full description of the tests made and the results thereof upon which the claims are based, or alternatively a citation to data that appear in the public literature or that previously had been submitted to the Administrator and that the Administrator may consider in accordance with the following provisions:

(i) With respect to pesticides containing active ingredients that are initially registered under this subchapter after September 30, 1978, data submitted to support the application for the original registration of the pesticide, or an application for an amendment adding any new use to the registration and that pertains solely to such new use, shall not, without the written permission of the original data submitter, be considered by the Administrator to support an application by another person during a period of ten years following the date the Administrator first registers the pesticide, except that such permission shall not be required in the case of defensive data.

(ii) The period of exclusive data use provided under clause (i) shall be extended 1 additional year for each 3 minor uses registered after August 3, 1996, and within 7 years of the commencement of the exclusive use period, up to a total of 3 additional years for all minor uses registered by the Administrator if the Administrator, in consultation with the Secretary of Agriculture, determines that, based on information provided by an applicant for registration or a registrant, that —

(I) there are insufficient efficacious alternative registered pesticides available for the use;

(II) the alternatives to the minor use pesticide pose greater risks to the environment or human health;

(III) the minor use pesticide plays or will play a significant part in managing pest resistance; or

(IV) the minor use pesticide plays or will play a significant part in an integrated pest management program.

The registration of a pesticide for a minor use on a crop grouping established by the Administrator shall be considered for purposes of this clause 1 minor use for each representative crop for which data are provided in the crop grouping. Any additional exclusive use period under this clause shall be modified as appropriate or terminated if the registrant voluntarily cancels the product or deletes from the registration the minor uses which formed the basis for the extension of the additional exclusive use period or if the Administrator determines that the registrant is not actually marketing the product for such minor uses.

(iii) Except as otherwise provided in clause (i), with respect to data submitted after December 31, 1969, by an applicant or registrant to support an application for registration, experimental use permit, or amendment adding a new use to an existing registration, to support or maintain in effect an existing registration, or for reregistration, the Administrator may, without the permission of the original data submitter, consider any such item of data in support of an application by any other person (hereinafter in this subparagraph referred to as the

"applicant") within the fifteen-year period following the date the data were originally submitted only if the applicant has made an offer to compensate the original data submitter and submitted such offer to the Administrator accompanied by evidence of delivery to the original data submitter of the offer. The terms and amount of compensation may be fixed by agreement between the original data submitter and the applicant, or, failing such agreement, binding arbitration under this subparagraph. If, at the end of ninety days after the date of delivery to the original data submitter of the offer to compensate, the original data submitter and the applicant have neither agreed on the amount and terms of compensation nor on a procedure for reaching an agreement on the amount and terms of compensation, either person may initiate binding arbitration proceedings by requesting the Federal Mediation and Conciliation Service to appoint an arbitrator from the roster of arbitrators maintained by such Service. The procedure and rules of the Service shall be applicable to the selection of such arbitrator and to such arbitration proceedings, and the findings and determination of the arbitrator shall be final and conclusive, and no official or court of the United States shall have power or jurisdiction to review any such findings and determination, except for fraud, misrepresentation, or other misconduct by one of the parties to the arbitration or the arbitrator where there is a verified complaint with supporting affidavits attesting to specific instances of such fraud, misrepresentation, or other misconduct. The parties to the arbitration shall share equally in the payment of the fee and expenses of the arbitrator. If the Administrator determines that an original data submitter has failed to participate in a procedure for reaching an agreement or in an arbitration proceeding as required by this subparagraph, or failed to comply with the terms of an agreement or arbitration decision concerning compensation under this subparagraph, the original data submitter shall forfeit the right to compensation for the use of the data in support of the application. Notwithstanding any other provision of this subchapter, if the Administrator determines that an applicant has failed to participate in a procedure for reaching an agreement or in an arbitration proceeding as required by this subparagraph, or failed to comply with the terms of an agreement or arbitration decision concerning compensation under this subparagraph, the Administrator shall deny the application or cancel the registration of the pesticide in support of which the data were used without further hearing. Before the Administrator takes action under either of the preceding two sentences, the Administrator shall furnish to the affected person, by certified mail, notice of intent to take action and allow fifteen days from the date of delivery of the notice for the affected person to respond. If a registration is denied or canceled under this subparagraph, the Administrator may make such order as the Administrator deems appropriate concerning the continued sale and use of existing stocks of such pesticide. Registration action by the Administrator shall not be delayed pending the fixing of compensation.

(iv) After expiration of any period of exclusive use and any period for which compensation is required for the use of an item of data under clauses (i), (ii), and (iii), the Administrator may consider such item of data in support of an application by any other applicant without the permission of the original data submitter and without an offer having been received to compensate the original data submitter for the use of such item of data.

(v) The period of exclusive use provided under clause (ii) shall not take effect until 1 year after August 3, 1996, except where an applicant or registrant is applying for the registration of a pesticide containing an active ingredient not previously registered.

(vi) With respect to data submitted after August 3, 1996, by an applicant or registrant to support an amendment adding a new use to an existing registration that does not retain any period of exclusive use, if such data relates solely to a minor use of a pesticide, such data shall not, without the written permission of the original data submitter, be considered by the Administrator to support an application for a minor use by another person during the period of 10 years following the date of submission of such data. The applicant or registrant at the time the new minor use is requested shall notify the Administrator that to the best of their knowledge the exclusive use period for the pesticide has expired and that the data pertaining solely to the minor use of a pesticide is eligible for the provisions of this paragraph. If the minor use registration which is supported by data submitted pursuant to this subsection is voluntarily canceled or if such data are subsequently

used to support a nonminor use, the data shall no longer be subject to the exclusive use provisions of this clause but shall instead be considered by the Administrator in accordance with the provisions of clause (i), as appropriate.

(G) If the applicant is requesting that the registration or amendment to the registration of a pesticide be expedited, an explanation of the basis for the request must be submitted, in accordance with paragraph (10) of this subsection.

(2) Data in support of registration

(A) In general — The Administrator shall publish guidelines specifying the kinds of information which will be required to support the registration of a pesticide and shall revise such guidelines from time to time. If thereafter the Administrator requires any additional kind of information under subparagraph (B) of this paragraph, the Administrator shall permit sufficient time for applicants to obtain such additional information. The Administrator, in establishing standards for data requirements for the registration of pesticides with respect to minor uses, shall make such standards commensurate with the anticipated extent of use, pattern of use, the public health and agricultural need for such minor use, and the level and degree of potential beneficial or adverse effects on man and the environment. The Administrator shall not require a person to submit, in relation to a registration or reregistration of a pesticide for minor agricultural use under this subchapter, any field residue data from a geographic area where the pesticide will not be registered for such use. In the development of these standards, the Administrator shall consider the economic factors of potential national volume of use, extent of distribution, and the impact of the cost of meeting the requirements on the incentives for any potential registrant to undertake the development of the required data. Except as provided by section 136h of this title, within 30 days after the Administrator registers a pesticide under this subchapter the Administrator shall make available to the public the data called for in the registration statement together with such other scientific information as the Administrator deems relevant to the Administrator's decision.

(B) Additional data

(i) If the Administrator determines that additional data are required to maintain in effect an existing registration of a pesticide, the Administrator shall notify all existing registrants of the pesticide to which the determination relates and provide a list of such registrants to any interested person.

(ii) Each registrant of such pesticide shall provide evidence within ninety days after receipt of notification that it is taking appropriate steps to secure the additional data that are required. Two or more registrants may agree to develop jointly, or to share in the cost of developing, such data if they agree and advise the Administrator of their intent within ninety days after notification. Any registrant who agrees to share in the cost of producing the data shall be entitled to examine and rely upon such data in support of maintenance of such registration. The Administrator shall issue a notice of intent to suspend the registration of a pesticide in accordance with the procedures prescribed by clause (iv) if a registrant fails to comply with this clause.

(iii) If, at the end of sixty days after advising the Administrator of their agreement to develop jointly, or share in the cost of developing, data, the registrants have not further agreed on the terms of the data development arrangement or on a procedure for reaching such agreement, any of such registrants may initiate binding arbitration proceedings by requesting the Federal Mediation and Conciliation Service to appoint an arbitrator from the roster of arbitrators maintained by such Service. The procedure and rules of the Service shall be applicable to the selection of such arbitrator and to such arbitration proceedings, and the findings and determination of the arbitrator shall be final and conclusive, and no official or court of the United States shall have power or jurisdiction to review any such findings and determination, except for fraud, misrepresentation, or other misconduct by one of the parties to the arbitration or the arbitrator where there is a verified complaint with supporting affidavits attesting to specific instances of such fraud, misrepresentation, or other misconduct. All parties to the arbitration shall share equally in the payment of the fee and expenses of the arbitrator. The Administrator shall issue a notice of intent to suspend the registration of a pesticide in accordance with the procedures prescribed by clause (iv) if a registrant fails to comply with this clause.

(iv) Notwithstanding any other provision of this subchapter, if the Administrator determines that a registrant, within the time required by the Administrator, has failed to take appropriate steps to secure the data required under this subparagraph, to participate in a procedure for reaching agreement concerning a joint data development arrangement under this subparagraph

or in an arbitration proceeding as required by this subparagraph, or to comply with the terms of an agreement or arbitration decision concerning a joint data development arrangement under this subparagraph, the Administrator may issue a notice of intent to suspend such registrant's registration of the pesticide for which additional data is required. The Administrator may include in the notice of intent to suspend such provisions as the Administrator deems appropriate concerning the continued sale and use of existing stocks of such pesticide. Any suspension proposed under this subparagraph shall become final and effective at the end of thirty days from receipt by the registrant of the notice of intent to suspend, unless during that time a request for hearing is made by a person adversely affected by the notice or the registrant has satisfied the Administrator that the registrant has complied fully with the requirements that served as a basis for the notice of intent to suspend. If a hearing is requested, a hearing shall be conducted under section 136d(d) of this title. The only matters for resolution at that hearing shall be whether the registrant has failed to take the action that served as the basis for the notice of intent to suspend the registration of the pesticide for which additional data is required, and whether the Administrator's determination with respect to the disposition of existing stocks is consistent with this subchapter. If a hearing is held, a decision after completion of such hearing shall be final. Notwithstanding any other provision of this subchapter, a hearing shall be held and a determination made within seventy-five days after receipt of a request for such hearing. Any registration suspended under this subparagraph shall be reinstated by the Administrator if the Administrator determines that the registrant has complied fully with the requirements that served as a basis for the suspension of the registration.

(v) Any data submitted under this subparagraph shall be subject to the provisions of paragraph (1)(D). Whenever such data are submitted jointly by two or more registrants, an agent shall be agreed on at the time of the joint submission to handle any subsequent data compensation matters for the joint submitters of such data.

(vi) Upon the request of a registrant the Administrator shall, in the case of a minor use, extend the deadline for the production of residue chemistry data under this subparagraph for data required solely to support that minor use until the final deadline for submission of data under section 136a-1 of this title for the other uses of the pesticide established as of August 3, 1996, if —

(I) the data to support other uses of the pesticide on a food are being provided;

(II) the registrant, in submitting a request for such an extension, provides a schedule, including interim dates to measure progress, to assure that the data production will be completed before the expiration of the extension period;

(III) the Administrator has determined that such extension will not significantly delay the Administrator's schedule for issuing a reregistration eligibility determination required under section 136a-1 of this title; and

(IV) the Administrator has determined that based on existing data, such extension would not significantly increase the risk of any unreasonable adverse effect on the environment. If the Administrator grants an extension under this clause, the Administrator shall monitor the development of the data and shall ensure that the registrant is meeting the schedule for the production of the data. If the Administrator determines that the registrant is not meeting or has not met the schedule for the production of such data, the Administrator may proceed in accordance with clause (iv) regarding the continued registration of the affected products with the minor use and shall inform the public of such action. Notwithstanding the provisions of this clause, the Administrator may take action to modify or revoke the extension under this clause if the Administrator determines that the extension for the minor use may cause an unreasonable adverse effect on the environment. In such circumstance, the Administrator shall provide, in writing to the registrant, a notice revoking the extension of time for submission of data. Such data shall instead be due in accordance with the date established by the Administrator for the submission of the data.

(vii) If the registrant does not commit to support a specific minor use of the pesticide, but is supporting and providing data in a timely and adequate fashion to support uses of the pesticide on a food, or if all uses of the pesticide are nonfood uses and the registrant does not commit to support a specific minor use of the pesticide but is supporting and providing data in a timely and adequate fashion to support other nonfood uses of the pesticide, the Administrator, at the written request of the registrant, shall not take any action pursuant to this clause in regard to such unsupported minor use until the final deadline established as of August 3, 1996, for the submission of data under section 136a-1 of this title for the supported uses identified pursuant to this clause unless the Administrator determines that the absence of the data is significant enough to cause human health or environmental concerns. On the basis of such determination, the Administrator may refuse the request for extension by the registrant. Upon receipt of the request from the registrant, the Administrator shall publish in the Federal Register a notice of the receipt of the request and the effective date upon which the uses not being supported will be voluntarily deleted from the registration pursuant to section 136d(f)(1) of this title. If the Administrator grants an extension under this clause, the Administrator shall monitor the development of the data for the uses being supported and shall ensure that the registrant is meeting the schedule for the production of such data. If the Administrator determines that the registrant is not meeting or has not met the schedule for the production of such data, the Administrator may proceed in accordance with clause (iv) of this subparagraph regarding the continued registration of the affected products with the minor and other uses and shall inform the public of such action in accordance with section 136d(f)(2) of this title. Notwithstanding the provisions of this clause, the Administrator may deny, modify, or revoke the temporary extension under this subparagraph if the Administrator determines that the continuation of the minor use may cause an unreasonable adverse effect on the environment. In the event of modification or revocation, the Administrator shall provide, in writing, to the registrant a notice revoking the temporary extension and establish a new effective date by which the minor use shall be deleted from the registration.

(viii)(I) If data required to support registration of a pesticide under subparagraph (A) is requested by a Federal or State regulatory authority, the Administrator shall, to the extent practicable, coordinate data requirements, test protocols, timetables, and standards of review and reduce burdens and redundancy caused to the registrant by multiple requirements on the registrant.

(II) The Administrator may enter into a cooperative agreement with a State to carry out subclause (I).

(III) Not later than 1 year after August 3, 1996, the Administrator shall develop a process to identify and assist in alleviating future disparities between Federal and State data requirements.

(C) Simplified procedures — Within nine months after September 30, 1978, the Administrator shall, by regulation, prescribe simplified procedures for the registration of pesticides, which shall include the provisions of subparagraph (D) of this paragraph.

(D) Exemption — No applicant for registration of a pesticide who proposes to purchase a registered pesticide from another producer in order to formulate such purchased pesticide into the pesticide that is the subject of the application shall be required to —

(i) submit or cite data pertaining to such purchased product; or

(ii) offer to pay reasonable compensation otherwise required by paragraph (1) (D) of this subsection for the use of any such data.

(E) Minor use waiver — In handling the registration of a pesticide for a minor use, the Administrator may waive otherwise applicable data requirements if the Administrator determines that the absence of such data will not prevent the Administrator from determining —

(i) the incremental risk presented by the minor use of the pesticide; and

(ii) that such risk, if any, would not be an unreasonable adverse effect on the environment.

(3) Application

(A) In general — The Administrator shall review the data after receipt of the application and shall, as expeditiously as possible, either register the pesticide in accordance with paragraph (5), or notify the applicant of the Administrator's determination that it does not comply with the provisions of the subchapter in accordance with paragraph (6).

(B) Identical or substantially similar

(i) The Administrator shall, as expeditiously as possible, review and act on any application received by the Administrator that —

(I) proposes the initial or amended registration of an end-use pesticide that, if registered as proposed, would be identical or substantially similar in composition and labeling to a currently-registered pesticide identified in the application, or that would differ in composition and labeling from such currently-registered pesticide only in ways that would not significantly increase the risk of unreasonable adverse effects on the environment; or

(II) proposes an amendment to the registration of a registered pesticide that does not require scientific review of data.

(ii) In expediting the review of an application for an action described in clause (i), the Administrator shall —

(I) review the application in accordance with section 136w-8(f)(4) (B) of this title and, if the application is found to be incomplete, reject the application;

(II) not later than the applicable decision review time established pursuant to section 136w-8(f)(4)(B) of this title, or, if no review time is established, not later than 90 days after receiving a complete application, notify the registrant if the application has been granted or denied; and

(III) if the application is denied, notify the registrant in writing of the specific reasons for the denial of the application.

(C) Minor use registration

(i) The Administrator shall, as expeditiously as possible, review and act on any complete application —

(I) that proposes the initial registration of a new pesticide active ingredient if the active ingredient is proposed to be registered solely for minor uses, or proposes a registration amendment solely for minor uses to an existing registration; or

(II) for a registration or a registration amendment that proposes significant minor uses.

(ii) For the purposes of clause (i) —

(I) the term "as expeditiously as possible" means that the Administrator shall, to the greatest extent practicable, complete a review and evaluation of all data, submitted with a complete application, within 12 months after the submission of the complete application, and the failure of the Administrator to complete such a review and evaluation under clause (i) shall not be subject to judicial review; and

(II) the term "significant minor uses" means 3 or more minor uses proposed for every nonminor use, a minor use that would, in the judgment of the Administrator, serve as a replacement for any use which has been canceled in the 5 years preceding the receipt of the application, or a minor use that in the opinion of the Administrator would avoid the reissuance of an emergency exemption under section 136p of this title for that minor use.

(D) Adequate time for submission of minor use data — If a registrant makes a request for a minor use waiver, regarding data required by the Administrator, pursuant to paragraph (2)(E), and if the Administrator denies in whole or in part such data waiver request, the registrant shall have a full-time period for providing such data. For purposes of this subparagraph, the term "full-time period" means the time period originally established by the Administrator for submission of such data, beginning with the date of receipt by the registrant of the Administrator's notice of denial.

(4) Notice of application — The Administrator shall publish in the Federal Register, promptly after receipt of the statement and other data required pursuant to paragraphs (1) and (2), a notice of each application for registration of any pesticide if it contains any new active ingredient or if it would entail a changed use pattern. The notice shall provide for a period of 30 days in which any Federal agency or any other interested person may comment.

(5) Approval of registration — The Administrator shall register a pesticide if the Administrator determines that, when considered with any restrictions imposed under subsection (d) of this section —

(A) its composition is such as to warrant the proposed claims for it;

(B) its labeling and other material required to be submitted comply with the requirements of this subchapter;

(C) it will perform its intended function without unreasonable adverse effects on the environment; and

(D) when used in accordance with widespread and commonly recognized practice it will not generally cause unreasonable adverse effects on the environment.

The Administrator shall not make any lack of essentiality a criterion for denying registration of any pesticide. Where two pesticides meet the requirements of this paragraph, one should not be registered in preference to the other. In considering an application for the registration of a pesticide, the Administrator may waive data requirements pertaining to efficacy, in which event the Administrator may register the pesticide without determining that the pesticide's composition is such as to warrant proposed claims of efficacy. If a pesticide is found to be efficacious by any State under section 136v(c) of this title, a presumption is established that the Administrator shall waive data requirements pertaining to efficacy for use of the pesticide in such State.

(6) Denial of registration — If the Administrator determines that the requirements of paragraph (5) for registration are not satisfied, the Administrator shall notify the applicant for registration of the Administrator's determination and of the Administrator's reasons (including the factual basis) therefor, and that, unless the applicant corrects the conditions and notifies the Administrator thereof during the 30-day period beginning with the day after the date on which the applicant receives the notice, the Administrator may refuse to register the pesticide. Whenever the Administrator refuses to register a pesticide, the Administrator shall notify the applicant of the Administrator's decision and of the Administrator's reasons (including the factual basis) therefor. The Administrator shall promptly publish in the Federal Register notice of such denial of registration and the reasons therefor. Upon such notification, the applicant for registration or other interested person with the concurrence of the applicant shall have the same remedies as provided for in section 136d of this title.

(7) Registration under special circumstances — Notwithstanding the provisions of paragraph (5) —

(A) The Administrator may conditionally register or amend the registration of a pesticide if the Administrator determines that (i) the pesticide and proposed use are identical or substantially similar to any currently registered pesticide and use thereof, or differ only in ways that would not significantly increase the risk of unreasonable adverse effects on the environment, and (ii) approving the registration or amendment in the manner proposed by the applicant would not significantly increase the risk of any unreasonable adverse effect on the environment. An applicant seeking conditional registration or amended registration under this subparagraph shall submit such data as would be required to obtain registration of a similar pesticide under paragraph (5). If the applicant is unable to submit an item of data because it has not yet been generated, the Administrator may register or amend the registration of the pesticide under such conditions as will require the submission of such data not later than the time such data are required to be submitted with respect to similar pesticides already registered under this subchapter.

(B) The Administrator may conditionally amend the registration of a pesticide to permit additional uses of such pesticide notwithstanding that data concerning the pesticide may be insufficient to support an unconditional amendment, if the Administrator determines that (i) the applicant has submitted satisfactory data pertaining to the proposed additional use, and (ii) amending the registration in the manner proposed by the applicant would not significantly increase the risk of any unreasonable adverse effect on the environment. Notwithstanding the foregoing provisions of this subparagraph, no registration of a pesticide may be amended to permit an additional use of such pesticide if the Administrator has issued a notice stating that such pesticide, or any ingredient thereof, meets or exceeds risk criteria associated in whole or in part with human dietary exposure enumerated in regulations issued under this subchapter, and during the pendency of any risk-benefit evaluation initiated by such notice, if (I) the additional use of such pesticide involves a major food or feed crop, or (II) the additional use of such pesticide involves a minor food or feed crop and the Administrator determines, with the concurrence of the Secretary of Agriculture, there is available an effective alternative pesticide that does not meet or exceed such risk criteria. An applicant seeking amended registration under this subparagraph shall submit such data as would be required to obtain registration of a similar pesticide under paragraph (5). If the applicant is unable to submit an item of data (other than data pertaining to the proposed additional use) because it has not yet been generated, the Administrator may amend the registration under such conditions as will require the submission of such data not later than the time such data are required to be submitted with respect to similar pesticides already registered under this subchapter.

(C) The Administrator may conditionally register a pesticide containing an active ingredient not contained in any currently registered pesticide for a period reasonably sufficient for the generation and submission of required data (which are lacking because a period reasonably sufficient for generation of the data has not elapsed since the Administrator first imposed the data requirement) on the condition that by the end of such period the Administrator receives such data and the data do not meet or exceed risk criteria enumerated in regulations issued under this subchapter, and on such other conditions as the Administrator may prescribe. A conditional registration under this subparagraph shall be granted only if the Administrator determines that use of the pesticide during such period will not cause any unreasonable adverse effect on the environment, and that use of the pesticide is in the public interest.

(8) Interim administrative review — Notwithstanding any other provision of this subchapter, the Administrator may not initiate a public interim administrative review process to develop a risk-benefit evaluation of the ingredients of a pesticide or any of its uses prior to initiating a formal action to cancel, suspend, or deny registration of such pesticide, required under this subchapter, unless such interim administrative process is based on a validated test or other significant evidence raising prudent concerns of unreasonable adverse risk to man or to the environment. Notice of the definition of the terms "validated test" and "other significant evidence" as used herein shall be published by the Administrator in the Federal Register.

(9) Labeling

(A) Additional statements — Subject to subparagraphs (B) and (C), it shall not be a violation of this subchapter for a registrant to modify the labeling of an antimicrobial pesticide product to include relevant information on product efficacy, product composition, container composition or design, or other characteristics that do not relate to any pesticidal claim or pesticidal activity.

(B) Requirements — Proposed labeling information under subparagraph (A) shall not be false or misleading, shall not conflict with or detract from any statement required by law or the Administrator as a condition of registration, and shall be substantiated on the request of the Administrator.

(C) Notification and disapproval

(i) Notification — A registration may be modified under subparagraph (A) if —

(I) the registrant notifies the Administrator in writing not later than 60 days prior to distribution or sale of a product bearing the modified labeling; and

(II) the Administrator does not disapprove of the modification under clause (ii).

(ii) Disapproval — Not later than 30 days after receipt of a notification under clause (i), the Administrator may disapprove the modification by sending the registrant notification in writing stating that the proposed language is not acceptable and stating the reasons why the Administrator finds the proposed modification unacceptable.

(iii) Restriction on sale — A registrant may not sell or distribute a product bearing a disapproved modification.

(iv) Objection — A registrant may file an objection in writing to a disapproval under clause (ii) not later than 30 days after receipt of notification of the disapproval.

(v) Final action — A decision by the Administrator following receipt and consideration of an objection filed under clause (iv) shall be considered a final agency action.

(D) Use dilution — The label or labeling required under this subchapter for an antimicrobial pesticide that is or may be diluted for use may have a different statement of caution or protective measures for use of the recommended diluted solution of the pesticide than for use of a concentrate of the pesticide if the Administrator determines that —

(i) adequate data have been submitted to support the statement proposed for the diluted solution uses; and

(ii) the label or labeling provides adequate protection for exposure to the diluted solution of the pesticide.

(10) Expedited registration of pesticides

(A) Not later than 1 year after August 3, 1996, the Administrator shall, utilizing public comment, develop procedures and guidelines, and expedite the review of an application for registration of a pesticide or an amendment to a registration that satisfies such guidelines.

(B) Any application for registration or an amendment, including biological and conventional pesticides, will be considered for expedited review under this paragraph. An application for registration or an amendment shall qualify for expedited review if use of the pesticide proposed by the application may reasonably be expected to accomplish 1 or more of the following:

(i) Reduce the risks of pesticides to human health.

(ii) Reduce the risks of pesticides to nontarget organisms.

(iii) Reduce the potential for contamination of groundwater, surface water, or other valued environmental resources.

(iv) Broaden the adoption of integrated pest management strategies, or make such strategies more available or more effective.

(C) The Administrator, not later than 30 days after receipt of an application for expedited review, shall notify the applicant whether the application is complete. If it is found to be incomplete, the Administrator may either reject the request for expedited review or ask the applicant for additional information to satisfy the guidelines developed under subparagraph (A).

(11) Interagency working group

(A) Definition of covered agency

In this paragraph, the term "covered agency" means any of the following:

(i) The Department of Agriculture.

(ii) The Department of Commerce.

(iii) The Department of the Interior.

(iv) The Council on Environmental Quality.

(v) The Environmental Protection Agency.

(B) Establishment

The Administrator shall establish an interagency working group, to be comprised of representatives from each covered agency, to provide recommendations regarding, and to implement a strategy for improving, the consultation process required under section 7 of the Endangered Species Act of 1973 (16 U.S.C. 1536) for pesticide registration and registration review.

(C) Duties

The interagency working group established under subparagraph (B) shall —

(i) analyze relevant Federal law (including regulations) and case law for purposes of providing an outline of the legal and regulatory framework for the consultation process referred to in that subparagraph, including —

(I) requirements under this subchapter and the Endangered Species Act of 1973 (16 U.S.C. 1531 et seq.);

(II) Federal case law regarding the intersection of this subchapter and the Endangered Species Act of 1973 (16 U.S.C. 1531 et seq.); and

(III) Federal regulations relating to the pesticide consultation process;

(ii) provide advice regarding methods of —

(I) defining the scope of actions of the covered agencies that are subject to the consultation requirement referred to in subparagraph (B); and

(II) properly identifying and classifying effects of actions of the covered agencies with respect to that consultation requirement;

(iii) identify the obligations and limitations under Federal law of each covered agency for purposes of providing a legal and regulatory framework for developing the recommendations referred to in subparagraph (B);

(iv) review practices for the consultation referred to in subparagraph (B) to identify problem areas, areas for improvement, and best practices for conducting that consultation among the covered agencies;

(v) develop scientific and policy approaches to increase the accuracy and timeliness of the process for that consultation, in accordance with requirements of this subchapter and the Endangered Species Act of 1973 (16 U.S.C. 1531 et seq.), including —

(I) processes to efficiently share data and coordinate analyses among the Department of Agriculture, the Department of Commerce, the Department of the Interior, and the Environmental Protection Agency;

(II) a streamlined process for identifying which actions require no consultation, informal consultation, or formal consultation;

(III) an approach that will provide clarity with respect to what constitutes the best scientific and commercial data available in the fields of pesticide use and ecological risk assessment, pursuant to section 7(a)(2) of the Endangered Species Act of 1973 (16 U.S.C. 1536(a)(2)); and

(IV) approaches that enable the Environmental Protection Agency to better assist the Department of the Interior and the Department of Commerce in carrying out obligations under that section in a timely and efficient manner; and

(vi) propose and implement a strategy to implement approaches to consultations under the Endangered Species Act of 1973 (16 U.S.C. 1531 et seq.) and document that strategy in a memorandum of understanding, revised regulations, or another appropriate format to promote durable cooperation among the covered agencies.

(D) Reports

(i) Progress reports

(I) In general

Not later than 18 months after December 20, 2018, the Administrator, in coordination with the head of each other covered agency, shall submit to the Committee on Agriculture of the House of Representatives and the Committee on Agriculture, Nutrition, and Forestry of the Senate a report describing the progress of the working group in developing the recommendations under subparagraph (B).

(II) Requirements

The report under this clause shall —

(aa) reflect the perspectives of each covered agency; and

(bb) identify areas of new consensus and continuing topics of disagreement and debate.

(ii) Results

(I) In general

Not later than 1 year after December 20, 2018, the Administrator, in coordination with the head of each other covered agency, shall submit to the Committee on Agriculture of the House of Representatives and the Committee on Agriculture, Nutrition, and Forestry of the Senate a report describing —

(aa) the recommendations developed under subparagraph (B); and

(bb) plans for implementation of those recommendations.

(II) Requirements

The report under this clause shall —

(aa) reflect the perspectives of each covered agency; and

(bb) identify areas of consensus and continuing topics of disagreement and debate, if any.

(iii) Implementation

Not later than 1 year after the date of submission of the report under clause (i), the Administrator, in coordination with the head of each other covered agency, shall submit to the Committee on Agriculture of the House of Representatives and the Committee on Agriculture, Nutrition, and Forestry of the Senate a report describing —

(I) the implementation of the recommendations referred to in that clause;

(II) the extent to which that implementation improved the consultation process referred to in subparagraph (B); and

(III) any additional recommendations for improvements to the process described in subparagraph (B).

(iv) Other reports

Not later than the date that is 180 days after the date of submission of the report under clause (iii), and not less frequently than once every 180 days thereafter during the 5-year period beginning on that date, the Administrator, in coordination with the head of each other covered agency, shall submit to the Committee on Agriculture of the House of Representatives and the Committee on Agriculture, Nutrition, and Forestry of the Senate a report describing —

(I) the implementation of the recommendations referred to in that clause;

(II) the extent to which that implementation improved the consultation process referred to in subparagraph (B); and

(III) any additional recommendations for improvements to the process described in subparagraph (B).

(E) Consultation with private sector

In carrying out the duties under this paragraph, the working group shall, as appropriate —

(i) consult with, representatives of interested industry stakeholders and non-governmental organizations; and

(ii) take into consideration factors, such as actual and potential differences in interest between, and the views of, those stakeholders and organizations.

(F) Federal Advisory Committee Act

The Federal Advisory Committee Act (5 U.S.C. App.) shall not apply to the working group established under this paragraph.

(G) Savings clause

Nothing in this paragraph supersedes any provision of —

(i) this subchapter; or

(ii) the Endangered Species Act of 1973 (16 U.S.C. 1531 et seq.), including the requirements under section 7 of that Act (16 U.S.C. 1536).

(d) Classification of pesticides

(1) Classification for general use, restricted use, or both

(A) As a part of the registration of a pesticide the Administrator shall classify it as being for general use or for restricted use. If the Administrator determines that some of the uses for which the pesticide is registered should be for general use and that other uses for which it is registered should be for restricted use, the Administrator shall classify it for both general use and restricted use. Pesticide uses may be classified by regulation on the initial classification, and registered pesticides may be classified prior to reregistration. If some of the uses of the pesticide are classified for general use, and other uses are classified for restricted use, the directions relating to its general uses shall be clearly separated and distinguished from those directions relating to its restricted uses. The Administrator may require that its packaging and labeling for restricted uses shall be clearly distinguishable from its packaging and labeling for general uses.

(B) If the Administrator determines that the pesticide, when applied in accordance with its directions for use, warnings and cautions and for the uses for which it is registered, or for one or more of such uses, or in accordance with a widespread and commonly recognized practice, will not generally cause unreasonable adverse effects on the environment, the Administrator will classify the pesticide, or the particular use or uses of the pesticide to which the determination applies, for general use.

(C) If the Administrator determines that the pesticide, when applied in accordance with its directions for use, warnings and cautions and for the uses for which it is registered, or for one or more of such uses, or in accordance with a widespread and commonly recognized practice, may generally cause, without additional regulatory restrictions, unreasonable adverse effects on the environment, including injury to the applicator, the Administrator shall classify the pesticide, or the particular use or uses to which the determination applies, for restricted use:

(i) If the Administrator classifies a pesticide, or one or more uses of such pesticide, for restricted use because of a determination that the acute dermal or inhalation toxicity of the pesticide presents a hazard to the applicator or other persons, the pesticide shall be applied for any use to which the restricted classification applies only by or under the direct supervision of a certified applicator.

(ii) If the Administrator classifies a pesticide, or one or more uses of such pesticide, for restricted use because of a determination that its use without additional regulatory restriction may cause unreasonable adverse effects on the environment, the pesticide shall be applied for any use to which the determination applies only by or under the direct supervision of a certified applicator, or subject to such other restrictions as the Administrator may provide by regulation. Any such regulation shall be reviewable in the appropriate court of appeals upon petition of a person adversely affected filed within 60 days of the publication of the regulation in final form.

(2) Change in classification — If the Administrator determines that a change in the classification of any use of a pesticide from general use to restricted use is necessary to prevent unreasonable adverse effects on the environment, the Administrator shall notify the registrant of such pesticide of such determination at least forty-five days before making the change and shall publish the proposed change in the Federal Register. The registrant, or other interested person with the concurrence of the registrant, may seek relief from such determination under section 136d(b) of this title.

(3) Change in classification from restricted use to general use — The registrant of any pesticide with one or more uses classified for restricted use may petition the Administrator to change any such classification from restricted to general use. Such petition shall set out the basis for the registrant's position that restricted use classification is unnecessary because classification of the pesticide for general use would not cause unreasonable adverse effects on the environment. The Administrator, within sixty days after receiving such petition, shall notify the registrant whether the petition has been granted or denied. Any denial shall contain

an explanation therefor and any such denial shall be subject to judicial review under section 136n of this title.

(e) Products with same formulation and claims — Products which have the same formulation, are manufactured by the same person, the labeling of which contains the same claims, and the labels of which bear a designation identifying the product as the same pesticide may be registered as a single pesticide; and additional names and labels shall be added to the registration by supplemental statements.

(f) Miscellaneous

(1) Effect of change of labeling or formulation — If the labeling or formulation for a pesticide is changed, the registration shall be amended to reflect such change if the Administrator determines that the change will not violate any provision of this subchapter.

(2) Registration not a defense — In no event shall registration of an article be construed as a defense for the commission of any offense under this subchapter. As long as no cancellation proceedings are in effect registration of a pesticide shall be prima facie evidence that the pesticide, its labeling and packaging comply with the registration provisions of the subchapter.

(3) Authority to consult other Federal agencies — In connection with consideration of any registration or application for registration under this section, the Administrator may consult with any other Federal agency.

(4) Mixtures of nitrogen stabilizers and fertilizer products — Any mixture or other combination of —

(A) 1 or more nitrogen stabilizers registered under this subchapter; and

(B) 1 or more fertilizer products, shall not be subject to the provisions of this section or sections 136a-1, 136c, 136e, 136m, and 136o(a)(2) of this title if the mixture or other combination is accompanied by the labeling required under this subchapter for the nitrogen stabilizer contained in the mixture or other combination, the mixture or combination is mixed or combined in accordance with such labeling, and the mixture or combination does not contain any active ingredient other than the nitrogen stabilizer.

(g) Registration review

(1) General rule

(A) Periodic review

(i) In general, the registrations of pesticides are to be periodically reviewed.

(ii) Regulations

In accordance with the subparagraph, the Administrator shall by regulation establish a procedure for accomplishing the periodic review of registrations.

(iii) Initial registration review

The Administrator shall complete the registration review of each pesticide or pesticide case, which may be composed of 1 or more active ingredients and the products associated with the active ingredients, not later than the later of —

(I) October 1, 2022; or

(II) the date that is 15 years after the date on which the first pesticide containing a new active ingredient is registered.

(iv) Subsequent registration review

Not later than 15 years after the date on which the initial registration review is completed under clause (iii) and each 15 years thereafter, the Administrator shall complete a subsequent registration review for each pesticide or pesticide case.

(v) Cancellation

No registration shall be canceled as a result of the registration review process unless the Administrator follows the procedures and substantive requirements of section 136d of this title.

(B) Docketing

(i) In general

Subject to clause (ii), after meeting with 1 or more individuals that are not government employees to discuss matters relating to a registration review, the Administrator shall place in the docket minutes of the meeting, a list of attendees, and any documents exchanged at the meeting, not later than the earlier of —

(I) the date that is 45 days after the meeting; or

(II) the date of issuance of the registration review decision.

(ii) Protected information

The Administrator shall identify, but not include in the docket, any confidential business information the disclosure of which is prohibited by section 136h of this title.

(C) Limitation

Nothing in this subsection shall prohibit the Administrator from undertaking any other review of a pesticide pursuant to this subchapter.

(2) Data

(A) Submission required

The Administrator shall use the authority in subsection (c)(2)(B) of this section to require the submission of data when such data are necessary for a registration review.

(B) Data submission, compensation, and exemption

For purposes of this subsection, the provisions of subsections (c)(1), (c)(2)(B), and (c)(2)(D) of this section shall be utilized for and be applicable to any data required for registration review.

(h) Registration requirements for antimicrobial pesticides

(1) Evaluation of process — To the maximum extent practicable consistent with the degrees of risk presented by an antimicrobial pesticide and the type of review appropriate to evaluate the risks, the Administrator shall identify and evaluate reforms to the antimicrobial registration process that would reduce review periods existing as of August 3, 1996, for antimicrobial pesticide product registration applications and applications for amended registration of antimicrobial pesticide products, including —

(A) new antimicrobial active ingredients;

(B) new antimicrobial end-use products;

(C) substantially similar or identical antimicrobial pesticides; and

(D) amendments to antimicrobial pesticide registrations.

(2) Review time period reduction goal — Each reform identified under paragraph (1) shall be designed to achieve the goal of reducing the review period following submission of a complete application, consistent with the degree of risk, to a period of not more than —

(A) 540 days for a new antimicrobial active ingredient pesticide registration;

(B) 270 days for a new antimicrobial use of a registered active ingredient;

(C) 120 days for any other new antimicrobial product;

(D) 90 days for a substantially similar or identical antimicrobial product;

(E) 90 days for an amendment to an antimicrobial registration that does not require scientific review of data; and

(F) 120 days for an amendment to an antimicrobial registration that requires scientific review of data and that is not otherwise described in this paragraph.

(3) Implementation

(A) Proposed rulemaking

(i) Issuance — Not later than 270 days after August 3, 1996, the Administrator shall publish in the Federal Register proposed regulations to accelerate and improve the review of antimicrobial pesticide products designed to implement, to the extent practicable, the goals set forth in paragraph (2).

(ii) Requirements — Proposed regulations issued under clause (i) shall —

(I) define the various classes of antimicrobial use patterns, including household, industrial, and institutional disinfectants and sanitizing pesticides, preservatives, water treatment, and pulp and paper mill additives, and other such products intended to disinfect, sanitize, reduce, or mitigate growth or development of microbiological organisms, or protect inanimate objects, industrial processes or systems, surfaces, water, or other chemical substances from contamination, fouling, or deterioration caused by bacteria, viruses, fungi, protozoa, algae, or slime;

(II) differentiate the types of review undertaken for antimicrobial pesticides;

(III) conform the degree and type of review to the risks and benefits presented by antimicrobial pesticides and the function of review under this subchapter, considering the use patterns of the product, toxicity, expected exposure, and product type;

(IV) ensure that the registration process is sufficient to maintain antimicrobial pesticide efficacy and that antimicrobial pesticide products continue to meet product performance standards and effectiveness levels for each type of label claim made; and

(V) implement effective and reliable deadlines for process management.

(iii) Comments — In developing the proposed regulations, the Administrator shall solicit the views from registrants and other affected parties to maximize the effectiveness of the rule development process.

(B) Final regulations

(i) Issuance — The Administrator shall issue final regulations not later than 240 days after the close of the comment period for the proposed regulations.

(ii) Failure to meet goal — If a goal described in paragraph (2) is not met by the final regulations, the Administrator shall identify the goal, explain why the goal was not attained, describe the element of the regulations included instead, and identify future steps to attain the goal.

(iii) Requirements — In issuing final regulations, the Administrator shall —

(I) consider the establishment of a certification process for regulatory actions involving risks that can be responsibly managed, consistent with the degree of risk, in the most cost-efficient manner;

(II) consider the establishment of a certification process by approved laboratories as an adjunct to the review process;

(III) use all appropriate and cost-effective review mechanisms, including —

(aa) expanded use of notification and non-notification procedures;

(bb) revised procedures for application review; and

(cc) allocation of appropriate resources to ensure streamlined management of antimicrobial pesticide registrations; and

(IV) clarify criteria for determination of the completeness of an application.

(C) Expedited review — This subsection does not affect the requirements or extend the deadlines or review periods contained in subsection (c)(3) of this section.

(D) Alternative review periods — If the final regulations to carry out this paragraph are not effective 630 days after August 3, 1996, until the final regulations become effective, the review period, beginning on the date of receipt by the Agency of a complete application, shall be —

(i) 2 years for a new antimicrobial active ingredient pesticide registration;

(ii) 1 year for a new antimicrobial use of a registered active ingredient;

(iii) 180 days for any other new antimicrobial product;

(iv) 90 days for a substantially similar or identical antimicrobial product;

(v) 90 days for an amendment to an antimicrobial registration that does not require scientific review of data; and

(vi) 120 days for an amendment to an antimicrobial registration that requires scientific review of data and that is not otherwise described in this subparagraph.

(E) Wood preservatives — An application for the registration, or for an amendment to the registration, of a wood preservative product for which a claim of pesticidal activity listed in section 136(mm) of this title is made (regardless of any other pesticidal claim that is made with respect to the product) shall be reviewed by the Administrator within the same period as that established under this paragraph for an antimicrobial pesticide product application, consistent with the degree of risk posed by the use of the wood preservative product, if the application requires the applicant to satisfy the same data requirements as are required to support an application for a wood preservative product that is an antimicrobial pesticide.

(F) Notification

(i) In general — Subject to clause (iii), the Administrator shall notify an applicant whether an application has been granted or denied not later than the final day of the appropriate review period under this paragraph, unless the applicant and the Administrator agree to a later date.

(ii) Final decision — If the Administrator fails to notify an applicant within the period of time required under clause (i), the failure shall be considered an agency action unlawfully withheld or unreasonably delayed for purposes of judicial review under chapter 7 of Title 5.

(iii) Exemption — This subparagraph does not apply to an application for an antimicrobial pesticide that is filed under subsection (c)(3)(B) of this section prior to 90 days after August 3, 1996.

(iv) Limitation — Notwithstanding clause (ii), the failure of the Administrator to notify an applicant for an amendment to a registration for an antimicrobial pesticide shall not be judicially reviewable in a Federal or State court if the amendment requires scientific review of data within —

(I) the time period specified in subparagraph (D)(vi), in the absence of a final regulation under subparagraph (B); or

(II) the time period specified in paragraph (2)(F), if adopted in a final regulation under subparagraph (B).

(4) Annual report

(A) Submission — Beginning on August 3, 1996, and ending on the date that the goals under paragraph (2) are achieved, the Administrator shall, not later than March 1 of each year, prepare and submit an annual report to the Committee on Agriculture of the House of Representatives and the Committee on Agriculture, Nutrition, and Forestry of the Senate.

(B) Requirements — A report submitted under subparagraph (A) shall include a description of —

(i) measures taken to reduce the backlog of pending registration applications;

(ii) progress toward achieving reforms under this subsection; and

(iii) recommendations to improve the activities of the Agency pertaining to antimicrobial registrations.

§136a-1. Reregistration of registered pesticides [FIFRA §4]

(a) General rule — The Administrator shall reregister, in accordance with this section, each registered pesticide containing any active ingredient contained in any pesticide first registered before November 1, 1984, except for any pesticide as to which the Administrator has determined, after November 1, 1984, and before the effective date of this section, that —

(1) there are no outstanding data requirements; and

(2) the requirements of section 136a(c)(5) of this title have been satisfied.

(b) Reregistration phases — Reregistrations of pesticides under this section shall be carried out in the following phases:

(1) The first phase shall include the listing under subsection (c) of this section of the active ingredients of the pesticides that will be reregistered.

(2) The second phase shall include the submission to the Administrator under subsection (d) of this section of notices by registrants respecting their intention to seek reregistration, identification by registrants of missing and inadequate data for such pesticides, and commitments by registrants to replace such missing or inadequate data within the applicable time period.

(3) The third phase shall include submission to the Administrator by registrants of the information required under subsection (e) of this section.

(4) The fourth phase shall include an independent, initial review by the Administrator under subsection (f) of this section of submissions under phases two and three, identification of outstanding data requirements, and the issuance, as necessary, of requests for additional data.

(5) The fifth phase shall include the review by the Administrator under subsection (g) of this section of data submitted for reregistration and appropriate regulatory action by the Administrator.

(c) Phase one

(1) Priority for reregistration — For purposes of the reregistration of the pesticides described in subsection (a) of this section, the Administrator shall list the active ingredients of pesticides and shall give priority to, among others, active ingredients (other than active ingredients for which registration standards have been issued before the effective date of this section) that —

(A) are in use on or in food or feed and may result in postharvest residues;

(B) may result in residues of potential toxicological concern in potable ground water, edible fish, or shellfish;

(C) have been determined by the Administrator before the effective date of this section to have significant outstanding data requirements; or

(D) are used on crops, including in greenhouses and nurseries, where worker exposure is most likely to occur.

(2) Reregistration lists — For purposes of reregistration under this section, the Administrator shall by order —

(A) not later than 70 days after the effective date of this section, list pesticide active ingredients for which registration standards have been issued before such effective date;

(B) not later than 4 months after such effective date, list the first 150 pesticide active ingredients, as determined under paragraph (1);

(C) not later than 7 months after such effective date, list the second 150 pesticide active ingredients, as determined under paragraph (1); and

(D) not later than 10 months after such effective date, list the remainder of the pesticide active ingredients, as determined under paragraph (1).

Each list shall be published in the Federal Register.

(3) Judicial review — The content of a list issued by the Administrator under paragraph (2) shall not be subject to judicial review.

(4) Notice to registrants — On the publication of a list of pesticide active ingredients under paragraph (2), the Administrator shall send by certified mail to the registrants of the pesticides containing such active ingredients a notice of the time by which the registrants are to notify the Administrator under subsection (d) of this section whether the registrants intend to seek or not to seek reregistration of such pesticides.

(d) Phase two

(1) In general — The registrant of a pesticide that contains an active ingredient listed under subparagraph (B), (C), or (D) of subsection (c)(2) of this section shall submit to the Administrator, within the time period prescribed by paragraph (4), the notice described in paragraph (2) and any information, commitment, or offer described in paragraph (3).

(2) Notice of intent to seek or not to seek reregistration

(A) The registrant of a pesticide containing an active ingredient listed under subparagraph (B), (C), or (D) of subsection (c)(2) of this section shall notify the Administrator by certified mail whether the registrant intends to seek or does not intend to seek reregistration of the pesticide.

(B) If a registrant submits a notice under subparagraph (A) of an intention not to seek reregistration of a pesticide, the Administrator shall publish a notice in the Federal Register stating that such a notice has been submitted.

(3) Missing or inadequate data — Each registrant of a pesticide that contains an active ingredient listed under subparagraph (B), (C), or (D) of subsection (c)(2) of this section and for which the registrant submitted a notice under paragraph (2) of an intention to seek reregistration of such pesticide shall submit to the Administrator —

(A) in accordance with regulations issued by the Administrator under section 136a of this title, an identification of —

(i) all data that are required by regulation to support the registration of the pesticide with respect to such active ingredient;

(ii) data that were submitted by the registrant previously in support of the registration of the pesticide that are inadequate to meet such regulations; and

(iii) data identified under clause (i) that have not been submitted to the Administrator; and

(B) either —

(i) a commitment to replace the data identified under subparagraph (A)(ii) and submit the data identified under subparagraph (A)(iii) within the applicable time period prescribed by paragraph (4)(B); or

(ii) an offer to share in the cost to be incurred by a person who has made a commitment under clause (i) to replace or submit the data and an offer to submit to arbitration as described by section 136a(c)(2)(B) of this title with regard to such cost sharing.

For purposes of a submission by a registrant under subparagraph (A)(ii), data are inadequate if the data are derived from a study with respect to which the registrant is unable to make the certification prescribed by subsection (e)(1)(G) of this section that the registrant possesses or has access to the raw data used in or generated by such study. For purposes of a submission by a registrant under such subparagraph, data shall be considered to be inadequate if the data are derived from a study submitted before January 1, 1970, unless it is demonstrated to the satisfaction of the Administrator that such data should be considered to support the registration of the pesticide that is to be reregistered.

(4) Time periods

(A) A submission under paragraph (2) or (3) shall be made —

(i) in the case of a pesticide containing an active ingredient listed under subsection (c)(2)(B) of this section, not later than 3 months after the date of publication of the listing of such active ingredient;

(ii) in the case of a pesticide containing an active ingredient listed under subsection (c)(2)(C) of this section, not later than 3 months after the date of publication of the listing of such active ingredient; and

(iii) in the case of a pesticide containing an active ingredient listed under subsection (c)(2)(D) of this section, not later than 3 months after the date of publication of the listing of such active ingredient.

On application, the Administrator may extend a time period prescribed by this subparagraph if the Administrator determines that factors beyond the control of the registrant prevent the registrant from complying with such period.

(B) A registrant shall submit data in accordance with a commitment entered into under paragraph (3)(B) within a reasonable period of time, as determined by the Administrator, but not more than 48 months after the date the registrant submitted the commitment. The Ad-

ministrator, on application of a registrant, may extend the period prescribed by the preceding sentence by no more than 2 years if extraordinary circumstances beyond the control of the registrant prevent the registrant from submitting data within such prescribed period. Upon application of a registrant, the Administrator shall, in the case of a minor use, extend the deadline for the production of residue chemistry data under this subparagraph for data required solely to support that minor use until the final deadline for submission of data under this section for the other uses of the pesticide established as of August 3, 1996, if —

(i) the data to support other uses of the pesticide on a food are being provided;

(ii) the registrant, in submitting a request for such an extension provides a schedule, including interim dates to measure progress, to assure that the data production will be completed before the expiration of the extension period;

(iii) the Administrator has determined that such extension will not significantly delay the Administrator's schedule for issuing a reregistration eligibility determination required under this section; and

(iv) the Administrator has determined that based on existing data, such extension would not significantly increase the risk of any unreasonable adverse effect on the environment. If the Administrator grants an extension under this subparagraph, the Administrator shall monitor the development of the data and shall ensure that the registrant is meeting the schedule for the production of the data. If the Administrator determines that the registrant is not meeting or has not met the schedule for the production of such data, the Administrator may proceed in accordance with clause (iv) of section 136a(c)(2)(B) of this title or other provisions of this section, as appropriate, regarding the continued registration of the affected products with the minor use and shall inform the public of such action. Notwithstanding the provisions of this subparagraph, the Administrator may take action to modify or revoke the extension under this subparagraph if the Administrator determines that the extension for the minor use may cause an unreasonable adverse effect on the environment. In such circumstance, the Administrator shall provide written notice to the registrant revoking the extension of time for submission of data. Such data shall instead be due in accordance with the date then established by the Administrator for submission of the data.

(5) Cancellation and removal

(A) If the registrant of a pesticide does not submit a notice under paragraph (2) or (3) within the time prescribed by paragraph (4)(A), the Administrator shall issue a notice of intent to cancel the registration of such registrant for such pesticide and shall publish the notice in the Federal Register and allow 60 days for the submission of comments on the notice. On expiration of such 60 days, the Administrator, by order and without a hearing, may cancel the registration or take such other action, including extension of applicable time periods, as may be necessary to enable reregistration of such pesticide by another person.

(B)(i) If —

(I) no registrant of a pesticide containing an active ingredient listed under subsection (c)(2) of this section notifies the Administrator under paragraph (2) that the registrant intends to seek reregistration of any pesticide containing that active ingredient;

(II) no such registrant complies with paragraph (3)(A); or

(III) no such registrant makes a commitment under paragraph (3)(B) to replace or submit all data described in clauses (ii) and (iii) of paragraph (3)(A);

the Administrator shall publish in the Federal Register a notice of intent to remove the active ingredient from the list established under subsection (c)(2) of this section and a notice of intent to cancel the registrations of all pesticides containing such active ingredient and shall provide 60 days for comment on such notice.

(ii) After the 60-day period has expired, the Administrator, by order, may cancel any such registration without hearing, except that the Administrator shall not cancel a registration under this subparagraph if —

(I) during the comment period a person acquires the rights of the registrant in that registration;

(II) during the comment period that person furnishes a notice of intent to reregister the pesticide in accordance with paragraph (2); and

(III) not later than 120 days after the publication of the notice under this subparagraph, that person has complied with paragraph (3) and the fee prescribed by subsection (i)(1) of this section has been paid.

(6) Suspensions and penalties — The Administrator shall issue a notice of intent to suspend the registration of a pesticide in accordance with

the procedures prescribed by section 136a(c)(2)(B)(iv) of this title if the Administrator determines that (A) progress is insufficient to ensure the submission of the data required for such pesticide under a commitment made under paragraph (3)(B) within the time period prescribed by paragraph (4)(B) or (B) the registrant has not submitted such data to the Administrator within such time period. If the registrant does not commit to support a specific minor use of the pesticide, but is supporting and providing data in a timely and adequate fashion to support uses of the pesticide on a food, or if all uses of the pesticide are nonfood uses and the registrant does not commit to support a specific minor use of the pesticide but is supporting and providing data in a timely and adequate fashion to support other nonfood uses of the pesticide, the Administrator, at the written request of the registrant, shall not take any action pursuant to this paragraph in regard to such unsupported minor use until the final deadline established as of August 3, 1996, for the submission of data under this section for the supported uses identified pursuant to this paragraph unless the Administrator determines that the absence of the data is significant enough to cause human health or environmental concerns. On such a determination the Administrator may refuse the request for extension by the registrant. Upon receipt of the request from the registrant, the Administrator shall publish in the Federal Register a notice of the receipt of the request and the effective date upon which the uses not being supported will be voluntarily deleted from the registration pursuant to section 136d(f)(1) of this title. If the Administrator grants an extension under this paragraph, the Administrator shall monitor the development of the data for the uses being supported and shall ensure that the registrant is meeting the schedule for the production of such data. If the Administrator determines that the registrant is not meeting or has not met the schedule for the production of such data, the Administrator may proceed in accordance with section 136a(c)(2)(B)(iv) of this title regarding the continued registration of the affected products with the minor and other uses and shall inform the public of such action in accordance with section 136d(f)(2) of this title. Notwithstanding this subparagraph, the Administrator may deny, modify, or revoke the temporary extension under this paragraph if the Administrator determines that the continuation of the minor use may cause an unreasonable adverse effect on the environment. In the event of modification or revocation, the Administrator shall provide, in writing, to the registrant a notice revoking the temporary extension and establish a new effective date by which the minor use shall be deleted from the registration.

(e) Phase three

(1) Information about studies — Each registrant of a pesticide that contains an active ingredient listed under subparagraph (B), (C), or (D) of subsection (c)(2) of this section who has submitted a notice under subsection (d)(2) of this section of an intent to seek the reregistration of such pesticide shall submit, in accordance with the guidelines issued under paragraph (4), to the Administrator —

(A) a summary of each study concerning the active ingredient previously submitted by the registrant in support of the registration of a pesticide containing such active ingredient and considered by the registrant to be adequate to meet the requirements of section 136a of this title and the regulations issued under such section;

(B) a summary of each study concerning the active ingredient previously submitted by the registrant in support of the registration of a pesticide containing such active ingredient that may not comply with the requirements of section 136a of this title and the regulations issued under such section but which the registrant asserts should be deemed to comply with such requirements and regulations;

(C) a reformat of the data from each study summarized under subparagraph (A) or (B) by the registrant concerning chronic dosing, oncogenicity, reproductive effects, mutagenicity, neurotoxicity, teratogenicity, or residue chemistry of the active ingredient that were submitted to the Administrator before January 1, 1982;

(D) where data described in subparagraph (C) are not required for the active ingredient by regulations issued under section 136a of this title, a reformat of acute and subchronic dosing data submitted by the registrant to the Administrator before January 1, 1982, that the registrant considers to be adequate to meet the requirements of section 136a of this title and the regulations issued under such section;

(E) an identification of data that are required to be submitted to the Administrator under section 136d(a)(2) of this title, indicating an adverse effect of the pesticide;

(F) an identification of any other information available that in the view of the registrant supports the registration;

(G) a certification that the registrant or the Administrator possesses or has access to the raw data used in or generated by the studies that the registrant summarized under subparagraph (A) or (B);

(H) either —

(i) a commitment to submit data to fill each outstanding data requirement identified by the registrant; or

(ii) an offer to share in the cost of developing such data to be incurred by a person who has made a commitment under clause (i) to submit such data, and an offer to submit to arbitration as described by section 136a(c)(2)(B) of this title with regard to such cost sharing; and

(I) evidence of compliance with section 136a(c)(1)(D)(ii) of this title and regulations issued thereunder with regard to previously submitted data as if the registrant were now seeking the original registration of the pesticide.

A registrant who submits a certification under subparagraph (G) that is false shall be considered to have violated this subchapter and shall be subject to the penalties prescribed by section 136l of this title.

(2) Time periods

(A) The information required by paragraph (1) shall be submitted to the Administrator —

(i) in the case of a pesticide containing an active ingredient listed under subsection (c)(2)(B) of this section, not later than 12 months after the date of publication of the listing of such active ingredient;

(ii) in the case of a pesticide containing an active ingredient listed under subsection (c)(2)(C) of this section, not later than 12 months after the date of publication of the listing of such active ingredient; and

(iii) in the case of a pesticide containing an active ingredient listed under subsection (c)(2)(D) of this section, not later than 12 months after the date of publication of the listing of such active ingredient.

(B) A registrant shall submit data in accordance with a commitment entered into under paragraph (1)(H) within a reasonable period of time, as determined by the Administrator, but not more than 48 months after the date the registrant submitted the commitment under such paragraph. The Administrator, on application of a registrant, may extend the period prescribed by the preceding sentence by no more than 2 years if extraordinary circumstances beyond the control of the registrant prevent the registrant from submitting data within such prescribed period. Upon application of a registrant, the Administrator shall, in the case of a minor use, extend the deadline for the production of residue chemistry data under this subparagraph for data required solely to support that minor use until the final deadline for submission of data under this section for the other uses of the pesticide established as of August 3, 1996, if —

(i) the data to support other uses of the pesticide on a food are being provided;

(ii) the registrant, in submitting a request for such an extension provides a schedule, including interim dates to measure progress, to assure that the data production will be completed before the expiration of the extension period;

(iii) the Administrator has determined that such extension will not significantly delay the Administrator's schedule for issuing a reregistration eligibility determination required under this section; and

(iv) the Administrator has determined that based on existing data, such extension would not significantly increase the risk of any unreasonable adverse effect on the environment. If the Administrator grants an extension under this subparagraph, the Administrator shall monitor the development of the data and shall ensure that the registrant is meeting the schedule for the production of the data. If the Administrator determines that the registrant is not meeting or has not met the schedule for the production of such data, the Administrator may proceed in accordance with clause (iv) of section 136a(c)(2)(B) of this title or other provisions of this section, as appropriate, regarding the continued registration of the affected products with the minor use and shall inform the public of such action. Notwithstanding the provisions of this subparagraph, the Administrator may take action to modify or revoke the extension under this subparagraph if the Administrator determines that the extension for the minor use may cause an unreasonable adverse effect on the environment. In such circumstance, the Administrator shall provide written notice to the registrant revoking the extension of time for submission of data. Such data shall instead be due in accordance with the date then established by the Administrator for submission of the data.

(3) Cancellation

(A) If the registrant of a pesticide fails to submit the information required by paragraph (1) within the time prescribed by paragraph (2), the Administrator, by order and without hearing, shall cancel the registration of such pesticide. If the registrant does not commit to support a specific minor use of the pesticide, but is supporting and providing data in a timely and adequate fashion to support uses of the pesticide on a food, or if all uses of the pesticide are nonfood uses and the registrant does not commit to support a specific minor use of the pesticide but is supporting and providing data in a timely

and adequate fashion to support other nonfood uses of the pesticide, the Administrator, at the written request of the registrant, shall not take any action pursuant to this subparagraph in regard to such unsupported minor use until the final deadline established as of August 3, 1996, for the submission of data under this section for the supported uses identified pursuant to this subparagraph unless the Administrator determines that the absence of the data is significant enough to cause human health or environmental concerns. On the basis of such determination, the Administrator may refuse the request for extension by the registrant. Upon receipt of the request from the registrant, the Administrator shall publish in the Federal Register a notice of the receipt of the request and the effective date upon which the uses not being supported will be voluntarily deleted from the registration pursuant to section 136d(f)(1) of this title. If the Administrator grants an extension under this subparagraph, the Administrator shall monitor the development of the data for the uses being supported and shall ensure that the registrant is meeting the schedule for the production of such data. If the Administrator determines that the registrant is not meeting or has not met the schedule for the production of such data, the Administrator may proceed in accordance with section 136a(c)(2)(B)(iv) of this title regarding the continued registration of the affected products with the minor and other uses and shall inform the public of such action in accordance with section 136d(f)(2) of this title. Notwithstanding this subparagraph, the Administrator may deny, modify, or revoke the temporary extension under this subparagraph if the Administrator determines that the continuation of the minor use may cause an unreasonable adverse effect on the environment. In the event of modification or revocation, the Administrator shall provide, in writing, to the registrant a notice revoking the temporary extension and establish a new effective date by which the minor use shall be deleted from the registration.

(B)(i) If the registrant of a pesticide submits the information required by paragraph (1) within the time prescribed by paragraph (2) and such information does not conform to the guidelines for submissions established by the Administrator, the Administrator shall determine whether the registrant made a good faith attempt to conform its submission to such guidelines.

(ii) If the Administrator determines that the registrant made a good faith attempt to conform its submission to such guidelines, the Administrator shall provide the registrant a reasonable period of time to make any necessary changes or corrections.

(iii)(I) If the Administrator determines that the registrant did not make a good faith attempt to conform its submission to such guidelines, the Administrator may issue a notice of intent to cancel the registration. Such a notice shall be sent to the registrant by certified mail.

(II) The registration shall be canceled without a hearing or further notice at the end of 30 days after receipt by the registrant of the notice unless during that time a request for a hearing is made by the registrant.

(III) If a hearing is requested, a hearing shall be conducted under section 136d(d) of this title, except that the only matter for resolution at the hearing shall be whether the registrant made a good faith attempt to conform its submission to such guidelines. The hearing shall be held and a determination made within 75 days after receipt of a request for hearing.

(4) Guidelines

(A) Not later than 1 year after the effective date of this section, the Administrator, by order, shall issue guidelines to be followed by registrants in —

(i)   summarizing studies;

(ii) reformatting studies;

(iii) identifying adverse information; and

(iv) identifying studies that have been submitted previously that may not meet the requirements of section 136a of this title or regulations issued under such section, under paragraph (1).

(B) Guidelines issued under subparagraph (A) shall not be subject to judicial review.

(5) Monitoring — The Administrator shall monitor the progress of registrants in acquiring and submitting the data required under paragraph (1).

(f) Phase four

(1) Independent review and identification of outstanding data requirements

(A) The Administrator shall review the submissions of all registrants of pesticides containing a particular active ingredient under subsections (d)(3) and (e)(1) of this section to determine if such submissions identified all the data that are missing or inadequate for such active ingredient. To assist the review of the Administrator under this subparagraph, the Administrator may require a registrant seeking reregistration to submit complete copies of studies summarized under subsection (e)(1) of this section.

(B) The Administrator shall independently identify and publish in the Federal Register the outstanding data requirements for each active ingredient that is listed under subparagraph (B), (C), or (D) of subsection (c)(2) of this section and that is contained in a pesticide to be reregistered under this section. The Administrator, at the same time, shall issue a notice under section 136a(c)(2)(B) of this title for the submission of the additional data that are required to meet such requirements.

(2) Time periods

(A) The Administrator shall take the action required by paragraph (1) —

(i)   in the case of a pesticide containing an active ingredient listed under subsection (c)(2)(B) of this section, not later than 18 months after the date of the listing of such active ingredient;

(ii) in the case of a pesticide containing an active ingredient listed under subsection (c)(2)(C) of this section, not later than 24 months after the date of the listing of such active ingredient; and

(iii) in the case of a pesticide containing an active ingredient listed under subsection (c)(2)(D) of this section, not later than 33 months after the date of the listing of such active ingredient.

(B) If the Administrator issues a notice to a registrant under paragraph (1)(B) for the submission of additional data, the registrant shall submit such data within a reasonable period of time, as determined by the Administrator, but not to exceed 48 months after the issuance of such notice. The Administrator, on application of a registrant, may extend the period prescribed by the preceding sentence by no more than 2 years if extraordinary circumstances beyond the control of the registrant prevent the registrant from submitting data within such prescribed period. Upon application of a registrant, the Administrator shall, in the case of a minor use, extend the deadline for the production of residue chemistry data under this subparagraph for data required solely to support that minor use until the final deadline for submission of data under this section for the other uses of the pesticide established as of August 3, 1996, if —

(i)   the data to support other uses of the pesticide on a food are being provided;

(ii) the registrant, in submitting a request for such an extension provides a schedule, including interim dates to measure progress, to assure that the data production will be completed before the expiration of the extension period;

(iii) the Administrator has determined that such extension will not significantly delay the Administrator's schedule for issuing a reregistration eligibility determination required under this section; and

(iv) the Administrator has determined that based on existing data, such extension would not significantly increase the risk of any unreasonable adverse effect on the environment. If the Administrator grants an extension under this subparagraph, the Administrator shall monitor the development of the data and shall ensure that the registrant is meeting the schedule for the production of the data. If the Administrator determines that the registrant is not meeting or has not met the schedule for the production of such data, the Administrator may proceed in accordance with clause (iv) of section 136a(c)(2)(B) of this title or other provisions of this section, as appropriate, regarding the continued registration of the affected products with the minor use and shall inform the public of such action. Notwithstanding the provisions of this subparagraph, the Administrator may take action to modify or revoke the extension under this subparagraph if the Administrator determines that the extension for the minor use may cause an unreasonable adverse effect on the environment. In such circumstance, the Administrator shall provide written notice to the registrant revoking the extension of time for submission of data. Such data shall instead be due in accordance with the date then established by the Administrator for submission of the data.

(3) **Suspensions and penalties** — The Administrator shall issue a notice of intent to suspend the registration of a pesticide in accordance with the procedures prescribed by section 136a(c)(2)(B)(iv) of this title if the Administrator determines that (A) tests necessary to fill an outstanding data requirement for such pesticide have not been initiated within 1 year after the issuance of a notice under paragraph (1)(B), or (B) progress is insufficient to ensure submission of the data referred to in clause (A) within the time period prescribed by paragraph (2)(B) or the required data have not been submitted to the Administrator within such time period. If the registrant does not commit to support a specific minor use of the pesticide, but is supporting and providing data in a timely and adequate fashion to support uses of the pesticide on a food, or if all uses of the pesticide are nonfood uses and the registrant does not commit to support a specific minor use of the pesticide but is supporting and providing data in a timely and adequate fashion to support other nonfood uses of the pesticide, the Administrator, at the written request of the registrant, shall not take

any action pursuant to this paragraph in regard to such unsupported minor use until the final deadline established as of August 3, 1996, for the submission of data under this section for the supported uses identified pursuant to this paragraph unless the Administrator determines that the absence of the data is significant enough to cause human health or environmental concerns. On such a determination the Administrator may refuse the request for extension by the registrant. Upon receipt of the request from the registrant, the Administrator shall publish in the Federal Register a notice of the receipt of the request and the effective date upon which the uses not being supported will be voluntarily deleted from the registration pursuant to section 136d(f)(1) of this title. If the Administrator grants an extension under this paragraph, the Administrator shall monitor the development of the data for the uses being supported and shall ensure that the registrant is meeting the schedule for the production of such data. If the Administrator determines that the registrant is not meeting or has not met the schedule for the production of such data, the Administrator may proceed in accordance with section 136a(c)(2)(B)(iv) of this title regarding the continued registration of the affected products with the minor and other uses and shall inform the public of such action in accordance with section 136d(f)(2) of this title. Notwithstanding this subparagraph, the Administrator may deny, modify, or revoke the temporary extension under this paragraph if the Administrator determines that the continuation of the minor use may cause an unreasonable adverse effect on the environment. In the event of modification or revocation, the Administrator shall provide, in writing, to the registrant a notice revoking the temporary extension and establish a new effective date by which the minor use shall be deleted from the registration.

(g) **Phase five**

(1) **Data review** — The Administrator shall conduct a thorough examination of all data submitted under this section concerning an active ingredient listed under subsection (c)(2) of this section and of all other available data found by the Administrator to be relevant.

(2) **Reregistration and other actions**
(A) **In general**
The Administrator shall make a determination as to eligibility for reregistration —

(i) for all active ingredients subject to reregistration under this section for which tolerances or exemptions from tolerances are required under the Federal Food, Drug, and Cosmetic Act (21 U.S.C. 301 *et seq.*), not later than the last date for tolerance reassessment established under section 408(q)(1)(C) of that Act (21 U.S.C. 346a(q)(1)(C)); and

(ii) for all other active ingredients subject to reregistration under this section, not later than October 3, 2008.

(B) Product-specific data

(i) In general

Before reregistering a pesticide, the Administrator shall obtain any needed product-specific data regarding the pesticide by use of section 136a(c)(2)(B) of this title and shall review such data within 90 days after its submission.

(ii) Timing

(I) In general

Subject to subclause (II), the Administrator shall require that data under this subparagraph be submitted to the Administrator not later than 8 months after a determination of eligibility under subparagraph (A) has been made for each active ingredient of the pesticide, unless the Administrator determines that a longer period is required for the generation of the data.

(II) Extraordinary circumstances

In the case of extraordinary circumstances, the Administrator may provide such a longer period, of not more than 2 additional years, for submission of data to the Administrator under this subparagraph.

(C) After conducting the review required by paragraph (1) for each active ingredient of a pesticide and the review required by subparagraph (B) of this paragraph, the Administrator shall determine whether to reregister a pesticide by determining whether such pesticide meets the requirements of section 136a(c)(5) of this title. If the Administrator determines that a pesticide is eligible to be reregistered, the Administrator shall reregister such pesticide within 6 months after the submission of the data concerning such pesticide under subparagraph (B).

(D) Determination to not reregister

(i) In general

If after conducting a review under paragraph (1) or subparagraph (B) of this paragraph the Administrator determines that a pesticide should not be reregistered, the Administrator shall take appropriate regulatory action.

(ii) Timing for regulatory action

Regulatory action under clause (i) shall be completed as expeditiously as possible.

(E) As soon as the Administrator has sufficient information with respect to the dietary risk of a particular active ingredient, but in any event no later than the time the Administrator makes a determination under subparagraph (C) or (D) with respect to pesticides containing a particular active ingredient, the Administrator shall —

(i) reassess each associated tolerance and exemption from the requirement for a tolerance issued under section 408 of the Federal Food, Drug, and Cosmetic Act (21 U.S.C. §346a);

(ii) determine whether such tolerance or exemption meets the requirements of that Act [21 U.S.C. §§301 *et seq.*];

(iii) determine whether additional tolerances or exemptions should be issued;

(iv) publish in the Federal Register a notice setting forth the determinations made under this subparagraph; and

(v) commence promptly such proceedings under this subchapter and section 408 of the Federal Food, Drug, and Cosmetic Act [21 U.S.C. §346a] as are warranted by such determinations.

(h) Compensation of data submitter — If data that are submitted by a registrant under subsection (d), (e), (f), or (g) of this section are used to support the application of another person under section 136a of this title, the registrant who submitted such data shall be entitled to compensation for the use of such data as prescribed by section 136a(c)(1)(D) of this title. In determining the amount of such compensation, the fees paid by the registrant under this section shall be taken into account.

(i) Fees

(1) Maintenance fee

(A) In general — Subject to other provisions of this paragraph, each registrant of a pesticide shall pay an annual fee by January 15 of each year for each registration, except that no fee shall be charged for more than 200 registrations held by any registrant.

(B) In the case of a pesticide that is registered for a minor agricultural use, the Administrator may reduce or waive the payment of the fee imposed under this paragraph if the Administrator determines that the fee would significantly reduce the availability of the pesticide for the use.

(C) Total amount of fees

The amount of each fee prescribed under subparagraph (A) shall be adjusted by the Administrator to a level that will result in the collection under this paragraph of, to the extent practicable, an average amount of $31,000,000 for each of fiscal years 2019 through 2023.

(D) Maximum amount of fees for registrants

The maximum annual fee payable under this paragraph by —

(i) a registrant holding not more than 50 pesticide registrations shall be $129,400 for each of fiscal years 2019 through 2023; and

(ii) a registrant holding over 50 registrations shall be $207,000 for each of fiscal years 2019 through 2023.

(E) Maximum amount of fees for small businesses

(i) In general

For a small business, the maximum annual fee payable under this paragraph by —

(I) a registrant holding not more than 50 pesticide registrations shall be $79,100 for each of fiscal years 2019 through 2023; and

(II) a registrant holding over 50 pesticide registrations shall be $136,800 for each of fiscal years 2019 through 2023.

(ii) Definition of small business

(I) In general

In clause (i), the term "small business" means a corporation, partnership, or unincorporated business that —

(aa) has 500 or fewer employees; and

(bb) during the 3-year period prior to the most recent maintenance fee billing cycle, had an average annual global gross revenue from pesticides that did not exceed $60,000,000.

(II) Affiliates

(aa) In general

In the case of a business entity with 1 or more affiliates, the gross revenue limit under subclause (I)(bb) shall apply to the gross revenue for the entity and all of the affiliates of the entity, including parents and subsidiaries, if applicable.

(bb) Affiliated persons

For the purpose of item (aa), persons are affiliates of each other if, directly or indirectly, either person controls or has the power to control the other person, or a third person controls or has the power to control both persons.

(cc) Indicia of control

For the purpose of item (aa), indicia of control include interlocking management or ownership, identity of interests among family members, shared facilities and equipment, and common use of employees.

(F) Fee reduction for certain small businesses

(i) Definition — In this subparagraph, the term "qualified small business entity" means a corporation, partnership, or unincorporated business that —

(I) has 500 or fewer employees;

(II) during the 3-year period prior to the most recent maintenance fee billing cycle, had an average annual global gross revenue from all sources that did not exceed $10,000,000; and

(III) holds not more than 5 pesticide registrations under this paragraph.

(ii) Waiver — Except as provided in clause (iii), the Administrator shall waive 25 percent of the fee under this paragraph applicable to the first registration of any qualified small business entity under this paragraph.

(iii) Limitation — The Administrator shall not grant a waiver under clause (ii) to a qualified small business entity if the Administrator determines that the entity has been formed or manipulated primarily for the purpose of qualifying for the waiver.

(G) The Administrator shall exempt any public health pesticide from the payment of the fee prescribed under this paragraph if, in consultation with the Secretary of Health and Human Services, the Administrator determines, based on information supplied by the registrant, that the economic return to the registrant from sales of the pesticide does not support the registration or reregistration of the pesticide.

(H) If any fee prescribed by this paragraph with respect to the registration of a pesticide is not paid by a registrant by the time prescribed, the Administrator, by order and without hearing, may cancel the registration.

(I) The authority provided under this paragraph shall terminate on September 30, 2017.

(2) Other fees — Except as provided in section 136w-8 of this title, during the period beginning on March 8, 2019, and ending on September 30, 2025, the Administrator may not levy any other fees for the registration of a pesticide under this subchapter or any other action covered under a table specified in section 136w-8(b)(3) of this title, except as provided in paragraph (1).

(j) Exemption of certain registrants The requirements of subsections (d), (e), (f), and (i) of this section (other than subsection (i)(1) of this section) regarding data concerning an active ingredient and fees for review of such data shall not apply to any person who is the registrant of a pesticide to the extent that, under section 136a(c)(2)(D) of this title, the person would not be required to submit or cite such data to obtain an initial registration of such pesticide.

(k) Reregistration and expedited processing fund —

(1) Establishment — There shall be established in the Treasury of the United States a reregistration and expedited processing fund which shall be known as the Reregistration and Expedited Processing Fund.

(2) Source and use

(A) All moneys derived from fees collected by the Administrator under subsection (i) shall be deposited in the Reregistration and Expedited Processing Fund and shall be available to the Administrator, without fiscal year limitation, specifically to offset the costs of reregistration and expedited processing of the applications specified in paragraph (3), to offset the costs of registration review under section 136a(g) of this title, including the costs associated with any review under the Endangered Species Act of 1973 (16 U.S.C. 1531 et seq.) required as part of the registration review, to offset the costs associated with tracking and implementing registration review decisions, including registration review decisions designed to reduce risk, for the purposes specified in paragraphs (4) and (5), and to enhance the information systems capabilities to improve the tracking of pesticide registration decisions. The Administrator shall, prior to expending any such moneys derived from fees —

(i) effective October 1, 1997, adopt specific and cost accounting rules and procedures as approved by the Government Accountability Office and the Inspector General of the Environmental Protection Agency to ensure that moneys derived from fees are allocated solely for the purposes specified in the first sentence of this subparagraph;

(ii) prohibit the use of such moneys derived from fees to pay for any costs other than those necessary to achieve the purposes specified in the first sentence of this subparagraph; and

(iii) ensure that personnel and facility costs associated with the functions to be carried out under this paragraph do not exceed agency averages for comparable personnel and facility costs.

(B) The Administrator shall also —

(i) complete the review of unreviewed reregistration studies required to support the reregistration eligibility decisions scheduled for completion in accordance with subsection (l) (2); and

(ii) contract for such outside assistance as may be necessary for review of required studies, using a generally accepted competitive process for the selection of vendors of such assistance.

(3) Review of inert ingredients; expedited processing of similar applications

(A) For each of fiscal years 2018 through 2023, the Administrator shall use between 1/9 and 1/8 of the maintenance fees collected in such fiscal year to obtain sufficient personnel and resources —

(i) to review and evaluate inert ingredients; and

(ii) to ensure the expedited processing and review of any application that —

(I) proposes the initial or amended registration of an end-use pesticide that, if registered as proposed, would be identical or substantially similar in composition and labeling to a currently-registered pesticide identified in the application, or that would differ in composition and labeling from any such currently-registered pesticide only in ways that would not significantly increase the risk of unreasonable adverse effects on the environment;

(II) proposes an amendment to the registration of a registered pesticide that does not require scientific review of data; or

(III) proposes the initial or amended registration of an end use pesticide that, if registered as proposed, would be used for a public health pesticide.

(B) Any amounts made available under subparagraph (A) shall be used to obtain sufficient personnel and resources to carry out the activities described in such subparagraph that are in addition to the personnel and resources available to carry out such activities on October 25, 1988.

(C) So long as the Administrator has not met the time frames specified in clause (ii) of section 136a(c)(3)(B) of this title with respect to any application subject to section 136a(c)(3)(B) of this title that was received prior to August 3, 1996, the Administrator shall use the full amount of the fees specified in subparagraph (A) for the purposes specified therein. Once all applications subject to section 136a(c)(3)(B of this title that were received prior to August 3, 1996, have been acted upon, no limitation shall be imposed by the preceding sentence of this subparagraph so long as the Administrator meets the time frames specified in clause (ii) of section 136a(c)(3)(B) of this title on 90 percent of affected applications in a fiscal year. Should the Administrator not meet such time frames in a fiscal year, the limitations imposed by the first sentence of this subparagraph shall apply until all overdue applications subject to section 136a(c)(3)(B) of this title have been acted upon.

(4) Expedited rulemaking and guidance development for certain product performance data requirements
(A) Set-aside

For each of fiscal years 2018 through 2023, the Administrator shall use not more than $500,000 of the amounts made available to the Administrator in the Reregistration and Expedited Processing Fund for the activities described in subparagraph (B).

(B) Products claiming efficacy against invertebrate pests of significant public health or economic importance

The Administrator shall use amounts made available under subparagraph (A) to develop, receive comments with respect to, finalize, and implement the necessary rulemaking and guidance for product performance data requirements to evaluate products claiming efficacy against the following invertebrate pests of significant public health or economic importance (in order of importance):

(i) Bed bugs.

(ii) Premise (including crawling insects, flying insects, and baits).

(iii) Pests of pets (including pet pests controlled by spot-ons, collars, shampoos, powders, or dips).

(iv) Fire ants.

(C) Deadlines for guidance

The Administrator shall develop, and publish guidance required by subparagraph (B), with respect to claims of efficacy against pests described in such subparagraph as follows:

(i) With respect to bed bugs, issue final guidance not later than 30 days after March 8, 2019.

(ii) With respect to pests specified in clause (ii) of such subparagraph —

(I) submit draft guidance to the Scientific Advisory Panel and for public comment not later than June 30, 2018; and

(II) complete any response to comments received with respect to such draft guidance and finalize the guidance not later than September 30, 2019.

(iii) With respect to pests specified in clauses (iii) and (iv) of such subparagraph —

(I) submit draft guidance to the Scientific Advisory Panel and for public comment not later than June 30, 2019; and

(II) complete any response to comments received with respect to such draft guidance and finalize the guidance not later than March 31, 2021.

(D) Revision

The Administrator shall revise the guidance required by subparagraph (B) from time to time, but shall permit applicants and registrants sufficient time to obtain data that meet the requirements specified in such revised guidance.

(E) Deadline for product performance data requirements

The Administrator shall, not later than September 30, 2021, issue regulations prescribing product performance data requirements for any pesticide intended for preventing, destroying, repelling, or mitigating any invertebrate pest of significant public health or economic importance specified in clauses (i) through (iv) of subparagraph (B).

(5) Good laboratory practices inspections
(A) Set-aside

For each of fiscal years 2018 through 2023, the Administrator shall use not more than $500,000 of the amounts made available to the Administrator in the Reregistration and Expedited Processing Fund for the activities described in subparagraph (B).

(B) Activities

The Administrator shall use amounts made available under subparagraph (A) for enhancements to the good laboratory practices standards compliance monitoring program established under part 160 of title 40 of the Code of Federal Regulations (or successor regulations), with respect to laboratory inspections and data audits conducted in support of pesticide product registrations under this subchapter. As part of such monitoring program, the Administrator shall make available to each laboratory inspected under such program in support of such registrations a preliminary summary of inspection observations not later than 60 days after the date on which such an inspection is completed.

(6) Unused funds — Money in the fund not currently needed to carry out this section shall be —

(A) maintained on hand or on deposit;

(B) invested in obligations of the United States or guaranteed thereby; or

(C) invested in obligations, participations, or other instruments that are lawful investments for fiduciary, trust, or public funds.

(7) Accounting and performance — The Administrator shall take all steps necessary to ensure that expenditures from fees authorized by subsection (i)(1)(C)(ii) of this section are used only for the purposes described in paragraphs (2), (3), (4), and (5) and to carry out the goals established under subsection (*l*) of this section. The Reregistration and Expedited Processing Fund shall be designated as an Environmental Protection Agency component for purposes of section 3515(c) of Title 31. The annual audit required under section 3521 of such title of the financial statements of activities under this subchapter under section 3515(b) of such title shall include an audit of the fees collected under subsection (i)(1)(C) of this section and disbursed, of the amount appropriated to match such fees, and of the Administrator's attainment of performance measures and goals established under subsection (*l*) of this section. Such an audit shall also include a review of the reasonableness of the overhead allocation and adequacy of disclosures of direct and indirect costs associated with carrying out the reregistration and expedited processing of the applications specified in paragraph (3), and the basis for and accuracy of all costs paid with moneys derived from such fees. The Inspector General shall conduct the annual audit and report the findings and recommendations of such audit to the Administrator and to the Committees on Agriculture of the House of Representatives and the Senate. The cost of such audit shall be paid for out of the fees collected under subsection (i)(1)(C) of this section.

(*l*) Performance measures and goals — The Administrator shall establish and publish annually in the Federal Register performance measures and goals. Such measures and goals shall include —

(1) the number of products reregistered, canceled, or amended, the status of reregistration, the number and type of data requests under section 136a(c)(2)(B) of this title issued to support product reregistration by active ingredient, the progress in reducing the number of unreviewed, required reregistration studies, the aggregate status of tolerances reassessed, and the number of applications for registration submitted under subsection (k)(3) of this section that were approved or disapproved;

(2) the future schedule for reregistrations, including the projection for such schedules that will be issued under subsection (g)(2)(A) and (B) of this section in the current fiscal year and the succeeding fiscal year; and

(3) the projected year of completion of the reregistrations under this section.

(m) Judicial review — Any failure of the Administrator to take any action required by this section shall be subject to judicial review under the procedures prescribed by section 136n(b) of this title.

(n) Authorization of funds to develop public health data

(1) "Secretary" defined — For the purposes of this section, "Secretary" means the Secretary of Health and Human Services, acting through the Public Health Service.

(2) Consultation — In the case of a pesticide registered for use in public health programs for vector control or for other uses the Administrator determines to be human health protection uses, the Administrator shall, upon timely request by the registrant or any other interested person, or on the Administrator's own initiative may, consult with the Secretary prior to taking final action to suspend registration under section 136a(c)(2)(B)(iv) of this title, or cancel a registration under section 136a-1, 136d(e), or 136d(f) of this title. In consultation with

the Secretary, the Administrator shall prescribe the form and content of requests under this section.

(3) **Benefits to support family** — The Administrator, after consulting with the Secretary, shall make a determination whether the potential benefits of continued use of the pesticide for public health or health protection purposes are of such significance as to warrant a commitment by the Secretary to conduct or to arrange for the conduct of the studies required by the Administrator to support continued registration under section 136a of this title or reregistration under this section.

(4) **Additional time** — If the Administrator determines that such a commitment is warranted and in the public interest, the Administrator shall notify the Secretary and shall, to the extent necessary, amend a notice issued under section 136a(c)(2)(B) of this title to specify additional reasonable time periods for submission of the data.

(5) **Arrangements** — The Secretary shall make such arrangements for the conduct of required studies as the Secretary finds necessary and appropriate to permit submission of data in accordance with the time periods prescribed by the Administrator. Such arrangements may include Public Health Service intramural research activities, grants, contracts, or cooperative agreements with academic, public health, or other organizations qualified by experience and training to conduct such studies.

(6) **Support** — The Secretary may provide for support of the required studies using funds authorized to be appropriated under this section, the Public Health Service Act [42 U.S.C. §§201 *et seq.*], or other appropriate authorities. After a determination is made under subsection (d) of this section, the Secretary shall notify the Committees on Appropriations of the House of Representatives and the Senate of the sums required to conduct the necessary studies.

(7) **Authorization of appropriations** — There is authorized to be appropriated to carry out the purposes of this section $12,000,000 for fiscal year 1997, and such sums as may be necessary for succeeding fiscal years.

§136b. Transferred
[FIFRA FORMER §4]

§136c. Experimental use permits
[FIFRA §5]

(a) Issuance — Any person may apply to the Administrator for an experimental use permit for a pesticide. An application for an experimental use permit for a covered application under section 136w-8(b) of this title shall conform with the requirements of that section. The Administrator shall review the application. After completion of the review, but not later than one hundred and twenty days after receipt of the application and all required supporting data (or in the case of an application for an experimental use permit for a covered application under section 136w-8(b) of this title, not later than the last day of the applicable timeframe for such application specified in such section), the Administrator shall either issue the permit or notify the applicant of the Administrator's determination not to issue the permit and the reasons therefor. The applicant may correct the application or request a waiver of the conditions for such permit within thirty days of receipt by the applicant of such notification. The Administrator may issue an experimental use permit only if the Administrator determines that the applicant needs such permit in order to accumulate information necessary to register a pesticide under section 136a of this title. An application for an experimental use permit may be filed at any time.

(b) Temporary tolerance level — If the Administrator determines that the use of a pesticide may reasonably be expected to result in any residue on or in food or feed, the Administrator may establish a temporary tolerance level for the residue of the pesticide before issuing the experimental use permit.

(c) Use under permit — Use of a pesticide under an experimental use permit shall be under the supervision of the Administrator, and shall be subject to such terms and conditions and be for such period of time as the Administrator may prescribe in the permit.

(d) Studies — When any experimental use permit is issued for a pesticide containing any chemical or combination of chemicals which has not been included in any previously registered pesticide, the Administrator may specify that studies be conducted to detect whether the use of the pesticide under the permit may cause unreasonable adverse effects on the environment. All results of such studies shall be reported to the Administrator before such pesticide may be registered under section 136a of this title.

(e) Revocation — The Administrator may revoke any experimental use permit, at any time, if the Administrator finds that its terms or conditions are being violated, or that its terms and conditions are inadequate to avoid unreasonable adverse effects on the environment.

(f) State issuance of permits — Notwithstanding the foregoing provisions of this section, the Administrator shall, under such terms and conditions as the Administrator may by regulations prescribe, authorize any State to issue an experimental use permit for a pesticide. All provisions of section 136i of this title relating to State plans shall apply with equal force to a State plan for the issuance of experimental use permits under this section.

(g) Exemption for agricultural research agencies — Notwithstanding the foregoing provisions of this section, the Administrator may issue an experimental use permit for a pesticide to any public or private agricultural research agency or educational institution which applies for such permit. Each permit shall not exceed more than a one-year period or such other specific time as the Administrator may prescribe. Such permit shall be issued under such terms and conditions restricting the use of the pesticide as the Administrator may require. Such pesticide may be used only by such research agency or educational institution for purposes of experimentation.

§136d. Administrative review; suspension
[FIFRA §6]
(a) Existing stocks and information

(1) Existing stocks — The Administrator may permit the continued sale and use of existing stocks of a pesticide whose registration is suspended or canceled under this section, or section 136a or 136a-1 of this title, to such extent, under such conditions, and for such uses as the Administrator determines that such sale or use is not inconsistent with the purposes of this subchapter.

(2) Information — If at any time after the registration of a pesticide the registrant has additional factual information regarding unreasonable adverse effects on the environment of the pesticide, the registrant shall submit such information to the Administrator.

(b) Cancellation and change in classification — If it appears to the Administrator that a pesticide or its labeling or other material required to be submitted does not comply with the provisions of this subchapter or, when used in accordance with widespread and commonly recognized practice, generally causes unreasonable adverse effects on the environment, the Administrator may issue a notice of the Administrator's intent either —

(1) to cancel its registration or to change its classification together with the reasons (including the factual basis) for the Administrator's action, or

(2) to hold a hearing to determine whether or not its registration should be canceled or its classification changed.

Such notice shall be sent to the registrant and made public. In determining whether to issue any such notice, the Administrator shall include among those factors to be taken into account the impact of the action proposed in such notice on production and prices of agricultural commodities, retail food prices, and otherwise on the agricultural economy. At least 60 days prior to sending such notice to the registrant or making public such notice, whichever occurs first, the Administrator shall provide the Secretary of Agriculture with a copy of such notice and an analysis of such impact on the agricultural economy. If the Secretary comments in writing to the Administrator regarding the notice and analysis within 30 days after receiving them, the Administrator shall publish in the Federal Register (with the notice) the comments of the Secretary and the response of the Administrator with regard to the Secretary's comments. If the Secretary does not comment in writing to the Administrator regarding the notice and analysis within 30 days after receiving them, the Administrator may notify the registrant and make public the notice at any time after such 30-day period notwithstanding the foregoing 60-day time requirement. The time requirements imposed by the preceding 3 sentences may be waived or modified to the extent agreed upon by the Administrator and the Secretary. Notwithstanding any other provision of this subsection and section 136w(d) of this title, in the event that the Administrator determines that suspension of a pesticide registration is necessary to prevent an imminent hazard to human health, then upon such a finding the Administrator may waive the requirement of notice to and consultation with the Secretary of Agriculture pursuant to this subsection and of submission to the Scientific Advisory Panel pursuant to section 136w(d) of this title and proceed in accordance with subsection (c) of this section. When a public health use is affected, the Secretary of Health and Human Services should provide available benefits and use information, or an analysis thereof, in accordance with the procedures followed and subject to the same conditions as the Secretary of Agriculture in the case of agricultural pesticides. The proposed action shall become final and effective at the end of 30 days from receipt by the registrant, or publication, of a notice issued under paragraph (1), whichever occurs later, unless within that time either (i) the registrant makes the necessary corrections, if possible, or (ii) a request for a hearing is made by a person adversely affected by the notice. In the event a hearing is held pursuant to such a request or to the Administrator's determination under paragraph (2), a decision pertaining to registration or classification issued after completion of such hearing shall be final. In taking any final action under this subsection, the Administrator shall consider restricting a pesticide's use or uses as an alternative to cancellation and shall fully explain the reasons for these restrictions, and shall include among those factors to be taken into account the impact of such final action on production and prices of agricultural commodities, retail food prices, and otherwise on the agricultural economy, and the Administrator shall publish in the Federal Register an analysis of such impact.

(c) Suspension

(1) Order — If the Administrator determines that action is necessary to prevent an imminent hazard during the time required for cancellation or change in classification proceedings, the Administrator may, by order, suspend the registration of the pesticide immediately. Except as provided in paragraph (3), no order of suspension may be issued under this subsection unless the Administrator has issued, or at the same time issues, a notice of intention to cancel the registration or change the classification of the pesticide under subsection (b) of this section. Except as provided in paragraph (3), the Administrator shall notify the registrant prior to issuing any suspension order. Such notice shall include findings pertaining to the question of "imminent hazard". The registrant shall then have an opportunity, in accordance with the provisions of paragraph (2), for an expedited hearing before the Administrator on the question of whether an imminent hazard exists.

(2) Expedite hearing — If no request for a hearing is submitted to the Administrator within five days of the registrant's receipt of the notification provided for by paragraph (1), the suspension order may be issued and shall take effect and shall not be reviewable by a court. If a hearing is requested, it shall commence within five days of the receipt of the request for such hearing unless the registrant and the Administrator agree that it shall commence at a later time. The hearing shall be held in accordance with the provisions of subchapter II of chapter 5 of Title 5, except that the presiding officer need not be a certified administrative law judge. The presiding officer shall have ten days from the conclusion of the presentation of evidence to submit recommended findings and conclusions to the Administrator, who shall then have seven days to render a final order on the issue of suspension.

(3) Emergency order — Whenever the Administrator determines that an emergency exists that does not permit the Administrator to hold a hearing before suspending, the Administrator may issue a suspension order in advance of notification to the registrant. The Administrator may issue an emergency order under this paragraph before issuing a notice of intention to cancel the registration or change the classification of the pesticide under subsection (b) of this section and the Administrator shall proceed to issue the notice under subsection (b) of this section within 90 days of issuing an emergency order. If the Administrator does not issue a notice under subsection (b) of this section within 90 days of issuing an emergency order, the emergency order shall expire. In the case of an emergency order, paragraph (2) shall apply except that (A) the order of suspension shall be in effect pending the expeditious completion of the remedies provided by that paragraph and the issuance of a final order on suspension, and (B) no party other than the registrant and the Administrator shall participate except that any person adversely affected may file briefs within the time allotted by the Agency's rules. Any person so filing briefs shall be considered a party to such proceeding for the purposes of section 136n(b) of this title.

(4) Judicial review — A final order on the question of suspension following a hearing shall be reviewable in accordance with section 136n of this title, notwithstanding the fact that any related cancellation proceedings have not been completed. Any order of suspension entered prior to a hearing before the Administrator shall be subject to immediate review in an action by the registrant or other interested person with the concurrence of the registrant in an appropriate district court, solely to determine whether the order of suspension was arbitrary, capricious or an abuse of discretion, or whether the order was issued in accordance with the

procedures established by law. The effect of any order of the court will be only to stay the effectiveness of the suspension order, pending the Administrator's final decision with respect to cancellation or change in classification. This action may be maintained simultaneously with any administrative review proceedings under this section. The commencement of proceedings under this paragraph shall not operate as a stay of order, unless ordered by the court.

(d) Public hearings and scientific review — In the event a hearing is requested pursuant to subsection (b) of this section or determined upon by the Administrator pursuant to subsection (b) of this section, such hearing shall be held after due notice for the purpose of receiving evidence relevant and material to the issues raised by the objections filed by the applicant or other interested parties, or to the issues stated by the Administrator, if the hearing is called by the Administrator rather than by the filing of objections. Upon a showing of relevance and reasonable scope of evidence sought by any party to a public hearing, the Hearing Examiner shall issue a subpoena to compel testimony or production of documents from any person. The Hearing Examiner shall be guided by the principles of the Federal Rules of Civil Procedure in making any order for the protection of the witness or the content of documents produced and shall order the payment of reasonable fees and expenses as a condition to requiring testimony of the witness. On contest, the subpoena may be enforced by an appropriate United States district court in accordance with the principles stated herein. Upon the request of any party to a public hearing and when in the Hearing Examiner's judgment it is necessary or desirable, the Hearing Examiner shall at any time before the hearing record is closed refer to a Committee of the National Academy of Sciences the relevant questions of scientific fact involved in the public hearing. No member of any committee of the National Academy of Sciences established to carry out the functions of this section shall have a financial or other conflict of interest with respect to any matter considered by such committee. The Committee of the National Academy of Sciences shall report in writing to the Hearing Examiner within 60 days after such referral on these questions of scientific fact. The report shall be made public and shall be considered as part of the hearing record. The Administrator shall enter into appropriate arrangements with the National Academy of Sciences to assure an objective and competent scientific review of the questions presented to Committees of the Academy and to provide such other scientific advisory services as may be required by the Administrator for carrying out the purposes of this subchapter. As soon as practicable after completion of the hearing (including the report of the Academy) but not later than 90 days thereafter, the Administrator shall evaluate the data and reports before the Administrator and issue an order either revoking the Administrator's

notice of intention issued pursuant to this section, or shall issue an order either canceling the registration, changing the classification, denying the registration, or requiring modification of the labeling or packaging of the article. Such order shall be based only on substantial evidence of record of such hearing and shall set forth detailed findings of fact upon which the order is based.

(e) Conditional registration

(1) The Administrator shall issue a notice of intent to cancel a registration issued under section 136a(c) (7) of this title if (A) the Administrator, at any time during the period provided for satisfaction of any condition imposed, determines that the registrant has failed to initiate and pursue appropriate action toward fulfilling any condition imposed, or (B) at the end of the period provided for satisfaction of any condition imposed, that condition has not been met. The Administrator may permit the continued sale and use of existing stocks of a pesticide whose conditional registration has been canceled under this subsection to such extent, under such conditions, and for such uses as the Administrator may specify if the Administrator determines that such sale or use is not inconsistent with the purposes of this subchapter and will not have unreasonable adverse effects on the environment.

(2) A cancellation proposed under this subsection shall become final and effective at the end of thirty days from receipt by the registrant of the notice of intent to cancel unless during that time a request for hearing is made by a person adversely affected by the notice. If a hearing is requested, a hearing shall be conducted under subsection (d) of this section. The only matters for resolution at that hearing shall be whether the registrant has initiated and pursued appropriate action to comply with the condition or conditions within the time provided or whether the condition or conditions have been satisfied within the time provided, and whether the Administrator's determination with respect to the disposition of existing stocks is consistent with this subchapter. A decision after completion of such hearing shall be final. Notwithstanding any other provision of this section, a hearing shall be held and a determination made within seventy-five days after receipt of a request for such hearing.

(f) General provisions

(1) Voluntary cancellation

(A) A registrant may, at any time, request that a pesticide registration of the registrant be canceled or amended to terminate one or more pesticide uses.

(B) Before acting on a request under subparagraph (A), the Administrator shall publish in the Federal Register a notice of the receipt of the request and provide for a 30-day period in which the public may comment.

(C) In the case of a pesticide that is registered for a minor agricultural use, if the

Administrator determines that the cancellation or termination of uses would adversely affect the availability of the pesticide for use, the Administrator —

(i) shall publish in the Federal Register a notice of the receipt of the request and make reasonable efforts to inform persons who so use the pesticide of the request; and

(ii) may not approve or reject the request until the termination of the 180-day period beginning on the date of publication of the notice in the Federal Register, except that the Administrator may waive the 180-day period upon the request of the registrant or if the Administrator determines that the continued use of the pesticide would pose an unreasonable adverse effect on the environment.

(D) Subject to paragraph (3)(B), after complying with this paragraph, the Administrator may approve or deny the request.

(2) Publication of notice — A notice of denial of registration, intent to cancel, suspension, or intent to suspend issued under this subchapter or a notice issued under subsection (c)(4) or (d)(5)(A) of section 136a-1 of this title shall be published in the Federal Register and shall be sent by certified mail, return receipt requested, to the registrant's or applicant's address of record on file with the Administrator. If the mailed notice is returned to the Administrator as undeliverable at that address, if delivery is refused, or if the Administrator otherwise is unable to accomplish delivery of the notice to the registrant or applicant after making reasonable efforts to do so, the notice shall be deemed to have been received by the registrant or applicant on the date the notice was published in the Federal Register.

(3) Transfer of registration of pesticides registered for minor agricultural uses

In the case of a pesticide that is registered for a minor agricultural use:

(A) During the 180-day period referred to in paragraph (1)(C)(ii), the registrant of the pesticide may notify the Administrator of an agreement between the registrant and a person or persons (including persons who so use the pesticide) to transfer the registration of the pesticide, in lieu of canceling or amending the registration to terminate the use.

(B) An application for transfer of registration, in conformance with any regulations the Administrator may adopt with respect to the transfer of the pesticide registrations, must be submitted to the Administrator within 30 days of the date of notification provided pursuant to subparagraph (A). If such an application is submitted, the Administrator shall approve the transfer and shall not approve the request for voluntary cancellation or amendment to termi-

nate use unless the Administrator determines that the continued use of the pesticide would cause an unreasonable adverse effect on the environment.

(C) If the Administrator approves the transfer and the registrant transfers the registration of the pesticide, the Administrator shall not cancel or amend the registration to delete the use or rescind the transfer of the registration, during the 180-day period beginning on the date of the approval of the transfer unless the Administrator determines that the continued use of the pesticide would cause an unreasonable adverse effect on the environment.

(D) The new registrant of the pesticide shall assume the outstanding data and other requirements for the pesticide that are pending at the time of the transfer.

(4) Utilization of data for voluntarily canceled pesticide — When an application is filed with the Administrator for the registration of a pesticide for a minor use and another registrant subsequently voluntarily cancels its registration for an identical or substantially similar pesticide for an identical or substantially similar use, the Administrator shall process, review, and evaluate the pending application as if the voluntary cancellation had not yet taken place except that the Administrator shall not take such action if the Administrator determines that such minor use may cause an unreasonable adverse effect on the environment. In order to rely on this subsection, the applicant must certify that it agrees to satisfy any outstanding data requirements necessary to support the reregistration of the pesticide in accordance with the data submission schedule established by the Administrator.

(g) Notice for stored pesticides with canceled or suspended registrations

(1) In general — Any producer or exporter of pesticides, registrant of a pesticide, applicant for registration of a pesticide, applicant for or holder of an experimental use permit, commercial applicator, or any person who distributes or sells any pesticide, who possesses any pesticide which has had its registration canceled or suspended under this section shall notify the Administrator and appropriate State and local officials of —

(A) such possession,

(B) the quantity of such pesticide such person possesses, and

(C) the place at which such pesticide is stored.

(2) Copies — The Administrator shall transmit a copy of each notice submitted under this subsection to the regional office of the Environmental Protection Agency which has jurisdiction over the place of pesticide storage identified in the notice.

(h) Judicial review — Final orders of the Administrator under this section shall be subject to judicial review pursuant to section 136n of this title.

§136e. Registration of establishments
[FIFRA §7]

(a) Requirement — No person shall produce any pesticide subject to this subchapter or active ingredient used in producing a pesticide subject to this subchapter in any State unless the establishment in which it is produced is registered with the Administrator. The application for registration of any establishment shall include the name and address of the establishment and of the producer who operates such establishment.

(b) Registration — Whenever the Administrator receives an application under subsection (a) of this section, the Administrator shall register the establishment and assign it an establishment number.

(c) Information required

(1) Any producer operating an establishment registered under this section shall inform the Administrator within 30 days after it is registered of the types and amounts of pesticides and, if applicable, active ingredients used in producing pesticides —

(A) which the producer is currently producing;

(B) which the producer has produced during the past year; and

(C) which the producer has sold or distributed during the past year.

The information required by this paragraph shall be kept current and submitted to the Administrator annually as required under such regulations as the Administrator may prescribe.

(2) Any such producer shall, upon the request of the Administrator for the purpose of issuing a stop sale order pursuant to section 136k of this title, inform the Administrator of the name and address of any recipient of any pesticide produced in any registered establishment which the producer operates.

(d) Confidential records and information — Any information submitted to the Administrator pursuant to subsection (c) of this section other than the names of the pesticides or active ingredients used in producing pesticides produced, sold, or distributed at an establishment shall be considered confidential and shall be subject to the provisions of section 136h of this title.

§136f. Books and records
[FIFRA §8]

(a) Requirements — The Administrator may prescribe regulations requiring producers, registrants, and applicants for registration to maintain such records with respect to their operations and the pesticides and devices produced as the Administrator determines are necessary for the effective enforcement of this subchapter and to make the records available for inspection and copying in the same manner as provided in subsection (b) of this section. No records required under this subsection shall extend to financial data, sales data other than shipment data, pricing data, personnel data, and research data (other than data relating to registered pesticides or to a pesticide for which an application for registration has been filed).

(b) Inspection — For the purposes of enforcing the provisions of this subchapter, any producer, distributor, carrier, dealer, or any other person who sells or offers for sale, delivers or offers for delivery any pesticide or device subject to this subchapter, shall, upon request of any officer or employee of the Environmental Protection Agency or of any State or political subdivision, duly designated by the Administrator, furnish or permit such person at all reasonable times to have access to, and to copy: (1) all records showing the delivery, movement, or holding of such pesticide or device, including the quantity, the date of shipment and receipt, and the name of the consignor and consignee; or (2) in the event of the inability of any person to produce records containing such information, all other records and information relating to such delivery, movement, or holding of the pesticide or device. Any inspection with respect to any records and information referred to in this subsection shall not extend to financial data, sales data other than shipment data, pricing data, personnel data; and research data (other than data relating to registered pesticides or to a pesticide for which an application for registration has been filed). Before undertaking an inspection under this subsection, the officer or employee must present to the owner, operator, or agent in charge of the establishment or other place where pesticides or devices are held for distribution or sale, appropriate credentials and a written statement as to the reason for the inspection, including a statement as to whether a violation of the law is suspected. If no violation is suspected, an alternate and sufficient reason shall be given in writing. Each such inspection shall be commenced and completed with reasonable promptness.

§136g. Inspection of establishments, etc.
[FIFRA §9]

(a) In general

(1) For purposes of enforcing the provisions of this subchapter, officers or employees of the Environmental Protection Agency or of any State duly designated by the Administrator are authorized to enter at reasonable times (A) any establishment or other place where pesticides or devices are held for distribution or sale for the purpose of inspecting and obtaining samples of any pesticides or devices, packaged, labeled, and released for shipment, and samples of any containers or labeling for such pesticides or devices, or (B) any place where there is being held any pesticide the registration of which has been suspended or canceled for the purpose of determining compliance with section 136q of this title.

(2) Before undertaking such inspection, the officers or employees must present to the owner,

operator, or agent in charge of the establishment or other place where pesticides or devices are held for distribution or sale, appropriate credentials and a written statement as to the reason for the inspection, including a statement as to whether a violation of the law is suspected. If no violation is suspected, an alternate and sufficient reason shall be given in writing. Each such inspection shall be commenced and completed with reasonable promptness. If the officer or employee obtains any samples, prior to leaving the premises, the officer or employee shall give to the owner, operator, or agent in charge a receipt describing the samples obtained and, if requested, a portion of each such sample equal in volume or weight to the portion retained. If an analysis is made of such samples, a copy of the results of such analysis shall be furnished promptly to the owner, operator, or agent in charge.

(b) Warrants — For purposes of enforcing the provisions of this subchapter and upon a showing to an officer or court of competent jurisdiction that there is reason to believe that the provisions of this subchapter have been violated, officers or employees duly designated by the Administrator are empowered to obtain and to execute warrants authorizing —

(1) entry, inspection, and copying of records for purposes of this section or section 136f of this title;

(2) inspection and reproduction of all records showing the quantity, date of shipment, and the name of consignor and consignee of any pesticide or device found in the establishment which is adulterated, misbranded, not registered (in the case of a pesticide) or otherwise in violation of this subchapter and in the event of the inability of any person to produce records containing such information, all other records and information relating to such delivery, movement, or holding of the pesticide or device; and

(3) the seizure of any pesticide or device which is in violation of this subchapter.

(c) Enforcement

(1) Certification of facts to Attorney General — The examination of pesticides or devices shall be made in the Environmental Protection Agency or elsewhere as the Administrator may designate for the purpose of determining from such examinations whether they comply with the requirements of this subchapter. If it shall appear from any such examination that they fail to comply with the requirements of this subchapter, the Administrator shall cause notice to be given to the person against whom criminal or civil proceedings are contemplated. Any person so notified shall be given an opportunity to present the person's views, either orally or in writing, with regard to such contemplated proceedings, and if in the opinion of the Administrator it appears that the provisions of this subchapter have been violated by such person, then the Administrator shall certify the facts to the Attorney General, with a copy of the results of the

analysis or the examination of such pesticide for the institution of a criminal proceeding pursuant to section 136*l*(b) of this title or a civil proceeding under section 136*l*(a) of this title, when the Administrator determines that such action will be sufficient to effectuate the purposes of this subchapter.

(2) Notice not required — The notice of contemplated proceedings and opportunity to present views set forth in this subsection are not prerequisites to the institution of any proceeding by the Attorney General.

(3) Warning notices — Nothing in this subchapter shall be construed as requiring the Administrator to institute proceedings for prosecution of minor violations of this subchapter whenever the Administrator believes that the public interest will be adequately served by a suitable written notice of warning.

§136h. Protection of trade secrets and other information
[FIFRA §10]

(a) In general — In submitting data required by this subchapter, the applicant may (1) clearly mark any portions thereof which in the applicant's opinion are trade secrets or commercial or financial information and (2) submit such market material separately from other material required to be submitted under this subchapter.

(b) Disclosure — Notwithstanding any other provision of this subchapter and subject to the limitations in subsections (d) and (e) of this section, the Administrator shall not make public information which in the Administrator's judgment contains or relates to trade secrets or commercial or financial information obtained from a person and privileged or confidential, except that, when necessary to carry out the provisions of this subchapter, information relating to formulas of products acquired by authorization of this subchapter may be revealed to any Federal agency consulted and may be revealed at a public hearing or in findings of fact issued by the Administrator.

(c) Disputes — If the Administrator proposes to release for inspection information which the applicant or registrant believes to be protected from disclosure under subsection (b) of this section, the Administrator shall notify the applicant or registrant, in writing, by certified mail. The Administrator shall not thereafter make available for inspection such data until thirty days after receipt of the notice by the applicant or registrant. During this period, the applicant or registrant may institute an action in an appropriate district court for a declaratory judgment as to whether such information is subject to protection under subsection (b) of this section.

(d) Limitations

(1) All information concerning the objectives, methodology, results, or significance of any test or experiment performed on or with a registered or previously registered pesticide or its separate ingredients, impurities, or degradation products, and any

223

information concerning the effects of such pesticide on any organism or the behavior of such pesticide in the environment, including, but not limited to, data on safety to fish and wildlife, humans and other mammals, plants, animals, and soil, and studies on persistence, translocation and fate in the environment, and metabolism, shall be available for disclosure to the public. The use of such data for any registration purpose shall be governed by section 136a of this title. This paragraph does not authorize the disclosure of any information that —

> (A) discloses manufacturing or quality control processes,
>
> (B) discloses the details of any methods for testing, detecting, or measuring the quantity of any deliberately added inert ingredient of a pesticide, or
>
> (C) discloses the identity or percentage quantity of any deliberately added inert ingredient of a pesticide,

unless the Administrator has first determined that disclosure is necessary to protect against an unreasonable risk of injury to health or the environment.

(2) Information concerning production, distribution, sale, or inventories of a pesticide that is otherwise entitled to confidential treatment under subsection (b) of this section may be publicly disclosed in connection with a public proceeding to determine whether a pesticide, or any ingredient of a pesticide, causes unreasonable adverse effects on health or the environment, if the Administrator determines that such disclosure is necessary in the public interest.

(3) If the Administrator proposes to disclose information described in clause (A), (B), or (C) of paragraph (1) or in paragraph (2) of this subsection, the Administrator shall notify by certified mail the submitter of such information of the intent to release such information. The Administrator may not release such information, without the submitter's consent, until thirty days after the submitter has been furnished such notice. Where the Administrator finds that disclosure of information described in clause (A), (B), or (C) of paragraph (1) of this subsection is necessary to avoid or lessen an imminent and substantial risk of injury to the public health, the Administrator may set such shorter period of notice (but not less than ten days) and such method of notice as the Administrator finds appropriate. During such period the data submitter may institute an action in an appropriate district court to enjoin or limit the proposed disclosure. The court may enjoin disclosure, or limit the disclosure or the parties to whom disclosure shall be made, to the extent that —

> (A) in the case of information described in clause (A), (B), or (C) of paragraph (1) of this subsection, the proposed disclosure is not required to protect against an unreasonable risk of injury to health or the environment; or

> (B) in the case of information described in paragraph (2) of this subsection, the public interest in availability of the information in the public proceeding does not outweigh the interests in preserving the confidentiality of the information.

(e) Disclosure to contractors — Information otherwise protected from disclosure to the public under subsection (b) of this section may be disclosed to contractors with the United States and employees of such contractors if, in the opinion of the Administrator, such disclosure is necessary for the satisfactory performance by the contractor of a contract with the United States for the performance of work in connection with this subchapter and under such conditions as the Administrator may specify. The Administrator shall require as a condition to the disclosure of information under this subsection that the person receiving it take such security precautions respecting the information as the Administrator shall by regulation prescribe.

(f) Penalty for disclosure by Federal employees

(1) Any officer or employee of the United States or former officer or employee of the United States who, by virtue of such employment or official position, has obtained possession of, or has access to, material the disclosure of which is prohibited by subsection (b) of this section, and who, knowing that disclosure of such material is prohibited by such subsection, willfully discloses the material in any manner to any person not entitled to receive it, shall be fined not more than $10,000 or imprisoned for not more than one year, or both. Section 1905 of Title 18 shall not apply with respect to the publishing, divulging, disclosure, or making known of, or making available, information reported or otherwise obtained under this subchapter. Nothing in this subchapter shall preempt any civil remedy under State or Federal law for wrongful disclosure of trade secrets.

(2) For the purposes of this section, any contractor with the United States who is furnished information as authorized by subsection (e) of this section, or any employee of any such contractor, shall be considered to be an employee of the United States.

(g) Disclosure to foreign and multinational pesticide producers

(1) The Administrator shall not knowingly disclose information submitted by an applicant or registrant under this subchapter to any employee or agent of any business or other entity engaged in the production, sale, or distribution of pesticides in countries other than the United States or in addition to the United States or to any other person who intends to deliver such data to such foreign or multinational business or entity unless the applicant or registrant has consented to such disclosure. The Administrator shall require an affirmation from any person who intends to

inspect data that such person does not seek access to the data for purposes of delivering it or offering it for sale to any such business or entity or its agents or employees and will not purposefully deliver or negligently cause the data to be delivered to such business or entity or its agents or employees. Notwithstanding any other provision of this subsection, the Administrator may disclose information to any person in connection with a public proceeding under law or regulation, subject to restrictions on the availability of information contained elsewhere in this subchapter, which information is relevant to a determination by the Administrator with respect to whether a pesticide, or any ingredient of a pesticide, causes unreasonable adverse effects on health or the environment.

(2) The Administrator shall maintain records of the names of persons to whom data are disclosed under this subsection and the persons or organizations they represent and shall inform the applicant or registrant of the names and affiliations of such persons.

(3) Section 1001 of Title 18 shall apply to any affirmation made under paragraph (1) of this subsection.

§136i. Use of restricted use pesticides; applicators
[FIFRA §11]
(a) Certification procedure

(1) Federal certification — In any State for which a State plan for applicator certification has not been approved by the Administrator, the Administrator, in consultation with the Governor of such State, shall conduct a program for the certification of applicators of pesticides. Such program shall conform to the requirements imposed upon the States under the provisions of subsection (a)(2) of this section and shall not require private applicators to take any examination to establish competency in the use of pesticides. Prior to the implementation of the program, the Administrator shall publish in the Federal Register for review and comment a summary of the Federal plan for applicator certification and shall make generally available within the State copies of the plan. The Administrator shall hold public hearings at one or more locations within the State if so requested by the Governor of such State during the thirty days following publication of the Federal Register notice inviting comment on the Federal plan. The hearings shall be held within thirty days following receipt of the request from the Governor. In any State in which the Administrator conducts a certification program, the Administrator may require any person engaging in the commercial application, sale, offering for sale, holding for sale, or distribution of any pesticide one or more uses of which have been classified for restricted use to maintain such records and submit such reports concerning the commercial application, sale, or distribution of such pesticide as the Administrator may by regulation prescribe. Subject to paragraph (2), the Administrator shall prescribe standards for the certification of applicators of pesticides. Such standards shall provide that to be certified, an individual must be determined to be competent with respect to the use and handling of the pesticides, or to the use and handling of the pesticide or class of pesticides covered by such individual's certification. The certification standard for a private applicator shall, under a State plan submitted for approval, be deemed fulfilled by the applicator completing a certification form. The Administrator shall further assure that such form contains adequate information and affirmations to carry out the intent of this subchapter, and may include in the form an affirmation that the private applicator has completed a training program approved by the Administrator so long as the program does not require the private applicator to take, pursuant to a requirement prescribed by the Administrator, any examination to establish competency in the use of the pesticide. The Administrator may require any pesticide dealer participating in a certification program to be licensed under a State licensing program approved by the Administrator.

(2) State certification — If any State, at any time, desires to certify applicators of pesticides, the Governor of such State shall submit a State plan for such purpose. The Administrator shall approve the plan submitted by any State, or any modification thereof, if such plan in the Administrator's judgment —

(A) designates a State agency as the agency responsible for administering the plan throughout the State;

(B) contains satisfactory assurances that such agency has or will have the legal authority and qualified personnel necessary to carry out the plan;

(C) gives satisfactory assurances that the State will devote adequate funds to the administration of the plan;

(D) provides that the State agency will make such reports to the Administrator in such form and containing such information as the Administrator may from time to time require; and

(E) contains satisfactory assurances that State standards for the certification of applicators of pesticides conform with those standards prescribed by the Administrator under paragraph (1).

Any State certification program under this section shall be maintained in accordance with the State plan approved under this section.

(b) State plans — If the Administrator rejects a plan submitted under subsection (a)(2) of this section, the Administrator shall afford the State submitting the plan due notice and opportunity for hearing before so doing. If the Administrator approves a plan submitted under subsection (a)(2) of this section, then such State shall certify applicators of pesticides with respect to such State. Whenever the Administrator determines that a State is not administering the certification program in accordance with the plan approved under this section, the Administrator shall so notify the State and provide for a hearing at the request of the State, and, if appropriate corrective action is not taken within a reasonable time, not to exceed ninety days, the Administrator shall withdraw approval of such plan.

(c) Instruction in integrated pest management techniques — Standards prescribed by the Administrator for the certification of applicators of pesticides under subsection (a) of this section, and State plans submitted to the Administrator under subsection (a) of this section, shall include provisions for making instructional materials concerning integrated pest management techniques available to individuals at their request in accordance with the provisions of section 136u(c) of this title, but such plans may not require that any individual receive instruction concerning such techniques or to be shown to be competent with respect to the use of such techniques. The Administrator and States implementing such plans shall provide that all interested individuals are notified on the availability of such instructional materials.

(d) In general — No regulations prescribed by the Administrator for carrying out the provisions of this subchapter shall require any private applicator to maintain any records or file any reports or other documents.

(e) Separate standards — When establishing or approving standards for licensing or certification, the Administrator shall establish separate standards for commercial and private applicators.

§136i-1. Pesticide recordkeeping
(a) Requirements

(1) The Secretary of Agriculture, in consultation with the Administrator of the Environmental Protection Agency, shall require certified applicators of restricted use pesticides (of the type described under section 136a(d)(1)(C) of this title) to maintain records comparable to records maintained by commercial applicators of pesticides in each State. If there is no State requirement for the maintenance of records, such applicator shall maintain records that contain the product name, amount, approximate date of application, and location of application of each such pesticide used for a 2-year period after such use.

(2) Within 30 days of a pesticide application, a commercial certified applicator shall provide a copy of records maintained under paragraph (1) to the person for whom such application was provided.

(b) Access — Records maintained under subsection (a) of this section shall be made available to any Federal or State agency that deals with pesticide use or any health or environmental issue related to the use of pesticides, on the request of such agency. Each such

Federal agency shall conduct surveys and record the data from individual applicators to facilitate statistical analysis for environmental and agronomic purposes, but in no case may a government agency release data, including the location from which the data was derived, that would directly or indirectly reveal the identity of individual producers. In the case of Federal agencies, such access to records maintained under subsection (a) of this section shall be through the Secretary of Agriculture, or the Secretary's designee. State agency requests for access to records maintained under subsection (a) of this section shall be through the lead State agency so designated by the State.

(c) Health care personnel — When a health professional determines that pesticide information maintained under this section is necessary to provide medical treatment or first aid to an individual who may have been exposed to pesticides for which the information is maintained, upon request persons required to maintain records under subsection (a) of this section shall promptly provide record and available label information to that health professional. In the case of an emergency, such record information shall be provided immediately.

(d) Penalty — The Secretary of Agriculture shall be responsible for the enforcement of subsections (a), (b), and (c) of this section. A violation of such subsection shall —

(1) in the case of the first offense, be subject to a fine of not more than $500; and

(2) in the case of subsequent offenses, be subject to a fine of not less than $1,000 for each violation, except that the penalty shall be less than $1,000 if the Secretary determines that the person made a good faith effort to comply with such subsection.

(e) Federal or State provisions — The requirements of this section shall not affect provisions of other Federal or State laws.

(f) Surveys and reports — The Secretary of Agriculture and the Administrator of the Environmental Protection Agency, shall survey the records maintained under subsection (a) of this section to develop and maintain a data base that is sufficient to enable the Secretary and the Administrator to publish annual comprehensive reports concerning agricultural and nonagricultural pesticide use. The Secretary and Administrator shall enter into a memorandum of understanding to define their respective responsibilities under this subsection in order to avoid duplication of effort. Such reports shall be transmitted to Congress not later than April 1 of each year.

(g) Regulations — The Secretary of Agriculture and the Administrator of the Environmental Protection Agency shall promulgate regulations on their respective areas of responsibility implementing this section within 180 days after November 28, 1990.

§136i-2. Collection of pesticide use information
(a) In general — The Secretary of Agriculture shall collect data of statewide or regional significance

on the use of pesticides to control pests and diseases of major crops and crops of dietary significance, including fruits and vegetables.

(b) Collection — The data shall be collected by surveys of farmers or from other sources offering statistically reliable data.

(c) Coordination — The Secretary of Agriculture shall, as appropriate, coordinate with the Administrator of the Environmental Protection Agency in the design of the surveys and make available to the Administrator the aggregate results of the surveys to assist the Administrator.

§136j. Unlawful acts
[FIFRA §12]
(a) In general

(1) Except as provided by subsection (b) of this section, it shall be unlawful for any person in any State to distribute or sell to any person —

(A) any pesticide that is not registered under section 136a of this title or whose registration has been canceled or suspended, except to the extent that distribution or sale otherwise has been authorized by the Administrator under this subchapter;

(B) any registered pesticide if any claims made for it as a part of its distribution or sale substantially differ from any claims made for it as a part of the statement required in connection with its registration under section 136a of this title;

(C) any registered pesticide the com-position of which differs at the time of its distribution or sale from its composition as described in the statement required in connection with its registration under section 136a of this title;

(D) any pesticide which has not been colored or discolored pursuant to the provisions of section 136w(c)(5) of this title;

(E) any pesticide which is adulterated or misbranded; or

(F) any device which is misbranded.

(2) It shall be unlawful for any person —

(A) to detach, alter, deface, or destroy, in whole or in part, any labeling required under this subchapter;

(B) to refuse to —

(i) prepare, maintain, or submit any records required by or under section 136c, 136e, 136f, 136i, or 136q of this title;

(ii) submit any reports required by or under section 136c, 136d, 136e, 136f, 136i, or 136q of this title; or

(iii) allow any entry, inspection, copying of records, or sampling authorized by this subchapter;

(C) to give a guaranty or undertaking provided for in subsection (b) of this sec-tion which is false in any particular, except that a person who receives and relies upon a guaranty authorized under subsection (b) of this section may give a guaranty to the same effect, which guaranty shall contain, in addition to the person's own name and address, the name and address of the person residing in the United States from whom the person received the guaranty or undertaking;

(D) to use for the person's own advantage or to reveal, other than to the Administrator, or officials or employees of the Environmental Protection Agency or other Federal executive agencies, or to the courts, or to physicians, pharmacists, and other qualified persons, needing such information for the performance of their duties, in accordance with such directions as the Administrator may prescribe, any information acquired by authority of this subchapter which is confidential under this subchapter;

(E) who is a registrant, wholesaler, dealer, retailer, or other distributor to advertise a product registered under this subchapter for restricted use without giving the classification of the product assigned to it under section 136a of this title;

(F) to distribute or sell, or to make available for use, or to use, any registered pesticide classified for restricted use for some or all purposes other than in accordance with section 136a(d) of this title and any regulations thereunder, except that it shall not be unlawful to sell, under regulations issued by the Administrator, a restricted use pesticide to a person who is not a certified applicator for application by a certified applicator;

(G) to use any registered pesticide in a manner inconsistent with its labeling;

(H) to use any pesticide which is under an experimental use permit contrary to the provisions of such permit;

(I) to violate any order issued under section 136k of this title;

(J) to violate any suspension order issued under section 136a(c)(2)(B), 136a-1, or 136d of this title;

(K) to violate any cancellation order issued under this subchapter or to fail to submit a notice in accordance with section 136d(g) of this title;

(L) who is a producer to violate any of the provisions of section 136e of this title;

(M) to knowingly falsify all or part of any application for registration, application for experimental use permit, any information submitted to the Administrator pursuant to section 136e of this title, any records required to be maintained pursuant to this subchapter, any report filed under this subchapter, or any information marked as confidential and submitted to the Administrator under any provision of this subchapter;

(N) who is a registrant, wholesaler, dealer, retailer, or other distributor to fail to file reports required by this subchapter;

(O) to add any substance to, or take any substance from, any pesticide in a manner that may defeat the purpose of this subchapter;

(P) to use any pesticide in tests on human beings unless such human beings (i) are fully informed of the nature and purposes of the test and of any physical and mental health consequences which are reasonably foreseeable therefrom, and (ii) freely volunteer to participate in the test;

(Q) to falsify all or part of any information relating to the testing of any pesticide (or any ingredient, metabolite, or degradation product thereof), including the nature of any protocol, procedure, substance, organism, or equipment used, observation made, or conclusion or opinion formed, submitted to the Administrator, or that the person knows will be furnished to the Administrator or will become a part of any records required to be maintained by this subchapter;

(R) to submit to the Administrator data known to be false in support of a registration; or

(S) to violate any regulation issued under section 136a(a) or 136q of this title.

(b) Exemptions — The penalties provided for a violation of paragraph (1) of subsection (a) of this section shall not apply to —

(1) any person who establishes a guaranty signed by, and containing the name and address of, the registrant or person residing in the United States from whom the person purchased or received in good faith the pesticide in the same unbroken package, to the effect that the pesticide was lawfully registered at the time of sale and delivery to the person, and that it complies with the other requirements of this subchapter, and in such case the guarantor shall be subject to the penalties which would otherwise attach to the person holding the guaranty under the provisions of this subchapter;

(2) any carrier while lawfully shipping, transporting, or delivering for shipment any pesticide or device, if such carrier upon request of any officer or employee duly designated by the Administrator shall permit such officer or employee to copy all of its records concerning such pesticide or device;

(3) any public official while engaged in the performance of the official duties of the public official;

(4) any person using or possessing any pesticide as provided by an experimental use permit in effect with respect to such pesticide and such use or possession; or

(5) any person who ships a substance or mixture of substances being put through tests in which the purpose is only to determine its value for pesticide purposes or to determine its toxicity or other properties and from which the user does not expect to receive any benefit in pest control from its use.

§136k. Stop sale, use, removal, and seizure [FIFRA §13]

(a) Stop sale, etc., orders — Whenever any pesticide or device is found by the Administrator in any State and there is reason to believe on the basis of inspection or tests that such pesticide or device is in violation of any of the provisions of this subchapter, or that such pesticide or device has been or is intended to be distributed or sold in violation of any such provisions, or when the registration of the pesticide has been canceled by a final order or has been suspended, the Administrator may issue a written or printed "stop sale, use, or removal" order to any person who owns, controls, or has custody of such pesticide or device, and after receipt of such order no person shall sell, use, or remove the pesticide or device described in the order except in accordance with the provisions of the order.

(b) Seizure — Any pesticide or device that is being transported or, having been transported, remains unsold or in original unbroken packages, or that is sold or offered for sale in any State, or that is imported from a foreign country, shall be liable to be proceeded against in any district court in the district where it is found and seized for confiscation by a process in rem for condemnation if —

(1) in the case of a pesticide —

(A) it is adulterated or misbranded;

(B) it is not registered pursuant to the provisions of section 136a of this title;

(C) its labeling fails to bear the information required by this subchapter;

(D) it is not colored or discolored and such coloring or discoloring is required under this subchapter; or

(E) any of the claims made for it or any of the directions for its use differ in substance from the representations made in connection with its registration;

(2) in the case of a device, it is misbranded; or

(3) in the case of a pesticide or device, when used in accordance with the requirements imposed under this subchapter and as directed by the labeling, it nevertheless causes unreasonable adverse effects on the environment.

In the case of a plant regulator, defoliant, or desiccant, used in accordance with the label claims and recommendations, physical or physiological effects on plants or parts thereof shall not be deemed to be injury, when such effects are the purpose for which the plant regulator, defoliant, or desiccant was applied.

(c) Disposition after condemnation — If the pesticide or device is condemned it shall, after entry of the decree, be disposed of by destruction or sale as the court may direct and the proceeds, if sold, less the court costs, shall be paid into the Treasury of the United States, but the pesticide or device shall not be sold contrary to the provisions of this subchapter or the laws of the jurisdiction in which it is sold. On payment of the costs of the condemnation proceedings and the execution and delivery of a good and sufficient bond conditioned that the pesticide or device shall not be sold or otherwise disposed of contrary to the provisions of the subchapter or the laws of any jurisdiction in which sold, the court may direct that such pesticide or device be delivered to the owner thereof. The proceedings of such condemnation cases shall conform, as near as may be to the proceedings in admiralty, except that either party may demand trial by jury of any issue of fact joined in any case, and all such proceedings shall be at the suit of and in the name of the United States.

(d) Court costs, etc. — When a decree of condemnation is entered against the pesticide or device, court costs and fees, storage, and other proper expenses shall be awarded against the person, if any, intervening as claimant of the pesticide or device.

§136*l*. Penalties
[FIFRA §14]
(a) Civil penalties

(1) In general — Any registrant, commercial applicator, wholesaler, dealer, retailer, or other distributor who violates any provision of this subchapter may be assessed a civil penalty by the Administrator of not more than $5,000 for each offense.

(2) Private applicator — Any private applicator or other person not included in paragraph (1) who violates any provision of this subchapter subsequent to receiving a written warning from the Administrator or following a citation for a prior violation, may be assessed a civil penalty by the Administrator of not more than $1,000 for each offense, except that any applicator not included under paragraph (1) of this subsection who holds or applies registered pesticides, or uses dilutions of registered pesticides, only to provide a service of controlling pests without delivering any unapplied pesticide to any person so served, and who violates any provision of this subchapter may be assessed a civil penalty by the Administrator of not more than $500 for the first offense nor more than $1,000 for each subsequent offense.

(3) Hearing — No civil penalty shall be assessed unless the person charged shall have been given notice and opportunity for a hearing on such charge in the county, parish, or incorporated city of the residence of the person charged.

(4) Determination of penalty — In determining the amount of the penalty, the Administrator shall consider the appropriateness of such penalty to the size of the business of the person charged, the effect on the person's ability to continue in business, and the gravity of the violation. Whenever the Administrator finds that the violation occurred despite the exercise of due care or did not cause significant harm to health or the environment, the Administrator may issue a warning in lieu of assessing a penalty.

(5) References to Attorney General — In case of inability to collect such civil penalty or failure of any person to pay all, or such portion of such civil penalty as the Administrator may determine, the Administrator shall refer the matter to the Attorney General, who shall recover such amount by action in the appropriate United States district court.

(b) Criminal penalties

(1) In general

(A) Any registrant, applicant for a registration, or producer who knowingly violates any provision of this subchapter shall be fined not more than $50,000 or imprisoned for not more than 1 year, or both.

(B) Any commercial applicator of a restricted use pesticide, or any other person not described in subparagraph (A) who distributes or sells pesticides or devices, who knowingly violates any provision of this subchapter shall be fined not more than $25,000 or imprisoned for not more than 1 year, or both.

(2) Private applicator — Any private applicator or other person not included in paragraph (1) who knowingly violates any provision of this subchapter shall be guilty of a misdemeanor and shall on conviction be fined not more than $1,000, or imprisoned for not more than 30 days, or both.

(3) Disclosure of information — Any person, who, with intent to defraud, uses or reveals information relative to formulas of products acquired under the authority of section 136a of this title, shall be fined not more than $10,000, or imprisoned for not more than three years, or both.

(4) Acts of officers, agents, etc. — When construing and enforcing the provisions of this subchapter, the act, omission, or failure of any officer, agent, or other person acting for or employed by any person shall in every case be also deemed to be the act, omission, or failure of such person as well as that of the person employed.

§136m. Indemnities
[FIFRA §15]
(a) General indemnification

(1) In general — Except as otherwise provided in this section, if —

(A) the Administrator notifies a registrant under section 136d(c)(1) of this title that the Administrator intends to suspend a registration or that an emergency order of suspension of a registration under section 136d(c)(3) of this title has been issued;

(B) the registration in question is suspended under section 136d(c) of this title, and thereafter is canceled under section 136d(b), 136d(d), or 136d(f) of this title; and

(C) any person who owned any quantity of the pesticide immediately before the notice to the registrant under subparagraph (A) suffered losses by reason of suspension or cancellation of the registration;

the Administrator shall make an indemnity payment to the person.

(2) Exception — Paragraph (1) shall not apply if the Administrator finds that the person —

(A) had knowledge of facts that, in themselves, would have shown that the pesticide did not meet the requirements of section 136a(c)(5) of this title for registration; and

(B) continued thereafter to produce the pesticide without giving timely notice of such facts to the Administrator.

(3) Report — If the Administrator takes an action under paragraph (1) that requires the payment of indemnification, the Administrator shall report to the Committee on Agriculture of the House of Representatives, the Committee on Agriculture, Nutrition, and Forestry of the Senate, and the Committees on Appropriations of the House of Representatives and the Senate on —

(A) the action taken that requires the payment of indemnification;

(B) the reasons for taking the action;

(C) the estimated cost of the payment; and

(D) a request for the appropriation of funds for the payment.

(4) Appropriation — The Administrator may not make a payment of indemnification under paragraph (1) unless a specific line item appropriation of funds has been made in advance for the payment.

(b) Indemnification of end users, dealers, and distributors

(1) End users — If —

(A) the Administrator notifies a registrant under section 136d(c)(1) of this title that the Administrator intends to suspend a registration or that an emergency order of suspension of a registration under section 136d(c)(3) of this title has been issued;

(B) the registration in question is suspended under section 136d(c) of this title, and thereafter is canceled under section 136d(b), 136d(d), or 136d(f) of this title; and

(C) any person who, immediately before the notice to the registrant under subparagraph (A), owned any quantity of the pesticide for purposes of applying or using the pesticide as an end user, rather than for purposes of distributing or selling it or further processing it for distribution or sale, suffered a loss by reason of the suspension

or cancellation of the pesticide;

the person shall be entitled to an indemnity payment under this subsection for such quantity of the pesticide.

(2) Dealers and distributors

(A) Any registrant, wholesaler, dealer, or other distributor (hereinafter in this paragraph referred to as a "seller") of a registered pesticide who distributes or sells the pesticide directly to any person not described as an end user in paragraph (1)(C) shall, with respect to any quantity of the pesticide that such person cannot use or resell as a result of the suspension or cancellation of the pesticide, reimburse such person for the cost of first acquiring the pesticide from the seller (other than the cost of transportation, if any), unless the seller provided to the person at the time of distribution or sale a notice, in writing, that the pesticide is not subject to reimbursement by the seller.

(B) If —

(i) the Administrator notifies a registrant under section 136d(c)(1) of this title that the Administrator intends to suspend a registration or that an emergency order of suspension of a registration under section 136d(c)(3) of this title has been issued;

(ii) the registration in question is suspended under section 136d(c) of this title, and thereafter is canceled under section 136d(b), 136d(d), or 136d(f) of this title;

(iii) any person who, immediately before the notice to the registrant under clause (i) —

(I) had not been notified in writing by the seller, as provided under subparagraph (A), that any quantity of the pesticide owned by such person is not subject to reimbursement by the seller in the event of suspension or cancellation of the pesticide; and

(II) owned any quantity of the pesticide for purposes of —

(aa) distributing or selling it; or

(bb) further processing it for distribution or sale directly to an end user;

suffered a loss by reason of the suspension or cancellation of the pesticide; and

(iv) the Administrator determines on the basis of a claim of loss submitted to the Administrator by the person, that the seller —

(I) did not provide the notice specified in subparagraph (A) to such person; and

(II) is and will continue to be unable to provide reimbursement to such person, as provided under sub-paragraph (A), for the loss referred to in clause (iii), as a result of the insolvency or bankruptcy of the seller and the seller's resulting inability to provide such reimbursement;

the person shall be entitled to an indemnity payment under this subsection for such quantity of the pesticide.

(C) If an indemnity payment is made by the United States under this paragraph, the United States shall be subrogated to any right that would otherwise be held under this paragraph by a seller who is unable to make a reimbursement in accordance with this paragraph with regard to reimbursements that otherwise would have been made by the seller.

(3) Source — Any payment required to be made under paragraph (1) or (2) shall be made from the appropriation provided under section 1304 of Title 31.

(4) Administrative settlement — An administrative settlement of a claim for such indemnity may be made in accordance with the third paragraph of section 2414 of Title 28 and shall be regarded as if it were made under that section for purposes of section 1304 of Title 31.

(c) Amount of payment

(1) In general — The amount of an indemnity payment under subsection (a) or (b) of this section to any person shall be determined on the basis of the cost of the pesticide owned by the person (other than the cost of transportation, if any) immediately before the issuance of the notice to the registrant referred to in subsection (a)(1)(A), (b)(1)(A), or (b)(2)(B)(i) of this section, except that in no event shall an indemnity payment to any person exceed the fair market value of the pesticide owned by the person immediately before the issuance of the notice.

(2) Special rule — Notwithstanding any other provision of this subchapter, the Administrator may provide a reasonable time for use or other disposal of the pesticide. In determining the quantity of any pesticide for which indemnity shall be paid under this section, proper adjustment shall be made for any pesticide used or otherwise disposed of by the owner.

§136n. Administrative procedure; judicial review

[FIFRA §16]

(a) District court review — Except as otherwise provided in this subchapter, the refusal of the Administrator to cancel or suspend a registration or to change a classification not following a hearing and other final actions of the Administrator not committed to the discretion of the Administrator by law are judicially reviewable by the district courts of the United States.

(b) Review by court of appeals — In the case of actual controversy as to the validity of any order issued by the Administrator following a public hearing, any person who will be adversely affected by such order and who had been a party to the proceedings may obtain judicial review by filing in the United States court of appeals for the circuit wherein such person resides or has a place of business, within 60 days after the entry of such order, a petition praying that the order be set aside in whole or in part. A copy of the petition shall be forthwith transmitted by the clerk of the court to the Administrator or any officer designated by the Administrator for that purpose, and thereupon the Administrator shall file in the court the record of the proceedings on which the Administrator based the Administrator's order, as provided in section 2112 of Title 28. Upon the filing of such petition the court shall have exclusive jurisdiction to affirm or set aside the order complained of in whole or in part. The court shall consider all evidence of record. The order of the Administrator shall be sustained if it is supported by substantial evidence when considered on the record as a whole. The judgment of the court affirming or setting aside, in whole or in part, any order under this section shall be final, subject to review by the Supreme Court of the United States upon certiorari or certification as provided in section 1254 of Title 28. The commencement of proceedings under this section shall not, unless specifically ordered by the court to the contrary, operate as a stay of an order.

(c) Jurisdiction of district courts — The district courts of the United States are vested with jurisdiction specifically to enforce, and to prevent and restrain violations of, this subchapter.

(d) Notice of judgments — The Administrator shall, by publication in such manner as the Administrator may prescribe, give notice of all judgments entered in actions instituted under the authority of this subchapter.

§136o. Imports and exports
[FIFRA §17]

(a) Pesticides and devices intended for export — Notwithstanding any other provision of this subchapter, no pesticide or device or active ingredient used in producing a pesticide intended solely for export to any foreign country shall be deemed in violation of this subchapter —

(1) when prepared or packed according to the specifications or directions of the foreign purchaser, except that producers of such pesticides and devices and active ingredients used in producing pesticides shall be subject to sections 136(p), 136(q)(1)(A), (C), (D), (E), (G), and (H), 136q(2)(A), (B), (C)(i) and (iii), and (D), 136e, and 136f of this title; and

(2) in the case of any pesticide other than a pesticide registered under section 136a or sold

under section 136d(a)(1) of this title, if, prior to export, the foreign purchaser has signed a statement acknowledging that the purchaser understands that such pesticide is not registered for use in the United States and cannot be sold in the United States under this subchapter.

A copy of that statement shall be transmitted to an appropriate official of the government of the importing country.

(b) Cancellation notices furnished to foreign governments — Whenever a registration, or a cancellation or suspension of the registration of a pesticide becomes effective, or ceases to be effective, the Administrator shall transmit through the State Department notification thereof to the governments of other countries and to appropriate international agencies. Such notification shall, upon request, include all information related to the cancellation or suspension of the registration of the pesticide and information concerning other pesticides that are registered under section 136a of this title and that could be used in lieu of such pesticide.

(c) Importation of pesticides and devices

(1) In general — The Secretary of the Treasury shall notify the Administrator of the arrival of pesticides and devices and shall deliver to the Administrator, upon the Administrator's request, samples of pesticides or devices which are being imported into the United States, giving notice to the owner or consignee, who may appear before the Administrator and have the right to introduce testimony. If it appears from the examination of a sample that it is adulterated, or misbranded or otherwise violated the provisions set forth in this subchapter, or is otherwise injurious to health or the environment, the pesticide or device may be refused admission, and the Secretary of the Treasury shall refuse delivery to the consignee and shall cause the destruction of any pesticide or device refused delivery which shall not be exported by the consignee within 90 days from the date of notice of such refusal under such regulations as the Secretary of the Treasury may prescribe. The Secretary of the Treasury may deliver to the consignee such pesticide or device pending examination and decision in the matter on execution of bond for the amount of the full invoice value of such pesticide or device, together with the duty thereon, and on refusal to return such pesticide or device for any cause to the custody of the Secretary of the Treasury, when demanded, for the purpose of excluding them from the country, or for any other purpose, said consignee shall forfeit the full amount of said bond. All charges for storage, cartage, and labor on pesticides or devices which are refused admission or delivery shall be paid by the owner or consignee, and in default of such payment shall constitute a lien against any future importation made by such owner or consignee.

(2) Importation of seed — Notwithstanding any other provision of law, no person is required to notify the Administrator of the arrival of a plant-incorporated protectant (as defined in section 174.3 of title 40, Code of Federal Regulations (or any successor regulation)) that is contained in a seed, if —

(A) that plant-incorporated protectant is registered under section 3;

(B) the Administrator has issued an experimental use permit for that plant-incorporated protectant under section 5; or

(C) the seed is covered by a permit (as defined in part 340 of title 7, Code of Federal Regulations (or any successor regulation)) or a notification.

(3) Cooperation —

(A) In general — in response to a request from the Administrator, the Secretary of Agriculture shall provide to the Administrator a list of seed containing plant-incorporated protectants (as defined in section 174.3 of title 40, Code of Federal Regulations (or any successor regulation)) if the importation of that seed into the United States has been approved under a permit or notification referred to in paragraph (2).

(B) Contents — The list under subparagraph (A) shall be provided in a form and at such intervals as may be agreed to by the Secretary and the Administrator.

(4) Applicability — Nothing in this subsection precludes or limits the authority of the Secretary of Agriculture with respect to the importation or movement of plants, plant products, or seeds under —

(A) the Plant Protection Act (7 U.S.C. 7701 *et seq.*); and

(B) the Federal Seed Act (7 U.S.C. 1551 *et seq.*).

(d) Cooperation in international efforts

(1) In general. The Administrator shall, in cooperation with the Department of State and any other appropriate Federal agency, participate and cooperate in any international efforts to develop improved pesticide research and regulations.

(2) Department of State expenses. Any expenses incurred by an employee of the Environmental Protection Agency who participates in any international technical, economic, or policy review board, committee, or other official body that is meeting in relation to an international treaty shall be paid by the Department of State.

(e) Regulations — The Secretary of the Treasury, in consultation with the Administrator, shall prescribe regulations for the enforcement of subsection (c) of this section.

§136p. Exemption of Federal and State agencies [FIFRA §18]

The Administrator may, at the Administrator's discretion, exempt any Federal or State agency from any provision of this subchapter if the Administrator determines that emergency conditions exist which require such exemption. The Administrator, in determining whether or not such emergency conditions exist, shall consult with the Secretary of Agriculture and the Governor of any State concerned if they request such determination.

§136q. Storage, disposal, transportation, and recall

[FIFRA §19]

(a) Storage, disposal, and transportation

(1) Data requirements and registration of pesticides — The Administrator may require under section 136a or 136d of this title that —

(A) the registrant or applicant for registration of a pesticide submit or cite data or information regarding methods for the safe storage and disposal of excess quantities of the pesticide to support the registration or continued registration of a pesticide;

(B) the labeling of a pesticide contain requirements and procedures for the transportation, storage, and disposal of the pesticide, any container of the pesticide, any rinsate containing the pesticide, or any other material used to contain or collect excess or spilled quantities of the pesticide; and

(C) the registrant of a pesticide provide evidence of sufficient financial and other resources to carry out a recall plan under subsection (b) of this section, and provide for the disposition of the pesticide, in the event of suspension and cancellation of the pesticide.

(2) Pesticides — The Administrator may by regulation, or as part of an order issued under section 136d of this title or an amendment to such an order —

(A) issue requirements and procedures to be followed by any person who stores or transports a pesticide the registration of which has been suspended or canceled;

(B) issue requirements and procedures to be followed by any person who disposes of stocks of a pesticide the registration of which has been suspended; and

(C) issue requirements and procedures for the disposal of any pesticide the registration of which has been canceled.

(3) Containers, rinsates, and other materials — The Administrator may by regulation, or as part of an order issued under section 136d of this title or an amendment to such an order —

(A) issue requirements and procedures to be followed by any person who stores or transports any container of a pesticide the registration of which has been suspended or canceled, any rinsate containing the pesticide, or any other material used to contain or collect excess or spilled quantities of the pesticide;

(B) issue requirements and procedures to be followed by any person who disposes of stocks of any container of a pesticide the

registration of which has been suspended, any rinsate containing the pesticide, or any other material used to contain or collect excess or spilled quantities of the pesticide; and

(C) issue requirements and procedures for the disposal of any container of a pesticide the registration of which has been canceled, any rinsate containing the pesticide, or any other material used to contain or collect excess or spilled quantities of the pesticide.

(4) Container recycling — The Secretary may promulgate a regulation for the return and recycling of disposable pesticide containers used for the distribution or sale of registered pesticide products in interstate commerce. Any such regulation requiring recycling of disposable pesticide containers shall not apply to antimicrobial pesticides (as defined in section 136 of this title) or other pesticide products intended for non-agricultural uses.

(b) Recalls

(1) In general — If the registration of a pesticide has been suspended and canceled under section 136d of this title, and if the Administrator finds that recall of the pesticide is necessary to protect health or the environment, the Administrator shall order a recall of the pesticide in accordance with this subsection.

(2) Voluntary recall — If, after determining under paragraph (1) that a recall is necessary, the Administrator finds that voluntary recall by the registrant and others in the chain of distribution may be as safe and effective as a mandatory recall, the Administrator shall request the registrant of the pesticide to submit, within 60 days of the request, a plan for the voluntary recall of the pesticide. If such a plan is requested and submitted, the Administrator shall approve the plan and order the registrant to conduct the recall in accordance with the plan unless the Administrator determines, after an informal hearing, that the plan is inadequate to protect health or the environment.

(3) Mandatory recall — If, after determining under paragraph (1) that a recall is necessary, the Administrator does not request the submission of a plan under paragraph (2) or finds such a plan to be inadequate, the Administrator shall issue a regulation that prescribes a plan for the recall of the pesticide. A regulation issued under this paragraph may apply to any person who is or was a registrant, distributor, or seller of the pesticide, or any successor in interest to such a person.

(4) Recall procedure — A regulation issued under this subsection may require any person that is subject to the regulation to —

(A) arrange to make available one or more storage facilities to receive and store the pesticide to which the recall program applies, and inform the Administrator of the location of each such facility;

(B) accept and store at such a facility those

existing stocks of such pesticide that are tendered by any other person who obtained the pesticide directly or indirectly from the person that is subject to such regulation;

(C) on the request of a person making such a tender, provide for proper transportation of the pesticide to a storage facility; and

(D) take such reasonable steps as the regulation may prescribe to inform persons who may be holders of the pesticide of the terms of the recall regulation and how those persons may tender the pesticide and arrange for transportation of the pesticide to a storage facility.

(5) Contents of recall plan — A recall plan established under this subsection shall include —

(A) the level in the distribution chain to which the recall is to extend, and a schedule for recall; and

(B) the means to be used to verify the effectiveness of the recall.

(6) Requirements or procedures — No requirement or procedure imposed in accordance with paragraph (2) of subsection (a) of this section may require the recall of existing stocks of the pesticide except as provided by this subsection.

(c) Storage costs

(1) Submission of plan — A registrant who wishes to become eligible for reimbursement of storage costs incurred as a result of a recall prescribed under subsection (b) of this section for a pesticide whose registration has been suspended and canceled shall, as soon as practicable after the suspension of the registration of the pesticide, submit to the Administrator a plan for the storage and disposal of the pesticide that meets criteria established by the Administrator by regulation.

(2) Reimbursement — Within a reasonable period of time after such storage costs are incurred and paid by the registrant, the Administrator shall reimburse the registrant, on request, for —

(A) none of the costs incurred by the registrant before the date of submission of the plan referred to in paragraph (1) to the Administrator;

(B) 100 percent of the costs incurred by the registrant after the date of submission of the plan to the Administrator or the date of cancellation of the registration of the pesticide, whichever is later, but before the approval of the plan by the Administrator;

(C) 50 percent of the costs incurred by the registrant during the 1-year period beginning on the date of the approval of the plan by the Administrator or the date of cancellation of the registration of the pesticide, whichever is later;

(D) none of the costs incurred by the registrant during the 3-year period beginning on the 366th day following approval of the plan by the Administrator or the date of can-

cellation of the registration of the pesticide, whichever is later; and

(E) 25 percent of the costs incurred by the registrant during the period beginning on the first day of the 5th year following the date of the approval of the plan by the Administrator or the date of cancellation of the registration of the pesticide, whichever is later, and ending on the date that a disposal permit for the pesticide is issued by a State or an alternative plan for disposal of the pesticide in accordance with applicable law has been developed.

(d) Administration of storage, disposal, transportation, and recall programs

(1) Voluntary agreements — Nothing in this section shall be construed as preventing or making unlawful any agreement between a seller and a buyer of any pesticide or other substance regarding the ultimate allocation of the costs of storage, transportation, or disposal of a pesticide.

(2) Rule and regulation review — Section 136w(a)(4) of this title shall not apply to any regulation issued under subsection (a)(2) or (b) of this section.

(3) Limitations — No registrant shall be responsible under this section for a pesticide the registration of which is held by another person. No distributor or seller shall be responsible under this section for a pesticide that the distributor or seller did not hold or sell.

(4) Seizure and penalties — If the Administrator finds that a person who is subject to a regulation or order under subsection (a)(2) or (b) of this section has failed substantially to comply with that regulation or order, the Administrator may take action under section 136k or 136l of this title or obtain injunctive relief under section 136n(c) of this title against such person or any successor in interest of any such person.

(e) Container design

(1) Procedures

(A) Not later than 3 years after the effective date of this subsection, the Administrator shall, in consultation with the heads of other interested Federal agencies, promulgate regulations for the design of pesticide containers that will promote the safe storage and disposal of pesticides.

(B) The regulations shall ensure, to the fullest extent practicable, that the containers —

(i) accommodate procedures used for the removal of pesticides from the containers and the rinsing of the containers;

(ii) facilitate the safe use of the containers, including elimination of splash and leakage of pesticides from the containers;

(iii) facilitate the safe disposal of the containers; and

(iv) facilitate the safe refill and reuse of the containers.

(2) Compliance — The Administrator shall require compliance with the regulations referred to in paragraph (1) not later than 5 years after the effective date of this subsection.

(f) Pesticide residue removal

(1) Procedures

(A) Not later than 3 years after the effective date of this subsection, the Administrator shall, in consultation with the heads of other interested Federal agencies, promulgate regulations prescribing procedures and standards for the removal of pesticides from containers prior to disposal.

(B) The regulations may —

(i) specify, for each major type of pesticide container, procedures and standards providing for, at a minimum, triple rinsing or the equivalent degree of pesticide removal;

(ii) specify procedures that can be implemented promptly and easily in various circumstances and conditions;

(iii) provide for reuse, whenever practicable, or disposal of rinse water and residue; and

(iv) be coordinated with requirements for the rinsing of containers imposed under the Solid Waste Disposal Act (42 U.S.C. §6901 et seq.).

(C) The Administrator may, at the discretion of the Administrator, exempt products intended solely for household use from the requirements of this subsection.

(2) Compliance — Effective beginning 5 years after the effective date of this subsection, a State may not exercise primary enforcement responsibility under section 136w-1 of this title, or certify an applicator under section 136i of this title, unless the Administrator determines that the State is carrying out an adequate program to ensure compliance with this subsection.

(3) Solid Waste Disposal Act — Nothing in this subsection shall affect the authorities or requirements concerning pesticide containers under the Solid Waste Disposal Act (42 U.S.C. §6901).

(g) Pesticide container study

(1) Study

(A) The Administrator shall conduct a study of options to encourage or require —

(i) the return, refill, and reuse of pesticide containers;

(ii) the development and use of pesticide formulations that facilitate the removal of pesticide residues from containers; and

(iii) the use of bulk storage facilities to reduce the number of pesticide containers requiring disposal.

(B) In conducting the study, the Administrator shall —

(i) consult with the heads of other interested Federal agencies, State agencies, industry groups, and environmental organizations; and

(ii) assess the feasibility, costs, and environmental benefits of encouraging or requiring various measures or actions.

(2) Report — Not later than 2 years after the effective date of this subsection, the Administrator shall submit to Congress a report describing the results of the study required under paragraph (1).

(h) Relationship to Solid Waste Disposal Act

(1) In general — Nothing in this section shall diminish the authorities or requirements of the Solid Waste Disposal Act (42 U.S.C. §6901 et seq.).

(2) Antimicrobial products — A household, industrial, or institutional antimicrobial product that is not subject to regulation under the Solid Waste Disposal Act (42 U.S.C. §6901 et seq.) shall not be subject to the provisions of subsections (a), (e), and (f) of this section, unless the Administrator determines that such product must be subject to such provisions to prevent an unreasonable adverse effect on the environment.

§136r. Research and monitoring
[FIFRA §20]

(a) Research — The Administrator shall undertake research including research by grant or contract with other Federal agencies, universities, or others as may be necessary to carry out the purposes of this subchapter, and the Administrator shall conduct research into integrated pest management in coordination with the Secretary of Agriculture. The Administrator shall also take care to ensure that such research does not duplicate research being undertaken by any other Federal agency.

(b) National monitoring plan — The Administrator shall formulate and periodically revise, in cooperation with other Federal, State, or local agencies, a national plan for monitoring pesticides.

(c) Monitoring — The Administrator shall undertake such monitoring activities, including, but not limited to monitoring in air, soil, water, man, plants, and animals, as may be necessary for the implementation of this subchapter and of the national pesticide monitoring plan. The Administrator shall establish procedures for the monitoring of man and animals and their environment for incidental pesticide exposure, including, but not limited to, the quantification of incidental human and environmental pesticide pollution and the secular trends thereof, and identification of the sources of contamination and their relationship to human and environmental effects. Such activities shall be carried out in cooperation with other Federal, State, and local agencies.

§136r-1. Integrated Pest Management

The Secretary of Agriculture, in cooperation with the Administrator, shall implement research, demonstration, and education programs to support adoption of Integrated Pest Management. Integrated Pest Management is a sustainable approach to managing pests by combining biological, cultural, physical, and chemical tools in a way that minimizes economic, health, and environmental risks. The Secretary of Agriculture and the Administrator shall make information on Integrated Pest Management widely available to pesticide users, including Federal agencies. Federal agencies shall use Integrated Pest Management techniques in carrying out pest management activities and shall promote Integrated Pest Management through procurement and regulatory policies, and other activities.

§136s. Solicitation of comments; notice of public hearings
[FIFRA §21]

(a) Secretary of Agriculture — The Administrator, before publishing regulations under this subchapter, shall solicit the views of the Secretary of Agriculture in accordance with the procedure described in section 136w(a) of this title.

(b) Secretary of Health and Human Services — The Administrator, before publishing regulations under this subchapter for any public health pesticide, shall solicit the views of the Secretary of Health and Human Services in the same manner as the views of the Secretary of Agriculture are solicited under section 136w(a)(2) of this title.

(c) Views — In addition to any other authority relating to public hearings and solicitation of views, in connection with the suspension or cancellation of a pesticide registration or any other actions authorized under this subchapter, the Administrator may, at the Administrator's discretion, solicit the views of all interested persons, either orally or in writing, and seek such advice from scientists, farmers, farm organizations, and other qualified persons as the Administrator deems proper.

(d) Notice — In connection with all public hearings under this subchapter the Administrator shall publish timely notice of such hearings in the Federal Register.

§136t. Delegation and cooperation
[FIFRA §22]

(a) Delegation — All authority vested in the Administrator by virtue of the provisions of this subchapter may with like force and effect be executed by such employees of the Environmental Protection Agency as the Administrator may designate for the purpose.

(b) Cooperation — The Administrator shall cooperate with Department of Agriculture, any other Federal agency, and any appropriate agency of any State or any political subdivision thereof, in carrying out the provisions of this subchapter, and in securing uniformity of regulations.

§136u. State cooperation, aid, and training
[FIFRA §23]

(a) Cooperative agreements — The Administrator may enter into cooperative agreements with States and Indian tribes —

(1) to delegate to any State or Indian tribe the authority to cooperate in the enforcement of this subchapter through the use of its personnel or facilities, to train personnel of the State or Indian tribe to cooperate in the enforcement of this subchapter, and to assist States and Indian tribes in implementing cooperative enforcement programs through grants-in-aid; and

(2) to assist States in developing and administering State programs, and Indian tribes that enter into cooperative agreements, to train and certify applicators consistent with the standards the Administrator prescribes.

Effective with the fiscal year beginning October 1, 1978, there are authorized to be appropriated annually such funds as may be necessary for the Administrator to provide through cooperative agreements an amount equal to 50 percent of the anticipated cost to each State or Indian tribe, as agreed to under such cooperative agreements, of conducting training and certification programs during such fiscal year. If funds sufficient to pay 50 percent of the costs for any year are not appropriated, the share of each State and Indian tribe shall be reduced in a like proportion in allocating available funds.

(b) Contracts for training — In addition, the Administrator may enter into contracts with Federal, State, or Indian tribal agencies for the purpose of encouraging the training of certified applicators.

(c) Information and education — The Administrator shall, in cooperation with the Secretary of Agriculture, use the services of the cooperative State extension services to inform and educate pesticide users about accepted uses and other regulations made under this subchapter.

§136v. Authority of States
[FIFRA §24]

(a) In general — A State may regulate the sale or use of any federally registered pesticide or device in the State, but only if and to the extent the regulation does not permit any sale or use prohibited by this subchapter.

(b) Uniformity — Such State shall not impose or continue in effect any requirements for labeling or packaging in addition to or different from those required under this subchapter.

(c) Additional uses —

(1) A State may provide registration for additional uses of federally registered pesticides formulated for distribution and use within that State to meet special local needs in accord with the purposes of this subchapter and if registration for such use has not previously been denied, disapproved, or canceled by the Administrator. Such registration shall be deemed registration under section 136a of this title for all purposes of this

subchapter, but shall authorize distribution and use only within such State.

(2) A registration issued by a State under this subsection shall not be effective for more than ninety days if disapproved by the Administrator within that period. Prior to disapproval, the Administrator shall, except as provided in paragraph (3) of this subsection, advise the State of the Administrator's intention to disapprove and the reasons therefor, and provide the State time to respond. The Administrator shall not prohibit or disapprove a registration issued by a State under this subsection (A) on the basis of lack of essentiality of a pesticide or (B) except as provided in paragraph (3) of this subsection, if its composition and use patterns are similar to those of a federally registered pesticide.

(3) In no instance may a State issue a registration for a food or feed use unless there exists a tolerance or exemption under the Federal Food, Drug, and Cosmetic Act [21 U.S.C. §§301 *et seq.*] that permits the residues of the pesticides on the food or feed. If the Administrator determines that a registration issued by a State is inconsistent with the Federal Food, Drug, and Cosmetic Act, or the use of, a pesticide under a registration issued by a State constitutes an imminent hazard, the Administrator may immediately disapprove the registration.

(4) If the Administrator finds, in accordance with standards set forth in regulations issued under section 136w of this title, that a State is not capable of exercising adequate controls to assure that State registration under this section will be in accord with the purposes of this subchapter or has failed to exercise adequate controls, the Administrator may suspend the authority of the State to register pesticides until such time as the Administrator is satisfied that the State can and will exercise adequate controls. Prior to any such suspension, the Administrator shall advise the State of the Administrator's intention to suspend and the reasons therefor and provide the State time to respond.

§136w. Authority of Administrator
[FIFRA §25]
(a) In general

(1) Regulations — The Administrator is authorized, in accordance with the procedure described in paragraph (2), to prescribe regulations to carry out the provisions of this subchapter. Such regulations shall take into account the difference in concept and usage between various classes of pesticides, including public health pesticides, and differences in environmental risk and the appropriate data for evaluating such risk between agricultural, nonagricultural, and public health pesticides.

(2) Procedure

(A) Proposed regulations — At least 60 days prior to signing any proposed regulation for publication in the Federal Register, the Administrator shall provide the Secretary of Agriculture with a copy of such regulation. If the Secretary comments in writing to the Administrator regarding any such regulation within 30 days after receiving it, the Administrator shall publish in the Federal Register (with the proposed regulation) the comments of the Secretary and the response of the Administrator with regard to the Secretary's comments. If the Secretary does not comment in writing to the Administrator regarding the regulation within 30 days after receiving it, the Administrator may sign such regulation for publication in the Federal Register any time after such 30-day period notwithstanding the foregoing 60-day time requirement.

(B) Final regulations — At least 30 days prior to signing any regulation in final form for publication in the Federal Register, the Administrator shall provide the Secretary of Agriculture with a copy of such regulation. If the Secretary comments in writing to the Administrator regarding any such final regulation within 15 days after receiving it, the Administrator shall publish in the Federal Register (with the final regulation) the comments of the Secretary, if requested by the Secretary, and the response of the Administrator concerning the Secretary's comments. If the Secretary does not comment in writing to the Administrator regarding the regulation within 15 days after receiving it, the Administrator may sign such regulation for publication in the Federal Register at any time after such 15-day period notwithstanding the foregoing 30-day time requirement. In taking any final action under this subsection, the Administrator shall include among those factors to be taken into account the effect of the regulation on production and prices of agricultural commodities, retail food prices, and otherwise on the agricultural economy, and the Administrator shall publish in the Federal Register an analysis of such effect.

(C) Time requirements — The time requirements imposed by subparagraphs (A) and (B) may be waived or modified to the extent agreed upon by the Administrator and the Secretary.

(D) Publication in the Federal Register — The Administrator shall, simultaneously with any notification to the Secretary of Agriculture under this paragraph prior to the issuance of any proposed or final regulation, publish such notification in the Federal Register.

(3) Congressional committees — At such time as the Administrator is required under paragraph (2) of this subsection to provide the Secretary of Agriculture with a copy of proposed regulations and a copy of the final form of regulations, the Administrator shall also furnish a copy of such regulations to the Committee on Agriculture of the House of Representatives and the Committee on Agriculture, Nutrition, and Forestry of the Senate.

(4) Congressional review of regulations — Simultaneously with the promulgation of any rule or regulation under this subchapter, the Administrator shall transmit a copy thereof to the Secretary of the Senate and the Clerk of the House of Representatives. The rule or regulation shall not become effective until the passage of 60 calendar days after the rule or regulation is so transmitted.

(b) Exemption of pesticides — The Administrator may exempt from the requirements of this subchapter by regulation any pesticide which the Administrator determines either (1) to be adequately regulated by another Federal agency, or (2) to be of a character which is unnecessary to be subject to this subchapter in order to carry out the purposes of this subchapter.

(c) Other authority — The Administrator, after notice and opportunity for hearing, is authorized —

(1) to declare a pest any form of plant or animal life (other than man and other than bacteria, virus, and other micro-organisms on or in living man or other living animals) which is injurious to health or the environment;

(2) to determine any pesticide which contains any substance or substances in quantities highly toxic to man;

(3) to establish standards (which shall be consistent with those established under the authority of the Poison Prevention Packaging Act (Public Law 91-601) [15 U.S.C. §§1471 *et seq.*]) with respect to the package, container, or wrapping in which a pesticide or device is enclosed for use or consumption, in order to protect children and adults from serious injury or illness resulting from accidental ingestion or contact with pesticides or devices regulated by this subchapter as well as to accomplish the other purposes of this subchapter;

(4) to specify those classes of devices which shall be subject to any provision of section 136(q)(1) or section 136e of this title upon the Administrator's determination that application of such provision is necessary to effectuate the purposes of this subchapter;

(5) to prescribe regulations requiring any pesticide to be colored or discolored if the Administrator determines that such requirement is feasible and is necessary for the protection of health and the environment; and

(6) to determine and establish suitable names to be used in the ingredient statement.

(d) Scientific advisory panel

(1) In general — The Administrator shall submit to an advisory panel for comment as to the impact on health and the environment of the action proposed in notices of intent issued under section 136d(b) of this title and of the proposed and final form of regulations issued under subsection (a) of this section within the same time periods as provided for the comments of the Secretary of Agriculture under such section 136d(b) and subsection (a) of this section. The time requirements for notices of intent and proposed and final forms of regulation may not be modified or waived unless in addition to meeting the requirements of section 136d(b) of this title or subsection (a) of this section, as applicable, the advisory panel has failed to comment on the proposed action within the prescribed time period or has agreed to the modification or waiver. The Administrator shall also solicit from the advisory panel comments, evaluations, and recommendations for operating guidelines to improve the effectiveness and quality of scientific analyses made by personnel of the Environmental Protection Agency that lead to decisions by the Administrator in carrying out the provisions of this subchapter. The comments, evaluations, and recommendations of the advisory panel submitted under this subsection and the response of the Administrator shall be published in the Federal Register in the same manner as provided for publication of the comments of the Secretary of Agriculture under such sections. The chairman of the advisory panel, after consultation with the Administrator, may create temporary subpanels on specific projects to assist the full advisory panel in expediting and preparing its evaluations, comments, and recommendations. The subpanels may be composed of scientists other than members of the advisory panel, as deemed necessary for the purpose of evaluating scientific studies relied upon by the Administrator with respect to proposed action. Such additional scientists shall be selected by the advisory panel. The panel referred to in this subsection shall consist of 7 members appointed by the Administrator from a list of 12 nominees, 6 nominated by the National Institutes of Health and 6 by the National Science Foundation, utilizing a system of staggered terms of appointment. Members of the panel shall be selected on the basis of their professional qualifications to assess the effects of the impact of pesticides on health and the environment. To the extent feasible to insure multidisciplinary representation, the panel membership shall include representation from the disciplines of toxicology, pathology, environmental biology, and related sciences. If a vacancy occurs on the panel due to expiration of a term, resignation, or any other reason, each replacement shall be selected by the Administrator from a group of 4 nominees, 2 submitted by each of the nominating entities named in this subsection. The Administrator may extend the term of a panel member until the new member is appointed to fill the vacancy. If a vacancy occurs due to resignation, or reason other than expiration of a term, the Administrator shall appoint a member to serve during the unexpired term utilizing the nomination process set forth in this subsection. Should the list of nominees provided under this subsection be unsatisfactory, the Administrator may request an additional set

of nominees from the nominating entities. The Administrator may require such information from the nominees to the advisory panel as the Administrator deems necessary, and the Administrator shall publish in the Federal Register the name, address, and professional affiliations of each nominee. Each member of the panel shall receive per diem compensation at a rate not in excess of that fixed for GS-18 of the General Schedule as may be determined by the Administrator, except that any such member who holds another office or position under the Federal Government the compensation for which exceeds such rate may elect to receive compensation at the rate provided for such other office or position in lieu of the compensation provided by this subsection. In order to assure the objectivity of the advisory panel, the Administrator shall promulgate regulations regarding conflicts of interest with respect to the members of the panel. The advisory panel established under this section shall be permanent. In performing the functions assigned by this subchapter, the panel shall consult and coordinate its activities with the Science Advisory Board established under the Environmental Research, Development, and Demonstration Authorization Act of 1978 [42 U.S.C. §4365]. Whenever the Administrator exercises authority under section 136d(c) of this title to immediately suspend the registration of any pesticide to prevent an imminent hazard, the Administrator shall promptly submit to the advisory panel for comment, as to the impact on health and the environment, the action taken to suspend the registration of such pesticide.

(2) Science Review Board — There is established a Science Review Board to consist of 60 scientists who shall be available to the Scientific Advisory Panel to assist in reviews conducted by the Panel. Members of the Board shall be selected in the same manner as members of temporary subpanels created under paragraph (1). Members of the Board shall be compensated in the same manner as members of the Panel.

(e) Peer review — The Administrator shall, by written procedures, provide for peer review with respect to the design, protocols, and conduct of major scientific studies conducted under this subchapter by the Environmental Protection Agency or by any other Federal agency, any State or political subdivision thereof, or any institution or individual under grant, contract, or cooperative agreement from or with the Environmental Protection Agency. In such procedures, the Administrator shall also provide for peer review, using the advisory panel established under subsection (d) of this section or appropriate experts appointed by the Administrator from a current list of nominees maintained by such panel, with respect to the results of any such scientific studies relied upon by the Administrator with respect to actions the Administrator may take relating to the change in classification, suspension, or cancellation of a pesticide. Whenever the Administrator determines that circumstances do not permit the peer review of the results of any such scientific study prior to the Administrator's exercising authority under section 136d(c) of this title to immediately suspend the registration of any pesticide to prevent an imminent hazard, the Administrator shall promptly thereafter provide for the conduct of peer review as provided in this sentence. The evaluations and relevant documentation constituting the peer review that relate to the proposed scientific studies and the results of the completed scientific studies shall be included in the submission for comment forwarded by the Administrator to the advisory panel as provided in subsection (d) of this section. As used in this subsection, the term "peer review" shall mean an independent evaluation by scientific experts, either within or outside the Environmental Protection Agency, in the appropriate disciplines.

§136w-1. State primary enforcement responsibility

[FIFRA §26]

(a) In general — For the purposes of this subchapter, a State shall have primary enforcement responsibility for pesticide use violations during any period for which the Administrator determines that such State —

(1) has adopted adequate pesticide use laws and regulations, except that the Administrator may not require a State to have pesticide use laws that are more stringent than this subchapter;

(2) has adopted and is implementing adequate procedures for the enforcement of such State laws and regulations; and

(3) will keep such records and make such reports showing compliance with paragraphs (1) and (2) of this subsection as the Administrator may require by regulation.

(b) Special rules — Notwithstanding the provisions of subsection (a) of this section, any State that enters into a cooperative agreement with the Administrator under section 136u of this title for the enforcement of pesticide use restrictions shall have the primary enforcement responsibility for pesticide use violations. Any State that has a plan approved by the Administrator in accordance with the requirements of section 136i of this title that the Administrator determines meets the criteria set out in subsection (a) of this section shall have the primary enforcement responsibility for pesticide use violations. The Administrator shall make such determinations with respect to State plans under section 136i of this title in effect on September 30, 1978, not later than six months after that date.

(c) Administrator — The Administrator shall have primary enforcement responsibility for those States that do not have primary enforcement responsibility under this subchapter. Notwithstanding the provisions of section 136(e)(1) of this title, during any period when the Administrator has such enforcement responsibility, section 136f(b) of this title shall apply to the books and records of commercial applicators and to any applicator who holds or applies pesticides, or uses dilutions of pesticides, only to provide a service of controlling pests without delivering any unapplied pesticide to any person so served, and section 136g(a) of this title shall apply to the establishment or other place where pesticides or devices are held for application by such persons with respect to pesticides or devices held for such application.

§136w-2. Failure by the State to assure enforcement of State pesticide use regulations
[FIFRA §27]

(a) Referral — Upon receipt of any complaint or other information alleging or indicating a significant violation of the pesticide use provisions of this subchapter, the Administrator shall refer the matter to the appropriate State officials for their investigation of the matter consistent with the requirements of this subchapter. If, within thirty days, the State has not commenced appropriate enforcement action, the Administrator may act upon the complaint or information to the extent authorized under this subchapter.

(b) Notice — Whenever the Administrator determines that a State having primary enforcement responsibility for pesticide use violations is not carrying out (or cannot carry out due to the lack of adequate legal authority) such responsibility, the Administrator shall notify the State. Such notice shall specify those aspects of the administration of the State program that are determined to be inadequate. The State shall have ninety days after receipt of the notice to correct any deficiencies. If after that time the Administrator determines that the State program remains inadequate, the Administrator may rescind, in whole or in part, the State's primary enforcement responsibility for pesticide use violations.

(c) Construction — Neither section 136w-1 of this title nor this section shall limit the authority of the Administrator to enforce this subchapter, where the Administrator determines that emergency conditions exist that require immediate action on the part of the Administrator and the State authority is unwilling or unable adequately to respond to the emergency.

§136w-3. Identification of pests; cooperation with Department of Agriculture's program
[FIFRA §28]

(a) In general — The Administrator, in coordination with the Secretary of Agriculture, shall identify those pests that must be brought under control. The Administrator shall also coordinate and cooperate with the Secretary of Agriculture's research and implementation programs to develop and improve the safe use and effectiveness of chemical, biological, and alternative methods to combat and control pests

that reduce the quality and economical production and distribution of agricultural products to domestic and foreign consumers.

(b) Pest control availability

(1) In general — The Administrator, in cooperation with the Secretary of Agriculture, shall identify —

(A) available methods of pest control by crop or animal;

(B) minor pest control problems, both in minor crops and minor or localized problems in major crops; and

(C) factors limiting the availability of specific pest control methods, such as resistance to control methods and regulatory actions limiting the availability of control methods.

(2) Report — The Secretary of Agriculture shall, not later than 180 days after November 28, 1990, and annually thereafter, prepare a report and send the report to the Administrator. The report shall —

(A) contain the information described in paragraph (1);

(B) identify the crucial pest control needs where a shortage of control methods is indicated by the information described in paragraph (1); and

(C) describe in detail research and extension efforts designed to address the needs identified in subparagraph (B).

(c) Integrated pest management — The Administrator, in cooperation with the Secretary of Agriculture, shall develop approaches to the control of pests based on integrated pest management that respond to the needs of producers, with a special emphasis on minor pests.

(d) Public health pests — The Administrator, in coordination with the Secretary of Agriculture and the Secretary of Health and Human Services, shall identify pests of significant public health importance and, in coordination with the Public Health Service, develop and implement programs to improve and facilitate the safe and necessary use of chemical, biological, and other methods to combat and control such pests of public health importance.

§136w-5. Minimum requirements for training of maintenance applicators and service technicians
[FIFRA §30]

Each State may establish minimum requirements for training of maintenance applicators and service technicians. Such training may include instruction in the safe and effective handling and use of pesticides in accordance with the Environmental Protection Agency approved labeling, and instruction in integrated pest management techniques. The authority of the Administrator with respect to minimum requirements for training of maintenance applicators and service technicians shall be limited to ensuring that each State understands the provisions of this section.

§136w-6. Environmental Protection Agency minor use program
[FIFRA §31]

(a) The Administrator shall assure coordination of minor use issues through the establishment of a minor use program within the Office of Pesticide Programs. Such office shall be responsible for coordinating the development of minor use programs and policies and consulting with growers regarding minor use issues and registrations and amendments which are submitted to the Environmental Protection Agency.

(b) The Office of Pesticide Programs shall prepare a public report concerning the progress made on the registration of minor uses, including implementation of the exclusive use as an incentive for registering new minor uses, within 3 years of the passage of the Food Quality Protection Act of 1996.

§136w-7. Department of Agriculture minor use program
[FIFRA §32]

(a) In general — The Secretary of Agriculture (hereinafter in this section referred to as the "Secretary") shall assure the coordination of the responsibilities of the Department of Agriculture related to minor uses of pesticides, including —

(1) carrying out the Inter-Regional Project Number 4 (IR-4) as described in section 2 of Public Law 89–106 (7 U.S.C. 450k(e)) and the national pesticide resistance monitoring program established under section 1651 of the Food, Agriculture, Conservation, and Trade Act of 1990 (7 U.S.C. §5882);

(2) supporting integrated pest management research;

(3) consulting with growers to develop data for minor uses; and

(4) providing assistance for minor use registrations, tolerances, and reregistrations with the Environmental Protection Agency.

(b) Minor use pesticide data and revolving fund

(1) Minor use pesticide data

(A) Grant authority — The Secretary, in consultation with the Administrator, shall establish a program to make grants for the development of data to support minor use pesticide registrations and reregistrations. The amount of any such grant shall not exceed 1/2 of the cost of the project for which the grant is made.

(B) Applicants — Any person who wants to develop data to support minor use pesticide registrations and reregistrations may apply for a grant under subparagraph (A). Priority shall be given to an applicant for such a grant who does not directly receive funds from the sale of pesticides registered for minor uses.

(C) Data ownership — Any data that is developed under a grant under subparagraph

(A) shall be jointly owned by the Department of Agriculture and the person who received the grant. Such a person shall enter into an agreement with the Secretary under which such person shall share any fee paid to such person under section 136a(c)(1)(F) of this title.

(2) Minor Use Pesticide Data Revolving Fund

(A) Establishment — There is established in the Treasury of the United States a revolving fund to be known as the Minor Use Pesticide Data Revolving Fund. The Fund shall be available without fiscal year limitation to carry out the authorized purposes of this subsection.

(B) Contents of the Fund — There shall be deposited in the Fund —

(i) such amounts as may be appropriated to support the purposes of this subsection; and

(ii) fees collected by the Secretary for any data developed under a grant under paragraph (1)(A).

(C) Authorizations of appropriations — There are authorized to be appropriated for each fiscal year to carry out the purposes of this subsection $10,000,000 to remain available until expended.

§136w-8. Pesticide registration service fees
[FIFRA §33]

(a) Definition of costs

In this section, the term "costs", when used with respect to review and decisionmaking pertaining to an application for which registration service fees are paid under this section, means —

(1) costs to the extent that —

(A) officers and employees provide direct support for the review and decisionmaking for covered pesticide applications, associated tolerances, and corresponding risk and benefits information and analyses;

(B) persons and organizations under contract with the Administrator engage in the review of the applications, and corresponding risk and benefits information and assessments; and

(C) advisory committees and other accredited persons or organizations, on the request of the Administrator, engage in the peer review of risk or benefits information associated with covered pesticide applications;

(2) costs of management of information, and the acquisition, maintenance, and repair of computer and telecommunication resources (including software), used to support review of pesticide applications, associated tolerances, and corresponding risk and benefits information and analyses; and

(3) costs of collecting registration service fees under subsections (b) and (c) and reporting, auditing, and accounting under this section.

(b) Fees
  (1) In general
    Effective beginning on the effective date of the Pesticide Registration Improvement Act of 2003, the Administrator shall assess and collect covered pesticide registration service fees in accordance with this section.
  (2) Covered applications
    (A) In general
      An application for the registration of a pesticide covered by this subchapter that is received by the Administrator on or after the effective date of the Pesticide Registration Improvement Act of 2003 or for any other action covered by a table specified in paragraph (3) shall be subject to a registration service fee under this section.
    (B) Existing applications
      (i) In general
        Subject to clause (ii), an application for the registration of a pesticide that was submitted to the Administrator before the effective date of the Pesticide Registration Improvement Act of 2003 and is pending on that effective date shall be subject to a service fee under this section if the application is for the registration of a new active ingredient that is not listed in the Registration Division 2003 Work Plan of the Office of Pesticide Programs of the Environmental Protection Agency.
      (ii) Tolerance or exemption fees
        The amount of any fee otherwise payable for an application described in clause (i) under this section shall be reduced by the amount of any fees paid to support the related petition for a pesticide tolerance or exemption under the Federal Food, Drug, and Cosmetic Act (21 U.S.C. 301 et seq.).
    (C) Documentation
      An application subject to a registration service fee under this section shall be submitted with documentation certifying —
      (i) payment of the registration service fee; or
      (ii) payment of at least 25 percent of the registration service fee and a request for

a waiver from or reduction of the remaining amount of the registration service fee.
    (D) Payment
      The registration service fee required under this subsection shall be due upon submission of the application.
    (E) Applications subject to additional fees
      An application may be subject to additional fees if —
      (i) the applicant identified the incorrect registration service fee and decision review period;
      (ii) after review of a waiver request, the Administrator denies the waiver request; or
      (iii) after review of the application, the Administrator determines that a different registration service fee and decision review period apply to the application.
    (F) Effect of failure to pay fees
      The Administrator shall reject any application submitted without the required registration service fee.
    (G) Non-refundable portion of fees
      (i) In general
        The Administrator shall retain 25 percent of the applicable registration service fee.
      (ii) Limitation
        Any waiver, refund, credit or other reduction in the registration service fee shall not exceed 75 percent of the registration service fee.
    (H) Collection of unpaid fees
      In any case in which the Administrator does not receive payment of a registration service fee (or applicable portion of the registration service fee) by the date that is 30 days after the fee is due, the fee shall be treated as a claim of the United States Government subject to subchapter II of chapter 37 of Title 31.
  (3) Schedule of covered applications and other actions and their registration service fees
    Subject to paragraph (6), the schedule of registration applications and other covered actions and their corresponding registration service fees shall be as follows:

EPA No.	New CR No.	Action	Decision Review Time (Months)(1)	Registration Service Fee ($)
		TABLE 1. — REGISTRATION DIVISION — NEW ACTIVE INGREDIENTS		
R010	1	New Active Ingredient, Food use. (2)(3)	24	753,082
R020	2	New Active Ingredient, Food use; reduced risk. (2)(3)	18	627,568
R040	3	New Active Ingredient, Food use; Experimental Use Permit application; establish temporary tolerance; submitted before application for registration; credit 45% of fee toward new active ingredient application that follows. (3)	18	462,502
R060	4	New Active Ingredient, Non-food use; outdoor. (2)(3)	21	523,205
R070	5	New Active Ingredient, Non-food use; outdoor; reduced risk. (2)(3)	16	436,004
R090	6	New Active Ingredient, Non-food use; outdoor; Experimental Use Permit application; submitted before application for registration; credit 45% of fee toward new active ingredient application that follows. (3)	16	323,690
R110	7	New Active Ingredient, Non-food use; indoor. (2)(3)	20	290,994
R120	8	New Active Ingredient, Non-food use; indoor; reduced risk. (2)(3)	14	242,495
R121	9	New Active Ingredient, Non-food use; indoor; Experimental Use Permit application; submitted before application for registration; credit 45% of fee toward new active ingredient application that follows. (3)	18	182,327
R122	10	Enriched isomer(s) of registered mixed-isomer active ingredient. (2)(3)	18	317,128
R123	11	New Active Ingredient, Seed treatment only; includes agricultural and non-agricultural seeds; residues not expected in raw agricultural commodities. (2)(3)	18	471,861
R125	12	New Active Ingredient, Seed treatment; Experimental Use Permit application; submitted before application for registration; credit 45% of fee toward new active ingredient application that follows. (3)	16	323,690

(1) A decision review time that would otherwise end on a Saturday, Sunday, or federal holiday, will be extended to end on the next business day.

(2) All requests for new uses (food and/or nonfood) contained in any application for a new active ingredient or a first food use are covered by the base fee for that new active ingredient or first food use application and retain the same decision time review period as the new active ingredient or first food use application. The application must be received by

the agency in one package. The base fee for the category covers a maximum of five new products. Each application for an additional new product registration and new inert approval that is submitted in the new active ingredient application package or first food use application package is subject to the registration service fee for a new product or a new inert approval. All such associated applications that are submitted together will be subject to the new active ingredient or first food use decision review time. In the case of a new active ingredient application, until that new active ingredient is approved, any subsequent application for another new product containing the same active ingredient or an amendment to the proposed labeling will be deemed a new active ingredient application, subject to the registration service fee and decision review time for a new active ingredient. In the case of a first food use application, until that first food use is approved, any subsequent application for an additional new food use or uses will be subject to the registration service fee and decision review time for a first food use. Any information that (a) was neither requested nor required by the Agency, and (b) is submitted by the applicant at the applicant's initiative to support the application after completion of the technical deficiency screening, and (c) is not itself a covered registration application, must be assessed 25% of the full registration service fee for the new active ingredient or first food use application.

(3) Where the action involves approval of a new or amended label, on or before the end date of the decision review time, the Agency shall provide to the applicant a draft accepted label, including any changes made by the Agency that differ from the applicant-submitted label and relevant supporting data reviewed by the Agency. The applicant will notify the Agency that the applicant either (a) agrees to all of the terms associated with the draft accepted label as amended by the Agency and requests that it be issued as the accepted final Agency-stamped label; or (b) does not agree to one or more of the terms of the draft accepted label as amended by the Agency and requests additional time to resolve the difference(s); or (c) withdraws the application without prejudice for subsequent resubmission, but forfeits the associated registration service fee. For cases described in (b), the applicant shall have up to 30 calendar days to reach agreement with the Agency on the final terms of the Agency-accepted label. If the applicant agrees to all of the terms of the accepted label as in (a), including upon resolution of differences in (b), the Agency shall provide an accepted final Agency-stamped label to the registrant within 2 business days following the registrant's written or electronic confirmation of agreement to the Agency.

		TABLE 2. — REGISTRATION DIVISION — NEW USES		
EPA No.	New CR No.	Action	Decision Review Time (Months)(1)	Registration Service Fee ($)
R130	13	First food use; indoor; food/food handling. (2) (3)	21	191,444
R140	14	Additional food use; Indoor; food/food handling. (3) (4)	**15**	44,672
R150	**15**	First food use. (2) (3)	21	317,104
R155	16 (new)	First food use, Experimental Use Permit application; a.i. registered for non-food outdoor use. (3) (4)	21	264,253
R160	17	First food use; reduced risk. (2) (3)	16	264,253
R170	18	Additional food use. (3) (4)	**15**	79,349
R175	19	Additional food uses covered within a crop group resulting from the conversion of existing approved crop group(s) to one or more revised crop groups. (3) (4)	10	66,124
R180	20	Additional food use; reduced risk. (3) (4)	10	66,124
R190	21	Additional food uses; 6 or more submitted in one application. (3) (4)	**15**	476,090
R200	22	Additional Food Use; 6 or more submitted in one application; Reduced Risk. (3) (4)	10	396,742
R210	23	Additional food use; Experimental Use Permit application; establish temporary tolerance; no credit toward new use registration. (3) (4)	12	48,986

R220	24	Additional food use; Experimental Use Permit application; crop destruct basis; no credit toward new use registration. (3) (4)	6	19,838
R230	25	Additional use; non-food; outdoor. (3) (4)	**15**	31,713
R240	26	Additional use; non-food; outdoor; reduced risk. (3) (4)	10	26,427
R250	27	Additional use; non-food; outdoor; Experimental Use Permit application; no credit toward new use registration. (3) (4)	6	19,838
R251	28	Experimental Use Permit application which requires no changes to the tolerance(s); non-crop destruct basis. (3)	8	19,838
R260	29	New use; non-food; indoor. (3) (4)	12	15,317
R270	30	New use; non-food; indoor; reduced risk. (3)(4)	9	12,764
R271	31	New use; non-food; indoor; Experimental Use Permit application; no credit toward new use registration. (3) (4)	6	9,725
R273	32	Additional use; seed treatment; limited uptake into Raw Agricultural Commodities; includes crops with established tolerances (e.g., for soil or foliar application); includes food and/or non-food uses. (3) (4)	12	50,445
R274	33	Additional uses; seed treatment only; 6 or more submitted in one application; limited uptake into raw agricultural commodities; includes crops with established tolerances (e.g., for soil or foliar application); includes food and/or non-food uses. (3) (4)	12	302,663

(1) A decision review time that would otherwise end on a Saturday, Sunday, or federal holiday, will be extended to end on the next business day.

(2) All requests for new uses (food and/or nonfood) contained in any application for a new active ingredient or a first food use are covered by the base fee for that new active ingredient or first food use application and retain the same decision time review period as the new active ingredient or first food use application. The application must be received by the agency in one package. The base fee for the category covers a maximum of five new products. Each application for an additional new product registration and new inert approval that is submitted in the new active ingredient application package or first food use application package is subject to the registration service fee for a new product or a new inert approval. All such associated applications that are submitted together will be subject to the new active ingredient or first food use decision review time. In the case of a new active ingredient application, until that new active ingredient is approved, any subsequent application for another new product containing the same active ingredient or an amendment to the proposed labeling will be deemed a new active ingredient application, subject to the registration service fee and decision review time for a new active ingredient. In the case of a first food use application, until that first food use is approved, any subsequent application for an additional new food use or uses will be subject to the registration service fee and decision review time for a first food use. Any information that (a) was neither requested nor required by the Agency, and (b) is submitted by the applicant at the applicant's initiative to support the application after completion of the technical deficiency screening, and (c) is not itself a covered registration application, must be assessed 25% of the full registration service fee for the new active ingredient or first food use application.

(3) Where the action involves approval of a new or amended label, on or before the end date of the decision review time, the Agency shall provide to the applicant a draft accepted label, including any changes made by the Agency that differ from the applicant-submitted label and relevant supporting data reviewed by the Agency. The applicant will notify the Agency that the applicant either (a) agrees to all of the terms associated with the draft accepted label as amended by the

Agency and requests that it be issued as the accepted final Agency-stamped label; or (b) does not agree to one or more of the terms of the draft accepted label as amended by the Agency and requests additional time to resolve the difference(s); or (c) withdraws the application without prejudice for subsequent resubmission, but forfeits the associated registration service fee. For cases described in (b), the applicant shall have up to 30 calendar days to reach agreement with the Agency on the final terms of the Agency-accepted label. If the applicant agrees to all of the terms of the accepted label as in (a), including upon resolution of differences in (b), the Agency shall provide an accepted final Agency-stamped label to the registrant within 2 business days following the registrant's written or electronic confirmation of agreement to the Agency. (4) Amendment applications to add the new use(s) to registered product labels are covered by the base fee for the new use(s). All items in the covered application must be submitted together in one package. Each application for an additional new product registration and new inert approval(s) that is submitted in the new use application package is subject to the registration service fee for a new product or a new inert approval. However, if a new use application only proposes to register the new use for a new product and there are no amendments in the application, then review of one new product application is covered by the new use fee. All such associated applications that are submitted together will be subject to the new use decision review time. Any application for a new product or an amendment to the proposed labeling (a) submitted subsequent to submission of the new use application and (b) prior to conclusion of its decision review time and (c) containing the same new uses, will be deemed a separate new-use application, subject to a separate registration service fee and new decision review time for a new use. If the new-use application includes non-food (indoor and/or outdoor), and food (outdoor and/or indoor) uses, the appropriate fee is due for each type of new use and the longest decision review time applies to all of the new uses requested in the application. Any information that (a) was neither requested nor required by the Agency, and (b) is submitted by the applicant at the applicant's initiative to support the application after completion of the technical deficiency screen, and (c) is not itself a covered registration application, must be assessed 25% of the full registration service fee for the new use application.

TABLE 3. — REGISTRATION DIVISION — IMPORT AND OTHER TOLERANCES				
EPA No.	New CR No.	Action	Decision Review Time (Months)(1)	Registration Service Fee ($)
R280	34	Establish import tolerance; new active ingredient or first food use. (2)	21	319,072
R290	35	Establish Import tolerance; Additional new food use.	**15**	63,816
R291	36	Establish import tolerances; additional food uses; 6 or more crops submitted in one petition.	**15**	382,886
R292	37	Amend an established tolerance (e.g., decrease or increase) and/or harmonize established tolerances with Codex MRLs; domestic or import; applicant-initiated.	11	45,341
R293	38	Establish tolerance(s) for inadvertent residues in one crop; applicant-initiated.	12	53,483
R294	39	Establish tolerances for inadvertent residues; 6 or more crops submitted in one application; applicant-initiated.	12	320,894
R295	40	Establish tolerance(s) for residues in one rotational crop in response to a specific rotational crop application; submission of corresponding label amendments which specify the necessary plant-back restrictions; applicant-initiated. (3) (4)	**15**	66,124

R296	41	Establish tolerances for residues in rotational crops in response to a specific rotational crop petition; 6 or more crops submitted in one application; submission of corresponding label amendments which specify the necessary plantback restrictions; applicant-initiated. (3) (4)	15	396,742
R297	42	Amend 6 or more established tolerances (e.g., decrease or increase) in one petition; domestic or import; applicant-initiated.	11	272,037
R298	43	Amend an established tolerance (e.g., decrease or increase); domestic or import; submission of corresponding amended labels (requiring science review). (3) (4)	13	58,565
R299	44	Amend 6 or more established tolerances (e.g., decrease or increase); domestic or import; submission of corresponding amended labels (requiring science review). (3) (4)	13	285,261

(1) A decision review time that would otherwise end on a Saturday, Sunday, or federal holiday, will be extended to end on the next business day.

(2) All requests for new uses (food and/or nonfood) contained in any application for a new active ingredient or a first food use are covered by the base fee for that new active ingredient or first food use application and retain the same decision time review period as the new active ingredient or first food use application. The application must be received by the agency in one package. The base fee for the category covers a maximum of five new products. Each application for an additional new product registration and new inert approval that is submitted in the new active ingredient application package or first food use application package is subject to the registration service fee for a new product or a new inert approval. All such associated applications that are submitted together will be subject to the new active ingredient or first food use decision review time. In the case of a new active ingredient application, until that new active ingredient is approved, any subsequent application for another new product containing the same active ingredient or an amendment to the proposed labeling will be deemed a new active ingredient application, subject to the registration service fee and decision review time for a new active ingredient. In the case of a first food use application, until that first food use is approved, any subsequent application for an additional new food use or uses will be subject to the registration service fee and decision review time for a first food use. Any information that (a) was neither requested nor required by the Agency, and (b) is submitted by the applicant at the applicant's initiative to support the application after completion of the technical deficiency screening, and (c) is not itself a covered registration application, must be assessed 25% of the full registration service fee for the new active ingredient or first food use application.

(3) Where the action involves approval of a new or amended label, on or before the end date of the decision review time, the Agency shall provide to the applicant a draft accepted label, including any changes made by the Agency that differ from the applicant-submitted label and relevant supporting data reviewed by the Agency. The applicant will notify the Agency that the applicant either (a) agrees to all of the terms associated with the draft accepted label as amended by the Agency and requests that it be issued as the accepted final Agency-stamped label; or (b) does not agree to one or more of the terms of the draft accepted label as amended by the Agency and requests additional time to resolve the difference(s); or (c) withdraws the application without prejudice for subsequent resubmission, but forfeits the associated registration service fee. For cases described in (b), the applicant shall have up to 30 calendar days to reach agreement with the Agency on the final terms of the Agency-accepted label. If the applicant agrees to all of the terms of

the accepted label as in (a), including upon resolution of differences in (b), the Agency shall provide an accepted final Agency-stamped label to the registrant within 2 business days following the registrant's written or electronic confirmation of agreement to the Agency.

(4) Amendment applications to add the revised use pattern(s) to registered product labels are covered by the base fee for the category. All items in the covered application must be submitted together in one package. Each application for an additional new product registration and new inert approval(s) that is submitted in the amendment application package is subject to the registration service fee for a new product or a new inert approval. However, if an amendment application only proposes to register the amendment for a new product and there are no amendments in the application, then review of one new product application is covered by the base fee. All such associated applications that are submitted together will be subject to the category decision review time.

		TABLE 4. — REGISTRATION DIVISION — NEW PRODUCTS		
EPA No.	New CR No.	Action	Decision Review Time (Months)(1)	Registration Service Fee ($)
R300	45	New product; or similar combination product (already registered) to an identical or substantially similar in composition and use to a registered product; registered source of active ingredient; no data review on acute toxicity, efficacy or CRP - only product chemistry data; cite-all data citation, or selective data citation where applicant owns all required data, or applicant submits specific authorization letter from data owner. Category also includes 100% re-package of registered end-use or manufacturing-use product that requires no data submission nor data matrix. (2)(3)	4	1,582
R301	46	New product; or similar combination product (already registered) to an identical or substantially similar in composition and use to a registered product; registered source of active ingredient; selective data citation only for data on product chemistry and/or acute toxicity and/or public health pest efficacy (identical data citation and claims to cited product(s)), where applicant does not own all required data and does not have a specific authorization letter from data owner. (2)(3)	4	1,897

R310	47	New end-use or manufacturing-use product with registered source(s) of active ingredient(s); includes products containing two or more registered active ingredients previously combined in other registered products; excludes products requiring or citing an animal safety study; requires review of data package within RD only; includes data and/or waivers of data for only: • product chemistry and/or • acute toxicity and/or • child resistant packaging and/ or • pest(s) requiring efficacy (4) - for up to 3 target pests. (2)(3)	7	7,301
R314	48	New end use product containing up to three registered active ingredients never before registered as this combination in a formulated product; new product label is identical or substantially similar to the labels of currently registered products which separately contain the respective component active ingredients; excludes products requiring or citing an animal safety study; requires review of data package within RD only; includes data and/or waivers of data for only: • product chemistry and/or • acute toxicity and/or • child resistant packaging and/ or • pest(s) requiring efficacy (4) - for up to 3 target pests. (2)(3)	8	8,626
R319	49	New end use product containing up to three registered active ingredients never before registered as this combination in a formulated product; new product label is identical or substantially similar to the labels of currently registered products which separately contain the respective component active ingredients; excludes products requiring or citing an animal safety study; requires review of data package within RD only; includes data and/or waivers of data for only: • product chemistry and/or • acute toxicity and/or • child resistant packaging and/ or • pest(s) requiring efficacy (4) - for 4 to 7 target pests. (2)(3)	10	12,626

R318	50 (new)	New end use product containing four or more registered active ingredients never before registered as this combination in a formulated product; new product label is identical or substantially similar to the labels of currently registered products which separately contain the respective component active ingredients; excludes products requiring or citing an animal safety study; requires review of data package within RD only; includes data and/or waivers of data for only: • product chemistry and/or • acute toxicity and/or • child resistant packaging and/ or • pest(s) requiring efficacy (4) - for up to 3 target pests. (2)(3)	9	13,252
R321	51 (new)	New end use product containing four or more registered active ingredients never before registered as this combination in a formulated product; new product label is identical or substantially similar to the labels of currently registered products which separately contain the respective component active ingredients; excludes products requiring or citing an animal safety study; requires review of data package within RD only; includes data and/or waivers of data for only: • product chemistry and/or • acute toxicity and/or • child resistant packaging and/ or • pest(s) requiring efficacy (4) - for 4 to 7 target pests. (2)(3)	11	17,252
R315	52	New end-use, on-animal product, registered source of active ingredient(s), with the submission of data and/or waivers for only: • animal safety and • pest(s) requiring efficacy (4) and/or • product chemistry and/or • acute toxicity and/or • child resistant packaging. (2) (3)	9	9,820
R316	53 (new)	New end-use or manufacturing product with registered source(s) of active ingredient(s) including products containing two or more registered active ingredients previously combined in other registered products; excludes products requiring or citing an animal safety study; and requires review of data and/or waivers for only: • product chemistry and/or • acute toxicity and/or • child resistant packaging and/ or • pest(s) requiring efficacy (4) - for greater than 3 and up to 7 target pests. (2)(3)	9	11,301

R317	54 (new)	New end-use or manufacturing product with registered source(s) of active ingredient(s) including products containing 2 or more registered active ingredients previously combined in other registered products; excludes products requiring or citing an animal safety study; and requires review of data and/or waivers for only: • product chemistry and/or • acute toxicity and/or • child resistant packaging and/ or • pest(s) requiring efficacy (4) - for greater than 7 target pests. (2)(3)	10	15,301
R320	55	New product; new physical form; requires data review in science divisions. (2)(3)	12	13,226
R331	56	New product; repack of identical registered end-use product as a manufacturing-use product, or identical registered manufacturing-use product as an end use product; same registered uses only. (2)(3)	3	2,530
R332	57	New manufacturing-use product; registered active ingredient; unregistered source of active ingredient; submission of completely new generic data package; registered uses only; requires review in RD and science divisions. (2)(3)	24	283,215
R333	58	New product; MUP or End use product with unregistered source of active ingredient; requires science data review; new physical form; etc. Cite-all or selective data citation where applicant owns all required data. (2)(3)	10	19,838
R334	59	New product; MUP or End use product with unregistered source of the active ingredient; requires science data review; new physical form; etc. Selective data citation. (2)(3)	11	23,100

(1) A decision review time that would otherwise end on a Saturday, Sunday, or federal holiday, will be extended to end on the next business day.

(2) An application for a new end-use product using a source of active ingredient that (a) is not yet registered but (b) has an application pending with the Agency for review, will be considered an application for a new product with an unregistered source of active ingredient.

(3) Where the action involves approval of a new or amended label, on or before the end date of the decision review time, the Agency shall provide to the applicant a draft accepted label, including any changes made by the Agency that differ from the applicant-submitted label and relevant supporting data reviewed by the Agency. The applicant will notify the Agency that the applicant either (a) agrees to all of the terms associated with the draft accepted label as amended by the Agency and requests that it be issued as the accepted final Agency-stamped label; or (b) does not agree to one or more of the terms of the draft accepted label as amended by the Agency and requests additional time to resolve the difference(s); or (c) withdraws the application without prejudice for subsequent resubmission, but forfeits the associated registration service fee. For cases described in (b), the applicant shall have up to 30 calendar days to reach agreement with the Agency on the final terms of the Agency-accepted label. If the applicant agrees to all of the terms of the accepted label as in (a), including upon resolution of differences in (b), the Agency shall provide an accepted final Agency-stamped label to the

registrant within 2 business days following the registrant's written or electronic confirmation of agreement to the Agency.
(4) For the purposes of classifying proposed registration actions into PRIA categories, "pest(s) requiring efficacy are: public health pests listed in PR Notice 2002-1, livestock pests (e.g. Horn flies, Stable flies), wood-destroying pests (e.g. termites, carpenter ants, wood-boring beetles) and certain invasive species (e.g. Asian Longhorned beetle, Emerald Ashborer). This list may be updated/refined as invasive pest needs arise. To determine the number of pests for the PRIA categories, pests have been placed into groups (general; e.g., cockroaches) and pest specific (specifically a test species). If seeking a label claim against a pest group (general), use the group listing below and each group will count as 1. The general pests groups are: mites, dust mites, chiggers, ticks, hard ticks, soft ticks, cattle ticks, scorpions, spiders, centipedes, lice, fleas, cockroaches, keds, bot flies, screwworms, filth flies, blow flies, house flies, flesh flies, mosquitoes, biting flies, horse flies, stable flies, deer flies, sand flies, biting midges, black flies, true bugs, bed bugs, stinging bees, wasps, yellow jackets, hornets, ants (excluding carpenter ants), fire and harvester ants, wood destroying beetles, carpenter ants, termites, subterranean termites, dry wood termites, arboreal termites, damp wood termites and invasive species. If seeking a claim against a specific pest without a general claim then each specific pest will count as 1.

TABLE 5. — REGISTRATION DIVISION — AMENDMENTS				
EPA No.	New CR No.	Action	Decision Review Time (Months)(1)	Registration Service Fee ($)
R340	60	Amendment requiring data review within RD (e.g., changes to precautionary label statements); includes adding/modifying pest(s) claims for up to 2 target pests, excludes products requiring or citing an animal safety study. (2)(3)(4)	4	4,988
R341	61	Amendment requiring data review within RD (e.g., changes to precautionary label statements), includes adding/modifying pest(s) claims for greater than 2 target pests, excludes products requiring or citing an animal safety study. (2)(3)(4)	6 (New)	5,988
R345	62	Amending on-animal products previously registered, with the submission of data and/or waivers for only: • animal safety and • pest(s) requiring efficacy (4) and/or • product chemistry and/or • acute toxicity and/ or • child resistant packaging. (2)(3)	7	8,820
R350	63	Amendment requiring data review in science divisions (e.g., changes to REI, or PPE, or PHI, or use rate, or number of applications; or add aerial application; or modify GW/SW advisory statement). (2)(3)	9	13,226
R351	64	Amendment adding a new unregistered source of active ingredient. (2)(3)	8	13,226

R352	65	Amendment adding already approved uses; selective method of support; does not apply if the applicant owns all cited data. (2) (3)	8	13,226
R371	66	Amendment to Experimental Use Permit; (does not include extending a permit's time period). (3)	6	10,090

(1) A decision review time that would otherwise end on a Saturday, Sunday, or federal holiday, will be extended to end on the next business day.

(2) (a) EPA-initiated amendments shall not be charged registration service fees. (b) Registrant-initiated fast-track amendments are to be completed within the timelines specified in FIFRA Section 3(c)(3)(B) and are not subject to registration service fees. (c) Registrant-initiated fast-track amendments handled by the Antimicrobials Division are to be completed within the timelines specified in FIFRA Section 3(h) and are not subject to registration service fees. (d) Registrant initiated amendments submitted by notification under PR Notices, such as PR Notice 98-10, continue under PR Notice timelines and are not subject to registration service fees. (e) Submissions with data and requiring data review are subject to registration service fees.

(3) Where the action involves approval of a new or amended label, on or before the end date of the decision review time, the Agency shall provide to the applicant a draft accepted label, including any changes made by the Agency that differ from the applicant-submitted label and relevant supporting data reviewed by the Agency. The applicant will notify the Agency that the applicant either (a) agrees to all of the terms associated with the draft accepted label as amended by the Agency and requests that it be issued as the accepted final Agency-stamped label; or (b) does not agree to one or more of the terms of the draft accepted label as amended by the Agency and requests additional time to resolve the difference(s); or (c) withdraws the application without prejudice for subsequent resubmission, but forfeits the associated registration service fee. For cases described in (b), the applicant shall have up to 30 calendar days to reach agreement with the Agency on the final terms of the Agency-accepted label. If the applicant agrees to all of the terms of the accepted label as in (a), including upon resolution of differences in (b), the Agency shall provide an accepted final Agency-stamped label to the registrant within 2 business days following the registrant's written or electronic confirmation of agreement to the Agency.

(4) For the purposes of classifying proposed registration actions into PRIA categories, "pest(s) requiring efficacy" are: public health pests listed in PR Notice 2002-1, livestock pests (e.g. Horn flies, Stable flies), wood-destroying pests (e.g. termites, carpenter ants, wood-boring beetles) and certain invasive species (e.g. Asian Longhorned beetle, Emerald Ashborer). This list may be updated/refined as invasive pest needs arise. To determine the number of pests for the PRIA categories, pests have been placed into groups (general; e.g., cockroaches) and pest specific (specifically a test species). If seeking a label claim against a pest group (general), use the group listing below and each group will count as 1. The general pests groups are: mites, dust mites, chiggers, ticks, hard ticks, soft ticks, cattle ticks, scorpions, spiders, centipedes, lice, fleas, cockroaches, keds, bot flies, screwworms, filth flies, blow flies, house flies, flesh flies, mosquitoes, biting flies, horse flies, stable flies, deer flies, sand flies, biting midges, black flies, true bugs, bed bugs, stinging bees, wasps, yellow jackets, hornets, ants (excluding carpenter ants), fire and harvester ants, wood destroying beetles, carpenter ants, termites, subterranean termites, dry wood termites, arboreal termites, damp wood termites and invasive species. If seeking a claim against a specific pest without a general claim then each specific pest will count as 1.

TABLE 6. — REGISTRATION DIVISION — OTHER ACTIONS

EPA No.	New CR No.	Action	Decision Review Time (Months)(1)	Registration Service Fee ($)
R124	67	Conditional Ruling on Pre-application Study Waivers; applicant-initiated.	6	2,530
R272	68	Review of Study Protocol applicant-initiated; excludes DART, pre-registration conference, Rapid Response review, DNT protocol review, protocol needing HSRB review.	3	2,530
R275	69	Rebuttal of agency reviewed protocol, applicant initiated.	3	2,530
R370	70	Cancer reassessment; applicant-initiated.	18	198,250

(1) A decision review time that would otherwise end on a Saturday, Sunday, or federal holiday, will be extended to end on the next business day.

TABLE 7. — ANTIMICROBIALS DIVISION — NEW ACTIVE INGREDIENTS

EPA No.	New CR No.	Action	Decision Review Time (Months)(1)	Registration Service Fee ($)
A380	71	New Active Ingredient; Indirect Food use; establish tolerance or tolerance exemption if required. (2)(3)	24	137,841
A390	72	New Active Ingredient; Direct Food use; establish tolerance or tolerance exemption if required. (2)(3)	24	229,733
A410	73	New Active Ingredient Non-food use.(2)(3)	21	229,733
A431	74	New Active Ingredient, Non-food use; low-risk. (2)(3)	12	80,225

(1) A decision review time that would otherwise end on a Saturday, Sunday, or federal holiday, will be extended to end on the next business day.

(2) All requests for new uses (food and/or nonfood) contained in any application for a new active ingredient or a first food use are covered by the base fee for that new active ingredient or first food use application and retain the same decision time review period as the new active ingredient or first food use application. The application must be received by the agency in one package. The base fee for the category covers a maximum of five new products. Each application for an additional new product registration and new inert approval that is submitted in the new active ingredient application package or first food use application package is subject to the registration service fee for a new product or a new inert approval. All such associated applications that are submitted together will be subject to the new active ingredient or first food use decision review time. In the case of a new active ingredient application, until that new active ingredient is approved, any subsequent application for another new product containing the same active ingredient or an amendment to the proposed labeling will be deemed a new active ingredient application, subject to the registration service fee and decision review time for a new active ingredient. In the case of a first food use application, until that first food use is approved, any subsequent application for an additional new food use or uses will be subject to the registration service fee and decision review time for a first food use. Any information that (a) was neither requested nor required by the Agency, and (b) is submitted by the applicant at the applicant's initiative to support the application after completion of the technical deficiency screening, and (c) is not itself a covered registration application, must be assessed 25% of the full registration service fee for the new active ingredient or first food use application.

(3) Where the action involves approval of a new or amended label, on or before the end date of the decision review time, the Agency shall provide to the applicant a draft accepted label, including any changes made by the Agency that differ from the applicant-submitted label and relevant supporting data reviewed by the Agency. The applicant will notify the Agency that the applicant either (a) agrees to all of the terms associated with the draft accepted label as amended by the Agency and requests that it be issued as the accepted final Agency-stamped label; or (b) does not agree to one or more of the terms of the draft accepted label as amended by the Agency and requests additional time to resolve the difference(s); or (c) withdraws the application without prejudice for subsequent resubmission, but forfeits the associated registration service fee. For cases described in (b), the applicant shall have up to 30 calendar days to reach agreement with the Agency

on the final terms of the Agency-accepted label. If the applicant agrees to all of the terms of the accepted label as in (a), including upon resolution of differences in (b), the Agency shall provide an accepted final Agency-stamped label to the registrant within 2 business days following the registrant's written or electronic confirmation of agreement to the Agency.

EPA No.	New CR No.	Action	Decision Review Time (Months)(1)	Registration Service Fee ($)
A440	75	New Use, Indirect Food Use, establish tolerance or tolerance exemption. (2)(3)(4)	21	31,910
A441	76	Additional Indirect food uses; establish tolerances or tolerance exemptions if required; 6 or more submitted in one application. (3)(4)(5)	21	114,870
A450	77	New use, Direct food use, establish tolerance or tolerance exemption. (2)(3)(4)	21	95,724
A451	78	Additional Direct food uses; establish tolerances or tolerance exemptions if required; 6 or more submitted in one application. (3)(4)(5)	21	182,335
A500	79	New use, non-food. (4)(5)	12	31,910
A501	80	New use, non-food; 6 or more submitted in one application. (4)(5)	**15**	76,583

TABLE 8. — ANTIMICROBIALS DIVISION — NEW USES

(1) A decision review time that would otherwise end on a Saturday, Sunday, or federal holiday, will be extended to end on the next business day.

(2) All requests for new uses (food and/or nonfood) contained in any application for a new active ingredient or a first food use are covered by the base fee for that new active ingredient or first food use application and retain the same decision time review period as the new active ingredient or first food use application. The application must be received by the agency in one package. The base fee for the category covers a maximum of five new products. Each application for an additional new product registration and new inert approval that is submitted in the new active ingredient application package or first food use application package is subject to the registration service fee for a new product or a new inert approval. All such associated applications that are submitted together will be subject to the new active ingredient or first food use decision review time. In the case of a new active ingredient application, until that new active ingredient is approved, any subsequent application for another new product containing the same active ingredient or an amendment to the proposed labeling will be deemed a new active ingredient application, subject to the registration service fee and decision review time for a new active ingredient. In the case of a first food use application, until that first food use is approved, any subsequent application for an additional new food use or uses will be subject to the registration service fee and decision review time for a first food use. Any information that (a) was neither requested nor required by the Agency, and (b) is submitted by the applicant at the applicant's initiative to support the application after completion of the technical deficiency screening, and (c) is not itself a covered registration application, must be assessed 25% of the full registration service fee for the new active ingredient or first food use application.

(3) If EPA data rules are amended to newly require clearance under section 408 of the FFDCA for an ingredient of an antimicrobial product where such ingredient was not previously subject to such a clearance, then review of the data for such clearance of such product is not subject to a registration service fee for the tolerance action for two years from the effective date of the rule.

(4) Where the action involves approval of a new or amended label, on or before the end date of the decision review time, the Agency shall provide to the applicant a draft accepted label, including any changes made by the Agency that differ from the applicant-submitted label and relevant supporting data reviewed by the Agency. The applicant will notify the Agency that the applicant either (a) agrees to all of the terms associated with the draft accepted label as amended by the Agency and requests that it be issued as the accepted final Agency-stamped label; or (b) does not agree to one or more of the terms of the draft accepted label as amended by the Agency and requests additional time to resolve the difference(s); or (c) withdraws the application without prejudice for subsequent resubmission, but forfeits the associated registration service fee. For cases described in (b), the applicant shall have up to 30 calendar days to reach agreement with the Agency on the final terms of the Agency-accepted label. If the applicant agrees to all of the terms of the accepted label as in (a),

including upon resolution of differences in (b), the Agency shall provide an accepted final Agency-stamped label to the registrant within 2 business days following the registrant's written or electronic confirmation of agreement to the Agency. (5) Amendment applications to add the new use(s) to registered product labels are covered by the base fee for the new use(s). All items in the covered application must be submitted together in one package. Each application for an additional new product registration and new inert approval(s) that is submitted in the new use application package is subject to the registration service fee for a new product or a new inert approval. However, if a new use application only proposes to register the new use for a new product and there are no amendments in the application, then review of one new product application is covered by the new use fee. All such associated applications that are submitted together will be subject to the new use decision review time. Any application for a new product or an amendment to the proposed labeling (a) submitted subsequent to submission of the new use application and (b) prior to conclusion of its decision review time and (c) containing the same new uses, will be deemed a separate new-use application, subject to a separate registration service fee and new decision review time for a new use. If the new-use application includes non-food (indoor and/or outdoor), and food (outdoor and/or indoor) uses, the appropriate fee is due for each type of new use and the longest decision review time applies to all of the new uses requested in the application. Any information that (a) was neither requested nor required by the Agency, and (b) is submitted by the applicant at the applicant's initiative to support the application after completion of the technical deficiency screen, and (c) is not itself a covered registration application, must be assessed 25% of the full registration service fee for the new use application.

TABLE 9. — ANTIMICROBIALS DIVISION — NEW PRODUCTS AND AMENDMENTS				
EPA No.	New CR No.	Action	Decision Review Time (Months)(1)	Registration Service Fee ($)
A530	81	New product, identical or substantially similar in composition and use to a registered product; no data review or only product chemistry data; cite all data citation or selective data citation where applicant owns all required data; or applicant submits specific authorization letter from data owner. Category also includes 100% re-package of registered end-use or manufacturing use product that requires no data submission nor data matrix. (2)(3)	4	1,278
A531	82	New product; identical or substantially similar in composition and use to a registered product; registered source of active ingredient: selective data citation only for data on product chemistry and/or acute toxicity and/or public health pest efficacy, where applicant does not own all required data and does not have a specific authorization letter from data owner. (2)(3)	4	1,824
A532	83	New product; identical or substantially similar in composition and use to a registered product; registered active ingredient; unregistered source of active ingredient; cite-all data citation except for product chemistry; product chemistry data submitted. (2)(3)	5	5,107
A540	84	New end use product; FIFRA §2(mm) uses only; up to 25 public health organisms. (2)(3)(5)(6)	5	5,107
A541	85 (new)	New end use product; FIFRA §2(mm) uses only; 26-50 public health organisms. (2)(3)(5)(6)	7	8,500
A542	86 (new)	New end use product; FIFRA §2(mm) uses only; ≥ 51 public health organisms. (2)(3)(5)	10	15,000

A550	87	New end-use product; uses other than FIFRA §2(mm); non-FQPA product. (2)(3)(5)	9	13,226
A560	88	New manufacturing use product; registered active ingredient; selective data citation. (2)(3)	6	12,596
A565	89 (new)	New manufacturing-use product; registered active ingredient; unregistered source of active ingredient; submission of new generic data package; registered uses only; requires science review. (2)(3)	12	18,234
A570	90	Label amendment requiring data review; up to 25 public health organisms. (3)(4)(5)(6)	4	3,831
A573	91 (new)	Label amendment requiring data review; 26-50 public health organisms. (2)(3)(5)(7)	6	6,350
A574	92 (new)	Label amendment requiring data review; ≥ 51 public health organisms. (2)(3)(5)(7)	9	11,000
A572	93	New Product or amendment requiring data review for risk assessment by Science Branch (e.g., changes to REI, or PPE, or use rate). (2)(3)(4)	9	13,226

(1) A decision review time that would otherwise end on a Saturday, Sunday, or federal holiday, will be extended to end on the next business day.

(2) An application for a new end-use product using a source of active ingredient that (a) is not yet registered but (b) has an application pending with the Agency for review, will be considered an application for a new product with an unregistered source of active ingredient.

(3) Where the action involves approval of a new or amended label, on or before the end date of the decision review time, the Agency shall provide to the applicant a draft accepted label, including any changes made by the Agency that differ from the applicant-submitted label and relevant supporting data reviewed by the Agency. The applicant will notify the Agency that the applicant either (a) agrees to all of the terms associated with the draft accepted label as amended by the Agency and requests that it be issued as the accepted final Agency-stamped label; or (b) does not agree to one or more of the terms of the draft accepted label as amended by the Agency and requests additional time to resolve the difference(s); or (c) withdraws the application without prejudice for subsequent resubmission, but forfeits the associated registration service fee. For cases described in (b), the applicant shall have up to 30 calendar days to reach agreement with the Agency on the final terms of the Agency-accepted label. If the applicant agrees to all of the terms of the accepted label as in (a), including upon resolution of differences in (b), the Agency shall provide an accepted final Agency-stamped label to the registrant within 2 business days following the registrant's written or electronic confirmation of agreement to the Agency.

(4) (a) EPA-initiated amendments shall not be charged registration service fees. (b) Registrant-initiated fast-track amendments are to be completed within the timelines specified in FIFRA Section 3(c)(3)(B) and are not subject to registration service fees. (c) Registrant-initiated fast-track amendments handled by the Antimicrobials Division are to be completed within the timelines specified in FIFRA Section 3(h) and are not subject to registration service fees. (d) Registrant initiated amendments submitted by notification under PR Notices, such as PR Notice 98-10, continue under PR Notice timelines and are not subject to registration service fees. (e) Submissions with data and requiring data review are subject to registration service fees.

(5) The applicant must identify the substantially similar product if opting to use cite-all or the selective method to support acute toxicity data requirements.

(6) Once a submission for a new product with public health organisms has been submitted and classified in either A540 or A541, additional organisms submitted for the same product before expiration of the first submission's original decision review time period will result in reclassification of both the original and subsequent submission into the appropriate new category based on the sum of the number of organisms in both submissions. A reclassification would result in a new PRIA start date and require additional fees to meet the fee of the new category.

(7) Once a submission for a label amendment with public health organisms has been submitted and classified in either A570 or A573, additional organisms submitted for the same product before expiration of the first submission's original decision review time period will result in reclassification of both the original and subsequent submission into the appropriate new category based on the sum of the number of organisms in both submissions. A reclassification would result in a new PRIA start date and require additional fees to meet the fee of the new category.

EPA No.	New CR No.	Action	Decision Review Time (Months)(1)	Registration Service Fee ($)

TABLE 10. — ANTIMICROBIALS DIVISION — EXPERIMENTAL USE PERMITS AND OTHER ACTIONS

EPA No.	New CR No.	Action	Decision Review Time (Months)(1)	Registration Service Fee ($)
A520	94	Experimental Use Permit application, non-food use. (2)	9	6,383
A521	95	Review of public health efficacy study protocol within AD, per AD Internal Guidance for the Efficacy Protocol Review Process; Code will also include review of public health efficacy study protocol and data review for devices making pesticidal claims; applicant-initiated; Tier 1.	4	4,726
A522	96	Review of public health efficacy study protocol outside AD by members of AD Efficacy Protocol Review Expert Panel; Code will also include review of public health efficacy study protocol and data review for devices making pesticidal claims; applicant-initiated; Tier 2.	12	12,156
A537	97 (new)	New Active Ingredient/New Use, Experimental Use Permit application; Direct food use; Establish tolerance or tolerance exemption if required. Credit 45% of fee toward new active ingredient/new use application that follows.	18	153,156
A538	98 (new)	New Active Ingredient/New Use, Experimental Use Permit application; Indirect food use; Establish tolerance or tolerance exemption if required Credit 45% of fee toward new active ingredient/new use application that follows.	18	95,724
A539	99 (new)	New Active Ingredient/New Use, Experimental Use Permit application; Nonfood use. Credit 45% of fee toward new active ingredient/new use application that follows.	15	92,163
A529	100	Amendment to Experimental Use Permit; requires data review or risk assessment. (2)	9	11,429
A523	101	Review of protocol other than a public health efficacy study (i.e., Toxicology or Exposure Protocols).	9	12,156
A571	102	Science reassessment: Cancer risk, refined ecological risk, and/or endangered species; applicant-initiated.	18	95,724
A533	103 (new)	Exemption from the requirement of an Experimental Use Permit. (2)	4	2,482
A534	104 (new)	Rebuttal of agency reviewed protocol, applicant initiated.	4	4,726
A535	105 (new)	Conditional Ruling on Pre-application Study Waiver or Data Bridging Argument; applicant-initiated.	6	2,409
A536	106 (new)	Conditional Ruling on Pre-application Direct Food, Indirect Food, Nonfood use determination; applicant-initiated.	4	2,482

(1) A decision review time that would otherwise end on a Saturday, Sunday, or federal holiday, will be extended to end on the next business day.

(2) Where the action involves approval of a new or amended label, on or before the end date of the decision review time, the Agency shall provide to the applicant a draft accepted label, including any changes made by the Agency that differ from the applicant-submitted label and relevant supporting data reviewed by the Agency. The applicant will notify the Agency that the applicant either (a) agrees to all of the terms associated with the draft accepted label as amended by the Agency and requests that it be issued as the accepted final Agency-stamped label; or (b) does not agree to one or more of the terms of the draft accepted label as amended by the Agency and requests additional time to resolve the difference(s); or (c) withdraws the application without prejudice for subsequent resubmission, but forfeits the associated registration service fee. For cases described in (b), the applicant shall have up to 30 calendar days to reach agreement with the Agency on the final terms of the Agency-accepted label. If the applicant agrees to all of the terms of the accepted label as in (a), including upon resolution of differences in (b), the Agency shall provide an accepted final Agency-stamped label to the registrant within 2 business days following the registrant's written or electronic confirmation of agreement to the Agency.

TABLE 11. — BIOPESTICIDES DIVISION — NEW ACTIVE INGREDIENTS				
EPA No.	New CR No.	Action	Decision Review Time (Months)(1)	Registration Service Fee ($)
B580	107	New active ingredient; food use; petition to establish a tolerance. (2)(3)	20	51,053
B590	108	New active ingredient; food use; petition to establish a tolerance exemption. (2)(3)	18	31,910
B600	109	New active ingredient; non-food use. (2)(3)	13	19,146
B610	110	New active ingredient; Experimental Use Permit application; petition to establish a temporary tolerance or temporary tolerance exemption. (3)	10	12,764
B611	111	New active ingredient; Experimental Use Permit application; petition to establish permanent tolerance exemption. (3)	12	12,764
B612	112	New active ingredient; no change to a permanent tolerance exemption. (2)(3)	10	17,550
B613	113	New active ingredient; petition to convert a temporary tolerance or a temporary tolerance exemption to a permanent tolerance or tolerance exemption. (2)(3)	11	17,550
B620	114	New active ingredient; Experimental Use Permit application; non-food use including crop destruct. (3)	7	6,383

(1) A decision review time that would otherwise end on a Saturday, Sunday, or federal holiday, will be extended to end on the next business day.

(2) All requests for new uses (food and/or nonfood) contained in any application for a new active ingredient or a first food use are covered by the base fee for that new active ingredient or first food use application and retain the same decision time review period as the new active ingredient or first food use application. The application must be received by the agency in one package. The base fee for the category covers a maximum of five new products. Each application for an additional new product registration and new inert approval that is submitted in the new active ingredient application package or first food use application package is subject to the registration service fee for a new product or a new inert approval. All such associated applications that are submitted together will be subject to the new active ingredient or first food use decision review time. In the case of a new active ingredient application, until that new active ingredient is approved, any subsequent application for another new product containing the same active ingredient or an amendment to the proposed labeling will be deemed a new active ingredient application, subject to the registration service fee and decision review time for a new active ingredient. In the case of a first food use application, until that first food use is approved, any subsequent application for an additional new food use or uses will be subject to the registration service fee and decision review time for a first food use. Any information that (a) was neither requested nor required by the Agency, and (b) is submitted by the applicant at the applicant's initiative to support the application after completion of the technical

deficiency screening, and (c) is not itself a covered registration application, must be assessed 25% of the full registration service fee for the new active ingredient or first food use application.

(3) Where the action involves approval of a new or amended label, on or before the end date of the decision review time, the Agency shall provide to the applicant a draft accepted label, including any changes made by the Agency that differ from the applicant-submitted label and relevant supporting data reviewed by the Agency. The applicant will notify the Agency that the applicant either (a) agrees to all of the terms associated with the draft accepted label as amended by the Agency and requests that it be issued as the accepted final Agency-stamped label; or (b) does not agree to one or more of the terms of the draft accepted label as amended by the Agency and requests additional time to resolve the difference(s); or (c) withdraws the application without prejudice for subsequent resubmission, but forfeits the associated registration service fee. For cases described in (b), the applicant shall have up to 30 calendar days to reach agreement with the Agency on the final terms of the Agency-accepted label. If the applicant agrees to all of the terms of the accepted label as in (a), including upon resolution of differences in (b), the Agency shall provide an accepted final Agency-stamped label to the registrant within 2 business days following the registrant's written or electronic confirmation of agreement to the Agency.

TABLE 12. — BIOPESTICIDES DIVISION — NEW USES				
EPA No.	New CR No.	Action	Decision Review Time (Months)(1)	Registration Service Fee ($)
B630	115	First food use; petition to establish a tolerance exemption. (2)(4)	13	12,764
B631	116	New food use; petition to amend an established tolerance. (3)(4)	12	12,764
B640	117	First food use; petition to establish a tolerance. (2)(4)	19	19,146
B643	118	New Food use; petition to amend an established tolerance exemption. (3)(4)	10	12,764
B642	119	First food use; indoor; food/food handling. (2)(4)	12	31,910
B644	120	New use, no change to an established tolerance or tolerance exemption. (3)(4)	8	12,764
B650	121	New use; non-food. (3)(4)	7	6,383
B645	122 (new)	New food use; Experimental Use Permit application; petition to amend or add a tolerance exemption. (4)	12	12,764
B646	123 (new)	New use; non-food use including crop destruct; Experimental Use Permit application. (4)	7	6,383

(1) A decision review time that would otherwise end on a Saturday, Sunday, or federal holiday, will be extended to end on the next business day.

(2) All requests for new uses (food and/or nonfood) contained in any application for a new active ingredient or a first food use are covered by the base fee for that new active ingredient or first food use application and retain the same decision time review period as the new active ingredient or first food use application. The application must be received by the agency in one package. The base fee for the category covers a maximum of five new products. Each application for

an additional new product registration and new inert approval that is submitted in the new active ingredient application package or first food use application package is subject to the registration service fee for a new product or a new inert approval. All such associated applications that are submitted together will be subject to the new active ingredient or first food use decision review time. In the case of a new active ingredient application, until that new active ingredient is approved, any subsequent application for another new product containing the same active ingredient or an amendment to the proposed labeling will be deemed a new active ingredient application, subject to the registration service fee and decision review time for a new active ingredient. In the case of a first food use application, until that first food use is approved, any subsequent application for an additional new food use or uses will be subject to the registration service fee and decision review time for a first food use. Any information that (a) was neither requested nor required by the Agency, and (b) is submitted by the applicant at the applicant's initiative to support the application after completion of the technical deficiency screening, and (c) is not itself a covered registration application, must be assessed 25% of the full registration service fee for the new active ingredient or first food use application.

(3) Amendment applications to add the new use(s) to registered product labels are covered by the base fee for the new use(s). All items in the covered application must be submitted together in one package. Each application for an additional new product registration and new inert approval(s) that is submitted in the new use application package is subject to the registration service fee for a new product or a new inert approval. However, if a new use application only proposes to register the new use for a new product and there are no amendments in the application, then review of one new product application is covered by the new use fee. All such associated applications that are submitted together will be subject to the new use decision review time. Any application for a new product or an amendment to the proposed labeling (a) submitted subsequent to submission of the new use application and (b) prior to conclusion of its decision review time and (c) containing the same new uses, will be deemed a separate new-use application, subject to a separate registration service fee and new decision review time for a new use. If the new-use application includes non-food (indoor and/or outdoor), and food (outdoor and/or indoor) uses, the appropriate fee is due for each type of new use and the longest decision review time applies to all of the new uses requested in the application. Any information that (a) was neither requested nor required by the Agency, and (b) is submitted by the applicant at the applicant's initiative to support the application after completion of the technical deficiency screen, and (c) is not itself a covered registration application, must be assessed 25% of the full registration service fee for the new use application.

(4) Where the action involves approval of a new or amended label, on or before the end date of the decision review time, the Agency shall provide to the applicant a draft accepted label, including any changes made by the Agency that differ from the applicant-submitted label and relevant supporting data reviewed by the Agency. The applicant will notify the Agency that the applicant either (a) agrees to all of the terms associated with the draft accepted label as amended by the Agency and requests that it be issued as the accepted final Agency-stamped label; or (b) does not agree to one or more of the terms of the draft accepted label as amended by the Agency and requests additional time to resolve the difference(s); or (c) withdraws the application without prejudice for subsequent resubmission, but forfeits the associated registration service fee. For cases described in (b), the applicant shall have up to 30 calendar days to reach agreement with the Agency on the final terms of the Agency-accepted label. If the applicant agrees to all of the terms of the accepted label as in (a), including upon resolution of differences in (b), the Agency shall provide an accepted final Agency-stamped label to the registrant within 2 business days following the registrant's written or electronic confirmation of agreement to the Agency.

TABLE 13. — BIOPESTICIDES DIVISION — NEW PRODUCTS				
EPA No.	New CR No.	Action	Decision Review Time (Months)(1)	Registration Service Fee ($)
B652	124	New product; registered source of active ingredient; requires petition to amend established tolerance or tolerance exemption; requires 1) submission of product specific data; or 2) citation of previously reviewed and accepted data; or 3) submission or citation of data generated at government expense; or 4) submission or citation of scientifically-sound rationale based on publicly available literature or other relevant information that addresses the data requirement; or 5) submission of a request for a data requirement to be waived supported by a scientifically-sound rationale explaining why the data requirement does not apply. (2)(3)	13	12,764
B660	125	New product; registered source of active ingredient(s); identical or substantially similar in composition and use to a registered product. No data review, or only product chemistry data; cite-all data citation, or selective data citation where applicant owns all required data or authorization from data owner is demonstrated. Category includes 100% re-package of registered end-use or manufacturing-use product that requires no data submission or data matrix. For microbial pesticides, the active ingredient(s) must not be re-isolated. (2)(3)	4	1,278
B670	126	New product; registered source of active ingredient(s); requires: 1) submission of product specific data; or 2) citation of previously reviewed and accepted data; or 3) submission or citation of data generated at government expense; or 4) submission or citation of a scientifically-sound rationale based on publicly available literature or other relevant information that addresses the data requirement; or 5) submission of a request for a data requirement to be waived supported by a scientifically-sound rationale explaining why the data requirement does not apply. (2)(3)	7	5,107

B671	127	New product; unregistered source of active ingredient(s); requires a petition to amend an established tolerance or tolerance exemption; requires: 1) submission of product specific data; or 2) citation of previously reviewed and accepted data; or 3) submission or citation of data generated at government expense; or 4) submission or citation of a scientifically-sound rationale based on publicly available literature or other relevant information that addresses the data requirement; or 5) submission of a request for a data requirement to be waived supported by a scientifically-sound rationale explaining why the data requirement does not apply. (2)(3)	17	12,764
B672	128	New product; unregistered source of active ingredient(s); non-food use or food use requires: 1) submission of product specific data; or 2) citation of previously reviewed and accepted data; or 3) submission or citation of data generated at government expense; or 4) submission or citation of a scientifically-sound rationale based on publicly available literature or other relevant information that addresses the data requirement; or 5) submission of a request for a data requirement to be waived supported by a scientifically-sound rationale explaining why the data requirement does not apply. (2)(3)	13	9,118
B673	129	New product MUP/EP; unregistered source of active ingredient(s); citation of Technical Grade Active Ingredient (TGAI) data previously reviewed and accepted by the Agency. Requires an Agency determination that the cited data supports the new product. (2)(3)	10	5,107
B674	130	New product MUP; Repack of identical registered end-use product as a manufacturing-use product; same registered uses only. (2)(3)	4	1,278
B675	131	New Product MUP; registered source of active ingredient; submission of completely new generic data package; registered uses only. (2)(3)	10	9,118

B676	132	New product; more than one active ingredient where one active ingredient is an unregistered source; product chemistry data must be submitted; requires: 1) submission of product specific data, and 2) citation of previously reviewed and accepted data; or 3) submission or citation of data generated at government expense; or 4) submission or citation of a scientifically-sound rationale based on publicly available literature or other relevant information that addresses the data requirement; or 5) submission of a request for a data requirement to be waived supported by a scientifically-sound rationale explaining why the data requirement does not apply. (2)(3)	13	9,118
B677	133	New end-use non-food animal product with submission of two or more target animal safety studies; includes data and/or waivers of data for only: • product chemistry and/or • acute toxicity and/or • public health pest efficacy and/or • animal safety studies and/or • child resistant packaging. (2)(3)	10	8,820

(1) A decision review time that would otherwise end on a Saturday, Sunday, or federal holiday, will be extended to end on the next business day.

(2) An application for a new end-use product using a source of active ingredient that (a) is not yet registered but (b) has an application pending with the Agency for review, will be considered an application for a new product with an unregistered source of active ingredient.

(3) Where the action involves approval of a new or amended label, on or before the end date of the decision review time, the Agency shall provide to the applicant a draft accepted label, including any changes made by the Agency that differ from the applicant-submitted label and relevant supporting data reviewed by the Agency. The applicant will notify the Agency that the applicant either (a) agrees to all of the terms associated with the draft accepted label as amended by the Agency and requests that it be issued as the accepted final Agency-stamped label; or (b) does not agree to one or more of the terms of the draft accepted label as amended by the Agency and requests additional time to resolve the difference(s); or (c) withdraws the application without prejudice for subsequent resubmission, but forfeits the associated registration service fee. For cases described in (b), the applicant shall have up to 30 calendar days to reach agreement with the Agency on the final terms of the Agency-accepted label. If the applicant agrees to all of the terms of the accepted label as in (a), including upon resolution of differences in (b), the Agency shall provide an accepted final Agency-stamped label to the registrant within 2 business days following the registrant's written or electronic confirmation of agreement to the Agency.

EPA No.	New CR No.	Action	Decision Review Time (Months)(1)	Registration Service Fee ($)
\multicolumn{5}{c}{TABLE 14. — BIOPESTICIDES DIVISION — AMENDMENTS}				
B621	134	Amendment; Experimental Use Permit; no change to an established temporary tolerance or tolerance exemption. (3)	7	5,107
B622	135	Amendment; Experimental Use Permit; petition to amend an established or temporary tolerance or tolerance exemption. (3)	11	12,764
B641	136	Amendment of an established tolerance or tolerance exemption.	13	12,764
B680	137	Amendment; registered sources of active ingredient(s); no new use(s); no changes to an established tolerance or tolerance exemption. Requires data submission. (2)(3)	5	5,107
B681	138	Amendment; unregistered source of active ingredient(s). Requires data submission. (2)(3)	7	6,079
B683	139	Label amendment; requires review/update of previous risk assessment(s) without data submission (e.g., labeling changes to REI, PPE, PHI). (2)(3)	6	5,107
B684	140	Amending non-food animal product that includes submission of target animal safety data; previously registered. (2)(3)	8	8,820
B685	141 (new)	Amendment; add a new biochemical unregistered source of active ingredient or a new microbial production site. Requires submission of analysis of samples data and source/production site-specific manufacturing process description. (3)	5	5,107

(1) A decision review time that would otherwise end on a Saturday, Sunday, or federal holiday, will be extended to end on the next business day.

(2) (a) EPA-initiated amendments shall not be charged registration service fees. (b) Registrant-initiated fast-track amendments are to be completed within the timelines specified in FIFRA Section 3(c)(3)(B) and are not subject to registration service fees. (c) Registrant-initiated fast-track amendments handled by the Antimicrobials Division are to be completed within the timelines specified in FIFRA Section 3(h) and are not subject to registration service fees. (d) Registrant initiated amendments submitted by notification under PR Notices, such as PR Notice 98-10, continue under PR Notice timelines and are not subject to registration service fees. (e) Submissions with data and requiring data review are subject to registration service fees.

(3) Where the action involves approval of a new or amended label, on or before the end date of the decision review time, the Agency shall provide to the applicant a draft accepted label, including any changes made by the Agency that differ from the applicant-submitted label and relevant supporting data reviewed by the Agency. The applicant will notify the Agency that the applicant either (a) agrees to all of the terms associated with the draft accepted label as amended by the Agency and requests that it be issued as the accepted final Agency-stamped label; or (b) does not agree to one or more of the terms of the draft accepted label as amended by the Agency and requests additional time to resolve the difference(s); or (c) withdraws the application without prejudice for subsequent resubmission, but forfeits the associated registration service fee. For cases described in (b), the applicant shall have up to 30 calendar days to reach agreement with the Agency on the final terms of the Agency-accepted label. If the applicant agrees to all of the terms of the accepted label as in (a), including upon resolution of differences in (b), the Agency shall provide an accepted final Agency-stamped label to the registrant within 2 business days following the registrant's written or electronic confirmation of agreement to the Agency.

		TABLE 15. — BIOPESTICIDES DIVISION — SCLP		
EPA No.	New CR No.	Action	Decision Review Time (Months)(1)	Registration Service Fee ($)
B690	142	New active ingredient; food or non-food use. (2)(6)	7	2,554
B700	143	Experimental Use Permit application; new active ingredient or new use. (6)	7	1,278
B701	144	Extend or amend Experimental Use Permit. (6)	4	1,278
B710	145	New product; registered source of active ingredient(s); identical or substantially similar in composition and use to a registered product; no change in an established tolerance or tolerance exemption. No data review, or only product chemistry data; cite-all data citation, or selective data citation where applicant owns all required data or authorization from data owner is demonstrated. Category includes 100% re-package of registered end-use or manufacturing-use product that requires no data submission or data matrix. (3)(6)	4	1,278
B720	146	New product; registered source of active ingredient(s); requires: 1) submission of product specific data; or 2) citation of previously reviewed and accepted data; or 3) submission or citation of data generated at government expense; or 4) submission or citation of a scientifically-sound rationale based on publicly available literature or other relevant information that addresses the data requirement; or 5) submission of a request for a data requirement to be waived supported by a scientifically-sound rationale explaining why the data requirement does not apply. (3)(6)	5	1,278
B721	147	New product; unregistered source of active ingredient. (3)(6)	7	2,676
B722	148	New use and/or amendment; petition to establish a tolerance or tolerance exemption. (4)(5)(6)	7	2,477
B730	149	Label amendment requiring data submission. (4)(6)	5	1,278

(1) A decision review time that would otherwise end on a Saturday, Sunday, or federal holiday, will be extended to end on the next business day.

(2) All requests for new uses (food and/or nonfood) contained in any application for a new active ingredient or a first food use are covered by the base fee for that new active ingredient or first food use application and retain the same decision time review period as the new active ingredient or first food use application. The application must be received by the agency in one package. The base fee for the category covers a maximum of five new products. Each application for an additional new product registration and new inert approval that is submitted in the new active ingredient application package or first food use application package is subject to the registration service fee for a new product or a new inert approval. All such associated applications that are submitted together will be subject to the new active ingredient or first food use decision review time. In the case of a new active ingredient application, until that new active ingredient is approved, any subsequent application for another new product containing the same active ingredient or an amendment to the proposed labeling will be deemed a new active ingredient application, subject to the registration service fee and decision review time for a new active ingredient. In the case of a first food use application, until that first food use is approved, any subsequent application for an additional new food use or uses will be subject to the registration service fee and

decision review time for a first food use. Any information that (a) was neither requested nor required by the Agency, and (b) is submitted by the applicant at the applicant's initiative to support the application after completion of the technical deficiency screening, and (c) is not itself a covered registration application, must be assessed 25% of the full registration service fee for the new active ingredient or first food use application.

(3) An application for a new end-use product using a source of active ingredient that (a) is not yet registered but (b) has an application pending with the Agency for review, will be considered an application for a new product with an unregistered source of active ingredient.

(4) (a) EPA-initiated amendments shall not be charged registration service fees. (b) Registrant-initiated fast-track amendments are to be completed within the timelines specified in FIFRA Section 3(c)(3)(B) and are not subject to registration service fees. (c) Registrant-initiated fast-track amendments handled by the Antimicrobials Division are to be completed within the timelines specified in FIFRA Section 3(h) and are not subject to registration service fees. (d) Registrant initiated amendments submitted by notification under PR Notices, such as PR Notice 98-10, continue under PR Notice timelines and are not subject to registration service fees. (e) Submissions with data and requiring data review are subject to registration service fees.

(5) Amendment applications to add the new use(s) to registered product labels are covered by the base fee for the new use(s). All items in the covered application must be submitted together in one package. Each application for an additional new product registration and new inert approval(s) that is submitted in the new use application package is subject to the registration service fee for a new product or a new inert approval. However, if a new use application only proposes to register the new use for a new product and there are no amendments in the application, then review of one new product application is covered by the new use fee. All such associated applications that are submitted together will be subject to the new use decision review time. Any application for a new product or an amendment to the proposed labeling (a) submitted subsequent to submission of the new use application and (b) prior to conclusion of its decision review time and (c) containing the same new uses, will be deemed a separate new-use application, subject to a separate registration service fee and new decision review time for a new use. If the new-use application includes non-food (indoor and/or outdoor), and food (outdoor and/or indoor) uses, the appropriate fee is due for each type of new use and the longest decision review time applies to all of the new uses requested in the application. Any information that (a) was neither requested nor required by the Agency, and (b) is submitted by the applicant at the applicant's initiative to support the application after completion of the technical deficiency screen, and (c) is not itself a covered registration application, must be assessed 25% of the full registration service fee for the new use application.

(6) Where the action involves approval of a new or amended label, on or before the end date of the decision review time, the Agency shall provide to the applicant a draft accepted label, including any changes made by the Agency that differ from the applicant-submitted label and relevant supporting data reviewed by the Agency. The applicant will notify the Agency that the applicant either (a) agrees to all of the terms associated with the draft accepted label as amended by the Agency and requests that it be issued as the accepted final Agency-stamped label; or (b) does not agree to one or more of the terms of the draft accepted label as amended by the Agency and requests additional time to resolve the difference(s); or (c) withdraws the application without prejudice for subsequent resubmission, but forfeits the associated registration service fee. For cases described in (b), the applicant shall have up to 30 calendar days to reach agreement with the Agency on the final terms of the Agency-accepted label. If the applicant agrees to all of the terms of the accepted label as in (a), including upon resolution of differences in (b), the Agency shall provide an accepted final Agency-stamped label to the registrant within 2 business days following the registrant's written or electronic confirmation of agreement to the Agency.

TABLE 16. — BIOPESTICIDES DIVISION — OTHER ACTIONS				
EPA No.	New CR No.	Action	Decision Review Time (Months)(1)	Registration Service Fee ($)
B614	150	Pre-application; Conditional Ruling on rationales for addressing a data requirement in lieu of data; applicant-initiated; applies to one rationale at a time.	3	2,530
B615	151	Rebuttal of agency reviewed protocol, applicant initiated.	3	2,530
B682	152	Protocol review; applicant initiated; excludes time for HSRB review.	3	2,432

(1) A decision review time that would otherwise end on a Saturday, Sunday, or federal holiday, will be extended to end on the next business day.

EPA No.	New CR No.	Action	Decision Review Time (Months)(1)	Registration Service Fee ($)
TABLE 17. — BIOPESTICIDES DIVISION — PIP				
B740	153	Experimental Use Permit application; no petition for tolerance/tolerance exemption. Includes:	6	95,724
		1. non-food/feed use(s) for a new (2) or registered (3) PIP (12);		
		2. food/feed use(s) for a new or registered PIP with crop destruct (12);		
		3. food/feed use(s) for a new or registered PIP in which an established tolerance/ tolerance exemption exists for the intended use(s). (4)(12)		
B741	154 (new)	Experimental Use Permit application; no petition for tolerance/tolerance exemption. Includes:	12	159,538
		1. non-food/feed use(s) for a new (2) or registered (3) PIP;		
		2. food/feed use(s) for a new or registered PIP with crop destruct;		
		3. food/feed use(s) for a new or registered PIP in which an established tolerance/ tolerance exemption exists for the intended use(s);		
		SAP Review. (12)		
B750	155	Experimental Use Permit application; with a petition to establish a temporary or permanent tolerance/tolerance exemption for the active ingredient. Includes new food/feed use for a registered (3) PIP. (4)(12)	9	127,630
B770	156	Experimental Use Permit application; new (2) PIP; with petition to establish a temporary tolerance/tolerance exemption for the active ingredient; credit 75% of B771 fee toward registration application for a new active ingredient that follows; SAP review. (5)(12)	15	191,444
B771	157	Experimental Use Permit application; new (2) PIP; with petition to establish a temporary tolerance/tolerance exemption for the active ingredient; credit 75% of B771 fee toward registration application for a new active ingredient that follows. (12)	10	127,630
B772	158	Application to amend or extend an Experimental Use Permit; no petition since the established tolerance/tolerance exemption for the active ingredient is unaffected. (12)	3	12,764
B773	159	Application to amend or extend an Experimental Use Permit; with petition to extend a temporary tolerance/tolerance exemption for the active ingredient. (12)	5	31,910
B780	160	Registration application; new (2) PIP; non-food/feed. (12)	12	159,537

B790	161	Registration application; new (2) PIP; non-food/feed; SAP review. (5)(12)	18	223,351
B800	162	Registration application; new (2) PIP; with petition to establish permanent tolerance/tolerance exemption for the active ingredient based on an existing temporary tolerance/tolerance exemption. (12)	13	172,300
B810	163	Registration application; new (2) PIP; with petition to establish permanent tolerance/tolerance exemption for the active ingredient based on an existing temporary tolerance/tolerance exemption. SAP review. (5)(12)	19	236,114
B820	164	Registration application; new (2) PIP; with petition to establish or amend a permanent tolerance/tolerance exemption of an active ingredient. (12)	**15**	204,208
B840	165	Registration application; new (2) PIP; with petition to establish or amend a permanent tolerance/tolerance exemption of an active ingredient. SAP review. (5)(12)	21	268,022
B851	166	Registration application; new event of a previously registered PIP active ingredient(s); no petition since permanent tolerance/tolerance exemption is already established for the active ingredient(s). (12)	9	127,630
B870	167	Registration application; registered (3) PIP; new product; new use; no petition since a permanent tolerance/tolerance exemption is already established for the active ingredient(s). (4) (12)	9	38,290
B880	168	Registration application; registered (3) PIP; new product or new terms of registration; additional data submitted; no petition since a permanent tolerance/tolerance exemption is already established for the active ingredient(s). (6) (7) (12)	9	31,910
B881	169	Registration application; registered (3) PIP; new product or new terms of registration; additional data submitted; no petition since a permanent tolerance/tolerance exemption is already established for the active ingredient(s). SAP review. (5)(6)(7)(12)	**15**	95,724
B882	170 (new)	Registration application; new (2) PIP, seed increase with negotiated acreage cap and time-limited registration; with petition to establish a permanent tolerance/tolerance exemption for the active ingredient based on an existing temporary tolerance/tolerance exemption; SAP Review. (8)(12)	**15**	191,444
B883	171	Registration application; new (2) PIP, seed increase with negotiated acreage cap and time-limited registration; with petition to establish a permanent tolerance/tolerance exemption for the active ingredient based on an existing temporary tolerance/tolerance exemption. (8) (12)	9	127,630

B884	172	Registration application; new (2) PIP, seed increase with negotiated acreage cap and time-limited registration; with petition to establish a permanent tolerance/tolerance exemption for the active ingredient. (8)(12)	12	159,537
B885	173	Registration application; registered (3) PIP, seed increase; breeding stack of previously approved PIPs, same crop; no petition since a permanent tolerance/tolerance exemption is already established for the active ingredient(s). (9)(12)	6	31,910
B886	174 (new)	Registration application; new (2) PIP, seed increase with negotiated acreage cap and time-limited registration; with petition to establish a permanent tolerance/tolerance exemption for the active ingredient. SAP Review. (8) (12)	18	223,351
B890	175	Application to amend a seed increase registration; converts registration to commercial registration; no petition since permanent tolerance/tolerance exemption is already established for the active ingredient(s). (12)	9	63,816
B891	176	Application to amend a seed increase registration; converts registration to a commercial registration; no petition since a permanent tolerance/tolerance exemption already established for the active ingredient(s); SAP review. (5)(12)	**15**	127,630
B900	177	Application to amend a registration, including actions such as extending an expiration date, modifying an IRM plan, or adding an insect to be controlled. (10)(11)(12)	6	12,764
B901	178	Application to amend a registration, including actions such as extending an expiration date, modifying an IRM plan, or adding an insect to be controlled. SAP review. (10) (11) (12)	12	76,578
B902	179	PIP Protocol review.	3	6,383
B903	180	Inert ingredient tolerance exemption; e.g., a marker such as NPT II; reviewed in BPPD.	6	63,816
B904	181	Import tolerance or tolerance exemption; processed commodities/food only (inert or active ingredient).	9	127,630
B905	182 (new)	SAP Review.	6	63,816
B906	183 (new)	Petition to establish a temporary tolerance/tolerance exemption for one or more active ingredients.	3	31,907
B907	184 (new)	Petition to establish a temporary tolerance/tolerance exemption for one or more active ingredients based on an existing temporary tolerance/tolerance exemption.	3	12,764
B908	185 (new)	Petition to establish a temporary tolerance/tolerance exemption for one or more active ingredients or inert ingredients.	3	44,671

(1) A decision review time that would otherwise end on a Saturday, Sunday, or federal holiday, will be extended to end on the next business day.

(2) New PIP = a PIP with an active ingredient that has not been registered.

(3) Registered PIP = a PIP with an active ingredient that is currently registered.

(4) Transfer registered PIP through conventional breeding for new food/ feed use, such as from field corn to sweet corn.

(5) The scientific data involved in this category are complex. EPA often seeks technical advice from the Scientific Advisory Panel on risks that pesticides pose to wildlife, farm workers, pesticide applicators, non-target species, as well as insect resistance, and novel scientific issues surrounding new technologies. The scientists of the SAP neither make nor recommend policy decisions. They provide advice on the science used to make these decisions. Their advice is invaluable to the EPA as it strives to protect humans and the environment from risks posed by pesticides. Due to the time it takes to schedule and prepare for meetings with the SAP, additional time and costs are needed.

(6) Registered PIPs stacked through conventional breeding.

(7) Deployment of a registered PIP with a different IRM plan (e.g., seed blend).

(8) The negotiated acreage cap will depend upon EPA's determination of the potential environmental exposure, risk(s) to non-target organisms, and the risk of targeted pest developing resistance to the pesticidal substance. The uncertainty of these risks may reduce the allowable acreage, based upon the quantity and type of non-target organism data submitted and the lack of insect resistance management data, which is usually not required for seed-increase registrations. Registrants are encouraged to consult with EPA prior to submission of a registration application in this category.

(9) Application can be submitted prior to or concurrently with an application for commercial registration.

(10) For example, IRM plan modifications that are applicant-initiated.

(11) EPA-initiated amendments shall not be charged fees.

(12) Where the action involves approval of a new or amended label, on or before the end date of the decision review time, the Agency shall provide to the applicant a draft accepted label, including any changes made by the Agency that differ from the applicant-submitted label and relevant supporting data reviewed by the Agency. The applicant will notify the Agency that the applicant either (a) agrees to all of the terms associated with the draft accepted label as amended by the Agency and requests that it be issued as the accepted final Agency-stamped label; or (b) does not agree to one or more of the terms of the draft accepted label as amended by the Agency and requests additional time to resolve the difference(s); or (c) withdraws the application without prejudice for subsequent resubmission, but forfeits the associated registration service fee. For cases described in (b), the applicant shall have up to 30 calendar days to reach agreement with the Agency on the final terms of the Agency-accepted label. If the applicant agrees to all of the terms of the accepted label as in (a), including upon resolution of differences in (b), the Agency shall provide an accepted final Agency-stamped label to the registrant within 2 business days following the registrant's written or electronic confirmation of agreement to the Agency.

TABLE 18. — INERT INGREDIENTS				
EPA No.	New CR No.	Action	Decision Review Time (Months)(1)	Registration Service Fee ($)
I001	186	Approval of new food use inert ingredient. (2)(3)	13	27,000
I002	187	Amend currently approved inert ingredient tolerance or exemption from tolerance; new data. (2)	11	7,500
I003	188	Amend currently approved inert ingredient tolerance or exemption from tolerance; no new data. (2)	9	3,308
I004	189	Approval of new non-food use inert ingredient. (2)	6	11,025
I005	190	Amend currently approved non-food use inert ingredient with new use pattern; new data. (2)	6	5,513
I006	191	Amend currently approved non-food use inert ingredient with new use pattern; no new data. (2)	3	3,308
I007	192	Approval of substantially similar non-food use inert ingredients when original inert is compositionally similar with similar use pattern. (2)	4	1,654
I008	193	Approval of new or amended polymer inert ingredient, food use. (2)	5	3,749

I009	194	Approval of new or amended polymer inert ingredient, non-food use. (2)	4	3,087
I010	195	Petition to amend a single tolerance exemption descriptor, or single non-food use descriptor, to add ≤ 10 CASRNs; no new data. (2)	6	1,654
I011	196 (new)	Approval of new food use safener with tolerance or exemption from tolerance. (2)(8)	24	597,683
I012	197 (new)	Approval of new non-food use safener. (2)(8)	21	415,241
I013	198 (new)	Approval of additional food use for previously approved safener with tolerance or exemption from tolerance. (2)	**15**	62,975
I014	199 (new)	Approval of additional non-food use for previously approved safener. (2)	**15**	25,168
I015	200 (new)	Approval of new generic data for previously approved food use safener. (2)	24	269,728
I016	201 (new)	Approval of amendment(s) to tolerance and label for previously approved safener. (2)	13	55,776

(1) A decision review time that would otherwise end on a Saturday, Sunday, or federal holiday, will be extended to end on the next business day.

(2) If another covered application is submitted that depends upon an application to approve an inert ingredient, each application will be subject to its respective registration service fee. The decision review time line for both submissions will be the longest of the associated applications. If the application covers multiple ingredients grouped by EPA into one chemical class, a single registration service fee will be assessed for approval of those ingredients.

(3) If EPA data rules are amended to newly require clearance under section 408 of the FFDCA for an ingredient of an antimicrobial product where such ingredient was not previously subject to such a clearance, then review of the data for such clearance of such product is not subject to a registration service fee for the tolerance action for two years from the effective date of the rule.

(4) Any other covered application that is associated with and dependent on the HSRB review will be subject to its separate registration service fee. The decision review times for the associated actions run concurrently, but will end at the date of the latest review time.

(5) Any other covered application that is associated with and dependent on the SAP review will be subject to its separate registration service fee. The decision review time for the associated action will be extended by the decision review time for the SAP review.

(6) An application for a new end-use product using a source of active ingredient that (a) is not yet registered but (b) has an application pending with the Agency for review, will be considered an application for a new product with an unregistered source of active ingredient.

(7) Where the action involves approval of a new or amended label, on or before the end date of the decision review time, the Agency shall provide to the applicant a draft accepted label, including any changes made by the Agency that differ from the applicant-submitted label and relevant supporting data reviewed by the Agency. The applicant will notify the Agency that the applicant either (a) agrees to all of the terms associated with the draft accepted label as amended by the Agency and requests that it be issued as the accepted final Agency-stamped label; or (b) does not agree to one or more of the terms of the draft accepted label as amended by the Agency and requests additional time to resolve the difference(s); or (c) withdraws the application without prejudice for subsequent resubmission, but forfeits the associated registration service fee. For cases described in (b), the applicant shall have up to 30 calendar days to reach agreement with the Agency on the final terms of the Agency-accepted label. If the applicant agrees to all of the terms of the accepted label as in (a), including upon resolution of differences in (b), the Agency shall provide an accepted final Agency-stamped label to the registrant within 2 business days following the registrant's written or electronic confirmation of agreement to the Agency.

(8) If a new safener is submitted in the same package as a new active ingredient, and that new active ingredient is determined to be reduced risk, then the safener would get the same reduced timeframe as the new active ingredient.

TABLE 19. — EXTERNAL REVIEW AND MISCELLANEOUS ACTIONS

EPA No.	New CR No.	Action	Decision Review Time (Months)(1)	Registration Service Fee ($)
M001	202	Study protocol requiring Human Studies Review Board review as defined in 40 CFR Part 26 in support of an active ingredient. (4)	9	7,938
M002	203	Completed study requiring Human Studies Review Board review as defined in 40 CFR Part 26 in support of an active ingredient. (4)	9	7,938
M003	204	External technical peer review of new active ingredient, product, or amendment (e.g., consultation with FIFRA Scientific Advisory Panel) for an action with a decision timeframe of less than 12 months. Applicant initiated request based on a requirement of the Administrator, as defined by FIFRA § 25(d), in support of a novel active ingredient, or unique use pattern or application technology. Excludes PIP active ingredients. (5)	12	63,945
M004	205	External technical peer review of new active ingredient, product, or amendment (e.g., consultation with FIFRA Scientific Advisory Panel) for an action with a decision timeframe of greater than 12 months. Applicant initiated request based on a requirement of the Administrator, as defined by FIFRA § 25(d), in support of a novel active ingredient, or unique use pattern or application technology. Excludes PIP active ingredients. (5)	18	63,945
M005	206	New Product: Combination, Contains a combination of active ingredients from a registered and/or unregistered source; conventional, antimicrobial and/or biopesticide. Requires coordination with other regulatory divisions to conduct review of data, label and/or verify the validity of existing data as cited. Only existing uses for each active ingredient in the combination product. (6)(7)	9	22,050
M006	207	Request for up to 5 letters of certification (Gold Seal) for one actively registered product (excludes distributor products). (8)	1	277
M007	208	Request to extend Exclusive Use of data as provided by FIFRA Section 3(c)(1)(F)(ii).	12	5,513
M008	209	Request to grant Exclusive Use of data as provided by FIFRA Section 3(c)(1)(F)(vi) for a minor use, when a FIFRA Section 2(ll)(2) determination is required.	**15**	1,654
M009	210 (new)	Non-FIFRA Regulated Determination: Applicant initiated, per product.	4	2,363
M010	211 (new)	Conditional ruling on pre-application, product substantial similarity.	4	2,363
M011	212 (new)	Label amendment to add the DfE logo; requires data review; no other label changes. (9)	4	3,648

(1) A decision review time that would otherwise end on a Saturday, Sunday, or federal holiday, will be extended to end on the next business day.

(2) If another covered application is submitted that depends upon an application to approve an inert ingredient, each

application will be subject to its respective registration service fee. The decision review time line for both submissions will be the longest of the associated applications. If the application covers multiple ingredients grouped by EPA into one chemical class, a single registration service fee will be assessed for approval of those ingredients.

(3) If EPA data rules are amended to newly require clearance under section 408 of the FFDCA for an ingredient of an antimicrobial product where such ingredient was not previously subject to such a clearance, then review of the data for such clearance of such product is not subject to a registration service fee for the tolerance action for two years from the effective date of the rule.

(4) Any other covered application that is associated with and dependent on the HSRB review will be subject to its separate registration service fee. The decision review times for the associated actions run concurrently, but will end at the date of the latest review time.

(5) Any other covered application that is associated with and dependent on the SAP review will be subject to its separate registration service fee. The decision review time for the associated action will be extended by the decision review time for the SAP review.

(6) An application for a new end-use product using a source of active ingredient that (a) is not yet registered but (b) has an application pending with the Agency for review, will be considered an application for a new product with an unregistered source of active ingredient.

(7) Where the action involves approval of a new or amended label, on or before the end date of the decision review time, the Agency shall provide to the applicant a draft accepted label, including any changes made by the Agency that differ from the applicant-submitted label and relevant supporting data reviewed by the Agency. The applicant will notify the Agency that the applicant either (a) agrees to all of the terms associated with the draft accepted label as amended by the Agency and requests that it be issued as the accepted final Agency-stamped label; or (b) does not agree to one or more of the terms of the draft accepted label as amended by the Agency and requests additional time to resolve the difference(s); or (c) withdraws the application without prejudice for subsequent resubmission, but forfeits the associated registration service fee. For cases described in (b), the applicant shall have up to 30 calendar days to reach agreement with the Agency on the final terms of the Agency-accepted label. If the applicant agrees to all of the terms of the accepted label as in (a), including upon resolution of differences in (b), the Agency shall provide an accepted final Agency-stamped label to the registrant within 2 business days following the registrant's written or electronic confirmation of agreement to the Agency.

(8) Due to low fee and short time frame this category is not eligible for small business waivers. Gold seal applies to one registered product.

(9) This category includes amendments the sole purpose of which is to add DfE (or equivalent terms that do not use "safe" or derivatives of "safe") logos to a label. DfE is a voluntary program. A label bearing a DfE logo is not considered an Agency endorsement because the ingredients in the qualifying product must meet objective, scientific criteria established and widely publicized by EPA.

(4) Pending pesticide registration applications

(A) In general

An applicant that submitted a registration application to the Administrator before the effective date of the Pesticide Registration Improvement Act of 2003, but that is not required to pay a registration service fee under paragraph (2)(B), may, on a voluntary basis, pay a registration service fee in accordance with paragraph (2)(B).

(B) Voluntary fee

The Administrator may not compel payment of a registration service fee for an application described in subparagraph (A).

(C) Documentation

An application for which a voluntary registration service fee is paid under this paragraph shall be submitted with documentation certifying —

(i) payment of the registration service fee; or

(ii) a request for a waiver from or reduction of the registration service fee.

(5) Resubmission of covered applications

If a covered application is submitted by a person that paid the fee for the application under paragraph (2), is determined by the Administrator to be complete, and is not approved or is withdrawn (without a waiver or refund), the submission of the same covered application by the same person (or a licensee, assignee, or successor of the person) shall not be subject to a fee under paragraph (2).

(6) Fee adjustment

(A) In general

Effective for a covered application received during the period beginning on October 1, 2019, and ending on September 30, 2021, the Administrator shall increase by 5 percent the registration service fee payable for the application under paragraph (3).

(B) Additional adjustment

Effective for a covered application received on or after October 1, 2021, the Administrator shall increase by an additional 5 percent the registration service fee in effect as of September 30, 2021.

(C) Publication

The Administrator shall publish in the Federal Register the service fee schedules revised pursuant to this paragraph.

(7) Waivers and reductions

(A) In general

An applicant for a covered application may request the Administrator to waive or reduce the amount of a registration service fee payable under this section under the circumstances described in subparagraphs (D) through (G), except that no waiver or fee reduction shall be provided in connection with a request for a letter of certification (commonly referred to as a Gold Seal letter).

(B) Documentation

(i) In general

A request for a waiver from or reduction of the registration service fee shall be accompanied by appropriate documentation demonstrating the basis for the waiver or reduction.

(ii) Certification

The applicant shall provide to the Administrator a written certification, signed by a responsible officer, that the documentation submitted to support the waiver or reduction request is accurate.

(iii) Inaccurate documentation

An application shall be subject to the applicable registration service fee payable under paragraph (3) if, at any time, the Administrator determines that —

(I) the documentation supporting the waiver or reduction request is not accurate; or

(II) based on the documentation or any other information, the waiver or reduction should not have been granted or should not be granted.

(C) Determination to grant or deny request

As soon as practicable, but not later than 60 days, after the date on which the Administrator receives a request for a waiver or reduction of a registration service fee under this paragraph, the Administrator shall —

(i) determine whether to grant or deny the request; and

(ii) notify the applicant of the determination.

(D) Minor uses

(i) In general

The Administrator may exempt from, or waive a portion of, the registration service fee for an application for minor uses for a pesticide.

(ii) Supporting documentation

An applicant requesting a waiver or exemption under this subparagraph shall provide supporting documentation that demonstrates, to the satisfaction of the Administrator, that anticipated revenues from the uses that are the subject of the application would be insufficient to justify imposition of the full application fee.

(E) IR-4 exemption

The Administrator shall exempt an application from the registration service fee if the Administrator determines that —

(i) the application is solely associated with a tolerance petition submitted in connection with the Inter-Regional Project Number 4 (IR-4) as described in section 2 of Public Law 89-106 (7 U.S.C. 450i(e));1 and

(ii) the exemption is in the public interest.

(F) Small businesses

(i) In general

The Administrator shall waive 50 percent of the registration service fees payable by an entity for a covered application under this section if the entity is a small business (as defined in section 136a-1(i)(1)(E)(ii) of this title) at the time of application.

(ii) Waiver of fees

The Administrator shall waive 75 percent of the registration service fees payable by an entity under this section if the entity —

(I) is a small business (as defined in section 136a-1(i)(1)(E)(ii) of this title) at the time of application; and

(II) has average annual global gross revenues described in section 136a-1(i)(1)(E)(ii)(I)(bb) of this title that does not exceed $10,000,000, at the time of application.

(iii) Formation for waiver

The Administrator shall not grant a waiver under this subparagraph if the Administrator determines that the entity submitting the application has been formed or manipulated primarily for the purpose of qualifying for the waiver.

(iv) Documentation

An entity requesting a waiver under this subparagraph shall provide to the Administrator —

(I) documentation demonstrating that the entity is a small business (as defined in section 136a-1(i)(1)(E)(ii) of this title) at the time of application; and

(II) if the entity is requesting a waiver of 75 percent of the applicable registration service fees payable under this section, documentation demonstrating that the entity has an average annual global gross revenue described in section 136a-1(i)(1)(E)(ii)

(I)(bb) of this title that does not exceed $10,000,000, at the time of application.

(G) Federal and State agency exemptions

An agency of the Federal Government or a State government shall be exempt from covered registration service fees under this section.

(8) Refunds

(A) Early withdrawals

If, during the first 60 days after the beginning of the applicable decision time review period under subsection (f)(3), a covered application is withdrawn by the applicant, the Administrator shall refund all but 25 percent.2 of the total registration service fee payable under paragraph (3) for the application.

(B) Withdrawals after the first 60 days of decision review time period

(i) In general

If a covered application is withdrawn after the first 60 days of the applicable decision time review period, the Administrator shall determine what portion, if any, of the total registration service fee payable under paragraph (3) for the application may be refunded based on the proportion of the work completed at the time of withdrawal.

(ii) Timing

The Administrator shall —

(I) make the determination described in clause (i) not later than 90 days after the date the application is withdrawn; and

(II) provide any refund as soon as practicable after the determination.

(C) Discretionary refunds

(i) In general

In the case of a covered application that has been filed with the Administrator and has not been withdrawn by the applicant, but for which the Administrator has not yet made a final determination, the Administrator may refund a portion of a covered registration service fee if the Administrator determines that the refund is justified.

(ii) Basis

The Administrator may provide a refund for an application under this subparagraph —

(I) on the basis that, in reviewing the application, the Administrator has considered data submitted in support of another covered application;

(II) on the basis that the Administrator completed portions of the review of the application before the effective date of this section; or

(III) on the basis that the Administrator rejected the application under subsection (f)(4)(B).

(D) Credited fees

In determining whether to grant a refund under this paragraph, the Administrator shall take into account any portion of the registration service fees credited under paragraph (2) or (4).

(c) Pesticide Registration Fund

(1) Establishment

There is established in the Treasury of the United States a Pesticide Registration Fund to be used in carrying out this section (referred to in this section as the "Fund"), consisting of —

(A) such amounts as are deposited in the Fund under paragraph (2);

(B) any interest earned on investment of amounts in the Fund under paragraph (5); and

(C) any proceeds from the sale or redemption of investments held in the Fund.

(2) Deposits in Fund

Subject to paragraph (4), the Administrator shall deposit fees collected under this section in the Fund.

(3) Expenditures from Fund

(A) In general

Subject to subparagraphs (B) and (C) and paragraph (4), the Administrator may make expenditures from the Fund —

(i) to cover the costs associated with the review and decisionmaking pertaining to all applications for which registration service fees have been paid under this section; and

(ii) to otherwise carry out this section.

(B) Worker protection, partnership grants, and pesticide safety education

(i) In general

For each of fiscal years 2013 through 2023, the Administrator shall use approximately 1/17 of the amount in the Fund (but not less than $1,000,000) to enhance scientific and regulatory activities relating to worker protection, with an emphasis on field-worker populations in the United States.

(ii) Partnership grants

Of the amounts in the Fund, the Administrator shall use for partnership grants, for each of fiscal years 2013 through 2023, $500,000.

(iii) Pesticide safety education program

Of the amounts in the Fund, the Administrator shall use $500,000 for each of fiscal years 2013 through 2023 to carry out the pesticide safety education program.

(4) Collections and appropriations Acts

The fees authorized by this section and amounts deposited in the Fund —

(A) shall be collected and made available for obligation only to the extent provided in advance in appropriations Acts; and

(B) shall be available without fiscal year limitation.

(5) Unused funds

(A) In general

Amounts in the Fund not currently needed to carry out this section shall be —

(i) maintained readily available or on deposit;

(ii) invested in obligations of the United States or guaranteed by the United States; or

(iii) invested in obligations, participations, or other instruments that are lawful investments for fiduciary, trust, or public funds.

(B) Use of investment income

After consultation with the Secretary of the Treasury, the Administrator may use income from investments described in clauses (ii) and (iii) of subparagraph (A) to carry out this section.

(d) Assessment of fees

(1) Definition of covered functions

In this subsection, the term "covered functions" means functions of the Office of Pesticide Programs of the Environmental Protection Agency, as identified in key programs and projects of the final operating plan for the Environmental Protection Agency submitted as part of the budget process for fiscal year 2002, regardless of any subsequent transfer of 1 or more of the functions to another office or agency or the subsequent transfer of a new function to the Office of Pesticide Programs.

(2) Minimum amount of appropriations

Registration service fees may not be assessed for a fiscal year under this section unless the amount of appropriations for salaries, contracts, and expenses for the functions (as in existence in fiscal year 2012) of the Office of Pesticide Programs of the Environmental Protection Agency for the fiscal year (excluding the amount of any fees appropriated for the fiscal year) are equal to or greater than the amount of appropriations for covered functions for fiscal year 2012 (excluding the amount of any fees appropriated for the fiscal year).

(3) Use of fees

Registration service fees authorized by this section shall be available, in the aggregate, only to defray increases in the costs associated with the review and decisionmaking for the review of pesticide registration applications and associated tolerances (including increases in the number of full-time equivalent positions in the Environmental Protection Agency engaged in those activities) over the costs for fiscal year 2002, excluding costs paid from fees appropriated for the fiscal year.

(4) Subsequent authority

If the Administrator does not assess registration service fees under subsection (b) during any portion of a fiscal year as the result of paragraph (2) and is subsequently permitted to assess the fees under subsection (b) during the fiscal year, the Administrator shall assess and collect the fees, without any modification in rate, at any time during the fiscal year, notwithstanding any provisions of subsection (b) relating to the date fees are to be paid.

(5) Redesignated (4)

(e) Reforms to reduce decision time review periods

To the maximum extent practicable consistent with the degrees of risk presented by pesticides and the type of review appropriate to evaluate risks, the Administrator shall identify and evaluate reforms to the pesticide registration process under this subchapter with the goal of reducing decision review periods in effect on the effective date of the Pesticide Registration Improvement Extension Act of 2018 for pesticide registration actions for covered pesticide registration applications (including reduced risk applications). Such reforms shall include identifying opportunities for streamlining review processes for applications for a new active ingredient or a new use and providing prompt feedback to applicants during such review process.

(f) Decision time review periods

(1) In general

Not later than 30 days after the effective date of the Pesticide Registration Improvement Extension Act of 2018, the Administrator shall make publicly available a schedule of decision review periods for covered pesticide registration actions or for any other action covered by a table specified in subsection (b)(3) and corresponding registration service fees under this subchapter.

(2) Report

The schedule shall be the same as the applicable schedule provided under subsection (b)(3).

(3) Applications subject to decision time review periods

The decision time review periods specified in paragraph (1) shall apply to —

(A) covered pesticide registration applications subject to registration service fees under subsection (b)(2);

(B) covered pesticide registration applications for which an applicant has voluntarily paid registration service fees under subsection (b)(4); and

(C) applications for any other action covered by a table specified in subsection (b)(3).

(4) Start of decision time review period

(A) In general

Except as provided in subparagraphs (C), (D), and (E), in the case of a covered application accompanied by the registration service fee required under this section, the decision time review period begins 21 days after the date on which the Administrator receives the covered application and fee.

(B) Initial content and preliminary technical screenings

(i) Screenings

(I) Initial content

Not later than 21 days after receiving an application and the required registration service fee, the Administrator shall conduct an initial screening of the contents of the application in accordance with clause (iii).

(II) Preliminary technical screening

After conducting the initial content screening described in subclause (I) and in accordance with clause (iv), the Administrator shall conduct a preliminary technical screening —

(aa) not later than 45 days after the date on which the decision time review period begins (for applications with decision time review periods of not more than 180 days); and

(bb) not later than 90 days after the date on which the decision time review period begins (for applications with decision time review periods greater than 180 days).

(ii) Rejection

(I) In general

If the Administrator determines at any time before the Administrator completes the preliminary technical screening under clause (i)(II) that the application failed the initial content or preliminary technical screening and the applicant does not correct the failure before the date that is 10 business days after the applicant receives a notification of the failure, the Administrator shall reject the application.

(II) Written notification

The Administrator shall make every effort to provide a written notification of a rejection under subclause (I) during the 10-day period that begins on the date the Administrator completes the preliminary technical screening.

(iii) Requirements of initial content screening

In conducting an initial content screening of an application, the Administrator shall determine whether —

(I)(aa) the applicable registration service fee has been paid; or

(bb) at least 25 percent of the applicable registration service fee has been paid and the application contains a waiver or refund request for the outstanding amount and documentation establishing the basis for the waiver request; and

(II) the application appears to contain all the necessary forms, data, and draft labeling, formatted in accordance with guidance published by the Administrator.

(iv) Requirements of preliminary technical screening

In conducting a preliminary technical screening of an application, the Administrator shall determine if —

(I) the application and the data and information submitted with the application are accurate and complete; and

(II) the application, data, and information are consistent with the proposed labeling and any proposal for a tolerance or exemption from the requirement for a tolerance under section 408 of the Federal Food, Drug, and Cosmetic Act (21 U.S.C. 346a), and are such that, subject to full review under the standards of this subchapter, could result in the granting of the application.

(C) Applications with waiver or reduction requests

(i) In general

In the case of an application submitted with a request for a waiver or reduction of registration service fees under subsection (b)(7), the decision time review period shall be determined in accordance with this subparagraph.

(ii) Request granted with no additional fees required

If the Administrator grants the waiver or reduction request and no additional fee is required, the decision time review period begins on the earlier of —

(I) the date on which the Administrator grants the request; or

(II) the date that is 60 days after the date of receipt of the application.

(iii) Request granted with additional fees required

If the Administrator grants the waiver or reduction request, in whole or in part, but an additional registration service fee is required, the decision time review period begins on the date on which the Administrator receives certification of payment of the applicable registration service fee.

(iv) Request denied

If the Administrator denies the waiver or reduction request, the decision time review period begins on the date on which the Administrator receives certification of payment of the applicable registration service fee.

(D) Pending applications

(i) In general

The start of the decision time review period for applications described in clause (ii) shall be the date on which the Administrator receives certification of payment of the applicable registration service fee.

(ii) Applications

Clause (i) applies to —

(I) covered pesticide registration applications for which voluntary fees have been paid under subsection (b)(4); and

(II) covered pesticide registration applications received on or after the effective date of the Pesticide Registration Improvement Act of 2003 but submitted without the applicable registration service fee required under this section due to the inability of the Administrator to assess fees under subsection (d)(1).

(E) 2003 work plan

In the case of a covered pesticide registration application listed in the Registration Division 2003 Work Plan of the Office of Pesticide Programs of the Environmental Protection Agency, the decision time review period begins on the date that is 30 days after the effective date of the Pesticide Registration Improvement Act of 2003.

(5) Extension of decision time review period

The Administrator and the applicant may mutually agree in writing to extend a decision time review period under this subsection.

(g) Judicial review

(1) In general

Any applicant adversely affected by the failure of the Administrator to make a determination on the application of the applicant for registration of a new active ingredient or new use for which a registration service fee is paid under this section may obtain judicial review of the failure solely under this section.

(2) Scope

(A) In general

In an action brought under this subsection, the only issue on review is whether the Administrator failed to make a determination on the application specified in paragraph (1) by the end of the applicable decision time review period required under subsection (f) for the application.

(B) Other actions

No other action authorized or required under this section shall be judicially reviewable by a Federal or State court.

(3) Timing

(A) In general

A person may not obtain judicial review of the failure of the Administrator to make a determination on the application specified in paragraph (1) before the expiration of the 2-year period that begins on the date on which the decision time review period for the application ends.

(B) Meeting with Administrator

To be eligible to seek judicial review under this subsection, a person seeking the review shall first request in writing, at least 120 days before filing the complaint for judicial review, a decision review meeting with the Administrator.

(4) Remedies

The Administrator may not be required or permitted to refund any portion of a registration service fee paid in response to a complaint that the Administrator has failed to make a determination on the covered pesticide registration application specified in paragraph (1) by the end of the applicable decision review period.

(h) Accounting

The Administrator shall —

(1) provide an annual accounting of the registration service fees paid to the Administrator and disbursed from the Fund, by providing financial statements in accordance with —

(A) the Chief Financial Officers Act of 1990 (Public Law 101-576; 104 Stat. 2838) and amendments made by that Act; and

(B) the Government Management Reform Act of 1994 (Public Law 103-356; 108 Stat. 3410) and amendments made by that Act;

(2) provide an accounting describing expenditures from the Fund authorized under subsection (c); and

(3) provide an annual accounting describing collections and expenditures authorized under subsection (d).

(i) Auditing

(1) Financial statements of agencies

For the purpose of section 3515(c) of Title 31, the Fund shall be considered a component of an executive agency.

(2) Components

The annual audit required under sections 3515(b) and 3521 of that title of the financial statements of activities under this section shall include an analysis of —

(A) the fees collected under subsection (b) and disbursed;

(B) compliance with subsection (f);

(C) the amount appropriated to meet the requirements of subsection (d)(1); and

(D) the reasonableness of the allocation of the overhead allocation of costs associated with the review and decisionmaking pertaining to applications under this section.

(3) Inspector General

The Inspector General of the Environmental Protection Agency shall —

(A) conduct the annual audit required under this subsection; and

(B) report the findings and recommendations of the audit to the Administrator and to the appropriate committees of Congress.

(j) Personnel levels

All full-time equivalent positions supported by fees authorized and collected under this section shall not be counted against the agency-wide personnel level goals of the Environmental Protection Agency.

(k) Reports

(1) In general

Not later than March 1, 2005, and each March 1 thereafter through March 1, 2023, the Administrator shall publish an annual report describing actions taken under this section.

(2) Contents

The report shall include —

(A) a review of the progress made in carrying out each requirement of subsections (e) and (f), including —

(i) the number of applications reviewed, including the decision times for each application specified in subsection (f);

(ii) the number of label amendments that have been reviewed using electronic means;

(iii) the amount of money from the Reregistration and Expedited Processing Fund used to carry out inert ingredient review and review of similar applications under section 136a-1(k)(3) of this title;

(iv) the number of applications completed for identical or substantially similar applications under section 136a(c)(3)(B) of this title, including the number of such applications completed within 90 days pursuant to that section;

(v) the number of actions pending in each category of actions described in subsection (f)(3), as well as the number of inert ingredients;

(vi) to the extent determined appropriate by the Administrator and consistent with the authorities of the Administrator and limitations on delegation of functions by the Administrator, recommendations for —

(I) expanding the use of self-certification in all appropriate areas of the registration process;

(II) providing for accreditation of outside reviewers and the use of outside reviewers to conduct the review of major portions of applications;

(III) reviewing the scope of use of the notification process to cover broader categories of registration actions;

(IV) providing for electronic submission and review of labels, including process improvements to further enhance the procedures used in electronic label review; and

(V) the allowance and use of summaries of acute toxicity studies;

(vii) the use of performance-based contracts, other contracts, and procurement to ensure that —

(I) the goals of this subchapter for the timely review of applications for registration are met; and

(II) the registration program is administered in the most productive and cost effective manner practicable; and

(viii) the number of extensions of decision time review periods agreed to under subsection (f)(5) along with a description of the reason that the Administrator was unable to make a decision within the initial decision time review period;

(B) a description of the staffing and resources relating to the costs associated with the review and decisionmaking pertaining to applications;

(C) a review of the progress in meeting the timeline requirements of section 136a-1(g) of this title;

(D) a review of the progress in carrying out section 136a(g) of this title, including —

(i) the number of pesticides or pesticide cases reviewed and the number of registration review decisions completed, including —

(I) the number of cases cancelled;

(II) the number of cases requiring risk mitigation measures;

(III) the number of cases removing risk mitigation measures;

(IV) the number of cases with no risk mitigation needed; and

(V) the number of cases in which risk mitigation has been fully implemented;

(ii) a description of the staffing and resources relating to the costs associated with the review and decision making relating to reregistration and registration review for compliance with the deadlines specified in this subchapter;

(iii) to the extent determined appropriate by the Administrator and consistent with the authorities of the Administrator and limitations on delegation of functions by the Administrator, recommendations for —

(I) process improvements in the handling of registration review under section 136a(g) of this title;

(II) providing for accreditation of outside reviewers and the use of outside reviewers in the registration review process; and

(III) streamlining the registration review process, consistent with section 136a(g) of this title;

(E) a review of the progress in meeting the timeline requirements for the review of antimicrobial pesticide products under section 136a(h) of this title;

(F) a review of the progress in carrying out the review of inert ingredients, including the number of applications pending, the number of new applications, the number of applications reviewed, staffing, and resources devoted to the review of inert ingredients and recommendations to improve the timeliness of review of inert ingredients;

(G) a review of the progress made toward —

(i) carrying out paragraphs (4) and (5) of section 136a-1(k) of this title and the amounts from the Reregistration and Expedited Processing Fund used for the purposes described in such paragraphs;

(ii) implementing enhancements to —

(I) the electronic tracking of covered applications;

(II) the electronic tracking of conditional registrations;

(III) the endangered species database;

(IV) the electronic review of labels submitted with covered applications; and

(V) the electronic review and assessment of confidential statements of formula submitted with covered applications; and

(iii) facilitating public participation in certain registration actions and the registration review process by providing electronic notification to interested parties of additions to the public docket;

(iv) Repealed. Pub.L. 116-8, § 5(e)(2) (B)(ii), Mar. 8, 2019, 133 Stat. 489

(v) Repealed. Pub.L. 116-8, § 5(e)(2)(B) (ii), Mar. 8, 2019, 133 Stat. 489

(vi) Repealed. Pub.L. 116-8, § 5(e)(2) (B)(ii), Mar. 8, 2019, 133 Stat. 489

(vii) Redesignated (iii)

(H) the number of applications rejected by the Administrator under the initial content and preliminary technical screening conducted under subsection (f)(4);

(I) a review of the progress made in updating the Pesticide Incident Data System, including progress toward making the information contained in the System available to the public (as the Administrator determines is appropriate);

(J) an assessment of the public availability of summary pesticide usage data;

(K) a review of the progress made in developing, updating, and implementing product performance test guidelines for pesticide products that are intended to control invertebrate pests of significant public health importance and, by regulation, prescribing product performance data requirements for such pesticide products registered under section 136a of this title;

(L) a review of the progress made in the priority review and approval of new pesticides to control invertebrate public health pests that may transmit vector-borne disease for use in the United States, including each territory or possession of the United States, and United States military installations globally;

(M) a review of the progress made in implementing enhancements to the good laboratory practices standards compliance monitoring program established under part 160 of title 40 of the Code of Federal Regulations (or successor regulations);

(N) the number of approvals for active ingredients, new uses, and pesticide end use products granted in connection with the Design for the Environment program (or any successor program) of the Environmental Protection Agency; and

(O) with respect to funds in the Pesticide Registration Fund reserved under subsection (c)(3), a review that includes —

(i) a description of the amount and use of such funds —

(I) to carry out activities relating to worker protection under clause (i) of subsection (c)(3)(B);

(II) to award partnership grants under clause (ii) of such subsection; and

(III) to carry out the pesticide safety education program under clause (iii) of such subsection;

(ii) an evaluation of the appropriateness and effectiveness of the activities, grants, and program described in clause (i);

(iii) a description of how stakeholders are engaged in the decision to fund such activities, grants, and program; and

(iv) with respect to activities relating to worker protection carried out under subparagraph (B)(i) of such subsection, a summary of the analyses from stakeholders, including from worker community-based organizations, on the appropriateness and effectiveness of such activities.

(3) Method

The Administrator shall publish a report required by this subsection by such method as the Administrator determines to be the most effective for efficiently disseminating the report, including publication of the report on the Internet site of the Environmental Protection Agency.

(4) Other report

(A) Scope

In addition to the annual report described in paragraph (1), not later than October 1, 2016, the Administrator shall submit to the Committee on Agriculture of the House of Representatives and the Committee on Agriculture, Nutrition, and Forestry of the Senate a report that includes an analysis of the impact of maintenance fees on small businesses that have —

(i) 10 or fewer employees; and

(ii) annual global gross revenue that does not exceed $2,000,000.

(B) Information required

In conducting the analysis described in subparagraph (A), the Administrator shall collect, and include in the report under that subparagraph, information on —

(i) the number of small businesses described in subparagraph (A) that are paying maintenance fees; and

(ii) the number of registrations each company holds.

(l) Savings clause

Nothing in this section affects any other duties, obligations, or authorities established by any other section of this subchapter, including the right to judicial review of duties, obligations, or authorities established by any other section of this subchapter.

(m) Termination of effectiveness

(1) In general

Except as provided in paragraph (2), the authority provided by this section terminates on September 30, 2023.

(2) Phase out

(A) Fiscal year 2024

During fiscal year 2024, the requirement to pay and collect registration service fees applies, except that the level of registration service fees payable under this section shall be reduced 40 percent below the level in effect on September 30, 2023.

(B) Fiscal year 2025

During fiscal year 2025, the requirement to pay and collect registration service fees applies, except that the level of registration service fees payable under this section shall be reduced 70 percent below

the level in effect on September 30, 2023.

(C) September 30, 2025

Effective September 30, 2025, the requirement to pay and collect registration service fees terminates.

(D) Decision review periods

(i) Pending applications

In the case of an application received under this section before September 30, 2023, the application shall be reviewed in accordance with subsection (f).

(ii) New applications

In the case of an application received under this section on or after September 30, 2023, subsection (f) shall not apply to the application.

§136x. Severability

[FIFRA §33]

If any provision of this subchapter or the application thereof to any person or circumstance is held invalid, the invalidity shall not affect other provisions or applications of this subchapter which can be given effect without regard to the invalid provision or application, and to this end the provisions of this subchapter are severable.

§136y. Authorization of appropriations

[FIFRA §34]

There is authorized to be appropriated to carry out this subchapter (other than section 136u(a) of this title) —

(1) $83,000,000 for fiscal year 1989, of which not more than $13,735,500 shall be available for research under this subchapter;

(2) $95,000,000 for fiscal year 1990, of which not more than $14,343,600 shall be available for research under this subchapter; and

(3) $95,000,000 for fiscal year 1991, of which not more than $14,978,200 shall be available for research under this subchapter.

C. SAFE DRINKING WATER ACT

A GUIDE TO MATERIALS AVAILABLE ON THE INTERNET PERTAINING TO THE SAFE DRINKING WATER ACT

EPA's regulations implementing the Safe Drinking Water Act are codified at 40 C.F.R. pts. 141 to 149. These CFR sections are available online through the National Archives and Records Administration's website, which includes a searchable version of the Code of Federal Regulations (*https://www.gpo.gov/fdsys/browse/collectionCfr.action?collectionCode=CFR*) and an electronic version ("e-CFR") that is continuously updated at *http://www.ecfr.gov*.

EPA's Office of Ground Water and Drinking Water is responsible for implementing the Safe Drinking Water Act. The office's webpage is at *https://www.epa.gov/ground-water-and-drinking-water*. It includes links to drinking water rules issued or proposed by EPA (arranged in chronological order) as well as copies of agency guidance and policy documents on drinking water issues at *http://water.epa.gov/lawsregs/*. A report by the Congressional Research Service that discusses the issues addressed by Congress during reauthorization of the SDWA and the implementation issues confronted by EPA is available at *https://fas.org/sgp/crs/misc/RL31243.pdf*.

The National Drinking Water Advisory Council, which advises EPA on drinking water policy issues, has a webpage located at *https://www.epa.gov/ndwac*.

The Natural Resources Defense Council (NRDC) has been the leading environmental organization working on issues involving safe drinking water. NRDC's webpage provides information about drinking water issues at *https://www.nrdc.org/issues/safe-drinking-water*. A coalition of environmental groups has produced a report on Source Water Stewardship available at *http://www.cleanwaterfund.org/files/publications/national/sourcewater-stewardship-guide.pdf*. Annotated links to websites providing information about drinking water issues may be found at *http://www.cyber-nook.com/water*.

The trade association that is most active on drinking water issues is the American Water Works Association (AWWA). AWWA website is located at *http://www.awwa.org*. The trade association for state officials who regulate drinking water quality is the Association of State Drinking Water Administrators. Their website, which has copies of their positions on various policy issues, is at *http://www.asdwa.org*.

SAFE DRINKING WATER ACT LEGISLATIVE HISTORY TIMELINE

December 17, 1974: President Ford signs the Safe Drinking Water Act into law, Pub. L. 93-523, 88 Stat. 1661, establishing a new national program to ensure the safety of drinking water supplied by public water supply systems. It requires EPA to adopt interim standards limiting levels of contaminants in drinking water within three months and, following a two-year study by the National Academy of Sciences, to promulgate revised drinking water regulations that are as close as feasible to levels fully protective of human health. The Act also requires EPA and the states to establish a program to control underground injection of fluids to protect groundwater supplies.

June 19, 1986: President Reagan signs the 1986 Amendments to the Safe Drinking Water Act into law, Pub. L. 99-339, 100 Stat. 642. The legislation requires EPA to issue drinking water standards for many unregulated contaminants by specified deadlines, strengthens EPA's enforcement powers, and bans the use of lead in plumbing materials.

October 31, 1988: The Lead Contamination Control Act of 1988, Pub. L. 100-572, 102 Stat. 2884, is enacted, requiring the recall of drinking water coolers with lead-lined tanks.

August 6, 1996: President Clinton signs the Safe Drinking Water Act Amendments of 1996 into law, Pub. L. 104-182, 110 Stat. 1615, making comprehensive revisions to the Act. The revisions provide new regulatory flexibility by repealing requirements that EPA regulate a certain number of contaminants per year and by giving EPA the authority to consider benefits and costs when setting standards.

June 12, 2002: President George W. Bush signs the Public Health Security and Bioterrorism Preparedness and Response Act of 2002, Pub. L. 107-188, 116 Stat. 682, which amends the Safe Drinking Water Act in an effort to increase the security of public water supply systems against terrorist attacks.

October 23, 2018: President Donald Trump signs into law America's Water Infrastructure Act of 2018, which provides federal funding for drinking water infrastructure improvements and mandates improvements in consumer confidence reports.

OUTLINE OF THE PRINCIPAL PROVISIONS OF THE
SAFE DRINKING WATER ACT

PART B — CONTROL OF CONTAMINANTS IN PUBLIC WATER SYSTEMS

§1412 (42 U.S.C. §300g-1) National Drinking Water Regulations: requires EPA to promulgate national drinking water regulations for public water systems. Regulations are to be issued for each contaminant that may have any adverse effect on health and that is known or anticipated to occur in such systems. Maximum contaminant level goals (MCLGs) are to be set "at the level at which no known or anticipated adverse effects on the health of persons occur and which allows an adequate margin of safety." Maximum contaminant levels (MCLs) are to be set as close to the MCLGs "as is feasible," unless after weighing the "quantifiable and nonquantifiable costs and benefits," the EPA determines that the benefits of that level would not justify the costs, in which case the MCL is to be set to "maximize health risk reduction benefits at a cost that is justified by the benefits."

§1413 (42 U.S.C. §300g-2) State Authority: authorizes the EPA Administrator to delegate primary enforcement responsibility under the Act to states that have drinking water regulations at least as stringent as federal standards and that have adequate procedures for enforcement.

§1414 (42 U.S.C. §300g-3) Enforcement: requires the EPA Administrator to notify states of violations of national primary drinking water regulations and to take enforcement action against violating public water systems if the states fail to do so. Owners and operators of public water systems are required to notify customers of violations and to mail them an annual consumer confidence report on the level of contaminants in the system's drinking water.

§§1415 & 1416 (42 U.S.C. §§300g-4 & 5) Variances and Exemptions: authorizes states to grant variances and exemptions from drinking water standards under certain circumstances.

§1417 (42 U.S.C. §300g-6) Prohibition on Use of Lead Pipes, Solder & Flux: prohibits the use of lead in pipes, solder, or flux in public water systems or in plumbing used to provide water for human consumption that is connected to such a system.

PART C — UNDERGROUND INJECTION CONTROL PROGRAM

§§1421-1429 (42 U.S.C. §§300h to 300h-8) Underground Injection Control: requires the EPA Administrator to establish minimum requirements for state programs to control underground injection to prevent danger to drinking water sources.

PART D — EMERGENCY POWERS

§1431 (42 U.S.C. §300i) Emergency Powers: grants EPA emergency powers to act against contamination of drinking water that may present an imminent and substantial endangerment to public health.

PART E — GENERAL PROVISIONS

§1448 (42 U.S.C. §300j-7) Judicial Review: authorizes judicial review of national primary drinking water regulations in the U.S. Court of Appeals for the D.C. Circuit; authorizes judicial review of any other EPA action under the Act in the U.S. Court of Appeals where the petitioner resides or transacts business.

§1449 (42 U.S.C. §300j-8) Citizen Suits: authorizes citizen suits against any person alleged to be in violation of the Act and against the EPA Administrator for failure to perform any nondiscretionary duty.

PART F — LEAD CONTAMINATION IN WATER COOLERS

§§1461-1465 (42 U.S.C. §§300j-21 to 26) Lead Contamination in Water Coolers: requires the Consumer Product Safety Commission to order the repair or recall of drinking water coolers with lead-lined tanks.

Safe Drinking Water Act

42 U.S.C. §§300f to 300j-26

SUBCHAPTER XII — SAFETY OF PUBLIC WATER SYSTEMS

PART A — DEFINITIONS

§300f. Definitions

[PHSA §1401]

For purposes of this subchapter:

(1) The term "primary drinking water regulation" means a regulation which —

(A) applies to public water systems;

(B) specifies contaminants which, in the judgment of the Administrator, may have any adverse effect on the health of persons;

(C) specifies for each such contaminant either —

(i) a maximum contaminant level, if, in the judgment of the Administrator, it is economically and technologically feasible to ascertain the level of such contaminant in water in public water systems, or

(ii) if, in the judgment of the Administrator, it is not economically or technologically feasible to so ascertain the level of such contaminant, each treatment technique known to the Administrator which leads to a reduction in the level of such contaminant sufficient to satisfy the requirements of section 300g-1 of this title; and

(D) contains criteria and procedures to assure a supply of drinking water which dependably complies with such maximum contaminant levels; including accepted methods for quality control and testing procedures to insure compliance with such levels and to insure proper operation and maintenance of the system, and requirements as to (i) the minimum quality of water which may be taken into the system and (ii) siting for new facilities for public water systems.

At any time after promulgation of a regulation referred to in this paragraph, the Administrator may add equally effective quality control and testing procedures by guidance published in the Federal Register. Such procedures shall be treated as an alternative for public water systems to the quality control and testing procedures listed in the regulation.

(2) The term "secondary drinking water regulation" means a regulation which applies to public water systems and which specifies the maximum contaminant levels which, in the judgment of the Administrator, are requisite to protect the public welfare. Such regulations may apply to any contaminant in drinking water (A) which may adversely affect the odor or appearance of such water and consequently may cause a substantial number of the persons served by the public water system providing such water to discontinue its use, or (B) which may otherwise adversely affect the public welfare. Such regulations may vary according to geographic and other circumstances.

(3) The term "maximum contaminant level" means the maximum permissible level of a contaminant in water which is delivered to any user of a public water system.

(4) Public water system —

(A) In general — The term "public water system" means a system for the provision to the public of water for human consumption through pipes or other constructed conveyances, if such system has at least fifteen service connections or regularly serves at least twenty-five individuals. Such term includes (i) any collection, treatment, storage, and distribution facilities under control of the operator of such system and used primarily in connection with such system, and (ii) any collection or pretreatment storage facilities not under such control which are used primarily in connection with such system.

(B) Connections —

(i) In general — For purposes of subparagraph (A), a connection to a system that delivers water by a constructed conveyance other than a pipe shall not be considered a connection, if —

(I) the water is used exclusively for purposes other than residential uses (consisting of drinking, bathing, and cooking, or other similar uses);

(II) the Administrator or the State (in the case of a State exercising primary enforcement responsibility for public water systems) determines that alternative water to achieve the equivalent level of public health protection provided by the applicable national primary drinking water regulation is provided for residential or similar uses for drinking and cooking; or

(III) the Administrator or the State (in the case of a State exercising primary enforcement responsibility for public water systems) determines that the water provided for residential or similar uses for drinking, cooking, and bathing is centrally treated or treated at the point of entry by the provider, a pass-through entity, or the user to achieve the equivalent level of protection provided by the applicable national primary drinking water regulations.

(ii) Irrigation districts — An irrigation district in existence prior to May 18, 1994, that provides primarily agricultural service through a piped water system with only incidental residential or similar use shall not be considered to be a public water system if the system or the residential or similar users of the system comply with subclause (II) or (III) of clause (i).

(C) Transition period — A water supplier that would be a public water system only as a result of modifications made to this paragraph by the Safe Drinking Water Act Amendments of 1996 shall not be considered a public water system for purposes of the Act until the date that is two years after August 6, 1996. If a water supplier does not serve 15 service connections (as defined in subparagraphs (A) and (B)) or 25 people at any time after the conclusion of the 2-year period, the water supplier shall not be considered a public water system.

(5) The term "supplier of water" means any person who owns or operates a public water system.

(6) The term "contaminant" means any physical, chemical, biological, or radiological substance or matter in water.

(7) The term "Administrator" means the Administrator of the Environmental Protection Agency.

(8) The term "Agency" means the Environmental Protection Agency.

(9) The term "Council" means the National Drinking Water Advisory Council established under section 300j-5 of this title.

(10) The term "municipality" means a city, town, or other public body created by or pursuant to State law, or an Indian Tribe.

(11) The term "Federal agency" means any department, agency, or instrumentality of the United States.

(12) The term "person" means an individual, corporation, company, association, partnership, State, municipality, or Federal agency (and includes officers, employees, and agents of any corporation, company, association, State, municipality, or Federal agency).

(13)(A) Except as provided in subparagraph (B), the term "State" includes, in addition to the several States, only the District of Columbia, Guam, the Commonwealth of Puerto Rico, the Northern Mariana Islands, the Virgin Islands, American Samoa, and the Trust Territory of the Pacific Islands.

(B) For purposes of section 300j-12 of this title, the term "State" means each of the 50 States, the District of Columbia, and the Commonwealth of Puerto Rico.

(14) The term "Indian Tribe" means any Indian tribe having a Federally recognized governing body

carrying out substantial governmental duties and powers over any area. For purposes of sections 300j-12, 300j-19a, and 300j-19b of this title, the term includes any Native village (as defined in section 1602(c) of Title 43).

(15) Community water system — The term "community water system" means a public water system that —

(A) serves at least 15 service connections used by year-round residents of the area served by the system; or

(B) regularly serves at least 25 year-round residents.

(16) Noncommunity water system — The term "noncommunity water system" means a public water system that is not a community water system.

PART B — PUBLIC WATER SYSTEMS

§300g. Coverage
[PHSA §1411]

Subject to sections 300g-4 and 300g-5 of this title, national primary drinking water regulations under this part shall apply to each public water system in each State; except that such regulations shall not apply to a public water system —

(1) which consists only of distribution and storage facilities (and does not have any collection and treatment facilities);

(2) which obtains all of its water from, but is not owned or operated by, a public water system to which such regulations apply;

(3) which does not sell water to any person; and

(4) which is not a carrier which conveys passengers in interstate commerce.

§300g-1. National drinking water regulations
[PHSA §1412]

(a) National primary drinking water regulations; maximum contaminant level goals; simultaneous publication of regulations and goals

(1) Effective on June 19, 1986, each national interim or revised primary drinking water regulation promulgated under this section before June 19, 1986, shall be deemed to be a national primary drinking water regulation under subsection (b) of this section. No such regulation shall be required to comply with the standards set forth in subsection (b)(4) of this section unless such regulation is amended to establish a different maximum contaminant level after June 19, 1986.

(2) After June 19, 1986, each recommended maximum contaminant level published before June 19, 1986, shall be treated as a maximum contaminant level goal.

(3) Whenever a national primary drinking water regulation is proposed under subsection

(b) of this section for any contaminant, the maximum contaminant level goal for such contaminant shall be proposed simultaneously. Whenever a national primary drinking water regulation is promulgated under subsection (b) of this section for any contaminant, the maximum contaminant level goal for such contaminant shall be published simultaneously.

(4) Paragraph (3) shall not apply to any recommended maximum contaminant level published before June 19, 1986.

(b) Standards

(1) Identification of contaminants for listing

(A) General authority — The Administrator shall, in accordance with the procedures established by this subsection, publish a maximum contaminant level goal and promulgate a national primary drinking water regulation for a contaminant (other than a contaminant referred to in paragraph (2) for which a national primary drinking water regulation has been promulgated as of August 6, 1996) if the Administrator determines that —

(i) the contaminant may have an adverse effect on the health of persons;

(ii) the contaminant is known to occur or there is a substantial likelihood that the contaminant will occur in public water systems with a frequency and at levels of public health concern; and

(iii) in the sole judgment of the Administrator, regulation of such contaminant presents a meaningful opportunity for health risk reduction for persons served by public water systems.

(B) Regulation of unregulated contaminants

(i) Listing of contaminants for consideration

(I) Not later than 18 months after August 6, 1996, and every 5 years thereafter, the Administrator, after consultation with the scientific community, including the Science Advisory Board, after notice and opportunity for public comment, and after considering the occurrence data base established under section 300j-4(g) of this title, shall publish a list of contaminants which, at the time of publication, are not subject to any proposed or promulgated national primary drinking water regulation, which are known or anticipated to occur in public water systems, and which may require regulation under this subchapter.

(II) The unregulated contaminants considered under subclause (I) shall include, but not be limited to, substances referred to in section 9601(14) of this title, and substances registered as pesticides under the Federal Insecticide, Fungicide, and Rodenticide Act [7 U.S.C. §§136 *et seq.*].

(III) The Administrator's decision whether or not to select an unregulated contaminant for a list under this clause shall not be subject to judicial review.

(ii) Determination to regulate

(I) Not later than 5 years after August 6, 1996, and every 5 years thereafter, the Administrator shall, after notice of the preliminary determination and opportunity for public comment, for not fewer than 5 contaminants included on the list published under clause (i), make determinations of whether or not to regulate such contaminants.

(II) A determination to regulate a contaminant shall be based on findings that the criteria of clauses (i), (ii), and (iii) of subparagraph (A) are satisfied. Such findings shall be based on the best available public health information, including the occurrence data base established under section 300j-4(g) of this title.

(III) The Administrator may make a determination to regulate a contaminant that does not appear on a list under clause (i) if the determination to regulate is made pursuant to subclause (II).

(IV) A determination under this clause not to regulate a contaminant shall be considered final agency action and subject to judicial review.

(iii) Review — Each document setting forth the determination for a contaminant under clause (ii) shall be available for public comment at such time as the determination is published.

(C) Priorities — In selecting unregulated contaminants for consideration under subparagraph (B), the Administrator shall select contaminants that present the greatest public health concern. The Administrator, in making such selection, shall take into consideration, among other factors of public health concern, the effect of such contaminants upon subgroups that comprise a meaningful portion of the general population (such as infants, children, pregnant women, the elderly, individuals with a history of serious illness, or other subpopulations) that are identifiable as being at greater risk of adverse health effects due to exposure to contaminants in drinking water than the general population.

(D) Urgent threats to public health — The administrator may promulgate an interim national primary drinking water regulation for a contaminant without making a determination for the contaminant under paragraph (4)(C), or completing the analysis under paragraph (3)(C), to address an urgent threat to public health as determined by the Administrator after consultation with and written response to any comments provided by the Secretary of Health and Human Services, acting through the director of the Centers for Disease Control and Prevention or the director of the National Institutes of Health. A determination for any contaminant in accordance with paragraph (4)(C) subject to an interim regulation under this subparagraph shall be issued, and a completed analysis meeting the requirements of paragraph (3)(C) shall be published, not later than 3 years after the date on which the regulation is promulgated and the regulation shall be repromulgated, or revised if appropriate, not later than 5 years after that date.

(E) Regulation — For each contaminant that the Administrator determines to regulate under subparagraph (B), the Administrator shall publish maximum contaminant level goals and promulgate, by rule, national primary drinking water regulations under this subsection. The Administrator shall propose the maximum contaminant level goal and national primary drinking water regulation for a contaminant not later than 24 months after the determination to regulate under subparagraph (B), and may publish such proposed regulation concurrent with the determination to regulate. The Administrator shall publish a maximum contaminant level goal and promulgate a national primary drinking water regulation within 18 months after the proposal thereof. The Administrator, by notice in the Federal Register, may extend the deadline for such promulgation for up to 9 months.

(F) Health advisories and other actions — The Administrator may publish health advisories (which are not regulations) or take other appropriate actions for contaminants not subject to any national primary drinking water regulation.

(2) Schedules and deadlines

(A) In general — In the case of the contaminants listed in the Advance Notice of Proposed Rulemaking published in volume 47, Federal Register, page 9352, and in volume 48, Federal Register, page 45502, the Administrator shall publish maximum contaminant level goals and promulgate national primary drinking water regulations —

(i) not later than 1 year after June 19, 1986, for not fewer than 9 of the listed contaminants;

(ii) not later than 2 years after June 19,

1986, for not fewer than 40 of the listed contaminants; and

(iii) not later than 3 years after June 19, 1986, for the remainder of the listed contaminants.

(B) Substitution of contaminants — If the Administrator identifies a drinking water contaminant the regulation of which, in the judgment of the Administrator, is more likely to be protective of public health (taking into account the schedule for regulation under subparagraph (A)) than a contaminant referred to in subparagraph (A), the Administrator may publish a maximum contaminant level goal and promulgate a national primary drinking water regulation for the identified contaminant in lieu of regulating the contaminant referred to in subparagraph (A). Substitutions may be made for not more than 7 contaminants referred to in subparagraph (A). Regulation of a contaminant identified under this subparagraph shall be in accordance with the schedule applicable to the contaminant for which the substitution is made.

(C) Disinfectants and disinfection byproducts — The Administrator shall promulgate an Interim Enhanced Surface Water Treatment Rule, a Final Enhanced Surface Water Treatment Rule, a Stage I Disinfectants and Disinfection Byproducts Rule, and a Stage II Disinfectants and Disinfection Byproducts Rule in accordance with the schedule published in volume 59, Federal Register, page 6361 (February 10, 1994), in table III.13 of the proposed Information Collection Rule. If a delay occurs with respect to the promulgation of any rule in the schedule referred to in this subparagraph, all subsequent rules shall be completed as expeditiously as practicable but no later than a revised date that reflects the interval or intervals for the rules in the schedule.

(3) Risk assessment, management, and communication

(A) Use of science in decisionmaking — In carrying out this section, and, to the degree that an Agency action is based on science, the Administrator shall use —

(i) the best available, peer-reviewed science and supporting studies conducted in accordance with sound and objective scientific practices; and

(ii) data collected by accepted methods or best available methods (if the reliability of the method and the nature of the decision justifies use of the data).

(B) Public information — In carrying out this section, the Administrator shall ensure that the presentation of information on public health effects is comprehensive, informative, and understandable. The Administrator shall, in a document made available to the public in support of a regulation promulgated under this section, specify, to the extent practicable —

(i) each population addressed by any estimate of public health effects;

(ii) the expected risk or central estimate of risk for the specific populations;

(iii) each appropriate upper-bound or lower-bound estimate of risk;

(iv) each significant uncertainty identified in the process of the assessment of public health effects and studies that would assist in resolving the uncertainty; and

(v) peer-reviewed studies known to the Administrator that support, are directly relevant to, or fail to support any estimate of public health effects and the methodology used to reconcile inconsistencies in the scientific data.

(C) Health risk reduction and cost analysis

(i) Maximum contaminant levels — When proposing any national primary drinking water regulation that includes a maximum contaminant level, the Administrator shall, with respect to a maximum contaminant level that is being considered in accordance with paragraph (4) and each alternative maximum contaminant level that is being considered pursuant to paragraph (5) or (6)(A), publish, seek public comment on, and use for the purposes of paragraphs (4), (5), and (6) an analysis of each of the following:

(I) Quantifiable and nonquantifiable health risk reduction benefits for which there is a factual basis in the rulemaking record to conclude that such benefits are likely to occur as the result of treatment to comply with each level.

(II) Quantifiable and nonquantifiable health risk reduction benefits for which there is a factual basis in the rulemaking record to conclude that such benefits are likely to occur from reductions in co-occurring contaminants that may be attributed solely to compliance with the maximum contaminant level, excluding benefits resulting from compliance with other proposed or promulgated regulations.

(III) Quantifiable and nonquantifiable costs for which there is a factual basis in the rulemaking record to conclude that such costs are likely to occur solely as a result of compliance with the maximum contaminant level, including monitoring, treatment, and other costs and excluding costs resulting from compliance with other proposed or promulgated regulations.

(IV) The incremental costs and benefits associated with each alternative maximum contaminant level considered.

(V) The effects of the contaminant on the general population and on groups within the general population such as infants, children, pregnant women, the elderly, individuals with a history of serious illness, or other subpopulations that are identified as likely to be at greater risk of adverse health effects due to exposure to contaminants in drinking water than the general population.

(VI) Any increased health risk that may occur as the result of compliance, including risks associated with co-occurring contaminants.

(VII) Other relevant factors, including the quality and extent of the information, the uncertainties in the analysis supporting subclauses (I) through (VI), and factors with respect to the degree and nature of the risk.

(ii) Treatment techniques — When proposing a national primary drinking water regulation that includes a treatment technique in accordance with paragraph (7)(A), the Administrator shall publish and seek public comment on an analysis of the health risk reduction benefits and costs likely to be experienced as the result of compliance with the treatment technique and alternative treatment techniques that are being considered, taking into account, as appropriate, the factors described in clause (i).

(iii) Approaches to measure and value benefits — The Administrator may identify valid approaches for the measurement and valuation of benefits under this subparagraph, including approaches to identify consumer willingness to pay for reductions in health risks from drinking water contaminants.

(iv) Authorization — There are authorized to be appropriated to the Administrator, acting through the Office of Ground Water and Drinking Water, to conduct studies, assessments, and analyses in support of regulations or the development of methods, $35,000,000 for each of fiscal years 1996 through 2003.

(4) Goals and standards

(A) Maximum contaminant level goals — Each maximum contaminant level goal established under this subsection shall be set at the level at which no known or anticipated adverse effects on the health of persons occur and which allows an adequate margin of safety.

(B) Maximum contaminant levels — Except as provided in paragraphs (5) and (6), each national primary drinking water regulation for a contaminant for which a maximum contaminant level goal is established under this subsection shall specify a maximum contaminant level for such contaminant which is as close to the maximum contaminant level goal as is feasible.

(C) Determination — At the time the Administrator proposes a national primary drinking water regulation under this paragraph, the Administrator shall publish a determination as to whether the benefits of the maximum contaminant level justify, or do not justify, the costs based on the analysis conducted under paragraph (3)(C).

(D) Definition of feasible — For the purposes of this subsection, the term "feasible" means feasible with the use of the best technology, treatment techniques and other means which the Administrator finds, after examination for efficacy under field conditions and not solely under laboratory conditions, are available (taking cost into consideration). For the purpose of this paragraph, granular activated carbon is feasible for the control of synthetic organic chemicals, and any technology, treatment technique, or other means found to be the best available for the control of synthetic organic chemicals must be at least as effective in controlling synthetic organic chemicals as granular activated carbon.

(E) Feasible technologies

(i) In general — Each national primary drinking water regulation which establishes a maximum contaminant level shall list the technology, treatment techniques, and other means which the Administrator finds to be feasible for purposes of meeting such maximum contaminant level, but a regulation under this subsection shall not require that any specified technology, treatment technique, or other means be used for purposes of meeting such maximum contaminant level.

(ii) List of technologies for small systems — The Administrator shall include in the list any technology, treatment technique, or other means that is affordable, as determined by the Administrator in consultation with the States, for small public water systems serving —

(I) a population of 10,000 or fewer but more than 3,300;

(II) a population of 3,300 or fewer but more than 500; and

(III) a population of 500 or fewer but more than 25; and that achieves compliance with the maximum contaminant level or treatment technique, including packaged or modular systems and point-of-entry or point-of-use treatment units. Point-of-entry and point-of-use treatment units shall be owned, controlled and maintained by the public water system or by a person under contract with the public water system to ensure proper operation and maintenance and compliance with the maximum contaminant level or treatment technique and equipped with mechanical warnings to ensure that customers are automatically notified of operational problems. The Administrator shall not include in the list any point-of-use treatment technology, treatment technique, or other means to achieve compliance with a maximum contaminant level or treatment technique requirement for a microbial contaminant (or an indicator of a microbial contaminant). If the American National Standards Institute has issued product standards applicable to a specific type of point-of-entry or point-of-use treatment unit, individual units of that type shall not be accepted for compliance with a maximum contaminant level or treatment technique requirement unless they are independently certified in accordance with such standards. In listing any technology, treatment technique, or other means pursuant to this clause, the Administrator shall consider the quality of the source water to be treated.

(iii) List of technologies that achieve compliance — Except as provided in clause (v), not later than 2 years after June 19, 1986, and after consultation with the States, the Administrator shall issue a list of technologies that achieve compliance with the maximum contaminant level or treatment technique for each category of public water systems described in subclauses (I), (II), and (III) of clause (ii) for each national primary drinking water regulation promulgated prior to August 6, 1996.

(iv) Additional technologies — The Administrator may, at any time after a national primary drinking water regulation has been promulgated, supplement the list of technologies describing additional or new or innovative treatment technologies that meet the requirements of this paragraph for categories of small public water systems described in subclauses (I), (II), and (III) of clause (ii) that are subject to the regulation.

(v) Technologies that meet surface water treatment rule — Within one year after August 6, 1996, the Administrator shall list technologies that meet the Surface Water Treatment Rule for each category of public water systems described in subclauses (I), (II), and (III) of clause (ii).

(5) Additional health risk considerations

(A) In general — Notwithstanding paragraph (4), the Administrator may establish a maximum contaminant level for a contaminant at a level other than the feasible level, if the technology, treatment techniques, and other means used to determine the feasible level would result in an increase in the health risk from drinking water by —

(i) increasing the concentration of other contaminants in drinking water; or

(ii) interfering with the efficacy of drinking water treatment techniques or processes that are used to comply with other national primary drinking water regulations.

(B) Establishment of level — If the Administrator establishes a maximum contaminant level or levels or requires the use of treatment techniques for any contaminant or contaminants pursuant to the authority of this paragraph —

(i) the level or levels or treatment techniques shall minimize the overall risk of adverse health effects by balancing the risk from the contaminant and the risk from other contaminants the concentrations of which may be affected by the use of a treatment technique or process that would be employed to attain the maximum contaminant level or levels; and

(ii) the combination of technology, treatment techniques, or other means required to meet the level or levels shall not be more stringent than is feasible (as defined in paragraph (4)(D)).

(6) Additional health risk reduction and cost considerations

(A) In general — Notwithstanding paragraph (4), if the Administrator determines based on an analysis conducted under paragraph (3)(C) that the benefits of a maximum contaminant level promulgated in accordance with paragraph (4) would not justify the costs of complying with the level, the Administrator may, after notice and opportunity for public comment, promulgate a maximum contaminant level for the contaminant that maximizes health risk reduction benefits at a cost that is justified by the benefits.

(B) Exception — The Administrator shall not use the authority of this paragraph to promulgate a maximum contaminant level for a contaminant, if the benefits of compliance with a national primary drinking water regulation for the contaminant that would be promulgated in accordance with paragraph (4) experienced by —

(i) persons served by large public water systems; and

(ii) persons served by such other systems as are unlikely, based on information provided by the States, to receive a variance under section 300g-4(e) of this title (relating to small system variances);
would justify the costs to the systems of complying with the regulation. This subparagraph shall not apply if the contaminant is found almost exclusively in small systems eligible under section 300g-4(e) of this title for a small system variance.

(C) Disinfectants and disinfection byproducts — The Administrator may not use the authority of this paragraph to establish a maximum contaminant level in a Stage I or Stage II national primary drinking water regulation (as described in paragraph (2) (C)) for contaminants that are disinfectants or disinfection byproducts, or to establish a maximum contaminant level or treatment technique requirement for the control of cryptosporidium. The authority of this paragraph may be used to establish regulations for the use of disinfection by systems relying on ground water sources as required by paragraph (8).

(D) Judicial review — A determination by the Administrator that the benefits of a maximum contaminant level or treatment requirement justify or do not justify the costs of complying with the level shall be reviewed by the court pursuant to section 300j-7 of this title only as part of a review of a final national primary drinking water regulation that has been promulgated based on the determination and shall not be set aside by the court under that section unless the court finds that the determination is arbitrary and capricious.

(7)(A) The Administrator is authorized to promulgate a national primary drinking water regulation that requires the use of a treatment technique in lieu of establishing a maximum contaminant level, if the Administrator makes a finding that it is not economically or technologically feasible to ascertain the level of the contaminant. In such case, the Administrator shall identify those treatment techniques which, in the Administrator's judgment, would prevent known or anticipated adverse effects on the health of persons to the extent feasible. Such regulations shall specify each treatment technique known to the Administrator which meets the requirements of this paragraph, but the Administrator may grant a variance from any specified treatment technique in accordance with section 300g-4(a)(3) of this title.

(B) Any schedule referred to in this subsection for the promulgation of a national primary drinking water regulation for any contaminant shall apply in the same manner if the regulation requires a treatment technique in lieu of establishing a maximum contaminant level.

(C)(i) Not later than 18 months after June 19, 1986, the Administrator shall propose and promulgate national primary drinking water regulations specifying criteria under which filtration (including coagulation and sedimentation, as appropriate) is required as a treatment technique for public water systems supplied by surface water sources. In promulgating such rules, the Administrator shall consider the quality of source waters, protection afforded by watershed management, treatment practices (such as disinfection and length of water storage) and other factors relevant to protection of health.

(ii) In lieu of the provisions of section 300g-4 of this title the Administrator shall specify procedures by which the State determines which public water systems within its jurisdiction shall adopt filtration under the criteria of clause (i). The State may require the public water system to provide studies or other information to assist in this determination. The procedures shall provide notice and opportunity for public hearing on this determination. If the State determines that filtration is required, the State shall prescribe a schedule for compliance by the public water system with the filtration requirement. A schedule shall require compliance within 18 months of a determination made under clause (iii).

(iii) Within 18 months from the time that the Administrator establishes the criteria and procedures under this subparagraph, a State with primary enforcement responsibility shall adopt any necessary regulations to implement this subparagraph. Within 12 months of adoption of such regulations the State shall make determinations regarding filtration for all the public water systems within its jurisdiction supplied by surface waters.

(iv) If a State does not have primary enforcement responsibility for public water systems, the Administrator shall have the same authority to make the determination in clause (ii) in such State as the State would have under that clause. Any filtration requirement or schedule under this subparagraph shall be treated as if it were a requirement of a national primary drinking water regulation.

(v) As an additional alternative to the regulations promulgated pursuant to clauses (i) and (iii), including the criteria for avoiding filtration contained in 40 CFR 141.71, a State exercising primary enforcement responsibility for public water systems may, on a case-by-case basis, and after notice and opportunity for public comment, establish treatment requirements as an alternative to filtration in the case of systems having uninhabited, undeveloped watersheds in consolidated ownership, and having control over access to, and activities in, those watersheds, if the State determines (and the Administrator concurs) that the quality of the source water and the alternative treatment requirements established by the State ensure greater removal or inactivation efficiencies of pathogenic organisms for which national primary drinking water regulations have been promulgated or that are of public health concern than would be achieved by the combination of filtration and chlorine disinfection (in compliance with this section).

(8) Disinfection — At any time after the end of the 3-year period that begins on August 6, 1996, but not later than the date on which the Administrator promulgates a Stage II rulemaking for disinfectants and disinfection byproducts (as described in paragraph (2)(C)), the Administrator shall also promulgate national primary drinking water regulations requiring disinfection as a treatment technique for all public water systems, including surface water systems and, as necessary, ground water systems. After consultation with the States, the Administrator shall (as part of the regulations) promulgate criteria that the Administrator, or a State that has primary enforcement responsibility under section 300g-2 of this title, shall apply to determine whether disinfection shall be required as a treatment technique for any public water system served by ground water. The Administrator shall simultaneously promulgate a rule specifying criteria that will be used by the Administrator (or delegated State authorities) to grant variances from this requirement according to the provisions of sections 300g-4(a)(1)(B) and 300g-4(a)(3) of this title. In implementing section 300j-1(e) of this title the Administrator or the delegated State authority shall, where appropriate, give special consideration to providing technical assistance to small public water systems in complying with the regulations promulgated under this paragraph.

(9) Review and revision — The Administrator shall, not less often than every 6 years, review and revise, as appropriate, each national primary drinking water regulation promulgated under this subchapter. Any revision of a national primary drinking water regulation shall be promulgated in accordance with this section, except that each revision shall maintain, or provide for greater, protection of the health of persons.

(10) Effective date — A national primary drinking water regulation promulgated under this section (and any amendment thereto) shall take effect on the date that is 3 years after the date on which the regulation is promulgated unless the Administrator determines that an earlier date is practicable, except that the Administrator, or a State (in the case of an individual system), may allow up to 2 additional years to comply with a maximum contaminant level or treatment technique if the Administrator or State (in the case of an individual system) determines that additional time is necessary for capital improvements.

(11) No national primary drinking water regulation may require the addition of any substance for preventive health care purposes unrelated to contamination of drinking water.

(12) Certain contaminants —

(A) Arsenic

(i) Schedule and standard — Notwithstanding the deadlines set forth in paragraph (1), the Administrator shall promulgate a national primary drinking water regulation for arsenic pursuant to this subsection, in accordance with the schedule established by this paragraph.

(ii) Study plan — Not later than 180 days after August 6, 1996, the Administrator shall develop a comprehensive plan for study in support of drinking water rulemaking to reduce the uncertainty in assessing health risks associated with exposure to low levels of arsenic. In conducting such study, the Administrator shall consult with the National Academy of Sciences, other Federal agencies, and interested public and private entities.

(iii) Cooperative agreements — In carrying out the study plan, the Administrator may enter into cooperative agreements with other Federal agencies, State and local governments, and other interested public and private entities.

(iv) Proposed regulations — The Administrator shall propose a national primary drinking water regulation for arsenic not later than January 1, 2000.

(v) Final regulations — Not later than January 1, 2001, after notice and opportunity for public comment, the Administrator shall promulgate a national primary drinking water regulation for arsenic.

(vi) Authorization — There are authorized to be appropriated $2,500,000 for each of fiscal years 1997 through 2000 for the studies required by this paragraph.

(B) Sulfate

(i) Additional study — Prior to promulgating a national primary drinking water regulation for sulfate, the Administrator and the Director of the Centers for Disease Control and Prevention shall jointly conduct an additional study to establish a reliable dose-response relationship for the adverse human health effects that may result from exposure to sulfate in drinking water, including the health effects that may be experienced by groups within the general population (including infants and travelers) that are potentially at greater risk of adverse health effects as the result of such exposure. The study shall be conducted in consultation with interested States, shall be based on the best available, peer-reviewed science and supporting studies conducted in accordance with sound and objective scientific practices, and shall be completed not later than 30 months after August 6, 1996.

(ii) Determination — The Administrator shall include sulfate among the 5 or more contaminants for which a determination is made pursuant to paragraph (3)(B) not later than 5 years after August 6, 1996.

(iii) Proposed and final rule — Notwithstanding the deadlines set forth in paragraph (2), the Administrator may, pursuant to the authorities of this subsection and after notice and opportunity for public comment, promulgate a final national primary drinking water regulation for sulfate. Any such regulation shall include requirements for public notification and options for the provision of alternative water supplies to populations at risk as a means of complying with the regulation in lieu of a best available treatment technology or other means.

(13) Radon in drinking water

(A) National primary drinking water regulation — Notwithstanding paragraph (2), the Administrator shall withdraw any national primary drinking water regulation for radon proposed prior to August 6, 1996, and shall propose and promulgate a regulation for radon under this section, as amended by the Safe Drinking Water Act Amendments of 1996.

(B) Risk assessment and studies —

(i) Assessment by NAS — Prior to proposing a national primary drinking water regulation for radon, the Administrator shall arrange for the National Academy of Sciences to prepare a risk assessment for radon in drinking water using the best available science in accordance with the requirements of paragraph (3). The risk assessment shall consider each of the risks associated with exposure to radon from drinking water and consider studies on the health effects of radon at levels and under conditions likely to be experienced through residential exposure. The risk assessment shall be peer-reviewed.

(ii) Study of other measures — The Administrator shall arrange for the National Academy of Sciences to prepare an assessment of the health risk reduction benefits associated with various mitigation measures to reduce radon levels in indoor air. The assessment may be conducted as part of the risk assessment authorized by clause (i) and shall be used by the Administrator to prepare the guidance and approve State programs under subparagraph (G).

(iii) Other organization — If the National Academy of Sciences declines to prepare the risk assessment or studies required by this subparagraph, the Administrator shall enter into a contract or cooperative agreement with another independent, scientific organization to prepare such assessments or studies.

(C) Health risk reduction and cost analysis — Not later than 30 months after August 6, 1996, the Administrator shall publish, and seek public comment on, a health risk reduction and cost analysis meeting the requirements of paragraph (3)(C) for potential maximum contaminant levels that are being considered for radon in drinking water. The Administrator shall include a response to all significant public comments received on the analysis with the preamble for the proposed rule published under subparagraph (D).

(D) Proposed regulation — Not later than 36 months after August 6, 1996, the Administrator shall propose a maximum contaminant level goal and a national primary drinking water regulation for radon pursuant to this section.

(E) Final regulation — Not later than 12 months after the date of the proposal under subparagraph (D), the Administrator shall publish a maximum contaminant level goal and promulgate a national primary drinking water regulation for radon pursuant to this section based on the risk assessment prepared pursuant to subparagraph (B) and the health risk reduction and cost analysis published pursuant to subparagraph (C). In considering the risk assessment and the health risk reduction and cost analysis in connection with the promulgation of such a standard, the Administrator shall take into account the costs and benefits of control programs for radon from other sources.

(F) Alternative maximum contaminant level — If the maximum contaminant level for radon in drinking water promulgated pursuant to subparagraph (E) is more stringent than necessary to reduce the contribution to radon in indoor air from drinking water to a concentration that is equivalent to the national average concentration of radon in outdoor air, the Administrator shall, simultaneously with the promulgation of such level, promulgate an alternative maximum contaminant level for radon that would result in a contribution of radon from drinking water to radon levels in indoor air equivalent to the national average concentration of radon in outdoor air. If the Administrator promulgates an alternative maximum contaminant level under this subparagraph, the Administrator shall, after notice and opportunity for public comment and in consultation with the States, publish guidelines for State programs, including criteria for multimedia measures to mitigate radon levels in indoor air, to be used by the States in preparing programs under subparagraph (G). The guidelines shall take into account data from existing radon mitigation programs and the assessment of mitigation measures prepared under subparagraph (B).

(G) Multimedia radon mitigation programs

(i) In general — A State may develop and submit a multimedia program to mitigate radon levels in indoor air for approval by the Administrator under this subparagraph. If, after notice and the opportunity for public comment, such program is approved by the Administrator, public water systems in the State may comply with the alternative maximum contaminant level promulgated under subparagraph (F) in lieu of the maximum contaminant level in the national primary drinking water regulation promulgated under subparagraph (E).

(ii) Elements of programs — State programs may rely on a variety of mitigation measures including public education, testing, training, technical assistance, remediation grant and loan or incentive programs, or other regulatory or nonregulatory measures. The effectiveness of elements in State programs shall be evaluated by the Administrator based on the assessment prepared by the National Academy of Sciences under subparagraph (B) and the guidelines published by the Administrator under subparagraph (F).

(iii) Approval — The Administrator shall approve a State program submitted under this paragraph if the health risk reduction benefits expected to be achieved by the program are equal to or greater than the health risk reduction benefits that would be achieved if each public water system in the State complied with the maximum contaminant level promulgated under subparagraph (E). The Administrator shall approve or disapprove a program submitted under this paragraph within 180 days of receipt. A program that is not disapproved during such period shall be deemed approved. A program that is disapproved may be modified to address the objections of the Administrator and be resubmitted for approval.

(iv) Review — The Administrator shall periodically, but not less often than every 5 years, review each multimedia mitigation program approved under this subparagraph to determine whether it continues to meet the requirements of clause (iii) and shall, after written notice to the State and an opportunity for the State to correct any deficiency in the program, withdraw approval of programs that no longer comply with such requirements.

(v) Extension — If, within 90 days after the promulgation of an alternative maximum contaminant level under subparagraph (F), the Governor of a State submits a letter to the Administrator committing to develop a multimedia mitigation program under this subparagraph, the effective date of the national primary drinking water regulation for radon in the State that would be applicable under paragraph (10) shall be extended for a period of 18 months.

(vi) Local programs — In the event that a State chooses not to submit a multimedia mitigation program for approval under this subparagraph or has submitted a program that has been disapproved, any public water system in the State may submit a program for approval by the Administrator according to the same criteria, conditions, and approval process that would apply to a State program. The Administrator shall approve a multimedia mitigation program if the health risk reduction benefits expected to be achieved by the program are equal to or greater than the health risk reduction benefits that would result from compliance by the public water system with the maximum contaminant level for radon promulgated under subparagraph (E).

(14) Recycling of filter backwash — The Administrator shall promulgate a regulation to govern the recycling of filter backwash water within the treatment process of a public water system. The Administrator shall promulgate such regulation not later than 4 years after August 6, 1996, unless such recycling has been addressed by the Administrator's Enhanced Surface Water Treatment Rule prior to such date.

(15) Variance technologies

(A) In general — At the same time as the Administrator promulgates a national primary drinking water regulation for a contaminant pursuant to this section, the Administrator shall issue guidance or regulations describing the best treatment technologies, treatment techniques, or other means (referred to in this paragraph as "variance technology") for the contaminant that the Administrator finds, after examination for efficacy under field conditions and not solely under laboratory conditions, are available and affordable, as determined by the Administrator in consultation with the States, for public water systems of varying size, considering the quality of the source water to be treated. The Administrator shall identify such variance technologies for public water systems serving —

(i) a population of 10,000 or fewer but more than 3,300;

(ii) a population of 3,300 or fewer but more than 500; and

(iii) a population of 500 or fewer but more than 25,

if, considering the quality of the source water to be treated, no treatment technology is listed for public water systems of that size under paragraph (4)(E). Variance technologies identified by the Administrator pursuant to this paragraph may not achieve compliance with the maximum contaminant level or treatment technique requirement of such regulation, but shall achieve the maximum reduction or inactivation efficiency that is affordable considering the size of the system and the quality of the source water. The guidance or regulations shall not require the use of a technology from a specific manufacturer or brand.

(B) Limitation — The Administrator shall not identify any variance technology under this paragraph, unless the Administrator has determined, considering the quality of the source water to be treated and the expected useful life of the technology, that the variance technology is protective of public health.

(C) Additional information — The Administrator shall include in the guidance or regulations identifying variance technologies under this paragraph any assumptions supporting the public health determination referred to in subparagraph (B), where such assumptions concern the public water system to which the technology may be applied, or its source waters. The Administrator shall provide any assumptions used in determining affordability, taking into consideration the number of persons served by such systems. The Administrator shall provide as much reliable information as practicable on performance, effectiveness, limitations, costs, and other relevant factors including the applicability of variance technology to waters from surface and underground sources.

(D) Regulations and guidance — Not later than 2 years after August 6, 1996, and after consultation with the States, the Administrator shall issue guidance or regulations under subparagraph (A) for each national primary drinking water regulation promulgated prior to August 6, 1996, for which a variance may be granted under section 300g-4(e) of this title. The Administrator may, at any time after a national primary drinking water regulation has been promulgated, issue guidance or regulations describing additional variance technologies. The Administrator shall, not less often than every 7 years, or upon receipt of a petition supported by substantial information, review variance technologies identified under this paragraph. The Administrator shall issue revised guidance or regulations if new or innovative variance technologies become available that meet the requirements of this paragraph and achieve an equal or greater reduction or inactivation efficiency than the variance technologies previously identified under this subparagraph. No public water system shall be required to replace a variance technology during the useful life of the technology for the sole reason that a more efficient variance technology has been listed under this subparagraph.

(c) **Secondary regulations; publication of proposed regulations; promulgation; amendments** — The Administrator shall publish proposed national secondary drinking water regulations within 270 days after December 16, 1974. Within 90 days after publication of any such regulation, he shall promulgate such regulation with such modifications as he deems appropriate. Regulations under this subsection may be amended from time to time.

(d) **Regulations; public hearings; administrative consultations** — Regulations under this section shall be prescribed in accordance with section 553 of Title 5 (relating to rulemaking), except that the Administrator shall provide opportunity for public hearing prior to promulgation of such regulations. In proposing and promulgating regulations under this section, the Administrator shall consult with the Secretary and the National Drinking Water Advisory Council.

(e) **Science Advisory Board comments** — The Administrator shall request comments from the Science Advisory Board (established under the Environmental Research, Development, and Demonstration Act of 1978) prior to proposal of a maximum contaminant level goal and national primary drinking water regulation. The Board shall respond, as it deems appropriate, within the time period applicable for promulgation of the national primary drinking water standard concerned. This subsection shall, under no circumstances, be used to delay final promulgation of any national primary drinking water standard.

§300g-2. State primary enforcement responsibility

[PHSA §1413]

(a) **In general** — For purposes of this subchapter, a State has primary enforcement responsibility for public water systems during any period for which the Administrator determines (pursuant to regulations prescribed under subsection (b) of this section) that such State —

(1) has adopted drinking water regulations that are no less stringent than the national primary drinking water regulations promulgated by the Administrator under subsections (a) and (b) of section 300g-1 of this title not later than 2 years after the date on which the regulations are promulgated by the Administrator, except that the Administrator may provide for an extension of not more than 2 years if, after submission and review of appropriate, adequate documentation from the State, the Administrator determines that the extension is necessary and justified;

(2) has adopted and is implementing adequate procedures for the enforcement of such State regulations, including conducting such monitoring and making such inspections as the Administrator may require by regulation;

(3) will keep such records and make such reports with respect to its activities under paragraphs (1) and (2) as the Administrator may require by regulation;

(4) if it permits variances or exemptions, or both, from the requirements of its drinking water regulations which meet the requirements of paragraph (1), permits such variances and exemptions under conditions and in a manner which is not less stringent than the conditions under, and the manner in which variances and exemptions may be granted under sections 300g-4 and 300g-5 of this title;

(5) has adopted and can implement an adequate plan for the provision of safe drinking water under emergency circumstances including earthquakes, floods, hurricanes, and other natural disasters, as appropriate;

(6) has adopted and is implementing procedures for requiring public water systems to assess options for consolidation or transfer of ownership or other actions in accordance with the regulations issued by the Administrator under section 300g-3(h)(6) of this title; and

(7) has adopted authority for administrative penalties (unless the constitution of the State prohibits the adoption of the authority) in a maximum amount —

(A) in the case of a system serving a population of more than 10,000, that is not less than $1,000 per day per violation; and

(B) in the case of any other system, that is adequate to ensure compliance (as determined by the State);

except that a State may establish a maximum limitation on the total amount of administrative penalties that may be imposed on a public water system per violation.

(b) Regulations

(1) The Administrator shall, by regulation (proposed within 180 days of December 16, 1974), prescribe the manner in which a State may apply to the Administrator for a determination that the requirements of paragraphs (1), (2), (3), and (4) of subsection (a) of this section are satisfied with respect to the State, the manner in which the determination is made, the period for which the determination will be effective, and the manner in which the Administrator may determine that such requirements are no longer met. Such regulations shall require that before a determination of the Administrator that such requirements are met or are no longer met with respect to a State may become effective, the Administrator shall notify such State of the determination and the reasons therefor and shall provide an opportunity for public hearing on the determination. Such regulations shall be promulgated (with such modifications as the Administrator deems appropriate) within 90 days of the publication of the proposed regulations in the Federal Register. The Administrator shall promptly notify in writing the chief executive officer of each State of the promulgation of regulations under this paragraph. Such notice shall contain a copy of the regulations and shall specify a State's authority under this subchapter when it is determined to have primary enforcement responsibility for public water systems.

(2) When an application is submitted in accordance with the Administrator's regulations under paragraph (1), the Administrator shall within 90 days of the date on which such application is submitted (A) make the determination applied for, or (B) deny the application and notify the applicant in writing of the reasons for his denial.

(c) Interim primary enforcement authority — A State that has primary enforcement authority under this section with respect to each existing national primary drinking water regulation shall be considered to have primary enforcement authority with respect to each new or revised national primary drinking water regulation during the period beginning on the effective date of a regulation adopted and submitted by the State with respect to the new or revised national primary drinking water regulation in accordance with subsection (b)(1) of this section and ending at such time as the Administrator makes a determination under subsection (b)(2)(B) of this section with respect to the regulation.

§300g-3. Enforcement of drinking water regulations

[PHSA §1414]

(a) Notice to State and public water system; issuance of administrative order; civil action

(1)(A) Whenever the Administrator finds during a period during which a State has primary enforcement responsibility for public water systems (within the meaning of section 300g-2(a) of this title) that any public water system —

    (i) for which a variance under section 300g-4 or an exemption under section 300g-5 of this title is not in effect, does not comply with any applicable requirement, or

    (ii) for which a variance under section 300g-4 or an exemption under section 300g-5 of this title is in effect, does not comply with any schedule or other requirement imposed pursuant thereto,

he shall so notify the State and such public water system and provide such advice and technical assistance to such State and public water system as may be appropriate to bring the system into compliance with the requirement by the earliest feasible time.

(B) If, beyond the thirtieth day after the Administrator's notification under subparagraph (A), the State has not commenced appropriate enforcement action, the Administrator shall issue an order under subsection (g) of this section requiring the public water system to comply with such applicable requirement or the Administrator shall commence a civil action under subsection (b) of this section.

(2) Enforcement in nonprimacy states

(A) In general — If, on the basis of information available to the Administrator, the Administrator finds, with respect to a period in which a State does not have primary enforcement responsibility for public water systems, that a public water system in the State —

    (i) for which a variance under section 300g-4 of this title or an exemption under section 300g-5 of this title is not in effect, does not comply with any applicable requirement; or

    (ii) for which a variance under section 300g-4 of this title or an exemption under section 300g-5 of this title is in effect, does not comply with any schedule or other requirement imposed pursuant to the variance or exemption;

the Administrator shall issue an order under subsection (g) of this section requiring the public water system to comply with the requirement, or commence a civil action under subsection (b) of this section.

(B) Notice — If the Administrator takes any action pursuant to this paragraph, the Administrator shall notify an appropriate local elected official, if any, with jurisdiction over the public water system of the action prior to the time that the action is taken.

(b) Judicial determinations in appropriate Federal district courts; civil penalties, separate violations — The Administrator may bring a civil action in the appropriate United States district court to require compliance with any applicable requirement with an order issued under subsection (g) of this section, or with any schedule or other requirement imposed pursuant to a variance or exemption granted under section 300g-4 or 300g-5 of this title if —

   (1) authorized under paragraph (1) or (2) of subsection (a) of this section, or

   (2) if requested by (A) the chief executive officer of the State in which is located the public water system which is not in compliance with such regulation or requirement, or (B) the agency of such State which has jurisdiction over compliance by public water systems in the State with national primary drinking water regulations or State drinking water regulations.

The court may enter, in an action brought under this subsection, such judgment as protection of public health may require, taking into consideration the time necessary to comply and the availability of alternative water supplies; and, if the court determines that there has been a violation of the regulation or schedule or other requirement with respect to which the action was brought, the court may, taking into account the seriousness of the violation, the population at risk, and other appropriate factors, impose on the violator a civil penalty of not to exceed $25,000 for each day in which such violation occurs.

(c) Notice to States, the Administrator, and persons served

   (1) In general — Each owner or operator of a public water system shall give notice of each of the following to the persons served by the system:

     (A) Notice of any failure on the part of the public water system to —

       (i) comply with an applicable maximum contaminant level or treatment technique requirement of, or a testing procedure prescribed by, a national primary drinking water regulation; or

       (ii) perform monitoring required by section 300j-4(a) of this title.

     (B) If the public water system is subject to a variance granted under subsection (a)(1)(A), (a)(2), or (e) of section 300g-4 of this title for an inability to meet a maximum contaminant level requirement or is subject to an exemption granted under section 300g-5 of this title, notice of —

       (i) the existence of the variance or exemption; and

       (ii) any failure to comply with the requirements of any schedule prescribed pursuant to the variance or exemption.

     (C) Notice of the concentration level of any unregulated contaminant for which the Administrator has required public notice pursuant to paragraph (2)(F).

     (D) Notice that the public water system exceeded the lead action level under section 141.80(c) of title 40, Code of Federal Regulations (or a prescribed level of lead that the Administrator establishes for public education or notification in a successor regulation promulgated pursuant to section 300g-1 of this title).

   (2) Form, manner, and frequency of notice

     (A) In general — The Administrator shall, by regulation, and after consultation with the States, prescribe the manner, frequency, form, and content for giving notice under this subsection. The regulations shall —

       (i) provide for different frequencies of notice based on the differences between violations that are intermittent or infrequent and violations that are continuous or frequent; and

       (ii) take into account the seriousness of any potential adverse health effects that may be involved.

     (B) State requirements

       (i) In general — A State may, by rule, establish alternative notification requirements —

         (I) with respect to the form and content of notice given under and in a manner in accordance with subparagraph (C); and

         (II) with respect to the form and content of notice given under subparagraph (E).

       (ii) Contents — The alternative requirements shall provide the same type and amount of information as required pursuant to this subsection and regulations issued under subparagraph (A).

       (iii) Relationship to section 300g-2 — Nothing in this subparagraph shall be construed or applied to modify the requirements of section 300g-2 of this title.

     (C) Notice of violations or exceedances with potential to have serious adverse effects on human health — Regulations issued under subparagraph (A) shall specify notification procedures for each violation, and each exceedance described in paragraph (1)(D), by a public water system that has the potential to have serious adverse effects on human health as a result of short-term exposure. Each notice of violation or exceedance provided under this subparagraph shall —

       (i) be distributed as soon as practicable, but not later than 24 hours, after the public water system learns of the violation or exceedance;

       (ii) provide a clear and readily understandable explanation of —

         (I) the violation or exceedance;

         (II) the potential adverse effects on human health;

         (III) the steps that the public water

system is taking to correct the violation or exceedance; and

(IV) the necessity of seeking alternative water supplies until the violation or exceedance is corrected;

(iii) be provided to the Administrator and the head of the State agency that has primary enforcement responsibility under section 300g-2 of this title, as applicable, as soon as practicable, but not later than 24 hours after the public water system learns of the violation or exceedance; and

(iv) as required by the State agency in general regulations of the State agency, or on a case-by-case basis after the consultation referred to in clause (iii), considering the health risks involved —

(I) be provided to appropriate media, including broadcast media;

(II) be prominently published in a newspaper of general circulation serving the area not later than 1 day after distribution of a notice pursuant to clause (i) or the date of publication of the next issue of the newspaper; or

(III) be provided by posting or door-to-door notification.

(D) Notice by the Administrator

If the State with primary enforcement responsibility or the owner or operator of a public water system has not issued a notice under subparagraph (C) for an exceedance of the lead action level under section 141.80(c) of title 40, Code of Federal Regulations (or a prescribed level of lead that the Administrator establishes for public education or notification in a successor regulation promulgated pursuant to section 300g-1 of this title) that has the potential to have serious adverse effects on human health as a result of short-term exposure, not later than 24 hours after the Administrator is notified of the exceedance, the Administrator shall issue the required notice under that subparagraph.

(E) Written notice

(i) In general

Regulations issued under subparagraph (A) shall specify notification procedures for violations other than the violations covered by subparagraph (C). The procedures shall specify that a public water system shall provide written notice to each person served by the system by notice (I) in the first bill (if any) prepared after the date of occurrence of the violation, (II) in an annual report issued not later than 1 year after the date of occurrence of the violation, or (III) by mail or direct delivery

as soon as practicable, but not later than 1 year after the date of occurrence of the violation.

(ii) Form and manner of notice

The Administrator shall prescribe the form and manner of the notice to provide a clear and readily understandable explanation of the violation, any potential adverse health effects, and the steps that the system is taking to seek alternative water supplies, if any, until the violation is corrected.

(F) Unregulated contaminants

The Administrator may require the owner or operator of a public water system to give notice to the persons served by the system of the concentration levels of an unregulated contaminant required to be monitored under section 300j-4(a) of this title.

(3) Reports

(A) Annual report by State

(i) In general

Not later than January 1, 1998, and annually thereafter, each State that has primary enforcement responsibility under section 300g-2 of this title shall prepare, make readily available to the public, and submit to the Administrator an annual report on violations of national primary drinking water regulations by public water systems in the State, including violations with respect to (I) maximum contaminant levels, (II) treatment requirements, (III) variances and exemptions, and (IV) monitoring requirements determined to be significant by the Administrator after consultation with the States.

(ii) Distribution

The State shall publish and distribute summaries of the report and indicate where the full report is available for review.

(B) Annual report by Administrator

Not later than July 1, 1998, and annually thereafter, the Administrator shall prepare and make available to the public an annual report summarizing and evaluating reports submitted by States pursuant to subparagraph (A), notices submitted by public water systems serving Indian Tribes provided to the Administrator pursuant to subparagraph (C) or (E) of paragraph (2), and notices issued by the Administrator with respect to public water systems serving Indian Tribes under subparagraph (D) of that paragraph and making recommendations concerning the resources needed to improve compliance with this subchapter. The report shall include information about public water system compliance on Indian reservations and about enforcement activities undertaken and financial assistance provided by the Administrator on Indian reservations, and shall make specific recommendations concerning the resources needed to improve compliance with this subchapter on Indian reservations.

(4) Consumer confidence reports by community water systems

(A) Reports to consumers

The Administrator, in consultation with public water systems, environmental groups, public interest groups, risk communication experts, and the States, and other interested parties, shall issue regulations within 24 months after August 6, 1996, to require each community water system to mail, or provide by electronic means, to each customer of the system at least once annually a report on the level of contaminants in the drinking water purveyed by that system (referred to in this paragraph as a "consumer confidence report"). Such regulations shall provide a brief and plainly worded definition of the terms "maximum contaminant level goal," "maximum contaminant level," "variances," and "exemptions" and brief statements in plain language regarding the health concerns that resulted in regulation of each regulated contaminant. The regulations shall also include a brief and plainly worded explanation regarding contaminants that may reasonably be expected to be present in drinking water, including bottled water. The regulations shall also provide for an Environmental Protection Agency toll-free hotline that consumers can call for more information and explanation.

(B) Contents of report

The consumer confidence reports under this paragraph shall include, but not be limited to, each of the following:

(i) Information on the source of the water purveyed.

(ii) A brief and plainly worded definition of the terms "action level," "maximum contaminant level goal," "maximum contaminant level," "variances," and "exemptions" as provided in the regulations of the Administrator.

(iii) If any regulated contaminant is detected in the water purveyed by the public water system, a statement describing, as applicable —

(I) the maximum contaminant level goal;

(II) the maximum contaminant level;

(III) the level of the contaminant in the water system;

(IV) the action level for the contaminant; and

(V) for any contaminant for which there has been a violation of the maximum contaminant level during the year concerned, a brief statement in plain language regarding the health concerns that resulted in regulation of the contaminant, as provided by the Administrator in regulations under subparagraph (A).

(iv) Information on compliance with national primary drinking water regulations, as required by the Administrator, including corrosion control efforts, and notice if the system is operating under a variance or exemption and the basis on which the variance or exemption was granted.

(v) Information on the levels of unregulated contaminants for which monitoring is required under section 300j-4(a)(2) of this title (including levels of cryptosporidium and radon where States determine they may be found).

(vi) A statement that the presence of contaminants in drinking water does not necessarily indicate that the drinking water poses a health risk and that more information about contaminants and potential health effects can be obtained by calling the Environmental Protection Agency hotline.

(vii) Identification of, if any —

(I) exceedances described in paragraph (1)(D) for which corrective action has been required by the Administrator or the State (in the case of a State exercising primary enforcement responsibility for public water systems) during the monitoring period covered by the consumer confidence report; and

(II) violations that occurred during the monitoring period covered by the consumer confidence report.

A public water system may include such additional information as it deems appropriate for public education. The Administrator may, for not more than 3 regulated contaminants other than those referred to in clause (iii)(V), require a consumer confidence report under this paragraph to include the brief statement in plain language regarding the health concerns that resulted in regulation of the contaminant or contaminants concerned, as provided by the Administrator in regulations under subparagraph (A).

(C) Coverage

The Governor of a State may determine not to apply the mailing requirement of subparagraph (A) to a community water system serving fewer than 10,000 persons. Any such system shall —

(i) inform, in the newspaper notice required by clause (iii) or by other means, its customers that the system will not be mailing the report as required by subparagraph (A);

(ii) make the consumer confidence report available upon request to the public; and

(iii) publish the report referred to in subparagraph (A) annually in one or more local newspapers serving the area in which customers of the system are located.

(D) Alternative to publication

For any community water system which, pursuant to subparagraph (C), is not required to meet the mailing requirement of subparagraph (A) and which serves 500 persons or fewer, the community water system may elect not to comply with clause (i) or (iii) of subparagraph (C). If the community water system so elects, the system shall, at a minimum —

(i) prepare an annual consumer confidence report pursuant to subparagraph (B); and

(ii) provide notice at least once per year to each of its customers by mail, by door-to-door delivery, by posting or by other means authorized by the regulations of the Administrator that the consumer confidence report is available upon request.

(E) Alternative form and content

A State exercising primary enforcement responsibility may establish, by rule, after notice and public comment, alternative requirements with respect to the form and content of consumer confidence reports under this paragraph.

(F) Revisions

(i) Understandability and frequency

Not later than 24 months after October 23, 2018, the Administrator, in consultation with the parties identified in subparagraph (A), shall issue revisions to the regulations issued under subparagraph (A) —

(I) to increase —

(aa) the readability, clarity, and understandability of the information presented in consumer confidence reports; and

(bb) the accuracy of information presented, and risk communication, in consumer confidence reports; and

(II) with respect to community water systems that serve 10,000 or more persons, to require each such community water system to provide, by mail, electronic means, or other methods described in clause (ii), a consumer confidence report to each customer of the system at least biannually.

(ii) Electronic delivery

Any revision of regulations pursuant to clause (i) shall allow delivery of consumer confidence reports by methods consistent with methods described in the memorandum "Safe Drinking Water Act-Consumer Confidence Report Rule Delivery Options" issued by the Environmental Protection Agency on January 3, 2013.

(5) Exceedance of lead level at households

(A) Strategic plan

Not later than 180 days after December 16, 2016, the Administrator shall, in collaboration with owners and operators of public water systems and States, establish a strategic plan for how the Administrator, a State with primary enforcement responsibility, and owners and operators of public water systems shall provide targeted outreach, education, technical assistance, and risk communication to populations affected by the concentration of lead in a public water system, including dissemination of information described in subparagraph (C).

(B) EPA initiation of notice

(i) Forwarding of data by employee of the Agency

If the Agency develops, or receives from a source other than a State or a public water system, data that meets the requirements of section 300g-1(b)(3)(A)(ii) of this title that indicates that the drinking water of a household served by a public water system contains a level of lead that exceeds the lead action level under section 141.80(c) of title 40, Code of Federal Regulations (or a prescribed level of lead that the Administrator establishes for public education or notification in a successor regulation promulgated pursuant to section 300g-1 of this title) (referred to in this paragraph as an "affected household"), the Administrator shall require an appropriate employee of the Agency to forward the data, and information on the sampling techniques used to obtain the data, to the owner or operator of the public water system and the State in which the affected household is located within a time period determined by the Administrator.

(ii) Dissemination of information by owner or operator

The owner or operator of a public water system shall disseminate to affected households the information described in subparagraph (C) within a time period established by the Administrator, if the owner or operator —

(I) receives data and information under clause (i); and

(II) has not, since the date of the test that developed the data, notified the affected households —

(aa) with respect to the concentration of lead in the drinking water of the affected households; and

(bb) that the concentration of lead in the drinking water of the affected households exceeds the lead action level under section 141.80(c) of title 40, Code of Federal Regulations (or a prescribed level of lead that the Administrator establishes for public education or notification in a successor regulation promulgated pursuant to section 300g-1 of this title).

(iii) Consultation

(I) Deadline

If the owner or operator of the public water system does not disseminate to the affected households the information described in subparagraph (C) as required under clause (ii) within the time period established by the Administrator, not later than 24 hours after the Administrator becomes aware of the failure by the owner or operator of the public water system to disseminate the information, the Administrator shall consult, within a period not to exceed 24 hours, with the applicable Governor to develop a plan, in accordance with the strategic plan, to disseminate the information to the affected households not later than 24 hours after the end of the consultation period.

(II) Delegation

The Administrator may only delegate the duty to consult under subclause (I) to an employee of the Agency who, as of the date of the delegation, works in the Office of Water at the headquarters of the Agency.

(iv) Dissemination by Administrator

The Administrator shall, as soon as practicable, disseminate to affected households the information described in subparagraph (C) if —

(I) the owner or operator of the public water system does not disseminate the information to the affected households within the time period determined by the Administrator, as required by clause (ii); and

(II)(aa) the Administrator and the applicable Governor do not agree on a plan described in clause (iii)(I) during the consultation period under that clause; or

(bb) the applicable Governor does not disseminate the information within 24 hours after the end of the consultation period.

(C) Information required

The information described in this subparagraph includes —

(i) a clear explanation of the potential adverse effects on human health of drinking water that contains a concentration of lead that exceeds the lead action level under section 141.80(c) of title 40, Code of Federal Regulations (or a prescribed level of lead that the Administrator establishes for public education or notification in a successor regulation promulgated pursuant to section 300g-1 of this title);

(ii) the steps that the owner or operator of the public water system is taking to mitigate the concentration of lead; and

(iii) the necessity of seeking alternative water supplies until the date on which the concentration of lead is mitigated.

(6) Privacy

Any notice to the public or an affected household under this subsection shall protect the privacy of individual customer information.

(d) Notice of noncompliance with secondary drinking water regulations — Whenever, on the basis of information available to him, the Administrator finds that within a reasonable time after national secondary drinking water regulations have been promulgated, one or more public water systems in a State do not comply with such secondary regulations, and that such noncompliance appears to result from a failure of such State to take reasonable action to assure that public water systems throughout such State meet such secondary regulations, he shall so notify the State.

(e) State authority to adopt or enforce laws or regulations respecting drinking water regulations or public water systems unaffected — Nothing in this subchapter shall diminish any authority of a State or political subdivision to adopt or enforce any law or regulation respecting drinking water regulations or public water systems, but no such law or regulation shall relieve any person of any requirement otherwise applicable under this subchapter.

(f) Notice and public hearing; availability of recommendations transmitted to State and public water system — If the Administrator makes a finding of noncompliance (described in subparagraph (A) or (B) of subsection (a)(1) of this section) with respect to a public water system in a State which has primary enforcement responsibility, the Administrator may, for the purpose of assisting that State in carrying out such responsibility and upon the petition of such State or public water system or persons served by such system, hold, after appropriate notice, public hearings for the purpose of gathering information from technical or other experts, Federal, State, or other public officials, representatives of such public water system, persons served by such system, and other interested persons on —

(1) the ways in which such system can within the earliest feasible time be brought into compliance with the regulation or requirement with respect to which such finding was made, and

(2) the means for the maximum feasible protection of the public health during any period in which such system is not in compliance with a national primary drinking water regulation or requirement applicable to a variance or exemption. On the basis of such hearings the Administrator shall issue recommendations which shall be sent to such State and public water system and shall be made available to the public and communications media.

(g) Administrative order requiring compliance; notice and hearing; civil penalty; civil actions

(1) In any case in which the Administrator is authorized to bring a civil action under this section or under section 300j-4 of this title with respect to any applicable requirement, the Administrator also may issue an order to require compliance with such applicable requirement.

(2) An order issued under this subsection shall not take effect, in the case of a State having primary enforcement responsibility for public water systems in that State, until after the Administrator has provided the State with an opportunity to confer with the Administrator regarding the order. A copy of any order issued under this subsection shall be sent to the appropriate State agency of the State involved if the State has primary enforcement responsibility for public water systems in that State. Any order issued under this subsection shall state with reasonable specificity the nature of the violation. In any case in which an order under this subsection is issued to a corporation, a copy of such order shall be issued to appropriate corporate officers.

(3)(A) Any person who violates, or fails or refuses to comply with, an order under this subsection shall be liable to the United States for a civil penalty of not more than $25,000 per day of violation.

(B) In a case in which a civil penalty sought by the Administrator under this paragraph does not exceed $5,000, the penalty shall be assessed by the Administrator after notice and opportunity for a public hearing (unless the person against whom the penalty is assessed requests a hearing on the record in accordance with section 554 of Title 5). In a case in which a civil penalty sought by the Administrator under this paragraph exceeds $5,000, but does not exceed $25,000, the penalty shall be assessed by the Administrator after notice and opportunity for a hearing on the record in accordance with section 554 of Title 5.

(C) Whenever any civil penalty sought by the Administrator under this subsection for a violation of an applicable requirement exceeds $25,000, the penalty shall be assessed by a civil action brought by the Administrator in the appropriate United States district court (as determined under the provisions of Title 28).

(D) If any person fails to pay an assessment of a civil penalty after it has become a final and unappealable order, or after the appropriate court of appeals has entered final judgment in favor of the Administrator, the Attorney General shall recover the amount for which such person is liable in any appropriate district court of the United States. In any such action, the validity and appropriateness of the final order imposing the civil penalty shall not be subject to review.

(h) Consolidation incentive

(1) In general — An owner or operator of a public water system may submit to the State in which the system is located (if the State has primary enforcement responsibility under section 300g-2 of this title) or to the Administrator (if the State does not have primary enforcement responsibility) a plan (including specific measures and schedules) for —

(A) the physical consolidation of the system with 1 or more other systems;

(B) the consolidation of significant management and administrative functions of the system with 1 or more other systems; or

(C) the transfer of ownership of the system that may reasonably be expected to improve drinking water quality; or

(D) entering into a contractual agreement for significant management or administrative functions of the system to correct violations identified in the plan.

(2) Consequences of approval — If the State or the Administrator approves a plan pursuant to paragraph (1), no enforcement action shall be taken pursuant to this part with respect to a specific violation identified in the approved plan prior to the date that is the earlier of the date on which consolidation is completed according to the plan or the date that is 2 years after the plan is approved.

(3) Authority for mandatory assessment

(A) Authority

A State with primary enforcement responsibility or the Administrator (if the State does not have primary enforcement responsibility) may require the owner or operator of a public water system to assess options for consolidation, or transfer of ownership of the system, as described in paragraph (1), or other actions expected to achieve compliance with national primary drinking water regulations described in clause (i)(I), if —

(i) the public water system —

(I) has repeatedly violated one or more national primary drinking water regulations and such repeated violations are likely to adversely affect human health; and

(II)(aa) is unable or unwilling to take feasible and affordable actions, as determined by the State with primary enforcement responsibility or the Administrator (if the State does not have primary enforcement responsibility), that will result in the public water system complying with the national primary drinking water regulations described in subclause (I), including accessing technical assistance and financial assistance through the State loan fund pursuant to section 300j-12 of this title; or

(bb) has already undertaken actions described in item (aa) without achieving compliance;

(ii) such consolidation, transfer, or other action is feasible; and

(iii) such consolidation, transfer, or other action could result in greater compliance with national primary drinking water regulations.

(B) Tailoring of assessments

Requirements for any assessment to be conducted pursuant to subparagraph (A) shall be tailored with respect to the size, type, and characteristics, of the public water system to be assessed.

(C) Approved entities

An assessment conducted pursuant to subparagraph (A) may be conducted by an entity approved by the State requiring such assessment (or the Administrator, if the State does not have primary enforcement responsibility), which may include such State (or the Administrator, as applicable), the public water system, or a third party.

(D) Burden of assessments

It is the sense of Congress that any assessment required pursuant to subparagraph (A) should not be overly burdensome on the public water system that is assessed.

(4) Financial assistance

Notwithstanding section 300j-12(a)(3) of this title, a public water system undertaking consolidation or transfer of ownership or other actions pursuant to an assessment completed under paragraph (3) may receive a loan described in section 300j-12(a)(2)(A) of this title to carry out such consolidation, transfer, or other action.

(5) Protection of nonresponsible system

(A) Identification of liabilities

(i) In general

An owner or operator of a public water system that submits a plan pursuant to paragraph (1) based on an assessment conducted with respect to such public water system under paragraph (3) shall identify as part of such plan —

(I) any potential and existing liability for penalties and damages arising from each specific violation identified in the plan of which the owner or operator is aware; and

(II) any funds or other assets that are available to satisfy such liability, as of the date of submission of such plan, to the public water system that committed such violation.

(ii) Inclusion

In carrying out clause (i), the owner or operator shall take reasonable steps to ensure that all potential and existing liabilities for penalties and damages arising from each specific violation identified in the plan are identified.

(B) Reservation of funds

A public water system that, consistent with the findings of an assessment conducted pursuant to paragraph (3), has completed the actions under a plan submitted and approved pursuant to this subsection shall not be liable under this subchapter for a violation of this subchapter identified in the plan, except to the extent to which funds or other assets are identified pursuant to subparagraph (A)(i)(II) as available to satisfy such liability.

(6) Regulations

Not later than 2 years after October 23, 2018, the Administrator shall promulgate regulations to implement paragraphs (3), (4), and (5).

(i) **"Applicable requirement" defined** — In this section, the term "applicable requirement" means —

(1) a requirement of section 300g-1, 300g-3, 300g-4, 300g-5, 300g-6, 300i-2, 300j, or 300j-4 of this title;

(2) a regulation promulgated pursuant to a section referred to in paragraph (1);

(3) a schedule or requirement imposed pursuant to a section referred to in paragraph (1); and

(4) a requirement of, or permit issued under, an applicable State program for which the

Administrator has made a determination that the requirements of section 300g-2 of this title have been satisfied, or an applicable State program approved pursuant to this part.

(j) Improved accuracy and availability of compliance monitoring data

(1) Strategic plan

Not later than 1 year after October 23, 2018, the Administrator, in coordination with States (including States without primary enforcement responsibility under section 300g-2 of this title), public water systems, and other interested stakeholders, shall develop and provide to Congress a strategic plan for improving the accuracy and availability of monitoring data collected to demonstrate compliance with national primary drinking water regulations and submitted —

(A) by public water systems to States; or

(B) by States to the Administrator.

(2) Evaluation

In developing the strategic plan under paragraph (1), the Administrator shall evaluate any challenges faced —

(A) in ensuring the accuracy and integrity of submitted data described in paragraph (1);

(B) by States and public water systems in implementing an electronic system for submitting such data, including the technical and economic feasibility of implementing such a system; and

(C) by users of such electronic systems in being able to access such data.

(3) Findings and recommendations

The Administrator shall include in the strategic plan provided to Congress under paragraph (1)—

(A) a summary of the findings of the evaluation under paragraph (2); and

(B) recommendations on practicable, cost-effective methods and means that can be employed to improve the accuracy and availability of submitted data described in paragraph (1).

(4) Consultation

In developing the strategic plan under paragraph (1), the Administrator may, as appropriate, consult with States or other Federal agencies that have experience using practicable methods and means to improve the accuracy and availability of submitted data described in such paragraph.

§300g-4. Variances
[PHSA §1415]

(a) Characteristics of raw water sources; specific treatment technique; notice to Administrator, reasons for variance; compliance, enforcement; approval or revision of schedules and revocation of variances; review of variances and schedules; publication in Federal Register, notice and results of review; notice to State; considerations respecting abuse of discretion in granting variances or failing to prescribe schedules; State corrective action; authority of Administrator in a State without primary enforcement responsibility; alternative treatment techniques — Notwithstanding any other provision of this part, variances from national primary drinking water regulations may be granted as follows:

(1)(A) A State which has primary enforcement responsibility for public water systems may grant one or more variances from an applicable national primary drinking water regulation to one or more public water systems within its jurisdiction which, because of characteristics of the raw water sources which are reasonably available to the systems, cannot meet the requirements respecting the maximum contaminant levels of such drinking water regulation. A variance may be issued to a system on condition that the system install the best technology, treatment techniques, or other means, which the Administrator finds are available (taking costs into consideration), and based upon an evaluation satisfactory to the State that indicates that alternative sources of water are not reasonably available to the system. The Administrator shall propose and promulgate his finding of the best available technology, treatment techniques or other means available for each contaminant for purposes of this subsection at the time he proposes and promulgates a maximum contaminant level for each such contaminant. The Administrator's finding of best available technology, treatment techniques or other means for purposes of this subsection may vary depending on the number of persons served by the system or for other physical conditions related to engineering feasibility and costs of compliance with maximum contaminant levels as considered appropriate by the Administrator. Before a State may grant a variance under this subparagraph, the State must find that the variance will not result in an unreasonable risk to health. If a State grants a public water system a variance under this subparagraph, the State shall prescribe at the the time the variance is granted, a schedule for —

(i) compliance (including increments of progress) by the public water system with each containment level requirement with respect to which the variance was granted, and

(ii) implementation by the public water system of such additional control measures as the State may require for each contaminant, subject to such contaminant level requirement, during the period ending on the date compliance with such requirement is required. Before a schedule prescribed by a State pursuant to this subparagraph may take effect, the State shall provide notice and opportunity for a public hearing on the schedule. A notice given pursuant to the preceding sentence may cover the prescribing of more than one such schedule and a hearing held pursuant to such notice shall include each of the schedules covered by the notice. A schedule prescribed pursuant to this subparagraph for a public water system granted a variance shall require compliance by the system with each contaminant level requirement with respect to which the variance was granted as expeditiously as practicable (as the State may reasonably determine).

(B) A State which has primary enforcement responsibility for public water systems may grant to one or more public water systems within its jurisdiction one or more variances from any provision of a national primary drinking water regulation which requires the use of a specified treatment technique with respect to a contaminant if the public water system applying for the variance demonstrates to the satisfaction of the State that such treatment technique is not necessary to protect the health of persons because of the nature of the raw water source of such system. A variance granted under this subparagraph shall be conditioned on such monitoring and other requirements as the Administrator may prescribe.

(C) Before a variance proposed to be granted by a State under subparagraph (A) or (B) may take effect, such State shall provide notice and opportunity for public hearing on the proposed variance. A notice given pursuant to the preceding sentence may cover the granting of more than one variance and a hearing held pursuant to such notice shall include each of the variances covered by the notice. The State shall promptly notify the Administrator of all variances granted by it. Such notification shall contain the reason for the variance (and in the case of a variance under subparagraph (A), the basis for the finding required by that subparagraph before the granting of the variance) and documentation of the need for the variance.

(D) Each public water system's variance granted by a State under subparagraph (A) shall be conditioned by the State upon compliance by the public water system with the schedule prescribed by the State pursuant to that subparagraph. The requirements of each schedule prescribed by a State pursuant to that subparagraph shall be enforceable by the State under its laws. Any requirement of a schedule on which a variance granted under that subparagraph is conditioned may be enforced under section 300g-3 of this title as if such requirement was part of a national primary drinking water regulation.

(E) Each schedule prescribed by a State pursuant to subparagraph (A) shall be deemed approved by the Administrator unless the variance for which it was prescribed is revoked by the Administrator under subparagraph (G) or the schedule is revised by the Administrator under such subparagraph.

(F) Not later than 18 months after the effective date of the interim national primary drinking water regulations the Administrator shall complete a comprehensive review of the variances granted under subparagraph (A) (and schedules prescribed pursuant thereto) and under subparagraph (B) by the States during the one-year period beginning on such effective date. The Administrator shall conduct such subsequent reviews of variances and schedules as he deems necessary to carry out the purposes of this subchapter, but each subsequent review shall be completed within each 3-year period following the completion of the first review under this subparagraph. Before conducting any review under this subparagraph, the Administrator shall publish notice of the proposed review in the Federal Register. Such notice shall (i) provide information respecting the location of data and other information respecting the variances to be reviewed (including data and other information concerning new scientific matters bearing on such variances), and (ii) advise of the opportunity to submit comments on the variances reviewed and on the need for continuing them. Upon completion of any such review, the Administrator shall publish in the Federal Register the results of his review together with findings responsive to comments submitted in connection with such review.

(G)(i) If the Administrator finds that a State has, in a substantial number of instances, abused its discretion in granting variances under subparagraph (A) or (B) or that in a substantial number of cases the State has failed to prescribe schedules in accordance with subparagraph (A), the Administrator shall notify the State of his findings. In determining if a State has abused its discretion in granting variances in a substantial number of instances, the Administrator shall consider the number of persons who are affected by the variances and if the requirements applicable to the granting of the variances were complied with. A notice under this clause shall —

(I) identify each public water system with respect to which the finding was made,

(II) specify the reasons for the finding, and

(III) as appropriate, propose revocations of specific variances or propose revised schedules or other requirements for specific public water systems granted variances, or both.

(ii) The Administrator shall provide reasonable notice and public hearing on the provisions of each notice given pursuant to clause (i) of this subparagraph. After a hearing on a notice pursuant to such clause, the Administrator shall (I) rescind the finding for which the notice was given and promptly notify the State of such rescission, or (II) promulgate (with such modifications as he deems appropriate) such variance revocations and revised schedules or other requirements proposed in such notice as he deems appropriate. Not later than 180 days after the date a notice is given pursuant to clause (i) of this subparagraph, the Administrator shall complete the hearing on the notice and take the action required by the preceding sentence.

(iii) If a State is notified under clause (i) of this subparagraph of a finding of the Administrator made with respect to a variance granted a public water system within that State or to a schedule or other requirement for a variance and if, before a revocation of such variance or a revision of such schedule or other requirement promulgated by the Administrator takes effect, the State takes corrective action with respect to such variance or schedule or other requirement which the Administrator determines makes his finding inapplicable to such variance or schedule or other requirement, the Administrator shall rescind the application of his finding to that variance or schedule or other requirement. No variance revocation or revised schedule or other requirement may take effect before the expiration of 90 days following the date of the notice in which the revocation or revised schedule or other requirement was proposed.

(2) If a State does not have primary enforcement responsibility for public water systems, the Administrator shall have the same authority to grant variances in such State as the State would have under paragraph (1) if it had primary enforcement responsibility.

(3) The Administrator may grant a variance from any treatment technique requirement of a national primary drinking water regulation upon a showing by any person that an alternative treatment technique not included in such requirement is at least as efficient in lowering the level of the contaminant with respect to which such requirement was prescribed. A variance under this paragraph shall be conditioned on the use of the alternative treatment technique which is the basis of the variance.

(b) Enforcement of schedule or other requirement — Any schedule or other requirement on which a variance granted under paragraph (1)(B) or (2) of subsection (a) of this section is conditioned may be enforced under section 300g-3 of this title as if such schedule or other requirement was part of a national primary drinking water regulation.

(c) Applications for variances; regulations: reasonable time for acting — If an application for a variance under subsection (a) of this section is made, the State receiving the application or the Administrator, as the case may be, shall act upon such application within a reasonable period (as determined under regulations prescribed by the Administrator) after the date of its submission.

(d) "Treatment technique requirement" defined — For purposes of this section, the term "treatment technique requirement" means a requirement in a national primary drinking water regulation which specifies for a contaminant (in accordance with section 300f(1)(C)(ii) of this title) each treatment technique known to the Administrator which leads to a reduction in the level of such contaminant sufficient to satisfy the requirements of section 300g-1(b) of this title.

(e) Small system variances

(1) In general — A State exercising primary enforcement responsibility for public water systems under section 300g-2 of this title (or the Administrator in nonprimacy States) may grant a variance under this subsection for compliance with a requirement specifying a maximum contaminant level or treatment technique contained in a national primary drinking water regulation to —

    (A) public water systems serving 3,300 or fewer persons; and

    (B) with the approval of the Administrator pursuant to paragraph (9), public water systems serving more than 3,300 persons but fewer than 10,000 persons,

if the variance meets each requirement of this subsection.

(2) Availability of variances — A public water system may receive a variance pursuant to paragraph (1), if —

    (A) the Administrator has identified a variance technology under section 300g-1(b)(15) of this title that is applicable to the size and source water quality conditions of the public water system;

    (B) the public water system installs, operates, and maintains, in accordance with guidance or regulations issued by the Administrator, such treatment technology, treatment technique, or other means; and

    (C) the State in which the system is located determines that the conditions of paragraph (3) are met.

(3) Conditions for granting variances — A variance under this subsection shall be available only to a system —

(A) that cannot afford to comply, in accordance with affordability criteria established by the Administrator (or the State in the case of a State that has primary enforcement responsibility under section 300g-2 of this title), with a national primary drinking water regulation, including compliance through —

(i) treatment;

(ii) alternative source of water supply; or

(iii) restructuring or consolidation (unless the Administrator (or the State in the case of a State that has primary enforcement responsibility under section 300g-2 of this title) makes a written determination that restructuring or consolidation is not practicable); and

(B) for which the Administrator (or the State in the case of a State that has primary enforcement responsibility under section 300g-2 of this title) determines that the terms of the variance ensure adequate protection of human health, considering the quality of the source water for the system and the removal efficiencies and expected useful life of the treatment technology required by the variance.

(4) Compliance schedules — A variance granted under this subsection shall require compliance with the conditions of the variance not later than 3 years after the date on which the variance is granted, except that the Administrator (or the State in the case of a State that has primary enforcement responsibility under section 300g-2 of this title) may allow up to 2 additional years to comply with a variance technology, secure an alternative source of water, restructure or consolidate if the Administrator (or the State) determines that additional time is necessary for capital improvements, or to allow for financial assistance provided pursuant to section 300j-12 of this title or any other Federal or State program.

(5) Duration of variances — The Administrator (or the State in the case of a State that has primary enforcement responsibility under section 300g-2 of this title) shall review each variance granted under this subsection not less often than every 5 years after the compliance date established in the variance to determine whether the system remains eligible for the variance and is conforming to each condition of the variance.

(6) Ineligibility for variances — A variance shall not be available under this subsection for —

(A) any maximum contaminant level or treatment technique for a contaminant with respect to which a national primary drinking water regulation was promulgated prior to January 1, 1986; or

(B) a national primary drinking water regulation for a microbial contaminant (including a bacterium, virus, or other organism) or an indicator or treatment technique for a microbial contaminant.

(7) Regulations and guidance

(A) In general — Not later than 2 years after August 6, 1996, and in consultation with the States, the Administrator shall promulgate regulations for variances to be granted under this subsection. The regulations shall, at a minimum, specify —

(i) procedures to be used by the Administrator or a State to grant or deny variances, including requirements for notifying the Administrator and consumers of the public water system that a variance is proposed to be granted (including information regarding the contaminant and variance) and requirements for a public hearing on the variance before the variance is granted;

(ii) requirements for the installation and proper operation of variance technology that is identified (pursuant to section 300g-1(b)(15) of this title) for small systems and the financial and technical capability to operate the treatment system, including operator training and certification;

(iii) eligibility criteria for a variance for each national primary drinking water regulation, including requirements for the quality of the source water (pursuant to section 300g-1(b)(15)(A) of this title); and

(iv) information requirements for variance applications.

(B) Affordability criteria — Not later than 18 months after August 6, 1996, the Administrator, in consultation with the States and the Rural Utilities Service of the Department of Agriculture, shall publish information to assist the States in developing affordability criteria. The affordability criteria shall be reviewed by the States not less often than every 5 years to determine if changes are needed to the criteria.

(8) Review by the Administrator

(A) In general — The Administrator shall periodically review the program of each State that has primary enforcement responsibility for public water systems under section 300g-2 of this title with respect to variances to determine whether the variances granted by the State comply with the requirements of this subsection. With respect to affordability, the determination of the Administrator shall be limited to whether the variances granted by the State comply with the affordability criteria developed by the State.

(B) Notice and publication — If the Administrator determines that variances granted by a State are not in compliance with affordability criteria developed by the State and the requirements of this subsection, the Administrator shall notify the State in writing of the deficiencies and make public the determination.

(9) Approval of variances — A State proposing to grant a variance under this subsection to a public water system serving more than 3,300 and fewer than 10,000 persons shall submit the variance to the Administrator for review and approval prior to the issuance of the variance. The Administrator shall approve the variance if it meets each of the requirements of this subsection. The Administrator shall approve or disapprove the variance within 90 days. If the Administrator disapproves a variance under this paragraph, the Administrator shall notify the State in writing of the reasons for disapproval and the variance may be resubmitted with modifications to address the objections stated by the Administrator.

(10) Objections to variances

(A) By the Administrator — The Administrator may review and object to any variance proposed to be granted by a State, if the objection is communicated to the State not later than 90 days after the State proposes to grant the variance. If the Administrator objects to the granting of a variance, the Administrator shall notify the State in writing of each basis for the objection and propose a modification to the variance to resolve the concerns of the Administrator. The State shall make the recommended modification or respond in writing to each objection. If the State issues the variance without resolving the concerns of the Administrator, the Administrator may overturn the State decision to grant the variance if the Administrator determines that the State decision does not comply with this subsection.

(B) Petition by consumers — Not later than 30 days after a State exercising primary enforcement responsibility for public water systems under section 300g-2 of this title proposes to grant a variance for a public water system, any person served by the system may petition the Administrator to object to the granting of a variance. The Administrator shall respond to the petition and determine whether to object to the variance under subparagraph (A) not later than 60 days after the receipt of the petition.

(C) Timing — No variance shall be granted by a State until the later of the following:

(i) 90 days after the State proposes to grant a variance.

(ii) If the Administrator objects to the variance, the date on which the State makes the recommended modifications or responds in writing to each objection.

§300g-5. Exemptions
[PHSA §1416]

(a) **Requisite findings** — A State which has primary enforcement responsibility may exempt any public water system within the State's jurisdiction from any requirement respecting a maximum contaminant level or any treatment technique requirement, or from both, of an applicable national primary drinking water regulation upon a finding that —

(1) due to compelling factors (which may include economic factors, including qualification of the public water system as a system serving a disadvantaged community pursuant to section 300j-12(d) of this title), the public water system is unable to comply with such contaminant level or treatment technique requirement, or to implement measures to develop an alternative source of water supply,

(2) the public water system was in operation on the effective date of such contaminant level or treatment technique requirement, or, for a system that was not in operation by that date, only if no reasonable alternative source of drinking water is available to such new system,

(3) the granting of the exemption will not result in an unreasonable risk to health; and

(4) management or restructuring changes (or both) cannot reasonably be made that will result in compliance with this subchapter or, if compliance cannot be achieved, improve the quality of the drinking water.

(b) Compliance schedule and implementation of control measures; notice and hearing; dates for compliance with schedule; extension for final date of compliance; compliance, enforcement; approval or revision of schedules and revocation of exemptions

(1) If a State grants a public water system an exemption under subsection (a) of this section, the State shall prescribe, at the time the exemption is granted, a schedule for —

(A) compliance (including increments of progress or measures to develop an alternative source of water supply) by the public water system with each contaminant level requirement or treatment technique requirement with respect to which the exemption was granted, and

(B) implementation by the public water system of such control measures as the State may require for each contaminant, subject to such contaminant level requirement or treatment technique requirement, during the period ending on the date compliance with such requirement is required.

Before a schedule prescribed by a State pursuant to this subsection may take effect, the State shall provide notice and opportunity for a public hearing on the schedule. A notice given pursuant to the preceding sentence may cover the prescribing of more than one such schedule and a hearing held pursuant to such notice shall include each of the schedules covered by the notice.

(2)(A) A schedule prescribed pursuant to this subsection for a public water system granted an exemption under subsection (a) of this section shall require compliance by the system with each contaminant level and treatment technique requirement with respect to which the exemption was granted as expeditiously as practicable (as the State may reasonably determine) but not later than 3 years after the otherwise applicable compliance date established in section 300g-1(b)(10) of this title.

(B) No exemption shall be granted unless the public water system establishes that —

(i) the system cannot meet the standard without capital improvements which cannot be completed prior to the date established pursuant to section 300g-1(b)(10) of this title;

(ii) in the case of a system which needs financial assistance for the necessary improvements, the system has entered into an agreement to obtain such financial assistance or assistance pursuant to section 300j-12 of this title, or any other Federal or State program is reasonably likely to be available within the period of the exemption; or

(iii) the system has entered into an enforceable agreement to become a part of a regional public water system; and the system is taking all practicable steps to meet the standard.

(C) In the case of a system which does not serve more than a population of 3,300 and which needs financial assistance for the necessary improvements, an exemption granted under clause (i) or (ii) of subparagraph (B) may be renewed for one or more additional 2-year periods, but not to exceed a total of 6 years, if the system establishes that it is taking all practicable steps to meet the requirements of subparagraph (B).

(D) Limitation — A public water system may not receive an exemption under this section if the system was granted a variance under section 300g-4(e) of this title.

(3) Each public water system's exemption granted by a State under subsection (a) of this section shall be conditioned by the State upon compliance by the public water system with the schedule prescribed by the State pursuant to this subsection. The requirements of each schedule prescribed by a State pursuant to this subsection shall be enforceable by the State under its laws. Any requirement of a schedule on which an exemption granted under this section is conditioned may be enforced under section 300g-3 of this title as if such requirement was part of a national primary drinking water regulation.

(4) Each schedule prescribed by a State pursuant to this subsection shall be deemed approved by the Administrator unless the exemption for which it was prescribed is revoked by the Administrator under subsection (d)(2) of this section or the schedule is revised by the Administrator under such subsection.

(c) **Notice to Administrator; reasons for exemption** — Each State which grants an exemption under subsection (a) of this section shall promptly notify the Administrator of the granting of such exemption. Such notification shall contain the reasons for the exemption (including the basis for the finding required by subsection (a)(3) of this section before the exemption may be granted) and document the need for the exemption.

(d) Review of exemptions and schedules; publication in Federal Register, notice and results of review; notice to State; considerations respecting abuse of discretion in granting exemptions or failing to prescribe schedules; State corrective action

(1) Not later than 18 months after the effective date of the interim national primary drinking water regulations the Administrator shall complete a comprehensive review of the exemptions granted (and schedules prescribed pursuant thereto) by the States during the one-year period beginning on such effective date. The Administrator shall conduct such subsequent reviews of exemptions and schedules as he deems necessary to carry out the purposes of this subchapter, but each subsequent review shall be completed within each 3-year period following the completion of the first review under this subparagraph. Before conducting any review under this subparagraph, the Administrator shall publish notice of the proposed review in the Federal Register. Such notice shall (A) provide information respecting the location of data and other information respecting the exemptions to be reviewed (including data and other information concerning new scientific matters bearing on such exemptions), and (B) advise of the opportunity to submit comments on the exemptions reviewed and on the need for continuing them. Upon completion of any such review, the Administrator shall publish in the Federal Register the results of his review, together with findings responsive to comments submitted in connection with such review.

(2)(A) If the Administrator finds that a State has, in a substantial number of instances, abused its discretion in granting exemptions under subsection (a) of this section or failed to prescribe schedules in accordance with subsection (b) of this section, the Administrator shall notify the State of his findings. In determining if a State has abused its discretion in granting exemptions in a substantial number of instances, the Administrator shall consider the number of persons who are affected by the exemptions and if the requirements applicable to the granting of the exemptions were complied with. A notice under this subparagraph shall —

(i) identify each exempt public water system with respect to which the finding was made,

(ii) specify the reasons for the finding, and

(iii) as appropriate, propose revocations of specific exemptions or propose revised schedules for specific exempt public water systems, or both.

(B) The Administrator shall provide reasonable notice and public hearing on the provisions of each notice given pursuant to subparagraph (A). After a hearing on notice pursuant to subparagraph (A), the Administrator shall (i) rescind the finding for which the notice was given and promptly notify the State of such rescission, or (ii) promulgate (with such modifications as he deems appropriate) such exemption revocations and revised schedules proposed in such notice as he deems appropriate. Not later than 180 days after the date a notice is given pursuant to subparagraph (A), the Administrator shall complete the hearing on the notice and take the action required by the preceding sentence.

(C) If a State is notified under subparagraph (A) of a finding of the Administrator made with respect to an exemption granted a public water system within that State or to a schedule prescribed pursuant to such an exemption and if before a revocation of such exemption or a revision of such schedule promulgated by the Administrator takes effect the State takes corrective action with respect to such exemption or schedule which the Administrator determines makes his finding inapplicable to such exemption or schedule, the Administrator shall rescind the application of his finding to that exemption or schedule. No exemption revocation or revised schedule may take effect before the expiration of 90 days following the date of the notice in which the revocation or revised schedule was proposed.

(e) "Treatment technique requirement" defined — For purposes of this section, the term "treatment technique requirement" means a requirement in a national primary drinking water regulation which specifies for a contaminant (in accordance with section 300f(1)(C)(ii) of this title) each treatment technique known to the Administrator which leads to a reduction in the level of such contaminant sufficient to satisfy the requirements of section 300g-1(b) of this title.

(f) Authority of Administrator in a State without primary enforcement responsibility — If a State does not have primary enforcement respon-

sibility for public water systems, the Administrator shall have the same authority to exempt public water systems in such State from maximum contaminant level requirements and treatment technique requirements under the same conditions and in the same manner as the State would be authorized to grant exemptions under this section if it had primary enforcement responsibility.

(g) Applications for exemptions; regulations; reasonable time for acting — If an application for an exemption under this section is made, the State receiving the application or the Administrator, as the case may be, shall act upon such application within a reasonable period (as determined under regulations prescribed by the Administrator) after the date of its submission.

§300g-6. Prohibition on use of lead pipes, solder, and flux
[PHSA §1417]

(a) In general

(1) Prohibitions

(A) In general — No person may use any pipe, any pipe or plumbing fitting or fixture, any solder, or any flux, after June 19, 1986, in the installation or repair of —

(i) any public water system; or

(ii) any plumbing in a residential or nonresidential facility providing water for human consumption, that is not lead free (within the meaning of subsection (d) of this section).

(B) Leaded joints — Subparagraph (A) shall not apply to leaded joints necessary for the repair of cast iron pipes.

(2) Public notice requirements

(A) In general — Each owner or operator of a public water system shall identify and provide notice to persons that may be affected by lead contamination of their drinking water where such contamination results from either or both of the following:

(i) The lead content in the construction materials of the public water distribution system.

(ii) Corrosivity of the water supply sufficient to cause leaching of lead.

The notice shall be provided in such manner and form as may be reasonably required by the Administrator. Notice under this paragraph shall be provided notwithstanding the absence of a violation of any national drinking water standard.

(B) Contents of notice — Notice under this paragraph shall provide a clear and readily understandable explanation of —

(i) the potential sources of lead in the drinking water,

(ii) potential adverse health effects,

(iii) reasonably available methods of mitigating known or potential lead content in drinking water,

(iv) any steps the system is taking to mitigate lead content in drinking water, and

(v) the necessity for seeking alternative water supplies, if any.

(3) Unlawful acts — Effective 2 years after August 6, 1996, it shall be unlawful —

(A) for any person to introduce into commerce any pipe, or any pipe or plumbing fitting or fixture, that is not lead free, except for a pipe that is used in manufacturing or industrial processing;

(B) for any person engaged in the business of selling plumbing supplies, except manufacturers, to sell solder or flux that is not lead free; or

(C) for any person to introduce into commerce any solder or flux that is not lead free unless the solder or flux bears a prominent label stating that it is illegal to use the solder or flux in the installation or repair of any plumbing providing water for human consumption.

(4) Exemptions

The prohibitions in paragraphs (1) and (3) shall not apply to —

(A) pipes, pipe fittings, plumbing fittings, or fixtures, including backflow preventers, that are used exclusively for nonpotable services such as manufacturing, industrial processing, irrigation, outdoor watering, or any other uses where the water is not anticipated to be used for human consumption; or

(B) toilets, bidets, urinals, fill valves, flushometer valves, tub fillers, shower valves, service saddles, or water distribution main gate valves that are 2 inches in diameter or larger.

(b) State enforcement

(1) Enforcement of prohibition — The requirements of subsection (a)(1) of this section shall be enforced in all States effective 24 months after June 19, 1986. States shall enforce such requirements through State or local plumbing codes, or such other means of enforcement as the State may determine to be appropriate.

(2) Enforcement of public notice requirements — The requirements of subsection (a)(2) of this section shall apply in all States effective 24 months after June 19, 1986.

(c) Penalties — If the Administrator determines that a State is not enforcing the requirements of subsection (a) of this section as required pursuant to subsection (b) of this section, the Administrator may withhold up to 5 percent of Federal funds available to that State for State program grants under section 300j-2(a) of this title.

(d) Definition of lead free

(1) In general

For the purposes of this section, the term "lead free" means —

(A) not containing more than 0.2 percent lead when used with respect to solder and flux; and

(B) not more than a weighted average of 0.25 percent lead when used with respect to the wetted surfaces of pipes, pipe fittings, plumbing fittings, and fixtures.

(2) Calculation

The weighted average lead content of a pipe, pipe fitting, plumbing fitting, or fixture shall be calculated by using the following formula: For each wetted component, the percentage of lead in the component shall be multiplied by the ratio of the wetted surface area of that component to the total wetted surface area of the entire product to arrive at the weighted percentage of lead of the component. The weighted percentage of lead of each wetted component shall be added together, and the sum of these weighted percentages shall constitute the weighted average lead content of the product. The lead content of the material used to produce wetted components shall be used to determine compliance with paragraph (1)(B). For lead content of materials that are provided as a range, the maximum content of the range shall be used.

(e) Plumbing fittings and fixtures

(1) In general — The Administrator shall provide accurate and timely technical information and assistance to qualified third-party certifiers in the development of voluntary standards and testing protocols for the leaching of lead from new plumbing fittings and fixtures that are intended by the manufacturer to dispense water for human ingestion.

(2) Standards

(A) In general — If a voluntary standard for the leaching of lead is not established by the date that is 1 year after August 6, 1996, the Administrator shall, not later than 2 years after August 6, 1996, promulgate regulations setting a health-effects-based performance standard establishing maximum leaching levels from new plumbing fittings and fixtures that are intended by the manufacturer to dispense water for human ingestion. The standard shall become effective on the date that is 5 years after the date of promulgation of the standard.

(B) Alternative requirement — If regulations are required to be promulgated under subparagraph (A) and have not been promulgated by the date that is 5 years after August 6, 1996, no person may import, manufacture, process, or distribute in commerce a new plumbing fitting or fixture, intended by the manufacturer to dispense water for human ingestion, that contains more than 4 percent lead by dry weight.

§300g-7. Monitoring of contaminants
[PHSA §1418]
(a) Interim monitoring relief authority

(1) In general — A State exercising primary enforcement responsibility for public water systems may modify the monitoring requirements for any regulated or unregulated contaminants for which monitoring is required other than microbial contaminants (or indicators thereof), disinfectants and disinfection byproducts or corrosion byproducts for an interim period to provide that any public water system serving 10,000 persons or fewer shall not be required to conduct additional quarterly monitoring during an interim relief period for such contaminants if —

(A) monitoring, conducted at the beginning of the period for the contaminant concerned and certified to the State by the public water system, fails to detect the presence of the contaminant in the ground or surface water supplying the public water system; and

(B) the State, considering the hydrogeology of the area and other relevant factors, determines in writing that the contaminant is unlikely to be detected by further monitoring during such period.

(2) Termination; timing of monitoring — The interim relief period referred to in paragraph (1) shall terminate when permanent monitoring relief is adopted and approved for such State, or at the end of 36 months after August 6, 1996, whichever comes first. In order to serve as a basis for interim relief, the monitoring conducted at the beginning of the period must occur at the time determined by the State to be the time of the public water system's greatest vulnerability to the contaminant concerned in the relevant ground or surface water, taking into account in the case of pesticides the time of application of the pesticide for the source water area and the travel time for the pesticide to reach such waters and taking into account, in the case of other contaminants, seasonality of precipitation and contaminant travel time.

(b) Permanent monitoring relief authority

(1) In general — Each State exercising primary enforcement responsibility for public water systems under this subchapter and having an approved source water assessment program may adopt, in accordance with guidance published by the Administrator, tailored alternative monitoring requirements for public water systems in such State (as an alternative to the monitoring requirements for chemical contaminants set forth in the applicable national primary drinking water regulations) where the State concludes that (based on data available at the time of adoption concerning susceptibility, use, occurrence, or wellhead protection, or from the State's drinking water source water assessment program) such alternative monitoring would provide assurance that it complies with the Administrator's guidelines. The State program must be adequate to assure compliance with, and enforcement of, applicable national primary drinking water regulations. Alternative monitoring shall not apply to regulated microbiological contaminants (or indicators thereof), disinfectants and disinfection byproducts, or corrosion byproducts. The preceding sentence is not intended to limit other authority of the Administrator under other provisions of this subchapter to grant monitoring flexibility.

(2) Guidelines

(A) In general — The Administrator shall issue, after notice and comment and at the same time as guidelines are issued for source water assessment under section 300j-13 of this title, guidelines for States to follow in proposing alternative monitoring requirements under paragraph (1) for chemical contaminants. The Administrator shall publish such guidelines in the Federal Register. The guidelines shall assure that the public health will be protected from drinking water contamination. The guidelines shall require that a State alternative monitoring program apply on a contaminant-by-contaminant basis and that, to be eligible for such alternative monitoring program, a public water system must show the State that the contaminant is not present in the drinking water supply or, if present, it is reliably and consistently below the maximum contaminant level.

(B) Definition — For purposes of subparagraph (A), the phrase "reliably and consistently below the maximum contaminant level" means that, although contaminants have been detected in a water supply, the State has sufficient knowledge of the contamination source and extent of contamination to predict that the maximum contaminant level will not be exceeded. In determining that a contaminant is reliably and consistently below the maximum contaminant level, States shall consider the quality and completeness of data, the length of time covered and the volatility or stability of monitoring results during that time, and the proximity of such results to the maximum contaminant level. Wide variations in the analytical results, or analytical results close to the maximum contaminant level, shall not be considered to be reliably and consistently below the maximum contaminant level.

(3) Effect of detection of contaminants — The guidelines issued by the Administrator under paragraph (2) shall require that if, after the monitoring program is in effect and operating, a contaminant covered by the alternative moni-

toring program is detected at levels at or above the maximum contaminant level or is no longer reliably or consistently below the maximum contaminant level, the public water system must either —

    (A) demonstrate that the contamination source has been removed or that other action has been taken to eliminate the contamination problem; or

    (B) test for the detected contaminant pursuant to the applicable national primary drinking water regulation.

(4) States not exercising primary enforcement responsibility — The Governor of any State not exercising primary enforcement responsibility under section 300g-2 of this title on August 6, 1996, may submit to the Administrator a request that the Administrator modify the monitoring requirements established by the Administrator and applicable to public water systems in that State. After consultation with the Governor, the Administrator shall modify the requirements for public water systems in that State if the request of the Governor is in accordance with each of the requirements of this subsection that apply to alternative monitoring requirements established by States that have primary enforcement responsibility. A decision by the Administrator to approve a request under this clause shall be for a period of 3 years and may subsequently be extended for periods of 5 years.

(c) Treatment as NPDWR — All monitoring relief granted by a State to a public water system for a regulated contaminant under subsection (a) or (b) of this section shall be treated as part of the national primary drinking water regulation for that contaminant.

(d) Other monitoring relief — Nothing in this section shall be construed to affect the authority of the States under applicable national primary drinking water regulations to alter monitoring requirements through waivers or other existing authorities. The Administrator shall periodically review and, as appropriate, revise such authorities.

§300g-8. Operator certification
[PHSA §1419]

(a) Guidelines — Not later than 30 months after August 6, 1996, and in cooperation with the States, the Administrator shall publish guidelines in the Federal Register, after notice and opportunity for comment from interested persons, including States and public water systems, specifying minimum standards for certification (and recertification) of the operators of community and nontransient noncommunity public water systems. Such guidelines shall take into account existing State programs, the complexity of the system, and other factors aimed at providing an effective program at reasonable cost to States and public water systems, taking into account the size of the system.

(b) State programs — Beginning 2 years after the date on which the Administrator publishes guidelines under subsection (a) of this section, the Administrator shall withhold 20 percent of the funds a State is otherwise entitled to receive under section 300j-12 of this title unless the State has adopted and is implementing a program for the certification of operators of community and nontransient noncommunity public water systems that meets the requirements of the guidelines published pursuant to subsection (a) of this section or that has been submitted in compliance with subsection (c) of this section and that has not been disapproved.

(c) Existing programs — For any State exercising primary enforcement responsibility for public water systems or any other State which has an operator certification program, the guidelines under subsection (a) of this section shall allow the State to enforce such program in lieu of the guidelines under subsection (a) of this section if the State submits the program to the Administrator within 18 months after the publication of the guidelines unless the Administrator determines (within 9 months after the State submits the program to the Administrator) that such program is not substantially equivalent to such guidelines. In making this determination, an existing State program shall be presumed to be substantially equivalent to the guidelines, notwithstanding program differences, based on the size of systems or the quality of source water, providing the State program meets the overall public health objectives of the guidelines. If disapproved, the program may be resubmitted within 6 months after receipt of notice of disapproval.

(d) Expense reimbursement

    (1) In general — The Administrator shall provide reimbursement for the costs of training, including an appropriate per diem for unsalaried operators, and certification for persons operating systems serving 3,300 persons or fewer that are required to undergo training pursuant to this section.

    (2) State grants — The reimbursement shall be provided through grants to States with each State receiving an amount sufficient to cover the reasonable costs for training all such operators in the State, as determined by the Administrator, to the extent required by this section. Grants received by a State pursuant to this paragraph shall first be used to provide reimbursement for training and certification costs of persons operating systems serving 3,300 persons or fewer. If a State has reimbursed all such costs, the State may, after notice to the Administrator, use any remaining funds from the grant for any of the other purposes authorized for grants under section 300j-12 of this title.

    (3) Authorization — There are authorized to be appropriated to the Administrator to provide grants for reimbursement under this section $30,000,000 for each of fiscal years 1997 through 2003.

(4) Reservation — If the appropriation made pursuant to paragraph (3) for any fiscal year is not sufficient to satisfy the requirements of paragraph (1), the Administrator shall, prior to any other allocation or reservation, reserve such sums as necessary from the funds appropriated pursuant to section 300j-12(m) of this title to provide reimbursement for the training and certification costs mandated by this subsection.

§300g-9. Capacity development
[PHSA §1420]

(a) State authority for new systems — A State shall receive only 80 percent of the allotment that the State is otherwise entitled to receive under section 300j-12 of this title (relating to State loan funds) unless the State has obtained the legal authority or other means to ensure that all new community water systems and new nontransient, noncommunity water systems commencing operation after October 1, 1999, demonstrate technical, managerial, and financial capacity with respect to each national primary drinking water regulation in effect, or likely to be in effect, on the date of commencement of operations.

(b) Systems in significant noncompliance

(1) List — Beginning not later than 1 year after August 6, 1996, each State shall prepare, periodically update, and submit to the Administrator a list of community water systems and nontransient, noncommunity water systems that have a history of significant noncompliance with this subchapter (as defined in guidelines issued prior to August 6, 1996, or any revisions of the guidelines that have been made in consultation with the States) and, to the extent practicable, the reasons for noncompliance.

(2) Report — Not later than 5 years after August 6, 1996, and as part of the capacity development strategy of the State, each State shall report to the Administrator on the success of enforcement mechanisms and initial capacity development efforts in assisting the public water systems listed under paragraph (1) to improve technical, managerial, and financial capacity.

(3) Withholding — The list and report under this subsection shall be considered part of the capacity development strategy of the State required under subsection (c) of this section for purposes of the withholding requirements of section 300j-12(a)(1)(G)(i) of this title (relating to State loan funds).

(c) Capacity development strategy

(1) In general — Beginning 4 years after August 6, 1996, a State shall receive only —

    (A) 90 percent in fiscal year 2001;

    (B) 85 percent in fiscal year 2002; and

    (C) 80 percent in each subsequent fiscal year,

of the allotment that the State is otherwise entitled to receive under section 300j-12 of this title (relating to State loan funds), unless the State is developing and implementing a strategy to assist public water systems in acquiring and maintaining technical, managerial, and financial capacity.

(2) Content — In preparing the capacity development strategy, the State shall consider, solicit public comment on, and include as appropriate —

    (A) the methods or criteria that the State will use to identify and prioritize the public water systems most in need of improving technical, managerial, and financial capacity;

    (B) a description of the institutional, regulatory, financial, tax, or legal factors at the Federal, State, or local level that encourage or impair capacity development;

    (C) a description of how the State will use the authorities and resources of this subchapter or other means to —

        (i) assist public water systems in complying with national primary drinking water regulations;

        (ii) encourage the development of partnerships between public water systems to enhance the technical, managerial, and financial capacity of the systems; and

        (iii) assist public water systems in the training and certification of operators;

    (D) a description of how the State will establish a baseline and measure improvements in capacity with respect to national primary drinking water regulations and State drinking water law; and

    (E) an identification of the persons that have an interest in and are involved in the development and implementation of the capacity development strategy (including all appropriate agencies of Federal, State, and local governments, private and nonprofit public water systems, and public water system customers); and

    (F) a description of how the State will, as appropriate —

        (i) encourage development by public water systems of asset management plans that include best practices for asset management; and

        (ii) assist, including through the provision of technical assistance, public water systems in training operators or other relevant and appropriate persons in implementing such asset management plans.

(3) Report — Not later than 2 years after the date on which a State first adopts a capacity development strategy under this subsection, and every 3 years thereafter, the head of the State agency that has primary responsibility to carry out this subchapter in the State shall submit to the Governor a report that shall also be available to the public on the efficacy of the strategy and progress made toward improving the technical, managerial, and financial capacity of public water systems in the State.

(4) Review — The decisions of the State under this section regarding any particular public water system are not subject to review by the Administrator and may not serve as the basis for withholding funds under section 300j-12 of this title, including efforts of the State to encourage development by public water systems of asset management plans and to assist public water systems in training relevant and appropriate persons in implementing such asset management plans.

(d) Federal assistance

(1) In general — The Administrator shall support the States in developing capacity development strategies.

(2) Informational assistance

(A) In general — Not later than 180 days after August 6, 1996, the Administrator shall —

(i) conduct a review of State capacity development efforts in existence on August 6, 1996, and publish information to assist States and public water systems in capacity development efforts; and

(ii) initiate a partnership with States, public water systems, and the public to develop information for States on recommended operator certification requirements.

(B) Publication of information — The Administrator shall publish the information developed through the partnership under subparagraph (A)(ii) not later than 18 months after August 6, 1996.

(3) Promulgation of drinking water regulations — In promulgating a national primary drinking water regulation, the Administrator shall include an analysis of the likely effect of compliance with the regulation on the technical, financial, and managerial capacity of public water systems.

(4) Guidance for new systems — Not later than 2 years after August 6, 1996, the Administrator shall publish guidance developed in consultation with the States describing legal authorities and other means to ensure that all new community water systems and new nontransient, noncommunity water systems demonstrate technical, managerial, and financial capacity with respect to national primary drinking water regulations.

(5) Information on asset management practices — Not later than 5 years after October 23, 2018, and not less often than every 5 years thereafter, the Administrator shall review and, if appropriate, update educational materials, including handbooks, training materials, and technical information, made available by the Administrator to owners, managers, and operators of public water systems, local officials, technical assistance providers (including nonprofit water associations), and State personnel concerning best practices for asset management strategies that may be used by public water systems.

(e) Variances and exemptions

(e) **Variances and exemptions** — Based on information obtained under subsection (c)(3) of this section, the Administrator shall, as appropriate, modify regulations concerning variances and exemptions for small public water systems to ensure flexibility in the use of the variances and exemptions. Nothing in this subsection shall be interpreted, construed, or applied to affect or alter the requirements of section 300g-4 or 300g-5 of this title.

(f) Small public water systems technology assistance centers

(1) Grant program — The Administrator is authorized to make grants to institutions of higher learning to establish and operate small public water system technology assistance centers in the United States.

(2) Responsibilities of the centers — The responsibilities of the small public water system technology assistance centers established under this subsection shall include the conduct of training and technical assistance relating to the information, performance, and technical needs of small public water systems or public water systems that serve Indian Tribes.

(3) Applications — Any institution of higher learning interested in receiving a grant under this subsection shall submit to the Administrator an application in such form and containing such information as the Administrator may require by regulation.

(4) Selection criteria — The Administrator shall select recipients of grants under this subsection on the basis of the following criteria:

(A) The small public water system technology assistance center shall be located in a State that is representative of the needs of the region in which the State is located for addressing the drinking water needs of small and rural communities or Indian Tribes.

(B) The grant recipient shall be located in a region that has experienced problems, or may reasonably be foreseen to experience problems, with small and rural public water systems.

(C) The grant recipient shall have access to expertise in small public water system technology management.

(D) The grant recipient shall have the capability to disseminate the results of small public water system technology and training programs.

(E) The projects that the grant recipient proposes to carry out under the grant are necessary and appropriate.

(F) The grant recipient has regional support beyond the host institution.

(5) Consortia of States — At least 2 of the grants under this subsection shall be made to consortia of States with low population densities.

(6) Authorization of appropriations — There are authorized to be appropriated to make grants

under this subsection $2,000,000 for each of the fiscal years 1997 through 1999, and $5,000,000 for each of the fiscal years 2000 through 2003.

(g) Environmental finance centers

(1) In general — The Administrator shall provide initial funding for one or more university-based environmental finance centers for activities that provide technical assistance to State and local officials in developing the capacity of public water systems. Any such funds shall be used only for activities that are directly related to this subchapter.

(2) National capacity development clearinghouse — The Administrator shall establish a national public water system capacity development clearinghouse to receive and disseminate information with respect to developing, improving, and maintaining financial and managerial capacity at public water systems. The Administrator shall ensure that the clearinghouse does not duplicate other federally supported clearinghouse activities.

(3) Capacity development techniques — The Administrator may request an environmental finance center funded under paragraph (1) to develop and test managerial, financial, and institutional techniques for capacity development. The techniques may include capacity assessment methodologies, manual and computer based public water system rate models and capital planning models, public water system consolidation procedures, and regionalization models.

(4) Authorization of appropriations — There are authorized to be appropriated to carry out this subsection $1,500,000 for each of the fiscal years 1997 through 2003.

(5) Limitation — No portion of any funds made available under this subsection may be used for lobbying expenses.

PART C — PROTECTION OF UNDERGROUND SOURCES OF DRINKING WATER

§300h. Regulations for State programs [PHSA §1421]

(a) Publication of proposed regulations; promulgation; amendments; public hearings; administrative consultations

(1) The Administrator shall publish proposed regulations for State underground injection control programs within 180 days after December 16, 1974. Within 180 days after publication of such proposed regulations, he shall promulgate such regulations with such modifications as he deems appropriate. Any regulation under this subsection may be amended from time to time.

(2) Any regulation under this section shall be proposed and promulgated in accordance with section 553 of Title 5 (relating to rulemaking), except

that the Administrator shall provide opportunity for public hearing prior to promulgation of such regulations. In proposing and promulgating regulations under this section, the Administrator shall consult with the Secretary, the National Drinking Water Advisory Council, and other appropriate Federal entities and with interested State entities.

(b) Minimum requirements; restrictions

(1) Regulations under subsection (a) of this section for State underground injection programs shall contain minimum requirements for effective programs to prevent underground injection which endangers drinking water sources within the meaning of subsection (d)(2) of this section. Such regulations shall require that a State program, in order to be approved under section 300h-1 of this title —

(A) shall prohibit, effective on the date on which the applicable underground injection control program takes effect, any underground injection in such State which is not authorized by a permit issued by the State (except that the regulations may permit a State to authorize underground injection by rule);

(B) shall require (i) in the case of a program which provides for authorization of underground injection by permit, that the applicant for the permit to inject must satisfy the State that the underground injection will not endanger drinking water sources, and (ii) in the case of a program which provides for such an authorization by rule, that no rule may be promulgated which authorizes any underground injection which endangers drinking water sources;

(C) shall include inspection, monitoring, recordkeeping, and reporting requirements; and

(D) shall apply (i) as prescribed by section 300j-6(b) of this title, to underground injections by Federal agencies, and (ii) to underground injections by any other person whether or not occurring on property owned or leased by the United States.

(2) Regulations of the Administrator under this section for State underground injection control programs may not prescribe requirements which interfere with or impede —

(A) the underground injection of brine or other fluids which are brought to the surface in connection with oil or natural gas production or natural gas storage operations, or

(B) any underground injection for the secondary or tertiary recovery of oil or natural gas, unless such requirements are essential to assure that underground sources of drinking water will not be endangered by such injection.

(3)(A) The regulations of the Administrator under this section shall permit or provide for consideration of varying geologic, hydrological, or historical conditions in different States and in different areas within a State.

(B)(i) In prescribing regulations under this section the Administrator shall, to the extent feasible, avoid promulgation of requirements which would unnecessarily disrupt State underground injection control programs which are in effect and being enforced in a substantial number of States.

(ii) For the purpose of this subparagraph, a regulation prescribed by the Administrator under this section shall be deemed to disrupt a State underground injection control program only if it would be infeasible to comply with both such regulation and the State underground injection control program.

(iii) For the purpose of this subparagraph, a regulation prescribed by the Administrator under this section shall be deemed unnecessary only if, without such regulation, underground sources of drinking water will not be endangered by an underground injection.

(C) Nothing in this section shall be construed to alter or affect the duty to assure that underground sources of drinking water will not be endangered by any underground injection.

(c) Temporary permits; notice and hearing

(1) The Administrator may, upon application of the Governor of a State which authorizes underground injection by means of permits, authorize such State to issue (without regard to subsection (b)(1)(B)(i) of this section) temporary permits for underground injection which may be effective until the, expiration of four years after December 16, 1974, if —

(A) the Administrator finds that the State has demonstrated that it is unable and could not reasonably have been able to process all permit applications within the time available;

(B) the Administrator determines the adverse effect on the environment of such temporary permits is not unwarranted;

(C) such temporary permits will be issued only with respect to injection wells in operation on the date on which such State's permit program approved under this part first takes effect and for which there was inadequate time to process its permit application; and

(D) the Administrator determines the temporary permits require the use of adequate safeguards established by rules adopted by him.

(2) The Administrator may, upon application of the Governor of a State which authorizes underground injection by means of permits, authorize such State to issue (without regard to subsection (b)(1)(B)(i) of this section), but after reasonable notice and hearing, one or more temporary permits each of which is applicable to a particular injection well and to the underground injection of a particular fluid and which may be effective until the expiration of four years after December 16, 1974, if the State finds, on the record of such hearing —

(A) that technology (or other means) to permit safe injection of the fluid in accordance with the applicable underground injection control program is not generally available (taking costs into consideration);

(B) that injection of the fluid would be less harmful to health than the use of other available means of disposing of waste or producing the desired product; and

(C) that available technology or other means have been employed (and will be employed) to reduce the volume and toxicity of the fluid and to minimize the potentially adverse effect of the injection on the public health.

(d) "Underground injection" defined; underground injection endangerment of drinking water sources — For purposes of this part:

(1) Underground injection — The term "underground injection" —

(A) means the subsurface emplacement of fluids by well injection; and

(B) excludes —

(i) the underground injection of natural gas for purposes of storage; and

(ii) the underground injection of fluids or propping agents (other than diesel fuels) pursuant to hydraulic fracturing operations related to oil, gas, or geothermal production activities.

(2) Underground injection endangers drinking water sources if such injection may result in the presence in underground water which supplies or can reasonably be expected to supply any public water system of any contaminant, and if the presence of such contaminant may result in such system's not complying with any national primary drinking water regulation or may otherwise adversely affect the health of persons.

§300h-1. State primary enforcement responsibility

[PHSA §1422]

(a) List of States in need of a control program; amendment of list — Within 180 days after December 16, 1974, the Administrator shall list in the Federal Register each State for which in his judgment a State underground injection control program may be necessary to assure that underground injection will not endanger drinking water sources. Such list may be amended from time to time.

(b) State applications; notice to Administrator of compliance with revised or added requirements; approval or disapproval by Administrator; duration of State primary enforcement responsibility; public hearing

(1)(A) Each State listed under subsection (a) of this section shall within 270 days after the date of promulgation of any regulation under section 300h of this title (or, if later, within 270 days after such State is first listed under subsection (a) of this section) submit to the Administrator an application which contains a showing satisfactory to the Administrator that the State —

 (i) has adopted after reasonable notice and public hearings, and will implement, an underground injection control program which meets the requirements of regulations in effect under section 300h of this title; and

 (ii) will keep such records and make such reports with respect to its activities under its underground injection control program as the Administrator may require by regulation.

The Administrator may, for good cause, extend the date for submission of an application by any State under this subparagraph for a period not to exceed an additional 270 days.

(B) Within 270 days of any amendment of a regulation under section 300h of this title revising or adding any requirement respecting State underground injection control programs, each State listed under subsection (a) of this section shall submit (in such form and manner as the Administrator may require) a notice to the Administrator containing a showing satisfactory to him that the State underground injection control program meets the revised or added requirement.

(2) Within ninety days after the State's application under paragraph (1)(A) or notice under paragraph (1)(B) and after reasonable opportunity for presentation of views, the Administrator shall by rule either approve, disapprove, or approve in part and disapprove in part, the State's underground injection control program.

(3) If the Administrator approves the State's program under paragraph (2), the State shall have primary enforcement responsibility for underground water sources until such time as the Administrator determines, by rule, that such State no longer meets the requirements of clause (i) or (ii) of paragraph (1)(A) of this subsection.

(4) Before promulgating any rule under paragraph (2) or (3) of this subsection, the Administrator shall provide opportunity for public hearing respecting such rule.

(c) Program by Administrator for State without primary enforcement responsibility; restrictions — If the Administrator disapproves a State's program (or part thereof) under subsection (b)(2) of this section, if the Administrator determines under subsection (b)(3) of this section that a State no longer meets the requirements of clause (i) or (ii) of subsection (b)(1)(A) of this section, or if a State fails to submit an application or notice before the date of expiration of the period specified in subsection (b)(1) of this section, the Administrator shall by regulation within 90 days after the date of such disapproval, determination, or expiration (as the case may be) prescribe (and may from time to time by regulation revise) a program applicable to such State meeting the requirements of section 300h(b) of this title. Such program may not include requirements which interfere with or impede —

 (1) the underground injection of brine or other fluids which are brought to the surface in connection with oil or natural gas production or natural gas storage operations, or

 (2) any underground injection for the secondary or tertiary recovery of oil or natural gas,

unless such requirements are essential to assure that underground sources of drinking water will not be endangered by such injection. Such program shall apply in such State to the extent that a program adopted by such State which the Administrator determines meets such requirements is not in effect. Before promulgating any regulation under this section, the Administrator shall provide opportunity for public hearing respecting such regulation.

(d) "Applicable underground injection control program" defined — For purposes of this subchapter, the term "applicable underground injection control program" with respect to a State means the program (or most recent amendment thereof) (1) which has been adopted by the State and which has been approved under subsection (b) of this section, or (2) which has been prescribed by the Administrator under subsection (c) of this section.

(e) Primary enforcement responsibility by Indian Tribe — An Indian Tribe may assume primary enforcement responsibility for underground injection control under this section consistent with such regulations as the Administrator has prescribed pursuant to this part and section 300j-11 of this title. The area over which such Indian Tribe exercises governmental jurisdiction need not have been listed under subsection (a) of this section, and such Tribe need not submit an application to assume primary enforcement responsibility within the 270-day deadline noted in subsection (b)(1)(A) of this section. Until an Indian Tribe assumes primary enforcement responsibility, the currently applicable underground injection control program shall continue to apply. If an applicable underground injection control program does not exist for an Indian Tribe, the Administrator shall prescribe such a program pursuant to subsection (c) of this section, and consistent with section 300h(b) of this title, within 270 days after June 19, 1986, unless an Indian Tribe first obtains approval to assume primary enforcement responsibility for underground injection control.

§300h-2. Enforcement of program
[PHSA §1423]
(a) Notice to State and violator; issuance of administrative order; civil action

(1) Whenever the Administrator finds during a period during which a State has primary enforcement responsibility for underground water sources (within the meaning of section 300h-1(b)(3) of this title or section 300h-4(c) of this title) that any person who is subject to a requirement of an applicable underground injection control program in such State is violating such requirement, he shall so notify the State and the person violating such requirement. If beyond the thirtieth day after the Administrator's notification the State has not commenced appropriate enforcement action, the Administrator shall issue an order under subsection (c) of this section requiring the person to comply with such requirement or the Administrator shall commence a civil action under subsection (b) of this section.

(2) Whenever the Administrator finds during a period during which a State does not have primary enforcement responsibility for underground water sources that any person subject to any requirement of any applicable underground injection control program in such State is violating such requirement, the Administrator shall issue an order under subsection (c) of this section requiring the person to comply with such requirement or the Administrator shall commence a civil action under subsection (b) of this section.

(b) Civil and criminal actions

— Civil actions referred to in paragraphs (1) and (2) of subsection (a) of this section shall be brought in the appropriate United States district court. Such court shall have jurisdiction to require compliance with any requirement of an applicable underground injection program or with an order issued under subsection (c) of this section. The court may enter such judgment as protection of public health may require. Any person who violates any requirement of an applicable underground injection control program or an order requiring compliance under subsection (c) of this section —

(1) shall be subject to a civil penalty of not more than $25,000 for each day of such violation, and

(2) if such violation is willful, such person may, in addition to or in lieu of the civil penalty authorized by paragraph (1), be imprisoned for not more than 3 years, or fined in accordance with Title 18, or both.

(c) Administrative orders

(1) In any case in which the Administrator is authorized to bring a civil action under this section with respect to any regulation or other requirement of this part other than those relating to —

(A) the underground injection of brine or other fluids which are brought to the surface in connection with oil or natural gas production, or

(B) any underground injection for the secondary or tertiary recovery of oil or natural gas,

the Administrator may also issue an order under this subsection either assessing a civil penalty of not more than $10,000 for each day of violation for any past or current violation, up to a maximum administrative penalty of $125,000, or requiring compliance with such regulation or other requirement, or both.

(2) In any case in which the Administrator is authorized to bring a civil action under this section with respect to any regulation, or other requirement of this part relating to —

(A) the underground injection of brine or other fluids which are brought to the surface in connection with oil or natural gas production, or

(B) any underground injection for the secondary or tertiary recovery of oil or natural gas,

the Administrator may also issue an order under this subsection either assessing a civil penalty of not more than $5,000 for each day of violation for any past or current violation, up to a maximum administrative penalty of $125,000, or requiring compliance with such regulation or other requirement, or both.

(3)(A) An order under this subsection shall be issued by the Administrator after opportunity (provided in accordance with this subparagraph) for a hearing. Before issuing the order, the Administrator shall give to the person to whom it is directed written notice of the Administrator's proposal to issue such order and the opportunity to request, within 30 days of the date the notice is received by such person, a hearing on the order. Such hearing shall not be subject to section 554 or 556 of Title 5, but shall provide a reasonable opportunity to be heard and to present evidence.

(B) The Administrator shall provide public notice of, and reasonable opportunity to comment on, any proposed order.

(C) Any citizen who comments on any proposed order under subparagraph (B) shall be given notice of any hearing under this subsection and of any order. In any hearing held under subparagraph (A), such citizen shall have a reasonable opportunity to be heard and to present evidence.

(D) Any order issued under this subsection shall become effective 30 days following its issuance unless an appeal is taken pursuant to paragraph (6).

(4)(A) Any order issued under this subsection shall state with reasonable specificity the nature of the violation and may specify a reasonable time for compliance.

(B) In assessing any civil penalty under this subsection, the Administrator shall take into account appropriate factors, including (i) the seriousness of the violation; (ii) the economic benefit (if any) resulting from the violation; (iii) any history of such violations; (iv) any good-faith efforts to comply with the applicable requirements; (v) the economic impact of the penalty on the violator; and (vi) such other matters as justice may require.

(5) Any violation with respect to which the Administrator has commenced and is diligently prosecuting an action, or has issued an order under this subsection assessing a penalty, shall not be subject to an action under subsection (b) of this section or section 300h-3(c) or 300j-8 of this title, except that the foregoing limitation on civil actions under section 300j-8 of this title shall not apply with respect to any violation for which —

    (A) a civil action under section 300j-8(a)(1) of this title has been filed prior to commencement of an action under this subsection, or

    (B) a notice of violation under section 300j-8(b)(1) of this title has been given before commencement of an action under this subsection and an action under section 300j-8(a)(1) of this title is filed before 120 days after such notice is given.

(6) Any person against whom an order is issued or who commented on a proposed order pursuant to paragraph (3) may file an appeal of such order with the United States District Court for the District of Columbia or the district in which the violation is alleged to have occurred. Such an appeal may only be filed within the 30-day period beginning on the date the order is issued. Appellant shall simultaneously send a copy of the appeal by certified mail to the Administrator and to the Attorney General. The Administrator shall promptly file in such court a certified copy of the record on which such order was imposed. The district court shall not set aside or remand such order unless there is not substantial evidence on the record, taken as a whole, to support the finding of a violation or, unless the Administrator's assessment of penalty or requirement for compliance constitutes an abuse of discretion. The district court shall not impose additional civil penalties for the same violation unless the Administrator's assessment of a penalty constitutes an abuse of discretion. Notwithstanding section 300j-7(a)(2) of this title, any order issued under paragraph (3) shall be subject to judicial review exclusively under this paragraph.

(7) If any person fails to pay an assessment of a civil penalty —

    (A) after the order becomes effective under paragraph (3), or

    (B) after a court, in an action brought under paragraph (6), has entered a final judgment in favor of the Administrator, the Administrator may request the Attorney General to bring a civil action in an appropriate district court to recover the amount assessed (plus costs, attorneys' fees, and interest at currently prevailing rates from the date the order is effective or the date of such final judgment, as the case may be). In such an action, the validity, amount, and appropriateness of such penalty shall not be subject to review.

(8) The Administrator may, in connection with administrative proceedings under this subsection, issue subpoenas compelling the attendance and testimony of witnesses and subpoenas duces tecum, and may request the Attorney General to bring an action to enforce any subpoena under this section. The district courts shall have jurisdiction to enforce such subpoenas and impose sanction.

(d) State authority to adopt or enforce laws or regulations respecting underground injection unaffected — Nothing in this subchapter shall diminish any authority of a State or political subdivision to adopt or enforce any law or regulation respecting underground injection but no such law or regulation shall relieve any person of any requirement otherwise applicable under this subchapter.

§300h-3. Interim regulation of underground injections
[PHSA §1424]
(a) Necessity for well operation permit; designation of one aquifer areas

(1) Any person may petition the Administrator to have an area of a State (or States) designated as an area in which no new underground injection well may be operated during the period beginning on the date of the designation and ending on the date on which the applicable underground injection control program covering such area takes effect unless a permit for the operation of such well has been issued by the Administrator under subsection (b) of this section. The Administrator may so designate an area within a State if he finds that the area has one aquifer which is the sole or principal drinking water source for the area and which, if contaminated, would create a significant hazard to public health.

(2) Upon receipt of a petition under paragraph (1) of this subsection, the Administrator shall publish it in the Federal Register and shall provide an opportunity to interested persons to submit written data, views, or arguments thereon. Not later than the 30th day following the date of the publication of a petition under this paragraph in the Federal Register, the Administrator shall either make the designation for which the petition is submitted or deny the petition.

323

(b) Well operation permits; publication in Federal Register; notice and hearing; issuance or denial; conditions for issuance

(1) During the period beginning on the date an area is designated under subsection (a) of this section and ending on the date the applicable underground injection control program covering such area takes effect, no new underground injection well may be operated in such area unless the Administrator has issued a permit for such operation.

(2) Any person may petition the Administrator for the issuance of a permit for the operation of such a well in such an area. A petition submitted under this paragraph shall be submitted in such manner and contain such information as the Administrator may require by regulation. Upon receipt of such a petition, the Administrator shall publish it in the Federal Register. The Administrator shall give notice of any proceeding on a petition and shall provide opportunity for agency hearing. The Administrator shall act upon such petition on the record of any hearing held pursuant to the preceding sentence respecting such petition. Within 120 days of the publication in the Federal Register of a petition submitted under this paragraph, the Administrator shall either issue the permit for which the petition was submitted or shall deny its issuance.

(3) The Administrator may issue a permit for the operation of a new underground injection well in an area designated under subsection (a) of this section only, if he finds that the operation of such well will not cause contamination of the aquifer of such area so as to create a significant hazard to public health. The Administrator may condition the issuance of such a permit upon the use of such control measures in connection with the operation of such well, for which the permit is to be issued, as he deems necessary to assure that the operation of the well will not contaminate the aquifer of the designated area in which the well is located so as to create a significant hazard to public health.

(c) Civil penalties; separate violations; penalties for willful violations; temporary restraining order or injunction — Any person who operates a new underground injection well in violation of subsection (b) of this section, (1) shall be subject to a civil penalty of not more than $5,000 for each day in which such violation occurs, or (2) if such violation is willful, such person may, in lieu of the civil penalty authorized by clause (1), be fined not more than $10,000 for each day in which such violation occurs. If the Administrator has reason to believe that any person is violating or will violate subsection (b) of this section, he may petition the United States district court to issue a temporary restraining order or injunction (including a mandatory injunction) to enforce such subsection.

(d) "New underground injection well" defined — For purposes of this section, the term "new underground injection well" means an underground injection well whose operation was not approved by appropriate State and Federal agencies before December 16, 1974.

(e) Areas with one aquifer; publication in Federal Register; commitments for Federal financial assistance — If the Administrator determines, on his own initiative or upon petition, that an area has an aquifer which is the sole or principal drinking water source for the area and which, if contaminated, would create a significant hazard to public health, he shall publish notice of that determination in the Federal Register. After the publication of any such notice, no commitment for Federal financial assistance (through a grant, contract, loan guarantee, or otherwise) may be entered into for any project which the Administrator determines may contaminate such aquifer through a recharge zone so as to create a significant hazard to public health, but a commitment for Federal financial assistance may, if authorized under another provision of law, be entered into to plan or design the project to assure that it will not so contaminate the aquifer.

§300h-4. Optional demonstration by States relating to oil or natural gas
[PHSA §1425]

(a) Approval of State underground injection control program; alternative showing of effectiveness of program by State — For purposes of the Administrator's approval or disapproval under section 300h-1 of this title of that portion of any State underground injection control program which relates to —

(1) the underground injection of brine or other fluids which are brought to the surface in connection with oil or natural gas production or natural gas storage operations, or

(2) any underground injection for the secondary or tertiary recovery of oil or natural gas,

in lieu of the showing required under subparagraph (A) of section 300h-1(b)(1) of this title the State may demonstrate that such portion of the State program meets the requirements of subparagraphs (A) through (D) of section 300h(b)(1) of this title and represents an effective program (including adequate recordkeeping and reporting) to prevent underground injection which endangers drinking water sources.

(b) Revision or amendment of requirements of regulation; showing of effectiveness of program by State — If the Administrator revises or amends any requirement of a regulation under section 300h of this title relating to any aspect of the underground injection referred to in subsection (a) of this section, in the case of that portion of a

State underground injection control program for which the demonstration referred to in subsection (a) of this section has been made, in lieu of the showing required under section 300h-1(b)(1)(B) of this title the State may demonstrate that, with respect to that aspect of such underground injection, the State program meets the requirements of subparagraphs (A) through (D) of section 300h(b)(1) of this title and represents an effective program (including adequate recordkeeping and reporting) to prevent underground injection which endangers drinking water sources.

(c) Primary enforcement responsibility of State; voiding by Administrator under duly promulgated rule

(1) Section 300h-1(b)(3) of this title shall not apply to that portion of any State underground injection control program approved by the Administrator pursuant to a demonstration under subsection (a) of this section (and under subsection (b) of this section where applicable).

(2) If pursuant to such a demonstration, the Administrator approves such portion of the State program, the State shall have primary enforcement responsibility with respect to that portion until such time as the Administrator determines, by rule, that such demonstration is no longer valid. Following such a determination, the Administrator may exercise the authority of subsection (c) of section 300h-1 of this title in the same manner as provided in such subsection with respect to a determination described in such subsection.

(3) Before promulgating any rule under paragraph (2), the Administrator shall provide opportunity for public hearing respecting such rule.

§300h-5. Regulation of State programs
[PHSA §1426]

Not later than 18 months after June 19, 1986, the Administrator shall modify regulations issued under this chapter for Class I injection wells to identify monitoring methods, in addition to those in effect on November 1, 1985, including groundwater monitoring. In accordance with such regulations, the Administrator, or delegated State authority, shall determine the applicability of such monitoring methods, wherever appropriate, at locations and in such a manner as to provide the earliest possible detection of fluid migration into, or in the direction of, underground sources of drinking water from such wells, based on its assessment of the potential for fluid migration from the injection zone that may be harmful to human health or the environment. For purposes of this subsection, a class I injection well is defined in accordance with 40 CFR 146.05 as in effect on November 1, 1985.

§300h-6. Sole source aquifer demonstration program
[PHSA §1427]

(a) Purpose — The purpose of this section is to establish procedures for development, implementation, and assessment of demonstration programs designed to protect critical aquifer protection areas located within areas designated as sole or principal source aquifers under section 300h-3(e) of this title.

(b) "Critical aquifer protection area" defined — For purposes of this section, the term "critical aquifer protection area" means either of the following:

(1) All or part of an area located within an area for which an application or designation as a sole or principal source aquifer pursuant to section 300h-3(e) of this title, has been submitted and approved by the Administrator and which satisfies the criteria established by the Administrator under subsection (d) of this section.

(2) All or part of an area which is within an aquifer designated as a sole source aquifer as of June 19, 1986, and for which an areawide ground water quality protection plan has been approved under section 208 of the Clean Water Act [33 U.S.C. §1288] prior to June 19, 1986.

(c) Application — Any State, municipal or local government or political subdivision thereof or any planning entity (including any interstate regional planning entity) that identifies a critical aquifer protection area over which it has authority or jurisdiction may apply to the Administrator for the selection of such area for a demonstration program under this section. Any applicant shall consult with other government or planning entities with authority or jurisdiction in such area prior to application. Applicants, other than the Governor, shall submit the application for a demonstration program jointly with the Governor.

(d) Criteria — Not later than 1 year after June 19, 1986, the Administrator shall, by rule, establish criteria for identifying critical aquifer protection areas under this section. In establishing such criteria, the Administrator shall consider each of the following:

(1) The vulnerability of the aquifer to contamination due to hydrogeologic characteristics.

(2) The number of persons or the proportion of population using the ground water as a drinking water source.

(3) The economic, social and environmental benefits that would result to the area from maintenance of ground water of high quality.

(4) The economic, social and environmental costs that would result from degradation of the quality of the ground water.

(e) Contents of application — An application submitted to the Administrator by any applicant for a demonstration program under this section shall meet each of the following requirements:

(1) The application shall propose boundaries for the critical aquifer protection area within its jurisdiction.

(2) The application shall designate or, if necessary, establish a planning entity (which shall be a public agency and which shall include representation of elected local and State governmental officials) to develop a comprehensive management plan (hereinafter in this section referred to as the "plan") for the critical protection area. Where a local government planning agency exists with adequate authority to carry out this section with respect to any proposed critical protection area, such agency shall be designated as the planning entity.

(3) The application shall establish procedures for public participation in the development of the plan, for review, approval, and adoption of the plan, and for assistance to municipalities and other public agencies with authority under State law to implement the plan.

(4) The application shall include a hydrogeologic assessment of surface and ground water resources within the critical protection area.

(5) The application shall include a comprehensive management plan for the proposed protection area.

(6) The application shall include the measures and schedule proposed for implementation of such plan.

(f) Comprehensive plan

(1) The objective of a comprehensive management plan submitted by an applicant under this section shall be to maintain the quality of the ground water in the critical protection area in a manner reasonably expected to protect human health, the environment and ground water resources. In order to achieve such objective, the plan may be designed to maintain, to the maximum extent possible, the natural vegetative and hydrogeological conditions. Each of the following elements shall be included in such a protection plan:

(A) A map showing the detailed boundary of the critical protection area.

(B) An identification of existing and potential point and nonpoint sources of ground water degradation.

(C) An assessment of the relationship between activities on the land surface and ground water quality.

(D) Specific actions and management practices to be implemented in the critical protection area to prevent adverse impacts on ground water quality.

(E) Identification of authority adequate to implement the plan, estimates of program costs, and sources of State matching funds.

(2) Such plan may also include the following:

(A) A determination of the quality of the existing ground water recharged through the special protection area and the natural recharge capabilities of the special protection area watershed.

(B) Requirements designed to maintain existing underground drinking water quality or improve underground drinking water quality if prevailing conditions fail to meet drinking water standards, pursuant to this chapter and State law.

(C) Limits on Federal, State, and local government, financially assisted activities and projects which may contribute to degradation of such ground water or any loss of natural surface and subsurface infiltration of purification capability of the special protection watershed.

(D) A comprehensive statement of land use management including emergency contingency planning as it pertains to the maintenance of the quality of underground sources of drinking water or to the improvement of such sources if necessary to meet drinking water standards pursuant to this chapter and State law.

(E) Actions in the special protection area which would avoid adverse impacts on water quality, recharge capabilities, or both.

(F) Consideration of specific techniques, which may include clustering, transfer of development rights, and other innovative measures sufficient to achieve the objectives of this section.

(G) Consideration of the establishment of a State institution to facilitate and assist funding a development transfer credit system.

(H) A program for State and local implementation of the plan described in this subsection in a manner that will insure the continued, uniform, consistent protection of the critical protection area in accord with the purposes of this section.

(I) Pollution abatement measures, if appropriate.

(g) Plans under section 208 of Clean Water Act — A plan approved before June 19, 1986, under section 208 of the Clean Water Act [33 U.S.C. §1288] to protect a sole source aquifer designated under section 300h-3(e) of this title shall be considered a comprehensive management plan for the purposes of this section.

(h) Consultation and hearings — During the development of a comprehensive management plan under this section, the planning entity shall consult with, and consider the comments of, appropriate officials of any municipality and State or Federal agency which has jurisdiction over lands and waters within the special protection area, other concerned organizations and technical and citizen advisory committees. The planning entity shall conduct public hearings at places within the special protection area for the purpose of providing the opportunity to comment on any aspect of the plan.

(i) Approval or disapproval — Within 120 days after receipt of an application under this section, the Administrator shall approve or disapprove the application. The approval or disapproval shall be based on a determination that the critical protection area satisfies the criteria established under subsection (d) of this section and that a demonstration program for the area would provide protection for ground water quality consistent with the objectives stated in subsection (f) of this section. The Administrator shall provide to the Governor a written explanation of the reasons for the disapproval of any such application. Any petitioner may modify and resubmit any application which is not approved. Upon approval of an application, the Administrator may enter into a cooperative agreement with the applicant to establish a demonstration program under this section.

(j) Grants and reimbursement — Upon entering a cooperative agreement under subsection (i) of this section, the Administrator may provide to the applicant, on a matching basis, a grant of 50 per centum of the costs of implementing the plan established under this section. The Administrator may also reimburse the applicant of an approved plan up to 50 per centum of the costs of developing such plan, except for plans approved under section 208 of the Clean Water Act [33 U.S.C. §1288]. The total amount of grants under this section for any one aquifer, designated under section 300h-3(e) of this title, shall not exceed $4,000,000 in any one fiscal year.

(k) Activities funded under other law — No funds authorized under this section may be used to fund activities funded under other sections of this chapter or the Clean Water Act [33 U.S.C. §§1251 *et seq.*], the Solid Waste Disposal Act [42 U.S.C. §§6901 *et seq.*], the Comprehensive Environmental Response, Compensation, and Liability Act of 1980 [42 U.S.C. §§9601 *et seq.*] or other environmental laws.

(*l*) Savings provision — Nothing under this section shall be construed to amend, supersede or abrogate rights to quantities of water which have been established by interstate water compacts, Supreme Court decrees, or State water laws; or any requirement imposed or right provided under any Federal or State environmental or public health statute.

(m) Authorization of appropriations — There are authorized to be appropriated to carry out this section not more than the following amounts:

Fiscal year:	Amount
1987	$10,000,000
1988	15,000,000
1989	17,500,000
1990	17,500,000
1991	17,500,000
1992-2003	15,000,000

Matching grants under this section may also be used to implement or update any water quality management plan for a sole or principal source aquifer approved (before June 19, 1986) by the Administrator under section 208 of the Federal Water Pollution Control Act [33 U.S.C. §1288].

§300h-7. State programs to establish wellhead protection areas
[PHSA §1428]

(a) State programs — The Governor or Governor's designee of each State shall, within 3 years of June 19, 1986, adopt and submit to the Administrator a State program to protect wellhead areas within their jurisdiction from contaminants which may have any adverse effect on the health of persons. Each State program under this section shall, at a minimum —

(1) specify the duties of State agencies, local governmental entities, and public water supply systems with respect to the development and implementation of programs required by this section;

(2) for each wellhead, determine the wellhead protection area as defined in subsection (e) of this section based on all reasonably available hydrogeologic information on ground water flow, recharge and discharge and other information the State deems necessary to adequately determine the wellhead protection area;

(3) identify within each wellhead protection area all potential anthropogenic sources of contaminants which may have any adverse effect on the health of persons;

(4) describe a program that contains, as appropriate, technical assistance, financial assistance, implementation of control measures, education, training, and demonstration projects to protect the water supply within wellhead protection areas from such contaminants;

(5) include contingency plans for the location and provision of alternate drinking water supplies for each public water system in the event of well or wellfield contamination by such contaminants; and

(6) include a requirement that consideration be given to all potential sources of such contaminants within the expected wellhead area of a new water well which serves a public water supply system.

(b) Public participation — To the maximum extent possible, each State shall establish procedures, including but not limited to the establishment of technical and citizens' advisory committees, to encourage the public to participate in developing the protection program for wellhead areas and source water assessment programs under section 300j-13 of this title. Such procedures shall include notice and opportunity for public hearing on the State program before it is submitted to the Administrator.

(c) Disapproval

(1) In general — If, in the judgment of the Administrator, a State program or portion thereof under subsection (a) of this section is not adequate to protect public water systems as required by subsection (a) of this section or a State program under section 300j-13 of this title or section 300g-7(b)

of this title does not meet the applicable requirements of section 300j-13 of this title or section 300g-7(b) of this title, the Administrator shall disapprove such program or portion thereof. A State program developed pursuant to subsection (a) of this section shall be deemed to be adequate unless the Administrator determines, within 9 months of the receipt of a State program, that such program (or portion thereof) is inadequate for the purpose of protecting public water systems as required by this section from contaminants that may have any adverse effect on the health of persons. A State program developed pursuant to section 300j-13 of this title or section 300g-7(b) of this title shall be deemed to meet the applicable requirements of section 300j-13 of this title or section 300g-7(b) of this title unless the Administrator determines within 9 months of the receipt of the program that such program (or portion thereof) does not meet such requirements. If the Administrator determines that a proposed State program (or any portion thereof) is disapproved, the Administrator shall submit a written statement of the reasons for such determination to the Governor of the State.

(2) Modification and resubmission — Within 6 months after receipt of the Administrator's written notice under paragraph (1) that any proposed State program (or portion thereof) is disapproved, the Governor or Governor's designee, shall modify the program based upon the recommendations of the Administrator and resubmit the modified program to the Administrator.

(d) Federal assistance — After the date 3 years after June 19, 1986, no State shall receive funds authorized to be appropriated under this section except for the purpose of implementing the program and requirements of paragraphs (4) and (6) of subsection (a) of this section.

(e) "Wellhead protection area" defined — As used in this section, the term "wellhead protection area" means the surface and subsurface area surrounding a water well or wellfield, supplying a public water system, through which contaminants are reasonably likely to move toward and reach such water well or wellfield. The extent of a wellhead protection area, within a State, necessary to provide protection from contaminants which may have any adverse effect on the health of persons is to be determined by the State in the program submitted under subsection (a) of this section. Not later than one year after June 19, 1986, the Administrator shall issue technical guidance which States may use in making such determinations. Such guidance may reflect such factors as the radius of influence around a well or wellfield, the depth of drawdown of the water table by such well or wellfield at any given point, the time or rate of travel of various contaminants in various hydrologic conditions, distance from the well or wellfield, or other factors affecting the likelihood of contaminants reaching the well or wellfield, taking into account available engineering pump tests or comparable data, field reconnaissance, topographic information, and the geology of the formation in which the well or wellfield is located.

(f) Prohibitions

(1) Activities under other laws — No funds authorized to be appropriated under this section may be used to support activities authorized by the Federal Water Pollution Control Act [33 U.S.C. §§1251 *et seq.*], the Solid Waste Disposal Act [42 U.S.C. §§6901 *et seq.*], the Comprehensive Environmental Response, Compensation, and Liability Act of 1980 [42 U.S.C. §§9601 *et seq.*], or other sections of this chapter.

(2) Individual sources — No funds authorized to be appropriated under this section may be used to bring individual sources of contamination into compliance.

(g) Implementation — Each State shall make every reasonable effort to implement the State wellhead area protection program under this section within 2 years of submitting the program to the Administrator. Each State shall submit to the Administrator a biennial status report describing the State's progress in implementing the program. Such report shall include amendments to the State program for water wells sited during the biennial period.

(h) Federal agencies — Each department, agency, and instrumentality of the executive, legislative, and judicial branches of the Federal Government having jurisdiction over any potential source of contaminants identified by a State program pursuant to the provisions of subsection (a)(3) of this section shall be subject to and comply with all requirements of the State program developed according to subsection (a)(4) of this section applicable to such potential source of contaminants, both substantive and procedural, in the same manner, and to the same extent, as any other person is subject to such requirements, including payment of reasonable charges and fees. The President may exempt any potential source under the jurisdiction of any department, agency, or instrumentality in the executive branch if the President determines it to be in the paramount interest of the United States to do so. No such exemption shall be granted due to the lack of an appropriation unless the President shall have specifically requested such appropriation as part of the budgetary process and the Congress shall have failed to make available such requested appropriations.

(i) Additional requirement

(1) In general — In addition to the provisions of subsection (a) of this section, States in which there are more than 2,500 active wells at which annular injection is used as of January 1, 1986, shall include in their State program a certification that a State program exists and is being adequately

enforced that provides protection from contaminants which may have any adverse effect on the health of persons and which are associated with the annular injection or surface disposal of brines associated with oil and gas production.

(2) "Annular injection" defined — For purposes of this subsection, the term "annular injection" means the reinjection of brines associated with the production of oil or gas between the production and surface casings of a conventional oil or gas producing well.

(3) Review — The Administrator shall conduct a review of each program certified under this subsection.

(4) Disapproval — If a State fails to include the certification required by this subsection or if in the judgment of the Administrator the State program certified under this subsection is not being adequately enforced, the Administrator shall disapprove the State program submitted under subsection (a) of this section.

(j) Coordination with other laws — Nothing in this section shall authorize or require any department, agency, or other instrumentality of the Federal Government or State or local government to apportion, allocate or otherwise regulate the withdrawal or beneficial use of ground or surface waters, so as to abrogate or modify any existing rights to water established pursuant to State or Federal law, including interstate compacts.

(k) Authorization of appropriations — Unless the State program is disapproved under this section, the Administrator shall make grants to the State for not less than 50 or more than 90 percent of the costs incurred by a State (as determined by the Administrator) in developing and implementing each State program under this section. For purposes of making such grants there is authorized to be appropriated not more than the following amounts:

Fiscal year:	Amount
1987	$20,000,000
1988	20,000,000
1989	35,000,000
1990	35,000,000
1991	35,000,000
1992-2003	30,000,000

§300h-8. State ground water protection grants
[PHSA §1429]

(a) In general — The Administrator may make a grant to a State for the development and implementation of a State program to ensure the coordinated and comprehensive protection of ground water resources within the State.

(b) Guidance — Not later than 1 year after August 6, 1996, and annually thereafter, the Administrator shall publish guidance that establishes procedures for application for State ground water protection program assistance and that identifies key elements of State ground water protection programs.

(c) Conditions of grants

(1) In general — The Administrator shall award grants to States that submit an application that is approved by the Administrator. The Administrator shall determine the amount of a grant awarded pursuant to this paragraph on the basis of an assessment of the extent of ground water resources in the State and the likelihood that awarding the grant will result in sustained and reliable protection of ground water quality.

(2) Innovative program grants — The Administrator may also award a grant pursuant to this subsection for innovative programs proposed by a State for the prevention of ground water contamination.

(3) Allocation of funds — The Administrator shall, at a minimum, ensure that, for each fiscal year, not less than 1 percent of funds made available to the Administrator by appropriations to carry out this section are allocated to each State that submits an application that is approved by the Administrator pursuant to this section.

(4) Limitation on grants — No grant awarded by the Administrator may be used for a project to remediate ground water contamination.

(d) Amount of grants — The amount of a grant awarded pursuant to paragraph (1) shall not exceed 50 percent of the eligible costs of carrying out the ground water protection program that is the subject of the grant (as determined by the Administrator) for the 1-year period beginning on the date that the grant is awarded. The State shall pay a State share to cover the costs of the ground water protection program from State funds in an amount that is not less than 50 percent of the cost of conducting the program.

(e) Evaluations and reports — Not later than 3 years after August 6, 1996, and every 3 years thereafter, the Administrator shall evaluate the State ground water protection programs that are the subject of grants awarded pursuant to this section and report to the Congress on the status of ground water quality in the United States and the effectiveness of State programs for ground water protection.

(f) Authorization of appropriations — There are authorized to be appropriated to carry out this section $15,000,000 for each of fiscal years 1997 through 2003.

PART D — EMERGENCY POWERS

§300i. Emergency powers
[PHSA §1431]

(a) Actions authorized against imminent and substantial endangerment to health — Notwithstanding any other provision of this subchapter the Administrator, upon receipt of information that a contaminant which is present in or is likely to enter a public water system or an underground source of drinking water, or that there is a threatened or potential terrorist attack (or other intentional act designed to disrupt the provision of safe drinking water or to impact adversely the safety of drinking water supplied to communities and individuals), which may present an imminent and substantial endangerment to the health of persons, and that appropriate State and local authorities have not acted to protect the health of such persons, may take such actions as he may deem necessary in order to protect the health of such persons. To the extent he determines it to be practicable in light of such imminent endangerment, he shall consult with the State and local authorities in order to confirm the correctness of the information on which action proposed to be taken under this subsection is based and to ascertain the action which such authorities are or will be taking. The action which the Administrator may take may include (but shall not be limited to) (1) issuing such orders as may be necessary to protect the health of persons who are or may be users of such system (including travelers), including orders requiring the provision of alternative water supplies by persons who caused or contributed to the endangerment, and (2) commencing a civil action for appropriate relief, including a restraining order or permanent or temporary injunction.

(b) Penalties for violations; separate offenses — Any person who violates or fails or refuses to comply with any order issued by the Administrator under subsection (a)(1) of this section may, in an action brought in the appropriate United States district court to enforce such order, be subject to a civil penalty of not to exceed $15,000 for each day in which such violation occurs or failure to comply continues.

§300i-1. Tampering with public water systems [PHSA §1432]

(a) Tampering — Any person who tampers with a public water system shall be imprisoned for not more than 20 years, or fined in accordance with Title 18, or both.

(b) Attempt or threat — Any person who attempts to tamper, or makes a threat to tamper, with a public drinking water system be imprisoned for not more than 10 years, or fined in accordance with Title 18, or both.

(c) Civil penalty — The Administrator may bring a civil action in the appropriate United States district court (as determined under the provisions of Title 28) against any person who tampers, attempts to tamper, or makes a threat to tamper with a public water system. The court may impose on such person a civil penalty of not more than $1,000,000 for such tampering or not more than $100,000 for such attempt or threat.

(d) "Tamper" defined — For purposes of this section, the term "tamper" means —

(1) to introduce a contaminant into a public water system with the intention of harming persons; or

(2) to otherwise interfere with the operation

of a public water system with the intention of harming persons.

§300i-2. Community water system risk and resilience

(a) Risk and resilience assessments

(1) In general

Each community water system serving a population of greater than 3,300 persons shall conduct an assessment of the risks to, and resilience of, its system. Such an assessment —

(A) shall include an assessment of —

(i) the risk to the system from malevolent acts and natural hazards;

(ii) the resilience of the pipes and constructed conveyances, physical barriers, source water, water collection and intake, pretreatment, treatment, storage and distribution facilities, electronic, computer, or other automated systems **(including the security of such systems)** which are utilized by the system;

(iii) the monitoring practices of the system;

(iv) the financial infrastructure of the system;

(v) the use, storage, or handling of various chemicals by the system; and

(vi) the operation and maintenance of the system; and

(B) may include an evaluation of capital and operational needs for risk and resilience management for the system.

(2) Baseline information

The Administrator, not later than August 1, 2019, after consultation with appropriate departments and agencies of the Federal Government and with State and local governments, shall provide baseline information on malevolent acts of relevance to community water systems, which shall include consideration of acts that may —

(A) substantially disrupt the ability of the system to provide a safe and reliable supply of drinking water; or

(B) otherwise present significant public health or economic concerns to the community served by the system.

(3) Certification

(A) Certification

Each community water system described in paragraph (1) shall submit to the Administrator a certification that the system has conducted an assessment complying with paragraph (1). Such certification shall be made prior to —

(i) March 31, 2020, in the case of systems serving a population of 100,000 or more;

(ii) December 31, 2020, in the case of systems serving a population of 50,000 or more but less than 100,000; and

(iii) June 30, 2021, in the case of systems serving a population greater than 3,300 but less than 50,000.

(B) Review and revision

Each community water system described in paragraph (1) shall review the assessment of such system conducted under such paragraph at least once every 5 years after the applicable deadline for submission of its certification under subparagraph (A) to determine whether such assessment should be revised. Upon completion of such a review, the community water system shall submit to the Administrator a certification that the system has reviewed its assessment and, if applicable, revised such assessment.

(4) Contents of certifications

A certification required under paragraph (3) shall contain only —

(A) information that identifies the community water system submitting the certification;

(B) the date of the certification; and

(C) a statement that the community water system has conducted, reviewed, or revised the assessment, as applicable.

(5) Provision to other entities

No community water system shall be required under State or local law to provide an assessment described in this section (or revision thereof) to any State, regional, or local governmental entity solely by reason of the requirement set forth in paragraph (3) that the system submit a certification to the Administrator.

(b) Emergency response plan

Each community water system serving a population greater than 3,300 shall prepare or revise, where necessary, an emergency response plan that incorporates findings of the assessment conducted under subsection (a) for such system (and any revisions thereto). Each community water system shall certify to the Administrator, as soon as reasonably possible after October 23, 2018, but not later than 6 months after completion of the assessment under subsection (a), that the system has completed such plan. The emergency response plan shall include —

(1) strategies and resources to improve the resilience of the system, including the physical security and cybersecurity of the system;

(2) plans and procedures that can be implemented, and identification of equipment that can be utilized, in the event of a malevolent act or natural hazard that threatens the ability of the community water system to deliver safe drinking water;

(3) actions, procedures, and equipment which can obviate or significantly lessen the impact of a malevolent act or natural hazard on the public health and the safety and supply of drinking water provided to communities and individuals, including the development of alternative source water options, relocation of water intakes, and construction of flood protection barriers; and

(4) strategies that can be used to aid in the detection of malevolent acts or natural hazards that threaten the security or resilience of the system.

(c) Coordination

Community water systems shall, to the extent possible, coordinate with existing local emergency planning committees established pursuant to the Emergency Planning and Community Right-To-Know Act of 1986 (42 U.S.C. 11001 et seq.) when preparing or revising an assessment or emergency response plan under this section.

(d) Record maintenance

Each community water system shall maintain a copy of the assessment conducted under subsection (a) and the emergency response plan prepared under subsection (b) (including any revised assessment or plan) for 5 years after the date on which a certification of such assessment or plan is submitted to the Administrator under this section.

(e) Guidance to small public water systems

The Administrator shall provide guidance and technical assistance to community water systems serving a population of less than 3,300 persons on how to conduct resilience assessments, prepare emergency response plans, and address threats from malevolent acts and natural hazards that threaten to disrupt the provision of safe drinking water or significantly affect the public health or significantly affect the safety or supply of drinking water provided to communities and individuals.

(f) Alternative preparedness and operational resilience programs

(1) Satisfaction of requirement

A community water system that is required to comply with the requirements of subsections (a) and (b) may satisfy such requirements by —

(A) using and complying with technical standards that the Administrator has recognized under paragraph (2); and

(B) submitting to the Administrator a certification that the community water system is complying with subparagraph (A).

(2) Authority to recognize

Consistent with section 12(d) of the National Technology Transfer and Advancement Act of 1995, the Administrator shall recognize technical standards that are developed or adopted by third-party organizations or voluntary consensus standards bodies that carry out the objectives or activities required by this section as a means of satisfying the requirements under subsection (a) or (b).

(g) Technical assistance and grants

(1) In general

The Administrator shall establish and implement a program, to be known as the Drinking

Water Infrastructure Risk and Resilience Program, under which the Administrator may award grants in each of fiscal years 2020 and 2021 to owners or operators of community water systems for the purpose of increasing the resilience of such community water systems.

(2) Use of funds

As a condition on receipt of a grant under this section, an owner or operator of a community water system shall agree to use the grant funds exclusively to assist in the planning, design, construction, or implementation of a program or project consistent with an emergency response plan prepared pursuant to subsection (b), which may include —

(A) the purchase and installation of equipment for detection of drinking water contaminants or malevolent acts;

(B) the purchase and installation of fencing, gating, lighting, or security cameras;

(C) the tamper-proofing of manhole covers, fire hydrants, and valve boxes;

(D) the purchase and installation of improved treatment technologies and equipment to improve the resilience of the system;

(E) improvements to electronic, computer, financial, or other automated systems and remote systems;

(F) participation in training programs, and the purchase of training manuals and guidance materials, relating to security and resilience;

(G) improvements in the use, storage, or handling of chemicals by the community water system;

(H) security screening of employees or contractor support services;

(I) equipment necessary to support emergency power or water supply, including standby and mobile sources; and

(J) the development of alternative source water options, relocation of water intakes, and construction of flood protection barriers.

(3) Exclusions

A grant under this subsection may not be used for personnel costs, or for monitoring, operation, or maintenance of facilities, equipment, or systems.

(4) Technical assistance

For each fiscal year, the Administrator may use not more than $5,000,000 from the funds made available to carry out this subsection to provide technical assistance to community water systems to assist in responding to and alleviating a vulnerability that would substantially disrupt the ability of the system to provide a safe and reliable supply of drinking water (including sources of water for such systems) which the Administrator determines to present an immediate and urgent need.

(5) Grants for small systems

For each fiscal year, the Administrator may use not more than $10,000,000 from the funds made available to carry out this subsection to make grants to community water systems serving a population of less than 3,300 persons, or nonprofit organizations receiving assistance under section 300j-1(e) of this title, for activities and projects undertaken in accordance with the guidance provided to such systems under subsection (e) of this section.

(6) Authorization of appropriations

To carry out this subsection, there are authorized to be appropriated $25,000,000 for each of fiscal years 2020 and 2021.

(h) Definitions

In this section —

(1) the term "resilience" means the ability of a community water system or an asset of a community water system to adapt to or withstand the effects of a malevolent act or natural hazard without interruption to the asset's or system's function, or if the function is interrupted, to rapidly return to a normal operating condition; and

(2) the term "natural hazard" means a natural event that threatens the functioning of a community water system, including an earthquake, tornado, flood, hurricane, wildfire, and hydrologic changes.

§300i-3. Contaminant prevention, detection and response

[PHSA §1434]

(a) In general

The Administrator, in consultation with the Centers for Disease Control and, after consultation with appropriate departments and agencies of the Federal Government and with State and local governments, shall review (or enter into contracts or cooperative agreements to provide for a review of) current and future methods to prevent, detect and respond to the intentional introduction of chemical, biological or radiological contaminants into community water systems and source water for community water systems, including each of the following:

(1) Methods, means and equipment, including real time monitoring systems, designed to monitor and detect various levels of chemical, biological, and radiological contaminants or indicators of contaminants and reduce the likelihood that such contaminants can be successfully introduced into public water systems and source water intended to be used for drinking water.

(2) Methods and means to provide sufficient notice to operators of public water systems, and individuals served by such systems, of the introduction of chemical, biological or radiological contaminants and the possible effect of such introduction on public health and the safety and supply of drinking water.

(3) Methods and means for developing educational and awareness programs for community water systems.

(4) Procedures and equipment necessary to prevent the flow of contaminated drinking water to individuals served by public water systems.

(5) Methods, means, and equipment which could negate or mitigate deleterious effects on public health and the safety and supply caused by the introduction of contaminants into water intended to be used for drinking water, including an examination of the effectiveness of various drinking water technologies in removing, inactivating, or neutralizing biological, chemical, and radiological contaminants.

(6) Biomedical research into the short-term and long-term impact on public health of various chemical, biological and radiological contaminants that may be introduced into public water systems through terrorist or other intentional acts.

(b) Funding

For the authorization of appropriations to carry out this section, see section 300i-4(e) of this title.

§300i-4. Supply disruption prevention, detection and response
[PHSA §1436]
(a) Disruption of supply or safety

The Administrator, in coordination with the appropriate departments and agencies of the Federal Government, shall review (or enter into contracts or cooperative agreements to provide for a review of) methods and means by which terrorists or other individuals or groups could disrupt the supply of safe drinking water or take other actions against water collection, pretreatment, treatment, storage and distribution facilities which could render such water significantly less safe for human consumption, including each of the following:

(1) Methods and means by which pipes and other constructed conveyances utilized in public water systems could be destroyed or otherwise prevented from providing adequate supplies of drinking water meeting applicable public health standards.

(2) Methods and means by which collection, pretreatment, treatment, storage and distribution facilities utilized or used in connection with public water systems and collection and pretreatment storage facilities used in connection with public water systems could be destroyed or otherwise prevented from providing adequate supplies of drinking water meeting applicable public health standards.

(3) Methods and means by which pipes, constructed conveyances, collection, pretreatment, treatment, storage and distribution systems that are utilized in connection with public water systems could be altered or affected so as to be subject to cross-contamination of drinking water supplies.

(4) Methods and means by which pipes, con-

structed conveyances, collection, pretreatment, treatment, storage and distribution systems that are utilized in connection with public water systems could be reasonably protected from terrorist attacks or other acts intended to disrupt the supply or affect the safety of drinking water.

(5) Methods and means by which information systems, including process controls and supervisory control and data acquisition and cyber systems at community water systems could be disrupted by terrorists or other groups.

(b) Alternative sources

The review under this section shall also include a review of the methods and means by which alternative supplies of drinking water could be provided in the event of the destruction, impairment or contamination of public water systems.

(c) Requirements and considerations

In carrying out this section and section 300i-3 of this title —

(1) the Administrator shall ensure that reviews carried out under this section reflect the needs of community water systems of various sizes and various geographic areas of the United States; and

(2) the Administrator may consider the vulnerability of, or potential for forced interruption of service for, a region or service area, including community water systems that provide service to the National Capital area.

(d) Information sharing

As soon as practicable after reviews carried out under this section or section 300i-3 of this title have been evaluated, the Administrator shall disseminate, as appropriate as determined by the Administrator, to community water systems information on the results of the project through the Information Sharing and Analysis Center, or other appropriate means.

(e) Funding

There are authorized to be appropriated to carry out this section and section 300i-3 of this title not more than $15,000,000 for the fiscal year 2002 and such sums as may be necessary for the fiscal years 2003 through 2005.

PART E — GENERAL PROVISIONS

§300j. Assurances of availability of adequate supplies of chemicals necessary for treatment of water
[PHSA §1441]

(a) Certification of need application — If any person who uses chlorine, activated carbon, lime, ammonia, soda ash, potassium permanganate, caustic soda, or other chemical or substance for the purpose of treating water in any public water system or in any public treatment works determines that the amount of such chemical or substance necessary to effectively treat such water is not reasonably available to him or will not be so available to him when required for the effective treatment of such water, such person may apply to the Administrator for a certification (hereinafter in this section referred to as a "certification of need") that the amount of such chemical or substance which such person requires to effectively treat such water is not reasonably available to him or will not be so available when required for the effective treatment of such water.

(b) Application requirements; publication in Federal Register; waiver; certification, issuance or denial

(1) An application for a certification of need shall be in such form and submitted in such manner as the Administrator may require and shall (A) specify the persons the applicant determines are able to provide the chemical or substance with respect to which the application is submitted, (B) specify the persons from whom the applicant has sought such chemical or substance, and (C) contain such other information as the Administrator may require.

(2) Upon receipt of an application under this section, the Administrator shall (A) publish in the Federal Register a notice of the receipt of the application and a brief summary of it, (B) notify in writing each person whom the President or his delegate (after consultation with the Administrator) determines could be made subject to an order required to be issued upon the issuance of the certification of need applied for in such application, and (C) provide an opportunity for the submission of written comments on such application. The requirements of the preceding sentence of this paragraph shall not apply when the Administrator for good cause finds (and incorporates the finding with a brief statement of reasons therefor in the order issued) that waiver of such requirements is necessary in order to protect the public health.

(3) Within 30 days after —

(A) the date a notice is published under paragraph (2) in the Federal Register with respect to an application submitted under this section for the issuance of a certification of need, or

(B) the date on which such application is received if as authorized by the second sentence of such paragraph no notice is published with respect to such application,

the Administrator shall take action either to issue or deny the issuance of a certification of need.

(c) Certification of need; issuance; executive orders; implementation of orders; equitable apportionment of orders; factors considered

(1) If the Administrator finds that the amount of a chemical or substance necessary for an applicant under an application submitted under this section to effectively treat water in a public water system or in a public treatment works is not reasonably available to the applicant or will not be so available to him when required for the effective treatment of such water, the Administrator shall

issue a certification of need. Not later than seven days following the issuance of such certification, the President or his delegate shall issue an order requiring the provision to such person of such amounts of such chemical or substance as the Administrator deems necessary in the certification of need issued for such person. Such order shall apply to such manufactures, producers, processors, distributors, and repackagers of such chemical or substance as the President or his delegate deems necessary and appropriate, except that such order may not apply to any manufacturer, producer, or processor of such chemical or substance who manufactures, produces, or processes (as the case may be) such chemical or substance solely for its own use. Persons subject to an order issued under this section shall be given a reasonable opportunity to consult with the President or his delegate with respect to the implementation of the order.

(2) Orders which are to be issued under paragraph (1) to manufacturers, producers, and processors of a chemical or substance shall be equitably apportioned, as far as practicable, among all manufacturers, producers, and processors of such chemical or substance; and orders which are to be issued under paragraph (1) to distributors and repackagers of a chemical or substance shall be equitably apportioned, as far as practicable, among all distributors and repackagers of such chemical or substance. In apportioning orders issued under paragraph (1) to manufacturers, producers, processors, distributors, and repackagers of chlorine, the President or his delegate shall, in carrying out the requirements of the preceding sentence, consider —

(A) the geographical relationships and established commercial relationships between such manufacturers, producers, processors, distributors, and repackagers and the persons for whom the orders are issued;

(B) in the case of orders to be issued to producers of chlorine, the (i) amount of chlorine historically supplied by each such producer to treat water in public water systems and public treatment works, and (ii) share of each such producer of the total annual production of chlorine in the United States; and

(C) such other factors as the President or his delegate may determine are relevant to the apportionment of orders in accordance with the requirements of the preceding sentence.

(3) Subject to subsection (f) of this section, any person for whom a certification of need has been issued under this subsection may upon the expiration of the order issued under paragraph (1) upon such certification apply under this section for additional certifications.

(d) Breach of contracts; defense — There shall be available as a defense to any action brought for breach of contract in a Federal or State court arising out of delay or failure to provide, sell, or offer for sale or exchange a chemical or substance subject to an order issued pursuant to subsection (c)(1) of this section, that such delay or failure was caused solely by compliance with such order.

(e) Penalties for noncompliance with orders; temporary restraining orders and preliminary or permanent injunctions

(1) Whoever knowingly fails to comply with any order issued pursuant to subsection (c)(1) of this section shall be fined not more than $5,000 for each such failure to comply.

(2) Whoever fails to comply with any order issued pursuant to subsection (c)(1) of this section shall be subject to a civil penalty of not more than $2,500 for each such failure to comply.

(3) Whenever the Administrator or the President or his delegate has reason to believe that any person is violating or will violate any order issued pursuant to subsection (c)(1) of this section, he may petition a United States district court to issue a temporary restraining order or preliminary or permanent injunction (including a mandatory injunction) to enforce the provision of such order.

(f) Termination date — No certification of need or order issued under this section may remain in effect for more than one year.

§300j-1. Research, technical assistance, information, training of personnel
[PHSA §1442]

(a) Specific powers and duties of Administrator

(1) The Administrator may conduct research, studies, and demonstrations relating to the causes, diagnosis, treatment, control, and prevention of physical and mental diseases and other impairments of man resulting directly or indirectly from contaminants in water, or to the provision of a dependably safe supply of drinking water, including —

(A) improved methods (i) to identify and measure the existence of contaminants in drinking water (including methods which may be used by State and local health and water officials), and (ii) to identify the source of such contaminants;

(B) improved methods to identify and measure the health effects of contaminants in drinking water;

(C) new methods of treating raw water to prepare it for drinking, so as to improve the efficiency of water treatment and to remove contaminants from water;

(D) improved methods for providing a dependably safe supply of drinking water, including improvements in water purification and distribution, and methods of assessing the health related hazards of drinking water; and

(E) improved methods of protecting underground water sources of public water

systems from contamination.

(2) Information and research facilities — In carrying out this subchapter, the Administrator is authorized to —

(A) collect and make available information pertaining to research, investigations, and demonstrations with respect to providing a dependably safe supply of drinking water, together with appropriate recommendations in connection with the information; and

(B) make available research facilities of the Agency to appropriate public authorities, institutions, and individuals engaged in studies and research relating to this subchapter.

(3) The Administrator shall carry out a study of polychlorinated biphenyl contamination of actual or potential sources of drinking water, contamination of such sources by other substances known or suspected to be harmful to public health, the effects of such contamination, and means of removing, treating, or otherwise controlling such contamination. To assist in carrying out this paragraph, the Administrator is authorized to make grants to public agencies and private nonprofit institutions.

(4) The Administrator shall conduct a survey and study of —

(A) disposal of waste (including residential waste) which may endanger underground water which supplies, or can reasonably be expected to supply, any public water systems, and

(B) means of control of such waste disposal. Not later than one year after December 16, 1974, he shall transmit to the Congress the results of such survey and study, together with such recommendations as he deems appropriate.

(5) The Administrator shall carry out a study of methods of underground injection which do not result in the degradation of underground drinking water sources.

(6) The Administrator shall carry out a study of methods of preventing, detecting, and dealing with surface spills of contaminants which may degrade underground water sources for public water systems.

(7) The Administrator shall carry out a study of virus contamination of drinking water sources and means of control of such contamination.

(8) The Administrator shall carry out a study of the nature and extent of the impact on underground water which supplies or can reasonably be expected to supply public water systems of (A) abandoned injection or extraction wells; (B) intensive application of pesticides and fertilizers in underground water recharge areas; and (C) ponds, pools, lagoons, pits, or other surface disposal of contaminants in underground water recharge areas.

(9) The Administrator shall conduct a comprehensive study of public water supplies and drinking water sources to determine the nature, extent, sources of and means of control of contamination by chemicals or other substances

suspected of being carcinogenic. Not later than six months after December 16, 1974, he shall transmit to the Congress the initial results of such study, together with such recommendations for further review and corrective action as he deems appropriate.

(10) The Administrator shall carry out a study of the reaction of chlorine and humic acids and the effects of the contaminants which result from such reaction on public health and on the safety of drinking water, including any carcinogenic effect.

(b) Emergency situations — The Administrator is authorized to provide technical assistance and to make grants to States, or publicly owned water systems to assist in responding to and alleviating any emergency situation affecting public water systems (including sources of water for such systems) which the Administrator determines to present substantial danger to the public health. Grants provided under this subsection shall be used only to support those actions which (i) are necessary for preventing, limiting or mitigating danger to the public health in such emergency situation and (ii) would not, in the judgment of the Administrator, be taken without such emergency assistance. The Administrator may carry out the program authorized under this subparagraph as part of, and in accordance with the terms and conditions of, any other program of assistance for environmental emergencies which the Administrator is authorized to carry out under any other provision of law. No limitation on appropriations for any such other program shall apply to amounts appropriated under this subsection.

(c) Establishment of training programs and grants for training; training fees

The Administrator shall —

(1) provide training for, and make grants for training (including postgraduate training) of (A) personnel of State agencies which have primary enforcement responsibility and of agencies or units of local government to which enforcement responsibilities have been delegated by the State, and (B) personnel who manage or operate public water systems, and

(2) make grants for postgraduate training of individuals (including grants to educational institutions for traineeships) for purposes of qualifying such individuals to work as personnel referred to in paragraph (1).

(3) make grants to, and enter into contracts with, any public agency, educational institution, and any other organization, in accordance with procedures prescribed by the Administrator, under which he may pay all or part of the costs (as may be determined by the Administrator) of any project or activity which is designed —

(A) to develop, expand, or carry out a program (which may combine training education and employment) for training persons for occupations involving the public health aspects of providing safe drinking water;

(B) to train inspectors and supervisory personnel to train or supervise persons in occupations involving the public health aspects of providing safe drinking water; or

(C) to develop and expand the capability of programs of States and municipalities to carry out the purposes of this subchapter (other than by carrying out State programs of public water system supervision or underground water source protection (as defined in section 300j-2(c) of this title)).

Reasonable fees may be charged for training provided under paragraph (1)(B) to persons other than personnel of State or local agencies but such training shall be provided to personnel of State or local agencies without charge.

(d) Authorization of appropriations — There are authorized to be appropriated to carry out subsection (b) of this section not more than $35,000,000 for the fiscal year 2002 and such sums as may be necessary for each fiscal year thereafter.

(e) Technical assistance

(1) The Administrator may provide technical assistance to small public water systems to enable such systems to achieve and maintain compliance with applicable national primary drinking water regulations.

(2) Such assistance may include circuit-rider and multi-State regional technical assistance programs, training, and preliminary engineering evaluations.

(3) The Administrator shall ensure that technical assistance pursuant to this subsection is available in each State.

(4) Each nonprofit organization receiving assistance under this subsection shall consult with the State in which the assistance is to be expended or otherwise made available before using assistance to undertake activities to carry out this subsection.

(5) There are authorized to be appropriated to the Administrator to be used for such technical assistance $15,000,000 for each of the fiscal years 2015 through 2020.

(6) No portion of any State loan fund established under section 300j-12 of this title (relating to State loan funds) and no portion of any funds made available under this subsection may be used for lobbying expenses.

(7) Of the total amount appropriated under this subsection, 3 percent shall be used for technical assistance to public water systems owned or operated by Indian Tribes.

(8) Nonprofit organizations. —

(A) In general. — The Administrator may use amounts made available to carry out this section to provide grants or cooperative agreements to nonprofit organizations that provide to small public water systems onsite technical assistance, circuit-rider technical assistance programs, multistate, regional technical assistance programs, onsite and regional training, assistance with implementing source water protection plans, and assistance with implementing monitoring plans, rules, regulations, and water security enhancements.

(B) Preference. — To ensure that technical assistance funding is used in a manner that is most beneficial to the small and rural communities of a State, the Administrator shall give preference under this paragraph to nonprofit organizations that, as determined by the Administrator, are the most qualified and experienced in providing training and technical assistance to small public water systems and that the small community water systems in that State find to be the most beneficial and effective.

(C) Limitation. — No grant or cooperative agreement provided or otherwise made available under this section may be used for litigation pursuant to section 300j-8 of this title.

§300j-1a. Innovative water technology grant program

(a) Definitions

In this section:

(1) Administrator

The term "Administrator" means the Administrator of the Environmental Protection Agency.

(2) Eligible entity

The term "eligible entity" means —

(A) a public water system (as defined under section 300f(4) of this title);

(B) an institution of higher education;

(C) a research institution or foundation;

(D) a regional water organization; or

(E) a nonprofit organization described in section 300j-1(e)(8) of this title.

(b) Grant program authorized

The Administrator shall carry out a grant program for the purpose of accelerating the development and deployment of innovative water technologies that address pressing drinking water supply, quality, treatment, or security challenges of public water systems, areas served by private wells, or source waters.

(c) Grants

In carrying out the program under subsection (b), the Administrator shall make grants to eligible entities —

(1) to develop, test, and deploy innovative water technologies; or

(2) to provide technical assistance to deploy demonstrated innovative water technologies.

(d) Selection criteria

In making grants under this section, the Administrator shall —

(1) award grants through a competitive process to eligible entities the Administrator determines are best able to carry out the purpose of the program; and

(2) give priority to projects that have the potential —

(A) to reduce ratepayer or community costs or costs of future capital investments;

(B) to significantly improve human health or the environment; or

(C) to provide additional drinking water supplies with minimal environmental impact.

(e) Cost-sharing

The Federal share of the cost of activities carried out using a grant under this section shall be not more than 65 percent.

(f) Limitation

The maximum amount of a grant under this section shall be $5,000,000.

(g) Report

Each year, the Administrator shall submit to Congress and make publicly available on the website of the Administrator a report that describes any advancements during the previous year in development of innovative water technologies made as a result of funding provided under this section.

(h) Partnerships

Grants awarded under this program may include projects that are carried out by an eligible entity in cooperation with a private entity, including a farmer, farmer cooperative, or manufacturer of water technologies.

(i) Authorization of appropriations

There is authorized to be appropriated to carry out this section $10,000,000 for each of fiscal years 2019 and 2020.

§300j-2. Grants for State programs
[PHSA §1443]

(a) Public water systems supervision programs; applications for grants; allotment of sums; waiver of grant restrictions; notice of approval or disapproval of application; authorization of appropriations

(1) From allotments made pursuant to paragraph (4), the Administrator may make grants to States to carry out public water system supervision programs.

(2) No grant may be made under paragraph (1) unless an application therefor has been submitted to the Administrator in such form and manner as he may require. The Administrator may not approve an application of a State for its first grant under paragraph (1) unless he determines that the State —

(A) has established or will establish within one year from the date of such grant a public water system supervision program, and

(B) will, within that one year, assume primary enforcement responsibility for public water systems within the State.

No grant may be made to a State under paragraph (1) for any period beginning more than one year after the date of the State's first grant unless the State has assumed and maintains primary enforcement responsibility for public water systems

337

within the State. The prohibitions contained in the preceding two sentences shall not apply to such grants when made to Indian Tribes.

(3) A grant under paragraph (1) shall be made to cover not more than 75 per centum of the grant recipient's costs (as determined under regulations of the Administrator) in carrying out, during the one-year period beginning on the date the grant is made, a public water system supervision program.

(4) In each fiscal year the Administrator shall, in accordance, with regulations, allot the sums appropriated for such year under paragraph (5) among the States on the basis of population, geographical area, number of public water systems, and other relevant factors. No State shall receive less than 1 per centum of the annual appropriation for grants under paragraph (1): *Provided,* That the Administrator may, by regulation, reduce such percentage in accordance with the criteria specified in this paragraph: *And provided further,* That such percentage shall not apply to grants allotted to Guam, American Samoa, or the Virgin Islands.

(5) The prohibition contained in the last sentence of paragraph (2) may be waived by the Administrator with respect to a grant to a State through fiscal year 1979 but such prohibition may only be waived if, in the judgment of the Administrator —

(A) the State is making a diligent effort to assume and maintain primary enforcement responsibility for public water systems within the State;

(B) the State has made significant progress toward assuming and maintaining such primary enforcement responsibility; and

(C) there is reason to believe the State will assume such primary enforcement responsibility by October 1, 1979.

The amount of any grant awarded for the fiscal years 1978 and 1979 pursuant to a waiver under this paragraph may not exceed 75 per centum of the allotment which the State would have received for such fiscal year if it had assumed and maintained such primary enforcement responsibility. The remaining 25 per centum of the amount allotted to such State for such fiscal year shall be retained by the Administrator, and the Administrator may award such amount to such State at such time as the State assumes such responsibility before the beginning of fiscal year 1980. At the beginning of each fiscal years 1979 and 1980 the amounts retained by the Administrator for any preceding fiscal year and not awarded by the beginning of fiscal year 1979 or 1980 to the States to which such amounts were originally allotted may be removed from the original allotment and reallotted for fiscal year 1979 or 1980 (as the case may be) to States which have assumed primary enforcement responsibility by the beginning of such fiscal year.

(6) The Administrator shall notify the State of the approval or disapproval of any application for a grant under this section —

(A) within ninety days after receipt of such application, or

(B) not later than the first day of the fiscal year for which the grant application is made, whichever is later.

(7) Authorization — For the purpose of making grants under paragraph (1), there are authorized to be $125,000,000 for each of the fiscal years 2020 and 2021.

(8) Reservation of funds by the administrator — If the Administrator assumes the primary enforcement responsibility of a State public water system supervision program, the Administrator may reserve from funds made available pursuant to this subsection an amount equal to the amount that would otherwise have been provided to the State pursuant to this subsection. The Administrator shall use the funds reserved pursuant to this paragraph to ensure the full and effective administration of a public water system supervision program in the State.

(9) State loan funds

(A) Reservation of funds — For any fiscal year for which the amount made available to the Administrator by appropriations to carry out this subsection is less than the amount that the Administrator determines is necessary to supplement funds made available pursuant to paragraph (8) to ensure the full and effective administration of a public water system supervision program in a State, the Administrator may reserve from the funds made available to the State under section 300j-12 of this title (relating to State loan funds) an amount that is equal to the amount of the shortfall. This paragraph shall not apply to any State not exercising primary enforcement responsibility for public water systems as of August 6, 1996.

(B) Duty of administrator — If the Administrator reserves funds from the allocation of a State under subparagraph (A), the Administrator shall carry out in the State each of the activities that would be required of the State if the State had primary enforcement authority under section 300g-2 of this title.

(b) Underground water source protection programs; applications for grants; allotment of sums; authorization of appropriations

(1) From allotments made pursuant to paragraph (4), the Administrator may make grants to States to carry out underground water source protection programs.

(2) No grant may be made under paragraph (1) unless an application therefor has been submitted

to the Administrator in such form and manner as he may require. No grant may be made to any State under paragraph (1) unless the State has assumed primary enforcement responsibility within two years after the date the Administrator promulgates regulations for State underground injection control programs under section 300h of this title. The prohibition contained in the preceding sentence shall not apply to such grants when made to Indian Tribes.

(3) A grant under paragraph (1) shall be made to cover not more than 75 per centum of the grant recipient's cost (as determined under regulations of the Administrator) in carrying out, during the one-year period beginning on the date the grant is made, and underground water source protection program.

(4) In each fiscal year the Administrator shall, in accordance with regulations, allot the sums appropriated for such year under paragraph (5) among the States on the basis of population, geographical area, and other relevant factors.

(5) For purposes of making grants under paragraph (1) there are authorized to be appropriated $5,000,000 for the fiscal year ending June 30, 1976, $7,500,000 for the fiscal year ending June 30, 1977, $10,000,000 for each of the fiscal years 1978 and 1979, $7,795,000 for the fiscal year ending September 30, 1980, $18,000,000 for the fiscal year ending September 30, 1981, and $21,000,000 for the fiscal year ending September 30, 1982. For the purpose of making grants under paragraph (1) there are authorized to be appropriated not more than the following amounts:

Fiscal year:	Amount
1987	$19,700,000
1988	19,700,000
1989	20,850,000
1990	20,850,000
1991	20,850,000
1992-2003	15,000,000

(c) **Definitions** — For purposes of this section:

(1) The term "public water system supervision program" means a program for the adoption and enforcement of drinking water regulations (with such variances and exemptions from such regulations under conditions and in a manner which is not less stringent than the conditions under, and the manner in, which variances and exemptions may be granted under sections 300g-4 and 300g-5 of this title) which are no less stringent than the national primary drinking water regulations under section 300g-1 of this title, and for keeping records and making reports required by section 300g-2(a)(3) of this title.

(2) The term "underground water source protection program" means a program for the adoption and enforcement of a program which meets the requirements of regulations under section 300h of this title, and for keeping records and making reports required by section 300h-1(b)(1)

(A)(ii) of this title. Such term includes, where applicable, a program which meets the requirements of section 300h-4 of this title.

(d) **New York City watershed protection program**

(1) In general — The Administrator is authorized to provide financial assistance to the State of New York for demonstration projects implemented as part of the watershed program for the protection and enhancement of the quality of source waters of the New York City water supply system, including projects that demonstrate, assess, or provide for comprehensive monitoring and surveillance and projects necessary to comply with the criteria for avoiding filtration contained in 40 CFR 141.71. Demonstration projects which shall be eligible for financial assistance shall be certified to the Administrator by the State of New York as satisfying the purposes of this subsection. In certifying projects to the Administrator, the State of New York shall give priority to monitoring projects that have undergone peer review.

(2) Report — Not later than 5 years after the date on which the Administrator first provides assistance pursuant to this paragraph, the Governor of the State of New York shall submit a report to the Administrator on the results of projects assisted.

(3) Matching requirements — Federal assistance provided under this subsection shall not exceed 50 percent of the total cost of the protection program being carried out for any particular watershed or ground water recharge area.

(4) Authorization — There are authorized to be appropriated to the Administrator to carry out this subsection for each of fiscal years 2003 through 2010, $15,000,000 for the purpose of providing assistance to the State of New York to carry out paragraph (1).

§300j-3. Special project grants and guaranteed loans

[PHSA §1444]

(a) **Special study and demonstration project grants** — The Administrator may make grants to any person for the purposes of —

(1) assisting in the development and demonstration (including construction) of any project which will demonstrate a new or improved method, approach, or technology, for providing a dependably safe supply of drinking water to the public; and

(2) assisting in the development and demonstration (including construction) of any project which will investigate and demonstrate health implications involved in the reclamation, recycling, and reuse of waste waters for drinking and the processes and methods for the preparation of safe and acceptable drinking water.

(b) **Limitations** — Grants made by the Administrator under this section shall be subject to the following limitations:

(1) Grants under this section shall not exceed 66 2/3 per centum of the total cost of construction of any facility and 75 per centum of any other costs, as determined by the Administrator.

(2) Grants under this section shall not be made for any project involving the construction or modification of any facilities for any public water system in a State unless such project has been approved by the State agency charged with the responsibility for safety of drinking water (or if there is no such agency in a State, by the State health authority).

(3) Grants under this section shall not be made for any project unless the Administrator determines, after consulting the National Drinking Water Advisory Council, that such project will serve a useful purpose relating to the development and demonstration of new or improved techniques, methods, or technologies for the provision of safe water to the public for drinking.

(4) Priority for grants under this section shall be given where there are known or potential public health hazards which require advanced technology for the removal of particles which are too small to be removed by ordinary treatment technology. ·

(c) **Authorization of appropriations** — For the purposes of making grants under subsections (a) and (b) of this section there are authorized to be appropriated $7,500,000 for the fiscal year ending June 30, 1975; and $7,500,000 for the fiscal year ending June 30, 1976; and $10,000,000 for the fiscal year ending June 30, 1977.

(d) **Loan guarantees to public water systems; conditions; indebtedness limitation; regulations** — The Administrator during the fiscal years ending June 30, 1975, and June 30, 1976, shall carry out a program of guaranteeing loans made by private lenders to small public water systems for the purpose of enabling such systems to meet national primary drinking water regulations prescribed under section 300g-1 of this title. No such guarantee may be made with respect to a system unless (1) such system cannot reasonably obtain financial assistance necessary to comply with such regulations from any other source, and (2) the Administrator determines that any facilities constructed with a loan guaranteed under this subsection is not likely to be made obsolete by subsequent changes in primary regulations. The aggregate amount of indebtedness guaranteed with respect to any system may not exceed $50,000. The aggregate amount of indebtedness guaranteed under this subsection may not exceed $50,000,000. The Administrator shall prescribe regulations to carry out this subsection.

§300j-3a. Grants to public sector agencies

(a) **Assistance for development and demonstration projects** — The Administrator of the Environmental Protection Agency shall offer grants to public sector agencies for the purposes of —

(1) assisting in the development and demonstration (including construction) of any project which will demonstrate a new or improved method, approach, or technology for providing a dependably safe supply of drinking water to the public; and

(2) assisting in the development and demonstration (including construction) of any project which will investigate and demonstrate health and conservation implications involved in the reclamation, recycling, and reuse of wastewaters for drinking and agricultural use or the processes and methods for the preparation of safe and acceptable drinking water.

(b) **Limitations** — Grants made by the Administrator under this section shall be subject to the following limitations:

(1) Grants under this section shall not exceed 66 2/3 per centum of the total cost of construction of any facility and 75 per centum of any other costs, as determined by the Administrator.

(2) Grants under this section shall not be made for any project involving the construction or modification of any facilities for any public water system in a State unless such project has been approved by the State agency charged with the responsibility for safety of drinking water (or if there is no such agency in a State, by the State health authority).

(3) Grants under this section shall not be made for any project unless the Administrator determines, after consultation, that such project will serve a useful purpose relating to the development and demonstration of new or improved techniques, methods, or technologies for the provision of safe water to the public for drinking.

(c) **Authorization of appropriations** — There are authorized to be appropriated for the purposes of this section $25,000,000 for fiscal year 1978.

§300j-3b. Contaminant standards or treatment technique guidelines

(1) Not later than nine months after October 18, 1978, the Administrator shall promulgate guidelines establishing supplemental standards or treatment technique requirements for microbiological, viral, radiological, organic, and inorganic contaminants, which guidelines shall be conditions, as provided in paragraph (2), of any grant for a demonstration project for water reclamation, recycling, and reuse funded under section 300j-3a of this title or under section 300j-3(a)(2) of this title, where such project involves direct human consumption of treated wastewater. Such guidelines shall provide for sufficient control of each such contaminant, such that in the Administrator's judgement, no adverse effects on the health of persons may reasonably be anticipated to occur, allowing an adequate margin of safety.

(2) A grant referred to in paragraph (1) for a project which involves direct human consumption of treated wastewater may be awarded on or after

the date of promulgation of guidelines under this section only if the applicant demonstrates to the satisfaction of the Administrator that the project —

(A) will comply with all national primary drinking water regulations under section 300g-1 of this title;

(B) will comply with all guidelines under this section; and

(C) will in other respects provide safe drinking water.

Any such grant awarded before the date of promulgation of such guidelines shall be conditioned on the applicant's agreement to comply to the maximum feasible extent with such guidelines as expeditiously as practicable following the date of promulgation thereof.

(3) Guidelines under this section may, in the discretion of the Administrator —

(A) be nationally and uniformly applicable to all projects funded under section 300j-3a of this title or section 300j-1(a)(2) of this title;

(B) vary for different classes or categories of such projects (as determined by the Administrator);

(C) be established and applicable on a project-by-project basis; or

(D) any combination of the above.

(4) Nothing in this section shall be construed to prohibit or delay the award of any grant referred to in paragraph (1) prior to the date of promulgation of such guidelines.

§300j-3c. National assistance program for water infrastructure and watersheds

(a) Technical and financial assistance — The Administrator of the Environmental Protection Agency may provide technical and financial assistance in the form of grants to States (1) for the construction, rehabilitation, and improvement of water supply systems, and (2) consistent with nonpoint source management programs established under section 1329 of Title 33, for source water quality protection programs to address pollutants in navigable waters for the purpose of making such waters usable by water supply systems.

(b) Limitation — Not more than 30 percent of the amounts appropriated to carry out this section in a fiscal year may be used for source water quality protection programs described in subsection (a)(2) of this section.

(c) Condition — As a condition to receiving assistance under this section, a State shall ensure that such assistance is carried out in the most cost-effective manner, as determined by the State.

(d) Authorization of appropriations

(1) Unconditional authorization — There are authorized to be appropriated to carry out this section $25,000,000 for each of fiscal years 1997 through 2003. Such sums shall remain available until expended.

(2) Conditional authorization — In addition to amounts authorized under paragraph (1), there

are authorized to be appropriated to carry out this section $25,000,000 for each of fiscal years 1997 through 2003, provided that such authorization shall be in effect for a fiscal year only if at least 75 percent of the total amount of funds authorized to be appropriated for such fiscal year by section 300j-12(m) of this title are appropriated.

(e) Acquisition of lands — Assistance provided with funds made available under this section may be used for the acquisition of lands and other interests in lands; however, nothing in this section authorizes the acquisition of lands or other interests in lands from other than willing sellers.

(f) Federal share — The Federal share of the cost of activities for which grants are made under this section shall be 50 percent.

(g) Definitions — In this section, the following definitions apply:

(1) State — The term "State" means a State, the District of Columbia, the Commonwealth of Puerto Rico, the Virgin Islands, Guam, American Samoa, and the Commonwealth of the Northern Mariana Islands.

(2) Water supply system — The term "water supply system" means a system for the provision to the public of piped water for human consumption if such system has at least 15 service connections or regularly serves at least 25 individuals and a draw and fill system for the provision to the public of water for human consumption. Such term does not include a system owned by a Federal agency. Such term includes (A) any collection, treatment, storage, and distribution facilities under control of the operator of such system and used primarily in connection with such system, and (B) any collection or pretreatment facilities not under such control that are used primarily in connection with such system.

§300j-3d. Water supply cost savings

(a) Drinking water technology clearing-house

The Administrator, in consultation with the Secretary of Agriculture, shall —

(1) develop a technology clearinghouse for information on the cost-effectiveness of innovative and alternative drinking water delivery systems, including wells and well systems; and

(2) disseminate such information to the public and to communities and not-for-profit organizations seeking Federal funding for drinking water delivery systems serving 500 or fewer persons.

(b) Water system assessment

In any application for a grant or loan for the purpose of construction, replacement, or rehabilitation of a drinking water delivery system serving 500 or fewer persons, the funding for which would come from the Federal Government (either directly or through a State), a unit of local government or not-for-profit organization shall self-certify that the unit of local government or organization has considered, as an alternative drinking water supply, drinking water delivery systems sourced by publicly owned —

(1) individual wells;

(2) shared wells; and

(3) community wells.

(c) Report to Congress

Not later than 3 years after December 16, 2016, the Comptroller General of the United States shall submit to Congress a report that describes —

(1) the use of innovative and alternative drinking water delivery systems described in this section;

(2) the range of cost savings for communities using innovative and alternative drinking water delivery systems described in this section; and

(3) the use of drinking water technical assistance programs operated by the Administrator and the Secretary of Agriculture.

§300j-4. Records and inspections
[PHSA §1445]
(a) Provision of information to Administrator; monitoring program for unregulated contaminants

(1)(A) Every person who is subject to any requirement of this subchapter or who is a grantee, shall establish and maintain such records, make such reports, conduct such monitoring, and provide such information as the Administrator may reasonably require by regulation to assist the Administrator in establishing regulations under this subchapter, in determining whether such person has acted or is acting in compliance with this subchapter, in administering any program of financial assistance under this subchapter, in evaluating the health risks of unregulated contaminants, or in advising the public of such risks. In requiring a public water system to monitor under this subsection, the Administrator may take into consideration the system size and the contaminants likely to be found in the system's drinking water.

(B) Every person who is subject to a national primary drinking water regulation under section 300g-1 of this title shall provide such information as the Administrator may reasonably require, after consultation with the State in which such person is located if such State has primary enforcement responsibility for public water systems, on a case-by-case basis, to determine whether such person has acted or is acting in compliance with this subchapter.

(C) Every person who is subject to a national primary drinking water regulation under section 300g-1 of this title shall provide such information as the Administrator may reasonably require to assist the Administrator in establishing regulations under section 300g-1 of this title, after consultation with States and suppliers of water. The Administrator may not require under this subparagraph the

installation of treatment equipment or process changes, the testing of treatment technology, or the analysis or processing of monitoring samples, except where the Administrator provides the funding for such activities. Before exercising this authority, the Administrator shall first seek to obtain the information by voluntary submission.

(D) The Administrator shall not later than 2 years after August 6, 1996, after consultation with public health experts, representatives of the general public, and officials of State and local governments, review the monitoring requirements for not fewer than 12 contaminants identified by the Administrator, and promulgate any necessary modifications.

(2) Monitoring program for unregulated contaminants —

(A) Establishment — The Administrator shall promulgate regulations establishing the criteria for a monitoring program for unregulated contaminants. The regulations shall require monitoring of drinking water supplied by public water systems and shall vary the frequency and schedule for monitoring requirements for systems based on the number of persons served by the system, the source of supply, and the contaminants likely to be found, ensuring that only a representative sample of systems serving 10,000 persons or fewer are required to monitor.

(B) Monitoring program for certain unregulated contaminants —

(i) Initial list — Not later than 3 years after August 6, 1996, and every 5 years thereafter, the Administrator shall issue a list pursuant to subparagraph (A) of not more than 30 unregulated contaminants to be monitored by public water systems and to be included in the national drinking water occurrence data base maintained pursuant to subsection (g) of this section.

(ii) Governors' petition — The Administrator shall include among the list of contaminants for which monitoring is required under this paragraph each contaminant recommended in a petition signed by the Governor of each of 7 or more States, unless the Administrator determines that the action would prevent the listing of other contaminants of a higher public health concern.

(C) Monitoring plan for small and medium systems —

(i) In general — Based on the regulations promulgated by the Administrator, each State may develop a representative monitoring plan to assess the occurrence of unregulated contaminants in public water systems that serve a population of 10,000 or fewer in that State. The plan shall require monitoring for systems representative of different sizes, types, and geographic locations in the State.

(ii) Grants for small system costs — From funds reserved under section 300j-12(o) of this title or appropriated under subparagraph (H), the Administrator shall pay the reasonable cost of such testing and laboratory analysis as are necessary to carry out monitoring under the plan.

(D) Monitoring results — Each public water system that conducts monitoring of unregulated contaminants pursuant to this paragraph shall provide the results of the monitoring to the primary enforcement authority for the system.

(E) Notification — Notification of the availability of the results of monitoring programs required under paragraph (2)(A) shall be given to the persons served by the system.

(F) Waiver of monitoring requirement — The Administrator shall waive the requirement for monitoring for a contaminant under this paragraph in a State, if the State demonstrates that the criteria for listing the contaminant do not apply in that State.

(G) Analytical methods — The State may use screening methods approved by the Administrator under subsection (i) of this section in lieu of monitoring for particular contaminants under this paragraph.

(H) Authorization of appropriations — There are authorized to be appropriated to carry out this paragraph $10,000,000 for each of the fiscal years 2019 through 2021.

(b) Entry of establishments, facilities, or other property; inspections; conduct of certain tests; audit and examination of records; entry restrictions; prohibition against informing of a proposed entry

(1) Except as provided in paragraph (2), the Administrator, or representatives of the Administrator duly designated by him, upon presenting appropriate credentials and a written notice to any supplier of water or other person subject to (A) a national primary drinking water regulation prescribed under section 300g-1 of this title, (B) an applicable underground injection control program, or (C) any requirement to monitor an unregulated contaminant pursuant to subsection (a) of this section, or person in charge of any of the property of such supplier or other person referred to in clause (A), (B), or (C), is authorized to enter any establishment, facility, or other property of such supplier or other person in order to determine whether such supplier or other person has acted or is acting in compliance with this subchapter, including for this purpose, inspection, at reasonable times, of records, files, papers, processes, controls, and facilities, or in order to test any feature of a public water system, including its raw water source. The

Administrator or the Comptroller General (or any representative designated by either) shall have access for the purpose of audit and examination to any records, reports, or information of a grantee which are required to be maintained under subsection (a) of this section or which are pertinent to any financial assistance under this subchapter.

(2) No entry may be made under the first sentence of paragraph (1) in an establishment, facility, or other property of a supplier of water or other person subject to a national primary drinking water regulation if the establishment, facility, or other property is located in a State which has primary enforcement responsibility for public water systems unless, before written notice of such entry is made, the Administrator (or his representative) notifies the State agency charged with responsibility for safe drinking water of the reasons for such entry. The Administrator shall, upon a showing by the State agency that such an entry will be detrimental to the administration of the State's program of primary enforcement responsibility, take such showing into consideration in determining whether to make such entry. No State agency which receives notice under this paragraph of an entry proposed to be made under paragraph (1) may use the information contained in the notice to inform the person whose property is proposed to be entered of the proposed entry; and if a State agency so uses such information, notice to the agency under this paragraph is not required until such time as the Administrator determines the agency has provided him satisfactory assurances that it will no longer so use information contained in a notice under this paragraph.

(c) Penalty — Whoever fails or refuses to comply with any requirement of subsection (a) of this section or to allow the Administrator, the Comptroller General, or representatives of either, to enter and conduct any audit or inspection authorized by subsection (b) of this section shall be subject to a civil penalty of not to exceed $25,000.

(d) Confidential information; trade secrets and secret processes; information disclosure; "information required under this section" defined

(1) Subject to paragraph (2), upon a showing satisfactory to the Administrator by any person that any information required under this section from such person, if made public, would divulge trade secrets or secret processes of such person, the Administrator shall consider such information confidential in accordance with the purposes of section 1905 of Title 18. If the applicant fails to make a showing satisfactory to the Administrator, the Administrator shall give such applicant thirty days' notice before releasing the information to which the application relates (unless the public health or safety requires an earlier release of such information).

(2) Any information required under this section (A) may be disclosed to other officers,

employees, or authorized representatives of the United States concerned with carrying out this subchapter or to committees of the Congress, or when relevant in any proceeding under this subchapter, and (B) shall be disclosed to the extent it deals with the level of contaminants in drinking water. For purposes of this subsection the term "information required under this section" means any papers, books, documents, or information, or any particular part thereof, reported to or otherwise obtained by the Administrator under this section.

(e) "Grantee" and "person" defined — For purposes of this section, (1) the term "grantee" means any person who applies for or receives financial assistance, by grant, contract, or loan guarantee under this subchapter, and (2) the term "person" includes a Federal agency.

(f) Information regarding drinking water coolers — The Administrator may utilize the authorities of this section for purposes of part F of this subchapter. Any person who manufactures, imports, sells, or distributes drinking water coolers in interstate commerce shall be treated as a supplier of water for purposes of applying the provisions of this section in the case of persons subject to part F of this subchapter.

(g) Occurrence data base

(1) In general — Not later than 3 years after August 6, 1996, the Administrator shall assemble and maintain a national drinking water contaminant occurrence data base, using information on the occurrence of both regulated and unregulated contaminants in public water systems obtained under subsection (a)(1)(A) of this section or subsection (a)(2) of this section and reliable information from other public and private sources.

(2) Public input — In establishing the occurrence data base, the Administrator shall solicit recommendations from the Science Advisory Board, the States, and other interested parties concerning the development and maintenance of a national drinking water contaminant occurrence data base, including such issues as the structure and design of the data base, data input parameters and requirements, and the use and interpretation of data.

(3) Use — The data shall be used by the Administrator in making determinations under section 300g-1(b)(1) of this title with respect to the occurrence of a contaminant in drinking water at a level of public health concern.

(4) Public recommendations — The Administrator shall periodically solicit recommendations from the appropriate officials of the National Academy of Sciences and the States, and any person may submit recommendations to the Administrator, with respect to contaminants that should be included in the national drinking water contaminant occurrence data base, including recommendations with respect to additional unregulated contaminants that should be listed under subsection (a) (2) of this section. Any recommendation submitted under this clause shall be accompanied by reasonable documentation that —

(A) the contaminant occurs or is likely to occur in drinking water; and

(B) the contaminant poses a risk to public health.

(5) Public availability — The information from the data base shall be available to the public in readily accessible form.

(6) Regulated contaminants — With respect to each contaminant for which a national primary drinking water regulation has been established, the data base shall include information on the detection of the contaminant at a quantifiable level in public water systems (including detection of the contaminant at levels not constituting a violation of the maximum contaminant level for the contaminant).

(7) Unregulated contaminants — With respect to contaminants for which a national primary drinking water regulation has not been established, the data base shall include —

(A) monitoring information collected by public water systems that serve a population of more than 10,000, as required by the Administrator under subsection (a) of this section;

(B) monitoring information collected from a representative sampling of public water systems that serve a population of 10,000 or fewer;

(C) if applicable, monitoring information collected by public water systems pursuant to subsection (j) that is not supplicative of monitoring information included in the data base under subparagraph (B) or (D); and

(D) other reliable and appropriate monitoring information on the occurrence of the contaminants in public water systems that is available to the Administrator.

(h) Availability of information on small system technologies — For purposes of sections 300g-1(b)(4)(E) and 300g-4(e) of this title (relating to small system variance program), the Administrator may request information on the characteristics of commercially available treatment systems and technologies, including the effectiveness and performance of the systems and technologies under various operating conditions. The Administrator may specify the form, content, and submission date of information to be submitted by manufacturers, States, and other interested persons for the purpose of considering the systems and technologies in the development of regulations or guidance under sections 300g-1(b)(4) (E) and 300g-4(e) of this title.

(i) Screening methods — The Administrator shall review new analytical methods to screen for regulated contaminants and may approve such methods as are more accurate or cost-effective than established reference methods for use in compliance monitoring.

(j) Monitoring by certain systems

(1) In general

Notwithstanding subsection (a)(2)(A), the Administrator shall, subject to the availability of appropriations for such purpose —

 (A) require public water systems serving between 3,300 and 10,000 persons to monitor for unregulated contaminants in accordance with this section; and

 (B) ensure that only a representative sample of public water systems serving fewer than 3,300 persons are required to monitor.

(2) Effective date

Paragraph (1) shall take effect 3 years after October 23, 2018.

(3) Limitation

Paragraph (1) shall take effect unless the Administrator determines that there is not sufficient laboratory capacity to accommodate the analysis necessary to carry out monitoring required under such paragraph.

(4) Limitation on enforcement

The Administrator may not enforce a requirement to monitor pursuant to paragraph (1) with respect to any public water system serving fewer than 3,300 persons, including by subjecting such a public water system to any civil penalty.

(5) Authorization of appropriations

There are authorized to be appropriated $15,000,000 in each fiscal year for which monitoring is required to be carried out under this subsection for the Administrator to pay the reasonable cost of such testing and laboratory analysis as are necessary to carry out monitoring required under this subsection.

§300j-5. National Drinking Water Advisory Council

[PHSA §1446]

(a) Establishment; membership; representation of interests; term of office, vacancies; reappointment — There is established a National Drinking Water Advisory Council which shall consist of fifteen members appointed by the Administrator after consultation with the Secretary. Five members shall be appointed from the general public; five members shall be appointed from appropriate State and local agencies concerned with water hygiene and public water supply; and five members shall be appointed from representatives of private organizations or groups demonstrating an active interest in the field of water hygiene and public water supply, of which two such members shall be associated with small, rural public water systems. Each member of the Council shall hold office for a term of three years, except that —

 (1) any member appointed to fill a vacancy occurring prior to the expiration of the term for which his predecessor was appointed shall be appointed for the remainder of such term; and

 (2) the terms of the members first taking office shall expire as follows: Five shall expire three years after December 16, 1974, five shall expire two years after such date, and five shall expire one year after such date, as designated by the Administrator at the time of appointment.

The members of the Council shall be eligible for reappointment.

(b) Functions — The Council shall advise, consult with, and make recommendations to, the Administrator on matters relating to activities, functions, and policies of the Agency under this subchapter.

(c) Compensation and allowances; travel expenses — Members of the Council appointed under this section shall, while attending meetings or conferences of the Council or otherwise engaged in business of the Council, receive compensation and allowances at a rate to be fixed by the Administrator, but not exceeding the daily equivalent of the annual rate of basic pay in effect for grade GS-18 of the General Schedule for each day (including travel time) during which they are engaged in the actual performance of duties vested in the Council. While away from their homes or regular places of business in the performance of services for the Council, members of the Council shall be allowed travel expenses, including per diem in lieu of subsistence, in the same manner as persons employed intermittently in the Government service are allowed expenses under section 5703(b) of Title 5.

(d) Advisory committee termination provision inapplicable — Section 14(a) of the Federal Advisory Committee Act (relating to termination) shall not apply to the Council.

§300j-6. Federal agencies

[PHSA §1447]

(a) In general — Each department, agency, and instrumentality of the executive, legislative, and judicial branches of the Federal Government —

 (1) owning or operating any facility in a wellhead protection area;

 (2) engaged in any activity at such facility resulting, or which may result, in the contamination of water supplies in any such area;

 (3) owning or operating any public water system; or

 (4) engaged in any activity resulting, or which may result in, underground injection which endangers drinking water (within the meaning of section 300h(d)(2) of this title),

shall be subject to, and comply with, all Federal, State, interstate, and local requirements, both substantive and procedural (including any requirement for permits or reporting or any provisions for injunctive relief and such sanctions as may be imposed by a court to enforce such relief), respecting the protection of such wellhead areas, respecting such public water systems, and respecting any underground injection in the same manner and to the same extent as any person is subject to such requirements, including the payment of reasonable service charges. The Federal, State, interstate, and local substantive and procedural requirements referred to in this subsection include, but are not limited to, all administrative orders and all civil and administrative penalties and fines, regardless of whether such penalties or fines are punitive or coercive in nature or are imposed for isolated, intermittent, or continuing violations. The United States hereby expressly waives any immunity otherwise applicable to the United States with respect to any such substantive or procedural requirement (including, but not limited to, any injunctive relief, administrative order or civil or administrative penalty or fine referred to in the preceding sentence, or reasonable service charge). The reasonable service charges referred to in this subsection include, but are not limited to, fees or charges assessed in connection with the processing and issuance of permits, renewal of permits, amendments to permits, review of plans, studies, and other documents, and inspection and monitoring of facilities, as well as any other nondiscriminatory charges that are assessed in connection with a Federal, State, interstate, or local regulatory program respecting the protection of wellhead areas or public water systems or respecting any underground injection. Neither the United States, nor any agent, employee, or officer thereof, shall be immune or exempt from any process or sanction of any State or Federal Court with respect to the enforcement of any such injunctive relief. No agent, employee, or officer of the United States shall be personally liable for any civil penalty under any Federal, State, interstate, or local law concerning the protection of wellhead areas or public water systems or concerning underground injection with respect to any act or omission within the scope of the official duties of the agent, employee, or officer. An agent, employee, or officer of the United States shall be subject to any criminal sanction (including, but not limited to, any fine or imprisonment) under any Federal or State requirement adopted pursuant to this subchapter, but no department, agency, or instrumentality of the executive, legislative, or judicial branch of the Federal Government shall be subject to any such sanction. The President may exempt any facility of any department, agency, or instrumentality in the executive branch from compliance with such a requirement if he determines it to be in the paramount interest of the United States to do so. No such exemption shall be granted due to lack of appropriation unless the President shall have specifically requested such appropriation as a part of the budgetary process and the Congress shall have failed to make available such requested appropriation. Any exemption shall be for a period not in excess of 1 year, but additional exemptions may be granted for periods not to exceed 1 year upon the President's making a new determination. The President shall report each January to the Congress all exemptions from the requirements of this section granted during the preceding calendar year, together with his reason for granting each such exemption.

(b) Administrative penalty orders

(1) In general — If the Administrator finds that a Federal agency has violated an applicable requirement under this subchapter, the Administrator may issue a penalty order assessing a penalty against the Federal agency.

(2) Penalties — The Administrator may, after notice to the agency, assess a civil penalty against the agency in an amount not to exceed $25,000 per day per violation.

(3) Procedure — Before an administrative penalty order issued under this subsection becomes final, the Administrator shall provide the agency an opportunity to confer with the Administrator and shall provide the agency notice and an opportunity for a hearing on the record in accordance with chapters 5 and 7 of Title 5.

(4) Public review

(A) In general — Any interested person may obtain review of an administrative penalty order issued under this subsection. The review may be obtained in the United States District Court for the District of Columbia or in the United States District Court for the district in which the violation is alleged to have occurred by the filing of a complaint with the court within the 30-day period beginning on the date the penalty order becomes final. The person filing the complaint shall simultaneously send a copy of the complaint by certified mail to the Administrator and the Attorney General.

(B) Record — The Administrator shall promptly file in the court a certified copy of the record on which the order was issued.

(C) Standard of review — The court shall not set aside or remand the order unless the court finds that there is not substantial evidence in the record, taken as a whole, to support the finding of a violation or that the assessment of the penalty by the Administrator constitutes an abuse of discretion.

(D) Prohibition on additional penalties — The court may not impose an additional civil penalty for a violation that is subject to the order unless the court finds that the assessment constitutes an abuse of discretion by the Administrator.

(c) Limitation on State use of funds collected from Federal Government — Unless a State law in effect on August 6, 1996, or a State constitution requires the funds to be used in a different manner, all funds collected by a State from the Federal Government from penalties and fines imposed for violation of any substantive or procedural requirement referred to in subsection (a) of this section shall be used by the State only for projects designed to improve or protect the environment or to defray the costs of environmental protection or enforcement.

(d) Indian rights and sovereignty as unaffected; "Federal agency" defined

(1) Nothing in the Safe Drinking Water Amendments of 1977 shall be construed to alter or affect the status of American Indian lands or water rights nor to waive any sovereignty over Indian lands guaranteed by treaty or statute.

(2) For the purposes of this chapter, the term "Federal agency" shall not be construed to refer to or include any American Indian tribe, nor to the Secretary of the Interior in his capacity as trustee of Indian lands.

(e) Washington Aqueduct — The Secretary of the Army shall not pass the cost of any penalty assessed under this subchapter on to any customer, user, or other purchaser of drinking water from the Washington Aqueduct system, including finished water from the Dalecarlia or McMillan treatment plant.

§300j-7. Judicial review
[PHSA §1448]

(a) Courts of appeals; petition for review: actions respecting regulations; filing period; grounds arising after expiration of filing period; exclusiveness of remedy — A petition for review of —

(1) actions pertaining to the establishment of national primary drinking water regulations (including maximum contaminant level goals) may be filed only in the United States Court of Appeals for the District of Columbia circuit; and

(2) any other final action of the Administrator under this chapter may be filed in the circuit in which the petitioner resides or transacts business which is directly affected by the action.

Any such petition shall be filed within the 45-day period beginning on the date of the promulgation of the regulation or any other final Agency action with respect to which review is sought or on the date of the determination with respect to which review is sought, and may be filed after the expiration of such 45-day period if the petition is based solely on grounds arising after the expiration of such period. Action of the Administrator with respect to which review could have been obtained under this subsection shall not be subject to judicial review in any civil or criminal proceeding for enforcement or in any civil action to enjoin enforcement. In any petition concerning the assessment of a civil penalty pursuant to section 300g-3(g)(3)(B) of this title, the petitioner shall simultaneously send a copy of the complaint by certified mail to the Administrator and the Attorney General. The court shall set aside and remand the penalty order if the court finds that there is not substantial evidence in the record to support the finding of a violation or that the assessment of the penalty by the Administrator constitutes an abuse of discretion.

(b) District courts; petition for review: actions respecting variances or exemptions; filing period; grounds arising after expiration of filing period; exclusiveness of remedy — The United States district courts shall have jurisdiction of actions brought to review (1) the granting of, or the refusing to grant, a variance or exemption under section 300g-4 or 300g-5 of this title or (2) the requirements of any schedule prescribed for a variance or exemption under such section or the failure to prescribe such a schedule. Such an action may only be brought upon a petition for review filed with the court within the 45-day period beginning on the date the action sought to be reviewed is taken or, in the case of a petition to review the refusal to grant a variance or exemption or the failure to prescribe a schedule, within the 45-day period beginning on the date action is required to be taken on the variance, exemption, or schedule, as the case may be. A petition for such review may be filed after the expiration of such period if the petition is based solely on grounds arising after the expiration of such period. Action with respect to which review could have been obtained under this subsection shall not be subject to judicial review in any civil or criminal proceeding for enforcement or in any civil action to enjoin enforcement.

(c) Judicial order for additional evidence before Administrator; modified or new findings; recommendation for modification or setting aside of original determination — In any judicial proceeding in which review is sought of a determination under this subchapter required to be made on the record after notice and opportunity for hearing, if any party applies to the court for leave to adduce additional evidence and shows to the satisfaction of the court that such additional evidence is material and that there were reasonable grounds for the failure to adduce such evidence in the proceeding before the Administrator, the court may order such additional evidence (and evidence in rebuttal thereof) to be taken before the Administrator, in such manner and upon such term and conditions as the court may deem proper. The Administrator may modify his findings as to the facts, or make new findings, by reason of the additional evidence so taken, and he shall file such modified or new findings, and his recommendation, if any, for the modification or setting aside of his original determination, with the return of such additional evidence.

§300j-8. Citizen's civil action
[PHSA §1449]

(a) Persons subject to civil action; jurisdiction of enforcement proceedings — Except as provided in subsection (b) of this section, any person may commence a civil action on his own behalf —

(1) against any person (including (A) the United States, and (B) any other governmental instrumentality or agency to the extent permitted by the eleventh amendment to the Constitution) who is alleged to be in violation of any requirement prescribed by or under this subchapter;

(2) against the Administrator where there is alleged a failure of the Administrator to perform

any act or duty under this subchapter which is not discretionary with the Administrator; or

(3) for the collection of a penalty by the United States Government (and associated costs and interest) against any Federal agency that fails, by the date that is 18 months after the effective date of a final order to pay a penalty assessed by the Administrator under section 300h-8(b) of this title, to pay the penalty.

No action may be brought under paragraph (1) against a public water system for a violation of a requirement prescribed by or under this subchapter which occurred within the 27-month period beginning on the first day of the month in which this subchapter is enacted. The United States district courts shall have jurisdiction, without regard to the amount in controversy or the citizenship of the parties, to enforce in an action brought under this subsection any requirement prescribed by or under this subchapter or to order the Administrator to perform an act or duty described in paragraph (2), as the case may be.

(b) Conditions for commencement of civil action; notice — No civil action may be commenced —

(1) under subsection (a)(1) of this section respecting violation of a requirement prescribed by or under this subchapter —

(A) prior to sixty days after the plaintiff has given notice of such violation (i) to the Administrator, (ii) to any alleged violator of such requirement and (iii) to the State in which the violation occurs, or

(B) if the Administrator, the Attorney General, or the State has commenced and is diligently prosecuting a civil action in a court of the United States to require compliance with such requirement, but in any such action in a court of the United States any person may intervene as a matter of right; or

(2) under subsection (a)(2) of this section prior to sixty days after the plaintiff has given notice of such action to the Administrator; or

(3) under subsection (a)(3) of this section prior to 60 days after the plaintiff has given notice of such action to the Attorney General and to the Federal agency.

Notice required by this subsection shall be given in such manner as the Administrator shall prescribe by regulation. No person may commence a civil action under subsection (a) of this section to require a State to prescribe a schedule under section 300g-4 or 300g-5 of this title for a variance or exemption, unless such person shows to the satisfaction of the court that the State has in a substantial number of cases failed to prescribe such schedules.

(c) Intervention of right — In any action under this section, the Administrator or the Attorney General, if not a party, may intervene as a matter of right.

(d) Costs; attorney fees; expert witness fees; filing of bond — The court, in issuing any final order in any action brought under subsection (a) of this section, may award costs of litigation (including reasonable attorney and expert witness fees) to any party whenever the court determines such an award is appropriate. The court may, if a temporary restraining order or preliminary injunction is sought, require the filing of a bond or equivalent security in accordance with the Federal Rules of Civil Procedure.

(e) Availability of other relief — Nothing in this section shall restrict any right which any person (or class of persons) may have under any statute or common law to seek enforcement of any requirement prescribed by or under this subchapter or to seek any other relief. Nothing in this section or in any other law of the United States shall be construed to prohibit, exclude, or restrict any State or local government from —

(1) bringing any action or obtaining any remedy or sanction in any State or local court, or

(2) bringing any administrative action or obtaining any administrative remedy or sanction,

against any agency of the United States under State or local law to enforce any requirement respecting the provision of safe drinking water or respecting any underground injection control program. Nothing in this section shall be construed to authorize judicial review of regulations or orders of the Administrator under this subchapter, except as provided in section 300j-7 of this title. For provisions providing for application of certain requirements to such agencies in the same manner as to nongovernmental entities, see section 300j-6 of this title.

§300j-9. General provisions
[PHSA §1450]
(a) Regulations; delegation of functions

(1) The Administrator is authorized to prescribe such regulations as are necessary or appropriate to carry out his functions under this subchapter.

(2) The Administrator may delegate any of his functions under this subchapter (other than prescribing regulations) to any officer or employee of the Agency.

(b) Utilization of officers and employees of Federal agencies — The Administrator, with the consent of the head of any other agency of the United States, may utilize such officers and employees of such agency as he deems necessary to assist him in carrying out the purposes of this subchapter.

(c) Assignment of Agency personnel to State or interstate agencies — Upon the request of a State or interstate agency, the Administrator may assign personnel of the Agency to such State or interstate agency for the purposes of carrying out the provisions of this subchapter.

(d) Payments of grants; adjustments; advances; reimbursement; installments; conditions; eligibility for grants; "nonprofit agency or institution" defined

(1) The Administrator may make payments of grants under this subchapter (after necessary adjustment on account of previously made underpayments or overpayments) in advance or by way of reimbursement, and in such installments and on such conditions as he may determine.

(2) Financial assistance may be made available in the form of grants only to individuals and nonprofit agencies or institutions. For purposes of this paragraph, the term "nonprofit agency or institution" means an agency or institution no part of the net earnings of which inure, or may lawfully inure, to the benefit of any private shareholder or individual.

(e) Labor standards — The Administrator shall take such action as may be necessary to assure compliance with provisions of sections 3141-3144, 3146 and 3147 of Title 40. The Secretary of Labor shall have, with respect to the labor standards specified in this subsection, the authority and functions set forth in Reorganization Plan Numbered 14 of 1950 (15 F.R. 3176; 64 Stat. 1267) and section 3145 of Title 40.

(f) Appearance and representation of Administrator through Attorney General or attorney appointees — The Administrator shall request the Attorney General to appear and represent him in any civil action instituted under this subchapter to which the Administrator is a party. Unless, within a reasonable time, the Attorney General notifies the Administrator that he will appear in such action, attorneys appointed by the Administrator shall appear and represent him.

(g) Authority of Administrator under other provisions unaffected — The provisions of this subchapter shall not be construed as affecting any authority of the Administrator under part G of subchapter II of this chapter.

(h) Reports to Congressional committees; review by Office of Management and Budget: submittal of comments to Congressional committees — Not later than April 1 of each year, the Administrator shall submit to the Committee on Commerce, Science, and Transportation of the Senate and the Committee on Energy and Commerce of the House of Representatives a report respecting the activities of the Agency under this subchapter and containing such recommendations for legislation as he considers necessary. The report of the Administrator under this subsection which is due not later than April 1, 1975, and each subsequent report of the Administrator under this subsection shall include a statement on the actual and anticipated cost to public water systems in each State of compliance with the requirements of this subchapter. The Office of Management and Budget may review any report required by this subsection before its submission to such committees of Congress, but the Office may not revise any such report, require any revision in any such report, or delay its submission beyond the day prescribed for its submission, and may submit to such committees of Congress its comments respecting any such report.

(i) Discrimination prohibition; filing of complaint; investigation; orders of Secretary; notice and hearing; settlements; attorneys' fees; judicial review; filing of petition; procedural requirements; stay of orders; exclusiveness of remedy; civil actions for enforcement of orders; appropriate relief; mandamus proceedings; prohibition inapplicable to undirected but deliberate violations

(1) No employer may discharge any employee or otherwise discriminate against any employee with respect to his compensation, terms, conditions, or privileges of employment because the employee (or any person acting pursuant to a request of the employee) has —

(A) commenced, caused to be commenced, or is about to commence or cause to be commenced a proceeding under this subchapter or a proceeding for the administration or enforcement of drinking water regulations or underground injection control programs of a State,

(B) testified or is about to testify in any such proceeding, or

(C) assisted or participated or is about to assist or participate in any manner in such a proceeding or in any other action to carry out the purposes of this subchapter.

(2)(A) Any employee who believes that he has been discharged or otherwise discriminated against by any person in violation of paragraph (1) may, within 30 days after such violation occurs, file (or have any person file on his behalf) a complaint with the Secretary of Labor (hereinafter in this subsection referred to as the "Secretary") alleging such discharge or discrimination. Upon receipt of such a complaint, the Secretary shall notify the person named in the complaint of the filing of the complaint.

(B)(i) Upon receipt of a complaint filed under subparagraph (A), the Secretary shall conduct an investigation of the violation alleged in the complaint. Within 30 days of the receipt of such complaint, the Secretary shall complete such investigation and shall notify in writing the complainant (and any person acting in his behalf) and the person alleged to have committed such violation of the results of the investigation conducted pursuant to this subparagraph. Within 90 days of the receipt of such complaint the Secretary shall, unless the proceeding on the complaint is terminated by the Secretary on the basis of a settlement entered into by the Secretary and the person alleged to have committed such violation, issue an order either providing the relief prescribed by clause (ii) or denying the complaint. An order of the Secretary shall be made on the record after notice and opportunity for agency hearing. The Secretary may not enter into a settlement terminating a proceeding on a complaint without the participation and consent of the complainant.

(ii) If in response to a complaint filed under subparagraph (A) the Secretary determines that a violation of paragraph (1) has occurred, the Secretary shall order (I) the person who committed such violation to take affirmative action to abate the violation, (II) such person to reinstate the complainant to his former position together with the compensation (including back pay), terms, conditions, and privileges of his employment, (III) compensatory damages, and (IV) where appropriate, exemplary damages. If such an order is issued, the Secretary, at the request of the complainant, shall assess against the person against whom the order is issued a sum equal to the aggregate amount of all costs and expenses (including attorneys' fees) reasonably incurred, as determined by the Secretary, by the complainant for, or in connection with, the bringing of the complaint upon which the order was issued.

(3)(A) Any person adversely affected or aggrieved by an order issued under paragraph (2) may obtain review of the order in the United States Court of Appeals for the circuit in which the violation, with respect to which the order was issued, allegedly occurred. The petition for review must be filed within sixty days from the issuance of the Secretary's order. Review shall conform to chapter 7 of Title 5. The commencement of proceedings under this subparagraph shall not, unless ordered by the court, operate as a stay of the Secretary's order.

(B) An order of the Secretary with respect to which review could have been obtained under subparagraph (A) shall not be subject to judicial review in any criminal or other civil proceeding.

(4) Whenever a person has failed to comply with an order issued under paragraph (2)(B), the Secretary shall file a civil action in the United States District Court for the district in which the violation was found to occur to enforce such order. In actions brought under this paragraph, the district courts shall have jurisdiction to grant all appropriate relief including, but not limited to, injunctive relief, compensatory, and exemplary damages.

(5) Any nondiscretionary duty imposed by this section is enforceable in mandamus proceeding brought under section 1361 of Title 28.

(6) Paragraph (1) shall not apply with respect to any employee who, acting without direction from his employer (or the employer's agent), deliberately causes a violation of any requirement of this subchapter.

§300j-10. Appointment of scientific, etc., personnel by Administrator of Environmental Protection Agency for implementation of responsibilities; compensation

To the extent that the Administrator of the Environmental Protection Agency deems such action necessary to the discharge of his functions under Title XIV of the Public Health Service Act [42 U.S.C. §§300f et seq.] (relating to safe drinking water) and under other provisions of law, he may appoint personnel to fill not more than thirty scientific, engineering, professional, legal, and administrative positions within the Environmental Protection Agency without regard to the civil service laws and may fix the compensation of such personnel not in excess of the maximum rate payable for GS-18 of the General Schedule under section 5332 of Title 5.

§300j-11. Indian Tribes
[PHSA §1451]

(a) In general — Subject to the provisions of subsection (b) of this section, the Administrator —

(1) is authorized to treat Indian Tribes as States under this subchapter,

(2) may delegate to such Tribes primary enforcement responsibility for public water systems and for underground injection control, and

(3) may provide such Tribes grant and contract assistance to carry out functions provided by this subchapter.

(b) EPA regulations

(1) Specific provisions — The Administrator shall, within 18 months after June 19, 1986, promulgate final regulations specifying those provisions of this subchapter for which it is appropriate to treat Indian Tribes as States. Such treatment shall be authorized only if:

(A) the Indian Tribe is recognized by the Secretary of the Interior and has a governing body carrying out substantial governmental duties and powers;

(B) the functions to be exercised by the Indian Tribe are within the area of the Tribal Government's jurisdiction; and

(C) the Indian Tribe is reasonably expected to be capable, in the Administrator's judgment, of carrying out the functions to be exercised in a manner consistent with the terms and purposes of this subchapter and of all applicable regulations.

(2) Provisions where treatment as State inappropriate — For any provision of this subchapter where treatment of Indian Tribes as identical to States is inappropriate, administratively infeasible or otherwise inconsistent with the purposes of this subchapter, the Administrator may include in the regulations promulgated under this section, other means for administering such provision in a manner that will achieve the purpose

of the provision. Nothing in this section shall be construed to allow Indian Tribes to assume or maintain primary enforcement responsibility for public water systems or for underground injection control in a manner less protective of the health of persons than such responsibility may be assumed or maintained by a State. An Indian tribe shall not be required to exercise criminal enforcement jurisdiction for purposes of complying with the preceding sentence.

§300j-12. State revolving loan funds
[PHSA §1452]
(a) General authority

(1) Grants to States to establish State loan funds

(A) In general — The Administrator shall offer to enter into agreements with eligible States to make capitalization grants, including letters of credit, to the States under this subsection to further the health protection objectives of this subchapter, promote the efficient use of fund resources, and for other purposes as are specified in this subchapter.

(B) Establishment of fund — To be eligible to receive a capitalization grant under this section, a State shall establish a drinking water treatment revolving loan fund (referred to in this section as a "State loan fund") and comply with the other requirements of this section. Each grant to a State under this section shall be deposited in the State loan fund established by the State, except as otherwise provided in this section and in other provisions of this subchapter. No funds authorized by other provisions of this subchapter to be used for other purposes specified in this subchapter shall be deposited in any State loan fund.

(C) Extended period — The grant to a State shall be available to the State for obligation during the fiscal year for which the funds are authorized and during the following fiscal year, except that grants made available from funds provided prior to fiscal year 1997 shall be available for obligation during each of the fiscal years 1997 and 1998.

(D) Allotment formula — Except as otherwise provided in this section, funds made available to carry out this section shall be allotted to States that have entered into an agreement pursuant to this section (other than the District of Columbia) in accordance with —

(i) for each of fiscal years 1995 through 1997, a formula that is the same as the formula used to distribute public water system supervision grant funds under section 300j-2 of this title in fiscal year 1995, except that the minimum proportionate share established in the formula shall be 1 percent of available funds and the formula

shall be adjusted to include a minimum proportionate share for the State of Wyoming and the District of Columbia; and

(ii) for fiscal year 1998 and each subsequent fiscal year, a formula that allocates to each State the proportional share of the State needs identified in the most recent survey conducted pursuant to subsection (h) of this section, except that the minimum proportionate share provided to each State shall be the same as the minimum proportionate share provided under clause (i).

(E) Reallotment — The grants not obligated by the last day of the period for which the grants are available shall be reallotted according to the appropriate criteria set forth in subparagraph (D), except that the Administrator may reserve and allocate 10 percent of the remaining amount for financial assistance to Indian Tribes in addition to the amount allotted under subsection (i) of this section and none of the funds reallotted by the Administrator shall be reallotted to any State that has not obligated all sums allotted to the State pursuant to this section during the period in which the sums were available for obligation.

(F) Nonprimacy States — The State allotment for a State not exercising primary enforcement responsibility for public water systems shall not be deposited in any such fund but shall be allotted by the Administrator under this subparagraph. Pursuant to section 300j-2(a)(9)(A) of this title such sums allotted under this subparagraph shall be reserved as needed by the Administrator to exercise primary enforcement responsibility under this subchapter in such State and the remainder shall be reallotted to States exercising primary enforcement responsibility for public water systems for deposit in such funds. Whenever the Administrator makes a final determination pursuant to section 300g-2(b) of this title that the requirements of section 300g-2(a) of this title are no longer being met by a State, additional grants for such State under this subchapter shall be immediately terminated by the Administrator. This subparagraph shall not apply to any State not exercising primary enforcement responsibility for public water systems as of August 6, 1996.

(G) Other programs

(i) New system capacity — Beginning in fiscal year 1999, the Administrator shall withhold 20 percent of each capitalization grant made pursuant to this section to a State unless the State has met the requirements of section 300g-9(a) of this title (relating to capacity development) and shall withhold 10 percent for fiscal year 2001, 15 percent for fiscal year 2002, and 20 percent for fiscal year 2003 if the State has not complied with the provisions of section 300g-9(c) of this title (relating to capacity development strategies). Not more than a total of 20 percent of the capitalization grants made to a State in any fiscal year may be withheld under the preceding provisions of this clause. All funds withheld by the Administrator pursuant to this clause shall be reallotted by the Administrator on the basis of the same ratio as is applicable to funds allotted under subparagraph (D). None of the funds reallotted by the Administrator pursuant to this paragraph shall be allotted to a State unless the State has met the requirements of section 300g-9 of this title (relating to capacity development).

(ii) Operator certification — The Administrator shall withhold 20 percent of each capitalization grant made pursuant to this section unless the State has met the requirements of 300g-8 of this title (relating to operator certification). All funds withheld by the Administrator pursuant to this clause shall be reallotted by the Administrator on the basis of the same ratio as applicable to funds allotted under subparagraph (D). None of the funds reallotted by the Administrator pursuant to this paragraph shall be allotted to a State unless the State has met the requirements of section 300g-8 of this title (relating to operator certification).

(2) Use of funds —
(A) In general
Except as otherwise authorized by this subchapter, amounts deposited in a State loan fund, including loan repayments and interest earned on such amounts, shall be used only for providing loans or loan guarantees, or as a source of reserve and security for leveraged loans, the proceeds of which are deposited in a State loan fund established under paragraph (1), or other financial assistance authorized under this section to community water systems and nonprofit noncommunity water systems, other than systems owned by Federal agencies.

(B) Limitation
Financial assistance under this section may be used by a public water system only for expenditures (including expenditures for planning, design, siting, and associated preconstruction activities, or for replacing or rehabilitating aging treatment, storage, or distribution facilities of public water systems, but not including monitoring, operation, and maintenance expenditures) of a type or category which the

Administrator has determined, through guidance, will facilitate compliance with national primary drinking water regulations applicable to the system under Section 300g-1 of this title or otherwise significantly further the health protection objectives of this subchapter.

(C) Sale of bonds
Funds may also be used by a public water system as a source of revenue (restricted solely to interest earnings of the applicable State loan fund) or security for payment of the principal and interest on revenue or general obligation bonds issued by the State to provide matching funds under subsection (e), if the proceeds of the sale of the bonds will be deposited in the State loan fund.

(D) Water treatment loans
The funds under this section may also be used to provide loans to a system referred to in section 300f(4)(B) of this title for the purpose of providing the treatment described in section 300f(4)(B)(i)(III) of this title.

(E) Acquisition of real property
The funds under this section shall not be used for the acquisition of real property or interests therein, unless the acquisition is integral to a project authorized by this paragraph and the purchase is from a willing seller.

(F) Loan assistance
Of the amount credited to any State loan fund established under this section in any fiscal year, 15 percent shall be available solely for providing loan assistance to public water systems which regularly serve fewer than 10,000 persons to the extent such funds can be obligated for eligible projects of public water systems.

(G) Emerging contaminants
(i) In general
Notwithstanding any other provision of law and subject to clause (ii), amounts deposited under subsection (t) in a State loan fund established under this section may only be used to provide grants for the purpose of addressing emerging contaminants, with a focus on perfluoroalkyl and polyfluoroalkyl substances.

(ii) Requirements
(I) Small and disadvantaged communities
Not less than 25 percent of the amounts described in clause (i) shall be used to provide grants to —
(aa) disadvantaged communities (as defined in subsection (d) (3)); or
(bb) public water systems serving fewer than 25,000 persons.

(II) Priorities
In selecting the recipient of a grant using amounts described in clause (i), a

State shall use the priorities described in subsection (b)(3)(A).

(iii) No increased bonding authority

The amounts deposited in the State loan fund of a State under subsection (t) may not be used as a source of payment of, or security for (directly or indirectly), in whole or in part, any obligation the interest on which is exempt from the tax imposed under chapter 1 of the Internal Revenue Code of 1986.

(3) Limitation

(A) In general — Except as provided in subparagraph (B), no assistance under this section shall be provided to a public water system that —

(i) does not have the technical, managerial, and financial capability to ensure compliance with the requirements of this subchapter; or

(ii) is in significant noncompliance with any requirement of a national primary drinking water regulation or variance.

(B) Restructuring — A public water system described in subparagraph (A) may receive assistance under this section if —

(i) the use of the assistance will ensure compliance; and

(ii) if subparagraph (A)(i) applies to the system, the owner or operator of the system agrees to undertake feasible and appropriate changes in operations (including ownership, management, accounting, rates, maintenance, consolidation, alternative water supply, or other procedures) if the State determines that the measures are necessary to ensure that the system has the technical, managerial, and financial capability to comply with the requirements of this subchapter over the long term.

(C) Review — Prior to providing assistance under this section to a public water system that is in significant noncompliance with any requirement of a national primary drinking water regulation or variance, the State shall conduct a review to determine whether subparagraph (A)(i) applies to the system.

(4) American iron and steel products

(A) In general

During fiscal years 2019 through 2023, funds made available from a State loan fund established pursuant to this section may not be used for a project for the construction, alteration, or repair of a public water system unless all of the iron and steel products used in the project are produced in the United States.

(B) Definition of iron and steel products

In this paragraph, the term "iron and steel products" means the following products made primarily of iron or steel:

(i) Lined or unlined pipes and fittings.

(ii) Manhole covers and other municipal castings.

(iii) Hydrants.

(iv) Tanks.

(v) Flanges.

(vi) Pipe clamps and restraints.

(vii) Valves.

(viii) Structural steel.

(ix) Reinforced precast concrete.

(x) Construction materials.

(C) Application

Subparagraph (A) shall be waived in any case or category of cases in which the Administrator finds that —

(i) applying subparagraph (A) would be inconsistent with the public interest;

(ii) iron and steel products are not produced in the United States in sufficient and reasonably available quantities and of a satisfactory quality; or

(iii) inclusion of iron and steel products produced in the United States will increase the cost of the overall project by more than 25 percent.

(D) Waiver

If the Administrator receives a request for a waiver under this paragraph, the Administrator shall make available to the public, on an informal basis, a copy of the request and information available to the Administrator concerning the request, and shall allow for informal public input on the request for at least 15 days prior to making a finding based on the request. The Administrator shall make the request and accompanying information available by electronic means, including on the official public Internet site of the Agency.

(E) International agreements

This paragraph shall be applied in a manner consistent with United States obligations under international agreements.

(F) Management and oversight

The Administrator may retain up to 0.25 percent of the funds appropriated for this section for management and oversight of the requirements of this paragraph.

(G) Effective date

This paragraph does not apply with respect to a project if a State agency approves the engineering plans and specifications for the project, in that agency's capacity to approve such plans and specifications prior to a project requesting bids, prior to December 16, 2016.

(5) Prevailing wages

The requirements of s of this title shall apply to any construction project carried out in whole or in part with assistance made available by a State loan fund.

(b) Intended use plans

(1) In general — After providing for public review and comment, each State that has entered into a capitalization agreement pursuant to this section shall annually prepare a plan that identifies the intended uses of the amounts available to the State loan fund of the State.

(2) Contents — An intended use plan shall include —

(A) a list of the projects to be assisted in the first fiscal year that begins after the date of the plan, including a description of the project, the expected terms of financial assistance, and the size of the community served;

(B) the criteria and methods established for the distribution of funds; and

(C) a description of the financial status of the State loan fund and the short-term and long-term goals of the State loan fund.

(3) Use of funds

(A) In general — An intended use plan shall provide, to the maximum extent practicable, that priority for the use of funds be given to projects that —

(i) address the most serious risk to human health;

(ii) are necessary to ensure compliance with the requirements of this subchapter (including requirements for filtration); and

(iii) assist systems most in need on a per household basis according to State affordability criteria.

(B) List of projects — Each State shall, after notice and opportunity for public comment, publish and periodically update a list of projects in the State that are eligible for assistance under this section, including the priority assigned to each project and, to the extent known, the expected funding schedule for each project.

(c) Fund management — Each State loan fund under this section shall be established, maintained, and credited with repayments and interest. The fund corpus shall be available in perpetuity for providing financial assistance under this section. To the extent amounts in the fund are not required for current obligation or expenditure, such amounts shall be invested in interest bearing obligations.

(d) Assistance for disadvantaged communities

(1) Loan subsidy — Notwithstanding any other provision of this section, in any case in which the State makes a loan pursuant to subsection (a)(2) of this section to a disadvantaged community or to a community that the State expects to become a disadvantaged community as the result of a proposed project, the State may provide additional subsidization (including forgiveness of principal).

(2) Total amount of subsidies — For each fiscal year, of the amount of the capitalization grant received by the State for the year, the total amount of loan subsidies made by a State pursuant to paragraph (1)—

(A) may not exceed 35 percent; and

(B) to the extent that there are sufficient applications for loans to communities described in paragraph (1), may not be less than 6 percent.

(3) "Disadvantaged community" defined — In this subsection, the term "disadvantaged community" means the service area of a public water system that meets affordability criteria established after public review and comment by the State in which the public water system is located. The Administrator may publish information to assist States in establishing affordability criteria.

(e) State contribution — Each agreement under subsection (a) of this section shall require that the State deposit in the State loan fund from State moneys an amount equal to at least 20 percent of the total amount of the grant to be made to the State on or before the date on which the grant payment is made to the State, except that a State shall not be required to deposit such amount into the fund prior to the date on which each grant payment is made for fiscal years 1994, 1995, 1996, and 1997 if the State deposits the State contribution amount into the State loan fund prior to September 30, 1999.

(f) Types of assistance — Except as otherwise limited by State law, the amounts deposited into a State loan fund under this section may be used only —

(1) to make loans, on the condition that —

(A) the interest rate for each loan is less than or equal to the market interest rate, including an interest free loan;

(B) principal and interest payments on each loan will commence not later than 18 months after completion of the project for which the loan was made;

(C) each loan will be fully amortized not later than 30 years after the completion of the project, except that in the case of a disadvantaged community (as defined in subsection (d)(3)) a State may provide an extended term for a loan, if the extended term —

(i) terminates not later than the date that is 40 years after the date of project completion; and

(ii) does not exceed the expected design life of the project;

(D) the recipient of each loan will establish a dedicated source of revenue (or, in the case of a privately owned system, demonstrate that there is adequate security) for the repayment of the loan; and

(E) the State loan fund will be credited with all payments of principal and interest on each loan;

(2) to buy or refinance the debt obligation of a municipality or an intermunicipal or interstate agency within the State at an interest rate that is less than or equal to the market interest rate in any case in which a debt obligation is incurred after July 1, 1993;

(3) to guarantee, or purchase insurance for, a local obligation (all of the proceeds of which finance a project eligible for assistance under this section) if the guarantee or purchase would improve credit market access or reduce the interest rate applicable to the obligation;

(4) as a source of revenue or security for the payment of principal and interest on revenue or general obligation bonds issued by the State if the proceeds of the sale of the bonds will be deposited into the State loan fund; and

(5) to earn interest on the amounts deposited into the State loan fund.

(g) Administration of State loan funds

(1) Combined financial administration — Notwithstanding subsection (c) of this section, a State may (as a convenience and to avoid unnecessary administrative costs) combine, in accordance with State law, the financial administration of a State loan fund established under this section with the financial administration of any other revolving fund established by the State if otherwise not prohibited by the law under which the State loan fund was established and if the Administrator determines that —

(A) the grants under this section, together with loan repayments and interest, will be separately accounted for and used solely for the purposes specified in subsection (a) of this section; and

(B) the authority to establish assistance priorities and carry out oversight and related activities (other than financial administration) with respect to assistance remains with the State agency having primary responsibility for administration of the State program under section 300g-2 of this title, after consultation with other appropriate State agencies (as determined by the State): *Provided,* That in nonprimacy States eligible to receive assistance under this section, the Governor shall determine which State agency will have authority to establish priorities for financial assistance from the State loan fund.

(2) Cost of administering fund — Each State may annually use up to 4 percent of the funds allotted to the State under this section to cover the reasonable costs of administration of the programs under this section, including the recovery of reasonable costs expended to establish a State loan fund which are incurred after August 6, 1996, and to provide technical assistance to public water

systems within the State. For fiscal year 1995 and each fiscal year thereafter, each State may use up to an additional 10 percent of the funds allotted to the State under this section —

(A) for public water system supervision programs under section 300j-2(a) of this title;

(B) to administer or provide technical assistance through source water protection programs;

(C) to develop and implement a capacity development strategy under section 300g-9(c) of this title; and

(D) for an operator certification program for purposes of meeting the requirements of section 300g-8 of this title,

if the State matches the expenditures with at least an equal amount of State funds. At least half of the match must be additional to the amount expended by the State for public water supervision in fiscal year 1993. An additional 2 percent of the funds annually allotted to each State under this section may be used by the State to provide technical assistance to public water systems serving 10,000 or fewer persons in the State. Funds utilized under subparagraph (B) shall not be used for enforcement actions.

(3) Guidance and regulations — The Administrator shall publish guidance and promulgate regulations as may be necessary to carry out the provisions of this section, including —

(A) provisions to ensure that each State commits and expends funds allotted to the State under this section as efficiently as possible in accordance with this subchapter and applicable State laws;

(B) guidance to prevent waste, fraud, and abuse; and

(C) guidance to avoid the use of funds made available under this section to finance the expansion of any public water system in anticipation of future population growth.

The guidance and regulations shall also ensure that the States, and public water systems receiving assistance under this section, use accounting, audit, and fiscal procedures that conform to generally accepted accounting standards.

(4) State report — Each State administering a loan fund and assistance program under this subsection shall publish and submit to the Administrator a report every 2 years on its activities under this section, including the findings of the most recent audit of the fund and the entire State allotment. The Administrator shall periodically audit all State loan funds established by, and all other amounts allotted to, the States pursuant to this section in accordance with procedures established by the Comptroller General.

(h) Needs survey —

(1) The Administrator shall conduct an assessment of water system capital improvement

needs of all eligible public water systems in the United States and submit a report to the Congress containing the results of the assessment within 180 days after August 6, 1996, and every 4 years thereafter.

(2) Any assessment conducted under paragraph (1) after October 23, 2018, shall include an assessment of costs to replace all lead service lines (as defined in section 300j-19b(a)(4) of this title) of all eligible public water systems in the United States, and such assessment shall describe separately the costs associated with replacing the portions of such lead service lines that are owned by an eligible public water system and the costs associated with replacing any remaining portions of such lead service lines, to the extent practicable.

(i) Indian Tribes

(1) In general — 1½ percent of the amounts appropriated annually to carry out this section may be used by the Administrator to make grants to Indian Tribes and Alaska Native villages that have not otherwise received either grants from the Administrator under this section or assistance from State loan funds established under this section. The grants may only be used for expenditures by tribes and villages for public water system expenditures referred to in subsection (a)(2) of this section.

(2) Use of funds — Funds reserved pursuant to paragraph (1) shall be used to address the most significant threats to public health associated with public water systems that serve Indian Tribes, as determined by the Administrator in consultation with the Director of the Indian Health Service and Indian Tribes.

(3) Alaska Native villages — In the case of a grant for a project under this subsection in an Alaska Native village, the Administrator is also authorized to make grants to the State of Alaska for the benefit of Native villages. An amount not to exceed 4 percent of the grant amount may be used by the State of Alaska for project management.

(4) Needs assessment — The Administrator, in consultation with the Director of the Indian Health Service and Indian Tribes, shall, in accordance with a schedule that is consistent with the needs surveys conducted pursuant to subsection (h) of this section, prepare surveys and assess the needs of drinking water treatment facilities to serve Indian Tribes, including an evaluation of the public water systems that pose the most significant threats to public health.

(j) Other areas — Of the funds annually available under this section for grants to States, the Administrator shall make allotments in accordance with section 300j-2(a)(4) of this title for the Virgin Islands, the Commonwealth of the Northern Mariana Islands, American Samoa, and Guam. The grants allotted as provided in this subsection may be provided by the Administrator to the governments of such areas, to

public water systems in such areas, or to both, to be used for the public water system expenditures referred to in subsection (a)(2) of this section. The grants, and grants for the District of Columbia, shall not be deposited in State loan funds. The total allotment of grants under this section for all areas described in this subsection in any fiscal year shall not exceed 0.33 percent of the aggregate amount made available to carry out this section in that fiscal year.

(k) Other authorized activities

(1) In general — Notwithstanding subsection (a)(2) of this section, a State may take each of the following actions:

(A) Provide assistance, only in the form of a loan, to one or more of the following:

(i) Any public water system described in subsection (a)(2) of this section to acquire land or a conservation easement from a willing seller or grantor, if the purpose of the acquisition is to protect the source water of the system from contamination and to ensure compliance with national primary drinking water regulations.

(ii) Any community water system to implement local, voluntary source water protection measures to protect source water in areas delineated pursuant to section 300j-13 of this title, in order to facilitate compliance with national primary drinking water regulations applicable to the system under section 300g-1 of this title or otherwise significantly further the health protection objectives of this subchapter. Funds authorized under this clause may be used to fund only voluntary, incentive-based mechanisms.

(iii) Any community water system to provide funding in accordance with section 300j-14(a)(1)(B)(i) of this title.

(B) Provide assistance, including technical and financial assistance, to any public water system as part of a capacity development strategy developed and implemented in accordance with section 300g-9(c) of this title.

(C) Make expenditures from the capitalization grant of the State to delineate, assess, and update assessments for source water protection areas in accordance with section 300j-13 of this title, except that funds set aside for such expenditure shall be obligated within 4 fiscal years.

(D) Make expenditures from the fund for the establishment and implementation of wellhead protection programs under section 300h-7 of this title and for the implementation of efforts (other than actions authorized under subparagraph (A)) to protect source water in areas delineated pursuant to section 300j-13 of this title.

(2) Limitation — For each fiscal year, the total amount of assistance provided and expenditures made by a State under this subsection may not exceed 15 percent of the amount of the capitalization grant received by the State for that year and may not exceed 10 percent of that amount for any one of the following activities:

(A) To acquire land or conservation easements pursuant to paragraph (1)(A)(i).

(B) To provide funding to implement voluntary, incentive-based source water quality protection measures pursuant to clauses (ii) and (iii) of paragraph (1)(A).

(C) To provide assistance through a capacity development strategy pursuant to paragraph (1)(B).

(D) To make expenditures to delineate or assess source water protection areas pursuant to paragraph (1)(C).

(E) To make expenditures to establish and implement wellhead protection programs, and to implement efforts to protect source water, pursuant to paragraph (1)(D).

(3) Statutory construction — Nothing in this section creates or conveys any new authority to a State, political subdivision of a State, or community water system for any new regulatory measure, or limits any authority of a State, political subdivision of a State or community water system.

(*l*) Savings — The failure or inability of any public water system to receive funds under this section or any other loan or grant program, or any delay in obtaining the funds, shall not alter the obligation of the system to comply in a timely manner with all applicable drinking water standards and requirements of this subchapter.

(m) Authorization of appropriations —

(1) There are authorized to be appropriated to carry out the purposes of this section, except for subsections (a)(2)(G) and (t)—

(A) $1,174,000,000 for fiscal year 2019;

(B) $1,300,000,000 for fiscal year 2020; and

(C) $1,950,000,000 for fiscal year 2021.

(2) To the extent amounts authorized to be appropriated under this subsection in any fiscal year are not appropriated in that fiscal year, such amounts are authorized to be appropriated in a subsequent fiscal year. Such sums shall remain available until expended.

(n) Health effects studies — From funds appropriated pursuant to this section for each fiscal year, the Administrator shall reserve $10,000,000 for health effects studies on drinking water contaminants authorized by the Safe Drinking Water Act Amendments of 1996. In allocating funds made available under this subsection, the Administrator shall give priority to studies concerning the health effects of cryptosporidium (as authorized by section 300j-18(c) of this title), disinfection byproducts (as authorized

by section 300j-18(c) of this title), and arsenic (as authorized by section 300g-1(b)(12)(A) of this title), and the implementation of a plan for studies of subpopulations at greater risk of adverse effects (as authorized by section 300j-18(a) of this title).

(o) Monitoring for unregulated contaminants — From funds appropriated pursuant to this section for each fiscal year beginning with fiscal year 1998, the Administrator shall reserve $2,000,000 to pay the costs of monitoring for unregulated contaminants under section 300j-4(a)(2)(C) of this title.

(p) Demonstration project for State of Virginia — Notwithstanding the other provisions of this section limiting the use of funds deposited in a State loan fund from any State allotment, the State of Virginia may, as a single demonstration and with the approval of the Virginia General Assembly and the Administrator, conduct a program to demonstrate alternative approaches to intergovernmental coordination to assist in the financing of new drinking water facilities in the following rural communities in southwestern Virginia where none exists on August 6, 1996, and where such communities are experiencing economic hardship: Lee County, Wise County, Scott County, Dickenson County, Russell County, Buchanan County, Tazewell County, and the city of Norton, Virginia. The funds allotted to that State and deposited in the State loan fund may be loaned to a regional endowment fund for the purpose set forth in this subsection under a plan to be approved by the Administrator. The plan may include an advisory group that includes representatives of such counties.

(q) Small system technical assistance — The Administrator may reserve up to 2 percent of the total funds appropriated pursuant to subsection (m) of this section for each of the fiscal years 1997 through 2003 to carry out the provisions of section 300j-1(e) of this title (relating to technical assistance for small systems), except that the total amount of funds made available for such purpose in any fiscal year through appropriations (as authorized by section 300j-1(e) of this title) and reservations made pursuant to this subsection shall not exceed the amount authorized by section 300j-1(e) of this title.

(r) Evaluation — The Administrator shall conduct an evaluation of the effectiveness of the State loan funds through fiscal year 2001. The evaluation shall be submitted to the Congress at the same time as the President submits to the Congress, pursuant to section 1108 of Title 31, an appropriations request for fiscal year 2003 relating to the budget of the Environmental Protection Agency.

(s) Best practices for State loan fund administration — The Administrator shall —

(1) collect information from States on administration of State loan funds established pursuant to subsection (a)(1), including —

(A) efforts to streamline the process for applying for assistance through such State loan funds;

(B) programs in place to assist with the completion of applications for assistance through such State loan funds;

(C) incentives provided to public water systems that partner with small public water systems to assist with the application process for assistance through such State loan funds;

(D) practices to ensure that amounts in such State loan funds are used to provide loans, loan guarantees, or other authorized assistance in a timely fashion;

(E) practices that support effective management of such State loan funds;

(F) practices and tools to enhance financial management of such State loan funds; and

(G) key financial measures for use in evaluating State loan fund operations, including —

(i) measures of lending capacity, such as current assets and current liabilities or undisbursed loan assistance liability; and

(ii) measures of growth or sustainability, such as return on net interest;

(2) not later than 3 years after October 23, 2018, disseminate to the States best practices for administration of such State loan funds, based on the information collected pursuant to this subsection; and

(3) periodically update such best practices, as appropriate.

(t) Emerging contaminants

(1) In general

Amounts made available under this subsection shall be allotted to a State as if allotted under subsection (a)(1)(D) as a capitalization grant, for deposit into the State loan fund of the State, for the purposes described in subsection (a)(2)(G).

(2) Authorization of appropriations

There is authorized to be appropriated to carry out this subsection $100,000,000 for each fiscal years 2020 through 2024, to remain available until expended.

§300j-13. Source water quality assessment [PHSA §1453]

(a) Source water assessment

(1) Guidance — Within 12 months after August 6, 1996, after notice and comment, the Administrator shall publish guidance for States exercising primary enforcement responsibility for public water systems to carry out directly or through delegation (for the protection and benefit of public water systems and for the support of monitoring flexibility) a source water assessment program within the State's boundaries. Each State adopting modifications to monitoring requirements pursuant to section 300g-7(b) of this title shall, prior to adopting such modifications, have an approved source water assessment program under this section and shall carry out the program either directly or through delegation.

(2) Program requirements — A source water assessment program under this subsection shall —

(A) delineate the boundaries of the assessment areas in such State from which one or more public water systems in the State receive supplies of drinking water, using all reasonably available hydrogeologic information on the sources of the supply of drinking water in the State and the water flow, recharge, and discharge and any other reliable information as the State deems necessary to adequately determine such areas; and

(B) identify for contaminants regulated under this subchapter for which monitoring is required under this subchapter (or any unregulated contaminants selected by the State, in its discretion, which the State, for the purposes of this subsection, has determined may present a threat to public health), to the extent practical, the origins within each delineated area of such contaminants to determine the susceptibility of the public water systems in the delineated area to such contaminants.

(3) Approval, implementation, and monitoring relief — A State source water assessment program under this subsection shall be submitted to the Administrator within 18 months after the Administrator's guidance is issued under this subsection and shall be deemed approved 9 months after the date of such submittal unless the Administrator disapproves the program as provided in section 300h-7(c) of this title. States shall begin implementation of the program immediately after its approval. The Administrator's approval of a State program under this subsection shall include a timetable, established in consultation with the State, allowing not more than 2 years for completion after approval of the program. Public water systems seeking monitoring relief in addition to the interim relief provided under section 300g-7(a) of this title shall be eligible for monitoring relief, consistent with section 300g-7(b) of this title, upon completion of the assessment in the delineated source water assessment area or areas concerned.

(4) Timetable — The timetable referred to in paragraph (3) shall take into consideration the availability to the State of funds under section 300j-12 of this title (relating to State loan funds) for assessments and other relevant factors. The Administrator may extend any timetable included in a State program approved under paragraph (3) to extend the period for completion by an additional 18 months.

(5) Demonstration project — The Administrator shall, as soon as practicable, conduct a demonstration project, in consultation with other Federal agencies, to demonstrate the most effective and protective means of assessing and protecting source waters serving large metropolitan areas and located on Federal lands.

(6) Use of other programs — To avoid duplication and to encourage efficiency, the program under this section may make use of any of the following:

(A) Vulnerability assessments, sanitary surveys, and monitoring programs.

(B) Delineations or assessments of ground water sources under a State wellhead protection program developed pursuant to this section.

(C) Delineations or assessments of surface or ground water sources under a State pesticide management plan developed pursuant to the Pesticide and Ground Water State Management Plan Regulation (subparts I and J of part 152 of title 40, Code of Federal Regulations), promulgated under section 136a(d) of Title 7.

(D) Delineations or assessments of surface water sources under a State watershed initiative or to satisfy the watershed criterion for determining if filtration is required under the Surface Water Treatment Rule (section 141.70 of title 40, Code of Federal Regulations).

(E) Delineations or assessments of surface or ground water sources under programs or plans pursuant to the Federal Water Pollution Control Act [33 U.S.C. §§1251 *et seq.*].·

(7) Public availability — The State shall make the results of the source water assessments conducted under this subsection available to the public.

(b) Approval and disapproval — For provisions relating to program approval and disapproval, see section 300h-7(c) of this title.

§300j-14. Source water petition program [PHSA §1454]

(a) Petition program

(1) In general

(A) Establishment — A State may establish a program under which an owner or operator of a community water system in the State, or a municipal or local government or political subdivision of a State, may submit a source water quality protection partnership petition to the State requesting that the State assist in the local development of a voluntary, incentive-based partnership, among the owner, operator, or government and other persons likely to be affected by the recommendations of the partnership, to —

(i) reduce the presence in drinking water of contaminants that may be addressed by a petition by considering the origins of the contaminants, including to the maximum extent practicable the specific activities that affect the drinking water supply of a community;

(ii) obtain financial or technical assistance necessary to facilitate establishment

of a partnership, or to develop and implement recommendations of a partnership for the protection of source water to assist in the provision of drinking water that complies with national primary drinking water regulations with respect to contaminants addressed by a petition; and

(iii) develop recommendations regarding voluntary and incentive-based strategies for the long-term protection of the source water of community water systems.

(B) Funding — Each State may —

(i) use funds set aside pursuant to section 300j-12(k)(1)(A)(iii) of this title by the State to carry out a program described in subparagraph (A), including assistance to voluntary local partnerships for the development and implementation of partnership recommendations for the protection of source water such as source water quality assessment, contingency plans, and demonstration projects for partners within a source water area delineated under section 300j-13(a) of this title; and

(ii) provide assistance in response to a petition submitted under this subsection using funds referred to in subsection (b) (2)(B) of this section.

(2) Objectives — The objectives of a petition submitted under this subsection shall be to —

(A) facilitate the local development of voluntary, incentive-based partnerships among owners and operators of community water systems, governments, and other persons in source water areas; and

(B) obtain assistance from the State in identifying resources which are available to implement the recommendations of the partnerships to address the origins of drinking water contaminants that may be addressed by a petition (including to the maximum extent practicable the specific activities contributing to the presence of the contaminants) that affect the drinking water supply of a community.

(3) Contaminants addressed by a petition — A petition submitted to a State under this subsection may address only those contaminants —

(A) that are pathogenic organisms for which a national primary drinking water regulation has been established or is required under section 300g-1 of this title; or

(B) for which a national primary drinking water regulation has been promulgated or proposed and that are detected by adequate monitoring methods in the source water at the intake structure or in any collection, treatment, storage, or distribution facilities by the community water systems at levels —

(i) above the maximum contaminant level; or

(ii) that are not reliably and consistently below the maximum contaminant level.

(4) Contents — A petition submitted under this subsection shall, at a minimum —

(A) include a delineation of the source water area in the State that is the subject of the petition;

(B) identify, to the maximum extent practicable, the origins of the drinking water contaminants that may be addressed by a petition (including to the maximum extent practicable the specific activities contributing to the presence of the contaminants) in the source water area delineated under section 300j-13 of this title;

(C) identify any deficiencies in information that will impair the development of recommendations by the voluntary local partnership to address drinking water contaminants that may be addressed by a petition;

(D) specify the efforts made to establish the voluntary local partnership and obtain the participation of —

(i) the municipal or local government or other political subdivision of the State with jurisdiction over the source water area delineated under section 300j-13 of this title; and

(ii) each person in the source water area delineated under section 300j-13 of this title —

(I) who is likely to be affected by recommendations of the voluntary local partnership; and

(II) whose participation is essential to the success of the partnership;

(E) outline how the voluntary local partnership has or will, during development and implementation of recommendations of the voluntary local partnership, identify, recognize and take into account any voluntary or other activities already being undertaken by persons in the source water area delineated under section 300j-13 of this title under Federal or State law to reduce the likelihood that contaminants will occur in drinking water at levels of public health concern; and

(F) specify the technical, financial, or other assistance that the voluntary local partnership requests of the State to develop the partnership or to implement recommendations of the partnership.

(b) Approval or disapproval of petitions

(1) In general — After providing notice and an opportunity for public comment on a petition submitted under subsection (a) of this section, the State shall approve or disapprove the petition, in whole or in part, not later than 120 days after the date of submission of the petition.

(2) Approval — The State may approve a petition if the petition meets the requirements established under subsection (a) of this section. The notice of approval shall, at a minimum, include for informational purposes —

(A) an identification of technical, financial, or other assistance that the State will provide to assist in addressing the drinking water contaminants that may be addressed by a petition based on —

(i) the relative priority of the public health concern identified in the petition with respect to the other water quality needs identified by the State;

(ii) any necessary coordination that the State will perform of the program established under this section with programs implemented or planned by other States under this section; and

(iii) funds available (including funds available from a State revolving loan fund established under Title VI of the Federal Water Pollution Control Act (33 U.S.C. §1381 *et seq.*)) or section 300j-12 of this title;

(B) a description of technical or financial assistance pursuant to Federal and State programs that is available to assist in implementing recommendations of the partnership in the petition, including —

(i) any program established under the Federal Water Pollution Control Act (33 U.S.C. §1251 *et seq.*);

(ii) the program established under section 1455b of Title 16;

(iii) the agricultural water quality protection program established under chapter 2 of subtitle D of Title XII of the Food Security Act of 1985 (16 U.S.C. §3838 *et seq.*);

(iv) the sole source aquifer protection program established under section 300h-6 of this title;

(v) the community wellhead protection program established under section 300h-7 of this title;

(vi) any pesticide or ground water management plan;

(vii) any voluntary agricultural resource management plan or voluntary whole farm or whole ranch management plan developed and implemented under a process established by the Secretary of Agriculture; and

(viii) any abandoned well closure program; and

(C) a description of activities that will be undertaken to coordinate Federal and State programs to respond to the petition.

(3) Disapproval — If the State disapproves a petition submitted under subsection (a) of this section, the State shall notify the entity submitting the petition in writing of the reasons for disapproval.

A petition may be resubmitted at any time if —

    (A) new information becomes available;

    (B) conditions affecting the source water that is the subject of the petition change; or

    (C) modifications are made in the type of assistance being requested.

(c) Grants to support State programs

(1) In general — The Administrator may make a grant to each State that establishes a program under this section that is approved under paragraph (2). The amount of each grant shall not exceed 50 percent of the cost of administering the program for the year in which the grant is available.

(2) Approval — In order to receive grant assistance under this subsection, a State shall submit to the Administrator for approval a plan for a source water quality protection partnership program that is consistent with the guidance published under subsection (d) of this section. The Administrator shall approve the plan if the plan is consistent with the guidance published under subsection (d) of this section.

(d) Guidance

(1) In general — Not later than 1 year after August 6, 1996, the Administrator, in consultation with the States, shall publish guidance to assist —

    (A) States in the development of a source water quality protection partnership program; and

    (B) municipal or local governments or political subdivisions of a State and community water systems in the development of source water quality protection partnerships and in the assessment of source water quality.

(2) Contents of the guidance — The guidance shall, at a minimum —

    (A) recommend procedures for the approval or disapproval by a State of a petition submitted under subsection (a) of this section;

    (B) recommend procedures for the submission of petitions developed under subsection (a) of this section;

    (C) recommend criteria for the assessment of source water areas within a State; and

    (D) describe technical or financial assistance pursuant to Federal and State programs that is available to address the contamination of sources of drinking water and to develop and respond to petitions submitted under subsection (a) of this section.

(e) Authorization of appropriations — There are authorized to be appropriated to carry out this section $5,000,000 for each of the fiscal years 2020 through 2021. Each State with a plan for a program approved under subsection (b) of this section shall receive an equitable portion of the funds available for any fiscal year.

(f) Statutory construction — Nothing in this section —

(1)(A) creates or conveys new authority to a State, political subdivision of a State, or

community water system for any new regulatory measure; or

    (B) limits any authority of a State, political subdivision, or community water system; or

(2) precludes a community water system, municipal or local government, or political subdivision of a government from locally developing and carrying out a voluntary, incentive-based, source water quality protection partnership to address the origins of drinking water contaminants of public health concern.

§300j-15. Water conservation plan
[PHSA §1455]

(a) Guidelines — Not later than 2 years after August 6, 1996, the Administrator shall publish in the Federal Register guidelines for water conservation plans for public water systems serving fewer than 3,300 persons, public water systems serving between 3,300 and 10,000 persons, and public water systems serving more than 10,000 persons, taking into consideration such factors as water availability and climate.

(b) Loans or grants — Within 1 year after publication of the guidelines under subsection (a) of this section, a State exercising primary enforcement responsibility for public water systems may require a public water system, as a condition of receiving a loan or grant from a State loan fund under section 300j-12 of this title, to submit with its application for such loan or grant a water conservation plan consistent with such guidelines.

§300j-16. Assistance to colonias
[PHSA §1456]

(a) Definitions — As used in this section:

(1) Border State — The term "border State" means Arizona, California, New Mexico, and Texas.

(2) Eligible community — The term "eligible community" means a low-income community with economic hardship that —

    (A) is commonly referred to as a colonia;

    (B) is located along the United States-Mexico border (generally in an unincorporated area); and

    (C) lacks a safe drinking water supply or adequate facilities for the provision of safe drinking water for human consumption.

(b) Grants to alleviate health risks — The Administrator of the Environmental Protection Agency and the heads of other appropriate Federal agencies are authorized to award grants to a border State to provide assistance to eligible communities to facilitate compliance with national primary drinking water regulations or otherwise significantly further the health protection objectives of this subchapter.

(c) Use of funds — Each grant awarded pursuant to subsection (b) of this section shall be used to provide assistance to one or more eligible communities with respect to which the residents are subject to a significant health risk (as determined by the Administrator or the head of the Federal agency making the grant) attributable to the lack of access to an adequate and affordable drinking water supply system.

(d) Cost sharing — The amount of a grant awarded pursuant to this section shall not exceed 50 percent of the costs of carrying out the project that is the subject of the grant.

(e) Authorization of appropriations — There are authorized to be appropriated to carry out this section $25,000,000 for each of the fiscal years 1997 through 1999.

§300j-17. Estrogenic substances screening program
[PHSA §1457]

In addition to the substances referred to in section 346a(p)(3)(B) of Title 21 the Administrator may provide for testing under the screening program authorized by section 346a(p) of Title 21, in accordance with the provisions of section 346a(p) of Title 21, of any other substance that may be found in sources of drinking water if the Administrator determines that a substantial population may be exposed to such substance.

§300j-18. Drinking water studies
[PHSA §1458]
(a) Subpopulations at greater risk

(1) In general — The Administrator shall conduct a continuing program of studies to identify groups within the general population that may be at greater risk than the general population of adverse health effects from exposure to contaminants in drinking water. The study shall examine whether and to what degree infants, children, pregnant women, the elderly, individuals with a history of serious illness, or other subpopulations that can be identified and characterized are likely to experience elevated health risks, including risks of cancer, from contaminants in drinking water.

(2) Report — Not later than 4 years after August 6, 1996, and periodically thereafter as new and significant information becomes available, the Administrator shall report to the Congress on the results of the studies.

(b) Biological mechanisms — The Administrator shall conduct biomedical studies to —

(1) understand the mechanisms by which chemical contaminants are absorbed, distributed, metabolized, and eliminated from the human body, so as to develop more accurate physiologically based models of the phenomena;

(2) understand the effects of contaminants and the mechanisms by which the contaminants cause adverse effects (especially noncancer and infectious effects) and the variations in the effects among humans, especially subpopulations at greater risk of adverse effects, and between test animals and humans; and

(3) develop new approaches to the study of complex mixtures, such as mixtures found in drinking water, especially to determine the prospects for synergistic or antagonistic interactions that may affect the shape of the dose-response relationship of the individual chemicals and microbes, and to examine noncancer endpoints and infectious diseases, and susceptible individuals and subpopulations.

(c) Studies on harmful substances in drinking water

(1) Development of studies — The Administrator shall, not later than 180 days after August 6, 1996, and after consultation with the Secretary of Health and Human Services, the Secretary of Agriculture, and, as appropriate, the heads of other Federal agencies, conduct the studies described in paragraph (2) to support the development and implementation of the most current version of each of the following:

(A) Enhanced Surface Water Treatment Rule (59 Fed. Reg. 38832 (July 29, 1994)).

(B) Disinfectant and Disinfection Byproducts Rule (59 Fed. Reg. 38668 (July 29, 1994)).

(C) Ground Water Disinfection Rule (availability of draft summary announced at (57 Fed. Reg. 33960 (July 31, 1992)).

(2) Contents of studies — The studies required by paragraph (1) shall include, at a minimum, each of the following:

(A) Toxicological studies and, if warranted, epidemiological studies to determine what levels of exposure from disinfectants and disinfection byproducts, if any, may be associated with developmental and birth defects and other potential toxic end points.

(B) Toxicological studies and, if warranted, epidemiological studies to quantify the carcinogenic potential from exposure to disinfection byproducts resulting from different disinfectants.

(C) The development of dose-response curves for pathogens, including cryptosporidium and the Norwalk virus.

(3) Authorization of appropriations — There are authorized to be appropriated to carry out this subsection $12,500,000 for each of fiscal years 1997 through 2003.

(d) Waterborne disease occurrence study

(1) System — The Director of the Centers for Disease Control and Prevention, and the Administrator shall jointly —

(A) within 2 years after August 6, 1996, conduct pilot waterborne disease occurrence studies for at least 5 major United States communities or public water systems; and

(B) within 5 years after August 6, 1996, prepare a report on the findings of the pilot studies, and a national estimate of waterborne disease occurrence.

(2) Training and education — The Director and Administrator shall jointly establish a national health care provider training and public education campaign to inform both the professional health care provider community and the general public about waterborne disease and the symptoms that may be caused by infectious agents, including microbial contaminants. In developing such a campaign, they shall seek comment from interested groups and individuals, including scientists, physicians, State and local governments, environmental groups, public water systems, and vulnerable populations.

(3) Funding — There are authorized to be appropriated for each of the fiscal years 1997 through 2001, $3,000,000 to carry out this subsection. To the extent funds under this subsection are not fully appropriated, the Administrator may use not more than $2,000,000 of the funds from amounts reserved under section 300j-12(n) of this title for health effects studies for purposes of this subsection. The Administrator may transfer a portion of such funds to the Centers for Disease Control and Prevention for such purposes.

§300j-19. Algal toxin risk assessment and management
[PHSA §1459]
(a) Strategic plan
(1) Development

Not later than 90 days after August 7, 2015, the Administrator shall develop and submit to Congress a strategic plan for assessing and managing risks associated with algal toxins in drinking water provided by public water systems. The strategic plan shall include steps and timelines to —

(A) evaluate the risk to human health from drinking water provided by public water systems contaminated with algal toxins;

(B) establish, publish, and update a comprehensive list of algal toxins which the Administrator determines may have an adverse effect on human health when present in drinking water provided by public water systems, taking into account likely exposure levels;

(C) summarize —

(i) the known adverse human health effects of algal toxins included on the list published under subparagraph (B) when present in drinking water provided by public water systems; and

(ii) factors that cause toxin-producing cyanobacteria and algae to proliferate and express toxins;

(D) with respect to algal toxins included on the list published under subparagraph (B), determine whether to —

(i) publish health advisories pursuant to section 300g-1(b)(1)(F) of this title for such algal toxins in drinking water provided by public water systems;

(ii) establish guidance regarding feasible analytical methods to quantify the presence of algal toxins; and

(iii) establish guidance regarding the frequency of monitoring necessary to determine if such algal toxins are present in drinking water provided by public water systems;

(E) recommend feasible treatment options, including procedures, equipment, and source water protection practices, to mitigate any adverse public health effects of algal toxins included on the list published under subparagraph (B); and

(F) enter into cooperative agreements with, and provide technical assistance to, affected States and public water systems, as identified by the Administrator, for the purpose of managing risks associated with algal toxins included on the list published under subparagraph (B).

(2) Updates

The Administrator shall, as appropriate, update and submit to Congress the strategic plan developed under paragraph (1).

(b) Information coordination

In carrying out this section the Administrator shall —

(1) identify gaps in the Agency's understanding of algal toxins, including —

(A) the human health effects of algal toxins included on the list published under subsection (a)(1)(B); and

(B) methods and means of testing and monitoring for the presence of harmful algal toxins in source water of, or drinking water provided by, public water systems;

(2) as appropriate, consult with —

(A) other Federal agencies that —

(i) examine or analyze cyanobacteria or algal toxins; or

(ii) address public health concerns related to harmful algal blooms;

(B) States;

(C) operators of public water systems;

(D) multinational agencies;

(E) foreign governments;

(F) research and academic institutions; and

(G) companies that provide relevant drinking water treatment options; and

(3) assemble and publish information from each Federal agency that has —

(A) examined or analyzed cyanobacteria or algal toxins; or

(B) addressed public health concerns related to harmful algal blooms.

(c) Use of science

The Administrator shall carry out this section in accordance with the requirements described in section 300g-1(b)(3)(A) of this title, as applicable.

(d) Feasible

For purposes of this section, the term "feasible" has the meaning given such term in section 300g-1(b)(4)(D) of this title.

§300j-19a. Assistance for small and disadvantaged communities

(a) Definition of underserved community

In this section:

(1) In general

The term "underserved community" means a political subdivision of a State that, as determined by the Administrator, has an inadequate system for obtaining drinking water.

(2) Inclusions

The term "underserved community" includes a political subdivision of a State that either, as determined by the Administrator —

(A) does not have household drinking water or wastewater services; or

(B) is served by a public water system that violates, or exceeds, as applicable, a requirement of a national primary drinking water regulation issued under section 300g-1 of this title, including —

(i) a maximum contaminant level;

(ii) a treatment technique; and

(iii) an action level.

(b) Establishment

(1) In general

The Administrator shall establish a program under which grants are provided to eligible entities for use in carrying out projects and activities the primary purposes of which are to assist public water systems in meeting the requirements of this subchapter.

(2) Inclusions

Projects and activities under paragraph (1) include —

(A) investments necessary for the public water system to comply with the requirements of this subchapter;

(B) assistance that directly and primarily benefits the disadvantaged community on a per-household basis; and

(C) programs to provide household water quality testing, including testing for unregulated contaminants.

(c) Eligible entities

An eligible entity under this section —

(1) is —

(A) a public water system;

(B) a water system that is located in an area governed by an Indian Tribe; or

(C) a State, on behalf of an underserved community; and

(2) serves a community —

(A) that, under affordability criteria established by the State under section 300j-12(d)

(3) of this title, is determined by the State —

(i) to be a disadvantaged community; or

(ii) to be a community that may become a disadvantaged community as a result of carrying out a project or activity under subsection (b); or

(B) with a population of less than 10,000 individuals that the Administrator determines does not have the capacity to incur debt sufficient to finance a project or activity under subsection (b).

(d) Priority

In prioritizing projects and activities for implementation under this section, the Administrator shall give priority to projects and activities that benefit underserved communities.

(e) Local participation

In prioritizing projects and activities for implementation under this section, the Administrator shall consult with and consider the priorities of States, Indian Tribes, and local governments in which communities described in subsection (c)(2) are located.

(f) Technical, managerial, and financial capability

The Administrator may provide assistance to increase the technical, managerial, and financial capability of an eligible entity receiving a grant under this section if the Administrator determines that the eligible entity lacks appropriate technical, managerial, or financial capability and is not receiving such assistance under another Federal program.

(g) Cost sharing

Before providing a grant to an eligible entity under this section, the Administrator shall enter into a binding agreement with the eligible entity to require the eligible entity —

(1) to pay not less than 45 percent of the total costs of the project or activity, which may include services, materials, supplies, or other in-kind contributions;

(2) to provide any land, easements, rights-of-way, and relocations necessary to carry out the project or activity; and

(3) to pay 100 percent of any operation and maintenance costs associated with the project or activity.

(h) Waiver

The Administrator may waive, in whole or in part, the requirement under subsection (g)(1) if the Administrator determines that an eligible entity is unable to pay, or would experience significant financial hardship if required to pay, the non-Federal share.

(i) Limitation on use of funds

Not more than 4 percent of funds made available for grants under this section may be used to pay the administrative costs of the Administrator.

(j) State response to contaminants

(1) In general

The Administrator may, subject to the terms and conditions of this section, issue a grant to a requesting State, on behalf of an underserved community, so the State may assist in, or otherwise carry out, necessary and appropriate activities related to a contaminant —

(A) that is determined by the State to —

(i) be present in, or likely to enter into, a public water system serving, or an underground source of drinking water for, such underserved community; and

(ii) potentially present an imminent and substantial endangerment to the health of persons; and

(B) with respect to which the State determines appropriate authorities have not acted sufficiently to protect the health of such persons.

(2) Recovery of funds

If, subsequent to the Administrator's award of a grant to a State under this subsection, any person or entity (including an eligible entity), is found by the Administrator or a court of competent jurisdiction to have caused or contributed to contamination that was detected as a result of testing conducted, or treated, with funds provided under this subsection, and such contamination violated a law administered by the Administrator, such person or entity shall, upon issuance of a final judgment or settlement and the exhaustion of all appellate and administrative remedies —

(A) notify the Administrator in writing not later than 30 days after such issuance of a final judgment or settlement and the exhaustion of all appellate and administrative remedies; and

(B) promptly pay the Administrator an amount equal to the amount of such funds.

(k) Authorization of appropriations

There are authorized to be appropriated to carry out subsections (a) through (j) of this section, $60,000,000 for each of fiscal years 2017 through 2021.

(l) Drinking water infrastructure resilience and sustainability

(1) Resilience and natural hazard

The terms "resilience" and "natural hazard" have the meaning given such terms in section 300i-2(h) of this title.

(2) In general

The Administrator may establish and carry out a program, to be known as the Drinking Water System Infrastructure Resilience and Sustainability Program, under which the Administrator, subject to the availability of appropriations for such purpose, shall award grants in each of fiscal years 2019 and 2020 to eligible entities for the purpose of increasing resilience to natural hazards.

(3) Use of funds

An eligible entity may only use grant funds received under this subsection to assist in the planning, design, construction, implementation, operation, or maintenance of a program or project that increases resilience to natural hazards through —

(A) the conservation of water or the enhancement of water use efficiency;

(B) the modification or relocation of existing drinking water system infrastructure made, or that is at risk of being, significantly impaired by natural hazards, including risks to drinking water from flooding;

(C) the design or construction of desalination facilities to serve existing communities;

(D) the enhancement of water supply through the use of watershed management and source water protection;

(E) the enhancement of energy efficiency or the use and generation of renewable energy in the conveyance or treatment of drinking water; or

(F) the development and implementation of measures to increase the resilience of the eligible entity to natural hazards.

(4) Application

To seek a grant under this subsection, the eligible entity shall submit to the Administrator an application that —

(A) includes a proposal of the program or project to be planned, designed, constructed, implemented, operated, or maintained by the eligible entity;

(B) identifies the natural hazard risk to be addressed by the proposed program or project;

(C) provides documentation prepared by a Federal, State, regional, or local government agency of the natural hazard risk to the area where the proposed program or project is to be located;

(D) includes a description of any recent natural hazard events that have affected the applicable water system;

(E) includes a description of how the proposed program or project would improve the performance of the system under the anticipated natural hazards; and

(F) explains how the proposed program or project is expected to enhance the resilience of the system to the anticipated natural hazards.

(5) Authorization of appropriations

There is authorized to be appropriated to carry out this subsection $4,000,000 for each of fiscal years 2019 and 2020.

§300j-19b. Reducing lead in drinking water

(a) Definitions

In this section:

(1) Eligible entity

The term "eligible entity" means —

(A) a community water system;

(B) a water system located in an area governed by an Indian Tribe;

(C) a nontransient noncommunity water system;

(D) a qualified nonprofit organization, as determined by the Administrator, servicing a public water system; and

(E) a municipality or State, interstate, or intermunicipal agency.

(2) Lead reduction project

(A) In general

The term "lead reduction project" means a project or activity the primary purpose of which is to reduce the concentration of lead in water for human consumption by —

(i) replacement of publicly owned lead service lines;

(ii) testing, planning, or other relevant activities, as determined by the Administrator, to identify and address conditions (including corrosion control) that contribute to increased concentration of lead in water for human consumption; and

(iii) providing assistance to low-income homeowners to replace lead service lines.

(B) Limitation

The term "lead reduction project" does not include a partial lead service line replacement if, at the conclusion of the service line replacement, drinking water is delivered to a household through a publicly or privately owned portion of a lead service line.

(3) Low-income

The term "low-income", with respect to an individual provided assistance under this section, has such meaning as may be given the term by the Governor of the State in which the eligible entity is located, based upon the affordability criteria established by the State under section 300j-12(d)(3) of this title.

(4) Lead service line

The term "lead service line" means a pipe and its fittings, which are not lead free (as defined in section 300g-6(d) of this title), that connect the drinking water main to the building inlet.

(5) Nontransient noncommunity water system

The term "nontransient noncommunity water system" means a public water system that is not a community water system and that regularly serves at least 25 of the same persons over 6 months per year.

(b) Grant program

(1) Establishment

The Administrator shall establish a grant program to provide assistance to eligible entities for lead reduction projects in the United States.

(2) Precondition

As a condition of receipt of assistance under this section, an eligible entity shall take steps to identify —

(A) the source of lead in the public water system that is subject to human consumption; and

(B) the means by which the proposed lead reduction project would meaningfully reduce the concentration of lead in water provided for human consumption by the applicable public water system.

(3) Priority application

In providing grants under this subsection, the Administrator shall give priority to an eligible entity that —

(A) the Administrator determines, based on affordability criteria established by the State under section 300j-12(d)(3) of this title, to be a disadvantaged community; and

(B) proposes to —

(i) carry out a lead reduction project at a public water system or nontransient noncommunity water system that has exceeded the lead action level established by the Administrator under section 300g-1 of this title at any time during the 3-year period preceding the date of submission of the application of the eligible entity; or

(ii) address lead levels in water for human consumption at a school, daycare, or other facility that primarily serves children or other vulnerable human subpopulation described in section 300j-18(a)(1) of this title.

(4) Cost sharing

(A) In general

Subject to subparagraph (B), the non-Federal share of the total cost of a project funded by a grant under this subsection shall be not less than 20 percent.

(B) Waiver

The Administrator may reduce or eliminate the non-Federal share under subparagraph (A) for reasons of affordability, as the Administrator determines to be appropriate.

(5) Low-income assistance

(A) In general

Subject to subparagraph (B), an eligible entity may use a grant provided under this subsection to provide assistance to low-income homeowners to replace the lead service lines of such homeowners.

(B) Limitation

The amount of a grant provided to a low-income homeowner under this paragraph shall not exceed the standard cost of replacement of the privately owned portion of the lead service line.

(6) Special consideration for lead service line replacement

In carrying out lead service line replacement using a grant under this subsection, an eligible entity —

(A) shall notify customers of the replacement of any publicly owned portion of the lead service line;

(B) may, in the case of a homeowner who is not low-income, offer to replace the privately owned portion of the lead service line at the cost of replacement for that homeowner's property;

(C) may, in the case of a low-income homeowner, offer to replace the privately owned portion of the lead service line at a cost that is equal to the difference between —

(i) the cost of replacement; and

(ii) the amount of assistance available to the low-income homeowner under paragraph (5);

(D) shall notify each customer that a planned replacement of any publicly owned portion of a lead service line that is funded by a grant made under this subsection will not be carried out unless the customer agrees to the simultaneous replacement of the privately owned portion of the lead service line; and

(E) shall demonstrate that the eligible entity has considered other options for reducing the concentration of lead in its drinking water, including an evaluation of options for corrosion control.

(c) Limitation on use of funds

Not more than 4 percent of funds made available for grants under this section may be used to pay the administrative costs of the Administrator.

(d) Authorization of appropriations

There is authorized to be appropriated to carry out this section $60,000,000 for each of fiscal years 2017 through 2021.

(e) Savings clause

Nothing in this section affects whether a public water system is responsible for the replacement of a lead service line that is —

(1) subject to the control of the public water system; and

(2) located on private property.

§300j-19c. Study on intractable water systems

(a) Definition of intractable water system

In this section, the term "intractable water system" means a community water system or a noncommunity water system —

(1) that serves fewer than 1,000 individuals;

(2) the owner or operator of which —

(A) is unable or unwilling to provide safe and adequate service to those individuals;

(B) has abandoned or effectively abandoned the community water system or noncommunity water system, as applicable;

(C) has defaulted on a financial obligation relating to the community water system or noncommunity water system, as applicable; or

(D) fails to maintain the facilities of the community water system or noncommunity water system, as applicable, in a manner so as to prevent a potential public health hazard; and

(3) that is, as of October 23, 2018—

(A) in significant noncompliance with this Act1 or any regulation promulgated pursuant to this Act1; or

(B) listed as having a history of significant noncompliance with this subchapter pursuant to section 300g-9(b)(1) of this title.

(b) Study required

(1) In general

Not later than 2 years after October 23, 2018, the Administrator, in consultation with the Secretary of Agriculture and the Secretary of Health and Human Services, shall complete a study that —

(A) identifies intractable water systems; and

(B) describes barriers to delivery of potable water to individuals served by an intractable water system.

(2) Report to Congress

Not later than 2 years after October 23, 2018, the Administrator shall submit to Congress a report describing findings and recommendations based on the study under this subsection.

§300j-19d. Review of technologies

(a) Review

The Administrator, after consultation with appropriate departments and agencies of the Federal Government and with State and local governments, shall review (or enter into contracts or cooperative agreements to provide for a review of) existing and potential methods, means, equipment, and technologies (including review of cost, availability, and efficacy of such methods, means, equipment, and technologies) that —

(1) ensure the physical integrity of community water systems;

(2) prevent, detect, and respond to any contaminant for which a national primary drinking water regulation has been promulgated in community water systems and source water for community water systems;

(3) allow for use of alternate drinking water supplies from nontraditional sources; and

(4) facilitate source water assessment and protection.

(b) Inclusions

The review under subsection (a) shall include review of methods, means, equipment, and technologies —

(1) that are used for corrosion protection, metering, leak detection, or protection against water loss;

(2) that are intelligent systems, including hardware, software, or other technology, used to assist in protection and detection described in paragraph (1);

(3) that are point-of-use devices or point-of-entry devices;

(4) that are physical or electronic systems that monitor, or assist in monitoring, contaminants in drinking water in real-time; and

(5) that allow for the use of nontraditional sources for drinking water, including physical separation and chemical and biological transformation technologies.

(c) Availability

The Administrator shall make the results of the review under subsection (a) available to the public.

(d) Authorization of appropriations

There is authorized to be appropriated to the Administrator to carry out this section $10,000,000 for fiscal year 2019, which shall remain available until expended.

§300j-19e. Water infrastructure and workforce investment

(a) Sense of Congress

It is the sense of Congress that —

(1) water and wastewater utilities provide a unique opportunity for access to stable, high-quality careers;

(2) as water and wastewater utilities make critical investments in infrastructure, water and wastewater utilities can invest in the development of local workers and local small businesses to strengthen communities and ensure a strong pipeline of skilled and diverse workers for today and tomorrow; and

(3) to further the goal of ensuring a strong pipeline of skilled and diverse workers in the water and wastewater utilities sector, Congress urges —

    (A) increased collaboration among Federal, State, and local governments; and

    (B) institutions of higher education, apprentice programs, high schools, and other community-based organizations to align workforce training programs and community resources with water and wastewater utilities to accelerate career pipelines and provide access to workforce opportunities.

(b) Innovative water infrastructure workforce development program

(1) Grants authorized

The Administrator of the Environmental Protection Agency (referred to in this section as the "Administrator"), in consultation with the Secretary of Agriculture, shall establish a competitive grant program —

    (A) to assist the development and utilization of innovative activities relating to workforce development and career opportunities in the water utility sector; and

    (B) to expand public awareness about water utilities and connect individuals to careers in the water utility sector.

(2) Selection of grant recipients

In awarding grants under paragraph (1), the Administrator shall, to the extent practicable, select nonprofit professional or service organizations, labor organizations, community colleges, institutions of higher education, or other training and educational institutions —

    (A) that have qualifications and experience —

        (i) in the development of training programs and curricula relevant to workforce needs of water utilities;

        (ii) working in cooperation with water utilities; or

        (iii) developing public education materials appropriate for communicating with groups of different ages and educational backgrounds; and

    (B) that will address the human resources and workforce needs of water utilities that —

        (i) are geographically diverse;

        (ii) are of varying sizes; and

        (iii) serve urban, suburban, and rural populations.

(3) Use of funds

Grants awarded under paragraph (1) may be used for activities such as —

    (A) targeted internship, apprenticeship, pre-apprenticeship, and post-secondary bridge programs for skilled water utility trades that provide —

        (i) on-the-job training;

        (ii) skills development;

        (iii) test preparation for skilled trade apprenticeships;

        (iv) advance training in the water utility sector relating to construction, utility operations, treatment and distribution, green infrastructure, customer service, maintenance, and engineering; or

        (v) other support services to facilitate post-secondary success;

    (B) education programs designed for elementary, secondary, and higher education students that —

        (i) inform people about the role of water and wastewater utilities in their communities;

        (ii) increase the awareness of career opportunities and exposure of students to water utility careers through various work-based learning opportunities inside and outside the classroom; and

        (iii) connect students to career pathways related to water utilities;

    (C) regional industry and workforce development collaborations to address water utility employment needs and coordinate candidate development, particularly in areas of high unemployment or for water utilities with a high proportion of retirement eligible employees;

(D) integrated learning laboratories in secondary educational institutions that provide students with —

    (i) hands-on, contextualized learning opportunities;

    (ii) dual enrollment credit for post-secondary education and training programs; and

    (iii) direct connection to industry employers; and

(E) leadership development, occupational training, mentoring, or cross-training programs that ensure that incumbent water and waste water utilities workers are prepared for higher level supervisory or management-level positions.

(4) Authorization of appropriations

There is authorized to be appropriated to carry out this subsection $1,000,000 for each of fiscal years 2019 and 2020.

PART F — ADDITIONAL REQUIREMENTS TO REGULATE SAFETY OF DRINKING WATER

§300j-21. Definitions
[PHSA §1461]

As used in this part —

(1) Drinking water cooler — The term "drinking water cooler" means any mechanical device affixed to drinking water supply plumbing which actively cools water for human consumption.

(2) Lead free — The term "lead free" means, with respect to a drinking water cooler, that each part or component of the cooler which may come in contact with drinking water contains not more than 8 percent lead, except that no drinking water cooler which contains any solder, flux, or storage tank interior surface which may come in contact with drinking water shall be considered lead free if the solder, flux, or storage tank interior surface contains more than 0.2 percent lead. The Administrator may establish more stringent requirements for treating any part or component of a drinking water cooler as lead free for purposes of this part whenever he determines that any such part may constitute an important source of lead in drinking water.

(3) Local educational agency — The term "local educational agency" means —

(A) any local educational agency as defined in section 7801 of Title 20,

(B) the owner of any private, nonprofit elementary or secondary school building, and

(C) the governing authority of any school operating under the defense dependent's education system provided for under the Defense Dependent's Education Act of 1978 (20 U.S.C. 921 and following).

(4) Repair — The term "repair" means, with respect to a drinking water cooler, to take such corrective action as is necessary to ensure that water cooler is lead free.

(5) Replacement — The term "replacement" when used with respect to a drinking water cooler or drinking water fountain, means the permanent removal of the water cooler or drinking water fountain and the installation of a lead free water cooler or drinking water fountain.

(6) School — The term "school" means any elementary school or secondary school as defined in section 7801 of Title 20 and any kindergarten or day care facility.

(7) Lead-lined tank — The term "lead-lined tank" means a water reservoir container in a drinking water cooler which container is constructed of lead or which has an interior surface which is not lead free.

§300j-22. Recall of drinking water coolers with lead-lined tanks
[PHSA §1462]

For purposes of the Consumer Product Safety Act [15 U.S.C. §§2051 *et seq.*], all drinking water coolers identified by the Administrator on the list under section 300j-23 of this title as having a lead-lined tank shall be considered to be imminently hazardous consumer products within the meaning of section 12 of such Act (15 U.S.C. §2061). After notice and opportunity for comment, including a public hearing, the Consumer Product Safety Commission shall issue an order requiring the manufacturers and importers of such coolers to repair, replace, or recall and provide a refund for such coolers within 1 year after October 31, 1988. For purposes of enforcement, such order shall be treated as an order under section 15(d) of that Act (15 U.S.C. §2064(d)).

§300j-23. Drinking water coolers containing lead
[PHSA §1463]

(a) Publication of lists — The Administrator shall, after notice and opportunity for public comment, identify each brand and model of drinking water cooler which is not lead free, including each brand and model of drinking water cooler which has a lead-lined tank. For purposes of identifying the brand and model of drinking water coolers under this subsection, the Administrator shall use the best information available to the Environmental Protection Agency. Within 100 days after October 31, 1988, the Administrator shall publish a list of each brand and model of drinking water cooler identified under this subsection. Such list shall separately identify each brand and model of cooler which has a lead-lined tank. The Administrator shall continue to gather information regarding lead in drinking water coolers and shall revise and republish the list from time to time as may be appropriate as new information or analysis becomes available regarding lead contamination in drinking water coolers.

(b) Prohibition — No person may sell in interstate commerce, or manufacture for sale in interstate commerce, any drinking water cooler listed under subsection (a) of this section or any other drinking water cooler which is not lead free, including a lead-lined drinking water cooler.

(c) Criminal penalty — Any person who knowingly violates the prohibition contained in subsection (b) of this section shall be imprisoned for not more than 5 years, or fined in accordance with Title 18, or both.

(d) Civil penalty — The Administrator may bring a civil action in the appropriate United States District Court (as determined under the provisions of Title 28) to impose a civil penalty on any person who violates subsection (b) of this section. In any such action the court may impose on such person a civil penalty of not more than $5,000 ($50,000 in the case of a second or subsequent violation).

§300j-24. Lead contamination in school drinking water

[PHSA §1464]

(a) Distribution of drinking water cooler list — Within 100 days after October 31, 1988, the Administrator shall distribute to the States a list of each brand and model of drinking water cooler identified and listed by the Administrator under section 300j-23(a) of this title.

(b) Guidance document and testing protocol — The Administrator shall publish a guidance document and a testing protocol to assist schools in determining the source and degree of lead contamination in school drinking water supplies and in remedying such contamination. The guidance document shall include guidelines for sample preservation. The guidance document shall also include guidance to assist States, schools, and the general public in ascertaining the levels of lead contamination in drinking water coolers and in taking appropriate action to reduce or eliminate such contamination. The guidance document shall contain a testing protocol for the identification of drinking water coolers which contribute to lead contamination in drinking water. Such document and protocol may be revised, republished and redistributed as the Administrator deems necessary. The Administrator shall distribute the guidance document and testing protocol to the States within 100 days after October 31, 1988.

(c) Dissemination to schools, etc. — Each State shall provide for the dissemination to local educational agencies, private nonprofi t elementary or secondary schools and to day care centers of the guidance document and testing protocol published under subsection (b) of this section, together with the list of drinking water coolers published under section 300j-23(a) of this title.

(d) Voluntary school and child care program lead testing grant program

(1) Definitions
In this subsection:
  (A) Child care program
The term "child care program" has the meaning given the term "early childhood education program" in section 1003(8) of Title 20.
  (B) Local educational agency
The term "local educational agency" means —
    (i) a local educational agency (as defined in section 7801 of Title 20);
    (ii) a tribal education agency (as defined in section 5502 of Title 20); and
    (iii) a person that owns or operates a child care program facility.
(2) Establishment
  (A) In general
Not later than 180 days after December 16, 2016, the Administrator shall establish a voluntary school and child care program lead testing grant program to make grants available to States to assist local educational agencies in voluntary testing for lead contamination in drinking water at schools and child care programs under the jurisdiction of the local educational agencies.
  (B) Direct grants to local educational agencies
The Administrator may make a grant for the voluntary testing described in subparagraph (A) directly available to —
    (i) any local educational agency described in clause (i) or (iii) of paragraph (1)(B) located in a State that does not participate in the voluntary grant program established under subparagraph (A); or
    (ii) any local educational agency described in clause (ii) of paragraph (1)(B).
  (C) Technical assistance
In carrying out the grant program under subparagraph (A), beginning not later than 1 year after October 23, 2018, the Administrator shall provide technical assistance to recipients of grants under this subsection —
    (i) to assist in identifying the source of lead contamination in drinking water at schools and child care programs under the jurisdiction of the grant recipient;
    (ii) to assist in identifying and applying for other Federal and State grant programs that may assist the grant recipient in eliminating lead contamination described in clause (i);
    (iii) to provide information on other financing options in eliminating lead contamination described in clause (i); and
    (iv) to connect grant recipients with nonprofit and other organizations that may be able to assist with the elimination of lead contamination described in clause (i).

(3) Application

To be eligible to receive a grant under this subsection, a State or local educational agency shall submit to the Administrator an application at such time, in such manner, and containing such information as the Administrator may require.

(4) Priority

In making grants under this subsection, the Administrator shall give priority to States and local educational agencies that will assist in voluntary testing for lead contamination in drinking water at schools and child care programs that are in low-income areas.

(5) Limitation on use of funds

Not more than 4 percent of grant funds accepted by a State or local educational agency for a fiscal year under this subsection shall be used to pay the administrative costs of carrying out this subsection.

(6) Guidance; public availability

As a condition of receiving a grant under this subsection, the recipient State or local educational agency shall ensure that each local educational agency to which grant funds are distributed shall —

　(A) expend grant funds in accordance with —

　　(i) the guidance of the Environmental Protection Agency entitled "3Ts for Reducing Lead in Drinking Water in Schools: Revised Technical Guidance" and dated October 2006 (or any successor guidance); or

　　(ii) applicable State regulations or guidance regarding reducing lead in drinking water in schools and child care programs that are not less stringent than the guidance referred to in clause (i); and

　(B)(i) make available, if applicable, in the administrative offices and, to the extent practicable, on the Internet website of the local educational agency for inspection by the public (including teachers, other school personnel, and parents) a copy of the results of any voluntary testing for lead contamination in school and child care program drinking water carried out using grant funds under this subsection; and

　　(ii) notify parent, teacher, and employee organizations of the availability of the results described in clause (i).

(7) Maintenance of effort

If resources are available to a State or local educational agency from any other Federal agency, a State, or a private foundation for testing for lead contamination in drinking water, the State or local educational agency shall demonstrate that the funds provided under this subsection will not displace those resources.

(8) Authorization of appropriations

There are authorized to be appropriated to carry out this subsection $20,000,000 for each of fiscal years 2017 through 2019, and $25,000,000 for each of fiscal years 2020 and 2021.

§300j-25. Drinking water fountain replacement for schools
[PHSA §1465]

(a) **Establishment** — Not later than 1 year after October 23, 2018, the Administrator shall establish a grant program to provide assistance to local educational agencies for the replacement of drinking water fountains manufactured prior to 1988.

(b) **Use of funds** — Funds awarded under the grant program —

　(1) shall be used to pay the costs of replacement of drinking water fountains in schools; and

　(2) may be used to pay the costs of monitoring and reporting of lead levels in the drinking water of schools of a local educational agency receiving such funds, as determined appropriate by the Administrator.

(c) **Priority** — In awarding funds under the grant program, the Administrator shall give priority to local educational agencies based on economic need.

(d) **Authorization of appropriations** — There are authorized to be appropriated to carry out this section $5,000,000 for each of fiscal years 2019 through 2021.

§300j-26. Certification of testing laboratories

The Administrator of the Environmental Protection Agency shall assure that programs for the certification of testing laboratories which test drinking water supplies for lead contamination certify only those laboratories which provide reliable accurate testing. The Administrator (or the State in the case of a State to which certification authority is delegated under this subsection) shall publish and make available to the public upon request the list of laboratories certified under this subsection.

D. EMERGENCY PLANNING AND COMMUNITY RIGHT-TO-KNOW ACT

A GUIDE TO MATERIALS AVAILABLE ON THE INTERNET PERTAINING TO THE EMERGENCY PLANNING AND COMMUNITY RIGHT-TO-KNOW ACT (EPCRA)

EPA's regulations implementing EPCRA are codified at 40 C.F.R. pts. 355-372. These CFR sections are available online through the National Archives and Records Administration's website, which includes a searchable version of the Code of Federal Regulations (*https://www.gpo.gov/fdsys/browse/collectionCfr.action?collectionCode=CFR*) and a continuously updated electronic CFR ("e-CFR") that can be found at *http://www.ecfr.gov.*

EPA's Office of Prevention, Pesticides, and Toxic Substances makes chemical release data from the agency's Toxics Release Inventory (TRI) available to the public online at its website at *https://www.epa.gov/toxics-release-inventory-tri-program.* The site allows visitors to search the TRI data.

When the TRI was first created, the Environmental Defense Fund created the "Scoreboard" website that allowed the public to obtain TRI data on chemical releases sorted by zipcodes and to send faxes to the largest dischargers objecting to the releases. This website has since closed down. The *Houston Chronicle* hosts "The Right-to-Know Network" website at: *https://rtk.rjifuture.org.*

EPCRA LEGISLATIVE HISTORY TIMELINE

October 17, 1986: The Emergency Planning and Community Right-to-Know Act, Pub. L. 99-499, 100 Stat. 1728, is enacted. It establishes a national program of planning for emergency response and it requires companies to report annually on their emissions of hazardous chemicals.

OUTLINE OF THE PRINCIPAL PROVISIONS OF THE EMERGENCY PLANNING AND COMMUNITY RIGHT-TO-KNOW ACT

TITLE I — EMERGENCY PLANNING AND NOTIFICATION

§301 (42 U.S.C. §11001) Establishment of State Commission and Local Committees: requires the establishment of state emergency response commissions and local emergency planning committees.

§302 (42 U.S.C. §11002) Substances and Facilities Covered and Notification: requires EPA to publish a list of extremely hazardous substances and to establish threshold planning quantities for these substances. Facilities where substances on the list are present in amounts in excess of the threshold quantities are required to notify the state emergency response commission and the local emergency planning committee.

§303 (42 U.S.C. §11003) Emergency Response Plans: requires local emergency planning committees to prepare a comprehensive emergency response plan and specifies minimum requirements for such plans.

§304 (42 U.S.C. §11004) Emergency Notification: requires owners and operators of facilities to notify community emergency response coordinators of releases of extremely hazardous substances.

TITLE II — REPORTING REQUIREMENTS

§§311 & 312 (42 U.S.C. §§11021 & 11022) Material Safety Data Sheets and Chemical Inventory Forms: requires owners and operators of facilities required by the Occupational Safety and Health Administration to prepare material safety data sheets (MSDSs) to submit them along with an emergency and hazardous chemical inventory form to the local emergency planning committee, the state emergency response commission, and the local fire department.

§313 (42 U.S.C. §11023) **Toxic Chemical Release Reports**: requires owners and operators of facilities that have ten or more full-time employees and that were in SIX Codes 20 through 39 as of July 1, 1985, to complete a toxic chemical release form reporting the quantities of releases of each of more than 600 toxic chemicals used in quantities that exceed established threshold quantities during the preceding calendar year. These forms must be submitted to EPA and state authorities by July 1 of each year to report data reflecting releases during the preceding calendar year. EPA is required to establish and maintain a national toxics release inventory (TRI) based on data submitted in these reports. The TRI must be maintained in a form accessible to the public online.

TITLE III – GENERAL PROVISIONS

§322 (42 U.S.C. §11042) **Trade Secrets**: authorizes the withholding of information on specific chemical identities if the information is a trade secret.

§324 (42 U.S.C. §11044) **Public Availability of Data**: requires that data reported under the Act generally be made available to the general public, consistent with §322.

§325 (42 U.S.C. §11045) **Enforcement**: provides civil, administrative, and criminal penalties for violations of the Act and authorizes enforcement actions by EPA.

§326 (42 U.S.C. §11046) **Citizen Suits**: authorizes any person to sue owners and operators of facilities that fail to comply with the Act and authorizes suits against the EPA Administrator and state officials for failure to perform certain duties required by the Act.

Emergency Planning and Community Right-to-Know Act

42 U.S.C. §§11001 to 11050

SUBCHAPTER I — EMERGENCY PLANNING AND NOTIFICATION

§11001. Establishment of State commissions, planning districts, and local committees
[EPCRA §301]

(a) Establishment of State emergency response commissions — Not later than six months after October 17, 1986, the Governor of each State shall appoint a State emergency response commission. The Governor may designate as the State emergency response commission one or more existing emergency response organizations that are State-sponsored or appointed. The Governor shall, to the extent practicable, appoint persons to the State emergency response commission who have technical expertise in the emergency response field. The State emergency response commission shall appoint local emergency planning committees under subsection (c) of this section and shall supervise and coordinate the activities of such committees. The State emergency response commission shall establish procedures for receiving and processing requests from the public for information under section 11044 of this title, including tier II information under section 11022 of this title. Such procedures shall include the designation of an official to serve as coordinator for information. If the Governor of any State does not designate a State emergency response commission within such period, the Governor shall operate as the State emergency response commission until the Governor makes such designation.

(b) Establishment of emergency planning districts — Not later than nine months after October 17, 1986, the State emergency response commission shall designate emergency planning districts in order to facilitate preparation and implementation of emergency plans. Where appropriate, the State emergency response commission may designate existing political subdivisions or multijurisdictional planning organizations as such districts. In emergency planning areas that involve more than one State, the State emergency response commissions of all potentially affected States may designate emergency planning districts and local emergency planning committees by agreement. In making such designation, the State emergency response commission shall indicate which facilities subject to the requirements of this subchapter are within such emergency planning district.

(c) Establishment of local emergency planning committees — Not later than 30 days after designation of emergency planning districts or 10 months after October 17, 1986, whichever is earlier, the State emergency response commission shall appoint members of a local emergency planning committee for each emergency planning district. Each committee shall include, at a minimum, representatives from each of the following groups or organizations: elected State and local officials; law enforcement, civil defense, firefighting, first aid, health, local environmental, hospital, and transportation personnel; broadcast and print media; community groups; and owners and operators of facilities subject to the requirements of this subchapter. Such committee shall appoint a chairperson and shall establish rules by which the committee shall function. Such rules shall include provisions for public notification of committee activities, public meetings to discuss the emergency plan, public comments, response to such comments by the committee, and distribution of the emergency plan. The local emergency planning committee shall establish procedures for receiving and processing requests from the public for information under section 11044 of this title, including tier II information under section 11022 of this title. Such procedures shall include the designation of an official to serve as coordinator for information.

(d) Revisions — A State emergency response commission may revise its designations and appointments under subsections (b) and (c) of this section as it deems appropriate. Interested persons may petition the State emergency response commission to modify the membership of a local emergency planning committee.

§11002. Substances and facilities covered and notification
[EPCRA §302]
(a) Substances covered

(1) In general — A substance is subject to the requirements of this subchapter if the substance is on the list published under paragraph (2).

(2) List of extremely hazardous substances — Within 30 days after October 17, 1986, the Administrator shall publish a list of extremely hazardous substances. The list shall be the same as the list of substances published in November 1985 by the Administrator in Appendix A of the "Chemical Emergency Preparedness Program Interim Guidance".

(3) Thresholds

(A) At the time the list referred to in paragraph (2) is published the Administrator shall —

(i) publish an interim final regulation establishing a threshold planning quantity for each substance on the list, taking into account the criteria described in paragraph (4), and

(ii) initiate a rulemaking in order to publish final regulations establishing a threshold planning quantity for each substance on the list.

(B) The threshold planning quantities may, at the Administrator's discretion, be based on classes of chemicals or categories of facilities.

(C) If the Administrator fails to publish an interim final regulation establishing a threshold planning quantity for a substance within 30 days after October 17, 1986, the threshold planning quantity for the substance shall be 2 pounds until such time as the Administrator publishes regulations establishing a threshold for the substance.

(4) Revisions — The Administrator may revise the list and thresholds under paragraphs (2) and (3) from time to time. Any revisions to the list shall take into account the toxicity, reactivity, volatility, dispersability, combustability, or flammability of a substance. For purposes of the preceding sentence, the term "toxicity" shall include any short- or long-term health effect which may result from a short-term exposure to the substance.

(b) Facilities covered

(1) Except as provided in section 11004 of this title, a facility is subject to the requirements of this subchapter if a substance on the list referred to in subsection (a) of this section is present at the facility in an amount in excess of the threshold planning quantity established for such substance.

(2) For purposes of emergency planning, a Governor or a State emergency response commission may designate additional facilities which shall be subject to the requirements of this subchapter, if such designation is made after public notice and opportunity for comment. The Governor or State emergency response commission shall notify the facility concerned of any facility designation under this paragraph.

(c) Emergency planning notification — Not later than seven months after October 17, 1986, the owner or operator of each facility subject to the requirements of this subchapter by reason of subsection (b)(1) of this section shall notify the State emergency response commission for the State in which such facility is located that such facility is subject to the requirements of this subchapter. Thereafter, if a substance on the list of extremely hazardous substances referred to in subsection (a) of this section first becomes present at such facility in excess of the threshold planning quantity established for such substance, or if there is a revision of such list and the facility has present a substance on the revised list in excess of the threshold planning quantity established for such substance, the owner or operator of the facility shall notify the State emergency response commission and the local emergency planning committee within 60 days after such acquisition or revision that such facility is subject to the requirements of this subchapter.

(d) Notification of Administrator — The State emergency response commission shall notify the Administrator of facilities subject to the requirements of this subchapter by notifying the Administrator of —

(1) each notification received from a facility under subsection (c) of this section, and

(2) each facility designated by the Governor or State emergency response commission under subsection (b)(2) of this section.

§11003. Comprehensive emergency response plans

[EPCRA §303]

(a) Plan required — Each local emergency planning committee shall complete preparation of an emergency plan in accordance with this section not later than two years after October 17, 1986. The committee shall review such plan once a year, or more frequently as changed circumstances in the community or at any facility may require.

(b) Resources — Each local emergency planning committee shall evaluate the need for resources necessary to develop, implement, and exercise the emergency plan, and shall make recommendations with respect to additional resources that may be required and the means for providing such additional resources.

(c) Plan provisions — Each emergency plan shall include (but is not limited to) each of the following:

(1) Identification of facilities subject to the requirements of this subchapter that are within the emergency planning district, identification of routes likely to be used for the transportation of substances on the list of extremely hazardous substances referred to in section 11002(a) of this title, and identification of additional facilities contributing or subjected to additional risk due to their proximity to facilities subject to the requirements of this subchapter, such as hospitals or natural gas facilities.

(2) Methods and procedures to be followed by facility owners and operators and local emergency and medical personnel to respond to any release of such substances.

(3) Designation of a community emergency coordinator and facility emergency coordinators, who shall make determinations necessary to implement the plan.

(4) Procedures providing reliable, effective, and timely notification by the facility emergency coordinators and the community emergency coordinator to persons designated in the emergency plan, and to the public, that a release has occurred (consistent with the emergency notification requirements of section 11004 of this title).

(5) Methods for determining the occurrence of a release, and the area or population likely to be affected by such release.

(6) A description of emergency equipment and facilities in the community and at each facility in the community subject to the requirements of this subchapter, and an identification of the persons responsible for such equipment and facilities.

(7) Evacuation plans, including provisions for a precautionary evacuation and alternative traffic routes.

(8) Training programs, including schedules for training of local emergency response and medical personnel.

(9) Methods and schedules for exercising the emergency plan.

(d) Providing of information — For each facility subject to the requirements of this subchapter:

(1) Within 30 days after establishment of a local emergency planning committee for the emergency planning district in which such facility is located, or within 11 months after October 17, 1986, whichever is earlier, the owner or operator of the facility shall notify the emergency planning committee (or the Governor if there is no committee) of a facility representative who will participate in the emergency planning process as a facility emergency coordinator.

(2) The owner or operator of the facility shall promptly inform the emergency planning committee of any relevant changes occurring at such facility as such changes occur or are expected to occur.

(3) Upon request from the emergency planning committee, the owner or operator of the facility shall promptly provide information to such committee necessary for developing and implementing the emergency plan.

(e) Review by State emergency response commission — After completion of an emergency plan under subsection (a) of this section for an emergency planning district, the local emergency planning committee shall submit a copy of the plan to the State emergency response commission of each State in which such district is located. The commission shall review the plan and make recommendations to the committee on revisions of the plan that may be necessary to ensure coordination of such plan with emergency response plans of other emergency planning districts. To the maximum extent practicable, such review shall not delay implementation of such plan.

(f) Guidance documents — The national response team, as established pursuant to the National Contingency Plan as established under section 9605 of this title, shall publish guidance documents for preparation and implementation of emergency plans. Such documents shall be published not later than five months after October 17, 1986.

(g) Review of plans by regional response teams — The regional response teams, as established pursuant to the National Contingency Plan as established under section 9605 of this title, may review and comment upon an emergency plan or other issues related to preparation, implementation, or exercise of such a plan upon request of a local emergency planning committee. Such review shall not delay implementation of the plan.

§11004. Emergency notification
[EPCRA §304]

(a) Types of releases

(1) 11002(a) substance which requires CERCLA notice — If a release of an extremely hazardous substance referred to in section 11002(a) of this title

occurs from a facility at which a hazardous chemical is produced, used, or stored, and such release requires a notification under section 103(a) of the Comprehensive Environmental Response, Compensation, and Liability Act of 1980 [42 U.S.C. §9603(a)] (hereafter in this section referred to as "CERCLA") (42 U.S.C. §9601 et seq.), the owner or operator of the facility shall immediately provide notice as described in subsection (b) of this section.

(2) Other 11002(a) substance — If a release of an extremely hazardous substance referred to in section 11002(a) of this title occurs from a facility at which a hazardous chemical is produced, used, or stored, and such release is not subject to the notification requirements under section 103(a) of CERCLA [42 U.S.C. §9603(a)], the owner or operator of the facility shall immediately provide notice as described in subsection (b) of this section, but only if the release —

(A) is not a federally permitted release as defined in section 101(10) of CERCLA [42 U.S.C. §§9601(10)],

(B) is in an amount in excess of a quantity which the Administrator has determined (by regulation) requires notice, and

(C) occurs in a manner which would require notification under section 103(a) of CERCLA [42 U.S.C. §9603(a)].

Unless and until superseded by regulations establishing a quantity for an extremely hazardous substance described in this paragraph, a quantity of 1 pound shall be deemed that quantity the release of which requires notice as described in subsection (b) of this section.

(3) Non-11002(a) substance which requires CERCLA notice — If a release of a substance which is not on the list referred to in section 11002(a) of this title occurs at a facility at which a hazardous chemical is produced, used, or stored, and such release requires notification under section 103(a) of CERCLA [42 U.S.C. §9603(a)], the owner or operator shall provide notice as follows:

(A) If the substance is one for which a reportable quantity has been established under section 102(a) of CERCLA [42 U.S.C. §9602(a)], the owner or operator shall provide notice as described in subsection (b) of this section.

(B) If the substance is one for which a reportable quantity has not been established under section 102(a) of CERCLA [42 U.S.C. §9602(a)] —

(i) Until April 30, 1988, the owner or operator shall provide, for releases of one pound or more of the substance, the same notice to the community emergency coordinator for the local emergency planning committee, at the same time and in the same form, as notice is provided to the National Response Center under section 103(a) of CERCLA [42 U.S.C. §9603(a)].

(ii) On and after April 30, 1988, the owner or operator shall provide, for releases of one pound or more of the substance, the notice as described in subsection (b) of this section.

(4) Exempted releases — This section does not apply to any release which results in exposure to persons solely within the site or sites on which a facility is located.

(b) Notification

(1) Recipients of notice — Notice required under subsection (a) of this section shall be given immediately after the release by the owner or operator of a facility (by such means as telephone, radio, or in person) to the community emergency coordinator for the local emergency planning committees, if established pursuant to section 11001(c) of this title, for any area likely to be affected by the release and to the State emergency response commission of any State likely to be affected by the release. With respect to transportation of a substance subject to the requirements of this section, or storage incident to such transportation, the notice requirements of this section with respect to a release shall be satisfied by dialing 911 or, in the absence of a 911 emergency telephone number, calling the operator.

(2) Contents — Notice required under subsection (a) of this section shall include each of the following (to the extent known at the time of the notice and so long as no delay in responding to the emergency results):

(A) The chemical name or identity of any substance involved in the release.

(B) An indication of whether the substance is on the list referred to in section 11002(a) of this title.

(C) An estimate of the quantity of any such substance that was released into the environment.

(D) The time and duration of the release.

(E) The medium or media into which the release occurred.

(F) Any known or anticipated acute or chronic health risks associated with the emergency and, where appropriate, advice regarding medical attention necessary for exposed individuals.

(G) Proper precautions to take as a result of the release, including evacuation (unless such information is readily available to the community emergency coordinator pursuant to the emergency plan).

(H) The name and telephone number of the person or persons to be contacted for further information.

(c) Followup emergency notice — As soon as practicable after a release which requires notice under subsection (a) of this section, such owner or operator shall provide a written followup emergency notice (or notices, as more information becomes available) setting forth and updating the information required under subsection (b) of this section, and including additional information with respect to —

(1) actions taken to respond to and contain the release,

(2) any known or anticipated acute or chronic health risks associated with the release, and

(3) where appropriate, advice regarding medical attention necessary for exposed individuals.

(d) Transportation exemption not applicable — The exemption provided in section 11047 of this title (relating to transportation) does not apply to this section.

(e) Addressing source water used for drinking water

(1) Applicable State agency notification — A State emergency response commission shall —

(A) promptly notify the applicable State agency of any release that requires notice under subsection (a);

(B) provide to the applicable State agency the information identified in subsection (b)(2); and

(C) provide to the applicable State agency a written followup emergency notice in accordance with subsection (c).

(2) Community water system notification

(A) In general

An applicable State agency receiving notice of a release under paragraph (1) shall —

(i) promptly forward such notice to any community water system the source waters of which are affected by the release;

(ii) forward to the community water system the information provided under paragraph (1)(B); and

(iii) forward to the community water system the written followup emergency notice provided under paragraph (1)(C).

(B) Direct notification

In the case of a State that does not have an applicable State agency, the State emergency response commission shall provide the notices and information described in paragraph (1) directly to any community water system the source waters of which are affected by a release that requires notice under subsection (a).

(3) Definitions — In this subsection:

(A) Community water system

The term "community water system" has the meaning given such term in section 300f (15) of this title.

(B) Applicable State agency

The term "applicable State agency" means the State agency that has primary responsibility to enforce the requirements of the Safe Drinking Water Act in the State.

§11005. Emergency training and review of emergency systems

[EPCRA §305]

(a) Emergency training

(1) Programs — Officials of the United States Government carrying out existing Federal programs for emergency training are authorized to specifically provide training and education programs for Federal, State, and local personnel in hazard mitigation, emergency preparedness, fire prevention and control, disaster response, long-term disaster recovery, national security, technological and natural hazards, and emergency processes. Such programs shall provide special emphasis for such training and education with respect to hazardous chemicals.

(2) State and local program support — There is authorized to be appropriated to the Federal Emergency Management Agency for each of the fiscal years 1987, 1988, 1989, and 1990, $5,000,000 for making grants to support programs of State and local governments, and to support university-sponsored programs, which are designed to improve emergency planning, preparedness, mitigation, response, and recovery capabilities. Such programs shall provide special emphasis with respect to emergencies associated with hazardous chemicals. Such grants may not exceed 80 percent of the cost of any such program. The remaining 20 percent of such costs shall be funded from non-Federal sources.

(3) Other programs — Nothing in this section shall affect the availability of appropriations to the Federal Emergency Management Agency for any programs carried out by such agency other than the programs referred to in paragraph (2).

(b) Review of emergency systems

(1) Review — The Administrator shall initiate, not later than 30 days after October 17, 1986, a review of emergency systems for monitoring, detecting, and preventing releases of extremely hazardous substances at representative domestic facilities that produce, use, or store extremely hazardous substances. The Administrator may select representative extremely hazardous substances from the substances on the list referred to in section 11002(a) of this title for the purposes of this review. The Administrator shall report interim findings to the Congress not later than seven months after October 17, 1986, and issue a final report of findings and recommendations to the Congress not later than 18 months after October 17, 1986. Such report shall be prepared in consultation with the States and appropriate Federal agencies.

(2) Report — The report required by this subsection shall include the Administrator's findings regarding each of the following:

(A) The status of current technological capabilities to (i) monitor, detect, and prevent, in a timely manner, significant releases of extremely hazardous substances, (ii) determine the magnitude and direction of the hazard posed by each release, (iii) identify specific substances, (iv) provide data on the specific chemical composition of such releases, and (v) determine the relative concentrations of the constituent substances.

(B) The status of public emergency alert devices or systems for providing timely and effective public warning of an accidental release of extremely hazardous substances into the environment, including releases into the atmosphere, surface water, or groundwater from facilities that produce, store, or use significant quantities of such extremely hazardous substances.

(C) The technical and economic feasibility of establishing, maintaining, and operating perimeter alert systems for detecting releases of such extremely hazardous substances into the atmosphere, surface water, or groundwater, at facilities that manufacture, use, or store significant quantities of such substances.

(3) Recommendations — The report required by this subsection shall also include the Administrator's recommendations for

(A) initiatives to support the development of new or improved technologies or systems that would facilitate the timely monitoring, detection, and prevention of releases of extremely hazardous substances, and

(B) improving devices or systems for effectively alerting the public in a timely manner, in the event of an accidental release of such extremely hazardous substances.

SUBCHAPTER II — REPORTING REQUIREMENTS

§11021. Material safety data sheets
[EPCRA §311]

(a) Basic requirement

(1) Submission of MSDS or list — The owner or operator of any facility which is required to prepare or have available a material safety data sheet for a hazardous chemical under the Occupational Safety and Health Act of 1970 [29 U.S.C. §§651 *et seq.*] and regulations promulgated under that Act shall submit a material safety data sheet for each such chemical, or a list of such chemicals as described in paragraph (2), to each of the following:

(A) The appropriate local emergency planning committee.

(B) The State emergency response commission.

(C) The fire department with jurisdiction over the facility.

(2) Contents of list

(A) The list of chemicals referred to in paragraph (1) shall include each of the following:

(i) A list of the hazardous chemicals for which a material safety data sheet is required under the Occupational Safety and Health Act of 1970 [29 U.S.C. §§651 *et seq.*] and regulations promulgated under that Act, grouped in categories of health and physical hazards as set forth under such Act and regulations promulgated under such Act, or in such other categories as the Administrator may prescribe under subparagraph (B).

(ii) The chemical name or the common name of each such chemical as provided on the material safety data sheet.

(iii) Any hazardous component of each such chemical as provided on the material safety data sheet.

(B) For purposes of the list under this paragraph, the Administrator may modify the categories of health and physical hazards as set forth under the Occupational Safety and Health Act of 1970 [29 U.S.C. §§651 *et seq.*] and regulations promulgated under that Act by requiring information to be reported in terms of groups of hazardous chemicals which present similar hazards in an emergency.

(3) Treatment of mixtures — An owner or operator may meet the requirements of this section with respect to a hazardous chemical which is a mixture by doing one of the following:

(A) Submitting a material safety data sheet for, or identifying on a list, each element or compound in the mixture which is a hazardous chemical. If more than one mixture has the same element or compound, only one material safety data sheet, or one listing, of the element or compound is necessary.

(B) Submitting a material safety data sheet for, or identifying on a list, the mixture itself.

(b) Thresholds — The Administrator may establish threshold quantities for hazardous chemicals below which no facility shall be subject to the provisions of this section. The threshold quantities may, in the Administrator's discretion, be based on classes of chemicals or categories of facilities.

(c) Availability of MSDS on request

(1) To local emergency planning committee — If an owner or operator of a facility submits a list of chemicals under subsection (a)(1) of this section, the owner or operator, upon request by the local emergency planning committee, shall submit the material safety data sheet for any chemical on the list to such committee.

(2) To public — A local emergency planning committee, upon request by any person, shall make available a material safety data sheet to the person in accordance with section 11044 of this title. If the local emergency planning committee does not have the requested material safety data sheet, the committee shall request the sheet from the facility owner or operator and then make the sheet available to the person in accordance with section 11044 of this title.

(d) Initial submission and updating

(1) The initial material safety data sheet or list required under this section with respect to a hazardous chemical shall be provided before the later of —

(A) 12 months after October 17, 1986, or

(B) 3 months after the owner or operator of a facility is required to prepare or have available a material safety data sheet for the chemical under the Occupational Safety and Health Act of 1970 [29 U.S.C. §§651 *et seq.*] and regulations promulgated under that Act.

(2) Within 3 months following discovery by an owner or operator of significant new information concerning an aspect of a hazardous chemical for which a material safety data sheet was previously submitted to the local emergency planning committee under subsection (a) of this section, a revised sheet shall be provided to such person.

(e) "Hazardous chemical" defined — For purposes of this section, the term "hazardous chemical" has the meaning given such term by section 1910.1200(c) of Title 29 of the Code of Federal Regulations, except that such term does not include the following:

(1) Any food, food additive, color additive, drug, or cosmetic regulated by the Food and Drug Administration.

(2) Any substance present as a solid in any manufactured item to the extent exposure to the substance does not occur under normal conditions of use.

(3) Any substance to the extent it is used for personal, family, or household purposes, or is present in the same form and concentration as a product packaged for distribution and use by the general public.

(4) Any substance to the extent it is used in a research laboratory or a hospital or other medical facility under the direct supervision of a technically qualified individual.

(5) Any substance to the extent it is used in routine agricultural operations or is a fertilizer held for sale by a retailer to the ultimate customer.

§11022. Emergency and hazardous chemical inventory forms
[EPCRA §312]

(a) Basic requirement

(1) The owner or operator of any facility which is required to prepare or have available a material safety data sheet for a hazardous chemical under the Occupational Safety and Health Act of 1970 [29 U.S.C. §§651 *et seq.*] and regulations promulgated under that Act shall prepare and submit an emergency and hazardous chemical inventory form (hereafter in this chapter referred to as an "inventory form") to each of the following:

(A) The appropriate local emergency planning committee.

(B) The State emergency response commission.

(C) The fire department with jurisdiction over the facility.

(2) The inventory form containing tier I information (as described in subsection (d)(1) of this section) shall be submitted on or before March 1, 1988, and annually thereafter on March 1, and shall contain data with respect to the preceding calendar year. The preceding sentence does not apply if an owner or operator provides, by the same deadline and with respect to the same calendar year, tier II information (as described in subsection (d)(2) of this section) to the recipients described in paragraph (1).

(3) An owner or operator may meet the requirements of this section with respect to a hazardous chemical which is a mixture by doing one of the following:

(A) Providing information on the inventory form on each element or compound in the mixture which is a hazardous chemical. If more than one mixture has the same element or compound, only one listing on the inventory form for the element or compound at the facility is necessary.

(B) Providing information on the inventory form on the mixture itself.

(b) Thresholds — The Administrator may establish threshold quantities for hazardous chemicals covered by this section below which no facility shall be subject to the provisions of this section. The threshold quantities may, in the Administrator's discretion, be based on classes of chemicals or categories of facilities.

(c) Hazardous chemicals covered — A hazardous chemical subject to the requirements of this section is any hazardous chemical for which a material safety data sheet or a listing is required under section 11021 of this title.

(d) Contents of form

(1) Tier I information

(A) Aggregate information by category — An inventory form shall provide the information described in subparagraph (B) in aggregate terms for hazardous chemicals in categories of health and physical hazards as set forth under the Occupational Safety and Health Act of 1970 [29 U.S.C. §§651 *et seq.*] and regulations promulgated under that Act.

(B) Required information — The information referred to in subparagraph (A) is the following:

(i) An estimate (in ranges) of the maximum amount of hazardous chemicals in each category present at the facility at any time during the preceding calendar year.

(ii) An estimate (in ranges) of the average daily amount of hazardous chemicals in each category present at the facility during the preceding calendar year.

(iii) The general location of hazardous chemicals in each category.

(C) Modifications — For purposes of reporting information under this paragraph, the Administrator may —

(i) modify the categories of health and physical hazards as set forth under the Occupational Safety and Health Act of 1970 [29 U.S.C. §§651 *et seq.*] and regulations promulgated under that Act by requiring information to be reported in terms of groups of hazardous chemicals which present similar hazards in an emergency, or

(ii) require reporting on individual hazardous chemicals of special concern to emergency response personnel.

(2) Tier II information — An inventory form shall provide the following additional information for each hazardous chemical present at the facility, but only upon request and in accordance with subsection (e) of this section:

(A) The chemical name or the common name of the chemical as provided on the material safety data sheet.

(B) An estimate (in ranges) of the maximum amount of the hazardous chemical present at the facility at any time during the preceding calendar year.

(C) An estimate (in ranges) of the average daily amount of the hazardouschemical present at the facility during the preceding calendar year.

(D) A brief description of the manner of storage of the hazardous chemical.

(E) The location at the facility of the hazardous chemical.

(F) An indication of whether the owner elects to withhold location information of a specific hazardous chemical from disclosure to the public under section 11044 of this title.

(e) Availability of tier II information

(1) Availability to State commissions, local committees, and fire departments — Upon request by a State emergency response commission, a local emergency planning committee, or a fire department with jurisdiction over the facility, the owner or operator of a facility shall provide tier II information, as described in subsection (d) of this section, to the person making the request. Any such request shall be with respect to a specific facility.

(2) Availability to other State and local officials — A State or local official acting in his or her official capacity may have access to tier II information by submitting a request to the State emergency response commission or the local emergency planning committee. Upon receipt of a request for tier II information, the State commission or local committee shall, pursuant to paragraph (1), request the facility owner or operator for the tier II information and make available such information to the official.

(3) Availability to public

(A) In general — Any person may request a State emergency response commission or local emergency planning committee for tier II information relating to the preceding calendar year with respect to a facility. Any such request shall be in writing and shall be with respect to a specific facility.

(B) Automatic provision of information to public — Any tier II information which a State emergency response commission or local emergency planning committee has in its possession shall be made available to a person making a request under this paragraph in accordance with section 11044 of this title. If the State emergency response commission or local emergency planning committee does not have the tier II information in its possession, upon a request for tier II information the State emergency response commission or local emergency planning committee shall, pursuant to paragraph (1), request the facility owner or operator for tier II information with respect to a hazardous chemical which a facility has stored in an amount in excess of 10,000 pounds present at the facility at any time during the preceding calendar year and make such information available in accordance with section 11044 of this title to the person making the request.

(C) Discretionary provision of information to public — In the case of tier II information which is not in the possession of a State emergency response commission or local emergency planning committee and which is with respect to a hazardous chemical which a facility has stored in an amount less than 10,000 pounds present at the facility at any time during the preceding calendar year, a request from a person must include the general need for the information. The State emergency response commission or local emergency planning committee may, pursuant to paragraph (1), request the facility owner or operator for the tier II information on behalf of the person making the request. Upon receipt of any information requested on behalf of such person, the State emergency response commission or local emergency planning committee shall make the information available in accordance with section 11044 of this title to the person.

(D) Response in 45 days — A State emergency response commission or local emergency planning committee shall respond to a request for tier II information under this paragraph no later than 45 days after the date of receipt of the request.

(4) Availability to community water systems

(A) In general — An affected community water system may have access to tier II information by submitting a request to the State emergency response commission or the local emergency planning committee. Upon receipt of a request for tier II information, the State commission or local committee shall, pursuant to paragraph (1), request the facility owner or operator for the tier II information and make available such information to the affected community water system.

(B) Definition — In this paragraph, the term "affected community water system" means a community water system (as defined in section 300f(15) of this title) that receives supplies of drinking water from a source water area, delineated under section 300j-13 of this title, in which a facility that is required to prepare and submit an inventory form under subsection (a)(1) is located.

(f) Fire department access — Upon request to an owner or operator of a facility which files an inventory form under this section by the fire department with jurisdiction over the facility, the owner or operator of the facility shall allow the fire department to conduct an on-site inspection of the facility and shall provide to the fire department specific location information on hazardous chemicals at the facility.

(g) Format of forms — The Administrator shall publish a uniform format for inventory forms within three months after October 17, 1986. If the Administrator does not publish such forms, owners and operators of facilities subject to the requirements of this section shall provide the information required under this section by letter.

§11023. Toxic chemical release forms
[EPCRA §313]

(a) Basic requirement — The owner or operator of a facility subject to the requirements of this section shall complete a toxic chemical release form as published under subsection (g) of this section for each toxic chemical listed under subsection (c) of this section that was manufactured, processed, or otherwise used in quantities exceeding the toxic chemical threshold quantity established by subsection (f) of this section during the preceding calendar year at such facility. Such form shall be submitted to the Administrator and to an official or officials of the State designated by the Governor on or before July 1, 1988, and annually thereafter on July 1 and shall contain data reflecting releases during the preceding calendar year.

(b) Covered owners and operators of facilities

(1) In general

(A) The requirements of this section shall apply to owners and operators of facilities that have 10 or more full-time employees and that are in Standard Industrial Classification Codes 20 through 39 (as in effect on July 1, 1985) and that manufactured, processed, or otherwise used a toxic chemical listed under subsection (c) of this section in excess of the quantity of that toxic chemical established under subsection (f) of this section during the calendar year for which a release form is required under this section.

(B) The Administrator may add or delete Standard Industrial Classification Codes for purposes of subparagraph (A), but only to the extent necessary to provide that each Standard Industrial Code to which this section applies is relevant to the purposes of this section.

(C) For purposes of this section —

(i) The term "manufacture" means to produce, prepare, import, or compound a toxic chemical.

(ii) The term "process" means the preparation of a toxic chemical, after its manufacture, for distribution in commerce —

(I) in the same form or physical state as, or in a different form or physical state from, that in which it was received by the person so preparing such chemical, or

(II) as part of an article containing the toxic chemical.

(2) Discretionary application to additional facilities — The Administrator, on his own motion or at the request of a Governor of a State (with regard to facilities located in that State), may apply the requirements of this section to the owners and operators of any particular facility that manufactures, processes, or otherwise uses a toxic chemical listed under subsection (c) of this section if the Administrator determines that such action is warranted on the basis of toxicity of the toxic chemical, proximity to other facilities that release the toxic chemical or to population centers, the history of releases of such chemical at such facility, or such other factors as the Administrator deems appropriate.

(c) Toxic chemicals covered

The toxic chemicals subject to the requirements of this section are —

(1) the chemicals on the list in Committee Print Number 99-169 of the Senate Committee on Environment and Public Works, titled "Toxic Chemicals Subject to Section 313 of the Emergency Planning and Community Right-To-Know Act of 1986" (including any revised version of the list as may be made pursuant to subsection (d) or (e)); and

(2) the chemicals included on such list under subsections (b)(1), (c)(1), and (d)(3) of section 8921 of Title 15.

(d) Revisions by Administrator

(1) In general — The Administrator may by rule add or delete a chemical from the list described in subsection (c) of this section at any time.

(2) Additions — A chemical may be added if the Administrator determines, in his judgment, that there is sufficient evidence to establish any one of the following:

(A) The chemical is known to cause or can reasonably be anticipated to cause significant adverse acute human health effects at concentration levels that are reasonably likely to exist beyond facility site boundaries as a result of continuous, or frequently recurring, releases.

(B) The chemical is known to cause or can reasonably be anticipated to cause in humans —

(i) cancer or teratogenic effects, or

(ii) serious or irreversible —

(I) reproductive dysfunctions,

(II) neurological disorders,

(III) heritable genetic mutations, or

(IV) other chronic health effects.

(C) The chemical is known to cause or can reasonably be anticipated to cause, because of —

(i) its toxicity,

(ii) its toxicity and persistence in the environment, or

(iii) its toxicity and tendency to bioaccumulate in the environment,

a significant adverse effect on the environment of sufficient seriousness, in the judgment of the Administrator, to warrant reporting under this section. The number of chemicals included on the list described in subsection (c) of this section on the basis of the preceding sentence may constitute in the aggregate no more than 25 percent of the total number of chemicals on the list.

A determination under this paragraph shall be based on generally accepted scientific principles or laboratory tests, or appropriately designed and conducted epidemiological or other population studies, available to the Administrator.

(3) Deletions — A chemical may be deleted if the Administrator determines there is not sufficient evidence to establish any of the criteria described in paragraph (2).

(4) Effective date — Any revision made on or after January 1 and before December 1 of any calendar year shall take effect beginning with the next calendar year. Any revision made on or after December 1 of any calendar year and before January 1 of the next calendar year shall take effect beginning with the calendar year following such next calendar year.

(e) Petitions

(1) In general — Any person may petition the Administrator to add or delete a chemical from the list described in subsection (c) of this section on the basis of the criteria in subparagraph (A) or (B) of subsection (d)(2) of this section. Within 180 days after receipt of a petition, the Administrator shall take one of the following actions:

(A) Initiate a rulemaking to add or delete the chemical to the list, in accordance with subsection (d)(2) or (d)(3) of this section.

(B) Publish an explanation of why the petition is denied.

(2) Governor petitions — A State Governor may petition the Administrator to add or delete a chemical from the list described in subsection (c) of this section on the basis of the criteria in subparagraph (A), (B), or (C) of subsection (d)(2) of this section. In the case of such a petition from a State Governor to delete a chemical, the petition shall be treated in the same manner as a petition received under paragraph (1) to delete a chemical. In the case of such a petition from a State Governor to add a chemical, the chemical will be added to the list within 180 days after receipt of the petition, unless the Administrator —

(A) initiates a rulemaking to add the chemical to the list, in accordance with subsection (d)(2) of this section, or

(B) publishes an explanation of why the Administrator believes the petition does not meet the requirements of subsection (d)(2) of this section for adding a chemical to the list.

(f) Threshold for reporting

(1) Toxic chemical threshold amount — The threshold amounts for purposes of reporting toxic chemicals under this section are as follows:

(A) With respect to a toxic chemical used at a facility, 10,000 pounds of the toxic chemical per year.

(B) With respect to a toxic chemical manufactured or processed at a facility —

(i) For the toxic chemical release form required to be submitted under this section on or before July 1, 1988, 75,000 pounds of the toxic chemical per year.

(ii) For the form required to be submitted on or before July 1, 1989, 50,000 pounds of the toxic chemical per year.

(iii) For the form required to be submitted on or before July 1, 1990, and for each form thereafter, 25,000 pounds of the toxic chemical per year.

(2) Revisions — The Administrator may establish a threshold amount for a toxic chemical different from the amount established by paragraph (1). Such revised threshold shall obtain reporting on a substantial majority of total releases of the chemical at all facilities subject to the requirements of this section. The amounts established under this paragraph may, at the Administrator's discretion, be based on classes of chemicals or categories of facilities.

(g) Form

(1) Information required — Not later than June 1, 1987, the Administrator shall publish a

uniform toxic chemical release form for facilities covered by this section. If the Administrator does not publish such a form, owners and operators of facilities subject to the requirements of this section shall provide the information required under this subsection by letter postmarked on or before the date on which the form is due. Such form shall —

(A) provide for the name and location of, and principal business activities at, the facility;

(B) include an appropriate certification, signed by a senior official with management responsibility for the person or persons completing the report, regarding the accuracy and completeness of the report; and

(C) provide for submission of each of the following items of information for each listed toxic chemical known to be present at the facility:

(i) Whether the toxic chemical at the facility is manufactured, processed, or otherwise used, and the general category or categories of use of the chemical.

(ii) An estimate of the maximum amounts (in ranges) of the toxic chemical present at the facility at any time during the preceding calendar year.

(iii) For each wastestream, the waste treatment or disposal methods employed, and an estimate of the treatment efficiency typically achieved by such methods for that wastestream.

(iv) The annual quantity of the toxic chemical entering each environmental medium.

(2) Use of available data — In order to provide the information required under this section, the owner or operator of a facility may use readily available data (including monitoring data) collected pursuant to other provisions of law, or, where such data are not readily available, reasonable estimates of the amounts involved. Nothing in this section requires the monitoring or measurement of the quantities, concentration, or frequency of any toxic chemical released into the environment beyond that monitoring and measurement required under other provisions of law or regulation. In order to assure consistency, the Administrator shall require that data be expressed in common units.

(h) Use of release form — The release forms required under this section are intended to provide information to the Federal, State, and local governments and the public, including citizens of communities surrounding covered facilities. The release form shall be available, consistent with section 11044(a) of this title, to inform persons about releases of toxic chemicals to the environment; to assist governmental agencies, researchers, and other persons in the conduct of research and data gathering; to aid in the development of appropriate regulations, guidelines, and standards; and for other similar purposes.

(i) Modifications in reporting frequency

(1) In general — The Administrator may modify the frequency of submitting a report under this section, but the Administrator may not modify the frequency to be any more often than annually. A modification may apply, either nationally or in a specific geographic area, to the following:

(A) All toxic chemical release forms required under this section.

(B) A class of toxic chemicals or a category of facilities.

(C) A specific toxic chemical.

(D) A specific facility.

(2) Requirements — A modification may be made under paragraph (1) only if the Administrator —

(A) makes a finding that the modification is consistent with the provisions of subsection (h) of this section, based on —

(i) experience from previously submitted toxic chemical release forms, and

(ii) determinations made under paragraph (3), and

(B) the finding is made by a rulemaking in accordance with section 553 of Title 5.

(3) Determinations — The Administrator shall make the following determinations with respect to a proposed modification before making a modification under paragraph (1):

(A) The extent to which information relating to the proposed modification provided on the toxic chemical release forms has been used by the Administrator or other agencies of the Federal Government, States, local governments, health professionals, and the public.

(B) The extent to which the information is (i) readily available to potential users from other sources, such as State reporting programs, and (ii) provided to the Administrator under another Federal law or through a State program.

(C) The extent to which the modification would impose additional and unreasonable burdens on facilities subject to the reporting requirements under this section.

(4) 5-year review — Any modification made under this subsection shall be reviewed at least once every 5 years. Such review shall examine the modification and ensure that the requirements of paragraphs (2) and (3) still justify continuation of the modification. Any change to a modification reviewed under this paragraph shall be made in accordance with this subsection.

(5) Notification to Congress — The Administrator shall notify Congress of an intention to initiate a rulemaking for a modification under this subsection. After such notification, the Administrator shall delay initiation of the rulemaking for at

least 12 months, but no more than 24 months, after the date of such notification.

(6) Judicial review — In any judicial review of a rulemaking which establishes a modification under this subsection, a court may hold unlawful and set aside agency action, findings, and conclusions found to be unsupported by substantial evidence.

(7) Applicability — A modification under this subsection may apply to a calendar year or other reporting period beginning no earlier than January 1, 1993.

(8) Effective date — Any modification made on or after January 1 and before December 1 of any calendar year shall take effect beginning with the next calendar year. Any modification made on or after December 1 of any calendar year and before January 1 of the next calendar year shall take effect beginning with the calendar year following such next calendar year.

(j) EPA management of data — The Administrator shall establish and maintain in a computer data base a national toxic chemical inventory based on data submitted to the Administrator under this section. The Administrator shall make these data accessible by computer telecommunication and other means to any person on a cost reimbursable basis.

(k) Report — Not later than June 30, 1991, the Comptroller General, in consultation with the Administrator and appropriate officials in the States, shall submit to the Congress a report including each of the following:

(1) A description of the steps taken by the Administrator and the States to implement the requirements of this section, including steps taken to make information collected under this section available to and accessible by the public.

(2) A description of the extent to which the information collected under this section has been used by the Environmental Protection Agency, other Federal agencies, the States, and the public, and the purposes for which the information has been used.

(3) An identification and evaluation of options for modifications to the requirements of this section for the purpose of making information collected under this section more useful.

(*l*) Mass balance study

(1) In general — The Administrator shall arrange for a mass balance study to be carried out by the National Academy of Sciences using mass balance information collected by the Administrator under paragraph (3). The Administrator shall submit to Congress a report on such study no later than 5 years after October 17, 1986.

(2) Purposes — The purposes of the study are as follows:

(A) To assess the value of mass balance analysis in determining the accuracy of information on toxic chemical releases.

(B) To assess the value of obtaining mass balance information, or portions thereof, to determine the waste reduction efficiency of different facilities, or categories of facilities, including the effectiveness of toxic chemical regulations promulgated under laws other than this chapter.

(C) To assess the utility of such information for evaluating toxic chemical management practices at facilities, or categories of facilities, covered by this section.

(D) To determine the implications of mass balance information collection on a national scale similar to the mass balance information collection carried out by the Administrator under paragraph (3), including implications of the use of such collection as part of a national annual quantity toxic chemical release program.

(3) Information collection

(A) The Administrator shall acquire available mass balance information from States which currently conduct (or during the 5 years after October 17, 1986 initiate) a mass balance-oriented annual quantity toxic chemical release program. If information from such States provides an inadequate representation of industry classes and categories to carry out the purposes of the study, the Administrator also may acquire mass balance information necessary for the study from a representative number of facilities in other States.

(B) Any information acquired under this section shall be available to the public, except that upon a showing satisfactory to the Administrator by any person that the information (or a particular part thereof) to which the Administrator or any officer, employee, or representative has access under this section if made public would divulge information entitled to protection under section 1905 of Title 18, such information or part shall be considered confidential in accordance with the purposes of that section, except that such information or part may be disclosed to other officers, employees, or authorized representatives of the United States concerned with carrying out this section.

(C) The Administrator may promulgate regulations prescribing procedures for collecting mass balance information under this paragraph.

(D) For purposes of collecting mass balance information under subparagraph (A), the Administrator may require the submission of information by a State or facility.

(4) Mass balance definition — For purposes of this subsection, the term "mass balance" means an accumulation of the annual quantities of chemicals transported to a facility, produced at a

facility, consumed at a facility, used at a facility, accumulated at a facility, released from a facility, and transported from a facility as a waste or as a commercial product or byproduct or component of a commercial product or byproduct.

SUBCHAPTER III — GENERAL PROVISIONS

§11041. Relationship to other law
[EPCRA §321]

(a) In general — Nothing in this chapter shall —

(1) preempt any State or local law,

(2) except as provided in subsection (b) of this section, otherwise affect any State or local law or the authority of any State or local government to adopt or enforce any State or local law, or

(3) affect or modify in any way the obligations or liabilities of any person under other Federal law.

(b) Effect on MSDS requirements — Any State or local law enacted after August 1, 1985, which requires the submission of a material safety data sheet from facility owners or operators shall require that the data sheet be identical in content and format to the data sheet required under subsection (a) of section 11021 of this title. In addition, a State or locality may require the submission of information which is supplemental to the information required on the data sheet (including information on the location and quantity of hazardous chemicals present at the facility), through additional sheets attached to the data sheet or such other means as the State or locality considers appropriate.

§11042. Trade secrets
[EPCRA §322]
(a) Authority to withhold information

(1) General authority

(A) With regard to a hazardous chemical, an extremely hazardous substance, or a toxic chemical, any person required under section 11003(d)(2), 11003(d)(3), 11021, 11022, or 11023 of this title to submit information to any other person may withhold from such submittal the specific chemical identity (including the chemical name and other specific identification), as defined in regulations prescribed by the Administrator under subsection (c) of this section, if the person complies with paragraph (2).

(B) Any person withholding the specific chemical identity shall, in the place on the submittal where the chemical identity would normally be included, include the generic class or category of the hazardous chemical, extremely hazardous substance, or toxic chemical (as the case may be).

(2) Requirements

(A) A person is entitled to withhold information under paragraph (1) if such person —

(i) claims that such information is a trade secret, on the basis of the factors enumerated in subsection (b) of this section,

(ii) includes in the submittal referred to in paragraph (1) an explanation of the reasons why such information is claimed to be a trade secret, based on the factors enumerated in subsection (b) of this section, including a specific description of why such factors apply, and

(iii) submits to the Administrator a copy of such submittal, and the information withheld from such submittal.

(B) In submitting to the Administrator the information required by subparagraph (A)(iii), a person withholding information under this subsection may —

(i) designate, in writing and in such manner as the Administrator may prescribe by regulation, the information which such person believes is entitled to be withheld under paragraph (1), and

(ii) submit such designated information separately from other information submitted under this subsection.

(3) Limitation — The authority under this subsection to withhold information shall not apply to information which the Administrator has determined, in accordance with subsection (c) of this section, is not a trade secret.

(b) Trade secret factors — No person required to provide information under this chapter may claim that the information is entitled to protection as a trade secret under subsection (a) of this section unless such person shows each of the following:

(1) Such person has not disclosed the information to any other person, other than a member of a local emergency planning committee, an officer or employee of the United States or a State or local government, an employee of such person, or a person who is bound by a confidentiality agreement, and such person has taken reasonable measures to protect the confidentiality of such information and intends to continue to take such measures.

(2) The information is not required to be disclosed, or otherwise made available, to the public under any other Federal or State law.

(3) Disclosure of the information is likely to cause substantial harm to the competitive position of such person.

(4) The chemical identity is not readily discoverable through reverse engineering.

(c) Trade secret regulations — As soon as practicable after October 17, 1986, the Administrator shall prescribe regulations to implement this section. With respect to subsection (b)(4) of this section, such regulations shall be equivalent to comparable provisions in the Occupational Safety and Health Administration Hazard Communication Standard (29 C.F.R. 1910.1200) and any revisions of such standard prescribed by the Secretary of Labor in accordance with the final ruling of the courts of the United States in United Steelworkers of America, AFL-CIO-CLC v. Thorne G. Auchter.

(d) Petition for review

(1) In general — Any person may petition the Administrator for the disclosure of the specific chemical identity of a hazardous chemical, an extremely hazardous substance, or a toxic chemical which is claimed as a trade secret under this section. The Administrator may, in the absence of a petition under this paragraph, initiate a determination, to be carried out in accordance with this subsection, as to whether information withheld constitutes a trade secret.

(2) Initial review — Within 30 days after the date of receipt of a petition under paragraph (1) (or upon the Administrator's initiative), the Administrator shall review the explanation filed by a trade secret claimant under subsection (a)(2) of this section and determine whether the explanation presents assertions which, if true, are sufficient to support a finding that the specific chemical identity is a trade secret.

(3) Finding of sufficient assertions

(A) If the Administrator determines pursuant to paragraph (2) that the explanation presents sufficient assertions to support a finding that the specific chemical identity is a trade secret, the Administrator shall notify the trade secret claimant that he has 30 days to supplement the explanation with detailed information to support the assertions.

(B) If the Administrator determines, after receipt of any supplemental supporting detailed information under subparagraph (A), that the assertions in the explanation are true and that the specific chemical identity is a trade secret, the Administrator shall so notify the petitioner and the petitioner may seek judicial review of the determination.

(C) If the Administrator determines, after receipt of any supplemental supporting detailed information under subparagraph (A), that the assertions in the explanation are not true and that the specific chemical identity is not a trade secret, the Administrator shall notify the trade secret claimant that the Administrator intends to release the specific chemical identity. The trade secret claimant has 30 days in which he may appeal the Administrator's determination under this subparagraph to the Administrator. If the Administrator does not reverse his determination under this subparagraph in such an appeal by the trade secret claimant, the trade secret claimaint may seek

judicial review of the determination.

(4) Finding of insufficient assertions

(A) If the Administrator determines pursuant to paragraph (2) that the explanation presents insufficient assertions to support a finding that the specific chemical identity is a trade secret, the Administrator shall notify the trade secret claimant that he has 30 days to appeal the determination to the Administrator, or, upon a showing of good cause, amend the original explanation by providing supplementary assertions to support the trade secret claim.

(B) If the Administrator does not reverse his determination under subparagraph (A) after an appeal or an examination of any supplementary assertions under subparagraph (A), the Administrator shall so notify the trade secret claimant and the trade secret claimant may seek judicial review of the determination.

(C) If the Administrator reverses his determination under subparagraph (A) after an appeal or an examination of any supplementary assertions under subparagraph (A), the procedures under paragraph (3) of this subsection apply.

(e) Exception for information provided to health professionals

— Nothing in this section, or regulations adopted pursuant to this section, shall authorize any person to withhold information which is required to be provided to a health professional, a doctor, or a nurse in accordance with section 11043 of this title.

(f) Providing information to Administrator; availability to public

— Any information submitted to the Administrator under subsection (a)(2) of this section or subsection (d)(3) of this section (except a specific chemical identity) shall be available to the public, except that upon a showing satisfactory to the Administrator by any person that the information (or a particular part thereof) to which the Administrator has access under this section if made public would divulge information entitled to protection under section 1905 of Title 18, such information or part shall be considered confidential in accordance with the purposes of that section, except that such information or part may be disclosed to other officers, employees, or authorized representatives of the United States concerned with carrying out this chapter.

(g) Information provided to State

— Upon request by a State, acting through the Governor of the State, the Administrator shall provide to the State any information obtained under subsection (a)(2) of this section and subsection (d)(3) of this section.

(h) Information on adverse effects

(1) In any case in which the identity of a hazardous chemical or an extremely hazardous substance is claimed as a trade secret, the Gov-

ernor or State emergency response commission established under section 11001 of this title shall identify the adverse health effects associated with the hazardous chemical or extremely hazardous substance and shall assure that such information is provided to any person requesting information about such hazardous chemical or extremely hazardous substance.

(2) In any case in which the identity of a toxic chemical is claimed as a trade secret, the Administrator shall identify the adverse health and environmental effects associated with the toxic chemical and shall assure that such information is included in the computer database required by section 11023(j) of this title and is provided to any person requesting information about such toxic chemical.

(i) Information provided to Congress — Notwithstanding any limitation contained in this section or any other provision of law, all information reported to or otherwise obtained by the Administrator (or any representative of the Administrator) under this chapter shall be made available to a duly authorized committee of the Congress upon written request by such a committee.

§11043. Provision of information to health professionals, doctors, and nurses
[EPCRA §323]

(a) Diagnosis or treatment by health professional — An owner or operator of a facility which is subject to the requirements of section 11021, 11022, or 11023 of this title shall provide the specific chemical identity, if known, of a hazardous chemical, extremely hazardous substance, or a toxic chemical to any health professional who requests such information in writing if the health professional provides a written statement of need under this subsection and a written confidentiality agreement under subsection (d) of this section. The written statement of need shall be a statement that the health professional has a reasonable basis to suspect that —

(1) the information is needed for purposes of diagnosis or treatment of an individual,

(2) the individual or individuals being diagnosed or treated have been exposed to the chemical concerned, and

(3) knowledge of the specific chemical identity of such chemical will assist in diagnosis or treatment.

Following such a written request, the owner or operator to whom such request is made shall promptly provide the requested information to the health professional. The authority to withhold the specific chemical identity of a chemical under section 11042 of this title when such information is a trade secret shall not apply to information required to be provided under this subsection, subject to the provisions of subsection (d) of this section.

(b) Medical emergency — An owner or operator of a facility which is subject to the requirements of section 11021, 11022, or 11023 of this title shall provide a copy of a material safety data sheet, an inventory form, or a toxic chemical release form, including the specific chemical identity, if known, of a hazardous chemical, extremely hazardous substance, or a toxic chemical, to any treating physician or nurse who requests such information if such physician or nurse determines that —

(1) a medical emergency exists,

(2) the specific chemical identity of the chemical concerned is necessary for or will assist in emergency or first-aid diagnosis or treatment, and

(3) the individual or individuals being diagnosed or treated have been exposed to the chemical concerned.

Immediately following such a request, the owner or operator to whom such request is made shall provide the requested information to the physician or nurse. The authority to withhold the specific chemical identity of a chemical from a material safety data sheet, an inventory form, or a toxic chemical release form under section 11042 of this title when such information is a trade secret shall not apply to information required to be provided to a treating physician or nurse under this subsection. No written confidentiality agreement or statement of need shall be required as a precondition of such disclosure, but the owner or operator disclosing such information may require a written confidentiality agreement in accordance with subsection (d) of this section and a statement setting forth the items listed in paragraphs (1) through (3) as soon as circumstances permit.

(c) Preventive measures by local health professionals

(1) Provision of information — An owner or operator of a facility subject to the requirements of section 11021, 11022, or 11023 of this title shall provide the specific chemical identity, if known, of a hazardous chemical, an extremely hazardous substance, or a toxic chemical to any health professional (such as a physician, toxicologist, or epidemiologist) —

(A) who is a local government employee or a person under contract with the local government, and

(B) who requests such information in writing and provides a written statement of need under paragraph (2) and a written confidentiality agreement under subsection (d) of this section.

Following such a written request, the owner or operator to whom such request is made shall promptly provide the requested information to the local health professional. The authority to withhold the specific chemical identity of a chemical under section 11042 of this title when such information is a trade secret shall not apply to information required to be provided under this subsection, subject to the provisions of subsection

(d) of this section.

(2) Written statement of need — The written statement of need shall be a statement that describes with reasonable detail one or more of the following health needs for the information:

(A) To assess exposure of persons living in a local community to the hazards of the chemical concerned.

(B) To conduct or assess sampling to determine exposure levels of various population groups.

(C) To conduct periodic medical surveillance of exposed population groups.

(D) To provide medical treatment to exposed individuals or population groups.

(E) To conduct studies to determine the health effects of exposure.

(F) To conduct studies to aid in the identification of a chemical that may reasonably be anticipated to cause an observed health effect.

(d) Confidentiality agreement — Any person obtaining information under subsection (a) or (c) of this section shall, in accordance with such subsection (a) or (c) of this section, be required to agree in a written confidentiality agreement that he will not use the information for any purpose other than the health needs asserted in the statement of need, except as may otherwise be authorized by the terms of the agreement or by the person providing such information. Nothing in this subsection shall preclude the parties to a confidentiality agreement from pursuing any remedies to the extent permitted by law.

(e) Regulations — As soon as practicable after October 17, 1986, the Administrator shall promulgate regulations describing criteria and parameters for the statement of need under subsection (a) and (c) of this section and the confidentiality agreement under subsection (d) of this section.

§11044. Public availability of plans, data sheets, forms, and followup notices
[EPCRA §324]

(a) Availability to public — Each emergency response plan, material safety data sheet, list described in section 11021(a)(2) of this title, inventory form, toxic chemical release form, and followup emergency notice shall be made available to the general public, consistent with section 11042 of this title, during normal working hours at the location or locations designated by the Administrator, Governor, State emergency response commission, or local emergency planning committee, as appropriate. Upon request by an owner or operator of a facility subject to the requirements of section 11022 of this title, the State emergency response commission and the appropriate local emergency planning committee shall withhold from disclosure under this section the location of any specific chemical required by section 11022(d)(2) of this title to be contained in an inventory form as tier II information.

(b) Notice of public availability — Each local emergency planning committee shall annually publish a notice in local newspapers that the emergency response plan, material safety data sheets, and inventory forms have been submitted under this section. The notice shall state that followup emergency notices may subsequently be issued. Such notice shall announce that members of the public who wish to review any such plan, sheet, form, or followup notice may do so at the location designated under subsection (a) of this section.

§11045. Enforcement
[EPCRA §325]
(a) Civil penalties for emergency planning
— The Administrator may order a facility owner or operator (except an owner or operator of a facility designated under section 11002(b)(2) of this title) to comply with section 11002(c) of this title and section 11003(d) of this title. The United States district court for the district in which the facility is located shall have jurisdiction to enforce the order, and any person who violates or fails to obey such an order shall be liable to the United States for a civil penalty of not more than $25,000 for each day in which such violation occurs or such failure to comply continues.

(b) Civil, administrative, and criminal penalties for emergency notification

(1) Class I administrative penalty

(A) A civil penalty of not more than $25,000 per violation may be assessed by the Administrator in the case of a violation of the requirements of section 11004 of this title.

(B) No civil penalty may be assessed under this subsection unless the person accused of the violation is given notice and opportunity for a hearing with respect to the violation.

(C) In determining the amount of any penalty assessed pursuant to this subsection, the Administrator shall take into account the nature, circumstances, extent and gravity of the violation or violations and, with respect to the violator, ability to pay, any prior history of such violations, the degree of culpability, economic benefit or savings (if any) resulting from the violation, and such other matters as justice may require.

(2) Class II administrative penalty — A civil penalty of not more than $25,000 per day for each day during which the violation continues may be assessed by the Administrator in the case of a violation of the requirements of section 11004 of this title. In the case of a second or subsequent violation the amount of such penalty may be not more than $75,000 for each day during which the violation continues. Any civil penalty under this subsection shall be assessed and collected in the same manner, and subject to the same provisions, as in the case of civil penalties assessed and

collected under section 2615 of Title 15. In any proceeding for the assessment of a civil penalty under this subsection the Administrator may issue subpoenas for the attendance and testimony of witnesses and the production of relevant papers, books, and documents and may promulgate rules for discovery procedures.

(3) Judicial assessment — The Administrator may bring an action in the United States District court for the appropriate district to assess and collect a penalty of not more than $25,000 per day for each day during which the violation continues in the case of a violation of the requirements of section 11004 of this title. In the case of a second or subsequent violation, the amount of such penalty may be not more than $75,000 for each day during which the violation continues.

(4) Criminal penalties — Any person who knowingly and willfully fails to provide notice in accordance with section 11004 of this title shall, upon conviction, be fined not more than $25,000 or imprisoned for not more than two years, or both (or in the case of a second or subsequent conviction, shall be fined not more than $50,000 or imprisoned for not more than five years, or both).

(c) Civil and administrative penalties for reporting requirements

(1) Any person (other than a governmental entity) who violates any requirement of section 11022 or 11023 of this title shall be liable to the United States for a civil penalty in an amount not to exceed $25,000 for each such violation.

(2) Any person (other than a governmental entity) who violates any requirement of section 11021 or 11043(b) of this title, and any person who fails to furnish to the Administrator information required under section 11042(a)(2) of this title shall be liable to the United States for a civil penalty in an amount not to exceed $10,000 for each such violation.

(3) Each day a violation described in paragraph (1) or (2) continues shall, for purposes of this subsection, constitute a separate violation.

(4) The Administrator may assess any civil penalty for which a person is liable under this subsection by administrative order or may bring an action to assess and collect the penalty in the United States district court for the district in which the person from whom the penalty is sought resides or in which such person's principal place of business is located.

(d) Civil, administrative, and criminal penalties with respect to trade secrets

(1) Civil and administrative penalty for frivolous claims — If the Administrator determines —

(A)(i) under section 11042(d)(4) of this title that an explanation submitted by a trade secret claimant presents insufficient assertions to support a finding that a specific chemical identity is a trade secret, or (ii) after receiving supplemental supporting detailed information under section 11042(d)(3)(A) of this title, that the specific chemical identity is not a trade secret; and

(B) that the trade secret claim is frivolous, the trade secret claimant is liable for a penalty of $25,000 per claim. The Administrator may assess the penalty by administrative order or may bring an action in the appropriate district court of the United States to assess and collect the penalty.

(2) Criminal penalty for disclosure of trade secret information — Any person who knowingly and willfully divulges or discloses any information entitled to protection under section 11042 of this title shall, upon conviction, be subject to a fine of not more than $20,000 or to imprisonment not to exceed one year, or both.

(e) Special enforcement provisions for section 11043 — Whenever any facility owner or operator required to provide information under section 11043 of this title to a health professional who has requested such information fails or refuses to provide such information in accordance with such section, such health professional may bring an action in the appropriate United States district court to require such facility owner or operator to provide the information. Such court shall have jurisdiction to issue such orders and take such other action as may be necessary to enforce the requirements of section 11043 of this title.

(f) Procedures for administrative penalties

(1) Any person against whom a civil penalty is assessed under this section may obtain review thereof in the appropriate district court of the United States by filing a notice of appeal in such court within 30 days after the date of such order and by simultaneously sending a copy of such notice by certified mail to the Administrator. The Administrator shall promptly file in such court a certified copy of the record upon which such violation was found or such penalty imposed. If any person fails to pay an assessment of a civil penalty after it has become a final and unappealable order or after the appropriate court has entered final judgment in favor of the United States, the Administrator may request the Attorney General of the United States to institute a civil action in an appropriate district court of the United States to collect the penalty, and such court shall have jurisdiction to hear and decide any such action. In hearing such action, the court shall have authority to review the violation and the assessment of the civil penalty on the record.

(2) The Administrator may issue subpoenas for the attendance and testimony of witnesses and the production of relevant papers, books, or documents in connection with hearings under this section. In case of contumacy or refusal to obey a

subpoena issued pursuant to this paragraph and served upon any person, the district court of the United States for any district in which such person is found, resides, or transacts business, upon application by the United States and after notice to such person, shall have jurisdiction to issue an order requiring such person to appear and give testimony before the administrative law judge or to appear and produce documents before the administrative law judge, or both, and any failure to obey such order of the court may be punished by such court as a contempt thereof.

§11046. Civil actions
[EPCRA §326]
(a) Authority to bring civil actions

(1) Citizen suits — Except as provided in subsection (e) of this section, any person may commence a civil action on his own behalf against the following:

(A) An owner or operator of a facility for failure to do any of the following:

(i) Submit a followup emergency notice under section 11004(c) of this title.

(ii) Submit a material safety data sheet or a list under section 11021(a) of this title.

(iii) Complete and submit an inventory form under section 11022(a) of this title containing tier I information as described in section 11022(d)(1) of this title unless such requirement does not apply by reason of the second sentence of section 11022(a)(2) of this title.

(iv) Complete and submit a toxic chemical release form under section 11023(a) of this title.

(B) The Administrator for failure to do any of the following:

(i) Publish inventory forms under section 11022(g) of this title.

(ii) Respond to a petition to add or delete a chemical under section 11023(e)(1) of this title within 180 days after receipt of the petition.

(iii) Publish a toxic chemical release form under 11023(g) of this title.

(iv) Establish a computer database in accordance with section 11023(j) of this title.

(v) Promulgate trade secret regulations under section 11042(c) of this title.

(vi) Render a decision in response to a petition under section 11042(d) of this title within 9 months after receipt of the petition.

(C) The Administrator, a State Governor, or a State emergency response commission, for failure to provide a mechanism for public availability of information in accordance with section 11044(a) of this title.

(D) A State Governor or a State emergency response commission for failure to respond to a request for tier II information under section 11022(e)(3) of this title within 120 days after the date of receipt of the request.

(2) State or local suits

(A) Any State or local government may commence a civil action against an owner or operator of a facility for failure to do any of the following:

(i) Provide notification to the emergency response commission in the State under section 11002(c) of this title.

(ii) Submit a material safety data sheet or a list under section 11021(a) of this title.

(iii) Make available information requested under section 11021(c) of this title.

(iv) Complete and submit an inventory form under section 11022(a) of this title containing tier I information unless such requirement does not apply by reason of the second sentence of section 11022(a)(2) of this title.

(B) Any State emergency response commission or local emergency planning committee may commence a civil action against an owner or operator of a facility for failure to provide information under section 11003(d) of this title or for failure to submit tier II information under section 11022(e)(1) of this title.

(C) Any State may commence a civil action against the Administrator for failure to provide information to the State under section 11042(g) of this title.

(b) Venue

(1) Any action under subsection (a) of this section against an owner or operator of a facility shall be brought in the district court for the district in which the alleged violation occurred.

(2) Any action under subsection (a) of this section against the Administrator may be brought in the United States District Court for the District of Columbia.

(c) Relief

— The district court shall have jurisdiction in actions brought under subsection (a) of this section against an owner or operator of a facility to enforce the requirement concerned and to impose any civil penalty provided for violation of that requirement. The district court shall have jurisdiction in actions brought under subsection (a) of this section against the Administrator to order the Administrator to perform the act or duty concerned.

(d) Notice

(1) No action may be commenced under subsection (a)(1)(A) of this section prior to 60 days after the plaintiff has given notice of the alleged violation to the Administrator, the State in which the alleged violation occurs, and the alleged violator. Notice under this paragraph shall be given in such manner as the Administrator shall prescribe by regulation.

(2) No action may be commenced under subsection (a)(1)(B) or (a)(1)(C) of this section prior to 60 days after the date on which the plaintiff gives notice to the Administrator, State Governor, or State emergency response commission (as the case may be) that the plaintiff will commence the action. Notice under this paragraph shall be given in such manner as the Administrator shall prescribe by regulation.

(e) Limitation — No action may be commenced under subsection (a) of this section against an owner or operator of a facility if the Administrator has commenced and is diligently pursuing an administrative order or civil action to enforce the requirement concerned or to impose a civil penalty under this Act with respect to the violation of the requirement.

(f) Costs — The court, in issuing any final order in any action brought pursuant to this section, may award costs of litigation (including reasonable attorney and expert witness fees) to the prevailing or the substantially prevailing party whenever the court determines such an award is appropriate. The court may, if a temporary restraining order or preliminary injunction is sought, require the filing of a bond or equivalent security in accordance with the Federal Rules of Civil Procedure.

(g) Other rights — Nothing in this section shall restrict or expand any right which any person (or class of persons) may have under any Federal or State statute or common law to seek enforcement of any requirement or to seek any other relief (including relief against the Administrator or a State agency).

(h) Intervention

(1) By the United States — In any action under this section the United States or the State, or both, if not a party, may intervene as a matter of right.

(2) By persons — In any action under this section, any person may intervene as a matter of right when such person has a direct interest which is or may be adversely affected by the action and the disposition of the action may, as a practical matter, impair or impede the person's ability to protect that interest unless the Administrator or the State shows that the person's interest is adequately represented by existing parties in the action.

§11047. Exemption
[EPCRA §327]

Except as provided in section 11004 of this title, this chapter does not apply to the transportation, including the storage incident to such transportation, of any substance or chemical subject to the requirements of this chapter, including the transportation and distribution of natural gas.

§11048. Regulations
[EPCRA §328]

The Administrator may prescribe such regulations as may be necessary to carry out this chapter.

§11049. Definitions
[EPCRA §329]

For purposes of this chapter —

(1) Administrator — The term "Administrator" means the Administrator of the Environmental Protection Agency.

(2) Environment — The term "environment" includes water, air, and land and the interrelationship which exists among and between water, air, and land and all living things.

(3) Extremely hazardous substance — The term "extremely hazardous substance" means a substance on the list described in section 11002(a)(2) of this title.

(4) Facility — The term "facility" means all buildings, equipment, structures, and other stationary items which are located on a single site or on contiguous or adjacent sites and which are owned or operated by the same person (or by any person which controls, is controlled by, or under common control with, such person). For purposes of section 11004 of this title, the term includes motor vehicles, rolling stock, and aircraft.

(5) Hazardous chemical — The term "hazardous chemical" has the meaning given such term by section 11021(e) of this title.

(6) Material safety data sheet — The term "material safety data sheet" means the sheet required to be developed under section 1910.1200(g) of Title 29 of the Code of Federal Regulations, as that section may be amended from time to time.

(7) Person — The term "person" means any individual, trust, firm, joint stock company, corporation (including a government corporation), partnership, association, State, municipality, commission, political subdivision of a State, or interstate body.

(8) Release — The term "release" means any spilling, leaking, pumping, pouring, emitting, emptying, discharging, injecting, escaping, leaching, dumping, or disposing into the environment (including the abandonment or discarding of barrels, containers, and other closed receptacles) of any hazardous chemical, extremely hazardous substance, or toxic chemical.

(9) State — The term "State" means any State of the United States, the District of Columbia, the Commonwealth of Puerto Rico, Guam, American Samoa, the United States Virgin Islands, the Northern Mariana Islands, and any other territory or possession over which the United States has jurisdiction.

(10) Toxic chemical — The term "toxic chemical" means a substance on the list described in section 11023(c) of this title.

§11050. Authorization of appropriations
[EPCRA §330]

There are authorized to be appropriated for fiscal years beginning after September 30, 1986, such sums as may be necessary to carry out this chapter.

E. CALIFORNIA'S PROPOSITION 65

A GUIDE TO MATERIALS PERTAINING TO CALIFORNIA'S PROPOSITION 65 AVAILABLE ON THE INTERNET

California's Office of Environmental Health Hazard Assessment (OEHHA), the state's lead agency for implementing Proposition 65, maintains a website that provides comprehensive information about the law, including links to the safe harbor regulations promulgated to implement the legislation and risk assessment information. The website is located at *http://oehha.ca.gov/proposition-65*. OEHHA's Proposition 65 Implementation Office also can be contacted by telephone at (916) 445-6900.

An updated list of chemicals covered by Proposition 65 can be found at *https://oehha.ca.gov/proposition-65/ proposition-65-list*. News about developments pertaining to Proposition 65 can be found at *https://oehha .ca.gov/news-and-events*. A new website with extensive information about Proposition 65 warnings, listed chemicals, facts sheets, and Proposition 65's application to various product categories can be found at *www .p65warnings.ca.gov*.

PROPOSITION 65 LEGISLATIVE HISTORY TIMELINE

November 4, 1986: The Safe Drinking Water and Toxic Enforcement Act of 1986 is enacted by California voters when they overwhelmingly approve Proposition 65 at a statewide election. The law requires the governor of California to publish a list of chemicals known to the state to cause cancer, birth defects, or other reproductive harm. It prohibits companies with ten or more employees from knowingly discharging listed chemicals into sources of drinking water and it requires them to provide a "clear and reasonable" warning before knowingly exposing anyone to a listed chemical unless the company can demonstrate that the exposure it causes poses no significant risk.

August 30, 2002: Governor Gray Davis signs amendments to the Safe Drinking Water and Toxic Enforcement Act that specify factors for courts to consider in assessing civil penalties and approving settlements under the Act and that require private parties involved in enforcement actions to report to the Attorney General the results of settlements they reach.

August 9, 2003: Governor Gray Davis signs amendments to the Safe Drinking Water and Toxic Enforcement Act that establish a Safe Drinking Water and Toxic Enforcement Fund funded by civil and criminal penalties assessed under the Act. A portion of these penalties are to be paid to city or state government entities that bring enforcement actions or to citizens who report violations that are the subject of such actions.

October 5, 2013: Governor Jerry Brown signs AB 227 into law, which provides that prior to filing an enforcement action, a plaintiff must first give the alleged violator notice and an opportunity to come into compliance. If the alleged violation is corrected within 14 days the offender will pay only a $500 civil penalty. Only 25 percent of the $500 civil penalty will be given to the party bringing the enforcement action, with the remainder deposited in the Safe Drinking Water and Toxic Enforcement Fund.

OUTLINE OF THE PRINCIPAL PROVISIONS OF PROPOSITION 65

§25249.5 Prohibition on Contaminating Drinking Water: prohibits private businesses employing 10 or more persons from releasing any chemical known to the state to cause cancer or reproductive toxicity into water or onto land where it probably will cause a significant amount of the chemical to pass into any source of drinking water.

§25249.6 Required Warning Before Exposure: requires private businesses employing 10 or more persons to provide a clear and reasonable warning prior to exposing any individual to a chemical known to the state to cause cancer or reproductive toxicity.

§25249.7 Enforcement: provides penalties of up to $2,500 per day for each violation, authorizes injunctive relief, and allows enforcement actions to be brought by the state Attorney General or any person in the public interest.

§25249.8 List of Chemicals: requires the governor to publish a list of chemicals known to the state to cause cancer or reproductive toxicity.

§25249.10 Exemptions from Warning Requirement: exempts from the warning requirement exposures to carcinogens for which the person responsible can show that the exposure poses no significant cancer risk assuming lifetime expose at the level in question; exempts exposures to reproductive toxins for which the person responsible can show that the exposure will have no observable effect assuming exposure at 1,000 times the level in question.

Safe Drinking Water and Toxic Enforcement Act (Proposition 65)

Ch. 6.6 Calif. Health & Safety Code §§25249.5 to 25249.13

DIVISION 20 — MISCELLANEOUS HEALTH AND SAFETY PROVISIONS

CHAPTER 6.6 SAFE DRINKING WATER AND TOXIC ENFORCEMENT

§25249.5. Prohibition on contaminating drinking water with chemicals known to cause cancer or reproductive toxicity — No person in the course of doing business shall knowingly discharge or release a chemical known to the state to cause cancer or reproductive toxicity into water or onto or into land where such chemical passes or probably will pass into any source of drinking water, notwithstanding any other provision or authorization of law except as provided in Section 25249.9.

§25249.6. Required warning before exposure to chemicals known to cause cancer or reproductive toxicity — No person in the course of doing business shall knowingly and intentionally expose any individual to a chemical known to the state to cause cancer or reproductive toxicity without first giving clear and reasonable warning to such individual, except as provided in Section 25249.10.

§25249.7. Enforcement

(a) A person who violates or threatens to violate Section 25249.5 or 25249.6 may be enjoined in any court of competent jurisdiction.

(b)(1) A person who has violated Section 25249.5 or 25249.6 is liable for a civil penalty not to exceed two thousand five hundred dollars ($2,500) per day for each violation in addition to any other penalty established by law. That civil penalty may be assessed and recovered in a civil action brought in any court of competent jurisdiction.

(2) In assessing the amount of a civil penalty for a violation of this chapter, the court shall consider all of the following:

(A) The nature and extent of the violation.

(B) The number of, and severity of, the violations.

(C) The economic effect of the penalty on the violator.

(D) Whether the violator took good faith measures to comply with this chapter and the time these measures were taken.

(E) The willfulness of the violator's misconduct.

(F) The deterrent effect that the imposition of the penalty would have on both the violator and the regulated community as a whole.

(G) Any other factor that justice may require.

(c) Actions pursuant to this section may be brought by the Attorney General in the name of the people of the State of California, by a district attorney, by a city attorney of a city having a population in excess of 750,000, or, with the consent of the district attorney, by a city prosecutor in a city or city and county having a full-time city prosecutor, or as provided in subdivision (d).

(d) Actions pursuant to this section may be brought by a person in the public interest if both of the following requirements are met:

(1) The private action is commenced more than 60 days from the date that the person has given notice of an alleged violation of Section 25249.5 or 25249.6 that is the subject of the private action to the Attorney General and the district attorney, city attorney, or prosecutor in whose jurisdiction the violation is alleged to have occurred, and to the alleged violator. If the notice

alleges a violation of Section 25249.6, the notice of the alleged violation shall include a certificate of merit executed by the attorney for the noticing party, or by the noticing party, if the noticing party is not represented by an attorney. The certificate of merit shall state that the person executing the certificate has consulted with one or more persons with relevant and appropriate experience or expertise who has reviewed facts, studies, or other data regarding the exposure to the listed chemical that is the subject of the action, and that, based on that information, the person executing the certificate believes there is a reasonable and meritorious case for the private action. Factual information sufficient to establish the basis of the certificate of merit, including the information identified in paragraph (2) of subdivision (h), shall be attached to the certificate of merit that is served on the Attorney General.

(2) The Attorney General, a district attorney, a city attorney, or a prosecutor has not commenced and is not diligently prosecuting an action against the violation.

(e) A person bringing an action in the public interest pursuant to subdivision (d) and a person filing an action in which a violation of this chapter is alleged shall notify the Attorney General that the action has been filed. Neither this subdivision nor the procedures provided in subdivisions (f) to (k), inclusive, affect the requirements imposed by statute or a court decision in existence on January 1, 2002, concerning whether a person filing an action in which a violation of this chapter is alleged is required to comply with the requirements of subdivision (d).

(f)(1) A person filing an action in the public interest pursuant to subdivision (d), a private person filing an action in which a violation of this chapter is alleged, or a private person settling a violation of this chapter alleged in a notice given pursuant to paragraph (1) of subdivision (d), shall, after the action or violation is subject either to a settlement or to a judgment, submit to the Attorney General a reporting form that includes the results of that settlement or judgment and the final disposition of the case, even if dismissed. At the time of the filing of a judgment pursuant to an action brought in the public interest pursuant to subdivision (d), or an action brought by a private person in which a violation of this chapter is alleged, the plaintiff shall file an affidavit verifying that the report required by this subdivision has been accurately completed and submitted to the Attorney General.

(2) A person bringing an action in the public interest pursuant to subdivision (d), or a private person bringing an action in which a violation of this chapter is alleged, shall, after the action is either subject to a settlement, with or without court approval, or to a judgment, submit to the Attorney General a report that includes informa-

tion on any corrective action being taken as a part of the settlement or resolution of the action.

(3) The Attorney General shall develop a reporting form that specifies the information that shall be reported, including, but not limited to, for purposes of subdivision (e), the date the action was filed, the nature of the relief sought, and for purposes of this subdivision, the amount of the settlement or civil penalty assessed, other financial terms of the settlement, and any other information the Attorney General deems appropriate.

(4) If there is a settlement of an action brought by a person in the public interest under subdivision (d), the plaintiff shall submit the settlement, other than a voluntary dismissal in which no consideration is received from the defendant, to the court for approval upon noticed motion, and the court may approve the settlement only if the court makes all of the following findings:

(A) The warning that is required by the settlement complies with this chapter.

(B) The award of attorney's fees is reasonable under California law.

(C) The penalty amount is reasonable based on the criteria set forth in paragraph (2) of subdivision (b).

(5) The plaintiff subject to paragraph (4) has the burden of producing evidence sufficient to sustain each required finding. The plaintiff shall serve the motion and all supporting papers on the Attorney General, who may appear and participate in a proceeding without intervening in the case.

(6) Neither this subdivision nor the procedures provided in subdivision (e) and subdivisions (g) to (k), inclusive, affect the requirements imposed by statute or a court decision in existence on January 1, 2002, concerning whether claims raised by a person or public prosecutor not a party to the action are precluded by a settlement approved by the court.

(g) The Attorney General shall maintain a record of the information submitted pursuant to subdivisions (e) and (f) and shall make this information available to the public.

(h)(1) Except as provided in paragraph (2), the basis for the certificate of merit required by subdivision (d) is not discoverable. However, nothing in this subdivision precludes the discovery of information related to the certificate of merit if that information is relevant to the subject matter of the action and is otherwise discoverable, solely on the ground that it was used in support of the certificate of merit.

(2) Upon the conclusion of an action brought pursuant to subdivision (d) with respect to a defendant, if the trial court determines that there was no actual or threatened exposure to a listed chemical, the court may, upon the motion of that alleged violator or upon the court's own motion, review the basis for the belief of the person executing the

certificate of merit, expressed in the certificate of merit, that an exposure to a listed chemical had occurred or was threatened. The information in the certificate of merit, including the identity of the persons consulted with and relied on by the certifier, and the facts, studies, or other data reviewed by those persons, shall be disclosed to the court in an in-camera proceeding at which the moving party shall not be present. If the court finds that there was no credible factual basis for the certifier's belief that an exposure to a listed chemical had occurred or was threatened, then the action shall be deemed frivolous within the meaning of Section 128.7 of the Code of Civil Procedure. The court shall not find a factual basis credible on the basis of a legal theory of liability that is frivolous within the meaning of Section 128.7 of the Code of Civil Procedure.

(i) The Attorney General may provide the factual information submitted to establish the basis of the certificate of merit on request to a district attorney, city attorney, or prosecutor within whose jurisdiction the violation is alleged to have occurred, or to any other state or federal government agency, but in all other respects the Attorney General shall maintain, and ensure that all recipients maintain, the submitted information as confidential official information to the full extent authorized in Section 1040 of the Evidence Code.

(j) In an action brought by the Attorney General, a district attorney, a city attorney, or a prosecutor pursuant to this chapter, the Attorney General, district attorney, city attorney, or prosecutor may seek and recover costs and attorney's fees on behalf of a party who provides a notice pursuant to subdivision (d) and who renders assistance in that action.

(k) A person who serves a notice of alleged violation pursuant to paragraph (1) of subdivision (d) for an exposure identified in subparagraph (A), (B), (C), or (D) of paragraph (1) shall complete, as appropriate, and provide to the alleged violator at the time the notice of alleged violation is served, a notice of special compliance procedure and proof of compliance form pursuant to subdivision (*l*) and shall not file an action for that exposure against the alleged violator or recover from the alleged violator in a settlement any payment in lieu of penalties or any reimbursement for costs and attorney's fees, if all of the following conditions have been met:

(1) The notice given pursuant to paragraph (1) of subdivision (d) was served on or after October 5, 2013 and alleges that the alleged violator failed to provide clear and reasonable warning as required under Section 25249.6 regarding one or more of the following:

(A) An exposure to alcoholic beverages that are consumed on the alleged violator's premises to the extent onsite consumption is permitted by law.

(B) An exposure to a chemical known to the state to cause cancer or reproductive toxicity in a food or beverage prepared and sold on the alleged violator's premises primarily intended for immediate consumption on or off premises, to the extent both of the following conditions apply:

(i) The chemical was not intentionally added.

(ii) The chemical was formed by cooking or similar preparation of food or beverage components necessary to render the food or beverage palatable or to avoid microbiological contamination.

(C) An exposure to environmental tobacco smoke caused by the entry of persons other than employees on premises owned or operated by the alleged violator where smoking is permitted at any location on the premises.

(D) An exposure to chemicals known to the state to cause cancer or reproductive toxicity in engine exhaust, to the extent the exposure occurs inside a facility owned or operated by the alleged violator and primarily intended for parking noncommercial vehicles.

(2) Within 14 days after service of the notice, the alleged violator has done all of the following:

(A) Corrected the alleged violation.

(B)(i) Agreed to pay a civil penalty for the alleged violation of Section 25249.6 in the amount of five hundred dollars ($500), to be adjusted quinquennially pursuant to clause (ii), per facility or premises where the alleged violation occurred, of which 75 percent shall be deposited in the Safe Drinking Water and Toxic Enforcement Fund, and 25 percent shall be paid to the person that served the notice as provided in Section 25249.12.

(ii) On April 1, 2019, and at each five-year interval thereafter, the dollar amount of the civil penalty provided pursuant to this subparagraph shall be adjusted by the Judicial Council based on the change in the annual California Consumer Price Index for All Urban Consumers, published by the Department of Industrial Relations, Division of Labor Statistics, for the most recent five-year period ending on December 31 of the year preceding the year in which the adjustment is made, rounded to the nearest five dollars ($5). The Judicial Council shall quinquennially publish the dollar amount of the adjusted civil penalty provided pursuant to this subparagraph, together with the date of the next scheduled adjustment.

(C) Notified, in writing, the person that served the notice of the alleged violation, that the violation has been corrected. The written notice shall include the notice of special compliance procedure and proof of compliance form specified in subdivision (*l*), which was provided by the person serving notice of the alleged violation and which shall be completed by the alleged violator as directed in the notice.

(3) The alleged violator shall deliver the civil penalty to the person that served the notice of the alleged violation within 30 days of service of that notice, and the person that served the notice of violation shall remit the portion of the penalty due to the Safe Drinking Water and Toxic Enforcement Fund within 30 days of receipt of the funds from the alleged violator.

(*l*) The notice required to be provided to an alleged violator pursuant to subdivision (k) shall be presented as follows:

Date: Page 1
Name of Noticing Party or attorney for Noticing Party:
Address:
Phone number:

SPECIAL COMPLIANCE PROCEDURE
PROOF OF COMPLIANCE

You are receiving this form because the Noticing Party listed above has alleged that you are violating California Health and Safety Code §25249.6 (Prop. 65).

The Noticing Party may not bring any legal proceedings against you for the alleged violation checked below if:
(1) You have actually taken the corrective steps that you have certified in this form.
(2) The Noticing Party has received this form at the address shown above, accurately completed by you, postmarked within 14 days of your receiving this notice.
(3) The Noticing Party receives the required $500 penalty payment from you at the address shown above postmarked within 30 days of your receiving this notice.
(4) This is the first time you have submitted a Proof of Compliance for a violation arising from the same exposure in the same facility on the same premises.

PART 1: TO BE COMPLETED BY THE NOTICING PARTY OR ATTORNEY FOR THE NOTICING PARTY

The alleged violation is for an exposure to: (check one)

___Alcoholic beverages that are consumed on the alleged violator's premises to the extent on-site consumption is permitted by law.

___A chemical known to the state to cause cancer or reproductive toxicity in a food or beverage prepared and sold on the alleged violator's premises for immediate consumption on or off premises to the extent: (1) the chemical was not intentionally added; and (2) the chemical was formed by cooking or similar preparation of food or beverage components necessary to render the food or beverage palatable or to avoid microbiological contamination.

___Environmental tobacco smoke caused by entry of persons (other than employees) on premises owned or operated by the alleged violator where smoking is permitted at any location on the premises.

___Chemicals known to the State to cause cancer or reproductive toxicity in engine exhaust, to the extent the exposure occurs inside a facility owned or operated by the alleged violator and primarily intended for parking noncommercial vehicles.

IMPORTANT NOTES:

(1) You have no potential liability under California Health and Safety Code § 25249.6 if your business has nine (9) or fewer employees.

(2) Using this form will NOT prevent the Attorney General, a district attorney, a city attorney, or a prosecutor in whose jurisdiction the violation is alleged to have occurred from filing an action over the same alleged violations, and that in any in such action, the amount of civil penalty shall be reduced to reflect any payment made at this time.

Date:
Name of Noticing Party or attorney for Noticing Party:
Address:
Phone number:

PART 2: TO BE COMPLETED BY THE ALLEGED VIOLATOR OR AUTHORIZED REPRESENTATIVE

Certification of Compliance

Accurate competition of this form will demonstrate that you are now in compliance with California Health and Safety Code § 25249.6 for the alleged violation listed above. You must complete and submit the form below to the Noticing Party at the address shown above, postmarked within 14 days of you receiving this notice.

I hereby agree to pay, within 30 days of completion of this notice, a civil penalty of $500 to the Noticing Party only and certify that I have complied with Health and Safety Code § 25249.6 by (check only one of the following):

[ ] Posting a warning or warnings about the alleged exposure that complies with the law, and attaching a copy of that warning and a photograph accurately showing its placement on my premises;

[ ] Posting the warning or warnings demanded in writing by the Noticing Party, and attaching a copy of that warning and a photograph accurately showing its placement on my premises; OR

[ ] Eliminating the alleged exposure, and attaching a statement accurately describing how the alleged exposure has been eliminated.

Certification

My statements on this form, and on any attachments to it, are true, complete, and correct to the best of my knowledge and belief and are made in good faith. I have carefully read the instructions to complete this form. I understand that if I make a false statement on this form, I may be subject to additional penalties under the Safe Drinking Water and Toxic Enforcement Act of 1986 (Proposition 65).

_____   _____
Signature of alleged violator or authorized   Date
representative

_____
Name and title of signatory

(m) An alleged violator may satisfy the conditions set forth in subdivision (k) only one time for a violation arising from the same exposure in the same facility or on the same premises.

(n) Subdivision (k) shall not prevent the Attorney General, a district attorney, a city attorney, or a prosecutor in whose jurisdiction the violation is alleged to have occurred from filing an action pursuant to subdivision (c) against an alleged violator. In any such action, the amount of any civil penalty for a violation shall be reduced to reflect any payment made by the alleged violator for the same alleged violation pursuant to subparagraph (B) of paragraph (2) of subdivision (k).

(o) If a violation of this chapter is alleged or the application or construction of provisions of this chapter is at issue in a proceeding in the Supreme Court, court of appeal, or the appellate division of the superior court, each party shall serve a copy of the party's brief or petition and brief, on the Attorney General. Service on the Attorney General shall be accomplished by serving the brief, or petition and brief, on the Proposition 65 coordinator at the service address designated on the Attorney General's internet website for Proposition 65 enforcement reporting. A brief shall not be accepted or filed unless the proof of service shows service on the Attorney General. A party failing to comply with this subdivision shall be given a reasonable opportunity to cure the failure before the court imposes sanction, and, in that instance, the court shall allow the Attorney General reasonable additional time to file a brief in the matter.

§25249.8. List of chemicals known to cause cancer or reproductive toxicity

(a) On or before March 1, 1987, the Governor shall cause to be published a list of those chemicals known to the state to cause cancer or reproductive toxicity within the meaning of this chapter, and he shall cause such list to be revised and republished in light of additional knowledge at least once per year thereafter. Such list shall include at a minimum those substances identified by reference in Labor Code Section 6382(b)(1) and those substances identified additionally by reference in Labor Code Section 6382(d).

(b) A chemical is known to the state to cause cancer or reproductive toxicity within the meaning of this chapter if in the opinion of the state's qualified experts it has been clearly shown through scientifically valid testing according to generally accepted principles to cause cancer or reproductive toxicity, or if a body considered to be authoritative by such experts has formally identified it as causing cancer or reproductive toxicity, or if an agency of the state or federal government has formally required it to be labeled or identified as causing cancer or reproductive toxicity.

(c) On or before January 1, 1989, and at least once per year thereafter, the Governor shall cause to be published a separate list of those chemicals that at the time of publication are required by state or federal law to have been tested for potential to cause cancer or reproductive toxicity but that the state's qualified experts have not found to have been adequately tested as required.

(d) The Governor shall identify and consult with the state's qualified experts as necessary to carry out his duties under this section.

(e) In carrying out the duties of the Governor under this section, the Governor and his designates shall not be considered to be adopting or amending a regulation within the meaning of the Administrative Procedure Act as defined in Government Code Section 11370.

§25249.9. Exemptions from discharge prohibition

(a) Section 25249.5 shall not apply to any discharge or release that takes places less than twenty months subsequent to the listing of the chemical in question on the list required to be published under subdivision (a) of Section 25249.8.

(b) Section 25249.5 shall not apply to any discharge or release that meets both of the following criteria:

(1) The discharge or release will not cause any significant amount of the discharged or released chemical to enter any source of drinking water.

(2) The discharge or release is in conformity with all other laws and with every applicable regulation, permit, requirement, and order.

In any action brought to enforce Section 25249.5, the burden of showing that a discharge or release meets the criteria of this subdivision shall be on the defendant.

§25249.10. Exemptions from warning requirement — Section 25249.6 shall not apply to any of the following:

(a) An exposure for which federal law governs warning in a manner that preempts state authority.

(b) An exposure that takes place less than twelve months subsequent to the listing of the chemical in question on the list required to be published under subdivision (a) of Section 25249.8.

(c) An exposure for which the person responsible can show that the exposure poses no significant risk assuming lifetime exposure at the level in question for substances known to the state to cause cancer, and that the exposure will have no observable effect assuming exposure at one thousand (1000) times the level in question for substances known to the state to cause reproductive toxicity, based on evidence and standards of comparable scientific validity to the evidence and standards which form the scientific basis for the listing of such chemical pursuant to subdivision (a) of Section 25249.8. In any action brought to enforce

Section 25249.6, the burden of showing that an exposure meets the criteria of this subdivision shall be on the defendant.

§25249.11. Definitions — For purposes of this chapter:

(a) "Person" means an individual, trust, firm, joint stock company, corporation, company, partnership, limited liability company, and association.

(b) "Person in the course of doing business" does not include any person employing fewer than 10 employees in his or her business; any city, county, or district or any department or agency thereof or the state or any department or agency thereof or the federal government or any department or agency thereof; or any entity in its operation of a public water system as defined in Section 116275.

(c) "Significant amount" means any detectable amount except an amount which would meet the exemption test in subdivision (c) of Section 25249.10 if an individual were exposed to such an amount in drinking water.

(d) "Source of drinking water" means either a present source of drinking water or water which is identified or designated in a water quality control plan adopted by a regional board as being suitable for domestic or municipal uses.

(e) "Threaten to violate" means to create a condition in which there is a substantial probability that a violation will occur.

(f) "Warning" within the meaning of Section 25249.6 need not be provided separately to each exposed individual and may be provided by general methods such as labels on consumer products, inclusion of notices in mailings to water customers, posting of notices, placing notices in public news media, and the like, provided that the warning accomplished is clear and reasonable. In order to minimize the burden on retail sellers of consumer products including foods, regulations implementing Section 25249.6 shall to the extent practicable place the obligation to provide any warning materials such as labels on the producer or packager rather than on the retail seller, except where the retail seller itself is responsible for introducing a chemical known to the state to cause cancer or reproductive toxicity into the consumer product in question.

§25249.12. Implementation; agency designation and authority; Safe Drinking Water and Toxic Enforcement Fund; recovery of prosecution costs

(a) The Governor shall designate a lead agency and other agencies that may be required to implement this chapter, including this section. Each agency so designated may adopt and modify regulations, standards, and permits as necessary to conform with and implement this chapter and to further its purposes.

(b) The Safe Drinking Water and Toxic Enforcement Fund is hereby established in the State Treasury. The director of the lead agency designated by the Governor to implement this chapter may expend the funds in the Safe Drinking Water and Toxic Enforcement Fund, upon appropriation by the Legislature, to implement and administer this chapter.

(c) In addition to any other money that may be deposited in the Safe Drinking Water and Toxic Enforcement Fund, all of the following amounts shall be deposited in the fund:

(1) Seventy-five percent of all civil and criminal penalties collected pursuant to this chapter.

(2) Any interest earned upon the money deposited into the Safe Drinking Water and Toxic Enforcement Fund.

(d) Twenty-five percent of all civil and criminal penalties collected pursuant to this chapter shall be paid to the office of the city attorney, city prosecutor, district attorney, or Attorney General, whichever office brought the action, or in the case of an action brought by a person under subdivision (d) of Section 25249.7, to that person.

§25249.13. Preservation of existing rights, obligations, and penalties — Nothing in this chapter shall alter or diminish any legal obligation otherwise required in common law or by statute or regulation, and nothing in this chapter shall create or enlarge any defense in any action to enforce such legal obligation. Penalties and sanctions imposed under this chapter shall be in addition to any penalties or sanctions otherwise prescribed by law.

4

WASTE MANAGEMENT AND POLLUTION PREVENTION

This chapter includes the principal federal statutes that regulate waste management. Management of hazardous waste is regulated "from cradle to grave" under federal law by the Resource Conservation and Recovery Act (RCRA), a statute adopted in 1976 as a comprehensive amendment to the Solid Waste Disposal Act (SWDA). While Congress thought that RCRA had closed the last remaining loophole in federal environmental law, it soon was confronted with the problem of abandoned toxic waste dumps. In response to this problem, Congress in 1980 adopted the Comprehensive Environmental Response, Compensation, and Liability Act (CERCLA). CERCLA created the Superfund program for cleaning up releases of hazardous substances and it imposed strict, joint and several liability for cleanup costs on broad classes of persons associated with the releases. In 1990 Congress adopted the Pollution Prevention Act, which declared source reduction to be the preferred policy for preventing pollution followed by recycling, treatment, and then disposal.

A. RESOURCE CONSERVATION AND RECOVERY ACT (RCRA)

A GUIDE TO MATERIALS ON RCRA AVAILABLE ON THE INTERNET

EPA's waste management regulations are codified at 40 C.F.R. pts. 239–282. Regulations governing hazardous waste begin at 40 C.F.R. pt. 260. Regulations governing underground storage tanks are found at 40 C.F.R. pts. 280-282. These CFR sections are available online through the National Archives and Records Administration's website, which includes a searchable version of the Code of Federal Regulations *(https://www.gpo.gov/fdsys/browse/collectionCfr.action?collectionCode=CFR)* and a continuously updated electronic CFR ("e-CFR") that can be found at *(http://www.ecfr.gov)*.

EPA's Office of Land and Emergency Management is responsible for implementing RCRA and CERCLA. Its webpage is located at *https://www.epa.gov/aboutepa/about-office-land-and-emergency-management-olem*. EPA's RCRA Docket and Information Center provides the public with access to documents concerning RCRA rulemakings including copies of all EPA generated documents associated with rulemaking activities, which are available to the public online at *https://www.epa.gov/dockets*. Information about EPA's regulation of underground storage tanks under RCRA is available from the agency's Underground Storage Tank (UST) Docket maintained by the agency's Office of Underground Storage Tanks at *http://www.epa.gov/ust*.

Detailed data on hazardous waste generation, management, and disposal is collected by EPA's RCRAInfo system. This comprehensive information system can be accessed online through the EPA site *(https://www.epa.gov/enviro/rcrainfo-overview)*.

Most states operate RCRA programs under delegated authority from EPA. Information about some of these state RCRA programs may be found on the internet. See, for example, the websites maintained by New York State's Department of Environmental Conservation at *http://www.dec.ny.gov*, and Florida's website at *http://www.dep.state.fl.us/waste*.

RCRA LEGISLATIVE HISTORY TIMELINE

October 21, 1976: Resource Conservation and Recovery Act, Pub. L. 94-580, 90 Stat. 2795, enacted as an amendment to the Solid Waste Disposal Act, adds Subchapter III (Subtitle C) to require EPA to establish a cradle-to-grave regulatory program for hazardous waste management.

October 15, 1980: Used Oil Recycling Act of 1980, Pub. L. 96-463, 94 Stat. 2055, makes minor amendments to RCRA.

October 21, 1980: Solid Waste Disposal Act Amendments of 1980, Pub. L. 96-482, 94 Stat. 2334, add Bevill amendment to §3001 of RCRA that temporarily suspends regulation of certain "special" wastes from oil and gas, mining, and utility industries.

November 8, 1984: Hazardous and Solid Waste Amendments of 1984, Pub. L. 98-616, 98 Stat. 3221, make comprehensive amendments to strengthen the RCRA program by adding a land disposal ban, imposing minimum technology standards on treatment, storage, and disposal facilities, and requiring permittees to undertake corrective action to clean up prior releases of toxics.

October 17, 1986: Superfund Amendments and Reauthorization Act, Pub. L. 99-499, 100 Stat. 1613, adds Subchapter IX (Subtitle I) program for regulating underground storage tanks.

November 1, 1988: Medical Waste Tracking Act of 1988, Pub. L. 100-582, 102 Stat. 2950, adds Subchapter X demonstration program for tracking medical wastes.

October 6, 1992: Federal Facility Compliance Act (FFCA), Pub. L. 102-386, 106 Stat. 1505, gives states the authority to levy civil penalties against federal entities who violate RCRA.

March 26, 1996: Land Disposal Program Flexibility Act of 1996, Pub. L. 104-119, 110 Stat. 830, makes minor changes relaxing portions of RCRA's land disposal ban and gives EPA the authority to exempt certain small municipal solid waste landfills from groundwater monitoring requirements.

August 8, 2005: The Underground Storage Tank Compliance Act of 2005 is enacted as Title XV, Subtitle B of the Energy Policy Act of 2005. It amends Subtitle I of the Solid Waste Disposal Act to require major changes in EPA's underground storage tank (UST) program. The amendments expand eligible uses of the Leaking Underground Storage Tank (LUST) Trust Fund, extend the LUST Trust Fund tax through 2011, and include provisions regarding inspections, operator training, delivery prohibition, secondary containment and financial responsibility, and cleanup of releases that contain oxygenated fuel additives.

October 5, 2012: The Hazardous Waste Electronic Manifest Establishment Act is added to Subtitle C of RCRA as Section 3024. It mandates that EPA implement a national electronic manifest system to track hazardous waste.

OUTLINE OF PRINCIPAL PROVISIONS OF THE
SOLID WASTE DISPOSAL ACT
(also known as the Resource Conservation and Recovery Act)

SUBTITLE C: HAZARDOUS WASTE MANAGEMENT (§§3001-3020)

§3001 (42 U.S.C. §6921) Identification and Listing of Hazardous Waste: requires EPA to develop criteria for determining what wastes are hazardous and to create lists of such waste.

§3002 (42 U.S.C. §6922) Regulation of Generators: requires EPA to establish regulations requiring generators to identify hazardous waste and to use a manifest system to track hazardous waste shipment.

§3003 (42 U.S.C. §6923) Regulation of Transporters: requires transporters of hazardous waste to use the manifest system to ensure that waste reaches its intended destination.

§3004 (42 U.S.C. §6924) Regulation of Treatment, Storage, and Disposal Facilities: requires EPA to set standards regulating waste management by facilities that treat, store, or dispose of hazardous waste (TSDs), mandates minimum technology standards for certain facilities, requires TSDs to clean up prior releases of hazardous wastes, and bans the land disposal of untreated hazardous waste unless EPA has specifically determined that such disposal is protective of human health and the environment.

§3005 (42 U.S.C. §6925) Permit Requirements for TSDs: requires TSDs to obtain permits from EPA or authorized states that incorporate the requirements of §3004.

SUBTITLE D: STATE OR REGIONAL SOLID WASTE PLANS (§§4001-4010)

Requires EPA to establish guidelines for state solid waste management plans that must include bans on open dumping and requires EPA to set minimum regulatory standards for municipal landfills.

ENFORCEMENT, CITIZEN SUIT, AND JUDICIAL REVIEW PROVISIONS

§3008 (42 U.S.C. §6928) Federal Enforcement: provides federal enforcement authorities including criminal, civil, and administrative penalties for violations of RCRA regulations.

§7002 (42 U.S.C. §6972) Citizen Suits: authorizes any person to sue anyone who violates RCRA, allows suits against anyone whose handling of waste causes imminent and substantial endangerment, and allows citizen suits against EPA for failure to perform nondiscretionary duties.

§7003 (42 U.S.C. §6973) Imminent Hazard: authorizes the EPA Administrator to issue cleanup orders and to sue for equitable relief against anyone who has contributed to past or present handling, storage, treatment, transportation, or disposal of waste that may present imminent and substantial endangerment.

§7006 (42 U.S.C. §6976) Judicial Review: authorizes judicial review of EPA's promulgation of RCRA regulations in the U.S. Court of Appeals for the District of Columbia Circuit.

SUBTITLE I: REGULATION OF UNDERGROUND STORAGE TANKS

§9002 (42 U.S.C. §6991a) Notification: requires owners of underground storage tanks containing petroleum or other hazardous substances that are not regulated under Subtitle C to notify state authorities.

§9003 (42 U.S.C. §6991b) Release Detection, Prevention and Correction: requires EPA to issue regulations governing prevention, detection, and remediation of leaks from underground storage tanks including financial responsibility requirements and new tank performance standards.

Solid Waste Disposal Act (as Amended by the Resource Conservation and Recovery Act)

42 U.S.C. §§6901 to 6992k

SUBCHAPTER I — GENERAL PROVISIONS

§6901. Congressional findings
[SWDA §1002]

(a) **Solid waste** — The Congress finds with respect to solid waste —

(1) that the continuing technological progress and improvement in methods of manufacture, packaging, and marketing of consumer products has resulted in an ever-mounting increase, and in a change in the characteristics, of the mass material discarded by the purchaser of such products;

(2) that the economic and population growth of our Nation, and the improvements in the standard of

living enjoyed by our population, have required increased industrial production to meet our needs, and have made necessary the demolition of old buildings, the construction of new buildings, and the provision of highways and other avenues of transportation, which, together with related industrial, commercial, and agricultural operations, have resulted in a rising tide of scrap, discarded, and waste materials;

(3) that the continuing concentration of our population in expanding metropolitan and other urban areas has presented these communities with serious financial, management, intergovernmental, and technical problems in the disposal of solid wastes resulting from the industrial, commercial, domestic, and other activities carried on in such areas;

(4) that while the collection and disposal of solid wastes should continue to be primarily the function of State, regional, and local agencies, the problems of waste disposal as set forth above have become a matter national in scope and in concern and necessitate Federal action through financial and technical assistance and leadership in the development, demonstration, and application of new and improved methods and processes to reduce the amount of waste and unsalvageable materials and to provide for proper and economical solid waste disposal practices.

(b) Environment and health — The Congress finds with respect to the environment and health, that —

(1) although land is too valuable a national resource to be needlessly polluted by discarded materials, most solid waste is disposed of on land in open dumps and sanitary landfills;

(2) disposal of solid waste and hazardous waste in or on the land without careful planning and management can present a danger to human health and the environment;

(3) as a result of the Clean Air Act [42 U.S.C. §§7401 et seq.], the Water Pollution Control Act [33 U.S.C. §§1251 et seq.], and other Federal and State laws respecting public health and the environment, greater amounts of solid waste (in the form of sludge and other pollution treatment residues) have been created. Similarly, inadequate and environmentally unsound practices for the disposal or use of solid waste have created greater amounts of air and water pollution and other problems for the environment and for health;

(4) open dumping is particularly harmful to health, contaminates drinking water from underground and surface supplies, and pollutes the air and the land;

(5) the placement of inadequate controls on hazardous waste management will result in substantial risks to human health and the environment;

(6) if hazardous waste management is improperly performed in the first instance, corrective

action is likely to be expensive, complex, and time consuming;

(7) certain classes of land disposal facilities are not capable of assuring long-term containment of certain hazardous wastes, and to avoid substantial risk to human health and the environment, reliance on land disposal should be minimized or eliminated, and land disposal, particularly landfill and surface impoundment, should be the least favored method for managing hazardous wastes; and

(8) alternatives to existing methods of land disposal must be developed since many of the cities in the United States will be running out of suitable solid waste disposal sites within five years unless immediate action is taken.

(c) Materials — The Congress finds with respect to materials, that —

(1) millions of tons of recoverable material which could be used are needlessly buried each year;

(2) methods are available to separate usable materials from solid waste; and

(3) the recovery and conservation of such materials can reduce the dependence of the United States on foreign resources and reduce the deficit in its balance of payments.

(d) Energy — The Congress finds with respect to energy, that —

(1) solid waste represents a potential source of solid fuel, oil, or gas that can be converted into energy;

(2) the need exists to develop alternative energy sources for public and private consumption in order to reduce our dependence on such sources as petroleum products, natural gas, nuclear and hydroelectric generation; and

(3) technology exists to produce usable energy from solid waste.

§6901a. Congressional findings: used oil recycling — The Congress finds and declares that —

(1) used oil is a valuable source of increasingly scarce energy and materials;

(2) technology exists to re-refine, reprocess, reclaim, and otherwise recycle used oil;

(3) used oil constitutes a threat to public health and the environment when reused or disposed of improperly; and

that, therefore, it is in the national interest to recycle used oil in a manner which does not constitute a threat to public health and the environment and which conserves energy and materials.

**§6902. Objectives and national policy
[SWDA §1003]**

(a) Objectives — The objectives of this chapter are to promote the protection of health and the environment and to conserve valuable material and energy resources by —

(1) providing technical and financial assistance to State and local governments and interstate agencies for the development of solid waste management plans (including resource recovery and resource conservation systems) which will promote improved solid waste management techniques (including more effective organizational arrangements), new and improved methods of collection, separation, and recovery of solid waste, and the environmentally safe disposal of nonrecoverable residues;

(2) providing training grants in occupations involving the design, operation, and maintenance of solid waste disposal systems;

(3) prohibiting future open dumping on the land and requiring the conversion of existing open dumps to facilities which do not pose a danger to the environment or to health;

(4) assuring that hazardous waste management practices are conducted in a manner which protects human health and the environment;

(5) requiring that hazardous waste be properly managed in the first instance thereby reducing the need for corrective action at a future date;

(6) minimizing the generation of hazardous waste and the land disposal of hazardous waste by encouraging process substitution, materials recovery, properly conducted recycling and reuse, and treatment;

(7) establishing a viable Federal-State partnership to carry out the purposes of this chapter and insuring that the Administrator will, in carrying out the provisions of subchapter III of this chapter, give a high priority to assisting and cooperating with States in obtaining full authorization of State programs under subchapter III of this chapter;

(8) providing for the promulgation of guidelines for solid waste collection, transport, separation, recovery, and disposal practices and systems;

(9) promoting a national research and development program for improved solid waste management and resource conservation techniques, more effective organizational arrangements, and new and improved methods of collection, separation, and recovery, and recycling of solid wastes and environmentally safe disposal of nonrecoverable residues;

(10) promoting the demonstration, construction, and application of solid waste management, resource recovery, and resource conservation systems which preserve and enhance the quality of air, water, and land resources; and

(11) establishing a cooperative effort among the Federal, State, and local governments and private enterprise in order to recover valuable materials and energy from solid waste.

(b) National policy — The Congress hereby declares it to be the national policy of the United States that, wherever feasible, the generation of hazardous waste is to be reduced or eliminated as expeditiously as possible. Waste that is nevertheless generated should be treated, stored, or disposed of so as to minimize the present and future threat to human health and the environment.

§6903. Definitions
[SWDA §1004]

As used in this chapter:

(1) The term "Administrator" means the Administrator of the Environmental Protection Agency.

(2) The term "construction," with respect to any project of construction under this chapter, means (A) the erection or building of new structures and acquisition of lands or interests therein, or the acquisition, replacement, expansion, remodeling, alteration, modernization, or extension of existing structures, and (B) the acquisition and installation of initial equipment of, or required in connection with, new or newly acquired structures or the expanded, remodeled, altered, modernized or extended part of existing structures (including trucks and other motor vehicles, and tractors, cranes, and other machinery) necessary for the proper utilization and operation of the facility after completion of the project; and includes preliminary planning to determine the economic and engineering feasibility and the public health and safety aspects of the project, the engineering, architectural, legal, fiscal, and economic investigations and studies, and any surveys, designs, plans, working drawings, specifications, and other action necessary for the carrying out of the project, and (C) the inspection and supervision of the process of carrying out the project to completion.

(2A) The term "demonstration" means the initial exhibition of a new technology process or practice or a significantly new combination or use of technologies, processes or practices, subsequent to the development stage, for the purpose of proving technological feasibility and cost effectiveness.

(3) The term "disposal" means the discharge, deposit, injection, dumping, spilling, leaking, or placing of any solid waste or hazardous waste into or on any land or water so that such solid waste or hazardous waste or any constituent thereof may enter the environment or be emitted into the air or discharged into any waters, including ground waters.

(4) The term "Federal agency" means any department, agency, or other instrumentality of the Federal Government, any independent agency or establishment of the Federal Government including any Government corporation, and the Government Publishing Office.

(5) The term "hazardous waste" means a solid waste, or combination of solid wastes, which

because of its quantity, concentration, or physical, chemical, or infectious characteristics may —

    (A) cause, or significantly contribute to an increase in mortality or an increase in serious irreversible, or incapacitating reversible, illness; or

    (B) pose a substantial present or potential hazard to human health or the environment when improperly treated, stored, transported, or disposed of, or otherwise managed.

(6) The term "hazardous waste generation" means the act or process of producing hazardous waste.

(7) The term "hazardous waste management" means the systematic control of the collection, source separation, storage, transportation, processing, treatment, recovery, and disposal of hazardous wastes.

(8) For purposes of Federal financial assistance (other than rural communities assistance), the term "implementation" does not include the acquisition, leasing, construction, or modification of facilities or equipment or the acquisition, leasing, or improvement of land.

(9) The term "intermunicipal agency" means an agency established by two or more municipalities with responsibility for planning or administration of solid waste.

(10) The term "interstate agency" means an agency of two or more municipalities in different States, or an agency established by two or more States, with authority to provide for the management of solid wastes and serving two or more municipalities located in different States.

(11) The term "long-term contract" means, when used in relation to solid waste supply, a contract of sufficient duration to assure the viability of a resource recovery facility (to the extent that such viability depends upon solid waste supply).

(12) The term "manifest" means the form used for identifying the quantity, composition, and the origin, routing, and destination of hazardous waste during its transportation from the point of generation to the point of disposal, treatment, or storage.

(13) The term "municipality" (A) means a city, town, borough, county, parish, district, or other public body created by or pursuant to State law, with responsibility for the planning or administration of solid waste management, or an Indian tribe or authorized tribal organization or Alaska Native village or organization, and (B) includes any rural community or unincorporated town or village or any other public entity for which an application for assistance is made by a State or political subdivision thereof.

(14) The term "open dump" means any facility or site where solid waste is disposed of which is not a sanitary landfill which meets the criteria promulgated under section 6944 of this title and which is not a facility for disposal of hazardous waste.

(15) The term "person" means an individual, trust, firm, joint stock company, corporation (including a government corporation), partnership, association, State, municipality, commission, political subdivision of a State, or any interstate body and shall include each department, agency, and instrumentality of the United States.

(16) The term "procurement item" means any device, good, substance, material, product, or other item whether real or personal property which is the subject of any purchase, barter, or other exchange made to procure such item.

(17) The term "procuring agency" means any Federal agency, or any State agency or agency of a political subdivision of a State which is using appropriated Federal funds for such procurement, or any person contracting with any such agency with respect to work performed under such contract.

(18) The term "recoverable" refers to the capability and likelihood of being recovered from solid waste for a commercial or industrial use.

(19) The term "recovered material" means waste material and byproducts which have been recovered or diverted from solid waste, but such term does not include those materials and byproducts generated from, and commonly reused within, an original manufacturing process.

(20) The term "recovered resources" means material or energy recovered from solid waste.

(21) The term "resource conservation" means reduction of the amounts of solid waste that are generated, reduction of overall resource consumption, and utilization of recovered resources.

(22) The term "resource recovery" means the recovery of material or energy from solid waste.

(23) The term "resource recovery system" means a solid waste management system which provides for collection, separation, recycling, and recovery of solid wastes, including disposal of nonrecoverable waste residues.

(24) The term "resource recovery facility" means any facility at which solid waste is processed for the purpose of extracting, converting to energy, or otherwise separating and preparing solid waste for reuse.

(25) The term "regional authority" means the authority established or designated under section 6946 of this title.

(26) The term "sanitary landfill" means a facility for the disposal of solid waste which meets the criteria published under section 6944 of this title.

(26A) The term "sludge" means any solid, semisolid or liquid waste generated from a municipal, commercial, or industrial wastewater treatment plant, water supply treatment plant, or air pollution control facility or any other such waste having similar characteristics and effects.

(27) The term "solid waste" means any garbage, refuse, sludge from a waste treatment plant, water supply treatment plant, or air pollution control facility and other discarded material, including solid, liquid, semisolid, or contained gaseous material resulting from industrial, commercial, mining, and agricultural operations, and from community activities, but does not include solid or dissolved material in domestic sewage, or solid or dissolved materials in irrigation return flows or industrial discharges which are point sources subject to permits under section 1342 of Title 33, or source, special nuclear, or byproduct material as defined by the Atomic Energy Act of 1954, as amended (68 Stat. 923) [42 U.S.C. §§2011 *et seq.*].

(28) The term "solid waste management" means the systematic administration of activities which provide for the collection, source separation, storage, transportation, transfer, processing, treatment, and disposal of solid waste.

(29) The term "solid waste management facility" includes —

(A) any resource recovery system or component thereof,

(B) any system, program, or facility for resource conservation, and

(C) any facility for the collection, source separation, storage, transportation, transfer, processing, treatment or disposal of solid wastes, including hazardous wastes, whether such facility is associated with facilities generating such wastes or otherwise.

(30) The terms "solid waste planning", "solid waste management", and "comprehensive planning" include planning or management respecting resource recovery and resource conservation.

(31) The term "State" means any of the several States, the District of Columbia, the Commonwealth of Puerto Rico, the Virgin Islands, Guam, American Samoa, and the Commonwealth of the Northern Mariana Islands.

(32) The term "State authority" means the agency established or designated under section 6947 of this title.

(33) The term "storage", when used in connection with hazardous waste, means the containment of hazardous waste, either on a temporary basis or for a period of years, in such a manner as not to constitute disposal of such hazardous waste.

(34) The term "treatment", when used in connection with hazardous waste, means any method, technique, or process, including neutralization, designed to change the physical, chemical, or biological character or composition of any hazardous waste so as to neutralize such waste or so as to render such waste nonhazardous, safer for transport, amenable for recovery, amenable for storage, or reduced in volume. Such term includes any activity or processing designed to change the physical form or chemical composition of hazardous waste so as to render it nonhazardous.

(35) The term "virgin material" means a raw material, including previously unused copper, aluminum, lead, zinc, iron, or other metal or metal ore, any undeveloped resource that is, or with new technology will become, a source of raw materials.

(36) The term "used oil" means any oil which has been —

(A) refined from crude oil,

(B) used, and

(C) as a result of such use, contaminated by physical or chemical impurities.

(37) The term "recycled oil" means any used oil which is reused, following its original use, for any purpose (including the purpose for which the oil was originally used). Such term includes oil which is re-refined, reclaimed, burned, or reprocessed.

(38) The term "lubricating oil" means the fraction of crude oil which is sold for purposes of reducing friction in any industrial or mechanical device. Such term includes re-refined oil.

(39) The term "re-refined oil" means used oil from which the physical and chemical contaminants acquired through previous use have been removed through a refining process.

(40) Except as otherwise provided in this paragraph, the term "medical waste" means any solid waste which is generated in the diagnosis, treatment, or immunization of human beings or animals, in research pertaining thereto, or in the production or testing of biologicals. Such term does not include any hazardous waste identified or listed under subchapter III or any household waste as defined in regulations under subchapter III.

(41) The term "mixed waste" means waste that contains both hazardous waste and source, special nuclear, or by-product material subject to the Atomic Energy Act of 1954 (42 U.S.C. §2011 *et seq.*).

§6904. Governmental cooperation
[SWDA §1005]

(a) **Interstate cooperation** — The provisions of this chapter to be carried out by States may be carried out by interstate agencies and provisions applicable to States may apply to interstate regions where such agencies and regions have been established by the respective States and approved by the Administrator. In any such case, action required to be taken by the Governor of a State, respecting regional designation shall be required to be taken by the Governor of each of the respective States with respect to so much of the interstate region as is within the jurisdiction of that State.

(b) **Consent of Congress to compacts** — The consent of the Congress is hereby given to two or more States to negotiate and enter into agreements or compacts, not in conflict with any law or treaty of the United States, for —

(1) cooperative effort and mutual assistance for the management of solid waste or hazardous waste (or both) and the enforcement of their respective laws relating thereto, and

(2) the establishment of such agencies, joint or otherwise, as they may deem desirable for making effective such agreements or compacts.

No such agreement or compact shall be binding or obligatory upon any State a party thereto unless it is agreed upon by all parties to the agreement and until it has been approved by the Administrator and the Congress.

§6905. Application of chapter and integration with other Acts
[SWDA §1006]

(a) Application of chapter — Nothing in this chapter shall be construed to apply to (or to authorize any State, interstate, or local authority to regulate) any activity or substance which is subject to the Federal Water Pollution Control Act [33 U.S.C. §§1251 *et seq.*], the Safe Drinking Water Act [42 U.S.C. §§300f *et seq.*], the Marine Protection, Research and Sanctuaries Act of 1972 [16 U.S.C. §§1431 *et seq.*, §§1447 *et seq.*, 33 U.S.C. §§1401 *et seq.*, §§2801 *et seq.*], or the Atomic Energy Act of 1954 [42 U.S.C. §§2011 *et seq.*] except to the extent that such application (or regulation) is not inconsistent with the requirements of such Acts.

(b) Integration with other Acts

(1) The Administrator shall integrate all provisions of this chapter for purposes of administration and enforcement and shall avoid duplication, to the maximum extent practicable, with the appropriate provisions of the Clean Air Act [42 U.S.C. §§7401 *et seq.*], the Federal Water Pollution Control Act [33 U.S.C. §§1251 *et seq.*], the Federal Insecticide, Fungicide, and Rodenticide Act [7 U.S.C. §§136 *et seq.*], the Safe Drinking Water Act [42 U.S.C. §§300f *et seq.*], the Marine Protection, Research and Sanctuaries Act of 1972 [16 U.S.C. §§1431 *et seq.*, §§1447 *et seq.*, 33 U.S.C. §§1401 *et seq.*, §§2801 *et seq.*], and such other Acts of Congress as grant regulatory authority to the Administrator. Such integration shall be effected only to the extent that it can be done in a manner consistent with the goals and policies expressed in this chapter and in the other acts referred to in this subsection.

(2)(A) As promptly as practicable after November 8, 1984, the Administrator shall submit a report describing —

(i) the current data and information available on emissions of polychlorinated dibenzo-p-dioxins from resource recovery facilities burning municipal solid waste;

(ii) any significant risks to human health posed by these emissions; and

(iii) operating practices appropriate for controlling these emissions.

(B) Based on the report under subparagraph (A) and on any future information on such emissions, the Administrator may publish advisories or guidelines regarding the control of dioxin emissions from such facilities. Nothing in this paragraph shall be construed to preempt or otherwise affect the authority of the Administrator to promulgate any regulations under the Clean Air Act [42 U.S.C. §§7401 *et seq.*] regarding emissions of polychlorinated dibenzo-p-dioxins.

(3) Notwithstanding any other provisions of law, in developing solid waste plans, it is the intention of this chapter that in determining the size of a waste-to-energy facility, adequate provisions shall be given to the present and reasonably anticipated future needs, including those needs created by thorough implementation of section 6962(h) of this title, of the recycling and resource recovery interests within the area encompassed by the solid waste plan.

(c) Integration with the Surface Mining Control and Reclamation Act of 1977

(1) No later than 90 days after October 21, 1980, the Administrator shall review any regulations applicable to the treatment, storage, or disposal of any coal mining wastes or overburden promulgated by the Secretary of the Interior under the Surface Mining and Reclamation Act of 1977 [30 U.S.C. §§1201 *et seq.*]. If the Administrator determines that any requirement of final regulations promulgated under any section of subchapter III of this chapter relating to mining wastes or overburden is not adequately addressed in such regulations promulgated by the Secretary, the Administrator shall promptly transmit such determination, together with suggested revisions and supporting documentation, to the Secretary.

(2) The Secretary of the Interior shall have exclusive responsibility for carrying out any requirement of subchapter III of this chapter with respect to coal mining wastes or overburden for which a surface coal mining and reclamation permit is issued or approved under the Surface Mining Control and Reclamation Act of 1977 [30 U.S.C. §§1201 *et seq.*]. The Secretary shall, with the concurrence of the Administrator, promulgate such regulations as may be necessary to carry out the purposes of this subsection and shall integrate such regulations with regulations promulgated under the Surface Mining Control and Reclamation Act of 1977.

§6906. Financial disclosure
[SWDA §1007]

(a) Statement — Each officer or employee of the Administrator who —

(1) performs any function or duty under this chapter; and

(2) has any known financial interest in any person who applies for or receives financial assistance under this chapter

shall, beginning on February 1, 1977, annually file with the Administrator a written statement concerning all such interests held by such officer or employee during the preceding calendar year. Such statement shall be available to the public.

(b) Action by Administrator — The Administrator shall —

(1) act within ninety days after October 21, 1976 —

(A) to define the term "known financial interest" for purposes of subsection (a) of this section; and

(B) to establish the methods by which the requirement to file written statements specified in subsection (a) of this section will be monitored and enforced, including appropriate provision for the filing by such officers and employees of such statements and the review by the Administrator of such statements; and

(2) report to the Congress on June 1, 1978, and of each succeeding calendar year with respect to such disclosures and the actions taken in regard thereto during the preceding calendar year.

(c) Exemption — In the rules prescribed under subsection (b) of this section, the Administrator may identify specific positions within the Environmental Protection Agency which are of a nonpolicy-making nature and provide that officers or employees occupying such positions shall be exempt from the requirements of this section.

(d) Penalty — Any officer or employee who is subject to, and knowingly violates, this section shall be fined not more than $2,500 or imprisoned not more than one year, or both.

§6907. Solid waste management information and guidelines
[SWDA §1008]

(a) Guidelines — Within one year of October 21, 1976, and from time to time thereafter, the Administrator shall, in cooperation with appropriate Federal, State, municipal, and intermunicipal agencies, and in consultation with other interested persons, and after public hearings, develop and publish suggested guidelines for solid waste management. Such suggested guidelines shall —

(1) provide a technical and economic description of the level of performance that can be attained by various available solid waste management practices (including operating practices) which provide for the protection of public health and the environment;

(2) not later than two years after October 21, 1976, describe levels of performance, including appropriate methods and degrees of control, that provide at a minimum for (A) protection of public health and welfare; (B) protection of the quality of ground waters and surface waters from leachates; (C) protection of the quality of surface waters from runoff through compliance with effluent limitations under the Federal Water Pollution Control Act, as amended [33 U.S.C. §§1251 *et seq.*]; (D) protection of ambient air quality through compliance with new source performance standards or requirements of air quality implementation plans under the Clean Air Act, as amended [42 U.S.C. §§7401 *et seq.*]; (E) disease and vector control; (F) safety; and (G) esthetics; and

(3) provide minimum criteria to be used by the States to define those solid waste management practices which constitute the open dumping of solid waste or hazardous waste and are to be prohibited under subchapter IV of this chapter.

Where appropriate, such suggested guidelines also shall include minimum information for use in deciding the adequate location, design, and construction of facilities associated with solid waste management practices, including the consideration of regional, geographic, demographic, and climatic factors.

(b) Notice — The Administrator shall notify the Committee on Environment and Public Works of the Senate and the Committee on Energy and Commerce of the House of Representatives a reasonable time before publishing any suggested guidelines or proposed regulations under this chapter of the content of such proposed suggested guidelines or proposed regulations under this chapter.

§6908. Small town environmental planning
[FFCA §109]

(a) Establishment — The Administrator of the Environmental Protection Agency (hereafter referred to as the "Administrator") shall establish a program to assist small communities in planning and financing environmental facilities. The program shall be known as the "Small Town Environmental Planning Program."

(b) Small Town Environmental Planning Task Force

(1) The Administrator shall establish a Small Town Environmental Planning Task Force which shall be composed of representatives of small towns from different areas of the United States, Federal and State governmental agencies, and public interest groups. The Administrator shall terminate the Task Force not later than 2 years after the establishment of the Task Force.

(2) The Task Force shall —

(A) identify regulations developed pursuant to Federal environmental laws which pose significant compliance problems for small towns;

(B) identify means to improve the working relationship between the Environmental Protection Agency (hereafter referred to as the Agency) and small towns;

(C) review proposed regulations for the protection of the environmental and public health and suggest revisions that could improve the ability of small towns to comply with such regulations;

(D) identify means to promote regionalization of environmental treatment systems and infrastructure serving small towns to improve the economic condition of such systems and infrastructure; and

(E) provide such other assistance to the Administrator as the Administrator deems appropriate.

(c) Identification of environmental requirements

(1) Not later than 6 months after October 6, 1992, the Administrator shall publish a list of requirements under Federal environmental and public health statutes (and the regulations developed pursuant to such statutes) applicable to small towns. Not less than annually, the Administrator shall make such additions and deletions to and from the list as the Administrator deems appropriate.

(2) The Administrator shall, as part of the Small Town Environmental Planning Program under this section, implement a program to notify small communities of the regulations identified under paragraph (1) and of future regulations and requirements through methods that the Administrator determines to be effective to provide information to the greatest number of small communities, including any of the following:

(A) Newspapers and other periodicals.

(B) Other news media.

(C) Trade, municipal, and other associations that the Administrator determines to be appropriate.

(D) Direct mail.

(d) Small Town Ombudsman — The Administrator shall establish and staff an Office of the Small Town Ombudsman. The Office shall provide assistance to small towns in connection with the Small Town Environmental Planning Program and other business with the Agency. Each regional office shall identify a small town contact. The Small Town Ombudsman and the regional contacts also may assist larger communities, but only if first priority is given to providing assistance to small towns.

(e) Multi-media permits

(1) The Administrator shall conduct a study of establishing a multi-media permitting program for small towns. Such evaluation shall include an analysis of —

(A) environmental benefits and liabilities of a multi-media permitting program;

(B) the potential of using such a program to coordinate a small town's environmental and public health activities; and

(C) the legal barriers, if any, to the establishment of such a program.

(2) Within 3 years after October 6, 1992, the Administrator shall report to Congress on the results of the evaluation performed in accordance with paragraph (1). Included in this report shall be a description of the activities conducted pursuant to subsections (a) through (d) of this section.

(f) "Small town" defined — For purposes of this section, the term "small town" means an incorporated or unincorporated community (as defined by the Administrator) with a population of less than 2,500 individuals.

(g) Authorization — There is authorized to be appropriated the sum of $500,000 to implement this section.

§6908a. Agreements with Indian Tribes

On and after October 21, 1998, the Administrator is authorized to enter into assistance agreements with Federally recognized Indian tribes on such terms and conditions as the Administrator deems appropriate for the development and implementation of programs to manage hazardous waste, and underground storage tanks.

SUBCHAPTER II — OFFICE OF SOLID WASTE; AUTHORITIES OF THE ADMINISTRATOR

§6911. Office of Solid Waste and Interagency Coordinating Committee
[SWDA §2001]

(a) Office of Solid Waste — The Administrator shall establish within the Environmental Protection Agency an Office of Solid Waste (hereinafter referred to as the "Office") to be headed by an Assistant Administrator of the Environmental Protection Agency. The duties and responsibilities (other than duties and responsibilities relating to research and development) of the Administrator under this chapter (as modified by applicable reorganization plans) shall be carried out through the Office.

(b) Interagency Coordinating Committee

(1) There is hereby established an Interagency Coordinating Committee on Federal Resource Conservation and Recovery Activities which shall have the responsibility for coordinating all activities dealing with resource conservation and recovery from solid waste carried out by the Environmental Protection Agency, the Department of Energy, the Department of Commerce, and all other Federal

agencies which conduct such activities pursuant to this chapter or any other Act. For purposes of this subsection, the term "resource conservation and recovery activities" shall include, but not be limited to, all research, development and demonstration projects on resource conservation or energy, or material, recovery from solid waste, and all technical or financial assistance for State or local planning for, or implementation of, projects related to resource conservation or energy or material, recovery from solid waste. The Committee shall be chaired by the Administrator of the Environmental Protection Agency or such person as the Administrator may designate. Members of the Committee shall include representatives of the Department of Energy, the Department of Commerce, the Department of the Treasury, and each other Federal agency which the Administrator determines to have programs or responsibilities affecting resource conservation or recovery.

(2) The Interagency Coordinating Committee shall include oversight of the implementation of —

(A) the May 1979 Memorandum of Understanding on Energy Recovery from Municipal Solid Waste between the Environmental Protection Agency and the Department of Energy;

(B) the May 30, 1978, Interagency Agreement between the Department of Commerce and the Environmental Protection Agency on the Implementation of the Resource Conservation and Recovery Act [42 U.S.C. §§6901 *et seq.*]; and

(C) any subsequent agreements between these agencies or other Federal agencies which address Federal resource recovery or conservation activities.

§6911a. Assistant Administrator of Environmental Protection Agency; appointment, etc.

The Assistant Administrator of the Environmental Protection Agency appointed to head the Office of Solid Waste shall be in addition to the five Assistant Administrators of the Environmental Protection Agency provided for in section 1(d) of Reorganization Plan Numbered 3 of 1970 and the additional Assistant Administrator provided by the Toxic Substances Control Act [15 U.S.C. §§2601 *et seq.*], shall be appointed by the President by and with the advice and consent of the Senate.

§6912. Authorities of Administrator
[SWDA §2002]

(a) Authorities — In carrying out this chapter, the Administrator is authorized to —

(1) prescribe, in consultation with Federal, State, and regional authorities, such regulations as are necessary to carry out his functions under this chapter;

(2) consult with or exchange information with other Federal agencies undertaking research, development, demonstration projects, studies, or investigations relating to solid waste;

(3) provide technical and financial assistance to States or regional agencies in the development and implementation of solid waste plans and hazardous waste management programs;

(4) consult with representatives of science, industry, agriculture, labor, environmental protection and consumer organizations, and other groups, as he deems advisable;

(5) utilize the information, facilities, personnel and other resources of Federal agencies, including the National Institute of Standards and Technology and the National Bureau of the Census, on a reimbursable basis, to perform research and analyses and conduct studies and investigations related to resource recovery and conservation and to otherwise carry out the Administrator's functions under this chapter; and

(6) to delegate to the Secretary of Transportation the performance of any inspection or enforcement function under this chapter relating to the transportation of hazardous waste where such delegation would avoid unnecessary duplication of activity and would carry out the objectives of this chapter and chapter 51 of Title 49 of the Hazardous Materials Transportation Act.

(b) Revision of regulations — Each regulation promulgated under this chapter shall be reviewed and, where necessary, revised not less frequently than every three years.

(c) Criminal investigations — In carrying out the provisions of this chapter, the Administrator, and duly-designated agents and employees of the Environmental Protection Agency, are authorized to initiate and conduct investigations under the criminal provisions of this chapter, and to refer the results of these investigations to the Attorney General for prosecution in appropriate cases.

§6913. Resource Recovery and Conservation Panels
[SWDA §2003]

The Administrator shall provide teams of personnel, including Federal, State, and local employees or contractors (hereinafter referred to as "Resource Conservation and Recovery Panels") to provide Federal agencies, States and local governments upon request with technical assistance on solid waste management, resource recovery, and resource conservation. Such teams shall include technical, marketing, financial, and institutional specialists, and the services of such teams shall be provided without charge to States or local governments.

§6914. Grants for discarded tire disposal
[SWDA §2004]

(a) Grants — The Administrator shall make available grants equal to 5 percent of the purchase price of tire shredders (including portable shredders attached to tire collection trucks) to those eligible applicants best meeting criteria promulgated under this section. An eligible applicant may be any private purchaser, public body, or public-private joint venture. Criteria for receiving grants shall be promulgated under this and shall include the policy to offer any private purchaser the first option to receive a grant, the policy to develop widespread geographic distribution of tire shredding facilities, the need for such facilities within a geographic area, and the projected risk and viability of any such venture. In the case of an application under this section from a public body, the Administrator shall first make a determination that there are no private purchasers interested in making an application before approving a grant to a public body.

(b) Authorization of appropriations — There is authorized to be appropriated $750,000 for each of the fiscal years 1978 and 1979 to carry out this section.

§6914a. Labeling of lubricating oil
[SWDA §2005]

For purposes of any provision of law which requires the labeling of commodities, lubricating oil shall be treated as lawfully labeled only if it bears the following statement, prominently displayed:

"DON'T POLLUTE — CONSERVE RESOURCES; RETURN USED OIL TO COLLECTION CENTERS".

§6914b. Degradable plastic ring carriers; definitions

As used in this title —

(1) the term "regulated item" means any plastic ring carrier device that contains at least one hole greater than 1¾ inches in diameter which is made, used, or designed for the purpose of packaging, transporting, or carrying multipackaged cans or bottles, and which is of a size, shape, design, or type capable, when discarded, of becoming entangled with fish or wildlife; and

(2) the term "naturally degradable material" means a material which, when discarded, will be reduced to environmentally benign subunits under the action of normal environmental forces, such as, among others, biological decomposition, photodegradation, or hydrolysis.

§6914b-1. Regulation of plastic ring carriers

Not later than 24 months after October 28, 1988 (unless the Administrator of the Environmental Protection Agency determines that it is not feasible or that the byproducts of degradable regulated items present a greater threat to the environment than nondegradable regulated items), the Administrator of the Environmental Protection Agency shall require, by regulation, that any regulated item intended for use in the United States shall be made of naturally degradable material which, when discarded, decomposes within a period established by such regulation. The period within which decomposition must occur after being discarded shall be the shortest period of time consistent with the intended use of the item and the physical integrity required for such use. Such regulation shall allow a reasonable time for affected parties to come into compliance, including the use of existing inventories.

§6915. Annual report
[SWDA §2006]

The Administrator shall transmit to the Congress and the President, not later than ninety days after the end of each fiscal year, a comprehensive and detailed report on all activities of the Office during the preceding fiscal year. Each such report shall include —

(1) a statement of specific and detailed objectives for the activities and programs conducted and assisted under this chapter;

(2) statements of the Administrator's conclusions as to the effectiveness of such activities and programs in meeting the stated objectives and the purposes of this chapter, measured through the end of such fiscal year;

(3) a summary of outstanding solid waste problems confronting the Administrator, in order of priority;

(4) recommendations with respect to such legislation which the Administrator deems necessary or desirable to assist in solving problems respecting solid waste;

(5) all other information required to be submitted to the Congress pursuant to any other provision of this chapter; and

(6) the Administrator's plans for activities and programs respecting solid waste during the next fiscal year.

§6916. General authorization
[SWDA §2007]

(a) General administration — There are authorized to be appropriated to the Administrator for the purpose of carrying out the provisions of this chapter, $35,000,000 for the fiscal year ending September 30, 1977, $38,000,000 for the fiscal year ending September 30, 1978, $42,000,000 for the fiscal year ending September 30, 1979, $70,000,000 for the fiscal year ending September 30, 1980, $80,000,000 for the fiscal year ending September 30, 1981, $80,000,000 for the fiscal year ending September 30, 1982, $70,000,000 for the fiscal year ending

September 30, 1985, $80,000,000 for the fiscal year ending September 30, 1986, $80,000,000 for the fiscal year ending September 30, 1987, and $80,000,000 for the fiscal year 1988.

(b) Resource Recovery and Conservation Panels — Not less than 20 percent of the amount appropriated under subsection (a) of this section, or $5,000,000 per fiscal year, whichever is less, shall be used only for purposes of Resource Recovery and Conservation Panels established under section 6913 of this title (including travel expenses incurred by such panels in carrying out their functions under this chapter).

(c) Hazardous waste — Not less than 30 percent of the amount appropriated under subsection (a) of this section shall be used only for purposes of carrying out subchapter III of this chapter (relating to hazardous waste) other than section 6931 of this title.

(d) State and local support — Not less than 25 per centum of the total amount appropriated under this chapter, up to the amount authorized in section 6948(a)(1) of this title, shall be used only for purposes of support to State, regional, local, and interstate agencies in accordance with subchapter IV of this chapter other than section 6948(a)(2) or 6949 of this title.

(e) Criminal investigators — There is authorized to be appropriated to the Administrator $3,246,000 for the fiscal year 1985, $2,408,300 for the fiscal year 1986, $2,529,000 for the fiscal year 1987, and $2,529,000 for the fiscal year 1988 to be used —

> (1) for additional officers or employees of the Environmental Protection Agency authorized by the Administrator to conduct criminal investigations (to investigate, or supervise the investigation of, any activity for which a criminal penalty is provided) under this chapter; and

> (2) for support costs for such additional officers or employees.

(f) Underground storage tanks

> (1) There are authorized to be appropriated to the Administrator for the purpose of carrying out the provisions of subchapter IX of this chapter (relating to regulation of underground storage tanks), $10,000,000 for each of the fiscal years 1985 through 1988.

> (2) There is authorized to be appropriated $25,000,000 for each of the fiscal years 1985 through 1988 to be used to make grants to the States for purposes of assisting the States in the development and implementation of approved State underground storage tank release detection, prevention, and correction programs under subchapter IX of this chapter.

§6917. Office of Ombudsman
[SWDA §2008]

(a) Establishment; functions — The Administrator shall establish an Office of Ombudsman, to be directed by an Ombudsman. It shall be the function of the Office of Ombudsman to receive individual complaints, grievances, requests for information submitted by any person with respect to any program or requirement under this chapter.

(b) Authority to render assistance — The Ombudsman shall render assistance with respect to the complaints, grievances, and requests submitted to the Office of Ombudsman, and shall make appropriate recommendations to the Administrator.

(c) Effect on procedures for grievances, appeals, or administrative matters — The establishment of the Office of Ombudsman shall not affect any procedures for grievances, appeals, or administrative matters in any other provision of this chapter, any other provision of law, or any Federal regulation.

(d) Termination — The Office of the Ombudsman shall cease to exist 4 years after November 8, 1984.

SUBCHAPTER III — HAZARDOUS WASTE MANAGEMENT

§6921. Identification and listing of hazardous waste
[SWDA §3001]

(a) Criteria for identification or listing — Not later than eighteen months after October 21, 1976, the Administrator shall, after notice and opportunity for public hearing, and after consultation with appropriate Federal and State agencies, develop and promulgate criteria for identifying the characteristics of hazardous waste, and for listing hazardous waste, which should be subject to the provisions of this subchapter, taking into account toxicity, persistence, and degradability in nature, potential for accumulation in tissue, and other related factors such as flammability, corrosiveness, and other hazardous characteristics. Such criteria shall be revised from time to time as may be appropriate.

(b) Identification and listing

> (1) Not later than eighteen months after October 21, 1976, and after notice and opportunity for public hearing, the Administrator shall promulgate regulations identifying the characteristics of hazardous waste, and listing particular hazardous wastes (within the meaning of section 6903(5) of this title), which shall be subject to the provisions of this subchapter. Such regulations shall be based on the criteria promulgated under subsection (a) of this section and shall be revised from time to time thereafter as may be appropriate. The Administrator, in cooperation with the Agency for Toxic Substances and Disease Registry and the National Toxicology Program, shall also identify or list those hazardous wastes

which shall be subject to the provisions of this subchapter solely because of the presence in such wastes of certain constituents (such as identified carcinogens, mutagens, or teratagens) at levels in excess of levels which endanger human health.

(2)(A) Notwithstanding the provisions of paragraph (1) of this subsection, drilling fluids, produced waters, and other wastes associated with the exploration, development, or production of crude oil or natural gas or geothermal energy shall be subject only to existing State or Federal regulatory programs in lieu of this subchapter until at least 24 months after October 21, 1980, and after promulgation of the regulations in accordance with subparagraphs (B) and (C) of this paragraph. It is the sense of the Congress that such State or Federal programs should include, for waste disposal sites which are to be closed, provisions requiring at least the following:

    (i) The identification through surveying, platting, or other measures, together with recordation of such information on the public record, so as to assure that the location where such wastes are disposed of can be located in the future; except however, that no such surveying, platting, or other measure identifying the location of a disposal site for drilling fluids and associated wastes shall be required if the distance from the disposal site to the surveyed or platted location to the associated well is less than two hundred lineal feet; and

    (ii) A chemical and physical analysis of a produced water and a composition of a drilling fluid suspected to contain a hazardous material, with such information to be acquired prior to closure and to be placed on the public record.

(B) Not later than six months after completion and submission of the study required by section 6982(m) of this title, the Administrator shall, after public hearings and opportunity for comment, determine either to promulgate regulations under this subchapter for drilling fluids, produced waters, and other wastes associated with the exploration, development, or production of crude oil or natural gas or geothermal energy or that such regulations are unwarranted. The Administrator shall publish his decision in the Federal Register accompanied by an explanation and justification of the reasons for it. In making the decision under this paragraph, the Administrator shall utilize the information developed or accumulated pursuant to the study required under section 6982(m) of this title.

(C) The Administrator shall transmit his decision, along with any regulations, if necessary, to both Houses of Congress. Such

regulations shall take effect only when authorized by Act of Congress.

(3)(A) Notwithstanding the provisions of paragraph (1) of this subsection, each waste listed below shall, except as provided in subparagraph (B) of this paragraph, be subject only to regulation under other applicable provisions of Federal or State law in lieu of this subchapter until at least six months after the date of submission of the applicable study required to be conducted under subsection (f), (n), (o), or (p) of section 6982 of this title and after promulgation of regulations in accordance with subparagraph (C) of this paragraph:

    (i) Fly ash waste, bottom ash waste, slag waste, and flue gas emission control waste generated primarily from the combustion of coal or other fossil fuels.

    (ii) Solid waste from the extraction, beneficiation, and processing of ores and minerals, including phosphate rock and overburden from the mining of uranium ore.

    (iii) Cement kiln dust waste.

(B)(i) Owners and operators of disposal sites for wastes listed in subparagraph (A) may be required by the Administrator, through regulations prescribed under authority of section 6912 of this title —

    (I) as to disposal sites for such wastes which are to be closed, to identify the locations of such sites through surveying, platting, or other measures, together with recordation of such information on the public record, to assure that the locations where such wastes are disposed of are known and can be located in the future, and

    (II) to provide chemical and physical analysis and composition of such wastes, based on available information, to be placed on the public record.

(ii)(I) In conducting any study under subsection (f), (n), (o), or (p), of section 6982 of this title, any officer, employee, or authorized representative of the Environmental Protection Agency, duly designated by the Administrator, is authorized, at reasonable times and as reasonably necessary for the purposes of such study, to enter any establishment where any waste subject to such study is generated, stored, treated, disposed of, or transported from; to inspect, take samples, and conduct monitoring and testing; and to have access to and copy records relating to such waste. Each such inspection shall be commenced and completed with reasonable promptness. If the officer, employee, or authorized representative obtains any samples prior to leaving the premises, he shall give to the owner, operator, or agent in charge a receipt describing the sample obtained and if requested a portion of each such sample equal in volume or weight to the portion retained. If any analysis is made of such samples, or monitoring and testing performed, a copy of the results shall be furnished promptly to the owner, operator, or agent in charge.

(II) Any records, reports, or information obtained from any person under subclause (I) shall be available to the public, except that upon a showing satisfactory to the Administrator by any person that records, reports, or information, or particular part thereof, to which the Administrator has access under this subparagraph is made public, would divulge information entitled to protection under section 1905 of Title 18, the Administrator shall consider such information or particular portion thereof confidential in accordance with the purposes of that section, except that such record, report, document, or information may be disclosed to other officers, employees, or authorized representatives of the United States concerned with carrying out this chapter. Any person not subject to the provisions of section 1905 of Title 18 who knowingly and willfully divulges or discloses any information entitled to protection under this subparagraph shall, upon conviction, be subject to a fine of not more than $5,000 or to imprisonment not to exceed one year, or both.

(iii) The Administrator may prescribe regulations, under the authority of this chapter, to prevent radiation exposure which presents an unreasonable risk to human health from the use in construction or land reclamation (with or without revegetation) of (I) solid waste from the extraction, beneficiation, and processing of phosphate rock or (II) overburden from the mining of uranium ore.

(iv) Whenever on the basis of any information the Administrator determines that any person is in violation of any requirement of this subparagraph, the Administrator shall give notice to the violator of his failure to comply with such requirement. If such violation extends beyond the thirtieth day after the Administrator's notification, the Administrator may issue an order requiring compliance within a specified time period or the Administrator may commence a civil action in the United States district court in the district in which the violation occurred for appropriate relief, including a temporary or permanent injunction.

(C) Not later than six months after the date of submission of the applicable study required to be conducted under subsection (f), (n), (o), or (p), of section 6982 of this title, the Administrator shall, after public hearings and opportunity for comment, either determine to promulgate regulations under this subchapter for each waste listed in subparagraph (A) of this paragraph or determine that such regulations are unwarranted. The Administrator shall publish his determination, which shall be based on information developed or accumulated pursuant to such study, public hearings, and comment, in the Federal Register accompanied by an explanation and justification of the reasons for it.

(c) Petition by State Governor — At any time after the date eighteen months after October 21, 1976, the Governor of any State may petition the Administrator to identify or list a material as a hazardous waste. The Administrator shall act upon such petition within ninety days following his receipt thereof and shall notify the Governor of such action. If the Administrator denies such petition because of financial considerations, in providing such notice to the Governor he shall include a statement concerning such considerations.

(d) Small quantity generator waste

(1) By March 31, 1986, the Administrator shall promulgate standards under sections 6922, 6923, and 6924 of this title for hazardous waste generated by a generator in a total quantity of hazardous waste greater than one hundred kilograms but less than one thousand kilograms during a calendar month.

(2) The standards referred to in paragraph (1), including standards applicable to the legitimate use, reuse, recycling, and reclamation of such wastes, may vary from the standards applicable to hazardous waste generated by larger quantity generators, but such standards shall be sufficient to protect human health and the environment.

(3) Not later than two hundred and seventy days after November 8, 1984, any hazardous waste which is part of a total quantity generated by a generator generating greater than one hundred kilograms but less than one thousand kilograms during one calendar month and which is shipped off the premises on which such waste is generated shall be accompanied by a copy of the Environmental Protection Agency Uniform Hazardous Waste Manifest form signed by the generator. This form shall contain the following information:

(A) the name and address of the generator of the waste;

(B) the United States Department of Transportation description of the waste, including the proper shipping name, hazard class, and identification number (UN/NA), if applicable;

(C) the number and type of containers;

(D) the quantity of waste being transported; and

(E) the name and address of the facility designated to receive the waste.

If subparagraph (B) is not applicable, in lieu of the description referred to in such subparagraph (B), the form shall contain the Environmental Protection Agency identification number, or a generic description of the waste, or a description of the waste by hazardous waste characteristic. Additional requirements related to the manifest form shall apply only if determined necessary by the Administrator to protect human health and the environment.

(4) The Administrator's responsibility under this subchapter to protect human health and the environment may require the promulgation of standards under this subchapter for hazardous wastes which are generated by any generator who does not generate more than one hundred kilograms of hazardous waste in a calendar month.

(5) Until the effective date of standards required to be promulgated under paragraph (1), any hazardous waste identified or listed under this section generated by any generator during any calendar month in a total quantity greater than one hundred kilograms but less than one thousand kilograms, which is not treated, stored, or disposed of at a hazardous waste treatment, storage, or disposal facility with a permit under section 6925 of this title, shall be disposed of only in a facility which is permitted, licensed, or registered by a State to manage municipal or industrial solid waste.

(6) Standards promulgated as provided in paragraph (1) shall, at a minimum, require that all treatment, storage, or disposal of hazardous wastes generated by generators referred to in paragraph (1) shall occur at a facility with interim status or a permit under this subchapter, except that onsite storage of hazardous waste generated by a generator generating a total quantity of hazardous waste greater than one hundred kilograms, but less than one thousand kilograms during a calendar month, may occur without the requirement of a permit for up to one hundred and eighty days. Such onsite storage may occur without the requirement of a permit for not more than six thousand kilograms for up to two hundred and seventy days if such generator must ship or haul such waste over two hundred miles.

(7)(A) Nothing in this subsection shall be construed to affect or impair the validity of regulations promulgated by the Secretary of Transportation pursuant to chapter 51 of Title 49 of the Hazardous Materials Transportation Act.

(B) Nothing in this subsection shall be construed to affect, modify, or render invalid any requirements in regulations promulgated prior to January 1, 1983 applicable to any acutely hazardous waste identified or listed under this section which is generated by any generator during any calendar month in a total quantity less than one thousand kilograms.

(8) Effective March 31, 1986, unless the Administrator promulgates standards as provided in paragraph (1) of this subsection prior to such date, hazardous waste generated by any generator in a total quantity greater than one hundred kilograms but less than one thousand kilograms during a calendar month shall be subject to the following requirements until the standards referred to in paragraph (1) of this subsection have become effective:

(A) the notice requirements of paragraph (3) of this subsection shall apply and in addition, the information provided in the form shall include the name of the waste transporters and the name and address of the facility designated to receive the waste;

(B) except in the case of the onsite storage referred to in paragraph (6) of this subsection, the treatment, storage, or disposal of such waste shall occur at a facility with interim status or a permit under this subchapter;

(C) generators of such waste shall file manifest exception reports as required of generators producing greater amounts of hazardous waste per month except that such reports shall be filed by January 31, for any waste shipment occurring in the last half of the preceding calendar year, and by July 31, for any waste shipment occurring in the first half of the calendar year; and

(D) generators of such waste shall retain for three years a copy of the manifest signed by the designated facility that has received the waste.

Nothing in this paragraph shall be construed as a determination of the standards appropriate under paragraph (1).

(9) The last sentence of section 6930(b) of this title shall not apply to regulations promulgated under this subsection.

(e) Specified wastes

(1) Not later than 6 months after November 8, 1984, the Administrator shall, where appropriate, list under subsection (b)(1) of this section, additional wastes containing chlorinated dioxins or chlorinated-dibenzofurans. Not later than one year after November 8, 1984, the Administrator shall, where appropriate, list under subsection (b)(1) of this section wastes containing remaining halogenated dioxins and halogenated-dibenzofurans.

(2) Not later than fifteen months after November 8, 1984, the Administrator shall make a determination of whether or not to list under subsection (b)(1) of this section the following wastes: Chlorinated Aliphatics, Dioxin, Dimethyl Hydrazine, TDI (toluene diisocyanate), Carbamates, Bromacil, Linuron, Organo-bromines, solvents, refining wastes, chlorinated aromatics, dyes and pigments, inorganic chemical industry wastes, lithium batteries, coke byproducts, paint production wastes, and coal slurry pipeline effluent.

(f) Delisting procedures

(1) When evaluating a petition to exclude a waste generated at a particular facility from listing under this section, the Administrator shall consider factors (including additional constituents) other than those for which the waste was listed if the Administrator has a reasonable basis to believe that such additional factors could cause the waste to be a hazardous waste. The Administrator shall provide notice and opportunity for comment on these additional factors before granting or denying such petition.

(2)(A) To the maximum extent practicable the Administrator shall publish in the Federal Register a proposal to grant or deny a petition referred to in paragraph (1) within twelve months after receiving a complete application to exclude a waste generated at a particular facility from being regulated as a hazardous waste and shall grant or deny such a petition within twenty-four months after receiving a complete application.

(B) The temporary granting of such a petition prior to November 8, 1984, without the opportunity for public comment and the full consideration of such comments shall not continue for more than twenty-four months after November 8, 1984. If a final decision to grant or deny such a petition has not been promulgated after notice and opportunity for public comment within the time limit prescribed by the preceding sentence, any such temporary granting of such petition shall cease to be in effect.

(g) EP toxicity — Not later than twenty-eight months after November 8, 1984, the Administrator shall examine the deficiencies of the extraction procedure toxicity characteristic as a predictor of the leaching potential of wastes and make changes in the extraction procedure toxicity characteristic, including changes in the leaching media, as are necessary to insure that it accurately predicts the leaching potential of wastes which pose a threat to human health and the environment when mismanaged.

(h) Additional characteristics — Not later than two years after November 8, 1984, the Administrator shall promulgate regulations under this section identifying additional characteristics of hazardous waste, including measures or indicators of toxicity.

(i) Clarification of household waste exclusion — A resource recovery facility recovering energy from the mass burning of municipal solid waste shall not be deemed to be treating, storing, disposing of, or otherwise managing hazardous wastes for the purposes of regulation under this subchapter, if —

(1) such facility —

(A) receives and burns only —

(i) household waste (from single and multiple dwellings, hotels, motels, and other residential sources), and

(ii) solid waste from commercial or industrial sources that does not contain hazardous waste identified or listed under this section, and

(B) does not accept hazardous wastes identified or listed under this section, and

(2) the owner or operator of such facility has established contractual requirements or other appropriate notification or inspection procedures to assure that hazardous wastes are not received at or burned in such facility.

(j) Methamphetamine production — Not later than every 24 months, the Administrator shall submit to the Committee on Energy and Commerce of the House of Representatives and the Committee on Environment and Public Works of the Senate a report setting forth information collected by the Administrator from law enforcement agencies, States, and other relevant stakeholders that identifies the byproducts of the methamphetamine production process and whether the Administrator considers each of the byproducts to be a hazardous waste pursuant to this section and relevant regulations.

§6922. Standards applicable to generators of hazardous waste
[SWDA §3002]

(a) In general — Not later than eighteen months after October 21, 1976, and after notice and opportunity for public hearings and after consultation with appropriate Federal and State agencies, the Administrator shall promulgate regulations establishing such standards, applicable to generators of hazardous waste identified or listed under this subchapter, as may be necessary to protect human health and the environment. Such standards shall establish requirements respecting —

(1) recordkeeping practices that accurately identify the quantities of such hazardous waste generated, the constituents thereof which are significant in quantity or in potential harm to human health or the environment, and the disposition of such wastes;

(2) labeling practices for any containers used for the storage, transport, or disposal of such

hazardous waste such as will identify accurately such waste;

(3) use of appropriate containers for such hazardous waste;

(4) furnishing of information on the general chemical composition of such hazardous waste to persons transporting, treating, storing, or disposing of such wastes;

(5) use of a manifest system and any other reasonable means necessary to assure that all such hazardous waste generated is designated for treatment, storage, or disposal in, and arrives at, treatment, storage, or disposal facilities (other than facilities on the premises where the waste is generated) for which a permit has been issued as provided in this subchapter, or pursuant to title I of the Marine Protection, Research, and Sanctuaries Act (86 Stat. 1052) [33 U.S.C. §§1411 *et seq.*]; and

(6) submission of reports to the Administrator (or the State agency in any case in which such agency carries out a permit program pursuant to this subchapter) at least once every two years, setting out —

(A) the quantities and nature of hazardous waste identified or listed under this subchapter that he has generated during the year;

(B) the disposition of all hazardous waste reported under subparagraph (A);

(C) the efforts undertaken during the year to reduce the volume and toxicity of waste generated; and

(D) the changes in volume and toxicity of waste actually achieved during the year in question in comparison with previous years, to the extent such information is available for years prior to November 8, 1984.

(b) Waste minimization — Effective September 1, 1985, the manifest required by subsection (a)(5) of this section shall contain a certification by the generator that —

(1) the generator of the hazardous waste has a program in place to reduce the volume or quantity and toxicity of such waste to the degree determined by the generator to be economically practicable; and

(2) the proposed method of treatment, storage, or disposal is that practicable method currently available to the generator which minimizes the present and future threat to human health and the environment.

§6923. Standards applicable to transporters of hazardous waste
[SWDA §3003]

(a) Standards — Not later than eighteen months after October 21, 1976, and after opportunity for public hearings, the Administrator, after consultation with the Secretary of Transportation and the States, shall promulgate regulations establishing such stan-dards, applicable to transporters of hazardous waste identified or listed under this subchapter, as may be necessary to protect human health and the environment. Such standards shall include but need not be limited to requirements respecting —

(1) recordkeeping concerning such hazardous waste transported, and their source and delivery points;

(2) transportation of such waste only if properly labeled;

(3) compliance with the manifest system referred to in section 6922(5) of this title; and

(4) transportation of all such hazardous waste only to the hazardous waste treatment, storage, or disposal facilities which the shipper designates on the manifest form to be a facility holding a permit issued under this subchapter, or pursuant to title I of the Marine Protection, Research, and Sanctuaries Act (86 Stat. 1052) [33 U.S.C. §§1411 *et seq.*].

(b) Coordination with regulations of Secretary of Transportation — In case of any hazardous waste identified or listed under this subchapter which is subject to chapter 51 of Title 49, the regulations promulgated by the Administrator under this section shall be consistent with the requirements of such Act and the regulations thereunder. The Administrator is authorized to make recommendations to the Secretary of Transportation respecting the regulations of such hazardous waste under the Hazardous Materials Transportation Act and for addition of materials to be covered by such Act.

(c) Fuel from hazardous waste — Not later than two years after November 8, 1984, and after opportunity for public hearing, the Administrator shall promulgate regulations establishing standards, applicable to transporters of fuel produced (1) from any hazardous waste identified or listed under section 6921 of this title, or (2) from any hazardous waste identified or listed under section 6921 of this title and any other material, as may be necessary to protect human health and the environment. Such standards may include any of the requirements set forth in paragraphs (1) through (4) of subsection (a) of this section as may be appropriate.

§6924. Standards applicable to owners and operators of hazardous waste treatment, storage, and disposal facilities
[SWDA §3004]

(a) In general — Not later than eighteen months after October 21, 1976, and after opportunity for public hearings and after consultation with appropriate Federal and State agencies, the Administrator shall promulgate regulations establishing such performance standards, applicable to owners and operators of facilities for the treatment, storage, or disposal of hazardous waste identified or listed under this subchapter, as may be necessary to protect human health and the environment. In establishing such standards the Administrator shall, where appropriate, distinguish in such standards between requirements appropriate for new facilities and for facilities in existence on the date of promulgation of such regulations. Such standards shall include, but need not be limited to, requirements respecting —

(1) maintaining records of all hazardous wastes identified or listed under this chapter which is treated, stored, or disposed of, as the case may be, and the manner in which such wastes were treated, stored, or disposed of;

(2) satisfactory reporting, monitoring, and inspection and compliance with the manifest system referred to in section 6922(5) of this title;

(3) treatment, storage, or disposal of all such waste received by the facility pursuant to such operating methods, techniques, and practices as may be satisfactory to the Administrator;

(4) the location, design, and construction of such hazardous waste treatment, disposal, or storage facilities;

(5) contingency plans for effective action to minimize unanticipated damage from any treatment, storage, or disposal of any such hazardous waste;

(6) the maintenance of operation of such facilities and requiring such additional qualifications as to ownership, continuity of operation, training for personnel, and financial responsibility (including financial responsibility for corrective action) as may be necessary or desirable; and

(7) compliance with the requirements of section 6925 of this title respecting permits for treatment, storage, or disposal.

No private entity shall be precluded by reason of criteria established under paragraph (6) from the ownership or operation of facilities providing hazardous waste treatment, storage, or disposal services where such entity can provide assurances of financial responsibility and continuity of operation consistent with the degree and duration of risks associated with the treatment, storage, or disposal of specified hazardous waste.

(b) Salt dome formations, salt bed formations, underground mines and caves

(1) Effective on November 8, 1984, the placement of any noncontainerized or bulk liquid hazardous waste in any salt dome formation, salt bed formation, underground mine, or cave is prohibited until such time as —

(A) the Administrator has determined, after notice and opportunity for hearings on the record in the affected areas, that such placement is protective of human health and the environment;

(B) the Administrator has promulgated performance and permitting standards for such facilities under this subchapter; and

(C) a permit has been issued under section 6925(c) of this title for the facility concerned.

(2) Effective on November 8, 1984, the placement of any hazardous waste other than a hazardous waste referred to in paragraph (1) in a salt dome formation, salt bed formation, underground mine, or cave is prohibited until such time as a permit has been issued under section 6925(c) of this title for the facility concerned.

(3) No determination made by the Administrator under subsection (d), (e), or (g) of this section regarding any hazardous waste to which such subsection (d), (e), or (g) of this section applies shall affect the prohibition contained in paragraph (1) or (2) of this subsection.

(4) Nothing in this subsection shall apply to the Department of Energy Waste Isolation Pilot Project in New Mexico.

(c) Liquids in landfills

(1) Effective 6 months after November 8, 1984, the placement of bulk or noncontainerized liquid hazardous waste or free liquids contained in hazardous waste (whether or not absorbents have been added) in any landfill is prohibited. Prior to such date the requirements (as in effect on April 30, 1983) promulgated under this section by the Administrator regarding liquid hazardous waste shall remain in force and effect to the extent such requirements are applicable to the placement of bulk or noncontainerized liquid hazardous waste, or free liquids contained in hazardous waste, in landfills.

(2) Not later than fifteen months after November 8, 1984, the Administrator shall promulgate final regulations which —

(A) minimize the disposal of containerized liquid hazardous waste in landfills, and

(B) minimize the presence of free liquids in containerized hazardous waste to be disposed of in landfills.

Such regulations shall also prohibit the disposal in landfills of liquids that have been absorbed in materials that biodegrade or that release liquids when compressed as might occur during routine landfill operations. Prior to the date on which such final regulations take effect, the requirements (as in effect on April 30, 1983) promulgated under this section by the Administrator shall remain in force and effect to the extent such requirements are applicable to the disposal of containerized liquid hazardous waste, or free liquids contained in hazardous waste, in landfills.

(3) Effective twelve months after November 8, 1984, the placement of any liquid which is not a hazardous waste in a landfill for which a permit is required under section 6925(c) of this title or which is operating pursuant to interim status granted under section 6925(e) of this title

is prohibited unless the owner or operator of such landfill demonstrates to the Administrator, or the Administrator determines, that —

(A) the only reasonably available alternative to the placement in such landfill is placement in a landfill or unlined surface impoundment, whether or not permitted under section 6925(c) of this title or operating pursuant to interim status under section 6925(e) of this title, which contains, or may reasonably be anticipated to contain, hazardous waste; and

(B) placement in such owner or operator's landfill will not present a risk of contamination of any underground source of drinking water.

As used in subparagraph (B), the term "underground source of drinking water" has the same meaning as provided in regulations under the Safe Drinking Water Act (title XIV of the Public Health Service Act) [42 U.S.C. §§300f et seq.].

(4) No determination made by the Administrator under subsection (d), (e), or (g) of this section regarding any hazardous waste to which such subsection (d), (e), or (g) of this section applies shall affect the prohibition contained in paragraph (1) of this subsection.

(d) Prohibitions on land disposal of specified wastes

(1) Effective 32 months after November 8, 1984 (except as provided in subsection (f) of this section with respect to underground injection into deep injection wells), the land disposal of the hazardous wastes referred to in paragraph (2) is prohibited unless the Administrator determines the prohibition on one or more methods of land disposal of such waste is not required in order to protect human health and the environment for as long as the waste remains hazardous, taking into account —

(A) the long-term uncertainties associated with land disposal,

(B) the goal of managing hazardous waste in an appropriate manner in the first instance, and

(C) the persistence, toxicity, mobility, and propensity to bioaccumulate of such hazardous wastes and their hazardous constituents.

For the purposes of this paragraph, a method of land disposal may not be determined to be protective of human health and the environment for a hazardous waste referred to in paragraph (2) (other than a hazardous waste which has complied with the pretreatment regulations promulgated under subsection (m) of this section), unless, upon application by an interested person, it has been demonstrated to the Administrator, to a reasonable degree of certainty, that there will be no migration of hazardous constituents from the disposal unit or injection zone for as long as the wastes remain hazardous.

(2) Paragraph (1) applies to the following hazardous wastes listed or identified under section 6921 of this title:

(A) Liquid hazardous wastes, including free liquids associated with any solid or sludge, containing free cyanides at concentrations greater than or equal to 1,000 mg/l.

(B) Liquid hazardous wastes, including free liquids associated with any solid or sludge, containing the following metals (or elements) or compounds of these metals (or elements) at concentrations greater than or equal to those specified below:

(i) arsenic and/or compounds (as As) 500 mg/l;

(ii) cadmium and/or compounds (as Cd) 100 mg/l;

(iii) chromium (VI and/or compounds (as Cr VI)) 500 mg/l;

(iv) lead and/or compounds (as Pb) 500 mg/l;

(v) mercury and/or compounds (as Hg) 20 mg/l;

(vi) nickel and/or compounds (as Ni) 134 mg/l;

(vii) selenium and/or compounds (as Se) 100 mg/l; and

(viii) thallium and/or compounds (as Th) 130 mg/l.

(C) Liquid hazardous waste having a pH less than or equal to two (2.0).

(D) Liquid hazardous wastes containing polychlorinated biphenyls at concentrations greater than or equal to 50 ppm.

(E) Hazardous wastes containing halogenated organic compounds in total concentration greater than or equal to 1,000 mg/kg.

When necessary to protect human health and the environment, the Administrator shall substitute more stringent concentration levels than the levels specified in subparagraphs (A) through (E).

(3) During the period ending forty-eight months after November 8, 1984, this subsection shall not apply to any disposal of contaminated soil or debris resulting from a response action taken under section 9604 or 9606 of this title or a corrective action required under this subchapter.

(e) Solvents and dioxins

(1) Effective twenty-four months after November 8, 1984 (except as provided in subsection (f) of this section with respect to underground injection into deep injection wells), the land disposal of the hazardous wastes referred to in paragraph (2) is prohibited unless the Administrator determines the prohibition of one or more methods of land disposal of such waste is not required in order to protect human health and the environment for as long as the waste remains

hazardous, taking into account the factors referred to in subparagraph (A) through (C) of subsection (d)(1) of this section. For the purposes of this paragraph, a method of land disposal may not be determined to be protective of human health and the environment for a hazardous waste referred to in paragraph (2) (other than a hazardous waste which has complied with the pretreatment regulations promulgated under subsection (m) of this section), unless upon application by an interested person it has been demonstrated to the Administrator, to a reasonable degree of certainty, that there will be no migration of hazardous constituents from the disposal unit or injection zone for as long as the wastes remain hazardous.

(2) The hazardous wastes to which the prohibition under paragraph (1) applies are as follows —

(A) dioxin-containing hazardous wastes numbered F020, F021, F022, and F023 (as referred to in the proposed rule published by the Administrator in the Federal Register for April 4, 1983), and

(B) those hazardous wastes numbered F001, F002, F003, F004, and F005 in regulations promulgated by the Administrator under section 6921 of this title (40 C.F.R. 261.31 (July 1, 1983)), as those regulations are in effect on July 1, 1983.

(3) During the period ending forty-eight months after November 8, 1984, this subsection shall not apply to any disposal of contaminated soil or debris resulting from a response action taken under section 9604 or 9606 of this title or a corrective action required under this subchapter.

(f) Disposal into deep injection wells; specified subsection (d) wastes; solvents and dioxins

(1) Not later than forty-five months after November 8, 1984, the Administrator shall complete a review of the disposal of all hazardous wastes referred to in paragraph (2) of subsection (d) of this section and in paragraph (2) of subsection (e) of this section by underground injection into deep injection wells.

(2) Within forty-five months after November 8, 1984, the Administrator shall make a determination regarding the disposal by underground injection into deep injection wells of the hazardous wastes referred to in paragraph (2) of subsection (d) of this section and the hazardous wastes referred to in paragraph (2) of subsection (e) of this section. The Administrator shall promulgate final regulations prohibiting the disposal of such wastes into such wells if it may reasonably be determined that such disposal may not be protective of human health and the environment for as long as the waste remains hazardous, taking into account the factors referred to in subparagraphs (A) through (C) of subsection (d)(1) of this section. In

promulgating such regulations, the Administrator shall consider each hazardous waste referred to in paragraph (2) of subsection (d) of this section or in paragraph (2) of subsection (e) of this section which is prohibited from disposal into such wells by any State.

(3) If the Administrator fails to make a determination under paragraph (2) for any hazardous waste referred to in paragraph (2) of subsection (d) of this section or in paragraph (2) of subsection (e) of this section within forty-five months after November 8, 1984, such hazardous waste shall be prohibited from disposal into any deep injection well.

(4) As used in this subsection, the term "deep injection well" means a well used for the underground injection of hazardous waste other than a well to which section 6979a(a) of this title applies.

(g) Additional land disposal prohibition determinations

(1) Not later than twenty-four months after November 8, 1984, the Administrator shall submit a schedule to Congress for —

(A) reviewing all hazardous wastes listed (as of November 8, 1984) under section 6921 of this title other than those wastes which are referred to in subsection (d) or (e) of this section; and

(B) taking action under paragraph (5) of this subsection with respect to each such hazardous waste.

(2) The Administrator shall base the schedule on a ranking of such listed wastes considering their intrinsic hazard and their volume such that decisions regarding the land disposal of high volume hazardous wastes with high intrinsic hazard shall, to the maximum extent possible, be made by the date forty-five months after November 8, 1984. Decisions regarding low volume hazardous wastes with lower intrinsic hazard shall be made by the date sixty-six months after November 8, 1984.

(3) The preparation and submission of the schedule under this subsection shall not be subject to the Paperwork Reduction Act of 1980. No hearing on the record shall be required for purposes of preparation or submission of the schedule. The schedule shall not be subject to judicial review.

(4) The schedule under this subsection shall require that the Administrator shall promulgate regulations in accordance with paragraph (5) or make a determination under paragraph (5) —

(A) for at least one-third of all hazardous wastes referred to in paragraph (1) by the date forty-five months after November 8, 1984;

(B) for at least two-thirds of all such listed wastes by the date fifty-five months after November 8, 1984; and

(C) for all such listed wastes and for all hazardous wastes identified under section 6921 of this title by the date sixty-six months after November 8, 1984.

In the case of any hazardous waste identified or listed under section 6921 of this title after November 8, 1984, the Administrator shall determine whether such waste shall be prohibited from one or more methods of land disposal in accordance with paragraph (5) within six months after the date of such identification or listing.

(5) Not later than the date specified in the schedule published under this subsection, the Administrator shall promulgate final regulations prohibiting one or more methods of land disposal of the hazardous wastes listed on such schedule except for methods of land disposal which the Administrator determines will be protective of human health and the environment for as long as the waste remains hazardous, taking into account the factors referred to in subparagraphs (A) through (C) of subsection (d)(1) of this section. For the purposes of this paragraph, a method of land disposal may not be determined to be protective of human health and the environment (except with respect to a hazardous waste which has complied with the pretreatment regulations promulgated under subsection (m) of this section) unless, upon application by an interested person, it has been demonstrated to the Administrator, to a reasonable degree of certainty, that there will be no migration of hazardous constituents from the disposal unit or injection zone for as long as the wastes remain hazardous.

(6)(A) If the Administrator fails (by the date forty-five months after November 8, 1984) to promulgate regulations or make a determination under paragraph (5) for any hazardous waste which is included in the first one-third of the schedule published under this subsection, such hazardous waste may be disposed of in a landfill or surface impoundment only if —

   (i) such facility is in compliance with the requirements of subsection (o) of this section which are applicable to new facilities (relating to minimum technological requirements); and

   (ii) prior to such disposal, the generator has certified to the Administrator that such generator has investigated the availability of treatment capacity and has determined that the use of such landfill or surface impoundment is the only practical alternative to treatment currently available to the generator.

The prohibition contained in this subparagraph shall continue to apply until the Administrator promulgates regulations or makes a determination under paragraph (5) for the waste concerned.

(B) If the Administrator fails (by the date 55 months after November 8, 1984) to promulgate regulations or make a determination under paragraph (5) for any hazardous waste which is included in the first two-thirds of the schedule published under this subsection, such hazardous waste may be disposed of in a landfill or surface impoundment only if —

   (i) such facility is in compliance with the requirements of subsection (o) of this section which are applicable to new facilities (relating to minimum technological requirements); and

   (ii) prior to such disposal, the generator has certified to the Administrator that such generator has investigated the availability of treatment capacity and has determined that the use of such landfill or surface impoundment is the only practical alternative to treatment currently available to the generator.

The prohibition contained in this subparagraph shall continue to apply until the Administrator promulgates regulations or makes a determination under paragraph (5) for the waste concerned.

(C) If the Administrator fails to promulgate regulations, or make a determination under paragraph (5) for any hazardous waste referred to in paragraph (1) within 66 months after November 8, 1984, such hazardous waste shall be prohibited from land disposal.

(7) Solid waste identified as hazardous based solely on one or more characteristics shall not be subject to this subsection, any prohibitions under subsection (d), (e), or (f) of this section, or any requirement promulgated under subsection (m) of this section (other than any applicable specific methods of treatment, as provided in paragraph (8)) if the waste —

   (A) is treated in a treatment system that subsequently discharges to waters of the United States pursuant to a permit issued under section 1342 of Title 33, treated for the purposes of the pretreatment requirements of section 1317 of Title 33, or treated in a zero discharge system that, prior to any permanent land disposal, engages in treatment that is equivalent to treatment required under section 1342 of Title 33 for discharges to waters of the United States, as determined by the Administrator; and

   (B) no longer exhibits a hazardous characteristic prior to management in any land-based solid waste management unit.

(8) Solid waste that otherwise qualifies under paragraph (7) shall nevertheless be required to meet any applicable specific methods of treatment specified for such waste by the Administrator

under subsection (m) of this section, including those specified in the rule promulgated by the Administrator June 1, 1990, prior to management in a land-based unit as part of a treatment system specified in paragraph (7)(A). No solid waste may qualify under paragraph (7) that would generate toxic gases, vapors, or fumes due to the presence of cyanide when exposed to pH conditions between 2.0 and 12.5.

(9) Solid waste identified as hazardous based on one or more characteristics alone shall not be subject to this subsection, any prohibitions under subsection (d), (e), or (f) of this section, or any requirement promulgated under subsection (m) of this section if the waste no longer exhibits a hazardous characteristic at the point of injection in any Class I injection well permitted under section 300h-1 of this title.

(10) Not later than five years after March 26, 1996, the Administrator shall complete a study of hazardous waste managed pursuant to paragraph (7) or (9) to characterize the risks to human health or the environment associated with such management. In conducting this study, the Administrator shall evaluate the extent to which risks are adequately addressed under existing State or Federal programs and whether unaddressed risks could be better addressed under such laws or programs. Upon receipt of additional information or upon completion of such study and as necessary to protect human health and the environment, the Administrator may impose additional requirements under existing Federal laws, including subsection (m)(1) of this section, or rely on other State or Federal programs or authorities to address such risks. In promulgating any treatment standards pursuant to subsection (m)(1) of this section under the previous sentence, the Administrator shall take into account the extent to which treatment is occurring in land-based units as part of a treatment system specified in paragraph (7)(A).

(11) Nothing in paragraph (7) or (9) shall be interpreted or applied to restrict any inspection or enforcement authority under the provisions of this chapter.

(h) Variance from land disposal prohibitions

(1) A prohibition in regulations under subsection (d), (e), (f), or (g) of this section shall be effective immediately upon promulgation.

(2) The Administrator may establish an effective date different from the effective date which would otherwise apply under subsection (d), (e), (f), or (g) of this section with respect to a specific hazardous waste which is subject to a prohibition under subsection (d), (e), (f), or (g) of this section or under regulations under subsection (d), (e), (f), or (g) of this section. Any such other effective date shall be established on the basis of the earliest date

on which adequate alternative treatment, recovery, or disposal capacity which protects human health and the environment will be available. Any such other effective date shall in no event be later than 2 years after the effective date of the prohibition which would otherwise apply under subsection (d), (e), (f), or (g) of this section.

(3) The Administrator, after notice and opportunity for comment and after consultation with appropriate State agencies in all affected States, may on a case-by-case basis grant an extension of the effective date which would otherwise apply under subsection (d), (e), (f), or (g) of this section or under paragraph (2) for up to one year, where the applicant demonstrates that there is a binding contractual commitment to construct or otherwise provide such alternative capacity but due to circumstances beyond the control of such applicant such alternative capacity cannot reasonably be made available by such effective date. Such extension shall be renewable once for no more than one additional year.

(4) Whenever another effective date (hereinafter referred to as a "variance") is established under paragraph (2), or an extension is granted under paragraph (3), with respect to any hazardous waste, during the period for which such variance or extension is in effect, such hazardous waste may be disposed of in a landfill or surface impoundment only if such facility is in compliance with the requirements of subsection (o) of this section.

(i) Publication of determination — If the Administrator determines that a method of land disposal will be protective of human health and the environment, he shall promptly publish in the Federal Register notice of such determination, together with an explanation of the basis for such determination.

(j) Storage of hazardous waste prohibited from land disposal — In the case of any hazardous waste which is prohibited from one or more methods of land disposal under this section (or under regulations promulgated by the Administrator under any provision of this section) the storage of such hazardous waste is prohibited unless such storage is solely for the purpose of the accumulation of such quantities of hazardous waste as are necessary to facilitate proper recovery, treatment or disposal.

(k) "Land disposal" defined — For the purposes of this section, the term "land disposal", when used with respect to a specified hazardous waste, shall be deemed to include, but not be limited to, any placement of such hazardous waste in a landfill, surface impoundment, waste pile, injection well, land treatment facility, salt dome formation, salt bed formation, or underground mine or cave.

(l) Ban on dust suppression — The use of waste or used oil or other material, which is contaminated or mixed with dioxin or any other hazardous waste identified or listed under section 6921 of this title (other than a waste identified solely on the basis of ignitability), for dust suppression or road treatment is prohibited.

(m) Treatment standards for wastes subject to land disposal prohibition

(1) Simultaneously with the promulgation of regulations under subsection (d), (e), (f), or (g) of this section prohibiting one or more methods of land disposal of a particular hazardous waste, and as appropriate thereafter, the Administrator shall, after notice and an opportunity for hearings and after consultation with appropriate Federal and State agencies, promulgate regulations specifying those levels or methods of treatment, if any, which substantially diminish the toxicity of the waste or substantially reduce the likelihood of migration of hazardous constituents from the waste so that short-term and long-term threats to human health and the environment are minimized.

(2) If such hazardous waste has been treated to the level or by a method specified in regulations promulgated under this subsection, such waste or residue thereof shall not be subject to any prohibition promulgated under subsection (d), (e), (f), or (g) of this section and may be disposed of in a land disposal facility which meets the requirements of this subchapter. Any regulation promulgated under this subsection for a particular hazardous waste shall become effective on the same date as any applicable prohibition promulgated under subsection (d), (e), (f), or (g) of this section.

(n) Air emissions — Not later than thirty months after November 8, 1984, the Administrator shall promulgate such regulations for the monitoring and control of air emissions at hazardous waste treatment, storage, and disposal facilities, including but not limited to open tanks, surface impoundments, and landfills, as may be necessary to protect human health and the environment.

(o) Minimum technological requirements

(1) The regulations under subsection (a) of this section shall be revised from time to time to take into account improvements in the technology of control and measurement. At a minimum, such regulations shall require, and a permit issued pursuant to section 6925(c) of this title after November 8, 1984, by the Administrator or a State shall require —

(A) for each new landfill or surface impoundment, each new landfill or surface impoundment unit at an existing facility, each replacement of an existing landfill or surface impoundment unit, and each lateral expansion of an existing landfill or surface impoundment unit, for which an application for a final determination regarding issuance of a permit under section 6925(c) of this title is received after November 8, 1984 —

(i) the installation of two or more liners and a leachate collection system above (in the case of a landfill) and between such liners; and

(ii) ground water monitoring; and

(B) for each incinerator which receives a permit under section 6925(c) of this title after November 8, 1984, the attainment of the minimum destruction and removal efficiency required by regulations in effect on June 24, 1982.

The requirements of this paragraph shall apply with respect to all waste received after the issuance of the permit.

(2) Paragraph (1)(A)(i) shall not apply if the owner or operator demonstrates to the Administrator, and the Administrator finds for such landfill or surface impoundment, that alternative design and operating practices, together with location characteristics, will prevent the migration of any hazardous constituents into the ground water or surface water at least as effectively as such liners and leachate collection systems.

(3) The double-liner requirement set forth in paragraph (1)(A)(i) may be waived by the Administrator for any monofill, if —

(A) such monofill contains only hazardous wastes from foundry furnace emission controls or metal casting molding sand,

(B) such wastes do not contain constituents which would render the wastes hazardous for reasons other than the Extraction Procedure ("EP") toxicity characteristics set forth in regulations under this subchapter, and

(C) such monofill meets the same requirements as are applicable in the case of a waiver under section 6925(j)(2) or (4) of this title.

(4)(A) Not later than thirty months after November 8, 1984, the Administrator shall promulgate standards requiring that new landfill units, surface impoundment units, waste piles, underground tanks and land treatment units for the storage, treatment, or disposal of hazardous waste identified or listed under section 6921 of this title shall be required to utilize approved leak detection systems.

(B) For the purposes of subparagraph (A) —

(i) the term "approved leak detection system" means a system or technology which the Administrator determines to be capable of detecting leaks of hazardous constituents at the earliest practicable time; and

(ii) the term "new units" means units on which construction commences after the date of promulgation of regulations under this paragraph.

(5)(A) The Administrator shall promulgate regulations or issue guidance documents implementing the requirements of paragraph (1) (A) within two years after November 8, 1984.

(B) Until the effective date of such regulations or guidance documents, the requirement for the installation of two or more liners may be satisfied by the installation of a top liner designed, operated, and constructed of materials to prevent the migration of any constituent into such liner during the period such facility remains in operation (including any post-closure monitoring period), and a lower liner designed, operated and constructed to prevent the migration of any constituent through such liner during such period. For the purpose of the preceding sentence, a lower liner shall be deemed to satisfy such requirement if it is constructed of at least a 3-foot thick layer of recompacted clay or other natural material with a permeability of no more than 1×10^7 centimeter per second.

(6) Any permit under section 6925 of this title which is issued for a landfill located within the State of Alabama shall require the installation of two or more liners and a leachate collection system above and between such liners, notwithstanding any other provision of this chapter.

(7) In addition to the requirements set forth in this subsection, the regulations referred to in paragraph (1) shall specify criteria for the acceptable location of new and existing treatment, storage, or disposal facilities as necessary to protect human health and the environment. Within 18 months after November 8, 1984, the Administrator shall publish guidance criteria identifying areas of vulnerable hydrogeology.

(p) Ground water monitoring — The standards under this section concerning ground water monitoring which are applicable to surface impoundments, waste piles, land treatment units, and landfills shall apply to such a facility whether or not —

(1) the facility is located above the seasonal high water table;

(2) two liners and a leachate collection system have been installed at the facility; or

(3) the owner or operator inspects the liner (or liners) which has been installed at the facility.

This subsection shall not be construed to affect other exemptions or waivers from such standards provided in regulations in effect on November 8, 1984, or as may be provided in revisions to those regulations, to the extent consistent with this subsection. The Administrator is authorized on a case-by-case basis to exempt from ground water monitoring requirements under this section (including subsection (o) of this section) any engineered structure which the Administrator finds does not receive or contain liquid waste (nor waste containing free liquids), is designed and operated to exclude liquid from precipitation or other runoff,

utilizes multiple leak detection systems within the outer layer of containment, and provides for continuing operation and maintenance of these leak detection systems during the operating period, closure, and the period required for post-closure monitoring and for which the Administrator concludes on the basis of such findings that there is a reasonable certainty hazardous constituents will not migrate beyond the outer layer of containment prior to the end of the period required for post-closure monitoring.

(q) Hazardous waste used as fuel

(1) Not later than two years after November 8, 1984, and after notice and opportunity for public hearing, the Administrator shall promulgate regulations establishing such —

(A) standards applicable to the owners and operators of facilities which produce a fuel —

(i) from any hazardous waste identified or listed under section 6921 of this title, or

(ii) from any hazardous waste identified or listed under section 6921 of this title and any other material;

(B) standards applicable to the owners and operators of facilities which burn, for purposes of energy recovery, any fuel produced as provided in subparagraph (A) or any fuel which otherwise contains any hazardous waste identified or listed under section 6921 of this title; and

(C) standards applicable to any person who distributes or markets any fuel which is produced as provided in subparagraph (A) or any fuel which otherwise contains any hazardous waste identified or listed under section 6921 of this title; as may be necessary to protect human health and the environment. Such standards may include any of the requirements set forth in paragraphs (1) through (7) of subsection (a) of this section as may be appropriate. Nothing in this subsection shall be construed to affect or impair the provisions of section 6921(b)(3) of this title. For purposes of this subsection, the term "hazardous waste listed under section 6921 of this title" includes any commercial chemical product which is listed under section 6921 of this title and which, in lieu of its original intended use, is (i) produced for use as (or as a component of) a fuel, (ii) distributed for use as a fuel, or (iii) burned as a fuel.

(2)(A) This subsection, subsection (r) of this section, and subsection (s) of this section shall not apply to petroleum refinery wastes containing oil which are converted into petroleum coke at the same facility at which such wastes were generated, unless the resulting coke product would exceed one or more characteristics by which a substance would be identified as a hazardous waste under section 6921 of this title.

(B) The Administrator may exempt from the requirements of this subsection, subsection (r) of this section, or subsection (s) of this section facilities which burn de minimis quantities of hazardous waste as fuel, as defined by the Administrator, if the wastes are burned at the same facility at which such wastes are generated; the waste is burned to recover useful energy, as determined by the Administrator on the basis of the design and operating characteristics of the facility and the heating value and other characteristics of the waste; and the waste is burned in a type of device determined by the Administrator to be designed and operated at a destruction and removal efficiency sufficient such that protection of human health and environment is assured.

(C)(i) After November 8, 1984, and until standards are promulgated and in effect under paragraph (2) of this subsection, no fuel which contains any hazardous waste may be burned in any cement kiln which is located within the boundaries of any incorporated municipality with a population greater than five hundred thousand (based on the most recent census statistics) unless such kiln fully complies with regulations (as in effect on November 8, 1984) under this subchapter which are applicable to incinerators.

(ii) Any person who knowingly violates the prohibition contained in clause (i) shall be deemed to have violated section 6928(d)(2) of this title.

(r) Labeling

(1) Notwithstanding any other provision of law, until such time as the Administrator promulgates standards under subsection (q) of this section specifically superceding this requirement, it shall be unlawful for any person who is required to file a notification in accordance with paragraph (1) or (3) of section 6930 of this title to distribute or market any fuel which is produced from any hazardous waste identified or listed under section 6921 of this title, or any fuel which otherwise contains any hazardous waste identified or listed under section 6921 of this title if the invoice or the bill of sale fails —

(A) to bear the following statement: "WARNING: THIS FUEL CONTAINS HAZARDOUS WASTES", and

(B) to list the hazardous wastes contained therein.

Beginning ninety days after November 8, 1984, such statement shall be located in a conspicuous place on every such invoice or bill of sale and shall appear in conspicuous and legible type in contrast by typography, layouts, or color with other printed matter on the invoice or bill of sale.

(2) Unless the Administrator determines otherwise as may be necessary to protect human health and the environment, this subsection shall not apply to fuels produced from petroleum refining waste containing oil if —

(A) such materials are generated and reinserted onsite into the refining process;

(B) contaminants are removed; and

(C) such refining waste containing oil is converted along with normal process streams into petroleum-derived fuel products at a facility at which crude oil is refined into petroleum products and which is classified as a number SIC 2911 facility under the Office of Management and Budget Standard Industrial Classification Manual.

(3) Unless the Administrator determines otherwise as may be necessary to protect human health and the environment, this subsection shall not apply to fuels produced from oily materials, resulting from normal petroleum refining, production and transportation practices, if (A) contaminants are removed; and (B) such oily materials are converted along with normal process streams into petroleum-derived fuel products at a facility at which crude oil is refined into petroleum products and which is classified as a number SIC 2911 facility under the Office of Management and Budget Standard Industrial Classification Manual.

(s) Recordkeeping — Not later than fifteen months after November 8, 1984, the Administrator shall promulgate regulations requiring that any person who is required to file a notification in accordance with subparagraph (1), (2), or (3), of section 6930(a) of this title shall maintain such records regarding fuel blending, distribution, or use as may be necessary to protect human health and the environment.

(t) Financial responsibility provisions

(1) Financial responsibility required by subsection (a) of this section may be established in accordance with regulations promulgated by the Administrator by any one, or any combination, of the following: insurance, guarantee, surety bond, letter of credit, or qualification as a self-insurer. In promulgating requirements under this section, the Administrator is authorized to specify policy or other contractual terms, conditions, or defenses which are necessary or are unacceptable in establishing such evidence of financial responsibility in order to effectuate the purposes of this chapter.

(2) In any case where the owner or operator is in bankruptcy, reorganization, or arrangement pursuant to the Federal Bankruptcy Code or where (with reasonable diligence) jurisdiction in any State court or any Federal Court cannot be obtained over an owner or operator likely to be solvent at the time of judgment, any claim arising

from conduct for which evidence of financial responsibility must be provided under this section may be asserted directly against the guarantor providing such evidence of financial responsibility. In the case of any action pursuant to this subsection, such guarantor shall be entitled to invoke all rights and defenses which would have been available to the owner or operator if any action had been brought against the owner or operator by the claimant and which would have been available to the guarantor if an action had been brought against the guarantor by the owner or operator.

(3) The total liability of any guarantor shall be limited to the aggregate amount which the guarantor has provided as evidence of financial responsibility to the owner or operator under this chapter. Nothing in this subsection shall be construed to limit any other State or Federal statutory, contractual or common law liability of a guarantor to its owner or operator including, but not limited to, the liability of such guarantor for bad faith either in negotiating or in failing to negotiate the settlement of any claim. Nothing in this subsection shall be construed to diminish the liability of any person under section 9607 or 9611 of this title or other applicable law.

(4) For the purpose of this subsection, the term "guarantor" means any person, other than the owner or operator, who provides evidence of financial responsibility for an owner or operator under this section.

(u) Continuing releases at permitted facilities — Standards promulgated under this section shall require, and a permit issued after November 8, 1984, by the Administrator or a State shall require, corrective action for all releases of hazardous waste or constituents from any solid waste management unit at a treatment, storage, or disposal facility seeking a permit under this subchapter, regardless of the time at which waste was placed in such unit. Permits issued under section 6925 of this title shall contain schedules of compliance for such corrective action (where such corrective action cannot be completed prior to issuance of the permit) and assurances of financial responsibility for completing such corrective action.

(v) Corrective action beyond facility boundary — As promptly as practicable after November 8, 1984, the Administrator shall amend the standards under this section regarding corrective action required at facilities for the treatment, storage, or disposal, of hazardous waste listed or identified under section 6921 of this title to require that corrective action be taken beyond the facility boundary where necessary to protect human health and the environment unless the owner or operator of the facility concerned demonstrates to the satisfaction of the Administrator that, despite the owner or operator's best efforts, the owner or operator was unable to obtain the necessary permission to undertake such action. Such regulations shall take effect immediately upon promulgation, notwithstanding section 6930(b) of this title, and shall apply to —

(1) all facilities operating under permits issued under subsection (c) of this section, and

(2) all landfills, surface impoundments, and waste pile units (including any new units, replacements of existing units, or lateral expansions of existing units) which receive hazardous waste after July 26, 1982.

Pending promulgation of such regulations, the Administrator shall issue corrective action orders for facilities referred to in paragraphs (1) and (2), on a case-by-case basis, consistent with the purposes of this subsection.

(w) Underground tanks — Not later than March 1, 1985, the Administrator shall promulgate final permitting standards under this section for underground tanks that cannot be entered for inspection. Within forty-eight months after November 8, 1984, such standards shall be modified, if necessary, to cover at a minimum all requirements and standards described in section 6991b of this title.

(x) Mining and other special wastes — If (1) solid waste from the extraction, beneficiation or processing of ores and minerals, including phosphate rock and overburden from the mining of uranium, (2) fly ash waste, bottom ash waste, slag waste, and flue gas emission control waste generated primarily from the combustion of coal or other fossil fuels, or (3) cement kiln dust waste, is subject to regulation under this subchapter, the Administrator is authorized to modify the requirements of subsections (c), (d), (e), (f), (g), (o), and (u) of this section and section 6925(j) of this title, in the case of landfills or surface impoundments receiving such solid waste, to take into account the special characteristics of such wastes, the practical difficulties associated with implementation of such requirements, and site-specific characteristics, including but not limited to the climate, geology, hydrology and soil chemistry at the site, so long as such modified requirements assure protection of human health and the environment.

(y) Munitions

(1) Not later than 6 months after October 6, 1992, the Administrator shall propose, after consulting with the Secretary of Defense and appropriate State officials, regulations identifying when military munitions become hazardous waste for purposes of this subchapter and providing for the safe transportation and storage of such waste. Not later than 24 months after October 6, 1992, and after notice and opportunity for comment, the Administrator shall promulgate such regulations. Any such regulations shall assure protection of human health and the environment.

(2) For purposes of this subsection, the term "military munitions" includes chemical and conventional munitions.

§6925. Permits for treatment, storage, or disposal of hazardous waste
[SWDA §3005]

(a) Permit requirements — Not later than eighteen months after October 21, 1976, the Administrator shall promulgate regulations requiring each person owning or operating an existing facility or planning to construct a new facility for the treatment, storage, or disposal of hazardous waste identified or listed under this subchapter to have a permit issued pursuant to this section. Such regulations shall take effect on the date provided in section 6930 of this title and upon and after such date the treatment, storage, or disposal of any such hazardous waste and the construction of any new facility for the treatment, storage, or disposal of any such hazardous waste is prohibited except in accordance with such a permit. No permit shall be required under this section in order to construct a facility if such facility is constructed pursuant to an approval issued by the Administrator under section 2605(e) of Title 15 for the incineration of polychlorinated biphenyls and any person owning or operating such a facility may, at any time after operation or construction of such facility has begun, file an application for a permit pursuant to this section authorizing such facility to incinerate hazardous waste identified or listed under this subchapter.

(b) Requirements of permit application — Each application for a permit under this section shall contain such information as may be required under regulations promulgated by the Administrator, including information respecting —

(1) estimates with respect to the composition, quantities, and concentrations of any hazardous waste identified or listed under this subchapter, or combinations of any such hazardous waste and any other solid waste, proposed to be disposed of, treated, transported, or stored, and the time, frequency, or rate of which such waste is proposed to be disposed of, treated, transported, or stored; and

(2) the site at which such hazardous waste or the products of treatment of such hazardous waste will be disposed of, treated, transported to, or stored.

(c) Permit issuance

(1) Upon a determination by the Administrator (or a State, if applicable), of compliance by a facility for which a permit is applied for under this section with the requirements of this section and section 6924 of this title, the Administrator (or the State) shall issue a permit for such facilities. In the event permit applicants propose modification of their facilities, or in the event the Administrator (or the State) determines that modifications are necessary to conform to the requirements under this section and section 6924 of this title, the permit shall specify the time allowed to complete the modifications.

(2)(A)(i) Not later than the date four years after November 8, 1984, in the case of each application under this subsection for a permit for a land disposal facility which was submitted before such date, the Administrator shall issue a final permit pursuant to such application or issue a final denial of such application.

(ii) Not later than the date five years after November 8, 1984, in the case of each application for a permit under this subsection for an incinerator facility which was submitted before such date, the Administrator shall issue a final permit pursuant to such application or issue a final denial of such application.

(B) Not later than the date eight years after November 8, 1984, in the case of each application for a permit under this subsection for any facility (other than a facility referred to in subparagraph (A)) which was submitted before such date, the Administrator shall issue a final permit pursuant to such application or issue a final denial of such application.

(C) The time periods specified in this paragraph shall also apply in the case of any State which is administering an authorized hazardous waste program under section 6926 of this title. Interim status under subsection (e) of this section shall terminate for each facility referred to in subparagraph (A)(ii) or (B) on the expiration of the five- or eight-year period referred to in subparagraph (A) or (B), whichever is applicable, unless the owner or operator of the facility applies for a final determination regarding the issuance of a permit under this subsection within —

(i) two years after November 8, 1984 (in the case of a facility referred to in subparagraph (A)(ii)), or

(ii) four years after November 8, 1984 (in the case of a facility referred to in subparagraph (B)).

(3) Any permit under this section shall be for a fixed term, not to exceed 10 years in the case of any land disposal facility, storage facility, or incinerator or other treatment facility. Each permit for a land disposal facility shall be reviewed five years after date of issuance or reissuance and shall be modified as necessary to assure that the facility continues to comply with the currently applicable requirements of this section and section 6924 of this title. Nothing in this subsection shall preclude the Administrator from reviewing and modifying a permit at any time during its term. Review of any application for a permit renewal shall consider improvements in the state of control and measurement technology as well as changes in applicable regulations. Each permit issued under this section

shall contain such terms and conditions as the Administrator (or the State) determines necessary to protect human health and the environment.

(d) Permit revocation — Upon a determination by the Administrator (or by a State, in the case of a State having an authorized hazardous waste program under section 6926 of this title) of noncompliance by a facility having a permit under this chapter with the requirements of this section or section 6924 of this title, the Administrator (or State, in the case of a State having an authorized hazardous waste program under section 6926 of this title) shall revoke such permit.

(e) Interim status

(1) Any person who —

(A) owns or operates a facility required to have a permit under this section which facility —

(i) was in existence on November 19, 1980, or

(ii) is in existence on the effective date of statutory or regulatory changes under this chapter that render the facility subject to the requirement to have a permit under this section,

(B) has complied with the requirements of section 6930(a) of this title, and

(C) has made an application for a permit under this section,

shall be treated as having been issued such permit until such time as final administrative disposition of such application is made, unless the Administrator or other plaintiff proves that final administrative disposition of such application has not been made because of the failure of the applicant to furnish information reasonably required or requested in order to process the application. This paragraph shall not apply to any facility which has been previously denied a permit under this section or if authority to operate the facility under this section has been previously terminated.

(2) In the case of each land disposal facility which has been granted interim status under this subsection before November 8, 1984, interim status shall terminate on the date twelve months after November 8, 1984, unless the owner or operator of such facility —

(A) applies for a final determination regarding the issuance of a permit under subsection (c) of this section for such facility before the date twelve months after November 8, 1984; and

(B) certifies that such facility is in compliance with all applicable groundwater monitoring and financial responsibility requirements.

(3) In the case of each land disposal facility which is in existence on the effective date of statutory or regulatory changes under this chapter that render the facility subject to the requirement to have a permit under this section and which is granted interim status under this subsection, interim status shall terminate on the date twelve months after the date on which the facility first becomes subject to such permit requirement unless the owner or operator of such facility —

(A) applies for a final determination regarding the issuance of a permit under subsection (c) of this section for such facility before the date twelve months after the date on which the facility first becomes subject to such permit requirement; and

(B) certifies that such facility is in compliance with all applicable groundwater monitoring and financial responsibility requirements.

(f) Coal mining wastes and reclamation permits — Notwithstanding subsection (a) through (e) of this section, any surface coal mining and reclamation permit covering any coal mining wastes or overburden which has been issued or approved under the Surface Mining Control and Reclamation Act of 1977 [30 U.S.C. §§1201 *et seq.*] shall be deemed to be a permit issued pursuant to this section with respect to the treatment, storage, or disposal of such wastes or overburden. Regulations promulgated by the Administrator under this subchapter shall not be applicable to treatment, storage, or disposal of coal mining wastes and overburden which are covered by such a permit.

(g) Research, development, and demonstration permits

(1) The Administrator may issue a research, development, and demonstration permit for any hazardous waste treatment facility which proposes to utilize an innovative and experimental hazardous waste treatment technology or process for which permit standards for such experimental activity have not been promulgated under this subchapter. Any such permit shall include such terms and conditions as will assure protection of human health and the environment. Such permits —

(A) shall provide for the construction of such facilities, as necessary, and for operation of the facility for not longer than one year (unless renewed as provided in paragraph (4)), and

(B) shall provide for the receipt and treatment by the facility of only those types and quantities of hazardous waste which the Administrator deems necessary for purposes of determining the efficacy and performance capabilities of the technology or process and the effects of such technology or process on human health and the environment, and

(C) shall include such requirements as the Administrator deems necessary to protect human health and the environment (including, but not limited to, requirements regarding monitoring, operation, insurance or bonding, financial reponsibility, closure, and remedial action), and such requirements as the Administrator deems necessary regarding testing and providing of information to the Administrator with respect to the operation of the facility. The Administrator may apply the criteria set forth in this paragraph in establishing the conditions of each permit without separate establishment of regulations implementing such criteria.

(2) For the purpose of expediting review and issuance of permits under this subsection, the Administrator may, consistent with the protection of human health and the environment, modify or waive permit application and permit issuance requirements established in the Administrator's general permit regulations except that there may be no modification or waiver of regulations regarding financial responsibility (including insurance) or of procedures established under section 6974(b)(2) of this title regarding public participation.

(3) The Administrator may order an immediate termination of all operations at the facility at any time he determines that termination is necessary to protect human health and the environment.

(4) Any permit issued under this subsection may be renewed not more than three times. Each such renewal shall be for a period of not more than 1 year.

(h) Waste minimization — Effective September 1, 1985, it shall be a condition of any permit issued under this section for the treatment, storage, or disposal of hazardous waste on the premises where such waste was generated that the permittee certify, no less often than annually, that —

(1) the generator of the hazardous waste has a program in place to reduce the volume or quantity and toxicity of such waste to the degree determined by the generator to be economically practicable; and

(2) the proposed method of treatment, storage, or disposal is that practicable method currently available to the generator which minimizes the present and future threat to human health and the environment.

(i) Interim status facilities receiving wastes after July 26, 1982 — The standards concerning ground water monitoring, unsaturated zone monitoring, and corrective action, which are applicable under section 6924 of this title to new landfills, surface impoundments, land treatment units, and waste-pile units required to be permitted under subsection (c) of this section shall also apply to any landfill, surface impoundment, land treatment unit, or waste-pile unit qualifying for the authorization to operate under subsection (e) of this section which receives hazardous waste after July 26, 1982.

(j) Interim status surface impoundments

(1) Except as provided in paragraph (2), (3), or (4), each surface impoundment in existence on November 8, 1984, and qualifying for the authorization to operate under subsection (e) of this section shall not receive, store, or treat hazardous waste after the date four years after November 8, 1984, unless such surface impoundment is in compliance with the requirements of section 6924(o)(1)(A) of this title which would apply to such impoundment if it were new.

(2) Paragraph (1) of this subsection shall not apply to any surface impoundment which (A) has at least one liner, for which there is no evidence that such liner is leaking; (B) is located more than one-quarter mile from an underground source of drinking water; and (C) is in compliance with generally applicable ground water monitoring requirements for facilities with permits under subsection (c) of this section.

(3) Paragraph (1) of this subsection shall not apply to any surface impoundment which (A) contains treated waste water during the secondary or subsequent phases of an aggressive biological treatment facility subject to a permit issued under section 1342 of Title 33 (or which holds such treated waste water after treatment and prior to discharge); (B) is in compliance with generally applicable ground water monitoring requirements for facilities with permits under subsection (c) of this section; and (C)(i) is part of a facility in compliance with section 1311(b)(2) of Title 33, or (ii) in the case of a facility for which no effluent guidelines required under section 1314(b)(2) of Title 33 are in effect and no permit under section 1342(a)(1) of Title 33 implementing section 1311(b)(2) of Title 33 has been issued, is part of a facility in compliance with a permit under section 1342 of Title 33, which is achieving significant degradation of toxic pollutants and hazardous constituents contained in the untreated waste stream and which has identified those toxic pollutants and hazardous constituents in the untreated waste stream to the appropriate permitting authority.

(4) The Administrator (or the State, in the case of a State with an authorized program), after notice and opportunity for comment, may modify the requirements of paragraph (1) for any surface impoundment if the owner or operator demonstrates that such surface impoundment is located, designed and operated so as to assure that there will be no migration of any hazardous constitutent into ground water or surface water at any future time. The Administrator or the State shall take into locational criteria established under section 6924(o)(7) of this title.

(5) The owner or operator of any surface impoundment potentially subject to paragraph

(1) who has reason to believe that on the basis of paragraph (2), (3), or (4) such surface impoundment is not required to comply with the requirements of paragraph (1), shall apply to the Administrator (or the State, in the case of a State with an authorized program) not later than twenty-four months after November 8, 1984, for a determination of the applicability of paragraph (1) (in the case of paragraph (2) or (3)) or for a modification of the requirements of paragraph (1) (in the case of paragraph (4)), with respect to such surface impoundment. Such owner or operator shall provide, with such application, evidence pertinent to such decision, including:

(A) an application for a final determination regarding the issuance of a permit under subsection (c) of this section for such facility, if not previously submitted;

(B) evidence as to compliance with all applicable ground water monitoring requirements and the information and analysis from such monitoring;

(C) all reasonably ascertainable evidence as to whether such surface impoundment is leaking; and

(D) in the case of applications under paragraph (2) or (3), a certification by a registered professional engineer with academic training and experience in ground water hydrology that —

(i) under paragraph (2), the liner of such surface impoundment is designed, constructed, and operated in accordance with applicable requirements, such surface impoundment is more than one-quarter mile from an underground source of drinking water and there is no evidence such liner is leaking; or

(ii) under paragraph (3), based on analysis of those toxic pollutants and hazardous constituents that are likely to be present in the untreated waste stream, such impoundment satisfies the conditions of paragraph (3).

In the case of any surface impoundment for which the owner or operator fails to apply under this paragraph within the time provided by this paragraph or paragraph (6), such surface impoundment shall comply with paragraph (1) notwithstanding paragraph (2), (3), or (4). Within twelve months after receipt of such application and evidence and not later than thirty-six months after November 8, 1984, and after notice and opportunity to comment, the Administrator (or, if appropriate, the State) shall advise such owner or operator on the applicability of paragraph (1) to such surface impoundment or as to whether and how the requirements of paragraph (1) shall be modified and applied to such surface impoundment.

(6)(A) In any case in which a surface impoundment becomes subject to paragraph (1) after November 8, 1984, due to the promulgation of additional listings or characteristics for the identification of hazardous waste under section 6921 of this title, the period for compliance in paragraph (1) shall be four years after the date of such promulgation, the period for demonstrations under paragraph (4) and for submission of evidence under paragraph (5) shall be not later than twenty-four months after the date of such promulgation, and the period for the Administrator (or if appropriate, the State) to advise such owners or operators under paragraph (5) shall be not later than thirty-six months after the date of promulgation.

(B) In any case in which a surface impoundment is initially determined to be excluded from the requirements of paragraph (1) but due to a change in condition (including the existence of a leak) no longer satisfies the provisions of paragraph (2), (3), or (4) and therefore becomes subject to paragraph (1), the period for compliance in paragraph (1) shall be two years after the date of discovery of such change of condition, or in the case of a surface impoundment excluded under paragraph (3) three years after such date of discovery.

(7)(A) The Administrator shall study and report to the Congress on the number, range of size, construction, likelihood of hazardous constituents migrating into ground water, and potential threat to human health and the environment of existing surface impoundments excluded by paragraph (3) from the requirements of paragraph (1). Such report shall address the need, feasibility, and estimated costs of subjecting such existing surface impoundments to the requirements of paragraph (1).

(B) In the case of any existing surface impoundment or class of surface impoundments from which the Administrator (or the State, in the case of a State with an authorized program) determines hazardous constituents are likely to migrate into ground water, the Administrator (or if appropriate, the State) is authorized to impose such requirements as may be necessary to protect human health and the environment, including the requirements of section 6924(o) of this title which would apply to such impoundments if they were new.

(C) In the case of any surface impoundment excluded by paragraph (3) from the requirements of paragraph (1) which is subsequently determined to be leaking, the Administrator (or, if appropriate, the State) shall require compliance with paragraph (1), unless the Administrator (or, if appropriate, the State) determines that such compliance is not necessary to protect human health and the environment.

(8) In the case of any surface impoundment in which the liners and leak detection system have been installed pursuant to the requirements of paragraph (1) and in good faith compliance with section 6924(o) of this title and the Administrator's regulations and guidance documents governing liners and leak detection systems, no liner or leak detection system which is different from that which was so installed pursuant to paragraph (1) shall be required for such unit by the Administrator when issuing the first permit under this section to such facility. Nothing in this paragraph shall preclude the Administrator from requiring installation of a new liner when the Administrator has reason to believe that any liner installed pursuant to the requirements of this subsection is leaking.

(9) In the case of any surface impoundment which has been excluded by paragraph (2) on the basis of a liner meeting the definition under paragraph (12)(A)(ii), at the closure of such impoundment the Administrator shall require the owner or operator of such impoundment to remove or decontaminate all waste residues, all contaminated liner material, and contaminated soil to the extent practicable. If all contaminated soil is not removed or decontaminated, the owner or operator of such impoundment shall be required to comply with appropriate post-closure requirements, including but not limited to ground water monitoring and corrective action.

(10) Any incremental cost attributable to the requirements of this subsection or section 6924(o) of this title shall not be considered by the Administrator (or the State, in the case of a State with an authorized program under section 1342 of Title 33) —

(A) in establishing effluent limitations and standards under section 1311, 1314, 1316, 1317, or 1342 of Title 33 based on effluent limitations guidelines and standards promulgated any time before twelve months after November 8, 1984; or

(B) in establishing any other effluent limitations to carry out the provisions of section 1311, 1317, or 1342 of Title 33 on or before October 1, 1986.

(11)(A) If the Administrator allows a hazardous waste which is prohibited from one or more methods of land disposal under subsection (d), (e), or (g) of section 6924 of this title (or under regulations promulgated by the Administrator under such subsections) to be placed in a surface impoundment (which is operating pursuant to interim status) for storage or treatment, such impoundment shall meet the requirements that are applicable to new surface impoundments

under section 6924(o)(1) of this title, unless such impoundment meets the requirements of paragraph (2) or (4).

(B) In the case of any hazardous waste which is prohibited from one or more methods of land disposal under subsection (d), (e), or (g) of section 6924 of this title (or under regulations promulgated by the Administrator under such subsection) the placement or maintenance of such hazardous waste in a surface impoundment for treatment is prohibited as of the effective date of such prohibition unless the treatment residues which are hazardous are, at a minimum, removed for subsequent management within one year of the entry of the waste into the surface impoundment.

(12)(A) For the purposes of paragraph (2)(A) of this subsection, the term "liner" means —

(i) a liner designed, constructed, installed, and operated to prevent hazardous waste from passing into the liner at any time during the active life of the facility; or

(ii) a liner designed, constructed, installed, and operated to prevent hazardous waste from migrating beyond the liner to adjacent subsurface soil, ground water, or surface water at any time during the active life of the facility.

(B) For the purposes of this subsection, the term "aggressive biological treatment facility" means a system of surface impoundments in which the initial impoundment of the secondary treatment segment of the facility utilizes intense mechanical aeration to enhance biological activity to degrade waste water pollutants and

(i) the hydraulic retention time in such initial impoundment is no longer than 5 days under normal operating conditions, on an annual average basis;

(ii) the hydraulic retention time in such initial impoundment is no longer than thirty days under normal operating conditions, on an annual average basis: *Provided,* That the sludge in such impoundment does not constitute a hazardous waste as identified by the extraction procedure toxicity characteristic in effect on November 8, 1984; or

(iii) such system utilizes activated sludge treatment in the first portion of secondary treatment.

(C) For the purposes of this subsection, the term "underground source or drinking water" has the same meaning as provided in regulations under the Safe Drinking Water Act (title XIV of the Public Health Service Act [42 U.S.C. §300f *et seq.*]).

(13) The Administrator may modify the requirements of paragraph (1) in the case of a surface impoundment for which the owner or operator, prior to October 1, 1984, has entered into, and is in compliance with, a consent order, decree, or agreement with the Administrator or a State with an authorized program mandating corrective action with respect to such surface impoundment that provides a degree of protection of human health and the environment which is at a minimum equivalent to that provided by paragraph (1).

§6926. Authorized State hazardous waste programs
[SWDA §3006]

(a) Federal guidelines — Not later than eighteen months after October 21, 1976, the Administrator, after consultation with State authorities, shall promulgate guidelines to assist States in the Development of State hazardous waste programs.

(b) Authorization of State program — Any State which seeks to administer and enforce a hazardous waste program pursuant to this subchapter may develop and, after notice and opportunity for public hearing, submit to the Administrator an application, in such form as he shall require, for authorization of such program. Within ninety days following submission of an application under this subsection, the Administrator shall issue a notice as to whether or not he expects such program to be authorized, and within ninety days following such notice (and after opportunity for public hearing) he shall publish his findings as to whether or not the conditions listed in items (1), (2), and (3) below have been met. Such State is authorized to carry out such program in lieu of the Federal program under this subchapter in such State and to issue and enforce permits for the storage, treatment, or disposal of hazardous waste (and to enforce permits deemed to have been issued under section 6935(d)(1) of this title) unless, within ninety days following submission of the application the Administrator notifies such State that such program may not be authorized and, within ninety days following such notice and after opportunity for public hearing, he finds that (1) such State program is not equivalent to the Federal program under this subchapter, (2) such program is not consistent with the Federal or State programs applicable in other States, or (3) such program does not provide adequate enforcement of compliance with the requirements of this subchapter. In authorizing a State program, the Administrator may base his findings on the Federal program in effect one year prior to submission of a State's application or in effect on January 26, 1983, whichever is later.

(c) Interim authorization

(1) Any State which has in existence a hazardous waste program pursuant to State law before the date ninety days after the date of promulgation of regulations under sections 6922, 6923, 6924, and 6925 of this title, may submit to the Administrator evidence of such existing program and may request a temporary authorization to carry out such program under this subchapter. The Administrator shall, if the evidence submitted shows the existing State program to be substantially equivalent to the Federal program under this subchapter, grant an interim authorization to the State to carry out such program in lieu of the Federal program pursuant to this subchapter for a period ending no later than January 31, 1986.

(2) The Administrator shall, by rule, establish a date for the expiration of interim authorization under this subsection.

(3) Pending interim or final authorization of a State program for any State which reflects the amendments made by the Hazardous and Solid Waste Amendments of 1984, the State may enter into an agreement with the Administrator under which the State may assist in the administration of the requirements and prohibitions which take effect pursuant to such Amendments.

(4) In the case of a State permit program for any State which is authorized under subsection (b) of this section or under this subsection, until such program is amended to reflect the amendments made by the Hazardous and Solid Waste Amendments of 1984 and such program amendments receive interim or final authorization, the Administrator shall have the authority in such State to issue or deny permits or those portions of permits affected by the requirements and prohibitions established by the Hazardous and Solid Waste Amendments of 1984. The Administrator shall coordinate with States the procedures for issuing such permits.

(d) Effect of State permit — Any action taken by a State under a hazardous waste program authorized under this section shall have the same force and effect as action taken by the Administrator under this subchapter.

(e) Withdrawal of authorization — Whenever the Administrator determines after public hearing that a State is not administering and enforcing a program authorized under this section in accordance with requirements of this section, he shall so notify the State and, if appropriate corrective action is not taken within a reasonable time, not to exceed ninety days, the Administrator shall withdraw authorization of such program and establish a Federal program pursuant to this subchapter. The Administrator shall not withdraw authorization of any such program unless he shall first have notified the State, and made public, in writing, the reasons for such withdrawal.

(f) Availability of information — No State program may be authorized by the Administrator under this section unless —

(1) such program provides for the public availability of information obtained by the State regarding facilities and sites for the treatment, storage, and disposal of hazardous waste; and

(2) such information is available to the public in substantially the same manner, and to the same degree, as would be the case if the Administrator was carrying out the provisions of this subchapter in such State.

(g) Amendments made by 1984 act

(1) Any requirement or prohibition which is applicable to the generation, transportation, treatment, storage, or disposal of hazardous waste and which is imposed under this subchapter pursuant to the amendments made by the Hazardous and Solid Waste Amendments of 1984 shall take effect in each State having an interim or finally authorized State program on the same date as such requirement takes effect in other States. The Administrator shall carry out such requirement directly in each such State unless the State program is finally authorized (or is granted interim authorization as provided in paragraph (2)) with respect to such requirement.

(2) Any State which, before November 8, 1984, has an existing hazardous waste program which has been granted interim or final authorization under this section may submit to the Administrator evidence that such existing program contains (or has been amended to include) any requirement which is substantially equivalent to a requirement referred to in paragraph (1) and may request interim authorization to carry out that requirement under this subchapter. The Administrator shall, if the evidence submitted shows the State requirement to be substantially equivalent to the requirement referred to in paragraph (1), grant an interim authorization to the State to carry out such requirement in lieu of direct administration in the State by the Administrator of such requirement.

(h) State programs for used oil — In the case of used oil which is not listed or identified under this subchapter as a hazardous waste but which is regulated under section 6935 of this title, the provisions of this section regarding State programs shall apply in the same manner and to the same extent as such provisions apply to hazardous waste identified or listed under this subchapter.

§6927. Inspections
[SWDA §3007]

(a) Access entry — For purposes of developing or assisting in the development of any regulation or enforcing the provisions of this chapter, any person who generates, stores, treats, transports, disposes of, or otherwise handles or has handled hazardous wastes shall, upon request of any officer, employee or representative of the Environmental Protection Agency, duly designated by the Administrator, or upon request of any duly designated officer, employee or representative of a State having an authorized hazardous waste program, furnish information relating to such wastes and permit such person at all reasonable times to have access to, and to copy all records relating to such wastes. For the purposes of developing or assisting in the development of any regulation or enforcing the provisions of this chapter, such officers, employees or representatives are authorized —

(1) to enter at reasonable times any establishment or other place where hazardous wastes are or have been generated, stored, treated, disposed of, or transported from;

(2) to inspect and obtain samples from any person of any such wastes and samples of any containers or labeling for such wastes.

Each such inspection shall be commenced and completed with reasonable promptness. If the officer, employee or representative obtains any samples, prior to leaving the premises, he shall give to the owner, operator, or agent in charge a receipt describing the sample obtained and if requested a portion of each such sample equal in volume or weight to the portion retained. If any analysis is made of such samples, a copy of the results of such analysis shall be furnished promptly to the owner, operator, or agent in charge.

(b) Availability to public

(1) Any records, reports, or information (including records, reports, or information obtained by representatives of the Environmental Protection Agency) obtained from any person under this section shall be available to the public, except that upon a showing satisfactory to the Administrator (or the State, as the case may be) by any person that records, reports, or information, or particular part thereof, to which the Administrator (or the State, as the case may be) or any officer, employee or representative thereof has access under this section if made public, would divulge information entitled to protection under section 1905 of Title 18, such information or particular portion thereof shall be considered confidential in accordance with the purposes of that section, except that such record, report, document, or information may be disclosed to other officers, employees, or authorized representatives of the United States concerned with carrying out this chapter, or when relevant in any proceeding under this chapter.

(2) Any person not subject to the provisions of section 1905 of Title 18 who knowingly and willfully divulges or discloses any information entitled to protection under this subsection shall, upon conviction, be subject to a fine of not more than $5,000 or to imprisonment not to exceed one year, or both.

(3) In submitting data under this chapter, a person required to provide such data may —

(A) designate the data which such person believes is entitled to protection under this subsection, and

(B) submit such designated data separately from other data submitted under this chapter.

A designation under this paragraph shall be made in writing and in such manner as the Administrator may prescribe.

(4) Notwithstanding any limitation contained in this section or any other provision of law, all information reported to, or otherwise obtained by, the Administrator (or any representative of the Administrator) under this chapter shall be made available, upon written request of any duly authorized committee of the Congress, to such committee.

(c) **Federal facility inspections** — The Administrator shall undertake on an annual basis a thorough inspection of each facility for the treatment, storage, or disposal of hazardous waste which is owned or operated by a department, agency, or instrumentality of the United States to enforce its compliance with this subchapter and the regulations promulgated thereunder. Any State with an authorized hazardous waste program also may conduct an inspection of any such facility for purposes of enforcing the facility's compliance with the State hazardous waste program. The records of such inspections shall be available to the public as provided in subsection (b) of this section. The department, agency, or instrumentality owning or operating each such facility shall reimburse the Environmental Protection Agency for the costs of the inspection of the facility. With respect to the first inspection of each such facility occurring after October 6, 1992, the Administrator shall conduct a comprehensive ground water monitoring evaluation at the facility, unless such an evaluation was conducted during the 12-month period preceding October 6, 1992.

(d) **State-operated facilities** — The Administrator shall annually undertake a thorough inspection of every facility for the treatment, storage, or disposal of hazardous waste which is operated by a State or local government for which a permit is required under section 6925 of this title. The records of such inspection shall be available to the public as provided in subsection (b) of this section.

(e) **Mandatory inspections**

(1) The Administrator (or the State in the case of a State having an authorized hazardous waste program under this subchapter) shall commence a program to thoroughly inspect every facility for the treatment, storage, or disposal of hazardous waste for which a permit is required under section 6925 of this title no less often than every two years as to its compliance with this subchapter (and the regulations promulgated under this subchapter). Such inspections shall commence not later than twelve months after November 8, 1984. The Administrator shall, after notice and opportunity for public comment, promulgate regulations governing the minimum frequency and manner of such inspections, including the manner in which records of such inspections shall be maintained and the manner in which reports of such inspections shall be filed. The Administrator may distinguish between classes and categories of facilities commensurate with the risks posed by each class or category.

(2) Not later than six months after November 8, 1984, the Administrator shall submit to the Congress a report on the potential for inspections of hazardous waste treatment, storage, or disposal facilities by nongovernmental inspectors as a supplement to inspections conducted by officers, employees, or representatives of the Environmental Protection Agency or States having authorized hazardous waste programs or operating under a cooperative agreement with the Administrator. Such report shall be prepared in cooperation with the States, insurance companies offering environmental impairment insurance, independent companies providing inspection services, and other such groups as appropriate. Such report shall contain recommendations on provisions and requirements for a program of private inspections to supplement governmental inspections.

§6928. Federal enforcement
[SWDA §3008]

(a) **Compliance orders**

(1) Except as provided in paragraph (2), whenever on the basis of any information the Administrator determines that any person has violated or is in violation of any requirement of this subchapter, the Administrator may issue an order assessing a civil penalty for any past or current violation, requiring compliance immediately or within a specified time period, or both, or the Administrator may commence a civil action in the United States district court in the district in which the violation occurred for appropriate relief, including a temporary or permanent injunction.

(2) In the case of a violation of any requirement of this subchapter where such violation occurs in a State which is authorized to carry out a hazardous waste program under section 6926 of this title, the Administrator shall give notice to the State in which such violation has occurred prior to issuing an order or commencing a civil action under this section.

(3) Any order issued pursuant to this subsection may include a suspension or revocation of any permit issued by the Administrator or a State under this subchapter and shall state with reasonable specificity the nature of the violation. Any penalty assessed in the order shall not ex-

ceed $25,000 per day of noncompliance for each violation of a requirement of this subchapter. In assessing such a penalty, the Administrator shall take into account the seriousness of the violation and any good faith efforts to comply with applicable requirements.

(b) Public hearing — Any order issued under this section shall become final unless, no later than thirty days after the order is served, the person or persons named therein request a public hearing. Upon such request the Administrator shall promptly conduct a public hearing. In connection with any proceeding under this section the Administrator may issue subpenas for the attendance and testimony of witnesses and the production of relevant papers, books, and documents, and may promulgate rules for discovery procedures.

(c) Violation of compliance orders — If a violator fails to take corrective action within the time specified in a compliance order, the Administrator may assess a civil penalty of not more than $25,000 for each day of continued noncompliance with the order and the Administrator may suspend or revoke any permit issued to the violator (whether issued by the Administrator or the State).

(d) Criminal penalties — Any person who —

(1) knowingly transports or causes to be transported any hazardous waste identified or listed under this subchapter to a facility which does not have a permit under this subchapter, or pursuant to title I of the Marine Protection, Research, and Sanctuaries Act (86 Stat. 1052) [33 U.S.C. §§1411 *et seq.*],

(2) knowingly treats, stores, or disposes of any hazardous waste identified or listed under this subchapter —

   (A) without a permit under this subchapter or pursuant to title I of the Marine Protection, Research, and Sanctuaries Act (86 Stat. 1052) [33 U.S.C. §§1411 *et seq.*]; or

   (B) in knowing violation of any material condition or requirement of such permit; or

   (C) in knowing violation of any material condition or requirement of any applicable interim status regulations or standards;

(3) knowingly omits material information or makes any false material statement or representation in any application, label, manifest, record, report, permit, or other document filed, maintained, or used for purposes of compliance with regulations promulgated by the Administrator (or by a State in the case of an authorized State program) under this subchapter;

(4) knowingly generates, stores, treats, transports, disposes of, exports, or otherwise handles any hazardous waste or any used oil not identified or listed as a hazardous waste under this subchapter (whether such activity took place before or takes place after November 8, 1984) and

who knowingly destroys, alters, conceals, or fails to file any record, application, manifest, report, or other document required to be maintained or filed for purposes of compliance with regulations promulgated by the Administrator (or by a State in the case of an authorized State program) under this subchapter;

(5) knowingly transports without a manifest, or causes to be transported without a manifest, any hazardous waste or any used oil not identified or listed as a hazardous waste under this subchapter required by regulations promulgated under this subchapter (or by a State in the case of a State program authorized under this subchapter) to be accompanied by a manifest;

(6) knowingly exports a hazardous waste identified or listed under this subchapter (A) without the consent of the receiving country or, (B) where there exists an international agreement between the United States and the government of the receiving country establishing notice, export, and enforcement procedures for the transportation, treatment, storage, and disposal of hazardous wastes, in a manner which is not in conformance with such agreement; or

(7) knowingly stores, treats, transports, or causes to be transported, disposes of, or otherwise handles any used oil not identified or listed as a hazardous waste under this subchapter —

   (A) in knowing violation of any material condition or requirement of a permit under this subchapter; or

   (B) in knowing violation of any material condition or requirement of any applicable regulations or standards under this chapter;

shall, upon conviction, be subject to a fine of not more than $50,000 for each day of violation, or imprisonment not to exceed two years (five years in the case of a violation of paragraph (1) or (2)), or both. If the conviction is for a violation committed after a first conviction of such person under this paragraph, the maximum punishment under the respective paragraph shall be doubled with respect to both fine and imprisonment.

(e) Knowing endangerment — Any person who knowingly transports, treats, stores, disposes of, or exports any hazardous waste identified or listed under this subchapter or used oil not identified or listed as a hazardous waste under this subchapter in violation of paragraph (1), (2), (3), (4), (5), (6), or (7) of subsection (d) of this section who knows at that time that he thereby places another person in imminent danger of death or serious bodily injury, shall, upon conviction, be subject to a fine of not more than $250,000 or imprisonment for not more than fifteen years, or both. A defendant that is an organization shall, upon conviction of violating this subsection, be subject to a fine of not more than $1,000,000.

(f) Special rules — For the purposes of subsection (e) of this section —

　(1) A person's state of mind is knowing with respect to —

　　(A) his conduct, if he is aware of the nature of his conduct;

　　(B) an existing circumstance, if he is aware or believes that the circumstance exists; or

　　(C) a result of his conduct, if he is aware or believes that his conduct is substantially certain to cause danger of death or serious bodily injury.

　(2) In determining whether a defendant who is a natural person knew that his conduct placed another person in imminent danger of death or serious bodily injury —

　　(A) the person is responsible only for actual awareness or actual belief that he possessed; and

　　(B) knowledge possessed by a person other than the defendant but not by the defendant himself may not be attributed to the defendant;

Provided, That in proving the defendant's possession of actual knowledge, circumstantial evidence may be used, including evidence that the defendant took affirmative steps to shield himself from relevant information.

　(3) It is an affirmative defense to a prosecution that the conduct charged was consented to by the person endangered and that the danger and conduct charged were reasonably foreseeable hazards of —

　　(A) an occupation, a business, or a profession; or

　　(B) medical treatment or medical or scientific experimentation conducted by professionally approved methods and such other person had been made aware of the risks involved prior to giving consent.

The defendant may establish an affirmative defense under this subsection by a preponderance of the evidence.

　(4) All general defenses, affirmative defenses, and bars to prosecution that may apply with respect to other Federal criminal offenses may apply under subsection (e) of this section and shall be determined by the courts of the United States according to the principles of common law as they may be interpreted in the light of reason and experience. Concepts of justification and excuse applicable under this section may be developed in the light of reason and experience.

　(5) The term "organization" means a legal entity, other than a government, established, or organized for any purpose, and such term includes a corporation, company, association, firm, partnership, joint stock company, foundation, institution, trust, society, union, or any other association of persons.

　(6) The term "serious bodily injury" means —

　　(A) bodily injury which involves a substantial risk of death;

　　(B) unconsciousness;

　　(C) extreme physical pain;

　　(D) protracted and obvious disfigurement; or

　　(E) protracted loss or impairment of the function of a bodily member, organ, or mental faculty.

(g) Civil penalty — Any person who violates any requirement of this subchapter shall be liable to the United States for a civil penalty in an amount not to exceed $25,000 for each such violation. Each day of such violation shall, for purposes of this subsection, constitute a separate violation.

(h) Interim status corrective action orders

　(1) Whenever on the basis of any information the Administrator determines that there is or has been a release of hazardous waste into the environment from a facility authorized to operate under section 6925(e) of this title, the Administrator may issue an order requiring corrective action or such other response measure as he deems necessary to protect human health or the environment or the Administrator may commence a civil action in the United States district court in the district in which the facility is located for appropriate relief, including a temporary or permanent injunction.

　(2) Any order issued under this subsection may include a suspension or revocation of authorization to operate under section 6925(e) of this title, shall state with reasonable specificity the nature of the required corrective action or other response measure, and shall specify a time for compliance. If any person named in an order fails to comply with the order, the Administrator may assess, and such person shall be liable to the United States for, a civil penalty in an amount not to exceed $25,000 for each day of noncompliance with the order.

§6929. Retention of State authority
[SWDA §3009]

Upon the effective date of regulations under this subchapter no State or political subdivision may impose any requirements less stringent than those authorized under this subchapter respecting the same matter as governed by such regulations, except that if application of a regulation with respect to any matter under this subchapter is postponed or enjoined by the action of any court, no State or political subdivision shall be prohibited from acting with respect to the same aspect of such matter until such time as such regulation takes effect. Nothing in this chapter shall be construed to prohibit any State or political subdivision thereof from imposing any requirements, including those for site selection, which are more stringent than those imposed by such regulations. Nothing in this chapter (or in any regulation adopted under this chapter) shall be construed to prohibit any State from requiring that the State be provided with a copy of each manifest used in connection with hazardous waste which is generated within that State or transported to a treatment, storage, or disposal facility within that State.

§6930. Effective date
[SWDA §3010]

(a) Preliminary notification — Not later than ninety days after promulgation of regulations under section 6921 of this title identifying by its characteristics or listing any substance as hazardous waste subject to this subchapter, any person generating or transporting such substance or owning or operating a facility for treatment, storage, or disposal of such substance shall file with the Administrator (or with States having authorized hazardous waste permit programs under section 6926 of this title) a notification stating the location and general description of such activity and the identified or listed hazardous wastes handled by such person. Not later than fifteen months after November 8, 1984 —

(1) the owner or operator of any facility which produces a fuel (A) from any hazardous waste identified or listed under section 6921 of this title, (B) from such hazardous waste identified or listed under section 6921 of this title and any other material, (C) from used oil, or (D) from used oil and any other material;

(2) the owner or operator of any facility (other than a single- or two-family residence) which burns for purposes of energy recovery any fuel produced as provided in paragraph (1) or any fuel which otherwise contains used oil or any hazardous waste identified or listed under section 6921 of this title; and

(3) any person who distributes or markets any fuel which is produced as provided in paragraph (1) or any fuel which otherwise contains used oil or any hazardous waste identified or listed under section 6921 of this title

shall file with the Administrator (and with the State in the case of a State with an authorized hazardous waste program) a notification stating the location and general description of the facility, together with a description of the identified or listed hazardous waste involved and, in the case of a facility referred to in paragraph (1) or (2), a description of the production or energy recovery activity carried out at the facility and such other information as the Administrator deems necessary. For purposes of the preceding provisions, the term "hazardous waste listed under section 6921 of this title" also includes any commercial chemical product which is listed under section 6921 of this title and which, in lieu of its original intended use, is (i) produced for use as (or as a component of) a fuel, (ii) distributed for use as a fuel, or (iii) burned as a fuel. Notification shall not be required under the second sentence of this subsection in the case of facilities (such as residential boilers) where the Administrator determines that such notification is not necessary in order for the Administrator to obtain sufficient information respecting current practices of facilities using hazardous waste for energy recovery. Nothing in this subsection shall be construed to affect or impair the provisions of section 6921(b)(3) of this title. Nothing in this subsection shall affect regulatory determinations under section 6935 of this title. In revising any regulation under section 6921 of this title identifying additional characteristics of hazardous waste or listing any additional substance as hazardous waste subject to this subchapter, the Administrator may require any person referred to in the preceding provisions to file with the Administrator (or with States having authorized hazardous waste permit programs under section 6926 of this title) the notification described in the preceding provisions. Not more than one such notification shall be required to be filed with respect to the same substance. No identified or listed hazardous waste subject to this subchapter may be transported, treated, stored, or disposed of unless notification has been given as required under this subsection.

(b) Effective date of regulation — The regulations under this subchapter respecting requirements applicable to the generation, transportation, treatment, storage, or disposal of hazardous waste (including requirements respecting permits for such treatment, storage, or disposal) shall take effect on the date six months after the date of promulgation thereof (or six months after the date of revision in the case of any regulation which is revised after the date required for promulgation thereof). At the time a regulation is promulgated, the Administrator may provide for a shorter period prior to the effective date, or an immediate effective date for:

(1) a regulation with which the Administrator finds the regulated community does not need six months to come into compliance;

(2) a regulation which responds to an emergency situation; or

(3) other good cause found and published with the regulation.

§6931. Authorization of assistance to States
[SWDA §3011]

(a) Authorization of appropriations — There is authorized to be appropriated $25,000,000 for each of the fiscal years 1978 and 1979 $20,000,000 for fiscal year 1980, $35,000,000 for fiscal year 1981, $40,000,000 for the fiscal year 1982, $55,000,000 for the fiscal year 1985, $60,000,000 for the fiscal year 1986, $60,000,000 for the fiscal year 1987, and

$60,000,000 for the fiscal year 1988 to be used to make grants to the States for purposes of assisting the States in the development and implementation of authorized State hazardous waste programs.

(b) Allocation — Amounts authorized to be appropriated under subsection (a) of this section shall be allocated among the States on the basis of regulations promulgated by the Administrator, after consultation with the States, which take into account, the extent to which hazardous waste is generated, transported, treated, stored, and disposed of within such State, the extent of exposure of human beings and the environment within such State to such waste, and such other factors as the Administrator deems appropriate.

(c) Activities included — State hazardous waste programs for which grants may be made under subsection (a) of this section may include (but shall not be limited to) planning for hazardous waste treatment, storage and disposal facilities, and the development and execution of programs to protect health and the environment from inactive facilities which may contain hazardous waste.

§6932. Transferred

§6933. Hazardous waste site inventory [SWDA §3012]

(a) State inventory programs — Each State shall, as expeditiously as practicable, undertake a continuing program to compile, publish, and submit to the Administrator an inventory describing the location of each site within such State at which hazardous waste has at any time been stored or disposed of. Such inventory shall contain —

(1) a description of the location of the sites at which any such storage or disposal has taken place before the date on which permits are required under section 6925 of this title for such storage or disposal;

(2) such information relating to the amount, nature, and toxicity of the hazardous waste at each such site as may be practicable to obtain and as may be necessary to determine the extent of any health hazard which may be associated with such site;

(3) the name and address, or corporate headquarters of, the owner of each such site, determined as of the date of preparation of the inventory;

(4) an identification of the types or techniques of waste treatment or disposal which have been used at each such site; and

(5) information concerning the current status of the site, including information respecting whether or not hazardous waste is currently being treated or disposed of at such site (and if not, the date on which such activity ceased) and information respecting the nature of any other activity currently carried out at such site.

For purposes of assisting the States in compiling information under this section, the Administrator shall make available to each State undertaking a program under this section such information as is available to him concerning the items specified in paragraphs (1) through (5) with respect to the sites within such State, including such information as the Administrator is able to obtain from other agencies or departments of the United States and from surveys and studies carried out by any committee or subcommittee of the Congress. Any State may exercise the authority of section 6927 of this title for purposes of this section in the same manner and to the same extent as provided in such section in the case of States having an authorized hazardous waste program, and any State may by order require any person to submit such information as may be necessary to compile the data referred to in paragraphs (1) through (5).

(b) Environmental Protection Agency program — If the Administrator determines that any State program under subsection (a) of this section is not adequately providing information respecting the sites in such State referred to in subsection (a) of this section, the Administrator shall notify the State. If within ninety days following such notification, the State program has not been revised or amended in such manner as will adequately provide such information, the Administrator shall carry out the inventory program in such State. In any such case —

(1) the Administrator shall have the authorities provided with respect to State programs under subsection (a) of this section;

(2) the funds allocated under subsection (c) of this section for grants to States under this section may be used by the Administrator for carrying out such program in such State; and

(3) no further expenditure may be made for grants to such State under this section until such time as the Administrator determines that such State is carrying out, or will carry out, an inventory program which meets the requirements of this section.

(c) Grants

(1) Upon receipt of an application submitted by any State to carry out a program under this section, the Administrator may make grants to the States for purposes of carrying out such a program. Grants under this section shall be allocated among the several States by the Administrator based upon such regulations as he prescribes to carry out the purposes of this section. The Administrator may make grants to any State which has conducted an inventory program which effectively carried out the purposes of this section before October 21, 1980, to reimburse such State for all, or any portion of, the costs incurred by such State in conducting such program.

(2) There are authorized to be appropriated to carry out this section $25,000,000 for each of the fiscal years 1985 through 1988.

(d) No impediment to immediate remedial action — Nothing in this section shall be construed to provide that the Administrator or any State should, pending completion of the inventory required under this section, postpone undertaking any enforcement or remedial action with respect to any site at which hazardous waste has been treated, stored, or disposed of.

§6934. Monitoring, analysis, and testing
[SWDA §3013]

(a) Authority of Administrator — If the Administrator determines, upon receipt of any information, that —

(1) the presence of any hazardous waste at a facility or site at which hazardous waste is, or has been, stored, treated, or disposed of, or

(2) the release of any such waste from such facility or site

may present a substantial hazard to human health or the environment, he may issue an order requiring the owner or operator of such facility or site to conduct such monitoring, testing, analysis, and reporting with respect to such facility or site as the Administrator deems reasonable to ascertain the nature and extent of such hazard.

(b) Previous owners and operators — In the case of any facility or site not in operation at the time a determination is made under subsection (a) of this section with respect to the facility or site, if the Administrator finds that the owner of such facility or site could not reasonably be expected to have actual knowledge of the presence of hazardous waste at such facility or site and of its potential for release, he may issue an order requiring the most recent previous owner or operator of such facility or site who could reasonably be expected to have such actual knowledge to carry out the actions referred to in subsection (a) of this section.

(c) Proposal — An order under subsection (a) or (b) of this section shall require the person to whom such order is issued to submit to the Administrator within 30 days from the issuance of such order a proposal for carrying out the required monitoring, testing, analysis, and reporting. The Administrator may, after providing such person with an opportunity to confer with the Administrator respecting such proposal, require such person to carry out such monitoring, testing, analysis, and reporting in accordance with such proposal, and such modifications in such proposal as the Administrator deems reasonable to ascertain the nature and extent of the hazard.

(d) Monitoring, etc., carried out by Administrator

(1) If the Administrator determines that no owner or operator referred to in subsection (a) or (b) of this section is able to conduct monitoring, testing, analysis, or reporting satisfactory to the Administrator, if the Administrator deems any such action carried out by an owner or operator to be unsatisfactory, or if the Administrator cannot initially determine that there is an owner or operator referred to in subsection (a) or (b) of this section who is able to conduct such monitoring, testing, analysis, or reporting, he may —

(A) conduct monitoring, testing, or analysis (or any combination thereof) which he deems reasonable to ascertain the nature and extent of the hazard associated with the site concerned, or

(B) authorize a State or local authority or other person to carry out any such action,

and require, by order, the owner or operator referred to in subsection (a) or (b) of this section to reimburse the Administrator or other authority or person for the costs of such activity.

(2) No order may be issued under this subsection requiring reimbursement of the costs of any action carried out by the Administrator which confirms the results of an order issued under subsection (a) or (b) of this section.

(3) For purposes of carrying out this subsection, the Administrator or any authority or other person authorized under paragraph (1), may exercise the authorities set forth in section 6927 of this title.

(e) Enforcement — The Administrator may commence a civil action against any person who fails or refuses to comply with any order issued under this section. Such action shall be brought in the United States district court in which the defendant is located, resides, or is doing business. Such court shall have jurisdiction to require compliance with such order and to assess a civil penalty of not to exceed $5,000 for each day during which such failure or refusal occurs.

§6935. Restrictions on recycled oil
[SWDA §3014]

(a) In general — Not later than one year after October 15, 1980, the Administrator shall promulgate regulations establishing such performance standards and other requirements as may be necessary to protect the public health and the environment from hazards associated with recycled oil. In developing such regulations, the Administrator shall conduct an analysis of the economic impact of the regulations on the oil recycling industry. The Administrator shall ensure that such regulations do not discourage the recovery or recycling of used oil, consistent with the protection of human health and the environment.

(b) Identification or listing of used oil as hazardous waste — Not later than twelve months after November 8, 1984, the Administrator shall propose whether to list or identify used automobile and truck crankcase oil as hazardous waste under section 6921 of this title. Not later than twenty-four months after November 8, 1984, the Administrator shall make a final determination whether to list or identify used automobile and truck crankcase oil and other used oil as hazardous wastes under section 6921 of this title.

(c) Used oil which is recycled

(1) With respect to generators and transporters of used oil identified or listed as a hazardous waste under section 6921 of this title, the standards promulgated under section 6921(d), 6922, and 6923 of this title shall not apply to such used oil if such used oil is recycled.

(2)(A) In the case of used oil which is exempt under paragraph (1), not later than twenty-four months after November 8, 1984, the Administrator shall promulgate such standards under this subsection regarding the generation and transportation of used oil which is recycled as may be necessary to protect human health and the environment. In promulgating such regulations with respect to generators, the Administrator shall take into account the effect of such regulations on environmentally acceptable types of used oil recycling and the effect of such regulations on small quantity generators and generators which are small businesses (as defined by the Administrator).

(B) The regulations promulgated under this subsection shall provide that no generator of used oil which is exempt under paragraph (1) from the standards promulgated under section 6921(d), 6922, and 6923 of this title shall be subject to any manifest requirement or any associated recordkeeping and reporting requirement with respect to such used oil if such generator —

 (i) either —

  (I) enters into an agreement or other arrangement (including an agreement or arrangement with an independent transporter or with an agent of the recycler) for delivery of such used oil to a recycling facility which has a permit under section 6925(c) of this title (or for which a valid permit is deemed to be in effect under subsection (d) of this section), or

  (II) recycles such used oil at one or more facilities of the generator which has such a permit under section 6925 of this title (or for which a valid permit is deemed to have been issued under subsection (d) of this section);

 (ii) such used oil is not mixed by the generator with other types of hazardous wastes; and

 (iii) the generator maintains such records relating to such used oil, including records of agreements or other arrangements for delivery of such used oil to any recycling facility referred to in clause (i)(I),

as the Administrator deems necessary to protect human health and the environment.

(3) The regulations under this subsection regarding the transportation of used oil which is exempt from the standards promulgated under section 6921(d), 6922, and 6923 of this title under paragraph (1) shall require the transporters of such used oil to deliver such used oil to a facility which has a valid permit under section 6925 of this title or which is deemed to have a valid permit under subsection (d) of this section. The Administrator shall also establish other standards for such transporters as may be necessary to protect human health and the environment.

(d) Permits

(1) The owner or operator of a facility which recycles used oil which is exempt under subsection (c)(1) of this section, shall be deemed to have a permit under this subsection for all such treatment or recycling (and any associated tank or container storage) if such owner and operator comply with standards promulgated by the Administrator under section 6924 of this title; except that the Administrator may require such owners and operators to obtain an individual permit under section 6925(c) of this title if he determines that an individual permit is necessary to protect human health and the environment.

(2) Notwithstanding any other provision of law, any generator who recycles used oil which is exempt under subsection (c)(1) of this section shall not be required to obtain a permit under section 6925(c) of this title with respect to such used oil until the Administrator has promulgated standards under section 6924 of this title regarding the recycling of such used oil.

§6936. Expansion during interim status [SWDA §3015]

(a) Waste piles — The owner or operator of a waste pile qualifying for the authorization to operate under section 6925(e) of this title shall be subject to the same requirements for liners and leachate collection systems or equivalent protection provided in regulations promulgated by the Administrator under section 6924 of this title before October 1, 1982, or revised under section 6924(o) of this title (relating to minimum technological requirements), for new facilities receiving individual permits under subsection (c) of section 6925 of this title, with respect to each new unit, replacement of an existing unit, or lateral expansion of an existing unit that is within the waste management area identified in the permit application submitted under section 6925 of this title, and with respect to waste received beginning six months after November 8, 1984.

(b) Landfills and surface impoundments

(1) The owner or operator of a landfill or surface impoundment qualifying for the authorization

to operate under section 6925(e) of this title shall be subject to the requirements of section 6924(o) of this title (relating to minimum technological requirements), with respect to each new unit, replacement of an existing unit, or lateral expansion of an existing unit that is within the waste management area identified in the permit application submitted under this section, and with respect to waste received beginning 6 months after November 8, 1984.

(2) The owner or operator of each unit referred to in paragraph (1) shall notify the Administrator (or the State, if appropriate) at least sixty days prior to receiving waste. The Administrator (or the State) shall require the filing, within six months of receipt of such notice, of an application for a final determination regarding the issuance of a permit for each facility submitting such notice.

(3) In the case of any unit in which the liner and leachate collection system has been installed pursuant to the requirements of this section and in good faith compliance with the Administrator's regulations and guidance documents governing liners and leachate collection systems, no liner or leachate collection system which is different from that which was so installed pursuant to this section shall be required for such unit by the Administrator when issuing the first permit under section 6925 of this title to such facility, except that the Administrator shall not be precluded from requiring installation of a new liner when the Administrator has reason to believe that any liner installed pursuant to the requirements of this section is leaking. The Administrator may, under section 6924 of this title, amend the requirements for liners and leachate collection systems required under this section as may be necessary to provide additional protection for human health and the environment.

§6937. Inventory of Federal agency hazardous waste facilities
[SWDA §3016]

(a) Program requirement; submission; availability; contents — Each Federal agency shall undertake a continuing program to compile, publish, and submit to the Administrator (and to the State in the case of sites in States having an authorized hazardous waste program) an inventory of each site which the Federal agency owns or operates or has owned or operated at which hazardous waste is stored, treated, or disposed of or has been disposed of at any time. The inventory shall be submitted every two years beginning January 31, 1986. Such inventory shall be available to the public as provided in section 6927(b) of this title. Information previously submitted by a Federal agency under section 9603 of this title, or under section 6925 or 6930 of this title, or under this section need not be resubmitted except that the agency shall update any previous submission

to reflect the latest available data and information. The inventory shall include each of the following:

(1) A description of the location of each site at which any such treatment, storage, or disposal has taken place before the date on which permits are required under section 6925 of this title for such storage, treatment, or disposal, and where hazardous waste has been disposed, a description of hydrogeology of the site and the location of withdrawal wells and surface water within one mile of the site.

(2) Such information relating to the amount, nature, and toxicity of the hazardous waste in each site as may be necessary to determine the extent of any health hazard which may be associated with any site.

(3) Information on the known nature and extent of environmental contamination at each site, including a description of the monitoring data obtained.

(4) Information concerning the current status of the site, including information respecting whether or not hazardous waste is currently being treated, stored, or disposed of at such site (and if not, the date on which such activity ceased) and information respecting the nature of any other activity currently carried out at such site.

(5) A list of sites at which hazardous waste has been disposed and environmental monitoring data has not been obtained, and the reasons for the lack of monitoring data at each site.

(6) A description of response actions undertaken or contemplated at contaminated sites.

(7) An identification of the types of techniques of waste treatment, storage, or disposal which have been used at each site.

(8) The name and address and responsible Federal agency for each site, determined as of the date of preparation of the inventory.

(b) Environmental Protection Agency program — If the Administrator determines that any Federal agency under subsection (a) of this section is not adequately providing information respecting the sites referred to in subsection (a) of this section, the Administrator shall notify the chief official of such agency. If within ninety days following such notification, the Federal agency has not undertaken a program to adequately provide such information, the Administrator shall carry out the inventory program for such agency.

§6938. Export of hazardous wastes
[SWDA §3017]

(a) In general — Beginning twenty-four months after November 8, 1984, no person shall export any hazardous waste identified or listed under this subchapter unless

(1)(A) such person has provided the notification required in subsection (c) of this section,

(B) the government of the receiving country

has consented to accept such hazardous waste,

    (C) a copy of the receiving country's written consent is attached to the manifest accompanying each waste shipment, and

    (D) the shipment conforms with the terms of the consent of the government of the receiving country required pursuant to subsection (e) of this section, or

  (2) the United States and the government of the receiving country have entered into an agreement as provided for in subsection (f) of this section and the shipment conforms with the terms of such agreement.

(b) Regulations — Not later than twelve months after November 8, 1984, the Administrator shall promulgate the regulations necessary to implement this section. Such regulations shall become effective one hundred and eighty days after promulgation.

(c) Notification — Any person who intends to export a hazardous waste identified or listed under this subchapter beginning twelve months after November 8, 1984, shall, before such hazardous waste is scheduled to leave the United States, provide notification to the Administrator. Such notification shall contain the following information:

  (1) the name and address of the exporter;

  (2) the types and estimated quantities of hazardous waste to be exported;

  (3) the estimated frequency or rate at which such waste is to be exported; and the period of time over which such waste is to be exported;

  (4) the ports of entry;

  (5) a description of the manner in which such hazardous waste will be transported to and treated, stored, or disposed in the receiving country; and

  (6) the name and address of the ultimate treatment, storage or disposal facility.

(d) Procedures for requesting consent of receiving country — Within thirty days of the Administrator's receipt of a complete notification under this section, the Secretary of State, acting on behalf of the Administrator, shall —

  (1) forward a copy of the notification to the government of the receiving country;

  (2) advise the government that United States law prohibits the export of hazardous waste unless the receiving country consents to accept the hazardous waste;

  (3) request the government to provide the Secretary with a written consent or objection to the terms of the notification; and

  (4) forward to the government of the receiving country a description of the Federal regulations which would apply to the treatment, storage, and disposal of the hazardous waste in the United States.

(e) Conveyance of written consent to exporter — Within thirty days of receipt by the Secretary of State of the receiving country's written consent or objection (or any subsequent communication withdrawing a prior consent or objection), the Administrator shall forward such a consent, objection, or other communication to the exporter.

(f) International agreements — Where there exists an international agreement between the United States and the government of the receiving country establishing notice, export, and enforcement procedures for the transportation, treatment, storage, and disposal of hazardous wastes, only the requirements of subsections (a)(2) and (g) of this section shall apply.

(g) Reports — After November 8, 1984, any person who exports any hazardous waste identified or listed under section 6921 of this title shall file with the Administrator no later than March 1 of each year, a report summarizing the types, quantities, frequency, and ultimate destination of all such hazardous waste exported during the previous calendar year.

(h) Other standards — Nothing in this section shall preclude the Administrator from establishing other standards for the export of hazardous wastes under section 6922 of this title or section 6923 of this title.

§6939. Domestic sewage
[SWDA §3018]

(a) Report — The Administrator shall, not later than 15 months after November 8, 1984, submit a report to the Congress concerning those substances identified or listed under section 6921 of this title which are not regulated under this subchapter by reason of the exclusion for mixtures of domestic sewage and other wastes that pass through a sewer system to a publicly owned treatment works. Such report shall include the types, size and number of generators which dispose of such substances in this manner, the types and quantities disposed of in this manner, and the identification of significant generators, wastes, and waste constituents not regulated under existing Federal law or regulated in a manner sufficient to protect human health and the environment.

(b) Revisions of regulations — Within eighteen months after submitting the report specified in subsection (a) of this section, the Administrator shall revise existing regulations and promulgate such additional regulations pursuant to this subchapter (or any other authority of the Administrator, including section 1317 of Title 33) as are necessary to assure that substances identified or listed under section 6921 of this title which pass through a sewer system to a publicly owned treatment works are adequately controlled to protect human health and the environment.

(c) Report on wastewater lagoons — The Administrator shall, within thirty-six months after November 8, 1984, submit a report to Congress concerning wastewater lagoons at publicly owned treatment works and their effect on groundwater quality. Such report shall include —

(1) the number and size of such lagoons;

(2) the types and quantities of waste contained in such lagoons;

(3) the extent to which such waste has been or may be released from such lagoons and contaminate ground water; and

(4) available alternatives for preventing or controlling such releases.

The Administrator may utilize the authority of sections 6927 and 6934 of this title for the purpose of completing such report.

(d) Application of sections 6927 and 6930 — The provisions of sections 6927 and 6930 of this title shall apply to solid or dissolved materials in domestic sewage to the same extent and in the same manner as such provisions apply to hazardous waste.

§6939a. Exposure information and health assessments
[SWDA §3019]

(a) Exposure information — Beginning on the date nine months after November 8, 1984, each application for a final determination regarding a permit under section 6925(c) of this title for a landfill or surface impoundment shall be accompanied by information reasonably ascertainable by the owner or operator on the potential for the public to be exposed to hazardous wastes or hazardous constituents through releases related to the unit. At a minimum, such information must address:

(1) reasonably foreseeable potential releases from both normal operations and accidents at the unit, including releases associated with transportation to or from the unit;

(2) the potential pathways of human exposure to hazardous wastes or constituents resulting from the releases described under paragraph (1); and

(3) the potential magnitude and nature of the human exposure resulting from such releases.

The owner or operator of a landfill or surface impoundment for which an application for such a final determination under section 6925(c) of this title has been submitted prior to November 8, 1984, shall submit the information required by this subsection to the Administrator (or the State, in the case of a State with an authorized program) no later than the date nine months after November 8, 1984.

(b) Health assessments

(1) The Administrator (or the State, in the case of a State with an authorized program) shall make the information required by subsection (a) of this section, together with other relevant information, available to the Agency for Toxic Substances and Disease Registry established by section 9604(i) of this title.

(2) Whenever in the judgment of the Administrator, or the State (in the case of a State with an authorized program), a landfill or a surface impoundment poses a substantial potential risk to human health, due to the existence of releases of hazardous constituents, the magnitude of contamination with hazardous constituents which may be the result of a release, or the magnitude of the population exposed to such release or contamination, the Administrator or the State (with the concurrence of the Administrator) may request the Administrator of the Agency for Toxic Substances and Disease Registry to conduct a health assessment in connection with such facility and take other appropriate action with respect to such risks as authorized by section 9604(b) and (i) of this title. If funds are provided in connection with such request the Administrator of such Agency shall conduct such health assessment.

(c) Members of the public — Any member of the public may submit evidence of releases of or exposure to hazardous constituents from such a facility, or as to the risks or health effects associated with such releases or exposure, to the Administrator of the Agency for Toxic Substances and Disease Registry, the Administrator, or the State (in the case of a State with an authorized program).

(d) Priority — In determining the order in which to conduct health assessments under this subsection, the Administrator of the Agency for Toxic Substances and Disease Registry shall give priority to those facilities or sites at which there is documented evidence of release of hazardous constituents, at which the potential risk to human health appears highest, and for which in the judgment of the Administrator of such Agency existing health assessment data is inadequate to assess the potential risk to human health as provided in subsection (f) of this section.

(e) Periodic reports — The Administrator of such Agency shall issue periodic reports which include the results of all the assessments carried out under this section. Such assessments or other activities shall be reported after appropriate peer review.

(f) "Health assessments" defined — For the purposes of this section, the term "health assessments" shall include preliminary assessments of the potential risk to human health posed by individual sites and facilities subject to this section, based on such factors as the nature and extent of contamination, the existence of potential for pathways of human exposure (including ground or surface water contamination, air emissions, and food chain contamination), the size and potential susceptibility of the community within the likely pathways of exposure, the comparison of expected human exposure levels to the short-term and long-term health effects associated with identified contaminants and any available recommended exposure or tolerance limits for such contaminants, and the comparison of existing morbidity and mortality data on diseases that may be associated with the observed levels of exposure. The assessment shall include an evaluation of the risks to the potentially affected population from all sources of such contaminants, including known point or nonpoint sources other than the site or facility in question. A purpose of such preliminary assessments shall be to help determine whether full-scale health or epidemiological studies and medical evaluations of exposed populations shall be undertaken.

(g) Cost recovery — In any case in which a health assessment performed under this section discloses the exposure of a population to the release of a hazardous substance, the costs of such health assessment may be recovered as a cost of response under section 9607 of this title from persons causing or contributing to such release of such hazardous substance or, in the case of multiple releases contributing to such exposure, to all such release.

§6939b. Interim control of hazardous waste injection

[SWDA §3020]

(a) Underground source of drinking water — No hazardous waste may be disposed of by underground injection —

    (1) into a formation which contains (within one-quarter mile of the well used for such underground injection) an underground source of drinking water; or

    (2) above such a formation.

The prohibitions established under this section shall take effect 6 months after November 8, 1984, except in the case of any State in which identical or more stringent prohibitions are in effect before such date under the Safe Drinking Water Act [42 U.S.C. §§300f *et seq.*].

(b) Actions under Comprehensive Environmental Response, Compensation, and Liability Act — Subsection (a) of this section shall not apply to the injection of contaminated ground water into the aquifer from which it was withdrawn, if —

    (1) such injection is —

        (A) a response action taken under section 9604 or 9606 of this title, or

        (B) part of corrective action required under this chapter intended to clean up such contamination;

    (2) such contaminated ground water is treated to substantially reduce hazardous constituents prior to such injection; and

    (3) such response action or corrective action will, upon completion, be sufficient to protect human health and the environment.

(c) Enforcement — In addition to enforcement under the provisions of this chapter, the prohibitions established under paragraphs (1) and (2) of subsection (a) of this section shall be enforceable under the Safe Drinking Water Act [42 U.S.C. §§300f *et seq.*] in any State —

    (1) which has adopted identical or more stringent prohibitions under part C of the Safe Drinking Water Act [42 U.S.C. §§300h *et seq.*] and which has assumed primary enforcement

responsibility under that Act [42 U.S.C. §§300f *et seq.*] for enforcement of such prohibitions; or

    (2) in which the Administrator has adopted identical or more stringent prohibitions under the Safe Drinking Water Act [42 U.S.C. §§300f *et seq.*] and is exercising primary enforcement responsibility under that Act [42 U.S.C. §§300f *et seq.*] for enforcement of such prohibitions.

(d) Definitions — The terms "primary enforcement responsibility", "underground source of drinking water", "formation" and "well" have the same meanings as provided in regulations of the Administrator under the Safe Drinking Water Act [42 U.S.C. §§300f *et seq.*]. The term "Safe Drinking Water Act" means title XIV of the Public Health Service Act.

§6939c. Mixed waste inventory reports and plan

[SWDA §3021]

(a) Mixed waste inventory reports

    (1) Requirement — Not later than 180 days after October 6, 1992, the Secretary of Energy shall submit to the Administrator and to the Governor of each State in which the Department of Energy stores or generates mixed wastes the following reports:

        (A) A report containing a national inventory of all such mixed wastes, regardless of the time they were generated, on a State-by-State basis.

        (B) A report containing a national inventory of mixed waste treatment capacities and technologies.

    (2) Inventory of wastes — The report required by paragraph (1)(A) shall include the following:

        (A) A description of each type of mixed waste at each Department of Energy facility in each State, including, at a minimum, the name of the waste stream.

        (B) The amount of each type of mixed waste currently stored at each Department of Energy facility in each State, set forth separately by mixed waste that is subject to the land disposal prohibition requirements of section 6924 of this title and mixed waste that is not subject to such prohibition requirements.

        (C) An estimate of the amount of each type of mixed waste the Department expects to generate in the next 5 years at each Department of Energy facility in each State.

        (D) A description of any waste minimization actions the Department has implemented at each Department of Energy facility in each State for each mixed waste stream.

        (E) The EPA hazardous waste code for each type of mixed waste containing waste that has been characterized at each Department of Energy facility in each State.

(F) An inventory of each type of waste that has not been characterized by sampling and analysis at each Department of Energy facility in each State.

(G) The basis for the Department's determination of the applicable hazardous waste code for each type of mixed waste at each Department of Energy facility and a description of whether the determination is based on sampling and analysis conducted on the waste or on the basis of process knowledge.

(H) A description of the source of each type of mixed waste at each Department of Energy facility in each State.

(I) The land disposal prohibition treatment technology or technologies specified for the hazardous waste component of each type of mixed waste at each Department of Energy facility in each State.

(J) A statement of whether and how the radionuclide content of the waste alters or affects use of the technologies described in subparagraph (I).

(3) Inventory of treatment capacities and technologies — The report required by paragraph (1)(B) shall include the following:

(A) An estimate of the available treatment capacity for each waste described in the report required by paragraph (1)(A) for which treatment technologies exist.

(B) A description, including the capacity, number and location, of each treatment unit considered in calculating the estimate under subparagraph (A).

(C) A description, including the capacity, number and location, of any existing treatment unit that was not considered in calculating the estimate under subparagraph (A) but that could, alone or in conjunction with other treatment units, be used to treat any of the wastes described in the report required by paragraph (1)(A) to meet the requirements of regulations promulgated pursuant to section 6924(m) of this title.

(D) For each unit listed in subparagraph (C), a statement of the reasons why the unit was not included in calculating the estimate under subparagraph (A).

(E) A description, including the capacity, number, location, and estimated date of availability, of each treatment unit currently proposed to increase the treatment capacities estimated under subparagraph (A).

(F) For each waste described in the report required by paragraph (1)(A) for which the Department has determined no treatment technology exists, information sufficient to support such determination and a description of the technological approaches the Department

anticipates will need to be developed to treat the waste.

(4) Comments and revisions — Not later than 90 days after the date of the submission of the reports by the Secretary of Energy under paragraph (1), the Administrator and each State which received the reports shall submit any comments they may have concerning the reports to the Department of Energy. The Secretary of Energy shall consider and publish the comments prior to publication of the final report.

(5) Requests for additional information — Nothing in this subsection limits or restricts the authority of States or the Administrator to request additional information from the Secretary of Energy.

(b) Plan for development of treatment capacities and technologies

(1) Plan requirement —

(A)(i) For each facility at which the Department of Energy generates or stores mixed wastes, except any facility subject to a permit, agreement, or order described in clause (ii), the Secretary of Energy shall develop and submit, as provided in paragraph (2), a plan for developing treatment capacities and technologies to treat all of the facility's mixed wastes, regardless of the time they were generated, to the standards promulgated pursuant to section 6924(m) of this title.

(ii) Clause (i) shall not apply with respect to any facility subject to any permit establishing a schedule for treatment of such wastes, or any existing agreement or administrative or judicial order governing the treatment of such wastes, to which the State is a party.

(B) Each plan shall contain the following:

(i) For mixed wastes for which treatment technologies exist, a schedule for submitting all applicable permit applications, entering into contracts, initiating construction, conducting systems testing, commencing operations, and processing backlogged and currently generated mixed wastes.

(ii) For mixed wastes for which no treatment technologies exist, a schedule for identifying and developing such technologies, identifying the funding requirements for the identification and development of such technologies, submitting treatability study exemptions, and submitting research and development permit applications.

(iii) For all cases where the Department proposes radionuclide separation of mixed wastes, or materials derived from mixed wastes, it shall provide an estimate of the volume of waste generated by each case of radionuclide separation, the volume of waste that would exist or be generated without radionuclide separation, the estimated costs of waste treatment and disposal if radionuclide separation is used compared to the estimated costs if it is not used, and the assumptions underlying such waste volume and cost estimates.

(C) A plan required under this subsection may provide for centralized, regional, or on-site treatment of mixed wastes, or any combination thereof.

(2) Review and approval of plan

(A) For each facility that is located in a State (i) with authority under State law to prohibit land disposal of mixed waste until the waste has been treated and (ii) with both authority under State law to regulate the hazardous components of mixed waste and authorization from the Environmental Protection Agency under section 6926 of this title to regulate the hazardous components of mixed waste, the Secretary of Energy shall submit the plan required under paragraph (1) to the appropriate State regulatory officials for their review and approval, modification, or disapproval. In reviewing the plan, the State shall consider the need for regional treatment facilities. The State shall consult with the Administrator and any other State in which a facility affected by the plan is located and consider public comments in making its determination on the plan. The State shall approve, approve with modifications, or disapprove the plan within 6 months after receipt of the plan.

(B) For each facility located in a State that does not have the authority described in subparagraph (A), the Secretary shall submit the plan required under paragraph (1) to the Administrator of the Environmental Protection Agency for review and approval, modification, or disapproval. A copy of the plan also shall be provided by the Secretary to the State in which such facility is located. In reviewing the plan, the Administrator shall consider the need for regional treatment facilities. The Administrator shall consult with the State or States in which any facility affected by the plan is located and consider public comments in making a determination on the plan. The Administrator shall approve, approve with modifications, or disapprove the plan within 6 months after receipt of the plan.

(C) Upon the approval of a plan under this paragraph by the Administrator or a State, the Administrator shall issue an order under section 6928(a) of this title, or the State shall issue an order under appropriate State authority, requiring compliance with the approved plan.

(3) Public participation — Upon submission of a plan by the Secretary of Energy to the Administrator or a State, and before approval of the plan by the Administrator or a State, the Administrator or State shall publish a notice of the availability of the submitted plan and make such submitted plan available to the public on request.

(4) Revisions of plan — If any revisions of an approved plan are proposed by the Secretary of Energy or required by the Administrator or a State, the provisions of paragraphs (2) and (3) shall apply to the revisions in the same manner as they apply to the original plan.

(5) Waiver of plan requirement

(A) A State may waive the requirement for the Secretary of Energy to develop and submit a plan under this subsection for a facility located in the State if the State (i) enters into an agreement with the Secretary of Energy that addresses compliance at that facility with section 6924(j) of this title with respect to mixed waste, and (ii) issues an order requiring compliance with such agreement and which is in effect.

(B) Any violation of an agreement or order referred to in subparagraph (A) is subject to the waiver of sovereign immunity contained in section 6961(a) of this title.

(c) Schedule and progress reports

(1) Schedule — Not later than 6 months after October 6, 1992, the Secretary of Energy shall publish in the Federal Register a schedule for submitting the plans required under subsection (b) of this section.

(2) Progress reports

(A) Not later than the deadlines specified in subparagraph (B), the Secretary of Energy shall submit to the Committee on Environment and Public Works of the Senate and the Committee on Energy and Commerce of the House of Representatives a progress report containing the following:

(i) An identification, by facility, of the plans that have been submitted to States or the Administrator of the Environmental Protection Agency pursuant to subsection (b) of this section.

(ii) The status of State and Environmental Protection Agency review and approval of each such plan.

(iii) The number of orders requiring compliance with such plans that are in effect.

(iv) For the first 2 reports required under this paragraph, an identification of the plans required under such subsection (b) of this section that the Secretary expects to submit in the 12-month period following submission of the report.

(B) The Secretary of Energy shall submit a report under subparagraph (A) not later than 12 months after October 6, 1992, 24 months after October 6, 1992, and 36 months after October 6, 1992.

§6939d. Public vessels
[SWDA §3022]

(a) Waste generated on public vessels — Any hazardous waste generated on a public vessel shall not be subject to the storage, manifest, inspection, or recordkeeping requirements of this chapter until such waste is transferred to a shore facility, unless —

(1) the waste is stored on the public vessel for more than 90 days after the public vessel is placed in reserve or is otherwise no longer in service; or

(2) the waste is transferred to another public vessel within the territorial waters of the United States and is stored on such vessel or another public vessel for more than 90 days after the date of transfer.

(b) Computation of storage period — For purposes of subsection (a) of this section, the 90-day period begins on the earlier of —

(1) the date on which the public vessel on which the waste was generated is placed in reserve or is otherwise no longer in service; or

(2) the date on which the waste is transferred from the public vessel on which the waste was generated to another public vessel within the territorial waters of the United States; and continues, without interruption, as long as the waste is stored on the original public vessel (if in reserve or not in service) or another public vessel.

(c) Definitions — For purposes of this section:

(1) The term "public vessel" means a vessel owned or bareboat chartered and operated by the United States, or by a foreign nation, except when the vessel is engaged in commerce.

(2) The terms "in reserve" and "in service" have the meanings applicable to those terms under section 8663 and sections 8674 through 8678 of Title 10 and regulations prescribed under those sections.

(d) Relationship to other law — Nothing in this section shall be construed as altering or otherwise affecting the provisions of section 8681 of Title 10.

§6939e. Federally owned treatment works
[SWDA §3023]

(a) In general — For purposes of section 6903(27) of this title, the phrase "but does not include solid or dissolved material in domestic sewage" shall apply to any solid or dissolved material introduced by a source into a federally owned treatment works if —

(1) such solid or dissolved material is subject to a pretreatment standard under section 1317 of Title 33, and the source is in compliance with such standard;

(2) for a solid or dissolved material for which a pretreatment standard has not been promulgated pursuant to section 1317 of Title 33, the Administrator has promulgated a schedule for establishing such a pretreatment standard which would be applicable to such solid or dissolved material not later than 7 years after October 6, 1992, such standard is promulgated on or before the date established in the schedule, and after the effective date of such standard the source is in compliance with such standard;

(3) such solid or dissolved material is not covered by paragraph (1) or (2) and is not prohibited from land disposal under subsections (d), (e), (f), or (g) of section 6924 of this title because such material has been treated in accordance with section 6924(m) of this title; or

(4) notwithstanding paragraphs (1), (2), or (3), such solid or dissolved material is generated by a household or person which generates less than 100 kilograms of hazardous waste per month unless such solid or dissolved material would otherwise be an acutely hazardous waste and subject to standards, regulations, or other requirements under this chapter notwithstanding the quantity generated.

(b) Prohibition — It is unlawful to introduce into a federally owned treatment works any pollutant that is a hazardous waste.

(c) Enforcement

(1) Actions taken to enforce this section shall not require closure of a treatment works if the hazardous waste is removed or decontaminated and such removal or decontamination is adequate, in the discretion of the Administrator or, in the case of an authorized State, of the State, to protect human health and the environment.

(2) Nothing in this subsection shall be construed to prevent the Administrator or an authorized State from ordering the closure of a treatment works if the Administrator or State determines such closure is necessary for protection of human health and the environment.

(3) Nothing in this subsection shall be construed to affect any other enforcement authorities available to the Administrator or a State under this subchapter.

(d) "Federally owned treatment works" defined — For purposes of this section, the term "federally owned treatment works" means a facility that is owned and operated by a department, agency, or instrumentality of the Federal Government treating wastewater, a majority of which is domestic sewage, prior to discharge in accordance with a permit issued under section 1342 of Title 33.

(e) Savings clause — Nothing in this section shall be construed as affecting any agreement, permit, or administrative or judicial order, or any condition or requirement contained in such an agreement, permit, or order, that is in existence on October 6, 1992, and that requires corrective action or closure at a federally owned treatment works or solid waste management unit or facility related to such a treatment works.

§6939f. Long-term storage
(a) Designation of facility
(1) In general
Not later than January 1, 2010, the Secretary of Energy (referred to in this section as the "Secretary") shall designate a facility or facilities of the Department of Energy, which shall not include the Y-12 National Security Complex or any other portion or facility of the Oak Ridge Reservation of the Department of Energy, for the purpose of long-term management and storage of elemental mercury generated within the United States.

(2) Operation of facility
Not later than January 1, 2019, the facility designated in paragraph (1) shall be operational and shall accept custody, for the purpose of long-term management and storage, of elemental mercury generated within the United States and delivered to such facility.

(b) Fees
(1) In general
(A) Assessment and collection
After consultation with persons who are likely to deliver elemental mercury to a designated facility for long-term management and storage under the program prescribed in subsection (a), and with other interested persons, the Secretary shall assess and collect a fee at the time of delivery for providing such management and storage, based on the pro rata cost of long-term management and storage of elemental mercury delivered to the facility.

(B) Amount
The amount of the fees described in subparagraph (A)—

(i) shall be made publicly available not later than October 1, 2018;

(ii) may be adjusted annually;

(iii) shall be set in an amount sufficient to cover the costs described in paragraph (2), subject to clause (iv); and

(iv) for generators temporarily accumulating elemental mercury in a facility subject to subparagraphs (B) and (D)(iv) of subsection (g)(2) if the facility designated in subsection (a) is not operational by January 1, 2019, shall be adjusted to subtract the cost of the temporary accumulation during the period in which the facility designated under subsection (a) is not operational.

(C) Conveyance of title and permitting
If the facility designated in subsection (a) is not operational by January 1, 2020, the Secretary—

(i) shall immediately accept the conveyance of title to all elemental mercury that has accumulated in facilities in accordance with subsection (g)(2)(D), before January 1, 2020, and deliver the accumulated mercury to the facility designated under subsection (a) on the date on which the facility becomes operational;

(ii) shall pay any applicable Federal permitting costs, including the costs for permits issued under section 3005(c) of the Solid Waste Disposal Act (42 U.S.C. 6925(c)); and

(iii) shall store, or pay the cost of storage of, until the time at which a facility designated in subsection (a) is operational, accumulated mercury to which the Secretary has title under this subparagraph in a facility that has been issued a permit under section 3005(c) of the Solid Waste Disposal Act (42 U.S.C. 6925(c)).

(2) Costs
The costs referred to in paragraph (1)(B)(iii) are the costs to the Department of Energy of providing such management and storage, including facility operation and maintenance, security, monitoring, reporting, personnel, administration, inspections, training, fire suppression, closure, and other costs required for compliance with applicable law. Such costs shall not include costs associated with land acquisition or permitting of a designated facility under the Solid Waste Disposal Act or other applicable law. Building design and building construction costs shall only be included to the extent that the Secretary finds that the management and storage of elemental mercury accepted under the program under this section cannot be accomplished without construction of a new building or buildings.

(c) Report — Not later than 60 days after the end of each Federal fiscal year, the Secretary shall transmit to the Committee on Energy and Commerce of the House of Representatives and the Committee on Environment and Public Works of the Senate a report on all of the costs incurred in the previous fiscal year associated with the long-term management and storage of elemental mercury. Such report shall set forth separately the costs associated with activities taken under this section.

(d) Management standards for a facility
(1) Guidance — Not later than October 1, 2009, the Secretary, after consultation with the Administrator of the Environmental Protection Agency and all appropriate State agencies in affected States, shall make available, including to potential users of the long-term management and storage program established under subsection (a), guidance that establishes procedures and standards for the receipt, management, and long-term storage of elemental mercury at a designated facility

or facilities, including requirements to ensure appropriate use of flasks or other suitable shipping containers. Such procedures and standards shall be protective of human health and the environment and shall ensure that the elemental mercury is stored in a safe, secure, and effective manner. In addition to such procedures and standards, elemental mercury managed and stored under this section at a designated facility shall be subject to the requirements of the Solid Waste Disposal Act, including the requirements of subtitle C of that Act, except as provided in subsection (g)(2) of this section. A designated facility in existence on or before January 1, 2013, is authorized to operate under interim status pursuant to section 6925(e) of this title until a final decision on a permit application is made pursuant to section 6925(c) of this title. Not later than January 1, 2015, the Administrator of the Environmental Protection Agency (or an authorized State) shall issue a final decision on the permit application.

(2) Training — The Secretary shall conduct operational training and emergency training for all staff that have responsibilities related to elemental mercury management, transfer, storage, monitoring, or response.

(3) Equipment — The Secretary shall ensure that each designated facility has all equipment necessary for routine operations, emergencies, monitoring, checking inventory, loading, and storing elemental mercury at the facility.

(4) Fire detection and suppression systems The Secretary shall —

(A) ensure the installation of fire detection systems at each designated facility, including smoke detectors and heat detectors; and

(B) ensure the installation of a permanent fire suppression system, unless the Secretary determines that a permanent fire suppression system is not necessary to protect human health and the environment.

(e) Indemnification of persons delivering elemental mercury

(1) In general

(A) Except as provided in subparagraph (B) and subject to paragraph (2), the Secretary shall hold harmless, defend, and indemnify in full any person who delivers elemental mercury to a designated facility under the program established under subsection (a) from and against any suit, claim, demand or action, liability, judgment, cost, or other fee arising out of any claim for personal injury or property damage (including death, illness, or loss of or damage to property or economic loss) that results from, or is in any manner predicated upon, the release or threatened release of elemental mercury as a result of acts or omissions occurring after such mercury is

delivered to a designated facility described in subsection (a).

(B) To the extent that a person described in subparagraph (A) contributed to any such release or threatened release, subparagraph (A) shall not apply.

(2) Conditions — No indemnification may be afforded under this subsection unless the person seeking indemnification —

(A) notifies the Secretary in writing within 30 days after receiving written notice of the claim for which indemnification is sought;

(B) furnishes to the Secretary copies of pertinent papers the person receives;

(C) furnishes evidence or proof of any claim, loss, or damage covered by this subsection; and

(D) provides, upon request by the Secretary, access to the records and personnel of the person for purposes of defending or settling the claim or action.

(3) Authority of Secretary

(A) In any case in which the Secretary determines that the Department of Energy may be required to make indemnification payments to a person under this subsection for any suit, claim, demand or action, liability, judgment, cost, or other fee arising out of any claim for personal injury or property damage referred to in paragraph (1)(A), the Secretary may settle or defend, on behalf of that person, the claim for personal injury or property damage.

(B) In any case described in subparagraph (A), if the person to whom the Department of Energy may be required to make indemnification payments does not allow the Secretary to settle or defend the claim, the person may not be afforded indemnification with respect to that claim under this subsection.

(f) Terms, conditions, and procedures —

The Secretary is authorized to establish such terms, conditions, and procedures as are necessary to carry out this section.

(g) Effect on other law

(1) In general — Except as provided in paragraph (2), nothing in this section changes or affects any Federal, State, or local law or the obligation of any person to comply with such law.

(2) Exception

(A) Elemental mercury that the Secretary is storing on a long-term basis shall not be subject to the storage prohibition of section 6924(j) of this title. For the purposes of section 6924(j) of this title, a generator accumulating elemental mercury destined for a facility designated by the Secretary under subsection (a) for 90 days or less shall be deemed to be accumulating the mercury to facilitate proper treatment, recovery, or disposal.

(B) Elemental mercury may be stored at a facility with respect to which any permit has been issued under section 6925(c) of this title, and shall not be subject to the storage prohibition of section 6924(j) of this title if —

(i) the Secretary is unable to accept the mercury at a facility designated by the Secretary under subsection (a) for reasons beyond the control of the owner or operator of the permitted facility;

(ii) the owner or operator of the permitted facility certifies in writing to the Secretary that it will ship the mercury to the designated facility when the Secretary is able to accept the mercury; and

(iii) the owner or operator of the permitted facility certifies in writing to the Secretary that it will not sell, or otherwise place into commerce, the mercury.

This subparagraph shall not apply to mercury with respect to which the owner or operator of the permitted facility fails to comply with a certification provided under clause (ii) or (iii).

(h) Study — Not later than July 1, 2014, the Secretary shall transmit to the Congress the results of a study, conducted in consultation with the Administrator of the Environmental Protection Agency, that—

(1) determines the impact of the long-term storage program under this section on mercury recycling; and

(2) includes proposals, if necessary, to mitigate any negative impact identified under paragraph (1).

§6939g. Hazardous Waste Electronic Manifest System
[SWDA §3024]
(a) Definitions
In this section:
(1) Board
The term "Board" means the Hazardous Waste Electronic Manifest System Advisory Board established under subsection (f).
(2) Fund
The term "Fund" means the Hazardous Waste Electronic Manifest System Fund established by subsection (d).
(3) Person
The term "person" includes an individual, corporation (including a Government corporation), company, association, firm, partnership, society, joint stock company, trust, municipality, commission, Federal agency, State, political subdivision of a State, or interstate body.
(4) System
The term "system" means the hazardous waste electronic manifest system established under subsection (b).
(5) User
The term "user" means a hazardous waste generator, a hazardous waste transporter, an owner or operator of a hazardous waste treatment, stor-

age, recycling, or disposal facility, or any other person that —

(A) is required to use a manifest to comply with any Federal or State requirement to track the shipment, transportation, and receipt of hazardous waste or other material that is shipped from the site of generation to an off-site facility for treatment, storage, disposal, or recycling; and

(B)(i) elects to use the system to complete and transmit an electronic manifest format; or

(ii) submits to the system for data processing purposes a paper copy of the manifest (or data from such a paper copy), in accordance with such regulations as the Administrator may promulgate to require such a submission.

(b) Establishment
Not later than 3 years after October 5, 2012, the Administrator shall establish a hazardous waste electronic manifest system that may be used by any user.

(c) User fees
(1) In general
In accordance with paragraph (4), the Administrator may impose on users such reasonable service fees as the Administrator determines to be necessary to pay costs incurred in developing, operating, maintaining, and upgrading the system, including any costs incurred in collecting and processing data from any paper manifest submitted to the system after the date on which the system enters operation.

(2) Collection of fees
The Administrator shall —

(A) collect the fees described in paragraph (1) from the users in advance of, or as reimbursement for, the provision by the Administrator of system-related services; and

(B) deposit the fees in the Fund.

(3) Fee structure
(A) In general
The Administrator, in consultation with information technology vendors, shall determine through the contract award process described in subsection (e) the fee structure that is necessary to recover the full cost to the Administrator of providing system-related services, including —

(i) contractor costs relating to —

(I) materials and supplies;

(II) contracting and consulting;

(III) overhead;

(IV) information technology (including costs of hardware, software, and related services);

(V) information management;

(VI) collection of service fees;

(VII) reporting and accounting; and

(VIII) project management; and

(ii) costs of employment of direct and indirect Government personnel dedicated to establishing, managing, and maintaining the system.

(B) Adjustments in fee amount

(i) In general

The Administrator, in consultation with the Board, shall increase or decrease the amount of a service fee determined under the fee structure described in subparagraph (A) to a level that will —

(I) result in the collection of an aggregate amount for deposit in the Fund that is sufficient and not more than reasonably necessary to cover current and projected system-related costs (including any necessary system upgrades); and

(II) minimize, to the maximum extent practicable, the accumulation of unused amounts in the Fund.

(ii) Exception for initial period of operation

The requirement described in clause (i) (II) shall not apply to any additional fees that accumulate in the Fund, in an amount that does not exceed $2,000, 000, during the 3-year period beginning on the date on which the system enters operation.

(iii) Timing of adjustments

Adjustments to service fees described in clause (i) shall be made —

(I) initially, at the time at which initial development costs of the system have been recovered by the Administrator such that the service fee may be reduced to reflect the elimination of the system development component of the fee; and

(II) periodically thereafter, upon receipt and acceptance of the findings of any annual accounting or auditing report under subsection (d)(3), if the report discloses a significant disparity for a fiscal year between the funds collected from service fees under this subsection for the fiscal year and expenditures made for the fiscal year to provide system-related services.

(4) Crediting and availability of fees

Fees authorized under this section shall be collected and available for obligation only to the extent and in the amount provided in advance in appropriations Acts.

(d) Hazardous Waste Electronic Manifest System Fund

(1) Establishment

There is established in the Treasury of the United States a revolving fund, to be known as the 'Hazardous Waste Electronic Manifest System Fund', consisting of such amounts as are deposited in the Fund under subsection (c)(2)(B).

(2) Expenditures from Fund

(A) In general

Only to the extent provided in advance in appropriations Acts, on request by the Administrator, the Secretary of the Treasury shall transfer from the Fund to the Administrator amounts appropriated to pay costs incurred in developing, operating, maintaining, and upgrading the system under subsection (c).

(B) Use of Funds by Administrator

Fees collected by the Administrator and deposited in the Fund under this section shall be available to the Administrator subject to appropriations Acts for use in accordance with this section without fiscal year limitation.

(C) Oversight of Funds

The Administrator shall carry out all necessary measures to ensure that amounts in the Fund are used only to carry out the goals of establishing, operating, maintaining, upgrading, managing, supporting, and overseeing the system.

(3) Accounting and auditing

(A) Accounting

For each 2-fiscal-year period, the Administrator shall prepare and submit to the Committee on Environment and Public Works and the Committee on Appropriations of the Senate and the Committee on Energy and Commerce and the Committee on Appropriations of the House of Representatives a report that includes —

(i) an accounting of the fees paid to the Administrator under subsection (c) and disbursed from the Fund for the period covered by the report, as reflected by financial statements provided in accordance with —

(I) the Chief Financial Officers Act of 1990 (Public Law 101-576; 104 Stat. 2838) and amendments made by that Act; and

(II) the Government Management Reform Act of 1994 (Public Law 103-356; 108 Stat. 3410) and amendments made by that Act; and

(ii) an accounting describing actual expenditures from the Fund for the period covered by the report for costs described in subsection (c)(1).

(B) Auditing

(i) In general

For the purpose of section 3515(c) of Title 31, the Fund shall be considered a component of an Executive agency.

(ii) Components of audit

The annual audit required in accordance with sections 3515(b) and 3521 of Title 31, of the financial statements of activities carried out using amounts from the Fund shall include an analysis of —

    (I) the fees collected and disbursed under this section;

    (II) the reasonableness of the fee structure in place as of the date of the audit to meet current and projected costs of the system;

    (III) the level of use of the system by users; and

    (IV) the success to date of the system in operating on a self-sustaining basis and improving the efficiency of tracking waste shipments and transmitting waste shipment data.

(iii) Federal responsibility

The Inspector General of the Environmental Protection Agency shall —

    (I) conduct the annual audit described in clause (ii); and

    (II) submit to the Administrator a report that describes the findings and recommendations of the Inspector General resulting from the audit.

(e) Contracts

(1) Authority to enter into contracts funded by service fees

After consultation with the Secretary of Transportation, the Administrator may enter into 1 or more information technology contracts with entities determined to be appropriate by the Administrator (referred to in this subsection as 'contractors') for the provision of system-related services.

(2) Term of contract

A contract awarded under this subsection shall have a term of not more than 10 years.

(3) Achievement of goals

The Administrator shall ensure, to the maximum extent practicable, that a contract awarded under this subsection —

    (A) is performance-based;

    (B) identifies objective outcomes; and

    (C) contains performance standards that may be used to measure achievement and goals to evaluate the success of a contractor in performing under the contract and the right of the contractor to payment for services under the contract, taking into consideration that a primary measure of successful performance shall be the development of a hazardous waste electronic manifest system that —

        (i) meets the needs of the user community (including States that rely on data contained in manifests);

        (ii) attracts sufficient user participation and service fee revenues to ensure the viability of the system;

        (iii) decreases the administrative burden on the user community; and

        (iv) provides the waste receipt data applicable to the biennial reports required by section 6922(a)(6) of this title.

(4) Payment structure

Each contract awarded under this subsection shall include a provision that specifies —

    (A) the service fee structure of the contractor that will form the basis for payments to the contractor; and

    (B) the fixed-share ratio of monthly service fee revenues from which the Administrator shall reimburse the contractor for system-related development, operation, and maintenance costs.

(5) Cancellation and termination

    (A) In general

If the Administrator determines that sufficient funds are not made available for the continuation in a subsequent fiscal year of a contract entered into under this subsection, the Administrator may cancel or terminate the contract.

    (B) Negotiation of amounts

The amount payable in the event of cancellation or termination of a contract entered into under this subsection shall be negotiated with the contractor at the time at which the contract is awarded.

(6) No effect on ownership

Regardless of whether the Administrator enters into a contract under this subsection, the system shall be owned by the Federal Government.

(f) Hazardous Waste Electronic Manifest System Advisory Board

(1) Establishment

Not later than 3 years after October 5, 2012, the Administrator shall establish a board to be known as the "Hazardous Waste Electronic Manifest System Advisory Board".

(2) Composition

The Board shall be composed of 9 members, of which —

    (A) 1 member shall be the Administrator (or a designee), who shall serve as Chairperson of the Board; and

    (B) 8 members shall be individuals appointed by the Administrator —

        (i) at least 2 of whom shall have expertise in information technology;

        (ii) at least 3 of whom shall have experience in using or represent users of the manifest system to track the transportation of hazardous waste under this subchapter (or an equivalent State program); and

        (iii) at least 3 of whom shall be a State representative responsible for processing those manifests.

(3) Duties

The Board shall meet annually to discuss, evaluate the effectiveness of, and provide recommendations to the Administrator relating to, the system.

(g) Regulations

(1) Promulgation

(A) In general

Not later than 1 year after October 5, 2012, after consultation with the Secretary of Transportation, the Administrator shall promulgate regulations to carry out this section.

(B) Inclusions

The regulations promulgated pursuant to subparagraph (A) may include such requirements as the Administrator determines to be necessary to facilitate the transition from the use of paper manifests to the use of electronic manifests, or to accommodate the processing of data from paper manifests in the electronic manifest system, including a requirement that users of paper manifests submit to the system copies of the paper manifests for data processing purposes.

(C) Requirements

The regulations promulgated pursuant to subparagraph (A) shall ensure that each electronic manifest provides, to the same extent as paper manifests under applicable Federal and State law, for —

(i) the ability to track and maintain legal accountability of —

(I) the person that certifies that the information provided in the manifest is accurately described; and

(II) the person that acknowledges receipt of the manifest;

(ii) if the manifest is electronically submitted, State authority to access paper printout copies of the manifest from the system; and

(iii) access to all publicly available information contained in the manifest.

(2) Effective date of regulations

Any regulation promulgated by the Administrator under paragraph (1) and in accordance with section 6923 of this title relating to electronic manifesting of hazardous waste shall take effect in each State as of the effective date specified in the regulation.

(3) Administration

The Administrator shall carry out regulations promulgated under this subsection in each State unless the State program is fully authorized to carry out such regulations in lieu of the Administrator.

(h) Requirement of compliance with respect to certain States

In any case in which the State in which waste is generated, or the State in which waste will be transported to a designated facility, requires that the waste be tracked through a hazardous waste manifest, the designated facility that receives the waste shall, regardless of the State in which the facility is located —

(1) complete the facility portion of the applicable manifest;

(2) sign and date the facility certification; and

(3) submit to the system a final copy of the manifest for data processing purposes.

(i) Authorization for start-up activities

There are authorized to be appropriated $2,000,000 for each of fiscal years 2013 through 2015 for start-up activities to carry out this section, to be offset by collection of user fees under subsection (c) such that all such appropriated funds are offset by fees as provided in subsection (c).

SUBCHAPTER IV — STATE OR REGIONAL SOLID WASTE PLANS

§6941. Objectives of subchapter
[SWDA §4001]

The objectives of this subchapter are to assist in developing and encouraging methods for the disposal of solid waste which are environmentally sound and which maximize the utilization of valuable resources including energy and materials which are recoverable from solid waste and to encourage resource conservation. Such objectives are to be accomplished through Federal technical and financial assistance to States or regional authorities for comprehensive planning pursuant to Federal guidelines designed to foster cooperation among Federal, State, and local governments and private industry. In developing such comprehensive plans, it is the intention of this chapter that in determining the size of the waste-to-energy facility, adequate provision shall be given to the present and reasonably anticipated future needs, including those needs created by thorough implementation of section 6962(h) of this title, of the recycling and resource recovery interest within the area encompassed by the planning process.

§6941a. Energy and materials conservation and recovery; Congressional findings

The Congress finds that —

(1) significant savings could be realized by conserving materials in order to reduce the volume or quantity of material which ultimately becomes waste;

(2) solid waste contains valuable energy and material resources which can be recovered and used thereby conserving increasingly scarce and expensive fossil fuels and virgin materials;

(3) the recovery of energy and materials from municipal waste, and the conservation of energy

and materials contributing to such waste streams, can have the effect of reducing the volume of the municipal waste stream and the burden of disposing of increasing volumes of solid waste;

(4) the technology to conserve resources exists and is commercially feasible to apply;

(5) the technology to recover energy and materials from solid waste is of demonstrated commercial feasibility; and

(6) various communities throughout the nation have different needs and different potentials for conserving resources and for utilizing techniques for the recovery of energy and materials from waste, and Federal assistance in planning and implementing such energy and materials conservation and recovery programs should be available to all such communities on an equitable basis in relation to their needs and potential.

§6942. Federal guidelines for plans
[SWDA §4002]

(a) Guidelines for identification of regions — For purposes of encouraging and facilitating the development of regional planning for solid waste management, the Administrator, within one hundred and eighty days after October 21, 1976, and after consultation with appropriate Federal, State, and local authorities, shall by regulation publish guidelines for the identification of those areas which have common solid waste management problems and are appropriate units for planning regional solid waste management services. Such guidelines shall consider —

(1) the size and location of areas which should be included,

(2) the volume of solid waste which should be included, and

(3) the available means of coordinating regional planning with other related regional planning and for coordination of such regional planning into the State plan.

(b) Guidelines for State plans — Not later than eighteen months after October 21, 1976, and after notice and hearing, the Administrator shall, after consultation with appropriate Federal, State, and local authorities, promulgate regulations containing guidelines to assist in the development and implementation of State solid waste management plans (hereinafter in this chapter referred to as "State plans"). The guidelines shall contain methods for achieving the objectives specified in section 6941 of this title. Such guidelines shall be reviewed from time to time, but not less frequently than every three years, and revised as may be appropriate.

(c) Considerations for State plan guidelines — The guidelines promulgated under subsection (b) of this section shall consider —

(1) the varying regional, geologic, hydrologic, climatic, and other circumstances under which different solid waste practices are required in order to insure the reasonable protection of the quality of the ground and surface waters from leachate contamination, the reasonable protection of the quality of the surface waters from surface runoff contamination, and the reasonable protection of ambient air quality;

(2) characteristics and conditions of collection, storage, processing, and disposal operating methods, techniques and practices, and location of facilities where such operating methods, techniques, and practices are conducted, taking into account the nature of the material to be disposed;

(3) methods for closing or upgrading open dumps for purposes of eliminating potential health hazards;

(4) population density, distribution, and projected growth;

(5) geographic, geologic, climatic, and hydrologic characteristics;

(6) the type and location of transportation;

(7) the profile of industries;

(8) the constituents and generation rates of waste;

(9) the political, economic, organizational, financial, and management problems affecting comprehensive solid waste management;

(10) types of resource recovery facilities and resource conservation systems which are appropriate; and

(11) available new and additional markets for recovered material and energy and energy resources recovered from solid waste as well as methods for conserving such materials and energy.

§6943. Requirements for approval of plans
[SWDA §4003]

(a) Minimum requirements — In order to be approved under section 6947 of this title, each State plan must comply with the following minimum requirements —

(1) The plan shall identify (in accordance with section 6946(b) of this title) (A) the responsibilities of State, local, and regional authorities in the implementation of the State plan, (B) the distribution of Federal funds to the authorities responsible for development and implementation of the State plan, and (C) the means for coordinating regional planning and implementation under the State plan.

(2) The plan shall, in accordance with sections 6944(b) and 6945(a) of this title, prohibit the establishment of new open dumps within the State, and contain requirements that all solid waste (including solid waste originating in other States, but not including hazardous waste) shall be (A) utilized for resource recovery or (B) disposed of in sanitary landfills (within the meaning of section 6944(a) of this title) or otherwise disposed of in an environmentally sound manner.

(3) The plan shall provide for the closing or upgrading of all existing open dumps within the State pursuant to the requirements of section 6945 of this title.

(4) The plan shall provide for the establishment of such State regulatory powers as may be necessary to implement the plan.

(5) The plan shall provide that no State or local government within the State shall be prohibited under State or local law from negotiating and entering into long-term contracts for the supply of solid waste to resource recovery facilities, from entering into long-term contracts for the operation of such facilities, or from securing long-term markets for material and energy recovered from such facilities or for conserving materials or energy by reducing the volume of waste.

(6) The plan shall provide for such resource conservation or recovery and for the disposal of solid waste in sanitary landfills or any combination of practices so as may be necessary to use or dispose of such waste in a manner that is environmentally sound.

(b) Discretionary plan provisions relating to recycled oil — Any State plan submitted under this subchapter may include, at the option of the State, provisions to carry out each of the following:

(1) Encouragement, to the maximum extent feasible and consistent with the protection of the public health and the environment, of the use of recycled oil in all appropriate areas of State and local government.

(2) Encouragement of persons contracting with the State to use recycled oil to the maximum extent feasible, consistent with protection of the public health and the environment.

(3) Informing the public of the uses of recycled oil.

(4) Establishment and implementation of a program (including any necessary licensing of persons and including the use, where appropriate, of manifests) to assure that used oil is collected, transported, treated, stored, reused, and disposed of, in a manner which does not present a hazard to the public health or the environment.

Any plan submitted under this chapter before October 15, 1980, may be amended, at the option of the State, at any time after such date to include any provision referred to in this subsection.

(c) Energy and materials conservation and recovery feasibility planning and assistance

(1) A State which has a plan approved under this subchapter or which has submitted a plan for such approval shall be eligible for assistance under section 6948(a)(3) of this title if the Administrator determines that under such plan the State will —

(A) analyze and determine the economic and technical feasibility of facilities and programs to conserve resources which contribute

to the waste stream or to recover energy and materials from municipal waste;

(B) analyze the legal, institutional, and economic impediments to the development of systems and facilities for conservation of energy or materials which contribute to the waste stream or for the recovery of energy and materials from municipal waste and make recommendations to appropriate governmental authorities for overcoming such impediments;

(C) assist municipalities within the State in developing plans, programs, and projects to conserve resources or recover energy and materials from municipal waste; and

(D) coordinate the resource conservation and recovery planning under subparagraph (C).

(2) The analysis referred to in paragraph (1)(A) shall include —

(A) the evaluation of, and establishment of priorities among, market opportunities for industrial and commercial users of all types (including public utilities and industrial parks) to utilize energy and materials recovered from municipal waste;

(B) comparisons of the relative costs of energy recovered from municipal waste in relation to the costs of energy derived from fossil fuels and other sources;

(C) studies of the transportation and storage problems and other problems associated with the development of energy and materials recovery technology, including curbside source separation;

(D) the evaluation and establishment of priorities among ways of conserving energy or materials which contribute to the waste stream;

(E) comparison of the relative total costs between conserving resources and disposing of or recovering such waste; and

(F) studies of impediments to resource conservation or recovery, including business practices, transportation requirements, or storage difficulties.

Such studies and analyses shall also include studies of other sources of solid waste from which energy and materials may be recovered or minimized.

(d) Size of waste-to-energy facilities — Notwithstanding any of the above requirements, it is the intention of this chapter and the planning process developed pursuant to this chapter that in determining the size of the waste-to-energy facility, adequate provision shall be given to the present and reasonably anticipated future needs of the recycling and resource recovery interest within the area encompassed by the planning process.

§6944. Criteria for sanitary landfills; sanitary landfills required for all disposal
[SWDA §4004]

(a) Criteria for sanitary landfills — Not later than one year after October 21, 1976, after consultation with the States, and after notice and public hearings, the Administrator shall promulgate regulations containing criteria for determining which facilities shall be classified as sanitary landfills and which shall be classified as open dumps within the meaning of this chapter. At a minimum, such criteria shall provide that a facility may be classified as a sanitary landfill and not an open dump only if there is no reasonable probability of adverse effects on health or the environment from disposal of solid waste at such facility. Such regulations may provide for the classification of the types of sanitary landfills.

(b) Disposal required to be in sanitary landfills, etc. — For purposes of complying with section 6943(2) of this title each State plan shall prohibit the establishment of open dumps and contain a requirement that disposal of all solid waste within the State shall be in compliance with such section 6943(2) of this title.

(c) Effective date — The prohibition contained in subsection (b) of this section shall take effect on the date six months after the date of promulgation of regulations under subsection (a) of this section.

§6945. Upgrading of open dumps
[SWDA §4005]

(a) Closing or upgrading of existing open dumps — Upon promulgation of criteria under section 6907(a)(3) of this title, any solid waste management practice or disposal of solid waste or hazardous waste which constitutes the open dumping of solid waste or hazardous waste is prohibited, except in the case of any practice or disposal of solid waste under a timetable or schedule for compliance established under this section. The prohibition contained in the preceding sentence shall be enforceable under section 6972 of this title against persons engaged in the act of open dumping. For purposes of complying with section 6943(a)(2) and 6943(a)(3) of this title, each State plan shall contain a requirement that all existing disposal facilities or sites for solid waste in such State which are open dumps listed in the inventory under subsection (b) shall comply with such measures as may be promulgated by the Administrator to eliminate health hazards and minimize potential health hazards. Each such plan shall establish, for any entity which demonstrates that it has considered other public or private alternatives for solid waste management to comply with the prohibition on open dumping and is unable to utilize such alternatives to so comply, a timetable or schedule for compliance for such practice or disposal of solid waste which specifies a schedule of remedial measures, including an enforceable sequence of actions or operations, leading to compliance with the prohibition on open dumping of solid waste within a reasonable time (not to exceed 5 years from the date of publication of criteria under section 6907(a) (3) of this title).

(b) Inventory — To assist the States in complying with section 6943(a)(3) of this title, not later than one year after promulgation of regulations under section 6944 of this title, the Administrator, with the cooperation of the Bureau of the Census shall publish an inventory of all disposal facilities or sites in the United States which are open dumps within the meaning of this chapter.

(c) Control of hazardous disposal

(1)(A) Not later than 36 months after November 8, 1984, each State shall adopt and implement a permit program or other system of prior approval and conditions to assure that each solid waste management facility within such State which may receive hazardous household waste or hazardous waste due to the provision of section 6921(d) of this title for small quantity generators (otherwise not subject to the requirement for a permit under section 6925 of this title) will comply with the applicable criteria promulgated under section 6944(a) and 6907(a) (3) of this title.

(B) Not later than eighteen months after the promulgation of revised criteria under subsection 6944(a) of this title (as required by section 6949a(c) of this title), each State shall adopt and implement a permit program or other system or prior approval and conditions, to assure that each solid waste management facility within such State which may receive hazardous household waste or hazardous waste due to the provision of section 6921(d) of this title for small quantity generators (otherwise not subject to the requirement for a permit under section 6925 of this title) will comply with the criteria revised under section 6944(a) of this title.

(C) The Administrator shall determine whether each State has developed an adequate program under this paragraph. The Administrator may make such a determination in conjunction with approval, disapproval or partial approval of a State plan under section 6947 of this title.

(2)(A) In any State that the Administrator determines has not adopted an adequate program for such facilities under paragraph (1)(B) by the date provided in such paragraph, the Administrator may use the authorities available under sections 6927 and 6928 of this title to enforce the prohibition contained in subsection (a) of this section with respect to such facilities.

(B) For purposes of this paragraph, the term "requirement of this subchapter" in section 6928 of this title shall be deemed to include criteria promulgated by the Administrator under sections 6907(a)(3) and 6944(a) of this title, and the term "hazardous wastes" in section 6927 of this title shall be deemed to include solid waste at facilities that may handle hazardous household wastes or hazardous wastes from small quantity generators.

(d) Management standards for a facility
(1) Guidance

Not later than October 1, 2009, the Secretary, after consultation with the Administrator of the Environmental Protection Agency and all appropriate State agencies in affected States, shall make available, including to potential users of the long-term management and storage program established under subsection (a), guidance that establishes procedures and standards for the receipt, management, and long-term storage of elemental mercury at a designated facility or facilities, including requirements to ensure appropriate use of flasks or other suitable shipping containers. Such procedures and standards shall be protective of human health and the environment and shall ensure that the elemental mercury is stored in a safe, secure, and effective manner. In addition to such procedures and standards, elemental mercury managed and stored under this section at a designated facility shall be subject to the requirements of the Solid Waste Disposal Act, including the requirements of subtitle C of that Act, except as provided in subsection (g)(2) of this section. A designated facility is authorized to operate under interim status pursuant to section 3005(e) of the Solid Waste Disposal Act until a final decision on a permit application is made pursuant to section 3005(c) of the Solid Waste Disposal Act. Not later than January 1, 2020, the Administrator of the Environmental Protection Agency (or an authorized State) shall issue a final decision on the permit application.

(2) Training

The Secretary shall conduct operational training and emergency training for all staff that have responsibilities related to elemental mercury management, transfer, storage, monitoring, or response.

(3) Equipment

The Secretary shall ensure that each designated facility has all equipment necessary for routine operations, emergencies, monitoring, checking inventory, loading, and storing elemental mercury at the facility.

(4) Fire detection and suppression systems

The Secretary shall—

(A) ensure the installation of fire detection systems at each designated facility, including smoke detectors and heat detectors; and

(B) ensure the installation of a permanent fire suppression system, unless the Secretary determines that a permanent fire suppression system is not necessary to protect human health and the environment.

(e) Indemnification of persons delivering elemental mercury
(1) In general

(A) Except as provided in subparagraph (B) and subject to paragraph (2), the Secretary shall hold harmless, defend, and indemnify in full any person who delivers elemental mercury to a designated facility under the program established under subsection (a) from and against any suit, claim, demand or action, liability, judgment, cost, or other fee arising out of any claim for personal injury or property damage (including death, illness, or loss of or damage to property or economic loss) that results from, or is in any manner predicated upon, the release or threatened release of elemental mercury as a result of acts or omissions occurring after such mercury is delivered to a designated facility described in subsection (a).

(B) To the extent that a person described in subparagraph (A) contributed to any such release or threatened release, subparagraph (A) shall not apply.

(2) Conditions

No indemnification may be afforded under this subsection unless the person seeking indemnification—

(A) notifies the Secretary in writing within 30 days after receiving written notice of the claim for which indemnification is sought;

(B) furnishes to the Secretary copies of pertinent papers the person receives;

(C) furnishes evidence or proof of any claim, loss, or damage covered by this subsection; and

(D) provides, upon request by the Secretary, access to the records and personnel of the person for purposes of defending or settling the claim or action.

(3) Authority of Secretary

(A) In any case in which the Secretary determines that the Department of Energy may be required to make indemnification payments to a person under this subsection for any suit, claim, demand or action, liability, judgment, cost, or other fee arising out of any claim for personal injury or property damage referred to in paragraph (1)(A), the Secretary may settle or defend, on behalf of that person, the claim for personal injury or property damage.

(B) In any case described in subparagraph (A), if the person to whom the Department of Energy may be required to make indemnification payments does not allow the Secretary to settle or defend the claim, the person may not be afforded indemnification with respect to that claim under this subsection.

(f) Terms, conditions, and procedures

The Secretary is authorized to establish such terms, conditions, and procedures as are necessary to carry out this section.

(g) Effect on other law
(1) In general

Except as provided in paragraph (2), nothing in this section changes or affects any Federal, State, or local law or the obligation of any person to comply with such law.

(2) Exception

(A) Elemental mercury that the Secretary is storing on a long-term basis shall not be subject to the storage prohibition of section 3004(j) of the Solid Waste Disposal Act (42 U.S.C. 6924(j)). For the purposes of section 3004(j) of the Solid Waste Disposal Act, a generator accumulating elemental mercury destined for a facility designated by the Secretary under subsection (a) for 90 days or less shall be deemed to be accumulating the mercury to facilitate proper treatment, recovery, or disposal.

(B) Elemental mercury may be stored at a facility with respect to which any permit has been issued under section 3005(c) of the Solid Waste Disposal Act (42 U.S.C. 6925(c)), and shall not be subject to the storage prohibition of section 3004(j) of the Solid Waste Disposal Act (42 U.S.C. 6924(j)) if—

(i) the Secretary is unable to accept the mercury at a facility designated by the Secretary under subsection (a) for reasons beyond the control of the owner or operator of the permitted facility;

(ii) the owner or operator of the permitted facility certifies in writing to the Secretary that it will ship the mercury to the designated facility when the Secretary is able to accept the mercury; and

(iii) the owner or operator of the permitted facility certifies in writing to the Secretary that it will not sell, or otherwise place into commerce, the mercury.

(C) Subparagraph (B) shall not apply to mercury with respect to which the owner or operator of the permitted facility fails to comply with a certification provided under clause (ii) or (iii) of that subparagraph.

(D) A generator producing elemental mercury incidentally from the beneficiation or processing of ore or related pollution control activities may accumulate the mercury produced onsite that is destined for a facility designated by the Secretary under subsection (a) for more than 90 days without a permit issued under section 3005(c) of the Solid Waste Disposal Act (42 U.S.C. 6925(c)), and shall not be subject to the storage prohibition of section 3004(j) of that Act (42 U.S.C. 6924(j)), if—

(i) the Secretary is unable to accept the mercury at a facility designated by the Secretary under subsection (a) for reasons beyond the control of the generator;

(ii) the generator certifies in writing to the Secretary that the generator will ship the mercury to a designated facility when the Secretary is able to accept the mercury;

(iii) the generator certifies in writing to the Secretary that the generator is storing only mercury the generator has produced or recovered onsite and will not sell, or otherwise place into commerce, the mercury; and

(iv) the generator has obtained an identification number under section 262.12 of title 40, Code of Federal Regulations, and complies with the requirements described in paragraphs (1) through (4) of section 262.34(a) of title 40, Code of Federal Regulations (as in effect on the date of enactment of this subparagraph).

(E) Management standards for temporary storage

Not later than January 1, 2017, the Secretary, after consultation with the Administrator of the Environmental Protection Agency and State agencies in affected States, shall develop and make available guidance that establishes procedures and standards for the management and short-term storage of elemental mercury at a generator covered under subparagraph (D), including requirements to ensure appropriate use of flasks or other suitable containers. Such procedures and standards shall be protective of health and the environment and shall ensure that the elemental mercury is stored in a safe, secure, and effective manner. A generator may accumulate mercury in accordance with subparagraph (D) immediately upon enactment of this subparagraph, and notwithstanding that guidance called for by this paragraph has not been developed or made available.

(h) Study

Not later than July 1, 2014, the Secretary shall transmit to the Congress the results of a study, conducted in consultation with the Administrator of the Environmental Protection Agency, that—

(1) determines the impact of the long-term storage program under this section on mercury recycling; and

(2) includes proposals, if necessary, to mitigate any negative impact identified under paragraph (1).

§6946. Procedure for development and implementation of State plan
[SWDA §4006]

(a) Identification of regions — Within one hundred and eighty days after publication of guidelines under section 6942(a) of this title (relating to identification of regions), the Governor of each State, after consultation with local elected officials, shall promulgate regulations based on such guidelines identifying the boundaries of each area within the State which, as a result of urban concentrations, geographic conditions, markets, and other factors, is appropriate for carrying out regional solid waste management. Such regulations may be modified from time to time (identifying additional or different regions) pursuant to such guidelines.

(b) Identification of State and local agencies and responsibilities

(1) Within one hundred and eighty days after the Governor promulgates regulations under subsection (a) of this section, for purposes of facilitating the development and implementation of a State plan which will meet the minimum requirements of section 6943 of this title, the State, together with appropriate elected officials of general purpose units of local government, shall jointly (A) identify an agency to develop the State plan and identify one or more agencies to implement such plan, and (B) identify which solid waste management activities will, under such State plan, be planned for and carried out by the State and which such management activities will, under such State plan, be planned for and carried out by a regional or local authority or a combination of regional or local and State authorities. If a multi-functional regional agency authorized by State law to conduct solid waste planning and management (the members of which are appointed by the Governor) is in existence on October 21, 1976, the Governor shall identify such authority for purposes of carrying out within such region clause (A) of this paragraph. Where feasible, designation of the agency for the affected area designated under section 1288 of Title 33 shall be considered. A State agency identified under this paragraph shall be established or designated by the Governor of such State. Local or regional agencies identified under this paragraph shall be composed of individuals at least a majority of whom are elected local officials.

(2) If planning and implementation agencies are not identified and designated or established as required under paragraph (1) for any affected area, the governor shall, before the date two hundred and seventy days after promulgation of regulations under subsection (a) of this section, establish or designate a State agency to develop and implement the State plan for such area.

(c) Interstate regions

(1) In the case of any region which, pursuant to the guidelines published by the Administrator under section 6942(a) of this title (relating to identification of regions), would be located in two or more States, the Governors of the respective States, after consultation with local elected officials, shall consult, cooperate, and enter into agreements identifying the boundaries of such region pursuant to subsection (a) of this section.

(2) Within one hundred and eighty days after an interstate region is identified by agreement under paragraph (1), appropriate elected officials of general purpose units of local government within such region shall jointly establish or designate an agency to develop a plan for such region. If no such agency is established or designated within such period by such officials, the Governors of the respective States may, by agreement, establish or designate for such purpose a single representative organization including elected officials of general purpose units of local government within such region.

(3) Implementation of interstate regional solid waste management plans shall be conducted by units of local government for any portion of a region within their jurisdiction, or by multijurisdictional agencies or authorities designated in accordance with State law, including those designated by agreement by such units of local government for such purpose. If no such unit, agency, or authority is so designated, the respective Governors shall designate or establish a single interstate agency to implement such plan.

(4) For purposes of this subchapter, so much of an interstate regional plan as is carried out within a particular State shall be deemed part of the State plan for such State.

§6947. Approval of State plan; Federal assistance

[SWDA §4007]

(a) Plan approval — The Administrator shall, within six months after a State plan has been submitted for approval, approve or disapprove the plan. The Administrator shall approve a plan if he determines that —

(1) it meets the requirements of paragraphs (1), (2), (3), and (5) of section 6943(a) of this title; and

(2) it contains provision for revision of such plan, after notice and public hearing, whenever the Administrator, by regulation, determines —

(A) that revised regulations respecting minimum requirements have been promulgated under paragraphs (1), (2), (3), and (5) of section 6943(a) of this title with which the State plan is not in compliance;

(B) that information has become available which demonstrates the inadequacy of the plan to effectuate the purposes of this subchapter; or

(C) that such revision is otherwise necessary.
The Administrator shall review approved plans from time to time and if he determines that revision or corrections are necessary to bring such plan into compliance with the minimum requirements promulgated under section 6943 of this title (including new or revised requirements), he shall, after notice and opportunity for public hearing, withdraw his approval of such plan. Such withdrawal of approval shall cease to be effective upon the Administrator's determination that such complies with such minimum requirements.

(b) Eligibility of States for Federal financial assistance

(1) The Administrator shall approve a State application for financial assistance under this subchapter, and make grants to such State, if such State and local and regional authorities within such State have complied with the requirements of section 6946 of this title within the period required under such section and if such State has a State plan which has been approved by the Administrator under this subchapter.

(2) The Administrator shall approve a State application for financial assistance under this subchapter, and make grants to such State, for fiscal years 1978 and 1979 if the Administrator determines that the State plan continues to be eligible for approval under subsection (a) of this section and is being implemented by the State.

(3) Upon withdrawal of approval of a State plan under subsection (a) of this section, the Administrator shall withhold Federal financial and technical assistance under this subchapter (other than such technical assistance as may be necessary to assist in obtaining the reinstatement of approval) until such time as such approval is reinstated.

(c) **Existing activities** — Nothing in this subchapter shall be construed to prevent or affect any activities respecting solid waste planning or management which are carried out by State, regional, or local authorities unless such activities are inconsistent with a State plan approved by the Administrator under this subchapter.

§6948. Federal assistance
[SWDA §4008]
(a) Authorization of Federal financial assistance

(1) There are authorized to be appropriated $30,000,000 for the fiscal year 1978, $40,000,000 for the fiscal year 1979, $20,000,000 for the fiscal year 1980, $15,000,000 for the fiscal year 1981, $20,000,000 for the fiscal year 1982, and $10,000,000 for each of the fiscal years 1985 through 1988 for purposes of financial assistance to States and local, regional, and interstate authorities for the development and implementation of plans approved by the Administrator under this subchapter (other than the provisions of such plans referred to in section 6943(b) of this title, relating to feasibility planning for municipal waste energy and materials conservation and recovery).

(2)(A) The Administrator is authorized to provide financial assistance to States, counties, municipalities, and intermunicipal agencies and State and local public solid waste management authorities for implementation of programs to provide solid waste management, resource recovery, and resource conservation services and hazardous waste management. Such assistance shall include assistance for facility planning and feasibility studies; expert consultation; surveys and analyses of market needs; marketing of recovered resources; technology assessments; legal expenses; construction feasibility studies; source separation

projects; and fiscal or economic investigations or studies; but such assistance shall not include any other element of construction, or any acquisition of land or interest in land, or any subsidy for the price of recovered resources. Agencies assisted under this subsection shall consider existing solid waste management and hazardous waste management services and facilities as well as facilities proposed for construction.

(B) An applicant for financial assistance under this paragraph must agree to comply with respect to the project or program assisted with the applicable requirements of section 6945 of this title and subchapter III of this chapter and apply applicable solid waste management practices, methods, and levels of control consistent with any guidelines published pursuant to section 6907 of this title. Assistance under this paragraph shall be available only for programs certified by the State to be consistent with any applicable State or areawide solid waste management plan or program. Applicants for technical and financial assistance under this section shall not preclude or foreclose consideration of programs for the recovery of recyclable materials through source separation or other resource recovery techniques.

(C) There are authorized to be appropriated $15,000,000 for each of the fiscal years 1978 and 1979 for purposes of this section. There are authorized to be appropriated $10,000,000 for fiscal year 1980, $10,000,000 for fiscal year 1981, $10,000,000 for fiscal year 1982, and $10,000,000 for each of the fiscal years 1985 through 1988 for purposes of this paragraph.

(D) There are authorized —

(i) to be made available $15,000,000 out of funds appropriated for fiscal year 1985, and

(ii) to be appropriated for each of the fiscal years 1986 though 1988, $20,000,000 for grants to States (and where appropriate to regional, local, and interstate agencies) to implement programs requiring compliance by solid waste management facilities with the criteria promulgated under section 6944(a) of this title and section 6907(a)(3) of this title and with the provisions of section 6945 of this title. To the extent practicable, such programs shall require such compliance not later than thirty-six months after November 8, 1984.

(3)(A) There is authorized to be appropriated for the fiscal year beginning October 1, 1981, and for each fiscal year thereafter before October 1, 1986, $4,000,000 for purposes of making grants to States to carry out section 6943(b) of this title. No amount may be appropriated for such purposes for the fiscal year beginning on October 1, 1986, or for any fiscal year thereafter.

(B) Assistance provided by the Administrator under this paragraph shall be used only for the purposes specified in section 6943(b) of this title. Such assistance may not be used for purposes of land acquisition, final facility design, equipment purchase, construction, startup or operation activities.

(C) Where appropriate, any State receiving assistance under this paragraph may make all or any part of such assistance available to municipalities within the State to carry out the activities specified in section 6943(b)(1)(A) and (B) of this title.

(b) State allotment — The sums appropriated in any fiscal year under subsection (a)(1) of this section shall be allotted by the Administrator among all States, in the ratio that the population in each State bears to the population in all of the States, except that no State shall receive less than one-half of 1 per centum of the sums so allotted in any fiscal year. No State shall receive any grant under this section during any fiscal year when its expenditures of non-Federal funds for other than non-recurrent expenditures for solid waste management control programs will be less than its expenditures were for such programs during fiscal year 1975, except that such funds may be reduced by an amount equal to their proportionate share of any general reduction of State spending ordered by the Governor or legislature of such State. No State shall receive any grant for solid waste management programs unless the Administrator is satisfied that such grant will be so used as to supplement and, to the extent practicable, increase the level of State, local, regional, or other non-Federal funds that would in the absence of such grant be made available for the maintenance of such programs.

(c) Distribution of Federal financial assistance within the State — The Federal assistance allotted to the States under subsection (b) of this section shall be allocated by the State receiving such funds to State, local, regional, and interstate authorities carrying out planning and implementation of the State plan. Such allocation shall be based upon the responsibilities of the respective parties as determined pursuant to section 6946(b) of this title.

(d) Technical assistance

(1) The Administrator may provide technical assistance to State and local governments for purposes of developing and implementing State plans. Technical assistance respecting resource recovery and conservation may be provided through resource recovery and conservation panels, established in the Environmental Protection Agency under subchapter II of this chapter, to assist the State and local governments with respect to particular resource recovery and conservation

projects under consideration and to evaluate their effect on the State plan.

(2) In carrying out this subsection, the Administrator may, upon request, provide technical assistance to States to assist in the removal or modification of legal, institutional, economic, and other impediments to the recycling of used oil. Such impediments may include laws, regulations, and policies, including State procurement policies, which are not favorable to the recycling of used oil.

(3) In carrying out this subsection, the Administrator is authorized to provide technical assistance to States, municipalities, regional authorities, and intermunicipal agencies upon request, to assist in the removal or modification of legal, institutional, and economic impediments which have the effect of impeding the development of systems and facilities to recovery energy and materials from municipal waste or to conserve energy or materials which contribute to the waste stream. Such impediments may include —

(A) laws, regulations, and policies, including State and local procurement policies, which are not favorable to resource conservation and recovery policies, systems, and facilities;

(B) impediments to the financing of facilities to conserve or recover energy and materials from municipal waste through the exercise of State and local authority to issue revenue bonds and the use of State and local credit assistance; and

(C) impediments to institutional arrangements necessary to undertake projects for the conservation or recovery of energy and materials from municipal waste, including the creation of special districts, authorities, or corporations where necessary having the power to secure the supply of waste of a project, to conserve resources, to implement the project, and to undertake related activities.

(e) Special communities

(1) The Administrator, in cooperation with State and local officials, shall identify local governments within the United States (A) having a solid waste disposal facility (i) which is owned by the unit of local government, (ii) for which an order has been issued by the State to cease receiving solid waste for treatment, storage, or disposal, and (iii) which is subject to a State-approved end-use recreation plan, and (B) which are located over an aquifer which is the source of drinking water for any person or public water system and which has serious environmental problems resulting from the disposal of such solid waste, including possible methane migration.

(2) There is authorized to be appropriated to the Administrator $2,500,000 for the fiscal year 1980 and $1,500,000 for each of the fiscal years 1981 and 1982 to make grants to be used for containment and

stabilization of solid waste located at the disposal sites referred to in paragraph (1). Not more than one community in any State shall be eligible for grants under this paragraph and not more than one project in any State shall be eligible for such grants. No unit of local government shall be eligible for grants under this paragraph with respect to any site which exceeds 65 acres in size.

(f) Assistance to States for discretionary program for recycled oil

(1) The Administrator may make grants to States, which have a State plan approved under section 6947 of this title, or which have submitted a State plan for approval under such section, if such plan includes the discretionary provisions described in section 6943(b) of this title. Grants under this subsection shall be for purposes of assisting the State in carrying out such discretionary provisions. No grant under this subsection may be used for construction or for the acquisition of land or equipment.

(2) Grants under this subsection shall be allotted among the States in the same manner as provided in the first sentence of subsection (b) of this section.

(3) No grant may be made under this subsection unless an application therefor is submitted to, and approved by, the Administrator. The application shall be in such form, be submitted in such manner, and contain such information as the Administrator may require.

(4) For purposes of making grants under this subsection, there are authorized to be appropriated $5,000,000 for fiscal year 1982, $5,000,000 for fiscal year 1983, and $5,000,000 for each of the fiscal years 1985 through 1988.

(g) Assistance to municipalities for energy and materials conservation and recovery planning activities

(1) The Administrator is authorized to make grants to municipalities, regional authorities, and intermunicipal agencies to carry out activities described in subparagraphs (A) and (B) of section 6943(b)(1) of this title. Such grants may be made only pursuant to an application submitted to the Administrator by the municipality which application has been approved by the State and determined by the State to be consistent with any State plan approved or submitted under this subchapter or any other appropriate planning carried out by the State.

(2) There is authorized to be appropriated for the fiscal year beginning October 1, 1981, and for each fiscal year thereafter before October 1, 1986, $8,000,000 for purposes of making grants to municipalities under this subsection. No amount may be appropriated for such purposes for the fiscal year beginning on October 1, 1986, or for any fiscal year thereafter.

(3) Assistance provided by the Administrator under this subsection shall be used only for the purposes specified in paragraph (1). Such assistance may not be used for purposes of land acquisition, final facility design, equipment purchase, construction, startup or operation activities.

§6949. Rural communities assistance
[SWDA §4009]

(a) In general — The Administrator shall make grants to States to provide assistance to municipalities with a population of five thousand or less, or counties with a population of ten thousand or less or less than twenty persons per square mile and not within a metropolitan area, for solid waste management facilities (including equipment) necessary to meet the requirements of section 6945 of this title or restrictions on open burning or other requirements arising under the Clean Air Act [42 U.S.C. §§7401 *et seq.*] or the Federal Water Pollution Control Act [33 U.S.C. §§1251 *et seq.*]. Such assistance shall only be available —

(1) to any municipality or county which could not feasibly be included in a solid waste management system or facility serving an urbanized, multijurisdictional area because of its distance from such systems;

(2) where existing or planned solid waste management services or facilities are unavailable or insufficient to comply with the requirements of section 6945 of this title; and

(3) for systems which are certified by the State to be consistent with any plans or programs established under any State or areawide planning process.

(b) Allotment — The Administrator shall allot the sums appropriated to carry out this section in any fiscal year among the States in accordance with regulations promulgated by him on the basis of the average of the ratio which the population of rural areas of each State bears to the total population of rural areas of all the States, the ratio which the population of counties in each State having less than twenty persons per square mile bears to the total population of such counties in all the States, and the ratio which the population of such low-density counties in each State having 33 per centum or more of all families with incomes not in excess of 125 per centum of the poverty level bears to the total population of such counties in all the States.

(c) Limit — The amount of any grant under this section shall not exceed 75 per centum of the costs of the project. No assistance under this section shall be available for the acquisition of land or interests in land.

(d) Authorization of appropriations — There are authorized to be appropriated $25,000,000 for each of the fiscal years 1978 and 1979 to carry out this section. There are authorized to be appropriated

467

$10,000,000 for the fiscal year 1980 and $15,000,000 for each of the fiscal years 1981 and 1982 to carry out this section.

(e) Additional appropriations

(1) In general — There are authorized to be appropriated to carry out this section for the Denali Commission to provide assistance to municipalities in the State of Alaska $1,500,000 for each of fiscal years 2008 through 2012.

(2) Administration — For the purpose of carrying out this subsection, the Denali Commission shall —

(A) be considered a State; and

(B) comply with all other requirements and limitations of this section.

§6949a. Adequacy of certain guidelines and criteria

[SWDA §4010]

(a) **Study** — The Administrator shall conduct a study of the extent to which the guidelines and criteria under this chapter (other than guidelines and criteria for facilities to which subchapter III of this chapter applies) which are applicable to solid waste management and disposal facilities, including, but not limited to landfills and surface impoundments, are adequate to protect human health and the environment from ground water contamination. Such study shall include a detailed assessment of the degree to which the criteria under section 6907(a) of this title and the criteria under section 6944 of this title regarding monitoring, prevention of contamination, and remedial action are adequate to protect ground water and shall also include recommendation with respect to any additional enforcement authorities which the Administrator, in consultation with the Attorney General, deems necessary for such purposes.

(b) **Report** — Not later than thirty-six months after November 8, 1984, the Administrator shall submit a report to the Congress setting forth the results of the study required under this section, together with any recommendations made by the Administrator on the basis of such study.

(c) Revisions of guidelines and criteria

(1) In general — Not later than March 31, 1988, the Administrator shall promulgate revisions of the criteria promulgated under paragraph (1) of section 6944(a) of this title and under section 6907(a)(3) of this title for facilities that may receive hazardous household wastes or hazardous wastes from small quantity generators under section 6921(d) of this title. The criteria shall be those necessary to protect human health and the environment and may take into account the practicable capability of such facilities. At a minimum such revisions for facilities potentially receiving such wastes should require ground water monitoring as necessary to detect contamination, establish criteria for the acceptable location of new

or existing facilities, and provide for corrective action as appropriate.

(2) Additional revisions — Subject to paragraph (3), the requirements of the criteria described in paragraph (1) relating to ground water monitoring shall not apply to an owner or operator of a new municipal solid waste landfill unit, an existing municipal solid waste landfill unit, or a lateral expansion of a municipal solid waste landfill unit, that disposes of less than 20 tons of municipal solid waste daily, based on an annual average, if —

(A) there is no evidence of ground water contamination from the municipal solid waste landfill unit or expansion; and

(B) the municipal solid waste landfill unit or expansion serves —

(i) a community that experiences an annual interruption of at least 3 consecutive months of surface transportation that prevents access to a regional waste management facility; or

(ii) a community that has no practicable waste management alternative and the landfill unit is located in an area that annually receives less than or equal to 25 inches of precipitation.

(3) Protection of ground water resources

(A) Monitoring requirement — A State may require ground water monitoring of a solid waste landfill unit that would otherwise be exempt under paragraph (2) if necessary to protect ground water resources and ensure compliance with a State ground water protection plan, where applicable.

(B) Methods — If a State requires ground water monitoring of a solid waste landfill unit under subparagraph (A), the State may allow the use of a method other than the use of ground water monitoring wells to detect a release of contamination from the unit.

(C) Corrective action — If a State finds a release from a solid waste landfill unit, the State shall require corrective action as appropriate.

(4) No-migration exemption

(A) In general — Ground water monitoring requirements may be suspended by the Director of an approved State for a landfill operator if the operator demonstrates that there is no potential for migration of hazardous constituents from the unit to the uppermost aquifer during the active life of the unit and the post-closure care period.

(B) Certification — A demonstration under subparagraph (A) shall be certified by a qualified ground-water scientist and approved by the Director of an approved State.

(C) Guidance — Not later than 6 months after March 26, 1996, the Administrator shall issue a guidance document to facilitate small community use of the no migration exemption under this paragraph.

(5) Alaska Native villages — Upon certification by the Governor of the State of Alaska that application of the requirements described in paragraph (1) to a solid waste landfill unit of a Native village (as defined in section 1602 of Title 43) or unit that is located in or near a small, remote Alaska village would be infeasible, or would not be cost-effective, or is otherwise inappropriate because of the remote location of the unit, the State may exempt the unit from some or all of those requirements. This paragraph shall apply only to solid waste landfill units that dispose of less than 20 tons of municipal solid waste daily, based on an annual average.

(6) Further revisions of guidelines and criteria — Recognizing the unique circumstances of small communities, the Administrator shall, not later than two years after March 26, 1996, promulgate revisions to the guidelines and criteria promulgated under this subchapter to provide additional flexibility to approved States to allow landfills that receive 20 tons or less of municipal solid waste per day, based on an annual average, to use alternative frequencies of daily cover application, frequencies of methane gas monitoring, infiltration layers for final cover, and means for demonstrating financial assurance: Provided, That such alternative requirements take into account climatic and hydrogeologic conditions and are protective of human health and environment.

SUBCHAPTER V — DUTIES OF THE SECRETARY OF COMMERCE IN RESOURCE AND RECOVERY

§6951. Functions
[SWDA §5001]

The Secretary of Commerce shall encourage greater commercialization of proven resource recovery technology by providing —

(1) accurate specifications for recovered materials;

(2) stimulation of development of markets for recovered materials;

(3) promotion of proven technology; and

(4) a forum for the exchange of technical and economic data relating to resource recovery facilities.

§6952. Development of specifications for secondary materials
[SWDA §5002]

The Secretary of Commerce, acting through the National Institute of Standards and Technology, and in conjunction with national standards-setting organizations in resource recovery, shall, after public hearings, and not later than two years after September 1, 1979, publish guidelines for the development of specifications for the classification of materials recovered from waste which were destined for disposal. The specifications shall pertain to the physical and chemical properties and characteristics of such materials with regard to their use in replacing virgin materials in various industrial, commercial, and governmental uses. In establishing such guidelines the Secretary shall also, to the extent feasible, provide such information as may be necessary to assist Federal agencies with procurement of items containing recovered materials. The Secretary shall continue to cooperate with national standards-setting organizations, as may be necessary, to encourage the publication, promulgation and updating of standards for recovered materials and for the use of recovered materials in various industrial, commercial, and governmental uses.

§6953. Development of markets for recovered materials
[SWDA §5003]

The Secretary of Commerce shall within two years after September 1, 1979, take such actions as may be necessary to —

(1) identify the geographical location of existing or potential markets for recovered materials;

(2) identify the economic and technical barriers to the use of recovered materials; and

(3) encourage the development of new uses for recovered materials.

§6954. Technology promotion
[SWDA §5004]

The Secretary of Commerce is authorized to evaluate the commercial feasibility of resource recovery facilities and to publish the results of such evaluation, and to develop a data base for purposes of assisting persons in choosing such a system.

§6955. Marketing policies, establishment; nondiscrimination requirement
[SWDA §5005]

In establishing any policies which may affect the development of new markets for recovered materials and in making any determination concerning whether or not to impose monitoring or other controls on any marketing or transfer of recovered materials, the Secretary of Commerce may consider whether to establish the same or similar policies or impose the same or similar monitoring or other controls on virgin materials.

§6956. Authorization of appropriations
[SWDA §5006]

There are authorized to be appropriated to the Secretary of Commerce $5,000,000 for each of fiscal years 1980, 1981, and 1982 and $1,500,000 for each of the fiscal years 1985 through 1988 to carry out the purposes of this subchapter.

SUBCHAPTER VI — FEDERAL RESPONSIBILITIES

§6961. Application of Federal, State, and local law to Federal facilities
[SWDA §6001]

(a) **In general** — Each department, agency, and instrumentality of the executive, legislative, and judicial branches of the Federal Government (1) having jurisdiction over any solid waste management facility or disposal site, or (2) engaged in any activity resulting, or which may result, in the disposal or management of solid waste or hazardous waste shall be subject to, and comply with, all Federal, State, interstate, and local requirements, both substantive and procedural (including any requirement for permits or reporting or any provisions for injunctive relief and such sanctions as may be imposed by a court to enforce such relief), respecting control and abatement of solid waste or hazardous waste disposal and management in the same manner, and to the same extent, as any person is subject to such requirements, including the payment of reasonable service charges. The Federal, State, interstate, and local substantive and procedural requirements referred to in this subsection include, but are not limited to, all administrative orders and all civil and administrative penalties and fines, regardless of whether such penalties or fines are punitive or coercive in nature or are imposed for isolated, intermittent, or continuing violations. The United States hereby expressly waives any immunity otherwise applicable to the United States with respect to any such substantive or procedural requirement (including, but not limited to, any injunctive relief, administrative order or civil or administrative penalty or fine referred to in the preceding sentence, or reasonable service charge). The reasonable service charges referred to in this subsection include, but are not limited to, fees or charges assessed in connection with the processing and issuance of permits, renewal of permits, amendments to permits, review of plans, studies, and other documents, and inspection and monitoring of facilities, as well as any other nondiscriminatory charges that are assessed in connection with a Federal, State, interstate, or local solid waste or hazardous waste regulatory program. Neither the United States, nor any agent, employee, or officer thereof, shall be immune or exempt from any process or sanction of any State or Federal Court with respect to the enforcement of any such injunctive relief. No agent, employee, or officer of the United States shall be personally liable for any civil penalty under any Federal, State, interstate, or local solid or hazardous waste law with respect to

any act or omission within the scope of the official duties of the agent, employee, or officer. An agent, employee, or officer of the United States shall be subject to any criminal sanction (including, but not limited to, any fine or imprisonment) under any Federal or State solid or hazardous waste law, but no department, agency, or instrumentality of the executive, legislative, or judicial branch of the Federal Government shall be subject to any such sanction. The President may exempt any solid waste management facility of any department, agency, or instrumentality in the executive branch from compliance with such a requirement if he determines it to be in the paramount interest of the United States to do so. No such exemption shall be granted due to lack of appropriation unless the President shall have specifically requested such appropriation as a part of the budgetary process and the Congress shall have failed to make available such requested appropriation. Any exemption shall be for a period not in excess of one year, but additional exemptions may be granted for periods not to exceed one year upon the President's making a new determination. The President shall report each January to the Congress all exemptions from the requirements of this section granted during the preceding calendar year, together with his reason for granting each such exemption.

(b) **Administrative enforcement actions**

(1) The Administrator may commence an administrative enforcement action against any department, agency, or instrumentality of the executive, legislative, or judicial branch of the Federal Government pursuant to the enforcement authorities contained in this chapter. The Administrator shall initiate an administrative enforcement action against such a department, agency, or instrumentality in the same manner and under the same circumstances as an action would be initiated against another person. Any voluntary resolution or settlement of such an action shall be set forth in a consent order.

(2) No administrative order issued to such a department, agency, or instrumentality shall become final until such department, agency, or instrumentality has had the opportunity to confer with the Administrator.

(c) **Limitation on State use of funds collected from Federal Government** — Unless a State law in effect on October 6, 1992, or a State constitution requires the funds to be used in a different manner, all funds collected by a State from the Federal Government from penalties and fines imposed for violation of any substantive or procedural requirement referred to in subsection (a) of this section shall be used by the State only for projects designed to improve or protect the environment or to defray the costs of environmental protection or enforcement.

§6962. Federal procurement
[SWDA §6002]

(a) Application of section — Except as provided in subsection (b) of this section, a procuring agency shall comply with the requirements set forth in this section and any regulations issued under this section, with respect to any purchase or acquisition of a procurement item where the purchase price of the item exceeds $10,000 or where the quantity of such items or of functionally equivalent items purchased or acquired in the course of the preceding fiscal year was $10,000 or more.

(b) Procurement subject to other law — Any procurement, by any procuring agency, which is subject to regulations of the Administrator under section 6964 of this title (as promulgated before October 21, 1976, under comparable provisions of prior law) shall not be subject to the requirements of this section to the extent that such requirements are inconsistent with such regulations.

(c) Requirements

(1) After the date specified in applicable guidelines prepared pursuant to subsection (e) of this section, each procuring agency which procures any items designated in such guidelines shall procure such items composed of the highest percentage of recovered materials practicable (and in the case of paper, the highest percentage of the postconsumer recovered materials referred to in subsection (h) (1) of this section practicable), consistent with maintaining a satisfactory level of competition, considering such guidelines. The decision not to procure such items shall be based on a determination that such procurement items —

(A) are not reasonably available within a reasonable period of time;

(B) fail to meet the performance standards set forth in the applicable specifications or fail to meet the reasonable performance standards of the procuring agencies; or

(C) are only available at an unreasonable price. Any determination under subparagraph (B) shall be made on the basis of the guidelines of the National Institute of Standards and Technology in any case in which such material is covered by such guidelines.

(2) Agencies that generate heat, mechanical, or electrical energy from fossil fuel in systems that have the technical capability of using energy or fuels derived from solid waste as a primary or supplementary fuel shall use such capability to the maximum extent practicable.

(3)(A) After the date specified in any applicable guidelines prepared pursuant to subsection (e) of this section, contracting officers shall require that vendors:

(i) certify that the percentage of recovered materials to be used in the performance of the contract will be at least the amount required by applicable specifications or other contractual requirements and

(ii) estimate the percentage of the total material utilized for the performance of the contract which is recovered materials.

(B) Clause (ii) of subparagraph (A) applies only to a contract in an amount greater than $100,000.

(d) Specifications — All Federal agencies that have the responsibility for drafting or reviewing specifications for procurement items procured by Federal agencies shall —

(1) as expeditiously as possible but in any event no later than eighteen months after November 8, 1984, eliminate from such specifications —

(A) any exclusion of recovered materials and

(B) any requirement that items be manufactured from virgin materials; and

(2) within one year after the date of publication of applicable guidelines under subsection (e) of this section, or as otherwise specified in such guidelines, assure that such specifications require the use of recovered materials to the maximum extent possible without jeopardizing the intended end use of the item.

(e) Guidelines — The Administrator, after consultation with the Administrator of General Services, the Secretary of Commerce (acting through the National Institute of Standards and Technology), and the Director of the Government Publishing Office, shall prepare, and from time to time revise, guidelines for the use of procuring agencies in complying with the requirements of this section. Such guidelines shall —

(1) designate those items which are or can be produced with recovered materials and whose procurement by procuring agencies will carry out the objectives of this section, and in the case of paper, provide for maximizing the use of post consumer recovered materials referred to in subsection (h) (1) of this section; and

(2) set forth recommended practices with respect to the procurement of recovered materials and items containing such materials and with respect to certification by vendors of the percentage of recovered materials used, and shall provide information as to the availability, relative price, and performance of such materials and items and where appropriate shall recommend the level of recovered material to be contained in the procured product. The Administrator shall prepare final guidelines for paper within one hundred and eighty days after November 8, 1984, and for three additional product categories (including tires) by October 1, 1985. In making the designation under paragraph (1), the Administrator shall consider, but is not limited in his considerations, to —

(A) the availability of such items;

471

(B) the impact of the procurement of such items by procuring agencies on the volume of solid waste which must be treated, stored or disposed of;

(C) the economic and technological feasibility of producing and using such items; and

(D) other uses for such recovered materials.

(f) Procurement of services — A procuring agency shall, to the maximum extent practicable, manage or arrange for the procurement of solid waste management services in a manner which maximizes energy and resource recovery.

(g) Executive Office — The Office of Procurement Policy in the Executive Office of the President, in cooperation with the Administrator, shall implement the requirements of this section. It shall be the responsibility of the Office of Procurement Policy to coordinate this policy with other policies for Federal procurement, in such a way as to maximize the use of recovered resources, and to, every two years beginning in 1984, report to the Congress on actions taken by Federal agencies and the progress made in the implementation of this section, including agency compliance with subsection (d) of this section.

(h) "Recovered materials" defined — As used in this section, in the case of paper products, the term "recovered materials" includes —

(1) postconsumer materials such as —

(A) paper, paperboard, and fibrous wastes from retail stores, office buildings, homes, and so forth, after they have passed through their end-usage as a consumer item, including: used corrugated boxes; old newspapers; old magazines; mixed waste paper; tabulating cards; and used cordage; and

(B) all paper, paperboard, and fibrous wastes that enter and are collected from municipal solid waste, and

(2) manufacturing, forest residues, and other wastes such as —

(A) dry paper and paperboard waste generated after completion of the papermaking process (that is, those manufacturing operations up to and including the cutting and trimming of the paper machine reel into smaller rolls or rough sheets) including: envelope cuttings, bindery trimmings, and other paper and paperboard waste, resulting from printing, cutting, forming, and other converting operations; bag, box, and carton manufacturing wastes; and butt rolls, mill wrappers, and rejected unused stock; and

(B) finished paper and paperboard from obsolete inventories of paper and paperboard manufacturers, merchants, wholesalers, dealers, printers, converters, or others;

(C) fibrous byproducts of harvesting, manufacturing, extractive, or wood-cutting processes, flax, straw, linters, bagasse, slash, and other forest residues;

(D) wastes generated by the conversion of goods made from fibrous material (that is, waste rope from cordage manufacture, textile mill waste, and cuttings); and

(E) fibers recovered from waste water which otherwise would enter the waste stream.

(i) Procurement program

(1) Within one year after the date of publication of applicable guidelines under subsection (e) of this section, each procuring agency shall develop an affirmative procurement program which will assure that items composed of recovered materials will be purchased to the maximum extent practicable and which is consistent with applicable provisions of Federal procurement law.

(2) Each affirmative procurement program required under this subsection shall, at a minimum, contain —

(A) a recovered materials preference program;

(B) an agency promotion program to promote the preference program adopted under subparagraph (A);

(C) a program for requiring estimates of the total percentage of recovered material utilized in the performance of a contract; certification of minimum recovered material content actually utilized, where appropriate; and reasonable verification procedures for estimates and certifications; and

(D) annual review and monitoring of the effectiveness of an agency's affirmative procurement program.

In the case of paper, the recovered materials preference program required under subparagraph (A) shall provide for the maximum use of the post consumer recovered materials referred to in subsection (h)(1) of this section.

(3) In developing the preference program, the following options shall be considered for adoption:

(A) Case-by-Case Policy Development: Subject to the limitations of subsection (c) (1)(A) through (C) of this section, a policy of awarding contracts to the vendor offering an item composed of the highest percentage of recovered materials practicable (and in the case of paper, the highest percentage of the post consumer recovered materials referred to in subsection (h)(1) of this section). Subject to such limitations, agencies may make an award to a vendor offering items with less than the maximum recovered materials content.

(B) Minimum Content Standards: Minimum recovered materials content specifications which are set in such a way as to assure that the recovered materials content (and in the case of paper, the content of post consumer materials referred to in subsection (h)(1) of this section) required is the maximum available without jeopardizing the intended end use of the item, or violating the limitations of subsection (c)(1)(A) through (C) of this section.

Procuring agencies shall adopt one of the options set forth in subparagraphs (A) and (B) or a substantially equivalent alternative, for inclusion in the affirmative procurement program.

§6963. Cooperation with Environmental Protection Agency
[SWDA §6003]

(a) General rule — All Federal agencies shall assist the Administrator in carrying out his functions under this chapter and shall promptly make available all requested information concerning past or present Agency waste management practices and past or present Agency owned, leased, or operated solid or hazardous waste facilities. This information shall be provided in such format as may be determined by the Administrator.

(b) Information relating to energy and materials conservation and recovery — The Administrator shall collect, maintain, and disseminate information concerning the market potential of energy and materials recovered from solid waste, including materials obtained through source separation, and information concerning the savings potential of conserving resources contributing to the waste stream. The Administrator shall identify the regions in which the increased substitution of such energy for energy derived from fossil fuels and other sources is most likely to be feasible, and provide information on the technical and economic aspects of developing integrated resource conservation or recovery systems which provide for the recovery of source-separated materials to be recycled or the conservation of resources. The Administrator shall utilize the authorities of subsection (a) of this section in carrying out this subsection.

§6964. Applicability of solid waste disposal guidelines to Executive agencies
[SWDA §6004]

(a) Compliance

(1) If —

(A) an Executive agency (as defined in section 105 of Title 5) or any unit of the legislative branch of the Federal Government has jurisdiction over any real property or facility the operation or administration of which involves such agency in solid waste management activities, or

(B) such an agency enters into a contract with any person for the operation by such person of any Federal property or facility, and the performance of such contract involves such person in solid waste management activities, then such agency shall insure compliance with the guidelines recommended under section 6907 of this title and the purposes of this chapter in the operation or administration of such property or facility, or the performance of such contract, as the case may be.

(2) Each Executive agency or any unit of the legislative branch of the Federal Government which conducts any activity —

(A) which generates solid waste, and

(B) which, if conducted by a person other than such agency, would require a permit or license from such agency in order to dispose of such solid waste, shall insure compliance with such guidelines and the purposes of this chapter in conducting such activity.

(3) Each Executive agency which permits the use of Federal property for purposes of disposal of solid waste shall insure compliance with such guidelines and the purposes of this chapter in the disposal of such waste.

(4) The President or the Committee on House Oversight of the House of Representatives and the Committee on Rules and Administration of the Senate with regard to any unit of the legislative branch of the Federal Government shall prescribe regulations to carry out this subsection.

(b) Licenses and permits — Each Executive agency which issues any license or permit for disposal of solid waste shall, prior to the issuance of such license or permit, consult with the Administrator to insure compliance with guidelines recommended under section 6907 of this title and the purposes of this chapter.

§6965. Chief Financial Officer report
[FFCA §110]

The Chief Financial Officer of each affected agency shall submit to Congress an annual report containing, to the extent practicable, a detailed description of the compliance activities undertaken by the agency for mixed waste streams, and an accounting of the fines and penalties imposed on the agency for violations involving mixed waste.

§6966. Increased use of recovered mineral component in Federally funded projects involving procurement of cement or concrete.

(a) Definitions — In this section:

(1) Agency head — The term "agency head" means —

(A) the Secretary of Transportation; and

(B) the head of any other Federal agency that, on a regular basis, procures, or provides Federal funds to pay or assist in paying the cost of procuring, material for cement or concrete projects.

(2) Cement or concrete project — The term "cement or concrete project" means a project for the construction or maintenance of a highway or other transportation facility or a Federal, State, or local government building or other public facility that—

    (A) involves the procurement of cement or concrete; and

    (B) is carried out, in whole or in part, using Federal funds.

(3) Recovered mineral component — The term "recovered mineral component" means—

    (A) ground granulated blast furnace slag, excluding lead slag;

    (B) coal combustion fly ash; and

    (C) any other waste material or byproduct recovered or diverted from solid waste that the Administrator, in consultation with an agency head, determines should be treated as recovered mineral component under this section for use in cement or concrete projects paid for, in whole or in part, by the agency head.

(b) Implementation of requirements

(1) In general — Not later than 1 year after August 8, 2005, the Administrator and each agency head shall take such actions as are necessary to implement fully all procurement requirements and incentives in effect as of the date of enactment of this section (including guidelines under section 6962 of this title) that provide for the use of cement and concrete incorporating recovered mineral component in cement or concrete projects.

(2) Priority — In carrying out paragraph (1), an agency head shall give priority to achieving greater use of recovered mineral component in cement or concrete projects for which recovered mineral components historically have not been used or have been used only minimally.

(3) Federal procurement requirements — The Administrator and each agency head shall carry out this subsection in accordance with section 6962 of this title.

(c) Full implementation study

(1) In general — The Administrator, in cooperation with the Secretary of Transportation and the Secretary of Energy, shall conduct a study to determine the extent to which procurement requirements, when fully implemented in accordance with subsection (b) of this section, may realize energy savings and environmental benefits attainable with substitution of recovered mineral component in cement used in cement or concrete projects.

(2) Matters to be addressed — The study shall—

    (A) quantify—

        (i) the extent to which recovered mineral components are being substituted for Portland cement, particularly as a result of procurement requirements; and

        (ii) the energy savings and environmental benefits associated with the substitution;

    (B) identify all barriers in procurement requirements to greater realization of energy savings and environmental benefits, including barriers resulting from exceptions from the law; and

    (C)(i) identify potential mechanisms to achieve greater substitution of recovered mineral component in types of cement or concrete projects for which recovered mineral components historically have not been used or have been used only minimally;

        (ii) evaluate the feasibility of establishing guidelines or standards for optimized substitution rates of recovered mineral component in those cement or concrete projects; and

        (iii) identify any potential environmental or economic effects that may result from greater substitution of recovered mineral component in those cement or concrete projects.

(3) Report — Not later than 30 months after August 8, 2005, the Administrator shall submit to Congress a report on the study.

(d) Additional procurement requirements — Unless the study conducted under subsection (c) of this section identifies any effects or other problems described in subsection (c)(2)(C)(iii) of this section that warrant further review or delay, the Administrator and each agency head shall, not later than 1 year after the date on which the report under subsection (c)(3) of this section is submitted, take additional actions under this Act to establish procurement requirements and incentives that provide for the use of cement and concrete with increased substitution of recovered mineral component in the construction and maintenance of cement or concrete projects —

    (1) to realize more fully the energy savings and environmental benefits associated with increased substitution; and

    (2) to eliminate barriers identified under subsection (c)(2)(B) of this section.

(e) Effect of section — Nothing in this section affects the requirements of section 6962 of this title (including the guidelines and specifications for implementing those requirements).

§6966a. Increased use of recovered mineral component in Federally funded projects involving procurement of cement or concrete

(a) Definitions

In this section:

(1) Agency head

The term "agency head" means —

(A) the Secretary of Transportation; and

(B) the head of each other Federal agency that on a regular basis procures, or provides Federal funds to pay or assist in paying the cost or procuring, material for cement or concrete projects.

(2) Cement or concrete project

The term "cement or concrete project" means a project for the construction or maintenance of a highway or other transportation facility or a Federal, State, or local government building or other public facility that —

(A) involves the procurement of cement or concrete; and

(B) is carried out in whole or in part using Federal funds.

(3) Recovered mineral component

The term "recovered mineral component" means —

(A) ground granulated blast furnace slag other than lead slag;

(B) coal combustion fly ash;

(C) blast furnace slag aggregate other than lead slag aggregate;

(D) silica fume; and

(E) any other waste material or byproduct recovered or diverted from solid waste that the Administrator, in consultation with an agency head, determines should be treated as recovered mineral component under this section for use in cement or concrete projects paid for, in whole or in part, by the agency head.

(b) Implementation of requirements

(1) In general

Not later than 1 year after August 10, 2005, the Administrator and each agency head shall take such actions as are necessary to implement fully all procurement requirements and incentives in effect as of August 10, 2005, (including guidelines under section 6962 of this title) that provide for the use of cement and concrete incorporating recovered mineral component in cement or concrete projects.

(2) Priority

In carrying out paragraph (1) an agency head shall give priority to achieving greater use of recovered mineral component in cement or concrete projects for which recovered mineral components historically have not been used or have been used only minimally.

(3) Conformance

The Administrator and each agency head shall carry out this subsection in accordance with section 6962 of this title.

(c) Full implementation study

(1) In general

The Administrator, in cooperation with the Secretary of Transportation and the Secretary of Energy, shall conduct a study to determine the extent to which current procurement requirements, when fully implemented in accordance with subsection (b) of this section, may realize energy savings and environmental benefits attainable with substitution of recovered mineral component in cement used in cement or concrete projects.

(2) Matters to be addressed

The study shall —

(A) quantify the extent to which recovered mineral components are being substituted for Portland cement, particularly as a result of current procurement requirements, and the energy savings and environmental benefits associated with that substitution;

(B) identify all barriers in procurement requirements to greater realization of energy savings and environmental benefits, including barriers resulting from exceptions from current law; and

(C)(i) identify potential mechanisms to achieve greater substitution of recovered mineral component in types of cement or concrete projects for which recovered mineral components historically have not been used or have been used only minimally;

(ii) evaluate the feasibility of establishing guidelines or standards for optimized substitution rates of recovered mineral component in those cement or concrete projects; and

(iii) identify any potential environmental or economic effects that may result from greater substitution of recovered mineral component in those cement or concrete projects.

(3) Report

Not later than 30 months after August 10, 2005, the Administrator shall submit to Congress a report on the study.

(d) Additional procurement requirements

Unless the study conducted under subsection (c) of this section identifies any effects or other problems described in subsection (c)(2)(C)(iii) of this section that warrant further review or delay, the Administrator and each agency head shall, not later than 1 year after the release of the report in accordance with subsection (c)(3) of this section, take additional actions authorized under this chapter to establish procurement requirements and incentives that provide for the use of cement and concrete with increased substitution of recovered mineral component in the construction and maintenance of cement or concrete projects, so as to —

    (1) realize more fully the energy savings and environmental benefits associated with increased substitution; and

    (2) eliminate barriers identified under subsection (c) of this section.

(e) Effect of section

Nothing in this section affects the requirements of section 6962 of this title (including the guidelines and specifications for implementing those requirements).

§6966b. Use of granular mine tailings
    (a) Mine tailings

    (1) In general — Not later than 180 days after August 10, 2005, the Administrator, in consultation with the Secretary of Transportation and heads of other Federal agencies, shall establish criteria (including an evaluation of whether to establish a numerical standard for concentration of lead and other hazardous substances) for the safe and environmentally protective use of granular mine tailings from the Tar Creek, Oklahoma Mining District, known as "chat," for—

    (A) cement or concrete projects; and

    (B) transportation construction projects (including transportation construction projects involving the use of asphalt) that are carried out, in whole or in part, using Federal funds.

    (2) Requirements — In establishing criteria under paragraph (1), the Administrator shall consider—

    (A) the current and previous uses of granular mine tailings as an aggregate for asphalt; and

    (B) any environmental and public health risks and benefits derived from the removal, transportation, and use in transportation projects of granular mine tailings.

    (3) Public participation — In establishing the criteria under paragraph (1), the Administrator shall solicit and consider comments from the public.

    (4) Applicability of criteria — On the establishment of the criteria under paragraph (1), any use of the granular mine tailings described in paragraph (1) in a transportation project that is carried out, in whole or in part, using Federal funds, shall meet the criteria established under paragraph (1).

    (b) Effect of sections — Nothing in this section or section 6966a of this title affects any requirement of any law (including a regulation) in effect on August 10, 2005.

SUBCHAPTER VII — MISCELLANEOUS PROVISIONS

§6971. Employee protection
[SWDA §7001]

    (a) General — No person shall fire, or in any other way discriminate against, or cause to be fired or discriminated against, any employee or any authorized representative of employees by reason of the fact that such employee or representative has filed, instituted, or caused to be filed or instituted any proceeding under this chapter or under any applicable implementation plan, or has testified or is about to testify in any proceeding resulting from the administration or enforcement of the provisions of this chapter or of any applicable implementation plan.

    (b) Remedy — Any employee or a representative of employees who believes that he has been fired or otherwise discriminated against by any person in violation of subsection (a) of this section may, within thirty days after such alleged violation occurs, apply to the Secretary of Labor for a review of such firing or alleged discrimination. A copy of the application shall be sent to such person who shall be the respondent. Upon receipt of such application, the Secretary of Labor shall cause such investigation to be made as he deems appropriate. Such investigation shall provide an opportunity for a public hearing at the request of any party to such review to enable the parties to present information relating to such alleged violation. The parties shall be given written notice of the time and place of the hearing at least five days prior to the hearing. Any such hearing shall be of record and shall be subject to section 554 of Title 5. Upon receiving the report of such investigation, the Secretary of Labor shall make findings of fact. If he finds that such violation did occur, he shall issue a decision, incorporating an order therein and his findings, requiring the party committing such violation to take such affirmative action to abate the violation as the Secretary of Labor deems appropriate, including, but not limited to, the rehiring or reinstatement of the employee or representative of employees to his former position with compensation. If he finds that there was no such violation, he shall issue an order denying the application. Such order issued by the Secretary of Labor under this subparagraph shall be subject to judicial review in the same manner as orders and decisions of the Administrator or subject to judicial review under this chapter.

    (c) Costs — Whenever an order is issued under this section to abate such violation, at the request of the applicant, a sum equal to the aggregate amount of all costs and expenses (including the attorney's fees) as determined by the Secretary of Labor, to have been reasonably incurred by the applicant for, or in connection with, the institution and prosecution of such proceedings, shall be assessed against the person committing such violation.

(d) Exception — This section shall have no application to any employee who, acting without direction from his employer (or his agent) deliberately violates any requirement of this chapter.

(e) Employment shifts and loss — The Administrator shall conduct continuing evaluations of potential loss or shifts of employment which may result from the administration or enforcement of the provisions of this chapter and applicable implementation plans, including, where appropriate, investigating threatened plant closures or reductions in employment allegedly resulting from such administration or enforcement. Any employee who is discharged, or laid off, threatened with discharge or layoff, or otherwise discriminated against by any person because of the alleged results of such administration or enforcement, or any representative of such employee, may request the Administrator to conduct a full investigation of the matter. The Administrator shall thereupon investigate the matter and, at the request of any party, shall hold public hearings on not less than five days' notice, and shall at such hearings require the parties, including the employer involved, to present information relating to the actual or potential effect of such administration or enforcement on employment and on any alleged discharge, layoff, or other discrimination and the detailed reasons or justification therefor. Any such hearing shall be of record and shall be subject to section 554 of Title 5. Upon receiving the report of such investigation, the Administrator shall make findings of fact as to the effect of such administration or enforcement on employment and on the alleged discharge, layoff, or discrimination and shall make such recommendations as he deems appropriate. Such report, findings, and recommendations shall be available to the public. Nothing in this subsection shall be construed to require or authorize the Administrator or any State to modify or withdraw any standard, limitation, or any other requirement of this chapter or any applicable implementation plan.

(f) Occupational safety and health — In order to assist the Secretary of Labor and the Director of the National Institute for Occupational Safety and Health in carrying out their duties under the Occupational Safety and Health Act of 1970 (29 U.S.C. 651 *et seq.*), the Administrator shall —

    (1) provide the following information, as such information becomes available, to the Secretary and the Director:

        (A) the identity of any hazardous waste generation, treatment, storage, disposal facility or site where cleanup is planned or underway;

        (B) information identifying the hazards to which persons working at a hazardous waste generation, treatment, storage, disposal facility or site or otherwise handling hazardous waste may be exposed, the nature and extent of the exposure, and methods to protect workers from such hazards; and

        (C) incidents of worker injury or harm at a hazardous waste generation, treatment, storage or disposal facility or site; and

    (2) notify the Secretary and the Director of the Administrator's receipt of notifications under section 6930 or reports under sections 6922, 6923, and 6924 of this title and make such notifications and reports available to the Secretary and the Director.

§6972. Citizen suits
[SWDA §7002]

(a) In general — Except as provided in subsection (b) or (c) of this section, any person may commence a civil action on his own behalf —

    (1)(A) against any person (including (a) the United States, and (b) any other governmental instrumentality or agency, to the extent permitted by the eleventh amendment to the Constitution) who is alleged to be in violation of any permit, standard, regulation, condition, requirement, prohibition, or order which has become effective pursuant to this chapter; or

        (B) against any person, including the United States and any other governmental instrumentality or agency, to the extent permitted by the eleventh amendment to the Constitution, and including any past or present generator, past or present transporter, or past or present owner or operator of a treatment, storage, or disposal facility, who has contributed or who is contributing to the past or present handling, storage, treatment, transportation, or disposal of any solid or hazardous waste which may present an imminent and substantial endangerment to health or the environment; or

    (2) against the Administrator where there is alleged a failure of the Administrator to perform any act or duty under this chapter which is not discretionary with the Administrator.

Any action under paragraph (a)(1) of this subsection shall be brought in the district court for the district in which the alleged violation occurred or the alleged endangerment may occur. Any action brought under paragraph (a)(2) of this subsection may be brought in the district court for the district in which the alleged violation occurred or in the District Court of the District of Columbia. The district court shall have jurisdiction, without regard to the amount in controversy or the citizenship of the parties, to enforce the permit, standard, regulation, condition, requirement, prohibition, or order, referred to in paragraph (1)(A), to restrain any person who has contributed or who is contributing to the past or present handling, storage, treatment, transportation, or disposal of any solid or hazardous waste referred to in paragraph (1)(B), to order such person to take such other action as may be necessary, or both, or to order the Administrator to perform the act or duty referred to in paragraph (2), as the case may be, and to apply any appropriate civil penalties under section 6928(a) and (g) of this title.

(b) Actions prohibited

(1) No action may be commenced under subsection (a)(1)(A) of this section —

(A) prior to 60 days after the plaintiff has given notice of the violation to —

(i) the Administrator;

(ii) the State in which the alleged violation occurs; and

(iii) to any alleged violator of such permit, standard, regulation, condition, requirement, prohibition, or order,

except that such action may be brought immediately after such notification in the case of an action under this section respecting a violation of subchapter III of this chapter; or

(B) if the Administrator or State has commenced and is diligently prosecuting a civil or criminal action in a court of the United States or a State to require compliance with such permit, standard, regulation, condition, requirement, prohibition, or order.

In any action under subsection (a)(1)(A) of this section in a court of the United States, any person may intervene as a matter of right.

(2)(A) No action may be commenced under subsection (a)(1)(B) of this section prior to ninety days after the plaintiff has given notice of the endangerment to —

(i) the Administrator;

(ii) the State in which the alleged endangerment may occur;

(iii) any person alleged to have contributed or to be contributing to the past or present handling, storage, treatment, transportation, or disposal of any solid or hazardous waste referred to in subsection (a)(1)(B) of this section,

except that such action may be brought immediately after such notification in the case of an action under this section respecting a violation of subchapter III of this chapter.

(B) No action may be commenced under subsection (a)(1)(B) of this section if the Administrator, in order to restrain or abate acts or conditions which may have contributed or are contributing to the activities which may present the alleged endangerment —

(i) has commenced and is diligently prosecuting an action under section 6973

of this title or under section 106 of the Comprehensive Environmental Response, Compensation and Liability Act of 1980 [42 U.S.C. §9606];

(ii) is actually engaging in a removal action under section 104 of the Comprehensive Environmental Response, Compensation and Liability Act of 1980 [42 U.S.C. §9604];

(iii) has incurred costs to initiate a Remedial Investigation and Feasibility Study under section 104 of the Comprehensive Environmental Response, Compensation and Liability Act of 1980 [42 U.S.C. §9604] and is diligently proceeding with a remedial action under that Act [42 U.S.C. §§9601 *et seq.*]; or

(iv) has obtained a court order (including a consent decree) or issued an administrative order under section 106 of the Comprehensive Environmental Response, Compensation and Liability Act of [1]980 (42 U.S.C. §9606) or section 6973 of this title pursuant to which a responsible party is diligently conducting a removal action, Remedial Investigation and Feasibility Study (RIFS), or proceeding with a remedial action.

In the case of an administrative order referred to in clause (iv), actions under subsection (a)(1)(B) of this section are prohibited only as to the scope and duration of the administrative order referred to in clause (iv).

(C) No action may be commenced under subsection (a)(1)(B) of this section if the State, in order to restrain or abate acts or conditions which may have contributed or are contributing to the activities which may present the alleged endangerment —

(i) has commenced and is diligently prosecuting an action under subsection (a)(1)(B) of this section;

(ii) is actually engaging in a removal action under section 104 of the Comprehensive Environmental Response, Compensation and Liability Act of 1980 [42 U.S.C. §9604]; or

(iii) has incurred costs to initiate a Remedial Investigation and Feasibility Study under section 104 of the Comprehensive Environmental Response, Compensation and Liability Act of 1980 [42 U.S.C. §9604] and is diligently proceeding with a remedial action under that Act [42 U.S.C. §§9601 *et seq.*].

(D) No action may be commenced under subsection (a)(1)(B) of this section by any person (other than a State or local government) with respect to the siting of a hazardous waste treatment, storage, or a disposal facility, nor to restrain or enjoin the issuance of a permit for such facility.

(E) In any action under subsection (a)(1)(B) of this section in a court of the United States, any person may intervene as a matter of right when the applicant claims an interest relating to the subject of the action and he is so situated that the disposition of the action may, as a practical matter, impair or impede his ability to protect that interest, unless the Administrator or the State shows that the applicant's interest is adequately represented by existing parties.

(F) Whenever any action is brought under subsection (a)(1)(B) of this section in a court of the United States, the plaintiff shall serve a copy of the complaint on the Attorney General of the United States and with the Administrator.

(c) Notice — No action may be commenced under paragraph (a)(2) of this section prior to sixty days after the plaintiff has given notice to the Administrator that he will commence such action, except that such action may be brought immediately after such notification in the case of an action under this section respecting a violation of subchapter III of this chapter. Notice under this subsection shall be given in such manner as the Administrator shall prescribe by regulation. Any action respecting a violation under this chapter may be brought under this section only in the judicial district in which such alleged violation occurs.

(d) Intervention — In any action under this section the Administrator, if not a party, may intervene as a matter of right.

(e) Costs — The court, in issuing any final order in any action brought pursuant to this section or section 6976 of this title, may award costs of litigation (including reasonable attorney and expert witness fees) to the prevailing or substantially prevailing party, whenever the court determines such an award is appropriate. The court may, if a temporary restraining order or preliminary injunction is sought, require the filing of a bond or equivalent security in accordance with the Federal Rules of Civil Procedure.

(f) Other rights preserved — Nothing in this section shall restrict any right which any person (or class of persons) may have under any statute or common law to seek enforcement of any standard or requirement relating to the management of solid waste or hazardous waste, or to seek any other relief (including relief against the Administrator or a State agency).

(g) Transporters — A transporter shall not be deemed to have contributed or to be contributing to the handling, storage, treatment, or disposal, referred to in subsection (a)(1)(B) of this section taking place after such solid waste or hazardous waste has left the possession or control of such transporter, if the transportation of such waste was under a sole contractual arrangement arising from a published tariff and acceptance for carriage by common carrier by rail and such transporter has exercised due care in the past or present handling, storage, treatment, transportation and disposal of such waste.

§6973. Imminent hazard
[SWDA §7003]

(a) Authority of Administrator — Notwithstanding any other provision of this chapter, upon receipt of evidence that the past or present handling, storage, treatment, transportation or disposal of any solid waste or hazardous waste may present an imminent and substantial endangerment to health or the environment, the Administrator may bring suit on behalf of the United States in the appropriate district court against any person (including any past or present generator, past or present transporter, or past or present owner or operator of a treatment, storage, or disposal facility) who has contributed or who is contributing to such handling, storage, treatment, transportation or disposal to restrain such person from such handling, storage, treatment, transportation, or disposal, to order such person to take such other action as may be necessary, or both. A transporter shall not be deemed to have contributed or to be contributing to such handling, storage, treatment, or disposal taking place after such solid waste or hazardous waste has left the possession or control of such transporter if the transportation of such waste was under a sole contractual arrangement arising from a published tariff and acceptance for carriage by common carrier by rail and such transporter has exercised due care in the past or present handling, storage, treatment, transportation and disposal of such waste. The Administrator shall provide notice to the affected State of any such suit. The Administrator may also, after notice to the affected State, take other action under this section including, but not limited to, issuing such orders as may be necessary to protect public health and the environment.

(b) Violations — Any person who willfully violates, or fails or refuses to comply with, any order of the Administrator under subsection (a) of this section may, in an action brought in the appropriate United States district court to enforce such order, be fined not more than $5,000 for each day in which such violation occurs or such failure to comply continues.

(c) Immediate notice — Upon receipt of information that there is hazardous waste at any site which has presented an imminent and substantial endangerment to human health or the environment, the Administrator shall provide immediate notice to the appropriate local government agencies. In addition, the Administrator shall require notice of such endangerment to be promptly posted at the site where the waste is located.

(d) Public participation in settlements — Whenever the United States or the Administrator proposes to covenant not to sue or to forbear from suit or to settle any claim arising under this section, notice, and opportunity for a public meeting in the affected area, and a reasonable opportunity to comment on the proposed settlement prior to its final entry shall be afforded to the public. The decision of the United States or the Administrator to enter into or not to enter into such Consent Decree, covenant or agreement shall not constitute a final agency action subject to judicial review under this chapter or chapter 7 of Title 5.

§6974. Petition for regulations; public participation
[SWDA §7004]

(a) Petition — Any person may petition the Administrator for the promulgation, amendment, or repeal of any regulation under this chapter. Within a reasonable time following receipt of such petition, the Administrator shall take action with respect to such petition and shall publish notice of such action in the Federal Register, together with the reasons therefor.

(b) Public participation

(1) Public participation in the development, revision, implementation, and enforcement of any regulation, guideline, information, or program under this chapter shall be provided for, encouraged, and assisted by the Administrator and the States. The Administrator, in cooperation with the States, shall develop and publish minimum guidelines for public participation in such processes.

(2) Before the issuing of a permit to any person with any respect to any facility for the treatment, storage, or disposal of hazardous wastes under section 6925 of this title, the Administrator shall —

    (A) cause to be published in major local newspapers of general circulation and broadcast over local radio stations notice of the agency's intention to issue such permit, and

    (B) transmit in writing notice of the agency's intention to issue such permit to each unit of local government having jurisdiction over the area in which such facility is proposed to be located and to each State agency having any authority under State law with respect to the construction or operation of such facility.

If within 45 days the Administrator receives written notice of opposition to the agency's intention to issue such permit and a request for a hearing, or if the Administrator determines on his own initiative, he shall hold an informal public hearing (including an opportunity for presentation of written and oral views) on whether he should issue a permit for the proposed facility. Whenever possible the Administrator shall schedule such hearing at a location convenient to the nearest population center to such proposed facility and give notice in the aforementioned manner of the date, time, and subject matter of such hearing. No State program which provides for the issuance of permits referred to in this paragraph may be authorized by the Administrator under section 6926 of this title unless such program provides for the notice and hearing required by the paragraph.

§6975. Separability
[SWDA §7005]

If any provision of this chapter, or the application of any provision of this chapter to any person or circumstance, is held invalid, the application of such provision to other persons or circumstances, and the remainder of this chapter, shall not be affected thereby.

§6976. Judicial review
[SWDA §7006]

(a) Review of final regulations and certain petitions — Any judicial review of final regulations promulgated pursuant to this chapter and the Administrator's denial of any petition for the promulgation, amendment, or repeal of any regulation under this chapter shall be in accordance with sections 701 through 706 of Title 5, except that —

(1) a petition for review of action of the Administrator in promulgating any regulation, or requirement under this chapter or denying any petition for the promulgation, amendment or repeal of any regulation under this chapter may be filed only in the United States Court of Appeals for the District of Columbia, and such petition shall be filed within ninety days from the date of such promulgation or denial, or after such date if such petition for review is based solely on grounds arising after such ninetieth day; action of the Administrator with respect to which review could have been obtained under this subsection shall not be subject to judicial review in civil or criminal proceedings for enforcement; and

(2) in any judicial proceeding brought under this section in which review is sought of a determination under this chapter required to be made on the record after notice and opportunity for hearing, if a party seeking review under this chapter applies to the court for leave to adduce additional evidence, and shows to the satisfaction of the court that the information is material and that there were reasonable grounds for the failure to adduce such evidence in the proceeding before the Administrator, the court may order such additional evidence (and evidence in rebuttal thereof) to be taken before the Administrator, and to be adduced upon the hearing in such manner and

upon such terms and conditions as the court may deem proper; the Administrator may modify his findings as to the facts, or make new findings, by reason of the additional evidence so taken, and he shall file with the court such modified or new findings and his recommendation, if any, for the modification or setting aside of his original order, with the return of such additional evidence.

(b) Review of certain actions under sections 6925 and 6926 of this title — Review of the Administrator's action (1) in issuing, denying, modifying, or revoking any permit under section 6925 of this title (or in modifying or revoking any permit which is deemed to have been issued under section 6935(d)(1) of this title), or (2) in granting, denying, or withdrawing authorization or interim authorization under section 6926 of this title, may be had by any interested person in the Circuit Court of Appeals of the United States for the Federal judicial district in which such person resides or transacts such business upon application by such person. Any such application shall be made within ninety days from the date of such issuance, denial, modification, revocation, grant, or withdrawal, or after such date only if such application is based solely on grounds which arose after such ninetieth day. Action of the Administrator with respect to which review could have been obtained under this subsection shall not be subject to judicial review in civil or criminal proceedings for enforcement. Such review shall be in accordance with sections 701 through 706 of Title 5.

§6977. Grants or contracts for training projects
[SWDA §7007]

(a) General authority — The Administrator is authorized to make grants to, and contracts with any eligible organization. For purposes of this section the term "eligible organization" means a State or interstate agency, a municipality, educational institution, and any other organization which is capable of effectively carrying out a project which may be funded by grant under subsection (b) of this section.

(b) Purposes

(1) Subject to the provisions of paragraph (2), grants or contracts may be made to pay all or a part of the costs, as may be determined by the Administrator, of any project operated or to be operated by an eligible organization, which is designed —

(A) to develop, expand, or carry out a program (which may combine training, education, and employment) for training persons for occupations involving the management, supervision, design, operation, or maintenance of solid waste management and resource recovery equipment and facilities; or

(B) to train instructors and supervisory personnel to train or supervise persons in occupations involving the design, operation, and maintenance of solid waste management and resource recovery equipment and facilities.

(2) A grant or contract authorized by paragraph (1) of this subsection may be made only upon application to the Administrator at such time or times and containing such information as he may prescribe, except that no such application shall be approved unless it provides for the same procedures and reports (and access to such reports and to other records) as required by section 3254a(b)(4) and (5) of this title (as in effect before October 21, 1976) with respect to applications made under such section (as in effect before October 21, 1976).

§6978. Payments
[SWDA §7008]

(a) General rule — Payments of grants under this chapter may be made (after necessary adjustment on account of previously made underpayments or overpayments) in advance or by way of reimbursement, and in such installments and on such conditions as the Administrator may determine.

(b) Prohibition — No grant may be made under this chapter to any private profitmaking organization.

§6979. Labor standards
[SWDA §7009]

No grant for a project of construction under this chapter shall be made unless the Administrator finds that the application contains or is supported by reasonable assurance that all laborers and mechanics employed by contractors or subcontractors on projects of the type covered by sections 3141-3144, 3146, 3147 of Title 40, will be paid wages at rates not less than those prevailing on similar work in the locality as determined by the Secretary of Labor in accordance with that Act; and the Secretary of Labor shall have with respect to the labor standards specified in this section the authority and functions set forth in Reorganization Plan Numbered 14 of 1950 (15 F.R. 3176) and section 3145 of Title 40.

§6979a. Transferred

§6979b. Law enforcement authority
[SWDA §7010]

The Attorney General of the United States shall, at the request of the Administrator and on the basis of a showing of need, deputize qualified employees of the Environmental Protection Agency to serve as special deputy United States marshals in criminal investigations with respect to violations of the criminal provisions of this chapter.

SUBCHAPTER VIII — RESEARCH, DEVELOPMENT, DEMONSTRATION, AND INFORMATION

§6981. Research, demonstration, training, and other activities
[SWDA §8001]

(a) **General authority** — The Administrator, alone or after consultation with the Secretary of Energy, shall conduct, and encourage, cooperate with, and render financial and other assistance to appropriate public (whether Federal, State, interstate, or local) authorities, agencies, and institutions, private agencies and institutions, and individuals in the conduct of, and promote the coordination of, research, investigations, experiments, training, demonstrations, surveys, public education programs, and studies relating to —

(1) any adverse health and welfare effects of the release into the environment of material present in solid waste, and methods to eliminate such effects;

(2) the operation and financing of solid waste management programs;

(3) the planning, implementation, and operation of resource recovery and resource conservation systems and hazardous waste management systems, including the marketing of recovered resources;

(4) the production of usable forms of recovered resources, including fuel, from solid waste;

(5) the reduction of the amount of such waste and unsalvageable waste materials;

(6) the development and application of new and improved methods of collecting and disposing of solid waste and processing and recovering materials and energy from solid wastes;

(7) the identification of solid waste components and potential materials and energy recoverable from such waste components;

(8) small scale and low technology solid waste management systems, including but not limited to, resource recovery source separation systems;

(9) methods to improve the performance characteristics of resources recovered from solid waste and the relationship of such performance characteristics to available and potentially available markets for such resources;

(10) improvements in land disposal practices for solid waste (including sludge) which may reduce the adverse environmental effects of such disposal and other aspects of solid waste disposal on land, including means for reducing the harmful environmental effects of earlier and existing landfills, means for restoring areas damaged by such earlier or existing landfills, means for rendering landfills safe for purposes of construction and other uses, and techniques of recovering materials and energy from landfills;

(11) methods for the sound disposal of, or recovery of resources, including energy, from, sludge (including sludge from pollution control and treatment facilities, coal slurry pipelines, and other sources);

(12) methods of hazardous waste management, including methods of rendering such waste environmentally safe; and

(13) any adverse effects on air quality (particularly with regard to the emission of heavy metals) which result from solid waste which is burned (either alone or in conjunction with other substances) for purposes of treatment, disposal or energy recovery.

(b) **Management program**

(1)(A) In carrying out his functions pursuant to this chapter, and any other Federal legislation respecting solid waste or discarded material research, development, and demonstrations, the Administrator shall establish a management program or system to insure the coordination of all such activities and to facilitate and accelerate the process of development of sound new technology (or other discoveries) from the research phase, through development, and into the demonstration phase.

(B) The Administrator shall (i) assist, on the basis of any research projects which are developed with assistance under this chapter or without Federal assistance, the construction of pilot plant facilities for the purpose of investigating or testing the technological feasibility of any promising new fuel, energy, or resource recovery or resource conservation method or technology; and (ii) demonstrate each such method and technology that appears justified by an evaluation at such pilot plant stage or at a pilot plant stage developed without Federal assistance. Each such demonstration shall incorporate new or innovative technical advances or shall apply such advances to different circumstances and conditions, for the purpose of evaluating design concepts or to test the performance, efficiency, and economic feasibility of a particular method or technology under actual operating conditions. Each such demonstration shall be so planned and designed that, if successful, it can be expanded or utilized directly as a full-scale operational fuel, energy, or resource recovery or resource conservation facility.

(2) Any energy-related research, development, or demonstration project for the conversion including bioconversion, of solid waste carried out by the Environmental Protection Agency or by the Secretary of Energy pursuant to this chapter or any other Act shall be administered in accordance with the May 7, 1976, Interagency Agreement between the Environmental Protection Agency

and the Energy Research and Development Administration on the Development of Energy from Solid Wastes and specifically, that in accordance with this agreement, (A) for those energy-related projects of mutual interest, planning will be conducted jointly by the Environmental Protection Agency and the Secretary of Energy, following which project responsibility will be assigned to one agency; (B) energy-related portions of projects for recovery of synthetic fuels or other forms of energy from solid waste shall be the responsibility of the Secretary of Energy; (C) the Environmental Protection Agency shall retain responsibility for the environmental, economic, and institutional aspects of solid waste projects and for assurance that such projects are consistent with any applicable suggested guidelines published pursuant to section 6907 of this title, and any applicable State or regional solid waste management plan; and (D) any activities undertaken under provisions of sections 6982 and 6983 of this title as related to energy; as related to energy or synthetic fuels recovery from waste; or as related to energy conservation shall be accomplished through coordination and consultation with the Secretary of Energy.

(c) Authorities

(1) In carrying out subsection (a) of this section respecting solid waste research, studies, development, and demonstration, except as otherwise specifically provided in section 6984(d) of this title, the Administrator may make grants to or enter into contracts (including contracts for construction) with, public agencies and authorities or private persons.

(2) Contracts for research, development, or demonstrations or for both (including contracts for construction) shall be made in accordance with and subject to the limitations provided with respect to research contracts of the military departments in section 2353 of Title 10, except that the determination, approval, and certification required thereby shall be made by the Administrator.

(3) Any invention made or conceived in the course of, or under, any contract under this chapter shall be subject to section 9 of the Federal Nonnuclear Energy Research and Development Act of 1974 (42 U.S.C. §5908) to the same extent and in the same manner as inventions made or conceived in the course of contracts under such Act (42 U.S.C. §§5901 *et seq.*), except that in applying such section, the Environmental Protection Agency shall be substituted for the Secretary of Energy and the words "solid waste" shall be substituted for the word "energy" where appropriate.

(4) For carrying out the purpose of this chapter the Administrator may detail personnel of the Environmental Protection Agency to agencies eligible for assistance under this section.

§6982. Special studies; plans for research, development, and demonstrations
[SWDA §8002]

(a) Glass and plastic — The Administrator shall undertake a study and publish a report on resource recovery from glass and plastic waste, including a scientific, technological, and economic investigation of potential solutions to implement such recovery.

(b) Composition of waste stream — The Administrator shall undertake a systematic study of the composition of the solid waste stream and of anticipated future changes in the composition of such stream and shall publish a report containing the results of such study and quantitatively evaluating the potential utility of such components.

(c) Priorities study — For purposes of determining priorities for research on recovery of materials and energy from solid waste and developing materials and energy recovery research, development, and demonstration strategies, the Administrator shall review, and make a study of, the various existing and promising techniques of energy recovery from solid waste (including, but not limited to, waterwall furnace incinerators, dry shredded fuel systems, pyrolysis, densified refuse-derived fuel systems, anerobic digestion, and fuel and feedstock preparation systems). In carrying out such study the Administrator shall investigate with respect to each such technique —

(1) the degree of public need for the potential results of such research, development, or demonstration,

(2) the potential for research, development, and demonstration without Federal action, including the degree of restraint on such potential posed by the risks involved, and

(3) the magnitude of effort and period of time necessary to develop the technology to the point where Federal assistance can be ended.

(d) Small-scale and low technology study — The Administrator shall undertake a comprehensive study and analysis of, and publish a report on, systems of small-scale and low technology solid waste management, including household resource recovery and resource recovery systems which have special application to multiple dwelling units and high density housing and office complexes. Such study and analysis shall include an investigation of the degree to which such systems could contribute to energy conservation.

(e) Front-end source separation — The Administrator shall undertake research and studies concerning the compatibility of front-end source separation systems with high technology resource recovery systems and shall publish a report containing the results of such research and studies.

(f) Mining waste — The Administrator, in consultation with the Secretary of the Interior, shall conduct a detailed and comprehensive study on the adverse effects of solid wastes from active and abandoned surface and underground mines on the environment, including, but not limited to, the effects of such wastes on humans, water, air, health, welfare, and natural resources, and on the adequacy of means and measures currently employed by the mining industry, Government agencies, and others to dispose of and utilize such solid wastes and to prevent or substantially mitigate such adverse effects. Such study shall include an analysis of —

(1) the sources and volume of discarded material generated per year from mining;

(2) present disposal practices;

(3) potential dangers to human health and the environment from surface runoff of leachate and air pollution by dust;

(4) alternatives to current disposal methods;

(5) the cost of those alternatives in terms of the impact on mine product costs; and

(6) potential for use of discarded material as a secondary source of the mine product.

In furtherance of this study, the Administrator shall, as he deems appropriate, review studies and other actions of other Federal agencies concerning such wastes with a view toward avoiding duplication of effort and the need to expedite such study. Not later than thirty-six months after October 21, 1980, the Administrator shall publish a report of such study and shall include appropriate findings and recommendations for Federal and non-Federal actions concerning such effects. Such report shall be submitted to the Committee on Environment and Public Works of the United States Senate and the Committee on Energy and Commerce of the United States House of Representatives.

(g) Sludge — The Administrator shall undertake a comprehensive study and publish a report on sludge. Such study shall include an analysis of —

(1) what types of solid waste (including but not limited to sewage and pollution treatment residues and other residues from industrial operations such as extraction of oil from shale, liquefaction and gasification of coal and coal slurry pipeline operations) shall be classified as sludge;

(2) the effects of air and water pollution legislation on the creation of large volumes of sludge;

(3) the amounts of sludge originating in each State and in each industry producing sludge;

(4) methods of disposal of such sludge, including the cost, efficiency, and effectiveness of such methods;

(5) alternative methods for the use of sludge, including agricultural applications of sludge and energy recovery from sludge; and

(6) methods to reclaim areas which have been used for the disposal of sludge or which have been damaged by sludge.

(h) Tires — The Administrator shall undertake a study and publish a report respecting discarded motor vehicle tires which shall include an analysis of the problems involved in the collection, recovery of resources including energy, and use of such tires.

(i) Resource recovery facilities — The Administrator shall conduct research and report on the economics of, and impediments, to the effective functioning of resource recovery facilities.

(j) Resource Conservation Committee

(1) The Administrator shall serve as Chairman of a Committee composed of himself, the Secretary of Commerce, the Secretary of Labor, the Chairman of the Council on Environmental Quality, the Secretary of Treasury, the Secretary of the Interior, the Secretary of Energy, the Chairman of the Council of Economic Advisors, and a representative of the Office of Management and Budget, which shall conduct a full and complete investigation and study of all aspects of the economic, social, and environmental consequences of resource conservation with respect to —

(A) the appropriateness of recommended incentives and disincentives to foster resource conservation;

(B) the effect of existing public policies (including subsidies and economic incentives and disincentives, percentage depletion allowances, capital gains treatment and other tax incentives and disincentives) upon resource conservation, and the likely effect of the modification or elimination of such incentives and disincentives upon resource conservation;

(C) the appropriateness and feasibility of restricting the manufacture or use of categories of consumer products as a resource conservation strategy;

(D) the appropriateness and feasibility of employing as a resource conservation strategy the imposition of solid waste management charges on consumer products, which charges would reflect the costs of solid waste management services, litter pickup, the value of recoverable components of such product, final disposal, and any social value associated with the nonrecycling or uncontrolled disposal of such product; and

(E) the need for further research, development, and demonstration in the area of resource conservation.

(2) The study required in paragraph (1)(D) may include pilot scale projects, and shall consider and evaluate alternative strategies with respect to —

(A) the product categories on which such charges would be imposed;

(B) the appropriate state in the production of such consumer product at which to levy such charge;

(C) appropriate criteria for establishing such charges for each consumer product category;

(D) methods for the adjustment of such charges to reflect actions such as recycling which would reduce the overall quantities of solid waste requiring disposal; and

(E) procedures for amending, modifying, or revising such charges to reflect changing conditions.

(3) The design for the study required in paragraph (1) of this subsection shall include timetables for the completion of the study. A preliminary report putting forth the study design shall be sent to the President and the Congress within six months following October 21, 1976, and followup reports shall be sent six months thereafter. Each recommendation resulting from the study shall include at least two alternatives to the proposed recommendation.

(4) The results of such investigation and study, including recommendations, shall be reported to the President and the Congress not later than two years after October 21, 1976.

(5) There are authorized to be appropriated not to exceed $2,000,000 to carry out this subsection.

(k) Airport landfills — The Administrator shall undertake a comprehensive study and analysis of and publish a report on systems to alleviate the hazards to aviation from birds congregating and feeding on landfills in the vicinity of airports.

(l) Completion of research and studies — The Administrator shall complete the research and studies, and submit the reports, required under subsections (b), (c), (d), (e), (f), (g), and (k) of this section not later that October 1, 1978. The Administrator shall complete the research and studies, and submit the reports, required under subsections (a), (h), and (i) of this section not later than October 1, 1979. Upon completion, each study specified in subsections (a) through (k) of this section, the Administrator shall prepare a plan for research, development, and demonstration respecting the findings of the study and shall submit any legislative recommendations resulting from such study to appropriate committees of Congress.

(m) Drilling fluids, produced waters, and other wastes associated with the exploration, development, or production of crude oil or natural gas or geothermal energy

(1) The Administrator shall conduct a detailed and comprehensive study and submit a report on the adverse effects, if any, of drilling fluids, produced waters, and other wastes associated with the exploration, development, or production of crude oil or natural gas or geothermal energy on human health and the environment, including, but not limited to, the effects of such wastes on humans, water, air, health, welfare, and natural resources and on the adequacy of means and measures currently employed by the oil and gas and geothermal drilling and production industry, Government agencies, and others to dispose of and utilize such wastes and to prevent or substantially mitigate such adverse effects. Such study shall include an analysis of —

(A) the sources and volume of discarded material generated per year from such wastes;

(B) present disposal practices;

(C) potential danger to human health and the environment from the surface runoff or leachate;

(D) documented cases which prove or have caused danger to human health and the environment from surface runoff or leachate;

(E) alternatives to current disposal methods;

(F) the cost of such alternatives; and

(G) the impact of those alternatives on the exploration for, and development and production of, crude oil and natural gas or geothermal energy.

In furtherance of this study, the Administrator shall, as he deems appropriate, review studies and other actions of other Federal agencies concerning such wastes with a view toward avoiding duplication of effort and the need to expedite such study. The Administrator shall publish a report of such study and shall include appropriate findings and recommendations for Federal and non-Federal actions concerning such effects.

(2) The Administrator shall complete the research and study and submit the report required under paragraph (1) not later than twenty-four months from October 21, 1980. Upon completion of the study, the Administrator shall prepare a summary of the findings of the study, a plan for research, development, and demonstration respecting the findings of the study, and shall submit the findings and the study, along with any recommendations resulting from such study, to the Committee on Environment and Public Works of the United States Senate and the Committee on Energy and Commerce of the United States House of Representatives.

(3) There are authorized to be appropriated not to exceed $1,000,000 to carry out the provisions of this subsection.

(n) Materials generated from the combustion of coal and other fossil fuels — The Administrator shall conduct a detailed and comprehensive study and submit a report on the adverse effects on human health and the environment, if any, of the disposal and utilization of fly ash waste, bottom ash waste, slag waste, flue gas emission control waste, and other byproduct materials generated primarily from the combustion of coal or other fossil fuels. Such study shall include an analysis of —

(1) the source and volumes of such material generated per year;

(2) present disposal and utilization practices;

(3) potential danger, if any, to human health and the environment from the disposal and reuse of such materials;

 (4) documented cases in which danger to human health or the environment from surface runoff or leachate has been proved;

 (5) alternatives to current disposal methods;

 (6) the costs of such alternatives;

 (7) the impact of those alternatives on the use of coal and other natural resources; and

 (8) the current and potential utilization of such materials.

In furtherance of this study, the Administrator shall, as he deems appropriate, review studies and other actions of other Federal and State agencies concerning such material and invite participation by other concerned parties, including industry and other Federal and State agencies, with a view toward avoiding duplication of effort. The Administrator shall publish a report on such study, which shall include appropriate findings, not later than twenty-four months after October 21, 1980. Such study and findings shall be submitted to the Committee on Environment and Public Works of the United States Senate and the Committee on Energy and Commerce of the United States House of Representatives.

(o) Cement kiln dust waste — The Administrator shall conduct a detailed and comprehensive study of the adverse effects on human health and the environment, if any, of the disposal of cement kiln dust waste. Such study shall include an analysis of —

 (1) the source and volumes of such materials generated per year;

 (2) present disposal practices;

 (3) potential danger, if any, to human health and the environment from the disposal of such materials;

 (4) documented cases in which danger to human health or the environment has been proved;

 (5) alternatives to current disposal methods;

 (6) the costs of such alternatives;

 (7) the impact of those alternatives on the use of natural resources; and

 (8) the current and potential utilization of such materials.

In furtherance of this study, the Administrator shall, as he deems appropriate, review studies and other actions of other Federal and State agencies concerning such waste or materials and invite participation by other concerned parties, including industry and other Federal and State agencies, with a view toward avoiding duplication of effort. The Administrator shall publish a report of such study, which shall include appropriate findings, not later than thirty-six months after October 21, 1980. Such report shall be submitted to the Committee on Environment and Public Works of the United States Senate

and the Committee on Energy and Commerce of the United States House of Representatives.

(p) Materials generated from extraction, beneficiation, and processing of ores and minerals, including phosphate rock and overburden from uranium mining — The Administrator shall conduct a detailed and comprehensive study on the adverse effects on human health and the environment, if any, of the disposal and utilization of solid waste from the extraction, beneficiation, and processing of ores and minerals, including phosphate rock and overburden from uranium mining. Such study shall be conducted in conjunction with the study of mining wastes required by subsection (f) of this section and shall include an analysis of —

 (1) the source and volumes of such materials generated per year;

 (2) present disposal and utilization practices;

 (3) potential danger, if any, to human health and the environment from the disposal and reuse of such materials;

 (4) documented cases in which danger to human health or the environment has been proved;

 (5) alternatives to current disposal methods;

 (6) the costs of such alternatives;

 (7) the impact of those alternatives on the use of phosphate rock and uranium ore, and other natural resources; and

 (8) the current and potential utilization of such materials.

In furtherance of this study, the Administrator shall, as he deems appropriate, review studies and other actions of other Federal and State agencies concerning such waste or materials and invite participation by other concerned parties, including industry and other Federal and State agencies, with a view toward avoiding duplication of effort. The Administrator shall publish a report of such study, which shall include appropriate findings, in conjunction with the publication of the report of the study of mining wastes required to be conducted under subsection (f) of this section. Such report and findings shall be submitted to the Committee on Environment and Public Works of the United States Senate and the Committee on Energy and Commerce of the United States House of Representatives.

(q) Authorization of appropriations — There are authorized to be appropriated not to exceed $8,000,000 for the fiscal years 1978 and 1979 to carry out this section other than subsection (j) of this section.

(r) Minimization of hazardous waste — The Administrator shall compile, and not later than October 1, 1986, submit to the Congress, a report on the feasibility and desirability of establishing standards of performance or of taking other additional actions under this chapter to require the generators of hazardous waste to reduce the volume or quantity and toxicity of the hazardous waste they generate, and of establishing with respect to hazardous wastes required management practices or other requirements to assure such wastes are managed in ways that minimize present and future risks to human health and the environment. Such report shall include any recommendations for legislative changes which the Administrator determines are feasible and desirable to implement the national policy established by section 6902 of this title.

(s) Extending landfill life and reusing landfilled areas — The Administrator shall conduct detailed, comprehensive studies of methods to extend the useful life of sanitary landfills and to better use sites in which filled or closed landfills are located. Such studies shall address —

(1) methods to reduce the volume of materials before placement in landfills;

(2) more efficient systems for depositing waste in landfills;

(3) methods to enhance the rate of decomposition of solid waste in landfills, in a safe and environmentally acceptable manner;

(4) methane production from closed landfill units;

(5) innovative uses of closed landfill sites, including use for energy production such as solar or wind energy and use for metals recovery;

(6) potential for use of sewage treatment sludge in reclaiming landfilled areas; and

(7) methods to coordinate use of a landfill owned by one municipality by nearby municipalities, and to establish equitable rates for such use, taking into account the need to provide future landfill capacity to replace that so used.

The Administrator is authorized to conduct demonstrations in the areas of study provided in this subsection. The Administrator shall periodically report on the results of such studies, with the first such report not later than October 1, 1986. In carrying out this subsection, the Administrator need not duplicate other studies which have been completed and may rely upon information which has previously been compiled.

§6983. Coordination, collection, and dissemination of information
[SWDA §8003]

(a) Information — The Administrator shall develop, collect, evaluate, and coordinate information on —

(1) methods and costs of the collection of solid waste;

(2) solid waste management practices, including data on the different management methods and the cost, operation, and maintenance of such methods;

(3) the amounts and percentages of resources (including energy) that can be recovered from solid

waste by use of various solid waste management practices and various technologies;

(4) methods available to reduce the amount of solid waste that is generated;

(5) existing and developing technologies for the recovery of energy or materials from solid waste and the costs, reliability, and risks associated with such technologies;

(6) hazardous solid waste, including incidents of damage resulting from the disposal of hazardous solid wastes; inherently and potentially hazardous solid wastes; methods of neutralizing or properly disposing of hazardous solid wastes; facilities that properly dispose of hazardous wastes;

(7) methods of financing resource recovery facilities or, sanitary landfills, or hazardous solid waste treatment facilities, whichever is appropriate for the entity developing such facility or landfill (taking into account the amount of solid waste reasonably expected to be available to such entity);

(8) the availability of markets for the purchase of resources, either materials or energy, recovered from solid waste; and

(9) research and development projects respecting solid waste management.

(b) Library

(1) The Administrator shall establish and maintain a central reference library for **(A)** the materials collected pursuant to subsection (a) of this section and **(B)** the actual performance and cost effectiveness records and other data and information with respect to —

(i) the various methods of energy and resource recovery from solid waste,

(ii) the various systems and means of resource conservation,

(iii) the various systems and technologies for collection, transport, storage, treatment, and final disposition of solid waste, and

(iv) other aspects of solid waste and hazardous solid waste management.

Such central reference library shall also contain, but not be limited to, the model codes and model accounting systems developed under this section, the information collected under subsection (d) of this section, and, subject to any applicable requirements of confidentiality, information respecting any aspect of solid waste provided by officers and employees of the Environmental Protection Agency which has been acquired by them in the conduct of their functions under this chapter and which may be of value to Federal, State, and local authorities and other persons.

(2) Information in the central reference library shall, to the extent practicable, be collated, analyzed, verified, and published and shall

be made available to State and local governments and other persons at reasonable times and subject to such reasonable charges as may be necessary to defray expenses of making such information available.

(c) Model accounting system — In order to assist State and local governments in determining the cost and revenues associated with the collection and disposal of solid waste and with resource recovery operations, the Administrator shall develop and publish a recommended model cost and revenue accounting system applicable to the solid waste management functions of State and local governments. Such system shall be in accordance with generally accepted accounting principles. The Administrator shall periodically, but not less frequently than once every five years, review such accounting system and revise it as necessary.

(d) Model codes — The Administrator is authorized, in cooperation with appropriate State and local agencies, to recommend model codes, ordinances, and statutes, providing for sound solid waste management.

(e) Information programs

(1) The Administrator shall implement a program for the rapid dissemination of information on solid waste management, hazardous waste management, resource conservation, and methods of resource recovery from solid waste, including the results of any relevant research, investigations, experiments, surveys, studies, or other information which may be useful in the implementation of new or improved solid waste management practices and methods and information on any other technical, managerial, financial, or market aspect of resource conservation and recovery facilities.

(2) The Administrator shall develop and implement educational programs to promote citizen understanding of the need for environmentally sound solid waste management practices.

(f) Coordination — In collecting and disseminating information under this section, the Administrator shall coordinate his actions and cooperate to the maximum extent possible with State and local authorities.

(g) Special restriction — Upon request, the full range of alternative technologies, programs or processes deemed feasible to meet the resource recovery or resource conservation needs of a jurisdiction shall be described in such a manner as to provide a sufficient evaluative basis from which the jurisdiction can make its decisions, but no officer or employee of the Environmental Protection Agency shall, in an official capacity, lobby for or otherwise represent an agency position in favor of resource recovery or resource conservation, as a policy alternative for adoption into ordinances, codes, regulations, or law by any State or political subdivision thereof.

§6984. Full-scale demonstration facilities [SWDA §8004]

(a) Authority — The Administrator may enter into contracts with public agencies or authorities or private persons for the construction and operation of a full-scale demonstration facility under this chapter, or provide financial assistance in the form of grants to a full-scale demonstration facility under this chapter only if the Administrator finds that —

(1) such facility or proposed facility will demonstrate at full scale a new or significantly improved technology or process, a practical and significant improvement in solid waste management practice, or the technological feasibility and cost effectiveness of an existing, but unproven technology, process, or practice, and will not duplicate any other Federal, State, local, or commercial facility which has been constructed or with respect to which construction has begun (determined as of the date action is taken by the Administrator under this chapter),

(2) such contract or assistance meets the requirements of section 6981 of this title and meets other applicable requirements of this chapter,

(3) such facility will be able to comply with the guidelines published under section 6907 of this title and with other laws and regulations for the protection of health and the environment,

(4) in the case of a contract for construction or operation, such facility is not likely to be constructed or operated by State, local, or private persons or in the case of an application for financial assistance, such facility is not likely to receive adequate financial assistance from other sources, and

(5) any Federal interest in, or assistance to, such facility will be disposed of or terminated, with appropriate compensation, within such period of time as may be necessary to carry out the basic objectives of this chapter.

(b) Time limitation — No obligation may be made by the Administrator for financial assistance under this subchapter for any full-scale demonstration facility after the date ten years after October 21, 1976. No expenditure of funds for any such full-scale demonstration facility under this subchapter may be made by the Administrator after the date fourteen years after October 21, 1976.

(c) Cost sharing

(1) Wherever practicable, in constructing, operating, or providing financial assistance under this subchapter to a full-scale demonstration facility, the Administrator shall endeavor to enter into agreements and make other arrangements for maximum practicable cost sharing with other Federal, State, and local agencies, private persons, or any combination thereof.

(2) The Administrator shall enter into arrangements, wherever practicable and desirable,

to provide monitoring of full-scale solid waste facilities (whether or not constructed or operated under this chapter) for purposes of obtaining information concerning the performance, and other aspects, of such facilities. Where the Administrator provides only monitoring and evaluation instruments or personnel (or both) or funds for such instruments or personnel and provides no other financial assistance to a facility, notwithstanding section 6981(c)(3) of this title, title to any invention made or conceived of in the course of developing, constructing, or operating such facility shall not be required to vest in the United States and patents respecting such invention shall not be required to be issued to the United States.

(d) Prohibition — After October 21, 1976, the Administrator shall not construct or operate any full-scale facility (except by contract with public agencies or authorities or private persons).

§6985. Special study and demonstration projects on recovery of useful energy and materials
[SWDA §8005]

(a) Studies — The Administrator shall conduct studies and develop recommendations for administrative or legislative action on —

(1) means of recovering materials and energy from solid waste, recommended uses of such materials and energy for national or international welfare, including identification of potential markets for such recovered resources, the impact of distribution of such resources on existing markets, and potentials for energy conservation through resource conservation and resource recovery;

(2) actions to reduce waste generation which have been taken voluntarily or in response to governmental action, and those which practically could be taken in the future, and the economic, social, and environmental consequences of such actions;

(3) methods of collection, separation, and containerization which will encourage efficient utilization of facilities and contribute to more effective programs of reduction, reuse, or disposal of wastes;

(4) the use of Federal procurement to develop market demand for recovered resources;

(5) recommended incentives (including Federal grants, loans, and other assistance) and disincentives to accelerate the reclamation or recycling of materials from solid wastes, with special emphasis on motor vehicle hulks;

(6) the effect of existing public policies, including subsidies and economic incentives and disincentives, percentage depletion allowances, capital gains treatment and other tax incentives and disincentives, upon the recycling and reuse of

materials, and the likely effect of the modification or elimination of such incentives and disincentives upon the reuse, recycling and conservation of such materials;

(7) the necessity and method of imposing disposal or other charges on packaging, containers, vehicles, and other manufactured goods, which charges would reflect the cost of final disposal, the value of recoverable components of the item, and any social costs associated with nonrecycling or uncontrolled disposal of such items; and

(8) the legal constraints and institutional barriers to the acquisition of land needed for solid waste management, including land for facilities and disposal sites;

(9) in consultation with the Secretary of Agriculture, agricultural waste management problems and practices, the extent of reuse and recovery of resources in such wastes, the prospects for improvement, Federal, State, and local regulations governing such practices, and the economic, social, and environmental consequences of such practices; and

(10) in consultation with the Secretary of the Interior, mining waste management problems, and practices, including an assessment of existing authorities, technologies, and economics, and the environmental and public health consequences of such practices.

(b) Demonstration — The Administrator is also authorized to carry out demonstration projects to test and demonstrate methods and techniques developed pursuant to subsection (a) of this section.

(c) Application of other sections — Section 6981(b) and (c) of this title shall be applicable to investigations, studies, and projects carried out under this section.

§6986. Grants for resource recovery systems and improved solid waste disposal facilities
[SWDA §8006]

(a) Authority — The Administrator is authorized to make grants pursuant to this section to any State, municipal, or interstate or intermunicipal agency for the demonstration of resource recovery systems or for the construction of new or improved solid waste disposal facilities.

(b) Conditions

(1) Any grant under this section for the demonstration of a resource recovery system may be made only if it (A) is consistent with any plans which meet the requirements of subchapter IV of this chapter; (B) is consistent with the guidelines recommended pursuant to section 6907 of this title; (C) is designed to provide area-wide resource recovery systems consistent with the purposes of this chapter, as determined by the Administrator, pursuant to regulations promulgated under subsection (d) of this section; and (D) provides an equitable system for distributing the costs associated

with construction, operation, and maintenance of any resource recovery system among the users of such system.

(2) The Federal share for any project to which paragraph (1) applies shall not be more than 75 percent.

(c) Limitations

(1) A grant under this section for the construction of a new or improved solid waste disposal facility may be made only if —

(A) a State or interstate plan for solid waste disposal has been adopted which applies to the area involved, and the facility to be constructed (i) is consistent with such plan, (ii) is included in a comprehensive plan for the area involved which is satisfactory to the Administrator for the purposes of this chapter, and (iii) is consistent with the guidelines recommended under section 6907 of this title, and

(B) the project advances the state of the art by applying new and improved techniques in reducing the environmental impact of solid waste disposal, in achieving recovery of energy or resources, or in recycling useful materials.

(2) The Federal share for any project to which paragraph (1) applies shall be not more than 50 percent in the case of a project serving an area which includes only one municipality, and not more than 75 percent in any other case.

(d) Regulations

(1) The Administrator shall promulgate regulations establishing a procedure for awarding grants under this section which —

(A) provides that projects will be carried out in communities of varying sizes, under such conditions as will assist in solving the community waste problems of urban-industrial centers, metropolitan regions, and rural areas, under representative geographic and environmental conditions; and

(B) provides deadlines for submission of, and action on, grant requests.

(2) In taking action on applications for grants under this section, consideration shall be given by the Administrator (A) to the public benefits to be derived by the construction and the propriety of Federal aid in making such grant; (B) to the extent applicable, to the economic and commercial viability of the project (including contractual arrangements with the private sector to market any resources recovered); (C) to the potential of such project for general application to community solid waste disposal problems; and (D) to the use by the applicant of comprehensive regional or metropolitan area planning.

(e) Additional limitations — A grant under this section —

(1) may be made only in the amount of the Federal share of (A) the estimated total design and construction costs, plus (B) in the case of a grant to which subsection (b)(1) of this section applies, the first-year operation and maintenance costs;

(2) may not be provided for land acquisition or (except as otherwise provided in paragraph (1)(B)) for operating or maintenance costs;

(3) may not be made until the applicant has made provision satisfactory to the Administrator for proper and efficient operation and maintenance of the project (subject to paragraph (1)(B)); and

(4) may be made subject to such conditions and requirements, in addition to those provided in this section, as the Administrator may require to properly carry out his functions pursuant to this chapter.

For purposes of paragraph (1), the non-Federal share may be in any form, including, but not limited to, lands or interests therein needed for the project or personal property or services, the value of which shall be determined by the Administrator.

(f) Single State

(1) Not more than 15 percent of the total of funds authorized to be appropriated for any fiscal year to carry out this section shall be granted under this section for projects in any one State.

(2) The Administrator shall prescribe by regulation the manner in which this subsection shall apply to a grant under this section for a project in an area which includes all or part of more than one State.

§6987. Authorization of appropriations [SWDA §8007]

There are authorized to be appropriated not to exceed $35,000,000 for the fiscal year 1978 to carry out the purposes of this subchapter (except for section 6982 of this title).

SUBCHAPTER IX — REGULATION OF UNDERGROUND STORAGE TANKS

§6991. Definitions and exemptions [SWDA §9001]

In this subchapter:

(1) Indian tribe

(A) In general — The term "Indian tribe" means any Indian tribe, band, nation, or other organized group or community that is recognized as being eligible for special programs and services provided by the United States to Indians because of their status as Indians.

(B) Inclusions — The term "Indian tribe" includes an Alaska Native village, as defined in or established under the Alaska Native Claims Settlement Act (43 U.S.C. 1601 *et seq.*); and

(2) The term "nonoperational storage tank" means any underground storage tank in which regulated

substances will not be deposited or from which regulated substances will not be dispensed after November 8, 1984.

(3) The term "operator" means any person in control of, or having responsibility for, the daily operation of the underground storage tank.

(4) The term "owner" means—

(A) in the case of an underground storage tank in use on November 8, 1984, or brought into use after that date, any person who owns an underground storage tank used for the storage, use, or dispensing of regulated substances, and

(B) in the case of any underground storage tank in use before November 8, 1984, but no longer in use on November 8, 1984, any person who owned such tank immediately before the discontinuation of its use.

(5) The term "person" has the same meaning as provided in section 6903(15) of this title, except that such term includes a consortium, a joint venture, and a commercial entity, and the United States Government.

(6) The term "petroleum" means petroleum, including crude oil or any fraction thereof which is liquid at standard conditions of temperature and pressure (60 degrees Fahrenheit and 14.7 pounds per square inch absolute).

(7) The term "regulated substance" means —

(A) any substance defined in section 9601(14) of this title (but not including any substance regulated as a hazardous waste under subchapter III of this chapter), and

(B) petroleum.

(8) The term "release" means any spilling, leaking, emitting, discharging, escaping, leaching, or disposing from an underground storage tank into ground water, surface water or subsurface soils.

(9) Trust fund — The term "Trust Fund" means the Leaking Underground Storage Tank Trust Fund established by section 9508 of Title 26.

(10) The term "underground storage tank" means any one or combination of tanks (including underground pipes connected thereto) which is used to contain an accumulation of regulated substances, and the volume of which (including the volume of the underground pipes connected thereto) is 10 per centum or more beneath the surface of the ground. Such term does not include any —

(A) farm or residential tank of 1,100 gallons or less capacity used for storing motor fuel for noncommercial purposes,

(B) tank used for storing heating oil for consumptive use on the premises where stored,

(C) septic tank,

(D) pipeline facility (including gathering lines) —

(i) which is regulated under chapter 601 of Title 49, or

(ii) which is an intrastate pipeline facility regulated under State laws as provided in chapter 601 of Title 49, and which is determined by the Secretary to be connected to a pipeline or to be operated or intended to be capable of operating at pipeline pressure or as an integral part of a pipeline,

(E) surface impoundment, pit, pond, or lagoon,

(F) storm water or waste water collection system,

(G) flow-through process tank,

(H) liquid trap or associated gathering lines directly related to oil or gas production and gathering operations, or

(I) storage tank situated in an underground area (such as a basement, cellar, mineworking, drift, shaft, or tunnel) if the storage tank is situated upon or above the surface of the floor.

The term "underground storage tank" shall not include any pipes connected to any tank which is described in subparagraphs (A) through (I).

§6991a. Notification
[SWDA §9002]
(a) Underground storage tanks

(1) Within 18 months after November 8, 1984, each owner of an underground storage tank shall notify the State or local agency or department designated pursuant to subsection (b)(1) of this section of the existence of such tank, specifying the age, size, type, location, and uses of such tank.

(2)(A) For each underground storage tank taken out of operation after January 1, 1974, the owner of such tank shall, within eighteen months after November 8, 1984, notify the State or local agency, or department designated pursuant to subsection (b)(1) of this section of the existence of such tanks (unless the owner knows the tank subsequently was removed from the ground). The owner of a tank taken out of operation on or before January 1, 1974, shall not be required to notify the State or local agency under this subsection.

(B) Notice under subparagraph (A) shall specify, to the extent known to the owner —

(i) the date the tank was taken out of operation,

(ii) the age of the tank on the date taken out of operation,

(iii) the size, type and location of the tank, and

(iv) the type and quantity of substances left stored in such tank on the date taken out of operation.

(3) Any owner which brings into use an underground storage tank after the initial notification period specified under paragraph (1), shall notify

the designated State or local agency or department within thirty days of the existence of such tank, specifying the age, size, type, location and uses of such tank.

(4) Paragraphs (1) through (3) of this subsection shall not apply to tanks for which notice was given pursuant to section 9603(c) of this title.

(5) Beginning thirty days after the Administrator prescribes the form of notice pursuant to subsection (b)(2) of this section and for eighteen months thereafter, any person who deposits regulated substances in an underground storage tank shall reasonably notify the owner or operator of such tank of the owner's notification requirements pursuant to this subsection.

(6) Beginning thirty days after the Administrator issues new tank performance standards pursuant to section 6991b(e) of this title, any person who sells a tank intended to be used as an underground storage tank shall notify the purchaser of such tank of the owner's notification requirements pursuant to this subsection.

(b) Agency designation

(1) Within one hundred and eighty days after November 8, 1984, the Governors of each State shall designate the appropriate State agency or department or local agencies or departments to receive the notifications under subsection (a)(1), (2), or (3) of this section.

(2) Within twelve months after November 8, 1984, the Administrator, in consultation with State and local officials designated pursuant to subsection (b)(1) of this section, and after notice and opportunity for public comment, shall prescribe the form of the notice and the information to be included in the notifications under subsection (a) (1), (2), or (3) of this section. In prescribing the form of such notice, the Administrator shall take into account the effect on small businesses and other owners and operators.

(c) State inventories

— Each State shall make 2 separate inventories of all underground storage tanks in such State containing regulated substances. One inventory shall be made with respect to petroleum and one with respect to other regulated substances. In making such inventories, the State shall utilize and aggregate the data in the notification forms submitted pursuant to subsections (a) and (b) of this section. Each State shall submit such aggregated data to the Administrator not later than 270 days after October 17, 1986.

(d) Public record

(1) In general — The Administrator shall require each State that receives Federal funds to carry out this subchapter to maintain, update at least annually, and make available to the public, in such manner and form as the Administrator shall prescribe (after consultation with States), a record of underground storage tanks regulated under this subchapter.

(2) Considerations — To the maximum extent practicable, the public record of a State, respectively, shall include, for each year —

(A) the number, sources, and causes of underground storage tank releases in the State;

(B) the record of compliance by underground storage tanks in the State with —

(i) this subchapter; or

(ii) an applicable State program approved under section 6991c of this title; and

(C) data on the number of underground storage tank equipment failures in the State.

§6991b. Release detection, prevention, and correction regulations
[SWDA §9003]

(a) Regulations — The Administrator, after notice and opportunity for public comment, and at least three months before the effective dates specified in subsection (f) of this section, shall promulgate release detection, prevention, and correction regulations applicable to all owners and operators of underground storage tanks, as may be necessary to protect human health and the environment.

(b) Distinctions in regulations — In promulgating regulations under this section, the Administrator may distinguish between types, classes, and ages of underground storage tanks. In making such distinctions, the Administrator may take into consideration factors, including, but not limited to: location of the tanks, soil and climate conditions, uses of the tanks, history of maintenance, age of the tanks, current industry recommended practices, national consensus codes, hydrogeology, water table, size of the tanks, quantity of regulated substances periodically deposited in or dispensed from the tank, the technical capability of the owners and operators, and the compatibility of the regulated substance and the materials of which the tank is fabricated.

(c) Requirements — The regulations promulgated pursuant to this section shall include, but need not be limited to, the following requirements respecting all underground storage tanks —

(1) requirements for maintaining a leak detection system, an inventory control system together with tank testing, or a comparable system or method designed to identify releases in a manner consistent with the protection of human health and the environment;

(2) requirements for maintaining records of any monitoring or leak detection system or inventory control system or tank testing or comparable system;

(3) requirements for reporting of releases and corrective action taken in response to a release from an underground storage tank;

(4) requirements for taking corrective action in response to a release from an underground storage tank;

(5) requirements for the closure of tanks to prevent future releases of regulated substances into the environment; and

(6) requirements for maintaining evidence of financial responsibility for taking corrective action and compensating third parties for bodily injury and property damage caused by sudden and nonsudden accidental releases arising from operating an underground storage tank.

(d) Financial responsibility

(1) Financial responsibility required by this subsection may be established in accordance with regulations promulgated by the Administrator by any one, or any combination, of the following: insurance, guarantee, surety bond, letter of credit, qualification as a self-insurer or any other method satisfactory to the Administrator. In promulgating requirements under this subsection, the Administrator is authorized to specify policy or other contractual terms, conditions, or defenses which are necessary or are unacceptable in establishing such evidence of financial responsibility in order to effectuate the purposes of this subchapter.

(2) In any case where the owner or operator is in bankruptcy, reorganization, or arrangement pursuant to the Federal Bankruptcy Code or where with reasonable diligence jurisdiction in any State court of the Federal courts cannot be obtained over an owner or operator likely to be solvent at the time of judgment, any claim arising from conduct for which evidence of financial responsibility must be provided under this subsection may be asserted directly against the guarantor providing such evidence of financial responsibility. In the case of any action pursuant to this paragraph such guarantor shall be entitled to invoke all rights and defenses which would have been available to the owner or operator if any action had been brought against the owner or operator by the claimant and which would have been available to the guarantor if an action had been brought against the guarantor by the owner or operator.

(3) The total liability of any guarantor shall be limited to the aggregate amount which the guarantor has provided as evidence of financial responsibility to the owner or operator under this section. Nothing in this subsection shall be construed to limit any other State or Federal statutory, contractual or common law liability of a guarantor to its owner or operator including, but not limited to, the liability of such guarantor for bad faith either in negotiating or in failing to negotiate the settlement of any claim. Nothing in this subsection shall be construed to diminish the liability of any person under section 9607 or 9611 of this title or other applicable law.

(4) For the purpose of this subsection, the term "guarantor" means any person, other than the owner or operator, who provides evidence of financial responsibility for an owner or operator under this subsection.

(5)(A) The Administrator, in promulgating financial responsibility regulations under this section, may establish an amount of coverage for particular classes or categories of underground storage tanks containing petroleum which shall satisfy such regulations and which shall not be less than $1,000,000 for each occurrence with an appropriate aggregate requirement.

(B) The Administrator may set amounts lower than the amounts required by subparagraph (A) of this paragraph for underground storage tanks containing petroleum which are at facilities not engaged in petroleum production, refining, or marketing and which are not used to handle substantial quantities of petroleum.

(C) In establishing classes and categories for purposes of this paragraph, the Administrator may consider the following factors:

(i) The size, type, location, storage, and handling capacity of underground storage tanks in the class or category and the volume of petroleum handled by such tanks.

(ii) The likelihood of release and the potential extent of damage from any release from underground storage tanks in the class or category.

(iii) The economic impact of the limits on the owners and operators of each such class or category, particularly relating to the small business segment of the petroleum marketing industry.

(iv) The availability of methods of financial responsibility in amounts greater than the amount established by this paragraph.

(v) Such other factors as the Administrator deems pertinent.

(D) The Administrator may suspend enforcement of the financial responsibility requirements for a particular class or category of underground storage tanks or in a particular State, if the Administrator makes a determination that methods of financial responsibility satisfying the requirements of this subsection are not generally available for underground storage tanks in that class or category, and —

(i) steps are being taken to form a risk retention group for such class of tanks; or

(ii) such State is taking steps to establish a fund pursuant to section 6991c(c)(1) of this title to be submitted as evidence of financial responsibility.

A suspension by the Administrator pursuant to this paragraph shall extend for a period not to exceed 180 days. A determination to suspend may be made with respect to the same class or category or for the same State at the end of such period, but only if substantial progress has been made in establishing a risk retention group, or the owners or operators in the class or category demonstrate, and the Administrator finds, that the formation of such a group is not possible and that the State is unable or unwilling to establish such a fund pursuant to clause (ii).

(e) New tank performance standards — The Administrator shall, not later than three months prior to the effective date specified in subsection (f) of this section, issue performance standards for underground storage tanks brought into use on or after the effective date of such standards. The performance standards for new underground storage tanks shall include, but need not be limited to, design, construction, installation, release detection, and compatibility standards.

(f) Effective dates

(1) Regulations issued pursuant to subsections (c) and (d) of this section, and standards issued pursuant to subsection (e) of this section, for underground storage tanks containing regulated substances defined in section 6991(7)(B) of this title (petroleum, including crude oil or any fraction thereof which is liquid at standard conditions of temperature and pressure) shall be effective not later than thirty months after November 8, 1984.

(2) Standards issued pursuant to subsection (e) of this section (entitled "New Tank Performance Standards") for underground storage tanks containing regulated substances defined in section 6991(7)(A) of this title shall be effective not later than thirty-six months after November 8, 1984.

(3) Regulations issued pursuant to subsection (c) of this section (entitled "Requirements") and standards issued pursuant to subsection (d) of this section (entitled "Financial Responsibility") for underground storage tanks containing regulated substances defined in section 6991(7)(A) of this title shall be effective not later than forty-eight months after November 8, 1984.

(g) Interim prohibition

(1) Until the effective date of the standards promulgated by the Administrator under subsection (e) of this section and after one hundred and eighty days after November 8, 1984, no person may install an underground storage tank for the purpose of storing regulated substances unless such tank (whether of single or double wall construction) —

(A) will prevent releases due to corrosion or structural failure for the operational life of the tank;

(B) is cathodically protected against corrosion, constructed of noncorrosive material, steel clad with a noncorrosive material, or designed in a manner to prevent the release or threatened release of any stored substance; and

(C) the material used in the construction or lining of the tank is compatible with the substance to be stored.

(2) Notwithstanding paragraph (1), if soil tests conducted in accordance with ASTM Standard G57-78, or another standard approved by the Administrator, show that soil resistivity in an installation location is 12,000 ohm/cm or more (unless a more stringent standard is prescribed by the Administrator by rule), a storage tank without corrosion protection may be installed in that location during the period referred to in paragraph (1).

(h) EPA response program for petroleum

(1) Before regulations — Before the effective date of regulations under subsection (c) of this section, the Administrator (or a State pursuant to paragraph (7)) is authorized to —

(A) require the owner or operator of an underground storage tank to undertake corrective action with respect to any release of petroleum when the Administrator (or the State) determines that such corrective action will be done properly and promptly by the owner or operator of the underground storage tank from which the release occurs; or

(B) undertake corrective action with respect to any release of petroleum into the environment from an underground storage tank if such action is necessary, in the judgment of the Administrator (or the State), to protect human health and the environment. The corrective action undertaken or required under this paragraph shall be such as may be necessary to protect human health and the environment. The Administrator shall use funds in the Leaking Underground Storage Tank Trust Fund for payment of costs incurred for corrective action under subparagraph (B), enforcement action under subparagraph (A), and cost recovery under paragraph (6) of this subsection. Subject to the priority requirements of paragraph (3), the Administrator (or the State) shall give priority in undertaking such actions under subparagraph (B) to cases where the Administrator (or the State) cannot identify a solvent owner or operator of the tank who will undertake action properly.

(2) After regulations — Following the effective date of regulations under subsection (c) of this section, all actions or orders of the Administrator (or a State pursuant to paragraph (7)) described in paragraph (1) of this subsection shall be in conformity with such regulations. Following such effective date, the Administrator (or the State) may undertake corrective action with respect to any release of petroleum into the environment from

an underground storage tank only if such action is necessary, in the judgment of the Administrator (or the State), to protect human health and the environment and one or more of the following situations exists:

(A) No person can be found, within 90 days or such shorter period as may be necessary to protect human health and the environment, who is —

(i) an owner or operator of the tank concerned,

(ii) subject to such corrective action regulations, and

(iii) capable of carrying out such corrective action properly.

(B) A situation exists which requires prompt action by the Administrator (or the State) under this paragraph to protect human health and the environment.

(C) Corrective action costs at a facility exceed the amount of coverage required by the Administrator pursuant to the provisions of subsections (c) and (d)(5) of this section and, considering the class or category of underground storage tank from which the release occurred, expenditures from the Leaking Underground Storage Tank Trust Fund are necessary to assure an effective corrective action.

(D) The owner or operator of the tank has failed or refused to comply with an order of the Administrator under this subsection or section 6991e of this title or with the order of a State under this subsection to comply with the corrective action regulations.

(3) Priority of corrective actions — The Administrator (or a State pursuant to paragraph (7)) shall give priority in undertaking corrective actions under this subsection, and in issuing orders requiring owners or operators to undertake such actions, to releases of petroleum from underground storage tanks which pose the greatest threat to human health and the environment.

(4) Corrective action orders — The Administrator is authorized to issue orders to the owner or operator of an underground storage tank to carry out subparagraph (A) of paragraph (1) or to carry out regulations issued under subsection (c)(4) of this section. A State acting pursuant to paragraph (7) of this subsection is authorized to carry out subparagraph (A) of paragraph (1) only until the State's program is approved by the Administrator under section 6991c of this title. Such orders shall be issued and enforced in the same manner and subject to the same requirements as orders under section 6991e of this title.

(5) Allowable corrective actions — The corrective actions undertaken by the Administrator (or a State pursuant to paragraph (7)) under paragraph (1) or

(2) may include temporary or permanent relocation of residents and alternative household water supplies. In connection with the performance of any corrective action under paragraph (1) or (2), the Administrator may undertake an exposure assessment as defined in paragraph (10) of this subsection or provide for such an assessment in a cooperative agreement with a State pursuant to paragraph (7) of this subsection. The costs of any such assessment may be treated as corrective action for purposes of paragraph (6), relating to cost recovery.

(6) Recovery of costs

(A) In general — Whenever costs have been incurred by the Administrator, or by a State pursuant to paragraph (7), for undertaking corrective action or enforcement action with respect to the release of petroleum from an underground storage tank, the owner or operator of such tank shall be liable to the Administrator or the State for such costs. The liability under this paragraph shall be construed to be the standard of liability which obtains under section 1321 of Title 33.

(B) Recovery — In determining the equities for seeking the recovery of costs under subparagraph (A), the Administrator (or a State pursuant to paragraph (7) of this subsection) may consider the amount of financial responsibility required to be maintained under subsections (c) and (d)(5) of this section and the factors considered in establishing such amount under subsection (d)(5) of this section.

(C) Effect on liability

(i) No transfers of liability — No indemnification, hold harmless, or similar agreement or conveyance shall be effective to transfer from the owner or operator of any underground storage tank or from any person who may be liable for a release or threat of release under this subsection, to any other person the liability imposed under this subsection. Nothing in this subsection shall bar any agreement to insure, hold harmless, or indemnify a party to such agreement for any liability under this section.

(ii) No bar to cause of action — Nothing in this subsection, including the provisions of clause (i) of this subparagraph, shall bar a cause of action that an owner or operator or any other person subject to liability under this section, or a guarantor, has or would have, by reason of subrogation or otherwise against any person.

(D) Facility — For purposes of this paragraph, the term "facility" means, with respect to any owner or operator, all underground storage tanks used for the storage of petroleum which are owned or operated by such owner or operator and located on a single parcel of property (or on any contiguous or adjacent property).

(E) Inability or limited ability to pay

(i) In general — In determining the level of recovery effort, or amount that should be recovered, the Administrator (or the State pursuant to paragraph (7)) shall consider the owner or operator's ability to pay. An inability or limited ability to pay corrective action costs must be demonstrated to the Administrator (or the State pursuant to paragraph (7)) by the owner or operator.

(ii) Considerations — In determining whether or not a demonstration is made under clause (i), the Administrator (or the State pursuant to paragraph (7)) shall take into consideration the ability of the owner or operator to pay corrective action costs and still maintain its basic business operations, including consideration of the overall financial condition of the owner or operator and demonstrable constraints on the ability of the owner or operator to raise revenues.

(iii) Information — An owner or operator requesting consideration under this subparagraph shall promptly provide the Administrator (or the State pursuant to paragraph (7)) with all relevant information needed to determine the ability of the owner or operator to pay corrective action costs.

(iv) Alternative payment methods — The Administrator (or the State pursuant to paragraph (7)) shall consider alternative payment methods as may be necessary or appropriate if the Administrator (or the State pursuant to paragraph (7)) determines that an owner or operator cannot pay all or a portion of the costs in a lump sum payment.

(v) Misrepresentation — If an owner or operator provides false information or otherwise misrepresents their financial situation under clause (ii), the Administrator (or the State pursuant to paragraph (7)) shall seek full recovery of the costs of all such actions pursuant to the provisions of subparagraph (A) without consideration of the factors in subparagraph (B).

(7) State authorities

(A) General — A State may exercise the authorities in paragraphs (1) and (2) of this subsection, subject to the terms and conditions of paragraphs (3), (5), (9), (10), and (11), and including the authorities of paragraphs (4), (6), and (8) of this subsection if —

(i) the Administrator determines that the State has the capabilities to carry out effective corrective actions and enforcement activities; and

(ii) the Administrator enters into a cooperative agreement with the State setting out the actions to be undertaken by the State.

The Administrator may provide funds from the Leaking Underground Storage Tank Trust Fund for the reasonable costs of the State's actions under the cooperative agreement.

(B) Cost share — Following the effective date of the regulations under subsection (c) of this section, the State shall pay 10 per centum of the cost of corrective actions undertaken either by the Administrator or by the State under a cooperative agreement, except that the Administrator may take corrective action at a facility where immediate action is necessary to respond to an imminent and substantial endangerment to human health or the environment if the State fails to pay the cost share.

(8) Emergency procurement powers — Notwithstanding any other provision of law, the Administrator may authorize the use of such emergency procurement powers as he deems necessary.

(9) Definition of owner or operator

(A) In general — As used in this subchapter, the terms "owner" and "operator" do not include a person that, without participating in the management of an underground storage tank and otherwise not engaged in petroleum production, refining, or marketing, holds indicia of ownership primarily to protect the person's security interest.

(B) Security interest holders — The provisions regarding holders of security interests in subparagraphs (E) through (G) of section 9601(20) of this title and the provisions regarding fiduciaries at section 9607(n) of this title shall apply in determining a person's liability as an owner or operator of an underground storage tank for the purposes of this subchapter.

(C) Effect on rule — Nothing in subparagraph (B) shall be construed as modifying or affecting the final rule issued by the Administrator on September 7, 1995 (60 Fed. Reg. 46,692), or as limiting the authority of the Administrator to amend the final rule, in accordance with applicable law. The final rule in effect on September 30, 1996, shall prevail over any inconsistent provision regarding holders of security interests in subparagraphs (E) through (G) of section 9601(20) of this title or any inconsistent provision regarding fiduciaries in section 9607(n) of this title. Any amendment to the final rule shall be consistent with the provisions regarding holders of security interests in subparagraphs (E) through (G) of section 9601(20) of this title and the provisions regarding fiduciaries in section 9607(n) of this title. This subparagraph does not preclude judicial review of any amendment of the final rule made after September 30, 1996.

(10) Definition of exposure assessment — As used in this subsection, the term "exposure assessment" means an assessment to determine the extent of exposure of, or potential for exposure of, individuals to petroleum from a release from an underground storage tank based on such factors as the nature and extent of contamination and the existence of or potential for pathways of human exposure (including ground or surface water contamination, air emissions, and food chain contamination), the size of the community within the likely pathways of exposure, and the comparison of expected human exposure levels to the short-term and long-term health effects associated with identified contaminants and any available recommended exposure or tolerance limits for such contaminants. Such assessment shall not delay corrective action to abate immediate hazards or reduce exposure.

(11) Facilities without financial responsibility — At any facility where the owner or operator has failed to maintain evidence of financial responsibility in amounts at least equal to the amounts established by subsection (d)(5)(A) of this section (or a lesser amount if such amount is applicable to such facility as a result of subsection (d)(5)(B) of this section) for whatever reason the Administrator shall expend no monies from the Leaking Underground Storage Tank Trust Fund to clean up releases at such facility pursuant to the provisions of paragraph (1) or (2) of this subsection. At such facilities the Administrator shall use the authorities provided in subparagraph (A) of paragraph (1) and paragraph (4) of this subsection and section 6991e of this title to order corrective action to clean up such releases. States acting pursuant to paragraph (7) of this subsection shall use the authorities provided in subparagraph (A) of paragraph (1) and paragraph (4) of this subsection to order corrective action to clean up such releases. Notwithstanding the provisions of this paragraph, the Administrator may use monies from the fund to take the corrective actions authorized by paragraph (5) of this subsection to protect human health at such facilities and shall seek full recovery of the costs of all such actions pursuant to the provisions of paragraph (6)(A) of this subsection and without consideration of the factors in paragraph (6)(B) of this subsection. Nothing in this paragraph shall

prevent the Administrator (or a State pursuant to paragraph (7) of this subsection) from taking corrective action at a facility where there is no solvent owner or operator or where immediate action is necessary to respond to an imminent and substantial endangerment of human health or the environment.

(12) Remediation of oxygenated fuel contamination

(A) In general — The Administrator and the States may use funds made available under section 6991m(2)(B) of this title to carry out corrective actions with respect to a release of a fuel containing an oxygenated fuel additive that presents a threat to human health or welfare or the environment.

(B) Applicable authority — The Administrator or a State shall carry out subparagraph (A) in accordance with paragraph (2), and in the case of a State, in accordance with a cooperative agreement entered into by the Administrator and the State under paragraph (7).

(i) Additional measures to protect groundwater from contamination — The Administrator shall require each State that receives funding under this subchapter to require one of the following:

(1) Tank and piping secondary containment

(A) Each new underground storage tank, or piping connected to any such new tank, installed after the effective date of this subsection, or any existing underground storage tank, or existing piping connected to such existing tank, that is replaced after the effective date of this subsection, shall be secondarily contained and monitored for leaks if the new or replaced underground storage tank or piping is within 1,000 feet of any existing community water system or any existing potable drinking water well.

(B) In the case of a new underground storage tank system consisting of one or more underground storage tanks and connected by piping, subparagraph (A) shall apply to all underground storage tanks and connected pipes comprising such system.

(C) In the case of a replacement of an existing underground storage tank or existing piping connected to the underground storage tank, subparagraph (A) shall apply only to the specific underground storage tank or piping being replaced, not to other underground storage tanks and connected pipes comprising such system.

(D) Each installation of a new motor fuel dispenser system, after the effective date of this subsection, shall include under-dispenser spill containment if the new dispenser is within 1,000 feet of any existing community water system or any existing potable drinking water well.

(E) This paragraph shall not apply to repairs to an underground storage tank, piping, or dispenser that are meant to restore a tank, pipe, or dispenser to operating condition.

(F) As used in this subsection:

(i) The term "secondarily contained" means a release detection and prevention system that meets the requirements of 40 CFR 280.43(g), but shall not include under-dispenser spill containment or control systems.

(ii) The term "underground storage tank" has the meaning given to it in section 6991 of this title, except that such term does not include tank combinations or more than a single underground pipe connected to a tank.

(iii) The term "installation of a new motor fuel dispenser system" means the installation of a new motor fuel dispenser and the equipment necessary to connect the dispenser to the underground storage tank system, but does not mean the installation of a motor fuel dispenser installed separately from the equipment need to connect the dispenser to the underground storage tank system.

(2) Evidence of financial responsibility and certification

(A) Manufacturer and installer financial responsibility — A person that manufactures an underground storage tank or piping for an underground storage tank system or that installs an underground storage tank system is required to maintain evidence of financial responsibility under subsec. (d) of this section in order to provide for the costs of corrective actions directly related to releases caused by improper manufacture or installation unless the person can demonstrate themselves to be already covered as an owner or operator of an underground storage tank under this section.

(B) Installer certification — The Administrator and each State that receives funding under this subchapter, as appropriate, shall require that a person that installs an underground storage tank system is—

(i) certified or licensed by the tank and piping manufacturer;

(ii) certified or licensed by the Administrator or a State, as appropriate;

(iii) has their underground storage tank system installation certified by a registered professional engineer with education and experience in underground storage tank system installation;

(iv) has had their installation of the underground storage tank inspected and approved by the Administrator or the State, as appropriate;

(v) compliant with a code of practice developed by a nationally recognized association or independent testing laboratory and in accordance with the manufacturer's instructions; or

(vi) compliant with another method that is determined by the Administrator or a State, as appropriate, to be no less protective of human health and the environment.

(C) Savings clause — Nothing in subparagraph (A) alters or affects the liability of any owner or operator of an underground storage tank.

(j) Government-owned tanks

(1) State compliance report

(A) Not later than 2 years after August 8, 2005, each State that receives funding under this subchapter shall submit to the Administrator a State compliance report that—

(i) lists the location and owner of each underground storage tank described in subparagraph (B) in the State that, as of the date of submission of the report, is not in compliance with this section; and

(ii) specifies the date of the last inspection and describes the actions that have been and will be taken to ensure compliance of the underground storage tank listed under clause (i) with this subchapter.

(B) An underground storage tank described in this subparagraph is an underground storage tank that is—

(i) regulated under this subchapter; and

(ii) owned or operated by the Federal, State, or local government.

(C) The Administrator shall make each report, received under subparagraph (A), available to the public through an appropriate media.

(2) Financial incentive — The Administrator may award to a State that develops a report described in paragraph (1), in addition to any other funds that the State is entitled to receive under this subchapter, not more than $50,000, to be used to carry out the report.

(3) Not a safe harbor — This subsection does not relieve any person from any obligation or requirement under this subchapter.

§6991c. Approval of State programs
[SWDA §9004]

(a) Elements of State program — Beginning 30 months after November 8, 1984, any State may, submit an underground storage tank release detection, prevention, and correction program for review and approval by the Administrator. The program may cover tanks used to store regulated substances referred to in subparagraph (A) or (B) of section 6991(7) this title. A State program may be approved by the Administrator under this section only if the State demonstrates that the State program includes the following requirements and standards and provides for adequate enforcement of compliance with such requirements and standards —

(1) requirements for maintaining a leak detection system, an inventory control system together with tank testing, or a comparable system or method designed to identify releases in a manner consistent with the protection of human health and the environment;

(2) requirements for maintaining records of any monitoring or leak detection system or inventory control system or tank testing system;

(3) requirements for reporting of any releases and corrective action taken in response to a release from an underground storage tank;

(4) requirements for taking corrective action in response to a release from an underground storage tank;

(5) requirements for the closure of tanks to prevent future releases of regulated substances into the environment;

(6) requirements for maintaining evidence of financial responsibility for taking corrective action and compensating third parties for bodily injury and property damage caused by sudden and nonsudden accidental releases arising from operating an underground storage tank;

(7) standards of performance for new underground storage tanks;

(8) requirements —

(A) for notifying the appropriate State agency or department (or local agency or department) designated according to section 6991a(b)(1) of this title of the existence of any operational or non-operational underground storage tank; and

(B) for providing the information required on the form issued pursuant to section 6991a(b)(2) of this title and

(9) State-specific training requirements as required by section 6991i.

(b) Federal standards

(1) A State program submitted under this section may be approved only if the requirements under paragraphs (1) through (7) of subsection (a) of this section are no less stringent than the corresponding requirements standards promulgated by the Administrator pursuant to section 6991b(a) of this title.

(2)(A) A State program may be approved without regard to whether or not the requirements referred to in paragraphs (1), (2), (3), and (5) of subsection (a) of this section are less stringent than the corresponding standards under section 6991b(a) of this title during the one-year period commencing on the date of promulgation of regulations under section 6991b(a) of this title if State regulatory action but no State legislative action is required in order to adopt a State program.

(B) If such State legislative action is required, the State program may be approved

without regard to whether or not the requirements referred to in paragraphs (1), (2), (3), and (5) of subsection (a) of this section are less stringent than the corresponding standards under section 6991b(a) of this title during the two-year period commencing on the date of promulgation of regulations under section 6991b(a) of this title (and during an additional one-year period after such legislative action if regulations are required to be promulgated by the State pursuant to such legislative action).

(c) Financial responsibility

(1) Corrective action and compensation programs administered by State or local agencies or departments may be submitted for approval under subsection (a)(6) of this section as evidence of financial responsibility.

(2) Financial responsibility required by this subsection may be established in accordance with regulations promulgated by the Administrator by any one, or any combination, of the following: insurance, guarantee, surety bond, letter of credit, qualification as a self-insurer or any other method satisfactory to the Administrator. In promulgating requirements under this subsection, the Administrator is authorized to specify policy or other contractual terms including the amount of coverage required for various classes and categories of underground storage tanks pursuant to section 6991b(d)(5) of this title, conditions, or defenses which are necessary or are unacceptable in establishing such evidence of financial responsibility in order to effectuate the purposes of this subchapter.

(3) In any case where the owner or operator is in bankruptcy, reorganization, or arrangement pursuant to the Federal Bankruptcy Code or where with reasonable diligence jurisdiction in any State court of the Federal courts cannot be obtained over an owner or operator likely to be solvent at the time of judgment, any claim arising from conduct for which evidence of financial responsibility must be provided under this subsection may be asserted directly against the guarantor providing such evidence of financial responsibility. In the case of any action pursuant to this paragraph such guarantor shall be entitled to invoke all rights and defenses which would have been available to the owner or operator if any action had been brought against the owner or operator by the claimant and which would have been available to the guarantor if an action had been brought against the guarantor by the owner or operator.

(4) The total liability of any guarantor shall be limited to the aggregate amount which the guarantor has provided as evidence of financial responsibility to the owner or operator under this section. Nothing in this subsection shall be construed to limit any other State or Federal

statutory, contractual or common law liability of a guarantor to its owner or operator including, but not limited to, the liability of such guarantor for bad faith either in negotiating or in failing to negotiate the settlement of any claim. Nothing in this subsection shall be construed to diminish the liability of any person under section 9607 or 9611 of this title or other applicable law.

(5) For the purpose of this subsection, the term "guarantor" means any person, other than the owner or operator, who provides evidence of financial responsibility for an owner or operator under this subsection.

(6) Withdrawal of approval — After an opportunity for good faith, collaborative efforts to correct financial deficiencies with a State fund, the Administrator may withdraw approval of any State fund or State assurance program to be used as a financial responsibility mechanism without withdrawing approval of a State underground storage tank program under subsection (a) of this section.

(d) EPA determination

(1) Within one hundred and eighty days of the date of receipt of a proposed State program, the Administrator shall, after notice and opportunity for public comment, make a determination whether the State's program complies with the provisions of this section and provides for adequate enforcement of compliance with the requirements and standards adopted pursuant to this section.

(2) If the Administrator determines that a State program complies with the provisions of this section and provides for adequate enforcement of compliance with the requirements and standards adopted pursuant to this section, he shall approve the State program in lieu of the Federal program and the State shall have primary enforcement responsibility with respect to requirements of its program.

(e) Withdrawal of authorization — When-

ever the Administrator determines after public hearing that a State is not administering and enforcing a program authorized under this subchapter in accordance with the provisions of this section, he shall so notify the State. If appropriate action is not taken within a reasonable time, not to exceed one hundred and twenty days after such notification, the Administrator shall withdraw approval of such program and reestablish the Federal program pursuant to this subchapter.

(f) Trust Fund distribution

(1) In general

(A) Amount and permitted uses of distribution — The Administrator shall distribute to States not less than 80 percent of the funds from the Trust Fund that are made available to the Administrator under section 6991m(2) (A) of this title for each fiscal year for use in paying the reasonable costs, incurred under a cooperative agreement with any State for—

(i) corrective actions taken by the State under section 6991b(h)(7)(A) of this title;

(ii) necessary administrative expenses, as determined by the Administrator, that are directly related to State fund or State assurance programs under subsection (c) (1) of this section; or

(iii) enforcement, by a State or a local government, of State or local regulations pertaining to underground storage tanks regulated under this subchapter.

(B) Use of funds for enforcement — In addition to the uses of funds authorized under subparagraph (A), the Administrator may use funds from the Trust Fund that are not distributed to States under subparagraph (A) for enforcement of any regulation promulgated by the Administrator under this subchapter.

(C) Prohibited uses — Funds provided to a State by the Administrator under subparagraph (A) shall not be used by the State to provide financial assistance to an owner or operator to meet any requirement relating to underground storage tanks under subparts B, C, D, H, and G of part 280 of title 40, Code of Federal Regulations (as in effect on August 8, 2005).

(2) Allocation

(A) Process — Subject to subparagraphs (B) and (C), in the case of a State with which the Administrator has entered into a cooperative agreement under section 6991b(h)(7)(A), the Administrator shall distribute funds from the Trust Fund to the State using an allocation process developed by the Administrator.

(B) Diversion of State funds — The Administrator shall not distribute funds under subparagraph (A)(iii) of subsection (f)(1) of this section to any State that has diverted funds from a State fund or State assurance program for purposes other than those related to the regulation of underground storage tanks covered by this subchapter, with the exception of those transfers that had been completed earlier than the date of enactment of this subsection.

(C) Revisions to process — The Administrator may revise the allocation process referred to in subparagraph (A) after —

(i) consulting with State agencies responsible for overseeing corrective action for releases from underground storage tanks; and

(ii) taking into consideration, at a minimum, each of the following:

(I) The number of confirmed releases from federally regulated leaking underground storage tanks in the States.

    (II) The number of federally regulated underground storage tanks in the States.

    (III) The performance of the States in implementing and enforcing the program.

    (IV) The financial needs of the States.

    (V) The ability of the States to use the funds referred to in subparagraph (A) in any year.

(3) Distributions to State agencies — Distributions from the Trust Fund under this subsection shall be made directly to a State agency that —

    (A) enters into a cooperative agreement referred to in paragraph (2)(A); or

    (B) is enforcing a State program approved under this section.

§6991d. Inspections, monitoring, testing, and corrective action
[SWDA §9005]

(a) Furnishing information — For the purposes of developing or assisting in the development of any regulation, conducting any study taking any corrective action, or enforcing the provisions of this subchapter, any owner or operator of an underground storage tank (or any tank subject to study under section 6991h of this title that is used for storing regulated substances) shall, upon request of any officer, employee or representative of the Environmental Protection Agency, duly designated by the Administrator, or upon request of any duly designated officer, employee, or representative of a State acting pursuant to subsection (h)(7) of section 6991b of this title or with an approved program, furnish information relating to such tanks, their associated equipment, their contents, conduct monitoring or testing, permit such officer at all reasonable times to have access to, and to copy all records relating to such tanks and permit such officer to have access for corrective action. For the purposes of developing or assisting in the development of any regulation, conducting any study, taking corrective action, or enforcing the provisions of this subchapter, such officers, employees, or representatives are authorized —

    (1) to enter at reasonable times any establishment or other place where an underground storage tank is located;

    (2) to inspect and obtain samples from any person of any regulated substances contained in such tank;

    (3) to conduct monitoring or testing of the tanks, associated equipment, contents, or surrounding soils, air, surface water or ground water; and

    (4) to take corrective action.

Each such inspection shall be commenced and completed with reasonable promptness.

(b) Confidentiality

    (1) Any records, reports, or information obtained from any persons under this section shall be available to the public, except that upon a showing satisfactory to the Administrator (or the State, as the case may be) by any person that records, reports, or information, or a particular part thereof, to which the Administrator (or the State, as the case may be) or any officer, employee, or representative thereof has access under this section if made public, would divulge information entitled to protection under section 1905 of Title 18, such information or particular portion thereof shall be considered confidential in accordance with the purposes of that section, except that such record, report, document, or information may be disclosed to other officers, employees, or authorized representatives of the United States concerned with carrying out this chapter, or when relevent in any proceeding under this chapter.

    (2) Any person not subject to the provisions of section 1905 of Title 18 who knowingly and willfully divulges or discloses any information entitled to protection under this subsection shall, upon conviction, be subject to a fine of not more than $5,000 or to imprisonment not to exceed one year, or both.

    (3) In submitting data under this subchapter, a person required to provide such data may —

        (A) designate the data which such person believes is entitled to protection under this subsection, and

        (B) submit such designated data separately from other data submitted under this subchapter.

A designation under this paragraph shall be made in writing and in such manner as the Administrator may prescribe.

    (4) Notwithstanding any limitation contained in this section or any other provision of law, all information reported to, or otherwise obtained, by the Administrator (or any representative of the Administrator) under this chapter shall be made available, upon written request of any duly authorized committee of the Congress, to such committee (including records, reports, or information obtained by representatives of the Evironmental Protection Agency).

(c) Inspection requirements

    (1) Uninspected tanks — In the case of underground storage tanks regulated under this subchapter that have not undergone an inspection since December 22, 1998, not later than 2 years after August 8, 2005, the Administrator or a State that receives funding under this subchapter, as appropriate, shall conduct on-site inspections of all such tanks to determine compliance with this subchapter and the regulations under this subchapter (40 CFR 280) or a requirement or standard of a State program developed under section 6991c of this title.

(2) Periodic inspections — After completion of all inspections required under paragraph (1), the Administrator or a State that receives funding under this subchapter, as appropriate, shall conduct on-site inspections of each underground storage tank regulated under this subchapter at least once every 3 years to determine compliance with this subchapter and the regulations under this subchapter (40 CFR 280) or a requirement or standard of a State program developed under section 6991c of this title. The Administrator may extend for up to one additional year the first 3-year inspection interval under this paragraph if the State demonstrates that it has insufficient resources to complete all such inspections within the first 3-year period.

(3) Inspection authority — Nothing in this section shall be construed to diminish the Administrator's or a State's authorities under subsection (a) of this section.

§6991e. Federal enforcement
[SWDA §9006]
(a) Compliance orders

(1) Except as provided in paragraph (2), whenever on the basis of any information, the Administrator determines that any person is in violation of any requirement of this subchapter, the Administrator may issue an order requiring compliance within a reasonable specified time period or the Administrator may commence a civil action in the United States district court in which the violation occurred for appropriate relief, including a temporary or permanent injunction.

(2) In the case of a violation of any requirement of this subchapter where such violation occurs in a State with a program approved under section 6991c of this title, the Administrator shall give notice to the State in which such violation has occurred prior to issuing an order or commencing a civil action under this section.

(3) If a violator fails to comply with an order under this subsection within the time specified in the order, he shall be liable for a civil penalty of not more than $25,000 for each day of continued noncompliance.

(b) **Procedure** — Any order issued under this section shall become final unless, no later than thirty days after the order is served, the person or persons named therein request a public hearing. Upon such request the Administrator shall promptly conduct a public hearing. In connection with any proceeding under this section the Administrator may issue subpoenas for the attendance and testimony of witnesses and the production of relevant papers, books, and documents, and may promulgate rules for discovery procedures.

(c) **Contents of order** — Any order issued under this section shall state with reasonable specificity the nature of the violation, specify a reasonable time for compliance, and assess a penalty, if any, which the Administrator determines is reasonable taking into account the seriousness of the violation and any good faith efforts to comply with the applicable requirements.

(d) **Civil penalties**

(1) Any owner who knowingly fails to notify or submits false information pursuant to section 6991a(a) of this title shall be subject to a civil penalty not to exceed $10,000 for each tank for which notification is not given or false information is submitted.

(2) Any owner or operator of an underground storage tank who fails to comply with —

(A) any requirement or standard promulgated by the Administrator under section 6991b of this title;

(B) any requirement or standard of a State program approved pursuant to section 6991c of this title; or

(C) the provisions of section 6991b(g) of this title (entitled "Interim Prohibition")

(D) the requirements established in section 6991b(i) of this title,

(D) the training requirements established by States pursuant to section 6991i of this title (relating to operator training); or

(E) the delivery prohibition requirement established by section 6991k of this title,

shall be subject to a civil penalty not to exceed $10,000 for each tank for each day of violation. Any person making or accepting a delivery or deposit of a regulated substance to an underground storage tank at an ineligible facility in violation of section 6991k of this title shall also be subject to the same civil penalty for each day of such violation.

(e) Incentive for performance — Both of the following may be taken into account in determining the terms of a civil penalty under subsection (d) of this section:

(1) The compliance history of an owner or operator in accordance with this subtitle or a program approved under section 6991c of this title.

(2) Any other factor the Administrator considers appropriate.

§6991f. Federal facilities

(a) **In general** — Each department, agency, and instrumentality of the executive, legislative, and judicial branches of the Federal Government (1) having jurisdiction over any underground storage tank or underground storage tank system, or (2) engaged in any activity resulting, or which may result, in the installation, operation, management, or closure of any underground storage tank, release response activities related thereto, or in the delivery, acceptance, or deposit of any regulated substance to an underground storage tank or underground storage tank system shall be subject to, and comply with, all Federal, State, interstate, and local requirements, both substantive and procedural (including any requirement for permits or reporting or any provisions for injunctive relief and such sanctions as may be imposed by a court to enforce such relief), respecting underground storage tanks in the same manner, and to the same extent, as any person is subject to such requirements, including the payment of reasonable service charges. The Federal, State, interstate, and local substantive and procedural requirements referred to in this subsection include, but are not limited to, all administrative orders and all civil and administrative penalties and fines, regardless of whether such penalties or fines are punitive or coercive in nature or are imposed for isolated, intermittent, or continuing violations. The United States hereby expressly waives any immunity otherwise applicable to the United States with respect to any such substantive or procedural requirement (including, but not limited to, any injunctive relief, administrative order or civil or administrative penalty or fine referred to in the preceding sentence, or reasonable service charge). The reasonable service charges referred to in this subsection include, but are not limited to, fees or charges assessed in connection with the processing and issuance of permits, renewal of permits, amendments to permits, review of plans, studies, and other documents, and inspection and monitoring of facilities, as well as any other nondiscriminatory charges that are assessed in connection with a Federal, State, interstate, or local underground storage tank regulatory program. Neither the United States, nor any agent, employee, or officer thereof, shall be immune or exempt from any process or sanction of any State or Federal Court with respect to the enforcement of any such injunctive relief. No agent, employee, or officer of the United States shall be personally liable for any civil penalty under any Federal, State, interstate, or local law concerning underground storage tanks with respect to any act or omission within the scope of the official duties of the agent, employee, or officer. An agent, employee, or officer of the United States shall be subject to any criminal sanction (including, but not limited to, any fine or imprisonment) under any Federal or State law concerning underground storage tanks, but no department, agency, or instrumentality of the executive, legislative, or judicial branch of the Federal Government shall be subject to any such sanction. The President may exempt any underground storage tank of any department, agency, or instrumentality in the executive branch from compliance with such a requirement if he determines it to be in the paramount interest of the United States to do so. No such exemption shall be granted due to lack of appropriation unless

the President shall have specifically requested such appropriation as a part of the budgetary process and the Congress shall have failed to make available such requested appropriation. Any exemption shall be for a period not in excess of 1 year, but additional exemptions may be granted for periods not to exceed 1 year upon the President's making a new determination. The President shall report each January to the Congress all exemptions from the requirements of this section granted during the preceding calendar year, together with his reason for granting each such exemption.

(b) Review of and report on Federal underground storage tanks

(1) Review — Not later than 12 months after August 8, 2005, each Federal agency that owns or operates one or more underground storage tanks, or that manages land on which one or more underground storage tanks are located, shall submit to the Administrator, the Committee on Energy and Commerce of the United States House of Representatives, and the Committee on the Environment and Public Works of the Senate a compliance strategy report that —

(A) lists the location and owner of each underground storage tank described in this paragraph;

(B) lists all tanks that are not in compliance with this subtitle that are owned or operated by the Federal agency;

(C) specifies the date of the last inspection by a State or Federal inspector of each underground storage tank owned or operated by the agency;

(D) lists each violation of this subchapter respecting any underground storage tank owned or operated by the agency;

(E) describes the operator training that has been provided to the operator and other persons having primary daily on-site management responsibility for the operation and maintenance of underground storage tanks owned or operated by the agency; and

(F) describes the actions that have been and will be taken to ensure compliance for each underground storage tank identified under subparagraph (B).

(2) Not a safe harbor — This subsection does not relieve any person from any obligation or requirement under this subchapter.

§6991g. State authority
[SWDA §9008]

Nothing in this subchapter shall preclude or deny any right of any State or political subdivision thereof to adopt or enforce any regulation, requirement, or standard of performance respecting underground storage tanks that is more stringent than a regulation, requirement, or standard of performance in effect under this subchapter or to impose any additional liability with respect to the release of regulated substances within such State or political subdivision.

§6991h. Study of underground storage tanks [SWDA §9009]

(a) Petroleum tanks — Not later than twelve months after November 8, 1984, the Administrator shall complete a study of underground storage tanks used for the storage of regulated substances defined in section 6991(7)(B) of this title.

(b) Other tanks — Not later than thirty-six months after November 8, 1984, the Administrator shall complete a study of all other underground storage tanks.

(c) Elements of studies — The studies under subsections (a) and (b) of this section shall include an assessment of the ages, types (including methods of manufacture, coatings, protection systems, the compatibility of the construction materials and the installation methods) and locations (including the climate of the locations) of such tanks; soil conditions, water tables, and the hydrogeology of tank locations; the relationship between the foregoing factors and the likelihood of releases from underground storage tanks; the effectiveness and costs of inventory systems, tank testing, and leak detection systems; and such other factors as the Administrator deems appropriate.

(d) Farm and heating oil tanks — Not later than thirty-six months after November 8, 1984, the Administrator shall conduct a study regarding the tanks referred to in subparagraphs (A) and (B) of section 6991(10) of this title. Such study shall include estimates of the number and location of such tanks and an analysis of the extent to which there may be releases or threatened releases from such tanks into the environment.

(e) Reports — Upon completion of the studies authorized by this section, the Administrator shall submit reports to the President and to the Congress containing the results of the studies and recommendations respecting whether or not such tanks should be subject to the preceding provisions of this subchapter.

(f) Reimbursement

(1) If any owner or operator (excepting an agency, department, or instrumentality of the United States Government, a State or a political subdivision thereof) shall incur costs, including the loss of business opportunity, due to the closure or interruption of operation of an underground storage tank solely for the purpose of conducting studies authorized by this section, the Administrator shall provide such person fair and equitable reimbursement for such costs.

(2) All claims for reimbursement shall be filed with the Administrator not later than ninety days after the closure or interruption which gives rise to the claim.

(3) Reimbursements made under this section shall be from funds appropriated by the Congress pursuant to the authorization contained in section 6916(g) of this title.

(4) For purposes of judicial review, a determination by the Administrator under this subsection shall be considered final agency action.

§6991i. Operator training
(a) Guidelines

(1) In general — Not later than 2 years after August 8, 2005, in consultation and cooperation with States and after public notice and opportunity for comment, the Administrator shall publish guidelines that specify training requirements for—

(A) persons having primary responsibility for on-site operation and maintenance of underground storage tank systems;

(B) persons having daily on-site responsibility for the operation and maintenance of underground storage tanks systems; and

(C) daily, on-site employees having primary responsibility for addressing emergencies presented by a spill or release from an underground storage tank system.

(2) Considerations — The guidelines described in paragraph (1) shall take into account —

(A) State training programs in existence as of the date of publication of the guidelines;

(B) training programs that are being employed by tank owners and tank operators as of August 8, 2005;

(C) the high turnover rate of tank operators and other personnel;

(D) the frequency of improvement in underground storage tank equipment technology;

(E) the nature of the businesses in which the tank operators are engaged;

(F) the substantial differences in the scope and length of training needed for the different classes of persons described in subparagraphs (A), (B), and (C) of paragraph (1); and

(G) such other factors as the Administrator determines to be necessary to carry out this section.

(b) State programs

(1) In general — Not later than 2 years after the date on which the Administrator publishes the guidelines under subsection (a)(1) of this section, each State that receives funding under this subchapter shall develop State-specific training requirements that are consistent with the guidelines developed under subsection (a)(1) of this section.

(2) Requirements — State requirements described in paragraph (1) shall —

(A) be consistent with subsection (a) of this section;

(B) be developed in cooperation with tank owners and tank operators;

(C) take into consideration training programs implemented by tank owners and tank operators as of August 8, 2005; and

(D) be appropriately communicated to tank owners and operators.

(3) Financial incentive — The Administrator may award to a State that develops and implements requirements described in paragraph (1), in addition to any funds that the State is entitled to receive under this subchapter, not more than $200,000, to be used to carry out the requirements.

(c) Training — All persons that are subject to the operator training requirements of subsection (a) of this section shall —

(1) meet the training requirements developed under subsection (b) of this section; and

(2) repeat the applicable requirements developed under subsection (b) of this section, if the tank for which they have primary daily on-site management responsibilities is determined to be out of compliance with —

(A) a requirement or standard promulgated by the Administrator under section 6991b of this title; or

(B) a requirement or standard of a State program approved under section 6991c of this title.

§6991j. Use of funds for release prevention and compliance

Funds made available under section 6991m(2)(D) of this title from the Trust Fund may be used to conduct inspections, issue orders, or bring actions under this subchapter—(1) by a State, in accordance with a grant or cooperative agreement with the Administrator, of State regulations pertaining to underground storage tanks regulated under this subchapter; and (2) by the Administrator, for tanks regulated under this subchapter (including under a State program approved under section 6991c of this title).

§6991k. Delivery prohibition
(a) Requirements

(1) Prohibition of delivery or deposit — Beginning 2 years after August 8, 2005, it shall be unlawful to deliver to, deposit into, or accept a regulated substance into an underground storage tank at a facility which has been identified by the Administrator or a State implementing agency to be ineligible for such delivery, deposit, or acceptance.

(2) Guidance — Within 1 year after August 8, 2005, the Administrator shall, in consultation with the States, underground storage tank owners, and product delivery industries, publish guidelines detailing the specific processes and procedures they will use to implement the provisions of this section. The processes and procedures include, at a minimum —

(A) the criteria for determining which underground storage tank facilities are ineligible for delivery, deposit, or acceptance of a regulated substance;

(B) the mechanisms for identifying which facilities are ineligible for delivery, deposit, or acceptance of a regulated substance to the underground storage tank owning and fuel delivery industries;

(C) the process for reclassifying ineligible facilities as eligible for delivery, deposit, or acceptance of a regulated substance;

(D) one or more processes for providing adequate notice to underground storage tank owners and operators and supplier industries that an underground storage tank has been determined to be ineligible for delivery, deposit, or acceptance of a regulated substance; and

(E) a delineation of, or a process for determining, the specified geographic areas subject to paragraph (4).

(3) Compliance — States that receive funding under this subchapter shall, at a minimum, comply with the processes and procedures published under paragraph (2).

(4) Consideration

(A) Rural and remote areas — Subject to subparagraph (B), the Administrator or a State may consider not treating an underground storage tank as ineligible for delivery, deposit, or acceptance of a regulated substance if such treatment would jeopardize the availability of, or access to, fuel in any rural and remote areas unless an urgent threat to public health, as determined by the Administrator, exists.

(B) Applicability — Subparagraph (A) shall apply only during the 180-day period following the date of a determination by the Administrator or the appropriate State under subparagraph (A).

(b) Effect on State authority — Nothing in this section shall affect or preempt the authority of a State to prohibit the delivery, deposit, or acceptance of a regulated substance to an underground storage tank.

(c) Defense to violation — A person shall not be in violation of subsection (a)(1) of this section if the person has not been provided with notice pursuant to subsection (a)(2)(D) of this section of the ineligibility of a facility for delivery, deposit, or acceptance of a regulated substance as determined by the Administrator or a State, as appropriate, under this section.

§6991l. Tanks on tribal lands
(a) Strategy — The Administrator, in coordination with Indian tribes, shall, not later than 1 year

after August 8, 2005, develop and implement a strategy —

(1) giving priority to releases that present the greatest threat to human health or the environment, to take necessary corrective action in response to releases from leaking underground storage tanks located wholly within the boundaries of —

(A) an Indian reservation; or

(B) any other area under the jurisdiction of an Indian tribe; and

(2) to implement and enforce requirements concerning underground storage tanks located wholly within the boundaries of —

(A) an Indian reservation; or

(B) any other area under the jurisdiction of an Indian tribe.

(b) Report — Not later than 2 years after August 8, 2005, the Administrator shall submit to Congress a report that summarizes the status of implementation and enforcement of this subchapter in areas located wholly within —

(1) the boundaries of Indian reservations; and

(2) any other areas under the jurisdiction of an Indian tribe.

The Administrator shall make the report under this subsection available to the public.

(c) Not a safe harbor — This section does not relieve any person from any obligation or requirement under this subchapter.

(d) State authority — Nothing in this section applies to any underground storage tank that is located in an area under the jurisdiction of a State, or that is subject to regulation by a State, as of August 8, 2005.

§6991m. Authorization of appropriations

There are authorized to be appropriated to the Administrator the following amounts:

(1) To carry out subchapter I (except sections 6991b(h), 6991d(c), 6991j and 6991k of this title) $50,000,000 for each of fiscal years 2006 through 2011.

(2) From the Trust Fund, notwithstanding section 9508(c)(1) of Title 26 —

(A) to carry out section 6991b(h) of this title (except section 6991b(h)(12) of this title) $200,000,000 for each of fiscal years 2006 through 2011;

(B) to carry out section 6991b(h)(12) of this title, $200,000,000 for each of fiscal years 2006 through 2011;

(C) to carry out sections 6991b(i), 6991c(f), and 6991d(c) of this title $100,000,000 for each of fiscal years 2006 through 2011; and

(D) to carry out sections 6991i, 6991j, 6991k, and 6991l of this title $55,000,000 for each of fiscal years 2006 through 2011.

SUBCHAPTER X — DEMONSTRATION MEDICAL WASTE TRACKING PROGRAM

§6992. Scope of demonstration program for medical waste
[SWDA §11001]

(a) Covered States — The States within the demonstration program established under this subchapter for tracking medical wastes shall be New York, New Jersey, Connecticut, the States contiguous to the Great Lakes and any State included in the program through the petition procedure described in subsection (c) of this section, except for any of such States in which the Governor notifies the Administrator under subsection (b) of this section that such State shall not be covered by the program.

(b) Opt out

(1) If the Governor of any State covered under subsection (a) of this section which is not contiguous to the Atlantic Ocean notifies the Administrator that such State elects not to participate in the demonstration program, the Administrator shall remove such State from the program.

(2) If the Governor of any other State covered under subsection (a) of this section notifies the Administrator that such State has implemented a medical waste tracking program that is no less stringent than the demonstration program under this subchapter and that such State elects not to participate in the demonstration program, the Administrator shall, if the Administrator determines that such State program is no less stringent than the demonstration program under this subchapter, remove such State from the demonstration program.

(3) Notifications under paragraphs (1) or (2) shall be submitted to the Administrator no later than 30 days after the promulgation of regulations implementing the demonstration program under this subchapter.

(c) Petition in — The Governor of any State may petition the Administrator to be included in the demonstration program and the Administrator may, in his discretion, include any such State. Such petition may not be made later than 30 days after promulgation of regulations establishing the demonstration program under this subchapter, and the Administrator shall determine whether to include the State within 30 days after receipt of the State's petition.

(d) Expiration of demonstration program — The demonstration program shall expire on the date 24 months after the effective date of the regulations under this subchapter.

§6992a. Listing of medical wastes
[SWDA §11002]

(a) List — Not later than 6 months after November 1, 1988, the Administrator shall promulgate regulations listing the types of medical waste to be tracked under the demonstration program. Except as provided in subsection (b) of this section, such list shall include, but need not be limited to, each of the following types of solid waste:

(1) Cultures and stocks of infectious agents and associated biologicals, including cultures from medical and pathological laboratories, cultures and stocks of infectious agents from research and industrial laboratories, wastes from the production of biologicals, discarded live and attenuated vaccines, and culture dishes and devices used to transfer, inoculate, and mix cultures.

(2) Pathological wastes, including tissues, organs, and body parts that are removed during surgery or autopsy.

(3) Waste human blood and products of blood, including serum, plasma, and other blood components.

(4) Sharps that have been used in patient care or in medical, research, or industrial laboratories, including hypodermic needles, syringes, pasteur pipettes, broken glass, and scalpel blades.

(5) Contaminated animal carcasses, body parts, and bedding of animals that were exposed to infectious agents during research, production of biologicals, or testing of pharmaceuticals.

(6) Wastes from surgery or autopsy that were in contact with infectious agents, including soiled dressings, sponges, drapes, lavage tubes, drainage sets, underpads, and surgical gloves.

(7) Laboratory wastes from medical, pathological, pharmaceutical, or other research, commercial, or industrial laboratories that were in contact with infectious agents, including slides and cover slips, disposable gloves, laboratory coats, and aprons.

(8) Dialysis wastes that were in contact with the blood of patients undergoing hemodialysis, including contaminated disposable equipment and supplies such as tubing, filters, disposable sheets, towels, gloves, aprons, and laboratory coats.

(9) Discarded medical equipment and parts that were in contact with infectious agents.

(10) Biological waste and discarded materials contaminated with blood, excretion, excudates or secretion from human beings or animals who are isolated to protect others from communicable diseases.

(11) Such other waste material that results from the administration of medical care to a patient by a health care provider and is found by the Administrator to pose a threat to human health or the environment.

(b) Exclusions from list — The Administrator may exclude from the list under this section any cat-

egories or items described in paragraphs (6) through (10) of subsection (a) of this section which he determines do not pose a substantial present or potential hazard to human health or the environment when improperly treated, stored, transported, disposed of, or otherwise managed.

§6992b. Tracking of medical waste
[SWDA §11003]

(a) Demonstration program — Not later than 6 months after November 1, 1988, the Administrator shall promulgate regulations establishing a program for the tracking of the medical waste listed in section 6992a of this title which is generated in a State subject to the demonstration program. The program shall (1) provide for tracking of the transportation of the waste from the generator to the disposal facility, except that waste that is incinerated need not be tracked after incineration, (2) include a system for providing the generator of the waste with assurance that the waste is received by the disposal facility, (3) use a uniform form for tracking in each of the demonstration States, and (4) include the following requirements:

(A) A requirement for segregation of the waste at the point of generation where practicable.

(B) A requirement for placement of the waste in containers that will protect waste handlers and the public from exposure.

(C) A requirement for appropriate labeling of containers of the waste.

(b) Small quantities — In the program under subsection (a) of this section, the Administrator may establish an exemption for generators of small quantities of medical waste listed under section 6992a of this title, except that the Administrator may not exempt from the program any person who, or facility that, generates 50 pounds or more of such waste in any calendar month.

(c) On-site incinerators — Concurrently with the promulgation of regulations under subsection (a) of this section, the Administrator shall promulgate a recordkeeping and reporting requirement for any generator in a demonstration State of medical waste listed in section 6992a of this title that (1) incinerates medical waste listed in section 6992a of this title on site and (2) does not track such waste under the regulations promulgated under subsection (a) of this section. Such requirement shall require the generator to report to the Administrator on the volume and types of medical waste listed in section 6992a of this title that the generator incinerated on site during the 6 months following the effective date of the requirements of this subsection.

(d) Type of medical waste and types of generators — For each of the requirements of this section, the regulations may vary for different types of medical waste and for different types of medical waste generators.

§6992c. Inspections
[SWDA §11004]

(a) Requirements for access — For purposes of developing or assisting in the development of any regulation or report under this subchapter or enforcing any provision of this subchapter, any person who generates, stores, treats, transports, disposes of, or otherwise handles or has handled medical waste shall, upon request of any officer, employee, or representative of the Environmental Protection Agency duly designated by the Administrator, furnish information relating to such waste, including any tracking forms required to be maintained under section 6992b of this title, conduct monitoring or testing, and permit such person at all reasonable times to have access to, and to copy, all records relating to such waste. For such purposes, such officers, employees, or representatives are authorized to —

    (1) enter at reasonable times any establishment or other place where medical wastes are or have been generated, stored, treated, disposed of, or transported from;

    (2) conduct monitoring or testing; and

    (3) inspect and obtain samples from any person of any such wastes and samples of any containers or labeling for such wastes.

(b) Procedures — Each inspection under this section shall be commenced and completed with reasonable promptness. If the officer, employee, or representative obtains any samples, prior to leaving the premises he shall give to the owner, operator, or agent in charge a receipt describing the sample obtained and, if requested, a portion of each such sample equal in volume or weight to the portion retained if giving such an equal portion is feasible. If any analysis is made of such samples, a copy of the results of such analysis shall be furnished promptly to the owner, operator, or agent in charge of the premises concerned.

(c) Availability to public — The provisions of section 6927(b) of this title shall apply to records, reports, and information obtained under this section in the same manner and to the same extent as such provisions apply to records, reports, and information obtained under section 6927 of this title.

§6992d. Enforcement
[SWDA §11005]

(a) Compliance orders

    (1) Violations — Whenever on the basis of any information the Administrator determines that any person has violated, or is in violation of, any requirement or prohibition in effect under this subchapter (including any requirement or prohibition in effect under regulations under this subchapter) (A) the Administrator may issue an order (i) assessing a civil penalty for any past or current violation, (ii) requiring compliance immediately or within a specified time period, or (iii) both, or (B) the Administrator may commence a civil action in the United States district court in the district in which the violation occurred for appropriate relief, including a temporary or permanent injunction. Any order issued pursuant to this subsection shall state with reasonable specificity the nature of the violation.

    (2) Orders assessing penalties — Any penalty assessed in an order under this subsection shall not exceed $25,000 per day of noncompliance for each violation of a requirement or prohibition in effect under this subchapter. In assessing such a penalty, the Administrator shall take into account the seriousness of the violation and any good faith efforts to comply with applicable requirements.

    (3) Public hearing — Any order issued under this subsection shall become final unless, not later than 30 days after issuance of the order, the persons named therein request a public hearing. Upon such request, the Administrator shall promptly conduct a public hearing. In connection with any proceeding under this section, the Administrator may issue subpoenas for the production of relevant papers, books, and documents, and may promulgate rules for discovery procedures.

    (4) Violation of compliance orders — In the case of an order under this subsection requiring compliance with any requirement of or regulation under this subchapter, if a violator fails to take corrective action within the time specified in an order, the Administrator may assess a civil penalty of not more than $25,000 for each day of continued noncompliance with the order.

(b) Criminal penalties — Any person who —

    (1) knowingly violates the requirements of or regulations under this subchapter;

    (2) knowingly omits material information or makes any false material statement or representation in any label, record, report, or other document filed, maintained, or used for purposes of compliance with this subchapter or regulations thereunder; or

    (3) knowingly generates, stores, treats, transports, disposes of, or otherwise handles any medical waste (whether such activity took place before or takes place after November 1, 1988) and who knowingly destroys, alters, conceals, or fails to file any record, report, or other document required to be maintained or filed for purposes of compliance with this subchapter or regulations thereunder

shall, upon conviction, be subject to a fine of not more than $50,000 for each day of violation, or imprisonment not to exceed 2 years (5 years in the case of a violation of paragraph (1)). If the conviction is for a violation committed after a first conviction of such person under this paragraph, the maximum punishment under the respective paragraph shall be doubled with respect to both fine and imprisonment.

(c) Knowing endangerment — Any person who knowingly violates any provision of subsection (b) of this section who knows at that time that he thereby places another person in imminent danger of death or serious bodily injury, shall upon conviction be subject to a fine of not more than $250,000 or imprisonment for not more than 15 years, or both. A defendant that is an organization shall, upon conviction under this subsection, be subject to a fine of not more than $1,000,000. The terms of this paragraph shall be interpreted in accordance with the rules provided under section 6928(f) of this title.

(d) Civil penalties — Any person who violates any requirement of or regulation under this subchapter shall be liable to the United States for a civil penalty in an amount not to exceed $25,000 for each such violation. Each day of such violation shall, for purposes of this section, constitute a separate violation.

(e) Civil penalty policy — Civil penalties assessed by the United States or by the States under this subchapter shall be assessed in accordance with the Administrator's "RCRA Civil Penalty Policy", as such policy may be amended from time to time.

§6992e. Federal facilities
[SWDA §11006]

(a) In general — Each department, agency, and instrumentality of the executive, legislative, and judicial branches of the Federal Government in a demonstration State (1) having jurisdiction over any solid waste management facility or disposal site at which medical waste is disposed of or otherwise handled, or (2) engaged in any activity resulting, or which may result, in the disposal, management, or handling of medical waste shall be subject to, and comply with, all Federal, State, interstate, and local requirements, both substantive and procedural (including any requirement for permits or reporting or any provisions for injunctive relief and such sanctions as may be imposed by a court to enforce such relief), respecting control and abatement of medical waste disposal and management in the same manner, and to the same extent, as any person is subject to such requirements, including the payment of reasonable service charges. The Federal, State, interstate, and local substantive and procedural requirements referred to in this subsection include, but are not limited to, all administrative orders, civil, criminal, and administrative penalties, and other sanctions, including injunctive relief, fines, and imprisonment. Neither the United States, nor any agent, employee, or officer thereof, shall be immune or exempt from any process or sanction of any State or Federal court with respect to the enforcement of any such order, penalty, or other sanction. For purposes of enforcing any such substantive or procedural requirement (including, but not limited to, any injunctive relief, administrative order, or civil, criminal, administrative penalty, or other sanction), against any such department, agency, or instrumentality, the United States hereby expressly waives any immunity otherwise applicable to the United States. The President may exempt any department, agency, or instrumentality in the executive branch from compliance with such a requirement if he determines it to be in the paramount interest of the United States to do so. No such exemption shall be granted due to lack of appropriation unless the President shall have specifically requested such appropriation as a part of the budgetary process and the Congress shall have failed to make available such requested appropriation. Any exemption shall be for a period not in excess of one year, but additional exemptions may be granted for periods not to exceed one year upon the President's making a new determination. The President shall report each January to the Congress all exemptions from the requirements of this section granted during the preceding calendar year, together with his reason for granting each such exemption.

(b) "Person" defined — For purposes of this chapter, the term "person" shall be treated as including each department, agency, and instrumentality of the United States.

§6992f. Relationship to State law
[SWDA §11007]

(a) State inspections and enforcement — A State may conduct inspections under 6992c of this title and take enforcement actions under section 6992d of this title against any person, including any person who has imported medical waste into a State in violation of the requirements of, or regulations under, this subchapter, to the same extent as the Administrator. At the time a State initiates an enforcement action under section 6992d of this title against any person, the State shall notify the Administrator in writing.

(b) Retention of State authority — Nothing in this subchapter shall —

    (1) preempt any State or local law; or

    (2) except as provided in subsection (c) of this section, otherwise affect any State or local law or the authority of any State or local government to adopt or enforce any State or local law.

(c) State forms — Any State or local law which requires submission of a tracking form from any person subject to this subchapter shall require that the form be identical in content and format to the form required under section 6992b of this title, except that a State may require the submission of other tracking information which is supplemental to the information required on the form required under section 6992b of this title through additional sheets or such other means as the State deems appropriate.

§6992g. Repealed. Pub. L. 105-362, title V, Sec. 501(h)(1)(A), Nov. 10, 1998, 112 Stat. 3284

§6992h. Health impacts report
[SWDA §11008]

Within 24 months after November 1, 1988, the Administrator of the Agency for Toxic Substances and Disease Registry shall prepare for Congress a report on the health effects of medical waste, including each of the following —

(1) A description of the potential for infection or injury from the segregation, handling, storage, treatment, or disposal of medical wastes.

(2) An estimate of the number of people injured or infected annually by sharps, and the nature and seriousness of those injuries or infections.

(3) An estimate of the number of people infected annually by other means related to waste segregation, handling, storage, treatment, or disposal, and the nature and seriousness of those infections.

(4) For diseases possibly spread by medical waste, including Acquired Immune Deficiency Syndrome and hepatitis B, an estimate of what percentage of the total number of cases nationally may be traceable to medical wastes.

§6992i. General provisions
[SWDA §11009]
(a) Consultation

(1) In promulgating regulations under this subchapter, the Administrator shall consult with the affected States and may consult with other interested parties.

(2) The Administrator shall also consult with the International Joint Commission to determine how to monitor the disposal of medical waste emanating from Canada.

(b) Public comment

In the case of the regulations required by this subchapter to be promulgated within 9 months after November 1, 1988, the Administrator may promulgate such regulations in interim final form without prior opportunity for public comment, but the Administrator shall provide an opportunity for public comment on the interim final rule. The promulgation of such regulations shall not be subject to the Paperwork Reduction Act of 1980.

(c) Relationship to subchapter III

Nothing in this subchapter shall affect the authority of the Administrator to regulate medical waste, including medical waste listed under section 6992a of this title, under subchapter III of this chapter.

§6992j. Effective date
[SWDA §11010]

The regulations promulgated under this subchapter shall take effect within 90 days after promulgation, except that, at the time of promulgation, the Administrator may provide for a shorter period prior to the effective date if he finds the regulated community does not need 90 days to come into compliance.

§6992k. Authorization of appropriations
[SWDA §11011]

There are authorized to be appropriated to the Administrator such sums as may be necessary for each of the fiscal years 1989 through 1991 for purposes of carrying out activities under this subchapter.

B. COMPREHENSIVE ENVIRONMENTAL RESPONSE, COMPENSATION, AND LIABILITY ACT (CERCLA)

A GUIDE TO CERCLA MATERIALS AVAILABLE ON THE INTERNET

EPA maintains dockets containing important information about sites eligible for cleanup under CERCLA. These include a National Priorities List Docket, a Federal Facilities Docket, and Superfund Administrative Records, which include Records of Decision (RODs) concerning site cleanups. Maps of sites on the National Priorities List and fact sheets describing conditions at them can be reviewed online at *https://www.epa.gov/superfund/superfund-national-priorities-list-npl*.

EPA's Office of Land and Emergency Management (OLEM) maintains a website that provides substantial information about its operation of the Superfund program at *http://www.epa.gov/superfund/*. A comprehensive set of EPA guidance and enforcement documents pertaining to the Superfund program are available online at *https://www.epa.gov/superfund/superfund-policy-guidance-and-laws*. These include guidance documents on a broad array of Superfund topics and cleanup enforcement documents from 1983 to the present. EPA's Brownfields program, which seeks to encourage redevelopment of contaminated sites, maintains a website that can be accessed at *http://www.epa.gov/brownfields*.

EPA's CERCLA regulations are codified at 40 C.F.R. pts. 300-312. The list of CERCLA hazardous substances appears at 40 C.F.R. pt. 302. These CFR sections may be accessed online through the National Archives and Records Administration's website, which includes a searchable version of the Code of Federal Regulations and a continuously updated electronic CFR ("e-CFR") that can be found at *http://www.ecfr.gov*. The report of the Natural Resource Damage Assessment and Restoration Federal Advisory Committee is available at *http://www.doi.gov/restoration/library/upload/faca_finalreport.pdf*.

The Agency for Toxic Substances and Disease Registry maintains a list, in order of priority, of the hazardous substances most commonly found at NPL sites. This list is available online at *http://www.atsdr.cdc.gov/SPL/index.html*.

Information about reporting releases of hazardous substances under CERCLA is provided at *https://www.epa.gov/pesticide-incidents/report-spills-and-environmental-violations#who*.

CERCLA LEGISLATIVE HISTORY TIMELINE

December 11, 1980: Comprehensive Environmental Response, Compensation, and Liability Act (CERCLA), Pub. L. 96-510, 94 Stat. 2767, signed into law. The legislation creates the Superfund, funded by a tax on feedstock chemicals, and imposes strict, joint and several liability for the costs of responding to releases of hazardous substances on various parties associated with such releases.

October 17, 1986: Comprehensive amendments to CERCLA contained in the Superfund Amendments and Reauthorization Act (SARA), Pub. L. 99-499, 100 Stat. 1613, signed into law. The amendments impose timetables for remediation of sites on the National Priorities List, add provisions authorizing contribution actions and encouraging de minimis settlements, provide defenses for innocent purchasers of contaminated property, and address how stringent site cleanups should be in light of existing environmental standards. They also repeal the post-closure liability trust fund and shift funding of the Superfund to general revenues.

September 30, 1996: The Asset Conservation, Lender Liability, and Deposit Insurance Protection Act of 1996, Pub. L. 104-208, 110 Stat. 3009-462, is signed into law, adding §107(n) to CERCLA to clarify that most routine lending activities do not constitute "participating in the management" of a facility that would make the lender liable as an "owner or operator" of a facility.

November 29, 1999: Legislation containing the Superfund Recycling Equity Act, Pub. L. 106-113, 113 Stat. 1501A-598, adopted as a rider to a rider of an omnibus appropriations act, signed into law, adding §127 to CERCLA to clarify that persons who arrange for recycling of certain recyclable materials are not liable as arrangers or transporters under §§107(a)(3) & (4) of CERCLA.

January 11, 2002: The Small Business Liability Relief and Brownfields Revitalization Act, Pub. L. 107-118, is signed into law, adding several sections to CERCLA, including §§107(q) & (r). The amendments encourage the cleanup and redevelopment of real property that may be contaminated by hazardous substances.

OUTLINE OF PRINCIPAL PROVISIONS OF CERCLA

§101 (42 U.S.C. §9601) Definitions: the term "hazardous substance" is defined in §101(14); "owner or operator" is defined in 101(20); "release" is defined in section 101(22); what innocent purchasers must do to qualify for §107(b)(3)'s third-party defense is specified in §101(35).

§103 (42 U.S.C. §9603) Notification Requirements: requires reporting of releases of hazardous substances to the National Response Center if they are in amounts that equal or exceed "reportable quantities" specified by regulation.

§104 (42 U.S.C. §9604) Response Authorities: authorizes the President to respond to actual or threatened releases of hazardous substances by undertaking removals or remedial actions consistent with the National Contingency Plan.

§105 (42 U.S.C. §9605) National Contingency Plan: requires revision of the National Contingency Plan for responding to releases of hazardous substances and requires the establishment of a National Priorities List (NPL) of facilities presenting the greatest dangers to health, welfare, or the environment based on a hazard ranking system (HRS).

§106 (42 U.S.C. §9606) Abatement Orders: authorizes the issuance of administrative orders requiring the abatement of actual or potential releases of hazardous substances that may create imminent and substantial endangerment to health, welfare, or the environment.

§107 (42 U.S.C. §9607) Liability: imposes liability on (1) current owners and operators of facilities where hazardous substances are released or threatened to be released, (2) owners and operators of facilities at the time substances were disposed, (3) persons who arranged for disposal or treatment of such substances, and (4) persons who accepted such substances for transport for disposal or treatment. These parties may be held strictly, jointly and severally liable for: (a) all costs of removal or remedial action incurred by the federal government that are not inconsistent with the NCP, (b) any other necessary costs of response incurred by persons that are consistent with the NCP, (c) damages for injury to natural resources, and (d) costs of health assessments.

§111 (42 U.S.C. §9611) Superfund: creates a Superfund which can be used to finance governmental response actions and to reimburse private parties for costs incurred in carrying out the NCP.

§113 (42 U.S.C. §9613) Judicial Review and Contribution: bars pre-enforcement judicial review of response actions and abatement orders, and authorizes private actions for contribution against potentially responsible parties.

§116 (42 U.S.C. §9616) Cleanup Schedules: establishes schedules for evaluating and listing sites on the NPL, for commencing remedial investigation and feasibility studies, and for commencing remedial action.

§121 (42 U.S.C. §9621) Cleanup Standards: establishes a preference for remedial actions that permanently and significantly reduce the volume, toxicity, or mobility of hazardous substances and requires selection of remedial actions that are protective of health and the environment and cost effective, using permanent solutions to the maximum extent practicable; requires cleanups to attain the level of any "legally applicable or relevant and appropriate standard, requirement, criteria or limitation" contained in any federal environmental law or in any more stringent state law.

§122 (42 U.S.C. §9622) Settlements: sets standards for settlements with potentially responsible parties and encourages settlements with de minimis contributors.

Comprehensive Environmental Response, Compensation, and Liability Act

42 U.S.C. §§9601 to 9675

SUBCHAPTER 1—HAZARDOUS SUBSTANCES RELEASES, LIABILITY, COMPENSATION

§9601. Definitions
[CERCLA §101]

For purpose of this subchapter —

(1) The term "act of God" means an unanticipated grave natural disaster or other natural phenomenon of an exceptional, inevitable, and irresistible character, the effects of which could not have been prevented or avoided by the exercise of due care or foresight.

(2) The term "Administrator" means the Administrator of the United States Environmental Protection Agency.

(3) The term "barrel" means forty-two United States gallons at sixty degrees Fahrenheit.

(4) The term "claim" means a demand in writing for a sum certain.

(5) The term "claimant" means any person who presents a claim for compensation under this chapter.

(6) The term "damages" means damages for injury or loss of natural resources as set forth in section 9607(a) or 9611(b) of this title.

(7) The term "drinking water supply" means any raw or finished water source that is or may be used by a public water system (as defined in the Safe Drinking Water Act (42 U.S.C. §§300f *et seq.*)) or as drinking water by one or more individuals.

(8) The term "environment" means (A) the navigable waters, the waters of the contiguous zone, and the ocean waters of which the natural resources are under the exclusive management authority of the United States under the Magnuson-Stevens Fishery Conservation and Management Act (16 U.S.C. §§1801 *et seq.*), and (B) any other surface water, ground water, drinking water supply, land surface or subsurface strata, or ambient air within the United States or under the jurisdiction of the United States.

(9) The term "facility" means (A) any building, structure, installation, equipment, pipe or pipeline (including any pipe into a sewer or publicly owned treatment works), well, pit, pond, lagoon, impoundment, ditch, landfill, storage container, motor vehicle, rolling stock, or aircraft, or (B) any site or area where a hazardous substance has been deposited, stored, disposed of, or placed, or otherwise come to be located; but does not include any consumer product in consumer use or any vessel.

(10) The term "federally permitted release" means (A) discharges in compliance with a permit under section 1342 of Title 33, (B) discharges resulting from circumstances identified and reviewed and made part of the public record with respect to a permit issued or modified under section 1342 of Title 33 and subject to a condition of such permit, (C) continuous or anticipated intermittent discharges from a point source, identified in a permit or permit application under section 1342 of Title 33, which are caused by events occurring within the scope of relevant operating or treatment systems, (D) discharges in compliance with a legally enforceable permit under section 1344 of Title 33, (E) releases in compliance with a legally enforceable final permit issued pursuant to section 3005(a) through (d) of the Solid Waste Disposal Act (42 U.S.C. §6925(a)-(d)) from a hazardous waste treatment, storage, or disposal facility when such permit specifically identifies the hazardous substances and makes such substances subject to a standard of practice, control procedure or bioassay limitation or condition, or other control on the hazardous substances in such releases, (F) any release in compliance with a legally enforceable permit issued under section 1412 of Title 33 of section 1413

of Title 33, (G) any injection of fluids authorized under Federal underground injection control programs or State programs submitted for Federal approval (and not disapproved by the Administrator of the Environmental Protection Agency) pursuant to part C of the Safe Drinking Water Act (42 U.S.C. §§300h *et seq.*), (H) any emission into the air subject to a permit or control regulation under section 111 (42 U.S.C. §7411), section 112 (42 U.S.C. §7412), Title I part C (42 U.S.C. §§7470 *et seq.*), Title I part D (42 U.S.C. §§7501 *et seq.*), or State implementation plans submitted in accordance with section 110 of the Clean Air Act (42 U.S.C. §7410) (and not disapproved by the Administrator of the Environmental Protection Agency), including any schedule or waiver granted, promulgated, or approved under these sections, (I) any injection of fluids or other materials authorized under applicable State law (i) for the purpose of stimulating or treating wells for the production of crude oil, natural gas, or water, (ii) for the purpose of secondary, tertiary, or other enhanced recovery of crude oil or natural gas, or (iii) which are brought to the surface in conjunction with the production of crude oil or natural gas and which are reinjected, (J) the introduction of any pollutant into a publicly owned treatment works when such pollutant is specified in and in compliance with applicable pretreatment standards of section 1317 (b) or (c) of Title 33 and enforceable requirements in a pretreatment program submitted by a State or municipality for Federal approval under section 1342 of Title 33, and (K) any release of source, special nuclear, or byproduct material, as those terms are defined in the Atomic Energy Act of 1954 (42 U.S.C. §§2011 *et seq.*), in compliance with a legally enforceable license, permit, regulation, or order issued pursuant to the Atomic Energy Act of 1954.

(11) The term "Fund" or "Trust Fund" means the Hazardous Substance Superfund established by section 9507 of Title 26.

(12) The term "ground water" means water in a saturated zone or stratum beneath the surface of land or water.

(13) The term "guarantor" means any person, other than the owner or operator, who provides evidence of financial responsibility for an owner or operator under this chapter.

(14) The term "hazardous substance" means (A) any substance designated pursuant to section 1321(b)(2)(A) of Title 33, (B) any element, compound, mixture, solution, or substance designated pursuant to section 9602 of this title, (C) any hazardous waste having the characteristics identified under or listed pursuant to section 3001 of the Solid Waste Disposal Act (42 U.S.C. §6921) (but not including any waste the regulation of which under the Solid Waste Disposal Act (42 U.S.C. §§6901 *et seq.*) has been suspended by Act of Congress), (D) any toxic pollutant listed under section 1317(a) of Title 33, (E) any hazardous air pollutant listed under section 112 of the Clean Air Act (42 U.S.C. §7412), and (F) any imminently hazardous chemical substance or mixture with respect to which the Administrator has taken action pursuant to section 2606 of Title 15. The term does not include petroleum, including crude oil or any fraction thereof which is not otherwise specifically listed or designated as a hazardous substance under subparagraphs (A) through (F) of this paragraph, and the term does not include natural gas, natural gas liquids, liquefied natural gas, or synthetic gas usable for fuel (or mixtures of natural gas and such synthetic gas).

(15) The term "navigable waters" or "navigable waters of the United States" means the waters of the United States, including the territorial seas.

(16) The term "natural resources" means land, fish, wildlife, biota, air, water, ground water, drinking water supplies, and other such resources belonging to, managed by, held in trust by, appertaining to, or otherwise controlled by the United States (including the resources of the fishery conservation zone established by the Magnuson-Stevens Fishery Conservation and Management Act (16 U.S.C. §§1801 *et seq.*)), any State or local government, any foreign government, any Indian tribe, or, if such resources are subject to a trust restriction on alienation, any member of an Indian tribe.

(17) The term "offshore facility" means any facility of any kind located in, on, or under, any of the navigable waters of the United States, and any facility of any kind which is subject to the jurisdiction of the United States and is located in, on, or under any other waters, other than a vessel or a public vessel.

(18) The term "onshore facility" means any facility (including, but not limited to, motor vehicles and rolling stock) of any kind located in, on, or under, any land or nonnavigable waters within the United States.

(19) The term "otherwise subject to the jurisdiction of the United States" means subject to the jurisdiction of the United States by virtue of United States citizenship, United States vessel documentation or numbering, or as provided by international agreement to which the United States is a party.

(20)(A) The term "owner or operator" means (i) in the case of a vessel, any person owning, operating, or chartering by demise, such vessel, (ii) in the case of an onshore facility or an offshore facility, any person owning or operating such facility, and (iii) in the case of any facility, title or control of which was conveyed due to bankruptcy, foreclosure, tax delinquency, abandonment, or similar means to a unit of State or local government,

any person who owned, operated, or otherwise controlled activities at such facility immediately beforehand. Such term does not include a person, who, without participating in the management of a vessel or facility, holds indicia of ownership primarily to protect his security interest in the vessel or facility.

(B) In the case of a hazardous substance which has been accepted for transportation by a common or contract carrier and except as provided in section 9607(a)(3) or (4) of this title, (i) the term "owner or operator" shall mean such common carrier or other bona fide for hire carrier acting as an independent contractor during such transportation, (ii) the shipper of such hazardous substance shall not be considered to have caused or contributed to any release during such transportation which resulted solely from circumstances or conditions beyond his control.

(C) In the case of a hazardous substance which has been delivered by a common or contract carrier to a disposal or treatment facility and except as provided in section 9607(a)(3) or (4) of this title, (i) the term "owner or operator" shall not include such common or contract carrier, and (ii) such common or contract carrier shall not be considered to have caused or contributed to any release at such disposal or treatment facility resulting from circumstances or conditions beyond its control.

(D) The term "owner or operator" does not include a unit of State or local government which acquired ownership or control through seizure or otherwise in connection with law enforcement activity, or through bankruptcy, tax delinquency, abandonment, or other circumstances in which the government involuntarily acquires title by virtue of its function as sovereign. The exclusion provided under this paragraph shall not apply to any State or local government which has caused or contributed to the release or threatened release of a hazardous substance from the facility, and such a State or local government shall be subject to the provisions of this chapter in the same manner and to the same extent, both procedurally and substantively, as any nongovernmental entity, including liability under section 9607 of this title.

(E) Exclusion of certain Alaska Native villages and Native Corporations

(i) In general—The term "owner or operator" does not include, with respect to a facility conveyed to a Native village or Native Corporation (as those terms are defined in section 1602 of Title 43) under the Alaska Native Claims Settlement Act—

(I) the Native village or Native Corporation that received the facility from the United States Government; or

(II) a successor in interest to which the facility was conveyed under section 1613(c) of Title 43.

(ii) Limitation—The exclusion provided under this subparagraph shall not apply to any entity described in clause (i) that causes or contributes to a release or threatened release of a hazardous substance from the facility conveyed as described in such clause.

(F) Exclusion of lenders not participants in management —

(i) Indicia of ownership to protect security — The term "owner or operator" does not include a person that is a lender that, without participating in the management of a vessel or facility, holds indicia of ownership primarily to protect the security interest of the person in the vessel or facility.

(ii) Foreclosure — The term "owner or operator" does not include a person that is a lender that did not participate in management of a vessel or facility prior to foreclosure, notwithstanding that the person —

(I) forecloses on the vessel or facility; and

(II) after foreclosure, sells, re-leases (in the case of a lease finance transaction), or liquidates the vessel or facility, maintains business activities, winds up operations, undertakes a response action under section 9607(d)(1) of this title or under the direction of an on-scene coordinator appointed under the National Contingency Plan, with respect to the vessel or facility, or takes any other measure to preserve, protect, or prepare the vessel or facility prior to sale or disposition,

if the person seeks to sell, re-lease (in the case of a lease finance transaction), or otherwise divest the person of the vessel or facility at the earliest practicable, commercially reasonable time, on commercially reasonable terms, taking into account market conditions and legal and regulatory requirements.

(G) Participation in management — For purposes of subparagraph (F) —

(i) the term "participate in management" —

(I) means actually participating in the management or operational affairs of a vessel or facility; and

(II) does not include merely having the capacity to influence, or the unexercised right to control, vessel or facility operations;

(ii) a person that is a lender and that holds indicia of ownership primarily to protect a security interest in a vessel or facility shall be considered to participate in management only if, while the borrower is still in possession of the vessel or facility encumbered by the security interest, the person —

(I) exercises decisionmaking control over the environmental compliance related to the vessel or facility, such that the person has undertaken responsibility for the hazardous substance handling or disposal practices related to the vessel or facility; or

(II) exercises control at a level comparable to that of a manager of the vessel or facility, such that the person has assumed or manifested responsibility —

(aa) for the overall management of the vessel or facility encompassing day-to-day decisionmaking with respect to environmental compliance; or

(bb) over all or substantially all of the operational functions (as distinguished from financial or administrative functions) of the vessel or facility other than the function of environmental compliance;

(iii) the term "participate in management" does not include performing an act or failing to act prior to the time at which a security interest is created in a vessel or facility; and

(iv) the term "participate in management" does not include —

(I) holding a security interest or abandoning or releasing a security interest;

(II) including in the terms of an extension of credit, or in a contract or security agreement relating to the extension, a covenant, warranty, or other term or condition that relates to environmental compliance;

(III) monitoring or enforcing the terms and conditions of the extension of credit or security interest;

(IV) monitoring or undertaking 1 or more inspections of the vessel or facility;

(V) requiring a response action or other lawful means of addressing the release or threatened release of a hazardous substance in connection with the vessel or facility prior to, during, or on the expiration of the term of the extension of credit;

(VI) providing financial or other advice or counseling in an effort to mitigate, prevent, or cure default or diminution in the value of the vessel or facility;

(VII) restructuring, renegotiating, or otherwise agreeing to alter the terms and conditions of the extension of credit or security interest, exercising forbearance;

(VIII) exercising other remedies that may be available under applicable law for the breach of a term or condition of the extension of credit or security agreement; or

(IX) conducting a response action under section 9607(d) of this title or under the direction of an on-scene coordinator appointed under the National Contingency Plan,

if the actions do not rise to the level of participating in management (within the meaning of clauses (i) and (ii)).

(H) Other terms — As used in this chapter:

(i) Extension of credit — The term "extension of credit" includes a lease finance transaction —

(I) in which the lessor does not initially select the leased vessel or facility and does not during the lease term control the daily operations or maintenance of the vessel or facility; or

(II) that conforms with regulations issued by the appropriate Federal banking agency or the appropriate State bank supervisor (as those terms are defined in section 1813 of Title 12 or with regulations issued by the National Credit Union Administration Board, as appropriate.

(ii) Financial or administrative function — The term "financial or administrative function" includes a function such as that of a credit manager, accounts payable officer, accounts receivable officer, personnel manager, comptroller, or chief financial officer, or a similar function.

(iii) Foreclosure; foreclose — The terms "foreclosure" and "foreclose" mean, respectively, acquiring, and to acquire, a vessel or facility through —

(I)(aa) purchase at sale under a judgment or decree, power of sale, or nonjudicial foreclosure sale;

(bb) a deed in lieu of foreclosure, or similar conveyance from a trustee; or

(cc) repossession, if the vessel or facility was security for an extension of credit previously contracted;

(II) conveyance pursuant to an extension of credit previously contracted, including the termination of a lease agreement; or

(III) any other formal or informal manner by which the person acquires, for subsequent disposition, title to or possession of a vessel or facility in order to protect the security interest of the person.

(iv) Lender — The term "lender" means —

(I) an insured depository institution (as defined in section 1813 of Title 12);

(II) an insured credit union (as defined in section 1752 of Title 12);

(III) a bank or association chartered under the Farm Credit Act of 1971 (12 U.S.C. 2001 *et seq.*);

(IV) a leasing or trust company that is an affiliate of an insured depository institution;

(V) any person (including a successor or assignee of any such person) that makes a bona fide extension of credit to or takes or acquires a security interest from a nonaffiliated person;

(VI) the Federal National Mortgage Association, the Federal Home Loan Mortgage Corporation, the Federal Agricultural Mortgage Corporation, or any other entity that in a bona fide manner buys or sells loans or interests in loans;

(VII) a person that insures or guarantees against a default in the repayment of an extension of credit, or acts as a surety with respect to an extension of credit, to a nonaffiliated person; and

(VIII) a person that provides title insurance and that acquires a vessel or facility as a result of assignment or conveyance in the course of underwriting claims and claims settlement.

(v) Operational function — The term "operational function" includes a function such as that of a facility or plant manager, operations manager, chief operating officer, or chief executive officer.

(vi) Security interest — The term "security interest" includes a right under a mortgage, deed of trust, assignment, judgment lien, pledge, security agreement, factoring agreement, or lease and any other right accruing to a person to secure the repayment of money, the performance of a duty, or any other obligation by a nonaffiliated person.

(21) The term "person" means an individual, firm, corporation, association, partnership, consortium, joint venture, commercial entity, United States Government, State, municipality, commission, political subdivision of a State, or any interstate body.

(22) The term "release" means any spilling, leaking, pumping, pouring, emitting, emptying, discharging, injecting, escaping, leaching, dumping, or disposing into the environment (including the abandonment or discarding of barrels, containers, and other closed receptacles containing any hazardous substance or pollutant or contaminant), but excludes (A) any release which results in exposure to persons solely within a workplace, with respect to a claim which such persons may assert against the employer of such persons, (B) emissions from the engine exhaust of a motor vehicle, rolling stock, aircraft, vessel, or pipeline pumping station engine, (C) release of source, byproduct, or special nuclear material from a nuclear incident, as those terms are defined in the Atomic Energy Act of 1954 [42 U.S.C. §§2011 *et seq.*], if such release is subject to requirements with respect to financial protection established by the Nuclear Regulatory Commission under section 170 of such Act (42 U.S.C. §2210), or, for the purposes of section 9604 of this title or any other response action, any release of source byproduct, or special nuclear material from any processing site designated under section 7912(a)(1) or 7942(a) of this title, and (D) the normal application of fertilizer.

(23) The terms "remove" or "removal" means the cleanup or removal of released hazardous substances from the environment, such actions as may be necessary taken in the event of the threat of release of hazardous substances into the environment, such actions as may be necessary to monitor, assess, and evaluate the release or threat of release of hazardous substances, the disposal of removed material, or the taking of such other actions as may be necessary to prevent, minimize, or mitigate damage to the public health or welfare or to the environment, which may otherwise result from a release or threat of release. The term includes, in addition, without being limited to, security fencing or other measures to limit access, provision of alternative water supplies, temporary evacuation and housing of threatened individuals not otherwise provided for, action taken under section 9604(b) of this title, and any emergency assistance which may be provided under the

Disaster Relief and Emergency Assistance Act [42 U.S.C. §§5121 *et seq.*].

(24) The terms "remedy" or "remedial action" means those actions consistent with permanent remedy taken instead of or in addition to removal actions in the event of a release or threatened release of a hazardous substance into the environment, to prevent or minimize the release of hazardous substances so that they do not migrate to cause substantial danger to present or future public health or welfare or the environment. The term includes, but is not limited to, such actions at the location of the release as storage, confinement, perimeter protection using dikes, trenches, or ditches, clay cover, neutralization, cleanup of released hazardous substances and associated contaminated materials, recycling or reuse, diversion, destruction, segregation of reactive wastes, dredging or excavations, repair or replacement of leaking containers, collection of leachate and runoff, onsite treatment or incineration, provision of alternative water supplies, and any monitoring reasonably required to assure that such actions protect the public health and welfare and the environment. The term includes the costs of permanent relocation of residents and businesses and community facilities where the President determines that, alone or in combination with other measures, such relocation is more cost-effective than and environmentally preferable to the transportation, storage, treatment, destruction, or secure disposition offsite of hazardous substances, or may otherwise be necessary to protect the public health or welfare; the term includes offsite transport and offsite storage, treatment, destruction, or secure disposition of hazardous substances and associated contaminated materials.

(25) The terms "respond" or "response" means remove, removal, remedy, and remedial action; all such terms (including the terms "removal" and "remedial action") include enforcement activities related thereto.

(26) The terms "transport" or "transportation" means the movement of a hazardous substance by any mode, including a hazardous liquid pipeline facility (as defined in section 60101(a) of Title 49), and in the case of a hazardous substance which has been accepted for transportation by a common or contract carrier, the term "transport" or "transportation" shall include any stoppage in transit which is temporary, incidental to the transportation movement, and at the ordinary operating convenience of a common or contract carrier, and any such stoppage shall be considered as a continuity of movement and not as the storage of a hazardous substance.

(27) The terms "United States" and "State" include the several States of the United States, the District of Columbia, the Commonwealth of Puerto

Rico, Guam, American Samoa, the United States Virgin Islands, the Commonwealth of the Northern Marianas, and any other territory or possession over which the United States has jurisdiction.

(28) The term "vessel" means every description of watercraft or other artificial contrivance used, or capable of being used, as a means of transportation on water.

(29) The terms "disposal", "hazardous waste", and "treatment" shall have the meaning provided in section 1004 of the Solid Waste Disposal Act [42 U.S.C. §6903].

(30) The terms "territorial sea" and "contiguous zone" shall have the meaning provided in section 1362 of Title 33.

(31) The term "national contingency plan" means the national contingency plan published under section 1321(c) of Title 33 or revised pursuant to section 9605 of this title.

(32) The terms "liable" or "liability" under this subchapter shall be construed to be the standard of liability which obtains under section 1321 of Title 33.

(33) The term "pollutant or contaminant" shall include, but not be limited to, any element, substance, compound, or mixture, including disease-causing agents, which after release into the environment and upon exposure, ingestion, inhalation, or assimilation into any organism, either directly from the environment or indirectly by ingestion through food chains, will or may reasonably be anticipated to cause death, disease, behavioral abnormalities, cancer, genetic mutation, physiological malfunctions (including malfunctions in reproduction) or physical deformations, in such organisms or their offspring; except that the term "pollutant or contaminant" shall not include petroleum, including crude oil or any fraction thereof which is not otherwise specifically listed or designated as a hazardous substance under subparagraphs (A) through (F) of paragraph (14) and shall not include natural gas, liquefied natural gas, or synthetic gas of pipeline quality (or mixtures of natural gas and such synthetic gas).

(34) The term "alternative water supplies" includes, but is not limited to, drinking water and household water supplies.

(35)(A) The term "contractual relationship", for the purpose of section 9607(b)(3) of this title, includes, but is not limited to, land contracts, deeds, easements, leases, or other instruments transferring title or possession, unless the real property on which the facility concerned is located was acquired by the defendant after the disposal or placement of the hazardous substance on, in, or at the facility, and one or more of the circumstances described in clause (i), (ii), or (iii) is also established by the defendant by a preponderance of the evidence:

(i) At the time the defendant acquired the facility the defendant did not know and had no reason to know that any hazardous substance which is the subject of the release or threatened release was disposed of on, in, or at the facility.

(ii) The defendant is a government entity which acquired the facility by escheat, or through any other involuntary transfer or acquisition, or through the exercise of eminent domain authority by purchase or condemnation.

(iii) The defendant acquired the facility by inheritance or bequest.

In addition to establishing the foregoing, the defendant must establish that the defendant has satisfied the requirements of section 9607(b)(3)(a) and (b) of this title provides full cooperation, assistance, and facility access to the persons that are authorized to conduct response actions at the facility (including the cooperation and access necessary for the installation, integrity, operation, and maintenance of any complete or partial response action at the facility), is in compliance with any land use restrictions established or relied on in connection with the response action at a facility, and does not impede the effectiveness or integrity of any institutional control employed at the facility in connection with a response action.

(B) Reason to know

(i) All appropriate inquiries to establish that the defendant had no reason to know of the matter described in subparagraph (A)(i), the defendant must demonstrate to a court that —

(I) on or before the date on which the defendant acquired the facility, the defendant carried out all appropriate inquiries, as provided in clauses (ii) and (iv), into the previous ownership and uses of the facility in accordance with generally accepted good commercial and customary standards and practices; and

(II) the defendant took reasonable steps to —

(aa) stop any continuing release;

(bb) prevent any threatened future release; and

(cc) prevent or limit any human, environmental, or natural resource exposure to any previously released hazardous substance.

(ii) Standards and practices

Not later than 2 years after January 11, 2002, the Administrator shall by regulation establish standards and practices for the purpose of satisfying the requirement to carry out all appropriate inquiries under clause (i).

(iii) Criteria

In promulgating regulations that establish the standards and practices referred to in clause (ii), the Administrator shall include each of the following:

(I) The results of an inquiry by an environmental professional.

(II) Interviews with past and present owners, operators, and occupants of the facility for the purpose of gathering information regarding the potential for contamination at the facility.

(III) Reviews of historical sources, such as chain of title documents, aerial photographs, building department records, and land use records, to determine previous uses and occupancies of the real property since the property was first developed.

(IV) Searches for recorded environmental cleanup liens against the facility that are filed under Federal, State, or local law.

(V) Reviews of Federal, State, and local government records, waste disposal records, underground storage tank records, and hazardous waste handling, generation, treatment, disposal, and spill records, concerning contamination at or near the facility.

(VI) Visual inspections of the facility and of adjoining properties.

(VII) Specialized knowledge or experience on the part of the defendant.

(VIII) The relationship of the purchase price to the value of the property, if the property was not contaminated.

(IX) Commonly known or reasonably ascertainable information about the property.

(X) The degree of obviousness of the presence or likely presence of contamination at the property, and the ability to detect the contamination by appropriate investigation.

(iv) Interim standards and practices

(I) Property purchased before May 31, 1997

With respect to property purchased before May 31, 1997, in making a determination with respect to a defendant described in clause (i), a court shall take into account—

(aa) any specialized knowledge or experience on the part of the defendant;

(bb) the relationship of the purchase price to the value of the property, if the property was not contaminated;

(cc) commonly known or reasonably ascertainable information about the property;

(dd) the obviousness of the presence or likely presence of contamination at the property; and

(ee) the ability of the defendant to detect the contamination by appropriate inspection.

(II) Property purchased on or after May 31, 1997

With respect to property purchased on or after May 31, 1997, and until the Administrator promulgates the regulations described in clause (ii), the procedures of the American Society for Testing and Materials, including the document known as 'Standard E1527-97', entitled 'Standard Practice for Environmental Site Assessment: Phase 1 Environmental Site Assessment Process', shall satisfy the requirements in clause (i).

(v) Site inspection and title search

In the case of property for residential use or other similar use purchased by a nongovernmental or noncommercial entity, a facility inspection and title search that reveal no basis for further investigation shall be considered to satisfy the requirements of this subparagraph.

(C) Nothing in this paragraph or in section 9607(b)(3) of this title shall diminish the liability of any previous owner or operator of such facility who would otherwise be liable under this chapter. Notwithstanding this paragraph, if the defendant obtained actual knowledge of the release or threatened release of a hazardous substance at such facility when the defendant owned the real property and then subsequently transferred ownership of the property to another person without disclosing such knowledge, such defendant shall be treated as liable under section 9607(a)(1) of this title and no defense under section 9607(b)(3) of this title shall be available to such defendant.

(D) Nothing in this paragraph shall affect the liability under this chapter of a defendant who, by any act or omission, caused or contributed to the release or threatened release of a hazardous substance which is the subject of the action relating to the facility.

(36) The term "Indian tribe" means any Indian tribe, band, nation, or other organized group or community, including any Alaska Native village but

not including any Alaska Native regional or village corporation, which is recognized as eligible for the special programs and services provided by the United States to Indians because of their status as Indians.

(37)(A) The term "service station dealer" means any person —

(i) who owns or operates a motor vehicle service station, filling station, garage, or similar retail establishment engaged in the business of selling, repairing, or servicing motor vehicles, where a significant percentage of the gross revenue of the establishment is derived from the fueling, repairing, or servicing of motor vehicles, and

(ii) who accepts for collection, accumulation, and delivery to an oil recycling facility, recycled oil that (I) has been removed from the engine of a light duty motor vehicle or household appliances by the owner of such vehicle or appliances, and (II) is presented, by such owner, to such person for collection, accumulation, and delivery to an oil recycling facility.

(B) For purposes of section 9614(c) of this title, the term "service station dealer" shall, notwithstanding the provisions of subparagraph (A), include any government agency that establishes a facility solely for the purpose of accepting recycled oil that satisfies the criteria set forth in subclauses (I) and (II) of subparagraph (A)(ii), and, with respect to recycled oil that satisfies the criteria set forth in subclauses (I) and (II), owners or operators of refuse collection services who are compelled by State law to collect, accumulate, and deliver such oil to an oil recycling facility.

(C) The President shall promulgate regulations regarding the determination of what constitutes a significant percentage of the gross revenues of an establishment for purposes of this paragraph.

(38) The term "incineration vessel" means any vessel which carries hazardous substances for the purpose of incineration of such substances, so long as such substances or residues of such substances are on board.

(39) Brownfield site

(A) In general

The term "brownfield site" means real property, the expansion, redevelopment, or reuse of which may be complicated by the presence or potential presence of a hazardous substance, pollutant, or contaminant.

(B) Exclusions

The term "brownfield site" does not include —

(i) a facility that is the subject of a planned or ongoing removal action under this subchapter;

(ii) a facility that is listed on the National Priorities List or is proposed for listing;

(iii) a facility that is the subject of a unilateral administrative order, a court order, an administrative order on consent or judicial consent decree that has been issued to or entered into by the parties under this chapter;

(iv) a facility that is the subject of a unilateral administrative order, a court order, an administrative order on consent or judicial consent decree that has been issued to or entered into by the parties, or a facility to which a permit has been issued by the United States or an authorized State under the Solid Waste Disposal Act (42 U.S.C. 6901 et seq.), the Federal Water Pollution Control Act (33 U.S.C. 1321), the Toxic Substances Control Act (15 U.S.C. 2601 et seq.), or the Safe Drinking Water Act (42 U.S.C. 300f et seq.);

(v) a facility that—

(I) is subject to corrective action under section 3004(u) or 3008(h) of the Solid Waste Disposal Act (42 U.S.C. 6924(u), 6928(h)); and

(II) to which a corrective action permit or order has been issued or modified to require the implementation of corrective measures;

(vi) a land disposal unit with respect to which—

(I) a closure notification under subtitle C of the Solid Waste Disposal Act (42 U.S.C. 6921 et seq.) has been submitted; and

(II) closure requirements have been specified in a closure plan or permit;

(vii) a facility that is subject to the jurisdiction, custody, or control of a department, agency, or instrumentality of the United States, except for land held in trust by the United States for an Indian tribe;

(viii) a portion of a facility —

(I) at which there has been a release of polychlorinated biphenyls; and

(II) that is subject to remediation under the Toxic Substances Control Act (15 U.S.C. 2601 et seq.); or

(ix) a portion of a facility, for which portion, assistance for response activity has been obtained under subtitle I of the Solid Waste Disposal Act (42 U.S.C. 6991 et seq.) from the Leaking Underground Storage Tank Trust Fund established under section 9508 of Title 26.

(C) Site-by-site determinations

Notwithstanding subparagraph (B) and on a site-by-site basis, the President may authorize financial assistance under section 9604(k) of this title to an eligible entity at a site included in clause (i), (iv), (v), (vi), (viii), or (ix) of subparagraph (B) if the President finds that financial assistance will protect human health and the environment, and either promote economic development or enable the creation of, preservation of, or addition to parks, greenways, undeveloped property, other recreational property, or other property used for nonprofit purposes.

(D) Additional areas

For the purposes of section 9604(k) of this title, the term "brownfield site" includes a site that—

    (i) meets the definition of "brownfield site" under subparagraphs (A) through (C); and

    (ii)(I) is contaminated by a controlled substance (as defined in section 802 of Title 21);

        (II)(aa) is contaminated by petroleum or a petroleum product excluded from the definition of "hazardous substance" under this section; and

            (bb) is a site for which there is no viable responsible party and that is determined by the Administrator or the State, as appropriate, to be a site that will be assessed, investigated, or cleaned up by a person that is not potentially liable for cleaning up the site under this chapter or any other law pertaining to the cleanup of petroleum products; and

            (cc) is not subject to any order issued under section 9003(h) of the Solid Waste Disposal Act (42 U.S.C.A. §6991b(h)); or

        (III) is mine-scarred land.

(40) Bona fide prospective purchaser

(A) In general

The term "bona fide prospective purchaser" means, with respect to a facility—

    (i) a person who—

        (I) acquires ownership of the facility after January 11, 2002; and

        (II) establishes by a preponderance of the evidence each of the criteria described in clauses (i) through (viii) of subparagraph (B); and

    (ii) a person—

        (I) who acquires a leasehold interest in the facility after January 11, 2002;

        (II) who establishes by a preponderance of the evidence that the leasehold interest is not designed to avoid liability under this chapter by any person; and

        (III) with respect to whom any of the following conditions apply:

            (aa) The owner of the facility that is subject to the leasehold interest is a person described in clause (i).

            (bb)(AA) The owner of the facility that is subject to the leasehold interest was a person described in clause (i) at the time the leasehold interest was acquired, but can no longer establish by a preponderance of the evidence each of the criteria described in clauses (i) through (viii) of subparagraph (B) due to circumstances unrelated to any action of the person who holds the leasehold interest; and

                (BB) the person who holds the leasehold interest establishes by a preponderance of the evidence each of the criteria described in clauses (i), (iii), (iv), (v), (vi), (vii), and (viii) of subparagraph (B).

            (cc) The person who holds the leasehold interest establishes by a preponderance of the evidence each of the criteria described in clauses (i) through (viii) of subparagraph (B).

(B) Criteria

The criteria described in this subparagraph are as follows:

    (i) Disposal prior to acquisition

All disposal of hazardous substances at the facility occurred before the person acquired the facility.

    (ii) Inquiries

        (I) In general

The person made all appropriate inquiries into the previous ownership and uses of the facility in accordance with generally accepted good commercial and customary standards and practices in accordance with subclauses (II) and (III).

        (II) Standards and practices

The standards and practices referred to in clauses (ii) and (iv) of paragraph (35)(B) shall be considered to satisfy the requirements of this clause.

        (III) Residential use

In the case of property in residential or other similar use at the time of purchase by a nongovernmental or noncommercial entity, a facility inspection and title search that reveal no basis for further investigation shall be considered to satisfy the requirements of this clause.

(iii) Notices

The person provides all legally required notices with respect to the discovery or release of any hazardous substances at the facility.

(iv) Care

The person exercises appropriate care with respect to hazardous substances found at the facility by taking reasonable steps to—

    (I) stop any continuing release;

    (II) prevent any threatened future release; and

    (III) prevent or limit human, environmental, or natural resource exposure to any previously released hazardous substance.

(v) Cooperation, assistance, and access

The person provides full cooperation, assistance, and access to persons that are authorized to conduct response actions or natural resource restoration at a vessel or facility (including the cooperation and access necessary for the installation, integrity, operation, and maintenance of any complete or partial response actions or natural resource restoration at the vessel or facility).

(vi) Institutional control

The person—

    (I) is in compliance with any land use restrictions established or relied on in connection with the response action at a vessel or facility; and

    (II) does not impede the effectiveness or integrity of any institutional control employed at the vessel or facility in connection with a response action.

(vii) Requests; subpoenas

The person complies with any request for information or administrative subpoena issued by the President under this chapter.

(viii) No affiliation

The person is not—

    (I) potentially liable, or affiliated with any other person that is potentially liable, for response costs at a facility through—

        (aa) any direct or indirect familial relationship; or

        (bb) any contractual, corporate, or financial relationship

(other than a contractual, corporate, or financial relationship that is created by the instruments by which title to the facility is conveyed or financed, by a tenancy, by the instruments by which a leasehold interest in the facility is created, or by a contract for the sale of goods or services); or

    (II) the result of a reorganization of a business entity that was potentially liable.

(41) Eligible response site

(A) In general

The term "eligible response site" means a site that meets the definition of a brownfield site in subparagraphs (A) and (B) of paragraph (39) of this section, as modified by subparagraphs (B) and (C) of this paragraph.

(B) Inclusions

The term "eligible response site" includes —

    (i) notwithstanding paragraph (39)(B)(ix) of this section, a portion of a facility, for which portion assistance for response activity has been obtained under subtitle I of the Solid Waste Disposal Act (42 U.S.C. 6991 *et seq.*) from the Leaking Underground Storage Tank Trust Fund established under section 9508 of Title 26; or

    (ii) a site for which, notwithstanding the exclusions provided in subparagraph (C) or paragraph (39)(B) of this section, the President determines, on a site-by-site basis and after consultation with the State, that limitations on enforcement under section 9628 of this title at sites specified in clause (iv), (v), (vi) or (viii) of paragraph (39)(B) of this section would be appropriate and will—

        (I) protect human health and the environment; and

        (II) promote economic development or facilitate the creation of, preservation of, or addition to a park, a greenway, undeveloped property, recreational property, or other property used for nonprofit purposes.

(C) Exclusions

The term "eligible response site" does not include—

    (i) a facility for which the President—

        (I) conducts or has conducted a preliminary assessment or site inspection; and

        (II) after consultation with the State, determines or has determined that the site obtains a preliminary score sufficient for possible listing on the National Priorities List, or that the site otherwise qualifies for listing on the National Priorities List; unless the President has made a determination that no further Federal action will be taken; or

(ii) facilities that the President determines warrant particular consideration as identified by regulation, such as sites posing a threat to a sole-source drinking water aquifer or a sensitive ecosystem.

§9602. Designation of additional hazardous substances and establishment of reportable released quantities; regulations
[CERCLA §102]

(a) Regulations — The Administrator shall promulgate and revise as may be appropriate, regulations designating as hazardous substances, in addition to those referred to in section 9601(14) of this title, such elements, compounds, mixtures, solutions, and substances which, when released into the environment may present substantial danger to the public health or welfare or the environment, and shall promulgate regulations establishing that quantity of any hazardous substance the release of which shall be reported pursuant to section 9603 of this title. The Administrator may determine that one single quantity shall be the reportable quantity for any hazardous substance, regardless of the medium into which the hazardous substance is released. For all hazardous substances for which proposed regulations establishing reportable quantities were published in the Federal Register under this subsection on or before March 1, 1986, the Administrator shall promulgate under this subsection final regulations establishing reportable quantities not later than December 31, 1986. For all hazardous substances for which proposed regulations establishing reportable quantities were not published in the Federal Register under this subsection on or before March 1, 1986, the Administrator shall publish under this subsection proposed regulations establishing reportable quantities not later than December 31, 1986, and promulgate final regulations under this subsection establishing reportable quantities not later than April 30, 1988."

(b) Reportable quantity — Unless and until superseded by regulations establishing a reportable quantity under subsection (a) of this section for any hazardous substance as defined in section 9601(14) of this title, (1) a quantity of one pound, or (2) for those hazardous substances for which reportable quantities have been established pursuant to section 1321(b)(4) of Title 33, such reportable quantity, shall be deemed that quantity, the release of which requires notification pursuant to section 9603(a) or (b) of this title.

§9603. Notification requirements respecting released substances
[CERCLA §103]

(a) Notice to National Response Center upon release from vessel or offshore or onshore facility by person in charge; conveyance of notice by Center — Any person in charge of a vessel or an offshore or an onshore facility shall, as soon as he has knowledge of any release (other than a federally permitted release) of a hazardous substance from such vessel or facility in quantities equal to or greater than those determined pursuant to section 9602 of this title, immediately notify the National Response Center established under the Clean Water Act [33 U.S.C. §§1251 et seq.] of such release. The National Response Center shall convey the notification expeditiously to all appropriate Government agencies, including the Governor of any affected State.

(b) Penalties for failure to notify; use of notice or information pursuant to notice in criminal case

Any person —

(1) in charge of a vessel from which a hazardous substance is released, other than a federally permitted release, into or upon the navigable waters of the United States, adjoining shorelines, or into or upon the waters of the contiguous zone, or

(2) in charge of a vessel from which a hazardous substance is released, other than a federally permitted release, which may affect natural resources belonging to, appertaining to, or under the exclusive management authority of the United States (including resources under the Magnuson-Stevens Fishery Conservation and Management Act (16 U.S.C. §§1801 et seq.)), and who is otherwise subject to the jurisdiction of the United States at the time of the release, or

(3) in charge of a facility from which a hazardous substance is released, other than a federally permitted release,

in a quantity equal to or greater than that determined pursuant to section 9602 of this title who fails to notify immediately the appropriate agency of the United States Government as soon as he has knowledge of such release or who submits in such a notification any information which he knows to be false or misleading shall, upon conviction, be fined in accordance with the applicable provisions of Title 18 or imprisoned for not more than 3 years (or not more than 5 years in the case of a second or subsequent conviction), or both. Notification received pursuant to this subsection or information obtained by the exploitation of such notification shall not be used against any such person in any criminal case, except a prosecution for perjury or for giving a false statement.

(c) Notice to Administrator of EPA of existence of storage, etc., facility by owner or operator; exception; time, manner, and form of notice; penalties for failure to notify; use of notice or information pursuant to notice in

criminal case — Within one hundred and eighty days after December 11, 1980, any person who owns or operates or who at the time of disposal owned or operated, or who accepted hazardous substances for transport and selected, a facility at which hazardous substances (as defined in section 9601(14)(C) of this title) are or have been stored, treated, or disposed of shall, unless such facility has a permit issued under, or has been accorded interim status under, subtitle C of the Solid Waste Disposal Act [42 U.S.C. §§6921 *et seq.*], notify the Administrator of the Environmental Protection Agency of the existence of such facility, specifying the amount and type of any hazardous substance to be found there, and any known, suspected, or likely releases of such substances from such facility. The Administrator may prescribe in greater detail the manner and form of the notice and the information included. The Administrator shall notify the affected State agency, or any department designated by the Governor to receive such notice, of the existence of such facility. Any person who knowingly fails to notify the Administrator of the existence of any such facility shall, upon conviction, be fined not more than $10,000, or imprisoned for not more than one year, or both. In addition, any such person who knowingly fails to provide the notice required by this subsection shall not be entitled to any limitation of liability or to any defenses to liability set out in section 9607 of this title: Provided, however, That notification under this subsection is not required for any facility which would be reportable hereunder solely as a result of any stoppage in transit which is temporary, incidental to the transportation movement, or at the ordinary operating convenience of a common or contract carrier, and such stoppage shall be considered as a continuity of movement and not as the storage of a hazardous substance. Notification received pursuant to this subsection or information obtained by the exploitation of such notification shall not be used against any such person in any criminal case, except a prosecution for perjury or for giving a false statement.

(d) Recordkeeping requirements; promulgation of rules and regulations by Administrator of EPA; penalties for violations; waiver of retention requirements

(1) The Administrator of the Environmental Protection Agency is authorized to promulgate rules and regulations specifying, with respect to —

(A) the location, title, or condition of a facility, and

(B) the identity, characteristics, quantity, origin, or condition (including containerization and previous treatment) of any hazardous substances contained or deposited in a facility; the records which shall be retained by any person required to provide the notification of a facility set out in subsection (c) of this section. Such specification shall be in accordance with the provisions of this subsection.

(2) Beginning with December 11, 1980, for fifty years thereafter or for fifty years after the date of establishment of a record (whichever is later), or at any such earlier time as a waiver if obtained under paragraph (3) of this subsection, it shall be unlawful for any such person knowingly to destroy, mutilate, erase, dispose of, conceal, or otherwise render unavailable or unreadable or falsify any records identified in paragraph (1) of this subsection. Any person who violates this paragraph shall, upon conviction, be fined in accordance with the applicable provisions of Title 18 or imprisoned for not more than 3 years (or not more than 5 years in the case of a second or subsequent conviction), or both.

(3) At any time prior to the date which occurs fifty years after December 11, 1980, any person identified under paragraph (1) of this subsection may apply to the Administrator of the Environmental Protection Agency for a waiver of the provisions of the first sentence of paragraph (2) of this subsection. The Administrator is authorized to grant such waiver if, in his discretion, such waiver would not unreasonably interfere with the attainment of the purposes and provisions of this chapter. The Administrator shall promulgate rules and regulations regarding such a waiver so as to inform parties of the proper application procedure and conditions for approval of such a waiver.

(4) Notwithstanding the provisions of this subsection, the Administrator of the Environmental Protection Agency may in his discretion require any such person to retain any record identified pursuant to paragraph (1) of this subsection for such a time period in excess of the period specified in paragraph (2) of this subsection as the Administrator determines to be necessary to protect the public health or welfare.

(e) Applicability to registered pesticide products and air emissions from animal waste at farms

(1) In general

This section shall not apply to—

(A) the application of a pesticide product registered under the Federal Insecticide, Fungicide, and Rodenticide Act (7 U.S.C. 136 et seq.) or the handling and storage of such a pesticide product by an agricultural producer; or

(B) air emissions from animal waste (including decomposing animal waste) at a farm.

(2) Definitions

In this subsection—

(A) Animal waste

(i) In general

The term "animal waste" means feces, urine, or other excrement, digestive emission, urea, or similar substances emitted by animals (including any form of livestock, poultry, or fish).

(ii) Inclusions

The term "animal waste" includes animal waste that is mixed or commingled with bedding, compost, feed, soil, or any other material typically found with such waste.

(B) Farm

The term "farm" means a site or area (including associated structures) that—

    (i) is used for—

        (I) the production of a crop; or

        (II) the raising or selling of animals (including any form of livestock, poultry, or fish); and

    (ii) under normal conditions, produces during a farm year any agricultural products with a total value equal to not less than $1,000.

(f) Exemptions from notice and penalty provisions for substances reported under other Federal law or is in continuous release, etc. — No notification shall be required under subsection (a) or (b) of this section for any release of a hazardous substance —

    (1) which is required to be reported (or specifically exempted from a requirement for reporting) under subtitle C of the Solid Waste Disposal Act [42 U.S.C. §§6921 *et seq.*] or regulations thereunder and which has been reported to the National Response Center, or

    (2) which is a continuous release, stable in quantity and rate, and is —

        (A) from a facility for which notification has been given under subsection (c) of this section, or

        (B) a release of which notification has been given under subsections (a) and (b) of this section for a period sufficient to establish the continuity, quantity, and regularity of such release: Provided, That notification in accordance with subsections (a) and (b) of this paragraph shall be given for releases subject to this paragraph annually, or at such time as there is any statistically significant increase in the quantity of any hazardous substance or constituent thereof released, above that previously reported or occurring.

§9604. Response authorities
[CERCLA §104]

(a) Removal and other remedial action by President; applicability of national contingency plan; response by potentially responsible parties; public health threats; limitations on response; exception

    (1) Whenever (A) any hazardous substance is released or there is a substantial threat of such a release into the environment, or (B) there is a release or substantial threat of release into the environment of any pollutant or contaminant which may present an imminent and substantial danger to the public health or welfare, the President is authorized to act, consistent with the national contingency plan, to remove or arrange for the removal of, and provide for remedial action relating to such hazardous substance, pollutant, or contaminant at any time (including its removal from any contaminated natural resource), or take any other response measure consistent with the national contingency plan which the President deems necessary to protect the public health or welfare or the environment. When the President determines that such action will be done properly and promptly by the owner or operator of the facility or vessel or by any other responsible party, the President may allow such person to carry out the action, conduct the remedial investigation, or conduct the feasibility study in accordance with section 9622 of this title. No remedial investigation or feasibility study (RI/FS) shall be authorized except on a determination by the President that the party is qualified to conduct the RI/FS and only if the President contracts with or arranges for a qualified person to assist the President in overseeing and reviewing the conduct of such RI/FS and if the responsible party agrees to reimburse the Fund for any cost incurred by the President under, or in connection with, the oversight contract or arrangement. In no event shall a potentially responsible party be subject to a lesser standard of liability, receive preferential treatment, or in any other way, whether direct or indirect, benefit from any such arrangements as a response action contractor, or as a person hired or retained by such a response action contractor, with respect to the release or facility in question. The President shall give primary attention to those releases which the President deems may present a public health threat.

    (2) Removal Action — Any removal action undertaken by the President under this subsection (or by any other person referred to in section 9622 of this title) should, to the extent the President deems practicable, contribute to the efficient performance of any long term remedial action with respect to the release or threatened release concerned.

    (3) Limitations on Response — The President shall not provide for a removal or remedial action under this section in response to a release or threat of release —

        (A) of a naturally occurring substance in its unaltered form, or altered solely through naturally occurring processes or phenomena, from a location where it is naturally found;

        (B) from products which are part of the structure of, and result in exposure within, residential buildings or business or community structures; or

        (C) into public or private drinking water supplies due to deterioration of the system through ordinary use.

(4) Exception to Limitations — Notwithstanding paragraph (3) of this subsection, to the extent authorized by this section, the President may respond to any release or threat of release if in the President's discretion, it constitutes a public health or environmental emergency and no other person with the authority and capability to respond to the emergency will do so in a timely manner.

(b) Investigations, monitoring, coordination, etc., by President

(1) Information; studies and investigations — Whenever the President is authorized to act pursuant to subsection (a) of this section, or whenever the President has reason to believe that a release has occurred or is about to occur, or that illness, disease, or complaints thereof may be attributable to exposure to a hazardous substance, pollutant, or contaminant and that a release may have occurred or be occurring, he may undertake such investigations, monitoring, surveys, testing, and other information gathering as he may deem necessary or appropriate to identify the existence and extent of the release or threat thereof, the source and nature of the hazardous substances, pollutants or contaminants involved, and the extent of danger to the public health or welfare or to the environment. In addition, the President may undertake such planning, legal, fiscal, economic, engineering, architectural, and other studies or investigations as he may deem necessary or appropriate to plan and direct response actions, to recover the costs thereof, and to enforce the provisions of this chapter.

(2) Coordination of investigations — The President shall promptly notify the appropriate Federal and State natural resource trustees of potential damages to natural resources resulting from releases under investigation pursuant to this section and shall seek to coordinate the assessments, investigations, and planning under this section with such Federal and State trustees.

(c) Criteria for continuance of obligations from Fund over specified amount for response actions; consultation by President with affected States; contracts or cooperative agreements by States with President prior to remedial actions; cost-sharing agreements; selection by President of remedial actions; State credits: granting of credit, expenses before listing or agreement, response actions between 1978 and 1980, State expenses after December 11, 1980, in excess of 10 percent of costs, item-by-item approval, use of credits; operation and maintenance; limitation on source of funds for O&M; recontracting; siting

(1) Unless

(A) the President finds that

(i) continued response actions are immediately required to prevent, limit, or mitigate an emergency,

(ii) there is an immediate risk to public health or welfare or the environment, and

(iii) such assistance will not otherwise be provided on a timely basis, or

(B) the President has determined the appropriate remedial actions pursuant to paragraph (2) of this subsection and the State or States in which the source of the release is located have complied with the requirements of paragraph (3) of this subsection, or

(C) continued response action is otherwise appropriate and consistent with the remedial action to be taken obligations from the Fund, other than those authorized by subsection (b) of this section, shall not continue after $2,000,000 has been obligated for response actions or 12 months has elapsed from the date of initial response to a release or threatened release of hazardous substances.

(2) The President shall consult with the affected State or States before determining any appropriate remedial action to be taken pursuant to the authority granted under subsection (a) of this section.

(3) The President shall not provide any remedial actions pursuant to this section unless the State in which the release occurs first enters into a contract or cooperative agreement with the President providing assurances deemed adequate by the President that

(A) the State will assure all future maintenance of the removal and remedial actions provided for the expected life of such actions as determined by the President;

(B) the State will assure the availability of a hazardous waste disposal facility acceptable to the President and in compliance with the requirements of subtitle C of the Solid Waste Disposal Act (42 U.S.C. §§6921 et seq.) for any necessary offsite storage, destruction, treatment, or secure disposition of the hazardous substances; and

(C) the State will pay or assure payment of

(i) 10 per centum of the costs of the remedial action, including all future maintenance, or

(ii) 50 percent (or such greater amount as the President may determine appropriate, taking into account the degree of responsibility of the State or political subdivision for the release) of any sums expended in response to a release at a facility, that was operated by the State or a political subdivision thereof, either directly or through a contractual relationship or otherwise, at the time of any disposal of hazardous substances therein. For the purpose of clause (ii) of this subparagraph, the term "facility" does not include navigable waters or the beds underlying those waters. In the case of remedial action to be taken on land or water held by an Indian tribe, held by the United States in trust for Indians, held by a member of an Indian tribe (if such land or water is subject to a trust restriction on alienation), or otherwise within the borders of an Indian reservation, the requirements of this paragraph for assurances regarding future maintenance and cost-sharing shall not apply, and the President shall provide the assurance required by this paragraph regarding the availability of a hazardous waste disposal facility.

(4) Selection of Remedial Action — The President shall select remedial actions to carry out this section in accordance with section 9621 of this title (relating to cleanup standards).

(5) State Credits —

(A) Granting of credit — The President shall grant a State a credit against the share of the costs, for which it is responsible under paragraph (3) with respect to a facility listed on the National Priorities List under the National Contingency Plan, for amounts expended by a State for remedial action at such facility pursuant to a contract or cooperative agreement with the President. The credit under this paragraph shall be limited to those State expenses which the President determines to be reasonable, documented, direct out-of-pocket expenditures of non-Federal funds.

(B) Expenses before listing or agreement — The credit under this paragraph shall include expenses for remedial action at a facility incurred before the listing of the facility on the National Priorities List or before a contract or cooperative agreement is entered into under subsection (d) of this section for the facility if —

(i) after such expenses are incurred the facility is listed on such list and a contract or cooperative agreement is entered into for the facility, and

(ii) the President determines that such expenses would have been credited to the State under subparagraph (A) had the expenditures been made after listing of the facility on such list and after the date on which such contract or cooperative agreement is entered into.

(C) Response actions between 1978 and 1980 — The credit under this paragraph shall include funds expended or obligated by the State or a political subdivision thereof after January 1, 1978, and before December 11, 1980, for cost-eligible response actions and claims for damages compensable under section 9611 of this title.

(D) State expenses after December 11, 1980, in excess of 10 percent of costs — The credit under this paragraph shall include 90 percent of State expenses incurred at a facility owned, but not operated, by such State or by a political subdivision thereof. Such credit applies only to expenses incurred pursuant to a contract or cooperative agreement under subsection (d) of this section and only to expenses incurred after December 11, 1980, but before October 17, 1986.

(E) Item-by-item approval — In the case of expenditures made after October 17, 1986, the President may require prior approval of each item of expenditure as a condition of granting a credit under this paragraph.

(F) Use of credits — Credits granted under this paragraph for funds expended with respect to a facility may be used by the State to reduce all or part of the share of costs otherwise required to be paid by the State under paragraph (3) in connection with remedial actions at such facility. If the amount of funds for which credit is allowed under this paragraph exceeds such share of costs for such facility, the State may use the amount of such excess to reduce all or part of the share of such costs at other facilities in that State. A credit shall not entitle the State to any direct payment.

(6) Operation and Maintenance — For the purposes of paragraph (3) of this subsection, in the case of ground or surface water contamination, completed remedial action includes the completion of treatment or other measures, whether taken onsite or offsite, necessary to restore ground and surface water quality to a level that assures protection of human health and the environment. With respect to such measures, the operation of such measures for a period of up to 10 years after the construction or installation and commencement of operation shall be considered remedial action. Activities required to maintain the effectiveness of such measures following such period or the completion of remedial action, whichever is earlier, shall be considered operation or maintenance.

(7) Limitation on Source of Funds for O&M — During any period after the availability of funds received by the Hazardous Substance Superfund established under subchapter A of chapter 98 of Title 26 from tax revenues or appropriations from general revenues, the Federal share of the payment of the cost of operation or maintenance pursuant to paragraph (3)(C)(i) or paragraph (6) of this subsection (relating to operation and maintenance) shall be from funds received by the Hazardous

Substance Superfund from amounts recovered on behalf of such fund under this chapter.

(8) Recontracting — The President is authorized to undertake or continue whatever interim remedial actions the President determines to be appropriate to reduce risks to public health or the environment where the performance of a complete remedial action requires recontracting because of the discovery of sources, types, or quantities of hazardous substances not known at the time of entry into the original contract. The total cost of interim actions undertaken at a facility pursuant to this paragraph shall not exceed $2,000,000.

(9) Siting — Effective 3 years after October 17, 1986, the President shall not provide any remedial actions pursuant to this section unless the State in which the release occurs first enters into a contract or cooperative agreement with the President providing assurances deemed adequate by the President that the State will assure the availability of hazardous waste treatment or disposal facilities which —

(A) have adequate capacity for the destruction, treatment, or secure disposition of all hazardous wastes that are reasonably expected to be generated within the State during the 20-year period following the date of such contract or cooperative agreement and to be disposed of, treated, or destroyed,

(B) are within the State or outside the State in accordance with an interstate agreement or regional agreement or authority,

(C) are acceptable to the President, and

(D) are in compliance with the requirements of subtitle C of the Solid Waste Disposal Act [42 U.S.C. §§6921 et seq.].

(d) Contracts or cooperative agreements by President with States or political subdivisions or Indian tribes; State applications, terms and conditions; reimbursements; cost-sharing provisions; enforcement requirements and procedures

(1) Cooperative Agreements —

(A) State applications — A State or political subdivision thereof or Indian tribe may apply to the President to carry out actions authorized in this section. If the President determines that the State or political subdivision or Indian tribe has the capability to carry out any or all of such actions in accordance with the criteria and priorities established pursuant to section 9605(a)(8) of this title and to carry out related enforcement actions, the President may enter into a contract or cooperative agreement with the State or political subdivision or Indian tribe to carry out such actions. The President shall make a determination regarding such an application within 90 days after the President receives the application.

(B) Terms and conditions — A contract or cooperative agreement under this paragraph shall be subject to such terms and conditions as the President may prescribe. The contract or cooperative agreement may cover a specific facility or specific facilities.

(C) Reimbursements — Any State which expended funds during the period beginning September 30, 1985, and ending on October 17, 1986, for response actions at any site included on the National Priorities List and subject to a cooperative agreement under this chapter shall be reimbursed for the share of costs of such actions for which the Federal Government is responsible under this chapter.

(2) If the President enters into a cost-sharing agreement pursuant to subsection (c) of this section or a contract or cooperative agreement pursuant to this subsection, and the State or political subdivision thereof fails to comply with any requirements of the contract, the President may, after providing sixty days notice, seek in the appropriate Federal district court to enforce the contract or to recover any funds advanced or any costs incurred because of the breach of the contract by the State or political subdivision.

(3) Where a State or a political subdivision thereof is acting in behalf of the President, the President is authorized to provide technical and legal assistance in the administration and enforcement of any contract or subcontract in connection with response actions assisted under this subchapter, and to intervene in any civil action involving the enforcement of such contract or subcontract.

(4) Where two or more noncontiguous facilities are reasonably related on the basis of geography, or on the basis of the threat, or potential threat to the public health or welfare or the environment, the President may, in his discretion, treat these related facilities as one for purposes of this section.

(e) Information gathering and access

(1) Action authorized — Any officer, employee, or representative of the President, duly designated by the President, is authorized to take action under paragraph (2), (3), or (4) (or any combination thereof) at a vessel, facility, establishment, place, property, or location or, in the case of paragraph (3) or (4), at any vessel, facility, establishment, place, property, or location which is adjacent to the vessel, facility, establishment, place, property, or location referred to in such paragraph (3) or (4). Any duly designated officer, employee, or representative of a State or political subdivision under a contract or cooperative agreement under subsection (d)(1) of this section is also authorized to take such action. The authority of paragraphs (3) and (4) may be exercised only if

there is a reasonable basis to believe there may be a release or threat of release of a hazardous substance or pollutant or contaminant. The authority of this subsection may be exercised only for the purposes of determining the need for response, or choosing or taking any response action under this subchapter, or otherwise enforcing the provisions of this subchapter.

(2) Access to information — Any officer, employee, or representative described in paragraph (1) may require any person who has or may have information relevant to any of the following to furnish, upon reasonable notice, information or documents relating to such matter:

(A) The identification, nature, and quantity of materials which have been or are generated, treated, stored, or disposed of at a vessel or facility or transported to a vessel or facility.

(B) The nature or extent of a release or threatened release of a hazardous substance or pollutant or contaminant at or from a vessel or facility.

(C) Information relating to the ability of a person to pay for or to perform a cleanup. In addition, upon reasonable notice, such person either (i) shall grant any such officer, employee, or representative access at all reasonable times to any vessel, facility, establishment, place, property, or location to inspect and copy all documents or records relating to such matters or (ii) shall copy and furnish to the officer, employee, or representative all such documents or records, at the option and expense of such person.

(3) Entry — Any officer, employee, or representative described in paragraph (1) is authorized to enter at reasonable times any of the following:

(A) Any vessel, facility, establishment, or other place or property where any hazardous substance or pollutant or contaminant may be or has been generated, stored, treated, disposed of, or transported from.

(B) Any vessel, facility, establishment, or other place or property from which or to which a hazardous substance or pollutant or contaminant has been or may have been released.

(C) Any vessel, facility, establishment, or other place or property where such release is or may be threatened.

(D) Any vessel, facility, establishment, or other place or property where entry is needed to determine the need for response or the appropriate response or to effectuate a response action under this subchapter.

(4) Inspection and samples

(A) Authority — Any officer, employee or representative described in paragraph (1) is authorized to inspect and obtain samples from any vessel, facility, establishment, or other place or property referred to in paragraph (3) or from any location of any suspected hazardous substance or pollutant or contaminant. Any such officer, employee, or representative is authorized to inspect and obtain samples of any containers or labeling for suspected hazardous substances or pollutants or contaminants. Each such inspection shall be completed with reasonable promptness.

(B) Samples — If the officer, employee, or representative obtains any samples, before leaving the premises he shall give to the owner, operator, tenant, or other person in charge of the place from which the samples were obtained a receipt describing the sample obtained and, if requested, a portion of each such sample. A copy of the results of any analysis made of such samples shall be furnished promptly to the owner, operator, tenant, or other person in charge, if such person can be located.

(5) Compliance orders

(A) Issuance — If consent is not granted regarding any request made by an officer, employee, or representative under paragraph (2), (3), or (4), the President may issue an order directing compliance with the request. The order may be issued after such notice and opportunity for consultation as is reasonably appropriate under the circumstances.

(B) Compliance — The President may ask the Attorney General to commence a civil action to compel compliance with a request or order referred to in subparagraph (A). Where there is a reasonable basis to believe there may be a release or threat of a release of a hazardous substance or pollutant or contaminant, the court shall take the following actions:

(i) In the case of interference with entry or inspection, the court shall enjoin such interference or direct compliance with orders to prohibit interference with entry or inspection unless under the circumstances of the case the demand for entry or inspection is arbitrary and capricious, an abuse of discretion, or otherwise not in accordance with law.

(ii) In the case of information or document requests or orders, the court shall enjoin interference with such information or document requests or orders or direct compliance with the requests or orders to provide such information or documents unless under the circumstances of the case the demand for information or documents is arbitrary and capricious, an abuse of discretion, or otherwise not in accordance with law.

The court may assess a civil penalty not to exceed $25,000 for each day of noncompliance against any person who unreasonably fails to comply with the provisions of paragraph (2), (3), or (4) or an order issued pursuant to subparagraph (A) of this paragraph.

(6) Other authority — Nothing in this subsection shall preclude the President from securing access or obtaining information in any other lawful manner.

(7) Confidentiality of information

(A) Any records, reports, or information obtained from any person under this section (including records, reports, or information obtained by representatives of the President) shall be available to the public, except that upon a showing satisfactory to the President (or the State, as the case may be) by any person that records, reports, or information, or particular part thereof (other than health or safety effects data), to which the President (or the State, as the case may be) or any officer, employee, or representative has access under this section if made public would divulge information entitled to protection under section 1905 of Title 18, such information or particular portion thereof shall be considered confidential in accordance with the purposes of that section, except that such record, report, document or information may be disclosed to other officers, employees, or authorized representatives of the United States concerned with carrying out this chapter, or when relevant in any proceeding under this chapter.

(B) Any person not subject to the provisions of section 1905 of Title 18 who knowingly and willfully divulges or discloses any information entitled to protection under this subsection shall, upon conviction, be subject to a fine of not more than $5,000 or to imprisonment not to exceed one year, or both.

(C) In submitting data under this chapter, a person required to provide such data may (i) designate the data which such person believes is entitled to protection under this subsection and (ii) submit such designated data separately from other data submitted under this chapter. A designation under this paragraph shall be made in writing and in such manner as the President may prescribe by regulation.

(D) Notwithstanding any limitation contained in this section or any other provision of law, all information reported to or otherwise obtained by the President (or any representative of the President) under this chapter shall be made available, upon written request of any duly authorized committee of the Congress, to such committee.

(E) No person required to provide information under this chapter may claim that the information is entitled to protection under this paragraph unless such person shows each of the following:

(i) Such person has not disclosed the information to any other person, other than a member of a local emergency planning committee established under Title III of the Amendments and Reauthorization Act of 1986 [42 U.S.C. §§11001 *et seq.*], an officer or employee of the United States or a State or local government, an employee of such person, or a person who is bound by a confidentiality agreement, and such person has taken reasonable measures to protect the confidentiality of such information and intends to continue to take such measures.

(ii) The information is not required to be disclosed, or otherwise made available, to the public under any other Federal or State law.

(iii) Disclosure of the information is likely to cause substantial harm to the competitive position of such person.

(iv) The specific chemical identity, if sought to be protected, is not readily discoverable through reverse engineering.

(F) The following information with respect to any hazardous substance at the facility or vessel shall not be entitled to protection under this paragraph:

(i) The trade name, common name, or generic class or category of the hazardous substance.

(ii) The physical properties of the substance, including its boiling point, melting point, flash point, specific gravity, vapor density, solubility in water, and vapor pressure at 20 degrees celsius.

(iii) The hazards to health and the environment posed by the substance, including physical hazards (such as explosion) and potential acute and chronic health hazards.

(iv) The potential routes of human exposure to the substance at the facility, establishment, place, or property being investigated, entered, or inspected under this subsection.

(v) The location of disposal of any waste stream.

(vi) Any monitoring data or analysis of monitoring data pertaining to disposal activities.

(vii) Any hydrogeologic or geologic data.

(viii) Any groundwater monitoring data.

(f) Contracts for response actions; compliance with Federal health and safety standards — In awarding contracts to any person engaged in response actions, the President or the State, in any case where it is awarding contracts pursuant to a contract entered into under subsection (d) of this section, shall require compliance with Federal health and safety standards established under section 9651(f) of this title by contractors and subcontractors as a condition of such contracts.

(g) Rates for wages and labor standards applicable to covered work

(1) All laborers and mechanics employed by contractors or subcontractors in the performance of construction, repair, or alteration work funded in whole or in part under this section or section 9628(a)(1)(B)(ii)(III) of this title shall be paid wages at rates not less than those prevailing on projects of a character similar in the locality as determined by the Secretary of Labor in accordance with the Davis-Bacon Act [40 U.S.C. §§276a *et seq.*]. The President shall not approve any such funding without first obtaining adequate assurance that required labor standards will be maintained upon the construction work.

(2) The Secretary of Labor shall have, with respect to the labor standards specified in paragraph (1), the authority and functions set forth in Reorganization Plan Numbered 14 of 1950 (15 F.R. 3176; 64 Stat. 1267) and section 3145 of Title 40.

(h) Emergency procurement powers; exercise by President — Notwithstanding any other provision of law, subject to the provisions of section 9611 of this title, the President may authorize the use of such emergency procurement powers as he deems necessary to effect the purpose of this chapter. Upon determination that such procedures are necessary, the President shall promulgate regulations prescribing the circumstances under which such authority shall be used and the procedures governing the use of such authority.

(i) Agency for Toxic Substances and Disease Registry; establishment, functions, etc.

(1) There is hereby established within the Public Health Service an agency, to be known as the Agency for Toxic Substances and Disease Registry, which shall report directly to the Surgeon General of the United States. The Administrator of said Agency shall, with the cooperation of the Administrator of the Environmental Protection Agency, the Commissioner of the Food and Drug Administration, the Directors of the National Institute of Medicine, National Institute of Environmental Health Sciences, National Institute of Occupational Safety and Health, Centers for Disease Control and Prevention, the Administrator of the Occupational Safety and Health Administration, the Administrator of the Social Security Administration, the Secretary of Transportation, and appropriate State and local health officials, and implement the health related authorities of this chapter. In addition, said Administrator shall —

(A) in cooperation with the States, establish and maintain a national registry of serious diseases and illnesses and a national registry of persons exposed to toxic substances;

(B) establish and maintain inventory of literature, research, and studies on the health effects of toxic substances;

(C) in cooperation with the States, and other agencies of the Federal Government, establish and maintain a complete listing of areas closed to the public or otherwise restricted in use because of toxic substance contamination;

(D) in cases of public health emergencies caused or believed to be caused by exposure to toxic substances, provide medical care and testing to exposed individuals, including but not limited to tissue sampling, chromosomal testing where appropriate, epidemiological studies, or any other assistance appropriate under the circumstances; and

(E) either independently or as part of other health status survey, conduct periodic survey and screening programs to determine relationships between exposure to toxic substances and illness. In cases of public health emergencies, exposed persons shall be eligible for admission to hospitals and other facilities and services operated or provided by the Public Health Service.

(2)(A) Within 6 months after October 17, 1986, the Administrator of the Agency for Toxic Substances and Disease Registry (ATSDR) and the Administrator of the Environmental Protection Agency ("EPA") shall prepare a list, in order of priority, of at least 100 hazardous substances which are most commonly found at facilities on the National Priorities List and which, in their sole discretion, they determine are posing the most significant potential threat to human health due to their known or suspected toxicity to humans and the potential for human exposure to such substances at facilities on the National Priorities List or at facilities to which a response to a release or a threatened release under this section is under consideration.

(B) Within 24 months after October 17, 1986, the Administrator of ATSDR and the Administrator of EPA shall revise the list prepared under subparagraph (A). Such revision shall include, in order of priority, the addition of 100 or more such hazardous substances. In each of the 3 consecutive 12-month periods that follow, the Administrator of ATSDR and the Administrator of EPA shall revise, in the same manner as provided in the 2 preceding sentences, such list to include not fewer than 25 additional hazardous substances per revision. The Administrator of ATSDR and the Administrator of EPA shall not less often than once every year thereafter revise such list to include additional hazardous substances in accordance with the criteria in subparagraph (A).

(3) Based on all available information, including information maintained under paragraph (1) (B) and data developed and collected on the health effects of hazardous substances under this paragraph, the Administrator of ATSDR shall prepare toxicological profiles of each of the substances listed pursuant to paragraph (2). The toxicological profiles shall be prepared in accordance with guidelines developed by the Administrator of ATSDR and the Administrator of EPA. Such profiles shall include, but not be limited to each of the following:

    (A) An examination, summary, and interpretation of available toxicological information and epidemiologic evaluations on a hazardous substance in order to ascertain the levels of significant human exposure for the substance and the associated acute, subacute, and chronic health effects.

    (B) A determination of whether adequate information on the health effects of each substance is available or in the process of development to determine levels of exposure which present a significant risk to human health of acute, subacute, and chronic health effects.

    (C) Where appropriate, an identification of toxicological testing needed to identify the types or levels of exposure that may present significant risk of adverse health effects in humans.

Any toxicological profile or revision thereof shall reflect the Administrator of ATSDR's assessment of all relevant toxicological testing which has been peer reviewed. The profiles required to be prepared under this paragraph for those hazardous substances listed under subparagraph (A) of paragraph (2) shall be completed, at a rate of no fewer than 25 per year, within 4 years after October 17, 1986. A profile required on a substance listed pursuant to subparagraph (B) of paragraph (2) shall be completed within 3 years after addition to the list. The profiles prepared under this paragraph shall be of those substances highest on the list of priorities under paragraph (2) for which profiles have not previously been prepared. Profiles required under this paragraph shall be revised and republished as necessary, but no less often than once every 3 years. Such profiles shall be provided to the States and made available to other interested parties.

(4) The Administrator of the ATSDR shall provide consultations upon request on health issues relating to exposure to hazardous or toxic substances, on the basis of available information, to the Administrator of EPA, State officials, and local officials. Such consultations to individuals may be provided by States under cooperative agreements established under this chapter.

(5)(A) For each hazardous substance listed pursuant to paragraph (2), the Administrator of ATSDR (in consultation with the Administrator of EPA and other agencies and programs of the Public Health Service) shall assess whether adequate information on the health effects of such substance is available. For any such substance for which adequate information is not available (or under development), the Administrator of ATSDR, in cooperation with the Director of the National Toxicology Program, shall assure the initiation of a program of research designed to determine the health effects (and techniques for development of methods to determine such health effects) of such substance. Where feasible, such program shall seek to develop methods to determine the health effects of such substance in combination with other substances with which it is commonly found. Before assuring the initiation of such program, the Administrator of ATSDR shall consider recommendations of the Interagency Testing Committee established under section 4(e) of the Toxic Substances Control Act [15 U.S.C. §2603(e)] on the types of research that should be done. Such program shall include, to the extent necessary to supplement existing information, but shall not be limited to —

    (i) laboratory and other studies to determine short, intermediate, and long-term health effects;

    (ii) laboratory and other studies to determine organ-specific, site-specific, and system-specific acute and chronic toxicity;

    (iii) laboratory and other studies to determine the manner in which such substances are metabolized or to otherwise develop an understanding of the biokinetics of such substances; and

    (iv) where there is a possibility of obtaining human data, the collection of such information.

(B) In assessing the need to perform laboratory and other studies, as required by subparagraph (A), the Administrator of ATSDR shall consider —

    (i) the availability and quality of existing test data concerning the substance on the suspected health effect in question;

    (ii) the extent to which testing already in progress will, in a timely fashion, provide data that will be adequate to support the preparation of toxicological profiles as required by paragraph (3); and

(iii) such other scientific and technical factors as the Administrator of ATSDR may determine are necessary for the effective implementation of this subsection.

(C) In the development and implementation of any research program under this paragraph, the Administrator of ATSDR and the Administrator of EPA shall coordinate such research program implemented under this paragraph with the National Toxicology Program and with programs of toxicological testing established under the Toxic Substances Control Act [15 U.S.C. §§2601 et seq.] and the Federal Insecticide, Fungicide and Rodenticide Act [7 U.S.C. §§136 et seq.]. The purpose of such coordination shall be to avoid duplication of effort and to assure that the hazardous substances listed pursuant to this subsection are tested thoroughly at the earliest practicable date. Where appropriate, consistent with such purpose, a research program under this paragraph may be carried out using such programs of toxicological testing.

(D) It is the sense of the Congress that the costs of research programs under this paragraph be borne by the manufacturers and processors of the hazardous substance in question, as required in programs of toxicological testing under the Toxic Substances Control Act [15 U.S.C. §§2601 et seq.]. Within 1 year after October 17, 1986, the Administrator of EPA shall promulgate regulations which provide, where appropriate, for payment of such costs by manufacturers and processors under the Toxic Substances Control Act, and registrants under the Federal Insecticide, Fungicide, and Rodenticide Act [7 U.S.C. §§136 et seq.], and recovery of such costs from responsible parties under this chapter.

(6)(A) The Administrator of ATSDR shall perform a health assessment for each facility on the National Priorities List established under section 9605 of this title. Such health assessment shall be completed not later than December 10, 1988, for each facility proposed for inclusion on such list prior to October 17, 1986, or not later than one year after the date of proposal for inclusion on such list for each facility proposed for inclusion on such list after October 17, 1986.

(B) The Administrator of ATSDR may perform health assessments for releases or facilities where individual persons or licensed physicians provide information that individuals have been exposed to a hazardous substance, for which the probable source of such exposure is a release. In addition to other methods (formal or informal) of providing such information, such individual persons or licensed physicians may submit a petition to the Administrator of ATSDR providing such information and requesting a health assessment. If such a petition is submitted and the Administrator of ATSDR does not initiate a health assessment, the Administrator of ATSDR shall provide a written explanation of why a health assessment is not appropriate.

(C) In determining the priority in which to conduct health assessments under this subsection, the Administrator of ATSDR, in consultation with the Administrator of EPA, shall give priority to those facilities at which there is documented evidence of the release of hazardous substances, at which the potential risk to human health appears highest, and for which in the judgment of the Administrator of ATSDR existing health assessment data are inadequate to assess the potential risk to human health as provided in subparagraph (f). In determining the priorities for conducting health assessments under this subsection, the Administrator of ATSDR shall consider the National Priorities List schedules and the needs of the Environmental Protection Agency and other Federal agencies pursuant to schedules for remedial investigation and feasibility studies.

(D) Where a health assessment is done at a site on the National Priorities List, the Administrator of ATSDR shall complete such assessment promptly and, to the maximum extent practicable, before the completion of the remedial investigation and feasibility study at the facility concerned.

(E) Any State or political subdivision carrying out a health assessment for a facility shall report the results of the assessment to the Administrator of ATSDR and the Administrator of EPA and shall include recommendations with respect to further activities which need to be carried out under this section. The Administrator of ATSDR shall state such recommendation in any report on the results of any assessment carried out directly by the Administrator of ATSDR for such facility and shall issue periodic reports which include the results of all the assessments carried out under this subsection.

(F) For the purposes of this subsection and section 9611(c)(4) of this title, the term "health assessments" shall include preliminary assessments of the potential risk to human health posed by individual sites and facilities, based on such factors as the nature and extent of contamination, the existence of potential pathways of human exposure (including ground or surface water contamination, air emissions, and food chain contamination), the size and potential susceptibility of the community within the likely pathways of exposure, the comparison of expected human exposure levels to the short-term and long-term health effects associated with identified hazardous substances and any available recommended exposure or tolerance limits for such hazardous substances, and the comparison of existing morbidity and mortality data on diseases that may be associated with the observed levels of exposure. The Administrator of ATSDR shall use appropriate data, risk assessments, risk evaluations and studies available from the Administrator of EPA.

(G) The purpose of health assessments under this subsection shall be to assist in determining whether actions under paragraph (11) of this subsection should be taken to reduce human exposure to hazardous substances from a facility and whether additional information on human exposure and associated health risks is needed and should be acquired by conducting epidemiological studies under paragraph (7), establishing a registry under paragraph (8), establishing a health surveillance program under paragraph (9), or through other means. In using the results of health assessments for determining additional actions to be taken under this section, the Administrator of ATSDR may consider additional information on the risks to the potentially affected population from all sources of such hazardous substances including known point or nonpoint sources other than those from the facility in question.

(H) At the completion of each health assessment, the Administrator of ATSDR shall provide the Administrator of EPA and each affected State with the results of such assessment, together with any recommendations for further actions under this subsection or otherwise under this chapter. In addition, if the health assessment indicates that the release or threatened release concerned may pose a serious threat to human health or the environment, the Administrator of ATSDR shall so notify the Administrator of EPA who shall promptly evaluate such release or threatened release in accordance with the hazard ranking system referred to in section 9605(a)(8)(A) of this title to determine whether the site shall be placed on the National Priorities List or, if the site is already on the list, the Administrator of ATSDR may recommend to the Administrator of EPA that the site be accorded a higher priority.

(7)(A) Whenever in the judgment of the Administrator of ATSDR it is appropriate on the basis of the results of a health assessment, the Administrator of ATSDR shall conduct a pilot study of health effects for selected groups of exposed individuals in order to determine the desirability

of conducting full scale epidemiological or other health studies of the entire exposed population.

(B) Whenever in the judgment of the Administrator of ATSDR it is appropriate on the basis of the results of such pilot study or other study or health assessment, the Administrator of ATSDR shall conduct such full scale epidemiological or other health studies as may be necessary to determine the health effects on the population exposed to hazardous substances from a release or threatened release. If a significant excess of disease in a population is identified, the letter of transmittal of such study shall include an assessment of other risk factors, other than a release, that may, in the judgment of the peer review group, be associated with such disease, if such risk factors were not taken into account in the design or conduct of the study.

(8) In any case in which the results of a health assessment indicate a potential significant risk to human health, the Administrator of ATSDR shall consider whether the establishment of a registry of exposed persons would contribute to accomplishing the purposes of this subsection, taking into account circumstances bearing on the usefulness of such a registry, including the seriousness or unique character of identified diseases or the likelihood of population migration from the affected area.

(9) Where the Administrator of ATSDR has determined that there is a significant increased risk of adverse health effects in humans from exposure to hazardous substances based on the results of a health assessment conducted under paragraph (6), an epidemiologic study conducted under paragraph (7), or an exposure registry that has been established under paragraph (8), and the Administrator of ATSDR has determined that such exposure is the result of a release from a facility, the Administrator of ATSDR shall initiate a health surveillance program for such population. This program shall include but not be limited to —

(A) periodic medical testing where appropriate of population subgroups to screen for diseases for which the population or subgroup is at significant increased risk; and

(B) a mechanism to refer for treatment those individuals within such population who are screened positive for such diseases.

(10) Two years after October 17, 1986, and every 2 years thereafter, the Administrator of ATSDR shall prepare and submit to the Administrator of EPA and to the Congress a report on the results of the activities of ATSDR regarding —

(A) health assessments and pilot health effects studies conducted;

(B) epidemiologic studies conducted;

(C) hazardous substances which have been listed under paragraph (2), toxicological profiles which have been developed, and toxicologic testing which has been conducted or which is being conducted under this subsection;

(D) registries established under paragraph (8); and

(E) an overall assessment, based on the results of activities conducted by the Administrator of ATSDR, of the linkage between human exposure to individual or combinations of hazardous substances due to releases from facilities covered by this chapter or the Solid Waste Disposal Act [42 U.S.C. §§6901 *et seq.*] and any increased incidence or prevalence of adverse health effects in humans.

(11) If a health assessment or other study carried out under this subsection contains a finding that the exposure concerned presents a significant risk to human health, the President shall take such steps as may be necessary to reduce such exposure and eliminate or substantially mitigate the significant risk to human health. Such steps may include the use of any authority under this chapter, including, but not limited to —

(A) provision of alternative water supplies, and

(B) permanent or temporary relocation of individuals.

In any case in which information is insufficient, in the judgment of the Administrator of ATSDR or the President to determine a significant human exposure level with respect to a hazardous substance, the President may take such steps as may be necessary to reduce the exposure of any person to such hazardous substance to such level as the President deems necessary to protect human health.

(12) In any case which is the subject of a petition, a health assessment or study, or a research program under this subsection, nothing in this subsection shall be construed to delay or otherwise affect or impair the authority of the President, the Administrator of ATSDR, or the Administrator of EPA to exercise any authority vested in the President, the Administrator of ATSDR or the Administrator of EPA under any other provision of law (including, but not limited to, the imminent hazard authority of section 7003 of the Solid Waste Disposal Act [42 U.S.C. §6973]) or the response and abatement authorities of this chapter.

(13) All studies and results of research conducted under this subsection (other than health assessments) shall be reported or adopted only after appropriate peer review. Such peer review shall be completed, to the maximum extent practicable, within a period of 60 days. In the case of research conducted under the National Toxicology Program, such peer review may be conducted by the Board of Scientific Counselors.

In the case of other research, such peer review shall be conducted by panels consisting of no less than three nor more than seven members, who shall be disinterested scientific experts selected for such purpose by the Administrator of ATSDR or the Administrator of EPA, as appropriate, on the basis of their reputation for scientific objectivity and the lack of institutional ties with any person involved in the conduct of the study or research under review. Support services for such panels shall be provided by the Agency for Toxic Substances and Disease Registry, or by the Environmental Protection Agency, as appropriate.

(14) In the implementation of this subsection and other health-related authorities of this chapter, the Administrator of ATSDR shall assemble, develop as necessary, and distribute to the States, and upon request to medical colleges, physicians, and other health professionals, appropriate educational materials (including short courses) on the medical surveillance, screening, and methods of diagnosis and treatment of injury or disease related to exposure to hazardous substances (giving priority to those listed in paragraph (2)), through such means as the Administrator of ATSDR deems appropriate.

(15) The activities of the Administrator of ATSDR described in this subsection and section 9611(c)(4) of this title shall be carried out by the Administrator of ATSDR, either directly or through cooperative agreements with States (or political subdivisions thereof) which the Administrator of ATSDR determines are capable of carrying out such activities. Such activities shall include provision of consultations on health information, the conduct of health assessments, including those required under section 3019(b) of the Solid Waste Disposal Act [42 U.S.C. §6939a(b)], health studies, registries, and health surveillance.

(16) The President shall provide adequate personnel for ATSDR, which shall not be fewer than 100 employees. For purposes of determining the number of employees under this subsection, an employee employed by ATSDR on a part-time career employment basis shall be counted as a fraction which is determined by dividing 40 hours into the average number of hours of such employee's regularly scheduled workweek.

(17) In accordance with section 9620 of this title (relating to Federal facilities), the Administrator of ATSDR shall have the same authorities under this section with respect to facilities owned or operated by a department, agency, or instrumentality of the United States as the Administrator of ATSDR has with respect to any nongovernmental entity.

(18) If the Administrator of ATSDR determines that it is appropriate for purposes of this section to treat a pollutant or contaminant as a hazard-

ous substance, such pollutant or contaminant shall be treated as a hazardous substance for such purpose.

(j) Acquisition of property

(1) Authority — The President is authorized to acquire, by purchase, lease, condemnation, donation, or otherwise, any real property or any interest in real property that the President in his discretion determines is needed to conduct a remedial action under this chapter. There shall be no cause of action to compel the President to acquire any interest in real property under this chapter.

(2) State assurance — The President may use the authority of paragraph (1) for a remedial action only if, before an interest in real estate is acquired under this subsection, the State in which the interest to be acquired is located assures the President, through a contract or cooperative agreement or otherwise, that the State will accept transfer of the interest following completion of the remedial action.

(3) Exemption — No Federal, State, or local government agency shall be liable under this chapter solely as a result of acquiring an interest in real estate under this subsection.

(k) Brownfields revitalization funding

(1) Definition of eligible entity. In this subsection, the term "eligible entity" means —

(A) a general purpose unit of local government;

(B) a land clearance authority or other quasi-governmental entity that operates under the supervision and control of or as an agent of a general purpose unit of local government;

(C) a government entity created by a State legislature;

(D) a regional council or group of general purpose units of local government;

(E) a redevelopment agency that is chartered or otherwise sanctioned by a State;

(F) a State;

(G) an Indian Tribe other than in Alaska;

(H) an Alaska Native Regional Corporation and an Alaska Native Village Corporation as those terms are defined in the Alaska Native Claims Settlement Act (43 U.S.C. 1601 and following) and the Metlakatla Indian community;

(I) an organization described in section 501(c)(3) of Title 26 and exempt from taxation under section 501(a) of that Title;

(J) a limited liability corporation in which all managing members are organizations described in subparagraph (I) or limited liability corporations whose sole members are organizations described in subparagraph (I);

(K) a limited partnership in which all general partners are organizations described in subparagraph (I) or limited liability corpora-

tions whose sole members are organizations described in subparagraph (I); or

(L) a qualified community development entity (as defined in section 45D(c)(1) of Title 26).

(2) Brownfield site characterization and assessment grant program.

(A) Establishment of program. The Administrator shall establish a program to —

(i) provide grants to inventory, characterize, assess, and conduct planning related to brownfield sites under subparagraph (B); and

(ii) perform targeted site assessments at brownfield sites.

(B) Assistance for site characterization and assessment.

(i) In general. On approval of an application made by an eligible entity, the Administrator may make a grant to the eligible entity to be used for programs to inventory, characterize, assess, and conduct planning related to one or more brownfield sites.

(ii) Site characterization and assessment. A site characterization and assessment carried out with the use of a grant under clause (i) shall be performed in accordance with section 101(35)(B) [42 USC §9601(35)(B)].

(C) Exemption for certain publicly owned brownfield sites—Notwithstanding paragraph (5)(B)(iii), an eligible entity described in any of subparagraphs (A) through (H) of paragraph (1) may receive a grant under this paragraph for property acquired by that eligible entity prior to January 11, 2002, even if the eligible entity does not qualify as a bona fide prospective purchaser, so long as the eligible entity has not caused or contributed to a release or threatened release of a hazardous substance at the property.

(3) Grants and loans for brownfield remediation.

(A) Grants provided by the president. Subject to paragraphs (4) and (5), the President shall establish a program to provide grants to —

(i) eligible entities, to be used for capitalization of revolving loan funds; and

(ii) eligible entities or nonprofit organizations, where warranted, as determined by the President based on considerations under subparagraph (C), to be used directly for remediation of one or more brownfield sites owned by the entity or organization that receives the grant and in amounts not to exceed $500,000 for each site to be remediated, which limit may be waived by the Administrator, but not to exceed a total of $650,000 for each site, based on the anticipated level of contamination, size, or ownership status of the site.

(B) Loans and grants provided by eligible entities. An eligible entity that receives a grant under subparagraph (A)(i) shall use the grant funds to provide assistance for the remediation of brownfield sites in the form of —

    (i) one or more loans to an eligible entity, a site owner, a site developer, or another person; or

    (ii) one or more grants to an eligible entity or other nonprofit organization, where warranted, as determined by the eligible entity that is providing the assistance, based on considerations under subparagraph (C), to remediate sites owned by the eligible entity or nonprofit organization that receives the grant.

(C) Considerations. In determining whether a grant under subparagraph (A)(ii) or (B)(ii) is warranted, the President or the eligible entity, as the case may be, shall take into consideration —

    (i) the extent to which a grant will facilitate the creation of, preservation of, or addition to a park, a greenway, undeveloped property, recreational property, or other property used for nonprofit purposes;

    (ii) the extent to which a grant will meet the needs of a community that has an inability to draw on other sources of funding for environmental remediation and subsequent redevelopment of the area in which a brownfield site is located because of the small population or low income of the community;

    (iii) the extent to which a grant will facilitate the use or reuse of existing infrastructure;

    (iv) the benefit of promoting the long-term availability of funds from a revolving loan fund for brownfield remediation; and

    (v) such other similar factors as the Administrator considers appropriate to consider for the purposes of this subsection.

(D) Transition. Revolving loan funds that have been established before January 11, 2002 may be used in accordance with this paragraph.

(E) Exemption for certain publicly owned brownfield sites

Notwithstanding paragraph (5)(B)(iii), an eligible entity described in any of subparagraphs (A) through (H) of paragraph (1) may receive a grant or loan under this paragraph

for property acquired by that eligible entity prior to January 11, 2002, even if the eligible entity does not qualify as a bona fide prospective purchaser, so long as the eligible entity has not caused or contributed to a release or threatened release of a hazardous substance at the property.

(4) Multipurpose brownfields grants.

    (A) In general.

Subject to subparagraph (D) and paragraphs (5) and (6), the Administrator shall establish a program to provide multipurpose grants to an eligible entity based on the criteria under subparagraph (C) and the considerations under paragraph (3)(C), to carry out inventory, characterization, assessment, planning, or remediation activities at 1 or more brownfield sites in an area proposed by the eligible entity.

    (B) Grant amounts.

        (i) Individual grant amounts

Each grant awarded under this paragraph shall not exceed $1,000,000.

        (ii) Cumulative grant amounts

The total amount of grants awarded for each fiscal year under this paragraph may not exceed 15 percent of the funds made available for the fiscal year to carry out this subsection.

(C) Criteria.

In awarding a grant under this paragraph, the Administrator shall consider the extent to which the eligible entity is able--

    (i) to provide an overall plan for revitalization of the 1 or more brownfield sites in the proposed area in which the multipurpose grant will be used;

    (ii) to demonstrate a capacity to conduct the range of eligible activities that will be funded by the multipurpose grant; and

    (iii) to demonstrate that a multipurpose grant will meet the needs of the 1 or more brownfield sites in the proposed area.

(D) Condition.

As a condition of receiving a grant under this paragraph, each eligible entity shall expend the full amount of the grant by not later than the date that is 5 years after the date on which the grant is awarded to the eligible entity, unless the Administrator provides an extension.

    (E) Ownership.

An eligible entity that receives a grant under this paragraph may not expend any of the grant funds for the remediation of a brownfield site unless the eligible entity owns the brownfield site.

(5) General provisions.

    (A) Maximum grant amount.

(i) Brownfield site characterization and assessment.

(I) In general. A grant under paragraph (2) may be awarded to an eligible entity on a community-wide or site-by-site basis, and shall not exceed, for any individual brownfield site covered by the grant, $200,000.

(II) Waiver. The Administrator may waive the $200,000 limitation under subclause (I) to permit the brownfield site to receive a grant of not to exceed $350,000, based on the anticipated level of contamination, size, or status of ownership of the site.

(ii) Brownfield remediation. A grant under paragraph (3)(A)(i) may be awarded to an eligible entity on a community-wide or site-by-site basis, not to exceed $1,000,000 per eligible entity. The Administrator may make an additional grant to an eligible entity described in the previous sentence for any year after the year for which the initial grant is made, taking into consideration—

(I) the number of sites and number of communities that are addressed by the revolving loan fund;

(II) the demand for funding by eligible entities that have not previously received a grant under this subsection;

(III) the demonstrated ability of the eligible entity to use the revolving loan fund to enhance remediation and provide funds on a continuing basis; and

(IV) such other similar factors as the Administrator considers appropriate to carry out this subsection.

(B) Prohibition.

No part of a grant or loan under this subsection may be used for the payment of—

(i) a penalty or fine;

(ii) a Federal cost-share requirement;

(iii) a response cost at a brownfield site for which the recipient of the grant or loan is potentially liable under section 107 [42 U.S.C. §9607]; or

(iv) a cost of compliance with any Federal law (including a Federal law specified in section 101(39)(B) [42 U.S.C. §9601(39)(B)]), excluding the cost of compliance with laws applicable to the cleanup.

(C) Assistance for development of local government site remediation programs. A local government that receives a grant under this subsection may use not to exceed 10 percent of the grant funds to develop and implement a brownfields program that may include —

(i) monitoring the health of populations exposed to one or more hazardous substances from a brownfield site; and

(ii) monitoring and enforcement of any institutional control used to prevent human exposure to any hazardous substance from a brownfield site.

(D) Insurance. A recipient of a grant or loan awarded under paragraph (2) or (3) that performs a characterization, assessment, or remediation of a brownfield site may use a portion of the grant or loan to purchase insurance for the characterization, assessment, or remediation of that site.

(E) Administrative costs.

(i) In general. An eligible entity may use up to 5 percent of the amounts made available under a grant or loan under this subsection for administrative costs.

(ii) Restriction. For purposes of clause (i), the term "administrative costs" does not include—

(I) investigation and identification of the extent of contamination of a brownfield site;

(II) design and performance of a response action; or

(III) monitoring of a natural resource.

(6) Grant applications.

(A) Submission.

(i) In general.

(I) Application. An eligible entity may submit to the Administrator, through a regional office of the Environmental Protection Agency and in such form as the Administrator may require, an application for a grant under this subsection for one or more brownfield sites (including information on the criteria used by the Administrator to rank applications under subparagraph (C), to the extent that the information is available).

(II) NCP requirements. The Administrator may include in any requirement for submission of an application under subclause (I) a requirement of the National Contingency Plan only to the extent that the requirement is relevant and appropriate to the program under this subsection.

(ii) Coordination. The Administrator shall coordinate with other Federal agencies to assist in making eligible entities aware of other available Federal resources.

(iii) Guidance. The Administrator shall publish guidance to assist eligible entities in applying for grants under this subsection.

(B) Approval. The Administrator shall—

(i) at least annually, complete a review of applications for grants that are received from eligible entities under this subsection; and

(ii) award grants under this subsection to eligible entities that the Administrator determines have the highest rankings under the ranking criteria established under subparagraph (C).

(C) Ranking criteria. The Administrator shall establish a system for ranking grant applications received under this paragraph that includes the following criteria:

(i) The extent to which a grant will stimulate the availability of other funds for environmental assessment or remediation, and subsequent reuse, of an area in which one or more brownfield sites are located.

(ii) The potential of the proposed project or the development plan for an area in which one or more brownfield sites are located to stimulate economic development of the area on completion of the cleanup.

(iii) The extent to which a grant would address or facilitate the identification and reduction of threats to human health and the environment, including threats in areas in which there is a greater-than-normal incidence of diseases or conditions (including cancer, asthma, or birth defects) that may be associated with exposure to hazardous substances, pollutants, or contaminants.

(iv) The extent to which a grant would facilitate the use or reuse of existing infrastructure.

(v) The extent to which a grant would facilitate the creation of, preservation of, or addition to a park, a greenway, undeveloped property, recreational property, or other property used for nonprofit purposes.

(vi) The extent to which a grant would meet the needs of a community that has an inability to draw on other sources of funding for environmental remediation and subsequent redevelopment of the area in which a brownfield site is located because of the small population or low income of the community.

(vii) The extent to which the applicant is eligible for funding from other sources.

(viii) The extent to which a grant will further the fair distribution of funding between urban and nonurban areas.

(ix) The extent to which the grant provides for involvement of the local community in the process of making decisions relating to cleanup and future use of a brownfield site.

(x) The extent to which a grant would address or facilitate the identification and reduction of threats to the health or welfare of children, pregnant women, minority or low-income communities, or other sensitive populations.

(xi) The extent to which a grant would address a site adjacent to a body of water or a federally designated flood plain.

(xii) The extent to which a grant would facilitate—

(I) the location at a brownfield site of a facility that generates renewable electricity from wind, solar, or geothermal energy; or

(II) any energy efficiency improvement project at a brownfield site, including a project for a combined heat and power system or a district energy system.

(D) Report on ranking criteria. Not later than September 30, 2022, the Administrator shall submit to Congress a report regarding the Administrator's use of the ranking criteria described in subparagraph (C) in awarding grants under this subsection.

(7) Implementation of brownfields programs.

(A) Establishment of program. The Administrator may provide, or fund eligible entities or nonprofit organizations to provide, training, research, and technical assistance to individuals and organizations, as appropriate, to facilitate the inventory of brownfield sites, site assessments, remediation of brownfield sites, community involvement, or site preparation.

(B) Funding restrictions. The total Federal funds to be expended by the Administrator under this paragraph shall not exceed 15 percent of the total amount appropriated to carry out this subsection in any fiscal year.

(8) Audits.

(A) In general. The Inspector General of the Environmental Protection Agency shall conduct such reviews or audits of grants and loans under this subsection as the Inspector General considers necessary to carry out this subsection.

(B) Procedure. An audit under this subparagraph shall be conducted in accordance with the auditing procedures of the General Accounting Office, including chapter 75 of Title 31, United States Code [31 U.S.C. §§7501 *et seq.*].

(C) Violations. If the Administrator determines that a person that receives a grant or loan under this subsection has violated or is in violation of a condition of the grant, loan, or applicable Federal law, the Administrator may —

    (i) terminate the grant or loan;

    (ii) require the person to repay any funds received; and

    (iii) seek any other legal remedies available to the Administrator.

(D) Report to Congress. Not later than September 30, 2022, the Inspector General of the Environmental Protection Agency shall submit to Congress a report that provides a description of the management of the program (including a description of the allocation of funds under this subsection).

(9) Leveraging. An eligible entity that receives a grant under this subsection may use the grant funds for a portion of a project at a brownfield site for which funding is received from other sources if the grant funds are used only for the purposes described in paragraph (2), (3), or (4).

(10) Agreements. Each grant or loan made under this subsection shall—

    (A) include a requirement of the National Contingency Plan only to the extent that the requirement is relevant and appropriate to the program under this subsection, as determined by the Administrator; and

    (B) be subject to an agreement that —

        (i) requires the recipient to —

            (I) comply with all applicable Federal and State laws; and

            (II) ensure that the cleanup protects human health and the environment;

        (ii) requires that the recipient use the grant or loan exclusively for purposes specified in paragraph (2), (3), or (4), as applicable;

        (iii) in the case of an application by an eligible entity under paragraph (3)(A), requires the eligible entity to pay a matching share (which may be in the form of a contribution of labor, material, or services) of at least 20 percent, from non-Federal sources of funding, unless the Administrator determines that the matching share would place an undue hardship on the eligible entity; and

        (iv) contains such other terms and conditions as the Administrator determines to be necessary to carry out this subsection.

(11) Facility other than brownfield site. The fact that a facility may not be a brownfield site within the meaning of section 101(39)(A) [42 U.S.C. §9601(39)(A)] has no effect on the eligibility of the facility for assistance under any other provision of Federal law.

(12) Effect on Federal laws. Nothing in this subsection affects any liability or response authority under any Federal law, including —

    (A) this Act (including the last sentence of section 101(14) [42 U.S.C. §9601(14)]);

    (B) the Solid Waste Disposal Act (42 U.S.C. 6901 *et seq.*);

    (C) the Federal Water Pollution Control Act (33 U.S.C. 1251 *et seq.*);

    (D) the Toxic Substances Control Act (15 U.S.C. 2601 *et seq.*); and

    (E) the Safe Drinking Water Act (42 U.S.C. 300f *et seq.*).

(13) Authorization of appropriations. There is authorized to be appropriated to carry out this subsection $200,000,000 for each of fiscal years 2019 through 2023.

§9605. National contingency plan [CERCLA §105]

(a) Revision and republication — Within one hundred and eighty days after December 11, 1980, the President shall, after notice and opportunity for public comments, revise and republish the national contingency plan for the removal of oil and hazardous substances, originally prepared and published pursuant to section 1321 of Title 33, to reflect and effectuate the responsibilities and powers created by this chapter, in addition to those matters specified in section 1321(c)(2) [1] of Title 33. Such revision shall include a section of the plan to be known as the national hazardous substance response plan which shall establish procedures and standards for responding to releases of hazardous substances, pollutants, and contaminants, which shall include at a minimum:

(1) methods for discovering and investigating facilities at which hazardous substances have been disposed of or otherwise come to be located;

(2) methods for evaluating, including analyses of relative cost, and remedying any releases or threats of releases from facilities which pose substantial danger to the public health or the environment;

(3) methods and criteria for determining the appropriate extent of removal, remedy, and other measures authorized by this chapter;

(4) appropriate roles and responsibilities for the Federal, State, and local governments and for interstate and nongovernmental entities in effectuating the plan;

(5) provision for identification, procurement, maintenance, and storage of response equipment and supplies;

(6) a method for and assignment of responsibility for reporting the existence of such facilities which may be located on federally owned or controlled properties and any releases of hazardous substances from such facilities;

(7) means of assuring that remedial action measures are cost-effective over the period of potential exposure to the hazardous substances or contaminated materials;

(8)(A) criteria for determining priorities among releases or threatened releases throughout the United States for the purpose of taking remedial action and, to the extent practicable taking into account the potential urgency of such action, for the purpose of taking removal action. Criteria and priorities under this paragraph shall be based upon relative risk or danger to public health or welfare or the environment, in the judgment of the President, taking into account to the extent possible the population at risk, the hazard potential of the hazardous substances at such facilities, the potential for contamination of drinking water supplies, the potential for direct human contact, the potential for destruction of sensitive ecosystems, the damage to natural resources which may affect the human food chain and which is associated with any release or threatened release, the contamination or potential contamination of the ambient air which is associated with the release or threatened release, State preparedness to assume State costs and responsibilities, and other appropriate factors;

(B) based upon the criteria set forth in subparagraph (A) of this paragraph, the President shall list as part of the plan national priorities among the known releases or threatened releases throughout the United States and shall revise the list no less often than annually. Within one year after December 11, 1980, and annually thereafter, each State shall establish and submit for consideration by the President priorities for remedial action among known releases and potential releases in that State based upon the criteria set forth in subparagraph (A) of this paragraph. In assembling or revising the national list, the President shall consider any priorities established by the States. To the extent practicable, the highest priority facilities shall be designated individually and shall be referred to as the "top priority among known response targets", and, to the extent practicable, shall include among the one hundred highest priority facilities one such facility from each State which shall be the facility designated by the State as presenting the greatest danger to public health or welfare or the environment among the known facilities in such State. State shall be allowed to designate its highest priority facility only once. Other priority facilities or incidents may be listed singly or grouped for response priority purposes;

(9) specified roles for private organizations and entities in preparation for response and in responding to releases of hazardous substances, including identification of appropriate qualifications and capacity therefor and including consideration of minority firms in accordance with subsection (f) of this section; and

(10) standards and testing procedures by which alternative or innovative treatment technologies can be determined to be appropriate for utilization in response actions authorized by this chapter. The plan shall specify procedures, techniques, materials, equipment, and methods to be employed in identifying, removing, or remedying releases of hazardous substances comparable to those required under section 1321(c)(2)(F) and (G) and (j)(1) of Title 33. Following publication of the revised national contingency plan, the response to and actions to minimize damage from hazardous substances releases shall, to the greatest extent possible, be in accordance with the provisions of the plan. The President may, from time to time, revise and republish the national contingency plan.

(b) Revision of plan — Not later than 18 months after the enactment of the Superfund Amendments and Reauthorization Act of 1986 (October 17, 1986), the President shall revise the National Contingency Plan to reflect the requirements of such amendments. The portion of such Plan known as "the National Hazardous Substance Response Plan" shall be revised to provide procedures and standards for remedial actions undertaken pursuant to this chapter which are consistent with amendments made by the Superfund Amendments and Reauthorization Act of 1986 relating to the selection of remedial action.

(c) Hazard ranking system

(1) Revision — Not later than 18 months after October 17, 1986, and after publication of notice and opportunity for submission of comments in accordance with section 553 of Title 5, the President shall by rule promulgate amendments to the hazard ranking system in effect on September 1, 1984. Such amendments shall assure, to the maximum extent feasible, that the hazard ranking system accurately assesses the relative degree of risk to human health and the environment posed by sites and facilities subject to review. The President shall establish an effective date for the amended hazard ranking system which is not later than 24 months after October 17, 1986. Such amended hazard ranking system shall be applied to any site or facility to be newly listed on the National Priorities List after the effective date established by the President. Until such effective date of the regulations, the hazard ranking system in effect on September 1, 1984, shall continue in full force and effect.

(2) Health assessment of water contamination risks — In carrying out this subsection, the President shall ensure that the human health risks associated with the contamination or potential contamination (either directly or as a result of the runoff of any

hazardous substance or pollutant or contaminant from sites or facilities) of surface water are appropriately assessed where such surface water is, or can be, used for recreation or potable water consumption. In making the assessment required pursuant to the preceding sentence, the President shall take into account the potential migration of any hazardous substance or pollutant or contaminant through such surface water to downstream sources of drinking water.

(3) Reevaluation not required — The President shall not be required to reevaluate, after October 17, 1986, the hazard ranking of any facility which was evaluated in accordance with the criteria under this section before the effective date of the amendments to the hazard ranking system under this subsection and which was assigned a national priority under the National Contingency Plan.

(4) New information — Nothing in paragraph (3) shall preclude the President from taking new information into account in undertaking response actions under this chapter.

(d) Petition for assessment of release — Any person who is, or may be, affected by a release or threatened release of a hazardous substance or pollutant or contaminant, may petition the President to conduct a preliminary assessment of the hazards to public health and the environment which are associated with such release or threatened release. If the President has not previously conducted a preliminary assessment of such release, the President shall, within 12 months after the receipt of any such petition, complete such assessment or provide an explanation of why the assessment is not appropriate. If the preliminary assessment indicates that the release or threatened release concerned may pose a threat to human health or the environment, the President shall promptly evaluate such release or threatened release in accordance with the hazard ranking system referred to in paragraph (8)(A) of subsection (a) of this section to determine the national priority of such release or threatened release.

(e) Releases from earlier sites — Whenever there has been, after January 1, 1985, a significant release of hazardous substances or pollutants or contaminants from a site which is listed by the President as a "Site Cleaned Up To Date" on the National Priorities List (revised edition, December 1984) the site shall be restored to the National Priorities List, without application of the hazard ranking system.

(f) Minority contractors — In awarding contracts under this chapter, the President shall consider the availability of qualified minority firms. The President shall describe, as part of any annual report submitted to the Congress under this chapter, the participation of minority firms in contracts carried out under this chapter. Such report shall contain a brief description of the contracts which have been awarded to minority firms under this chapter and of the efforts made by the President to encourage the participation of such firms in programs carried out under this chapter.

(g) Special study wastes

(1) Application — This subsection applies to facilities —

(A) which as of October 17, 1986, were not included on, or proposed for inclusion on, the National Priorities List; and

(B) at which special study wastes described in paragraph (2), (3)(A)(ii) or (3)(A)(iii) of section 6921(b) of this title are present in significant quantities, including any such facility from which there has been a release of a special study waste.

(2) Considerations in adding facilities to NPL — Pending revision of the hazard ranking system under subsection (c) of this section, the President shall consider each of the following factors in adding facilities covered by this section to the National Priorities List:

(A) The extent to which hazard ranking system score for the facility is affected by the presence of any special study waste at, or any release from, such facility.

(B) Available information as to the quantity, toxicity, and concentration of hazardous substances that are constituents of any special study waste at, or released from such facility, the extent of or potential for release of such hazardous constituents, the exposure or potential exposure to human population and the environment, and the degree of hazard to human health or the environment posed by the release of such hazardous constituents at such facility. This subparagraph refers only to available information on actual concentrations of hazardous substances and not on the total quantity of special study waste at such facility.

(3) Savings provisions — Nothing in this subsection shall be construed to limit the authority of the President to remove any facility which as of October 17, 1986, is included on the National Priorities List from such List, or not to list any facility which as of such date is proposed for inclusion on such list.

(4) Information gathering and analysis — Nothing in this chapter shall be construed to preclude the expenditure of monies from the Fund for gathering and analysis of information which will enable the President to consider the specific factors required by paragraph (2).

(h) NPL deferral

(1) Deferral to State voluntary cleanups. At the request of a State and subject to paragraphs (2) and (3), the President generally shall defer final listing of an eligible response site on the National Priorities List if the President determines that—

(A) the State, or another party under an agreement with or order from the State, is conducting a response action at the eligible response site—

    (i) in compliance with a State program that specifically governs response actions for the protection of public health and the environment; and

    (ii) that will provide long-term protection of human health and the environment; or

(B) the State is actively pursuing an agreement to perform a response action described in subparagraph (A) at the site with a person that the State has reason to believe is capable of conducting a response action that meets the requirements of subparagraph (A).

(2) Progress toward cleanup. If, after the last day of the 1-year period beginning on the date on which the President proposes to list an eligible response site on the National Priorities List, the President determines that the State or other party is not making reasonable progress toward completing a response action at the eligible response site, the President may list the eligible response site on the National Priorities List.

(3) Cleanup agreements. With respect to an eligible response site under paragraph (1)(B), if, after the last day of the 1-year period beginning on the date on which the President proposes to list the eligible response site on the National Priorities List, an agreement described in paragraph (1)(B) has not been reached, the President may defer the listing of the eligible response site on the National Priorities List for an additional period of not to exceed 180 days if the President determines deferring the listing would be appropriate based on—

    (A) the complexity of the site;

    (B) substantial progress made in negotiations; and

    (C) other appropriate factors, as determined by the President.

(4) Exceptions. The President may decline to defer, or elect to discontinue a deferral of, a listing of an eligible response site on the National Priorities List if the President determines that—

    (A) deferral would not be appropriate because the State, as an owner or operator or a significant contributor of hazardous substances to the facility, is a potentially responsible party;

    (B) the criteria under the National Contingency Plan for issuance of a health advisory have been met; or

    (C) the conditions in paragraphs (1) through (3), as applicable, are no longer being met.

§9606. Abatement actions
[CERCLA §106]

(a) Maintenance, jurisdiction, etc. — In addition to any other action taken by a State or local government, when the President determines that there may be an imminent and substantial endangerment to the public health or welfare or the environment because of an actual or threatened release of a hazardous substance from a facility, he may require the Attorney General of the United States to secure such relief as may be necessary to abate such danger or threat, and the district court of the United States in the district in which the threat occurs shall have jurisdiction to grant such relief as the public interest and the equities of the case may require. The President may also, after notice to the affected State, take other action under this section including, but not limited to, issuing such orders as may be necessary to protect public health and welfare and the environment.

(b) Fines; reimbursement

(1) Any person who, without sufficient cause, willfully violates, or fails or refuses to comply with, any order of the President under subsection (a) of this section may, in an action brought in the appropriate United States district court to enforce such order, be fined not more than $25,000 for each day in which such violation occurs or such failure to comply continues.

(2)(A) Any person who receives and complies with the terms of any order issued under subsection (a) of this section may, within 60 days after completion of the required action, petition the President for reimbursement from the Fund for the reasonable costs of such action, plus interest. Any interest payable under this paragraph shall accrue on the amounts expended from the date of expenditure at the same rate as specified for interest on investments of the Hazardous Substance Superfund established under subchapter A of chapter 98 of Title 26.

    (B) If the President refuses to grant all or part of a petition made under this paragraph, the petitioner may within 30 days of receipt of such refusal file an action against the President in the appropriate United States district court seeking reimbursement from the Fund.

    (C) Except as provided in subparagraph (D), to obtain reimbursement, the petitioner shall establish by a preponderance of the evidence that it is not liable for response costs under section 9607(a) of this title and that costs for which it seeks reimbursement are reasonable in light of the action required by the relevant order.

    (D) A petitioner who is liable for response costs under section 9607(a) of this title may also recover its reasonable costs of response to the extent that it can demonstrate, on the administrative record, that the President's decision in selecting the response action ordered was arbitrary and capricious or was otherwise not in accordance with law. Reimbursement awarded under this subparagraph shall include all reasonable response costs incurred by the petitioner pursuant to the portions of the order found to be arbitrary and capricious or otherwise not in accordance with law.

(E) Reimbursement awarded by a court under subparagraph (C) or (D) may include appropriate costs, fees, and other expenses in accordance with subsections (a) and (d) of section 2412 of Title 28.

(c) Guidelines for using imminent hazard, enforcement, and emergency response authorities; promulgation by Administrator of EPA, scope, etc. — Within one hundred and eighty days after December 11, 1980, the Administrator of the Environmental Protection Agency shall, after consultation with the Attorney General, establish and publish guidelines for using the imminent hazard, enforcement, and emergency response authorities of this section and other existing statutes administered by the Administrator of the Environmental Protection Agency to effectuate the responsibilities and powers created by this chapter. Such guidelines shall to the extent practicable be consistent with the national hazardous substance response plan, and shall include, at a minimum, the assignment of responsibility for coordinating response actions with the issuance of administrative orders, enforcement of standards and permits, the gathering of information, and other imminent hazard and emergency powers authorized by (1) sections 1321(c)(2), 1318, 1319, and 1364(a) of Title 33, (2) sections 6927, 6928, 6934, and 6973 of this title, (3) sections 300j-4 and 300i of this title, (4) sections 7413, 7414, and 7603 of this title, and (5) section 2606 of Title 15.

§9607. Liability
[CERCLA §107]

(a) Covered persons; scope; recoverable costs and damages; interest rate; "comparable maturity" date — Notwithstanding any other provision or rule of law, and subject only to the defenses set forth in subsection (b) of this section —

(1) the owner and operator of a vessel or a facility,

(2) any person who at the time of disposal of any hazardous substance owned or operated any facility at which such hazardous substances were disposed of,

(3) any person who by contract, agreement, or otherwise arranged for disposal or treatment, or arranged with a transporter for transport for disposal or treatment, of hazardous substances owned or possessed by such person, by any other party or entity, at any facility or incineration vessel owned or operated by another party or entity and containing such hazardous substances, and

(4) any person who accepts or accepted any hazardous substances for transport to disposal or treatment facilities, incineration vessels or sites selected by such person, from which there is a release, or a threatened release which causes the incurrence of response costs, of a hazardous substance, shall be liable for —

(A) all costs of removal or remedial action incurred by the United States Government or a State or an Indian tribe not inconsistent with the national contingency plan;

(B) any other necessary costs of response incurred by any other person consistent with the national contingency plan;

(C) damages for injury to, destruction of, or loss of natural resources, including the reasonable costs of assessing such injury, destruction, or loss resulting from such a release; and

(D) the costs of any health assessment or health effects study carried out under section 9604(i) of this title.

The amounts recoverable in an action under this section shall include interest on the amounts recoverable under subparagraphs (A) through (D). Such interest shall accrue from the later of (i) the date payment of a specified amount is demanded in writing, or (ii) the date of the expenditure concerned. The rate of interest on the outstanding unpaid balance of the amounts recoverable under this section shall be the same rate as is specified for interest on investments of the Hazardous Substance Superfund established under subchapter A of chapter 98 of Title 26. For purposes of applying such amendments to interest under this subsection, the term "comparable maturity" shall be determined with reference to the date on which interest accruing under this subsection commences.

(b) Defenses — There shall be no liability under subsection (a) of this section for a person otherwise liable who can establish by a preponderance of the evidence that the release or threat of release of a hazardous substance and the damages resulting therefrom were caused solely by —

(1) an act of God;

(2) an act of war;

(3) an act or omission of a third party other than an employee or agent of the defendant, or than one whose act or omission occurs in connection with a contractual relationship, existing directly or indirectly, with the defendant (except where the sole contractual arrangement arises from a published tariff and acceptance for carriage by a common carrier by rail), if the defendant establishes by a preponderance of the evidence that (a) he exercised due care with respect to the hazardous substance concerned, taking into consideration the characteristics of such hazardous substance,

in light of all relevant facts and circumstances, and (b) he took precautions against foreseeable acts or omissions of any such third party and the consequences that could foreseeably result from such acts or omissions; or

(4) any combination of the foregoing paragraphs.

(c) Determination of amounts

(1) Except as provided in paragraph (2) of this subsection, the liability under this section of an owner or operator or other responsible person for each release of a hazardous substance or incident involving release of a hazardous substance shall not exceed —

(A) for any vessel, other than an incineration vessel, which carries any hazardous substance as cargo or residue, $300 per gross ton, or $5,000,000, whichever is greater;

(B) for any other vessel, other than an incineration vessel, $300 per gross ton, or $500,000, whichever is greater;

(C) for any motor vehicle, aircraft, hazardous liquid pipeline facility (as defined in section 60101(a) of Title 49), or rolling stock, $50,000,000 or such lesser amount as the President shall establish by regulation, but in no event less than $5,000,000 (or, for releases of hazardous substances as defined in section 9601(14)(A) of this title into the navigable waters, $8,000,000). Such regulations shall take into account the size, type, location, storage, and handling capacity and other matters relating to the likelihood of release in each such class and to the economic impact of such limits on each such class; or

(D) for any incineration vessel or any facility other than those specified in subparagraph (C) of this paragraph, the total of all costs of response plus $50,000,000 for any damages under this subchapter.

(2) Notwithstanding the limitations in paragraph (1) of this subsection, the liability of an owner or operator or other responsible person under this section shall be the full and total costs of response and damages, if (A)(i) the release or threat of release of a hazardous substance was the result of willful misconduct or willful negligence within the privity or knowledge of such person, or (ii) the primary cause of the release was a violation (within the privity or knowledge of such person) of applicable safety, construction, or operating standards or regulations;or (B) such person fails or refuses to provide all reasonable cooperation and assistance requested by a responsible public official in connection with response activities under the national contingency plan with respect to regulated carriers subject to the provisions of Title 49 or vessels subject to the provisions of Title 33, 46, or 46 Appendix, subparagraph (A)(ii) of this paragraph

shall be deemed to refer to Federal standards or regulations.

(3) If any person who is liable for a release or threat of release of a hazardous substance fails without sufficient cause to properly provide removal or remedial action upon order of the President pursuant to section 9604 or 9606 of this title, such person may be liable to the United States for punitive damages in an amount at least equal to, and not more than three times, the amount of any costs incurred by the Fund as a result of such failure to take proper action. The President is authorized to commence a civil action against any such person to recover the punitive damages, which shall be in addition to any costs recovered from such person pursuant to section 9612(c) of this title. Any moneys received by the United States pursuant to this subsection shall be deposited in the Fund.

(d) Rendering care or advice

(1) In general — Except as provided in paragraph (2), no person shall be liable under this subchapter for costs or damages as a result of actions taken or omitted in the course of rendering care, assistance, or advice in accordance with the National Contingency Plan ("NCP") or at the direction of an onscene coordinator appointed under such plan, with respect to an incident creating a danger to public health or welfare or the environment as a result of any releases of a hazardous substance or the threat thereof. This paragraph shall not preclude liability for costs or damages as the result of negligence on the part of such person.

(2) State and local governments — No State or local government shall be liable under this subchapter for costs or damages as a result of actions taken in response to an emergency created by the release or threatened release of a hazardous substance generated by or from a facility owned by another person. This paragraph shall not preclude liability for costs or damages as a result of gross negligence or intentional misconduct by the State or local government. For the purpose of the preceding sentence, reckless, willful, or wanton misconduct shall constitute gross negligence.

(3) Savings provision — This subsection shall not alter the liability of any person covered by the provisions of paragraph (1), (2), (3), or (4) of subsection (a) of this section with respect to the release or threatened release concerned.

(e) Indemnification, hold harmless, etc., agreements or conveyances; subrogation rights

(1) No indemnification, hold harmless, or similar agreement or conveyance shall be effective to transfer from the owner or operator of any vessel or facility or from any person who may be liable for a release or threat of release under this section, to any other person the liability imposed

under this section. Nothing in this subsection shall bar any agreement to insure, hold harmless, or indemnify a party to such agreement for any liability under this section.

(2) Nothing in this subchapter, including the provisions of paragraph (1) of this subsection, shall bar a cause of action that an owner or operator or any other person subject to liability under this section, or a guarantor, has or would have, by reason of subrogation or otherwise against any person.

(f) Natural resources liability; designation of public trustees of natural resources

(1) Natural resources liability — In the case of an injury to, destruction of, or loss of natural resources under subparagraph (C) of subsection (a) liability shall be to the United States Government and to any State for natural resources within the State or belonging to, managed by, controlled by, or appertaining to such State and to any Indian tribe for natural resources belonging to, managed by, controlled by, or appertaining to such tribe, or held in trust for the benefit of such tribe, or belonging to a member of such tribe if such resources are subject to a trust restriction on alienation: Provided, however, That no liability to the United States or State or Indian tribe shall be imposed under subparagraph (C) of subsection (a) where the party sought to be charged has demonstrated that the damages to natural resources complained of were specifically identified as an irreversible and irretrievable commitment of natural resources in an environmental impact statement, or other comparable environment analysis, and the decision to grant a permit or license authorizes such commitment of natural resources, and the facility or project was otherwise operating within the terms of its permit or license, so long as, in the case of damages to an Indian tribe occurring pursuant to a Federal permit or license, the issuance of that permit or license was not inconsistent with the fiduciary duty of the United States with respect to such Indian tribe. The President, or the authorized representative of any State, shall act on behalf of the public as trustee of such natural resources to recover for such damages. Sums recovered by the United States Government as trustee under this subsection shall be retained by the trustee, without further appropriation, for use only to restore, replace, or acquire the equivalent of such natural resources. Sums recovered by a State as trustee under this subsection shall be available for use only to restore, replace, or acquire the equivalent of such natural resources by the State. The measure of damages in any action under subparagraph (C) of subsection (a) shall not be limited by the sums which can be used to restore or replace such resources. There shall be no double recovery under this chapter for

natural resource damages, including the costs of damage assessment or restoration, rehabilitation, or acquisition for the same release and natural resource. There shall be no recovery under the authority of subparagraph (C) of subsection (a) where such damages and the release of a hazardous substance from which such damages resulted have occurred wholly before December 11, 1980.

(2) Designation of Federal and State officials

(A) Federal — The President shall designate in the National Contingency Plan published under section 9605 of this title the Federal officials who shall act on behalf of the public as trustees for natural resources under this chapter and section 1321 of Title 33. Such officials shall assess damages for injury to, destruction of, or loss of natural resources for purposes of this chapter and such section 1321 of Title 33 for those resources under their trusteeship and may, upon request of and reimbursement from a State and at the Federal officials' discretion, assess damages for those natural resources under the State's trusteeship.

(B) State — The Governor of each State shall designate State officials who may act on behalf of the public as trustees for natural resources under this chapter and section 1321 of Title 33 and shall notify the President of such designations. Such State officials shall assess damages to natural resources for the purposes of this chapter and such section 1321 of Title 33 for those natural resources under their trusteeship.

(C) Rebuttable presumption — Any determination or assessment of damages to natural resources for the purposes of this chapter and section 1321 of Title 33 made by a Federal or State trustee in accordance with the regulations promulgated under section 9651(c) of this title shall have the force and effect of a rebuttable presumption on behalf of the trustee in any administrative or judicial proceeding under this chapter or section 1321 of Title 33.

(g) Federal agencies — For provisions relating to Federal agencies, see section 9620 of this title.

(h) Owner or operator of vessel — The owner or operator of a vessel shall be liable in accordance with this section, under maritime tort law, and as provided under section 9614 of this title notwithstanding any provision of the Act of March 3, 1851 (46 U.S.C. §183ff) [46 App. U.S.C. §§182, 183, 184-188] or the absence of any physical damage to the proprietary interest of the claimant.

(i) Application of a registered pesticide product — No person (including the United States or any State or Indian tribe) may recover under the authority of this section for any response costs or damages resulting from the application of a pesticide product registered under the Federal Insecticide, Fungicide, and Rodenticide Act [7 U.S.C. §§136 *et seq.*]. Nothing in this paragraph shall affect or modify in any way the obligations or liability of any person under any other provision of State or Federal law, including common law, for damages, injury, or loss resulting from a release of any hazardous substance or for removal or remedial action or the costs of removal or remedial action of such hazardous substance.

(j) Obligations or liability pursuant to federally permitted release — Recovery by any person (including the United States or any State or Indian tribe) for response costs or damages resulting from a federally permitted release shall be pursuant to existing law in lieu of this section. Nothing in this paragraph shall affect or modify in any way the obligations or liability of any person under any other provision of State or Federal law, including common law, for damages, injury, or loss resulting from a release of any hazardous substance or for removal or remedial action or the costs of removal or remedial action of such hazardous substance. In addition, costs of response incurred by the Federal Government in connection with a discharge specified in section 9601(10)(B) or (C) of this title shall be recoverable in an action brought under section 1319(b) of Title 33.

(k) Transfer to, and assumption by, Post-Closure Liability Fund of liability of owner or operator of hazardous waste disposal facility in receipt of permit under applicable solid waste disposal law; time, criteria applicable, procedures, etc.; monitoring costs; reports

(1) The liability established by this section or any other law for the owner or operator of a hazardous waste disposal facility which has received a permit under subtitle C of the Solid Waste Disposal Act [42 U.S.C. §§6921 *et seq.*], shall be transferred to and assumed by the Post-closure Liability Fund established by section 9641 of this title when —

(A) such facility and the owner and operator thereof has complied with the requirements of subtitle C of the Solid Waste Disposal Act [42 U.S.C. §§6921 *et seq.*] and regulations issued thereunder, which may affect the performance of such facility after closure; and

(B) such facility has been closed in accordance with such regulations and the conditions of such permit, and such facility and the surrounding area have been monitored as required by such regulations and permit conditions for a period not to exceed five years after closure to demonstrate that there is no substantial likelihood that any migration offsite or release from confinement of any hazardous substance or other risk to public health or welfare will occur.

(2) Such transfer of liability shall be effective ninety days after the owner or operator of such facility notifies the Administrator of the Environmental Protection Agency (and the State where it has an authorized program under section 3006(b) of the Solid Waste Disposal Act (42 U.S.C. §6926(b))) that the conditions imposed by this subsection have been satisfied. If within such ninety-day period the Administrator of the Environmental Protection Agency or such State determines that any such facility has not complied with all the conditions imposed by this subsection or that insufficient information has been provided to demonstrate such compliance, the Administrator or such State shall so notify the owner and operator of such facility and the administrator of the Fund established by section 9641 of this title, and the owner and operator of such facility shall continue to be liable with respect to such facility under this section and other law until such time as the Administrator and such State determines that such facility has complied with all conditions imposed by this subsection. A determination by the Administrator or such State that a facility has not complied with all conditions imposed by this subsection or that insufficient information has been supplied to demonstrate compliance, shall be a final administrative action for purposes of judicial review. A request for additional information shall state in specific terms the data required.

(3) In addition to the assumption of liability of owners and operators under paragraph (1) of this subsection, the Post-closure Liability Fund established by section 9641 of this title may be used to pay costs of monitoring and care and maintenance of a site incurred by other persons after the period of monitoring required by regulations under subtitle C of the Solid Waste Disposal Act [42 U.S.C. §§6921 *et seq.*] for hazardous waste disposal facilities meeting the conditions of paragraph (1) of this subsection.

(4)(A) Not later than one year after December 11, 1980, the Secretary of the Treasury shall conduct a study and shall submit a report thereon to the Congress on the feasibility of establishing or qualifying an optional system of private insurance for postclosure financial responsibility for hazardous waste disposal facilities to which this subsection applies. Such study shall include a specification of adequate and realistic minimum standards to assure that any such privately placed insurance will carry out the purposes of this subsection in a reliable, enforceable, and practical manner. Such a study shall include an examination of the public and private incentives, programs, and actions necessary to make privately placed insurance a practical and effective option to the financing system for the Post-closure Liability Fund provided in subchapter II of this chapter.

(B) Not later than eighteen months after December 11, 1980, and after a public hearing, the President shall by rule determine whether or not it is feasible to establish or qualify an optional system of private insurance for post-closure financial responsibility for hazardous waste disposal facilities to which this subsection applies. If the President determines the establishment or qualification of such a system would be infeasible, he shall promptly publish an explanation of the reasons for such a determination. If the President determines the establishment or qualification of such a system would be feasible, he shall promptly publish notice of such determination. Not later than six months after an affirmative determination under the preceding sentence and after a public hearing, the President shall by rule promulgate adequate and realistic minimum standards which must be met by any such privately placed insurance, taking into account the purposes of this chapter and this subsection. Such rules shall also specify reasonably expeditious procedures by which privately placed insurance plans can qualify as meeting such minimum standards.

(C) In the event any privately placed insurance plan qualifies under subparagraph (B), any person enrolled in, and complying with the terms of, such plan shall be excluded from the provisions of paragraphs (1), (2), and (3) of this subsection and exempt from the requirements to pay any tax or fee to the Post-closure Liability Fund under subchapter II of this chapter.

(D) The President may issue such rules and take such other actions as are necessary to effectuate the purposes of this paragraph.

(5) Suspension of liability transfer — Notwithstanding paragraphs (1), (2), (3), and (4) of this subsection and subsection (j) of section 9611 of this title, no liability shall be transferred to or assumed by the Post-Closure Liability Trust Fund established by section 9641 of this title prior to completion of the study required under paragraph (6) of this subsection, transmission of a report of such study to both Houses of Congress, and authorization of such a transfer or assumption by Act of Congress following receipt of such study and report.

(6) Study of options for post-closure program —

(A) Study — The Comptroller General shall conduct a study of options for a program for the management of the liabilities associated with hazardous waste treatment, storage, and disposal sites after their closure which complements the policies set forth in the Hazardous and Solid Waste Amendments of 1984 and assures the protection of human health and the environment.

(B) Program elements — The program referred to in subparagraph (A) shall be designed to assure each of the following:

(i) Incentives are created and maintained for the safe management and disposal of hazardous wastes so as to assure protection of human health and the environment.

(ii) Members of the public will have reasonable confidence that hazardous wastes will be managed and disposed of safely and that resources will be available to address any problems that may arise and to cover costs of long-term monitoring, care, and maintenance of such sites.

(iii) Persons who are or seek to become owners and operators of hazardous waste disposal facilities will be able to manage their potential future liabilities and to attract the investment capital necessary to build, operate, and close such facilities in a manner which assures protection of human health and the environment.

(C) Assessments — The study under this paragraph shall include assessments of treatment, storage, and disposal facilities which have been or are likely to be issued a permit under section 3005 of the Solid Waste Disposal Act (42 U.S.C. §6925) and the likelihood of future insolvency on the part of owners and operators of such facilities. Separate assessments shall be made for different classes of facilities and for different classes of land disposal facilities and shall include but not be limited to —

(i) the current and future financial capabilities of facility owners and operators;

(ii) the current and future costs associated with facilities, including the costs of routine monitoring and maintenance, compliance monitoring, corrective action, natural resource damages, and liability for damages to third parties; and

(iii) the availability of mechanisms by which owners and operators of such facilities can assure that current and future costs, including post-closure costs, will be financed.

(D) Procedures — In carrying out the responsibilities of this paragraph, the Comptroller General shall consult with the Administrator, the Secretary of Commerce, the Secretary of the Treasury, and the heads of other appropriate Federal agencies.

(E) Consideration of options — In conducting the study under this paragraph, the Comptroller General shall consider various mechanisms and combinations of mechanisms to complement the policies set forth in the Hazardous and Solid Waste Amendments of 1984 to serve the purposes set forth in subparagraph (B) and to assure that the current and future costs associated with hazardous waste facilities, including post-closure costs, will be adequately financed and, to the greatest extent possible, borne by the owners and operators of such facilities. Mechanisms to be considered include, but are not limited to —

(i) revisions to closure, post-closure, and financial responsibility requirements under subtitles C and I of the Solid Waste Disposal Act [42 U.S.C. §§6921 *et seq.*, §§6991 *et seq.*];

(ii) voluntary risk pooling by owners and operators;

(iii) legislation to require risk pooling by owners and operators;

(iv) modification of the Post-Closure Liability Trust Fund previously established by section 9641 of this title, and the conditions for transfer of liability under this subsection, including limiting the transfer of some or all liability under this subsection only in the case of insolvency of owners and operators;

(v) private insurance;

(vi) insurance provided by the Federal Government;

(vii) coinsurance, reinsurance, or pooled-risk insurance, whether provided by the private sector or provided or assisted by the Federal Government; and

(viii) creation of a new program to be administered by a new or existing Federal agency or by a federally chartered corporation.

(F) Recommendations — The Comptroller General shall consider options for funding any program under this section and shall, to the extent necessary, make recommendations to the appropriate committees of Congress for additional authority to implement such program.

(l) Federal lien

(1) In general — All costs and damages for which a person is liable to the United States under subsection (a) of this section (other than the owner or operator of a vessel under paragraph (1) of subsection (a) shall constitute a lien in favor of the United States upon all real property and rights to such property which —

(A) belong to such person; and

(B) are subject to or affected by a removal or remedial action.

(2) Duration — The lien imposed by this subsection shall arise at the later of the following:

(A) The time costs are first incurred by the United States with respect to a response action under this chapter.

(B) The time that the person referred to in paragraph (1) is provided (by certified or registered mail) written notice of potential liability.

Such lien shall continue until the liability for the costs (or a judgment against the person arising out of such liability) is satisfied or becomes unenforceable through operation of the statute of limitations provided in section 9613 of this title.

(3) Notice and validity — The lien imposed by this subsection shall be subject to the rights of any purchaser, holder of a security interest, or judgment lien creditor whose interest is perfected under applicable State law before notice of the lien has been filed in the appropriate office within the State (or county or other governmental subdivision), as designated by State law, in which the real property subject to the lien is located. Any such purchaser, holder of a security interest, or judgment lien creditor shall be afforded the same protections against the lien imposed by this subsection as are afforded under State law against a judgment lien which arises out of an unsecured obligation and which arises as of the time of the filing of the notice of the lien imposed by this subsection. If the State has not by law designated one office for the receipt of such notices of liens, the notice shall be filed in the office of the clerk of the United States district court for the district in which the real property is located. For purposes of this subsection, the terms "purchaser" and "security interest" shall have the definitions provided under section 6323(h) of Title 26.

(4) Action in rem — The costs constituting the lien may be recovered in an action in rem in the United States district court for the district in which the removal or remedial action is occurring or has occurred. Nothing in this subsection shall affect the right of the United States to bring an action against any person to recover all costs and damages for which such person is liable under subsection (a) of this section.

(m) Maritime lien — All costs and damages for which the owner or operator of a vessel is liable under subsection (a)(1) with respect to a release or threatened release from such vessel shall constitute a maritime lien in favor of the United States on such vessel. Such costs may be recovered in an action in rem in the district court of the United States for the district in which the vessel may be found. Nothing in this subsection shall affect the right of the United States to bring an action against the owner or operator of such vessel in any court of competent jurisdiction to recover such costs.

(n) Liability of fiduciaries

(1) In general — The liability of a fiduciary under any provision of this chapter for the release or threatened release of a hazardous substance at, from, or in connection with a vessel or facility held in a fiduciary capacity shall not exceed the assets held in the fiduciary capacity.

(2) Exclusion — Paragraph (1) does not apply to the extent that a person is liable under this chapter independently of the person's ownership of a vessel or facility as a fiduciary or actions taken in a fiduciary capacity.

(3) Limitation — Paragraphs (1) and (4) do not limit the liability pertaining to a release or threatened release of a hazardous substance if negligence of a fiduciary causes or contributes to the release or threatened release.

(4) Safe harbor — A fiduciary shall not be liable in its personal capacity under this chapter for —

(A) undertaking or directing another person to undertake a response action under subsection (d)(1) or under the direction of an on scene coordinator designated under the National Contingency Plan;

(B) undertaking or directing another person to undertake any other lawful means of addressing a hazardous substance in connection with the vessel or facility;

(C) terminating the fiduciary relationship;

(D) including in the terms of the fiduciary agreement a covenant, warranty, or other term or condition that relates to compliance with an environmental law, or monitoring, modifying or enforcing the term or condition;

(E) monitoring or undertaking 1 or more inspections of the vessel or facility;

(F) providing financial or other advice or counseling to other parties to the fiduciary relationship, including the settlor or beneficiary;

(G) restructuring, renegotiating, or otherwise altering the terms and conditions of the fiduciary relationship;

(H) administering, as a fiduciary, a vessel or facility that was contaminated before the fiduciary relationship began; or

(I) declining to take any of the actions described in subparagraphs (B) through (H).

(5) Definitions — As used in this chapter:

(A) Fiduciary — The term "fiduciary" —

(i) means a person acting for the benefit of another party as a bona fide —

(I)　trustee;

(II)　executor;

(III) administrator;

(IV) custodian;

(V)　guardian of estates or guardian ad litem;

(VI) receiver;

(VII) conservator;

(VIII) committee of estates of incapacitated persons;

(IX)　personal representative;

(X)　trustee (including a successor to a trustee) under an indenture agreement, trust agreement, lease, or similar financing agreement, for debt securities, certificates of interest or certificates of participation in debt securities, or other forms of indebtedness as to which the trustee is not, in the capacity of trustee, the lender; or

(XI) representative in any other capacity that the Administrator, after providing public notice, determines to be similar to the capacities described in subclauses (I) through (X); and

(ii) does not include —

(I) a person that is acting as a fiduciary with respect to a trust or other fiduciary estate that was organized for the primary purpose of, or is engaged in, actively carrying on a trade or business for profit, unless the trust or other fiduciary estate was created as part of, or to facilitate, 1 or more estate plans or because of the incapacity of a natural person; or

(II)　a person that acquires ownership or control of a vessel or facility with the objective purpose of avoiding liability of the person or of any other person.

(B) Fiduciary capacity — The term "fiduciary capacity" means the capacity of a person in holding title to a vessel or facility, or otherwise having control of or an interest in the vessel or facility, pursuant to the exercise of the responsibilities of the person as a fiduciary.

(6) Savings clause — Nothing in this subsection —

(A) affects the rights or immunities or other defenses that are available under this chapter or other law that is applicable to a person subject to this subsection; or

(B) creates any liability for a person or a private right of action against a fiduciary or any other person.

(7) No effect on certain persons — Nothing in this subsection applies to a person if the person —

(A)(i) acts in a capacity other than that of a fiduciary or in a beneficiary capacity; and

(ii) in that capacity, directly or indirectly benefits from a trust or fiduciary relationship; or

(B)(i) is a beneficiary and a fiduciary with respect to the same fiduciary estate; and

(ii) as a fiduciary, receives benefits that exceed customary or reasonable compensation, and incidental benefits, permitted under other applicable law.

(8) Limitation — This subsection does not preclude a claim under this chapter against —

(A) the assets of the estate or trust administered by the fiduciary; or

(B) a nonemployee agent or independent contractor retained by a fiduciary.

(o) De micromis exemption

(1) In general. Except as provided in paragraph (2), a person shall not be liable, with respect to response costs at a facility on the National Priorities List, under this Act if liability is based solely on paragraph (3) or (4) of subsection (a), and the person, except as provided in paragraph (4) of this subsection, can demonstrate that—

(A) the total amount of the material containing hazardous substances that the person arranged for disposal or treatment of, arranged with a transporter for transport for disposal or treatment of, or accepted for transport for disposal or treatment, at the facility was less than 110 gallons of liquid materials or less than 200 pounds of solid materials (or such greater or lesser amounts as the Administrator may determine by regulation); and

(B) all or part of the disposal, treatment, or transport concerned occurred before April 1, 2001.

(2) Exceptions. Paragraph (1) shall not apply in a case in which—

(A) the President determines that —

(i) the materials containing hazardous substances referred to in paragraph (1) have contributed significantly or could contribute significantly, either individually or in the aggregate, to the cost of the response action or natural resource restoration with respect to the facility; or

(ii) the person has failed to comply with an information request or administrative subpoena issued by the President under this Act or has impeded or is impeding, through action or inaction, the performance of a response action or natural resource restoration with respect to the facility; or

(B) a person has been convicted of a criminal violation for the conduct to which the exemption would apply, and that conviction has not been vitiated on appeal or otherwise.

(3) No judicial review. A determination by the President under paragraph (2)(A) shall not be subject to judicial review.

(4) Nongovernmental third-party contribution actions. In the case of a contribution action, with respect to response costs at a facility on the National Priorities List, brought by a party, other than a Federal, State, or local government, under this Act, the burden of proof shall be on the party bringing the action to demonstrate that the conditions described in paragraph (1)(A) and (B) of this subsection are not met.

(p) Municipal solid waste exemption

(1) In general. Except as provided in paragraph (2) of this subsection, a person shall not be liable, with respect to response costs at a facility on the National Priorities List, under paragraph (3) of subsection (a) for municipal solid waste disposed of at a facility if the person, except as provided in paragraph (5) of this subsection, can demonstrate that the person is—

(A) an owner, operator, or lessee of residential property from which all of the person's municipal solid waste was generated with respect to the facility;

(B) a business entity (including a parent, subsidiary, or affiliate of the entity) that, during its 3 taxable years preceding the date of transmittal of written notification from the President of its potential liability under this section, employed on average not more than 100 full-time individuals, or the equivalent thereof, and that is a small business concern (within the meaning of the Small Business Act (15 U.S.C. 631 *et seq.*)) from which was generated all of the municipal solid waste attributable to the entity with respect to the facility; or

(C) an organization described in section 501(c)(3) of the Internal Revenue Code of 1986 [26 U.S.C. §501(c)(3)] and exempt from tax under section 501(a) of such Code [26 U.S.C. §501(a)] that, during its taxable year preceding the date of transmittal of written notification from the President of its potential liability under this section, employed not more than 100 paid individuals at the location from which was generated all of the municipal solid waste attributable to the organization with respect to the facility. For purposes of this subsection, the term "affiliate" has the meaning of that term provided in the definition of "small business concern" in regulations promulgated by the Small Business Administration in accordance with the Small Business Act (15 U.S.C. 631 *et seq.*).

(2) Exception. Paragraph (1) shall not apply in a case in which the President determines that—

(A) the municipal solid waste referred to in paragraph (1) has contributed significantly or could contribute significantly, either individually or in the aggregate, to the cost of the response action or natural resource restoration with respect to the facility;

(B) the person has failed to comply with an information request or administrative subpoena issued by the President under this Act; or

(C) the person has impeded or is impeding, through action or inaction, the performance of a response action or natural resource restoration with respect to the facility.

(3) No judicial review. A determination by the President under paragraph (2) shall not be subject to judicial review.

(4) Definition of municipal solid waste.

(A) In general. For purposes of this subsection, the term "municipal solid waste" means waste material—

    (i) generated by a household (including a single or multifamily residence); and

    (ii) generated by a commercial, industrial, or institutional entity, to the extent that the waste material—

        (I) is essentially the same as waste normally generated by a household;

        (II) is collected and disposed of with other municipal solid waste as part of normal municipal solid waste collection services; and

        (III) contains a relative quantity of hazardous substances no greater than the relative quantity of hazardous substances contained in waste material generated by a typical single-family household.

(B) Examples. Examples of municipal solid waste under subparagraph (A) include food and yard waste, paper, clothing, appliances, consumer product packaging, disposable diapers, office supplies, cosmetics, glass and metal food containers, elementary or secondary school science laboratory waste, and household hazardous waste.

(C) Exclusions. The term "municipal solid waste" does not include—

    (i) combustion ash generated by resource recovery facilities or municipal incinerators; or

    (ii) waste material from manufacturing or processing operations (including pollution control operations) that is not essentially the same as waste normally generated by households.

(5) Burden of proof. In the case of an action, with respect to response costs at a facility on the National Priorities List, brought under section 107 or 113 [this section or 42 U.S.C. §9613] by—

(A) a party, other than a Federal, State, or local government, with respect to municipal solid waste disposed of on or after April 1, 2001; or

(B) any party with respect to municipal solid waste disposed of before April 1, 2001, the burden of proof shall be on the party bringing the action to demonstrate that the conditions described in paragraphs (1) and (4) for exemption for entities and organizations described in paragraph (1)(B) and (C) are not met.

(6) Certain actions not permitted. No contribution action may be brought by a party, other than a Federal, State, or local government, under this Act with respect to circumstances described in paragraph (1)(A).

(7) Costs and fees. A nongovernmental entity that commences, after the date of the enactment of this subsection, a contribution action under this Act shall be liable to the defendant for all reasonable costs of defending the action, including all reasonable attorney's fees and expert witness fees, if the defendant is not liable for contribution based on an exemption under this subsection or subsection (o).

(q) Contiguous properties

(1) Not considered to be an owner or operator.

(A) In general. A person that owns real property that is contiguous to or otherwise similarly situated with respect to, and that is or may be contaminated by a release or threatened release of a hazardous substance from, real property that is not owned by that person shall not be considered to be an owner or operator of a vessel or facility under paragraph (1) or (2) of subsection (a) solely by reason of the contamination if—

    (i) the person did not cause, contribute, or consent to the release or threatened release;

    (ii) the person is not—

        (I) potentially liable, or affiliated with any other person that is potentially liable, for response costs at a facility through any direct or indirect familial relationship or any contractual, corporate, or financial relationship (other than a contractual, corporate, or financial relationship that is created by a contract for the sale of goods or services); or

        (II) the result of a reorganization of a business entity that was potentially liable;

    (iii) the person takes reasonable steps to —

        (I) stop any continuing release;

        (II) prevent any threatened future release; and

        (III) prevent or limit human, environmental, or natural resource exposure to any hazardous substance released on or from property owned by that person;

    (iv) the person provides full cooperation, assistance, and access to persons that are authorized to conduct response actions or natural resource restoration at the vessel or facility from which there has been a release or threatened release (including the cooperation and access necessary for the installation, integrity, operation, and maintenance of any complete or partial response action or natural resource restoration at the vessel or facility);

    (v) the person—

(I) is in compliance with any land use restrictions established or relied on in connection with the response action at the facility; and

(II) does not impede the effectiveness or integrity of any institutional control employed in connection with a response action;

(vi) the person is in compliance with any request for information or administrative subpoena issued by the President under this Act;

(vii) the person provides all legally required notices with respect to the discovery or release of any hazardous substances at the facility; and

(viii) at the time at which the person acquired the property, the person—

(I) conducted all appropriate inquiry within the meaning of section 101(35)(B) [42 U.S.C. §9601(35)(B)] with respect to the property; and

(II) did not know or have reason to know that the property was or could be contaminated by a release or threatened release of one or more hazardous substances from other real property not owned or operated by the person.

(B) Demonstration. To qualify as a person described in subparagraph (A), a person must establish by a preponderance of the evidence that the conditions in clauses (i) through (viii) of subparagraph (A) have been met.

(C) Bona fide prospective purchaser. Any person that does not qualify as a person described in this paragraph because the person had, or had reason to have, knowledge specified in subparagraph (A)(viii) at the time of acquisition of the real property may qualify as a bona fide prospective purchaser under section 101(40) [42 U.S.C. 9601(40)] if the person is otherwise described in that section.

(D) Ground water. With respect to a hazardous substance from one or more sources that are not on the property of a person that is a contiguous property owner that enters ground water beneath the property of the person solely as a result of subsurface migration in an aquifer, subparagraph (A)(iii) shall not require the person to conduct ground water investigations or to install ground water remediation systems, except in accordance with the policy of the Environmental Protection Agency concerning owners of property containing contaminated aquifers, dated May 24, 1995.

(2) Effect of law. With respect to a person described in this subsection, nothing in this subsection—

(A) limits any defense to liability that may be available to the person under any other provision of law; or

(B) imposes liability on the person that is not otherwise imposed by subsection (a).

(3) Assurances. The Administrator may—

(A) issue an assurance that no enforcement action under this Act will be initiated against a person described in paragraph (1); and

(B) grant a person described in paragraph (1) protection against a cost recovery or contribution action under section 113(f) [42 U.S.C. §9613(f)].

(r) Prospective purchaser and windfall lien

(1) Limitation on liability. Notwithstanding subsection (a)(1), a bona fide prospective purchaser whose potential liability for a release or threatened release is based solely on the bona fide prospective purchaser being considered to be an owner or operator of a facility shall not be liable as long as the bona fide prospective purchaser does not impede the performance of a response action or natural resource restoration.

(2) Lien. If there are unrecovered response costs incurred by the United States at a facility for which an owner of the facility is not liable by reason of paragraph (1), and if each of the conditions described in paragraph (3) is met, the United States shall have a lien on the facility, or may by agreement with the owner, obtain from the owner a lien on any other property or other assurance of payment satisfactory to the Administrator, for the unrecovered response costs.

(3) Conditions. The conditions referred to in paragraph (2) are the following:

(A) Response action. A response action for which there are unrecovered costs of the United States is carried out at the facility.

(B) Fair market value. The response action increases the fair market value of the facility above the fair market value of the facility that existed before the response action was initiated.

(4) Amount; duration. A lien under paragraph (2) —

(A) shall be in an amount not to exceed the increase in fair market value of the property attributable to the response action at the time of a sale or other disposition of the property;

(B) shall arise at the time at which costs are first incurred by the United States with respect to a response action at the facility;

(C) shall be subject to the requirements of subsection (*l*)(3); and

(D) shall continue until the earlier of—

(i) satisfaction of the lien by sale or other means; or

(ii) notwithstanding any statute of limitations under section 113 [42 U.S.C. §§9613], recovery of all response costs incurred at the facility.

§9608. Financial responsibility
[CERCLA §108]

(a) Establishment and maintenance by owner or operator of vessel; amount; failure to obtain certification of compliance

(1) The owner or operator of each vessel (except a nonself-propelled barge that does not carry hazardous substances as cargo) over three hundred gross tons that uses any port or place in the United States or the navigable waters or any offshore facility, shall establish and maintain, in accordance with regulations promulgated by the President, evidence of financial responsibility of $300 per gross ton (or for a vessel carrying hazardous substances as cargo, or $5,000,000, whichever is greater) to cover the liability prescribed under paragraph (1) of section 9607(a) of this title. Financial responsibility may be established by any one, or any combination, of the following: insurance, guarantee, surety bond, or qualification as a self-insurer. Any bond filed shall be issued by a bonding company authorized to do business in the United States. In cases where an owner or operator owns, operates, or charters more than one vessel subject to this subsection, evidence of financial responsibility need be established only to meet the maximum liability applicable to the largest of such vessels.

(2) The Secretary of the Treasury shall withhold or revoke the clearance required by section 91 of Title 46, Appendix, of any vessel subject to this subsection that does not have certification furnished by the President that the financial responsibility provisions of paragraph (1) of this subsection have been complied with.

(3) The Secretary of Transportation, in accordance with regulations issued by him, shall (A) deny entry to any port or place in the United States or navigable waters to, and (B) detain at the port or place in the United States from which it is about to depart for any other port or place in the United States, any vessel subject to this subsection that, upon request, does not produce certification furnished by the President that the financial responsibility provisions of paragraph (1) of this subsection have been complied with.

(4) In addition to the financial responsibility provisions of paragraph (1) of this subsection, the President shall require additional evidence of financial responsibility for incineration vessels in such amounts, and to cover such liabilities recognized by law, as the President deems appropriate, taking into account the potential risks posed by incineration and transport for incineration, and any other factors deemed relevant.

(b) Establishment and maintenance by owner or operator of production, etc., facilities; amount; adjustment; consolidated form of responsibility; coverage of motor carriers

(1) Beginning not earlier than five years after December 11, 1980, the President shall promulgate requirements (for facilities in addition to those under subtitle C of the Solid Waste Disposal Act [42 U.S.C. §§6921 *et seq.*] and other Federal law) that classes of facilities establish and maintain evidence of financial responsibility consistent with the degree and duration of risk associated with the production, transportation, treatment, storage, or disposal of hazardous substances. Not later than three years after December 11, 1980, the President shall identify those classes for which requirements will be first developed and publish notice of such identification in the Federal Register. Priority in the development of such requirements shall be accorded to those classes of facilities, owners, and operators which the President determines present the highest level of risk of injury.

(2) The level of financial responsibility shall be initially established, and, when necessary, adjusted to protect against the level of risk which the President in his discretion believes is appropriate based on the payment experience of the Fund, commercial insurers, courts settlements and judgments, and voluntary claims satisfaction. To the maximum extent practicable, the President shall cooperate with and seek the advice of the commercial insurance industry in developing financial responsibility requirements. Financial responsibility may be established by any one, or any combination, of the following: insurance, guarantee, surety bond, letter of credit, or qualification as a self-insurer. In promulgating requirements under this section, the President is authorized to specify policy or other contractual terms, conditions, or defenses which are necessary, or which are unacceptable, in establishing such evidence of financial responsibility in order to effectuate the purposes of this chapter.

(3) Regulations promulgated under this subsection shall incrementally impose financial responsibility requirements as quickly as can reasonably be achieved but in no event more than 4 years after the date of promulgation. Where possible, the level of financial responsibility which the President believes appropriate as a final requirement shall be achieved through incremental, annual increases in the requirements.

(4) Where a facility is owned or operated by more than one person, evidence of financial responsibility covering the facility may be established and maintained by one of the owners or operators, or, in consolidated form, by or on behalf of two or more owners or operators. When evidence of financial responsibility is established in a consolidated form, the proportional share of each participant shall be shown. The evidence shall be accompanied by a statement authorizing the applicant to act for and in behalf of each participant in submitting and maintaining the evidence of financial responsibility.

(5) The requirements for evidence of financial responsibility for motor carriers covered by this chapter shall be determined under section 31139 of Title 49.

(c) Direct action

(1) Releases from vessels — In the case of a release or threatened release from a vessel, any claim authorized by section 9607 or 9611 of this title may be asserted directly against any guarantor providing evidence of financial responsibility for such vessel under subsection (a) of this section. In defending such a claim, the guarantor may invoke all rights and defenses which would be available to the owner or operator under this subchapter. The guarantor may also invoke the defense that the incident was caused by the willful misconduct of the owner or operator, but the guarantor may not invoke any other defense that the guarantor might have been entitled to invoke in a proceeding brought by the owner or operator against him.

(2) Releases from facilities — In the case of a release or threatened release from a facility, any claim authorized by section 9607 or 9611 of this title may be asserted directly against any guarantor providing evidence of financial responsibility for such facility under subsection (b) of this section, if the person liable under section 9607 of this title is in bankruptcy, reorganization, or arrangement pursuant to the Federal Bankruptcy Code, or if, with reasonable diligence, jurisdiction in the Federal courts cannot be obtained over a person liable under section 9607 of this title who is likely to be solvent at the time of judgment. In the case of any action pursuant to this paragraph, the guarantor shall be entitled to invoke all rights and defenses which would have been available to the person liable under section 9607 of this title if any action had been brought against such person by the claimant and all rights and defenses which would have been available to the guarantor if an action had been brought against the guarantor by such person.

(d) Limitation of guarantor liability

(1) Total liability — The total liability of any guarantor in a direct action suit brought under this section shall be limited to the aggregate amount of the monetary limits of the policy of insurance, guarantee, surety bond, letter of credit, or similar instrument obtained from the guarantor by the person subject to liability under section 9607 of this title for the purpose of satisfying the requirement for evidence of financial responsibility.

(2) Other liability — Nothing in this subsection shall be construed to limit any other State or Federal statutory, contractual, or common law liability of a guarantor, including, but not limited to, the liability of such guarantor for bad faith either in negotiating or in failing to negotiate the settlement of any claim. Nothing in this subsec-

tion shall be construed, interpreted, or applied to diminish the liability of any person under section 9607 of this title or other applicable law.

§9609. Civil penalties and awards
[CERCLA §109]

(a) Class I administrative penalty

(1) Violations — A civil penalty of not more than $25,000 per violation may be assessed by the President in the case of any of the following —

(A) A violation of the requirements of section 9603(a) or (b) of this title (relating to notice).

(B) A violation of the requirements of section 9603(d)(2) of this title (relating to destruction of records, etc.).

(C) A violation of the requirements of section 9608 of this title (relating to financial responsibility, etc.), the regulations issued under section 9608 of this title, or with any denial or detention order under section 9608 of this title.

(D) A violation of an order under section 9622(d)(3) of this title (relating to settlement agreements for action under section 9604(b) of this title).

(E) Any failure or refusal referred to in section 9622(l) of this title (relating to violations of administrative orders, consent decrees, or agreements under section 9620 of this title).

(2) Notice and hearings — No civil penalty may be assessed under this subsection unless the person accused of the violation is given notice and opportunity for a hearing with respect to the violation.

(3) Determining amount — In determining the amount of any penalty assessed pursuant to this subsection, the President shall take into account the nature, circumstances, extent and gravity of the violation or violations and, with respect to the violator, ability to pay, any prior history of such violations, the degree of culpability, economic benefit or savings (if any) resulting from the violation, and such other matters as justice may require.

(4) Review — Any person against whom a civil penalty is assessed under this subsection may obtain review thereof in the appropriate district court of the United States by filing a notice of appeal in such court within 30 days from the date of such order and by simultaneously sending a copy of such notice by certified mail to the President. The President shall promptly file in such court a certified copy of the record upon which such violation was found or such penalty imposed. If any person fails to pay an assessment of a civil penalty after it has become a final and unappealable order or after the appropriate court has entered final judgment in favor of the United States, the President may request the Attorney General of the United States to institute a civil action in an appropriate district court of the United States to collect the penalty, and such court shall have jurisdiction to hear and decide any such action. In hearing such action, the court shall have authority to review the violation and the assessment of the civil penalty on the record.

(5) Subpoenas — The President may issue subpoenas for the attendance and testimony of witnesses and the production of relevant papers, books, or documents in connection with hearings under this subsection. In case of contumacy or refusal to obey a subpoena issued pursuant to this paragraph and served upon any person, the district court of the United States for any district in which such person is found, resides, or transacts business, upon application by the United States and after notice to such person, shall have jurisdiction to issue an order requiring such person to appear and give testimony before the administrative law judge or to appear and produce documents before the administrative law judge, or both, and any failure to obey such order of the court may be punished by such court as a contempt thereof.

(b) Class II administrative penalty — A civil penalty of not more than $25,000 per day for each day during which the violation continues may be assessed by the President in the case of any of the following —

(1) A violation of the notice requirements of section 9603(a) or (b) of this title.

(2) A violation of section 9603(d)(2) of this title (relating to destruction of records, etc.).

(3) A violation of the requirements of section 9608 of this title (relating to financial responsibility, etc.), the regulations issued under section 9608 of this title, or with any denial or detention order under section 9608 of this title.

(4) A violation of an order under section 9622(d)(3) of this title (relating to settlement agreements for action under section 9604(b) of this title).

(5) Any failure or refusal referred to in section 9622(*l*) of this title (relating to violations of administrative orders, consent decrees, or agreements under section 9620 of this title).

In the case of a second or subsequent violation the amount of such penalty may be not more than $75,000 for each day during which the violation continues. Any civil penalty under this subsection shall be assessed and collected in the same manner, and subject to the same provisions, as in the case of civil penalties assessed and collected after notice and opportunity for hearing on the record in accordance with section 554 of title 5. In any proceeding for the assessment of a civil penalty under this subsection the President may issue subpoenas for the attendance and testimony of witnesses and the production of relevant papers, books, and documents and may

promulgate rules for discovery procedures. Any person who requested a hearing with respect to a civil penalty under this subsection and who is aggrieved by an order assessing the civil penalty may file a petition for judicial review of such order with the United States Court of Appeals for the District of Columbia Circuit or for any other circuit in which such person resides or transacts business. Such a petition may only be filed within the 30-day period beginning on the date the order making such assessment was issued.

(c) Judicial assessment — The President may bring an action in the United States district court for the appropriate district to assess and collect a penalty of not more than $25,000 per day for each day during which the violation (or failure or refusal) continues in the case of any of the following —

(1) A violation of the notice requirements of section 9603(a) or (b) of this title.

(2) A violation of section 9603(d)(2) of this title (relating to destruction of records, etc.).

(3) A violation of the requirements of section 9608 of this title (relating to financial responsibility, etc.), the regulations issued under section 9608 of this title, or with any denial or detention order under section 9608 of this title.

(4) A violation of an order under section 9622(d)(3) of this title (relating to settlement agreements for action under section 9604(b) of this title).

(5) Any failure or refusal referred to in section 9622(*l*) of this title (relating to violations of administrative orders, consent decrees, or agreements under section 9620 of this title).

In the case of a second or subsequent violation (or failure or refusal), the amount of such penalty may be not more than $75,000 for each day during which the violation (or failure or refusal) continues. For additional provisions providing for judicial assessment of civil penalties for failure to comply with a request or order under section 9604(e) of this title (relating to information gathering and access authorities), see section 9604(e) of this title.

(d) Awards — The President may pay an award of up to $10,000 to any individual who provides information leading to the arrest and conviction of any person for a violation subject to a criminal penalty under this chapter, including any violation of section 9603 of this title and any other violation referred to in this section. The President shall, by regulation, prescribe criteria for such an award and may pay any award under this subsection from the Fund, as provided in section 9611 of this title.

(e) Procurement procedures — Notwithstanding any other provision of law, any executive agency may use competitive procedures or procedures other than competitive procedures to procure the services of experts for use in preparing or prosecuting a civil or criminal action under this chapter, whether or not the expert is expected to testify at trial. The executive agency need not provide any written justification for the use of procedures other than competitive procedures when procuring such expert services under this chapter and need not furnish for publication in the Commerce Business Daily or otherwise any notice of solicitation or synopsis with respect to such procurement.

(f) Savings clause — Action taken by the President pursuant to this section shall not affect or limit the President's authority to enforce any provisions of this chapter.

§9610. Employee protection
[CERCLA §110]

(a) Activities of employee subject to protection — No person shall fire or in any other way discriminate against, or cause to be fired or discriminated against, any employee or any authorized representative of employees by reason of the fact that such employee or representative has provided information to a State or to the Federal Government, filed, instituted, or caused to be filed or instituted any proceeding under this chapter, or has testified or is about to testify in any proceeding resulting from the administration or enforcement of the provisions of this chapter.

(b) Administrative grievance procedure in cases of alleged violations — Any employee or a representative of employees who believes that he has been fired or otherwise discriminated against by any person in violation of subsection (a) of this section may, within thirty days after such alleged violation occurs, apply to the Secretary of Labor for a review of such firing or alleged discrimination. A copy of the application shall be sent to such person, who shall be the respondent. Upon receipt of such application, the Secretary of Labor shall cause such investigation to be made as he deems appropriate. Such investigation shall provide an opportunity for a public hearing at the request of any party to such review to enable the parties to present information relating to such alleged violation. The parties shall be given written notice of the time and place of the hearing at least five days prior to the hearing. Any such hearing shall be of record and shall be subject to section 554 of Title 5. Upon receiving the report of such investigation, the Secretary of Labor shall make findings of fact. If he finds that such violation did occur, he shall issue a decision, incorporating an order therein and his findings, requiring the party committing such violation to take such affirmative action to abate the violation as the Secretary of Labor deems appropriate, including, but not limited to, the rehiring or reinstatement of the employee or representative of employees to his former position with compensation. If he finds that there was no such violation, he shall issue an order denying the application. Such order issued by the Secretary of Labor under this subparagraph shall be subject to judicial review in the same manner as orders and

decisions are subject to judicial review under this chapter.

(c) Assessment of costs and expenses against violator subsequent to issuance of order of abatement — Whenever an order is issued under this section to abate such violation, at the request of the applicant a sum equal to the aggregate amount of all costs and expenses (including the attorney's fees) determined by the Secretary of Labor to have been reasonably incurred by the applicant for, or in connection with, the institution and prosecution of such proceedings, shall be assessed against the person committing such violation.

(d) Defenses — This section shall have no application to any employee who acting without discretion from his employer (or his agent) deliberately violates any requirement of this chapter.

(e) Presidential evaluations of potential loss of shifts of employment resulting from administration or enforcement of provisions; investigations; procedures applicable, etc. — The President shall conduct continuing evaluations of potential loss of shifts of employment which may result from the administration or enforcement of the provisions of this chapter, including, where appropriate, investigating threatened plant closures or reductions in employment allegedly resulting from such administration or enforcement. Any employee who is discharged, or laid off, threatened with discharge or layoff, or otherwise discriminated against by any person because of the alleged results of such administration or enforcement, or any representative of such employee, may request the President to conduct a full investigation of the matter and, at the request of any party, shall hold public hearings, require the parties, including the employer involved, to present information relating to the actual or potential effect of such administration or enforcement on employment and any alleged discharge, layoff, or other discrimination, and the detailed reasons or justification therefore. Any such hearing shall be of record and shall be subject to section 554 of Title 5. Upon receiving the report of such investigation, the President shall make findings of fact as to the effect of such administration or enforcement on employment and on the alleged discharge, layoff, or discrimination and shall make such recommendations as he deems appropriate. Such report, findings, and recommendations shall be available to the public. Nothing in this subsection shall be construed to require or authorize the President or any State to modify or withdraw any action, standard, limitation, or any other requirement of this chapter.

§9611. Uses of Fund
[CERCLA §111]

(a) In general — For the purposes specified in this section there is authorized to be appropriated from the Hazardous Substance Superfund established under subchapter A of chapter 98 of Title 26 not more than $8,500,000,000 for the 5-year period beginning on October 17, 1986, and not more than $5,100,000,000 for the period commencing October 1, 1991, and ending September 30, 1994, and such sums shall remain available until expended. The preceding sentence constitutes a specific authorization for the funds appropriated under Title II of Pub. L. 99-160 (relating to payment to the Hazardous Substances Trust Fund). The President shall use the money in the Fund for the following purposes:

　(1) Payment of governmental response costs incurred pursuant to section 9604 of this title, including costs incurred pursuant to the Intervention on the High Seas Act [33 U.S.C. §§1471 *et seq.*].

　(2) Payment of any claim for necessary response costs incurred by any other person as a result of carrying out the national contingency plan established under section 1321(c) of Title 33 and amended by section 9605 of this title: Provided, however, That such costs must be approved under said plan and certified by the responsible Federal official.

　(3) Payment of any claim authorized by subsection (b) of this section and finally decided pursuant to section 9612 of this title, including those costs set out in subsection 9612(c)(3) of this title.

　(4) Payment of costs specified under subsection (c) of this section.

　(5) Grants for technical assistance — The cost of grants under section 9617(e) of this title (relating to public participation grants for technical assistance).

　(6) Lead contaminated soil — Payment of not to exceed $15,000,000 for the costs of a pilot program for removal, decontamination, or other action with respect to lead-contaminated soil in one to three different metropolitan areas.

The President shall not pay for any administrative costs or expenses out of the Fund unless such costs and expenses are reasonably necessary for and incidental to the implementation of this subchapter.

(b) Additional authorized purposes

　(1) In general — Claims asserted and compensable but unsatisfied under provisions of section 1321 of Title 33, which are modified by section 304 of this Act may be asserted against the Fund under this subchapter; and other claims resulting from a release or threat of release of a hazardous substance from a vessel or a facility may be asserted against the Fund under this subchapter for injury to, or destruction or loss of, natural resources, including cost for damage assessment: Provided, however, That any such claim may be asserted only by the President, as trustee, for natural resources over which the United States has sovereign rights, or natural resources within

the territory or the fishery conservation zone of the United States to the extent they are managed or protected by the United States, or by any State for natural resources within the boundary of that State belonging to, managed by, controlled by, or appertaining to the State, or by any Indian tribe or by the United States acting on behalf of any Indian tribe for natural resources belonging to, managed by, controlled by, or appertaining to such tribe, or held in trust for the benefit of such tribe, or belonging to a member of such tribe if such resources are subject to a trust restriction on alienation.

　(2) Limitation on payment of natural resource claims

　　(A) General requirements — No natural resource claim may be paid from the Fund unless the President determines that the claimant has exhausted all administrative and judicial remedies to recover the amount of such claim from persons who may be liable under section 9607 of this title.

　　(B) Definition — As used in this paragraph, the term "natural resource claim" means any claim for injury to, or destruction or loss of, natural resources. The term does not include any claim for the costs of natural resource damage assessment.

(c) Peripheral matters and limitations — Uses of the Fund under subsection (a) of this section include —

　(1) The costs of assessing both short-term and long-term injury to, destruction of, or loss of any natural resources resulting from a release of a hazardous substance.

　(2) The costs of Federal or State or Indian tribe efforts in the restoration, rehabilitation, or replacement or acquiring the equivalent of any natural resources injured, destroyed, or lost as a result of a release of a hazardous substance.

　(3) Subject to such amounts as are provided in appropriation Acts, the costs of a program to identify, investigate, and take enforcement and abatement action against releases of hazardous substances.

　(4) Any costs incurred in accordance with subsection (m) of this section (relating to ATSDR) and section 9604(i) of this title, including the costs of epidemiologic and laboratory studies, health assessments, preparation of toxicologic profiles, development and maintenance of a registry of persons exposed to hazardous substances to allow long-term health effect studies, and diagnostic services not otherwise available to determine whether persons in populations exposed to hazardous substances in connection with a release or a suspected release are suffering from long-latency diseases.

　(5) Subject to such amounts as are provided in appropriation Acts, the costs of providing equipment

and similar overhead, related to the purposes of this chapter and section 1321 of Title 33, and needed to supplement equipment and services available through contractors or other non-Federal entities, and of establishing and maintaining damage assessment capability, for any Federal agency involved in strike forces, emergency task forces, or other response teams under the national contingency plan.

(6) Subject to such amounts as are provided in appropriation Acts, the costs of a program to protect the health and safety of employees involved in response to hazardous substance releases. Such program shall be developed jointly by the Environmental Protection Agency, the Occupational Safety and Health Administration, and the National Institute for Occupational Safety and Health and shall include, but not be limited to, measures for identifying and assessing hazards to which persons engaged in removal, remedy, or other response to hazardous substances may be exposed, methods to protect workers from such hazards, and necessary regulatory and enforcement measures to assure adequate protection of such employees.

(7) Evaluation costs under petition provisions of section 9605(d) — Costs incurred by the President in evaluating facilities pursuant to petitions under section 9605(d) of this title (relating to petitions for assessment of release).

(8) Contract costs under section 9604(a)(1) — The costs of contracts or arrangements entered into under section 9604(a)(1) of this title to oversee and review the conduct of remedial investigations and feasibility studies undertaken by persons other than the President and the costs of appropriate Federal and State oversight of remedial activities at National Priorities List sites resulting from consent orders or settlement agreements.

(9) Acquisition costs under section 9604(j) — The costs incurred by the President in acquiring real estate or interests in real estate under section 9604(j) of this title (relating to acquisition of property).

(10) Research, development, and demonstration costs under section 9660 — The cost of carrying out section 9660 of this title (relating to research, development, and demonstration), except that the amounts available for such purposes shall not exceed the amounts specified in subsection (n) of this section.

(11) Local government reimbursement — Reimbursements to local governments under section 9623 of this title, except that during the 8-fiscal year period beginning October 1, 1986, not more than 0.1 percent of the total amount appropriated from the Fund may be used for such reimbursements.

(12) Worker training and education grants — The costs of grants under section 9660a of this title for training and education of workers to the extent that such costs do not exceed $20,000,000

for each of the fiscal years 1987, 1988, 1989, 1990, 1991, 1992, 1993, and 1994.

(13) Awards under section 9609 — The costs of any awards granted under section 9609(d) of this title.

(14) Lead poisoning study — The cost of carrying out the study under subsection (f) of section 118 of the Superfund Amendments and Reauthorization Act of 1986 (relating to lead poisoning in children).

(d) Additional limitations

(1) No money in the Fund may be used under subsection (c)(1) and (2) of this section, nor for the payment of any claim under subsection (b) of this section, where the injury, destruction, or loss of natural resources and the release of a hazardous substance from which such damages resulted have occurred wholly before December 11, 1980.

(2) No money in the Fund may be used for the payment of any claim under subsection (b) of this section where such expenses are associated with injury or loss resulting from long-term exposure to ambient concentrations of air pollutants from multiple or diffuse sources.

(e) Funding requirements respecting moneys in Fund; limitation on certain claims; Fund use outside Federal property boundaries

(1) Claims against or presented to the Fund shall not be valid or paid in excess of the total money in the Fund at any one time. Such claims become valid only when additional money is collected, appropriated, or otherwise added to the Fund. Should the total claims outstanding at any time exceed the current balance of the Fund, the President shall pay such claims, to the extent authorized under this section, in full in the order in which they were finally determined.

(2) In any fiscal year, 85 percent of the money credited to the Fund under subchapter II of this chapter shall be available only for the purposes specified in paragraphs (1), (2), and (4) of subsection (a) of this section. No money in the Fund may be used for the payment of any claim under subsection (a)(3) or subsection (b) of this section in any fiscal year for which the President determines that all of the Fund is needed for response to threats to public health from releases or threatened releases of hazardous substances.

(3) No money in the Fund shall be available for remedial action, other than actions specified in subsection (c) of this section, with respect to federally owned facilities; except that money in the Fund shall be available for the provision of alternative water supplies (including the reimbursement of costs incurred by a municipality) in any case involving groundwater contamination outside the boundaries of a federally owned facility in which the federally owned facility is not the only potentially responsible party.

(4) Paragraphs (1) and (4) of subsection (a) of this section shall in the aggregate be subject to such amounts as are provided in appropriation Acts.

(f) Obligation of moneys by Federal officials; obligation of moneys or settlement of claims by State officials or Indian tribe — The President is authorized to promulgate regulations designating one or more Federal officials who may obligate money in the Fund in accordance with this section or portions thereof. The President is also authorized to delegate authority to obligate money in the Fund or to settle claims to officials of a State or Indian tribe operating under a contract or cooperative agreement with the Federal Government pursuant to section 9604(d) of this title.

(g) Notice to potential injured parties by owner and operator of vessel or facility causing release of substance; rules and regulations — The President shall provide for the promulgation of rules and regulations with respect to the notice to be provided to potential injured parties by an owner and operator of any vessel, or facility from which a hazardous substance has been released. Such rules and regulations shall consider the scope and form of the notice which would be appropriate to carry out the purposes of this subchapter. Upon promulgation of such rules and regulations, the owner and operator of any vessel or facility from which a hazardous substance has been released shall provide notice in accordance with such rules and regulations. With respect to releases from public vessels, the President shall provide such notification as is appropriate to potential injured parties. Until the promulgation of such rules and regulations, the owner and operator of any vessel or facility from which a hazardous substance has been released shall provide reasonable notice to potential injured parties by publication in local newspapers serving the affected area.

(h) Repealed. Pub. L. 99-499, Title I, Sec. 111(c)(2), Oct. 17, 1986, 100 Stat. 1643

(i) Restoration, etc., of natural resources — Except in a situation requiring action to avoid an irreversible loss of natural resources or to prevent or reduce any continuing danger to natural resources or similar need for emergency action, funds may not be used under this chapter for the restoration, rehabilitation, or replacement or acquisition of the equivalent of any natural resources until a plan for the use of such funds for such purposes has been developed and adopted by affected Federal agencies and the Governor or Governors of any State having sustained damage to natural resources within its borders, belonging to, managed by or appertaining to such State, and by the governing body of any Indian tribe having sustained damage to natural resources belonging to, managed by, controlled by, or appertaining to such tribe, or held in trust for the benefit of such tribe, or belonging to a member of such tribe if such resources are subject to a trust restriction on alienation, after adequate public notice and opportunity for hearing and consideration of all public comment.

(j) Use of Post-closure Liability Fund — The President shall use the money in the Post-closure Liability Fund for any of the purposes specified in subsection (a) of this section with respect to a hazardous waste disposal facility for which liability has transferred to such fund under section 9607(k) of this title, and, in addition, for payment of any claim or appropriate request for costs of response, damages, or other compensation for injury or loss under section 9607 of this title or any other State or Federal law, resulting from a release of a hazardous substance from such a facility.

(k) Inspector General — In each fiscal year, the Inspector General of each department, agency, or instrumentality of the United States which is carrying out any authority of this chapter shall conduct an annual audit of all payments, obligations, reimbursements, or other uses of the Fund in the prior fiscal year, to assure that the Fund is being properly administered and that claims are being appropriately and expeditiously considered. The audit shall include an examination of a sample of agreements with States (in accordance with the provisions of the Single Audit Act [31 U.S.C. §§7501 *et seq.*]) carrying out response actions under this subchapter and an examination of remedial investigations and feasibility studies prepared for remedial actions. The Inspector General shall submit to the Congress an annual report regarding the audit report required under this subsection. The report shall contain such recommendations as the Inspector General deems appropriate. Each department, agency, or instrumentality of the United States shall cooperate with its inspector general in carrying out this subsection.

(l) Foreign claimants — To the extent that the provisions of this chapter permit, a foreign claimant may assert a claim to the same extent that a United States claimant may assert a claim if —

(1) the release of a hazardous substance occurred (A) in the navigable waters or (B) in or on the territorial sea or adjacent shoreline of a foreign country of which the claimant is a resident;

(2) the claimant is not otherwise compensated for his loss;

(3) the hazardous substance was released from a facility or from a vessel located adjacent to or within the navigable waters or was discharged in connection with activities conducted under the Outer Continental Shelf Lands Act, as amended [43 U.S.C. §§1331 *et seq.*] or the Deepwater Port Act of 1974, as amended [33 U.S.C. §§1501 *et seq.*]; and

(4) recovery is authorized by a treaty or an executive agreement between the United States and foreign country involved, or if the Secretary of State, in consultation with the Attorney General and other appropriate officials, certifies that such country provides a comparable remedy for United States claimants.

(m) Agency for Toxic Substances and Disease Registry — There shall be directly available to the Agency for Toxic Substances and Disease Registry to be used for the purpose of carrying out activities described in subsection (c)(4) of this section and section 9604(i) of this title not less than $50,000,000 per fiscal year for each of fiscal years 1987 and 1988, not less than $55,000,000 for fiscal year 1989, and not less than $60,000,000 per fiscal year for each of fiscal years 1990, 1991, 1992, 1993, and 1994. Any funds so made available which are not obligated by the end of the fiscal year in which made available shall be returned to the Fund.

(n) Limitations on research, development, and demonstration program

(1) Section 9660(b) — For each of the fiscal years 1987, 1988, 1989, 1990, 1991, 1992, 1993, and 1994, not more than $20,000,000 of the amounts available in the Fund may be used for the purposes of carrying out the applied research, development, and demonstration program for alternative or innovative technologies and training program authorized under section 9660(b) of this title (relating to research, development, and demonstration) other than basic research. Such amounts shall remain available until expended.

(2) Section 9660(a) — From the amounts available in the Fund, not more than the following amounts may be used for the purposes of section 9660(a) of this title (relating to hazardous substance research, demonstration, and training activities):

(A) For the fiscal year 1987, $3,000,000.

(B) For the fiscal year 1988, $10,000,000.

(C) For the fiscal year 1989, $20,000,000.

(D) For the fiscal year 1990, $30,000,000.

(E) For each of the fiscal years 1991, 1992, 1993, and 1994, $35,000,000. No more than 10 percent of such amounts shall be used for training under section 9660(a) of this title in any fiscal year.

(3) Section 9660(d) — For each of the fiscal years 1987, 1988, 1989, 1990, 1991, 1992, 1993, and 1994, not more than $5,000,000 of the amounts available in the Fund may be used for the purposes of section 9660(d) of this title (relating to university hazardous substance research centers).

(o) Notification procedures for limitations on certain payments — Not later than 90 days after October 17, 1986, the President shall develop and implement procedures to adequately notify, as soon as practicable after a site is included on the National Priorities List, concerned local and State officials and

other concerned persons of the limitations, set forth in subsection (a)(2) of this section, on the payment of claims for necessary response costs incurred with respect to such site.

(p) General revenue share of Superfund

(1) In general — The following sums are authorized to be appropriated, out of any money in the Treasury not otherwise appropriated, to the Hazardous Substance Superfund:

(A) For fiscal year 1987, $212,500,000.

(B) For fiscal year 1988, $212,500,000.

(C) For fiscal year 1989, $212,500,000.

(D) For fiscal year 1990, $212,500,000.

(E) For fiscal year 1991, $212,500,000.

(F) For fiscal year 1992, $212,500,000.

(G) For fiscal year 1993, $212,500,000.

(H) For fiscal year 1994, $212,500,000.

In addition there is authorized to be appropriated to the Hazardous Substance Superfund for each fiscal year an amount equal to so much of the aggregate amount authorized to be appropriated under this subsection (and paragraph (2) of section 9631(b) of this title) as has not been appropriated before the beginning of the fiscal year involved.

(2) Computation — The amounts authorized to be appropriated under paragraph (1) of this subsection in a given fiscal year shall be available only to the extent that such amount exceeds the amount determined by the Secretary under section 9507(b)(2) of Title 26 for the prior fiscal year.

§9612. Claims procedure
[CERCLA §112]

(a) Claims against Fund for response costs — No claim may be asserted against the Fund pursuant to section 9611(a) of this title unless such claim is presented in the first instance to the owner, operator, or guarantor of the vessel or facility from which a hazardous substance has been released, if known to the claimant, and to any other person known to the claimant who may be liable under section 9607 of this title. In any case where the claim has not been satisfied within 60 days of presentation in accordance with this subsection, the claimant may present the claim to the Fund for payment. No claim against the Fund may be approved or certified during the pendency of an action by the claimant in court to recover costs which are the subject of the claim.

(b) Forms and procedures applicable

(1) Prescribing forms and procedures — The President shall prescribe appropriate forms and procedures for claims filed hereunder, which shall include a provision requiring the claimant to make a sworn verification of the claim to the best of his knowledge. Any person who knowingly gives or causes to be given any false information as a part of any such claim shall, upon conviction, be fined in accordance with the applicable provisions of Title 18 or imprisoned for not more than 3 years (or not more than 5 years in the

case of a second or subsequent conviction), or both.

(2) Payment or request for hearing — The President may, if satisfied that the information developed during the processing of the claim warrants it, make and pay an award of the claim, except that no claim may be awarded to the extent that a judicial judgment has been made on the costs that are the subject of the claim. If the President declines to pay all or part of the claim, the claimant may, within 30 days after receiving notice of the President's decision, request an administrative hearing.

(3) Burden of proof — In any proceeding under this subsection, the claimant shall bear the burden of proving his claim.

(4) Decisions — All administrative decisions made hereunder shall be in writing, with notification to all appropriate parties, and shall be rendered within 90 days of submission of a claim to an administrative law judge, unless all the parties to the claim agree in writing to an extension or unless the President, in his discretion, extends the time limit for a period not to exceed sixty days.

(5) Finality and appeal — All administrative decisions hereunder shall be final, and any party to the proceeding may appeal a decision within 30 days of notification of the award or decision. Any such appeal shall be made to the Federal district court for the district where the release or threat of release took place. In any such appeal, the decision shall be considered binding and conclusive, and shall not be overturned except for arbitrary or capricious abuse of discretion.

(6) Payment — Within 20 days after the expiration of the appeal period for any administrative decision concerning an award, or within 20 days after the final judicial determination of any appeal taken pursuant to this subsection, the President shall pay any such award from the Fund. The President shall determine the method, terms, and time of payment.

(c) Subrogation rights; actions maintainable

(1) Payment of any claim by the Fund under this section shall be subject to the United States Government acquiring by subrogation the rights of the claimant to recover those costs of removal or damages for which it has compensated the claimant from the person responsible or liable for such release.

(2) Any person, including the Fund, who pays compensation pursuant to this chapter to any claimant for damages or costs resulting from a release of a hazardous substance shall be subrogated to all rights, claims, and causes of action for such damages and costs of removal that the claimant has under this chapter or any other law.

(3) Upon request of the President, the Attorney General shall commence an action on behalf of

the Fund to recover any compensation paid by the Fund to any claimant pursuant to this subchapter, and, without regard to any limitation of liability, all interest, administrative and adjudicative costs, and attorney's fees incurred by the Fund by reason of the claim. Such an action may be commenced against any owner, operator, or guarantor, or against any other person who is liable, pursuant to any law, to the compensated claimant or to the Fund, for the damages or costs for which compensation was paid.

(d) Statute of limitations

(1) Claims for recovery of costs — No claim may be presented under this section for recovery of the costs referred to in section 9607(a) of this title after the date 6 years after the date of completion of all response action.

(2) Claims for recovery of damages — No claim may be presented under this section for recovery of the damages referred to in section 9607(a) of this title unless the claim is presented within 3 years after the later of the following:

(A) The date of the discovery of the loss and its connection with the release in question.

(B) The date on which final regulations are promulgated under section 9651(c) of this title.

(3) Minors and incompetents — The time limitations contained herein shall not begin to run —

(A) against a minor until the earlier of the date when such minor reaches 18 years of age or the date on which a legal representative is duly appointed for the minor, or

(B) against an incompetent person until the earlier of the date on which such person's incompetency ends or the date on which a legal representative is duly appointed for such incompetent person.

(e) Other statutory or common law claims not waived, etc. — Regardless of any State statutory or common law to the contrary, no person who asserts a claim against the Fund pursuant to this subchapter shall be deemed or held to have waived any other claim not covered or assertable against the Fund under this subchapter arising from the same incident, transaction, or set of circumstances, nor to have split a cause of action. Further, no person asserting a claim against the Fund pursuant to this subchapter shall as a result of any determination of a question of fact or law made in connection with that claim be deemed or held to be collaterally estopped from raising such question in connection with any other claim not covered or assertable against the Fund under this subchapter arising from the same incident, transaction, or set of circumstances.

(f) Double recovery prohibited — Where the President has paid out of the Fund for any response costs or any costs specified under section 9611(c)(1) or (2) of this title, no other claim may be paid out of the Fund for the same costs.

§9613. Civil proceedings
[CERCLA §113]

(a) Review of regulations in Circuit Court of Appeals of the United States for the District of Columbia — Review of any regulation promulgated under this chapter may be had upon application by any interested person only in the Circuit Court of Appeals of the United States for the District of Columbia. Any such application shall be made within ninety days from the date of promulgation of such regulations. Any matter with respect to which review could have been obtained under this subsection shall not be subject to judicial review in any civil or criminal proceeding for enforcement or to obtain damages or recovery of response costs.

(b) Jurisdiction; venue — Except as provided in subsections (a) and (h) of this section, the United States district courts shall have exclusive original jurisdiction over all controversies arising under this chapter, without regard to the citizenship of the parties or the amount in controversy. Venue shall lie in any district in which the release or damages occurred, or in which the defendant resides, may be found, or has his principal office. For the purposes of this section, the Fund shall reside in the District of Columbia.

(c) Controversies or other matters resulting from tax collection or tax regulation review — The provisions of subsections (a) and (b) of this section shall not apply to any controversy or other matter resulting from the assessment of collection of any tax, as provided by subchapter II of this chapter, or to the review of any regulation promulgated under Title 26.

(d) Litigation commenced prior to December 11, 1980 — No provision of this chapter shall be deemed or held to moot any litigation concerning any release of any hazardous substance, or any damages associated therewith, commenced prior to December 11, 1980.

(e) Nationwide service of process — In any action by the United States under this chapter, process may be served in any district where the defendant is found, resides, transacts business, or has appointed an agent for the service of process.

(f) Contribution

(1) Contribution — Any person may seek contribution from any other person who is liable or potentially liable under section 9607(a) of this title, during or following any civil action under section 9606 of this title or under section 9607(a) of this title. Such claims shall be brought in accordance with this section and the Federal Rules of Civil Procedure, and shall be governed by Federal law. In resolving contribution claims, the court may allocate response costs among liable parties using such equitable factors as the court determines are appropriate. Nothing in this subsection shall diminish the right of any person to bring an action for contribution in the absence of a civil action under section 9606 of this title or section 9607 of this title.

(2) Settlement — A person who has resolved its liability to the United States or a State in an administrative or judicially approved settlement shall not be liable for claims for contribution regarding matters addressed in the settlement. Such settlement does not discharge any of the other potentially liable persons unless its terms so provide, but it reduces the potential liability of the others by the amount of the settlement.

(3) Persons not party to settlement

(A) If the United States or a State has obtained less than complete relief from a person who has resolved its liability to the United States or the State in an administrative or judicially approved settlement, the United States or the State may bring an action against any person who has not so resolved its liability.

(B) A person who has resolved its liability to the United States or a State for some or all of a response action or for some or all of the costs of such action in an administrative or judicially approved settlement may seek contribution from any person who is not party to a settlement referred to in paragraph (2).

(C) In any action under this paragraph, the rights of any person who has resolved its liability to the United States or a State shall be subordinate to the rights of the United States or the State. Any contribution action brought under this paragraph shall be governed by Federal law.

(g) Period in which action may be brought

(1) Actions for natural resource damages — Except as provided in paragraphs (3) and (4), no action may be commenced for damages (as defined in section 9601(6) of this title) under this chapter, unless that action is commenced within 3 years after the later of the following:

(A) The date of the discovery of the loss and its connection with the release in question.

(B) The date on which regulations are promulgated under section 9651(c) of this title. With respect to any facility listed on the National Priorities List (NPL), any Federal facility identified under section 9620 of this title (relating to Federal facilities), or any vessel or facility at which a remedial action under this chapter is otherwise scheduled, an action for damages under this chapter must be commenced within 3 years after the completion of the remedial action (excluding operation and maintenance activities) in lieu of the dates referred to in subparagraph (A) or (B). In no event may an action for damages under this chapter with respect to such a vessel or facility be commenced (i) prior to 60 days after the Federal or State natural resource trustee provides to the President and the potentially responsible party a notice of intent to file suit, or (ii) before selection of the remedial action if the President is diligently proceeding with a remedial investigation and feasibility study under section 9604(b) of this title or section 9620 of this title (relating to Federal facilities). The limitation in the preceding sentence on commencing an action before giving notice or before selection of the remedial action does not apply to actions filed on or before October 17, 1986.

(2) Actions for recovery of costs — An initial action for recovery of the costs referred to in section 9607 of this title must be commenced —

(A) for a removal action, within 3 years after completion of the removal action, except that such cost recovery action must be brought within 6 years after a determination to grant a waiver under section 9604(c)(1)(C) of this title for continued response action; and

(B) for a remedial action, within 6 years after initiation of physical on-site construction of the remedial action, except that, if the remedial action is initiated within 3 years after the completion of the removal action, costs incurred in the removal action may be recovered in the cost recovery action brought under this subparagraph.

In any such action described in this subsection, the court shall enter a declaratory judgment on liability for response costs or damages that will be binding on any subsequent action or actions to recover further response costs or damages. A subsequent action or actions under section 9607 of this title for further response costs at the vessel or facility may be maintained at any time during the response action, but must be commenced no later than 3 years after the date of completion of all response action. Except as otherwise provided in this paragraph, an action may be commenced under section 9607 of this title for recovery of costs at any time after such costs have been incurred.

(3) Contribution — No action for contribution for any response costs or damages may be commenced more than 3 years after —

(A) the date of judgment in any action under this chapter or recovery of such costs or damages, or

(B) the date of an administrative order under section 9622(g) of this title (relating to de minimis settlements) or 9622(h) of this title relating to cost recovery settlements) or entry of a judicially approved settlement with respect to such costs or damages.

(4) Subrogation — No action based on rights subrogated pursuant to this section by reason of payment of a claim may be commenced under this subchapter more than 3 years after the date of payment of such claim.

(5) Actions to recover indemnification payments — Notwithstanding any other provision of this subsection, where a payment pursuant to an indemnification agreement with a response action contractor is made under section 9619 of this title, an action under section 9607 of this title for recovery of such indemnification payment from a potentially responsible party may be brought at any time before the expiration of 3 years from the date on which such payment is made.

(6) Minors and incompetents — The time limitations contained herein shall not begin to run —

(A) against a minor until the earlier of the date when such minor reaches 18 years of age or the date on which a legal representative is duly appointed for such minor, or

(B) against an incompetent person until the earlier of the date on which such incompetent's incompetency ends or the date on which a legal representative is duly appointed for such incompetent.

(h) **Timing of review** — No Federal court shall have jurisdiction under Federal law other than under section 1332 of Title 28 (relating to diversity of citizenship jurisdiction) or under State law which is applicable or relevant and appropriate under section 9621 of this title (relating to cleanup standards) to review any challenges to removal or remedial action selected under section 9604 of this title, or to review any order issued under section 9606(a) of this title, in any action except one of the following:

(1) An action under section 9607 of this title to recover response costs or damages or for contribution.

(2) An action to enforce an order issued under section 9606(a) of this title or to recover a penalty for violation of such order.

(3) An action for reimbursement under section 9606(b)(2) of this title.

(4) An action under section 9659 of this title (relating to citizens suits) alleging that the removal or remedial action taken under section 9604 of this title or secured under section 9606 of this title was in violation of any requirement of this chapter. Such an action may not be brought with regard to a removal where a remedial action is to be undertaken at the site.

(5) An action under section 9606 of this title in which the United States has moved to compel a remedial action.

(i) **Intervention** — In any action commenced under this chapter or under the Solid Waste Disposal Act [42 U.S.C. §§6901 *et seq.*] in a court of the United States, any person may intervene as a matter of right when such person claims an interest relating to the subject of the action and is so situated that the disposition of the action may, as a practical matter, impair or impede the person's ability to protect that interest, unless the President or the State shows that the person's interest is adequately represented by existing parties.

(j) Judicial review

(1) Limitation — In any judicial action under this chapter, judicial review of any issues concerning the adequacy of any response action taken or ordered by the President shall be limited to the administrative record. Otherwise applicable principles of administrative law shall govern whether any supplemental materials may be considered by the court.

(2) Standard — In considering objections raised in any judicial action under this chapter, the court shall uphold the President's decision in selecting the response action unless the objecting party can demonstrate, on the administrative record, that the decision was arbitrary and capricious or otherwise not in accordance with law.

(3) Remedy — If the court finds that the selection of the response action was arbitrary and capricious or otherwise not in accordance with law, the court shall award (A) only the response costs or damages that are not inconsistent with the national contingency plan, and (B) such other relief as is consistent with the National Contingency Plan.

(4) Procedural errors — In reviewing alleged procedural errors, the court may disallow costs or damages only if the errors were so serious and related to matters of such central relevance to the action that the action would have been significantly changed had such errors not been made.

(k) Administrative record and participation procedures

(1) Administrative record — The President shall establish an administrative record upon which the President shall base the selection of a response action. The administrative record shall be available to the public at or near the facility at issue. The President also may place duplicates of the administrative record at any other location.

(2) Participation procedures

(A) Removal action — The President shall promulgate regulations in accordance with chapter 5 of Title 5 establishing procedures for the appropriate participation of interested persons in the development of the administrative record on which the President will base the selection of removal actions and on which judicial review of removal actions will be based.

(B) Remedial action — The President shall provide for the participation of interested persons, including potentially responsible parties, in the development of the administrative record on which the President will base the selection of remedial actions and on which judicial review of remedial actions will be based. The procedures developed under this subparagraph shall include, at a minimum, each of the following:

(i) Notice to potentially affected persons and the public, which shall be accompanied by a brief analysis of the plan and alternative plans that were considered.

(ii) A reasonable opportunity to comment and provide information regarding the plan.

(iii) An opportunity for a public meeting in the affected area, in accordance with section 9617(a)(2) of this title (relating to public participation).

(iv) A response to each of the significant comments, criticisms, and new data submitted in written or oral presentations.

(v) A statement of the basis and purpose of the selected action. For purposes of this subparagraph, the administrative record shall include all items developed and received under this subparagraph and all items described in the second sentence of section 9617(d) of this title. The President shall promulgate regulations in accordance with chapter 5 of Title 5 to carry out the requirements of this subparagraph.

(C) Interim record — Until such regulations under subparagraphs (A) and (B) are promulgated, the administrative record shall consist of all items developed and received pursuant to current procedures for selection of the response action, including procedures for the participation of interested parties and the public. The development of an administrative record and the selection of response action under this chapter shall not include an adjudicatory hearing.

(D) Potentially responsible parties — The President shall make reasonable efforts to identify and notify potentially responsible parties as early as possible before selection of a response action. Nothing in this paragraph shall be construed to be a defense to liability.

(*l*) Notice of actions — Whenever any action is brought under this chapter in a court of the United States by a plaintiff other than the United States, the plaintiff shall provide a copy of the complaint to the Attorney General of the United States and to the Administrator of the Environmental Protection Agency.

§9614. Relationship to other law
[CERCLA §114]

(a) Additional State liability or requirements with respect to release of substances within

State — Nothing in this chapter shall be construed or interpreted as preempting any State from imposing any additional liability or requirements with respect to the release of hazardous substances within such State.

(b) Recovery under other State or Federal law of compensation for removal costs or damages, or payment of claims — Any person who receives compensation for removal costs or damages or claims pursuant to this chapter shall be precluded from recovering compensation for the same removal costs or damages or claims pursuant to any other State or Federal law. Any person who receives compensation for removal costs or damages or claims pursuant to any other Federal or State law shall be precluded from receiving compensation for the same removal costs or damages or claims as provided in this chapter.

(c) Recycled oil

(1) Service station dealers, etc. — No person (including the United States or any State) may recover, under the authority of subsection (a)(3) or (a)(4) of section 9607 of this title, from a service station dealer for any response costs or damages resulting from a release or threatened release of recycled oil, or use the authority of section 9606 of this title against a service station dealer other than a person described in subsection (a)(1) or (a)(2) of section 9607 of this title, if such recycled oil —

(A) is not mixed with any other hazardous substance, and

(B) is stored, treated, transported, or otherwise managed in compliance with regulations or standards promulgated pursuant to section 3014 of the Solid Waste Disposal Act (42 U.S.C. §6935) and other applicable authorities.

Nothing in this paragraph shall affect or modify in any way the obligations or liability of any person under any other provision of State or Federal law, including common law, for damages, injury, or loss resulting from a release or threatened release of any hazardous substance or for removal or remedial action or the costs of removal or remedial action.

(2) Presumption — Solely for the purposes of this subsection, a service station dealer may presume that a small quantity of used oil is not mixed with other hazardous substances if it —

(A) has been removed from the engine of a light duty motor vehicle or household appliances by the owner of such vehicle or appliances, and

(B) is presented, by such owner, to the dealer for collection, accumulation, and delivery to an oil recycling facility.

(3) Definition — For purposes of this subsection, the terms "used oil" and "recycled oil" have the same meanings as set forth in sections 1004(36)

and 1004(37) of the Solid Waste Disposal Act (42 U.S.C. §6903(36), (37)) and regulations promulgated pursuant to that Act [42 U.S.C. §§6901 *et seq.*].

(4) Effective date — The effective date of paragraphs (1) and (2) of this subsection shall be the effective date of regulations or standards promulgated under section 3014 of the Solid Waste Disposal Act (42 U.S.C. §6935) that include, among other provisions, a requirement to conduct corrective action to respond to any releases of recycled oil under subtitle C or subtitle I of such Act [42 U.S.C. §§6921 *et seq.*, §§6991 *et seq.*].

(d) Financial responsibility of owner or operator of vessel or facility under State or local law, rule, or regulation — Except as provided in this subchapter, no owner or operator of a vessel or facility who establishes and maintains evidence of financial responsibility in accordance with this subchapter shall be required under any State or local law, rule, or regulation to establish or maintain any other evidence of financial responsibility in connection with liability for the release of a hazardous substance from such vessel or facility. Evidence of compliance with the financial responsibility requirements of this subchapter shall be accepted by a State in lieu of any other requirement of financial responsibility imposed by such State in connection with liability for the release of a hazardous substance from such vessel or facility.

§9615. Presidential delegation and assignment of duties or powers and promulgation of regulations
[CERCLA §115]

The President is authorized to delegate and assign any duties or powers imposed upon or assigned to him and to promulgate any regulations necessary to carry out the provisions of this subchapter.

§9616. Schedules
[CERCLA §116]

(a) Assessment and listing of facilities — It shall be a goal of this chapter that, to the maximum extent practicable —

(1) not later than January 1, 1988, the President shall complete preliminary assessments of all facilities that are contained (as of October 17, 1986) on the Comprehensive Environmental Response, Compensation, and Liability Information System (CERCLIS) including in each assessment a statement as to whether a site inspection is necessary and by whom it should be carried out; and

(2) not later than January 1, 1989, the President shall assure the completion of site inspections at all facilities for which the President has stated a site inspection is necessary pursuant to paragraph (1).

(b) Evaluation — Within 4 years after October 17, 1986, each facility listed (as of October 7, 1986) in the CERCLIS shall be evaluated if the President determines that such evaluation is warranted on the basis of a site inspection or preliminary assessment. The evaluation shall be in accordance with the criteria established in section 9605 of this title under the National Contingency Plan for determining priorities among release for inclusion on the National Priorities List. In the case of a facility listed in the CERCLIS after October 17, 1986, the facility shall be evaluated within 4 years after the date of such listing if the President determines that such evaluation is warranted on the basis of a site inspection or preliminary assessment.

(c) Explanations — If any of the goals established by subsection (a) or (b) of this section are not achieved, the President shall publish an explanation of why such action could not be completed by the specified date.

(d) Commencement of RI/FS — The President shall assure that remedial investigations and feasibility studies (RI/FS) are commenced for facilities listed on the National Priorities List, in addition to those commenced prior to October 17, 1986, in accordance with the following schedule:

(1) not fewer than 275 by the date 36 months after October 17, 1986, and

(2) if the requirement of paragraph (1) is not met, not fewer than an additional 175 by the date 4 years after October 17, 1986, an additional 200 by the date 5 years after October 17, 1986, and a total of 650 by the date 5 years after October 17, 1986.

(e) Commencement of remedial action — The President shall assure that substantial and continuous physical on-site remedial action commences at facilities on the National Priorities List, in addition to those facilities on which remedial action has commenced prior to October 17, 1986, at a rate not fewer than:

(1) 175 facilities during the first 36-month period after October 17, 1986; and

(2) 200 additional facilities during the following 24 months after such 36-month period.

§9617. Public participation
[CERCLA §117]

(a) Proposed plan — Before adoption of any plan for remedial action to be undertaken by the President, by a State, or by any other person, under section 9604, 9606, 9620, or 9622 of this title, the President or State, as appropriate, shall take both of the following actions:

(1) Publish a notice and brief analysis of the proposed plan and make such plan available to the public.

(2) Provide a reasonable opportunity for submission of written and oral comments and an opportunity for a public meeting at or near the facility at issue regarding the proposed plan and regarding any proposed findings under section 9621(d)(4) of this title (relating to cleanup standards). The President or the State shall keep a transcript of the meeting and make such transcript available to the public.

The notice and analysis published under paragraph (1) shall include sufficient information as may be necessary to provide a reasonable explanation of the proposed plan and alternative proposals considered.

(b) Final plan — Notice of the final remedial action plan adopted shall be published and the plan shall be made available to the public before commencement of any remedial action. Such final plan shall be accompanied by a discussion of any significant changes (and the reasons for such changes) in the proposed plan and a response to each of the significant comments, criticisms, and new data submitted in written or oral presentations under subsection (a) of this section.

(c) Explanation of differences — After adoption of a final remedial action plan —

(1) if any remedial action is taken,

(2) if any enforcement action under section 9606 of this title is taken, or

(3) if any settlement or consent decree under section 9606 of this title or section 9622 of this title is entered into,

and if such action, settlement, or decree differs in any significant respects from the final plan, the President or the State shall publish an explanation of the significant differences and the reasons such changes were made.

(d) Publication — For the purposes of this section, publication shall include, at a minimum, publication in a major local newspaper of general circulation. In addition, each item developed, received, published, or made available to the public under this section shall be available for public inspection and copying at or near the facility at issue.

(e) Grants for technical assistance

(1) Authority — Subject to such amounts as are provided in appropriations Acts and in accordance with rules promulgated by the President, the President may make grants available to any group of individuals which may be affected by a release or threatened release at any facility which is listed on the National Priorities List under the National Contingency Plan. Such grants may be used to obtain technical assistance in interpreting information with regard to the nature of the hazard, remedial investigation and feasibility study, record of decision, remedial design, selection and construction of remedial action, operation and maintenance, or removal action at such facility.

(2) Amount — The amount of any grant under this subsection may not exceed $50,000 for a single grant recipient. The President may waive the $50,000 limitation in any case where such waiver is necessary to carry out the purposes of this subsection. Each grant recipient shall be required, as a condition of the grant, to contribute at least

20 percent of the total of costs of the technical assistance for which such grant is made. The President may waive the 20 percent contribution requirement if the grant recipient demonstrates financial need and such waiver is necessary to facilitate public participation in the selection of remedial action at the facility. Not more than one grant may be made under this subsection with respect to a single facility, but the grant may be renewed to facilitate public participation at all stages of remedial action.

§9618. High priority for drinking water supplies
[CERCLA §118]

For purposes of taking action under section 9604 or 9606 of this title and listing facilities on the National Priorities List, the President shall give a high priority to facilities where the release of hazardous substances or pollutants or contaminants has resulted in the closing of drinking water wells or has contaminated a principal drinking water supply.

§9619. Response action contractors
[CERCLA §119]
(a) Liability of response action contractors

(1) Response action contractors — A person who is a response action contractor with respect to any release or threatened release of a hazardous substance or pollutant or contaminant from a vessel or facility shall not be liable under this subchapter or under any other Federal law to any person for injuries, costs, damages, expenses, or other liability (including but not limited to claims for indemnification or contribution and claims by third parties for death, personal injury, illness or loss of or damage to property or economic loss) which results from such release or threatened release.

(2) Negligence, etc. — Paragraph (1) shall not apply in the case of a release that is caused by conduct of the response action contractor which is negligent, grossly negligent, or which constitutes intentional misconduct.

(3) Effect on warranties; employer liability — Nothing in this subsection shall affect the liability of any person under any warranty under Federal, State, or common law. Nothing in this subsection shall affect the liability of an employer who is a response action contractor to any employee of such employer under any provision of law, including any provision of any law relating to worker's compensation.

(4) Governmental employees — A state employee or an employee of a political subdivision who provides services relating to response action while acting within the scope of his authority as a governmental employee shall have the same exemption from liability (subject to the other provisions of this section) as is provided to the response action contractor under this section.

(b) Savings provisions

(1) Liability of other persons — The defense provided by section 9607(b)(3) of this title shall not be available to any potentially responsible party with respect to any costs or damages caused by any act or omission of a response action contractor. Except as provided in subsection (a)(4) of this section and the preceding sentence, nothing in this section shall affect the liability under this chapter or under any other Federal or State law of any person, other than a response action contractor.

(2) Burden of plaintiff — Nothing in this section shall affect the plaintiff's burden of establishing liability under this subchapter.

(c) Indemnification

(1) In general — The President may agree to hold harmless and indemnify any response action contractor meeting the requirements of this subsection against any liability (including the expenses of litigation or settlement) for negligence arising out of the contractor's performance in carrying out response action activities under this subchapter, unless such liability was caused by conduct of the contractor which was grossly negligent or which constituted intentional misconduct.

(2) Applicability — This subsection shall apply only with respect to a response action carried out under written agreement with —

(A) the President;

(B) any Federal agency;

(C) a State or political subdivision which has entered into a contract or cooperative agreement in accordance with section 9604(d)(1) of this title; or

(D) any potentially responsible party carrying out any agreement under section 9622 of this title (relating to settlements) or section 9606 of this title (relating to abatement).

(3) Source of funding — This subsection shall not be subject to section 1301 or 1341 of Title 31 or section 11 of Title 41 or to section 9662 of this title. For purposes of section 9611 of this title, amounts expended pursuant to this subsection for indemnification of any response action contractor (except with respect to federally owned or operated facilities) shall be considered governmental response costs incurred pursuant to section 9604 of this title. If sufficient funds are unavailable in the Hazardous Substance Superfund established under subchapter A of chapter 98 of Title 26 to make payments pursuant to such indemnification or if the Fund is repealed, there are authorized to be appropriated such amounts as may be necessary to make such payments.

(4) Requirements — An indemnification agreement may be provided under this subsection only if the President determines that each of the following requirements are met:

(A) The liability covered by the indemnification agreement exceeds or is not covered by insurance available, at a fair and reasonable price, to the contractor at the time the contractor enters into the contract to provide response action, and adequate insurance to cover such liability is not generally available at the time the response action contract is entered into.

(B) The response action contractor has made diligent efforts to obtain insurance coverage from non-Federal sources to cover such liability.

(C) In the case of a response action contract covering more than one facility, the response action contractor agrees to continue to make such diligent efforts each time the contractor begins work under the contract at a new facility.

(5) Limitations

(A) Liability covered — Indemnification under this subsection shall apply only to response action contractor liability which results from a release of any hazardous substance or pollutant or contaminant if such release arises out of response action activities.

(B) Deductibles and limits — An indemnification agreement under this subsection shall include deductibles and shall place limits on the amount of indemnification to be made available.

(C) Contracts with potentially responsible parties

(i) Decision to indemnify — In deciding whether to enter into an indemnification agreement with a response action contractor carrying out a written contract or agreement with any potentially responsible party, the President shall determine an amount which the potentially responsible party is able to indemnify the contractor. The President may enter into such an indemnification agreement only if the President determines that such amount of indemnification is inadequate to cover any reasonable potential liability of the contractor arising out of the contractor's negligence in performing the contract or agreement with such party. The President shall make the determinations in the preceding sentences (with respect to the amount and the adequacy of the amount) taking into account the total net assets and resources of potentially responsible parties with respect to the facility at the time of such determinations.

(ii) Conditions — The President may pay a claim under an indemnification agreement referred to in clause (i) for the amount determined under clause (i) only

if the contractor has exhausted all administrative, judicial, and common law claims for indemnification against all potentially responsible parties participating in the clean-up of the facility with respect to the liability of the contractor arising out of the contractor's negligence in performing the contract or agreement with such party. Such indemnification agreement shall require such contractor to pay any deductible established under subparagraph (B) before the contractor may recover any amount from the potentially responsible party or under the indemnification agreement.

(D) RCRA facilities — No owner or operator of a facility regulated under the Solid Waste Disposal Act [42 U.S.C. §§6901 *et seq.*] may be indemnified under this subsection with respect to such facility.

(E) Persons retained or hired — A person retained or hired by a person described in subsection (e)(2)(B) of this section shall be eligible for indemnification under this subsection only if the President specifically approves of the retaining or hiring of such person.

(6) Cost recovery — For purposes of section 9607 of this title, amounts expended pursuant to this subsection for indemnification of any person who is a response action contractor with respect to any release or threatened release shall be considered a cost of response incurred by the United States Government with respect to such release.

(7) Regulations — The President shall promulgate regulations for carrying out the provisions of this subsection. Before promulgation of the regulations, the President shall develop guidelines to carry out this section. Development of such guidelines shall include reasonable opportunity for public comment.

(8) Study — The Comptroller General shall conduct a study in the fiscal year ending September 30, 1989, on the application of this subsection, including whether indemnification agreements under this subsection are being used, the number of claims that have been filed under such agreements, and the need for this subsection. The Comptroller General shall report the findings of the study to Congress no later than September 30, 1989.

(d) Exception — The exemption provided under subsection (a) of this section and the authority of the President to offer indemnification under subsection (c) of this section shall not apply to any person covered by the provisions of paragraph (1), (2), (3), or (4) of section 9607(a) of this title with respect to the release or threatened release concerned if such person would be covered by such provisions even if such person had not carried out any actions referred to in subsection (e) of this section.

(e) Definitions — For purposes of this section —

(1) Response action contract — The term "response action contract" means any written contract or agreement entered into by a response action contractor (as defined in paragraph (2)(A) of this subsection) with —

(A) the President;

(B) any Federal agency;

(C) a State or political subdivision which has entered into a contract or cooperative agreement in accordance with section 9604(d)(1) of this title; or

(D) any potentially responsible party carrying out an agreement under section 9606 or 9622 of this title;

to provide any remedial action under this chapter at a facility listed on the National Priorities List, or any removal under this chapter, with respect to any release or threatened release of a hazardous substance or pollutant or contaminant from the facility or to provide any evaluation, planning, engineering, surveying and mapping, design, construction, equipment, or any ancillary services thereto for such facility.

(2) Response action contractor — The term "response action contractor" means —

(A) any —

(i) person who enters into a response action contract with respect to any release or threatened release of a hazardous substance or pollutant or contaminant from a facility and is carrying out such contract; and

(ii) person, public or nonprofit private entity, conducting a field demonstration pursuant to section 9660(b) of this title; and

(iii) recipients of grants (including sub-grantees) under section 9660a of this title for the training and education of workers who are or may be engaged in activities related to hazardous waste removal, containment, or emergency response under this chapter; and

(B) any person who is retained or hired by a person described in subparagraph (A) to provide any services relating to a response action; and

(C) any surety who after October 16, 1990, provides a bid, performance or payment bond to a response action contractor, and begins activities to meet its obligations under such bond, but only in connection with such activities or obligations.

(3) Insurance — The term "insurance" means liability insurance which is fair and reasonably priced, as determined by the President, and which is made available at the time the contractor enters into the response action contract to provide response action.

(f) Competition — Response action contractors and subcontractors for program management, construction management, architectural and engineering, surveying and mapping, and related services shall be selected in accordance with Title IX of the Federal Property and Administrative Services Act of 1949 [40 U.S.C. §§541 *et seq.*]. The Federal selection procedures shall apply to appropriate contracts negotiated by all Federal governmental agencies involved in carrying out this chapter. Such procedures shall be followed by response action contractors and subcontractors.

(g) Surety bonds

(1) If under sections 3131 to 3133 of Title 40, surety bonds are required for any direct Federal procurement of any response action contract and are not waived pursuant to section 3134 of Title 40, they shall be issued in accordance with such sections 3131 to 3133 of Title 40.

(2) If under applicable Federal law surety bonds are required for any direct Federal procurement of any response action contract, no right of action shall accrue on the performance bond issued on such response action contract to or for the use of any person other than the obligee named in the bond.

(3) If under applicable Federal law surety bonds are required for any direct Federal procurement of any response action contract, unless otherwise provided for by the procuring agency in the bond, in the event of a default, the surety's liability on a performance bond shall be only for the cost of completion of the contract work in accordance with the plans and specifications less the balance of funds remaining to be paid under the contract, up to the penal sum of the bond. The surety shall in no event be liable on bonds to indemnify or compensate the obligee for loss or liability arising from personal injury or property damage whether or not caused by a breach of the bonded contract.

(4) Nothing in this subsection shall be construed as preempting, limiting, superseding, affecting, applying to, or modifying any State laws, regulations, requirements, rules, practices or procedures. Nothing in this subsection shall be construed as affecting, applying to, modifying, limiting, superseding, or preempting any rights, authorities, liabilities, demands, actions, causes of action, losses, judgments, claims, statutes of limitation, or obligations under Federal or State law, which do not arise on or under the bond.

(5) This subsection shall not apply to bonds executed before October 17, 1990.

§9620. Federal facilities
[CERCLA §120]

(a) Application of chapter to Federal Government

(1) In general — Each department, agency,

and instrumentality of the United States (including the executive, legislative, and judicial branches of government) shall be subject to, and comply with, this chapter in the same manner and to the same extent, both procedurally and substantively, as any nongovernmental entity, including liability under section 9607 of this title. Nothing in this section shall be construed to affect the liability of any person or entity under sections 9606 and 9607 of this title.

(2) Application of requirements to Federal facilities — All guidelines, rules, regulations, and criteria which are applicable to preliminary assessments carried out under this chapter for facilities at which hazardous substances are located, applicable to evaluations of such facilities under the National Contingency Plan, applicable to inclusion on the National Priorities List, or applicable to remedial actions at such facilities shall also be applicable to facilities which are owned or operated by a department, agency, or instrumentality of the United States in the same manner and to the extent as such guidelines, rules, regulations, and criteria are applicable to other facilities. No department, agency, or instrumentality of the United States may adopt or utilize any such guidelines, rules, regulations, or criteria which are inconsistent with the guidelines, rules, regulations, and criteria established by the Administrator under this chapter.

(3) Exceptions — This subsection shall not apply to the extent otherwise provided in this section with respect to applicable time periods. This subsection shall also not apply to any requirements relating to bonding, insurance, or financial responsibility. Nothing in this chapter shall be construed to require a State to comply with section 9604(c)(3) of this title in the case of a facility which is owned or operated by any department, agency, or instrumentality of the United States.

(4) State laws — State laws concerning removal and remedial action, including State laws regarding enforcement, shall apply to removal and remedial action at facilities owned or operated by a department, agency, or instrumentality of the United States or facilities that are the subject of a deferral under subsection (h)(3)(C) of this section when such facilities are not included on the National Priorities List. The preceding sentence shall not apply to the extent a State law would apply any standard or requirement to such facilities which is more stringent than the standards and requirements applicable to facilities which are not owned or operated by any such department, agency, or instrumentality.

(b) Notice — Each department, agency, and instrumentality of the United States shall add to the inventory of Federal agency hazardous waste facilities required to be submitted under section 3016 of the Solid Waste Disposal Act (42 U.S.C. §6937) (in addition to the information required under section 3016(a)(3) of such Act (42 U.S.C. §6937(a)(3))) information on contamination from each facility owned or operated by the department, agency, or instrumentality if such contamination affects contiguous or adjacent property owned by the department, agency, or instrumentality or by any other person, including a description of the monitoring data obtained.

(c) Federal Agency Hazardous Waste Compliance Docket — The Administrator shall establish a special Federal Agency Hazardous Waste Compliance Docket (hereinafter in this section referred to as the "docket") which shall contain each of the following:

(1) All information submitted under section 3016 of the Solid Waste Disposal Act [42 U.S.C. §6937] and subsection (b) of this section regarding any Federal facility and notice of each subsequent action taken under this chapter with respect to the facility.

(2) Information submitted by each department, agency, or instrumentality of the United States under section 3005 or 3010 of such Act [42 U.S.C. §§6925, 6930].

(3) Information submitted by the department, agency, or instrumentality under section 9603 of this title. The docket shall be available for public inspection at reasonable times. Six months after establishment of the docket and every 6 months thereafter, the Administrator shall publish in the Federal Register a list of the Federal facilities which have been included in the docket during the immediately preceding 6-month period. Such publication shall also indicate where in the appropriate regional office of the Environmental Protection Agency additional information may be obtained with respect to any facility on the docket. The Administrator shall establish a program to provide information to the public with respect to facilities which are included in the docket under this subsection.

(d) Assessment and evaluation

(1) In general — The Administrator shall take steps to assure that a preliminary assessment is conducted for each facility on the docket. Following such preliminary assessment, the Administrator shall, where appropriate —

(A) evaluate such facilities in accordance with the criteria established in accordance with section 9605 of this title under the National Contingency Plan for determining priorities among releases; and

(B) include such facilities on the National Priorities List maintained under such plan if the facility meets such criteria.

(2) Application of criteria

(A) In general — Subject to subparagraph (B), the criteria referred to in paragraph (1) shall be applied in the same manner as the criteria are applied to facilities that are owned or operated by persons other than the United States.

(B) Response under other law — It shall be an appropriate factor to be taken into consideration for the purposes of section 9605(a)(8)(A) of this title that the head of the department, agency, or instrumentality that owns or operates a facility has arranged with the Administrator or appropriate State authorities to respond appropriately, under authority of a law other than this chapter, to a release or threatened release of a hazardous substance.

(3) Completion — Evaluation and listing under this subsection shall be completed in accordance with a reasonable schedule established by the Administrator.

(e) Required action by department

(1) RI/FS — Not later than 6 months after the inclusion of any facility on the National Priorities List, the department, agency, or instrumentality which owns or operates such facility shall, in consultation with the Administrator and appropriate State authorities, commence a remedial investigation and feasibility study for such facility. In the case of any facility which is listed on such list before October 17, 1986, the department, agency, or instrumentality which owns or operates such facility shall, in consultation with the Administrator and appropriate State authorities, commence such an investigation and study for such facility within one year after October 17, 1986. The Administrator and appropriate State authorities shall publish a timetable and deadlines for expeditious completion of such investigation and study.

(2) Commencement of remedial action; interagency agreement — The Administrator shall review the results of each investigation and study conducted as provided in paragraph (1). Within 180 days thereafter, the head of the department, agency, or instrumentality concerned shall enter into an interagency agreement with the Administrator for the expeditious completion by such department, agency, or instrumentality of all necessary remedial action at such facility. Substantial continuous physical onsite remedial action shall be commenced at each facility not later than 15 months after completion of the investigation and study. All such interagency agreements, including review of alternative remedial action plans and selection of remedial action, shall comply with the public participation requirements of section 9617 of this title.

(3) Completion of remedial actions — Remedial actions at facilities subject to interagency agreements under this section shall be completed as expeditiously as practicable. Each agency shall include in its annual budget submissions to the Congress a review of alternative agency funding which could be used to provide for the costs of remedial action. The budget submission shall also include a statement of the hazard posed by the facility to human health, welfare, and the environment and identify the specific consequences of failure to begin and complete remedial action.

(4) Contents of agreement — Each interagency agreement under this subsection shall include, but shall not be limited to, each of the following:

(A) A review of alternative remedial actions and selection of a remedial action by the head of the relevant department, agency, or instrumentality and the Administrator or, if unable to reach agreement on selection of a remedial action, selection by the Administrator.

(B) A schedule for the completion of each such remedial action.

(C) Arrangements for long-term operation and maintenance of the facility.

(5) Annual report — Each department, agency, or instrumentality responsible for compliance with this section shall furnish an annual report to the Congress concerning its progress in implementing the requirements of this section. Such reports shall include, but shall not be limited to, each of the following items:

(A) A report on the progress in reaching interagency agreements under this section.

(B) The specific cost estimates and budgetary proposals involved in each interagency agreement.

(C) A brief summary of the public comments regarding each proposed interagency agreement.

(D) A description of the instances in which no agreement was reached.

(E) A report on progress in conducting investigations and studies under paragraph (1).

(F) A report on progress in conducting remedial actions.

(G) A report on progress in conducting remedial action at facilities which are not listed on the National Priorities List.

With respect to instances in which no agreement was reached within the required time period, the department, agency, or instrumentality filing the report under this paragraph shall include in such report an explanation of the reasons why no agreement was reached. The annual report required by this paragraph shall also contain a detailed description on a State-by-State basis of the status of each facility subject to this section, including a description of the hazard presented by each facility, plans and schedules for initiating and completing response action, enforcement status (where appropriate), and an explanation of any postponements or failure to complete response action. Such reports shall also be submitted to the affected States.

(6) Settlements with other parties — If the Administrator, in consultation with the head of the relevant department, agency, or instrumentality of the United States, determines that remedial investigations and feasibility studies or remedial action will be done properly at the Federal facility by another potentially responsible party within the deadlines provided in paragraphs (1), (2), and (3) of this subsection, the Administrator may enter into an agreement with such party under section 9622 of this title (relating to settlements). Following approval by the Attorney General of any such agreement relating to a remedial action, the agreement shall be entered in the appropriate United States district court as a consent decree under section 9606 of this title.

(f) State and local participation — The Administrator and each department, agency, or instrumentality responsible for compliance with this section shall afford to relevant State and local officials the opportunity to participate in the planning and selection of the remedial action, including but not limited to the review of all applicable data as it becomes available and the development of studies, reports, and action plans. In the case of State officials, the opportunity to participate shall be provided in accordance with section 9621 of this title.

(g) Transfer of authorities — Except for authorities which are delegated by the Administrator to an officer or employee of the Environmental Protection Agency, no authority vested in the Administrator under this section may be transferred, by executive order of the President or otherwise, to any other officer or employee of the United States or to any other person.

(h) Property transferred by Federal agencies

(1) Notice — After the last day of the 6-month period beginning on the effective date of regulations under paragraph (2) of this subsection, whenever any department, agency, or instrumentality of the United States enters into any contract for the sale or other transfer of real property which is owned by the United States and on which any hazardous substance was stored for one year or more, known to have been released, or disposed of, the head of such department, agency, or instrumentality shall include in such contract notice of the type and quantity of such hazardous substance and notice of the time at which such storage, release, or disposal took place, to the extent such information is available on the basis of a complete search of agency files.

(2) Form of notice; regulations — Notice under this subsection shall be provided in such form and manner as may be provided in regulations promulgated by the Administrator. As promptly as practicable after October 17, 1986, but not later than 18 months after October 17,

1986, and after consultation with the Administrator of the General Services Administration, the Administrator shall promulgate regulations regarding the notice required to be provided under this subsection.

(3) Contents of certain deeds

(A) In general — After the last day of the 6-month period beginning on the effective date of regulations under paragraph (2) of this subsection, in the case of any real property owned by the United States on which any hazardous substance was stored for one year or more, known to have been released, or disposed of, each deed entered into for the transfer of such property by the United States to any other person or entity shall contain —

(i) to the extent such information is available on the basis of a complete search of agency files —

(I) a notice of the type and quantity of such hazardous substances,

(II) notice of the time at which such storage, release, or disposal took place, and

(III) a description of the remedial action taken, if any;

(ii) a covenant warranting that —

(I) all remedial action necessary to protect human health and the environment with respect to any such substance remaining on the property has been taken before the date of such transfer, and

(II) any additional remedial action found to be necessary after the date of such transfer shall be conducted by the United States; and

(iii) a clause granting the United States access to the property in any case in which remedial action or corrective action is found to be necessary after the date of such transfer.

(B) Covenant requirements — For purposes of subparagraphs (A)(ii)(I) and (C)(iii), all remedial action described in such subparagraph has been taken if the construction and installation of an approved remedial design has been completed, and the remedy has been demonstrated to the Administrator to be operating properly and successfully. The carrying out of long-term pumping and treating, or operation and maintenance, after the remedy has been demonstrated to the Administrator to be operating properly and successfully does not preclude the transfer of the property. The requirements of subparagraph (A)(ii) shall not apply in any case in which the person or entity to whom the real property is transferred is a potentially responsible party with respect to such property. The requirements of subparagraph (A)(ii) shall not apply in any case in which the transfer of the property occurs or has occurred by means of a lease, without regard to whether the lessee has agreed to purchase the property or whether the duration of the lease is longer than 55 years. In the case of a lease entered into after September 30, 1995, with respect to real property located at an installation approved for closure or realignment under a base closure law, the agency leasing the property, in consultation with the Administrator, shall determine before leasing the property that the property is suitable for lease, that the uses contemplated for the lease are consistent with protection of human health and the environment, and that there are adequate assurances that the United States will take all remedial action referred to in subparagraph (A)(ii) that has not been taken on the date of the lease.

(C) Deferral

(i) In general — The Administrator, with the concurrence of the Governor of the State in which the facility is located (in the case of real property at a Federal facility that is listed on the National Priorities List), or the Governor of the State in which the facility is located (in the case of real property at a Federal facility not listed on the National Priorities List) may defer the requirement of subparagraph (A)(ii)(I) with respect to the property if the Administrator or the Governor, as the case may be, determines that the property is suitable for transfer, based on a finding that —

(I) the property is suitable for transfer for the use intended by the transferee, and the intended use is consistent with protection of human health and the environment;

(II) the deed or other agreement proposed to govern the transfer between the United States and the transferee of the property contains the assurances set forth in clause (ii).

(III) the Federal agency requesting deferral has provided notice, by publication in a newspaper of general circulation in the vicinity of the property, of the proposed transfer and of the opportunity for the public to submit, within a period of not less than 30 days after the date of the notice, written comments on the suitability of the property for transfer; and

(IV) the deferral and the transfer of the property will not substantially delay any necessary response action at the property.

(ii) Response action assurances — With regard to a release or threatened release of a hazardous substance for which a Federal agency is potentially responsible under this section, the deed or other agreement proposed to govern the transfer shall contain assurances that —

(I) provide for any necessary restrictions on the use of the property to ensure the protection of human health and the environment;

(II) provide that there will be restrictions on use necessary to ensure that required remedial investigations, response action, and oversight activities will not be disrupted;

(III) provide that all necessary response action will be taken and identify the schedules for investigation and completion of all necessary response action as approved by the appropriate regulatory agency; and

(IV) provide that the Federal agency responsible for the property subject to transfer will submit a budget request to the Director of the Office of Management and Budget that adequately addresses schedules for investigation and completion of all necessary response action, subject to congressional authorizations and appropriations.

(iii) Warranty — When all response action necessary to protect human health and the environment with respect to any substance remaining on the property on the date of transfer has been taken, the United States shall execute and deliver to the transferee an appropriate document containing a warranty that all such response action has been taken, and the making of the warranty shall be considered to satisfy the requirement of subparagraph (A)(ii)(I).

(iv) Federal responsibility — A deferral under this subparagraph shall not increase, diminish, or affect in any manner any rights or obligations of a Federal agency (including any rights or obligations under this section and sections 9606 and 9607 of this title existing prior to transfer) with respect to a property transferred under this subparagraph.

(4) Identification of uncontaminated property

(A) In the case of real property to which this paragraph applies (as set forth in subparagraph (E)), the head of the department, agency, or instrumentality of the United States with jurisdiction over the property shall identify the real property on which no hazardous substances and no petroleum products or their derivatives were known to have been released or disposed of. Such identification shall be based on an investigation of the real property to determine or discover the obviousness of the presence or likely presence of a release or threatened release of any hazardous substance or any petroleum product or its derivatives, including aviation fuel and motor oil, on the real property. The identification shall consist, at a minimum, of a review of each of the following sources of information concerning the current and previous uses of the real property:

(i) A detailed search of Federal Government records pertaining to the property.

(ii) Recorded chain of title documents regarding the real property.

(iii) Aerial photographs that may reflect prior uses of the real property and that are reasonably obtainable through State or local government agencies.

(iv) A visual inspection of the real property and any buildings, structures, equipment, pipe, pipeline, or other improvements on the real property, and a visual inspection of properties immediately adjacent to the real property.

(v) A physical inspection of property adjacent to the real property, to the extent permitted by owners or operators of such property.

(vi) Reasonably obtainable Federal, State, and local government records of each adjacent facility where there has been a release of any hazardous substance or any petroleum product or its derivatives, including aviation fuel and motor oil, and which is likely to cause or contribute to a release or threatened release of any hazardous substance or any petroleum product or its derivatives, including aviation fuel and motor oil, on the real property.

(vii) Interviews with current or former employees involved in operations on the real property. Such identification shall also be based on sampling, if appropriate under the circumstances. The results of the identification shall be provided immediately to the Administrator and State and local government officials and made available to the public.

(B) The identification required under subparagraph (A) is not complete until concurrence in the results of the identification is obtained, in the case of real property that is part of a facility on the National Priorities List, from the Administrator, or, in the case of real property that is not part of a facility on the National Priorities List, from the appropriate State official. In the case of a concurrence which is required from a State official, the concurrence is deemed to be obtained if, within 90 days after receiving a request for the concurrence, the State official has not acted (by either concurring or declining to concur) on the request for concurrence.

(C)(i) Except as provided in clauses (ii), (iii), and (iv), the identification and concurrence required under subparagraphs (A) and (B), respectively, shall be made at least 6 months before the termination of operations on the real property.

(ii) In the case of real property described in subparagraph (E)(i)(II) on which operations have been closed or realigned or scheduled for closure or realignment pursuant to a base closure law described in subparagraph (E)(ii)(I) or (E)(ii)(II) by October 19, 1992, the identification and concurrence required under subparagraphs (A) and (B), respectively, shall be made not later than 18 months after October 19, 1992.

(iii) In the case of real property described in subparagraph (E)(i)(II) on which operations are closed or realigned or become scheduled for closure or realignment pursuant to the base closure law described in subparagraph (E)(ii)(II) after October 19, 1992, the identification and concurrence required under subparagraphs (A) and (B), respectively, shall be made not later than 18 months after the date by which a joint resolution disapproving the closure or realignment of the real property under section 2904(b) of such base closure law must be enacted, and such a joint resolution has not been enacted.

(iv) In the case of real property described in subparagraphs (E)(i)(II) on which operations are closed or realigned pursuant to a base closure law described in subparagraph (E)(ii)(III) or (E)(ii)(IV), the identification and concurrence required under subparagraphs (A) and (B), respectively, shall be made not later than 18 months after the date on which the real property is selected for closure or realignment pursuant to such a base closure law.

(D) In the case of the sale or other transfer of any parcel of real property identified under subparagraph (A), the deed entered into for the sale or transfer of such property by the United States to any other person or entity shall contain —

(i) a covenant warranting that any response action or corrective action found to be necessary after the date of such sale or transfer shall be conducted by the United States; and

(ii) a clause granting the United States access to the property in any case in which a response action or corrective action is found to be necessary after such date at such property, or such access is necessary to carry out a response action or corrective action on adjoining property.

(E)(i) This paragraph applies to —

(I) real property owned by the United States and on which the United States plans to terminate Federal Government operations, other than real property described in subclause (II); and

(II) real property that is or has been used as a military installation and on which the United States plans to close or realign military operations pursuant to a base closure law.

(ii) For purposes of this paragraph, the term "base closure law" includes the following:

(I) Title II of the Defense Authorization Amendments and Base Closure and Realignment Act (Pub. L. 100-526; 10 U.S.C. §2687 note).

(II) The Defense Base Closure and Realignment Act of 1990 (part A of Title XXIX of Pub. L. 101-510; 10 U.S.C. §2687 note).

(III) Section 2687 of Title 10.

(IV) Any provision of law authorizing the closure or realignment of a military installation enacted on or after October 19, 1992.

(F) Nothing in this paragraph shall affect, preclude, or otherwise impair the termination of Federal Government operations on real property owned by the United States.

(5) Notification of States regarding certain leases — In the case of real property owned by the United States, on which any hazardous substance or any petroleum product or its derivatives (including aviation fuel and motor oil) was stored for one year or more, known to have been released, or disposed of, and on which the United States plans to terminate Federal Government operations, the head of the department, agency, or instrumentality of the United States with jurisdiction over the property shall notify the State in which the property is located of any lease entered into by the United States that will encumber the property beyond the date of termination of operations on the property. Such notification shall be made before entering into the lease and shall include the length of the lease, the name of person to whom the property is leased, and a description of the

uses that will be allowed under the lease of the property and buildings and other structures on the property.

(i) Obligations under Solid Waste Disposal Act — Nothing in this section shall affect or impair the obligation of any department, agency, or instrumentality of the United States to comply with any requirement of the Solid Waste Disposal Act [42 U.S.C. §§6901 *et seq.*] (including corrective action requirements).

(j) National security

(1) Site specific Presidential orders — The President may issue such orders regarding response actions at any specified site or facility of the Department of Energy or the Department of Defense as may be necessary to protect the national security interests of the United States at that site or facility. Such orders may include, where necessary to protect such interests, an exemption from any requirement contained in this subchapter or under Title III of the Superfund Amendments and Reauthorization Act of 1986 [42 U.S.C. §§11001 *et seq.*] with respect to the site or facility concerned. The President shall notify the Congress within 30 days of the issuance of an order under this paragraph providing for any such exemption. Such notification shall include a statement of the reasons for the granting of the exemption. An exemption under this paragraph shall be for a specified period which may not exceed one year. Additional exemptions may be granted, each upon the President's issuance of a new order under this paragraph for the site or facility concerned. Each such additional exemption shall be for a specified period which may not exceed one year. It is the intention of the Congress that whenever an exemption is issued under this paragraph the response action shall proceed as expeditiously as practicable. The Congress shall be notified periodically of the progress of any response action with respect to which an exemption has been issued under this paragraph. No exemption shall be granted under this paragraph due to lack of appropriation unless the President shall have specifically requested such appropriation as a part of the budgetary process and the Congress shall have failed to make available such requested appropriation.

(2) Classified information — Notwithstanding any other provision of law, all requirements of the Atomic Energy Act [42 U.S.C. §§2011 *et seq.*] and all Executive orders concerning the handling of restricted data and national security information, including "need to know" requirements, shall be applicable to any grant of access to classified information under the provisions of this chapter or under Title III of the Superfund Amendments and Reauthorization Act of 1986 [42 U.S.C. §§11001 *et seq.*].

§9621. Cleanup standards
[CERCLA §121]

(a) Selection of remedial action — The President shall select appropriate remedial actions determined to be necessary to be carried out under section 9604 of this title or secured under section 9606 of this title which are in accordance with this section and, to the extent practicable, the national contingency plan, and which provide for cost-effective response. In evaluating the cost effectiveness of proposed alternative remedial actions, the President shall take into account the total short- and long-term costs of such actions, including the costs of operation and maintenance for the entire period during which such activities will be required.

(b) General rules

(1) Remedial actions in which treatment which permanently and significantly reduces the volume, toxicity or mobility of the hazardous substances, pollutants, and contaminants is a principal element, are to be preferred over remedial actions not involving such treatment. The offsite transport and disposal of hazardous substances or contaminated materials without such treatment should be the least favored alternative remedial action where practicable treatment technologies are available. The President shall conduct an assessment of permanent solutions and alternative treatment technologies or resource recovery technologies that, in whole or in part, will result in a permanent and significant decrease in the toxicity, mobility, or volume of the hazardous substance, pollutant, or contaminant. In making such assessment, the President shall specifically address the long-term effectiveness of various alternatives. In assessing alternative remedial actions, the President shall, at a minimum, take into account:

(A) the long-term uncertainties associated with land disposal;

(B) the goals, objectives, and requirements of the Solid Waste Disposal Act [42 U.S.C. §§6901 *et seq.*];

(C) the persistence, toxicity, mobility, and propensity to bioaccumulate of such hazardous substances and their constituents;

(D) short- and long-term potential for adverse health effects from human exposure;

(E) long-term maintenance costs;

(F) the potential for future remedial action costs if the alternative remedial action in question were to fail; and

(G) the potential threat to human health and the environment associated with excavation, transportation, and redisposal, or containment.

The President shall select a remedial action that is protective of human health and the environment, that is cost effective, and that utilizes permanent solutions and alternative treatment technologies or resource recovery technologies to the maximum extent practicable. If the President selects a remedial action not appropriate for a preference under this subsection, the President shall publish an explanation as to why a remedial action involving such reductions was not selected.

(2) The President may select an alternative remedial action meeting the objectives of this subsection whether or not such action has been achieved in practice at any other facility or site that has similar characteristics. In making such a selection, the President may take into account the degree of support for such remedial action by parties interested in such site.

(c) Review — If the President selects a remedial action that results in any hazardous substances, pollutants, or contaminants remaining at the site, the President shall review such remedial action no less often than each 5 years after the initiation of such remedial action to assure that human health and the environment are being protected by the remedial action being implemented. In addition, if upon such review it is the judgment of the President that action is appropriate at such site in accordance with section 9604 or 9606 of this title, the President shall take or require such action. The President shall report to the Congress a list of facilities for which such review is required, the results of all such reviews, and any actions taken as a result of such reviews.

(d) Degree of cleanup

(1) Remedial actions selected under this section or otherwise required or agreed to by the President under this chapter shall attain a degree of cleanup of hazardous substances, pollutants, and contaminants released into the environment and of control of further release at a minimum which assures protection of human health and the environment. Such remedial actions shall be relevant and appropriate under the circumstances presented by the release or threatened release of such substance, pollutant, or contaminant.

(2)(A) With respect to any hazardous substance, pollutant or contaminant that will remain onsite, if —

(i) any standard, requirement, criteria, or limitation under any Federal environmental law, including, but not limited to, the Toxic Substances Control Act [15 U.S.C. §§2601 *et seq.*], the Safe Drinking Water Act [42 U.S.C. §§300f *et seq.*], the Clean Air Act (42 U.S.C. §§7401 *et seq.*), the Clean Water Act [33 U.S.C. §§1251 *et seq.*], the Marine Protection, Research and Sanctuaries Act [16 U.S.C. §§1431 *et seq.*, §§1447 *et seq.*, 33 U.S.C. §§1401 *et seq.*, §§2801 *et seq.*], or the Solid Waste Disposal Act [42 U.S.C. §§6901 *et seq.*]; or

(ii) any promulgated standard, requirement, criteria, or limitation under a

State environmental or facility siting law that is more stringent than any Federal standard, requirement, criteria, or limitation, including each such State standard, requirement, criteria, or limitation contained in a program approved, authorized or delegated by the Administrator under a statute cited in subparagraph (A), and that has been identified to the President by the State in a timely manner, is legally applicable to the hazardous substance or pollutant or contaminant concerned or is relevant and appropriate under the circumstances of the release or threatened release of such hazardous substance or pollutant or contaminant, the remedial action selected under section 9604 of this title or secured under section 9606 of this title shall require, at the completion of the remedial action, a level or standard of control for such hazardous substance or pollutant or contaminant which at least attains such legally applicable or relevant and appropriate standard, requirement, criteria, or limitation. Such remedial action shall require a level or standard of control which at least attains Maximum Contaminant Level Goals established under the Safe Drinking Water Act [42 U.S.C. §§300f *et seq.*] and water quality criteria established under section 304 or 303 of the Clean Water Act (33 U.S.C. §1314, 1313), where such goals or criteria are relevant and appropriate under the circumstances of the release or threatened release.

(B)(i) In determining whether or not any water quality criteria under the Clean Water Act (33 U.S.C. 1251 *et seq.*) is relevant and appropriate under the circumstances of the release or threatened release, the President shall consider the designated or potential use of the surface or groundwater, the environmental media affected, the purposes for which such criteria were developed, and the latest information available.

(ii) For the purposes of this section, a process for establishing alternate concentration limits to those otherwise applicable for hazardous constituents in groundwater under subparagraph (A) may not be used to establish applicable standards under this paragraph if the process assumes a point of human exposure beyond the boundary of the facility, as defined at the conclusion of the remedial investigation and feasibility study, except where —

(I) there are known and projected points of entry of such groundwater into surface water; and

(II) on the basis of measurements or projections, there is or will be no statistically significant increase of such constituents from such groundwater in such surface water at the point of entry or at any point where there is reason to believe accumulation of constituents may occur downstream; and

(III) the remedial action includes enforceable measures that will preclude human exposure to the contaminated groundwater at any point between the facility boundary and all known and projected points of entry of such groundwater into surface water then the assumed point of human exposure may be at such known and projected points of entry.

(C)(i) Clause (ii) of this subparagraph shall be applicable only in cases where, due to the President's selection, in compliance with subsection (b)(1) of this section, of a proposed remedial action which does not permanently and significantly reduce the volume, toxicity, or mobility of hazardous substances, pollutants, or contaminants, the proposed disposition of waste generated by or associated with the remedial action selected by the President is land disposal in a State referred to in clause (ii).

(ii) Except as provided in clauses (iii) and (iv), a State standard, requirement, criteria, or limitation (including any State siting standard or requirement) which could effectively result in the statewide prohibition of land disposal of hazardous substances, pollutants, or contaminants shall not apply.

(iii) Any State standard, requirement, criteria, or limitation referred to in clause (ii) shall apply where each of the following conditions is met:

(I) The State standard, requirement, criteria, or limitation is of general applicability and was adopted by formal means.

(II) The State standard, requirement, criteria, or limitation was adopted on the basis of hydrologic, geologic, or other relevant considerations and was not adopted for the purpose of precluding onsite remedial actions or other land disposal for reasons unrelated to protection of human health and the environment.

(III) The State arranges for, and assures payment of the incremental costs of utilizing, a facility for disposition of the hazardous substances, pollutants, or contaminants concerned.

(iv) Where the remedial action selected by the President does not conform to a State standard and the State has initiated a law suit against the Environmental Protection Agency prior to May 1, 1986, to seek to have the remedial action conform to such standard, the President shall conform the remedial action to the State standard. The State shall assure the availability of an offsite facility for such remedial action.

(3) In the case of any removal or remedial action involving the transfer of any hazardous substance or pollutant or contaminant offsite, such hazardous substance or pollutant or contaminant shall only be transferred to a facility which is operating in compliance with section 3004 and 3005 of the Solid Waste Disposal Act [42 U.S.C. §§6924, 6925] (or, where applicable, in compliance with the Toxic Substances Control Act [15 U.S.C. §§2601 *et seq.*] or other applicable Federal law) and all applicable State requirements. Such substance or pollutant or contaminant may be transferred to a land disposal facility only if the President determines that both of the following requirements are met:

(A) The unit to which the hazardous substance or pollutant or contaminant is transferred is not releasing any hazardous waste, or constituent thereof, into the groundwater or surface water or soil.

(B) All such releases from other units at the facility are being controlled by a corrective action program approved by the Administrator under subtitle C of the Solid Waste Disposal Act [42 U.S.C. §§6921 *et seq.*]. The President shall notify the owner or operator of such facility of determinations under this paragraph.

(4) The President may select a remedial action meeting the requirements of paragraph (1) that does not attain a level or standard of control at least equivalent to a legally applicable or relevant and appropriate standard, requirement, criteria, or limitation as required by paragraph (2) (including subparagraph (B) thereof), if the President finds that —

(A) the remedial action selected is only part of a total remedial action that will attain such level or standard of control when completed;

(B) compliance with such requirement at that facility will result in greater risk to human health and the environment than alternative options;

(C) compliance with such requirements is technically impracticable from an engineering perspective;

(D) the remedial action selected will attain a standard of performance that is equivalent to that required under the otherwise applicable standard, requirement, criteria, or limitation, through use of another method or approach;

(E) with respect to a State standard, requirement, criteria, or limitation, the State has not consistently applied (or demonstrated the intention to consistently apply) the standard, requirement, criteria, or limitation in similar circumstances at other remedial actions within the State; or

(F) in the case of a remedial action to be undertaken solely under section 9604 of this title using the Fund, selection of a remedial action that attains such level or standard of control will not provide a balance between the need for protection of public health and welfare and the environment at the facility under consideration, and the availability of amounts from the Fund to respond to other sites which present or may present a threat to public health or welfare or the environment, taking into consideration the relative immediacy of such threats.

The President shall publish such findings, together with an explanation and appropriate documentation.

(e) Permits and enforcement

(1) No Federal, State, or local permit shall be required for the portion of any removal or remedial action conducted entirely onsite, where such remedial action is selected and carried out in compliance with this section.

(2) A State may enforce any Federal or State standard, requirement, criteria, or limitation to which the remedial action is required to conform under this chapter in the United States district court for the district in which the facility is located. Any consent decree shall require the parties to attempt expeditiously to resolve disagreements concerning implementation of the remedial action informally with the appropriate Federal and State agencies. Where the parties agree, the consent decree may provide for administrative enforcement. Each consent decree shall also contain stipulated penalties for violations of the decree in an amount not to exceed $25,000 per day, which may be enforced by either the President or the State. Such stipulated penalties shall not be construed to impair or affect the authority of the court to order compliance with the specific terms of any such decree.

(f) State involvement

(1) The President shall promulgate regulations providing for substantial and meaningful involvement by each State in initiation, development, and selection of remedial actions to be undertaken in that State. The regulations, at a minimum, shall include each of the following:

(A) State involvement in decisions whether to perform a preliminary assessment and site inspection.

(B) Allocation of responsibility for hazard ranking system scoring.

(C) State concurrence in deleting sites from the National Priorities List.

(D) State participation in the long-term planning process or all remedial sites within the State.

(E) A reasonable opportunity for States to review and comment on each of the following:

　　(i) The remedial investigation and feasibility study and all data and technical documents leading to its issuance.

　　(ii) The planned remedial action identified in the remedial investigation and feasibility study.

　　(iii) The engineering design following selection of the final remedial action.

　　(iv) Other technical data and reports relating to implementation of the remedy.

　　(v) Any proposed finding or decision by the President to exercise the authority of subsection (d)(4) of this section.

(F) Notice to the State of negotiations with potentially responsible parties regarding the scope of any response action at a facility in the State and an opportunity to participate in such negotiations and, subject to paragraph (2), be a party to any settlement.

(G) Notice to the State and an opportunity to comment on the President's proposed plan for remedial action as well as on alternative plans under consideration. The President's proposed decision regarding the selection of remedial action shall be accompanied by a response to the comments submitted by the State, including an explanation regarding any decision under subsection (d)(4) of this section on compliance with promulgated State standards. A copy of such response shall also be provided to the State.

(H) Prompt notice and explanation of each proposed action to the State in which the facility is located. Prior to the promulgation of such regulations, the President shall provide notice to the State of negotiations with potentially responsible parties regarding the scope of any response action at a facility in the State, and such State may participate in such negotiations and, subject to paragraph (2), any settlements.

(2)(A) This paragraph shall apply to remedial actions secured under section 9606 of this title. At least 30 days prior to the entering of any consent decree, if the President proposes to select a remedial action that does not attain a legally applicable or relevant and appropriate standard, requirement, criteria, or limitation, under the authority of subsection (d)(4) of this section, the President shall provide an opportunity for the State to concur or not concur

in such selection. If the State concurs, the State may become a signatory to the consent decree.

(B) If the State does not concur in such selection, and the State desires to have the remedial action conform to such standard, requirement, criteria, or limitation, the State shall intervene in the action under section 9606 of this title before entry of the consent decree, to seek to have the remedial action so conform. Such intervention shall be a matter of right. The remedial action shall conform to such standard, requirement, criteria, or limitation if the State establishes, on the administrative record, that the finding of the President was not supported by substantial evidence. If the court determines that the remedial action shall conform to such standard, requirement, criteria, or limitation, the remedial action shall be so modified and the State may become a signatory to the decree. If the court determines that the remedial action need not conform to such standard, requirement, criteria, or limitation, and the State pays or assures the payment of the additional costs attributable to meeting such standard, requirement, criteria, or limitation, the remedial action shall be so modified and the State shall become a signatory to the decree.

(C) The President may conclude settlement negotiations with potentially responsible parties without State concurrence.

(3)(A) This paragraph shall apply to remedial actions at facilities owned or operated by a department, agency, or instrumentality of the United States. At least 30 days prior to the publication of the President's final remedial action plan, if the President proposes to select a remedial action that does not attain a legally applicable or relevant and appropriate standard, requirement, criteria, or limitation, under the authority of subsection (d)(4) of this section, the President shall provide an opportunity for the State to concur or not concur in such selection. If the State concurs, or does not act within 30 days, the remedial action may proceed.

(B) If the State does not concur in such selection as provided in subparagraph (A), and desires to have the remedial action conform to such standard, requirement, criteria, or limitation, the State may maintain an action as follows:

　　(i) If the President has notified the State of selection of such a remedial action, the State may bring an action within 30 days of such notification for the sole purpose of determining whether the finding of the President is supported by substantial evidence. Such action shall be brought in the United States district court for the district in which the facility is located.

(ii) If the State establishes, on the administrative record, that the President's finding is not supported by substantial evidence, the remedial action shall be modified to conform to such standard, requirement, criteria, or limitation.

(iii) If the State fails to establish that the President's finding was not supported by substantial evidence and if the State pays, within 60 days of judgment, the additional costs attributable to meeting such standard, requirement, criteria, or limitation, the remedial action shall be selected to meet such standard, requirement, criteria, or limitation. If the State fails to pay within 60 days, the remedial action selected by the President shall proceed through completion.

(C) Nothing in this section precludes, and the court shall not enjoin, the Federal agency from taking any remedial action unrelated to or not inconsistent with such standard, requirement, criteria, or limitation.

§9622. Settlements
[CERCLA §122]
(a) Authority to enter into agreements — The President, in his discretion, may enter into an agreement with any person (including the owner or operator of the facility from which a release or substantial threat of release emanates, or any other potentially responsible person), to perform any response action (including any action described in section 9604(b) of this title) if the President determines that such action will be done properly by such person. Whenever practicable and in the public interest, as determined by the President, the President shall act to facilitate agreements under this section that are in the public interest and consistent with the National Contingency Plan in order to expedite effective remedial actions and minimize litigation. If the President decides not to use the procedures in this section, the President shall notify in writing potentially responsible parties at the facility of such decision and the reasons why use of the procedures is inappropriate. A decision of the President to use or not to use the procedures in this section is not subject to judicial review.

(b) Agreements with potentially responsible parties

(1) Mixed funding — An agreement under this section may provide that the President will reimburse the parties to the agreement from the Fund, with interest, for certain costs of actions under the agreement that the parties have agreed to perform but which the President has agreed to finance. In any case in which the President

provides such reimbursement, the President shall make all reasonable efforts to recover the amount of such reimbursement under section 9607 of this title or under other relevant authorities.

(2) Reviewability — The President's decisions regarding the availability of fund financing under this subsection shall not be subject to judicial review under subsection (d) of this section.

(3) Retention of funds — If, as part of any agreement, the President will be carrying out any action and the parties will be paying amounts to the President, the President may, notwithstanding any other provision of law, retain and use such amounts for purposes of carrying out the agreement.

(4) Future obligation of Fund — In the case of a completed remedial action pursuant to an agreement described in paragraph (1), the Fund shall be subject to an obligation for subsequent remedial actions at the same facility but only to the extent that such subsequent actions are necessary by reason of the failure of the original remedial action. Such obligation shall be in a proportion equal to, but not exceeding, the proportion contributed by the Fund for the original remedial action. The Fund's obligation for such future remedial action may be met through Fund expenditures or through payment, following settlement or enforcement action, by parties who were not signatories to the original agreement.

(c) Effect of agreement

(1) Liability — Whenever the President has entered into an agreement under this section, the liability to the United States under this chapter of each party to the agreement, including any future liability to the United States, arising from the release or threatened release that is the subject of the agreement shall be limited as provided in the agreement pursuant to a covenant not to sue in accordance with subsection (f) of this section. A covenant not to sue may provide that future liability to the United States of a settling potentially responsible party under the agreement may be limited to the same proportion as that established in the original settlement agreement. Nothing in this section shall limit or otherwise affect the authority of any court to review in the consent decree process under subsection (d) of this section any covenant not to sue contained in an agreement under this section. In determining the extent to which the liability of parties to an agreement shall be limited pursuant to a covenant not to sue, the President shall be guided by the principle that a more complete covenant not to sue shall be provided for a more permanent remedy undertaken by such parties.

(2) Actions against other persons — If an agreement has been entered into under this section, the President may take any action under section 9606 of this title against any person who

is not a party to the agreement, once the period for submitting a proposal under subsection (e)(2)(B) of this section has expired. Nothing in this section shall be construed to affect either of the following:

(A) The liability of any person under section 9606 or 9607 of this title with respect to any costs or damages which are not included in the agreement.

(B) The authority of the President to maintain an action under this chapter against any person who is not a party to the agreement.

(d) Enforcement

(1) Cleanup agreements

(A) Consent decree — Whenever the President enters into an agreement under this section with any potentially responsible party with respect to remedial action under section 9606 of this title, following approval of the agreement by the Attorney General, except as otherwise provided in the case of certain administrative settlements referred to in subsection (g) of this section, the agreement shall be entered in the appropriate United States district court as a consent decree. The President need not make any finding regarding an imminent and substantial endangerment to the public health or the environment in connection with any such agreement or consent decree.

(B) Effect — The entry of any consent decree under this subsection shall not be construed to be an acknowledgment by the parties that the release or threatened release concerned constitutes an imminent and substantial endangerment to the public health or welfare or the environment. Except as otherwise provided in the Federal Rules of Evidence, the participation by any party in the process under this section shall not be considered an admission of liability for any purpose, and the fact of such participation shall not be admissible in any judicial or administrative proceeding, including a subsequent proceeding under this section.

(C) Structure — The President may fashion a consent decree so that the entering of such decree and compliance with such decree or with any determination or agreement made pursuant to this section shall not be considered an admission of liability for any purpose.

(2) Public participation

(A) Filing of proposed judgment — At least 30 days before a final judgment is entered under paragraph (1), the proposed judgment shall be filed with the court.

(B) Opportunity for comment — The Attorney General shall provide an opportunity to persons who are not named as parties to the action to comment on the proposed judgment before its entry by the court as a final judgment. The Attorney General shall consider, and file with the court, any written comments, views, or allegations relating to the proposed judgment. The Attorney General may withdraw or withhold its consent to the proposed judgment if the comments, views, and allegations concerning the judgment disclose facts or considerations which indicate that the proposed judgment is inappropriate, improper, or inadequate.

(3) 9604(b) agreements — Whenever the President enters into an agreement under this section with any potentially responsible party with respect to action under section 9604(b) of this title, the President shall issue an order or enter into a decree setting forth the obligations of such party. The United States district court for the district in which the release or threatened release occurs may enforce such order or decree.

(e) Special notice procedures

(1) Notice — Whenever the President determines that a period of negotiation under this subsection would facilitate an agreement with potentially responsible parties for taking response action (including any action described in section 9604(b) of this title) and would expedite remedial action, the President shall so notify all such parties and shall provide them with information concerning each of the following:

(A) The names and addresses of potentially responsible parties (including owners and operators and other persons referred to in section 9607(a) of this title), to the extent such information is available.

(B) To the extent such information is available, the volume and nature of substances contributed by each potentially responsible party identified at the facility.

(C) A ranking by volume of the substances at the facility, to the extent such information is available.

The President shall make the information referred to in this paragraph available in advance of notice under this paragraph upon the request of a potentially responsible party in accordance with procedures provided by the President. The provisions of subsection (e) of section 9604 of this title regarding protection of confidential information apply to information provided under this paragraph. Disclosure of information generated by the President under this section to persons other than the Congress, or any duly authorized Committee thereof, is subject to other privileges or protections provided by law, including (but not limited to) those applicable to attorney work product. Nothing contained in this paragraph or in other provisions of this chapter shall be construed, interpreted, or applied to diminish the required disclosure of information under other provisions of this or other Federal or State laws.

(2) Negotiation

(A) Moratorium — Except as provided in this subsection, the President may not commence action under section 9604(a) of this title or take any action under section 9606 of this title for 120 days after providing notice and information under this subsection with respect to such action. Except as provided in this subsection, the President may not commence a remedial investigation and feasibility study under section 9604(b) of this title for 90 days after providing notice and information under this subsection with respect to such action. The President may commence any additional studies or investigations authorized under section 9604(b) of this title, including remedial design, during the negotiation period.

(B) Proposals — Persons receiving notice and information under paragraph (1) of this subsection with respect to action under section 9606 of this title shall have 60 days from the date of receipt of such notice to make a proposal to the President for undertaking or financing the action under section 9606 of this title. Persons receiving notice and information under paragraph (1) of this subsection with respect to action under section 9604(b) of this title shall have 60 days from the date of receipt of such notice to make a proposal to the President for undertaking or financing the action under section 9604(b) of this title.

(C) Additional parties — If an additional potentially responsible party is identified during the negotiation period or after an agreement has been entered into under this subsection concerning a release or threatened release, the President may bring the additional party into the negotiation or enter into a separate agreement with such party.

(3) Preliminary allocation of responsibility

(A) In general — The President shall develop guidelines for preparing nonbinding preliminary allocations of responsibility. In developing these guidelines the President may include such factors as the President considers relevant, such as: volume, toxicity, mobility, strength of evidence, ability to pay, litigative risks, public interest considerations, precedential value, and inequities and aggravating factors. When it would expedite settlements under this section and remedial action, the President may, after completion of the remedial investigation and feasibility study, provide a nonbinding preliminary allocation of responsibility which allocates percentages of the total cost of response among potentially responsible parties at the facility.

(B) Collection of information — To collect information necessary or appropriate for performing the allocation under subparagraph (A) or for otherwise implementing this section, the President may by subpoena require the attendance and testimony of witnesses and the production of reports, papers, documents, answers to questions, and other information that the President deems necessary. Witnesses shall be paid the same fees and mileage that are paid witnesses in the courts of the United States. In the event of contumacy or failure or refusal of any person to obey any such subpoena, any district court of the United States in which venue is proper shall have jurisdiction to order any such person to comply with such subpoena. Any failure to obey such an order of the court is punishable by the court as a contempt thereof.

(C) Effect — The nonbinding preliminary allocation of responsibility shall not be admissible as evidence in any proceeding, and no court shall have jurisdiction to review the nonbinding preliminary allocation of responsibility. The nonbinding preliminary allocation of responsibility shall not constitute an apportionment or other statement on the divisibility of harm or causation.

(D) Costs — The costs incurred by the President in producing the nonbinding preliminary allocation of responsibility shall be reimbursed by the potentially responsible parties whose offer is accepted by the President. Where an offer under this section is not accepted, such costs shall be considered costs of response.

(E) Decision to reject offer — Where the President, in his discretion, has provided a nonbinding preliminary allocation of responsibility and the potentially responsible parties have made a substantial offer providing for response to the President which he rejects, the reasons for the rejection shall be provided in a written explanation. The President's decision to reject such an offer shall not be subject to judicial review.

(4) Failure to propose — If the President determines that a good faith proposal for undertaking or financing action under section 9606 of this title has not been submitted within 60 days of the provision of notice pursuant to this subsection, the President may thereafter commence action under section 9604(a) of this title or take an action against any person under section 9606 of this title. If the President determines that a good faith proposal for undertaking or financing action under section 9604(b) of this title has not been submitted within 60 days after the provision of notice pursuant to this subsection, the President

may thereafter commence action under section 9604(b) of this title.

(5) Significant threats — Nothing in this subsection shall limit the President's authority to undertake response or enforcement action regarding a significant threat to public health or the environment within the negotiation period established by this subsection.

(6) Inconsistent response action — When either the President, or a potentially responsible party pursuant to an administrative order or consent decree under this chapter, has initiated a remedial investigation and feasibility study for a particular facility under this chapter, no potentially responsible party may undertake any remedial action at the facility unless such remedial action has been authorized by the President.

(f) Covenant not to sue

(1) Discretionary covenants — The President may, in his discretion, provide any person with a covenant not to sue concerning any liability to the United States under this chapter, including future liability, resulting from a release or threatened release of a hazardous substance addressed by a remedial action, whether that action is onsite or offsite, if each of the following conditions is met:

(A) The covenant not to sue is in the public interest.

(B) The covenant not to sue would expedite response action consistent with the National Contingency Plan under section 9605 of this title.

(C) The person is in full compliance with a consent decree under section 9606 of this title (including a consent decree entered into in accordance with this section) for response to the release or threatened release concerned.

(D) The response action has been approved by the President.

(2) Special covenants not to sue — In the case of any person to whom the President is authorized under paragraph (1) of this subsection to provide a covenant not to sue, for the portion of remedial action —

(A) which involves the transport and secure disposition offsite of hazardous substances in a facility meeting the requirements of sections 6924(c), (d), (e), (f), (g), (m), (o), (p), (u), and (v) and 6925(c) of this title, where the President has rejected a proposed remedial action that is consistent with the National Contingency Plan that does not include such offsite disposition and has thereafter required offsite disposition; or

(B) which involves the treatment of hazardous substances so as to destroy, eliminate, or permanently immobilize the hazardous constituents of such substances, such that, in

the judgment of the President, the substances no longer present any current or currently foreseeable future significant risk to public health, welfare or the environment, no byproduct of the treatment or destruction process presents any significant hazard to public health, welfare or the environment, and all byproducts are themselves treated, destroyed, or contained in a manner which assures that such byproducts do not present any current or currently foreseeable future significant risk to public health, welfare or the environment,

the President shall provide such person with a covenant not to sue with respect to future liability to the United States under this chapter for a future release or threatened release of hazardous substances from such facility, and a person provided such covenant not to sue shall not be liable to the United States under section 9606 or 9607 of this title with respect to such release or threatened release at a future time.

(3) Requirement that remedial action be completed — A covenant not to sue concerning future liability to the United States shall not take effect until the President certifies that remedial action has been completed in accordance with the requirements of this chapter at the facility that is the subject of such covenant.

(4) Factors — In assessing the appropriateness of a covenant not to sue under paragraph (1) and any condition to be included in a covenant not to sue under paragraph (1) or (2), the President shall consider whether the covenant or condition is in the public interest on the basis of such factors as the following:

(A) The effectiveness and reliability of the remedy, in light of the other alternative remedies considered for the facility concerned.

(B) The nature of the risks remaining at the facility.

(C) The extent to which performance standards are included in the order or decree.

(D) The extent to which the response action provides a complete remedy for the facility, including a reduction in the hazardous nature of the substances at the facility.

(E) The extent to which the technology used in the response action is demonstrated to be effective.

(F) Whether the Fund or other sources of funding would be available for any additional remedial actions that might eventually be necessary at the facility.

(G) Whether the remedial action will be carried out, in whole or in significant part, by the responsible parties themselves.

(5) Satisfactory performance — Any covenant not to sue under this subsection shall be subject

to the satisfactory performance by such party of its obligations under the agreement concerned.

(6) Additional condition for future liability

(A) Except for the portion of the remedial action which is subject to a covenant not to sue under paragraph (2) or under subsection (g) of this section (relating to de minimis settlements), a covenant not to sue a person concerning future liability to the United States shall include an exception to the covenant that allows the President to sue such person concerning future liability resulting from the release or threatened release that is the subject of the covenant where such liability arises out of conditions which are unknown at the time the President certifies under paragraph (3) that remedial action has been completed at the facility concerned.

(B) In extraordinary circumstances, the President may determine, after assessment of relevant factors such as those referred to in paragraph (4) and volume, toxicity, mobility, strength of evidence, ability to pay, litigative risks, public interest considerations, precedential value, and inequities and aggravating factors, not to include the exception referred to in subparagraph (A) if other terms, conditions, or requirements of the agreement containing the covenant not to sue are sufficient to provide all reasonable assurances that public health and the environment will be protected from any future releases at or from the facility.

(C) The President is authorized to include any provisions allowing future enforcement action under section 9606 or 9607 of this title that in the discretion of the President are necessary and appropriate to assure protection of public health, welfare, and the environment.

(g) De minimis settlements

(1) Expedited final settlement — Whenever practicable and in the public interest, as determined by the President, the President shall as promptly as possible reach a final settlement with a potentially responsible party in an administrative or civil action under section 9606 or 9607 of this title if such settlement involves only a minor portion of the response costs at the facility concerned and, in the judgment of the President, the conditions in either of the following subparagraph (A) or (B) are met:

(A) Both of the following are minimal in comparison to other hazardous substances at the facility:

(i) The amount of the hazardous substances contributed by that party to the facility.

(ii) The toxic or other hazardous effects of the substances contributed by that party to the facility.

(B) The potentially responsible party —

(i) is the owner of the real property on or in which the facility is located;

(ii) did not conduct or permit the generation, transportation, storage, treatment, or disposal of any hazardous substance at the facility; and

(iii) did not contribute to the release or threat of release of a hazardous substance at the facility through any action or omission.

This subparagraph (B) does not apply if the potentially responsible party purchased the real property with actual or constructive knowledge that the property was used for the generation, transportation, storage, treatment, or disposal of any hazardous substance.

(2) Covenant not to sue — The President may provide a covenant not to sue with respect to the facility concerned to any party who has entered into a settlement under this subsection unless such a covenant would be inconsistent with the public interest as determined under subsection (f) of this section.

(3) Expedited agreement — The President shall reach any such settlement or grant any such covenant not to sue as soon as possible after the President has available the information necessary to reach such a settlement or grant such a covenant.

(4) Consent decree or administrative order — A settlement under this subsection shall be entered as a consent decree or embodied in an administrative order setting forth the terms of the settlement. In the case of any facility where the total response costs exceed $500,000 (excluding interest), if the settlement is embodied as an administrative order, the order may be issued only with the prior written approval of the Attorney General. If the Attorney General or his designee has not approved or disapproved the order within 30 days of this referral, the order shall be deemed to be approved unless the Attorney General and the Administrator have agreed to extend the time. The district court for the district in which the release or threatened release occurs may enforce any such administrative order.

(5) Effect of agreement — A party who has resolved its liability to the United States under this subsection shall not be liable for claims for contribution regarding matters addressed in the settlement. Such settlement does not discharge any of the other potentially responsible parties unless its terms so provide, but it reduces the potential liability of the others by the amount of the settlement.

(6) Settlements with other potentially responsible parties — Nothing in this subsection shall be construed to affect the authority of the President

to reach settlements with other potentially responsible parties under this chapter.

(7) Reduction in settlement amount based on limited ability to pay

(A) In general. The condition for settlement under this paragraph is that the potentially responsible party is a person who demonstrates to the President an inability or a limited ability to pay response costs.

(B) Considerations. In determining whether or not a demonstration is made under subparagraph (A) by a person, the President shall take into consideration the ability of the person to pay response costs and still maintain its basic business operations, including consideration of the overall financial condition of the person and demonstrable constraints on the ability of the person to raise revenues.

(C) Information. A person requesting settlement under this paragraph shall promptly provide the President with all relevant information needed to determine the ability of the person to pay response costs.

(D) Alternative payment methods. If the President determines that a person is unable to pay its total settlement amount at the time of settlement, the President shall consider such alternative payment methods as may be necessary or appropriate.

(8) Additional conditions for expedited settlements

(A) Waiver of claims. The President shall require, as a condition for settlement under this subsection, that a potentially responsible party waive all of the claims (including a claim for contribution under this Act) that the party may have against other potentially responsible parties for response costs incurred with respect to the facility, unless the President determines that requiring a waiver would be unjust.

(B) Failure to comply. The President may decline to offer a settlement to a potentially responsible party under this subsection if the President determines that the potentially responsible party has failed to comply with any request for access or information or an administrative subpoena issued by the President under this Act or has impeded or is impeding, through action or inaction, the performance of a response action with respect to the facility.

(C) Responsibility to provide information and access. A potentially responsible party that enters into a settlement under this subsection shall not be relieved of the responsibility to provide any information or access requested in accordance with subsection (e)(3)(B) or section 104(e) [42 U.S.C. §9604(e)].

(9) Basis of determination. If the President determines that a potentially responsible party is not eligible for settlement under this subsection, the President shall provide the reasons for the determination in writing to the potentially responsible party that requested a settlement under this subsection.

(10) Notification. As soon as practicable after receipt of sufficient information to make a determination, the President shall notify any person that the President determines is eligible under paragraph (1) of the person's eligibility for an expedited settlement.

(11) No judicial review. A determination by the President under paragraph (7), (8), (9), or (10) shall not be subject to judicial review.

(12) Notice of settlement. After a settlement under this subsection becomes final with respect to a facility, the President shall promptly notify potentially responsible parties at the facility that have not resolved their liability to the United States of the settlement.

(h) Cost recovery settlement authority

(1) Authority to settle — The head of any department or agency with authority to undertake a response action under this chapter pursuant to the national contingency plan may consider, compromise, and settle a claim under section 9607 of this title for costs incurred by the United States Government if the claim has not been referred to the Department of Justice for further action. In the case of any facility where the total response costs exceed $500,000 (excluding interest), any claim referred to in the preceding sentence may be compromised and settled only with the prior written approval of the Attorney General.

(2) Use of arbitration — Arbitration in accordance with regulations promulgated under this subsection may be used as a method of settling claims of the United States where the total response costs for the facility concerned do not exceed $500,000 (excluding interest). After consultation with the Attorney General, the department or agency head may establish and publish regulations for the use of arbitration or settlement under this subsection.

(3) Recovery of claims — If any person fails to pay a claim that has been settled under this subsection, the department or agency head shall request the Attorney General to bring a civil action in an appropriate district court to recover the amount of such claim, plus costs, attorneys' fees, and interest from the date of the settlement. In such an action, the terms of the settlement shall not be subject to review.

(4) Claims for contribution — A person who has resolved its liability to the United States under this subsection shall not be liable for claims for contribution regarding matters addressed in the settlement. Such settlement shall not discharge any of the other potentially liable persons unless its terms so provide,

but it reduces the potential liability of the others by the amount of the settlement.

(i) Settlement procedures

(1) Publication in Federal Register — At least 30 days before any settlement (including any settlement arrived at through arbitration) may become final under subsection (h) of this section, or under subsection (g) of this section in the case of a settlement embodied in an administrative order, the head of the department or agency which has jurisdiction over the proposed settlement shall publish in the Federal Register notice of the proposed settlement. The notice shall identify the facility concerned and the parties to the proposed settlement.

(2) Comment period — For a 30-day period beginning on the date of publication of notice under paragraph (1) of a proposed settlement, the head of the department or agency which has jurisdiction over the proposed settlement shall provide an opportunity for persons who are not parties to the proposed settlement to file written comments relating to the proposed settlement.

(3) Consideration of comments — The head of the department or agency shall consider any comments filed under paragraph (2) in determining whether or not to consent to the proposed settlement and may withdraw or withhold consent to the proposed settlement if such comments disclose facts or considerations which indicate the proposed settlement is inappropriate, improper, or inadequate.

(j) Natural resources

(1) Notification of trustee — Where a release or threatened release of any hazardous substance that is the subject of negotiations under this section may have resulted in damages to natural resources under the trusteeship of the United States, the President shall notify the Federal natural resource trustee of the negotiations and shall encourage the participation of such trustee in the negotiations.

(2) Covenant not to sue — An agreement under this section may contain a covenant not to sue under section 9607(a)(4)(C) of this title for damages to natural resources under the trusteeship of the United States resulting from the release or threatened release of hazardous substances that is the subject of the agreement, but only if the Federal natural resource trustee has agreed in writing to such covenant. The Federal natural resource trustee may agree to such covenant if the potentially responsible party agrees to undertake appropriate actions necessary to protect and restore the natural resources damaged by such release or threatened release of hazardous substances.

(k) Section not applicable to vessels — The provisions of this section shall not apply to releases from a vessel.

(l) Civil penalties — A potentially responsible party which is a party to an administrative order or consent decree entered pursuant to an agreement under this section or section 9620 of this title (relating to Federal facilities) or which is a party to an agreement under section 9620 of this title and which fails or refuses to comply with any term or condition of the order, decree or agreement shall be subject to a civil penalty in accordance with section 9609 of this title.

(m) Applicability of general principles of law — In the case of consent decrees and other settlements under this section (including covenants not to sue), no provision of this chapter shall be construed to preclude or otherwise affect the applicability of general principles of law regarding the setting aside or modification of consent decrees or other settlements.

§9623. Reimbursement to local governments [CERCLA §123]

(a) Application — Any general purpose unit of local government for a political subdivision which is affected by a release or threatened release at any facility may apply to the President for reimbursement under this section.

(b) Reimbursement

(1) Temporary emergency measures — The President is authorized to reimburse local community authorities for expenses incurred (before or after October 17, 1986) in carrying out temporary emergency measures necessary to prevent or mitigate injury to human health or the environment associated with the release or threatened release of any hazardous substance or pollutant or contaminant. Such measures may include, where appropriate, security fencing to limit access, response to fires and explosions, and other measures which require immediate response at the local level.

(2) Local funds not supplanted — Reimbursement under this section shall not supplant local funds normally provided for response.

(c) Amount — The amount of any reimbursement to any local authority under subsection (b)(1) of this section may not exceed $25,000 for a single response. The reimbursement under this section with respect to a single facility shall be limited to the units of local government having jurisdiction over the political subdivision in which the facility is located.

(d) Procedure — Reimbursements authorized pursuant to this section shall be in accordance with rules promulgated by the Administrator within one year after October 17, 1986.

§9624. Methane recovery [CERCLA §124]

(a) In general — In the case of a facility at which equipment for the recovery or processing (including recirculation of condensate) of methane has been installed, for purposes of this chapter:

    (1) The owner or operator of such equipment shall not be considered an "owner or operator", as defined in section 9601(20) of this title, with respect to such facility.

    (2) The owner or operator of such equipment shall not be considered to have arranged for disposal or treatment of any hazardous substance at such facility pursuant to section 9607 of this title.

    (3) The owner or operator of such equipment shall not be subject to any action under section 9606 of this title with respect to such facility.

(b) Exceptions — Subsection (a) of this section does not apply with respect to a release or threatened release of a hazardous substance from a facility described in subsection (a) of this section if either of the following circumstances exist:

    (1) The release or threatened release was primarily caused by activities of the owner or operator of the equipment described in subsection (a) of this section.

    (2) The owner or operator of such equipment would be covered by paragraph (1), (2), (3), or (4) of subsection (a) of section 9607 of this title with respect to such release or threatened release if he were not the owner or operator of such equipment.

In the case of any release or threatened release referred to in paragraph (1), the owner or operator of the equipment described in subsection (a) of this section shall be liable under this chapter only for costs or damages primarily caused by the activities of such owner or operator.

§9625. Section 6921(b)(3)(A)(i) waste
[CERCLA §125]

(a) Revision of hazard ranking system — This section shall apply only to facilities which are not included or proposed for inclusion on the National Priorities List and which contain substantial volumes of waste described in section 6921(b)(3)(A)(i) of this title. As expeditiously as practicable, the President shall revise the hazard ranking system in effect under the National Contingency Plan with respect to such facilities in a manner which assures appropriate consideration of each of the following site-specific characteristics of such facilities:

    (1) The quantity, toxicity, and concentrations of hazardous constituents which are present in such waste and a comparison thereof with other wastes.

    (2) The extent of, and potential for, release of such hazardous constituents into the environment.

    (3) The degree of risk to human health and the environment posed by such constituents.

(b) Inclusion prohibited — Until the hazard ranking system is revised as required by this section,

the President may not include on the National Priorities List any facility which contains substantial volumes of waste described in section 6921(b)(3)(A)(i) of this title on the basis of an evaluation made principally on the volume of such waste and not on the concentrations of the hazardous constituents of such waste. Nothing in this section shall be construed to affect the President's authority to include any such facility on the National Priorities List based on the presence of other substances at such facility or to exercise any other authority of this chapter with respect to such other substances.

§9626. Indian tribes
[CERCLA §126]

(a) Treatment generally — The governing body of an Indian tribe shall be afforded substantially the same treatment as a State with respect to the provisions of section 9603(a) of this title (regarding notification of releases), section 9604(c)(2) of this title (regarding consultation on remedial actions), section 9604(e) of this title (regarding access to information), section 9604(i) of this title (regarding health authorities) and section 9605 of this title (regarding roles and responsibilities under the national contingency plan and submittal of priorities for remedial action, but not including the provision regarding the inclusion of at least one facility per State on the National Priorities List).

(b) Community relocation — Should the President determine that proper remedial action is the permanent relocation of tribal members away from a contaminated site because it is cost effective and necessary to protect their health and welfare, such finding must be concurred in by the affected tribal government before relocation shall occur. The President, in cooperation with the Secretary of the Interior, shall also assure that all benefits of the relocation program are provided to the affected tribe and that alternative land of equivalent value is available and satisfactory to the tribe. Any lands acquired for relocation of tribal members shall be held in trust by the United States for the benefit of the tribe.

(c) Study — The President shall conduct a survey, in consultation with the Indian tribes, to determine the extent of hazardous waste sites on Indian lands. Such survey shall be included within a report which shall make recommendations on the program needs of tribes under this chapter, with particular emphasis on how tribal participation in the administration of such programs can be maximized. Such report shall be submitted to Congress along with the President's budget request for fiscal year 1988.

(d) Limitation — Notwithstanding any other provision of this chapter, no action under this chapter by an Indian tribe shall be barred until the later of the following:

    (1) The applicable period of limitations has expired.

(2) 2 years after the United States, in its capacity as trustee for the tribe, gives written notice to the governing body of the tribe that it will not present a claim or commence an action on behalf of the tribe or fails to present a claim or commence an action within the time limitations specified in this chapter.

§9627. Recycling transactions
[CERCLA §127]
(a) Liability clarification

(1) As provided in subsections (b), (c), (d), and (e), a person who arranged for recycling of recyclable material shall not be liable under sections 9607(a)(3) and 9607(a)(4) of this title with respect to such material.

(2) A determination whether or not any person shall be liable under section 9607(a)(3) or section 9607(a)(4) of this title for any material that is not a recyclable material as that term is used in subsections (b) and (c), (d), or (e) of this section shall be made, without regard to subsections (b), (c), (d), or (e) of this section.

(b) **Recyclable material defined** — For purposes of this section, the term "recyclable material" means scrap paper, scrap plastic, scrap glass, scrap textiles, scrap rubber (other than whole tires), scrap metal, or spent lead-acid, spent nickel-cadmium, and other spent batteries, as well as minor amounts of material incident to or adhering to the scrap material as a result of its normal and customary use prior to becoming scrap; except that such term shall not include —

(1) shipping containers of a capacity from 30 liters to 3,000 liters, whether intact or not, having any hazardous substance (but not metal bits and pieces or hazardous substance that form an integral part of the container) contained in or adhering thereto; or

(2) any item of material that contained polychlorinated biphenyls at a concentration in excess of 50 parts per million or any new standard promulgated pursuant to applicable Federal laws.

(c) **Transactions involving scrap paper, plastic, glass, textiles, or rubber** — Transactions involving scrap paper, scrap plastic, scrap glass, scrap textiles, or scrap rubber (other than whole tires) shall be deemed to be arranging for recycling if the person who arranged for the transaction (by selling recyclable material or otherwise arranging for the recycling of recyclable material) can demonstrate by a preponderance of the evidence that all of the following criteria were met at the time of the transaction:

(1) The recyclable material met a commercial specification grade.

(2) A market existed for the recyclable material.

(3) A substantial portion of the recyclable material was made available for use as feedstock for the manufacture of a new saleable product.

(4) The recyclable material could have been a replacement or substitute for a virgin raw material, or the product to be made from the recyclable material could have been a replacement or substitute for a product made, in whole or in part, from a virgin raw material.

(5) For transactions occurring 90 days or more after November 29, 1999, the person exercised reasonable care to determine that the facility where the recyclable material was handled, processed, reclaimed, or otherwise managed by another person (hereinafter in this section referred to as a "consuming facility") was in compliance with substantive (not procedural or administrative) provisions of any Federal, State, or local environmental law or regulation, or compliance order or decree issued pursuant thereto, applicable to the handling, processing, reclamation, storage, or other management activities associated with recyclable material.

(6) For purposes of this subsection, "reasonable care" shall be determined using criteria that include (but are not limited to) —

(A) the price paid in the recycling transaction;

(B) the ability of the person to detect the nature of the consuming facility's operations concerning its handling, processing, reclamation, or other management activities associated with recyclable material; and

(C) the result of inquiries made to the appropriate Federal, State, or local environmental agency (or agencies) regarding the consuming facility's past and current compliance with substantive (not procedural or administrative) provisions of any Federal, State, or local environmental law or regulation, or compliance order or decree issued pursuant thereto, applicable to the handling, processing, reclamation, storage, or other management activities associated with the recyclable material. For the purposes of this paragraph, a requirement to obtain a permit applicable to the handling, processing, reclamation, or other management activity associated with the recyclable materials shall be deemed to be a substantive provision.

(d) Transactions involving scrap metal

(1) Transactions involving scrap metal shall be deemed to be arranging for recycling if the person who arranged for the transaction (by selling recyclable material or otherwise arranging for the recycling of recyclable material) can demonstrate by a preponderance of the evidence that at the time of the transaction —

(A) the person met the criteria set forth in subsection (c) with respect to the scrap metal;

(B) the person was in compliance with any applicable regulations or standards regarding the storage, transport, management, or other activities associated with the recycling of scrap metal that the Administrator promulgates under the Solid Waste Disposal Act [42 U.S.C.A. §§6901 *et seq.*] subsequent to the enactment of this section and with regard to transactions occurring after the effective date of such regulations or standards; and

(C) the person did not melt the scrap metal prior to the transaction.

(2) For purposes of paragraph (1)(C), melting of scrap metal does not include the thermal separation of 2 or more materials due to differences in their melting points (referred to as "sweating").

(3) For purposes of this subsection, the term "scrap metal" means bits and pieces of metal parts (e.g., bars, turnings, rods, sheets, wire) or metal pieces that may be combined together with bolts or soldering (e.g., radiators, scrap automobiles, railroad box cars), which when worn or superfluous can be recycled, except for scrap metals that the Administrator excludes from this definition by regulation.

(e) Transactions involving batteries

Transactions involving spent lead-acid batteries, spent nickel-cadmium batteries, or other spent batteries shall be deemed to be arranging for recycling if the person who arranged for the transaction (by selling recyclable material or otherwise arranging for the recycling of recyclable material) can demonstrate by a preponderance of the evidence that at the time of the transaction —

(1) the person met the criteria set forth in subsection (c) with respect to the spent lead-acid batteries, spent nickel-cadmium batteries, or other spent batteries, but the person did not recover the valuable components of such batteries; and

(2)(A) with respect to transactions involving lead-acid batteries, the person was in compliance with applicable Federal environmental regulations or standards, and any amendments thereto, regarding the storage, transport, management, or other activities associated with the recycling of spent lead-acid batteries;

(B) with respect to transactions involving nickel-cadmium batteries, Federal environmental regulations or standards are in effect regarding the storage, transport, management, or other activities associated with the recycling of spent nickel-cadmium batteries, and the person was in compliance with applicable regulations or standards or any amendments thereto; or

(C) with respect to transactions involving other spent batteries, Federal environmental regulations or standards are in effect regarding the storage, transport, management, or other activities associated with the recycling of such batteries, and the person was in compliance

with applicable regulations or standards or any amendments thereto.

(f) Exclusions

(1) The exemptions set forth in subsections (c), (d), and (e) shall not apply if —

(A) the person had an objectively reasonable basis to believe at the time of the recycling transaction —

(i) that the recyclable material would not be recycled;

(ii) that the recyclable material would be burned as fuel, or for energy recovery or incineration; or

(iii) for transactions occurring before 90 days after November 29, 1999, that the consuming facility was not in compliance with a substantive (not procedural or administrative) provision of any Federal, State, or local environmental law or regulation, or compliance order or decree issued pursuant thereto, applicable to the handling, processing, reclamation, or other management activities associated with the recyclable material;

(B) the person had reason to believe that hazardous substances had been added to the recyclable material for purposes other than processing for recycling; or

(C) the person failed to exercise reasonable care with respect to the management and handling of the recyclable material (including adhering to customary industry practices current at the time of the recycling transaction designed to minimize, through source control, contamination of the recyclable material by hazardous substances).

(2) For purposes of this subsection, an objectively reasonable basis for belief shall be determined using criteria that include (but are not limited to) the size of the person's business, customary industry practices (including customary industry practices current at the time of the recycling transaction designed to minimize, through source control, contamination of the recyclable material by hazardous substances), the price paid in the recycling transaction, and the ability of the person to detect the nature of the consuming facility's operations concerning its handling, processing, reclamation, or other management activities associated with the recyclable material.

(3) For purposes of this subsection, a requirement to obtain a permit applicable to the handling, processing, reclamation, or other management activities associated with recyclable material shall be deemed to be a substantive provision.

(g) Effect on other liability — Nothing in this section shall be deemed to affect the liability of a person under paragraph (1) or (2) of section 9607(a) of this title.

(h) Regulations — The Administrator has the authority, under section 9615 of this title, to promulgate additional regulations concerning this section.

(i) Effect on pending or concluded actions — The exemptions provided in this section shall not affect any concluded judicial or administrative action or any pending judicial action initiated by the United States prior to enactment of this section.

(j) Liability for attorney's fees for certain actions — Any person who commences an action in contribution against a person who is not liable by operation of this section shall be liable to that person for all reasonable costs of defending that action, including all reasonable attorney's and expert witness fees.

(k) Relationship to liability under other laws — Nothing in this section shall affect —

(1) liability under any other Federal, State, or local statute or regulation promulgated pursuant to any such statute, including any requirements promulgated by the Administrator under the Solid Waste Disposal Act [42 U.S.C.A. §§6901 *et seq.*]; or

(2) the ability of the Administrator to promulgate regulations under any other statute, including the Solid Waste Disposal Act [42 U.S.C.A. §§6901 *et seq.*].

(*l*) Limitation on statutory construction — Nothing in this section shall be construed to —

(1) affect any defenses or liabilities of any person to whom subsection (a)(1) does not apply; or

(2) create any presumption of liability against any person to whom subsection (a)(1) does not apply.

§9628. State response programs
[CERCLA §128]

(a) Assistance to States

(1) In general

(A) States. The Administrator may award a grant to a State or Indian tribe that —

(i) has a response program that includes each of the elements, or is taking reasonable steps to include each of the elements, listed in paragraph (2); or

(ii) is a party to a memorandum of agreement with the Administrator for voluntary response programs.

(B) Use of grants by States

(i) In general. A State or Indian tribe may use a grant under this subsection to establish or enhance the response program of the State or Indian tribe.

(ii) Additional uses. In addition to the uses under clause (i), a State or Indian tribe may use a grant under this subsection to —

(I) capitalize a revolving loan fund for brownfield remediation under section 104(k)(3) [42 U.S.C. §9604(k)(3)];

(II) purchase insurance or develop a risk sharing pool, an indemnity pool, or insurance mechanism to provide financing for response actions under a State response program; or

(III) assist small communities, Indian tribes, rural areas, or disadvantaged areas in carrying out activities described in section 9604(k)(7)(A) of this title with respect to brownfield sites.

(iii) Small communities, Indian tribes, rural areas, and disadvantaged areas

(I) In general

To make grants to States or Indian tribes under clause (ii)(III), the Administrator may use, in addition to amounts available to carry out this subsection, not more than $1,500,000 of the amounts made available to carry out section 9604(k)(7) of this title in each fiscal year.

(II) Limitation

Each grant made under subclause (I) may be not more than $20,000.

(III) Inclusion in other grants

The Administrator may, at the request of a State or Indian tribe, include a grant under this clause in any other grant to the State or Indian tribe made under this subsection.

(iv) Definitions. In this subparagraph:

(I) Disadvantaged area

The term "disadvantaged area" means a community with an annual median household income that is less than 80 percent of the statewide annual median household income, as determined by the President based on the latest available decennial census.

(II) Small community

The term "small community" means a community with a population of not more than 15,000 individuals, as determined by the President based on the latest available decennial census.

(2) Elements. The elements of a State or Indian tribe response program referred to in paragraph (1)(A)(i) are the following:

(A) Timely survey and inventory of brownfield sites in the State.

(B) Oversight and enforcement authorities or other mechanisms, and resources, that are adequate to ensure that—

(i) a response action will—

(I) protect human health and the environment; and

(II) be conducted in accordance with applicable Federal and State law; and

(ii) if the person conducting the response action fails to complete the necessary response activities, including operation and maintenance or long-term monitoring activities, the necessary response activities are completed.

(C) Mechanisms and resources to provide meaningful opportunities for public participation, including—

(i) public access to documents that the State, Indian tribe, or party conducting the cleanup is relying on or developing in making cleanup decisions or conducting site activities;

(ii) prior notice and opportunity for comment on proposed cleanup plans and site activities; and

(iii) a mechanism by which—

(I) a person that is or may be affected by a release or threatened release of a hazardous substance, pollutant, or contaminant at a brownfield site located in the community in which the person works or resides may request the conduct of a site assessment; and

(II) an appropriate State official shall consider and appropriately respond to a request under subclause (I).

(D) Mechanisms for approval of a cleanup plan, and a requirement for verification by and certification or similar documentation from the State, an Indian tribe, or a licensed site professional to the person conducting a response action indicating that the response is complete.

(3) Funding. There is authorized to be appropriated to carry out this subsection $50,000,000 for each of fiscal years 2019 through 2023.

(b) Enforcement in cases of a release subject to State program

(1) Enforcement.

(A) In general. Except as provided in subparagraph (B) and subject to subparagraph (C), in the case of an eligible response site at which—

(i) there is a release or threatened release of a hazardous substance, pollutant, or contaminant; and

(ii) a person is conducting or has completed a response action regarding the specific release that is addressed by the response action that is in compliance with the State program that specifically governs response actions for the protection of public health and the environment,

the President may not use authority under this chapter to take an administrative or judicial enforcement action under section 106(a) [42

U.S.C. §9606(a)] or to take a judicial enforcement action to recover response costs under section 107(a) [42 U.S.C. §9607(a)] against the person regarding the specific release that is addressed by the response action.

(B) Exceptions. The President may bring an administrative or judicial enforcement action under this Act during or after completion of a response action described in subparagraph (A) with respect to a release or threatened release at an eligible response site described in that subparagraph if—

(i) the State requests that the President provide assistance in the performance of a response action;

(ii) the Administrator determines that contamination has migrated or will migrate across a State line, resulting in the need for further response action to protect human health or the environment, or the President determines that contamination has migrated or is likely to migrate onto property subject to the jurisdiction, custody, or control of a department, agency, or instrumentality of the United States and may impact the authorized purposes of the Federal property;

(iii) after taking into consideration the response activities already taken, the Administrator determines that—

(I) a release or threatened release may present an imminent and substantial endangerment to public health or welfare or the environment; and

(II) additional response actions are likely to be necessary to address, prevent, limit, or mitigate the release or threatened release; or

(iv) the Administrator, after consultation with the State, determines that information, that on the earlier of the date on which cleanup was approved or completed, was not known by the State, as recorded in documents prepared or relied on in selecting or conducting the cleanup, has been discovered regarding the contamination or conditions at a facility such that the contamination or conditions at the facility present a threat requiring further remediation to protect public health or welfare or the environment. Consultation with the State shall not limit the ability of the Administrator to make this determination.

(C) Public record. The limitations on the authority of the President under subparagraph (A) apply only at sites in States that maintain, update not less than annually, and make available to the public a record of sites, by name and location, at which response actions have been completed in the previous year and are planned to be addressed under the State program that specifically governs response actions for the protection of public health and the environment in the upcoming year. The public record shall identify whether or not the site, on completion of the response action, will be suitable for unrestricted use and, if not, shall identify the institutional controls relied on in the remedy. Each State and tribe receiving financial assistance under subsection (a) shall maintain and make available to the public a record of sites as provided in this paragraph.

(D) EPA notification

(i) In general. In the case of an eligible response site at which there is a release or threatened release of a hazardous substance, pollutant, or contaminant and for which the Administrator intends to carry out an action that may be barred under subparagraph (A), the Administrator shall —

(I) notify the State of the action the Administrator intends to take; and

(II) (aa) wait 48 hours for a reply from the State under clause (ii); or

(bb) if the State fails to reply to the notification or if the Administrator makes a determination under clause (iii), take immediate action under that clause.

(ii) State reply. Not later than 48 hours after a State receives notice from the Administrator under clause (i), the State shall notify the Administrator if—

(I) the release at the eligible response site is or has been subject to a cleanup conducted under a State program; and

(II) the State is planning to abate the release or threatened release, any actions that are planned.

(iii) Immediate Federal action. The Administrator may take action immediately after giving notification under clause (i) without waiting for a State reply under clause (ii) if the Administrator determines that one or more exceptions under subparagraph (B) are met.

(E) Report to Congress. Not later than 90 days after the date of initiation of any enforcement action by the President under clause (ii), (iii), or (iv) of subparagraph (B), the President shall submit to Congress a report describing the basis for the enforcement action, including specific references to the facts demonstrating that enforcement action is permitted under subparagraph (B).

(2) Savings provision.

(A) Costs incurred prior to limitations. Nothing in paragraph (1) precludes the President from seeking to recover costs incurred prior to the date of the enactment of this section or during a period in which the limitations of paragraph (1)(A) were not applicable.

(B) Effect on agreements between States and EPA. Nothing in paragraph (1)—

(i) modifies or otherwise affects a memorandum of agreement, memorandum of understanding, or any similar agreement relating to this chapter between a State agency or an Indian tribe and the Administrator that is in effect on or before the date of the enactment of this section (which agreement shall remain in effect, subject to the terms of the agreement); or

(ii) limits the discretionary authority of the President to enter into or modify an agreement with a State, an Indian tribe, or any other person relating to the implementation by the President of statutory authorities.

(3) Effective date. This subsection applies only to response actions conducted after February 15, 2001.

(c) Effect on Federal laws. Nothing in this section affects any liability or response authority under any Federal law, including—

(1) this chapter, except as provided in subsection (b);

(2) the Solid Waste Disposal Act (42 U.S.C. 6901 *et seq.*);

(3) the Federal Water Pollution Control Act (33 U.S.C. 1251 *et seq.*);

(4) the Toxic Substances Control Act (15 U.S.C. 2601 *et seq.*); and

(5) the Safe Drinking Water Act (42 U.S.C. 300f *et seq.*).

SUBCHAPTER II — HAZARDOUS SUBSTANCE RESPONSE REVENUE

PART A — HAZARDOUS SUBSTANCE RESPONSE TRUST FUND

§§9631 to 9633. Repealed.

PART B — POST-CLOSURE LIABILITY TRUST FUND

§9641. Repealed. Pub. L. 99-499, title V, Sec. 514(b), Oct. 17, 1986, 100 Stat. 1767

SUBCHAPTER III — MISCELLANEOUS PROVISIONS

§9651. Reports and studies
[CERCLA §301]
(a) Implementation experiences; identification and disposal of waste

(1) The President shall submit to the Congress, within four years after December 11, 1980, a comprehensive report on experience with the implementation of this chapter including, but not limited to —

(A) the extent to which the chapter and Fund are effective in enabling Government to respond to and mitigate the effects of releases of hazardous substances;

(B) a summary of past receipts and disbursements from the Fund;

(C) a projection of any future funding needs remaining after the expiration of authority to collect taxes, and of the threat to public health, welfare, and the environment posed by the projected releases which create any such needs;

(D) the record and experience of the Fund in recovering Fund disbursements from liable parties;

(E) the record of State participation in the system of response, liability, and compensation established by this chapter;

(F) the impact of the taxes imposed by subchapter II of this chapter on the Nation's balance of trade with other countries;

(G) an assessment of the feasibility and desirability of a schedule of taxes which would take into account one or more of the following: the likelihood of a release of a hazardous substance, the degree of hazard and risk of harm to public health, welfare, and the environment resulting from any such release, incentives to proper handling, recycling, incineration, and neutralization of hazardous wastes, and disincentives to improper or illegal handling or disposal of hazardous materials, administrative and reporting burdens on Government and industry, and the extent to which the tax burden falls on the substances and parties which create the problems addressed by this chapter. In preparing the report, the President shall consult with appropriate Federal, State, and local agencies, affected industries and claimants, and such other interested parties as he may find useful. Based upon the analyses and consultation required by this subsection, the President shall also include in the report any recommendations for legislative changes he may deem necessary for the better effectuation of the purposes of this chapter, including but not limited to recommendations concerning authorization levels,

taxes, State participation, liability and liability limits, and financial responsibility provisions for the Response Trust Fund and the Post-closure Liability Trust Fund;

(H) an exemption from or an increase in the substances or the amount of taxes imposed by section 4661 of Title 26 for copper, lead, and zinc oxide, and for feedstocks when used in the manufacture and production of fertilizers, based upon the expenditure experience of the Response Trust Fund;

(I) the economic impact of taxing coal-derived substances and recycled metals.

(2) The Administrator of the Environmental Protection Agency (in consultation with the Secretary of the Treasury) shall submit to the Congress (i) within four years after December 11, 1980, a report identifying additional wastes designated by rule as hazardous after the effective date of this chapter and pursuant to section 3001 of the Solid Waste Disposal Act (42 U.S.C. §6921) and recommendations on appropriate tax rates for such wastes for the Post-closure Liability Trust Fund. The report shall, in addition, recommend a tax rate, considering the quantity and potential danger to human health and the environment posed by the disposal of any wastes which the Administrator, pursuant to subsection 3001(b)(2)(B) and subsection 3001(b)(3)(A) of the Solid Waste Disposal Act of 1980 [42 U.S.C. §6921(b)(2)(B) and 6921(b)(3)(A)], has determined should be subject to regulation under subtitle C of such Act [42 U.S.C. §§6921 et seq.], (ii) within three years after December 11, 1980, a report on the necessity for and the adequacy of the revenue raised, in relation to estimated future requirements, of the Post-closure Liability Trust Fund.

(b) Private insurance protection — The President shall conduct a study to determine (1) whether adequate private insurance protection is available on reasonable terms and conditions to the owners and operators of vessels and facilities subject to liability under section 9607 of this title, and (2) whether the market for such insurance is sufficiently competitive to assure purchasers of features such as a reasonable range of deductibles, coinsurance provisions, and exclusions. The President shall submit the results of his study, together with his recommendations, within two years of December 11, 1980, and shall submit an interim report on his study within one year of December 11, 1980.

(c) Regulations respecting assessment of damages to natural resources

(1) The President, acting through Federal officials designated by the National Contingency Plan published under section 9605 of this title, shall study and, not later than two years after December 11, 1980, shall promulgate regulations for the assessment of damages for injury to, destruction of,

or loss of natural resources resulting from a release of oil or a hazardous substance for the purposes of this chapter and section 1321(f)(4) and (5) of Title 33. Notwithstanding the failure of the President to promulgate the regulations required under this subsection on the required date, the President shall promulgate such regulations not later than 6 months after October 17, 1986.

(2) Such regulations shall specify (A) standard procedures for simplified assessments requiring minimal field observation, including establishing measures of damages based on units of discharge or release or units of affected area, and (B) alternative protocols for conducting assessments in individual cases to determine the type and extent of short- and long-term injury, destruction, or loss. Such regulations shall identify the best available procedures to determine such damages, including both direct and indirect injury, destruction, or loss and shall take into consideration factors including, but not limited to, replacement value, use value, and ability of the ecosystem or resource to recover.

(3) Such regulations shall be reviewed and revised as appropriate every two years.

(d) Issues, alternatives, and policy considerations involving selection of locations for waste treatment, storage, and disposal facilities — The Administrator of the Environmental Protection Agency shall, in consultation with other Federal agencies and appropriate representatives of State and local governments and nongovernmental agencies, conduct a study and report to the Congress within two years of December 11, 1980, on the issues, alternatives, and policy considerations involved in the selection of locations for hazardous waste treatment, storage, and disposal facilities.

This study shall include —

(A) an assessment of current and projected treatment, storage, and disposal capacity needs and shortfalls for hazardous waste by management category on a State-by-State basis;

(B) an evaluation of the appropriateness of a regional approach to siting and designing hazardous waste management facilities and the identification of hazardous waste management regions, interstate or intrastate, or both, with similar hazardous waste management needs;

(C) solicitation and analysis of proposals for the construction and operation of hazardous waste management facilities by nongovernmental entities, except that no proposal solicited under terms of this subsection shall be analyzed if it involves cost to the United States Government or fails to comply with the requirements of subtitle C of the Solid Waste Disposal Act [42 U.S.C. §§6921 et seq.] and other applicable provisions of law;

(D) recommendations on the appropriate balance between public and private sector involvement in the siting, design, and operation of new hazardous waste management facilities;

(E) documentation of the major reasons for public opposition to new hazardous waste management facilities; and

(F) an evaluation of the various options for overcoming obstacles to siting new facilities, including needed legislation for implementing the most suitable option or options.

(e) Adequacy of existing common law and statutory remedies

(1) In order to determine the adequacy of existing common law and statutory remedies in providing legal redress for harm to man and the environment caused by the release of hazardous substances into the environment, there shall be submitted to the Congress a study within twelve months of December 11, 1980.

(2) This study shall be conducted with the assistance of the American Bar Association, the American Law Institute, the Association of American Trial Lawyers, and the National Association of State Attorneys General with the President of each entity selecting three members from each organization to conduct the study. The study chairman and one reporter shall be elected from among the twelve members of the study group.

(3) As part of their review of the adequacy of existing common law and statutory remedies, the study group shall evaluate the following:

(A) the nature, adequacy, and availability of existing remedies under present law in compensating for harm to man from the release of hazardous substances;

(B) the nature of barriers to recovery (particularly with respect to burdens of going forward and of proof and relevancy) and the role such barriers play in the legal system;

(C) the scope of the evidentiary burdens placed on the plaintiff in proving harm from the release of hazardous substances, particularly in light of the scientific uncertainty over causation with respect to —

(i) carcinogens, mutagens, and teratogens, and

(ii) the human health effects of exposure to low doses of hazardous substances over long periods of time;

(D) the nature and adequacy of existing remedies under present law in providing compensation for damages to natural resources from the release of hazardous substances;

(E) the scope of liability under existing law and the consequences, particularly with respect to obtaining insurance, of any changes in such liability;

(F) barriers to recovery posed by existing statutes of limitations.

(4) The report shall be submitted to the Congress with appropriate recommendations. Such recommendations shall explicitly address —

(A) the need for revisions in existing statutory or common law, and

(B) whether such revisions should take the form of Federal statutes or the development of a model code which is recommended for adoption by the States.

(5) The Fund shall pay administrative expenses incurred for the study. No expenses shall be available to pay compensation, except expenses on a per diem basis for the one reporter, but in no case shall the total expenses of the study exceed $300,000.

(f) Modification of national contingency plan — The President, acting through the Administrator of the Environmental Protection Agency, the Secretary of Transportation, the Administrator of the Occupational Safety and Health Administration, and the Director of the National Institute for Occupational Safety and Health shall study and, not later than two years after December 11, 1980, shall modify the national contingency plan to provide for the protection of the health and safety of employees involved in response actions.

(g) Insurability study

(1) Study by Comptroller General — The Comptroller General of the United States, in consultation with the persons described in paragraph (2), shall undertake a study to determine the insurability, and effects on the standard of care, of the liability of each of the following:

(A) Persons who generate hazardous substances: liability for costs and damages under this chapter.

(B) Persons who own or operate facilities: liability for costs and damages under this chapter.

(C) Persons liable for injury to persons or property caused by the release of hazardous substances into the environment.

(2) Consultation — In conducting the study under this subsection, the Comptroller General shall consult with the following:

(A) Representatives of the Administrator.

(B) Representatives of persons described in subparagraphs (A) through (C) of the preceding paragraph.

(C) Representatives (i) of groups or organizations comprised generally of persons adversely affected by releases or threatened releases of hazardous substances and (ii) of groups organized for protecting the interests of consumers.

(D) Representatives of property and casualty insurers.

(E) Representatives of reinsurers.

(F) Persons responsible for the regulation of insurance at the State level.

(3) Items evaluated — The study under this section shall include, among other matters, an evaluation of the following:

(A) Current economic conditions in, and the future outlook for, the commercial market for insurance and reinsurance.

(B) Current trends in statutory and common law remedies.

(C) The impact of possible changes in traditional standards of liability, proof, evidence, and damages on existing statutory and common law remedies.

(D) The effect of the standard of liability and extent of the persons upon whom it is imposed under this chapter on the protection of human health and the environment and on the availability, underwriting, and pricing of insurance coverage.

(E) Current trends, if any, in the judicial interpretation and construction of applicable insurance contracts, together with the degree to which amendments in the language of such contracts and the description of the risks assumed, could affect such trends.

(F) The frequency and severity of a representative sample of claims closed during the calendar year immediately preceding October 17, 1986.

(G) Impediments to the acquisition of insurance or other means of obtaining liability coverage other than those referred to in the preceding subparagraphs.

(H) The effects of the standards of liability and financial responsibility requirements imposed pursuant to this chapter on the cost of, and incentives for, developing and demonstrating alternative and innovative treatment technologies, as well as waste generation minimization.

(4) Submission — The Comptroller General shall submit a report on the results of the study to Congress with appropriate recommendations within 12 months after October 17, 1986.

§9652. Effective dates; savings provisions [CERCLA §302]

(a) Unless otherwise provided, all provisions of this chapter shall be effective on December 11, 1980.

(b) Any regulation issued pursuant to any provisions of section 1321 of Title 33 which is repealed or superseded by this chapter and which is in effect on the date immediately preceding the effective date of this chapter shall be deemed to be a regulation issued pursuant to the authority of this chapter and shall remain in full force and effect unless or until superseded by new regulations issued thereunder.

(c) Any regulation —
    (1) respecting financial responsibility,
    (2) issued pursuant to any provision of law repealed or superseded by this chapter, and
    (3) in effect on the date immediately preceding the effective date of this chapter shall be deemed to be a regulation issued pursuant to the authority of this chapter and shall remain in full force and effect unless or until superseded by new regulations issued thereunder.

(d) Nothing in this chapter shall affect or modify in any way the obligations or liabilities of any person under other Federal or State law, including common law, with respect to releases of hazardous substances or other pollutants or contaminants. The provisions of this chapter shall not be considered, interpreted, or construed in any way as reflecting a determination, in part or whole, of policy regarding the inapplicability of strict liability, or strict liability doctrines, to activities relating to hazardous substances, pollutants, or contaminants or other such activities.

§9653. Repealed. Pub. L. 99-499, Title V, Sec. 511(b), Oct. 17, 1986, 100 Stat. 1761

§9654. Applicability of Federal water pollution control funding, etc., provisions
[CERCLA §304]

(a) Omitted

(b) One-half of the unobligated balance remaining before December 11, 1980, under subsection (k)[1] of section 1321 of Title 33 and all sums appropriated under section 1364(b) of Title 33 shall be transferred to the Fund established under subchapter II of this chapter.

(c) In any case in which any provision of section 1321 of Title 33 is determined to be in conflict with any provisions of this chapter, the provisions of this chapter shall apply.

§9655. Legislative veto of rule or regulation
[CERCLA §305]

(a) **Transmission to Congress upon promulgation or repromulgation of rule or regulation; disapproval procedures** — Notwithstanding any other provision of law, simultaneously with promulgation or repromulgation of any rule or regulation under authority of subchapter I of this chapter, the head of the department, agency, or instrumentality promulgating such rule or regulation shall transmit a copy thereof to the Secretary of the Senate and the Clerk of the House of Representatives. Except as provided in subsection (b) of this section, the rule or regulation shall not become effective, if —
    (1) within ninety calendar days of continuous session of Congress after the date of promulgation, both Houses of Congress adopt a concurrent

resolution, the matter after the resolving clause of which is as follows: "That Congress disapproves the rule or regulation promulgated by the _____ dealing with the matter of _____, which rule or regulation was transmitted to Congress on _____.", the blank spaces therein being appropriately filled; or
    (2) within sixty calendar days of continuous session of Congress after the date of promulgation, one House of Congress adopts such a concurrent resolution and transmits such resolution to the other House, and such resolution is not disapproved by such other House within thirty calendar days of continuous session of Congress after such transmittal.

(b) **Approval; effective dates** — If, at the end of sixty calendar days of continuous session of Congress after the date of promulgation of a rule or regulation, no committee of either House of Congress has reported or been discharged from further consideration of a concurrent resolution disapproving the rule or regulation and neither House has adopted such a resolution, the rule or regulation may go into effect immediately. If, within such sixty calendar days, such a committee has reported or been discharged from further consideration of such a resolution, or either House has adopted such a resolution, the rule or regulation may go into effect not sooner than ninety calendar days of continuous session of Congress after such rule is prescribed unless disapproved as provided in subsection (a) of this section.

(c) **Sessions of Congress as applicable** — For purposes of subsections (a) and (b) of this section —
    (1) continuity of session is broken only by an adjournment of Congress sine die; and
    (2) the days on which either House is not in session because of an adjournment of more than three days to a day certain are excluded in the computation of thirty, sixty, and ninety calendar days of continuous session of Congress.

(d) **Congressional inaction on, or rejection of, resolution of disapproval** — Congressional inaction on, or rejection of, a resolution of disapproval shall not be deemed an expression of approval of such rule or regulation.

§9656. Transportation of hazardous substances; listing as hazardous material; liability for release
[CERCLA §306]

(a) **Listing as hazardous material** — Each hazardous substance which is listed or designated as provided in section 9601(14) of this title shall, within 30 days after October 17, 1986, or at the time of such listing or designation, whichever is later, be listed and regulated as a hazardous material under chapter 51 of Title 49.

(b) Liability for releases — A common or contract carrier shall be liable under other law in lieu of section 9607 of this title for damages or remedial action resulting from the release of a hazardous substance during the course of transportation which commenced prior to the effective date of the listing and regulation of such substance as a hazardous material under chapter 51 of Title 49, or for substances listed pursuant to subsection (a) of this section, prior to the effective date of such listing: Provided, however, That this subsection shall not apply where such a carrier can demonstrate that he did not have actual knowledge of the identity or nature of the substance released.

§9657. Separability; contribution
[CERCLA §308]

If any provision of this chapter, or the application of any provision of this chapter to any person or circumstance, is held invalid, the application of such provision to other persons or circumstances and the remainder of this chapter shall not be affected thereby. If an administrative settlement under section 9622 of this title has the effect of limiting any person's right to obtain contribution from any party to such settlement, and if the effect of such limitation would constitute a taking without just compensation in violation of the fifth amendment of the Constitution of the United States, such person shall not be entitled, under other laws of the United States, to recover compensation from the United States for such taking, but in any such case, such limitation on the right to obtain contribution shall be treated as having no force and effect.

§9658. Actions under State law for damages from exposure to hazardous substances
[CERCLA §309]
(a) State statutes of limitations for hazardous substance cases

(1) Exception to State statutes — In the case of any action brought under State law for personal injury, or property damages, which are caused or contributed to by exposure to any hazardous substance, or pollutant or contaminant, released into the environment from a facility, if the applicable limitations period for such action (as specified in the State statute of limitations or under common law) provides a commencement date which is earlier than the federally required commencement date, such period shall commence at the federally required commencement date in lieu of the date specified in such State statute.

(2) State law generally applicable — Except as provided in paragraph (1), the statute of limitations established under State law shall apply in all actions brought under State law for personal injury, or property damages, which are caused

or contributed to by exposure to any hazardous substance, or pollutant or contaminant, released into the environment from a facility.

(3) Actions under section 9607 — Nothing in this section shall apply with respect to any cause of action brought under section 9607 of this title.

(b) Definitions — As used in this section —

(1) Subchapter I terms — The terms used in this section shall have the same meaning as when used in subchapter I of this chapter.

(2) Applicable limitations period — The term "applicable limitations period" means the period specified in a statute of limitations during which a civil action referred to in subsection (a)(1) of this section may be brought.

(3) Commencement date — The term "commencement date" means the date specified in a statute of limitations as the beginning of the applicable limitations period.

(4) Federally required commencement date

(A) In general — Except as provided in subparagraph (B), the term "federally required commencement date" means the date the plaintiff knew (or reasonably should have known) that the personal injury or property damages referred to in subsection (a)(1) of this section were caused or contributed to by the hazardous substance or pollutant or contaminant concerned.

(B) Special rules — In the case of a minor or incompetent plaintiff, the term "federally required commencement date" means the later of the date referred to in subparagraph (A) or the following:

(i) In the case of a minor, the date on which the minor reaches the age of majority, as determined by State law, or has a legal representative appointed.

(ii) In the case of an incompetent individual, the date on which such individual becomes competent or has had a legal representative appointed.

§9659. Citizens suits
[CERCLA §310]

(a) Authority to bring civil actions — Except as provided in subsections (d) and (e) of this section and in section 9613(h) of this title (relating to timing of judicial review), any person may commence a civil action on his own behalf —

(1) against any person (including the United States and any other governmental instrumentality or agency, to the extent permitted by the eleventh amendment to the Constitution) who is alleged to be in violation of any standard, regulation, condition, requirement, or order which has become effective pursuant to this chapter (including any provision of an agreement under section 9620 of this title, relating to Federal facilities); or

(2) against the President or any other officer of the United States (including the Administrator of the Environmental Protection Agency and the Administrator of the ATSDR) where there is alleged a failure of the President or of such other officer to perform any act or duty under this chapter, including an act or duty under section 9620 of this title (relating to Federal facilities), which is not discretionary with the President or such other officer.

Paragraph (2) shall not apply to any act or duty under the provisions of section 9660 of this title (relating to research, development, and demonstration).

(b) Venue

(1) Actions under subsection (a)(1) — Any action under subsection (a)(1) of this section shall be brought in the district court for the district in which the alleged violation occurred.

(2) Actions under subsection (a)(2) — Any action brought under subsection (a)(2) of this section may be brought in the United States District Court for the District of Columbia.

(c) Relief — The district court shall have jurisdiction in actions brought under subsection (a)(1) of this section to enforce the standard, regulation, condition, requirement, or order concerned (including any provision of an agreement under section 9620 of this title), to order such action as may be necessary to correct the violation, and to impose any civil penalty provided for the violation. The district court shall have jurisdiction in actions brought under subsection (a)(2) of this section to order the President or other officer to perform the act or duty concerned.

(d) Rules applicable to subsection (a)(1) actions

(1) Notice — No action may be commenced under subsection (a)(1) of this section before 60 days after the plaintiff has given notice of the violation to each of the following:

(A) The President.

(B) The State in which the alleged violation occurs.

(C) Any alleged violator of the standard, regulation, condition, requirement, or order concerned (including any provision of an agreement under section 9620 of this title).

Notice under this paragraph shall be given in such manner as the President shall prescribe by regulation.

(2) Diligent prosecution — No action may be commenced under paragraph (1) of subsection (a) of this section if the President has commenced and is diligently prosecuting an action under this chapter, or under the Solid Waste Disposal Act [42 U.S.C. §§6901 *et seq*.] to require compliance with the standard, regulation, condition, requirement, or order concerned (including any provision of an agreement under section 9620 of this title).

(e) Rules applicable to subsection (a)(2) actions — No action may be commenced under paragraph (2) of subsection (a) of this section before the 60th day following the date on which the plaintiff gives notice to the Administrator or other department, agency, or instrumentality that the plaintiff will commence such action. Notice under this subsection shall be given in such manner as the President shall prescribe by regulation.

(f) Costs — The court, in issuing any final order in any action brought pursuant to this section, may award costs of litigation (including reasonable attorney and expert witness fees) to the prevailing or the substantially prevailing party whenever the court determines such an award is appropriate. The court may, if a temporary restraining order or preliminary injunction is sought, require the filing of a bond or equivalent security in accordance with the Federal Rules of Civil Procedure.

(g) Intervention — In any action under this section, the United States or the State, or both, if not a party may intervene as a matter of right. For other provisions regarding intervention, see section 9613 of this title.

(h) Other rights — This chapter does not affect or otherwise impair the rights of any person under Federal, State, or common law, except with respect to the timing of review as provided in section 9613(h) of this title or as otherwise provided in section 9658 of this title (relating to actions under State law).

(i) Definitions — The terms used in this section shall have the same meanings as when used in subchapter I of this chapter.

§9660. Research, development, and demonstration

[CERCLA §311]

(a) Hazardous substance research and training

(1) Authorities of Secretary — The Secretary of Health and Human Services (hereinafter in this subsection referred to as the Secretary), in consultation with the Administrator, shall establish and support a basic research and training program (through grants, cooperative agreements, and contracts) consisting of the following:

(A) Basic research (including epidemiologic and ecologic studies) which may include each of the following:

(i) Advanced techniques for the detection, assessment, and evaluation of the effects on human health of hazardous substances.

(ii) Methods to assess the risks to human health presented by hazardous substances.

(iii) Methods and technologies to detect hazardous substances in the environment and basic biological, chemical, and physical methods to reduce the amount and toxicity of hazardous substances.

(B) Training, which may include each of the following:

    (i) Short courses and continuing education for State and local health and environment agency personnel and other personnel engaged in the handling of hazardous substances, in the management of facilities at which hazardous substances are located, and in the evaluation of the hazards to human health presented by such facilities.

    (ii) Graduate or advanced training in environmental and occupational health and safety and in the public health and engineering aspects of hazardous waste control.

    (iii) Graduate training in the geosciences, including hydrogeology, geological engineering, geophysics, geochemistry, and related fields necessary to meet professional personnel needs in the public and private sectors and to effectuate the purposes of this chapter.

(2) Director of NIEHS — The Director of the National Institute for Environmental Health Sciences shall cooperate fully with the relevant Federal agencies referred to in subparagraph (A) of paragraph (5) in carrying out the purposes of this section.

(3) Recipients of grants, etc. — A grant, cooperative agreement, or contract may be made or entered into under paragraph (1) with an accredited institution of higher education. The institution may carry out the research or training under the grant, cooperative agreement, or contract through contracts, including contracts with any of the following:

    (A) Generators of hazardous wastes.

    (B) Persons involved in the detection, assessment, evaluation, and treatment of hazardous substances.

    (C) Owners and operators of facilities at which hazardous substances are located.

    (D) State and local governments.

(4) Procedures — In making grants and entering into cooperative agreements and contracts under this subsection, the Secretary shall act through the Director of the National Institute for Environmental Health Sciences. In considering the allocation of funds for training purposes, the Director shall ensure that at least one grant, cooperative agreement, or contract shall be awarded for training described in each of clauses (i), (ii), and (iii) of paragraph (1)(B). Where applicable, the Director may choose to operate training activities in cooperation with the Director of the National Institute for Occupational Safety and Health. The procedures applicable to grants and contracts under Title IV of the Public Health Service Act [42

U.S.C. §§281 *et seq.*] shall be followed under this subsection.

(5) Advisory council — To assist in the implementation of this subsection and to aid in the coordination of research and demonstration and training activities funded from the Fund under this section, the Secretary shall appoint an advisory council (hereinafter in this subsection referred to as the "Advisory Council") which shall consist of representatives of the following:

    (A) The relevant Federal agencies.

    (B) The chemical industry.

    (C) The toxic waste management industry.

    (D) Institutions of higher education.

    (E) State and local health and environmental agencies.

    (F) The general public.

(6) Planning — Within nine months after October 17, 1986, the Secretary, acting through the Director of the National Institute for Environmental Health Sciences, shall issue a plan for the implementation of paragraph (1). The plan shall include priorities for actions under paragraph (1) and include research and training relevant to scientific and technological issues resulting from site specific hazardous substance response experience. The Secretary shall, to the maximum extent practicable, take appropriate steps to coordinate program activities under this plan with the activities of other Federal agencies in order to avoid duplication of effort. The plan shall be consistent with the need for the development of new technologies for meeting the goals of response actions in accordance with the provisions of this chapter. The Advisory Council shall be provided an opportunity to review and comment on the plan and priorities and assist appropriate coordination among the relevant Federal agencies referred to in subparagraph (A) of paragraph (5).

(b) Alternative or innovative treatment technology research and demonstration program

    (1) Establishment — The Administrator is authorized and directed to carry out a program of research, evaluation, testing, development, and demonstration of alternative or innovative treatment technologies (hereinafter in this subsection referred to as the "program") which may be utilized in response actions to achieve more permanent protection of human health and welfare and the environment.

    (2) Administration — The program shall be administered by the Administrator, acting through an office of technology demonstration and shall be coordinated with programs carried out by the Office of Solid Waste and Emergency Response and the Office of Research and Development.

    (3) Contracts and grants — In carrying out the program, the Administrator is authorized to enter into contracts and cooperative agreements with, and make grants to, persons, public entities, and nonprofit private entities which are exempt from tax under section 501(c)(3) of Title 26. The Administrator shall, to the maximum extent possible, enter into appropriate cost sharing arrangements under this subsection.

(4) Use of sites — In carrying out the program, the Administrator may arrange for the use of sites at which a response may be undertaken under section 9604 of this title for the purposes of carrying out research, testing, evaluation, development, and demonstration projects. Each such project shall be carried out under such terms and conditions as the Administrator shall require to assure the protection of human health and the environment and to assure adequate control by the Administrator of the research, testing, evaluation, development, and demonstration activities at the site.

(5) Demonstration assistance

(A) Program components — The demonstration assistance program shall include the following:

(i) The publication of a solicitation and the evaluation of applications for demonstration projects utilizing alternative or innovative technologies.

(ii) The selection of sites which are suitable for the testing and evaluation of innovative technologies.

(iii) The development of detailed plans for innovative technology demonstration projects.

(iv) The supervision of such demonstration projects and the providing of quality assurance for data obtained.

(v) The evaluation of the results of alternative innovative technology demonstration projects and the determination of whether or not the technologies used are effective and feasible.

(B) Solicitation — Within 90 days after October 17, 1986, and no less often than once every 12 months thereafter, the Administrator shall publish a solicitation for innovative or alternative technologies at a stage of development suitable for full-scale demonstrations at sites at which a response action may be undertaken under section 9604 of this title. The purpose of any such project shall be to demonstrate the use of an alternative or innovative treatment technology with respect to hazardous substances or pollutants or contaminants which are located at the site or which are to be removed from the site. The solicitation notice shall prescribe information to be included in the application, including technical and economic data derived from the applicant's own research and development efforts, and other information sufficient

to permit the Administrator to assess the technology's potential and the types of remedial action to which it may be applicable.

(C) Applications — Any person and any public or private nonprofit entity may submit an application to the Administrator in response to the solicitation. The application shall contain a proposed demonstration plan setting forth how and when the project is to be carried out and such other information as the Administrator may require.

(D) Project selection — In selecting technologies to be demonstrated, the Administrator shall fully review the applications submitted and shall consider at least the criteria specified in paragraph (7). The Administrator shall select or refuse to select a project for demonstration under this subsection within 90 days of receiving the completed application for such project. In the case of a refusal to select the project, the Administrator shall notify the applicant within such 90-day period of the reasons for his refusal.

(E) Site selection — The Administrator shall propose 10 sites at which a response may be undertaken under section 9604 of this title to be the location of any demonstration project under this subsection within 60 days after the close of the public comment period. After an opportunity for notice and public comment, the Administrator shall select such sites and projects. In selecting any such site, the Administrator shall take into account the applicant's technical data and preferences either for onsite operation or for utilizing the site as a source of hazardous substances or pollutants or contaminants to be treated offsite.

(F) Demonstration plan — Within 60 days after the selection of the site under this paragraph to be the location of a demonstration project, the Administrator shall establish a final demonstration plan for the project, based upon the demonstration plan contained in the application for the project. Such plan shall clearly set forth how and when the demonstration project will be carried out.

(G) Supervision and testing — Each demonstration project under this subsection shall be performed by the applicant, or by a person satisfactory to the applicant, under the supervision of the Administrator. The Administrator shall enter into a written agreement with each applicant granting the Administrator the responsibility and authority for testing procedures, quality control, monitoring, and other measurements necessary to determine and evaluate the results of the demonstration project. The Administrator may pay the costs of testing, monitoring, quality control, and other measurements required by the Administrator to determine and evaluate the results of the demonstration project, and the limitations established by subparagraph (j) shall not apply to such costs.

(H) Project completion — Each demonstration project under this subsection shall be completed within such time as is established in the demonstration plan.

(I) Extensions — The Administrator may extend any deadline established under this paragraph by mutual agreement with the applicant concerned.

(J) Funding restrictions — The Administrator shall not provide any Federal assistance for any part of a full-scale field demonstration project under this subsection to any applicant unless such applicant can demonstrate that it cannot obtain appropriate private financing on reasonable terms and conditions sufficient to carry out such demonstration project without such Federal assistance. The total Federal funds for any full-scale field demonstration project under this subsection shall not exceed 50 percent of the total cost of such project estimated at the time of the award of such assistance. The Administrator shall not expend more than $10,000,000 for assistance under the program in any fiscal year and shall not expend more than $3,000,000 for any single project.

(6) Field demonstrations — In carrying out the program, the Administrator shall initiate or cause to be initiated at least 10 field demonstration projects of alternative or innovative treatment technologies at sites at which a response may be undertaken under section 9604 of this title, in fiscal year 1987 and each of the succeeding three fiscal years. If the Administrator determines that 10 field demonstration projects under this subsection cannot be initiated consistent with the criteria set forth in paragraph (7) in any of such fiscal years, the Administrator shall transmit to the appropriate committees of Congress a report explaining the reasons for his inability to conduct such demonstration projects.

(7) Criteria — In selecting technologies to be demonstrated under this subsection, the Administrator shall, consistent with the protection of human health and the environment, consider each of the following criteria:

(A) The potential for contributing to solutions to those waste problems which pose the greatest threat to human health, which cannot be adequately controlled under present technologies, or which otherwise pose significant management difficulties.

(B) The availability of technologies which have been sufficiently developed for field demonstration and which are likely to be cost-effective and reliable.

(C) The availability and suitability of sites for demonstrating such technologies, taking into account the physical, biological, chemical, and geological characteristics of the sites, the extent and type of contamination found at the site, and the capability to conduct demonstration projects in such a manner as to assure the protection of human health and the environment.

(D) The likelihood that the data to be generated from the demonstration project at the site will be applicable to other sites.

(8) Technology transfer — In carrying out the program, the Administrator shall conduct a technology transfer program including the development, collection, evaluation, coordination, and dissemination of information relating to the utilization of alternative or innovative treatment technologies for response actions. The Administrator shall establish and maintain a central reference library for such information. The information maintained by the Administrator shall be made available to the public, subject to the provisions of section 552 of Title 5 and section 1905 of Title 18, and to other Government agencies in a manner that will facilitate its dissemination; except, that upon a showing satisfactory to the Administrator by any person that any information or portion thereof obtained under this subsection by the Administrator directly or indirectly from such person, would, if made public, divulge —

(A) trade secrets; or

(B) other proprietary information of such person,

the Administrator shall not disclose such information and disclosure thereof shall be punishable under section 1905 of Title 18. This subsection is not authority to withhold information from Congress or any committee of Congress upon the request of the chairman of such committee.

(9) Training — The Administrator is authorized and directed to carry out, through the Office of Technology Demonstration, a program of training and an evaluation of training needs for each of the following:

(A) Training in the procedures for the handling and removal of hazardous substances for employees who handle hazardous substances.

(B) Training in the management of facilities at which hazardous substances are located and in the evaluation of the hazards to human health presented by such facilities for State and local health and environment agency personnel.

(10) Definition — For purposes of this subsection, the term "alternative or innovative treatment technologies" means those technologies, including proprietary or patented methods, which permanently alter the composition of hazardous waste through chemical, biological, or physical means so as to significantly reduce the toxicity, mobility, or volume (or any combination thereof) of the hazardous waste or contaminated materials being treated. The term also includes technologies that characterize or assess the extent of contamination, the chemical and physical character of the contaminants, and the stresses imposed by the contaminants on complex ecosystems at sites.

(c) Hazardous substance research — The Administrator may conduct and support, through grants, cooperative agreements, and contracts, research with respect to the detection, assessment, and evaluation of the effects on and risks to human health of hazardous substances and detection of hazardous substances in the environment. The Administrator shall coordinate such research with the Secretary of Health and Human Services, acting through the advisory council established under this section, in order to avoid duplication of effort.

(d) University hazardous substance research centers

(1) Grant program — The Administrator shall make grants to institutions of higher learning to establish and operate not fewer than 5 hazardous substance research centers in the United States. In carrying out the program under this subsection, the Administrator should seek to have established and operated 10 hazardous substance research centers in the United States.

(2) Responsibilities of centers — The responsibilities of each hazardous substance research center established under this subsection shall include, but not be limited to, the conduct of research and training relating to the manufacture, use, transportation, disposal, and management of hazardous substances and publication and dissemination of the results of such research.

(3) Applications — Any institution of higher learning interested in receiving a grant under this subsection shall submit to the Administrator an application in such form and containing such information as the Administrator may require by regulation.

(4) Selection criteria — The Administrator shall select recipients of grants under this subsection on the basis of the following criteria:

(A) The hazardous substance research center shall be located in a State which is representative of the needs of the region in which such State is located for improved hazardous waste management.

(B) The grant recipient shall be located in an area which has experienced problems with hazardous substance management.

(C) There is available to the grant recipient for carrying out this subsection demonstrated research resources.

(D) The capability of the grant recipient to provide leadership in making national and regional contributions to the solution of both long-range and immediate hazardous substance management problems.

(E) The grant recipient shall make a commitment to support ongoing hazardous substance research programs with budgeted institutional funds of at least $100,000 per year.

(F) The grant recipient shall have an interdisciplinary staff with demonstrated expertise in hazardous substance management and research.

(G) The grant recipient shall have a demonstrated ability to disseminate results of hazardous substance research and educational programs through an interdisciplinary continuing education program.

(H) The projects which the grant recipient proposes to carry out under the grant are necessary and appropriate.

(5) Maintenance of effort — No grant may be made under this subsection in any fiscal year unless the recipient of such grant enters into such agreements with the Administrator as the Administrator may require to ensure that such recipient will maintain its aggregate expenditures from all other sources for establishing and operating a regional hazardous substance research center and related research activities at or above the average level of such expenditures in its 2 fiscal years preceding October 17, 1986.

(6) Federal share — The Federal share of a grant under this subsection shall not exceed 80 percent of the costs of establishing and operating the regional hazardous substance research center and related research activities carried out by the grant recipient.

(7) Limitation on use of funds — No funds made available to carry out this subsection shall be used for acquisition of real property (including buildings) or construction of any building.

(8) Administration through the Office of the Administrator — Administrative responsibility for carrying out this subsection shall be in the Office of the Administrator.

(9) Equitable distribution of funds — The Administrator shall allocate funds made available to carry out this subsection equitably among the regions of the United States.

(10) Technology transfer activities — Not less than five percent of the funds made available to carry out this subsection for any fiscal year shall be available to carry out technology transfer activities.

(e) Report to Congress — At the time of the submission of the annual budget request to Congress, the Administrator shall submit to the appropriate committees of the House of Representatives and the Senate and to the advisory council established under subsection (a) of this section, a report on the progress of the research, development, and demonstration program authorized by subsection (b) of this section, including an evaluation of each demonstration project completed in the preceding fiscal year, findings with respect to the efficacy of such demonstrated technologies in achieving permanent and significant reductions in risk from hazardous wastes, the costs of such demonstration projects, and the potential applicability of, and projected costs for, such technologies at other hazardous substance sites.

(f) Saving provision — Nothing in this section shall be construed to affect the provisions of the Solid Waste Disposal Act [42 U.S.C. §§6901 *et seq.*].

(g) Small business participation — The Administrator shall ensure, to the maximum extent practicable, an adequate opportunity for small business participation in the program established by subsection (b) of this section.

§9660a. Grant program

(1) Grant purposes — Grants for the training and education of workers who are or may be engaged in activities related to hazardous waste removal or containment or emergency response may be made under this section.

(2) Administration — Grants under this section shall be administered by the National Institute of Environmental Health Sciences.

(3) Grant recipients — Grants shall be awarded to nonprofit organizations which demonstrate experience in implementing and operating worker health and safety training and education programs and demonstrate the ability to reach and involve in training programs target populations of workers who are or will be engaged in hazardous waste removal or containment or emergency response operations.

§9661. Love Canal property acquisition [CERCLA §312]

(a) Acquisition of property in Emergency Declaration Area — The Administrator of the Environmental Protection Agency (hereinafter referred to as the "Administrator") may make grants not to exceed $2,500,000 to the State of New York (or to any duly constituted public agency or authority thereof) for purposes of acquisition of private property in the Love Canal Emergency Declaration Area. Such acquisition shall include (but shall not be limited to) all private property within the Emergency Declaration Area, including non-owner occupied residential properties, commercial, industrial, public, religious, non-profit, and vacant properties.

(b) Procedures for acquisition — No property shall be acquired pursuant to this section unless the property owner voluntarily agrees to such acquisition. Compensation for any property acquired pursuant to this section shall be based upon the fair market value of the property as it existed prior to the emergency declaration. Valuation procedures for property acquired with funds provided under this section shall be in accordance with those set forth in the agreement entered into between the New York State Disaster Preparedness Commission and the Love Canal Revitalization Agency on October 9, 1980.

(c) State ownership — The Administrator shall not provide any funds under this section for the acquisition of any properties pursuant to this section unless a public agency or authority of the State of New York first enters into a cooperative agreement with the Administrator providing assurances deemed adequate by the Administrator that the State or an agency created under the laws of the State shall take title to the properties to be so acquired.

(d) Maintenance of property — The Administrator shall enter into a cooperative agreement with an appropriate public agency or authority of the State of New York under which the Administrator shall maintain or arrange for the maintenance of all properties within the Emergency Declaration Area that have been acquired by any public agency or authority of the State. Ninety (90) percent of the costs of such maintenance shall be paid by the Administrator. The remaining portion of such costs shall be paid by the State (unless a credit is available under section 9604(c) of this title). The Administrator is authorized, in his discretion, to provide technical assistance to any public agency or authority of the State of New York in order to implement the recommendations of the habitability and land-use study in order to put the land within the Emergency Declaration Area to its best use.

(e) Habitability and land use study — The Administrator shall conduct or cause to be conducted a habitability and land-use study. The study shall —

(1) assess the risks associated with inhabiting of the Love Canal Emergency Declaration Area;

(2) compare the level of hazardous waste contamination in that Area to that present in other comparable communities; and

(3) assess the potential uses of the land within the Emergency Declaration Area, including but not limited to residential, industrial, commercial and recreational, and the risks associated with such potential uses.

The Administrator shall publish the findings of such study and shall work with the State of New York to develop recommendations based upon the results of such study.

(f) Funding — For purposes of section 9611 of this title [and 9631(c) of this title], the expenditures authorized by this section shall be treated as a cost specified in section 9611(c) of this title.

(g) Response — The provisions of this section shall not affect the implementation of other response actions within the Emergency Declaration Area that the Administrator has determined (before October 17,

1986) to be necessary to protect the public health or welfare or the environment.

(h) Definitions — For purposes of this section:

(1) Emergency Declaration Area — The terms "Emergency Declaration Area" and "Love Canal Emergency Declaration Area" mean the Emergency Declaration Area as defined in section 950, paragraph (2) of the General Municipal Law of the State of New York, Chapter 259, Laws of 1980 [McKinney's N.Y., General Municipal Law, S950, par. 2], as in effect on October 17, 1986.

(2) Private property — As used in subsection (a) of this section, the term "private property" means all property which is not owned by a department, agency, or instrumentality of —

(A) the United States, or

(B) the State of New York (or any public agency or authority thereof).

§9662. Limitation on contract and borrowing authority

Any authority provided by this Act, including any amendment made by this Act, to enter into contracts to obligate the United States or to incur indebtedness for the repayment of which the United States is liable shall be effective only to such extent or in such amounts as are provided in appropriation Acts.

SUBCHAPTER IV — POLLUTION INSURANCE

§9671. Definitions
[CERCLA §401]

As used in this subchapter —

(1) Insurance — The term "insurance" means primary insurance, excess insurance, reinsurance, surplus lines insurance, and any other arrangement for shifting and distributing risk which is determined to be insurance under applicable State or Federal law.

(2) Pollution liability — The term "pollution liability" means liability for injuries arising from the release of hazardous substances or pollutants or contaminants.

(3) Risk retention group — The term "risk retention group" means any corporation or other limited liability association taxable as a corporation, or as an insurance company, formed under the laws of any State —

(A) whose primary activity consists of assuming and spreading all, or any portion, of the pollution liability of its group members;

(B) which is organized for the primary purpose of conducting the activity described under subparagraph (A);

(C) which is chartered or licensed as an insurance company and authorized to engage in the business of insurance under the laws of any State; and

(D) which does not exclude any person from membership in the group solely to provide for members of such a group a competitive advantage over such a person.

(4) Purchasing group — The term "purchasing group" means any group of persons which has as one of its purposes the purchase of pollution liability insurance on a group basis.

(5) State — The term "State" means any State of the United States, the District of Columbia, the Commonwealth of Puerto Rico, Guam, American Samoa, the Virgin Islands, the Commonwealth of the Northern Marianas, and any other territory or possession over which the United States has jurisdiction.

§9672. State laws; scope of subchapter
[CERCLA §402]

(a) State laws — Nothing in this subchapter shall be construed to affect either the tort law or the law governing the interpretation of insurance contracts of any State. The definitions of pollution liability and pollution liability insurance under any State law shall not be applied for the purposes of this subchapter, including recognition or qualification of risk retention groups or purchasing groups.

(b) Scope of subchapter — The authority to offer or to provide insurance under this subchapter shall be limited to coverage of pollution liability risks and this subchapter does not authorize a risk retention group or purchasing group to provide coverage of any other line of insurance.

§9673. Risk retention groups
[CERCLA §403]

(a) Exemption — Except as provided in this section, a risk retention group shall be exempt from the following:

(1) A State law, rule, or order which makes unlawful, or regulates, directly or indirectly, the operation of a risk retention group.

(2) A State law, rule, or order which requires or permits a risk retention group to participate in any insurance insolvency guaranty association to which an insurer licensed in the State is required to belong.

(3) A State law, rule, or order which requires any insurance policy issued to a risk retention group or any member of the group to be countersigned by an insurance agent or broker residing in the State.

(4) A State law, rule, or order which otherwise discriminates against a risk retention group or any of its members.

(b) Exceptions

(1) State laws generally applicable — Nothing in subsection (a) of this section shall be construed to affect the applicability of State laws generally

applicable to persons or corporations. The State in which a risk retention group is chartered may regulate the formation and operation of the group.

(2) State regulations not subject to exemption — Subsection (a) of this section shall not apply to any State law which requires a risk retention group to do any of the following:

(A) Comply with the unfair claim settlement practices law of the State.

(B) Pay, on a nondiscriminatory basis, applicable premium and other taxes which are levied on admitted insurers and surplus line insurers, brokers, or policyholders under the laws of the State.

(C) Participate, on a nondiscriminatory basis, in any mechanism established or authorized under the law of the State for the equitable apportionment among insurers of pollution liability insurance losses and expenses incurred on policies written through such mechanism.

(D) Submit to the appropriate authority reports and other information required of licensed insurers under the laws of a State relating solely to pollution liability insurance losses and expenses.

(E) Register with and designate the State insurance commissioner as its agent solely for the purpose of receiving service of legal documents or process.

(F) Furnish, upon request, such commissioner a copy of any financial report submitted by the risk retention group to the commissioner of the chartering or licensing jurisdiction.

(G) Submit to an examination by the State insurance commissioner in any State in which the group is doing business to determine the group's financial condition, if —

(i) the commissioner has reason to believe the risk retention group is in a financially impaired condition; and

(ii) the commissioner of the jurisdiction in which the group is chartered has not begun or has refused to initiate an examination of the group.

(H) Comply with a lawful order issued in a delinquency proceeding commenced by the State insurance commissioner if the commissioner of the jurisdiction in which the group is chartered has failed to initiate such a proceeding after notice of a finding of financial impairment under subparagraph (G).

(c) **Application of exemptions** — The exemptions specified in subsection (a) of this section apply to —

(1) pollution liability insurance coverage provided by a risk retention group for —

(A) such group; or

(B) any person who is a member of such group;

(2) the sale of pollution liability insurance coverage for a risk retention group; and

(3) the provision of insurance related services or management services for a risk retention group or any member of such a group.

(d) **Agents or brokers** — A State may require that a person acting, or offering to act, as an agent or broker for a risk retention group obtain a license from that State, except that a State may not impose any qualification or requirement which discriminates against a nonresident agent or broker.

§9674. Purchasing groups
[CERCLA §404]

(a) **Exemption** — Except as provided in this section, a purchasing group is exempt from the following:

(1) A State law, rule, or order which prohibits the establishment of a purchasing group.

(2) A State law, rule, or order which makes it unlawful for an insurer to provide or offer to provide insurance on a basis providing, to a purchasing group or its member, advantages, based on their loss and expense experience, not afforded to other persons with respect to rates, policy forms, coverages, or other matters.

(3) A State law, rule, or order which prohibits a purchasing group or its members from purchasing insurance on the group basis described in paragraph (2) of this subsection.

(4) A State law, rule, or order which prohibits a purchasing group from obtaining insurance on a group basis because the group has not been in existence for a minimum period of time or because any member has not belonged to the group for a minimum period of time.

(5) A State law, rule, or order which requires that a purchasing group must have a minimum number of members, common ownership or affiliation, or a certain legal form.

(6) A State law, rule, or order which requires that a certain percentage of a purchasing group must obtain insurance on a group basis.

(7) A State law, rule, or order which requires that any insurance policy issued to a purchasing group or any members of the group be countersigned by an insurance agent or broker residing in that State.

(8) A State law, rule, or order which otherwise discriminate against a purchasing group or any of its members.

(b) **Application of exemptions** — The exemptions specified in subsection (a) of this section apply to the following:

(1) Pollution liability insurance, and comprehensive general liability insurance which includes this coverage, provided to —

(A) a purchasing group; or

(B) any person who is a member of a purchasing group.

(2) The sale of any one of the following to a purchasing group or a member of the group:

(A) Pollution liability insurance and comprehensive general liability coverage.

(B) Insurance related services.

(C) Management services.

(c) **Agents or brokers** — A State may require that a person acting, or offering to act, as an agent or broker for a purchasing group obtain a license from that State, except that a State may not impose any qualification or requirement which discriminates against a nonresident agent or broker.

§9675. Applicability of securities laws
[CERCLA §405]

(a) **Ownership interests** — The ownership interests of members of a risk retention group shall be considered to be —

(1) exempted securities for purposes of section 77e of Title 15 and for purposes of section 78*l* of Title 15; and

(2) securities for purposes of the provisions of section 77q of Title 15 and the provisions of section 78j of Title 15.

(b) **Investment Company Act** — A risk retention group shall not be considered to be an investment company for purposes of the Investment Company Act of 1940 (15 U.S.C. §§80a-1 *et seq.*).

(c) **Blue sky law** — The ownership interests of members in a risk retention group shall not be considered securities for purposes of any State blue sky law.

C. POLLUTION PREVENTION ACT (PPA)

A GUIDE TO MATERIALS ON POLLUTION PREVENTION AVAILABLE ON THE INTERNET

The homepage of EPA's Office of Pollution Prevention and Toxics (OPPT) is located at *https://www.epa. gov/aboutepa/about-office-chemical-safety-and-pollution-prevention-ocspp#oppt*. It includes links to the agency's Safer Choice Program *(https://www.epa.gov/saferchoice)*, which encourages the incorporation of environmental considerations into product design decisions, and to EPA's Green Chemistry Program *(https://www.epa.gov/ greenchemistry)*, which encourages the use of technologies that reduce or eliminate the use or generation of hazardous substances.

OPPT maintains a webpage devoted entirely to Pollution Prevention ("P2") issues. The webpage is located at *http://www.epa.gov/p2*. It explains EPA's use of "P2" principles as a vehicle for reinventing traditional agency programs and for developing innovative new strategies to promote environmental protection. The webpage provides information about EPA's P2 practices and programs, and it includes links to technical assistance resources and to information about P2 programs undertaken by others.

EPA funds the Pollution Prevention Resource Exchange, a consortium of eight regional centers offering information, training, referrals, and research on pollution prevention principles. The consortium's website is located at *https://www.epa.gov/p2/pollution-prevention-resource-exchange-p2rx*. EPA also maintains a Pollution Prevention Information Clearinghouse (PPIC), as required by Congress in the Pollution Prevention Act (PPA).

POLLUTION PREVENTION ACT LEGISLATIVE HISTORY TIMELINE

November 5, 1990: The Pollution Prevention Act, Pub. L. 101-508, 104 Stat. 1388, is signed into law by President Bush. The legislation declares a national policy to prevent or reduce pollution at the source whenever feasible and requires EPA to establish a pollution prevention strategy to promote source reduction and recycling.

OUTLINE OF PRINCIPAL PROVISIONS OF THE PPA

§6602 (42 U.S.C. §13101) National Policy: declares a national policy to prevent or reduce pollution at the source whenever feasible.

§6604 (42 U.S.C. §13103) EPA Activities: requires EPA to establish a source reduction strategy, to establish standard methods of measuring source reduction, and to promote source reduction by businesses.

§6605 (42 U.S.C. §13104) Grants to State Technical Assistance Programs: authorizes EPA to make matching grants to states for programs to promote the use of source reduction techniques by businesses.

§6606 (42 U.S.C. §13105) Source Reduction Clearinghouse: requires EPA to establish a Source Reduction Clearinghouse including a computer database containing information on approaches to source reduction.

§6607 (42 U.S.C. §13106) Reporting of Source Reduction and Recycling: requires facilities filing annual toxic chemical release forms to also file annual reports on their progress in source reduction and recycling.

§6608 (42 U.S.C. §13107) EPA Reports: requires the EPA Administrator to report to Congress biennially on actions taken to implement the agency's source reduction strategy.

Pollution Prevention Act
42 U.S.C. §§13101 to 13109

§13101. Findings and policy
[PPA §6602]

(a) Findings — The Congress finds that:

(1) The United States of America annually produces millions of tons of pollution and spends tens of billions of dollars per year controlling this pollution.

(2) There are significant opportunities for industry to reduce or prevent pollution at the source through cost-effective changes in production, operation, and raw materials use. Such changes offer industry substantial savings in reduced raw material, pollution control, and liability costs as well as help protect the environment and reduce risks to worker health and safety.

(3) The opportunities or source reduction are often not realized because existing regulations, and the industrial resources they require for compliance, focus upon treatment and disposal, rather than source reduction; existing regulations do not emphasize multi-media management of pollution; and businesses need information and technical assistance to overcome institutional barriers to the adoption of source reduction practices.

(4) Source reduction is fundamentally different and more desirable than waste management and pollution control. The Environmental Protection Agency needs to address the historical lack of attention to source reduction.

(5) As a first step in preventing pollution through source reduction, the Environmental Protection Agency must establish a source reduction program which collects and disseminates information, provides financial assistance to States, and implements the other activities provided for in this chapter.

(b) Policy — The Congress hereby declares it to be the national policy of the United States that pollution should be prevented or reduced at the source whenever feasible; pollution that cannot be prevented should be recycled in an environmentally safe manner, whenever feasible; pollution that cannot be prevented or recycled should be treated in an environmentally safe manner whenever feasible; and disposal or other release into the environment should be employed only as a last resort and should be conducted in an environmentally safe manner.

§13102. Definitions
[PPA §6603]

For purposes of this chapter —

(1) The term "Administrator" means the Administrator of the Environmental Protection Agency.

(2) The term "Agency" means the Environmental Protection Agency.

(3) The term "toxic chemical" means any substance on the list described in section 11023(c) of this title.

(4) The term "release" has the same meaning as provided by section 11049(8) of this title.

(5)(A) The term "source reduction" means any practice which —

(i) reduces the amount of any hazardous substance, pollutant, or contaminant entering any waste stream or otherwise released into the environment (including fugitive emissions) prior to recycling, treatment, or disposal; and

(ii) reduces the hazards to public health and the environment associated with the release of such substances, pollutants, or contaminants. The term includes equipment or technology modifications, process or procedure modifications, reformulation or redesign of products, substitution of raw materials, and improvements in housekeeping, maintenance, training, or inventory control.

(B) The term "source reduction" does not include any practice which alters the physical, chemical, or biological characteristics or the volume of a hazardous substance, pollutant, or contaminant through a process or activity which itself is not integral to and necessary for the production of a product or the providing of a service.

(6) The term "multi-media" means water, air, and land.

(7) The term "SIC codes" refers to the 2-digit code numbers used for classification of economic activity in the Standard Industrial Classification Manual.

§13103. EPA activities
[PPA §6604]

(a) Authorities — The Administrator shall establish in the Agency an office to carry out the functions of the Administrator under this chapter. The office shall be independent of the Agency's single-medium program offices but shall have the authority to review and advise such offices on their activities to promote a multi-media approach to source reduction. The office shall be under the direction of such officer of the Agency as the Administrator shall designate.

(b) Functions — The Administrator shall develop and implement a strategy to promote source reduction. As part of the strategy, the Administrator shall —

(1) establish standard methods of measurement of source reduction;

(2) ensure that the Agency considers the effect of its existing and proposed programs on source reduction efforts and shall review regulations of the Agency prior and subsequent to their proposal to determine their effect on source reduction;

(3) coordinate source reduction activities in each Agency Office and coordinate with appropriate offices to promote source reduction practices in other Federal agencies, and generic research and development on techniques and processes which have broad applicability;

(4) develop improved methods of coordinating, streamlining and assuring public access to data collected under Federal environmental statutes;

(5) facilitate the adoption of source reduction techniques by businesses. This strategy shall include the use of the Source Reduction Clearinghouse and State matching grants provided in this chapter to foster the exchange of information regarding source reduction techniques, the dissemination of such information to businesses, and the provision of technical assistance to businesses. The strategy shall also consider the capabilities of various businesses to make use of source reduction techniques;

(6) identify, where appropriate, measurable goals which reflect the policy of this chapter, the tasks necessary to achieve the goals, dates at which the principal tasks are to be accomplished, required resources, organizational responsibilities, and the means by which progress in meeting the goals will be measured;

(8)[2] establish an advisory panel of technical experts comprised of representatives from industry, the States, and public interest groups, to advise the Administrator on ways to improve collection and dissemination of data;

(9) establish a training program on source reduction opportunities, including workshops and guidance documents, for State and Federal permit issuance, enforcement, and inspection officials working within all agency program offices.

(10) identify and make recommendations to Congress to eliminate barriers to source reduction including the use of incentives and disincentives;

(11) identify opportunities to use Federal procurement to encourage source reduction;

(12) develop, test and disseminate model source reduction auditing procedures designed to highlight source reduction opportunities; and

(13) establish an annual award program to recognize a company or companies which operate outstanding or innovative source reduction programs.

§13104. Grants to States for State technical assistance programs
[PPA §6605]

(a) General authority — The Administrator shall make matching grants to States for programs to promote the use of source reduction techniques by businesses.

(b) Criteria — When evaluating the requests for grants under this section, the Administrator shall consider, among other things, whether the proposed State program would accomplish the following:

(1) Make specific technical assistance available to businesses seeking information about source reduction opportunities, including funding for experts to provide onsite technical advice to business seeking assistance and to assist in the development of source reduction plans.

(2) Target assistance to businesses for whom lack of information is an impediment to source reduction.

(3) Provide training in source reduction techniques. Such training may be provided through local engineering schools or any other appropriate means.

(c) Matching funds — Federal funds used in any State program under this section shall provide no more than 50 per centum of the funds made available to a State in each year of that State's participation in the program.

(d) Effectiveness — The Administrator shall establish appropriate means for measuring the effectiveness of the State grants made under this section in promoting the use of source reduction techniques by businesses.

(e) Information — States receiving grants under this section shall make information generated under the grants available to the Administrator.

§13105. Source Reduction Clearinghouse
[PPA §6606]

(a) Authority — The Administrator shall establish a Source Reduction Clearinghouse to compile information including a computer data base which contains information on management, technical, and operational approaches to source reduction. The Administrator shall use the clearinghouse to —

(1) serve as a center for source reduction technology transfer;

---

2. So in original. Subsec. (b) enacted without a par. (7).

(2) mount active outreach and education programs by the States to further the adoption of source reduction technologies; and

(3) collect and compile information reported by States receiving grants under section 13104 of this title on the operation and success of State source reduction programs.

(b) Public availability — The Administrator shall make available to the public such information on source reduction as is gathered pursuant to this chapter and such other pertinent information and analysis regarding source reduction as may be available to the Administrator. The data base shall permit entry and retrieval of information to any person.

§13106. Source reduction and recycling data collection

[PPA §6607]

(a) Reporting requirements — Each owner or operator of a facility required to file an annual toxic chemical release form under section 11023 of this title for any toxic chemical shall include with each such annual filing a toxic chemical source reduction and recycling report for the preceeding calendar year. The toxic chemical source reduction and recycling report shall cover each toxic chemical required to be reported in the annual toxic chemical release form filed by the owner or operator under section 11023(c) of this title. This section shall take effect with the annual report filed under section 11023 of this title for the first full calendar year beginning after November 5, 1990.

(b) Items included in report — The toxic chemical source reduction and recycling report required under subsection (a) of this section shall set forth each of the following on a facility-by-facility basis for each toxic chemical:

(1) The quantity of the chemical entering any waste stream (or otherwise released into the environment) prior to recycling, treatment, or disposal during the calendar year for which the report is filed and the percentage change from the previous year. The quantity reported shall not include any amount reported under paragraph (7). When actual measurements of the quantity of a toxic chemical entering the waste streams are not readily available, reasonable estimates should be made based on best engineering judgment.

(2) The amount of the chemical from the facility which is recycled (at the facility or elsewhere) during such calendar year, the percentage change from the previous year, and the process of recycling used.

(3) The source reduction practices used with respect to that chemical during such year at the facility. Such practices shall be reported in accordance with the following categories unless the Administrator finds other categories to be more appropriate.

(A) Equipment, technology, process, or procedure modifications.

(B) Reformulation or redesign of products.

(C) Substitution of raw materials.

(D) Improvement in management, training, inventory control, materials handling, or other general operational phases of industrial facilities.

(4) The amount expected to be reported under paragraph (1) and (2) for the two calendar years immediately following the calendar year for which the report is filed. Such amount shall be expressed as a percentage change from the amount reported in paragraphs (1) and (2).

(5) A ratio of production in the reporting year to production in the previous year. The ratio should be calculated to most closely reflect all activities involving the toxic chemical. In specific industrial classifications subject to this section, where a feedstock or some variable other than production is the primary influence on waste characteristics or volumes, the report may provide an index based on that primary variable for each toxic chemical. The Administrator is encouraged to develop production indexes to accommodate individual industries for use on a voluntary basis.

(6) The techniques which were used to identify source reduction opportunities. Techniques listed should include, but are not limited to, employee recommendations, external and internal audits, participative team management, and material balance audits. Each type of source reduction listed under paragraph (3) should be associated with the techniques or multiples of techniques used to identify the source reduction technique.

(7) The amount of any toxic chemical released into the environment which resulted from a catastrophic event, remedial action, or other one-time event, and is not associated with production processes during the reporting year.

(8) The amount of the chemical from the facility which is treated (at the facility or elsewhere) during such calendar year and the percentage change from the previous year. For the first year of reporting under this subsection, comparison with the previous year is required only to the extent such information is available.

(c) SARA provisions — The provisions of sections 11042, 11045(c), and 11046 of this title shall apply to the reporting requirements of this section in the same manner as to the reports required under section 11023 of this title. The Administrator may modify the form required for purposes of reporting information under section 11023 of this title to the extent he deems necessary to include the additional information required under this section.

(d) Additional optional information — Any person filing a report under this section for any year may include with the report additional information regarding source reduction, recycling, and other pollution control techniques in earlier years.

(e) Availability of data — Subject to section 11042 of this title, the Administrator shall make data collected under this section publicly available in the same manner as the data collected under section 11023 of this title.

§13107. EPA report
[PPA §6608]

(a) Biennial reports — The Administrator shall provide Congress with a report within eighteen months after November 5, 1990, and biennially thereafter, containing a detailed description of the actions taken to implement the strategy to promote source reduction developed under section 13103(b) of this title and of the results of such actions. The report shall include an assessment of the effectiveness of the clearinghouse and grant program established under this chapter in promoting the goals of the strategy, and shall evaluate data gaps and data duplication with respect to data collected under Federal environmental statutes.

(b) Subsequent reports — Each biennial report submitted under subsection (a) of this section after the first report shall contain each of the following:

(1) An analysis of the data collected under section 13106 of this title on an industry-by-industry basis for not less than five SIC codes or other categories as the Administrator deems appropriate. The analysis shall begin with those SIC codes or other categories of facilities which generate the largest quantities of toxic chemical waste. The analysis shall include an evaluation of trends in source reduction by industry, firm size, production, or other useful means. Each such subsequent report shall cover five SIC codes or other categories which were not covered in a prior report until all SIC codes or other categories have been covered.

(2) An analysis of the usefulness and validity of the data collected under section 13106 of this title for measuring trends in source reduction and the adoption of source reduction by business.

(3) Identification of regulatory and nonregulatory barriers to source reduction, and of opportunities for using existing regulatory programs, and incentives and disincentives to promote and assist source reduction.

(4) Identification of industries and pollutants that require priority assistance in multi-media source reduction.

(5) Recommendations as to incentives needed to encourage investment and research and development in source reduction.

(6) Identification of opportunities and development of priorities for research and development in source reduction methods and techniques.

(7) An evaluation of the cost and technical feasibility, by industry and processes, of source reduction opportunities and current activities and an identification of any industries for which there are significant barriers to source reduction with an analysis of the basis of this identification.

(8) An evaluation of methods of coordinating, streamlining, and improving public access to data collected under Federal environmental statutes.

(9) An evaluation of data gaps and data duplication with respect to data collected under Federal environmental statutes.

In the report following the first biennial report provided for under this subsection, paragraphs (3) through (9) may be included at the discretion of the Administrator.

§13108. Savings provisions
[PPA §6609]

(a) Nothing in this chapter shall be construed to modify or interfere with the implementation of title III of the Superfund Amendments and Reauthorization Act of 1986 (42 U.S.C. §§11001 *et seq.*).

(b) Nothing contained in this chapter shall be construed, interpreted or applied to supplant, displace, preempt or otherwise diminish the responsibilities and liabilities under other State or Federal law, whether statutory or common.

§13109. Authorization of appropriations
[PPA §6610]

There is authorized to be appropriated to the Administrator $8,000,000 for each of the fiscal years 1991, 1992, and 1993 for functions carried out under this chapter (other than State Grants), and $8,000,000 for each of the fiscal years 1991, 1992, and 1993, for grant programs to States issued pursuant to section 13104 of this title.

5

AIR POLLUTION CONTROL

National concern over air pollution spawned the first comprehensive federal regulatory program to protect the environment: the Clean Air Act of 1970. While the Act initially was enacted in 1963, it did not provide for comprehensive national regulation until it was amended in 1970. The 1970 Amendments established the basic program for controlling air pollution that remains in effect today. As amended in comprehensive fashion in 1977 and 1990, the Clean Air Act now represents the longest-standing and most complex scheme of national environmental regulation.

A GUIDE TO MATERIALS ON AIR POLLUTION CONTROL AVAILABLE ON THE INTERNET

EPA's regulations implementing the Clean Air Act are codified at 40 C.F.R. pts. 50-98. These CFR sections are available online through the National Archives and Records Administration's website, which includes a searchable version of the Code of Federal Regulations (*http://www.ecfr.gov*) and an electronic version of the CFR ("e-CFR") updated continuously.

EPA's Office of Air and Radiation (OAR) is the office responsible for implementing the Clean Air Act. OAR's website is located at *https://www.epa.gov/aboutepa/about-office-air-and-radiation-oar*. The website serves as a gateway for access to a tremendous amount of information about the Clean Air Act and the agency's complex air pollution control regulations. Information about ongoing EPA rulemaking proceedings can be obtained from the agency's Air and Radiation Docket and Information Center (*https://www.epa.gov/dockets/view-dockets-open-public-comment-program-office*).

EPA has published a "Plain English Guide to the Clean Air Act" to make its complex provisions easier for laypersons to understand. Copies of this document, issued shortly after enactment of the 1990 Clean Air Act Amendments, are available on the web at: *https://www.epa.gov/clean-air-act-overview*. Data on air quality trends are available at *http://www.epa.gov/airdata/*.

Specific air pollution control initiatives are explained on OAR's website. Information on new source review is available at *http://www.epa.gov/nsr*. National emissions standards to control hazardous air pollutants (NESHAPs) under §112 of the Act are described at: *http://www.epa.gov/ttn/atw/eparules.html*. The agency's acid deposition control program is explained at *http://www.epa.gov/acidrain*.

EPA maintains a Technology Transfer Network (TTN Web) website that provides technical information about air pollution control at *https://www.epa.gov/technical-air-pollution-resources*. The TTN Web includes detailed information about air quality monitoring programs and methods, trends in air quality, control technologies, and legal requirements under the Act. EPA has prepared reports to Congress that review estimates of the benefits and costs of the Clean Air Act, both retrospectively and prospectively. Copies of these reports are now available on the web at *https://www.epa.gov/clean-air-act-overview/benefits-and-costs-clean-air-act*.

The Congressional Research Service has prepared several reports for Congress evaluating various proposals to amend the Clean Air Act and efforts to stimulate the development of new technologies to reduce air pollution. See, e.g., "Clean Air Issues in the 114th Congress," at *https://fas.org/sgp/crs/misc/R43851.pdf*.

The National Association of Clean Air Agencies (formerly the Association of State and Territorial Air Pollution Program Administrators (STAPPA) and the Association of Local Air Pollution Control Officials (ALAPCO)) have a website located at *http://www.4cleanair.org*. The American Lung Association, a nonprofit group active on air pollution issues, maintains a website that provides information about the Clean Air Act, the state of air quality, and various programs to control air pollution at *http://www.lung.org*.

CLEAN AIR ACT LEGISLATIVE HISTORY TIMELINE

July 14, 1955: President Eisenhower signs into law the Air Pollution Control Act of 1955, Pub. L. 84-159, 69 Stat. 322, which provided funds for the U.S. Public Health Service to conduct research into the causes and consequences of air pollution and to provide technical assistance to state and local governments relating to air pollution control. In 1960 and 1962, this research program was renewed by Congress, which also directed the U.S. Surgeon General to study the health effects of pollution from motor vehicles.

December 17, 1963: President Johnson signs into law the Clean Air Act of 1963, Pub. L. 88-206, 77 Stat. 392, which increased federal funding for research on air pollution control while providing new financial assistance to state and local governments to encourage them to adopt emissions standards to control air pollution.

October 20, 1965: President Johnson signs into law the Motor Vehicle Air Pollution Control Act of 1965, Pub. L. 89-272, 79 Stat. 992, which required the Secretary of Health Education and Welfare to establish standards limiting tailpipe emissions of pollutants from each new motor vehicle manufactured for sale in the United States.

November 21, 1967: President Johnson signs into law the Air Quality Act of 1967, Pub. L. 90-148, 81 Stat. 485, which in addition to devoting more federal research funding to air pollution, also directed the Secretary of Health, Education and Welfare to define air quality control regions (ACQRs) for purpose of developing air pollution controls based upon each region's meteorological and topographical features.

December 31, 1970: President Nixon signs into law the Clean Air Act Amendments of 1970, Pub. L. 91-604, 84 Stat. 1676, which create the first comprehensive, national regulatory program to control air pollution. The legislation required the EPA Administrator to promulgate uniform, national, health-based, ambient air quality standards for criteria pollutants, to issue national emission standards for hazardous air pollutants, and to issue technology-based new source performance standards. It required auto manufacturers to reduce tailpipe emissions of pollutants by 90 percent between model years 1970 and 1975, and it authorized citizen suits to enforce the requirements of the Act.

August 7, 1977: President Carter signs the Clean Air Act Amendments of 1977, Pub. L. 95-95, 91 Stat. 685, which extend the deadlines for achieving the NAAQSs in areas of the country that had failed to do so, while imposing stringent new requirements for air pollution control on such nonattainment areas. The Amendments also ratified EPA's program to prevent significant deterioration of air quality (PSD program) in areas where air quality already met the NAAQSs.

July 17, 1981: President Reagan signs the Steel Industry Compliance Extension Act of 1981, Pub. L. 97-23, 95 Stat. 139, which extends the deadlines for certain sources to comply with provisions of the Act.

November 15, 1990: President Bush signs the Clean Air Act Amendments of 1990, Pub. L. 101-549, 104 Stat. 2399, which revise and strengthen the provisions of the Act in comprehensive fashion. The Amendments mandate cleaner burning fuels and lower emission vehicles. They added Title IV to the Act, a new program to control pollutants that cause acid rain by requiring a 10 million ton/year reduction in emissions of sulfur dioxide while authorizing trading of emission allowances to reduce compliance costs. The Amendments also added Title V, which establishes a new national permit program for major sources, and Title VI, which phases out the use of substances that contribute to depletion of the ozone layer.

December 23, 1995: President Clinton signs legislation, Pub. L. 104-70, 109 Stat. 773, that repeals provisions of the 1990 Amendments requiring certain employers to implement an employee trip reduction program to reduce vehicle emissions in nonattainment areas.

October 27, 1998: President Clinton signs the Border Smog Reduction Act of 1998, Pub. L. 105-286, 112 Stat. 2773, which adds §183(h) to the Clean Air Act, limiting entries into the United States of vehicles from Mexico that do not comply with state inspection and maintenance programs.

August 5, 1999: President Clinton signs the Chemical Safety Information, Site Security and Fuels Regulatory Relief Act, Pub. L. 106-40, 113 Stat. 207, which requires the EPA Administrator to assess the consequences of allowing public access to information about the off-site consequences of potential chemical accidents.

August 8, 2005: The Energy Policy Act of 2005, Pub. L. 109-58, 119 Stat. 1067, amends §211 of the Clean Air Act by adding new §§211(o), (q) & (r) and §212, to create incentives to encourage greater use of renewable fuels.

December 19, 2007: The Energy Independence and Security Act of 2007, Pub. L. 110-140, 121 Stat. 1492, amends §211(o) of the Clean Air Act to increase the production of biofuels through the year 2022.

A NOTE ON THE 1990 AMENDMENTS TO SECTION 111(d)

When Congress adopted the 1990 Amendments to the Clean Air Act, it fundamentally restructured the regulation of hazardous air pollutants under Section 112. It specified a list of 189 substances to be regulated as hazardous air pollutants, and it required EPA to set emissions standards for every industrial source category that emits these pollutants. In doing so Congress deleted a provision — Section 112(b)(1)(4) — that formerly had been cross-referenced in Section 111(d). However, it did so in two different versions of the legislation, both of which were included in the final bill approved by Congress.

The Senate version deleted "112(b)(1)(A)" and replaced it with "112(b)," which now contains the list of hazardous air pollutants specified by Congress. The House version struck the words "or 112(b)(1)(A)" and replaced it with the phrase "or emitted from a source category which is regulated under section 112." Neither version was discussed in committee hearings, floor debates, or the House/Senate conference, but they both were included in the final bill approved by Congress.

This has become an important issue because industry groups challenging EPA efforts to use §111(d) to regulate greenhouse gas emissions from existing powerplants maintain that the House version precludes their regulation because powerplants emit hazardous air pollutants. EPA argues that the conflicting versions of §111(d) create a statutory ambiguity that entitles the agency's interpretation of the Act — that the Senate version controls — to judicial deference.

OUTLINE OF THE PRINCIPAL PROVISIONS OF THE CLEAN AIR ACT

TITLE I — PROGRAMS AND ACTIVITIES

PART A — AIR QUALITY AND EMISSIONS LIMITATIONS

§108 (42 U.S.C. §7408) Air Quality Criteria: requires EPA to identify air pollutants anticipated to endanger public health or welfare and to publish air quality criteria.

§109 (42 U.S.C. §7409) National Ambient Air Quality Standards: requires EPA to adopt nationally uniform standards limiting levels of criteria air pollutants in the ambient air, known as national ambient air quality standards (NAAQSs). Primary standards are to protect public health with an adequate margin of safety while secondary standards are to protect public welfare.

§110 (42 U.S.C. §7410) State Implementation Plans: requires state to develop and to submit to EPA for approval state implementation plans (SIPs) specifying measures to assure that air quality within their jurisdictions attains the NAAQSs.

§111 (42 U.S.C. §7411) New Source Performance Standards: requires the EPA Administrator to establish nationally uniform, technology-based standards controlling emissions from major new stationary sources of air pollution, known as new source performance standards (NSPSs).

§112 (42 U.S.C. §7412) National Emission Standards for Hazardous Air Pollutants: requires the EPA Administrator to establish nationally uniform, technology-based standards to control emissions of an initial list of 189 toxic air pollutants. The standards initially are to impose levels of emissions control that reflect use of the maximum achievable control technology (MACT), with more stringent standards to be imposed later if necessary to protect public health with an "ample margin of safety."

§113 (42 U.S.C. §7413) Federal Enforcement: Authorizes federal enforcement actions against violators of state implementation plans or air emissions permits, provides civil and criminal penalties for violations, and authorizes administrative enforcement and field citations for less significant violations.

§115 (42 U.S.C. §7415) International Air Pollution: Authorizes the EPA Administrator to require states to revise their SIPs upon a finding that they are inadequate to prevent air pollution emitted from their jurisdiction from endangering public health or welfare in a foreign country.

PART C — PREVENTION OF SIGNIFICANT DETERIORATION OF AIR QUALITY

SUBPART 1 — Clean Air

§§160-169 (42 U.S.C. §§7470-7479) Prevention of Significant Deterioration: establishes a national permit program limiting the extent to which new sources or major modifications of existing sources can deteriorate air quality in areas of the country in which air quality already meets levels required by the NAAQSs (attainment areas).

§§169A & 169B (42 U.S.C. §§7491 & 7492) **Visibility Protection**: authorizes the EPA Administrator to issue regulations to prevent air pollution from impairing visibility in national parks and wilderness areas.

PART D—PLAN REQUIREMENTS FOR NONATTAINMENT AREAS

SUBPART 1 — Nonattainment Areas in General
§§171-179B (42 U.S.C. §§7501-7509a) **Nonattainment Provisions**: specifies more stringent requirements to control air pollution that must be employed in areas of the country that have failed to achieve the NAAQSs (nonattainment areas) including use of all reasonably available control technology (RACT) by existing sources and a preconstruction permitting program for new or modified major stationary sources that requires them to obtain offsetting emissions reductions to achieve reasonable further progress toward achieving the NAAQSs.

SUBPART 2 — Additional Provisions for Ozone Nonattainment Areas
§§181-185B (42 U.S.C. §§7511-7511f): Classifies areas of the country that have failed to attain the ozone NAAQS into five categories (marginal, moderate, serious, severe and extreme) based on the extent of their nonattainment and requires progressively more stringent control measures in areas further away from attainment in return for extending the deadlines for achieving it.

SUBPART 3 — Additional Provisions for CO Nonattainment Areas
§§186-187 (42 U.S.C. §§7512-7512a): Classifies areas of the country that have failed to attain the carbon monoxide NAAQS into two categories (moderate and serious) based on the extent of their nonattainment and requires progressively more stringent control measures in areas further away from attainment in return for extending the deadlines for achieving it.

SUBPART 4 — Additional Provisions for PM-10 in Nonattainment Areas
§§188-189 (42 U.S.C. §§7513-7513a): Classifies areas of the country that have failed to attain the particulate matter NAAQS into two categories (moderate and serious) based on the extent of their nonattainment and requires progressively more stringent control measures in areas further away from attainment in return for achieving the deadlines for achieving it.

SUBCHAPTER II — EMISSION STANDARDS FOR MOVING SOURCES

PART A — MOTOR VEHICLE EMISSIONS AND FUEL STANDARDS

§202 (42 U.S.C. §7521) **Emission Standards for New Motor Vehicles**: Establishes standards limiting tailpipe emission of air pollutants from new motor vehicles, mandating reductions in emissions of hydrocarbons, carbon monoxide, and nitrogen oxide. Authorizes the EPA Administrator to require further reductions in such emissions if necessary to attain or maintain the NAAQSs.

§211 (42 U.S.C. §7545) **Regulation of Fuels**: Authorizes the EPA Administrator to regulate fuel additives whose emission products contribute to air pollution that may reasonably be anticipated to endanger public health or welfare.

PART C — CLEAN FUEL VEHICLES

§§241-250 (42 U.S.C. §§7581-7590): Establishes standards requiring the production, sale, and distribution of certain numbers of lower-emission vehicles in the state of California, while authorizing other states with nonattainment problems to adopt identical programs.

TITLE III — GENERAL PROVISIONS

§304 (42 U.S.C. §7604) Citizen Suits: authorizes citizens to sue both violators of emissions standards and the EPA Administrator if she fails to perform nondiscretionary duties under the Act.

§307 (42 U.S.C. §7607) Rulemaking and Judicial Review: establishes procedural requirements for EPA's issuance of regulations under the Act and authorizes judicial review of nationally applicable EPA actions exclusively in the U.S. Court of Appeals for the District of Columbia Circuit.

TITLE IV — ACID DEPOSITION CONTROL

§§401-416 (42 U.S.C. §§7651-7651o) Acid Deposition Control and Emissions Trading: requires substantial reductions in emissions of sulfur dioxide and nitrogen oxide, pollutants that contribute to acid deposition, and creates a system of marketable allowances to achieve the reductions at reduced cost.

TITLE V — PERMITS

§§501-507 (42 U.S.C. §§7661-7661f) National Permit Program: requires permits for all major industrial sources of air pollution to be administered by state authorities subject to federal oversight.

TITLE VI — STRATOSPHERIC OZONE PROTECTION

§§601-617 (42 U.S.C. §§7671-7671q) Phaseout of Ozone Depleting Substances: requires the phaseout of the production, use and consumption of certain substances that contribute to depletion of the earth's stratospheric ozone layer.

Clean Air Act

42 U.S.C. §§7401 to 7671q

SUBCHAPTER I — PROGRAMS AND ACTIVITIES

PART A — AIR QUALITY AND EMISSIONS LIMITATIONS

§7401. Congressional findings and declaration of purpose
[CAA §101]

(a) Findings — The Congress finds —

(1) that the predominant part of the Nation's population is located in its rapidly expanding metropolitan and other urban areas, which generally cross the boundary lines of local jurisdictions and often extend into two or more States;

(2) that the growth in the amount and complexity of air pollution brought about by urbanization, industrial development, and the increasing use of motor vehicles, has resulted in mounting dangers to the public health and welfare, including injury to agricultural crops and livestock, damage to and the deterioration of property, and hazards to air and ground transportation;

(3) that air pollution prevention (that is, the reduction or elimination, through any measures, of the amount of pollutants produced or created at the source) and air pollution control at its source is the primary responsibility of States and local governments; and

(4) that Federal financial assistance and leadership is essential for the development of cooperative Federal, State, regional, and local programs to prevent and control air pollution.

(b) Declaration — The purposes of this subchapter are —

(1) to protect and enhance the quality of the Nation's air resources so as to promote the public health and welfare and the productive capacity of its population;

(2) to initiate and accelerate a national research and development program to achieve the prevention and control of air pollution;

(3) to provide technical and financial assistance to State and local governments in connection with the development and execution of their air pollution prevention and control programs; and

(4) to encourage and assist the development and operation of regional air pollution prevention and control programs.

(c) Pollution prevention — A primary goal of this Act is to encourage or otherwise promote reasonable Federal,

State, and local governmental actions, consistent with the provisions of this Act, for pollution prevention.

§7402. Cooperative activities
[CAA §102]

(a) Interstate cooperation; uniform State laws; State compacts — The Administrator shall encourage cooperative activities by the States and local governments for the prevention and control of air pollution; encourage the enactment of improved and, so far as practicable in the light of varying conditions and needs, uniform State and local laws relating to the prevention and control of air pollution; and encourage the making of agreements and compacts between States for the prevention and control of air pollution.

(b) Federal cooperation — The Administrator shall cooperate with and encourage cooperative activities by all Federal departments and agencies having functions relating to the prevention and control of air pollution, so as to assure the utilization in the Federal air pollution control program of all appropriate and available facilities and resources within the Federal Government.

(c) Consent of Congress to compacts — The consent of the Congress is hereby given to two or more States to negotiate and enter into agreements or compacts, not in conflict with any law or treaty of the United States, for (1) cooperative effort and mutual assistance for the prevention and control of air pollution and the enforcement of their respective laws relating thereto, and (2) the establishment of such agencies, joint or otherwise, as they may deem desirable for making effective such agreements or compacts. No such agreement or compact shall be binding or obligatory upon any State a party thereto unless and until it has been approved by Congress. It is the intent of Congress that no agreement or compact entered into between States after the date of enactment of the Air Quality Act of 1967, which relates to the control and abatement of air pollution in an air quality control region, shall provide for participation by a State which is not included (in whole or in part) in such air quality control region.

§7403. Research, investigation, training, and other activities
[CAA §103]

(a) Research and development program for prevention and control of air pollution — The Administrator shall establish a national research and development program for the prevention and control of air pollution and as part of such program shall —

(1) conduct, and promote the coordination and acceleration of, research, investigations, experiments, demonstrations, surveys, and studies relating to the causes, effects (including health and welfare effects), extent, prevention, and control of air pollution;

(2) encourage, cooperate with, and render technical services and provide financial assistance to air pollution control agencies and other appropriate public or private agencies, institutions, and organizations, and individuals in the conduct of such activities;

(3) conduct investigations and research and make surveys concerning any specific problem of air pollution in cooperation with any air pollution control agency with a view to recommending a solution of such problem, if he is requested to do so by such agency or if, in his judgment, such problem may affect any community or communities in a State other than that in which the source of the matter causing or contributing to the pollution is located;

(4) establish technical advisory committees composed of recognized experts in various aspects of air pollution to assist in the examination and evaluation of research progress and proposals and to avoid duplication of research; and

(5) conduct and promote coordination and acceleration of training for individuals relating to the causes, effects, extent, prevention, and control of air pollution.

(b) Authorized activities of Administrator in establishing research and development program — In carrying out the provisions of the preceding subsection the Administrator is authorized to —

(1) collect and make available, through publications and other appropriate means, the results of and other information, including appropriate recommendations by him in connection therewith, pertaining to such research and other activities;

(2) cooperate with other Federal departments and agencies, with air pollution control agencies, with other public and private agencies, institutions, and organizations, and with any industries involved, in the preparation and conduct of such research and other activities;

(3) make grants to air pollution control agencies, to other public or nonprofit private agencies, institutions, and organizations, and to individuals, for purposes stated in subsection (a)(1) of this section;

(4) contract with public or private agencies, institutions, and organizations, and with individuals, without regard to section 3324(a) and (b) of Title 31 and section 5 of Title 41;

(5) establish and maintain research fellowships, in the Environmental Protection Agency and at public or nonprofit private educational institutions or research organizations;

(6) collect and disseminate, in cooperation with other Federal departments and agencies, and with other public or private agencies, institutions, and organizations having related responsibilities, basic data on chemical, physical, and biological effects of varying air quality and other information pertaining to air pollution and the prevention and control thereof;

(7) develop effective and practical processes, methods, and prototype devices for the prevention or control of air pollution; and

(8) construct facilities, provide equipment, and employ staff as necessary to carry out this Act.

In carrying out the provisions of subsection (a), the Administrator shall provide training for, and make training grants to, personnel of air pollution control agencies and other persons with suitable qualifications and make grants to such agencies, to other public or nonprofit private agencies, institutions, and organizations for the purposes stated in subsection (a)(5). Reasonable fees may be charged for such training provided to persons other than personnel of air pollution control agencies but such training shall be provided to such personnel of air pollution control agencies without charge.

(c) Air pollutant monitoring, analysis, modeling, and inventory research — In carrying out subsection (a) of this section, the Administrator shall conduct a program of research, testing, and development of methods for sampling, measurement, monitoring, analysis, and modeling of air pollutants. Such program shall include the following elements:

(1) Consideration of individual, as well as complex mixtures of, air pollutants and their chemical transformations in the atmosphere.

(2) Establishment of a national network to monitor, collect, and compile data with quantification of certainty in the status and trends of air emissions, deposition, air quality, surface water quality, forest condition, and visibility impairment, and to ensure the comparability of air quality data collected in different States and obtained from different nations.

(3) Development of improved methods and technologies for sampling, measurement, monitoring, analysis, and modeling to increase understanding of the sources of ozone precursors, ozone formation, ozone transport, regional influences on urban ozone, regional ozone trends, and interactions of ozone with other pollutants. Emphasis shall be placed on those techniques which —

(A) improve the ability to inventory emissions of volatile organic compounds and nitrogen oxides that contribute to urban air pollution, including anthropogenic and natural sources;

(B) improve the understanding of the mechanism through which anthropogenic and biogenic volatile organic compounds react to form ozone and other oxidants; and

(C) improve the ability to identify and evaluate region-specific prevention and control options for ozone pollution.

(4) Submission of periodic reports to the Congress, not less than once every 5 years, which evaluate and assess the effectiveness of air pollution control regulations and programs using monitoring and modeling data obtained pursuant to this subsection.

(d) Environmental health effects research

(1) The Administrator, in consultation with the Secretary of Health and Human Services, shall conduct a research program on the short-term and long-term effects of air pollutants, including wood smoke, on human health. In conducting such research program the Administrator —

(A) shall conduct studies, including epidemiological, clinical, and laboratory and field studies, as necessary to identify and evaluate exposure to and effects of air pollutants on human health;

(B) may utilize, on a reimbursable basis, the facilities of existing Federal scientific laboratories and research centers; and

(C) shall consult with other Federal agencies to ensure that similar research being conducted in other agencies is coordinated to avoid duplication.

(2) In conducting the research program under this subsection, the Administrator shall develop methods and techniques necessary to identify and assess the risks to human health from both routine and accidental exposures to individual air pollutants and combinations thereof. Such research program shall include the following elements:

(A) The creation of an Interagency Task Force to coordinate such program. The Task Force shall include representatives of the National Institute for Environmental Health Sciences, the Environmental Protection Agency, the Agency for Toxic Substances and Disease Registry, the National Toxicology Program, the National Institute of Standards and Technology, the National Science Foundation, the Surgeon General, and the Department of Energy. This Interagency Task Force shall be chaired by a representative of the Environmental Protection Agency and shall convene its first meeting within 60 days after the date of enactment of this subparagraph.

(B) An evaluation, within 12 months after the date of enactment of this paragraph, of each of the hazardous air pollutants listed under section 112(b) of this Act, to decide, on the basis of available information, their relative priority for preparation of environmental health assessments pursuant to subparagraph (C). The evaluation shall be based on reasonably anticipated toxicity to humans and exposure factors such as frequency of occurrence as an air pollutant and volume of emissions in populated areas. Such evaluation shall be reviewed by the Interagency Task Force established pursuant to subparagraph (A).

(C) Preparation of environmental health assessments for each of the hazardous air pollutants referred to in subparagraph (B), beginning 6 months after the first meeting of the Interagency Task Force and to be completed within 96 months thereafter. No fewer than 24 assessments shall be completed and published annually. The assessments shall be prepared in accordance with guidelines developed by the Administrator in consultation with the Interagency Task Force and the Science Advisory Board of the Environmental Protection Agency. Each such assessment shall include —

(i) an examination, summary, and evaluation of available toxicological and epidemiological information for the pollutant to ascertain the levels of human exposure which pose a significant threat to human health and the associated acute, subacute, and chronic adverse health effects;

(ii) a determination of gaps in available information related to human health effects and exposure levels; and

(iii) where appropriate, an identification of additional activities, including toxicological and inhalation testing, needed to identify the types or levels of exposure which may present significant risk of adverse health effects in humans.

(e) Ecosystem research — In carrying out subsection (a), the Administrator, in cooperation, where appropriate, with the Under Secretary of Commerce for Oceans and Atmosphere, the Director of the Fish and Wildlife Service, and the Secretary of Agriculture, shall conduct a research program to improve understanding of the short-term and long-term causes, effects, and trends of ecosystems damage from air pollutants on ecosystems. Such program shall include the following elements:

(1) Identification of regionally representative and critical ecosystems for research.

(2) Evaluation of risks to ecosystems exposed to air pollutants, including characterization of the causes and effects of chronic and episodic exposures to air pollutants and determination of the reversibility of those effects.

(3) Development of improved atmospheric dispersion models and monitoring systems and networks for evaluating and quantifying exposure to and effects of multiple environmental stresses associated with air pollution.

(4) Evaluation of the effects of air pollution on water quality, including assessments of the short-term and long-term ecological effects of acid deposition and other atmospherically derived pollutants on surface water (including wetlands and estuaries) and groundwater.

(5) Evaluation of the effects of air pollution on forests, materials, crops, biological diversity, soils, and other terrestrial and aquatic systems exposed to air pollutants.

(6) Estimation of the associated economic costs of ecological damage which have occurred as a result of exposure to air pollutants.

Consistent with the purpose of this program, the Administrator may use the estuarine research reserves established pursuant to section 315 of the Coastal Zone Management Act of 1972 (16 U.S.C. §1461) to carry out this research.

(f) Liquefied gaseous fuels spill test facility

(1) The Administrator, in consultation with the Secretary of Energy and the Federal Coordinating Council for Science, Engineering, and Technology, shall oversee an experimental and analytical research effort, with the experimental research to be carried out at the Liquefied Gaseous Fuels Spill Test Facility. In consultation with the Secretary of Energy, the Administrator shall develop a list of chemicals and a schedule for field testing at the Facility. Analysis of a minimum of 10 chemicals per year shall be carried out, with the selection of a minimum of 2 chemicals for field testing each year. Highest priority shall be given to those chemicals that would present the greatest potential risk to human health as a result of an accidental release —

(A) from a fixed site; or

(B) related to the transport of such chemicals.

(2) The purpose of such research shall be to —

(A) develop improved predictive models for atmospheric dispersion which at a minimum —

(i) describe dense gas releases in complex terrain including man-made structures or obstacles with variable winds;

(ii) improve understanding of the effects of turbulence on dispersion patterns; and

(iii) consider realistic behavior of aerosols by including physicochemical reactions with water vapor, ground deposition, and removal by water spray;

(B) evaluate existing and future atmospheric dispersion models by —

(i) the development of a rigorous, standardized methodology for dense gas models; and

(ii) the application of such methodology to current dense gas dispersion models using data generated from field experiments; and

(C) evaluate the effectiveness of hazard mitigation and emergency response technology for fixed site and transportation related accidental releases of toxic chemicals.

Models pertaining to accidental release shall be evaluated and improved periodically for their utility in planning and implementing evacuation procedures and other mitigative strategies designed to minimize human exposure to hazardous air pollutants released accidentally.

(3) The Secretary of Energy shall make available to interested persons (including other Federal agencies and businesses) the use of the Liquefied Gaseous Fuels Spill Test Facility to conduct research and other activities in connection with the activities described in this subsection.

(g) Pollution prevention and emissions control

(1) In general

In carrying out subsection (a), the Administrator shall conduct a basic engineering research and technology program to develop, evaluate, and demonstrate nonregulatory strategies and technologies for air pollution prevention.

(2) Participation requirement

Such strategies and technologies described in paragraph (1) shall be developed with priority on those pollutants which pose a significant risk to human health and the environment, and with opportunities for participation by industry, public interest groups, scientists, States, institutions of higher education, and other interested persons in the development of such strategies and technologies.

(3) Program inclusions

The program under this subsection shall include the following elements:

(A) Improvements in nonregulatory strategies and technologies for preventing or reducing multiple air pollutants, including sulfur oxides, nitrogen oxides, heavy metals, PM-10 (particulate matter), carbon monoxide, and carbon dioxide, from stationary sources, including fossil fuel power plants. Such strategies and technologies shall include improvements in the relative cost effectiveness and long-range implications of various air pollutant reduction and nonregulatory control strategies such as energy conservation, including end-use efficiency, and fuel-switching to cleaner fuels. Such strategies and technologies shall be considered for existing and new facilities.

(B) Improvements in nonregulatory strategies and technologies for reducing air emissions from area sources.

(C) Improvements in nonregulatory strategies and technologies for preventing, detecting, and correcting accidental releases of hazardous air pollutants.

(D) Improvements in nonregulatory strategies and technologies that dispose of tires in ways that avoid adverse air quality impacts.

(4) Effect of subsection

Nothing in this subsection shall be construed to authorize the imposition on any person of air pollution control requirements.

(5) Coordination and avoidance of duplication

The Administrator shall consult with other appropriate Federal agencies to ensure coordination and to avoid duplication of activities authorized under this subsection.

(6) Certain carbon dioxide activities

(A) In general

In carrying out paragraph (3)(A) with respect to carbon dioxide, the Administrator—

(i) is authorized to carry out the activities described in subparagraph (B); and

(ii) shall carry out the activities described in subparagraph (C).

(B) Direct air capture research

(i) Definitions

In this subparagraph:

(I) Board

The term "Board" means the Direct Air Capture Technology Advisory Board established by clause (iii)(I).

(II) Dilute

The term "dilute" means a concentration of less than 1 percent by volume.

(III) Direct air capture

(aa) In general

The term "direct air capture", with respect to a facility, technology, or system, means that the facility, technology, or system uses carbon capture equipment to capture carbon dioxide directly from the air.

(bb) Exclusion

The term "direct air capture" does not include any facility, technology, or system that captures carbon dioxide—

(AA) that is deliberately released from a naturally occurring subsurface spring; or

(BB) using natural photosynthesis.

(IV) Intellectual property

The term "intellectual property" means—

(aa) an invention that is patentable under Title 35; and

(bb) any patent on an invention described in item (aa).

(ii) Technology prizes

(I) In general

Not later than 1 year after December 27, 2020, the Administrator, in consultation with the Secretary of Energy, is authorized to establish a program to provide financial awards on a competitive basis for direct air capture from media in which the concentration of carbon dioxide is dilute.

(II) Duties

In carrying out this clause, the Administrator shall—

(aa) subject to subclause (III), develop specific requirements for—

(AA) the competition process; and

(BB) the demonstration of performance of approved projects;

(bb) offer financial awards for a project designed—

(AA) to the maximum extent practicable, to capture more than 10,000 tons of carbon dioxide per year;

(BB) to operate in a manner that would be commercially viable in the foreseeable future (as determined by the Board); and

(CC) to improve the technologies or information systems that enable monitoring and verification methods for direct air capture projects; and

(cc) to the maximum extent practicable, make financial awards to geographically diverse projects, including at least—

(AA) 1 project in a coastal State; and

(BB) 1 project in a rural State.

(III) Public participation

In carrying out subclause (II)(aa), the Administrator shall—

(aa) provide notice of and, for a period of not less than 60 days, an opportunity for public comment on, any draft or proposed version of the requirements described in subclause (II)(aa); and

(bb) take into account public comments received in developing the final version of those requirements.

(iii) Direct Air Capture Technology Advisory Board

(I) Establishment

The Administrator may establish an advisory board to be known as the "Direct Air Capture Technology Advisory Board".

(II) Composition

The Board, on the establishment of the Board, shall be composed of 9 members appointed by the Administrator, who shall provide expertise in—

(aa) climate science;

(bb) physics;

(cc) chemistry;

(dd) biology;

(ee) engineering;

(ff) economics;

(gg) business management; and

(hh) such other disciplines as the Administrator determines to be necessary to achieve the purposes of this subparagraph.

(III) Term; vacancies

(aa) Term

A member of the Board shall serve for a term of 6 years.

(bb) Vacancies

A vacancy on the Board—

(AA) shall not affect the powers of the Board; and

(BB) shall be filled in the same manner as the original appointment was made.

(IV) Initial meeting

Not later than 30 days after the date on which all members of the Board have been appointed, the Board shall hold the initial meeting of the Board.

(V) Meetings

The Board shall meet at the call of the Chairperson or on the request of the Administrator.

(VI) Quorum

A majority of the members of the Board shall constitute a quorum, but a lesser number of members may hold hearings.

(VII) Chairperson and Vice Chairperson

The Board shall select a Chairperson and Vice Chairperson from among the members of the Board.

(VIII) Compensation

Each member of the Board may be compensated at not to exceed the daily equivalent of the annual rate of basic pay in effect for a position at level V of the Executive Schedule under section 5316 of Title 5 for each day during which the member is engaged in the actual performance of the duties of the Board.

(IX) Duties

The Board shall—

(aa) advise the Administrator on carrying out the duties of the Administrator under this subparagraph; and

(bb) provide other assistance and advice as requested by the Administrator.

(iv) Intellectual property

(I) In general

As a condition of receiving a financial award under this subparagraph, an applicant shall agree to vest the intellectual property of the applicant derived from the technology in 1 or more entities that are incorporated in the United States.

(II) Reservation of license

The United States—

(aa) may reserve a nonexclusive, nontransferable, irrevocable, paid-up license, to have practiced for or on behalf of the United States, in connection with any intellectual property described in subclause (I); but

(bb) shall not, in the exercise of a license reserved under item (aa), publicly disclose proprietary information relating to the license.

(III) Transfer of title

Title to any intellectual property described in subclause (I) shall not be transferred or passed, except to an entity that is incorporated in the United States, until the expiration of the first patent obtained in connection with the intellectual property.

(v) Authorization of appropriations

There is authorized to be appropriated to carry out this subparagraph $35,000,000, to remain available until expended.

(vi) Termination of authority

Notwithstanding section 14 of the Federal Advisory Committee Act (5 U.S.C. App.), the Board and all authority provided under this subparagraph shall terminate not later than 12 years after December 27, 2020.

(C) Deep saline formation report

(i) Definition of deep saline formation

(I) In general

In this subparagraph, the term "deep saline formation" means a formation of subsurface geographically extensive sedimentary rock layers saturated with waters or brines that have a high total dissolved solids content and that are below the depth where carbon dioxide can exist in the formation as a supercritical fluid.

(II) Clarification

In this subparagraph, the term "deep saline formation" does not include oil and gas reservoirs.

(ii) Report

In consultation with the Secretary of Energy, and, as appropriate, with the head of any other relevant Federal agency and relevant stakeholders, not later than 1 year after December 27, 2020, the Administrator shall prepare, submit to Congress, and make publicly available a report that includes—

(I) a comprehensive identification of potential risks and benefits to project developers associated with increased storage of carbon dioxide captured from stationary sources in deep saline formations, using existing research;

(II) recommendations for managing the potential risks identified under subclause (I), including potential risks unique to public land; and

(III) recommendations for Federal legislation or other policy changes to mitigate any potential risks identified under subclause (I).

(D) GAO report

Not later than 5 years after December 27, 2020, the Comptroller General of the United States shall submit to Congress a report that—

(i) identifies all Federal grant programs in which a purpose of a grant under the program is to perform research on carbon capture and utilization technologies, including direct air capture technologies; and

(ii) examines the extent to which the Federal grant programs identified pursuant to clause (i) overlap or are duplicative.

(h) NIEHS studies

(1) The Director of the National Institute of Environmental Health Sciences may conduct a program of basic research to identify, characterize, and quantify risks to human health from air pollutants. Such research shall be conducted primarily through a combination of university and medical school-based grants, as well as through intramural studies and contracts.

(2) The Director of the National Institute of Environmental Health Sciences shall conduct a program for the education and training of physicians in environmental health.

(3) The Director shall assure that such programs shall not conflict with research undertaken by the Administrator.

(4) There are authorized to be appropriated to the National Institute of Environmental Health Sciences such sums as may be necessary to carry out the purposes of this subsection.

(i) Coordination of research — The Administrator shall develop and implement a plan for identifying areas in which activities authorized under this section can be carried out in conjunction with other Federal ecological and air pollution research efforts. The plan, which shall be submitted to Congress within 6 months after the date of enactment of this subsection, shall include —

(1) an assessment of ambient monitoring stations and networks to determine cost effective ways to expand monitoring capabilities in both urban and rural environments;

(2) a consideration of the extent of the feasibility and scientific value of conducting the research program under subsection (e) to include consideration of the effects of atmospheric processes and air pollution effects; and

(3) a methodology for evaluating and ranking pollution prevention technologies, such as those developed under subsection (g), in terms of their ability to reduce cost effectively the emissions of air pollutants and other airborne chemicals of concern.

Not later than 2 years after the date of enactment of this subsection, and every 4 years thereafter, the Administrator shall report to Congress on the progress made in implementing the plan developed under this subsection, and shall include in such report any revisions of the plan.

(j) Continuation of the National Acid Precipitation Assessment Program

(1) The acid precipitation research program set forth in the Acid Precipitation Act of 1980 shall be continued with modifications pursuant to this subsection.

(2) The Acid Precipitation Task Force shall consist of the Administrator of the Environmental Protection Agency, the Secretary of Energy, the Secretary of the Interior, the Secretary of Agriculture, the Administrator of the National Oceanic and Atmospheric Administration, the Administrator of the National Aeronautics and Space Administration, and such additional members as the President may select. The President shall appoint a chairman for the Task Force from among its members within 30 days after the date of enactment of this subsection.

(3) The responsibilities of the Task Force shall include the following:

(A) Review of the status of research activities conducted to date under the comprehensive research plan developed pursuant to the Acid Precipitation Act of 1980, and development of a revised plan that identifies significant research gaps and establishes a coordinated program to address current and future research priorities. A draft of the revised plan shall be submitted by the Task Force to Congress within 6 months after the date of enactment of this subsection. The plan shall be available for public comment during the 60 day period after its submission, and a final plan shall be submitted by the President to the Congress within 45 days after the close of the comment period.

(B) Coordination with participating Federal agencies, augmenting the agencies' research and monitoring efforts and sponsoring additional research in the scientific community as necessary to ensure the availability and quality of data and methodologies needed to evaluate the status and effectiveness of the acid deposition control program. Such research and monitoring efforts shall include, but not be limited to —

(i) continuous monitoring of emissions of precursors of acid deposition;

(ii) maintenance, upgrading, and application of models, such as the Regional Acid Deposition Model, that describe the interactions of emissions with the atmosphere, and models that describe the response of ecosystems to acid deposition; and

(iii) analysis of the costs, benefits, and effectiveness of the acid deposition control program.

(C) Publication and maintenance of a National Acid Lakes Registry that tracks the condition and change over time of a statistically representative sample of lakes in regions that are known to be sensitive to surface water acidification.

(D) Submission every two years of a unified budget recommendation to the President for activities of the Federal Government in connection with the research program described in this subsection.

(E) Beginning in 1992 and biennially thereafter, submission of a report to Congress describing the results of its investigations and analyses. The reporting of technical information about acid deposition shall be provided in a format that facilitates communication with policymakers and the public. The report shall include —

(i) actual and projected emissions and acid deposition trends;

(ii) average ambient concentrations of acid deposition percursors and their transformation products;

(iii) the status of ecosystems (including forests and surface waters), materials, and visibility affected by acid deposition;

(iv) the causes and effects of such deposition, including changes in surface water quality and forest and soil conditions;

(v) the occurrence and effects of episodic acidification, particularly with respect to high elevation watersheds; and

(vi) the confidence level associated with each conclusion to aid policymakers in use of the information.

(F) Beginning in 1996, and every 4 years thereafter, the report under subparagraph (E) shall include —

(i) the reduction in deposition rates that must be achieved in order to prevent adverse ecological effects; and

(ii) the costs and benefits of the acid deposition control program created by title IV of this Act.

(k) Air pollution conferences — If, in the judgment of the Administrator, an air pollution problem of substantial significance may result from discharge or discharges into the atmosphere, the Administrator may call a conference concerning this potential air pollution problem to be held in or near one or more of the places where such discharge or discharges are occurring or will occur. All interested persons shall be given an opportunity to be heard at such conference, either orally or in writing, and shall be permitted to appear in person or by representative in accordance with procedures prescribed by the Administrator. If the Administrator finds, on the basis of the evidence presented at such conference, that the discharge or discharges if permitted to take place or continue are likely to cause or contribute to air pollution subject to abatement under part A of Title I, the Administrator shall send such findings, together with recommendations concerning the measures which the Administrator finds reasonable and suitable to prevent such pollution, to the person or persons whose actions will result in the discharge or discharges involved; to air pollution agencies of the State or States and of the municipality or municipalities where such discharge or discharges will originate; and to the interstate air pollution control agency, if any, in the jurisdictional area of which any such municipality is located. Such findings and recommendations shall be advisory only, but shall be admitted together with the record of the conference, as part of the proceedings under subsections (b), (c), (d), (e), and (f) of section 108.

§7404. Research relating to fuels and vehicles [CAA §104]

(a) Research programs; grants; contracts; pilot and demonstration plants; byproducts research — The Administrator shall give special emphasis to research and development into new and improved methods, having industry wide application, for the prevention and control of air pollution resulting from the combustion of fuels. In furtherance of such research and development he shall —

(1) conduct and accelerate research programs directed toward development of improved, cost-effective techniques for —

(A) control of combustion byproducts of fuels,

(B) removal of potential air pollutants from fuels prior to combustion,

(C) control of emissions from the evaporation of fuels,

(D) improving the efficiency of fuels combustion so as to decrease atmospheric emissions, and

(E) producing synthetic or new fuels which, when used, result in decreased atmospheric emissions.

(2) provide for Federal grants to public or non-profit agencies, institutions, and organizations and to individuals, and contracts with public or private agencies, institutions or persons, for payment of — (A) part of the cost of acquiring, constructing, or otherwise securing for research and development purposes, new or improved devices or methods having industry wide application of preventing or controlling discharges into the air of various types of pollutants; (B) part of the cost of programs to develop low emission alternatives to the present internal combustion engine; (C) the cost to purchase vehicles and vehicle engines, or portions thereof,

for research, development, and testing purposes; and (D) carrying out the other provisions of this section, without regard to sections 3648 and 3709 of the Revised Statutes (31 U.S.C. §529; 41 U.S.C. §5): *Provided*, That research or demonstration contracts awarded pursuant to this subsection or demonstration contracts awarded pursuant to this subsection (including contracts for construction) may be made in accordance with, and subject to the limitations provided with respect to research contracts of the military departments in, section 2353 of Title 10, United States Code, except that the determination, approval, and certification required thereby shall be made by the Administrator: *Provided further*, That no grant may be made under this paragraph in excess of $1,500,000;

(3) determine, by laboratory and pilot plant testing, the results of air pollution research and studies in order to develop new or improved processes and plant designs to the point where they can be demonstrated on a large and practical scale;

(4) construct, operate, and maintain, or assist in meeting the cost of the construction, operation, and maintenance of new or improved demonstration plants or processes which have promise of accomplishing the purposes of this Act;

(5) study new or improved methods for the recovery and marketing of commercially valuable byproducts resulting from the removal of pollutants.

(b) Powers of Administrator in establishing research and development programs — In carrying out the provisions of this section, the Administrator may —

(1) conduct and accelerate research and development of cost-effective instrumentation techniques to facilitate determination of quantity and quality of air pollutant emissions, including, but not limited to, automotive emissions;

(2) utilize, on a reimbursable basis, the facilities of existing Federal scientific laboratories;

(3) establish and operate necessary facilities and test sites at which to carry on the research, testing, development, and programing necessary to effectuate the purposes of this section;

(4) acquire secret processes, technical data, inventions, patent applications, patents, licenses, and an interest in lands, plants, and facilities, and other property or rights by purchase, license, lease, or donation; and

(5) cause on-site inspections to be made of promising domestic and foreign projects, and cooperate and participate in their development in instances in which the purposes of the Act will be served thereby.

(c) Clean alternative fuels — The Administrator shall conduct a research program to identify, characterize, and predict air emissions related to the production, distribution, storage, and use of clean alternative fuels to determine the risks and benefits to human health and the environment relative to those from using conventional gasoline and diesel fuels. The Administrator shall consult with other Federal agencies to ensure coordination and to avoid duplication of activities authorized under this subsection.

§7405. Grants for support of air pollution planning and control programs
[CAA §105]
(a) Amounts; limitations; assurances of plan development capability

(1)(A) The Administrator may make grants to air pollution control agencies, within the meaning of paragraph (1), (2), (3), (4), or (5) of section 302, in an amount up to three-fifths of the cost of implementing programs for the prevention and control of air pollution or implementation of national primary and secondary ambient air quality standards. For the purpose of this section, "implementing" means any activity related to the planning, developing, establishing, carrying-out, improving, or maintaining of such programs.

(B) Subject to subsections (b) and (c) of this section, an air pollution control agency which receives a grant under subparagraph (A) and which contributes less than the required two-fifths minimum shall have 3 years following the date of the enactment of the Clean Air Act Amendments of 1990 in which to contribute such amount. If such an agency fails to meet and maintain this required level, the Administrator shall reduce the amount of the Federal contribution accordingly.

(C) With respect to any air quality control region or portion thereof for which there is an applicable implementation plan under section 110, grants under subparagraph (A) may be made only to air pollution control agencies which have substantial responsibilities for carrying out such applicable implementation plan.

(2) Before approving any grant under this subsection to any air pollution control agency within the meaning of sections 302(b)(2) and 302(b)(4) of this title, the Administrator shall receive assurances that such agency provides for adequate representation of appropriate State, interstate, local, and (when appropriate) international, interests in the air quality control region.

(3) Before approving any planning grant under this subsection to any air pollution control agency within the meaning of sections 302(b)(2) and 302(b)(4), the Administrator shall receive assurances that such agency has the capability of developing a comprehensive air quality plan for the air quality control region, which plan shall include (when appropriate) a recommended system of alerts to avert and reduce the risk of situations in which there may be imminent and serious danger to the public health or welfare from air pollutants and the various aspects relevant to the establishment of air quality standards for such air quality control region, includ-

ing the concentration of industries, other commercial establishments, population and naturally occurring factors which shall affect such standards.

(b) Terms and conditions; regulations; factors for consideration; State expenditure limitations

(1) From the sums available for the purposes of subsection (a) of this section for any fiscal year, the Administrator shall from time to time make grants to air pollution control agencies upon such terms and conditions as the Administrator may find necessary to carry out the purpose of this section. In establishing regulations for the granting of such funds the Administrator shall, so far as practicable, give due consideration to (A) the population, (B) the extent of the actual or potential air pollution problem, and (C) the financial need of the respective agencies.

(2) Not more than 10 per centum of the total of funds appropriated or allocated for the purposes of subsection (a) of this section shall be granted for air pollution control programs in any one State. In the case of a grant for a program in an area crossing State boundaries, the Administrator shall determine the portion of such grant that is chargeable to the percentage limitation under this subsection for each State into which such area extends. Subject to the provisions of paragraph (1) of this subsection, no State shall have made available to it for application less than one-half of 1 per centum of the annual appropriation for grants under this section for grants to agencies within such State.

(c) Maintenance of effort

(1) No agency shall receive any grant under this section during any fiscal year when its expenditures of non-Federal funds for recurrent expenditures for air pollution control programs will be less than its expenditures were for such programs during the preceding fiscal year. In order for the Administrator to award grants under this section in a timely manner each fiscal year, the Administrator shall compare an agency's prospective expenditure level to that of its second preceding fiscal year. The Administrator shall revise the current regulations which define applicable nonrecurrent and recurrent expenditures, and in so doing, give due consideration to exempting an agency from the limitations of this paragraph and subsection (a) due to periodic increases experienced by that agency from time to time in its annual expenditures for purposes acceptable to the Administrator for that fiscal year.

(2) The Administrator may still award a grant to an agency not meeting the requirements of paragraph (l) of this subsection if the Administrator, after notice and opportunity for public hearing, determines that a reduction in expenditures is attributable to a non-selective reduction in the expenditures in the programs of all Executive branch agencies of the applicable unit of Government. No agency shall receive any grant under

this section with respect to the maintenance of a program for the prevention and control of air pollution unless the Administrator is satisfied that such a grant will be so used to supplement and, to the extent practicable, increase the level of State, local, or other non-Federal funds. No grants shall be made under this section until the Administrator has consulted with the appropriate official as designated by the Governor or Governors of the State or States affected.

(d) Reduction of payments; availability of reduced amounts; reduced amount as deemed paid to agency for purpose of determining amount of grant — The Administrator, with the concurrence of any recipient of a grant under this section may reduce the payments to such recipient by the amount of the pay, allowances, traveling expenses, and any other costs in connection with the detail of any officer or employee to the recipient under section 301 of the Act, when such detail is for the convenience of, and at the request of, such recipient and for the purpose of carrying out the provisions of this Act. The amount by which such payments have been reduced shall be available for payment of such costs by the Administrator, but shall, for the purpose of determining the amount of any grant to a recipient under subsection (a) of this section, be deemed to have been paid to such agency.

(e) Notice and opportunity for hearing when affected by adverse action — No application by a State for a grant under this section may be disapproved by the Administrator without prior notice and opportunity for a public hearing in the affected State, and no commitment or obligation of any funds under any such grant may be revoked or reduced without prior notice and opportunity for a public hearing in the affected State (or in one of the affected States if more than one State is affected).

§7406. Interstate air quality agencies; program cost limitations
[CAA §106]

For the purpose of developing implementation plans for any interstate air quality control region designated pursuant to section 107 or of implementing section 176A (relating to control of interstate air pollution) or section 184 (relating to control of interstate ozone pollution), the Administrator is authorized to pay, for two years, up to 100 per centum of the air quality planning program costs of any commission established under section 176A (relating to control of interstate air pollution) or section 184 (relating to control of interstate ozone pollution) or any agency designated by the Governors of the affected States, which agency shall be capable of recommending to the Governors plans for implementation of national primary and secondary ambient air quality standards and shall include representation from the States and appropriate political subdivisions within the air quality control region. After the initial two-year period

the Administrator is authorized to make grants to such agency or such commission in an amount up to three-fifths of the air quality implementation program costs of such agency or commission.

§7407. Air quality control regions
[CAA §107]

(a) Responsibility of each State for air quality; submission of implementation plan — Each State shall have the primary responsibility for assuring air quality within the entire geographic area comprising such State by submitting an implementation plan for such State which will specify the manner in which national primary and secondary ambient air quality standards will be achieved and maintained within each air quality control region in such State.

(b) Designated regions — For purposes of developing and carrying out implementation plans under section 110 —

(1) an air quality control region designated under this section before the date of enactment of the Clean Air Amendments of 1970, or a region designated after such date under subsection (c), shall be an air quality control region; and

(2) the portion of such State which is not part of any such designated region shall be an air quality control region, but such portion may be subdivided by the State into two or more air quality control regions with the approval of the Administrator.

(c) Authority of Administrator to designate regions; notification of Governors of affected States — The Administrator shall, within 90 days after the date of enactment of the Clean Air Amendments of 1970, after consultation with appropriate State and local authorities, designate as an air quality control region any interstate area or major intrastate area which he deems necessary or appropriate for the attainment and maintenance of ambient air quality standards. The Administrator shall immediately notify the Governors of the affected States of any designation made under this subsection.

(d) Designations

(1) Designations generally

(A) Submission by governors of initial designations following promulgation of new or revised standards — By such date as the Administrator may reasonably require, but not later than 1 year after promulgation of a new or revised national ambient air quality standard for any pollutant under section 109, the Governor of each State shall (and at any other time the Governor of a State deems appropriate the Governor may) submit to the Administrator a list of all areas (or portions thereof) in the State, designating as —

(i) nonattainment, any area that does not meet (or that contributes to ambient air quality in a nearby area that does not meet) the national primary or secondary ambient air quality standard for the pollutant,

(ii) attainment, any area (other than an area identified in clause (i)) that meets the national primary or secondary ambient air quality standard for the pollutant, or

(iii) unclassifiable, any area that cannot be classified on the basis of available information as meeting or not meeting the national primary or secondary ambient air quality standard for the pollutant.

The Administrator may not require the Governor to submit the required list sooner than 120 days after promulgating a new or revised national ambient air quality standard.

(B) Promulgation by EPA of designations

(i) Upon promulgation or revision of a national ambient air quality standard, the Administrator shall promulgate the designations of all areas (or portions thereof) submitted under subparagraph (A) as expeditiously as practicable, but in no case later than 2 years from the date of promulgation of the new or revised national ambient air quality standard. Such period may be extended for up to one year in the event the Administrator has insufficient information to promulgate the designations.

(ii) In making the promulgations required under clause (i), the Administrator may make such modifications as the Administrator deems necessary to the designations of the areas (or portions thereof) submitted under subparagraph (A) (including to the boundaries of such areas or portions thereof). Whenever the Administrator intends to make a modification, the Administrator shall notify the State and provide such State with an opportunity to demonstrate why any proposed modification is inappropriate. The Administrator shall give such notification no later than 120 days before the date the Administrator promulgates the designation, including any modification thereto. If the Governor fails to submit the list in whole or in part, as required under subparagraph (A), the Administrator shall promulgate the designation that the Administrator deems appropriate for any area (or portion thereof) not designated by the State.

(iii) If the Governor of any State, on the Governor's own motion, under subparagraph (A), submits a list of areas (or portions thereof) in the State designated as nonattainment, attainment, or unclassifiable, the Administrator shall act on such designations in accordance with the procedures under paragraph (3) (relating to redesignation).

(iv) A designation for an area (or portion thereof) made pursuant to this subsection shall remain in effect until the area (or portion thereof) is redesignated pursuant to paragraph (3) or (4).

(C) Designations by operation of law

(i) Any area designated with respect to any air pollutant under the provisions of paragraph (1)(A), (B), or (C) of this subsection (as in effect immediately before the date of the enactment of the Clean Air Act Amendments of 1990) is designated, by operation of law, as a nonattainment area for such pollutant within the meaning of subparagraph (A)(i).

(ii) Any area designated with respect to any air pollutant under the provisions of paragraph (1)(E) (as in effect immediately before the date of the enactment of the Clean Air Act Amendments of 1990) is designated by operation of law, as an attainment area for such pollutant within the meaning of subparagraph (A)(ii).

(iii) Any area designated with respect to any air pollutant under the provisions of paragraph (1)(D) (as in effect immediately before the date of the enactment of the Clean Air Act Amendments of 1990) is designated, by operation of law, as an unclassifiable area for such pollutant within the meaning of subparagraph (A)(iii).

(2) Publication of designations and redesignations

(A) The Administrator shall publish a notice in the Federal Register promulgating any designation under paragraph (1) or (5), or announcing any designation under paragraph (4), or promulgating any redesignation under paragraph (3).

(B) Promulgation or announcement of a designation under paragraph (1), (4) or (5) shall not be subject to the provisions of sections 553 through 557 of title 5 of the United States Code (relating to notice and comment), except nothing herein shall be construed as precluding such public notice and comment whenever possible.

(3) Redesignation

(A) Subject to the requirements of subparagraph (E), and on the basis of air quality data, planning and control considerations, or any other air quality-related considerations the Administrator deems appropriate, the Administrator may at any time notify the Governor of any State that available information indicates that the designation of any area or portion of an area within the State or interstate area should be revised. In issuing such notification, which shall be public, to the Governor, the Administrator shall provide such information as the Administrator may have available explaining the basis for the notice.

(B) No later than 120 days after receiving a notification under subparagraph (A), the Governor shall submit to the Administrator such redesignation, if any, of the appropriate area (or areas) or portion thereof within the State or inter-state area, as the Governor considers appropriate.

(C) No later than 120 days after the date described in subparagraph (B) (or paragraph (1)(B)(iii)), the Administrator shall promulgate the re-designation, if any, of the area or portion thereof, submitted by the Governor in accordance with subparagraph (B), making such modifications as the Administrator may deem necessary, in the same manner and under the same procedure as is applicable under clause (ii) of paragraph (1)(B), except that the phrase "60 days" shall be substi-tuted for the phrase "120 days" in that clause. If the Governor does not submit, in accordance with subparagraph (B), a redesignation for an area (or portion thereof) identified by the Administra-tor under subparagraph (A), the Administrator shall promulgate such redesignation, if any, that the Administrator deems appropriate.

(D) The Governor of any State may, on the Governor's own motion, submit to the Administrator a revised designation of any area or portion thereof within the State. Within 18 months of receipt of a complete State redesignation submittal, the Administrator shall approve or deny such redesignation. The submission of a redesignation by a Governor shall not affect the effectiveness or enforce-ability of the applicable implementation plan for the State.

(E) The Administrator may not promulgate a redesignation of a nonattainment area (or portion thereof) to attainment unless —

　(i) the Administrator determines that the area has attained the national ambient air quality standard;

　(ii) the Administrator has fully ap-proved the applicable implementation plan for the area under section 110(k);

　(iii) the Administrator determines that the improvement in air quality is due to permanent and enforceable reductions in emissions resulting from implementation of the applicable implementation plan and applicable Federal air pollutant con-trol regulations and other permanent and enforceable reductions;

　(iv) the Administrator has fully ap-proved a maintenance plan for the area as meeting the requirements of section 175A; and

　(v) the State containing such area has met all requirements applicable to the area under section 110 and part D.

(F) The Administrator shall not promulgate any redesignation of any area (or portion there-of) from nonattainment to unclassifiable.

(4) Nonattainment designations for ozone, car-bon monoxide and particulate matter (PM-10) —

(A) Ozone and carbon monoxide

　(i) Within 120 days after the date of the enactment of the Clean Air Act Amend-ments of 1990, each Governor of each State shall submit to the Administrator a list that designates, affirms or reaffirms the designation of, or redesignates (as the case may be), all areas (or portions thereof) of the Governor's State as attainment, nonat-tainment, or unclassifiable with respect to the national ambient air quality standards for ozone and carbon monoxide.

　(ii) No later than 120 days after the date the Governor is required to submit the list of areas (or portions thereof) required under clause (i) of this subparagraph, the Administrator shall promulgate such designations, making such modifications as the Administrator may deem necessary, in the same manner, and under the same procedure, as is applicable under clause (ii) of paragraph (1)(B), except that the phrase "60 days" shall be substituted for the phrase "120 days" in that clause. If the Governor does not submit, in accordance with clause (i) of this subparagraph, a des-ignation for an area (or portion thereof), the Administrator shall promulgate the designation that the Administrator deems appropriate.

　(iii) No nonattainment area may be redesignated as an attainment area under this subparagraph.

　(iv) Notwithstanding paragraph (1)(C)(ii) of this subsection, if an ozone or carbon monoxide nonattainment area located within a metropolitan statistical area or consolidated metropolitan statistical area (as established by the Bureau of the Census) is classified under part D of this title as a Serious, Severe, or Extreme Area, the bound-aries of such area are hereby revised (on the date 45 days after such classification) by operation of law to include the entire metropolitan statistical area or consolidat-ed metropolitan statistical area, as the case may be, unless within such 45-day period the Governor (in consultation with State and local air pollution control agencies) notifies the Administrator that additional time is necessary to evaluate the application of clause (v). Whenever a Governor has sub-mitted such a notice to the Administrator, such boundary revision shall occur on the later of the date 8 months after such clas-sification or 14 months after the date of the enactment of the Clean Air Act Amend-ments of 1990 unless the Governor makes the finding referred to in clause (v), and the Administrator concurs in such finding, within such period. Except as otherwise provided in this paragraph, a boundary revision under this clause or clause (v) shall apply for purposes of any State implementation plan revision required to be submitted after the date of the enactment of the Clean Air Act Amendments of 1990.

(v) Whenever the Governor of a State has submitted a notice under clause (iv), the Governor, in consultation with State and local air pollution control agencies, shall undertake a study to evaluate whether the entire metropolitan statistical area or consolidated metropolitan statistical area should be included within the nonattainment area. Whenever a Governor finds and demonstrates to the satisfaction of the Administrator, and the Administrator concurs in such finding, that with respect to a portion of a metropolitan statistical area or consolidated metropolitan statistical area, sources in the portion do not contribute significantly to violation of the national ambient air quality standard, the Administrator shall approve the Governor's request to exclude such portion from the nonattainment area. In making such finding, the Governor and the Administrator shall consider factors such as population density, traffic congestion, commercial development, industrial development, meteorological conditions, and pollution transport.

(B) PM-10 designations — By operation of law, until redesignation by the Administrator pursuant to paragraph (3) —

    (i) each area identified in 52 Federal Register 29383 (Aug. 7, 987) as a Group I area (except to the extent that such identification was modified by the Administrator before the date of the enactment of the Clean Air Act Amendments of 1990) is designated nonattainment for PM-10;

    (ii) any area containing a site for which air quality monitoring data show a violation of the national ambient air quality standard for PM-10 before January 1, 1989 (as determined under part 50, appendix K of title 40 of the Code of Federal Regulations) is hereby designated nonattainment for PM-10; and

    (iii) each area not described in clause (i) or (ii) is hereby designated unclassifiable for PM-10.

Any designation for particulate matter (measured in terms of total suspended particulates) that the Administrator promulgated pursuant to this subsection (as in effect immediately before the date of the enactment of the Clean Air Act Amendments of 1990) shall remain in effect for purposes of implementing the maximum allowable increases in concentrations of particulate matter (measured in terms of total suspended particulates) pursuant to section 163(b), until the Administrator determines that such designation is no longer necessary for that purpose.

(5) Designations for lead — The Administrator may, in the Administrator's discretion at any time the Administrator deems appropriate, require a State to designate areas (or portions thereof) with respect to the national ambient air quality standard for lead in effect as of the date of the enactment of the Clean Air Act Amendments of 1990, in accordance with the procedures under subparagraphs (A) and (B) of paragraph (1), except that in applying subparagraph (B)(i) of paragraph (1) the phrase "2 years from the date of promulgation of the new or revised national ambient air quality standard" shall be replaced by the phrase "1 year from the date the Administrator notifies the State of the requirement to designate areas with respect to the standard for lead".

(6) Designations

    (A) Submission — Notwithstanding any other provision of law, not later than February 15, 2004, the Governor of each State shall submit designations referred to in paragraph (1) for the July 1997 $PM_{2.5}$ national ambient air quality standards for each area within the State, based on air quality monitoring data collected in accordance with any applicable Federal reference methods for the relevant areas.

    (B) Promulgation — Notwithstanding any other provision of law, not later than December 31, 2004, the Administrator shall, consistent with paragraph (1), promulgate the designations referred to in subparagraph (A) for each area of each State for the July 1997 $PM_{2.5}$ national ambient air quality standards.

(7) Implementation plan for regional haze

    (A) In general — Notwithstanding any other provision of law, not later than 3 years after the date on which the Administrator promulgates the designations referred to in paragraph (6)(B) for a State, the State shall submit, for the entire State, the State implementation plan revisions to meet the requirements promulgated by the Administrator under section 169B(e)(1) (referred to in this paragraph as "regional haze requirements").

    (B) No preclusion of other provisions — Nothing in this paragraph precludes the implementation of the agreements and recommendations stemming from the Grand Canyon Visibility Transport Commission Report dated June 1996, including the submission of State implementation plan revisions by the States of Arizona, California, Colorado, Idaho, Nevada, New Mexico, Oregon, Utah, or Wyoming by

December 31, 2003, for implementation of regional haze requirements applicable to those States.

(e) Redesignation of air quality control regions

(1) Except as otherwise provided in paragraph (2), the Governor of each State is authorized, with the approval of the Administrator, to redesignate from time to time the air quality control regions within such State for purposes of efficient and effective air quality management. Upon such redesignation, the list under subsection (d) shall be modified accordingly.

(2) In the case of an air quality control region in a State, or part of such region, which the Administrator finds may significantly affect air pollution concentrations in another State, the Governor of the State in which such region, or part of a region, is located may redesignate from time to time the boundaries of so much of such air quality control region as is located within such State only with the approval of the Administrator and with the consent of all Governors of all States which the Administrator determines may be significantly affected.

(3) No compliance date extension granted under section 113(d)(5) (relating to coal conversion) shall cease to be effective by reason of the regional limitation provided in section 113(d)(5) if the violation of such limitation is due solely to a redesignation of a region under this subsection.

§7408. Air quality criteria and control techniques

[CAA §108]

(a) Air pollutant list; publication and revision by Administrator; issuance of air quality criteria for air pollutants

(1) For the purpose of establishing national primary and secondary ambient air quality standards, the Administrator shall within 30 days after the date of enactment of the Clean Air Amendments of 1970 publish, and shall from time to time thereafter revise, a list which includes each air pollutant —

(A) emissions of which, in his judgment, cause or contribute to air pollution which may reasonably be anticipated to endanger public health or welfare;

(B) the presence of which in the ambient air results from numerous or diverse mobile or stationary sources; and

(C) for which air quality criteria had not been issued before the date of enactment of the Clean Air Amendments of 1970, but for which he plans to issue air quality criteria under this section.

(2) The Administrator shall issue air quality criteria for an air pollutant within 12 months after he has included such pollutant in a list under paragraph (1). Air quality criteria for an air pollutant shall accurately reflect the latest scientific knowledge useful in indicating the kind and extent of all identifiable effects on public health or welfare which may be expected from the presence of such pollutant in the ambient air, in varying quantities. The criteria for an air pollutant, to the extent practicable, shall include information on —

(A) those variable factors (including atmospheric conditions) which of themselves or in combination with other factors may alter the effects on public health or welfare of such air pollutant;

(B) the types of air pollutants which, when present in the atmosphere, may interact with such pollutant to produce an adverse effect on public health or welfare; and

(C) any known or anticipated adverse effects on welfare.

(b) Issuance by Administrator of information on air pollution control techniques; standing consulting committees for air pollutants; establishment; membership

(1) Simultaneously with the issuance of criteria under subsection (a), the Administrator shall, after consultation with appropriate advisory committees and Federal departments and agencies, issue to the States and appropriate air pollution control agencies information on air pollution control techniques, which information shall include data relating to the cost of installation and operation, energy requirements, emission reduction benefits, and environmental impact of the emission control technology. Such information shall include such data as are available on available technology and alternative methods of prevention and control of air pollution. Such information shall also include data on alternative fuels, processes, and operating methods which will result in elimination or significant reduction of emissions.

(2) In order to assist in the development of information on pollution control techniques, the Administrator may establish a standing consulting committee for each air pollutant included in a list published pursuant to subsection (a)(1), which shall be comprised of technically qualified individuals representative of State and local governments, industry, and the economic community. Each such committee shall submit, as appropriate, to the Administrator information related to that required by paragraph (1).

(c) Review, modification, and reissuance of criteria or information
— The Administrator shall from time to time review, and, as appropriate, modify, and reissue any criteria or information on control techniques issued pursuant to this section. Not later than six months after the date of the enactment of the Clean Air Act Amendments of 1977, the Administrator shall revise and reissue criteria relating to concentrations of NO_2 over such period (not more than three hours) as

he deems appropriate. Such criteria shall include a discussion of nitric and nitrous acids, nitrites, nitrates, nitrosamines, and other carcinogenic and potentially carcinogenic derivatives of oxides of nitrogen.

(d) Publication in Federal Register; availability of copies for general public — The issuance of air quality criteria and information on air pollution control techniques shall be announced in the Federal Register and copies shall be made available to the general public.

(e) Transportation planning and guidelines — The Administrator shall, after consultation with the Secretary of Transportation, and after providing public notice and opportunity for comment, and with State and local officials, within nine months after enactment of the Clean Air Act Amendments of 1990 and periodically thereafter as necessary to maintain a continuous transportation-air quality planning process, update the June 1978 Transportation-Air Quality Planning Guidelines and publish guidance on the development and implementation of transportation and other measures necessary to demonstrate and maintain attainment of national ambient air quality standards. Such guidelines shall include information on —

(1) methods to identify and evaluate alternative planning and control activities;

(2) methods of reviewing plans on a regular basis as conditions change or new information is presented;

(3) identification of funds and other resources necessary to implement the plan, including interagency agreements on providing such funds and resources;

(4) methods to assure participation by the public in all phases of the planning process; and

(5) such other methods as the Administrator determines necessary to carry out a continuous planning process.

(f) Information regarding processes, procedures, and methods to reduce or control pollutants in transportation; reduction of mobile source related pollutants; reduction of impact on public health

(1) The Administrator shall publish and make available to appropriate Federal, State, and local environmental and transportation agencies not later than one year after enactment of the Clean Air Act Amendments of 1990, and from time to time thereafter —

(A) information prepared, as appropriate, in consultation with the Secretary of Transportation, and after providing public notice and opportunity for comment, regarding the formulation and emission reduction potential of transportation control measures related to criteria pollutants and their precursors, including, but not limited to —

(i) programs for improved public transit;

(ii) restriction of certain roads or lanes to, or construction of such roads or lanes

for use by, passenger buses or high occupancy vehicles;

(iii) employer-based transportation management plans, including incentives;

(iv) trip-reduction ordinances;

(v) traffic flow improvement programs that achieve emission reductions;

(vi) fringe and transportation corridor parking facilities serving multiple occupancy vehicle programs or transit service;

(vii) programs to limit or restrict vehicle use in downtown areas or other areas of emission concentration particularly during periods of peak use;

(viii) programs for the provision of all forms of high-occupancy, shared-ride services;

(ix) programs to limit portions of road surfaces or certain sections of the metropolitan area to the use of non-motorized vehicles or pedestrian use, both as to time and place;

(x) programs for secure bicycle storage facilities and other facilities, including bicycle lanes, for the convenience and protection of bicyclists, in both public and private areas;

(xi) programs to control extended idling of vehicles;

(xii) programs to reduce motor vehicle emissions, consistent with title II, which are caused by extreme cold start conditions;

(xiii) employer-sponsored programs to permit flexible work schedules;

(xiv) programs and ordinances to facilitate non-automobile travel, provision and utilization of mass transit, and to generally reduce the need for single-occupant vehicle travel, as part of transportation planning and development efforts of a locality, including programs and ordinances applicable to new shopping centers, special events, and other centers of vehicle activity;

(xv) programs for new construction and major reconstructions of paths, tracks or areas solely for the use by pedestrian or other non-motorized means of transportation when economically feasible and in the public interest. For purposes of this clause, the Administrator shall also consult with the Secretary of the Interior; and

(xvi) program to encourage the voluntary removal from use and the marketplace of pre-1980 model year light duty vehicles and pre-1980 model light duty trucks.

(B) information on additional methods or strategies that will contribute to the reduction of mobile source related pollutants during periods in which any primary ambient air quality standard will be exceeded and during episodes for which an air pollution alert, warning, or emergency has been declared;

(C) information on other measures which may be employed to reduce the impact on public health or protect the health of sensitive or susceptible individuals or groups; and

(D) information on the extent to which any process, procedure, or method to reduce or control such air pollutant may cause an increase in the emissions or formation of any other pollutant.

(2) In publishing such information the Administrator shall also include an assessment of —

(A) the relative effectiveness of such processes, procedures, and methods;

(B) the potential effect of such processes, procedures, and methods on transportation system and the provision of transportation services; and

(C) the environmental, energy, and economic impact of such processes, procedures, and methods.

(3) Repealed, Pub. L. 105-362, Title XV, §1501(b), Nov. 10, 1998, 112 Stat. 3294.

(4) Repealed. Pub. L. 105-362, Title XV, §1501(b), Nov. 10, 1998, 112 Stat. 3294.

(g) Assessment of Risks to Ecosystems — The Administrator may assess the risks to ecosystems from exposure to criteria air pollutants (as identified by the Administrator in the Administrator's sole discretion).

(h) RACT/BACT/LAER Clearinghouse — The Administrator shall make information regarding emission control technology available to the States and to the general public through a central database. Such information shall include all control technology information received pursuant to State plan provisions requiring permits for sources, including operating permits for existing sources.

§7409. National primary and secondary ambient air quality standards
[CAA §109]
(a) Promulgation

(1) The Administrator —

(A) within 30 days after the date of enactment of the Clean Air Amendments of 1970, shall publish proposed regulations prescribing a national primary ambient air quality standard and a national secondary ambient air quality standard for each air pollutant for which air quality criteria have been issued prior to such date of enactment; and

(B) after a reasonable time for interested persons to submit written comments thereon (but no later than 90 days after the initial publication of such proposed standards) shall by regulation promulgate such proposed national primary and secondary ambient air

quality standards with such modifications as he deems appropriate.

(2) With respect to any air pollutant for which air quality criteria are issued after the date of enactment of the Clean Air Amendments of 1970, the Administrator shall publish, simultaneously with the issuance of such criteria and information, proposed national primary and secondary ambient air quality standards for any such pollutant. The procedure provided for in paragraph (1)(B) of this subsection shall apply to the promulgation of such standards.

(b) Protection of public health and welfare

(1) National primary ambient air quality standards, prescribed, under subsection (a) shall be ambient air quality standards the attainment and maintenance of which in the judgment of the Administrator, based on such criteria and allowing an adequate margin of safety, are requisite to protect the public health. Such primary standards may be revised in the same manner as promulgated.

(2) Any national secondary ambient air quality standard prescribed, under subsection (a) shall specify a level of air quality the attainment and maintenance of which in the judgment of the Administrator, based on such criteria, is requisite to protect the public welfare from any known or anticipated adverse effects associated with the presence of such air pollutant in the ambient air. Such secondary standards may be revised in the same manner as promulgated.

(c) National primary ambient air quality standard for nitrogen dioxide — The Administrator shall, not later than one year after the date of the enactment of the Clean Air Act Amendments of 1977, promulgate a national primary ambient air quality standard for NO_2 concentrations over a period of not more than 3 hours unless, based on the criteria issued under section 108(c), he finds that there is no significant evidence that such a standard for such a period is requisite to protect public health.

(d) Review and revision of criteria and standards; independent scientific review committee; appointment; advisory functions

(1) Not later than December 31, 1980, and at five-year intervals thereafter, the Administrator shall complete a thorough review of the criteria published under section 108 and the national ambient air quality standards promulgated under this section and shall make such revisions in such criteria and standards and promulgate such new standards as may be appropriate in accordance with section 108 and subsection (b) of this section. The Administrator may review and revise criteria or promulgate new standards earlier or more frequently than required under this paragraph.

(2)(A) The Administrator shall appoint an independent scientific review committee composed of seven members including at least one member of the National Academy of Sciences, one physician, and one person representing State air pollution control agencies.

(B) Not later than January 1, 1980, and at five-year intervals thereafter, the committee referred to in subparagraph (A) shall complete a review of the criteria published under section 108 and the national primary and secondary ambient air quality standards promulgated under this section and shall recommend to the Administrator any new national ambient air quality standards and revisions of existing criteria and standards as may be appropriate under section 108 and subsection (b) of this section.

(C) Such committee shall also (i) advise the Administrator of areas in which additional knowledge is required to appraise the adequacy and basis of existing, new, or revised national ambient air quality standards, (ii) describe the research efforts necessary to provide the required information, (iii) advise the Administrator on the relative contribution to air pollution concentrations of natural as well as anthropogenic activity, and (iv) advise the Administrator of any adverse public health, welfare, social, economic, or energy effects which may result from various strategies for attainment and maintenance of such national ambient air quality standards.

§7410. State implementation plans for national primary and secondary ambient air quality standards
[CAA §110]
(a) Adoption of plan by State; submission to Administrator; content of plan; revision; new sources; indirect source review program; supplemental or intermittent control systems

(1) Each State shall, after reasonable notice and public hearings, adopt and submit to the Administrator, within 3 years (or such shorter period as the Administrator may prescribe) after the promulgation of a national primary ambient air quality standard (or any revision thereof) under section 109 for any air pollutant, a plan which provides for implementation, maintenance, and enforcement of such primary standard in each air quality control region (or portion thereof) within such State. In addition, such State shall adopt and submit to the Administrator (either as a part of a plan submitted under the preceding sentence or separately) within 3 years (or such shorter period as the Administrator may prescribe) after the promulgation of a national ambient air quality secondary standard (or revision thereof), a plan which provides for implementation, maintenance,

and enforcement of such secondary standard in each air quality control region (or portion thereof) within such State. Unless a separate public hearing is provided, each State shall consider its plan implementing such secondary standard at the hearing required by the first sentence of this paragraph.

(2) Each implementation plan submitted by a State under this Act shall be adopted by the State after reasonable notice and public hearing. Each such plan shall —

(A) include enforceable emission limitations and other control measures, means, or techniques (including economic incentives such as fees, marketable permits, and auctions of emissions rights), as well as schedules and timetables for compliance, as may be necessary or appropriate to meet the applicable requirements of this Act;

(B) provide for establishment and operation of appropriate devices, methods, systems, and procedures necessary to —

(i) monitor, compile, and analyze data on ambient air quality, and

(ii) upon request, make such data available to the Administrator;

(C) include a program to provide for the enforcement of the measures described in subparagraph (A), and regulation of the modification and construction of any stationary source within the areas covered by the plan as necessary to assure that national ambient air quality standards are achieved, including a permit program as required in parts C and D;

(D) contain adequate provisions —

(i) prohibiting, consistent with the provisions of this title, any source or other type of emissions activity within the State from emitting any air pollutant in amounts which will —

(I) contribute significantly to nonattainment in, or interfere with maintenance by, any other State with respect to any such national primary or secondary ambient air quality standard, or

(II) interfere with measures required to be included in the applicable implementation plan for any other State under part C to prevent significant deterioration of air quality or to protect visibility,

(ii) insuring compliance with the applicable requirements of sections 126 and 115 (relating to interstate and international pollution abatement);

(E) provide (i) necessary assurances that the State (or, except where the Administrator deems inappropriate, the general purpose local government or governments, or a regional agency designated by the State or general purpose local governments for such purpose) will have adequate personnel, funding, and authority under State (and, as appropriate, local) law to carry out such implementation plan (and is not prohibited by any provision of Federal or State law from carrying out such implementation plan or portion thereof), (ii) requirements that the State comply with the requirements respecting State boards under section 128, and (iii) necessary assurances that, where the State has relied on a local or regional government, agency, or instrumentality for the implementation of any plan provision, the State has responsibility for ensuring adequate implementation of such plan provision;

(F) require, as may be prescribed by the Administrator —

(i) the installation, maintenance, and replacement of equipment, and the implementation of other necessary steps, by owners or operators of stationary sources to monitor emissions from such sources,

(ii) periodic reports on the nature and amounts of emissions and emissions-related data from such sources, and

(iii) correlation of such reports by the State agency with any emission limitations or standards established pursuant to this Act, which reports shall be available at reasonable times for public inspection;

(G) provide for authority comparable to that in section 303 and adequate contingency plans to implement such authority;

(H) provide for revision of such plan —

(i) from time to time as may be necessary to take account of revisions of such national primary or secondary ambient air quality standard or the availability of improved or more expeditious methods of attaining such standard, and

(ii) except as provided in paragraph (3)(C), whenever the Administrator finds on the basis of information available to the Administrator that the plan is substantially inadequate to attain the national ambient air quality standard which it implements or to otherwise comply with any additional requirements established under this Act;

(I) in the case of a plan or plan revision for an area designated as a nonattainment area, meet the applicable requirements of part D (relating to nonattainment areas);

(J) meet the applicable requirements of section 121 (relating to consultation), section 127 (relating to public notification), and part C (relating to prevention of significant deterioration of air quality and visibility protection);

(K) provide for —

(i) the performance of such air quality modeling as the Administrator may prescribe for the purpose of predicting the effect on ambient air quality of any emissions of any air pollutant for which the Administrator has established a national ambient air quality standard, and

(ii) the submission, upon request, of data related to such air quality modeling to the Administrator;

(L) require the owner or operator of each major stationary source to pay to the permitting authority, as a condition of any permit required under this Act, a fee sufficient to cover —

(i) the reasonable costs of reviewing and acting upon any application for such a permit, and

(ii) if the owner or operator receives a permit for such source, the reasonable costs of implementing and enforcing the terms and conditions of any such permit (not including any court costs or other costs associated with any enforcement action), until such fee requirement is superseded with respect to such sources by the Administrator's approval of a fee program under title V; and

(M) provide for consultation and participation by local political subdivisions affected by the plan.

(3)[(A)] Repealed. Pub. L. 101-549. Title I §101(d)(1). Nov. 15, 1990, 104 Stat. 2409

(B) As soon as practicable, the Administrator shall, consistent with the purposes of this Act and the Energy Supply and Environmental Coordination Act of 1974, review each State's applicable implementation plans and report to the State on whether such plans can be revised in relation to fuel burning stationary sources (or persons supplying fuel to such sources) without interfering with the attainment and maintenance of any national ambient air quality standard within the period permitted in this section. If the Administrator determines that any such plan can be revised, he shall notify the State that a plan revision may be submitted by the State. Any plan revision which is submitted by the State shall, after public notice and opportunity for public hearing, be approved by the Administrator if the revision relates only to fuel burning stationary ources (or persons supplying fuel to such sources), and the plan as revised complies with paragraph (2) of this subsection. The Administrator shall approve or disapprove any revision no later than three months after its submission.

(C) Neither the State, in the case of a plan (or portion thereof) approved under this subsection, nor the Administrator, in the case of a plan (or portion thereof) promulgated under subsection (c), shall be required to revise an applicable implementation plan because one or more exemptions under section 118 (relating to Federal facilities), enforcement orders under section 113(d), suspensions under section 110 (f) or (g) (relating to temporary energy or economic authority), orders under section 119 (relating to primary nonferrous smelters), or extensions of compliance in decrees entered under section 113(e) (relating to iron- and steel-producing operations) have been granted, if such plan would have met the requirements of this section if no such exemptions, orders, or extensions had been granted.

(D) Repealed. Pub. L. 101-549, Title I, §101(d)(1), Nov. 15, 1990, 104 Stat. 2409

[(4)] Repealed. Pub. L. 101-549. Title I, §101(d)(2), Nov. 15, 1990, 104 Stat. 2409

(5)(A)(i) Any State may include in a State implementation plan, but the Administrator may not require as a condition of approval of such plan under this section, any indirect source review program. The Administrator may approve and enforce, as part of an applicable implementation plan, an indirect source review program which the State chooses to adopt and submit as part of its plan.

(ii) Except as provided in subparagraph (B), no plan promulgated by the Administrator shall include any indirect source review program for any air quality control region, or portion thereof.

(iii) Any State may revise an applicable implementation plan approved under section 110(a) to suspend or revoke any such program included in such plan, provided that such plan meets the requirements of this section.

(B) The Administrator shall have the authority to promulgate, implement and enforce regulations under section 110(c) respecting indirect source review programs which apply only to federally assisted highways, airports, and other major federally assisted indirect sources and federally owned or operated indirect sources.

(C) For purposes of this paragraph, the term "indirect source" means a facility, building, structure, installation, real property, road, or highway which attracts, or may attract, mobile sources of pollution. Such term includes parking lots, parking garages, and other facilities subject to any measure for management of parking supply (within the meaning of section 110(c)(2)(D)(ii)), including regulation of existing off-street parking but such term does not include new or existing on-street parking. Direct emissions sources or facilities at, within, or associated with, any indirect source shall not be deemed indirect sources for the purpose of this paragraph.

(D) For purposes of this paragraph the term "indirect source review program" means the facility-by-facility review of indirect sources of air pollution, including such measures as are necessary to assure, or assist in assuring, that a new or modified indirect source will not attract mobile sources of air pollution, the emissions from which would cause or contribute to air pollution concentrations —

(i) exceeding any national primary ambient air quality standard for a mobile source-related air pollutant after the primary standard attainment date, or

(ii) preventing maintenance of any such standard after such date.

(E) For purposes of this paragraph and paragraph (2)(B), the term "transportation control measure" does not include any measure which is an "indirect source review program".

(6) No State plan shall be treated as meeting the requirements of this section unless such plan provides that in the case of any source which uses a supplemental, or intermittent control system for purposes of meeting the requirements of an order under section 113(d) or section 119 (relating to primary nonferrous smelter orders), the owner or operator of such source may not temporarily reduce the pay of any employee by reason of the use of such supplemental or intermittent or other dispersion dependent control system.

(b) Extension of period for submission of plans — The Administrator may, wherever he determines necessary, extend the period for submission of any plan or portion thereof which implements a national secondary ambient air quality standard for a period not to exceed eighteen months from the date otherwise required for submission of such plan.

(c) Preparation and publication by Administrator of proposed regulations setting forth implementation plan; transportation regulations study and report; parking surcharge; suspension authority; plan implementation

(1) The Administrator shall promulgate a Federal implementation plan at any time within 2 years after the Administrator —

(A) finds that a State has failed to make a required submission or finds that the plan or plan revision submitted by the State does not satisfy the minimum criteria established under section 110(k)(1)(A), or

(B) disapproves a State implementation plan submission in whole or in part,

unless the State corrects the deficiency, and the Administrator approves the plan or plan revision, before the Administrator promulgates such Federal implementation plan.

(2)[(A)] Repealed. Pub. L. 101-549, Title I, §101(d)(3)(A), Nov. 15, 1990, 104 Stat. 2409.

(B) No parking surcharge regulation may be required by the Administrator under paragraph (1) of this subsection as a part of an applicable implementation plan. All parking surcharge regulations previously required by the Administrator shall be void upon the date of enactment of this subparagraph. This subparagraph shall not prevent the Administrator from approving parking surcharges if they are adopted and submitted by a State as part of an applicable implementation plan. The Administrator may not condition approval of any implementation plan submitted by a State on such plan's including a parking surcharge regulation.

[(C)] Repealed. Pub. L. 101-549, Title I, §101(d)(3)(B), Nov. 15, 1990, 104 Stat. 2409.

(D) For purposes of this paragraph —

(i) The term "parking surcharge regulation" means a regulation imposing or requiring the imposition of any tax, surcharge, fee, or other charge on parking spaces, or any other area used for the temporary storage of motor vehicles.

(ii) The term "management of parking supply" shall include any requirement providing that any new facility containing a given number of parking spaces shall receive a permit or other prior approval, issuance of which is to be conditioned on air quality considerations.

(iii) The term "preferential bus/carpool lane" shall include any requirement for the setting aside of one or more lanes of a street or highway on a permanent or temporary basis for the exclusive use of buses or carpools, or both.

(E) No standard, plan, or requirement, relating to management of parking supply or preferential bus/carpool lanes shall be promulgated after the date of enactment of this paragraph by the Administrator pursuant to this section, unless such promulgation has been subjected to at least one public hearing which has been held in the area affected and for which reasonable notice has been given in such area. If substantial changes are made following public hearings, one or more additional hearings shall be held in such area after such notice.

(3) Upon application of the chief executive officer of any general purpose unit of local government, if the Administrator determines that such unit has adequate authority under State or local law, the Administrator may delegate to such unit the authority to implement and enforce within the jurisdiction of such unit any part of a plan promulgated under this subsection. Nothing in this paragraph shall prevent the Administrator from implementing or enforcing any applicable provision of a plan promulgated under this subsection.

(4) Repealed. Pub. L. 101-549, Title I, §101(d)(3)(C), Nov. 15, 1990, 104 Stat. 2409.

(5)(A) Any measure in an applicable implementation plan which requires a toll or other charge for the use of a bridge located entirely within one city shall be eliminated from such plan by the Administrator upon application by the Governor of the State, which application shall include a certification by the Governor that he will revise such plan in accordance with subparagraph (B).

(B) In the case of any applicable implementation plan with respect to which a measure has been eliminated under subparagraph (A), such plan shall, not later than one year after the date of the enactment of this subparagraph, be revised to include comprehensive measures to:

(i) establish, expand, or improve public transportation measures to meet basic transportation needs, as expeditiously as is practicable; and

(ii) implement transportation control measures necessary to attain and maintain national ambient air quality standards,

and such revised plan shall, for the purpose of implementing such comprehensive public transportation measures, include requirements to use (insofar as is necessary) Federal grants, State or local funds, or any combination of such grants and funds as may be consistent with the terms of the legislation providing such grants and funds. Such measures shall, as a substitute for the tolls or charges eliminated under subparagraph (A), provide for emissions reductions equivalent to the reductions which may reasonably be expected to be achieved through the use of the tolls or charges eliminated.

(C) Any revision of any implementation plan for purposes of meeting the requirements of subparagraph (B) shall be submitted in coordination with any plan revision required under part D.

(d), (e) Repealed. Pub. L. 101-549, Title I, §101(d)(4), (5), Nov. 15, 1990, 104 Stat. 2409.

(f) National or regional energy emergencies; determination by President

(1) Upon application by the owner or operator of a fuel burning stationary source, and after notice and opportunity for public hearing, the Governor of the State in which such source is located may petition the President to determine that a national or regional energy emergency exists of such severity that —

(A) a temporary suspension of any part of the applicable implementation plan or any requirement under section 411 (concerning excess emissions penalties or offsets) of title IV of the Act may be necessary, and

(B) other means of responding to the energy emergency may be inadequate.

Such determination shall not be delegable by the President to any other person. If the President determines that a national or regional energy emergency of such severity exists, a temporary emergency suspension of any part of an applicable implementation plan or any requirement under section 411 (concerning excess emissions penalties or offsets) of title IV of the Act adopted by the State may be issued by the Governor of any State covered by the President's determination under the condition specified in paragraph (2) and may take effect immediately.

(2) A temporary emergency suspension under this subsection shall be issued to a source only if the Governor of such State finds that —

(A) there exists in the vicinity of such source a temporary energy emergency involving high levels of unemployment or loss of necessary energy supplies for residential dwellings; and

(B) such unemployment or loss can be totally or partially alleviated by such emergency suspension.

Not more than one such suspension may be issued for any source on the basis of the same set of circumstances or on the basis of the same emergency.

(3) A temporary emergency suspension issued by a Governor under this subsection shall remain in effect for a maximum of four months or such lesser period as may be specified in a disapproval order of the Administrator, if any. The Administrator may disapprove such suspension if he determines that it does not meet the requirements of paragraph (2).

(4) This subsection shall not apply in the case of a plan provision or requirement promulgated by the Administrator under subsection (c) of this section, but in any such case the President may grant a temporary emergency suspension for a four month period of any such provision or requirement if he makes the determinations and findings specified in paragraphs (1) and (2).

(5) The Governor may include in any temporary emergency suspension issued under this subsection a provision delaying for a period identical to the period of such suspension any compliance schedule (or increment of progress) to which such source is subject under section 119, as in effect before the date of the enactment of this paragraph or section 113(d) of this Act, upon a finding that such source is unable to comply with such schedule (or increment) solely because of the conditions on the basis of which a suspension was issued under this subsection.

(g) Governor's authority to issue temporary emergency suspensions

(1) In the case of any State which has adopted and submitted to the Administrator a proposed plan revision which the State determines —

(A) meets the requirements of this section, and

(B) is necessary

(i) to prevent the closing for one year or more of any source of air pollution, and

(ii) to prevent substantial increases in unemployment which would result from such closing, and

which the Administrator has not approved or disapproved under this section within 12 months of submission of the proposed plan revision, the Governor may issue a temporary emergency suspension of the part of the applicable implementation plan for such State which is proposed to be revised with respect to such source. The determination under subparagraph (B) may not be made with respect to a source which would close without regard whether or not the proposed plan revision is approved.

(2) A temporary emergency suspension issued by a Governor under this subsection shall remain in effect for a maximum of four months or such lesser period as may be specified in a disapproval order of the Administrator. The Administrator may disapprove such suspension if he determines that it does not meet the requirements of this subsection.

(3) The Governor may include in any temporary emergency suspension issued under this subsection a provision delaying for a period identical to the period of such suspension any compliance schedule (or increment of progress) to which such source is subject under section 119 as in effect before the date of the enactment of this paragraph, or under section 113(d) upon a finding that such source is unable to comply with such schedule (or increment) solely because of the conditions on the basis of which a suspension was issued under this subsection.

(h) Publication of comprehensive document for each State setting forth requirements of applicable implementation plan

(1) Not later than 5 years after the date of enactment of the Clean Air Act Amendments of 1990, and every three years thereafter, the Administrator shall assemble and publish a comprehensive document for each State setting forth all requirements of the applicable implementation plan for such State and shall publish notice in the Federal Register of the availability of such documents.

(2) The Administrator may promulgate such regulations as may be reasonably necessary to carry out the purpose of this subsection.

(i) Modification of requirements prohibited — Except for a primary nonferrous smelter order under section 119, a suspension under section 110 (f) or (g) (relating to emergency suspensions), an exemption under section 118 (relating to certain Federal facilities), an order under section 113(d) (relating to compliance orders), a plan promulgation under section 110(c), or a plan revision under section 110(a)(3), no order, suspension, plan revision, or other action modifying any requirement of an applicable implementation plan may be taken with respect to any stationary source by the State or by the Administrator.

(j) Technological systems of continuous emission reduction on new or modified stationary sources; compliance with performance standards — As a condition for issuance of any permit required under this title, the owner or operator of each new or modified stationary source which is required to obtain such a permit must show to the satisfaction of the permitting authority that the technological system of continuous emission reduction which is to be used will enable such source to comply with the standards of performance which are to apply to such source and that the construction or modification and operation of such source will be in compliance with all other requirements of this Act.

(k) Environmental Protection Agency action on plan submissions

   (1) Completeness of plan submissions

      (A) Completeness criteria — Within 9 months after the date of the enactment of the Clean Air Act Amendments of 1990, the Administrator shall promulgate minimum criteria that any plan submission must meet before the Administrator is required to act on such submission under this subsection. The criteria shall be limited to the information necessary to enable the Administrator to determine whether the plan submission complies with the provisions of this Act.

      (B) Completeness finding — Within 60 days of the Administrator's receipt of a plan or plan revision, but no later than 6 months after the date, if any, by which a State is required to submit the plan or revision, the Administrator shall determine whether the minimum criteria established pursuant to subparagraph (A) have been met. Any plan or plan revision that a State submits to the Administrator, and that has not been determined by the Administrator (by the date 6 months after receipt of the submission) to have failed to meet the minimum criteria established pursuant to subparagraph (A), shall on that date be deemed by operation of law to meet such minimum criteria.

      (C) Effect of finding of incompleteness — Where the Administrator determines that a plan submission (or part thereof) does not meet the minimum criteria established pursuant to subparagraph (A), the State shall be treated as not having made the submission (or, in the Administrator's discretion, part thereof).

   (2) Deadline for action — Within 12 months of a determination by the Administrator (or a determination deemed by operation of law) under paragraph (1) that a State has submitted a plan or plan revision (or, in the Administrator's discretion, part thereof) that meets the minimum criteria established pursuant to paragraph (1), if applicable (or, if those criteria are not applicable, within 12 months of submission of the plan or revision), the Administrator shall act on the submission in accordance with paragraph (3).

   (3) Full and partial approval and disapproval — In the case of any submittal on which the Administrator is required to act under paragraph (2), the Administrator shall approve such submittal as a whole if it meets all of the applicable requirements of this Act. If a portion of the plan revision meets all the applicable requirements of this Act, the Administrator may approve the plan revision in part and disapprove the plan revision in part. The plan revision shall not be treated as meeting the requirements of this Act until the Administrator approves the entire plan revision as complying with the applicable requirements of this Act.

   (4) Conditional approval — The Administrator may approve a plan revision based on a commitment of the State to adopt specific enforceable measures by a date certain, but not later than 1 year after the date of approval of the plan revision. Any such conditional approval shall be treated as a disapproval if the State fails to comply with such commitment.

   (5) Calls for plan revisions — Whenever the Administrator finds that the applicable implementation plan for any area is substantially inadequate to attain or maintain the relevant national ambient air quality standard, to mitigate adequately the interstate pollutant transport described in section 176A or section 184, or to otherwise comply with any requirement of this Act, the Administrator shall require the State to revise the plan as necessary to correct such inadequacies. The Administrator shall notify the State of the inadequacies, and may establish reasonable deadlines (not to exceed 18 months after the date of such notice) for the submission of such plan revisions. Such findings and notice shall be public. Any finding under this paragraph shall, to the extent the Administrator deems appropriate, subject the State to the requirements of this Act to which the State was subject when it developed and submitted the plan for which such finding was made, except that the Administrator may adjust any dates applicable under such requirements as appropriate (except that the Administrator may not adjust any attainment date prescribed under part D, unless such date has elapsed).

   (6) Corrections — Whenever the Administrator determines that the Administrator's action approving, disapproving, or promulgating any plan or plan revision (or part thereof), area designation, redesignation, classification, or reclassification was in error, the Administrator may in the same manner as the approval, disapproval, or promulgation revise such action as appropriate without requiring any further submission from the State. Such determination and the basis thereof shall be provided to the State and public.

(l) Plan revisions — Each revision to an implementation plan submitted by a State under this Act shall be adopted by such State after reasonable notice and public hearing. The Administrator shall not approve a revision of a plan if the revision would interfere with any applicable requirement concerning attainment and reasonable further progress (as defined in section 171), or any other applicable requirement of this Act.

(m) Sanctions — The Administrator may apply any of the sanctions listed in section 179(b) at any time (or at any time after) the Administrator makes a finding, disapproval, or determination under paragraphs (1) through (4), respectively, of section 179(a) in relation to any plan or plan item (as that term is defined by the Administrator) required under this Act, with respect to any portion of the State the Administrator determines reasonable and appropriate, for the purpose of ensuring that the requirements of this Act relating to such plan or plan item are met. The Administrator shall, by rule, establish criteria for exercising his authority under the previous sentence with respect to any deficiency referred to in section 179(a) to ensure that, during the 24-month period following the finding, disapproval, or determination referred to in section 179(a), such sanctions are not applied on a statewide basis where one or more political subdivisions covered by the applicable implementation plan are principally responsible for such deficiency.

(n) Savings clauses

(1) Existing plan provisions — Any provision of any applicable implementation plan that was approved or promulgated by the Administrator pursuant to this section as in effect before the date of the enactment of the Clean Air Act Amendments of 1990 shall remain in effect as part of such applicable implementation plan, except to the extent that a revision to such provision is approved or promulgated by the Administrator pursuant to this Act.

(2) Attainment dates — For any area not designated nonattainment, any plan or plan revision submitted or required to be submitted by a State —

(A) in response to the promulgation or revision of a national primary ambient air quality standard in effect on the date of the enactment of the Clean Air Act Amendments of 1990, or

(B) in response to a finding of substantial inadequacy under subsection (a)(2) (as in effect immediately before the date of the enactment of the Clean Air Act Amendments of 1990), shall provide for attainment of the national primary ambient air quality standards within 3 years of the date of the enactment of the Clean Air Act Amendments of 1990 or within 5 years of issuance of such finding of substantial inadequacy, whichever is later.

(3) Retention of construction moratorium in certain areas — In the case of an area to which, immediately before the date of the enactment of the Clean Air Act Amendments of 1990, the prohibition on construction or modification of major stationary sources prescribed in subsection (a)(2) (i) (as in effect immediately before the date of the enactment of the Clean Air Act Amendments of 1990) applied by virtue of a finding of the Administrator that the State containing such area had not submitted an implementation plan meeting the requirements of section 172(c)(6) (relating to establishment of a permit program) (as in effect immediately before the date of enactment of the Clean Air Act Amendments of 1990) or 172(a)(1) (to the extent such requirements relate to provision for attainment of the primary national ambient air quality standard for sulfur oxides by December 31, 1982) as in effect immediately before the date of the enactment of the Clean Air Act Amendments of 1990, no major stationary source of the relevant air pollutant or pollutants shall be constructed or modified in such area until the Administrator finds that the plan for such area meets the applicable requirements of section 172(c)(5) (relating to permit programs) or subpart 5 of part D (relating to attainment of the primary national ambient air quality standard for sulfur dioxide), respectively.

(o) Indian tribes — If an Indian tribe submits an implementation plan to the Administrator pursuant to section 301(d), the plan shall be reviewed in accordance with the provisions for review set forth in this section for State plans, except as otherwise provided by regulation promulgated pursuant to section 301(d)(2). When such plan becomes effective in accordance with the regulations promulgated under section 301(d), the plan shall become applicable to all areas (except as expressly provided otherwise in the plan) located within the exterior boundaries of the reservation, notwithstanding the issuance of any patent and including rights-of-way running through the reservation.

(p) Reports — Any State shall submit, according to such schedule as the Administrator may prescribe, such reports as the Administrator may require relating to emission reductions, vehicle miles traveled, congestion levels, and any other information the Administrator may deem necessary to assess the development effectiveness, need for revision, or implementation of any plan or plan revision required under this Act.

§7411. Standards of performance for new stationary sources
[CAA §111]

(a) Definitions — For purposes of this section:

(1) The term "standard of performance" means a standard for emissions of air pollutants which reflects the degree of emission limitation achievable through the application of the best system of emission reduction which (taking into account the cost of achieving such reduction and any non air quality health and environmental impact and energy requirements) the Administrator determines has been adequately demonstrated.

(2) The term "new source" means any stationary source, the construction or modification of which is commenced after the publication of regulations (or, if earlier, proposed regulations)

prescribing a standard of performance under this section which will be applicable to such source.

(3) The term "stationary source" means any building, structure, facility, or installation which emits or may emit any air pollutant. Nothing in title II of this Act relating to nonroad engines shall be construed to apply to stationary internal combustion engines.

(4) The term "modification" means any physical change in, or change in the method of operation of, a stationary source which increases the amount of any air pollutant emitted by such source or which results in the emission of any air pollutant not previously emitted.

(5) The term "owner or operator" means any person who owns, leases, operates, controls, or supervises a stationary source.

(6) The term "existing source" means any stationary source other than a new source.

(7) The term "technological system of continuous emission reduction" means —

(A) a technological process for production or operation by any source which is inherently low-polluting or nonpolluting, or

(B) a technological system for continuous reduction of the pollution generated by a source before such pollution is emitted into the ambient air, including precombustion cleaning or treatment of fuels.

(8) A conversion to coal (A) by reason of an order under section 2(a) of the Energy Supply and Environmental Coordination Act of 1974 or any amendment thereto, or any subsequent enactment which supersedes such Act, or (B) which qualifies under section 113(d)(5)(A)(ii) of this Act, shall not be deemed to be a modification for purposes of paragraphs (2) and (4) of this subsection.

(b) List of categories of stationary sources; standards of performance; information on pollution control techniques; sources owner or operated by United States; particular systems; revised standards

(1)(A) The Administrator shall, within 90 days after the date of enactment of the Clean Air Amendments of 1970, publish (and from time to time thereafter shall revise) a list of categories of stationary sources. He shall include a category of sources in such list if in his judgment it causes, or contributes significantly to, air pollution which may reasonably be anticipated to endanger public health or welfare.

(B) Within one year after the inclusion of a category of stationary sources in a list under subparagraph (A), the Administrator shall publish proposed regulations, establishing Federal standards of performance for new sources within such category. The Administrator shall afford interested persons an opportunity for written comment on such proposed regulations. After considering such comments, he shall

promulgate, within one year after such publication, such standards with such modifications as he deems appropriate. The Administrator shall, at least every 8 years, review and, if appropriate, revise such standards following the procedure required by this subsection for promulgation of such standards. Notwithstanding the requirements of the previous sentence, the Administrator need not review any such standard if the Administrator determines that such review is not appropriate in light of readily available information on the efficacy of such standard. Standards of performance or revisions thereof shall become effective upon promulgation. When implementation and enforcement of any requirement of this Act indicate that emission limitations and percent reductions beyond those required by the standards promulgated under this section are achieved in practice, the Administrator shall, when revising standards promulgated under this section, consider the emission limitations and percent reductions achieved in practice.

(2) The Administrator may distinguish among classes, types, and sizes within categories of new sources for the purpose of establishing such standards.

(3) The Administrator shall, from time to time, issue information on pollution control techniques for categories of new sources and air pollutants subject to the provisions of this section.

(4) The provisions of this section shall apply to any new source owned or operated by the United States.

(5) Except as otherwise authorized under subsection (h), nothing in this section shall be construed to require, or to authorize the Administrator to require, any new or modified source to install and operate any particular technological system of continuous emission reduction to comply with any new source standard of performance.

(6) The revised standards of performance required by enactment of subsection (a)(1)(A)(i) and (ii) shall be promulgated not later than one year after enactment of this paragraph. Any new or modified fossil fuel fired stationary source which commences construction prior to the date of publication of the proposed revised standards shall not be required to comply with such revised standards.

(c) State implementation and enforcement of standards of performance

(1) Each State may develop and submit to the Administrator a procedure for implementing and enforcing standards of performance for new sources located in such State. If the Administrator finds the State procedure is adequate, he shall delegate to such State any authority he has under this Act to implement and enforce such standards.

(2) Nothing in this subsection shall prohibit the Administrator from enforcing any applicable standard of performance under this section.

(d) Standards of performance for existing sources; remaining useful life of source

(1) The Administrator shall prescribe regulations which shall establish a procedure similar to that provided by section 110 under which each State shall submit to the Administrator a plan which (A) establishes standards of performance for any existing source for any air pollutant (i) for which air quality criteria have not been issued or which is not included on a list published under section 108(a) [or emitted from a source category which is regulated under section 112] [or 112(b)]* but (ii) to which a standard of performance under this section would apply if such existing source were a new source, and (B) provides for the implementation and enforcement of such standards of performance. Regulations of the Administrator under this paragraph shall permit the State in applying a standard of performance to any particular source under a plan submitted under this paragraph to take into consideration, among other factors, the remaining useful life of the existing source to which such standard applies.

(2) The Administrator shall have the same authority —

(A) to prescribe a plan for a State in cases where the State fails to submit a satisfactory plan as he would have under section 110(c) in the case of failure to submit an implementation plan, and

(B) to enforce the provisions of such plan in cases where the State fails to enforce them as he would have under sections 113 and 114 with respect to an implementation plan.

In promulgating a standard of performance under a plan prescribed under this paragraph, the Administrator shall take into consideration, among other factors, remaining useful lives of the sources in the category of sources to which such standard applies.

(e) Prohibited acts
— After the effective date of standards of performance promulgated under this section, it shall be unlawful for any owner or operator of any new source to operate such source in violation of any standard of performance applicable to such source.

(f) New source standards of performance

(1) For those categories of major stationary sources that the Administrator listed under subsection (b)(1)(A) before the date of the enactment of the Clean Air Act Amendments of 1990 and for which regulations had not been proposed by the Administrator by such date, the Administrator shall —

(A) propose regulations establishing standards of performance for at least 25 percent of such categories of sources within 2 years after the date of the enactment of the Clean Air Act Amendments of 1990;

(B) propose regulations establishing standards of performance for at least 50 percent of such categories of sources within 4 years after the date of the enactment of the Clean Air Act Amendments of 1990; and

(C) propose regulations for the remaining categories of sources within 6 years after the date of the enactment of the Clean Air Act Amendments of 1990.

(2) In determining priorities for promulgating standards for categories of major stationary sources for the purpose of paragraph (1), the Administrator shall consider —

(A) the quantity of air pollutant emissions which each such category will emit, or will be designed to emit;

(B) the extent to which each such pollutant may reasonably be anticipated to endanger public health or welfare; and

(C) the mobility and competitive nature of each such category of sources and the consequent need for nationally applicable new source standards of performance.

(3) Before promulgating any regulations under this subsection or listing any category of major stationary sources as required under this subsection, the Administrator shall consult with appropriate representatives of the Governors and of State air pollution control agencies.

(g) Revision of regulations

(1) Upon application by the Governor of a State showing that the Administrator has failed to specify in regulations under subsection (f)(1) any category of major stationary sources required to be specified under such regulations, the Administrator shall revise such regulations, to specify any such category.

(2) Upon application of the Governor of a State, showing that any category of stationary sources which is not included in the list under subsection (b)(1)(A) contributes significantly to air pollution which may reasonably be anticipated to endanger public health or welfare (notwithstanding that such category is not a category of major stationary sources), the Administrator shall revise such regulations to specify such category of stationary sources.

(3) Upon application of the Governor of a State showing that the Administrator has failed to apply properly the criteria required to be considered under subsection (f)(2), the Administrator shall revise the list under subsection (b)(1)(A) to apply properly such criteria.

(4) Upon application of the Governor of a State showing that —

(A) a new, innovative, or improved technology or process which achieves greater continuous emission reduction has been adequately demonstrated for any category of stationary sources, and

---

* See "A Note on the 1990 Amendments and Section 111(d)," which appears after the Legislative History Timeline at the beginning of this chapter.

(B) as a result of such technology or process, the new source standard of performance in effect under this section for such category no longer reflects the greatest degree of emission limitation achievable through application of the best technological system of continuous emission reduction which (taking into consideration the cost of achieving such emission reduction, and any non-air quality health and environmental impact and energy requirements) has been adequately demonstrated,

the Administrator shall revise such standard of performance for such category accordingly.

(5) Unless later deadlines for action of the Administrator are otherwise prescribed under this section, the Administrator shall, not later than three months following the date of receipt of any application by a Governor of a State, either —

(A) find that such application does not contain the requisite showing and deny such application, or

(B) grant such application and take the action required under this subsection.

(6) Before taking any action required by subsection (f) or by this subsection, the Administrator shall provide notice and opportunity for public hearing.

(h) Design, equipment, work practice, or operational standard; alternative emission limitation

(1) For purposes of this section, if in the judgment of the Administrator, it is not feasible to prescribe or enforce a standard of performance, he may instead promulgate a design, equipment, work practice, or operational standard, or combination thereof, which reflects the best technological system of continuous emission reduction which (taking into consideration the cost of achieving such emission reduction, and any non-air quality health and environmental impact and energy requirements) the Administrator determines has been adequately demonstrated. In the event the Administrator promulgates a design or equipment standard under this subsection, he shall include as part of such standard such requirements as will assure the proper operation and maintenance of any such element of design or equipment.

(2) For the purpose of this subsection, the phrase "not feasible to prescribe or enforce a standard of performance" means any situation in which the Administrator determines that (A) a pollutant or pollutants cannot be emitted through a conveyance designed and constructed to emit or capture such pollutant, or that any requirement for, or use of, such a conveyance would be inconsistent with any Federal, State, or local law, or (B) the application of measurement methodology to

a particular class of sources is not practicable due to technological or economic limitations.

(3) If after notice and opportunity for public hearing, any person establishes to the satisfaction of the Administrator that an alternative means of emission limitation will achieve a reduction in emissions of any air pollutant at least equivalent to the reduction in emissions of such air pollutant achieved under the requirements of paragraph (1), the Administrator shall permit the use of such alternative by the source for purposes of compliance with this section with respect to such pollutant.

(4) Any standard promulgated under paragraph (1) shall be promulgated in terms of standard of performance whenever it becomes feasible to promulgate and enforce such standard in such terms.

(5) Any design, equipment, work practice, or operational standard, or any combination thereof, described in this subsection shall be treated as a standard of performance for purposes of the provisions of this Act (other than the provisions of subsection (a) and this subsection).

(i) Country elevators — Any regulations promulgated by the Administrator under this section applicable to grain elevators shall not apply to country elevators (as defined by the Administrator) which have a storage capacity of less than two million five hundred thousand bushels.

(j) Innovative technological systems of continuous emissions reduction

(1)(A) Any person proposing to own or operate a new source may request the Administrator for one or more waivers from the requirements of this section for such source or any portion thereof with respect to any air pollutant to encourage the use of an innovative technological system or systems of continuous emission reduction. The Administrator may, with the consent of the Governor of the State in which the source is to be located, grant a waiver under this paragraph, if the Administrator determines after notice and opportunity for public hearing, that —

(i) the proposed system or systems have not been adequately demonstrated,

(ii) the proposed system or systems will operate effectively and there is a substantial likelihood that such system or systems will achieve greater continuous emission reduction than that required to be achieved under the standards of performance which would otherwise apply, or achieve at least an equivalent reduction at lower cost in terms of energy, economic, or nonair quality environmental impact.

(iii) the owner or operator of the proposed source has demonstrated to the satisfaction of the Administrator that the proposed system will not cause or contribute to an unreasonable risk to public health, welfare, or safety in its operation, function, or malfunction, and

(iv) the granting of such waiver is consistent with the requirements of subparagraph (C).

In making any determination under clause (ii), the Administrator shall take into account any previous failure of such system or systems to operate effectively or to meet any requirement of the new source performance standards. In determining whether an unreasonable risk exists under clause (iii), the Administrator shall consider, among other factors, whether and to what extent the use of the proposed technological system will cause, increase, reduce, or eliminate emissions of any unregulated pollutants; available methods for reducing or eliminating any risk to public health, welfare, or safety which may be associated with the use of such system; and the availability of other technological systems which may be used to conform to standards under this section without causing or contributing to such unreasonable risk. The Administrator may conduct such tests and may require the owner or operator of the proposed source to conduct such tests and provide such information as is necessary to carry out clause (iii) of this subparagraph. Such requirements shall include a requirement for prompt reporting of the emission of any unregulated pollutant from a system if such pollutant was not emitted, or was emitted in significantly lesser amounts without use of such system.

(B) A waiver under this paragraph shall be granted on such terms and conditions as the Administrator determines to be necessary to assure —

(i) emissions from the source will not prevent attainment and maintenance of any national ambient air quality standards, and

(ii) proper functioning of the technological system or systems authorized.

Any such term or condition shall be treated as a standard of performance for the purposes of subsection (e) of this section and section 113.

(C) The number of waivers granted under this paragraph with respect to a proposed technological system of continuous emission reduction shall not exceed such number as the Administrator finds necessary to ascertain whether or not such system will achieve the conditions specified in clauses (ii) and (iii) of subparagraph (A).

(D) A waiver under this paragraph shall extend to the sooner of —

(i) the date determined by the Administrator, after consultation with the owner or operator of the source, taking into consideration the design, installation, and capital cost of the technological system or systems being used, or

(ii) the date on which the Administrator determines that such system has failed to —

(I) achieve at least an equivalent continuous emission reduction to that required to be achieved under the standards of performance which would otherwise apply, or

(II) comply with the condition specified in paragraph (1)(A)(iii), and that such failure cannot be corrected.

(E) In carrying out subparagraph (D)(i), the Administrator shall not permit any waiver for a source or portion thereof to extend beyond the date —

(i) seven years after the date on which any waiver is granted to such source or portion thereof, or

(ii) four years after the date on which such source or portion thereof commences operation, whichever is earlier.

(F) No waiver under this subsection shall apply to any portion of a source other than the portion on which the innovative technological system or systems of continuous emission reduction is used.

(2)(A) If a waiver under paragraph (1) is terminated under clause (ii) of paragraph (1)(D), the Administrator shall grant an extension of the requirements of this section for such source for such minimum period as may be necessary to comply with the applicable standard of performance under this section. Such period shall not extend beyond the date three years from the time such waiver is terminated.

(B) An extension granted under this paragraph shall set forth emission limits and a compliance schedule containing increments of progress which require compliance with the applicable standards of performance as expeditiously as practicable and include such measures as are necessary and practicable in the interim to minimize emissions. Such schedule shall be treated as a standard of performance for purposes of subsection (e) of this section and section 7413 of this title.

§7412. Hazardous air pollutants
[CAA §112]

(a) Definitions — For purposes of this section, except subsection (r) —

(1) Major source — The term "major source" means any stationary source or group of stationary sources located within a contiguous area and under common control that emits or has the potential to emit considering controls, in the aggregate, 10 tons per year or more of any hazardous air pollutant or 25 tons per year or more of any combination of hazardous air pollutants. The Administrator may establish a lesser quantity, or in the case of radionuclides different criteria, for a major source than that specified in the previous sentence, on the basis of the potency of the air pollutant, persistence, potential for bioaccumulation, other characteristics of the air pollutant, or other relevant factors.

(2) Area source — The term "area source" means any stationary source of hazardous air pollutants that is not a major source. For purposes of this section, the term "area source" shall not include motor vehicles or nonroad vehicles subject to regulation under title II.

(3) Stationary source — The term "stationary source" shall have the same meaning as such term has under section 111(a).

(4) New source — The term "new source" means a stationary source the construction or reconstruction of which is commenced after the Administrator first proposes regulations under this section establishing an emission standard applicable to such source.

(5) Modification — The term "modification" means any physical change in, or change in the method of operation of, a major source which increases the actual emissions of any hazardous air pollutant emitted by such source by more than a de minimis amount or which results in the emission of any hazardous air pollutant not previously emitted by more than a de minimis amount.

(6) Hazardous air pollutant — The term "hazardous air pollutant" means any air pollutant listed pursuant to subsection (b).

(7) Adverse environmental effect — The term "adverse environmental effect" means any significant and widespread adverse effect, which may reasonably be anticipated, to wildlife, aquatic life, or other natural resources, including adverse impacts on populations of endangered or threatened species or significant degradation of environmental quality over broad areas.

(8) Electric utility steam generating unit — The term "electric utility steam generating unit" means any fossil fuel fired combustion unit of more than 25 megawatts that serves a generator that produces electricity for sale. A unit that cogenerates steam and electricity and supplies more than one-third of its potential electric output capacity and more than 25 megawatts electrical output to any utility power distribution system for sale shall be considered an electric utility steam generating unit.

(9) Owner or operator — The term "owner or operator" means any person who owns, leases, operates, controls, or supervises a stationary source.

(10) Existing source — The term "existing source" means any stationary source other than a new source.

(11) Carcinogenic effect — Unless revised, the term "carcinogenic effect" shall have the meaning provided by the Administrator under Guidelines for Carcinogenic Risk Assessment as of the date of enactment. Any revisions in the existing Guidelines shall be subject to notice and opportunity for comment.

(b) List of pollutants

(1) Initial list — The Congress establishes for purposes of this section a list of hazardous air pollutants as follows:

CAS number	Chemical name
75070	Acetaldehyde
60355	Acetamide
75058	Acetonitrile
98862	Acetophenone
53963	2-Acetylaminofluorene
107028	Acrolein
79061	Acrylamide
79107	Acrylic acid
107131	Acrylonitrile
107051	Allyl chloride
92671	4-Aminobiphenyl
62533	Aniline
90040	o-Anisidine
1332214	Asbestos
71432	Benzene (including benzene from gasoline)
92875	Benzidine
98077	Benzotrichloride
100447	Benzyl chloride
92524	Biphenyl
117817	Bis(2-ethylhexyl)phthalate (DEHP)
542881	Bis(chloromethyl)ether
75252	Bromoform
106990	1,3-Butadiene
156627	Calcium cyanamide
105602	Caprolactam
133062	Captan
63252	Carbaryl
75150	Carbon disulfide
56235	Carbon tetrachloride
463581	Carbonyl sulfide
120809	Catechol
133904	Chloramben
57749	Chlordane
7782505	Chlorine
79118	Chloroacetic acid
532274	2-Chloroacetophenone
108907	Chlorobenzene
510156	Chlorobenzilate
67663	Chloroform
107302	Chloromethyl methyl ether
126998	Chloroprene
1319773	Cresols/Cresylic acid (isomers and mixture)
95487	o-Cresol
108394	m-Cresol
106445	p-Cresol
98828	Cumene
94757	2,4-D, salts and esters
3547044	DDE
334883	Diazomethane
132649	Dibenzofurans
96128	1,2-Dibromo-3-chloropropane

84742	Dibutylphthalate		72435	Methoxychlor
106467	1,4-Dichlorobenzene(p)		74839	Methyl bromide (Bromomethane)
91941	3,3-Dichlorobenzidene		74873	Methyl chloride (Chloromethane)
111444	Dichloroethyl ether (Bis(2-chloro-ethyl)ether)		71556	Methyl chloroform (1,1,1 Trichloroethane)
542756	1,3-Dichloropropene		78933	Methyl ethyl ketone (2-Butanone)
62737	Dichlorvos		60344	Methyl hydrazine
111422	Diethanolamine		74884	Methyl iodide (Iodomethane)
121697	N,N-Diethyl aniline (N,N-Dimethy-laniline)		108101	Methyl isobutyl ketone (Hexone)
64675	Diethyl sulfate		624839	Methyl isocyanate
119904	3,3-Dimethoxybenzidine		80626	Methyl methacrylate
60117	Dimethyl aminoazobenzene		1634044	Methyl tert butyl ether
119937	3,3-Dimethyl benzidine		101144	4,4-Methylene bis(2-chloroaniline)
79447	Dimethyl carbamoyl chloride		75092	Methylene chloride (Dichloromethane)
68122	Dimethyl formamide		101688	Methylene diphenyl diisocyanate (MDI)
57147	1,1-Dimethyl hydrazine			
131113	Dimethyl phthalate		101779	4,4-Methylenedianiline
77781	Dimethyl sulfate		91203	Naphthalene
534521	4,6-Dinitro-o-cresol, and salts		98953	Nitrobenzene
51285	2,4-Dinitrophenol		92933	4-Nitrobiphenyl
121142	2,4-Dinitrotoluene		100027	4-Nitrophenol
123911	1,4-Dioxane (1,4-Diethyleneoxide)		79469	2-Nitropropane
122667	1,2-Diphenylhydrazine		684935	N-Nitroso-N-methylurea
106898	Epichlorohydrin (l-Chloro-2,3-epoxypropane)		62759	N-Nitrosodimethylamine
			59892	N-Nitrosomorpholine
106887	1,2-Epoxybutane		56382	Parathion
140885	Ethyl acrylate		82688	Pentachloronitrobenzene (Quintobenzene)
100414	Ethyl benzene			
51796	Ethyl carbamate (Urethane)		87865	Pentachlorophenol
75003	Ethyl chloride (Chloroethane)		108952	Phenol
106934	Ethylene dibromide (Dibromoethane)		106503	p-Phenylenediamine
			75445	Phosgene
107062	Ethylene dichloride (1,2 Dichloroethane)		7803512	Phosphine
			7723140	Phosphorus
107211	Ethylene glycol		85449	Phthalic anhydride
151564	Ethylene imine (Aziridine)		1336363	Polychlorinated biphenyls (Aroclors)
75218	Ethylene oxide			
96457	Ethylene thiourea		1120714	1,3-Propane sultone
75343	Ethylidene dichloride (1,1 Dichloroethane)		57578	beta-Propiolactone
			123386	Propionaldehyde
50000	Formaldehyde		114261	Propoxur (Baygon)
76448	Heptachlor		78875	Propylene dichloride (1,2 Dichloropropane)
118741	Hexachlorobenzene			
87683	Hexachlorobutadiene		75569	Propylene oxide
77474	Hexachlorocyclopentadiene		75558	1,2-Propylenimine (2-Methyl aziridine)
67721	Hexachloroethane			
822060	Hexamethylene-1,6-diisocyanate		91225	Quinoline
680319	Hexamethylphosphoramide		106514	Quinone
110543	Hexane		100425	Styrene
302012	Hydrazine		96093	Styrene oxide
7647010	Hydrochloric acid		1746016	2,3,7,8-Tetrachlorodibenzo-p-dioxin
7664393	Hydrogen fluoride (Hydrofluoric acid)			
			79345	1,1,2,2-Tetrachloroethane
7783064	Hydrogen sulfide		127184	Tetrachloroethylene (Perchloroeth-ylene)
123319	Hydroquinone			
78591	Isophorone		7550450	Titanium tetrachloride
58899	Lindane (all isomers)		108883	Toluene
108316	Maleic anhydride		95807	2,4-Toluene diamine
67561	Methanol		584849	2,4-Toluene diisocyanate

95534	o-Toluidine
8001352	Toxaphene (chlorinated camphene)
120821	1,2,4-Trichlorobenzene
79005	1,1,2-Trichloroethane
79016	Trichloroethylene
95954	2,4,5-Trichlorophenol
88062	2,4,6-Trichlorophenol
121448	Triethylamine
1582098	Trifluralin
540841	2,2,4-Trimethylpentane
108054	Vinyl acetate
593602	Vinyl bromide
75014	Vinyl chloride
75354	Vinylidene chloride (1,1 Dichloroethylene)
1330207	Xylenes (isomers and mixture)
95476	o-Xylenes
108383	m-Xylenes
106423	p-Xylenes
0	Antimony Compounds
0	Arsenic Compounds (inorganic including arsine)
0	Beryllium Compounds
0	Cadmium Compounds
0	Chromium Compounds
0	Cobalt Compounds
0	Coke Oven Emissions
0	Cyanide Compounds
0	Glycol ethers
0	Lead Compounds
0	Manganese Compounds
0	Mercury Compounds
0	Fine mineral fibers
0	Nickel Compounds
0	Polycylic Organic Matter
0	Radionuclides (including radon)
0	Selenium Compounds

NOTE: For all listings above which contain the word "compounds" and for glycol ethers, the following applies: Unless otherwise specified, these listings are defined as including any unique chemical substance that contains the named chemical (i.e., antimony, arsenic, etc.) as part of that chemical's infrastructure.

(2) Revision of the list — The Administrator shall periodically review the list established by this subsection and publish the results thereof and, where appropriate, revise such list by rule, adding pollutants which present, or may present, through inhalation or other routes of exposure, a threat of adverse human health effects (including, but not limited to, substances which are known to be, or may reasonably be anticipated to be, carcinogenic, mutagenic, teratogenic, neurotoxic, which cause reproductive dysfunction, or which are acutely or chronically toxic) or adverse environmental effects whether through ambient concentrations, bioacumulation, deposition, or otherwise, but not including releases subject to regulation under

subsection (r) as a result of emissions to the air. No air pollutant which is listed under section 108(a) may be added to the list under this section, except that the prohibition of this sentence shall not apply to any pollutant which independently meets the listing criteria of this paragraph and is a precursor to a pollutant which is listed under section 108(a) or to any pollutant which is in a class of pollutants listed under such section. No substance, practice, process or activity regulated under subchapter VI of this chapter shall be subject to regulation under this section solely due to its adverse effects on the environment.

(3) Petitions to modify the list

(A) Beginning at any time after 6 months after the date of enactment of the Clean Air Act Amendments of 1990, any person may petition the Administrator to modify the list of hazardous air pollutants under this subsection by adding or deleting a substance or, in case of listed pollutants without CAS numbers (other than coke oven emissions, mineral fibers, or polycyclic organic matter) removing certain unique substances. Within 18 months after receipt of a petition, the Administrator shall either grant or deny the petition by publishing a written explanation of the reasons for the Administrator's decision. Any such petition shall include a showing by the petitioner that there is adequate data on the health or environmental defects of the pollutant or other evidence adequate to support the petition. The Administrator may not deny a petition solely on the basis of inadequate resources or time or review.

(B) The Administrator shall add a substance to the list upon a showing by the petitioner or on the Administrator's own determination that the substance is an air pollutant and that emissions, ambient concentrations, bioaccumulation or deposition of the substance are known to cause or may reasonably be anticipated to cause adverse effects to human health or adverse environmental effects.

(C) The Administrator shall delete a substance from the list upon a showing by the petitioner or on the Administrator's own determination that there is adequate data on the health and environmental effects of the substance to determine that emissions, ambient concentrations, bioaccumulation or deposition of the substance may not reasonably be anticipated to cause any adverse effects to the human health or adverse environmental effects.

(D) The Administrator shall delete one or more unique chemical substances that contain a listed hazardous air pollutant not having a CAS number (other than coke oven emissions, mineral fibers, or polycyclic organic matter) upon a showing by the petitioner or on the dministrator's own determination that such unique chemical substances that contain the named chemical of such listed hazardous air pollutant meet the deletion requirements of subparagraph (C). The Administrator must grant or deny a deletion petition prior to promulgating any emission standards pursuant to subsection (d) applicable to any source category or subcategory of a listed hazardous air pollutant without a CAS number listed under subsection (b) for which a deletion petition has been filed within 12 months of the date of enactment of the Clean Air Act Amendments of 1990.

(4) Further information — If the Administrator determines that information on the health or environmental effects of a substance is not sufficient to make a determination required by this subsection, the Administrator may use any authority available to the Administrator to acquire such information.

(5) Test methods — The Administrator may establish, by rule, test measures and other analytic procedures for monitoring and measuring emissions, ambient concentrations, deposition, and bioaccumulation of hazardous air pollutants.

(6) Prevention of significant deterioration — The provisions of part C (prevention of significant deterioration) shall not apply to pollutants listed under this section.

(7) Lead — The Administrator may not list elemental lead as a hazardous air pollutant under this subsection.

(c) List of source categories

(1) In general — Not later than 12 months after the date of enactment of the Clean Air Act Amendments of 1990, the Administrator shall publish, and shall from time to time, but no less often than every 8 years, revise, if appropriate, in response to public comment or new information, a list of all categories and subcategories of major sources and area sources (listed under paragraph (3)) of the air pollutants listed pursuant to subsection (b). To the extent practicable, the categories and subcategories listed under this subsection shall be consistent with the list of source categories established pursuant to section 111 and part C. Nothing in the preceding sentence limits the Administrator's authority to establish subcategories under this section, as appropriate.

(2) Requirement for emissions standards — For the categories and subcategories the Administrator lists, the Administrator shall establish emissions standards under subsection (d), according to the schedule in this subsection and subsection (e).

(3) Area sources — The Administrator shall list under this subsection each category or subcategory of area sources which the Administrator finds presents a threat of adverse effects to human health or the environment (by such sources individually or in the aggregate) warranting regulation under this section. The Administrator shall, not later than

5 years after the date of enactment of the Clean Air Act Amendments of 1990 and pursuant to subsection (k)(3)(B), list, based on actual or estimated aggregate emissions of a listed pollutant or pollutants, sufficient categories or subcategories of area sources to ensure that area sources representing 90 percent of the area source emissions of the 30 hazardous air pollutants that present the greatest threat to public health in the largest number of urban areas are subject to regulation under this section. Such regulations shall be promulgated not later than 10 years after such date of enactment.

(4) Previously regulated categories — The Administrator may, in the Administrator's discretion, list any category or subcategory of sources previously regulated under this section as in effect before the date of enactment of the Clean Air Act Amendments of 1990.

(5) Additional categories — In addition to those categories and subcategories of sources listed for regulation pursuant to paragraphs (1) and (3), the Administrator may at any time list additional categories and subcategories of sources of hazardous air pollutants according to the same criteria for listing applicable under such paragraphs. In the case of source categories and subcategories listed after publication of the initial list required under paragraph (1) or (3), emission standards under subsection (d) for the category or subcategory shall be promulgated within 10 years after the date of enactment of the Clean Air Act Amendments of 1990, or within 2 years after the date on which such category or subcategory is listed, whichever is later.

(6) Specific pollutants — With respect to alkylated lead compounds, polycyclic organic matter, hexachlorobenzene, mercury, polychlorinated biphenyls, 2,3,7,8-tetrachlorodi-benzofurans and 2,3,7,8-tetrachlorodibenzo-p-dioxin, the Administrator shall, not later than 5 years after the date of enactment of the Clean Air Act Amendments of 1990, list categories and subcategories of sources assuring that sources accounting for not less than 90 per centum of the aggregate emissions of each such pollutant are subject to standards under subsection (d)(2) or (d)(4). Such standards shall be promulgated not later than 10 years after such date of enactment. This paragraph shall not be construed to require the Administrator to promulgate standards for such pollutants emitted by electric utility steam generating units.

(7) Research facilities — The Administrator shall establish a separate category covering research or laboratory facilities, as necessary to assure the equitable treatment of such facilities. For purposes of this section, "research or laboratory facility" means any stationary source whose primary purpose is to conduct research and development into new processes and products, where such source is operated under the close supervision of techni-

cally trained personnel and is not engaged in the manufacture of products for commercial sale in commerce, except in a de minimis manner.

(8) Boat manufacturing — When establishing emissions standards for styrene, the Administrator shall list boat manufacturing as a separate subcategory unless the Administrator finds that such listing would be inconsistent with the goals and requirements of this Act.

(9) Deletions from the list

(A) Where the sole reason for the inclusion of a source category on the list required under this subsection is the emission of a unique chemical substance, the Administrator shall delete the source category from the list if it is appropriate because of action taken under either subparagraphs (C) or (D) of subsection (b)(3).

(B) The Administrator may delete any source category from the list under this subsection, on petition of any person or on the Administrator's own motion, whenever the Administrator makes the following determination or determinations, as applicable:

(i) In the case of hazardous air pollutants emitted by sources in the category that may result in cancer in humans, a determination that no source in the category (or group of sources in the case of area sources) emits such hazardous air pollutants in quantities which may cause a lifetime risk of cancer greater than one in one million to the individual in the population who is most exposed to emissions of such pollutants from the source (or group of sources in the case of area sources).

(ii) In the case of hazardous air pollutants that may result in adverse health effects in humans other than cancer or adverse environmental effects, a determination that emissions from no source in the category or subcategory concerned (or group of sources in the case of area sources) exceed a level which is adequate to protect public health with an ample margin of safety and no adverse environmental effect will result from emissions from any source (or from a group of sources in the case of area sources).

The Administrator shall grant or deny a petition under this paragraph within 1 year after the petition is filed.

(d) Emission standards

(1) In general — The Administrator shall promulgate regulations establishing emission standards for each category or subcategory of major sources and area sources of hazardous air pollutants listed for regulation pursuant to subsection (c) in accordance with the schedules provided in subsections (c) and (e). The Administrator may dis-

tinguish among classes, types, and sizes of sources within a category or subcategory in establishing such standards except that, there shall be no delay in the compliance date for any standard applicable to any source under subsection (i) as the result of the authority provided by this sentence.

(2) Standards and methods — Emissions standards promulgated under this subsection and applicable to new or existing sources of hazardous air pollutants shall require the maximum degree of reduction in emissions of the hazardous air pollutants subject to this section (including a prohibition on such emissions, where achievable) that the Administrator, taking into consideration the cost of achieving such emission reduction, and any non-air quality health and environmental impacts and energy requirements, determines is achievable for new or existing sources in the category or subcategory to which such emission standard applies, through application of measures, processes, methods, systems or techniques including, but not limited to, measures which —

(A) reduce the volume of, or eliminate emissions of, such pollutants through process changes, substitution of materials or other modifications,

(B) enclose systems or processes to eliminate emissions,

(C) collect, capture or treat such pollutants when released from a process, stack, storage or fugitive emissions point,

(D) are design, equipment, work practice, or operational standards (including requirements for operator training or certification) as provided in subsection (h), or

(E) are a combination of the above.

None of the measures described in subparagraphs (A) through (D) shall, consistent with the provisions of section 114(c), in any way compromise any United States patent or United States trademark right, or any confidential business information, or any trade secret or any other intellectual property right.

(3) New and existing sources — The maximum degree of reduction in emissions that is deemed achievable for new sources in a category or subcategory shall not be less stringent than the emission control that is achieved in practice by the best controlled similar source, as determined by the Administrator. Emission standards promulgated under this subsection for existing sources in a category or subcategory may be less stringent than standards for new sources in the same category or subcategory but shall not be less stringent, and may be more stringent than —

(A) the average emission limitation achieved by the best performing 12 percent of the existing sources (for which the Administrator has emissions information), excluding those sources that have, within 18 months before the emission standard is proposed or within 30 months before such standard is promulgated, whichever is later, first achieved a level of emission rate or emission reduction which complies, or would comply if the source is not subject to such standard, with the lowest achievable emission rate (as defined by section 171) applicable to the source category and prevailing at the time, in the category or subcategory for categories and subcategories with 30 or more sources, or

(B) the average emission limitation achieved by the best performing 5 sources (for which the Administrator has or could reasonably obtain emissions information) in the category or subcategory for categories or subcategories with fewer than 30 sources.

(4) Health threshold — With respect to pollutants for which a health threshold has been established, the Administrator may consider such threshold level, with an ample margin of safety, when establishing emission standards under this subsection.

(5) Alternative standard for area sources — With respect only to categories and subcategories of area sources listed pursuant to subsection (c), the Administrator may, in lieu of the authorities provided in paragraph (2) and subsection (f), elect to promulgate standards or requirements applicable to sources in such categories or subcategories which provide for the use of generally available control technologies or management practices by such sources to reduce emissions of hazardous air pollutants.

(6) Review and revision — The Administrator shall review, and revise as necessary (taking into account developments in practices, processes, and control technologies), emission standards promulgated under this section no less often than every 8 years.

(7) Other requirements preserved — No emission standard or other requirement promulgated under this section shall be interpreted, construed or applied to diminish or replace the requirements of a more stringent emission limitation or other applicable requirement established pursuant to section 111, part C or D, or other authority of this Act or a standard issued under State authority.

(8) Coke ovens

(A) Not later than December 31, 1992, the Administrator shall promulgate regulations establishing emission standards under paragraphs (2) and (3) of this subsection for coke oven batteries. In establishing such standards, the Administrator shall evaluate —

    (i) the use of sodium silicate (or equivalent) luting compounds to prevent door leaks, and other operating practices and technologies for their effectiveness in reducing coke oven emissions, and their suitability for use on new and existing coke oven batteries, taking into account costs and reasonable

commercial door warranties; and

    (ii) as a basis for emission standards under this subsection for new coke oven batteries that begin construction after the date of proposal of such standards, the Jewell design Thompson non-recovery coke oven batteries and other non-recovery coke oven technologies, and other appropriate emission control and coke production technologies, as to their effectiveness in reducing coke oven emissions and their capability for production of steel quality coke.

Such regulations shall require at a minimum that coke oven batteries will not exceed 8 per centum leaking doors, 1 per centum leaking lids, 5 per centum leaking offtakes, and 16 seconds visible emissions per charge, with no exclusion for emissions during the period after the closing of self-sealing oven doors. Notwithstanding subsection (i), the compliance date for such emission standards for existing coke oven batteries shall be December 31, 1995.

(B) The Administrator shall promulgate work practice regulations under this subsection for coke oven batteries requiring, as appropriate —

    (i) the use of sodium silicate (or equivalent) luting compounds, if the Administrator determines that use of sodium silicate is an effective means of emissions control and is achievable, taking into account costs and reasonable commercial warranties for doors and related equipment; and

    (ii) door and jam cleaning practices.

Notwithstanding subsection (i), the compliance date for such work practice regulations for coke oven batteries shall be not later than the date 3 years after the date of enactment of the Clean Air Act Amendments of 1990.

(C) For coke oven batteries electing to qualify for an extension of the compliance date for standards promulgated under subsection (f) in accordance with subsection (i)(8), the emission standards under this subsection for coke oven batteries shall require that coke oven batteries not exceed 8 per centum leaking doors, 1 per centum leaking lids, 5 per centum leaking offtakes, and 16 seconds visible emissions per charge, with no exclusion for emissions during the period after the closing of self-sealing doors. Notwithstanding subsection (i), the compliance date for such emission standards for existing coke oven batteries seeking an extension shall be not later than the date 3 years after November 15, 1990.

(9) Sources licensed by the nuclear regulatory commission — No standard for radionuclide emissions from any category or subcategory of facilities licensed by the Nuclear Regulatory Commission (or an Agreement State) is required to be promulgated under this section if the Administrator determines, by rule, and after consultation with the Nuclear Regulatory Commission, that the regulatory program established by the Nuclear Regulatory Commission pursuant to the Atomic Energy Act for such category or subcategory provides an ample margin of safety to protect the public health. Nothing in this subsection shall preclude or deny the right of any State or political subdivision thereof to adopt or enforce any standard or limitation respecting emissions of radionuclides which is more stringent than the standard or limitation in effect under section 7411 of this title or this section.

(10) Effective date — Emission standards or other regulations promulgated under this subsection shall be effective upon promulgation.

(e) Schedule for standards and review

(1) In general — The Administrator shall promulgate regulations establishing emission standards for categories and subcategories of sources initially listed for regulation pursuant to subsection (c)(1) as expeditiously as practicable, assuring that —

(A) emission standards for not less than 40 categories and subcategories (not counting coke oven batteries) shall be promulgated not later than 2 years after the date of enactment of the Clean Air Act Amendments of 1990;

(B) emission standards for coke oven batteries shall be promulgated not later than December 31, 1992;

(C) emission standards for 25 per centum of the listed categories and subcategories shall be promulgated not later than 4 years after the date of enactment of the Clean Air Act Amendments of 1990;

(D) emission standards for an additional 25 per centum of the listed categories and subcategories shall be promulgated not later than 7 years after the date of enactment of the Clean Air Act Amendments of 1990; and

(E) emission standards for all categories and subcategories shall be promulgated not later than 10 years after the date of enactment of the Clean Air Act Amendments of 1990.

(2) Priorities — In determining priorities for promulgating standards under subsection (d), the Administrator shall consider —

(A) the known or anticipated adverse effects of such pollutants on public health and the environment;

(B) the quantity and location of emissions or reasonably anticipated emissions of hazardous air pollutants that each category or subcategory will emit; and

(C) the efficiency of grouping categories or subcategories according to the pollutants emitted, or the processes or technologies used.

(3) Published schedule — Not later than 24 months after the date of enactment of the Clean Air

Act Amendments of 1990 and after opportunity for comment, the Administrator shall publish a schedule establishing a date for the promulgation of emission standards for each category and subcategory of sources listed pursuant to subsection (c)(1) and (3) which shall be consistent with the requirements of paragraphs (1) and (2). The determination of priorities for the promulgation of standards pursuant to this paragraph is not a rulemaking and shall not be subject to judicial review, except that, failure to promulgate any standard pursuant to the schedule established by this paragraph shall be subject to review under section 304 of this Act.

(4) Judicial review — Notwithstanding section 307 of this Act, no action of the Administrator adding a pollutant to the list under subsection (b) or listing a source category or subcategory under subsection (c) shall be a final agency action subject to judicial review, except that any such action may be reviewed under such section 307 when the Administrator issues emission standards for such pollutant or category.

(5) Publicly owned treatment works — The Administrator shall promulgate standards pursuant to subsection (d) of this section applicable to publicly owner treatment works (as defined in title II of the Federal Water Pollution Control Act) not later than 5 years after November 15, 1990.

(f) Standard to protect health and the environment

(1) Report — Not later than 6 years after November 15, 1990, the Administrator shall investigate and report, after consultation with the Surgeon General and after opportunity for public comment, to Congress on —

(A) methods of calculating the risk to public health remaining, or likely to remain, from sources subject to regulation under this section after the application of standards under subsection (d);

(B) the public health significance of such estimated remaining risk and the technologically and commercially available methods and costs of reducing such risks;

(C) the actual health effects with respect to persons living in the vicinity of sources, any available epidemiological or other health studies, risks presented by background concentrations of hazardous air pollutants, any uncertainties in risk assessment methodology or other health assessment technique, and any negative health or environmental consequences to the community of efforts to reduce such risks; and

(D) recommendations as to legislation regarding such remaining risk.

(2) Emission standards

(A) If Congress does not act on any recommendation submitted under paragraph (1), the Administrator shall, within 8 years after promulgation of standards for each category or subcategory of sources pursuant to subsection (d), promulgate standards for such category or subcategory if promulgation of such standards is required in order to provide an ample margin of safety to protect public health in accordance with this section (as in effect before the date of enactment of the Clean Air Act Amendments of 1990) or to prevent, taking into consideration costs, energy, safety, and other relevant factors, an adverse environmental effect. Emission standards promulgated under this subsection shall provide an ample margin of safety to protect public health in accordance with this section (as in effect before the date of enactment of the Clean Air Act Amendments of 1990), unless the Administrator determines that a more stringent standard is necessary to prevent, taking into consideration costs, energy, safety, and other relevant factors, an adverse environmental effect. If standards promulgated pursuant to subsection (d) and applicable to a category or subcategory of sources emitting a pollutant (or pollutants) classified as a known, probable or possible human carcinogen do not reduce lifetime excess cancer risks to the individual most exposed to emissions from a source in the category or subcategory to less than one in one million, the Administrator shall promulgate standards under this subsection for such source category.

(B) Nothing in subparagraph (A) or in any other provision of this section shall be construed as affecting, or applying to the Administrator's interpretation of this section, as in effect before the date of enactment of the Clean Air Act Amendments of 1990 and set forth in the Federal Register of September 14, 1989 (54 Fed. Reg. 38044).

(C) The Administrator shall determine whether or not to promulgate such standards and, if the Administrator decides to promulgate such standards, shall promulgate the standards 8 years after promulgation of the standards under subsection (d) for each source category or subcategory concerned. In the case of categories or subcategories for which standards under subsection (d) are required to be promulgated within 2 years after the date of enactment of the Clean Air Act Amendments of 1990, the Administrator shall have 9 years after promulgation of the standards under subsection (d) to make the determination under the preceding sentence and, if required, to promulgate the standards under this paragraph.

(3) Effective date — Any emission standard established pursuant to this subsection shall become effective upon promulgation.

(4) Prohibition — No air pollutant to which a standard under this subsection applies may be emitted from any stationary source in violation of such standard, except that in the case of an existing source —

 (A) such standard shall not apply until 90 days after its effective date, and

 (B) the Administrator may grant a waiver permitting such source a period of up to 2 years after the effective date of a standard to comply with the standard if the Administrator finds that such period is necessary for the installation of controls and that steps will be taken during the period of the waiver to assure that the health of persons will be protected from imminent endangerment.

(5) Area sources — The Administrator shall not be required to conduct any review under this subsection or promulgate emission limitations under this subsection for any category or subcategory of area sources that is listed pursuant to subsection (c)(3) and for which an emission standard is promulgated pursuant to subsection (d)(5).

(6) Unique chemical substances — In establishing standards for the control of unique chemical substances of listed pollutants without CAS numbers under this subsection, the Administrator shall establish such standards with respect to the health and environmental effects of the substances actually emitted by sources and direct transformation byproducts of such emissions in the categories and subcategories.

(g) Modifications

 (1) Offsets

  (A) A physical change in, or change in the method of operation of, a major source which results in a greater than de minimis increase in actual emissions of a hazardous air pollutant shall not be considered a modification, if such increase in the quantity of actual emissions of any hazardous air pollutant from such source will be offset by an equal or greater decrease in the quantity of emissions of another hazardous air pollutant (or pollutants) from such source which is deemed more hazardous, pursuant to guidance issued by the Administrator under subparagraph (B). The owner or operator of such source shall submit a showing to the Administrator (or the State) that such increase has been offset under the preceding sentence.

  (B) The Administrator shall, after notice and opportunity for comment and not later than 18 months after the date of enactment of the Clean Air Act Amendments of 1990, publish guidance with respect to implementation of this subsection. Such guidance shall include an identification, to the extent practicable, of the relative hazard to human health resulting from emissions to the ambient air of each of the pollutants listed under subsection (b) sufficient to facilitate the offset showing authorized by subparagraph (A). Such guidance shall not authorize offsets between pollutants where the increased pollutant (or more than one pollutant in a stream of pollutants) causes adverse effects to human health for which no safety threshold for exposure can be determined unless there are corresponding decreases in such types of pollutant(s).

(2) Construction, reconstruction and modifications

(A) After the effective date of a permit program under subchapter V of this chapter in any State, no person may modify a major source of hazardous air pollutants in such State, unless the Administrator (or the State) determines that the maximum achievable control technology emission limitation under this section for existing sources will be met. Such determination shall be made on a case-by-case basis where no applicable emissions limitations have been established by the Administrator.

(B) After the effective date of a permit program under title V in any State, no person may construct or reconstruct any major source of hazardous air pollutants, unless the Administrator (or the State) determines that the maximum achievable control technology emission limitation under this section for new sources will be met. Such determination shall be made on a case-by-case basis where no applicable emission limitations have been established by the Administrator.

(3) Procedures for modifications — The Administrator (or the State) shall establish reasonable procedures for assuring that the requirements applying to modifications under this section are reflected in the permit.

(h) Work practice standards and other requirements

(1) In general — For purposes of this section, if it is not feasible in the judgment of the Administrator to prescribe or enforce an emission standard for control of a hazardous air pollutant or pollutants, the Administrator may, in lieu thereof, promulgate a design, equipment, work practice, or operational standard, or combination thereof, which in the Administrator's judgment is consistent with the provisions of subsection (d) or (f). In the event the Administrator promulgates a design or equipment standard under this subsection, the Administrator shall include as part of such standard such requirements as will assure the proper operation and maintenance of any such element of design or equipment.

(2) Definition — For the purpose of this subsection, the phrase "not feasible to prescribe or enforce an emission standard" means any situation in which the Administrator determines that —

(A) a hazardous air pollutant or pollutants cannot be emitted through a conveyance designed and constructed to emit or capture

such pollutant, or that any requirement for, or use of, such a conveyance would be inconsistent with any Federal, State or local law, or

(B) the application of measurement methodology to a particular class of sources is not practicable due to technological and economic limitations.

(3) Alternative standard — If after notice and opportunity for comment, the owner or operator of any source establishes to the satisfaction of the Administrator that an alternative means of emission limitation will achieve a reduction in emissions of any air pollutant at least equivalent to the reduction in emissions of such pollutant achieved under the requirements of paragraph (1), the Administrator shall permit the use of such alternative by the source for purposes of compliance with this section with respect to such pollutant.

(4) Numerical standard required — Any standard promulgated under paragraph (1) shall be promulgated in terms of an emission standard whenever it is feasible to promulgate and enforce a standard in such terms.

(i) Schedule for compliance

(1) Preconstruction and operating requirements — After the effective date of any emission standard, limitation, or regulation under subsection (d), (f) or (h), no person may construct any new major source or reconstruct any existing major source subject to such emission standard, regulation or limitation unless the Administrator (or a State with a permit program approved under title V) determines that such source, if properly constructed, reconstructed and operated, will comply with the standard, regulation or limitation.

(2) Special rule — Notwithstanding the requirements of paragraph (1), a new source which commences construction or reconstruction after a standard, limitation or regulation applicable to such source is proposed and before such standard, limitation or regulation is promulgated shall not be required to comply with such promulgated standard until the date 3 years after the date of promulgation if —

(A) the promulgated standard, limitation or regulation is more stringent than the standard, limitation or regulation proposed; and

(B) the source complies with the standard, limitation, or regulation as proposed during the 3-year period immediately after promulgation.

(3) Compliance schedule for existing sources

(A) After the effective date of any emissions standard, limitation or regulation promulgated under this section and applicable to a source, no person may operate such source in violation of such standard, limitation or regulation except, in the case of an existing source, the Administrator shall establish a compliance date or dates for each category or subcategory of existing sources, which shall provide for compliance as expeditiously as practicable, but in no event later than 3 years after the effective date of such standard, except as provided in subparagraph (B) and paragraphs (4) through (8).

(B) The Administrator (or a State with a program approved under title V) may issue a permit that grants an extension permitting an existing source up to 1 additional year to comply with standards under subsection (d) if such additional period is necessary for the installation of controls. An additional extension of up to 3 years may be added for mining waste operations, if the 4-year compliance time is insufficient to dry and cover mining waste in order to reduce emissions of any pollutant listed under subsection (b).

(4) Presidential exemption — The President may exempt any stationary source from compliance with any standard or limitation under this section or period of not more than 2 years if the President determines that the technology to implement such standard is not available and that it is in the national security interests of the United States to do so. An exemption under this paragraph may be extended for 1 or more additional periods, each period not to exceed 2 years. The President shall report to Congress with respect to each exemption (or extension thereof) made under this paragraph.

(5) Early reduction

(A) The Administrator (or a State acting pursuant to a permit program approved under title V) shall issue a permit allowing an existing source, for which the owner or operator demonstrates that the source has achieved a reduction of 90 per centum or more in emissions of hazardous air pollutants (95 per centum in the case of hazardous air pollutants which are particulates) from the source, to meet an alternative emission limitation reflecting such reduction in lieu of an emission limitation promulgated under subsection (d) for a period of 6 years from the compliance date for the otherwise applicable standard, provided that such reduction is achieved before the otherwise applicable standard under subsection (d) is first proposed. Nothing in this paragraph shall preclude a State from requiring reductions in excess of those specified in this subparagraph as a condition of granting the extension authorized by the previous sentence.

(B) An existing source which achieves the reduction referred to in subparagraph (A) after the proposal of an applicable standard but before January 1, 1994, may qualify under subparagraph (A), if the source makes an enforceable commitment to achieve such reduction before the proposal of the standard. Such commitment shall be enforceable to the same extent as a regulation under this section.

(C) The reduction shall be determined with respect to verifiable and actual emissions in a base year not earlier than calendar year 1987, provided that, there is no evidence that emissions in the base year are artificially or substantially greater than emissions in other years prior to implementation of emissions reduction measures. The Administrator may allow a source to use a baseline year of 1985 or 1986 provided that the source can demonstrate to the satisfaction of the Administrator that emissions data for the source reflects verifiable data based on information for such source, received by the Administrator prior to the enactment of the Clean Air Act Amendments of 1990, pursuant to an information request issued under section 114.

(D) For each source granted an alternative emission limitation under this paragraph there shall be established by a permit issued pursuant to title V an enforceable emission limitation for hazardous air pollutants reflecting the reduction which qualifies the source for an alternative emission limitation under this paragraph. An alternative emission limitation under this paragraph shall not be available with respect to standards or requirements promulgated pursuant to subsection (f) and the Administrator shall, for the purpose of determining whether a standard under subsection (f) is necessary, review emissions from sources granted an alternative emission limitation under this paragraph at the same time that other sources in the category or subcategory are reviewed.

(E) With respect to pollutants for which high risks of adverse public health effects may be associated with exposure to small quantities including, but not limited to, chlorinated dioxins and furans, the Administrator shall by regulation limit the use of offsetting reductions in emissions of other hazardous air pollutants from the source as counting toward the 90 per centum reduction in such high-risk pollutants qualifying for an alternative emissions limitation under this paragraph.

(6) Other reductions — Notwithstanding the requirements of this section, no existing source that has installed —

(A) best available control technology (as defined in section 7479(3) of this title), or

(B) technology required to meet a lowest achievable emission rate (as defined in section 7501 of this title),

prior to the promulgation of a standard under this section applicable to such source and the same pollutant (or stream of pollutants) controlled pursuant to an action described in subparagraph (A) or (B) shall be required to comply with such standard under this section until the date 5 years after the date on which such installation or reduction has been achieved, as determined by the Administrator. The Administrator may issue such rules and guidance as are necessary to implement this paragraph.

(7) Extension for new sources — A source for which construction or reconstruction is commenced after the date an emission standard applicable to such source is proposed pursuant to subsection (d) but before the date an emission standard applicable to such source is proposed pursuant to subsection (f) shall not be required to comply with the emission standard under subsection (f) until the date 10 years after the date construction or reconstruction is commenced.

(8) Coke ovens

(A) Any coke oven battery that complies with the emission limitations established under subsection (d)(8)(C), subparagraph (B), and subparagraph (C), and complies with the provisions of subparagraph (E), shall not be required to achieve emission limitations promulgated under subsection (f) until January 1, 2020.

(B)(i) Not later than December 31, 1992, the Administrator shall promulgate emission limitations for coke oven emissions from coke oven batteries. Notwithstanding paragraph (3) of this subsection, the compliance date for such emission limitations for existing coke oven batteries shall be January 1, 1998. Such emission limitations shall reflect the lowest achievable emission rate as defined in section 171 for a coke oven battery that is rebuilt or a replacement at a coke oven plant for an existing battery. Such emission limitations shall be no less stringent than —

> **(I)** 3 per centum leaking doors (5 per centum leaking doors for six meter batteries);
>
> **(II)** 1 per centum leaking lids;
>
> **(III)** 4 per centum leaking offtakes; and
>
> **(IV)** 16 seconds visible emissions per charge,

with an exclusion for emissions during the period after the closing of self-sealing oven doors (or the total mass emissions equivalent). The rulemaking in which such emission limitations are promulgated shall also establish an appropriate measurement methodology for determining compliance with such emission limitations, and shall establish such emission limitations in terms of an equivalent level of mass emissions reduction from a coke oven battery, unless the Administrator finds that such a mass emissions standard would not be practicable or enforceable. Such measurement methodology, to the extent it measures leaking doors, shall take into consideration alternative test methods that reflect the best technology and practices actually applied in the affected industries, and shall assure that the final test methods are consistent with the performance of such best technology and practices.

> **(ii)** If the Administrator fails to promulgate such emission limitations under this subparagraph prior to the effective date of such emission limitations, the emission limitations applicable to coke oven batteries under this subparagraph shall be —

> **(I)** 3 per centum leaking doors (5 per centum leaking doors for six meter batteries);
>
> **(II)** 1 per centum leaking lids;
>
> **(III)** 4 per centum leaking offtakes; and
>
> **(IV)** 16 seconds visible emissions per charge,

or the total mass emissions equivalent (if the total mass emissions equivalent is determined to be practicable and enforceable), with no exclusion for emissions during the period after the closing of self-sealing oven doors.

(C) Not later than January 1, 2007, the Administrator shall review the emission limitations promulgated under subparagraph (B) and revise, as necessary, such emission limitations to reflect the lowest achievable emission rate as defined in section 171 at the time for a coke oven battery that is rebuilt or a replacement at a coke oven plant for an existing battery. Such emission limitations shall be no less stringent than the emission limitation promulgated under subparagraph (B). Notwithstanding paragraph (2) of this subsection, the compliance date for such emission limitations for existing coke oven batteries shall be January 1, 2010.

(D) At any time prior to January 1, 1998, the owner or operator of any coke oven battery may elect to comply with emission limitations promulgated under subsection (f) by the date such emission limitations would otherwise apply to such coke oven battery, in lieu of the emission limitations and the compliance dates provided under subparagraphs (B) and (C) of this paragraph. Any such owner or operator shall be legally bound to comply with such emission limitations promulgated under subsection (f) with respect to such coke oven battery as of January 1, 2003. If no such emission limitations have been promulgated for such coke oven battery, the Administrator shall promulgate such emission limitations in accordance with subsection (f) for such coke oven battery.

(E) Coke oven batteries qualifying for an extension under subparagraph (A) shall make available not later than January 1, 2000, to the surrounding communities the results of any risk assessment performed by the Administrator to determine the appropriate level of any emission standard established by the Administrator pursuant to subsection (f).

(F) Notwithstanding the provisions of this section, reconstruction of any source of coke oven emissions qualifying for an extension under this paragraph shall not subject such source to emission limitations under subsection (f) more stringent than those established under subparagraphs (B) and (C) until January 1, 2020. For the purposes of this subparagraph, the term "reconstruction" includes the replacement of existing coke oven battery capacity with new coke oven batteries of comparable or lower capacity and lower potential emissions.

(j) Equivalent emission limitation by permit

(1) Effective date — The requirements of this subsection shall apply in each State beginning on the effective date of a permit program established pursuant to title V in such State, but not prior to the date 42 months after the date of enactment of the Clean Air Act Amendments of 1990.

(2) Failure to promulgate a standard — In the event that the Administrator fails to promulgate a standard for a category or subcategory of major sources by the date established pursuant to subsection (e)(1) and (3), and beginning 18 months after such date (but not prior to the effective date of a permit program under title V), the owner or operator of any major source in such category or subcategory shall submit a permit application under paragraph (3) and such owner or operator shall also comply with paragraphs (5) and (6).

(3) Applications — By the date established by paragraph (2), the owner or operator of a major source subject to this sub-section shall file an application for a permit. If the owner or operator of a source has submitted a timely and complete application for a permit required by this subsection, any failure to have a permit shall not be a violation of paragraph (2), unless the delay in final action is due to the failure of the applicant to timely submit information required or requested to process the application. The Administrator shall not later than 18 months after November 15, 1990, and after notice and opportunity for comment, establish requirements for applications under this subsection including a standard application form and criteria for determining in a timely manner the completeness of applications.

(4) Review and approval — Permit applications submitted under this subsection shall be reviewed and approved or disapproved according to the provisions of section 505. In the event that the Administrator (or the State) disapproves a permit application submitted under this subsection or determines that the application is incomplete, the applicant shall have up to 6 months to revise the application to meet the objections of the Administrator (or the State).

(5) Emission limitation — The permit shall be issued pursuant to title V and shall contain emission limitations for the hazardous air pollutants subject to regulation under this section and emitted by the source that the Administrator (or the State) determines, on a case-by-case basis, to

be equivalent to the limitation that would apply to such source if an emission standard had been promulgated in a timely manner under subsection (d). In the alternative, if the applicable criteria are met, the permit may contain an emissions limitation established according to the provisions of subsection (i)(5). For purposes of the preceding sentence, the reduction required by subsection (i)(5)(A) shall be achieved by the date on which the relevant standard should have been promulgated under subsection (d). No such pollutant may be emitted in amounts exceeding an emission limitation contained in a permit immediately for new sources and, as expeditiously as practicable, but not later than the date 3 years after the permit is issued for existing sources or such other compliance date as would apply under subsection (i).

(6) Applicability of subsequent standards — If the Administrator promulgates an emission standard that is applicable to the major source prior to the date on which a permit application is approved, the emission limitation in the permit shall reflect the promulgated standard rather than the emission limitation determined pursuant to paragraph (5), provided that the source shall have the compliance period provided under subsection (i). If the Administrator promulgates a standard under subsection (d) that would be applicable to the source in lieu of the emission limitation established by permit under this subsection after the date on which the permit has been issued, the Administrator (or the State) shall revise such permit upon the next renewal to reflect the standard promulgated by the Administrator providing such source a reasonable time to comply, but no longer than 8 years after such standard is promulgated or 8 years after the date on which the source is first required to comply with the emissions limitation established by paragraph (5), whichever is earlier.

(k) Area source program

(1) Findings and purpose — The Congress finds that emissions of hazardous air pollutants from area sources may individually, or in the aggregate, present significant risks to public health in urban areas. Considering the large number of persons exposed and the risks of carcinogenic and other adverse health effects from hazardous air pollutants, ambient concentrations characteristic of large urban areas should be reduced to levels substantially below those currently experienced. It is the purpose of this subsection to achieve a substantial reduction in emissions of hazardous air pollutants from area sources and an equivalent reduction in the public health risks associated with such sources including a reduction of not less than 75 per centum in the incidence of cancer attributable to emissions from such sources.

(2) Research program — The Administrator shall, after consultation with State and local air

pollution control officials, conduct a program of research with respect to sources of hazardous air pollutants in urban areas and shall include within such program —

(A) ambient monitoring for a broad range of hazardous air pollutants (including, but not limited to, volatile organic compounds, metals, pesticides and products of incomplete combustion) in a representative number of urban locations;

(B) analysis to characterize the sources of such pollution with a focus on area sources and the contribution that such sources make to public health risks from hazardous air pollutants; and

(C) consideration of atmospheric transformation and other factors which can elevate public health risks from such pollutants.

Health effects considered under this program shall include, but not be limited to, carcinogenicity, mutagenicity, teratogenicity, neurotoxicity, reproductive dysfunction and other acute and chronic effects including the role of such pollutants as precursors of ozone or acid aerosol formation. The Administrator shall report the preliminary results of such research not later than 3 years after the date of enactment of the Clean Air Act Amendments of 1990.

(3) National strategy

(A) Considering information collected pursuant to the monitoring program authorized by paragraph (2), the Administrator shall, not later than 5 years after November 15, 1990, and after notice and opportunity for public comment, prepare and transmit to the Congress a comprehensive strategy to control emissions of hazardous air pollutants from area sources in urban areas.

(B) The strategy shall —

(i) identify not less than 30 hazardous air pollutants which, as the result of emissions from area sources, present the greatest threat to public health in the largest number of urban areas and that are or will be listed pursuant to subsection (b), and

(ii) identify the source categories or subcategories emitting such pollutants that are or will be listed pursuant to subsection (c). When identifying categories and subcategories of sources under this subparagraph, the Administrator shall assure that sources accounting for 90 per centum or more of the aggregate emissions of each of the 30 identified hazardous air pollutants are subject to standards pursuant to subsection (d).

(C) The strategy shall include a schedule of specific actions to substantially reduce the public health risks posed by the release of hazardous air pollutants from area sources that will be implemented by the Administrator under the authority of this or other laws (including, but not limited to, the Toxic Substances Control

Act, the Federal Insecticide, Fungicide and Rodenticide Act and the Resource Conservation and Recovery Act) or by the States. The strategy shall achieve a reduction in the incidence of cancer attributable to exposure to hazardous air pollutants emitted by stationary sources of not less than 75 per centum, considering control of emissions of hazardous air pollutants from all stationary sources and resulting from measures implemented by the Administrator or by the States under this or other laws.

(D) The strategy may also identify research needs in monitoring, analytical methodology, modeling or pollution control techniques and recommendations for changes in law that would further the goals and objectives of this subsection.

(E) Nothing in this subsection shall be interpreted to preclude or delay implementation of actions with respect to area sources of hazardous air pollutants under consideration pursuant to this or any other law and that may be promulgated before the strategy is prepared.

(F) The Administrator shall implement the strategy as expeditiously as practicable assuring that all sources are in compliance with all requirements not later than 9 years after the date of enactment of the Clean Air Act Amendments of 1990.

(G) As part of such strategy the Administrator shall provide for ambient monitoring and emissions modeling in urban areas as appropriate to demonstrate that the goals and objectives of the strategy are being met.

(4) Areawide activities — In addition to the national urban air toxics strategy authorized by paragraph (3), the Administrator shall also encourage and support areawide strategies developed by State or local air pollution control agencies that are intended to reduce risks from emissions by area sources within a particular urban area. From the funds available for grants under this section, the Administrator shall set aside not less than 10 per centum to support areawide strategies addressing hazardous air pollutants emitted by area sources and shall award such funds on a demonstration basis to those States with innovative and effective strategies. At the request of State or local air pollution control officials, the Administrator shall prepare guidelines for control technologies or management practices which may be applicable to various categories or subcategories of area sources.

(5) Report — The Administrator shall report to the Congress at intervals not later than 8 and 12 years after November 15, 1990, on actions taken under this subsection and other parts of this Act to reduce the risk to public health posed by the release of hazardous air pollutants from area sources. The reports shall also identify specific metropolitan areas that continue to experience high risks to

public health as the result of emissions from area sources.

(*l*) State programs

(1) In general — Each State may develop and submit to the Administrator for approval a program for the implementation and enforcement (including a review of enforcement delegations previously granted) of emission standards and other requirements for air pollutants subject to this section or requirements for the prevention and mitigation of accidental releases pursuant to subsection (r). A program submitted by a State under this subsection may provide for partial or complete delegation of the Administrator's authorities and responsibilities to implement and enforce emissions standards and prevention requirements but shall not include authority to set standards less stringent than those promulgated by the Administrator under this Act.

(2) Guidance — Not later than 12 months after November 15, 1990, the Administrator shall publish guidance that would be useful to the States in developing programs for submittal under this subsection. The guidance shall also provide for the registration of all facilities producing, processing, handling or storing any substance listed pursuant to subsection (r) in amounts greater than the threshold quantity. The Administrator shall include as an element in such guidance an optional program begun in 1986 for the review of high-risk point sources of air pollutants including, but not limited to, hazardous air pollutants listed pursuant to subsection (b).

(3) Technical assistance — The Administrator shall establish and maintain an air toxics clearinghouse and center to provide technical information and assistance to State and local agencies and, on a cost recovery basis, to others on control technology, health and ecological risk assessment, risk analysis, ambient monitoring and modeling, and emissions measurement and monitoring. The Administrator shall use the authority of section 7403 to examine methods for preventing, measuring, and controlling emissions and evaluating associated health and ecological risks. Where appropriate, such activity shall be conducted with not-for-profit organizations. The Administrator may conduct research on methods for preventing, measuring and controlling emissions and evaluating associated health and environment risks. All information collected under this paragraph shall be available to the public.

(4) Grants — Upon application of a State, the Administrator may make grants, subject to such terms and conditions as the Administrator deems appropriate, to such State for the purpose of assisting the State in developing and implementing a program for submittal and approval under this subsection. Programs assisted under this paragraph may include program elements addressing air pollutants or extremely hazardous substances other than those specifically subject to this section. Grants under this paragraph may include support for high-risk point source review as provided in paragraph (2) and support for the development and implementation of areawide area source programs pursuant to subsection (k).

(5) Approval or disapproval — Not later than 180 days after receiving a program submitted by a State, and after notice and opportunity for public comment, the Administrator shall either approve or disapprove such program. The Administrator shall disapprove any program submitted by a State, if the Administrator determines that —

(A) the authorities contained in the program are not adequate to assure compliance by all sources within the State with each applicable standard, regulation or requirement established by the Administrator under this section;

(B) adequate authority does not exist, or adequate resources are not available, to implement the program;

(C) the schedule for implementing the program and assuring compliance by affected sources is not sufficiently expeditious; or

(D) the program is otherwise not in compliance with the guidance issued by the Administrator under paragraph (2) or is not likely to satisfy, in whole or in part, the objectives of this Act.

If the Administrator disapproves a State program, the Administrator shall notify the State of any revisions or modifications necessary to obtain approval. The State may revise and resubmit the proposed program for review and approval pursuant to the provisions of this subsection.

(6) Withdrawal — Whenever the Administrator determines, after public hearing, that a State is not administering and enforcing a program approved pursuant to this subsection in accordance with the guidance published pursuant to paragraph (2) or the requirements of paragraph (5), the Administrator shall so notify the State and, if action which will assure prompt compliance is not taken within 90 days, the Administrator shall withdraw approval of the program. The Administrator shall not withdraw approval of any program unless the State shall have been notified and the reasons for withdrawal shall have been stated in writing and made public.

(7) Authority to enforce — Nothing in this subsection shall prohibit the Administrator from enforcing any applicable emission standard or requirement under this section.

(8) Local program — The Administrator may, after notice and opportunity for public comment, approve a program developed and submitted by a local air pollution control agency (after consultation with the State) pursuant to this subsection and any such agency implementing an approved program may take any action authorized to be taken by a State under this section.

(9) Permit authority — Nothing in this subsection shall affect the authorities and obligations of the Administrator or the State under title V.

(m) Atmospheric deposition to Great Lakes and coastal waters

(1) Deposition assessment — The Administrator, in cooperation with the Under Secretary of Commerce for Oceans and Atmosphere, shall conduct a program to identify and assess the extent of atmospheric deposition of hazardous air pollutants (and in the discretion of the Administrator, other air pollutants) to the Great Lakes, the Chesapeake Bay, Lake Champlain and coastal waters. As part of such program, the Administrator shall —

(A) monitor the Great Lakes, the Chesapeake Bay, Lake Champlain and coastal waters, including monitoring of the Great Lakes through the monitoring network established pursuant to paragraph (2) of this subsection and designing and deploying an atmospheric monitoring network for coastal waters pursuant to paragraph (4);

(B) investigate the sources and deposition rates of atmospheric deposition of air pollutants (and their atmospheric transformation precursors);

(C) conduct research to develop and improve monitoring methods and to determine the relative contribution of atmospheric pollutants to total pollution loadings to the Great Lakes, the Chesapeake Bay, Lake Champlain, and coastal waters;

(D) evaluate any adverse effects to public health or the environment caused by such deposition (including effects resulting from indirect exposure pathways) and assess the contribution of such deposition to violations of water quality standards established pursuant to the Federal Water Pollution Control Act and drinking water standards established pursuant to the Safe Drinking Water Act; and

(E) sample for such pollutants in biota, fish, and wildlife of the Great Lakes, the Chesapeake Bay, Lake Champlain and coastal waters and characterize the sources of such pollutants.

(2) Great lakes monitoring network — The Administrator shall oversee, in accordance with Annex 15 of the Great Lakes Water Quality Agreement, the establishment and operation of a Great Lakes atmospheric deposition network to monitor atmospheric deposition of hazardous air pollutants (and in the Administrator's discretion, other air pollutants) to the Great Lakes.

(A) As part of the network provided for in this paragraph, and not later than December 31, 1991, the Administrator shall establish in each of the 5 Great Lakes at least 1 facility capable of monitoring the atmospheric deposition of hazardous air pollutants in both dry and wet conditions.

(B) The Administrator shall use the data provided by the network to identify and track the movement of hazardous air pollutants through the Great Lakes, to determine the portion of water pollution loadings attributable to atmospheric deposition of such pollutants, and to support development of remedial action plans and other management plans as required by the Great Lakes Water Quality Agreement.

(C) The Administrator shall assure that the data collected by the Great Lakes atmospheric deposition monitoring network is in a format compatible with databases sponsored by the International Joint Commission, Canada, and the several States of the Great Lakes region.

(3) Monitoring for the Chesapeake Bay and Lake Champlain — The Administrator shall establish at the Chesapeake Bay and Lake Champlain atmospheric deposition stations to monitor deposition of hazardous air pollutants (and in the Administrator's discretion, other air pollutants) within the Chesapeake Bay and Lake Champlain watersheds. The Administrator shall determine the role of air deposition in the pollutant loadings of the Chesapeake Bay and Lake Champlain, investigate the sources of air pollutants deposited in the watersheds, evaluate the health and environmental effects of such pollutant loadings, and shall sample such pollutants in biota, fish and wildlife within the watersheds, as necessary to characterize such effects.

(4) Monitoring for coastal waters — The Administrator shall design and deploy atmospheric deposition monitoring networks for coastal waters and their watersheds and shall make any information collected through such networks available to the public. As part of this effort, the Administrator shall conduct research to develop and improve deposition monitoring methods, and to determine the relative contribution of atmospheric pollutants to pollutant loadings. For purposes of this subsection, "coastal waters" shall mean estuaries selected pursuant to section 320(a)(2)(A) of the Federal Water Pollution Control Act or listed pursuant to section 320(a)(2)(B) of such Act or estuarine research reserves designated pursuant to section 315 of the Coastal Zone Management Act (16 U.S.C. §1461).

(5) Report — Within 3 years of November 15, 1990, and biennially thereafter, the Administrator, in cooperation with the Under Secretary of Commerce for Oceans and Atmosphere, shall submit to the Congress a report on the results of any monitoring, studies, and investigations conducted pursuant to this subsection. Such report shall include, at a minimum, an assessment of —

(A) the contribution of atmospheric deposition to pollution loadings in the Great Lakes, the Chesapeake Bay, Lake Champlain and coastal waters;

(B) the environmental and public health effects of any pollution which is attributable to atmospheric deposition to the Great Lakes, the Chesapeake Bay, Lake Champlain and coastal waters;

(C) the source or sources of any pollution to the Great Lakes, the Chesapeake Bay, Lake Champlain and coastal waters which is attributable to atmospheric deposition;

(D) whether pollution loadings in the Great Lakes, the Chesapeake Bay, Lake Champlain or coastal waters cause or contribute to exceedances of drinking water standards pursuant to the Safe Drinking Water Act or water quality standards pursuant to the Federal Water Pollution Control Act or, with respect to the Great Lakes, exceedances of the specific objectives of the Great Lakes Water Quality Agreement; and

(E) a description of any revisions of the requirements, standards, and limitations pursuant to this Act and other applicable Federal laws as are necessary to assure protection of human health and the environment.

(6) Additional regulation — As part of the report to Congress, the Administrator shall determine whether the other provisions of this section are adequate to prevent serious adverse effects to public health and serious or widespread environmental effects, including such effects resulting from indirect exposure pathways, associated with atmospheric deposition to the Great Lakes, the Chesapeake Bay, Lake Champlain and coastal waters of hazardous air pollutants (and their atmospheric transformation products). The Administrator shall take into consideration the tendency of such pollutants to bioaccumulate. Within 5 years after the date of enactment of the Clean Air Act Amendments of 1990, the Administrator shall, based on such report and determination, promulgate, in accordance with this section, such further emission standards or control measures as may be necessary and appropriate to prevent such effects, including effects due to bioaccumulation and indirect exposure pathways. Any requirements promulgated pursuant to this paragraph with respect to coastal waters shall only apply to the coastal waters of the States which are subject to section 328(a).

(n) Other provisions

(1) Electric utility steam generating units

(A) The Administrator shall perform a study of the hazards to public health reasonably anticipated to occur as a result of emissions by electric utility steam generating units of pollutants listed under subsection (b) after imposition of the requirements of this Act. The Administrator shall report the results of this study to the Congress within 3 years after the date of the enactment of the Clean Air Act Amendments of 1990. The Administrator shall develop and describe in the Administrator's report to Congress alternative control strategies for emissions which may warrant regulation under this section. The Administrator shall regulate electric utility steam generating units under this section, if the Administrator finds such regulation is appropriate and necessary after considering the results of the study required by this subparagraph.

(B) The Administrator shall conduct, and transmit to the Congress not later than 4 years after the date of enactment of the Clean Air Act Amendments of 1990, a study of mercury emissions from electric utility steam generating units, municipal waste combustion units, and other sources, including area sources. Such study shall consider the rate and mass of such emissions, the health and environmental effects of such emissions, technologies which are available to control such emissions, and the costs of such technologies.

(C) The National Institute of Environmental Health Sciences shall conduct, and transmit to the Congress not later than 3 years after the date of enactment of the Clean Air Act Amendments of 1990, a study to determine the threshold level of mercury exposure below which adverse human health effects are not expected to occur. Such study shall include a threshold for mercury concentrations in the tissue of fish which may be consumed (including consumption by sensitive populations) without adverse effects to public health.

(2) Coke oven production technology study

(A) The Secretary of the Department of Energy and the Administrator shall jointly undertake a 6-year study to assess coke oven production emission control technologies and to assist in the development and commercialization of technically practicable and economically viable control technologies which have the potential to significantly reduce emissions of hazardous air pollutants from coke oven production facilities. In identifying control technologies, the Secretary and the Administrator shall consider the range of existing coke oven operations and battery design and the availability of sources of materials for such coke ovens as well as alternatives to existing coke oven production design.

(B) The Secretary and the Administrator are authorized to enter into agreements with persons who propose to develop, install and operate coke production emission control technologies which have the potential for significant emissions reductions of hazardous air pollutants provided that Federal funds shall not exceed 50 per centum of the cost of any project assisted pursuant to this paragraph.

(C) On completion of the study, the Secretary shall submit to Congress a report on the results of the study and shall make recommendations to the Administrator identifying practicable and economically viable control technologies for coke oven production facilities to reduce residual risks remaining after implementation of the standard under subsection (d) of this section.

(D) There are authorized to be appropriated $5,000,000 for each of the fiscal years 1992 through 1997 to carry out the program authorized by this paragraph.

(3) Publicly owned treatment works — The Administrator may conduct, in cooperation with the owners and operators of publicly owned treatment works, studies to characterize emissions of hazardous air pollutants emitted by such facilities, to identify industrial, commercial and residential discharges that contribute to such emissions and to demonstrate control measures for such emissions. When promulgating any standard under this section applicable to publicly owned treatment works, the Administrator may provide for control measures that include pretreatment of discharges causing emissions of hazardous air pollutants and process or product substitutions or limitations that may be effective in reducing such emissions. The Administrator may prescribe uniform sampling, modeling and risk assessment methods for use in implementing this subsection.

(4) Oil and gas wells; pipeline facilities

(A) Notwithstanding the provisions of subsection (a), emissions from any oil or gas exploration or production well (with its associated equipment) and emissions from any pipeline compressor or pump station shall not be aggregated with emissions from other similar units, whether or not such units are in a contiguous area or under common control, to determine whether such units or stations are major sources, and in the case of any oil or gas exploration or production well (with its associated equipment), such emissions shall not be aggregated for any purpose under this section.

(B) The Administrator shall not list oil and gas production wells (with its associated equipment) as an area source category under subsection (c), except that the Administrator may establish an area source category for oil and gas production wells located in any metropolitan statistical area or consolidated metropolitan statistical area with a population in excess of 1 million, if the Administrator determines that emissions of hazardous air pollutants from such wells present more than a negligible risk of adverse effects to public health.

(5) Hydrogen sulfide — The Administrator is directed to assess the hazards to public health and the environment resulting from the emission of hydrogen sulfide associated with the extraction of oil and natural gas resources. To the extent practicable, the assessment shall build upon and not

duplicate work conducted for an assessment pursuant to section 8002(m) of the Solid Waste Disposal Act and shall reflect consultation with the States. The assessment shall include a review of existing State and industry control standards, techniques and enforcement. The Administrator shall report to the Congress within 24 months after November 15, 1990, with the findings of such assessment, together with any recommendations, and shall, as appropriate, develop and implement a control strategy for emissions of hydrogen sulfide to protect human health and the environment, based on the findings of such assessment, using authorities under this Act including sections 111 and this section.

(6) Hydrofluoric acid — Not later than 2 years after November 15, 1990, the Administrator shall, for those regions of the country which do not have comprehensive health and safety regulations with respect to hydrofluoric acid, complete a study of the potential hazards of hydrofluoric acid and the uses of hydrofluoric acid in industrial and commercial applications to public health and the environment considering a range of events including worst-case accidental releases and shall make recommendations to the Congress for the reduction of such hazards, if appropriate.

(7) RCRA facilities — In the case of any category or subcategory of sources the air emissions of which are regulated under subtitle C of the Solid Waste Disposal Act, the Administrator shall take into account any regulations of such emissions which are promulgated under such subtitle and shall, to the maximum extent practicable and consistent with the provisions of this section, ensure that the requirements of such subtitle and this section are consistent.

(o) National Academy of Sciences study

(1) Request of the academy — Within 3 months of the date of enactment of the Clean Air Act Amendments of 1990, the Administrator shall enter into appropriate arrangements with the National Academy of Sciences to conduct a review of —

(A) risk assessment methodology used by the Environmental Protection Agency to determine the carcinogenic risk associated with exposure to hazardous air pollutants from source categories and subcategories subject to the requirements of this section; and

(B) improvements in such methodology.

(2) Elements to be studied — In conducting such review, the National Academy of Sciences should consider, but not be limited to, the following —

(A) the techniques used for estimating and describing the carcinogenic potency to humans of hazardous air pollutants; and

(B) the techniques used for estimating exposure to hazardous air pollutants (for hypothetical and actual maximally exposed individuals as well as other exposed individuals).

(3) Other health effects of concern — To the extent practicable, the Academy shall evaluate and report on the methodology for assessing the risk of adverse human health effects other than cancer for which safe thresholds of exposure may not exist, including, but not limited to, inheritable genetic mutations, birth defects, and reproductive dysfunctions.

(4) Report — A report on the results of such review shall be submitted to the Senate Committee on Environment and Public Works, the House Committee on Energy and Commerce, the Risk Assessment and Management Commission established by section 303 of the Clean Air Act Amendments of 1990 and the Administrator not later than 30 months after the date of enactment of the Clean Air Act Amendments of 1990.

(5) Assistance — The Administrator shall assist the Academy in gathering any information the Academy deems necessary to carry out this subsection. The Administrator may use any authority under this Act to obtain information from any person, and to require any person to conduct tests, keep and produce records, and make reports respecting research or other activities conducted by such person as necessary to carry out this subsection.

(6) Authorization — Of the funds authorized to be appropriated to the Administrator by this Act, such amounts as are required shall be available to carry out this subsection.

(7) Guidelines for carcinogenic risk assessment — The Administrator shall consider, but need not adopt, the recommendations contained in the report of the National Academy of Sciences prepared pursuant to this subsection and the views of the Science Advisory Board, with respect to such report. Prior to the promulgation of any standard under subsection (f), and after notice and opportunity for comment, the Administrator shall publish revised Guidelines for Carcinogenic Risk Assessment or a detailed explanation of the reasons that any recommendations contained in the report of the National Academy of Sciences will not be implemented. The publication of such revised Guidelines shall be a final Agency action for purposes of section 307.

(p) Mickey Leland Urban Air Toxics Research Center

(1) Establishment — The Administrator shall oversee the establishment of a National Urban Air Toxics Research Center, to be located at a university, a hospital, or other facility capable of undertaking and maintaining similar research capabilities in the areas of epidemiology, oncology, toxicology, pulmonary medicine, pathology, and biostatistics. The center shall be known as the Mickey Leland National Urban Air Toxics Research Center. The geographic site of the National Urban Air Toxics Research Center should be further directed to Harris County, Texas, in order to take full advantage of the well developed scientific community presence

on-site at the Texas Medical Center as well as the extensive data previously compiled for the comprehensive monitoring system currently in place.

(2) Board of Directors — The National Urban Air Toxics Research Center shall be governed by a Board of Directors to be comprised of 9 members, the appointment of which shall be allocated pro rata among the Speaker of the House, the Majority Leader of the Senate and the President. The members of the Board of Directors shall be selected based on their respective academic and professional backgrounds and expertise in matters relating to public health, environmental pollution and industrial hygiene. The duties of the Board of Directors shall be to determine policy and research guidelines, submit views from center sponsors and the public and issue periodic reports of center findings and activities.

(3) Scientific Advisory Panel — The Board of Directors shall be advised by a Scientific Advisory Panel, the 13 members of which shall be appointed by the Board, and to include eminent members of the scientific and medical communities. The Panel membership may include scientists with relevant experience from the National Institute of Environmental Health Sciences, the Center for Disease Control, the Environmental Protection Agency, the National Cancer Institute, and others, and the Panel shall conduct peer review and evaluate research results. The Panel shall assist the Board in developing the research agenda, reviewing proposals and applications, and advise on the awarding of research grants.

(4) Funding — The center shall be established and funded with both Federal and private source funds.

(q) Savings provision

(1) Standards previously promulgated — Any standard under this section in effect before the date of enactment of the Clean Air Act Amendments of 1990 shall remain in force and effect after such date unless modified as provided in this section before the date of enactment of such Amendments or under such Amendments. Except as provided in paragraph (4), any standard under this section which has been promulgated, but has not taken effect, before such date shall not be affected by such Amendments unless modified as provided in this section before such date or under such Amendments. Each such standard shall be reviewed and, if appropriate, revised, to comply with the requirements of subsection (d) within 10 years after the date of enactment of the Clean Air Act Amendments of 1990. If a timely petition for review of any such standard under section 7607 is pending on such date of enactment, the standard shall be upheld if it complies with this section as in effect before that date. If any such standard is remanded to the Administrator, the Administrator may in the Administrator's discretion apply either the requirements of this section, or those of this

section as in effect before the date of enactment of the Clean Air Act Amendments of 1990.

(2) Special rule — Notwithstanding paragraph (1), no standard shall be established under this section, as amended by the Clean Air Act Amendments of 1990, for radionuclide emissions from (A) elemental phosphorous plants, (B) grate alcinations elemental phosphorous plants, (C) phosphogypsum stacks, or (D) any subcategory of the foregoing. This section, as in effect prior to the date of enactment of the Clean Air Act Amendments of 1990, shall remain in effect for radionuclide emissions from such plants and stacks.

(3) Other categories — Notwithstanding paragraph (1), this section, as in effect prior to the date of enactment of the Clean Air Act Amendments of 1990, shall remain in effect for radionuclide emissions from non-Department of Energy Federal facilities that are not licensed by the Nuclear Regulatory Commission, coal-fired utility and industrial boilers, underground uranium mines, surface uranium mines, and disposal of uranium mill tailings piles, unless the Administrator, in the Administrator's discretion, applies the requirements of this section as modified by the Clean Air Act Amendments of 1990 to such sources of radionuclides.

(4) Medical facilities — Notwithstanding paragraph (1), no standard promulgated under this section prior to the date of enactment of the Clean Air Act Amendments of 1990 with respect to medical research or treatment facilities shall take effect for two years following the date of enactment of the Clean Air Act Amendments of 1990, unless the Administrator makes a determination pursuant to a rulemaking under subsection (d)(9) of this section. If the Administrator determines that the regulatory program established by the Nuclear Regulatory Commission for such facilities does not provide an ample margin of safety to protect public health, the requirements of this section shall fully apply to such facilities. If the Administrator determines that such regulatory program does provide an ample margin of safety to protect the public health, the Administrator is not required to promulgate a standard under this section for such facilities, as provided in subsection (d)(9) of this section.

(r) Prevention of accidental releases

(1) Purpose and general duty — It shall be the objective of the regulations and programs authorized under this subsection to prevent the accidental release and to minimize the consequences of any such release of any substance listed pursuant to paragraph (3) or any other extremely hazardous substance. The owners and operators of stationary sources producing, processing, handling or storing such substances have a general duty in the same manner and to the same extent as section 654, Title 29 to identify hazards which may result from such releases using appropriate hazard assessment techniques, to design and maintain a safe facility taking such steps as are necessary to prevent releases, and to minimize the consequences of accidental releases which do occur. For purposes of this paragraph, the provisions of section 7604 shall not be available to any person or otherwise be construed to be applicable to this paragraph. Nothing in this section shall be interpreted, construed, implied or applied to create any liability or basis for suit for compensation for bodily injury or any other injury or property damages to any person which may result from accidental releases of such substances.

(2) Definitions

(A) The term "accidental release" means an unanticipated emission of a regulated substance or other extremely hazardous substance into the ambient air from a stationary source.

(B) The term "regulated substance" means a substance listed under paragraph (3).

(C) The term "stationary source" means any buildings, structures, equipment, installations or substance emitting stationary activities (i) which belong to the same industrial group, (ii) which are located on one or more contiguous properties, (iii) which are under the control of the same person (or persons under common control), and (iv) from which an accidental release may occur.

(D) The term "retail facility" means a stationary source at which more than one-half of the income is obtained from direct sales to end users or at which more than one-half of the fuel sold, by volume, is sold through a cylinder exchange program.

(3) List of substances — The Administrator shall promulgate not later than 24 months after November 15, 1990, an initial list of 100 substances which, in the case of an accidental release, are known to cause or may reasonably be anticipated to cause death, injury, or serious adverse effects to human health or the environment. For purposes of promulgating such list, the Administrator shall use, but is not limited to, the list of extremely hazardous substances published under the Emergency Planning and Community Right-to-Know Act of 1986, with such modifications as the Administrator deems appropriate. The initial list shall include chlorine, anhydrous ammonia, methyl chloride, ethylene oxide, vinyl chloride, methyl isocyanate, hydrogen cyanide, ammonia, hydrogen sulfide, toluene diisocyanate, phosgene, bromine, anhydrous hydrogen chloride, hydrogen fluoride, anhydrous sulfur dioxide, and sulfur trioxide. The initial list shall include at least 100 substances which pose the greatest risk of causing death, injury, or serious adverse effects to human health or the environment from accidental releases. Regulations establishing the list shall include an explanation of the basis for establishing the list. The list may be revised from time to time by the Administrator on the Administrator's own motion or by petition and shall be reviewed at least every 5 years. No air

pollutant for which a national primary ambient air quality standard has been established shall be included on any such list. No substance, practice, process, or activity regulated under subchapter VI of this chapter shall be subject to regulations under this subsection. The Administrator shall establish procedures for the addition and deletion of substances from the list established under this paragraph consistent with those applicable to the list in subsection (b) of this section.

(4) Factors to be considered — In listing substances under paragraph (3), the Administrator

(A) shall consider —

(i) the severity of any acute adverse health effects associated with accidental releases of the substance;

(ii) the likelihood of accidental releases of the substance; and

(iii) the potential magnitude of human exposure to accidental releases of the substance; and

(B) shall not list a flammable substance when used as a fuel or held for sale as a fuel at a retail facility under this subsection solely because of the explosive or flammable properties of the substance, unless a fire or explosion caused by the substance will result in acute adverse health effects from human exposure to the substance, including the unburned fuel or its combustion byproducts, other than those caused by the heat of the fire or impact of the explosion.

(5) Threshold quantity — At the time any substance is listed pursuant to paragraph (3), the Administrator shall establish by rule, a threshold quantity for the substance, taking into account the toxicity, eactivity, volatility, dispersibility, combustibility, or flammability of the substance and the amount of the substance which, as a result of an accidental release, is known to cause or may reasonably be anticipated to cause death, injury or serious adverse effects to human health for which the substance was listed. The Administrator is authorized to establish a greater threshold quantity for, or to exempt entirely, any substance that is a nutrient used in agriculture when held by a farmer.

(6) Chemical Safety Board

(A) There is hereby established an independent safety board to be known as the Chemical Safety and Hazard Investigation Board.

(B) The Board shall consist of 5 members, including a Chairperson, who shall be appointed by the President, by and with the advice and consent of the Senate. Members of the Board shall be appointed on the basis of technical qualification, professional standing, and demonstrated knowledge in the fields of accident reconstruction, safety engineering, human factors, toxicology, or air pollution regulation. The terms of office of members of the Board shall be 5 years. Any member of the Board, including the Chairperson, may be removed for inefficiency, neglect of duty, or malfeasance in office. The Chairperson shall be the Chief Executive Officer of the Board and shall exercise the executive and administrative functions of the Board.

(C) The Board shall —

(i) investigate (or cause to be investigated), determine and report to the public in writing the facts, conditions, and circumstances and the cause or probable cause of any accidental release resulting in a fatality, serious injury or substantial property damages;

(ii) issue periodic reports to the Congress, Federal, State and local agencies, including the Environmental Protection Agency and the Occupational Safety and Health Administration, concerned with the safety of chemical production, processing, handling and storage, and other interested persons recommending measures to reduce the likelihood or the consequences of accidental releases and proposing corrective steps to make chemical production, processing, handling and storage as safe and free from risk of injury as is possible and may include in such reports proposed rules or orders which should be issued by the Administrator under the authority of this section or the Secretary of Labor under the Occupational Safety and Health Act to prevent or minimize the consequences of any release of substances that may cause death, injury or other serious adverse effects on human health or substantial property damage as the result of an accidental release; and

(iii) establish by regulation requirements binding on persons for reporting accidental releases into the ambient air subject to the Board's investigatory jurisdiction. Reporting releases to the National Response Center, in lieu of the Board directly, shall satisfy such regulations. The National Response Center shall promptly notify the Board of any releases which are within the Board's jurisdiction.

(D) The Board may utilize the expertise and experience of other agencies.

(E) The Board shall coordinate its activities with investigations and studies conducted by other agencies of the United States having a responsibility to protect public health and safety. The Board shall enter into a memorandum of understanding with the National Transportation Safety Board to assure coordination of functions and to limit duplication of activities which shall designate the National Transportation Safety Board as the lead agency for the investigation of releases which are transportation related. The Board shall not be authorized to investigate marine oil spills, which the National Transportation Safety Board is authorized to investigate. The Board shall enter into a memorandum of understanding with the Occupational Safety and Health Administration so as to limit duplication of activities. In no event shall the Board forego an investigation where an accidental release causes a fatality or serious injury among the general public, or had the potential to cause substantial property damage or a number of deaths or injuries among the general public.

(F) The Board is authorized to conduct research and studies with respect to the potential for accidental releases, whether or not an accidental release has occurred, where there is evidence which indicates the presence of a potential hazard or hazards. To the extent practicable, the Board shall conduct such studies in cooperation with other Federal agencies having emergency response authorities, State and local governmental agencies and associations and organizations from the industrial, commercial, and nonprofit sectors.

(G) No part of the conclusions, findings, or recommendations of the Board relating to any accidental release or the investigation thereof shall be admitted as evidence or used in any action or suit for damages arising out of any matter mentioned in such report.

(H) Not later than 18 months after November 15, 1990, the Board shall publish a report accompanied by recommendations to the Administrator on the use of hazard assessments in preventing the occurrence and minimizing the consequences of accidental releases of extremely hazardous substances. The recommendations shall include a list of extremely hazardous substances which are not regulated substances (including threshold quantities for such substances) and categories of stationary sources for which hazard assessments would be an appropriate measure to aid in the prevention of accidental releases and to minimize the consequences of those releases that do occur. The recommendations shall also include a description of the information and analysis which would be appropriate to include in any hazard assessment. The Board shall also make recommendations with respect to the role of risk management plans as required by paragraph (8)(B) in preventing accidental releases. The Board may from time to time review and revise its recommendations under this subparagraph.

(I) Whenever the Board submits a recommendation with respect to accidental releases to the Administrator, the Administrator shall respond to such recommendation formally and in writing not later than 180 days after receipt thereof. The response to the Board's recommendation by the Administrator shall indicate whether the Administrator will —

(i) initiate a rulemaking or issue such orders as are necessary to implement the recommendation in full or in part, pursuant to any timetable contained in the recommendation;

(ii) decline to initiate a rulemaking or issue orders as recommended.

Any determination by the Administrator not to implement a recommendation of the Board or to implement a recommendation only in part, including any variation from the schedule contained in the recommendation, shall be accompanied by a statement from the Administrator setting forth the reasons for such determination.

(J) The Board may make recommendations with respect to accidental releases to the Secretary of Labor. Whenever the Board submits such recommendation, the Secretary shall respond to such recommendation formally and in writing not later than 180 days after receipt thereof. The response to the Board's recommendation by the Administrator shall indicate whether the Secretary will —

(i) initiate a rulemaking or issue such orders as are necessary to implement the recommendation in full or in part, pursuant to any timetable contained in the recommendation;

(ii) decline to initiate a rulemaking or issue orders as recommended.

Any determination by the Secretary not to implement a recommendation or to implement a recommendation only in part, including any variation from the schedule contained in the recommendation, shall be accompanied by a statement from the Secretary setting forth the reasons for such determination.

(K) Within 2 years after November 15, 1990, the Board shall issue a report to the Administrator of the Environmental Protection Agency and to the Administrator of the Occupational Safety and Health Administration recommending the adoption of regulations for the preparation of risk management plans and general requirements for the prevention of accidental releases of regulated substances into the ambient air (including recommendations for listing substances under paragraph (3)) and for the mitigation of the potential adverse effect on human health or the environment as a result of accidental releases which should be applicable to any stationary source handling any regulated substance in more than threshold amounts. The Board may include proposed rules or orders which should be issued by the Administrator under authority of this subsection or by the Secretary of Labor under the Occupational Safety and

Health Act. Any such recommendations shall be specific and shall identify the regulated substance or class of regulated substances (or other substances) to which the recommendations apply. The Administrator shall consider such recommendations before promulgating regulations required by paragraph (7)(B).

(L) The Board, or upon authority of the Board, any member thereof, any administrative law judge employed by or assigned to the Board, or any officer or employee duly designated by the Board, may for the purpose of carrying out duties authorized by subparagraph (C) —

(i) hold such hearings, sit and act at such times and places, administer such oaths, and require by subpoena or otherwise attendance and testimony of such witnesses and the production of evidence and may require by order that any person engaged in the production, processing, handling, or storage of extremely hazardous substances submit written reports and responses to requests and questions within such time and in such form as the Board may require; and

(ii) upon presenting appropriate credentials and a written notice of inspection authority, enter any property where an accidental release causing a fatality, serious injury or substantial property damage has occurred and do all things therein necessary for a proper investigation pursuant to subparagraph (C) and inspect at reasonable times records, files, papers, processes, controls, and facilities and take such samples as are relevant to such investigation.

Whenever the Administrator or the Board conducts an inspection of a facility pursuant to this subsection, employees and their representatives shall have the same rights to participate in such inspections as provided in the Occupational Safety and Health Act.

(M) In addition to that described in subparagraph (L), the Board may use any information gathering authority of the Administrator under this Act, including the subpoena power provided in section 7607(a)(1) of this title.

(N) The Board is authorized to establish such procedural and administrative rules as are necessary to the exercise of its functions and duties. The Board is authorized without regard to section 5 of Title 41 to enter into contracts, leases, cooperative agreements or other transactions as may be necessary in the conduct of the duties and functions of the Board with any other agency, institution, or person.

(O) After the effective date of any reporting requirement promulgated pursuant to subparagraph (C)(iii) it shall be unlawful for any person to fail to report any release of any extremely hazardous substance as required by such subparagraph. The Administrator is authorized to enforce any regulation or requirements established by the Board pursuant to subparagraph (C)(iii) using the authorities of sections 7413 and 7414. Any request for information from the owner or operator of a stationary source made by the Board or by the Administrator under this section shall be treated, for purposes of sections 7413, 7414, 7416, 7420, 7603, 7604 and 7607 and any other enforcement provisions of this Act, as a request made by the Administrator under section 7414 of this title and may be enforced by the Chairperson of the Board or by the Administrator as provided in such section.

(P) The Administrator shall provide to the Board such support and facilities as may be necessary for operation of the Board.

(Q) Consistent with subsection (G) and section 7414(c) of this title any records, reports or information obtained by the Board shall be available to the Administrator, the Secretary of Labor, the Congress and the public, except that upon a showing satisfactory to the Board by any person that records, reports, or information, or particular part thereof (other than release or emissions data) to which the Board has access, if made public, is likely to cause substantial harm to the person's competitive position, the Board shall consider such record, report, or information or particular portion thereof confidential in accordance with section 1905 of Title 18, except that such record, report, or information may be disclosed to other officers, employees, and authorized representatives of the United States concerned with carrying out this Act or when relevant under any proceeding under this Act. This subparagraph does not constitute authority to withhold records, reports, or information from the Congress.

(R) Whenever the Board submits or transmits any budget estimate, budget request, supplemental budget request, or other budget information, legislative recommendation, prepared testimony for congressional hearings, recommendation or study to the President, the Secretary of Labor, the Administrator, or the Director of the Office of Management and Budget, it shall concurrently transmit a copy thereof to the Congress. No report of the Board shall be subject to review by the Administrator or any Federal agency or to judicial review in any court. No officer or agency of the United States shall have authority to require the Board to submit its budget requests or estimates, legislative recommendations, prepared testimony, comments, recommendations or reports to any officer or agency of the United States for approval or review prior to the submission of such recommendations, testimony, comments or reports to the Congress. In the performance of their functions as established by this Act, the members, officers and employees of the Board shall not be responsible to or subject to supervision or direction, in carrying out any duties under this subsection, of any officer or employee or agent of the Environmental Protection Agency, the Department of Labor or any other agency of the United States except that the President may remove any member, officer or employee of the Board for inefficiency, neglect of duty or malfeasance in office. Nothing in this section shall affect the application of Title 5 to officers or employees of the Board.

(S) The Board shall submit an annual report to the President and to the Congress which shall include, but not be limited to, information on accidental releases which have been investigated by or reported to the Board during the previous year, recommendations for legislative or administrative action which the Board has made, the actions which have been taken by the Administrator or the Secretary of Labor or the heads of other agencies to implement such recommendations, an identification of priorities for study and investigation in the succeeding year, progress in the development of risk-reduction technologies and the response to and implementation of significant research findings on chemical safety in the public and private sector.

(7) Accident prevention

(A) In order to prevent accidental releases of regulated substances, the Administrator is authorized to promulgate release prevention, detection, and correction requirements which may include monitoring, record-keeping, reporting, training, vapor recovery, secondary containment, and other design, equipment, work practice, and operational requirements. Regulations promulgated under this paragraph may make distinctions between various types, classes, and kinds of facilities, devices and systems taking into consideration factors including, but not limited to, the size, location, process, process controls, quantity of substances handled, potency of substances, and response capabilities present at any stationary source. Regulations promulgated pursuant to this subparagraph shall have an effective date, as determined by the Administrator, assuring compliance as expeditiously as practicable.

(B)(i) Within 3 years after the date of enactment of the Clean Air Act Amendments of 1990, the Administrator shall promulgate reasonable regulations and appropriate guidance to provide, to the greatest extent practicable, for the prevention and detection of accidental releases of regulated substances and for response to such releases by the owners or operators of the sources of such releases. The Administrator shall utilize the expertise of the Secretaries of Transportation and Labor in promulgating such regulations. As appropriate, such regulations shall cover the use, operation, repair, replacement, and maintenance of equipment to monitor, detect, inspect, and control such releases, including training of persons in the use and maintenance of such equipment and in the conduct of periodic inspections. The regulations shall include procedures and measures for emergency response after an accidental release of a regulated substance in order to protect human health and the environment. The regulations shall cover storage, as well as operations. The regulations shall, as appropriate, recognize differences in size, operations, processes, class and categories of sources and the voluntary actions of such sources to prevent such releases and respond to such releases. The regulations shall be applicable to a stationary source 3 years after the date of promulgation, or 3 years after the date on which a regulated substance present at the source in more than threshold amounts is first listed under paragraph (3), whichever is later.

(ii) The regulations under this subparagraph shall require the owner or operator of stationary sources at which a regulated substance is present in more than a threshold quantity to prepare and implement a risk management plan to detect and prevent or minimize accidental releases of such substances from the stationary source, and to provide a prompt emergency response to any such releases in order to protect human health and the environment. Such plan shall provide for compliance with the requirements of this subsection and shall also include each of the following:

(I) a hazard assessment to assess the potential effects of an accidental release of any regulated substance. This assessment shall include an estimate of potential release quantities and a determination of downwind effects, including potential exposures to affected populations. Such assessment shall include a previous release history of the past 5 years, including the size, concentration, and duration of releases, and shall include an evaluation of worst case accidental releases;

(II) a program for preventing accidental releases of regulated substances, including safety precautions and maintenance, monitoring and employee training measures to be used at the source; and

      (III) a response program providing for specific actions to be taken in response to an accidental release of a regulated substance so as to protect human health and the environment, including procedures for informing the public and local agencies responsible for responding to accidental releases, emergency health care, and employee training measures.

At the time regulations are promulgated under this subparagraph, the Administrator shall promulgate guidelines to assist stationary sources in the preparation of risk management plans. The guidelines shall, to the extent practicable, include model risk management plans.

    (iii) The owner or operator of each stationary source covered by clause (ii) shall register a risk management plan prepared under this subparagraph with the Administrator before the effective date of regulations under clause (i) in such form and manner as the Administrator shall, by rule, require. Plans prepared pursuant to this subparagraph shall also be submitted to the Chemical Safety and Hazard Investigation Board, to the State in which the stationary source is located, and to any local agency or entity having responsibility for planning for or responding to accidental releases which may occur at such source, and shall be available to the public under section 7414(c) of this title. The Administrator shall establish, by rule, an auditing system to regularly review and, if necessary, require revision in risk management plans to assure that the plans comply with this subparagraph. Each such plan shall be updated periodically as required by the Administrator, by rule

(C) Any regulations promulgated pursuant to this subsection shall to the maximum extent practicable, consistent with this subsection, be consistent with the recommendations and standards established by the American Society of Mechanical Engineers (ASME), the American National Standards Institute (ANSI) or the American Society of Testing Materials (ASTM). The Administrator shall take into consideration the concerns of small business in promulgating regulations under this subsection.

(D) In carrying out the authority of this paragraph, the Administrator shall consult with the Secretary of Labor and the Secretary of Transportation and shall coordinate any requirements under this paragraph with any requirements established for comparable purposes by the Occupational Safety and Health Administration or the Department of Transportation. Nothing in this subsection shall be interpreted, construed or applied to impose requirements affecting, or to grant the Administrator, the Chemical Safety and Hazard Investigation Board, or any other agency any authority to regulate (including requirements for hazard assessment), the accidental release of radionuclides arising from the construction and operation of facilities licensed by the Nuclear Regulatory Commission.

(E) After the effective date of any regulation or requirement imposed under this subsection, it shall be unlawful for any person to operate any stationary source subject to such regulation or requirement in violation of such regulation or requirement. Each regulation or requirement under this subsection shall for purposes of sections 7413, 7414, 7416, 7420, 7604, and 7607 and other enforcement provisions of this Act, be treated as a standard in effect under subsection (d) of this section.

(F) Notwithstanding the provisions of subchapter V of this chapter or this section, no stationary source shall be required to apply for, or operate pursuant to, a permit issued under such title solely because such source is subject to regulations or requirements under this subsection.

(G) In exercising any authority under this subsection, the Administrator shall not, for purposes of section 653(b)(1) of Title 29, be deemed to be exercising statutory authority to prescribe or enforce standards or regulations affecting occupational safety and health.

(H) Public access to off-site consequence analysis information —

    (i) Definitions — In this subparagraph:

      (I)   Covered person — The term "covered person" means —

        (aa) an officer or employee of the United States;

        (bb) an officer or employee of an agent or contractor of the Federal Government;

        (cc) an officer or employee of a State or local government;

        (dd) an officer or employee of an agent or contractor of a State or local government;

        (ee) an individual affiliated with an entity that has been given, by a State or local government, responsibility for preventing, planning for, or responding to accidental releases;

        (ff)   an officer or employee or an agent or contractor of an entity described in item (ee); and

(gg) a qualified researcher under clause (vii).

(II) Official use — The term "official use" means an action of a Federal, State, or local government agency or an entity referred to in subclause (I) (ee) intended to carry out a function relevant to preventing, planning for, or responding to accidental releases.

(III) Off-site consequence analysis information — The term "off-site consequence analysis information" means those portions of a risk management plan, excluding the executive summary of the plan, consisting of an evaluation of 1 or more worst-case release scenarios or alternative release scenarios, and any electronic data base created by the Administrator from those portions.

(IV) Risk management plan — The term "risk management plan" means a risk management plan submitted to the Administrator by an owner or operator of a stationary source under subparagraph (B)(iii).

(ii) Regulations — Not later than 1 year after the date of enactment of this subparagraph, the President shall

(I) assess —

(aa) the increased risk of terrorist and other criminal activity associated with the posting of off-site consequence analysis information on the Internet; and

(bb) the incentives created by public disclosure of off-site consequence analysis information for reduction in the risk of accidental releases; and

(II) based on the assessment under subclause (I), promulgate regulations governing the distribution of off-site consequence analysis information in a manner that, in the opinion of the President, minimizes the likelihood of accidental releases and the risk described in subclause (I)(aa) and the likelihood of harm to public health and welfare, and —

(aa) allows access by any member of the public to paper copies of off-site consequence analysis information for a limited number of stationary sources located anywhere in the United States, without any geographical restriction;

(bb) allows other public access to off-site consequence analysis information as appropriate;

(cc) allows access for official use by a covered person described in any of items (cc) through (ff) of clause (i)(I) (referred to in this subclause as a "State or local covered person") to off-site consequence analysis information relating to stationary sources located in the person's State;

(dd) allows a State or local covered person to provide, for official use, off-site consequence analysis information relating to stationary sources located in the person's State to a State or local covered person in a contiguous State; and

(ee) allows a State or local covered person to obtain for official use, by request to the Administrator, off-site consequence analysis information that is not available to the person under item (cc).

(iii) Availability under freedom of information act

(I) First year — Off-site consequence analysis information, and any ranking of stationary sources derived from the information, shall not be made available under section 552 of Title 5, United States Code, during the 1-year period beginning on the date of enactment of this subparagraph.

(II) After first year — If the regulations under clause (ii) are promulgated on or before the end of the period described in subclause (I), off-site consequence analysis information covered by the regulations, and any ranking of stationary sources derived from the information, shall not be made available under section 552 of Title 5, United States Code, after the end of that period.

(III) Applicability — Subclauses (I) and (II) apply to off-site consequence analysis information submitted to the Administrator before, on, or after the date of enactment of this subparagraph.

(iv) Availability of information during transition period — The Administrator shall make off-site consequence analysis information available to covered persons for official use in a manner that meets the requirements of items (cc) through (ee) of clause (ii)(II), and to the public in a form that does not make available any information concerning the identity or location of stationary sources, during the period —

(I) beginning on the date of enactment of this subparagraph; and

(II) ending on the earlier of the date of promulgation of the regulations under clause (ii) or the date that is 1 year after the date of enactment of this subparagraph.

(v) Prohibition on unauthorized disclosure of information by covered persons —

(I) In general — Beginning on the date of enactment of this subparagraph, a covered person shall not disclose to the public off-site consequence analysis information in any form, or any statewide or national ranking of identified stationary sources derived from such information, except as authorized by this subparagraph (including the regulations promulgated under clause (ii)). After the end of the 1-year period beginning on the date of enactment of this subparagraph, if regulations have not been promulgated under clause (ii), the preceding sentence shall not apply.

(II) Criminal penalties — Notwithstanding section 113, a covered person that willfully violates a restriction or prohibition established by this subparagraph (including the regulations promulgated under clause (ii)) shall, upon conviction, be fined for an infraction under section 3571 of Title 18, United States Code, (but shall not be subject to imprisonment) for each unauthorized disclosure of off-site consequence analysis information, except that subsection (d) of such section 3571 shall not apply to a case in which the offense results in pecuniary loss unless the defendant knew that such loss would occur. The disclosure of off-site consequence analysis information for each specific stationary source shall be considered a separate offense. The total of all penalties that may be imposed on a single person or organization under this item shall not exceed $1,000,000 for violations committed during any 1 calendar year.

(III) Applicability — If the owner or operator of a stationary source makes off-site consequence analysis information relating to that stationary source available to the public without restriction —

(aa) subclauses (I) and (II) shall not apply with respect to the information; and

(bb) the owner or operator shall notify the Administrator of the public availability of the information.

(IV) List — The Administrator shall maintain and make publicly available a list of all stationary sources that have provided notification under subclause (III)(bb).

(vi) Notice — The Administrator shall provide notice of the definition of official use as provided in clause (i)(III) and examples of actions that would and would not meet that definition, and notice of the restrictions on further dissemination and the penalties established by this Act to each covered person who receives off-site consequence analysis information under clause (iv) and each covered person who receives off-site consequence analysis information for an official use under the regulations promulgated under clause (ii).

(vii) Qualified researchers

(I) In general — Not later than 180 days after the date of enactment of this subparagraph, the Administrator, in consultation with the Attorney General, shall develop and implement a system for providing off-site consequence analysis information, including facility identification, to any qualified researcher, including a qualified researcher from industry or any public interest group.

(II) Limitation on dissemination — The system shall not allow the researcher to disseminate, or make available on the Internet, the off-site consequence analysis information, or any portion of the off-site consequence analysis information, received under this clause.

(viii) Read-only information technology system — In consultation with the Attorney General and the heads of other appropriate Federal agencies, the Administrator shall establish an information technology system that provides for the availability to the public of off-site consequence analysis information by means of a central data base under the control of the Federal Government that contains information that users may read, but that provides no means by which an electronic or mechanical copy of the information may be made.

(ix) Voluntary industry accident prevention standards — The Environmental Protection Agency, the Department of Justice, and other appropriate agencies may provide technical assistance to owners and operators of stationary sources and participate in the development of voluntary industry standards that will help achieve the objectives set forth in paragraph (1).

(x) Effect on state or local law

(I) In general — Subject to subclause (II), this subparagraph (including the regulations promulgated under this subparagraph) shall supersede any provision of State or local law that is inconsistent with this subparagraph (including the regulations).

(II) Availability of information under state law — Nothing in this subparagraph precludes a State from making available data on the off-site consequences of chemical releases collected in accordance with State law.

(xi) Report

(I) In general — Not later than 3 years after the date of enactment of this subparagraph, the Attorney General, in consultation with appropriate State, local, and Federal Government agencies, affected industry, and the public, shall submit to Congress a report that describes the extent to which regulations promulgated under this paragraph have resulted in actions, including the design and maintenance of safe facilities, that are effective in detecting, preventing, and minimizing the consequences of releases of regulated substances that may be caused by criminal activity. As part of this report, the Attorney General, using available data to the extent possible, and a sampling of covered stationary sources selected at the discretion of the Attorney General, and in consultation with appropriate State, local, and Federal governmental agencies, affected industry, and the public, shall review the vulnerability of covered stationary sources to criminal and terrorist activity, current industry practices regarding site security, and security of transportation of regulated substances. The Attorney General shall submit this report, containing the results of the review, together with recommendations, if any, for reducing vulnerability of covered stationary sources to criminal and terrorist activity, to the Committee on Commerce of the United States House of Representatives and the Committee on Environment and Public Works of the United States Senate and other relevant committees of Congress.

(II) Interim report — Not later than 12 months after the date of enactment of this subparagraph, the Attorney General shall submit to the Committee on Commerce of the United States House of Representatives and the Committee on Environment and Public Works of the United States Senate, and other relevant committees of Congress, an interim report that includes, at a minimum —

(aa) the preliminary findings under subclause (I);

(bb) the methods used to develop the findings; and

(cc) an explanation of the activities expected to occur that could cause the findings of the report under subclause (I) to be different than the preliminary findings.

(III) Availability of information — Information that is developed by the Attorney General or requested by the Attorney General and received from a covered stationary source for the purpose of conducting the review under subclauses (I) and (II) shall be exempt from disclosure under section 552 of Title 5, United States Code, if such information would pose a threat to national security.

(xii) Scope — This subparagraph —

(I) applies only to covered persons; and

(II) does not restrict the dissemination of off-site consequence analysis information by any covered person in any manner or form except in the form of a risk management plan or an electronic data base created by the Administrator from off-site consequence analysis information.

(xiii) Authorization of appropriations — There are authorized to be appropriated to the Administrator and the Attorney General such sums as are necessary to carry out this subparagraph (including the regulations promulgated under clause (ii)), to remain available until expended.

(8) Research on hazard assessments — The Administrator may collect and publish information on accident scenarios and consequences covering a range of possible events for substances listed under paragraph (3). The Administrator shall establish a program of long-term research to develop and disseminate information on methods and techniques for hazard assessment which may be useful in improving and validating the procedures employed in the preparation of hazard assessments under this subsection.

(9) Order authority

(A) In addition to any other action taken, when the Administrator determines that there may be an imminent and substantial endangerment to the human health or welfare or the environment because of an actual or threatened accidental release of a regulated substance, the Administrator may secure such relief as may be necessary to abate such danger or threat, and the district court of the United States in the district in which the threat occurs shall have jurisdiction to grant such relief as the public interest and the equities of the case may require. The Administrator may also, after notice to the State in which the stationary source is located, take other action under this paragraph including, but not limited to, issuing such orders as may be necessary to protect human health. The Administrator shall take action under section 7603 rather than this paragraph whenever the authority of such section is adequate to protect human health and the environment.

(B) Orders issued pursuant to this paragraph may be enforced in an action brought in the appropriate United States district court as if the order were issued under section 7603.

(C) Within 180 days after November 15, 1990, the Administrator shall publish guidance for using the order authorities established by this paragraph. Such guidance shall provide for the coordinated use of the authorities of this paragraph with other emergency powers authorized by section 9606 of this title [§106 of the Comprehensive Environmental Response, Compensation and Liability Act], sections 311(c), 308, 309 and 504(a) of the Federal Water Pollution Control Act, sections 3007, 3008, 3013, and 7003 of the Solid Waste Disposal Act, sections 1445 and 1431 of the Safe Drinking Water Act, sections 5 and 7 of the Toxic Substances Control Act, and sections 7313, 7314, and 7603 of this title.

(10) Presidential review — The President shall conduct a review of release prevention, mitigation and response authorities of the various Federal agencies and shall clarify and coordinate agency responsibilities to assure the most effective and efficient implementation of such authorities and to identify any deficiencies in authority or resources which may exist. The President may utilize the resources and solicit the recommendations of the Chemical Safety and Hazard Investigation Board in conducting such review. At the conclusion of such review, but not later than 24 months after November 15, 1990, the President shall transmit a message to the Congress on the release prevention, mitigation and response activities of the Federal Government making such recommendations for change in law as the President may deem appropri-

ate. Nothing in this paragraph shall be interpreted, construed or applied to authorize the President to modify or reassign release prevention, mitigation or response authorities otherwise established by law.

(11) State authority — Nothing in this subsection shall preclude, deny or limit any right of a State or political subdivision thereof to adopt or enforce any regulation, requirement, limitation or standard (including any procedural requirement) that is more stringent than a regulation, requirement, limitation or standard in effect under this subsection or that applies to a substance not subject to this subsection.

(s) Periodic report — Not later than January 15, 1993 and every 3 years thereafter, the Administrator shall prepare and transmit to the Congress a comprehensive report on the measures taken by the Agency and by the States to implement the provisions of this section. The Administrator shall maintain a database on pollutants and sources subject to the provisions of this section and shall include aggregate information from the database in each annual report. The report shall include, but not be limited to —

(1) a status report on standard-setting under subsections (d) and (f);

(2) information with respect to compliance with such standards including the costs of compliance experienced by sources in various categories and subcategories;

(3) development and implementation of the national urban air toxics program; and

(4) recommendations of the Chemical Safety and Hazard Investigation Board with respect to the prevention and mitigation of accidental releases.

§7413. Federal enforcement
[CAA §113]

(a) In general

(1) Order to comply with SIP — Whenever, on the basis of any information available to the Administrator, the Administrator finds that any person has violated or is in violation of any requirement or prohibition of an applicable implementation plan or permit, the Administrator shall notify the person and the State in which the plan applies of such finding. At any time after the expiration of 30 days following the date on which such notice of a violation is issued, the Administrator may, without regard to the period of violation (subject to section 2462 of Title 28 of the United States Code) —

(A) issue an order requiring such person to comply with the requirements or prohibitions of such plan or permit,

(B) issue an administrative penalty order in accordance with subsection (d), or

(C) bring a civil action in accordance with subsection (b).

(2) State failure to enforce SIP or permit program — Whenever, on the basis of information

available to the Administrator, the Administrator finds that violations of an applicable implementation plan or an approved permit program under title V are so widespread that such violations appear to result from a failure of the State in which the plan or permit program applies to enforce the plan or permit program effectively, the Administrator shall so notify the State. In the case of a permit program, the notice shall be made in accordance with title V. If the Administrator finds such failure extends beyond the 30th day after such notice (90 days in the case of such permit program), the Administrator shall give public notice of such finding. During the period beginning with such public notice and ending when such State satisfies the Administrator that it will enforce such plan or permit program (hereafter referred to in this section as "period of federally assumed enforcement"), the Administrator may enforce any requirement or prohibition of such plan or permit program with respect to any person by —

(A) issuing an order requiring such person to comply with such requirement or prohibition,

(B) issuing an administrative penalty order in accordance with subsection (d), or

(C) bringing a civil action in accordance with subsection (b).

(3) EPA enforcement of other requirements — Except for a requirement or prohibition enforceable under the preceding provisions of this subsection, whenever, on the basis of any information available to the Administrator, the Administrator finds that any person has violated, or is in violation of, any other requirement or prohibition of this title, section 7603 of this title, subchapter IV-A, subchapter V, or subchapter VI, of this chapter, including, but not limited to, a requirement or prohibition of any rule, plan, order, waiver, or permit promulgated, issued, or approved under those provisions or titles, or for the payment of any fee owed to the United States under this Act (other than subchapter II of this chapter), the Administrator may —

(A) issue an administrative penalty order in accordance with subsection (d),

(B) issue an order requiring such person to comply with such requirement or prohibition,

(C) bring a civil action in accordance with subsection (b) or section 305, or

(D) request the Attorney General to commence a criminal action in accordance with subsection (c).

(4) Requirements for orders — An order issued under this subsection (other than an order relating to a violation of section 7412 of this title) shall not take effect until the person to whom it is issued has had an opportunity to confer with the Administrator concerning the alleged violation. A copy of any order issued under this subsection shall be sent to the State air pollution control agency of any State

in which the violation occurs. Any order issued under this subsection shall state with reasonable specificity the nature of the violation and specify a time for compliance which the Administrator determines is reasonable, taking into account the seriousness of the violation and any good faith efforts to comply with applicable requirements. In any case in which an order under this subsection (or notice to a violator under paragraph (1)) is issued to a corporation, a copy of such order (or notice) shall be issued to appropriate corporate officers. An order issued under this subsection shall require the person to whom it was issued to comply with the requirement as expeditiously as practicable, but in no event longer than one year after the date the order was issued, and shall be nonrenewable. No order issued under this subsection shall prevent the State or the Administrator from assessing any penalties nor otherwise affect or limit the State's or the United States authority to enforce under other provisions of this Act, nor affect any person's obligations to comply with any section of this Act or with a term or condition of any permit or applicable implementation plan promulgated or approved under this Act.

(5) Failure to comply with new source requirements — Whenever, on the basis of any available information, the Administrator finds that a State is not acting in compliance with any requirement or prohibition of the Act relating to the construction of new sources or the modification of existing sources, the Administrator may —

(A) issue an order prohibiting the construction or modification of any major stationary source in any area to which such requirement applies;

(B) issue an administrative penalty order in accordance with subsection (d); or

(C) bring a civil action under subsection (b).

Nothing in this subsection shall preclude the United States from commencing a criminal action under section 113(c) at any time for any such violation.

(b) Civil judicial enforcement — The Administrator shall, as appropriate, in the case of any person that is the owner or operator of an affected source, a major emitting facility, or a major stationary source, and may, in the case of any other person, commence a civil action for a permanent or temporary injunction, or to assess and recover a civil penalty of not more than $25,000 per day for each violation, or both, in any of the following instances:

(1) Whenever such person has violated, or is in violation of, any requirement or prohibition of an applicable implementation plan or permit. Such an action shall be commenced (A) during any period of federally assumed enforcement, or (B) more than 30 days following the date of the Administrator's notification under subsection (a)(1) that such person has violated, or is in violation of, such requirement or prohibition.

(2) Whenever such person has violated, or is in violation of, any other requirement or prohibition of this title, section 303 of title III, title IV, title V, or title VI, including, but not limited to, a requirement or prohibition of any rule, order, waiver or permit promulgated, issued, or approved under this Act, or for the payment of any fee owed the United States under this Act (other than title II).

(3) Whenever such person attempts to construct or modify a major stationary source in any area with respect to which a finding under subsection (a)(5) has been made.

Any action under this subsection may be brought in the district court of the United States for the district in which the violation is alleged to have occurred, or is occurring, or in which the defendant resides, or where the defendant's principal place of business is located, and such court shall have jurisdiction to restrain such violation, to require compliance, to assess such civil penalty, to collect any fees owed the United States under this Act (other than title II) and any noncompliance assessment and nonpayment penalty owed under section 120, and to award any other appropriate relief. Notice of the commencement of such action shall be given to the appropriate State air pollution control agency. In the case of any action brought by the Administrator under this subsection, the court may award costs of litigation (including reasonable attorney and expert witness fees) to the party or parties against whom such action was brought if the court finds that such action was unreasonable.

(c) Criminal penalties

(1) Any person who knowingly violates any requirement or prohibition of an applicable implementation plan (during any period of federally assumed enforcement or more than 30 days after having been notified under subsection (a)(1) by the Administrator that such person is violating such requirement or prohibition), any order under subsection (a) of this section, requirement or prohibition of section 111(e) of this title (relating to new source performance standards), section 112 of this title, section 114 of this title (relating to inspections, etc.), section 129 of this title (relating to solid waste combustion), section 165(a) of this title (relating to preconstruction requirements), an order under section 167 of this title (relating to preconstruction requirements), an order under section 303 of title III (relating to emergency orders), section 502(a) or 503(c) of title V (relating to permits), or any requirement or prohibition of title IV (relating to acid deposition control), or title VI (relating to stratospheric ozone control), including a requirement of any rule, order, waiver, or permit promulgated or approved under such sections or titles, and including any requirement for the payment of any fee owed the United States under this Act (other than title II) shall, upon conviction, be punished by a fine pursuant to Title 18 of the

United States Code, or by imprisonment for not to exceed 5 years, or both. If a conviction of any person under this paragraph is for a violation committed after a first conviction of such person under this paragraph, the maximum punishment shall be doubled with respect to both the fine and imprisonment.

(2) Any person who knowingly —

    (A) makes any false material statement, representation, or certification in, or omits material information from, or knowingly alters, conceals, or fails to file or maintain any notice, application, record, report, plan, or other document required pursuant to this Act to be either filed or maintained (whether with respect to the requirements imposed by the Administrator or by a State);

    (B) fails to notify or report as required under this Act; or

    (C) falsifies, tampers with, renders inaccurate, or fails to install any monitoring device or method required to be maintained or followed under this Act

shall, upon conviction, be punished by a fine pursuant to title 18 of the United States Code, or by imprisonment for not more than 2 years, or both. If a conviction of any person under this paragraph is for a violation committed after a first conviction of such person under this paragraph, the maximum punishment shall be doubled with respect to both the fine and imprisonment.

(3) Any person who knowingly fails to pay any fee owed the United States under this subchapter, subchapter III, IV-A, V, or VI of this chapter shall, upon conviction, be punished by a fine pursuant to Title 18 of the United States Code, or by imprisonment for not more than 1 year, or both. If a conviction of any person under this paragraph is for a violation committed after a first conviction of such person under this paragraph, the maximum punishment shall be doubled with respect to both the fine and imprisonment.

(4) Any person who negligently releases into the ambient air any hazardous air pollutant listed pursuant to section 7412 of this title or any extremely hazardous substance listed pursuant to section 11002(a)(2) of this title that is not listed in section 7412 of this title, and who at the time negligently places another person in imminent danger of death or serious bodily injury shall, upon conviction, be punished by a fine under title 18 of the United States Code, or by imprisonment for not more than 1 year, or both. If a conviction of any person under this paragraph is for a violation committed after a first conviction of such person under this paragraph, the maximum punishment shall be doubled with respect to both the fine and imprisonment.

(5)(A) Any person who knowingly releases into the ambient air any hazardous air pollutant listed pursuant to section 7412 of this title or any extremely hazardous substance listed pursuant to section 11002(a)(2) of this title that is not listed in section 7412 of this title, and who knows at the time that he thereby places another person in imminent danger of death or serious bodily injury shall, upon conviction, be punished by a fine under Title 18 of the United States Code, or by imprisonment of not more than 15 years, or both. Any person committing such violation which is an organization shall, upon conviction under this paragraph, be subject to a fine of not more than $1,000,000 for each violation. If a conviction of any person under this paragraph is for a violation committed after a first conviction of such person under this paragraph, the maximum punishment shall be doubled with respect to both the fine and imprisonment. For any air pollutant for which the Administrator has set an emissions standard or for any source for which a permit has been issued under subchapter V of this chapter, a release of such pollutant in accordance with that standard or permit shall not constitute a violation of this paragraph or paragraph (4).

(B) In determining whether a defendant who is an individual knew that the violation placed another person in imminent danger of death or serious bodily injury —

(i) the defendant is responsible only for actual awareness or actual belief possessed; and

(ii) knowledge possessed by a person other than the defendant, but not by the defendant, may not be attributed to the defendant; except that in proving a defendant's possession of actual knowledge, circumstantial evidence may be used, including evidence that the defendant took affirmative steps to be shielded from relevant information.

(C) It is an affirmative defense to a prosecution that the conduct charged was freely consented to by the person endangered and that the danger and conduct charged were reasonably foreseeable hazards of —

(i) an occupation, a business, or a profession; or

(ii) medical treatment or medical or scientific experimentation conducted by professionally approved methods and such other person had been made aware of the risks involved prior to giving consent.

The defendant may establish an affirmative defense under this subparagraph by a preponderance of the evidence.

(D) All general defenses, affirmative defenses, and bars to prosecution that may apply with respect to other Federal criminal offenses may apply under subparagraph (A) of this paragraph and shall be determined by the courts of the United States according to the principles of common law as they may be interpreted in the light of reason and experience. Concepts of justification and excuse applicable under this section may be developed in the light of reason and experience.

(E) The term "organization" means a legal entity, other than a government, established or organized for any purpose, and such term includes a corporation, company, association, firm, partnership, joint stock company, foundation, institution, trust, society, union, or any other association of persons.

(F) The term "serious bodily injury" means bodily injury which involves a substantial risk of death, unconsciousness, extreme physical pain, protracted and obvious disfigurement or protracted loss or impairment of the function of a bodily member, organ, or mental faculty.

(6) For the purpose of this subsection, the term "person" includes, in addition to the entities referred to in section 7602(e), of this title any responsible corporate officer.

(d) Administrative assessment of civil penalties

(1) The Administrator may issue an administrative order against any person assessing a civil administrative penalty of up to $25,000, per day of violation, whenever, on the basis of any available information, the Administrator finds that such person —

(A) has violated or is violating any requirement or prohibition of an applicable implementation plan (such order shall be issued (i) during any period of federally assumed enforcement, or (ii) more than thirty days following the date of the Administrator's notification under subsection (a)(1) of this section of a finding that such person has violated or is violating such requirement or prohibition); or

(B) has violated or is violating any other requirement or prohibition of this subchapter or subchapter III, IV-A, V, or VI of this chapter, including, but not limited to, a requirement or prohibition of any rule, order, waiver, permit, or plan promulgated, issued, or approved under this Act, or for the payment of any fee owed the United States under this Act (other than subchapter II of this chapter); or

(C) attempts to construct or modify a major stationary source in any area with respect to which a finding under subsection (a)(5) of this section has been made.

The Administrator's authority under this paragraph shall be limited to matters where the total penalty sought does not exceed $200,000 and the first alleged date of violation occurred no more than 12 months prior to the initiation of the administrative action, except where the Administrator and the Attorney General jointly determine that a matter involving a larger penalty amount or longer period of violation is appropriate for administrative penalty action. Any such determination by the Administrator and the Attorney General shall not be subject to judicial review.

(2)(A) An administrative penalty assessed under paragraph (1) shall be assessed by the Administrator by an order made after opportunity for a hearing on the record in accordance with sections 554 and 556 of Title 5 of the United States Code. The Administrator shall issue reasonable rules for discovery and other procedures for hearings under this paragraph. Before issuing such an order, the Administrator shall give written notice to the person to be assessed an administrative penalty of the Administrator's proposal to issue such order and provide such person an opportunity to request such a hearing on the order, within 30 days of the date the notice is received by such person.

(B) The Administrator may compromise, modify, or remit, with or without conditions, any administrative penalty which may be imposed under this subsection.

(3) The Administrator may implement, after consultation with the Attorney General and the States, a field citation program through regulations establishing appropriate minor violations for which field citations assessing civil penalties not to exceed $5,000 per day of violation may be issued by officers or employees designated by the Administrator. Any person to whom a field citation is assessed may, within a reasonable time as prescribed by the Administrator through regulation, elect to pay the penalty assessment or to request a hearing on the field citation. If a request for a hearing is not made within the time specified in the regulation, the penalty assessment in the field citation shall be final. Such hearing shall not be subject to section 554 or 556 of Title 5 of the United States Code, but shall provide a reasonable opportunity to be heard and to present evidence. Payment of a civil penalty required by a field citation shall not be a defense to further enforcement by the United States or a State to correct a violation, or to assess the statutory maximum penalty pursuant to other authorities in the Act, if the violation continues.

(4) Any person against whom a civil penalty is assessed under paragraph (3) of this subsection or to whom an administrative penalty order is issued under paragraph (1) of this subsection may seek review of such assessment in the United States District Court for the District of Columbia or for the district in which the violation is alleged to have occurred, in which such person resides, or where such person's principal place of business is located, by filing in such court within 30 days following the date the administrative penalty order becomes final under paragraph (2), the assessment becomes final under paragraph (3), or a final decision following a hearing under paragraph (3) is rendered, and by simultaneously sending a copy of the filing by certified mail to the Administrator and the Attorney General. Within 30 days thereafter, the Administrator shall file in such court a certified copy, or certified index, as appropriate, of the record on which the administrative penalty order or assessment was issued. Such court shall not set aside or remand such order or assessment unless there is not substantial evidence in the record, taken as a whole, to support the finding of a violation or unless the order or penalty assessment constitutes an abuse of discretion. Such order or penalty assessment shall not be subject to review by any court except as provided in this paragraph. In any such proceedings, the United States may seek to recover civil penalties ordered or assessed under this section.

(5) If any person fails to pay an assessment of a civil penalty or fails to comply with an administrative penalty order —

(A) after the order or assessment has become final, or

(B) after a court in an action brought under paragraph (4) has entered final judgment in favor of the Administrator,

the Administrator shall request the Attorney General to bring a civil action in an appropriate district court to enforce the order or to recover the amount ordered or assessed (plus interest at rates established pursuant to section 6621(a)(2) of Title 26 from the date of the final order or decision or the date of the final judgment, as the case may be). In such an action, the validity, amount, and appropriateness of such order or assessment shall not be subject to review. Any person who fails to pay on a timely basis a civil penalty ordered or assessed under this section shall be required to pay, in addition to such penalty and interest, the United States enforcement expenses, including but not limited to attorneys fees and costs incurred by the United States for collection proceedings and a quarterly nonpayment penalty for each quarter during which such failure to pay persists. Such nonpayment penalty shall be 10 percent of the aggregate amount of such person's outstanding penalties and nonpayment penalties accrued as of the beginning of such quarter.

(e) Penalty assessment criteria

(1) In determining the amount of any penalty to be assessed under this section or section 304(a), the Administrator or the court, as appropriate, shall take into consideration (in addition to such other factors as justice may require) the size of the business, the economic impact of the penalty on the business, the violator's full compliance history and good faith efforts to comply, the duration of the violation as established by any credible evidence (including evidence other than the applicable test method), payment by the violator of penalties previously assessed for the same violation, the economic benefit of noncompliance, and the seriousness of the violation. The court shall not assess penalties for noncompliance with administrative subpoenas under section 307(a), or actions

under section 114 of this Act, where the violator had sufficient cause to violate or fail or refuse to comply with such subpoena or action.

(2) A penalty may be assessed for each day of violation. For purposes of determining the number of days of violation for which a penalty may be assessed under subsection (b) or (d)(1) of this section, or section 7604(a) of this title, or an assessment may be made under section 7420, where the Administrator or an air pollution control agency has notified the source of the violation, and the plaintiff makes a prima facie showing that the conduct or events giving rise to the violation are likely to have continued or recurred past the date of notice, the days of violation shall be presumed to include the date of such notice and each and every day thereafter until the violator establishes that continuous compliance has been achieved, except to the extent that the violator can prove by a preponderance of the evidence that there were intervening days during which no violation occurred or that the violation was not continuing in nature.

(f) **Awards** — The Administrator may pay an award, not to exceed $10,000, to any person who furnishes information or services which lead to a criminal conviction or a judicial or administrative civil penalty for any violation of this title or title III, IV, V, or VI of this Act enforced under this section. Such payment is subject to available appropriations for such purposes as provided in annual appropriation Acts. Any officer, or employee of the United States or any State or local government who furnishes information or renders service in the performance of an official duty is ineligible for payment under this subsection. The Administrator may, by regulation, prescribe additional criteria for eligibility for such an award.

(g) **Settlements; public participation** — At least 30 days before a consent order or settlement agreement of any kind under this Act to which the United States is a party (other than enforcement actions under this section, section 7420 of this title, or subchapter II of this chapter, whether or not involving civil or criminal penalties, or judgments subject to Department of Justice policy on public participation) is final or filed with a court, the Administrator shall provide a reasonable opportunity by notice in the Federal Register to persons who are not named as parties or intervenors to the action or matter to comment in writing. The Administrator or the Attorney General, as appropriate, shall promptly consider any such written comments and may withdraw or withhold his consent to the proposed order or agreement if the comments disclose facts or considerations which indicate that such consent is inappropriate, improper, inadequate, or inconsistent with the requirements of this Act. Nothing in this subsection shall apply to civil or criminal penalties under this Act.

(h) **Operator** — For purposes of the provisions of this section and section 7420, the term "opera-tor", as used in such provisions, shall include any person who is senior management personnel or a corporate officer. Except in the case of knowing and willful violations, such term shall not include any person who is a stationary engineer or technician responsible for the operation, maintenance, repair, or monitoring of equipment and facilities and who often has supervisory and training duties but who is not senior management personnel or a corporate officer. Except in the case of knowing and willful violations, for purposes of subsection (c)(4) of this section, the term "a person" shall not include an employee who is carrying out his normal activities and who is not a part of senior management personnel or a corporate officer. Except in the case of knowing and willful violations, for purposes of paragraphs (1), (2), (3), and (5) of subsection (c) of this section the term "a person" shall not include an employee who is carrying out his normal activities and who is acting under orders from the employer.

§7414. Recordkeeping, inspections, monitoring, and entry

[CAA §114]

(a) **Authority of Administrator or authorized representative** — For the purpose (i) of developing or assisting in the development of any implementation plan under section 7410 or 7411(d) of this title, any standard of performance under section 7411 of this title, or any emission standard under section 7412 of this title, or any regulation of solid waste combustion under section 7429 of this title, or any regulation under section 7429 of this title (relating to solid waste combustion), (ii) of determining whether any person is in violation of any such standard or any requirement of such a plan, or (iii) carrying out any provision of this Act (except a provision of subchapter II of this chapter with respect to a manufacturer of new motor vehicles or new motor vehicle engines) —

(1) the Administrator may require any person who owns or operates any emission source, who manufactures emission control equipment or process equipment, who the Administrator believes may have information necessary for the purposes set forth in this subsection, or who is subject to any requirement of this Act (other than a manufacturer subject to the provisions of section 7525(c) or 7542 of this title with respect to a provision of subchapter II of this chapter) on a one-time, periodic or continuous basis to —

(A) establish and maintain such records;

(B) make such reports;

(C) install, use, and maintain such monitoring equipment, and use such audit procedures, or methods;

(D) sample such emissions (in accordance with such procedures or methods, at such locations, at such intervals, during such periods and in such manner as the Administrator shall prescribe);

(E) keep records on control equipment parameters, production variables or other indirect data when direct monitoring of emissions is impractical;

(F) submit compliance certifications in accordance with section 114(a)(3); and

(G) provide such other information as the Administrator may reasonably require; and

(2) the Administrator or his authorized representative, upon presentation of his credentials —

(A) shall have a right of entry to, upon, or through any premises of such person or in which any records required to be maintained under paragraph (1) of this section are located, and

(B) may at reasonable times have access to and copy any records, inspect any monitoring equipment and method required under paragraph (1), and sample any emissions which such person is required to sample under paragraph (1).

(3) The Administrator shall in the case of any person which is the owner or operator of a major stationary source, and may, in the case of any other person, require enhanced monitoring and submission of compliance certifications. Compliance certifications shall include (A) identification of the applicable requirement that is the basis of the certification, (B) the method used for determining the compliance status of the source, (C) the compliance status, (D) whether compliance is continuous or intermittent, (E) such other facts as the Administrator may require. Compliance certifications and monitoring data shall be subject to subsection (c) of this section. Submission of a compliance certification shall in no way limit the Administrator's authorities to investigate or otherwise implement this Act. The Administrator shall promulgate rules to provide guidance and to implement this paragraph within 2 years after November 15, 1990.

(b) State enforcement

(1) Each State may develop and submit to the Administrator a procedure for carrying out this section in such State. If the Administrator finds the State procedure is adequate, he may delegate to such State any authority he has to carry out this section.

(2) Nothing in this subsection shall prohibit the Administrator from carrying out this section in a State.

(c) Availability of records, reports, and information to public; disclosure of trade secrets

— Any records, reports, or information obtained under subsection (a) shall be available to the public, except that upon a showing satisfactory to the Administrator by any person that records, reports, or information, or particular part thereof (other than emission data), to which the Administrator has access under this section if made public, would divulge methods or processes entitled to protection as trade secrets of such person, the Administrator shall consider such record, report, or information or particular portion thereof confidential in accordance with the purposes of section 1905 of Title 18 of the United States Code, except that such record, report, or information may be disclosed to other officers, employees, or authorized representatives of the United States concerned with carrying out this Act or when relevant in any proceeding under this Act.

(d) Notice of proposed entry, inspection, or monitoring

(1) In the case of any emission standard or limitation or other requirement which is adopted by a State, as part of an applicable implementation plan or as part of an order under section 7413(d), of this title, before carrying out an entry, inspection, or monitoring under paragraph (2) of subsection (a) of this section with respect to such standard, limitation, or other requirement, the Administrator (or his representatives) shall provide the State air pollution control agency with reasonable prior notice of such action, indicating the purpose of such action. No State agency which receives notice under this paragraph of an action proposed to be taken may use the information contained in the notice to inform the person whose property is proposed to be affected of the proposed action. If the Administrator has reasonable basis for believing that a State agency is so using or will so use such information, notice to the agency under this paragraph is not required until such time as the Administrator determines the agency will no longer so use information contained in a notice under this paragraph. Nothing in this section shall be construed to require notification to any State agency of any action taken by the Administrator with respect to any standard, limitation, or other requirement which is not part of an applicable implementation plan or which was promulgated by the Administrator under section 7410(c) of this title.

(2) Nothing in paragraph (1) shall be construed to provide that any failure of the Administrator to comply with the requirements of such paragraph shall be a defense in any enforcement action brought by the Administrator or shall make inadmissible as evidence in any such action any information or material obtained notwithstanding such failure to comply with such requirements.

§7415. International air pollution
[CAA §115]

(a) **Endangerment of public health or welfare in foreign countries from pollution emitted in United States** — Whenever the Administrator, upon receipt of reports, surveys or studies from any duly constituted international agency has reason to believe that any air pollutant or pollutants emitted in the United States cause or contribute to air pollution which may reasonably be anticipated to endanger public health or welfare in a foreign country or whenever the Secretary of State requests him to do so with respect to such pollution which the Secretary of State alleges is of such a nature, the Administrator shall give formal notification thereof to the Governor of the State in which such emissions originate.

(b) Prevention or elimination of endangerment — The notice of the Administrator shall be deemed to be a finding under section 7410(a)(2)(H)(ii) of this title which requires a plan revision with respect to so much of the applicable implementation plan as is inadequate to prevent or eliminate the endangerment referred to in subsection (a). Any foreign country so affected by such emission of pollutant or pollutants shall be invited to appear at any public hearing associated with any revision of the appropriate portion of the applicable implementation plan.

(c) Reciprocity — This section shall apply only to a foreign country which the Administrator determines has given the United States essentially the same rights with respect to the prevention or control of air pollution occurring in that country as is given that country by this section.

(d) Recommendations — Recommendations issued following any abatement conference conducted prior to August 7, 1977, shall remain in effect with respect to any pollutant for which no national ambient air quality standard has been established under section 7409 of this title unless the Administrator, after consultation with all agencies which were party to the conference, rescinds any such recommendation on grounds of obsolescence.

§7416. Retention of State authority
[CAA §116]

Except as otherwise provided in sections 1857c-10(c), (e), and (f) (as in effect before August 7, 1977), 7543, 7545(c)(4) and 7573 of this title (preempting certain State regulation of moving sources) nothing in this Act shall preclude or deny the right of any State or political subdivision thereof to adopt or enforce (1) any standard or limitation respecting emissions of air pollutants or (2) any requirement respecting control or abatement of air pollution; except that if an emission standard or limitation is in effect under an applicable implementation plan or under section 7411 or section 7412 of this title, such State or political subdivision may not adopt or enforce any emission standard or limitation which is less stringent than the standard or limitation under such plan or section.

§7417. Advisory committees
[CAA 117]

(a) Establishment; membership — In order to obtain assistance in the development and implementation of the purposes of this chapter including air quality criteria, recommended control techniques, standards, research and development, and to encourage the continued efforts on the part of industry to improve air quality and to develop economically feasible methods for the control and abatement of air pollution, the Administrator shall from time to time establish advisory committees. Committee members shall include, but not be limited to, persons who are knowledgeable concerning air quality from the standpoint of health, welfare, economics, or technology.

(b) Compensation — The members of any other advisory committees appointed pursuant to this Act who are not officers or employees of the United States while attending conferences or meetings or while otherwise serving at the request of the Administrator, shall be entitled to receive compensation at a rate to be fixed by the Administrator, but not exceeding $100 per diem, including travel time, and while away from their homes or regular places of business they may be allowed travel expenses, including per diem in lieu of subsistence, as authorized by section 5703 of Title 5 of the United States Code for persons in the Government service employed intermittently.

(c) Consultations by Administrator — Prior to —

    (1) issuing criteria for an air pollutant under section 7408(a)(2) of this title,

    (2) publishing any list under section 7411(b)(1)(A) or 7412(b)(1)(A) of this title,

    (3) publishing any standard under section 7411 or section 7412 of this title, or

    (4) publishing any regulation under section 7521(a) of this title,

the Administrator shall, to the maximum extent practicable within the time provided, consult with appropriate advisory committees, independent experts, and Federal departments and agencies.

§7418. Control of pollution from Federal facilities
[CAA §118]

(a) General compliance — Each department, agency, and instrumentality of executive, legislative, and judicial branches of the Federal Government (1) having jurisdiction over any property or facility, or (2) engaged in any activity resulting, or which may result, in the discharge of air pollutants, and each officer, agent, or employee thereof, shall be subject to, and comply with, all Federal, State, interstate, and local requirements, administrative authority, and process and sanctions respecting the control and abatement of air pollution in the same manner, and to the same extent as any nongovernmental entity. The preceding sentence shall apply (A) to any requirement whether substantive or procedural (including any record keeping or reporting requirement, any requirement respecting permits and any other requirement whatsoever), (B) to any requirement to pay a fee or charge imposed by any State or local agency to defray the costs of its air pollution regulatory program, (C) to the exercise of any Federal, State, or local administrative authority, and (D) to any process and sanction, whether enforced in Federal, State, or local courts, or in any other manner. This subsection shall apply notwithstanding any immunity of such agencies, officers, agents, or employees under any law or rule of law. No officer, agent, or employee of the United States shall be personally liable for any civil penalty for which he is not otherwise liable.

(b) Exemption — The President, may exempt any emission source of any department, agency, or instrumentality in the executive branch from compliance with such a requirement if he determines it to be in the paramount interest of the United States to do so, except that no exemption may be granted from section 7411 of this title, and an exemption from section 7412 of this title may be granted only in accordance with section 7412(i)(4) of this title. No such exemption shall be granted due to lack of appropriation unless the President shall have specifically requested such appropriation as a part of the budgetary process and the Congress shall have failed to make available such requested appropriation. Any exemption shall be for a period not in excess of one year, but additional exemptions may be granted for periods of not to exceed one year upon the President's making a new determination. In addition to any such exemption of a particular emission source, the President may, if he determines it to be in the paramount interest of the United States to do so, issue regulations exempting from compliance with the requirements of this section any weaponry, equipment, aircraft, vehicles, or other classes or categories of property which are owned or operated by the Armed Forces of the United States (including the Coast Guard) or by the National Guard of any State and which are uniquely military in nature. The President shall reconsider the need for such regulations at three-year intervals. The President shall report each January to the Congress all exemptions from the requirements of this section granted during the preceding calendar year, together with his reason for granting each such exemption.

(c) Government vehicles — Each department, agency, and instrumentality of executive, legislative, and judicial branches of the Federal Government shall comply with all applicable provisions of a valid inspection and maintenance program established under the provisions of subpart 2 of part D of this subchapter or subpart 3 of part D of this subchapter except for such vehicles that are considered military tactical vehicles.

(d) Vehicles operated on Federal installations — Each department, agency, and instrumentality of executive, legislative, and judicial branches of the Federal Government having jurisdiction over any property or facility shall require all employees which operate motor vehicles on the property or facility to furnish proof of compliance with the applicable requirements of any vehicle inspection and maintenance program established under the provisions of subpart 2 of part D of this subchapter or subpart 3 of part D of this subchapter for the State in which such property or facility is located (without regard to whether such vehicles are registered in the State). The installation shall use one of the following methods to establish proof of compliance —

(1) presentation by the vehicle owner of a valid certificate of compliance from the vehicle inspection and maintenance program;

(2) presentation by the vehicle owner of proof of vehicle registration within the geographic area covered by the vehicle inspection and maintenance program (except for any program whose enforcement mechanism is not through the denial of vehicle registration);

(3) another method approved by the vehicle inspection and maintenance program administrator.

§7419. Primary nonferrous smelter orders
[CAA §119]
(a) Issuance; hearing; enforcement orders; statement of grounds for application; findings

(1) Upon application by the owner or operator of a primary nonferrous smelter, a primary nonferrous smelter order under subsection (b) may be issued —

(A) by the Administrator, after thirty days' notice to the State, or

(B) by the State in which such source is located, but no such order issued by the State shall take effect until the Administrator determines that such order has been issued in accordance with the requirements of this chapter.

Not later than ninety days after submission by the State to the Administrator of notice of the issuance of a primary nonferrous smelter order under this section, the Administrator shall determine whether or not such order has been issued by the State in accordance with the requirements of this Act. If the Administrator determines that such order has not been issued in accordance with such requirements, he shall conduct a hearing respecting the reasonably available control technology for primary nonferrous smelters.

(2)(A) An order issued under this section to a primary nonferrous smelter shall be referred to as a "primary nonferrous smelter order". No primary nonferrous smelter may receive both an enforcement order under section 7413(d) of this title and a primary nonferrous smelter order under this section.

(B) Before any hearing conducted under this section, in the case of an application made by the owner or operator of a primary nonferrous smelter for a second order under this section, the applicant shall furnish the Administrator (or the State as the case may be) with a statement of the grounds on which such application is based (including all supporting documents and information). The statement of the grounds for the proposed order shall be provided by the Administrator or the State in any case in which such State or Administrator is acting on its own initiative. Such statement (including such documents and information) shall be made available to the public for a thirty-day period before such hearing and shall be considered as part of such hearing. No primary nonferrous smelter order may be granted unless the applicant establishes that he meets the conditions required for the issuance of such order (or the Administrator or State establishes the meeting of such conditions when acting on their own initiative).

(C) Any decision with respect to the issuance of a primary nonferrous smelter order shall be accompanied by a concise statement of the findings and of the basis of such findings.

(3) For the purposes of section 7410, 7604, and 7607 of this title, any order issued by the State and in effect pursuant to this subsection shall become part of the applicable implementation plan.

(b) Prerequisites to issuance of orders — A primary nonferrous smelter order under this section may be issued to a primary nonferrous smelter if —

(1) such smelter is in existence on August 7, 1977;

(2) the requirement of the applicable implementation plan with respect to which the order is issued is an emission limitation or standard for sulfur oxides which is necessary and intended to be itself sufficient to enable attainment and maintenance of national primary and secondary ambient air quality standards for sulfur oxides; and

(3) such smelter is unable to comply with such requirement by the applicable date for compliance because no means of emission limitation applicable to such smelter which will enable it to achieve compliance with such requirement has been adequately demonstrated to be reasonably available (as determined by the Administrator, taking into account the cost of compliance, non-air quality health and environmental impact, and energy consideration).

(c) Second orders

(1) A second order issued to a smelter under this section shall set forth compliance schedules containing increments of progress which require compliance with the requirement postponed as expeditiously as practicable. The increments of progress shall be limited to requiring compliance with subsection (d) and, in the case of a second order, to procuring, installing, and operating the necessary means of emission limitation as expeditiously as practicable after the Administrator determines such means have been adequately demonstrated to be reasonably available within the meaning of subsection (b)(3) of this section.

(2) Not in excess of two primary nonferrous smelter orders may be issued under this section to any primary nonferrous smelter. The first such order issued to a smelter shall not result in the postponement of the requirement with respect to which such order is issued beyond January 1, 1983. The second such order shall not result in

the postponement of such requirement beyond January 1, 1988.

(d) Interim measures; continuous emission reduction technology

(1)(A) Each primary nonferrous smelter to which an order is issued under this section shall be required to use such interim measures for the period during which such order is in effect as may be necessary in the judgment of the Administrator to assure attainment and maintenance of the national primary and secondary ambient air quality standards during such period, taking into account the aggregate effect on air quality of such order together with all variances, extensions, waivers, enforcement orders, delayed compliance orders and primary nonferrous smelter orders previously issued under this chapter.

(B) Such interim requirements shall include —

(i) a requirement that the source to which the order applies comply with such reporting requirements and conduct such monitoring as the Administrator determines may be necessary, and

(ii) such measures as the Administrator determines are necessary to avoid an imminent and substantial endangerment to health of persons.

(C) Such interim measures shall also, except as provided in paragraph (2), include continuous emission reduction technology. The Administrator shall condition the use of any such interim measures upon the agreement of the owner or operator of the smelter —

(i) to comply with such conditions as the Administrator determines are necessary to maximize the reliability and enforceability of such interim measures, as applied to the smelter, in attaining and maintaining the national ambient air quality standards to which the order relates, and

(ii) to commit reasonable resources to research and development of appropriate emission control technology.

(2) The requirement of paragraph (1) for the use of continuous emission reduction technology may be waived with respect to a particular smelter by the State or the Administrator, after notice and a hearing on the record, and upon a showing by the owner or operator of the smelter that such requirement would be so costly as to necessitate permanent or prolonged temporary cessation of operations of the smelter. Upon application for such waiver, the Administrator shall be notified and shall, within ninety days, hold a hearing on the record in accordance with section 554 of Title 5 of the United States Code. At such hearing the Administrator shall require the smelter involved to present information relating to any alleged cessation of operations and the detailed reasons or

justifications therefor. On the basis of such hearing the Administrator shall make findings of fact as to the effect of such requirement and on the alleged cessation of operations and shall make such recommendations as he deems appropriate. Such report, findings, and recommendations shall be available to the public, and shall be taken into account by the State or the Administrator in making the decision whether or not to grant such waiver.

(3) In order to obtain information for purposes of a waiver under paragraph (2), the Administrator may, on his own motion, conduct an investigation and use the authority of section 7621 of this title.

(4) In the case of any smelter which on August 7, 1977, uses continuous emission reduction technology and supplemental controls and which receives an initial primary nonferrous smelter order under this section, no additional continuous emission reduction technology shall be required as a condition of such order unless the Administrator determines, at any time, after notice and public hearing, that such additional continuous emission reduction technology is adequately demonstrated to be reasonably available for the primary nonferrous smelter industry.

(e) Termination of orders — At any time during which an order under this section applies, the Administration may enter upon a public hearing respecting the availability of technology. Any order under this section shall be terminated if the Administrator determines on the record, after notice and public hearing, that the conditions upon which the order was based no longer exist. If the owner or operator of the smelter to which the order is issued demonstrates that prompt termination of such order would result in undue hardship, the termination shall become effective at the earliest practicable date on which such undue hardship would not result, but in no event later than the date required under subsection (c).

(f) Violation of requirements — If the Administrator determines that a smelter to which an order is issued under this section is in violation of any requirement of subsection (c) or (d), he shall —

(1) enforce such requirement under section 113,

(2) (after notice and opportunity for public hearing) revoke such order and enforce compliance with the requirement with respect to which such order was granted,

(3) give notice of noncompliance and commence action under section 7420 of this title, or

(4) take any appropriate combination of such action.

§7420. Noncompliance penalty
[CAA §120]
(a) Assessment and collection

(1)(A) Not later than 6 months after August 7, 1977, and after notice and opportunity for a public hearing, the Administrator shall promulgate regulations requiring the assessment and collection of a noncompliance penalty against persons referred to in paragraph (2)(A).

(B)(i) Each State may develop and submit to the Administrator a plan for carrying out this section in such State. If the Administrator finds that the State plan meets the requirements of this section, he may delegate to such State any authority he has to carry out this action.

(ii) Notwithstanding a delegation to a State under clause (i), the Administrator may carry out this section in such State under the circumstances described in subsection (b)(2)(B) of this section.

(2)(A) Except as provided in subparagraph (B) or (C) of this Paragraph, the State or the Administrator shall assess and collect a noncompliance penalty against every person who owns or operates —

(i) a major stationary source (other than a primary nonferrous smelter which has received a primary nonferrous smelter order under section 7419 of this title) which is not in compliance with any emission limitation, emission standard or compliance schedule under any applicable implementation plan (whether or not such source is subject to a Federal or State consent decree), or

(ii) a stationary source which is not in compliance with an emission limitation, emission standard, standard of performance, or other requirement established under section 7411, 7477, 7603, or 7412 of this title, or

(iii) a stationary source which is not in compliance with any requirement of subchapter IV-A, V, or VI of this chapter, or

(iv) any source referred to in clause (i), (ii), or (iii) (for which an extension, order, or suspension referred to in subparagraph (B), or Federal or State consent decree is in effect), or a primary nonferrous smelter which has received a primary nonferrous smelter order under section 7419 which is not in compliance with any interim emission control requirement or schedule of compliance under such extension, order, suspension, or consent decree.

For purposes of subsection (d)(2) of this section, in the case of a penalty assessed with respect to a source referred to in clause (iii) of this subparagraph, the costs referred to in such subsection (d)(2) shall be the economic value of noncompliance with the interim emission control requirement or the remaining steps in the schedule of compliance referred to in such clause.

(B) Notwithstanding the requirements of subparagraph (A)(i) and (ii), the owner or operator of any source shall be exempted from the duty to pay a noncompliance penalty under such requirements with respect to that source if, in accordance with the procedures in subsection (b)(5) of this section, the owner or operator demonstrates that the failure of such source to comply with any such requirement is due solely to —

    (i) a conversion by such source from the burning of petroleum products or natural gas, or both, as the permanent primary energy source to the burning of coal pursuant to an order under section 7413(d)(5) of this title or section 1857c-10 (as in effect before August 7, 1977);

    (ii) in the case of a coal-burning source granted an extension under the second sentence of section 1857c-10(c)(1) (as in effect before August 7, 1977), a prohibition from using petroleum products or natural gas or both, by reason of an order under the provisions of section 792(a) and (b) of Title 15 or under any legislation which amends or supersedes such provisions;

    (iii) the use of innovative technology sanctioned by an enforcement order under section 7413(d)(4) of this title;

    (iv) an inability to comply with any such requirement, for which inability the source has received an order under section 7413(d) of this title (or an order under section 7413 of this title issued before August 7, 1977) which has the effect of permitting a delay or violation of any requirement of this Act (including a requirement of an applicable implementation plan) which inability results from reasons entirely beyond the control of the owner or operator of such source or of any entity controlling, controlled by, or under common control with the owner or operator of such source; or

    (v) the conditions by reason of which a temporary emergency suspension is authorized under section 7410 (f) or (g) of this title.

An exemption under this subparagraph shall cease to be effective if the source fails to comply with the interim emission control requirements or schedules of compliance (including increments of progress) under any such extension, order, or suspension.

    (C) The Administrator may, after notice and opportunity for public hearing, exempt any source from the requirements of this section with respect to a particular instance of noncompliance if he finds that such instance of noncompliance is de minimis in nature and in duration.

  (b) Regulations — Regulations under subsection (a) shall —

    (1) permit the assessment and collection of such penalty by the State if the State has a delegation of authority in effect under subsection (a)(1)(B)(i) of this section;

    (2) provide for the assessment and collection of such penalty by the Administrator, if —

      (A) the State does not have a delegation of authority in effect under subsection (a)(1)(B)(i) of this section, or

      (B) the State has such a delegation in effect but fails with respect to any particular person or source to assess or collect the penalty in accordance with the requirements of this section;

    (3) require the States, or in the event the States fail to do so, the Administrator, to give a brief but reasonably specific notice of noncompliance under this section to each person referred to in subsection (a)(2)(A) of this section with respect to each source owned or operated by such person which is not in compliance as provided in such subsection, not later than July 1, 1979, or thirty days after the discovery of such noncompliance, whichever is later;

    (4) require each person to whom notice is given under paragraph (3) to —

      (A) calculate the amount of the penalty owed (determined in accordance with subsection (d)(2) of this section) and the schedule of payments (determined in accordance with subsection (d)(3) of this section) for each such source and, within forty-five days after the issuance of such notice or after the denial of a petition under subparagraph (B), to submit that calculation and proposed schedule, together with the information necessary for an independent verification thereof, to the State and to the Administrator, or

      (B) submit a petition, within forty-five days after the issuance of such notice, challenging such notice of noncompliance or alleging entitlement to an exemption under subsection (a)(2)(B) of this section with respect to a particular source;

    (5) require the Administrator to provide a hearing on the record (within the meaning of subchapter II of chapter 5 of Title 5, United States Code) and to make a decision on such petition (including findings of fact and conclusions of law) not later than ninety days after the receipt of any petition under paragraph (4)(B), unless the State agrees to provide a hearing which is substantially similar to such a hearing on the record and to make a decision on such petition (including such findings and conclusions) within such ninety day period;

    (6)(A) authorize the Administrator on his own initiative to review the decision of the State under paragraph (5) and disapprove it if it is not in accordance with the requirements of this section, and (B) require the Administrator to do so not later than sixty days after receipt of a petition under this subparagraph, notice, and public hearing and a showing by such petitioner that the State decision under paragraph (5) is not in accordance with the requirements of this section;

(7) require payment, in accordance with subsection (d), of the penalty by each person to whom notice of noncompliance is given under paragraph (3) with respect to each noncomplying source for which such notice is given unless there has been a final determination granting a petition under paragraph (4)(B) with respect to such source;

(8) authorize the State or the Administrator to adjust (and from time to time to readjust) the amount of the penalty assessment calculated or the payment schedule proposed by such owner or operator under paragraph (4), if the Administrator finds after notice and opportunity for a hearing on the record that the penalty or schedule does not meet the requirements of this section; and

(9) require a final adjustment of the penalty within 180 days after such source comes into compliance in accordance with subsection (d)(4) of this section.

In any case in which the State establishes a non-compliance penalty under this section, the State shall provide notice thereof to the Administrator. A noncompliance penalty established by a State under this section shall apply unless the Administrator, within ninety days after the date of receipt of notice of the State penalty assessment under this section, objects in writing to the amount of the penalty as less than would be required to comply with guidelines established by the Administrator. If the Administrator objects, he shall immediately establish a substitute noncompliance penalty applicable to such source.

(c) Contract to assist in determining amount of penalty assessment or payment schedule —

If the owner or operator of any stationary source to whom a notice is issued under subsection (b)(3) —

(1) does not submit a timely petition under subsection (b)(4)(B) of this section, or

(2) submits a petition under subsection (b)(4)(B) of this section which is denied, and

fails to submit a calculation of the penalty assessment, a schedule for payment, and the information necessary for independent verification thereof, the State (or the Administrator, as the case may be) may enter into a contract with any person who has no financial interest in the owner or operator of the source (or in any person controlling, controlled by or under common control with such source) to assist in determining the amount of the penalty assessment or payment schedule with respect to such source. The cost of carrying out such contract may be added to the penalty to be assessed against the owner or operator of such source.

(d) Payment

(1) All penalties assessed by the Administrator under this section shall be paid to the United States Treasury. All penalties assessed by the State under this section shall be paid to such State.

(2) The amount of the penalty which shall be assessed and collected with respect to any source under this section shall be equal to —

(A) the amount determined in accordance with regulations promulgated by the Administrator under subsection (a), which is no less than the economic value which a delay in compliance beyond July 1, 1979, may have for the owner of such source, including the quarterly equivalent of the capital costs of compliance and debt service over a normal amortization period, not to exceed ten years, operation and maintenance costs foregone as a result of non-compliance, and any additional economic value which such a delay may have for the owner or operator of such source, minus

(B) the amount of any expenditure made by the owner or operator of that source during any such quarter for the purpose of bringing that source into, and maintaining compliance with, such requirement, to the extent that such expenditures have not been taken into account in the calculation of the penalty under subparagraph (A).

To the extent that any expenditure under subparagraph (B) made during any quarter is not subtracted for such quarter from the costs under subparagraph (A), such expenditure may be subtracted for any subsequent quarter from such costs. In no event shall the amount paid be less than the quarterly payment minus the amount attributed to actual cost of construction.

(3)(A) The assessed penalty required under this section shall be paid in quarterly installments for the period of covered noncompliance. All quarterly payments (determined without regard to any adjustment or any subtraction under paragraph (2)(B)) after the first payment shall be equal.

(B) The first payment shall be due on the date six months after the date of issuance of the notice of noncompliance under subsection (b)(3) of this section with respect to any source or on January 1, 1980, whichever is later. Such first payment shall be in the amount of the quarterly installment for the upcoming quarter, plus the amount owed for any preceding period within the period of covered noncompliance for such source.

(C) For the purpose of this section, the term "period of covered noncompliance" means the period which begins —

(i) two years after August 7, 1977, in the case of a source for which notice of noncompliance under subsection (b)(3) of this section is issued on or before the date two years August 7, 1977, or

(ii) on the date of issuance of the notice of noncompliance under subsection (b)(3) of this section, in the case of a source for which such notice is issued after July 1, 1979,

and ending on the date on which such source comes into (or for the purpose of establishing the schedule of payments, is estimated to come into) compliance with such requirement.

(4) Upon making a determination that a source with respect to which a penalty has been paid under this section is in compliance and is maintaining compliance with the applicable requirement, the State (or the Administrator as the case may be) shall review the actual expenditures made by the owner or operator of such source for the purpose of attaining and maintaining compliance, and shall within 180 days after such source comes into compliance —

(A) provide reimbursement with interest (to be paid by the State or Secretary of the Treasury, as the case may be) at appropriate prevailing rates (as determined by the Secretary of the Treasury) for any overpayment by such person, or

(B) assess and collect an additional payment with interest at appropriate prevailing rates (as determined by the Secretary of the Treasury) for any underpayment by such person.

(5) Any person who fails to pay the amount of any penalty with respect to any source under this section on a timely basis shall be required to pay in addition a quarterly nonpayment penalty for each quarter during which such failure to pay persists. Such nonpayment penalty shall be in an amount equal to 20 percent of the aggregate amount of such person's penalties and nonpayment penalties with respect to such source which are unpaid as of the beginning of such quarter.

(e) **Judicial review** — Any action pursuant to this section, including any objection of the Administrator under the last sentence of subsection (b), shall be considered a final action for purposes of judicial review of any penalty under section 7607 of this title.

(f) **Other orders, payments, sanctions, or requirements** — Any orders, payments, sanctions, or other requirements under this section shall be in addition to any other permits, orders, payments, sanctions, or other requirements established under this chapter, and shall in no way affect any civil or criminal enforcement proceedings brought under any provisions of this Act or State or local law.

(g) **More stringent emission limitations or other requirements** — In the case of any emission limitation or other requirement approved or promulgated by the Administrator under this chapter after August 7, 1977 which is more stringent than the emission limitation or requirement for the source in effect prior to such approval or promulgation, if any, or where there was no emission limitation or requirement approved or promulgated before August 7, 1977, the date for imposition of the non-compliance penalty under this section, shall be either July 1, 1979, or the date on which the source is required to be in full compliance with such emission limitation or requirement, whichever is later, but in no event later than three years after the approval or promulgation of such emission limitation or requirement.

§7421. Consultation
[CAA §121]

In carrying out the requirements of this chapter requiring applicable implementation plans to contain —

(1) any transportation controls, air quality maintenance plan requirements or preconstruction review of direct sources of air pollution, or

(2) any measure referred to —

(A) in part D of this subchapter (pertaining to nonattainment requirements), or

(B) in part C of this subchapter (pertaining to prevention of significant deterioration),

and in carrying out the requirements of section 7413(d) (relating to certain enforcement orders), the State shall provide a satisfactory process of consultation with general purpose local governments, designated organizations of elected officials of local governments and any Federal and manager having authority over Federal land to which the State plan applies, effective with respect to any such requirement which is adopted more than one year after August 7, 1977, as part of such plan. Such process shall be in accordance with regulations promulgated by the Administrator to assure adequate consultation. The Administrator shall update as necessary the original regulations required and promulgated under this section (as in effect immediately before November 15, 1990) to ensure adequate consultation. Only a general purpose unit of local government, regional agency, or council of governments adversely affected by action of the Administrator approving any portion of a plan referred to in this subsection may petition for judicial review of such action on the basis of a violation of the requirements of this section.

§7422. Listing of certain unregulated pollutants
[CAA §122]

(a) **Radioactive pollutants, cadmium, arsenic, and polycyclic organic matter** — Not later than one year after August 7, 1977 (two years for radioactive pollutants) and after notice and opportunity for public hearing, the Administrator shall review all available relevant information and determine whether or not emissions of radioactive pollutants (including source material, special nuclear material, and byproduct material), cadmium, arsenic and polycyclic organic matter into the ambient air will cause, or contribute to, air pollution which may reasonably be anticipated to endanger public health. If the Administrator makes an affirmative determination with respect to any such substance, he shall simultaneously with such determination include such substance in the list published under section 7408(a)(1) or 7412(b)(1)(A) of this title (in the case of a substance which, in the judgment of the Administrator, causes, or contributes to, air pollution which may reasonably be anticipated to result in an increase in mortality or an increase in serious irreversible, or incapacitating reversible, illness), or shall include each category of stationary sources emitting such substance in significant mounts in the list published under section 7411(b)(1)(A) of this title, or take any combination of such actions.

(b) Revision authority — Nothing in subsection (a) of this section shall be construed to affect the authority of the Administrator to revise any list referred to in subsection (a) of this section with respect to any substance (whether or not enumerated in subsection (a)).

(c) Consultation with Nuclear Regulatory Commission; interagency agreement; notice and hearing

(1) Before listing any source material, special nuclear, or byproduct material (or component or derivative thereof) as provided in subsection (a) of this section, the Administrator shall consult with the Nuclear Regulatory Commission.

(2) Not later than six months after listing any such material (or component or derivative thereof) the Administrator and the Nuclear Regulatory Commission shall enter into an interagency agreement with respect to those sources or facilities which are under the jurisdiction of the Commission. This agreement shall, to the maximum extent practicable consistent with this Act, minimize duplication of effort and conserve administrative resources in the establishment, implementation, and enforcement of emission limitations, standards of performance, and other requirements and authorities (substantive and procedural) under this Act respecting the emission of such material (or component or derivative thereof) from such sources or facilities.

(3) In case of any standard or emission limitation promulgated by the Administrator, under this Act or by any State (or the Administrator) under any applicable implementation plan under this Act, if the Nuclear Regulatory Commission determines, after notice and opportunity for public hearing that the application of such standard or limitation to a source or facility within the jurisdiction of the Commission would endanger public health or safety, such standard or limitation shall not apply to such facilities or sources unless the President determines otherwise within ninety days from the date of such finding.

§7423. Stack heights
[CAA §123]

(a) Heights in excess of good engineering practice; other dispersion techniques — The degree of emission limitation required for control of any air pollutant under an applicable implementation plan under this title shall not be affected in any manner by —

(1) so much of the stack height of any source as exceeds good engineering practice (as determined under regulations promulgated by the Administrator), or

(2) any other dispersion technique.

The preceding sentence shall not apply with respect to stack heights in existence before December 31, 1970, or dispersion techniques implemented before such date. In establishing an emission limitation for coal-fired steam electric generating units which are subject to the provisions of section 7418 of this title and which commenced operation before July 1, 1957, the effect of the entire stack height of stacks for which a construction contract was awarded before February 8, 1974, may be taken into account.

(b) Dispersion technique — For the purpose of this section, the term "dispersion technique" includes any intermittent or supplemental control of air pollutants varying with atmospheric conditions.

(c) Regulations; good engineering practice — Not later than six months after August 7, 1977, the Administrator, shall after notice and opportunity for public hearing, promulgate regulations to carry out this section. For purposes of this section, good engineering practice means, with respect to stack heights, the height necessary to insure that emissions from the stack do not result in excessive concentrations of any air pollutant in the immediate vicinity of the source as a result of atmospheric downwash, eddies and wakes which may be created by the source itself, nearby structures or nearby terrain obstacles (as determined by the Administrator). For purposes of this section such height shall not exceed two and a half times the height of such source unless the owner or operator of the source demonstrates, after notice and opportunity for public hearing, to the satisfaction of the Administrator, that a greater height is necessary as provided under the preceding sentence. In no event may the Administrator prohibit any increase in any stack height or restrict in any manner the stack height of any source.

§7424. Assurance of adequacy of State plans
[CAA §124]

(a) State review of implementation plans which relate to major fuel burning sources — As expeditiously as practicable but not later than one year after August 7, 1977, each State shall review the provisions of its implementation plan which relate to major fuel burning sources and shall determine —

(1) the extent to which compliance with requirements of such plan is dependent upon the use by major fuel burning stationary sources of petroleum products or natural gas,

(2) the extent to which such plan may reasonably be anticipated to be inadequate to meet the requirements of this Act in such State on a reliable and long-term basis by reason of its dependence upon the use of such fuels, and

(3) the extent to which compliance with the requirements of such plan is dependent upon use of coal or coal derivatives which is not locally or regionally available.

Each State shall submit the results of its review and its determination under this paragraph to the Administrator promptly upon completion thereof.

(b) Plan revision

(1) Not later than eighteen months after August 7, 1977, the Administrator shall review the submissions of the States under subsection (a) and shall require each State to revise its plan if, in the judgment of the Administrator, such plan revision is necessary to assure that such plan will be adequate to assure compliance with the requirements of this Act in such State on a reliable and long-term basis, taking into account the actual or potential prohibitions on use of petroleum products or natural gas, or both, under any other authority of law.

(2) Before requiring a plan revision under this subsection, with respect to any State the Administrator shall take into account the report of the review conducted by such State under paragraph (1) and shall consult with the Governor of the State respecting such required revision.

§7425. Measures to prevent economic disruption or unemployment
[CAA §125]

(a) Determination that action is necessary —
After notice and opportunity for a public hearing —

(1) the Governor of any State in which a major fuel burning stationary source referred to in this subsection (or class or category thereof) is located,

(2) the Administrator, or

(3) the President (or his designee), may determine that action under subsection (b) is necessary to prevent or minimize significant local or regional economic disruption or unemployment which would otherwise result from use by such source (or class or category) of —

    (A) coal or coal derivatives other than locally or regionally available coal,

    (B) petroleum products,

    (C) natural gas, or

    (D) any combination of fuels referred to in subparagraphs (A) through (C),

to comply with the requirements of a State implementation plan.

(b) Use of locally or regionally available coal or coal derivatives to comply with implementation plan requirements — Upon a determination under subsection (a) —

(1) such Governor, with the written consent of the President or his designee,

(2) the President's designee with the written consent of such Governor, or

(3) the President

may by rule or order prohibit any such major fuel burning stationary source (or class or category thereof) from using fuels other than locally or regionally available coal or coal derivatives to comply with implementation plan requirements. In taking any action under this subsection, the Governor, the President, or the President's

designee as the case may be, shall take into account the final cost to the consumer of such an action.

(c) Contracts; schedules — The Governor, in the case of action under subsection (b)(1) of this section, or the Administrator, in the case of an action under subsection (b)(2) or (3) of this section shall, by rule or order, require each source to which such action applies to —

(1) enter into long-term contracts of at least ten years in duration (except as the President or his designee may otherwise permit or require by rule or order for good cause) for supplies of regionally available coal or coal derivatives,

(2) enter into contracts to acquire any additional means of emission limitation which the Administrator or the State determines may be necessary to comply with the requirements of this Act while using such coal or coal derivatives as fuel, and

(3) comply with such schedules (including increments of progress), timetables and other requirements as may be necessary to assure compliance with the requirements of this chapter.

Requirements under this subsection shall be established simultaneously with, and as a condition of, any action under subsection (b).

(d) Existing or new major fuel burning stationary sources — This section applies only to existing or new major fuel burning stationary sources —

(1) which have the design capacity to produce 250,000,000 Btu's per hour (or its equivalent), as determined by the Administrator, and

(2) which are not in compliance with the requirements of an applicable implementation plan or which are prohibited from burning oil or natural gas, or both, under any other authority of law.

(e) Actions not to be deemed modifications of major fuel burning stationary sources —
Except as may otherwise be provided by rule by the State or the Administrator for good cause, any action required to be taken by a major fuel burning stationary source under this section shall not be deemed to constitute a modification for purposes of section 7411(a)(2) and (4) of this title.

(f) Treatment of prohibitions, rules, or orders as requirements or parts of plans under other provisions — For purposes of sections 7413 and 7420 of this title a prohibition under subsection (b) of this section, and a corresponding rule or order under subsection (c) of this section, shall be treated as a requirement of section 7413 of this title. For purposes of any plan (or portion thereof) promulgated under section 7410(c) of this title, any rule or order under subsection (c) of this section corresponding to a prohibition under subsection (b) of this section, shall be treated as a part of such plan. For purposes of section 7413 of this title, a prohibition under subsection (b) of this section, applicable to any source, and a corresponding rule or order under subsection (c) of this section, shall be treated as part of the applicable implementation plan for the State in which subject source is located.

(g) Delegation of Presidential authority — The President may delegate his authority under this section to an officer or employee of the United States designated by him on a case-by-case basis or in any other manner he deems suitable.

(h) "Locally or regionally available coal or coal derivatives" defined — For the purpose of this section the term "locally or regionally available coal or coal derivatives" means coal or coal derivatives which is, or can in the judgment of the State or the Administrator feasibly be, mined or produced in the local or regional area (as determined by the Administrator) in which the major fuel burning stationary source is located.

§7426. Interstate pollution abatement
[CAA §126]

(a) Written notice to all nearby States — Each applicable implementation plan shall —

(1) require each major proposed new (or modified) source —

(A) subject to part C (relating to significant deterioration of air quality) or

(B) which may significantly contribute to levels of air pollution in excess of the national ambient air quality standards in any air quality control region outside the State in which such source intends to locate (or make such modification),

to provide written notice to all nearby States the air pollution levels of which may be affected by such source at least sixty days prior to the date on which commencement of construction is to be permitted by the State providing notice, and

(2) identify all major existing stationary sources which may have the impact described in paragraph (1) with respect to new or modified sources and provide notice to all nearby States of the identity of such sources not later than three months after August 7, 1977.

(b) Petition for finding that major sources emit or would emit prohibited air pollutants — Any State or political subdivision may petition the Administrator for a finding that any major source or group of stationary sources emits or would emit any air pollutant in violation of the prohibition of section 110(a)(2)(D)(ii) or this section. Within 60 days after receipt of any petition under this subsection and after public hearing, the Administrator shall make such a finding or deny the petition.

(c) Violations; allowable continued operation — Notwithstanding any permit which may have been granted by the State in which the source is located (or intends to locate), it shall be a violation of [this section and] the applicable implementation plan in such State —

(1) for any major proposed new (or modified) source with respect to which a finding has been made under subsection (b) to be constructed or to operate in violation of [this section and] the

prohibition of section 110(a)(2)(D)(ii) or this section, or

(2) for any major existing source to operate more than three months after such finding has been made with respect to it.

The Administrator may permit the continued operation of a source referred to in paragraph (2) beyond the expiration of such three-month period if such source complies with such emission limitations and compliance schedules (containing increments of progress) as may be provided by the Administrator to bring about compliance with the requirements contained in section 7410(a)(2)(D)(ii) of this title or this section as expeditiously as practicable, but in no case later than three years after the date of such finding. Nothing in the preceding sentence shall be construed to preclude any such source from being eligible for an enforcement order under section 7413(d) of this title after the expiration of such period during which the Administrator has permitted continuous operation.

§7427. Public notification
[CAA §127]

(a) Warning signs; television, radio, or press notices or information — Each State plan shall contain measures which will be effective to notify the public during any calendar on a regular basis of instances or areas in which any national primary ambient air quality standard is exceeded or was exceeded during any portion of the preceding calendar year to advise the public of the health hazards associated with such pollution, and to enhance public awareness of the measures which can be taken to prevent such standards from being exceeded and the ways in which the public can participate in regulatory and other efforts to improve air quality. Such measures may include the posting of warning signs on interstate highway access points to metropolitan areas or television, radio, or press notices or information.

(b) Grants — The Administrator is authorized to make grants to States to assist in carrying out the requirements of subsection (a).

§7428. State boards
[CAA §128]

Not later than the date one year after the date of the enactment of this section, each applicable implementation plan shall contain requirements that —

(1) any board or body which approves permits or enforcement orders under this chapter shall have at least a majority of members who represent the public interest and do not derive any significant portion of their income from persons subject to permits or enforcement orders under this Act, and

(2) any potential conflicts of interest by members of such board or body or the head of an executive agency with similar powers be adequately disclosed.

A State may adopt any requirements respecting conflicts of interest for such boards or bodies or heads of executive agencies, or any other entities which are more stringent than the requirements of paragraphs (1) and (2), and the Administrator shall approve any such more stringent requirements submitted as part of an implementation plan.

§7429. Solid waste combustion
[CAA §129]
(a) New source performance standards

(1) In general —

(A) The Administrator shall establish performance standards and other requirements pursuant to section 7411 of this title and this section for each category of solid waste incineration units. Such standards shall include emissions limitations and other requirements applicable to new units and guidelines (under section 7411(d) of this title and this section) and other requirements applicable to existing units.

(B) Standards under section 7411 of this title and this section applicable to solid waste incineration units with capacity greater than 250 tons per day combusting municipal waste shall be promulgated not later than 12 months after November 15, 1990. Nothing in this subparagraph shall alter any schedule for the promulgation of standards applicable to such units under section 7411 of this title pursuant to any settlement and consent decree entered by the Administrator before November 15, 1990: *Provided*, That, such standards are subsequently modified pursuant to the schedule established in this subparagraph to include each of the requirements of this section.

(C) Standards under section 7411 of this title and this section applicable to solid waste incineration units with capacity equal to or less than 250 tons per day combusting municipal waste and units combusting hospital waste, medical waste and infectious waste shall be promulgated not later than 24 months after November 15, 1990.

(D) Standards under section 7411 of this title and this section applicable to solid waste incineration units combusting commercial or industrial waste shall be proposed not later than 36 months after November 15, 1990 and promulgated not later than 48 months after November 15, 1990.

(E) Not later than 18 months after November 15, 1990, the Administrator shall publish a schedule for the promulgation of standards under section 7411 of this title and this section applicable to other categories of solid waste incineration units.

(2) Emissions standard — Standards applicable to solid waste incineration units promulgated under section 7411 of this title and this section shall reflect the maximum degree of reduction in emissions of air pollutants listed under section (a)(4) that the Administrator, taking into consideration the cost of achieving such emission reduction, and any non-air quality health and environmental impacts and energy requirements, determines is achievable for new or existing units in each category. The Administrator may distinguish among classes, types (including mass-burn, refuse-derived fuel, modular and other types of units), and sizes of units within a category in establishing such standards. The degree of reduction in emissions that is deemed achievable for new units in a category shall not be less stringent than the emissions control that is achieved in practice by the best controlled similar unit, as determined by the Administrator. Emissions standards for existing units in a category may be less stringent than standards for new units in the same category but shall not be less stringent than the average emissions limitation achieved by the best performing 12 percent of units in the category (excluding units which first met lowest achievable emissions rates 18 months before the date such standards are proposed or 30 months before the date such standards are promulgated, whichever is later).

(3) Control methods and technologies — Standards under section 7411 of this title and this section applicable to solid waste incineration units shall be based on methods and technologies for removal or destruction of pollutants before, during, or after combustion, and shall incorporate for new units siting requirements that minimize, on a site specific basis, to the maximum extent practicable, potential risks to public health or the environment.

(4) Numerical emissions limitations — The performance standards promulgated under section 7411 of this title and this section and applicable to solid waste incineration units shall specify numerical emission limitations for the following substances or mixtures: particulate matter (total and fine), opacity (as appropriate), sulfur dioxide, hydrogen chloride, oxides of nitrogen, carbon monoxide, lead, cadmium, mercury, and dioxins and dibenzofurans. The Administrator may promulgate numerical emissions limitations or provide for the monitoring of post combustion concentrations of surrogate substances, parameters or periods of residence time in excess of stated temperatures with respect to pollutants other than those listed in this paragraph.

(5) Review and revision — Not later than 5 years following the initial promulgation of any performance standards and other requirements under this section and section 7411 of this title applicable to a category of solid waste incineration units, and at 5 year intervals thereafter, the Administrator shall review, and in accordance with this section and section 7411 of this title, revise such standards and requirements.

(b) Existing units

(1) Guidelines — Performance standards under this section and section 7411 of this title for solid waste incineration units shall include guidelines promulgated pursuant to section 7411(d) of this title and this section applicable to existing units. Such guidelines shall include, as provided in this section, each of the elements required by subsection (a) (emissions limitations, notwithstanding any restriction in section 7411(d) of this title regarding issuance of such limitations), subsection (c) of this section (monitoring), subsection (d) of this section (operator training), subsection (e) of this section (permits), and subsection (h)(4) of this section (residual risk).

(2) State plans — Not later than 1 year after the Administrator promulgates guidelines for a category of solid waste incineration units, each State in which units in the category are operating shall submit to the Administrator a plan to implement and enforce the guidelines with respect to such units. The State plan shall be at least as protective as the guidelines promulgated by the Administrator and shall provide that each unit subject to the guidelines shall in compliance with all requirements of this section not later than 3 years after the State plan is approved by the Administrator but not later than 5 years after the guidelines were promulgated. The Administrator shall approve or disapprove any State plan within 180 days of the submission, and if a plan is disapproved, the Administrator shall state the reasons for disapproval in writing. Any State may modify and resubmit a plan which has been disapproved by the Administrator.

(3) Federal plan — The Administrator shall develop, implement and enforce a plan for existing solid waste incineration units within any category located in any State which has not submitted an approvable plan under this subsection with respect to units in such category within 2 years after the date on which the Administrator promulgated the relevant guidelines. Such plan shall assure that each unit subject to the plan is in compliance with all pro-visions of the guidelines not later than 5 years after the date the relevant guidelines are promulgated.

(c) Monitoring

— The Administrator shall, as part of each performance standard promulgated pursuant to subsection (a) and section 7411 of this title, promulgate regulations requiring the owner or operator of each solid waste incineration unit —

(1) to monitor emissions from the unit at the point at which such emissions are emitted into the ambient air (or within the stack, combustion chamber or pollution control equipment, as appropriate) and at such other points as necessary to protect public health and the environment;

(2) to monitor such other parameters relating to the operation of the unit and its pollution con-trol technology as the Administrator determines are appropriate; and

(3) to report the results of such monitoring. Such regulations shall contain provisions regarding the frequency of monitoring, test methods and procedures validated on solid waste incineration units, and the form and frequency of reports containing the results of monitoring and shall require that any monitoring reports or test results indicating an exceedance of any standard under this section shall be reported separately and in a manner that facilitates review for purposes of enforcement actions. Such regulations shall require that copies of the results of such monitoring be maintained on file at the facility concerned and that copies shall be made available for inspection and copying by interested members of the public during business hours.

(d) Operator training

— Not later than 24 months after November 15, 1990, the Administrator shall develop and promote a model State program for the training and certification of solid waste incineration unit operators and high-capacity fossil fuel fired plant operators. The Administrator may authorize any State to implement a model program for the training of solid waste incineration unit operators and high-capacity fossil fuel fired plant operators, if the State has adopted a program which is at least as effective as the model program developed by the Administrator. Beginning on the date 36 months after the date on which performance standards and guidelines are promulgated under subsection (a) of this section and section 7411 of this title for any category of solid waste incineration units it shall be unlawful to operate any unit in the category unless each person with control over processes affecting emissions from such unit has satisfactorily completed a training program meeting the requirements established by the Administrator under this subsection.

(e) Permits

— Beginning (1) 36 months after the promulgation of a performance standard under subsection (a) of this section and section 7411 of this title applicable to a category of solid waste incineration units, or (2) the effective date of a permit program under subchapter V of this chapter in the State in which the unit is located, whichever is later, each unit in the category shall operate pursuant to a permit issued under this subsection and subchapter V. Permits required by this subsection may be renewed according to the provisions of title V. Notwithstanding any other provision of this Act, each permit for a solid waste incineration unit combusting municipal waste issued under this Act shall be issued for a period of up to 12 years and shall be reviewed every 5 years after date of issuance or reissuance. Each permit shall continue in effect after the date of issuance until the date of termination, unless the Administrator or State determines that the unit is not in compliance with all standards and conditions contained in the permit. Such determination shall be made at regular intervals during the term of the permit, such intervals not to exceed 5 years, and only after public comment and public hearing. No permit for a solid waste incineration unit may be issued under this chapter by an agency, instrumentality or person that is also responsible, in whole or part, for the design and construction or operation of the unit. Notwithstanding any other provision of this subsection, the Administrator or the State shall require the owner or operator of any unit to comply with emissions limitations or implement any other measures, if the Administrator or the State determines that emissions in the absence of such limitations or measures may reasonably be anticipated to endanger public health or the environment. The Administrator's determination under the preceding sentence is a discretionary decision.

(f) Effective date and enforcement

(1) New units — Performance standards and other requirements promulgated pursuant to this section and section 7411 of this title and applicable to new solid waste incineration units shall be effective as of the date 6 months after the date of promulgation.

(2) Existing units — Performance standards and other requirements promulgated pursuant to this section and section 7411 of this title and applicable to existing solid waste incineration units shall be effective as expeditiously as practicable after approval of a State plan under subsection (b)(2) of this section (or promulgation of a plan by the Administrator under subsection (b)(3) of this section) but in no event later than 3 years after the State plan is approved or 5 years after the date such standards or requirements are promulgated, whichever is earlier.

(3) Prohibition — After the effective date of any performance standard, emission limitation or other requirement promulgated pursuant to this section and section 7411 of this title, it shall be unlawful for any owner or operator of any solid waste incineration unit to which such standard, limitation or requirement applies to operate such unit in violation of such limitation, standard or requirement or for any other person to violate an applicable requirement of this section.

(4) Coordination with other authorities — For purposes of sections 7411(e), 7413, 7414, 7416, 7420, 7603, 7604, 7607 of this title and other provisions for the enforcement of this chapter, each performance standard, emission limitation or other requirement established pursuant to this section by the Administrator or a State or local government, shall be treated in the same manner as a standard of performance under section 7411 of this title which is an emission limitation.

(g) Definitions — For purposes of section 306 of the Clean Air Act Amendments of 1990 and this section only —

(1) Solid waste incineration unit — The term "solid waste incineration unit" means a distinct operating unit of any facility which combusts any solid waste material from commercial or industrial establishments or the general public (including single and multiple residences, hotels, and motels). Such term does not include incinerators or other units required to have a permit under section 3005 of the Solid Waste Disposal Act. The term "solid waste incineration unit" does not include (A) materials recovery facilities (including primary or secondary smelters) which combust waste for the primary purpose of recovering metals, (B) qualifying small power production facilities, as defined in section 796(17)(C) of Title 16, or qualifying cogeneration facilities, as defined in section 796(18)(B) Title 16, which burn homogeneous waste (such as units which burn tires or used oil, but not including refuse-derived fuel) for the production of electric energy or in the case of qualifying cogeneration facilities which burn homogeneous waste for the production of electric energy and steam or forms of useful energy (such as heat) which are used for industrial, commercial, heating or cooling purposes, or (C) air curtain incinerators provided that such incinerators only burn wood wastes, yard wastes and clean lumber and that such air curtain incinerators comply with opacity limitations to be established by the Administrator by rule.

(2) New solid waste incineration unit — The term "new solid waste incineration unit" means a solid waste incineration unit the construction of which is commenced after the Administrator proposes requirements under this section establishing emissions standards or other requirements which would be applicable to such unit or a modified solid waste incineration unit.

(3) Modified solid waste incineration unit — The term "modified solid waste incineration unit" means a solid waste incineration unit at which modifications have occurred after the effective date of a standard under subsection (a) if (A) the cumulative cost of the modifications, over the life of the unit, exceed 50 per centum of the original cost of construction and installation of the unit (not including the cost of any land purchased in connection with such construction or installation) updated to current costs, or (B) the modification is a physical change in or change in the method of operation of the unit which increases the amount of any air pollutant emitted by the unit for which standards have been established under this section or section 7411 of this title.

(4) Existing solid waste incineration unit — The term "existing solid waste incineration unit" means a solid waste unit which is not a new or modified solid waste incineration unit.

(5) Municipal waste — The term "municipal waste" means refuse (and refuse-derived fuel) collected from the general public and from residential, commercial, institutional, and industrial sources consisting of paper, wood, yard wastes,

food wastes, plastics, leather, rubber, and other combustible materials and non-combustible materials such as metal, glass and rock, provided that: (A) the term does not include industrial process wastes or medical wastes that are segregated from such other wastes; and (B) an incineration unit shall not be considered to be combusting municipal waste for purposes of section 7411 of this title or this section if it combusts a fuel feed stream, 30 percent or less of the weight of which is comprised, in aggregate, of municipal waste.

(6) Other terms — The terms "solid waste" and "medical waste" shall have the meanings established by the Administrator pursuant to the Solid Waste Disposal Act.

(h) Other authority

(1) State authority — Nothing in this section shall preclude or deny the right of any State or political subdivision thereof to adopt or enforce any regulation, requirement, limitation or standard relating to solid waste incineration units that is more stringent than a regulation, requirement, limitation or standard in effect under this section or under any other provision of this Act.

(2) Other authority under this chapter — Nothing in this section shall diminish the authority of the Administrator or a State to establish any other requirements applicable to solid waste incineration units under any other authority of law, including the authority to establish for any air pollutant a national ambient air quality standard, except that no solid waste incineration unit subject to performance standards under this section and section 7411 of this title shall be subject to standards under section 7412(d) of this title.

(3) Residual risk — The Administrator shall promulgate standards under section 7412(f) of this title for a category of solid waste incineration units, if promulgation of such standards is required under section 7412(f) of this title. For purposes of this preceding sentence only —

(A) the performance standards under subsection (a) of this section and section 7411 of this title applicable to a category of solid waste incineration units shall be deemed standards under section 7412(d)(2) of this title, and

(B) the Administrator shall consider and regulate, if required, the pollutants listed under subsection (a)(4) of this section and no others.

(4) Acid rain — A solid waste incineration unit shall not be a utility unit as defined in subchapter IV-A of this chapter: *Provided*, That, more than 80 per centum of its annual average fuel consumption measured on a Btu basis, during a period or periods to be determined by the Administrator, is from a fuel (including any waste burned as a fuel) other than a fossil fuel.

(5) Requirements of parts C and D — No requirement of an applicable implementation plan under section 7475 of this title (relating to construction of facilities in regions identified pursuant to section 7407(d)(1)(A)(ii) or (iii) of this title) or under section 7502(c)(5) of this title (relating to permits for construction and operation in nonattainment areas) may be used to weaken the standards in effect under this section.

§7430. Emission factors
[CAA §130]

Within 6 months after November 15, 1990, and at least every 3 years thereafter, the Administrator shall review and, if necessary, revise, the methods ("emission factors") used for purposes of this Act to estimate the quantity of emissions of carbon monoxide, volatile organic compounds, and oxides of nitrogen from sources of such air pollutants (including area sources and mobile sources). In addition, the Administrator shall establish emission factors for sources for which no such methods have previously been established by the Administrator. The Administrator shall permit any person to demonstrate improved emissions estimating techniques, and following approval of such techniques, the Administrator shall authorize the use of such techniques. Any such technique may be approved only after appropriate public participation. Until the Administrator has completed the revision required by this section, nothing in this section shall be construed to affect the validity of emission factors established by the Administrator before November 15, 1990.

§7431. Land use authority
[CAA §131]

Nothing in this Act constitutes an infringement on the existing authority of counties and cities to plan or control land use, and nothing in this Act provides or transfers authority over such land use.

PART B — OZONE PROTECTION

§§7450 to 7459. Repealed. Pub. L. 101-549, Title VI §601, Nov. 15, 1990, 104 Stat. 2648

PART C — PREVENTION OF SIGNIFICANT DETERIORATION OF AIR QUALITY

SUBPART I — CLEAN AIR

§7470. Congressional declaration of purpose
[CAA §160]

The purposes of this part are as follows:

(1) to protect public health and welfare from any actual or potential adverse effect which in the Administrator's judgment may reasonably be anticipated to occur from air pollution or from exposures to pollutants in other media, which pollutants originate as emissions to the ambient air),

notwithstanding attainment and maintenance of all national ambient air quality standards;

(2) to preserve, protect, and enhance the air quality in national parks, national wilderness areas, national monuments, national seashores, and other areas of special national or regional natural, recreational, scenic, or historic value;

(3) to insure that economic growth will occur in a manner consistent with the preservation of existing clean air resources;

(4) to assure that emissions from any source in any State will not interfere with any portion of the applicable implementation plan to prevent significant deterioration of air quality for any other State; and

(5) to assure that any decision to permit increased air pollution in any area to which this section applies is made only after careful evaluation of all the consequences of such a decision and after adequate procedural opportunities for informed public participation in the decisionmaking process.

§7471. Plan requirements
[CAA §161]

In accordance with the policy of section 7401(b)(1) of this title, each applicable implementation plan shall contain emission limitations and such other measures as may be necessary, as determined under regulations promulgated under this part, to prevent significant deterioration of air quality in each region (or portion thereof) designated pursuant to section 7407 of this title as attainment or unclassifiable.

§7472. Initial classifications
[CAA §162]

(a) Areas designated as class I —Upon the enactment of this part, all —

(1) international parks,

(2) national wilderness areas which exceed 5,000 acres in size,

(3) national memorial parks which exceed 5,000 acres in size, and

(4) national parks which exceed six thousand acres in size,

and which are in existence on August 7, 1977 shall be class I areas and may not be redesignated. All areas which were redesignated as class I under regulations promulgated before such date of enactment shall be class I areas which may be redesignated as provided in this part. The extent of the areas designated as Class I under this section shall conform to any changes in the boundaries of such areas which have occurred subsequent to August 7, 1977, or which may occur subsequent to November 15, 1990.

(b) Areas designated as class II — All areas in such State designated pursuant to section 7407(d) of this title as attainment or unclassifiable which are not established as class I under subsection (a) shall be class II areas unless redesignated under section 7474 of this title.

§7473. Increments and ceilings
[CAA §163]

(a) Sulfur oxide and particulate matter; requirement that maximum allowable increases and maximum allowable concentrations not be exceeded — In the case of sulfur oxide and particulate matter, each applicable implementation plan shall contain measures assuring that maximum allowable increases over baseline concentrations of, and maximum allowable concentrations of, such pollutant shall not be exceeded. In the case of any maximum allowable increase (except an allowable increase specified under section 7475(d)(2)(C)(iv) of this title) for a pollutant based on concentrations permitted under national ambient air quality standards for any period other than an annual period, such regulations shall permit such maximum allowable increase to be exceeded during one such period per year.

(b) Maximum allowable increases in concentrations over baseline concentrations

(1) For any class I area, the maximum allowable increase in concentrations of sulfur dioxide and particulate matter over the baseline concentration of such pollutants shall not exceed the following amounts:

Maximum allowable increase
[Micrograms per cubic meter]

Pollutant	
Particulate matter:	
Annual geometric mean	5
Twenty-four-hour maximum	10
Sulfur dioxide:	
Annual arithmetic mean	2
Twenty-four-hour maximum	5
Three-hour maximum	25

(2) For any class II area, the maximum allowable increase in concentrations of sulfur dioxide and particulate matter over the baseline concentration of such pollutants shall not exceed the following amounts:

Maximum allowable increase
[Micrograms per cubic meter]

Pollutant	
Particulate matter:	
Annual geometric mean	19
Twenty-four-hour maximum	37
Sulfur dioxide:	
Annual arithmetic mean	20
Twenty-four-hour maximum	91
Three-hour maximum	512

(3) For any class III area, the maximum allowable increase in concentrations of sulfur dioxide and particulate matter over the baseline concentration of such pollutants shall not exceed the following amounts:

Maximum allowable increase
[Micrograms per cubic meter]

Pollutant

Particulate matter:
Annual geometric mean	37
Twenty-four-hour maximum	75

Sulfur dioxide:
Annual arithmetic mean	40
Twenty-four-hour maximum	182
Three-hour maximum	700

(4) The maximum allowable concentration of any air pollutant in any area to which this part applies shall not exceed a concentration for such pollutant for each period of exposure equal to —

(A) the concentration permitted under the national secondary ambient air quality standard, or

(B) the concentration permitted under the national primary ambient air quality standard,

whichever concentration is lowest for such pollutant for such period of exposure.

(c) Orders or rules for determining compliance with maximum allowable increases in ambient concentrations of air pollutants

(1) In the case of any State which has a plan approved by the Administrator for purposes of carrying out this part, the Governor of such State may, after notice and opportunity for public hearing, issue orders or promulgate rules providing that for purposes of determining compliance with the maximum allowable increases in ambient concentrations of an air pollutant, the following concentrations of such pollutant shall not be taken into account:

(A) concentrations of such pollutant attributable to the increase in emissions from stationary sources which have converted from the use of petroleum products, or natural gas, or both, by reason of an order which is in effect under the provisions of sections 792(a) and (b) of Title 15 (or any subsequent legislation which supersedes such provisions) over the emissions from such sources before the effective date of such order.

(B) the concentrations of such pollutant attributable to the increase in emissions from stationary sources which have converted from using natural gas by reason of a natural gas curtailment pursuant to a natural gas curtailment plan in effect pursuant to the Federal Power Act over the emissions from such sources before the effective date of such plan,

(C) concentrations of particulate matter attributable to the increase in emissions from construction or other temporary emission-related activities, and

(D) the increase in concentrations attributable to new sources outside the United States over the concentrations attributable to existing sources which are included in the baseline

concentration determined in accordance with section 7479(4) of this title.

(2) No action taken with respect to a source under paragraph (1)(A) or (1)(B) shall apply more than five years after the effective date of the order referred to in paragraph (1)(A) or the plan referred to in paragraph (1)(B), whichever is applicable. If both such order and plan are applicable, no such action shall apply more than five years after the later of such effective dates.

(3) No action under this subsection shall take effect unless the Governor submits the order or rule providing for such exclusion to the Administrator and the Administrator determines that such order or rule is in compliance with the provisions of this subsection.

§7474. Area redesignation
[CAA §164]
(a) Authority of States to redesignate areas — Except as otherwise provided under subsection (c), a State may redesignate such areas as it deems appropriate as class I areas. The following areas may be redesignated only as class I or II:

(1) an area which exceeds ten thousand acres in size and is a national monument, a national primitive area, a national preserve, a national recreation area, a national wild and scenic river, a national wildlife refuge, a national lakeshore or seashore, and

(2) a national park or national wilderness area established after August 7, 1977, which exceeds ten thousand acres in size.

The extent of the areas referred to in paragraph (1) and (2) shall conform to any changes in the boundaries of such areas which have occurred subsequent to August 7, 1977, or which may occur subsequent to November 15, 1990. Any area (other than an area referred to in paragraph (1) or (2) or an area established as class I under the first sentence of section 162(a)) may be redesignated by the State as class III if —

(A) such redesignation has been specifically approved by the Governor of the State, after consultation with the appropriate Committees of the legislature if it is in session or with the leadership of the legislature if it is not in session (unless State law provides that such redesignation must be specifically approved by State legislation) and if general purpose units of local government representing a majority of the residents of the area so redesignated enact legislation (including for such units of local government resolutions where appropriate) concurring in the State's redesignation;

(B) such redesignation will not cause, or contribute to, concentrations of any air pollutant which exceed any maximum allowable increase or maximum allowable concentration permitted under the classification of any other area; and

(C) such redesignation otherwise meets the requirements of this part.

Subparagraph (A) of this paragraph shall not apply to area redesignations by Indian tribes.

(b) Notice and hearing; notice to Federal land manager; written comments and recommendations; regulations; disapproval of redesignation

(1)(A) Prior to redesignation of any area under this part, notice shall be afforded and public hearings shall be conducted in areas proposed to be redesignated and in areas which may be affected by the proposed redesignation. Prior to any such public hearing a satisfactory description and analysis of the health, environmental, economic, social, and energy effects of the proposed redesignation shall be prepared and made available for public inspection and prior to any such redesignation, the description and analysis of such effects shall be reviewed and examined by the redesignating authorities.

(B) Prior to the issuance of notice under subparagraph (A) respecting the redesignation of any area under this subsection, if such area includes any Federal lands, the State shall provide written notice to the appropriate Federal land manager and afford adequate opportunity (but not in excess of 60 days) to confer with the State respecting the intended notice of redesignation and to submit written comments and recommendations with respect to such intended notice of redesignation. In redesignating any area under this section with respect to which any Federal land manager has submitted written comments and recommendations, the State shall publish a list of any inconsistency between such redesignation and such recommendations and an explanation of such inconsistency (together with the reasons for making such redesignation against the recommendation of the Federal land manager).

(C) The Administrator shall promulgate regulations not later than six months after August 7, 1977, to assure, insofar as practicable, that prior to any public hearing on redesignation of any area, there shall be available for public inspection any specific plans for any new or modified major emitting facility which may be permitted to be constructed and operated only if the area in question is designated or redesignated as class III.

(2) The Administrator may disapprove the redesignation of any area only if he finds, after notice and opportunity for public hearing, that such redesignation does not meet the procedural requirements of this section or is inconsistent with the requirements of section 7472(a) of this title or of subsection (a) of this section. If any such disapproval occurs, the classification of the area shall be that which was in effect prior to the redesignation which was disapproved.

(c) Indian reservations — Lands within the exterior boundaries of reservations of federally recognized Indian tribes may be redesignated only by the appropriate Indian governing body. Such Indian governing body shall be subject in all respect to the provisions of subsection (e) of this section.

(d) Review of national monuments, primitive areas, and national preserves — The Federal Land Manager shall review all national monuments, primitive areas, and national preserves, and shall recommend any appropriate areas for redesignation as class I where air quality related values are important attributes of the area. The Federal Land Manager shall report such recommendations, within supporting analysis, to the Congress and the affected States within one year after enactment of this section. The Federal Land Manager shall consult with the appropriate States before making such recommendations.

(e) Resolution of disputes between State and Indian tribes — If any State affected by the redesign-ation of any area by an Indian tribe or any Indian tribe affected by the redesignation of an area by a State disagrees with such redesignation of any area, or if a permit is proposed to be issued for any new major emitting facility proposed for construction in any State which the Governor of an affected State or governing body of an affected Indian tribe determines will cause or contribute to a cumulative change in air quality in excess of that allowed in this part within the affected State or tribal reservation, the Governor or Indian ruling body may request the Administrator to enter into negotiations with the parties involved to resolve such dispute. If requested by any State or Indian tribe involved, the Administrator shall make a recommendation to resolve the dispute and protect the air quality related values of the lands involved. If the parties involved do not reach agreement, the Administrator shall resolve the dispute and his determination, or the results of agreements reached through other means, shall become part of the applicable plan and shall be enforceable as part of such plan. In resolving such disputes relating to area redesignation, the Administrator shall consider the extent to which the lands involved are of sufficient size to allow effective air quality management or have air quality related values of such an area.

§7475. Preconstruction requirements
[CAA §165]

(a) Major emitting facilities on which construction is commenced — No major emitting facility on which construction is commenced after August 7, 1977, may be constructed in any area to which this part applies unless —

(1) a permit has been issued for such proposed facility in accordance with this part setting forth emission limitations for such facility which conform to the requirements of this part;

(2) the proposed permit has been subject to a review in accordance with this section, the

required analysis has been conducted in accordance with regulations promulgated by the Administrator, and a public hearing as been held with opportunity for interested persons including representatives of the Administrator to appear and submit written or oral presentations on the air quality impact of such source, alternatives thereto, control technology requirements, and other appropriate considerations;

(3) the owner or operator of such facility demonstrates, as required pursuant to section 7410(j) of this title, that emissions from construction or operation of such facility will not cause, or contribute to, air pollution in excess of any (A) maximum allowable increase or maximum allowable concentration for any pollutant in any area to which this part applies more than one time per year, (B) national ambient air quality standard in any air quality control region, or (C) any other applicable emission standard or standard of performance under this Act;

(4) the proposed facility is subject to the best available control technology for each pollutant subject to regulation under this Act emitted from, or which results from, such facility;

(5) the provisions of subsection (d) of this section with respect to protection of class I areas have been complied with for such facility;

(6) there has been an analysis of any air quality impacts projected for the area as a result of growth associated with such facility;

(7) the person who owns or operates, or proposes to own or operate, a major emitting facility for which a permit is required under this part agrees to conduct such monitoring as may be necessary to determine the effect which emissions from any such facility may have, or is having, on air quality in any area which may be affected by emissions from such source; and

(8) in the case of a source which proposes to construct in a class III area, emissions from which would cause or contribute to exceeding the maximum allowable increments applicable in a class II area and where no standard under section 7411 of this title has been promulgated subsequent to August 7, 1977, for such source category, the Administrator has approved the determination of best available technology as set forth in the permit.

(b) Exception — The demonstration pertaining to maximum allowable increases required under subsection (a)(3) of this section shall not apply to maximum allowable increases for class II areas in the case of an expansion or modification of a major emitting facility which is in existence on August 7, 1977, whose allowable emissions of air pollutants, after compliance with subsection (a)(4) of this section, will be less than fifty tons per year and for which the owner or operator of such facility demonstrates that emissions of particulate matter and sulfur oxides will not cause or contribute to ambient air quality levels in excess of the national secondary ambient air quality standard for either of such pollutants.

(c) Permit applications — Any completed permit application under section 7410 of this title for a major emitting facility in any area to which this part applies shall be granted or denied not later than one year after the date of filing of such completed application.

(d) Action taken on permit applications; notice; adverse impact on air quality related values; variance; emission limitations

(1) Each State shall transmit to the Administrator a copy of each permit application relating to a major emitting facility received by such State and provide notice to the Administrator of every action related to the consideration of such permit.

(2)(A) The Administrator shall provide notice of the permit application to the Federal Land Manager and the Federal official charged with direct responsibility for management of any lands within a class I area which may be affected by emissions from the proposed facility.

(B) The Federal Land Manager and the Federal official charged with direct responsibility for management of such lands shall have an affirmative responsibility to protect the air quality related values (including visibility) of any such lands within a class I area and to consider, in consultation with the Administrator, whether a proposed major emitting facility will have an adverse impact on such values.

(C)(i) In any case where the Federal official charged with direct responsibility for management of any lands within a class I area or the Federal Land Manager of such lands, or the Administrator, or the Governor of an adjacent State containing such a class I area files a notice alleging that emissions from a proposed major emitting facility may cause or contribute to a change in the air quality in such area and identifying the potential adverse impact of such change, a permit shall not be issued unless the owner or operator of such facility demonstrates that emissions of particulate matter and sulfur dioxide will not cause or contribute to concentrations which exceed the maximum allowable increases for a class I area.

(ii) In any case where the Federal Land Manager demonstrates to the satisfaction of the State that the emissions from such facility will have an adverse impact on the air quality-related values (including visibility) of such lands, notwithstanding the fact that the change in air quality resulting from emissions from such facility will not cause or contribute to concentrations which exceed the maximum allowable increases for a class I area, a permit shall not be issued.

(iii) In any case where the owner or operator of such facility demonstrates to the

701

satisfaction of the Federal Land Manager, and the Federal Land Manager so certifies, that the emissions from such facility will have no adverse impact on the air quality-related values of such lands (including visibility) notwithstanding the fact that the change in air quality resulting from emissions from such facility will cause or contribute to concentrations which exceed the maximum allowable increases for class I areas, the State may issue a permit.

(iv) In the case of a permit issued pursuant to clause (iii), such facility shall comply with such emission limitations under such permit as may be necessary to assure that emissions of sulfur oxides and particulates from such facility, will not cause or contribute to concentrations of such pollutant which exceed the following maximum allowable increases over the baseline concentration for such pollutants:

Maximum allowable increase
[Micrograms per cubic meter]

Particulate matter:

Annual geometric mean	19
Twenty-four-hour maximum	37

Sulfur dioxide:

Annual arithmetic mean	20
Twenty-four-hour maximum	91
Three-hour maximum	325

(D)(i) In any case where the owner or operator of a proposed major emitting facility who has been denied a certification under subparagraph (C)(iii) demonstrates to the satisfaction of the Governor, after notice and public hearing, and the Governor finds, that the facility cannot be constructed by reason of any maximum allowable increase for sulfur dioxide for periods of twenty-four hours or less applicable to any class I area and, in the case of Federal mandatory class I areas, that a variance under this clause will not adversely affect the air quality related values of the area (including visibility), the Governor, after consideration of the Federal Land Manager's recommendation (if any) and subject to his concurrence, may grant a variance from such maximum allowable increase. If such variance is granted, a permit may be issued to such source pursuant to the requirements of this subparagraph.

(ii) In any case in which the Governor recommends a variance under this subparagraph in which the Federal Land Manager does not concur, the recommendations of the Governor and the Federal

Land Manager shall be transmitted to the President. The President may approve the Governor's recommendation if he finds that such variance is in the national interest. No Presidential finding shall be reviewable in any court. The variance shall take effect if the President approves the Governor's recommendations. The President shall approve or disapprove such recommendation within ninety days after his receipt of the recommendations of the Governor and the Federal Land Manager.

(iii) In the case of a permit issued pursuant to this subparagraph, such facility shall comply with such emission limitations under such permit as may be necessary to assure that emissions of sulfur oxides from such facility will not (during any day on which the otherwise applicable maximum allowable increases are exceeded) cause or contribute to concentrations which exceed the following maximum allowable increases for such areas over the baseline concentration for such pollutant and to assure that such emissions will not cause or contribute to concentrations which exceed the otherwise applicable maximum allowable increases for periods of exposure of 24 hours or less on more than 18 days during any annual period:

Maximum allowable increase
[Micrograms per cubic meter]

Period of exposure:	Low terrain areas	High terrain areas
24-hr maximum	36	62
3-hr maximum	130	221

(iv) For purposes of clause (iii), the term "high terrain area" means with respect to any facility, any area having an elevation of 900 feet or more above the base of the stack of such facility, and the term "low terrain area" means any area other than a high terrain area.

(e) Analysis; continuous air quality monitoring data; regulations; model adjustments

(1) The review provided for in subsection (a) of this section shall be preceded by an analysis in accordance with regulations of the Administrator, promulgated under this subsection, which may be conducted by the State (or any general purpose unit of local government) or by the major emitting facility applying for such permit, of the ambient air quality at the proposed site and in areas which may be affected by emissions from such facility for each pollutant subject to regulation under this Act which will be emitted from such facility.

(2) Effective one year after August 7, 1977, the analysis required by this subsection shall include continuous air quality monitoring data gathered

for purposes of determining whether emissions from such facility will exceed the maximum allowable increases or the maximum allowable concentration permitted under this part. Such data shall be gathered over a period of one calendar year preceding the date of application for a permit under this part unless the State, in accordance with regulations promulgated by the Administrator, determines that a complete and adequate analysis for such purposes may be accomplished in a shorter period. The results of such analysis shall be available at the time of the public hearing on the application for such permit.

(3) The Administrator shall within six months after August 7, 1977, promulgate regulations respecting the analysis required under this subsection which regulations —

(A) shall not require the use of any automatic or uniform buffer zone or zones,

(B) shall require an analysis of the ambient air quality, climate and meteorology, terrain, soils and vegetation, and visibility at the site of the proposed major emitting facility and in the area potentially affected by the emissions from such facility for each pollutant regulated under this Act which will be emitted from, or which results from the construction or operation of, such facility, the size and nature of the proposed facility, the degree of continuous emission reduction which could be achieved by such facility, and such other factors as may be relevant in determining the effect of emissions from a proposed facility on any air quality control region,

(C) shall require the results of such analysis shall be available at the time of the public hearing on the application for such permit, and

(D) shall specify with reasonable particularity each air quality model or models to be used under specified sets of conditions for purposes of this part.

Any model or models designated under such regulations may be adjusted upon a determination, after notice and opportunity for public hearing, by the Administrator that such adjustment is necessary to take into account unique terrain or meteorological characteristics of an area potentially affected by emissions from a source applying for a permit required under this part.

§7476. Other pollutants
[CAA §166]

(a) Hydrocarbons, carbon monoxide, photochemical oxidants, and nitrogen oxides — In the case of the pollutants hydrocarbons, carbon monoxide, photochemical oxidants, and nitrogen oxides, the Administrator shall conduct a study and not later than two years after August 7, 1977, promulgate regulations to prevent the significant deterioration of air quality which would result from the emissions of such pollutants. In the case of pollutants for which

national ambient air quality standards are promulgated after August 7, 1977, he shall promulgate such regulations not more than 2 years after the date of promulgation of such standards.

(b) Effective date of regulations — Regulations referred to in subsection (a) of this section shall become effective one year after the date of promulgation. Within 21 months after such date of promulgation such plan revision shall be submitted to the Administrator who shall approve or disapprove the plan within 25 months after such date or promulgation in the same manner as required under section 7410 of this title.

(c) Contents of regulations — Such regulations shall provide specific numerical measures against which permit applications may be evaluated, a framework for stimulating improved control technology, protection of air quality values, and fulfill the goals and purposes set forth in section 101 and section 160.

(d) Specific measures to fulfill goals and purposes — The regulations of the Administrator under subsection (a) shall provide specific measures at least as effective as the increments established in section 163 to fulfill such goals and purposes, and may contain air quality increments, emission density requirements, or other measures.

(e) Area classification plan not required — With respect to any air pollutant for which a national ambient air quality standard is established other than sulfur oxides or particulate matter, an area classification plan shall not be required under this section if the implementation plan adopted by the State and submitted for the Administrator's approval or promulgated by the Administrator under section 7410(c) of this title contains other provisions which when considered as a whole, the Administrator finds will carry out the purposes in section 7470 of this title at least as effectively as an area classification plan for such pollutant. Such other provisions referred to in the preceding sentence need not require the establishment of maximum allowable increases with respect to such pollutant for any area to which this section applies.

(f) PM-10 increments — The Administrator is authorized to substitute, for the maximum allowable increases in particulate matter specified in section 7473(b) of this title and section 7475(d)(2)(C)(iv) of this title, maximum allowable increases in particulate matter with an aerodynamic diameter smaller than or equal to 10 micrometers. Such substituted maximum allowable increases shall be of equal stringency in effect as those specified in the provisions for which they are substituted. Until the Administrator promulgates regulations under the authority of this subsection, the current maximum allowable increases in concentrations of particulate matter shall remain in effect.

§7477. Enforcement
[CAA §167]

The Administrator shall, and a State may, take such measures, including issuance of an order, or seeking injunctive relief, as necessary to prevent the construction or modification of a major emitting facility which does not conform to the requirements of this part, or which is proposed to be constructed in any area designated pursuant to section 7407(d) of this title as attainment or unclassifiable and which is not subject to an implementation plan which meets the requirements of this part.

§7478. Period before plan approval
[CAA §168]

(a) Existing regulations to remain in effect — Until such time as an applicable implementation plan is in effect for any area, which plan meets the requirements of this part to prevent significant deterioration of air quality with respect to any air pollutant, applicable regulations under this chapter prior to August 7, 1977, shall remain in effect to prevent significant deterioration of air quality in any such area for any such pollutant except as otherwise provided in subsection (b) of this section.

(b) Regulations deemed amended; construction commenced after June 1, 1975 — If any regulation in effect prior to August 7, 1977, to prevent significant deterioration of air quality would be inconsistent with the requirements of section 7472(a), section 7473(b) or section 7474(a) of this title, then such regulations shall be deemed amended so as to conform with such requirements. In the case of a facility on which construction was commenced (in accordance with this definition of "commenced" in section 7479(2) of this title) after June 1, 1975, and prior to August 7, 1977, the review and permitting of such facility shall be in accordance with the regulations for the prevention of significant deterioration in effect prior to August 7, 1977.

§7479. Definitions
[CAA §169]

For purposes of this part —

(1) The term "major emitting facility" means any of the following stationary sources of air pollutants which emit, or have the potential to emit, one hundred tons per year or more of any air pollutant from the following types of stationary sources: fossil-fuel fired steam electric plants of more than two hundred and fifty million British thermal units per hour heat input, coal cleaning plants (thermal dryers), kraft pulp mills, Portland Cement plants, primary zinc smelters, iron and steel plants, primary aluminum ore reduction plants, primary copper smelters, municipal incinerators capable of charging more than fifty tons of refuse per day, hydrofluoric, sulfuric, and nitric acid plants, petroleum refineries, lime plants, phosphate rock processing plants, coke oven batteries, sulfur recovery plants, carbon black plants (furnace process) primary lead smelters, fuel conversion plants, sintering plants, secondary metal production facilities, chemical process plants, fossil-fuel boilers of more than two hundred and

fifty million British thermal units per hour heat input, petroleum storage and transfer facilities with a capacity exceeding three hundred thousand barrels, taconite ore processing facilities, glass fiber processing plants, charcoal production facilities. Such term also includes any other source with the potential to emit two hundred and fifty tons per year or more of any air pollutant. This term shall not include new or modified facilities which are nonprofit health or education institutions which have been exempted by the State.

(2)(A) The term "commenced" as applied to construction of a major emitting facility means that the owner or operator has obtained all necessary preconstruction approvals or permits required by Federal, State, or local air pollution emissions and air quality laws or regulations and either has (i) begun, or caused to begin, a continuous program of physical on-site construction of the facility or (ii) entered into binding agreements or contractual obligations, which cannot be canceled or modified without substantial loss to the owner or operator, to undertake a program of construction of the facility to be completed within a reasonable time.

(B) The term "necessary preconstruction approvals or permits" means those permits or approvals required by the permitting authority as a precondition to undertaking any activity under clauses (i) or (ii) of subparagraph (A) of this paragraph.

(C) The term "construction" when used in connection with any source or facility, includes the modification (as defined in section 7411(a) of this title) of any source or facility.

(3) The term "best available control technology" means an emission limitation based on the maximum degree of reduction of each pollutant subject to regulation under this chapter emitted from or which results from any major emitting facility, which the permitting authority, on a case-by-case basis, taking into account energy, environmental, and economic impacts and other costs, determines is achievable for such facility through application of production processes and available methods, systems, and techniques, including fuel cleaning, clean fuels, or treatment or innovative fuel combustion techniques for control of each such pollutant. In no event shall application of "best available control technology" result in emissions of any pollutants which will exceed the emissions allowed by any applicable standard established pursuant to section 7411 or 7412 of this title. Emissions from any source utilizing clean fuels, or any other means, to comply with this paragraph shall not be allowed to increase above levels that would have been required under this paragraph as it existed prior to enactment of the Clean Air Act Amendments of 1990.

(4) The term "baseline concentration" means, with respect to a pollutant, the ambient concentra-

tion levels which exist at the time of the first application for a permit in an area subject to this part, based on air quality data available in the Environmental Protection Agency or a State air pollution control agency and on such monitoring data as the permit applicant is required to submit. Such ambient concentration levels shall take into account all projected emissions in, or which may affect, such area from any major emitting facility on which construction commenced prior to January 6, 1975, but which has not begun operation by the date of the baseline air quality concentration determination. Emissions of sulfur oxides and particulate matter from any major emitting facility on which construction commenced after January 6, 1975, shall not be included in the baseline and shall be counted against the maximum allowable increases in pollutant concentrations established under this part.

SUBPART II — VISIBILITY PROTECTION

§7491. Visibility protection for Federal class I areas

[CAA §169A]

(a) Impairment of visibility; list of areas; study and report

(1) Congress hereby declares as a national goal the prevention of any future, and the remedying of any existing, impairment of visibility in mandatory class I Federal areas which impairment results from manmade air pollution.

(2) Not later than six months after August 7, 1977, the Secretary of the Interior in consultation with other Federal land managers shall review all mandatory class I Federal areas and identify those where visibility is an important value of the area. From time to time the Secretary of the Interior may revise such identifications. Not later than one year after August 7, 1977, the Administrator shall, after consultation with the Secretary of the Interior, promulgate a list of mandatory class I Federal areas in which he determines visibility is an important value.

(3) Not later than eighteen months after August 7, 1977, the Administrator shall complete a study and report to Congress on available methods for implementing the national goal set forth in paragraph (1). Such report shall include recommendations for —

(A) methods for identifying, characterizing, determining, quantifying, and measuring visibility impairment in Federal areas referred to in paragraph (1), and

(B) modeling techniques (or other methods) for determining the extent to which manmade air pollution may reasonably be anticipated to cause or contribute to such impairment, and

(C) methods for preventing and remedying such manmade air pollution and resulting visibility impairment.

Such report shall also identify the classes or categories of sources and the types of air pollutants which, alone or in conjunction with other sources or pollutants, may reasonably be anticipated to cause or contribute significantly to impairment of visibility.

(4) Not later than twenty-four months after August 7, 1977, and after notice and public hearing, the Administrator shall promulgate regulations to assure (A) reasonable progress toward meeting the national goal specified in paragraph (1), and (B) compliance with the requirements of this section.

(b) Regulations — Regulations under subsection (a)(4) shall —

(1) provide guidelines to the States, taking into account the recommendations under subsection (a)(3) of this section on appropriate techniques and methods for implementing this section (as provided in subparagraphs (A) through (C) of such subsection (a)(3)), and

(2) require each applicable implementation plan for a State in which any area listed by the Administrator under subsection (a)(2) of this section is located (or for a State the emissions from which may reasonably be anticipated to cause or contribute to any impairment of visibility in any such area) to contain such emission limits, schedules of compliance and other measures as may be necessary to make reasonable progress toward meeting the national goal specified in subsection (a), including —

(A) except as otherwise provided pursuant to subsection (c), a requirement that each major stationary source which is in existence on August 7, 1977, but which has not been in operation for more than fifteen years as of such date, and which, as determined by the State (or the Administrator in the case of a plan promulgated under section 7410(c) of this title) emits any air pollutant which may reasonably be anticipated to cause or contribute to any impairment of visibility in any such area, shall procure, install, and operate, as expeditiously as practicable (and maintain thereafter) the best available retrofit technology, as determined by the State (or the Administrator in the case of a plan promulgated under section 7410(c) of this title) for controlling emissions from such source for the purpose of eliminating or reducing any such impairment, and

(B) a long-term (ten to fifteen years) strategy for making reasonable progress toward meeting the national goal specified in subsection (a) of this section.

In the case of a fossil-fuel fired generating powerplant having a total generating capacity in excess of 750 megawatts, the emission limitations required under this paragraph shall be determined pursuant to guidelines, promulgated by the Administrator under paragraph (1).

(c) Exemptions

(1) The Administrator may, by rule, after notice and opportunity for public hearing, exempt any major stationary source from the requirement of subsection (b)(2)(A) of this section, upon his determination that such source does not or will not, by itself or in combination with other sources, emit any air pollutant which may reasonably be anticipated to cause or contribute to a significant impairment of visibility in any mandatory class I Federal area.

(2) Paragraph (1) of this subsection shall not be applicable to any fossil-fuel fired powerplant with total design capacity of 750 megawatts or more, unless the owner or operator of any such plant demonstrates to the satisfaction of the Administrator that such powerplant is located at such distance from all areas listed by the Administrator under subsection (a)(2) of this section that such powerplant does not or will not, by itself or in combination with other sources, emit any air pollutant which may reasonably be anticipated to cause or contribute to significant impairment of visibility in any such area.

(3) An exemption under this subsection shall be effective only upon concurrence by the appropriate Federal land manager or managers with the Administrator's determination under this subsection.

(d) Consultation with appropriate Federal land managers

— Before holding the public hearing on the proposed revision of an applicable implementation plan to meet the requirements of this section, the State (or the Administrator, in the case of a plan promulgated under section 7410(c) of this title) shall consult in person with the appropriate Federal land manager or managers and shall include a summary of the conclusions and recommendations of the Federal land managers in the notice to the public.

(e) Buffer zones

— In promulgating regulations under this section, the Administrator shall not require the use of any automatic or uniform buffer zone or zones.

(f) Nondiscretionary duty

— For purposes of section 7604(a)(2), of this title the meeting of the national goal specified in subsection (a)(1) of this section by any specific date or dates shall not be considered a "nondiscretionary duty" of the Administrator.

(g) Definitions

— For the purpose of this section —

(1) in determining reasonable progress there shall be taken into consideration the costs of compliance, the time necessary for compliance, and the energy and nonair quality environmental impacts of compliance, and the remaining useful life of any existing source subject to such requirements;

(2) in determining best available retrofit technology the State (or the Administrator in determining emission limitations which reflect such technology) shall take into consideration the costs of compliance, the energy and nonair quality environmental impacts of compliance, any existing pollution control technology in use at the source, the remaining useful life of the source, and the degree of improvement in visibility which may reasonably be anticipated to result from the use of such technology;

(3) the term "manmade air pollution" means air pollution which results directly or indirectly from human activities;

(4) the term "as expeditiously as practicable" means as expeditiously as practicable but in no event later than five years after the date of approval of a plan revision under this section (or the date of promulgation of such a plan revision in the case of action by the Administrator under section 110(c) for purposes of this section);

(5) the term "mandatory class I Federal areas" means Federal areas which may not be designated as other than class I under this part;

(6) the terms "visibility impairment" and "impairment of visibility" shall include reduction in visual range and atmospheric discoloration; and

(7) the term "major stationary source" means the following types of stationary sources with the potential to emit 250 tons or more of any pollutant; fossil-fuel fired steam electric plants of more than 250 million British thermal units per hour heat input, coal cleaning plants (thermal dryers), kraft pulp mills, Portland Cement plants, primary zinc smelters, iron and steel mill plants, primary aluminum ore reduction plants, primary copper smelters, municipal incinerators capable of charging more than 250 tons of refuse per day, hydrofluoric, sulfuric, and nitric acid plants, petroleum refineries, lime plants, phosphate rock processing plants, coke oven batteries, sulfur recovery plants, carbon black plants (furnace process), primary lead smelters, fuel conversion plants, sintering plants, secondary metal production facilities, chemical process plants, fossil-fuel boilers of more than 250 million British thermal units per hour heat input, petroleum storage and transfer facilities with a capacity exceeding 300,000 barrels, taconite ore processing facilities, glass fiber processing plants, charcoal production facilities.

§7492. Visibility
[CAA §169B]

(a) Studies

(1) The Administrator, in conjunction with the National Park Service and other appropriate Federal agencies, shall conduct research to identify and evaluate sources and source regions of both visibility impairment and regions that provide predominantly clean air in class I areas. A total of $8,000,000 per year for 5 years is authorized to be appropriated for the Environmental Protection Agency and the other Federal agencies to conduct this research. The research shall include —

(A) expansion of current visibility related monitoring in class I areas;

(B) assessment of current sources of visibility impairing pollution and clean air corridors;

(C) adaptation of regional air quality models for the assessment of visibility;

(D) studies of atmospheric chemistry and physics of visibility.

(2) Based on the findings available from the research required in subsection (a)(1) of this section as well as other available scientific and technical data, studies, and other available information pertaining to visibility source receptor relationships, the Administrator shall conduct an assessment and evaluation that identifies, to the extent possible, sources and source regions of visibility impairment including natural sources as well as source regions of clear air for class I areas. The Administrator shall produce interim findings from this study within 3 years after enactment of the Clean Air Act Amendments of 1990.

(b) Impacts of other provisions — Within 24 months after November 15, 1990, the Administrator shall conduct an assessment of the progress and improvements in visibility in class I areas that are likely to result from the implementation of the provisions of the Clean Air Act Amendments of 1990 other than the provisions of this section. Every 5 years thereafter the Administrator shall conduct an assessment of actual progress and improvement in visibility in class I areas. The Administrator shall prepare a written report on each assessment and transmit copies of these reports to the appropriate committees of Congress.

(c) Establishment of visibility transport regions and commissions

(1) Authority to establish visibility transport regions — Whenever, upon the Administrator's motion or by petition from the Governors of at least two affected States, the Administrator has reason to believe that the current or projected interstate transport of air pollutants from one or more States contributes significantly to visibility impairment in class I areas located in the affected States, the Administrator may establish a transport region for such pollutants that includes such States. The Administrator, upon the Administrator's own motion or upon petition from the Governor of any affected State, or upon the recommendations of a transport commission established under subsection (b) of this section may —

(A) add any State or portion of a State to a visibility transport region when the Administrator determines that the interstate transport of air pollutants from such State significantly contributes to visibility impairment in a class I area located within the transport region, or

(B) remove any State or portion of a State from the region whenever the Administrator has reason to believe that the control of emissions in that State or portion of the State pursuant to this section will not significantly contribute

to the protection or enhancement of visibility in any class I area in the region.

(2) Visibility transport commissions — Whenever the Administrator establishes a transport region under subsection (c)(1) of this section, the Administrator shall establish a transport commission comprised of (as a minimum) each of the following members:

(A) the Governor of each State in the Visibility Transport Region, or the Governor's designee;

(B) The Administrator or the Administrator's designee; and

(C) A representative of each Federal agency charged with the direct management of each class I area or areas within the Visibility Transport Region.

(3) Ex officio members — All representatives of the Federal Government shall be ex officio members.

(4) Federal Advisory Committee Act — The visibility transport commissions shall be exempt from the requirements of the Federal Advisory Committee Act (5 U.S.C. Appendix 2, Section 1).

(d) Duties of visibility transport commissions — A Visibility Transport Commission —

(1) shall assess the scientific and technical data, studies, and other currently available information, including studies conducted pursuant to subsection (a)(1) of this section, pertaining to adverse impacts on visibility from potential or projected growth in emissions from sources located in the Visibility Transport Region; and

(2) shall, within 4 years of establishment, issue a report to the Administrator recommending what measures, if any, should be taken under the Clean Air Act to remedy such adverse impacts. The report required by this subsection shall address at least the following measures:

(A) the establishment of clean air corridors, in which additional restrictions on increases in emissions may be appropriate to protect visibility in affected class I areas;

(B) the imposition of the requirements of part D of this title affecting the construction of new major stationary sources or major modifications to existing sources in such clean air corridors specifically including the alternative siting analysis provisions of section 7503(a)(5) of this title; and

(C) the promulgation of regulations under section 7491 of this title to address long range strategies for addressing regional haze which impairs visibility in affected class I areas.

(e) Duties of Administrator

(1) The Administrator shall, taking into account the studies pursuant to subsection (a)(1) of this section and the reports pursuant to subsection (d)(2) of this section and any other relevant information, within eighteen months of receipt of the report referred to in subsection (d)(2) of

this section, carry out the Administrator's regulatory responsibilities under section 7491 of this title, including criteria for measuring "reasonable progress" toward the national goal.

(2) Any regulations promulgated under section 7491 of this title pursuant to this subsection shall require affected States to revise within 12 months their implementation plans under section 7410 of this title to contain such emission limits, schedules of compliance, and other measures as may be necessary to carry out regulations promulgated pursuant to this subsection.

(f) Grand Canyon visibility transport commission — The Administrator pursuant to subsection (c)(1) of this section shall, within 12 months, establish a visibility transport commission for the region affecting the visibility of the Grand Canyon National Park.

PART D — PLAN REQUIREMENTS FOR NONATTAINMENT AREAS

SUBPART 1 — NONATTAINMENT AREAS IN GENERAL
[CAA§171]
§7501. Definitions —

For the purpose of this part —

(1) Reasonable further progress — The term "reasonable further progress" means such annual incremental reductions in emissions of the relevant air pollutant as are required by this part or may reasonably be required by the Administrator for the purpose of ensuring attainment of the applicable national ambient air quality standard by the applicable date.

(2) Nonattainment area — The term "nonattainment area" means, for any air pollutant, an area which is designated "nonattainment" with respect to that pollutant within the meaning of section 7407(d) of this title.

(3) Lowest achievable emission rate — The term "lowest achievable emission rate" means for any source, that rate of emissions which reflects —

(A) the most stringent emission limitation which is contained in the implementation plan of any State for such class or category of source, unless the owner or operator of the proposed source demonstrates that such limitations are not achievable, or

(B) the most stringent emission limitation which is achieved in practice by such class or category of source, whichever is more stringent.

In no event shall the application of this term permit a proposed new or modified source to emit any pollutant in excess of the amount allowable under applicable new source standards of performance.

(4) Modifications; modified — The terms "modifications" and "modified" mean the same as the term "modification" as used in section 7411(a)(4) of this title.

§7502. Nonattainment plan provisions in general
[CAA §172]
(a) Classifications and attainment dates

(1) Classifications

(A) On or after the date the Administrator promulgates the designation of an area as a non-attainment area pursuant to section 7407(d) of this title with respect to any national ambient air quality standard (or any revised standard, including a revision of any standard in effect on November 15, 1990), the Administrator may classify the area for the purpose of applying an attainment date pursuant to paragraph (2), and for other purposes. In determining the appropriate classification, if any, for nonattainment area, the Administrator may consider such factors as the severity of nonattainment in such area and the availability and feasibility of the pollution control measures that the Administrator believes may be necessary to provide for attainment of such standard in such area.

(B) The Administrator shall publish a notice in the Federal Register announcing each classification under subparagraph (A), except the Administrator shall provide an opportunity for at least 30 days for written comment. Such classification shall not be subject to the provisions of sections 553 through 557 of Title 5 of the United States Code (concerning notice and comment) and shall not be subject to judicial review until the Administrator takes final action under subsection (k) or (l) of section 7410 of this title (concerning action on plan submissions) or section 7509 of this title (concerning sanctions) with respect to any plan submissions required by virtue of such classification.

(C) This paragraph shall not apply with respect to nonattainment areas for which classifications are specifically provided under other provisions of this part.

(2) Attainment dates for nonattainment areas

(A) The attainment date for an area designated nonattainment with respect to a national primary ambient air quality standard shall be the date by which attainment can be achieved as expeditiously as practicable, but no later than 5 years from the date such area was designated nonattainment under section 7407(d) of this title, except that the Administrator may extend the attainment date to the extent the

Administrator determines appropriate, for a period no greater than 10 years from the date of designation as nonattainment, considering the severity of nonattainment and the availability and feasibility of pollution control measures.

(B) The attainment date for an area designated nonattainment with respect to a secondary national ambient air quality standard shall be the date by which attainment can be achieved as expeditiously as practicable after the date such area was designated nonattainment under section 7407(d) of this title.

(C) Upon application by any State, the Administrator may extend for 1 additional year (hereinafter referred to as the "Extension Year") the attainment date determined by the Administrator under subparagraph (A) or (B) if —

    (i) the State has complied with all requirements and commitments pertaining to the area in the applicable implementation plan, and

    (ii) in accordance with guidance published by the Administrator, no more than a minimal number of exceedances of the relevant national ambient air quality standard has occurred in the area in the year preceding the Extension Year.

No more than 2 one-year extensions may be issued under this subparagraph for a single nonattainment area.

(D) This paragraph shall not apply with respect to nonattainment areas for which attainment dates are specifically provided under other provisions of this part.

(b) Schedule for plan submissions — At the time the Administrator promulgates the designation of an area as nonattainment with respect to a national ambient air quality standard under section 7407(d), of this title the Administrator shall establish a schedule according to which the State containing such area shall submit a plan or plan revision (including the plan items) meeting the applicable requirements of subsection (c) of this section and section 7410(a)(2) of this title. Such schedule shall at a minimum, include a date or dates, extending no later than 3 years from the date of the nonattainment designation, for the submission of a plan or plan revision (including the plan items) meeting the applicable requirements of subsection (c) of this section and section 7410(a)(2) of this title.

(c) Nonattainment plan provisions — The plan provisions (including plan items) required to be submitted under this part shall comply with each of the following:

    (1) In general — Such plan provisions shall provide for the implementation of all reasonably available control measures as expeditiously as practicable (including such reductions in emissions from existing sources in the area as may be obtained through the adoption, at a minimum, of reasonably available control technology) and shall provide for attainment of the national primary ambient air quality standards.

    (2) RFP — Such plan provisions shall require reasonable further progress.

    (3) Inventory — Such plan provisions shall include a comprehensive, accurate, current inventory of actual emissions from all sources of the relevant pollutant or pollutants in such area, including such periodic revisions as the Administrator may determine necessary to assure that the requirements of this part are met.

    (4) Identification and quantification — Such plan provisions shall expressly identify and quantify the emissions, if any, of any such pollutant or pollutants which will be allowed, in accordance with section 7503(a)(1)(B) of this title, from the construction and operation of major new or modified stationary sources in each such area. The plan shall demonstrate to the satisfaction of the Administrator that the emissions quantified for this purpose will be consistent with the achievement of reasonable further progress and will not interfere with attainment of the applicable national ambient air quality standard by the applicable attainment date.

    (5) Permits for new and modified major stationary sources — Such plan provisions shall require permits for the construction and operation of new or modified major stationary sources anywhere in the nonattainment area, in accordance with section 7503 of this title.

    (6) Other measures — Such plan provisions shall include enforceable emission limitations, and such other control measures, means or techniques (including economic incentives such as fees, marketable permits, and auctions of emission rights), as well as schedules and timetables for compliance, as may be necessary or appropriate to provide for attainment of such standard in such area by the applicable attainment date specified in this part.

    (7) Compliance with section 7410(a)(2) — Such plan provisions shall also meet the applicable provisions of section 7410(a)(2) of this title.

    (8) Equivalent techniques — Upon application by any State, the Administrator may allow the use of equivalent modeling, emission inventory, and planning procedures, unless the Administrator determines that the proposed techniques are, in the aggregate, less effective than the methods specified by the Administrator.

    (9) Contingency measures — Such plan shall provide for the implementation of specific measures to be undertaken if the area fails to make reasonable further progress, or to attain the national primary ambient air quality standard by the attainment date applicable under this part. Such measures shall be included in the plan revision as contingency measures to take effect in any such case without further action by the State or the Administrator.

(d) Plan revisions required in response to finding of plan inadequacy — Any plan revision for a nonattainment area which is required to be submitted in response to a finding by the Administrator pursuant to section 7410(k)(5) of this title (relating to calls for plan revisions) must correct the plan deficiency (or deficiencies) specified by the Administrator and meet all other applicable plan requirements of section 7410 of this title and this part. The Administrator may reasonably adjust the dates otherwise applicable under such requirements to such revision (except for attainment dates that have not yet elapsed), to the extent necessary to achieve a consistent application of such requirements. In order to facilitate submittal by the States of adequate and approvable plans consistent with the applicable requirements of this Act, the Administrator shall, as appropriate and from time to time, issue written guidelines, interpretations, and information to the States which shall be available to the public, taking into consideration any such guidelines, interpretations, or information provided before November 15, 1990.

(e) Future modification of standard — If the Administrator relaxes a national primary ambient air quality standard after November 15, 1990, the Administrator shall, within 12 months after the relaxation, promulgate requirements applicable to all areas which have not attained that standard as of the date of such relaxation. Such requirements shall provide for controls which are not less stringent than the controls applicable to areas designated nonattainment before such relaxation.

§7503. Permit requirements
[CAA §173]

(a) In general — The permit program required by section 7502(b)(6) of this title shall provide that permits to construct and operate may be issued if —

(1) in accordance with regulations issued by the Administrator for the determination of baseline emissions in a manner consistent with the assumptions underlying the applicable implementation plan approved under section 7410 of this title and this part, the permitting agency determines that —

(A) by the time the source is to commence operation, sufficient offsetting emissions reductions have been obtained, such that total allowable emissions from existing sources in the region, from new or modified sources which are not major emitting facilities, and from the proposed source will be sufficiently less than total emissions from existing sources (as determined in accordance with the regulations under this paragraph) prior to the application for such permit to construct or modify so as to represent (when considered together with the plan provisions required under section 7502

of this title) reasonable further progress (as defined in section 7501 of this title); or

(B) in the case of a new or modified major stationary source which is located in a zone (within the nonattainment area) identified by the Administrator, in consultation with the Secretary of Housing and Urban Development, as a zone to which economic development should be targeted, that emissions of such pollutant resulting from the proposed new or modified major stationary source will not cause or contribute to emissions levels which exceed the allowance permitted for such pollutant for such area from new or modified major stationary sources under section 7502(c) of this title;

(2) the proposed source is required to comply with the lowest achievable emission rate;

(3) the owner or operator of the proposed new or modified source has demonstrated that all major stationary sources owned or operated by such person (or by any entity controlling, controlled by, or under common control with such person) in such State are subject to emission limitations and are in compliance, or on a schedule for compliance, with all applicable emission limitations and standards under this Act;

(4) the Administrator has not determined that the applicable implementation plan is not being adequately implemented for the nonattainment area in which the proposed source is to be constructed or modified in accordance with the requirements of this part; and

(5) an analysis of alternative sites, sizes, production processes, and environmental control techniques for such proposed source demonstrates that benefits of the proposed source significantly outweigh the environmental and social costs imposed as a result of its location, construction, or modification.

Any emission reductions required as a precondition of the issuance of a permit under paragraph (1) shall be federally enforceable before such permit may be issued.

(b) Prohibition on use of old growth allowances — Any growth allowance included in an applicable implementation plan to meet the requirements of section 7502(b)(5) of this title (as in effect immediately before November 15, 1990) shall not be valid for use in any area that received or receives a notice under section 7410(a)(2)(H)(ii) of this title (as in effect immediately before November 15, 1990) or under section 7410(k)(1) of this title that its applicable implementation plan containing such allowance is substantially inadequate.

(c) Offsets

(1) The owner or operator of a new or modified major stationary source may comply with any offset requirement in effect under this part for increased emissions of any air pollutant only by obtaining emission reductions of such air pollut-

ant from the same source or other sources in the same nonattainment area, except that the State may allow the owner or operator of a source to obtain such emission reductions in another nonattainment area if (A) the other area has an equal or higher nonattainment classification than the area in which the source is located and (B) emissions from such other area contribute to a violation of the national ambient air quality standard in the nonattainment area in which the source is located. Such emission reductions shall be, by the time a new or modified source commences operation, in effect and enforceable and shall assure that the total tonnage of increased emissions of the air pollutant from the new or modified source shall be offset by an equal or greater reduction, as applicable, in the actual emissions of such air pollutant from the same or other sources in the area.

(2) Emission reductions otherwise required by this Act shall not be creditable as emissions reductions for purposes of any such offset requirement. Incidental emission reductions which are not otherwise required by this Act shall be creditable as emission reductions for such purposes if such emission reductions meet the requirements of paragraph (1).

(d) Control technology information — The State shall provide that control technology information from permits issued under this section will be promptly submitted to the Administrator for purposes of making such information available through the RACT/BACT/LAER clearinghouse to other States and to the general public.

(e) Rocket engines or motors — The permitting authority of a State shall allow a source to offset by alternative or innovative means emission increases from rocket engine and motor firing, and cleaning related to such firing, at an existing or modified major source that tests rocket engines or motors under the following conditions:

(1) Any modification proposed is solely for the purpose of expanding the testing of rocket engines or motors at an existing source that is permitted to test such engines on the date of enactment of this subsection.

(2) The source demonstrates to the satisfaction of the permitting authority of the State that it has used all reasonable means to obtain and utilize offsets, as determined on an annual basis, for the emissions increases beyond allowable levels, that all available offsets are being used, and that sufficient offsets are not available to the source.

(3) The source has obtained a written finding from the Department of Defense, Department of Transportation, National Aeronautics and Space Administration or other appropriate Federal agency, that the testing of rocket motors or engines at the facility is required for a program essential to the national security.

(4) The source will comply with an alternative measure, imposed by the permitting authority, designed to offset any emission increases beyond permitted levels not directly offset by the source. In lieu of imposing any alternative offset measures, the permitting authority may impose an emissions fee to be paid to such authority of a State which shall be an amount no greater than 1.5 times the average cost of stationary source control measures adopted in that area during the previous 3 years. The permitting authority shall utilize the fees in a manner that maximizes the emissions reductions in that area.

§7504. Planning procedures
[CAA §174]

(a) In general — For any ozone, carbon monoxide, or PM-10 nonattainment area, the State containing such area and elected officials of affected local governments shall, before the date required for submittal of the inventory described under sections 7511(a)(1) and 7512(a)(1) of this title, jointly review and update as necessary the planning procedures adopted pursuant to this subsection as in effect immediately before November 15, 1990, or develop new planning procedures pursuant to this subsection, as appropriate. In preparing such procedures the State and local elected officials shall determine which elements of a revised implementation plan will be developed, adopted, and implemented (through means including enforcement) by the State and which by local governments or regional agencies, or any combination of local governments, regional agencies, or the State. The implementation plan required by this part shall be prepared by an organization certified by the State, in consultation with elected officials of local governments and in accordance with the determination under the second sentence of this subsection. Such organization shall include elected officials of local governments in the affected area, and representatives of the State air quality planning agency, the State transportation planning agency, the metropolitan planning organization designated to conduct the continuing, cooperative and comprehensive transportation planning process for the area under section 134 of Title 23, United States Code, the organization responsible for the air quality maintenance planning process under regulations implementing this Act, and any other organization with responsibilities for developing, submitting, or implementing the plan required by this part. Such organization may be one that carried out these functions before November 15, 1990.

(b) Coordination — The preparation of implementation plan provisions and subsequent plan revisions under the continuing transportation-air quality planning process described in section 108(e) shall be coordinated with the continuing, cooperative and comprehensive transportation planning process required under section 134 of Title 23, United States Code, and such planning processes shall take into account the requirements of this part.

(c) Joint planning — In the case of a nonattainment area that is included within more than one State, the affected States may jointly, through interstate compact or otherwise, undertake and implement all or part of the planning procedures described in this section.

§7505. Environmental Protection Agency grants
[CAA §175]

(a) Plan revision development cost — The Administrator shall make grants to any organization of local elected officials with transportation or air quality maintenance planning responsibilities recognized by the State under section 7504(a) of this title for payment of the reasonable costs of developing a plan revision under this part.

(b) Uses of grant funds — The amount granted to any organization under subsection (a) shall be 100 percent of any additional costs of developing a plan revision under this part for the first two fiscal years following receipt of the grant under this paragraph, and shall supplement any funds available under Federal law to such organization for transportation or air quality maintenance planning. Grants under this section shall not be used for construction.

§7505a. Maintenance plans
[CAA §175A]

(a) Plan revision — Each State which submits a request under section 7407(d) of this title for redesignation of a nonattainment area for any air pollutant as an area which has attained the national primary ambient air quality standard for that air pollutant shall also submit a revision of the applicable State implementation plan to provide for the maintenance of the national primary ambient air quality standard for such air pollutant in the area concerned for at least 10 years after the redesignation. The plan shall contain such additional measures, if any, as may be necessary to ensure such maintenance.

(b) Subsequent plan revisions — 8 years after redesignation of any area as an attainment area under section 7407(d) of this title, the State shall submit to the Administrator an additional revision of the applicable State implementation plan for maintaining the national primary ambient air quality standard for 10 years after the expiration of the 10-year period referred to in subsection (a) of this section.

(c) Nonattainment requirements applicable pending plan approval — Until such plan revision is approved and an area is redesignated as attainment for any area designated as a nonattainment area, the requirements of this part shall continue in force and effect with respect to such area.

(d) Contingency provisions — Each plan revision submitted under this section shall contain such contingency provisions as the Administrator deems necessary to assure that the State will promptly correct any violation of the standard which occurs after the redesignation of the area as an attainment area. Such provisions shall include a requirement that the State will implement all measures with respect to the control of the air pollutant concerned which were contained in the State implementation plan for the area before redesignation of the area as an attainment area. The failure of any area redesignated as an attainment area to maintain the national ambient air quality standard concerned shall not result in a requirement that the State revise its State implementation plan unless the Administrator, in the Administrator's discretion, requires the State to submit a revised State implementation plan.

§7506. Limitations on certain Federal assistance
[CAA §176]

Subsections (a) and (b), repealed by Pub. L. 101-549, Title I, §110(4), 104 Stat. 2470

(c) Activities not conforming to approved or promulgated plans

(1) No department, agency, or instrumentality of the Federal Government shall engage in, support in any way or provide financial assistance for, license or permit, or approve, any activity which does not conform to an implementation plan after it has been approved or promulgated under section 7410 of this title. No metropolitan planning organization designated under section 134 of Title 23, United States Code, shall give its approval to any project, program, or plan which does not conform to an implementation plan approved or promulgated under section 7410 of this title. The assurance of conformity to such an implementation plan shall be an affirmative responsibility of the head of such department, agency, or instrumentality. Conformity to an implementation plan means —

(A) conformity to an implementation plan's purpose of eliminating or reducing the severity and number of violations of the national ambient air quality standards and achieving expeditious attainment of such standards; and

(B) that such activities will not —

(i) cause or contribute to any new violation of any standard in any area;

(ii) increase the frequency or severity of any existing violation of any standard in any area; or

(iii) delay timely attainment of any standard or any required interim emission reductions or other milestones in any area.

The determination of conformity shall be based on the most recent estimates of emissions, and such estimates shall be determined from the most recent population, employment, travel and congestion estimates as determined by the metropolitan planning organization or other agency authorized to make such estimates.

(2) Any transportation plan or program developed pursuant to Title 23, United States Code, or the Urban Mass Transportation Act shall implement the transportation provisions of any applicable implementation plan approved under this Act applicable to all or part of the area covered by such transportation plan or program. No Federal agency may approve, accept or fund any transportation plan, program or project unless such plan, program or project has been found to conform to any applicable implementation plan in effect under this Act. In particular —

(A) no transportation plan or transportation improvement program may be adopted by a metropolitan planning organization designated under Title 23, United States Code, or the Urban Mass Transportation Act, or be found to be in conformity by a metropolitan planning organization until a final determination has been made that emissions expected from implementation of such plans and programs are consistent with estimates of emissions from motor vehicles and necessary emissions reductions contained in the applicable implementation plan, and that the plan or program will conform to the requirements of paragraph (1)(B);

(B) no metropolitan planning organization or other recipient of funds under Title 23, United States Code, or the Urban Mass Transportation Act shall adopt or approve a transportation improvement program of projects until it determines that such program provides for timely implementation of transportation control measures consistent with schedules included in the applicable implementation plan;

(C) a transportation project may be adopted or approved by a metropolitan planning organization or any recipient of funds designated under Title 23, United States Code, or the Urban Mass Transportation Act, or found in conformity by a metropolitan planning organization or approved, accepted, or funded by the Department of Transportation only if it meets either the requirements of subparagraph (D) or the following requirements —

(i) such a project comes from a conforming plan and program;

(ii) the design concept and scope of such project have not changed significantly since the conformity finding regarding the plan and program from which the project derived; and

(iii) the design concept and scope of such project at the time of the conformity determination for the program was adequate to determine emissions.

(D) Any project not referred to in subparagraph (C) shall be treated as conforming to the applicable implementation plan only if it is demonstrated that the projected emissions from such project, when considered together with emissions projected for the conforming transportation plans and programs within the nonattainment area, do not cause such plans and programs to exceed the emission reduction projections and schedules assigned to such plans and programs in the applicable implementation plan.

(E) The appropriate metropolitan planning organization shall redetermine conformity of existing transportation plans and programs not later than 2 years after the date on which the Administrator —

(i) finds a motor vehicle emissions budget to be adequate in accordance with section 93.118(e)(4) of title 40, Code of Federal Regulations (as in effect on October 1, 2004);

(ii) approves an implementation plan that establishes a motor vehicle emissions budget if that budget has not yet been determined to be adequate in accordance with clause (i); or

(iii) promulgates an implementation plan that establishes or revises a motor vehicle emissions budget.

(3) Until such time as the implementation plan revision referred to in paragraph (4)(C) is approved, conformity of such plans, programs, and projects will be demonstrated if —

(A) the transportation plans and programs —

(i) are consistent with the most recent estimates of mobile source emissions;

(ii) provide for the expeditious implementation of transportation control measures in the applicable implementation plan; and

(iii) with respect to ozone and carbon monoxide nonattainment areas, contribute to annual emissions reductions consistent with sections 7511(b)(1) and 7512(a)(7) of this title; and

(B) the transportation projects —

(i) come from a conforming transportation plan and program as defined in subparagraph (A) or for 12 months after November 15, 1990, from a transportation program found to conform within 3 years prior November 15, 1990; and

(ii) in carbon monoxide nonattainment areas, eliminate or reduce the severity and number of violations of the carbon monoxide standards in the area substantially affected by the project.

With regard to subparagraph (B)(ii), such determination may be made as part of either the conformity determination for the transportation program or for the individual project taken as a whole during the environmental review phase of project development.

(4) Criteria and procedures for determining conformity

(A) In general — The Administrator shall promulgate, and periodically update, criteria and procedures for determining conformity (except in the case of transportation plans, programs, and projects) of, and for keeping the Administrator informed about, the activities referred to in paragraph (1).

(B) Transportation plans, programs, and projects — The Administrator, with the concurrence of the Secretary of Transportation, shall promulgate, and periodically update, criteria and procedures for demonstrating and assuring conformity in the case of transportation plans, programs, and projects.

(C) Civil action to compel promulgation — A civil action may be brought against the Administrator and the Secretary of Transportation under section 7604 of this title to compel promulgation of such criteria and procedures and the Federal district court shall have jurisdiction to order such promulgation.

(D) The procedures and criteria shall, at a minimum —

(i) address the consultation procedures to be undertaken by metropolitan planning organizations and the Secretary of Transportation with State and local air quality agencies and State departments of transportation before such organizations and the Secretary make conformity determinations;

(ii) address the appropriate frequency for making conformity determinations, but the frequency for making conformity determinations on updated transportation plans and programs shall be every 4 years, except in a case in which —

(I) the metropolitan planning organization elects to update a transportation plan or program more frequently; or

(II) the metropolitan planning organization is required to determine conformity in accordance with paragraph (2)(E); and

(iii) address how conformity determinations will be made with respect to maintenance plans.

(E) Inclusion of criteria and procedures in SIP — Not later than 2 years after August 10, 2005, the procedures under subparagraph (A) shall include a requirement that each State include in the State implementation plan criteria and procedures for consultation required by subparagraph (D)(i), and enforcement and

enforceability (pursuant to sections 93.125(c) and 93.122(a)(4)(ii) of title 40, Code of Federal Regulations) in accordance with the Administrator's criteria and procedures for consultation, enforcement and enforceability.

(F) Compliance with the rules of the Administrator for determining the conformity of transportation plans, programs, and projects funded or approved under Title 23 or chapter 53 of Title 49 to State or Federal implementation plans shall not be required for traffic signal synchronization projects prior to the funding, approval or implementation of such projects. The supporting regional emissions analysis for any conformity determination made with respect to a transportation plan, program, or project shall consider the effect on emissions of any such project funded, approved, or implemented prior to the conformity determination.

(5) Applicability

This subsection shall apply only with respect to —

(A) a nonattainment area and each pollutant for which the area is designated as a nonattainment area; and

(B) an area that was designated as a nonattainment area but that was later redesignated by the Administrator as an attainment area and that is required to develop a maintenance plan under section 7505a of this title with respect to the specific pollutant for which the area was designated nonattainment.

(6) Notwithstanding paragraph 5, this subsection shall not apply with respect to an area designated nonattainment under section 7407(d)(1) of this title until 1 year after that area is first designated nonattainment for a specific national ambient air quality standard. This paragraph only applies with respect to the national ambient air quality standard for which an area is newly designated nonattainment and does not affect the area's requirements with respect to all other national ambient air quality standards for which the area is designated nonattainment or has been redesignated from nonattainment to attainment with a maintenance plan pursuant to section 175(A) (including any pre-existing national ambient air quality standard for a pollutant for which a new or revised standard has been issued).

(7) Conformity horizon for transportation plans

(A) In general — Each conformity determination required under this section for a transportation plan under section 134(i) of Title 23 or section 5303(i) of Title 49 shall require a demonstration of conformity for the period ending on either the final year of the transportation plan, or at the election of the metropolitan planning organization, after consultation with the air pollution control agency and solicitation of public comments and consideration of such comments, the longest of the following periods:

(i) The first 10-year period of any such transportation plan.

(ii) The latest year in the implementation plan applicable to the area that contains a motor vehicle emission budget.

(iii) The year after the completion date of a regionally significant project if the project is included in the transportation improvement program or the project requires approval before the subsequent conformity determination.

(B) Regional emissions analysis — The conformity determination shall be accompanied by a regional emissions analysis for the last year of the transportation plan and for any year shown to exceed emission budgets by a prior analysis, if such year extends beyond the applicable period as determined under subparagraph (A).

(C) Exception — In any case in which an area has a revision to an implementation plan under section 7505a(b) of this title and the Administrator has found the motor vehicles emissions budgets from that revision to be adequate in accordance with section 93.118(e)(4) of title 40, Code of Federal Regulations (as in effect on October 1, 2004), or has approved the revision, the demonstration of conformity at the election of the metropolitan planning organization, after consultation with the air pollution control agency and solicitation of public comments and consideration of such comments, shall be required to extend only through the last year of the implementation plan required under section 7505a(b) of this title.

(D) Effect of election — Any election by a metropolitan planning organization under this paragraph shall continue in effect until the metropolitan planning organization elects otherwise.

(E) Air pollution control agency defined — In this paragraph, the term "air pollution control agency" means an air pollution control agency (as defined in section 7602(b) of this title) that is responsible for developing plans or controlling air pollution within the area covered by a transportation plan.

(8) Substitution of transportation control measures

(A) In general — Transportation control measures that are specified in an implementation plan may be replaced or added to the implementation plan with alternate or additional transportation control measures —

(i) if the substitute measures achieve equivalent or greater emissions reductions than the control measure to be replaced, as demonstrated with an emissions impact analysis that is consistent with the current methodology used for evaluating the replaced control measure in the implementation plan;

(ii) if the substitute control measures are implemented —

(I) in accordance with a schedule that is consistent with the schedule provided for control measures in the implementation plan; or

(II) if the implementation plan date for implementation of the control measure to be replaced has passed, as soon as practicable after the implementation plan date but not later than the date on which emission reductions are necessary to achieve the purpose of the implementation plan;

(iii) if the substitute and additional control measures are accompanied with evidence of adequate personnel and funding and authority under State or local law to implement, monitor, and enforce the control measures;

(iv) if the substitute and additional control measures were developed through a collaborative process that included —

(I) participation by representatives of all affected jurisdictions (including local air pollution control agencies, the State air pollution control agency, and State and local transportation agencies);

(II) consultation with the Administrator; and

(III) reasonable public notice and opportunity for comment; and

(v) if the metropolitan planning organization, State air pollution control agency, and the Administrator concur with the equivalency of the substitute or additional control measures.

(B) Adoption

(i) Concurrence by the metropolitan planning organization, State air pollution control agency and the Administrator as required by subparagraph (A)(v) shall constitute adoption of the substitute or additional control measures so long as the requirements of subparagraphs (A)(i), (A)(ii), (A)(iii) and (A)(iv) are met.

(ii) Once adopted, the substitute or additional control measures become, by operation of law, part of the State implementation plan and become federally enforceable.

(iii) Within 90 days of its concurrence under subparagraph (A)(v), the State air pollution control agency shall submit the substitute or additional control measure to the Administrator for incorporation in the codification of the applicable implementation plan. Nothwithstanding any other provision of this chapter, no additional State process shall be necessary to support such revision to the applicable plan.

(C) No requirement for express permission — The substitution or addition of a transportation control measure in accordance with this paragraph and the funding or approval of such a control measure shall not be contingent on the existence of any provision in the applicable implementation plan that expressly permits such a substitution or addition.

(D) No requirement for new conformity determination — The substitution or addition of a transportation control measure in accordance with this paragraph shall not require —

(i) a new conformity determination for the transportation plan; or

(ii) a revision of the implementation plan.

(E) Continuation of control measure being replaced — A control measure that is being replaced by a substitute control measure under this paragraph shall remain in effect until the substitute control measure is adopted by the State pursuant to subparagraph (B).

(F) Effect of adoption — Adoption of a substitute control measure shall constitute rescission of the previously applicable control measure.

(9) Lapse of conformity — If a conformity determination required under this subsection for a transportation plan under section 134(i) of Title 23, or section 5303(i) of Title 49, or a transportation improvement program under section 134(j) of such title 23 or under section 5303(j) of such title 49 is not made by the applicable deadline and such failure is not corrected by additional measures to either reduce motor vehicle emissions sufficient to demonstrate compliance with the requirements of this subsection within 12 months after such deadline or other measures sufficient to correct such failures, the transportation plan shall lapse.

(10) Lapse — In this subsection, the term "lapse" means that the conformity determination for a transportation plan or transportation improvement program has expired, and thus there is no currently conforming transportation plan or transportation improvement program.

(d) **Priority of achieving and maintaining national primary ambient air quality standards** — Each department, agency, or instrumentality of the Federal Government having authority to conduct or support any program with air-quality related transportation consequences shall give priority in the exercise of such authority, consistent with statutory requirements for allocation among States or other jurisdictions, to the implementation of those portions of plans prepared under this section to achieve and maintain the national primary ambient air quality standard. This paragraph extends to, but is not limited to, authority exercised under the Urban Mass Transportation Act, Title 23 of the United States Code, and the Housing and Urban Development Act.

§7506a. Interstate transport commissions
[CAA §176A]

(a) **Authority to establish interstate transport regions** — Whenever, on the Administrator's own motion or by petition from the Governor of any State, the Administrator has reason to believe that the interstate transport of air pollutants from one or more States contributes significantly to a violation of a national ambient air quality standard in one or more other States, the Administrator may establish, by rule, a transport region for such pollutant that includes such States. The Administrator, on the Administrator's own motion or upon petition from the Governor of any State, or upon the recommendation of a transport commission established under subsection (b), may —

(1) add any State or portion of a State to any region established under this subsection whenever the Administrator has reason to believe that the interstate transport of air pollutants from such State significantly contributes to a violation of the standard in the transport region, or

(2) remove any State or portion of a State from the region whenever the Administrator has reason to believe that the control of emissions in that State or portion of the State pursuant to this section will not significantly contribute to the attainment of the standard in any area in the region.

The Administrator shall approve or disapprove any such petition recommendation within 18 months of its receipt. The Administrator shall establish appropriate proceedings for public participation regarding such petitions and motions, including notice and comment.

(b) **Transport commissions**

(1) Establishment — Whenever the Administrator establishes a transport region under subsection (a) of this section, the Administrator shall establish a transport commission comprised of (at a minimum) each of the following members:

(A) The Governor of each State in the region or the designee of each such Governor.

(B) The Administrator or the Administrator's designee.

(C) The Regional Administrator (or the Administrator's designee) for each Regional Office for each Environmental Protection Agency Region affected by the transport region concerned.

(D) An air pollution control official representing each State in the region, appointed by the Governor.

Decisions of, and recommendations and requests to, the Administrator by each transport commission may be made only by a majority vote of all members other than the Administrator and the Regional Administrators (or designees thereof).

(2) Recommendations — The transport commission shall assess the degree of interstate transport of the pollutant or precursors to the pollutant throughout the transport region, assess strategies for mitigating the interstate pollution, and recommend to the Administrator such measures as the Commission determines to be necessary to ensure that the plans for the relevant States meet the requirements of section 7410(a)(2)(D) of this title. Such commission shall not be subject to the provisions of the Federal Advisory Committee Act (5 U.S.C. App.).

(c) Commission requests — A transport commission established under subsection (b) may request the Administrator to issue a finding under section 7410(k)(5) of this title that the implementation plan for one or more of the States in the transport region is substantially inadequate to meet the requirements of section 7410(a)(2)(D) of this title. The Administrator shall approve, disapprove, or partially approve and partially disapprove such a request within 18 months of its receipt and, to the extent the Administrator approves such request, issue the finding under section 7410(k)(5) of this title at the time of such approval. In acting on such request, the Administrator shall provide an opportunity for public participation and shall address each specific recommendation made by the commission. Approval or disapproval of such a request shall constitute final agency action within the meaning of section 7607(b) of this title.

§7507. New motor vehicle emission standards in nonattainment areas
[CAA §177]

Notwithstanding section 7543(a) of this title, any State which has plan provisions approved under this part may adopt and enforce for any model year standards relating to control of emissions from new motor vehicles or new motor vehicle engines and take such other actions as are referred to in section 7543(a) of this title respecting such vehicles if —

(1) such standards are identical to the California standards for which a waiver has been granted for such model year, and

(2) California and such State adopt such standards at least two years before commencement of such model year (as determined by regulations of the Administrator).

Nothing in this section or in title II of this Act shall be construed as authorizing any such State to prohibit or limit, directly or indirectly, the manufacture or sale of a new motor vehicle or motor vehicle engine that is certified in California as meeting California standards, or to take any action of any kind to create, or have the effect of creating, a motor vehicle or motor vehicle engine different than a motor vehicle or engine certified in California under California standards (a "third vehicle") or otherwise create such a "third vehicle".

§7508. Guidance documents
[CAA §178]

The Administrator shall issue guidance documents under section 7408 of this title for purposes of assisting States in implementing requirements of this part respecting the lowest achievable emission rate. Such a document shall be published not later than nine months after the date of enactment of this part and shall be revised at least every two years thereafter.

§7509. Sanctions and consequences of failure to attain
[CAA §179]

(a) State failure — For any implementation plan or plan revision required under this part (or required in response to a finding of substantial inadequacy as described in section 7410(k)(5) of this title), if the Administrator —

(1) finds that a State has failed, for an area designated nonattainment under section 7407(d) of this title, to submit a plan, or to submit 1 or more of the elements (as determined by the Administrator) required by the provisions of this Act applicable to such an area, or has failed to make a submission for such an area that satisfies the minimum criteria established in relation to any such element under section 7410(k), of this title,

(2) disapproves a submission under section 7410(k) of this title, for an area designated nonattainment under section 7407 of this title, based on the submission's failure to meet one or more of the elements required by the provisions of this Act applicable to such an area,

(3)(A) determines that a State has failed to make any submission as may be required under this Act, other than one described under paragraph (1) or (2), including an adequate maintenance plan, or has failed to make any submission, as may be required under this Act, other than one described under paragraph (1) or (2), that satisfies the minimum criteria established in relation to such submission under section 7410(k)(1)(A) of this title, or

(B) disapproves in whole or in part a submission described under subparagraph (A), or

(4) finds that any requirement of an approved plan (or approved part of a plan) is not being implemented,

unless such deficiency has been corrected within 18 months after the finding, disapproval, or determination referred to in paragraphs (1), (2), (3), and (4), one of the sanctions referred to in subsection (b) shall apply, as selected by the Administrator, until the Administrator determines that the State has come into compliance, except that if the Administrator finds a lack of good faith, sanctions under both paragraph (1) and paragraph (2) of subsection (b) shall apply until the Administrator determines that the State has come into compliance. If the Administrator has selected one of such sanctions and the deficiency has not been corrected within 6 months thereafter, sanctions under both paragraph (1) and paragraph (2) of subsection (b) shall apply until the Administrator determines that the State has come into compliance. In addition to any other sanction applicable as provided in this section, the Administrator may withhold all or part of the grants for support of air pollution planning and control programs that the Administrator may award under section 7405 of this title.

(b) Sanctions — The sanctions available to the Administrator as provided in subsection (a) are as follows:

(1) Highway sanctions —

(A) The Administrator may impose a prohibition, applicable to a nonattainment area, on the approval by the Secretary of Transportation of any projects or the awarding by the Secretary of any grants, under Title 23, United States Code, other than projects or grants for safety where the Secretary determines, based on accident or other appropriate data submitted by the State, that the principal purpose of the project is an improvement in safety to resolve a demonstrated safety problem and likely will result in a significant reduction in, or avoidance of, accidents. Such prohibition shall become effective upon the selection by the Administrator of this sanction.

(B) In addition to safety, projects or grants that may be approved by the Secretary, notwithstanding the prohibition in subparagraph (A), are the following —

(i) capital programs for public transit;

(ii) construction or restriction of certain roads or lanes solely for the use of passenger buses or high occupancy vehicles;

(iii) planning for requirements for employers to reduce employee work-trip-related vehicle emissions;

(iv) highway ramp metering, traffic signalization, and related programs that improve traffic flow and achieve a net emission reduction;

(v) fringe and transportation corridor parking facilities serving multiple occupancy vehicle programs or transit operations;

(vi) programs to limit or restrict vehicle use in downtown areas or other areas of emission concentration particularly during periods of peak use, through road use charges, tolls, parking surcharges, or other pricing mechanisms, vehicle restricted zones or periods, or vehicle registration programs;

(vii) programs for breakdown and accident scene management, nonrecurring congestion, and vehicle information systems, to reduce congestion and emissions; and

(viii) such other transportation-related programs as the Administrator, in consultation with the Secretary of Transportation, finds would improve air quality and would not encourage single occupancy vehicle capacity.

In considering such measures, the State should seek to ensure adequate access to downtown, other commercial, and residential areas, and avoid increasing or relocating emissions and congestion rather than reducing them.

(2) Offsets — In applying the emissions offset requirements of section 7503 of this title to new or modified sources or emissions units for which a permit is required under this part, the ratio of emission reductions to increased emissions shall be at least 2 to 1.

(c) Notice of failure to attain

(1) As expeditiously as practicable after the applicable attainment date for any nonattainment area, but not later than 6 months after such date, the Administrator shall determine, based on the area's air quality as of the attainment date, whether the area attained the standard by that date.

(2) Upon making the determination under paragraph (1), the Administrator shall publish a notice in the Federal Register containing such determination and identifying each area that the Administrator has determined to have failed to attain. The Administrator may revise or supplement such determination at any time based on more complete information or analysis concerning the area's air quality as of the attainment date.

(d) Consequences for failure to attain

(1) Within 1 year after the Administrator publishes the notice under subsection (c)(2) of this section (relating to notice of failure to attain), each State containing a nonattainment area shall submit a revision to the applicable implementation plan meeting the requirements of paragraph (2) of this subsection.

(2) The revision required under paragraph (1) shall meet the requirements of section 7410 of this title and section 7502 of this title. In addition, the revision shall include such additional measures as the Administrator may reasonably prescribe, including all measures that can be feasibly implemented in the area in light of technological achievability, costs, and any nonair quality and other air quality-related health and environmental impacts.

(3) The attainment date applicable to the revision required under paragraph (1) shall be the same as provided in the provisions of section

7502(a)(2) of this title, except that in applying such provisions the phrase "from the date of the notice under section 7509(c)(2) of this title" shall be substituted for the phrase "from the date such area was designated nonattainment under section 7407(d) of this title" and for the phrase "from the date of designation as nonattainment".

§7509a. International border areas
[CAA §179B]

(a) Implementation plans and revisions — Notwithstanding any other provision of law, an implementation plan or plan revision required under this Act shall be approved by the Administrator if —

(1) such plan or revision meets all the requirements applicable to it under the Act other than a requirement that such plan or revision demonstrate attainment and maintenance of the relevant national ambient air quality standards by the attainment date specified under the applicable provision of this Act, or in a regulation promulgated under such provision, and

(2) the submitting State establishes to the satisfaction of the Administrator that the implementation plan of such State would be adequate to attain and maintain the relevant national ambient air quality standards by the attainment date specified under the applicable provision of this Act, or in a regulation promulgated under such provision, but for emissions emanating from outside of the United States.

(b) Attainment of ozone levels — Notwithstanding any other provision of law, any State that establishes to the satisfaction of the Administrator that, with respect to an ozone nonattainment area in such State, such State would have attained the national ambient air quality standard for ozone by the applicable attainment date, but for emissions emanating from outside of the United States, shall not be subject to the provisions of section 7511(a)(2) or (5) of this title or section 7511d of this title.

(c) Attainment of carbon monoxide levels — Notwithstanding any other provision of law, any State that establishes to the satisfaction of the Administrator, with respect to a carbon monoxide nonattainment area in such State, that such State has attained the national ambient air quality standard for carbon monoxide by the applicable attainment date, but for emissions emanating from outside of the United States, shall not be subject to the provisions of section 7513(b)(2) or (9) of this title.

(d) Attainment of PM-10 levels — Notwithstanding any other provision of law, any State that establishes to the satisfaction of the Administrator that, with respect to a PM-10 nonattainment area in such State, such State would have attained the national ambient air quality standard for carbon monoxide by the applicable attainment date, but for emissions emanating from outside the United States, shall not be subject to the provisions of section 7513(b)(2) of this title.

SUBPART 2 — ADDITIONAL PROVISIONS FOR OZONE NONATTAINMENT AREAS

§7511. Classifications and attainment dates
[CAA §181]
(a) Classification and attainment dates for 1989 nonattainment areas

(1) Each area designated nonattainment for ozone pursuant to section 7407(d) of this title shall be classified at the time of such designation, under table 1, by operation of law, as a Marginal Area, a Moderate Area, a Serious Area, a Severe Area, or an Extreme Area based on the design value for the area. The design value shall be calculated according to the interpretation methodology issued by the Administrator most recently before November 15, 1990. For each area classified under this subsection, the primary standard attainment date for ozone shall be as expeditiously as practicable but not later than the date provided in table 1.

TABLE 1

Area class	Design value*	Primary standard attainment date**
Marginal	0.121 up to 0.138	3 years after enactment
Moderate	0.138 up to 0.160	6 years after enactment
Serious	0.160 up to 0.180	9 years after enactment
Severe	0.180 up to 0.280	15 years after enactment
Extreme	0.280 and above	20 years after enactment

* The design value is measured in parts per million (ppm).
** The primary standard attainment date is measured from November 15, 1990.

(2) Notwithstanding table 1, in the case of a severe area with a 1988 ozone design value between 0.190 and 0.280 ppm, the attainment date shall be 17 years (in lieu of 15 years) after November 15, 1990.

(3) At the time of publication of the notice under section 7407(d)(4) of this title (relating to area designations) for each ozone nonattainment area, the Administrator shall publish a notice announcing the classification of such ozone nonattainment area. The provisions of section 7502(a)(1)(B) of this title (relating to lack of notice and comment and judicial review) shall apply to such classification.

(4) If an area classified under paragraph (1) (Table 1) would have been classified in another category if the design value in the area were 5 percent greater or 5 percent less than the level on which such classification was based, the Administrator may, in the Administrator's discretion, within 90 days after the

initial classification, by the procedure required under paragraph (3), adjust the classification to place the area in such other category. In making such adjustment, the Administrator may consider the number of exceedances of the national primary ambient air quality standard for ozone in the area, the level of pollution transport between the area and other affected areas, including both intrastate and interstate transport, and the mix of sources and air pollutants in the area.

(5) Upon application by any State, the Administrator may extend for 1 additional year (hereinafter referred to as the "Extension Year") the date specified in table 1 of paragraph (1) of this subsection if —

(A) the State has complied with all requirements and commitments pertaining to the area in the applicable implementation plan, and

(B) no more than 1 exceedance of the national ambient air quality standard level for ozone has occurred in the area in the year preceding the Extension Year.

No more than 2 one-year extensions may be issued under this paragraph for a single nonattainment area.

(b) New designations and reclassifications

(1) New designations to nonattainment — Any area that is designated attainment or unclassifiable for ozone under section 7407(d)(4) of this title, and that is subsequently redesignated to nonattainment for ozone under section 7407(d)(3) of this title, shall, at the time of the redesignation, be classified by operation of law in accordance with table 1 under subsection (a). Upon its classification, the area shall be subject to the same requirements under section 110, subpart 1 of this part, and this subpart that would have applied had the area been so classified at the time of the notice under subsection (a)(3), except that any absolute, fixed date applicable in connection with any such requirement is extended by operation of law by a period equal to the length of time between the date of the enactment of the Clean Air Act Amendments of 1990 and the date the area is classified under this paragraph.

(2) Reclassification upon failure to attain

(A) Within 6 months following the applicable attainment date (including any extension thereof) for an ozone nonattainment area, the Administrator shall determine, based on the area's design value (as of the attainment date), whether the area attained the standard by that date. Except for any Severe or Extreme area, any area that the Administrator finds has not attained the standard by that date shall be reclassified by operation of law in accordance with table 1 of subsection (a) to the higher of —

(i) the next higher classification for the area, or

(ii) the classification applicable to the area's design value as determined at the time of the notice required under subparagraph (B).

No area shall be reclassified as Extreme under clause (ii).

(B) The Administrator shall publish a notice in the Federal Register, no later than 6 months following the attainment date, identifying each area that the Administrator has determined under subparagraph (A) as having failed to attain and identifying the reclassification, if any, described under subparagraph (A).

(3) Voluntary reclassification — The Administrator shall grant the request of any State to reclassify a nonattainment area in that State in accordance with table 1 of subsection (a) to a higher classification. The Administrator shall publish a notice in the Federal Register of any such request and of action by the Administrator granting the request.

(4) Failure of severe areas to attain standard

(A) If any Severe Area fails to achieve the national primary ambient air quality standard for ozone by the applicable attainment date (including any extension thereof), the fee provisions under section 7511d of this title shall apply within the area, the percent reduction requirements of section 7511a(c)(2)(B) and (C) of this title (relating to reasonable further progress demonstration and NOx control) shall continue to apply to the area, and the State shall demonstrate that such percent reduction has been achieved in each 3-year interval after such failure until the standard is attained. Any failure to make such a demonstration shall be subject to the sanctions provided under this part.

(B) In addition to the requirements of subparagraph (A), if the ozone design value for a Severe Area referred to in subparagraph (A) is above 0.140 ppm for the year of the applicable attainment date, or if the area has failed to achieve its most recent milestone under section 7511a(g) of this title, the new source review requirements applicable under this subpart in Extreme Areas shall apply in the area and the term "major source" and "major stationary source" shall have the same meaning as in Extreme Areas.

(C) In addition to the requirements of subparagraph (A) for those areas referred to in subparagraph (A) and not covered by subparagraph (B), the provisions referred to in subparagraph (B) shall apply after 3 years from the applicable attainment date unless the area has attained the standard by the end of such 3-year period.

(D) If, after November 15, 1990, the Administrator modifies the method of determining compliance with the national primary ambient air quality standard, a design value or other indicator comparable to 0.140 in terms of its relationship to the standard shall be used in lieu of 0.140 for purposes of applying the provisions of subparagraphs (B) and (C).

(c) References to terms

(1) Any reference in this subpart to a "Marginal Area", a "Moderate Area", a "Serious Area", a "Severe Area", or an "Extreme Area" shall be considered a reference to a Marginal Area, a Moderate Area, a Serious Area, a Severe Area, or an Extreme Area as respectively classified under this section.

(2) Any reference in this subpart to "next higher classification" or comparable terms shall be considered a reference to the classification related to the next higher set of design values in table 1.

§7511a. Plan submissions and requirements [CAA §182]

(a) **Marginal Areas** — Each State in which all or part of a Marginal Area is located shall, with respect to the Marginal Area (or portion thereof, to the extent specified in this subsection), submit to the Administrator the State implementation plan revisions (including the plan items) described under this subsection except to the extent the State has made such submissions as of November 15, 1990.

(1) Inventory — Within 2 years after November 15, 1990, the State shall submit a comprehensive, accurate, current inventory of actual emissions from all sources, as described in section 7502(c)(3) of this title, in accordance with guidance provided by the Administrator.

(2) Corrections to the state implementation plan — Within the periods prescribed in this paragraph, the State shall submit a revision to the State implementation plan that meets the following requirements —

(A) Reasonably available control technology corrections — For any Marginal Area (or, within the Administrator's discretion, portion thereof) the State shall submit, within 6 months of the date of classification under section 7511(a) of this title, a revision that includes such provisions to correct requirements in (or add requirements to) the plan concerning reasonably available control technology as were required under section 7502(b) of this title (as in effect immediately before November 15, 1990), as interpreted in guidance issued by the Administrator under section 7408 of this title before November 15, 1990.

(B) Savings clause for vehicle inspection and maintenance

(i) For any Marginal Area (or, within the Administrator's discretion, portion thereof), the plan for which already includes, or was required by section 7502(b)(11)(B) of this title (as in effect immediately before November 15, 1990) to have included, a specific schedule for implementation of a vehicle emission control inspection and maintenance program, the State shall submit, immediately after November 15, 1990, a revision that includes any provisions necessary to provide for a vehicle inspection and maintenance program of no less stringency than that of either the program defined in House Report Numbered 95-294, 95th Congress, 1st Session, 281-291 (1977) as interpreted in guidance of the Administrator issued pursuant to section 7502(b)(11)(B) of this title (as in effect immediately before November 15, 1990) or the program already included in the plan, whichever is more stringent.

(ii) Within 12 months after November 15, 1990, the Administrator shall review, revise, update, and republish in the Federal Register the guidance for the States for motor vehicle inspection and maintenance programs required by this Act, taking into consideration the Administrator's investigations and audits of such program. The guidance shall, at a minimum, cover the frequency of inspections, the types of vehicles to be inspected (which shall include leased vehicles that are registered in the nonattainment area), vehicle maintenance by owners and operators, audits by the State, the test method and measures, including whether centralized or decentralized, inspection methods and procedures, quality of inspection, components covered, assurance that a vehicle subject to a recall notice from a manufacturer has complied with that notice, and effective implementation and enforcement, including ensuring that any retesting of a vehicle after a failure shall include proof of corrective action and providing for denial of vehicle registration in the case of tampering or misfueling. The guidance which shall be incorporated in the applicable State implementation plans by the States shall provide the States with continued reasonable flexibility to fashion effective, reasonable, and fair programs for the affected consumer. No later than 2 years after the Administrator promulgates regulations under section 7521(m)(3) of this title (relating to emission control diagnostics), the State shall submit a revision to such program to meet any requirements that the Administrator may prescribe under that section.

(C) Permit programs — Within 2 years after November 15, 1990, the State shall submit a revision that includes each of the following:

(i) Provisions to require permits, in accordance with sections 7502(c)(5) and 7503 of this title, for the construction and operation of each new or modified major stationary source (with respect to ozone) to be located in the area.

(ii) Provisions to correct requirements in (or add requirements to) the plan concerning permit programs as were required under section 7502(b)(6) (as in effect immediately before November 15, 1990), as interpreted in regulations of the Administrator promulgated as of November 15, 1990.

(3) Periodic inventory

(A) General requirement — No later than the end of each 3-year period after submission of the inventory under paragraph (1) until the area is redesignated to attainment, the State shall submit a revised inventory meeting the requirements of subsection (a)(1).

(B) Emissions statements

(i) Within 2 years after November 15, 1990, the State shall submit a revision to the State implementation plan to require that the owner or operator of each stationary source of oxides of nitrogen or volatile organic compounds provide the State with a statement, in such form as the Administrator may prescribe (or accept an equivalent alternative developed by the State), for classes or categories of sources, showing the actual emissions of oxides of nitrogen and volatile organic compounds from that source. The first such statement shall be submitted within 3 years after November 15, 1990. Subsequent statements shall be submitted at least every year thereafter. The statement shall contain a certification that the information contained in the statement is accurate to the best knowledge of the individual certifying the statement.

(ii) The State may waive the application of clause (i) to any class or category of stationary sources which emit less than 25 tons per year of volatile organic compounds or oxides of nitrogen if the State, in its submissions under subparagraphs (1) or (3)(A), provides an inventory of emissions from such class or category of sources, based on the use of the emission factors established by the Administrator or other methods acceptable to the Administrator.

(4) General offset requirement — For purposes of satisfying the emission offset requirements of this part, the ratio of total emission reductions of volatile organic compounds to total increased emissions of such air pollutant shall be at least 1.1 to 1.

The Administrator may, in the Administrator's discretion, require States to submit a schedule for submitting any of the revisions or other items required under this subsection. The requirements of this subsection shall apply in lieu of any requirement that the State submit a demonstration that the applicable implementation plan provides for attainment of the ozone standard by the applicable attainment date

in any Marginal Area. Section 7502(c)(9) of this title (relating to contingency measures) shall not apply to Marginal Areas.

(b) **Moderate Areas** — Each State in which all or part of a Moderate Area is located shall, with respect to the Moderate Area, make the submissions described under subsection (a) (relating to Marginal Areas), and shall also submit the revisions to the applicable implementation plan described under this subsection.

(1) Plan provisions for reasonable further progress —

(A) General rule

(i) By no later than 3 years after November 15, 1990, the State shall submit a revision to the applicable implementation plan to provide for volatile organic compound emission reductions, within 6 years after November 15, 1990, of at least 15 percent from baseline emissions, accounting for any growth in emissions after 1990. Such plan shall provide for such specific annual reductions in emissions of volatile organic compounds and oxides of nitrogen as necessary to attain the national primary ambient air quality standard for ozone by the attainment date applicable under this Act. This subparagraph shall not apply in the case of oxides of nitrogen for those areas for which the Administrator determines (when the Administrator approves the plan or plan revision) that additional reductions of oxides of nitrogen would not contribute to attainment.

(ii) A percentage less than 15 percent may be used for purposes of clause (i) in the case of any State which demonstrates to the satisfaction of the Administrator that —

(I) new source review provisions are applicable in the nonattainment areas in the same manner and to the same extent as required under subsection (e) of this section in the case of Extreme Areas (with the exception that, in applying such provisions, the terms "major source" and "major stationary source" shall include (in addition to the sources described in section 7602 of this title) any stationary source or group of sources located within a contiguous area and under common control that emits, or has the potential to emit, at least 5 tons per year of volatile organic compounds);

(II) reasonably available control technology is required for all existing major sources (as defined in subclause (I)); and

(III) the plan reflecting a lesser percentage than 15 percent includes all measures that can feasibly be implemented in the area, in light of technological achievability.

To qualify for a lesser percentage under this clause, a State must demonstrate to the satisfaction of the Administrator that the plan for the area includes the measures that are achieved in practice by sources in the same source category in nonattainment areas of the next higher category.

(B) Baseline emissions — For purposes of subparagraph (A), the term "baseline emissions" means the total amount of actual VOC or NOx emissions from all anthropogenic sources in the area during the calendar year 1990, excluding emissions that would be eliminated under the regulations described in clauses (i) and (ii) of subparagraph (D).

(C) General rule for creditability of reductions — Except as provided under subparagraph (D), emissions reductions are creditable toward the 15 percent required under subparagraph (A) to the extent they have actually occurred, as of 6 years after November 15, 1990, from the implementation of measures required under the applicable implementation plan, rules promulgated by the Administrator, or a permit under subchapter V of this chapter.

(D) Limits on creditability of reductions — Emission reductions from the following measures are not creditable toward the 15 percent reductions required under subparagraph (A):

(i) Any measure relating to motor vehicle exhaust or evaporative emissions promulgated by the Administrator by January 1, 1990.

(ii) Regulations concerning Reid Vapor Pressure promulgated by the Administrator by November 15, 1990 or required to be promulgated under section 7545(h) of this title.

(iii) Measures required under subsection (a)(2)(A) of this section (concerning corrections to implementation plans prescribed under guidance by the Administrator).

(iv) Measures required under subsection (a)(2)(B) of this section to be submitted immediately after the date of the enactment of the Clean Air Act Amendments of 1990 (concerning corrections to motor vehicle inspection and maintenance programs).

(2) Reasonably available control technology — The State shall submit a revision to the applicable implementation plan to include provisions to require the implementation of reasonably available control technology under section 7502(c)(1) of this title with respect to each of the following:

(A) Each category of VOC sources in the area covered by a CTG document issued by the Administrator between the date of the enactment of the Clean Air Act Amendments

of 1990 and the date of attainment.

(B) All VOC sources in the area covered by any CTG issued before November 15, 1990.

(C) All other major stationary sources of VOCs that are located in the area.

Each revision described in subparagraph (A) shall be submitted within the period set forth by the Administrator in issuing the relevant CTG document. The revisions with respect to sources described in subparagraphs (B) and (C) shall be submitted by 2 years after November 15, 1990, and shall provide for the implementation of the required measures as expeditiously as practicable but no later than May 31, 1995.

(3) Gasoline vapor recovery

(A) General rule — Not later than 2 years after November 15, 1990, the State shall submit a revision to the applicable implementation plan to require all owners or operators of gasoline dispensing systems to install and operate, by the date prescribed under subparagraph (B), a system for gasoline vapor recovery of emissions from the fueling of motor vehicles. The Administrator shall issue guidance as appropriate as to the effectiveness of such system. This subparagraph shall apply only to facilities which sell more than 10,000 gallons of gasoline per month (50,000 gallons per month in the case of an independent small business marketer of gasoline as defined in section 7625-1 of this title).

(B) Effective date — The date required under subparagraph (A) shall be —

(i) 6 months after the adoption date, in the case of gasoline dispensing facilities for which construction commenced after November 15, 1990;

(ii) one year after the adoption date, in the case of gasoline dispensing facilities which dispense at least 100,000 gallons of gasoline per month, based on average monthly sales for the 2-year period before the adoption date; or

(iii) 2 years after the adoption date, in the case of all other gasoline dispensing facilities.

Any gasoline dispensing facility described under both clause (i) and clause (ii) shall meet the requirements of clause (i).

(C) Reference to terms — For purposes of this paragraph, any reference to the term "adoption date" shall be considered a reference to the date of adoption by the State of requirements for the installation and operation of a system for gasoline vapor recovery of emissions from the fueling of motor vehicles.

(4) Motor vehicle inspection and maintenance — For all Moderate Areas, the State shall submit, immediately after November 15, 1990, a revision to the applicable implementation plan that includes provisions necessary to provide for a vehicle inspection and maintenance program as described in subsection (a)(2)(B) of this section (without regard to whether or not the area was required by section 7502(b)(11)(B) of this title (as in effect immediately before November 15, 1990) to have included a specific schedule for implementation of such a program).

(5) General offset requirement — For purposes of satisfying the emission offset requirements of this part, the ratio of total emission reductions of volatile organic compounds to total increase emissions of such air pollutant shall be at least 1.15 to 1.

(c) Serious Areas — Except as otherwise specified in paragraph (4), each State in which all or part of a Serious Area is located shall, with respect to the Serious Area (or portion thereof, to the extent specified in this subsection), make the submissions described under subsection (b) (relating to Moderate Areas), and shall also submit the revisions to the applicable implementation plan (including the plan items) described under this subsection. For any Serious Area, the terms "major source" and "major stationary source" include (in addition to the sources described in section 7602 of this title) any stationary source or group of sources located within a contiguous area and under common control that emits, or has the potential to emit, at least 50 tons per year of volatile organic compounds.

(1) Enhanced monitoring — In order to obtain more comprehensive and representative data on ozone air pollution, not later than 18 months after November 15, 1990 the Administrator shall promulgate rules, after notice and public comment, for enhanced monitoring of ozone, oxides of nitrogen, and volatile organic compounds. The rules shall, among other things, cover the location and maintenance of monitors. Immediately following the promulgation of rules by the Administrator relating to enhanced monitoring, the State shall commence such actions as may be necessary to adopt and implement a program based on such rules, to improve monitoring for ambient concentrations of ozone, oxides of nitrogen and volatile organic compounds and to improve monitoring of emissions of oxides of nitrogen and volatile organic compounds. Each State implementation plan for the area shall contain measures to improve the ambient monitoring of such air pollutants.

(2) Attainment and reasonable further progress demonstrations — Within 4 years after November 15, 1990, the State shall submit a revision to the applicable implementation plan that includes each of the following:

(A) Attainment demonstration — A demonstration that the plan, as revised, will provide for attainment of the ozone national ambient air quality standard by the applicable attainment date. This attainment demonstration must be based on photochemical grid modeling or any other analytical method determined by the Administrator, in the Administrator's discretion, to be at least as effective.

(B) Reasonable further progress demonstration — A demonstration that the plan, as revised, will result in VOC emissions reductions from the baseline emissions described in subsection (b)(1)(B) equal to the following amount averaged over each consecutive 3-year period beginning 6 years after November 15, 1990, until the attainment date:

(i) at least 3 percent of baseline emissions each year; or

(ii) an amount less than 3 percent of such baseline emissions each year, if the State demonstrates to the satisfaction of the Administrator that the plan reflecting such lesser amount includes all measures that can feasibly be implemented in the area, in light of technological achievability.

To lessen the 3 percent requirement under clause (ii), a State must demonstrate to the satisfaction of the Administrator that the plan for the area includes the measures that are achieved in practice by sources in the same source category in nonattainment areas of the next higher classification. Any determination to lessen the 3 percent requirement shall be reviewed at each milestone under subsection (g) of this section and revised to reflect such new measures (if any) achieved in practice by sources in the same category in any State, allowing a reasonable time to implement such measures. The emission reductions described in this subparagraph shall be calculated in accordance with subsection (b)(1)(C) and (D) of this section (concerning creditability of reductions). The reductions creditable for the period beginning 6 years after the date of the enactment of the Clean Air Act Amendments of 1990, shall include reductions that occurred before such period, computed in accordance with subsection (b)(1) of this section, that exceed the 15-percent amount of reductions required under subsection (b)(1)(A) of this section.

(C) NOx control — The revision may contain, in lieu of the demonstration required under subparagraph (B), a demonstration to the satisfaction of the Administrator that the applicable implementation plan, as revised, provides for reductions of emissions of VOC's and oxides of nitrogen (calculated according to the creditability provisions of subsection (b)(1)(C) and (D)), that would result in a reduction in ozone concentrations at least equivalent to that which would result from the amount of VOC emission reductions required under subparagraph (B). Within 1 year after November 15, 1990, the Administrator shall issue guidance concerning the conditions under which NOx control may be substituted for VOC control or may be combined with VOC control in order to maximize the reduction in ozone air pollution. In accord with such guidance, a lesser percentage of VOCs may be accepted as an adequate demonstration for purposes of this subsection.

(3) Enhanced vehicle inspection and maintenance program

(A) Requirement for submission — Within 2 years after November 15, 1990, theState shall submit a revision to the applicable implementation plan to provide for an enhanced program to reduce hydrocarbon emissions and NOx emissions from in-use motor vehicles registered in each urbanized area (in the nonattainment area), as defined by the Bureau of the Census, with a 1980 population of 200,000 or more.

(B) Effective date of state programs; guidance — The State program required under subparagraph (A) shall take effect no later than 2 years from November 15,1990, and shall comply in all respects with guidance published in the Federal Register (and from time to time revised) by the Administrator for enhanced vehicle inspection and maintenance programs. Such guidance shall include —

(i) a performance standard achievable by a program combining emission testing, including on-road emission testing, with inspection to detect tampering with emission control devices and misfueling for all light-duty vehicles and all light-duty trucks subject to standards under section 7521 of this title; and

(ii) program administration features necessary to reasonably assure that adequate management resources, tools, and practices are in place to attain and maintain the performance standard.

Compliance with the performance standard under clause (i) shall determined using a method to be established by the Administrator.

(C) State program — The State program required under subparagraph (A) shall include, at a minimum, each of the following elements —

(i) Computerized emission analyzers, including on-road testing devices.

(ii) No waivers for vehicles and parts covered by the emission control performance warranty as provided for in section 7541(b) of this title unless a warranty remedy has been denied in writing, or for tampering-related repairs.

(iii) In view of the air quality purpose of the program, if, for any vehicle, waivers are permitted for emissions related repairs not covered by warranty, an expenditure to qualify for the waiver of an amount of $450 or more for such repairs (adjusted annually as determined by the Administrator on the basis of the Consumer Price Index in the same manner as provided in subchapter V of this chapter).

(iv) Enforcement through denial of vehicle registration (except for any program in operation before November 15, 1990 whose enforcement mechanism is demonstrated to the Administrator to be more effective than the applicable vehicle registration program in assuring that noncomplying vehicles are not operated on public roads).

(v) Annual emission testing and necessary adjustment, repair, and maintenance, unless the State demonstrates to the satisfaction of the Administrator that a biennial inspection, in combination with other features of the program which exceed the requirements of this Act, will result in emission reductions which equal or exceed the reductions which can be obtained through such annual inspections.

(vi) Operation of the program on a centralized basis, unless the State demonstrates to the satisfaction of the Administrator that a decentralized program will be equally effective. An electronically connected testing system, a licensing system, or other measures (or any combination thereof) may be considered, in accordance with criteria established by the Administrator, as equally effective for such purposes.

(vii) Inspection of emission control diagnostic systems and the maintenance or repair of malfunctions or system deterioration identified by or affecting such diagnostics systems.

Each State shall biennially prepare a report to the Administrator which assesses the emission reductions achieved by the program required under this paragraph based on data collected during inspection and repair of vehicles. The methods used to assess the emission reductions shall be those established by the Administrator.

(4) Clean-fuel vehicle programs

(A) Except to the extent that substitute provisions have been approved by the Adminis-trator under subparagraph (B), the State shall submit to the Administrator, within 42 months of November 15, 1990, a revision to the applicable implementation plan for each area described under part C of subchapter II of this chapter to include such measures as may be necessary to ensure the effectiveness of the applicable provisions of the clean-fuel vehicle program prescribed under part C of subchapter II of this chapter, including all measures necessary to make the use of clean alternative fuels in clean-fuel vehicles (as defined in part C of subchapter II of this chapter) economic from the standpoint of vehicle owners. Such a revision shall also be submitted for each area that opts into the clean fuel-vehicle program as provided in part C of subchapter II of this chapter.

(B) The Administrator shall approve, as a substitute for all or a portion of the clean-fuel vehicle program prescribed under part C of subchapter II of this chapter, any revision to the relevant applicable implementation plan that in the Administrator's judgment will achieve long-term reductions in ozone-producing and toxic air emissions equal to those achieved under part C of subchapter II of this chapter, or the percentage thereof attributable to the portion of the clean-fuel vehicle program for which the revision is to substitute. The Administrator may approve such revision only if it consists exclusively of provisions other than those required under this Act for the area. Any State seeking approval of such revision must submit the revision to the Administrator within 24 months of November 15, 1990. The Administrator shall approve or disapprove any such revision within 30 months of the date of the enactment of the Clean Air Act Amendments of 1990. The Administrator shall publish the revision submitted by a State in the Federal Register upon receipt. Such notice shall constitute a notice of proposed rulemaking on whether or not to approve such revision and shall be deemed to comply with the requirements concerning notices of proposed rulemaking contained in sections 553 through 557 of Title 5 of the United States Code (related to notice and comment). Where the Administrator approves such revision for any area, the State need not submit the revision required by subparagraph (A) for the area with respect to the portions of the Federal clean-fuel vehicle program for which the Administrator has approved the revision as a substitute.

(C) If the Administrator determines, under section 7509 of this title, that the State has failed to submit any portion of the program required under subparagraph (A), then, in addition to any sanctions available under section 7509 of this title, the State may not receive credit, in any demonstration of attainment or reasonable further progress for the area, for any emission reductions from implementation of the corresponding aspects of the Federal clean-fuel vehicle requirements established in part C of subchapter II of this chapter.

(5) Transportation control

(A) Beginning 6 years after November 15, 1990 and each third year thereafter, the State shall submit a demonstration as to whether current aggregate vehicle mileage, aggregate vehicle emissions, congestion levels, and other relevant parameters are consistent with those used for the area's demonstration of attainment. Where such parameters and emissions levels exceed the levels projected for purposes of the area's attainment demonstration, the State shall within 18 months develop and submit a revision of the applicable implementation plan that includes a transportation control measures program consisting of measures from, but not limited to, section 7408(f) of this title that will reduce emissions to levels that are consistent with emission levels projected in such demonstration. In considering such measures, the State should ensure adequate access to downtown, other commercial, and residential areas and should avoid measures that increase or relocate emissions and congestion rather than reduce them. Such revision shall be developed in accordance with guidance issued by the Administrator pursuant to section 7408(e) of this title and with the requirements of section 7504(b) of this title and shall include implementation and funding schedules that achieve expeditious emissions reductions in accordance with implementation plan projections.

(6) De minimis rule — The new source review provisions under this part shall ensure that increased emissions of volatile organic compounds resulting from any physical change in, or change in the method of operation of, a stationary source located in the area shall not be considered de minimis for purposes of determining the applicability of the permit requirements established by this Act unless the increase in net emissions of such air pollutant from such source does not exceed 25 tons when aggregated with all other net increases in emissions from the source over any period of 5 consecutive calendar years which includes the calendar year in which such increase occurred.

(7) Special rule for modifications of sources emitting less than 100 tons — In the case of any major stationary source of volatile organic compounds located in the area (other than a source which emits or has the potential to emit 100 tons or more of volatile organic compounds per year), whenever any change (as described in section 7411(a)(4) of this title) at that source results in any increase (other than a de minimis increase) in emissions of volatile organic compounds from any discrete operation, unit, or other pollutant emitting activity at the source, such increase shall be considered a modification for purposes of section 7502(c)(5) of this title and section 7503(a) of this title, except that such increase shall

not be considered a modification for such purposes if the owner or operator of the source elects to offset the increase by a greater reduction in emissions of volatile organic compounds concerned from other operations, units, or activities within the source at an internal offset ratio of at least 1.3 to 1. If the owner or operator does not make such election, such change shall be considered a modification for such purposes, but in applying section 7503(a)(2) of this title in the case of any such modification, the best available control technology (BACT), as defined in section 7479 of this title, shall be substituted for the lowest achievable emission rate (LAER). The Administrator shall establish and publish policies and procedures for implementing the provisions of this paragraph.

(8) Special rule for modifications of sources emitting 100 tons or more — In the case of any major stationary source of volatile organic compounds located in the area which emits or has the potential to emit 100 tons or more of volatile organic compounds per year, whenever any change (as described in section 7411(a)(4) of this title) at that source results in any increase (other than a de minimis increase) in emissions of volatile organic compounds from any discrete operation, unit, or other pollutant emitting activity at the source, such increase shall be considered a modification for purposes of section 7502(c)(5) of this title and section 7503(a) of this title, except that if the owner or operator of the source elects to offset the increase by a greater reduction in emissions of volatile organic compounds from other operations, units, or activities within the source at an internal offset ratio of at least 1.3 to 1, the requirements of section 7503(a)(2) of this title (concerning the lowest achievable emission rate (LAER)) shall not apply.

(9) Contingency provisions — In addition to the contingency provisions required under section 7502(c)(9) of this title, the plan revision shall provide for the implementation of specific measures to be undertaken if the area fails to meet any applicable milestone. Such measures shall be included in the plan revision as contingency measures to take effect without further action by the State or the Administrator upon a failure by the State to meet the applicable milestone.

(10) General offset requirement — For purposes of satisfying the emission offset requirements of this part, the ratio of total emission reductions of volatile organic compounds to total increase emissions of such air pollutant shall be at least 1.2 to 1.

Any reference to "attainment date" in subsection (b) of this section, which is incorporated by reference into this subsection, shall refer to the attainment date for serious areas.

(d) Severe Areas — Each State in which all or part of a Severe Area is located shall, with respect to the Severe Area, make the submissions described under subsection (c) of this section (relating to Serious Areas), and shall also submit the revisions to the applicable implementation plan (including the plan items) described under this subsection. For any Severe Area, the terms "major source" and "major stationary source" include (in addition to the sources described in section 7602 of this title) any stationary source or group of sources located within a contiguous area and under common control that emits, or has the potential to emit, at least 25 tons per year of volatile organic compounds.

(1) Vehicle miles traveled

(A) Within 2 years after November 15, 1990, the State shall submit a revision that identifies and adopts specific enforceable transportation control strategies and transportation control measures to offset any growth in emissions from growth in vehicle miles traveled or numbers of vehicle trips in such area and to attain reduction in motor vehicle emissions as necessary, in combination with other emission reduction requirements of this subpart, to comply with the requirements of subsection (b)(2)(B) and (c)(2)(B) of this section (pertaining to periodic emissions reduction requirements). The State shall consider measures specified in section 7408(f) of this title, and choose from among and implement such measures as necessary to demonstrate attainment with the national ambient air quality standards; in considering such measures, the State should ensure adequate access to downtown, other commercial, and residential areas and should avoid measures that increase or relocate emissions and congestion rather than reduce them.

(B) The State may also, in its discretion, submit a revision at any time requiring employers in such area to implement programs to reduce work-related vehicle trips and miles traveled by employees. Such revision shall be developed in accordance with guidance issued by the Administrator pursuant to section 7408(f) of this title and shall, at a minimum, require that each employer of 100 or more persons in such area increase average passenger occupancy per vehicle in commuting trips between home and the workplace during peak travel periods by not less than 25 percent above the average vehicle occupancy for all such trips in the area at the time the revision is submitted. The guidance of the Administrator may specify average vehicle occupancy rates which vary for locations within a nonattainment area (suburban, center city, business district) or among nonattainment areas reflecting existing occupancy rates and the availability of high occupancy modes. Any State required to submit a revision under this subparagraph (as in effect before December

23, 1995) containing provisions requiring employers to reduce work-related vehicle trips and miles travelled by employees may, in accordance with State law, remove such provisions from the implementation plan, or withdraw its submission, if the State notifies the Administrator, in writing, that the State has undertaken, or will undertake, one or more alternative methods that will achieve emission reductions equivalent to those to be achieved by the removed or withdrawn provision.

(2) Offset requirement — For purposes of satisfying the offset requirements pursuant to this part, the ratio of total emission reductions of VOCs to total increased emissions of such air pollutant shall be at least 1.3 to 1, except that if the State plan requires all existing major sources in the nonattainment area to use best available control technology (as defined in section 169(3)) for the control of volatile organic compounds, the ratio shall be at least 1.2 to 1.

(3) Enforcement under section 7511d — By December 31, 2000, the State shall submit a plan revision which includes the provisions required under section 7511d of this title.

Any reference to the term "attainment date" in subsection (b) or (c) of this section, which is incorporated by reference into this subsection (d), shall refer to the attainment date for Severe Areas.

(e) Extreme Areas — Each State in which all or part of an Extreme Area is located shall, with respect to the Extreme Area, make the submissions described under subsection (d) (relating to Severe Areas), and shall also submit the revisions to the applicable implementation plan (including the plan items) described under this subsection. The provisions of clause (ii) of subsection (c)(2)(B) of this section (relating to reductions of less than 3 percent), the provisions of paragaphs (6), (7) and (8) of subsection (c) of this section (relating to de minimis rule and modification of sources), and the provisions of clause (ii) of subsection (b)(1)(A) of this section (relating to reductions of less than 15 percent) shall not apply in the case of an Extreme Area. For any Extreme Area, the terms "major source" and "major stationary source" includes (in addition to the sources described in section 7602 of this title) any stationary source or group of sources located within a contiguous area and under common control that emits, or has the potential to emit, at least 10 tons per year of volatile organic compounds.

(1) Offset requirement — For purposes of satisfying the offset requirements pursuant to this part, the ratio of total emission reductions of VOCs to total increased emissions of such air pollutant shall be at least 1.5 to 1, except that if the State plan requires all existing major sources in the nonat-tainment area to use best available control technology (as defined in section 7479(3)

of this title) for the control of volatile organic compounds, the ratio shall be at least 1.2 to 1.

(2) Modifications — Any change (as described in section 7411(a)(4) of this title) at a major stationary source which results in any increase in emissions from any discrete operation, unit, or other pollutant emitting activity at the source shall be considered a modification for purposes of section 7502(c)(5) of this title and section 7503(a) of this title, except that for purposes of complying with the offset requirement pursuant to section 7503(a)(1) of this title, any such increase shall not be considered a modification if the owner or operator of the source elects to offset the increase by a greater reduction in emissions of the air pollutant concerned from other discrete operations, units, or activities within the source at an internal offset ratio of at least 1.3 to 1. The offset requirements of this part shall not be applicable in Extreme Areas to a modification of an existing source if such modification consists of installation of equipment required to comply with the applicable implementation plan, permit, or this Act.

(3) Use of clean fuels or advanced control technology — For Extreme Areas, a plan revision shall be submitted within 3 years after the date of the enactment of the Clean Air Act Amendments of 1990 to require, effective 8 years after such date, that each new, modified, and existing electric utility and industrial and commercial boiler which emits more than 25 tons per year of oxides of nitrogen —

(A) burn as its primary fuel natural gas, methanol, or ethanol (or a comparably low polluting fuel), or

(B) use advanced control technology (such as catalytic control technology or other comparably effective control methods) for reduction of emissions of oxides of nitrogen.

For purposes of this subsection, the term "primary fuel" means the fuel which is used 90 percent or more of the operating time. This paragraph shall not apply during any natural gas supply emergency (as defined in title III of the Natural Gas Policy Act of 1978).

(4) Traffic control measures during heavy traffic hours — For Extreme Areas, each implementation plan revision under this subsection may contain provisions establishing traffic control measures applicable during heavy traffic hours to reduce the use of high polluting vehicles or heavy-duty vehicles, notwithstanding any other provision of law.

(5) New technologies — The Administrator may, in accordance with section 7410 of this title, approve provisions of an implementation plan for an Extreme Area which anticipate development of new control techniques or improvement of existing control technologies, and an attainment demonstration based on such provisions, if the State demonstrates to the satisfaction of the Administrator that —

(A) such provisions are not necessary to achieve the incremental emission reductions required during the first 10 years after November 15, 1990; and

(B) the State has submitted enforceable commitments to develop and adopt contingency measures to be implemented as set forth herein if the anticipated technologies do not achieve planned reductions.

Such contingency measures shall be submitted to the Administrator no later than 3 years before proposed implementation of the plan provisions and approved or disapproved by the Administrator in accordance with section 7410 of this title. The contingency measures shall be adequate to produce emission reductions sufficient, in conjunction with other approved plan provisions, to achieve the periodic emission reductions required by subsection (b)(1) or (c)(2) of this section and attainment by the applicable dates. If the Administrator determines that an Extreme Area has failed to achieve an emission reduction requirement set forth in subsection (b)(1) or (c)(2) of this section, and that such failure is due in whole or part to an inability to fully implement provisions approved pursuant to this subsection, the Administrator shall require the State to implement the contingency measures to the extent necessary to assure compliance with subsections (b)(1) and (c)(2) of this section.

Any reference to the term "attainment date" in subsection (b), (c), or (d) of this section which is incorporated by reference into this subsection, shall refer to the attainment date for Extreme Areas.

(f) NOx requirements

(1) The plan provisions required under this subpart for major stationary sources of volatile organic compounds shall also apply to major stationary sources (as defined in section 7602 of this title and subsections (c), (d), and (e) of this section) of oxides of nitrogen. This subsection shall not apply in the case of oxides of nitrogen for those sources for which the Administrator determines (when the Administrator approves a plan or plan revision) that net air quality benefits are greater in the absence of reductions of oxides of nitrogen from the sources concerned. This subsection shall also not apply in the case of oxides of nitrogen for —

(A) nonattainment areas not within an ozone transport region under section 7511c of this title if the Administrator determines (when the Administrator approves a plan or plan revision) that additional reductions of oxides of nitrogen would not contribute to attainment of the national ambient air quality standard for ozone in the area, or

(B) nonattainment areas within such an ozone transport region if the Administrator determines (when the Administrator approves

a plan or plan revision) that additional reductions of oxides of nitrogen would not produce net ozone air quality benefits in such region. The Administrator shall, in the Administrator's determinations, consider the study required under section 7511f of this title.

(2)(A) If the Administrator determines that excess reductions in emissions of NOx would be achieved under paragraph (1), the Administrator may limit the application of paragraph (1) to the extent necessary to avoid achieving such excess reductions.

(B) For purposes of this paragraph, excess reductions in emissions of NOx are emission reductions for which the Administrator determines that net air quality benefits are greater in the absence of such reductions. Alternatively, for purposes of this paragraph, excess reductions in emissions of NOx are, for —

(i) nonattainment areas not within an ozone transport region under section 7511c of this title, emission reductions that the Administrator determines would not contribute to attainment of the national ambient air quality standard for ozone in the area, or

(ii) nonattainment areas within such ozone transport region, emission reductions that the Administrator determines would not produce net ozone air quality benefits in such region.

(3) At any time after the final report under section 7511f of this title is submitted to Congress, a person may petition the Administrator for a determination under paragraph (1) or (2) with respect to any nonattainment area or any ozone transport region under section 7511c of this title. The Administrator shall grant or deny such petition within 6 months after its filing with the Administrator.

(g) Milestones

(1) Reductions in emissions — 6 years after November 15, 1990 and at intervals of every 3 years thereafter, the State shall determine whether each nonattainment area (other than an area classified as Marginal or Moderate) has achieved a reduction in emissions during the preceding intervals equivalent to the total emission reductions required to be achieved by the end of such interval pursuant to subsection (b)(1) of this section and the corresponding requirements of subsections (c)(2)(B) and (C), (d), and (e) of this section. Such reduction shall be referred to in this section as an applicable milestone.

(2) Compliance demonstration — For each nonattainment area referred to in paragraph (1), not later than 90 days after the date on which an applicable milestone occurs (not including an attainment date on which a milestone occurs in cases where the standard has been attained), each State in which all or part of such area is located shall submit to the Administrator a demonstration

that the milestone has been met. A demonstration under this paragraph shall be submitted in such form and manner, and shall contain such information and analysis, as the Administrator shall require, by rule. The Administrator shall determine whether or not a State's demonstration is adequate within 90 days after the Administrator's receipt of a demonstration which contains the information and analysis required by the Administrator.

(3) Serious and severe areas; state election — If a State fails to submit a demonstration under paragraph (2) for any Serious or Severe Area within the required period or if the Administrator determines that the area has not met any applicable milestone, the State shall elect, within 90 days after such failure or determination —

    (A) to have the area reclassified to the next higher classification,

    (B) to implement specific additional measures adequate, as determined by the Administrator, to meet the next milestone as provided in the applicable contingency plan, or

    (C) to adopt an economic incentive program as described in paragraph (4).

If the State makes an election under subparagraph (B), the Administrator shall, within 90 days after the election, review such plan and shall, if the Administrator finds the contingency plan inadequate, require further measures necessary to meet such milestone. Once the State makes an election, it shall be deemed accepted by the Administrator as meeting the election requirement. If the State fails to make an election required under this paragraph within the required 90-day period or within 6 months thereafter, the area shall be reclassified to the next higher classification by operation of law at the expiration of such 6-month period. Within 12 months after the date required for the State to make an election, the State shall submit a revision of the applicable implementation plan for the area that meets the requirements of this paragraph. The Administrator shall review such plan revision and approve or disapprove the revision within 9 months after the date of its submission.

(4) Economic incentive program

    (A) An economic incentive program under this paragraph shall be consistent with rules published by the Administrator and sufficient, in combination with other elements of the State plan, to achieve the next milestone. The State program may include a nondiscriminatory system, consistent with applicable law regarding interstate commerce, of State established emissions fees or a system of marketable permits, or a system of State fees on sale or manufacture of products the use of which contributes to ozone formation, or any combination of the foregoing or other similar measures. The program may also in-

clude incentives and requirements to reduce vehicle emissions and vehicle miles traveled in the area, including any of the transportation control measures identified in section 7408(f) of this title.

    (B) Within 2 years after November 15, 1990, the Administrator shall publish rules for the programs to be adopted pursuant to subparagraph (A). Such rules shall include model plan provisions which may be adopted for reducing emissions from permitted stationary sources, area sources, and mobile sources. The guidelines shall require that any revenues generated by the plan provisions adopted pursuant to subparagraph (A) shall be used by the State for any of the following:

      (i) Providing incentives for achieving emission reductions.

      (ii) Providing assistance for the development of innovative technologies for the control of ozone air pollution and for the development of lower-polluting solvents and surface coatings. Such assistance shall not provide for the payment of more than 75 percent of either the costs of any project to develop such a technology or the costs of development of a lower-polluting solvent or surface coating.

      (iii) Funding the administrative costs of State programs under this Act. Not more than 50 percent of such revenues may be used for purposes of this clause.

(5) Extreme areas — If a State fails to submit a demonstration under paragraph (2) for any Extreme Area within the required period, or if the Administrator determines that the area has not met any applicable milestone, the State shall, within 9 months after such failure or determination, submit a plan revision to implement an economic incentive program which meets the requirements of paragraph (4). The Administrator shall review such plan revision and approve or disapprove the revision within 9 months after the date of its submission.

(h) Rural transport areas

(1) Notwithstanding any other provision of section 7511 of this title or this section, a State containing an ozone nonattainment area that does not include, and is not adjacent to, any part of a Metropolitan Statistical Area or, where one exists, a Consolidated Metropolitan Statistical Area (as defined by the United States Bureau of the Census), which area is treated by the Administrator, in the Administrator's discretion, as a rural transport area within the meaning of paragraph (2), shall be treated by operation of law as satisfying the requirements of this section if it makes the submissions required under subsection (a) of this section (relating to marginal areas).

(2) The Administrator may treat an ozone nonattainment area as a rural transport area if the Administrator finds that sources of VOC (and, where the Administrator determines relevant, NOx) emissions within the area do not make a significant contribution to the ozone concentrations measured in the area or in other areas.

(i) Reclassified areas — Each State containing an ozone nonattainment area reclassified under section 7511(b)(2) of this title shall meet such requirements of subsections (b) through (d) of this section as may be applicable to the area as reclassified, according to the schedules prescribed in connection with such requirements, except that the Administrator may adjust any applicable deadlines (other than attainment dates) to the extent such adjustment is necessary or appropriate to assure consistency among the required submissions.

(j) Multi-State ozone nonattainment areas

(1) Coordination among states — Each State in which there is located a portion of a single ozone nonattainment area which covers more than one State (hereinafter in this section referred to as a "multi-State ozone nonattainment area") shall —

(A) take all reasonable steps to coordinate, substantively and procedurally, the revisions and implementation of State implementation plans applicable to the nonattainment area concerned; and

(B) use photochemical grid modeling or any other analytical method determined by the Administrator, in his discretion, to be at least as effective.

The Administrator may not approve any revision of a State implementation plan submitted under this part for a State in which part of a multi-State ozone nonattainment area is located if the plan revision for that State fails to comply with the requirements of this subsection.

(2) Failure to demonstrate attainment — If any State in which there is located a portion of a multi-State ozone non-attainment area fails to provide a demonstration of attainment of the national ambient air quality standard for zone in that portion within the required period, the State may petition the Administrator to make a finding that the State would have been able to make such demonstration but for the failure of one or more other States in which other portions of the area are located to commit to the implementation of all measures required under section 182 (relating to plan submissions and requirements for ozone nonattainment areas). If the Administrator makes such finding, the provisions of section 7509 of this title (relating to sanctions) shall not apply, by reason of the failure to make such demonstration, in the portion of the multi-State ozone nonattainment area within the State submitting such petition.

§7511b. Federal ozone measures
[CAA §183]

(a) Control techniques guidelines for VOC sources — Within 3 years after November 15, 1990, the Administrator shall issue control techniques guidelines, in accordance with section 7408 of this title, for 11 categories of stationary sources of VOC emissions for which such guidelines have not been issued as of November 15, 1990, not including the categories referred to in paragraphs (3) and (4) of subsection (b) of this section. The Administrator may issue such additional control techniques guidelines as the Administrator deems necessary.

(b) Existing and new CTGS

(1) Within 36 months after November 15, 1990, and periodically thereafter, the Administrator shall review and, if necessary, update control technique guidance issued under section 7408 of this title before November 15, 1990.

(2) In issuing the guidelines the Administrator shall give priority to those categories which the Administrator considers to make the most significant contribution to the formation of ozone air pollution in ozone nonattainment areas, including hazardous waste treatment, storage, and disposal facilities which are permitted under subtitle C of the Solid Waste Disposal Act. Thereafter the Administrator shall periodically review and, if necessary, revise such guidelines.

(3) Within 3 years after November 15, 1990, the Administrator shall issue control techniques guidelines in accordance with section 7408 of this title to reduce the aggregate emissions of volatile organic compounds into the ambient air from aerospace coatings and solvents. Such control techniques guidelines shall, at minimum, be adequate to reduce aggregate emissions of volatile organic compounds into the ambient air from the application of such coatings and solvents to such level as the Administrator determines may be achieved through the adoption of best available control measures. Such control technology guidance shall provide for such reductions in such increments and on such schedules as the Administrator determines to be reasonable, but in no event later than 10 years after the final issuance of such control technology guidance. In developing control technology guidance under this subsection, the Administrator shall consult with the Secretary of Defense, the Secretary of Transportation, and the Administrator of the National Aeronautics and Space Administration with regard to the establishment of specifications for such coatings. In evaluating VOC reduction strategies, the guidance shall take into account the applicable requirements of section 7412 of this title and the need to protect stratospheric ozone.

(4) Within 3 years after November 15, 1990, the Administrator shall issue control techniques

guidelines in accordance with section 7408 of this title to reduce the aggregate emissions of volatile organic compounds and PM-10 into the ambient air from paints, coatings, and solvents used in shipbuilding operations and ship repair. Such control techniques guidelines shall, at a minimum, be adequate to reduce aggregate emissions of volatile organic compounds and PM-10 into the ambient air from the removal or application of such paints, coatings, and solvents to such level as the Administrator determines may be achieved through the adoption of the best available control measures. Such control techniques guidelines shall provide for such reductions in such increments and on such schedules as the Administrator determines to be reasonable, but in no event later than 10 years after the final issuance of such control technology guidance. In developing control techniques guidelines under this subsection, the Administrator shall consult with the appropriate Federal agencies.

(c) Alternative control techniques — Within 3 years after November 15, 1990, the Administrator shall issue technical documents which identify alternative controls for all categories of stationary sources of volatile organic compounds and oxides of nitrogen which emit, or have the potential to emit 25 tons per year or more of such air pollutant. The Administrator shall revise and update such documents as the Administrator determines necessary.

(d) Guidance for evaluating cost-effectiveness — Within 1 year after November 15, 1990, the Administrator shall provide guidance to the States to be used in evaluating the relative cost-effectiveness of various options for the control of emissions from existing stationary sources of air pollutants which contribute to nonattainment of the national ambient air quality standards for ozone.

(e) Control of emissions from certain sources

(1) Definitions — For purposes of this subsection —

(A) Best available controls — The term "best available controls" means the degree of emissions reduction that the Administrator determines, on the basis of technological and economic feasibility, health, environmental, and energy impacts, is achievable through the application of the most effective equipment, measures, processes, methods, systems or techniques, including chemical reformulation, product or feedstock substitution, repackaging, and directions for use, consumption, storage, or disposal.

(B) Consumer or commercial product — The term "consumer or commercial product" means any substance, product (including paints, coatings, and solvents), or article (including any container or packaging) held by any person, the use, consumption, storage, disposal, destruction, or decomposition of which may result in the release of volatile organic compounds. The term does not include fuels or fuel additives regulated under section 7545 of this title, or motor vehicles, non-road vehicles, and non-road engines as defined under section 7550 of this title.

(C) Regulated entities — The term "regulated entities" means —

(i) manufacturers, processors, wholesale distributors, or importers of consumer or commercial products for sale or distribution in interstate commerce in the United States; or

(ii) manufacturers, processors, wholesale distributors, or importers that supply the entities listed under clause (i) with such products for sale or distribution in interstate commerce in the United States.

(2) Study and report

(A) Study — The Administrator shall conduct a study of the emissions of volatile organic compounds into the ambient air from consumer and commercial products (or any combination thereof) in order to —

(i) determine their potential to contribute to ozone levels which violate the national ambient air quality standard for ozone; and

(ii) establish criteria for regulating consumer and commercial products or classes or categories thereof which shall be subject to control under this subsection.

The study shall be completed and a report submitted to Congress not later than 3 years after November 15, 1990.

(B) Consideration of certain factors — In establishing the criteria under subparagraph (A)(ii), the Administrator shall take into consideration each of the following:

(i) The uses, benefits, and commercial demand of consumer and commercial products.

(ii) The health or safety functions (if any) served by such consumer and commercial products.

(iii) Those consumer and commercial products which emit highly reactive volatile organic compounds into the ambient air.

(iv) Those consumer and commercial products which are subject to the most cost-effective controls.

(v) The availability of alternatives (if any) to such consumer and commercial products which are of comparable costs, considering health, safety, and environmental impacts.

(3) Regulations to require emission reductions

(A) In general — Upon submission of the final report under paragraph (2), the Administrator shall list those categories of consumer or commercial products that the Administrator determines, based on the study, account for at least 80 percent of the VOC emissions, on a reactivity-adjusted basis, from consumer or commercial products in areas that violate the NAAQS for ozone. Credit toward the 80 percent emissions calculation shall be given for emission reductions from consumer or commercial products made after November 15, 1990. At such time, the Administrator shall divide the list into 4 groups establishing priorities for regulation based on the criteria established in paragraph (2). Every 2 years after promulgating such list, the Administrator shall regulate one group of categories until all 4 groups are regulated. The regulations shall require best available controls as defined in this section. Such regulations may exempt health use products for which the Administrator determines there is no suitable substitute. In order to carry out this section, the Administrator may, by regulation, control or prohibit any activity, including the manufacture or introduction into commerce, offering for sale, or sale of any consumer or commercial product which results in emission of volatile organic compounds into the ambient air.

(B) Regulated entities — Regulations under this subsection may be imposed only with respect to regulated entities.

(C) Use of CTGS — For any consumer or commercial product the Administrator may issue control techniques guidelines under this Act in lieu of regulations required under subparagraph (A) if the Administrator determines that such guidance will be substantially as effective as regulations in reducing emissions of volatile organic compounds which contribute to ozone levels in areas which violate the national ambient air quality standard for ozone.

(4) Systems of regulation — The regulations under this subsection may include any system or systems of regulation as the Administrator may deem appropriate, including requirements for registration and labeling, self-monitoring and reporting, prohibitions, limitations, or economic incentives (including marketable permits and auctions of emissions rights) concerning the manufacture, processing, distribution, use, consumption, or disposal of the product.

(5) Special fund — Any amounts collected by the Administrator under such regulations shall be deposited in a special fund in the United States Treasury for licensing and other services, which thereafter shall be available until expended, subject to annual appropriation Acts, solely to carry out the activities of the Administrator for which such fees, charges, or collections are established or made.

(6) Enforcement — Any regulation established under this subsection shall be treated, for purposes of enforcement of this Act, as a standard under section 7411 of this title and any violation of such regulation shall be treated as a violation of a requirement of section 7411(e) of this title.

(7) State administration — Each State may develop and submit to the Administrator a procedure under State law for implementing and enforcing regulations promulgated under this subsection. If the Administrator finds the State procedure is adequate, the Administrator shall approve such procedure. Nothing in this paragraph shall prohibit the Administrator from enforcing any applicable regulations under this subsection.

(8) Size, etc. — No regulations regarding the size, shape, or labeling of a product may be promulgated, unless the Administrator determines such regulations to be useful in meeting any national ambient air quality standard.

(9) State consultation — Any State which proposes regulations other than those adopted under this subsection shall consult with the Administrator regarding whether any other State or local subdivision has promulgated or is promulgating regulations on any products covered under this part. The Administrator shall establish a clearinghouse of information, studies, and regulations proposed and promulgated regarding products covered under this subsection and disseminate such information collected as requested by State or local subdivisions.

(f) Tank vessel standards

(1) Schedule for standards

(A) Within 2 years after November 15, 1990, the Administrator, in consultation with the Secretary of the Department in which the Coast Guard is operating, shall promulgate standards applicable to the emission of VOCs and any other air pollutant from loading and unloading of tank vessels (as that term is defined in section 2101 of Title 46 of the United States Code) which the Administrator finds causes, or contributes to, air pollution that may be reasonably anticipated to endanger public health or welfare. Such standards shall require the application of reasonably available control technology, considering costs, any nonair quality benefits, environmental impacts, energy requirements and safety factors associated with alternative control techniques. To the extent practicable such standards shall apply to loading and unloading facilities and not to tank vessels.

(B) Any regulation prescribed under this subsection (and any revision thereof) shall take effect after such period as the Administrator finds (after consultation with the Secretary of the department in which the Coast Guard is operating) necessary to permit the development and application of the requisite technology, giving appropriate consideration to the cost of compliance within such period, except that the effective date shall not be more than 2 years after promulgation of such regulations.

(2) Regulations on equipment safety — Within 6 months after November 15, 1990, the Secretary of the Department in which the Coast Guard is operating shall issue regulations to ensure the safety of the equipment and operations which are to control emissions from the loading and unloading of tank vessels, under section 3703 of Title 46 of the United States Code and section 1225 of Title 33. The standards promulgated by the Administrator under paragraph (1) and the regulations issued by a State or political subdivision regarding emissions from the loading and unloading of tank vessels shall be consistent with the regulations regarding safety of the Department in which the Coast Guard is operating.

(3) Agency authority

(A) The Administrator shall ensure compliance with the tank vessel emission standards prescribed under paragraph (1)(A). The Secretary of the Department in which the Coast Guard is operating shall also ensure compliance with the tank vessel standards prescribed under paragraph (1)(A).

(B) The Secretary of the Department in which the Coast Guard is operating shall ensure compliance with the regulations issued under paragraph (2).

(4) State or local standards — After the Administrator promulgates standards under this section, no State or political subdivision thereof may adopt or attempt to enforce any standard respecting emissions from tank vessels subject to regulation under paragraph (1) unless such standard is no less stringent than the standards promulgated under paragraph (1).

(5) Enforcement — Any standard established under paragraph (1)(A) shall be treated, for purposes of enforcement of this Act, as a standard under section 7411 of this title and any violation of such standard shall be treated as a violation of a requirement of section 7411(e) of this title.

(g) **Ozone design value study** — The Administrator shall conduct a study of whether the methodology in use by the Environmental Protection Agency as of November 15, 1990, for establishing a design value for ozone provides a reasonable indicator of the ozone air quality of ozone nonattainment areas. The Administrator shall obtain input from States, local subdivisions thereof, and others. The study shall be completed and a report submitted to Congress not later than 3 years after November 15, 1990. The results of the study shall be subject to peer and public review before submitting it to Congress.

(h) **Vehicles entering ozone nonattainment areas**

(1) Authority regarding ozone inspection and maintenance testing

(A) In general

No noncommercial motor vehicle registered in a foreign country and operated by a United States citizen or by an alien who is a permanent resident of the United States, or who holds a visa for the purposes of employment or educational study in the United States, may enter a covered ozone nonattainment area from a foreign country bordering the United States and contiguous to the nonattainment area more than twice in a single calendar-month period, if State law has requirements for the inspection and maintenance of such vehicles under the applicable implementation plan in the nonattainment area.

(B) Applicability

Subparagraph (A) shall not apply if the operator presents documentation at the United States border entry point establishing that the vehicle has complied with such inspection and maintenance requirements as are in effect and are applicable to motor vehicles of the same type and model year.

(2) Sanctions for violations

The President may impose and collect from the operator of any motor vehicle who violates, or attempts to violate, paragraph (1) a civil penalty of not more than $200 for the second violation or attempted violation and $400 for the third and each subsequent violation or attempted violation.

(3) State election

The prohibition set forth in paragraph (1) shall not apply in any State that elects to be exempt from the prohibition. Such an election shall take effect upon the President's receipt of written notice from the Governor of the State notifying the President of such election.

(4) Alternative approach

The prohibition set forth in paragraph (1) shall not apply in a State, and the President may implement an alternative approach, if —

(A) The Governor of the State submits to the President a written description of an alternative approach to facilitate the compliance, by some or all foreign-registered motor vehicles, with the motor vehicle inspection and maintenance requirements that are —

(i) related to emissions of air pollutants;

(ii) in effect under the applicable implementation plan in the covered ozone non-attainment area; and

(iii) applicable to motor vehicles of the same types and model years as the foreign-registered motor vehicles; and

(B) the President approves the alternative approach as facilitating compliance with the motor vehicle inspection and maintenance requirements referred to in subparagraph (A).

(5) Definition of covered ozone nonattainment area

In this section, the term "covered ozone nonattainment area" means a Serious Area, as classified under section 7511 of this title as of October 27, 1998.

§7511c. Control of interstate ozone pollution [CAA §184]

(a) Ozone transport regions — A single transport region for ozone (within the meaning of section 7506(a) of this title), comprised of the States of Connecticut, Delaware, Maine, Maryland, Massachusetts, New Hampshire, New Jersey, New York, Pennsylvania, Rhode Island, Vermont, and the Consolidated Metropolitan Statistical Area that includes the District of Columbia, is hereby established by operation of law. The provisions of section 7506a(a)(1) and (2) of this title shall apply with respect to the transport region established under this section and any other transport region established for ozone, except to the extent inconsistent with the provisions of this section. The Administrator shall convene the commission required (under section 7506a(b) of this title) as a result of the establishment of such region within 6 months of November 15, 1990.

(b) Plan provisions for States in ozone transport regions

(1) In accordance with section 7410 of this title, not later than 2 years after November 15, 1990 (or 9 months after the subsequent inclusion of a State in a transport region established for ozone), each State included within a transport region established for ozone shall submit a State implementation plan or revision thereof to the Administrator which requires the following —

(A) that each area in such State that is in an ozone transport region, and that is a metropolitan statistical area or part thereof with a population of 100,000 or more comply with the provisions of section 7511a(c)(2)(A) of this title (pertaining to enhanced vehicle inspection and maintenance programs); and

(B) implementation of reasonably available control technology with respect to all sources of volatile organic compounds in the State covered by a control techniques guideline issued before or after November 15, 1990.

(2) Within 3 years after November 15, 1990, the Administrator shall complete a study identifying control measures capable of achieving emission reductions comparable to those achievable through vehicle refueling controls contained in section 7511a(b)(3) of this title, and such measures or such vehicle refueling controls shall be implemented in accordance with the provisions of this section. Notwithstanding other deadlines in this section, the applicable implementation plan shall be revised to reflect such measures within 1 year of completion of the study. For purposes of

this section any stationary source that emits or has the potential to emit at least 50 tons per year of volatile organic compounds shall be considered a major stationary source and subject to the requirements which would be applicable to major stationary sources if the area were classified as a Moderate nonattainment area.

(c) Additional control measures

(1) Recommendations — Upon petition of any State within a transport region established for ozone, and based on a majority vote of the Governors on the Commission (or their designees), the Commission may, after notice and opportunity for public comment, develop recommendations for additional control measures to be applied within all or a part of such transport region if the commission determines such measures are necessary to bring any area in such region into attainment by the dates provided by this subpart. The commission shall transmit such recommendations to the Administrator.

(2) Notice and review — Whenever the Administrator receives recommendations prepared by a commission pursuant to paragraph (1) (the date of receipt of which shall hereinafter in this section be referred to as the "receipt date"), the Administrator shall —

(A) immediately publish in the Federal Register a notice stating that the recommendations are available and provide an opportunity for public hearing within 90 days beginning on the receipt date; and

(B) commence a review of the recommendations to determine whether the control measures in the recommendations are necessary to bring any area in such region into attainment by the dates provided by this subpart and are otherwise consistent with this Act.

(3) Consultation — In undertaking the review required under paragraph (2)(B), the Administrator shall consult with members of the commission of the affected States and shall take into account the data, views, and comments received pursuant to paragraph (2)(A).

(4) Approval and disapproval — Within 9 months after the receipt date, the Administrator shall (A) determine whether to approve, disapprove, or partially disapprove and partially approve the recommendations; (B) notify the commission in writing of such approval, disapproval, or partial disapproval; and (C) publish such determination in the Federal Register. If the Administrator disapproves or partially disapproves the recommendations, the Administrator shall specify —

(i) why any disapproved additional control measures are not necessary to bring any area in such region into attainment by the dates provided by this subpart or are otherwise not consistent with the Act; and

(ii) recommendations concerning equal or more effective actions that could be taken by the commission to conform the disapproved portion of the recommendations to the requirements of this section.

(5) Finding — Upon approval or partial approval of recommendations submitted by a commission, the Administrator shall issue to each State which is included in the transport region and to which a requirement of the approved plan applies, a finding under section 7410(k)(5) of this title that the implementation plan for such State is inadequate to meet the requirements of section 7410(a)(2)(D) of this title. Such finding shall require each such State to revise its implementation plan to include the approved additional control measures within one year after the finding is issued.

(d) Best available air quality monitoring and modeling — For purposes of this section, not later than 6 months after November 15, 1990, the Administrator shall promulgate criteria for purposes of determining the contribution of sources in one area to concentrations of ozone in another area which is a nonattainment area for ozone. Such criteria shall require that the best available air quality monitoring and modeling techniques be used for purposes of making such determinations.

§7511d. Enforcement for Severe and Extreme ozone nonattainment areas for failure to attain
[CAA §185]

(a) General rule — Each implementation plan revision required under section 182 (d) and (e) (relating to the attainment plan for Severe and Extreme ozone nonattainment areas) shall provide that, if the area to which such plan revision applies has failed to attain the national primary ambient air quality standard for ozone by the applicable attainment date, each major stationary source of VOCs located in the area shall, except as otherwise provided under subsection (c), pay a fee to the State as a penalty for such failure, computed in accordance with subsection (b), for each calendar year beginning after the attainment date, until the area is redesignated as an attainment area for ozone. Each such plan revision should include procedures for assessment and collection of such fees.

(b) Computation of fee

(1) Fee amount — The fee shall equal $5,000, adjusted in accordance with paragraph (3), per ton of VOC emitted by the source during the calendar year in excess of 80 percent of the baseline amount, computed under paragraph (2).

(2) Baseline amount — For purposes of this section, the baseline amount shall be computed, in accordance with such guidance as the Administrator may provide, as the lower of the amount of actual VOC emissions ("actuals") or VOC emissions allowed under the permit applicable to the source (or, if no such permit has been issued for the attainment

year, the amount of VOC emissions allowed under the applicable implementation plan ("allowables")) during the attainment year. Notwithstanding the preceding sentence, the Administrator may issue guidance authorizing the baseline amount to be determined in accordance with the lower of average actuals or average allowables, determined over a period of more than one calendar year. Such guidance may provide that such average calculation for a specific source may be used if that source's emissions are irregular, cyclical, or otherwise vary significantly from year to year.

(3) Annual adjustment — The fee amount under paragraph (1) shall be adjusted annually, beginning in the year beginning after the year of enactment, in accordance with section 7661a(b)(3)(B)(v) of this section (relating to inflation adjustment).

(c) Exception — Notwithstanding any provision of this section, no source shall be required to pay any fee under subsection (a) with respect to emissions during any year that is treated as an Extension Year under section 7511(a)(5) of this title.

(d) Fee collection by Administrator — If the Administrator has found that the fee provisions of the implementation plan do not meet the requirements of this section, or if the Administrator makes a finding that the State is not administering and enforcing the fee required under this section, the Administrator shall, in addition to any other action authorized under this title, collect, in accordance with procedures promulgated by the Administrator, the unpaid fees required under subsection (a). If the Administrator makes such a finding under section 179(a)(4), the Administrator may collect fees for periods before the determination, plus interest computed in accordance with section 6621(a)(2) of the Internal Revenue Code of 1986 (relating to computation of interest on underpayment of Federal taxes), to the extent the Administrator finds such fees have not been paid to the State. The provisions of clauses (ii) through (iii) of section 502(b)(3)(C) (relating to penalties and use of the funds, respectively) shall apply with respect to fees collected under this subsection.

(e) Exemptions for certain small areas — For areas with a total population under 200,000 which fail to attain the standard by the applicable attainment date, no sanction under this section or under any other provision of this Act shall apply if the area can demonstrate, consistent with guidance issued by the Administrator, that attainment in the area is prevented because of ozone or ozone precursors transported from other areas. The prohibition applies only in cases in which the area has met all requirements and implemented all measures applicable to the area under this Act.

§7511e. Transitional areas
[CAA §185A]

If an area designated as an ozone nonattainment area as of November 15, 1990 has not violated the national primary ambient air quality standard for ozone for the

36-month period commencing on January 1, 1987, and ending on December 31, 1989, the Administrator shall suspend the application of the requirements of this subpart to such area until December 31, 1991. By June 30, 1992, the Administrator shall determine by order, based on the area's design value as of the attainment date, whether the area attained such standard by December 31, 1991. If the Administrator determines that the area attained the standard, the Administrator shall require, as part of the order, the State to submit a maintenance plan for the area within 12 months of such determination. If the Administrator determines that the area failed to attain the standard, the Administrator shall, by June 30, 1992, designate the area as non-attainment under section 7407(d)(4) of this title.

§7511f. NOx and VOC study
[CAA §185B]

The Administrator, in conjunction with the National Academy of Sciences, shall conduct a study on the role of ozone precursors in tropospheric ozone formation and control. The study shall examine the roles of NOx and VOC emission reductions, the extent to which NOx reductions may contribute (or be counter-productive) to achievement of attainment in different nonattainment areas, the sensitivity of ozone to the control of NOx, the availability and extent of controls for NOx, the role of biogenic VOC emissions, and the basic information required for air quality models. The study shall be completed and a proposed report made public for 30 days comment within 1 year of No-vember 15, 1990, and a final report shall be submitted to Congress within 15 months after November 15, 1990. The Administrator shall utilize all available information and studies, as well as develop additional information, in conducting the study required by this section.

SUBPART 3 — ADDITIONAL PROVISIONS FOR CARBON MONOXIDE NONATTAINMENT AREAS

§7512. Classification and attainment dates
[CAA §186]

(a) Classification by operation of law and attainment dates for nonattainment areas

(1) Each area designated nonattainment for carbon monoxide pursuant to section 7407(d) of this title shall be classified at the time of such designation under table 1, by operation of law, as a Moderate Area or a Serious Area based on the design value for the area. The design value shall be calculated according to the interpretation methodology issued by the Administrator most recently before November 15, 1990. For each area classified under this subsection, the primary standard

attainment date for carbon monoxide shall be as expeditiously as practicable but not later than the date provided in table 1:

TABLE 3*

Area classification	Design value	Primary standard attainment date
Moderate	9.1 – 16.4 ppm	December 31, 1995
Serious	16.5 and above	December 31, 2000

*So in original. Probably should read Table 1. — Eds.

(2) At the time of publication of the notice required under section 7407 of this title (designating carbon monoxide nonattainment areas), the Administrator shall publish a notice announcing the classification of each such carbon monoxide nonattainment area. The provisions of section 7502(a)(1)(B) of this title (relating to lack of notice-and-comment and judicial review) shall apply with respect to such classification.

(3) If an area classified under paragraph (1), table 1, would have been classified in another category if the design value in the area were 5 percent greater or 5 percent less than the level on which such classification was based, the Administrator may, in the Administrator's discretion, within 90 days after November 15, 1990 by the procedure required under paragraph (2), adjust the classification of the area. In making such adjustment, the Administrator may consider the number of exceedances of the national primary ambient air quality standard for carbon monoxide in the area, the level of pollution transport between the area and the other affected areas, and the mix of sources and air pollutants in the area. The Administrator may make the same adjustment for purposes of paragraphs (2), (3), (6), and (7) of section 7512a(a) of this title.

(4) Upon application by any State, the Administrator may extend for 1 additional year (hereinafter in this subpart referred to as the "Extension Year") the date specified in table 1 of subsection (a) if —

(A) the State has complied with all requirements and commitments pertaining to the area in the applicable implementation plan, and

(B) no more than one exceedance of the national ambient air quality standard level for carbon monoxide has occurred in the area in the year preceding the Extension Year.

No more than 2 one-year extensions may be issued under this paragraph for a single nonattainment area.

(b) New designations and reclassifications

(1) New designations to nonattainment — Any area that is designated attainment or unclassifiable for carbon monoxide under section 7407(d)(4) of this title, and that is subsequently redesignated to nonattainment for carbon monoxide under section 7407(d)(3) of this title, shall, at the time of the redesignation, be classified by

operation of law in accordance with table 1 under subsections (a)(1) and (a)(4) of this section. Upon its classification, the area shall be subject to the same requirements under section 110, subpart 1 of this part, and this subpart that would have applied had the area been so classified at the time of the notice under subsection (a)(2) of this section, except that any absolute, fixed date applicable in connection with any such requirement is extended by operation of law by a period equal to the length of time between November 15, 1990 and the date the area is classified.

(2) Reclassification of moderate areas upon failure to attain

(A) General rule — Within 6 months following the applicable attainment date for a carbon monoxide nonattainment area, the Administrator shall determine, based on the area's design value as of the attainment date, whether the area has attained the standard by that date. Any Moderate Area that the Administrator finds has not attained the standard by that date shall be reclassified by operation of law in accordance with table 1 of subsection (a)(1) of this section as a Serious Area.

(B) Publication of notice — The Administrator shall publish a notice in the Federal Register, no later than 6 months following the attainment date, identifying each area that the Administrator has determined, under subparagraph (A), as having failed to attain and identifying the reclassification, if any, described under subparagraph (A).

(c) **References to terms** — Any reference in this subpart to a "Moderate Area" or a "Serious Area" shall be considered a reference to a Moderate Area or a Serious Area, respectively, as classified under this section.

§7512a. Plan submissions and requirements [CAA §187]

(a) **Moderate Areas** — Each State in which all or part of a Moderate Area is located shall, with respect to the Moderate Area (or portion thereof, to the extent specified in guidance of the Administrator issued before November 15, 1990), submit to the Administrator the State implementation plan revisions (including the plan items) described under this subsection, within such periods as are prescribed under this subsection, except to the extent the State has made such submissions as of November 15, 1990:

(1) Inventory — No later than 2 years from November 15, 1990, the State shall submit a comprehensive, accurate, current inventory of actual emissions from all sources, as described in section 7502(c)(3), of this title in accordance with guidance provided by the Administrator.

(2)(A) Vehicle miles traveled — No later than 2 years after November 15, 1990, for areas with a design value above 12.7 ppm at the time of classification, the plan revision shall contain a forecast of vehicle miles traveled in the nonattainment area concerned for each year before the year in which the plan projects the national ambient air quality standard for carbon monoxide to be attained in the area. The forecast shall be based on guidance which shall be published by the Administrator, in consultation with the Secretary of Transportation, within 6 months after November 15, 1990. The plan revision shall provide for annual updates of the forecasts to be submitted to the Administrator together with annual reports regarding the extent to which such forecasts proved to be accurate. Such annual reports shall contain estimates of actual vehicle miles traveled in each year for which a forecast was required.

(B) Special rule for Denver — Within 2 years after November 15, 1990, in the case of Denver, the State shall submit a revision that includes the transportation control measures as required in section 7511a(d)(1)(A) of this title except that such revision shall be for the purpose of reducing CO emissions rather than volatile organic compound emissions. If the State fails to include any such measure, the implementation plan shall contain an explanation of why such measure was not adopted and what emissions reduction measure was adopted to provide a comparable reduction in emissions, or reasons why such reduction is not necessary to attain the national primary ambient air quality standard for carbon monoxide.

(3) Contingency provisions — No later than 2 years after November 15, 1990, for areas with a design value above 12.7 ppm at the time of classification, the plan revision shall provide for the implementation of specific measures to be undertaken if any estimate of vehicle miles traveled in the area which is submitted in an annual report under paragraph (2) exceeds the number predicted in the most recent prior forecast or if the area fails to attain the national primary ambient air quality standard for carbon monoxide by the primary standard attainment date. Such measures shall be included in the plan revision as contingency measures to take effect without further action by the State or the Administrator if the prior forecast has been exceeded by an updated forecast or if the national standard is not attained by such deadline.

(4) Savings clause for vehicle inspection and maintenance provisions of the state implementation plan — Immediately after November 15, 1990, for any Moderate Area (or, within the Administrator's discretion, portion thereof), the plan for which is of the type described in section 7511a(a)(2)(B) of this title any provisions necessary to ensure that the applicable implementation plan includes the vehicle inspection and maintenance program described in section 7511a(a)(2)(B) of this title.

(5) Periodic inventory — No later than September 30, 1995, and no later than the end of each 3 year period thereafter, until the area is redesignated to attainment, a revised inventory meeting the requirements of subsection (a)(1) of this section.

(6) Enhanced vehicle inspection and maintenance — No later than 2 years after November 15, 1990 in the case of Moderate Areas with a design value greater than 12.7 ppm at the time of classification, a revision that includes provisions for an enhanced vehicle inspection and maintenance program as required in section 7511a(c)(3) of this title (concerning serious ozone nonattainment areas), except that such program shall be for the purpose of reducing carbon monoxide rather than hydrocarbon emissions.

(7) Attainment demonstration and specific annual emission reductions — In the case of Moderate Areas with a design value greater than 12.7 ppm at the time of classification, no later than 2 years after November 15, 1990, a revision to provide, and a demonstration that the plan as revised will provide, for attainment of the carbon monoxide NAAQS by the applicable attainment date and provisions for such specific annual emission reductions as are necessary to attain the standard by that date.

The Administrator may, in the Administrator's discretion, require States to submit a schedule for submitting any of the revisions or other items required under this subsection. In the case of Moderate Areas with a design value of 12.7 ppm or lower at the time of classification, the requirements of this subsection shall apply in lieu of any requirement that the State submit a demonstration that the applicable implementation plan provides for attainment of the carbon monoxide standard by the applicable attainment date.

(b) Serious Areas

(1) In general — Each State in which all or part of a Serious Area is located shall, with respect to the Serious Area, make the submissions (other than those required under subsection (a)(1)(B)) of this section applicable under subsection (a) of this section to Moderate Areas with a design value of 12.7 ppm or greater at the time of classification, and shall also submit the revision and other items described under this subsection.

(2) Vehicle miles traveled — Within 2 years after November 15, 1990 the State shall submit a revision that includes the transportation control measures as required in section 7511a(d)(1) of this title except that such revision shall be for the purpose of reducing CO emissions rather than volatile organic compound emissions. In the case of any such area (other than an area in New York State) which is a covered area (as defined in section 7586(a)(2)(B) of this title) for purposes of the Clean Fuel Fleet program under part C of subchapter II of this chapter, if the State fails to include any such measure, the implementation plan shall contain an explanation of why such measure was not adopted and what emissions reduction measure was adopted to provide a comparable reduction in emissions, or reasons why such reduction is not necessary to attain the national primary ambient air quality standard for carbon monoxide.

(3) Oxygenated gasoline

(A) Within 2 years after November 15, 1990, the State shall submit a revision to require that gasoline sold, supplied, offered for sale or supply, dispensed, transported or introduced into commerce in the larger of —

(i) the Consolidated Metropolitan Statistical Area (as defined by the United States Office of Management and Budget) (CMSA) in which the area is located, or

(ii) if the area is not located in a CMSA, the Metropolitan Statistical Area (as defined by the United States Office of Management and Budget) in which the area is located,

be blended, during the portion of the year in which the area is prone to high ambient concentrations of carbon monoxide (as determined by the Administrator), with fuels containing such level of oxygen as is necessary, in combination with other measures, to provide for attainment of the carbon monoxide national ambient air quality standard by the applicable attainment date and maintenance of the national ambient air quality standard thereafter in the area. The revision shall provide that such requirement shall take effect no later than October 1, 1993, and shall include a program for implementation and enforcement of the requirement consistent with guidance to be issued by the Administrator.

(B) Notwithstanding subparagraph (A), the revision described in this paragraph shall not be required for an area if the State demonstrates to the satisfaction of the Administrator that the revision is not necessary to provide for attainment of the carbon monoxide national ambient air quality standard by the applicable attainment date and maintenance of the national ambient air quality standard thereafter in the area.

(c) Areas with significant stationary source emissions of CO

(1) Serious Areas — In the case of Serious Areas in which stationary sources contribute significantly to carbon monoxide levels (as determined under rules issued by the Administrator), the State shall submit a plan revision within 2 years after November 15, 1990, which provides that the term "major stationary source" includes (in addition to the sources described in section 7602 of this title) any stationary source which emits, or has the potential to emit, 50 tons per year or more of carbon monoxide.

(2) Waivers for certain areas — The Administrator may, on a case-by-case basis, waive any requirements that pertain to transportation controls, inspection and maintenance, or oxygenated fuels where the Administrator determines by rule that mobile sources of carbon monoxide do not contribute significantly to carbon monoxide levels in the area.

(3) Guidelines — Within 6 months after November 15, 1990, the Administrator shall issue guidelines for and rules determining whether stationary sources contribute significantly to carbon monoxide levels in an area.

(d) CO milestone

(1) Milestone demonstration — By March 31, 1996, each State in which all or part of a Serious Area is located shall submit to the Administrator a demonstration that the area has achieved a reduction in emissions of CO equivalent to the total of the specific annual emission reductions required by December 31, 1995. Such reductions shall be referred to in this subsection as the milestone.

(2) Adequacy of demonstration — A demonstration under this paragraph shall be submitted in such form and manner, and shall contain such information and analysis, as the Administrator shall require. The Administrator shall determine whether or not a State's demonstration is adequate within 90 days after the Administrator's receipt of a demonstration which contains the information and analysis required by the Administrator.

(3) Failure to meet emission reduction milestone — If a State fails to submit a demonstration under paragraph (1) within the required period, or if the Administrator notifies the State that the State has not met the milestone, the State shall, within 9 months after such a failure or notification, submit a plan revision to implement an economic incentive and transportation control program as described in section 7511a(g)(4) of this title. Such revision shall be sufficient to achieve the specific annual reductions in carbon monoxide emissions set forth in the plan by the attainment date.

(e) Multi-State CO nonattainment areas

(1) Coordination among states — Each State in which there is located a portion of a single nonattainment area for carbon monoxide which covers more than one State ("multi-State nonattainment area") shall take all reasonable steps to coordinate, substantively and procedurally, the revisions and implementation of State implementation plans applicable to the nonattainment area concerned. The Administrator may not approve any revision of a State implementation plan submitted under this part for a State in which part of a multi-State nonattainment area is located if the plan revision for that State fails to comply with the requirements of this subsection.

(2) Failure to demonstrate attainment — If any State in which there is located a portion of a multi-State nonattainment area fails to provide a demonstration of attainment of the national ambient air quality standard for carbon monoxide in that portion within the period required under this part the State may petition the Administrator to make a finding that the State would have been able to make such demonstration but for the failure of one or more other States in which other portions of the area are located to commit to the implementation of all measures required under this section (relating to plan submissions for carbon monoxide nonattainment areas). If the Administrator makes such finding, in the portion of the nonattainment area within the State submitting such petition, no sanction shall be imposed under section 7509 of this title or under any other provision of this chapter, by reason of the failure to make such demonstration.

(f) Reclassified areas — Each State containing a carbon monoxide nonattainment area reclassified under section 7512(b)(2) of this title shall meet the requirements of subsection (b) of this section, as may be applicable to the area as reclassified, according to the schedules prescribed in connection with such requirements, except that the Administrator may adjust any applicable deadlines (other than the attainment date) where such deadlines are shown to be infeasible.

(g) Failure of Serious Area to attain standard — If the Administrator determines under section 7512(b)(2) of this title that the national primary ambient air quality standard for carbon monoxide has not been attained in a Serious Area by the applicable attainment date, the State shall submit a plan revision for the area within 9 months after the date of such determination. The plan revision shall provide that a program of incentives and requirements as described in section 7511a(g)(4) of this title shall be applicable in the area, and such program, in combination with other elements of the revised plan, shall be adequate to reduce the total tonnage of emissions of carbon monoxide in the area by at least 5 percent per year in each year after approval of the plan revision and before attainment of the national primary ambient air quality standard for carbon monoxide.

SUBPART 4 — ADDITIONAL PROVISIONS FOR PARTICULATE MATTER NONATTAINMENT AREAS

§7513. Classifications and attainment dates [CAA §188]

(a) Initial classifications — Every area designated nonattainment for PM-10 pursuant to section 7407(d) of this ttitle shall be classified at the time of such designation, by operation of law, as a moderate PM-10 nonattainment area (also referred to in this subpart as a "Moderate Area") at the time of such designation. At the time of publication of the notice under section 107(d)(4) (relating to area designations) for each PM-10 nonattainment area, the Administrator shall publish a notice announcing the classification of such area. The provisions of section 7502(a)(1)(B) of this title (relating to lack of notice-and-comment and judicial review) shall apply with respect to such classification.

(b) Reclassification as Serious

(1) Reclassification before attainment date — The Administrator may reclassify as a Serious PM-10 nonattainment area (identified in this subpart also as a "Serious Area") any area that the Administrator determines cannot practicably attain the national ambient air quality standard for PM-10 by the attainment date (as prescribed in subsection (c)) for Moderate Areas. The Administrator shall reclassify appropriate areas as Serious by the following dates:

(A) For areas designated nonattainment for PM-10 under section 7407(d)(4) of this title, the Administrator shall propose to reclassify appropriate areas by June 30, 1991, and take final action by December 31, 1991.

(B) For areas subsequently designated nonattainment, the Administrator shall reclassify appropriate areas within 18 months after the required date for the State's submission of a SIP for the Moderate Area.

(2) Reclassification upon failure to attain — Within 6 months following the applicable attainment date for a PM-10 nonattainment area, the Administrator shall determine whether the area attained the standard by that date. If the Administrator finds that any Moderate Area is not in attainment after the applicable attainment date —

(A) the area shall be reclassified by operation of law as a Serious Area; and

(B) the Administrator shall publish a notice in the Federal Register no later than 6 months following the attainment date, identifying the area as having failed to attain and identifying the reclassification described under subparagraph (A).

(c) Attainment dates

— Except as provided under subsection (d) of this section, the attainment dates for PM-10 nonattainment areas shall be as follows:

(1) Moderate areas — For a Moderate Area, the attainment date shall be as expeditiously as practicable but no later than the end of the sixth calendar year after the area's designation as nonattainment, except that, for areas designated nonattainment for PM-10 under section 7407(d)(4) of this title, the attainment date shall not extend beyond December 31, 1994.

(2) Serious areas — For a Serious Area, the attain-ment date shall be as expeditiously as practicable but no later than the end of the tenth calendar year beginning after the area's designation as nonattainment, except that, for areas designated nonattainment for PM-10 under section 7407(d)(4) of this title, the date shall not extend beyond December 31, 2001.

(d) Extension of attainment date for Moderate Areas

— Upon application by any State, the Administrator may extend for 1 additional year (hereinafter referred to as the "Extension Year") the date specified in paragraph (c)(1) if —

(1) the State has complied with all requirements and commitments pertaining to the area in the applicable implementation plan; and

(2) no more than one exceedance of the 24-hour national ambient air quality standard level for PM-10 has occurred in the area in the year preceding the Extension Year, and the annual mean concentration of PM-10 in the area for such year is less than or equal to the standard level.

No more than 2 one-year extensions may be issued under the subsection for a single nonattainment area.

(e) Extension of attainment date for Serious Areas

— Upon application by any State, the Administrator may extend the attainment date for a Serious Area beyond the date specified under subsection (c), if attainment by the date established under subsection (c) would be impracticable, the State has complied with all requirements and commitments pertaining to that area in the implementation plan, and the State demonstrates to the satisfaction of the Administrator that the plan for that area includes the most stringent measures that are included in the implementation plan of any State or are achieved in practice in any State, and can feasibly be implemented in the area. At the time of such application, the State must submit a revision to the implementation plan that includes a demonstration of attainment by the most expeditious alternative date practicable. In determining whether to grant an extension, and the appropriate length of time for any such extension, the Administrator may consider the nature and extent of nonattainment, the types and numbers of sources or other emitting activities in the area (including the influence of uncontrollable natural sources and transboundary emissions from foreign countries), the population exposed to concentrations in excess of the standard, the presence and concentration of potentially toxic substances in the mix of particulate emissions in the area, and the technological and economic feasibility of various control measures. The Administrator may not approve an extension until the State submits an attainment demonstration for the area. The Administrator may grant at most one such extension for an area, of no more than 5 years.

(f) Waivers for certain areas

— The Administrator may, on a case-by-case basis, waive any requirement applicable to any Serious Area under this subpart where the Administrator determines that anthropogenic sources of PM-10 do not contribute significantly to the violation of the PM-10 standard in the area. The Administrator may also waive a specific date for attainment of the standard where the Administrator determines that nonanthropogenic sources of PM-10 contribute significantly to the violation of the PM-10 standard in the area.

§7513a. Plan provisions and schedules for plan submissions
[CAA §189]
(a) Moderate Areas

(1) Plan provisions — Each State in which all or part of a Moderate Area is located shall submit, according to the applicable schedule under paragraph (2), an implementation plan that includes each of the following:

(A) For the purpose of meeting the requirements of section 7502(c)(5) of this title, a permit program providing that permits meeting the requirements of section 7503 of this title are required for the construction and operation of new and modified major stationary sources of PM-10.

(B) Either (i) a demonstration (including air quality modeling) that the plan will provide for attainment by the applicable attainment date; or (ii) a demonstration that attainment by such date is impracticable.

(C) Provisions to assure that reasonably available control measures for the control of PM-10 shall be implemented no later than December 10, 1993, or 4 years after designation in the case of an area classified as moderate after November 15, 1990.

(2) Schedule for plan submissions — A State shall submit the plan required under subparagraph (1) no later than the following:

(A) Within 1 year of November 15, 1990, for areas designated nonattainment under section 7407(d)(4) of this title, except that the provision required under subparagraph (1)(A) shall be submitted no later than June 30, 1992.

(B) 18 months after the designation as nonattainment, for those areas designated nonattainment after the designations prescribed under section 7407 (d)(4) of this title.

(b) Serious Areas

(1) Plan provisions — In addition to the provisions submitted to meet the requirements of paragraph (a)(1) (relating to Moderate Areas), each State in which all or part of a Serious Area is located shall submit an implementation plan for such area that includes each of the following:

(A) A demonstration (including air quality modeling) —

(i) that the plan provides for attainment of the PM-10 national ambient air quality standard by the applicable attainment date, or

(ii) for any area for which the State is seeking, pursuant to section 7513(e) of this title, an extension of the attainment date beyond the date set forth in section 7513(c) of this title, that attainment by that date would be impracticable, and that the plan provides for attainment by the most expeditious alternative date practicable.

(B) Provisions to assure that the best available control measures for the control of PM-10 shall be implemented no later than 4 years after the date the area is classified (or reclassified) as a Serious Area.

(2) Schedule for plan submissions — A State shall submit the demonstration required for an area under paragraph (1)(A) no later than 4 years after reclassification of the area to Serious, except that for areas reclassified under section 7513(b)(2) of this title, the State shall submit the attainment demonstration within 18 months after reclassification to Serious. A State shall submit the provisions described under paragraph (1)(B) no later than 18 months after reclassification of the area as a Serious Area.

(3) Major sources — For any Serious Area, the terms "major source" and "major stationary source" include any stationary source or group of stationary sources located within a contiguous area and under common control that emits, or has the potential to emit, at least 70 tons per year of PM-10.

(c) Milestones

(1) Plan revisions demonstrating attainment submitted to the Administrator for approval under this subpart shall contain quantitative milestones which are to be achieved every 3 years until the area is redesignated attainment and which demonstrate reasonable further progress, as defined in section 7501(1) of this title, toward attainment by the applicable date.

(2) Not later than 90 days after the date on which a milestone applicable to the area occurs, each State in which all or part of such area is located shall submit to the Administrator a demonstration that all measures in the plan approved under this section have been implemented and that the milestone has been met. A demonstration under this subsection shall be submitted in such form and manner, and shall contain such information and analysis, as the Administrator shall require. The Administrator shall determine whether or not a State's demonstration under this subsection is adequate within 90 days after the Administrator's receipt of a demonstration which contains the information and analysis required by the Administrator.

(3) If a State fails to submit a demonstration under paragraph (2) with respect to a milestone

within the required period or if the Administrator determines that the area has not met any applicable milestone, the Administrator shall require the State, within 9 months after such failure or determination to submit a plan revision that assures that the State will achieve the next milestone (or attain the national ambient air quality standard for PM-10, if there is no next milestone) by the applicable date.

(d) Failure to attain — In the case of a Serious PM-10 nonattainment area in which the PM-10 standard is not attained by the applicable attainment date, the State in which such area is located shall, after notice and opportunity for public comment, submit within 12 months after the applicable attainment date, plan revisions which provide for attainment of the PM-10 air quality standard and, from the date of such submission until attainment, for an annual reduction in PM-10 or PM-10 precursor emissions within the area of not less than 5 percent of the amount of such emissions as reported in the most recent inventory prepared for such area.

(e) PM-10 precursors — The control requirements applicable under plans in effect under this part for major stationary sources of PM-10 shall also apply to major stationary sources of PM-10 precursors, except where the Administrator determines that such sources do not contribute significantly to PM-10 levels which exceed the standard in the area. The Administrator shall issue guidelines regarding the application of the preceding sentence.

§7513b. Issuance of RACM and BACM guidance
[CAA §190]

The Administrator shall issue, in the same manner and according to the same procedure as guidance is issued under section 7408(c) of this title, technical guidance on reasonably available control measures and best available control measures for urban fugitive dust, and emissions from residential wood combustion (including curtailments and exemptions from such curtailments) and prescribed silvicultural and agricultural burning, no later than 18 months following November 15, 1990. The Administrator shall also examine other categories of sources contributing to nonattainment of the PM-10 standard, and determine whether additional guidance on reasonably available control measures and best available control measures is needed, and issue any such guidance no later than 3 years after November 15, 1990. In issuing guidelines and making determinations under this section, the Administrator (in consultation with the State) shall take into account emission reductions achieved, or expected to be achieved, under subchapter IV of this chapter and other provisions of this chapter.

SUBPART 5 — ADDITIONAL PROVISIONS FOR AREAS DESIGNATED NONATTAINMENT FOR SULFUR OXIDES, NITROGEN DIOXIDE, OR LEAD

§7514. Plan submission deadlines
[CAA §191]

(a) Submission — Any State containing an area designated or redesignated under section 7407(d) of this title as nonattainment with respect to the national primary ambient air quality standards for sulfur oxides, nitrogen dioxide, or lead subsequent to November 15, 1990 shall submit to the Administrator, within 18 months of the designation, an applicable implementation plan meeting the requirements of this part.

(b) States lacking fully approved State implementation plans — Any State containing an area designated nonattainment with respect to national primary ambient air quality standards for sulfur oxides or nitrogen dioxide under section 7407(d)(1)(C)(i) of this title, but lacking a fully approved implementation plan complying with the requirements of this chapter (including this part) as in effect immediately before November 15, 1990, shall submit to the Administrator, within 18 months of November 15, 1990, an implementation plan meeting the requirements of subpart 1 (except as otherwise prescribed by section 7514a of this title).

§7514a. Attainment dates
[CAA §192]

(a) Plans under section 7514(a) — Implementation plans required under section 7514(a) of this title shall provide for attainment of the relevant primary standard as expeditiously as practicable but no later than 5 years from the date of the nonattainment designation.

(b) Plans under section 7514(b) — Implementation plans required under section 7514(b) shall provide for attainment of the relevant primary national ambient air quality standard within 5 years after November 15, 1990.

(c) Inadequate plans — Implementation plans for nonattainment areas for sulfur oxides or nitrogen dioxide with plans that were approved by the Administrator before November 15, 1990 but, subsequent to such approval, were found by the Administrator to be substantially inadequate, shall provide for attainment of the relevant primary standard within 5 years from the date of such finding.

SUBPART 6 — SAVINGS PROVISIONS

§7515. General savings clause
[CAA §193]

Each regulation, standard, rule, notice, order and guidance promulgated or issued by the Administrator under this Act, as in effect before November 15, 1990 shall remain in effect according to its terms, except to the extent otherwise provided under this Act, inconsistent with any provision of this Act, or revised by the Administrator. No control requirement in effect, or required to be adopted by an order, settlement agreement, or plan in effect before November 15, 1990 in any area which is a nonattainment area for any air pollutant may be modified after November 15, 1990, in any manner unless the modification insures equivalent or greater emission reductions of such air pollutant.

SUBCHAPTER II — EMISSION STANDARDS FOR MOVING SOURCES

PART A — MOTOR VEHICLE EMISSION AND FUEL STANDARDS

§7521. Emission standards for new motor vehicles or new motor vehicle engines
[CAA §202]

(a) Authority of Administrator to prescribe by regulation — Except as otherwise provided in subsection (b) —

(1) The Administrator shall by regulation prescribe (and from time to time revise) in accordance with the provisions of this section, standards applicable to the emission of any air pollutant from any class or classes of new motor vehicles or new motor vehicle engines, which in his judgment cause, or contribute to, air pollution which may reasonably be anticipated to endanger public health or welfare. Such standards shall be applicable to such vehicles and engines for their useful life (as determined under subsection (d), of this section relating to useful life of vehicles for purposes of certification), whether such vehicles and engines are designed as complete systems or incorporate devices to prevent or control such pollution.

(2) Any regulation prescribed under paragraph (1) of this subsection (and any revision thereof) shall take effect after such period as the Administrator finds necessary to permit the development and application of the requisite technology, giving appropriate consideration to the cost of compliance within such period.

(3)(A) In General —

(i) Unless the standard is changed as provided in subparagraph (B), regulations under paragraph (1) of this subsection applicable to emissions of hydrocarbons, carbon monoxide, oxides of nitrogen, and particulate matter from classes or categories of heavy-duty vehicles or engines manufactured during or after model year 1983 shall contain standards

which reflect the greatest degree of emission reduction achievable through the application of technology which the Administrator determines will be available for the model year to which such standards apply, giving appropriate consideration to cost, energy, and safety factors associated with the application of such technology.

(ii) In establishing classes or categories of vehicles or engines for purposes of regulations under this paragraph, the Administrator may base such classes or categories on gross vehicle weight, horsepower, type of fuel used or other appropriate factors.

(B) Revised standards for heavy duty trucks

(i) On the basis of information available to the Administrator concerning the effects of air pollutants emitted from heavy-duty vehicles or engines and from other sources of mobile source related pollutants on the public health and welfare, and taking costs into account, the Administrator may promulgate regulations under paragraph (1) of this subsection revising any standard promulgated under, or before the date of, the enactment of the Clean Air Act Amendments of 1990 (or previously revised under this subparagraph) and applicable to classes or categories of heavy-duty vehicles or engines.

(ii) Effective for the model year 1998 and thereafter, the regulations under paragraph (1) of this subsection applicable to emissions of oxides of nitrogen (NOx) from gasoline and diesel-fueled heavy duty trucks shall contain standards which provide that such emissions may not exceed 4.0 grams per brake horsepower hour (gbh).

(C) Lead time and stability — Any standard promulgated or revised under this paragraph and applicable to classes or categories of heavy-duty vehicles or engines shall apply for a period of no less than 3 model years beginning no earlier than the model year commencing 4 years after such revised standard is promulgated.

(D) Rebuilding practices — The Administrator shall study the practice of rebuilding heavy-duty engines and the impact rebuilding has on engine emissions. On the basis of that study and other information available to the Administrator, the Administrator may prescribe requirements to control rebuilding practices, including standards applicable to emissions from any rebuilt heavy-duty engines (whether or not the engine is past its statutory useful life), which in the Administrator's judgment cause, or contribute to, air pollution which may reasonably be anticipated to endanger public health or welfare taking costs into account. Any regulation shall take effect after a period the Administrator finds necessary to permit the development and application of the requisite control measures, giving appropriate consideration to the cost of compliance within the period and energy and safety factors.

(E) Motorcycles — For purposes of this paragraph, motorcycles and motorcycle engines shall be treated in the same manner as heavy-duty vehicles and engines (except as otherwise permitted under section 7525(f)(1) of this title) unless the the Administrator promulgates a rule reclassifying motorcycles as light-duty vehicles within the meaning of this section or unless the Administrator promulgates regulations under subsection (a) applying standards applicable to the emission of air pollutants from motorcycles as a separate class or category. In any case in which such standards are promulgated for such emissions from motorcycles as a separate class or category, the Administrator, in promulgating such standards, shall consider the need to achieve equivalency of emission reductions between motorcycles and other motor vehicles to the maximum extent practicable.

(4)(A) Effective with respect to vehicles and engines manufactured after model year 1978, no emission control device, system, or element of design shall be used in a new motor vehicle or new motor vehicle engine for purposes of complying with requirements prescribed under this title if such device, system, or element of design will cause or contribute to an unreasonable risk to public health, welfare, or safety in its operation or function.

(B) In determining whether an unreasonable risk exists under subparagraph (A), the Administrator shall consider, among other factors, (i) whether and to what extent the use of any device, system, or element of design causes, increases, reduces, or eliminates emissions of any unregulated pollutants; (ii) available methods for reducing or eliminating any risk to public health, welfare, or safety which may be associated with the use of such device, system, or element of design, and (iii) the availability of other devices, systems, or elements of design which may be used to conform to requirements prescribed under this title without causing or contributing to such unreasonable risk. The Administrator shall include in the consideration required by this paragraph all relevant information developed pursuant to section 7548 of this title.

(5)(A) If the Administrator promulgates final regulations which define the degree of control required and the test procedures by which compliance could be determined for gasoline vapor recovery of uncontrolled emissions from the fueling of motor vehicles, the Administrator shall, after consultation with the Secretary of Transportation with respect to motor vehicle safety, prescribe, by regulation, fill pipe standards for new motor vehicles in order to insure effective connection between such fill pipe and any vapor recovery system which the Administrator determines may be required to comply with such vapor recovery regulations. In promulgating such standards the Administrator shall take into consideration limits on fill pipe diameter, minimum design criteria for nozzle retainer lips, limits on the location of the unleaded fuel restrictors, a minimum access zone surrounding a fill pipe, a minimum pipe or nozzle insertion angle, and such other factors as he deems pertinent.

(B) Regulations prescribing standards under subparagraph (A) shall not become effective until the introduction of the model year for which it would be feasible to implement such standards, taking into consideration the restraints of an adequate lead time for design and production.

(C) Nothing in subparagraph (A) shall (i) prevent the Administrator from specifying different nozzle and fill neck sizes for gasoline with additives and gasoline without additives or (ii) permit the Administrator to require a specific location, configuration, modeling, or styling of the motor vehicle body with respect to the fuel tank fill neck or fill nozzle clearance envelope.

(D) For the purpose of this paragraph, the term "fill pipe" shall include the fuel tank fill pipe, fill neck, fill inlet, and closure.

(6) Onboard vapor recovery — Within 1 year after November 15, 1990, the Administrator shall, after consultation with the Secretary of Transportation regarding the safety of vehicle-based ("onboard") systems for the control of vehicle refueling emissions, promulgate standards under this section requiring that new light-duty vehicles manufactured beginning in the fourth model year after the model year in which the standards are promulgated and thereafter shall be equipped with such systems. The standards required under this paragraph shall apply to a percentage of each manufacturer's fleet of new light-duty vehicles beginning with the fourth model year after the model year in which the standards are promulgated. The percentage shall be as specified in the following table:

IMPLEMENTATION SCHEDULE FOR ONBOARD
VAPOR RECOVERY REQUIREMENTS

Model year commencing after standards promulgated	Percentage*
Fourth	40
Fifth	80
After Fifth	100

* Percentages in the table refer to a percentage of the manufacturer's sales volume.

The standards shall require that such systems provide a minimum evaporative emission capture efficiency of 95 percent. The requirements of section 7511a(b)(3) of this title (relating to stage II gasoline vapor recovery) for areas classified under section 7511 of this title as moderate for ozone shall not apply after promulgation of such standards and the Administrator may, by rule, revise or waive the application of the requirements of such section 7511a(b)(3) of this title for areas classified under section 7511 of this title as Serious, Severe, or Extreme for ozone, as appropriate, after such time as the Administrator determines that onboard emissions control systems required under this paragraph are in widespread use throughout the motor vehicle fleet.

(b) Emissions of carbon monoxide, hydrocarbons, and oxides of nitrogen; annual report to Congress; waiver of emission standards; research objectives

(1)(A) The regulations under subsection (a) applicable to emissions of carbon monoxide and hydrocarbons from light-duty vehicles and engines manufactured during model years 1977 through 1979 shall contain standards which provide that such emissions from such vehicles and engines may not exceed 1.5 grams per vehicle mile of hydrocarbons and 15.0 grams per vehicle mile of carbon monoxide. The regulations under subsection (a) applicable to emissions of carbon monoxide from light-duty vehicles and engines manufactured during the model year 1980 shall contain standards which provide that such emissions may not exceed 7.0 grams per vehicle mile. The regulations under subsection (a) applicable to emissions of hydrocarbons from light-duty vehicles and engines manufactured during or after model year 1980 shall contain standards which require a reduction of at least 90 percent from emissions of such pollutant allowable under the standards under this section applicable to light-duty vehicles and engines manufactured in model year 1970. Unless waived as provided in paragraph (5), regulations under subsection (a) of this section applicable to emissions of carbon monoxide from light-duty vehicles and engines manufactured during or after the model year 1981 shall contain standards which require a reduction of at least 90

percent from emissions of such pollutant allowable under the standards under this section applicable to light-duty vehicles and engines manufactured in model year 1970.

(B) The regulations under subsection (a) applicable to emissions of oxides of nitrogen from light-duty vehicles and engines manufactured during model years 1977 through 1980 shall contain standards which provide that such emissions from such vehicles and engines may not exceed 2.0 grams per vehicle mile. The regulations under subsection (a) applicable to emissions of oxides of nitrogen from light-duty vehicles and engines manufactured during the model year 1981 and thereafter shall contain standards which provide that such emissions from such vehicles and engines may not exceed 1.0 gram per vehicle mile. The Administrator shall prescribe standards in lieu of those required by the preceding sentence which provide that emissions of oxides of nitrogen may not exceed 2.0 grams per vehicle mile for any light-duty vehicle manufactured during model years 1981 and 1982 by any manufacturer whose production, by corporate identity, for calendar year 1976 was less than three hundred thousand light-duty motor vehicles worldwide if the Administrator determines that —

(i) the ability of such manufacturer to meet emission standards in the 1975 and subsequent model years was, and is, primarily dependent upon technology developed by other manufacturers and purchased from such manufacturers; and

(ii) such manufacturer lacks the financial resources and technological ability to develop such technology.

(C) The Administrator may promulgate regulations under subsection (a)(1) of this section revising any standard prescribed or previously revised under this subsection, as needed to protect public health or welfare, taking costs, energy, and safety into account. Any revised standard shall require a reduction of emissions from the standard that was previously applicable. Any such revision under this title may provide for a phase-in of the standard. It is the intent of Congress that the numerical emission standards specified in subsections (a)(3)(B)(ii), (g), (h), and (i) of this section shall not be modified by the Administrator after November 15, 1990 for any model year before the model year 2004.

(2) Emission standards under paragraph (1), and measurement techniques on which such standards are based (if not promulgated prior to

November 15, 1990), shall be promulgated by regulation within 180 days after such date.

(3) For purposes of this part —

(A)(i) The term "model year" with reference to any specific calendar year means the manufacturer's annual production period (as determined by the Administrator) which includes January 1 of such calendar year. If the manufacturer has no annual production period, the term "model year" shall mean the calendar year.

(ii) For the purpose of assuring that vehicles and engines manufactured before the beginning of a model year were not manufactured for purposes of circumventing the effective date of a standard required to be prescribed by subsection (b), the Administrator may prescribe regulations defining "model year" otherwise than as provided in clause (i).

(B) Repealed. Pub. L. 101-549, Title II, §230(1), Nov. 15, 1990, 104 Stat. 2529

(C) The term "heavy duty vehicle" means a truck, bus, or other vehicle manufactured primarily for use on the public streets, roads, and highways (not including any vehicle operated exclusively on a rail or rails) which has a gross vehicle weight (as determined under regulations promulgated by the Administrator) in excess of six thousand pounds. Such term includes any such vehicle which has special features enabling off-street or off-highway operation and use.

(3) Upon the petition of any manufacturer, the Administrator, after notice and opportunity for public hearing, may waive the standard required under subparagraph (B) of paragraph (1) to not exceed 1.5 grams of oxides of nitrogen per vehicle mile for any class or category of light-duty vehicles or engines manufactured by such manufacturer during any period of up to four model years beginning after the model year 1980 if the manufacturer demonstrates that such waiver is necessary to permit the use of an innovative power train technology, or innovative emission control device or system, in such class or category of vehicles or engines and that such technology or system was not utilized by more than 1 percent of the light-duty vehicles sold in the United States in the 1975 model year. Such waiver may be granted only if the Administrator determines —

(A) that such waiver would not endanger public health,

(B) that there is a substantial likelihood that the vehicles or engines will be able to comply with the applicable standard under this section at the expiration of the waiver, and

(C) that the technology or system has a potential for longterm air quality benefit and

has the potential to meet or exceed the average fuel economy standard applicable under the Energy Policy and Conservation Act upon the expiration of the waiver.

No waiver under this subparagraph granted to any manufacturer shall apply to more than 5 percent of such manufacturer's production or more than fifty thousand vehicles or engines, whichever is greater.

(c) Feasibility study and investigation by National Academy of Sciences; reports to Administrator and Congress; availability of information

(1) The Administrator shall undertake to enter into appropriate arrangements with the National Academy of Sciences to conduct a comprehensive study and investigation of the technological feasibility of meeting the emissions standards required to be prescribed by the Administrator by subsection (b) of this section.

(2) Of the funds authorized to be appropriated to the Administrator by this Act, such amounts as are required shall be available to carry out the study and investigation authorized by paragraph (1) of this subsection.

(3) In entering into any arrangement with the National Academy of Sciences for conducting the study and investigation authorized by paragraph (1) of this subsection, the Administrator shall request the National Academy of Sciences to submit semiannual reports on the progress of its study and investigation to the Administrator and the Congress, beginning not later than July 1, 1971, and continuing until such study and investigation is completed.

(4) The Administrator shall furnish to such Academy at its request any information which the Academy deems necessary for the purpose of conducting the investigation and study authorized by paragraph (1) of this subsection. For the purpose of furnishing such information, the Administrator may use any authority he has under this chapter (A) to obtain information from any person, and (B) to require such person to conduct such tests, keep such records, and make such reports respecting research or other activities conducted by such person as may be reasonably necessary to carry out this subsection.

(d) Useful life of vehicles — The Administrator shall prescribe regulations under which the useful life of vehicles and engines shall be determined for purposes of subsection (a)(1) of this section and section 7541 of this title. Such regulations shall provide that except where different useful life period is specified in this title useful life shall —

(1) in the case of light duty vehicles and light duty vehicle engines and light-duty trucks up to 3,750 lbs. LVW and up to 6,000 lbs. GVWR, be a period of use of five years or of fifty thousand

miles (or the equivalent), whichever first occurs, except that in the case of any requirement of this section which first becomes applicable after the enactment of the Clean Air Act Amendments of 1990 where the useful life period is not otherwise specified for such vehicles and engines, the period shall be 10 years or 100,000 miles (or the equivalent), whichever first occurs, with testing for purposes of in-use compliance under section 207 up to (but not beyond) 7 years or 75,000 miles (or the equivalent), whichever first occurs;

(2) in the case of any other motor vehicle or motor vehicle engine (other than motorcycles or motorcycle engines) be a period of use set forth in paragraph (1) unless the Administrator determines that a period of use of greater duration or mileage is appropriate; and

(3) in the case of any motorcycle or motorcycle engine, be a period of use the Administrator shall determine.

(e) New power sources or propulsion systems — In the event a new power source or propulsion system for new motor vehicles or new motor vehicle engines is submitted for certification pursuant to section 7525(a) of this title, the Administrator may postpone certification until he has prescribed standards for any air pollutants emitted by such vehicle or engine which in his judgment cause or contribute to, air pollution which may reasonably be anticipated to endanger the public health or welfare but for which standards have not been prescribed under subsection (a) of this section.

(f) High altitude regulations

(1) The high altitude regulation in effect with respect to model year 1977 motor vehicles shall not apply to the manufacture, distribution, or sale of 1978 and later model year motor vehicles. Any future regulation affecting the sale or distribution of motor vehicles or engines manufactured before the model year 1984 in high altitude areas of the country shall take effect no earlier than model year 1981.

(2) Any such future regulation applicable to high altitude vehicles or engines shall not require a percentage of reduction in the emissions of such vehicles which is greater than the required percentage of reduction in emissions from motor vehicles as set forth in subsection (b) of this section. This percentage reduction shall be determined by comparing any proposed high altitude emission standards to high altitude emissions from vehicles manufactured during model year 1970. In no event shall regulations applicable to high altitude vehicles manufactured before the model year 1984 establish a numerical standard which is more stringent than that applicable to vehicles certified under non-high altitude conditions.

(3) Section 7607(d) of this title shall apply to any high altitude regulation referred to in

paragraph (2) and before promulgating any such regulation, the Administrator shall consider and make a finding with respect to —

(A) the economic impact upon consumers, individual high altitude dealers, and the automobile industry of any such regulation, including the economic impact which was experienced as a result of the regulation imposed during model year 1977 with respect to high altitude certification requirements;

(B) the present and future availability of emission control technology capable of meeting the applicable vehicle and engine emission requirements without reducing model availability; and

(C) the likelihood that the adoption of such a high altitude regulation will result in any significant improvement in air quality in any area to which it shall apply.

(g) Light-duty trucks up to 6,000 lbs. GVWR and light-duty vehicles; standards for model years after 1993

(1) NMHC, CO, and NOx — Effective with respect to the model year 1994 and thereafter, the regulations under subsection (a) applicable to emissions of nonmethane hydrocarbons (NMHC), carbon monoxide (CO), and oxides of nitrogen (NOx) from light-duty trucks (LDTs) of up to 6,000 lbs. gross vehicle weight rating (GVWR) and light-duty vehicles (LDVs) shall contain standards which provide that emissions from a percentage of each manufacturer's sales volume of such vehicles and trucks shall comply with the levels specified in table G. The percentage shall be as specified in the implementation schedule below:

TABLE G — EMISSION STANDARDS FOR NMHC, CO, AND NOx FROM LIGHT-DUTY TRUCKS OF UP TO 6,000 LBS. GVWR AND LIGHT-DUTY VEHICLES

Vehicle type	Column A (5 yrs/50,000 mi)		
	NMHC	CO	NOx
LDTs (0–3,750 lbs. LVW) and light-duty vehicles	0.25	3.5	0.4*
LDTs (3,751–5,750 lbs. LVW)	0.32	4.4	0.7**

Vehicle type	Column B (10 yrs/100,000 mi)		
	NMHC	CO	NOx
LDTs (0–3,750 lbs. LVW) and light-duty vehicles	0.31	4.2	0.6*
LDTs (3,751–5,750 lbs. LVW)	0.40	5.5	0.97**

Standards are expressed in grams per mile (gpm). For standards under column A, for purposes of certification under section 206, the applicable useful life shall be 5 years or 50,000 miles (or the equivalent), whichever first occurs. For standards under column B, for purposes of certification under section 206, the applicable useful life shall be 10 years or 100,000 miles (or the equivalent), whichever first occurs.

    * In the case of diesel-fueled LDTs (0-3,750 LVW) and light-duty vehicles, before the model year 2004, in lieu of the 0.4 and 0.6 standards for NOx, the applicable standards for NOx shall be 1.0 gpm for a useful life of 5 years or 50,000 miles (or the equivalent), whichever first occurs, and 1.25 gpm for a useful life of 10 years or 100,000 miles (or the equivalent) whichever first occurs.

    ** This standard does not apply to diesel-fueled LDTs (3,751-5,750 lbs. LVW).

IMPLEMENTATION SCHEDULE
FOR TABLE G STANDARDS

Model year	Percentage*
1994	40
1995	80
After 1995	100

* Percentages in the table refer to a percentage of the manufacturer's sales volume.

    (2) PM Standard — Effective with respect to model year 1994 and thereafter in the case of light-duty vehicles, and effective with respect to the model year 1995 and thereafter in the case of light-duty trucks (LDTs) of up to 6,000 lbs. Gross vehicle weight rating (GVWR), the regulations under subsection (a) applicable to emissions of particulate matter (PM) from such vehicles and trucks shall contain standards which provide that such emissions from a percentage of each manufacturer's sales volume of such vehicles and trucks shall not exceed the levels specified in the table below. The percentage shall be as specified in the Implementation Schedule below.

PM STANDARD FOR LDTS OF UP
TO 6,000 LBS. GVWR

Useful life period	Standard
5/50,000	0.8 gpm
10/100,000	0.10 gpm

The applicable useful life, for purposes of certification under section 206 and for purposes of in-use compliance under section 7525 of this title, shall be 5 years or 50,000 miles (or the equivalent), whichever first occurs, in the case of the 5/50,000 standard.

    The applicable useful life, for purposes of certification under section 206 and for purposes of in-use compliance under section 7541 of this title, shall be 10 years or 100,000 miles (or the equivalent), whichever first occurs in the case of the 10/100,000 standard.

IMPLEMENTATION SCHEDULE
FOR PM STANDARDS

Model year	Light-duty vehicles	Standard LDTs
1994	40%*	
1995	80%*	40%*
1996	100%*	80%*
After 1996	100%*	100%*

* Percentages in the table refer to a percentage of each manufacturer's sales volume.

    (h) Light-duty trucks of more than 6,000 lbs. GVWR; standards for model years after 1995 — Effective with respect to the model year 1996 and thereafter, the regulations under subsection (a) applicable to emissions of nonmethane hydrocarbons (NMHC), carbon monoxide (CO), oxides of nitrogen (NOx), and particulate matter (PM) from light-duty trucks (LDTs) of more than 6,000 lbs. Gross vehicle weight rating (GVWR) shall contain standards which provide that emissions from a specified percentage of each manufacturer's sales volume of such trucks shall comply with the levels specified in table H. The specified percentage shall be 50 percent in model year 1996 and 100 percent thereafter.

TABLE H — EMISSION STANDARDS
FOR NMHC AND CO FROM GASOLINE AND
DIESEL FUELED LIGHT-DUTY TRUCKS OF
MORE THAN 6,000 LBS. GVWR

	Column A (5 yrs/50,000 mi)		
	NMHC	CO	NOx
3,751–5,750 lbs. TW	0.32	4.4	0.7*
Over 5,750 lbs. TW	0.39	5.0	1.1*

	Column B (11 yrs/120,000 mi)			
	NMHC	CO	NOx	PM
3,751–5,750 lbs. TW	0.46	6.4	0.98	0.10
Over 5,750 lbs. TW	0.56	7.3	1.53	0.12

Standards are expressed in grams per mile (GPM). For standards under column A, for purposes of certification under section 7525 of this title, the applicable useful life shall be 5 years or 50,000 miles (or the equivalent), whichever first occurs. For standards under column B, for purposes of certification under section 7525 of this title, the applicable useful life shall be 11 years or 120,000 miles (or the equivalent), whichever first occurs.

* Not applicable to diesel-fueled LDTs.

(i) Phase II study for certain light-duty vehicles and light-duty trucks

(1) The Administrator, with the participation of the Office of Technology Assessment, shall study whether or not further reductions in emissions from light-duty vehicles and light-duty trucks should be required pursuant to this title. The study shall consider whether to establish with respect to model years commencing after January 1, 2003, the standards and useful life period for gasoline and diesel-fueled light-duty vehicles and light-duty trucks with a loaded vehicle weight (LVW) of 3,750 lbs. or less specified in the following table:

TABLE 3 — PENDING EMISSION STANDARDS FOR GASOLINE AND DIESEL FUELED LIGHT-DUTY VEHICLES AND LIGHT-DUTY TRUCKS 3,750 LBS. LVW OR LESS

Pollutant	Emission level*
NMHC	0.125 GPM
Nox	0.2 GPM
CO	1.7 GPM

* Emission levels are expressed in grams per mile (GPM). For vehicles and engines subject to this subsection for purposes of section 202(d) and any reference thereto, the useful life of such vehicles and engines shall be a period of 10 years or 100,000 miles (or the equivalent), whichever first occurs.

Such study shall also consider other standards and useful life periods which are more stringent or less stringent than those set forth in table 3 (but more stringent than those referred to in subsections (g) and (h) of this section).

(2)(A) As part of the study under paragraph (1), the Administrator shall examine the need for further reductions in emissions in order to attain or maintain the national ambient air quality standards, taking into consideration the waiver provisions of section 7543(b) of this title. As part of such study, the Administrator shall also examine —

(i) the availability of technology (including the costs thereof), in the case of light-duty vehicles and light-duty trucks with a loaded vehicle weight (LVW) of 3,750 lbs. Or less, for meeting more stringent emission standards than those provided in subsections (g) and (h) of this section for model years commencing not earlier than after January 1, 2003, and not later than model year 2006, including the lead time

and safety and energy impacts of meeting more stringent emission standards; and

(ii) the need for, and cost effectiveness of, obtaining further reductions in emissions from such light-duty vehicles and light-duty trucks, taking into consideration alternative means of attaining or maintaining the national primary ambient air quality standards pursuant to State implementation plans and other requirements of this chapter, including their feasibility and cost effectiveness.

(B) The Administrator shall submit a report to Congress no later than June 1, 1997, containing the results of the study under this subsection, including the results of the examination conducted under subparagraph (A). Before submittal of such report the Administrator shall provide a reasonable opportunity for public comment and shall include a summary of such comments in the report to Congress.

(3)(A) Based on the study under paragraph (1) the Administrator shall determine, by rule, within 3 calendar years after the report is submitted to Congress, but not later than December 31, 1999, whether —

(i) there is a need for further reductions in emissions as provided in paragraph (2)(A);

(ii) the technology for meeting more stringent emission standards will be available, as provided in paragraph (2)(A)(i), in the case of light-duty vehicles and light-duty trucks with a loaded vehicle weight (LVW) of 3,750 lbs. or less, for model years commencing not earlier than January 1, 2003 and not later than model year 2006, considering the factors listed in paragraph (2)(A)(i); and

(iii) obtaining further reductions in emissions from such vehicles will be needed and cost effective, taking into consideration alternatives as provided in paragraph (2)(A)(ii).

The rulemaking under this paragraph shall commence within 3 months after submission of the report to Congress under paragraph (2)(B).

(B) If the Administrator determines under subparagraph (A) that —

(i) there is no need for further reductions in emissions as provided in paragraph (2)(A);

(ii) the technology for meeting more stringent emission standards will not be available as provided in paragraph (2)(A)(i), in the case of light-duty vehicles and light-duty trucks with a loaded vehicle weight (LVW) of 3,750 lbs. or less, for model years commencing not earlier than January 1, 2003, and not later than model year 2006, considering the factors listed in paragraph (2)(A)(i); or

(iii) obtaining further reductions in emissions from such vehicles will not be needed or cost effective, taking into consideration alternatives as provided in paragraph (2)(A)(ii),

the Administrator shall not promulgate more stringent standards than those in effect pursuant to subsections (g) and (h) of this section. Nothing in this paragraph shall prohibit the Administrator from exercising the Administrator's authority under subsection (a) to promulgate more stringent standards for light-duty vehicles and light-duty trucks with a loaded vehicle weight (LVW) of 3,750 lbs. or less at any other time thereafter in accordance with subsection (a) of this section.

(C) If the Administrator determines under subparagraph (A) that —

(i) there is a need for further reductions in emissions as provided in paragraph (2)(A);

(ii) the technology for meeting more stringent emission standards will be available, as provided in paragraph (2)(A)(i), in the case of light-duty vehicles and light-duty trucks with a loaded vehicle weight (LVW) of 3,750 lbs. or less, for model years commencing not earlier than January 1, 2003, and not later than model year 2006, considering the factors listed in paragraph (2)(A)(i); and

(iii) obtaining further reductions in emissions from such vehicles will be needed and cost effective, taking into consideration alternatives as provided in paragraph (2)(A)(ii),

the Administrator shall either promulgate the standards (and useful life periods) set forth in Table 3 in paragraph (1) or promulgate alternative standards (and useful life periods) which are more stringent than those referred to in subsections (g) and (h) of this section. Any such standards (or useful life periods) promulgated by the Administrator shall take effect with respect to any such vehicles or engines no earlier than the model year 2003 but not later than model year 2006, as determined by the Administrator in the rule.

(D) Nothing in this paragraph shall be construed by the Administrator or by a court as a presumption that any standards (or useful life period) set forth in Table 3 shall be promulgated in the rulemaking required under this paragraph. The action required of the Administrator in accordance with this paragraph shall be treated as a nondiscretionary duty for purposes of section 7604(a)(2) of this title (relating to citizen suits).

(E) Unless the Administrator determines not to promulgate more stringent standards as provided in subparagraph (B) or to postpone the effective date of standards referred to in Table 3 in paragraph (1) or to establish alternative standards as provided in subparagraph (C), effective with respect to model years commencing after January 1, 2003, the regulations under subsection (a) applicable to emissions of non-methane hydrocarbons (NMHC), oxides of nitrogen (NOx), and carbon monoxide (CO) from motor vehicles and motor vehicle engines in the classes specified in Table 3 in paragraph (1) above shall contain standards which provide that emissions may not exceed the pending emission levels specified in Table 3 in paragraph (1).

(j) Cold CO standard

(1) Phase I — Not later than 12 months after November 15, 1990, the Administrator shall promulgate regulations under subsection (a) of this section applicable to emissions of carbon monoxide from 1994 and later model year light-duty vehicles and light-duty trucks when operated at 20 degrees Fahrenheit. The regulations shall contain standards which provide that emissions of carbon monoxide from a manufacturer's vehicles when operated at 20 degrees Fahrenheit may not exceed, in the case of light-duty vehicles, 10.0 grams per mile, and in the case of light-duty trucks, a level comparable in stringency to the standard applicable to light-duty vehicles. The standards shall take effect after model year 1993 according to a phase-in schedule which requires a percentage of each manufacturer's sales volume of light-duty vehicles and light-duty trucks to comply with applicable standards after model year 1993. The percentage shall be as specified in the following table:

PHASE-IN SCHEDULE FOR COLD
START STANDARDS

Model Year	Percentage
1994	40
1995	80
1996	100

(2) Phase II

(A) Not later than June 1, 1997, the Administrator shall complete a study assessing the need for further reductions in emissions of carbon monoxide and the maximum reductions in such emissions achievable from model year 2001 and later model year light-duty vehicles and light-duty trucks when operated at 20 degrees Fahrenheit.

(B)(i) If as of June 1, 1997, 6 or more nonattainment areas have a carbon monoxide design value of 9.5 ppm or greater, the regulations under subsection (a)(1) of this section applicable to emissions of carbon monoxide from model year 2002 and later model year light-duty vehicles and light-duty trucks shall contain standards which provide that emissions of carbon monoxide from such vehicles and trucks when operated at 20 degrees Fahrenheit may not exceed 3.4 grams per mile (gpm) in the case of light-duty vehicles and 4.4 grams per mile (gpm) in the case of light-duty trucks up to 6,000 GVWR and a level comparable in stringency in the case of light-duty trucks 6,000 GVWR and above.

(ii) In determining for purposes of this subparagraph whether 6 or more nonattainment areas have a carbon monoxide design value of 9.5 ppm or greater, the Administrator shall exclude the areas of Steubenville, Ohio, and Oshkosh, Wisconsin.

(3) Useful-life for phase I and phase II standards — In the case of the standards referred to in paragraphs (1) and (2), for purposes of certification under section 7525 of this title and in-use compliance under section 7541 of this title, the applicable useful life period shall be 5 years or 50,000 miles, whichever first occurs, except that the Administrator may extend such useful life period (for purposes of section 7525 of this title, or section 7541 of this title, or both) if he determines that it is feasible for vehicles and engines subject to such standards to meet such standards for a longer useful life. If the Administrator extends such useful life period, the Administrator may make an appropriate adjustment of applicable standards for such extended useful life. No such extended useful life shall extend beyond the useful life period provided in regulations under subsection (d) of this section.

(4) Heavy-duty vehicles and engines — The Administrator may also promulgate regulations under subsection (a)(1) of this section applicable to emissions of carbon monoxide from heavy-duty vehicles and engines when operated at cold temperatures.

(k) Control of evaporative emissions — The Administrator shall promulgate (and from time to time revise) regulations applicable to evaporative emissions of hydrocarbons from all gasoline-fueled motor vehicles —

(1) during operation; and

(2) over 2 or more days of nonuse;

under ozone-prone summertime conditions (as determined by regulations of the Administrator). The regulations shall take effect as expeditiously as possible and shall require the greatest degree of emission reduction achievable by means reasonably expected to be available for production during any model year to which the regulations apply, giving appropriate consideration to fuel volatility, and to cost, energy,

and safety factors associated with the application of the appropriate technology. The Administrator shall commence a rulemaking under this subsection within 12 months after November 15, 1990. If final regulations are not promulgated under this subsection within 18 months after November 15, 1990, the Administrator shall submit a statement to the Congress containing an explanation of the reasons for the delay and a date certain for promulgation of such final regulations in accordance with this Act. Such date certain shall not be later than 15 months after the expiration of such 18 month deadline.

(l) Mobile source-related air toxics

(1) Study — Not later than 18 months after November 15, 1990, the Administrator shall complete a study of the need for, and feasibility of, controlling emissions of toxic air pollutants which are unregulated under this Act and associated with motor vehicles and motor vehicle fuels, and the need for, and feasibility of, controlling such emissions and the means and measures for such controls. The study shall focus on those categories of emissions that pose the greatest risk to human health or about which significant uncertainties remain, including emissions of benzene, formaldehyde, and 1,3 butadiene. The proposed report shall be available for public review and comment and shall include a summary of all comments.

(2) Standards — Within 54 months after November 15, 1990, the Administrator shall, based on the study under paragraph (1), promulgate (and from time to time revise) regulations under subsection (a)(1) of this section or section 7545(c)(1) of this title containing reasonable requirements to control hazardous air pollutants from motor vehicles and motor vehicle fuels. The regulations shall contain standards for such fuels or vehicles, or both, which the Administrator determines reflect the greatest degree of emission reduction achievable through the application of technology which will be available, taking into consideration the standards established under subsection (a), the availability and costs of the technology, and noise, energy, and safety factors, and lead time. Such regulations shall not be inconsistent with standards under subsection (a) of this section. The regulations shall, at a minimum, apply to emissions of benzene and formaldehyde.

(m) Emissions control diagnostics

(1) Regulations — Within 18 months after November 15, 1990, the Administrator shall promulgate regulations under subsection (a) requiring manufacturers to install on all new light-duty vehicles and light-duty trucks diagnostics systems capable of —

(A) accurately identifying for the vehicle's useful life as established under this section, emission-related systems deterioration or malfunction, including, at a minimum, the catalytic converter and oxygen sensor, which could cause or result in failure of the vehicles to comply with emission standards established under this section,

(B) alerting the vehicle's owner or operator to the likely need for emission-related components or systems maintenance or repair,

(C) storing and retrieving fault codes specified by the Administrator, and

(D) providing access to stored information in a manner specified by the Administrator. The Administrator may, in the Administrator's discretion, promulgate regulations requiring manufacturers to install such onboard diagnostic systems on heavy-duty vehicles and engines.

(2) Effective date — The regulations required under paragraph (1) of this subsection shall take effect in model year 1994, except that the Administrator may waive the application of such regulations for model year 1994 or 1995 (or both) with respect to any class or category of motor vehicles if the Administrator determines that it would be infeasible to apply the regulations to that class or category in such model year or years, consistent with corresponding regulations or policies adopted by the California Air Resources Board for such systems.

(3) State inspection — The Administrator shall by regulation require States that have implementation plans containing motor vehicle inspection and maintenance programs to amend their plans within 2 years after promulgation of such regulations to provide for inspection of onboard diagnostics systems (as prescribed by regulations under paragraph (1) of this subsection) and for the maintenance or repair of malfunctions or system deterioration identified by or affecting such diagnostics systems. Such regulations shall not be inconsistent with the provisions for warranties promulgated under section 7541(a) and (b) of this title.

(4) Specific requirements — In promulgating regulations under this subsection, the Administrator shall require —

(A) that any connectors through which the emission control diagnostics system is accessed for inspection, diagnosis, service, or repair shall be standard and uniform on all motor vehicles and motor vehicle engines;

(B) that access to the emission control diagnostics system through such connectors shall be unrestricted and shall not require any access code or any device which is only available from a vehicle manufacturer; and

(C) that the output of the data from the emission control diagnostics system through such connectors shall be usable without the need for any unique decoding information or device.

(5) Information availability — The Administrator, by regulation, shall require (subject to the provisions of section 7542(c) of this title regarding the protection of methods or processes entitled to protection as trade secrets) manufacturers to provide promptly to any person engaged in the repairing or servicing of motor vehicles or motor vehicle engines, and the Administrator for use by any such persons, with any and all information needed to make use of the emission control diagnostics system prescribed under this subsection and such other information including instructions for making emission related diagnosis and repairs. No such information may be withheld under section 7542(c) of this title if that information is provided (directly or indirectly) by the manufacturer to franchised dealers or other persons engaged in the repair, diagnosing, or servicing of motor vehicles or motor vehicle engines. Such information shall also be available to the Administrator, subject to section 7542(c) of this title, in carrying out the Administrator's responsibilities under this section.

(f)* Model years after 1990 [* So in original. Probably should be (n)] — For model years prior to model year 1994, the regulations under subsection (a) of this section applicable to buses other than those subject to standards under section 7554 of this title shall contain a standard which provides that emissions of particulate matter (PM) from such buses may not exceed the standards set forth in the following table:

PM STANDARD FOR BUSES

Model year	Standard*
1991	0.25
1992	0.25
1993 and thereafter	0.10

* Standards are expressed in grams per brake horsepower hour (g/bhp/hr).

§7522. Prohibited acts
[CAA §203]

(a) Enumerated prohibitions — The following acts and the causing thereof are prohibited —

(1) in the case of a manufacturer of new motor vehicles or new motor vehicle engines for distribution in commerce, the sale, or the offering for sale, or the introduction, or delivery for introduction, into commerce, or (in the case of any person, except as provided by regulation of the Administrator), the importation into the United States, of any new motor vehicle or new motor vehicle engine, manufactured after the effective date of regulations under this part which are applicable to such vehicle or engine unless such vehicle or engine is covered by a certificate of conformity issued (and in effect) under regulations prescribed under this part or part C in the case of clean-fuel vehicles (except as provided in subsection (b) of this section);

(2)(A) for any person to fail or refuse to permit access to or copying of records or to fail to make reports or provide information required under section 7542 of this title;

(B) for any person to fail or refuse to permit entry, testing or inspection authorized under section 7525(c) of this title or section 7542 of this title;

(C) for any person to fail or refuse to perform tests, or have tests performed as required under section 7542 of this title;

(D) for any manufacturer to fail to make information available as provided by regulation under section 7521(m)(5) of this title;

(3)(A) for any person to remove or render inoperative any device or element of design installed on or in a motor vehicle or motor vehicle engine in compliance with regulations under this title prior to its sale and delivery to the ultimate purchaser, or for any person knowingly to remove or render inoperative any such device or element of design after such sale and delivery to the ultimate purchaser; or

(B) for any person to manufacture or sell, or offer to sell, or install, any part or component intended for use with, or as part of, any motor vehicle or motor vehicle engine, where a principal effect of the part or component is to bypass, defeat, or render inoperative any device or element of design installed on or in a motor vehicle or motor vehicle engine in compliance with regulations under this title, and where the person knows or should know that such part or component is being offered for sale or installed for such use or put to such use; or

(4) for any manufacturer of a new motor vehicle or new motor vehicle engine subject to standards prescribed under section 7521 of this title or part C of this subchapter —

(A) to sell or lease any such vehicle or engine unless such manufacturer has complied with (i) the requirements of section 7541(a) and (b) of this title with respect to such vehicle or engine, and unless a label or tag is affixed to such vehicle or engine in accordance with section 7541(c)(3) of this title, or (ii) the corresponding requirements of part C of this subchapter in the case of clean fuel vehicles unless the manufacturer has complied with the corresponding requirements of part C of this subchapter;

(B) to fail or refuse to comply with the requirements of section 7541(c) or (e) of this title, or the corresponding requirements of part C of this subchapter in the case of clean fuel vehicles;

(C) except as provided in subsection (c)(3) of section 7541 of this title and the corresponding requirements of part C of this subchapter in the case of clean fuel vehicles, to provide directly or indirectly in any communication to the ultimate purchaser or any subsequent purchaser that the coverage of any warranty under this Act is conditioned upon use of any part, component, or system manufactured by such manufacturer or any person acting for such manufacturer or under his control, or conditioned upon service performed by any such person; or

(D) to fail or refuse to comply with the terms and conditions of the warranty under section 7541 (a) or (b) of this title or the corresponding requirements of part C of this subchapter in the case of clean fuel vehicles with respect to any vehicle; or

(5) for any person to violate section 7553 of this title, 7554 of this title, or part C of this subchapter or any regulations under section 7553 of this title, 7554 of this title, or part C of this subchapter.

No action with respect to any element of design referred to in paragraph (3) (including any adjustment or alteration of such element) shall be treated as a prohibited Act under such paragraph (3) if such action is in accordance with section 7549 of this title. Nothing in paragraph (3) shall be construed to require the use of manufacturer parts in maintaining or repairing any motor vehicle or motor vehicle engine. For the purposes of the preceding sentence, the term "manufacturer parts" means, with respect to a motor vehicle engine, parts produced or sold by the manufacturer of the motor vehicle or motor vehicle engine. No action with respect to any device or element of design referred to in paragraph (3) shall be treated as a prohibited act under that paragraph if (i) the action is for the purpose of repair or replacement of the device or element, or is a necessary and temporary procedure to repair or replace any other item and the device or element is replaced upon completion of the procedure, and (ii) such action thereafter results in the proper functioning of the device or element referred to in paragraph (3). No action with respect to any device or element of design referred to in paragraph (3) shall be treated as a prohibited act under that paragraph if the action is for the purpose of a conversion of a motor vehicle for use of a clean alternative fuel (as defined in this title) and if such vehicle complies with the applicable standard under section 7521 of this title when operating on such fuel, and if in the case of a clean alternative fuel vehicle (as defined by rule by the Administrator), the device or element is replaced upon completion of the conversion procedure and such action results in proper functioning of the device or element when the motor vehicle operates on conventional fuel.

(b) Exemptions; refusal to admit vehicle or engine into United States; vehicles or engines intended for export

(1) The Administrator may exempt any new motor vehicle or new motor vehicle engine from subsection (a), upon such terms and conditions as he may find necessary for the purpose of research, investigations, studies, demonstrations, or training, or for reasons of national security.

(2) A new motor vehicle or new motor vehicle engine offered for importation or imported by any person in violation of subsection (a) shall be refused admission into the United States, but the Secretary of the Treasury and the Administrator may, by joint regulation, provide for deferring final determination as to admission and authorizing the delivery of such a motor vehicle or engine offered for import to the owner or consignee thereof upon such terms and conditions (including the furnishing of a bond) as may appear to them appropriate to insure that any such motor vehicle or engine will be brought into conformity with the standards, requirements, and limitations applicable to it under this part. The Secretary of the Treasury shall, if a motor vehicle or engine is finally refused admission under this paragraph, cause disposition thereof in accordance with the customs laws unless it is exported, under regulations prescribed by such Secretary, within ninety days of the date of notice of such refusal or such additional time as may be permitted pursuant to such regulations, except that disposition in accordance with the customs laws may not be made in such manner as may result, directly or indirectly, in the sale, to the ultimate consumer, of a new motor vehicle or new motor vehicle engine that fails to comply with applicable standards of the Administrator under this part.

(3) A new motor vehicle or new motor vehicle engine intended solely for export, and so labeled or tagged on the outside of the container and on the vehicle or engine itself, shall be subject to the provisions of subsection (a), except that if the country which is to receive such vehicle or engine has emission standards which differ from the standards prescribed under section 7521 of this title, then such vehicle or engine shall comply with the standards of such country which is to receive such vehicle or engine.

§7523. Actions to restrain violations
[CAA §204]

(a) Jurisdiction — The district courts of the United States shall have jurisdiction to restrain violations of section 7522(a) of this title.

(b) Actions brought by or in name of United States; subpoenas — Actions to restrain such violations shall be brought by and in the name of the United States. In any such action, subpoenas for witnesses who are required to attend a district court in any district may run into any other district.

§7524. Civil penalties
[CAA §205]

(a) Violations — Any person who violates sections 7522(a)(1), 7522(a)(4), or 7522(a)(5) or any manufacturer or dealer who violates section 7522(a)(3)(A) of this title shall be subject to a civil penalty of not more than $25,000. Any person other than a manufacturer or dealer who violates section 7522(a)(3)(A) of this title or any person who violates section 7522(a)(3)(B) of this title shall be subject to a civil penalty of not more than $2,500. Any such violation with respect to paragraph (1), (3)(A), or (4) of section 7522(a) of this title shall constitute a separate offense with respect to each motor vehicle or motor vehicle engine. Any such violation with respect to section 7522(a)(3)(B) of this title shall constitute a separate offense with respect to each part or component. Any person who violates section 7522(a)(2) of this title shall be subject to a civil penalty of not more than $25,000 per day of violation.

(b) Civil actions — The Administrator may commence a civil action to assess and recover any civil penalty under subsection (a) of this section, section 7545(d) of this title, or section 7547(d) of this title. Any action under this subsection may be brought in the district court of the United States for the district in which the violation is alleged to have occurred or in which the defendant resides or has the Administrator's principal place of business, and the court shall have jurisdiction to assess a civil penalty. In determining the amount of any civil penalty to be assessed under this subsection, the court shall take into account the gravity of the violation, the economic benefit or savings (if any) resulting from the violation, the size of the violator's business, the violator's history of compliance with this title, action taken to remedy the violation, the effect of the penalty on the violator's ability to continue in business, and such other matters as justice may require. In any such action, subpoenas for witnesses who are required to attend a district court in any district may run into any other district.

(c) Administrative assessment of certain penalties

(1) Administrative penalty authority — In lieu of commencing a civil action under subsection (b) of this section, the Administrator may assess any civil penalty prescribed in subsection (a) of this section, section 7545(d) of this title, or section 7547(d), of this title except that the maximum amount of penalty sought against each violator in a penalty assessment proceeding shall not exceed $200,000, unless the Administrator and the Attorney General jointly determine that a matter involving a larger penalty amount is appropriate for administrative penalty assessment. Any such determination by the Administrator and the Attorney General shall not be subject to judicial review. Assessment of a civil penalty under this subsection shall be by an order made on the record after opportunity for a hearing in accordance with sections 554 and 556 of Title 5. The Administrator shall issue reasonable rules for discovery and other procedures for hearings under this paragraph. Before issuing such an order, the Administrator shall give written notice to the person to be assessed an administrative penalty of the Administrator's proposal to issue such order and provide such person an

opportunity to request such a hearing on the order, within 30 days of the date the notice is received by such person. The Administrator may compromise, or remit, with or without conditions, any administrative penalty which may be imposed under this section.

(2) Determining amount — In determining the amount of any civil penalty assessed under this subsection, the Administrator shall take into account the gravity of the violation, the economic benefit or savings (if any) resulting from the violation, the size of the violator's business, the violator's history of compliance with this title, action taken to remedy the violation, the effect of the penalty on the violator's ability to continue in business, and such other matters as justice may require.

(3) Effect of administrator's action —

(A) Action by the Administrator under this subsection shall not affect or limit the Administrator's authority to enforce any provision of this Act; except that any violation,

(i) with respect to which the Administrator has commenced and is diligently prosecuting an action under this subsection, or

(ii) for which the Administrator has issued a final order not subject to further judicial review and the violator has paid a penalty assessment under this subsection,

shall not be the subject of civil penalty action under subsection (b) of this section.

(B) No action by the Administrator under this subsection shall affect any person's obligation to comply with any section of this chapter.

(4) Finality of order — An order issued under this subsection shall become final 30 days after its issuance unless a petition for judicial review is filed under paragraph (5).

(5) Judicial review — Any person against whom a civil penalty is assessed in accordance with this subsection may seek review of the assessment in the United States District Court for the District of Columbia, or for the district in which the violation is alleged to have occurred, in which such person resides, or where such person's principal place of business is located, within the 30-day period beginning on the date a civil penalty order is issued. Such person shall simultaneously send a copy of the filing by certified mail to the Administrator and the Attorney General. The Administrator shall file in the court a certified copy, or certified index, as appropriate, of the record on which the order was issued within 30 days. The court shall not set aside or remand any order issued in accordance with the requirements of this subsection unless there is not substantial evidence in the record, taken as a whole, to support the finding of a violation or unless the Administrator's assessment of the penalty constitutes an abuse of discretion, and the court shall not impose additional civil penal-

ties unless the Administrator's assessment of the penalty constitutes an abuse of discretion. In any proceedings, the United States may seek to recover civil penalties assessed under this section.

(6) Collection — If any person fails to pay an assessment of a civil penalty imposed by the Administrator as provided in this subsection —

(A) after the order making the assessment has become final, or

(B) after a court in an action brought under paragraph (5) has entered a final judgment in favor of the Administrator,

the Administrator shall request the Attorney General to bring a civil action in an appropriate district court to recover the amount assessed (plus interest at rates established pursuant to section 6621(a)(2) of Title 26 from the date of the final order or the date of the final judgment, as the case may be). In such an action, the validity, amount, and appropriateness of the penalty shall not be subject to review. Any person who fails to pay on a timely basis the amount of an assessment of a civil penalty as described in the first sentence of this paragraph shall be required to pay, in addition to that amount and interest, the United States' enforcement expenses, including attorneys fees and costs for collection proceedings, and a quarterly nonpayment penalty for each quarter during which such failure to pay persists. The nonpayment penalty shall be in an amount equal to 10 percent of the aggregate amount of that person's penalties and nonpayment penalties which are unpaid as of the beginning of such quarter.

§7525. Motor vehicle and motor vehicle engine compliance testing and certification
[CAA §206]
(a) Testing and issuance of certificate of conformity

(1) The Administrator shall test, or require to be tested in such manner as he deems appropriate, any new motor vehicle or new motor vehicle engine submitted by a manufacturer to determine whether such vehicle or engine conforms with the regulations prescribed under section 7521 of this title. If such vehicle or engine conforms to such regulations, the Administrator shall issue a certificate of conformity upon such terms, and for such period (not in excess of one year) as he may prescribe. In the case of any original equipment manufacturer (as defined by the Administrator in regulations promulgated before November 15, 1990) of vehicles or vehicle engines whose projected sales in the United States for any model year (as determined by the Administrator) will not exceed 300, the Administrator shall not require, for purposes of determining compliance with regulations under section 202 for the useful life of

the vehicle or engine, operation of any vehicle or engine manufactured during such model year for more than 5,000 miles or 160 hours, respectively, unless the Administrator, by regulation, prescribes otherwise. The Administrator shall apply any adjustment factors that the Administrator deems appropriate to assure that each vehicle or engine will comply during its useful life (as determined under section 7521(d) of this title) with the regulations prescribed under section 7521 of this title.

(2) The Administrator shall test any emission control system incorporated in a motor vehicle or motor vehicle engine submitted to him by any person, in order to determine whether such system enables such vehicle or engine to conform to the standards required to be prescribed under section 7521(b) of this title. If the Administrator finds on the basis of such tests that such vehicle or engine conforms to such standards, the Administrator shall issue a verification of compliance with emission standards for such system when incorporated in vehicles of a class of which the tested vehicle is representative. He shall inform manufacturers and the National Academy of Sciences, and make available to the public, the results of such tests. Tests under this paragraph shall be conducted under such terms and conditions (including requirements for preliminary testing by qualified independent laboratories) as the Administrator may prescribe by regulations.

(3)(A) A certificate of conformity may be issued under this section only if the Administrator determines that the manufacturer (or in the case of a vehicle or engine for import, any person) has established to the satisfaction of the Administrator that any emission control device, system, or element of design installed on, or incorporated in, such vehicle or engine conforms to applicable requirements of section 7521(a)(4) of this title.

(B) The Administrator may conduct such tests and may require the manufacturer (or any such person) to conduct such tests and provide such information as is necessary to carry out subparagraph (A) of this paragraph. Such requirements shall include a requirement for prompt reporting of the emission of any unregulated pollutant from a system, device, or element of design if such pollutant was not emitted, or was emitted in significantly lesser amounts, from the vehicle or engine without use of the system, device, or element of design.

(4)(A) Not later than 12 months after November 15, 1990, the Administrator shall revise the regulations promulgated under this subsection to add test procedures capable of determining whether model year 1994 and later model year light-duty vehicles and light-duty trucks, when properly maintained and used, will pass the inspection methods and procedures established

under section 7541(b) of this title for that model year, under conditions reasonably likely to be encountered in the conduct of inspection and maintenance programs, but which those programs cannot reasonably influence or control. The conditions shall include fuel characteristics, ambient temperature, and short (30 minutes or less) waiting periods before tests are conducted. The Administrator shall not grant a certificate of conformity under this subsection for any 1994 or later model year vehicle or engine that the Administrator concludes cannot pass the test procedures established under this paragraph.

(B) From time to time, the Administrator may revise the regulations promulgated under subparagraph (A), as the Administrator deems appropriate.

(5)(A) A motor vehicle engine (including all engine emission controls) may be installed in an exempted specially produced motor vehicle if the motor vehicle engine is from a motor vehicle that is covered by a certificate of conformity issued by the Administrator for the model year in which the exempted specially produced motor vehicle is produced, or the motor vehicle engine is covered by an Executive order subject to regulations promulgated by the California Air Resources Board for the model year in which the exempted specially produced motor vehicle is produced, and—

(i) the manufacturer of the engine supplies written instructions to the Administrator and the manufacturer of the exempted specially produced motor vehicle explaining how to install the engine and maintain functionality of the engine's emission control system and the on-board diagnostic system (commonly known as "OBD"), except with respect to evaporative emissions;

(ii) the manufacturer of the exempted specially produced motor vehicle installs the engine in accordance with such instructions and certifies such installation in accordance with subparagraph (E);

(iii) the installation instructions include emission control warranty information from the engine manufacturer in compliance with section 7541 of this title, including where warranty repairs can be made, emission control labels to be affixed to the vehicle, and the certificate of conformity number for the applicable vehicle in which the engine was originally intended or the applicable Executive order number for the engine; and

(iv) the manufacturer of the exempted specially produced motor vehicle does not produce more than 325 such vehicles in the calendar year in which the vehicle is produced.

(B) A motor vehicle containing an engine compliant with the requirements of subparagraph (A) shall be treated as meeting the requirements of section 7521 of this title applicable to new vehicles produced or imported in the model year in which the exempted specially produced motor vehicle is produced or imported.

(C) Engine installations that are not performed in accordance with installation instructions provided by the manufacturer and alterations to the engine not in accordance with the installation instructions shall—

　(i) be treated as prohibited acts by the installer under section 7522 of this title and any applicable regulations; and

　(ii) subject to civil penalties under section 7524(a) of this title, civil actions under section 7524(b) of this title, and administrative assessment of penalties under section 7524(c) of this title.

(D) The manufacturer of an exempted specially produced motor vehicle that has an engine compliant with the requirements of subparagraph (A) shall provide to the purchaser of such vehicle all information received by the manufacturer from the engine manufacturer, including information regarding emissions warranties from the engine manufacturer and all emissions-related recalls by the engine manufacturer.

(E) To qualify to install an engine under this paragraph, and sell, offer for sale, introduce into commerce, deliver for introduction into commerce or import an exempted specially produced motor vehicle, a manufacturer of exempted specially produced motor vehicles shall register with the Administrator at such time and in such manner as the Administrator determines appropriate. The manufacturer shall submit an annual report to the Administrator that includes—

　(i) a description of the exempted specially produced motor vehicles and engines installed in such vehicles;

　(ii) the certificate of conformity number issued to the motor vehicle in which the engine was originally intended or the applicable Executive order number for the engine; and

　(iii) a certification that it produced all exempted specially produced motor vehicles according to the written instructions from the engine manufacturer, and otherwise that the engine conforms in all material respects to the description in the application for the applicable certificate of conformity or Executive order.

(F) Exempted specially produced motor vehicles compliant with this paragraph shall be exempted from—

　(i) motor vehicle certification testing under this section; and

　(ii) vehicle emission control inspection and maintenance programs required under section 7410 of this title.

(G)(i) Except as provided in subparagraphs (A) through (F), a person engaged in the manufacturing or assembling of exempted specially produced motor vehicles shall be considered a manufacturer for purposes of this chapter.

(ii) Nothing in this paragraph shall be construed to exempt any person from the prohibitions in section 7522(a)(3) of this title or the requirements in sections 7542, 7525(c), or 7521(m)(5) of this title.

(H) In this paragraph:

(i) The term "exempted specially produced motor vehicle" means a light-duty vehicle or light-duty truck produced by a low-volume manufacturer and that—

　(I) is intended to resemble the body of another motor vehicle that was manufactured not less than 25 years before the manufacture of the exempted specially produced motor vehicle; and

　(II) is manufactured under a license for the product configuration, trade dress, trademark, or patent, for the motor vehicle that is intended to be replicated from the original manufacturer, its successors or assignees, or current owner of such product configuration, trade dress, trademark, or patent rights.

(ii) The term "low-volume manufacturer" means a motor vehicle manufacturer, other than a person who is registered as an importer under section 30141 of title 49, whose annual worldwide production, including by a parent or subsidiary of the manufacturer, if applicable, is not more than 5,000 motor vehicles.

(b) Testing procedures; hearing; judicial review; additional evidence — **(1)** In order to determine whether new motor vehicles or new motor vehicle engines being manufactured by a manufacturer do in fact conform with the regulations with respect to which the certificate of conformity was issued, the Administrator is authorized to test such vehicles or engines. Such tests may be conducted by the Administrator directly or, in accordance with conditions specified by the Administrator, by the manufacturer.

(2)(A)(i) If, based on tests conducted under paragraph (1) on a sample of new vehicles or engines covered by a certificate of conformity, the Administrator determines that all or part of the vehicles or engines so covered do not conform with the regulations with respect to which the certificate of conformity was issued and with the requirements of section 7521(a)(4) of this title, he may suspend or revoke such certificate in whole or in part, and shall so notify the manufacturer. Such suspension or revocation shall apply in the case of any new motor vehicles or new motor vehicle engines manufactured after the date of such notification (or manufactured before such date if still in the hands of the manufacturer), and shall apply until such time as the Administrator finds that vehicles and engines manufactured by the manufacturer do conform to such regulations and requirements. If, during any period of suspension or revocation, the Administrator finds that a vehicle or engine actually conforms to such regulations and requirements, he shall issue a certificate of conformity applicable to such vehicle or engine.

(ii) If, based on tests conducted under paragraph (1) on any new vehicle or engine, the Administrator determines that such vehicle or engine does not conform with such regulations, he may suspend or revoke such certificate insofar as it applies to such vehicle or engine until such time as he finds such vehicle or engine actually so conforms with such regulations, and he shall so notify the manufacturer.

(B)(i) At the request of any manufacturer the Administrator shall grant such manufacturer a hearing as to whether the tests have been properly conducted or any sampling methods have been properly applied, and make a determination on the record with respect to any suspension or revocation under subparagraph (A); but suspension or revocation under subparagraph (A) shall not be stayed by reason of such hearing.

(ii) In any case of actual controversy as to the validity of any determination under clause (i), the manufacturer may at any time prior to the 60th day after such determination is made file a petition with the United States court of appeals for the circuit wherein such manufacturer resides or has his principal place of business for a judicial review of such determination. A copy of the petition shall be forthwith transmitted by the clerk of the court to the Administrator or other officer designated by him for that purpose. The Administrator thereupon shall file in the court the record of the proceedings on which the Administrator based his determination, as provided in section 2112 of Title 28.

(iii) If the petitioner applies to the court for leave to adduce additional evidence, and shows to the satisfaction of the court that such additional evidence is material and that there were reasonable grounds for the failure to adduce such evidence in the proceeding before the Administrator, the court may order such additional evidence (and evidence in rebuttal thereof) to be taken before the Administrator, in such manner and upon such terms and conditions as the court may deem proper. The Administrator may modify his findings as to the facts, or make new findings, by reason of the additional evidence so taken and he shall file such modified or new findings, and his recommendation, if any, for the modification or setting aside of his original determination, with the return of such additional evidence.

(iv) Upon the filing of the petition referred to in clause (ii), the court shall have jurisdiction to review the order in accordance with chapter 7 of Title 5, and to grant appropriate relief as provided in such chapter.

(c) Inspection — For purposes of enforcement of this section, officers or employees duly designated by the Administrator, upon presenting appropriate credentials to the manufacturer or person in charge, are authorized (1) to enter, at reasonable times, any plant or other establishment of such manufacturers, for the purpose of conducting tests of vehicles of engines in the hands of the manufacturer, or (2) to inspect at reasonable times, records, files, papers, processes, controls, and facilities used by such manufacturer in conducting tests under regulations of the Administrator. Each such inspection shall be commenced and completed with reasonable promptness.

(d) Rules and regulations — The Administrator shall by regulation establish methods and procedures for making tests under this section.

(e) Publication of test results — The Administrator shall make available to the public the results of his tests of any motor vehicle or motor vehicle engine submitted by a manufacturer under subsection (a) as promptly as possible after the enactment of the Clean Air Amendments of 1970 and at the beginning of each model year which begins thereafter. Such results shall be described in such nontechnical manner as will reasonably disclose to prospective ultimate purchasers of new motor vehicles and new motor vehicle engines the comparative performance of the vehicles and engines tested in meeting the standards prescribed under section 7521 of this title.

(f) High altitude regulations — All light-duty vehicles and engines manufactured during or after model year 1984 and all light-duty trucks manufactured during or after model year 1995 shall comply with the requirements of section 7521 of this title regardless of the altitude at which they are sold.

(g) Nonconformance penalty

(1) In the case of any class or category of heavy-duty vehicles or engines to which a standard promulgated under section 7521(a) of this title applies, except as provided in paragraph (2), a certificate of conformity shall be issued under

subsection (a) and shall not be suspended or re- voked under subsection (b) for such vehicles or engines manufactured by a manufacturer notwith- standing the failure of such vehicles or engines to meet such standard if such manufacturer pays a nonconformance penalty as provided under regulations promulgated by the Administrator after notice and opportunity for public hear- ing. In the case of motorcycles to which such a standard applies, such a certificate may be issued notwithstanding such failure if the manufacturer pays such a penalty.

(2) No certificate of conformity may be issued under paragraph (1) with respect to any class or category of vehicle or engine if the degree by which the manufacturer fails to meet any standard promulgated under section 7521(a) of this title with respect to such class or category exceeds the percentage determined under regulations promul- gated by the Administrator to be practicable. Such regulations shall require such testing of vehicle or engines being produced as may be necessary to determine the percentage of the classes or cat- egories of vehicles or engines which are not in compliance with the regulations with respect to which a certificate of conformity was issued and shall be promulgated not later than one year after August 7, 1977.

(3) The regulations promulgated under para- graph (1) shall, not later than one year after August 7, 1977, provide for nonconformance penalties in amounts determined under a formula established by the Administrator. Such penalties under such formula —

    (A) may vary from pollutant-to-pollutant;

    (B) may vary by class or category or vehicle or engine;

    (C) shall take into account the extent to which actual emissions of any air pollutant ex- ceed allowable emissions under the standards promulgated under section 7521 of this title;

    (D) shall be increased periodically in order to create incentives for the development of production vehicles or engines which achieve the required degree of emission reduction; and

    (E) shall remove any competitive disadvan- tage to manufacturers whose engines or vehicles achieve the required degree of emission reduc- tion (including any such disadvantage arising from the application of paragraph (4)).

(4) In any case in which a certificate of con- formity has been issued under this subsection, any warranty required under section 7541(b)(2) of this title and any action under section 7541(c) of this title shall be required to be effective only for the emission levels which the Administrator determines that such certificate was issued and not for the emission levels required under the applicable standard.

(5) The authorities of section 7542(a) of this title shall apply, subject to the conditions of section 7542(b) of this title, for purposes of this subsection.

(h) Review and revision of regulations — Within 18 months after November 15, 1990, the Administrator shall review and revise as necessary the regulations under subsection (a) and (b) of this section regarding the testing of motor vehicles and motor vehicle engines to insure that vehicles are tested under circumstances which reflect the actual current driving conditions under which motor ve- hicles are used, including conditions relating to fuel, temperature, acceleration, and altitude.

§7541. Compliance by vehicles and engines in actual use
[CAA §207]
(a) Warranty; certification; payment of replacement costs of parts, devices, or compo- nents designed for emission control

(1) Effective with respect to vehicles and engines manufactured in model years beginning more than 60 days after December 31, 1970, the manufacturer of each new motor vehicle and new motor vehicle engine shall warrant to the ultimate purchaser and each subsequent purchaser that such vehicle or engine is (A) designed, built, and equipped so as to conform at the time of sale with applicable regulations under section 7521 of this title, and (B) free from defects in materials and workmanship which cause such vehicle or engine to fail to conform with applicable regulations for its useful life (as determined under section 202(d). In the case of vehicles and engines manufactured in the model year 1995 and thereafter such war- ranty shall require that the vehicle or engine is free from any such defects for the warranty period provided under subsection (i) of this section.

(2) In the case of a motor vehicle part or motor vehicle engine part, the manufacturer or rebuilder of such part may certify that use of such part will not result in a failure of the vehicle or engine to comply with emission standards promulgated under section 7521 of this title. Such certification shall be made only under such regulations as may be promulgated by the Administrator to carry out the purposes of subsection (b) of this section. The Administrator shall promulgate such regulations no later than two years following August 7, 1977.

(3) The cost of any part, device, or component of any light-duty vehicle that is designed for emis- sion control and which in the instructions issued pursuant to subsection (c)(3) of this section is scheduled for replacement during the useful life of the vehicle in order to maintain compliance with regulations under section 7521 of this title, the failure of which shall not interfere with the nor-

mal performance of the vehicle, and the expected retail price of which, including installation costs, is greater than 2 percent of the suggested retail price of such vehicle, shall be borne or reimbursed at the time of replacement by the vehicle manufacturer and such replacement shall be provided without cost to the ultimate purchaser, subsequent purchaser, or dealer. The term "designed for emission control" as used in the preceding sentence means a catalytic converter, thermal reactor, or other component installed on or in a vehicle for the sole or primary purpose of reducing vehicle emissions (not including those vehicle components which were in general use prior to model year 1968 and the primary function of which is not related to emission control).

(b) Testing methods and procedures — If the Administrator determines that (i) there are available testing methods and procedures to ascertain whether, when in actual use throughout its the warranty period (as determined under subsection (i)), each vehicle and engine to which regulations under section 7521 of this title apply complies with the emission standards of such regulations, (ii) such methods and procedures are in accordance with good engineering practices, and (iii) such methods and procedures are reasonably capable of being correlated with tests conducted under section 7525(a)(1) of this title, then —

(1) he shall establish such methods and procedures by regulation, and

(2) at such time as he determines that inspection facilities or equipment are available for purposes of carrying out testing methods and procedures established under paragraph (1), he shall prescribe regulations which shall require manufacturers to warrant the emission control device or system of each new motor vehicle or new motor vehicle engine to which a regulation under section 7521 of this title applies and which is manufactured in a model year beginning after the Administrator first prescribes warranty regulations under this paragraph. The warranty under such regulations shall run to the ultimate purchaser and each subsequent purchaser and shall provide that if —

(A) the vehicle or engine is maintained and operated in accordance with instructions under subsection (c)(3) of this section,

(B) it fails to conform at any time during its the warranty period (as determined under subsection (i)) to the regulations prescribed under section 7521 of this title, and

(C) such nonconformity results in the ultimate purchaser (or any subsequent purchaser) of such vehicle or engine having to bear any penalty or other sanction (including the denial of the right to use such vehicle or engine) under State or Federal law,

then such manufacturer shall remedy such non-conformity under such warranty with the cost thereof to be borne by the manufacturer. No such warranty shall be invalid on the basis of any part used in the maintenance or repair of a vehicle or engine if such part was certified as provided under subsection (a)(2) of this section.

(c) Nonconforming vehicles; plan for remedying nonconformity; instructions for maintenance and use; label or tag
Effective with respect to vehicles and engines manufactured during model years beginning more than 60 days after December 31, 1970 —

(1) If the Administrator determines that a substantial number of any class or category of vehicles or engines, although properly maintained and used, do not conform to the regulations prescribed under section 7521 of this title, when in actual use throughout their useful life (as determined under section 7521(d) of this title), he shall immediately notify the manufacturer thereof of such nonconformity, and he shall require the manufacturer to submit a plan for remedying the nonconformity of the vehicles or engines with respect to which such notification is given. The plan shall provide that the nonconformity of any such vehicles or engines which are properly used and maintained will be remedied at the expense of the manufacturer. If the manufacturer disagrees with such determination of nonconformity and so advises the Administrator, the Administrator shall afford the manufacturer and other interested persons an opportunity to present their views and evidence in support thereof at a public hearing. Unless, as a result of such hearing the Administrator withdraws such determination of nonconformity, he shall, within 60 days after the completion of such hearing, order the manufacturer to provide prompt notification of such nonconformity in accordance with paragraph (2).

(2) Any notification required by paragraph (1) with respect to any class or category of vehicles or engines shall be given to dealers, ultimate purchasers, and subsequent purchasers (if known) in such manner and containing such information as the Administrator may by regulations require.

(3)(A) The manufacturer shall furnish with each new motor vehicle or motor vehicle engine written instructions for the proper maintenance and use of the vehicle or engine by the ultimate purchaser and such instructions shall correspond to regulations which the Administrator shall promulgate. The manufacturer shall provide in boldface type on the first page of the written maintenance instructions notice that maintenance, replacement, or repair of the emission control devices and systems may be performed by any automotive repair establishment or individual using any automotive part which has been certified as provided in subsection (a)(2) of this section.

(B) The instruction under subparagraph (A) of this paragraph shall not include any condition on the ultimate purchaser's using, in connection with such vehicle or engine, any component or service (other than a component or service provided without charge under the terms of the purchase agreement) which is identified by brand, trade, or corporate name; or directly or indirectly distinguishing between service performed by the franchised dealers of such manufacturer or any other service establishments with which such manufacturer has a commercial relationship, and service performed by independent automotive repair facilities with which such manufacturer has no commercial relationship; except that the prohibition of this subsection may be waived by the Administrator if —

　(i) the manufacturer satisfies the Administrator that the vehicle or engine will function properly only if the component or service so identified is used in connection with such vehicle or engine, and

　(ii) the Administrator finds that such a waiver is in the public interest.

(C) In addition, the manufacturer shall indicate by means of a label or tag permanently affixed to such vehicle or engine that such vehicle or engine is covered by a certificate of conformity issued for the purpose of assuring achievement of emissions standards prescribed under section 7521 of this title. Such label or tag shall contain such other information relating to control of motor vehicle emissions as the Administrator shall prescribe by regulation.

(4) Intermediate in-use standards

(A) Model years 1994 and 1995 — For light-duty trucks of up to 6,000 lbs. gross vehicle weight rating (GVWR) and light-duty vehicles which are subject to standards under table G of section 7521(g)(1) of this title in model years 1994 and 1995 (40 percent of the manufacturer's sales volume in model year 1994 and 80 percent in model year 1995), the standards applicable to NMHC, CO, and NOx for purposes of this subsection shall be those set forth in table A below in lieu of the standards for such air pollutants otherwise applicable under this title.

TABLE A — INTERMEDIATE IN-USE
STANDARDS LDTS UP TO 6,000 LBS.
GVWR AND LIGHT-DUTY VEHICLES

Vehicle type	NMHC	CO	NOx
Light-duty vehicles	0.32	3.4	0.4*
LDTs (0–3,750 LVW)	0.32	5.2	0.4*
LDTs (3,751–5,750 LVW)	0.41	6.7	0.7*

* Not applicable to diesel-fueled vehicles.

(B) Model years 1996 and thereafter —

　(i) In the model years 1996 and 1997, light-duty trucks (LDTs) up to 6,000 lbs. gross vehicle weight rating (GVWR) and light-duty vehicles which are not subject to final in-use standards under paragraph (5) (60 percent of the manufacturer's sales volume in model year 1996 and 20 percent in model year 1997) shall be subject to the standards set forth in table A of subparagraph (A) for NMHC, CO, and NOx for purposes of this subsection in lieu of those set forth in paragraph (5).

　(ii) For LDTs of more than 6,000 lbs. GVWR —

　　(I) in model year 1996 which are subject to the standards set forth in Table H of section 202(h) (50%);

　　(II) in model year 1997 (100%); and

　　(III) in model year 1998 which are not subject to final in use standards under paragraph (5) (50%);

the standards for NMHC, CO, and NOx for purposes of this subsection shall be those set forth in Table B below in lieu of the standards for such air pollutants otherwise applicable under this title.

TABLE B — INTERMEDIATE IN-USE
STANDARDS LDTS
MORE THAN 6,000 LBS. GVWR

Vehicle type	NMHC	CO	NOx
LDTs (3,751–5,750 lbs. TW)	0.40	5.5	0.88*
LDTs (over 5,750 lbs. TW)	0.49	6.2	1.38*

* Not applicable to diesel-fueled vehicles.

(C) Useful life — In the case of the in-use standards applicable under this paragraph, for purposes of applying this subsection, the applicable useful life shall be 5 years or 50,000 miles or the equivalent (whichever first occurs).

(5) Final in-use standards

(A) After the model year 1995, for purposes of applying this subsection, in the case of the percentage specified in the implementation schedule below of each manufacturer's sales volume of light-duty trucks of up to 6,000 lbs. gross vehicle weight rating (GVWR) and light duty vehicles, the standards for NMHC, CO, and NOx shall be as provided in Table G in section 7521(g) of this title, except that in applying the standards set forth in Table G for purposes of determining compliance with this subsection, the applicable useful life shall be (i) 5 years or 50,000 miles (or the equivalent) whichever first occurs in the case of standards applicable for purposes of certification at 50,000 miles; and (ii)10 years or 100,000 miles (or the equivalent), whichever first occurs in the case of standards applicable for purposes of certification at 100,000 miles, except that no testing shall be done beyond 7 years or 75,000 miles, or the equivalent whichever first occurs.

LDTS UP TO 6,000 LBS. GVWR AND LIGHT-DUTY VEHICLE SCHEDULE FOR IMPLEMENTATION OF FINAL IN-USE STANDARDS

Model year	Percent
1996	40
1997	80
1998	100

(B) After the model year 1997, for purposes of applying this subsection, in the case of the percentage specified in the implementation schedule below of each manufacturer's sales volume of light-duty trucks of more than 6,000 lbs. gross vehicle weight rating (GVWR), the standards for NMHC, CO, and NOx shall be as provided in Table H in section 202(h), except that in applying the standards set forth in Table H for purposes of determining compliance with this subsection, the applicable useful life shall be (i) 5 years or 50,000 miles (or the equivalent) whichever first occurs in the case of standards applicable for purposes of certification at 50,000 miles; and (ii) 11 years or 120,000 miles (or the equivalent), whichever first occurs in the case of standards applicable for purposes of certification at 120,000 miles, except that no testing shall be done beyond 7 years or 90,000 miles (or the equivalent) whichever first occurs.

LDTS OF MORE THAN 6,000 LBS. GVWR IMPLEMENTATION SCHEDULE FOR IMPLEMENTATION OF FINAL IN-USE STANDARDS

Model year	Percent
1998	50
1999	100

(6) Diesel vehicles; in-use useful life and testing.

(A) In the case of diesel-fueled light-duty trucks up to 6,000 lbs. GVWR and light-duty vehicles, the useful life for purposes of determining in-use compliance with the standards under section 7521(g) of this title for NOx shall be a period of 10 years or 100,000 miles (or the

equivalent), whichever first occurs, in the case of standards applicable for purposes of certification at 100,000 miles, except that testing shall not be done for a period beyond 7 years or 75,000 miles (or the equivalent) whichever first occurs.

(B) In the case of diesel-fueled light-duty trucks of 6,000 lbs. GVWR or more, the useful life for purposes of determining in-use compliance with the standards under section 7521(h) of this title for NOx shall be a period of 11 years or 120,000 miles (or the equivalent), whichever first occurs, in the case of standards applicable for purposes of certification at 120,000 miles, except that testing shall not be done for a period beyond 7 years or 90,000 miles (or the equivalent) whichever first occurs.

(d) Dealer costs borne by manufacturer — Any cost obligation of any dealer incurred as a result of any requirement imposed by subsection (a), (b), or (c) of this section shall be borne by the manufacturer. The transfer of any such cost obligation from a manufacturer to any dealer through franchise or other agreement is prohibited.

(e) Cost statement — If a manufacturer includes in any advertisement a statement respecting the cost or value of emission control devices or systems, such manufacturer shall set forth in such statement the cost or value attributed to such devices or systems by the Secretary of Labor (through the Bureau of Labor Statistics). The Secretary of Labor, and his representatives, shall have the same access for this purpose to the books, documents, papers, and records of a manufacturer as the Comptroller General has to those of a recipient of assistance for purposes of section 7611 of this title.

(f) Inspection after sale to ultimate purchaser — Any inspection of a motor vehicle or a motor vehicle engine for purposes of subsection (c)(1) of this section, after its sale to the ultimate purchaser, shall be made only if the owner of such vehicle or engine voluntarily permits such inspection to be made, except as may be provided by any State or local inspection program.

(g) Replacement and maintenance costs borne by owner — For the purposes of this section, the owner of any motor vehicle or motor vehicle engine warranted under this section is responsible in the proper maintenance of such vehicle or engine to replace and to maintain, at his expense at any service establishment or facility of his choosing, such items as spark plugs, points, condensers, and any other part, item, or device related to emission control (but not designed for emission control under the terms of the last sentence of subsection (a)(3) of this section)), unless such part, item, or device is covered by any warranty not mandated by this chapter.

(h) Dealer certification

(1) If at any time during the period for which the warranty applies under subsection (b), a motor vehicle fails to conform to the applicable regulations under section 7521 of this title as determined under subsection (b) of this section such nonconformity shall be remedied by the manufacturer at the cost of the manufacturer pursuant to such warranty as provided in subsection (b)(2) of this section (without regard to subparagraph (C) thereof).

(2) Nothing in section 7543(a) of this title shall be construed to prohibit a State from testing, or requiring testing of, a motor vehicle after the date of sale of such vehicle to the ultimate purchaser (except that no new motor vehicle manufacturer or dealer may be required to conduct testing under this paragraph).

(i) Warranty period

(1) In general — For purposes of subsection (a)(1) of this section and subsection (b) of this section, the warranty period, effective with respect to new light-duty trucks and new light-duty vehicles and engines, manufactured in the model year 1995 and thereafter, shall be the first 2 years or 24,000 miles of use (whichever first occurs), except as provided in paragraph (2). For purposes of subsection (a)(1) of this section and subsection (b), of this section for other vehicles and engines the warranty period shall be the period established by the Administrator by regulation (promulgated prior to November 15, 1990) for such purposes unless the Administrator subsequently modifies such regulation.

(2) Specified major emission control components — In the case of a specified major emission control component, the warranty period for new light-duty trucks and new light-duty vehicles and engines manufactured in the model year 1995 and thereafter for purposes of subsection (a)(1) of this section and subsection (b) of this section shall be 8 years or 80,000 miles of use (whichever first occurs). As used in this paragraph, the term "specified major emission control component" means only a catalytic converter, an electronic emissions control unit, and an onboard emissions diagnostic device, except that the Administrator may designate any other pollution control device or component as a specified major emission control component if —

(A) the device or component was not in general use on vehicles and engines manufactured prior to the model year 1990; and

(B) the Administrator determines that the retail cost (exclusive of installation costs) of such device or component exceeds $200 (in 1989 dollars), adjusted for inflation or deflation as calculated by the Administrator at the time of such determination.

For purposes of this paragraph, the term "onboard emissions diagnostic device" means any device installed for the purpose of storing or processing emissions related diagnostic information, but not including any parts or other systems which it monitors except specified major emissions

control components. Nothing in this Act shall be construed to provide that any part (other than a part referred to in the preceding sentence) shall be required to be warranted under this Act for the period of 8 years or 80,000 miles referred to in this paragraph.

(3) Instructions — Subparagraph (A) of subsection (b)(2) of this section shall apply only where the Administrator has made a determination that the instructions concerned conform to the requirements of subsection (c)(3) of this section.

§7542. Information collection
[CAA §208]

(a) **Manufacturer's responsibility** — Every manufacturer of new motor vehicles or new motor vehicle engines, and every manufacturer of new motor vehicle or engine parts or components, and other persons subject to the requirements of this part or part C, of this subchapter shall establish and maintain records, perform tests where such testing is not otherwise reasonably available under this part and part C of this subchapter (including fees for testing), make reports and provide information the Administrator may reasonably require to determine whether the manufacturer or other person has acted or is acting in compliance with this part and part C of this subchapter and regulations there under, or to otherwise carry out the provision of this part and part C, and shall, upon request of an officer or employee duly designated by the Administrator, permit such officer or employee at reasonable times to have access to and copy such records.

(b) **Enforcement authority** — For the purposes of enforcement of this section, officers or employees duly designated by the Administrator upon presenting appropriate credentials are authorized —

(1) to enter, at reasonable times, any establishment of the manufacturer, or of any person whom the manufacturer engages to perform any activity required by subsection (a), for the purposes of inspecting or observing any activity conducted pursuant to subsection (a), and

(2) to inspect records, files, papers, processes, controls, and facilities used in performing any activity required by subsection (a), by such manufacturer or by any person whom the manufacturer engages to perform any such activity.

(c) **Availability to the public; trade secrets** — Any records, reports, or information obtained under this part or part C of this subchapter shall be available to the public, except that upon a showing satisfactory to the Administrator by any person that records, reports, or information, or a particular portion thereof (other than emission data), to which the Administrator has access under this section, if made public, would divulge methods or processes entitled to protection as trade secrets of that person, the Administrator shall consider the record, report, or information or particular portion thereof confidential in accordance with the purposes of section 1905 of Title 18. Any authorized representative of the Administrator shall be considered an employee of the United States for purposes of section 1905 of Title 18. Nothing in this section shall prohibit the Administrator or authorized representative of the Administrator from disclosing records, reports or information to other officers, employees or authorized representatives of the United States concerned with carrying out this Act or when relevant in any proceeding under this Act. Nothing in this section shall authorize the withholding of information by the Administrator or any officer or employee under the Administrator's control from the duly authorized committees of the Congress.

§7543. State standards
[CAA §209]

(a) Prohibition — No State or any political subdivision thereof shall adopt or attempt to enforce any standard relating to the control of emissions from new motor vehicles or new motor vehicle engines subject to this part. No State shall require certification, inspection, or any other approval relating to the control of emissions from any new motor vehicle or new motor vehicle engine as condition precedent to the initial retail sale, titling (if any), or registration of such motor vehicle, motor vehicle engine, or equipment.

(b) Waiver

(1) The Administrator shall, after notice and opportunity for public hearing, waive application of this section to any State which has adopted standards (other than crankcase emission standards) for the control of emissions from new motor vehicles or new motor vehicle engines prior to March 30, 1966, if the State determines that the State standards will be, in the aggregate, at least as protective of public health and welfare as applicable Federal standards. No such waiver shall be granted if the Administrator finds that —

(A) the determination of the State is arbitrary and capricious,

(B) such State does not need such State standards to meet compelling and extraordinary conditions, or

(C) such State standards and accompanying enforcement procedures are not consistent with section 7521(a) of this title.

(2) If each State standard is at least as stringent as the comparable applicable Federal standard, such State standard shall be deemed to be at least as protective of health and welfare as such Federal standards for purposes of paragraph (1).

(3) in the case of any new motor vehicle or new motor vehicle engine to which State standards apply pursuant to a waiver granted under paragraph (1), compliance with such State standards shall be treated as compliance with applicable Federal standards for purposes of this subchapter.

(c) Certification of vehicle parts or engine parts — Whenever a regulation with respect to any motor vehicle part or motor vehicle engine part is in effect under section 7541(a)(2) of this title, no State or political subdivision thereof shall adopt or attempt to enforce any standard or any requirement of certification, inspection, or approval which relates to motor vehicle emissions and is applicable to the same aspect of such part. The preceding sentence shall not apply in the case of a State with respect to which a waiver is in effect under subsection (b) of this section.

(d) Control, regulation, or restrictions on registered or licensed motor vehicles — Nothing in this part shall preclude or deny to any State or political subdivision thereof the right otherwise to control, regulate, or restrict the use, operation, or movement of registered or licensed motor vehicles.

(e) Nonroad engines or vehicles

(1) Prohibition on certain state standards — No State or any political subdivision thereof shall adopt or attempt to enforce any standard or other requirement relating to the control of emissions from either of the following new nonroad engines or nonroad vehicles subject to regulation under this chapter —

(A) New engines which are used in construction equipment or vehicles or used in farm equipment or vehicles and which are smaller than 175 horsepower.

(B) New locomotives or new engines used in locomotives.

Subsection (b) of this section shall not apply for purposes of this paragraph.

(2) Other nonroad engines or vehicles

(A) In the case of any nonroad vehicles or engines other than those referred to in subparagraph (A) or (B) of paragraph (1), the Administrator shall, after notice and opportunity for public hearing, authorize California to adopt and enforce standards and other requirements relating to the control of emissions from such vehicles or engines if California determines that California standards will be, in the aggregate, at least as protective of public health and welfare as applicable Federal standards. No such authorization shall be granted if the Administrator finds that —

(i) the determination of California is arbitrary and capricious,

(ii) California does not need such California standards to meet compelling and extraordinary conditions, or

(iii) California standards and accompanying enforcement procedures are not consistent with this section.

(B) Any State other than California which has plan provisions approved under part D of subchapter I of this chapter may adopt and enforce, after notice to the Administrator, for any period, standards relating to control of emissions from nonroad vehicles or engines (other than those referred to in subparagraph (A) or (B) of paragraph (1)) and take such other actions as are referred to in subparagraph (A) of this paragraph respecting such vehicles or engines if —

(i) such standards and implementation and enforcement are identical, for the period concerned, to the California standards authorized by the Administrator under subparagraph (A), and

(ii) California and such State adopt such standards at least 2 years before commencement of the period for which the standards take effect.

The Administrator shall issue regulations to implement this subsection.

§7544. State grants
[CAA §210]

The Administrator is authorized to make grants to appropriate State agencies in an amount up to two-thirds of the cost of developing and maintaining effective vehicle emission devices and systems inspection and emission testing and control programs, except that —

(1) no such grant shall be made for any part of any State vehicle inspection program which does not directly relate to the cost of the air pollution control aspects of such a program;

(2) no such grant shall be made unless the Secretary of Transportation has certified to the Administrator that such program is consistent with any highway safety program developed pursuant to section 402 of Title 23; and

(3) no such grant shall be made unless the program includes provisions designed to insure that emission control devices and systems on vehicles in actual use have not been discontinued or rendered inoperative.

Grants may be made under this section by way of reimbursement in any case in which amounts have been expended by the State before the date on which any such grant was made.

§7545. Regulation of fuels
[CAA §211]

(a) Authority of Administrator to regulate — The Administrator may by regulation designate any fuel or fuel additive (including any fuel or fuel additive used exclusively in nonroad engines or nonroad vehicles) and, after such date or dates as may be prescribed by him, no manufacturer or processor of any such fuel or additive may sell, offer for sale, or introduce into commerce such fuel or additive unless the Administrator has registered such fuel or additive in accordance with subsection (b) of this section.

(b) Registration requirement

(1) For the purpose of registration of fuels and fuel additives, the Administrator shall require —

(A) the manufacturer of any fuel to notify him as to the commercial identifying name and manufacturer of any additive contained in such fuel; the range of concentration of any additive in the fuel; and the purpose-in-use of any such additive; and

(B) the manufacturer of any additive to notify him as to the chemical composition of such additive.

(2) For the purpose of registration of fuels and fuel additives, the Administrator shall, on a regular basis, require the manufacturer of any fuel or fuel additive—

(A) to conduct tests to determine potential public health and environmental effects of the fuel or additive (including carcinogenic, teratogenic, or mutagenic effects); and

(B) to furnish the description of any analytical technique that can be used to detect and measure any additive in such fuel, the recommended range of concentration of such additive, and the recommended purpose-in-use of such additive, and such other information as is reasonable and necessary to determine the emissions resulting from the use of the fuel or additive contained in such fuel, the effect of such fuel or additive on the emission control performance of any vehicle, vehicle engine, nonroad engine or nonroad vehicle, or the extent to which such emissions affect the public health or welfare.

Tests under subparagraph (A) shall be conducted in conformity with test procedures and protocols established by the Administrator. The results of such tests shall not be considered confidential.

(3) Upon compliance with the provisions of this subsection, including assurances that the Administrator will receive changes in the information required, the Administrator shall register such fuel or fuel additive.

(4) Study on certain fuel additives and blendstocks

(A) In general — Not later than 2 years after August 8, 2005, the Administrator shall —

(i) conduct a study on the effects on public health (including the effects on children, pregnant women, minority or low-income communities, and other sensitive populations), air quality, and water resources of increased use of, and the feasibility of using as substitutes for methyl tertiary butyl ether in gasoline —

(I) ethyl tertiary butyl ether;

(II) tertiary amyl methyl ether;

(III) di-isopropyl ether;

(IV) tertiary butyl alcohol;

(V) other ethers and heavy alcohols, as determined by then Administrator;

(VI) ethanol;

(VII) iso-octane; and

(VIII) alkylates; and

(ii) conduct a study on the effects on public health (including the effects on children, pregnant women, minority or low-income communities, and other sensitive populations), air quality, and water resources of the adjustment for ethanol-blended reformulated gasoline to the volatile organic compounds performance requirements that are applicable under paragraphs (1) and (3) of subsection (k) of this section; and

(iii) submit to the Committee on Environment and Public Works of the Senate and the Committee on Energy and Commerce of the House of Representatives a report describing the results of the studies under clauses (i) and (ii).

(B) Contracts for study — In carrying out this paragraph, the Administrator may enter into one or more contracts with nongovernmental entities such as —

(i) the national energy laboratories; and

(ii) institutions of higher education (as defined in section 1001 of Title 20).

(c) Offending fuels and fuel additives; control; prohibition

(1) The Administrator may, from time to time on the basis of information obtained under subsection (b) of this section or other information available to him, by regulation, control or prohibit the manufacture, introduction into commerce, offering for sale, or sale of any fuel or fuel additive for use in a motor vehicle, motor vehicle engine, or nonroad engine or nonroad vehicle if, in the judgment of the Administrator, any fuel or fuel additive or any emission product of such fuel or fuel additive causes, or contributes, to air pollution or water pollution (including any degradation in the quality of groundwater) that may reasonably be anticipated to endanger the public health or welfare, or (B) if emission products of such fuel or fuel additive will impair to a significant degree the performance of any emission control device or system which is in general use, or which the Administrator finds has been developed to a point where in a reasonable time it would be in general use were such regulation to be promulgated.

(2)(A) No fuel, class of fuels, or fuel additive may be controlled or prohibited by the Administrator pursuant to clause (A) of paragraph (1) except after consideration of all relevant medical and scientific evidence available to him, including consideration of other technologically or economically feasible means of achieving emission standards under section 7521 of this title.

(B) No fuel or fuel additive may be controlled or prohibited by the Administrator pursuant to clause (B) of paragraph (1) except after consideration of available scientific and economic data, including a cost benefit analysis comparing emission control devices or systems which are or will be in general use and require the proposed control or prohibition with emission control devices or systems which are or will be in general use and do not require the proposed control or prohibition. On request of a manufacturer of motor vehicles, motor vehicle engines, fuels, or fuel additives submitted within 10 days of notice of proposed rule-making, the Administrator shall hold a public hearing and publish findings with respect to any matter he is required to consider under this subparagraph. Such findings shall be published at the time of promulgation of final regulations.

(C) No fuel or fuel additive may be prohibited by the Administrator under paragraph (1) unless he finds, and publishes such finding, that in his judgment such prohibition will not cause the use of ny other fuel or fuel additive which will produce emissions which will endanger the public health or welfare to the same or greater degree than the use of the fuel or fuel additive proposed to be prohibited.

(3)(A) For the purpose of obtaining evidence and data to carry out paragraph (2), the Administrator may require the manufacturer of any motor vehicle or motor vehicle engine to furnish any information which has been developed concerning the emissions from motor vehicles resulting from the use of any fuel or fuel additive, or the effect of such use on the performance of any emission control device or system.

(B) In obtaining information under subparagraph (A), section 7607(a) of this title (relating to subpoenas) shall be applicable.

(4)(A) Except as otherwise provided in subparagraph (B) or (C), no State (or political subdivision thereof) may prescribe or attempt to enforce, for the purposes of motor vehicle emission control, any control or prohibition respecting any characteristic or component of a fuel or fuel additive in a motor vehicle or motor vehicle engine —

(i) if the Administrator has found that no control or prohibition of the characteristic or component of a fuel or fuel additive under paragraph (1) is necessary and has published his finding in the Federal Register, or

(ii) if the Administrator has prescribed under paragraph (1) a control or prohibition applicable to such characteristic or component of a fuel or fuel additive, unless State prohibition or control is identical to the prohibition or control prescribed by the Administrator.

(B) Any State for which application of section 7543(a) of this title has at any time been waived under section 7543(b) of this title may at any time prescribe and enforce, for the purpose of motor vehicle emission control, a control or prohibition respecting any fuel or fuel additive.

(C)(i) A State may prescribe and enforce, for purposes of motor vehicle emission control, a control or prohibition respecting the use of a fuel or fuel additive in a motor vehicle or motor vehicle engine if an applicable implementation plan for such State under section 7410 of this title so provides. The Administrator may approve such provision in an implementation plan, or promulgate an implementation plan containing such a provision, only if he finds that the State control or prohibition is necessary to achieve the national primary or secondary ambient air quality standard which the plan implements. The Administrator may find that a State control or prohibition is necessary to achieve that standard if no other measures that would bring about timely attainment exist, or if other measures exist and are technically possible to implement, but are unreasonable or impracticable. The Administrator may make a finding of necessity under this subparagraph even if the plan for the area does not contain an approved demonstration of timely attainment.

(ii) The Administrator may temporarily waive a control or prohibition respecting the use of a fuel or fuel additive required or regulated by the Administrator pursuant to subsection (c), (h), (i), (k), or (m) of this section or prescribed in an applicable implementation plan under section 7410 of this title approved by the Administrator under clause (i) of this subparagraph if, after consultation with, and concurrence by, the Secretary of Energy, the Administrator determines that —

(I) extreme and unusual fuel or fuel additive supply circumstances exist in a State or region of the Nation which prevent the distribution of an adequate supply of the fuel or fuel additive to consumers;

(II) such extreme and unusual fuel and fuel additive supply circumstances are the result of a natural disaster, an Act of God, a pipeline or refinery equipment failure, or another event that could not reasonably have been foreseen or prevented and not the lack of prudent planning on the part of the suppliers of the fuel or fuel additive to such State or region; and

(III) it is in the public interest to grant the waiver (for example, when a waiver is necessary to meet projected temporary shortfalls in the supply of the fuel or fuel additive in a State or region of the Nation which cannot otherwise be compensated for).

(iii) If the Administrator makes the determinations required under clause (ii), such a temporary extreme and unusual fuel and fuel additive supply circumstances waiver shall be permitted only if —

(I) the waiver applies to the smallest geographic area necessary to address the extreme and unusual fuel and fuel additive supply circumstances;

(II) the waiver is effective for a period of 20 calendar days or, if the Administrator determines that a shorter waiver period is adequate, for the shortest practicable time period necessary to permit the correction of the extreme and unusual fuel and fuel additive supply circumstances and to mitigate impact on air quality;

(III) the waiver permits a transitional period, the exact duration of which shall be determined by the Administrator (but which shall be for the shortest practicable period), after the termination of the temporary waiver to permit wholesalers and retailers to blend down their wholesale and retail inventory;

(IV) the waiver applies to all persons in the motor fuel distribution system; and

(V) the Administrator has given public notice to all parties in the motor fuel distribution system, and local and State regulators, in the State or region to be covered by the waiver.

The term "motor fuel distribution system" as used in this clause shall be defined by the Administrator through rulemaking.

(iv) Within 180 days of August 8, 2005, the Administrator shall promulgate regulations to implement clauses (ii) and (iii).

(v) Nothing in this subparagraph shall —

(I) limit or otherwise affect the application of any other waiver authority of the Administrator pursuant to this section or pursuant to a regulation promulgated pursuant to this section; and

(II) subject any State or person to an enforcement action, penalties, or liability solely arising from actions taken pursuant to the issuance of a waiver under this subparagraph.

(v)(I) The Administrator shall have no authority, when considering a State implementation plan or a State implementation plan revision, to approve under this paragraph any fuel included in such plan or revision if the effect of such approval increases the total number of fuels approved under this paragraph as of September 1, 2004, in all State implementation plans.

(II) The Administrator, in consultation with the Secretary of Energy, shall determine the total number of fuels approved under this paragraph as of September 1, 2004, in all State implementation plans and shall publish a list of such fuels, including the States and Petroleum Administration for Defense District in which they are used, in the Federal Register for public review and comment no later than 90 days after enactment.

(III) The Administrator shall remove a fuel from the list published under subclause (II) if a fuel ceases to be included in a State implementation plan or if a fuel in a State implementation plan is identical to a Federal fuel formulation implemented by the Administrator, but the Administrator shall not reduce the total number of fuels authorized under the list published under subclause (II).

(IV) Subclause (i) shall not limit the Administrator's authority to approve a control or prohibition respecting any new fuel under this paragraph in a State implementation plan or revision to a State implementation plan if such new fuel—

    (aa) completely replaces a fuel on the list published under subclause (II); or

    (bb) does not increase the total number of fuels on the list published under subclause (II) as of September 1, 2004.

In the event that the total number of fuels on the list published under subclause (II) at the time of the Administrator's consideration of a control or prohibition respecting a new fuel is lower than the total number of fuels on such list as of September 1, 2004, the Administrator may approve a control or prohibition respecting a new fuel under this subclause if the Administrator, after consultation with the Secretary of Energy, publishes in the Federal Register after notice and comment a finding that, in the Administrator's judgment, such control or prohibition respecting a new fuel will not cause fuel supply or distribution interruptions or have a significant adverse impact on fuel producibility in the affected area or contiguous areas.

(V) The Administrator shall have no authority under this paragraph, when considering any particular State's implementation plan or a revision to that State's implementation plan, to approve any fuel unless that fuel was, as of the date of such consideration, approved in at least one State implementation plan in the applicable Petroleum Administration for Defense District. However, the Administrator may approve as part of a State implementation plan or State implementation plan revision a fuel with a summertime Reid Vapor Pressure of 7.0 psi. In no event shall such approval by the Administrator cause an increase in the total number of fuels on the list published under subclause (II).

(VI) Nothing in this clause shall be construed to have any effect regarding any available authority of States to require the use of any fuel additive registered in accordance with subsection (b) of this section, including any fuel additive registered in accordance with subsection (b) of this section after the enactment of this subclause.

(d) Penalties and injunctions

(1) Civil penalties — Any person who violates subsection (a), (f), (g), (k), (*l*), (m), (n) or (o) of this section or the regulations prescribed under subsection (c), (h), (i), (k), (*l*), (m), (n) or (o) of this section or who fails to furnish any information or conduct any tests required by the Administrator under subsection (b) of this section shall be liable to the United States for a civil penalty of not more than the sum of $25,000 for every day of such violation and the amount of economic benefit or savings resulting from the violation. Any violation with respect to a regulation prescribed under subsection (c), (k), (*l*), (m) or (o) of this section which establishes a regulatory standard based upon a multiday averaging period shall constitute a separate day of violation for each and every day in the averaging period. Civil penalties shall be assessed in accordance with subsections (b) and (c) of section 7524 of this title.

(2) Injunctive authority — The district courts of the United States shall have jurisdiction to restrain violations of subsections (a), (f), (g), (k), (*l*), (m), (n)[, and (o)] of this section and of the regulations prescribed under subsections (c), (h), (i), (k), (*l*), (m), (n)[, and (o)] of this section, to award other appropriate relief, and to compel the furnishing of information and the conduct of tests required by the Administrator under subsection (b) of this section. Actions to restrain such violations and compel such actions shall be brought by and in the name of the United States. In any such action, subpoenas for witnesses who are required to attend a district court in any district may run into any other district.

(e) Testing of fuels and fuel additives

(1) Not later than one year after August 7, 1977, and after notice and opportunity for a public hearing, the Administrator shall promulgate regulations which implement the authority under subsection (b)(2)(A) and (B) of this section with respect to each fuel or fuel additive which is registered on the date of promulgation of such regulations and with respect to each fuel or fuel additive for which an application for registration is filed thereafter.

(2) Regulations under subsection (b) of this section to carry out this subsection shall require that the requisite information be provided to the Administrator by each such manufacturer —

  (A) prior to registration, in the case of any fuel or fuel additive which is not registered on the date of promulgation of such regulations; or

  (B) not later than three years after the date of promulgation of such regulations, in the case of any fuel or fuel additive which is registered on such date.

(3) In promulgating such regulations, the Administrator may —

  (A) exempt any small business (as defined in such regulations) from or defer or modify the requirements of, such regulations with respect to any such small business;

  (B) provide for cost-sharing with respect to the testing of any fuel or fuel additive which is manufactured or processed by two or more persons or otherwise provide for shared responsibility to meet the requirements of this section without duplication; or

  (C) exempt any person from such regulations with respect to a particular fuel or fuel additive upon a finding that any additional testing of such fuel or fuel additive would be duplicative of adequate existing testing.

(f) New fuels and fuel additives

(1)(A) Effective upon March 31, 1977, it shall be unlawful for any manufacturer of any fuel or fuel additive to first introduce into commerce, or to increase the concentration in use of, any fuel or fuel additive for general use in light duty motor vehicles manufactured after model year 1974 which is not substantially similar to any fuel or fuel additive utilized in the certification of any model year 1975, or subsequent model year, vehicle or engine under section 7525 of this title.

  (B) Effective upon November 15, 1990, it shall be unlawful for any manufacturer of any fuel or fuel additive to first introduce into commerce, or to increase the concentration in use of, any fuel or fuel additive for use by any person in motor vehicles manufactured after model year 1974 which is not substantially similar to any fuel or fuel additive utilized in the certification of any model year 1975, or subsequent model year, vehicle or engine under section 7525 of this title.

(2) Effective November 30, 1977, it shall be unlawful for any manufacturer of any fuel to introduce into commerce any gasoline which contains a concentration of manganese in excess of .0625 grams per gallon of fuel, except as otherwise provided pursuant to a waiver under paragraph (4).

(3) Any manufacturer of any fuel or fuel additive which prior to March 31, 1977, and after January 1, 1974, first introduced into commerce or increased the concentration in use of a fuel or fuel additive that would otherwise have been prohibited under paragraph (1)(A) if introduced on or after March 31, 1977 shall, not later than September 15, 1978, cease to distribute such fuel or fuel additive in commerce. During the period beginning 180 days after the date of the enactment of this subsection and before September 15, 1978, the Administrator shall prohibit, or restrict the concentration of any fuel additive which he determines will cause or contribute to the failure of an emission control device or system (over the useful life of any vehicle in which such device or system is used) to achieve compliance by the vehicle with the emission standards with respect to which it has been certified under section 7525 of this title.

(4) The Administrator, upon application of any manufacturer of any fuel or fuel additive, may waive the prohibitions established under paragraph (1) or (3) of this subsection or the limitation specified in paragraph (2) of this subsection, if he determines that the applicant has established that such fuel or fuel additive or a specified concentration thereof, and the emission products of such fuel or additive or specified concentration thereof, will not cause or contribute to a failure of any emission control device or system (over the useful life of the motor vehicle, motor vehicle engine, nonroad engine or nonroad vehicle in which such device or system is used) to achieve compliance by the vehicle or engine with the emission standards with respect to which it has been certified pursuant to sections 7525 and 7547(a) of this title. The Administrator shall take final action to grant or deny an application submitted under this paragraph, after public notice and comment, within

270 days of the receipt of such an application

(5) No action of the Administrator under this section may be stayed by any court pending judicial review of such action.

(g) Misfueling

(1) No person shall introduce, or cause or allow the introduction of, leaded gasoline into any motor vehicle which is labeled "unleaded gasoline only," which is equipped with a gasoline tank filler inlet designed for the introduction of unleaded gasoline, which is a 1990 or later model year motor vehicle, or which such person knows or should know is a vehicle designed solely for the use of unleaded gasoline.

(2) Beginning October 1, 1993, no person shall introduce or cause or allow the introduction into any motor vehicle of diesel fuel which such person knows or should know contains a concentration of sulfur in excess of 0.05 percent (by weight) or which fails to meet acetane index minimum of 40 or such equivalent alternative aromatic level as prescribed by the Administrator under subsection (i)(2) of this section.

(h) Reid Vapor Pressure requirements

(1) Prohibition — Not later than 6 months after November 15, 1990, the Administrator shall promulgate regulations making it unlawful for any person during the high ozone season (as defined by the Administrator) to sell, offer for sale, dispense, supply, offer for supply, transport, or introduce into commerce gasoline with a Reid Vapor Pressure in excess of 9.0 pounds per square inch (psi). Such regulations shall also establish more stringent Reid Vapor Pressure standards in a nonattainment area as the Administrator finds necessary to generally achieve comparable evaporative emissions (on a per-vehicle basis) in nonattainment areas, taking into consideration the enforceability of such standards, the need of an area for emission control, and economic factors.

(2) Attainment areas — The regulations under this subsection shall not make it unlawful for any person to sell, offer for supply, transport, or introduce into commerce gasoline with a Reid Vapor Pressure of 9.0 pounds per square inch (psi) or lower in any area designated under section 7407 of this title as an attainment area. Notwithstanding the preceding sentence, the Administrator may impose a Reid vapor pressure requirement lower than 9.0 pounds per square inch (psi) in any area, formerly an ozone nonattainment area, which has been redesignated as an attainment area.

(3) Effective date; enforcement — The regulations under this subsection shall provide that the requirements of this subsection shall take effect not later than the high ozone season for 1992, and shall include such provisions as the Administrator determines are necessary to implement and enforce the requirements of this subsection.

(4) Ethanol waiver — For fuel blends containing gasoline and 10 percent denatured anhydrous ethanol, the Reid vapor pressure limitation under this subsection shall be one pound per square inch (psi) greater than the applicable Reid vapor pressure limitations established under paragraph (1); *Provided*, however, That a distributor, blender, marketer, reseller, carrier, retailer, or wholesale purchaser-consumer shall be deemed to be in full compliance with the provisions of this subsection and the regulations promulgated thereunder if it can demonstrate (by showing receipt of a certification or other evidence acceptable to the Administrator) that —

(A) the gasoline portion of the blend complies with the Reid vapor pressure limitations promulgated pursuant to this subsection;

(B) the ethanol portion of the blend does not exceed its waiver condition under subsection (f)(4); and

(C) no additional alcohol or other additive has been added to increase the Reid Vapor Pressure of the ethanol portion of the blend.

(5) Exclusion from ethanol waiver

(A) Promulgation of regulations — Upon notification, accompanied by supporting documentation, from the Governor of a State that the Reid vapor pressure limitation established by paragraph (4) will increase emissions that contribute to air pollution in any area in the State, the Administrator shall, by regulation, apply, in lieu of the Reid vapor pressure limitation established by paragraph (4), the Reid vapor pressure limitation established by paragraph (1) to all fuel blends containing gasoline and 10 percent denatured anhydrous ethanol that are sold, offered for sale, dispensed, supplied, offered for supply, transported, or introduced into commerce in the area during the high ozone season.

(B) Deadline for promulgation — The Administrator shall promulgate regulations under subparagraph (A) not later than 90 days after the date of receipt of a notification from a Governor under that subparagraph.

(C) Effective date

(i) In general — With respect to an area in a State for which the Governor submits a notification under subparagraph (A), the regulations under that subparagraph shall take effect on the later of —

(I) the first day of the first high ozone season for the area that begins after the date of receipt of the notification; or

(II) 1 year after the date of receipt of the notification.

(ii) Extension of effective date based on determination of insufficient supply

(I) In general — If, after receipt of a notification with respect to an area from a Governor of a State under subparagraph (A), the Administrator determines, on the Administrator's own motion or on petition of any person and after consultation with the Secretary of Energy, that the promulgation of regulations described in subparagraph (A) would result in an insufficient supply of gasoline in the State, the Administrator, by regulation—

(aa) shall extend the effective date of the regulations under clause (i) with respect to the area for not more than 1 year; and

(bb) may renew the extension under item (aa) for two additional periods, each of which shall not exceed 1 year.

(II) Deadline for action on petitions — The Administrator shall act on any petition submitted under subclause (I) not later than 180 days after the date of receipt of the petition.

(6) Areas covered — The provisions of this subsection shall apply only to the 48 contiguous States and the District of Columbia.

(i) Sulfur content requirements for diesel fuel

(1) Effective October 1, 1993, no person shall manufacture, sell, supply, offer for sale or supply, dispense, transport, or introduce into commerce motor vehicle diesel fuel which contains a concentration of sulfur in excess of 0.05 percent (by weight) or which fails to meet a cetane index minimum of 40.

(2) Not later than 12 months after November 15, 1990, the Administrator shall promulgate regulations to implement and enforce the requirements of paragraph (1). The Administrator may require manufacturers and importers of diesel fuel not intended for use in motor vehicles to dye such fuel in a particular manner in order to segregate it from motor vehicle diesel fuel. The Administrator may establish an equivalent alternative aromatic level to the cetane index specification in paragraph (1).

(3) The sulfur content of fuel required to be used in the certification of 1991 through 1993 model year heavy-duty diesel vehicles and engines shall be 0.10 percent (by weight). The sulfur content and cetane index minimum of fuel required to be used in the certification of 1994 and later model year heavy-duty diesel vehicles and engines shall comply with the regulations promulgated under paragraph (2).

(4) The States of Alaska and Hawaii may be exempted from the requirements of this subsection in the same manner as provided in section 7625 of this title. The Administrator shall take final action on any petition filed under section 7625 of this title or this paragraph for an exemption from the requirements of this subsection, within 12 months from the date of the petition.

(j) Lead substitute gasoline additives

(1) After November 15, 1990, any person proposing to register any gasoline additive under subsection (a) or to use any previously registered additive as a lead substitute may also elect to register the additive as a lead substitute gasoline additive for reducing valve seat wear by providing the Administrator with such relevant information regarding product identity and composition as the Administrator deems necessary for carrying out the responsibilities of paragraph (2) of this subsection (in addition to other information which may be required under subsection (b) of this section).

(2) In addition to the other testing which may be required under subsection (b), in the case of the lead substitute gasoline additives referred to in paragraph (1), the Administrator shall develop and publish a test procedure to determine the additives' effectiveness in reducing valve seat wear and the additives' tendencies to produce engine deposits and other adverse side effects. The test procedures shall be developed in cooperation with the Secretary of Agriculture and with the input of additive manufacturers, engine and engine components manufacturers, and other interested persons. The Administrator shall enter into arrangements with an independent laboratory to conduct tests of each additive using the test procedures developed and published pursuant to this paragraph. The Administrator shall publish the results of the tests by company and additive name in the Federal Register along with, for comparison purposes, the results of applying the same test procedures to gasoline containing 0.1 gram of lead per gallon in lieu of the lead substitute gasoline additive. The Administrator shall not rank or otherwise rate the lead substitute additives. Test procedures shall be established within 1 year after November 15, 1990. Additives shall be tested within 18 months of November 15, 1990 or 6 months after the lead substitute additives are identified to the Administrator, whichever is later.

(3) The Administrator may impose a user fee to recover the costs of testing of any fuel additive referred to in this subsection. The fee shall be paid by the person proposing to register the fuel additive concerned. Such fee shall not exceed $20,000 for a single fuel additive.

(4) There are authorized to be appropriated to the Administrator not more than $1,000,000 for the second full fiscal year after November 15, 1990 to establish test procedures and conduct engine tests as provided in this subsection. Not more than $500,000 per year is authorized to be appropriated for each of the 5 subsequent fiscal years.

(5) Any fees collected under this subsection shall be deposited in a special fund in the United States

Treasury for licensing and other services which thereafter shall be available for appropriation, to remain available until expended, to carry out the Agency's activities for which the fees were collected.

(k) Reformulated gasoline for conventional vehicles

(1) EPA regulations

(A) In general — Not later than November 15, 1991, the Administrator shall promulgate regulations under this section establishing requirements for reformulated gasoline to be used in gasoline fueled vehicles in specified nonattainment areas. Such regulations shall require the greatest reduction in emissions of ozone forming volatile organic compounds (during the high ozone season) and emissions of toxic air pollutants (during the entire year) achievable through the reformulation of conventional gasoline, taking into consideration the cost of achieving such emission reductions, any nonair quality and other air-quality related health and environmental impacts and energy requirements.

(B) Maintenance of toxic air pollutant emissions reductions from reformulated gasoline

(i) Definition of PADD — In this subparagraph the term "PADD" means a Petroleum Administration for Defense District.

(ii) Regulations concerning emissions of toxic air pollutants — Not later than 270 days after August 8, 2005, the Administrator shall establish by regulation, for each refinery or importer (other than a refiner or importer in a State that has received a waiver under section 7543(b) of this title with respect to gasoline produced for use in that State), standards for toxic air pollutants from use of the reformulated gasoline produced or distributed by the refiner or importer that maintain the reduction of the average annual aggregate emissions of toxic air pollutants for reformulated gasoline produced or distributed by the refiner or importer during calendar years 2001 and 2002 (as determined on the basis of data collected by the Administrator with respect to the refiner or importer).

(iii) Standards applicable to specific refineries or importers

(I) Applicability of standards — For any calendar year, the standards applicable to a refiner or importer under clause (ii) shall apply to the quantity of gasoline produced or distributed by the refiner or importer in the calendar year only to the extent that the quantity is less than or equal to the average annual quantity of reformulated gasoline produced or distributed by the refiner or importer during calendar years 2001 and 2002.

(II) Applicability of other standards — For any calendar year, the quantity of gasoline produced or distributed by a refiner or importer that is in excess of the quantity subject to subclause (I) shall be subject to standards for emissions of toxic air pollutants promulgated under subparagraph (A) and paragraph (3)(B).

(iv) Credit program — The Administrator shall provide for the granting and use of credits for emissions of toxic air pollutants in the same manner as provided in paragraph (7).

(v) Regional protection of toxics reduction baselines

(I) In general — Not later than 60 days after August 8, 2005, and not later than April 1 of each calendar year that begins after that date of enactment, the Administrator shall publish in the Federal Register a report that specifies, with respect to the previous calendar year—

(aa) the quantity of reformulated gasoline produced that is in excess of the average annual quantity of reformulated gasoline produced in 2001 and 2002; and

(bb) the reduction of the average annual aggregate emissions of toxic air pollutants in each PADD, based on retail survey data or data from other appropriate sources.

(II) Effect of failure to maintain aggregate toxics reductions — If, in any calendar year, the reduction of the average annual aggregate emissions of toxic air pollutants in a PADD fails to meet or exceed the reduction of the average annual aggregate emissions of toxic air pollutants in the PADD in calendar years 2001 and 2002, the Administrator, not later than 90 days after the date of publication of the report for the calendar year under subclause (I), shall—

(aa) identify, to the maximum extent practicable, the reasons for the failure, including the sources, volumes, and characteristics of reformulated gasoline that contributed to the failure; and

(bb) promulgate revisions to the regulations promulgated under clause (ii), to take effect not earlier than 180 days but not later than 270 days after the date of promulgation, to provide that, notwithstanding clause (iii)(II), all reformulated gasoline produced or distributed at each refiner or importer shall meet the standards applicable under clause (iii)(I) beginning not later than April 1 of the calendar year following publication of the report under subclause (I) and in each calendar year thereafter.

(vi) Not later than July 1, 2007, the Administrator shall promulgate final regulations to control hazardous air pollutants from motor vehicles and motor vehicle fuels, as provided for in section 80.1045 of title 40, Code of Federal Regulations (as in effect on August 8, 2005), and as authorized under section 7521(a)(1) of this title. If the Administrator promulgates by such date, final regulations to control hazardous air pollutants from motor vehicles and motor vehicle fuels that achieve and maintain greater overall reductions in emissions of air toxics from reformulated gasoline than the reductions that would be achieved under subsection (k)(1)(B) as amended by this clause, then subsections (k)(1)(B)(i) through (k)(1)(B)(v) of this section shall be null and void and regulations promulgated thereunder shall be rescinded and have no further effect.

(2) General requirements — The regulations referred to in paragraph (1) shall require that reformulated gasoline comply with paragraph (3) and with each of the following requirements (subject to paragraph (7)):

(A) NOx emissions — The emissions of oxides of nitrogen (NOx) from baseline vehicles when using the reformulated gasoline shall be no greater than the level of such emissions from such vehicles when using baseline gasoline. If the Administrator determines that compliance with the limitation on emissions of oxides of nitrogen under the preceding sentence is technically infeasible, considering the other requirements applicable under this subsection to such gasoline, the Administrator may, as appropriate to ensure compliance with this subparagraph, adjust (or waive entirely), any other requirements of this paragraph or any requirements applicable under paragraph (3)(A).

(B) Benzene content — The benzene content of the gasoline shall not exceed 1.0 percent by volume.

(C) Heavy metals — The gasoline shall have no heavy metals, including lead or manganese. The Administrator may waive the prohibition contained in this subparagraph for a heavy metal (other than lead) if the Admin-istrator determines that addition of the heavy metal to the gasoline will not increase, on an aggregate mass or cancer-risk basis, toxic air pollutant emissions from motor vehicles.

(3) More stringent of formula or performance standards — The regulations referred to in paragraph (1) shall require compliance with the more stringent of either the requirements set forth in subparagraph (A) or the requirements of subparagraph (B) of this paragraph. For purposes of determining the more stringent provision, clause (i) and clause (ii) of subparagraph (B) shall be considered independently.

(A) Formula

(i) Benzene — The benzene content of the reformulated gasoline shall not exceed 1.0 percent by volume.

(ii) Aromatics — The aromatic hydrocarbon content of the reformulated gasoline shall not exceed 25 percent by volume.

(iii) Lead — The reformulated gasoline shall have no lead content.

(iv) Detergents — The reformulated gasoline shall contain additives to prevent the accumulation of deposits in engines or vehicle fuel supply systems.

(B) Performance standard

(i) VOC emissions — During the high ozone season (as defined by the Administrator), the aggregate emissions of ozone forming volatile organic compounds from baseline vehicles when using the reformulated gasoline shall be 15 percent below the aggregate emissions of ozone forming volatile organic compounds from such vehicles when using baseline gasoline. Effective in calendar year 2000 and thereafter, 25 percent shall be substituted for 15 percent in applying this clause, except that the Administrator may adjust such 25 percent requirement to provide for a lesser or greater reduction based on technological feasibility, considering the cost of achieving such reductions in VOC emissions. No such adjustment shall provide for less than a 20 percent reduction below the aggregate emissions of such air pollutants from such vehicles when using baseline gasoline. The reductions required under this clause shall be on a mass basis.

(ii) Toxics — During the entire year, the aggregate emissions of toxic air pollutants from baseline vehicles when using the reformulated gasoline shall be 15 percent below the aggregate emissions of toxic air pollutants from such vehicles when using baseline gasoline. Effective in calendar year 2000 and thereafter, 25 percent shall be substituted for 15 percent in applying this clause, except that the Administrator may adjust such 25 percent requirement to provide for a lesser or greater reduction based on technological feasibility, considering the cost of achieving such reductions in toxic air pollutants. No such adjustment shall provide for less than a 20 percent reduction below the aggregate emissions of such air pollutants from such vehicles when using baseline gasoline. The reductions required under this clause shall be on a mass basis.

Any reduction greater than a specific percentage reduction required under this subparagraph shall be treated as satisfying such percentage reduction requirement.

(4) Certification procedures

(A) Regulations — The regulations under this subsection shall include procedures under which the Administrator shall certify reformulated gasoline as complying with the requirements established pursuant to this subsection. Under such regulations, the Administrator shall establish procedures for any person to petition the Administrator to certify a fuel formulation, or slate of fuel formulations. Such procedures shall further require that the Administrator shall approve or deny such petition within 180 days of receipt. If the Administrator fails to act within such 180-day period, the fuel shall be deemed certified until the Administrator completes action on the petition.

(B) Certification; equivalency — The Administrator shall certify a fuel formulation or slate of fuel formulations as complying with this subsection if such fuel or fuels —

(i) comply with the requirements of paragraph (2), and

(ii) achieve equivalent or greater reductions in emissions of ozone forming volatile organic compounds and emissions of toxic air pollutants than are achieved by a reformulated gasoline meeting the applicable requirements of paragraph (3).

(C) EPA determination of emissions level — Within 1 year after November 15, 1990, the Administrator shall determine the level of emissions of ozone forming volatile organic compounds and emissions of toxic air pollutants emitted by baseline vehicles when operating on baseline gasoline. For purposes of this subsection, within 1 year after November 15, 1990, the Administrator shall, by rule, determine appropriate measures of, and methodology for, ascertaining the emissions of air pollutants (including calculations, equipment, and testing tolerances).

(5) Prohibition — Effective beginning January 1, 1995, each of the following shall be a violation of this subsection:

(A) The sale or dispensing by any person of conventional gasoline to ultimate consumers in any covered area.

(B) The sale or dispensing by any refiner, blender, importer, or marketer of conventional gasoline for resale in any covered area, without (i) segregating such gasoline from reformulated gasoline, and (ii) clearly marking such conventional gasoline as "conventional gasoline, not for sale to ultimate consumer in a covered area."

Any refiner, blender, importer or marketer who purchases property segregated and marked conventional gasoline, and thereafter labels, represents, or wholesales such gasoline as reformulated gasoline shall also be in violation of this subsection. The Administrator may impose sampling, testing, and recordkeeping requirements upon any refiner, blender, importer, or marketer to prevent violations of this section.

(6) Opt-in areas

(A) Classified areas

(i) In general — Upon the application of the Governor of a State, the Administrator shall apply the prohibition set forth in paragraph (5) in any area in the State classified under subpart 2 of part D of subchapter I of this chapter as a Marginal, Moderate, Serious, or Severe Area (without regard to whether or not the 1980 population of the area exceeds 250,000). In any such case, the Administrator shall establish an effective date for such prohibition as he deems appropriate, not later than January 1, 1995, or 1 year after such application is received, whichever is later. The Administrator shall publish such application in the Federal Register upon receipt.

(ii) Effect of insufficient domestic capacity to produce reformulated gasoline — If the Administrator determines, on the Administrator's own motion or on petition of any person, after consultation with the Secretary of Energy, that there is insufficient domestic capacity to produce gasoline certified under this subsection, the Administrator shall, by rule, extend the effective date of such prohibition in Marginal, Moderate, Serious, or Severe Areas referred to in clause (i) for one additional year, and may, by rule, renew such extension for 2 additional one-year periods. The Administrator shall act on any petition submitted under this subparagraph within 6 months after receipt of the petition. The Administrator shall issue such extensions for areas with a lower ozone classification before issuing any such extension for areas with a higher classification.

(B) Ozone transport region

(i) Application of prohibition

(I) In general — On application of the Governor of a State in the ozone transport region established by section

7511c(a) of this title, the Administrator, not later than 180 days after the date of receipt of the application, shall apply the prohibition specified in paragraph (5) to any area in the State (other than an area classified as a marginal, moderate, serious, or severe ozone nonattainment area under subpart 2 of part D of subchapter I of this chapter) unless the Administrator determines under clause (iii) that there is insufficient capacity to supply reformulated gasoline.

(II) Publication of application — As soon as practicable after the date of receipt of an application under subclause (I), the Administrator shall publish the application in the Federal Register.

(ii) Period of applicability — Under clause (i), the prohibition specified in paragraph (5) shall apply in a State —

(I) commencing as soon as practicable but not later than 2 years after the date of approval by the Administrator of the application of the Governor of the State; and

(II) ending not earlier than 4 years after the commencement date determined under subclause (I).

(iii) Extension of commencement date based on insufficient capacity

(I) In general — If, after receipt of an application from a Governor of a State under clause (i), the Administrator determines, on the Administrator's own motion or on petition of any person, after consultation with the Secretary of Energy, that there is insufficient capacity to supply reformulated gasoline, the Administrator, by regulation —

(aa) shall extend the commencement date with respect to the State under clause (ii)(I) for not more than 1 year; and

(bb) may renew the extension under item (aa) for 2 additional periods, each of which shall not exceed 1 year.

(II) Deadline for action on petitions — The Administrator shall act on any petition submitted under subclause (I) not later than 180 days after the date of receipt of the petition.

(7) Credits

(A) The regulations promulgated under this subsection shall provide for the granting of an appropriate amount of credits to a person who refines, blends, or imports and certifies a gasoline or slate of gasoline that —

(i) has an aromatic hydrocarbon content (by volume) that is less than the maximum aromatic hydrocarbon content required to comply with paragraph (3); or

(ii) has a benzene content (by volume) that is less than the maximum benzene content specified in paragraph (2).

(B) The regulations described in subparagraph (A) shall also provide that a person who is granted credits may use such credits, or transfer all or a portion of such credits to another person for use within the same nonattainment area, for the purpose of complying with this subsection.

(C) The regulations promulgated under subparagraphs (A) and (B) shall ensure the enforcement of the requirements for the issuance, application, and transfer of the credits. Such regulations shall prohibit the granting or transfer of such credits for use with respect to any gasoline in a nonattainment area, to the extent the use of such credits would result in any of the following:

(i) An average gasoline aromatic hydrocarbon content (by volume) for the nonattainment (taking into account all gasoline sold for use in conventional gasoline-fueled vehicles in the nonattainment area) higher than the average fuel aromatic hydrocarbon content (by volume) that would occur in the absence of using any such credits.

(ii) An average benzene content (by volume) for the nonattainment area (taking into account all gasoline sold for use in conventional gasoline-fueled vehicles in the nonattainment area) higher than the average benzene content (by volume) that would occur in the absence of using any such credits.

(8) Anti-dumping rules

(A) In general — Within 1 year after November 15, 1990, the Administrator shall promulgate regulations applicable to each refiner, blender, or importer of gasoline ensuring that gasoline sold or introduced into commerce by such refiner, blender, or importer (other than reformulated gasoline subject to the requirements of paragraph (1)) does not result in average per gallon emissions (measured on a mass basis) of (i) volatile organic compounds, (ii) oxides of nitrogen, (iii) carbon monoxide, and (iv) toxic air pollutants in excess of such emissions of such pollutants attributable to gasoline sold or introduced into commerce in calendar year 1990 by that refiner, blender, or importer. Such regulations shall take effect beginning January 1, 1995.

(B) Adjustments — In evaluating compliance with the requirements of subparagraph (A), the Administrator shall make appropriate adjustments to insure that no credit is provided for improvement in motor vehicle emissions control in motor vehicles sold after the calendar year 1990.

(C) Compliance determined for each pollutant independently — In determining whether there is an increase in emissions in violation of the prohibition contained in subparagraph (A) the Administrator shall consider an increase in each air pollutant referred to in clauses (i) through (iv) as a separate violation of such prohibition, except that the Administrator shall promulgate regulations to provide that any increase in emissions of oxides of nitrogen resulting from adding oxygenates to gasoline may be offset by an equivalent or greater reduction (on a mass basis) in emissions of volatile organic compounds, carbon monoxide, or toxic air pollutants, or any combination of the foregoing.

(D) Compliance period — The Administrator shall promulgate an appropriate compliance period or appropriate compliance periods to be used for assessing compliance with the prohibition contained in subparagraph (A).

(E) Baseline for determining compliance — If the Administrator determines that no adequate and reliable data exists regarding the composition of gasoline sold or introduced into commerce by a refiner, blender, or importer in calendar year 1990, for such refiner, blender, or importer, baseline gasoline shall be substituted for such 1990 gasoline in determining compliance with subparagraph (A).

(9) Emissions from entire vehicle — In applying the requirements of this subsection, the Administrator shall take into account emissions from the entire motor vehicle, including evaporative, running, refueling, and exhaust emissions.

(10) Definitions — For purposes of this subsection —

(A) Baseline vehicles — The term "baseline vehicles" mean representative model year 1990 vehicles.

(B) Baseline gasoline

(i) Summertime — The term "baseline gasoline" means in the case of gasoline sold during the high ozone period (as defined by the Administrator) a gasoline which meets the following specifications:

BASELINE GASOLINE FUEL PROPERTIES

API Gravity	57.4
Sulfur, ppm	339
Benzene, %	1.53
RVP, psi	8.7
Octane, R+M/2	87.3
IBP, F	91
10%, F	128
50%, F	218
90%, F	330
End Point, F	415
Aromatics, %	32.0
Olefins, %	9.2
Saturates, %	58.8

(ii) Wintertime — The Administrator shall establish the specifications of "baseline gasoline" for gasoline sold at times other than the high ozone period (as defined by the Administrator). Such specifications shall be the specifications of 1990 industry average gasoline sold during such period.

(C) Toxic air pollutants — The term "toxic air pollutants" means the aggregate emissions of the following:

> Benzene
> 1,3 Butadiene
> Polycyclic organic matter (POM)
> Acetaldehyde
> Formaldehyde.

(D) Covered area — The 9 ozone nonattainment areas having a 1980 population in excess of 250,000 and having the highest ozone design value during the period 1987 through 1989 shall be "covered areas" for purposes of this subsection. Effective one year after the reclassification of any ozone nonattainment area as a Severe ozone nonattainment area under section 7511(b) of this title, such Severe area shall also be a "covered area" for purposes of this subsection.

(E) Reformulated gasoline — The term "reformulated gasoline" means any gasoline which is certified by the Administrator under this section as complying with this subsection.

(F) Conventional gasoline — The term "conventional gasoline" means any gasoline which does not meet specifications set by a certification under this subsection.

(*l*) Detergents — Effective beginning January 1, 1995, no person may sell or dispense to an ultimate consumer in the United States, and no refiner or marketer may directly or indirectly sell or dispense to persons who sell or dispense to ultimate consumers in the United States any gasoline which does not contain additives to prevent the accumulation of deposits in engines or fuel supply systems. Not later than 2 years after November 15, 1990, the Administrator shall promulgate a rule establishing specifications for such additives.

(m) Oxygenated fuels

(1) Plan revisions for CO nonattainment areas

(A) Each State in which there is located all or part of an area which is designated under title I as a nonattainment area for carbon monoxide and which has a carbon monoxide design value of 9.5 parts per million (ppm) or above based on data for the 2-year period of 1988 and 1989 and calculated according to the most recent interpretation methodology issued by the Administrator prior to November 15, 1990 shall submit to the Administrator a State implementation plan revision under section 7410 of this title and part D of subchapter I of this chapter for such area which shall contain the provisions specified under this subsection regarding oxygenated gasoline.

(B) A plan revision which contains such provisions shall also be submitted by each State in which there is located any area which, for any 2-year period after 1989 has a carbon monoxide design value of 9.5 ppm or above. The revision shall be submitted within 18 months after such 2-year period.

(2) Oxygenated gasoline in CO nonattainment areas — Each plan revision under this subsection shall contain provisions to require that any gasoline sold, or dispensed, to the ultimate consumer in the carbon monoxide nonattainment area or sold or dispensed directly or indirectly by fuel refiners or marketers to persons who sell or dispense to ultimate consumers, in the larger of —

(A) the Consolidated Metropolitan Statistical Area (CMSA) in which the area is located, or

(B) if the area is not located in a CMSA, the Metropolitan Statistical Area in which the area is located,

be blended, during the portion of the year in which the area is prone to high ambient concentrations of carbon monoxide to contain not less than 2.7 percent oxygen by weight (subject to a testing tolerance established by the Administrator). The portion of the year in which the area is prone to high ambient concentrations of carbon monoxide shall be as determined by the Administrator, but shall not be less than 4 months. At the request of a State with respect to any area designated as nonattainment for carbon monoxide, the Administrator may reduce the period specified in the preceding sentence if the State can demonstrate that because of meteorological conditions, a reduced period will assure that there will be no exceedances of the carbon monoxide standard outside of such reduced period. For areas with a carbon monoxide design value of 9.5 ppm or more of November 15, 1990, the revision shall provide that such requirement shall take effect no later than November 1, 1992, (or at such other date during 1992 as the Administrator establishes under the preceding provisions of this paragraph). For other areas, the revision shall provide that such requirement shall take effect no later than November 1 of the third year after the last year of the applicable 2-year period referred to in paragraph (1) (or at such other date during such third year as the Administrator establishes under the preceding provisions of this paragraph) and shall include a program for implementation and enforcement of the requirement consistent with guidance to be issued by the Administrator.

(3) Waivers

(A) The Administrator shall waive, in whole or in part, the requirements of paragraph (2) upon a demonstration by the State to the satisfaction of the Administrator that the use of oxygenated gasoline would prevent or interfere with the attainment by the area of a national primary ambient air quality standard (or a State or local ambient air quality standard) for any air pollutant other than carbon monoxide.

(B) The Administrator shall, upon demonstration by the State satisfactory to the Administrator, waive the requirement of paragraph (2) where the Administrator determines that mobile sources of carbon monoxide do not contribute significantly to carbon monoxide levels in an area.

(C)(i) Any person may petition the Administrator to make a finding that there is, or is likely to be, for any area, an inadequate domestic supply of, or distribution capacity for, oxygenated gasoline meeting the requirements of paragraph (2) or fuel additives (oxygenates) necessary to meet such requirements. The Administrator shall act on such petition within 6 months after receipt of the petition.

(ii) If the Administrator determines, in response to a petition under clause (i), that there is an inadequate supply or capacity described in clause (i), the Administrator shall delay the effective date of paragraph (2) for 1 year. Upon petition, the Administrator may extend such effective date for one additional year. No partial delay or lesser waiver may be granted under this clause.

(iii) In granting waivers under this subparagraph the Administrator shall consider distribution capacity separately from the adequacy of domestic supply and shall grant such waivers in such manner as will assure that, if supplies of oxygenated gasoline are limited, areas having the highest design value for carbon monoxide will have a priority in obtaining oxygenated gasoline which meets the requirements of paragraph (2).

(iv) As used in this subparagraph, the term distribution capacity includes capacity for transportation, storage, and blending.

(4) Fuel dispensing systems — Any person selling oxygenated gasoline at retail pursuant to this subsection shall be required under regulations promulgated by the Administrator to label the fuel dispensing system with a notice that the gasoline is oxygenated and will reduce the carbon monoxide emissions from the motor vehicle.

(5) Guidelines for credit — The Administrator shall promulgate guidelines, within 9 months after November 15, 1990, allowing the use of marketable oxygen credits from gasolines during that portion of the year specified in paragraph (2) with higher oxygen content than required to offset the sale or use of gasoline with a lower oxygen content than required. No credits may be transferred between nonattainment areas.

(6) Attainment areas — Nothing in this subsection shall be interpreted as requiring an oxygenated gasoline program in an area which is in attainment for carbon monoxide, except that in a carbon monoxide nonattainment area which is redesignated as attainment for carbon monoxide, the requirements of this subsection shall remain in effect to the extent such program is necessary to maintain such standard thereafter in the area.

(7) Failure to attain CO standard — If the Administrator determines under section 7512(b)(2) of this title that the national primary ambient air quality standard for carbon monoxide has not been attained in a Serious Area by the applicable attainment date, the State shall submit a plan revision for the area within 9 months after the date of such determination. The plan revision shall provide that the minimum oxygen content of gasoline referred to in paragraph (2) shall be 3.1 percent by weight unless such requirement is waived in accordance with the provisions of this subsection.

(n) Prohibition on leaded gasoline for highway use — After December 31, 1995, it shall be unlawful for any person to sell, offer for sale, supply, offer for supply, dispense, transport, or introduce into commerce, for use as fuel in any motor vehicle (as defined in section 7554(2) of this title) any gasoline which contains lead or lead additives.

(o) Renewable fuel program

(1) Definitions — In this section:

(A) Additional renewable fuel

The term "additional renewable fuel" means fuel that is produced from renewable biomass and that is used to replace or reduce the quantity of fossil fuel present in home heating oil or jet fuel.

(B) Advanced biofuel

(i) In general

The term "advanced biofuel" means renewable fuel, other than ethanol derived from corn starch, that has lifecycle greenhouse gas emissions, as determined by the Administrator, after notice and opportunity for comment, that are at least 50 percent less than baseline lifecycle greenhouse gas emissions.

(ii) Inclusions

The types of fuels eligible for consideration as "advanced biofuel" may include any of the following:

(I) Ethanol derived from cellulose, hemicellulose, or lignin.

(II) Ethanol derived from sugar or starch (other than corn starch).

(III) Ethanol derived from waste material, including crop residue, other vegetative waste material, animal waste, and food waste and yard waste.

(IV) Biomass-based diesel.

(V) Biogas (including landfill gas and sewage waste treatment gas) produced through the conversion of organic matter from renewable biomass.

(VI) Butanol or other alcohols produced through the conversion of organic matter from renewable biomass.

(VII) Other fuel derived from cellulosic biomass.

(C) Baseline lifecycle greenhouse gas emissions

The term "baseline lifecycle greenhouse gas emissions" means the average lifecycle greenhouse gas emissions, as determined by the Administrator, after notice and opportunity for comment, for gasoline or diesel (whichever is being replaced by the renewable fuel) sold or distributed as transportation fuel in 2005.

(D) Biomass-based diesel

The term "biomass-based diesel" means renewable fuel that is biodiesel as defined in section 13220(f) of this title and that has lifecycle greenhouse gas emissions, as determined by the Administrator, after notice and opportunity for comment, that are at least 50 percent less than the baseline lifecycle greenhouse gas emissions. Notwithstanding the preceding sentence, renewable fuel derived from co-processing biomass with a petroleum feedstock shall be advanced biofuel if it meets the requirements of subparagraph (B), but is not biomass-based diesel.

(E) Cellulosic biofuel

The term "cellulosic biofuel" means renewable fuel derived from any cellulose, hemicellulose, or lignin that is derived from renewable biomass and that has lifecycle greenhouse gas emissions, as determined by the Administrator, that are at least 60 percent less than the baseline lifecycle greenhouse gas emissions.

(F) Conventional biofuel

The term "conventional biofuel" means renewable fuel that is ethanol derived from corn starch.

(G) Greenhouse gas

The term "greenhouse gas" means carbon dioxide, hydrofluorocarbons, methane, nitrous oxide, perfluorocarbons, sulfur hexafluoride. The Administrator may include any other anthropogenically-emitted gas that is determined by the Administrator, after notice and comment, to contribute to global warming.

(H) Lifecycle greenhouse gas emissions

The term "lifecycle greenhouse gas emissions" means the aggregate quantity of greenhouse gas emissions (including direct emissions and significant indirect emissions such as significant emissions from land use changes), as determined by the Administrator, related to the full fuel lifecycle, including all stages of fuel and feedstock production and distribution, from feedstock generation or extraction through the distribution and delivery and use of the finished fuel to the ultimate consumer, where the mass values for all greenhouse gases are adjusted to account for their relative global warming potential.

(I) Renewable biomass

The term "renewable biomass" means each of the following:

(i) Planted crops and crop residue harvested from agricultural land cleared or cultivated at any time prior to the enactment of this sentence that is either actively managed or fallow, and nonforested.

(ii) Planted trees and tree residue from actively managed tree plantations on non-federal land cleared at any time prior to enactment of this sentence, including land belonging to an Indian tribe or an Indian individual, that is held in trust by the United States or subject to a restriction against alienation imposed by the United States.

(iii) Animal waste material and animal byproducts.

(iv) Slash and pre-commercial thinnings that are from non-federal forestlands, including forestlands belonging to an Indian tribe or an Indian individual, that are held in trust by the United States or subject to a restriction against alienation imposed by the United States, but not forests or forestlands that are ecological communities with a global or State ranking of critically imperiled, imperiled, or rare pursuant to a State Natural Heritage Program, old growth forest, or late successional forest.

(v) Biomass obtained from the immediate vicinity of buildings and other areas regularly occupied by people, or of public infrastructure, at risk from wildfire.

(vi) Algae.

(vii) Separated yard waste or food waste, including recycled cooking and trap grease.

(J) Renewable fuel

The term "renewable fuel" means fuel that is produced from renewable biomass and that is used to replace or reduce the quantity of fossil fuel present in a transportation fuel.

(K) Small refinery

The term "small refinery" means a refinery for which the average aggregate daily crude oil throughput for a calendar year (as determined by dividing the aggregate throughput for the calendar year by the number of days in the calendar year) does not exceed 75,000 barrels.

(L) Transportation fuel

The term "transportation fuel" means fuel for use in motor vehicles, motor vehicle engines, nonroad vehicles, or nonroad engines (except for ocean-going vessels).

(2) Renewable fuel program

(A) Regulations

(i) In general — Not later than 1 year after August 8, 2005, the Administrator shall promulgate regulations to ensure that gasoline sold or introduced into commerce in the United States (except in noncontiguous States or territories), on an annual average basis, contains the applicable volume of renewable fuel determined in accordance with subparagraph (B).

Not later than 1 year after December 19, 2007, the Administrator shall revise the regulations under this paragraph to ensure that transportation fuel sold or introduced into commerce in the United States (except in noncontiguous States or territories), on an annual average basis, contains at least the applicable volume of renewable fuel, advanced biofuel, cellulosic biofuel, and biomass-based diesel, determined in accordance with subparagraph (B) and, in the case of any such renewable fuel produced from new facilities that commence construction after December 19, 2007, achieves at least a 20 percent reduction in lifecycle greenhouse gas emissions compared to baseline lifecycle greenhouse gas emissions.

(ii) Noncontiguous State opt-in

(I) In general — On the petition of a noncontiguous State or territory, the Administrator may allow the renewable fuel program established under this subsection to apply in the noncontiguous State or territory at the same time or any time after the Administrator promulgates regulations under this subparagraph.

(II) Other actions — In carrying out this clause, the Administrator may —

(aa) issue or revise regulations under this paragraph;

(bb) establish applicable percentages under paragraph (3);

(cc) provide for the generation of credits under paragraph (5); and

(dd) take such other actions as are necessary to allow for the application of the renewable fuels program in a noncontiguous State or territory.

(iii) Provisions of regulations — Regardless of the date of promulgation, the regulations promulgated under clause (i) —

　(I) shall contain compliance provisions applicable to refineries, blenders, distributors, and importers, as appropriate, to ensure that the requirements of this paragraph are met; but

　(II) shall not —

　　(aa) restrict geographic areas in which renewable fuel may be used; or

　　(bb) impose any per-gallon obligation for the use of renewable fuel.

(iv) Requirement in case of failure to promulgate regulations — If the Administrator does not promulgate regulations under clause (i), the percentage of renewable fuel in gasoline sold or dispensed to consumers in the United States, on a volume basis, shall be 2.78 percent for calendar year 2006.

(B) Applicable volumes

(i) Calendar years after 2005

　(I) Renewable fuel

For the purpose of subparagraph (A), the applicable volume of renewable fuel for the calendar years 2006 through 2022 shall be determined in accordance with the following table:

Calendar year:	Applicable volume of renewable fuel (in billions of gallons):
2006	4.0
2007	4.7
2008	9.0
2009	11.1
2010	12.95
2011	13.95
2012	15.2
2013	16.55
2014	18.15
2015	20.5
2016	22.25
2017	24.0
2018	26.0
2019	28.0
2020	30.0
2021	33.0
2022	36.0

　(II) Advanced biofuel

For the purpose of subparagraph (A), of the volume of renewable fuel required under subclause (I), the applicable volume of advanced biofuel for the calendar years 2009 through 2022 shall be determined in accordance with the following table:

Calendar year:	Applicable volume of advanced biofuel (in billions of gallons):
2009	0.6
2010	0.95
2011	1.35
2012	2.0
2013	2.75
2014	3.75
2015	5.5
2016	7.25
2017	9.0
2018	11.0
2019	13.0
2020	15.0
2021	18.0
2022	21.0

　(III) Cellulosic biofuel

For the purpose of subparagraph (A), of the volume of advanced biofuel required under subclause (II), the applicable volume of cellulosic biofuel for the calendar years 2010 through 2022 shall be determined in accordance with the following table:

Calendar year:	Applicable volume of cellulosic biofuel (in billions of gallons):
2010	0.1
2011	0.25
2012	0.5
2013	1.0
2014	1.75
2015	3.0
2016	4.25
2017	5.5
2018	7.0
2019	8.5
2020	10.5
2021	13.5
2022	16.0

　(IV) Biomass-based diesel

For the purpose of subparagraph (A), of the volume of advanced biofuel required under subclause (II), the applicable volume of biomass-based diesel for the calendar years 2009 through 2012 shall be determined in accordance with the following table:

Calendar year:	Applicable volume of biomass-based diesel (in billions of gallons):
2009	0.5
2010	0.65
2011	0.80
2012	1.0

(ii) Other calendar years

For the purposes of subparagraph (A), the applicable volumes of each fuel specified in the tables in clause (i) for calendar years after the calendar years specified in the tables shall be determined by the Administrator, in coordination with the Secretary of Energy and the Secretary of Agriculture, based on a review of the implementation of the program during calendar years specified in the tables, and an analysis of —

(I) the impact of the production and use of renewable fuels on the environment, including on air quality, climate change, conversion of wetlands, ecosystems, wildlife habitat, water quality, and water supply;

(II) the impact of renewable fuels on the energy security of the United States;

(III) the expected annual rate of future commercial production of renewable fuels, including advanced biofuels in each category (cellulosic biofuel and biomass-based diesel);

(IV) the impact of renewable fuels on the infrastructure of the United States, including deliverability of materials, goods, and products other than renewable fuel, and the sufficiency of infrastructure to deliver and use renewable fuel;

(V) the impact of the use of renewable fuels on the cost to consumers of transportation fuel and on the cost to transport goods; and

(VI) the impact of the use of renewable fuels on other factors, including job creation, the price and supply of agricultural commodities, rural economic development, and food prices.

The Administrator shall promulgate rules establishing the applicable volumes under this clause no later than 14 months before the first year for which such applicable volume will apply.

(iii) Applicable volume of advanced biofuel

For the purpose of making the determinations in clause (ii), for each calendar year, the applicable volume of advanced biofuel shall be at least the same percentage of the applicable volume of renewable fuel as in calendar year 2022.

(iv) Applicable volume of cellulosic biofuel

For the purpose of making the determinations in clause (ii), for each calendar year, the applicable volume of cellulosic biofuel established by the Administrator shall be based on the assumption that the Administrator will not need to issue a waiver for such years under paragraph (7)(D).

(v) Minimum applicable volume of biomass-based diesel

For the purpose of making the determinations in clause (ii), the applicable volume of biomass-based diesel shall not be less than the applicable volume listed in clause (i)(IV) for calendar year 2012.

(3) Applicable percentages

(A) Provision of estimate of volumes of gasoline sales — Not later than October 31 of each of calendar years 2005 through 2021, the Administrator of the Energy Information Administration shall provide to the Administrator of the Environmental Protection Agency an estimate, with respect to the following calendar year, of the volumes of transportation fuel, biomass-based diesel and cellulosic biofuel projected to be sold or introduced into commerce in the United States.

(B) Determination of applicable percentages

(i) In general — Not later than November 30 of each of calendar years 2005 through 2012, based on the estimate provided under subparagraph (A), the Administrator of the Environmental Protection

Agency shall determine and publish in the Federal Register, with respect to the following calendar year, the renewable fuel obligation that ensures that the requirements of paragraph (2) are met.

(ii) Required elements — The renewable fuel obligation determined for a calendar year under clause (i) shall—

(I) be applicable to refineries, blenders, and importers, as appropriate;

(II) be expressed in terms of a volume percentage of transportation fuel sold or introduced into commerce in the United States; and

(III) subject to subparagraph (C)(i), consist of a single applicable percentage that applies to all categories of persons specified in subclause (I).

(C) Adjustments — In determining the applicable percentage for a calendar year, the Administrator shall make adjustments —

(i) to prevent the imposition of redundant obligations on any person specified in subparagraph (B)(ii)(I); and

(ii) to account for the use of renewable fuel during the previous calendar year by small refineries that are exempt under paragraph (9).

(4) Modification of greenhouse gas reduction percentages

(A) In general

The Administrator may, in the regulations under the last sentence of paragraph (2)(A)(i), adjust the 20 percent, 50 percent, and 60 percent reductions in lifecycle greenhouse gas emissions specified in paragraphs (2)(A)(i) (relating to renewable fuel), (1)(D) (relating to biomass-based diesel), (1)(B)(i) (relating to advanced biofuel), and (1)(E) (relating to cellulosic biofuel) to a lower percentage. For the 50 and 60 percent reductions, the Administrator may make such an adjustment only if he determines that generally such reduction is not commercially feasible for fuels made using a variety of feedstocks, technologies, and processes to meet the applicable reduction.

(B) Amount of adjustment

In promulgating regulations under this paragraph, the specified 50 percent reduction in greenhouse gas emissions from advanced biofuel and in biomass-based diesel may not be reduced below 40 percent. The specified 20 percent reduction in greenhouse gas emissions from renewable fuel may not be reduced below 10 percent, and the specified 60 percent reduction in greenhouse gas emissions from cellulosic biofuel may not be reduced below 50 percent.

(C) Adjusted reduction levels

An adjustment under this paragraph to a percent less than the specified 20 percent

greenhouse gas reduction for renewable fuel shall be the minimum possible adjustment, and the adjusted greenhouse gas reduction shall be established by the Administrator at the maximum achievable level, taking cost in consideration, for natural gas fired corn-based ethanol plants, allowing for the use of a variety of technologies and processes. An adjustment in the 50 or 60 percent greenhouse gas levels shall be the minimum possible adjustment for the fuel or fuels concerned, and the adjusted greenhouse gas reduction shall be established at the maximum achievable level, taking cost in consideration, allowing for the use of a variety of feedstocks, technologies, and processes.

(D) 5-year review

Whenever the Administrator makes any adjustment under this paragraph, not later than 5 years thereafter he shall review and revise (based upon the same criteria and standards as required for the initial adjustment) the regulations establishing the adjusted level.

(E) Subsequent adjustments

After the Administrator has promulgated a final rule under the last sentence of paragraph (2)(A)(i) with respect to the method of determining lifecycle greenhouse gas emissions, except as provided in subparagraph (D), the Administrator may not adjust the percent greenhouse gas reduction levels unless he determines that there has been a significant change in the analytical methodology used for determining the lifecycle greenhouse gas emissions. If he makes such determination, he may adjust the 20, 50, or 60 percent reduction levels through rulemaking using the criteria and standards set forth in this paragraph.

(F) Limit on upward adjustments

If, under subparagraph (D) or (E), the Administrator revises a percent level adjusted as provided in subparagraphs (A), (B), and (C) to a higher percent, such higher percent may not exceed the applicable percent specified in paragraph (2)(A)(i), (1)(D), (1)(B)(i), or (1)(E).

(G) Applicability of adjustments

If the Administrator adjusts, or revises, a percent level referred to in this paragraph or makes a change in the analytical methodology used for determining the lifecycle greenhouse gas emissions, such adjustment, revision, or change (or any combination thereof) shall only apply to renewable fuel from new facilities that commence construction after the effective date of such adjustment, revision, or change.

(5) Credit program

(A) In general — The regulations promulgated under paragraph (2)(A) shall provide—

(i) for the generation of an appropriate amount of credits by any person that refines, blends, or imports gasoline that con-tains a quantity of renewable fuel that is greater than the quantity required under paragraph (2);

(ii) for the generation of an appropriate amount of credits for biodiesel; and

(iii) for the generation of credits by small refineries in accordance with paragraph (9)(C).

(B) Use of credits — A person that generates credits under subparagraph (A) may use the credits, or transfer all or a portion of the credits to another person, for the purpose of complying with paragraph (2).

(C) Duration of credits — A credit generated under this paragraph shall be valid to show compliance for the 12 months as of the date of generation.

(D) Inability to generate or purchase sufficient credits — The regulations promulgated under paragraph (2)(A) shall include provisions allowing any person that is unable to generate or purchase sufficient credits to meet the requirements of paragraph (2) to carry forward a renewable fuel deficit on condition that the person, in the calendar year following the year in which the renewable fuel deficit is created—

(i) achieves compliance with the renewable fuel requirement under paragraph (2); and

(ii) generates or purchases additional renewable fuel credits to offset the renewable fuel deficit of the previous year.

(E) Credits for additional renewable fuel The Administrator may issue regulations providing: (i) for the generation of an appropriate amount of credits by any person that refines, blends, or imports additional renewable fuels specified by the Administrator; and (ii) for the use of such credits by the generator, or the transfer of all or a portion of the credits to another person, for the purpose of complying with paragraph (2).

(6) Seasonal variations in renewable fuel use

(A) Study — For each of calendar years 2006 through 2012, the Administrator of the Energy Information Administration shall conduct a study of renewable fuel blending to determine whether there are excessive seasonal variations in the use of renewable fuel.

(B) Regulation of excessive seasonal variations — If, for any calendar year, the Administrator of the Energy Information Administration, based on the study under subparagraph (A), makes the determinations specified in subparagraph (C), the Administrator of the Environmental Protection Agency shall promulgate regulations to ensure that 25 percent or more of the quantity of renewable fuel necessary to meet the requirements

of paragraph (2) is used during each of the 2 periods specified in subparagraph (D) of each subsequent calendar year.

(C) Determinations — The determinations referred to in subparagraph (B) are that —

(i) less than 25 percent of the quantity of renewable fuel necessary to meet the requirements of paragraph (2) has been used during 1 of the 2 periods specified in subparagraph (D) of the calendar year;

(ii) a pattern of excessive seasonal variation described in clause (i) will continue in subsequent calendar years; and

(iii) promulgating regulations or other requirements to impose a 25 percent or more seasonal use of renewable fuels will not prevent or interfere with the attainment of national ambient air quality standards or significantly increase the price of motor fuels to the consumer.

(D) Periods — The 2 periods referred to in this paragraph are —

(i) April through September; and

(ii) January through March and October through December.

(E) Exclusion — Renewable fuel blended or consumed in calendar year 2006 in a State that has received a waiver under section 7543(b) of this title shall not be included in the study under subparagraph (A).

(F) State exemption from seasonality requirements — Notwithstanding any other provision of law, the seasonality requirement relating to renewable fuel use established by this paragraph shall not apply to any State that has received a waiver under section 7543(b) or any State dependent on refineries in such State for gasoline supplies.

(7) Waivers

(A) In general — The Administrator, in consultation with the Secretary of Agriculture and the Secretary of Energy, may waive the requirements of paragraph (2) in whole or in part on petition by one or more States, by any person subject to the requirements of this subsection, or by the Administrator on his own motion by reducing the national quantity of renewable fuel required under paragraph (2) —

(i) based on a determination by the Administrator, after public notice and opportunity for comment, that implementation of the requirement would severely harm the economy or environment of a State, a region, or the United States; or

(ii) based on a determination by the Administrator, after public notice and opportunity for comment, that there is an inadequate domestic supply.

(B) Petitions for waivers — The Administrator, in consultation with the Secretary of Agriculture and the Secretary of Energy, shall approve or disapprove a State petition for a waiver of the requirements of paragraph (2) within 90 days after the date on which the petition is received by the Administrator.

(C) Termination of waivers — A waiver granted under subparagraph (A) shall terminate after 1 year, but may be renewed by the Administrator after consultation with the Secretary of Agriculture and the Secretary of Energy.

(D) Cellulosic biofuel

(i) For any calendar year for which the projected volume of cellulosic biofuel production is less than the minimum applicable volume established under paragraph (2)(B), as determined by the Administrator based on the estimate provided under paragraph (3)(A), not later than November 30 of the preceding calendar year, the Administrator shall reduce the applicable volume of cellulosic biofuel required under paragraph (2)(B) to the projected volume available during that calendar year. For any calendar year in which the Administrator makes such a reduction, the Administrator may also reduce the applicable volume of renewable fuel and advanced biofuels requirement established under paragraph (2)(B) by the same or a lesser volume.

(ii) Whenever the Administrator reduces the minimum cellulosic biofuel volume under this subparagraph, the Administrator shall make available for sale cellulosic biofuel credits at the higher of $0.25 per gallon or the amount by which $3.00 per gallon exceeds the average wholesale price of a gallon of gasoline in the United States. Such amounts shall be adjusted for inflation by the Administrator for years after 2008.

(iii) Eighteen months after December 19, 2007, the Administrator shall promulgate regulations to govern the issuance of credits under this subparagraph. The regulations shall set forth the method for determining the exact price of credits in the event of a waiver. The price of such credits shall not be changed more frequently than once each quarter. These regulations shall include such provisions, including limiting the credits' uses and useful life, as the Administrator deems appropriate to assist market liquidity and transparency, to provide appropriate certainty for regulated entities and renewable fuel producers, and to limit any potential misuse of cellulosic biofuel credits to reduce

the use of other renewable fuels, and for such other purposes as the Administrator determines will help achieve the goals of this subsection. The regulations shall limit the number of cellulosic biofuel credits for any calendar year to the minimum applicable volume (as reduced under this subparagraph) of cellulosic biofuel for that year.

(E) Biomass-based diesel

(i) Market evaluation

The Administrator, in consultation with the Secretary of Energy and the Secretary of Agriculture, shall periodically evaluate the impact of the biomass-based diesel requirements established under this paragraph on the price of diesel fuel.

(ii) Waiver

If the Administrator determines that there is a significant renewable feedstock disruption or other market circumstances that would make the price of biomass-based diesel fuel increase significantly, the Administrator, in consultation with the Secretary of Energy and the Secretary of Agriculture, shall issue an order to reduce, for up to a 60-day period, the quantity of biomass-based diesel required under subparagraph (A) by an appropriate quantity that does not exceed 15 percent of the applicable annual requirement for biomass-based diesel. For any calendar year in which the Administrator makes a reduction under this subparagraph, the Administrator may also reduce the applicable volume of renewable fuel and advanced biofuels requirement established under paragraph (2)(B) by the same or a lesser volume.

(iii) Extensions

If the Administrator determines that the feedstock disruption or circumstances described in clause (ii) is continuing beyond the 60-day period described in clause (ii) or this clause, the Administrator, in consultation with the Secretary of Energy and the Secretary of Agriculture, may issue an order to reduce, for up to an additional 60-day period, the quantity of biomass-based diesel required under subparagraph (A) by an appropriate quantity that does not exceed an additional 15 percent of the applicable annual requirement for biomass-based diesel.

(F) Modification of applicable volumes

For any of the tables in paragraph (2)(B), if the Administrator waives —

(i) at least 20 percent of the applicable volume requirement set forth in any such table for 2 consecutive years; or

(ii) at least 50 percent of such volume requirement for a single year, the Administrator shall promulgate a rule (within 1 year after issuing such waiver) that modifies the applicable volumes set forth in the table concerned for all years following the final year to which the waiver applies, except that no such modification in applicable volumes shall be made for any year before 2016. In promulgating such a rule, the Administrator shall comply with the processes, criteria, and standards set forth in paragraph (2)(B)(ii).

(8) Study and waiver for initial year of program

(A) In general — Not later than 180 days after August 8, 2005, the Secretary of Energy shall conduct for the Administrator a study assessing whether the renewable fuel requirement under paragraph (2) will likely result in significant adverse impacts on consumers in 2006, on a national, regional, or State basis.

(B) Required evaluations — The study shall evaluate renewable fuel —

    (i) supplies and prices;

    (ii) blendstock supplies; and

    (iii) supply and distribution system capabilities.

(C) Recommendations by the Secretary — Based on the results of the study, the Secretary of Energy shall make specific recommendations to the Administrator concerning waiver of the requirements of paragraph (2), in whole or in part, to prevent any adverse impacts described in subparagraph (A).

(D) Waiver

    (i) In general — Not later than 270 days after August 8, 2005, the Administrator shall, if and to the extent recommended by the Secretary of Energy under subparagraph (C), waive, in whole or in part, the renewable fuel requirement under paragraph (2) by reducing the national quantity of renewable fuel required under paragraph (2) in calendar year 2006.

    (ii) No effect on waiver authority — Clause (i) does not limit the authority of the Administrator to waive the requirements of paragraph (2) in whole, or in part, under paragraph (7).

(9) Small refineries

(A) Temporary exemption

    (i) In general — The requirements of paragraph (2) shall not apply to small refineries until calendar year 2011.

    (ii) Extension of exemption

        (I) Study by Secretary of Energy — Not later than December 31, 2008, the Secretary of Energy shall conduct for the Administrator a study to determine whether compliance with the requirements of paragraph (2) would impose a disproportionate economic hardship on small refineries.

        (II) Extension of exemption — In the case of a small refinery that the Secretary of Energy determines under subclause (I) would be subject to a disproportionate economic hardship if required to comply with paragraph (2), the Administrator shall extend the exemption under clause (i) for the small refinery for a period of not less than 2 additional years.

(B) Petitions based on disproportionate economic hardship

    (i) Extension of exemption — A small refinery may at any time petition the Administrator for an extension of the exemption under subparagraph (A) for the reason of disproportionate economic hardship.

    (ii) Evaluation of petitions — In evaluating a petition under clause (i), the Administrator, in consultation with the Secretary of Energy, shall consider the findings of the study under subparagraph (A)(ii) and other economic factors.

    (iii) Deadline for action on petitions — The Administrator shall act on any petition submitted by a small refinery for a hardship exemption not later than 90 days after the date of receipt of the petition.

(C) Credit program — If a small refinery notifies the Administrator that the small refinery waives the exemption under subparagraph (A), the regulations promulgated under paragraph (2)(A) shall provide for the generation of credits by the small refinery under paragraph (5) beginning in the calendar year following the date of notification.

(D) Opt-in for small refineries — A small refinery shall be subject to the requirements of paragraph (2) if the small refinery notifies the Administrator that the small refinery waives the exemption under subparagraph (A).

(10) Ethanol market concentration analysis

(A) Analysis

    (i) In general — Not later than 180 days after August 8, 2005, and annually thereafter, the Federal Trade Commission shall perform a market concentration analysis of the ethanol production industry using the Herfindahl-Hirschman Index to determine whether there is sufficient competition among industry participants to avoid price-setting and other anticompetitive behavior.

    (ii) Scoring — For the purpose of scoring under clause (i) using the Herfindahl-Hirschman Index, all marketing arrangements among industry participants shall be considered.

(B) Report — Not later than December 1, 2005, and annually thereafter, the Federal Trade Commission shall submit to Congress and the Administrator a report on the results of the market concentration analysis performed under subparagraph (A)(i).

(11) Periodic reviews

To allow for the appropriate adjustment of the requirements described in subparagraph (B) of paragraph (2), the Administrator shall conduct periodic reviews of —

(A) existing technologies;

(B) the feasibility of achieving compliance with the requirements; and

(C) the impacts of the requirements described in subsection (a)(2) of this section on each individual and entity described in paragraph (2).

(12) Effect on other provisions

Nothing in this subsection, or regulations issued pursuant to this subsection, shall affect or be construed to affect the regulatory status of carbon dioxide or any other greenhouse gas, or to expand or limit regulatory authority regarding carbon dioxide or any other greenhouse gas, for purposes of other provisions (including section 7475 of this title) of this chapter. The previous sentence shall not affect implementation and enforcement of this subsection.

(q) Analyses of motor vehicle fuel changes and emissions model

(1) Anti-backsliding analysis

(A) Draft analysis — Not later than 4 years after August 8, 2005, the Administrator shall publish for public comment a draft analysis of the changes in emissions of air pollutants and air quality due to the use of motor vehicle fuel and fuel additives resulting from implementation of the amendments made by the Energy Policy Act of 2005.

(B) Final analysis — After providing a reasonable opportunity for comment but not later than 5 years after August 8, 2005, the Administrator shall publish the analysis in final form.

(2) Emissions model — For the purposes of this section, not later than 4 years after August 8, 2005, the Administrator shall develop and finalize an emissions model that reflects, to the maximum extent practicable, the effects of gasoline characteristics or components on emissions from vehicles in the motor vehicle fleet during calendar year 2007.

(3) Permeation effects study

(A) In general — Not later than 1 year after August 8, 2005, the Administrator shall conduct a study, and report to Congress the results of the study, on the effects of ethanol content in gasoline on permeation, the process by which fuel molecules migrate through the elastomeric materials (rubber and plastic parts) that make up the fuel and fuel vapor systems of a motor vehicle.

(B) Evaporative emissions — The study shall include estimates of the increase in total evaporative emissions likely to result from the use of gasoline with ethanol content in a motor vehicle, and the fleet of motor vehicles, due to permeation.

(r) Fuel and fuel additive importers and importation — For the purposes of this section, the term "manufacturer" includes an importer and the term "manufacture" includes importation.

(s) Conversion assistance for cellulosic biomass, waste-derived ethanol, approved renewable fuels

(1) In general — The Secretary of Energy may provide grants to merchant producers of cellulosic biomass ethanol, waste-derived ethanol, and approved renewable fuels in the United States to assist the producers in building eligible production facilities described in paragraph (2) for the production of ethanol or approved renewable fuels.

(2) Eligible production facilities — A production facility shall be eligible to receive a grant under this subsection if the production facility—

(A) is located in the United States; and

(B) uses cellulosic or renewable biomass or waste-derived feedstocks derived from agricultural residues, wood residues, municipal solid waste, or agricultural byproducts.

(3) Authorization of appropriations — There are authorized to be appropriated the following amounts to carry out this subsection:

(A) $100,000,000 for fiscal year 2006.

(B) $250,000,000 for fiscal year 2007.

(C) $400,000,000 for fiscal year 2008.

(4) Definitions — For the purposes of this subsection:

(A) The term "approved renewable fuels" are fuels and components of fuels that have been approved by the Department of Energy, as defined in section 13211 of this title, which have been made from renewable biomass.

(B) The term "renewable biomass" is, as defined in Presidential Executive Order 13134, published in the Federal Register on August 16, 1999, any organic matter that is available on a renewable or recurring basis (excluding old-growth timber), including dedicated energy crops and trees, agricultural food and feed crop residues, aquatic plants, animal wastes, wood and wood residues, paper and paper residues, and other vegetative waste materials. Old-growth timber means timber of a forest from the late successional stage of forest development.

(t) Blending of compliant reformulated gasolines

(1) In general — Notwithstanding subsections (h) and (k) of this section and subject to the limitations in paragraph (2) of this subsection, it shall not be a violation of this subtitle for a gasoline retailer, during any month of the year, to blend at a retail location batches of ethanol-blended and non-ethanol-blended reformulated gasoline, provided that—

(A) each batch of gasoline to be blended has been individually certified as in compliance with subsections (h) and (k) of this section prior to being blended;

(B) the retailer notifies the Administrator prior to such blending, and identifies the exact location of the retail station and the specific tank in which such blending will take place;

(C) the retailer retains and, as requested by the Administrator or the Administrator's designee, makes available for inspection such certifications accounting for all gasoline at the retail outlet; and

(D) the retailer does not, between June 1 and September 15 of each year, blend a batch of VOC-controlled, or "summer", gasoline with a batch of non-VOC-controlled, or "winter", gasoline (as these terms are defined under subsections (h) and (k) of this section).

(2) Limitations

(A) Frequency limitation — A retailer shall only be permitted to blend batches of compliant reformulated gasoline under this subsection a maximum of two blending periods between May 1 and September 15 of each calendar year.

(B) Duration of blending period — Each blending period authorized under subparagraph (A) shall extend for a period of no more than 10 consecutive calendar days.

(3) Surveys — A sample of gasoline taken from a retail location that has blended gasoline within the past 30 days and is in compliance with subparagraphs (A), (B), (C), and (D) of paragraph (1) shall not be used in a VOC survey mandated by 40 CFR Part 80.

(4) State implementation plans — A State shall be held harmless and shall not be required to revise its State implementation plan under section 7410 of this title to account for the emissions from blended gasoline authorized under paragraph (1).

(5) Preservation of State law — Nothing in this subsection shall—

(A) preempt existing State laws or regulations regulating the blending of compliant gasolines; or

(B) prohibit a State from adopting such restrictions in the future.

(6) Regulations — The Administrator shall promulgate, after notice and comment, regulations implementing this subsection within 1 year after August 8, 2005.

(7) Effective date — This subsection shall become effective 15 months after August 8, 2005, and shall apply to blended batches of reformulated gasoline on or after that date, regardless of whether the implementing regulations required by paragraph (6) have been promulgated by the Administrator by that date.

(8) Liability — No person other than the person responsible for blending under this subsection shall be subject to an enforcement action or penalties under subsection (d) of this section solely arising from the blending of compliant reformulated gasolines by the retailers.

(9) Formulation of gasoline — This subsection does not grant authority to the Administrator or any State (or any subdivision thereof) to require reformulation of gasoline at the refinery to adjust for potential or actual emissions increases due to the blending authorized by this subsection.

(u) Standard specifications for biodiesel

(1) Unless the American Society for Testing and Materials has adopted a standard for diesel fuel containing 20 percent biodiesel (commonly known as "B20") within 1 year after the date of enactment of this subsection [enacted Dec. 19, 2007], the Administrator shall initiate a rulemaking to establish a uniform per gallon fuel standard for such fuel and designate an identification number so that vehicle manufacturers are able to design engines to use fuel meeting such standard.

(2) Unless the American Society for Testing and Materials has adopted a standard for diesel fuel containing 5 percent biodiesel (commonly known as "B5") within 1 year after the date of enactment of this subsection [enacted Dec. 19, 2007], the Administrator shall initiate a rulemaking to establish a uniform per gallon fuel standard for such fuel and designate an identification so that vehicle manufacturers are able to design engines to use fuel meeting such standard.

(3) Whenever the Administrator is required to initiate a rulemaking under paragraph (1) or (2), the Administrator shall promulgate a final rule within 18 months after the date of the enactment of this subsection [enacted Dec. 19, 2007].

(4) Not later than 180 days after the enactment of this subsection [enacted Dec. 19, 2007], the Administrator shall establish an annual inspection and enforcement program to ensure that diesel fuel containing biodiesel sold or distributed in interstate commerce meets the standards established under regulations under this section, including testing and certification for compliance with applicable standards of the American Society for Testing and Materials. There are authorized to be appropriated

to carry out the inspection and enforcement program under this paragraph $3,000,000 for each of fiscal years 2008 through 2010.

(5) For purposes of this subsection, the term "biodiesel" has the meaning provided by section 312(f) of Energy Policy Act of 1992 (42 U.S.C. 13220(f)).

(v) Prevention of air quality deterioration

(1) Study

(A) In general — Not later than 18 months after the date of enactment of this subsection [enacted Dec. 19, 2007], the Administrator shall complete a study to determine whether the renewable fuel volumes required by this section will adversely impact air quality as a result of changes in vehicle and engine emissions of air pollutants regulated under this Act.

(B) Considerations — The study shall include consideration of —

(i) different blend levels, types of renewable fuels, and available vehicle technologies; and

(ii) appropriate national, regional, and local air quality control measures.

(2) Regulations — Not later than 3 years after the date of enactment of this subsection [enacted Dec. 19, 2007], the Administrator shall —

(A) promulgate fuel regulations to implement appropriate measures to mitigate, to the greatest extent achievable, considering the results of the study under paragraph (1), any adverse impacts on air quality, as the result of the renewable volumes required by this section; or

(B) make a determination that no such measures are necessary.

§7546. Renewable fuel

(a) Definitions — In this section:

(1) Municipal solid waste — The term "municipal solid waste" has the meaning given the term "solid waste" in section 6903 of this title.

(2) RFG State — The term "RFG State" means a State in which is located one or more covered areas (as defined in section 7545(k)(10)(D) of this title).

(3) Secretary — The term "Secretary" means the Secretary of Energy.

(b) Cellulosic biomass ethanol and municipal solid waste loan guarantee program

(1) In general — Funds may be provided for the cost (as defined in the Federal Credit Reform Act of 1990 (2 U.S.C. 661 *et seq.*)) of loan guarantees issued under title XIV of the Energy Policy Act to carry out commercial demonstration projects for celluosic biomass and sucrose-derived ethanol.

(2) Demonstration projects

(A) In general — The Secretary shall issue loan guarantees under this section to carry out not more than 4 projects to commercially demonstrate the feasibility and viability of producing cellulosic biomass ethanol or sucrose-derived ethanol, including at least 1 project that uses cereal straw as a feedstock and 1 project that uses municipal solid waste as a feedstock.

(B) Design capacity — Each project shall have a design capacity to produce at least 30,000,000 gallons of cellulosic biomass ethanol each year.

(3) Applicant assurances — An applicant for a loan guarantee under this section shall provide assurances, satisfactory to the Secretary, that—

(A) the project design has been validated through the operation of a continuous process facility with a cumulative output of at least 50,000 gallons of ethanol;

(B) the project has been subject to a full technical review;

(C) the project is covered by adequate project performance guarantees;

(D) the project, with the loan guarantee, is economically viable; and

(E) there is a reasonable assurance of repayment of the guaranteed loan.

(4) Limitations

(A) Maximum guarantee — Except as provided in subparagraph (B), a loan guarantee under this section may be issued for up to 80 percent of the estimated cost of a project, but may not exceed $250,000,000 for a project.

(B) Additional guarantees

(i) In general — The Secretary may issue additional loan guarantees for a project to cover up to 80 percent of the excess of actual project cost over estimated project cost but not to exceed 15 percent of the amount of the original guarantee.

(ii) Principal and interest — Subject to subparagraph (A), the Secretary shall guarantee 100 percent of the principal and interest of a loan made under subparagraph (A).

(5) Equity contributions — To be eligible for a loan guarantee under this section, an applicant for the loan guarantee shall have binding commitments from equity investors to provide an initial equity contribution of at least 20 percent of the total project cost.

(6) Insufficient amounts — If the amount made available to carry out this section is insufficient to allow the Secretary to make loan guarantees for 3 projects described in subsection (b) of this section, the Secretary shall issue loan guarantees for one or more qualifying projects under this section in the order in which the applications for the projects are received by the Secretary.

(7) Approval — An application for a loan guarantee under this section shall be approved or disapproved by the Secretary not later than 90 days after the application is received by the Secretary.

(c) Authorization of appropriations for resource center — There is authorized to be appropriated, for a resource center to further develop bioconversion technology using low-cost biomass for the production of ethanol at the Center for Biomass-Based Energy at the Mississippi State University and the Oklahoma State University, $4,000,000 for each of fiscal years 2005 through 2007.

(d) Renewable fuel production research and development grants

(1) In general — The Administrator shall provide grants for the research into, and development and implementation of, renewable fuel production technologies in RFG States with low rates of ethanol production, including low rates of production of cellulosic biomass ethanol.

(2) Eligibility

(A) In general — The entities eligible to receive a grant under this subsection are academic institutions in RFG States, and consortia made up of combinations of academic institutions, industry, State government agencies, or local government agencies in RFG States, that have proven experience and capabilities with relevant technologies.

(B) Application — To be eligible to receive a grant under this subsection, an eligible entity shall submit to the Administrator an application in such manner and form, and accompanied by such information, as the Administrator may specify.

(3) Authorization of appropriations — There is authorized to be appropriated to carry out this subsection $25,000,000 for each of fiscal years 2006 through 2010.

(e) Cellulosic biomass ethanol conversion assistance

(1) In general — The Secretary may provide grants to merchant producers of cellulosic biomass ethanol in the United States to assist the producers in building eligible production facilities described in paragraph (2) for the production of cellulosic biomass ethanol.

(2) Eligible production facilities — A production facility shall be eligible to receive a grant under this subsection if the production facility —

(A) is located in the United States; and

(B) uses cellulosic biomass feedstocks derived from agricultural residues or municipal solid waste.

(3) Authorization of appropriations — There is authorized to be appropriated to carry out this subsection—

(A) $250,000,000 for fiscal year 2006; and

(B) $400,000,000 for fiscal year 2007.

§7547. Nonroad engines and vehicles
[CAA §213]

(a) Emissions standards

(1) The Administrator shall conduct a study of emissions from nonroad engines and nonroad vehicles (other than locomotives or engines used in locomotives) to determine if such emissions cause, or significantly contribute to, air pollution which may reasonably be anticipated to endanger public health or welfare. Such study shall be completed within 12 months of November 15, 1990.

(2) After notice and opportunity for public hearing, the Administrator shall determine within 12 months after completion of the study under paragraph (1), based upon the results of such study, whether emissions of carbon monoxide, oxides of nitrogen, and volatile organic compounds from new and existing nonroad engines or nonroad vehicles (other than locomotives or engines used in locomotives) are significant contributors to ozone or carbon monoxide concentrations in more than 1 area which has failed to attain the national ambient air quality standards for ozone or carbon monoxide. Such determination shall be included in the regulations under paragraph (3).

(3) If the Administrator makes an affirmative determination under paragraph (2) the Administrator shall, within 12 months after completion of the study under paragraph (1), promulgate (and from time to time revise) regulations containing standards applicable to emissions from those classes or categories of new nonroad engines and new nonroad vehicles (other than locomotives or engines used in locomotives) which in the Administrator's judgment cause, or contribute to, such air pollution. Such standards shall achieve the greatest degree of emission reduction achievable through the application of technology which the Administrator determines will be available for the engines or vehicles to which such standards apply, giving appropriate consideration to the cost of applying such technology within the period of time available to manufacturers and to noise, energy, and safety factors associated with the application of such technology. In determining what degree of reduction will be available, the Administrator shall first consider standards equivalent in stringency to standards for comparable motor vehicles or engines (if any) regulated under section 7521 of this title, taking into account the technological feasibility, costs, safety, noise, and energy factors associated with achieving, as appropriate, standards of such stringency and lead time. The regulations shall apply to the useful life of the engines or vehicles (as determined by the Administrator).

(4) If the Administrator determines that any emissions not referred to in paragraph (2) from new nonroad engines or vehicles significantly contribute to air pollution which may reasonably be anticipated to endanger public health or welfare, the Administrator may promulgate

(and from time to time revise) such regulations as the Administrator deems appropriate containing standards applicable to emissions from those classes or categories of new nonroad engines and new nonroad vehicles (other than locomotives or engines used in locomotives) which in the Administrator's judgment cause, or contribute to, such air pollution, taking into account costs, noise, safety, and energy factors associated with the application of technology which the Administrator determines will be available for the engines and vehicles to which such standards apply. The regulations shall apply to the useful life of the engines or vehicles (as determined by the Administrator).

(5) Within 5 years after November 15, 1990, the Administrator shall promulgate regulations containing standards applicable to emissions from new locomotives and new engines used in locomotives. Such standards shall achieve the greatest degree of emission reduction achievable through the application of technology which the Administrator determines will be available for the locomotives or engines to which such standards apply, giving appropriate consideration to the cost of applying such technology within the period of time available to manufacturers and to noise, energy, and safety factors associated with the application of such technology.

(b) Effective date — Standards under this section shall take effect at the earliest possible date considering the lead time necessary to permit the development and application of the requisite technology, giving appropriate consideration to the cost of compliance within such period and energy and safety.

(c) Safe controls — Effective with respect to new engines or vehicles to which standards under this section apply, no emission control device, system, or element of design shall be used in such a new nonroad engine or new nonroad vehicle for purposes of complying with such standards if such device, system, or element of design will cause or contribute to an unreasonable risk to public health, welfare, or safety in its operation or function. In determining whether an unreasonable risk exists, the Administrator shall consider factors including those described in section 7521(a)(4)(B) of this title.

(d) Enforcement — The standards under this section shall be subject to sections 7525, 7541, 7542, and 7543 of this title, with such modifications of the applicable regulations implementing such sections as the Administrator deems appropriate, and shall be enforced in the same manner as standards prescribed under section 7521 of this title. The Administrator shall revise or promulgate regulations as may be necessary to determine compliance with, and enforce, standards in effect under this section.

§7548. Study of particulate emissions from motor vehicles
[CAA §214]
(a) Study and analysis

(1) The Administrator shall conduct a study concerning the effects on health and welfare of particulate emissions from motor vehicles or motor vehicle engines to which section 7521 of this title applies. Such study shall characterize and quantify such emissions and analyze the relationship of such emissions to various fuels and fuel additives.

(2) The study shall also include an analysis of particulate emissions from mobile sources which are not related to engine emissions (including, but not limited to tire debris, and asbestos from brake lining).

(b) Report to Congress — The Administrator shall report to the Congress the findings and results of the study conducted under subsection (a) not later than two years after August 7, 1977. Such report shall also include recommendations for standards or methods to regulate particulate emissions described in paragraph (2) of subsection (a) of this section.

§7549. High altitude performance adjustments
[CAA §215]
(a) Instruction of the manufacturer

(1) Any action taken with respect to any element of design installed on or in a motor vehicle or motor vehicle engine in compliance with regulations under this title (including any alteration or adjustment of such element), shall be treated as not in violation of section 7522(a) of this title if such action is performed in accordance with high altitude adjustment instructions provided by the manufacturer under subsection (b) of this section and approved by the Administrator.

(2) If the Administrator finds that adjustments or modifications made pursuant to instructions of the manufacturer under paragraph (1) will not insure emission control performance with respect to each standard under section 7521 of this title at least equivalent to that which would result if no such adjustments or modifications were made, he shall disapprove such instructions. Such findings shall be based upon minimum engineering evaluations consistent with good engineering practice.

(b) Regulations

(1) Instructions respecting each class or category of vehicles or engines to which this title applies providing for such vehicle and engine adjustments and modifications as may be necessary to insure emission control performance at different altitudes shall be submitted by the manufacturer to the Administrator pursuant to regulations promulgated by the Administrator.

(2) Any knowing violation by a manufacturer of requirements of the Administrator under paragraph (1) shall be treated as a violation by such manufacturer of section 7522(a)(3) of this title for purposes of the penalties contained in section 7524 of this title.

(3) Such instruction shall provide, in addition to other adjustments, for adjustments for vehicles moving from high altitude areas to low altitude areas after the initial registration of such vehicles.

(c) Manufacturer parts — No instructions under this section respecting adjustments or modifications may require the use of any manufacturer parts (as defined in section 7522(a) of this title) unless the manufacturer demonstrates to the satisfaction of the Administrator that the use of such manufacturer parts is necessary to insure emission control performance.

(d) State inspection and maintenance programs — Before January 1, 1981 the authority provided by this section shall be available in any high altitude State (as determined under regulations of the Administrator under regulations promulgated before August 7, 1977) but after December 31, 1980, such authority shall be available only in any such State in which an inspection and maintenance program for the testing of motor vehicle emissions has been instituted for the portions of the State where any national ambient air quality standard for auto-related pollutants has not been attained.

(e) High altitude testing

(1) The Administrator shall promptly establish at least one testing center (in addition to the testing centers existing on November 15, 1990) located at a site that represents high altitude conditions, to ascertain in a reasonable manner whether, when in actual use throughout their useful life (as determined under section 7521(d) of this title), each class or category of vehicle and engines to which regulations under section 7521 of this title apply conforms to the emissions standards established by such regulations. For purposes of this subsection, the term "high altitude conditions" refers to high altitude as defined in regulations of the Administrator in effect as of November 15, 1990.

(2) The Administrator, in cooperation with the Secretary of Energy and the Administrator of the Urban Mass Transportation Administration, and such other agencies as the Administrator deems appropriate, shall establish a research and technology assessment center to provide for the development and evaluation of less-polluting heavy-duty engines and fuels for use in buses, heavy-duty trucks, and non-road engines and vehicles, which shall be located at a high-altitude site that represents high-altitude conditions. In establishing and funding such a center, the Administrator shall give preference to proposals which provide for local cost-sharing of facilities and recovery of costs of operation through utilization of such facility for the purposes of this section.

(3) The Administrator shall designate at least one center at high-altitude conditions to provide research on after-market emission components, dual-fueled vehicles and conversion kits, the effects of tampering on emissions equipment, testing of alternate fuels and conversion kits, and the development of curricula, training courses, and materials to maximize the effectiveness of inspection and maintenance programs as they relate to promoting effective control of vehicle emissions at high-altitude elevations. Preference shall be given to existing vehicle emissions testing and research centers that have established reputations for vehicle emissions research and development and training, and that possess in-house Federal Test Procedure capacity.

§7550. Definitions
[CAA §216]

As used in this part —

(1) The term "manufacturer" as used in sections 7521, 7522, 7525, 7541, and 7542 of this title means any person engaged in the manufacturing or assembling of new motor vehicles, new motor vehicle engines, new non-road vehicles or new nonroad engines, or importing such vehicles or engines for resale, or who acts for and is under the control of any such person in connection with the distribution of new motor vehicles, new motor vehicle engines, new nonroad vehicles or new nonroad engines, but shall not include any dealer with respect to new motor vehicles, new motor vehicle engines, new nonroad vehicles or new nonroad engines received by him in commerce.

(2) The term "motor vehicle" means any self-propelled vehicle designed for transporting persons or property on a street or highway.

(3) Except with respect to vehicles or engines imported or offered for importation, the term "new motor vehicle" means a motor vehicle the equitable or legal title to which has never been transferred to an ultimate purchaser; and the term "new motor vehicle engine" means an engine in a new motor vehicle or a motor vehicle engine the equitable or legal title to which has never been transferred to the ultimate purchaser; and with respect to imported vehicles or engines, such terms mean a motor vehicle and engine, respectively, manufactured after the effective date of a regulation issued under section 7521 of this title which is applicable to such vehicle or engine (or which would be applicable to such vehicle or engine had it been manufactured for importation into the United States).

(4) The term "dealer" means any person who is engaged in the sale or the distribution of new

motor vehicles or new motor vehicle engines to the ultimate purchaser.

(5) The term "ultimate purchaser" means, with respect to any new motor vehicle or new motor vehicle engine, the first person who in good faith purchases such new motor vehicle or new engine for purposes other than resale.

(6) The term "commerce" means (A) commerce between any place in any State and any place outside thereof; and (B) commerce wholly within the District of Columbia.

(7) Vehicle curb weight, gross vehicle weight rating, light-duty truck, light-duty vehicle, and loaded vehicle weight — The terms "vehicle curb weight", "gross vehicle weight rating" (GVWR), "light-duty truck" (LDT), light-duty vehicle, and "loaded vehicle weight" (LVW) have the meaning provided in regulations promulgated by the Administrator and in effect as of November 15, 1990. The abbreviations in parentheses corresponding to any term referred to in this paragraph shall have the same meaning as the corresponding term.

(8) Test weight — The term "test weight" and the abbreviation "tw" mean the vehicle curb weight added to the gross vehicle weight rating (gvwr) and divided by 2.

(9) Motor vehicle or engine part manufacturer — The term "motor vehicle or engine part manufacturer" as used in sections 7541 and 7542 of this title means any person engaged in the manufacturing, assembling or rebuilding of any device, system, part, component or element of design which is installed in or on motor vehicles or motor vehicle engines.

(10) Nonroad engine — The term "nonroad engine" means an internal combustion engine (including the fuel system) that is not used in a motor vehicle or a vehicle used solely for competition, or that is not subject to standards promulgated under section 7411 of this title or section 7521 of this title.

(11) Nonroad vehicle — The term "nonroad vehicle" means a vehicle that is powered by a nonroad engine and that is not a motor vehicle or a vehicle used solely for competition.

§7552. Motor vehicle compliance program fees
[CAA §217]

(a) Fee collection — Consistent with section 9701 of Title 31, the Administrator may promulgate (and from time to time revise) regulations establishing fees to recover all reasonable costs to the Administrator associated with —

(1) new vehicle or engine certification under section 7525(a) of this title or part C of this subchapter,

(2) new vehicle or engine compliance monitoring and testing under section 7525(b) of this title or part C, of this subchapter, and

(3) in-use vehicle or engine compliance monitoring and testing under section 7541(c) of this title or part C of this subchapter.

The Administrator may establish for all foreign and domestic manufacturers a fee schedule based on such factors as the Administrator finds appropriate and equitable and nondiscriminatory, including the number of vehicles or engines produced under a certificate of conformity. In the case of heavy-duty engine and vehicle manufacturers, such fees shall not exceed a reasonable amount to recover an appropriate portion of such reasonable costs.

(b) Special Treasury fund — Any fees collected under this section shall be deposited in a special fund in the United States Treasury for licensing and other services which thereafter shall be available for appropriation, to remain available until expended, to carry out the Agency's activities for which the fees were collected.

(c) Limitation on fund use — Moneys in the special fund referred to in subsection (b) shall not be used until after the first fiscal year commencing after the first July 1 when fees are paid into the fund.

(d) Administrator's testing authority — Nothing in this subsection shall be construed to limit the Administrator's authority to require manufacturer or confirmatory testing as provided in this part.

§7553. Prohibition on production of engines requiring leaded gasoline
[CAA §218]

The Administrator shall promulgate regulations applicable to motor vehicle engines and nonroad engines manufactured after model year 1992 that prohibit the manufacture, sale, or introduction into commerce of any engine that requires leaded gasoline.

§7554. Urban bus standards
[CAA §219]

(a) Standards for model years after 1993 — Not later than January 1, 1992, the Administrator shall promulgate regulations under section 7521(a) of this title applicable to urban buses for the model year 1994 and thereafter. Such standards shall be based on the best technology that can reasonably be anticipated to be available at the time such measures are to be implemented, taking costs, safety, energy, lead time, and other relevant factors into account. Such regulations shall require that such urban buses comply with the provisions of subsection (b) of this section (and subsection (c) of this subsection, if applicable) in addition to compliance with the standards applicable under section 7521(a) of this title for heavy-duty vehicles of the same type and model year.

(b) PM standard

(1) 50 percent reduction — The standards under section 7521(a) of this title applicable to urban buses shall require that, effective for the model year 1994 and thereafter, emissions of particulate matter (PM) from urban buses shall not exceed 50 percent of the emissions of particulate matter (PM) allowed under the emission standard applicable under section 7521(a) of this title as of November 15, 1990, for particulate matter (PM) in the case of heavy-duty diesel vehicles and engines manufactured in the model year 1994.

(2) Revised reduction — The Administrator shall increase the level of emissions of particulate matter allowed under the standard referred to in paragraph (1) if the Administrator determines that the 50 percent reduction referred to in paragraph (1) is not technologically achievable, taking into account durability, costs, lead time, safety, and other relevant factors. The Administrator may not increase such level of emissions above 70 percent of the emissions of particulate matter (PM) allowed under the emission standard applicable under section 7521(a) as of November 15, 1990 for particulate matter (PM) in the case of heavy-duty diesel vehicles and engines manufactured in the model year 1994.

(3) Determination as part of rule — As part of the rulemaking under subsection (a), the Administrator shall make a determination as to whether the 50 percent reduction referred to in paragraph (1) is technologically achievable, taking into account durability, costs, lead time, safety, and other relevant factors.

(c) Low-polluting fuel requirement

(1) Annual testing — Beginning with model year 1994 buses, the Administrator shall conduct annual tests of a representative sample of operating urban buses subject to the particulate matter (PM) standard applicable pursuant to subsection (b) to determine whether such buses comply with such standard in use over their full useful life.

(2) Promulgation of additional low-polluting fuel requirement

(A) If the Administrator determines, based on the testing under paragraph (1), that urban buses subject to the particulate matter (PM) standard applicable pursuant to subsection (b) do not comply with such standard in use over their full useful life, he shall revise the standards applicable to such buses to require (in addition to compliance with the PM standard applicable pursuant to subsection (b)) that all new urban buses purchased or placed into service by owners or operators of urban buses in all metropolitan statistical areas or consolidated metropolitan statistical areas with a 1980 population of 750,000 or more shall be capable of operating, and shall be exclusively operated, on low-polluting fuels. The Administrator shall establish the pass-fail rate for purposes of testing under this subparagraph.

(B) The Administrator shall promulgate a schedule phasing in any low-polluting fuel requirement established pursuant to this paragraph to an increasing percentage of new urban buses purchased or placed into service in each of the first 5 model years commencing 3 years after the determination under subparagraph (A). Under such schedule 100 percent of new urban buses placed into service in the fifth model year commencing 3 years after the determination under subparagraph (A) shall comply with the low-polluting fuel requirement established pursuant to this paragraph.

(C) The Administrator may extend the requirements of this paragraph to metropolitan statistical areas or consolidated metropolitan statistical areas with a 1980 population of less than 750,000, if the Administrator determines that a significant benefit to public health could be expected to result from such extension.

(d) Retrofit requirements — Not later than 12 months after November 15, 1990, the Administrator shall promulgate regulations under section 7521(a) of this title requiring that urban buses which —

(1) are operating in areas referred to in subparagraph (A) of subsection (c)(2) (or subparagraph (C) of subsection (c)(2) if the Administrator has taken action under that subparagraph);

(2) were not subject to standards in effect under the regulations under subsection (a); and

(3) have their engines replaced or rebuilt after January 1, 1995,

shall comply with an emissions standard or emissions control technology requirement established by the Administrator in such regulations. Such emissions standard or emissions control technology requirement shall reflect the best retrofit technology and maintenance practices reasonably achievable.

(e) Procedures for administration and enforcement — The Administrator shall establish, within 18 months after November 15, 1990, and in accordance with section 7525(h) of this title, procedures for the administration and enforcement of standards for buses subject to standards under this section, testing procedures, sampling protocols, in-use compliance requirements, and criteria governing evaluation of buses. Procedures for testing (including, but not limited to, certification testing) shall reflect actual operating conditions.

(f) Definitions — For purposes of this section —

(1) Urban bus — The term "urban bus" has the meaning provided under regulations of the Administrator promulgated under section 7521(a) of this title.

(2) Low-polluting fuel — The term "low-polluting fuel" means methanol, ethanol, propane, or natural gas, or any comparably low-polluting fuel. In determining whether a fuel is comparably low-polluting, the Administrator shall consider both the level of emissions of air pollutants from vehicles using the fuel and the contribution of such emissions to ambient levels of air pollutants. For purposes of this paragraph, the term "methanol" includes any fuel which contains at least 85 percent methanol unless the Administrator increases such percentage as he deems appropriate to protect public health and welfare.

PART B — AIRCRAFT EMISSION STANDARDS

§7571. Establishment of standards
[CAA §231]
(a) Study; proposed standards; hearings; issuance of regulations

(1) Within 90 days after December 31, 1970, the Administrator shall commence a study and investigation of emissions of air pollutants from aircraft in order to determine —

(A) the extent to which such emissions affect air quality in air quality control regions throughout the United States, and

(B) the technological feasibility of controlling such emissions.

(2)(A) The Administrator shall, from time to time, issue proposed emission standards applicable to the emission of any air pollutant from any class or classes of aircraft engines which in his judgment causes, or contributes to, air pollution which may reasonably be anticipated to endanger public health or welfare.

(B)(i) The Administrator shall consult with the Administrator of the Federal Aviation Administration on aircraft engine emission standards.

(ii) The Administrator shall not change the aircraft engine emission standards if such change would significantly increase noise and adversely affect safety.

(3) The Administrator shall hold public hearings with respect to such proposed standards. Such hearings shall, to the extent practicable, be held in air quality control regions which are most seriously affected by aircraft emissions. Within 90 days after the issuance of such proposed regulations, he shall issue such regulation with such modifications as he deems appropriate. Such regulations may be revised from time to time.

(b) Effective date of regulations — Any regulation prescribed under this section (and any revision thereof) shall take effect after such period as the Administrator finds necessary (after consultation with the Secretary of Transportation) to permit the development and application of the requisite technology, giving appropriate consideration to the cost of compliance within such period.

(c) Regulations which create hazards to aircraft safety — Any regulations in effect under this section on August 7, 1977 or proposed or promulgated thereafter, or amendments thereto, with respect to aircraft shall not apply if disapproved by the President, after notice and opportunity for public hearing, on the basis of a finding by the Secretary of Transportation that any such regulation would create a hazard to aircraft safety. Any such finding shall include a reasonably specific statement of the basis upon which the finding was made.

§7572. Enforcement of standards
[CAA §232]
(a) Regulations to insure compliance with standards — The Secretary of Transportation, after consultation with the Administrator, shall prescribe regulations to insure compliance with all standards prescribed under section 7571 of this title by the Administrator. The regulations of the Secretary of Transportation shall include provisions making such standards applicable in the issuance, amendment, modification, suspension, or revocation of any certificate authorized by the Federal Aviation Act or the Department of Transportation Act. Such Secretary shall insure that all necessary inspections are accomplished, and may execute any power or duty vested in him by any other provision of law in the execution of all powers and duties vested in him under this section.

(b) Notice and appeal rights — In any action to amend, modify, suspend, or revoke a certificate in which violation of an emission standard prescribed under section 7571 of this title or of a regulation prescribed under subsection (a) of this section is at issue, the certificate holder shall have the same notice and appeal rights as are prescribed for such holders in the Federal Aviation Act of 1958 or the Department of Transportation Act, except that in any appeal to the National Transportation Safety Board, the Board may amend, modify, or revoke the order of the Secretary of Transportation only if it finds no violation of such standard or regulation and that such amendment, modification, or revocation is consistent with safety in air transportation.

§7573. State standards and controls
[CAA §233]

No State or political subdivision thereof may adopt or attempt to enforce any standard respecting emissions of any air pollutant from any aircraft or engine thereof unless such standard is identical to a standard applicable to such aircraft under this part.

§7574. Definitions
[CAA §234]

Terms used in this part (other than Administrator) shall have the same meaning as such terms have under section 101 of the Federal Aviation Act of 1958.

PART C — CLEAN FUEL VEHICLES

§7581. Definitions
[CAA §241]

For purposes of this part —

(1) Terms defined in part A — The definitions applicable to part A under section 7550 of this title shall also apply for purposes of this part.

(2) Clean alternative fuel — The term "clean alternative fuel" means any fuel (including methanol, ethanol, or other alcohols (including any mixture thereof containing 85 percent or more by volume of such alcohol with gasoline or other fuels), reformulated gasoline, diesel, natural gas, liquefied petroleum gas, and hydrogen) or power source (including electricity) used in a clean-fuel vehicle that complies with the standards and requirements applicable to such vehicle under this title when using such fuel or power source. In the case of any flexible fuel vehicle or dual fuel vehicle, the term "clean alternative fuel" means only a fuel with respect to which such vehicle was certified as a clean-fuel vehicle meeting the standards applicable to clean-fuel vehicles under section 7583(d)(2) of this title when operating on clean alternative fuel (or any CARB standards which replaces such standards pursuant to section 7583(e) of this title).

(3) NMOG — The term nonmethane organic gas ("NMOG") means the sum of nonoxygenated and oxygenated hydrocarbons contained in a gas sample, including, at a minimum, all oxygenated organic gases containing 5 or fewer carbon atoms (i.e., aldehydes, ketones, alcohols, ethers, etc.), and all known alkanes, alkenes, alkynes, and aromatics containing 12 or fewer carbon atoms. To demonstrate compliance with a NMOG standard, NMOG emissions shall be measured in accordance with the "California Non-Methane Organic Gas Test Procedures". In the case of vehicles using fuels other than base gasoline, the level of NMOG emissions shall be adjusted based on the reactivity of the emissions relative to vehicles using base gasoline.

(4) Base gasoline — The term "base gasoline" means gasoline which meets the following specifications:

SPECIFICATIONS OF BASE GASOLINE USED AS BASIS FOR REACTIVITY READJUSTMENT:

API gravity	57.8
Sulfur, ppm	317
Color	Purple
Benzene, vol. %	1.35
Reid vapor pressure	8.7
Drivability	1195
Antiknock index	87.3
Distillation, D-86° F	
IBP	92
10%	126
50%	219
90%	327
EP	414
Hydrocarbon Type, Vol. % FIA:	
Aromatics	30.9
Olefins	8.2
Saturates	60.9

The Administrator shall modify the definitions of NMOG, base gasoline, and the methods for making reactivity adjustments, to conform to the definitions and method used in California under the Low-Emission Vehicle and Clean Fuel Regulations of the California Air Resources Board, so long as the California definitions are, in the aggregate, at least as protective of public health and welfare as the definitions in this section.

(5) Covered fleet — The term "covered fleet" means 10 or more motor vehicles which are owned or operated by a single person. In determining the number of vehicles owned or operated by a single person for purposes of this paragraph, all motor vehicles owned or operated, leased or otherwise controlled by such person, by any person who controls such person, by any person controlled by such person, and by any person under common control with such person shall be treated as owned by such person. The term "covered fleet" shall not include motor vehicles held for lease or rental to the general public, motor vehicles held for sale by motor vehicle dealers (including demonstration vehicles), motor vehicles used for motor vehicle manufacturer product evaluations or tests, law enforcement and other emergency vehicles, or nonroad vehicles (including farm and construction vehicles).

(6) Covered fleet vehicle — The term "covered fleet vehicle" means only a motor vehicle which is —

(i) in a vehicle class for which standards are applicable under this part; and

(ii) in a covered fleet which is centrally fueled (or capable of being centrally fueled).

No vehicle which under normal operations is garaged at a personal residence at night shall be considered to be a vehicle which is capable of being centrally fueled within the meaning of this paragraph.

(7) Clean-fuel vehicle — The term "clean-fuel vehicle" means a vehicle in a class or category of vehicles which has been certified to meet for any model year the clean-fuel vehicle standards applicable under this part for that model year to clean-fuel vehicles in that class or category.

§7582. Requirements applicable to clean-fuel vehicles
[CAA §242]

(a) Promulgation of standards — Not later than 24 months after November 15, 1990, the Administrator shall promulgate regulations under this part containing clean-fuel vehicle standards for the clean-fuel vehicles specified in this part.

(b) Other requirements — Clean-fuel vehicles of up to 8,500 gvwr subject to standards set forth in this part shall comply with all motor vehicle requirements of this subchapter (such as requirements relating to on-board diagnostics, evaporative emissions, etc.) which are applicable to conventional gasoline-fueled vehicles of the same category and model year, except as provided in section 7584 of this title with respect to administration and enforcement, and except to the extent that any such requirement is in conflict with the provisions of this part. Clean-fuel vehicles of 8,500 gvwr or greater subject to standards set forth in this part shall comply with all requirements of this title which are applicable in the case of conventional gasoline-fueled or diesel fueled vehicles of the same category and model year, except as provided in section 244 with respect to administration and enforcement, and except to the extent that any such requirement is in conflict with the provisions of this part.

(c) In-use useful life and testing

(1) In the case of light-duty vehicles and light-duty trucks up to 6,000 lbs gvwr, the useful life for purposes of determining in-use compliance with the standards under section 7583 of this title shall be —

(A) a period of 5 years or 50,000 miles (or the equivalent) whichever first occurs, in the case of standards applicable for purposes of certification at 50,000 miles; and

(B) a period of 10 years or 100,000 miles (or the equivalent) whichever first occurs, in the case of standards applicable for purposes of certification at 100,000 miles, except that in-use testing shall not be done for a period beyond 7 years or 75,000 miles (or the equivalent) whichever first occurs.

(2) In the case of light-duty trucks of more than 6,000 lbs gvwr, the useful life for purposes of determining in-use compliance with the standards under section 7583 of this title shall be —

(A) a period of 5 years or 50,000 miles (or the equivalent) whichever first occurs in the case of standards applicable for purposes of certification at 50,000 miles; and

(B) a period of 11 years or 120,000 miles (or the equivalent) whichever first occurs in the case of standards applicable for purposes of certification at 120,000 miles, except that in-use testing shall not be done for a period beyond 7 years or 90,000 miles (or the equivalent) whichever first occurs.

§7583. Standards for light-duty clean-fuel vehicles and certain light-duty trucks
[CAA §243]

(a) Exhaust standards for light-duty vehicles and certain light-duty trucks — The standards set forth in this subsection shall apply in the case of clean-fuel vehicles which are light-duty trucks of up to 6,000 lbs. gross vehicle weight rating (gvwr) (but not including light-duty trucks of more than 3,750 lbs. loaded vehicle weight (lvw)) or light-duty vehicles:

(1) Phase I — Beginning with model year 1996, for the air pollutants specified in the following table, the clean-fuel vehicle standards under this section shall provide that vehicle exhaust emissions shall not exceed the levels specified in the following table:

PHASE I CLEAN FUEL VEHICLE EMISSION
STANDARDS FOR LIGHT-DUTY TRUCKS
OF UP TO 3,750 LBS. LVW AND UP TO 6,000
LBS. GVWR AND LIGHT-DUTY VEHICLES

Pollutant	NMOG	CO	NOx	PM	HCHO (formal-dehyde)
50,000 mile standard	0.125	3.4	0.4	. . .	0.015
100,000 mile standard	0.156	4.2	0.6	0.08	0.018

Standards are expressed in grams per mile (gpm)
*Standards for particulates (PM) shall apply only to diesel-fueled vehicles.

In the case of the 50,000 mile standards and the 100,000 mile standards, for purposes of certification, the applicable useful life shall be 50,000 miles or 100,000 miles, respectively.

(2) Phase II

Beginning with model year 2001, for air pollutants specified in the following table, the clean-fuel vehicle standards under this section shall provide that vehicle exhaust emissions shall not exceed the levels specified in the following table.

PHASE II CLEAN FUEL VEHICLE EMISSION
STANDARDS FOR LIGHT-DUTY TRUCKS
OF UP TO 3,750 LBS. LVW AND UP TO 6,000
LBS. GVWR AND LIGHT-DUTY VEHICLES

Pollutant	NMOG	CO	NOx	PM	HCHO (formaldehyde)
50,000 mile standard	0.075	3.4	0.2	. . .	0.015
100,000 mile standard	0.090	4.2	0.3	0.08	0.018

Standards are expressed in grams per mile (gpm)
*Standards for particulates (PM) shall apply only to diesel-fueled vehicles.

In the case of the 50,000 mile standards and the 100,000 mile standards, for purposes of certification, the applicable useful life shall be 50,000 miles or 100,000 miles, respectively.

(b) Exhaust standards for light-duty trucks of more than 3,750 lbs. LVW and up to 5,750 lbs. LVW and up to 6,000 lbs. GVWR — The standards set forth in this paragraph shall apply in the case of clean-fuel vehicles which are light-duty trucks of more than 3,750 lbs. loaded vehicle weight (LVW) but not more than 5,750 lbs. LVW and not more than 6,000 lbs. gross weight rating (GVWR):

(1) Phase I — Beginning with model year 1996, for the air pollutants specified in the following table, the clean-fuel vehicle standards under this section shall provide that vehicle exhaust emissions shall not exceed the levels specified in the following table.

PHASE I CLEAN FUEL VEHICLE EMISSION
STANDARDS FOR LIGHT-DUTY TRUCKS
OF MORE THAN 3,750 LBS. AND UP TO 5,750 LBS.
LVW AND UP TO 6,000 LBS. GVWR

Pollutant	NMOG	CO	NOx	PM*	HCHO (formaldehyde)
50,000 mile standard	0.160	4.4	0.7	. . .	0.018
100,000 mile standard	0.200	5.5	0.9	0.08	0.023

Standards are expressed in grams per mile (gpm)
*Standards for particulates (PM) shall apply only to diesel-fueled vehicles.

In the case of the 50,000 mile standards and the 100,000 mile standards, for purposes of certification, the applicable useful life shall be 50,000 miles or 100,000 miles, respectively.

(2) Phase II — Beginning with model year 2001, for the air pollutants specified in the following table, the clean-fuel vehicle standards under this section shall provide that vehicle exhaust emissions shall not exceed the levels specified in the following table.

PHASE II CLEAN FUEL VEHICLE EMISSION
STANDARDS FOR LIGHT-DUTY TRUCKS
OF MORE THAN 3,750 LBS. LVW AND UP TO 5,750 LBS.
LVW AND UP TO 6,000 LBS. GVWR

Pollutant	NMOG	CO	NOx	PM	HCHO (formaldehyde)
50,000 mile standard	0.100	4.4	0.4	. . .	0.018
100,000 mile standard	0.130	5.5	0.5	0.08	0.023

Standards are expressed in grams per mile (gpm)
*Standards for particulates (PM) shall apply only to diesel-fueled vehicles.

In the case of the 50,000 mile standards and the 100,000 mile standards, for purposes of certification, the applicable useful life shall be 50,000 miles or 100,000 miles, respectively.

(c) Exhaust standards for light-duty trucks greater than 6,000 lbs. GVWR — The standards set forth in this subsection shall apply in the case of clean-fuel vehicles which are light-duty trucks of more than 6,000 lbs. gross weight rating (GVWR) and less than or equal to 8,500 lbs. GVWR, beginning with model year 1998. For the air pollutants specified in the following table, the clean fuel vehicle standards under this section shall provide that vehicle exhaust emissions of vehicles within the test weight categories specified in the following table shall not exceed the levels specified in such table.

CLEAN FUEL VEHICLE EMISSION
STANDARDS FOR LIGHT-DUTY TRUCKS
GREATER THAN 6,000 LBS. GVWR

Test Weight Category: Up to 3,750 lbs. tw

Pollutant	NMOG	CO	NOx	PM	HCHO (formaldehyde)
50,000 mile standard	0.125	3.4	0.4**	. . .	0.015
100,000 mile standard	0.180	5.0	0.6	0.08	0.022

Test Weight Category: Above 3,750 but not above 5,750 lbs. tw

Pollutant	NMOG	CO	NOx	PM*	HCHO (formaldehyde)
50,000 mile standard	0.160	4.4	0.7**	. . .	0.018
100,000 mile standard	0.230	6.4	1.0	0.10	0.027

Test Weight Category: Above 5,750
but not above 8,500 lbs. gvwr

Pollutant	NMOG	CO	NOx	PM	HCHO (formaldehyde)
50,000 mile standard	0.195	5.0	1.1**	...	0.022
100,000 mile standard	0.280	7.3	1.5	0.12*	0.032

Standards are expressed in grams per mile (gpm)
*Standards for particulates (PM) shall apply only to diesel-fueled vehicles.
**Standard not applicable to diesel-fueled vehicles.
For the 50,000 mile standards and the 120,000 mile standards set forth in the table, the applicable useful life for purposes of certification shall be 50,000 miles or 120,000 miles, respectively.

(d) Flexible and dual-fuel vehicles

(1) In general — The Administrator shall establish standards and requirements under this section for the model year 1996 and thereafter for vehicles weighing not more than 8,500 lbs. gvwr which are capable of operating on more than one fuel. Such standards shall require that such vehicles meet the exhaust standards applicable under subsection (a), (b), and (c) for CO, NOx , and HCHO, and if appropriate, PM for single-fuel vehicles of the same vehicle category and model year.

(2) Exhaust NMOG standard for operation on clean alternative fuel — In addition to standards for the pollutants referred to in paragraph (1), the standards established under paragraph (1) shall require that vehicle exhaust emissions of NMOG not exceed the levels (expressed in grams per mile) specified in the tables below when the vehicle is operated on the clean alternative fuel for which such vehicle is certified:

NMOG STANDARDS FOR FLEXIBLE- AND
DUAL-FUELED VEHICLES WHEN OPERATING ON
CLEAN ALTERNATIVE FUEL

Light-duty Trucks up to 6,000 lbs.
GVWR and Light-duty vehicles

Vehicle Type	Column A (50,000 mi.) Standard (gpm)	Column B (100,000 mi.) Standard (gpm)
Beginning MY 1996:		
LDT's (0-3.750 lbs. LVW) and light-duty vehicles	0.125	0.156
LDT's (3,751-5.750 lbs. LVW)	0.160	0.200
Beginning MY 2001:		
LDT's (0-3.750 lbs. LVW) and light-duty vehicles	0.075	0.090
LDT's (3,751-5.750 lbs. LVW)	0.100	0.130

For standards under column A, for purposes of certification under section 7525 of this title, the applicable useful life shall be 50,000 miles.
For standards under column B, for purposes of certification under section 7525 of this title, the applicable useful life shall be 100,000 miles.

Light-duty Trucks more than 6,000 lbs. GVWR

Vehicle Type	Column A (50,000 mi.) Standard (gpm)	Column B (100,000 mi.) Standard (gpm)
Beginning MY 1998:		
LDT's (0-3.750 lbs. TW)	0.125	0.180
LDT's (3,751-5.750 lbs. TW)	0.160	0.230
LDT's (above 5,750 lbs. TW)	0.195	0.280

For standards under column A, for purposes of certification under section 7525 of this title, the applicable useful life shall be 50,000 miles.
For standards under column B, for purposes of certification under section 7525 of this title, the applicable useful life shall be 120,000 miles.

(3) NMOG standard for operation on conventional fuel — In addition to the standards referred to in paragraph (1), the standards established under paragraph (1) shall require that vehicle exhaust emissions of NMOG not exceed the levels (expressed in grams per mile) specified in the tables below:

NMOG STANDARDS FOR FLEXIBLE- AND
DUAL-FUELED VEHICLES WHEN OPERATING ON
CONVENTIONAL FUEL

Light-duty Trucks of up to 6,000 lbs.
GVWR and Light-duty vehicles

Vehicle Type	Column A (50,000 mi.) Standard (gpm)	Column B (100,000 mi.) Standard (gpm)
Beginning MY 1996:		
LDT's (0-3.750 lbs. LVW) and light-duty vehicles	0.25	0.31
LDT's (3,751-5.750 lbs. LVW)	0.32	0.40
Beginning MY 2001:		
LDT's (0-3.750 lbs. LVW) and light-duty vehicles	0.125	0.156
LDT's (3,751-5.750 lbs. LVW)	0.160	0.200

For standards under column A, for purposes of certification under section 7525 of this title, the applicable useful life shall be 50,000 miles.
For standards under column B, for purposes of certification under section 7525 of this title, the applicable useful life shall be 100,000 miles.

Light-duty Trucks of up to 6,000 lbs. GVWR

Vehicle Type	Column A (50,000 mi.) Standard (gpm)	Column B (120,000 mi.) Standard (gpm)
Beginning MY 1998:		
LDT's (0-3.750 lbs. TW)	0.25	0.36
LDT's (3,751-5.750 lbs. TW)	0.32	0.46
LDT's (above 5,750 lbs. TW)	0.39	0.56

For standards under column A, for purposes of certification under section 7525 of this title, the applicable useful life shall be 50,000 miles.

For standards under column B, for purposes of certification under section 7525 of this title, the applicable useful life shall be 120,000 miles.

(e) Replacement by CARB standards

(1) Single set of CARB standards — If the State of California promulgates regulations establishing and implementing a single set of standards applicable in California pursuant to a waiver approved under section 7543 of this title to any category of vehicles referred to in subsection (a), (b), (c), or (d) of this section and such set of standards is, in the aggregate, at least as protective of public health and welfare as the otherwise applicable standards set forth in section 7582 of this title and subsection (a), (b), (c), or (d) of this section, such set of California standards shall apply to clean-fuel vehicles in such category in lieu of the standards otherwise applicable under section 7582 of this title and subsection (a), (b), (c), or (d) of this section, as the case may be.

(2) Multiple sets of CARB standards — If the State of California promulgates regulations establishing and implementing several different sets of standards applicable in California pursuant to a waiver approved under section 7543 of this title to any category of vehicles referred to in subsection (a), (b), (c), or (d) of this section and each of such sets of California standards is, in the aggregate, at least as protective of public health and welfare as the otherwise applicable standards set forth in section 7582 of this title and subsection (a), (b), (c), or (d) of this section, such standards shall be treated as "qualifying California standards" for purposes of this paragraph. Where more than one set of qualifying standards are established and adminis-tered by the State of California, the least stringent set of qualifying California standards shall apply to the clean-fuel vehicles concerned in lieu of the standards otherwise applicable to such vehicles under section 7582 of this title and this section.

(f) Less stringent CARB standards — If the

Low-Emission Vehicle and Clean Fuels Regulations of the California Air Resources Board applicable to any category of vehicles referred to in subsection (a), (b), (c), or (d) of this section are modified after November 15, 1990 to provide an emissions standard which is less stringent than the otherwise applicable standard set forth in subsection (a), (b), (c), or (d), or if any ef-fective date contained in such regulations is delayed, such modified standards or such delay (or both, as the case may be) shall apply, for an interim period, in lieu of the standard or effective date otherwise applicable under subsection (a), (b), (c), or (d) to any vehicles covered by such modified standard or delayed effective date. The interim period shall be a period of not more than 2 model years from the effective date otherwise applicable under subsection (a), (b), (c), or (d). After such interim period, the otherwise applicable standard set forth in subsection (a), (b), (c), or (d) shall take ef-fect with respect to such vehicles (unless subsequently replaced under subsection (e) of this section).

(g) Not applicable to heavy-duty vehicles —

Notwithstanding any provision of the Low-Emission Vehicle and Clean Fuels Regulations of the California Air Resources Board nothing in this section shall ap-ply to heavy-duty engines in vehicles of more than 8,500 lbs. GVWR.

§7584. Administration and enforcement as per California standards
[CAA §244]

Where the numerical clean-fuel vehicle standards applicable under this part to vehicles of not more than 8,500 lbs. GVWR are the same as numerical emission standards applicable in California under the Low-Emission Vehicle and Clean Fuels Regulations of the California Air Resources Board ("CARB"), such standards shall be administered and enforced by the Administrator —

(1) in the same manner and with the same flexibility as the State of California administers and enforces corresponding standards applicable under the Low-Emission Vehicle and Clean Fuels Regulations of the California Air Resources Board ("CARB"); and

(2) subject to the same requirements, and utilizing the same interpretations and policy judgments, as are applicable in the case of such CARB standards, including, but not limited to, requirements regarding certification, production-line testing, and in-use compliance,

unless the Administrator determines (in promulgating the rules establishing the clean fuel vehicle program under this section) that any such administration and enforcement would not meet the criteria for a waiver under section 7543 of this title. Nothing in this sec-tion shall apply in the case of standards under section 7585 of this title for heavy-duty vehicles.

§7585. Standards for heavy-duty clean-fuel ve-hicles (GVWR above 8,500 up to 26,000 lbs.)
[CAA §245]

(a) Model years after 1997; combined NOx and NMHC standard — For classes or categories of heavy-duty vehicles or engines manufactured for the model year 1998 or thereafter and having a GVWR greater than 8,500 lbs. and up to 26,000 lbs. GVWR, the standards under this part for clean-fuel vehicles shall require that combined emissions of oxides of nitrogen (NOx) and non-methane hydrocarbons (NMHC) shall not exceed 3.15 grams per brake horse-power hour (equivalent to 50 percent of the combined emission standards applicable under section 7521 of this title for such air pollutants in the case of a conventional model year 1994 heavy-duty diesel-fueled vehicle or engine). No standard shall be promulgated as provided in this section for any heavy-duty vehicle of more than 26,000 lbs. GVWR.

(b) Revised standards that are less stringent

(1) The Administrator may promulgate a revised less stringent standard for the vehicles or engines referred to in subsection (a) if the Administrator determines that the 50 percent reduction required under subsection (a) is not technologically feasible for clean diesel-fueled vehicles and engines, taking into account durability, costs, lead time, safety, and other relevant factors. To provide adequate lead time the Administrator shall make a determination with regard to the technological feasibility of such 50 percent reduction before December 31, 1993.

(2) Any person may at any time petition the Administrator to make a determination under paragraph (1). The Administrator shall act on such a petition within 6 months after the petition is filed.

(3) Any revised less stringent standards promulgated as provided in this subsection shall require at least a 30 percent reduction in lieu of the 50 percent reduction referred to in paragraph (1).

§7586. Centrally fueled fleets
[CAA §246]
(a) Fleet program required for certain non-attainment areas

(1) SIP revision — Each State in which there is located all or part of a covered area (as defined in paragraph (2)) shall submit, within 42 months after November 15, 1990, a State implementation plan revision under section 7410 of this title and part D of subchapter I to establish a clean-fuel vehicle program for fleets under this section.

(2) Covered areas — For purposes of this subsection, each of the following shall be a "covered area":

(A) Ozone nonattainment areas — Any ozone nonattainment area with a 1980 population of 250,000 or more classified under subpart 2 of part D of subchapter I of this chapter as Serious, Severe, or Extreme based on data for the calendar years 1987, 1988, and 1989. In determining the ozone nonattainment areas to be treated as covered areas pursuant to this subparagraph, the Administrator shall use the most recent interpretation methodology issued by the Administrator prior to November 15, 1990.

(B) Carbon monoxide nonattainment areas — Any carbon monoxide nonattainment area with a 1980 population of 250,000 or more and a carbon monoxide design value at or above 16.0 parts per million based on data for calendar years 1988 and 1989 (as calculated according to the most recent interpretation methodology issued prior to November 15, 1990 by the United States Environmental Protection Agency), excluding those carbon monoxide nonattainment areas in which mobile sources do not contribute significantly to carbon monoxide exceedances.

(3) Plan revisions for reclassified areas — In the case of ozone nonattainment areas reclassified as Serious, Severe, or Extreme under part D of title I with a 1980 population of 250,000 or more, the State shall submit a plan revision meeting the requirements of this subsection within 1 year after reclassification. Such plan revision shall implement the requirements applicable under this subsection at the time of reclassification and thereafter, except that the Administrator may adjust for a limited period the deadlines for compliance where compliance with such deadlines would be infeasible.

(4) Consultation; consideration of factors — Each State required to submit an implementation plan revision under this subsection shall develop such revision in consultation with fleet operators, vehicle manufacturers, fuel producers and distributors, motor vehicle fuel, and other interested parties, taking into consideration operational range, specialty uses, vehicle and fuel availability, costs, safety, resale values of vehicles and equipment and other relevant factors.

(b) Phase-in of requirements — The plan revision required under this section shall contain provisions requiring that at least a specified percentage of all new covered fleet vehicles in model year 1998 and thereafter purchased by each covered fleet operator in each covered area shall be clean-fuel vehicles and shall use clean alternative fuels when operating in the covered area. For the applicable model years (MY) specified in the following table and thereafter, the specified percentage shall be as provided in the table for the vehicle types set forth in the table:

CLEAN FUEL VEHICLE PHASE-IN
REQUIREMENTS FOR FLEETS

Vehicle Type	MY1998	MY1999	MY2000
Light-duty trucks up to 6,000 lbs. GVWR and light-duty vehicles	30%	50%	70%
Heavy-duty trucks above 8,500 lbs. GVWR	50%	50%	50%

The term MY refers to model year.

(c) Accelerated standard for light-duty trucks up to 6,000 lbs. GVWR and light-duty vehicles — Notwithstanding the model years for which clean-fuel vehicle standards are applicable as provided in section 7583 of this title, for purposes of this section, light duty trucks of up to 6,000 lbs. GVWR and light-duty vehicles manufactured in model years 1998 through model year 2000 shall be treated as clean-fuel vehicles only if such vehicles comply with the standards applicable under section 7583 of this title for vehicles in the same class for the model year 2001. The requirements of subsection (b) of this section shall take effect on the earlier of the following:

(1) The first model year after model year 1997 in which new light-duty trucks up to 6,000 lbs. GVWR and light-duty vehicles which comply with the model year 2001 standards under section 7583 are offered for sale in California.

(2) Model year 2001 — Whenever the effective date of subsection (b) is delayed pursuant to paragraph (1) of this subsection, the phase-in schedule under subsection (b) shall be modified to commence with the model year referred to in paragraph (1) in lieu of model year 1998.

(d) Choice of vehicles and fuel — The plan revision under this subsection shall provide that the choice of clean-fuel vehicles and clean alternative fuels shall be made by the covered fleet operator subject to the requirements of this subsection.

(e) Availability of clean alternative fuel — The plan revision shall require fuel providers to make clean alternative fuel available to covered fleet operators at locations at which covered fleet vehicles are centrally fueled.

(f) Credits

(1) Issuance of credits — The State plan revision required under this section shall provide for the issuance by the State of appropriate credits to a fleet operator for any of the following (or any combination thereof):

(A) The purchase of more clean-fuel vehicles than required under this section.

(B) The purchase of clean fuel vehicles which meet more stringent standards established by the Administrator pursuant to paragraph (4).

(C) The purchase of vehicles in categories which are not covered by this section but which meet standards established for such vehicles under paragraph (4).

(2) Use of credits; limitations based on weight classes

(A) Use of credits — Credits under this subsection may be used by the person holding such credits to demonstrate compliance with this section or may be traded or sold for use by any other person to demonstrate compliance with other requirements applicable under this section in the same nonattainment area.

Credits obtained at any time may be held or banked for use at any later time, and when so used, such credits shall maintain the same value as if used at an earlier date.

(B) Limitations based on weight classes — Credits issued with respect to the purchase of vehicles of up to 8,500 lbs. GVWR may not be used to demonstrate compliance by any person with the requirements applicable under this subsection to vehicles of more than 8,500 lbs. GVWR. Credits issued with respect to the purchase of vehicles of more than 8,500 lbs. GVWR may not be used to demonstrate compliance by any person with the requirements applicable under this subsection to vehicles weighing up to 8,500 lbs. GVWR.

(C) Weighting — Credits issued for purchase of a clean fuel vehicle under this subsection shall be adjusted with appropriate weighting to reflect the level of emission reduction achieved by the vehicle.

(3) Regulations and administration — Within 12 months after November 15, 1990, the Administrator shall promulgate regulations for such credit program. The State shall administer the credit program established under this subsection.

(4) Standards for issuing credits for cleaner vehicles — Solely for purposes of issuing credits under paragraph (1)(B), the Administrator shall establish under this paragraph standards for Ultra-Low Emission Vehicles ("ULEV"s) and Zero Emissions Vehicles ("ZEV"s) which shall be more stringent than those otherwise applicable to clean-fuel vehicles under this part. The Administrator shall certify clean fuel vehicles as complying with such more stringent standards, and administer and enforce such more stringent standards, in the same manner as in the case of the otherwise applicable clean-fuel vehicle standards established under this section. The standards established by the Administrator under this paragraph for vehicles under 8,500 lbs. GVWR or greater shall conform as closely as possible to standards which are established by the State of California for ULEV and ZEV vehicles in the same class. For vehicles of 8,500 lbs. GVWR or more, the Administrator shall promulgate comparable standards for purposes of this subsection.

(5) Early fleet credits — The State plan revision shall provide credits under this subsection to fleet operators that purchase vehicles certified to meet clean-fuel vehicle standards under this part during any period after approval of the plan revision and prior to the effective date of the fleet program under this section.

(g) Availability to public — At any facility owned or operated by a department, agency, or instrumentality of the United States where vehicles subject to this subsection are supplied with clean alternative fuel, such fuel shall be offered for sale to the public for use in other vehicles during reasonable business times and subject to national security concerns, unless such fuel is commercially available for vehicles in the vicinity of such Federal facilities.

(h) Transportation control measures — The Administrator shall by rule, within 1 year after November 15, 1990, ensure that certain transportation control measures including time-of-day or day-of-week restrictions, and other similar measures that restrict vehicle usage, do not apply to any clean-fuel vehicle that meets the requirements of this section. This subsection shall apply notwithstanding subchapter I of this chapter.

§7587. Vehicle conversions
[CAA §247]

(a) Conversion of existing and new conventional vehicles to clean-fuel vehicles — The requirements of section 7586 of this title may be met through the conversion of existing or new gasoline or diesel-powered vehicles to clean-fuel vehicles which comply with the applicable requirements of that section. For purposes of such provisions the conversion of a vehicle to clean fuel vehicle shall be treated as the purchase of a clean fuel vehicle. Nothing in this part shall be construed to provide that any covered fleet operator subject to fleet vehicle purchase requirements under section 7586 of this title shall be required to convert existing or new gasoline or diesel-powered vehicles to clean-fuel vehicles or to purchase converted vehicles.

(b) Regulations — The Administrator shall, within 24 months after November 15, 1990, consistent with the requirements of this title applicable to new vehicles, promulgate regulations governing conversions of conventional vehicles to clean-fuel vehicles. Such regulations shall establish criteria for such conversions which will ensure that a converted vehicle will comply with the standards applicable under this part to clean-fuel vehicles. Such regulations shall provide for the application to such conversions of the same provisions of this title (including provisions relating to administration enforcement) as are applicable to standards under section 7582, 7583, 7584, and 7585 of this title, except that in the case of conversions the Administrator may modify the applicable regulations implementing such provisions as the Administrator deems necessary to implement this part.

(c) Enforcement — Any person who converts conventional vehicles to clean-fuel vehicles pursuant to subsection (b) of this section, shall be considered a manufacturer for purposes of sections 7525 and 7541 of this title and related enforcement provisions. Nothing in the preceding sentence shall require a person who performs such conversions to warrant any part or operation of a vehicle other than as required under this part. Nothing in this paragraph shall limit the applicability of any other warranty to unrelated parts or operations.

(d) Tampering — The conversion from a vehicle capable of operating on gasoline or diesel fuel only to a clean-fuel vehicle shall not be considered a violation of section 7522(a)(3) of this title if such conversion complies with the regulations promulgated under subsection (b) of this section.

(e) Safety — The Secretary of Transportation shall, if necessary, promulgate rules under applicable motor vehicle laws regarding the safety of vehicles converted from existing and new vehicles to clean-fuel vehicles.

§7588. Federal agency fleets
[CAA §248]

(a) Additional provisions applicable — The provisions of this section shall apply, in addition to the other provisions of this part, in the case of covered fleet vehicles owned or operated by an agency, department, or instrumentality of the United States, except as otherwise provided in subsection (e) of this section.

(b) Cost of vehicles to Federal agency — Notwithstanding the provisions of section 491 of Title 40, the Administrator of General Services shall not include the incremental costs of clean-fuel vehicles in the amount to be reimbursed by Federal agencies if the Administrator of General Services determines that appropriations provided pursuant to this paragraph are sufficient to provide for the incremental cost of such vehicles over the cost of comparable conventional vehicles.

(c) Limitations on appropriations — Funds appropriated pursuant to the authorization under this paragraph shall be applicable only —

(1) to the portion of the cost of acquisition, maintenance and operation of vehicles acquired under this subparagraph which exceeds the cost of acquisition, maintenance and operation of comparable conventional vehicles;

(2) to the portion of the costs of fuel storage and dispensing equipment attributable to such vehicles which exceeds the costs for such purposes required for conventional vehicles; and

(3) to the portion of the costs of acquisition of clean-fuel vehicles which represents a reduction in revenue from the disposal of such vehicles as compared to revenue resulting from the disposal of comparable conventional vehicles.

(d) Vehicle costs — The incremental cost of vehicles acquired under this part over the cost of comparable conventional vehicles shall not be applied to any calculation with respect to a limitation under law on the maximum cost of individual vehicles which may be required by the United States.

(e) Exemptions — The requirements of this part shall not apply to vehicles with respect to which the Secretary of Defense has certified to the Administrator that an exemption is needed based on national security consideration.

(f) Acquisition requirement — Federal agencies, to the extent practicable, shall obtain clean-fuel vehicles from original equipment manufacturers.

(g) Authorization of appropriations — There are authorized to be appropriated such sums as may be required to carry out the provisions of this section: *Provided*, That such sums as are appropriated for the Administrator of General Services pursuant to the authorization under this section shall be added to the General Supply Fund established in section 756 of Title 40.

§7589. California pilot test program
[CAA §249]

(a) Establishment — The Administrator shall establish a pilot program in the State of California to demonstrate the effectiveness of clean-fuel vehicles in controlling air pollution in ozone nonattainment areas.

(b) Applicability — The provisions of this section shall only apply to light duty trucks and light-duty vehicles, and such provisions shall apply only in the State of California, except as provided in subsection (f) of this section.

(c) Program requirements — Not later than 24 months after November 15, 1990, the Administrator shall promulgate regulations establishing requirements under this section applicable in the State of California. The regulations shall provide the following:

(1) Clean-fuel vehicles — Clean-fuel vehicles shall be produced, sold, and distributed (in accordance with normal business practices and applicable franchise agreements) to ultimate purchasers in California (including owners of covered fleets referred to in section 7586 of this title) in numbers that meet or exceed the following schedule:

Model Years	Number of Clean-Fuel Vehicles
1996, 1997, 1998	150,000 vehicles
1999 and thereafter	300,000 vehicles

(2) Clean alternative fuels

(A) Within 2 years after November 15, 1990, the State of California shall submit a revision of the applicable implementation plan under part D of subchapter I of this chapter and section 7410 of this title containing a clean fuel plan that requires that clean alternative fuels on which the clean-fuel vehicles required under this paragraph can operate shall be produced and distributed by fuel suppliers and made available in California. At a minimum, sufficient clean alternative fuels shall be produced, distributed and made available to assure that all clean-fuel vehicles required under this section can operate, to the maximum extent practicable, exclusively on such fuels in California. The State shall require that clean alternative fuels be made available and offered for sale at an adequate number of locations with sufficient geographic distribution to ensure convenient refueling with clean alternative fuels, considering the number of, and type of, such vehicles sold and the geographic distribution of such vehicles within the State. The State shall determine the clean alternative fuels to be produced, distributed, and made available based on motor vehicle manufacturers' projections of future sales of such vehicles and consultations with the affected local governments and fuel suppliers.

(B) The State may by regulation grant persons subject to the requirements prescribed under this paragraph an appropriate amount of credits for exceeding such requirements, and any person granted credits may transfer some or all of the credits for use by one or more persons in demonstrating compliance with such requirements. The State may make the credits available for use after consideration of enforceability, environmental, and economic factors and upon such terms and conditions as the State finds appropriate.

(C) The State may also by regulation establish specifications for any clean alternative fuel produced and made available under this paragraph as the State finds necessary to reduce or eliminate an unreasonable risk to public health, welfare, or safety associated with its use or to ensure acceptable vehicle maintenance and performance characteristics.

(D) If a retail gasoline dispensing facility would have to remove or replace one or more motor vehicle fuel underground storage tanks and accompanying piping in order to comply with the provisions of this section, and it had removed and replaced such tank or tanks and accompanying piping in order to comply with subtitle I of the Solid Waste Disposal Act prior to November 15, 1990, it shall not be required to comply with this subsection until a period of 7 years has passed from the date of the removal and replacement of such tank or tanks.

(E) Nothing in this section authorizes any State other than California to adopt provisions regarding clean alternative fuels.

(F) If the State of California fails to adopt a clean fuel program that meets the requirements of this paragraph, the Administrator shall, within 4 years after November 15, 1990, establish a clean fuel program for the State of California under this paragraph and section 7410(c) of this title that meets the requirements of this paragraph.

(d) Credits for motor vehicle manufacturers

(1) The Administrator may (by regulation) grant a motor vehicle manufacturer an appropriate amount of credits toward fulfillment of such manufacturer's share of the requirements of subsection (c)(1) of this section for any of the following (or any combination thereof):

(A) The sale of more clean-fuel vehicles than required under subsection (c)(1) of this section.

(B) The sale of clean fuel vehicles which meet standards established by the Administrator as provided in paragraph (3) which are more stringent than the clean-fuel vehicle standards otherwise applicable to such clean-fuel vehicle. A manufacturer granted credits under this paragraph may transfer some or all of the credits for use by one or more other manufacturers in demonstrating compliance with the requirements prescribed under this paragraph. The Administrator may make the credits available for use after consideration of enforceability, environmental, and economic factors and upon such terms and conditions as he finds appropriate. The Administrator shall grant credits in accordance with this paragraph, notwithstanding any requirements of State law or any credits granted with respect to the same vehicles under any State law, rule, or regulation.

(2) Regulations and administration — The Administrator shall administer the credit program established under this subsection. Within 12 months after November 15, 1990, the Administrator shall promulgate regulations for such credit program.

(3) Standards for issuing credits for cleaner vehicles — The more stringent standards and other requirements (including requirements relating to the weighting of credits) established by the Administrator for purposes of the credit program under 7585(e) of this title (relating to credits for clean fuel vehicles in the fleets program) shall also apply for purposes of the credit program under this paragraph.

(e) Program evaluation

(1) Not later than June 30, 1994 and again in connection with the report under paragraph (2), the Administrator shall provide a report to the Congress on the status of the California Air Resources Board Low-Emissions Vehicles and Clean Fuels Program. Such report shall examine the capability, from a technological standpoint, of motor vehicle manufacturers and motor vehicle fuel suppliers to comply with the requirements of such program and with the requirements of the California Pilot Program under this section.

(2) Not later than June 30, 1998, the Administrator shall complete and submit a report to Congress on the effectiveness of the California pilot program under this section. The report shall evaluate the level of emission reductions achieved under the program, the costs of the program, the advantages and disadvantages of extending the program to other nonattainment areas, and desirability of continuing or expanding the program in California.

(3) The program under this section cannot be extended or terminated by the Administrator

except by Act of Congress enacted after November 15, 1990. Section 7507 of this title does not apply to the program under this section.

(f) Voluntary opt-in for other states

(1) EPA regulations — Not later than 2 years after November 15, 1990, the Administrator shall promulgate regulations establishing a voluntary opt-in program under this subsection pursuant to which —

(A) clean-fuel vehicles which are required to be produced, sold, and distributed in the State of California under this section, and

(B) clean alternative fuels required to be produced and distributed under this section by fuel suppliers and made available in California may also be sold and used in other States which submit plan revisions under paragraph (2).

(2) Plan revisions — Any State in which there is located all or part of an ozone nonattainment area classified under subpart D of title I as Serious, Severe, or Extreme may submit a revision of the applicable implementation plan under part D of title I and section 7410 of this title to provide incentives for the sale or use in such an area or State of clean-fuel vehicles which are required to be produced, sold, and distributed in the State of California, and for the use in such an area or State of clean alternative fuels required to be produced and distributed by fuel suppliers and made available in California. Such plan provisions shall not take effect until 1 year after the State has provided notice of such provisions to motor vehicle manufacturers and to fuel suppliers.

(3) Incentives — The incentives referred to in paragraph (2) may include any or all of the following:

(A) A State registration fee on new motor vehicles registered in the State which are not clean-fuel vehicles in the amount of at least 1 percent of the cost of the vehicle. The proceeds of such fee shall be used to provide financial incentives to purchasers of clean-fuel vehicles and to vehicle dealers who sell high volumes or high percentages of clean-fuel vehicles and to defray the administrative costs of the incentive program.

(B) Provisions to exempt clean-fuel vehicles from high occupancy vehicle or trip reduction requirements.

(C) Provisions to provide preference in the use of existing parking spaces for clean-fuel vehicles.

The incentives under this paragraph shall not apply in the case of covered fleet vehicles.

(4) No sales or production mandate — The regulations and plan revisions under paragraphs (1) and (2) shall not include any production or sales mandate for clean-fuel vehicles or clean alternative fuels. Such regulations and plan revisions shall also provide that vehicle manufacturers and fuel suppliers may not be subject to penalties or sanctions for failing to produce or sell clean-fuel vehicles or clean alternative fuels.

§7590. General provisions
[CAA §250]

(a) State refueling facilities — If any State adopts enforceable provisions in an implementation plan applicable to a nonattainment area which provides that existing State refueling facilities will be made available to the public for the purchase of clean alternative fuels or that State-operated refueling facilities for such fuels will be constructed and operated by the State and made available to the public at reasonable times, taking into consideration safety, costs, and other relevant factors, in approving such plan under section 7410 of this title and part D, the Administrator may credit a State with the emission reductions for purposes of part D attributable to such actions.

(b) No production mandate — The Administrator shall have no authority under this part to mandate the production of clean-fuel vehicles except as provided in the California pilot test program or to specify as applicable the models, lines, or types of, or marketing or price practices, policies, or strategies for, vehicles subject to this part. Nothing in this part shall be construed to give the Administrator authority to mandate marketing or pricing practices, policies, or strategies for fuels.

(c) Tank and fuel system safety — The Secretary of Transportation shall, in accordance with the National Motor Vehicle Traffic Safety Act of 1966, promulgate applicable regulations regarding the safety and use of fuel storage cylinders and fuel systems, including appropriate testing and retesting, in conversions of motor vehicles.

(d) Consultation with Department of Energy and Department of Transportation — The Administrator shall coordinate with the Secretaries of the Department of Energy and the Department of Transportation in carrying out the Administrator's duties under this part.

SUBCHAPTER III — GENERAL PROVISIONS

§7601. Administration
[CAA §301]

(a) Regulations; delegation of powers and duties; regional officers and employees

(1) The Administrator is authorized to prescribe such regulations as are necessary to carry out his functions under this Act. The Administrator may delegate to any officer or employee of the Environmental Protection Agency such of his powers and duties under this Act, except the making of regulations subject to section 7607(d) of this title, as he may deem necessary or expedient.

(2) Not later than one year after August 7, 1977, the Administrator shall promulgate regulations establishing general applicable procedures and policies for regional officers and employees (including the Regional Administrator) to follow in carrying out a delegation under paragraph (1), if any. Such regulations shall be designed —

(A) to assure fairness and uniformity in the criteria, procedures, and policies applied by the various regions in implementing and enforcing the Act;

(B) to assure at least an adequate quality audit of each State's performance and adherence to the requirements of this Act in implementing and enforcing the Act, particularly in the review of new sources and in enforcement of the Act; and

(C) to provide a mechanism for identifying and standardizing inconsistent or varying criteria, procedures, and policies being employed by such officers and employees in implementing and enforcing the chapter.

(b) Detail of Environmental Protection Agency personnel to air pollution control agencies — Upon the request of an air pollution control agency, personnel of the Environmental Protection Agency may be detailed to such agency for the purpose of carrying out the provisions of this chapter.

(c) Payments under grants; installments; advances or reimbursements — Payments under grants made under this Act may be made in installments, and in advance or by way of reimbursement, as may be determined by the Administrator.

(d) Tribal authority

(1) Subject to the provisions of paragraph (2), the Administrator —

(A) is authorized to treat Indian tribes as States under this Act, except for purposes of the requirement that makes available for application by each State no less than one-half of 1 percent of annual appropriations under section 7405 of this title; and

(B) may provide any such Indian tribe grant and contract assistance to carry out functions provided by this chapter.

(2) The Administrator shall promulgate regulations within 18 months after November 15, 1990, specifying those provisions of this chapter for which it is appropriate to treat Indian tribes as States. Such treatment shall be authorized only if —

(A) the Indian tribe has a governing body carrying out substantial governmental duties and powers;

(B) the functions to be exercised by the Indian tribe pertain to the management and protection of air resources within the exterior boundaries of the reservation or other areas within the tribe's jurisdiction; and

(C) the Indian tribe is reasonably expected to be capable, in the judgment of the Administrator, of carrying out the functions to be exercised in a manner consistent with the terms and purposes of this Act and all applicable regulations.

(3) The Administrator may promulgate regulations which establish the elements of tribal implementation plans and procedures for approval or disapproval of tribal implementation plans and portions thereof.

(4) In any case in which the Administrator determines that the treatment of Indian tribes as identical to States is inappropriate or administratively infeasible, the Administrator may provide, by regulation, other means by which the Administrator will directly administer such provisions so as to achieve the appropriate purpose.

(5) Until such time as the Administrator promulgates regulations pursuant to this subsection, the Administrator may continue to provide financial assistance to eligible Indian tribes under section 7405 of this title.

§7602. Definitions
[CAA §302]

When used in this Act —

(a) The term "Administrator" means the Administrator of the Environmental Protection Agency.

(b) The term "air pollution control agency" means any of the following:

(1) A single State agency designated by the Governor of that State as the official State air pollution control agency for purposes of this chapter.

(2) An agency established by two or more States and having substantial powers or duties pertaining to the prevention and control of air pollution.

(3) A city, county, or other local government health authority, or, in the case of any city, county, or other local government in which there is an agency other than the health authority charged with responsibility for enforcing ordinances or laws relating to the prevention and control of air pollution, such other agency.

(4) An agency of two or more municipalities located in the same State or in different States and having substantial powers or duties pertaining to the prevention and control of air pollution.

(5) An agency of an Indian tribe.

(c) The term "interstate air pollution control agency" means —

(1) an air pollution control agency established by two or more States, or

(2) an air pollution control agency of two or more municipalities located in different States.

(d) The term "State" means a State, the District of Columbia, the Commonwealth of Puerto Rico, the Virgin Islands, Guam, and American Samoa and includes the Commonwealth of the Northern Mariana Islands.

(e) The term "person" includes an individual, corporation, partnership, association, State, municipality, political subdivision of a State, and any agency, department, or instrumentality of the United States and any officer, agent, or employee thereof.

(f) The term "municipality" means a city, town, borough, county, parish, district, or other public body created by or pursuant to State law.

(g) The term "air pollutant" means any air pollution agent or combination of such agents, including any physical, chemical, biological, radioactive (including source material, special nuclear material, and byproduct material) substance or matter which is emitted into or otherwise enters the ambient air. Such term includes any precursors to the formation of any air pollutant, to the extent the Administrator has identified such precursor or precursors for the particular purpose for which the term "air pollutant" is used.

(h) All language referring to effects on welfare includes, but is not limited to, effects on soils, water, crops, vegetation, man-made materials, animals, wildlife, weather, visibility, and climate, damage to and deterioration of property, and hazards to transportation, as well as effects on economic values and on personal comfort and well-being, whether caused by transformation, conversion, or combination with other air pollutants.

(i) The term "Federal land manager" means, with respect to any lands in the United States, the Secretary of the department with authority over such lands.

(j) Except as otherwise expressly provided, the terms "major stationary source" and "major emitting facility" mean any stationary facility or source of air pollutants which directly emits, or has the potential to emit, one hundred tons per year or more of any air pollutant (including any major emitting facility or source of fugitive emissions of any such pollutant, as determined by rule by the Administrator).

(k) The terms "emission limitation" and "emission standard" mean a requirement established by the State or the Administrator which limits the quantity, rate, or concentration of emissions of air pollutants on a continuous basis, including any requirement relating to the operation or maintenance of a source to assure continuous emission reduction, and any design, equipment, work practice or operational standard promulgated under this chapter.

(*l*) The term "standard of performance" means a requirement of continuous emission reduction, including any requirement relating to the operation or maintenance of a source to assure continuous emission reduction.

(m) The term "means of emission limitation" means a system of continuous emission reduction (including the use of specific technology or fuels with specified pollution characteristics).

(n) The term "primary standard attainment date" means the date specified in the applicable implementation plan for the attainment of a national primary ambient air quality standard for any air pollutant.

(o) The term "delayed compliance order" means an order issued by the State or by the Administrator to an existing stationary source, postponing the date required under an applicable implementation plan for compliance by such source with any requirement of such plan.

(p) The term "schedule and timetable of compliance" means a schedule of required measures including an enforceable sequence of actions or operations leading to compliance with an emission limitation, other limitation, prohibition, or standard.

(q) For purposes of this Act, the term "applicable implementation plan" means the portion (or portions) of the implementation plan, or most recent revision thereof, which has been approved under section 7410 of this title, or promulgated under section 7410(c) of this title, or promulgated or approved pursuant to regulations promulgated under section 7601(d) of this title and which implements the relevant requirements of this chapter.

(r) Indian Tribe — The term "Indian tribe" means any Indian tribe, band, nation, or other organized group or community, including any Alaska Native village, which is Federally recognized as eligible for the special programs and services provided by the United States to Indians because of their status as Indians.

(s) VOC — The term "VOC" means volatile organic compound, as defined by the Administrator.

(t) PM-10 — The term "PM-10" means particulate matter with an aerodynamic diameter less than or equal to a nominal ten micrometers, as measured by such method as the Administrator may determine.

(u) NAAQS and CTG — The term "NAAQS" means national ambient air quality standard. The term "CTG" means a Control Technique Guideline published by the Administrator under section 7408 of this title.

(v) NOx — The term "NOx" means oxides of nitrogen.

(w) CO — The term "CO" means carbon monoxide.

(x) Small source — The term "small source" means a source that emits less than 100 tons of regulated pollutants per year, or any class of persons that the Administrator determines, through regulation, generally lack technical ability or knowledge regarding control of air pollution.

(y) Federal implementation plan — The term "Federal implementation plan" means a plan (or portion thereof) promulgated by the Administrator to fill all or a portion of a gap or otherwise correct all or a portion of an inadequacy in a State implementation plan, and which includes enforceable emission limitations or other control measures, means or techniques (including economic incentives, such as marketable permits or auctions of emissions allowances), and

provides for attainment of the relevant national ambient air quality standard.

(z) Stationary source — The term "stationary source" means generally any source of an air pollutant except those emissions resulting directly from an internal combustion engine for transportation purposes or from a nonroad engine or nonroad vehicle as defined in section 7550 of this title.

§7603. Emergency powers
[CAA §303]

Notwithstanding any other provisions of this Act, the Administrator upon receipt of evidence that a pollution source or combination of sources (including moving sources) is presenting an imminent and substantial endangerment to public health or welfare, or the environment, may bring suit on behalf of the United States in the appropriate United States district court to immediately restrain any person causing or contributing to the alleged pollution to stop the emission of air pollutants causing or contributing to such pollution or to take such other action as may be necessary. If it is not practicable to assure prompt protection of public health or welfare or the environment by commencement of such a civil action, the Administrator may issue such orders as may be necessary to protect public health or welfare or the environment. Prior to taking any action under this section, the Administrator shall consult with appropriate State and local authorities and attempt to confirm the accuracy of the information on which the action proposed to be taken is based. Any order issued by the Administrator under this section shall be effective upon issuance and shall remain in effect for a period of not more than 60 days, unless the Administrator brings an action pursuant to the first sentence of this section before the expiration of that period. Whenever the Administrator brings such an action within the 60-day period, such order shall remain in effect for an additional 14 days or for such longer period as may be authorized by the court in which such action is brought.

§7604. Citizen suits
[CAA §304]

(a) Authority to bring civil action; jurisdiction — Except as provided in subsection (b) of this section, any person may commence a civil action on his own behalf —

(1) against any person (including (i) the United States, and (ii) any other governmental instrumentality or agency to the extent permitted by the Eleventh Amendment to the Constitution) who is alleged to have violated (if there is evidence that the alleged violation has been repeated) or to be in violation of (A) an emission standard or limitation under this Act or (B) an order issued by the Administrator or a State with respect to such a standard or limitation,

(2) against the Administrator where there is alleged a failure of the Administrator to perform any

act or duty under this Act which is not discretionary with the Administrator, or

(3) against any person who proposes to construct or constructs any new or modified major emitting facility without a permit required under part C of subchapter I of this chapter (relating to significant deterioration of air quality) or part D of subchapter I of this chapter (relating to nonattainment) or who is alleged to be in violation of any condition of such permit.

The district courts shall have jurisdiction, without regard to the amount in controversy or the citizenship of the parties, to enforce such an emission standard or limitation, or such an order, or to order the Administrator to perform such act or duty, as the case may be, and to apply any appropriate civil penalties (except for actions under paragraph (2)). The district courts of the United States shall have jurisdiction to compel (consistent with paragraph (2) of this subsection) agency action unreasonably delayed, except that an action to compel agency action referred to in section 7607(b) of this title which is unreasonably delayed may only be filed in a United States District Court within the circuit in which such action would be reviewable under section 7607(b) of this title. In any such action for unreasonable delay, notice to the entities referred to in subsection (b)(1)(A) shall be provided 180 days before commencing such action.

(b) Notice — No action may be commenced —

(1) under subsection (a)(1) —

(A) prior to 60 days after the plaintiff has given notice of the violation (i) to the Administrator, (ii) to the State in which the violation occurs, and (iii) to any alleged violator of the standard, limitation, or order, or

(B) if the Administrator or State has commenced and is diligently prosecuting a civil action in a court of the United States or a State to require compliance with the standard, limitation, or order, but in any such action in a court of the United States any person may intervene as a matter of right.

(2) under subsection (a)(2) prior to 60 days after the plaintiff has given notice of such action to the Administrator,

except that such action may be brought immediately after such notification in the case of an action under this section respecting a violation of section 7412(i)(3)(A) or (f)(4) of this title or an order issued by the Administrator pursuant to section 7413(a) of this title. Notice under this subsection shall be given in such manner as the Administrator shall prescribe by regulation.

(c) Venue; intervention by Administrator; service of complaint; consent judgment

(1) Any action respecting a violation by a stationary source of an emission standard or limitation or an order respecting such standard or limitation may be brought only in the judicial district in which such source is located.

(2) In any action under this section, the Administrator, if not a party, may intervene as a matter of right at any time in the proceeding. A judgment in an action under this section to which the United States is not a party shall not, however, have any binding effect upon the United States.

(3) Whenever any action is brought under this section the plaintiff shall serve a copy of the complaint on the Attorney General of the United States and on the Administrator. No consent judgment shall be entered in an action brought under this section in which the United States is not a party prior to 45 days following the receipt of a copy of the proposed consent judgment by the Attorney General and the Administrator during which time the Government may submit its comments on the proposed consent judgment to the court and parties or may intervene as a matter of right.

(d) Award of costs; security — The court, in issuing any final order in any action brought pursuant to subsection (a) of this section, may award costs of litigation (including reasonable attorney and expert witness fees) to any party, whenever the court determines such award is appropriate. The court may, if a temporary restraining order or preliminary injunction is sought, require the filing of a bond or equivalent security in accordance with the Federal Rules of Civil Procedure.

(e) Nonrestriction of other rights — Nothing in this section shall restrict any right which any person (or class of persons) may have under any statute or common law to seek enforcement of any emission standard or limitation or to seek any other relief (including relief against the Administrator or a State agency). Nothing in this section or in any other law of the United States shall be construed to prohibit, exclude, or restrict any State, local, or interstate authority from —

(1) bringing any enforcement action or obtaining any judicial remedy or sanction in any State or local court, or

(2) bringing any administrative enforcement action or obtaining any administrative remedy or sanction in any State or local administrative agency, department or instrumentality,

against the United States, any department, agency, or instrumentality thereof, or any officer, agent, or employee thereof under State or local law respecting control and abatement of air pollution. For provisions requiring compliance by the United States, departments, agencies, instrumentalities, officers, agents, and employees in the same manner as nongovernmental entities, see section 7418 of this title.

(f) "Emission standard or limitation under this chapter" defined — For purposes of this section, the term "emission standard or limitation under this Act" means —

(1) a schedule or timetable of compliance, emission limitation, standard of performance or emission standard,

(2) a control or prohibition respecting a motor vehicle fuel or fuel additive, or

(3) any condition or requirement of a permit under part C of subchapter I of this chapter (relating to significant deterioration of air quality) or part D of subchapter I of this chapter (relating to nonattainment), section 7419 of this title (relating to primary nonferrous smelter orders), any condition or requirement under an applicable implementation plan relating to transportation control measures, air quality maintenance plans, vehicle inspection and maintenance programs or vapor recovery requirements, section 7545(e) and (f) of this title (relating to fuels and fuel additives), section 7491 of this title (relating to visibility protection), any condition or requirement under subchapter VI of this chapter (relating to ozone protection), or any requirement under section 7411 or 7412 of this title (without regard to whether such requirement is expressed as an emission standard or otherwise); or

(4) any other standard, limitation, or schedule established under any permit issued pursuant to subchapter V of this chapter or under any applicable State implementation plan approved by the Administrator, any permit term or condition, and any requirement to obtain a permit as a condition of operations.

which is in effect under this Act (including a requirement applicable by reason of section 7418 of this title) or under an applicable implementation plan.

(g) Penalty fund

(1) Penalties received under subsection (a) shall be deposited in a special fund in the United States Treasury for licensing and other services. Amounts in such fund are authorized to be appropriated and shall remain available until expended, for use by the Administrator to finance air compliance and enforcement activities. The Administrator shall annually report to the Congress about the sums deposited into the fund, the sources thereof, and the actual and proposed uses thereof.

(2) Notwithstanding paragraph (1) the court in any action under this subsection to apply civil penalties shall have discretion to order that such civil penalties, in lieu of being deposited in the fund referred to in paragraph (1), be used in beneficial mitigation projects which are consistent with this Act and enhance the public health or the environment. The court shall obtain the view of the Administrator in exercising such discretion and selecting any such projects. The amount of any such payment in any such action shall not exceed $100,000.

§7605. Representation in litigation
[CAA §305]

(a) Attorney General; attorneys appointed by Administrator — The Administrator shall request the Attorney General to appear and represent him in any civil action instituted under this Act to which the Administrator is a party. Unless the Attorney General notifies the Administrator that he will appear in such action, within a reasonable time, attorneys appointed by the Administrator shall appear and represent him.

(b) Memorandum of understanding regarding legal representation — In the event the Attorney General agrees to appear and represent the Administrator in any such action, such representation shall be conducted in accordance with, and shall include participation by, attorneys appointed by the Administrator to the extent authorized by, the memorandum of understanding between the Department of Justice and the Environmental Protection Agency, dated June 13, 1977, respecting representation of the agency by the department in civil litigation.

§7606. Federal procurement
[CAA §306]

(a) Contracts with violators prohibited — No Federal agency may enter into any contract with any person who is convicted of any offense under section 7413(c) of this title for the procurement of goods, materials, and services to perform such contract at any facility at which the violation which gave rise to such conviction occurred if such facility is owned, leased, or supervised by such person. The prohibition in the preceding sentence shall continue until the Administrator certifies that the condition giving rise to such a conviction has been corrected. For convictions arising under section 7413(c)(2) of this title, the condition giving rise to the conviction also shall be considered to include any substantive violation of this chapter associated with the violation of 7413(c)(2) of this title. The Administrator may extend this prohibition to other facilities owned or operated by the convicted person

(b) Notification procedures — The Administrator shall establish procedures to provide all Federal agencies with the notification necessary for the purposes of subsection (a) of this section.

(c) Federal agency contracts — In order to implement the purposes and policy of this Act to protect and enhance the quality of the Nation's air, the President shall, not more than 180 days after December 31, 1970, cause to be issued an order (1) requiring each Federal agency authorized to enter into contracts and each Federal agency which is empowered to extend Federal assistance by way of grant, loan, or contract to effectuate the purpose and policy of this Act in such contracting or assistance activities, and (2) setting forth procedures, sanctions, penalties, and such other provisions, as the President determines necessary to carry out such requirement.

(d) Exemptions; notification to Congress — The President may exempt any contract, loan, or grant from all or part of the provisions of this section where he determines such exemption is necessary in the paramount interest of the United States and he shall notify the Congress of such exemption.

§7607. Administrative proceedings and judicial review

[CAA §307]

(a) Administrative subpoenas; confidentiality; witnesses — In connection with any determination under section 7410(f), of this title or for purposes of obtaining information under section 7521(b)(4) or 7545(c)(3) of this title, any investigation, monitoring, reporting requirement, entry, compliance inspection, or administrative enforcement proceeding under the chapter (including but not limited to section 7413, section 7414, section 7420, section 7429, section 7477, section 7524, section 7525, section 7603, section 7606 of this title), the Administrator may issue subpoenas for the attendance and testimony of witnesses and the production of relevant papers, books, and documents, and he may administer oaths. Except for emission data, upon a showing satisfactory to the Administrator by such owner or operator that such papers, books, documents, or information or particular part thereof, if made public, would divulge trade secrets or secret processes of such owner or operator, the Administrator shall consider such record, report, or information or particular portion thereof confidential in accordance with the purposes of section 1905 of Title 18, except that such paper, book, document, or information may be discussed to other officers, employees, or authorized representatives of the United States concerned with carrying out this chapter, to persons carrying out the National Academy of Sciences' study and investigation provided for in section 7521(c) of this title, or when relevant in any proceeding under this chapter. Witnesses summoned shall be paid the same fees and mileage that are paid witnesses in the courts of the United States. In cases of contumacy or refusal to obey a subpena served upon any person under this subparagraph, the district court of the United States for any district in which such person is found or resides or transacts business, upon application by the United States and after notice to such person, shall have jurisdiction to issue an order requiring such person to appear and give testimony before the Administrator to appear and produce papers, books, and documents before the Administrator, or both, and any failure to obey such order of the court may be punished by such court as a contempt thereof.

(b) Judicial review

(1) A petition for review of action of the Administrator in promulgating any national primary or secondary ambient air quality standard, any emission standard or requirement under section 7412 of this title, any standard of performance or requirement under section 7411 of this title, any standard under section 7521 of this title (other than a standard required to be prescribed under section 7521(b)(1) of this title), any determination under section 7521(b)(5) of this title, any control or prohibition under section 7545 of this title, any standard under section 7571 of this title, any rule issued under section 7413, 7419, or under section 7420 of this title, or any other nationally applicable regulations promulgated, or final action taken, by the Administrator under this Act may be filed only in the United States Court of Appeals for the District of Columbia. A petition for review of the Administrator's action in approving or promulgating any implementation plan under section 7410 of this title or section 7411(d) of this title, any order under section 7411(j) of this title, under section 7412 of this title, under section 7419 of this title, or under section 7420 of this title, or his action under section 1857c-10(c)(2)(A), (B), or (C) of this title (as in effect before the date of enactment of the Clean Air Act Amendments of 1977) or under regulations thereunder, or revising regulations for enhanced monitoring and compliance certification programs under section 7414(a)(3) of this title, or any other final action of the Administrator under this Act (including any denial or disapproval by the Administrator under subchapter I of this chapter) which is local or regionally applicable may be filed only in the United States Court of Appeals for the appropriate circuit. Notwithstanding the preceding sentence a petition for review of any action referred to in such sentence may be filed only in the United States Court of Appeals for the District of Columbia if such action is based on a determination of nationwide scope or effect and if in taking such action the Administrator finds and publishes that such action is based on such a determination. Any petition for review under this subsection shall be filed within sixty days from the date notice of such promulgation, approval, or action appears in the Federal Register, except that if such petition is based solely on grounds arising after such sixtieth day, then any petition for review under this subsection shall be filed within sixty days after such grounds arise. The filing of a petition for reconsideration by the Administrator of any otherwise final rule or action shall not affect the finality of such rule or action for purposes of judicial review nor extend the time within which a petition for judicial review of such rule or action under this section may be filed, and shall not postpone the effectiveness of such rule or action.

(2) Action of the Administrator with respect to which review could have been obtained under paragraph (1) shall not be subject to judicial review in civil or criminal proceedings for enforcement. Where a final decision by the Administrator defers performance of any nondiscretionary statutory action to a later time, any person may challenge the deferral pursuant to paragraph (1).

(c) Additional evidence — In any judicial proceeding in which review is sought of a determination under this Act required to be made on the record after notice and opportunity for hearing, if any party applies to the court for leave to adduce additional evidence, and shows to the satisfaction of the court that such additional evidence is material and that there were reasonable grounds for the failure to adduce such evidence in the proceeding before the Administrator, the court may order such additional evidence (and evidence in rebuttal thereof) to be taken before the Administrator, in such manner and upon such terms and conditions as to the court may deem proper. The Administrator may modify his findings as to the facts, or make new findings, by reason of the additional evidence so taken and he shall file such modified or new findings, and his recommendation, if any, for the modification or setting aside of his original determination, with the return of such additional evidence.

(d) Rulemaking

(1) This subsection applies to —

(A) the promulgation or revision of any national ambient air quality standard under section 7409 of this title,

(B) the promulgation or revision of an implementation plan by the Administrator under section 7410(c) of this title,

(C) the promulgation or revision of any standard of performance under section 7411 of this title, or emission standard or limitation under section 7412(d) of this title, any standard under section 7412(f), of this title, or any regulation under section 7412(g)(1)(D) and (F) of this title, or any regulation under section 7412(m) or (n) of this title,

(D) the promulgation of any requirement for solid waste combustion under section 7429 of this title,

(E) the promulgation or revision of any regulation pertaining to any fuel or fuel additive under section 7545 of this title,

(F) the promulgation or revision of any aircraft emission standard under section 7571 of this title,

(G) the promulgation or revision of any regulation under subchapter IV-A of this chapter (relating to control of acid deposition),

(H) promulgation or revision of regulations pertaining to primary nonferrous smelter orders under section 7419 of this title (but not including the granting or denying of any such order),

(I) promulgation or revision of regulations under subchapter VI of this chapter (relating to stratosphere and ozone protection),

(J) promulgation or revision of regulations under part C of subchapter I of this chapter (relating to prevention of significant deterioration of air quality and protection of visibility),

(K) promulgation or revision of regulations under section 7521 of this title and test procedures for new motor vehicles or engines under section 7525 of this title, and the revision of a standard under section 7521(a)(3) of this title,

(L) promulgation or revision of regulations for noncompliance penalties under section 7420 of this title,

(M) promulgation or revision of any regulations promulgated under section 7541 of this title (relating to warranties and compliance by vehicles in actual use),

(N) action of the Administrator under section 7426 of this title (relating to interstate pollution abatement),

(O) the promulgation or revision of any regulation pertaining to consumer and commercial products under section 7511b(e) of this title,

(P) the promulgation or revision of any regulation pertaining to field citations under section 7413(d)(3) of this title,

(Q) the promulgation or revision of any regulation pertaining to urban buses or the clean-fuel vehicle, clean-fuel fleet, and clean fuel programs under part C of subchapter II of this chapter,

(R) the promulgation or revision of any regulation pertaining to nonroad engines or nonroad vehicles under section 7547 of this title,

(S) the promulgation or revision of any regulation relating to motor vehicle compliance program fees under section 7552 of this title,

(T) the promulgation or revision of any regulation under subchapter IV-A of this chapter (relating to acid deposition),

(U) the promulgation or revision of any regulation under section 7511b(f) of this title pertaining to marine vessels, and

(V) such other actions as the Administrator may determine.

The provisions of section 553 through 557 and section 706 of Title 5 shall not, except as expressly provided in this subsection, apply to action to which this subsection applies. This subsection shall not apply in the case of any rule or circumstance referred to in subparagraphs (A) or (B) of subsection 553(b) of Title 5.

(2) Not later than the date of proposal of any action to which this subsection applies, the Administrator shall establish a rulemaking docket for such action (hereinafter in this subsection referred to as a "rule"). Whenever a rule applies only within a particular State, a second (identical) docket shall be established in the appropriate regional office of the Environmental Protection Agency.

(3) In the case of any rule to which this subsection applies, notice of proposed rulemaking shall

be published in the Federal Register, as provided under section 553(b) of Title 5, shall be accompanied by a statement of its basis and purpose and shall specify the period available for public comment (hereinafter referred to as the "comment period"). The notice of proposed rulemaking shall also state the docket number, the location or locations of the docket, and the times it will be open to public inspection. The statement of basis and purpose shall include a summary of —

(A) the factual data on which the proposed rule is based;

(B) the methodology used in obtaining the data and in analyzing the data; and

(C) the major legal interpretations and policy considerations underlying the proposed rule.

The statement shall also set forth or summarize and provide a reference to any pertinent findings, recommendations, and comments by the Scientific Review Committee established under section 109(d) and the National Academy of Sciences, and, if the proposal differs in any important respect from any of these recommendations, an explanation of the reasons for such differences. All data, information, and documents referred to in this paragraph on which the proposed rule relies shall be included in the docket on the date of publication of the proposed rule.

(4)(A) The rulemaking docket required under paragraph (2) shall be open for inspection by the public at reasonable times specified in the notice of proposed rulemaking. Any person may copy documents contained in the docket. The Administrator shall provide copying facilities which may be used at the expense of the person seeking copies, but the Administrator may waive or reduce such expenses in such instances as the public interest requires. Any person may request copies by mail if the person pays the expenses, including personnel costs to do the copying.

(B)(i) Promptly upon receipt by the agency, all written comments and documentary information on the proposed rule received from any person for inclusion in the docket during the comment period shall be placed in the docket. The transcript of public hearings, if any, on the proposed rule shall also be included in the docket promptly upon receipt from the person who transcribed such hearings. All documents which become available after the proposed rule has been published and which the Administrator determines are of central relevance to the rulemaking shall be placed in the docket as soon as possible after their availability.

(ii) The drafts of proposed rules submitted by the Administrator to the Office of Management and Budget for any interagency review process prior to proposal of any such rule, all documents accompanying such drafts, and all written comments thereon by other agencies and all written responses to such written comments by the Administrator shall be placed in the docket no later than the date of proposal of the rule. The drafts of the final rule submitted for such review process prior to promulgation and all such written comments thereon, all documents accompanying such drafts, and written responses thereto shall be placed in the docket no later than the date of promulgation.

(5) In promulgating a rule to which this subsection applies (i) the Administrator shall allow any person to submit written comments, data, or documentary information; (ii) the Administrator shall give interested persons an opportunity for the oral presentation of data, views, or arguments, in addition to an opportunity to make written submissions; (iii) a transcript shall be kept of any oral presentation; and (iv) the Administrator shall keep the record of such proceeding open for thirty days after completion of the proceeding to provide an opportunity for submission of rebuttal and supplementary information.

(6)(A) The promulgated rule shall be accompanied by (i) a statement of basis and purpose like that referred to in paragraph (3) with respect to a proposed rule and (ii) an explanation of the reasons for any major changes in the promulgated rule from the proposed rule.

(B) The promulgated rule shall also be accompanied by a response to each of the significant comments, criticisms, and new data submitted in written or oral presentations during the comment period.

(C) The promulgated rule may not be based (in part or whole) on any information or data which has not been placed in the docket as of the date of such promulgation.

(7)(A) The record for judicial review shall consist exclusively of the material referred to in paragraph (3), clause (i) of paragraph (4)(B), and subparagraphs (A) and (B) of paragraph (6).

(B) Only an objection to a rule or procedure which was raised with reasonable specificity during the period for public comment (including any public hearing) may be raised during judicial review. If the person raising an objection can demonstrate to the Administrator that it was impracticable to raise such objection within such time or if the grounds for such objection arose after the period for public comment (but within the time specified for judicial review) and if such objection is of central relevance to the outcome of the rule, the Administrator shall convene a proceeding for reconsideration of the rule and provide the same procedural rights as would have been afforded had the information been available at the time the rule was proposed. If the Administrator refuses to convene such a proceeding, such person may seek review of such refusal in the United States court of appeals for the appro-priate circuit (as provided in subsection (b) of this section). Such reconsideration shall not postpone the effectiveness of the rule. The effectiveness of the rule may be stayed during such reconsideration, however, by the Administrator or the court for a period not to exceed three months.

(8) The sole forum for challenging procedural determinations made by the Administrator under this subsection shall be in the United States court of appeals for the appropriate circuit (as provided in subsection (b)) at the time of the substantive review of the rule. No interlocutory appeals shall be permitted with respect to such procedural determinations. In reviewing alleged procedural errors, the court may invalidate the rule only if the errors were so serious and related to matters of such central relevance to the rule that there is a substantial likelihood that the rule would have been significantly changed if such errors had not been made.

(9) In the case of review of any action of the Administrator to which this subsection applies, the court may reverse any such action found to be —

(A) arbitrary, capricious, an abuse of discretion, or otherwise not in accordance with law;

(B) contrary to constitutional right, power, privilege, or immunity;

(C) in excess of statutory jurisdiction, authority, or limitations, or short of statutory right; or

(D) without observance of procedure required by law, if (i) such failure to observe such procedure is arbitrary or capricious, (ii) the requirement of paragraph (7)(B) has been met, and (iii) the condition of the last sentence of paragraph (8) is met.

(10) Each statutory deadline for promulgation of rules to which this subsection applies which requires promulgation less than six months after date of proposal may be extended to not more than six months after date of proposal by the Administrator upon a determination that such extension is necessary to afford the public, and the agency, adequate opportunity to carry out the purposes of this subsection.

(11) The requirements of this subsection shall take effect with respect to any rule the proposal of which occurs after ninety days after August 7, 1977.

(e) Other methods of judicial review not authorized — Nothing in this Act shall be construed to authorize judicial review of regulation or orders of the Administrator under this Act, except as provided in this section.

(f) Costs — In any judicial proceeding under this section, the court may award costs of litigation (including reasonable attorney and expert witness fees) whenever it determines that such award is appropriate.

(g) Stay, injunction, or similar relief in proceedings relating to noncompliance penalties — In any action respecting the promulgation of regulations under section 7420 of this title or the administration or enforcement of section 7420 of this title no court shall grant any stay, injunctive, or similar relief before final judgment by such court in such action.

(h) Public participation — It is the intent of Congress that, consistent with the policy of subchapter II of chapter 5 of Title 5 [the Administrative Procedures Act], the Administrator in promulgating any regulation under this Act, including a regulation subject to a deadline, shall ensure a reasonable period for public participation of at least 30 days, except as otherwise expressly provided in section 7407(d), 7502(a), 7511(a) and (b), and 7512(a) and (b) of this title.

§7608. Mandatory licensing
[CAA §308]

Whenever the Attorney General determines upon application of the Administrator —

(1) that —

(A) in the implementation of the requirements of section 7411, 7412, or 7521 of this title, a right under any United States letters patent, which is being used or intended for public or commercial use and not otherwise reasonably available, is necessary to enable any person required to comply with such limitation to so comply, and

(B) there are no reasonable alternative methods to accomplish such purpose, and

(2) that the unavailability of such right may result in a substantial lessening of competition or tendency to create a monopoly in any line of commerce in any section of the country, the Attorney General may so certify to a district court of the United States, which may issue an order requiring the person who owns such patent to license it on such reasonable terms and conditions as the court, after hearing, may determine. Such certification may be made to the district court for the district in which the person owning the patent resides, does business, or is found.

§7609. Policy review
[CAA §309]

(a) Environmental impact — The Administrator shall review and comment in writing on the environmental impact of any matter relating to duties and responsibilities granted pursuant to this Act or other provisions of the authority of the Administrator, contained in any (1) legislation proposed by any Federal department or agency, (2) newly authorized Federal projects for construction and any major Federal agency action (other than a project for construction) to which section 4332(2)(C) of this title applies, and (3) proposed regulations published by any department or agency of the Federal Government. Such written comment shall be made public at the conclusion of any such review.

(b) Unsatisfactory legislation, action, or regulation — In the event the Administrator determines that any such legislation, action, or regulation is unsatisfactory from the standpoint of public health or welfare or environmental quality, he shall publish his determination and the matter shall be referred to the Council on Environmental Quality.

§7610. Other authority
[CAA §310]

(a) Authority and responsibilities under other laws not affected — Except as provided in subsection (b) of this section, this chapter shall not be construed as superseding or limiting the authorities and responsibilities, under any other provision of law, of the Administrator or any other Federal officer, department, or agency.

(b) Nonduplication of appropriations — No appropriation shall be authorized or made under section 241, 243, or 246 of this title for any fiscal year after the fiscal year ending June 30, 1964, for any purpose for which appropriations may be made under authority of this chapter.

§7611. Records and audit
[CAA §311]

(a) Recipients of assistance to keep prescribed records — Each recipient of assistance under this Act shall keep such records as the Administrator shall prescribe, including records which fully disclose the amount and disposition by such recipient of the proceeds of such assistance, the total cost of the project or undertaking in connection with which such assistance is given or used, and the amount of that portion of the cost of the project or undertaking supplied by other sources, and such other records as will facilitate an effective audit.

(b) Audits — The Administrator and the Comptroller General of the United States, or any of their duly authorized representatives, shall have access for the purpose of audit and examinations to any books, documents, papers, and records of the recipients that are pertinent to the grants received under this chapter.

§7612. Economic impact analyses
[CAA §312]

(a) Cost-benefit analysis — The Administrator, in consultation with the Secretary of Commerce, the Secretary of Labor, and the Council on Clean Air Compliance Analysis (as established under subsection (f) of this section), shall conduct a comprehensive analysis of the impact of this Act on the public health, economy, and environment of the United States. In performing such analysis, the Administrator should consider the costs, benefits and other effects associated with compliance with each standard issued for —

(1) a criteria air pollutant subject to a standard issued under section 7409 of this title;

(2) a hazardous air pollutant listed under section 7412 of this title, including any technology-based standard and any risk-based standard for such pollutant;

(3) emissions from mobile sources regulated under subchapter II of this chapter;

(4) a limitation under this chapter for emissions of sulfur dioxide or nitrogen oxides;

(5) a limitation under subchapter VI of this chapter on the production of any ozone-depleting substance; and

(6) any other section of this chapter.

(b) Benefits — In describing the benefits of a standard described in subsection (a) of this section, the Administrator shall consider all of the economic, public health, and environmental benefits of efforts to comply with such standard. In any case where numerical values are assigned to such benefits, a default assumption of zero value shall not be assigned to such benefits unless supported by specific data. The Administrator shall assess how benefits are measured in order to assure that damage to human health and the environment is more accurately measured and taken into account.

(c) Costs — In describing the costs of a standard described in subsection (a) of this section, the Administrator shall consider the effects of such standard on employment, productivity, cost of living, economic growth, and the overall economy of the United States.

(d) Initial report — Not later than 12 months after November 15, 1990, the Administrator, in consultation with the Secretary of Commerce, the Secretary of Labor, and the Council on Clean Air Compliance Analysis, shall submit a report to the Congress that summarizes the results of the analysis described in subsection (a), which reports —

(1) all costs incurred previous to November 15, 1990 in the effort to comply with such standards; and

(2) all benefits that have accrued to the United States as a result of such costs.

(f) Appointment of Advisory Council on Clean Air Compliance Analysis — Not later than 6 months after November 15, 1990, the Administrator, in consultation with the Secretary of Commerce and the Secretary of Labor, shall appoint an Advisory Council on Clean Air Compliance Analysis of not less than nine members (hereafter in this section referred to as the "Council"). In appointing such members, the Administrator shall appoint recognized experts in the fields of the health and environmental effects of air pollution, economic analysis, environmental sciences, and such other fields that the Administrator determines to be appropriate.

(g) Duties of Advisory Council — The Council shall —

(1) review the data to be used for any analysis required under this section and make

recommendations to the Administrator on the use of such data;

(2) review the methodology used to analyze such data and make recommendations to the Administrator on the use of such methodology; and

(3) prior to the issuance of a report required under subsection (d) or (e), review the findings of such report, and make recommendations to the Administrator concerning the validity and utility of such findings.

§7613. Repealed. Pub. L. 101-549, §803, Nov. 15, 1990, 104 Stat. 2689

§7614. Labor standards
[CAA §314]

The Administrator shall take such action as may be necessary to insure that all laborers and mechanics employed by contractors or subcontractors on projects assisted under this Act shall be paid wages at rates not less than those prevailing for the same type of work on similar construction in the locality as determined by the Secretary of Labor, in accordance with the Act of March 3, 1931, as amended, known as the Davis-Bacon Act (46 Stat. 1494; 40 U.S.C. 276a-276a(5). The Secretary of Labor shall have, with respect to the labor standards specified in this subsection, the authority and functions set forth in Reorganization Plan Numbered 14 of 1950 (15 F.R. 3176; 64 Stat. 1267) and section 276c of Title 40.

§7615. Separability
[CAA §315]

If any provision of this Act, or the application of any provision of this Act to any person or circumstance, is held invalid, the application of such provision to other persons or circumstances, and the remainder of this Act, shall not be affected thereby.

§7616. Sewage treatment grants
[CAA §316]

(a) Construction — No grant which the Administrator is authorized to make to any applicant for construction of sewage treatment works in any area in any State may be withheld, conditioned, or restricted by the Administrator on the basis of any requirement of this Act except as provided in subsection (b) of this section.

(b) Withholding, conditioning, or restriction of construction grants — The Administrator may withhold, condition, or restrict the making of any grant for construction referred to in subsection (a) of this section only if he determines that —

(1) such treatment works will not comply with applicable standards under section 7411 or 7412 of this title,

(2) the State does not have in effect, or is not carrying out, a State implementation plan

approved by the Administrator which expressly quantifies and provides for the increase in emissions of each air pollutant (from stationary and mobile sources in any area to which either part C or part D of subchapter I of this chapter applies for such pollutant) which increase may reasonably be anticipated to result directly or indirectly from the new sewage treatment capacity which would be created by such construction.

(3) the construction of such treatment works would create new sewage treatment capacity which —

(A) may reasonably be anticipated to cause or contribute to, directly or indirectly, an increase in emissions of any air pollutant in excess of the increase provided for under the provisions referred to in paragraph (2) for any such area, or

(B) would otherwise not be in conformity with the applicable implementation plan, or

(4) such increase in emissions would interfere with, or be inconsistent with, the applicable implementation plan for any other State.

In the case of construction of a treatment works which would result, directly or indirectly, in an increase in emissions of any air pollutant from stationary and mobile sources in an area to which part D of subchapter I of this chapter applies, the quantification of emissions referred to in paragraph (2) shall include the emissions of any such pollutant resulting directly or indirectly from areawide and nonmajor stationary source growth (mobile and stationary) for each such area.

(c) National Environmental Policy Act — Nothing in this section shall be construed to amend or alter any provision of the National Environmental Policy Act or to affect any determination as to whether or not the requirements of such Act have been met in the case of the construction of any sewage treatment works.

§7617. Economic impact assessment
[CAA §317]

(a) Notice of proposed rulemaking; substantial revisions — This section applies to action of the Administrator in promulgating or revising —

(1) any new source standard of performance under section 7411 of this title,

(2) any regulation under section 7411(d) of this title,

(3) any regulation under part B of subchapter I of this chapter (relating to ozone and stratosphere protection),

(4) any regulation under part C of subchapter I of this chapter (relating to prevention of significant deterioration of air quality),

(5) any regulation establishing emission standards under section 7521 of this title and any other regulation promulgated under that section,

(6) any regulation controlling or prohibiting any fuel or fuel additive under section 7545(c), and

(7) any aircraft emission standard under section 7571 of this title.

Nothing in this section shall apply to any standard or regulation described in paragraphs (1) through (7) of this subsection unless the notice of proposed rule-making in connection with such standard or regulation is published in the Federal Register after the date ninety days after the date of enactment of this section. In the case of revisions of such standards or regulations, this section shall apply only to revisions which the Administrator determines to be substantial revisions.

(b) Preparation of assessment by Administrator — Before publication of notice of proposed rulemaking with respect to any standard or regulation to which this section applies, the Administrator shall prepare an economic impact assessment respecting such standard or regulation. Such assessment shall be included in the docket required under section 7607(d)(2) of this title and shall be available to the public as provided in section 7607(d)(4) of this title. Notice of proposed rulemaking shall include notice of such availability together with an explanation of the extent and manner in which the Administrator has considered the analysis contained in such economic impact assessment in proposing the action. The Administrator shall also provide such an explanation in his notice of promulgation of any regulation or standard referred to in subsection (a). Each such explanation shall be part of the statements of basis and purpose required under sections 7607(d)(3) and 7607(d)(6) of this title.

(c) Analysis — Subject to subsection (d), the assessment required under this section with respect to any standard or regulation shall contain an analysis of —

(1) costs of compliance with any such standard or regulation, including extent to which the costs of compliance will vary depending on (A) the effective date of the standard or regulation, and (B) the development of less expensive, more efficient means or methods of compliance with the standard or regulation;

(2) the potential inflationary or recessionary effects of the standard or regulation;

(3) the effects on competition of the standard or regulation with respect to small business;

(4) the effects of the standard or regulation on consumer costs; and

(5) the effects of the standard or regulation on energy use.

Nothing in this section shall be construed to provide that the analysis of the factors specified in this subsection affects or alters the factors which the Administrator is required to consider in taking any action referred to in subsection of this section.

(d) Extensiveness of assessment — The assessment required under this section shall be as extensive as practicable, in the judgment of the Administrator taking into account the time and resources available to the Environmental Protection Agency and other duties and authorities which the Administrator is required to carry out under this chapter.

(e) Limitations on construction of section — Nothing in this section shall be construed —

(1) to alter the basis on which a standard or regulation is promulgated under this chapter;

(2) to preclude the Administrator from carrying out his responsibility under this Act to protect public health and welfare; or

(3) to authorize or require any judicial review of any such standard or regulation, or any stay or injunction of the proposal, promulgation, or effectiveness of such standard or regulation on the basis of failure to comply with this section.

(f) Citizen suits — The requirements imposed on the Administrator under this section shall be treated as nondiscretionary duties for purposes of section 7604(a)(2) of this title, relating to citizen suits. The sole method for enforcement of the Administrator's duty under this section shall be by bringing a citizen suit under such section 7604(a)(2) for a court order to compel the Administrator to perform such duty. Violation of any such order shall subject the Administrator to penalties for contempt of court.

(g) Costs — In the case of any provision of this Act in which costs are expressly required to be taken into account, the adequacy or inadequacy of any assessment required under this section may be taken into consideration, but shall not be treated for purposes of judicial review of any such provision as conclusive with respect to compliance or noncompliance with the requirement of such provision to take cost into account.

§7618. Repealed. Pub. L. 101-549, Title I, §108(q), Nov. 15, 1990, 104 Stat. 2469

§7619. Air quality monitoring
[CAA §319]

(a) In general — After notice and opportunity for public hearing, the Administrator shall promulgate regulations establishing an air quality monitoring system throughout the United States which —

(1) utilizes uniform air quality monitoring criteria and methodology and measures such air quality according to a uniform air quality index,

(2) provides for air quality monitoring stations in major urban areas and other appropriate areas throughout the United States to provide monitoring such as will supplement (but not duplicate) air quality monitoring carried out by the States required under any applicable implementation plan,

(3) provides for daily analysis and reporting of air quality based upon such uniform air quality index, and

(4) provides for recordkeeping with respect to such monitoring data and for periodic analysis and reporting to the general public by the Administrator with respect to air quality based upon such data. The operation of such air quality monitoring system may be carried out by the Administrator or by such other departments, agencies, or entities of the Federal Government (including the National Weather Service) as the President may deem appropriate. Any air quality monitoring system required under any applicable implementation plan under section 7410 of this title shall, as soon as practicable following promulgation of regulations under this section, utilize the standard criteria and methodology, and measure air quality according to the standard index, established under such regulations.

(b) Air quality monitoring data influenced by exceptional events

(1) Definition of exceptional event — In this section:

(A) In general — The term "exceptional event" means an event that —

(i) affects air quality;

(ii) is not reasonably controllable or preventable;

(iii) is an event caused by human activity that is unlikely to recur at a particular location or a natural event; and

(iv) is determined by the Administrator through the process established in the regulations promulgated under paragraph (2) to be an exceptional event.

(B) Exclusions — In this subsection, the term "exceptional event" does not include —

(i) stagnation of air masses or meteorological inversions;

(ii) a meteorological event involving high temperatures or lack of precipitation; or

(iii) air pollution relating to source noncompliance.

(2) Regulations

(A) Proposed regulations — Not later than March 1, 2006, after consultation with Federal land managers and State air pollution control agencies, the Administrator shall publish in the Federal Register proposed regulations governing the review and handling of air quality monitoring data influenced by exceptional events.

(B) Final regulations — Not later than 1 year after the date on which the Administrator publishes proposed regulations under subparagraph (A), and after providing an opportunity for interested persons to make oral presentations of views, data, and arguments regarding the proposed regulations, the Administrator shall promulgate final regulations governing the review and handling or air quality monitoring data influenced by an exceptional event that are consistent with paragraph (3).

(3) Principles and requirements

(A) Principles — In promulgating regulations under this section, the Administrator shall follow—

(i) the principle that protection of public health is the highest priority;

(ii) the principle that timely information should be provided to the public in any case in which the air quality is unhealthy;

(iii) the principle that all ambient air quality data should be included in a timely manner, an appropriate Federal air quality database that is accessible to the public;

(iv) the principle that each State must take necessary measures to safeguard public health regardless of the source of the air pollution; and

(v) the principle that air quality data should be carefully screened to ensure that events not likely to recur are represented accurately in all monitoring data and analyses.

(B) Requirements — Regulations promulgated under this section shall, at a minimum, provide that —

(i) the occurrence of an exceptional event must be demonstrated by reliable, accurate data that is promptly produced and provided by Federal, State, or local government agencies;

(ii) a clear causal relationship must exist between the measured exceedances of a national ambient air quality standard and the exceptional event to demonstrate that the exceptional event caused a specific air pollution concentration at a particular air quality monitoring location;

(iii) there is a public process for determining whether an event is exceptional; and

(iv) there are criteria and procedures for the Governor of a State to petition the Administrator to exclude air quality monitoring data that is directly due to exceptional events from use in determinations by the Administrator with respect to exceedances or violations of the national ambient air quality standards.

(4) Interim provision — Until the effective date of a regulation promulgated under paragraph (2), the following guidance issued by the Administrator shall continue to apply:

(A) Guidance on the identification and use of air quality data affected by exceptional events (July 1986).

(B) Areas affected by PM-10 natural events, May 30, 1996.

(C) Appendices I, K, and N to part 50 of title 40, Code of Federal Regulations.

§7620. Standardized air quality modeling
[CAA §320]

(a) Conferences — Not later than six months after August 7, 1977, and at least every three years thereafter, the Administrator shall conduct a conference on air quality modeling. In conducting such conference, special attention shall be given to appropriate modeling necessary for carrying out part C of subchapter I of this chapter (relating to prevention of significant deterioration of air quality).

(b) Conferees — The conference conducted under this section shall provide for participation by the National Academy of Sciences, representatives of State and local air pollution control agencies, and appropriate Federal agencies, including the National Science Foundation; the National Oceanic and Atmospheric Administration, and the National Institute of Standards and Technology.

(c) Comments; transcripts — Interested persons shall be permitted to submit written comments and a verbatim transcript of the conference proceedings shall be maintained.

(d) Promulgation and revision of regulation relating to air quality monitoring — The comments submitted and the transcript maintained pursuant to subsection (c) of this section shall be included in the docket required to be established for purposes of promulgating or revising any regulation relating to air quality modeling under part C of subchapter I of this chapter.

§7621. Employment effects
[CAA §321]

(a) Continuous evaluation of potential loss or shifts of employment — The Administrator shall conduct continuing evaluations of potential loss or shifts of employment which may result from the administration or enforcement of the provision of this chapter and applicable implementation plans, including where appropriate, investigating threatened plant closures or reductions in employment allegedly resulting from such administration or enforcement.

(b) Request for investigation; hearings; record; report — Any employee, or any representative of such employee, who is discharged or laid off, threatened with discharge or layoff, or whose employment is otherwise adversely affected or threatened to be adversely affected because of the alleged results of any requirement imposed or proposed to be imposed under this Act, including any requirement applicable to Federal facilities and any requirement imposed by a State or political subdivision thereof, may request the Administrator to conduct a full investigation of the matter. Any such request shall be reduced to writing, shall set forth with reasonable particularity the grounds for the request, and shall be signed by the employee, or representative of such employee, making the request. The Administrator shall thereupon investigate the matter and, at the request of any party, shall hold public hearings on not less than five days' notice. At such hearings, the Administrator shall require the parties, including the employer involved, to present information relating to the actual or potential effect of such requirements on employment and the detailed reasons or justification therefor. If the Administrator determines that there are no reasonable grounds for conducting a public hearing he shall notify (in writing) the party requesting such hearing of such a determination and the reasons therefor. If the Administrator does convene such a hearing, the hearing shall be on the record. Upon receiving the report of such investigation, the Administrator shall make findings of fact as to the effect of such requirements on employment and on the alleged actual or potential discharge, layoff, or other adverse effect on employment, and shall make such recommendations as he deems appropriate. Such report, findings, and recommendations shall be available to the public.

(c) Subpoenas; confidential information; witnesses; penalty — In connection with any investigation or public hearing conducted under subsection (b) of this section or as authorized in section 7419 of this title (relating to primary nonferrous smelter orders), the Administrator may issue subpenas for the attendance and testimony of witnesses and the production of relevant papers, books and documents, and he may administer oaths. Except for emission data, upon a showing satisfactory to the Administrator by such owner or operator that such papers, books, documents, or information or particular part thereof, if made public, would divulge trade secrets or secret processes of such owner, or operator, the Administrator shall consider such record, report, or information or particular portion thereof confidential in accordance with the purposes of section 1905 of Title 18, except that such paper, book, document, or information may be disclosed to other officers, employees, or authorized representatives of the United States concerned with carrying out this Act, or when relevant in any proceeding under this Act. Witnesses summoned shall be paid the same fees and mileage that are paid witnesses in the courts of the United States. In cases of contumacy or refusal to obey a subpena served upon any person under this subparagraph, the district court of the United States for any district in which such person is found or resides or transacts business, upon application by the United States and after notice to such person, shall have jurisdiction to issue an order requiring such person to appear and give testimony before the Administrator, to appear and produce papers, books, and documents before the Administrator, or both, and any failure to obey such order of the court may be punished by such court as a contempt thereof.

(d) Limitations on construction of section — Nothing in this section shall be construed to require or authorize the Administrator, the States, or political subdivisions thereof, to modify or withdraw any requirement imposed or proposed to be imposed under this chapter.

§7622. Employee protection
[CAA §322]
(a) Discharge or discrimination prohibited — No employer may discharge any employee or otherwise discriminate against any employee with respect to his compensation, terms, conditions, or privileges of employment because the employee (or any person acting pursuant to a request of the employee) —

(1) commenced, caused to be commenced, or is about to commence or cause to be commenced a proceeding under this Act or a proceeding for the administration or enforcement of any requirement imposed under this Act or under any applicable implementation plan,

(2) testified or is about to testify in any such proceeding, or

(3) assisted or participated or is about to assist or participate in any manner in such a proceeding or in any other action to carry out the purposes of this chapter.

(b) Complaint charging unlawful discharge or discrimination; investigation; order

(1) Any employee who believes that he has been discharged or otherwise discriminated against by any person in violation of subsection (a) of this section may, within thirty days after such violation occurs, file (or have any person file on his behalf) a complaint with the Secretary of Labor (hereinafter in this subsection referred to as the "Secretary") alleging such discharge or discrimination. Upon receipt of such a complaint, the Secretary shall notify the person named in the complaint of the filing of the complaint.

(2)(A) Upon receipt of a complaint filed under paragraph (1), the Secretary shall conduct an investigation of the violation alleged in the complaint. Within thirty days of the receipt of such complaint, the Secretary shall complete such investigation and shall notify in writing the complainant (and any person acting in his behalf) and the person alleged to have committed such violation of the results of the investigation conducted pursuant to this subparagraph. Within ninety days of the receipt of such complaint the Secretary shall, unless the proceeding on the complaint is terminated by the Secretary on the basis of a settlement entered into by the Secretary and the person alleged to have committed such violation, issue an order either providing the relief prescribed by subparagraph (B) or denying the complaint. An order of the Secretary shall be made on the record after notice and opportunity for public hearing. The Secretary may not enter into a settlement terminating a proceeding on a complaint without the participation and consent of the complainant.

(B) If, in response to a complaint filed under paragraph (1), the Secretary determines that a violation of subsection (a) has occurred, the Secretary shall order the person who committed such violation to (i) take affirmative action to abate the violation, and (ii) reinstate the complainant to his former position together with the compensation (including back pay), terms, conditions, and privileges of his employment, and the Secretary may order such person to provide compensatory damages to the complainant. If an order is issued under this paragraph, the Secretary, at the request of the complainant, shall assess against the person against whom the order is issued a sum equal to the aggregate amount of all costs and expenses (including attorneys' and expert witness fees) reasonably incurred, as determined by the Secretary, by the complainant for, or in connection with, the bringing of the complaint upon which the order was issued.

(c) Review

(1) Any person adversely affected or aggrieved by an order issued under subsection (b) may obtain review of the order in the United States court of appeals for the circuit in which the violation, with respect to which the order was issued, allegedly occurred. The petition for review must be filed within sixty days from the issuance of the Secretary's order. Review shall conform to chapter 7 of Title 5. The commencement of proceedings under this subparagraph shall not, unless ordered by the court, operate as a stay of the Secretary's order.

(2) An order of the Secretary with respect to which review could have been obtained under paragraph (1) shall not be subject to judicial review in any criminal or other civil proceeding.

(d) Enforcement of order by Secretary — Whenever a person has failed to comply with an order issued under subsection (b)(2) of this section, the Secretary may file a civil action in the United States district court for the district in which the violation was found to occur to enforce such order. In actions brought under this subsection, the district courts shall have jurisdiction to grant all appropriate relief including, but not limited to, injunctive relief, compensatory, and exemplary damages.

(e) Enforcement of order by person on whose behalf order was issued

(1) Any person on whose behalf an order was issued under paragraph (2) of subsection (b) of this section may commence a civil action against the person to whom such order was issued to require compliance with such order. The appropriate United States district court shall have jurisdiction, without regard to the amount in controversy or the citizenship of the parties, to enforce such order.

(2) The court, in issuing any final order under this subsection, may award costs of litigation (including reasonable attorney and expert witness

fees) to any party whenever the court determines such award is appropriate.

(f) Mandamus — Any nondiscretionary duty imposed by this section shall be enforceable in a mandamus proceeding brought under section 1361 of Title 28.

(g) Deliberate violation by employee — Subsection (a) of this section shall not apply with respect to any employee who, acting without direction from his employer (or the employer's agent), deliberately causes a violation of any requirement of this chapter.

§7623. Repealed. Pub. L. 96-300, §1(c), July 2, 1980, 94 Stat. 831

§7624. Cost of vapor recovery equipment
[CAA §323]

(a) Costs to be borne by owner of retail outlet — The regulations under this Act applicable to vapor recovery with respect to mobile source fuels at retail outlets of such fuels shall provide that the cost of procurement and installation of such vapor recovery shall be borne by the owner of such outlet (as determined under such regulations). Except as provided in subsection (b) of this section, such regulations shall provide that no lease of a retail outlet by the owner thereof which is entered into or renewed after August 7, 1977, may provide for a payment by the lessee of the cost of procurement and installation of vapor recovery equipment. Such regulations shall also provide that the cost of procurement and installation of vapor recovery equipment may be recovered by the owner of such outlet by means of price increases in the cost of any product sold by such owner, notwithstanding any provision of law.

(b) Payment by lessee — The regulations of the Administrator referred to in subsection (a) shall permit a lease of a retail outlet to provide for payment by the lessee of the cost of procurement and installation of vapor recovery requirement over a reasonable period (as determined in accordance with such regulations), if the owner of such outlet does not sell, trade in, or otherwise dispense any product at wholesale or retail at such outlet.

§7625. Vapor recovery for small business marketers of petroleum products
[CAA §324]

(a) Marketers of gasoline — The regulations under this Act applicable to vapor recovery from fueling of motor vehicles at retail outlets of gasoline shall not apply to any outlet owned by an independent small business marketer of gasoline having monthly sales of less than 50,000 gallons. In the case of any other outlet owned by an independent small business marketer, such regulations shall provide, with respect to independent small business marketers of gasoline, for a three-year phase-in period for the installation of such vapor recovery equipment at such outlets

under which such marketers shall have —

(1) 33 percent of such outlets in compliance at the end of the first year during which such regulations apply to such marketers,

(2) 66 percent at the end of such second year, and

(3) 100 percent at the end of the third year.

(b) State requirements — Nothing in subsection (a) of this section shall be construed to prohibit any State from adopting or enforcing, with respect to independent small business marketers of gasoline having monthly sales of less than 50,000 gallons, any vapor recovery requirements for mobile source fuels at retail outlets. Any vapor recovery requirement which is adopted by a State and submitted to the Administrator as part of its implementation plan may be approved and enforced by the Administrator as part of the applicable implementation plan for that State.

(c) Refiners — For purposes of this section, an independent small business marketer of gasoline is a person engaged in the marketing of gasoline who would be required to pay for procurement and installation of vapor recovery equipment under section 7624 of this title or under regulations of the Administrator, unless such person —

(1)(A) is a refiner, or

(B) controls, is controlled by, or is under common control with, a refiner.

(C) is otherwise directly or indirectly affiliated (as determined under the regulations of the Administrator) with a refiner or with a person who controls, is controlled by, or is under a common control with a refiner (unless the sole affiliation referred to herein is by means of a supply contract or an agreement or contract to use a trademark, trade name, service mark, or other identifying symbol or name owned by such refiner or any such person), or

(2) receives less than 50 percent of his annual income from refining or marketing of gasoline. For the purpose of this section, the term "refiner" shall not include any refiner whose total refinery capacity (including the refinery capacity of any person who controls, is controlled by, or is under common control with, such refiner) does not exceed 65,000 barrels per day. For purposes of this section, "control" of a corporation means ownership of more than 50 percent of its stock.

§7625-1. Exemptions for certain territories
[CAA §325]
(a) In general

(1) Upon petition by the governor of Guam, American Samoa, [the Virgin Islands,] or the Commonwealth of the Northern Mariana Islands, the Administrator is authorized to exempt any person or source or class of persons or sources in such territory from any requirement under this Act other than section 7412 of this title or any requirement

under section 7410 of this title or part D of subchapter I of this chapter necessary to attain or maintain a national primary ambient air quality standard. Such exemption may be granted if the Administrator finds that compliance with such requirement is not feasible or is unreasonable due to unique geographical, meteorological, or economic factors of such territory, or such other local factors as the Administrator deems significant. Any such petition shall be considered in accordance with section 307(d) and any exemption under this subsection shall be considered final action by the Administrator for the purposes of section 7607(b) of this title.

(2) The Administrator shall promptly notify the Committees on Energy and Commerce and on Interior and Insular Affairs of the House of Representatives and the Committees on Environment and Public Works and on Energy and Natural Resources of the Senate upon receipt of any petition under this subsection and of the approval or rejection of such petition and the basis for such action.

(b) Power plant operating within Guam as of December 8, 1983 — Notwithstanding any other provision of this Act, any fossil fuel fired steam electric power plant operating within Guam as of the date of enactment of this section is hereby exempted from:

(1) any requirement of the new source performance standards relating to sulfur dioxide promulgated under section 7411 of this title as of December 8, 1983; and

(2) any regulation relating to sulfur dioxide standards or limitations contained in a State implementation plan approved under section 7410 as of such date of enactment: *Provided,* That such exemption shall expire eighteen months after such date of enactment unless the Administrator determines that such plant is making all emissions reductions practicable to prevent exceedances of the national ambient air quality standards for sulfur dioxide.

§7625a. Statutory construction
[CAA §326]

The parenthetical cross references in any provision of this Act to other provisions of the Act, or other provisions of law, where the words "relating to" or "pertaining to" are used, are made only for convenience, and shall be given no legal effect.

§7626. Authorization of appropriations
[CAA §327]

(a) In general — There are authorized to be appropriated to carry out this Act such sums as may be necessary for the 7 fiscal years commencing after November 15, 1990.

(b) Grants for planning — There are authorized to be appropriated (1) not more than $50,000,000 to carry out section 7505 of this title beginning in fiscal year 1991, to be available until expended, to develop plan revisions required by subpart 2, 3, or 4 of part D

of subchapter I of this chapter, and (2) not more than $15,000,000 for each of the 7 fiscal years commencing after November 15, 1990 to make grants to the States to prepare implementation plans as required by subpart 2, 3, or 4 of part D of subchapter I of this chapter.

§7627. Air pollution from Outer Continental Shelf activities
[CAA §328]
(a) Applicable requirements for certain areas

(1) In general — Not later than 12 months after November 15, 1990, following consultation with the Secretary of the Interior and the Commandant of the United States Coast Guard, the Administrator, by rule, shall establish requirements to control air pollution from Outer Continental Shelf sources located offshore of the States along the Pacific, Arctic and Atlantic Coasts (other than Outer Continental Shelf sources located offshore of the North Slope Borough of the State of Alaska), and along the United States Gulf Coast off the State of Florida eastward of longitude 87 degrees and 30 minutes ("OCS sources") to attain and maintain Federal and State ambient air quality standards and to comply with the provisions of part C of subchapter I of this chapter. For such sources located within 25 miles of the seaward boundary of such States, such requirements shall be the same as would be applicable if the source were located in the corresponding onshore area, and shall include, but not be limited to, State and local requirements for emission controls, emission limitations, offsets, permitting, monitoring, testing, and reporting. New OCS sources shall comply with such requirements on the date of promulgation and existing OCS sources shall comply on the date 24 months thereafter. The Administrator shall update such requirements as necessary to maintain consistency with onshore regulations. The authority of this subsection shall supersede section 5(a)(8) of the Outer Continental Shelf Lands Act but shall not repeal or modify any other Federal, State, or local authorities with respect to air quality. Each requirement established under this section shall be treated, for purposes of sections 7413, 7414, 7416, 7420, and 7604 of this title, as a standard under section 7411 of this title and a violation of any such requirement shall be considered a violation of section 7411(e) of this title.

(2) Exemptions — The Administrator may exempt an OCS source from a specific requirement in effect under regulations under this subsection if the Administrator finds that compliance with a pollution control technology requirement is technically infeasible or will cause an unreasonable threat to health and safety. The Administrator shall make written findings explaining the basis of any exemption issued pursuant to this subsection and shall impose another requirement equal to or as

close in stringency to the original requirement as possible. The Administrator shall ensure that any increase in emissions due to the granting of an exemption is offset by reductions in actual emissions, not otherwise required by this Act, from the same source or other sources in the area or in the corresponding onshore area. The Administrator shall establish procedures to provide for public notice and comment on exemptions proposed pursuant to this subsection.

(3) State procedures — Each State adjacent to an OCS source included under this subsection may promulgate and submit to the Administrator regulations for implementing and enforcing the requirements of this subsection. If the Administrator finds that the State regulations are adequate, the Administrator shall delegate to that State any authority the Administrator has under this Act to implement and enforce such requirements. Nothing in this subsection shall prohibit the Administrator from enforcing any requirement of this section.

(4) Definitions — For purposes of subsections (a) and (b) of this section —

(A) Outer Continental Shelf — The term "Outer Continental Shelf" has the meaning provided by section 2 of the Outer Continental Shelf Lands Act (43 U.S.C. §1331).

(B) Corresponding onshore area — The term "corresponding onshore area" means, with respect to any OCS source, the onshore attainment or nonattainment area that is closest to the source, unless the Administrator determines that another area with more stringent requirements with respect to the control and abatement of air pollution may reasonably be expected to be affected by such emissions. Such determination shall be based on the potential for air pollutants from the OCS source to reach the other onshore area and the potential of such air pollutants to affect the efforts of the other onshore area to attain or maintain any Federal or State ambient air quality standard or to comply with the provisions of part C of subchapter I of this chapter.

(C) Outer continental shelf source — The terms "Outer Continental Shelf source" and "OCS source" include any equipment, activity, or facility which —

(i) emits or has the potential to emit any air pollutant,

(ii) is regulated or authorized under the Outer Continental Shelf Lands Act, [43 U.S.C. §§1331 et seq.] and

(iii) is located on the Outer Continental Shelf or in or on waters above the Outer Continental Shelf.

Such activities include, but are not limited to, platform and drill ship exploration, construction, development, production, processing,

and transportation. For purposes of this subsection, emissions from any vessel servicing or associated with an OCS source, including emissions while at the OCS source or en route to or from the OCS source within 25 miles of the OCS source, shall be considered direct emissions from the OCS source.

(D) New and existing OCS sources — The term "new OCS source" means an OCS source which is a new source within the meaning of section 7411(a) of this title. The term "existing OCS source" means any OCS source other than a new OCS source.

(b) Requirements for other offshore areas —
For portions of the United States Outer Continental Shelf that are adjacent to the States not covered by subsection (a) which are Texas, Louisiana, Mississippi, and Alabama or are adjacent to the North Slope Borough of the State of Alaska, the Secretary shall consult with the Administrator to assure coordination of air pollution control regulation for Outer Continental Shelf emissions and emissions in adjacent onshore areas. Concurrently with this obligation, the Secretary shall complete within 3 years of November 15, 1990, a research study examining the impacts of emissions from Outer Continental Shelf activities in such areas that fail to meet the national ambient air quality standards for either ozone or nitrogen dioxide. Based on the results of this study, the Secretary shall consult with the Administrator and determine if any additional actions are necessary. There are authorized to be appropriated such sums as may be necessary to provide funding for the study required under this section.

(c) Coastal waters

(1) The study report of section 7412(n) of the Clean Air Act shall apply to the coastal waters of the United States to the same extent and in the same manner as such requirements apply to the Great Lakes, the Chesapeake Bay, and their tributary waters.

(2) The regulatory requirements of section 7412(n) of of this title shall apply to the coastal waters of the States which are subject to subsection (a) of this section, to the same extent and in the same manner as such requirements apply to the Great Lakes, the Chesapeake Bay, and their tributary waters.

§7628. Demonstration grant program for local governments

[CAA 329]

(a) Grant program

(1) In general — The Administrator shall establish a demonstration program under which the Administrator shall provide competitive grants to assist local governments (such as municipalities and counties), with respect to local government buildings —

(A) to deploy cost-effective technologies and practices; and

(B) to achieve operational cost savings, through the application of cost-effective technologies and practices, as verified by the Administrator.

(2) Cost sharing

(A) In general—The Federal share of the cost of an activity carried out using a grant provided under this section shall be 40 percent.

(B) Waiver of non-federal share — The Administrator may waive up to 100 percent of the local share of the cost of any grant under this section should the Administrator determine that the community is economically distressed, pursuant to objective economic criteria established by the Administrator in published guidelines.

(3) Maximum amount — The amount of a grant provided under this subsection shall not exceed $1,000,000.

(b) Guidelines

(1) In general — Not later than 1 year after the date of enactment of this section [enacted Dec. 19, 2007], the Administrator shall issue guidelines to implement the grant program established under subsection (a).

(2) Requirements — The guidelines under paragraph (1) shall establish —

(A) standards for monitoring and verification of operational cost savings through the application of cost-effective technologies and practices reported by grantees under this section;

(B) standards for grantees to implement training programs, and to provide technical assistance and education, relating to the retrofit of buildings using cost-effective technologies and practices; and

(C) a requirement that each local government that receives a grant under this section shall achieve facility-wide cost savings, through renovation of existing local government buildings using cost-effective technologies and practices, of at least 40 percent as compared to the baseline operational costs of the buildings before the renovation (as calculated assuming a 3-year, weather-normalized average).

(c) Compliance with State and local law — Nothing in this section or any program carried out using a grant provided under this section supersedes or otherwise affects any State or local law, to the extent that the State or local law contains a requirement that is more stringent than the relevant requirement of this section.

(d) Authorization of appropriations — There is authorized to be appropriated to carry out this section $20,000,000 for each of fiscal years 2007 through 2012.

(e) Reports

(1) In general — The Administrator shall provide annual reports to Congress on cost savings achieved and actions taken and recommendations made under this section, and any recommendations for further action.

(2) Final report — The Administrator shall issue a final report at the conclusion of the program, including findings, a summary of total cost savings achieved, and recommendations for further action.

(f) Termination — The program under this section shall terminate on September 30, 2012.

(g) Definitions — In this section, the terms "cost-effective technologies and practices" and "operating cost savings" shall have the meanings defined in section 401 of the Energy Independence and Security Act of 2007 [42 U.S.C. §17061].

SUBCHAPTER IV — NOISE POLLUTION

§7641. Noise abatement
[CAA §402]

(a) Office of Noise Abatement and Control — The Administrator shall establish within the the the Environmental Protection Agency an Office of Noise Abatement and Control, and shall carry out through such Office a full and complete investigation and study of noise and its effect on the public health and welfare in order to (1) identify and classify causes and sources of noise, and (2) determine —

(A) effects at various levels;

(B) projected growth of noise levels in urban areas through the year 2000;

(C) the psychological and physiological effect on humans;

(D) effects of sporadic extreme noise (such as jet noise near airports) as compared with constant noise;

(E) effect on wildlife and property (including values);

(F) effect of sonic booms on property (including values); and

(G) such other matters as may be of interest in the public welfare.

(b) Investigation techniques; report and recommendations — In conducting such investigation, the Administrator shall hold public hearings, conduct research, experiments, demonstrations, and studies. The Administrator shall report the results of such investigation and study, together with his recommendations for legislation or other action, to the President and the Congress not later than one year after the date of enactment of this title.

(c) Abatement of noise from federal activities — In any case where any Federal department or a agency is carrying out or sponsoring any activity resulting in noise which the administrator determines amounts to a public nuisance or is otherwise objectionable, such department or agency shall consult with the Administrator to determine possible means of abating such noise.

§7642. Authorization of appropriations
[CAA §403]

There is authorized to be appropriated such amount, not to exceed $30,000,000, as may be necessary for the purposes of this title.

SUBCHAPTER IV-A — ACID DEPOSITION CONTROL

§7651. Findings and purposes
[CAA §401]

(a) Findings — The Congress finds that —

(1) the presence of acidic compounds and their precursors in the atmosphere and in deposition from the atmosphere represents a threat to natural resources, ecosystems, materials, visibility, and public health;

(2) the principal sources of the acidic compounds and their precursors in the atmosphere are emissions of sulfur and nitrogen oxides from the combustion of fossil fuels;

(3) the problem of acid deposition is of national and international significance;

(4) strategies and technologies for the control of precursors to acid deposition exist now that are economically feasible, and improved methods are expected to become increasingly available over the next decade;

(5) current and future generations of Americans will be adversely affected by delaying measures to remedy the problem;

(6) reduction of total atmospheric loading of sulfur dioxide and nitrogen oxides will enhance protection of the public health and welfare and the environment; and

(7) control measures to reduce precursor emissions from steam-electric generating units should be initiated without delay.

(b) Purposes — The purpose of this title is to reduce the adverse effects of acid deposition through reductions in annual emissions of sulfur dioxide of ten million tons from 1980 emission levels, and, in combination with other provisions of this Act, of nitrogen oxides emissions of approximately two million tons from 1980 emission levels, in the forty-eight contiguous States and the District of Columbia. It is the intent of this title to effectuate such reductions by requiring compliance by affected sources with prescribed emission limitations by specified deadlines, which limitations may be met through alternative methods of compliance provided by an emission allocation and transfer system. It is also the purpose of this title to encourage energy conservation, use of renewable and clean alternative technologies, and pollution prevention as a long-range strategy, consistent with the provisions of this title, for reducing air pollution and other adverse impacts of energy production and use.

§7651a. Definitions
[CAA §402]

As used in this title:

(1) The term "affected source" means a source that includes one or more affected units.

(2) The term "affected unit" means a unit that is subject to emission reduction requirements or limitations under this title.

(3) The term "allowance" means an authorization, allocated to an affected unit by the Administrator under this title, to emit, during or after a specified calendar year, one ton of sulfur dioxide.

(4) The term "baseline" means the annual quantity of fossil fuel consumed by an affected unit, measured in millions of British Thermal Units ("mmBtu's"), calculated as follows:

(A) For each utility unit that was in commercial operation prior to January 1, 1985, the baseline shall be the annual average quantity of mmBtu's consumed in fuel during calendar years 1985, 1986, and 1987, as recorded by the Department of Energy pursuant to Form 767. For any utility unit for which such form was not filed, the baseline shall be the level specified for such unit in the 1985 National Acid Precipitation Assessment Program (NAPAP) Emissions Inventory, Version 2, National Utility Reference File (NURF) or in a corrected data base as established by the Administrator pursuant to paragraph (3). For nonutility units, the baseline is the NAPAP Emissions Inventory, Version 2. The Administrator, in the Administrator's sole discretion, may exclude periods during which a unit is shutdown for a continuous period of four calendar months or longer, and make appropriate adjustments under this paragraph. Upon petition of the owner or operator of any unit, the Administrator may make appropriate baseline adjustments for accidents that caused prolonged outages.

(B) For any other nonutility unit that is not included in the NAPAP Emissions Inventory, Version 2, or a corrected data base as established by the Administrator pursuant to paragraph (3), the baseline shall be the annual average quantity, in mmBtu consumed in fuel by that unit, as calculated pursuant to a method which the administrator shall prescribe by regulation to be promulgated not later than eighteen months after November 15, 1990.

(C) The Administrator shall, upon application or on his own motion, by December 31, 1991, supplement data needed in support of this title and correct any factual errors in data from which affected Phase II units' baselines or actual 1985 emission rates have been calculated. Corrected data shall be used for purposes of issuing allowances under the title. Such corrections shall not be subject to judicial review, nor shall the failure of the Administrator to correct an alleged factual error in such reports be subject to judicial review.

(5) The term "capacity factor" means the ratio between the actual electric output from a unit and the potential electric output from that unit.

(6) The term "compliance plan" means, for purposes of the requirements of this title, either —

(A) a statement that the source will comply with all applicable requirements under this title, or

(B) where applicable, a schedule and description of the method or methods for compliance and certification by the owner or operator that the source is in compliance with the requirements of this title.

(7) The term "continuous emission monitoring system" (CEMS) means the equipment as required by section 7651K of this title, used to sample, analyze, measure, and provide on a continuous basis a permanent record of emissions and flow (expressed in pounds per million British thermal units (lbs/mmBtu), pounds per hour (lbs/hr) or such other form as the Administrator may prescribe by regulations under section 412).

(8) The term "existing unit" means a unit (including units subject to section 7411 of this title) that commenced commercial operation before the date of enactment of the Clean Air Act Amendments of 1990. Any unit that commenced commercial operation before November 15, 1990, which is modified, reconstructed, or repowered after November 15, 1990, shall continue to be an existing unit for the purposes of this title. For the purposes of this title, existing units shall not include simple combustion turbines, or units which serve a generator with a nameplate capacity of 25 MWe or less.

(9) The term "generator" means a device that produces electricity and which is reported as a generating unit pursuant to Department of Energy Form 860.

(10) The term "new unit" means a unit that commences commercial operation on or after November 15, 1990.

(11) The term "permitting authority" means the Administrator, or the State or local air pollution control agency, with an approved permitting program under part B of title III of the Act.

(12) The term "repowering" means replacement of an existing coal-fired boiler with one of the following clean coal technologies: atmospheric or pressurized fluidized bed combustion, integrated gasification combined cycle, magneto-hydrodynamics, direct and indirect coal-fired turbines, integrated gasification fuel cells, or as determined by the

Administrator, in consultation with the Secretary of Energy, a derivative of one or more of these technologies, and any other technology capable of controlling multiple combustion emissions simultaneously with improved boiler or generation efficiency and with significantly greater waste reduction relative to the performance of technology in widespread commercial use as November 15, 1990. Notwithstanding the provisions of section 7651h(a) of this title, for the purpose of this subchapter, the term "repowering" shall also include any oil and/or gas-fired unit which has been awarded clean coal technology demonstration funding as of January 1, 1991, by the Department of Energy.

(13) The term "reserve" means any bank of allowances established by the Administrator under this title.

(14) The term "State" means one of the 48 contiguous States and the District of Columbia.

(15) The term "unit" means a fossil fuel-fired combustion device.

(16) The term "actual 1985 emission rate", for electric utility units means the annual sulfur dioxide or nitrogen oxides emission rate in pounds per million Btu as reported in the NAPAP Emissions Inventory, Version 2, National Utility Reference File. For nonutility units, the term "actual 1985 emission rate" means the annual sulfur dioxide or nitrogen oxides emission rate in pounds per million Btu as reported in the NAPAP Emission Inventory, Version 2.

(17)(A) The term "utility unit" means —

(i) a unit that serves a generator in any State that produces electricity for sale, or

(ii) a unit that, during 1985, served a generator in any State that produced electricity for sale.

(B) Notwithstanding subparagraph (A), a unit described in subparagraph (A) that —

(i) was in commercial operation during 1985, but

(ii) did not, during 1985, serve a generator in any State that produced electricity for sale shall not be a utility unit for purposes of this title.

(C) A unit that cogenerates steam and electricity is not a "utility unit" for purposes of this title unless the unit is constructed for the purpose of supplying, or commences construction after November 15, 1990, and supplies, more than one-third of its potential electric output capacity and more than 25 megawatts electrical output to any utility power distribution system for sale.

(18) The term "allowable 1985 emissions rate" means a federally enforceable emissions limitation for sulfur dioxide or oxides of nitrogen, applicable to the unit in 1985 or the limitation applicable in such other subsequent year as determined by the Administrator if such a limitation for 1985 does not exist. Where the emissions limitation for a

unit is not expressed in pounds of emissions per million Btu, or the averaging period of that emissions limitation is not expressed on an annual basis, the Administrator shall calculate the annual equivalent of that emissions limitation in pounds per million Btu to establish the allowable 1985 emissions rate.

(19) The term "qualifying phase I technology" means a technological system of continuous emission reduction which achieves a 90 percent reduction in emissions of sulfur dioxide from the emissions that would have resulted from the use of fuels which were not subject to treatment prior to combustion.

(20) The term "alternative method of compliance" means a method of compliance in accordance with one or more of the following authorities:

(A) a substitution plan submitted and approved in accordance with subsections 7651c(b) and (c) of this title;

(B) a Phase I extension plan approved by the Administrator under section 7651c(d), of this title using qualifying phase I technology as determined by the Administrator in accordance with that section; or

(C) repowering with a qualifying clean coal technology under section 7651h of this title.

(21) The term "commenced" as applied to construction of any new electric utility unit means that an owner or operator has undertaken a continuous program of construction or that an owner or operator has entered into a contractual obligation to undertake and complete, within a reasonable time, a continuous program of construction.

(22) The term "commenced commercial operation" means to have begun to generate electricity for sale.

(23) The term "construction" means fabrication, erection, or installation of an affected unit.

(24) The term "industrial source" means a unit that does not serve a generator that produces electricity, a "nonutility unit" as defined in this section, or a process source as defined in section 7651(e) of this title.

(25) The term "nonutility unit" means a unit other than a utility unit.

(26) The term "designated representative" means a responsible person or official authorized by the owner or operator of a unit to represent the owner or operator in matters pertaining to the holding, transfer, or disposition of allowances allocated to a unit, and the submission of and compliance with permits, permit applications, and compliance plans for the unit.

(27) The term "life-of-the-unit, firm power contractual arrangement" means a unit participation power sales agreement under which a utility or industrial customer reserves, or is entitled to receive, a specified amount or percentage of capac-

ity and associated energy generated by a specified generating unit (or units) and pays its proportional amount of such unit's total costs, pursuant to a contract either —

(A) for the life of the unit;

(B) for a cumulative term of no less than 30 years, including contracts that permit an election for early termination; or

(C) for a period equal to or greater than 25 years or 70 percent of the economic useful life of the unit determined as of the time the unit was built, with option rights to purchase or release some portion of the capacity and associated energy generated by the unit (or units) at the end of the period.

(28) The term "basic Phase II allowance allocations" means:

(A) For calendar years 2000 through 2009 inclusive, allocations of allowances made by the Administrator pursuant to section 7651b of this title and subsections (b)(1), (3), and (4); (c)(1), (2), (3), and (5); (d)(1), (2), (4), and (5); (e); (f); (g)(1), (2), (3), (4), and (5); (h)(1); (i) and (j) of section 7651d of this title.

(B) For each calendar year beginning in 2010, allocations of allowances made by the Administrator pursuant to section 7651b and subsections (b)(1), (3), and (4); (c)(1), (2), (3), and (5); (d)(1), (2), (4), and (5); (e); (f); (g)(1), (2), (3), (4), and (5); (h)(1) and (3); (i) and (j) of section 7651d of this title.

(29) The term "Phase II bonus allowance allocations" means, for calendar year 2000 through 2009, inclusive, and only for such years, allocations made by the Administrator pursuant to section 7651b of this title, subsections (a)(2), (b)(2), (c)(4), (d)(3) (except as otherwise provided therein), and (h)(2) of section 7651d of this title, and section 7651e of this title.

§7651b. Sulfur dioxide allowance program for existing and new units
[CAA §403]
(a) Allocations of annual allowances for existing and new units

(1) For the emission limitation programs under this subchapter, the Administrator shall allocate annual allowances for the unit, to be held or distributed by the designated representative of the owner or operator of each affected unit at an affected source in accordance with this subchapter, in an amount equal to the annual tonnage emission limitation calculated under section 7651c, 7651d, 7651e, 7651h, or 7651I of this title except as otherwise specifically provided elsewhere in this subchapter. Except as provided in sections 7651d(a)(2), 7651d(a)(3), 7651h and 7651I of this title, beginning January 1, 2000, the Administrator shall not allocate annual allowances to emit sulfur dioxide pursuant

to section 405 in such an amount as would result in total annual emissions of sulfur dioxide from utility units in excess of 8.90 million tons except that the Administrator shall not take into account unused allowances carried forward by owners and operators of affected units or by other persons holding such allowances, following the year for which they were allocated. If necessary to meeting the restrictions imposed in the preceding sentence, the Administrator shall reduce, pro rata, the basic Phase II allowance allocations for each unit subject to the requirements of section 7651d of this title. Subject to the provisions of section 7651o of this title, the Administrator shall allocate allowances for each affected unit at an affected source annually, as provided in paragraphs (2) and (3) and section 7651g. Except as provided in sections 7651h and 7651I of this title, the removal of an existing affected unit or source from commercial operation at any time after November 15, 1990 (whether before or after January 1, 1995, or January 1, 2000) shall not terminate or otherwise affect the allocation of allowances pursuant to section 7651c or 7651d of this title to which the unit is entitled. Allowances shall be allocated by the Administrator without cost to the recipient, except for allowances sold by the Administrator pursuant to section 7651o of this title. Not later than December 31, 1991, the Administrator shall publish a proposed list of the basic Phase II allowance allocations, the Phase II bonus allowance allocations and, if applicable, allocations pursuant to section 7651d(a)(3) of this title for each unit subject to the emissions limitation requirements of section 7651d for the year 2000 and the year 2010. After notice and opportunity for public comment, but not later than December 31, 1992, the Administrator shall publish a final list of such allocations, subject to the provisions of section 7651d(a)(2) of this title. Any owner or operator of an existing unit subject to the requirements of section 7651d(b) or (c) of this title who is considering applying for an extension of the emission limitation requirement compliance deadline for that unit from January 1, 2000, until not later than December 31, 2000, pursuant to section 409, shall notify the Administrator no later than March 31, 1991. Such notification shall be used as the basis for estimating the basic Phase II allowances under this subsection. Prior to June 1, 1998, the Administrator shall publish a revised final statement of allowance allocations, subject to the provisions of section 7651d(a)(2) of this title and taking into account the effect of any compliance date extensions granted pursuant to section 7651h of this title on such allocations. Any person who may make an election concerning the amount of allowances to be allocated to a unit or units shall make such election and so inform the Administrator not later than March 31, 1991, in the case of an election under section 7651d of this title (or June 30, 1991, in the case of an election under section 7651e

of this title). If such person fails to make such election, the Administrator shall set forth for each unit owned or operated by such person, the amount of allowances reflecting the election that would, in the judgment of the Administrator, provide the greatest benefit for the owner or operator of the unit. If such person is a Governor who may make an election under section 7651e of this title and the Governor fails to make an election, the Administrator shall set forth for each unit in the State the amount of allowances reflecting the election that would, in the judgment of the Administrator, provide the greatest benefit for units in the State.

(b) Allowance transfer system — Allowances allocated under this title may be transferred among designated representatives of the owners or operators of affected sources under this title and any other person who holds such allowances, as provided by the allowance system regulations to be promulgated by the Administrator not later than eighteen months after November 15,1990. Such regulations shall establish the allowance system prescribed under this section, including, but not limited to, requirements for the allocation, transfer, and use of allowances under this title. Such regulations shall prohibit the use of any allowance prior to the calendar year for which the allowance was allocated, and shall provide, consistent with the purposes of this title, for the identification of unused allowances, and for such unused allowances to be carried forward and added to allowances allocated in subsequent years, including allowances allocated to units subject to Phase I requirements (as described in section 7651c of this title) which are applied to emissions limitations requirements in Phase II (as described in section 7651d of this title). Transfers of allowances shall not be effective until written certification of the transfer, signed by a responsible official of each party to the transfer, is received and recorded by the Administrator. Such regulations shall permit the transfer of allowances prior to the issuance of such allowances. Recorded pre-allocation transfers shall be deducted by the Administrator from the number of allowances which would otherwise be allocated to the transferor, and added to those allowances allocated to the transferee. Pre-allocation transfers shall not affect the prohibition contained in this subsection against the use of allowances prior to the year for which they are allocated.

(c) Interpollutant trading — Not later than January 1, 1994, the Administrator shall furnish to the Congress a study evaluating the environmental and economic consequences of amending this title to permit trading sulfur dioxide allowances for nitrogen oxides allowances.

(d) Allowance tracking system

(1) The Administrator shall promulgate, not later than 18 months after November 15, 1990, a system for issuing, recording, and tracking allowances, which shall specify all necessary procedures and requirements for an orderly and competitive functioning of the allowance system. All allowance

allocations and transfers shall, upon recordation by the Administrator, be deemed a part of each unit's permit requirements pursuant to section 7651g of this title, without any further permit review and revision.

(2) In order to insure electric reliability, such regulations shall not prohibit or affect temporary increases and decreases in emissions within utility systems, power pools, or utilities entering into allowance pool agreements, that result from their operations, including emergencies and central dispatch, and such temporary emissions increases and decreases shall not require transfer of allowances among units nor shall it require recordation. The owners or operators of such units shall act through a designated representative. Notwithstanding the preceding sentence, the total tonnage of emissions in any calendar year (calculated at the end thereof) from all units in such a utility system, power pool, or allowance pool agreements shall not exceed the total allowances for such units for the calendar year concerned.

(e) New utility units — After January 1, 2000, it shall be unlawful for a new utility unit to emit an annual tonnage of sulfur dioxide in excess of the number of allowances to emit held for the unit by the unit's owner or operator. Such new utility units shall not be eligible for an allocation of sulfur dioxide allowances under subsection (a)(1), unless the unit is subject to the provisions of subsection (g)(2) or (3) of section 7651d of this title. New utility units may obtain allowances from any person, in accordance with this title. The owner or operator of any new utility unit in violation of this subsection shall be liable for fulfilling the obligations specified in section 7651j of this title.

(f) Nature of allowances — An allowance allocated under this title is a limited authorization to emit sulfur dioxide in accordance with the provisions of this title. Such allowance does not constitute a property right. Nothing in this title or in any other provision of law shall be construed to limit the authority of the United States to terminate or limit such authorization. Nothing in this section relating to allowances shall be construed as affecting the application of, or compliance with, any other provision of this Act to an affected unit or source, including the provisions related to applicable National Ambient Air Quality Standards and State implementation plans. Nothing in this section shall be construed as requiring a change of any kind in any State law regulating electric utility rates and charges or affecting any State law regarding such State regulation or as limiting State regulation (including any prudency review) under such a State law. Nothing in this section shall be construed as modifying the Federal Power Act or as affecting the authority of the Federal Energy Regulatory Commission under that Act. Nothing in this title shall be construed to interfere with or impair any program for competitive bidding for power supply in a State in which such program is established. Allowances, once allocated to a person by the Administrator, may be received,

held, and temporarily or permanently transferred in accordance with this title and the regulations of the Administrator without regard to whether or not a permit is in effect under subchapter V of this chapter or section 7651g of this title with respect to the unit for which such allowance was originally allocated and recorded. Each permit under this subchapter and each permit issued under subchapter V of this chapter for any affected unit shall provide that the affected unit may not emit an annual tonnage of sulfur dioxide in excess of the allowances held for that unit.

(g) Prohibition — It shall be unlawful for any person to hold, use, or transfer any allowance allocated under this title, except in accordance with regulations promulgated by the Administrator. It shall be unlawful for any affected unit to emit sulfur dioxide in excess of the number of allowances held for that unit for that year by the owner or operator of the unit. Upon the allocation of allowances under this subchapter the prohibition contained in the preceding sentence shall supersede any other emission limitation applicable under this subchapter to the units for which such allowances are allocated. Allowances may not be used prior to the calendar year for which they are allocated. Nothing in this section or in the allowance system regulations shall relieve the Administrator of the Administrator's permitting, monitoring and enforcement obligations under this Act, nor relieve affected sources of their requirements and liabilities under this Act.

(h) Competitive bidding for power supply — Nothing in this title shall be construed to interfere with or impair any program for competitive bidding for power supply in a State in which such program is established.

(i) Applicability of antitrust laws

(1) Nothing in this section affects —

(A) the applicability of the antitrust laws to the transfer, use, or sale of allowances, or

(B) the authority of the Federal Energy Regulatory Commission under any provision of law respecting unfair methods of competition or anticompetitive acts or practices.

(2) As used in this section, "antitrust laws" means those Acts set forth in section 12 of Title 15, as amended.

(j) Public Utility Holding Company Act — The acquisition or disposition of allowances pursuant to this subchapter including the issuance of securities or the undertaking of any other financing transaction in connection with such allowances shall not be subject to the provisions of the Public Utility Holding Company Act of 1935.

§7651c. Phase I sulfur dioxide requirements
[CAA §404]
(a) Emission limitations

(1) After January 1, 1995, each source that includes one or more affected units listed in table A is an affected source under this section. After

January 1, 1995, it shall be unlawful for any affected unit (other than an eligible phase I unit under subsection (d)(2) of this section) to emit sulfur dioxide in excess of the tonnage limitation stated as a total number of allowances in table A for phase I, unless (A) the emissions reduction requirements applicable to such unit have been achieved pursuant to subsection (b) or (d), or (B) the owner or operator of such unit holds allowances to emit not less than the unit's total annual emissions, except that, after January 1, 2000, the emissions limitations established in this section shall be superseded by those established in section 7651d of this title. The owner or operator of any unit in violation of this section shall be fully liable for such violation including, but not limited to, liability for fulfilling the obligations specified in section 7651j of this title.

(2) Not later than December 31, 1991, the Administrator shall determine the total tonnage of reductions in the emissions of sulfur dioxide from all utility units in calendar year 1995 that will occur as a result of compliance with the emissions limitation requirements of this section, and shall establish a reserve of allowances equal in amount to the number of tons determined thereby not to exceed a total of 3.50 million tons. In making such determination, the Administrator shall compute for each unit subject to the emissions limitation requirements of this section the difference between:

(A) the product of its baseline multiplied by the lesser of each unit's allowable 1985 emissions rate and its actual 1985 emissions rate, divided by 2,000, and

(B) the product of each unit's baseline multiplied by 2.50 lbs/mmBtu divided by 2,000, and sum the computations. The Administrator shall adjust the foregoing calculation to reflect projected calendar year 1995 utilization of the units subject to the emissions limitations of this title that the Administrator finds would have occurred in the absence of the imposition of such requirements. Pursuant to subsection (d) of this section, the Administrator shall allocate allowances from the reserve established herein under until the earlier of such time as all such allowances in the reserve are allocated or December 31, 1999.

(3) In addition to allowances allocated pursuant to paragraph (1), in each calendar year beginning in 1995 and ending in 1999, inclusive, the Administrator shall allocate for each unit on Table A that is located in the States of Illinois, Indiana, or Ohio (other than units at Kyger Creek, Clifty Creek and Joppa Steam), allowances in an amount equal to 200,000 multiplied by the unit's pro rata share of the total number of allowances allocated for all units on Table A in the 3 States (other than units at Kyger Creek, Clifty Creek, and Joppa Steam) pursuant to paragraph (1). Such allowances shall be excluded from the calculation of the reserve under paragraph (2).

(b) Substitutions — The owner or operator of an affected unit under subsection (a) may include in its section 7651g of this title permit application and proposed compliance plan a proposal to reassign, in whole or in part, the affected unit's sulfur dioxide reduction requirements to any other unit(s) under the control of such owner or operator. Such proposal shall specify —

(1) the designation of the substitute unit or units to which any part of the reduction obligations of subsection (a) shall be required, in addition to, or in lieu of, any original affected units designated under such subsection;

(2) the original affected unit's baseline, the actual and allowable 1985 emissions rate for sulfur dioxide, and the authorized annual allowance allocation stated in table A;

(3) calculation of the annual average tonnage for calendar years 1985, 1986, and 1987, emitted by the substitute unit or units, based on the baseline for each unit, as defined in section 7651a(d) of this title, multiplied by the lesser of the unit's actual or allowable 1985 emissions rate;

(4) the emissions rates and tonnage limitations that would be applicable to the original and substitute affected units under the substitution proposal;

(5) documentation, to the satisfaction of the Administrator, that the reassigned tonnage limits will, in total, achieve the same or greater emissions reduction than would have been achieved by the original affected unit and the substitute unit or units without such substitution; and

(6) such other information as the Administrator may require.

(c) Administrator's action on substitution proposals

(1) The Administrator shall take final action on such substitution proposal in accordance with section 7651g(c) of this title if the substitution proposal fulfills the requirements of this subsection. The Administrator may approve a substitution proposal in whole or in part and with such modifications or conditions as may be consistent with the orderly functioning of the allowance system and which will ensure the emissions reductions contemplated by this title. If a proposal does not meet the requirements of subsection (b), the Administrator shall disapprove it. The owner or operator of a unit listed in table A shall not substitute another unit or units without the prior approval of the Administrator.

(2) Upon approval of a substitution proposal, each substitute unit, and each source with such unit, shall be deemed affected under this title, and the Administrator shall issue a permit to the original and substitute affected source and unit in accordance with the approved substitution plan and section 408. The Administrator shall allocate allowances for the original and substitute affected

units in accordance with the approved substitution proposal pursuant to section 7651b of this title. It shall be unlawful for any source or unit that is allocated allowances pursuant to this section to emit sulfur dioxide in excess of the emissions limitation provided for in the approved substitution permit and plan unless the owner or operator of each unit governed by the permit and approved substitution plan holds allowances to emit not less than the units total annual emissions. The owner or operator of any original or substitute affected unit operated in violation of this subsection shall be fully liable for such violation, including liability for fulfilling the obligations specified in section 7651j of this title. If a substitution proposal is disapproved, the Administrator shall allocate allowances to the original affected unit or units in accordance with subsection (a) of this section.

(d) Eligible phase I extension units

(1) The owner or operator of any affected unit subject to an emissions limitation requirement under this section may petition the Administrator in its permit application under section 7651g of this title for an extension of 2 years of the deadline for meeting such requirement, provided that the owner or operator of any such unit holds allowances to emit not less than the unit's total annual emissions for each of the 2 years of the period of extension. To qualify for such an extension, the affected unit must either employ a qualifying phase I technology, or transfer its phase I emissions reduction obligation to a unit employing a qualifying phase I technology. Such transfer shall be accomplished in accordance with a compliance plan, submitted and approved under section 7651g of this title, that shall govern operations at all units included in the transfer, and that specifies the emissions reduction requirements imposed pursuant to this title.

(2) Such extension proposal shall —

(A) specify the unit or units proposed for designation as an eligible phase I extension unit;

(B) provide a copy of an executed contract, which may be contingent upon the Administrator approving the proposal, for the design engineering, and construction of the qualifying phase I technology for the extension unit, or for the unit or units to which the extension unit's emission reduction obligation is to be transferred;

(C) specify the unit's or units' baseline, actual 1985 emissions rate, allowable 1985 emissions rate, and projected utilization for calendar years 1995 through 1999;

(D) require CEMS on both the eligible phase I extension unit or units and the transfer unit or units beginning no later than January 1, 1995; and

(E) specify the emission limitation and number of allowances expected to be neces-

sary for annual operation after the qualifying phase I technology has been installed.

(3) The Administrator shall review and take final action on each extension proposal in order of receipt, consistent with section 7651g of this title, and for an approved proposal shall designate the unit or units as an eligible phase I extension unit. The Administrator may approve an extension proposal in whole or in part, and with such modifications or conditions as may be necessary, consistent with the orderly functioning of the allowance system, and to ensure the emissions reductions contemplated by the subchapter.

(4) In order to determine the number of proposals eligible for allocations from the reserve under subsection (a)(2) of this section and the number of allowances remaining available after each proposal is acted upon, the Administrator shall reduce the total number of allowances remaining available in the reserve by the number of allowances calculated according to subparagraphs (A), (B) and (C) until either no allowances remain available in the reserve for further allocation or all approved proposals have been acted upon. If no allowances remain available in the reserve for further allocation before all proposals have been acted upon by the Administrator, any pending proposals shall be disapproved. The Administrator shall calculate allowances equal to —

(A) the difference between the lesser of the average annual emissions in calendar years 1988 and 1989 or the projected emissions tonnage for calendar year 1995 of each eligible phase I extension unit, as designated under paragraph (3), and the product of the unit's baseline multiplied by an emission rate of 2.50 lbs/mmBtu, divided by 2,000;

(B) the difference between the lesser of the average annual emissions in calendar years 1988 and 1989 or the projected emissions tonnage for calendar year 1996 of each eligible phase I extension unit, as designated under paragraph (3), and the product of the unit's baseline multiplied by an emission rate of 2.50 lbs/mmBtu, divided by 2,000; and

(C) the amount by which (i) the product of each unit's baseline multiplied by an emission rate of 1.20 lbs/mmBtu, divided by 2,000, exceeds (ii) the tonnage level specified under subparagraph (E) of paragraph (2) of this subsection multiplied by a factor of 3.

(5) Each eligible Phase I extension unit shall receive allowances determined under subsection (a)(1) or (c) of this section. In addition, for calendar year 1995, the Administrator shall allocate to each eligible Phase I extension unit, from the allowance reserve created pursuant to subsection (a)(2) of this section, allowances equal to the difference between the lesser of the average annual

emissions in calendar years 1988 and 1989 or its projected emissions tonnage for calendar year 1995 and the product of the unit's baseline multiplied by an emission rate of 2.50 lbs/mmBtu, divided by 2,000. In calendar year 1996, the Administrator shall allocate for each eligible unit, from the allowance reserve created pursuant to subsection (a)(2) of this section, allowances equal to the difference between the lesser of the average annual emissions in calendar years 1988 and 1989 or its projected emissions tonnage for calendar year 1996 and the product of the unit's baseline multiplied by an emission rate of 2.50 lbs/mmBtu, divided by 2,000. It shall be unlawful for any source or unit subject to an approved extension plan under this subsection to emit sulfur dioxide in excess of the emissions limitations provided for in the permit and approved extension plan, unless the owner or operator of each unit governed by the permit and approved plan holds allowances to emit not less than the unit's total annual emissions.

(6) In addition to allowances specified in paragraph (5), the Administrator shall allocate for each eligible Phase I extension unit employing qualifying Phase I technology, for calendar years 1997, 1998, and 1999, additional allowances, from any remaining allowances in the reserve created pursuant to subsection (a)(2), following the reduction in the reserve provided for in paragraph (4), not to exceed the amount by which (A) the product of each eligible unit's baseline times an emission rate of 1.20 lbs/mmBtu, divided by 2,000, exceeds (B) the tonnage level specified under subparagraph (E) of paragraph (2) of this subsection.

(7) After January 1, 1997, in addition to any liability under this chapter, including under section 7651j of this title, if any eligible phase I extension unit employing qualifying phase I technology or any transfer unit under this subsection emits sulfur dioxide in excess of the annual tonnage limitation specified in the extension plan, as approved in paragraph (3) of this subsection, the Administrator shall, in the calendar year following such excess, deduct allowances equal to the amount of such excess from such unit's annual allowance allocation.

(e) Allocation of allowances

(1) In the case of a unit that receives authorization from the Governor of the State in which such unit is located to make reductions in the emissions of sulfur dioxide prior to calendar year 1995 and that is part of a utility system that meets the following requirements: (A) the total coal-fired generation within the utility system as a percentage of total system generation decreased by more than 20 percent between January 1, 1980, and December 31, 1985; and (B) the weighted capacity factor of all coal-fired units within the utility system averaged over the period from January 1, 1985, through December 31, 1987, was below 50 percent, the

Administrator shall allocate allowances under this paragraph for the unit pursuant to this subsection. The Administrator shall allocate allowances for a unit that is an affected unit pursuant to section 7651d of this title (but is not also an affected unit under this section) and part of a utility system that includes 1 or more affected units under section 7651d of this title for reductions in the emissions of sulfur dioxide made during the period 1995-1999 if the unit meets the requirements of this subsection and the requirements of the preceding sentence, except that for the purposes of applying this subsection to any such unit, the prior year concerned as specified below, shall be any year after January 1, 1995 but prior to January 1, 2000.

(2) In the case of an affected unit under this section described in subparagraph (A), the allowances allocated under this subsection for early reductions in any prior year may not exceed the amount which (A) the product of the unit's baseline multiplied by the unit's 1985 actual sulfur dioxide emission rate (in lbs. per mmBtu), divided by 2,000, exceeds (B) the allowances specified for such unit in Table A. In the case of an affected unit under section 7651d of this title described in subparagraph (A), the allowances awarded under this subsection for early reductions in any prior year may not exceed the amount by which (i) the product of the quantity of fossil fuel consumed by the unit (in mmBtu) in the prior year multiplied by the lesser of 2.50 or the most stringent emission rate (in lbs. per mmBtu) applicable to the unit under the applicable implementation plan, divided by 2,000, exceeds (ii) the unit's actual tonnage of sulfur dioxide emission for the prior year concerned. Allowances allocated under this subsection for units referred to in subparagraph (A) may be allocated only for emission reductions achieved as a result of physical changes or changes in the method of operation made after November 15, 1990, including changes in the type or quality of fossil fuel consumed.

(3) In no event shall the provisions of this paragraph be interpreted as an event of force majeure or a commercial impractibility or in any other way as a basis for excused nonperformance by a utility system under a coal sales contract in effect before November 15, 1990.

TABLE A — AFFECTED SOURCES AND UNITS IN PHASE I AND THEIR SULFUR DIOXIDE ALLOWANCES (TONS)

State	Plant Name	Ga.	Phase I Allowances
Alabama	Colbert	1	13,570
		2	15,310
		3	15,400
		4	15,410

State	Plant	Unit	Value
		5	37,180
	E.C. Gaston	1	18,100
		2	18,540
		3	18,310
		4	19,280
		5	59,840
Florida	Big Ben	1	28,410
		2	27,100
		3	26,740
	Crist	6	19,200
		7	31,680
Georgia	Bowen	1	56,320
		2	54,770
		3	71,550
		4	71,740
	Hammond	1	8,780
		2	9,220
		3	8,910
		4	37,640
	J. McDonough	1	19,910
		2	20,600
	Wansley	1	70,770
		2	65,430
	Yates	1	7,210
		2	7,040
		3	6,950
		4	8,910
		5	9,410
		6	24,760
		7	21,480
Illinois	Baldwin	1	42,010
		2	44,420
		3	42,550
	Coffeen	1	11,790
		2	35,670
	Grand Tower	4	5,910
	Henepin	2	18,410
	Joppa Steam	1	12,590
		2	10,770
		3	12,270
		4	11,360
		5	11,420
		6	10,620
	Kincaid	1	31,530
		2	33,810
	Meredosia	3	13,890
	Vermilion	2	8,880
Indiana	Bailly	7	11,180
	Breed	8	15,630
	Cayuga	1	18,500
		1	33,370
		2	34,130
	Clifty Creek	1	20,150
		2	19,810
		3	20,410
		4	20,080
		5	19,360
		6	20,380
	E.W. Stout	5	3,880

State	Plant	Unit	Value
		6	4,770
		7	23,610
	F.B. Culley	2	4,290
		3	16,970
	F.E. Ratts	1	8,330
		2	8,480
	Gibson	1	40,400
		2	41,010
		3	41,080
		4	40,320
	H.T. Prichard	6	5,770
	Michigan City	12	23,310
	Petersburg	1	16,430
		2	32,380
	R. Gallagher	1	6,490
		2	7,280
		3	6,530
		4	7,650
	Tanners Creek	4	24,820
	Wabash River	1	4,000
		2	2,860
		3	3,750
		5	3,670
		6	12,280
	Warrick	4	26,980
Iowa	Burlington	1	10,710
	Des Moines	7	2,320
	George Neal	1	1,290
	M.L. Kapp	2	13,800
	Prairie Creek	4	8,180
	Riverside	5	3,990
Kansas	Quindaro	2	4,220
Kentucky	Coleman	1	11,250
		2	12,840
		3	12,340
	Cooper	1	7,450
		2	15,320
	E.W. Brown	1	7,110
		2	10,910
		3	26,100
	Elmer Smith	1	6,520
		2	14,410
	Ghent	1	28,410
	Green River	4	7,820
	H.L. Spurlock	1	22,780
	Henderson II	1	13,340
		2	12,310
	Paradise	3	59,170
	Shawnee	10	10,170
Maryland	Chalk Point	1	21,910
		2	24,330
	C.P. Crane	1	10,330
		2	9,230
	Morgantown	1	35,260
		2	38,480
Michigan	J.H. Campbell	1	19,280
		2	23,060
Minnesota	High Bridge	6	4,270
Mississippi	Jack Watson	4	17,910

State	Plant	Unit	Value	State	Plant	Unit	Value
		5	36,700			5	40,470
Missouri	Asbury	1	16,190		Niles	1	6,940
	James River	5	4,850			2	9,100
	Labadie	1	40,110		Pickway	5	4,930
		2	37,710		R.E. Burger	3	6,150
		3	40,310			4	10,780
		4	35,940			5	12,430
	Montrose	1	7,390		W.H. Sammis	5	24,170
		2	8,200			6	39,930
		3	10,090			7	43,220
	New Madrid	1	28,240		W.C. Beckjord	5	8,950
		2	32,480			6	23,020
	Sibley	3	15,580	Penn-sylvania	Armstrong	1	14,410
	Sioux	1	22,570			2	15,430
		2	23,690		Brunner Island	1	27,760
	Thomas Hill	1	10,250			2	31,100
		2	19,390			3	53,820
New Hampshire	Merrimack	1	10,190		Cheswick	1	39,170
		2	22,000		Conemaugh	1	59,790
New Jersey	B.L. England	1	9,060			2	66,450
		2	11,720		Hatfield's Ferry	1	37,830
New York	Dunkirk	3	12,600			2	37,320
		4	14,060			3	40,270
	Greenbridge	4	7,540		Martins Creek	1	12,660
	Milliken	1	11,170			2	12,820
		2	12,410		Portland	1	5,940
	Northport	1	19,810			2	10,230
		2	24,110		Shawville	1	10,320
		3	26,480			2	10,320
	Port Jefferson	3	10,470			3	14,220
		4	12,330			4	14,070
Ohio	Ashtabula	5	16,740		Sanbury	3	8,760
	Avon Lake	8	11,650			4	11,450
	Cardinal	1	34,270	Tennessee	Allen	1	15,320
		2	38,320			2	16,770
	Conesville	1	4,210			3	15,670
		2	4,890		Cumberland	1	86,700
		3	5,500			2	94,840
		4	48,770		Gallatin	1	17,870
	Eastlake	1	7,800			2	17,310
		2	8,640			3	20,020
		3	10,020			4	21,260
		4	14,510		Johnsonville	1	7,790
		5	34,070			2	8,040
	Edgewater	4	5,050			3	8,410
	Gen. J.M. Gavin	1	79,080			4	7,990
		2	80,560			5	8,240
	Kyger Creek	1	19,280			6	7,890
		2	18,560			7	8,980
		3	17,910			8	8,700
		4	18,710			9	7,080
		5	18,740			10	7,550
	Miami Fort	5	760	West Virginia	Albright	3	12,000
		6	11,380		Fort Martin	1	41,590
		7	38,510			2	41,200
	Muskingum	1	14,880		Harrison	1	48,620
		2	14,170			2	46,150
		3	13,950			3	41,500
		4	11,780		Kammer	1	18,740

		2	19,460
		3	17,390
	Mitchell	1	43,980
		2	45,510
	Mount Storm	1	43,720
		2	35,580
		3	42,430
Wisconsin	Edgewater	4	24,750
	La Crosse/		
	Genoa	3	22,700
	Nelson Dewey	1	6,010
		2	6,680
	N. Oak Creek	1	5,220
		2	5,140
		3	5,370
		4	6,320
	Pulliam	8	7,510
	S. Oak Creek	5	9,670
		6	12,040
		7	16,180
		8	15,790

(f) Energy conservation and renewable energy

(1) Definitions — As used in this subsection:

(A) Qualified energy conservation measure — The term "qualified energy conservation measure" means a cost effective measure, as identified by the Administrator in consultation with the Secretary of Energy, that increases the efficiency of the use of electricity provided by an electric utility to its customers.

(B) Qualified renewable energy — The term "qualified renewable energy" means energy derived from biomass, solar, geothermal, or wind as identified by the Administrator in consultation with the Secretary of Energy.

(C) Electric utility — The term "electric utility" means any person, State agency, or Federal agency, which sells electric energy.

(2) Allowances for emissions avoided through energy conservation and renewable energy

(A) In general — The regulations under paragraph (4) of this subsection shall provide that for each ton of sulfur dioxide emissions avoided by an electric utility, during the applicable period, through the use of qualified energy conservation measures or qualified renewable energy, the Administrator shall allocate a single allowance to such electric utility, on a first-come-first-served basis from the Conservation and Renewable Energy Reserve established under subsection (g) of this section, up to total of 300,000 allowances for allocation from such Reserve.

(B) Requirements for issuance — The Administrator shall allocate allowances to an electric utility under this subsection only if all of the following requirements are met:

(i) Such electric utility is paying for the qualified energy conservation measures or qualified renewable energy directly or through purchase from another person.

(ii) The emissions of sulfur dioxide avoided through the use of qualified energy conservation measures or qualified renewable energy are quantified in accordance with regulations promulgated by the Administrator under this subsection.

(iii)(I) Such electric utility has adopted and is implementing a least cost energy conservation and electric power plan which evaluates a range of resources, including new power supplies, energy conservation, and renewable energy resources, in order to meet expected future demand at the lowest system cost.

(II) The qualified energy conservation measures or qualified renewable energy, or both, are consistent with that plan.

(III) Electric utilities subject to the jurisdiction of a State regulatory authority must have such plan approved by such authority. For electric utilities not subject to the jurisdiction of a State regulatory authority such plan shall be approved by the entity with rate-making authority for such utility.

(iv) In the case of qualified energy conservation measures undertaken by a State regulated electric utility, the Secretary of Energy certifies that the State regulatory authority with jurisdiction over the electric rates of such electric utility has established rates and charges which ensure that the net income of such electric utility after implementation of specific cost effective energy conservation measures is at least as high as such net income would have been if the energy conservation measures had not been implemented. Upon the date of any such certification by the Secretary of Energy, all allowances which, but for this paragraph, would have been allocated under subparagraph (A) before such date, shall be allocated to the electric utility. This clause is not a requirement for qualified renewable energy.

(v) Such utility or any subsidiary of the utility's holding company owns or operates at least one affected unit.

(C) Period of applicability — Allowances under this subsection shall be allocated only with respect to kilowatt hours of electric energy saved by qualified energy conservation measures or generated by qualified renewable energy after January 1, 1992 and before the earlier of (i) December 31, 2000, or (ii) the date on which any electric utility steam generating unit owned or operated by the electric utility to which the allowances are allocated becomes subject to this title (including those sources that elect to become affected by this title, pursuant to section 7651i of this title).

(D) Determination of avoided emissions

(i) Application — In order to receive allowances under this subsection, an electric utility shall make an application which —

(I) designates the qualified energy conservation measures implemented and the qualified renewable energy sources used for purposes of avoiding emissions,

(II) calculates, in accordance with subparagraphs (F) and (G), the number of tons of emissions avoided by reason of the implementation of such measures or the use of such renewable energy sources; and

(III) demonstrates that the requirements of subparagraph (B) have been met.

Such application for allowances by a State-regulated electric utility shall require approval by the State regulatory authority with jurisdiction over such electric utility. The authority shall review the application for accuracy and compliance with this subsection and the rules under this subsection. Electric utilities whose retail rates are not subject to the jurisdiction of a State regulatory authority shall apply directly to the Administrator for such approval.

(E) Avoided emissions from qualified energy conservation measures — For the purposes of this subsection, the emission tonnage deemed avoided by reason of the implementation of qualified energy conservation measures for any calendar year shall be a tonnage equal to the product of multiplying —

(i) the kilowatt hours that would otherwise have been supplied by the utility during such year in the absence of such qualified energy conservation measures, by

(ii) 0.004,

and dividing by 2,000.

(F) Avoided emissions from the use of qualified renewable energy — The emissions tonnage deemed avoided by reason of the use of qualified renewable energy by an electric utility for any calendar year shall be a tonnage equal to the product of multiplying —

(i) the actual kilowatt hours generated by, or purchased from, qualified renewable energy, by

(ii) 0.004,

and dividing by 2,000.

(G) Prohibitions

(i) No allowances shall be allocated under this subsection for the implementation of programs that are exclusively informational or educational in nature.

(ii) No allowances shall be allocated for energy conservation measures or renewable energy that were operational before January 1, 1992.

(3) Savings provision — Nothing in this subsection precludes a State or State regulatory authority from providing additional incentives to utilities to encourage investment in demand-side resources.

(4) Regulations — Not later than 18 months after November 15, 1990 and in conjunction with the regulations required to be promulgated under subsections (b) and (c) of this section, the Administrator shall, in consultation with the Secretary of Energy, promulgate regulations under this subsection. Such regulations shall list energy conservation measures and renewable energy sources which may be treated as qualified energy conservation measures and qualified renewable energy for purposes of this subsection. Allowances shall only be allocated if all requirements of this subsection and the rules promulgated to implement this subsection are complied with. The Administrator shall review the determinations of each State regulatory authority under this subsection to encourage consistency from electric utility to electric utility and from State to State in accordance with the Administrator's rules. The Administrator shall publish the findings of this review no less than annually.

(g) Conservation and renewable energy reserve — The Administrator shall establish a Conservation and Renewable Energy Reserve under this subsection. Beginning on January 1, 1995, the Administrator may allocate from the Conservation and Renewable Energy Reserve an amount equal to a total of 300,000 allowances for emissions of sulfur dioxide pursuant to section 403. In order to provide 300,000 allowances for such reserve, in each year beginning in calendar year 2000 and until calendar year 2009, inclusive, the Administrator shall reduce each unit's basic Phase II allowance allocation on the basis of its pro rata share of 30,000 allowances. If allowances remain in the reserve after January 2, 2010, the Administrator shall allocate such allowances for affected units under section 405 on a pro rata basis. For purposes of this subsection, for any unit subject to the emissions limitation requirements of section 405, the term "pro rata basis" refers to the ratio which the reductions made in such unit's allowances in order to establish the reserve under this subsection bears to the total of such reductions for all such units.

(h) Alternative allowance allocation for units in certain utility systems with optional baseline

(1) Optional baseline for units in certain systems — In the case of a unit subject to the emissions limitation requirements of this section which (as of November 15, 1990) —

　(A) has an emission rate below 1.0 lbs/mmBtu,

　(B) has decreased its sulfur dioxide emissions rate by 60 percent or greater since 1980, and

　(C) is part of a utility system which has a weighted average sulfur dioxide emissions rate for all fossil fueled-fired units below 1.0 lbs/mmBtu,

at the election of the owner or operator of such unit, the unit's baseline may be calculated (i) as provided under section 7651a(d) of this title, or (ii) by utilizing the unit's average annual fuel consumption at a 60 percent capacity factor. Such election shall be made no later than March 1, 1991.

(2) Allowance allocation — Whenever a unit referred to in paragraph (1) elects to calculate its baseline as provided in clause (ii) of paragraph (1), the Administrator shall allocate allowances for the unit pursuant to section 7651b(a)(1) of this title, this section, and section 7651d of this title (as basic Phase II allowance allocations) in an amount equal to the baseline selected multiplied by the lower of the average annual emission rate for such unit in 1989, or 1.0lbs/mmBtu. Such allowance allocation shall be in lieu of any allocation of allowances under this section and section 7651d of this title.

§7651d. Phase II sulfur dioxide requirements
[CAA §405]

(a) Applicability

(1) After January 1, 2000, each existing utility unit as provided below is subject to the limitations or requirements of this section. Each utility unit subject to an annual sulfur dioxide tonnage emission limitation under this section is an affected unit under this title. Each source that includes one or more affected units is an affected source. In the case of an existing unit that was not in operation during calendar year 1985, the emission rate for a calendar year after 1985, as determined by the Administrator, shall be used in lieu of the 1985 rate. The owner or operator of any unit operated in violation of this section shall be fully liable under this Act for fulfilling the obligations specified in section 7651j of this title.

(2) In addition to basic Phase II allowance allocations, in each year beginning in calendar year 2000 and ending in calendar year 2009, inclusive, the Administrator shall allocate up to 530,000 Phase II bonus allowances pursuant to subsections (b)(2), (c)(4), (d)(3)(A) and (B), and (h)(2) of this section and section 7651e of this title. Not later than June 1, 1998, the Administrator shall calculate, for each unit granted an extension pursuant to section 7651h of this title the

difference between (A) the number of allowances allocated for the unit in calendar year 2000, and (B) the product of the unit's baseline multiplied by 1.20 lbs/mmBtu, divided by 2000, and sum the computations. In each year, beginning in calendar year 2000 and ending in calendar year 2009, inclusive, the Administrator shall deduct from each unit's basic Phase II allowance allocation its pro rata share of 10 percent of the sum calculated pursuant to the preceding sentence.

(3) In addition to basic Phase II allowance allocations and Phase II bonus allowance allocations, beginning January 1, 2000, the Administrator shall allocate for each unit listed on Table A in section 404 (other than units at Kyger Creek, Clifty Creek, and Joppa Steam) and located in the States of Illinois, Indiana, Ohio, Georgia, Alabama, Missouri, Pennsylvania, West Virginia, Kentucky, or Tennessee allowances in an amount equal to 50,000 multiplied by the unit's pro rata share of the total number of basic allowances allocated for all units listed on Table A (other than units at Kyger Creek, Clifty Creek, and Joppa Steam). Allowances allocated pursuant to this paragraph shall not be subject to the 8,900,000 ton limitation in section 7651b(a) of this title.

(b) Units equal to, or above, 75 MWe and 1.20 lbs/mmBtu

(1) Except as otherwise provided in paragraph (3), after January 1, 2000, it shall be unlawful for any existing utility unit that serves a generator with nameplate capacity equal to, or greater, than 75 MWe and an actual 1985 emission rate equal to or greater than 1.20 lbs/mmBtu to exceed an annual sulfur dioxide tonnage emission limitation equal to the product of the unit's baseline multiplied by an emission rate equal to 1.20 lbs/mmBtu, divided by 2,000, unless the owner or operator of such unit holds allowances to emit not less than the unit's total annual emissions.

(2) In addition to allowances allocated pursuant to paragraph (1) and section 7651b(a)(1) of this title as basic Phase II allowance allocations, beginning January 1, 2000, and for each calendar year thereafter until and including 2009, the Administrator shall allocate annually for each unit subject to the emissions limitation requirements of paragraph (1) with an actual 1985 emissions rate greater than 1.20 lbs/mmBtu and less than 2.50 lbs/mmBtu and a baseline capacity factor of less than 60 percent, allowances from the reserve created pursuant to subsection (a)(2) in an amount equal to 1.20 lbs/mmBtu multiplied by 50 percent of the difference, on a Btu basis, between the unit's baseline and the unit's fuel consumption at a 60 percent capacity factor.

(3) After January 1, 2000, it shall be unlawful for any existing utility unit with an actual 1985 emissions rate equal to or greater than 1.20 lbs/mmBtu whose annual average fuel consumption during 1985, 1986, and 1987 on a Btu basis exceeded

90 percent in the form of lignite coal which is located in a State in which, as of July 1, 1989, no county or portion of a county was designated nonattainment under section 7407 of this title for any pollutant subject to the requirements of section 7409 of this title to exceed an annual sulfur dioxide tonnage limitation equal to the product of the unit's baseline multiplied by the lesser of the unit's actual 1985 emissions rate or its allowable 1985 emissions rate, divided by 2,000, unless the owner or operator of such unit holds allowances to emit not less than the unit's total annual emissions.

(4) After January 1, 2000, the Administrator shall allocate annually for each unit, subject to the emissions limitation requirements of paragraph (1), which is located in a State with an installed electrical generating capacity of more than 30,000,000 kw in 1988 and for which was issued a prohibition order or a proposed prohibition order (from burning oil), which unit subsequently converted to coal between January 1, 1980 and December 31, 1985, allowances equal to the difference between (A) the product of the unit's annual fuel consumption, on a Btu basis, at a 65 percent capacity factor multiplied by the lesser of its actual or allowable emissions rate during the first full calendar year after conversion, divided by 2,000, and (B) the number of allowances allocated for the unit pursuant to paragraph (1): *Provided*, That the number of allowances allocated pursuant to this paragraph shall not exceed an annual total of five thousand. If necessary to meeting the restriction imposed in the preceding sentence the Administrator shall reduce, pro rata, the annual allowances allocated for each unit under this paragraph.

(c) Coal or oil-fired units below 75 MWe and above 1.20 lbs/mmBtu

(1) Except as otherwise provided in paragraph (3), after January 1, 2000, it shall be unlawful for a coal or oil-fired existing utility unit that serves a generator with nameplate capacity of less than 75 MWe and an actual 1985 emission rate equal to, or greater than, 1.20 lbs/mmBtu and which is a unit owned by a utility operating company whose aggregate nameplate fossil fuel steam-electric capacity is, as of December 31, 1989, equal to, or greater than, 250 MWe to exceed an annual sulfur dioxide emissions limitation equal to the product of the unit's baseline multiplied by an emission rate equal to 1.20 lbs/mmBtu, divided by 2,000, unless the owner or operator of such unit holds allowances to emit not less than the unit's total annual emissions.

(2) After January 1, 2000, it shall be unlawful for a coal or oil-fired existing utility unit that serves a generator with nameplate capacity of less than 75 MWe and an actual 1985 emission rate equal to, or greater than, 1.20 lbs/mmBtu (excluding units subject to section 7411 of this title or to a federally enforceable emissions limitation for sulfur dioxide equivalent to an annual rate of less than 1.20 lbs/

mmBtu) and which is a unit owned by a utility operating company whose aggregate nameplate fossil fuel steam-electric capacity is, as of December 31, 1989, less than 250 MWe, to exceed an annual sulfur dioxide tonnage emissions limitation equal to the product of the unit's baseline multiplied by the lesser of its actual 1985 emissions rate or its allowable 1985 emissions rate, divided by 2,000, unless the owner or operator of such unit holds allowances to emit not less than the unit's total annual emissions.

(3) After January 1, 2000 it shall be unlawful for any existing utility unit with a nameplate capacity below 75 MWe and an actual 1985 emissions rate equal to, or greater than, 1.20 lbs/mmBtu which became operational on or before December 31, 1965, which is owned by a utility operating company with, as of December 31, 1989, a total fossil fuel steam-electric generating capacity greater than 250 MWe, and less than 450 MWe which serves fewer than 78,000 electrical customers as of November 15, 1990 to exceed an annual sulfur dioxide emissions tonnage limitation equal to the product of its baseline multiplied by the lesser of its actual or allowable 1985 emission rate, divided by 2,000, unless the owner or operator holds allowances to emit not less than the units total annual emissions. After January 1, 2010, it shall be unlawful for each unit subject to the emissions limitation requirements of this paragraph to exceed an annual emissions tonnage limitation equal to the product of its baseline multiplied by an emissions rate of 1.20 lbs/mmBtu, divided by 2,000, unless the owner or operator holds allowances to emit not less than the unit's total annual emissions.

(4) In addition to allowances allocated pursuant to paragraph (1) and section 7651b(a)(1) of this title as basic Phase II allowance allocations, beginning January 1, 2000, and for each calendar year thereafter until and including 2009, inclusive, the Administrator shall allocate annually for each unit subject to the emissions limitation requirements of paragraph (1) with an actual 1985 emissions rate equal to, or greater than, 1.20 lbs/mmBtu and less than 2.50 lbs/mmBtu and a baseline capacity factor of less than 60 percent, allowances from the reserve created pursuant to subsection (a)(2) of this section in an amount equal to 1.20 lbs/mmBtu multiplied by 50 percent of the difference, on a Btu basis, between the unit's baseline and the unit's fuel consumption at a 60 percent capacity factor.

(5) After January 1, 2000, it shall be unlawful for any existing utility unit with a nameplate capacity below 75 MWe and an actual 1985 emissions rate equal to, or greater than, 1.20 lbs/mmBtu which is part of an electric utility system which, as of the date of the enactment of the Clean Air Act Amendments of 1990, (A) has at least 20 percent of its fossil-fuel capacity controlled by flue gas desulfurization devices, (B) has more than 10 percent of its fossil-fuel capacity consisting of coal-fired units of

less than 75 MWe, and (C) has large units (greater than 400 MWe) all of which have difficult or very difficult FGD Retrofit Cost Factors (according to the Emissions and the FGD Retrofit Feasibility at the 200 Top Emitting Generating Stations, prepared for the United States Environmental Protection Agency on January 10, 1986) to exceed an annual sulfur dioxide emissions tonnage limitation equal to the product of its baseline multiplied by an emissions rate of 2.5 lbs/mmBtu, divided by 2,000, unless the owner or operator holds allowances to emit not less than the unit's total annual emissions. After January 1, 2010, it shall be unlawful for each unit subject to the emissions limitation requirements of this paragraph to exceed an annual emissions tonnage limitation equal to the product of its baseline multiplied by an emissions rate of 1.20 lbs/mmBtu, divided by 2,000, unless the owner or operator holds for use allowances to emit not less than the unit's total annual emissions.

(d) Coal-fired units below 1.20 lbs/mmBtu

(1) After January 1, 2000, it shall be unlawful for any existing coal-fired utility unit the lesser of whose actual or allowable 1985 sulfur dioxide emissions rate is less than 0.60 lbs/mmBtu to exceed an annual sulfur dioxide tonnage emission limitation equal to the product of the unit's baseline multiplied by (A) the lesser of 0.60 lbs/mmBtu or the unit's allowable 1985 emissions rate, and (B) a numerical factor of 120 percent, divided by 2,000, unless the owner or operator of such unit holds allowances to emit not less than the unit's total annual emissions.

(2) After January 1, 2000, it shall be unlawful for any existing coal-fired utility unit the lesser of whose actual or allowable 1985 sulfur dioxide emissions rate is equal to, or greater than, 0.60 lbs/mmBtu and less than 1.20 lbs/mmBtu to exceed an annual sulfur dioxide tonnage emissions limitation equal to the product of the unit's baseline multiplied by (A) the lesser of its actual 1985 emissions rate or its allowable 1985 emissions rate, and (B) a numerical factor of 120 percent, divided by 2,000, unless the owner or operator of such unit holds allowances to emit not less than the unit's total annual emissions.

(3)(A) In addition to allowances allocated pursuant to paragraph (1) and section 7651b(a)(1) of this title as basic Phase II allowance allocations, at the election of the designated representative of the operating company, beginning January 1, 2000, and for each calendar year thereafter until and including 2009, the Administrator shall allocate annually for each unit subject to the emissions limitation requirements of paragraph (1) allowances from the reserve created pursuant to subsection (a)(2) in an amount equal to the amount by which (i) the product of the lesser of 0.60 lbs/mmBtu or the unit's allowable 1985 emissions rate multiplied by the unit's baseline adjusted to reflect operation at a 60 percent capacity factor, divided by 2,000, exceeds

(ii) the number of allowances allocated for the unit pursuant to paragraph (1) and section 7651(a)(1) of this title as basic Phase II allowance allocations.

(B) In addition to allowances allocated pursuant to paragraph (2) and section 7651b(a)(1) of this title as basic Phase II allowance allocations, at the election of the designated representative of the operating company, beginning January 1, 2000, and for each calendar year thereafter until and including 2009, the Administrator shall allocate annually for each unit subject to the emissions limitation requirements of paragraph (2) allowances from the reserve created pursuant to subsection (a)(2) of this section in an amount equal to the amount by which (i) the product of the lesser of the unit's actual 1985 emissions rate or its allowable 1985 emissions rate multiplied by the unit's baseline adjusted to reflect operation at a 60 percent capacity factor, divided by 2,000, exceeds (ii) the number of allowances allocated for the unit pursuant to paragraph (2) and section 7651b(a)(1) of this title as basic Phase II allowance allocations.

(C) An operating company with units subject to the emissions limitation requirements of this subsection may elect the allocation of allowances as provided under subparagraphs (A) and (B). Such election shall apply to the annual allowance allocation for each and every unit in the operating company subject to the emissions limitation requirements of this subsection. The Administrator shall allocate allowances pursuant to subparagraphs (A) and (B) only in accordance with this subparagraph.

(4) Notwithstanding any other provision of this section, at the election of the owner or operator, after January 1, 2000, the Administrator shall allocate in lieu of allocation, pursuant to paragraph (1), (2), (3), (5), or (6), allowances for a unit subject to the emissions limitation requirements of this subsection which commenced commercial operation on or after January 1, 1981 and before December 31, 1985, which was subject to, and in compliance with, section 7411 of the title in an amount equal to the unit's annual fuel consumption, on a Btu basis, at a 65 percent capacity factor multiplied by the unit's allowable 1985 emissions rate, divided by 2,000.

(5) For the purposes of this section, in the case of an oil- and gas-fired unit which has been awarded a clean coal technology demonstration grant as of January 1, 1991, by the United States Department of Energy, beginning January 1, 2000, the Administrator shall allocate for the unit allowances in an amount equal to the unit's baseline multiplied by 1.20 lbs/mmbtu, divided by 2,000.

(e) Oil and gas-fired units equal to or greater than 0.60 lbs/mmBtu and less than 1.20 lbs/mmBtu — After January 1, 2000, it shall be unlawful for any existing oil and gas-fired utility unit the lesser of whose actual or allowable 1985 sulfur dioxide emission rate is equal to, or greater than, 0.60 lbs/mmBtu, but less than 1.20 lbs/mmBtu to exceed an annual sulfur dioxide tonnage limitation equal to the product of the unit's baseline multiplied by (A) the lesser of the unit's allowable 1985 emissions rate or its actual 1985 emissions rate and (B) a numerical factor of 120 percent divided by 2,000, unless the owner or operator of such unit holds allowances to emit not less than the unit's total annual emissions.

(f) Oil and gas-fired units less than 0.60 lbs/mmBtu

(1) After January 1, 2000, it shall be unlawful for any oil and gas-fired existing utility unit the lesser of whose actual or allowable 1985 emission rate is less than 0.60 lbs/mmBtu and whose average annual fuel consumption during the period 1980 through 1989 on a Btu basis was 90 percent or less in the form of natural gas to exceed an annual sulfur dioxide tonnage emissions limitation equal to the product of the unit's baseline multiplied by (A) the lesser of 0.60 lbs/mmBtu or the unit's allowable 1985 emissions, and (B) a numerical factor of 120 percent, divided by 2,000, unless the owner or operator of such unit holds allowances to emit not less than the unit's total annual emissions.

(2) In addition to allowances allocated pursuant to paragraph (1) as basic Phase II allowance allocations and section 7651b(a)(1) of this title, beginning January 1, 2000, the Administrator shall, in the case of any unit operated by a utility that furnishes electricity, electric energy, steam, and natural gas within an area consisting of a city and 1 contiguous county, and in the case of any unit owned by a State authority, the output of which unit is furnished within that same area consisting of a city and 1 contiguous county, the Administrator shall allocate for each unit in the utility its pro rata share of 7,000 allowances and for each unit in the State authority its pro rata share of 2,000 allowances.

(g) Units that commence operation between 1986 and December 31, 1995

(1) After January 1, 2000, it shall be unlawful for any utility unit that has commenced commercial operation on or after January 1, 1986, but not later than September 30, 1990 to exceed an annual tonnage emission limitation equal to the product of the unit's annual fuel consumption, on a Btu basis, at a 65 percent capacity factor multiplied by the unit's allowable 1985 sulfur dioxide emissions rate (converted, if necessary, to pounds per mmBtu), divided by 2,000 unless the owner or operator of such unit holds allowances to emit not less than the unit's total annual emissions.

(2) After January 1, 2000, the Administrator shall allocate allowances pursuant to section 7651b to each unit which is listed in table B of this paragraph in an annual amount equal to the amount specified in Table B.

TABLE B

Unit	Allowances
Brandon Shores	8,907
Miller 4	9,197
TNP One 2	4,000
Zimmer 1	18,458
Spruce 1	7,647
Clover 1	2,796
Clover 2	2,796
Twin Oak 2	1,760
Twin Oak 1	9,158
Cross 1	6,401
Malakoff 1	1,759

Notwithstanding any other paragraph of this subsection, for units subject to this paragraph, the Administrator shall not allocate allowances pursuant to any other paragraph of this subsection, *Provided* that the owner or operator of a unit listed on Table B may elect an allocation of allowances under another paragraph of this subsection in lieu of an allocation under this paragraph.

(3) Beginning January 1, 2000, the Administrator shall allocate to the owner or operator of any utility unit that commences commercial operation, or has commenced commercial operation, on or after October 1, 1990, but not later than December 31, 1992 allowances in an amount equal to the product of the unit's annual fuel consumption, on a Btu basis, at a 65 percent capacity factor multiplied by the lesser of 0.30 lbs/mmBtu or the unit's allowable sulfur dioxide emission rate (converted, if necessary, to pounds per mmBtu), divided by 2,000.

(4) Beginning January 1, 2000, the Administrator shall allocate to the owner or operator of any utility unit that has commenced construction before December 31, 1990 and that commences commercial operation between January 1, 1993 and December 31, 1995, allowances in an amount equal to the product of the unit's annual fuel consumption, on a Btu basis, at a 65 percent capacity factor multiplied by the lesser of 0.30 lbs/mmBtu or the unit's allowable sulfur dioxide emission rate (converted, if necessary, to pounds per mmBtu), divided by 2,000.

(5) After January 1, 2000, it shall be unlawful for any existing utility unit that has completed conversion from predominantly gas fired existing operation to coal fired operation between January 1, 1985 and December 31, 1987, for which there has been allocated a proposed or final prohibition order pursuant to section 301(b) of the Powerplant and Industrial Fuel Use Act of 1978 (42 U.S.C. §§8301 *et seq.*, repealed 1987) to exceed an annual sulfur dioxide tonnage emissions limitation equal to the product of the unit's annual fuel consumption, on a Btu basis, at a 65 percent capacity factor multiplied by the lesser of 1.20 lbs/mmBtu or the

unit's allowable 1987 sulfur dioxide emissions rate, divided by 2,000, unless the owner or operator of such unit has obtained allowances equal to its actual emissions.

(6)(A) Unless the Administrator has approved a designation of such facility under section 7651i of this title, the provisions of this title shall not apply to a "qualifying small power production facility" or "qualifying cogeneration facility" (within the meaning of section 796(17)(C) or 796(18)(B) of Title 16 [the Federal Power Act]) or to a "new independent power production facility" as defined in section 7651o of this title except that clause (iii) of such definition in section 7651o of this title shall not apply for purposes of this paragraph if, as of November 15, 1990,

    (i) an applicable power sales agreement has been executed;

    (ii) the facility is the subject of a State regulatory authority order requiring an electric utility to enter into a power sales agreement with, purchase capacity from, or (for purposes of establishing terms and conditions of the electric utility's purchase of power) enter into arbitration concerning, the facility;

    (iii) an electric utility has issued a letter of intent or similar instrument committing to purchase power from the facility at a previously offered or lower price and a power sales agreement is executed within a reasonable period of time; or

    (iv) the facility has been selected as a winning bidder in a utility competitive bid solicitation.

(h) Oil and gas-fired units less than 10 percent oil consumed

(1) After January 1, 2000, it shall be unlawful for any oil and gas-fired utility unit whose average annual fuel consumption during the period 1980 through 1989 on a Btu basis exceeded 90 percent in the form of natural gas to exceed an annual sulfur dioxide tonnage limitation equal to the product of the unit's baseline multiplied by the unit's actual 1985 emissions rate divided by 2,000 unless the owner or operator of such unit holds allowances to emit not less than the unit's total annual emissions.

(2) In addition to allowances allocated pursuant to paragraph (1) and section 7651b(a)(1) of this title as basic Phase II allowance allocations, beginning January 1, 2000, and for each calendar year thereafter until and including 2009, the Administrator shall allocate annually for each unit subject to the emissions limitation requirements of paragraph (1) allowances from the reserve created pursuant to subsection (a)(2) in an amount equal to the unit's baseline multiplied by 0.050 lbs/mmBtu, divided by 2,000.

(3) In addition to allowances allocated pursuant to paragraph (1) and section 7651b(a)(1) of this title, beginning January 1, 2010, the Administrator shall allocate annually for each unit subject to the emissions limitation requirements of paragraph (1) allowances in an amount equal to the unit's baseline multiplied by 0.050 lbs/mmBtu, divided by 2,000.

(i) Units in high growth States — (1) In addition to allowances allocated pursuant to this section and section 7651b(a)(1) of this title as basic Phase II allowance allocations, beginning January 1, 2000, the Administrator shall allocate annually allowances for each unit, subject to an emissions limitation requirement under this section, and located in a State that —

    (A) has experienced a growth in population in excess of 25 percent between 1980 and 1988 according to State Population and Household Estimates, With Age, Sex, and Components of Change: 1981-1988 allocated by the United States Department of Commerce, and

    (B) had an installed electrical generating capacity of more than 30,000,000 kw in 1988,

in an amount equal to the difference between (A) the number of allowances that would be allocated for the unit pursuant to the emissions limitation requirements of this section applicable to the unit adjusted to reflect the unit's annual average fuel consumption on a Btu basis of any three consecutive calendar years between 1980 and 1989 (inclusive) as elected by the owner or operator and (B) the number of allowances allocated for the unit pursuant to the emissions limitation requirements of this section: *Provided*, That the number of allowances allocated pursuant to this subsection shall not exceed an annual total of 40,000. If necessary to meeting the 40,000 allowance restriction imposed under this subsection the Administrator shall reduce, pro rata, the additional annual allowances allocated to each unit under this subsection.

(2) Beginning January 1, 2000, in addition to allowances allocated pursuant to this section and section 7651b(a)(1) of this title as basic Phase II allowance allocations, the Administrator shall allocate annually for each unit subject to the emissions limitation requirements of subsection (b)(1), (A) the lesser of whose actual or allowable 1980 emissions rate has declined by 50 percent or more as of November 15, 1990, (B) whose actual emissions rate is less than 1.2 lbs/mmBtu as of January 1, 2000, (C) which commenced operation after January 1, 1970, (D) which is owned by a utility company whose combined commercial and industrial kilowatt-hour sales have increased by more than 20 percent between calendar year 1980 and November 15, 1990, and (E) whose company-wide fossil-fuel sulfur dioxide emissions rate has declined 40 per centum or more from 1980 to 1988, allowances in an amount equal to

the difference between (i) the number of allowances that would be allocated for the unit pursuant to the emissions limitation requirements of subsection (b)(1) adjusted to reflect the unit's annual average fuel consumption on a Btu basis for any three consecutive years between 1980 and 1989 (inclusive) as elected by the owner or operator and (ii) the number of allowances allocated for the unit pursuant to the emissions limitation requirements of subsection (b)(1): *Provided*, That the number of allowances allocated pursuant to this paragraph shall not exceed an annual total of 5,000. If necessary to meeting the 5,000 allowance restriction imposed in the last clause of the preceding sentence the Administrator shall reduce, pro rata, the additional allowances allocated to each unit pursuant to this paragraph.

(j) Certain municipally owned power plants — Beginning January 1, 2000, in addition to allowances allocated pursuant to this section and section 7651b(a)(1) of this title as basic Phase II allowance allocations, the Administrator shall allocate annually for each existing municipally owned oil and gas-fired utility unit with nameplate capacity equal to, or less than, 40 MWe, the lesser of whose actual or allowable 1985 sulfur dioxide emission rate is less than 1.20 lbs/mmBtu, allowances in an amount equal to the product of the unit's annual fuel consumption on a Btu basis at a 60 percent capacity factor multiplied by the lesser of its allowable 1985 emission rate or its actual 1985 emission rate, divided by 2,000.

§7651e. Allowances for States with emissions rates at or below 0.80 lbs/mmBtu
[CAA §406]

(a) Election of Governor — In addition to basic Phase II allowance allocations, upon the election of the Governor of any State, with a 1985 state-wide annual sulfur dioxide emissions rate equal to or less than, 0.80 lbs/mmBtu, averaged over all fossil fuel-fired utility steam generating units, beginning January 1, 2000, and for each calendar year thereafter until and including 2009, the Administrator shall allocate, in lieu of other Phase II bonus allowance allocations, allowances from the reserve created pursuant to section 7651d(a)(2) of this title to all such units in the State in an amount equal to 125,000 multiplied by the unit's pro rata share of electricity generated in calendar year 1985 at fossil fuel-fired utility steam units in all States eligible for the election.

(b) Notification of Administrator — Pursuant to section 7651b(a)(1) of this title, each Governor of a State eligible to make an election under paragraph (a) shall notify the Administrator of such election. In the event that the Governor of any such State fails to notify the Administrator of the Governor's elections, the Administrator shall allocate allowances pursuant to section 7651d of this title.

(c) Allowances after January 1, 2010 — After January 1, 2010, the Administrator shall allocate allowances to units subject to the provisions of this section pursuant to section 7651d of this title.

§7651f. Nitrogen oxides emission reduction program
[CAA §407]

(a) Applicability — On the date that a coal-fired utility unit becomes an affected unit pursuant to sections 7651c, 7651d, 7651h of this title, or on the date a unit subject to the provisions of section 7651c(d) or 7651h(b), must meet the SO_2 reduction requirements, each such unit shall become an affected unit for purposes of this section and shall be subject to the emission limitations for nitrogen oxides set forth herein.

(b) Emission limitations

(1) Not later than eighteen months after November 15, 1990, the Administrator shall by regulation establish annual allowable emission limitations for nitrogen oxides for the types of utility boilers listed below, which limitations shall not exceed the rates listed below: *Provided*, That the Administrator may set a rate higher than that listed for any type of utility boiler if the Administrator finds that the maximum listed rate for that boiler type cannot be achieved using low NOx burner technology. The maximum allowable emission rates are as follows:

(A) for tangentially fired boilers, 0.45 lb/mmBtu;

(B) for dry bottom wall-fired boilers (other than units applying cell burner technology), 0.50 lb/mmBtu.

After January 1, 1995, it shall be unlawful for any unit that is an affected unit on that date and is of the type listed in this paragraph to emit nitrogen oxides in excess of the emission rates set by the Administrator pursuant to this paragraph.

(2) Not later than January 1, 1997, the Administrator shall, by regulation, establish allowable emission limitations on a lb/mmBtu, annual average basis, for nitrogen oxides for the following types of utility boilers:

(A) wet bottom wall-fired boilers;

(B) cyclones;

(C) units applying cell burner technology;

(D) all other types of utility boilers. The Administrator shall base such rates on the degree of reduction achievable through the retrofit application of the best system of continuous emission reduction, taking into account available technology, costs and energy and environmental impacts; and which is comparable to the costs of nitrogen oxides controls set pursuant to subsection (b)(1) of this section. Not later than January 1, 1997, the Administrator may revise the applicable emission limitations for tangentially fired and dry bottom, wall-fired boilers (other than cell burners) to be more stringent if the Administrator determines that more effective low NOx burner technology is available: *Provided*, That, no unit that is an affected unit pursuant to section 7651c and that is subject to the requirements of subsection (b)(1) of this section, shall be subject to the revised emission limitations, if any.

(c) Revised performance standards

(1) Not later than January 1, 1993, the Administrator shall propose revised standards of performance to section 7411 of this title for nitrogen oxides emissions from fossil-fuel fired steam generating units, including both electric utility and nonutility units. Not later than January 1, 1994, the Administrator shall promulgate such revised standards of performance. Such revised standards of performance shall reflect improvements in methods for the reduction of emissions of oxides of nitrogen.

(d) Alternative emission limitations — The permitting authority shall, upon request of an owner or operator of a unit subject to this section, authorize an emission limitation less stringent than the applicable limitation established under subsection (b)(1) or (b)(2) of this section upon a determination that —

(1) a unit subject to subsection (b)(1) of this section cannot meet the applicable limitation using low NOx burner technology; or

(2) a unit subject to subsection (b)(2) of this section cannot meet the applicable rate using the technology on which the Administrator based the applicable emission limitation.

The permitting authority shall base such determination upon a showing satisfactory to the permitting authority, in accordance with regulations established by the Administrator not later than eighteen months after November 15, 1990, that the owner or operator —

(1) has properly installed appropriate control equipment designed to meet the applicable emission rate;

(2) has properly operated such equipment for a period of fifteen months (or such other period of time as the Administrator determines through the regulations), and provides operating and monitoring data for such period demonstrating that the unit cannot meet the applicable emission rate; and

(3) has specified an emission rate that such unit can meet on an annual average basis.

The permitting authority shall issue an operating permit for the unit in question, in accordance with section 7651g of this title and part B of title III —

(i) that permits the unit during the demonstration period referred to in subparagraph (2) above, to emit at a rate in excess of the applicable emission rate;

(ii) at the conclusion of the demonstration period to revise the operating permit to reflect the alternative emission rate demonstrated in paragraphs (2) and (3) above.

Units subject to subsection (b)(1) of this section for which an alternative emission limitation is established shall not be required to install any additional control technology beyond low NOx burners. Nothing in this section shall preclude an owner or operator from installing and operating an alternative NOx control technology capable of achieving the applicable emission limitation. If the owner or operator of a unit subject to the emissions limitation requirements of subsection (b)(1) of this section demonstrates to the satisfaction of the Administrator that the technology necessary to meet such requirements is not in adequate supply to enable its installation and operation at the unit, consistent with system reliability, by January 1, 1995, then the Administrator shall extend the deadline for compliance for the unit by a period of 15 months. Any owner or operator may petition the Administrator to make a determination under the previous sentence. The Administrator shall grant or deny such petition within 3 months of submittal.

(e) Emissions averaging — In lieu of complying with the applicable emission limitations under subsection (b)(1), (2), or (d) of this section, the owner or operator of two or more units subject to one or more of the applicable emission limitations set pursuant to these sections, may petition the permitting authority for alternative contemporaneous annual emission limitations for such units that ensure that (1) the actual annual emission rate in pounds of nitrogen oxides per million Btu averaged over the units in question is a rate that is less than or equal to (2) the Btu-weighted average annual emission rate for the same units if they had been operated, during the same period of time, in compliance with limitations set in accordance with the applicable emission rates set pursuant to subsections (b)(1) and (2) of this section.

If the permitting authority determines, in accordance with regulations issued by the Administrator not later than eighteen months after November 15, 1990; that the conditions in the paragraph above can be met, the permitting authority shall issue operating permits for such units, in accordance with section 7651g of this title and part B of title III, that allow alternative contemporaneous annual emission limitations. Such emission limitations shall only remain in effect while both units continue operation under the conditions specified in their respective operating permits.

§7651g. Permits and compliance plans
[CAA §408]

(a) Permit program — The provisions of this title shall be implemented, subject to section 7651b of this title, by permits issued to units subject to this subchapter (and enforced) in accordance with the provisions of subchapter V of this chapter, as modified by this subchapter. Any such permit issued by the Administrator, or by a State with an approved permit program, shall prohibit —

843

(1) annual emissions of sulfur dioxide in excess of the number of allowances to emit sulfur dioxide the owner or operator, or the designated representative of the owners or operators, of the unit hold for the unit,

(2) exceedances of applicable emissions rates,

(3) the use of any allowance prior to the year for which it was allocated, and

(4) contravention of any other provision of the permit.

Permits issued to implement this subchapter shall be issued for a period of 5 years, notwithstanding subchapter V of this chapter. No permit shall be issued that is inconsistent with the requirements of this subchapter, and subchapter V of this chapter as applicable.

(b) Compliance plan — Each initial permit application shall be accompanied by a compliance plan for the source to comply with its requirements under this title. Where an affected source consists of more than one affected unit, such plan shall cover all such units, and for purposes of section 7661a(c) of this title, such source shall be considered a "facility". Nothing in this section regarding compliance plans or in subchapter V of this chapter shall be construed as affecting allowances. Except as provided under subsection (c)(1)(B) of this section, submission of a statement by the owner or operator, or the designated representative of the owners and operators, of a unit subject to the emissions limitation requirements of sections 7651c, 7651d, and 7651f of this title, that the unit will meet the applicable emissions limitation requirements of such sections in a timely manner or that, in the case of the emissions limitation requirements of sections 7651c and 7651d of this title, the owners and operators will hold allowances to emit not less than the total annual emissions of the unit, shall be deemed to meet the proposed and approved compliance planning requirements of this section and subchapter V of this chapter, except that, for any unit that will meet the requirements of this title by means of an alternative method of compliance authorized under section 7651c(b), (c), (d), or (f) of this title section 7651f(d) or (e) of this title, section 7651h of this title and section 7651i of this title, the proposed and approved compliance plan, permit application and permit shall include, pursuant to regulations promulgated by the Administrator, for each alternative method of compliance a comprehensive description of the schedule and means by which the unit will rely on one or more alternative methods of compliance in the manner and time authorized under this title. Recordation by the Administrator of transfers of allowances shall amend automatically all applicable proposed or approved permit applications, compliance plans and permits. The Administrator may also require —

(1) for a source, a demonstration of attainment of national ambient air quality standards, and

(2) from the owner or operator of two or more affected sources, an integrated compliance plan

providing an overall plan for achieving compliance at the affected sources.

(c) First phase permits — The Administrator shall issue permits to affected sources under sections 7651c and 7651f of this title.

(1) Permit application and compliance plan

(A) Not later than 27 months after November 15, 1990, the designated representative of the owners or operators, or the owner and operator, of each affected source under sections 7651c and 7651f shall submit a permit application and compliance plan for that source in accordance with regulations issued by the Administrator under paragraph (3). The permit application and the compliance plan shall be binding on the owner or operator or the designated representative of owners and operators for purposes of this subchapter and section 7651a(a) of this title, and shall be enforceable in lieu of a permit until a permit is issued by the Administrator for the source.

(B) In the case of a compliance plan for an affected source under sections 7651c and 7651f of this title for which the owner or operator proposes to meet the requirements of that section by reducing utilization of the unit as compared with its baseline or by shutting down the unit, the owner or operator shall include in the proposed compliance plan a specification of the unit or units that will provide electrical generation to compensate for the reduced output at the affected source, or a demonstration that such reduced utilization will be accomplished through energy conservation or improved unit efficiency. The unit to be used for such compensating generation, which is not otherwise an affected unit under sections 7651c and 7651f of this title, shall be deemed an affected unit under section 7651c of this title, subject to all of the requirements for such units under this title, except that allowances shall be allocated to such compensating unit in the amount of an annual limitation equal to the product of the unit's baseline multiplied by the lesser of the unit's actual 1985 emissions rate or its allowable 1985 emissions rate, divided by 2,000.

(2) EPA action on compliance plans — The Administrator shall review each proposed compliance plan to determine whether it satisfies the requirements of this title, and shall approve or disapprove such plan within months after receipt of a complete submission. If a plan is disapproved, it may be resubmitted for approval with such changes as the Administrator shall require consistent with the requirements of this title and within such period as the Administrator prescribes as part of such disapproval.

(3) Regulations; issuance of permits — Not later than 18 months after November 15, 1990, the Administrator shall promulgate regulations, in

accordance with subchapter V of this chapter, to implement a Federal permit program to issue permits for affected sources under this title. Following promulgation, the Administrator shall issue a permit to implement the requirements of section 7651c of this title and the allowances provided under section 7651b of this title to the owner or operator of each affected source under section 404. Such a permit shall supersede any permit application and compliance plan submitted under paragraph (1).

(4) Fees — During the years 1995 through 1999 inclusive, no fee shall be required to be paid under section 7661a(b)(3) of this title or under section 7410(a)(2)(L) of this title with respect to emissions from any unit which is an affected unit under section 404.

(d) Second phase permits

(1) To provide for permits for (A) new electric utility steam generating units required under section 7651b(e) of this title to have allowances, (B) affected units or sources under section 7651d of this title, and (C) existing units subject to nitrogen oxide emission reductions under section 7651f of this title, each State in which one or more such units or sources are located shall submit in accordance with subchapter V of this chapter, a permit program for approval as provided by that title. Upon approval of such program, for the units or sources subject to such approved program the Administrator shall suspend the issuance of permits as provided in subchapter V of this chapter.

(2) The owner or operator or the designated representative of each affected source under section 405 shall submit a permit application and compliance plan for that source to the permitting authority, not later than January 1, 1996.

(3) Not later than December 31, 1997, each State with an approved permit program shall issue permits to the owner or operator, or the designated representative of the owners and operators, of affected sources under section 7651d of this title that satisfy the requirements of subchapter V of this chapter and this subchapter and that submitted to such State a permit application and compliance plan pursuant to paragraph (2). In the case of a State without an approved permit program by July 1, 1996, the Administrator shall, not later than January 1, 1998, issue a permit to the owner or operator or the designated representative of each such affected source. In the case of affected sources for which applications and plans are timely received under paragraph (2), the permit application and the compliance plan, including amendments thereto, shall be binding on the owner or operator or the designated representative of the owners or operators and shall be enforceable as a permit for purposes of this subchapter and subchapter V of this chapter until a permit is issued by the permitting authority for the affected source. The provisions of section 558(c) of Title 5 (relating to renewals) shall apply

to permits issued by a permitting authority under this title and subchapter V of this chapter.

(4) The permit issued in accordance with this subsection for an affected source shall provide that the affected units at the affected source may not emit an annual tonnage of sulfur dioxide in excess of the number of allowances to emit sulfur dioxide the owner or operator or designated representative hold for the unit.

(e) New units — The owner or operator of each source that includes a new electric utility steam generating unit shall submit a permit application and compliance plan to the permitting authority not later than 24 months before the later of (1) January 1, 2000, or (2) the date on which the unit commences operation. The permitting authority shall issue a permit to the owner or operator, or the designated representative thereof, of the unit that satisfies the requirements of subchapter V of this chapter and this subchapter.

(f) Units subject to certain other limits — The owner or operator, or designated representative thereof, of any unit subject to an emission rate requirement under section 7651f of this title shall submit a permit application and compliance plan for such unit to the permitting authority, not later than January 1, 1998. The permitting authority shall issue a permit to the owner or operator that satisfies the requirements of subchapter V of this chapter and this subchapter, including any appropriate monitoring and reporting requirements.

(g) Amendment of application and compliance plan — At any time after the submission of an application and compliance plan under this section, the applicant may submit a revised application and compliance plan, in accordance with the requirements of this section. In considering any permit application and compliance plan under this title, the permitting authority shall ensure coordination with the applicable electric ratemaking authority, in the case of regulated utilities, and with unregulated public utilities.

(h) Prohibition

(1) It shall be unlawful for an owner or operator, or designated representative, required to submit a permit application or compliance plan under this subchapter to fail to submit such application or plan in accordance with the deadlines specified in this section or to otherwise fail to comply with regulations implementing this section.

(2) It shall be unlawful for any person to operate any source subject to this subchapter except in compliance with the terms and requirements of a permit application and compliance plan (including amendments thereto) or permit issued by the Administrator or a State with an approved permit program. For purposes of this subsection, compliance, as provided in section 7661e(f) of this title, with a permit issued under subchapter V of this chapter which complies with this title for sources subject to this title shall be deemed compliance with this subsection as well as section 7661a(a) of this title.

(3) In order to ensure reliability of electric power, nothing in this subchapter or subchapter V of this chapter shall be construed as requiring termination of operations of an electric utility steam generating unit for failure to have an approved permit or compliance plan, except that any such unit may be subject to the applicable enforcement provisions of section 7413 of this title.

(i) Multiple owners — No permit shall be issued under this section to an affected unit until the designated representative of the owners or operators has filed a certificate of representation with regard to matters under this title, including the holding and distribution of allowances and the proceeds of transactions involving allowances. Where there are multiple holders of a legal or equitable title to, or a leasehold interest in, such a unit, or where a utility or industrial customer purchases power from an affected unit (or units) under life-of-the-unit, firm power contractual arrangements, the certificate shall state (1) that allowances and the proceeds of transactions involving allowances will be deemed to be held or distributed in proportion to each holder's legal, equitable, leasehold, or contractual reservation or entitlement, or (2) if such multiple holders have expressly provided for a different distribution of allowances by contract, that allowances and the proceeds of transactions involving allowances will be deemed to be held or distributed in accordance with the contract. A passive lessor, or a person who has an equitable interest through such lessor, whose rental payments are not based, either directly or indirectly, upon the revenues or income from the affected unit shall not be deemed to be a holder of a legal, equitable, leasehold, or contractual interest for the purpose of holding or distributing allowances as provided in this subsection, during either the term of such leasehold or thereafter, unless expressly provided for in the leasehold agreement. Except as otherwise provided in this subsection, where all legal or equitable title to or interest in an affected unit is held by a single person, the certification shall state that all allowances received by the unit are deemed to be held for that person.

§7651h. Repowered sources
[CAA §409]

(a) Availability — Not later than December 31, 1997, the owner or operator of an existing unit subject to the emissions limitation requirements of section 7651d(b) and (c) of this title may demonstrate to the permitting authority that one or more units will be repowered with a qualifying clean coal technology to comply with the requirements under section 405. The owner or operator shall, as part of any such demonstration, provide, not later than January 1, 2000, satisfactory documentation of a preliminary design and engineering effort for such repowering and an executed and binding contract for the majority of the equipment to repower such unit and such other information as the Administrator may require by regulation.

The replacement of an existing utility unit with a new utility unit using a repowering technology referred to in section 7651a(2) of this title which is located at a different site, shall be treated as repowering of the existing unit for purposes of this title, if —

(1) the replacement unit is designated by the owner or operator to replace such existing unit, and

(2) the existing unit is retired from service on or before the date on which the designated replacement unit enters commercial operation.

(b) Extension

(1) An owner or operator satisfying the requirements of subsection (a) shall be granted an extension of the emission limitation requirement compliance date for that unit from January 1, 2000, to December 31, 2003. The extension shall be specified in the permit issued to the source under section 7651g of this title, together with any compliance schedule and other requirements necessary to meet second phase requirements by the extended date. Any unit that is granted an extension under this section shall not be eligible for a waiver under section 7411(j) of this title, and shall continue to be subject to requirements under this title as if it were a unit subject to section 7651d of this title.

(2) If (A) the owner or operator of an existing unit has been granted an extension under paragraph (1) in order to repower such unit with a clean coal unit, and (B) such owner or operator demonstrates to the satisfaction of the Administrator that the repowering technology to be utilized by such unit has been properly constructed and tested on such unit, but nevertheless has been unable to achieve the emission reduction limitations and is economically or technologically infeasible, such existing unit may be retrofitted or repowered with equipment or facilities utilizing another clean coal technology or other available control technology.

(c) Allowances

(1) For the period of the extension under this section, the Administrator shall allocate to the owner or operator of the affected unit, annual allowances for sulfur dioxide equal to the affected unit's baseline multiplied by the lesser of the unit's federally approved State Implementation Plan emissions limitation or its actual emission rate for 1995 in lieu of any other allocation. Such allowances may not be transferred or used by any other source to meet emission requirements under this title. The source owner or operator shall notify the Administrator sixty days in advance of the date on which the affected unit for which the extension has been granted is to be removed from operation to install the repowering technology.

(2) Effective on that date, the unit shall be subject to the requirements of section 7651d of this title. Allowances for the year in which the unit is removed from operation to install the repowering technology shall be calculated as the product of

the unit's baseline multiplied by 1.20 lbs/mmBtu, divided by 2,000, and prorated accordingly, and are transferable.

(3) Allowances for such existing utility units for calendar years after the year the repowering is complete shall be calculated as the product of the existing unit's baseline multiplied by 1.20 lbs/mmBtu, divided by 2,000.

(4) Notwithstanding the provisions of section 7651b(a) and (e) of this title, allowances shall be allocated under this section for a designated replacement unit which replaces an existing unit (as provided in the last sentence of subsection (a)) in lieu of any further allocations of allowances for the existing unit.

(5) For the purpose of meeting the aggregate emissions limitation requirement set forth in section 403(a)(1), the units with an extension under this subsection shall be treated in each calendar year during the extension period as holding allowances allocated under paragraph (3).

(d) Control requirements — Any unit qualifying for an extension under this section that does not increase actual hourly emissions for any pollutant regulated under the Act shall not be subject to any standard of performance under section 7411 of this title. Notwithstanding the provisions of this subsection, no new unit (1) designated as a replacement for an existing unit, (2) qualifying for the extension under subsection (b), and (3) located at a different site than the existing unit shall receive an exemption from the requirements imposed under section 7411 of this title.

(e) Expedited permitting — State permitting authorities and, where applicable, the Administrator, are encouraged to give expedited consideration to permit applications under parts C and D of subchapter I of this chapter for any source qualifying for an extension under this section.

(f) Prohibition — It shall be unlawful for the owner or operator of a repowered source to fail to comply with the requirement of this section, or any regulations of permit requirements to implement this section, including the prohibition against emitting sulfur dioxide in excess of allowances held.

§7651i. Election for additional sources [CAA §410]

(a) Applicability — The owner or operator of any unit that is not, nor will become, an affected unit under section 7651b(e), 7651c, or 7651d of this title, or that is a process source under subsection (d) of this section, that emits sulfur dioxide, may elect to designate that unit or source to become an affected unit and to receive allowances under this title. An election shall be submitted to the Administrator for approval, along with a permit application and proposed compliance plan in accordance with section 7651g of this title. The Administrator shall approve a designation that meets the requirements of this

section, and such designated unit, or source, shall be allocated allowances, and be an affected unit for purposes of this title.

(b) Establishment of baseline — The baseline for a unit designated under this section shall be established by the Administrator by regulation, based on fuel consumption and operating data for the unit for calendar years 1985, 1986, and 1987, or if such data is not available, the Administrator may prescribe a baseline based on alternative representative data.

(c) Emission limitations — Annual emissions limitations for sulfur dioxide shall be equal to the product of the baseline multiplied by the lesser of the unit's 1985 actual or allowable emission rate in lbs/mmBtu, or, if the unit did not operate in 1985, by the lesser of the unit's actual or allowable emission rate for a calendar year after 1985 (as determined by the Administrator), divided by 2,000.

(d) Process sources — Not later than 18 months after November 15, 1990, the Administrator shall establish a program under which the owner or operator of a process source that emits sulfur dioxide may elect to designate that source as an affected unit for the purpose of receiving allowances under this title. The Administrator shall, by regulation, define the sources that may be designated; specify the emissions limitation; specify the operating, emission baseline, and other data requirements; prescribe CEMS or other monitoring requirements; and promulgate permit, reporting, and any other requirements necessary to implement such a program.

(e) Allowances and permits — The Administrator shall issue allowances to an affected unit under this section in an amount equal to the emissions limitation calculated under subsection (c) or (d), in accordance with section 7651b of this title. Such allowance may be used in accordance with, and shall be subject to, the provisions of section 7651b of this title. Affected sources under this section shall be subject to the requirements of sections 7651b, 7651g, 7651j, 7651k, 7651l, and 7651m of this title.

(f) Limitation — Any unit designated under this section shall not transfer or bank allowances produced as a result of reduced utilization or shutdown, except that, such allowances may be transferred or carried forward for use in subsequent years to the extent that the reduced utilization or shutdown results from the replacement of thermal energy from the unit designated under this section, with thermal energy generated by any other unit or units subject to the requirements of this title, and the designated unit's allowances are transferred or carried forward for use at such other replacement unit or units. In no case may the Administrator allocate to a source designated under this section allowances in an amount greater than the emissions resulting from operation of the source in full compliance with the requirements of this Act. No such allowances shall authorize operation of a unit in violation of any other requirements of this Act.

(g) Implementation — The Administrator shall issue regulations to implement this section not later than eighteen months after November 15, 1990.

(h) Small diesel refineries — The Administrator shall issue allowances to owners or operators of small diesel refineries who produce diesel fuel after October 1, 1993, meeting the requirements of subsection 7545(i) of this title.

(1) Allowance period — Allowances may be allocated under this subsection only for the period from October 1, 1993, through December 31, 1999.

(2) Allowance determination — The number of allowances allocated pursuant to this paragraph shall equal the annual number of pounds of sulfur dioxide reduction attributable to desulfurization by a small refinery divided by 2,000. For the purposes of this calculation, the concentration of sulfur removed from diesel fuel shall be the difference between 0.274 percent (by weight) and 0.050 percent (by weight).

(3) Refinery eligibility — As used in this subsection, the term "small refinery" shall mean a refinery or portion of a refinery —

(A) which, as of November 15, 1990, has bona fide crude oil throughput of less than 18,250,000 barrels per year, as reported to the Department of Energy, and

(B) which, as of November 15, 1990, is owned or controlled by a refiner with a total combined bona fide crude oil throughput of less than 50,187,500 barrels per year, as reported to the Department of Energy.

(4) Limitation per refinery — The maximum number of allowances that can be annually allocated to a small refinery pursuant to this subsection is one thousand and five hundred.

(5) Limitation on total — In any given year, the total number of allowances allocated pursuant to this subsection shall not exceed thirty-five thousand.

(6) Required certification — The Administrator shall not allocate any allowances pursuant to this subsection unless the owner or operator of a small diesel refinery shall have certified, at a time and in a manner prescribed by the Administrator, that all motor diesel fuel produced by the refinery for which allowances are claimed, including motor diesel fuel for off-highway use, shall have met the requirements of subsection 7545(i) of this title.

§7651j. Excess emissions penalty
[CAA §411]

(a) Excess emissions penalty — The owner or operator of any unit or process source subject to the requirements of sections 7651b, 7651c, 7651d, 7651e, 7651f, or 7651h of this title, or designated under section 7651i of this title, that emits sulfur dioxide or nitrogen oxides for any calendar year in excess of the unit's emissions limitation requirement or, in the case of sulfur dioxide, of the allowances the owner or operator holds for use for the unit for that calendar year shall be liable for the payment of an excess emissions penalty, except where such emissions were authorized pursuant to section 7410(f) of this title. That penalty shall be calculated on the basis of the number of tons emitted in excess of the unit's emissions limitation requirement or, in the case of sulfur dioxide, of the allowances the operator holds for use for the unit for that year, multiplied by $2,000. Any such penalty shall be due and payable without demand to the Administrator as provided in regulations to be issued by the Administrator by no later than eighteen months after November 15, 1990. Any such payment shall be deposited in the United States Treasury pursuant to the Miscellaneous Receipts Act. Any penalty due and payable under this section shall not diminish the liability of the unit's owner or operator for any fine, penalty or assessment against the unit for the same violation under any other section of this Act.

(b) Excess emissions offset — The owner or operator of any affected source that emits sulfur dioxide during any calendar year in excess of the unit's emissions limitation requirement or of the allowances held for the unit for the calendar year, shall be liable to offset the excess emissions by an equal tonnage amount in the following calendar year, or such longer period as the Administrator may prescribe. The owner or operator of the source shall, within sixty days after the end of the year in which the excess emissions occurred, submit to the Administrator, and to the State in which the source is located, a proposed plan to achieve the required offsets. Upon approval of the proposed plan by the Administrator, as submitted, modified or conditioned, the plan shall be deemed at a condition of the operating permit for the unit without further review or revision of the permit. The Administrator shall also deduct allowances equal to the excess tonnage from those allocated for the source for the calendar year, or succeeding years during which offsets are required, following the year in which the excess emissions occurred.

(c) Penalty adjustment — The Administrator shall, by regulation, adjust the penalty specified in subsection (a) of this section for inflation, based on the Consumer Price Index, on November 15, 1990, and annually thereafter.

(d) Prohibition — It shall be unlawful for the owner or operator of any source liable for a penalty and offset under this section to fail (1) to pay the penalty under subsection (a) of this section, (2) to provide, and thereafter comply with, a compliance plan as required by subsection (b), or (3) to offset excess emissions as required by subsection (b).

(e) Savings provision — Nothing in this title shall limit or otherwise affect the application of section 7413, 7414, 7420, or 7604 of this title except as otherwise explicitly provided in this title.

§7651k. Monitoring, reporting, and record-keeping requirements
[CAA §412]

(a) Applicability — The owner and operator of any source subject to this title shall be required to install and operate CEMS on each affected unit at the source, and to quality assure the data for sulfur dioxide, nitrogen oxides, opacity and volumetric flow at each such unit. The Administrator shall, by regulations issued not later than eighteen months after November 15, 1990, specify the requirements for CEMS, for any alternative monitoring system that is demonstrated as providing information with the same precision, reliability, accessibility, and timeliness as that provided by CEMS, and for recordkeeping and reporting of information from such systems. Such regulations may include limitations or the use of alternative compliance methods by units equipped with an alternative monitoring system as may be necessary to preserve the orderly functioning of the allowance system, and which will ensure the emissions reductions contemplated by this title. Where 2 or more units utilize a single stack, a separate CEMS shall not be required for each unit, and for such units the regulations shall require that the owner or operator collect sufficient information to permit reliable compliance determinations for each such unit.

(b) First phase requirements — Not later than thirty-six months after November 15, 1990, the owner or operator of each affected unit under section 7651c of this title, including, but not limited to, units that become affected units pursuant to subsections (b) and (c) of this section and eligible units under subsection (d) of this section, shall install and operate CEMS, quality assure the data, and keep records and reports in accordance with the regulations issued under subsection (a) of this section.

(c) Second phase requirements — Not later than January 1, 1995, the owner or operator of each affected unit that has not previously met the requirements of subsections (a) and (b) of this section shall install and operate CEMS, quality assure the data, and keep records and reports in accordance with the regulations issued under subsection (a) of this section. Upon commencement of commercial operation of each new utility unit, the unit shall comply with the requirements of subsection (a) of this section.

(d) Unavailability of emissions data — If CEMS data or data from an alternative monitoring system approved by the Administrator under subsection (a) is not available for any affected unit during any period of a calendar year in which such data is required under this title, and the owner or operator cannot provide information, satisfactory to the Administrator, on emissions during that period, the Administrator shall deem the unit to be operating in an uncontrolled manner during the entire period for which the data was not available and shall, by regulation which shall be issued not later than eighteen

months after November 15, 1990, prescribe means to calculate emissions for that period. The owner or operator shall be liable for excess emissions fees and offsets under section 7651j of this section in accordance with such regulations. Any fee due and payable under this subsection shall not diminish the liability of the unit's owner or operator for any fine, penalty, fee or assessment against the unit for the same violation under any other section of this chapter.

(e) Prohibition — It shall be unlawful for the owner or operator of any source subject to this title to operate a source without complying with the requirements of this section, and any regulations implementing this section.

§7651l. General compliance with other provisions
[CAA §413]

Except as expressly provided, compliance with the requirements of this subchapter shall not exempt or exclude the owner or operator of any source subject to this subchapter from compliance with any other applicable requirements of this chapter.

§7651m. Enforcement
[CAA §414]

It shall be unlawful for any person subject to this title to violate any prohibition of, requirement of, or regulation promulgated pursuant to this title shall be a violation of this Act. In addition to the other requirements and prohibitions provided for in this subchapter, the operation of any affected unit to emit sulfur dioxide in excess of allowances held for such unit shall be deemed a violation, with each ton emitted in excess of allowances held constituting a separate violation.

§7651n. Clean coal technology regulatory incentives
[CAA §415]

(a) "Clean coal technology" defined — For purposes of this section, "clean coal technology" means any technology, including technologies applied at the precombustion, combustion, or post combustion stage, at a new or existing facility which will achieve significant reductions in air emissions of sulfur dioxide or oxides of nitrogen associated with the utilization of coal in the generation of electricity, process steam, or industrial products, which is not in widespread use as of November 15, 1990.

(b) Revised regulations for clean coal technology demonstrations

(1) Applicability — This subsection applies to physical or operational changes to existing facilities for the sole purpose of installation, operation, cessation, or removal of a temporary or permanent clean coal technology demonstration project. For the purposes of this section, a clean coal technology demonstration project shall mean a project using funds appropriated under the heading "Department

849

of Energy-Clean Coal Technology", up to a total amount of $2,500,000,000 for commercial demonstration of clean coal technology, or similar projects funded through appropriations for the Environmental Protection Agency. The Federal contribution for a qualifying project shall be at least 20 percent of the total cost of the demonstration project.

(2) Temporary projects — Installation, operation, cessation, or removal of a temporary clean coal technology demonstration project that is operated for a period of five years or less, and which complies with the State implementation plans for the State in which the project is located and other requirements necessary to attain and maintain the national ambient air quality standards during and after the project is terminated, shall not subject such facility to the requirements of section 7411 of this title or part C or D of subchapter I of this chapter.

(3) Permanent projects — For permanent clean coal technology demonstration projects that constitute repowering as defined in section 7651a(*l*) of this title, any qualifying project shall not be subject to standards of performance under section 7411 of this title or to the review and permitting requirements of part C for any pollutant the potential emissions of which will not increase as a result of the demonstration project.

(4) EPA regulations — Not later than 12 months after November 15, 1990, the Administrator shall promulgate regulations or interpretive rulings to revise requirements under section 7411 of this title and parts C and D, as appropriate, to facilitate projects consistent in this subsection. With respect to parts C and D, such regulations or rulings shall apply to all areas in which EPA is the permitting authority. In those instances in which the State is the permitting authority under part C or D, any State may adopt and submit to the Administrator for approval revisions to its implementation plan to apply the regulations or rulings promulgated under this subsection.

(c) **Exemption for reactivation of very clean units** — Physical changes or changes in the method of operation associated with the commencement of commercial operations by a coal-fired utility unit after a period of discontinued operation shall not subject the unit to the requirements of section 7411 of this title or part C of the Act where the unit (1) has not been in operation for the two-year period prior to the enactment of the Clean Air Act Amendments of 1990, and the emissions from such unit continue to be carried in the permitting authority's emissions inventory at the time of enactment, (2) was equipped prior to shut-down with a continuous system of emissions control that achieves a removal efficiency for sulfur dioxide of no less than 85 percent and a removal efficiency for particulates of no less than 98 percent, (3) is equipped with low-NOx burners prior to the time of commencement, and (4) is otherwise in compliance with the requirements of this chapter.

§7651o. Contingency guarantee, auctions, reserve

[CAA §416]

(a) **Definitions** — For purposes of this section —

(1) The term "independent power producer" means any person who owns or operates, in whole or in part, one or more new independent power production facilities.

(2) The term "new independent power production facility" means a facility that —

(A) is used for the generation of electric energy, 80 percent or more of which is sold at wholesale;

(B) is nonrecourse project-financed (as such term is defined by the Secretary of Energy within 3 months of November 15,1990);

(C) does not generate electric energy sold to any affiliate (as defined in section 79b(a)(11) of Title 15 [The Public Utility Holding Company Act of 1935] of the facility's owner or operator unless the owner or operator of the facility demonstrates that it cannot obtain allowances from the affiliate; and

(D) is a new unit required to hold allowances under this title.

(3) The term "required allowances" means the allowances required to operate such unit for so much of the unit's useful life as occurs after January 1, 2000.

(b) **Special reserve of allowances** — Within 36 months after November 15, 1990, the Administrator shall promulgate regulations establishing a Special Allowance Reserve containing allowances to be sold under this section. For purposes of establishing the Special Allowance Reserve, the Administrator shall withhold —

(1) 2.8 percent of the allocation of allowances for each year from 1995 through 1999 inclusive; and

(2) 2.8 percent of the basic Phase II allowance allocation of allowances for each year beginning in the year 2000

which would (but for this subsection) be issued for each affected unit at an affected source. The Administrator shall record such withholding for purposes of transferring the proceeds of the allowance sales under this subsection. The allowances so withheld shall be deposited in the Reserve under this section.

(c) **Direct sale at $1,500 per ton**

(1) Subaccount for direct sales — In accordance with regulations under this section, the Administrator shall establish a Direct Sale Subaccount in the Special Allowance Reserve established under this section. The Direct Sale Subaccount shall contain allowances in the amount of 50,000 tons per year for each year beginning in the year 2000.

(2) Sales — Allowances in the subaccount shall be offered for direct sale to any person at the times and in the amounts specified in table 1 at a price of $1,500 per allowance, adjusted by the Consumer Price Index in the same manner as

provided in paragraph (3). Requests to purchase allowances from the Direct Sale Subaccount established under paragraph (1) shall be approved in the order of receipt until no allowances remain in such subaccount, except that an opportunity to purchase such allowances shall be provided to the independent power producers referred to in this subsection before such allowances are offered to any other person. Each applicant shall be required to pay 50 percent of the total purchase price of the allowances within 6 months after the approval of the request to purchase. The remainder shall be paid on or before the transfer of the allowances.

TABLE 1 — NUMBER OF ALLOWANCES
AVAILABLE FOR SALE AT $1,500 PER TON

Year of Sale	Spot Sale	Advance Sale
1993-1999		25,000
2000 and after	25,000	25,000

Allowances sold in the spot sale in any year are allowances which may only be used in that year (unless banked for use in a later year). Allowances sold in the advance sale in any year are allowances which may only be used in the 7th year after the year in which they are first offered for sale unless banked for use in a later year).

(3) Entitlement to written guarantee — Any independent power producer that submits an application to the Administrator establishing that such independent power producer —

(A) proposes to construct a new independent power production facility for which allowances are required under this title;

(B) will apply for financing to construct such facility after January 1, 1990, and before the date of the first auction under this section;

(C) has submitted to each owner or operator of an affected unit listed in table A (in section 7651c of this title) a written offer to purchase the required allowances for $750 per ton; and

(D) has not received (within 180 days after submitting offers to purchase under subparagraph (C)) an acceptance of the offer to purchase the required allowances,

shall, within 30 days after submission of such application, be entitled to receive the Administrator's written guarantee (subject to the eligibility requirements set forth in paragraph (4)) that such required allowances will be made available for purchase from the Direct Sale Subaccount established under this subsection and at a guaranteed price. The guaranteed price at which such allowances shall be made available for purchase shall be $1,500 per ton, adjusted by the percentage, if any, by which the Consumer Price Index (as determined under section 7661a(b)(3)(B)(v) of this title) for the year in which the allowance is

purchased exceeds the Consumer Price Index for the calendar year 1990.

(4) Eligibility requirements — The guarantee issued by the Administrator under paragraph (3) shall be subject to a demonstration by the independent power producer, satisfactory to the Administrator, that —

(A) the independent power producer has —

(i) made good faith efforts to purchase the required allowances from the owners or operators of affected units to which allowances will be allocated, including efforts to purchase at annual auctions under this section, and from industrial sources that have elected to become affected units pursuant to section 7651i of this title; and

(ii) such bids and efforts were unsuccessful in obtaining the required allowances; and

(B) the independent power producer will continue to make good faith efforts to purchase the required allowances from the owners or operators of affected units and from industrial sources.

(5) Issuance of guaranteed allowances from Direct Sale Subaccount under this section — From the allowances available in the Direct Sale Subaccount established under this subsection, upon payment of the guaranteed price, the Administrator shall issue to any person exercising the right to purchase allowances pursuant to a guarantee under this subsection the allowances covered by such guarantee. Persons to which guarantees under this subsection have been issued shall have the opportunity to purchase allowances pursuant to such guarantee from such subaccount before the allowances in such reserve are offered for sale to any other person.

(6) Proceeds — Notwithstanding section 3302 of Title 31 or any other provision of law, the Administrator shall require that the proceeds of any sale under this subsection be transferred, within 90 days after the sale, without charge, on a pro rata basis to the owners or operators of the affected units from whom the allowances were withheld under subsection (b) and that any unsold allowances be transferred to the Subaccount for Auction Sales established under subsection (d) of this section. No proceeds of any sale under this subsection shall be held by any officer or employee of the United States or treated for any purpose as revenue to the United States or to the Administrator.

(7) Termination of subaccount — If the Administrator determines that, during any period of 2 consecutive calendar years, less than 20 percent of the allowances available in the subaccount for direct sales established under this subsection have been purchased under this paragraph, the Administrator shall terminate the subaccount and transfer such allowances to the Auction Subaccount under subsection (d) of this section.

(d) Auction sales

(1) Subaccount for auctions — The Administrator shall establish an Auction Subaccount in the Special Reserve established under this section. The Auction Subaccount shall contain allowances to be sold at auction under this section in the amount of 150,000 tons per year for each year from 1995 through 1999, inclusive and 250,000 tons per year for each year beginning in the calendar year 2000.

(2) Annual auctions — Commencing in 1993 and in each year thereafter, the Administrator shall conduct auctions at which the allowances referred to in paragraph (1) shall be offered for sale in accordance with regulations promulgated by the Administrator, in consultation with the Secretary of the Treasury, within 12 months of November 15, 1990. The allowances referred to in paragraph (1) shall be offered for sale at auction in the amounts specified in table 2. The auction shall be open to any person. A person wishing to bid for such allowances shall submit (by a date set by the Administrator) to the Administrator (on a sealed bid schedule provided by the Administrator) offers to purchase specified numbers of allowances at specified prices. Such regulations shall specify that the auctioned allowances shall be allocated and sold on the basis of bid price, starting with the highest-priced bid and continuing until all allowances for sale at such auction have been allocated. The regulations shall not permit that a minimum price be set for the purchase of withheld allowances. Allowances purchased at the auction may be used for any purpose and at any time after the auction, subject to the provisions of this title.

TABLE 2 — NUMBER OF ALLOWANCES
AVAILABLE FOR AUCTION

Year of Sale	Spot Auction (same year)	Advance Auction
1993	50,000*	100,000
1994	50,000*	100,000
1995	50,000*	100,000
1996	150,000	100,000
1997	150,000	100,000
1998	150,000	100,000
1999	150,000	100,000
2000 and after	100,000	100,000

Allowances sold in the spot sale in any year are allowances which may only be used in that year (unless banked for use in a later year), except as otherwise noted. Allowances sold in the advance auction in any year are allowances which may only be used in the 7th year after the year in which they are first offered for sale (unless banked for use in a later year).

*Available for use only in 1995 (unless banked for use in a later year).

(3) Proceeds

(A) Notwithstanding section 3302 of Title 31 or any other provision of law, within 90 days of receipt, the Administrator shall transfer the proceeds from the auction under this section, on a pro rata basis, to the owners or operators of the affected units at an affected source from whom allowances were withheld under subsection (b) of this section. No funds transferred from a purchaser to a seller of allowances under this paragraph shall be held by any officer or employee of the United States or treated for any purpose as revenue to the United States or the Administrator.

(B) At the end of each year, any allowances offered for sale but not sold at the auction shall be returned without charge, on a pro rata basis, to the owner or operator of the affected units from whose allocation the allowances were withheld.

(4) Additional auction participants — Any person holding allowances or to whom allowances are allocated by the Administrator may submit those allowances to the Administrator to be offered for sale at auction under this subsection. The proceeds of any such sale shall be transferred at the time of sale by the purchaser to the person submitting such allowances for sale. The holder of allowances offered for sale under this paragraph may specify a minimum sale price. Any person may purchase allowances offered for auction under this paragraph. Such allowances shall be allocated and sold to purchasers on the basis of bid price after the auction under paragraph (2) is complete. No funds transferred from a purchaser to a seller of allowances under this paragraph shall be held by any officer or employee of the United States or treated for any purpose as revenue to the United States or the Administrator.

(5) Recording by EPA — The Administrator shall record and publicly report the nature, prices and results of each auction under this subsection, including the prices of successful bids, and shall record the transfers of allowances as a result of each auction in accordance with the requirements of this section. The transfer of allowances at such auction shall be recorded in accordance with the regulations promulgated by the Administrator under this title.

(e) Changes in sales, auctions, and withholding — Pursuant to rulemaking after public notice and comment the Administrator may at any time after the year 1998 (in the case of advance sales or advance auctions) and 2005 (in the case of spot sales or spot auctions) decrease the number of allowances withheld and sold under this section.

(f) Termination of auctions — The Administrator may terminate the withholding of allowances and the auction sales under this section if the Administrator determines that, during any period of 3 consecutive calendar years after 2002, less than 20 percent of the allowances available in the auction subaccount have been purchased. Pursuant to regulations under this section, the Administrator may by delegation or contract provide for the conduct of sales or auctions under the Administrator's supervision by other departments or agencies of the United States Government or by nongovernmental agencies, groups, or organizations.

SUBCHAPTER V — PERMITS

§7661. Definitions
[CAA §501]
As used in this title —

(1) Affected source — The term "affected source" shall have the meaning given such term in subchapter IV-A of this chapter.

(2) Major source — The term "major source" means any stationary source (or any group of stationary sources located within a contiguous area and under common control) that is either of the following:

(A) A major source as defined in section 7412 of this title.

(B) A major stationary source as defined in section 7602 of this title or part D of subchapter I of this chapter.

(3) Schedule of compliance — The term "schedule of compliance" means a schedule of remedial measures, including an enforceable sequence of actions or operations, leading to compliance with an applicable implementation plan, emission standard, emission limitation, or emission prohibition.

(4) Permitting authority — The term "permitting authority" means the Administrator or the air pollution control agency authorized by the Administrator to carry out a permit program under this title.

§7661a. Permit programs
[CAA §502]
(a) Violations — After the effective date of any permit program approved or promulgated under this title, it shall be unlawful for any person to violate any requirement of a permit issued under this title, or to operate an affected source (as provided in subchapter IV-A of this chapter), a major source, any other source (including an area source) subject to standards or regulations under section 7411 or 7412 of this title, any other source required to have a permit under parts C or D of subchapter I of this chapter, or any other stationary source in a category designated (in whole or in part) by regulations promulgated by the Administrator (after notice and public comment) which shall include a finding setting forth the basis for such designation, except in compliance with a permit issued by a permitting authority under this title. (Nothing in this subsection shall be construed to alter the applicable requirements of this Act that a permit be obtained before construction or modification.) The Administrator may, in the Administrator's discretion and consistent with the applicable provisions of this Act, promulgate regulations to

exempt one or more source categories (in whole or in part) from the requirements of this subsection if the Administrator finds that compliance with such requirements is impracticable, infeasible, or unnecessarily burdensome on such categories, except that the Administrator may not exempt any major source from such requirements.

(b) Regulations — The Administrator shall promulgate within 12 months after November 15, 1990 regulations establishing the minimum elements of a permit program to be administered by any air pollution control agency. These elements shall include each of the following:

(1) Requirements for permit applications, including a standard application form and criteria for determining in a timely fashion the completeness of applications.

(2) Monitoring and reporting requirements.

(3)(A) A requirement under State or local law or interstate compact that the owner or operator of all sources subject to the requirement to obtain a permit under this title pay an annual fee, or the equivalent over some other period, sufficient to cover all reasonable (direct and indirect) costs required to develop and administer the permit program requirements of this title, including section 7661f of this title, including the reasonable costs of —

(i) reviewing and acting upon any application for such a permit,

(ii) if the owner or operator receives a permit for such source, whether before or after the date of the enactment of the Clean Air Act Amendments of 1990, implementing and enforcing the terms and conditions of any such permit (not including any court costs or other costs associated with any enforcement action),

(iii) emissions and ambient monitoring,

(iv) preparing generally applicable regulations, or guidance,

(v) modeling, analyses, and demonstrations, and

(vi) preparing inventories and tracking emissions.

(B) The total amount of fees collected by the permitting authority shall conform to the following requirements:

(i) The Administrator shall not approve a program as meeting the requirements of this paragraph unless the State demonstrates that, except as otherwise provided in subparagraphs (ii) through (v) of this subparagraph, the program will result in the collection, in the aggregate, from all sources subject to subparagraph (A), of an amount not less than $25 per ton of each regulated pollutant, or such other amount as the Administrator may determine adequately reflects the reasonable costs of the permit program.

(ii) As used in this subparagraph, the term "regulated pollutant" shall mean (I) a volatile organic compound; (II) each pollutant regulated under section 7411 or 7412 of this title; and (III) each pollutant for which a national primary ambient air quality standard has been promulgated (except that carbon monoxide shall be excluded from this reference).

(iii) In determining the amount under clause (i), the permitting authority is not required to include any amount of regulated pollutant emitted by any source in excess of 4,000 tons per year of that regulated pollutant.

(iv) The requirements of clause (i) shall not apply if the permitting authority demonstrates that collecting an amount less than the amount specified under clause (i) will meet the requirements of subparagraph (A).

(v) The fee calculated under clause (i) shall be increased (consistent with the need to cover the reasonable costs authorized by subparagraph (A)) in each year beginning after the year of the enactment of the Clean Air Act Amendments of 1990 by the percentage, if any, by which the Consumer Price Index for the most recent calendar year ending before the beginning of such year exceeds the Consumer Price Index for the calendar year 1989. For purposes of this clause —

    (I) the Consumer Price Index for any calendar year is the average of the Consumer Price Index for all-urban consumers published by the Department of Labor, as of the close of the 12-month period ending on August 31 of each calendar year, and

    (II) the revision of the Consumer Price Index which is most consistent with the Consumer Price Index for calendar year 1989 shall be used.

(C)(i) If the Administrator determines, under subsection (d) of this section, that the fee provisions of the operating permit program do not meet the requirements of this paragraph, or if the Administrator makes a determination, under subsection (i), that the permitting authority is not adequately administering or enforcing an approved fee program, the Administrator may, in addition to taking any other action authorized under this title, collect reasonable fees from the sources identified under subparagraph (A). Such fees shall be designed solely to cover the Administrator's costs of administering the provisions of the permit program promulgated by the Administrator.

(ii) Any source that fails to pay fees lawfully imposed by the Administrator under this subparagraph shall pay a penalty of 50 percent of the fee amount, plus interest on the fee amount computed in accordance with section 6621(a)(2) of Title 26 [the Internal Revenue Code of 1986] (relating to computation of interest on underpayment of Federal taxes).

(iii) Any fees, penalties, and interest collected under this subparagraph shall be deposited in a special fund in the United States Treasury for licensing and other services, which thereafter shall be available for appropriation, to remain available until expended, subject to appropriation, to carry out the Agency's activities for which the fees were collected. Any fee required to be collected by a State, local, or interstate agency under this subsection shall be utilized solely to cover all reasonable (direct and indirect) costs required to support the permit program as set forth in subparagraph (A).

(4) Requirements for adequate personnel and funding to administer the program.

(5) A requirement that the permitting authority have adequate authority to:

    (A) issue permits and assure compliance by all sources required to have a permit under this title with each applicable standard, regulation or requirement under this Act;

    (B) issue permits for a fixed term, not to exceed 5 years;

    (C) assure that upon issuance or renewal permits incorporate emission limitations and other requirements in an applicable implementation plan;

    (D) terminate, modify, or revoke and reissue permits for cause;

    (E) enforce permits, permit fee requirements, and the requirement to obtain a permit, including authority to recover civil penalties in a maximum amount of not less than $10,000 per day for each violation, and provide appropriate criminal penalties; and

    (F) assure that no permit will be issued if the Administrator objects to its issuance in a timely manner under this title.

(6) Adequate, streamlined, and reasonable procedures for expeditiously determining when applications are complete, for processing such applications, for public notice, including offering an opportunity for public comment and a hearing, and for expeditious review of permit actions, including applications, renewals, or revisions, and including an opportunity for judicial review in State court of the final permit action by the applicant, any person who participated in the public comment process, and any other person who could obtain judicial review of that action under applicable law.

(7) To ensure against unreasonable delay by the permitting authority, adequate authority and procedures to provide that a failure of such permitting authority to act on a permit application or permit renewal application (in accordance with the time periods specified in section 7661b of this title or, as appropriate, subchapter IV-A of this chapter) shall be treated as a final permit action solely for purposes of obtaining judicial review in State court of an action brought by any person referred to in paragraph (6) to require that action be taken by the permitting authority on such application without additional delay.

(8) Authority, and reasonable procedures consistent with the need for expeditious action by the permitting authority on permit applications and related matters, to make available to the public any permit application, compliance plan, permit, and monitoring or compliance report under section 7661b(e) of this title, subject to the provisions of section 7414(c) of this title.

(9) A requirement that the permitting authority, in the case of permits with a term of 3 or more years for major sources, shall require revisions to the permit to incorporate applicable standards and regulations promulgated under this Act after the issuance of such permit. Such revisions shall occur as expeditiously as practicable and consistent with the procedures established under paragraph (6) but not later than 18 months after the promulgation of such standards and regulations. No such revision shall be required if the effective date of the standards or regulations is a date after the expiration of the permit term. Such permit revision shall be treated as a permit renewal if it complies with the requirements of this title regarding renewals.

(10) Provisions to allow changes within a permitted facility (or one operating pursuant to section 7661b(d)) without requiring a permit revision, if the changes are not modifications under any provision of title I and the changes do not exceed the emissions allowable under the permit (whether expressed therein as a rate of emissions or in terms of total emissions: Provided, That the facility provides the Administrator and the permitting authority with written notification in advance of the proposed changes which shall be a minimum of 7 days, unless the permitting authority provides in its regulations a different timeframe for emergencies.

(c) **Single Permit** — A single permit may be issued for a facility with multiple sources.

(d) **Submission and approval**

(1) Not later than 3 years after November 15, 1990, the Governor of each State shall develop and submit to the Administrator a permit program under State or local law or under an interstate compact meeting the requirements of this title. In addition, the Governor shall submit a legal opinion from the attorney general (or the attorney for those State air pollution control agencies that have independent legal counsel), or from the chief legal officer of an interstate agency, that the laws of the State, locality, or the interstate compact provide adequate authority to carry out the program. Not later than 1 year after receiving a program, and after notice and opportunity for public comment, the Administrator shall approve or disapprove such program, in whole or in part. The Administrator may approve a program to the extent that the program meets the requirements of this Act, including the regulations issued under subsection (b). If the program is disapproved, in whole or in part, the Administrator shall notify the Governor of any revisions or modifications necessary to obtain approval. The Governor shall revise and resubmit the program for review under this section within 180 days after receiving notification.

(2)(A) If the Governor does not submit a program as required under paragraph (1) or if the Administrator disapproves a program submitted by the Governor under paragraph (1), in whole or in part, the Administrator may, prior to the expiration of the 18-month period referred to in subparagraph (B), in the Administrator's discretion, apply any of the sanctions specified in section 7509(b) of this title.

(B) If the Governor does not submit a program as required under paragraph (1), or if the Administrator disapproves any such program submitted by the Governor under paragraph (1), in whole or in part, 18 months after the date required for such submittal or the date of such disapproval, as the case may be, the Administrator shall apply sanctions under section 7509(b) of this title in the same manner and subject to the same deadlines and other conditions as are applicable in the case of a determination, disapproval, or finding under section 7509(a) of this title.

(C) The sanctions under section 7509(b)(2) of this title shall not apply pursuant to this paragraph in any area unless the failure to submit or the disapproval referred to in subparagraph (A) or (B) relates to an air pollutant for which such area has been designated a nonattainment area (as defined in part D of subchapter I of this chapter).

(3) If a program meeting the requirements of this title has not been approved in whole for any State, the Administrator shall, 2 years after the date required for submission of such a program under paragraph (1), promulgate, administer, and enforce a program under this title for that State.

(e) **Suspension** — The Administrator shall suspend the issuance of permits promptly upon publication of notice of approval of a permit program under this section, but may, in such notice, retain jurisdiction over permits that have been federally issued, but for which the administrative or judicial review process is not complete. The Administrator shall continue to administer and enforce federally issued permits under this title until they are replaced by a permit issued by a permitting program. Nothing in this subsection should be construed to limit the Administrator's ability to enforce permits issued by a State.

(f) Prohibition — No partial permit program shall be approved unless, at a minimum, it applies, and ensures compliance with, this title and each of the following:

(1) All requirements established under subchapter IV-A of this chapter applicable to "affected sources".

(2) All requirements established under section 7412 of this title applicable to "major sources", "area sources," and "new sources".

(3) All requirements of subchapter I of this chapter (other than section 7412 of this title) applicable to sources required to have a permit under this title.

Approval of a partial program shall not relieve the State of its obligation to submit a complete program, nor from the application of any sanctions under this Act for failure to submit an approvable permit program.

(g) Interim approval — If a program (including a partial permit program) submitted under this title substantially meets the requirements of this title, but is not fully approvable, the Administrator may by rule grant the program interim approval. In the notice of final rulemaking, the Administrator shall specify the changes that must be made before the program can receive full approval. An interim approval under this subsection shall expire on a date set by the Administrator not later than 2 years after such approval, and may not be renewed. For the period of any such interim approval, the provisions of subsection (d)(2) of this section, and the obligation of the Administrator to promulgate a program under this title or the State pursuant to subsection (d)(3) of this section, shall be suspended. Such provisions and such obligation of the Administrator shall apply after the expiration of such interim approval.

(h) Effective date — The effective date of a permit program, or partial or interim program, approved under this title, shall be the effective date of approval by the Administrator. The effective date of a permit program, or partial permit program, promulgated by the Administrator shall be the date of promulgation.

(i) Administration and enforcement

(1) Whenever the Administrator makes a determination that a permitting authority is not adequately administering and enforcing a program, or portion thereof, in accordance with the requirements of this title, the Administrator shall provide notice to the State and may, prior to the expiration of the 18-month period referred to in paragraph (2), in the Administrator's discretion, apply any of the sanctions specified in section 7509(b) of this title.

(2) Whenever the Administrator makes a determination that a permitting authority is not adequately administering and enforcing a program, or portion thereof, in accordance with the requirements of this title, 18 months after the date of the notice under paragraph (1), the Administrator shall apply the sanctions under section 7509(b) of this title in the same manner and subject to the same deadlines and other conditions as are applicable in the case of a determination, disapproval, or finding under section 7509(a) of this title.

(3) The sanctions under section 7509(b)(2) of this title shall not apply pursuant to this subsection in any area unless the failure to adequately enforce and administer the program relates to an air pollutant for which such area has been designated a nonattainment area.

(4) Whenever the Administrator has made a finding under paragraph (1) with respect to any State, unless the State has corrected such deficiency within 18 months after the date of such finding, the Administrator shall, 2 years after the date of such finding, promulgate, administer, and enforce a program under this title for that State. Nothing in this paragraph shall be construed to affect the validity of a program which has been approved under this title or the authority of any permitting authority acting under such program until such time as such program is promulgated by the Administrator under this paragraph.

§7661b. Permit applications
[CAA §503]

(a) Applicable date — Any source specified in section 7661a(a) of this title shall become subject to a permit program, and required to have a permit, on the later of the following dates —

(1) the effective date of a permit program or partial or interim permit program applicable to the source; or

(2) the date such source becomes subject to section 7661a(a) of this title.

(b) Compliance plan

(1) The regulations required by section 7661a(b) of this title shall include a requirement that the applicant submit with the permit application a compliance plan describing how the source will comply with all applicable requirements under this Act. The compliance plan shall include a schedule of compliance, and a schedule under which the permittee will submit progress reports to the permitting authority no less frequently than every 6 months.

(2) The regulations shall further require the permittee to periodically (but no less frequently than annually) certify that the facility is in compliance with any applicable requirements of the

permit, and to promptly report any deviations from permit requirements to the permitting authority.

(c) Deadline — Any person required to have a permit shall, not later than 12 months after the date on which the source becomes subject to a permit program approved or promulgated under this title, or such earlier date as the permitting authority may establish, submit to the permitting authority a compliance plan and an application for a permit signed by a responsible official, who shall certify the accuracy of the information submitted. The permitting authority shall approve or disapprove a completed application (consistent with the procedures established under this title for consideration of such applications), and shall issue or deny the permit, within 18 months after the date of receipt thereof, except that the permitting authority shall establish a phased schedule for acting on permit applications submitted within the first full year after the effective date of a permit program (or a partial or interim program). Any such schedule shall assure that at least one-third of such permits will be acted on by such authority annually over a period of not to exceed 3 years after such effective date. Such authority shall establish reasonable procedures to prioritize such approval or disapproval actions in the case of applications for construction or modification under the applicable requirements of this chapter.

(d) Timely and complete applications — Except for sources required to have a permit before construction or modification under the applicable requirements of this Act, if an applicant has submitted a timely and complete application for a permit required by this title (including renewals), but final action has not been taken on such application, the source's failure to have a permit shall not be a violation of this Act, unless the delay in final action was due to the failure of the applicant timely to submit information required or requested to process the application. No source required to have a permit under this title shall be in violation of section 7661a(a) of this title before the date on which the source is required to submit an application under subsection (c).

(e) Copies; availability — A copy of each permit application, compliance plan (including the schedule of compliance), emissions or compliance monitoring report, certification, and each permit issued under this title, shall be available to the public. If an applicant or permittee is required to submit information entitled to protection from disclosure under section 7414(c) of this title, the applicant or permittee may submit such information separately. The requirements of section 7414(c) of this title shall apply to such information. The contents of a permit shall not be entitled to protection under section 7414(c) of this title.

§7661c. Permit requirements and conditions

[CAA §504]

(a) Conditions — Each permit issued under this title shall include enforceable emission limitations and standards, a schedule of compliance, a requirement that the permittee submit to the permitting authority, no less often than every 6 months, the results of any required monitoring, and such other conditions as are necessary to assure compliance with applicable requirements of this Act, including the requirements of the applicable implementation plan.

(b) Monitoring and analysis — The Administrator may by rule prescribe procedures and methods for determining compliance and for monitoring and analysis of pollutants regulated under this Act, but continuous emissions monitoring need not be required if alternative methods are available that provide sufficiently reliable and timely information for determining compliance. Nothing in this subsection shall be construed to affect any continuous emissions monitoring requirement of subchapter IV-A of this chapter, or where required elsewhere in this Act.

(c) Inspection, entry, monitoring, certification, and reporting — Each permit issued under this title shall set forth inspection, entry, monitoring, compliance certification, and reporting requirements to assure compliance with the permit terms and conditions. Such monitoring and reporting requirements shall conform to any applicable regulation under subsection (b) of this section. Any report required to be submitted by a permit issued to a corporation under this title shall be signed by a responsible corporate official, who shall certify its accuracy.

(d) General permits — The permitting authority may, after notice and opportunity for public hearing, issue a general permit covering numerous similar sources. Any general permit shall comply with all requirements applicable to permits under this title. No source covered by a general permit shall thereby be relieved from the obligation to file an application under section 7661b of this title.

(e) Temporary sources — The permitting authority may issue a single permit authorizing emissions from similar operations at multiple temporary locations. No such permit shall be issued unless it includes conditions that will assure compliance with all the requirements of this chapter at all authorized locations, including, but not limited to, ambient standards and compliance with any applicable increment or visibility requirements under part C of subchapter I of this chapter. Any such permit shall in addition require the owner or operator to notify the permitting authority in advance of each change in location. The permitting authority may require a separate permit fee for operations at each location.

(f) Permit shield — Compliance with a permit issued in accordance with this title shall be deemed compliance with section 7661a of this title. Except as otherwise provided by the Administrator by rule, the permit may also provide that compliance with the permit shall be deemed compliance with other applicable provisions of this Act that relate to the permittee if —

    (1) the permit includes the applicable requirements of such provisions, or

    (2) the permitting authority in acting on the permit application makes a determination relating to the permittee that such other provisions (which shall be referred to in such determination) are not applicable and the permit includes the determination or a concise summary thereof.

Nothing in the preceding sentence shall alter or affect the provisions of section 7603 of this title, including the authority of the Administrator under that section.

§7661d. Notification to Administrator and contiguous States

[CAA §505]

(a) Transmission and notice

    (1) Each permitting authority —

    (A) shall transmit to the Administrator a copy of each permit application (and any application for a permit modification or renewal) or such portion thereof, including any compliance plan, as the Administrator may require to effectively review the application and otherwise to carry out the Administrator's responsibilities under this Act, and

    (B) shall provide to the Administrator a copy of each permit proposed to be issued and issued as a final permit.

    (2) The permitting authority shall notify all States —

    (A) whose air quality may be affected and that are contiguous to the State in which the emission originates, or

    (B) that are within 50 miles of the source, of each permit application or proposed permit forwarded to the Administrator under this section, and shall provide an opportunity for such States to submit written recommendations respecting the issuance of the permit and its terms and conditions. If any part of those recommendations are not accepted by the permitting authority, such authority shall notify the State submitting the recommendations and the Administrator in writing of its failure to accept those recommendations and the reasons therefor.

(b) Objection by EPA

    (1) If any permit contains provisions that are determined by the Administrator as not in compliance with the applicable requirements of this Act, including the requirements of an applicable implementation plan, the Administrator shall, in accordance with this subsection, object to its issuance. The permitting authority shall respond in writing if the Administrator (A) within 45 days after receiving a copy of the proposed permit under subsection (a)(1) of this section, or (B) within 45 days after receiving notification under subsection (a)(2)of this section, objects in writing to its issuance as not in compli-

ance with such requirements. With the objection, the Administrator shall provide a statement of the reasons for the objection. A copy of the objection and statement shall be provided to the applicant.

    (2) If the Administrator does not object in writing to the issuance of a permit pursuant to paragraph (1), any person may petition the Administrator within 60 days after the expiration of the 45-day review period specified in paragraph (1) to take such action. A copy of such petition shall be provided to the permitting authority and the applicant by the petitioner. The petition shall be based only on objections to the permit that were raised with reasonable specificity during the public comment period provided by the permitting agency (unless the petitioner demonstrates in the petition to the Administrator that it was impracticable to raise such objections within such period or unless the grounds for such objection arose after such period). The petition shall identify all such objections. If the permit has been issued by the permitting agency, such petition shall not postpone the effectiveness of the permit. The Administrator shall grant or deny such petition within 60 days after the petition is filed. The Administrator shall issue an objection within such period if the petitioner demonstrates to the Administrator that the permit is not in compliance with the requirements of this Act, including the requirements of the applicable implementation plan. Any denial of such petition shall be subject to judicial review under section 7607 of this title. The Administrator shall include in regulations under this title provisions to implement this paragraph. The Administrator may not delegate the requirements of this paragraph.

    (3) Upon receipt of an objection by the Administrator under this subsection, the permitting authority may not issue the permit unless it is revised and issued in accordance with subsection (c). If the permitting authority has issued a permit prior to receipt of an objection by the Administrator under paragraph (2) of this subsection, the Administrator shall modify, terminate, or revoke such permit and the permitting authority may thereafter only issue a revised permit in accordance with subsection (c) of this section.

(c) Issuance or denial — If the permitting authority fails, within 90 days after the date of an objection under subsection (b) of this section, to submit a permit revised to meet the objection, the Administrator shall issue or deny the permit in accordance with the requirements of this title. No objection shall be subject to judicial review until the Administrator takes final action to issue or deny a permit under this subsection.

(d) Waiver of notification requirements

    (1) The Administrator may waive the requirements of subsections (a) and (b) of this section at the time of approval of a permit program under this

title for any category (including any class, type, or size within such category) of sources covered by the program other than major sources.

(2) The Administrator may, by regulation, establish categories of sources (including any class, type, or size within such category) to which the requirements of subsections (a) and (b) of this section shall not apply. The preceding sentence shall not apply to major sources.

(3) The Administrator may exclude from any waiver under this subsection notification under subsection (a)(2) of this section. Any waiver granted under this subsection may be revoked or modified by the Administrator by rule.

(e) Refusal of permitting authority to terminate, modify, or revoke and reissue — If the Administrator finds that cause exists to terminate, modify, or revoke and reissue a permit under this title, the Administrator shall notify the permitting authority and the source of the Administrator's finding. The permitting authority shall, within 90 days after receipt of such notification, forward to the Administrator under this section a proposed determination of termination, modification, or revocation and reissuance, as appropriate. The Administrator may extend such 90 day period for an additional 90 days if the Administrator finds that a new or revised permit application is necessary, or that the permitting authority must require the permittee to submit additional information. The Administrator may review such proposed determination under the provisions of subsections (a) and (b). If the permitting authority fails to submit the required proposed determination, or if the Administrator objects and the permitting authority fails to resolve the objection within 90 days, the Administrator may, after notice and in accordance with fair and reasonable procedures, terminate, modify, or revoke and reissue the permit.

§7661e. Other authorities
[CAA §506]

(a) In general — Nothing in this title shall prevent a State, or interstate permitting authority, from establishing additional permitting requirements not inconsistent with this Act.

(b) Permits implementing acid rain provisions — The provisions of this title, including provisions regarding schedules for submission and approval or disapproval of permit applications, shall apply to permits implementing the requirements of subchapter IV-A of this chapter except as modified by that subchapter.

§7661f. Small business stationary source technical and environmental compliance assistance program
[CAA §507]

(a) Plan revisions — Consistent with sections 7410 and 7412 of this title, each State shall, after reasonable notice and public hearings, adopt and submit to the Administrator as part of the State implementation plan for such State or as a revision to such State implementation plan under section 7410 of this title, plans for establishing a small business stationary source technical and environmental compliance assistance program. Such submission shall be made within 24 months after November 15, 1990. The Administrator shall approve such program if it includes each of the following:

(1) Adequate mechanisms for developing, collecting, and coordinating information concerning compliance methods and technologies for small business stationary sources, and programs to encourage lawful cooperation among such sources and other persons to further compliance with this chapter.

(2) Adequate mechanisms for assisting small business stationary sources with pollution prevention and accidental release detection and prevention, including providing information concerning alternative technologies, process changes, products, and methods of operation that help reduce air pollution.

(3) A designated State office within the relevant State agency to serve as ombudsman for small business stationary sources in connection with the implementation of this chapter.

(4) A compliance assistance program for small business stationary sources which assists small business stationary sources in determining applicable requirements and in receiving permits under this Act in a timely and efficient manner.

(5) Adequate mechanisms to assure that small business stationary sources receive notice of their rights under this Act in such manner and form as to assure reasonably adequate time for such sources to evaluate compliance methods and any relevant or applicable proposed or final regulation or standard issued under this chapter.

(6) Adequate mechanisms for informing small business stationary sources of their obligations under this Act, including mechanisms for referring such sources to qualified auditors or, at the option of the State, for providing audits of the operations of such sources to determine compliance with this chapter.

(7) Procedures for consideration of requests from a small business stationary source for modification of —

(A) any work practice or technological method of compliance, or

(B) the schedule of milestones for implementing such work practice or method of compliance preceding any applicable compliance date,

based on the technological and financial capability of any such small business stationary source. No such modification may be granted unless it is in compliance with the applicable requirements of this chapter, including the requirements of the applicable implementation plan. Where such applicable requirements are set forth in Federal regulations, only modifications authorized in such regulations may be allowed.

(b) Program — The Administrator shall establish within 9 months after November 15, 1990 a small business stationary source technical and environmental compliance assistance program. Such program shall —

    (1) assist the States in the development of the program required under subsection (a) (relating to assistance for small business stationary sources);

    (2) issue guidance for the use of the States in the implementation of these programs that includes alternative control technologies and pollution prevention methods applicable to small business stationary sources; and

    (3) provide for implementation of the program provisions required under subsection (a)(4) of this section in any State that fails to submit such a program under that subsection.

(c) Eligibility

    (1) Except as provided in paragraphs (2) and (3), for purposes of this section, the term "small business stationary source" means a stationary source that —

        (A) is owned or operated by a person that employs 100 or fewer individuals,

        (B) is a small business concern as defined in the Small Business Act;

        (C) is not a major stationary source;

        (D) does not emit 50 tons or more per year of any regulated pollutant; and

        (E) emits less than 75 tons per year of all regulated pollutants.

    (2) Upon petition by a source, the State may, after notice and opportunity for public comment, include as a small business stationary source for purposes of this section any stationary source which does not meet the criteria of subparagraphs (C), (D), or (E) of paragraph (1) but which does not emit more than 100 tons per year of all regulated pollutants.

    (3)(A) The Administrator, in consultation with the Administrator of the Small Business Administration and after providing notice and opportunity for public comment, may exclude from the small business stationary source definition under this section any category or subcategory of sources that the Administrator determines to have sufficient technical and financial capabilities to meet the requirements of this Act without the application of this subsection.

        (B) The State, in consultation with the Administrator and the Administrator of the Small Business Administration and after providing notice and opportunity for public hearing, may exclude from the small business stationary source definition under this section any category or subcategory of sources that the State determines to have sufficient technical and financial capabilities to meet the requirements of this Act without the application of this subsection.

(d) Monitoring — The Administrator shall direct the Agency's Office of Small and Disadvantaged Business Utilization through the Small Business Ombudsman (hereinafter in this section referred to as the "Ombudsman") to monitor the small business stationary source technical and environmental compliance assistance program under this section. In carrying out such monitoring activities, the Ombudsman shall —

    (1) render advisory opinions on the overall effectiveness of the Small Business Stationary Source Technical and Environmental Compliance Assistance Program, difficulties encountered, and degree and severity of enforcement;

    (2) make periodic reports to the Congress on the compliance of the Small Business Stationary Source Technical and Environmental Compliance Assistance Program with the requirements of the Paperwork Reduction Act, the Regulatory Flexibility Act, and the Equal Access to Justice Act;

    (3) review information to be issued by the Small Business Stationary Source Technical and Environmental Compliance Assistance Program for small business stationary sources to ensure that the information is understandable by the layperson; and

    (4) have the Small Business Stationary Source Technical and Environmental Compliance Assistance Program serve as the secretariat for the development and dissemination of such reports and advisory opinions.

(e) Compliance Advisory Panel

    (1) There shall be created a Compliance Advisory Panel (hereinafter referred to as the "Panel") on the State level of not less than 7 individuals. This Panel shall —

        (A) render advisory opinions concerning the effectiveness of the small business stationary source technical and environmental compliance assistance program, difficulties encountered, and degree and severity of enforcement;

        (B) make periodic reports to the Administrator concerning the compliance of the State Small Business Stationary Source Technical and Environmental Compliance Assistance Program with the requirements of the Paperwork Reduction Act, the Regulatory Flexibility Act, and the Equal Access to Justice Act;

        (C) review information for small business stationary sources to assure such information is understandable by the layperson; and

        (D) have the Small Business Stationary Source Technical and Environmental Compliance Assistance Program serve as the secretariat for the development and dissemination of such reports and advisory opinions.

    (2) The Panel shall consist of —

        (A) 2 members, who are not owners, or representatives of owners, of small business stationary sources, selected by the Governor to represent the general public;

(B) 2 members selected by the State legislature who are owners, or who represent owners, of small business stationary sources (1 member each by the majority and minority leadership of the lower house, or in the case of a unicameral State legislature, 2 members each shall be selected by the majority leadership and the minority leadership, respectively, of such legislature, and subparagraph (C) shall not apply);

(C) 2 members selected by the State legislature who are owners, or who represent owners, of small business stationary sources (1 member each by the majority and minority leadership of the upper house, or the equivalent State entity); and

(D) 1 member selected by the head of the department or agency of the State responsible for air pollution permit programs to represent that agency.

(f) Fees — The State (or the Administrator) may reduce any fee required under this Act to take into account the financial resources of small business stationary sources.

(g) Continuous emission monitors — In developing regulations and CTGs under this Act that contain continuous emission monitoring requirements, the Administrator, consistent with the requirements of this Act, before applying such requirements to small business stationary sources, shall consider the necessity and appropriateness of such requirements for such sources. Nothing in this subsection shall affect the applicability of subchapter IV-A of this chapter provisions relating to continuous emissions monitoring.

(h) Control technique guidelines — The Administrator shall consider, consistent with the requirements of this Act, the size, type, and technical capabilities of small business stationary sources (and sources which are eligible under subsection (c)(2) of this section to be treated as small business stationary sources) in developing CTGs applicable to such sources under this chapter.

SUBCHAPTER VI —STRATOSPHERIC OZONE PROTECTION

§7671. Definitions
[CAA §601]
As used in this title —

(1) Appliance — The term "appliance" means any device which contains and uses a class I or class II substance as a refrigerant and which is used for household or commercial purposes, including any air conditioner, refrigerator, chiller, or freezer.

(2) Baseline year — The term "baseline year" means —

(A) the calendar year 1986, in the case of any class I substance listed in Group I or II under section 7671a(a) of this title,

(B) the calendar year 1989, in the case of any class I substance listed in Group III, IV, or V under section 7671a(a) of this title, and

(C) a representative calendar year selected by the Administrator, in the case of —

(i) any substance added to the list of class I substances after thepublication of the initial list under section 7671a(a) of this title, and

(ii) any class II substance.

(3) Class I substance — The term "class I substance" means each of the substances listed as provided in section 7671a(a) of this title.

(4) Class II substance — The term "class II substance" means each of the substances listed as provided in section 7671a(b) of this title.

(5) Commissioner — The term "Commissioner" means the Commissioner of the Food and Drug Administration.

(6) Consumption — The term "consumption" means, with respect to any substance, the amount of that substance produced in the United States, plus the amount imported, minus the amount exported to Parties to the Montreal Protocol. Such term shall be construed in a manner consistent with the Montreal Protocol.

(7) Import — The term "import" means to land on, bring into, or introduce into, or attempt to land on, bring into, or introduce into, any place subject to the jurisdiction of the United States, whether or not such landing, bringing, or introduction constitutes an importation within the meaning of the customs laws of the United States.

(8) Medical device — The term "medical device" means any device (as defined in the Federal Food, Drug, and Cosmetic Act (21 U.S.C. §321)), diagnostic product, drug (as defined in the Federal Food, Drug, and Cosmetic Act), and drug delivery system —

(A) if such device, product, drug, or drug delivery system utilizes a class I or class II substance for which no safe and effective alternative has been developed, and where necessary, approved by the Commissioner; and

(B) if such device, product, drug, or drug delivery system, has, after notice and opportunity for public comment, been approved and determined to be essential by the Commissioner in consultation with the Administrator.

(9) Montreal Protocol — The terms "Montreal Protocol" and "the Protocol" mean the Montreal Protocol on Substances that Deplete the Ozone Layer, a protocol to the Vienna Convention for the Protection of the Ozone Layer, including adjustments adopted by Parties thereto and amendments that have entered into force.

(10) Ozone-depletion potential — The term "ozone-depletion potential" means a factor established by the Administrator to reflect the

ozone-depletion potential of a substance, on a mass per kilogram basis, as compared to chlorofluorocarbon-11 (CFC-11). Such factor shall be based upon the substance's atmospheric lifetime, the molecular weight of bromine and chlorine, and the substance's ability to be photolytically disassociated, and upon other factors determined to be an accurate measure of relative ozone-depletion potential.

(11) Produce, produced, and production — The terms "produce", "produced", and "production", refer to the manufacture of a substance from any raw material or feedstock chemical, but such terms do not include —

    (A) the manufacture of a substance that is used and entirely consumed (except for trace quantities) in the manufacture of other chemicals, or

    (B) the reuse or recycling of a substance.

§7671a. Listing of class I and class II substances [CAA §602]

(a) List of class I substances — Within 60 days after November 15, 1990, the Administrator shall publish an initial list of class I substances, which list shall contain the following substances:

Group I
chlorofluorocarbon — 11 (CFC-11)
chlorofluorocarbon — 12 (CFC-12)
chlorofluorocarbon — 113 (CFC-113)
chlorofluorocarbon — 114 (CFC-114)
chlorofluorocarbon — 115 (CFC-115)

Group II
halon — 1211
halon — 1301
halon — 2402

Group III
chlorofluorocarbon-13 (CFC-13)
chlorofluorocarbon-111 (CFC-111)
chlorofluorocarbon-112 (CFC-112)
chlorofluorocarbon-211 (CFC-211)
chlorofluorocarbon-212 (CFC-212)
chlorofluorocarbon-213 (CFC-213)
chlorofluorocarbon-214 (CFC-214)
chlorofluorocarbon-215 (CFC-215)
chlorofluorocarbon-216 (CFC-216)
chlorofluorocarbon-217 (CFC-217)

Group IV
carbon tetrachloride

Group V
methyl chloroform

The initial list under this subsection shall also include the isomers of the substances listed above, other than 1,1,2-trichloroethane (an isomer of methyl chloroform). Pursuant to subsection (c), the Administrator shall add to the list of class I substances any other substance that the Admin-

istrator finds causes or contributes significantly to harmful effects on the stratospheric ozone layer. The Administrator shall, pursuant to subsection (c) of this section, add to such list all substances that the Administrator determines have an ozone depletion potential of 0.2 or greater.

(b) List of class II substances — Simultaneously with publication of the initial list of class I substances, the Administrator shall publish an initial list of class II substances, which shall contain the following substances:

hydrochlorofluorocarbon-21 (HCFC-21)
hydrochlorofluorocarbon-22 (HCFC-22)
hydrochlorofluorocarbon-31 (HCFC-31)
hydrochlorofluorocarbon-121 (HCFC-121)
hydrochlorofluorocarbon-122 (HCFC-122)
hydrochlorofluorocarbon-123 (HCFC-123)
hydrochlorofluorocarbon-124 (HCFC-124)
hydrochlorofluorocarbon-131 (HCFC-131)
hydrochlorofluorocarbon-132 (HCFC-132)
hydrochlorofluorocarbon-133 (HCFC-133)
hydrochlorofluorocarbon-141 (HCFC-141)
hydrochlorofluorocarbon-142 (HCFC-142)
hydrochlorofluorocarbon-221 (HCFC-221)
hydrochlorofluorocarbon-222 (HCFC-222)
hydrochlorofluorocarbon-223 (HCFC-223)
hydrochlorofluorocarbon-224 (HCFC-224)
hydrochlorofluorocarbon-225 (HCFC-225)
hydrochlorofluorocarbon-226 (HCFC-226)
hydrochlorofluorocarbon-231 (HCFC-231)
hydrochlorofluorocarbon-232 (HCFC-232)
hydrochlorofluorocarbon-233 (HCFC-233)
hydrochlorofluorocarbon-234 (HCFC-234)
hydrochlorofluorocarbon-235 (HCFC-235)
hydrochlorofluorocarbon-241 (HCFC-241)
hydrochlorofluorocarbon-242 (HCFC-242)
hydrochlorofluorocarbon-243 (HCFC-243)
hydrochlorofluorocarbon-244 (HCFC-244)
hydrochlorofluorocarbon-251 (HCFC-251)
hydrochlorofluorocarbon-252 (HCFC-252)
hydrochlorofluorocarbon-253 (HCFC-253)
hydrochlorofluorocarbon-261 (HCFC-261)
hydrochlorofluorocarbon-262 (HCFC-262)
hydrochlorofluorocarbon-271 (HCFC-271)

The initial list under this subsection shall also include the isomers of the substances listed above. Pursuant to subsection (c) of this section, the Administrator shall add to the list of class II substances any other substance that the Administrator finds is known or may reasonably be anticipated to cause or contribute to harmful effects on the stratospheric ozone layer.

(c) Additions to the lists

(1) The Administrator may add, by rule, in accordance with the criteria set forth in subsection (a) or (b) of this section, as the case may be, any substance to the list of class I or class II substances under subsection (a) or (b) of this section. For purposes of exchanges under section 7661f of this title,

whenever a substance is added to the list of class I substances the Administrator shall, to the extent consistent with the Montreal Protocol, assign such substance to existing Group I, II, III, IV, or V or place such substance in a new Group.

(2) Periodically, but not less frequently than every 3 years after November 15, 1990, the Administrator shall list, by rule, as additional class I or class II substances those substances which the Administrator finds meet the criteria of subsection (a) or (b) of this section, as the case may be.

(3) At any time, any person may petition the Administrator to add a substance to the list of class I or class II substances. Pursuant to the criteria set forth in subsection (a) or (b) of this section as the case may be, within 180 days after receiving such a petition, the Administrator shall either propose to add the substance to such list or publish an explanation of the petition denial. In any case where the Administrator proposes to add a substance to such list, the Administrator shall add, by rule, (or make a final determination not to add) such substance to such list within 1 year after receiving such petition. Any petition under this paragraph shall include a showing by the petitioner that there are data on the substance adequate to support the petition. If the Administrator determines that information on the substance is not sufficient to make a determination under this paragraph, the Administrator shall use any authority available to the Administrator, under any law administered by the Administrator, to acquire such information.

(4) Only a class II substance which is added to the list of class I substances may be removed from the list of class II substances. No substance referred to in subsection (a) of this section, including methyl chloroform, may be removed from the list of class I substances.

(d) New listed substances — In the case of any substance added to the list of class I or class II substances after publication of the initial list of such substances under this section, the Administrator may extend any schedule or compliance deadline contained in section 604 or 605 to a later date than specified in such sections if such schedule or deadline is unattainable, considering when such substance is added to the list. No extension under this subsection may extend the date for termination of production of any class I substance to a date more than 7 years after January 1 of the year after the year in which the substance is added to the list of class I substances. No extension under this subsection may extend the date for termination of production of any class II substance to a date more than 10 years after January 1 of the year after the year in which the substance is added to the list of class II substances.

(e) Ozone-depletion and global warming potential — Simultaneously with publication of the lists under this section and simultaneously with any addition to either of such lists, the Administrator shall assign to each listed substance a numerical value representing the substance's ozone-depletion potential. In addition, the Administrator shall publish the chlorine and bromine loading potential and the atmospheric lifetime of each listed substance. One year after November 15, 1990 (one year after the addition of a substance to either of such lists in the case of a substance added after the publication of the initial lists of such substances), and after notice and opportunity for public comment, the Administrator shall publish the global warming potential of each listed substance. The preceding sentence shall not be construed to be the basis of any additional regulation under this Act. In the case of the substances referred to in table 1, the ozone-depletion potential shall be as specified in table 1, unless the Administrator adjusts the substance's ozone-depletion potential based on criteria referred to in section 7671(10) of this title:

TABLE 1

Substance	Ozone-depletion Potential
chlorofluorocarbon-11 (CFC-11)	1.0
chlorofluorocarbon-12 (CFC-12)	1.0
chlorofluorocarbon-13 (CFC-13)	1.0
chlorofluorocarbon-111 (CFC-111)	1.0
chlorofluorocarbon-112 (CFC-112)	1.0
chlorofluorocarbon-113 (CFC-113)	0.8
chlorofluorocarbon-114 (CFC-114)	1.0
chlorofluorocarbon-115 (CFC-115)	0.6
chlorofluorocarbon-211 (CFC-211)	1.0
chlorofluorocarbon-212 (CFC-212)	1.0
chlorofluorocarbon-213 (CFC-213)	1.0
chlorofluorocarbon-214 (CFC-214)	1.0
chlorofluorocarbon-215 (CFC-215)	1.0
chlorofluorocarbon-216 (CFC-216)	1.0
chlorofluorocarbon-217 (CFC-217)	1.0
halon-1211	3.0
halon-1301	10.0
halon-2402	6.0
carbon tetrachloride	1.1
methyl chloroform	0.1
hydrochlorofluorocarbon-22 (HCFC-22)	0.05
hydrochlorofluorocarbon-123 (HCFC-123)	0.02
hydrochlorofluorocarbon-124 (HCFC-124)	0.02
hydrochlorofluorocarbon-141(b) (HCFC-141(b))	0.1
hydrochlorofluorocarbon-142(b) (HCFC-142(b))	0.06

Where the ozone-depletion potential of a substance is specified in the Montreal Protocol, the ozone-depletion potential specified for that substance under this section shall be consistent with the Montreal Protocol.

863

§7671b. Monitoring and reporting requirements

[CAA §603]

(a) Regulations — Within 270 days after November 15, 1990, the Administrator shall amend the regulations of the Administrator in effect on such date regarding monitoring and reporting of class I and class II substances. Such amendments shall conform to the requirements of this section. The amended regulations shall include requirements with respect to the time and manner of monitoring and reporting as required under this section.

(b) Production, import, and export level reports — On a quarterly basis, or such other basis (not less than annually) as determined by the Administrator, each person who produced, imported, or exported a class I or class II substance shall file a report with the Administrator setting forth the amount of the substance that such person produced, imported, and exported during the preceding reporting period. Each such report shall be signed and attested by a responsible officer. No such report shall be required from a person after April 1 of the calendar year after such person permanently ceases production, importation, and exportation of the substance and so notifies the Administrator in writing.

(c) Baseline reports for Class I substances — Unless such information has previously been reported to the Administrator, on the date on which the first report under subsection (b) of this section is required to be filed, each person who produced, imported, or exported a class I substance (other than a substance added to the list of class I substances after the publication of the initial list of such substances under this section) shall file a report with the Administrator setting forth the amount of such substance that such person produced, imported, and exported during the baseline year. In the case of a substance added to the list of class I substances after publication of the initial list of such substances under this section, the regulations shall require that each person who produced, imported, or exported such substance shall file a report with the Administrator within 180 days after the date on which such substance is added to the list, setting forth the amount of the substance that such person produced, imported, and exported in the baseline year.

(d) Monitoring and reports to Congress

(1) The Administrator shall monitor and, not less often than every 3 years following November 15, 1990, submit a report to Congress on the production, use and consumption of class I and class II substances. Such report shall include data on domestic production, use and consumption, and an estimate of worldwide production, use and consumption of such substances. Not less frequently than every 6 years the Administrator shall report to Congress on the environmental and economic effects of any stratospheric ozone depletion.

(2) The Administrators of the National Aeronautics and Space Administration and the National Oceanic and Atmospheric Administration shall monitor, and not less often than every 3 years following November 15, 1990, submit a report to Congress on the current average tropospheric concentration of chlorine and bromine and on the level of stratospheric ozone depletion. Such reports shall include updated projections of —

(A) peak chlorine loading;

(B) the rate at which the atmospheric abundance of chlorine is projected to decrease after the year 2000; and

(C) the date by which the atmospheric abundance of chlorine is projected to return to a level of two parts per billion.

Such updated projections shall be made on the basis of current international and domestic controls on substances covered by this title as well as on the basis of such controls supplemented by a year 2000 global phase out of all halocarbon emissions (the base case). It is the purpose of the Congress through the provisions of this section to monitor closely the production and consumption of class II substances to assure that the production and consumption of such substances will not:

(i) increase significantly the peak chlorine loading that is projected to occur under the base case established for purposes of this section;

(ii) reduce significantly the rate at which the atmospheric abundance of chlorine is projected to decrease under the base case; or

(iii) delay the date by which the average atmospheric concentration of chlorine is projected under the base case to return to a level of two parts per billion.

(e) Technology status report in 2015 — The Administrator shall review, on a periodic basis, the progress being made in the development of alternative systems or products necessary to manufacture and operate appliances without class II substances. If the Administrator finds, after notice and opportunity for public comment, that as a result of technological development problems, the development of such alternative systems or products will not occur within the time necessary to provide for the manufacture of such equipment without such substances prior to the applicable deadlines under section 7671d of this title, the Administrator shall, not later than January 1, 2015, so inform the Congress.

(f) Emergency report — If, in consultation with the Administrators of the National Aeronautics and Space Administration and the National Oceanic and Atmospheric Administration, and after notice and opportunity for public comment, the Administrator determines that the global production, consumption, and use of class II substances are projected to contribute to an atmospheric chlorine loading in excess of the base case projections by more than 5/10ths parts per billion, the Administrator shall so inform the Congress immediately. The determination referred to in the preceding sentence shall be based on the monitoring under subsection (d) of this section and updated not less often than every 3 years.

§7671c. Phase-out of production and consumption of class I substances
[CAA §604]

(a) Production phase-out — Effective on January 1 of each year specified in Table 2, it shall be unlawful for any person to produce any class I substance in an annual quantity greater than the relevant percentage specified in Table 2. The percentages in Table 2 refer to a maximum allowable production as a percentage of the quantity of the substance produced by the person concerned in the baseline year.

TABLE 2

Date	Carbon tetrachloride	Methyl Chloroform	Other class I substance
1991	100%	100%	85%
1992	90%	100%	80%
1993	80%	90%	75%
1994	70%	85%	65%
1995	15%	70%	50%
1996	15%	50%	40%
1997	15%	50%	15%
1998	15%	50%	15%
1999	15%	50%	15%
2000		20%	
2001		20%	

(b) Termination of production of class I substances — Effective January 1, 2000 (January 1, 2002 in the case of methyl chloroform), it shall be unlawful for any person to produce any amount of a class I substance.

(c) Regulations regarding production and consumption of class I substances — The Administrator shall promulgate regulations within 10 months after November 15, 1990 phasing out the production of class I substances in accordance with this section and other applicable provisions of this title. The Administrator shall also promulgate regulations to insure that the consumption of class I substances in the United States is phased out and terminated in accordance with the same schedule (subject to the same exceptions and other provisions) as is applicable to the phase-out and termination of production of class I substances under this title.

(d) Exceptions for essential uses of methyl chloroform, medical devices, and aviation safety

(1) Essential uses of methyl chloroform — Notwithstanding the termination of production required by subsection (b), during the period beginning on January 1, 2002, and ending on January 1, 2005, the Administrator, after notice and opportunity for public comment, may, to the extent such action is consistent with the Montreal Protocol, authorize the production of limited quantities of methyl chloroform solely for use in essential applications (such as nondestructive testing for metal fatigue and corrosion of existing airplane engines and airplane parts susceptible to metal fatigue) for which no safe and effective substitute is available. Notwithstanding this paragraph, the authority to produce methyl chloroform for use in medical devices shall be provided in accordance with paragraph (2).

(2) Medical devices — Notwithstanding the termination of production required by subsection (b), the Administrator, after notice and opportunity for public comment, shall, to the extent such action is consistent with the Montreal Protocol, authorize the production of limited quantities of class I substances solely for use in medical devices if such authorization is determined by the Commissioner, in consultation with the Administrator, to be necessary for use in medical devices.

(3) Aviation safety

(A) Notwithstanding the termination of production required by subsection (b) of this section, the Administrator, after notice and opportunity for public comment, may, to the extent such action is consistent with the Montreal Protocol, authorize the production of limited quantities of halon-1211 (bromochlorodifluoro-methane), halon-1301 (bromotrifluoro-methane), and halon-2402 (dibromotetrafluoro-ethane) solely for purposes of aviation safety if the Administrator of the Federal Aviation Administration, in consultation with the Administrator, determines that no safe and effective substitute has been developed and that such authorization is necessary for aviation safety purposes.

(B) The Administrator of the Federal Aviation Administration shall, in consultation with the Administrator, examine whether safe and effective substitutes for methyl chloroform or alternative techniques will be available for nondestructive testing for metal fatigue and corrosion of existing airplane engines and airplane parts susceptible to metal fatigue and whether an exception for such uses of methyl chloroform under this paragraph will be necessary for purposes of airline safety after January 1, 2005 and provide a report to Congress in 1998.

(4) Cap on certain exceptions — Under no circumstances may the authority set forth in paragraphs (1), (2), and (3) of subsection (d) of this section be applied to authorize any person to produce a class I substance in annual quantities greater than 10 percent of that produced by such person during the baseline year.

(5) Sanitation and food protection — To the extent consistent with the Montreal Protocol's quarantine and pre-shipment provisions, the Administrator shall exempt the production, importation, and consumption of methyl bromide to fumigate commodities entering or leaving the United States or any State (or political subdivision thereof) for purposes of compliance with Animal and Plant Health Inspection Service requirements or with any international, Federal, State, or local sanitation or food protection standard.

(6) Critical uses — To the extent consistent with the Montreal Protocol, the Administrator, after notice and the opportunity for public comment, and after consultation with other departments or instrumentalities of the Federal Government having regulatory authority related to methyl bromide, including the Secretary of the Agriculture, may exempt the production, importation, and consumption of methyl bromide for critical uses.

(e) Developing countries

(1) Exception — Notwithstanding the phase-out and termination of production required under subsections (a) and (b) of this section, the Administrator, after notice and opportunity for public comment, may, consistent with the Montreal Protocol, authorize the production of limited quantities of a class I substance in excess of the amounts otherwise allowable under subsection (a) or (b) of this section, or both, solely for export to, and use in, developing countries that are Parties to the Montreal Protocol and are operating under article 5 of such Protocol. Any production authorized under this paragraph shall be solely for purposes of satisfying the basic domestic needs of such countries.

(2) Cap on exception

(A) Under no circumstances may the authority set forth in paragraph (1) be applied to authorize any person to produce a class I substance in any year for which a production percentage is specified in Table 2 of subsection (a) in an annual quantity greater than the specified percentage, plus an amount equal to 10 percent of the amount produced by such person in the baseline year.

(B) Under no circumstances may the authority set forth in paragraph (1) be applied to authorize any person to produce a class I substance in the applicable termination year referred to in subsection (b), or in any year thereafter, in an annual quantity greater than 15 percent of the baseline quantity of such substance produced by such person.

(C) An exception authorized under this subsection shall terminate no later than January 1, 2010 (2012 in the case of methyl chloroform).

(3) Methyl bromide — Notwithstanding the phase-out and termination of production of methyl bromide pursuant to section 604(h) [subsection (h) of this section], the Administrator may, consistent with the Montreal Protocol, authorize the production of limited quantities of methyl bromide, solely for use in developing countries that are Parties to the Copenhagen Amendments to the Montreal Protocol.

(f) National security — The President may, to the extent such action is consistent with the Montreal Protocol, issue such orders regarding production and use of CFC-114 (chlorofluorocarbon-114), halon-1211, halon-1301, and halon-2402, at any specified site or facility or on any vessel as may be necessary to protect the national security interests of the United States if the President finds that adequate substitutes are not available and that the production and use of such substance are necessary to protect such national security interest. Such orders may include, where necessary to protect such interests, an exemption from any prohibition or requirement contained in this title. The President shall notify the Congress within 30 days of the issuance of an order under this paragraph providing for any such exemption. Such notification shall include a statement of the reasons for the granting of the exemption. An exemption under this paragraph shall be for a specified period which may not exceed one year. Additional exemptions may be granted, each upon the President's issuance of a new order under this paragraph. Each such additional exemption shall be for a specified period which may not exceed one year. No exemption shall be granted under this paragraph due to lack of appropriation unless the President shall have specifically requested such appropriation as a part of the budgetary process and the Congress shall have failed to make available such requested appropriation.

(g) Fire suppression and explosion prevention

(1) Notwithstanding the production phase-out set forth in subsection (a) of this section, the Administrator, after notice and opportunity for public comment, may, to the extent such action is consistent with the Montreal Protocol, authorize the production of limited quantities of halon-1211, halon-1301, and halon-2402 in excess of the amount otherwise permitted pursuant to the schedule under subsection (a) solely for purposes of fire suppression or explosion prevention if the Administrator, in consultation with the Administrator of the United States Fire Administration, determines that no safe and effective substitute has been developed and that such authorization is necessary for fire suppression or explosion prevention purposes. The Administrator shall not authorize production under this paragraph for purposes of fire safety or explosion prevention training or testing of fire suppression or explosion prevention equipment. In no event shall the Administrator grant an exception under this paragraph that permits production after December 31, 1999.

(2) The Administrator shall periodically monitor and assess the status of efforts to obtain substitutes for the substances referred to in paragraph (1) for purposes of fire suppression or explosion prevention and the probability of such substitutes being available by December 31, 1999. The Administrator, as part of such assessment, shall consider any relevant assessments under the Montreal Protocol and the actions of the Parties pursuant to Article 2B of the Montreal Protocol in identifying essential uses and in permitting a level of production or consumption that is necessary to satisfy such uses for which no adequate alternatives are available after December 31, 1999. The Administrator shall report to Congress the results of such assessment in 1994 and again in 1998.

(3) Notwithstanding the termination of production set forth in subsection (b) of this section, the Administrator, after notice and opportunity for public comment, may, to the extent consistent with the Montreal Protocol, authorize the production of limited quantities of halon-1211, halon-1301, and halon-2402 in the period after December 31, 1999, and before December 31, 2004, solely for purposes of fire suppression or explosion prevention in association with domestic production of crude oil and natural gas energy supplies on the North Slope of Alaska, if the Administrator, in consultation with the Administrator of the United States Fire Administration, determines that no safe and effective substitute has been developed and that such authorization is necessary for fire suppression and explosion prevention purposes. The Administrator shall not authorize production under the paragraph for purposes of fire safety or explosion prevention training or testing of fire suppression or explosion prevention equipment. In no event shall the Administrator authorize under this paragraph any person to produce any such halon in an amount greater than 3 percent of that produced by such person during the baseline year.

(h) Methyl bromide — Notwithstanding subsection (d) and section 604(b) [subsection (b) of this section], the Administrator shall not terminate production of methyl bromide prior to January 1, 2005. The Administrator shall promulgate rules for reductions in, and terminate the production, importation, and consumption of, methyl bromide under a schedule that is in accordance with, but not more stringent than, the phaseout of the Montreal Protocol Treaty as in effect on October 21, 1998.

§7671d. Phase-out of production and consumption of class II substances
[CAA §605]
(a) Restriction of use of class II substances — Effective January 1, 2015, it shall be unlawful for any person to introduce into interstate commerce or use any class II substance unless such substance —

(1) has been used, recovered, and recycled;

(2) is used and entirely consumed (except for trace quantities) in the production of other chemicals; or

(3) is used as a refrigerant in appliances manufactured prior to January 1, 2020.

As used in this subsection, the term "refrigerant" means any class II substance used for heat transfer in a refrigerating system.

(b) Production phase-out

(1) Effective January 1, 2015, it shall be unlawful for any person to produce any class II substance in an annual quantity greater than the quantity of such substance produced by such person during the baseline year.

(2) Effective January 1, 2030, it shall be unlawful for any person to produce any class II substance.

(c) Regulations regarding production and consumption of class II substances — By December 31, 1999, the Administrator shall promulgate regulations phasing out the production, and restricting the use, of class II substances in accordance with this section, subject to any acceleration of the phase-out of production under section 7671e of this title. The Administrator shall also promulgate regulations to insure that the consumption of class II substances in the United States is phased out and terminated in accordance with the same schedule (subject to the same exceptions and other provisions) as is applicable to the phase-out and termination of production of class II substances under this title.

(d) Exceptions

(1) Medical devices

(A) In general — Notwithstanding the termination of production required under subsection (b)(2) of this section and the restriction on use referred to in subsection (a) of this section, the Administrator, after notice and opportunity for public comment, shall, to the extent such action is consistent with the Montreal Protocol, authorize the production and use of limited quantities of class II substances solely for purposes of use in medical devices if such authorization is determined by the Commissioner, in consultation with the Administrator, to be necessary for use in medical devices.

(B) Cap on exception — Under no circumstances may the authority set forth in subparagraph (A) be applied to authorize any person to produce a class II substance in annual quantities greater than 10 percent of that produced by such person during the baseline year.

(2) Developing countries

(A) In general— Notwithstanding the provisions of subsection (a) or (b) of this section, the Administrator, after notice and opportunity for public comment, may authorize the production of limited quantities of a class II substance in excess of the quantities otherwise permitted under such provisions solely for export to and use in developing countries that are Parties to the Montreal Protocol, as determined by the Administrator. Any production authorized under this subsection shall be solely for purposes of satisfying the basic domestic needs of such countries.

(B) Cap on exception

(i) Under no circumstances may the authority set forth in subparagraph (A) be applied to authorize any person to produce a class II substance in any year following the effective date of subsection (b)(1) of this section and before the year 2030 in annual quantities greater than 110 percent of the quantity of such substance produced by such person during the baseline year.

(ii) Under no circumstances may the authority set forth in subparagraph (A) be applied to authorize any person to produce a class II substance in the year 2030, or any year thereafter, in an annual quantity greater than 15 percent of the quantity of such substance produced by such person during the baseline year.

(iii) Each exception authorized under this paragraph shall terminate no later than January 1, 2040.

§7671e. Accelerated schedule
[CAA §606]

(a) In general — The Administrator shall promulgate regulations, after notice and opportunity for public comment, which establish a schedule for phasing out the production and consumption of class I and class II substances (or use of class II substances) that is more stringent than set forth in section 7671c or 7671d of this title, or both, if —

(1) based on an assessment of credible current scientific information (including any assessment under the Montreal Protocol) regarding harmful effects on the stratospheric ozone layer associated with a class I or class II substance, the Administrator determines that such more stringent schedule may be necessary to protect human health and the environment against such effects,

(2) based on the availability of substitutes for listed substances, the Administrator determines that such more stringent schedule is practicable, taking into account technological achievability, safety, and other relevant factors, or

(3) the Montreal Protocol is modified to include a schedule to control or reduce production, consumption, or use of any substance more rapidly than the applicable schedule under this title.

In making any determination under paragraphs (1) and (2), the Administrator shall consider the status of the period remaining under the applicable schedule under this subchapter.

(b) Petition — Any person may petition the Administrator to promulgate regulations under this section. The Administrator shall grant or deny the petition within 180 days after receipt of any such petition. If the Administrator denies the petition, the Administrator shall publish an explanation of why the petition was denied. If the Administrator grants such petition, such final regulations shall be promulgated within 1 year. Any petition under this subsection shall include a showing by the petitioner that there are data adequate to support the petition. If the Administrator determines that information is not sufficient to make a determination under this subsection, the Administrator shall use any authority available to the Administrator, under any law administered by the Administrator, to acquire such information.

§7671f. Exchange authority
[CAA §607]

(a) Transfers — The Administrator shall, within 10 months after November 15, 1990, promulgate rules under this title providing for the issuance of allowances for the production of class I and II substances in accordance with the requirements of this title and governing the transfer of such allowances. Such rules shall insure that the transactions under the authority of this section will result in greater total reductions in the production in each year of class I and class II substances than would occur in that year in the absence of such transactions.

(b) Interpollutant transfers

(1) The rules under this section shall permit a production allowance for a substance for any year to be transferred for a production allowance for another substance for the same year on an ozone depletion weighted basis.

(2) Allowances for substances in each group of class I substances (as listed pursuant to section 7671a of this title) may only be transferred for allowances for other substances in the same Group.

(3) The Administrator shall, as appropriate, establish groups of class II substances for trading purposes and assign class II substances to such groups. In the case of class II substances, allowances may only be transferred for allowances for other class II substances that are in the same Group.

(c) Trades with other persons — The rules under this section shall permit 2 or more persons to transfer production allowances (including interpollutant transfers which meet the requirements of subsections (a) and (b) of this section) if the transferor of such allowances will be subject, under such rules, to an enforceable and quantifiable reduction in annual production which —

(1) exceeds the reduction otherwise applicable to the transferor under this title,

(2) exceeds the production allowances transferred to the transferee, and

(3) would not have occurred in the absence of such transaction.

(d) Consumption — The rules under this section shall also provide for the issuance of consumption allowances in accordance with the requirements of this title and for the trading of such allowances in the same manner as is applicable under this section to the trading of production allowances under this section.

§7671g. National recycling and emission reduction program

[CAA §608]

(a) In general

(1) The Administrator shall, by not later than January 1, 1992, promulgate regulations establishing standards and requirements regarding the use and disposal of class I substances during the service, repair, or disposal of appliances and industrial process refrigeration. Such standards and requirements shall become effective not later than July 1, 1992.

(2) The Administrator shall, within 4 years after November 15, 1990, promulgate regulations establishing standards and requirements regarding use and disposal of class I and II substances not covered by paragraph (1), including the use and disposal of class II substances during service, repair, or disposal of appliances and industrial process refrigeration. Such standards and requirements shall become effective not later than 12 months after promulgation of the regulations.

(3) The regulations under this subsection shall include requirements that —

(A) reduce the use and emission of such substances to the lowest achievable level, and

(B) maximize the recapture and recycling of such substances.

Such regulations may include requirements to use alternative substances (including substances which are not class I or class II substances) or to minimize use of class I or class II substances, or to promote the use of safe alternatives pursuant to section 7671k of this title or any combination of the foregoing.

(b) Safe disposal — The regulations under subsection (a) of this section shall establish standards and requirements for the safe disposal of class I and II substances. Such regulations shall include each of the following —

(1) Requirements that class I or class II substances contained in bulk in appliances, machines or other goods shall be removed from each such appliance, machine or other good prior to the disposal of such items or their delivery for recycling.

(2) Requirements that any appliance, machine or other good containing a class I or class II substance in bulk shall not be manufactured, sold, or distributed in interstate commerce or offered for sale or distribution in interstate commerce unless it is equipped with a servicing aperture or an equally effective design feature which will facilitate the recapture of such substance during service and repair or disposal of such item.

(3) Requirements that any product in which a class I or class II substance is incorporated so as to constitute an inherent element of such product shall be disposed of in a manner that reduces, to the maximum extent practicable, the release of such substance into the environment. If the Administrator determines that the application of this paragraph to any product would result in producing only insignificant environmental benefits, the Administrator shall include in such regulations an exception for such product.

(c) Prohibitions

(1) Effective July 1, 1992, it shall be unlawful for any person, in the course of maintaining, servicing, repairing, or disposing of an appliance or industrial process refrigeration, to knowingly vent or otherwise knowingly release or dispose of any class I or class II substance used as a refrigerant in such appliance (or industrial process refrigeration) in a manner which permits such substance to enter the environment. De minimis releases associated with good faith attempts to recapture and recycle or safely dispose of any such substance shall not be subject to the prohibition set forth in the preceding sentence.

(2) Effective 5 years after November 15, 1990, paragraph (1) shall also apply to the venting, release, or disposal of any substitute substance for a class I or class II substance by any person maintaining, servicing, repairing, or disposing of an appliance or industrial process refrigeration which contains and uses as a refrigerant any such substance, unless the Administrator determines that venting, releasing, or disposing of such substance does not pose a threat to the environment. For purposes of this paragraph, the term "appliance" includes any device which contains and uses as a refrigerant a substitute substance and which is used for household or commercial purposes, including any air conditioner, refrigerator, chiller, or freezer.

§7671h. Servicing of motor vehicle air conditioners

[CAA §609]

(a) Regulations — Within 1 year after November 15, 1990, the Administrator shall promulgate regulations in accordance with this section establishing standards and requirements regarding the servicing of motor vehicle air conditioners.

(b) Definitions — As used in this section —

(1) The term "refrigerant" means any class I or class II substance used in a motor vehicle air conditioner. Effective 5 years after November 15, 1990, the term "refrigerant" shall also include any substitute substance.

(2)(A) The term "approved refrigerant recycling equipment" means equipment certified by the Administrator (or an independent standards testing organization approved by the Administrator) to meet the standards established by the Administrator and applicable to equipment for the extraction and reclamation of refrigerant from motor vehicle air conditioners. Such standards shall, at a minimum, be at least as stringent as the standards of the Society of Automotive Engineers in effect as of November 15, 1990 and applicable to such equipment (SAE standard J-1990).

(B) Equipment purchased before the proposal of regulations under this section shall be considered certified if it is substantially identical to equipment certified as provided in subparagraph (A).

(3) The term "properly using" means, with respect to approved refrigerant recycling equipment, using such equipment in conformity with standards established by the Administrator and applicable to the use of such equipment. Such standards shall, at a minimum, be at least as stringent as the standards of the Society of Automotive Engineers in effect as of November 15, 1990 and applicable to the use of such equipment (SAE standard J-1989).

(4) The term "properly trained and certified" means training and certification in the proper use of approved refrigerant recycling equipment for motor vehicle air conditioners in conformity with standards established by the Administrator and applicable to the performance of service on motor vehicle air conditioners. Such standards shall, at a minimum, be at least as stringent as specified, as of November 15, 1990, in SAE standard J-1989 under the certification program of the National Institute for Automotive Service Excellence (ASE) or under a similar program such as the training and certification program of the Mobile Air Conditioning Society (MACS).

(c) Servicing motor vehicle air conditioners — Effective January 1, 1992, no person repairing or servicing motor vehicles for consideration may perform any service on a motor vehicle air conditioner involving the refrigerant for such air conditioner without properly using approved refrigerant recycling equipment and no such person may perform such service unless such person has been properly trained and certified. The requirements of the previous sentence shall not apply until January 1, 1993 in the case of a person repairing or servicing motor vehicles for consideration at an entity which performed service on fewer than 100 motor vehicle air conditioners during calendar year 1990 and if such person so certifies, pursuant to subsection (d)(2) of this section, to the Administrator by January 1, 1992.

(d) Certification

(1) Effective 2 years after November 15, 1990, each person performing service on motor vehicle air conditioners for consideration shall certify to the Administrator either —

(A) that such person has acquired, and is properly using, approved refrigerant recycling equipment in service on motor vehicle air conditioners involving refrigerant and that each individual authorized by such person to perform such service is properly trained and certified; or

(B) that such person is performing such service at an entity which serviced fewer than 100 motor vehicle air conditioners in 1991.

(2) Effective January 1, 1993, each person who certified under paragraph (1)(B) shall submit a certification under paragraph (1)(A).

(3) Each certification under this subsection shall contain the name and address of the person certifying under this subsection and the serial number of each unit of approved recycling equipment acquired by such person and shall be signed and attested by the owner or another responsible officer. Certifications under paragraph (1)(A) may be made by submitting the required information to the Administrator on a standard form provided by the manufacturer of certified refrigerant recycling equipment.

(e) Small containers of class I or class II substances — Effective 2 years after November 15, 1990, it shall be unlawful for any person to sell or distribute, or offer for sale or distribution, in interstate commerce to any person (other than a person performing service for consideration on motor vehicle air-conditioning systems in compliance with this section) any class I or class II substance that is suitable for use as a refrigerant in a motor vehicle air-conditioning system and that is in a container which contains less than 20 pounds of such refrigerant.

§7671i. Nonessential products containing chlorofluorocarbons
[CAA §610]

(a) Regulations — The Administrator shall promulgate regulations to carry out the requirements of this section within 1 year after the enactment of the Clean Air Act Amendments of 1990.

(b) Nonessential products — The regulations under this section shall identify nonessential products that release class I substances into the environment (including any release occurring during manufacture, use, storage, or disposal) and prohibit any person from selling or distributing any such product, or offering any such product for sale or distribution, in interstate commerce. At a minimum, such prohibition shall apply to —

(1) chlorofluorocarbon-propelled plastic party streamers and noise horns,

(2) chlorofluorocarbon-containing cleaning fluids for noncommercial electronic and photographic equipment, and

(3) other consumer products that are determined by the Administrator —

(A) to release class I substances into the environment (including any release occurring during manufacture, use, storage, or disposal), and

　　(B) to be nonessential.

In determining whether a product is nonessential, the Administrator shall consider the purpose or intended use of the product, the technological availability of substitutes for such product and for such class I substance, safety, health, and other relevant factors.

(c) Effective date — Effective 24 months after November 15, 1990, it shall be unlawful for any person to sell or distribute, or offer for sale or distribution, in interstate commerce any nonessential product to which regulations under subsection (a) of this section implementing subsection (b) of this section are applicable.

(d) Other products

　　(1) Effective January 1, 1994, it shall be unlawful for any person to sell or distribute, or offer for sale or distribution, in interstate commerce —

　　　　(A) any aerosol product or other pressurized dispenser which contains a class II substance; or

　　　　(B) any plastic foam product which contains, or is manufactured with, a class II substance.

　　(2) The Administrator is authorized to grant exceptions from the prohibition under subparagraph (A) of paragraph (1) where —

　　　　(A) the use of the aerosol product or pressurized dispenser is determined by the Administrator to be essential as a result of flammability or worker safety concerns, and

　　　　(B) the only available alternative to use of a class II substance is use of a class I substance which legally could be substituted for such class II substance.

　　(3) Subparagraph (B) of paragraph (1) shall not apply to —

　　　　(A) a foam insulation product, or

　　　　(B) an integral skin, rigid, or semi-rigid foam utilized to provide for motor vehicle safety in accordance with Federal Motor Vehicle Safety Standards where no adequate substitute substance (other than a class I or class II substance) is practicable for effectively meeting such Standards.

(e) Medical devices — Nothing in this section shall apply to any medical device as defined in section 7671(8) of this title.

§7671j. Labeling

[CAA §611]

(a) Regulations — The Administrator shall promulgate regulations to implement the labeling requirements of this section within 18 months after November 15, 1990, after notice and opportunity for public comment.

(b) Containers containing class I or class II substances and products containing class I

substances — Effective 30 months after November 15, 1990, no container in which a class I or class II substance is stored or transported, and no product containing a class I substance, shall be introduced into interstate commerce unless it bears a clearly legible and conspicuous label stating:

> "Warning: Contains [insert name of substance], a substance which harms public health and environment by destroying ozone in the upper atmosphere".

(c) Products containing class II substances

　　(1) After 30 months after November 15, 1990, and before January 1, 2015, no product containing a class II substance shall be introduced into interstate commerce unless it bears the label referred to in subsection (b) of this section if the Administrator determines, after notice and opportunity for public comment, that there are substitute products or manufacturing processes (A) that do not rely on the use of such class II substance, (B) that reduce the overall risk to human health and the environment, and (C) that are currently or potentially available.

　　(2) Effective January 1, 2015, the requirements of subsection (b) of this section shall apply to all products containing a class II substance.

(d) Products manufactured with class I and class II substances

　　(1) In the case of a class II substance, after 30 months after November 15, 1990, and before January 1, 2015, if the Administrator, after notice and opportunity for public comment, makes the determination referred to in subsection (c) of this section with respect to a product manufactured with a process that uses such class II substance, no such product shall be introduced into interstate commerce unless it bears a clearly legible and conspicuous label stating:

> "Warning: Manufactured with [insert name of substance], a substance which harms public health and environment by destroying ozone in the upper atmosphere".

　　(2) In the case of a class I substance, effective 30 months after November 15, 1990, and before January 1, 2015, the labeling requirements of this subsection shall apply to all products manufactured with a process that uses such class I substance unless the Administrator determines that there are no substitute products or manufacturing processes that (A) do not rely on the use of such class I substance, (B) reduce the overall risk to human health and the environment, and (C) are currently or potentially available.

(e) Petitions

　　(1) Any person may, at any time after 18 months after November 15, 1990, petition the Administrator to apply the requirements of this section to a product containing a class II substance or a product manu-

factured with a class I or II substance which is not otherwise subject to such requirements. Within 180 days after receiving such petition, the Administrator shall, pursuant to the criteria set forth in subsection (c), either propose to apply the requirements of this section to such product or publish an explanation of the petition denial. If the Administrator proposes to apply such requirements to such product, the Administrator shall, by rule, render a final determination pursuant to such criteria within 1 year after receiving such petition.

(2) Any petition under this paragaph shall include a showing by the petitioner that there are data on the product adequate to support the petition.

(3) If the Administrator determines that information on the product is not sufficient to make the required determination the Administrator shall use any authority available to the Administrator under any law administered by the Administrator to acquire such information.

(4) In the case of a product determined by the Administrator, upon petition or on the Administrator's own motion, to be subject to the requirements of this section, the Administrator shall establish an effective date for such requirements. The effective date shall be 1 year after such determination or 30 months after November 15, 1990, whichever is later.

(5) Effective January 1, 2015, the labeling requirements of this subsection shall apply to all products manufactured with a process that uses a class I or class II substance.

(f) Relationship to other law

(1) The labeling requirements of this section shall not constitute, in whole or part, a defense to liability or a cause for reduction in damages in any suit, whether civil or criminal, brought under any law, whether Federal or State, other than a suit for failure to comply with the labeling requirements of this section.

(2) No other approval of such label by the Administrator under any other law administered by the Administrator shall be required with respect to the labeling requirements of this section.

§7671k. Safe alternatives policy
[CAA §612]

(a) Policy — To the maximum extent practicable, class I and class II substances shall be replaced by chemicals, product substitutes, or alternative manufacturing processes that reduce overall risks to human health and the environment.

(b) Reviews and reports — The Administrator shall —

(1) in consultation and coordination with interested members of the public and the heads of relevant Federal agencies and departments, recommend Federal research programs and other activities to assist in identifying alternatives to the use of class I and class II substances as refrigerants, solvents, fire retardants, foam blowing agents, and

other commercial applications and in achieving a transition to such alternatives, and, where appropriate, seek to maximize the use of Federal research facilities and resources to assist users of class I and class II substances in identifying and developing alternatives to the use of such substances as refrigerants, solvents, fire retardants, foam blowing agents, and other commercial applications;

(2) examine in consultation and coordination with the Secretary of Defense and the heads of other relevant Federal agencies and departments, including the General Services Administration, Federal procurement practices with respect to class I and class II substances and recommend measures to promote the transition by the Federal Government, as expeditiously as possible, to the use of safe substitutes;

(3) specify initiatives, including appropriate intergovernmental, international, and commercial information and technology transfers, to promote the development and use of safe substitutes for class I and class II substances, including alternative chemicals, product substitutes, and alternative manufacturing processes; and

(4) maintain a public clearinghouse of alternative chemicals, product substitutes, and alternative manufacturing processes that are available for products and manufacturing processes which use class I and class II substances.

(c) Alternatives for class I or II substances — Within 2 years after November 15, 1990, the Administrator shall promulgate rules under this section providing that it shall be unlawful to replace any class I or class II substance with any substitute substance which the Administrator determines may present adverse effects to human health or the environment, where the Administrator has identified an alternative to such replacement that —

(1) reduces the overall risk to human health and the environment; and

(2) is currently or potentially available.

The Administrator shall publish a list of (A) the substitutes prohibited under this subsection for specific uses and (B) the safe alternatives identified under this subsection for specific uses.

(d) Right to petition — Any person may petition the Administrator to add a substance to the lists under subsection (c) or to remove a substance from either of such lists. The Administrator shall grant or deny the petition within 90 days after receipt of any such petition. If the Administrator denies the petition, the Administrator shall publish an explanation of why the petition was denied. If the Administrator grants such petition the Administrator shall publish such revised list within 6 months thereafter. Any petition under this subsection shall include a showing by the petitioner that there are data on the substance adequate to support the petition. If the Administrator determines that information on the substance is not sufficient to make a determination under this subsection, the Administrator shall use any authority available to the Administrator, under any law administered by the Administrator, to acquire such information.

(e) Studies and notification — The Administrator shall require any person who produces a chemical substitute for a class I substance to provide the Administrator with such person's unpublished health and safety studies on such substitute and require producers to notify the Administrator not less than 90 days before new or existing chemicals are introduced into interstate commerce for significant new uses as substitutes for a class I substance. This subsection shall be subject to section 7414(c) of this title.

§7671*l*. Federal procurement
[CAA §613]

Not later than 18 months after November 15, 1990, the Administrator, in consultation with the Administrator of the General Services Administration and the Secretary of Defense, shall promulgate regulations requiring each department, agency, and instrumentality of the United States to conform its procurement regulations to the policies and requirements of this title and to maximize the substitution of safe alternatives identified under section 7671k of this title for class I and class II substances. Not later than 30 months after November 15, 1990, each department, agency, and instrumentality of the United States shall so conform its procurement regulations and certify to the President that its regulations have been modified in accordance with this section.

§7671m. Relationship to other laws
[CAA §614]

(a) State laws — Notwithstanding section 7416 of this title, during the 2-year period beginning on November 15, 1990, no State or local government may enforce any requirement concerning the design of any new or recalled appliance for the purpose of protecting the stratospheric ozone layer.

(b) Montreal Protocol — This subchapter as added by the Clean Air Act Amendments of 1990 shall be construed, interpreted, and applied as a supplement to the terms and conditions of the Montreal Protocol, as provided in Article 2, paragraph 11 thereof, and shall not be construed, interpreted, or applied to abrogate the responsibilities or obligations of the United States to implement fully the provisions of the Montreal Protocol. In the case of conflict between any provision of this title and any provision of the Montreal Protocol, the more stringent provision shall govern. Nothing in this title shall be construed, interpreted, or applied to affect the authority or responsibility of the Administrator to implement Article 4 of the Montreal Protocol with other appropriate agencies.

(c) Technology export and overseas investment — Upon enactment of this title, the President shall —

(1) prohibit the export of technologies used to produce a class I substance;

(2) prohibit direct or indirect investments by any person in facilities designed to produce a class I or class II substance in nations that are not parties to the Montreal Protocol; and

(3) direct that no agency of the government provide bilateral or multilateral subsidies, aids, credits, guarantees, or insurance programs, for the purpose of producing any class I substance.

§7671n. Authority of Administrator
[CAA §615]

If, in the Administrator's judgment, any substance, practice, process, or activity may reasonably be anticipated to affect the stratosphere, especially ozone in the stratosphere, and such effect may reasonably be anticipated to endanger public health or welfare, the Administrator shall promptly promulgate regulations respecting the control of such substance, practice, process, or activity, and shall submit notice of the proposal and promulgation of such regulation to Congress.

§7671o. Transfers among Parties to Montreal Protocol
[CAA §616]

(a) In general — Consistent with the Montreal Protocol, the United States may engage in transfers with other Parties to the Protocol under the following conditions:

(1) The United States may transfer production allowances to another Party if, at the time of such transfer, the Administrator establishes revised production limits for the United States such that the aggregate national United States production permitted under the revised production limits equals the lesser of (A) the maximum production level permitted for the substance or substances concerned in the transfer year under the Protocol minus the production allowances transferred, (B) the maximum production level permitted for the substance or substances concerned in the transfer year under applicable domestic law minus the production allowances transferred, or (C) the average of the actual national production level of the substance or substances concerned for the 3 years prior to the transfer minus the production allowances transferred.

(2) The United States may acquire production allowances from another Party if, at the time of such transfer, the Administrator finds that the other Party has revised its domestic production limits in the same manner as provided with respect to transfers by the United States in this subsection.

(b) Effect of transfers on production limits — The Administrator is authorized to reduce the production limits established under this Act as required as a prerequisite to transfers under paragraph (1) of subsection (a) of this section or to increase production limits established under this Act to reflect production allowances acquired under a transfer under paragraph (2) of subsection (a) of this section.

(c) Regulations — The Administrator shall promulgate, within 2 years after November 15, 1990, regulations to implement this section.

(d) "Applicable domestic law" defined — In the case of the United States, the term "applicable domestic law" means this chapter.

§7671p. International cooperation
[CAA §617]

(a) In general — The President shall undertake to enter into international agreements to foster cooperative research which complements studies and research authorized by this title, and to develop standards and regulations which protect the stratosphere consistent with regulations applicable within the United States. For these purposes the President through the Secretary of State and the Assistant Secretary of State for Oceans and International Environmental and Scientific Affairs, shall negotiate multilateral treaties, conventions, resolutions, or other agreements, and formulate, present, or support proposals at the United Nations and other appropriate international forums and shall report to the Congress periodically on efforts to arrive at such agreements.

(b) Assistance to developing countries — The Administrator, in consultation with the Secretary of State, shall support global participation in the Montreal Protocol by providing technical and financial assistance to developing countries that are Parties to the Montreal Protocol and operating under article 5 of the Protocol. There are authorized to be appropriated not more than $30,000,000 to carry out this section in fiscal years 1991, 1992 and 1993 and such sums as may be necessary in fiscal years 1994 and 1995. If China and India become Parties to the Montreal Protocol, there are authorized to be appropriated not more than an additional $30,000,000 to carry out this section in fiscal years 1991, 1992, and 1993.

§7671q. Miscellaneous provisions
[CAA §618]

For purposes of section 7416 of this title, requirements concerning the areas addressed by this subchapter for the protection of the stratosphere against ozone layer depletion shall be treated as requirements for the control and abatement of air pollution. For purposes of section 7418 of this title, the requirements of this title and corresponding State, interstate, and local requirements, administrative authority, and process, and sanctions respecting the protection of the stratospheric ozone layer shall be treated as requirements for the control and abatement of air pollution within the meaning of section 7418 of this title.

6

WATER POLLUTION CONTROL

While several statutes regulate pollutants that may affect water quality, the Federal Water Pollution Control Act, also known as the Clean Water Act (CWA), is the most comprehensive federal regulatory program for controlling discharges to surface waters. The Act bans all discharges of pollutants from point sources unless a permit has been obtained. Discharges to marine waters require a permit under the Marine Protection, Research, and Sanctuaries Act (MPRSA), also known as the Ocean Dumping Act. Special regulations govern oil spills of water and land under the Oil Pollution Act (OPA).

A. THE CLEAN WATER ACT (CWA)

A GUIDE TO MATERIALS ON WATER POLLUTION CONTROL AVAILABLE ON THE INTERNET

The U.S. Environmental Protection Agency's regulations implementing the Clean Water Act are codified at 40 C.F.R. pts. 100-140. Effluent guidelines and standards and general pretreatment regulations are located at 40 C.F.R. pts. 400-471. EPA's regulations governing the issuance of permits under §404 of the Act can be found at 40 C.F.R. pts. 230-233; the regulations governing the U.S. Army Corps of Engineers' section 404 permit program are found at 33 C.F.R. pts. 323-331. These CFR sections are available online through the National Archives and Records Administration's website, which includes a searchable version of the Code of Federal Regulations and an electronic version of the CFR ("e-CFR") updated continuously, which can be found at *http://www.ecfr.gov*.

EPA's Office of Water (OW) is responsible for implementing the Clean Water Act. OW's website is located at *https://www.epa.gov/environmental-topics/water-topics*. A webpage describing the laws and regulations pertinent to EPA's water programs is located at *https://www.epa.gov/regulatory-information-topic/regulatory-information-topic-water*. EPA's Strategic Plan and Guidance for the National Water Program is located at *https://www.epa.gov/water-planning-evaluation*. EPA's efforts to encourage action to control nonpoint sources of pollution are described at *https://www.epa.gov/nps*. The activities of the agency's Office of Wastewater Management are explained at *https://www.epa.gov/environmental-topics/water-topics*.

EPA's Office of Water allows the public to subscribe to a variety of water newsletters, including Water Headlines, a Climate and Water E-Newsletter, a Water Quality Standards News Listserv, a Fish Advisory Newsletter, NPDES News, and a Water Research Updates Newsletter. Information on how to subscribe is located at *https://www.epa.gov/aboutepa/about-office-water*.

To enable citizens to obtain more information about their watersheds and the groups working to preserving them, EPA maintains a "Surf Your Watershed" webpage that has a search function for locating watersheds by zip code, city, river, county or state. The page is located at *http://cfpub.epa.gov/surf/locate/index.cfm*.

EPA operates a toll-free Wetlands Helpline that provides information about wetlands issues and regulatory requirements concerning development in wetlands areas. The Army Corps of Engineers has a website with links to regulatory documents concerning its §404 permit program at *http://www.usace.army.mil/Missions/Civil-Works/Regulatory-Program-and-Permits/Obtain-a-Permit/*.

The Natural Resources Defense Council's webpage includes an extensive set of links to other nonprofit organizations working on various aspects of clean water issues. It can be accessed at *https://www.nrdc.org/issues/water*.

CLEAN WATER ACT LEGISLATIVE HISTORY TIMELINE

June 30, 1948: President Truman signs the Water Pollution Control Act, Pub. L. 80-845, 62 Stat. 1155, which provides federal funds to assist state and local efforts to protect water quality.

July 9, 1956: Congress enacts the Federal Water Pollution Control Act of 1956, Pub. L. 84-660, 70 Stat. 498, overriding President Eisenhower's veto. The legislation creates a program of federal construction grants to municipalities for the construction of sewage treatment plants.

October 2, 1965: President Johnson signs into law the Water Quality Act of 1965, Pub. L. 89-234, 79 Stat. 403, which requires states to adopt water quality standards for interstate waters subject to the approval of the newly created Federal Water Pollution Control Administration.

October 18, 1972: Congress enacts the Federal Water Pollution Control Act Amendments of 1972 (FWPCA), Pub. L. 92-500, 86 Stat. 816, over President Nixon's veto. They create a comprehensive national regulatory program to control water pollution. They require EPA to set technology-based effluent standards and they require that a permit be obtained for all discharges from point sources.

December 27, 1977: President Carter signs into law the Clean Water Act Amendments of 1977, Pub. L. 95-217, 91 Stat. 1566, which mandate a new technology-based program for controlling discharges of toxic water pollutants.

February 4, 1987: Congress enacts the Water Quality Act of 1987, Pub. L. 100-4, 101 Stat. 7, overriding President Reagan's veto. The Act establishes a new program for controlling hot spots of toxic water pollution and it strengthens efforts to control nonpoint source pollution.

October 10, 2000: President Clinton signs into law the Beaches Environmental Assessment and Coastal Health Act of 2000, Pub. L. 106-284, 114 Stat. 870, which requires new efforts to assess human health risks from exposure to pathogens in coastal recreation waters and the development of new water quality criteria and standards to protect against them.

July 29, 2008: President George W. Bush signs into law the Clean Boating Act of 2008, Pub. L. 110-288, 122 Stat. 2650, which adds §402(r) to the Clean Water Act to exempt discharges incidental to the normal operation of recreational vessels from the Act's NPDES permit program. It also adds §312(o) to require EPA to develop management practices and performance standards to mitigate such discharges.

PRINCIPAL PROVISIONS OF THE CLEAN WATER ACT

TITLE I — RESEARCH AND RELATED PROGRAMS

§101 (33 U.S.C. §1251) Congressional Declaration of Goals and Policy: declares national goals of fishable/swimmable waters by 1983, the elimination of pollutant discharges into navigable waters by 1985, and the control of nonpoint sources of water pollution.

§§102-120 (33 U.S.C. §§1252-1274) Comprehensive Programs for Water Pollution Control: authorizes federal financial support for a broad array of research and policy initiatives including efforts to clean up the Chesapeake Bay and the Great Lakes.

TITLE II — GRANTS FOR CONSTRUCTION OF SEWAGE TREATMENT WORKS

§§201-219 (33 U.S.C. §§1281-1301) Construction Grants: establishes a program of federal financial assistance to municipalities for the construction of sewage treatment works.

TITLE III — STANDARDS AND ENFORCEMENT

§301 (33 U.S.C. §1311) Effluent Limitations: prohibits the discharge to navigable waters of any pollutant from any point source without a permit. Imposes technology-based effluent limitations on discharges from industrial point sources and publicly owned treatment works.

§302 (33 U.S.C. §1312) Water Quality Related Effluent Limitations: authorizes the imposition of more stringent effluent limitations when necessary to meet water quality standards.

§303 (33 U.S.C. §1313) Water Quality Standards and TMDLs: requires states and tribes to adopt and to review triennially water quality criteria and standards subject to EPA approval, to identify waters where effluent limitations are insufficient to achieve such standards, and to establish total maximum daily loadings (TMDLs) for such waters.

§304 (33 U.S.C. §1314) Water Quality Criteria and Effluent Limitation Guidelines, Toxic Hotspots: requires the EPA Administrator to adopt water quality criteria and effluent limitation guidelines. Section 304(*l*) requires states and EPA to develop individual control strategies for waters with toxic pollution in excess of water quality standards.

§306 (33 U.S.C. §1316) New Source Performance Standards: requires the EPA Administrator to promulgate performance standards for new sources that reflect the best demonstrated control technology.

§307 (33 U.S.C. §1317) Toxic and Pretreatment Effluent Standards: requires dischargers of toxic pollutants to meet effluent limits reflecting the best available technology economically achievable. Requires the EPA Administrator to establish pretreatment standards to prevent discharges to sewers from interfering with sewage treatment.

§309 (33 U.S.C. §1319) Enforcement Authorities: authorizes the imposition of administrative, civil, and criminal penalties for violations of the Act.

§319 (33 U.S.C. §1329) Nonpoint Source Management Programs: requires states and tribes to identify waters that do not meet water quality standards due to pollution from nonpoint sources and to prepare management plans identifying controls for specific sources.

TITLE IV — PERMITS AND LICENSES

§401 (33 U.S.C. §1341) Certification: requires applicants for federal licenses or permits for projects resulting in discharges to obtain certifications from states that their discharges will comply with provisions of the Act.

§402 (33 U.S.C. §1342) NPDES Permits: establishes a national permit program, the pollutant discharge elimination system (NPDES), which may be administered by states or tribes under delegated authority from EPA.

§404 (33 U.S.C. §1344) Dredge and Fill Permits: requires a permit from the Army Corps of Engineers, subject to EPA concurrence, for the discharge of dredged or fill material into navigable waters including wetlands.

TITLE V — GENERAL PROVISIONS

§505 (33 U.S.C. §1365) Citizen Suits: authorizes citizens to sue any person who violates the Act, including the EPA Administrator if she fails to perform a nondiscretionary duty.

§509 (33 U.S.C. §1369) Judicial Review: authorizes judicial review of EPA rulemaking actions in the U.S. Courts of Appeal.

§518 (33 U.S.C. §1377) Indian Tribes: allows Indian tribes that have governing bodies performing substantial governmental duties to be treated as states for purposes of the Act.

Federal Water Pollution Control Act (Clean Water Act [CWA])

33 U.S.C. §§1251 to 1388

SUBCHAPTER I — RESEARCH AND RELATED PROGRAMS

§1251. Congressional declaration of goals and policy

[CWA §101]

(a) Restoration and maintenance of chemical, physical and biological integrity of Nation's waters; national goals for achievement of objective — The objective of this chapter is to restore and maintain the chemical, physical, and biological integrity of the Nation's waters. In order to achieve this objective it is hereby declared that, consistent with the provisions of this chapter —

(1) it is the national goal that the discharge of pollutants into the navigable waters be eliminated by 1985;

(2) it is the national goal that wherever attainable, an interim goal of water quality which provides for the protection and propagation of fish, shellfish, and wildlife and provides for recreation in and on the water be achieved by July 1, 1983;

(3) it is the national policy that the discharge of toxic pollutants in toxic amounts be prohibited;

(4) it is the national policy that Federal financial assistance be provided to construct publicly owned waste treatment works;

(5) it is the national policy that areawide waste treatment management planning processes be developed and implemented to assure adequate control of sources of pollutants in each State;

(6) it is the national policy that a major research and demonstration effort be made to develop technology necessary to eliminate the discharge of pollutants into the navigable waters, waters of the contiguous zone, and the oceans; and

(7) it is the national policy that programs for the control of nonpoint sources of pollution be developed and implemented in an expeditious manner so as to enable the goals of this chapter to be met through the control of both point and nonpoint sources of pollution.

(b) Congressional recognition, preservation, and protection of primary responsibilities and rights of States — It is the policy of the Congress to recognize, preserve, and protect the primary responsibilities and rights of States to prevent, reduce, and eliminate pollution, to plan the development and use (including restoration, preservation, and enhancement) of land and water resources, and to consult with the Administrator in the exercise of his authority under this chapter. It is the policy of Congress that the States manage the construction grant program under this chapter and implement the permit programs under sections 1342 and 1344 of this title. It is further the policy of the Congress to support and aid research relating to the prevention, reduction, and elimination of pollution, and to provide Federal technical services and financial aid to State and interstate agencies and municipalities in connection with the prevention, reduction, and elimination of pollution.

(c) Congressional policy toward Presidential activities with foreign countries — It is further the policy of Congress that the President, acting through the Secretary of State and such national and international organizations as he determines appropriate, shall take such action as may be necessary to insure that to the fullest extent possible all foreign countries shall take meaningful action for the prevention, reduction, and elimination of pollution in their waters and in international waters and for the achievement of goals regarding the elimination of discharge of pollutants and the improvement of water quality to at least the same extent as the United States does under its laws.

(d) Administrator of Environmental Protection Agency to administer chapter — Except as otherwise expressly provided in this chapter, the Administrator of the Environmental Protection Agency (hereinafter in this chapter called "Administrator") shall administer this chapter.

(e) Public participation in development, revision, and enforcement of any regulation, etc. — Public participation in the development, revision, and enforcement of any regulation, standard, effluent limitation, plan, or program established by the Administrator or any State under this chapter shall be provided for, encouraged, and assisted by the Administrator and the States. The Administrator, in cooperation with the States, shall develop and publish regulations specifying minimum guidelines for public participation in such processes.

(f) Procedures utilized for implementing chapter — It is the national policy that to the maximum extent possible the procedures utilized for implementing this chapter shall encourage the drastic minimization of paperwork and interagency decision procedures, and the best use of available manpower and funds, so as to prevent needless duplication and unnecessary delays at all levels of government.

(g) Authority of States over water — It is the policy of Congress that the authority of each State to allocate quantities of water within its jurisdiction shall not be superseded, abrogated or otherwise impaired by this chapter. It is the further policy of Congress that nothing in this chapter shall be construed to supersede or abrogate rights to quantities of water which have been established by any State. Federal agencies shall co-operate with State and local agencies to develop comprehensive solutions to prevent, reduce and eliminate pollution in concert with programs for managing water resources.

§1252. Comprehensive programs for water pollution control
[CWA §102]

(a) Preparation and development — The Administrator shall, after careful investigation, and in cooperation with other Federal agencies, State water pollution control agencies, interstate agencies, and the municipalities and industries involved, prepare or develop comprehensive programs for preventing, reducing, or eliminating the pollution of the navigable waters and ground waters and improving the sanitary condition of surface and underground waters. In the development of such comprehensive programs due regard shall be given to the improvements which are necessary to conserve such waters for the protection and propagation of fish and aquatic life and wildlife, recreational purposes, and the withdrawal of such waters for public water supply, agricultural, industrial, and other purposes. For the purpose of this section, the Administrator is authorized to make joint investigations with any such agencies of the condition of any waters in any State or States, and of the discharges of any sewage, industrial wastes, or substance which may adversely affect such waters.

(b) Planning for reservoirs; storage for regulation of streamflow

(1) In the survey or planning of any reservoir by the Corps of Engineers, Bureau of Reclamation, or other Federal agency, consideration shall be given to inclusion of storage for regulation of streamflow, except that any such storage and water releases shall not be provided as a substitute for adequate treatment or other methods of controlling waste at the source.

(2) The need for and the value of storage for regulation of streamflow (other than for water quality) including but not limited to navigation, salt water intrusion, recreation, esthetics, and fish and wildlife, shall be determined by the Corps of Engineers, Bureau of Reclamation, or other Federal agencies.

(3) The need for, the value of, and the impact of, storage for water quality control shall be determined by the Administrator, and his views on these matters shall be set forth in any report or presentation to Congress proposing authorization or construction of any reservoir including such storage.

(4) The value of such storage shall be taken into account in determining the economic value of the entire project of which it is a part, and costs shall be allocated to the purpose of regulation of

streamflow in a manner which will insure that all project purposes, share equitably in the benefit of multiple-purpose construction.

(5) Costs of regulation of streamflow features incorporated in any Federal reservoir or other impoundment under the provisions of this chapter shall be determined and the beneficiaries identified and if the benefits are widespread or national in scope, the costs of such features shall be nonreimbursable.

(6) No license granted by the Federal Energy Regulatory for a hydroelectric power project shall include storage for regulation of streamflow for the purpose of water quality control unless the Administrator shall recommend its inclusion and such reservoir storage capacity shall not exceed such proportion of the total storage required for the water quality control plan as the drainage area of such reservoir bears to the drainage area of the river basin or basins involved in such water quality control plan.

(c) Basins; grants to State agencies

(1) The Administrator shall, at the request of the Governor of a State, or a majority of the Governors when more than one State is involved, make a grant to pay not to exceed 50 per centum of the administrative expenses of a planning agency for a period not to exceed three years, which period shall begin after October 18, 1972, if such agency provides for adequate representation of appropriate State, interstate, local, or (when appropriate) international interests in the basin or portion thereof involved and is capable of developing an effective, comprehensive water quality control plan for a basin or portion thereof.

(2) Each planning agency receiving a grant under this subsection shall develop a comprehensive pollution control plan for the basin or portion thereof which —

(A) is consistent with any applicable water quality standards, effluent and other limitations, and thermal discharge regulations established pursuant to current law within the basin;

(B) recommends such treatment works as will provide the most effective and economical means of collection, storage, treatment, and elimination of pollutants and recommends means to encourage both municipal and industrial use of such works;

(C) recommends maintenance and improvement of water quality within the basin or portion thereof and recommends methods of adequately financing those facilities as may be necessary to implement the plan; and

(D) as appropriate, is developed in cooperation with, and is consistent with any comprehensive plan prepared by the Water Resources Council, any areawide waste management plans developed pursuant to section 1288 of

this title, and any State plan developed pursuant to section 1313(e) of this title.

(3) For the purposes of this subsection the term "basin" includes, but is not limited to, rivers and their tributaries, streams, coastal waters, sounds, estuaries, bays, lakes, and portions thereof as well as the lands drained thereby.

§1252a. Reservoir projects, water storage; modification; storage for other than for water quality, opinion of Federal agency, committee resolutions of approval; provisions inapplicable to projects with certain prescribed water quality benefits in relation to total project benefits [CWA §102A]

In the case of any reservoir project authorized for construction by the Corps of Engineers, Bureau of Reclamation, or other Federal agency when the Administrator of the Environmental Protection Agency determines pursuant to section 1252(b) of this title that any storage in such project for regulation of streamflow for water quality is not needed, or is needed in a different amount, such project may be modified accordingly by the head of the appropriate agency, and any storage no longer required for water quality may be utilized for other authorized purposes of the project when, in the opinion of the head of such agency, such use is justified. Any such modification of a project where the benefits attributable to water quality are 15 per centum or more but not greater than 25 per centum of the total project benefits shall take effect only upon the adoption of resolutions approving such modification by the appropriate committees of the Senate and House of Representatives. The provisions of the section shall not apply to any project where the benefits attributable to water quality exceed 25 per centum of the total project benefits.

§1253. Interstate cooperation and uniform laws [CWA §103]

(a) The Administrator shall encourage cooperative activities by the States for the prevention, reduction, and elimination of pollution, encourage the enactment of improved and, so far as practicable, uniform State laws relating to the prevention, reduction, and elimination of pollution; and encourage compacts between States for the prevention and control of pollution.

(b) The consent of the Congress is hereby given to two or more States to negotiate and enter into agreements or compacts, not in conflict with any law or treaty of the United States, for (1) cooperative effort and mutual assistance for the prevention and control of pollution and the enforcement of their respective laws relating thereto, and (2) the establishment of such agencies, joint or otherwise, as they may deem desirable for making effective such agreements and compacts. No such agreement or compact shall be binding or obligatory upon any State a party thereto unless and until it has been approved by the Congress.

§1254. Research, investigations, training, and information

[CWA §104]

(a) Establishment of national programs; cooperation; investigations; water quality surveillance system; reports — The Administrator shall establish national programs for the prevention, reduction, and elimination of pollution and as part of such programs shall —

(1) in cooperation with other Federal, State, and local agencies, conduct and promote the coordination and acceleration of, research, investigations, experiments, training, demonstrations, surveys, and studies relating to the causes, effects, extent, prevention, reduction, and elimination of pollution;

(2) encourage, cooperate with, and render technical services to pollution control agencies and other appropriate public or private agencies, institutions, and organizations, and individuals, including the general public, in the conduct of activities referred to in paragraph (1) of this subsection;

(3) conduct, in cooperation with State water pollution control agencies and other interested agencies, organizations and persons, public investigations concerning the pollution of any navigable waters, and report on the results of such investigations;

(4) establish advisory committees composed of recognized experts in various aspects of pollution and representatives of the public to assist in the examination and evaluation of research progress and proposals and to avoid duplication of research;

(5) in cooperation with the States, and their political subdivisions, and other Federal agencies establish, equip, and maintain a water quality surveillance system for the purpose of monitoring the quality of the navigable waters and ground waters and the contiguous zone and the oceans and the Administrator shall, to the extent practicable, conduct such surveillance by utilizing the resources of the National Aeronautics and Space Administration, the National Oceanic and Atmospheric Administration, the United States Geological Survey, and the Coast Guard, and shall report on such quality in the report required under subsection (a) of section 1375 of this title; and

(6) initiate and promote the coordination and acceleration of research designed to develop the most effective practicable tools and techniques for measuring the social and economic costs and benefits of activities which are subject to regulation under this chapter; and shall transmit a report on the results of such research to the Congress not later than January 1, 1974.

(b) Authorized activities of Administrator — In carrying out the provisions of subsection (a) of this section the Administrator is authorized to —

(1) collect and make available, through publications and other appropriate means, the results of and other information, including appropriate recommen-dations by him in connection therewith, pertaining to such research and other activities referred to in paragraph (1) of subsection (a) of this section;

(2) cooperate with other Federal departments and agencies, State water pollution control agencies, interstate agencies, other public and private agencies, institutions, organizations, industries involved, and individuals, in the preparation and conduct of such research and other activities referred to in paragraph (1) of subsection (a) of this section;

(3) make grants to State water pollution control agencies, interstate agencies, other public or nonprofit private agencies, institutions, organizations, and individuals, for purposes stated in paragraph (1) of subsection (a) of this section;

(4) contract with public or private agencies, institutions, organizations, and individuals, without regard to section 3324(a) and (b) of Title 31 and section 5 of Title 41, referred to in paragraph (1) of subsection (a) of this section;

(5) establish and maintain research fellowships at public or nonprofit private educational institutions or research organizations;

(6) collect and disseminate, in cooperation with other Federal departments and agencies, and with other public or private agencies, institutions, and organizations having related responsibilities, basic data on chemical, physical, and biological effects of varying water quality and other information pertaining to pollution and the prevention, reduction, and elimination thereof; and

(7) develop effective and practical processes, methods, and prototype devices for the prevention, reduction, and elimination of pollution.

(8) make grants to nonprofit organizations —

(A) to provide technical assistance to rural, small, and tribal municipalities for the purpose of assisting, in consultation with the State in which the assistance is provided, such municipalities and tribal governments in the planning, developing, and acquisition of financing for eligible projects and activities described in section 1383(c) of this title;

(B) to provide technical assistance and training for rural, small, and tribal publicly owned treatment works and decentralized wastewater treatment systems to enable such treatment works and systems to protect water quality and achieve and maintain compliance with the requirements of this chapter; and

(C) to disseminate information to rural, small, and tribal municipalities and municipalities that meet the affordability criteria established under section 1383(i)(2) of this title by the State in which the municipality is located with respect to planning, design, construction, and operation of publicly owned treatment works and decentralized wastewater treatment systems.

(c) Research and studies on harmful effects of pollutants; cooperation with Secretary of Health and Human Services — In carrying out the provisions of subsection (a) of this section the Administrator shall conduct research on, and survey the results of other scientific studies on, the harmful effects on the health or welfare of persons caused by pollutants. In order to avoid duplication of effort, the Administrator shall, to the extent practicable, conduct such research in cooperation with and through the facilities of the Secretary of Health and Human Services.

(d) Sewage treatment; identification and measurement of effects of pollutants; augmented streamflow — In carrying out the provisions of this section the Administrator shall develop and demonstrate under varied conditions (including conducting such basic and applied research, studies, and experiments as may be necessary):

(1) Practicable means of treating municipal sewage, and other waterborne wastes to implement the requirements of section 1281 of this title;

(2) Improved methods and procedures to identify and measure the effects of pollutants, including those pollutants created by new technological developments; and

(3) Methods and procedures for evaluating the effects on water quality of augmented streamflows to control pollution not susceptible to other means of prevention, reduction, or elimination.

(e) Field laboratory and research facilities — The Administrator shall establish, equip, and maintain field laboratory and research facilities, including, but not limited to, one to be located in the northeastern area of the United States, one in the Middle Atlantic area, one in the southeastern area, one in the midwestern area, one in the southwestern area, one in the Pacific Northwest, and one in the State of Alaska, for the conduct of research, investigations, experiments, field demonstrations and studies, and training relating to the prevention, reduction and elimination of pollution. Insofar as practicable, each such facility shall be located near institutions of higher learning in which graduate training in such research might be carried out. In conjunction with the development of criteria under section 1343 of this title, the Administrator shall construct the facilities authorized for the National Marine Water Quality Laboratory established under this subsection.

(f) Great Lakes water quality research — The Administrator shall conduct research and technical development work, and make studies, with respect to the quality of the waters of the Great Lakes, including an analysis of the present and projected future water quality of the Great Lakes under varying conditions of waste treatment and disposal, an evaluation of the water quality needs of those to be served by such waters, an evaluation of municipal, industrial, and vessel waste treatment and disposal practices with respect to such waters, and a study of alternate means of solving pollution problems (including additional waste treatment measures) with respect to such waters.

(g) Treatment works pilot training programs; employment needs forecasting; training projects and grants; research fellowships; technical training; report to the President and transmittal to Congress

(1) For the purpose of providing an adequate supply of trained personnel to operate and maintain existing and future treatment works and related activities, and for the purpose of enhancing substantially the proficiency of those engaged in such activities, the Administrator shall finance pilot programs, in cooperation with State and interstate agencies, municipalities, educational institutions, and other organizations and individuals, of manpower development and training and retraining of persons in, on entering into, the field of operation and maintenance of treatment works and related activities. Such program and any funds expended for such a program shall supplement, not supplant, other manpower and training programs and funds available for the purposes of this paragraph. The Administrator is authorized, under such terms and conditions as he deems appropriate, to enter into agreements with one or more States, acting jointly or severally, or with other public or private agencies or institutions for the development and implementation of such a program.

(2) The Administrator is authorized to enter into agreements with public and private agencies and institutions, and individuals to develop and maintain an effective system for forecasting the supply of, and demand for, various professional and other occupational categories needed for the prevention, reduction, and elimination of pollution in each region, State, or area of the United States and, from time to time, to publish the results of such forecasts.

(3) In furtherance of the purposes of this chapter, the Administrator is authorized to —

(A) make grants to public or private agencies and institutions and to individuals for training projects, and provide for the conduct of training by contract with public or private agencies and institutions and with individuals without regard to section 3324(a) and (b) of Title 31 and section 5 of Title 41;

(B) establish and maintain research fellowships in the Environmental Protection Agency with such stipends and allowances, including traveling and subsistence expenses, as he may deem necessary to procure the assistance of the most promising research fellows; and

(C) provide, in addition to the program established under paragraph (1) of this subsection, training in technical matters relating to the causes, prevention, reduction, and elimination of pollution for personnel of public agencies and other persons with suitable qualifications.

(4) The Administrator shall submit, through the President, a report to the Congress not later than December 31, 1973, summarizing the actions taken under this subsection and the effectiveness of such actions, and setting forth the number of persons trained, the occupational categories for which training was provided, the effectiveness of other Federal, State, and local training programs in this field, together with estimates of future needs, recommendations on improving training programs, and such other information and recommendations, including legislative recommendations, as he deems appropriate.

(h) **Lake pollution** — The Administrator is authorized to enter into contracts with, or make grants to, public or private agencies and organizations and individuals for (A) the purpose of developing and demonstrating new or improved methods for the prevention, removal, reduction, and elimination of pollution in lakes, including the undesirable effects of nutrients and vegetation, and (B) the construction of publicly owned research facilities for such purpose.

(i) **Oil pollution control studies** — The Administrator, in cooperation with the Secretary of the Department in which the Coast Guard is operating, shall —

(1) engage in such research, studies, experiments, and demonstrations as he deems appropriate, relative to the removal of oil from any waters and to the prevention, control, and elimination of oil and hazardous substances pollution;

(2) publish from time to time the results of such activities; and

(3) from time to time, develop and publish in the Federal Register specifications and other technical information on the various chemical compounds used in the control of oil and hazardous substances spills.

In carrying out this subsection, the Administrator may enter into contracts with, or make grants to, public or private agencies and organizations and individuals.

(j) **Solid waste disposal equipment for vessels** — The Secretary of the department in which the Coast Guard is operating shall engage in such research, studies, experiments, and demonstrations as he deems appropriate relative to equipment which is to be installed on board a vessel and is designed to receive, retain, treat, or discharge human body wastes and the wastes from toilets and other receptacles intended to receive or retain body wastes with particular emphasis on equipment to be installed on small recreational vessels. The Secretary of the department in which the Coast Guard is operating shall report to Congress the results of such research, studies, experiments, and demonstrations prior to the effective date of any regulations established under section 1322 of this title. In carrying out this subsection the Secretary of the department in which the Coast Guard is operating may enter into contracts with, or make grants to, public or private organizations and individuals.

(k) **Land acquisition** — In carrying out the provisions of this section relating to the conduct by the Administrator of demonstration projects and the development of field laboratories and research facilities, the Administrator may acquire land and interests therein by purchase, with appropriated or donated funds, by donation, or by exchange for acquired or public lands under his jurisdiction which he classifies as suitable for disposition. The values of the properties so exchanged either shall be approximately equal, or if they are not approximately equal, the values shall be equalized by the payment of cash to the grantor or to the Administrator as the circumstances require.

(*l*) **Collection and dissemination of scientific knowledge on effects and control of pesticides in water**

(1) The Administrator shall, after consultation with appropriate local, State, and Federal agencies, public and private organizations, and interested individuals, as soon as practicable but not later than January 1, 1973, develop and issue to the States for the purpose of carrying out this chapter the latest scientific knowledge available in indicating the kind and extent of effects on health and welfare which may be expected from the presence of pesticides in the water in varying quantities. He shall revise and add to such information whenever necessary to reflect developing scientific knowledge.

(2) The President shall, in consultation with appropriate local, State, and Federal agencies, public and private organizations, and interested individuals, conduct studies and investigations of methods to control the release of pesticides into the environment which study shall include examination of the persistency of pesticides in the water environment and alternatives thereto. The President shall submit reports, from time to time, on such investigations to Congress together with his recommendations for any necessary legislation.

(m) **Waste oil disposal study**

(1) The Administrator shall, in an effort to prevent degradation of the environment from the disposal of waste oil, conduct a study of (A) the generation of used engine, machine, cooling, and similar waste oil, including quantities generated, the nature and quality of such oil, present collecting methods and disposal practices, and alternate uses of such oil; (B) the long-term, chronic biological effects of the disposal of such waste oil; and (C) the potential market for such oils, including the economic and legal factors relating to the sale of products made from such oils, the

level of subsidy, if any, needed to encourage the purchase by public and private nonprofit agencies of products from such oil, and the practicability of Federal procurement, on a priority basis, of products made from such oil. In conducting such study, the Administrator shall consult with affected industries and other persons.

(2) The Administrator shall report the preliminary results of such study to Congress within six months after October 18, 1972, and shall submit a final report to Congress within 18 months after such date.

(n) Comprehensive studies of effects of pollution on estuaries and estuarine zones

(1) The Administrator shall, in cooperation with the Secretary of the Army, the Secretary of Agriculture, the Water Resources Council, and with other appropriate Federal, State, interstate, or local public bodies and private organizations, institutions, and individuals, conduct and promote, and encourage contributions to, continuing comprehensive studies of the effects of pollution, including sedimentation, in the estuaries and estuarine zones of the United States on fish and wildlife, on sport and commercial fishing, on recreation, on water supply and water power, and on other beneficial purposes. Such studies shall also consider the effect of demographic trends, the exploitation of mineral resources and fossil fuels, land and industrial development, navigation, flood and erosion control, and other uses of estuaries and estuarine zones upon the pollution of the waters therein.

(2) In conducting such studies, the Administrator shall assemble, coordinate, and organize all existing pertinent information on the Nation's estuaries and estuarine zones; carry out a program of investigations and surveys to supplement existing information in representative estuaries and estuarine zones; and identify the problems and areas where further research and study are required.

(3) The Administrator shall submit to Congress, from time to time, reports of the studies authorized by this subsection but at least one such report during any six-year period. Copies of each such report shall be made available to all interested parties, public and private.

(4) For the purpose of this subsection, the term "estuarine zones" means an environmental system consisting of an estuary and those transitional areas which are consistently influenced or affected by water from an estuary such as, but not limited to, salt marshes, coastal and intertidal areas, bays, harbors, lagoons, inshore waters, and channels, and the term "estuary" means all or part of the mouth of a river or stream or other body of water having unimpaired natural connection with open sea and within which the sea water is measurably diluted with fresh water derived from land drainage.

(o) Methods of reducing total flow of sewage and unnecessary water consumption; reports

(1) The Administrator shall conduct research and investigations on devices, systems, incentives, pricing policy, and other methods of reducing the total flow of sewage, including, but not limited to, unnecessary water consumption in order to reduce the requirements for, and the costs of, sewage and waste treatment services. Such research and investigations shall be directed to develop devices, systems, policies, and methods capable of achieving the maximum reduction of unnecessary water consumption.

(2) The Administrator shall report the preliminary results of such studies and investigations to the Congress within one year after October 18, 1972, and annually thereafter in the report required under subsection (a) of section 1375 of this title. Such report shall include recommendations for any legislation that may be required to provide for the adoption and use of devices, systems, policies, or other methods of reducing water consumption and reducing the total flow of sewage. Such report shall include an estimate of the benefits to be derived from adoption and use of such devices, systems, policies, or other methods and also shall reflect estimates of any increase in private, public, or other cost that would be occasioned thereby.

(p) Agricultural pollution — In carrying out the provisions of subsection (a) of this section the Administrator shall, in cooperation with the Secretary of Agriculture, other Federal agencies, and the States, carry out a comprehensive study and research program to determine new and improved methods and the better application of existing methods of preventing, reducing, and eliminating pollution from agriculture, including the legal, economic, and other implications of the use of such methods.

(q) Sewage in rural areas; national clearinghouse for alternative treatment information; clearinghouse on small flows

(1) The Administrator shall conduct a comprehensive program of research and investigation and pilot project implementation into new and improved methods of preventing, reducing, storing, collecting, treating, or otherwise eliminating pollution from sewage in rural and other areas where collection of sewage in conventional, communitywide sewage collection systems is impractical, uneconomical, or otherwise infeasible, or where soil conditions or other factors preclude the use of septic tank and drainage field systems.

(2) The Administrator shall conduct a comprehensive program of research and investigation and pilot project implementation into new and

improved methods for the collection and treatment of sewage and other liquid wastes combined with the treatment and disposal of solid wastes.

(3) The Administrator shall establish, either within the Environmental Protection Agency, or through contract with an appropriate public or private non-profit organization, a national clearinghouse which shall (A) receive reports and information resulting from research, demonstrations, and other projects funded under this chapter related to paragraph (1) of this subsection and to subsection (e)(2) of section 1255 of this title; (B) coordinate and disseminate such reports and information for use by Federal and State agencies, municipalities, institutions, and persons in developing new and improved methods pursuant to this subsection; and (C) provide for the collection and dissemination of reports and information relevant to this subsection from other Federal and State agencies, institutions, universities, and persons.

(4) Small flows clearinghouse — Notwithstanding section 1285(d) of this title, from amounts that are set aside for a fiscal year under section 1285(i) of this title and are not obligated by the end of the 24-month period of availability for such amounts under section 1285(d) of this title, the Administrator shall make available $1,000,000 or such unobligated amount, whichever is less, to support a national clearinghouse within the Environmental Protection Agency to collect and disseminate information on small flows of sewage and innovative or alternative wastewater treatment processes and techniques, consistent with paragraph (3). This paragraph shall apply with respect to amounts set aside under section 1285(i) of this title for which the 24-month period of availability referred to in the preceding sentence ends on or after September 30, 1986.

(r) **Research grants to colleges and universities** — The Administrator is authorized to make grants to colleges and universities to conduct basic research into the structure and function of freshwater aquatic ecosystems, and to improve understanding of the ecological characteristics necessary to the maintenance of the chemical, physical, and biological integrity of freshwater aquatic ecosystems.

(s) **River Study Centers** — The Administrator is authorized to make grants to one or more institutions of higher education (regionally located and to be designated as "River Study Centers") for the purpose of conducting and reporting on interdisciplinary studies on the nature of river systems, including hydrology, biology, ecology, economics, the relationship between river uses and land uses, and the effects of development within river basins on river systems and on the value of water resources and water related activities. No such grant in any fiscal year shall exceed $1,000,000.

(t) **Thermal discharges** — The Administrator shall, in cooperation with State and Federal agencies and public and private organizations, conduct continuing comprehensive studies of the effects and methods of control of thermal discharges. In evaluating alternative methods of control the studies shall consider (1) such data as are available on the latest available technology, economic feasibility including cost-effectiveness analysis, and (2) the total impact on the environment, considering not only water quality but also air quality, land use, and effective utilization and conservation of freshwater and other natural resources. Such studies shall consider methods of minimizing adverse effects and maximizing beneficial effects of thermal discharges. The results of these studies shall be reported by the Administrator as soon as practicable, but not later than 270 days after October 18, 1972, and shall be made available to the public and the States, and considered as they become available by the Administrator in carrying out section 1326 of this title and by the States in proposing thermal water quality standards.

(u) **Authorization of appropriations** — There is authorized to be appropriated (1) not to exceed $100,000,000 per fiscal year for the fiscal year ending June 30, 1973, the fiscal year ending June 30, 1974, and the fiscal year ending June 30, 1975, not to exceed $14,039,000 for the fiscal year ending September 30, 1980, not to exceed $20,697,000 for the fiscal year ending September 30, 1981, not to exceed $22,770,000 for the fiscal year ending September 30, 1982, such sums as may be necessary for fiscal years 1983 through 1985, and not to exceed $22,770,000 per fiscal year for each of the fiscal years 1986 through 1990, for carrying out the provisions of this section, other than subsections (g)(1) and (2), (p), (r), and (t) of this section, except that such authorizations are not for any research, development, or demonstration activity pursuant to such provisions; (2) not to exceed $7,500,000 for fiscal years 1973, 1974, and 1975, $2,000,000 for fiscal year 1977, $3,000,000 for fiscal year 1978, $3,000,000 for fiscal year 1979, $3,000,000 for fiscal year 1980, $3,000,000 for fiscal year 1981, $3,000,000 for fiscal year 1982, such sums as may be necessary for fiscal years 1983 through 1985, and $3,000,000 per fiscal year for each of the fiscal years 1986 through 1990, for carrying out the provisions of subsection (g)(1) of this section; (3) not to exceed $2,500,000 for fiscal years 1973, 1974, and 1975, $1,000,000 for fiscal year 1977, $1,500,000 for fiscal year 1978, $1,500,000 for fiscal year 1979, $1,500,000 for fiscal year 1980, $1,500,000 for fiscal year 1981, $1,500,000 for fiscal year 1982, such sums as may be necessary for fiscal years 1983 through 1985, and $1,500,000 per fiscal year for each of the fiscal years 1986 through 1990, for carrying out the provisions of subsection (g)(2) of this section; (4) not to exceed $10,000,000 for each of the fiscal years ending June 30, 1973, June 30, 1974, and June 30, 1975, for carrying out the provisions of subsection (p) of this section; (5) not to exceed $15,000,000 per fiscal year for the fiscal years ending June 30, 1973, June 30, 1974, and June 30, 1975, for carrying out the provisions of subsection

(r) of this section; (6) not to exceed $10,000,000 per fiscal year for the fiscal years ending June 30, 1973, June 30, 1974, and June 30, 1975, for carrying out the provisions of subsection (t); and (7) not to exceed $25,000,000 for each of fiscal years 2019 through 2023 for carrying out subsections (b)(3), (b)(8), and (g).

(v) Studies concerning pathogen indicators in coastal recreation waters — Not later than 18 months after October 10, 2000, after consultation and in cooperation with appropriate Federal, State, tribal, and local officials (including local health officials), the Administrator shall initiate, and, not later than 3 years after October 10, 2000, shall complete, in cooperation with the heads of other Federal agencies, studies to provide additional information for use in developing —

(1) an assessment of potential human health risks resulting from exposure to pathogens in coastal recreation waters, including nongastrointestinal effects;

(2) appropriate and effective indicators for improving detection in a timely manner in coastal recreation waters of the presence of pathogens that are harmful to human health;

(3) appropriate, accurate, expeditious, and cost-effective methods (including predictive models) for detecting in a timely manner in coastal recreation waters the presence of pathogens that are harmful to human health; and

(4) guidance for State application of the criteria for pathogens and pathogen indicators to be published under section 1314(a)(9) of this title to account for the diversity of geographic and aquatic conditions.

(w) Nonprofit organization — For purposes of subsection (b)(8), the term "nonprofit organization" means a nonprofit organization that the Administrator determines, after consultation with the States regarding what small publicly owned treatments works in the State find to be most beneficial and effective, is qualified and experienced in providing on-site training and technical assistance to small publicly owned treatment works.

§1254a. Research on effects of pollutants

In carrying out the provisions of section 1254(a) of this title, the Administrator shall conduct research on the harmful effects on the health and welfare of persons caused by pollutants in water, in conjunction with the United States Fish and Wildlife Service, the National Oceanic and Atmospheric Administration, and other Federal, State, and interstate agencies carrying on such research. Such research shall include, and shall place special emphasis on, the effect that bioaccumulation of these pollutants in aquatic species has upon reducing the value of aquatic commercial and sport industries. Such research shall further study methods to reduce and remove these pollutants from the relevant affected aquatic species so as to restore and enhance these valuable resources.

§1255. Grants for research and development [CWA §105]

(a) Demonstration projects covering storm waters, advanced waste treatment and water purification methods, and joint treatment systems for municipal and industrial wastes — The Administrator is authorized to conduct in the Environmental Protection Agency, and to make grants to any State, municipality, or intermunicipal or interstate agency for the purpose of assisting in the development of —

(1) any project which will demonstrate a new or improved method of preventing, reducing, and eliminating the discharge into any waters of pollutants from sewers which carry storm water or both storm water and pollutants; or

(2) any project which will demonstrate advanced waste treatment and water purification methods (including the temporary use of new or improved chemical additives which provide substantial immediate improvements to existing treatment processes), or new or improved methods of joint treatment systems for municipal and industrial wastes;

and to include in such grants such amounts as are necessary for the purpose of reports, plans, and specifications in connection therewith.

(b) Demonstration projects for advanced treatment and environmental enhancement techniques to control pollution in river basins — The Administrator is authorized to make grants to any State or States or interstate agency to demonstrate, in river basins or portions thereof, advanced treatment and environmental enhancement techniques to control pollution from all sources, within such basins or portions thereof, including nonpoint sources, together with in stream water quality improvement techniques.

(c) Research and demonstration projects for prevention of water pollution by industry — In order to carry out the purposes of section 1311 of this title, the Administrator is authorized to (1) conduct in the Environmental Protection Agency, (2) make grants to persons, and (3) enter into contracts with persons, for research and demonstration projects for prevention of pollution of any waters by industry including, but not limited to, the prevention, reduction, and elimination of the discharge of pollutants. No grant shall be made for any project under this subsection unless the Administrator determines that such project will develop or demonstrate a new or improved method of treating industrial wastes or otherwise prevent pollution by industry, which method shall have industrywide application.

(d) Accelerated and priority development of waste management and waste treatment methods and identification and measurement methods — In carrying out the provisions of this section, the Administrator shall conduct, on a priority basis, an accelerated effort to develop, refine, and achieve practical application of:

(1) waste management methods applicable to point and nonpoint sources of pollutants to eliminate the discharge of pollutants, including, but not limited to, elimination of runoff of pollutants and the effects of pollutants from inplace or accumulated sources;

(2) advanced waste treatment methods applicable to point and nonpoint sources, including inplace or accumulated sources of pollutants, and methods for reclaiming and recycling water and confining pollutants so they will not migrate to cause water or other environmental pollution; and

(3) improved methods and procedures to identify and measure the effects of pollutants on the chemical, physical, and biological integrity of water, including those pollutants created by new technological developments.

(e) Research and demonstration projects covering agricultural pollution and pollution from sewage in rural areas; dissemination of information

(1) The Administrator is authorized to (A) make, in consultation with the Secretary of Agriculture, grants to persons for research and demonstration projects with respect to new and improved methods of preventing, reducing, and eliminating pollution from agriculture, and (B) disseminate, in cooper- ation with the Secretary of Agriculture, such information obtained under this subsection, section 1254(p) of this title, and section 1314 of this title as will encourage and enable the adoption of such methods in the agricultural industry.

(2) The Administrator is authorized, (A) in consultation with other interested Federal agencies, to make grants for demonstration projects with respect to new and improved methods of preventing, reducing, storing, collecting, treating, or otherwise eliminating pollution from sewage in rural and other areas where collection of sewage in conventional, community-wide sewage collection systems is impractical, uneconomical, or otherwise infeasible, or where soil conditions or other factors preclude the use of septic tank and drainage field systems, and (B) in cooperation with other interested Federal and State agencies, to disseminate such information obtained under this subsection as will encourage and enable the adoption of new and improved methods developed pursuant to this subsection.

(f) Limitations — Federal grants under subsection (a) of this section shall be subject to the following limitations:

(1) No grant shall be made for any project unless such project shall have been approved by the appropriate State water pollution control agency or agencies and by the Administrator;

(2) No grant shall be made for any project in an amount exceeding 75 per centum of cost thereof as determined by the Administrator; and

(3) No grant shall be made for any project unless the Administrator determines that such project will serve as a useful demonstration for the purpose set forth in clause (1) or (2) of subsection (a) of this section.

(g) Maximum grants — Federal grants under subsections (c) and (d) of this section shall not exceed 75 per centum of the cost of the project.

(h) Authorization of appropriations — For the purpose of this section there is authorized to be appropriated $75,000,000 per fiscal year for the fiscal year ending June 30, 1973, the fiscal year ending June 30, 1974, and the fiscal year ending June 30, 1975, and from such appropriations at least 10 per centum of the funds actually appropriated in each fiscal year shall be available only for the purposes of subsection (e) of this section.

(i) Assistance for research and demonstration projects — The Administrator is authorized to make grants to a municipality to assist in the costs of operating and maintaining a project which received a grant under this section, section 1254 of this title, or section 1263 of this title prior to December 27, 1977, so as to reduce the operation and maintenance costs borne by the recipients of services from such project to costs comparable to those for projects assisted under subchapter II of this chapter.

(j) Assistance for recycle, reuse, and land treatment projects — The Administrator is authorized to make a grant to any grantee who received an increased grant pursuant to section 1282(a)(2) of this title. Such grant may pay up to 100 per centum of the costs of technical evaluation of the operation of the treatment works, costs of training of persons (other than employees of the grantee), and costs of disseminating technical information on the operation of the treatment works.

§1256. Grants for pollution control programs [CWA §106]

(a) Authorization of appropriations for State and interstate programs — There are hereby authorized to be appropriated the following sums, to remain available until expended, to carry out the purpose of this section —

(1) $60,000,000 for the fiscal year ending June 30, 1973; and

(2) $75,000,000 for the fiscal year ending June 30, 1974, and the fiscal year ending June 30, 1975, $100,000,000 per fiscal year for the fiscal years 1977, 1978, 1979, and 1980, $75,000,000 per fiscal year for the fiscal years 1981 and 1982, such sums as may be necessary for fiscal years 1983 through 1985, and $75,000,000 per fiscal year for each of the fiscal years 1986 through 1990;

for grants to States and to interstate agencies to assist

them in administering programs for the prevention, reduction, and elimination of pollution, including enforcement directly or through appropriate State law enforcement officers or agencies.

(b) Allotments — From the sums appropriated in any fiscal year, the Administrator shall make allotments to the several States and interstate agencies in accordance with regulations promulgated by him on the basis of the extent of the pollution problem in the respective States.

(c) Maximum annual payments — The Administrator is authorized to pay to each State and interstate agency each fiscal year either —

(1) the allotment of such State or agency for such fiscal year under subsection (b) of this section, or

(2) the reasonable costs as determined by the Administrator of developing and carrying out a pollution program by such State or agency during such fiscal year,

which ever amount is the lesser.

(d) Limitations — No grant shall be made under this section to any State or interstate agency for any fiscal year when the expenditure of non-Federal funds by such State or interstate agency during such fiscal year for the recurrent expenses of carrying out its pollution control program are less than the expenditure by such State or interstate agency of non-Federal funds for such recurrent program expenses during the fiscal year ending June 30, 1971.

(e) Grants prohibited to States not establishing water quality monitoring procedures or adequate emergency and contingency plans — Beginning in fiscal year 1974 the Administrator shall not make any grant under this section to any State which has not provided or is not carrying out as a part of its program —

(1) the establishment and operation of appropriate devices, methods, systems, and procedures necessary to monitor, and to compile and analyze data on (including classification according to eutrophic condition), the quality of navigable waters and to the extent practicable, ground waters including biological monitoring; and provision for annually updating such data and including it in the report required under section 1315 of this title;

(2) authority comparable to that in section 1364 of this title and adequate contingency plans to implement such authority.

(f) Conditions — Grants shall be made under this section on condition that —

(1) Such State (or interstate agency) files with the Administrator within one hundred and twenty days after October 18, 1972:

(A) a summary report of the current status of the State pollution control program, including the criteria used by the State in determining priority of treatment works; and

(B) such additional information, data, and reports as the Administrator may require.

(2) No federally assumed enforcement as defined in section 1319(a)(2) of this title is in effect with respect to such State or interstate agency.

(3) Such State (or interstate agency) submits within one hundred and twenty days after October 18, 1972, and before October 1 of each year thereafter for the Administrator's approval of its program for the prevention, reduction, and elimination of pollution in accordance with purposes and provisions of this chapter in such form and content as the Administrator may prescribe.

(g) Reallotment of unpaid allotments — Any sums allotted under subsection (b) of this section in any fiscal year which are not paid shall be reallotted by the Administrator in accordance with regulations promulgated by him.

§1257. Mine water pollution control demonstrations
[CWA §107]

(a) Comprehensive approaches to elimination or control of mine water pollution — The Administrator in cooperation with the Appalachian Regional Commission and other Federal agencies is authorized to conduct, to make grants for, or to contract for, projects to demonstrate comprehensive approaches to the elimination or control of acid or other mine water pollution resulting from active or abandoned mining operations and other environmental pollution affecting water quality within all or part of a watershed or river basin, including siltation from surface mining. Such projects shall demonstrate the engineering and economic feasibility and practicality of various abatement techniques which will contribute substantially to effective and practical methods of acid or other mine water pollution elimination or control, and other pollution affecting water quality, including techniques that demonstrate the engineering and economic feasibility and practicality of using sewage sludge materials and other municipal wastes to diminish or prevent pollution affecting water quality from acid, sedimentation, or other pollutants and in such projects to restore affected lands to usefulness for forestry, agriculture, recreation, or other beneficial purposes.

(b) Consistency of projects with objectives of Appalachian Regional Development Act of 1965 — Prior to undertaking any demonstration project under this section in the Appalachian region (as defined in section 14102 of Title 40), the Appalachian Regional Commission shall determine that such demonstration project is consistent with the objectives of subtitle IV of Title 40.

(c) Watershed selection — The Administrator, in selecting watersheds for the purposes of this section, shall be satisfied that the project area will not be affected adversely by the influx of acid or other mine water pollution from nearby sources.

(d) Conditions upon Federal participation — Federal participation in such projects shall be subject to the conditions —

　　(1) that the State shall acquire any land or interests therein necessary for such project; and

　　(2) that the State shall provide legal and practical protection to the project area to insure against any activities which will cause future acid or other mine water pollution.

(e) Authorization of appropriations — There is authorized to be appropriated $30,000,000 to carry out the provisions of this section, which sum shall be available until expended.

§1257a. State demonstration programs for cleanup of abandoned mines for use as waste disposal sites; authorization of appropriations — The Administrator of the Environmental Protection Agency is authorized to make grants to States to undertake a demonstration program for the cleanup of State-owned abandoned mines which can be used as hazardous waste disposal sites. The State shall pay 10 per centum of project costs. At a minimum, the Administrator shall undertake projects under such program in the States of Ohio, Illinois, and West Virginia. There are authorized to be appropriated $10,000,000 per fiscal year for each of the fiscal years ending September 30, 1982, September 30, 1983, and September 30, 1984, to carry out this section. Such projects shall be undertaken in accordance with all applicable laws and regulations.

§1258. Pollution control in the Great Lakes
[CWA §108]

(a) Demonstration projects — The Administrator, in cooperation with other Federal departments, agencies, and instrumentalities is authorized to enter into agreements with any State, political subdivision, interstate agency, or other public agency, or combination thereof, to carry out one or more projects to demonstrate new methods and techniques and to develop preliminary plans for the elimination or control of pollution, within all or any part of the watersheds of the Great Lakes. Such projects shall demonstrate the engineering and economic feasibility and practicality of removal of pollutants and prevention of any polluting matter from entering into the Great Lakes in the future and other reduction and remedial techniques which will contribute substantially to effective and practical methods of pollution prevention, reduction, or elimination.

(b) Conditions of Federal participation — Federal participation in such projects shall be subject to the condition that the State, political subdivision, interstate agency, or other public agency, or combination thereof, shall pay not less than 25 per centum of the actual project costs, which payment may be in any form, including, but not limited to, land or interests therein that is needed for the project, and

personal property or services the value of which shall be determined by the Administrator.

(c) Authorization of appropriations — There is authorized to be appropriated $20,000,000 to carry out the provisions of subsections (a) and (b) of this section, which sum shall be available until expended.

(d) Lake Erie demonstration program

　　(1) In recognition of the serious conditions which exist in Lake Erie, the Secretary of the Army, acting through the Chief of Engineers, is directed to design and develop a demonstration waste water management program for the rehabilitation and environmental repair of Lake Erie. Prior to the initiation of detailed engineering and design, the program, along with the specific recommendations of the Chief of Engineers, and recommendations for its financing, shall be submitted to the Congress for statutory approval. This authority is in addition to, and not in lieu of, other waste water studies aimed at eliminating pollution emanating from select sources around Lake Erie.

　　(2) This program is to be developed in cooperation with the Environmental Protection Agency, other interested departments, agencies, and instrumentalities of the Federal Government, and the States and their political subdivisions. This program shall set forth alternative systems for managing waste water on a regional basis and shall provide local and State governments with a range of choice as to the type of system to be used for the treatment of waste water. These alternative systems shall include both advanced waste treatment technology and land disposal systems including aerated treatment-spray irrigation technology and will also include provisions for the disposal of solid wastes, including sludge. Such program should include measures to control point sources of pollution, area sources of pollution, including acid-mine drainage, urban runoff and rural runoff, and in place sources of pollution, including bottom loads, sludge banks, and polluted harbor dredgings.

(e) Authorization of appropriations for Lake Erie demonstration program — There is authorized to be appropriated $5,000,000 to carry out the provisions of subsection (d) of this section, which sum shall be available until expended.

§1259. Training grants and contracts
[CWA §109]

(a) The Administrator is authorized to make grants to or contracts with institutions of higher education, or combinations of such institutions, to assist them in planning, developing, strengthening, improving, or carrying out programs or projects for the preparation of undergraduate students to enter an occupation which involves the design, operation, and maintenance of treatment works, and other facilities whose purpose is water quality control. Such grants or contracts may include payment of all or part of the cost of programs or projects such as —

(A) planning for the development or expansion of programs or projects for training persons in the operation and maintenance of treatment works;

(B) training and retraining of faculty members;

(C) conduct of short-term or regular session institutes for study by persons engaged in, or preparing to engage in, the preparation of students preparing to enter an occupation involving the operation and maintenance of treatment works;

(D) carrying out innovative and experimental programs of cooperative education involving alternate periods of full-time or part-time academic study at the institution and periods of full-time or part-time employment involving the operation and maintenance of treatment works; and

(E) research into, and development of, methods of training students or faculty, including the preparation of teaching materials and the planning of curriculum.

(b)(1) The Administrator may pay 100 per centum of any additional cost of construction of treatment works required for a facility to train and upgrade waste treatment works operation and maintenance personnel and for the costs of other State treatment works operator training programs, including mobile training units, classroom rental, specialized instructors, and instructional material.

(2) The Administrator shall make no more than one grant for such additional construction in any State (to serve a group of States, where, in his judgment, efficient training programs require multi-State programs), and shall make such grant after consultation with and approval by the State or States on the basis of (A) the suitability of such facility for training operation and maintenance personnel for treatment works throughout such State or States; and (B) a commitment by the State agency or agencies to carry out at such facility a program of training approved by the Administrator. In any case where a grant is made to serve two or more States, the Administrator is authorized to make an additional grant for a supplemental facility in each such State.

(3) The Administrator may make such grant out of the sums allocated to a State under section 1285 of this title, except that in no event shall the Federal cost of any such training facilities exceed $500,000.

(4) The Administrator may exempt a grant under this section from any requirement under section 1284(a)(3) of this title. Any grantee who received a grant under this section prior to enactment of the Clean Water Act of 1977 shall be eligible to have its grant increased by funds made available under such Act.

§1260. Applications; allocation
[CWA §110]

(1) A grant or contract authorized by section 1259 of this title may be made only upon application to the Administrator at such time or times and containing such information as he may prescribe, except that no such application shall be approved unless it —

(A) sets forth programs, activities, research, or development for which a grant is authorized under section 1259 of this title and describes the relation to any program set forth by the applicant in an application, if any, submitted pursuant to section 1261 of this title;

(B) provides such fiscal control and fund accounting procedures as may be necessary to assure proper disbursement of and accounting for Federal funds paid to the applicant under this section; and

(C) provides for making such reports, in such form and containing such information, as the Administrator may require to carry out his functions under this section, and for keeping such records and for affording such access thereto as the Administrator may find necessary to assure the correctness and verification of such reports.

(2) The Administrator shall allocate grants or contracts under section 1259 of this title in such manner as will most nearly provide an equitable distribution of the grants or contracts throughout the United States among institutions of higher education which show promise of being able to use funds effectively for the purpose of this section.

(3)(A) Payments under this section may be used in accordance with regulations of the Administrator, and subject to the terms and conditions set forth in an application approved under paragraph (1), to pay part of the compensation of students employed in connection with the operation and maintenance of treatment works, other than as an employee in connection with the operation and maintenance of treatment works or as an employee in any branch of the Government of the United States, as part of a program for which a grant has been approved pursuant to this section.

(B) Departments and agencies of the United States are encouraged, to the extent consistent with efficient administration, to enter into arrangements with institutions of higher education for the full-time, part-time, or temporary employment, whether in the competitive or excepted service, of students enrolled in programs set forth in applications approved under paragraph (1).

§1261. Scholarships
[CWA §111]

(1) The Administrator is authorized to award scholarships in accordance with the provisions of

this section for undergraduate study by persons who plan to enter an occupation involving the operation and maintenance of treatment works. Such scholarships shall be awarded for such periods as the Administrator may determine but not to exceed four academic years.

(2) The Administrator shall allocate scholarships under this section among institutions of higher education with programs approved under the provisions of this section for the use of individuals accepted into such programs in such manner and according to such plan as will insofar as practicable —

(A) provide an equitable distribution of such scholarships throughout the United States; and

(B) attract recent graduates of secondary schools to enter an occupation involving the operation and maintenance of treatment works.

(3) The Administrator shall approve a program of any institution of higher education for the purposes of this section only upon application by the institution and only upon his finding —

(A) that such program has a principal objective the education and training of persons in the operation and maintenance of treatment works;

(B) that such program is in effect and of high quality, or can be readily put into effect and may reasonably be expected to be of high quality;

(C) that the application describes the relation of such program to any program, activity, research, or development set forth by the applicant in an application, if any, submitted pursuant to section 1260 of this title; and

(D) that the application contains satisfactory assurances that (i) the institution will recommend to the Administrator for the award of scholarships under this section, for study in such program, only persons who have demonstrated to the satisfaction of the institution a serious intent, upon completing the program, to enter an occupation involving the operation and maintenance of treatment works, and (ii) the institution will make reasonable continuing efforts to encourage recipients of scholarships under this section, enrolled in such program, to enter occupations involving the operation and maintenance of treatment works upon completing the program.

(4)(A) The Administrator shall pay to persons awarded scholarships under this section such stipends (including such allowances for subsistence and other expenses for such persons and their dependents) as he may determine to be consistent with prevailing practices under comparable federally supported programs.

(B) The Administrator shall (in addition to the stipends paid to persons under paragraph (1)) pay to the institution of higher education at which such person is pursuing his course of study such amount as he may determine to be consistent with prevailing practices under comparable federally supported programs.

(5) A person awarded a scholarship under the provisions of this section shall continue to receive the payments provided in this section only during such periods as the Administrator finds that he is maintaining satisfactory proficiency and devoting full time to study or research in the field in which such scholarship was awarded in an institution of higher education, and is not engaging in gainful employment other than employment approved by the Administrator by or pursuant to regulation.

(6) The Administrator shall by regulation provide that any person awarded a scholarship under this section shall agree in writing to enter and remain in an occupation involving the design, operation, or maintenance of treatment works for such period after completion of his course of studies as the Administrator determines appropriate.

§1262. Definitions and authorizations [CWA §112]

(a) As used in sections 1259 through 1262 of this title —

(1) The term "institution of higher education" means an educational institution described in the first sentence of section 1001 of Title 20 (other than an institution of any agency of the United States) which is accredited by a nationally recognized accrediting agency or association approved by the Administrator for this purpose. For purposes of this subsection, the Administrator shall publish a list of nationally recognized accrediting agencies or associations which he determines to be reliable authority as to the quality of training offered.

(2) The term "academic year" means an academic year or its equivalent, as determined by the Administrator.

(b) The Administrator shall annually report his activities under sections 1259 through 1262 of this title, including recommendations for needed revisions in the provisions thereof.

(c) There are authorized to be appropriated $25,000,000 per fiscal year for the fiscal years ending June 30, 1973, June 30, 1974, and June 30, 1975, $6,000,000 for the fiscal year ending September 30, 1977, $7,000,000 for the fiscal year ending September 30, 1978, $7,000,000 for the fiscal year ending September 30, 1979, $7,000,000 for the fiscal year ending September 30, 1980, $7,000,000 for the fiscal year ending September 30, 1981, $7,000,000 for the fiscal year ending September 30, 1982, such sums as may be necessary for fiscal years 1983 through 1985, and $7,000,000 per fiscal year for each of the fiscal years 1986 through 1990, to carry out sections 1259 through 1262 of this title.

§1263. Alaska village demonstration projects [CWA §113]

(a) Central community facilities for safe water; elimination or control of pollution — The Administrator is authorized to enter into agreements with the State of Alaska to carry out one or more projects to demonstrate methods to provide for central community facilities for safe water and eliminate or control of pollution in those native villages of Alaska without such facilities. Such project shall include provisions for community safe water supply systems, toilets, bathing and laundry facilities, sewage disposal facilities, and other similar facilities, and educational and informational facilities and programs relating to health and hygiene. Such demonstration projects shall be for the further purpose of developing preliminary plans for providing such safe water and such elimination or control of pollution for all native villages in such State.

(b) Utilization of personnel and facilities of Department of Health and Human Services — In carrying out this section the Administrator shall cooperate with the Secretary of Health and Human Services for the purpose of utilizing such of the personnel and facilities of that Department as may be appropriate.

(c) Omitted

(d) Authorization of appropriations — There is authorized to be appropriated not to exceed $2,000,000 to carry out this section. In addition, there is authorized to be appropriated to carry out this section not to exceed $200,000 for the fiscal year ending September 30, 1978, and $220,000 for the fiscal year ending September 30, 1979.

(e) Study to develop comprehensive program for achieving sanitation services; report to Congress — The Administrator is authorized to coordinate with the Secretary of the Department of Health and Human Services, the Secretary of the Department of Housing and Urban Development, the Secretary of the Department of the Interior, the Secretary of the Department of Agriculture, and the heads of any other departments or agencies he may deem appropriate to conduct a joint study with representatives of the State of Alaska and the appropriate Native organizations (as defined in Public Law 92-203) to develop a comprehensive program for achieving adequate sanitation services in Alaska villages. This study shall be coordinated with the programs and projects authorized by sections 1254(q) and 1255(e)(2) of this title. The Administrator shall submit a report of the results of the study, together with appropriate

supporting data and such recommendations as he deems desirable, to the Committee on Environment and Public Works of the Senate and to the Committee on Public Works and Transportation of the House of Representatives not later than December 31, 1979. The Administrator shall also submit recommended administrative actions, procedures, and any proposed legislation necessary to implement the recommendations of the study no later than June 30, 1980.

(f) Technical, financial, and management assistance — The Administrator is authorized to provide technical, financial and management assistance for operation and maintenance of the demonstration projects constructed under this section, until such time as the recommendations of subsection (e) of this section are implemented.

(g) "Village" and "sanitation services" defined — For the purpose of this section, the term "village" shall mean an incorporated or unincorporated community with a population of ten to six hundred people living within a two-mile radius. The term "sanitation services" shall mean water supply, sewage disposal, solid waste disposal and other services necessary to maintain generally accepted standards of personal hygiene and public health.

§1263a. Grants to Alaska to improve sanitation in rural and Native villages

(a) In general — The Administrator of the Environmental Protection Agency may make grants to the State of Alaska for the benefit of rural and Native villages in Alaska to pay the Federal share of the cost of —

(1) the development and construction of public water systems and wastewater systems to improve the health and sanitation conditions in the villages; and

(2) training, technical assistance, and educational programs relating to the operation and management of sanitation services in rural and Native villages.

(b) Federal share — The Federal share of the cost of the activities described in subsection (a) of this section shall be 50 percent.

(c) Administrative expenses — The State of Alaska may use an amount not to exceed 4 percent of any grant made available under this subsection for administrative expenses necessary to carry out the activities described in subsection (a) of this section.

(d) Consultation with the State of Alaska — The Administrator shall consult with the State of Alaska on a method of prioritizing the allocation of grants under subsection (a) of this section according to the needs of, and relative health and sanitation conditions in, each eligible village.

(e) Authorization of appropriations — There are authorized to be appropriated to carry out this section $40,00,000 for each of fiscal years 2001 through 2005.

§1264. Omitted

§1265. In-place toxic pollutants
[CWA §115]

The Administrator is directed to identify the location of in-place pollutants with emphasis on toxic pollutants in harbors and navigable waterways and is authorized, acting through the Secretary of the Army, to make contracts for the removal and appropriate disposal of such materials from critical port and harbor areas. There is authorized to be appropriated $15,000,000 to carry out the provisions of this section, which sum shall be available until expended.

§1266. Hudson River reclamation demonstration project
[CWA §116]

(a) The Administrator is authorized to enter into contracts and other agreements with the State of New York to carry out a project to demonstrate methods for the selective removal of polychlorinated biphenyls contaminating bottom sediments of the Hudson River, treating such sediments as required, burying such sediments in secure landfills, and installing monitoring systems for such landfills. Such demonstration project shall be for the purpose of determining the feasibility of indefinite storage in secure landfills of toxic substances and of ascertaining the improvement of the rate of recovery of a toxic contaminated national waterway. No pollutants removed pursuant to this paragraph shall be placed in any landfill unless the Administrator first determines that disposal of the pollutants in such landfill would provide a higher standard of protection of the public health, safety, and welfare than disposal of such pollutants by any other method including, but not limited to, incineration or a chemical destruction process.

(b) The Administrator is authorized to make grants to the State of New York to carry out this section from funds allotted to such State under section 1285(a) of this title, except that the amount of any such grant shall be equal to 75 per centum of the cost of the project and such grant shall be made on condition that non-Federal sources provide the remainder of the cost of such project. The authority of this section shall be available until September 30, 1983. Funds allotted to the State of New York under section 1285(a) of this title shall be available under this subsection only to the extent that funds are not available, as determined by the Administrator, to the State of New York for the work authorized by this section under section 1265 or 1321 of this title or a comprehensive hazardous substance response and clean up fund. Any funds used under the authority of this subsection shall be deducted from any estimate of the needs of the State of New York prepared under section 1375(b) of this title. The Administrator may not obligate or expend more than $20,000,000 to carry out this section.

§1267. Chesapeake Bay
[CWA §117]

(a) Definitions — In this section, the following definitions apply:

(1) Administrative cost — The term "administrative cost" means the cost of salaries and fringe benefits incurred in administering a grant under this section.

(2) Chesapeake Bay Agreement — The term "Chesapeake Bay Agreement" means the formal, voluntary agreements executed to achieve the goal of restoring and protecting the Chesapeake Bay ecosystem and the living resources of the Chesapeake Bay ecosystem and signed by the Chesapeake Executive Council.

(3) Chesapeake Bay ecosystem — The term "Chesapeake Bay ecosystem" means the ecosystem of the Chesapeake Bay and its watershed.

(4) Chesapeake Bay Program — The term "Chesapeake Bay Program" means the program directed by the Chesapeake Executive Council in accordance with the Chesapeake Bay Agreement.

(5) Chesapeake Executive Council — The term "Chesapeake Executive Council" means the signatories to the Chesapeake Bay Agreement.

(6) Signatory jurisdiction — The term "signatory jurisdiction" means a jurisdiction of a signatory to the Chesapeake Bay Agreement.

(b) Continuation of Chesapeake Bay Program

(1) In general — In cooperation with the Chesapeake Executive Council (and as a member of the Council), the Administrator shall continue the Chesapeake Bay Program.

(2) Program Office —

(A) In general — The Administrator shall maintain in the Environmental Protection Agency a Chesapeake Bay Program Office.

(B) Function — The Chesapeake Bay Program Office shall provide support to the Chesapeake Executive Council by —

(i) implementing and coordinating science, research, modeling, support services, monitoring, data collection, and other activities that support the Chesapeake Bay Program;

(ii) developing and making available, through publications, technical assistance, and other appropriate means, information pertaining to the environmental quality and living resources of the Chesapeake Bay ecosystem;

(iii) in cooperation with appropriate Federal, State, and local authorities, assisting the signatories to the Chesapeake Bay Agreement in developing and implementing specific action plans to carry out the responsibilities of the signatories to the Chesapeake Bay Agreement;

(iv) coordinating the actions of the Environmental Protection Agency with the actions of the appropriate officials of other Federal agencies and State and local authorities in developing strategies to —

(I) improve the water quality and living resources in the Chesapeake Bay ecosystem; and

(II) obtain the support of the appropriate officials of the agencies and authorities in achieving the objectives of the Chesapeake Bay Agreement; and

(v) implementing outreach programs for public information, education, and participation to foster stewardship of the resources of the Chesapeake Bay.

(c) **Interagency agreements** — The Administrator may enter into an interagency agreement with a Federal agency to carry out this section.

(d) **Technical assistance and assistance grants**

(1) In general — In cooperation with the Chesapeake Executive Council, the Administrator may provide technical assistance, and assistance grants, to nonprofit organizations, State and local governments, colleges, universities, and interstate agencies to carry out this section, subject to such terms and conditions as the Administrator considers appropriate.

(2) Federal share —

(A) In general — Except as provided in subparagraph (B), the Federal share of an assistance grant provided under paragraph (1) shall be determined by the Administrator in accordance with guidance issued by the Administrator.

(B) Small watershed grants program — The Federal share of an assistance grant provided under paragraph (1) to carry out an implementing activity under subsection (g)(2) of this section shall not exceed 75 percent of eligible project costs, as determined by the Administrator.

(3) Non-Federal share — An assistance grant under paragraph (1) shall be provided on the condition that non-Federal sources provide the remainder of eligible project costs, as determined by the Administrator.

(4) Administrative costs — Administrative costs shall not exceed 10 percent of the annual grant award.

(e) **Implementation and monitoring grants**

(1) In general — If a signatory jurisdiction has approved and committed to implement all or substantially all aspects of the Chesapeake Bay Agreement, on the request of the chief executive of the jurisdiction, the Administrator —

(A) shall make a grant to the jurisdiction for the purpose of implementing the management mechanisms established under the Chesapeake Bay Agreement, subject to such terms and conditions as the Administrator considers appropriate; and

(B) may make a grant to a signatory jurisdiction for the purpose of monitoring the Chesapeake Bay ecosystem.

(2) Proposals —

(A) In general — A signatory jurisdiction described in paragraph (1) may apply for a grant under this subsection for a fiscal year by submitting to the Administrator a comprehensive proposal to implement management mechanisms established under the Chesapeake Bay Agreement.

(B) Contents — A proposal under subparagraph (A) shall include —

(i) a description of proposed management mechanisms that the jurisdiction commits to take within a specified time period, such as reducing or preventing pollution in the Chesapeake Bay and its watershed or meeting applicable water quality standards or established goals and objectives under the Chesapeake Bay Agreement; and

(ii) the estimated cost of the actions proposed to be taken during the fiscal year.

(3) Approval — If the Administrator finds that the proposal is consistent with the Chesapeake Bay Agreement and the national goals established under section 1251(a) of this title, the Administrator may approve the proposal for an award.

(4) Federal share — The Federal share of a grant under this subsection shall not exceed 50 percent of the cost of implementing the management mechanisms during the fiscal year.

(5) Non-Federal share — A grant under this subsection shall be made on the condition that non-Federal sources provide the remainder of the costs of implementing the management mechanisms during the fiscal year.

(6) Administrative costs — Administrative costs shall not exceed 10 percent of the annual grant award.

(7) Reporting — On or before October 1 of each fiscal year, the Administrator shall make available to the public a document that lists and describes, in the greatest practicable degree of detail —

(A) all projects and activities funded for the fiscal year;

(B) the goals and objectives of projects funded for the previous fiscal year; and

(C) the net benefits of projects funded for previous fiscal years.

(f) **Federal facilities and budget coordination**

(1) Subwatershed planning and restoration — A Federal agency that owns or operates a facility (as defined by the Administrator) within the Chesapeake Bay watershed shall participate in regional and subwatershed planning and restoration programs.

(2) Compliance with Agreement — The head of each Federal agency that owns or occupies real

property in the Chesapeake Bay watershed shall ensure that the property, and actions taken by the agency with respect to the property, comply with the Chesapeake Bay Agreement, the Federal Agencies Chesapeake Ecosystem Unified Plan, and any subsequent agreements and plans.

(3) Budget coordination

(A) In general — As part of the annual budget submission of each Federal agency with projects or grants related to restoration, planning, monitoring, or scientific investigation of the Chesapeake Bay ecosystem, the head of the agency shall submit to the President a report that describes plans for the expenditure of the funds under this section.

(B) Disclosure to the Council — The head of each agency referred to in subparagraph (A) shall disclose the report under that subparagraph with the Chesapeake Executive Council as appropriate.

(g) Chesapeake Bay Program

(1) Management strategies — The Administrator, in coordination with other members of the Chesapeake Executive Council, shall ensure that management plans are developed and implementation is begun by signatories to the Chesapeake Bay Agreement to achieve and maintain —

(A) the nutrient goals of the Chesapeake Bay Agreement for the quantity of nitrogen and phosphorus entering the Chesapeake Bay and its watershed;

(B) the water quality requirements necessary to restore living resources in the Chesapeake Bay ecosystem;

(C) the Chesapeake Bay Basinwide Toxins Reduction and Prevention Strategy goal of reducing or eliminating the input of chemical contaminants from all controllable sources to levels that result in no toxic or bioaccumulative impact on the living resources of the Chesapeake Bay ecosystem or on human health;

(D) habitat restoration, protection, creation, and enhancement goals established by Chesapeake Bay Agreement signatories for wetlands, riparian forests, and other types of habitat associated with the Chesapeake Bay ecosystem; and

(E) the restoration, protection, creation, and enhancement goals established by the Chesapeake Bay Agreement signatories for living resources associated with the Chesapeake Bay ecosystem.

(2) Small watershed grants program — The Administrator, in cooperation with the Chesapeake Executive Council, shall —

(A) establish a small watershed grants program as part of the Chesapeake Bay Program; and

(B) offer technical assistance and assistance grants under subsection (d) to local

governments and nonprofit organizations and individuals in the Chesapeake Bay region to implement —

(i) cooperative tributary basin strategies that address the water quality and living resource needs in the Chesapeake Bay ecosystem; and

(ii) locally based protection and restoration programs or projects within a watershed that complement the tributary basin strategies, including the creation, restoration, protection, or enhancement of habitat associated with the Chesapeake Bay ecosystem.

(h) Study of Chesapeake Bay Program

(1) In general — Not later than April 22, 2003, and every 5 years thereafter, the Administrator, in coordination with the Chesapeake Executive Council, shall complete a study and submit to Congress a comprehensive report on the results of the study.

(2) Requirements — The study and report shall —

(A) assess the state of the Chesapeake Bay ecosystem;

(B) compare the current state of the Chesapeake Bay ecosystem with its state in 1975, 1985, and 1995;

(C) assess the effectiveness of management strategies being implemented on November 7, 2000, and the extent to which the priority needs are being met;

(D) make recommendations for the improved management of the Chesapeake Bay Program either by strengthening strategies being implemented on November 7, 2000, or by adopting new strategies; and

(E) be presented in such a format as to be readily transferable to and usable by other watershed restoration programs.

(i) Special study of living resource response

(1) In general — Not later than 180 days after November 7, 2000, the Administrator shall commence a 5-year special study with full participation of the scientific community of the Chesapeake Bay to establish and expand understanding of the response of the living resources of the Chesapeake Bay ecosystem to improvements in water quality that have resulted from investments made through the Chesapeake Bay Program.

(2) Requirements — The study shall —

(A) determine the current status and trends of living resources, including grasses, benthos, phytoplankton, zooplankton, fish, and shellfish;

(B) establish to the extent practicable the rates of recovery of the living resources in response to improved water quality condition;

(C) evaluate and assess interactions of species, with particular attention to the impact of changes within and among trophic levels; and

(D) recommend management actions to optimize the return of a healthy and balanced ecosystem in response to improvements in the quality and character of the waters of the Chesapeake Bay.

(3) Annual survey — The Administrator shall carry out an annual survey of sea grasses in the Chesapeake Bay.

(j) Authorization of appropriations — There are authorized to be appropriated to carry out this section

    (1) for fiscal year 2021, $90,000,000
    (2) for fiscal year 2022, $90,500,000
    (3) for fiscal year 2023, $91,000,000
    (4) for fiscal year 2024, $91,500,000
    (5) for fiscal year 2025, $92,000,000

§1268. Great Lakes
[CWA §118]
(a) Findings, purpose, and definitions

(1) Findings — The Congress finds that —

(A) the Great Lakes are a valuable national resource, continuously serving the people of the United States and other nations as an important source of food, fresh water, recreation, beauty, and enjoyment;

(B) the United States should seek to attain the goals embodied in the Great Lakes Water Quality Agreement of 1978, as amended by the Water Quality Agreement of 1987 and any other agreements and amendments, with particular emphasis on goals related to toxic pollutants; and

(C) the Environmental Protection Agency should take the lead in the effort to meet those goals, working with other Federal agencies and State and local authorities.

(2) Purpose — It is the purpose of this section to achieve the goals embodied in the Great Lakes Water Quality Agreement of 1978, as amended by the Water Quality Agreement of 1987 and any other agreements and amendments, through improved organization and definition of mission on the part of the Agency, funding of State grants for pollution control in the Great Lakes area, and improved accountability for implementation of such agreement.

(3) Definitions — For purposes of this section, the term —

(A) "Agency" means the Environmental Protection Agency;

(B) "Great Lakes" means Lake Ontario, Lake Erie, Lake Huron including Lake St. Clair), Lake Michigan, and Lake Superior, and the connecting channels (Saint Mary's River, Saint Clair River, Detroit River, Niagara River, and Saint Lawrence River to the Canadian Border);

(C) "Great Lakes System" means all the streams, rivers, lakes, and other bodies of water within the drainage basin of the Great Lakes;

(D) "Program Office" means the Great Lakes National Program Office established by this section;

(E) "Research Office" means the Great Lakes Research Office established by subsection (d) of this section;

(F) "area of concern" means a geographic area located within the Great Lakes, in which beneficial uses are impaired and which has been officially designated as such under Annex 2 of the Great Lakes Water Quality Agreement;

(G) "Great Lakes States" means the States of Illinois, Indiana, Michigan, Minnesota, New York, Ohio, Pennsylvania, and Wisconsin;

(H) "Great Lakes Water Quality Agreement" means the bilateral agreement, between the United States and Canada which was signed in 1978 and amended by the Protocol of 1987;

(I) "Lakewide Management Plan" means a written document which embodies a systematic and comprehensive ecosystem approach to restoring and protecting the beneficial uses of the open waters of each of the Great Lakes, in accordance with article VI and Annex 2 of the Great Lakes Water Quality Agreement;

(J) "Remedial Action Plan" means a written document which embodies a systematic and comprehensive ecosystem approach to restoring and protecting the beneficial uses of areas of concern, in accordance with article VI and Annex 2 of the Great Lakes Water Quality Agreement;

(K) "site characterization" means a process for monitoring and evaluating the nature and extent of sediment contamination in accordance with the Environmental Protection Agency's guidance for the assessment of contaminated sediment in an area of concern located wholly or partially within the United States; and

(L) "potentially responsible party" means an individual or entity that may be liable under any Federal or State authority that is being used or may be used to facilitate the cleanup and protection of the Great Lakes.

(b) Great Lakes National Program Office
— The Great Lakes National Program Office (previously established by the Administrator) is hereby established within the Agency. The Program Office shall be headed by a Director who, by reason of management experience and technical expertise relating to the Great Lakes, is highly qualified to direct the development of programs and plans on a variety of Great Lakes issues. The Great Lakes National Program Office shall be located in a Great Lakes State.

(c) Great Lakes management

(1) Functions — The Program Office shall —

(A) in cooperation with appropriate Federal, State, tribal, and international agencies, and in accordance with section 1251(e) of this title, develop and implement specific action plans to carry out the responsibilities of the United States under the Great Lakes Water Quality Agreement of 1978, as amended by the Water Quality Agreement of 1987 and any other agreements and amendments;

(B) establish a Great Lakes system-wide surveillance network to monitor the water quality of the Great Lakes, with specific emphasis on the monitoring of toxic pollutants;

(C) serve as the liaison with, and provide information to, the Canadian members of the International Joint Commission and the Canadian counterpart to the Agency;

(D) coordinate actions of the Agency (including actions by headquarters and regional offices thereof) aimed at improving Great Lakes water quality; and

(E) coordinate actions of the Agency with the actions of other Federal agencies and State and local authorities, so as to ensure the input of those agencies and authorities in developing water quality strategies and obtain the support of those agencies and authorities in achieving the objectives of such agreement.

(2) Great Lakes water quality guidance

(A) By June 30, 1991, the Administrator, after consultation with the Program Office, shall publish in the Federal Register for public notice and comment proposed water quality guidance for the Great Lakes System. Such guidance shall conform with the objectives and provisions of the Great Lakes Water Quality Agreement, shall be no less restrictive than the provisions of this chapter and national water quality criteria and guidance, shall specify numerical limits on pollutants in ambient Great Lakes waters to protect human health, aquatic life, and wildlife, and shall provide guidance to the Great Lakes States on minimum water quality standards, antidegradation policies, and implementation procedures for the Great Lakes System.

(B) By June 30, 1992, the Administrator, in consultation with the Program Office, shall publish in the Federal Register, pursuant to this section and the Administrator's authority under this chapter, final water quality guidance for the Great Lakes System.

(C) Within two years after such Great Lakes guidance is published, the Great Lakes States shall adopt water quality standards, antidegradation policies, and implementation procedures for waters within the Great Lakes System which are consistent with such guidance. If a Great Lakes State fails to adopt such standards, policies, and procedures, the Administrator shall promulgate them not later than the end of such two-year period. When

reviewing any Great Lakes State's water quality plan, the agency shall consider the extent to which the State has complied with the Great Lakes guidance issued pursuant to this section.

(3) Remedial Action Plans

(A) For each area of concern for which the United States has agreed to draft a Remedial Action Plan, the Program Office shall ensure that the Great Lakes State in which such area of concern is located —

(i) submits a Remedial Action Plan to the Program Office by June 30, 1991;

(ii) submits such Remedial Action Plan to the International Joint Commission by January 1, 1992; and

(iii) includes such Remedial Action Plans within the State's water quality plan by January 1, 1993.

(B) For each area of concern for which Canada has agreed to draft a Remedial Action Plan, the Program Office shall, pursuant to subparagraph (c)(1)(C) of this section, work with Canada to assure the submission of such Remedial Action Plans to the International Joint Commission by June 30, 1991, and to finalize such Remedial Action Plans by January 1, 1993.

(C) For any area of concern designated as such subsequent to November 16, 1990, the Program Office shall (i) if the United States has agreed to draft the Remedial Action Plan, ensure that the Great Lakes State in which such area of concern is located submits such Plan to the Program Office within two years of the area's designation, submits it to the International Joint Commission no later than six months after submitting it to the Program Office, and includes such Plan in the State's water quality plan no later than one year after submitting it to the Commission; and (ii) if Canada has agreed to draft the Remedial Action Plan, work with Canada, pursuant to subparagraph (c)(1)(C) of this section, to ensure the submission of such Plan to the International Joint Commission within two years of the area's designation and the finalization of such Plan no later than eighteen months after submitting it to such Commission.

(D) The Program Office shall compile formal comments on individual Remedial Action Plans made by the International Joint Commission pursuant to section 4(d) of Annex 2 of the Great Lakes Water Quality Agreement and, upon request by a member of the public, shall make such comments available for inspection and copying. The Program Office shall also make available, upon request, formal comments made by the Environmental Protection Agency on individual Remedial Action Plans.

(E) Report — Not later than 1 year after the date of enactment of this subparagraph, the Administrator shall submit to Congress a report on such actions, time periods, and resources as are necessary to fulfill the duties of the Agency relating to oversight of Remedial Action Plans under —

    (i) this paragraph; and

    (ii) the Great Lakes Water Quality Agreement.

(4) Lakewide Management Plans — The Administrator, in consultation with the Program Office shall —

    (A) by January 1, 1992, publish in the Federal Register a proposed Lakewide Management Plan for Lake Michigan and solicit public comments;

    (B) by January 1, 1993, submit a proposed Lakewide Management Plan for Lake Michigan to the International Joint Commission for review; and

    (C) by January 1, 1994, publish in the Federal Register a final Lakewide Management Plan for Lake Michigan and begin implementation.

Nothing in this subparagraph shall preclude the simultaneous development of Lakewide Management Plans for the other Great Lakes.

(5) Spills of oil and hazardous materials — The Program Office, in consultation with the Coast Guard, shall identify areas within the Great Lakes which are likely to experience numerous or voluminous spills of oil or other hazardous materials from land based facilities, vessels, or other sources and, in consultation with the Great Lakes States, shall identify weaknesses in Federal and State programs and systems to prevent and respond to such spills. This information shall be included on at least a biennial basis in the report required by this section.

(6) 5-year plan and program — The Program Office shall develop, in consultation with the States, a five-year plan and program for reducing the amount of nutrients introduced into the Great Lakes. Such program shall incorporate any management program for reducing nutrient runoff from nonpoint sources established under section 1329 of this title and shall include a program for monitoring nutrient runoff into, and ambient levels in, the Great Lakes.

(7) Great Lakes Restoration Initiative

    (A) Establishment

    There is established in the Agency a Great Lakes Restoration Initiative (referred to in this paragraph as the "Initiative") to carry out programs and projects for Great Lakes protection and restoration.

    (B) Focus areas

    In carrying out the Initiative, the Administrator shall prioritize programs and projects, to be carried out in coordination with non-Federal partners, that address the priority areas described in the Initiative Action Plan, including —

    (i) the remediation of toxic substances and areas of concern;

    (ii) the prevention and control of invasive species and the impacts of invasive species;

    (iii) the protection and restoration of nearshore health and the prevention and mitigation of nonpoint source pollution;

    (iv) habitat and wildlife protection and restoration, including wetlands restoration and preservation; and

    (v) accountability, monitoring, evaluation, communication, and partnership activities.

(C) Projects

    (i) In general

    In carrying out the Initiative, the Administrator shall collaborate with other Federal partners, including the Great Lakes Interagency Task Force established by Executive Order No. 13340 (69 Fed. Reg. 29043), to select the best combination of programs and projects for Great Lakes protection and restoration using appropriate principles and criteria, including whether a program or project provides —

    (I) the ability to achieve strategic and measurable environmental outcomes that implement the Initiative Action Plan and the Great Lakes Water Quality Agreement;

    (II) the feasibility of —

      (aa) prompt implementation;

      (bb) timely achievement of results; and

      (cc) resource leveraging; and

    (III) the opportunity to improve interagency, intergovernmental, and interorganizational coordination and collaboration to reduce duplication and streamline efforts.

    (ii) Outreach

    In selecting the best combination of programs and projects for Great Lakes protection and restoration under clause (i), the Administrator shall consult with the Great Lakes States and Indian tribes and solicit input from other non-Federal stakeholders.

    (iii) Harmful algal bloom coordinator

    The Administrator shall designate a point person from an appropriate Federal partner to coordinate, with Federal partners and Great Lakes States, Indian tribes, and other non-Federal stakeholders, projects and activities under the Initiative involving harmful algal blooms in the Great Lakes.

(D) Implementation of projects

(i) In general

Subject to subparagraph (J)(ii), funds made available to carry out the Initiative shall be used to strategically implement —

　(I) Federal projects;

　(II) projects carried out in coordination with States, Indian tribes, municipalities, institutions of higher education, and other organizations; and

　(III) operations and activities of the Program Office, including remediation of sediment contamination in areas of concern.

(ii) Transfer of funds

With amounts made available for the Initiative each fiscal year, the Administrator may —

　(I) transfer not more than the total amount appropriated under subparagraph (J)(i) for the fiscal year to the head of any Federal department or agency, with the concurrence of the department or agency head, to carry out activities to support the Initiative and the Great Lakes Water Quality Agreement; and

　(II) enter into an interagency agreement with the head of any Federal department or agency to carry out activities described in subclause (I).

(iii) Agreements with non-Federal entities

　(I) In general

　The Administrator, or the head of any other Federal department or agency receiving funds under clause (ii)(I), may make a grant to, or otherwise enter into an agreement with, a qualified non-Federal entity, as determined by the Administrator or the applicable head of the other Federal department or agency receiving funds, for planning, research, monitoring, outreach, or implementation of a project selected under subparagraph (C), to support the Initiative Action Plan or the Great Lakes Water Quality Agreement.

　(II) Qualified non-Federal entity

　For purposes of this clause, a qualified non-Federal entity may include a governmental entity, nonprofit organization, institution, or individual.

(E) Scope

(i) In general

Projects may be carried out under the Initiative on multiple levels, including —

　(I) locally;

　(II) Great Lakes-wide; or

　(III) Great Lakes basin-wide.

(ii) Limitation

No funds made available to carry out the Initiative may be used for any water infrastructure activity (other than a green infrastructure project that improves habitat and other ecosystem functions in the Great Lakes) for which financial assistance is received —

　(I) from a State water pollution control revolving fund established under subchapter VI;

　(II) from a State drinking water revolving loan fund established under section 300j-12 of title 42; or

　(III) pursuant to the Water Infrastructure Finance and Innovation Act of 2014 (33 U.S.C. 3901 et seq.).

(F) Activities by other Federal agencies

Each relevant Federal department or agency shall, to the maximum extent practicable —

(i) maintain the base level of funding for the Great Lakes activities of that department or agency without regard to funding under the Initiative; and

(ii) identify new activities and projects to support the environmental goals of the Initiative.

(G) Revision of Initiative Action Plan

(i) In general

Not less often than once every 5 years, the Administrator, in conjunction with the Great Lakes Interagency Task Force, shall review, and revise as appropriate, the Initiative Action Plan to guide the activities of the Initiative in addressing the restoration and protection of the Great Lakes system.

(ii) Outreach

In reviewing and revising the Initiative Action Plan under clause (i), the Administrator shall consult with the Great Lakes States and Indian tribes and solicit input from other non-Federal stakeholders.

(H) Monitoring and reporting

The Administrator shall —

(i) establish and maintain a process for monitoring and periodically reporting to the public on the progress made in implementing the Initiative Action Plan;

(ii) make information about each project carried out under the Initiative Action Plan available on a public website; and

(iii) provide to the Committee on Transportation and Infrastructure of the House of Representatives and the

Committee on Environment and Public Works of the Senate a yearly detailed description of the progress of the Initiative and amounts transferred to participating Federal departments and agencies under subparagraph (D)(ii).

(I) Initiative Action Plan defined

In this paragraph, the term "Initiative Action Plan" means the comprehensive, multiyear action plan for the restoration of the Great Lakes, first developed pursuant to the Joint Explanatory Statement of the Conference Report accompanying the Department of the Interior, Environment, and Related Agencies Appropriations Act, 2010 (Public Law 111-88).

(J) Funding

There are authorized to be appropriated to carry out this paragraph—

　　(I) $300,000,000 for each of fiscal years 2017 through 2021;

　　(II) $375,000,000 for fiscal year 2022;

　　(III) $400,000,000 for fiscal year 2023;

　　(IV) $425,000,000 for fiscal year 2024;

　　(V) $450,000,000 for fiscal year 2025; and

　　(VI) $475,000,000 for fiscal year 2026.

(8) Administrator's responsibility — The Administrator shall ensure that the Program Office enters into agreements with the various organizational elements of the Agency involved in Great Lakes activities and the appropriate State agencies specifically delineating —

(A) the duties and responsibilities of each such element in the Agency with respect to the Great Lakes;

(B) the time periods for carrying out such duties and responsibilities; and

(C) the resources to be committed to such duties and responsibilities.

(9) Budget item — The Administrator shall, in the Agency's annual budget submission to Congress, include a funding request for the Program Office as a separate budget line item.

(10) Confined disposal facilities

(A) The Administrator, in consultation with the Assistant Secretary of the Army for Civil Works, shall develop and implement, within one year of November 16, 1990, management plans for every Great Lakes confined disposal facility.

(B) The plan shall provide for monitoring of such facilities, including

　　(i) water quality at the site and in the area of the site;

　　(ii) sediment quality at the site and in the area of the site;

　　(iii) the diversity, productivity, and stability of aquatic organisms at the site and in the area of the site; and

　　(iv) such other conditions as the Administrator deems appropriate.

(C) The plan shall identify the anticipated use and management of the site over the following twenty-year period including the expected termination of dumping at the site, the anticipated need for site management, including pollution control, following the termination of the use of the site.

(D) The plan shall identify a schedule for review and revision of the plan which shall not be less frequent than five years after adoption of the plan and every five years thereafter.

(11) Remediation of sediment contamination in areas of concern

(A) In general

In accordance with this paragraph, the Administrator, acting through the Program Office, may carry out projects that meet the requirements of subparagraph (B).

(B) Eligible projects

A project meets the requirements of this subparagraph if the project is to be carried out in an area of concern located wholly or partially in the United States and the project —

　　(i) monitors or evaluates contaminated sediment;

　　(ii) subject to subparagraph (D), implements a plan to remediate contaminated sediment, including activities to restore aquatic habitat that are carried out in conjunction with a project for the remediation of contaminated sediment; or

　　(iii) prevents further or renewed contamination of sediment.

(C) Priority

In selecting projects to carry out under this paragraph, the Administrator shall give priority to a project that —

　　(i) constitutes remedial action for contaminated sediment;

　　(ii)(I) has been identified in a Remedial Action Plan submitted under paragraph (3); and

　　　　(II)　is ready to be implemented;

　　(iii) will use an innovative approach, technology, or technique that may provide greater environmental benefits, or equivalent environmental benefits at a reduced cost; or

　　(iv) includes remediation to be commenced not later than 1 year after the date of receipt of funds for the project.

(D) Limitations

The Administrator may not carry out a project under this paragraph for remediation of contaminated sediments located in an area of concern —

(i) if an evaluation of remedial alternatives for the area of concern has not been conducted, including a review of the short-term and long-term effects of the alternatives on human health and the environment;

(ii) if the Administrator determines that the area of concern is likely to suffer significant further or renewed contamination from existing sources of pollutants causing sediment contamination following completion of the project;

(iii) unless each non-Federal sponsor for the project has entered into a written project agreement with the Administrator under which the party agrees to carry out its responsibilities and requirements for the project; or

(iv) unless the Administrator provides assurance that the Agency has conducted a reasonable inquiry to identify potentially responsible parties connected with the site.

(E) Non-Federal share

(i) In general

The non-Federal share of the cost of a project carried out under this paragraph shall be at least 35 percent.

(ii) In-kind contributions

(I) In general

The non-Federal share of the cost of a project carried out under this paragraph may include the value of an in-kind contribution provided by a non-Federal sponsor.

(II) Credit — A project agreement described in subparagraph (D)(iii) may provide, with respect to a project, that the Administrator shall credit toward the non-Federal share of the cost of the project the value of an in-kind contribution made by the non-Federal sponsor, if the Administrator determines that the material or service provided as the in-kind contribution is integral to the project.

(III) Work performed before project agreement — In any case in which a non-Federal sponsor is to receive credit under subclause (II) for the cost of work carried out by the non-Federal sponsor and such work has not been carried out by the non-Federal sponsor as of October 8, 2008, the Administrator and the non-Federal sponsor shall enter into an agreement under which the non-Federal sponsor shall carry out such work, and only work carried out following the execution of the agreement shall be eligible for credit.

(IV) Limitation — Credit authorized under this clause for a project carried out under this paragraph —

(aa) shall not exceed the non-Federal share of the cost of the project; and

(bb) shall not exceed the actual and reasonable costs of the materials and services provided by the non-Federal sponsor, as determined by the Administrator.

(V) Inclusion of certain contributions — In this subparagraph, the term "in-kind contribution" may include the costs of planning (including data collection), design, construction, and materials that are provided by the non-Federal sponsor for implementation of a project under this paragraph.

(iii) Treatment of credit between projects

Any credit provided under this subparagraph towards the non-Federal share of the cost of a project carried out under this paragraph may be applied towards the non-Federal share of the cost of any other project carried out under this paragraph by the same non-Federal sponsor for a site within the same area of concern.

(iv) Non-Federal share

The non-Federal share of the cost of a project carried out under this paragraph —

(I) may include monies paid pursuant to, or the value of any in-kind contribution performed under, an administrative order on consent or judicial consent decree; but

(II) may not include any funds paid pursuant to, or the value of any in-kind contribution performed under, a unilateral administrative order or court order.

(v) Operation and maintenance

The non-Federal share of the cost of the operation and maintenance of a project carried out under this paragraph shall be 100 percent.

(F) Site characterization

(i) In general

The Administrator, in consultation with any affected State or unit of local government, shall carry out at Federal expense the site characterization of a project under this paragraph for the remediation of contaminated sediment.

(ii) Limitation

For purposes of clause (i), the Administrator may carry out one site assessment per discrete site within a project at Federal expense.

(G) Coordination

In carrying out projects under this paragraph, the Administrator shall coordinate with the Secretary of the Army, and with the Governors of States in which the projects are located, to ensure that Federal and State assistance for remediation in areas of concern is used as efficiently as practicable.

(H) Authorization of appropriations

(i) In general

In addition to other amounts authorized under this section, there is authorized to be appropriated to carry out this paragraph $50,000,000 for each of fiscal years 2004 through 2010.

(ii) Availability

Funds made available under clause (i) shall remain available until expended.

(iii) Allocation of funds

Not more than 20 percent of the funds appropriated pursuant to clause (i) for a fiscal year may be used to carry out subparagraph (F).

(12) Public information program

(A) In general

The Administrator, acting through the Program Office and in coordination with States, Indian tribes, local governments, and other entities, may carry out a public information program to provide information relating to the remediation of contaminated sediment to the public in areas of concern that are located wholly or partially in the United States.

(B) Authorization of appropriations

There is authorized to be appropriated to carry out this paragraph $1,000,000 for each of fiscal years 2004 through 2010.

(d) Great Lakes research

(1) Establishment of Research Office — There is established within the National Oceanic and Atmospheric Administration the Great Lakes Research Office.

(2) Identification of issues — The Research Office shall identify issues relating to the Great Lakes resources on which research is needed. The Research Office shall submit a report to Congress on such issues before the end of each fiscal year which shall identify any changes in the Great Lakes system with respect to such issues.

(3) Inventory — The Research Office shall identify and inventory Federal, State, university, and tribal environmental research programs (and, to the extent feasible, those of private organizations and other nations) relating to the Great Lakes system, and shall update that inventory every four years.

(4) Research exchange — The Research Office shall establish a Great Lakes research exchange for the purpose of facilitating the rapid identification, acquisition, retrieval, dissemination, and use of information concerning research projects which are ongoing or completed and which affect the Great Lakes System.

(5) Research program — The Research Office shall develop, in cooperation with the Coordination Office, a comprehensive environmental research program and data base for the Great Lakes system. The data base shall include, but not be limited to, data relating to water quality, fisheries, and biota.

(6) Monitoring — The Research Office shall conduct, through the Great Lakes Environmental Research Laboratory, the National Sea Grant College program, other Federal laboratories, and the private sector, appropriate research and monitoring activities which address priority issues and current needs relating to the Great Lakes.

(7) Location — The Research Office shall be located in a Great Lakes State.

(e) Research and management coordination

(1) Joint plan — Before October 1 of each year, the Program Office and the Research Office shall prepare a joint research plan for the fiscal year which begins in the following calendar year.

(2) Contents of plan — Each plan prepared under paragraph (1) shall —

(A) identify all proposed research dedicated to activities conducted under the Great Lakes Water Quality Agreement of 1978, as amended by the Water Quality Agreement of 1987 and any other agreements and amendments;

(B) include the Agency's assessment of priorities for research needed to fulfill the terms of such Agreement; and

(C) identify all proposed research that may be used to develop a comprehensive environmental data base for the Great Lakes System and establish priorities for development of such data base.

(3) Health research report

(A) Not later than September 30, 1994, the Program Office, in consultation with the Research Office, the Agency for Toxic Substances and Disease Registry, and Great Lakes States shall submit to the Congress a report assessing the adverse effects of water pollutants in the Great Lakes System on the health of persons in Great Lakes States and the health of fish, shellfish, and wildlife in the Great Lakes System. In conducting research in support of this report, the Administrator may, where appropriate, provide for research to be conducted under cooperative agreements with Great Lakes States.

(B) There is authorized to be appropriated to the Administrator to carry out this section not to exceed $3,000,000 for each of fiscal years 1992, 1993, and 1994.

(f) Interagency cooperation — The head of each department, agency, or other instrumentality of the Federal Government which is engaged in, is concerned with, or has authority over programs relating to research, monitoring, and planning to maintain, enhance, preserve, or rehabilitate the environmental quality and natural resources of the Great Lakes, including the Chief of Engineers of the Army, the Chief of the Soil Conservation Service, the Commandant of the Coast Guard, the Director of the Fish and Wildlife Service, and the Administrator of the National Oceanic and Atmospheric Administration, shall submit an annual report to the Administrator with respect to the activities of that agency or office affecting compliance with the Great Lakes Water Quality Agreement of 1978, as amended by the Water Quality Agreement of 1987 and any other agreements and amendments.

(g) Relationship to existing Federal and State laws and international treaties — Nothing in this section shall be construed (1) to affect the jurisdiction, powers, or prerogatives of any department, agency, or officer of the Federal Government or of any State government, or of any tribe, nor any powers, jurisdiction, or prerogatives of any international body created by treaty with authority relating to the Great Lakes; or (2) to affect any other Federal or State authority that is being used or may be used to facilitate the cleanup and protection of the Great Lakes.

(h) Authorizations of Great Lakes appropriations — There are authorized to be appropriated to the Administrator to carry out this section not to exceed (1) $11,000,000 per fiscal year for the fiscal years 1987, 1988, 1989, and 1990, and $25,000,000 for fiscal year 1991; (2) such sums as are necessary for each of fiscal years 1992 through 2003; and (3) $25,000,000 for each of fiscal years 2004 through 2008.

§1268a. Great Lakes restoration activities report

(a) For purposes of this section the following definitions apply:

(1) The terms "Great Lakes" and "Great Lakes State" have the same meanings as such terms have in section 1962d-22 of title 42.

(2) The term "Great Lakes restoration activities" means any Federal or State activity primarily or entirely within the Great Lakes watershed that seeks to improve the overall health of the Great Lakes ecosystem.

(b) Hereafter, not later than 45 days after submission of the budget of the President to Congress, the Director of the Office of Management and Budget, in coordination with the Governor of each Great Lakes State and the Great Lakes Interagency Task Force, shall submit to the appropriate authorizing and appropriating committees of the Senate and the House of Representatives a financial report, certified by the Secretary of each agency that has budget authority for Great Lakes restoration activities, containing —

(1) an interagency budget crosscut report that —

(A) displays the budget proposed, including any planned interagency or intra-agency transfer, for each of the Federal agencies that carries out Great Lakes restoration activities in the upcoming fiscal year, separately reporting the amount of funding to be provided under existing laws pertaining to the Great Lakes ecosystem; and

(B) identifies all expenditures in each of the 5 prior fiscal years by the Federal Government and State governments for Great Lakes restoration activities.

§1269. Long Island Sound
[CWA §119]

(a) Office of Management Conference of the Long Island Sound Study — The Administrator shall continue the Management Conference of the Long Island Sound Study (hereinafter referred to as the "Conference") as established pursuant to section 1330 of this title, and shall establish an office (hereinafter referred to as the "Office") to be located on or near Long Island Sound.

(b) Administration and staffing of Office — The Office shall be headed by a Director, who shall be detailed by the Administrator, following consultation with the Administrators of EPA regions I and II, from among the employees of the Agency who are in civil service. The Administrator shall delegate to the Director such authority and detail such additional staff as may be necessary to carry out the duties of the Director under this section.

(c) Duties of Office — The Office shall assist the conference study in carrying out its goals. Specifically, the Office shall —

(1) assist and support the implementation of the Comprehensive Conservation and Management Plan for Long Island Sound developed pursuant to section 1330 of this title, including efforts to establish, within the process for granting watershed general permits, a system for promoting innovative methodologies and technologies that are cost-effective and consistent with the goals of the Plan;

(2) conduct or commission studies deemed necessary for strengthened implementation of the Comprehensive Conservation and Management Plan including, but not limited to —

(A) population growth and the adequacy of wastewater treatment facilities,

(B) the use of biological methods for nutrient removal in sewage treatment plants,

(C) contaminated sediments, and dredging activities,

(D) nonpoint source pollution abatement and land use activities in the Long Island Sound watershed,

(E) wetland protection and restoration,

(F) atmospheric deposition of acidic and other pollutants into Long Island Sound,

(G) water quality requirements to sustain fish, shellfish, and wildlife populations, and the use of indicator species to assess environmental quality,

(H) State water quality programs, for their adequacy pursuant to implementation of the Comprehensive Conservation and Management Plan,

(I) options for long-term financing of wastewater treatment projects and water pollution control programs.

(J) environmental vulnerabilities of the Long Island Sound watershed, including —

(i) the identification and assessment of such vulnerabilities in the watershed;

(ii) the development and implementation of adaptation strategies to reduce such vulnerabilities; and

(iii) the identification and assessment of the effects of sea level rise on water quality, habitat, and infrastructure; and

(3) coordinate the grant, research and planning programs authorized under this section;

(4) develop and implement strategies to increase public education and awareness with respect to the ecological health and water quality conditions of Long Island Sound;

(5) provide administrative and technical support to the conference study;

(6) collect and make available to the public (including on a publicly accessible website) publications, and other forms of information the conference study determines to be appropriate, relating to the environmental quality of Long Island Sound;

(7) monitor the progress made toward meeting the identified goals, actions, and schedules of the Comprehensive Conservation and Management Plan, including through the implementation and support of a monitoring system for the ecological health and water quality conditions of Long Island Sound; and

(8) convene conferences and meetings for legislators from State governments and political subdivisions thereof for the purpose of making recommendations for coordinating legislative efforts to facilitate the environmental restoration of Long Island Sound and the implementation of the Comprehensive Conservation and Management Plan.

(d) Grants

(1) The Administrator is authorized to make grants for projects and studies which will help implement the Long Island Sound Comprehensive Conservation and Management Plan. Special emphasis shall be given to implementation, research and planning, enforcement, and citizen involvement and education.

(2) State, interstate, and regional water pollution control agencies, and other public or nonprofit private agencies, institutions, and organizations held to be eligible for grants pursuant to this subsection.

(3) Citizen involvement and citizen education grants under this subsection shall not exceed 95 per centum of the costs of such work. All other grants under this subsection shall not exceed 60 per cent of the research, studies, or work. All grants shall be made on the condition that the non-Federal share of such costs are provided from non-Federal sources.

(e) Assistance to distressed communities

(1) Eligible communities — For the purposes of this subsection, a distressed community is any community that meets affordability criteria established by the State in which the community is located, if such criteria are developed after public review and comment.

(2) Priority — In making assistance available under this section for the upgrading of wastewater treatment facilities, the Administrator may give priority to a distressed community.

(f) Report

(1) In general

Not later than 2 years after October 23, 2018, and biennially thereafter, the Director of the Office, in consultation with the Governor of each Long Island Sound State, shall submit to Congress a report that —

(A) summarizes and assesses the progress made by the Office and the Long Island Sound States in implementing the Long Island Sound Comprehensive Conservation and Management Plan, including an assessment of the progress made toward meeting the performance goals and milestones contained in the Plan;

(B) assesses the key ecological attributes that reflect the health of the ecosystem of the Long Island Sound watershed;

(C) describes any substantive modifications to the Long Island Sound Comprehensive Conservation and Management Plan made during the 2-year period preceding the date of submission of the report;

(D) provides specific recommendations to improve progress in restoring and protecting the Long Island Sound watershed, including, as appropriate, proposed modifications to the Long Island Sound Comprehensive Conservation and Management Plan;

(E) identifies priority actions for implementation of the Long Island Sound Comprehensive Conservation and Management Plan for the 2-year period following the date of submission of the report; and

(F) describes the means by which Federal funding and actions will be coordinated with the actions of the Long Island Sound States and other entities.

(2) Public availability

The Administrator shall make the report described in paragraph (1) available to the public, including on a publicly accessible website.

(g) Federal entities

(1) Coordination

The Administrator shall coordinate the actions of all Federal departments and agencies that affect water quality in the Long Island Sound watershed in order to improve the water quality and living resources of the watershed.

(2) Methods

In carrying out this section, the Administrator, acting through the Director of the Office, may —

(A) enter into interagency agreements; and

(B) make intergovernmental personnel appointments.

(4) Consistency with Comprehensive Conservation and Management Plan

To the maximum extent practicable, the head of each Federal department or agency that owns or occupies real property, or carries out activities, within the Long Island Sound watershed shall ensure that the property and all activities carried out by the department or agency are consistent with the Long Island Sound Comprehensive Conservation and Management Plan (including any related subsequent agreements and plans).

(h) Authorization of appropriations — There is authorized to be appropriated to the Administrator to carry out this section $40,000,000 for each of fiscal years 2019 through 2023.

§1270. Lake Champlain Basin Program
[CWA §120]

(a) Establishment

(1) In general — There is established a Lake Champlain Management Conference to develop a comprehensive pollution prevention, control, and restoration plan for Lake Champlain. The Administrator shall convene the management conference within ninety days of November 16, 1990.

(2) Implementation —

The Administrator —

(A) may provide support to the state of Vermont, the state of New York, and the New England Interstate Water Pollution Commission for the implementation of the Lake Champlain Basic Program; and

(B) shall coordinate actions of the Environmental Protection Agency under subparagraph (a) with the actions of other appropriate Federal agencies.

(b) Membership — The Members of the Management Conference shall be comprised of —

(1) the Governors of the States of Vermont and New York;

(2) each interested Federal agency, not to exceed a total of five members;

(3) the Vermont and New York Chairpersons of the Vermont, New York, Quebec Citizens Advisory Committee for the Environmental Management of Lake Champlain;

(4) four representatives of the State legislature of Vermont;

(5) four representatives of the State legislature of New York;

(6) six persons representing local governments having jurisdiction over any land or water within the Lake Champlain basin, as determined appropriate by the Governors; and

(7) eight persons representing affected industries, nongovernmental organizations, public and private educational institutions, and the general public, as determined appropriate by the trigovernmental Citizens Advisory Committee for the Environmental Management of Lake Champlain, but not to be current members of the Citizens Advisory Committee.

(c) Technical Advisory Committee

(1) The Management Conference shall, not later than one hundred and twenty days after November 16, 1990, appoint a Technical Advisory Committee.

(2) Such Technical Advisory Committee shall consist of officials of: appropriate departments and agencies of the Federal Government; the State governments of New York and Vermont; and governments of political subdivisions of such States; and public and private research institutions.

(d) Research program

(1) The Management Conference shall establish a multi-disciplinary environmental research program for Lake Champlain. Such research program shall be planned and conducted jointly with the Lake Champlain Research Consortium.

(e) Pollution prevention, control, and restoration plan

(1) Not later than three years after November 16, 1990, the Management Conference shall publish a pollution prevention, control, and restoration plan for Lake Champlain.

(2) The Plan developed pursuant to this section shall —

(A) identify corrective actions and compliance schedules addressing point and nonpoint sources of pollution necessary to restore and maintain the chemical, physical, and biological integrity of water quality, a balanced, indigenous population of shellfish, fish and wildlife, recreational, and economic activities in and on the lake;

(B) incorporate environmental management concepts and programs established in State and Federal plans and programs in effect at the time of the development of such plan;

(C) clarify the duties of Federal and State agencies in pollution prevention and control activities, and to the extent allowable by law, suggest a timetable for adoption by the appropriate Federal and State agencies to accomplish such duties within a reasonable period of time;

(D) describe the methods and schedules for funding of programs, activities, and projects identified in the Plan, including the use of Federal funds and other sources of funds; and

(E) include a strategy for pollution prevention and control that includes the promotion of pollution prevention and management practices to reduce the amount of pollution generated in the Lake Champlain basin.

(F) be reviewed and revised, as necessary, at least once every 5 years, in consultation with the Administrator and other appropriate Federal agencies.

(3) The Administrator, in cooperation with the Management Conference, shall provide for public review and comment on the draft Plan. At a minimum, the Management Conference shall conduct one public meeting to hear comments on the draft plan in the State of New York and one such meeting in the State of Vermont.

(4) Not less than one hundred and twenty days after the publication of the Plan required pursuant to this section, the Administrator shall approve such plan if the plan meets the requirements of this section and the Governors of the States of New York and Vermont concur.

(5) Upon approval of the plan, such plan shall be deemed to be an approved management program for the purposes of section 1329(h) of this title and such plan shall be deemed to be an approved comprehensive conservation and management plan pursuant to section 1330 of this title.

(f) Grant assistance

(1) The Administrator may, in consultation with participants in the Lake Champlain Basin Program, make grants to State, interstate, and regional water pollution control agencies, and public or nonprofit agencies, institutions, and organizations.

(2) Grants under this subsection shall be made for assisting research, surveys, studies, and modeling and technical and supporting work necessary for the development and implementation of the Plan.

(3) The amount of grants to any person under this subsection for a fiscal year shall not exceed 75 per centum of the costs of such research, survey, study and work and shall be made available on the condition that non-Federal share of such costs are provided from non-Federal sources.

(4) The Administrator may establish such requirements for the administration of grants as he determines to be appropriate.

(g) Definitions

In this section:

(1) Lake Champlain Basin Program

The term "Lake Champlain Basin Program" means the coordinated efforts among the Federal Government, State governments, and local governments to implement the Plan.

(2) Lake Champlain drainage basin

The term "Lake Champlain drainage basin" means all or part of Clinton, Franklin, Hamilton, Warren, Essex, and Washington counties in the State of New York and all or part of Franklin, Grand Isle, Chittenden, Addison, Rutland, Bennington, Lamoille, Orange, Washington, Orleans, and Caledonia counties in Vermont, that contain all of the streams, rivers, lakes, and other bodies of water, including wetlands, that drain into Lake Champlain.

(3) Plan

The term "Plan" means the plan developed under subsection (e) of this section.

(h) No effect on certain authority

Nothing in this section —

(1) affects the jurisdiction or powers of —

(A) any department or agency of the Federal Government or any State government; or

(B) any international organization or entity related to Lake Champlain created by treaty or memorandum to which the United States is a signatory;

(2) provides new regulatory authority for the Environmental Protection Agency; or

(3) affects section 304 of the Great Lakes Critical Programs Act of 1990 (Public Law 101-596; 33 U.S.C. 1270 note).

(i) Authorization

There are authorized to be appropriated to the Environmental Protection Agency to carry out this section —

(1) $2,000,000 for each of fiscal years 1991, 1992, 1993, 1994, and 1995;

(2) such sums as are necessary for each of fiscal years 1996 through 2003; and

(3) $11,000,000 for each of fiscal years 2004 through 2008.

§1271. Sediment survey and monitoring

(a) Survey

(1) In general — The Administrator, in consultation with the Administrator of the National Oceanic and Atmospheric Administration and the Secretary, shall conduct a comprehensive national survey of data regarding aquatic sediment quality in the United States. The Administrator shall compile all existing information on the quantity, chemical and physical composition, and geographic location of pollutants in aquatic sediment, including the probable source of such pollutants and identification of those sediments which are contaminated pursuant to section 501(b)(4).

(2) Report — Not later than 24 months after October 31, 1992, the Administrator shall report to the Congress the findings, conclusions, and recommendations of such survey, including recommendations for actions necessary to prevent contamination of aquatic sediments and to control sources of contamination.

(b) Monitoring

(1) In general — The Administrator, in consultation with the Administrator of the National Oceanic and Atmospheric Administration and the Secretary, shall conduct a comprehensive and continuing program to assess aquatic sediment quality. The program conducted pursuant to this subsection shall, at a minimum —

(A) identify the location of pollutants in aquatic sediment;

(B) identify the extent of pollutants in sediment and those sediments which are contaminated pursuant to section 501(b)(4);

(C) establish methods and protocols for monitoring the physical, chemical, and biological effects of pollutants in aquatic sediment and of contaminated sediment;

(D) develop a system for the management, storage, and dissemination of data concerning aquatic sediment quality;

(E) provide an assessment of aquatic sediment quality trends over time;

(F) identify locations where pollutants in sediment may pose a threat to the quality of drinking water supplies, fisheries resources, and marine habitats; and

(G) establish a clearing house for information on technology, methods, and practices available for the remediation, decontamination, and control of sediment contamination.

(2) Report — The Administrator shall submit to Congress a report on the findings of the monitoring under paragraph (1) on the date that is 2 years after the date specified in subsection (a)(2) of this section and biennially thereafter.

§1271a. Research and development program

(a) In general

In coordination with other Federal, State, and local officials, the Administrator of the Environmental Protection Agency may conduct research on the development and use of innovative approaches, technologies, and techniques for the remediation of sediment contamination in areas of concern that are located wholly or partially in the United States.

(b) Authorization of appropriations

(1) In general

In addition to amounts authorized under other laws, there is authorized to be appropriated to carry out this section $3,000,000 for each of fiscal years 2004 through 2010.

(2) Availability

Funds appropriated under paragraph (1) shall remain available until expended.

§1272. Environmental dredging

(a) Operation and maintenance of navigation projects — Whenever necessary to meet the requirements of the Federal Water Pollution Control Act (33 U.S.C. §§1251 *et seq.*), the Secretary,

in consultation with the Administrator of the Environmental Protection Agency, may remove and remediate, as part of operation and maintenance of a navigation project, contaminated sediments outside the boundaries of and adjacent to the navigation channel.

(b) Nonproject specific

(1) In general — The Secretary may remove and remediate contaminated sediments from the navigable waters of the United States for the purpose of environmental enhancement and water quality improvement if such removal and remediation is requested by a non-Federal sponsor and the sponsor agrees to pay 35 percent of the cost of such removal and remediation.

(2) Maximum amount — The Secretary may not expend more than $50,000,000 in a fiscal year to carry out this subsection.

(c) Joint plan requirement — The Secretary may only remove and remediate contaminated sediments under subsection (b) of this section in accordance with a joint plan developed by the Secretary and interested Federal, State, and local government officials. Such plan must include an opportunity for public comment, a description of the work to be undertaken, the method to be used for dredged material disposal, the roles and responsibilities of the Secretary and non-Federal sponsors, and identification of sources of funding.

(d) Disposal costs — Costs of disposal of contaminated sediments removed under this section shall be a shared as a cost of construction.

(e) Limitation on statutory construction — Nothing in this section shall be construed to affect the rights and responsibilities of any person under the Comprehensive Environmental Response, Compensation, and Liability Act of 1980 (42 U.S.C. §§9601 *et seq.*).

(f) Priority work — In carrying out this section, the Secretary shall give priority to work in the following areas:

(1) Brooklyn Waterfront, New York

(2) Buffalo Harbor and River, New York

(3) Ashtabula River, Ohio

(4) Mahoning River, Ohio

(5) Lower Fox River, Wisconsin

(6) Passaic River and Newark Bay, New Jersey

(7) Snake Creek, Bixby, Oklahoma

(8) Willamette River, Oregon

(g) Nonprofit entities — Notwithstanding section 1962d-5b of Title 42, for any project carried out under this section, a non-Federal sponsor may include a nonprofit entity, with the consent of the affected local government.

§1273. Lake Pontchartrain Basin

(a) Establishment of Restoration Program — The Administrator shall establish within the Environmental Protection Agency the Lake Pontchartrain Basin Restoration Program.

(b) Purpose — The purpose of the program shall be to restore the ecological health of the Basin by developing and funding restoration projects and related scientific and public education projects.

(c) Duties — In carrying out the program, the Administrator shall —

(1) provide administrative and technical assistance to a management conference convened for the Basin under section 1330 of this title;

(2) assist and support the activities of the management conference, including the implementation of recommendations of the management conference;

(3) support environmental monitoring of the Basin and research to provide necessary technical and scientific information;

(4) develop a comprehensive research plan to address the technical needs of the program;

(5) coordinate the grant, research, and planning programs authorized under this section; and

(6) collect and make available to the public publications, and other forms of information the management conference determines to be appropriate, relating to the environmental quality of the Basin.

(d) Grants — The Administrator may make grants to pay not more than 75 percent of the costs —

(1) for restoration projects and studies recommended by a management conference convened for the Basin under section 1330 of this title; and

(2) for public education projects recommended by the management conference.

(e) Definitions — In this section, the following definitions apply:

(1) Basin — The term "Basin" means the Lake Pontchartrain Basin, a 5,000 square mile watershed encompassing 16 parishes in the State of Louisiana and 4 counties in the State of Mississippi.

(2) Program — The term "program" means the Lake Pontchartrain Basin Restoration Program established under subsection (a) of this section.

(f) Authorization of appropriations

(1) In general — There is authorized to be appropriated to carry out this section $20,000,000 for each of fiscal years 2001 through 2012 and the amount appropriated for fiscal year 2009 for each of fiscal years 2013 through 2017. Such sums shall remain available until expended.

(2) Public education projects — Not more than 15 percent of the amount appropriated pursuant to paragraph (1) in a fiscal year may be expended on grants for public education projects under subsection (d)(2) of this section.

§1274. Watershed pilot projects

(a) In general — The Administrator, in coordination with the States, may provide technical assistance and grants to a municipality or municipal entity to carry out pilot projects relating to the following areas:

(1) Watershed management of wet weather discharges — The management of municipal combined sewer overflows, sanitary sewer overflows, and stormwater discharges, on an integrated watershed or subwatershed basis for the purpose of demonstrating the effectiveness of a unified wet weather approach.

(2) Stormwater best management practices — The control of pollutants from municipal separate storm sewer systems for the purpose of demonstrating and determining controls that are cost-effective and that use innovative technologies to manage, reduce, treat, recapture, or reuse municipal stormwater, including techniques that utilize infiltration, evapotranspiration, and reuse of stormwater onsite.

(3) Watershed partnerships — Efforts of municipalities and property owners to demonstrate cooperative ways to address nonpoint sources of pollution to reduce adverse impacts on water quality.

(4) Integrated water resource plan — The development of an integrated water resource plan for the coordinated management and protection of surface water, ground water, and stormwater resources on a watershed or subwatershed basis to meet the objectives, goals, and policies of this chapter.

(5) Municipality-wide stormwater management planning — The development of a municipality-wide plan that identifies the most effective placement of stormwater technologies and management approaches, to reduce water quality impairments from stormwater on a municipality-wide basis.

(6) Increased resilience of treatment works — Efforts to assess future risks and vulnerabilities of publicly owned treatment works to manmade or natural disasters, including extreme weather events and sea-level rise, and to carry out measures, on a systemwide or area-wide basis, to increase the resiliency of publicly owned treatment works.

(b) Administration — The Administrator, in coordination with the States, shall provide municipalities participating in a pilot project under this section the ability to engage in innovative practices, including the ability to unify separate wet weather control efforts under a single permit.

(c) Report to Congress — Not later than October 1, 2015, the Administrator shall transmit to Congress a report on the results of the pilot projects conducted under this section and their possible application nationwide.

§1275. Columbia River Basin Restoration

(a) Definitions

In this section, the following definitions apply:

(1) Columbia River Basin

The term "Columbia River Basin" means the entire United States portion of the Columbia River watershed.

(2) Estuary Partnership

The term "Estuary Partnership" means the Lower Columbia Estuary Partnership, an entity created by the States of Oregon and Washington and the Environmental Protection Agency under section 1330 of this title.

(3) Estuary Plan

(A) In general

The term "Estuary Plan" means the Estuary Partnership Comprehensive Conservation and Management Plan adopted by the Environmental Protection Agency and the Governors of Oregon and Washington on October 20, 1999, under section 1330 of this title.

(B) Inclusion

The term "Estuary Plan" includes any amendments to the plan.

(4) Lower Columbia River Estuary

The term "Lower Columbia River Estuary" means the mainstem Columbia River from the Bonneville Dam to the Pacific Ocean and tidally influenced portions of tributaries to the Columbia River in that region.

(5) Middle and Upper Columbia River Basin

The term "Middle and Upper Columbia River Basin" means the region consisting of the United States portion of the Columbia River Basin above Bonneville Dam.

(6) Program

The term "Program" means the Columbia River Basin Restoration Program established under subsection (b)(1)(A).

(b) Columbia River Basin Restoration Program

(1) Establishment

(A) In general

The Administrator shall establish within the Environmental Protection Agency a Columbia River Basin Restoration Program.

(B) Effect

(i) The establishment of the Program does not modify any legal or regulatory authority or program in effect as of December 16, 2016, including the roles of Federal agencies in the Columbia River Basin.

(ii) This section does not create any new regulatory authority.

(2) Scope of Program

The Program shall consist of a collaborative stakeholder-based program for environmental protection and restoration activities throughout the Columbia River Basin.

(3) Duties

The Administrator shall —

(A) assess trends in water quality, including trends that affect uses of the water of the Columbia River Basin;

(B) collect, characterize, and assess data on water quality to identify possible causes of environmental problems; and

(C) provide grants in accordance with subsection (d) for projects that assist in —

(i) eliminating or reducing pollution;

(ii) cleaning up contaminated sites;

(iii) improving water quality;

(iv) monitoring to evaluate trends;

(v) reducing runoff;

(vi) protecting habitat; or

(vii) promoting citizen engagement or knowledge.

(c) Stakeholder Working Group

(1) Establishment

The Administrator shall establish a Columbia River Basin Restoration Working Group (referred to in this subsection as the "Working Group").

(2) Membership

(A) In general

Membership in the Working Group shall be on a voluntary basis and any person invited by the Administrator under this subsection may decline membership.

(B) Invited representatives

The Administrator shall invite, at a minimum, representatives of —

(i) each State located in whole or in part in the Columbia River Basin;

(ii) the Governors of each State located in whole or in part in the Columbia River Basin;

(iii) each federally recognized Indian tribe in the Columbia River Basin;

(iv) local governments in the Columbia River Basin;

(v) industries operating in the Columbia River Basin that affect or could affect water quality;

(vi) electric, water, and wastewater utilities operating in the Columba 1 River Basin;

(vii) private landowners in the Columbia River Basin;

(viii) soil and water conservation districts in the Columbia River Basin;

(ix) nongovernmental organizations that have a presence in the Columbia River Basin;

(x) the general public in the Columbia River Basin; and

(xi) the Estuary Partnership.

(3) Geographic representation

The Working Group shall include representatives from —

(A) each State located in whole or in part in the Columbia River Basin; and

(B) each of the lower, middle, and upper basins of the Columbia River.

(4) Duties and responsibilities

The Working Group shall —

(A) recommend and prioritize projects and actions; and

(B) review the progress and effectiveness of projects and actions implemented.

(5) Lower Columbia River Estuary

(A) Estuary Partnership

The Estuary Partnership shall perform the duties and fulfill the responsibilities of the Working Group described in paragraph (4) as those duties and responsibilities relate to the Lower Columbia River Estuary for such time as the Estuary Partnership is the management conference for the Lower Columbia River National Estuary Program under section 1330 of this title.

(B) Designation

If the Estuary Partnership ceases to be the management conference for the Lower Columbia River National Estuary Program under section 1330 of this title, the Administrator may designate the new management conference to assume the duties and responsibilities of the Working Group described in paragraph (4) as those duties and responsibilities relate to the Lower Columbia River Estuary.

(C) Incorporation

If the Estuary Partnership is removed from the National Estuary Program, the duties and responsibilities for the lower 146 miles of the Columbia River pursuant to this section shall be incorporated into the duties of the Working Group.

(d) Grants

(1) In general

The Administrator shall establish a voluntary, competitive Columbia River Basin program to provide grants to State governments, tribal governments, regional water pollution control agencies and entities, local government entities, nongovernmental entities, or soil and water conservation districts to develop or implement projects authorized under this section for the purpose of environmental protection and restoration activities throughout the Columbia River Basin.

(2) Federal share

(A) In general

Except as provided in subparagraph (B), the Federal share of the cost of any project or activity carried out using funds from a grant provided to any person (including a State, tribal, or local government or interstate or regional agency) under this subsection for a fiscal year —

(i) shall not exceed 75 percent of the total cost of the project or activity; and

(ii) shall be made on condition that the non-Federal share of such total cost shall be provided from non-Federal sources.

(B) Exceptions

With respect to cost-sharing for a grant provided under this subsection —

(i) a tribal government may use Federal funds for the non-Federal share; and

(ii) the Administrator may increase the Federal share under such circumstances as the Administrator determines to be appropriate.

(3) Allocation

In making grants using funds appropriated to carry out this section, the Administrator shall —

(A) provide not less than 25 percent of the funds to make grants for projects, programs, and studies in the Lower Columbia River Estuary;

(B) provide not less than 25 percent of the funds to make grants for projects, programs, and studies in the Middle and Upper Columbia River Basin, including the Snake River Basin; and

(C) retain not more than 5 percent of the funds for the Environmental Protection Agency for purposes of implementing this section.

(4) Reporting

(A) In general

Each grant recipient under this subsection shall submit to the Administrator reports on progress being made in achieving the purposes of this section.

(B) Requirements

The Administrator shall establish requirements and timelines for recipients of grants under this subsection to report on progress made in achieving the purposes of this section.

(5) Relationship to other funding

(A) In general

Nothing in this subsection limits the eligibility of the Estuary Partnership to receive funding under section 1330(g) of this title.

(B) Limitation

None of the funds made available under this subsection may be used for the administration of a management conference under section 1330 of this title.

(6) Authorization of appropriations

There is authorized to be appropriated to carry out this subsection $30,000,000 for each of fiscal years 2020 and 2021.

(e) Annual budget plan

The President, as part of the annual budget submission of the President to Congress under section 1105(a) of title 31, shall submit information regarding each Federal agency involved in protection and restoration of the Columbia River Basin, including an interagency crosscut budget that displays for each Federal agency —

(1) the amounts obligated for the preceding fiscal year for protection and restoration projects, programs, and studies relating to the Columbia River Basin;

(2) the estimated budget for the current fiscal year for protection and restoration projects, programs, and studies relating to the Columbia River Basin; and

(3) the proposed budget for protection and restoration projects, programs, and studies relating to the Columbia River Basin.

SUBCHAPTER II — GRANTS FOR CONSTRUCTION OF TREATMENT WORKS

§1281. Congressional declaration of purpose [CWA §201]

(a) Development and implementation of waste treatment management plans and practices — It is the purpose of this subchapter to require and to assist the development and implementation of waste treatment management plans and practices which will achieve the goals of this chapter.

(b) Application of technology: confined disposal of pollutants; consideration of advanced techniques — Waste treatment management plans and practices shall provide for the application of the best practicable waste treatment technology before any discharge into receiving waters, including reclaiming and recycling of water, and confined disposal of pollutants so they will not migrate to cause water or other environmental pollution and shall provide for consideration of advanced waste treatment techniques.

(c) Waste treatment management area and scope — To the extent practicable, waste treatment management shall be on an areawide basis and provide control or treatment of all point and nonpoint sources of pollution, including in place or accumulated pollution sources.

(d) Waste treatment management construction of revenue producing facilities — The Administrator shall encourage waste treatment management which results in the construction of revenue producing facilities providing for —

(1) the recycling of potential sewage pollutants through the production of agriculture, silviculture, or aquaculture products, or any combination thereof;

(2) the confined and contained disposal of pollutants not recycled;

(3) the reclamation of wastewater; and

(4) the ultimate disposal of sludge in a manner that will not result in environmental hazards.

(e) Waste treatment management integration of facilities — The Administrator shall encourage waste treatment management which results in integrating facilities for sewage treatment and recycling with facilities to treat, dispose of, or utilize other industrial and municipal wastes, including but not limited to solid waste and waste heat and thermal discharges. Such integrated facilities shall be designed and operated to produce revenues in excess of capital and operation and maintenance costs and such revenues shall be used by the designated regional management agency to aid in financing other environmental improvement programs.

(f) Waste treatment management "open space" and recreational considerations — The Administrator shall encourage waste treatment management which combines "open space" and recreational considerations with such management.

(g) Grants to construct publicly owned treatment works

(1) The Administrator is authorized to make grants to any State, municipality, or intermunicipal or interstate agency for the construction of publicly owned treatment works. On and after October 1, 1984, grants under this subchapter shall be made only for projects for secondary treatment or more stringent treatment, or any cost effective alternative thereto, new interceptors and appurtenances, and infiltration-in-flow correction. Notwithstanding the preceding sentences, the Administrator may make grants on and after October 1, 1984, for (A) any project within the definition set forth in section 1292(2) of this title, other than for a project referred to in the preceding sentence, and (B) any purpose for which a grant may be made under sections 1329(h) and (i) of this title (including any innovative and alternative approaches for the control of nonpoint sources of pollution), except that not more than 20 per centum (as determined by the Governor of the State) of the amount allotted to a State under section 1285 of this title for any fiscal year shall be obligated in such State under authority of this sentence.

(2) The Administrator shall not make grants from funds authorized for any fiscal year beginning after June 30, 1974, to any State, municipality, or intermunicipal or interstate agency for the erection, building, acquisition, alteration, remodeling, improvement, or extension of treatment works unless the grant applicant has satisfactorily demonstrated to the Administrator that —

(A) alternative waste management techniques have been studied and evaluated and the works proposed for grant assistance will provide for the application of the best practicable waste treatment technology over the life of the works consistent with the purposes of this subchapter; and

(B) as appropriate, the works proposed for grant assistance will take into account and allow to the extent practicable the application of technology at a later date which will provide for the reclaiming or recycling of water or otherwise eliminate the discharge of pollutants.

(3) The Administrator shall not approve any grant after July 1, 1973, for treatment works under this section unless the applicant shows to the satisfaction of the Administrator that each sewer

collection system discharging into such treatment works is not subject to excessive infiltration.

(4) The Administrator is authorized to make grants to applicants for treatment works grants under this section for such sewer system evaluation studies as may be necessary to carry out the requirements of paragraph (3) of this subsection. Such grants shall be made in accordance with rules and regulations promulgated by the Administrator. Initial rules and regulations shall be promulgated under this paragraph not later than 120 days after October 18, 1972.

(5) The Administrator shall not make grants from funds authorized for any fiscal year beginning after September 30, 1978, to any State, municipality, or intermunicipal or interstate agency for the erection, building, acquisition, alteration, remodeling, improvement, or extension of treatment works unless the grant applicant has satisfactorily demonstrated to the Administrator that innovative and alternative wastewater treatment processes and techniques which provide for the reclaiming and reuse of water, otherwise eliminate the discharge of pollutants, and utilize recycling techniques, land treatment, new or improved methods of waste treatment management for municipal and industrial waste (discharged into municipal systems) and the confined disposal of pollutants, so that pollutants will not migrate to cause water or other environmental pollution, have been fully studied and evaluated by the applicant taking into account subsection (d) of this section and taking into account and allowing to the extent practicable the more efficient use of energy and resources.

(6) The Administrator shall not make grants from funds authorized for any fiscal year beginning after September 30, 1978, to any State, municipality, or intermunicipal or interstate agency for the erection, building, acquisition, alteration, remodeling, improvement, or extension of treatment works unless the grant applicant has satisfactorily demonstrated to the Administrator that the applicant has analyzed the potential recreation and open space opportunities in the planning of the proposed treatment works.

(h) Grants to construct privately owned treatment works — A grant may be made under this section to construct a privately owned treatment works serving one or more principal residences or small commercial establishments constructed prior to, and inhabited on, December 27, 1977, where the Administrator finds that —

(1) a public body otherwise eligible for a grant under subsection (g) of this section has applied on behalf of a number of such units and certified that public ownership of such works is not feasible;

(2) such public body has entered into an agreement with the Administrator which guarantees that such treatment works will be properly operated and maintained and will comply with all other requirements of section 1284 of this title and includes a system of charges to assure that each recipient of waste treatment services under such a grant will pay its proportionate share of the cost of operation and maintenance (including replacement); and

(3) the total cost and environmental impact of providing waste treatment services to such residences or commercial establishments will be less than the cost of providing a system of collection and central treatment of such wastes.

(i) Waste treatment management methods, processes, and techniques to reduce energy requirements — The Administrator shall encourage waste treatment management methods, processes, and techniques which will reduce total energy requirements.

(j) Grants for treatment works utilizing processes and techniques of guidelines under section 1314(d)(3) of this title — The Administrator is authorized to make a grant for any treatment works utilizing processes and techniques meeting the guidelines promulgated under section 1314(d)(3) of this title, if the Administrator determines it is in the public interest and if in the cost effectiveness study made of the construction grant application for the purpose of evaluating alternative treatment works, the life cycle cost of the treatment works for which the grant is to be made does not exceed the life cycle cost of the most cost effective alternative by more than 15 per centum.

(k) Limitation on use of grants for publicly owned treatment works — No grant made after November 15, 1981, for a publicly owned treatment works, other than for facility planning and the preparation of construction plans and specifications, shall be used to treat, store, or convey the flow of any industrial user into such treatment works in excess of a flow per day equivalent to fifty thousand gallons per day of sanitary waste. This subsection shall not apply to any project proposed by a grantee which is carrying out an approved project to prepare construction plans and specifications for a facility to treat wastewater, which received its grant approval before May 15, 1980. This subsection shall not be in effect after November 15, 1981.

(l) Grants for facility plans, or plans, specifications, and estimates for proposed project for construction of treatment works; limitations, allotments, advances, etc.

(1) After December 29, 1981, Federal grants shall not be made for the purpose of providing assistance solely for facility plans, or plans, specifications, and estimates for any proposed project for the construction of treatment works. In the event that the proposed project receives a grant under this section for construction, the Administrator shall make an allowance in such grant for non-Federal funds expended during the facility planning and advanced engineering and design phase at the prevailing Federal share under section 1282(a) of this title, based on the percentage of total project costs which the Administrator determines is the general experience for such projects.

(2)(A) Each State shall use a portion of the funds allotted to such State each fiscal year, but not to exceed 10 per centum of such funds, to advance to potential grant applicants under this subchapter the costs of facility planning or the preparation of plans, specifications, and estimates.

(B) Such an advance shall be limited to the allowance for such costs which the Administrator establishes under paragraph (1) of this subsection, and shall be provided only to a potential grant applicant which is a small community and which in the judgment of the State would otherwise be unable to prepare a request for a grant for construction costs under this section.

(C) In the event a grant for construction costs is made under this section for a project for which an advance has been made under this paragraph, the Administrator shall reduce the amount of such grant by the allowance established under paragraph (1) of this subsection. In the event no such grant is made, the State is authorized to seek repayment of such advance on such terms and conditions as it may determine.

(m) Grants for State of California projects

(1) Notwithstanding any other provisions of this subchapter, the Administrator is authorized to make a grant from any funds otherwise allotted to the State of California under section 1285 of this title to the project (and in the amount) specified in Order WQG 81-1 of the California State Water Resources Control Board.

(2) Notwithstanding any other provision of this chapter, the Administrator shall make a grant from any funds otherwise allotted to the State of California to the city of Eureka, California, in connection with project numbered C-06-2772, for the purchase of one hundred and thirty-nine acres of property as environmental mitigation for siting of the proposed treatment plant.

(3) Notwithstanding any other provision of this chapter, the Administrator shall make a grant from any funds otherwise allotted to the State of California to the city of San Diego, California, in connection with that city's aquaculture sewage process (total resources recovery system) as an innovative and alternative waste treatment process.

(n) Water quality problems; funds, scope, etc.

(1) On and after October 1, 1984, upon the request of the Governor of an affected State, the Administrator is authorized to use funds available to such State under section 1285 of this title to address water quality problems due to the impacts of discharges from combined storm water and

sanitary sewer overflows, which are not otherwise eligible under this subsection, where correction of such discharges is a major priority for such State.

(2) Beginning fiscal year 1983, the Administrator shall have available $200,000,000 per fiscal year in addition to those funds authorized in section 1287 of this title to be utilized to address water quality problems of marine bays and estuaries subject to lower levels of water quality due to the impacts of discharges from combined storm water and sanitary sewer overflows from adjacent urban complexes, not otherwise eligible under this subsection. Such sums may be used as deemed appropriate by the Administrator as provided in paragraphs (1) and (2) of this subsection, upon the request of and demonstration of water quality benefits by the Governor of an affected State.

(o) Capital financing plan — The Administrator shall encourage and assist applicants for grant assistance under this subchapter to develop and file with the Administrator a capital financing plan which, at a minimum —

(1) projects the future requirements for waste treatment services within the applicant's jurisdiction for a period of no less than ten years;

(2) projects the nature, extent, timing, and costs of future expansion and reconstruc- tion of treatment works which will be necessary to satisfy the applicant's projected future requirements for waste treatment services; and

(3) sets forth with specificity the manner in which the applicant intends to finance such future expansion and reconstruction.

(p) Time limit on resolving certain disputes — In any case in which a dispute arises with respect to the awarding of a contract for construction of treatment works by a grantee of funds under this subchapter and a party to such dispute files an appeal with the Administrator under this subchapter for resolution of such dispute, the Administrator shall make a final decision on such appeal within 90 days of the filing of such appeal.

§1281a. Total treatment system funding — Notwithstanding any other provision of law, in any case where the Administrator of the Environmental Protection Agency finds that the total of all grants made under section 1281 of this title for the same treatment works exceeds the actual construction costs for such treatment works (as defined in this chapter) such excess amount shall be a grant of the Federal share (as defined in this chapter) of the cost of construction of a sewage collection system if —

(1) such sewage collection system was constructed as part of the same total treatment system as the treatment works for which such grants under section 1281 of this title were approved, and

(2) an application for assistance for the construction of such sewage collection system was

filed in accordance with section 3102 of Title 42 before all such grants under section 1281 of this title were made and such grant under section 3102 of Title 42 could not be approved due to lack of funding under such section 3102 of Title 42. The total of all grants for sewage collection systems made under this section shall not exceed $2,800,000.

§1281b. Availability of Farmers Home Administration funds for non-Federal share —

Notwithstanding any other provision of law, Federal assistance made available by the Farmers Home Administration to any political subdivision of a State may be used to provide the non-Federal share of the cost of any construction project carried out under section 1281 of this title.

§1282. Federal share
[CWA §202]
(a) Amount of grants for treatment works

(1) The amount of any grant for treatment works made under this chapter from funds authorized for any fiscal year beginning after June 30, 1971, and ending before October 1, 1984, shall be 75 per centum of the cost of construction thereof (as approved by the Administrator), and for any fiscal year beginning on or after October 1, 1984, shall be 55 per centum of the cost of construction thereof (as approved by the Administrator), unless modified to a lower percentage rate uniform throughout a State by the Governor of that State with the concurrence of the Administrator. Within ninety days after October 21, 1980, the Administrator shall issue guidelines for concurrence in any such modification, which shall provide for the consideration of the unobligated balance of sums allocated to the State under section 1285 of this title, the need for assistance under this subchapter in such State, and the availability of State grant assistance to replace the Federal share reduced by such modification. The payment of any such reduced Federal share shall not constitute an obligation on the part of the United States or a claim on the part of any State or grantee to reimbursement for the portion of the Federal share reduced in any such State. Any grant (other than for reimbursement) made prior to October 18, 1972, from any funds authorized for any fiscal year beginning after June 30, 1971, shall, upon the request of the applicant, be increased to the applicable percentage under this section. Notwithstanding the first sentence of this paragraph, in any case where a primary, secondary, or advanced waste treatment facility or its related interceptors or a project for infiltration-in-flow correction has received a grant for erection, building, acquisition, alteration, remodeling, improvement, extension, or correction before October 1, 1984, all segments and phases of such facility, interceptors, and project for infiltration-in-flow correction shall be

eligible for grants at 75 per centum of the cost of construction thereof for any grant made pursuant to a State obligation which obligation occurred before October 1, 1990. Notwithstanding the first sentence of this paragraph, in the case of a project for which an application for a grant under this subchapter has been made to the Administrator before October 1, 1984, and which project is under judicial injunction on such date prohibiting its construction, such project shall be eligible for grants at 75 percent of the cost of construction thereof. Notwithstanding the first sentence of this paragraph, in the case of the Wyoming Valley Sanitary Authority project mandated by judicial order under a proceeding begun prior to October 1, 1984, and a project for wastewater treatment for Altoona, Pennsylvania, such projects shall be eligible for grants at 75 percent of the cost of construction thereof.

(2) The amount of any grant made after September 30, 1978, and before October 1, 1981, for any eligible treatment works or significant portion thereof utilizing innovative or alternative wastewater treatment processes and techniques referred to in section 1281(g)(5) of this title shall be 85 per centum of the cost of construction thereof, unless modified by the Governor of the State with the concurrence of the Administrator to a percentage rate no less than 15 per centum greater than the modified uniform percentage rate in which the Administrator has concurred pursuant to paragraph (1) of this subsection. The amount of any grant made after September 30, 1981, for any eligible treatment works or unit processes and techniques thereof utilizing innovative or alternative wastewater treatment processes and techniques referred to in section 1281(g)(5) of this title shall be a percentage of the cost of construction thereof equal to 20 per centum greater than the percentage in effect under paragraph (1) of this subsection for such works or unit processes and techniques, but in no event greater than 85 per centum of the cost of construction thereof. No grant shall be made under this paragraph for construction of a treatment works in any State unless the proportion of the State contribution to the non-Federal share of construction costs for all treatment works in such State receiving a grant under this paragraph is the same as or greater than the proportion of the State contribution (if any) to the non-Federal share of construction costs for all treatment works receiving grants in such State under paragraph (1) of this subsection.

(3) In addition to any grant made pursuant to paragraph (2) of this subsection, the Administrator is authorized to make a grant to fund all of the costs of the modification or replacement of any facilities constructed with a grant made pursuant to paragraph (2) if the Administrator finds that such facilities have not met design performance

specifications unless such failure is attributable to negligence on the part of any person and if such failure has significantly increased capital or operating and maintenance expenditures. In addition, the Administrator is authorized to make a grant to fund all of the costs of the modification or replacement of biodisc equipment (rotating biological contactors) in any publicly owned treatment works if the Administrator finds that such equipment has failed to meet design performance specifications, unless such failure is attributable to negligence on the part of any person, and if such failure has significantly increased capital or operating and maintenance expenditures.

(4) For the purposes of this section, the term "eligible treatment works" means those treatment works in each State which meet the requirements of section 1281(g)(5) of this title and which can be fully funded from funds available for such purpose in such State.

(b) Amount of grants for construction of treatment works not commenced prior to July 1, 1971 — The amount of the grant for any project approved by the Administrator after January 1, 1971, and before July 1, 1971, for the construction of treatment works, the actual erection, building or acquisition of which was not commenced prior to July 1, 1971, shall, upon the request of the applicant, be increased to the applicable percentage under subsection (a) of this section for grants for treatment works from funds for fiscal years beginning after June 30, 1971, with respect to the cost of such actual erection, building, or acquisition. Such increased amount shall be paid from any funds allocated to the State in which the treatment works is located without regard to the fiscal year for which such funds were authorized. Such increased amount shall be paid for such project only if —

(1) a sewage collection system that is a part of the same total waste treatment system as the treatment works for which such grant was approved is under construction or is to be constructed for use in conjunction with such treatment works, and if the cost of such sewage collection system exceeds the cost of such treatment works, and

(2) the State water pollution control agency or other appropriate State authority certifies that the quantity of available ground water will be insufficient, inadequate, or unsuitable for public use, including the ecological preservation and recreational use of surface water bodies, unless effluents from publicly-owned treatment works after adequate treatment are returned to the ground water consistent with acceptable technological standards.

(c) Availability of sums allotted to Puerto Rico — Notwithstanding any other provision of law, sums allotted to the Commonwealth of Puerto Rico under section 1285 of this title for fiscal year 1981 shall remain available for obligation for the fiscal year for which authorized and for the period of the next succeeding twenty-four months. Such sums and any unobligated funds available to Puerto Rico from allotments for fiscal years ending prior to October 1, 1981, shall be available for obligation by the Administrator of the Environmental Protection Agency only to fund the following systems: Aguadilla, Arecibo, Mayaguez, Carolina, and Camuy Hatillo. These funds may be used by the commonwealth of Puerto Rico to fund the non-Federal share of the costs of such projects. To the extent that these funds are used to pay the non-Federal share, the Commonwealth of Puerto Rico shall repay to the Environmental Protection Agency such amounts on terms and conditions developed and approved by the Administrator in consultation with the Governor of the Commonwealth of Puerto Rico. Agreement on such terms and conditions, including the payment of interest to be determined by the Secretary of the Treasury, shall be reached prior to the use of these funds for the Commonwealth's non-Federal share. No Federal funds awarded under this provision shall be used to replace local governments funds previously expended on these projects.

§1283. Plans, specifications, estimates, and payments

[CWA §203]

(a) Submission; contractual nature of approval by Administrator; agreement on eligible costs; single grant

(1) Each applicant for a grant shall submit to the Administrator for his approval, plans, specifications, and estimates for each proposed project for the construction of treatment works for which a grant is applied for under section 1281(g)(1) of this title from funds allotted to the State under section 1285 of this title and which otherwise meets the requirements of this chapter. The Administrator shall act upon such plans, specifications, and estimates as soon as practicable after the same have been submitted, and his approval of any such plans, specifications, and estimates shall be deemed a contractual obligation of the United States for the payment of its proportional contribution to such project.

(2) **Agreement on eligible costs**

(A) Limitation on modifications — Before taking final action on any plans, specifications, and estimates submitted under this subsection after the 60th day following February 4, 1987, the Administrator shall enter into a written agreement with the applicant which establishes and specifies which items of the proposed project are eligible for Federal payments under this section. The Administrator may not later modify such eligibility determinations unless they are found to have been made in violation of applicable Federal statutes and regulations.

(B) Limitation on effect — Eligibility determinations under this paragraph shall not preclude the Administrator from auditing a project pursuant to section 1361 of this title, or other authority, or from withholding or recovering Federal funds for costs which are found to be unreasonable, unsupported by adequate documentation, or otherwise unallowable under applicable Federal cost principles, or which are incurred on a project which fails to meet the design specifications or effluent limitations contained in the grant agreement and permit pursuant to section 1342 of this title for such project.

(3) In the case of a treatment works that has an estimated total cost of $8,000,000 or less (as determined by the Administrator), and the population of the applicant municipality is twenty-five thousand or less (according to the most recent United States census), upon completion of an approved facility plan, a single grant may be awarded for the combined Federal share of the cost of preparing construction plans and specifications, and the building and erection of the treatment works.

(b) Periodic payments — The Administrator shall, from time to time as the work progresses, make payments to the recipient of a grant for costs of construction incurred on a project. These payments shall at no time exceed the Federal share of the cost of construction incurred to the date of the voucher covering such payment plus the Federal share of the value of the materials which have been stockpiled in the vicinity of such construction in conformity to plans and specifications for the project.

(c) Final payments — After completion of a project and approval of the final voucher by the Administrator, he shall pay out of the appropriate sums the unpaid balance of the Federal share payable on account of such project.

(d) Projects eligible — Nothing in this chapter shall be construed to require, or to authorize the Administrator to require, that grants under this chapter for construction of treatment works be made only for projects which are operable units usable for sewage collection, transportation, storage, waste treatment, or for similar purposes without additional construction.

(e) Technical and legal assistance in administration and enforcement of contracts; intervention in civil actions — At the request of a grantee under this subchapter, the Administrator is authorized to provide technical and legal assistance in the administration and enforcement of any contract in connection with treatment works assisted under this subchapter, and to intervene in any civil action involving the enforcement of such a contract.

(f) Design/build projects

(1) Agreement — Consistent with State law, an applicant who proposes to construct waste water treatment works may enter into an agreement with the Administrator under this subsection providing for the preparation of construction plans and specifications and the erection of such treatment works, in lieu of proceeding under the other provisions of this section.

(2) Limitation on projects Agreements under this subsection shall be limited to projects under an approved facility plan which projects are —

(A) treatment works that have an estimated total cost of $8,000,000 or less; and

(B) any of the following types of waste water treatment systems: aerated lagoons, trickling filters, stabilization ponds, land application systems, sand filters, and subsurface disposal systems.

(3) Required terms — An agreement entered into under this subsection shall —

(A) set forth an amount agreed to as the maximum Federal contribution to the project, based upon a competitively bid document of basic design data and applicable standard construction specifications and a determination of the federally eligible costs of the project at the applicable Federal share under section 1282 of this title;

(B) set forth dates for the start and completion of construction of the treatment works by the applicant and a schedule of payments of the Federal contribution to the project;

(C) contain assurances by the applicant that (i) engineering and management assistance will be provided to manage the project; (ii) the proposed treatment works will be an operable unit and will meet all the requirements of this subchapter; and (iii) not later than 1 year after the date specified as the date of completion of construction of the treatment works, the treatment works will be operating so as to meet the requirements of any applicable permit for such treatment works under section 1342 of this title;

(D) require the applicant to obtain a bond from the contractor in an amount determined necessary by the Administrator to protect the Federal interest in the project; and

(E) contain such other terms and conditions as are necessary to assure compliance with this subchapter (except as provided in paragraph (4) of this subsection).

(4) Limitation on application — Subsections (a), (b), and (c) of this section shall not apply to grants made pursuant to this subsection.

(5) Reservation to assure compliance — The Administrator shall reserve a portion of the grant to assure contract compliance until final project approval as defined by the Administrator. If the amount agreed to under paragraph (3)(A) exceeds the cost of designing and constructing the treatment works, the Administrator shall reallot the amount of the excess to the State in which such treatment works are located for the fiscal year in which such audit is completed.

(6) Limitation on obligations — The Administrator shall not obligate more than 20 percent of the amount allotted to a State for a fiscal year under section 1285 of this title for grants pursuant to this subsection.

(7) Allowance — The Administrator shall determine an allowance for facilities planning for projects constructed under this subsection in accordance with section 1281(*l*) of this title.

(8) Limitation on Federal contributions — In no event shall the Federal contribution for the cost of preparing construction plans and specifications and the building and erection of treatment works pursuant to this subsection exceed the amount agreed upon under paragraph (3).

(9) Recovery action — In any case in which the recipient of a grant made pursuant to this subsection does not comply with the terms of the agreement entered into under paragraph (3), the Administrator is authorized to take such action as may be necessary to recover the amount of the Federal contribution to the project.

(10) Prevention of double benefits — A recipient of a grant made pursuant to this subsection shall not be eligible for any other grants under this subchapter for the same project.

§1284. Limitations and conditions
[CWA §204]

(a) Determinations by Administrator — Before approving grants for any project for any treatment works under section 1281(g)(1) of this title the Administrator shall determine —

(1) that any required areawide waste treatment management plan under section 1288 of this title (A) is being implemented for such area and the proposed treatment works are included in such plan, or (B) is being developed for such area and reasonable progress is being made toward its implementation and the proposed treatment works will be included in such plan;

(2) that (A) the State in which the project is to be located (i) is implementing any required plan under section 1313(e) of this title and the proposed treatment works are in conformity with such plan, or (ii) is developing such a plan and the proposed treatment works will be in conformity with such plan, and (B) such State is in compliance with section 1315(b) of this title;

(3) that such works have been certified by the appropriate State water pollution control agency as entitled to priority over such other works in the State in accordance with any applicable State plan under section 1313(e) of this title, except that any priority list developed pursuant to section 1313(e)(3)(H) of this title may be modified by such State in accordance with regulations promulgated by the Administrator to give higher priority for grants for the Federal share of the cost of preparing construction drawings and specifications for any treatment works utilizing processes and techniques meeting the guidelines promulgated under section 1314(d)(3) of this title and for grants for the combined Federal share of the cost of preparing construction drawings and specifications and the building and erection of any treatment works meeting the requirements of the next to the last sentence of section 1283(a) of this title which utilizes processes and techniques meeting the guidelines promulgated under section 1314(d)(3) of this title.

(4) that the applicant proposing to construct such works agrees to pay the non-Federal costs of such works and has made adequate provisions satisfactory to the Administrator for assuring proper and efficient operation, including the employment of trained management and operations personnel, and the maintenance of such works in accordance with a plan of operation approved by the State water pollution control agency or, as appropriate, the interstate agency, after construction thereof;

(5) that the size and capacity of such works relate directly to the needs to be served by such works, including sufficient reserve capacity. The amount of reserve capacity provided shall be approved by the Administrator on the basis of a comparison of the cost of constructing such reserves as a part of the works to be funded and the anticipated cost of providing expanded capacity at a date when such capacity will be required, after taking into account, in accordance with regulations promulgated by the Administrator, efforts to reduce total flow of sewage and unnecessary water consumption. The amount of reserve capacity eligible for a grant under this subchapter shall be determined by the Administrator taking into account the projected population and associated commercial and industrial establishments within the jurisdiction of the applicant to be served by such treatment works as identified in an approved facilities plan, an areawide plan under section 1288 of this title, or an applicable municipal master plan of development. For the purpose of this paragraph, section 1288 of this title, and any such plan, projected population shall be determined on the basis of the latest information available from the United States Department of Commerce or from the States as the Administrator, by regulation, determines appropriate. Beginning October 1, 1984, no grant shall be made under this subchapter to construct that portion of any treatment works providing reserve capacity in excess of existing needs (including existing needs of residential, commercial, industrial, and other users) on the date of approval of a grant for the erection, building, acquisition, alteration, remodeling, improvement, or extension of a project for secondary treatment or more stringent treatment or new interceptors and appurtenances, except that in no event shall reserve capacity of a facility and its related interceptors to which this subsection applies be in excess of existing needs on October 1, 1990. In any case in which an applicant proposes to provide reserve capacity greater than that eligible for Federal financial assistance under this subchapter, the incremental costs of the additional reserve capacity shall be paid by the applicant;

(6) that no specification for bids in connection with such works shall be written in such a manner as to contain proprietary, exclusionary, or discriminatory requirements other than those based upon performance, unless such requirements are necessary to test or demonstrate a specific thing or to provide for necessary interchangeability of parts and equipment. When in the judgment of the grantee, it is impractical or uneconomical to make a clear and accurate description of the technical requirements, a "brand name or equal" description may be used as a means to define the performance or other salient requirements of a procurement, and in doing so the grantee need not establish the existence of any source other than the brand or source so named.

(b) Additional determinations; issuance of guidelines; approval by Administrator; system of charges

(1) Notwithstanding any other provision of this subchapter, the Administrator shall not approve any grant for any treatment works under section 1281(g)(1) of this title after March 1, 1973, unless he shall first have determined that the applicant (A) has adopted or will adopt a system of charges to assure that each recipient of waste treatment services within the applicant's jurisdiction, as determined by the Administrator, will pay its proportionate share (except as otherwise provided in this paragraph) of the costs of operation and maintenance (including replacement) of any waste treatment services provided by the applicant; and (B) has legal, institutional, managerial, and financial capability to insure adequate construction, operation, and maintenance of treatment works throughout the applicant's jurisdiction, as determined by the Administrator. In any case where an applicant which, as of December 27, 1977, uses a system of dedicated ad valorem taxes and the Administrator determines that the applicant has a system of charges which results in the distribution of operation and maintenance costs for treatment works within the applicant's jurisdiction, to each user class, in proportion to the contribution to the total cost of operation and maintenance of such works by each user class (taking into account total waste water loading of such works, the constituent elements of the wastes, and other appropriate factors), and such applicant is otherwise in compliance with clause (A) of this paragraph with respect to each industrial user, then such dedicated ad valorem tax system shall

be deemed to be the user charge system meeting the requirements of clause (A) of this paragraph for the residential user class and such small non-residential user classes as defined by the Administrator. In defining small non-residential users, the Administrator shall consider the volume of wastes discharged into the treatment works by such users and the constituent elements of such wastes as well as such other factors as he deems appropriate. A system of user charges which imposes a lower charge for low-income residential users (as defined by the Administrator) shall be deemed to be a user charge system meeting the requirements of clause (A) of this paragraph if the Administrator determines that such system was adopted after public notice and hearing.

(2) The Administrator shall, within one hundred and eighty days after October 18, 1972, and after consultation with appropriate State, interstate, municipal, and intermunicipal agencies, issue guidelines applicable to payment of waste treatment costs by industrial and nonindustrial recipients of waste treatment services which shall establish (A) classes of users of such services, including categories of industrial users; (B) criteria against which to determine the adequacy of charges imposed on classes and categories of users reflecting all factors that influence the cost of waste treatment, including strength, volume, and delivery flow rate characteristics of waste; and (C) model systems and rates of user charges typical of various treatment works serving municipal-industrial communities.

(3) Approval by the Administrator of a grant to an interstate agency established by interstate compact for any treatment works shall satisfy any other requirement that such works be authorized by Act of Congress.

(4) A system of charges which meets the requirement of clause (A) of paragraph (1) of this subsection may be based on something other than metering the sewage or water supply flow of residential recipients of waste treatment services, including ad valorem taxes. If the system of charges is based on something other than metering the Administrator shall require (A) the applicant to establish a system by which the necessary funds will be available for the proper operation and maintenance of the treatment works; and (B) the applicant to establish a procedure under which the residential user will be notified as to that portion of his total payment which will be allocated to the cost of the waste treatment services.

(c) Applicability of reserve capacity restrictions to primary, secondary, or advanced waste treatment facilities or related interceptors — The next to the last sentence of paragraph (5) of subsection (a) of this section shall not apply in any case where a primary, secondary, or advanced waste treatment facility or its related interceptors has received a grant for erection, building, acquisition, alteration, remodeling, improvement, or extension before October 1, 1984, and all segments and phases of such facility and interceptors shall be funded based on a 20-year reserve capacity in the case of such facility and a 20-year reserve capacity in the case of such interceptors, except that, if a grant for such interceptors has been approved prior to December 29, 1981, such interceptors shall be funded based on the approved reserve capacity not to exceed 40 years.

(d) Engineering requirements; certification by owner and operator; contractual assurances, etc.

(1) A grant for the construction of treatment works under this subchapter shall provide that the engineer or engineering firm supervising construction or providing architect engineering services during construction shall continue its relationship to the grant applicant for a period of one year after the completion of construction and initial operation of such treatment works. During such period such engineer or engineering firm shall supervise operation of the treatment works, train operating personnel, and prepare curricula and training material for operating personnel. Costs associated with the implementation of this paragraph shall be eligible for Federal assistance in accordance with this subchapter.

(2) On the date one year after the completion of construction and initial operation of such treatment works, the owner and operator of such treatment works shall certify to the Administrator whether or not such treatment works meet the design specifications and effluent limitations contained in the grant agreement and permit pursuant to section 1342 of this title for such works. If the owner and operator of such treatment works cannot certify that such treatment works meet such design specifications and effluent limitations, any failure to meet such design specifications and effluent limitations shall be corrected in a timely manner, to allow such affirmative certification, at other than Federal expense.

(3) Nothing in this section shall be construed to prohibit a grantee under this subchapter from requiring more assurances, guarantees, or indemnity or other contractual requirements from any party to a contract pertaining to a project assisted under this subchapter, than those provided under this subsection.

§1285. Allotment of grant funds
[CWA §205]

(a) Funds for fiscal years during period June 30, 1972, and September 30, 1977; determination of amount — Sums authorized to be appropriated pursuant to section 1287 of this title for each fiscal year beginning after June 30, 1972, and before September 30, 1977, shall be allotted by the Administrator not later than the January 1st immediately preceding the beginning of the fiscal year for which authorized, except that the allotment for fiscal year 1973 shall be made not later than 30 days after October 18, 1972. Such sums shall be allotted among the States by the Administrator in accordance with regulations promulgated by him, in the ratio that the estimated cost of constructing all needed publicly owned treatment works in each State bears to the estimated cost of construction of all needed publicly owned treatment works in all of the States. For the fiscal years ending June 30, 1973, and June 30, 1974, such ratio shall be determined on the basis of table III of House Public Works Committee Print No. 92-50. For the fiscal year ending June 30, 1975, such ratio shall be determined one-half on the basis of table I of House Public Works Committee Print Numbered 93-28 and one-half on the basis of table II of such print, except that no State shall receive an allotment less than that which it received for the fiscal year ending June 30, 1972, as set forth in table III of such print. Allotments for fiscal years which begin after the fiscal year ending June 30, 1975, shall be made only in accordance with a revised cost estimate made and submitted to Congress in accordance with section 1375(b) of this title and only after such revised cost estimate shall have been approved by law specifically enacted after October 18, 1972.

(b) Availability and use of funds allotted for fiscal years during period June 30, 1972, and September 30, 1977; reallotment

(1) Any sums allotted to a State under subsection (a) of this section shall be available for obligation under section 1283 of this title on and after the date of such allotment. Such sums shall continue available for obligation in such State for a period of one year after the close of the fiscal year for which such sums are authorized. Any amounts so allotted which are not obligated by the end of such one-year period shall be immediately reallotted by the Administrator, in accordance with regulations promulgated by him, generally on the basis of the ratio used in making the last allotment of sums under this section. Such reallotted sums shall be added to the last allotments made to the States. Any sum made available to a State by reallotment under this subsection shall be in addition to any funds otherwise allotted to such State for grants under this subchapter during any fiscal year.

(2) Any sums which have been obligated under section 1283 of this title and which are released by the payment of the final voucher for the project shall be immediately credited to the State to which such sums were last allotted. Such released sums shall be added to the amounts last allotted to such State and shall be immediately available for obligation in the same manner and to the same extent as such last allotment.

(c) Funds for fiscal years during period October 1, 1977, and September 30, 1981; funds for fiscal years 1982 to 1990; determination of amount

(1) Sums authorized to be appropriated pursuant to section 1287 of this title for the fiscal years during the period beginning October 1, 1977, and ending September 30, 1981, shall be allotted for each such year by the Administrator not later than the tenth day which begins after December 27, 1977. Notwithstanding any other provision of law, sums authorized for the fiscal years ending September 30, 1978, September 30, 1979, September 30, 1980, and September 30, 1981, shall be allotted in accordance with table 3 of Committee Print Numbered 95-30 of the Committee on Public Works and Transportation of the House of Representatives.

(2) Sums authorized to be appropriated pursuant to section 1287 of this title for the fiscal years 1982, 1983, 1984, and 1985 shall be allotted for each such year by the Administrator not later than the tenth day which begins after December 29, 1981. Notwithstanding any other provision of law, sums authorized for the fiscal year ending September 30, 1982, shall be allotted in accordance with table 3 of Committee Print Numbered 95-30 of the Committee on Public Works and Transportation of the House of Representatives. Sums authorized for the fiscal years ending September 30, 1983, September 30, 1984, September 30, 1985, and September 30, 1986, shall be allotted in accordance with the following table:

States	Fiscal years 1983 through 1985
Alabama	.011398
Alaska	.006101
Arizona	.006885
Arkansas	.006668
California	.072901
Colorado	.008154
Connecticut	.012487
Delaware	.004965
District of Columbia	.004965
Florida	.034407
Georgia	.017234
Hawaii	.007895
Idaho	.004965
Illinois	.046101
Indiana	.024566
Iowa	.013796
Kansas	.009201
Kentucky	.012973
Louisiana	.011205
Maine	.007788
Maryland	.024653
Massachusetts	.034608
Michigan	.043829
Minnesota	.018735
Mississippi	.009184
Missouri	.028257
Montana	.004965
Nebraska	.005214
Nevada	.004965
New Hampshire	.010186
New Jersey	.041654
New Mexico	.004965
New York	.113097
North Carolina	.018396
North Dakota	.004965
Ohio	.057383
Oklahoma	.008235
Oregon	.011515
Pennsylvania	.040377
Rhode Island	.006750
South Carolina	.010442
South Dakota	.004965
Tennessee	.014807
Texas	.038726
Utah	.005371
Vermont	.004965
Virginia	.020861
Washington	.017726
West Virginia	.015890
Wisconsin	.027557
Wyoming	.004965
[American] Samoa	.000915
Guam	.000662
Northern Marianas	.000425
Puerto Rico	.013295
Pacific Trust Territories	.001305
Virgin Islands	.000531
United States totals	.999996

(3) Fiscal years 1987-1990 — Sums authorized to be appropriated pursuant to section 1287 of this title for the fiscal years 1987, 1988, 1989, and 1990 shall be allotted for each such year by the Administra- tor not later than the 10th day which begins after February 4, 1987. Sums authorized for such fiscal years shall be allotted in accordance with the following table:

States	Fiscal years 1983 through 1985
Alabama	.011309
Alaska	.006053
Arizona	.006831
Arkansas	.006616
California	.072333
Colorado	.008090
Connecticut	.012390
Delaware	.004965
District of Columbia	.004965
Florida	.034139

Georgia	.017100
Hawaii	.007833
Idaho	.004965
Illinois	.045741
Indiana	.024374
Iowa	.013688
Kansas	.009129
Kentucky	.012872
Louisiana	.011118
Maine	.007829
Maryland	.024461
Massachusetts	.034338
Michigan	.043487
Minnesota	.018589
Mississippi	.009112
Missouri	.028037
Montana	.004965
Nebraska	.005173
Nevada	.004965
New Hampshire	.010107
New Jersey	.041329
New Mexico	.004965
New York	.111632
North Carolina	.018253
North Dakota	.004965
Ohio	.056936
Oklahoma	.008171
Oregon	.011425
Pennsylvania	.040062
Rhode Island	.006791
South Carolina	.010361
South Dakota	.004965
Tennessee	.014692
Texas	.046226
Utah	.005329
Vermont	.004965
Virginia	.020698
Washington	.017588
West Virginia	.015766
Wisconsin	.027342
Wyoming	.004965
American Samoa	.000908
Guam	.000657
Northern Marianas	.000422
Puerto Rico	.013191
Pacific Trust Territories	.001295
Virgin Islands	.000527

(d) Availability and use of funds; reallotment — Sums allotted to the States for a fiscal year shall remain available for obligation for the fiscal year for which authorized and for the period of the next succeeding twelve months. The amount of any allotment not obligated by the end of such twenty-four-month period shall be immediately reallotted by the Administrator on the basis of the same ratio as applicable to sums allotted for the then current fiscal year, except that none of the funds reallotted by the Administrator for fiscal year 1978 and for fiscal years

thereafter shall be allotted to any State which failed to obligate any of the funds being reallotted. Any sum made available to a State by reallotment under this subsection shall be in addition to any funds otherwise allotted to such State for grants under this subchapter during any fiscal year.

(e) Minimum allotment; additional appropriations; ratio of amount available — For the fiscal years 1978, 1979, 1980, 1981, 1982, 1983, 1984, 1985, 1986, 1987, 1988, 1989, and 1990, no State shall receive less than one-half of 1 per centum of the total allotment under subsection (c) of this section, except that in the case of Guam, Virgin Islands, American Samoa, and the Trust Territories not more than thirty-three one-hundredths of 1 per centum in the aggregate shall be allotted to all four of these jurisdictions. For the purpose of carrying out this subsection there are authorized to be appropriated, subject to such amounts as are provided in appropriation Acts, not to exceed $75,000,000 for each of fiscal years 1978, 1979, 1980, 1981, 1982, 1983, 1984, 1985, 1986, 1987, 1988, 1989, and 1990. If for any fiscal year the amount appropriated under authority of this subsection is less than the amount necessary to carry out this subsection, the amount each State receives under this subsection for such year shall bear the same ratio to the amount such State would have received under this subsection in such year if the amount necessary to carry it out had been appropriated as the amount appropriated for such year bears to the amount necessary to carry out this subsection for such year.

(f) Omitted

(g) Reservation of funds; State management assistance

(1) The Administrator is authorized to reserve each fiscal year not to exceed 2 per centum of the amount authorized under section 1287 of this title for purposes of the allotment made to each State under this section on or after October 1, 1977, except in the case of any fiscal year beginning on or after October 1, 1981, and ending before October 1, 1994, in which case the percentage authorized to be reserved shall not exceed 4 per centum or $400,000 whichever amount is the greater. Sums so reserved shall be available for making grants to such State under paragraph (2) of this subsection for the same period as sums are available from such allotment under subsection (d) of this section, and any such grant shall be available for obligation only during such period. Any grant made from sums reserved under this subsection which has not been obligated by the end of the period for which available shall be added to the amount last allotted to such State under this section and shall be immediately available for obligation in the same manner and to the same extent as such last allotment. Sums authorized to be reserved by this paragraph shall be in addition to and not in lieu of any other funds which may be authorized

to carry out this subsection.

(2) The Administrator is authorized to grant to any State from amounts reserved to such State under this subsection, the reasonable costs of administering any aspects of sections 1281, 1283, 1284, and 1292 of this title the responsibility for administration of which the Administrator has delegated to such State. The Administrator may increase such grant to take into account the reasonable costs of administering an approved program under section 1342 or 1344 of this title, administering a statewide waste treatment management planning program under section 1288(b)(4) of this title, and managing waste treatment construction grants for small communities.

(h) Alternate systems for small communities — The Administrator shall set aside from funds authorized for each fiscal year beginning on or after October 1, 1978, a total (as determined by the Governor of the State) of not less than 4 percent nor more than 7 1/2 percent of the sums allotted to any State with a rural population of 25 per centum or more of the total population of such State, as determined by the Bureau of the Census. The Administrator may set aside no more than 7 1/2 percent of the sums allotted to any other State for which the Governor requests such action. Such sums shall be available only for alternatives to conventional sewage treatment works for municipalities having a population of three thousand five hundred or less, or for the highly dispersed sections of larger municipalities, as defined by the Administrator.

(i) Set-aside for innovative and alternative projects — Not less than 1/2 of 1 percent of funds allotted to a State for each of the fiscal years ending September 30, 1979, through September 30, 1990, under subsection (c) of this section shall be expended only for increasing the Federal share of grants for construction of treatment works utilizing innovative processes and techniques pursuant to section 1282(a)(2) of this title. Including the expenditures authorized by the preceding sentence, a total of 2 percent of the funds allotted to a State for each of the fiscal years ending September 30, 1979, and September 30, 1980, and 3 percent of the funds allotted to a State for the fiscal year ending September 30, 1981, under subsection (c) of this section shall be expended only for increasing grants for construction of treatment works pursuant to section 1282(a)(2) of this title. Including the expenditures authorized by the first sentence of this subsection, a total (as determined by the Governor of the State) of not less than 4 percent nor more than 7 1/2 percent of the funds allotted to such State under subsection (c) of this section for each of the fiscal years ending September 30, 1982, through September 30, 1990, shall be expended only for increasing the Federal share of grants for construction of treatment works pursuant to section 1282(a)(2) of this title.

(j) Water quality management plan; reservation of funds for nonpoint source management

(1) The Administrator shall reserve each fiscal year not to exceed 1 per centum of the sums allotted and available for obligation to each State under this section for each fiscal year beginning on or after October 1, 1981, or $100,000, whichever amount is the greater.

(2) Such sums shall be used by the Administrator to make grants to the States to carry out water quality management planning, including, but not limited to —

(A) identifying most cost effective and locally acceptable facility and non-point measures to meet and maintain water quality standards;

(B) developing an implementation plan to obtain State and local financial and regulatory commitments to implement measures developed under subparagraph (A);

(C) determining the nature, extent, and causes of water quality problems in various areas of the State and interstate region, and reporting on these annually; and

(D) determining those publicly owned treatment works which should be constructed with assistance under this subchapter, in which areas and in what sequence, taking into account the relative degree of effluent reduction attained, the relative contributions to water quality of other point or nonpoint sources, and the consideration of alternatives to such construction, and implementing section 1313(e) of this title.

(3) In carrying out planning with grants made under paragraph (2) of this subsection, a State shall develop jointly with local, regional, and interstate entities, a plan for carrying out the program and give funding priority to such entities and designated or undesignated public comprehensive planning organizations to carry out the purposes of this subsection. In giving such priority, the State shall allocate at least 40 percent of the amount granted to such State for a fiscal year under paragraph (2) of this subsection to regional public comprehensive planning organizations in such State and appropriate interstate organizations for the development and implementation of the plan described in this paragraph. In any fiscal year for which the Governor, in consultation with such organizations and with the approval of the Administrator, determines that allocation of at least 40 percent of such amount to such organizations will not result in significant participation by such organizations in water quality management planning and not significantly assist in development and implementation of the plan described in this paragraph and achieving the goals of this

chapter, the allocation to such organization may be less than 40 percent of such amount.

(4) All activities undertaken under this subsection shall be in coordination with other related provisions of this chapter.

(5) Nonpoint source reservation — In addition to the sums reserved under paragraph (1), the Administrator shall reserve each fiscal year for each State 1 percent of the sums allotted and available for obligation to such State under this section for each fiscal year beginning on or after October 1, 1986, or $100,000, whichever is greater, for the purpose of carrying out section 1329 of this title. Sums so reserved in a State in any fiscal year for which such State does not request the use of such sums, to the extent such sums exceed $100,000, may be used by such State for other purposes under this subchapter.

(k) New York City Convention Center — The Administrator shall allot to the State of New York from sums authorized to be appropriated for the fiscal year ending September 30, 1982, an amount necessary to pay the entire cost of conveying sewage from the Convention Center of the city of New York to the Newtown sewage treatment plant, Brooklyn-Queens area, New York. The amount allotted under this subsection shall be in addition to and not in lieu of any other amounts authorized to be allotted to such State under this chapter.

(*l*) Marine estuary reservation

(1) Reservation of funds

(A) General rule — Prior to making allotments among the States under subsection (c) of this section, the Administrator shall reserve funds from sums appropriated pursuant to section 1287 of this title for each fiscal year beginning after September 30, 1986.

(B) Fiscal years 1987 and 1988 — For each of fiscal years 1987 and 1988 the reservation shall be 1 percent of the sums appropriated pursuant to section 1287 of this title for such fiscal year.

(C) Fiscal years 1989 and 1990 — For each of fiscal years 1989 and 1990 the reservation shall be 1 1/2 percent of the funds appropriated pursuant to section 1287 of this title for such fiscal year.

(2) Use of funds — Of the sums reserved under this subsection, two-thirds shall be available to address water quality problems of marine bays and estuaries subject to lower levels of water quality due to the impacts of discharges from combined storm water and sanitary sewer overflows from adjacent urban complexes, and one-third shall be available for the implementation of section 1330 of this title, relating to the national estuary program.

(3) Period of availability — Sums reserved under this subsection shall be subject to the period of availability for obligation established by subsection (d) of this section.

(4) Treatment of certain body of water — For purposes of this section and section 1281(n) of this title, Newark Bay, New Jersey, and the portion of the Passaic River up to Little Falls, in the vicinity of Beatties Dam, shall be treated as a marine bay and estuary.

(m) Discretionary deposits into State water pollution control revolving funds

(1) From construction grant allotments — In addition to any amounts deposited in a water pollution control revolving fund established by a State under subchapter VI of this chapter, upon request of the Governor of such State, the Administrator shall make available to the State for deposit, as capitalization grants, in such fund in any fiscal year beginning after September 30, 1986, such portion of the amounts allotted to such State under this section for such fiscal year as the Governor considers appropriate; except that (A) in fiscal year 1987, such deposit may not exceed 50 percent of the amounts allotted to such State under this section for such fiscal year, and (B) in fiscal year 1988, such deposit may not exceed 75 percent of the amounts allotted to such State under this section for this fiscal year.

(2) Notice requirement — The Governor of a State may make a request under paragraph (1) for a deposit into the water pollution control revolving fund of such State —

(A) in fiscal year 1987 only if no later than 90 days after February 4, 1987, and

(B) in each fiscal year thereafter only if 90 days before the first day of such fiscal year, the State provides notice of its intent to make such deposit.

(3) Exception — Sums reserved under section 1285(j) of this title shall not be available for obligation under this subsection.

§1286. Reimbursement and advanced construction

[CWA §206]

(a) Publicly owned treatment works construction initiated after June 30, 1966, but before July 1, 1973; reimbursement formula — Any publicly owned treatment works in a State on which construction was initiated after June 30, 1966, but before July 1, 1973, which was approved by the appropriate State water pollution control agency and which the Administrator finds meets the requirements of section 1158 of this title in effect at the time of the initiation of construction shall be reimbursed a total amount equal to the difference between the amount of Federal financial assistance, if any, received under such section 1158 of this title for such project and 50 per centum of the cost of such project, or 55 per centum of the project cost where the Administrator also determines that such treatment works was constructed in conformity with a comprehensive metropolitan treatment plan as described in section 1158(f) of this title as in effect immediately prior to October 18, 1972. Nothing in this subsection shall result in any such works receiving Federal grants from all sources in excess of 80 per centum of the cost of such project.

(b) Publicly owned treatment works construction initiated between June 30, 1956, and June 30, 1966; reimbursement formula — Any publicly owned treatment works constructed with or eligible for Federal financial assistance under this Act in a State between June 30, 1956, and June 30, 1966, which was approved by the State water pollution control agency and which the Administrator finds meets the requirements of section 1158 of this title prior to October 18, 1972 but which was constructed without assistance under such section 1158 of this title or which received such assistance in an amount less than 30 per centum of the cost of such project shall qualify for payments and reimbursement of State or local funds used for such project from sums allocated to such State under this section in an amount which shall not exceed the difference between the amount of such assistance, if any, received for such project and 30 per centum of the cost of such project.

(c) Application for reimbursement — No publicly owned treatment works shall receive any payment or reimbursement under subsection (a) or (b) of this section unless an application for such assistance is filed with the Administrator within the one year period which begins on October 18, 1972. Any application filed within such one year period may be revised from time to time, as may be necessary.

(d) Allocation of funds — The Administrator shall allocate to each qualified project under subsection (a) of this section each fiscal year for which funds are appropriated under subsection (e) of this section an amount which bears the same ratio to the unpaid balance of the reimbursement due such project as the total of such funds for such year bears to the total unpaid balance of reimbursement due all such approved projects on the date of enactment of such appropriation. The Administrator shall allocate to each qualified project under subsection (b) of this section each fiscal year for which funds are appropriated under subsection (e) of this section an amount which bears the same ratio to the unpaid balance of the reimbursement due such project as the total of such funds for such year bears to the total unpaid balance of reimbursement due all such approved projects on the date of enactment of such appropriation.

(e) Authorization of appropriations — There is authorized to be appropriated to carry out subsection (a) of this section not to exceed $2,600,000,000 and, to carry out subsection (b) of this section, not to exceed $750,000,000. The authorizations contained in this subsection shall be the sole source of funds for reimbursements authorized by this section.

(f) Additional funds

(1) In any case where a substantial portion of the funds allotted to a State for the current fiscal year under this subchapter have been obligated under section 1281(g) of this title, or will be so obligated in a timely manner (as determined by the Administrator), and there is construction of any treatment works project without the aid of Federal funds and in accordance with all procedures and all requirements applicable to treatment works projects, except those procedures and requirements which limit construction of projects to those constructed with the aid of previously allotted Federal funds, the Administrator, upon his approval of an application made under this subsection therefor, is authorized to pay the Federal share of the cost of construction of such project when additional funds are allotted to the State under this subchapter if prior to the construction of the project the Administrator approves plans, specifications, and estimates therefor in the same manner as other treatment works projects. The Administrator may not approve an application under this subsection unless an authorization is in effect for the first fiscal year in the period for which the application requests payment and such requested payment for that fiscal year does not exceed the State's expected allotment from such authorization. The Administrator shall not be required to make such requested payment for any fiscal year —

(A) to the extent that such payment would exceed such State's allotment of the amount appropriated for such fiscal year; and

(B) unless such payment is for a project which, on the basis of an approved funding priority list of such State, is eligible to receive such payment based on the allotment and appropriation for such fiscal year.

To the extent that sufficient funds are not appropriated to pay the full Federal share with respect to a project for which obligations under the provisions of this subsection have been made, the Administrator shall reduce the Federal share to such amount less than 75 per centum as such appropriations do provide.

(2) In determining the allotment for any fiscal year under this subchapter, any treatment works project constructed in accordance with this section and without the aid of Federal funds shall not be considered completed until an application under the provisions of this subsection with respect to such project has been approved by the Administrator, or the availability of funds from which this project is eligible for reimbursement has expired, whichever first occurs.

§1287. Authorization of appropriations
[CWA §207]

There is authorized to be appropriated to carry out this subchapter, other than sections 1286(e), 1288 and 1289 of this title, for the fiscal year ending June 30, 1973, not to exceed $5,000,000,000, for the fiscal year ending June 30, 1974, not to exceed $6,000,000,000, and for the fiscal year ending June 30, 1975, not to exceed $7,000,000,000, and subject to such amounts as are provided in appropriation Acts, for the fiscal year ending September 30, 1977, $1,000,000,000 for the fiscal year ending September 30, 1978, $4,500,000,000 and for the fiscal years ending September 30, 1979, September 30, 1980, not to exceed $5,000,000,000; for the fiscal year ending September 30, 1981, not to exceed $2,548,837,000; and for the fiscal years ending September 30, 1982, September 30, 1983, September 30, 1984, and September 30, 1985, not to exceed $2,400,000,000 per fiscal year; and for each of the fiscal years ending September 30, 1986, September 30, 1987, and September 30, 1988, not to exceed $2,400,000,000; and for each of the fiscal years ending September 30, 1989, and September 30, 1990, not to exceed $1,200,000,000.

§1288. Areawide waste treatment management
[CWA §208]

(a) Identification and designation of areas having substantial water quality control problems — For the purpose of encouraging and facilitating the development and implementation of areawide waste treatment management plans —

(1) The Administrator, within ninety days after October 18, 1972, and after consultation with appropriate Federal, State, and local authorities, shall by regulation publish guidelines for the identification of those areas which, as a result of urban-industrial concentrations or other factors, have substantial water quality control problems.

(2) The Governor of each State, within sixty days after publication of the guidelines issued pursuant to paragraph (1) of this subsection, shall identify each area within the State which, as a result of urban-industrial concentrations or other factors, has substantial water quality control problems. Not later than one hundred and twenty days following such identification and after consultation with appropriate elected and other officials of local governments having jurisdiction in such areas, the Governor shall designate (A) the boundaries of each such area, and (B) a single representative organization, including elected officials from local governments or their designees, capable of developing effective areawide waste treatment management plans for such area. The Governor may in the same manner at any later time identify any additional area (or modify an existing area) for which he determines areawide waste treatment management to be appropriate, designate the boundaries of such area, and designate an organization capable of developing effective areawide waste treatment management plans for such area.

(3) With respect to any area which, pursuant to the guidelines published under paragraph (1) of this subsection, is located in two or more States, the Governors of the respective States shall consult and cooperate in carrying out the provisions of paragraph (2), with a view toward designating the boundaries of the interstate area having common water quality control problems and for which areawide waste treatment management plans would be most effective, and toward designating, within one hundred and eighty days after publication of guidelines issued pursuant to paragraph (1) of this subsection, of a single representative organization capable of developing effective areawide waste treatment management plans for such area.

(4) If a Governor does not act, either by designating or determining not to make a designation under paragraph (2) of this subsection, within the time required by such paragraph, or if, in the case of an interstate area, the Governors of the States involved do not designate a planning organization within the time required by paragraph (3) of this subsection, the chief elected officials of local governments within an area may by agreement designate (A) the boundaries for such an area, and (B) a single representative organization including elected officials from such local governments, or their designees, capable of developing an areawide waste treatment management plan for such area.

(5) Existing regional agencies may be designated under paragraphs (2), (3), and (4) of this subsection.

(6) The State shall act as a planning agency for all portions of such State which are not designated under paragraphs (2), (3), or (4) of this subsection.

(7) Designations under this subsection shall be subject to the approval of the Administrator.

(b) Planning process

(1)(A) Not later than one year after the date of designation of any organization under subsection (a) of this section such organization shall have in operation a continuing areawide waste treatment management planning process consistent with section 1281 of this title. Plans prepared in accordance with this process shall contain alternatives for waste treatment management, and be applicable to all wastes generated within the area involved. The initial plan prepared in accordance with such process shall be certified by the Governor and submitted to the Administrator not later than two years after the planning process is in operation.

(B) For any agency designated after 1975 under subsection (a) of this section and for all portions of a State for which the State is required to act as the planning agency in accordance with subsection (a)(6) of this section, the initial plan prepared in accordance with such process shall be certified by the Governor and submitted to the Administrator not later than three years after the receipt of the initial grant award authorized under subsection (f) of this section.

(2) Any plan prepared under such process shall include, but not be limited to —

(A) the identification of treatment works necessary to meet the anticipated municipal and industrial waste treatment needs of the area over a twenty-year period, annually updated (including an analysis of alternative waste treatment systems), including any requirements for the acquisition of land for treatment purposes; the necessary waste water collection and urban storm water runoff systems; and a program to provide the necessary financial arrangements for the development of such treatment works, and an identification of open space and recreation opportunities that can be expected to result from improved water quality, including consideration of potential use of lands associated with treatment works and increased access to water-based recreation;

(B) the establishment of construction priorities for such treatment works and time schedules for the initiation and completion of all treatment works;

(C) the establishment of a regulatory program to —

(i) implement the waste treatment management requirements of section 1281(c) of this title,

(ii) regulate the location, modification, and construction of any facilities within such area which may result in any discharge in such area, and

(iii) assure that any industrial or commercial wastes discharged into any treatment works in such area meet applicable pretreatment requirements;

(D) the identification of those agencies necessary to construct, operate, and maintain all facilities required by the plan and otherwise to carry out the plan;

(E) the identification of the measures necessary to carry out the plan (including financing), the period of time necessary to carry out the plan, the costs of carrying out the plan within such time, and the economic, social, and environmental impact of carrying out the plan within such time;

(F) a process to (i) identify, if appropriate, agriculturally and silviculturally related nonpoint sources of pollution, including return flows from irrigated agriculture, and their cumulative effects, runoff from manure disposal areas, and from land used for livestock and crop production, and (ii) set forth procedures and methods (including land use requirements) to control to the extent feasible such sources;

(G) a process to (i) identify, if appropriate, mine-related sources of pollution including new, current, and abandoned surface and underground mine runoff, and (ii) set forth procedures and methods (including land use requirements) to control to the extent feasible such sources;

(H) a process to (i) identify construction activity related sources of pollution, and (ii) set forth procedures and methods (including land use requirements) to control to the extent feasible such sources;

(I) a process to (i) identify, if appropriate, salt water intrusion into rivers, lakes, and estuaries resulting from reduction of fresh water flow from any cause, including irrigation, obstruction, ground water extraction, and diversion, and (ii) set forth procedures and methods to control such intrusion to the extent feasible where such procedures and methods are otherwise a part of the waste treatment management plan;

(J) a process to control the disposition of all residual waste generated in such area which could affect water quality; and

(K) a process to control the disposal of pollutants on land or in subsurface excavations within such area to protect ground and surface water quality.

(3) Areawide waste treatment management plans shall be certified annually by the Governor or his designee (or Governors or their designees, where more than one State is involved) as being consistent with applicable basin plans and such areawide waste treatment management plans shall be submitted to the Administrator for his approval.

(4)(A) Whenever the Governor of any State determines (and notifies the Administrator) that consistency with a statewide regulatory program under section 1313 of this title so requires, the requirements of clauses (F) through (K) of paragraph (2) of this subsection shall be developed and submitted by the Governor to the Administrator for approval for application to a class or category of activity throughout such State.

(B) Any program submitted under subparagraph (A) of this paragraph which, in whole or in part, is to control the discharge or other placement of dredged or fill material into the navigable waters shall include the following:

(i) A consultation process which includes the State agency with primary jurisdiction over fish and wildlife resources.

(ii) A process to identify and manage the discharge or other placement of dredged or fill material which adversely affects navigable waters, which shall complement and be coordinated with a State program under section 1344 of this title conducted pursuant to this chapter.

(iii) A process to assure that any activity conducted pursuant to a best management practice will comply with the guidelines established under section 1344(b)(1) of this title, and sections 1317 and 1343 of this title.

(iv) A process to assure that any activity conducted pursuant to a best management practice can be terminated or modified for cause including, but not limited to, the following:

(I) violation of any condition of the best management practice;

(II) change in any activity that requires either a temporary or permanent reduction or elimination of the discharge pursuant to the best management practice.

(v) A process to assure continued coordination with Federal and Federal-State water-related planning and reviewing processes, including the National Wetlands Inventory.

(C) If the Governor of a State obtains approval from the Administrator of a statewide regulatory program which meets the requirements of subparagraph (B) of this paragraph and if such State is administering a permit program under section 1344 of this title, no person shall be required to obtain an individual permit pursuant to such section, or to comply with a general permit issued pursuant to such section, with respect to any appropriate activity within such State for which a best management practice has been approved by the Administrator under the program approved by the Administrator pursuant to this paragraph.

(D)(i) Whenever the Administrator determines after public hearing that a State is not administering a program approved under this section in accordance with the requirements of this section, the Administrator shall so notify the State, and if appropriate corrective action is not taken within a reasonable time, not to exceed ninety days, the Administrator shall withdraw approval of such program. The Administrator shall not withdraw approval of any such program unless he shall first have notified the State, and made public, in writing, the reasons for such withdrawal.

(ii) In the case of a State with a program submitted and approved under this paragraph, the Administrator shall withdraw approval of such program under this subparagraph only for a substantial failure of the State to administer its program in accordance with the requirements of this paragraph.

(c) Regional operating agencies

(1) The Governor of each State, in consultation with the planning agency designated under subsection (a) of this section, at the time a plan is submitted to the Administrator, shall designate one or more waste treatment management agencies (which may be an existing or newly created local, regional, or State agency or political subdivision) for each area designated under subsection (a) of this section and submit such designations to the Administrator.

(2) The Administrator shall accept any such designation, unless, within 120 days of such designation, he finds that the designated management agency (or agencies) does not have adequate authority —

(A) to carry out appropriate portions of an areawide waste treatment management plan developed under subsection (b) of this section;

(B) to manage effectively waste treatment works and related facilities serving such area in conformance with any plan required by subsection (b) of this section;

(C) directly or by contract, to design and construct new works, and to operate and maintain new and existing works as required by any plan developed pursuant to subsection (b) of this section;

(D) to accept and utilize grants, or other funds from any source, for waste treatment management purposes;

(E) to raise revenues, including the assessment of waste treatment charges;

(F) to incur short- and long-term indebtedness;

(G) to assure in implementation of an areawide waste treatment management plan that each participating community pays its proportionate share of treatment costs;

(H) to refuse to receive any wastes from any municipality or subdivision thereof, which does not comply with any provisions of an approved plan under this section applicable to such area; and

(I) to accept for treatment industrial wastes.

(d) Conformity of works with area plan — After a waste treatment management agency having the authority required by subsection (c) of this section has been designated under such subsection for an area and a plan for such area has been approved under subsection (b) of this section, the Administrator shall not make any grant for construction of a publicly owned treatment works under section 1281(g)(1) of this title within such area except to such designated agency and for works in conformity with such plan.

(e) Permits not to conflict with approved plans — No permit under section 1342 of this title shall be issued for any point source which is in conflict with a plan approved pursuant to subsection (b) of this section.

(f) Grants

(1) The Administrator shall make grants to any agency designated under subsection (a) of this section for payment of the reasonable costs of developing and operating a continuing areawide waste treatment management planning process under subsection (b) of this section.

(2) For the two-year period beginning on the date the first grant is made under paragraph (1) of this subsection to an agency, if such first grant is made before October 1, 1977, the amount of each such grant to such agency shall be 100 per centum of the costs of developing and operating a continuing areawide waste treatment management planning process under subsection (b) of this section, and thereafter the amount granted to such agency shall not exceed 75 per centum of such costs in each succeeding one-year period. In the case of any other grant made to an agency under such paragraph (1) of this subsection, the amount of such grant shall not exceed 75 per centum of the costs of developing and operating a continuing areawide waste treatment management planning process in any year.

(3) Each applicant for a grant under this subsection shall submit to the Administrator for his approval each proposal for which a grant is applied for under this subsection. The Administrator shall act upon such proposal as soon as practicable after it has been submitted, and his approval of that proposal shall be deemed a contractual obligation of the United States for the payment of its contribution to such proposal, subject to such amounts as are provided in appropriation Acts. There is authorized to be appropriated to carry out this subsection not to exceed $50,000,000 for the fiscal year ending June 30, 1973, not to exceed $100,000,000 for the fiscal year ending June 30, 1974, not to exceed $150,000,000 per fiscal year for the fiscal years ending June 30, 1975, September 30, 1977, September 30, 1978, September 30, 1979, and September 30, 1980, not to exceed $100,000,000 per fiscal year for the fiscal years ending September 30, 1981, and September

30, 1982, and such sums as may be necessary for fiscal years 1983 through 1990.

(g) Technical assistance by Administrator — The Administrator is authorized, upon request of the Governor or the designated planning agency, and without reimbursement, to consult with, and provide technical assistance to, any agency designated under subsection (a) of this section in the development of areawide waste treatment management plans under subsection (b) of this section.

(h) Technical assistance by Secretary of the Army

(1) The Secretary of the Army, acting through the Chief of Engineers, in cooperation with the Administrator is authorized and directed, upon request of the Governor or the designated planning organization, to consult with, and provide technical assistance to, any agency designed under subsection (a) of this section in developing and operating a continuing areawide waste treatment management planning process under subsection (b) of this section.

(2) There is authorized to be appropriated to the Secretary of the Army, to carry out this subsection, not to exceed $50,000,000 per fiscal year for the fiscal years ending June 30, 1973, and June 30, 1974.

(i) State best management practices program

(1) The Secretary of the Interior, acting through the Director of the United States Fish and Wildlife Service, shall, upon request of the Governor of a State, and without reimbursement, provide technical assistance to such State in developing a statewide program for submission to the Administrator under subsection (b)(4)(B) of this section and in implementing such program after its approval.

(2) There is authorized to be appropriated to the Secretary of the Interior $6,000,000 to complete the National Wetlands Inventory of the United States, by December 31, 1981, and to provide information from such Inventory to States as it becomes available to assist such States in the development and operation of programs under this chapter.

(j) Agricultural cost sharing

(1) The Secretary of Agriculture, with the concurrence of the Administrator, and acting through the Soil Conservation Service and such other agencies of the Department of Agriculture as the Secretary may designate, is authorized and directed to establish and administer a program to enter into contracts, subject to such amounts as are provided in advance by appropriation acts, of not less than five years nor more than ten years with owners and operators having control of rural land for the purpose of installing and maintaining measures incorporating best management practices to control nonpoint source pollution for improved

water quality in those States or areas for which the Administrator has approved a plan under subsection (b) of this section where the practices to which the contracts apply are certified by the management agency designated under subsection (c)(1) of this section to be consistent with such plans and will result in improved water quality. Such contracts may be entered into during the period ending not later than September 31, 1988. Under such contracts the land owner or operator shall agree —

    (i) to effectuate a plan approved by a soil conservation district, where one exists, under this section for his farm, ranch, or other land substantially in accordance with the schedule outlined therein unless any requirement thereof is waived or modified by the Secretary;

    (ii) to forfeit all rights to further payments or grants under the contract and refund to the United States all payments and grants received thereunder, with interest, upon his violation of the contract at any stage during the time he has control of the land if the Secretary, after considering the recommendations of the soil conservation district, where one exists, and the Administrator, determines that such violation is of such a nature as to warrant termination of the contract, or to make refunds or accept such payment adjustments as the Secretary may deem appropriate if he determines that the violation by the owner or operator does not warrant termination of the contract;

    (iii) upon transfer of his right and interest in the farm, ranch, or other land during the contract period to forfeit all rights to further payments or grants under the contract and refund to the United States all payments or grants received thereunder, with interest, unless the transferee of any such land agrees with the Secretary to assume all obligations of the contract;

    (iv) not to adopt any practice specified by the Secretary on the advice of the Administrator in the contract as a practice which would tend to defeat the purposes of the contract;

    (v) to such additional provisions as the Secretary determines are desirable and includes in the contract to effectuate the purposes of the program or to facilitate the practical administration of the program.

(2) In return for such agreement by the landowner or operator the Secretary shall agree to provide technical assistance and share the cost of carrying out those conservation practices and measures set forth in the contract for which he determines that cost sharing is appropriate and in the public interest and which are approved for cost sharing by the agency designated to implement the plan developed under subsection (b) of this section. The portion of such cost (including labor) to be shared shall be that part which the Secretary determines is necessary and appropriate to effectuate the installation of the water quality management practices and measures under the contract, but not to exceed 50 per centum of the total cost of the measures set forth in the contract; except the Secretary may increase the matching cost share where he determines that (1) the main benefits to be derived from the measures are related to improving offsite water quality, and (2) the matching share requirement would place a burden on the landowner which would probably prevent him from participating in the program.

(3) The Secretary may terminate any contract with a landowner or operator by mutual agreement with the owner or operator if the Secretary determines that such termination would be in the public interest, and may agree to such modification of contracts previously entered into as he may determine to be desirable to carry out the purposes of the program or facilitate the practical administration thereof or to accomplish equitable treatment with respect to other conservation, land use, or water quality programs.

(4) In providing assistance under this subsection the Secretary will give priority to those areas and sources that have the most significant effect upon water quality. Additional investigations or plans may be made, where necessary, to supplement approved water quality management plans, in order to determine priorities.

(5) The Secretary shall, where practicable, enter into agreements with soil conservation districts, State soil and water conservation agencies, or State water quality agencies to administer all or part of the program established in this subsection under regulations developed by the Secretary. Such agreements shall provide for the submission of such reports as the Secretary deems necessary, and for payment by the United States of such portion of the costs incurred in the administration of the program as the Secretary may deem appropriate.

(6) The contracts under this subsection shall be entered into only in areas where the management agency designated under subsection (c)(1) of this section assures an adequate level of participation by owners and operators having control of rural land in such areas. Within such areas the local soil conservation district, where one exists, together with the Secretary of Agriculture, will determine the priority of assistance among individual land owners and operators to assure that the most critical water quality problems are addressed.

(7) The Secretary, in consultation with the Administrator and subject to section 1314(k)

of this title, shall, not later than September 30, 1978, promulgate regulations for carrying out this subsection and for support and cooperation with other Federal and non-Federal agencies for implementation of this subsection.

(8) This program shall not be used to authorize or finance projects that would otherwise be eligible for assistance under the terms of Public Law 83-566 (16 U.S.C. §§1001 *et seq.*).

(9) There are hereby authorized to be appropriated to the Secretary of Agriculture $200,000,000 for fiscal year 1979, 400,000,000 for fiscal year 1980, $100,000,000 for fiscal year 1981, $100,000,000 for fiscal year 1982, and such sums as may be necessary for fiscal years 1983 through 1990, to carry out this subsection. The program authorized under this subsection shall be in addition to, and not in substitution of, other programs in such area authorized by this or any other public law.

§1289. Basin planning
[CWA §209]

(a) **Preparation of Level B plans** — The President, acting through the Water Resources Council, shall, as soon as practicable, prepare a Level B plan under the Water Resources Planning Act (42 U.S.C. §§1962 *et seq.*) for all basins in the United States. All such plans shall be completed not later than January 1, 1980, except that priority in the preparation of such plans shall be given to those basins and portions thereof which are within those areas designated under paragraphs (2), (3), and (4) of subsection (a) of section 1288 of this title.

(b) **Reporting requirements.** The President, acting through the Water Resources Council, shall report annually to Congress on progress being made in carrying out this section. The first such report shall be submitted not later than January 31, 1973.

(c) **Authorization of appropriations** — There is authorized to be appropriated to carry out this section not to exceed $200,000,000.

§1290. Annual survey
[CWA §210]

The Administrator shall annually make a survey to determine the efficiency of the operation and maintenance of treatment works constructed with grants made under this chapter, as compared to the efficiency planned at the time the grant was made. The results of such annual survey shall be included in the report required under section 1375(a) of this title.

§1291. Sewage collection systems
[CWA §211]

(a) **Existing and new systems** — No grant shall be made for a sewage collection system under this subchapter unless such grant (1) is for replacement or major rehabilitation of an existing collection system and is necessary to the total integrity and performance

of the waste treatment works servicing such community, or (2) is for a new collection system in an existing community with sufficient existing or planned capacity adequately to treat such collected sewage and is consistent with section 1281 of this title.

(b) **Use of population density as test** — If the Administrator uses population density as a test for determining the eligibility of a collector sewer for assistance it shall be only for the purpose of evaluating alternatives and determining the needs for such system in relation to ground or surface water quality impact.

(c) **Pollutant discharges from separate storm sewer systems** — No grant shall be made under this subchapter from funds authorized for any fiscal year during the period beginning October 1, 1977, and ending September 30, 1990, for treatment works for control of pollutant discharges from separate storm sewer systems.

§1292. Definitions
[CWA §212]

As used in this subchapter —

(1) The term "construction" means any one or more of the following: preliminary planning to determine the feasibility of treatment works, engineering, architectural, legal, fiscal, or economic investigations or studies, surveys, designs, plans, working drawings, specifications, procedures, field testing of innovative or alternative waste water treatment processes and techniques meeting guidelines promulgated under section 1314(d)(3) of this title, or other necessary actions, erection, building, acquisition, alteration, remodeling, improvement, or extension of treatment works, or the inspection or supervision of any of the foregoing items.

(2)(A) The term "treatment works" means any devices and systems used in the storage, treatment, recycling, and reclamation of municipal sewage or industrial wastes of a liquid nature to implement section 1281 of this title, or necessary to recycle or reuse water at the most economical cost over the estimated life of the works, including intercepting sewers, outfall sewers, sewage collection systems, pumping, power, and other equipment, and their appurtenances; extensions, improvements, remodeling, additions, and alterations thereof; elements essential to provide a reliable recycled supply such as standby treatment units and clear well facilities; and acquisition of the land that will be an integral part of the treatment process (including land used for the storage of treated wastewater in land treatment systems prior to land application) or will be used for ultimate disposal of residues resulting from such treatment and acquisition of other land, and interests in land, that are necessary for construction.

(B) In addition to the definition contained in subparagraph (A) of this paragraph, "treatment works" means any other method or system for preventing, abating, reducing, storing, treating, separating, or disposing of municipal waste, including storm water runoff, or industrial waste, including waste in combined storm water and sanitary sewer systems. Any application for construction grants which includes wholly or in part such methods or systems shall, in accordance with guidelines published by the Administrator pursuant to subparagraph (C) of this paragraph, contain adequate data and analysis demonstrating such proposal to be, over the life of such works, the most cost efficient alternative to comply with sections 1311 or 1312 of this title, or the requirements of section 1281 of this title.

(C) For the purposes of subparagraph (B) of this paragraph, the Administrator shall, within one hundred and eighty days after October 18, 1972, publish and thereafter revise no less often than annually, guidelines for the evaluation of methods, including cost-effective analysis, described in subparagraph (B) of this paragraph.

(3) The term "replacement" as used in this subchapter means those expenditures for obtaining and installing equipment, accessories, or appurtenances during the useful life of the treatment works necessary to maintain the capacity and performance for which such works are designed and constructed.

§1293. Loan guarantees
[CWA §213]

(a) State or local obligations issued exclusively to Federal Financing Bank for publicly owned treatment works; determination of eligibility of project by Administrator — Subject to the conditions of this section and to such terms and conditions as the Administrator determines to be necessary to carry out the purposes of this subchapter, the Administrator is authorized to guarantee, and to make commitments to guarantee, the principal and interest (including interest accruing between the date of default and the date of the payment in full of the guarantee) of any loan, obligation, or participation therein of any State, municipality, or intermunicipal or interstate agency issued directly and exclusively to the Federal Financing Bank to finance that part of the cost of any grant-eligible project for the construction of publicly owned treatment works not paid for with Federal financial assistance under this subchapter (other than this section), which project the Administrator has determined to be eligible for such financial assistance under this subchapter, including, but not limited to, projects eligible for reimbursement under section 1286 of this title.

(b) Conditions for issuance — No guarantee, or commitment to make a guarantee, may be made pursuant to this section —

(1) unless the Administrator certifies that the issuing body is unable to obtain on reasonable terms sufficient credit to finance its actual needs without such guarantee; and

(2) unless the Administrator determines that there is a reasonable assurance of repayment of the loan, obligation, or participation therein.

A determination of whether financing is available at reasonable rates shall be made by the Secretary of the Treasury with relationship to the current average yield on outstanding marketable obligations of municipalities of comparable maturity.

(c) Fees for application investigation and issuance of commitment guarantee — The Administrator is authorized to charge reasonable fees for the investigation of an application for a guarantee and for the issuance of a commitment to make a guarantee.

(d) Commitment for repayment — The Administrator, in determining whether there is a reasonable assurance of repayment, may require a commitment which would apply to such repayment. Such commitment may include, but not be limited to, any funds received by such grantee from the amounts appropriated under section 1286 of this title.

§1293a. Contained spoil disposal facilities

(a) Construction, operation, and maintenance; period; conditions; requirements — The Secretary of the Army, acting through the Chief of Engineers, is authorized to construct, operate, and maintain, subject to the provisions of subsection (c) of this section, contained spoil disposal facilities of sufficient capacity for a period not to exceed ten years, to meet the requirements of this section. Before establishing each such facility, the Secretary of the Army shall obtain the concurrence of appropriate local governments and shall consider the views and recommendations of the Administrator of the Environmental Protection Agency and shall comply with requirements of section 1171 of this title, and of the National Environmental Policy Act of 1969 (42 U.S.C. §§4321 et seq.). Section 401 of this title shall not apply to any facility authorized by this section.

(b) Time for establishment; consideration of area needs; requirements — The Secretary of the Army, acting through the Chief of Engineers, shall establish the contained spoil disposal facilities authorized in subsection (a) of this section at the earliest practicable date, taking into consideration the views and recommendations of the Administrator of the Environmental Protection Agency as to those areas which, in the Administrator's judgment, are most urgently in need of such facilities and pursuant to the requirements of the National Environmental Policy Act of 1969 (42 U.S.C. §§4321 et seq.) and the

Federal Water Pollution Control Act (33 U.S.C. §§1251 *et seq.*).

(c) Written agreement requirement; terms of agreement — Prior to construction of any such facility, the appropriate State or States, interstate agency, municipality, or other appropriate political subdivision of the State shall agree in writing to (1) furnish all lands, easements, and rights-of-way necessary for the construction, operation, and maintenance of the facility; (2) contribute to the United States 25 per centum of the construction costs, such amount to be payable either in cash prior to construction, in installments during construction, or in installments, with interest at a rate to be determined by the Secretary of the Treasury, as of the beginning of the fiscal year in which construction is initiated, on the basis of the computed average interest rate payable by the Treasury upon its outstanding marketable public obligations, which are neither due or callable for redemption for fifteen years from date of issue; (3) hold and save the United States free from damages due to construction, operation, and maintenance of the facility; and (4) except as provided in subsection (f) of this section, maintain the facility after completion of its use for disposal purposes in a manner satisfactory to the Secretary of the Army.

(d) Waiver of construction costs contribution from non-Federal interests; findings of participation in waste treatment facilities for general geographical area and compliance with water quality standards; waiver of payments in event of written agreement before occurrence of findings — The requirement for appropriate non-Federal interest or interests to furnish an agreement to contribute 25 per centum of the construction costs as set forth in subsection (c) of this section shall be waived by the Secretary of the Army upon a finding by the Administrator of the Environmental Protection Agency that for the area to which such construction applies, the State or States involved, interstate agency, municipality, and other appropriate political subdivision of the State and industrial concerns are participating in and in compliance with an approved plan for the general geographical area of the dredging activity for construction, modification, expansion, or rehabilitation of waste treatment facilities and the Administrator has found that applicable water quality standards are not being violated. In the event such findings occur after the appropriate non-Federal interest or interests have entered into the agreement required by subsection (c) of this section, any payments due after the date of such findings as part of the required local contribution of 25 per centum of the construction costs shall be waived by the Secretary of the Army.

(e) Federal payment of costs for disposal of dredged spoil from project — Notwithstanding any other provision of law, all costs of disposal of dredged spoil from the project for the Great Lakes connecting channels, Michigan, shall be borne by the United States.

(f) Title to lands, easements, and rights-of-way; retention by non-Federal interests; conveyance of facilities; agreement of transferee — The participating non-Federal interest or interests shall retain title to all lands, easements, and rights-of-way furnished by it pursuant to subsection (c) of this section. A spoil disposal facility owned by a non-Federal interest or interests may be conveyed to another party only after completion of the facility's use for disposal purposes and after the transferee agrees in writing to use or maintain the facility in a manner which the Secretary of the Army determines to be satisfactory.

(g) Federal licenses or permits; charges; remission of charge — Any spoil disposal facilities constructed under the provisions of this section shall be made available to Federal licensees or permittees upon payment of an appropriate charge for such use. Twenty-five per centum of such charge shall be remitted to the participating non-Federal interest or interests except for those excused from contributing to the construction costs under subsections (d) and (e) of this section.

(h) Provisions applicable to Great Lakes and their connecting channels — This section, other than subsection (i), shall be applicable only to the Great Lakes and their connecting channels.

(i) Research, study, and experimentation program relating to dredged spoil extended to navigable waters, etc.; cooperative program; scope of program; utilization of facilities and personnel of Federal agency — The Chief of Engineers, under the direction of the Secretary of the Army, is hereby authorized to extend to all navigable waters, connecting channels, tributary streams, other waters of the United States and waters contiguous to the United States, a comprehensive program of research, study, and experimentation relating to dredged spoil. This program shall be carried out in cooperation with other Federal and State agencies, and shall include, but not be limited to, investigations on the characteristics of dredged spoil, and alternative methods of its disposal. To the extent that such study shall include the effects of such dredge spoil on water quality, the facilities and personnel of the Environmental Protection Agency shall be utilized.

(j) Period for depositing dredged materials — The Secretary of the Army, acting through the Chief of Engineers, is authorized to continue to deposit dredged materials into a contained spoil disposal facility constructed under this section until the Secretary determines that such facility is no longer needed for such purpose or that such facility is completely full.

(k) Study and monitoring program

(1) Study — The Secretary of the Army, acting through the Chief of Engineers, shall conduct a

study of the materials disposed of in contained spoil disposal facilities constructed under this section for the purpose of determining whether or not toxic pollutants are present in such facilities and for the purpose of determining the concentration levels of each of such pollutants in such facilities.

(2) Report — Not later than 1 year after November 17, 1988, the Secretary shall transmit to Congress a report on the results of the study conducted under paragraph (1).

(3) Inspection and monitoring program — The Secretary shall conduct a program to inspect and monitor contained spoil disposal facilities constructed under this section for the purpose of determining whether or not toxic pollutants are leaking from such facilities.

(4) Toxic pollutant defined — For purposes of this subsection, the term "toxic pollutant" means those toxic pollutants referred to in section 1311(b)(2)(C) and 1311(b)(2)(D) of this title and such other pollutants as the Secretary, in consultation with the Administrator of the Environmental Protection Agency, determines are appropriate based on their effects on human health and the environment.

§1294. Public information and education on recycling and reuse of wastewater, use of land treatment, and reduction of wastewater volume
[CWA §214]

The Administrator shall develop and operate within one year of December 27, 1977, a continuing program of public information and education on recycling and reuse of wastewater (including sludge), the use of land treatment, and methods for the reduction of wastewater volume.

§1295. Requirements for American materials
[CWA §215]

Notwithstanding any other provision of law, no grant for which application is made after February 1, 1978, shall be made under this subchapter for any treatment works unless only such unmanufactured articles, materials, and supplies as have been mined or produced in the United States, and only such manufactured articles, materials, and supplies as have been manufactured in the United States, substantially all from articles, materials, or supplies mined, produced, or manufactured, as the case may be, in the United States will be used in such treatment works. This section shall not apply in any case where the Administrator determines, based upon those factors the Administrator deems relevant, including the available resources of the agency, it to be inconsistent with the public interest (including multilateral government procurement agreements) or the cost to be unreasonable, or if articles, materials, or supplies of the class or kind to be used or the articles, materials,

or supplies from which they are manufactured are not mined, produced, or manufactured, as the case may be, in the United States in sufficient and reasonably available commercial quantities and of a satisfactory quality.

§1296. Determination of priority of projects
[CWA §216]

Notwithstanding any other provision of this chapter, the determination of the priority to be given each category of projects for construction of publicly owned treatment works within each State shall be made solely by that State, except that if the Administrator, after a public hearing, determines that a specific project will not result in compliance with the enforceable requirements of this chapter, such project shall be removed from the State's priority list and such State shall submit a revised priority list. These categories shall include, but not be limited to (A) secondary treatment, (B) more stringent treatment, (C) infiltration-in-flow correction, (D) major sewer system rehabilitation, (E) new collector sewers and appurtenances, (F) new interceptors and appurtenances, and (G) correction of combined sewer overflows. Not less than 25 per centum of funds allocated to a State in any fiscal year under this subchapter for construction of publicly owned treatment works in such State shall be obligated for those types of projects referred to in clauses (D), (E), (F), and (G) of this section, if such projects are on such State's priority list for that year and are otherwise eligible for funding in that fiscal year. It is the policy of Congress that projects for wastewater treatment and management undertaken with Federal financial assistance under this chapter by any State, municipality, or intermunicipal or interstate agency shall be projects which, in the estimation of the State, are designed to achieve optimum water quality management, consistent with the public health and water quality goals and requirements of this chapter.

§1297. Guidelines for cost-effectiveness analysis
[CWA §217]

Any guidelines for cost-effectiveness analysis published by the Administrator under this subchapter shall provide for the identification and selection of cost effective alternatives to comply with the objectives and goals of this chapter and sections 1281(b), 1281(d), 1281(g)(2)(A), and 1311(b)(2)(B) of this title.

§1298. Cost effectiveness
[CWA §218]

(a) Congressional statement of policy — It is the policy of Congress that a project for waste treatment and management undertaken with Federal financial assistance under this chapter by any State, municipality, or intermunicipal or interstate agency shall be considered as an overall waste treatment system for waste treatment and management, and shall be that system which constitutes the most economical and cost-effective combination of devices and systems used in the storage, treatment, recycling, and reclamation of municipal sewage or industrial wastes of a liquid nature to implement section 1281 of this title, or necessary to recycle or reuse water at the most economical cost over the estimated life of the works, including intercepting sewers, outfall sewers, sewage collection systems, pumping power, and other equipment, and their appurtenances; extension, improvements, remodeling, additions, and alterations thereof; elements essential to provide a reliable recycled supply such as standby treatment units and clear well facilities; and any works, including site acquisition of the land that will be an integral part of the treatment process (including land use for the storage of treated wastewater in land treatment systems prior to land application) or which is used for ultimate disposal of residues resulting from such treatment; water efficiency measures and devices; and any other method or system for preventing, abating, reducing, storing, treating, separating, or disposing of municipal waste, including storm water runoff, or industrial waste, including waste in combined storm water and sanitary sewer systems; to meet the requirements of this chapter.

(b) Determination by Administrator as prerequisite to approval of grant — In accordance with the policy set forth in subsection (a) of this section, before the Administrator approves any grant to any State, municipality, or intermunicipal or interstate agency for the erection, building, acquisition, alteration, remodeling, improvement, or extension of any treatment works the Administrator shall determine that the facilities plan of which such treatment works are a part constitutes the most economical and cost-effective combination of treatment works over the life of the project to meet the requirements of this chapter, including, but not limited to, consideration of construction costs, operation, maintenance, and replacement costs.

(c) Value engineering review — In furtherance of the policy set forth in subsection (a) of this section, the Administrator shall require value engineering review in connection with any treatment works, prior to approval of any grant for the erection, building, acquisition, alteration, remodeling, improvement, or extension of such treatment works, in any case in which the cost of such erection, building, acquisition, alteration, remodeling, improvement, or extension is projected to be in excess of $10,000,000. For purposes of this subsection, the term "value engineering review" means a specialized cost control technique which uses a systematic and creative approach to identify and to focus on unnecessarily high cost in a project in order to arrive at a cost saving without sacrificing the reliability or efficiency of the project.

(d) Projects affected — This section applies to projects for waste treatment and management for which no treatment works including a facilities plan for such project have received Federal financial assistance for the preparation of construction plans and specifications under this chapter before December 29, 1981.

§1299. State certification of projects
[CWA §219]

Whenever the Governor of a State which has been delegated sufficient authority to administer the construction grant program under this subchapter in that State certifies to the Administrator that a grant application meets applicable requirements of Federal and State law for assistance under this subchapter, the Administrator shall approve or disapprove such application within 45 days of the date of receipt of such application. If the Administrator does not approve or disapprove such application within 45 days of receipt, the application shall be deemed approved. If the Administrator disapproves such application the Administrator shall state in writing the reasons for such disapproval. Any grant approved or deemed approved under this section shall be subject to amounts provided in appropriation Acts.

§1300. Pilot program for alternative water source projects
[CWA §220]

(a) Policy — Nothing in this section shall be construed to affect the application of section 1251(g) of this title and all of the provisions of this section shall be carried out in accordance with the provisions of section 1251(g) of this title.

(b) In general — The Administrator may establish a pilot program to make grants to State, interstate, and intrastate water resource development agencies (including water management districts and water supply authorities), local government agencies, private utilities, and nonprofit entities for alternative water source projects to meet critical water supply needs.

(c) Eligible entity — The Administrator may make grants under this section to an entity only if the entity has authority under State law to develop or provide water for municipal, industrial, and agricultural uses in an area of the State that is experiencing critical water supply needs.

(d) Selection of projects

(1) Limitation — A project that has received funds under the reclamation and reuse program conducted under the Reclamation Projects Authorization and Adjustment Act of 1992 (43 U.S.C. 390h *et seq.*) shall not be eligible for grant assistance under this section.

(2) Additional consideration — In making grants under this section, the Administrator shall consider whether the project is located within the

boundaries of a State or area referred to in section 391 of Title 43, and within the geographic scope of the reclamation and reuse program conducted under the Reclamation Projects Authorization and Adjustment Act of 1992 (43 U.S.C. 390h *et seq.*).

(3) Geographical distribution — Alternative water source projects selected by the Administrator under this section shall reflect a variety of geographical and environmental conditions.

(e) Committee resolution procedure

(1) In general — No appropriation shall be made for any alternative water source project under this section, the total Federal cost of which exceeds $3,000,000, if such project has not been approved by a resolution adopted by the Committee on Transportation and Infrastructure of the House of Representatives or the Committee on Environment and Public Works of the Senate.

(2) Requirements for securing consideration — For purposes of securing consideration of approval under paragraph (1), the Administrator shall provide to a committee referred to in paragraph (1) such information as the committee requests and the non-Federal sponsor shall provide to the committee information on the costs and relative needs for the alternative water source project.

(f) Uses of grants — Amounts from grants received under this section may be used for engineering, design, construction, and final testing of alternative water source projects designed to meet critical water supply needs. Such amounts may not be used for planning, feasibility studies or for operation, maintenance, replacement, repair, or rehabilitation.

(g) Cost sharing — The Federal share of the eligible costs of an alternative water source project carried out using assistance made available under this section shall not exceed 50 percent.

(h) Reports — On or before September 30, 2004, the Administrator shall transmit to Congress a report on the results of the pilot program established under this section, including progress made toward meeting the critical water supply needs of the participants in the pilot program.

(i) Definitions — In this section, the following definitions apply:

(1) Alternative water source project — The term "alternative water source project" means a project designed to provide municipal, industrial, and agricultural water supplies in an environmentally sustainable manner by conserving, managing, reclaiming, or reusing water or wastewater or by treating wastewater. Such term does not include water treatment or distribution facilities.

(2) Critical water supply needs — The term "critical water supply needs" means existing or reasonably anticipated future water supply needs that cannot be met by existing water supplies, as identified in a comprehensive statewide or regional water supply plan or assessment projected over a planning period of at least 20 years.

(j) Authorization of appropriations — There is authorized to be appropriated to carry out this section a total of $75,000,000 for fiscal years 2002 through 2004. Such sums shall remain available until expended.

§1301. Sewer overflow control grants
[CWA §221]

(a) In general

(1) Grants to States — The Administrator may make grants to States for the purpose of providing grants to a municipality or municipal entity for planning, design, and construction of —

(A) treatment works to intercept, transport, control, treat, or reuse municipal combined sewer overflows, sanitary sewer overflows, or stormwater; and

(B) any other measures to manage, reduce, treat, or recapture stormwater or subsurface drainage water eligible for assistance under section 1383(c) of this title.

(2) Direct municipal grants — Subject to subsection (g), the Administrator may make a direct grant to a municipality or municipal entity for the purposes described in paragraph (1).

(b) Prioritization — In selecting from among municipalities applying for grants under subsection (a), a State or the Administrator shall give priority to an applicant that —

(1) is a municipality that is a financially distressed community under subsection (c) of this section;

(2) has implemented or is complying with an implementation schedule for the nine minimum controls specified in the CSO control policy referred to in section 1342(q)(1) of this title and has begun implementing a long-term municipal combined sewer overflow control plan or a separate sanitary sewer overflow control plan;

(3) is requesting a grant for a project that is on a State's intended use plan pursuant to section 1386(c) of this title; or

(4) is an Alaska Native Village.

(c) Financially distressed community —

(1) Definition — In subsection (b), the term "financially distressed community" means a community that meets affordability criteria established by the State in which the community is located, if such criteria are developed after public review and comment.

(2) Consideration of impact on water and sewer rates — In determining if a community is a distressed community for the purposes of subsection (b), the State shall consider, among other factors, the extent to which the rate of growth of a community's tax base has been historically slow such that implementing a plan described in subsection

(b)(2) would result in a significant increase in any water or sewer rate charged by the community's publicly owned wastewater treatment facility.

(3) Information to assist States — The Administrator may publish information to assist States in establishing affordability criteria under paragraph (1).

(d) Cost-sharing — The Federal share of the cost of activities carried out using amounts from a grant made under subsection (a) shall be not less than 55 percent of the cost. The non-Federal share of the cost may include, in any amount, public and private funds and in-kind services, and may include, notwithstanding section 1383(h) of this title, financial assistance, including loans, from a State water pollution control revolving fund.

(e) Administrative requirements — A project that receives assistance under this section shall be carried out subject to the same requirements as a project that receives assistance from a State water pollution control revolving fund under subchapter VI, except to the extent that the Governor of the State in which the project is located determines that a requirement of subchapter VI is inconsistent with the purposes of this section. For the purposes of this subsection, a Governor may not determine that the requirements of subchapter VI relating to the application of section 1372 of this title are inconsistent with the purposes of this section.

(f) Authorization of appropriations

(1) In general — There is authorized to be appropriated to carry out this section $225,000,000 for each of fiscal years 2019 through 2020.

(2) Minimum allocations — To the extent there are sufficient eligible project applications, the Administrator shall ensure that a State uses not less than 20 percent of the amount of the grants made to the State under subsection (a) in a fiscal year to carry out projects to intercept, transport, control, treat, or reuse municipal combined sewer overflows, sanitary sewer overflows, or stormwater through the use of green infrastructure, water and energy efficiency improvements, and other environmentally innovative activities.

(g) Allocation of funds

(1) Fiscal year 2019 — Subject to subsection (h), the Administrator shall use the amounts appropriated to carry out this section for fiscal year 2019 for making grants to municipalities and municipal entities under subsection (a)(2) in accordance with the criteria set forth in subsection (b).

(2) Fiscal year 2020 and thereafter — Subject to subsection (h), the Administrator shall use the amounts appropriated to carry out this section for fiscal year 2020 and each fiscal year thereafter for making grants to States under subsection (a)(1) in accordance with a formula to be established by the Administrator, after providing notice and an opportunity for public comment, that allocates to each State a proportional share of such amounts based on the total needs of the State for municipal combined sewer overflow controls, sanitary sewer overflow controls, and stormwater identified in the most recent detailed estimate and comprehensive study submitted pursuant to section 1375 of this title and any other information the Administrator considers appropriate.

(h) Administrative expenses — Of the amounts appropriated to carry out this section for each fiscal year —

(1) the Administrator may retain an amount not to exceed 1 percent for the reasonable and necessary costs of administering this section; and

(2) the Administrator, or a State, may retain an amount not to exceed 4 percent of any grant made to a municipality or municipal entity under subsection (a), for the reasonable and necessary costs of administering the grant.

(i) Reports — Not later than December 31, 2003, and periodically thereafter, the Administrator shall transmit to Congress a report containing recommended funding levels for grants under this section. The recommended funding levels shall be sufficient to ensure the continued expeditious implementation of municipal combined sewer overflow and sanitary sewer overflow controls nationwide.

SUBCHAPTER III — STANDARDS AND ENFORCEMENT

§1311. Effluent limitations
[CWA §301]

(a) Illegality of pollutant discharges except in compliance with law — Except as in compliance with this section and sections 1312, 1316, 1317, 1328, 1342, and 1344 of this title, the discharge of any pollutant by any person shall be unlawful.

(b) Timetable for achievement of objectives — In order to carry out the objective of this chapter there shall be achieved —

(1)(A) not later than July 1, 1977, effluent limitations for point sources, other than publicly owned treatment works, (i) which shall require the application of the best practicable control technology currently available as defined by the Administrator pursuant to section 1314(b) of this title, or (ii) in the case of a discharge into a publicly owned treatment works which meets the requirements of subparagraph (B) of this paragraph, which shall require compliance with any applicable pretreatment requirements and any requirements under section 1317 of this title; and

(B) for publicly owned treatment works in existence on July 1, 1977, or approved pursuant to section 1283 of this title prior to June 30, 1974 (for which construction must be completed within four years of approval), effluent limitations based upon secondary treatment as defined by the Administrator pursuant to section 1314(d)(1) of this title; or,

(C) not later than July 1, 1977, any more stringent limitation, including those necessary to meet water quality standards, treatment standards, or schedules of compliance, established pursuant to any State law or regulations (under authority preserved by section 1370 of this title) or any other Federal law or regulation, or required to implement any applicable water quality standard established pursuant to this chapter.

(2)(A) for pollutants identified in subparagraphs (C), (D), and (F) of this paragraph, effluent limitations for categories and classes of point sources, other than publicly owned treatment works, which (i) shall require application of the best available technology economically achievable for such category or class, which will result in reasonable further progress toward the national goal of eliminating the discharge of all pollutants, as determined in accordance with regulations issued by the Administrator pursuant to section 1314(b)(2) of this title, which such effluent limitations shall require the elimination of discharges of all pollutants if the Administrator finds, on the basis of information available to him (including information developed pursuant to section 1325 of this title), that such elimination is technologically and economically achievable for a category or class of point sources as determined in accordance with regulations issued by the Administrator pursuant to section 1314(b)(2) of this title, or (ii) in the case of the introduction of a pollutant into a publicly owned treatment works which meets the requirements of subparagraph (B) of this paragraph, shall require compliance with any applicable pretreatment requirements and any other requirement under section 1317 of this title;

(B) Repealed. Pub. L. 97-117, Sec. 21(b), Dec. 29, 1981, 95 Stat. 1632.

(C) with respect to all toxic pollutants referred to in table 1 of Committee Print Numbered 95-30 of the Committee on Public Works and Transportation of the House of Representatives compliance with effluent limitations in accordance with subparagraph (A) of this paragraph as expeditiously as practicable but in no case later than three years after the date such limitations are promulgated under section 1314(b) of this title, and in no case later than March 31, 1989;

(D) for all toxic pollutants listed under paragraph (1) of subsection (a) of section 1317 of this title which are not referred to in subparagraph (C) of this paragraph compliance with effluent limitations in accordance

with subparagraph (A) of this paragraph as expeditiously as practicable, but in no case later than three years after the date such limitations are promulgated under section 1314(b) of this title, and in no case later than March 31, 1989;

(E) as expeditiously as practicable but in no case later than three years after the date such limitations are promulgated under section 1314(b) of this title, and in no case later than March 31, 1989, compliance with effluent limitations for categories and classes of point sources, other than publicly owned treatment works, which in the case of pollutants identified pursuant to section 1314(a)(4) of this title shall require application of the best conventional pollutant control technology as determined in accordance with regulations issued by the Administrator pursuant to section 1314(b)(4) of this title; and

(F) for all pollutants (other than those subject to subparagraphs (C), (D), or (E) of this paragraph) compliance with effluent limitations in accordance with subparagraph (A) of this paragraph as expeditiously as practicable but in no case later than 3 years after the date such limitations are established, and in no case later than March 31, 1989.

(3)(A) for effluent limitations under paragraph (1)(A)(i) of this subsection promulgated after January 1, 1982, and requiring a level of control substantially greater or based on fundamentally different control technology than under permits for an industrial category issued before such date, compliance as expeditiously as practicable but in no case later than three years after the date such limitations are promulgated under section 1314(b) of this title, and in no case later than March 31, 1989; and

(B) for any effluent limitation in accordance with paragraph (1)(A)(i), (2)(A)(i), or (2)(E) of this subsection established only on the basis of section 1342(a)(1) of this title in a permit issued after February 4, 1987, compliance as expeditiously as practicable but in no case later than three years after the date such limitations are established, and in no case later than March 31, 1989.

(c) **Modification of timetable** — The Administrator may modify the requirements of subsection (b)(2)(A) of this section with respect to any point source for which a permit application is filed after July 1, 1977, upon a showing by the owner or operator of such point source satisfactory to the Administrator that such modified requirements (1) will represent the maximum use of technology within the economic capability of the owner or operator; and (2) will result in reasonable further progress toward the elimination of the discharge of pollutants.

(d) Review and revision of effluent limitations — Any effluent limitation required by paragraph (2) of subsection (b) of this section shall be reviewed at least every five years and, if appropriate, revised pursuant to the procedure established under such paragraph.

(e) All point discharge source application of effluent limitations — Effluent limitations established pursuant to this section or section 1312 of this title shall be applied to all point sources of discharge of pollutants in accordance with the provisions of this chapter.

(f) Illegality of discharge of radiological, chemical, or biological warfare agents, high-level radioactive waste, or medical waste — Notwithstanding any other provisions of this chapter it shall be unlawful to discharge any radiological, chemical, or biological warfare agent, any high-level radioactive waste, or any medical waste, into the navigable waters.

(g) Modifications for certain nonconventional pollutants

(1) General authority — The Administrator, with the concurrence of the State, may modify the requirements of subsection (b)(2)(A) of this section with respect to the discharge from any point source of ammonia, chlorine, color, iron, and total phenols (4AAP) (when determined by the Administrator to be a pollutant covered by subsection (b)(2)(F) of this section) and any other pollutant which the Administrator lists under paragraph (4) of this subsection.

(2) Requirements for granting modifications — A modification under this subsection shall be granted only upon a showing by the owner or operator of a point source satisfactory to the Administrator that —

(A) such modified requirements will result at a minimum in compliance with the requirements of subsection (b)(1)(A) or (C) of this section, whichever is applicable;

(B) such modified requirements will not result in any additional requirements on any other point or nonpoint source; and

(C) such modification will not interfere with the attainment or maintenance of that water quality which shall assure protection of public water supplies, and the protection and propagation of a balanced population of shellfish, fish, and wildlife, and allow recreational activities, in and on the water and such modification will not result in the discharge of pollutants in quantities which may reasonably be anticipated to pose an unacceptable risk to human health or the environment because of bioaccumulation, persistency in the environment, acute toxicity, chronic toxicity (including carcinogenicity, mutagenicity or teratogenicity), or synergistic propensities.

(3) Limitation on authority to apply for subsection (c) modification — If an owner or operator of a point source applies for a modification under this subsection with respect to the discharge of any pollutant, such owner or operator shall be eligible to apply for modification under subsection (c) of this section with respect to such pollutant only during the same time period as he is eligible to apply for a modification under this subsection.

(4) Procedures for listing additional pollutants

(A) General authority — Upon petition of any person, the Administrator may add any pollutant to the list of pollutants for which modification under this section is authorized (except for pollutants identified pursuant to section 1314(a)(4) of this title, toxic pollutants subject to section 1317(a) of this title, and the thermal component of discharges) in accordance with the provisions of this paragraph.

(B) Requirements for listing

(i) Sufficient information — The person petitioning for listing of an additional pollutant under this subsection shall submit to the Administrator sufficient information to make the determinations required by this subparagraph.

(ii) Toxic criteria determination — The Administrator shall determine whether or not the pollutant meets the criteria for listing as a toxic pollutant under section 1317(a) of this title.

(iii) Listing as toxic pollutant — If the Administrator determines that the pollutant meets the criteria for listing as a toxic pollutant under section 1317(a) of this title, the Administrator shall list the pollutant as a toxic pollutant under section 1317(a) of this title.

(iv) Nonconventional criteria determination — If the Administrator determines that the pollutant does not meet the criteria for listing as a toxic pollutant under such section and determines that adequate test methods and sufficient data are available to make the determinations required by paragraph (2) of this subsection with respect to the pollutant, the Administrator shall add the pollutant to the list of pollutants specified in paragraph (1) of this subsection for which modifications are authorized under this subsection.

(C) Requirements for filing of petitions — A petition for listing of a pollutant under this paragraph —

(i) must be filed not later than 270 days after the date of promulgation of an applicable effluent guideline under section 1314 of this title;

(ii) may be filed before promulgation of such guideline; and

(iii) may be filed with an application for a modification under paragraph (1) with respect to the discharge of such pollutant.

(D) Deadline for approval of petition — A decision to add a pollutant to the list of pollutants for which modifications under this subsection are authorized must be made within 270 days after the date of promulgation of an applicable effluent guideline under section 1314 of this title.

(E) Burden of proof — The burden of proof for making the determinations under subparagraph (B) shall be on the petitioner.

(5) Removal of pollutants — The Administrator may remove any pollutant from the list of pollutants for which modifications are authorized under this subsection if the Administrator determines that adequate test methods and sufficient data are no longer available for determining whether or not modifications may be granted with respect to such pollutant under paragraph (2) of this subsection.

(h) **Modification of secondary treatment requirements** — The Administrator, with the concurrence of the State, may issue a permit under section 1342 of this title which modifies the requirements of subsection (b)(1)(B) of this section with respect to the discharge of any pollutant from a publicly owned treatment works into marine waters, if the applicant demonstrates to the satisfaction of the Administrator that —

(1) there is an applicable water quality standard specific to the pollutant for which the modification is requested, which has been identified under section 1314(a)(6) of this title;

(2) the discharge of pollutants in accordance with such modified requirements will not interfere, alone or in combination with pollutants from other sources, with the attainment or maintenance of that water quality which assures protection of public water supplies and the protection and propagation of a balanced, indigenous population of shellfish, fish, and wildlife, and allows recreational activities, in and on the water;

(3) the applicant has established a system for monitoring the impact of such discharge on a representative sample of aquatic biota, to the extent practicable, and the scope of such monitoring is limited to include only those scientific investigations which are necessary to study the effects of the proposed discharge;

(4) such modified requirements will not result in any additional requirements on any other point or nonpoint source;

(5) all applicable pretreatment requirements for sources introducing waste into such treatment works will be enforced;

(6) in the case of any treatment works serving a population of 50,000 or more, with respect to any toxic pollutant introduced into such works by an industrial discharger for which pollutant there is no applicable pretreatment requirement in effect, sources introducing waste into such works are in compliance with all applicable pretreatment requirements, the applicant will enforce such requirements, and the applicant has in effect a pretreatment program which, in combination with the treatment of discharges from such works, removes the same amount of such pollutant as would be removed if such works were to apply secondary treatment to discharges and if such works had no pretreatment program with respect to such pollutant;

(7) to the extent practicable, the applicant has established a schedule of activities designed to eliminate the entrance of toxic pollutants from nonindustrial sources into such treatment works;

(8) there will be no new or substantially increased discharges from the point source of the pollutant to which the modification applies above that volume of discharge specified in the permit;

(9) the applicant at the time such modification becomes effective will be discharging effluent which has received at least primary or equivalent treatment and which meets the criteria established under section 1314(a)(1) of this title after initial mixing in the waters surrounding or adjacent to the point at which such effluent is discharged.

For the purposes of this subsection the phrase "the discharge of any pollutant into marine waters" refers to a discharge into deep waters of the territorial sea or the waters of the contiguous zone, or into saline estuarine waters where there is strong tidal movement and other hydrological and geological characteristics which the Administrator determines necessary to allow compliance with paragraph (2) of this subsection, and section 1251(a)(2) of this title. For the purposes of paragraph (9), "primary or equivalent treatment" means treatment by screening, sedimentation, and skimming adequate to remove at least 30 percent of the biological oxygen demanding material and of the suspended solids in the treatment works influent, and disinfection, where appropriate. A municipality which applies secondary treatment shall be eligible to receive a permit pursuant to this subsection which modifies the requirements of subsection (b)(1)(B) of this section with respect to the discharge of any pollutant from any treatment works owned by such municipality into marine waters. No permit issued under this subsection shall authorize the discharge of sewage sludge into marine waters. In order for a permit to be issued under this subsection for the discharge of a pollutant into marine waters, such marine waters must exhibit characteristics assuring that water providing dilution does not contain significant amounts of previously discharged effluent from such treatment works. No permit issued under this subsection shall authorize the discharge of any pollutant into saline estuarine waters which at the time of application do not support a balanced indigenous population of shellfish, fish and wildlife, or allow recreation in and on the waters or which exhibit ambient water quality below applicable water quality standards adopted for the protection of public water supplies, shellfish, fish and wildlife or recreational activities or such other standards necessary to assure support and protection of such uses. The prohibition contained in the preceding sentence shall apply without regard to the presence or absence of a causal relationship between such characteristics and the applicant's current or proposed discharge. Notwithstanding any other provisions of this subsection, no permit may be issued under this subsection for discharge of a pollutant into the New York Bight Apex consisting of the ocean waters of the Atlantic Ocean westward of 73 degrees 30 minutes west longitude and northward of 40 degrees 10 minutes north latitude.

(i) Municipal time extensions

(1) Where construction is required in order for a planned or existing publicly owned treatment works to achieve limitations under subsection (b)(1)(B) or (b)(1)(C) of this section, but (A) construction cannot be completed within the time required in such subsection, or (B) the United States has failed to make financial assistance under this chapter available in time to achieve such limitations by the time specified in such subsection, the owner or operator of such treatment works may request the Administrator (or if appropriate the State) to issue a permit pursuant to section 1342 of this title or to modify a permit issued pursuant to that section to extend such time for compliance. Any such request shall be filed with the Administrator (or if appropriate the State) within 180 days after February 4, 1987. The Administrator (or if appropriate the State) may grant such request and issue or modify such a permit, which shall contain a schedule of compliance for the publicly owned treatment works based on the earliest date by which such financial assistance will be available from the United States and construction can be completed, but in no event later than July 1, 1988, and shall contain such other terms and conditions, including those necessary to carry out subsections (b) through (g) of section 1281 of this title, section 1317 of this title, and such interim effluent limitations applicable to that treatment works as the Administrator determines are necessary to carry out the provisions of this chapter.

(2)(A) Where a point source (other than a publicly owned treatment works) will not achieve the requirements of subsections (b)(1)(A) and (b)(1)(C) of this section and —

(i) if a permit issued prior to July 1, 1977, to such point source is based upon a discharge into a publicly owned treatment works; or

(ii) if such point source (other than a publicly owned treatment works) had before July 1, 1977, a contract (enforceable against such point source) to discharge into a publicly owned treatment works; or

(iii) if either an application made before July 1, 1977, for a construction grant under this chapter for a publicly owned treatment works, or engineering or architectural plans or working drawings made before July 1, 1977, for a publicly owned treatment works, show that such point source was to discharge into such publicly owned treatment works,

and such publicly owned treatment works is presently unable to accept such discharge without construction, and in the case of a discharge to an existing publicly owned treatment works, such treatment works has an extension pursuant to paragraph (1) of this subsection, the owner or operator of such point source may request the Administrator (or if appropriate the State) to issue or modify such a permit pursuant to such section 1342 of this title to extend such time for compliance. Any such request shall be filed with the Administrator (or if appropriate the State) within 180 days after December 27, 1977, or the filing of a request by the appropriate publicly owned treatment works under paragraph (1) of this subsection, whichever is later. If the Administrator (or if appropriate the State) finds that the owner or operator of such point source has acted in good faith, he may grant such request and issue or modify such a permit, which shall contain a schedule of compliance for the point source to achieve the requirements of subsections (b)(1)(A) and (C) of this section and shall contain such other terms and conditions, including pretreatment and interim effluent limitations and water conservation requirements applicable to that point source, as the Administrator determines are necessary to carry out the provisions of this chapter.

(B) No time modification granted by the Administrator (or if appropriate the State) pursuant to paragraph (2)(A) of this subsection shall extend beyond the earliest date practicable for compliance or beyond the date of any extension granted to the appropriate publicly owned treatment works pursuant to paragraph (1) of this subsection, but in no event shall it extend beyond July 1, 1988; and no such time modification shall be granted unless (i) the publicly owned treatment works will be in operation and available to the point source before July 1, 1988, and will meet the requirements of subsections

941

(b)(1)(B) and (C) of this section after receiving the discharge from that point source; and (ii) the point source and the publicly owned treatment works have entered into an enforceable contract requiring the point source to discharge into the publicly owned treatment works, the owner or operator of such point source to pay the costs required under section 1284 of this title, and the publicly owned treatment works to accept the discharge from the point source; and (iii) the permit for such point source requires that point source to meet all requirements under section 1317(a) and (b) of this title during the period of such time modification.

(j) Modification procedures

(1) Any application filed under this section for a modification of the provisions of —

(A) subsection (b)(1)(B) of this section under subsection (h) of this section shall be filed not later that the 365th day which begins after December 29, 1981, except that a publicly owned treatment works which prior to December 31, 1982, had a contractual arrangement to use a portion of the capacity of an ocean outfall operated by another publicly owned treatment works which has applied for or received modification under subsection (h) of this section, may apply for a modification of subsection (h) of this section in its own right not later than 30 days after February 4, 1987, and except as provided in paragraph (5);

(B) subsection (b)(2)(A) of this section as it applies to pollutants identified in subsection (b)(2)(F) of this section shall be filed not later than 270 days after the date of promulgation of an applicable effluent guideline under section 1314 of this title or not later than 270 days after December 27, 1977, whichever is later.

(2) Subject to paragraph (3) of this section, any application for a modification filed under subsection (g) of this section shall not operate to stay any requirement under this chapter, unless in the judgment of the Administrator such a stay or the modification sought will not result in the discharge of pollutants in quantities which may reasonably be anticipated to pose an unacceptable risk to human health or the environment because of bioaccumulation, persistency in the environment, acute toxicity, chronic toxicity (including carcinogenicity, mutagenicity, or teratogenicity), or synergistic propensities, and that there is a substantial likelihood that the applicant will succeed on the merits of such application. In the case of an application filed under subsection (g) of this section, the Administrator may condition any stay granted under this paragraph on requiring the filing of a bond or other appropriate security to assure timely compliance with the requirements from which a modification is sought.

(3) Compliance requirements under subsection (g)

(A) Effect of filing — An application for a modification under subsection (g) of this section and a petition for listing of a pollutant as a pollutant for which modifications are authorized under such subsection shall not stay the requirement that the person seeking such modification or listing comply with effluent limitations under this chapter for all pollutants not the subject of such application or petition.

(B) Effect of disapproval — Disapproval of an application for a modification under subsection (g) of this section shall not stay the requirement that the person seeking such modification comply with all applicable effluent limitations under this chapter.

(4) Deadline for subsection (g) decision — An application for a modification with respect to a pollutant filed under subsection (g) of this section must be approved or disapproved not later than 365 days after the date of such filing; except that in any case in which a petition for listing such pollutant as a pollutant for which modifications are authorized under such subsection is approved, such application must be approved or disapproved not later than 365 days after the date of approval of such petition.

(5) Extension of application deadline

(A) In general — In the 180-day period beginning on October 31, 1994, the city of San Diego, California, may apply for a modification pursuant to subsection (h) of this section of the requirements of subsection (b)(1)(B) of this section with respect to biological oxygen demand and total suspended solids in the effluent discharged into marine waters.

(B) Application — An application under this paragraph shall include a commitment by the applicant to implement a waste water reclamation program that, at a minimum, will —

(i) achieve a system capacity of 45,000,000 gallons of reclaimed waste water per day by January 1, 2010; and

(ii) result in a reduction in the quantity of suspended solids discharged by the applicant into the marine environment during the period of the modification.

(C) Additional conditions — The Administrator may not grant a modification pursuant to an application submitted under this paragraph unless the Administrator determines that such modification will result in removal of not less than 58 percent of the biological oxygen demand (on an annual average) and not less than 80 percent of total suspended solids (on a monthly average) in the discharge to which the application applies.

(D) Preliminary decision deadline — The Administrator shall announce a preliminary decision on an application submitted under this paragraph not later than 1 year after the date the application is submitted.

(k) Innovative technology — In the case of any facility subject to a permit under section 1342 of this title which proposes to comply with the requirements of subsection (b)(2)(A) or (b)(2)(E) of this section by replacing existing production capacity with an innovative production process which will result in an effluent reduction significantly greater than that required by the limitation otherwise applicable to such facility and moves toward the national goal of eliminating the discharge of all pollutants, or with the installation of an innovative control technique that has a substantial likelihood for enabling the facility to comply with the applicable effluent limitation by achieving a significantly greater effluent reduction than that required by the applicable effluent limitation and moves toward the national goal of eliminating the discharge of all pollutants, or by achieving the required reduction with an innovative system that has the potential for significantly lower costs than the systems which have been determined by the Administrator to be economically achievable, the Administrator (or the State with an approved program under section 1342 of this title, in consultation with the Administrator) may establish a date for compliance under subsection (b)(2)(A) or (b)(2)(E) of this section no later than two years after the date for compliance with such effluent limitation which would otherwise be applicable under such subsection, if it is also determined that such innovative system has the potential for industrywide application.

(*l*) Toxic pollutants — Other than as provided in subsection (n) of this section, the Administrator may not modify any requirement of this section as it applies to any specific pollutant which is on the toxic pollutant list under section 1317(a)(1) of this title.

(m) Modification of effluent limitation requirements for point sources

(1) The Administrator, with the concurrence of the State, may issue a permit under section 1342 of this title which modifies the requirements of subsections (b)(1)(A) and (b)(2)(E) of this section, and of section 1343 of this title, with respect to effluent limitations to the extent such limitations relate to biochemical oxygen demand and pH from discharges by an industrial discharger in such State into deep waters of the territorial seas, if the applicant demonstrates and the Administrator finds that —

    (A) the facility for which modification is sought is covered at the time of the enactment of this subsection by National Pollutant Discharge Elimination System permit number CA0005894 or CA0005282;

    (B) the energy and environmental costs of meeting such requirements of subsections (b)(1)(A) and (b)(2)(E) of this section and section 1343 of this title exceed by an unreasonable amount the benefits to be obtained, including the objectives of this chapter;

    (C) the applicant has established a system for monitoring the impact of such discharges on a representative sample of aquatic biota;

    (D) such modified requirements will not result in any additional requirements on any other point or nonpoint source;

    (E) there will be no new or substantially increased discharges from the point source of the pollutant to which the modification applies above that volume of discharge specified in the permit;

    (F) the discharge is into waters where there is strong tidal movement and other hydrological and geological characteristics which are necessary to allow compliance with this subsection and section 1251(a)(2) of this title;

    (G) the applicant accepts as a condition to the permit a contractual obligation to use funds in the amount required (but not less than $250,000 per year for ten years) for research and development of water pollution control technology, including but not limited to closed cycle technology;

    (H) the facts and circumstances present a unique situation which, if relief is granted, will not establish a precedent or the relaxation of the requirements of this chapter applicable to similarly situated discharges; and

    (I) no owner or operator of a facility comparable to that of the applicant situated in the United States has demonstrated that it would be put at a competitive disadvantage to the applicant (or the parent company or any subsidiary thereof) as a result of the issuance of a permit under this subsection.

(2) The effluent limitations established under a permit issued under paragraph (1) shall be sufficient to implement the applicable State water quality standards, to assure the protection of public water supplies and protection and propagation of a balanced, indigenous population of shellfish, fish, fauna, wildlife, and other aquatic organisms, and to allow recreational activities in and on the water. In setting such limitations, the Administrator shall take into account any seasonal variations and the need for an adequate margin of safety, considering the lack of essential knowledge concerning the relationship between effluent limitations and water quality and the lack of essential knowledge of the effects of discharges on beneficial uses of the receiving waters.

(3) A permit under this subsection may be issued for a period not to exceed five years, and such a permit may be renewed for one additional period not to exceed five years upon a demonstration by the applicant and a finding by the Administrator at the time of application for any such renewal that the provisions of this subsection are met.

(4) The Administrator may terminate a permit issued under this subsection if the Administrator determines that there has been a decline in ambient water quality of the receiving waters during the period of the permit even if a direct cause and effect relationship cannot be shown: *Provided,* That if the effluent from a source with a permit issued under this subsection is contributing to a decline in ambient water quality of the receiving waters, the Administrator shall terminate such permit.

(n) Fundamentally different factors

(1) General rule — The Administrator, with the concurrence of the State, may establish an alternative requirement under subsection (b)(2) of this section or section 1317(b) of this title for a facility that modifies the requirements of national effluent limitation guidelines or categorical pretreatment standards that would otherwise be applicable to such facility, if the owner or operator of such facility demonstrates to the satisfaction of the Administrator that —

(A) the facility is fundamentally different with respect to the factors (other than cost) specified in section 1314(b) or 1314(g) of this title and considered by the Administrator in establishing such national effluent limitation guidelines or categorical pretreatment standards;

(B) the application —

(i) is based solely on information and supporting data submitted to the Administrator during the rulemaking for establishment of the applicable national effluent limitation guidelines or categorical pretreatment standard specifically raising the factors that are fundamentally different for such facility; or

(ii) is based on information and supporting data referred to in clause (i) and information and supporting data the applicant did not have a reasonable opportunity to submit during such rulemaking;

(C) the alternative requirement is no less stringent than justified by the fundamental difference; and

(D) the alternative requirement will not result in a non-water quality environmental impact which is markedly more adverse than the impact considered by the Administrator in establishing such national effluent limitation guideline or categorical pretreatment standard.

(2) Time limit for applications — An application for an alternative requirement which modifies the requirements of an effluent limitation or pretreatment standard under this subsection must be submitted to the Administrator within 180 days after the date on which such limitation or standard is established or revised, as the case may be.

(3) Time limit for decision — The Administrator shall approve or deny by final agency action an application submitted under this subsection within 180 days after the date such application is filed with the Administrator.

(4) Submission of information — The Administrator may allow an applicant under this subsection to submit information and supporting data until the earlier of the date the application is approved or denied or the last day that the Administrator has to approve or deny such application.

(5) Treatment of pending applications — For the purposes of this subsection, an application for an alternative requirement based on fundamentally different factors which is pending on February 4, 1987, shall be treated as having been submitted to the Administrator on the 180th day following February 4, 1987. The applicant may amend the application to take into account the provisions of this subsection.

(6) Effect of submission of application — An application for an alternative requirement under this subsection shall not stay the applicant's obligation to comply with the effluent limitation guideline or categorical pretreatment standard which is the subject of the application.

(7) Effect of denial — If an application for an alternative requirement which modifies the requirements of an effluent limitation or pretreatment standard under this subsection is denied by the Administrator, the applicant must comply with such limitation or standard as established or revised, as the case may be.

(8) Reports — By January 1, 1997, and January 1 of every odd-numbered year thereafter, the Administrator shall submit to the Committee on Environment and Public Works of the Senate and the Committee on Transportation and Infrastructure of the House of Representatives a report on the status of applications for alternative requirements which modify the requirements of effluent limitations under section 1311 or 1314 of this title or any national categorical pretreatment standard under section 1317(b) of this title filed before, on, or after February 4, 1987.

(o) Application fees — The Administrator shall prescribe and collect from each applicant fees reflecting the reasonable administrative costs incurred in reviewing and processing applications for modifications submitted to the Administrator pursuant to subsections (c), (g), (i), (k), (m) and (n) of this section, section 1314(d)(4) of this title, and section 1326(a) of this title. All amounts collected by the Administrator under this subsection shall be deposited into a special fund of the Treasury entitled "Water Permits and Related Services" which shall thereafter be available for appropriation to carry out activities of the Environmental Protection Agency for which such fees were collected.

(p) Modified permit for coal remining operations

(1) In general — Subject to paragraphs (2) through (4) of this subsection, the Administrator, or the State in any case which the State has an approved permit program under section 1342(b) of this title, may issue a permit under section 1342 of this title which modifies the requirements of subsection (b)(2)(A) of this section with respect to the pH level of any pre-existing discharge, and with respect to pre-existing discharges of iron and manganese from the remined area of any coal remining operation or with respect to the pH level or level of iron or manganese in any pre-existing discharge affected by the remining operation. Such modified requirements shall apply the best available technology economically achievable on a case-by-case basis, using best professional judgment, to set specific numerical effluent limitations in each permit.

(2) Limitations — The Administrator or the State may only issue a permit pursuant to paragraph (1) if the applicant demonstrates to the satisfaction of the Administrator or the State, as the case may be, that the coal remining operation will result in the potential for improved water quality from the remining operation but in no event shall such a permit allow the pH level of any discharge, and in no event shall such a permit allow the discharges of iron and manganese, to exceed the levels being discharged from the remined area before the coal remining operation begins. No discharge from, or affected by, the remining operation shall exceed State water quality standards established under section 1313 of this title.

(3) Definitions — For purposes of this subsection —

(A) Coal remining operation — The term "coal remining operation" means a coal mining operation which begins after February 4, 1987 at a site on which coal mining was conducted before August 3, 1977.

(B) Remined area — The term "remined area" means only that area of any coal remining operation on which coal mining was conducted before August 3, 1977.

(C) Pre-existing discharge — The term "pre-existing discharge" means any discharge at the time of permit application under this subsection.

(4) Applicability of strip mining laws — Nothing in this subsection shall affect the application of the Surface Mining Control and Reclamation Act of 1977 (30 U.S.C. §1201 *et seq.*) to any coal remining operation, including the application of such Act to suspended solids.

§1312. Water quality related effluent limitations

[CWA §302]

(a) **Establishment** — Whenever, in the judgment of the Administrator or as identified under section 1314(*l*) of this title, discharges of pollutants from a point source or group of point sources, with the application of effluent limitations required under section 1311(b)(2) of this title, would interfere with the attainment or maintenance of that water quality in a specific portion of the navigable waters which shall assure protection of public health, public water supplies, agricultural and industrial uses, and the protection and propagation of a balanced population of shellfish, fish and wildlife, and allow recreational activities in and on the water, effluent limitations (including alternative effluent control strategies) for such point source or sources shall be established which can reasonably be expected to contribute to the attainment or maintenance of such water quality.

(b) Modifications of effluent limitations

(1) Notice and hearing — Prior to establishment of any effluent limitation pursuant to subsection (a) of this section, the Administrator shall publish such proposed limitation and within 90 days of such publication hold a public hearing.

(2) Permits

(A) No reasonable relationship — The Administrator, with the concurrence of the State, may issue a permit which modifies the effluent limitations required by subsection (a) of this section for pollutants other than toxic pollutants if the applicant demonstrates at such hearing that (whether or not technology or other alternative control strategies are available) there is no reasonable relationship between the economic and social costs and the benefits to be obtained (including attainment of the objective of this chapter) from achieving such limitation.

(B) Reasonable progress — The Administrator, with the concurrence of the State, may issue a permit which modifies the effluent limitations required by subsection (a) of this section for toxic pollutants for a single period not to exceed 5 years if the applicant demonstrates to the satisfaction of the Administrator that such modified requirements (i) will represent the maximum degree of control within the economic capability of the owner and operator of the source, and (ii) will result in reasonable further progress beyond the requirements of section 1311(b)(2) of this title toward the requirements of subsection (a) of this section.

(c) Delay in application of other limitations — The establishment of effluent limitations under this section shall not operate to delay the application of any effluent limitation established under section 1311 of this title.

§1313. Water quality standards and implementation plans
[CWA §303]
(a) Existing water quality standards

(1) In order to carry out the purpose of this chapter, any water quality standard applicable to interstate waters which was adopted by any State and submitted to, and approved by, or is a waiting approval by, the Administrator pursuant to this Act as in effect immediately prior to October 18, 1972, shall remain in effect unless the Administrator determined that such standard is not consistent with the applicable requirements of this Act as in effect immediately prior to October 18, 1972. If the Administrator makes such a determination he shall, within three months after October 18, 1972, notify the State and specify the changes needed to meet such requirements. If such changes are not adopted by the State within ninety days after the date of such notification, the Administrator shall promulgate such changes in accordance with subsection (b) of this section.

(2) Any State which, before October 18, 1972, has adopted, pursuant to its own law, water quality standards applicable to intrastate waters shall submit such standards to the Administrator within thirty days after October 18, 1972. Each such standard shall remain in effect, in the same manner and to the same extent as any other water quality standard established under this chapter unless the Administrator determines that such standard is inconsistent with the applicable requirements of this Act as in effect immediately prior to October 18, 1972. If the Administrator makes such a determination he shall not later than the one hundred and twentieth day after the date of submission of such standards, notify the State and specify the changes needed to meet such requirements. If such changes are not adopted by the State within ninety days after such notification, the Administrator shall promulgate such changes in accordance with subsection (b) of this section.

(3)(A) Any State which prior to October 18, 1972, has not adopted pursuant to its own laws water quality standards applicable to intrastate waters shall, not later than one hundred and eighty days after October 18, 1972, adopt and submit such standards to the Administrator.

(B) If the Administrator determines that any such standards are consistent with the applicable requirements of this Act as in effect immediately prior to October 18, 1972, he shall approve such standards.

(C) If the Administrator determines that any such standards are not consistent with the applicable requirements of this Act as in effect immediately prior to October 18, 1972, he shall, not later than the ninetieth day after the date of submission of such standards, notify the State and specify the changes to meet such requirements. If such changes are not adopted by the State within ninety days after the date of notification, the Administrator shall promulgate such standards pursuant to subsection (b) of this section.

(b) Proposed regulations

(1) The Administrator shall promptly prepare and publish proposed regulations setting forth water quality standards for a State in accordance with the applicable requirements of this Act as in effect immediately prior to October 18, 1972, if —

(A) the State fails to submit water quality standards within the times prescribed in subsection (a) of this section.

(B) a water quality standard submitted by such State under subsection (a) of this section is determined by the Administrator not to be consistent with the applicable requirements of subsection (a) of this section.

(2) The Administrator shall promulgate any water quality standard published in a proposed regulation not later than one hundred and ninety days after the date he publishes any such proposed standard, unless prior to such promulgation, such State has adopted a water quality standard which the Administrator determines to be in accordance with subsection (a) of this section.

(c) Review; revised standards; publication

(1) The Governor of a State or the State water pollution control agency of such State shall from time to time (but at least once each three year period beginning with October 18, 1972) hold public hearings for the purpose of reviewing applicable water quality standards and, as appropriate, modifying and adopting standards. Results of such review shall be made available to the Administrator.

(2)(A) Whenever the State revises or adopts a new standard, such revised or new standard shall be submitted to the Administrator. Such revised or new water quality standard shall consist of the designated uses of the navigable waters involved and the water quality criteria for such waters based upon such uses. Such standards shall be such as to protect the public health or welfare, enhance the quality of water and serve the purposes of this chapter. Such standards shall be established taking into consideration their use and value for public water supplies, propagation of fish and wildlife, recreational purposes, and agricultural, industrial, and other purposes, and also taking into consideration their use and value for navigation.

(B) Whenever a State reviews water quality standards pursuant to paragraph (1) of this subsection, or revises or adopts new standards pursuant to this paragraph, such State shall adopt criteria for all toxic pollutants listed pursuant to section 1317(a)(1) of this title for which criteria have been published under section 1314(a) of this title, the discharge or presence of which in the affected waters could reasonably be expected to interfere with those designated uses adopted by the State, as necessary to support such designated uses. Such criteria shall be specific numerical criteria for such toxic pollutants. Where such numerical criteria are not available, whenever a State reviews water quality standards pursuant to paragraph (1), or revises or adopts new standards pursuant to this paragraph, such State shall adopt criteria based on biological monitoring or assessment methods consistent with information published pursuant to section 1314(a)(8) of this title. Nothing in this section shall be construed to limit or delay the use of effluent limitations or other permit conditions based on or involving biological monitoring or assessment methods or previously adopted numerical criteria.

(3) If the Administrator, within sixty days after the date of submission of the revised or new standard, determines that such standard meets the requirements of this chapter, such standard shall thereafter be the water quality standard for the applicable waters of that State. If the Administrator determines that any such revised or new standard is not consistent with the applicable requirements of this chapter, he shall not later than the ninetieth day after the date of submission of such standard notify the State and specify the changes to meet such requirements. If such changes are not adopted by the State within ninety days after the date of notification, the Administrator shall promulgate such standard pursuant to paragraph (4) of this subsection.

(4) The Administrator shall promptly prepare and publish proposed regulations setting forth a revised or new water quality standard for the navigable waters involved —

(A) if a revised or new water quality standard submitted by such State under paragraph (3) of this subsection for such waters is determined by the Administrator not to be consistent with the applicable requirements of this chapter, or

(B) in any case where the Administrator determines that a revised or new standard is necessary to meet the requirements of this chapter.

The Administrator shall promulgate any revised or new standard under this paragraph not later than ninety days after he publishes such proposed standards, unless prior to such promulgation, such State has adopted a revised or new water quality standard which the Administrator determines to be in accordance with this chapter.

(d) Identification of areas with insufficient controls; maximum daily load; certain effluent limitations revision

(1)(A) Each State shall identify those waters within its boundaries for which the effluent limitations required by section 1311(b)(1)(A) and section 1311(b)(1)(B) of this title are not stringent enough to implement any water quality standard applicable to such waters. The State shall establish a priority ranking for such waters, taking into account the severity of the pollution and the uses to be made of such waters.

(B) Each State shall identify those waters or parts thereof within its boundaries for which controls on thermal discharges under section 1311 of this title are not stringent enough to assure protection and propagation of a balanced indigenous population of shellfish, fish, and wildlife.

(C) Each State shall establish for the waters identified in paragraph (1)(A) of this subsection, and in accordance with the priority ranking, the total maximum daily load, for those pollutants which the Administrator identifies under section 1314(a)(2) of this title as suitable for such calculation. Such load shall be es- tablished at a level necessary to implement the applicable water quality standards with seasonal variations and a margin of safety which takes into account any lack of knowledge concerning the relationship between effluent limitations and water quality.

(D) Each State shall estimate for the waters identified in paragraph (1)(B) of this subsection the total maximum daily thermal load required to assure protection and propagation of a balanced, indigenous population of shellfish, fish, and wildlife. Such estimates shall take into account the normal water tempera- tures, flow rates, seasonal variations, existing sources of heat input, and the dissipative capacity of the identified waters or parts thereof. Such estimates shall include a calculation of the maximum heat input that can be made into each such part and shall include a margin of safety which takes into account any lack of knowledge concerning the development of thermal water quality criteria for such protection and propagation in the identified waters or parts thereof.

(2) Each State shall submit to the Administrator from time to time, with the first such submission not later than one hundred and eighty days after the date of publication of the first identification of pollutants under section 1314(a)(2)(D)

of this title, for his approval the waters identified and the loads established under paragraphs (1)(A), (1)(B), (1)(C), and (1)(D) of this subsection. The Administrator shall either approve or disapprove such identification and load not later than thirty days after the date of submission. If the Administrator approves such identification and load, such State shall incorporate them into its current plan under subsection (e) of this section. If the Administrator disapproves such identification and load, he shall not later than thirty days after the date of such disapproval identify such waters in such State and establish such loads for such waters as he determines necessary to implement the water quality standards applicable to such waters and upon such identification and establishment the State shall incorporate them into its current plan under subsection (e) of this section.

(3) For the specific purpose of developing information, each State shall identify all waters within its boundaries which it has not identified under paragraph (1)(A) and (1)(B) of this subsection and estimate for such waters the total maximum daily load with seasonal variations and margins of safety, for those pollutants which the Administrator identifies under section 1314(a)(2) of this title as suitable for such calculation and for thermal discharges, at a level that would assure protection and propagation of a balanced indigenous population of fish, shellfish, and wildlife.

(4) Limitations on revision of certain effluent limitations —

(A) Standard not attained — For waters identified under paragraph (1)(A) where the applicable water quality standard has not yet been attained, any effluent limitation based on a total maximum daily load or other waste load allocation established under this section may be revised only if (i) the cumulative effect of all such revised effluent limitations based on such total maximum daily load or waste load allocation will assure the attainment of such water quality standard, or (ii) the designated use which is not being attained is removed in accordance with regulations established under this section.

(B) Standard attained — For waters identified under paragraph (1)(A) where the quality of such waters equals or exceeds levels necessary to protect the designated use for such waters or otherwise required by applicable water quality standards, any effluent limitation based on a total maximum daily load or other waste load allocation established under this section, or any water quality standard established under this section, or any other permitting standard may be revised only if such revision is subject to and consistent with the antidegradation policy established under this section.

(e) Continuing planning process

(1) Each State shall have a continuing planning process approved under paragraph (2) of this subsection which is consistent with this chapter.

(2) Each State shall submit not later than 120 days after October 18, 1972, to the Administrator for his approval a proposed continuing planning process which is consistent with this chapter. Not later than thirty days after the date of submission of such a process the Administrator shall either approve or disapprove such process. The Administrator shall from time to time review each State's approved planning process for the purpose of insuring that such planning process is at all times consistent with this chapter. The Administrator shall not approve any State permit program under subchapter IV of this chapter for any State which does not have an approved continuing planning process under this section.

(3) The Administrator shall approve any continuing planning process submitted to him under this section which will result in plans for all navigable waters within such State, which include, but are not limited to, the following:

(A) effluent limitations and schedules of compliance at least as stringent as those required by section 1311(b)(1), section 1311(b)(2), section 1316, and section 1317 of this title, and at least as stringent as any requirements contained in any applicable water quality standard in effect under authority of this section;

(B) the incorporation of all elements of any applicable area-wide waste management plans under section 1288 of this title, and applicable basin plans under section 1289 of this title;

(C) total maximum daily load for pollutants in accordance with subsection (d) of this section;

(D) procedures for revision;

(E) adequate authority for intergovernmental cooperation;

(F) adequate implementation, including schedules of compliance, for revised or new water quality standards, under subsection (c) of this section;

(G) controls over the disposition of all residual waste from any water treatment processing;

(H) an inventory and ranking, in order of priority, of needs for construction of waste treatment works required to meet the applicable requirements of sections 1311 and 1312 of this title.

(f) Earlier compliance — Nothing in this section shall be construed to affect any effluent limitation, or schedule of compliance required by any State to be implemented prior to the dates set forth in sections 1311(b)(1) and 1311(b)(2) of this title nor to preclude any State from requiring compliance with any effluent limitation or schedule of compliance at dates earlier than such dates.

(g) Heat standards — Water quality standards relating to heat shall be consistent with the requirements of section 1326 of this title.

(h) Thermal water quality standards — For the purposes of this chapter the term "water quality standards" includes thermal water quality standards.

(i) Coastal recreation water quality criteria

(1) Adoption by States

(A) Initial criteria and standards — Not later than 42 months after October 10, 2000, each State having coastal recreation waters shall adopt and submit to the Administrator water quality criteria and standards for the coastal recreation waters of the State for those pathogens and pathogen indicators for which the Administrator has published criteria under section 1314(a) of this title.

(B) New or revised criteria and standards — Not later than 36 months after the date of publication by the Administrator of new or revised water quality criteria under section 1314(a)(9), each State having coastal recreation waters shall adopt and submit to the Administrator new or revised water quality standards for the coastal recreation waters of the State for all pathogens and pathogen indicators to which the new or revised water quality criteria are applicable.

(2) Failure of States to adopt

(A) In general — If a State fails to adopt water quality criteria and standards in accordance with paragraph (1)(A) that are as protective of human health as the criteria for pathogens and pathogen indicators for coastal recreation waters published by the Administrator, the Administrator shall promptly propose regulations for the State setting forth revised or new water quality standards for pathogens and pathogen indicators described in paragraph (1)(A) for coastal recreation waters of the State.

(B) Exception — If the Administrator proposes regulations for a State described in subparagraph (A) under subsection (c)(4)(B), the Administrator shall publish any revised or new standard under this subsection not later than 42 months after October 10, 2000.

(3) Applicability — Except as expressly provided by this subsection, the requirements and procedures of subsection (c) apply to this subsection, including the requirement in subsection (c)(2)(A) that the criteria protect public health and welfare.

§1313a. Revised water quality standards

The review, revision, and adoption or promulgation of revised or new water quality standards pursuant to section 303(c) of the Federal Water Pollution Control Act (33 U.S.C. §1313(c)) shall be completed by the date three years after December 29, 1981. No grant shall be made under title II of the Federal Water Pollution Control Act (33 U.S.C. §1281 *et seq.*) after such date until water quality standards are reviewed and revised pursuant to section 303(c), except where the State has in good faith submitted such revised water quality standards and the Administrator has not acted to approve or disapprove such submission within one hundred and twenty days of receipt.

§1314. Information and guidelines
[CWA §304]

(a) Criteria development and publication

(1) The Administrator, after consultation with appropriate Federal and State agencies and other interested persons, shall develop and publish, within one year after October 18, 1972 (and from time to time thereafter revise) criteria for water quality accurately reflecting the latest scientific knowledge (A) on the kind and extent of all identifiable effects on health and welfare including, but not limited to, plankton, fish, shellfish, wildlife, plant life, shorelines, beaches, esthetics, and recreation which may be expected from the presence of pollutants in any body of water, including ground water; (B) on the concentration and dispersal of pollutants, or their byproducts, through biological, physical, and chemical processes; and (C) on the effects of pollutants on biological community diversity, productivity, and stability, including information on the factors affecting rates of eutrophication and rates of organic and inorganic sedimentation for varying types of receiving waters.

(2) The Administrator, after consultation with appropriate Federal and State agencies and other interested persons, shall develop and publish, within one year after October 18, 1972 (and from time to time thereafter revise) information (A) on the factors necessary to restore and maintain the chemical, physical, and biological integrity of all navigable waters, ground waters, waters of the contiguous zone, and the oceans; (B) on the factors necessary for the protection and propagation of shellfish, fish, and wildlife for classes and categories of receiving waters and to allow recreational activities in and on the water; and (C) on the measurement and classification of water quality; and (D) for the purpose of section 1313 of this title, on and the identification of pollutants suitable for maximum daily load measurement correlated with the achievement of water quality objectives.

(3) Such criteria and information and revisions thereof shall be issued to the States and shall be published in the Federal Register and otherwise made available to the public.

(4) The Administrator shall, within 90 days after December 27, 1977, and from time to time thereafter, publish and revise as appropriate information identifying conventional pollutants, including but not limited to, pollutants classified as biological oxygen demanding, suspended solids, fecal coliform, and pH. The thermal component of any discharge shall not be identified as a conventional pollutant under this paragraph.

(5)(A) The Administrator, to the extent practicable before consideration of any request under section 1311(g) of this title and within six months after December 27, 1977, shall develop and publish information on the factors necessary for the protection of public water supplies, and the protection and propagation of a balanced population of shellfish, fish and wildlife, and to allow recreational activities, in and on the water.

(B) The Administrator, to the extent practicable before consideration of any application under section 1311(h) of this title and within six months after December 27, 1977, shall develop and publish information on the factors necessary for the protection of public water supplies, and the protection and propagation of a balanced indigenous population of shellfish, fish and wildlife, and to allow recreational activities, in and on the water.

(6) The Administrator shall, within three months after December 27, 1977, and annually thereafter, for purposes of section 1311(h) of this title publish and revise as appropriate information identifying each water quality standard in effect under this chapter or State law, the specific pollutants associated with such water quality standard, and the particular waters to which such water quality standard applies.

(7) Guidance to states — The Administrator, after consultation with appropriate State agencies and on the basis of criteria and information published under paragraphs (1) and (2) of this subsection, shall develop and publish, within 9 months after February 4, 1987, guidance to the States on performing the identification required by subsection (*l*)(1) of this section.

(8) Information on water quality criteria — The Administrator, after consultation with appropriate State agencies and within 2 years after February 4, 1987, shall develop and publish information on methods for establishing and measuring water quality criteria for toxic pollutants on other bases than pollutant-by-pollutant criteria, including biological monitoring and assessment methods.

(9) Revised criteria for coastal recreation waters

(A) In general — Not later than 5 years after October 10, 2000, after consultation and in cooperation with appropriate Federal, State, tribal, and local officials (including local health officials), the Administrator shall publish new or revised water quality criteria for pathogens and pathogen indicators (including a revised list of testing methods, as appropriate), based on the results of the studies conducted under section 1254(v) of this title, for the purpose of protecting human health in coastal recreation waters.

(B) Reviews — Not later than the date that is 5 years after the date of publication of water quality criteria under this paragraph, and at least once every 5 years thereafter, the Administrator shall review and, as necessary, revise the water quality criteria.

(b) Effluent limitation guidelines — For the purpose of adopting or revising effluent limitations under this chapter the Administrator shall, after consultation with appropriate Federal and State agencies and other interested persons, publish within one year of October 18, 1972, regulations, providing guidelines for effluent limitations, and, at least annually thereafter, revise, if appropriate, such regulations. Such regulations shall —

(1)(A) identify, in terms of amounts of constituents and chemical, physical, and biological characteristics of pollutants, the degree of effluent reduction attainable through the application of the best practicable control technology currently available for classes and categories of point sources (other than publicly owned treatment works); and

(B) specify factors to be taken into account in determining the control measures and practices to be applicable to point sources (other than publicly owned treatment works) within such categories or classes. Factors relating to the assessment of best practicable control technology currently available to comply with subsection (b)(1) of section 1311 of this title shall include consideration of the total cost of application of technology in relation to the effluent reduction benefits to be achieved from such application, and shall also take into account the age of equipment and facilities involved, the process employed, the engineering aspects of the application of various types of control techniques, process changes, non-water quality environmental impact (including energy requirements), and such other factors as the Administrator deems appropriate;

(2)(A) identify, in terms of amounts of constituents and chemical, physical, and biological characteristics of pollutants, the degree of effluent reduction attainable through the application of the best control measures and practices achievable including treatment techniques, process and procedure innovations, operating methods, and other alternatives for classes and categories of point sources (other than publicly owned treatment works); and

    (B) specify factors to be taken into account in determining the best measures and practices available to comply with subsection (b)(2) of section 1311 of this title to be applicable to any point source (other than publicly owned treatment works) within such categories or classes. Factors relating to the assessment of best available technology shall take into account the age of equipment and facilities involved, the process employed, the engineering aspects of the application of various types of control techniques, process changes, the cost of achieving such effluent reduction, non-water quality environmental impact (including energy requirements), and such other factors as the Administrator deems appropriate;

(3) identify control measures and practices available to eliminate the discharge of pollutants from categories and classes of point sources, taking into account the cost of achieving such elimination of the discharge of pollutants; and

(4)(A) identify, in terms of amounts of constituents and chemical, physical, and biological characteristics of pollutants, the degree of effluent reduction attainable through the application of the best conventional pollutant control technology (including measures and practices) for classes and categories of point sources (other than publicly owned treatment works); and

    (B) specify factors to be taken into account in determining the best conventional pollutant control technology measures and practices to comply with section 1311(b)(2)(E) of this title to be applicable to any point source (other than publicly owned treatment works) within such categories or classes. Factors relating to the assessment of best conventional pollutant control technology (including measures and practices) shall include consideration of the reasonableness of the relationship between the costs of attaining a reduction in effluents and the effluent reduction benefits derived, and the comparison of the cost and level of reduction of such pollutants from the discharge from publicly owned treatment works to the cost and level of reduction of such pollutants from a class or category of industrial sources, and shall take into account the age of equipment and facilities involved, the process employed, the engineering aspects of the application of various types of control techniques, process changes, non-water quality environmental impact (including energy requirements), and such other factors as the Administrator deems appropriate.

(c) Pollution discharge elimination procedures — The Administrator, after consultation, with

appropriate Federal and State agencies and other interested persons, shall issue to the States and appropriate water pollution control agencies within 270 days after October 18, 1972 (and from time to time thereafter) information on the processes, procedures, or operating methods which result in the elimination or reduction of the discharge of pollutants to implement standards of performance under section 1316 of this title. Such information shall include technical and other data, including costs, as are available on alternative methods of elimination or reduction of the discharge of pollutants. Such information, and revisions thereof, shall be published in the Federal Register and otherwise shall be made available to the public.

(d) Secondary treatment information; alternative waste treatment management techniques; innovative and alternative wastewater treatment processes; facilities deemed equivalent of secondary treatment

    (1) The Administrator, after consultation with appropriate Federal and State agencies and other interested persons, shall publish within sixty days after October 18, 1972 (and from time to time thereafter) information, in terms of amounts of constituents and chemical, physical, and biological characteristics of pollutants, on the degree of effluent reduction attainable through the application of secondary treatment.

    (2) The Administrator, after consultation with appropriate Federal and State agencies and other interested persons, shall publish within nine months after October 18, 1972 (and from time to time thereafter) information on alternative waste treatment management techniques and systems available to implement section 1281 of this title.

    (3) The Administrator, after consultation with appropriate Federal and State agencies and other interested persons, shall promulgate within one hundred and eighty days after December 27, 1977, guidelines for identifying and evaluating innovative and alternative wastewater treatment processes and techniques referred to in section 1281(g)(5) of this title.

    (4) For the purposes of this subsection, such biological treatment facilities as oxidation ponds, lagoons, and ditches and trickling filters shall be deemed the equivalent of secondary treatment. The Administrator shall provide guidance under paragraph (1) of this subsection on design criteria for such facilities, taking into account pollutant removal efficiencies and, consistent with the objectives of this chapter, assuring that water quality will not be adversely affected by deeming such facilities as the equivalent of secondary treatment.

(e) Best management practices for industry — The Administrator, after consultation with appropriate Federal and State agencies and other interested persons, may publish regulations, supplemental to any effluent limitations specified under subsections (b) and (c) of this section for a class or category of point sources, for any specific pollutant which the Administrator is charged with a duty to regulate as a toxic or hazardous pollutant under section 1317(a)(1) or 1321 of this title, to control plant site runoff, spillage or leaks, sludge or waste disposal, and drainage from raw material storage which the Administrator determines are associated with or ancillary to the industrial manufacturing or treatment process within such class or category of point sources and may contribute significant amounts of such pollutants to navigable waters. Any applicable controls established under this subsection shall be included as a requirement for the purposes of section 1311, 1312, 1316, 1317, or 1343 of this title, as the case may be, in any permit issued to a point source pursuant to section 1342 of this title.

(f) Identification and evaluation of non-point sources of pollution; processes, procedures, and methods to control pollution — The Administrator, after consultation with appropriate Federal and State agencies and other interested persons, shall issue to appropriate Federal agencies, the States, water pollution control agencies, and agencies designated under section 1288 of this title, within one year after October 18, 1972 (and from time to time thereafter) information including (1) guidelines for identifying and evaluating the nature and extent of nonpoint sources of pollutants, and (2) processes, procedures, and methods to control pollution resulting from —

　　(A) agricultural and silvicultural activities, including runoff from fields and crop and forest lands;

　　(B) mining activities, including runoff and siltation from new, currently operating, and abandoned surface and underground mines;

　　(C) all construction activity, including runoff from the facilities resulting from such construction;

　　(D) the disposal of pollutants in wells or in subsurface excavations;

　　(E) salt water intrusion resulting from reductions of fresh water flow from any cause, including extraction of ground water, irrigation, obstruction, and diversion; and

　　(F) changes in the movement, flow, or circulation of any navigable waters or ground waters, including changes caused by the construction of dams, levees, channels, causeways, or flow diversion facilities.

Such information and revisions thereof shall be published in the Federal Register and otherwise made available to the public.

(g) Guidelines for pretreatment of pollutants

　　(1) For the purpose of assisting States in carrying out programs under section 1342 of this title, the Administrator shall publish, within one hundred and twenty days after October 18, 1972, and review at least annually thereafter and, if appropriate, revise guidelines for pretreatment of pollutants which he determines are not susceptible to treatment by publicly owned treatment works. Guidelines under this subsection shall be established to control and prevent the discharge into the navigable waters, the contiguous zone, or the ocean (either directly or through publicly owned treatment works) of any pollutant which interferes with, passes through, or otherwise is incompatible with such works.

　　(2) When publishing guidelines under this subsection, the Administrator shall designate the category or categories of treatment works to which the guidelines shall apply.

(h) Test procedures guidelines — The Administrator shall, within one hundred and eighty days from October 18, 1972, promulgate guidelines establishing test procedures for the analysis of pollutants that shall include the factors which must be provided in any certification pursuant to section 1341 of this title or permit application pursuant to section 1342 of this title.

(i) Guidelines for monitoring, reporting, enforcement, funding, personnel, and manpower — The Administrator shall (1) within sixty days after October 18, 1972, promulgate guidelines for the purpose of establishing uniform application forms and other minimum requirements for the acquisition of information from owners and operators of point-sources of discharge subject to any State program under section 1342 of this title, and (2) within sixty days from October 18, 1972, promulgate guidelines establishing the minimum procedural and other elements of any State program under section 1342 of this title, which shall include:

　　(A) monitoring requirements;

　　(B) reporting requirements (including procedures to make information available to the public);

　　(C) enforcement provisions; and

　　(D) funding, personnel qualifications, and manpower requirements (including a requirement that no board or body which approves permit applications or portions thereof shall include, as a member, any person who receives, or has during the previous two years received, a significant portion of his income directly or indirectly from permit holders or applicants for a permit).

(j) Lake restoration guidance manual — The Administrator shall, within 1 year after February 4, 1987, and biennially thereafter, publish and disseminate a lake restoration guidance manual describing methods, procedures, and processes to guide State and local efforts to improve, restore, and enhance water quality in the Nation's publicly owned lakes.

(k) Agreements with Secretaries of Agriculture, Army, and the Interior to provide maximum utilization of programs to achieve and maintain water quality; transfer of funds; authorization of appropriations

(1) The Administrator shall enter into agreements with the Secretary of Agriculture, the Secretary of the Army, and the Secretary of the Interior, and the heads of such other departments, agencies, and instrumentalities of the United States as the Administrator determines, to provide for the maximum utilization of other Federal laws and programs for the purpose of achieving and maintaining water quality through appropriate implementation of plans approved under section 1288 of this title and nonpoint source pollution management programs approved under section 1329 of this title.

(2) The Administrator is authorized to transfer to the Secretary of Agriculture, the Secretary of the Army, and the Secretary of the Interior and the heads of such other departments, agencies, and instrumentalities of the United States as the Administrator determines, any funds appropriated under paragraph (3) of this subsection to supplement funds otherwise appropriated to programs authorized pursuant to any agreement under paragraph (1).

(3) There is authorized to be appropriated to carry out the provisions of this subsection, $100,000,000 per fiscal year for the fiscal years 1979 through 1983 and such sums as may be necessary for fiscal years 1984 through 1990.

(l) Individual control strategies for toxic pollutants

(1) State list of navigable waters and development of strategies — Not later than 2 years after February 4, 1987, each State shall submit to the Administrator for review, approval, and implementation under this subsection —

(A) a list of those waters within the State which after the application of effluent limitations required under section 1311(b)(2) of this title cannot reasonably be anticipated to attain or maintain (i) water quality standards for such waters reviewed, revised, or adopted in accordance with section 1313(c)(2)(B) of this title, due to toxic pollutants, or (ii) that water quality which shall assure protection of public health, public water supplies, agricultural and industrial uses, and the protection and propagation of a balanced population of shellfish, fish and wildlife, and allow recreational activities in and on the water;

(B) a list of all navigable waters in such State for which the State does not expect the applicable standard under section 1313 of this title will be achieved after the requirements of sections 1311(b), 1316, and 1317(b) of this title are met, due entirely or substantially to discharges from point sources of any toxic pollutants listed pursuant to section 1317(a) of this title;

(C) for each segment of the navigable waters included on such lists, a determination of the specific point sources discharging any such toxic pollutant which is believed to be preventing or impairing such water quality and the amount of each such toxic pollutant discharged by each such source; and

(D) for each such segment, an individual control strategy which the State determines will produce a reduction in the discharge of toxic pollutants from point sources identified by the State under this paragraph through the establishment of effluent limitations under section 1342 of this title and water quality standards under section 1313(c)(2)(B) of this title, which reduction is sufficient, in combination with existing controls on point and nonpoint sources of pollution, to achieve the applicable water quality standard as soon as possible, but not later than 3 years after the date of the establishment of such strategy.

(2) Approval or disapproval — Not later than 120 days after the last day of the 2-year period referred to in paragraph (1), the Administrator shall approve or disapprove the control strategies submitted under paragraph (1) by any State.

(3) Administrator's action — If a State fails to submit control strategies in accordance with paragraph (1) or the Administrator does not approve the control strategies submitted by such State in accordance with paragraph (1), then, not later than 1 year after the last day of the period referred to in paragraph (2), the Administrator, in cooperation with such State and after notice and opportunity for public comment, shall implement the requirements of paragraph (1) in such State. In the implementation of such requirements, the Administrator shall, at a minimum, consider for listing under this subsection any navigable waters for which any person submits a petition to the Administrator for listing not later than 120 days after such last day.

(m) Schedule for review of guidelines

(1) Publication — Within 12 months after February 4, 1987, and biennially thereafter, the Administrator shall publish in the Federal Register a plan which shall —

(A) establish a schedule for the annual review and revision of promulgated effluent guidelines, in accordance with subsection (b) of this section;

(B) identify categories of sources discharging toxic or nonconventional pollutants for which guidelines under subsection (b)(2) of this section and section 1316 of this title have not previously been published; and

(C) establish a schedule for promulgation of effluent guidelines for categories identified in subparagraph (B), under which promulgation of such guidelines shall be no later than 4 years after February 4, 1987, for categories identified in the first published plan or 3 years after the publication of the plan for categories identified in later published plans.

(2) Public review — The Administrator shall provide for public review and comment on the plan prior to final publication.

§1315. State reports on water quality [CWA §305]

(a) Omitted.

(b)(1) Each State shall prepare and submit to the Administrator by April 1, 1975, and shall bring up to date by April 1, 1976, and biennially thereafter, a report which shall include —

(A) a description of the water quality of all navigable waters in such State during the preceding year, with appropriate supplemental descriptions as shall be required to take into account seasonal, tidal, and other variations, correlated with the quality of water required by the objective of this chapter (as identified by the Administrator pursuant to criteria published under section 1314(a) of this title) and the water quality described in subparagraph (B) of this paragraph;

(B) an analysis of the extent to which all navigable waters of such State provide for the protection and propagation of a balanced population of shellfish, fish, and wildlife, and allow recreational activities in and on the water;

(C) an analysis of the extent to which the elimination of the discharge of pollutants and a level of water quality which provides for the protection and propagation of a balanced population of shellfish, fish, and wildlife and allows recreational activities in and on the water, have been or will be achieved by the requirements of this chapter, together with recommendations as to additional action necessary to achieve such objectives and for what waters such additional action is necessary;

(D) an estimate of (i) the environmental impact, (ii) the economic and social costs necessary to achieve the objective of this chapter in such State, (iii) the economic and social benefits of such achievement, and (iv) an estimate of the date of such achievement; and

(E) a description of the nature and extent of nonpoint sources of pollutants, and recommendations as to the programs which must be undertaken to control each category of such sources, including an estimate of the costs of implementing such programs.

(2) The Administrator shall transmit such State reports, together with an analysis thereof, to Congress on or before October 1, 1975, and October 1, 1976, and biennially thereafter.

§1316. National standards of performance [CWA §306]

(a) **Definitions** — For purposes of this section:

(1) The term "standard of performance" means a standard for the control of the discharge of pollutants which reflects the greatest degree of effluent reduction which the Administrator determines to be achievable through application of the best available demonstrated control technology, processes, operating methods, or other alternatives, including, where practicable, a standard permitting no discharge of pollutants.

(2) The term "new source" means any source, the construction of which is commenced after the publication of proposed regulations prescribing a standard of performance under this section which will be applicable to such source, if such standard is thereafter promulgated in accordance with this section.

(3) The term "source" means any building, structure, facility, or installation from which there is or may be the discharge of pollutants.

(4) The term "owner or operator" means any person who owns, leases, operates, controls, or supervises a source.

(5) The term "construction" means any placement, assembly, or installation of facilities or equipment (including contractual obligations to purchase such facilities or equipment) at the premises where such equipment will be used, including preparation work at such premises.

(b) **Categories of sources; Federal standards of performance for new sources**

(1)(A) The Administrator shall, within ninety days after October 18, 1972, publish (and from time to time thereafter shall revise) a list of categories of sources, which shall, at the minimum, include:

pulp and paper mills;
paperboard, builders paper and board mills;
meat product and rendering processing;
dairy product processing;
grain mills;
canned and preserved fruits and vegetables processing;
canned and preserved seafood processing;
sugar processing;
textile mills;
cement manufacturing;
feedlots;
electroplating;
organic chemicals manufacturing;
inorganic chemicals manufacturing;

plastic and synthetic materials manufacturing;
soap and detergent manufacturing;
fertilizer manufacturing;
petroleum refining;
iron and steel manufacturing;
nonferrous metals manufacturing;
phosphate manufacturing;
steam electric powerplants;
ferroalloy manufacturing;
leather tanning and finishing;
glass and asbestos manufacturing;
rubber processing; and
timber products processing.

(B) As soon as practicable, but in no case more than one year, after a category of sources is included in a list under subparagraph (A) of this paragraph, the Administrator shall propose and publish regulations establishing Federal standards of performance for new sources within such category. The Administrator shall afford interested persons an opportunity for written comment on such proposed regulations. After considering such comments, he shall promulgate, within one hundred and twenty days after publication of such proposed regulations, such standards with such adjustments as he deems appropriate. The Administrator shall, from time to time, as technology and alternatives change, revise such standards following the procedure required by this subsection for promulgation of such standards. Standards of performance, or revisions thereof, shall become effective upon promulgation. In establishing or revising Federal standards of performance for new sources under this section, the Administrator shall take into consideration the cost of achieving such effluent reduction, and any non-water quality, environmental impact and energy requirements.

(2) The Administrator may distinguish among classes, types, and sizes within categories of new sources for the purpose of establishing such standards and shall consider the type of process employed (including whether batch or continuous).

(3) The provisions of this section shall apply to any new source owned or operated by the United States.

(c) State enforcement of standards of performance — Each State may develop and submit to the Administrator a procedure under State law for applying and enforcing standards of performance for new sources located in such State. If the Administrator finds that the procedure and the law of any State require the application and enforcement of standards of performance to at least the same extent as required by this section, such State is authorized to apply and enforce such standards of performance (except with respect to new sources owned or operated by the United States).

(d) Protection from more stringent standards — Notwithstanding any other provision of this chapter, any point source the construction of which is commenced after October 18, 1972, and which is so constructed as to meet all applicable standards of performance shall not be subject to any more stringent standard of performance during a ten-year period beginning on the date of completion of such construction or during the period of depreciation or amortization of such facility for the purposes of section 167 or 169 (or both) of Title 26, whichever period ends first.

(e) Illegality of operation of new sources in violation of applicable standards of performance — After the effective date of standards of performance promulgated under this section, it shall be unlawful for any owner or operator of any new source to operate such source in violation of any standard of performance applicable to such source.

§1317. Toxic and pretreatment effluent standards

[CWA §307]

(a) Toxic pollutant list; revision; hearing; promulgation of standards; effective date; consultation

(1) On and after December 27, 1977, the list of toxic pollutants or combination of pollutants subject to this chapter shall consist of those toxic pollutants listed in table 1 of Committee Print Numbered 95-30 of the Committee on Public Works and Transportation of the House of Representatives, and the Administrator shall publish, not later than the thirtieth day after December 27, 1977, that list. From time to time thereafter, the Administrator may revise such list and the Administrator is authorized to add to or remove from such list any pollutant. The Administrator in publishing any revised list, including the addition or removal of any pollutant from such list, shall take into account toxicity of the pollutant, its persistence, degradability, the usual or potential presence of the affected organisms in any waters, the importance of the affected organisms, and the nature and extent of the effect of the toxic pollutant on such organisms. A determination of the Administrator under this paragraph shall be final except that if, on judicial review, such determination was based on arbitrary and capricious action of the Administrator, the Administrator shall make a redetermination.

(2) Each toxic pollutant listed in accordance with paragraph (1) of this subsection shall be subject to effluent limitations resulting from the application of the best available technology economically achievable for the applicable category or class of point sources established in accordance with sections 1311(b)(2)(A) and 1314(b)(2) of this title. The Administrator, in his discretion, may publish in the Federal Register a proposed effluent standard (which may include a prohibition) establishing requirements for a toxic pollutant which, if an effluent limitation is applicable to a class or category of point sources, shall be applicable to such category or class only if such standard imposes more stringent requirements. Such published effluent standard (or prohibition) shall take into account the toxicity of the pollutant, its persistence, degradability, the usual or potential presence of the affected organisms in any waters, the importance of the affected organisms and the nature and extent of the effect of the toxic pollutant on such organisms, and the extent to which effective control is being or may be achieved under other regulatory authority. The Administrator shall allow a period of not less than sixty days following publication of any such proposed effluent standard (or prohibition) for written comment by interested persons on such proposed standard. In addition, if within thirty days of publication of any such proposed effluent standard (or prohibition) any interested person so requests, the Administrator shall hold a public hearing in connection therewith. Such a public hearing shall provide an opportunity for oral and written presentations, such cross-examination as the Administrator determines is appropriate on disputed issues of material fact, and the transcription of a verbatim record which shall be available to the public. After consideration of such comments and any information and material presented at any public hearing held on such proposed standard or prohibition, the Administrator shall promulgate such standard (or prohibition) with such modification as the Administrator finds are justified. Such promulgation by the Administrator shall be made within two hundred and seventy days after publication of proposed standard (or prohibition). Such standard (or prohibition) shall be final except that if, on judicial review, such standard was not based on substantial evidence, the Administrator shall promulgate a revised standard. Effluent limitations shall be established in accordance with sections 1311(b)(2)(A) and 1314(b)(2) of this title for every toxic pollutant referred to in table 1 of Committee Print Numbered 95-30 of the Committee on Public Works and Transportation of the House of Representatives as soon as practicable after December 27, 1977, but no later than July 1, 1980. Such effluent limitations or effluent standards (or prohibitions) shall be established for every other toxic pollutant listed under paragraph (1) of this subsection as soon as practicable after it is so listed.

(3) Each such effluent standard (or prohibition) shall be reviewed and, if appropriate, revised at least every three years.

(4) Any effluent standard promulgated under this section shall be at that level which the Administrator determines provides an ample margin of safety.

(5) When proposing or promulgating any effluent standard (or prohibition) under this section, the Administrator shall designate the category or categories of sources to which the effluent standard (or prohibition) shall apply. Any disposal of dredged material may be included in such a category of sources after consultation with the Secretary of the Army.

(6) Any effluent standard (or prohibition) established pursuant to this section shall take effect on such date or dates as specified in the order promulgating such standard, but in no case, more than one year from the date of such promulgation. If the Administrator determines that compliance within one year from the date of promulgation is technologically infeasible for a category of sources, the Administrator may establish the effective date of the effluent standard (or prohibition) for such category at the earliest date upon which compliance can be feasibly attained by sources within such category, but in no event more than three years after the date of such promulgation.

(7) Prior to publishing any regulations pursuant to this section the Administrator shall, to the maximum extent practicable within the time provided, consult with appropriate advisory committees, States, independent experts, and Federal departments and agencies.

(b) Pretreatment standards; hearing; promulgation; compliance period; revision; application to State and local laws

(1) The Administrator shall, within one hundred and eighty days after October 18, 1972, and from time to time thereafter, publish proposed regulations establishing pretreatment standards for introduction of pollutants into treatment works (as defined in section 1292 of this title) which are publicly owned for those pollutants which are determined not to be susceptible to treatment by such treatment works or which would interfere with the operation of such treatment works. Not later than ninety days after such publication, and after opportunity for public hearing, the Administrator shall promulgate such pretreatment standards. Pretreatment standards under this subsection shall specify a time for compliance not to exceed three years from the date of promulgation and shall be established to prevent the discharge of any pollutant through treatment works (as defined in section 1292 of this title) which are publicly owned, which pollutant interferes with, passes through, or otherwise is incompatible with such works. If, in the case of any toxic pollutant under subsection (a) of this section introduced by a source into a publicly owned treatment works, the

treatment by such works removes all or any part of such toxic pollutant and the discharge from such works does not violate that effluent limitation or standard which would be applicable to such toxic pollutant if it were discharged by such source other than through a publicly owned treatment works, and does not prevent sludge use or disposal by such works in accordance with section 1345 of this title, then the pretreatment requirements for the sources actually discharging such toxic pollutant into such publicly owned treatment works may be revised by the owner or operator of such works to reflect the removal of such toxic pollutant by such works.

(2) The Administrator shall, from time to time, as control technology, processes, operating methods, or other alternatives change, revise such standards following the procedure established by this subsection for promulgation of such standards.

(3) When proposing or promulgating any pretreatment standard under this section, the Administrator shall designate the category or categories of sources to which such standard shall apply.

(4) Nothing in this subsection shall affect any pretreatment requirement established by any State or local law not in conflict with any pretreatment standard established under this subsection.

(c) New sources of pollutants into publicly owned treatment works — In order to insure that any source introducing pollutants into a publicly owned treatment works, which source would be a new source subject to section 1316 of this title if it were to discharge pollutants, will not cause a violation of the effluent limitations established for any such treatment works, the Administrator shall promulgate pretreatment standards for the category of such sources simultaneously with the promulgation of standards of performance under section 1316 of this title for the equivalent category of new sources. Such pretreatment standards shall prevent the discharge of any pollutant into such treatment works, which pollutant may interfere with, pass through, or otherwise be incompatible with such works.

(d) Operation in violation of standards unlawful — After the effective date of any effluent standard or prohibition or pretreatment standard promulgated under this section, it shall be unlawful for any owner or operator of any source to operate any source in violation of any such effluent standard or prohibition or pretreatment standard.

(e) Compliance date extension for innovative pretreatment systems — In the case of any existing facility that proposes to comply with the pretreatment standards of subsection (b) of this section by applying an innovative system that meets the requirements of section 1311(k) of this title, the owner or operator of the publicly owned treatment works receiving the treated effluent from such facility may extend the date for compliance with the applicable pretreatment standard established under this section for a period not to exceed 2 years —

(1) if the Administrator determines that the innovative system has the potential for industry-wide application, and

(2) if the Administrator (or the State in consultation with the Administrator, in any case in which the State has a pretreatment program approved by the Administrator) —

(A) determines that the proposed extension will not cause the publicly owned treatment works to be in violation of its permit under section 1342 of this title or of section 1345 of this title or to contribute to such a violation, and

(B) concurs with the proposed extension.

§1318. Records and reports; inspections [CWA §308]

(a) Maintenance; monitoring equipment; entry; access to information — Whenever required to carry out the objective of this chapter, including but not limited to (1) developing or assisting in the development of any effluent limitation, or other limitation, prohibition, or effluent standard, pretreatment standard, or standard of performance under this chapter; (2) determining whether any person is in violation of any such effluent limitation, or other limitation, prohibition or effluent standard, pretreatment standard, or standard of performance; (3) any requirement established under this section; or (4) carrying out sections 1315, 1321, 1342, 1344 (relating to State permit programs), 1345, and 1364 of this title —

(A) the Administrator shall require the owner or operator of any point source to (i) establish and maintain such records, (ii) make such reports, (iii) install, use, and maintain such monitoring equipment or methods (including where appropriate, biological monitoring methods), (iv) sample such effluents (in accordance with such methods, at such locations, at such intervals, and in such manner as the Administrator shall prescribe), and (v) provide such other information as he may reasonably require; and

(B) the Administrator or his authorized representative (including an authorized contractor acting as a representative of the Administrator), upon presentation of his credentials —

(i) shall have a right of entry to, upon, or through any premises in which an effluent source is located or in which any records required to be maintained under clause (A) of this subsection are located, and

(ii) may at reasonable times have access to and copy any records, inspect any monitoring equipment or method required under clause (A), and sample any effluents which the owner or operator of such source is required to sample under such clause.

(b) Availability to public; trade secrets exception; penalty for disclosure of confidential information — Any records, reports, or information obtained under this section (1) shall, in the case of effluent data, be related to any applicable effluent limitations, toxic, pretreatment, or new source performance standards, and (2) shall be available to the public, except that upon a showing satisfactory to the Administrator by any person that records, reports, or information, or particular part thereof (other than effluent data), to which the Administrator has access under this section, if made public would divulge methods or processes entitled to protection as trade secrets of such person, the Administrator shall consider such record, report, or information, or particular portion thereof confidential in accordance with the purposes of section 1905 of Title 18. Any authorized representative of the Administrator (including an authorized contractor acting as a representative of the Administrator) who knowingly or willfully publishes, divulges, discloses, or makes known in any manner or to any extent not authorized by law any information which is required to be considered confidential under this subsection shall be fined not more than $1,000 or imprisoned not more than 1 year, or both. Nothing in this subsection shall prohibit the Administrator or an authorized representative of the Administrator (including any authorized contractor acting as a representative of the Administrator) from disclosing records, reports, or information to other officers, employees, or authorized representatives of the United States concerned with carrying out this chapter or when relevant in any proceeding under this chapter.

(c) Application of State law — Each State may develop and submit to the Administrator procedures under State law for inspection, monitoring, and entry with respect to point sources located in such State. If the Administrator finds that the procedures and the law of any State relating to inspection, monitoring, and entry are applicable to at least the same extent as those required by this section, such State is authorized to apply and enforce its procedures for inspection, monitoring, and entry with respect to point sources located in such State (except with respect to point sources owned or operated by the United States).

(d) Access by Congress — Notwithstanding any limitation contained in this section or any other provision of law, all information reported to or otherwise obtained by the Administrator (or any representative of the Administrator) under this chapter shall be made available, upon written request of any duly authorized committee of Congress, to such committee.

§1319. Enforcement
[CWA §309]
(a) State enforcement; compliance orders

(1) Whenever, on the basis of any information available to him, the Administrator finds that any person is in violation of any condition or limitation which implements section 1311, 1312, 1316, 1317, 1318, 1328, or 1345 of this title in a permit issued by a State under an approved permit program under section 1342 or 1344 of this title he shall proceed under his authority in paragraph (3) of this subsection or he shall notify the person in alleged violation and such State of such finding. If beyond the thirtieth day after the Administrator's notification the State has not commenced appropriate enforcement action, the Administrator shall issue an order requiring such person to comply with such condition or limitation or shall bring a civil action in accordance with subsection (b) of this section.

(2) Whenever, on the basis of information available to him, the Administrator finds that violations of permit conditions or limitations as set forth in paragraph (1) of this subsection are so widespread that such violations appear to result from a failure of the State to enforce such permit conditions or limitations effectively, he shall so notify the State. If the Administrator finds such failure extends beyond the thirtieth day after such notice, he shall give public notice of such finding. During the period beginning with such public notice and ending when such State satisfies the Administrator that it will enforce such conditions and limitations (hereafter referred to in this section as the period of "federally assumed enforcement"), except where an extension has been granted under paragraph (5)(B) of this subsection, the Administrator shall enforce any permit condition or limitation with respect to any person —

    (A) by issuing an order to comply with such condition or limitation, or

    (B) by bringing a civil action under subsection (b) of this section.

(3) Whenever on the basis of any information available to him the Administrator finds that any person is in violation of section 1311, 1312, 1316, 1317, 1318, 1328, or 1345 of this title, or is in violation of any permit condition or limitation implementing any of such sections in a permit issued under section 1342 of this title by him or by a State or in a permit issued under section 1344 of this title by a State, he shall issue an order requiring such person to comply with such section or requirement, or he shall bring a civil action in accordance with subsection (b) of this section.

(4) A copy of any order issued under this subsection shall be sent immediately by the Administrator to the State in which the violation occurs and other affected States. In any case in

which an order under this subsection (or notice to a violator under paragraph (1) of this subsection) is issued to a corporation, a copy of such order (or notice) shall be served on any appropriate corporate officers. An order issued under this subsection relating to a violation of section 1318 of this title shall not take effect until the person to whom it is issued has had an opportunity to confer with the Administrator concerning the alleged violation.

(5)(A) Any order issued under this subsection shall be by personal service, shall state with reasonable specificity the nature of the violation, and shall specify a time for compliance not to exceed thirty days in the case of a violation of an interim compliance schedule or operation and maintenance requirement and not to exceed a time the Administrator determines to be reasonable in the case of a violation of a final deadline, taking into account the seriousness of the violation and any good faith efforts to comply with applicable requirements.

(B) The Administrator may, if he determines (i) that any person who is a violator of, or any person who is otherwise not in compliance with, the time requirements under this chapter or in any permit issued under this chapter, has acted in good faith, and has made a commitment (in the form of contracts or other securities) of necessary resources to achieve compliance by the earliest possible date after July 1, 1977, but not later than April 1, 1979; (ii) that any extension under this provision will not result in the imposition of any additional controls on any other point or nonpoint source; (iii) that an application for a permit under section 1342 of this title was filed for such person prior to December 31, 1974; and (iv) that the facilities necessary for compliance with such requirements are under construction, grant an extension of the date referred to in section 1311(b)(1)(A) of this title to a date which will achieve compliance at the earliest time possible but not later than April 1, 1979.

(6) Whenever, on the basis of information available to him, the Administrator finds (A) that any person is in violation of section 1311(b)(1)(A) or (C) of this title, (B) that such person cannot meet the requirements for a time extension under section 1311(i)(2) of this title, and (C) that the most expeditious and appropriate means of compliance with this chapter by such person is to discharge into a publicly owned treatment works, then, upon request of such person, the Administrator may issue an order requiring such person to comply with this chapter at the earliest date practicable, but not later than July 1, 1983, by discharging into a publicly owned treatment works if such works concur with such order. Such order shall include a schedule of compliance.

(b) Civil actions — The Administrator is authorized to commence a civil action for appropriate relief, including a permanent or temporary injunction, for any violation for which he is authorized to issue a compliance order under subsection (a) of this section. Any action under this subsection may be brought in the district court of the United States for the district in which the defendant is located or resides or is doing business, and such court shall have jurisdiction to restrain such violation and to require compliance. Notice of the commencement of such action shall be given immediately to the appropriate State.

(c) Criminal penalties

(1) Negligent violations — Any person who —

(A) negligently violates section 1311, 1312, 1316, 1317, 1318, 1321(b)(3), 1328, or 1345 of this title, or any permit condition or limitation implementing any of such sections in a permit issued under section 1342 of this title by the Administrator or by a State, or any requirement imposed in a pretreatment program approved under section 1342(a)(3) or 1342(b)(8) of this title or in a permit issued under section 1344 of this title by the Secretary of the Army or by a State; or

(B) negligently introduces into a sewer system or into a publicly owned treatment works any pollutant or hazardous substance which such person knew or reasonably should have known could cause personal injury or property damage or, other than in compliance with all applicable Federal, State, or local requirements or permits, which causes such treatment works to violate any effluent limitation or condition in any permit issued to the treatment works under section 1342 of this title by the Administrator or a State;

shall be punished by a fine of not less than $2,500 nor more than $25,000 per day of violation, or by imprisonment for not more than 1 year, or by both. If a conviction of a person is for a violation committed after a first conviction of such person under this paragraph, punishment shall be by a fine of not more than $50,000 per day of violation, or by imprisonment of not more than 2 years, or by both.

(2) Knowing violations — Any person who —

(A) knowingly violates section 1311, 1312, 1316, 1317, 1318, 1321(b)(3), 1328, or 1345 of this title, or any permit condition or limitation implementing any of such sections in a permit issued under section 1342 of this title by the Administrator or by a State, or any requirement imposed in a pretreatment program approved under section 1342(a)(3) or 1342(b)(8) of this title or in a permit issued under section 1344 of this title by the Secretary of the Army or by a State; or

(B) knowingly introduces into a sewer system or into a publicly owned treatment works any pollutant or hazardous substance which such person knew or reasonably should have known could cause personal injury or property damage or, other than in compliance with all applicable Federal, State, or local requirements or permits, which causes such treatment works to violate any effluent limitation or condition in a permit issued to the treatment works under section 1342 of this title by the Administrator or a State;

shall be punished by a fine of not less than $5,000 nor more than $50,000 per day of violation, or by imprisonment for not more than 3 years, or by both. If a conviction of a person is for a violation committed after a first conviction of such person under this paragraph, punishment shall be by a fine of not more than $100,000 per day of violation, or by imprisonment of not more than 6 years, or by both.

(3) Knowing endangerment

(A) General rule — Any person who knowingly violates section 1311, 1312, 1313, 1316, 1317, 1318, 1321(b)(3), 1328, or 1345 of this title, or any permit condition or limitation implementing any of such sections in a permit issued under section 1342 of this title by the Administrator or by a State, or in a permit issued under section 1344 of this title by the Secretary of the Army or by a State, and who knows at that time that he thereby places another person in imminent danger of death or serious bodily injury, shall, upon conviction, be subject to a fine of not more than $250,000 or imprisonment of not more than 15 years, or both. A person which is an organization shall, upon conviction of violating this subparagraph, be subject to a fine of not more than $1,000,000. If a conviction of a person is for a violation committed after a first conviction of such person under this paragraph, the maximum punishment shall be doubled with respect to both fine and imprisonment.

(B) Additional provisions — For the purpose of subparagraph (A) of this paragraph —

(i) in determining whether a defendant who is an individual knew that his conduct placed another person in imminent danger of death or serious bodily injury —

(I) the person is responsible only for actual awareness or actual belief that he possessed; and

(II) knowledge possessed by a person other than the defendant but not by the defendant himself may not be attributed to the defendant;

except that in proving the defendant's possession of actual knowledge, circumstantial evidence may be used, including evidence that the defendant took affirmative steps to shield himself from relevant information;

(ii) it is an affirmative defense to prosecution that the conduct charged was consented to by the person endangered and that the danger and conduct charged were reasonably foreseeable hazards of —

(I) an occupation, a business, or a profession; or

(II) medical treatment or medical or scientific experimentation conducted by professionally approved methods and such other person had been made aware of the risks involved prior to giving consent;

and such defense may be established under this subparagraph by a preponderance of the evidence;

(iii) the term "organization" means a legal entity, other than a government, established or organized for any purpose, and such term includes a corporation, company, association, firm, partnership, joint stock company, foundation, institution, trust, society, union, or any other association of persons; and

(iv) the term "serious bodily injury" means bodily injury which involves a substantial risk of death, unconsciousness, extreme physical pain, protracted and obvious disfigurement, or protracted loss or impairment of the function of a bodily member, organ, or mental faculty.

(4) False statements — Any person who knowingly makes any false material statement, representation, or certification in any application, record, report, plan, or other document filed or required to be maintained under this chapter or who knowingly falsifies, tampers with, or renders inaccurate any monitoring device or method required to be maintained under this chapter, shall upon conviction, be punished by a fine of not more than $10,000, or by imprisonment for not more than 2 years, or by both. If a conviction of a person is for a violation committed after a first conviction of such person under this paragraph, punishment shall be by a fine of not more than $20,000 per day of violation, or by imprisonment of not more than 4 years, or by both.

(5) Treatment of single operational upset — For purposes of this subsection, a single operational upset which leads to simultaneous violations of more than one pollutant parameter shall be treated as a single violation.

(6) Responsible corporate officer as "person" — For the purpose of this subsection, the term

"person" means, in addition to the definition contained in section 1362(5) of this title, any responsible corporate officer.

(7) Hazardous substance defined — For the purpose of this subsection, the term "hazardous substance" means (A) any substance designated pursuant to section 1321(b)(2)(A) of this title, (B) any element, compound, mixture, solution, or substance designated pursuant to section 9602 of Title 42, (C) any hazardous waste having the characteristics identified under or listed pursuant to section 3001 of the Solid Waste Disposal Act (42 U.S.C. §6921) (but not including any waste the regulation of which under the Solid Waste Disposal Act (42 U.S.C. §6901 *et seq.*) has been suspended by Act of Congress), (D) any toxic pollutant listed under section 1317(a) of this title, and (E) any imminently hazardous chemical substance or mixture with respect to which the Administrator has taken action pursuant to section 2606 of Title 15.

(d) **Civil penalties; factors considered in determining amount** — Any person who violates section 1311, 1312, 1316, 1317, 1318, 1328, or 1345 of this title, or any permit condition or limitation implementing any of such sections in a permit issued under section 1342 of this title by the Administrator, or by a State, or in a permit issued under section 1344 of this title by a State, or any requirement imposed in a pretreatment program approved under section 1342(a)(3) or 1342(b)(8) of this title, and any person who violates any order issued by the Administrator under subsection (a) of this section, shall be subject to a civil penalty not to exceed $25,000 per day for each violation. In determining the amount of a civil penalty the court shall consider the seriousness of the violation or violations, the economic benefit (if any) resulting from the violation, any history of such violations, any good-faith efforts to comply with the applicable requirements, the economic impact of the penalty on the violator, and such other matters as justice may require. For purposes of this subsection, a single operational upset which leads to simultaneous violations of more than one pollutant parameter shall be treated as a single violation.

(e) **State liability for judgments and expenses** — Whenever a municipality is a party to a civil action brought by the United States under this section, the State in which such municipality is located shall be joined as a party. Such State shall be liable for payment of any judgment, or any expenses incurred as a result of complying with any judgment, entered against the municipality in such action to the extent that the laws of that State prevent the municipality from raising revenues needed to comply with such judgment.

(f) **Wrongful introduction of pollutant into treatment works** — Whenever, on the basis of any information available to him, the Administrator finds that an owner or operator of any source is introducing a pollutant into a treatment works in violation of subsection (d) of section 1317 of this title, the Administrator may notify the owner or operator of such treatment works and the State of such violation. If the owner or operator of the treatment works does not commence appropriate enforcement action within 30 days of the date of such notification, the Administrator may commence a civil action for appropriate relief, including but not limited to, a permanent or temporary injunction, against the owner or operator of such treatment works. In any such civil action the Administrator shall join the owner or operator of such source as a party to the action. Such action shall be brought in the district court of the United States in the district in which the treatment works is located. Such court shall have jurisdiction to restrain such violation and to require the owner or operator of the treatment works and the owner or operator of the source to take such action as may be necessary to come into compliance with this chapter. Notice of commencement of any such action shall be given to the State. Nothing in this subsection shall be construed to limit or prohibit any other authority the Administrator may have under this chapter.

(g) **Administrative penalties**

(1) Violations — Whenever on the basis of any information available —

(A) the Administrator finds that any person has violated section 1311, 1312, 1316, 1317, 1318, 1328, or 1345 of this title, or has violated any permit condition or limitation implementing any of such sections in a permit issued under section 1342 of this title by the Administrator or by a State, or in a permit issued under section 1344 of this title by a State, or

(B) the Secretary of the Army (hereinafter in this subsection referred to as the "Secretary") finds that any person has violated any permit condition or limitation in a permit issued under section 1344 of this title by the Secretary, the Administrator or Secretary, as the case may be, may, after consultation with the State in which the violation occurs, assess a class I civil penalty or a class II civil penalty under this subsection.

(2) Classes of penalties

(A) Class I — The amount of a class I civil penalty under paragraph (1) may not exceed $10,000 per violation, except that the maximum amount of any class I civil penalty under this subparagraph shall not exceed $25,000. Before issuing an order assessing a civil penalty under this subparagraph, the Administrator or the Secretary, as the case may be, shall give to the person to be assessed such penalty written notice of the Administrator's or Secretary's proposal to issue such order and the opportunity to request, within 30 days of the date the notice is received by such person, a hearing on the proposed order. Such hearing shall not be subject to section 554 or 556 of Title 5, but shall provide a reasonable opportunity to be heard and to present evidence.

(B) Class II — The amount of a class II civil penalty under paragraph (1) may not exceed $10,000 per day for each day during which the violation continues; except that the maximum amount of any class II civil penalty under this subparagraph shall not exceed $125,000. Except as otherwise provided in this subsection, a class II civil penalty shall be assessed and collected in the same manner, and subject to the same provisions, as in the case of civil penalties assessed and collected after notice and opportunity for a hearing on the record in accordance with section 554 of Title 5. The Administrator and the Secretary may issue rules for discovery procedures for hearings under this subparagraph.

(3) Determining amount — In determining the amount of any penalty assessed under this subsection, the Administrator or the Secretary, as the case may be, shall take into account the nature, circumstances, extent and gravity of the violation, or violations, and, with respect to the violator, ability to pay, any prior history of such violations, the degree of culpability, economic benefit or savings (if any) resulting from the violation, and such other matters as justice may require. For purposes of this subsection, a single operational upset which leads to simultaneous violations of more than one pollutant parameter shall be treated as a single violation.

(4) Rights of interested persons

(A) Public notice — Before issuing an order assessing a civil penalty under this subsection the Administrator or Secretary, as the case may be, shall provide public notice of and reasonable opportunity to comment on the proposed issuance of such order.

(B) Presentation of evidence — Any person who comments on a proposed assessment of a penalty under this subsection shall be given notice of any hearing held under this subsection and of the order assessing such penalty. In any hearing held under this subsection, such person shall have a reasonable opportunity to be heard and to present evidence.

(C) Rights of interested persons to a hearing — If no hearing is held under paragraph (2) before issuance of an order assessing a penalty under this subsection, any person who commented on the proposed assessment may petition, within 30 days after the issuance of such order, the Administrator or Secretary, as the case may be, to set aside such order and to provide a hearing on the penalty. If the

evidence presented by the petitioner in support of the petition is material and was not considered in the issuance of the order, the Administrator or Secretary shall immediately set aside such order and provide a hearing in accordance with paragraph (2)(A) in the case of a class I civil penalty and paragraph (2)(B) in the case of a class II civil penalty. If the Administrator or Secretary denies a hearing under this subparagraph, the Administrator or Secretary shall provide to the petitioner, and publish in the Federal Register, notice of and the reasons for such denial.

(5) Finality of order — An order issued under this subsection shall become final 30 days after its issuance unless a petition for judicial review is filed under paragraph (8) or a hearing is requested under paragraph (4)(C). If such a hearing is denied, such order shall become final 30 days after such denial.

(6) Effect of order

(A) Limitation on actions under other sections — Action taken by the Administrator or the Secretary, as the case may be, under this subsection shall not affect or limit the Administrator's or Secretary's authority to enforce any provision of this chapter; except that any violation —

(i) with respect to which the Administrator or the Secretary has commenced and is diligently prosecuting an action under this subsection,

(ii) with respect to which a State has commenced and is diligently prosecuting an action under a State law comparable to this subsection, or

(iii) for which the Administrator, the Secretary, or the State has issued a final order not subject to further judicial review and the violator has paid a penalty assessed under this subsection, or such comparable State law, as the case may be,

shall not be the subject of a civil penalty action under subsection (d) of this section or section 1321(b) of this title or section 1365 of this title.

(B) Applicability of limitation with respect to citizen suits — The limitations contained in subparagraph (A) on civil penalty actions under section 1365 of this title shall not apply with respect to any violation for which —

(i) a civil action under section 1365(a)(1) of this title has been filed prior to commencement of an action under this subsection, or

(ii) notice of an alleged violation of section 1365(a)(1) of this title has been given in accordance with section 1365(b)(1)(A) of this title prior to commencement of an action under this subsection and an action under section 1365(a)(1) of this title with respect to such alleged violation is filed before the 120th day after the date on which such notice is given.

(7) Effect of action on compliance — No action by the Administrator or the Secretary under this subsection shall affect any person's obligation to comply with any section of this chapter or with the terms and conditions of any permit issued pursuant to section 1342 or 1344 of this title.

(8) Judicial review — Any person against whom a civil penalty is assessed under this subsection or who commented on the proposed assessment of such penalty in accordance with paragraph (4) may obtain review of such assessment —

(A) in the case of assessment of a class I civil penalty, in the United States District Court for the District of Columbia or in the district in which the violation is alleged to have occurred, or

(B) in the case of assessment of a class II civil penalty, in United States Court of Appeals for the District of Columbia Circuit or for any other circuit in which such person resides or transacts business,

by filing a notice of appeal in such court within the 30-day period beginning on the date the civil penalty order is issued and by simultaneously sending a copy of such notice by certified mail to the Administrator or the Secretary, as the case may be, and the Attorney General. The Administrator or the Secretary shall promptly file in such court a certified copy of the record on which the order was issued. Such court shall not set aside or remand such order unless there is not substantial evidence in the record, taken as a whole, to support the finding of a violation or unless the Administrator's or Secretary's assessment of the penalty constitutes an abuse of discretion and shall not impose additional civil penalties for the same violation unless the Administrator's or Secretary's assessment of the penalty constitutes an abuse of discretion.

(9) Collection — If any person fails to pay an assessment of a civil penalty —

(A) after the order making the assessment has become final, or

(B) after a court in an action brought under paragraph (8) has entered a final judgment in favor of the Administrator or the Secretary, as the case may be,

the Administrator or the Secretary shall request the Attorney General to bring a civil action in an appropriate district court to recover the amount assessed (plus interest at currently prevailing rates from the date of the final order or the date of the final judgment, as the case may be). In such an action, the validity, amount, and appropriateness of such penalty shall not be subject to review. Any person

who fails to pay on a timely basis the amount of an assessment of a civil penalty as described in the first sentence of this paragraph shall be required to pay, in addition to such amount and interest, attorneys fees and costs for collection proceedings and a quarterly nonpayment penalty for each quarter during which such failure to pay persists. Such nonpayment penalty shall be in an amount equal to 20 percent of the aggregate amount of such person's penalties and nonpayment penalties which are unpaid as of the beginning of such quarter.

(10) Subpoenas — The Administrator or Secretary, as the case may be, may issue subpoenas for the attendance and testimony of witnesses and the production of relevant papers, books, or documents in connection with hearings under this subsection. In case of contumacy or refusal to obey a subpoena issued pursuant to this paragraph and served upon any person, the district court of the United States for any district in which such person is found, resides, or transacts business, upon application by the United States and after notice to such person, shall have jurisdiction to issue an order requiring such person to appear and give testimony before the administrative law judge or to appear and produce documents before the administrative law judge, or both, and any failure to obey such order of the court may be punished by such court as a contempt thereof.

(11) Protection of existing procedures — Nothing in this subsection shall change the procedures existing on the day before February 4, 1987, under other subsections of this section for issuance and enforcement of orders by the Administrator.

(h) Implementation of integrated plans

(1) In general — In conjunction with an enforcement action under subsection (a) or (b) relating to municipal discharges, the Administrator shall inform a municipality of the opportunity to develop an integrated plan, as defined in section 1342(s) of this title.

(2) Modification — Any municipality under an administrative order under subsection (a) or settlement agreement (including a judicial consent decree) under subsection (b) that has developed an integrated plan consistent with section 1342(s) of this title may request a modification of the administrative order or settlement agreement based on that integrated plan.

§1320. International pollution abatement
[CWA §310]

(a) Hearing; participation by foreign nations — Whenever the Administrator, upon receipts of reports, surveys, or studies from any duly constituted international agency, has reason to believe that pollution is occurring which endangers the health or welfare of persons in a foreign country, and the Secretary of State requests him to abate such pollution, he shall give formal notification thereof to the State water pollution control agency of the State or States in which such discharge or discharges originate and to the appropriate interstate agency, if any. He shall also promptly call such a hearing, if he believes that such pollution is occurring in sufficient quantity to warrant such action, and if such foreign country has given the United States essentially the same rights with respect to the prevention and control of pollution occurring in that country as is given that country by this subsection. The Administrator, through the Secretary of State, shall invite the foreign country which may be adversely affected by the pollution to attend and participate in the hearing, and the representative of such country shall, for the purpose of the hearing and any further proceeding resulting from such hearing, have all the rights of a State water pollution control agency. Nothing in this subsection shall be construed to modify, amend, repeal, or otherwise affect the provisions of the 1909 Boundary Waters Treaty between Canada and the United States or the Water Utilization Treaty of 1944 between Mexico and the United States (59 Stat. 1219), relative to the control and abatement of pollution in waters covered by those treaties.

(b) Functions and responsibilities of Administrator not affected — The calling of a hearing under this section shall not be construed by the courts, the Administrator, or any person as limiting, modifying, or otherwise affecting the functions and responsibilities of the Administrator under this section to establish and enforce water quality requirements under this chapter.

(c) Hearing board; composition; findings of fact; recommendations; implementation of board's decision — The Administrator shall publish in the Federal Register a notice of a public hearing before a hearing board of five or more persons appointed by the Administrator. A majority of the members of the board and the chairman who shall be designated by the Administrator shall not be officers or employees of Federal, State, or local governments. On the basis of the evidence presented at such hearing, the board shall within sixty days after completion of the hearing make findings of fact as to whether or not such pollution is occurring and shall thereupon by decision, incorporating its findings therein, make such recommendations to abate the pollution as may be appropriate and shall transmit such decision and the record of the hearings to the Administrator. All such decisions shall be public. Upon receipt of such decision, the Administrator shall promptly implement the board's decision in accordance with the provisions of this chapter.

(d) Report by alleged polluter — In connection with any hearing called under this subsection, the board is authorized to require any person whose alleged activities result in discharges causing or contributing to pollution to file with it in such forms as it may prescribe, a report based on existing data, furnishing such information as may reasonably be required as to the character, kind, and quantity of such discharges and the use of facilities or other means to prevent or reduce such discharges by the person filing such a report. Such report shall be made under oath or otherwise, as the board may prescribe, and shall be filed with the board within such reasonable period as it may prescribe, unless additional time is granted by it. Upon a showing satisfactory to the board by the person filing such report that such report or portion thereof (other than effluent data), to which the Administrator has access under this section, if made public would divulge trade secrets or secret processes of such person, the board shall consider such report or portion thereof confidential for the purposes of section 1905 of Title 18. If any person required to file any report under this paragraph shall fail to do so within the time fixed by the board for filing the same, and such failure shall continue for thirty days after notice of such default, such person shall forfeit to the United States the sum of $1,000 for each and every day of the continuance of such failure, which forfeiture shall be payable into the Treasury of the United States, and shall be recoverable in a civil suit in the name of the United States in the district court of the United States where such person has his principal office or in any district in which he does business. The Administrator may upon application therefor remit or mitigate any forfeiture provided for under this subsection.

(e) Compensation of board members — Board members, other than officers or employees of Federal, State, or local governments, shall be for each day (including travel-time) during which they are performing board business, entitled to receive compensation at a rate fixed by the Administrator but not in excess of the maximum rate of pay for grade GS-18, as provided in the General Schedule under section 5332 of Title 5, and shall, notwithstanding the limitations of sections 5703 and 5704 of Title 5, be fully reimbursed for travel, subsistence and related expenses.

(f) Enforcement proceedings — When any such recommendation adopted by the Administrator involves the institution of enforcement proceedings against any person to obtain the abatement of pollution subject to such recommendation, the Administrator shall institute such proceedings if he believes that the evidence warants such proceedings. The district court of the United States shall consider and determine de novo all relevant issues, but shall receive in evidence the record of the proceedings before the conference or hearing board. The court shall have jurisdiction to enter such judgment and orders enforcing such judgment as it deems appropriate or to remand such proceedings to the Administrator for such further action as it may direct.

§1321. Oil and hazardous substance liability [CWA §311]

(a) Definitions — For the purpose of this section, the term —

(1) "oil" means oil of any kind or in any form, including, but not limited to, petroleum, fuel oil, sludge, oil refuse, and oil mixed with wastes other than dredged spoil;

(2) "discharge" includes, but is not limited to, any spilling, leaking, pumping, pouring, emitting, emptying or dumping, but excludes (A) discharges in compliance with a permit under section 1342 of this title, (B) discharges resulting from circumstances identified and reviewed and made a part of the public record with respect to a permit issued or modified under section 1342 of this title, and subject to a condition in such permit, (C) continuous or anticipated intermittent discharges from a point source, identified in a permit or permit application under section 1342 of this title, which are caused by events occurring within the scope of relevant operating or treatment systems, and (D) discharges incidental to mechanical removal authorized by the President under subsection (c) of this section;

(3) "vessel" means every description of watercraft or other artificial contrivance used, or capable of being used, as a means of transportation on water other than a public vessel;

(4) "public vessel" means a vessel owned or bareboat-chartered and operated by the United States, or by a State or political subdivision thereof, or by a foreign nation, except when such vessel is engaged in commerce;

(5) "United States" means the States, the District of Columbia, the Commonwealth of Puerto Rico, the Commonwealth of the Northern Mariana Islands, Guam, American Samoa, the Virgin Islands, and the Trust Territory of the Pacific Islands;

(6) "owner or operator" means (A) in the case of a vessel, any person owning, operating, or chartering by demise, such vessel, and (B) in the case of an onshore facility, and an offshore facility, any person owning or operating such onshore facility or offshore facility, and (C) in the case of any abandoned offshore facility, the person who owned or operated such facility immediately prior to such abandonment;

(7) "person" includes an individual, firm, corporation, association, and a partnership;

(8) "remove" or "removal" refers to containment and removal of the oil or hazardous substances from the water and shorelines or the taking of such other actions as may be necessary to prevent, minimize or mitigate damage to the public health or welfare, including, but not limited to, fish, shellfish, wildlife, and public and private property, shorelines, and beaches;

(9) "contiguous zone" means the entire zone established or to be established by the United States under article 24 of the Convention on the Territorial Sea and the Contiguous Zone;

(10) "onshore facility" means any facility (including, but not limited to, motor vehicles and rolling stock) of any kind located in, on, or under, any land within the United States other than submerged land;

(11) "offshore facility" means any facility of any kind located in, on, or under, any of the navigable waters of the United States, any facility of any kind which is subject to the jurisdiction of the United States and is located in, on, or under any other waters, other than a vessel or public vessel, and, for the purposes of applying subsections (b), (c), (e), and (o), any foreign offshore unit (as defined in section 1001 of the Oil Pollution Act) or any other facility located seaward of the exclusive economic zone;

(12) "act of God" means an act occasioned by an unanticipated grave natural disaster;

(13) "barrel" means 42 United States gallons at 60 degrees Fahrenheit;

(14) "hazardous substance" means any substance designated pursuant to subsection (b)(2) of this section;

(15) "inland oil barge" means a non-self-propelled vessel carrying oil in bulk as cargo and certificated to operate only in the inland waters of the United States, while operating in such waters;

(16) "inland waters of the United States" means those waters of the United States lying inside the baseline from which the territorial sea is measured and those waters outside such baseline which are a part of the Gulf Intracoastal Waterway;

(17) "otherwise subject to the jurisdiction of the United States" means subject to the jurisdiction of the United States by virtue of United States citizenship, United States vessel documentation or numbering, or as provided for by international agreement to which the United States is a party;

(18) "Area Committee" means an Area Committee established under subsection (j) of this section;

(19) "Area Contingency Plan" means an Area Contingency Plan prepared under subsection (j) of this section;

(20) "Coast Guard District Response Group" means a Coast Guard District Response Group established under subsection (j) of this section;

(21) "Federal On-Scene Coordinator" means a Federal On-Scene Coordinator designated in the National Contingency Plan;

(22) "National Contingency Plan" means the National Contingency Plan prepared and published under subsection (d) of this section;

(23) "National Response Unit" means the National Response Unit established under subsection (j) of this section;

(24) "worst case discharge" means —

(A) in the case of a vessel, a discharge in adverse weather conditions of its entire cargo; and

(B) in the case of an offshore facility or onshore facility, the largest foreseeable discharge in adverse weather conditions;

(25) "removal costs" means —

(A) the costs of removal of oil or a hazardous substance that are incurred after it is discharged; and

(B) in any case in which there is a substantial threat of a discharge of oil or a hazardous substance, the costs to prevent, minimize or mitigate that threat; and

(26) "nontank vessel" means a self-propelled vessel that —

(A) is at least 400 gross tons as measured under section 14302 of title 46, United States Code [46 §14302], or, for vessels not measured under that section, as measured under section 14502 of that title [46 §14502];

(B) is not a tank vessel;

(C) carries oil of any kind as fuel for main propulsion; and

(D) operates on the navigable waters of the United States, as defined in section 2101(23) of that title.

(27) the term "best available science" means science that —

(A) maximizes the quality, objectivity, and integrity of information, including statistical information;

(B) uses peer-reviewed and publicly available data; and

(C) clearly documents and communicates risks and uncertainties in the scientific basis for such projects;

(28) the term "Chairperson" means the Chairperson of the Council;

(29) the term "coastal political subdivision" means any local political jurisdiction that is immediately below the State level of government, including a county, parish, or borough, with a coastline that is contiguous with any portion of the United States Gulf of Mexico;

(30) the term "Comprehensive Plan" means the comprehensive plan developed by the Council pursuant to subsection (t);

(31) the term "Council" means the Gulf Coast Ecosystem Restoration Council established pursuant to subsection (t);

(32) the term "Deepwater Horizon oil spill" means the blowout and explosion of the mobile offshore drilling unit Deepwater Horizon that occurred on April 20, 2010, and resulting hydrocarbon releases into the environment;

(33) the term "Gulf Coast region" means —

(A) in the Gulf Coast States, the coastal zones ((as that term is defined in section 1453

of Title 16), except that, in this section, the term "coastal zones" includes land within the coastal zones that is held in trust by, or the use of which is by law subject solely to the discretion of, the Federal Government or officers or agents of the Federal Government) that border the Gulf of Mexico;

(B) any adjacent land, water, and watersheds, that are within 25 miles of the coastal zones described in subparagraph (A) of the Gulf Coast States; and

(C) all Federal waters in the Gulf of Mexico;

(34) the term "Gulf Coast State" means any of the States of Alabama, Florida, Louisiana, Mississippi, and Texas; and

(35) the term "Trust Fund" means the Gulf Coast Restoration Trust Fund established pursuant to section 1602 of the Resources and Ecosystems Sustainability, Tourist Opportunities, and Revived Economies of the Gulf Coast States Act of 2012.

(b) Congressional declaration of policy against discharges of oil or hazardous substances; designation of hazardous substances; study of higher standard of care incentives and report to Congress; liability; penalties; civil actions: penalty limitations, separate offenses, jurisdiction, mitigation of damages and costs, recovery of removal costs, alternative remedies, and withholding clearance of vessels

(1) The Congress hereby declares that it is the policy of the United States that there should be no discharges of oil or hazardous substances into or upon the navigable waters of the United States, adjoining shorelines, or into or upon the waters of the contiguous zone, or in connection with activities under the Outer Continental Shelf Lands Act (43 U.S.C. §1331 *et seq.*) or the Deepwater Port Act of 1974 (33 U.S.C. §1501 *et seq.*), or which may affect natural resources belonging to, appertaining to, or under the exclusive management authority of the United States (including resources under the Magnuson-Stevens Fishery Conservation and Management Act (16 U.S.C. §1801 *et seq.*)).

(2)(A) The Administrator shall develop, promulgate, and revise as may be appropriate, regulations designating as hazardous substances, other than oil as defined in this section, such elements and compounds which, when discharged in any quantity into or upon the navigable waters of the United States or adjoining shorelines or the waters of the contiguous zone or in connection with activities under the Outer Continental Shelf Lands Act (43 U.S.C. §1331 *et seq.*) or the Deepwater Port Act of 1974 (33 U.S.C. §1501 *et seq.*), or which may affect natural resources belonging to, appertaining to, or under the exclusive management authority of the United States (including resources under the Magnuson-Stevens Fishery Conservation and Management Act (16 U.S.C. §1801 *et seq.*)), present an imminent and substantial danger to the public health or welfare, including, but not limited to, fish, shellfish, wildlife, shorelines, and beaches.

(B) The Administrator shall within 18 months after the date of enactment of this paragraph, conduct a study and report to the Congress on methods, mechanisms, and procedures to create incentives to achieve a higher standard of care in all aspects of the management and movement of hazardous substances on the part of owners, operators, or persons in charge of onshore facilities, offshore facilities, or vessels. The Administrator shall include in such study (1) limits of liability, (2) liability for third party damages, (3) penalties and fees, (4) spill prevention plans, (5) current practices in the insurance and banking industries, and (6) whether the penalty enacted in subclause (bb) of clause (iii) of subparagraph (B) of subsection (b)(2) of section 311 of Public Law 92-500 should be enacted.

(3) The discharge of oil or hazardous substances (i) into or upon the navigable waters of the United States, adjoining shorelines, or into or upon the waters of the contiguous zone, or (ii) in connection with activities under the Outer Continental Shelf Lands Act (43 U.S.C. §1331 *et seq.*) or the Deepwater Port Act of 1974 (33 U.S.C. §1501 *et seq.*), or which may affect natural resources belonging to, appertaining to, or under the exclusive management authority of the United States (including resources under the Magnuson-Stevens Fishery Conservation and Management Act (16 U.S.C. §1801 *et seq.*)), in such quantities as may be harmful as determined by the President under paragraph (4) of this subsection, is prohibited, except (A) in the case of such discharges into the waters of the contiguous zone or which may affect natural resources belonging to, appertaining to, or under the exclusive management authority of the United States (including resources under the Magnuson-Stevens Fishery Conservation and Management Act), where permitted under the Protocol of 1978 Relating to the International Convention for the Prevention of Pollution from Ships, 1973, and (B) where permitted in quantities and at times and locations or under such circumstances or conditions as the President may, by regulation, determine not to be harmful. Any regulations issued under this subsection shall be consistent with maritime safety and with marine and navigation laws and regulations and applicable water quality standards.

(4) The President shall by regulation determine for the purposes of this section those quantities of oil and any hazardous substances the discharge of which may be harmful to the public health or welfare or the environment of the United States, including but not limited to fish, shellfish, wildlife, and public and private property, shorelines, and beaches.

(5) Any person in charge of a vessel or of an onshore facility or an offshore facility shall, as soon as he has knowledge of any discharge of oil or a hazardous substance from such vessel or facility in violation of paragraph (3) of this subsection, immediately notify the appropriate agency of the United States Government of such discharge. The Federal agency shall immediately notify the appropriate State agency of any State which is, or may reasonably be expected to be, affected by the discharge of oil or a hazardous substance. Any such person (A) in charge of a vessel from which oil or a hazardous substance is discharged in violation of paragraph (3)(i) of this subsection, or (B) in charge of a vessel from which oil or a hazardous substance is discharged in violation of paragraph (3)(ii) of this subsection and who is otherwise subject to the jurisdiction of the United States at the time of the discharge, or (C) in charge of an onshore facility or an offshore facility, who fails to notify immediately such agency of such discharge shall, upon conviction, be fined in accordance with Title 18, or imprisoned for not more than 5 years, or both. Notification received pursuant to this paragraph shall not be used against any such natural person in any criminal case, except a prosecution for perjury or for giving a false statement.

(6) Administrative penalties

(A) Violations — Any owner, operator, or person in charge of any vessel, onshore facility, or offshore facility —

(i) from which oil or a hazardous substance is discharged in violation of paragraph (3), or

(ii) who fails or refuses to comply with any regulation issued under subsection (j) of this section to which that owner, operator, or person in charge is subject,

may be assessed a class I or class II civil penalty by the Secretary of the department in which the Coast Guard is operating or the Administrator.

(B) Classes of penalties

(i) Class I — The amount of a class I civil penalty under subparagraph (A) may not exceed $10,000 per violation, except that the maximum amount of any class I civil penalty under this subparagraph shall not exceed $25,000. Before assessing a civil penalty under this clause, the Administrator or Secretary, as the case may be, shall give to the person to be assessed such penalty written notice of the Administrator's or Secretary's proposal to assess the penalty and the opportunity to request, within 30 days of the date the notice is received by such person, a hearing on the proposed penalty. Such hearing shall not be subject to section 554 or 556 of Title 5, but shall provide a reasonable opportunity to be heard and to present evidence.

(ii) Class II — The amount of a class II civil penalty under subparagraph (A) may not exceed $10,000 per day for each day during which the violation continues; except that the maximum amount of any class II civil penalty under this subparagraph shall not exceed $125,000. Except as otherwise provided in this subsection, a class II civil penalty shall be assessed and collected in the same manner, and subject to the same provisions, as in the case of civil penalties assessed and collected after notice and opportunity for a hearing on the record in accordance with section 554 of Title 5. The Administrator and Secretary may issue rules for discovery procedures for hearings under this paragraph.

(C) Rights of interested persons

(i) Public notice — Before issuing an order assessing a class II civil penalty under this paragraph the Administrator or Secretary, as the case may be, shall provide public notice of and reasonable opportunity to comment on the proposed issuance of such order.

(ii) Presentation of evidence — Any person who comments on a proposed assessment of a class II civil penalty under this paragraph shall be given notice of any hearing held under this paragraph and of the order assessing such penalty. In any hearing held under this paragraph, such person shall have a reasonable opportunity to be heard and to present evidence.

(iii) Rights of interested persons to a hearing — If no hearing is held under subparagraph (B) before issuance of an order assessing a class II civil penalty under this paragraph, any person who commented on the proposed assessment may petition, within 30 days after the issuance of such order, the Administrator or Secretary, as the case may be, to set aside such order and to provide a hearing on the penalty. If the evidence presented by the petitioner in support of the petition is material and was not considered in the issuance of the order, the Administrator or Secretary shall immediately set aside such order and provide a hearing in accordance with subparagraph (B)(ii). If the Administrator or Secretary denies a hearing under this clause, the Administrator or Secretary shall provide to the petitioner, and publish in the Federal Register, notice of and the reasons for such denial.

(D) Finality of order — An order assessing a class II civil penalty under this paragraph shall become final 30 days after its issuance unless a petition for judicial review is filed under subparagraph (G) or a hearing is requested under subparagraph (C)(iii). If such a hearing is denied, such order shall become final 30 days after such denial.

(E) Effect of order — Action taken by the Administrator or Secretary, as the case may be, under this paragraph shall not affect or limit the Administrator's or Secretary's authority to enforce any provision of this chapter; except that any violation —

(i) with respect to which the Administrator or Secretary has commenced and is diligently prosecuting an action to assess a class II civil penalty under this paragraph, or

(ii) for which the administrator or Secretary has issued a final order assessing a class II civil penalty not subject to further judicial review and the violator has paid a penalty assessed under this paragraph,

shall not be the subject of a civil penalty action under section 1319(d), 1319(g), or 1365 of this title or under paragraph (7).

(F) Effect of action on compliance — No action by the Administrator or Secretary under this paragraph shall affect any person's obligation to comply with any section of this chapter.

(G) Judicial review — Any person against whom a civil penalty is assessed under this paragraph or who commented on the proposed assessment of such penalty in accordance with subparagraph (C) may obtain review of such assessment —

(i) in the case of assessment of a class I civil penalty, in the United States District Court for the District of Columbia or in the district in which the violation is alleged to have occurred, or

(ii) in the case of assessment of a class II civil penalty, in United States Court of Appeals for the District of Columbia Circuit or for any other circuit in which such person resides or transacts business,

by filing a notice of appeal in such court within the 30-day period beginning on the date the civil penalty order is issued and by simultaneously sending a copy of such notice by certified mail to the Administrator or Secretary, as the case may be, and the Attorney General. The Administrator or Secretary shall promptly file in such court a certified copy of the record on which the order was issued. Such court shall not set aside or remand such order unless there is not substantial evidence in the record, taken as a whole, to support the finding of a violation or unless the Administrator's or Secretary's assessment of the penalty constitutes an abuse of discretion and shall not impose additional civil penalties for the same violation unless the Administrator's or Secretary's assessment of the penalty constitutes an abuse of discretion.

(H) Collection — If any person fails to pay an assessment of a civil penalty —

　　(i) after the assessment has become final, or

　　(ii) after a court in an action brought under subparagraph (G) has entered a final judgment in favor of the Administrator or Secretary, as the case may be,

the Administrator or Secretary shall request the Attorney General to bring a civil action in an appropriate district court to recover the amount assessed (plus interest at currently prevailing rates from the date of the final order or the date of the final judgment, as the case may be). In such an action, the validity, amount, and appropriateness of such penalty shall not be subject to review. Any person who fails to pay on a timely basis the amount of an assessment of a civil penalty as described in the first sentence of this subparagraph shall be required to pay, in addition to such amount and interest, attorneys fees and costs for collection proceedings and a quarterly nonpayment penalty for each quarter during which such failure to pay persists. Such nonpayment penalty shall be in an amount equal to 20 percent of the aggregate amount of such person's penalties and nonpayment penalties which are unpaid as of the beginning of such quarter.

(I) Subpoenas — The Administrator or Secretary, as the case may be, may issue subpoenas for the attendance and testimony of witnesses and the production of relevant papers, books, or documents in connection with hearings under this paragraph. In case of contumacy or refusal to obey a subpoena issued pursuant to this subparagraph and served upon any person, the district court of the United States for any district in which such person is found, resides, or transacts business, upon application by the United States and after notice to such person, shall have jurisdiction to issue an order requiring such person to appear and give testimony before the administrative law judge or to appear and produce documents before the administrative law judge, or both, and any failure to obey such order of the court may be punished by such court as a contempt thereof.

(7) Civil penalty action —

(A) Discharge, generally — Any person who is the owner, operator, or person in charge of any vessel, onshore facility, or offshore facility from which oil or a hazardous substance is discharged in violation of paragraph (3), shall be subject to a civil penalty in an amount up to $25,000 per day of violation or an amount up to $1,000 per barrel of oil or unit of reportable quantity of hazardous substances discharged.

(B) Failure to remove or comply — Any person described in subparagraph (A) who, without sufficient cause —

　　(i) fails to properly carry out removal of the discharge under an order of the President pursuant to subsection (c) of this section; or

　　(ii) fails to comply with an order pursuant to subsection (e)(1)(B) of this section;

shall be subject to a civil penalty in an amount up to $25,000 per day of violation or an amount up to 3 times the costs incurred by the Oil Spill Liability Trust Fund as a result of such failure.

(C) Failure to comply with regulation — Any person who fails or refuses to comply with any regulation issued under subsection (j) of this section shall be subject to a civil penalty in an amount up to $25,000 per day of violation.

(D) Gross negligence — In any case in which a violation of paragraph (3) was the result of gross negligence or willful misconduct of a person described in subparagraph (A), the person shall be subject to a civil penalty of not less than $100,000, and not more than $3,000 per barrel of oil or unit of reportable quantity of hazardous substance discharged.

(E) Jurisdiction — An action to impose a civil penalty under this paragraph may be brought in the district court of the United States for the district in which the defendant is located, resides, or is doing business, and such court shall have jurisdiction to assess such penalty.

(F) Limitation — A person is not liable for a civil penalty under this paragraph for a discharge if the person has been assessed a civil penalty under paragraph (6) for the discharge.

(8) Determination of amount — In determining the amount of a civil penalty under paragraphs (6) and (7), the Administrator, Secretary, or the court, as the case may be, shall consider the seriousness of the violation or violations, the economic benefit to the violator, if any, resulting from the violation, the degree of culpability involved, any other penalty for the same incident, any history of prior violations, the nature, extent, and degree of success of any efforts of the violator to minimize or mitigate the effects of the discharge, the economic impact of the penalty on the violator, and any other matters as justice may require.

(9) Mitigation of damage — In addition to establishing a penalty for the discharge of oil or a hazardous substance, the Administrator or the Secretary of the department in which the Coast Guard is operating may act to mitigate the damage to the public health or welfare caused by such discharge. The cost of such mitigation shall be deemed a cost incurred under subsection (c) of this section for the removal of such substance by the United States Government.

(10) Recovery of removal costs — Any costs of removal incurred in connection with a discharge excluded by subsection (a)(2)(C) of this section shall be recoverable from the owner or operator of the source of the discharge in an action brought under section 1319(b) of this title.

(11) Limitation — Civil penalties shall not be assessed under both this section and section 1319 of this Title for the same discharge.

(12) Withholding clearance — If any owner, operator, or person in charge of a vessel is liable for a civil penalty under this subsection, or if reasonable cause exists to believe that the owner, operator, or person in charge may be subject to a civil penalty under this subsection, the Secretary of the Treasury, upon the request of the Secretary of the department in which the Coast Guard is operating or the Administrator, shall with respect to such vessel refuse or revoke —

　(A) the clearance required by section 91 of the Appendix to Title 46;

　(B) a permit to proceed under section 4367 of the Revised Statutes of the United States (46 U.S.C. App. 313); and

　(C) a permit to depart required under section 1443 of Title 19;

as applicable. Clearance or a permit refused or revoked under this paragraph may be granted upon the filing of a bond or other surety satisfactory to the Secretary of the department in which the Coast Guard is operating or the Administrator.

(c) Federal removal authority

(1) General removal requirement

　(A) The President shall, in accordance with the National Contingency Plan and any appropriate Area Contingency Plan, ensure effective and immediate removal of a discharge, and mitigation or prevention of a substantial threat of a discharge, of oil or a hazardous substance —

　　(i)　into or on the navigable waters;

　　(ii)　on the adjoining shorelines to the navigable waters;

　　(iii) into or on the waters of the exclusive economic zone; or

　　(iv) that may affect natural resources belonging to, appertaining to, or under the exclusive management authority of the United States.

　(B) In carrying out this paragraph, the President may —

　　(i)　remove or arrange for the removal of a discharge, and mitigate or prevent a substantial threat of a discharge, at any time;

　　(ii)　direct or monitor all Federal, State, and private actions to remove a discharge; and

　　(iii) remove and, if necessary, destroy a vessel discharging, or threatening to discharge, by whatever means are available.

(2) Discharge posing substantial threat to public health or welfare

　(A) If a discharge, or a substantial threat of a discharge, of oil or a hazardous substance from a vessel, offshore facility, or onshore facility is of such a size or character as to be a substantial threat to the public health or welfare of the United States (including but not limited to fish, shellfish, wildlife, other natural resources, and the public and private beaches and shorelines of the United States), the President shall direct all Federal, State, and private actions to remove the discharge or to mitigate or prevent the threat of the discharge.

　(B) In carrying out this paragraph, the President may, without regard to any other provision of law governing contracting procedures or employment of personnel by the Federal Government —

　　(i)　remove or arrange for the removal of the discharge, or mitigate or prevent the substantial threat of the discharge; and

　　(ii)　remove and, if necessary, destroy a vessel discharging, or threatening to discharge, by whatever means are available.

(3) Actions in accordance with National Contingency Plan

　(A) Each Federal agency, State, owner or operator, or other person participating in efforts under this subsection shall act in accordance with the National Contingency Plan or as directed by the President.

　(B) An owner or operator participating in efforts under this subsection shall act in accordance with the National Contingency Plan and the applicable response plan required under subsection (j) of this section, or as directed by the President, except that the owner or operator may deviate from the applicable response plan if the President or the Federal On-Scene Coordinator determines that deviation from the response plan would provide for a more expeditious or effective response to the spill or mitigation of its environmental effects.

(4) Exemption from liability

　(A) A person is not liable for removal costs or damages which result from actions taken or omitted to be taken in the course of rendering care, assistance, or advice consistent with the National Contingency Plan or as otherwise directed by the President relating to a discharge or a substantial threat of a discharge of oil or a hazardous substance.

(B) Subparagraph (A) does not apply —

    (i) to a responsible party;

    (ii) to a response under the Comprehensive Environmental Response, Compensation, and Liability Act of 1980 (42 U.S.C. §9601 *et seq.*);

    (iii) with respect to personal injury or wrongful death; or

    (iv) if the person is grossly negligent or engages in willful misconduct.

(C) A responsible party is liable for any removal costs and damages that another person is relieved of under subparagraph (A).

(5) Obligation and liability of owner or operator not affected — Nothing in this subsection affects —

    (A) the obligation of an owner or operator to respond immediately to a discharge, or the threat of a discharge, of oil; or

    (B) the liability of a responsible party under the Oil Pollution Act of 1990 (33 U.S.C. §2701 *et seq.*).

(6) "Responsible party" defined — For purposes of this subsection, the term "responsible party" has the meaning given that term under section 1001 of the Oil Pollution Act of 1990 (33 U.S.C. §2701).

(d) National Contingency Plan

(1) Preparation by President — The President shall prepare and publish a National Contingency Plan for removal of oil and hazardous substances pursuant to this section.

(2) Contents — The National Contingency Plan shall provide for efficient, coordinated, and effective action to minimize damage from oil and hazardous substance discharges, including containment, dispersal, and removal of oil and hazardous substances, and shall include, but not be limited to, the following:

    (A) Assignment of duties and responsibilities among Federal departments and agencies in coordination with State and local agencies and port authorities including, but not limited to, water pollution control and conservation and trusteeship of natural resources (including conservation of fish and wildlife).

    (B) Identification, procurement, maintenance, and storage of equipment and supplies.

    (C) Establishment or designation of Coast Guard strike teams, consisting of —

        (i) personnel who shall be trained, prepared, and available to provide necessary services to carry out the National Contingency Plan;

        (ii) adequate oil and hazardous substance pollution control equipment and material; and

        (iii) a detailed oil and hazardous substance pollution and prevention plan, including measures to protect fisheries and wildlife.

    (D) A system of surveillance and notice designed to safeguard against as well as ensure earliest possible notice of discharges of oil and hazardous substances and imminent threats of such discharges to the appropriate State and Federal agencies.

    (E) Establishment of a national center to provide coordination and direction for operations in carrying out the Plan.

    (F) Procedures and techniques to be employed in identifying, containing, dispersing, and removing oil and hazardous substances.

    (G) A schedule, prepared in cooperation with the States, identifying —

        (i) dispersants, other chemicals, and other spill mitigating devices and substances, if any, that may be used in carrying out the Plan,

        (ii) the waters in which such dispersants, other chemicals, and other spill mitigating devices and substances may be used, and

        (iii) the quantities of such dispersant, other chemicals, or other spill mitigating device or substance which can be used safely in such waters,

which schedule shall provide in the case of any dispersant, chemical, spill mitigating device or substance, or waters not specifically identified in such schedule that the President, or his delegate, may, on a case-by-case basis, identify the dispersants, other chemicals, and other spill mitigating devices and substances which may be used, the waters in which they may be used, and the quantities which can be used safely in such waters.

    (H) A system whereby the State or States affected by a discharge of oil or hazardous substance may act where necessary to remove such discharge and such State or States may be reimbursed in accordance with the Oil Pollution Act of 1990 (33 U.S.C. §2701 *et seq.*), in the case of any discharge of oil from a vessel or facility, for the reasonable costs incurred for that removal, from the Oil Spill Liability Trust Fund.

    (I) Establishment of criteria and procedures to ensure immediate and effective Federal identification of, and response to, a discharge, or the threat of a discharge, that results in a substantial threat to the public health or welfare of the United States, as required under subsection (c)(2) of this section.

(J) Establishment of procedures and standards for removing a worst case discharge of oil, and for mitigating or preventing a substantial threat of such a discharge.

(K) Designation of the Federal official who shall be the Federal On-Scene Coordinator for each area for which an Area Contingency Plan is required to be prepared under subsection (j) of this section.

(L) Establishment of procedures for the coordination of activities of —

    (i) Coast Guard strike teams established under subparagraph (C);

    (ii) Federal On-Scene Coordinators designated under subparagraph (K);

    (iii) District Response Groups established under subsection (j) of this section; and

    (iv) Area Committees established under subsection (j) of this section.

(M) A fish and wildlife response plan, developed in consultation with the United States Fish and Wildlife Service, the National Oceanic and Atmospheric Administration, and other interested parties (including State fish and wildlife conservation officials), for the immediate and effective protection, rescue, and rehabilitation of, and the minimization of risk of damage to, fish and wildlife resources and their habitat that are harmed or that may be jeopardized by a discharge.

(3) Revisions and amendments — The President may, from time to time, as the President deems advisable, revise or otherwise amend the National Contingency Plan.

(4) Actions in accordance with National Contingency Plan — After publication of the National Contingency Plan, the removal of oil and hazardous substances and actions to minimize damage from oil and hazardous substance discharges shall, to the greatest extent possible, be in accordance with the National Contingency Plan.

(e) Civil enforcement

(1) Orders protecting public health — In addition to any action taken by a State or local government, when the President determines that there may be an imminent and substantial threat to the public health or welfare of the United States, including fish, shellfish, and wildlife, public and private property, shorelines, beaches, habitat, and other living and nonliving natural resources under the jurisdiction or control of the United States, because of an actual or threatened discharge of oil or a hazardous substance from a vessel or facility in violation of subsection (b) of this section, the President may —

    (A) require the Attorney General to secure any relief from any person, including the owner or operator of the vessel or facility, as may be necessary to abate such endangerment; or

    (B) after notice to the affected State, take any other action under this section, including issuing administrative orders, that may be necessary to protect the public health and welfare.

(2) Jurisdiction of district courts — The district courts of the United States shall have jurisdiction to grant any relief under this subsection that the public interest and the equities of the case may require.

(f) Liability for actual costs of removal

(1) Except where an owner or operator can prove that a discharge was caused solely by (A) an act of God, (B) an act of war, (C) negligence on the part of the United States Government, or (D) an act or omission of a third party without regard to whether any such act or omission was or was not negligent, or any combination of the foregoing clauses, such owner or operator of any vessel from which oil or a hazardous substance is discharged in violation of subsection (b)(3) of this section shall, notwithstanding any other provision of law, be liable to the United States Government for the actual costs incurred under subsection (c) of this section for the removal of such oil or substance by the United States Government in an amount not to exceed, in the case of an inland oil barge $125 per gross ton of such barge, or $125,000, whichever is greater, and in the case of any other vessel, $150 per gross ton of such vessel (or, for a vessel carrying oil or hazardous substances as cargo, $250,000), whichever is greater, except that where the United States can show that such discharge was the result of willful negligence or willful misconduct within the privity and knowledge of the owner, such owner or operator shall be liable to the United States Government for the full amount of such costs. Such costs shall constitute a maritime lien on such vessel which may be recovered in an action in rem in the district court of the United States for any district within which any vessel may be found. The United States may also bring an action against the owner or operator of such vessel in any court of competent jurisdiction to recover such costs.

(2) Except where an owner or operator of an onshore facility can prove that a discharge was caused solely by (A) an act of God, (B) an act of war, (C) negligence on the part of the United States Government, or (D) an act or omission of a third party without regard to whether any such act or omission was or was not negligent, or any combination of the foregoing clauses, such owner or operator of any such facility from which oil or a hazardous substance is discharged in violation of subsection (b)(3) of this section shall be liable to the United States Government for the actual costs incurred under subsection (c) of this section for the removal of such oil or substance by the

United States Government in an amount not to exceed $50,000,000, except that where the United States can show that such discharge was the result of willful negligence or willful misconduct within the privity and knowledge of the owner, such owner or operator shall be liable to the United States Government for the full amount of such costs. The United States may bring an action against the owner or operator of such facility in any court of competent jurisdiction to recover such costs. The Administrator is authorized, by regulation, after consultation with the Secretary of Commerce and the Small Business Administration, to establish reasonable and equitable classifications of those onshore facilities having a total fixed storage capacity of 1,000 barrels or less which he determines because of size, type, and location do not present a substantial risk of the discharge of oil or a hazardous substance in violation of subsection (b)(3) of this section, and apply with respect to such classifications differing limits of liability which may be less than the amount contained in this paragraph.

(3) Except where an owner or operator of an offshore facility can prove that a discharge was caused solely by (A) an act of God, (B) an act of war, (C) negligence on the part of the United States Government, or (D) an act or omission of a third party without regard to whether any such act or omission was or was not negligent, or any combination of the foregoing clauses, such owner or operator of any such facility from which oil or a hazardous substance is discharged in violation of subsection (b)(3) of this section shall, notwithstanding any other provision of law, be liable to the United States Government for the actual costs incurred under subsection (c) of this section for the removal of such oil or substance by the United States Government in an amount not to exceed $50,000,000, except that where the United States can show that such discharge was the result of willful negligence or willful misconduct within the privity and knowledge of the owner, such owner or operator shall be liable to the United States Government for the full amount of such costs. The United States may bring an action against the owner or operator of such a facility in any court of competent jurisdiction to recover such costs.

(4) The costs of removal of oil or a hazardous substance for which the owner or operator of a vessel or onshore or offshore facility is liable under subsection (f) of this section shall include any costs or expenses incurred by the Federal Government or any State government in the restoration or replacement of natural resources damaged or destroyed as a result of a discharge of oil or a hazardous substance in violation of subsection (b) of this section.

(5) The President, or the authorized representative of any State, shall act on behalf of the public as trustee of the natural resources to recover for the costs of replacing or restoring such resources. Sums recovered shall be used to restore, rehabilitate, or acquire the equivalent of such natural resources by the appropriate agencies of the Federal Government, or the State government.

(g) Third party liability — Where the owner or operator of a vessel (other than an inland oil barge) carrying oil or hazardous substances as cargo or an onshore or offshore facility which handles or stores oil or hazardous substances in bulk, from which oil or a hazardous substance is discharged in violation of subsection (b) of this section, alleges that such discharge was caused solely by an act or omission of a third party, such owner or operator shall pay to the United States Government the actual costs incurred under subsection (c) of this section for removal of such oil or substance and shall be entitled by subrogation to all rights of the United States Government to recover such costs from such third party under this subsection. In any case where an owner or operator of a vessel, of an onshore facility, or of an offshore facility, from which oil or a hazardous substance is discharged in violation of subsection (b)(3) of this section, proves that such discharge of oil or hazardous substance was caused solely by an act or omission of a third party, or was caused solely by such an act or omission in combination with an act of God, an act of war, or negligence on the part of the United States Government, such third party shall, notwithstanding any other provision of law, be liable to the United States Government for the actual costs incurred under subsection (c) of this section for removal of such oil or substance by the United States Government, except where such third party can prove that such discharge was caused solely by (A) an act of God, (B) an act of war, (C) negligence on the part of the United States Government, or (D) an act or omission of another party without regard to whether such act or omission was or was not negligent, or any combination of the foregoing clauses. If such third party was the owner or operator of a vessel which caused the discharge of oil or a hazardous substance in violation of subsection (b)(3) of this section, the liability of such third party under this subsection shall not exceed, in the case of an inland oil barge $125 per gross ton of such barge, or $125,000, whichever is greater, and in the case of any other vessel, $150 per gross ton of such vessel (or, for a vessel carrying oil or hazardous substances as cargo, $250,000), whichever is greater. In any other case the liability of such third party shall not exceed the limitation which would have been applicable to the owner or operator of the vessel or the onshore or offshore facility from which the discharge actually occurred if such owner or operator were liable. If the United States can show that the discharge of oil or a hazardous substance in violation of subsection (b)(3) of this section was the result of willful negligence or willful misconduct within the privity and knowledge of such third party, such third party shall be liable to the United States Government for the full amount of such removal costs. The United States may bring an action against the third party in any court of competent jurisdiction to recover such removal costs.

(h) Rights against third parties who caused or contributed to discharge — The liabilities established by this section shall in no way affect any rights which (1) the owner or operator of a vessel or of an onshore facility or an offshore facility may have against any third party whose acts may in any way have caused or contributed to such discharge, or (2) the United States Government may have against any third party whose actions may in any way have caused or contributed to the discharge of oil or hazardous substance.

(i) Recovery of removal costs — In any case where an owner or operator of a vessel or an onshore facility or an offshore facility from which oil or a hazardous substance is discharged in violation of subsection (b)(3) of this section acts to remove such oil or substance in accordance with regulations promulgated pursuant to this section, such owner or operator shall be entitled to recover the reasonable costs incurred in such removal upon establishing, in a suit which may be brought against the United States Government in the United States Court of Federal Claims, that such discharge was caused solely by (A) an act of God, (B) an act of war, (C) negligence on the part of the United States Government, or (D) an act or omission of a third party without regard to whether such act or omission was or was not negligent, or of any combination of the foregoing causes.

(j) National Response System

(1) In general — Consistent with the National Contingency Plan required by subsection (c)(2) of this section, as soon as practicable after October 18, 1972, and from time to time thereafter, the President shall issue regulations consistent with maritime safety and with marine and navigation laws (A) establishing methods and procedures for removal of discharged oil and hazardous substances, (B) establishing criteria for the development and implementation of local and regional oil and hazardous substance removal contingency plans, (C) establishing procedures, methods, and equipment and other requirements for equipment to prevent discharges of oil and hazardous substances from vessels and from onshore facilities and offshore facilities, and to contain such discharges, and (D) governing the inspection of vessels carrying cargoes of oil and hazardous substances and the inspection of such cargoes in order to reduce the likelihood of discharges of oil from vessels in violation of this section.

(2) National Response Unit — The Secretary of the department in which the Coast Guard is operating shall establish a National Response Unit at Elizabeth City, North Carolina. The Secretary, acting through the National Response Unit —

(A) shall compile and maintain a comprehensive computer list of spill removal resources, personnel, and equipment that is available worldwide and within the areas designated by the President pursuant to paragraph (4), and of information regarding previous spills, including data from universities, research institutions, State governments, and other nations, as appropriate, which shall be disseminated as appropriate to response groups and area committees, and which shall be available to Federal and State agencies and the public;

(B) shall provide technical assistance, equipment, and other resources requested by a Federal On-Scene Coordinator;

(C) shall coordinate use of private and public personnel and equipment to remove a worst case discharge, and to mitigate or prevent a substantial threat of such a discharge, from a vessel, offshore facility, or onshore facility operating in or near an area designated by the President pursuant to paragraph (4);

(D) may provide technical assistance in the preparation of Area Contingency Plans required under paragraph (4);

(E) shall administer Coast Guard strike teams established under the National Contingency Plan;

(F) shall maintain on file all Area Contingency Plans approved by the President under this subsection; and

(G) shall review each of those plans that affects its responsibilities under this subsection.

(3) Coast Guard District Response Groups

(A) The Secretary of the department in which the Coast Guard is operating shall establish in each Coast Guard district a Coast Guard District Response Group.

(B) Each Coast Guard District Response Group shall consist of —

(i) the Coast Guard personnel and equipment, including firefighting equipment, of each port within the district;

(ii) additional prepositioned equipment; and

(iii) a district response advisory staff.

(C) Coast Guard district response groups —

(i) shall provide technical assistance, equipment, and other resources when required by a Federal On-Scene Coordinator;

(ii) shall maintain all Coast Guard response equipment within its district;

(iii) may provide technical assistance in the preparation of Area Contingency Plans required under paragraph (4); and

(iv) shall review each of those plans that affect its area of geographic responsibility.

(4) Area Committees and Area Contingency Plans

(A) There is established for each area designated by the President an Area Committee comprised of members appointed by the President from qualified —

(i) personnel of Federal, State, and local agencies; and

(ii) members of federally recognized Indian tribes, where applicable.

(B) Each Area Committee, under the direction of the Federal On-Scene Coordinator for its area, shall —

(i) prepare for its area the Area Contingency Plan required under subparagraph (C);

(ii) work with State, local, and tribal officials to enhance the contingency planning of those officials and to assure preplanning of joint response efforts, including appropriate procedures for mechanical recovery, dispersal, shoreline cleanup, protection of sensitive environmental areas, and protection, rescue, and rehabilitation of fisheries and wildlife, including advance planning with respect to the closing and reopening of fishing areas following a discharge; and

(iii) work with State, local, and tribal officials to expedite decisions for the use of dispersants and other mitigating substances and devices.

(C) Each Area Committee shall prepare and submit to the President for approval an Area Contingency Plan for its area. The Area Contingency Plan shall —

(i) when implemented in conjunction with the National Contingency Plan, be adequate to remove a worst case discharge, and to mitigate or prevent a substantial threat of such a discharge, from a vessel, offshore facility, or onshore facility operating in or near the area;

(ii) describe the area covered by the plan, including the areas of special economic or environmental importance that might be damaged by a discharge;

(iii) describe in detail the responsibilities of an owner or operator and of Federal, State, and local agencies in removing a discharge, and in mitigating or preventing a substantial threat of a discharge;

(iv) list the equipment (including firefighting equipment), dispersants or other mitigating substances and devices, and personnel available to an owner or operator

and Federal, State, and local agencies, and tribal governments, to ensure an effective and immediate removal of a discharge, and to ensure mitigation or prevention of a substantial threat of a discharge;

(v) compile a list of local scientists, both inside and outside Federal Government service, with expertise in the environmental effects of spills of the types of oil typically transported in the area, who may be contacted to provide information or, where appropriate, participate in meetings of the scientific support team convened in response to a spill, and describe the procedures to be followed for obtaining an expedited decision regarding the use of dispersants;

(vi) describe in detail how the plan is integrated into other Area Contingency Plans and vessel, offshore facility, and onshore facility response plans approved under this subsection, and into operating procedures of the National Response Unit;

(vii) include a framework for advance planning and decisionmaking with respect to the closing and reopening of fishing areas following a discharge, including protocols and standards for the closing and reopening of fishing areas;

(viii) include any other information the President requires; and

(ix) be updated periodically by the Area Committee.

(D) The President shall —

(i) review and approve Area Contingency Plans under this paragraph; and

(ii) periodically review Area Contingency Plans so approved.

(5) Tank vessel, nontank vessel, and facility response plans

(A)(i) The President shall issue regulations which require an owner or operator of a tank vessel or facility described in subparagraph (C) to prepare and submit to the President a plan for responding, to the maximum extent practicable, to a worst case discharge, and to a substantial threat of such a discharge, of oil or a hazardous substance.

(ii) The President shall also issue regulations which require an owner or operator of a nontank vessel to prepare and submit to the President a plan for responding, to the maximum extent practicable, to a worst case discharge, and to a substantial threat of such a discharge, of oil.

(B) The Secretary of the Department in which the Coast Guard is operating may issue regulations which require an owner or operator of a tank vessel, a nontank vessel, or a facility described in subparagraph (C) that transfers noxious liquid substances in bulk to or from a vessel to prepare and submit to the Secretary a plan for responding, to the maximum extent practicable, to a worst case discharge, and to a substantial threat of such a discharge, of a noxious liquid substance that is not designated as a hazardous substance or regulated as oil in any other law or regulation. For purposes of this paragraph, the term "noxious liquid substance" has the same meaning when that term is used in the MARPOL Protocol described in section 1901(a)(3) of this title.

(C) The tank vessels, nontank vessels, and facilities referred to in subparagraphs (A) and (B) are the following:

(i) A tank vessel, as defined under section 2101 of Title 46.

(ii) A nontank vessel.

(iii) An offshore facility.

(iv) An onshore facility that, because of its location, could reasonably be expected to cause substantial harm to the environment by discharging into or on the navigable waters, adjoining shorelines, or the exclusive economic zone.

(D) A response plan required under this paragraph shall —

(i) be consistent with the requirements of the National Contingency Plan and Area Contingency Plans;

(ii) identify the qualified individual having full authority to implement removal actions, and require immediate communications between that individual and the appropriate Federal official and the persons providing personnel and equipment pursuant to clause (iii);

(iii) identify, and ensure by contract or other means approved by the President the availability of, private personnel and equipment necessary to remove to the maximum extent practicable a worst case discharge (including a discharge resulting from fire or explosion), and to mitigate or prevent a substantial threat of such a discharge;

(iv) describe the training, equipment testing, periodic unannounced drills, and response actions of persons on the vessel or at the facility, to be carried out under the plan to ensure the safety of the vessel or facility and to mitigate or prevent the discharge, or the substantial threat of a discharge;

(v) be updated periodically; and

(vi) be resubmitted for approval of each significant change.

(E) With respect to any response plan submitted under this paragraph for an onshore facility that, because of its location, could reasonably be expected to cause significant and substantial harm to the environment by discharging into or on the navigable waters or adjoining shorelines or the exclusive economic zone, and with respect to each response plan submitted under this paragraph for a tank vessel, nontank vessel, or offshore facility, the President shall —

(i) promptly review such response plan;

(ii) require amendments to any plan that does not meet the requirements of this paragraph;

(iii) approve any plan that meets the requirements of this paragraph;

(iv) review each plan periodically thereafter; and

(v) in the case of a plan for a nontank vessel, consider any applicable State-mandated response plan in effect on August 9, 2004 and ensure consistency to the extent practicable.

(F) A tank vessel, nontank vessel, offshore facility, or onshore facility required to prepare a response plan under this subsection may not handle, store, or transport oil unless —

(i) in the case of a tank vessel, nontank vessel, offshore facility, or onshore facility for which a response plan is reviewed by the President under subparagraph (E), the plan has been approved by the President; and

(ii) the vessel or facility is operating in compliance with the plan.

(G) Notwithstanding subparagraph (E), the President may authorize a tank vessel, nontank vessel, offshore facility, or onshore facility to operate without a response plan approved under this paragraph, until not later than 2 years after the date of the submission to the President of a plan for the tank vessel, nontank vessel, or facility, if the owner or operator certifies that the owner or operator has ensured by contract or other means approved by the President the availability of private personnel and equipment necessary to respond, to the maximum extent practicable, to a worst case discharge or a substantial threat of such a discharge.

(H) The owner or operator of a tank vessel, nontank vessel, offshore facility, or onshore facility may not claim as a defense to liability under title I of the Oil Pollution Act of 1990 [33 U.S.C.A. §§2701 et seq.] that the owner or operator was acting in accordance with an approved response plan.

(I) The Secretary shall maintain, in the Vessel Identification System established under chapter 125 of Title 46, the dates of approval and review of a response plan under this paragraph for each tank vessel and nontank vessel that is a vessel of the United States.

(6) Equipment requirements and inspection

The President may require —

(A) periodic inspection of containment booms, skimmers, vessels, and other major equipment used to remove discharges; and

(B) vessels operating on navigable waters and carrying oil or a hazardous substance in bulk as cargo, and nontank vessels carrying oil of any kind as fuel for main propulsion, to carry appropriate removal equipment that employs the best technology economically feasible and that is compatible with the safe operation of the vessel.

(7) Area drills — The President shall periodically conduct drills of removal capability, without prior notice, in areas for which Area Contingency Plans are required under this subsection and under relevant tank vessel, nontank vessel, and facility response plans. The drills may include participation by Federal, State, and local agencies, the owners and operators of vessels and facilities in the area, and private industry. The President may publish annual reports on these drills, including assessments of the effectiveness of the plans and a list of amendments made to improve plans.

(8) United States Government not liable

The United States Government is not liable for any damages arising from its actions or omissions relating to any response plan required by this section.

(k) Repealed. Pub. L. 101-380, Title I, Sec. 2002(b)(2), Aug. 18, 1990, 104 Stat. 507

(*l*) **Administration** — The President is authorized to delegate the administration of this section to the heads of those Federal departments, agencies, and instrumentalities which he determines to be appropriate. Each such department, agency, and instrumentality, in order to avoid duplication of effort, shall, whenever appropriate, utilize the personnel, services, and facilities of other Federal departments, agencies, and instrumentalities.

(m) Administrative provisions

(1) For vessels — Anyone authorized by the President to enforce the provisions of this section with respect to any vessel may, except as to public vessels —

(A) board and inspect any vessel upon the navigable waters of the United States or the waters of the contiguous zone;

(B) with or without a warrant, arrest any person who in the presence or view of the authorized person violates the provisions of this section or any regulation issued thereunder, and

(C) execute any warrant or other process issued by an officer or court of competent jurisdiction.

(2) For facilities

(A) Recordkeeping — Whenever required to carry out the purposes of this section, the Administrator or the Secretary of the Department in which the Coast Guard is operating shall require the owner or operator of a facility to which this section applies to establish and maintain such records, make such reports, install, use, and maintain such monitoring equipment and methods, and provide such other information as the Administrator or Secretary, as the case may be, may require to carry out the objectives of this section.

(B) Entry and inspection — Whenever required to carry out the purposes of this section, the Administrator or the Secretary of the Department in which the Coast Guard is operating or an authorized representative of the Administrator or Secretary, upon presentation of appropriate credentials, may —

(i) enter and inspect any facility to which this section applies, including any facility at which any records are required to be maintained under subparagraph (A); and

(ii) at reasonable times, have access to and copy any records, take samples, and inspect any monitoring equipment or methods required under subparagraph (A).

(C) Arrests and execution of warrants — Anyone authorized by the Administrator or the Secretary of the department in which the Coast Guard is operating to enforce the provisions of this section with respect to any facility may —

(i) with or without a warrant, arrest any person who violates the provisions of this section or any regulation issued thereunder in the presence or view of the person so authorized; and

(ii) execute any warrant or process issued by an officer or court of competent jurisdiction.

(D) Public access — Any records, reports, or information obtained under this paragraph shall be subject to the same public access and disclosure requirements which are applicable to records, reports, and information obtained pursuant to section 1318 of this title.

(n) Jurisdiction — The several district courts of the United States are invested with jurisdiction for any actions, other than actions pursuant to subsection (i) (1) of this section, arising under this section. In the case of Guam and the Trust Territory of the Pacific Islands, such actions may be brought in the district court of Guam, and in the case of the Virgin Islands such actions may be brought in the district court of the Virgin Islands. In the case of American Samoa and the Trust Territory of the Pacific Islands, such actions may be brought in the District Court of the United States for the District of Hawaii and such court shall have jurisdiction of such actions. In the case of the Canal Zone, such actions may be brought in the United States District Court for the District of the Canal Zone.

(o) Obligation for damages unaffected; local authority not preempted; existing Federal authority not modified or affected

(1) Nothing in this section shall affect or modify in any way the obligations of any owner or operator of any vessel, or of any owner or operator of any onshore facility or offshore facility to any person or agency under any provision of law for damages to any publicly owned or privately owned property resulting from a discharge of any oil or hazardous substance or from the removal of any such oil or hazardous substance.

(2) Nothing in this section shall be construed as preempting any State or political subdivision thereof from imposing any requirement or liability with respect to the discharge of oil or hazardous substance into any waters within such State, or with respect to any removal activities related to such discharge.

(3) Nothing in this section shall be construed as affecting or modifying any other existing authority of any Federal department, agency, or instrumentality, relative to onshore or offshore facilities under this chapter or any other provision of law, or to affect any State or local law not in conflict with this section.

(p) Repealed. Pub. L. 101-380, Title II, Sec. 2002(b)(4), Aug. 18, 1990, 104 Stat. 507

(q) Establishment of maximum limit of liability with respect to onshore or offshore facilities — The President is authorized to establish, with respect to any class or category of onshore or offshore facilities, a maximum limit of liability under subsections (f)(2) and (3) of this section of less than $50,000,000, but not less than $8,000,000.

(r) Liability limitations not to limit liability under other legislation — Nothing in this section shall be construed to impose, or authorize the imposition of, any limitation on liability under the Outer Continental Shelf Lands Act (43 U.S.C. §1331 *et seq.*) or the Deepwater Port Act of 1974 (33 U.S.C. §1501 *et seq.*).

(s) Oil Spill Liability Trust Fund — The Oil Spill Liability Trust Fund established under section 9509 of Title 26 shall be available to carry out subsections (b), (c), (d), (j), and (*l*) of this section as those subsections apply to discharges, and substantial threats of discharges, of oil. Any amounts received by the United States under this section shall be deposited in the Oil Spill Liability Trust Fund.

(t) Gulf Coast restoration and recovery —

(1) State allocation and expenditures —

(A) In general — Of the total amounts made available in any fiscal year from the Trust Fund, 35 percent shall be available, in accordance with the requirements of this sec-

tion, to the Gulf Coast States in equal shares for expenditure for ecological and economic restoration of the Gulf Coast region in accordance with this subsection.

(B) Use of funds —

(i) Eligible activities in the Gulf Coast region — Subject to clause (iii), amounts provided to the Gulf Coast States under this subsection may only be used to carry out 1 or more of the following activities in the Gulf Coast region:

(I) Restoration and protection of the natural resources, ecosystems, fisheries, marine and wildlife habitats, beaches, and coastal wetlands of the Gulf Coast region.

(II) Mitigation of damage to fish, wildlife, and natural resources.

(III) Implementation of a federally approved marine, coastal, or comprehensive conservation management plan, including fisheries monitoring.

(IV) Workforce development and job creation.

(V) Improvements to or on State parks located in coastal areas affected by the Deepwater Horizon oil spill.

(VI) Infrastructure projects benefitting the economy or ecological resources, including port infrastructure.

(VII) Coastal flood protection and related infrastructure.

(VIII) Planning assistance.

(IX) Administrative costs of complying with this subsection.

(ii) Activities to promote tourism and seafood in the Gulf Coast region — Amounts provided to the Gulf Coast States under this subsection may be used to carry out 1 or more of the following activities:

(I) Promotion of tourism in the Gulf Coast Region, including recreational fishing.

(II) Promotion of the consumption of seafood harvested from the Gulf Coast Region.

(iii) Limitation —

(I) **In general** — Of the amounts received by a Gulf Coast State under this subsection, not more than 3 percent may be used for administrative costs eligible under clause (i)(IX).

(II) **Claims for compensation** — Activities funded under this subsection may not be included in any claim for compensation paid out by the Oil Spill Liability Trust Fund after the date of enactment of this subsection.

(C) Coastal political subdivisions —

(i) Distribution — In the case of a State where the coastal zone includes the entire State —

    (I) 75 percent of funding shall be provided directly to the 8 disproportionately affected counties impacted by the Deepwater Horizon oil spill; and

    (II) 25 percent shall be provided directly to nondisproportionately impacted counties within the State.

(ii) Nondisproportionately impacted counties — The total amounts made available to coastal political subdivisions in the State of Florida under clause (i)(II) shall be distributed according to the following weighted formula:

    (I) 34 percent based on the weighted average of the population of the county.

    (II) 33 percent based on the weighted average of the county per capita sales tax collections estimated for fiscal year 2012.

    (III) 33 percent based on the inverse proportion of the weighted average distance from the Deepwater Horizon oil rig to each of the nearest and farthest points of the shoreline.

(D) Louisiana —

(i) In general — Of the total amounts made available to the State of Louisiana under this paragraph:

    (I) 70 percent shall be provided directly to the State in accordance with this subsection.

    (II) 30 percent shall be provided directly to parishes in the coastal zone (as defined in section 304 of the Coastal Zone Management Act of 1972 (16 U.S.C. 1453)) of the State of Louisiana according to the following weighted formula:

        (aa) 40 percent based on the weighted average of miles of the parish shoreline oiled.

        (bb) 40 percent based on the weighted average of the population of the parish.

        (cc) 20 percent based on the weighted average of the land mass of the parish.

(ii) Conditions —

    (I) Land use plan — As a condition of receiving amounts allocated under this paragraph, the chief executive of the eligible parish shall certify to the Governor of the State that the parish has completed a comprehensive land use plan.

    (II) Other conditions — A coastal political subdivision receiving funding under this paragraph shall meet all of the conditions in subparagraph (E).

(E) Conditions — As a condition of receiving amounts from the Trust Fund, a Gulf Coast State, including the entities described in subparagraph (F), or a coastal political subdivision shall —

    (i) agree to meet such conditions, including audit requirements, as the Secretary of the Treasury determines necessary to ensure that amounts disbursed from the Trust Fund will be used in accordance with this subsection;

    (ii) certify in such form and in such manner as the Secretary of the Treasury determines necessary that the project or program for which the Gulf Coast State or coastal political subdivision is requesting amounts —

        (I) is designed to restore and protect the natural resources, ecosystems, fisheries, marine and wildlife habitats, beaches, coastal wetlands, or economy of the Gulf Coast;

        (II) carries out 1 or more of the activities described in clauses (i) and (ii) of subparagraph (B);

        (III) was selected based on meaningful input from the public, including broad-based participation from individuals, businesses, and nonprofit organizations; and

        (IV) in the case of a natural resource protection or restoration project, is based on the best available science;

    (iii) certify that the project or program and the awarding of a contract for the expenditure of amounts received under this paragraph are consistent with the standard procurement rules and regulations governing a comparable project or program in that State, including all applicable competitive bidding and audit requirements; and

    (iv) develop and submit a multiyear implementation plan for the use of such amounts, which may include milestones, projected completion of each activity, and a mechanism to evaluate the success of each activity in helping to restore and protect the Gulf Coast region impacted by the Deepwater Horizon oil spill.

(F) Approval by State entity, task force, or agency — The following Gulf Coast State entities, task forces, or agencies shall carry out the duties of a Gulf Coast State pursuant to this paragraph:

(i) Alabama —

(I) In general — In the State of Alabama, the Alabama Gulf Coast Recovery Council, which shall be comprised of only the following:

(aa) The Governor of Alabama, who shall also serve as Chairperson and preside over the meetings of the Alabama Gulf Coast Recovery Council.

(bb) The Director of the Alabama State Port Authority, who shall also serve as Vice Chairperson and preside over the meetings of the Alabama Gulf Coast Recovery Council in the absence of the Chairperson.

(cc) The Chairman of the Baldwin County Commission.

(dd) The President of the Mobile County Commission.

(ee) The Mayor of the city of Bayou La Batre.

(ff) The Mayor of the town of Dauphin Island.

(gg) The Mayor of the city of Fairhope.

(hh) The Mayor of the city of Gulf Shores.

(ii) The Mayor of the city of Mobile.

(jj) The Mayor of the city of Orange Beach.

(II) Vote — Each member of the Alabama Gulf Coast Recovery Council shall be entitled to 1 vote.

(III) Majority vote — All decisions of the Alabama Gulf Coast Recovery Council shall be made by majority vote.

(IV) Limitation on administrative expenses — Administrative duties for the Alabama Gulf Coast Recovery Council may only be performed by public officials and employees that are subject to the ethics laws of the State of Alabama.

(ii) Louisiana — In the State of Louisiana, the Coastal Protection and Restoration Authority of Louisiana.

(iii) Mississippi — In the State of Mississippi, the Mississippi Department of Environmental Quality.

(iv) Texas — In the State of Texas, the Office of the Governor or an appointee of the Office of the Governor.

(G) Compliance with eligible activities — If the Secretary of the Treasury determines that an expenditure by a Gulf Coast State or coastal political subdivision of amounts made available under this subsection does not meet one of the activities described in clauses (i) and (ii) of subparagraph (B), the Secretary shall make no additional amounts from the Trust Fund available to that Gulf Coast State or coastal political subdivision until such time as an amount equal to the amount expended for the unauthorized use —

(i) has been deposited by the Gulf Coast State or coastal political subdivision in the Trust Fund; or

(ii) has been authorized by the Secretary of the Treasury for expenditure by the Gulf Coast State or coastal political subdivision for a project or program that meets the requirements of this subsection.

(H) Compliance with conditions — If the Secretary of the Treasury determines that a Gulf Coast State or coastal political subdivision does not meet the requirements of this paragraph, including the conditions of subparagraph (E), where applicable, the Secretary of the Treasury shall make no amounts from the Trust Fund available to that Gulf Coast State or coastal political subdivision until all conditions of this paragraph are met.

(I) Public input — In meeting any condition of this paragraph, a Gulf Coast State may use an appropriate procedure for public consultation in that Gulf Coast State, including consulting with one or more established task forces or other entities, to develop recommendations for proposed projects and programs that would restore and protect the natural resources, ecosystems, fisheries, marine and wildlife habitats, beaches, coastal wetlands, and economy of the Gulf Coast.

(J) Previously approved projects and programs — A Gulf Coast State or coastal political subdivision shall be considered to have met the conditions of subparagraph (E) for a specific project or program if, before the date of enactment of the Resources and Ecosystems Sustainability, Tourist Opportunities, and Revived Economies of the Gulf Coast States Act of 2012 —

(i) the Gulf Coast State or coastal political subdivision has established conditions for carrying out projects and programs that are substantively the same as the conditions described in subparagraph (E); and

(ii) the applicable project or program carries out 1 or more of the activities described in clauses (i) and (ii) of subparagraph (B).

(K) Local preference — In awarding contracts to carry out a project or program under this paragraph, a Gulf Coast State or coastal political subdivision may give a preference to individuals and companies that reside in, are headquartered in, or are principally engaged in business in the State of project execution.

(L) Unused funds — Funds allocated to a State or coastal political subdivision under this paragraph shall remain in the Trust Fund until such time as the State or coastal political subdivision develops and submits a plan identifying uses for those funds in accordance with subparagraph (E)(iv).

(M) Judicial review — If the Secretary of the Treasury determines that a Gulf Coast State or coastal political subdivision does not meet the requirements of this paragraph, including the conditions of subparagraph (E), the Gulf Coast State or coastal political subdivision may obtain expedited judicial review within 90 days after that decision in a district court of the United States, of appropriate jurisdiction and venue, that is located within the State seeking the review.

(N) Cost-sharing —

　(i) In general — A Gulf Coast State or coastal political subdivision may use, in whole or in part, amounts made available under this paragraph to that Gulf Coast State or coastal political subdivision to satisfy the non-Federal share of the cost of any project or program authorized by Federal law that is an eligible activity described in clauses (i) and (ii) of subparagraph (B).

　(ii) Effect on other funds — The use of funds made available from the Trust Fund to satisfy the non-Federal share of the cost of a project or program that meets the requirements of clause (i) shall not affect the priority in which other Federal funds are allocated or awarded.

(2) Council establishment and allocation —

　(A) In general — Of the total amount made available in any fiscal year from the Trust Fund, 30 percent shall be disbursed to the Council to carry out the Comprehensive Plan.

　(B) Council expenditures —

　　(i) In general — In accordance with this paragraph, the Council shall expend funds made available from the Trust Fund to undertake projects and programs, using the best available science, that would restore and protect the natural resources, ecosystems, fisheries, marine and wildlife habitats, beaches, coastal wetlands, and economy of the Gulf Coast.

　　(ii) Allocation and expenditure procedures — The Secretary of the Treasury shall develop such conditions, including audit requirements, as the Secretary of the Treasury determines necessary to ensure that amounts disbursed from the Trust Fund to the Council to implement the Comprehensive Plan will be used in accordance with this paragraph.

　　(iii) Administrative expenses — Of the amounts received by the Council under this paragraph, not more than 3 percent may be used for administrative expenses, including staff.

(C) Gulf Coast Ecosystem Restoration Council —

　(i) Establishment — There is established as an independent entity in the Federal Government a council to be known as the "Gulf Coast Ecosystem Restoration Council".

　(ii) Membership — The Council shall consist of the following members, or in the case of a Federal agency, a designee at the level of the Assistant Secretary or the equivalent:

　　(I) The Secretary of the Interior.

　　(II) The Secretary of the Army.

　　(III) The Secretary of Commerce.

　　(IV) The Administrator of the Environmental Protection Agency.

　　(V) The Secretary of Agriculture.

　　(VI) The head of the department in which the Coast Guard is operating.

　　(VII) The Governor of the State of Alabama.

　　(VIII) The Governor of the State of Florida.

　　(IX) The Governor of the State of Louisiana.

　　(X) The Governor of the State of Mississippi.

　　(XI) The Governor of the State of Texas.

　(iii) Alternate — A Governor appointed to the Council by the President may designate an alternate to represent the Governor on the Council and vote on behalf of the Governor.

　(iv) Chairperson — From among the Federal agency members of the Council, the representatives of States on the Council shall select, and the President shall appoint, 1 Federal member to serve as Chairperson of the Council.

　(v) Presidential appointment — All Council members shall be appointed by the President.

　(vi) Council actions —

　　(I) In general — The following actions by the Council shall require the affirmative vote of the Chairperson and a majority of the State members to be effective:

(aa) Approval of a Comprehensive Plan and future revisions to a Comprehensive Plan.

(bb) Approval of State plans pursuant to paragraph (3)(B)(iv).

(cc) Approval of reports to Congress pursuant to clause (vii)(VII).

(dd) Approval of transfers pursuant to subparagraph (E)(ii)(I).

(ee) Other significant actions determined by the Council.

(II) Quorum — A majority of State members shall be required to be present for the Council to take any significant action.

(III) Affirmative vote requirement considered met — For approval of State plans pursuant to paragraph (3)(B)(iv), the certification by a State member of the Council that the plan satisfies all requirements of clauses (i) and (ii) of paragraph (3)(B), when joined by an affirmative vote of the Federal Chairperson of the Council, shall be considered to satisfy the requirements for affirmative votes under subclause (I).

(IV) Public transparency — Appropriate actions of the Council, including significant actions and associated deliberations, shall be made available to the public via electronic means prior to any vote.

(vii) Duties of Council — The Council shall —

(I) develop the Comprehensive Plan and future revisions to the Comprehensive Plan;

(II) identify as soon as practicable the projects that —

(aa) have been authorized prior to the date of enactment of this subsection but not yet commenced; and

(bb) if implemented quickly, would restore and protect the natural resources, ecosystems, fisheries, marine and wildlife habitats, beaches, barrier islands, dunes, and coastal wetlands of the Gulf Coast region;

(III) establish such other 1 or more advisory committees as may be necessary to assist the Council, including a scientific advisory committee and a committee to advise the Council on public policy issues;

(IV) collect and consider scientific and other research associated with restoration of the Gulf Coast ecosystem, including research, observation, and monitoring carried out pursuant to sections 1604 and 1605 of the Resources and Ecosystems Sustainability, Tourist Opportunities, and Revived Economies of the Gulf Coast States Act of 2012;

(V) develop standard terms to include in contracts for projects and programs awarded pursuant to the Comprehensive Plan that provide a preference to individuals and companies that reside in, are headquartered in, or are principally engaged in business in a Gulf Coast State;

(VI) prepare an integrated financial plan and recommendations for coordinated budget requests for the amounts proposed to be expended by the Federal agencies represented on the Council for projects and programs in the Gulf Coast States; and

(VII) submit to Congress an annual report that —

(aa) summarizes the policies, strategies, plans, and activities for addressing the restoration and protection of the Gulf Coast region;

(bb) describes the projects and programs being implemented to restore and protect the Gulf Coast region, including —

(AA) a list of each project and program;

(BB) an identification of the funding provided to projects and programs identified in subitem (AA);

(CC) an identification of each recipient for funding identified in subitem (BB); and

(DD) a description of the length of time and funding needed to complete the objectives of each project and program identified in subitem (AA);

(cc) makes such recommendations to Congress for modifications of existing laws as the Council determines necessary to implement the Comprehensive Plan;

(dd) reports on the progress on implementation of each project or program —

(AA) after 3 years of ongoing activity of the project or program, if applicable; and

(BB) on completion of the project or program;

(ee) includes the information required to be submitted under section 1605(c)(4) of the Resources and Ecosystems Sustainability, Tourist Opportunities, and Revived Economies of the Gulf Coast States Act of 2012; and

(ff) submits the reports required under item (dd) to —

(AA) the Committee on Science, Space, and Technology, the Committee on Natural Resources, the Committee on Transportation and Infrastructure, and the Committee on Appropriations of the House of Representatives; and

(BB) the Committee on Environment and Public Works, the Committee on Commerce, Science, and Transportation, the Committee on Energy and Natural Resources, and the Committee on Appropriations of the Senate.

(viii) Application of Federal Advisory Committee Act — The Council, or any other advisory committee established under this subparagraph, shall not be considered an advisory committee under the Federal Advisory Committee Act (5 U.S.C. App.).

(ix) Sunset — The authority for the Council, and any other advisory committee established under this subparagraph, shall terminate on the date all funds in the Trust Fund have been expended.

(D) Comprehensive plan —

(i) Proposed plan —

(I) In general — Not later than 180 days after the date of enactment of the Resources and Ecosystems Sustainability, Tourist Opportunities, and Revived Economies of the Gulf Coast States Act of 2012, the Chairperson, on behalf of the Council and after appropriate public input, review, and comment, shall publish a proposed plan to restore and protect the natural resources, ecosystems, fisheries, marine and wildlife habitats, beaches, and coastal wetlands of the Gulf Coast region.

(II) Inclusions — The proposed plan described in subclause (I) shall include and incorporate the findings and information prepared by the President's Gulf Coast Restoration Task Force.

(ii) Publication —

(I) Initial plan — Not later than 1 year after the date of enactment of the Resources and Ecosystems Sustainability, Tourist Opportunities, and Revived Economies of the Gulf Coast States Act of 2012 and after notice and opportunity for public comment, the Chairperson, on behalf of the Council and after approval by the Council, shall publish in the Federal Register the initial Comprehensive Plan to restore and protect the natural resources, ecosystems, fisheries, marine and wildlife habitats, beaches, and coastal wetlands of the Gulf Coast region.

(II) Cooperation with Gulf Coast Restoration Task Force — The Council shall develop the initial Comprehensive Plan in close coordination with the President's Gulf Coast Restoration Task Force.

(III) Considerations — In developing the initial Comprehensive Plan and subsequent updates, the Council shall consider all relevant findings, reports, or research prepared or funded under section 1604 or 1605 of the Resources and Ecosystems Sustainability, Tourist Opportunities, and Revived Economies of the Gulf Coast States Act of 2012.

(IV) Contents — The initial Comprehensive Plan shall include —

(aa) such provisions as are necessary to fully incorporate in the Comprehensive Plan the strategy, projects, and programs recommended by the President's Gulf Coast Restoration Task Force;

(bb) a list of any project or program authorized prior to the date of enactment of this subsection but not yet commenced, the completion of which would further the purposes and goals of this subsection and of the Resources and Ecosystems Sustainability, Tourist Opportunities, and Revived Economies of the Gulf Coast States Act of 2012;

(cc) a description of the manner in which amounts from the Trust Fund projected to be made available to the Council for the succeeding 10 years will be allocated; and

(dd) subject to available funding in accordance with clause (iii), a prioritized list of specific projects and programs to be funded and carried out during the 3-year period immediately following the date of publication of the initial Comprehensive Plan, including a table that illustrates the distribution of projects and programs by the Gulf Coast State.

(V) Plan updates — The Council shall update —

(aa) the Comprehensive Plan every 5 years in a manner comparable to the manner established in this subparagraph for each 5-year period for which amounts are expected to be made available to the Gulf Coast States from the Trust Fund; and

(bb) the 3-year list of projects and programs described in subclause (IV)(dd) annually.

(iii) Restoration priorities — Except for projects and programs described in clause (ii)(IV)(bb), in selecting projects and programs to include on the 3-year list described in clause (ii)(IV)(dd), based on the best available science, the Council shall give highest priority to projects that address 1 or more of the following criteria:

(I) Projects that are projected to make the greatest contribution to restoring and protecting the natural resources, ecosystems, fisheries, marine and wildlife habitats, beaches, and coastal wetlands of the Gulf Coast region, without regard to geographic location within the Gulf Coast region.

(II) Large-scale projects and programs that are projected to substantially contribute to restoring and protecting the natural resources, ecosystems, fisheries, marine and wildlife habitats, beaches, and coastal wetlands of the Gulf Coast ecosystem.

(III) Projects contained in existing Gulf Coast State comprehensive plans for the restoration and protection of natural resources, ecosystems, fisheries, marine and wildlife habitats, beaches, and coastal wetlands of the Gulf Coast region.

(IV) Projects that restore long-term resiliency of the natural resources, ecosystems, fisheries, marine and wildlife habitats, beaches, and coastal wetlands most impacted by the Deepwater Horizon oil spill.

(E) Implementation —

(i) In general — The Council, acting through the Federal agencies represented on the Council and Gulf Coast States, shall expend funds made available from the Trust Fund to carry out projects and programs adopted in the Comprehensive Plan.

(ii) Administrative responsibility

(I) In general — Primary authority and responsibility for each project and program included in the Comprehensive Plan shall be assigned by the Council to a Gulf Coast State represented on the Council or a Federal agency.

(II) Transfer of amounts — Amounts necessary to carry out each project or program included in the Comprehensive Plan shall be transferred by the Secretary of the Treasury from the Trust Fund to that Federal agency or Gulf Coast State as the project or program is implemented, subject to such conditions as the Secretary of the Treasury, in consultation with the Secretary of the Interior and the Secretary of Commerce, established pursuant to section 1602 of the Resources and Ecosystems Sustainability, Tourist Opportunities, and Revived Economies of the Gulf Coast States Act of 2012.

(III) Limitation on transfers —

(aa) Grants to nongovernmental entities — In the case of funds transferred to a Federal or State agency under subclause (II), the agency shall not make 1 or more grants or cooperative agreements to a nongovernmental entity if the total amount provided to the entity would equal or exceed 10 percent of the total amount provided to the agency for that particular project or program, unless the 1 or more grants have been reported in accordance with item (bb).

(bb) Reporting of grantees — At least 30 days prior to making a grant or entering into a cooperative agreement described in item (aa), the name of each grantee, including the amount and purpose of each grant or cooperative agreement, shall be published in the Federal Register and delivered to the congressional committees listed in subparagraph (C)(vii)(VII)(ff).

(cc) Annual reporting of grantees — Annually, the name of each grantee, including the amount and purposes of each grant or cooperative agreement, shall be published in the Federal Register and delivered to Congress as part of the report submitted pursuant to subparagraph (C)(vii)(VII).

(IV) Project and program limitation — The Council, a Federal agency, or a State may not carry out a project or program funded under this paragraph outside of the Gulf Coast region.

(F) Coordination — The Council and the Federal members of the Council may develop memoranda of understanding establishing integrated funding and implementation plans among the member agencies and authorities.

(3) Oil spill restoration impact allocation —

(A) In general —

(i) Disbursement — Of the total amount made available from the Trust Fund, 30 percent shall be disbursed pursuant to the formula in clause (ii) to the Gulf Coast States on the approval of the plan described in subparagraph (B)(i).

(ii) Formula — Subject to subparagraph (B), for each Gulf Coast State, the amount disbursed under this paragraph shall be based on a formula established by the Council by regulation that is based on a weighted average of the following criteria:

(I) 40 percent based on the proportionate number of miles of shoreline in each Gulf Coast State that experienced oiling on or before April 10, 2011, compared to the total number of miles of shoreline that experienced oiling as a result of the Deepwater Horizon oil spill.

(II) 40 percent based on the inverse proportion of the average distance from the mobile offshore drilling unit Deepwater Horizon at the time of the explosion to the nearest and farthest point of the shoreline that experienced oiling of each Gulf Coast State.

(III) 20 percent based on the average population in the 2010 decennial census of coastal counties bordering the Gulf of Mexico within each Gulf Coast State.

(iii) Minimum allocation — The amount disbursed to a Gulf Coast State for each fiscal year under clause (ii) shall be at least 5 percent of the total amounts made available under this paragraph.

(B) Disbursement of funds

(i) In general — The Council shall disburse amounts to the respective Gulf Coast States in accordance with the formula developed under subparagraph (A)

for projects, programs, and activities that will improve the ecosystems or economy of the Gulf Coast region, subject to the condition that each Gulf Coast State submits a plan for the expenditure of amounts disbursed under this paragraph that meets the following criteria:

(I) All projects, programs, and activities included in the plan are eligible activities pursuant to clauses (i) and (ii) of paragraph (1)(B).

(II) The projects, programs, and activities included in the plan contribute to the overall economic and ecological recovery of the Gulf Coast.

(III) The plan takes into consideration the Comprehensive Plan and is consistent with the goals and objectives of the Plan, as described in paragraph (2)(B)(i).

(ii) Funding —

(I) In general — Except as provided in subclause (II), the plan described in clause (i) may use not more than 25 percent of the funding made available for infrastructure projects eligible under subclauses (VI) and (VII) of paragraph (1)(B)(i).

(II) Exception — The plan described in clause (i) may propose to use more than 25 percent of the funding made available for infrastructure projects eligible under subclauses (VI) and (VII) of paragraph (1)(B)(i) if the plan certifies that —

(aa) ecosystem restoration needs in the State will be addressed by the projects in the proposed plan; and

(bb) additional investment in infrastructure is required to mitigate the impacts of the Deepwater Horizon Oil Spill to the ecosystem or economy.

(iii) Development — The plan described in clause (i) shall be developed by —

(I) in the State of Alabama, the Alabama Gulf Coast Recovery Council established under paragraph (1)(F)(i);

(II) in the State of Florida, a consortia of local political subdivisions that includes at a minimum 1 representative of each affected county;

(III) in the State of Louisiana, the Coastal Protection and Restoration Authority of Louisiana;

(IV) in the State of Mississippi, the Office of the Governor or an appointee of the Office of the Governor; and

(V) in the State of Texas, the Office of the Governor or an appointee of the Office of the Governor.

(iv) **Approval** — Not later than 60 days after the date on which a plan is submitted under clause (i), the Council shall approve or disapprove the plan based on the conditions of clause (i).

(C) **Disapproval** — If the Council disapproves a plan pursuant to subparagraph (B)(iv), the Council shall —

(i) provide the reasons for disapproval in writing; and

(ii) consult with the State to address any identified deficiencies with the State plan.

(D) **Failure to submit adequate plan** — If a State fails to submit an adequate plan under this paragraph, any funds made available under this paragraph shall remain in the Trust Fund until such date as a plan is submitted and approved pursuant to this paragraph.

(E) **Judicial review** — If the Council fails to approve or take action within 60 days on a plan, as described in subparagraph (B)(iv), the State may obtain expedited judicial review within 90 days of that decision in a district court of the United States, of appropriate jurisdiction and venue, that is located within the State seeking the review.

(F) **Cost-sharing** —

(i) **In general** — A Gulf Coast State or coastal political subdivision may use, in whole or in part, amounts made available to that Gulf Coast State or coastal political subdivision under this paragraph to satisfy the non-Federal share of any project or program that —

(I) is authorized by other Federal law; and

(II) is an eligible activity described in clause (i) or (ii) of paragraph (1)(B).

(ii) **Effect on other funds** — The use of funds made available from the Trust Fund under this paragraph to satisfy the non-Federal share of the cost of a project or program described in clause (i) shall not affect the priority in which other Federal funds are allocated or awarded.

(4) **Authorization of interest transfers** — Of the total amount made available for any fiscal year from the Trust Fund that is equal to the interest earned by the Trust Fund and proceeds from investments made by the Trust Fund in the preceding fiscal year —

(A) 50 percent shall be divided equally between —

(i) the Gulf Coast Ecosystem Restoration Science, Observation, Monitoring, and Technology program authorized in section 1604 of the Resources and Ecosystems Sustainability, Tourist Opportunities, and Revived Economies of the Gulf Coast States Act of 2012; and

(ii) the centers of excellence research grants authorized in section 1605 of that Act; and

(B) 50 percent shall be made available to the Gulf Coast Ecosystem Restoration Council to carry out the Comprehensive Plan pursuant to paragraph (2).

§1321a. Prevention of small oil spills [CWA §311a]

(a) **Prevention and education program** — The Under Secretary of Commerce for Oceans and Atmosphere, in consultation with the Secretary of the Department in which the Coast Guard is operating and other appropriate agencies, shall establish an oil spill prevention and education program for small vessels. The program shall provide for assessment, outreach, and training and voluntary compliance activities to prevent and improve the effective response to oil spills from vessels and facilities not required to prepare a vessel response plan under the Federal Water Pollution Control Act (33 U.S.C. 1251 *et seq.*), including recreational vessels, commercial fishing vessels, marinas, and aquaculture facilities. The Under Secretary may provide grants to sea grant colleges and institutes designated under section 1126 of this title and to State agencies, tribal governments, and other appropriate entities to carry out —

(1) regional assessments to quantify the source, incidence and volume of small oil spills, focusing initially on regions in the country where, in the past 10 years, the incidence of such spills is estimated to be the highest;

(2) voluntary, incentive-based clean marina programs that encourage marina operators, recreational boaters, and small commercial vessel operators to engage in environmentally sound operating and maintenance procedures and best management practices to prevent or reduce pollution from oil spills and other sources;

(3) cooperative oil spill prevention education programs that promote public understanding of the impacts of spilled oil and provide useful information and techniques to minimize pollution, including methods to remove oil and reduce oil contamination of bilge water, prevent accidental spills during maintenance and refueling and properly cleanup and dispose of oil and hazardous substances; and

(4) support for programs, including outreach and education to address derelict vessels and the threat of such vessels sinking and discharging oil and other hazardous substances, including outreach and education to involve efforts to the owners of such vessels.

(b) Authorization of appropriations — They are authorized to be appropriated to the Under Secretary of Commerce for Oceans and Atmosphere to carry out this section, $10,000,000 for each of fiscal years 2010 through 2014.

§1321b. Improved coordination with tribal governments
[CWA §311b]

(a) In general — Within 6 months after October 15, 2010, the Secretary of the Department in which the Coast Guard is operating shall complete the development of a tribal consultation policy, which recognizes and protects to the maximum extent practicable tribal treaty rights and trust assets in order to improve the Coast Guard's consultation and coordination with the tribal governments of federally recognized Indian tribes with respect to oil spill prevention, preparedness, response and natural resource damage assessment.

(b) Inclusion of tribal government — The Secretary of the Department in which the Coast Guard is operating shall ensure that, as soon as practicable after identifying an oil spill that is likely to have a significant impact on natural or cultural resources owned or directly utilized by a federally recognized Indian tribe, the Coast Guard will —

(1) ensure that representatives of the tribal government of the affected tribes are included as part of the incident command system established by the Coast Guard to respond to the spill;

(2) share information about the oil spill with the tribal government of the affected tribe; and

(3) to the extent practicable, involve tribal governments in deciding how to respond to the spill.

(c) Cooperative arrangements — The Coast Guard may enter into memoranda of agreement and associated protocols with Indian tribal governments in order to establish cooperative arrangements for oil pollution prevention, preparedness, and response. Such memoranda may be entered into prior to the development of the tribal consultation and coordination policy to provide Indian tribes grant and contract assistance. Such memoranda of agreement and associated protocols with Indian tribal governments may include —

(1) arrangements for the assistance of the tribal government to participate in the development of the National Contingency Plan and local Area Contingency Plans to the extent they affect tribal lands, cultural and natural resources;

(2) arrangements for the assistance of the tribal government to develop the capacity to implement the National Contingency Plan and local Area Contingency Plans to the extent they affect tribal lands, cultural and natural resources;

(3) provisions on coordination in the event of a spill, including agreements that representatives of the tribal government will be included as part of the regional response team co-chaired by the Coast Guard and the Environmental Protection Agency to establish policies for responding to oil spills;

(4) arrangements for the Coast Guard to provide training of tribal incident commanders and spill responders for oil spill preparedness and response;

(5) demonstration projects to assist tribal governments in building the capacity to protect tribal treaty rights and trust assets from oil spills; and

(6) such additional measures the Coast Guard determines to be necessary for oil pollution prevention, preparedness, and response.

(d) Funding for tribal participation — Subject to the availability of appropriations, the Commandant of the Coast Guard shall provide assistance to participating tribal governments in order to facilitate the implementation of cooperative arrangements under subsection (c) and ensure the participation of tribal governments in such arrangements. There are authorized to be appropriated to the Commandant $500,000 for each of fiscal years 2010 through 2014 to be used to carry out this section.

§1321c. International efforts on enforcement
[CWA §311c]

The Secretary of the department in which the Coast Guard is operating, in consultation with the heads of other appropriate Federal agencies, shall ensure that the Coast Guard pursues stronger enforcement in the International Maritime Organization of agreements related to oil discharges, including joint enforcement operations, training, and stronger compliance mechanisms.

§1322. Marine sanitation devices; discharges incidental to the normal operation of vessels
[CWA §312]

(a) Definitions — In this section, the term —

(1) "new vessel" includes every description of watercraft or other artificial contrivance used, or capable of being used, as a means of transportation on the navigable waters, the construction of which is initiated after promulgation of standards and regulations under this section;

(2) "existing vessel" includes every description of watercraft or other artificial contrivance used, or capable of being used, as a means of transportation on the navigable waters, the construction of which is initiated before promulgation of standards and regulations under this section;

(3) "public vessel" means a vessel owned or bareboat chartered and operated by the United States, by a State or political subdivision thereof, or by a foreign nation, except when such vessel is engaged in commerce;

(4) "United States" includes the States, the District of Columbia, the Commonwealth of Puerto Rico, the Virgin Islands, Guam, American Samoa, the Canal Zone, and the Trust Territory of the Pacific Islands;

(5) "marine sanitation device" includes any equipment for installation on board a vessel which is designed to receive, retain, treat, or discharge sewage, and any process to treat such sewage;

(6) "sewage" means human body wastes and the wastes from toilets and other receptacles intended to receive or retain body wastes except that, with respect to commercial vessels on the Great Lakes, such term shall include graywater;

(7) "manufacturer" means any person engaged in the manufacturing, assembling, or importation of marine sanitation devices, marine pollution control device equipment, or vessels subject to standards and regulations promulgated under this section;

(8) "person" means an individual, partnership, firm, corporation, association, or agency of the United States, but does not include an individual on board a public vessel;

(9) "discharge" includes, but is not limited to, any spilling, leaking, pumping, pouring, emitting, emptying or dumping;

(10) "commercial vessels" means those vessels used in the business of transporting property for compensation or hire, or in transporting property in the business of the owner, lessee, or operator of the vessel;

(11) "graywater" means galley, bath, and shower water;

(12) "discharge incidental to the normal operation of a vessel" —

(A) means a discharge, including —

(i) graywater, bilge water, cooling water, weather deck runoff, ballast water, oil water separator effluent, and any other pollutant discharge from the operation of a marine propulsion system, shipboard maneuvering system, crew habitability system, or installed major equipment, such as an aircraft carrier elevator or a catapult, or from a protective, preservative, or absorptive application to the hull of the vessel; and

(ii) a discharge in connection with the testing, maintenance, and repair of a system described in clause (i) whenever the vessel is waterborne; and

(B) does not include —

(i) a discharge of rubbish, trash, garbage, or other such material discharged overboard;

(ii) an air emission resulting from the operation of a vessel propulsion system, motor driven equipment, or incinerator; or

(iii) a discharge that is not covered by part 122.3 of title 40, Code of Federal Regulations (as in effect on February 10, 1996);

(13) "marine pollution control device" means, except as provided in subsection (p), any equip-

ment or management practice, for installation or use on board a vessel of the Armed Forces, that is —

(A) designed to receive, retain, treat, control, or discharge a discharge incidental to the normal operation of a vessel; and

(B) determined by the Administrator and the Secretary of Defense to be the most effective equipment or management practice to reduce the environmental impacts of the discharge consistent with the considerations set forth in subsection (n)(2)(B) of this section; and

(14) "vessel of the Armed Forces" means —

(A) any vessel owned or operated by the Department of Defense, other than a time or voyage chartered vessel; and

(B) any vessel owned or operated by the Department of Transportation that is designated by the Secretary of the department in which the Coast Guard is operating as a vessel equivalent to a vessel described in subparagraph (A).

(b) Federal standards of performance

(1) As soon as possible, after October 18, 1972, and subject to the provisions of section 1254(j) of this title, the Administrator, after consultation with the Secretary of the department in which the Coast Guard is operating, after giving appropriate consideration to the economic costs involved, and within the limits of available technology, shall promulgate Federal standards of performance for marine sanitation devices (hereafter in this section referred to as "standards") which shall be designed to prevent the discharge of untreated or inadequately treated sewage into or upon the navigable waters from new vessels and existing vessels, except vessels not equipped with installed toilet facilities. Such standards and standards established under subsection (c)(1)(B) of this section shall be consistent with maritime safety and the marine and navigation laws and regulations and shall be coordinated with the regulations issued under this subsection by the Secretary of the department in which the Coast Guard is operating. The Secretary of the department in which the Coast Guard is operating shall promulgate regulations, which are consistent with standards promulgated under this subsection and subsection (c) of this section and with maritime safety and the marine and navigation laws and regulations governing the design, construction, installation, and operation of any marine sanitation device on board such vessels.

(2) Any existing vessel equipped with a marine sanitation device on the date of promulgation of initial standards and regulations under this section, which device is in compliance with such initial standards and regulations, shall be deemed in compliance with this section until such time as the

device is replaced or is found not to be in compliance with such initial standards and regulations.

(c) Initial standards; effective dates; revision; waiver

(1)(A) Initial standards and regulations under this section shall become effective for new vessels two years after promulgation; and for existing vessels five years after promulgation. Revisions of standards and regulations shall be effective upon promulgation, unless another effective date is specified, except that no revision shall take effect before the effective date of the standard or regulation being revised.

(B) The Administrator shall, with respect to commercial vessels on the Great Lakes, establish standards which require at a minimum the equivalent of secondary treatment as defined under section 1314(d) of this title. Such standards and regulations shall take effect for existing vessels after such time as the Administrator determines to be reasonable for the upgrading of marine sanitation devices to attain such standard.

(2) The Secretary of the department in which the Coast Guard is operating with regard to his regulatory authority established by this section, after consultation with the Administrator, may distinguish among classes, type, and sizes of vessels as well as between new and existing vessels, and may waive applicability of standards and regulations as necessary or appropriate for such classes, types, and sizes of vessels (including existing vessels equipped with marine sanitation devices on the date of promulgation of the initial standards required by this section), and, upon application, for individual vessels.

(d) Vessels owned and operated by the United States

— The provisions of this section and the standards and regulations promulgated hereunder apply to vessels owned and operated by the United States unless the Secretary of Defense finds that compliance would not be in the interest of national security. With respect to vessels owned and operated by the Department of Defense, regulations under the last sentence of subsection (b)(1) of this section and certifications under subsection (g)(2) of this section shall be promulgated and issued by the Secretary of Defense.

(e) Pre-promulgation consultation

— Before the standards and regulations under this section are promulgated, the Administrator and the Secretary of the department in which the Coast Guard is operating shall consult with the Secretary of State; the Secretary of Health and Human Services; the Secretary of Defense; the Secretary of the Treasury; the Secretary of Commerce; other interested Federal agencies; and the States and industries interested; and otherwise comply with the requirements of section 553 of Title 5.

(f) Regulation by States or political subdivisions thereof; complete prohibition upon discharge of sewage

(1)(A) Except as provided in subparagraph (B), after the effective date of the initial standards and regulations promulgated under this section, no State or political subdivision thereof shall adopt or enforce any statute or regulation of such State or political subdivision with respect to the design, manufacture, or installation or use of any marine sanitation device on any vessel subject to the provisions of this section.

(B) A State may adopt and enforce a statute or regulation with respect to the design, manufacture, or installation or use of any marine sanitation device on a houseboat, if such statute or regulation is more stringent than the standards and regulations promulgated under this section. For purposes of this paragraph, the term "houseboat" means a vessel which, for a period of time determined by the State in which the vessel is located, is used primarily as a residence and is not used primarily as a means of transportation.

(2) If, after promulgation of the initial standards and regulations and prior to their effective date, a vessel is equipped with a marine sanitation device in compliance with such standards and regulations and the installation and operation of such device is in accordance with such standards and regulations, such standards and regulations shall, for the purposes of paragraph (1) of this subsection, become effective with respect to such vessel on the date of such compliance.

(3) After the effective date of the initial standards and regulations promulgated under this section, if any State determines that the protection and enhancement of the quality of some or all of the waters within such State require greater environmental protection, such State may completely prohibit the discharge from all vessels of any sewage, whether treated or not, into such waters, except that no such prohibition shall apply until the Administrator determines that adequate facilities for the safe and sanitary removal and treatment of sewage from all vessels are reasonably available for such water to which such prohibition would apply. Upon application of the State, the Administrator shall make such determination within 90 days of the date of such application.

(4)(A) If the Administrator determines upon application by a State that the protection and enhancement of the quality of specified waters within such State requires such a prohibition, he shall by regulation completely prohibit the discharge from a vessel of any sewage (whether treated or not) into such waters.

(B) Upon application by a State, the Administrator shall, by regulation, establish a drinking water intake zone in any waters within such State and prohibit the discharge of sewage from vessels within that zone.

(g) Sales limited to certified devices; certification of test device; recordkeeping; reports

(1) No manufacturer of a marine sanitation device or marine pollution control device equipment shall sell, offer for sale, or introduce or deliver for introduction in interstate commerce, or import into the United States for sale or resale any marine sanitation device or marine pollution control device equipment manufactured after the effective date of the standards and regulations promulgated under this section unless such device or equipment is in all material respects substantially the same as a test device or equipment certified under this subsection.

(2) Upon application of the manufacturer, the Secretary of the department in which the Coast Guard is operating shall so certify a marine sanitation device or marine pollution control device equipment if he determines, in accordance with the provisions of this paragraph, that it meets the appropriate standards and regulations promulgated under this section. The Secretary of the department in which the Coast Guard is operating shall test or require such testing of the device or equipment in accordance with procedures set forth by the Administrator as to standards of performance and for such other purposes as may be appropriate. If the Secretary of the department in which the Coast Guard is operating determines that the device or equipment is satisfactory from the standpoint of safety and any other requirements of maritime law or regulation, and after consideration of the design, installation, operation, material, or other appropriate factors, he shall certify the device or equipment. Any device or equipment manufactured by such manufacturer which is in all material respects substantially the same as the certified test device or equipment shall be deemed to be in conformity with the appropriate standards and regulations established under this section.

(3) Every manufacturer shall establish and maintain such records, make such reports, and provide such information as the Administrator or the Secretary of the department in which the Coast Guard is operating may reasonably require to enable him to determine whether such manufacturer has acted or is acting in compliance with this section and regulations issued thereunder and shall, upon request of an officer or employee duly designated by the Administrator or the Secretary of the department in which the Coast Guard is operating, permit such officer or employee at reasonable times to have access to and copy such records. All information reported to or otherwise obtained by the Administrator or the Secretary

of the Department in which the Coast Guard is operating or their representatives pursuant to this subsection which contains or relates to a trade secret or other matter referred to in section 1905 of Title 18 shall be considered confidential for the purpose of that section, except that such information may be disclosed to other officers or employees concerned with carrying out this section. This paragraph shall not apply in the case of the construction of a vessel by an individual for his own use.

(h) Sale and resale of properly equipped vessels; operability of certified marine sanitation devices

(1) In general

Subject to paragraph (2), after the effective date of standards and regulations promulgated under this section, it shall be unlawful —

(A) for the manufacturer of any vessel subject to such standards and regulations to manufacture for sale, to sell or offer for sale, or to distribute for sale or resale any such vessel unless it is equipped with a marine sanitation device and marine pollution control device equipment which is in all material respects substantially the same as the appropriate test device certified pursuant to this section;

(B) for any person, prior to the sale or delivery of a vessel subject to such standards and regulations to the ultimate purchaser, wrongfully to remove or render inoperative any certified marine sanitation device or element of design of such device or any certified marine pollution control device equipment or element of design of such equipment installed in such vessel;

(C) for any person to fail or refuse to permit access to or copying of records or to fail to make reports or provide information required under this section; and

(D) for a vessel subject to such standards and regulations to operate on the navigable waters of the United States, if such vessel is not equipped with an operable marine sanitation device certified pursuant to this section.

(2) Effect of subsection

Nothing in this subsection requires certification of a marine pollution control device for use on any vessel of the Armed Forces.

(i) Jurisdiction to restrain violations; contempts

The district courts of the United States shall have jurisdictions to restrain violations of subsection (g)(1) of this section and subsections (h)(1) through (3) of this section. Actions to restrain such violations shall be brought by, and in, the name of the United States. In case of contumacy or refusal to obey a subpena served upon any person under this subsection, the district court of the United States for any district in which such person is found or resides or transacts business, upon application by the United States and after notice to such person, shall have jurisdiction to issue an order requiring such person to appear and give testimony or to appear and produce documents, and any failure to obey such order of the court may be punished by such court as a contempt thereof.

(j) Penalties

Any person who violates subsection (g)(1), clause (1) or (2) of subsection (h), or subsection (n)(8) shall be liable to a civil penalty of not more than $5,000 for each violation. Any person who violates clause (4) of subsection (h) of this section or any regulation issued pursuant to this section shall be liable to a civil penalty of not more than $2,000 for each violation. Each violation shall be a separate offense. The Secretary of the department in which the Coast Guard is operating may assess and compromise any such penalty. No penalty shall be assessed until the person charged shall have been given notice and an opportunity for a hearing on such charge. In determining the amount of the penalty, or the amount agreed upon in compromise, the gravity of the violation, and the demonstrated good faith of the person charged in attempting to achieve rapid compliance, after notification of a violation, shall be considered by said Secretary.

(k) Enforcement authority

(1) Administrator

This section shall be enforced by the Administrator, to the extent provided in section 1319 of this title.

(2) Secretary

(A) In general

This section shall be enforced by the Secretary of the department in which the Coast Guard is operating, who may use, by agreement, with or without reimbursement, law enforcement officers or other personnel and facilities of the Administrator, other Federal agencies, or the States to carry out the provisions of this section.

(B) Inspections

For purposes of ensuring compliance with this section, the Secretary —

(i) may carry out an inspection (including the taking of ballast water samples) of any vessel at any time; and

(ii) shall —

(I) establish procedures for —

(aa) reporting violations of this section; and

(bb) accumulating evidence regarding those violations; and

(II) use appropriate and practicable measures of detection and environmental monitoring of vessels.

(C) Detention

The Secretary may detain a vessel if the Secretary —

(i) has reasonable cause to believe that the vessel —

(I) has failed to comply with an applicable requirement of this section; or

(II) is being operated in violation of such a requirement; and

(ii) the Secretary provides to the owner or operator of the vessel a notice of the intent to detain.

(3) States

(A) In general

This section may be enforced by a State or political subdivision of a State (including the attorney general of a State), including by filing a civil action in an appropriate Federal district court to enforce any violation of subsection (p).

(B) Jurisdiction

The appropriate Federal district court shall have jurisdiction with respect to a civil action filed pursuant to subparagraph (A), without regard to the amount in controversy or the citizenship of the parties —

(i) to enforce the requirements of this section; and

(ii) to apply appropriate civil penalties under this section or section 1319(d) of this title, as appropriate.

(*l*) Boarding and inspection of vessels; execution of warrants and other process — Anyone authorized by the Secretary of the department in which the Coast Guard is operating to enforce the provisions of this section may, except as to public vessels, (1) board and inspect any vessel upon the navigable waters of the United States and (2) execute any warrant or other process issued by an officer or court of competent jurisdiction.

(m) Enforcement in United States possessions — In the case of Guam and the Trust Territory of the Pacific Islands, actions arising under this section may be brought in the district court of Guam, and in the case of the Virgin Islands such actions may be brought in the district court of the Virgin Islands. In the case of American Samoa and the Trust Territory of the Pacific Islands, such actions may be brought in the District Court of the United States for the District of Hawaii and such court shall have jurisdiction of such actions. In the case of the Canal Zone, such actions may be brought in the District Court for the District of the Canal Zone.

(n) Uniform national discharge standards for vessels of Armed Forces

(1) Applicability — This subsection shall apply to vessels of the Armed Forces and discharges, other than sewage, incidental to the normal operation of a vessel of the Armed Forces, unless the Secretary of Defense finds that compliance with this subsection would not be in the national security interests of the United States.

(2) Determination of discharges required to be controlled by marine pollution control devices

(A) In general — The Administrator and the Secretary of Defense, after consultation with the Secretary of the department in which the Coast Guard is operating, the Secretary of Commerce, and interested States, shall jointly determine the discharges incidental to the normal operation of a vessel of the Armed Forces for which it is reasonable and practicable to require use of a marine pollution control device to mitigate adverse impacts on the marine environment. Notwithstanding subsection (a)(1) of section 553 of Title 5, the Administrator and the Secretary of Defense shall promulgate the determinations in accordance with such section. The Secretary of Defense shall require the use of a marine pollution control device on board a vessel of the Armed Forces in any case in which it is determined that the use of such a device is reasonable and practicable.

(B) Considerations — In making a determination under subparagraph (A), the Administrator and the Secretary of Defense shall take into consideration —

　　(i) the nature of the discharge;

　　(ii) the environmental effects of the discharge;

　　(iii) the practicability of using the marine pollution control device;

　　(iv) the effect that installation or use of the marine pollution control device would have on the operation or operational capability of the vessel;

　　(v) applicable United States law;

　　(vi) applicable international standards; and

　　(vii) the economic costs of the installation and use of the marine pollution control device.

(3) Performance standards for marine pollution control devices

(A) In general — For each discharge for which a marine pollution control device is determined to be required under paragraph (2), the Administrator and the Secretary of Defense, in consultation with the Secretary of the department in which the Coast Guard is operating, the Secretary of State, the Secretary of Commerce, other interested Federal agencies, and interested States, shall jointly promulgate Federal standards of performance for each marine pollution control device required with respect to the discharge. Notwithstanding subsection (a)(1) of section 553 of Title 5, the Administrator and the Secretary of Defense shall promulgate the standards in accordance with such section.

(B) Considerations — In promulgating standards under this paragraph, the Adminis-

trator and the Secretary of Defense shall take into consideration the matters set forth in paragraph (2)(B).

(C) Classes, types, and sizes of vessels — The standards promulgated under this paragraph may —

　　(i) distinguish among classes, types, and sizes of vessels;

　　(ii) distinguish between new and existing vessels; and

　　(iii) provide for a waiver of the applicability of the standards as necessary or appropriate to a particular class, type, age, or size of vessel.

(4) Regulations for use of marine pollution control devices — The Secretary of Defense, after consultation with the Administrator and the Secretary of the department in which the Coast Guard is operating, shall promulgate such regulations governing the design, construction, installation, and use of marine pollution control devices on board vessels of the Armed Forces as are necessary to achieve the standards promulgated under paragraph (3).

(5) Deadlines; effective date

(A) Determinations — The Administrator and the Secretary of Defense shall —

　　(i) make the initial determinations under paragraph (2) not later than 2 years after February 10, 1996; and

　　(ii) every 5 years —

　　　　(I) review the determinations; and

　　　　(II) if necessary, revise the determinations based on significant new information.

(B) Standards — The Administrator and the Secretary of Defense shall —

　　(i) promulgate standards of performance for a marine pollution control device under paragraph (3) not later than 2 years after the date of a determination under paragraph (2) that the marine pollution control device is required; and

　　(ii) every 5 years —

　　　　(I) review the standards; and

　　　　(II) if necessary, revise the standards, consistent with paragraph (3)(B) and based on significant new information.

(C) Regulations — The Secretary of Defense shall promulgate regulations with respect to a marine pollution control device under paragraph (4) as soon as practicable after the Administrator and the Secretary of Defense promulgate standards with respect to the device under paragraph (3), but not later than 1 year after the Administrator and the Secretary of Defense promulgate the standards. The regulations promulgated by the Secretary of Defense under paragraph (4) shall become effective upon promulgation unless another effective date is specified in the regulations.

(D) Petition for review — The Governor of any State may submit a petition requesting that the Secretary of Defense and the Administrator review a determination under paragraph (2) or a standard under paragraph (3), if there is significant new information, not considered previously, that could reasonably result in a change to the particular determination or standard after consideration of the matters set forth in paragraph (2)(B). The petition shall be accompanied by the scientific and technical information on which the petition is based. The Administrator and the Secretary of Defense shall grant or deny the petition not later than 2 years after the date of receipt of the petition.

(6) Effect on other laws

(A) Prohibition on regulation by States or political subdivisions of States — Beginning on the effective date of —

    (i) a determination under paragraph (2) that it is not reasonable and practicable to require use of a marine pollution control device regarding a particular discharge incidental to the normal operation of a vessel of the Armed Forces; or

    (ii) regulations promulgated by the Secretary of Defense under paragraph (4);

except as provided in paragraph (7), neither a State nor a political subdivision of a State may adopt or enforce any statute or regulation of the State or political subdivision with respect to the discharge or the design, construction, installation, or use of any marine pollution control device required to control discharges from a vessel of the Armed Forces.

(B) Federal laws — This subsection shall not affect the application of section 1321 of this title to discharges incidental to the normal operation of a vessel.

(7) Establishment of State no-discharge zones

    (A) State prohibition

        (i) In general — After the effective date of —

            (I) a determination under paragraph (2) that it is not reasonable and practicable to require use of a marine pollution control device regarding a particular discharge incidental to the normal operation of a vessel of the Armed Forces; or

            (II) regulations promulgated by the Secretary of Defense under paragraph (4);

if a State determines that the protection and enhancement of the quality of some or all of the waters within the State require

greater environmental protection, the State may prohibit 1 or more discharges incidental to the normal operation of a vessel, whether treated or not treated, into the waters. No prohibition shall apply until the Administrator makes the determinations described in subclauses (II) and (III) of subparagraph (B)(i).

        (ii) Documentation — To the extent that a prohibition under this paragraph would apply to vessels of the Armed Forces and not to other types of vessels, the State shall document the technical or environmental basis for the distinction.

    (B) Prohibition by the Administrator

        (i) In general — Upon application of a State, the Administrator shall by regulation prohibit the discharge from a vessel of 1 or more discharges incidental to the normal operation of a vessel, whether treated or not treated, into the waters covered by the application if the Administrator determines that —

            (I) the protection and enhancement of the quality of the specified waters within the State require a prohibition of the discharge into the waters;

            (II) adequate facilities for the safe and sanitary removal of the discharge incidental to the normal operation of a vessel are reasonably available for the waters to which the prohibition would apply; and

            (III) the prohibition will not have the effect of discriminating against a vessel of the Armed Forces by reason of the ownership or operation by the Federal Government, or the military function, of the vessel.

        (ii) Approval or disapproval — The Administrator shall approve or disapprove an application submitted under clause (i) not later than 90 days after the date on which the application is submitted to the Administrator. Notwithstanding clause (i) (II), the Administrator shall not disapprove an application for the sole reason that there are not adequate facilities to remove any discharge incidental to the normal operation of a vessel from vessels of the Armed Forces.

    (C) Applicability to foreign flagged vessels — A prohibition under this paragraph —

        (i) shall not impose any design, construction, manning, or equipment standard on a foreign flagged vessel engaged in innocent passage unless the prohibition implements a generally accepted international rule or standard; and

(ii) that relates to the prevention, reduction, and control of pollution shall not apply to a foreign flagged vessel engaged in transit passage unless the prohibition implements an applicable international regulation regarding the discharge of oil, oily waste, or any other noxious substance into the waters.

(8) Prohibition relating to vessels of the Armed Forces — After the effective date of the regulations promulgated by the Secretary of Defense under paragraph (4), it shall be unlawful for any vessel of the Armed Forces subject to the regulations to —

(A) operate in the navigable waters of the United States or the waters of the contiguous zone, if the vessel is not equipped with any required marine pollution control device meeting standards established under this subsection; or

(B) discharge overboard any discharge incidental to the normal operation of a vessel in waters with respect to which a prohibition on the discharge has been established under paragraph (7).

(9) Enforcement — This subsection shall be enforceable, as provided in subsections (j) and (k) of this section, against any agency of the United States responsible for vessels of the Armed Forces notwithstanding any immunity asserted by the agency.

(o) **Management practices for recreational vessels**

(1) Applicability

This subsection applies to any discharge, other than a discharge of sewage, from a recreational vessel that is —

(A) incidental to the normal operation of the vessel; and

(B) exempt from permitting requirements under section 1342(r) of this title.

(2) Determination of discharges subject to management practices

(A) Determination

(i) In general

The Administrator, in consultation with the Secretary of the department in which the Coast Guard is operating, the Secretary of Commerce, and interested States, shall determine the discharges incidental to the normal operation of a recreational vessel for which it is reasonable and practicable to develop management practices to mitigate adverse impacts on the waters of the United States.

(ii) Promulgation

The Administrator shall promulgate the determinations under clause (i) in accordance with section 553 of Title 5.

(iii) Management practices

The Administrator shall develop management practices for recreational vessels in any case in which the Administrator determines that the use of those practices is reasonable and practicable.

(B) Considerations

In making a determination under subparagraph (A), the Administrator shall consider —

(i) the nature of the discharge;

(ii) the environmental effects of the discharge;

(iii) the practicability of using a management practice;

(iv) the effect that the use of a management practice would have on the operation, operational capability, or safety of the vessel;

(v) applicable Federal and State law;

(vi) applicable international standards; and

(vii) the economic costs of the use of the management practice.

(C) Timing

The Administrator shall —

(i) make the initial determinations under subparagraph (A) not later than 1 year after July 29, 2008; and

(ii) every 5 years thereafter —

(I) review the determinations; and

(II) if necessary, revise the determinations based on any new information available to the Administrator.

(3) Performance standards for management practices

(A) In general

For each discharge for which a management practice is developed under paragraph (2), the Administrator, in consultation with the Secretary of the department in which the Coast Guard is operating, the Secretary of Commerce, other interested Federal agencies, and interested States, shall promulgate, in accordance with section 553 of Title 5, Federal standards of performance for each management practice required with respect to the discharge.

(B) Considerations

In promulgating standards under this paragraph, the Administrator shall take into account the considerations described in paragraph (2)(B).

(C) Classes, types, and sizes of vessels

The standards promulgated under this paragraph may —

(i) distinguish among classes, types, and sizes of vessels;

(ii) distinguish between new and existing vessels; and

(iii) provide for a waiver of the applicability of the standards as necessary or appropriate to a particular class, type, age, or size of vessel.

(D) Timing

The Administrator shall —

(i) promulgate standards of performance for a management practice under subparagraph (A) not later than 1 year after the date of a determination under paragraph (2) that the management practice is reasonable and practicable; and

(ii) every 5 years thereafter —

(I) review the standards; and

(II) if necessary, revise the standards, in accordance with subparagraph (B) and based on any new information available to the Administrator.

(4) Regulations for the use of management practices

(A) In general

The Secretary of the department in which the Coast Guard is operating shall promulgate such regulations governing the design, construction, installation, and use of management practices for recreational vessels as are necessary to meet the standards of performance promulgated under paragraph (3).

(B) Regulations

(i) In general

The Secretary shall promulgate the regulations under this paragraph as soon as practicable after the Administrator promulgates standards with respect to the practice under paragraph (3), but not later than 1 year after the date on which the Administrator promulgates the standards.

(ii) Effective date

The regulations promulgated by the Secretary under this paragraph shall be effective upon promulgation unless another effective date is specified in the regulations.

(iii) Consideration of time

In determining the effective date of a regulation promulgated under this paragraph, the Secretary shall consider the period of time necessary to communicate the existence of the regulation to persons affected by the regulation.

(5) Effect of other laws

This subsection shall not affect the application of section 1321 of this title to discharges incidental to the normal operation of a recreational vessel.

(6) Prohibition relating to recreational vessels

After the effective date of the regulations promulgated by the Secretary of the department in which the Coast Guard is operating under paragraph (4), the owner or operator of a recreational vessel shall neither operate in nor discharge any discharge incidental to the normal operation of the vessel into, the waters of the United States or the waters of the contiguous zone, if the owner or operator of the vessel is not using any applicable management practice meeting standards established under this subsection.

(p) Uniform national standards for discharges incidental to normal operation of vessels

(1) Definitions

In this subsection:

(A) Aquatic nuisance species

The term "aquatic nuisance species" means a nonindigenous species that threatens —

(i) the diversity or abundance of a native species;

(ii) the ecological stability of —

(I) waters of the United States; or

(II) waters of the contiguous zone; or

(iii) a commercial, agricultural, aquacultural, or recreational activity that is dependent on —

(I) waters of the United States; or

(II) waters of the contiguous zone.

(B) Ballast water

(i) In general

The term "ballast water" means any water, suspended matter, and other materials taken onboard a vessel —

(I) to control or maintain trim, draught, stability, or stresses of the vessel, regardless of the means by which any such water or suspended matter is carried; or

(II) during the cleaning, maintenance, or other operation of a ballast tank or ballast water management system of the vessel.

(ii) Exclusion

The term "ballast water" does not include any substance that is added to the water described in clause (i) that is directly related to the operation of a properly functioning ballast water management system.

(C) Ballast water discharge standard

The term "ballast water discharge standard" means —

(i) the numerical ballast water discharge standard established by section 151.1511 or 151.2030 of title 33, Code of Federal Regulations (or successor regulations); or

(ii) if a standard referred to in clause (i) is superseded by a numerical standard of performance under this subsection, that superseding standard.

(D) Ballast water exchange

The term "ballast water exchange" means the replacement of water in a ballast water tank using 1 of the following methods:

(i) Flow-through exchange, in which ballast water is flushed out by pumping in midocean water at the bottom of the tank if practicable, and continuously overflowing the tank from the top, until 3 full volumes of water have been changed to minimize the number of original organisms remaining in the tank.

(ii) Empty and refill exchange, in which ballast water taken on in ports, estuarine waters, or territorial waters is pumped out until the pump loses suction, after which the ballast tank is refilled with midocean water.

(E) Ballast water management system

The term "ballast water management system" means any marine pollution control device (including all ballast water treatment equipment, ballast tanks, pipes, pumps, and all associated control and monitoring equipment) that processes ballast water —

(i) to kill, render nonviable, or remove organisms; or

(ii) to avoid the uptake or discharge of organisms.

(F) Best available technology economically achievable

The term "best available technology economically achievable" means —

(i) best available technology economically achievable (within the meaning of section 1311(b)(2)(A) of this title);

(ii) best available technology (within the meaning of section 1314(b)(2)(B) of this title); and

(iii) best available technology, as determined in accordance with section 125.3(d)(3) of title 40, Code of Federal Regulations (or successor regulations).

(G) Best conventional pollutant control technology

The term "best conventional pollutant control technology" means —

(i) best conventional pollutant control technology (within the meaning of section 1311(b)(2)(E) of this title);

(ii) best conventional pollutant control technology (within the meaning of section 1314(b)(4) of this title); and

(iii) best conventional pollutant control technology, as determined in accordance with section 125.3(d)(2) of title 40, Code of Federal Regulations (or successor regulations).

(H) Best management practice

(i) In general

The term "best management practice" means a schedule of activities, prohibitions of practices, maintenance procedures, and other management practices to prevent or reduce the pollution of —

(I) the waters of the United States; or

(II) the waters of the contiguous zone.

(ii) Inclusions

The term "best management practice" includes any treatment requirement, operating procedure, or practice to control —

(I) vessel runoff;

(II) spillage or leaks;

(III) sludge or waste disposal; or

(IV) drainage from raw material storage.

(I) Best practicable control technology currently available

The term "best practicable control technology currently available" means —

(i) best practicable control technology currently available (within the meaning of section 1311(b)(1)(A) of this title);

(ii) best practicable control technology currently available (within the meaning of section 1314(b)(1) of this title); and

(iii) best practicable control technology currently available, as determined in accordance with section 125.3(d)(1) of title 40, Code of Federal Regulations (or successor regulations).

(J) Captain of the Port Zone

The term "Captain of the Port Zone" means a Captain of the Port Zone established by the Secretary pursuant to sections 92, 93, and 633 of Title 14.1

(K) Empty ballast tank

The term "empty ballast tank" means a tank that —

(i) has previously held ballast water that has been drained to the limit of the functional or operational capabilities of the tank (such as loss of suction);

(ii) is recorded as empty on a vessel log; and

(iii) contains unpumpable residual ballast water and sediment.

(L) Great Lakes Commission

The term "Great Lakes Commission" means the Great Lakes Commission established by article IV A of the Great Lakes Compact2 to which Congress granted consent in the Act of July 24, 1968 (Public Law 90-419; 82 Stat. 414).

(M) Great Lakes State

The term "Great Lakes State" means any of the States of —

(i) Illinois;

(ii) Indiana;

(iii) Michigan;

(iv) Minnesota;

(v) New York;

(vi) Ohio;

(vii) Pennsylvania; and

(viii) Wisconsin.

(N) Great Lakes System

The term "Great Lakes System" has the meaning given the term in section 1268(a)(3) of this title.

(O) Internal waters

The term "internal waters" has the meaning given the term in section 2.24 of title 33, Code of Federal Regulations (or a successor regulation).

(P) Marine pollution control device

The term "marine pollution control device" means any equipment or management practice (or combination of equipment and a management practice), for installation or use onboard a vessel, that is —

(i) designed to receive, retain, treat, control, or discharge a discharge incidental to the normal operation of a vessel; and

(ii) determined by the Administrator and the Secretary to be the most effective equipment or management practice (or combination of equipment and a management practice) to reduce the environmental impacts of the discharge, consistent with the factors for consideration described in paragraphs (4) and (5).

(Q) Nonindigenous species

The term "nonindigenous species" means an organism of a species that enters an ecosystem beyond the historic range of the species.

(R) Organism

The term "organism" includes —

(i) an animal, including fish and fish eggs and larvae;

(ii) a plant;

(iii) a pathogen;

(iv) a microbe;

(v) a virus;

(vi) a prokaryote (including any archean or bacterium);

(vii) a fungus; and

(viii) a protist.

(S) Pacific Region

(i) In general

The term "Pacific Region" means any Federal or State water —

(I) adjacent to the State of Alaska, California, Hawaii, Oregon, or Washington; and

(II) extending from shore.

(ii) Inclusion

The term "Pacific Region" includes the entire exclusive economic zone (as defined in section 2701 of this title) adjacent to each State described in clause (i)(I).

(T) Port or place of destination

The term "port or place of destination" means a port or place to which a vessel is bound to anchor or moor.

(U) Render nonviable

The term "render nonviable", with respect to an organism in ballast water, means the action of a ballast water management system that renders the organism permanently incapable of reproduction following treatment.

(V) Saltwater flush

(i) In general

The term "saltwater flush" means —

(I)(aa) the addition of as much midocean water into each empty ballast tank of a vessel as is safe for the vessel and crew; and

(bb) the mixing of the flushwater with residual ballast water and sediment through the motion of the vessel; and

(II) the discharge of that mixed water, such that the resultant residual water remaining in the tank —

(aa) has the highest salinity possible; and

(bb) is at least 30 parts per thousand.

(ii) Multiple sequences

For purposes of clause (i), a saltwater flush may require more than 1 fill-mix-empty sequence, particularly if only small quantities of water can be safely taken onboard a vessel at 1 time.

(W) Secretary

The term "Secretary" means the Secretary of the department in which the Coast Guard is operating.

(X) Small Vessel General Permit

The term "Small Vessel General Permit" means the permit that is the subject of the notice of final permit issuance entitled "Final National Pollutant Discharge Elimination System (NPDES) Small Vessel General Permit for Discharges Incidental to the Normal Operation of Vessels Less Than 79 Feet" (79 Fed. Reg. 53702 (September 10, 2014)).

(Y) Small vessel or fishing vessel

The term "small vessel or fishing vessel" means a vessel that is —

(i) less than 79 feet in length; or

(ii) a fishing vessel, fish processing vessel, or fish tender vessel (as those terms are defined in section 2101 of Title 46), regardless of the length of the vessel.

(Z) Vessel General Permit

The term "Vessel General Permit" means the permit that is the subject of the notice of final permit issuance entitled "Final

National Pollutant Discharge Elimination System (NPDES) General Permit for Discharges Incidental to the Normal Operation of a Vessel" (78 Fed. Reg. 21938 (April 12, 2013)).

(2) Applicability

  (A) In general

Except as provided in subparagraph (B), this subsection applies to —

    (i) any discharge incidental to the normal operation of a vessel; and

    (ii) any discharge incidental to the normal operation of a vessel (such as most graywater) that is commingled with sewage, subject to the conditions that —

      (I) nothing in this subsection prevents a State from regulating sewage discharges; and

      (II) any such commingled discharge shall comply with all applicable requirements of —

        (aa) this subsection; and

        (bb) any law applicable to discharges of sewage.

  (B) Exclusion

This subsection does not apply to any discharge incidental to the normal operation of a vessel —

    (i) from —

      (I) a vessel of the Armed Forces subject to subsection (n);

      (II) a recreational vessel subject to subsection (o);

      (III) a small vessel or fishing vessel, except that this subsection shall apply to any discharge of ballast water from a small vessel or fishing vessel; or

      (IV) a floating craft that is permanently moored to a pier, including a "floating" casino, hotel, restaurant, or bar;

    (ii) of ballast water from a vessel —

      (I) that continuously takes on and discharges ballast water in a flow-through system, if the Administrator determines that system cannot materially contribute to the spread or introduction of an aquatic nuisance species into waters of the United States;

      (II) in the National Defense Reserve Fleet that is scheduled for disposal, if the vessel does not have an operable ballast water management system;

      (III) that discharges ballast water consisting solely of water taken onboard from a public or commercial source that, at the time the water is taken onboard, meets the applicable requirements or permit requirements of the Safe Drinking Water Act (42 U.S.C. 300f et seq.);

      (IV) that carries all permanent ballast water in sealed tanks that are not subject to discharge; or

      (V) that only discharges ballast water into a reception facility; or

    (iii) that results from, or contains material derived from, an activity other than the normal operation of the vessel, such as material resulting from an industrial or manufacturing process onboard the vessel.

(3) Continuation in effect of existing requirements

  (A) Vessel General Permit

Notwithstanding the expiration date of the Vessel General Permit or any other provision of law, all provisions of the Vessel General Permit shall remain in force and effect, and shall not be modified, until the applicable date described in subparagraph (C).

  (B) Nonindigenous Aquatic Nuisance Prevention and Control Act regulations

Notwithstanding section 903(a)(2)(A) of the Vessel Incidental Discharge Act of 2018, all regulations promulgated by the Secretary pursuant to section 1101 of the Nonindigenous Aquatic Nuisance Prevention and Control Act of 1990 (16 U.S.C. 4711) (as in effect on the day before December 4, 2018), including the regulations contained in subparts C and D of part 151 of title 33, Code of Federal Regulations, and subpart 162.060 of part 162 of title 46, Code of Federal Regulations (as in effect on the day before December 4, 2018), shall remain in force and effect until the applicable date described in subparagraph (C).

  (C) Repeal on existence of final, effective, and enforceable requirements

Effective beginning on the date on which the requirements promulgated by the Secretary under subparagraphs (A), (B), and (C) of paragraph (5) with respect to every discharge incidental to the normal operation of a vessel that is subject to regulation under this subsection are final, effective, and enforceable, the requirements of the Vessel General Permit and the regulations described in subparagraph (B) shall have no force or effect.

(4) National standards of performance for marine pollution control devices and water quality orders

  (A) Establishment

    (i) In general

Not later than 2 years after December 4, 2018, the Administrator, in concurrence with the Secretary (subject to clause (ii)), and in consultation with interested Governors (subject to clause (iii)), shall promulgate Federal standards of performance for marine pollution control devices for each type of discharge incidental to the normal operation of a vessel that is subject to regulation under this subsection.

(ii) Concurrence with Secretary

(I) Request

The Administrator shall submit to the Secretary a request for written concurrence with respect to a proposed standard of performance under clause (i).

(II) Effect of failure to concur

A failure by the Secretary to concur with the Administrator under clause (i) by the date that is 60 days after the date on which the Administrator submits a request for concurrence under subclause (I) shall not prevent the Administrator from promulgating the relevant standard of performance in accordance with the deadline under clause (i), subject to the condition that the Administrator shall include in the administrative record of the promulgation —

(aa) documentation of the request submitted under subclause (I); and

(bb) the response of the Administrator to any written objections received from the Secretary relating to the proposed standard of performance during the 60-day period beginning on the date of submission of the request.

(iii) Consultation with Governors

(I) In general

The Administrator, in promulgating a standard of performance under clause (i), shall develop the standard of performance —

(aa) in consultation with interested Governors; and

(bb) in accordance with the deadlines under that clause.

(II) Process

The Administrator shall develop a process for soliciting input from interested Governors, including information sharing relevant to such process, to allow interested Governors to inform the development of standards of performance under clause (i).

(III) Objection by Governors

(aa) Submission

An interested Governor that objects to a proposed standard of performance under clause (i) may submit to the Administrator in writing a detailed objection to the proposed standard of performance, describing the scientific, technical, or operational factors that form the basis of the objection.

(bb) Response

Before finalizing a standard of performance under clause (i) that is subject to an objection under item (aa) from 1 or more interested Governors, the Administrator shall provide a written response to each interested Governor that submitted an objection under that item that details the scientific, technical, or operational factors that form the basis for that standard of performance.

(cc) Judicial review

A response of the Administrator under item (bb) shall not be subject to judicial review.

(iv) Procedure

The Administrator shall promulgate the standards of performance under this subparagraph in accordance with —

(I) this paragraph; and

(II) section 553 of Title 5.

(B) Stringency

(i) In general

Subject to clause (iii), the standards of performance promulgated under this paragraph shall require —

(I) with respect to conventional pollutants, toxic pollutants, and nonconventional pollutants (including aquatic nuisance species), the application of the best practicable control technology currently available;

(II) with respect to conventional pollutants, the application of the best conventional pollutant control technology; and

(III) with respect to toxic pollutants and nonconventional pollutants (including aquatic nuisance species), the application of the best available technology economically achievable for categories and classes of vessels, which shall result in reasonable progress toward the national goal of eliminating discharges of all pollutants.

(ii) Best management practices

The Administrator shall require the use of best management practices to control or abate any discharge incidental to the normal operation of a vessel if —

(I) numeric standards of performance are infeasible under clause (i); or

(II) the best management practices are reasonably necessary —

(aa) to achieve the standards of performance; or

(bb) to carry out the purpose and intent of this subsection.

(iii) Minimum requirements

Subject to subparagraph (D)(ii)(II), the combination of any equipment or best management practice comprising a marine pollution control device shall not be less stringent than the following provisions of the Vessel General Permit:

(I) All requirements contained in parts 2.1 and 2.2 (relating to effluent limits and related requirements), including with respect to waters subject to Federal protection, in whole or in part, for conservation purposes.

(II) All requirements contained in part 5 (relating to vessel class-specific requirements) that concern effluent limits and authorized discharges (within the meaning of that part), including with respect to waters subject to Federal protection, in whole or in part, for conservation purposes.

(C) Classes, types, and sizes of vessels

The standards promulgated under this paragraph may distinguish —

(i) among classes, types, and sizes of vessels; and

(ii) between new vessels and existing vessels.

(D) Review and revision

(i) In general

Not less frequently than once every 5 years, the Administrator, in consultation with the Secretary, shall —

(I) review the standards of performance in effect under this paragraph; and

(II) if appropriate, revise those standards of performance —

(aa) in accordance with subparagraphs (A) through (C); and

(bb) as necessary to establish requirements for any discharge that is subject to regulation under this subsection.

(ii) Maintaining protectiveness

(I) In general

Except as provided in subclause (II), the Administrator shall not revise a standard of performance under this subsection to be less stringent than an applicable existing requirement.

(II) Exceptions

The Administrator may revise a standard of performance to be less stringent than an applicable existing requirement —

(aa) if information becomes available that —

(AA) was not reasonably available when the Administrator promulgated the initial standard of performance or comparable requirement of the Vessel General Permit, as applicable (including the subsequent scarcity or unavailability of materials used to control the relevant discharge); and

(BB) would have justified the application of a less-stringent standard of performance at the time of promulgation; or

(bb) if the Administrator determines that a material technical mistake or misinterpretation of law occurred when promulgating the existing standard of performance or comparable requirement of the Vessel General Permit, as applicable.

(E) Best management practices for aquatic nuisance species emergencies and further protection of water quality

(i) In general

Notwithstanding any other provision of this subsection, the Administrator, in concurrence with the Secretary (subject to clause (ii)), and in consultation with States, may require, by order, the use of an emergency best management practice for any region or category of vessels in any case in which the Administrator determines that such a best management practice —

(I) is necessary to reduce the reasonably foreseeable risk of introduction or establishment of an aquatic nuisance species; or

(II) will mitigate the adverse effects of a discharge that contributes to a violation of a water quality requirement under section 1313 of this title, other than a requirement based on the presence of an aquatic nuisance species.

(ii) Concurrence with Secretary

(I) Request

The Administrator shall submit to the Secretary a request for written concurrence with respect to an order under clause (i).

(II) Effect of failure to concur

A failure by the Secretary to concur with the Administrator under clause (i) by the date that is 60 days after the date on which the Administrator submits a request for concurrence under subclause (I) shall not prevent the Administrator from issuing the relevant order, subject to the condition that the Administrator shall include in the administrative record of the issuance —

    (aa) documentation of the request submitted under subclause (I); and

    (bb) the response of the Administrator to any written objections received from the Secretary relating to the proposed order during the 60-day period beginning on the date of submission of the request.

(iii) Duration

An order issued by the Administrator under clause (i) shall expire not later than the date that is 4 years after the date of issuance.

(iv) Extensions

The Administrator may reissue an order under clause (i) for such subsequent periods of not longer than 4 years as the Administrator determines to be appropriate.

(5) Implementation, compliance, and enforcement requirements

(A) Establishment

(i) In general

As soon as practicable, but not later than 2 years, after the date on which the Administrator promulgates any new or revised standard of performance under paragraph (4) with respect to a discharge, the Secretary, in consultation with States, shall promulgate the regulations required under this paragraph with respect to that discharge.

(ii) Minimum requirements

Subject to subparagraph (C)(ii)(II), the regulations promulgated under this paragraph shall not be less stringent with respect to ensuring, monitoring, and enforcing compliance than —

    (I) the requirements contained in part 3 of the Vessel General Permit (relating to corrective actions);

    (II) the requirements contained in part 4 of the Vessel General Permit (relating to inspections, monitoring, reporting, and recordkeeping), including with respect to waters subject to Federal protection, in whole or in part, for conservation purposes;

    (III) the requirements contained in part 5 of the Vessel General Permit

(relating to vessel class-specific requirements) regarding monitoring, inspection, and educational and training requirements (within the meaning of that part), including with respect to waters subject to Federal protection, in whole or in part, for conservation purposes; and

    (IV) any comparable, existing requirements promulgated under the Nonindigenous Aquatic Nuisance Prevention and Control Act of 1990 (16 U.S.C. 4701 et seq.) (including section 1101 of that Act (16 U.S.C. 4711) (as in effect on the day before December 4, 2018)) applicable to that discharge.

(iii) Coordination with States

The Secretary, in coordination with the Governors of the States, shall develop, publish, and periodically update inspection, monitoring, data management, and enforcement procedures for the enforcement by States of Federal standards and requirements under this subsection.

(iv) Effective date

In determining the effective date of a regulation promulgated under this paragraph, the Secretary shall take into consideration the period of time necessary —

    (I) to communicate to affected persons the applicability of the regulation; and

    (II) for affected persons reasonably to comply with the regulation.

(v) Procedure

The Secretary shall promulgate the regulations under this subparagraph in accordance with —

    (I) this paragraph; and

    (II) section 553 of Title 5.

(B) Implementation regulations for marine pollution control devices

The Secretary shall promulgate such regulations governing the design, construction, testing, approval, installation, and use of marine pollution control devices as are necessary to ensure compliance with the standards of performance promulgated under paragraph (4).

(C) Compliance assurance

(i) In general

The Secretary shall promulgate requirements (including requirements for vessel owners and operators with respect to inspections, monitoring, reporting, sampling, and recordkeeping) to ensure, monitor, and enforce compliance with —

    (I) the standards of performance promulgated by the Administrator under paragraph (4); and

(II) the implementation regulations promulgated by the Secretary under subparagraph (B).

(ii) Maintaining protectiveness

(I) In general

Except as provided in subclause (II), the Secretary shall not revise a requirement under this subparagraph or subparagraph (B) to be less stringent with respect to ensuring, monitoring, or enforcing compliance than an applicable existing requirement.

(II) Exceptions

The Secretary may revise a requirement under this subparagraph or subparagraph (B) to be less stringent than an applicable existing requirement —

(aa) in accordance with this subparagraph or subparagraph (B), as applicable;

(bb) if information becomes available that —

(AA) the Administrator determines was not reasonably available when the Administrator promulgated the existing requirement of the Vessel General Permit, or that the Secretary determines was not reasonably available when the Secretary promulgated the existing requirement under the Nonindigenous Aquatic Nuisance Prevention and Control Act of 1990 (16 U.S.C. 4701 et seq.) or the applicable existing requirement under this subparagraph, as applicable (including subsequent scarcity or unavailability of materials used to control the relevant discharge); and

(BB) would have justified the application of a less-stringent requirement at the time of promulgation; or

(cc) if the Administrator determines that a material technical mistake or misinterpretation of law occurred when promulgating an existing requirement of the Vessel General Permit, or if the Secretary determines that a material mistake or misinterpretation of law occurred when promulgating an existing requirement under the Nonindigenous Aquatic Nuisance Prevention and Control Act of 1990 (16 U.S.C. 4701 et seq.) or this subsection.

(D) Data availability

Beginning not later than 1 year after December 4, 2018, the Secretary shall provide to the Governor of a State, on request by the Governor, access to Automated Identification System arrival data for inbound vessels to specific ports or places of destination in the State.

(6) Additional provisions regarding ballast water

(A) In general

In addition to the other applicable requirements of this subsection, the requirements of this paragraph shall apply with respect to any discharge incidental to the normal operation of a vessel that is a discharge of ballast water.

(B) Empty ballast tanks

(i) Requirements

Except as provided in clause (ii), the owner or operator of a vessel with empty ballast tanks bound for a port or place of destination subject to the jurisdiction of the United States shall, prior to arriving at that port or place of destination, conduct a ballast water exchange or saltwater flush —

(I) not less than 200 nautical miles from any shore for a voyage originating outside the United States or Canadian exclusive economic zone; or

(II) not less than 50 nautical miles from any shore for a voyage originating within the United States or Canadian exclusive economic zone.

(ii) Exceptions

Clause (i) shall not apply —

(I) if the unpumpable residual waters and sediments of an empty ballast tank were subject to treatment, in compliance with applicable requirements, through a type-approved ballast water management system approved by the Secretary;

(II) except as otherwise required under this subsection, if the unpumpable residual waters and sediments of an empty ballast tank were sourced within —

(aa) the same port or place of destination; or

(bb) contiguous portions of a single Captain of the Port Zone;

(III) if complying with an applicable requirement of clause (i) —

(aa) would compromise the safety of the vessel; or

(bb) is otherwise prohibited by any Federal, Canadian, or international law (including regulations) pertaining to vessel safety;

(IV) if design limitations of the vessel prevent a ballast water exchange or saltwater flush from being conducted in accordance with clause (i); or

(V) if the vessel is operating exclusively within the internal waters of the United States or Canada.

(C) Period of use of installed ballast water management systems

(i) In general

Except as provided in clause (ii), a vessel shall be deemed to be in compliance with a standard of performance for a marine pollution control device that is a ballast water management system if the ballast water management system —

(I) is maintained in proper working condition, as determined by the Secretary;

(II) is maintained and used in accordance with manufacturer specifications;

(III) continues to meet the ballast water discharge standard applicable to the vessel at the time of installation, as determined by the Secretary; and

(IV) has in effect a valid type-approval certificate issued by the Secretary.

(ii) Limitation

Clause (i) shall cease to apply with respect to any vessel on, as applicable —

(I) the expiration of the service life, as determined by the Secretary, of —

(aa) the ballast water management system; or

(bb) the vessel;

(II) the completion of a major conversion (as defined in section 2101 of Title 46) of the vessel; or

(III) a determination by the Secretary that there are other type-approved systems for the vessel or category of vessels, with respect to the use of which the environmental, health, and economic benefits would exceed the costs.

(D) Review of ballast water management system type-approval testing methods

(i) Definition of live; living

Notwithstanding any other provision of law (including regulations), for purposes of section 151.1511 of title 33, and part 162 of title 46, Code of Federal Regulations (or successor regulations), the terms "live" and "living" shall not —

(I) include an organism that has been rendered nonviable; or

(II) preclude the consideration of any method of measuring the concentration of organisms in ballast water that are capable of reproduction.

(ii) Draft policy

Not later than 180 days after December 4, 2018, the Secretary, in coordination with the Administrator, shall publish a draft policy letter, based on the best available science, describing type-approval testing methods and protocols for ballast water management systems, if any, that —

(I) render nonviable organisms in ballast water; and

(II) may be used in addition to the methods established under subpart 162.060 of title 46, Code of Federal Regulations (or successor regulations) —

(aa) to measure the concentration of organisms in ballast water that are capable of reproduction;

(bb) to certify the performance of each ballast water management system under this subsection; and

(cc) to certify laboratories to evaluate applicable treatment technologies.

(iii) Public comment

The Secretary shall provide a period of not more than 60 days for public comment regarding the draft policy letter published under clause (ii).

(iv) Final policy

(I) In general

Not later than 1 year after December 4, 2018, the Secretary, in coordination with the Administrator, shall publish a final policy letter describing type-approval testing methods, if any, for ballast water management systems that render nonviable organisms in ballast water.

(II) Method of evaluation

The ballast water management systems under subclause (I) shall be evaluated by measuring the concentration of organisms in ballast water that are capable of reproduction based on the best available science that may be used in addition to the methods established under subpart 162.060 of title 46, Code of Federal Regulations (or successor regulations).

(III) Revisions

The Secretary shall revise the final policy letter under subclause (I) in any case in which the Secretary, in coordination with the Administrator, determines that additional testing methods are capable of measuring the concentration of organisms in ballast water that have not been rendered nonviable.

(v) Factors for consideration

In developing a policy letter under this subparagraph, the Secretary, in coordination with the Administrator —

(I) shall take into consideration a testing method that uses organism grow-out and most probable number statistical analysis to determine the concentration of organisms in ballast water that are capable of reproduction; and

(II) shall not take into consideration a testing method that relies on a staining method that measures the concentration of —

(aa) organisms greater than or equal to 10 micrometers; and

(bb) organisms less than or equal to 50 micrometers.

(E) Intergovernmental response framework

(i) In general

The Secretary, in consultation with the Administrator and acting in coordination with, or through, the Aquatic Nuisance Species Task Force established by section 1201(a) of the Nonindigenous Aquatic Nuisance Prevention and Control Act of 1990 (16 U.S.C. 4721(a)), shall establish a framework for Federal and intergovernmental response to aquatic nuisance species risks from discharges from vessels subject to ballast water and incidental discharge compliance requirements under this subsection, including the introduction, spread, and establishment of aquatic nuisance species populations.

(ii) Ballast discharge risk response

The Administrator, in coordination with the Secretary and taking into consideration information from the National Ballast Information Clearinghouse developed under section 1102(f) of the Nonindigenous Aquatic Nuisance Prevention and Control Act of 1990 (16 U.S.C. 4712(f)), shall establish a risk assessment and response framework using ballast water discharge data and aquatic nuisance species monitoring data for the purposes of —

(I) identifying and tracking populations of aquatic invasive species;

(II) evaluating the risk of any aquatic nuisance species population tracked under subclause (I) establishing and spreading in waters of the United States or waters of the contiguous zone; and

(III) establishing emergency best management practices that may be deployed rapidly, in a local or regional manner, to respond to emerging aquatic nuisance species threats.

(7) Petitions by Governors for review

(A) In general

The Governor of a State (or a designee) may submit to the Administrator or the Secretary a petition —

(i) to issue an order under paragraph (4)(E); or

(ii) to review any standard of performance, regulation, or policy promulgated under paragraph (4), (5), or (6), respectively, if there exists new information that could reasonably result in a change to —

(I) the standard of performance, regulation, or policy; or

(II) a determination on which the standard of performance, regulation, or policy was based.

(B) Inclusion

A petition under subparagraph (A) shall include a description of any applicable scientific or technical information that forms the basis of the petition.

(C) Determination

(i) Timing

The Administrator or the Secretary, as applicable, shall grant or deny -

(I) a petition under subparagraph (A)(i) by not later than the date that is 180 days after the date on which the petition is submitted; and

(II) a petition under subparagraph (A)(ii) by not later than the date that is 1 year after the date on which the petition is submitted.

(ii) Effect of grant

If the Administrator or the Secretary determines under clause (i) to grant a petition —

(I) in the case of a petition under subparagraph (A)(i), the Administrator shall immediately issue the relevant order under paragraph (4)(E); or

(II) in the case of a petition under subparagraph (A)(ii), the Administrator or Secretary shall publish in the Federal Register, by not later than 30 days after the date of that determination, a notice of proposed rulemaking to revise the relevant standard, requirement, regulation, or policy under paragraph (4), (5), or (6), as applicable.

(iii) Notice of denial

If the Administrator or the Secretary determines under clause (i) to deny a petition, the Administrator or Secretary shall publish in the Federal Register, by not later than 30 days after the date of that determination, a detailed explanation of the scientific, technical, or operational factors that form the basis of the determination.

(iv) Review

A determination by the Administrator or the Secretary under clause (i) to deny a petition shall be —

(I) considered to be a final agency action; and

(II) subject to judicial review in accordance with section 1369 of this title, subject to clause (v).

(v) Exceptions

(I) Venue

Notwithstanding section 1369(b) of this title, a petition for review of a determination by the Administrator or the Secretary under clause (i) to deny a petition submitted by the Governor of a State under subparagraph (A) may be filed in any United States district court of competent jurisdiction.

(II) Deadline for filing

Notwithstanding section 1369(b) of this title, a petition for review of a determination by the Administrator or the Secretary under clause (i) shall be filed by not later than 180 days after the date on which the justification for the determination is published in the Federal Register under clause (iii).

(8) Prohibition

(A) In general

It shall be unlawful for any person to violate —

(i) a provision of the Vessel General Permit in force and effect under paragraph (3)(A);

(ii) a regulation promulgated pursuant to section 1101 of the Nonindigenous Aquatic Nuisance Prevention and Control Act of 1990 (16 U.S.C. 4711) (as in effect on the day before December 4, 2018) in force and effect under paragraph (3)(B); or

(iii) an applicable requirement or regulation under this subsection.

(B) Compliance with regulations

Effective beginning on the effective date of a regulation promulgated under paragraph (4), (5), (6), or (10), as applicable, it shall be unlawful for the owner or operator of a vessel subject to the regulation —

(i) to discharge any discharge incidental to the normal operation of the vessel into waters of the United States or waters of the contiguous zone, except in compliance with the regulation; or

(ii) to operate in waters of the United States or waters of the contiguous zone, if the vessel is not equipped with a required marine pollution control device that complies with the requirements established under this subsection, unless —

(I) the owner or operator of the vessel denotes in an entry in the official logbook of the vessel that the equipment was not operational; and

(II) either —

(aa) the applicable discharge was avoided; or

(bb) an alternate compliance option approved by the Secretary as meeting the applicable standard was employed.

(C) Affirmative defense

No person shall be found to be in violation of this paragraph if —

(i) the violation was in the interest of ensuring the safety of life at sea, as determined by the Secretary; and

(ii) the applicable emergency circumstance was not the result of negligence or malfeasance on the part of —

(I) the owner or operator of the vessel;

(II) the master of the vessel; or

(III) the person in charge of the vessel.

(D) Treatment

Each day of continuing violation of an applicable requirement of this subsection shall constitute a separate offense.

(E) In rem liability

A vessel operated in violation of this subsection is liable in rem for any civil penalty assessed for the violation.

(F) Revocation of clearance

The Secretary shall withhold or revoke the clearance of a vessel required under section 60105 of Title 46 if the owner or operator of the vessel is in violation of this subsection.

(9) Effect on other laws

(A) State authority

(i) In general

Except as provided in clauses (ii) through (v) and paragraph (10), effective beginning on the date on which the requirements promulgated by the Secretary under subparagraphs (A), (B), and (C) of paragraph (5) with respect to every discharge incidental to the normal operation of a vessel that is subject to regulation under this subsection are final, effective, and enforceable, no State, political subdivision of a State, or interstate agency may adopt or enforce any law, regulation, or other requirement of the State, political subdivision, or interstate agency with respect to any such discharge.

(ii) Identical or lesser State laws

Clause (i) shall not apply to any law, regulation, or other requirement of a State, political subdivision of a State, or interstate agency in effect on or after December 4, 2018 —

(I) that is identical to a Federal requirement under this subsection applicable to the relevant discharge; or

(II) compliance with which would be achieved concurrently in achieving compliance with a Federal requirement under this subsection applicable to the relevant discharge.

(iii) State enforcement of Federal requirements

A State may enforce any standard of performance or other Federal requirement of this subsection in accordance with subsection (k) or other applicable Federal authority.

(iv) Exception for certain fees

(I) In general

Subject to subclauses (II) and (III), a State that assesses any fee pursuant to any State or Federal law relating to the regulation of a discharge incidental to the normal operation of a vessel before December 4, 2018, may assess or retain a fee to cover the costs of administration, inspection, monitoring, and enforcement activities by the State to achieve compliance with the applicable requirements of this subsection.

(II) Maximum amount

(aa) In general

Except as provided in item (bb), a State may assess a fee for activities under this clause equal to not more than $1,000 against the owner or operator of a vessel that —

(AA) has operated outside of that State; and

(BB) arrives at a port or place of destination in the State (excluding movement entirely within a single port or place of destination).

(bb) Vessels engaged in coastwise trade

A State may assess against the owner or operator of a vessel registered in accordance with applicable Federal law and lawfully engaged in the coastwise trade not more than $5,000 in fees under this clause per vessel during a calendar year.

(III) Adjustment for inflation

(aa) In general

A State may adjust the amount of a fee authorized under this clause not more frequently than once every 5 years to reflect the percentage by which the Consumer Price Index for All Urban Consumers published by the Department of Labor for the month of October immediately preceding the date of adjustment exceeds the Consumer Price Index for All Urban Consumers published by the Department of Labor for the month of October that immediately precedes the date that is 5 years before the date of adjustment.

(bb) Effect of subclause

Nothing in this subclause prevents a State from adjusting a fee in effect before December 4, 2018, to the applicable maximum amount under subclause (II).

(cc) Applicability

This subclause applies only to increases in fees to amounts greater than the applicable maximum amount under subclause (II).

(v) Alaska graywater

Clause (i) shall not apply with respect to any discharge of graywater (as defined in section 1414 of the Consolidated Appropriations Act, 2001 (Public Law 106-554; 114 Stat. 2763A-323)) from a passenger vessel (as defined in section 2101 of Title 46) in the State of Alaska (including all waters in the Alexander Archipelago) carrying 50 or more passengers.

(vi) Preservation of authority

Nothing in this subsection preempts any State law, public initiative, referendum, regulation, requirement, or other State action, except as expressly provided in this subsection.

(B) Established regimes

Except as expressly provided in this subsection, nothing in this subsection affects the applicability to a vessel of any other provision of Federal law, including —

    (i) this section;

    (ii) section 1321 of this title;

    (iii) the Act to Prevent Pollution from Ships (33 U.S.C. 1901 et seq.); and

    (iv) title X of the Coast Guard Authorization Act of 2010 (33 U.S.C. 3801 et seq.).

(C) Permitting

Effective beginning on December 4, 2018 —

    (i) the Small Vessel General Permit is repealed; and

    (ii) the Administrator, or a State in the case of a permit program approved under section 1342 of this title, shall not require, or in any way modify, a permit under that section for —

        (I) any discharge that is subject to regulation under this subsection;

        (II) any discharge incidental to the normal operation of a vessel from a small vessel or fishing vessel, regardless of whether that discharge is subject to regulation under this subsection; or

        (III) any discharge described in paragraph (2)(B)(ii).

(D) No effect on civil or criminal actions

Nothing in this subsection, or any standard, regulation, or requirement established under this subsection, modifies or otherwise affects, preempts, or displaces —

    (i) any cause of action; or

    (ii) any provision of Federal or State law establishing a remedy for civil relief or criminal penalty.

(E) No effect on certain secretarial authority

Nothing in this subsection affects the authority of the Secretary of Commerce or the Secretary of the Interior to administer any land or waters under the administrative control of the Secretary of Commerce or the Secretary of the Interior, respectively.

(F) No limitation on State inspection authority

Nothing in this subsection limits the authority of a State to inspect a vessel pursuant to paragraph (5)(A)(iii) in order to monitor compliance with an applicable requirement of this section.

(10) Additional regional requirements

(A) Minimum Great Lakes System requirements

    (i) In general

Except as provided in clause (ii), the owner or operator of a vessel entering the St. Lawrence Seaway through the mouth of the St. Lawrence River shall conduct a complete ballast water exchange or saltwater flush —

        (I) not less than 200 nautical miles from any shore for a voyage originating outside the United States or Canadian exclusive economic zone; or

        (II) not less than 50 nautical miles from any shore for a voyage originating within the United States or Canadian exclusive economic zone.

    (ii) Exceptions

Clause (i) shall not apply to a vessel if —

        (I) complying with an applicable requirement of clause (i) —

            (aa) would compromise the safety of the vessel; or

            (bb) is otherwise prohibited by any Federal, Canadian, or international law (including regulations) pertaining to vessel safety;

        (II) design limitations of the vessel prevent a ballast water exchange from being conducted in accordance with an applicable requirement of clause (i);

        (III) the vessel —

            (aa) is certified by the Secretary as having no residual ballast water or sediments onboard; or

            (bb) retains all ballast water while in waters subject to the requirement; or

        (IV) empty ballast tanks on the vessel are sealed and certified by the Secretary in a manner that ensures that —

            (aa) no discharge or uptake occurs; and

            (bb) any subsequent discharge of ballast water is subject to the requirement.

(B) Enhanced Great Lakes System requirements

    (i) Petitions by Governors for proposed enhanced standards and requirements

        (I) In general

The Governor of a Great Lakes State (or a State employee designee) may submit a petition in accordance with subclause (II) to propose that other Governors of Great Lakes States endorse an enhanced standard of performance or other requirement with respect to any discharge that —

            (aa) is subject to regulation under this subsection; and

            (bb) occurs within the Great Lakes System.

(II) Submission

A Governor shall submit a petition under subclause (I), in writing, to —

(aa) the Executive Director of the Great Lakes Commission, in such manner as may be prescribed by the Great Lakes Commission;

(bb) the Governor of each other Great Lakes State; and

(cc) the Director of the Great Lakes National Program Office established by section 1268(b) of this title.

(III) Preliminary assessment by Great Lakes Commission

(aa) In general

After the date of receipt of a petition under subclause (II)(aa), the Great Lakes Commission (acting through the Great Lakes Panel on Aquatic Nuisance Species, to the maximum extent practicable) may develop a preliminary assessment regarding each enhanced standard of performance or other requirement described in the petition.

(bb) Provisions

The preliminary assessment developed by the Great Lakes Commission under item (aa) —

(AA) may be developed in consultation with relevant experts and stakeholders;

(BB) may be narrative in nature;

(CC) may include the preliminary views, if any, of the Great Lakes Commission on the propriety of the proposed enhanced standard of performance or other requirement;

(DD) shall be submitted, in writing, to the Governor of each Great Lakes State and the Director of the Great Lakes National Program Office and published on the internet website of the Great Lakes National Program Office; and

(EE) except as provided in clause (iii), shall not be taken into consideration, or provide a basis for review, by the Administrator or the Secretary for purposes of that clause.

(ii) Proposed enhanced standards and requirements

(I) Publication in Federal Register

(aa) Request by Governor

Not earlier than the date that is 90 days after the date on which the Executive Director of the Great Lakes Commission receives from a Governor of a Great Lakes State a petition under clause (i)(II)(aa), the Governor may request the Director of the Great Lakes National Program Office to publish, for a period requested by the Governor of not less than 30 days, and the Director shall so publish, in the Federal Register for public comment —

(AA) a copy of the petition; and

(BB) if applicable as of the date of publication, any preliminary assessment of the Great Lakes Commission developed under clause (i)(III) relating to the petition.

(bb) Review of public comments

On receipt of a written request of a Governor of a Great Lakes State, the Director of the Great Lakes National Program Office shall make available all public comments received in response to the notice under item (aa).

(cc) No response required

Notwithstanding any other provision of law, a Governor of a Great Lakes State or the Director of the Great Lakes National Program Office shall not be required to provide a response to any comment received in response to the publication of a petition or preliminary assessment under item (aa).

(dd) Purpose

Any public comments received in response to the publication of a petition or preliminary assessment under item (aa) shall be used solely for the purpose of providing information and feedback to the Governor of each Great Lakes State regarding the decision to endorse the proposed standard or requirement.

(ee) Effect of petition

A proposed standard or requirement developed under subclause (II) may differ from the proposed standard or requirement described in a petition published under item (aa).

(II) Coordination to develop proposed standard or requirement

After the expiration of the public comment period for the petition under subclause (I), any interested Governor of a Great Lakes State may work in coordination with the Great Lakes Commission to develop a proposed standard of performance or other requirement applicable to a discharge referred to in the petition.

(III) Requirements

A proposed standard of performance or other requirement under subclause (II) —

(aa) shall be developed —

(AA) in consultation with representatives from the Federal and provincial governments of Canada;

(BB) after notice and opportunity for public comment on the petition published under subclause (I); and

(CC) taking into consideration the preliminary assessment, if any, of the Great Lakes Commission under clause (i)(III);

(bb) shall be specifically endorsed in writing by —

(AA) the Governor of each Great Lakes State, if the proposed standard or requirement would impose any additional equipment requirement on a vessel; or

(BB) not fewer than 5 Governors of Great Lakes States, if the proposed standard or requirement would not impose any additional equipment requirement on a vessel; and

(cc) in the case of a proposed requirement to prohibit 1 or more types of discharge regulated under this subsection, whether treated or not treated, into waters within the Great Lakes System, shall not apply outside the waters of the Great Lakes States of the Governors endorsing the proposed requirement under item (bb).

(iii) Promulgation by Administrator and Secretary

(I) Submission

(aa) In general

The Governors endorsing a proposed standard or requirement

under clause (ii)(III)(bb) may jointly submit to the Administrator and the Secretary for approval each proposed standard of performance or other requirement developed and endorsed pursuant to clause (ii).

(bb) Inclusion

Each submission under item (aa) shall include an explanation regarding why the applicable standard of performance or other requirement is —

(AA) at least as stringent as a comparable standard of performance or other requirement under this subsection;

(BB) in accordance with maritime safety; and

(CC) in accordance with applicable maritime and navigation laws and regulations.

(cc) Withdrawal

(AA) In general

The Governor of any Great Lakes State that endorses a proposed standard or requirement under clause (ii)(III) (bb) may withdraw the endorsement by not later than the date that is 90 days after the date on which the Administrator and the Secretary receive the proposed standard or requirement.

(BB) Effect on Federal review

If, after the withdrawal of an endorsement under subitem (AA), the proposed standard or requirement does not have the applicable number of endorsements under clause (ii)(III)(bb), the Administrator and the Secretary shall terminate the review under this clause.

(dd) Dissenting opinions

The Governor of a Great Lakes State that does not endorse a proposed standard or requirement under clause (ii)(III)(bb) may submit to the Administrator and the Secretary any dissenting opinions of the Governor.

(II) Joint notice

On receipt of a proposed standard of performance or other requirement under subclause (I), the Administrator and the Secretary shall publish in the

Federal Register a joint notice that, at minimum —

(aa) states that the proposed standard or requirement is publicly available; and

(bb) provides an opportunity for public comment regarding the proposed standard or requirement during the 90-day period beginning on the date of receipt by the Administrator and the Secretary of the proposed standard or requirement.

(III) Review

(aa) In general

As soon as practicable after the date of publication of a joint notice under subclause (II) —

(AA) the Administrator shall commence a review of each proposed standard of performance or other requirement covered by the notice to determine whether that standard or requirement is at least as stringent as comparable standards and requirements under this subsection; and

(BB) the Secretary shall commence a review of each proposed standard of performance or other requirement covered by the notice to determine whether that standard or requirement is in accordance with maritime safety and applicable maritime and navigation laws and regulations.

(bb) Consultation

In carrying out item (aa), the Administrator and the Secretary —

(AA) shall consult with the Governor of each Great Lakes State and representatives from the Federal and provincial governments of Canada;

(BB) shall take into consideration any relevant data or public comments received under subclause (II)(bb); and

(CC) shall not take into consideration any preliminary assessment by the Great Lakes Commission under clause (i)(III), or any dissenting opinion under subclause (I)(dd), except to the extent that such an assessment or opinion is relevant to the criteria for the applicable determination under item (aa).

(IV) Approval or disapproval

Not later than 180 days after the date of receipt of each proposed standard of performance or other requirement under subclause (I), the Administrator and the Secretary shall —

(aa) determine, as applicable, whether each proposed standard or other requirement satisfies the criteria under subclause (III)(aa);

(bb) approve each proposed standard or other requirement, unless the Administrator or the Secretary, as applicable, determines under item (aa) that the proposed standard or other requirement does not satisfy the criteria under subclause (III)(aa); and

(cc) submit to the Governor of each Great Lakes State, and publish in the Federal Register, a notice of the determination under item (aa).

(V) Action on disapproval

(aa) Rationale and recommendations

If the Administrator and the Secretary disapprove a proposed standard of performance or other requirement under subclause (IV)(bb), the notices under subclause (IV)(cc) shall include —

(AA) a description of the reasons why the standard or requirement is, as applicable, less stringent than a comparable standard or requirement under this subsection, inconsistent with maritime safety, or inconsistent with applicable maritime and navigation laws and regulations; and

(BB) any recommendations regarding changes the Governors of the Great Lakes States could make to conform the disapproved portion of the standard or requirement to the requirements of this subparagraph.

(bb) Review

Disapproval of a proposed standard or requirement by the Administrator and the Secretary under this subparagraph shall be considered to be a final agency action subject to judicial review under section 1369 of this title.

(VI) Action on approval

On approval by the Administrator and the Secretary of a proposed standard of performance or other requirement under subclause (IV)(bb) —

(aa) the Administrator shall establish, by regulation, the proposed standard or requirement within the Great Lakes System in lieu of any comparable standard or other requirement promulgated under paragraph (4); and

(bb) the Secretary shall establish, by regulation, any requirements necessary to implement, ensure compliance with, and enforce the standard or requirement under item (aa), or to apply the proposed requirement, within the Great Lakes System in lieu of any comparable requirement promulgated under paragraph (5).

(VII) No judicial review for certain actions

An action or inaction of a Governor of a Great Lakes State or the Great Lakes Commission under this subparagraph shall not be subject to judicial review.

(VIII) Great Lakes Compact

Nothing in this subsection limits, alters, or amends the Great Lakes Compact2 to which Congress granted consent in the Act of July 24, 1968 (Public Law 90-419; 82 Stat. 414).

(IX) Authorization of appropriations

There is authorized to be appropriated to the Great Lakes Commission $5,000,000, to be available until expended.

(C) Minimum Pacific Region requirements

(i) Definition of commercial vessel

In this subparagraph, the term "commercial vessel" means a vessel operating between —

(I) 2 ports or places of destination within the Pacific Region; or

(II) a port or place of destination within the Pacific Region and a port or place of destination on the Pacific Coast of Canada or Mexico north of parallel 20 degrees north latitude, inclusive of the Gulf of California.

(ii) Ballast water exchange

(I) In general

Except as provided in subclause (II) and clause (iv), the owner or operator of a commercial vessel shall conduct a complete ballast water exchange in waters more than 50 nautical miles from shore.

(II) Exemptions

Subclause (I) shall not apply to a commercial vessel —

(aa) using, in compliance with applicable requirements, a type-approved ballast water management system approved by the Secretary; or

(bb) voyaging —

(AA) between or to a port or place of destination in the State of Washington, if the ballast water to be discharged from the commercial vessel originated solely from waters located between the parallel 46 degrees north latitude, including the internal waters of the Columbia River, and the internal waters of Canada south of parallel 50 degrees north latitude, including the waters of the Strait of Georgia and the Strait of Juan de Fuca;

(BB) between ports or places of destination in the State of Oregon, if the ballast water to be discharged from the commercial vessel originated solely from waters located between the parallel 40 degrees north latitude and the parallel 50 degrees north latitude;

(CC) between ports or places of destination in the State of California within the San Francisco Bay area east of the Golden Gate Bridge, including the Port of Stockton and the Port of Sacramento, if the ballast water to be discharged from the commercial vessel originated solely from ports or places within that area;

(DD) between the Port of Los Angeles, the Port of Long Beach, and the El Segundo offshore marine oil terminal, if the ballast water to be discharged from the commercial vessel originated solely from the Port of Los Angeles, the Port of Long Beach, or the El

Segundo offshore marine oil terminal;

(EE) between a port or place of destination in the State of Alaska within a single Captain of the Port Zone;

(FF) between ports or places of destination in different counties of the State of Hawaii, if the vessel may conduct a complete ballast water exchange in waters that are more than 10 nautical miles from shore and at least 200 meters deep; or

(GG) between ports or places of destination within the same county of the State of Hawaii, if the vessel does not transit outside State marine waters during the voyage.

(iii) Low-salinity ballast water

(I) In general

Except as provided in subclause (II) and clause (iv), the owner or operator of a commercial vessel that transports ballast water sourced from waters with a measured salinity of less than 18 parts per thousand and voyages to a Pacific Region port or place of destination with a measured salinity of less than 18 parts per thousand shall conduct a complete ballast water exchange —

(aa) not less than 50 nautical miles from shore, if the ballast water was sourced from a Pacific Region port or place of destination; or

(bb) more than 200 nautical miles from shore, if the ballast water was not sourced from a Pacific Region port or place of destination.

(II) Exception

Subclause (I) shall not apply to a commercial vessel voyaging to a port or place of destination in the Pacific Region that is using, in compliance with applicable requirements, a type-approved ballast water management system approved by the Secretary to achieve standards of performance of —

(aa) less than 1 organism per 10 cubic meters, if that organism —

(AA) is living, or has not been rendered nonviable; and

(BB) is 50 or more micrometers in minimum dimension;

(bb) less than 1 organism per 10 milliliters, if that organism —

(AA) is living, or has not been rendered nonviable; and

(BB) is more than 10, but less than 50, micrometers in minimum dimension;

(cc) concentrations of indicator microbes that are less than —

(AA) 1 colony-forming unit of toxicogenic Vibrio cholera (serotypes O1 and O139) per 100 milliliters or less than 1 colony-forming unit of that microbe per gram of wet weight of zoological samples;

(BB) 126 colony-forming units of escherichia coli per 100 milliliters; and

(CC) 33 colony-forming units of intestinal enterococci per 100 milliliters; and

(dd) concentrations of such additional indicator microbes and viruses as may be specified in the standards of performance established by the Administrator under paragraph (4).

(iv) General exceptions

The requirements of clauses (ii) and (iii) shall not apply to a commercial vessel if —

(I) complying with the requirement would compromise the safety of the commercial vessel;

(II) design limitations of the commercial vessel prevent a ballast water exchange from being conducted in accordance with clause (ii) or (iii), as applicable;

(III) the commercial vessel —

(aa) is certified by the Secretary as having no residual ballast water or sediments onboard; or

(bb) retains all ballast water while in waters subject to those requirements; or

(IV) empty ballast tanks on the commercial vessel are sealed and certified by the Secretary in a manner that ensures that —

(aa) no discharge or uptake occurs; and

(bb) any subsequent discharge of ballast water is subject to those requirements.

(D) Establishment of State no-discharge zones

(i) State prohibition

Subject to clause (ii), after the effective date of regulations promulgated by the Secretary under paragraph (5), if any State determines that the protection and enhancement of the quality of some or all of the waters within the State require greater environmental protection, the State may prohibit 1 or more types of discharge regulated under this subsection, whether treated or not treated, into such waters.

(ii) Applicability

A prohibition by a State under clause (i) shall not apply until the date on which the Administrator makes the applicable determinations described in clause (iii).

(iii) Prohibition by Administrator

(I) Determination

On application of a State, the Administrator, in concurrence with the Secretary (subject to subclause (II)), shall, by regulation, prohibit the discharge from a vessel of 1 or more discharges subject to regulation under this subsection, whether treated or not treated, into the waters covered by the application if the Administrator determines that —

(aa) prohibition of the discharge would protect and enhance the quality of the specified waters within the State;

(bb) adequate facilities for the safe and sanitary removal and treatment of the discharge are reasonably available for the water and all vessels to which the prohibition would apply;

(cc) the discharge can be safely collected and stored until a vessel reaches a discharge facility or other location; and

(dd) in the case of an application for the prohibition of discharges of ballast water in a port (or in any other location where cargo, passengers, or fuel are loaded and unloaded) —

(AA) the adequate facilities described in item (bb) are reasonably available for commercial vessels, after considering, at a minimum, water depth, dock size, pumpout facility capacity and flow rate, availability of year-round operations, proximity to navigation routes, and the ratio of pumpout facilities to the population and discharge capacity of commercial vessels operating in those waters; and

(BB) the prohibition will not unreasonably interfere with the safe loading and unloading of cargo, passengers, or fuel.

(II) Concurrence with Secretary

(aa) Request

The Administrator shall submit to the Secretary a request for written concurrence with respect to a prohibition under subclause (I).

(bb) Effect of failure to concur

A failure by the Secretary to concur with the Administrator under subclause (I) by the date that is 60 days after the date on which the Administrator submits a request for concurrence under item (aa) shall not prevent the Administrator from prohibiting the relevant discharge in accordance with subclause (III), subject to the condition that the Administrator shall include in the administrative record of the promulgation —

(AA) documentation of the request submitted under item (aa); and

(BB) the response of the Administrator to any written objections received from the Secretary relating to the proposed standard of performance during the 60-day period beginning on the date of submission of the request.

(III) Timing

The Administrator shall approve or disapprove an application submitted under subclause (I) by not later than 90 days after the date on which the application is submitted to the Administrator.

(E) Maintenance in effect of more-stringent standards

In any case in which a requirement established under this paragraph is more stringent or environmentally protective than a comparable requirement established under paragraph (4), (5), or (6), the more-stringent or more-protective requirement shall control.

§1323. Federal facilities pollution control [CWA §313]

(a) Compliance with pollution control requirements by Federal entities

Each department, agency, or instrumentality of the executive, legislative, and judicial branches of the Federal Government (1) having jurisdiction over any property or facility, or (2) engaged in any activity resulting, or which may result, in the discharge or run-off of pollutants, and each officer, agent, or employee thereof in the performance of his official duties, shall be subject to, and comply with, all Federal, State, inter-state, and local requirements, administrative authority, and process and sanctions respecting the control and abatement of water pollution in the same manner, and to the same extent as any nongovernmental entity including the payment of reasonable service charges. The preceding sentence shall apply (A) to any require-ment whether substantive or procedural (including any recordkeeping or reporting requirement, any requirement respecting permits and any other require-ment, whatsoever), (B) to the exercise of any Federal, State, or local administrative authority, and (C) to any process and sanction, whether enforced in Federal, State, or local courts or in any other manner. This subsection shall apply notwithstanding any immunity of such agencies, officers, agents, or employees under any law or rule of law. Nothing in this section shall be construed to prevent any department, agency, or instrumentality of the Federal Government, or any officer, agent, or employee thereof in the performance of his official duties, from removing to the appropri-ate Federal district court any proceeding to which the department, agency, or instrumentality or officer, agent, or employee thereof is subject pursuant to this section, and any such proceeding may be removed in accordance with sections 1441 *et seq.* of Title 28. No officer, agent, or employee of the United States shall be personally liable for any civil penalty arising from the performance of his official duties, for which he is not otherwise liable, and the United States shall be li-able only for those civil penalties arising under Federal law or imposed by a State or local court to enforce an order or the process of such court. The President may exempt any effluent source of any department, agency, or instrumentality in the executive branch from compliance with any such a requirement if he determines it to be in the paramount interest of the United States to do so; except that no exemption may be granted from the requirements of section 1316 or 1317 of this title. No such exemptions shall be granted due to lack of appropriation unless the President shall have specifically requested such appropriation as a part of the budgetary process and the Congress shall have failed to make available such requested appropriation. Any exemption shall be for a period not in excess of one year, but additional exemptions may be granted for periods of not to exceed one year upon the President's making a new determination. The President shall report each January to the Congress all exemptions from the requirements of this section granted during the preceding calendar year, together with his reason for granting such exemption. In ad-dition to any such exemption of a particular effluent source, the President may, if he determines it to be in the paramount interest of the United States to do so, issue regulations exempting from compliance with the requirements of this section any weaponry, equipment, aircraft, vessels, vehicles, or other classes or categories of property, and access to such property, which are owned or operated by the Armed Forces of the United States (including the Coast Guard) or by the National Guard of any State and which are uniquely military in nature. The President shall reconsider the need for such regulations at three-year intervals.

(b) Cooperation with Federal entities and limitation on facility construction

(1) The Administrator shall coordinate with the head of each department, agency, or instru-mentality of the Federal Government having jurisdiction over any property or facility utilizing federally owned wastewater facilities to develop a program of cooperation for utilizing wastewa-ter control systems utilizing those innovative treatment processes and techniques for which guidelines have been promulgated under section 1314(d)(3) of this title. Such program shall include an inventory of property and facilities which could utilize such processes and techniques.

(2) Construction shall not be initiated for facilities for treatment of wastewater at any Fed-eral property or facility after September 30, 1979, if alternative methods for wastewater treatment at such property or facility utilizing innovative treatment processes and techniques, including but not limited to methods utilizing recycle and reuse techniques and land treatment are not utilized, un-less the life cycle cost of the alternative treatment works exceeds the life cycle cost of the most cost effective alternative by more than 15 per centum. The Administrator may waive the application of this paragraph in any case where the Administrator determines it to be in the public interest, or that compliance with this paragraph would interfere with the orderly compliance with conditions of a permit issued pursuant to section 1342 of this title.

(c) Reasonable service charges

(1) In general — For the purposes of this chapter, reasonable service charges described in subsection (a) include any reasonable nondis-criminatory fee, charge, or assessment that is —

(A) based on some fair approximation of the proportionate contribution of the property or facil-ity to stormwater pollution (in terms of quantities of pollutants, or volume or rate of stormwater dis-charge or runoff from the property or facility); and

(B) used to pay or reimburse the costs associ-ated with any stormwater management program (whether associated with a separate storm sewer system or a sewer system that manages a combina-tion of stormwater and sanitary waste), including the full range of programmatic and structural costs attributable to collecting stormwater, reducing pol-lutants in stormwater, and reducing the volume and rate of stormwater discharge, regardless of whether that reasonable fee, charge, or assessment is denominated a tax.

(2) Limitation on accounts

(A) Limitation — The payment or reimbursement of any fee, charge, or assessment described in paragraph (1) shall not be made using funds from any permanent authorization account in the Treasury.

(B) Reimbursement or payment obligation of Federal Government — Each department, agency, or instrumentality of the executive, legislative, and judicial branches of the Federal Government, as described in subsection (a), shall not be obligated to pay or reimburse any fee, charge, or assessment described in paragraph (1), except to the extent and in an amount provided in advance by any appropriations Act to pay or reimburse the fee, charge, or assessment.

§1324. Clean lakes
[CWA §314]
(a) Establishment and scope of program

(1) State program requirements — Each State on a biennial basis shall prepare and submit to the Administrator for his approval —

(A) an identification and classification according to eutrophic condition of all publicly owned lakes in such State;

(B) a description of procedures, processes, and methods (including land use requirements), to control sources of pollution of such lakes;

(C) a description of methods and procedures, in conjunction with appropriate Federal agencies, to restore the quality of such lakes;

(D) methods and procedures to mitigate the harmful effects of high acidity, including innovative methods of neutralizing and restoring buffering capacity of lakes and methods of removing from lakes toxic metals and other toxic substances mobilized by high acidity;

(E) a list and description of those publicly owned lakes in such State for which uses are known to be impaired, including those lakes which are known not to meet applicable water quality standards or which require implementation of control programs to maintain compliance with applicable standards and those lakes in which water quality has deteriorated as a result of high acidity that may reasonably be due to acid deposition; and

(F) an assessment of the status and trends of water quality in lakes in such State, including but not limited to, the nature and extent of pollution loading from point and nonpoint sources and the extent to which the use of lakes is impaired as a result of such pollution, particularly with respect to toxic pollution.

(2) Submission as part of 1315(b)(1) report — The information required under paragraph (1) shall be included in the report required under section 1315(b)(1) of this title, beginning with the report required under such section by April 1, 1988.

(3) Report of Administrator — Not later than 180 days after receipt from the States of the biennial information required under paragraph (1), the Administrator shall submit to the Committee on Public Works and Transportation of the House of Representatives and the Committee on Environment and Public Works of the Senate a report on the status of water quality in lakes in the United States, including the effectiveness of the methods and procedures described in paragraph (1)(D).

(4) Eligibility requirement — Beginning after April 1, 1988, a State must have submitted the information required under paragraph (1) in order to receive grant assistance under this section.

(b) Financial assistance to States — The
Administrator shall provide financial assistance to States in order to carry out methods and procedures approved by him under subsection (a) of this section. The Administrator shall provide financial assistance to States to prepare the identification and classification surveys required in subsection (a)(1) of this section.

(c) Maximum amount of grant; authorization of appropriations

(1) The amount granted to any State for any fiscal year under subsection (b) of this section shall not exceed 70 per centum of the funds expended by such State in such year for carrying out approved methods and procedures under subsection (a) of this section.

(2) There is authorized to be appropriated $50,000,000 for each of the fiscal years 2001 through 2005 for grants to States under subsection (b) of this section which such sums shall remain available until expended. The Administrator shall provide for an equitable distribution of such sums to the States with approved methods and procedures under subsection (a) of this section.

(d) Demonstration program

(1) General requirements — The Administrator is authorized and directed to establish and conduct at locations throughout the Nation a lake water quality demonstration program. The program shall, at a minimum —

(A) develop cost effective technologies for the control of pollutants to preserve or enhance lake water quality while optimizing multiple lakes uses;

(B) control nonpoint sources of pollution which are contributing to the degradation of water quality in lakes;

(C) evaluate the feasibility of implementing regional consolidated pollution control strategies;

(D) demonstrate environmentally preferred techniques for the removal and disposal of contaminated lake sediments;

(E) develop improved methods for the removal of silt, stumps, aquatic growth, and other obstructions which impair the quality of lakes;

(F) construct and evaluate silt traps and other devices or equipment to prevent or abate the deposit of sediment in lakes; and

(G) demonstrate the costs and benefits of utilizing dredged material from lakes in the reclamation of despoiled land.

(2) Geographical requirements — Demonstration projects authorized by this subsection shall be undertaken to reflect a variety of geographical and environmental conditions. As a priority, the Administrator shall undertake demonstration projects at Lake Champlain, New York and Vermont; Lake Houston, Texas; Beaver Lake, Arkansas; Greenwood Lake and Belcher Creek, New Jersey; Deal Lake, New Jersey; Alcyon Lake, New Jersey; Gorton's Pond, Rhode Island; Lake Washington, Rhode Island; Lake Bomoseen, Vermont; Sauk Lake, Minnesota; Otsego Lake, New York; Oneida Lake, New York; Raystown Lake, Pennsylvania; Swan Lake, Itasca County, Minnesota; Walker Lake, Nevada; Lake Tahoe, California and Nevada; Ten Mile Lakes, Oregon; Woahink Lake, Oregon; Highland Lake, Connecticut; Lily Lake, New Jersey; Strawbridge Lake, New Jersey; Baboosic Lake, New Hampshire; French Pond, New Hampshire; Dillon Reservoir, Ohio; Tohopekaliga Lake, Florida; Lake Apopka, Florida; Lake George, New York; Lake Wallenpaupack, Pennsylvania; Lake Allatoona, Georgia; and Lake Worth, Texas.

(3) Reports — Notwithstanding section 3003 of the Federal Reports Elimination and Sunset Act of 1995 (31 U.S.C. §1113 note; 109 Stat. 734-736), by January 1, 1997, and January 1 of every odd-numbered year thereafter, the Administrator shall report to the Committee on Transportation and Infrastructure of the House of Representatives and the Committee on Environment and Public Works of the Senate on work undertaken pursuant to this subsection. Upon completion of the program authorized by this subsection, the Administrator shall submit to such committees a final report on the results of such program, along with recommendations for further measures to improve the water quality of the Nation's lakes.

(4) Authorization of appropriations

(A) In general — There is authorized to be appropriated to carry out this subsection not to exceed $40,000,000 for fiscal years beginning after September 30, 1986, to remain available until expended.

(B) Special authorizations

    (i) Amount — There is authorized to be appropriated to carry out subsection (b) of this section with respect to subsection (a)(1)(D) of this section not to exceed $25,000,000 for fiscal years beginning after September 30, 1986, to remain available until expended.

    (ii) Distribution of funds — The Administrator shall provide for an equitable distribution of sums appropriated pursuant to this subparagraph among States carrying out approved methods and procedures. Such distribution shall be based on the relative needs of each such State for the mitigation of the harmful effects on lakes and other surface waters of high acidity that may reasonably be due to acid deposition or acid mine drainage.

    (iii) Grants as additional assistance — The amount of any grant to a State under this subparagraph shall be in addition to, and not in lieu of, any other Federal financial assistance.

§1325. National Study Commission [CWA §315]

(a) Establishment — There is established a National Study Commission, which shall make a full and complete investigation and study of all of the technological aspects of achieving, and all aspects of the total economic, social, and environmental effects of achieving or not achieving, the effluent limitations and goals set forth for 1983 in section 1311(b)(2) of this title.

(b) Membership; chairman — Such Commission shall be composed of fifteen members, including five members of the Senate, who are members of the Environment and Public Works committee, appointed by the President of the Senate, five members of the House, who are members of the Public Works and Transportation committee, appointed by the Speaker of the House, and five members of the public appointed by the President. The Chairman of such Commission shall be elected from among its members.

(c) Contract authority — In the conduct of such study, the Commission is authorized to contract with the National Academy of Sciences and the National Academy of Engineering (acting through the National Research Council), the National Institute of Ecology, Brookings Institution, and other nongovernmental entities, for the investigation of matters within their competence.

(d) Cooperation of departments, agencies, and instrumentalities of executive branch — The heads of the departments, agencies and instrumentalities of the executive branch of the Federal Government shall cooperate with the Commission in carrying out the requirements of this section, and shall furnish to the Commission such information as the Commission deems necessary to carry out this section.

(e) Report to Congress — A report shall be submitted to the Congress of the results of such investigation and study, together with recommendations, not later than three years after October 18, 1972.

(f) Compensation and allowances — The members of the Commission who are not officers or employees of the United States, while attending conferences or meetings of the Commission or while otherwise serving at the request of the Chairman shall be entitled to receive compensation at a rate not in excess of the maximum rate of pay for Grade GS-18, as provided in the General Schedule under section 5332 of Title 5, including travel time and while away from their homes or regular places of business they may be allowed travel expenses, including per diem in lieu of subsistence as authorized by law for persons in the Government service employed intermittently.

(g) Appointment of personnel — In addition to authority to appoint personnel subject to the provisions of Title 5 governing appointments in the competitive service, and to pay such personnel in accordance with the provisions of chapter 51 and subchapter III of chapter 53 of such title relating to classification and General Schedule pay rates, the Commission shall have authority to enter into contracts with private or public organizations who shall furnish the Commission with such administrative and technical personnel as may be necessary to carry out the purpose of this section. Personnel furnished by such organizations under this subsection are not, and shall not be considered to be, Federal employees for any purposes, but in the performance of their duties shall be guided by the standards which apply to employees of the legislative branches under rules 41 and 43 of the Senate and House of Representatives, respectively.

(h) Authorization of appropriation — There is authorized to be appropriated, for use in carrying out this section, not to exceed $17,250,000.

§1326. Thermal discharges
[CWA §316]

(a) Effluent limitations that will assure protection and propagation of balanced, indigenous population of shellfish, fish, and wildlife — With respect to any point source otherwise subject to the provisions of section 1311 of this title or section 1316 of this title, whenever the owner or operator of any such source, after opportunity for public hearing, can demonstrate to the satisfaction of the Administrator (or, if appropriate, the State) that any effluent limitation proposed for the control of the thermal component of any discharge from such source will require effluent limitations more stringent than necessary to assure the projection and propagation of a balanced, indigenous population of shellfish, fish, and wildlife in and on the body of water into which the discharge is to be made, the Administrator (or, if appropriate, the State) may impose an effluent limitation under such sections for such plant, with respect to the thermal component of such discharge (taking into account the interaction of such thermal component with other pollutants), that will assure the protection and propagation of a balanced, indigenous

population of shellfish, fish, and wildlife in and on that body of water.

(b) Cooling water intake structures — Any standard established pursuant to section 1311 of this title or section 1316 of this title and applicable to a point source shall require that the location, design, construction, and capacity of cooling water intake structures reflect the best technology available for minimizing adverse environmental impact.

(c) Period of protection from more stringent effluent limitations following discharge point source modification commenced after October 18, 1972 — Notwithstanding any other provision of this chapter, any point source of a discharge having a thermal component, the modification of which point source is commenced after October 18, 1972, and which, as modified, meets effluent limitations established under section 1311 of this title or, if more stringent, effluent limitations established under section 1313 of this title and which effluent limitations will assure protection and propagation of a balanced, indigenous population of shellfish, fish, and wildlife in or on the water into which the discharge is made, shall not be subject to any more stringent effluent limitation with respect to the thermal component of its discharge during a ten year period beginning on the date of completion of such modification or during the period of depreciation or amortization of such facility for the purpose of section 167 or 169 (or both) of Title 26, whichever period ends first.

§1327. Omitted

§1328. Aquaculture
[CWA §318]

(a) Authority to permit discharge of specific pollutants — The Administrator is authorized, after public hearings, to permit the discharge of a specific pollutant or pollutants under controlled conditions associated with an approved aquaculture project under Federal or State supervision pursuant to section 1342 of this title.

(b) Procedures and guidelines — The Administrator shall by regulation establish any procedures and guidelines which the Administrator deems necessary to carry out this section. Such regulations shall require the application to such discharge of each criterion, factor, procedure, and requirement applicable to a permit issued under section 1342 of this title, as the Administrator determines necessary to carry out the objective of this chapter.

(c) State administration — Each State desiring to administer its own permit program within its jurisdiction for discharge of a specific pollutant or pollutants under controlled conditions associated with an approved aquaculture project may do so if upon submission of such program the Administrator determines such program is adequate to carry out the objective of this chapter.

§1329. Nonpoint source management programs

[CWA §319]

(a) State assessment reports

(1) Contents — The Governor of each State shall, after notice and opportunity for public comment, prepare and submit to the Administrator for approval, a report which —

(A) identifies those navigable waters within the State which, without additional action to control nonpoint sources of pollution, cannot reasonably be expected to attain or maintain applicable water quality standards or the goals and requirements of this chapter;

(B) identifies those categories and subcategories of nonpoint sources or, where appropriate, particular nonpoint sources which add significant pollution to each portion of the navigable waters identified under subparagraph (A) in amounts which contribute to such portion not meeting such water quality standards or such goals and requirements;

(C) describes the process, including intergovernmental coordination and public participation, for identifying best management practices and measures to control each category and subcategory of nonpoint sources and, where appropriate, particular nonpoint sources identified under subparagraph (B) and to reduce, to the maximum extent practicable, the level of pollution resulting from such category, subcategory, or source; and

(D) identifies and describes State and local programs for controlling pollution added from nonpoint sources to, and improving the quality of, each such portion of the navigable waters, including but not limited to those programs which are receiving Federal assistance under subsections (h) and (i) of this section.

(2) Information used in preparation — In developing the report required by this section, the State (A) may rely upon information developed pursuant to sections 1288, 1313(e), 1314(f), 1315(b), and 1324 of this title, and other information as appropriate, and (B) may utilize appropriate elements of the waste treatment management plans developed pursuant to sections 1288(b) and 1313 of this title, to the extent such elements are consistent with and fulfill the requirements of this section.

(b) State management programs

(1) In general — The Governor of each State, for that State or in combination with adjacent States, shall, after notice and opportunity for public comment, prepare and submit to the Administrator for approval a management program which such State proposes to implement in the first four fiscal years beginning after the date of submission of such management program for controlling pollution added from nonpoint sources to the navigable waters within the State and improving the quality of such waters.

(2) Specific contents — Each management program proposed for implementation under this subsection shall include each of the following:

(A) An identification of the best management practices and measures which will be undertaken to reduce pollutant loadings resulting from each category, subcategory, or particular nonpoint source designated under paragraph (1)(B), taking into account the impact of the practice on ground water quality.

(B) An identification of programs (including, as appropriate, nonregulatory or regulatory programs for enforcement, technical assistance, financial assistance, education, training, technology transfer, and demonstration projects) to achieve implementation of the best management practices by the categories, subcategories, and particular nonpoint sources designated under subparagraph (A).

(C) A schedule containing annual milestones for (i) utilization of the program implementation methods identified in subparagraph (B), and (ii) implementation of the best management practices identified in subparagraph (A) by the categories, subcategories, or particular nonpoint sources designated under paragraph (1)(B). Such schedule shall provide for utilization of the best management practices at the earliest practicable date.

(D) A certification of the attorney general of the State or States (or the chief attorney of any State water pollution control agency which has independent legal counsel) that the laws of the State or States, as the case may be, provide adequate authority to implement such management program or, if there is not such adequate authority, a list of such additional authorities as will be necessary to implement such management program. A schedule and commitment by the State or States to seek such additional authorities as expeditiously as practicable.

(E) Sources of Federal and other assistance and funding (other than assistance provided under subsections (h) and (i) of this section) which will be available in each of such fiscal years for supporting implementation of such practices and measures and the purposes for which such assistance will be used in each of such fiscal years.

(F) An identification of Federal financial assistance programs and Federal development projects for which the State will review individual assistance applications or development projects for their effect on water quality pursuant to the procedures set forth in Executive

Order 12372 as in effect on September 17, 1983, to determine whether such assistance applications or development projects would be consistent with the program prepared under this subsection; for the purposes of this subparagraph, identification shall not be limited to the assistance programs or development projects subject to Executive Order 12372 but may include any programs listed in the most recent Catalog of Federal Domestic Assistance which may have an effect on the purposes and objectives of the State's nonpoint source pollution management program.

(3) Utilization of local and private experts — In developing and implementing a management program under this subsection, a State shall, to the maximum extent practicable, involve local public and private agencies and organizations which have expertise in control of nonpoint sources of pollution.

(4) Development on watershed basis — A State shall, to the maximum extent practicable, develop and implement a management program under this subsection on a watershed-by-watershed basis within such State.

(c) Administrative provisions

(1) Cooperation requirement — Any report required by subsection (a) of this section and any management program and report required by subsection (b) of this section shall be developed in cooperation with local, substate regional, and interstate entities which are actively planning for the implementation of nonpoint source pollution controls and have either been certified by the Administrator in accordance with section 1288 of this title, have worked jointly with the State on water quality management planning under section 1285(j) of this title, or have been designated by the State legislative body or Governor as water quality management planning agencies for their geographic areas.

(2) Time period for submission of reports and management programs — Each report and management program shall be submitted to the Administrator during the 18-month period beginning on February 4, 1987.

(d) Approval or disapproval of reports and management programs

(1) Deadline — Subject to paragraph (2), not later than 180 days after the date of submission to the Administrator of any report or management program under this section (other than subsections (h), (i), and (k) of this section), the Administrator shall either approve or disapprove such report or management program, as the case may be. The Administrator may approve a portion of a management program under this subsection. If the Administrator does not disapprove a report, management program, or portion of a management program in

such 180-day period, such report, management program, or portion shall be deemed approved for purposes of this section.

(2) Procedure for disapproval — If, after notice and opportunity for public comment and consultation with appropriate Federal and State agencies and other interested persons, the Administrator determines that —

(A) the proposed management program or any portion thereof does not meet the requirements of subsection (b)(2) of this section or is not likely to satisfy, in whole or in part, the goals and requirements of this chapter;

(B) adequate authority does not exist, or adequate resources are not available, to implement such program or portion;

(C) the schedule for implementing such program or portion is not sufficiently expeditious; or

(D) the practices and measures proposed in such program or portion are not adequate to reduce the level of pollution in navigable waters in the State resulting from nonpoint sources and to improve the quality of navigable waters in the State;

the Administrator shall within 6 months of the receipt of the proposed program notify the State of any revisions or modifications necessary to obtain approval. The State shall thereupon have an additional 3 months to submit its revised management program and the Administrator shall approve or disapprove such revised program within three months of receipt.

(3) Failure of State to submit report — If a Governor of a State does not submit the report required by subsection (a) of this section within the period specified by subsection (c)(2) of this section, the Administrator shall, within 30 months after February 4, 1987, prepare a report for such State which makes the identifications required by paragraphs (1)(A) and (1)(B) of subsection (a) of this section. Upon completion of the requirement of the preceding sentence and after notice and opportunity for comment, the Administrator shall report to Congress on his actions pursuant to this section.

(e) Local management programs; technical assistance — If a State fails to submit a management program under subsection (b) of this section or the Administrator does not approve such a management program, a local public agency or organization which has expertise in, and authority to, control water pollution resulting from nonpoint sources in any area of such State which the Administrator determines is of sufficient geographic size may, with approval of such State, request the Administrator to provide, and the Administrator shall provide, technical assistance to such agency or organization in developing for such area a management program which is described in subsection (b) of this section and can be approved

pursuant to subsection (d) of this section. After development of such management program, such agency or organization shall submit such management program to the Administrator for approval. If the Administrator approves such management program, such agency or organization shall be eligible to receive financial assistance under subsection (h) of this section for implementation of such management program as if such agency or organization were a State for which a report submitted under subsection (a) of this section and a management program submitted under subsection (b) of this section were approved under this section. Such financial assistance shall be subject to the same terms and conditions as assistance provided to a State under subsection (h) of this section.

(f) Technical assistance for States — Upon request of a State, the Administrator may provide technical assistance to such State in developing a management program approved under subsection (b) of this section for those portions of the navigable waters requested by such State.

(g) Interstate management conference

(1) Convening of conference; notification; purpose — If any portion of the navigable waters in any State which is implementing management program approved under this section is not meeting applicable water quality standards or the goals and requirements of this chapter as a result, in whole or in part, of pollution from nonpoint sources in another State, such State may petition the Administrator to convene, and the Administrator shall convene, a management conference of all States which contribute significant pollution resulting from nonpoint sources to such portion. If, on the basis of information available, the Administrator determines that a State is not meeting applicable water quality standards or the goals and requirements of this chapter as a result, in whole or in part, of significant pollution from nonpoint sources in another State, the Administrator shall notify such States. The Administrator may convene a management conference under this paragraph not later than 180 days after giving such notification, whether or not the State which is not meeting such standards requests such conference. The purpose of such conference shall be to develop an agreement among such States to reduce the level of pollution in such portion resulting from nonpoint sources and to improve the water quality of such portion. Nothing in such agreement shall supersede or abrogate rights to quantities of water which have been established by interstate water compacts, Supreme Court decrees, or State water laws. This subsection shall not apply to any pollution which is subject to the Colorado River Basin Salinity Control Act (43 U.S.C. §1571 *et seq.*). The requirement that the Administrator convene a management conference shall not be subject to the provisions of section 1365 of this title.

(2) State management program requirement — To the extent that the States reach agreement through such conference, the management programs of the States which are parties to such agreements and which contribute significant pollution to the navigable waters or portions thereof not meeting applicable water quality standards or goals and requirements of this chapter will be revised to reflect such agreement. Such management programs shall be consistent with Federal and State law.

(h) Grant program

(1) Grants for implementation of management programs — Upon application of a State for which a report submitted under subsection (a) of this section and a management program submitted under subsection (b) of this section is approved under this section, the Administrator shall make grants, subject to such terms and conditions as the Administrator considers appropriate, under this subsection to such State for the purpose of assisting the State in implementing such management program. Funds reserved pursuant to section 1285(j)(5) of this title may be used to develop and implement such management program.

(2) Applications — An application for a grant under this subsection in any fiscal year shall be in such form and shall contain such other information as the Administrator may require, including an identification and description of the best management practices and measures which the State proposes to assist, encourage, or require in such year with the Federal assistance to be provided under the grant.

(3) Federal share — The Federal share of the cost of each management program implemented with Federal assistance under this subsection in any fiscal year shall not exceed 60 percent of the cost incurred by the State in implementing such management program and shall be made on condition that the non-Federal share is provided from non-Federal sources.

(4) Limitation on grant amounts — Notwithstanding any other provision of this subsection, not more than 15 percent of the amount appropriated to carry out this subsection may be used to make grants to any one State, including any grants to any local public agency or organization with authority to control pollution from nonpoint sources in any area of such State.

(5) Priority for effective mechanisms — For each fiscal year beginning after September 30, 1987, the Administrator may give priority in making grants under this subsection, and shall give consideration in determining the Federal share of any such grant, to States which have implemented or are proposing to implement management programs which will —

(A) control particularly difficult or serious nonpoint source pollution problems, including, but not limited to, problems resulting from mining activities;

(B) implement innovative methods or practices for controlling nonpoint sources of pollution, including regulatory programs where the Administrator deems appropriate;

(C) control interstate nonpoint source pollution problems; or

(D) carry out ground water quality protection activities which the Administrator determines are part of a comprehensive nonpoint source pollution control program, including research, planning, ground water assessments, demonstration programs, enforcement, technical assistance, education, and training to protect ground water quality from nonpoint sources of pollution.

(6) Availability for obligation — The funds granted to each State pursuant to this subsection in a fiscal year shall remain available for obligation by such State for the fiscal year for which appropriated. The amount of any such funds not obligated by the end of such fiscal year shall be available to the Administrator for granting to other States under this subsection in the next fiscal year.

(7) Limitation on use of funds — States may use funds from grants made pursuant to this section for financial assistance to persons only to the extent that such assistance is related to the costs of demonstration projects.

(8) Satisfactory progress — No grant may be made under this subsection in any fiscal year to a State which in the preceding fiscal year received a grant under this subsection unless the Administrator determines that such State made satisfactory progress in such preceding fiscal year in meeting the schedule specified by such State under subsection (b)(2) of this section.

(9) Maintenance of effort — No grant may be made to a State under this subsection in any fiscal year unless such State enters into such agreements with the Administrator as the Administrator may require to ensure that such State will maintain its aggregate expenditures from all other sources for programs for controlling pollution added to the navigable waters in such State from nonpoint sources and improving the quality of such waters at or above the average level of such expenditures in its two fiscal years preceding February 4, 1987.

(10) Request for information — The Administrator may request such information, data, and reports as he considers necessary to make the determination of continuing eligibility for grants under this section.

(11) Reporting and other requirements — Each State shall report to the Administrator on an annual basis concerning (A) its progress in meeting the schedule of milestones submitted pursuant to subsection (b)(2)(C) of this section, and (B) to the extent that appropriate information is available, reductions in nonpoint source pollutant loading and improvements in water quality for those navigable waters or watersheds within the State which were identified pursuant to subsection (a)(1)(A) of this section resulting from implementation of the management program.

(12) Limitation on administrative costs — For purposes of this subsection, administrative costs in the form of salaries, overhead, or indirect costs for services provided and charged against activities and programs carried out with a grant under this subsection shall not exceed in any fiscal year 10 percent of the amount of the grant in such year, except that costs of implementing enforcement and regulatory activities, education, training, technical assistance, demonstration projects, and technology transfer programs shall not be subject to this limitation.

(i) Grants for protecting groundwater quality

(1) Eligible applicants and activities — Upon application of a State for which a report submitted under subsection (a) of this section and a plan submitted under subsection (b) of this section is approved under this section, the Administrator shall make grants under this subsection to such State for the purpose of assisting such State in carrying out groundwater quality protection activities which the Administrator determines will advance the State toward implementation of a comprehensive nonpoint source pollution control program. Such activities shall include, but not be limited to, research, planning, groundwater assessments, demonstration programs, enforcement, technical assistance, education and training to protect the quality of groundwater and to prevent contamination of groundwater from nonpoint sources of pollution.

(2) Applications — An application for a grant under this subsection shall be in such form and shall contain such information as the Administrator may require.

(3) Federal share; maximum amount — The Federal share of the cost of assisting a State in carrying out groundwater protection activities in any fiscal year under this subsection shall be 50 percent of the costs incurred by the State in carrying out such activities, except that the maximum amount of Federal assistance which any State may receive under this subsection in any fiscal year shall not exceed $150,000.

(4) Report — The Administrator shall include in each report transmitted under subsection (m) of this section a report on the activities and programs implemented under this subsection during the preceding fiscal year.

(j) Authorization of appropriations — There is authorized to be appropriated to carry out subsections (h) and (i) of this section not to exceed $70,000,000 for fiscal year 1988, $100,000,000 per fiscal year for each of fiscal years 1989 and 1990, and $130,000,000 for fiscal year 1991; except that for each of such fiscal years not to exceed $7,500,000 may be made available to carry out subsection (i) of this section. Sums appropriated pursuant to this subsection shall remain available until expended.

(k) Consistency of other programs and projects with management programs — The Administrator shall transmit to the Office of Management and Budget and the appropriate Federal departments and agencies a list of those assistance programs and development projects identified by each State under subsection (b)(2)(F) of this section for which individual assistance applications and projects will be reviewed pursuant to the procedures set forth in Executive Order 12372 as in effect on September 17, 1983. Beginning not later than sixty days after receiving notification by the Administrator, each Federal department and agency shall modify existing regulations to allow States to review individual development projects and assistance applications under the identified Federal assistance programs and shall accommodate, according to the requirements and definitions of Executive Order 12372, as in effect on September 17, 1983, the concerns of the State regarding the consistency of such applications or projects with the State nonpoint source pollution management program.

(l) Collection of information — The Administrator shall collect and make available, through publications and other appropriate means, information pertaining to management practices and implementation methods, including, but not limited to, (1) information concerning the costs and relative efficiencies of best management practices for reducing nonpoint source pollution; and (2) available data concerning the relationship between water quality and implementation of various management practices to control nonpoint sources of pollution.

(m) Reports of Administrator

(1) Annual reports

Not later than January 1, 1988, and each January 1 thereafter, the Administrator shall transmit to the Committee on Public Works and Transportation of the House of Representatives and the Committee on Environment and Public Works of the Senate, a report for the preceding fiscal year on the activities and programs implemented under this section and the progress made in reducing pollution in the navigable waters resulting from nonpoint sources and improving the quality of such waters.

(2) Final report

Not later than January 1, 1990, the Administrator shall transmit to Congress a final report on the activities carried out under this section. Such report, at a minimum, shall —

(A) describe the management programs being implemented by the States by types and amount of affected navigable waters, categories and subcategories of nonpoint sources, and types of best management practices being implemented;

(B) describe the experiences of the States in adhering to schedules and implementing best management practices;

(C) describe the amount and purpose of grants awarded pursuant to subsections (h) and (i) of this section;

(D) identify, to the extent that information is available, the progress made in reducing pollutant loads and improving water quality in the navigable waters;

(E) indicate what further actions need to be taken to attain and maintain in those navigable waters (i) applicable water quality standards, and (ii) the goals and requirements of this chapter;

(F) include recommendations of the Administrator concerning future programs (including enforcement programs) for controlling pollution from nonpoint sources; and

(G) identify the activities and programs of departments, agencies, and instrumentalities of the United States which are inconsistent with the management programs submitted by the States and recommend modifications so that such activities and programs are consistent with and assist the States in implementation of such management programs.

(n) Set aside for administrative personnel — Not less than 5 percent of the funds appropriated pursuant to subsection (j) of this section for any fiscal year shall be available to the Administrator to maintain personnel levels at the Environmental Protection Agency at levels which are adequate to carry out this section in such year.

§1330. National estuary program
[CWA §320]

(a) Management conference

(1) Nomination of estuaries — The Governor of any State may nominate to the Administrator an estuary lying in whole or in part within the State as an estuary of national significance and request a management conference to develop a comprehensive management plan for the estuary. The nomination shall document the need for the conference, the likelihood of success, and information relating to the factors in paragraph (2).

(2) Convening of conference

(A) In general — In any case where the Administrator determines, on his own initiative or upon nomination of a State under paragraph (1), that the attainment or maintenance of that water quality in an estuary which assures protection of public water supplies and the protection and propagation of a balanced, indigenous population of shellfish, fish, and wildlife, and allows recreational activities, in and on the water, requires the control of point and nonpoint sources of pollution to supplement existing controls of pollution in more than one State, the Administrator shall select such estuary and convene a management conference.

(B) Priority consideration — The Administrator shall give priority consideration under this section to Long Island Sound, New York and Connecticut; Narragansett Bay, Rhode Island; Buzzards Bay, Massachusetts; Massachusetts Bay, Massachusetts (including Cape Cod Bay and Boston Harbor); Puget Sound, Washington; New York-New Jersey Harbor, New York and New Jersey; Delaware Bay, Delaware and New Jersey; Delaware Inland Bays, Delaware; Albemarle Sound, North Carolina; Sarasota Bay, Florida; San Francisco Bay, California; Santa Monica Bay, California; Galveston Bay, Texas; Barataria-Terrebonne Bay estuary complex, Louisiana; Indian River Lagoon, Florida; Lake Pontchartrain Basin, Louisiana and Mississippi; Casco Bay, Maine; Tampa Bay, Florida; Coastal Bend, Texas; San Juan Bay, Puerto Rico; Tillamook Bay, Oregon; Piscataqua Region, New Hampshire; Barnegat Bay, New Jersey; Maryland Coastal Bays; Maryland; Charlotte Harbor, Florida; Mobile Bay, Alabama; Morro Bay, California' and Lower Columbia River, Oregon and Washington.

(3) Boundary dispute exception — In any case in which a boundary between two States passes through an estuary and such boundary is disputed and is the subject of an action in any court, the Administrator shall not convene a management conference with respect to such estuary before a final adjudication has been made of such dispute.

(b) Purposes of conference — The purposes of any management conference convened with respect to an estuary under this subsection shall be to —

(1) assess trends in water quality, natural resources, and uses of the estuary;

(2) collect, characterize, and assess data on toxics, nutrients, and natural resources within the estuarine zone to identify the causes of environmental problems;

(3) develop the relationship between the in-place loads and point and nonpoint loadings of pollutants to the estuarine zone and the potential uses of the zone, water quality, and natural resources;

(4) develop a comprehensive conservation and management plan that —

(A) recommends priority corrective actions and compliance schedules addressing point and nonpoint sources of pollution to restore and maintain the chemical, physical, and biological integrity of the estuary, including restoration and maintenance of water quality, a balanced indigenous population of shellfish, fish and wildlife, and recreational activities in the estuary, and assure that the designated uses of the estuary are protected;

(B) addresses the effects of recurring extreme weather events on the estuary, including the identification and assessment of vulnerabilities in the estuary and the development and implementation of adaptation strategies; and

(C) increases public education and awareness of the ecological health and water quality conditions of the estuary;

(5) develop plans for the coordinated implementation of the plan by the States as well as Federal and local agencies participating in the conference;

(6) monitor the effectiveness of actions taken pursuant to the plan; and

(7) review all Federal financial assistance programs and Federal development projects in accordance with the requirements of Executive Order 12372, as in effect on September 17, 1983, to determine whether such assistance program or project would be consistent with and further the purposes and objectives of the plan prepared under this section.

For purposes of paragraph (7), such programs and projects shall not be limited to the assistance programs and development projects subject to Executive Order 12372, but may include any programs listed in the most recent Catalog of Federal Domestic Assistance which may have an effect on the purposes and objectives of the plan developed under this section.

(c) Members of conference — The members of a management conference convened under this section shall include, at a minimum, the Administrator and representatives of —

(1) each State and foreign nation located in whole or in part in the estuarine zone of the estuary for which the conference is convened;

(2) international, interstate, or regional agencies or entities having jurisdiction over all or a significant part of the estuary;

(3) each interested Federal agency, as determined appropriate by the Administrator;

(4) local governments having jurisdiction over any land or water within the estuarine zone, as determined appropriate by the Administrator; and

(5) affected industries, public and private educational institutions, nonprofit organizations, and the general public, as determined appropriate by the Administrator.

(d) Utilization of existing data — In developing a conservation and management plan under this section, the management conference shall survey and utilize existing reports, data, and studies relating to the estuary that have been developed by or made available to Federal, interstate, State, and local agencies.

(e) Period of conference — A management conference convened under this section shall be convened for a period not to exceed 5 years. Such conference may be extended by the Administrator, and if terminated after the initial period, may be reconvened by the Administrator at any time thereafter, as may be necessary to meet the requirements of this section.

(f) Approval and implementation of plans

(1) Approval — Not later than 120 days after the completion of a conservation and management plan and after providing for public review and comment, the Administrator shall approve such plan if the plan meets the requirements of this section and the affected Governor or Governors concur.

(2) Implementation — Upon approval of a conservation and management plan under this section, such plan shall be implemented. Funds authorized to be appropriated under subchapters II and VI of this chapter and section 1329 of this title may be used in accordance with the applicable requirements of this chapter to assist States with the implementation of such plan.

(g) Grants

(1) Recipients — The Administrator is authorized to make grants to State, interstate, and regional water pollution control agencies and entities, State coastal zone management agencies, interstate agencies, other public or nonprofit private agencies, institutions, organizations, and individuals.

(2) Purposes — Grants under this subsection shall be made to pay for activities necessary for the development and implementation of a comprehensive conservation and management plan under this section.

(3) Federal share — The Federal share of a grant to any person (including a State, interstate, or regional agency or entity) under this subsection for a fiscal year —

(A) shall not exceed —

(i) 75 percent of the annual aggregate costs of the development of a comprehensive conservation and management plan; and

(ii) 50 percent of the annual aggregate costs of the implementation of the plan; and

(B) shall be made on condition that the non-Federal share of the costs are provided from non-Federal sources.

(4) Competitive Awards —

(A) In general — Using the amounts made available under subsection (i)(2)(B), the Administrator shall make competitive awards under this paragraph.

(B) Application for awards — The Administrator shall solicit applications for awards under this paragraph from State, interstate, and regional water pollution control agencies and entities, State coastal zone management agencies, interstate agencies, other public or nonprofit private agencies, institutions, organizations, and individuals.

(C) Selection of recipients — In selecting award recipients under this paragraph, the Administrator shall select recipients that are best able to address urgent, emerging, and challenging issues that threaten the ecological and economic well-being of the estuaries selected by the Administrator under subsection (a)(2), or that relate to the coastal resiliency of such estuaries. Such issues shall include —

(i) extensive seagrass habitat losses resulting in significant impacts on fisheries and water quality;

(ii) recurring harmful algae blooms;

(iii) unusual marine mammal mortalities;

(iv) invasive exotic species that may threaten wastewater systems and cause other damage;

(v) jellyfish proliferation limiting community access to water during peak tourism seasons;

(vi) stormwater runoff;

(vii) accelerated land loss;

(viii) flooding that may be related to sea level rise, extreme weather, or wetland degradation or loss; and

(ix) low dissolved oxygen conditions in estuarine waters and related nutrient management.

(h) Grant reporting — Any person (including a State, interstate, or regional agency or entity) that receives a grant under subsection (g) of this section shall report to the Administrator not later than 18 months after receipt of such grant and biennially thereafter on the progress being made under this section.

(i) Authorization of appropriations —

(1) In general — There is authorized to be appropriated to the Administrator $26,500,000 for each of fiscal years 2017 through 2021, and $50,000,000 for each of fiscal years 2022 through 2026, for —

(A) expenses relating to the administration of grants or awards by the Administrator under this section, including the award and oversight of grants and awards, except that such expenses may not exceed 5 percent of the amount appropriated under this subsection for a fiscal year; and

(B) making grants and awards under subsection (g).

(2) Allocations —

(A) Conservation and management plans — Not less than 80 percent of the amount made available under this subsection for a fiscal year shall be used by the Administrator to provide grant assistance for the development, implementation, and monitoring of each of the conservation and management plans eligible for grant assistance under subsection (g)(2).

(B) Competitive awards — Not less than 15 percent of the amount made available under this subsection for a fiscal year shall be used by the Administrator for making competitive awards described in subsection (g)(4).

(j) Research

(1) Programs — In order to determine the need to convene a management conference under this section or at the request of such a management conference, the Administrator shall coordinate and implement, through the National Marine Pollution Program Office and the National Marine Fisheries Service of the National Oceanic and Atmospheric Administration, as appropriate, for one or more estuarine zones —

　(A) a long-term program of trend assessment monitoring measuring variations in pollutant concentrations, marine ecology, and other physical or biological environmental parameters which may affect estuarine zones, to provide the Administrator the capacity to determine the potential and actual effects of alternative management strategies and measures;

　(B) a program of ecosystem assessment assisting in the development of (i) baseline studies which determine the state of estuarine zones and the effects of natural and anthropogenic changes, and (ii) predictive models capable of translating information on specific discharges or general pollutant loadings within estuarine zones into a set of probable effects on such zones;

　(C) a comprehensive water quality sampling program for the continuous monitoring of nutrients, chlorine, acid precipitation dissolved oxygen, and potentially toxic pollutants (including organic chemicals and metals) in estuarine zones, after consultation with interested State, local, interstate, or international agencies and review and analysis of all environmental sampling data presently collected from estuarine zones; and

　(D) a program of research to identify the movements of nutrients, sediments and pollutants through estuarine zones and the impact of nutrients, sediments, and pollutants on water quality, the ecosystem, and designated or potential uses of the estuarine zones.

(2) Reports

The Administrator, in cooperation with the Administrator of the National Oceanic and Atmospheric Administration, shall submit to the Congress no less often than biennially a comprehensive report on the activities authorized under this subsection including —

　(A) a listing of priority monitoring and research needs;

　(B) an assessment of the state and health of the Nation's estuarine zones, to the extent evaluated under this subsection;

　(C) a discussion of pollution problems and trends in pollutant concentrations with a direct or indirect effect on water quality, the ecosystem, and designated or potential uses of each estuarine zone, to the extent evaluated under this subsection; and

　(D) an evaluation of pollution abatement activities and management measures so far implemented to determine the degree of improvement toward the objectives expressed in subsection (b)(4) of this section.

(k) Definitions — For purposes of this section, the terms "estuary" and "estuarine zone" have the meanings such terms have in section 1254(n)(3) of this title, except that the term "estuarine zone" shall also include associated aquatic ecosystems and those portions of tributaries draining into the estuary up to the historic height of migration of anadromous fish or the historic head of tidal influence, whichever is higher.

SUBCHAPTER IV — PERMITS AND LICENSES

§1341. Certification
[CWA §401]

(a) Compliance with applicable requirements; application; procedures; license suspension

(1) Any applicant for a Federal license or permit to conduct any activity including, but not limited to, the construction or operation of facilities, which may result in any discharge into the navigable waters, shall provide the licensing or permitting agency a certification from the State in which the discharge originates or will originate, or, if appropriate, from the interstate water pollution control agency having jurisdiction over the navigable waters at the point where the discharge originates or will originate, that any such discharge will comply with the applicable provisions of sections 1311, 1312, 1313, 1316, and 1317 of this title. In the case of any such activity for which there is not an applicable effluent limitation or other limitation under sections 1311(b) and 1312 of this title, and there is not an applicable standard under sections 1316 and 1317 of this title, the State shall so certify, except that any such certification shall not be deemed to satisfy section 1371(c) of this title. Such State or interstate agency shall establish procedures for public notice in the case of all applications for certification by it and, to the extent it deems appropriate, procedures for public hearings in connection with specific applications. In any case where a State or interstate agency has no authority to give such a certification, such certification shall be from the Administrator. If the State, interstate agency, or Administrator, as the case may be, fails or refuses to act on a request for certification, within a reasonable period of time (which shall not exceed

one year) after receipt of such request, the certification requirements of this subsection shall be waived with respect to such Federal application. No license or permit shall be granted until the certification required by this section has been obtained or has been waived as provided in the preceding sentence. No license or permit shall be granted if certification has been denied by the State, interstate agency, or the Administrator, as the case may be.

(2) Upon receipt of such application and certification the licensing or permitting agency shall immediately notify the Administrator of such application and certification. Whenever such a discharge may affect, as determined by the Administrator, the quality of the waters of any other State, the Administrator within thirty days of the date of notice of application for such Federal license or permit shall so notify such other State, the licensing or permitting agency, and the applicant. If, within sixty days after receipt of such notification, such other State determines that such discharge will affect the quality of its waters so as to violate any water quality requirements in such State, and within such sixty-day period notifies the Administrator and the licensing or permitting agency in writing of its objection to the issuance of such license or permit and requests a public hearing on such objection, the licensing or permitting agency shall hold such a hearing. The Administrator shall at such hearing submit his evaluation and recommendations with respect to any such objection to the licensing or permitting agency. Such agency, based upon the recommendations of such State, the Administrator, and upon any additional evidence, if any, presented to the agency at the hearing, shall condition such license or permit in such manner as may be necessary to insure compliance with applicable water quality requirements. If the imposition of conditions cannot insure such compliance such agency shall not issue such license or permit.

(3) The certification obtained pursuant to paragraph (1) of this subsection with respect to the construction of any facility shall fulfill the requirements of this subsection with respect to certification in connection with any other Federal license or permit required for the operation of such facility unless, after notice to the certifying State, agency, or Administrator, as the case may be, which shall be given by the Federal agency to whom application is made for such operating license or permit, the State, or if appropriate, the interstate agency or the Administrator, notifies such agency within sixty days after receipt of such notice that there is no longer reasonable assurance that there will be compliance with the applicable provisions of sections 1311, 1312, 1313, 1316, and 1317 of this title because of changes since the construction license or permit certification was issued in (A) the construction or operation of the facility, (B)

the characteristics of the waters into which such discharge is made, (C) the water quality criteria applicable to such waters or (D) applicable effluent limitations or other requirements. This paragraph shall be inapplicable in any case where the applicant for such operating license or permit has failed to provide the certifying State, or, if appropriate, the interstate agency or the Administrator, with notice of any proposed changes in the construction or operation of the facility with respect to which a construction license or permit has been granted, which changes may result in violation of section 1311, 1312, 1313, 1316, or 1317 of this title.

(4) Prior to the initial operation of any federally licensed or permitted facility or activity which may result in any discharge into the navigable waters and with respect to which a certification has been obtained pursuant to paragraph (1) of this subsection, which facility or activity is not subject to a Federal operating license or permit, the licensee or permittee shall provide an opportunity for such certifying State, or, if appropriate, the interstate agency or the Administrator to review the manner in which the facility or activity shall be operated or conducted for the purposes of assuring that applicable effluent limitations or other limitations or other applicable water quality requirements will not be violated. Upon notification by the certifying State, or if appropriate, the interstate agency or the Administrator that the operation of any such federally licensed or permitted facility or activity will violate applicable effluent limitations or other limitations or other water quality requirements such Federal agency may, after public hearing, suspend such license or permit. If such license or permit is suspended, it shall remain suspended until notification is received from the certifying State, agency, or Administrator, as the case may be, that there is reasonable assurance that such facility or activity will not violate the applicable provisions of section 1311, 1312, 1313, 1316, or 1317 of this title.

(5) Any Federal license or permit with respect to which a certification has been obtained under paragraph (1) of this subsection may be suspended or revoked by the Federal agency issuing such license or permit upon the entering of a judgment under this chapter that such facility or activity has been operated in violation of the applicable provisions of section 1311, 1312, 1313, 1316, or 1317 of this title.

(6) Except with respect to a permit issued under section 1342 of this title, in any case where actual construction of a facility has been lawfully commenced prior to April 3, 1970, no certification shall be required under this subsection for a license or permit issued after April 3, 1970, to operate such facility, except that any such license or permit issued without certification shall terminate April 3,

1973, unless prior to such termination date the person having such license or permit submits to the Federal agency which issued such license or permit a certification and otherwise meets the requirements of this section.

(b) Compliance with other provisions of law setting applicable water quality requirements — Nothing in this section shall be construed to limit the authority of any department or agency pursuant to any other provision of law to require compliance with any applicable water quality requirements. The Administrator shall, upon the request of any Federal department or agency, or State or interstate agency, or applicant, provide, for the purpose of this section, any relevant information on applicable effluent limitations, or other limitations, standards, regulations, or requirements, or water quality criteria, and shall, when requested by any such department or agency or State or interstate agency, or applicant, comment on any methods to comply with such limitations, standards, regulations, requirements, or criteria.

(c) Authority of Secretary of the Army to permit use of spoil disposal areas by Federal licensees or permittees — In order to implement the provisions of this section, the Secretary of the Army, acting through the Chief of Engineers, is authorized, if he deems it to be in the public interest, to permit the use of spoil disposal areas under his jurisdiction by Federal licensees or permittees, and to make an appropriate charge for such use. Moneys received from such licensees or permittees shall be deposited in the Treasury as miscellaneous receipts.

(d) Limitations and monitoring requirements of certification — Any certification provided under this section shall set forth any effluent limitations and other limitations, and monitoring requirements necessary to assure that any applicant for a Federal license or permit will comply with any applicable effluent limitations and other limitations, under section 1311 or 1312 of this title, standard of performance under section 1316 of this title, or prohibition, effluent standard, or pretreatment standard under section 1317 of this title, and with any other appropriate requirement of State law set forth in such certification, and shall become a condition on any Federal license or permit subject to the provisions of this section.

§1342. National pollutant discharge elimination system

[CWA §402]

(a) Permits for discharge of pollutants

(1) Except as provided in sections 1328 and 1344 of this title, the Administrator may, after opportunity for public hearing issue a permit for the discharge of any pollutant, or combination of pollutants, notwithstanding section 1311(a) of this title, upon condition that such discharge will meet either (A) all applicable requirements under sections 1311, 1312, 1316, 1317, 1318, and 1343 of this title, or (B) prior to the taking of necessary implementing actions relating to all such requirements, such conditions as the Administrator determines are necessary to carry out the provisions of this chapter.

(2) The Administrator shall prescribe conditions for such permits to assure compliance with the requirements of paragraph (1) of this subsection, including conditions on data and information collection, reporting, and such other requirements as he deems appropriate.

(3) The permit program of the Administrator under paragraph (1) of this subsection, and permits issued thereunder, shall be subject to the same terms, conditions, and requirements as apply to a State permit program and permits issued thereunder under subsection (b) of this section.

(4) All permits for discharges into the navigable waters issued pursuant to section 407 of this title shall be deemed to be permits issued under this subchapter, and permits issued under this subchapter shall be deemed to be permits issued under section 407 of this title, and shall continue in force and effect for their term unless revoked, modified, or suspended in accordance with the provisions of this chapter.

(5) No permit for a discharge into the navigable waters shall be issued under section 407 of this title after October 18, 1972. Each application for a permit under section 407 of this title, pending on October 18, 1972, shall be deemed to be an application for a permit under this section. The Administrator shall authorize a State, which he determines has the capability of administering a permit program which will carry out the objectives of this chapter to issue permits for discharges into the navigable waters within the jurisdiction of such State. The Administrator may exercise the authority granted him by the preceding sentence only during the period which begins on October 18, 1972, and ends either on the ninetieth day after the date of the first promulgation of guidelines required by section 1314(i)(2) of this title, or the date of approval by the Administrator of a permit program for such State under subsection (b) of this section, whichever date first occurs, and no such authorization to a State shall extend beyond the last day of such period. Each such permit shall be subject to such conditions as the Administrator determines are necessary to carry out the provisions of this chapter. No such permit shall issue if the Administrator objects to such issuance.

(b) State permit programs — At any time after the promulgation of the guidelines required by subsection (i)(2) of section 1314 of this title, the Governor of each State desiring to administer its own permit program for discharges into navigable waters within its jurisdiction may submit to the

Administrator a full and complete description of the program it proposes to establish and administer under State law or under an interstate compact. In addition, such State shall submit a statement from the attorney general (or the attorney for those State water pollution control agencies which have independent legal counsel), or from the chief legal officer in the case of an interstate agency, that the laws of such State, or the interstate compact, as the case may be, provide adequate authority to carry out the described program. The Administrator shall approve each submitted program unless he determines that adequate authority does not exist:

(1) To issue permits which —

(A) apply, and insure compliance with, any applicable requirements of sections 1311, 1312, 1316, 1317, and 1343 of this title;

(B) are for fixed terms not exceeding five years; and

(C) can be terminated or modified for cause including, but not limited to, the following:

(i) violation of any condition of the permit;

(ii) obtaining a permit by misrepresentation, or failure to disclose fully all relevant facts;

(iii) change in any condition that requires either a temporary or permanent reduction or elimination of the permitted discharge;

(D) control the disposal of pollutants into wells;

(2)(A) To issue permits which apply, and insure compliance with, all applicable requirements of section 1318 of this title; or

(B) To inspect, monitor, enter, and require reports to at least the same extent as required in section 1318 of this title;

(3) To insure that the public, and any other State the waters of which may be affected, receive notice of each application for a permit and to provide an opportunity for public hearing before a ruling on each such application;

(4) To insure that the Administrator receives notice of each application (including a copy thereof) for a permit;

(5) To insure that any State (other than the permitting State), whose waters may be affected by the issuance of a permit may submit written recommendations to the permitting State (and the Administrator) with respect to any permit application and, if any part of such written recommendations are not accepted by the permitting State, that the permitting State will notify such affected State (and the Administrator) in writing of its failure to so accept such recommendations together with its reasons for so doing;

(6) To insure that no permit will be issued if, in the judgment of the Secretary of the Army acting through the Chief of Engineers, after consultation with the Secretary of the department in which the Coast Guard is operating, anchorage and navigation of any of the navigable waters would be substantially impaired thereby;

(7) To abate violations of the permit or the permit program, including civil and criminal penalties and other ways and means of enforcement;

(8) To insure that any permit for a discharge from a publicly owned treatment works includes conditions to require the identification in terms of character and volume of pollutants of any significant source introducing pollutants subject to pretreatment standards under section 1317(b) of this title into such works and a program to assure compliance with such pretreatment standards by each such source, in addition to adequate notice to the permitting agency of (A) new introductions into such works of pollutants from any source which would be a new source as defined in section 1316 of this title if such source were discharging pollutants, (B) new introductions of pollutants into such works from a source which would be subject to section 1311 of this title if it were discharging such pollutants, or (C) a substantial change in volume or character of pollutants being introduced into such works by a source introducing pollutants into such works at the time of issuance of the permit. Such notice shall include information on the quality and quantity of effluent to be introduced into such treatment works and any anticipated impact of such change in the quantity or quality of effluent to be discharged from such publicly owned treatment works; and

(9) To insure that any industrial user of any publicly owned treatment works will comply with sections 1284(b), 1317, and 1318 of this title.

(c) Suspension of Federal program upon submission of State program; withdrawal of approval of State program; return of State program to Administrator

(1) Not later than ninety days after the date on which a State has submitted a program (or revision thereof) pursuant to subsection (b) of this section, the Administrator shall suspend the issuance of permits under subsection (a) of this section as to those discharges subject to such program unless he determines that the State permit program does not meet the requirements of subsection (b) of this section or does not conform to the guidelines issued under section 1314(i)(2) of this title. If the Administrator so determines, he shall notify the State of any revisions or modifications necessary to conform to such requirements or guidelines.

(2) Any State permit program under this section shall at all times be in accordance with this section and guidelines promulgated pursuant to section 1314(i)(2) of this title.

(3) Whenever the Administrator determines after public hearing that a State is not administering a program approved under this section in accordance with requirements of this section, he shall so notify the State and, if appropriate corrective action is not taken within a reasonable time, not to exceed ninety days, the Administrator shall withdraw approval of such program. The Administrator shall not withdraw approval of any such program unless he shall first have notified the State, and made public, in writing, the reasons for such withdrawal.

(4) Limitations on partial permit program returns and withdrawals — A State may return to the Administrator administration, and the Administrator may withdraw under paragraph (3) of this subsection approval, of —

(A) a State partial permit program approved under subsection (n)(3) of this section only if the entire permit program being administered by the State department or agency at the time is returned or withdrawn; and

(B) a State partial permit program approved under subsection (n)(4) of this section only if an entire phased component of the permit program being administered by the State at the time is returned or withdrawn.

(d) Notification of Administrator

(1) Each State shall transmit to the Administrator a copy of each permit application received by such State and provide notice to the Administrator of every action related to the consideration of such permit application, including each permit proposed to be issued by such State.

(2) No permit shall issue (A) if the Administrator within ninety days of the date of his notification under subsection (b)(5) of this section objects in writing to the issuance of such permit, or (B) if the Administrator within ninety days of the date of transmittal of the proposed permit by the State objects in writing to the issuance of such permit as being outside the guidelines and requirements of this chapter. Whenever the Administrator objects to the issuance of a permit under this paragraph such written objection shall contain a statement of the reasons for such objection and the effluent limitations and conditions which such permit would include if it were issued by the Administrator.

(3) The Administrator may, as to any permit application, waive paragraph (2) of this subsection.

(4) In any case where, after December 27, 1977, the Administrator, pursuant to paragraph (2) of this subsection, objects to the issuance of a permit, on request of the State, a public hearing shall be held by the Administrator on such objection. If the State does not resubmit such permit revised to meet such objection within 30 days after completion of the hearing, or, if no hearing is requested within 90 days after the date of such objection, the Administrator may issue the permit pursuant to subsection (a) of this section for such source in accordance with the guidelines and requirements of this chapter.

(e) Waiver of notification requirement — In accordance with guidelines promulgated pursuant to subsection (i)(2) of section 1314 of this title, the Administrator is authorized to waive the requirements of subsection (d) of this section at the time he approves a program pursuant to subsection (b) of this section for any category (including any class, type, or size within such category) of point sources within the State submitting such program.

(f) Point source categories — The Administrator shall promulgate regulations establishing categories of point sources which he determines shall not be subject to the requirements of subsection (d) of this section in any State with a program approved pursuant to subsection (b) of this section. The Administrator may distinguish among classes, types, and sizes within any category of point sources.

(g) Other regulations for safe transportation, handling, carriage, storage, and stowage of pollutants — Any permit issued under this section for the discharge of pollutants into the navigable waters from a vessel or other floating craft shall be subject to any applicable regulations promulgated by the Secretary of the department in which the Coast Guard is operating, establishing specifications for safe transportation, handling, carriage, storage, and stowage of pollutants.

(h) Violation of permit conditions; restriction or prohibition upon introduction of pollutant by source not previously utilizing treatment works — In the event any condition of a permit for discharges from a treatment works (as defined in section 1292 of this title) which is publicly owned is violated, a State with a program approved under subsection (b) of this section or the Administrator, where no State program is approved or where the Administrator determines pursuant to section 1319(a) of this title that a State with an approved program has not commenced appropriate enforcement action with respect to such permit, may proceed in a court of competent jurisdiction to restrict or prohibit the introduction of any pollutant into such treatment works by a source not utilizing such treatment works prior to the finding that such condition was violated.

(i) Federal enforcement not limited — Nothing in this section shall be construed to limit the authority of the Administrator to take action pursuant to section 1319 of this title.

(j) Public information — A copy of each permit application and each permit issued under this section shall be available to the public. Such permit application or permit, or portion thereof, shall further be available on request for the purpose of reproduction.

(k) Compliance with permits — Compliance with a permit issued pursuant to this section shall be deemed compliance, for purposes of sections 1319 and 1365 of this title, with sections 1311, 1312, 1316, 1317, and 1343 of this title, except any standard imposed under section 1317 of this title for a toxic pollutant injurious to human health. Until December 31, 1974, in any case where a permit for discharge has been applied for pursuant to this section, but final administrative disposition of such application has not been made, such discharge shall not be a violation of (1) section 1311, 1316, or 1342 of this title, or (2) section 407 of this title, unless the Administrator or other plaintiff proves that final administrative disposition of such application has not been made because of the failure of the applicant to furnish information reasonably required or requested in order to process the application. For the 180-day period beginning on October 18, 1972, in the case of any point source discharging any pollutant or combination of pollutants immediately prior to such date which source is not subject to section 407 of this title, the discharge by such source shall not be a violation of this chapter if such a source applies for a permit for discharge pursuant to this section within such 180-day period.

(l) Limitation on permit requirement

(1) Agricultural return flows — The Administrator shall not require a permit under this section for discharges composed entirely of return flows from irrigated agriculture, nor shall the Administrator directly or indirectly, require any State to require such a permit.

(2) Stormwater runoff from oil, gas, and mining operations — The Administrator shall not require a permit under this section, nor shall the Administrator directly or indirectly require any State to require a permit, for discharges of stormwater runoff from mining operations or oil and gas exploration, production, processing, or treatment operations or transmission facilities, composed entirely of flows which are from conveyances or systems of conveyances (including but not limited to pipes, conduits, ditches, and channels) used for collecting and conveying precipitation runoff and which are not contaminated by contact with, or do not come into contact with, any overburden, raw material, intermediate products, finished product, byproduct, or waste products located on the site of such operations.

(3) Silvicultural activities

(A) NPDES permit requirements for silvicultural activities — The Administrator shall not require a permit under this section nor directly or indirectly require any State to require a permit under this section for a discharge from runoff resulting from the conduct of the following silviculture activities conducted in accordance with standard industry practice: nursery operations, site preparation, reforestation and subsequent cultural treatment, thinning, prescribed burning, pest and fire control, harvesting operations, surface drainage, or road construction and maintenance.

(B) Other requirements — Nothing in this paragraph exempts a discharge from silvicultural activity from any permitting requirement under section 1344 of this title, existing permitting requirements under section 1342 of this title, or from any other federal law.

(C) The authorization provided in Section 1365(a) of this title does not apply to any nonpermitting program established under 1342(p)(6) of this title for the silviculture activities listed in 1342(l)(3)(A) of this title, or to any other limitations that might be deemed to apply to the silviculture activities listed in 1342(l)(3)(A) of this title.

(m) Additional pretreatment of conventional pollutants not required — To the extent a treatment works (as defined in section 1292 of this title) which is publicly owned is not meeting the requirements of a permit issued under this section for such treatment works as a result of inadequate design or operation of such treatment works, the Administrator, in issuing a permit under this section, shall not require pretreatment by a person introducing conventional pollutants identified pursuant to section 1314(a)(4) of this title into such treatment works other than pretreatment required to assure compliance with pretreatment standards under subsection (b)(8) of this section and section 1317(b)(1) of this title. Nothing in this subsection shall affect the Administrator's authority under sections 1317 and 1319 of this title, affect State and local authority under sections 1317(b)(4) and 1370 of this title, relieve such treatment works of its obligations to meet requirements established under this chapter, or otherwise preclude such works from pursuing whatever feasible options are available to meet its responsibility to comply with its permit under this section.

(n) Partial permit program

(1) State submission — The Governor of a State may submit under subsection (b) of this section a permit program for a portion of the discharges into the navigable waters in such State.

(2) Minimum coverage — A partial permit program under this subsection shall cover, at a minimum, administration of a major category of the discharges into the navigable waters of the State or a major component of the permit program required by subsection (b) of this section.

(3) Approval of major category partial permit programs — The Administrator may approve a partial permit program covering administration of a major category of discharges under this subsection if —

(A) such program represents a complete permit program and covers all of the discharges under the jurisdiction of a department or agency of the State; and

(B) the Administrator determines that the partial program represents a significant and identifiable part of the State program required by subsection (b) of this section.

(4) Approval of major component partial permit programs — The Administrator may approve under this subsection a partial and phased permit program covering administration of a major component (including discharge categories) of a State permit program required by subsection (b) of this section if —

    (A) the Administrator determines that the partial program represents a significant and identifiable part of the State program required by subsection (b) of this section; and

    (B) the State submits, and the Administrator approves, a plan for the State to assume administration by phases of the remainder of the State program required by subsection (b) of this section by a specified date not more than 5 years after submission of the partial program under this subsection and agrees to make all reasonable efforts to assume such administration by such date.

(o) Anti-backsliding

(1) General prohibition — In the case of effluent limitations established on the basis of subsection (a)(1)(B) of this section, a permit may not be renewed, reissued, or modified on the basis of effluent guidelines promulgated under section 1314(b) of this title subsequent to the original issuance of such permit, to contain effluent limitations which are less stringent than the comparable effluent limitations in the previous permit. In the case of effluent limitations established on the basis of section 1311(b)(1)(C) or section 1313(d) or (e) of this title, a permit may not be renewed, reissued, or modified to contain effluent limitations which are less stringent than the comparable effluent limitations in the previous permit except in compliance with section 1313(d)(4) of this title.

(2) Exceptions — A permit with respect to which paragraph (1) applies may be renewed, reissued, or modified to contain a less stringent effluent limitation applicable to a pollutant if —

    (A) material and substantial alterations or additions to the permitted facility occurred after permit issuance which justify the application of a less stringent effluent limitation;

    (B)(i) information is available which was not available at the time of permit issuance (other than revised regulations, guidance, or test methods) and which would have justified the application of a less stringent effluent limitation at the time of permit issuance; or

        (ii) the Administrator determines that technical mistakes or mistaken interpretations of law were made in issuing the permit under subsection (a)(1)(B) of this section;

    (C) a less stringent effluent limitation is necessary because of events over which the permittee has no control and for which there is no reasonably available remedy;

    (D) the permittee has received a permit modification under section 1311(c), 1311(g), 1311(h), 1311(i), 1311(k), 1311(n), or 1326(a) of this title; or

    (E) the permittee has installed the treatment facilities required to meet the effluent limitations in the previous permit and has properly operated and maintained the facilities but has nevertheless been unable to achieve the previous effluent limitations, in which case the limitations in the reviewed, reissued, or modified permit may reflect the level of pollutant control actually achieved (but shall not be less stringent than required by effluent guidelines in effect at the time of permit renewal, reissuance, or modification).

Subparagraph (B) shall not apply to any revised waste load allocations or any alternative grounds for translating water quality standards into effluent limitations, except where the cumulative effect of such revised allocations results in a decrease in the amount of pollutants discharged into the concerned waters, and such revised allocations are not the result of a discharger eliminating or substantially reducing its discharge of pollutants due to complying with the requirements of this chapter or for reasons otherwise unrelated to water quality.

(3) Limitations — In no event may a permit with respect to which paragraph (1) applies be renewed, reissued, or modified to contain an effluent limitation which is less stringent than required by effluent guidelines in effect at the time the permit is renewed, reissued, or modified. In no event may such a permit to discharge into waters be renewed, reissued, or modified to contain a less stringent effluent limitation if the implementation of such limitation would result in a violation of a water quality standard under section 1313 of this title applicable to such waters.

(p) Municipal and industrial stormwater discharges

(1) General rule — Prior to October 1, 1994, the Administrator or the State (in the case of a permit program approved under this section) shall not require a permit under this section for discharges composed entirely of stormwater.

(2) Exceptions — Paragraph (1) shall not apply with respect to the following stormwater discharges:

    (A) A discharge with respect to which a permit has been issued under this section before February 4, 1987.

    (B) A discharge associated with industrial activity.

    (C) A discharge from a municipal separate storm sewer system serving a population of 250,000 or more.

(D) A discharge from a municipal separate storm sewer system serving a population of 100,000 or more but less than 250,000.

(E) A discharge for which the Administrator or the State, as the case may be, determines that the stormwater discharge contributes to a violation of a water quality standard or is a significant contributor of pollutants to waters of the United States.

(3) Permit requirements

(A) Industrial discharges — Permits for discharges associated with industrial activity shall meet all applicable provisions of this section and section 1311 of this title.

(B) Municipal discharge — Permits for discharges from municipal storm sewers —

(i) may be issued on a system- or jurisdiction-wide basis;

(ii) shall include a requirement to effectively prohibit non-stormwater discharges into the storm sewers; and

(iii) shall require controls to reduce the discharge of pollutants to the maximum extent practicable, including management practices, control techniques and system, design and engineering methods, and such other provisions as the Administrator or the State determines appropriate for the control of such pollutants.

(4) Permit application requirements

(A) Industrial and large municipal discharges — Not later than 2 years after February 4, 1987, the Administrator shall establish regulations setting forth the permit application requirements for stormwater discharges described in paragraphs (2)(B) and (2)(C). Applications for permits for such discharges shall be filed no later than 3 years after February 4, 1987. Not later than 4 years after February 4, 1987, the Administrator or the State, as the case may be, shall issue or deny each such permit. Any such permit shall provide for compliance as expeditiously as practicable, but in no event later than 3 years after the date of issuance of such permit.

(B) Other municipal discharges — Not later than 4 years after February 4, 1987, the Administrator shall establish regulations setting forth the permit application requirements for stormwater discharges described in paragraph (2)(D). Applications for permits for such discharges shall be filed no later than 5 years after February 4, 1987. Not later than 6 years after February 4, 1987, the Administrator or the State, as the case may be, shall issue or deny each such permit. Any such permit shall provide for compliance as expeditiously as practicable, but in no event later than 3 years after the date of issuance of such permit.

(5) Studies — The Administrator, in consultation with the States, shall conduct a study for the purposes of —

(A) identifying those stormwater discharges or classes of stormwater discharges for which permits are not required pursuant to paragraphs (1) and (2) of this subsection;

(B) determining, to the maximum extent practicable, the nature and extent of pollutants in such discharges; and

(C) establishing procedures and methods to control stormwater discharges to the extent necessary to mitigate impacts on water quality. Not later than October 1, 1988, the Administrator shall submit to Congress a report on the results of the study described in subparagraphs (A) and (B). Not later than October 1, 1989, the Administrator shall submit to Congress a report on the results of the study described in subparagraph (C).

(6) Regulations — Not later than October 1, 1993, the Administrator, in consultation with State and local officials, shall issue regulations (based on the results of the studies conducted under paragraph (5)) which designate stormwater discharges, other than those discharges described in paragraph (2), to be regulated to protect water quality and shall establish a comprehensive program to regulate such designated sources. The program shall, at a minimum, (A) establish priorities, (B) establish requirements for State stormwater management programs, and (C) establish expeditious deadlines. The program may include performance standards, guidelines, guidance, and management practices and treatment requirements, as appropriate.

(q) Combined sewer overflows

(1) Requirement for permits, orders, and decrees — Each permit, order, or decree issued pursuant to this chapter after December 21, 2000 for a discharge from a municipal combined storm and sanitary sewer shall conform to the Combined Sewer Overflow Control Policy signed by the Administrator on April 11, 1994 (in this subsection referred to as the "CSO control policy").

(2) Water quality and designated use review guidance — Not later than July 31, 2001, and after providing notice and opportunity for public comment, the Administrator shall issue guidance to facilitate the conduct of water quality and designated use reviews for municipal combined sewer overflow receiving waters.

(3) Report — Not later than September 1, 2001, the Administrator shall transmit to Congress a report on the progress made by the Environmental Protection Agency, States, and municipalities in implementing and enforcing the CSO control policy.

(r) Discharges incidental to the normal operation of recreational vessels —

No permit shall be required under this chapter by the Administrator (or a State, in the case of a permit program approved under subsection (b)) for the discharge of any graywater, bilge water, cooling water, weather deck runoff, oil water separator effluent, or effluent from properly functioning marine engines, or any other discharge that is incidental to the normal operation of a vessel, if the discharge is from a recreational vessel.

(s) Integrated plans

(1) Definition of integrated plan

In this subsection, the term "integrated plan" means a plan developed in accordance with the Integrated Municipal Stormwater and Wastewater Planning Approach Framework, issued by the Environmental Protection Agency and dated June 5, 2012.

(2) In general

The Administrator (or a State, in the case of a permit program approved by the Administrator) shall inform municipalities of the opportunity to develop an integrated plan that may be incorporated into a permit under this section.

(3) Scope

(A) Scope of permit incorporating integrated plan

A permit issued under this section that incorporates an integrated plan may integrate all requirements under this chapter addressed in the integrated plan, including requirements relating to —

(i)   a combined sewer overflow;

(ii) a capacity, management, operation, and maintenance program for sanitary sewer collection systems;

(iii) a municipal stormwater discharge;

(iv) a municipal wastewater discharge; and

(v)   a water quality-based effluent limitation to implement an applicable wasteload allocation in a total maximum daily load.

(B) Inclusions in integrated plan

An integrated plan incorporated into a permit issued under this section may include the implementation of —

(i)   projects, including innovative projects, to reclaim, recycle, or reuse water; and

(ii) green infrastructure.

(4) Compliance schedules

(A) In general

A permit issued under this section that incorporates an integrated plan may include a schedule of compliance, under which actions taken to meet any applicable water quality-based effluent limitation may be implemented over more than 1 permit term if the schedule of compliance —

(i)   is authorized by State water quality standards; and

(ii) meets the requirements of section 122.47 of title 40, Code of Federal Regulations (as in effect on January 14, 2019).

(B) Time for compliance

For purposes of subparagraph (A)(ii), the requirement of section 122.47 of title 40, Code of Federal Regulations, for compliance by an applicable statutory deadline under this chapter does not prohibit implementation of an applicable water quality-based effluent limitation over more than 1 permit term.

(C) Review

A schedule of compliance incorporated into a permit issued under this section may be reviewed at the time the permit is renewed to determine whether the schedule should be modified.

(5) Existing authorities retained

(A) Applicable standards

Nothing in this subsection modifies any obligation to comply with applicable technology and water quality-based effluent limitations under this chapter.

(B) Flexibility

Nothing in this subsection reduces or eliminates any flexibility available under this chapter, including the authority of a State to revise a water quality standard after a use attainability analysis under section 131.10(g) of title 40, Code of Federal Regulations (or a successor regulation), subject to the approval of the Administrator under section 1313(c) of this title.

(6) Clarification of State authority

(A) In general

Nothing in section 1311(b)(1)(C) of this title precludes a State from authorizing in the water quality standards of the State the issuance of a schedule of compliance to meet water quality-based effluent limitations in permits that incorporate provisions of an integrated plan.

(B) Transition rule

In any case in which a discharge is subject to a judicial order or consent decree, as of January 14, 2019, resolving an enforcement action under this chapter, any schedule of compliance issued pursuant to an authorization in a State water quality standard may not revise a schedule of compliance in that order or decree to be less stringent, unless the order or decree is modified by agreement of the parties and the court.

§1343. Ocean discharge criteria
[CWA §403]

(a) Issuance of permits — No permit under section 1342 of this title for a discharge into the territorial sea, the waters of the contiguous zone, or the oceans shall be issued, after promulgation of guidelines established under subsection (c) of this section, except in compliance with such guidelines. Prior to the promulgation of such guidelines, a permit may be issued under such section 1342 of this title if the Administrator determines it to be in the public interest.

(b) Waiver — The requirements of subsection (d) of section 1342 of this title may not be waived in the case of permits for discharges into the territorial sea.

(c) Guidelines for determining degradation of waters

(1) The Administrator shall, within one hundred and eighty days after October 18, 1972 (and from time to time thereafter), promulgate guidelines for determining the degradation of the waters of the territorial seas, the contiguous zone, and the oceans, which shall include:

(A) the effect of disposal of pollutants on human health or welfare, including but not limited to plankton, fish, shellfish, wildlife, shorelines, and beaches;

(B) the effect of disposal of pollutants on marine life including the transfer, concentration, and dispersal of pollutants or their byproducts through biological, physical, and chemical processes; changes in marine ecosystem diversity, productivity, and stability; and species and community population changes;

(C) the effect of disposal, of pollutants on esthetic, recreation, and economic values;

(D) the persistence and permanence of the effects of disposal of pollutants;

(E) the effect of the disposal of varying rates, of particular volumes and concentrations of pollutants;

(F) other possible locations and methods of disposal or recycling of pollutants including land-based alternatives; and

(G) the effect on alternate uses of the oceans, such as mineral exploitation and scientific study.

(2) In any event where insufficient information exists on any proposed discharge to make a reasonable judgment on any of the guidelines established pursuant to this subsection no permit shall be issued under section 1342 of this title.

§1344. Permits for dredged or fill material
[CWA §404]

(a) Discharge into navigable waters at specified disposal sites — The Secretary may issue permits, after notice and opportunity for public hearings for the discharge of dredged or fill material into the navigable waters at specified disposal sites. Not

later than the fifteenth day after the date an applicant submits all the information required to complete an application for a permit under this subsection, the Secretary shall publish the notice required by this subsection.

(b) Specification for disposal sites — Subject to subsection (c) of this section, each such disposal site shall be specified for each such permit by the Secretary (1) through the application of guidelines developed by the Administrator, in conjunction with the Secretary, which guidelines shall be based upon criteria comparable to the criteria applicable to the territorial seas, the contiguous zone, and the ocean under section 1343(c) of this title, and (2) in any case where such guidelines under clause (1) alone would prohibit the specification of a site, through the application additionally of the economic impact of the site on navigation and anchorage.

(c) Denial or restriction of use of defined areas as disposal sites — The Administrator is authorized to prohibit the specification (including the withdrawal of specification) of any defined area as a disposal site, and he is authorized to deny or restrict the use of any defined area for specification (including the withdrawal of specification) as a disposal site, whenever he determines, after notice and opportunity for public hearings, that the discharge of such materials into such area will have an unacceptable adverse effect on municipal water supplies, shellfish beds and fishery areas (including spawning and breeding areas), wildlife, or recreational areas. Before making such determination, the Administrator shall consult with the Secretary. The Administrator shall set forth in writing and make public his findings and his reasons for making any determination under this subsection.

(d) "Secretary" defined — The term "Secretary" as used in this section means the Secretary of the Army, acting through the Chief of Engineers.

(e) General permits on State, regional, or nationwide basis

(1) In carrying out his functions relating to the discharge of dredged or fill material under this section, the Secretary may, after notice and opportunity for public hearing, issue general permits on a State, regional, or nationwide basis for any category of activities involving discharges of dredged or fill material if the Secretary determines that the activities in such category are similar in nature, will cause only minimal adverse environmental effects when performed separately, and will have only minimal cumulative adverse effect on the environment. Any general permit issued under this subsection shall (A) be based on the guidelines described in subsection (b)(1) of this section, and (B) set forth the requirements and standards which shall apply to any activity authorized by such general permit.

(2) No general permit issued under this subsection shall be for a period of more than five years

after the date of its issuance and such general permit may be revoked or modified by the Secretary if, after opportunity for public hearing, the Secretary determines that the activities authorized by such general permit have an adverse impact on the environment or such activities are more appropriately authorized by individual permits.

(f) Non-prohibited discharge of dredged or fill material

(1) Except as provided in paragraph (2) of this subsection, the discharge of dredged or fill material —

(A) from normal farming, silviculture, and ranching activities such as plowing, seeding, cultivating, minor drainage, harvesting for the production of food, fiber, and forest products, or upland soil and water conservation practices;

(B) for the purpose of maintenance, including emergency reconstruction of recently damaged parts, of currently serviceable structures such as dikes, dams, levees, groins, riprap, breakwaters, causeways, and bridge abutments or approaches, and transportation structures;

(C) for the purpose of construction or maintenance of farm or stock ponds or irrigation ditches, or the maintenance of drainage ditches;

(D) for the purpose of construction of temporary sedimentation basins on a construction site which does not include placement of fill material into the navigable waters;

(E) for the purpose of construction or maintenance of farm roads or forest roads, or temporary roads for moving mining equipment, where such roads are constructed and maintained, in accordance with best management practices, to assure that flow and circulation patterns and chemical and biological characteristics of the navigable waters are not impaired, that the reach of the navigable waters is not reduced, and that any adverse effect on the aquatic environment will be otherwise minimized;

(F) resulting from any activity with respect to which a State has an approved program under section 1288(b)(4) of this title which meets the requirements of sub-paragraphs (B) and (C) of such section,

is not prohibited by or otherwise subject to regulation under this section or section 1311(a) or 1342 of this title (except for effluent standards or prohibitions under section 1317 of this title).

(2) Any discharge of dredged or fill material into the navigable waters incidental to any activity having as its purpose bringing an area of the navigable waters into a use to which it was not previously subject, where the flow or circulation of navigable waters may be impaired or the reach of

such waters be reduced, shall be required to have a permit under this section.

(g) State administration

(1) The Governor of any State desiring to administer its own individual and general permit program for the discharge of dredged or fill material into the navigable waters (other than those waters which are presently used, or are susceptible to use in their natural condition or by reasonable improvement as a means to transport interstate or foreign commerce shoreward to their ordinary high water mark, including all waters which are subject to the ebb and flow of the tide shoreward to their mean high water mark, or mean higher high water mark on the west coast, including wetlands adjacent thereto) within its jurisdiction may submit to the Administrator a full and complete description of the program it proposes to establish and administer under State law or under an interstate compact. In addition, such State shall submit a statement from the attorney general (or the attorney for those State agencies which have independent legal counsel), or from the chief legal officer in the case of an interstate agency, that the laws of such State, or the interstate compact, as the case may be, provide adequate authority to carry out the described program.

(2) Not later than the tenth day after the date of the receipt of the program and statement submitted by any State under paragraph (1) of this subsection, the Administrator shall provide copies of such program and statement to the Secretary and the Secretary of the Interior, acting through the Director of the United States Fish and Wildlife Service.

(3) Not later than the ninetieth day after the date of the receipt by the Administrator of the program and statement submitted by any State, under paragraph (1) of this subsection, the Secretary and the Secretary of the Interior, acting through the Director of the United States Fish and Wildlife Service, shall submit any comments with respect to such program and statement to the Administrator in writing.

(h) Determination of State's authority to issue permits under State program; approval; notification; transfers to State program

(1) Not later than the one-hundred-twentieth day after the date of the receipt by the Administrator of a program and statement submitted by any State under paragraph (1) of this subsection, the Administrator shall determine, taking into account any comments submitted by the Secretary and the Secretary of the Interior, acting through the Director of the United States Fish and Wildlife Service, pursuant to subsection (g) of this section, whether such State has the following authority with respect to the issuance of permits pursuant to such program:

(A) To issue permits which —

(i) apply, and assure compliance with, any applicable requirements of this section, including, but not limited to, the guidelines established under subsection (b)(1) of this section, and sections 1317 and 1343 of this title;

(ii) are for fixed terms not exceeding five years; and

(iii) can be terminated or modified for cause including, but not limited to, the following:

(I) violation of any condition of the permit;

(II) obtaining a permit by misrepresentation, or failure to disclose fully all relevant facts;

(III) change in any condition that requires either a temporary or permanent reduction or elimination of the permitted discharge.

(B) To issue permits which apply, and assure compliance with, all applicable requirements of section 1318 of this title, or to inspect, monitor, enter, and require reports to at least the same extent as required in section 1318 of this title.

(C) To assure that the public, and any other State the waters of which may be affected, receive notice of each application for a permit and to provide an opportunity for public hearing before a ruling on each such application.

(D) To assure that the Administrator receives notice of each application (including a copy thereof) for a permit.

(E) To assure that any State (other than the permitting State), whose waters may be affected by the issuance of a permit may submit written recommendations to the permitting State (and the Administrator) with respect to any permit application and, if any part of such written recommendations are not accepted by the permitting State, that the permitting State will notify such affected State (and the Administrator) in writing of its failure to so accept such recommendations together with its reasons for so doing.

(F) To assure that no permit will be issued if, in the judgment of the Secretary, after consultation with the Secretary of the department in which the Coast Guard is operating, anchorage and navigation of any of the navigable waters would be substantially impaired thereby.

(G) To abate violations of the permit or the permit program, including civil and criminal penalties and other ways and means of enforcement.

(H) To assure continued coordination with Federal and Federal-State water-related planning and review processes.

(2) If, with respect to a State program submitted under subsection (g)(1) of this section, the Administrator determines that such State —

(A) has the authority set forth in paragraph (1) of this subsection, the Administrator shall approve the program and so notify (i) such State and (ii) the Secretary, who upon subsequent notification from such State that it is administering such program, shall suspend the issuance of permits under subsections (a) and (e) of this section for activities with respect to which a permit may be issued pursuant to such State program; or

(B) does not have the authority set forth in paragraph (1) of this subsection, the Administrator shall so notify such State, which notification shall also describe the revisions or modifications necessary so that such State may resubmit such program for a determination by the Administrator under this subsection.

(3) If the Administrator fails to make a determination with respect to any program submitted by a State under subsection (g)(1) of this section within one-hundred-twenty days after the date of the receipt of such program, such program shall be deemed approved pursuant to paragraph (2)(A) of this subsection and the Administrator shall so notify such State and the Secretary who, upon subsequent notification from such State that it is administering such program, shall suspend the issuance of permits under subsection (a) and (e) of this section for activities with respect to which a permit may be issued by such State.

(4) After the Secretary receives notification from the Administrator under paragraph (2) or (3) of this subsection that a State permit program has been approved, the Secretary shall transfer any applications for permits pending before the Secretary for activities with respect to which a permit may be issued pursuant to such State program to such State for appropriate action.

(5) Upon notification from a State with a permit program approved under this subsection that such State intends to administer and enforce the terms and conditions of a general permit issued by the Secretary under subsection (e) of this section with respect to activities in such State to which such general permit applies, the Secretary shall suspend the administration and enforcement of such general permit with respect to such activities.

(i) **Withdrawal of approval** — Whenever the Administrator determines after public hearing that a State is not administering a program approved under subsection (h)(2)(A) of this section, in accordance with this section, including, but not limited to, the guidelines established under subsection (b)(1) of this section, the Administrator shall so notify the State, and, if appropriate corrective action is not taken within a reasonable time, not to exceed ninety days after the date of the receipt of such notification, the Administrator shall (1) withdraw approval of such program until the Administrator determines such corrective action has been taken, and (2) notify the Secretary that the Secretary shall resume the program for the issuance of permits under subsections (a) and (e) of this section for activities with respect to which the State was issuing permits and that such authority of the Secretary shall continue in effect until such time as the Administrator makes the determination described in clause (1) of this subsection and such State again has an approved program.

(j) Copies of applications for State permits and proposed general permits to be transmitted to Administrator — Each State which is administering a permit program pursuant to this section shall transmit to the Administrator (1) a copy of each permit application received by such State and provide notice to the Administrator of every action related to the consideration of such permit application, including each permit proposed to be issued by such State, and (2) a copy of each proposed general permit which such State intends to issue. Not later than the tenth day after the date of the receipt of such permit application or such proposed general permit, the Administrator shall provide copies of such permit application or such proposed general permit to the Secretary and the Secretary of the Interior, acting through the Director of the United States Fish and Wildlife Service. If the Administrator intends to provide written comments to such State with respect to such permit application or such proposed general permit, he shall so notify such State not later than the thirtieth day after the date of the receipt of such application or such proposed general permit and provide such written comments to such State, after consideration of any comments made in writing with respect to such application or such proposed general permit by the Secretary and the Secretary of the Interior, acting through the Director of the United States Fish and Wildlife Service, not later than the ninetieth day after the date of such receipt. If such State is so notified by the Administrator, it shall not issue the proposed permit until after the receipt of such comments from the Administrator, or after such ninetieth day, whichever first occurs. Such State shall not issue such proposed permit after such ninetieth day if it has received such written comments in which the Administrator objects (A) to the issuance of such proposed permit and such proposed permit is one that has been submitted to the Administrator pursuant to subsection (h)(1)(E) of this section, or (B) to the issuance of such proposed permit as being outside the requirements of this section, including, but not limited to, the guidelines developed under subsection (b)(1) of this section unless it modifies such proposed permit in accordance with such comments. Whenever the Administrator objects to the issuance of a permit under the preceding sentence such written objection shall contain a statement of the reasons for such objection and the conditions which such permit would include if it were issued by the Administrator. In any case where the Administrator objects to the issuance of a permit, on request of the State, a public hearing shall be held by the Administrator on such objection. If the State does not resubmit such permit revised to meet such objection within 30 days after completion of the hearing or, if no hearing is requested within 90 days after the date of such objection, the Secretary may issue the permit pursuant to subsection (a) or (e) of this section, as the case may be, for such source in accordance with the guidelines and requirements of this chapter.

(k) Waiver — In accordance with guidelines promulgated pursuant to subsection (i)(2) of section 1314 of this title, the Administrator is authorized to waive the requirements of subsection (j) of this section at the time of the approval of a program pursuant to subsection (h)(2)(A) of this section for any category (including any class, type, or size within such category) of discharge within the State submitting such program.

(l) Categories of discharges not subject to requirements — The Administrator shall promulgate regulations establishing categories of discharges which he determines shall not be subject to the requirements of subsection (j) of this section in any State with a program approved pursuant to subsection (h)(2)(A) of this section. The Administrator may distinguish among classes, types, and sizes within any category of discharges.

(m) Comments on permit applications or proposed general permits by Secretary of the Interior acting through Director of United States Fish and Wildlife Service — Not later than the ninetieth day after the date on which the Secretary notifies the Secretary of the Interior, acting through the Director of the United States Fish and Wildlife Service that (1) an application for a permit under subsection (a) of this section has been received by the Secretary, or (2) the Secretary proposes to issue a general permit under subsection (e) of this section, the Secretary of the Interior, acting through the Director of the United States Fish and Wildlife Service, shall submit any comments with respect to such application or such proposed general permit in writing to the Secretary.

(n) Enforcement authority not limited — Nothing in this section shall be construed to limit the authority of the Administrator to take action pursuant to section 1319 of this title.

(o) Public availability of permits and permit applications — A copy of each permit application and each permit issued under this section shall be available to the public. Such permit application or portion thereof, shall further be available on request for the purpose of reproduction.

(p) Compliance — Compliance with a permit issued pursuant to this section, including any activity carried out pursuant to a general permit issued under this section, shall be deemed compliance, for purposes of sections 1319 and 1365 of this title, with sections 1311, 1317, and 1343 of this title.

(q) Minimization of duplication, needless paperwork, and delays in issuance; agreements — Not later than the one-hundred-eightieth day after December 27, 1977, the Secretary shall enter into agreements with the Administrator, the Secretaries of the Departments of Agriculture, Commerce, Interior, and Transportation, and the heads of other appropriate Federal agencies to minimize, to the maximum extent practicable, duplication, needless paperwork, and delays in the issuance of permits under this section. Such agreements shall be developed to assure that, to the maximum extent practicable, a decision with respect to an application for a permit under subsection (a) of this section will be made not later than the ninetieth day after the date the notice for such application is published under subsection (a) of this section.

(r) Federal projects specifically authorized by Congress — The discharge of dredged or fill material as part of the construction of a Federal project specifically authorized by Congress, whether prior to or on or after December 27, 1977, is not prohibited by or otherwise subject to regulation under this section, or a State program approved under this section, or section 1311(a) or 1342 of this title (except for effluent standards or prohibitions under section 1317 of this title), if information on the effects of such discharge, including consideration of the guidelines developed under subsection (b)(1) of this section, is included in an environmental impact statement for such project pursuant to the National Environmental Policy Act of 1969 (42 U.S.C. §§4321 *et seq.*) and such environmental impact statement has been submitted to Congress before the actual discharge of dredged or fill material in connection with the construction of such project and prior to either authorization of such project or an appropriation of funds for such construction.

(s) Violation of permits

(1) Whenever on the basis of any information available to him the Secretary finds that any person is in violation of any condition or limitation set forth in a permit issued by the Secretary under this section, the Secretary shall issue an order requiring such person to comply with such condition or limitation, or the Secretary shall bring a civil action in accordance with paragraph (3) of this subsection.

(2) A copy of any order issued under this subsection shall be sent immediately by the Secretary to the State in which the violation occurs and other affected States. Any order issued under this subsection shall be by personal service and shall state with reasonable specificity the nature of the violation, specify a time for compliance, not to exceed thirty days, which the Secretary determines is reasonable, taking into account the seriousness of the violation and any good faith efforts to comply with applicable requirements. In any case in which an order under this subsection is issued to a corporation, a copy of such order shall be served on any appropriate corporate officers.

(3) The Secretary is authorized to commence a civil action for appropriate relief, including a permanent or temporary injunction for any violation for which he is authorized to issue a compliance order under paragraph (1) of this subsection. Any action under this paragraph may be brought in the district court of the United States for the district in which the defendant is located or resides or is doing business, and such court shall have jurisdiction to restrain such violation and to require compliance. Notice of the commencement of such action shall be given immediately to the appropriate State.

(4) Any person who violates any condition or limitation in a permit issued by the Secretary under this section, and any person who violates any order issued by the Secretary under paragraph (1) of this subsection, shall be subject to a civil penalty not to exceed $25,000 per day for each violation. In determining the amount of a civil penalty the court shall consider the seriousness of the violation or violations, the economic benefit (if any) resulting from the violation, any history of such violations, any good-faith efforts to comply with the applicable requirements, the economic impact of the penalty on the violator, and such other matters as justice may require.

(t) Navigable waters within State jurisdiction — Nothing in this section shall preclude or deny the right of any State or interstate agency to control the discharge of dredged or fill material in any portion of the navigable waters within the jurisdiction of such State, including any activity of any Federal agency, and each such agency shall comply with such State or interstate requirements both substantive and procedural to control the discharge of dredged or fill material to the same extent that any person is subject to such requirements. This section shall not be construed as affecting or impairing the authority of the Secretary to maintain navigation.

§1345. Disposal or use of sewage sludge [CWA §405]

(a) Permit — Notwithstanding any other provision of this chapter or of any other law, in any case where the disposal of sewage sludge resulting from the operation of a treatment works as defined in section 1292 of this title (including the removal of in-place sewage sludge from one location and its deposit at another location) would result in any pollutant from such sewage sludge entering the navigable waters, such disposal is prohibited except in accordance with a permit issued by the Administrator under section 1342 of this title.

(b) Issuance of permit; regulations — The Administrator shall issue regulations governing the issuance of permits for the disposal of sewage sludge subject to subsection (a) of this section and section 1342 of this title. Such regulations shall require the application to such disposal of each criterion, factor, procedure, and requirement applicable to a permit issued under section 1342 of this title.

(c) State permit program — Each State desiring to administer its own permit program for disposal of sewage sludge subject to subsection (a) of this section within its jurisdiction may do so in accordance with section 1342 of this title.

(d) Regulations

(1) Regulations — The Administrator, after consultation with appropriate Federal and State agencies and other interested persons, shall develop and publish, within one year after December 27, 1977, and from time to time thereafter, regulations providing guidelines for the disposal of sludge and the utilization of sludge for various purposes. Such regulations shall —

(A) identify uses for sludge, including disposal;

(B) specify factors to be taken into account in determining the measures and practices applicable to each such use or disposal (including publication of information on costs);

(C) identify concentrations of pollutants which interfere with each such use or disposal.

The Administrator is authorized to revise any regulation issued under this subchapter.

(2) Identification and regulation of toxic pollutants

(A) On basis of available information

(i) Proposed regulations — Not later than November 30, 1986, the Administrator shall identify those toxic pollutants which, on the basis of available information on their toxicity, persistence, concentration, mobility, or potential for exposure, may be present in sewage sludge in concentrations which may adversely affect public health or the environment, and propose regulations specifying acceptable management practices for sewage sludge containing each such toxic pollutant and establishing numerical limitations for each such pollutant for each use identified under paragraph (1)(A).

(ii) Final regulations — Not later than August 31, 1987, and after opportunity for public hearing, the Administrator shall promulgate the regulations required by subparagraph (A)(i).

(B) Others

(i) Proposed regulations — Not later than July 31, 1987, the Administrator shall identify those toxic pollutants not identified under subparagraph (A)(i) which may be present in sewage sludge in concentrations which may adversely affect public health or the environment, and propose regulations specifying acceptable management practices for sewage sludge containing each such toxic pollutant and establishing numerical limitations for each pollutant for each such use identified under paragraph (1)(A).

(ii) Final regulations — Not later than June 15, 1988, the Administrator shall promulgate the regulations required by subparagraph (B)(i).

(C) Review — From time to time, but not less often than every 2 years, the Administrator shall review the regulations promulgated under this paragraph for the purpose of identifying additional toxic pollutants and promulgating regulations for such pollutants consistent with the requirements of this paragraph.

(D) Minimum standards; compliance date — The management practices and numerical criteria established under subparagraphs (A), (B), and (C) shall be adequate to protect public health and the environment from any reasonably anticipated adverse effects of each pollutant. Such regulations shall require compliance as expeditiously as practicable but in no case later than 12 months after their publication, unless such regulations require the construction of new pollution control facilities, in which case the regulations shall require compliance as expeditiously as practicable but in no case later than two years from the date of their publication.

(3) Alternative standards — For purposes of this subsection, if, in the judgment of the Administrator, it is not feasible to prescribe or enforce a numerical limitation for a pollutant identified under paragraph (2), the Administrator may instead promulgate a design, equipment, management practice, or operational standard, or combination thereof, which in the Administrator's judgment is adequate to protect public health and the environment from any reasonably anticipated adverse effects of such pollutant. In the event the Administrator promulgates a design or equipment standard under this subsection, the Administrator shall include as part of such standard such requirements as will assure the proper operation and maintenance of any such element of design or equipment.

(4) Conditions on permits — Prior to the promulgation of the regulations required by paragraph (2), the Administrator shall impose conditions in permits issued to publicly owned treatment works under section 1342 of this title or take such other measures as the Administrator deems appropriate to protect public health and the environment from any adverse effects which may occur from toxic pollutants in sewage sludge.

(5) Limitation on statutory construction — Nothing in this section is intended to waive more stringent requirements established by this chapter or any other law.

(e) Manner of sludge disposal — The determination of the manner of disposal or use of sludge is a local determination, except that it shall be unlawful for any person to dispose of sludge from a publicly owned treatment works or any other treatment works treating domestic sewage for any use for which regulations have been established pursuant to subsection (d) of this section, except in accordance with such regulations.

(f) Implementation of regulations

(1) Through section 1342 permits — Any permit issued under section 1342 of this title to a publicly owned treatment works or any other treatment works treating domestic sewage shall include requirements for the use and disposal of sludge that implement the regulations established pursuant to subsection (d) of this section, unless such requirements have been included in a permit issued under the appropriate provisions of subtitle C of the Solid Waste Disposal Act (42 U.S.C. §§6921 *et seq.*), part C of the Safe Drinking Water Act (42 U.S.C. §§300h *et seq.*), the Marine Protection, Research, and Sanctuaries Act of 1972 (33 U.S.C. §§1401 *et seq.*), or the Clean Air Act (42 U.S.C. §§7401 *et seq.*), or under State permit programs approved by the Administrator, where the Administrator determines that such programs assure compliance with any applicable requirements of this section. Not later than December 15, 1986, the Administrator shall promulgate procedures for approval of State programs pursuant to this paragraph.

(2) Through other permits — In the case of a treatment works described in paragraph (1) that is not subject to section 1342 of this title and to which none of the other above listed permit programs nor approved State permit authority apply, the Administrator may issue a permit to such treatment works solely to impose requirements for the use and disposal of sludge that implement the regulations established pursuant to subsection (d) of this section. The Administrator shall include in the permit appropriate requirements to assure compliance with the regulations established pursuant to subsection (d) of this section. The Administrator shall establish procedures for issuing permits pursuant to this paragraph.

(g) Studies and projects

(1) Grant program; information gathering — The Administrator is authorized to conduct or initiate scientific studies, demonstration projects, and public information and education projects which are designed to promote the safe and beneficial management or use of sewage sludge for such purposes as aiding the restoration of abandoned mine sites, conditioning soil for parks and recreation areas, agricultural and horticultural uses, and other beneficial purposes. For the purposes of carrying out this subsection, the Administrator may make grants to State water pollution control agencies, other public or nonprofit agencies, institutions, organizations, and individuals. In cooperation with other Federal departments and agencies, other public and private agencies, institutions, and organizations, the Administrator is authorized to collect and disseminate information pertaining to the safe and beneficial use of sewage sludge.

(2) Authorization of appropriations — For the purposes of carrying out the scientific studies, demonstration projects, and public information and education projects authorized in this section, there is authorized to be appropriated for fiscal years beginning after September 30, 1986, not to exceed $5,000,000.

§1346. Coastal recreation water quality monitoring and notification

(a) Monitoring and notification

(1) In general — Not later than 18 months after October 10, 2000, after consultation and in cooperation with appropriate Federal, State, tribal, and local officials (including local health officials), and after providing public notice and an opportunity for comment, the Administrator shall publish performance criteria for —

(A) monitoring and assessment (including specifying available methods for monitoring) of coastal recreation waters adjacent to beaches or similar points of access that are used by the public for attainment of applicable water quality standards for pathogens and pathogen indicators; and

(B) the prompt notification of the public, local governments, and the Administrator of any exceeding of or likelihood of exceeding applicable water quality standards for coastal recreation waters described in subpara- graph (A).

(2) Level of protection — The performance criteria referred to in paragraph (1) shall provide that the activities described in subparagraphs (A) and (B) of that paragraph shall be carried out as necessary for the protection of public health and safety.

(b) Program development and implementation grants

(1) In general — The Administrator may make grants to States and local governments to develop and implement programs for monitoring and notification for coastal recreation waters adjacent to beaches or similar points of access that are used by the public.

(2) Limitations

(A) In general — The Administrator may award a grant to a State or a local government to implement a monitoring and notification program if —

(i) the program is consistent with the performance criteria published by the Administrator under subsection (a);

(ii) the State or local government prioritizes the use of grant funds for particular coastal recreation waters based on the use of the water and the risk to human health presented by pathogens or pathogen indicators;

(iii) the State or local government makes available to the Administrator the factors used to prioritize the use of funds under clause (ii);

(iv) the State or local government provides a list of discrete areas of coastal recreation waters that are subject to the program for monitoring and notification for which the grant is provided that specifies any coastal recreation waters for which fiscal constraints will prevent consistency with the performance criteria under subsection (a) of this section; and

(v) the public is provided an opportunity to review the program through a process that provides for public notice and an opportunity for comment.

(B) Grants to local governments — The Administrator may make a grant to a local government under this subsection for implementation of a monitoring and notification program only if, after the 1-year period beginning on the date of publication of performance criteria under subsection (a)(1), the Administrator determines that the State is not implementing a program that meets the requirements of this subsection, regardless of whether the State has received a grant under this subsection.

(3) Other requirements

(A) Report — A State recipient of a grant under this subsection shall submit to the Administrator, in such format and at such intervals as the Administrator determines to be appropriate, a report that describes —

(i) data collected as part of the program for monitoring and notification as described in subsection (c) of this section; and

(ii) actions taken to notify the public when water quality standards are exceeded.

(B) Delegation — A State recipient of a grant under this subsection shall identify each local government to which the State has delegated or intends to delegate responsibility for implementing a monitoring and notification program consistent with the performance criteria published under subsection (a) (including any coastal recreation waters for which the authority to implement a monitoring and notification program would be subject to the delegation).

(4) Federal share

(A) In general — The Administrator, through grants awarded under this section, may pay up to 100 percent of the costs of developing and implementing a program for monitoring and notification under this subsection.

(B) Non-Federal share — The non-Federal share of the costs of developing and implementing a monitoring and notification program may be —

(i) in an amount not to exceed 50 percent, as determined by the Administrator in consultation with State, tribal, and local government representatives; and

(ii) provided in cash or in kind.

(c) Content of State and local government programs — As a condition of receipt of a grant under subsection (b), a State or local government program for monitoring and notification under this section shall identify —

(1) lists of coastal recreation waters in the State, including coastal recreation waters adjacent to beaches or similar points of access that are used by the public;

(2) in the case of a State program for monitoring and notification, the process by which the State may delegate to local governments responsibility for implementing the monitoring and notification program;

(3) the frequency and location of monitoring and assessment of coastal recreation waters based on —

(A) the periods of recreational use of the waters;

(B) the nature and extent of use during certain periods;

(C) the proximity of the waters to known point sources and nonpoint sources of pollution; and

(D) any effect of storm events on the waters;

(4)(A) the methods to be used for detecting levels of pathogens and pathogen indicators that are harmful to human health; and

(B) the assessment procedures for identifying short-term increases in pathogens and pathogen indicators that are harmful to human health in coastal recreation waters (including increases in relation to storm events);

(5) measures for prompt communication of the occurrence, nature, location, pollutants involved, and extent of any exceeding of, or likelihood of exceeding, applicable water quality standards for pathogens and pathogen indicators to —

(A) the Administrator, in such form as the Administrator determines to be appropriate; and

(B) a designated official of a local government having jurisdiction over land adjoining the coastal recreation waters for which the failure to meet applicable standards is identified;

(6) measures for the posting of signs at beaches or similar points of access, or functionally equivalent communication measures that are sufficient to give notice to the public that the coastal recreation waters are not meeting or are not expected to meet applicable water quality standards for pathogens and pathogen indicators; and

(7) measures that inform the public of the potential risks associated with water contact activities in the coastal recreation waters that do not meet applicable water quality standards.

(d) Federal agency programs — Not later than 3 years after October 10, 2000, each Federal agency that has jurisdiction over coastal recreation waters adjacent to beaches or similar points of access that are used by the public shall develop and implement, through a process that provides for public notice and an opportunity for comment, a monitoring and notification program for the coastal recreation waters that —

(1) protects the public health and safety;

(2) is consistent with the performance criteria published under subsection (a) of this section;

(3) includes a completed report on the information specified in subsection (b)(3)(A) of this section, to be submitted to the Administrator; and

(4) addresses the matters specified in subsection (c) of this section.

(e) Database — The Administrator shall establish, maintain, and make available to the public by electronic and other means a national coastal recreation water pollution occurrence database that provides —

(1) the data reported to the Administrator under subsections (b)(3)(A)(i) and (d)(3) of this section; and

(2) other information concerning pathogens and pathogen indicators in coastal recreation waters that —

(A) is made available to the Administrator by a State or local government, from a coastal water quality monitoring program of the State or local government; and

(B) the Administrator determines should be included.

(f) Technical assistance for monitoring floatable material — The Administrator shall provide technical assistance to States and local governments for the development of assessment and monitoring procedures for floatable material to protect public health and safety in coastal recreation waters.

(g) List of waters

(1) In general — Beginning not later than 18 months after the date of publication of performance criteria under subsection (a), based on information made available to the Administrator, the Administrator shall identify, and maintain a list of, discrete coastal recreation waters adjacent to beaches or similar points of access that are used by the public that —

(A) specifies any waters described in this paragraph that are subject to a monitoring and notification program consistent with the performance criteria established under subsection (a) of this section; and

(B) specifies any waters described in this paragraph for which there is no monitoring and notification program (including waters for which fiscal constraints will prevent the State or the Administrator from performing monitoring and notification consistent with the performance criteria established under subsection (a) of this section).

(2)   Availability — The Administrator shall make the list described in paragraph (1) available to the public through —

(A) publication in the Federal Register; and

(B) electronic media.

(3) Updates — The Administrator shall update the list described in paragraph (1) periodically as new information becomes available.

(h) EPA implementation — In the case of a State that has no program for monitoring and notification that is consistent with the performance criteria published under subsection (a) after the last day of the 3-year period beginning on the date on which the Administrator lists waters in the State under subsection (g)(1)(B), the Administrator shall conduct a monitoring and notification program for the listed waters based on a priority ranking established by the Administrator using funds appropriated for grants under subsection (i) of this section —

(1) to conduct monitoring and notification; and

(2) for related salaries, expenses, and travel.

(i) Authorization of appropriations — There is authorized to be appropriated for making grants under subsection (b), including implementation of monitoring and notification programs by the Administrator under subsection (h), $30,000,000 for each of fiscal years 2001 through 2005.

SUBCHAPTER V — GENERAL PROVISIONS

§1361. Administration
[CWA §501]

(a) Authority of Administrator to prescribe regulations — The Administrator is authorized to prescribe such regulations as are necessary to carry out his functions under this chapter.

(b) Utilization of other agency officers and employees — The Administrator, with the consent of the head of any other agency of the United States, may utilize such officers and employees of such agency as may be found necessary to assist in carrying out the purposes of this chapter.

(c) Recordkeeping — Each recipient of financial assistance under this chapter shall keep such records as the Administrator shall prescribe, including records which fully disclose the amount and disposition by such recipient of the proceeds of such assistance, the total cost of the project or undertaking in connection with which such assistance is given or used, and the amount of that portion of the cost of the project or undertaking supplied by other sources, and such other records as will facilitate effective audit.

(d) Audit — The Administrator and the Comptroller General of the United States, or any of their duly authorized representatives, shall have access, for the purpose of audit and examination, to any books, documents, papers, and records of the recipients that are pertinent to the grants received under this chapter. For the purpose of carrying out audits and examinations with respect to recipients of Federal assistance under this chapter, the Administrator is authorized to enter into noncompetitive procurement contracts with independent State audit organizations, consistent with chapter 75 of Title 31. Such contracts may only be entered into to the extent and in such amounts as may be provided in advance in appropriation Acts.

(e) Awards for outstanding technological achievement or innovative processes, methods, or devices in waste treatment and pollution abatement programs

(1) It is the purpose of this subsection to authorize a program which will provide official recognition by the United States Government to those industrial organizations and political subdivisions of States which during the preceding year demonstrated an outstanding technological achievement or an innovative process, method, or device in their waste treatment and pollution abatement programs. The Administrator shall, in consultation with the appropriate State water pollution control agencies, establish regulations under which such recognition may be applied for and granted, except that no applicant shall be eligible for an award under this subsection if such applicant is not in total compliance with all applicable water quality requirements under this chapter, or otherwise does not have a satisfactory record with respect to environmental quality.

(2) The Administrator shall award a certificate or plaque of suitable design to each industrial organization or political subdivision which qualifies for such recognition under regulations established under this subsection.

(3) The President of the United States, the Governor of the appropriate State, the Speaker of the House of Representatives, and the President pro tempore of the Senate shall be notified of the award by the Administrator and the awarding of such recognition shall be published in the Federal Register.

(f) Detail of Environmental Protection Agency personnel to State water pollution control agencies — Upon the request of a State water pollution control agency, personnel of the Environmental Protection Agency may be detailed to such agency for the purpose of carrying out the provisions of this chapter.

§1362. Definitions
[CWA §502]

Except as otherwise specifically provided, when used in this chapter:

(1) The term "State water pollution control agency" means the State agency designated by the Governor having responsibility for enforcing State laws relating to the abatement of pollution.

(2) The term "interstate agency" means an agency of two or more States established by or pursuant to an agreement or compact approved by the Congress, or any other agency of two or more States, having substantial powers or duties pertaining to the control of pollution as determined and approved by the Administrator.

(3) The term "State" means a State, the District of Columbia, the Commonwealth of Puerto Rico, the Virgin Islands, Guam, American Samoa, the Commonwealth of the Northern Mariana Islands, and the Trust Territory of the Pacific Islands.

(4) The term "municipality" means a city, town, borough, county, parish, district, association, or other public body created by or pursuant to State law and having jurisdiction over disposal of sewage, industrial wastes, or other wastes, or an Indian tribe or an authorized Indian tribal organization, or a designated and approved management agency under section 1288 of this title.

(5) The term "person" means an individual, corporation, partnership, association, State, municipality, commission, or political subdivision of a State, or any interstate body.

(6) The term "pollutant" means dredged spoil, solid waste, incinerator residue, sewage, garbage, sewage sludge, munitions, chemical wastes, biolog-

ical materials, radioactive materials, heat, wrecked or discarded equipment, rock, sand, cellar dirt and industrial, municipal, and agricultural waste discharged into water. This term does not mean (A) "sewage from vessels or a discharge incidental to the normal operation of a vessel of the Armed Forces" within the meaning of section 1322 of this title; or (B) water, gas, or other material which is injected into a well to facilitate production of oil or gas, or water derived in association with oil or gas production and disposed of in a well, if the well used either to facilitate production or for disposal purposes is approved by authority of the State in which the well is located, and if such State determines that such injection or disposal will not result in the degradation of ground or surface water resources.

(7) The term "navigable waters" means the waters of the United States, including the territorial seas.

(8) The term "territorial seas" means the belt of the seas measured from the line of ordinary low water along that portion of the coast which is in direct contact with the open sea and the line marking the seaward limit of inland waters, and extending seaward a distance of three miles.

(9) The term "contiguous zone" means the entire zone established or to be established by the United States under article 24 of the Convention of the Territorial Sea and the Contiguous Zone.

(10) The term "ocean" means any portion of the high seas beyond the contiguous zone.

(11) The term "effluent limitation" means any restriction established by a State or the Administrator on quantities, rates, and concentrations of chemical, physical, biological, and other constituents which are discharged from point sources into navigable waters, the waters of the contiguous zone, or the ocean, including schedules of compliance.

(12) The term "discharge of a pollutant" and the term "discharge of pollutants" each means (A) any addition of any pollutant to navigable waters from any point source, (B) any addition of any pollutant to the waters of the contiguous zone or the ocean from any point source other than a vessel or other floating craft.

(13) The term "toxic pollutant" means those pollutants, or combinations of pollutants, including disease-causing agents, which after discharge and upon exposure, ingestion, inhalation or assimilation into any organism, either directly from the environment or indirectly by ingestion through food chains, will, on the basis of information available to the Administrator, cause death, disease, behavioral abnormalities, cancer, genetic mutations, physiological malfunctions (including malfunctions in reproduction) or physical deformations, in such organisms or their offspring.

(14) The term "point source" means any discernible, confined and discrete conveyance, including but not limited to any pipe, ditch, channel, tunnel, conduit, well, discrete fissure, container, rolling stock, concentrated animal feeding operation, or vessel or other floating craft, from which pollutants are or may be discharged. This term does not include agricultural stormwater discharges and return flows from irrigated agriculture.

(15) The term "biological monitoring" shall mean the determination of the effects on aquatic life, including accumulation of pollutants in tissue, in receiving waters due to the discharge of pollutants (A) by techniques and procedures, including sampling of organisms representative of appropriate levels of the food chain appropriate to the volume and the physical, chemical, and biological characteristics of the effluent, and (B) at appropriate frequencies and locations.

(16) The term "discharge" when used without qualification includes a discharge of a pollutant, and a discharge of pollutants.

(17) The term "schedule of compliance" means a schedule of remedial measures including an enforceable sequence of actions or operations leading to compliance with an effluent limitation, other limitation, prohibition, or standard.

(18) The term "industrial user" means those industries identified in the Standard Industrial Classification Manual, Bureau of the Budget, 1967, as amended and supplemented, under the category of "Division D — Manufacturing" and such other classes of significant waste producers as, by regulation, the Administrator deems appropriate.

(19) The term "pollution" means the manmade or man-induced alteration of the chemical, physical, biological, and radiological integrity of water.

(20) The term "medical waste" means isolation wastes; infectious agents; human blood and blood products; pathological wastes; sharps; body parts; contaminated bedding; surgical wastes and potentially contaminated laboratory wastes; dialysis wastes; and such additional medical items as the Administrator shall prescribe by regulation.

(21) Coastal recreation waters

(A) In general — The term "coastal recreation waters" means —

(i) the Great Lakes; and

(ii) marine coastal waters (including coastal estuaries) that are designated under section 1313(c) by a State for use for swimming, bathing, surfing, or similar water contact activities.

(B) Exclusions — The term "coastal recreation waters" does not include —

(i) inland waters; or

(ii) waters upstream of the mouth of

a river or stream having an unimpaired natural connection with the open sea.

(22) Floatable material

(A) In general — The term "floatable material" means any foreign matter that may float or remain suspended in the water column.

(B) Inclusions — The term "floatable material" includes —

(i) plastic;

(ii) aluminum cans;

(iii) wood products;

(iv) bottles; and

(v) paper products.

(23) Pathogen indicator — The term "pathogen indicator" means a substance that indicates the potential for human infectious disease.

(24) Oil and gas exploration and production. The term "oil and gas exploration, production, processing, or treatment operations or transmission facilities" means all field activities or operations associated with exploration, production, processing, or treatment operations, or transmission facilities, including activities necessary to prepare a site for drilling and for the movement and placement of drilling equipment, whether or not such field activities or operations may be considered to be construction activities.

(25) Recreational vessel

(A) In general

The term "recreational vessel" means any vessel that is —

(i) manufactured or used primarily for pleasure; or

(ii) leased, rented, or chartered to a person for the pleasure of that person.

(B) Exclusion

The term "recreational vessel" does not include a vessel that is subject to Coast Guard inspection and that —

(i) is engaged in commercial use; or

(ii) carries paying passengers.

(26) Treatment works — The term "treatment works" has the meaning given the term in section 1292 of this title.

(27) Green infrastructure — The term "green infrastructure" means the range of measures that use plant or soil systems, permeable pavement or other permeable surfaces or substrates, stormwater harvest and reuse, or landscaping to store, infiltrate, or evapotranspirate stormwater and reduce flows to sewer systems or to surface waters.

§1363. Water Pollution Control Advisory Board
[CWA §503]
(a) Establishment; composition; terms of office

(1) There is hereby established in the Environmental Protection Agency a Water Pollution Control Advisory Board, composed of the Administrator or his designee, who shall be Chairman, and nine members appointed by the President, none of whom shall be Federal officers or employees. The appointed members, having due regard for the purposes of this chapter, shall be selected from among representatives of various State, interstate, and local governmental agencies, of public or private interests contributing to, affected by, or concerned with pollution, and of other public and private agencies, organizations, or groups demonstrating an active interest in the field of pollution prevention and control, as well as other individuals who are expert in this field.

(2)(A) Each member appointed by the President shall hold office for a term of three years, except that (i) any member appointed to fill a vacancy occurring prior to the expiration of the term for which his predecessor was appointed shall be appointed for the remainder of such term, and (ii) the terms of office of the members first taking office after June 30, 1956, shall expire as follows: three at the end of one year after such date, three at the end of two years after such date, and three at the end of three years after such date, as designated by the President at the time of appointment, and (iii) the term of any member under the preceding provisions shall be extended until the date on which his successor's appointment is effective. None of the members appointed by the President shall be eligible for reappointment within one year after the end of his preceding term.

(B) The members of the Board who are not officers or employees of the United States, while attending conferences or meetings of the Board or while serving at the request of the Administrator, shall be entitled to receive compensation at a rate to be fixed by the Administrator, but not exceeding $100 per diem, including travel-time, and while away from their homes or regular places of business they may be allowed travel expenses, including per diem in lieu of subsistence, as authorized by law for persons in the Government service employed intermittently.

(b) Functions — The Board shall advise, consult with, and make recommendations to the Administrator on matters of policy relating to the activities and functions of the Administrator under this chapter.

(c) Clerical and technical assistance — Such clerical and technical assistance as may be necessary to discharge the duties of the Board shall be provided from the personnel of the Environmental Protection Agency.

§1364. Emergency powers
[CWA §504]
(a) Emergency powers — Notwithstanding any other provision of this chapter, the Administrator

upon receipt of evidence that a pollution source or combination of sources is presenting an imminent and substantial endangerment to the health of persons or to the welfare of persons where such endangerment is to the livelihood of such persons, such as inability to market shellfish, may bring suit on behalf of the United States in the appropriate district court to immediately restrain any person causing or contributing to the alleged pollution to stop the discharge of pollutants causing or contributing to such pollution or to take such other action as may be necessary.

(b) Repealed. Pub. L. 96-510, Title III, Sec. 304(a), Dec. 11, 1980, 94 Stat. 2809

§1365. Citizen suits
[CWA §505]

(a) Authorization; jurisdiction — Except as provided in subsection (b) of this section and section 1319(g)(6) of this title, any citizen may commence a civil action on his own behalf —

(1) against any person (including (i) the United States, and (ii) any other governmental instrumentality or agency to the extent permitted by the eleventh amendment to the Constitution) who is alleged to be in violation of (A) an effluent standard or limitation under this chapter or (B) an order issued by the Administrator or a State with respect to such a standard or limitation, or

(2) against the Administrator where there is alleged a failure of the Administrator to perform any act or duty under this chapter which is not discretionary with the Administrator.

The district courts shall have jurisdiction, without regard to the amount in controversy or the citizenship of the parties, to enforce such an effluent standard or limitation, or such an order, or to order the Administrator to perform such act or duty, as the case may be, and to apply any appropriate civil penalties under section 1319(d) of this title.

(b) Notice — No action may be commenced —

(1) under subsection (a)(1) of this section —

(A) prior to sixty days after the plaintiff has given notice of the alleged violation (i) to the Administrator, (ii) to the State in which the alleged violation occurs, and (iii) to any alleged violator of the standard, limitation, or order, or

(B) if the Administrator or State has commenced and is diligently prosecuting a civil or criminal action in a court of the United States, or a State to require compliance with the standard, limitation, or order, but in any such action in a court of the United States any citizen may intervene as a matter of right.

(2) under subsection (a)(2) of this section prior to sixty days after the plaintiff has given notice of such action to the Administrator,

except that such action may be brought immediately after such notification in the case of an action under this section respecting a violation of sections 1316 and 1317(a) of this title. Notice under this subsection shall be given in such manner as the Administrator shall prescribe by regulation.

(c) Venue; intervention by Administrator; United States interests protected

(1) Any action respecting a violation by a discharge source of an effluent standard or limitation or an order respecting such standard or limitation may be brought under this section only in the judicial district in which such source is located.

(2) In such action under this section, the Administrator, if not a party, may intervene as a matter of right.

(3) Protection of interests of United States — Whenever any action is brought under this section in a court of the United States, the plaintiff shall serve a copy of the complaint on the Attorney General and the Administrator. No consent judgment shall be entered in an action in which the United States is not a party prior to 45 days following the receipt of a copy of the proposed consent judgment by the Attorney General and the Administrator.

(d) Litigation costs — The court, in issuing any final order in any action brought pursuant to this section, may award costs of litigation (including reasonable attorney and expert witness fees) to any prevailing or substantially prevailing party, whenever the court determines such award is appropriate. The court may, if a temporary restraining order or preliminary injunction is sought, require the filing of a bond or equivalent security in accordance with the Federal Rules of Civil Procedure.

(e) Statutory or common law rights not restricted — Nothing in this section shall restrict any right which any person (or class of persons) may have under any statute or common law to seek enforcement of any effluent standard or limitation or to seek any other relief (including relief against the Administrator or a State agency).

(f) Effluent standard or limitation — For purposes of this section, the term "effluent standard or limitation under this chapter" means (1) effective July 1, 1973, an unlawful act under subsection (a) of section 1311 of this title; (2) an effluent limitation or other limitation under section 1311 or 1312 of this title; (3) standard of performance under section 1316 of this title; (4) prohibition, effluent standard or pretreatment standards under section 1317 of this title; (5) a standard of performance or requirement under section 1322(p) of this title; (6) a certification under section 1341 of this title; (7) a permit or condition of a permit issued under section 1342 of this title that is in effect under this chapter (including a requirement applicable by reason of section 1323 of this title); or (8) a regulation under section 1345(d) of this title.

(g) "Citizen" defined — For the purposes of this section the term "citizen" means a person or persons having an interest which is or may be adversely affected.

(h) Civil action by State Governors — A Governor of a State may commence a civil action under subsection (a) of this section, without regard to the limitations of subsection (b) of this section, against the Administrator where there is alleged a failure of the Administrator to enforce an effluent standard or limitation under this chapter the violation of which is occurring in another State and is causing an adverse effect on the public health or welfare in his State, or is causing a violation of any water quality requirement in his State.

§1366. Appearance
[CWA §506]

The Administrator shall request the Attorney General to appear and represent the United States in any civil or criminal action instituted under this chapter to which the Administrator is a party. Unless the Attorney General notifies the Administrator within a reasonable time, that he will appear in a civil action, attorneys who are officers or employees of the Environ-mental Protection Agency shall appear and represent the United States in such action.

§1367. Employee protection
[CWA §507]

(a) Discrimination against persons filing, instituting, or testifying in proceedings under this chapter prohibited — No person shall fire, or in any other way discriminate against, or cause to be fired or discriminated against, any employee or any authorized representative of employees by reason of the fact that such employee or representative has filed, instituted, or caused to be filed or instituted any proceeding under this chapter, or has testified or is about to testify in any proceeding resulting from the administration or enforcement of the provisions of this chapter.

(b) Application for review; investigation; hearing; review — Any employee or a representative of employees who believes that he has been fired or otherwise discriminated against by any person in violation of subsection (a) of this section may, within thirty days after such alleged violation occurs, apply to the Secretary of Labor for a review of such firing or alleged discrimination. A copy of the application shall be sent to such person who shall be the respondent. Upon receipt of such application, the Secretary of Labor shall cause such investigation to be made as he deems appropriate. Such investigation shall provide an opportunity for a public hearing at the request of any party to such review to enable the parties to present information relating to such alleged violation. The parties shall be given written notice of the time and place of the hearing at least five days prior to the hearing. Any such hearing shall be of record and shall be subject to section 554 of title 5. Upon receiving the report of such investigation, the Secretary of Labor shall make findings of fact. If he finds that such violation did occur, he shall issue a decision, incorporating an order therein and his findings, requiring the party committing such violation to take such affirmative action to abate the violation as the Secretary of Labor deems appropriate, including, but not limited to, the rehiring or reinstatement of the employee or representative of employees to his former position with compensation. If he finds that there was no such violation, he shall issue an order denying the application. Such order issued by the Secretary of Labor under this subparagraph shall be subject to judicial review in the same manner as orders and decisions of the Administrator are subject to judicial review under this chapter.

(c) Costs and expenses — Whenever an order is issued under this section to abate such violation, at the request of the applicant, a sum equal to the aggregate amount of all costs and expenses (including the attorney's fees), as determined by the Secretary of Labor, to have been reasonably incurred by the applicant for, or in connection with, the institution and prosecution of such proceedings, shall be assessed against the person committing such violation.

(d) Deliberate violations by employee acting without direction from his employer or his agent — This section shall have no application to any employee who, acting without direction from his employer (or his agent) deliberately violates any prohibition of effluent limitation or other limitation under section 1311 or 1312 of this title, standards of performance under section 1316 of this title, effluent standard, prohibition or pretreatment standard under section 1317 of this title, or any other prohibition or limitation established under this chapter.

(e) Investigations of employment reductions — The Administrator shall conduct continuing evaluations of potential loss or shifts of employment which may result from the issuance of any effluent limitation or order under this chapter, including, where appropriate, investigating threatened plant closures or reductions in employment allegedly resulting from such limitation or order. Any employee who is discharged or laid-off, threatened with discharge or lay-off, or otherwise discriminated against by any person because of the alleged results of any effluent limitation or order issued under this chapter, or any representative of such employee, may request the Administrator to conduct a full investigation of the matter. The Administrator shall thereupon investigate the matter and, at the request of any party, shall hold public hearings on not less than five days notice, and shall at such hearings require the parties, including the employer involved, to present information relating to the actual or potential effect of such limitation or order on employment and on any alleged discharge, lay-off, or other discrimination and the detailed reasons or justification therefor. Any such hearing shall be of record and shall be subject to section 554 of Title 5. Upon receiving the report of such investigation, the Administrator shall make findings of fact as to the effect of such effluent limitation or order on employment and on the alleged discharge, lay-off, or discrimination and shall make such recommendations as he deems appropriate. Such report, findings, and recommendations shall be available to the public. Nothing in this subsection shall be construed to require or authorize the Administrator to modify or withdraw any effluent limitation or order issued under this chapter.

§1368. Federal procurement
[CWA §508]

(a) Contracts with violators prohibited — No Federal agency may enter into any contract with any person, who has been convicted of any offense under section 1319(c) of this title, for the procurement of goods, materials, and services if such contract is to be performed at any facility at which the violation which gave rise to such conviction occurred, and if such facility is owned, leased, or supervised by such person. The prohibition in the preceding sentence shall continue until the Administrator certifies that the condition giving rise to such conviction has been corrected.

(b) Notification of agencies — The Administrator shall establish procedures to provide all Federal agencies with the notification necessary for the purposes of subsection (a) of this section.

(c) Omitted

(d) Exemptions — The President may exempt any contract, loan, or grant from all or part of the provisions of this section where he determines such exemption is necessary in the paramount interest of the United States and he shall notify the Congress of such exemption.

(e) Annual report to Congress —
The President shall annually report to the Congress on measures taken in compliance with the purpose and intent of this section, including, but not limited to, the progress and problems associated with such compliance.

(f) Contractor certification or contract clause in acquisition of commercial items

(1) No certification by a contractor, and no contract clause, may be required in the case of a contract for the acquisition of commercial products or commercial services in order to implement a prohibition or requirement of this section or a prohibition or requirement issued in the implementation of this section.

(2) In paragraph (1), the terms "commercial product" and "commercial service" have the meanings given those terms in sections 103 and 103a, respectively, of Title 41.

§1369. Administrative procedure and judicial review
[CWA §509]

(a) Subpoenas

(1) For purposes of obtaining information under section 1315 of this title, or carrying out section 1367(e) of this title, the Administrator may issue subpoenas for the attendance and testimony of witnesses and the production of relevant papers, books, and documents, and he may administer oaths. Except for effluent data, upon a showing satisfactory to the Administrator that such papers, books, documents, or information or particular part thereof, if made public, would divulge trade secrets or secret processes, the Administrator shall consider such record, report, or information or particular portion thereof confidential in accordance with the purposes of section 1905 of Title 18, except that such paper, book, document, or information may be disclosed to other officers, employees, or authorized representatives of the United States concerned with carrying out this chapter, or when relevant in any proceeding under this chapter. Witnesses summoned shall be paid the same fees and mileage that are paid witnesses in the courts of the United States. In case of contumacy or refusal to obey a subpoena served upon any person under this subsection, the district court of the United States for any district in which such person is found or resides or transacts business, upon application by the United States and after notice to such person, shall have jurisdiction to issue an order requiring such person to appear and give testimony before the Administrator, to appear and produce papers, books, and documents before the Administrator, or both, and any failure to obey such order of the court may be punished by such court as a contempt thereof.

(2) The district courts of the United States are authorized, upon application by the Administrator, to issue subpoenas for attendance and testimony of witnesses and the production of relevant papers, books, and documents, for purposes of obtaining information under sections 1314(b) and (c) of this title. Any papers, books, documents, or other information or part thereof, obtained by reason of such a subpoena shall be subject to the same requirements as are provided in paragraph (1) of this subsection.

(b) Review of Administrator's actions; selection of court; fees

(1) Review of the Administrator's action (A) in promulgating any standard of performance under section 1316 of this title, (B) in making any determination pursuant to section 1316(b)(1)(C) of this title, (C) in promulgating any effluent standard, prohibition, or pretreatment standard under section 1317 of this title, (D) in making any determination as to a State permit program

submitted under section 1342(b) of this title, (E) in approving or promulgating any effluent limitation or other limitation under section 1311, 1312, 1316, or 1345 of this title, (F) in issuing or denying any permit under section 1342 of this title, and (G) in promulgating any individual control strategy under section 1314(*l*) of this title, may be had by any interested person in the Circuit Court of Appeals of the United States for the Federal judicial district in which such person resides or transacts business which is directly affected by such action upon application by such person. Any such application shall be made within 120 days from the date of such determination, approval, promulgation, issuance or denial, or after such date only if such application is based solely on grounds which arose after such 120th day.

(2) Action of the Administrator with respect to which review could have been obtained under paragraph (1) of this subsection shall not be subject to judicial review in any civil or criminal proceeding for enforcement.

(3) Award of fees — In any judicial proceeding under this subsection, the court may award costs of litigation (including reasonable attorney and expert witness fees) to any prevailing or substantially prevailing party whenever it determines that such award is appropriate.

(4) Discharges incidental to normal operation of vessels

(A) In general

Except as provided in subparagraph (B), any interested person may file a petition for review of a final agency action under section 1322(p) of this title of the Administrator or the Secretary of the department in which the Coast Guard is operating in accordance with the requirements of this subsection.

(B) Venue exception

Subject to section 1322(p)(7)(C)(v) of this title, a petition for review of a final agency action under section 1322(p) of this title of the Administrator or the Secretary of the department in which the Coast Guard is operating may be filed only in the United States Court of Appeals for the District of Columbia Circuit.

(c) **Additional evidence** — In any judicial proceeding brought under subsection (b) of this section in which review is sought of a determination under this chapter required to be made on the record after notice and opportunity for hearing, if any party applies to the court for leave to adduce additional evidence, and shows to the satisfaction of the court that such additional evidence is material and that there were reasonable grounds for the failure to adduce such evidence in the proceeding before the Administrator, the court may order such additional evidence (and

evidence in rebuttal thereof) to be taken before the Administrator, in such manner and upon such terms and conditions as the court may deem proper. The Administrator may modify his findings as to the facts, or make new findings, by reason of the additional evidence so taken and he shall file such modified or new findings, and his recommendation, if any, for the modification or setting aside of his original determination, with the return of such additional evidence.

§1370. State authority
[CWA §510]

Except as expressly provided in this chapter, nothing in this chapter shall (1) preclude or deny the right of any State or political subdivision thereof or interstate agency to adopt or enforce (A) any standard or limitation respecting discharges of pollutants, or (B) any requirement respecting control or abatement of pollution; except that if an effluent limitation, or other limitation, effluent standard, prohibition, pretreatment standard, or standard of performance is in effect under this chapter, such State or political subdivision or interstate agency may not adopt or enforce any effluent limitation, or other limitation, effluent standard, prohibition, pretreatment standard, or standard of performance which is less stringent than the effluent limitation, or other limitation, effluent standard, prohibition, pretreatment standard, or standard of performance under this chapter; or (2) be construed as impairing or in any manner affecting any right or jurisdiction of the States with respect to the waters (including boundary waters) of such States.

§1371. Authority under other laws and regulations
[CWA §511]

(a) **Impairment of authority or functions of officials and agencies; treaty provisions** — This chapter shall not be construed as (1) limiting the authority or functions of any officer or agency of the United States under any other law or regulation not inconsistent with this chapter; (2) affecting or impairing the authority of the Secretary of the Army (A) to maintain navigation or (B) under the Act of March 3, 1899; (30 Stat. 1112); except that any permit issued under section 1344 of this title shall be conclusive as to the effect on water quality of any discharge resulting from any activity subject to section 403 of this title; or (3) affecting or impairing the provisions of any treaty of the United States.

(b) **Discharges of pollutants into navigable waters** — Discharges of pollutants into the navigable waters subject to the Rivers and Harbors Act of 1910 (36 Stat. 593; 33 U.S.C. §421) and the Supervisory Harbors Act of 1888 (25 Stat. 209; 33 U.S.C. §§441-451b) shall be regulated pursuant to this chapter, and not subject to such Act of 1910 and the Act of 1888 except as to effect on navigation and anchorage.

(c) Action of the Administrator deemed major Federal action; construction of the National Environmental Policy Act of 1969

(1) Except for the provision of Federal financial assistance for the purpose of assisting the construction of publicly owned treatment works as authorized by section 1281 of this title, and the issuance of a permit under section 1342 of this title for the discharge of any pollutant by a new source as defined in section 1316 of this title, no action of the Administrator taken pursuant to this chapter shall be deemed a major Federal action significantly affecting the quality of the human environment within the meaning of the National Environmental Policy Act of 1969 (83 Stat. 852) (42 U.S.C. 4321 *et seq.*); and

(2) Nothing in the National Environmental Policy Act of 1969 (83 Stat. 852) shall be deemed to —

(A) authorize any Federal agency authorized to license or permit the conduct of any activity which may result in the discharge of a pollutant into the navigable waters to review any effluent limitation or other requirement established pursuant to this chapter or the adequacy of any certification under section 1341 of this title; or

(B) authorize any such agency to impose, as a condition precedent to the issuance of any license or permit, any effluent limitation other than any such limitation established pursuant to this chapter.

(d) Consideration of international water pollution control agreements — Notwithstanding this chapter or any other provision of law, the Administrator (1) shall not require any State to consider in the development of the ranking in order of priority of needs for the construction of treatment works (as defined in subchapter II of this chapter), any water pollution control agreement which may have been entered into between the United States and any other nation, and (2) shall not consider any such agreement in the approval of any such priority ranking.

§1372. Labor standards
[CWA §513]

The Administrator shall take such action as may be necessary to insure that all laborers and mechanics employed by contractors or subcontractors on treatment works for which grants are made under this chapter shall be paid wages at rates not less than those prevailing for the same type of work on similar construction in the immediate locality, as determined by the Secretary of Labor, in accordance with sections 3141-3144, 3146, and 3147 of Title 40. The Secretary of Labor shall have, with respect to the labor standards specified in this subsection, the authority and functions set forth in Reorganization Plan Numbered 14 of 1950 (15 F.R. 3176) and section 3145 of Title 40.

§1373. Public health agency coordination
[CWA §514]

The permitting agency under section 1342 of this title shall assist the applicant for a permit under such section in coordinating the requirements of this chapter with those of the appropriate public health agencies.

§1374. Effluent Standards and Water Quality Information Advisory Committee
[CWA §515]
(a) Establishment; membership; term

(1) There is established an Effluent Standards and Water Quality Information Advisory Committee, which shall be composed of a Chairman and eight members who shall be appointed by the Administrator within sixty days after October 18, 1972.

(2) All members of the Committee shall be selected from the scientific community, qualified by education, training, and experience to provide, assess, and evaluate scientific and technical information on effluent standards and limitations.

(3) Members of the Committee shall serve for a term of four years, and may be reappointed.

(b) Action on proposed regulations

(1) No later than one hundred and eighty days prior to the date on which the Administrator is required to publish any proposed regulations required by section 1314(b) of this title, any proposed standard of performance for new sources required by section 1316 of this title, or any proposed toxic effluent standard required by section 1317 of this title, he shall transmit to the Committee a notice of intent to propose such regulations. The Chairman of the Committee within ten days after receipt of such notice may publish a notice of a public hearing by the Committee, to be held within thirty days.

(2) No later than one hundred and twenty days after receipt of such notice, the Committee shall transmit to the Administrator such scientific and technical information as is in its possession, including that presented at any public hearing, related to the subject matter contained in such notice.

(3) Information so transmitted to the Administrator shall constitute a part of the administrative record and comments on any proposed regulations or standards as information to be considered with other comments and information in making any final determinations.

(4) In preparing information for transmittal, the Committee shall avail itself of the technical and scientific services of any Federal agency, including the United States Geological Survey and any national environmental laboratories which may be established.

(c) Secretary; legal counsel; compensation

(1) The Committee shall appoint and prescribe the duties of a Secretary, and such legal counsel as it

deems necessary. The Committee shall appoint such other employees as it deems necessary to exercise and fulfill its powers and responsibilities. The compensation of all employees appointed by the Committee shall be fixed in accordance with chapter 51 and subchapter III of chapter 53 of Title 5.

(2) Members of the Committee shall be entitled to receive compensation at a rate to be fixed by the President but not in excess of the maximum rate of pay for grade GS-18, as provided in the General Schedule under section 5332 of Title 5.

(d) Quorum; special panel — Five members of the Committee shall constitute a quorum, and official actions of the Committee shall be taken only on the affirmative vote of at least five members. A special panel composed of one or more members upon order of the Committee shall conduct any hearing authorized by this section and submit the transcript of such hearing to the entire Committee for its action thereon.

(e) Rules — The Committee is authorized to make such rules as are necessary for the orderly transaction of its business.

§1375. Reports to Congress; detailed estimates and comprehensive study on costs; state estimates

[CWA §516]

(a) Implementation of chapter objectives; status and progress of programs

Within ninety days following the convening of each session of Congress, the Administrator shall submit to the Congress a report, in addition to any other report required by this chapter, on measures taken toward implementing the objective of this chapter, including, but not limited to, (1) the progress and problems associated with developing comprehensive plans under section 1252 of this title, areawide plans under section 1288 of this title, basin plans under section 1289 of this title, and plans under section 1313(e) of this title; (2) a summary of actions taken and results achieved in the field of water pollution control research, experiments, studies, and related matters by the Administrator and other Federal agencies and by other persons and agencies under Federal grants or contracts; (3) the progress and problems associated with the development of effluent limitations and recommended control techniques; (4) the status of State programs, including a detailed summary of the progress obtained as compared to that planned under State program plans for development and enforcement of water quality requirements; (5) the identification and status of enforcement actions pending or completed under this chapter during the preceding year; (6) the status of State, interstate, and local pollution control programs established pursuant to, and assisted by, this chapter; (7) a summary of the results of the survey required to be taken under section 1290 of this title; (8) his activities including recommendations under sections 1259 through 1261

of this title; and (9) all reports and recommendations made by the Water Pollution Control Advisory Board.

(b)(1) The Administrator, in cooperation with the States, including water pollution control agencies and other water pollution control planning agencies, shall make (A) a detailed estimate of the cost of carrying out the provisions of this chapter; (B) a detailed estimate, biennially revised, of the cost of construction of all needed publicly owned treatment works in all of the States and of the cost of construction of all needed publicly owned treatment works in each of the States; (C) a comprehensive study of the economic impact on affected units of government of the cost of installation of treatment facilities; and (D) a comprehensive analysis of the national requirements for and the cost of treating municipal, industrial, and other effluent to attain the water quality objectives as established by this chapter or applicable State law. The Administrator shall submit such detailed estimate and such comprehensive study of such cost to the Congress no later than February 10 of each odd-numbered year. Whenever the Administrator, pursuant to this subsection, requests and receives an estimate of cost from a State, he shall furnish copies of such estimate together with such detailed estimate to Congress.

(2) Notwithstanding the second sentence of paragraph (1) of this subsection, the Administrator shall make a preliminary detailed estimate called for by subparagraph (B) of such paragraph and shall submit such preliminary detailed estimate to the Congress no later than September 3, 1974. The Administrator shall require each State to prepare an estimate of cost for such State, and shall utilize the survey form EPA-1, O.M.B. No. 158-R0017, prepared for the 1973 detailed estimate, except that such estimate shall include all costs of compliance with section 1281(g)(2)(A) of this title and water quality standards established pursuant to section 1313 of this title, and all costs of treatment works as defined in section 1292(2) of this title, including all eligible costs of constructing sewage collection systems and correcting excessive infiltration or inflow and all eligible costs of correcting combined storm and sanitary sewer problems and treating storm water flows. The survey form shall be distributed by the Administrator to each State no later than January 31, 1974.

(c) Status of combined sewer overflows in municipal treatment works operations

The Administrator shall submit to the Congress by October 1, 1978, a report on the status of combined sewer overflows in municipal treatment works operations. The report shall include (1) the status of any projects funded under this chapter to address combined sewer overflows, (2) a listing by State of combined sewer overflow needs identified in the 1977 State priority listings, (3) an estimate for each applicable municipality of the number of years necessary, assuming an annual authorization and appropriation for the construction grants program of $5,000,000,000, to correct combined sewer overflow problems, (4) an analysis using representative municipalities faced with major combined sewer overflow needs, of the annual discharges of pollutants from overflows in comparison to treated effluent discharges, (5) an analysis of the technological alternatives available to municipalities to correct major combined sewer overflow problems, and (6) any recommendations of the Administrator for legislation to address the problem of combined sewer overflows, including whether a separate authorization and grant program should be established by the Congress to address combined sewer overflows.

(d) Legislative recommendations on program requiring coordination between water supply and wastewater control plans as condition for construction grants; public hearing

The Administrator, in cooperation with the States, including water pollution control agencies, and other water pollution control planning agencies, and water supply and water resources agencies of the States and the United States shall submit to Congress, within two years of December 27, 1977, a report with recommendations for legislation on a program to require coordination between water supply and wastewater control plans as a condition to grants for construction of treatment works under this chapter. No such report shall be submitted except after opportunity for public hearings on such proposed report.

(e) State revolving fund report

(1) In general

Not later than February 10, 1990, the Administrator shall submit to Congress a report on the financial status and operations of water pollution control revolving funds established by the States under subchapter VI of this chapter. The Administrator shall prepare such report in cooperation with the States, including water pollution control agencies and other water pollution control planning and financing agencies.

(2) Content

The report under this subsection shall also include the following:

(A) an inventory of the facilities that are in significant noncompliance with the enforceable requirements of this chapter;

(B) an estimate of the cost of construction necessary to bring such facilities into compliance with such requirements;

(C) an assessment of the availability of sources of funds for financing such needed construction, including an estimate of the amount of funds available for providing assistance for such construction through September 30, 1999, from the water pollution control revolving funds established by the States under subchapter VI of this chapter;

(D) an assessment of the operations, loan portfolio, and loan conditions of such revolving funds;

(E) an assessment of the effect on user charges of the assistance provided by such revolving funds compared to the assistance provided with funds appropriated pursuant to section 1287 of this title; and

(F) an assessment of the efficiency of the operation and maintenance of treatment works constructed with assistance provided by such revolving funds compared to the efficiency of the operation and maintenance of treatment works constructed with assistance provided under section 1281 of this title.

§1375a. Report on coastal recreation waters

(a) In general — Not later than 4 years after October 10, 2000, and every 4 years thereafter, the Administrator of the Environmental Protection Agency shall submit to Congress a report that includes —

(1) recommendations concerning the need for additional water quality criteria for pathogens and pathogen indicators and other actions that should be taken to improve the quality of coastal recreation waters;

(2) an evaluation of Federal, State, and local efforts to implement this Act, including the amendments made by this Act; and

(3) recommendations on improvements to methodologies and techniques for monitoring of coastal recreation waters.

(b) Coordination — The Administrator of the Environmental Protection Agency may coordinate the report under this section with other reporting requirements under the Federal Water Pollution Control Act (33 U.S.C. §§1251 et seq.).

§1376. Authorization of appropriations
[CWA §517]

There are authorized to be appropriated to carry out this chapter, other than sections 1254, 1255, 1256(a), 1257, 1258, 1262, 1263, 1264, 1265, 1286, 1287, 1288(f) and (h), 1289, 1314, 1321(c), (d), (i), (*l*) and (k), 1324, 1325 and 1327 of this title, $250,000,000 for the fiscal year ending June 30, 1973, $300,000,000 for the fiscal year ending June 30, 1974, $350,000,000 for the fiscal year ending June 30, 1975, $100,000,000 for the fiscal year ending September 30, 1977, $150,000,000 for the fiscal year ending September 30, 1978, $150,000,000 for the fiscal year ending September 30, 1979, $150,000,000 for the fiscal year ending September 30, 1980, $150,000,000 for the fiscal year ending September 30, 1981, $161,000,000 for the fiscal year ending September 30, 1982, such sums as may be necessary for fiscal years 1983 through 1985, and $135,000,000 per fiscal year for each of the fiscal years 1986 through 1990.

§1377. Indian tribes
[CWA §518]

(a) Policy — Nothing in this section shall be construed to affect the application of section 1251(g) of this title, and all of the provisions of this section shall be carried out in accordance with the provisions of such section 1251(g) of this title. Indian tribes shall be treated as States for purposes of such section 1251(g) of this title.

(b) Assessment of sewage treatment needs; report — The Administrator, in cooperation with the Director of the Indian Health Service, shall assess the need for sewage treatment works to serve Indian tribes, the degree to which such needs will be met through funds allotted to States under section 1285 of this title and priority lists under section 1296 of this title, and any obstacles which prevent such needs from being met. Not later than one year after February 4, 1987, the Administrator shall submit a report to Congress on the assessment under this subsection, along with recommendations specifying (1) how the Administrator intends to provide assistance to Indian tribes to develop waste treatment management plans and to construct treatment works under this chapter, and (2) methods by which the participation in and administration of programs under this chapter by Indian tribes can be maximized.

(c) Reservation of funds

(1) Fiscal years 1987-2014

The Administrator shall reserve each of fiscal years 1987 through 2014, before allotments to the States under section 1285(e) of this title, one-half of one percent of the sums appropriated under section 1287 of this title.

(2) Fiscal year 2015 and thereafter

For fiscal year 2015 and each fiscal year thereafter, the Administrator shall reserve, before allotments to the States under section 1384(a) of this title, not less than 0.5 percent and not more than 2.0 percent of the funds made available to carry out subchapter VI.

(3) Use of funds

Funds reserved under this subsection shall be available only for grants for projects and activities eligible for assistance under section 1383(c) of this title to serve —

(A) Indian tribes (as defined in subsection (h));

(B) former Indian reservations in Oklahoma (as determined by the Secretary of the Interior); and

(C) Native villages (as defined in section 1602 of Title 43).

(d) Cooperative agreements — In order to ensure the consistent implementation of the requirements of this chapter, an Indian tribe and the State or States in which the lands of such tribe are located may enter into a cooperative agreement, subject to the review and approval of the Administrator, to jointly plan and administer the requirements of this chapter.

(e) Treatment as States — The Administrator is authorized to treat an Indian tribe as a State for purposes of subchapter II of this chapter and sections 1254, 1256, 1313, 1315, 1318, 1319, 1324, 1329, 1341, 1342, 1344, and 1346 of this title to the degree necessary to carry out the objectives of this section, but only if —

(1) the Indian tribe has a governing body carrying out substantial governmental duties and powers;

(2) the functions to be exercised by the Indian tribe pertain to the management and protection of water resources which are held by an Indian tribe, held by the United States in trust for Indians, held by a member of an Indian tribe if such property interest is subject to a trust restriction on alienation, or otherwise within the borders of an Indian reservation; and

(3) the Indian tribe is reasonably expected to be capable, in the Administrator's judgment, of carrying out the functions to be exercised in a manner consistent with the terms and purposes of this chapter and of all applicable regulations.

Such treatment as a State may include the direct provision of funds reserved under subsection (c) of this section to the governing bodies of Indian tribes, and the determination of priorities by Indian tribes, where not determined by the Administrator in cooperation with the Director of the Indian Health Service. The Administrator, in cooperation with the Director of the Indian Health Service, is authorized to make grants under subchapter II of this chapter in an amount not to exceed 100 percent of the cost of a project. Not later than 18 months after February 4, 1987, the Administrator shall, in consultation with Indian tribes, promulgate final regulations which specify how Indian tribes shall be treated as States for purposes of this chapter. The Administrator shall, in promulgating such regulations, consult affected States sharing common water bodies and provide a mechanism for the resolution of any unreasonable consequences that may arise as a result of differing water quality standards that may be set by States and Indian tribes located on common bodies of water. Such mechanism shall provide for explicit consideration of relevant factors including, but not limited to, the effects of differing water quality permit requirements on upstream and downstream dischargers, economic impacts, and present and historical uses and quality of the waters subject to such standards. Such mechanism should provide for the avoidance of such unreasonable consequences in a manner consistent with the objective of this chapter.

(f) Grants for nonpoint source programs — The Administrator shall make grants to an Indian tribe under section 1329 of this title as though such tribe was a State. Not more than one-third of one percent of the amount appropriated for any fiscal year under section 1329 of this title may be used to make grants under this subsection. In addition to the requirements of section 1329 of this title, an Indian tribe shall be required to meet the requirements of paragraphs (1), (2), and (3) of subsection (d) of this section in order to receive such a grant.

(g) Alaska Native organizations — No provision of this chapter shall be construed to —

(1) grant, enlarge, or diminish, or in any way affect the scope of the governmental authority, if any, of any Alaska Native organization, including any federally-recognized tribe, traditional Alaska Native council, or Native council organized pursuant to the Act of June 18, 1934 (48 Stat. 987), over lands or persons in Alaska;

(2) create or validate any assertion by such organization or any form of governmental authority over lands or persons in Alaska; or

(3) in any way affect any assertion that Indian country, as defined in section 1151 of title 18, exists or does not exist in Alaska.

(h) Definitions — For purposes of this section, the term —

(1) "Federal Indian reservation" means all land within the limits of any Indian reservation under the jurisdiction of the United States Government, notwithstanding the issuance of any patent, and including rights-of-way running through the reservation; and

(2) "Indian tribe" means any Indian tribe, band, group, or community recognized by the Secretary of the Interior and exercising governmental authority over a Federal Indian reservation.

§ 1377a. Green infrastructure promotion

(a) In general — The Administrator shall promote the use of green infrastructure in, and coordinate the integration of green infrastructure into, permitting and enforcement under this chapter, planning efforts, research, technical assistance, and funding guidance of the Environmental Protection Agency.

(b) Coordination of efforts — The Administrator shall ensure that the Office of Water coordinates efforts to increase the use of green infrastructure with —

(1) other Federal departments and agencies;

(2) State, tribal, and local governments; and

(3) the private sector.

(c) Regional green infrastructure promotion — The Administrator shall direct each regional office of the Environmental Protection Agency, as appropriate based on local factors, and consistent with the requirements of this chapter, to promote and integrate the use of green infrastructure within the region, including through —

(1) outreach and training regarding green infrastructure implementation for State, tribal,

and local governments, tribal communities, and the private sector; and

(2) the incorporation of green infrastructure into permitting and other regulatory programs, codes, and ordinance development, including the requirements under consent decrees and settlement agreements in enforcement actions.

(d) Green infrastructure information-sharing — The Administrator shall promote green infrastructure information-sharing, including through an internet website, to share information with, and provide technical assistance to, State, tribal, and local governments, tribal communities, the private sector, and the public, regarding green infrastructure approaches for —

(1) reducing water pollution;

(2) protecting water resources;

(3) complying with regulatory requirements; and

(4) achieving other environmental, public health, and community goals.

SUBCHAPTER VI — STATE WATER POLLUTION CONTROL REVOLVING FUNDS

§1381. Grants to States for establishment of revolving funds
[CWA §601]

(a) General authority — Subject to the provisions of this subchapter, the Administrator shall make capitalization grants to each State for the purpose of establishing a water pollution control revolving fund to accomplish the objectives, goals and policies of this chapter by providing assistance for projects and activities identified in section 1383(c) of this title.

(b) Schedule of grant payments — The Administrator and each State shall jointly establish a schedule of payments under which the Administrator will pay to the State the amount of each grant to be made to the State under this subchapter. Such schedule shall be based on the State's intended use plan under section 1386(c) of this title, except that —

(1) such payments shall be made in quarterly installments, and

(2) such payments shall be made as expeditiously as possible, but in no event later than the earlier of —

(A) 8 quarters after the date such funds were obligated by the State, or

(B) 12 quarters after the date such funds were allotted to the State.

§1382. Capitalization grant agreements
[CWA §602]

(a) General rule — To receive a capitalization grant with funds made available under this subchapter and section 1285(m) of this title, a State shall enter into an agreement with the Administrator which shall include but not be limited to the specifications set forth in subsection (b) of this section.

(b) Specific requirements — The Administrator shall enter into an agreement under this section with a State only after the State has established to the satisfaction of the Administrator that —

(1) the State will accept grant payments with funds to be made available under this subchapter and section 1285(m) of this title in accordance with a payment schedule established jointly by the Administrator under section 1381(b) of this title and will deposit all such payments in the water pollution control revolving fund established by the State in accordance with this subchapter;

(2) the State will deposit in the fund from State moneys an amount equal to at least 20 percent of the total amount of all capitalization grants which will be made to the State with funds to be made available under this subchapter and section 1285(m) of this title on or before the date on which each quarterly grant payment will be made to the State under this subchapter;

(3) the State will enter into binding commitments to provide assistance in accordance with the requirements of this subchapter in an amount equal to 120 percent of the amount of each such grant payment within 1 year after the receipt of such grant payment;

(4) all funds in the fund will be expended in an expeditious and timely manner;

(5) all funds in the fund as a result of capitalization grants under this subchapter and section 1285(m) of this title will first be used to assure maintenance of progress, as determined by the Governor of the State, toward compliance with enforceable deadlines, goals, and requirements of this chapter, including the municipal compliance deadline;

(6) treatment works eligible under this chapter which will be constructed in whole or in part with assistance made available by a State water pollution control revolving fund authorized under this subchapter, or section 1285(m) of this title, or both, will meet the requirements of, or otherwise be treated (as determined by the Governor of the State) under sections 1371(c)(1) and 1372 of this title in the same manner as treatment works constructed with assistance under subchapter II of this chapter;

(7) in addition to complying with the requirements of this subchapter, the State will commit or expend each quarterly grant payment which it will receive under this subchapter in accordance with laws and procedures applicable to the commitment or expenditure of revenues of the State;

(8) in carrying out the requirements of section 1386 of this title, the State will use account-ing, audit, and fiscal procedures conforming to generally accepted government accounting standards;

(9) the State will require as a condition of making a loan or providing other assistance, as described in section 1383(d) of this title, from the fund that the recipient of such assistance will maintain project accounts in accordance with generally accepted government accounting standards, including standards relating to the reporting of infrastructure assets; and

(10) the State will make annual reports to the Administrator on the actual use of funds in accordance with section 1386(d) of this title.

(11) the State will establish, maintain, invest, and credit the fund with repayments, such that the fund balance will be available in perpetuity for activities under this chapter;

(12) any fees charged by the State to recipients of assistance that are considered program income will be used for the purpose of financing the cost of administering the fund or financing projects or activities eligible for assistance from the fund;

(13) beginning in fiscal year 2016, the State will require as a condition of providing assistance to a municipality or intermunicipal, interstate, or State agency that the recipient of such assistance certify, in a manner determined by the Governor of the State, that the recipient —

(A) has studied and evaluated the cost and effectiveness of the processes, materials, techniques, and technologies for carrying out the proposed project or activity for which assistance is sought under this subchapter; and

(B) has selected, to the maximum extent practicable, a project or activity that maximizes the potential for efficient water use, reuse, recapture, and conservation, and energy conservation, taking into account —

(i) the cost of constructing the project or activity;

(ii) the cost of operating and maintaining the project or activity over the life of the project or activity; and

(iii) the cost of replacing the project or activity; and

(14) a contract to be carried out using funds directly made available by a capitalization grant under this subchapter for program management, construction management, feasibility studies, preliminary engineering, design, engineering, surveying, mapping, or architectural related services shall be negotiated in the same manner as a contract for architectural and engineering services is negotiated under chapter 11 of Title 40 or an equivalent State qualifications-based requirement (as determined by the Governor of the State).

§1383. Water pollution control revolving loan funds

[CWA §603]

(a) Requirements for obligation of grant funds — Before a State may receive a capitalization grant with funds made available under this subchapter and section 1285(m) of this title, the State shall first establish a water pollution control revolving fund which complies with the requirements of this section.

(b) Administration

Each State water pollution control revolving fund shall be administered by an instrumentality of the State with such powers and limitations as may be required to operate such fund in accordance with the requirements and objectives of this chapter.

(c) Projects and activities eligible for assistance

The amounts of funds available to each State water pollution control revolving fund shall be used only for providing financial assistance —

(1) to any municipality or intermunicipal, interstate, or State agency for construction of publicly owned treatment works (as defined in section 1292 of this title);

(2) for the implementation of a management program established under section 1329 of this title;

(3) for development and implementation of a conservation and management plan under section 1330 of this title;

(4) for the construction, repair, or replacement of decentralized wastewater treatment systems that treat municipal wastewater or domestic sewage;

(5) for measures to manage, reduce, treat, or recapture stormwater or subsurface drainage water;

(6) to any municipality or intermunicipal, interstate, or State agency for measures to reduce the demand for publicly owned treatment works capacity through water conservation, efficiency, or reuse;

(7) for the development and implementation of watershed projects meeting the criteria set forth in section 1274 of this title;

(8) to any municipality or intermunicipal, interstate, or State agency for measures to reduce the energy consumption needs for publicly owned treatment works;

(9) for reusing or recycling wastewater, stormwater, or subsurface drainage water;

(10) for measures to increase the security of publicly owned treatment works;

(11) to any qualified nonprofit entity, as determined by the Administrator, to provide assistance to owners and operators of small and medium publicly owned treatment works —

(A) to plan, develop, and obtain financing for eligible projects under this subsection, including planning, design, and associated preconstruction activities; and

(B) to assist such treatment works in achieving compliance with this chapter; and

(12) to any qualified nonprofit entity, as determined by the Administrator, to provide assistance to an eligible individual (as defined in subsection (j)) —

(A) for the repair or replacement of existing individual household decentralized wastewater treatment systems; or

(B) in a case in which an eligible individual resides in a household that could be cost-effectively connected to an available publicly owned treatment works, for the connection of the applicable household to such treatment works.

(d) Types of assistance — Except as otherwise limited by State law, a water pollution control revolving fund of a State under this section may be used only —

(1) to make loans, on the condition that —

(A) such loans are made at or below market interest rates, including interest free loans, at terms not to exceed the lesser of 30 years and the projected useful life (as determined by the State) of the project to be financed with the proceeds of the loan;

(B) annual principal and interest payments will commence not later than 1 year after completion of any project and all loans will be fully amortized upon the expiration of the term of the loan;

(C) the recipient of a loan will establish a dedicated source of revenue for repayment of loans;

(D) the fund will be credited with all payments of principal and interest on all loans; and

(E) for a treatment works proposed for repair, replacement, or expansion, and eligible for assistance under subsection (c)(1), the recipient of the loan shall —

(i) develop and implement a fiscal sustainability plan that includes —

(I) an inventory of critical assets that are a part of the treatment works;

(II) an evaluation of the condition and performance of inventoried assets or asset groupings;

(III) a certification that the recipient has evaluated and will be implementing water and energy conservation efforts as part of the plan; and

(IV) a plan for maintaining, repairing, and, as necessary, replacing the treatment works and a plan for funding such activities; or

(ii) certify that the recipient has developed and implemented a plan that meets the requirements under clause (i);

(2) to buy or refinance the debt obligation of municipalities and intermunicipal and interstate agencies within the State at or below market rates, where such debt obligations were incurred after March 7, 1985;

(3) to guarantee, or purchase insurance for, local obligations where such action would improve credit market access or reduce interest rates;

(4) as a source of revenue or security for the payment of principal and interest on revenue or general obligation bonds issued by the State if the proceeds of the sale of such bonds will be deposited in the fund;

(5) to provide loan guarantees for similar revolving funds established by municipalities or intermunicipal agencies;

(6) to earn interest on fund accounts; and

(7) for the reasonable costs of administering the fund and conducting activities under this subchapter, except that such amounts shall not exceed 4 percent of all grant awards to such fund under this subchapter, $400,000 per year, or 1/5 percent per year of the current valuation of the fund, whichever amount is greatest, plus the amount of any fees collected by the State for such purpose regardless of the source.

(e) Limitation to prevent double benefits

If a State makes, from its water pollution revolving fund, a loan which will finance the cost of facility planning and the preparation of plans, specifications, and estimates for construction of publicly owned treatment works, the State shall ensure that if the recipient of such loan receives a grant under section 1281(g) of this title for construction of such treatment works and an allowance under section 1281(*l*)(1) of this title for non-Federal funds expended for such planning and preparation, such recipient will promptly repay such loan to the extent of such allowance.

(f) Consistency with planning requirements — A State may provide financial assistance from its water pollution control revolving fund only with respect to a project which is consistent with plans, if any, developed under sections 1285(j), 1288, 1313(e), 1329, and 1330 of this title.

(g) Priority list requirement — The State may provide financial assistance from its water pollution control revolving fund only with respect to a project for construction of a treatment works described in subsection (c)(1) of this section if such project is on the State's priority list under section 1296 of this title. Such assistance may be provided regardless of the rank of such project on such list.

(h) Eligibility of non-Federal share of construction grant projects — A State water pollution control revolving fund may provide assistance (other than under subsection (d)(1) of this section) to a municipality or intermunicipal or interstate

agency with respect to the non-Federal share of the costs of a treatment works project for which such municipality or agency is receiving assistance from the Administrator under any other authority only if such assistance is necessary to allow such project to proceed.

(i) Additional subsidization

(1) In general

In any case in which a State provides assistance to an eligible recipient under subsection (d), the State may provide additional subsidization, including forgiveness of principal and negative interest loans —

(A) in assistance to a municipality or intermunicipal, interstate, or State agency to benefit a municipality that —

(i) meets the affordability criteria of the State established under paragraph (2); or

(ii) does not meet the affordability criteria of the State if the recipient —

(I) seeks additional subsidization to benefit individual ratepayers in the residential user rate class;

(II) demonstrates to the State that such ratepayers will experience a significant hardship from the increase in rates necessary to finance the project or activity for which assistance is sought; and

(III) ensures, as part of an assistance agreement between the State and the recipient, that the additional subsidization provided under this paragraph is directed through a user charge rate system (or other appropriate method) to such ratepayers; or

(B) to implement a process, material, technique, or technology —

(i) to address water-efficiency goals;

(ii) to address energy-efficiency goals;

(iii) to mitigate stormwater runoff; or

(iv) to encourage sustainable project planning, design, and construction.

(2) Affordability criteria

(A) Establishment

(i) In general

Not later than September 30, 2015, and after providing notice and an opportunity for public comment, a State shall establish affordability criteria to assist in identifying municipalities that would experience a significant hardship raising the revenue necessary to finance a project or activity eligible for assistance under subsection (c)(1) if additional subsidization is not provided.

(ii) Contents

The criteria under clause (i) shall be based on income and unemployment data, population trends, and other data determined relevant by the State, including whether the project or activity is to be carried out in an economically distressed area, as described in section 3161 of Title 42.

(B) Existing criteria

If a State has previously established, after providing notice and an opportunity for public comment, affordability criteria that meet the requirements of subparagraph (A)—

 (i) the State may use the criteria for the purposes of this subsection; and

 (ii) those criteria shall be treated as affordability criteria established under this paragraph.

(C) Information to assist States

The Administrator may publish information to assist States in establishing affordability criteria under subparagraph (A).

(3) Limitations

(A) In general

A State may provide additional subsidization in a fiscal year under this subsection only if the total amount appropriated for making capitalization grants to all States under this subchapter for the fiscal year exceeds $1,000,000,000.

(B) Additional limitation

 (i) General rule

Subject to clause (ii), a State may use not more than 30 percent of the total amount received by the State in capitalization grants under this subchapter for a fiscal year for providing additional subsidization under this subsection.

 (ii) Exception

If, in a fiscal year, the amount appropriated for making capitalization grants to all States under this subchapter exceeds $1,000,000,000 by a percentage that is less than 30 percent, clause (i) shall be applied by substituting that percentage for 30 percent.

(C) Applicability

The authority of a State to provide additional subsidization under this subsection shall apply to amounts received by the State in capitalization grants under this subchapter for fiscal years beginning after September 30, 2014.

(D) Consideration

If the State provides additional subsidization to a municipality or intermunicipal, interstate, or State agency under this subsection that meets the criteria under paragraph (1)(A), the State shall take the criteria set forth in section 1382(b)(5) of this title into consideration.

(j) Definition of eligible individual — In subsection (c)(12), the term "eligible individual" means a member of a household, the members of which have a combined income (for the most recent 12-month period for which information is available) equal to not more than 50 percent of the median nonmetropolitan household income for the State in which the household is located, according to the most recent decennial census.

§1384. Allotment of funds
[CWA §604]

(a) Formula — Sums authorized to be appropriated to carry out this section for each of fiscal years 1989 and 1990 shall be allotted by the Administrator in accordance with section 1285(c) of this title.

(b) Reservation of funds for planning — Each State shall reserve each fiscal year 1 percent of the sums allotted to such State under this section for such fiscal year, or $100,000, whichever amount is greater, to carry out planning under sections 1285(j) and 1313(e) of this title.

(c) Allotment period

(1) Period of availability for grant award — Sums allotted to a State under this section for a fiscal year shall be available for obligation by the State during the fiscal year for which sums are authorized and during the following fiscal year.

(2) Reallotment of unobligated funds — The amount of any allotment not obligated by the State by the last day of the 2-year period of availability established by paragraph (1) shall be immediately reallotted by the Administrator on the basis of the same ratio as is applicable to sums allotted under subchapter II of this chapter for the second fiscal year of such 2-year period. None of the funds reallotted by the Administrator shall be reallotted to any State which has not obligated all sums allotted to such State in the first fiscal year of such 2-year period.

§1385. Corrective action
[CWA §605]

(a) Notification of noncompliance — If the Administrator determines that a State has not complied with its agreement with the Administrator under section 1382 of this title or any other requirement of this subchapter, the Administrator shall notify the State of such noncompliance and the necessary corrective action.

(b) Withholding of payments — If a State does not take corrective action within 60 days after the date a State receives notification of such action under subsection (a) of this section, the Administrator shall withhold additional payments to the State until the Administrator is satisfied that the State has taken the necessary corrective action.

(c) Reallotment of withheld payments — If the Administrator is not satisfied that adequate corrective actions have been taken by the State within 12 months after the State is notified of such actions under subsection (a) of this section, the payments withheld from the State by the Administrator under subsection (b) of this section shall be made available for reallotment in accordance with the most recent formula for allotment of funds under this subchapter.

§1386. Audits, reports, and fiscal controls; intended use plan
[CWA §606]
(a) Fiscal control and auditing procedures — Each State electing to establish a water pollution control revolving fund under this subchapter shall establish fiscal controls and accounting procedures sufficient to assure proper accounting during appropriate accounting periods for —

(1) payments received by the fund;

(2) disbursements made by the fund; and

(3) fund balances at the beginning and end of the accounting period.

(b) Annual Federal audits — The Administrator shall, at least on an annual basis, conduct or require each State to have independently conducted reviews and audits as may be deemed necessary or appropriate by the Administrator to carry out the objectives of this section. Audits of the use of funds deposited in the water pollution revolving fund established by such State shall be conducted in accordance with the auditing procedures of the General Accounting Office, including chapter 75 of Title 31.

(c) Intended use plan — After providing for public comment and review, each State shall annually prepare a plan identifying the intended uses of the amounts available to its water pollution control revolving fund. Such intended use plan shall include, but not be limited to —

(1) a list of those projects for construction of publicly owned treatment works on the State's priority list developed pursuant to section 1296 of this title and a list of activities eligible for assistance under sections 1329 and 1330 of this title;

(2) a description of the short- and long-term goals and objectives of its water pollution control revolving fund;

(3) information on the activities to be supported, including a description of project categories, discharge requirements under subchapters III and IV of this chapter, terms of financial assistance, and communities served;

(4) assurances and specific proposals for meeting the requirements of paragraphs (3), (4), (5), and (6) of section 1382(b) of this title; and

(5) the criteria and method established for the distribution of funds.

(d) Annual report — Beginning the first fiscal year after the receipt of payments under this subchapter, the State shall provide an annual report to the Administrator describing how the State has met the goals and objectives for the previous fiscal year as identified in the plan prepared for the previous fiscal year pursuant to subsection (c) of this section, including identification of loan recipients, loan amounts, and loan terms and similar details on other forms of financial assistance provided from the water pollution control revolving fund.

(e) Annual Federal oversight review — The Administrator shall conduct an annual oversight review of each State plan prepared under subsection (c) of this section, each State report prepared under subsection (d) of this section, and other such materials as are considered necessary and appropriate in carrying out the purposes of this subchapter. After reasonable notice by the Administrator to the State or the recipient of a loan from a water pollution control revolving fund, the State or loan recipient shall make available to the Administrator such records as the Administrator reasonably requires to review and determine compliance with this subchapter.

(f) Applicability of subchapter II provisions — Except to the extent provided in this subchapter, the provisions of subchapter II of this chapter shall not apply to grants under this subchapter.

§1387. Authorization of appropriations
[CWA §607]
There is authorized to be appropriated to carry out the purposes of this subchapter the following sums:

(1) $1,200,000,000 per fiscal year for each of fiscal years 1989 and 1990;

(2) $2,400,000,000 for fiscal year 1991;

(3) $1,800,000,000 for fiscal year 1992;

(4) $1,200,000,000 for fiscal year 1993; and

(5) $600,000,000 for fiscal year 1994.

§1388. Requirements
[CWA §608]
(a) In general

Funds made available from a State water pollution control revolving fund established under this subchapter may not be used for a project for the construction, alteration, maintenance, or repair of treatment works unless all of the iron and steel products used in the project are produced in the United States.

(b) Definition of iron and steel products

In this section, the term "iron and steel products" means the following products made primarily of iron or steel: lined or unlined pipes and fittings, manhole covers and other municipal castings, hydrants, tanks, flanges, pipe clamps and restraints, valves, structural steel, reinforced precast concrete, construction materials.

(c) Application

Subsection (a) shall not apply in any case or category of cases in which the Administrator finds that —

(1) applying subsection (a) would be inconsistent with the public interest;

(2) iron and steel products are not produced in the United States in sufficient and reasonably available quantities and of a satisfactory quality; or

(3) inclusion of iron and steel products produced in the United States will increase the cost of the overall project by more than 25 percent.

(d) Waiver

If the Administrator receives a request for a waiver under this section, the Administrator shall make available to the public, on an informal basis, a copy of the request and information available to the Administrator concerning the request, and shall allow for informal public input on the request for at least 15 days prior to making a finding based on the request. The Administrator shall make the request and accompanying information available by electronic means, including on the official public Internet site of the Environmental Protection Agency.

(e) International agreements

This section shall be applied in a manner consistent with United States obligations under international agreements.

(f) Management and oversight

The Administrator may retain up to 0.25 percent of the funds appropriated for this subchapter for management and oversight of the requirements of this section.

(g) Effective date

This section does not apply with respect to a project if a State agency approves the engineering plans and specifications for the project, in that agency's capacity to approve such plans and specifications prior to a project requesting bids, prior to June 10, 2014.

B. OIL POLLUTION ACT (OPA)

A GUIDE TO MATERIALS ON THE CONTROL AND PREVENTION OF OIL POLLUTION AVAILABLE ON THE INTERNET

The U.S. Environmental Protection Agency's regulations implementing the Oil Pollution Act are codified at 40 C.F.R. Part 112. They are available online through the National Archives and Records Administration's website, which includes a searchable version of the Code of Federal Regulations and an electronic version of the CFR ("e-CFR") updated continuously, which can be found at *http://www.ecfr.gov.*

EPA's Oil Spill Program has a webpage at *https://www.epa.gov/oil-spills-prevention-and-preparedness-regulations* with links to relevant statutes and regulations and an explanation of EPA's spill prevention efforts. The U.S. National Response Team (NRT), which is responsible for federal emergency responses to oil spills, has a webpage at *http://www.nrt.org.* It describes NRT's activities and lessons learned from multi-agency response exercises, and it has links to information about the latest spills.

The National Oceanic and Atmospheric Administration (NOAA) promulgated regulations on assessment of natural resource damages. NOAA's guidance document for such assessments can be located at *https://darrp.noaa.gov/legal-context.* The Department of Transportation's Pipeline and Hazardous Materials Safety Administration is responsible for implementing the Oil Pollution Act as it applies to onshore oil pipelines. Their website is at *http://phmsa.dot.gov.*

When it adopted regulations requiring double hulls on oil tankers operating in U.S. waters, Congress asked the National Research Council (NRC) of the National Academy of Sciences to study the effects of this requirement. Copies of the NRC's report "Double-Hull Tanker Legislation: An Assessment of the Oil Pollution Act of 1990" are available online at *http://www.nap.edu/openbook.php?isbn=0309063701.*

The Exxon Valdez Oil Spill Trustee Council provides continuing information about the impact of the massive oil spill in Prince William Sound in March 1989. Its website, located at *http://www.evostc.state.ak.us,* provides links to information on the restoration plan, how money received from the oil spill settlement is being used, and the impact of the spill on people, beaches, and habitat.

Information about the response to the massive oil spill in the Gulf of Mexico caused by the April 20, 2010 explosion of the Deepwater Horizon drilling rig is available at *https://obamawhitehouse.archives.gov/deepwater-bp-oil-spill.*

OIL POLLUTION ACT LEGISLATIVE HISTORY TIMELINE

August 18, 1990: President Bush signs the Oil Pollution Act of 1990, Pub. L. 101-380, 104 Stat. 484, which makes owners and operators of vessels, facilities, and pipelines that discharge oil strictly liable for the costs of cleaning up spills and for damages to natural resources and real and personal property. The law raises liability limits eight-fold, requires vessels and facilities operating in the U.S. to maintain evidence of financial responsibility up to the liability limits, and creates a new $1 billion Oil Spill Liability Trust Fund funded by a five cent/barrel tax on crude oil (26 U.S.C. §9509) to fund responses in excess of liability limits. It also requires oil tankers operating in U.S. waters to have double-hulls, a requirement to be phased in over a 20-year period (46 U.S.C. §3703a).

November 13, 1998: President Clinton signs the Coast Guard Authorization Act of 1998, Pub. L. 105-383, 112 Stat. 3421, which reduces the amount of liability insurance offshore drilling operations must carry and exempts from the financial responsibility requirements facilities transporting, storing, or otherwise handling 1,000 barrels of oil or less at any one time.

August 9, 2004: President George W. Bush signs the Coast Guard and Maritime Transportation Act of 2004, Pub. L. 108-293, 118 Stat. 1069. The Act amends the definitions of "owner" and "operator" in the Oil Pollution Act to exclude from liability secondary lenders (those without management participation) and state or local governments that involuntarily acquire control or ownership of a vessel or facility involved in an oil spill. It also requires non-tank vessels of 400 gross tons and greater to prepare oil spill response plans similar to those required now of tank vessels.

PRINCIPAL PROVISIONS OF THE OIL POLLUTION ACT

§1002 (33 U.S.C. §2702) Liability for Oil Spills: holds owners and operators of vessels, facilities, and pipelines from which oil is discharged liable for all cleanup costs resulting from the discharge, as well as for damages to natural resources, loss of subsistence use of resources, damages to real or personal property and economic losses resulting from their destruction.

§1003 (33 U.S.C. §2703) Defenses to Liability: provides a defense to liability if the oil discharge was caused solely by an act of God, an act of war, or the act or omission of a non-employee or non-agent third party when due care and precautions were taken against foreseeable acts of such third party.

§1004 (33 U.S.C. §2704) Limits on Liability: establishes limits on the liability of responsible parties based on the size of their vessel or facility that apply only if the oil spill was not caused by gross negligence, willful misconduct, or the violation of applicable regulations.

§1006 (33 U.S.C. §2706) Natural Resources Damages: establishes procedures for assessing natural resource damages and for the recovery of them by federal, state, and tribal trustees.

§1009 (33 U.S.C. §2709) Contribution: authorizes suits seeking contribution from responsible parties.

§1012 (33 U.S.C. §2712) Uses of Trust Fund: specifies how funds in the Oil Spill Liability Trust Fund may be used.

§1013 (33 U.S.C. §2713) Claims Procedure: specifies procedures for making claims for removal costs or damages from the Oil Spill Liability Trust Fund.

§1016 (33 U.S.C. §2716) Financial Responsibility: requires owners and operators of vessels and facilities to carry evidence of financial responsibility to meet the maximum liability limits to which they are subject under the Act.

§1017 (33 U.S.C. §2717) Jurisdiction and Judicial Review: gives federal district courts exclusive jurisdiction over controversies arising under the Act except for claims for removal costs or damages, which also may be heard by state trial courts of competent jurisdiction, and for judicial review of regulations promulgated under the Act, which is authorized only in the U.S. Court of Appeals for the District of Columbia Circuit.

§1018 (33 U.S.C. §2718) Preservation of State Authorities and Funds: specifies that nothing in the Act preempts state liability requirements or state oil spill trust funds.

§4115 (46 U.S.C. §3703a) Oil Tanker Construction Standards: requires that oil tankers operating in U.S. waters have double hulls, a requirement that applies to all new oil tankers and that is phased in over a 20-year period for existing ships. The phase-in schedule is dependent upon a tanker's size and age with older and larger ships having to comply more quickly than newer and smaller tankers.

Oil Pollution Act

33 U.S.C. §§2701 to 2762
46 U.S.C. §§3703a to 3719

SUBCHAPTER I — OIL POLLUTION LIABILITY AND COMPENSATION

§2701. Definitions
[OPA §1001]

For the purposes of this Act, the term —

(1) "act of God" means an unanticipated grave natural disaster or other natural phenomenon of an exceptional, inevitable, and irresistible character the effects of which could not have been prevented or avoided by the exercise of due care or foresight;

(2) "barrel" means 42 United States gallons at 60 degrees Fahrenheit;

(3) "claim" means a request, made in writing for a sum certain, for compensation for damages or removal costs resulting from an incident;

(4) "claimant" means any person or government who presents a claim for compensation under this subchapter;

(5) "damages" means damages specified in section 2702(b) of this title, and includes the cost of assessing these damages;

(6) "deepwater port" is a facility licensed under the Deepwater Port Act of 1974 (33 U.S.C. §§1501-1524);

(7) "discharge" means any emission (other than natural seepage), intentional or unintentional, and includes, but is not limited to, spilling, leaking, pumping, pouring, emitting, emptying, or dumping;

(8) "exclusive economic zone" means the zone established by Presidential Proclamation Numbered 5030, dated March 10, 1983, including the ocean waters of the areas referred to as "eastern special areas" in Article 3(1) of the Agreement between the United States of America and the Union of Soviet Socialist Republics on the Maritime Boundary, signed June 1, 1990;

(9) "facility" means any structure, group of structures, equipment, or device (other than a vessel) which is used for one or more of the following purposes: exploring for, drilling for, producing, storing, handling, transferring, processing, or transporting oil. This term includes any motor vehicle, rolling stock, or pipeline used for one or more of these purposes;

(10) "foreign offshore unit" means a facility which is located, in whole or in part, in the territorial sea or on the continental shelf of a foreign country and which is or was used for one or more of the following purposes: exploring for, drilling for, producing, storing, handling, transferring, processing, or transporting oil produced from the seabed beneath the foreign country's territorial sea or from the foreign country's continental shelf;

(11) "Fund" means the Oil Spill Liability Trust Fund, established by section 9509 of title 26;

(12) "gross ton" has the meaning given that term by the Secretary under part J of title 46;

(13) "guarantor" means any person, other than the responsible party, who provides evidence of financial responsibility for a responsible party under this Act;

(14) "incident" means any occurrence or series of occurrences having the same origin, involving one or more vessels, facilities, or any combination thereof, resulting in the discharge or substantial threat of discharge of oil;

(15) "Indian tribe" means any Indian tribe, band, nation, or other organized group or community, but not including any Alaska Native regional or village corporation, which is recognized as eligible for the special programs and services provided by the United States to Indians because of their status as Indians and has governmental authority over lands belonging to or controlled by the tribe;

(16) "lessee" means a person holding a leasehold interest in an oil or gas lease on lands beneath navigable waters (as that term is defined in section 1301(a) of title 43) or on submerged lands of the Outer Continental Shelf, granted or maintained under applicable State law or the Outer Continental Shelf Lands Act (43 U.S.C. §§1331 *et seq.*);

(17) "liable" or "liability" shall be construed to be the standard of liability which obtains under section 1321 of this title;

(18) "mobile offshore drilling unit" means a vessel (other than a self-elevating lift vessel) capable of use as an offshore facility;

(19) "National Contingency Plan" means the National Contingency Plan prepared and published under section 1321(d) of this title or revised under section 105 of the Comprehensive Environmental Response, Compensation, and Liability Act (42 U.S.C. §9605);

(20) "natural resources" includes land, fish, wildlife, biota, air, water, ground water, drinking water supplies, and other such resources belonging to, managed by, held in trust by, appertaining to, or otherwise controlled by the United States (including the resources of the exclusive economic zone), any State or local government or Indian tribe, or any foreign government;

(21) "navigable waters" means the waters of the United States, including the territorial sea;

(22) "offshore facility" means any facility of any kind located in, on, or under any of the navigable waters of the United States, and any facility of any kind which is subject to the jurisdiction of the United States and is located in, on, or under any other waters, other than a vessel or a public vessel;

(23) "oil" means oil of any kind or in any form, including petroleum, fuel oil, sludge, oil refuse, and oil mixed with wastes other than dredged spoil, but does not include any substance which is specifically listed or designated as a hazardous substance under subparagraphs (A) through (F) of section 101(14) of the Comprehensive Environmental Response, Compensation, and Liability Act (42 U.S.C. §9601) and which is subject to the provisions of that Act (42 U.S.C. §§9601 *et seq.*);

(24) "onshore facility" means any facility (including, but not limited to, motor vehicles and rolling stock) of any kind located in, on, or under, any land within the United States other than submerged land;

(25) the term "Outer Continental Shelf facility" means an offshore facility which is located, in whole or in part, on the Outer Continental Shelf and is or was used for one or more of the

following purposes: exploring for, drilling for, producing, storing, handling, transferring, processing, or transporting oil produced from the Outer Continental Shelf;

(26) "owner or operator" —

(A) means —

(i) in the case of a vessel, any person owning, operating, or chartering by demise, the vessel;

(ii) in the case of an onshore facility, offshore facility, or foreign offshore unit or other facility located seaward of the exclusive economic zone, any person or entity owning or operating such facility;

(iii) in the case of any abandoned offshore facility or foreign offshore unit or other facility located seaward of the exclusive economic zone, the person or entity that owned or operated such facility immediately prior to such abandonment;

(iv) in the case of any facility, title or control of which was conveyed due to bankruptcy, foreclosure, tax delinquency, abandonment, or similar means to a unit of State or local government, any person who owned, operated, or otherwise controlled activities at such facility immediately beforehand;

(v) notwithstanding subparagraph (B)(i), and in the same manner and to the same extent, both procedurally and substantively, as any nongovernmental entity, including for purposes of liability under section 2702 of this title, any State or local government that has caused or contributed to a discharge or substantial threat of a discharge of oil from a vessel or facility ownership or control of which was acquired involuntarily through —

(I) seizure or otherwise in connection with law enforcement activity;

(II) bankruptcy;

(III) tax delinquency;

(IV) abandonment; or

(V) other circumstances in which the government involuntarily acquires title by virtue of its function as sovereign;

(vi) notwithstanding subparagraph (B) (ii), a person that is a lender and that holds indicia of ownership primarily to protect a security interest in a vessel or facility if, while the borrower is still in possession of the vessel or facility encumbered by the security interest, the person —

(I) exercises decision making control over the environmental compliance related to the vessel or facility, such that the person has undertaken responsibility for oil handling or disposal practices related to the vessel or facility; or

(II) exercises control at a level comparable to that of a manager of the vessel or facility, such that the person has assumed or manifested responsibility —

(aa) for the overall management of the vessel or facility encompassing day-to-day decision making with respect to environmental compliance; or

(bb) over all or substantially all of the operational functions (as distinguished from financial or administrative functions) of the vessel or facility other than the function of environmental compliance; and

(B) does not include —

(i) A unit of state or local government that acquired ownership or control of a vessel or facility involuntarily through —

(I) seizure or otherwise in connection with law enforcement activity;

(II) bankruptcy;

(III) tax delinquency;

(IV) abandonment; or

(V) other circumstances in which the government involuntarily acquires title by virtue of its function as sovereign;

(ii) a person that is a lender that does not participate in management of a vessel or facility, but holds indicia of ownership primarily to protect the security interest of the person in the vessel or facility; or

(iii) a person that is a lender that did not participate in management of a vessel or facility prior to foreclosure, notwithstanding that the person —

(I) forecloses on the vessel or facility; and

(II) after foreclosure, sells, re-leases (in the case of a lease finance transaction), or liquidates the vessel or facility, maintains business activities, winds up operations, undertakes a removal action under section 1321(c) of this title or under the direction of an on-scene coordinator appointed under the National Contingency Plan, with respect to the vessel or facility, or takes any other measure to preserve, protect, or prepare the vessel or facility prior to sale or disposition,

if the person seeks to sell, re-lease (in the case of a lease finance transaction), or otherwise divest the person of the vessel or facility at the earliest practicable, commercially reasonable time, on commercially reasonable terms, taking into account market conditions and legal and regulatory requirements;

(27) "person" means an individual, corporation, partnership, association, State, municipality, commission, or political subdivision of a State, or any interstate body;

(28) "permittee" means a person holding an authorization, license, or permit for geological exploration issued under section 11 of the Outer Continental Shelf Lands Act (43 U.S.C. §1340) or applicable State law;

(29) "public vessel" means a vessel owned or bareboat chartered and operated by the United States, or by a State or political subdivision thereof, or by a foreign nation, except when the vessel is engaged in commerce;

(30) "remove" or "removal" means containment and removal of oil or a hazardous substance from water and shorelines or the taking of other actions as may be necessary to minimize or mitigate damage to the public health or welfare, including, but not limited to, fish, shellfish, wildlife, and public and private property, shorelines, and beaches;

(31) "removal costs" means the costs of removal that are incurred after a discharge of oil has occurred or, in any case in which there is a substantial threat of a discharge of oil, the costs to prevent, minimize, or mitigate oil pollution from such an incident;

(32) "responsible party" means the following:

(A) Vessels — In the case of a vessel, any person owning, operating, or demise chartering the vessel. In the case of a vessel, the term "responsible party" also includes the owner of oil being transported in a tank vessel with a single hull after December 31, 2010.

(B) Onshore facilities — In the case of an onshore facility (other than a pipeline), any person owning or operating the facility, except a Federal agency, State, municipality, commission, or political subdivision of a State, or any interstate body, that as the owner transfers possession and right to use the property to another person by lease, assignment, or permit.

(C) Offshore facilities — In the case of an offshore facility (other than a pipeline or a deepwater port licensed under the Deepwater Port Act of 1974 (33 U.S.C. §§1501 et seq.)), the lessee or permittee of the area in which the facility is located or the holder of a right of use and easement granted under applicable State law or the Outer Continental Shelf Lands Act (43 U.S.C. 1301-1356) for the area in which the facility is located (if the holder is a different person than the lessee or permittee), except a Federal agency, State, municipality, commission, or political subdivision of a State,

or any interstate body, that as owner transfers possession and right to use the property to another person by lease, assignment, or permit.

(D) Foreign facilities. — In the case of a foreign offshore unit or other facility located seaward of the exclusive economic zone, any person or other entity owning or operating the facility, and any leaseholder, permit holder, assignee, or holder of a right of use and easement granted under applicable foreign law for the area in which the facility is located;

(E) Deepwater ports — In the case of a deep-water port licensed under the Deepwater Port Act of 1974 (33 U.S.C. 1501-1524), the licensee.

(F) Pipelines — In the case of a pipeline, any person owning or operating the pipeline.

(G) Abandonment — In the case of an abandoned vessel, onshore facility, deepwater port, pipeline, offshore facility, or foreign offshore unit or other facility located seaward of the exclusive economic zone, the persons or entities that would have been responsible parties immediately prior to the abandonment of the vessel or facility.

(33) "Secretary" means the Secretary of the department in which the Coast Guard is operating;

(34) "tank vessel" means a vessel that is constructed or adapted to carry, or that carries, oil or hazardous material in bulk as cargo or cargo residue, and that —

(A) is a vessel of the United States;

(B) operates on the navigable waters; or

(C) transfers oil or hazardous material in a place subject to the jurisdiction of the United States;

(35) "territorial seas" means the belt of the seas measured from the line of ordinary low water along that portion of the coast which is in direct contact with the open sea and the line marking the seaward limit of inland waters, and extending seaward a distance of 3 miles;

(36) "United States" and "State" mean the several States of the United States, the District of Columbia, the Commonwealth of Puerto Rico, Guam, American Samoa, the United States Virgin Islands, the Commonwealth of the Northern Marianas, and any other territory or possession of the United States;

(37) "vessel" means every description of watercraft or other artificial contrivance used, or capable of being used, as a means of transportation on water, other than a public vessel;

(38) "participate in management" —

(A)(i) means actually participating in the management or operational affairs of a vessel or facility; and

(ii) does not include merely having the capacity to influence, or the unexercised right to control, vessel or facility operations; and

(B) does not include —

(i) performing an act or failing to act prior to the time at which a security interest is created in a vessel or facility;

(ii) holding a security interest or abandoning or releasing a security interest;

(iii) including in the terms of an extension of credit, or in a contract or security agreement relating to the extension, a covenant, warranty, or other term or condition that relates to environmental compliance;

(iv) monitoring or enforcing the terms and conditions of the extension of credit or security interest;

(v) monitoring or undertaking one or more inspections of the vessel or facility;

(vi) requiring a removal action or other lawful means of addressing a discharge or substantial threat of a discharge of oil in connection with the vessel or facility prior to, during, or on the expiration of the term of the extension of credit;

(vii) providing financial or other advice or counseling in an effort to mitigate, prevent, or cure default or diminution in the value of the vessel or facility;

(viii) restructuring, renegotiating, or otherwise agreeing to alter the terms and conditions of the extension of credit or security interest, exercising forbearance;

(ix) exercising other remedies that may be available under applicable law for the breach of a term or condition of the extension of credit or security agreement; or

(x) conducting a removal action under section 1321(c) of this title or under the direction of an on-scene coordinator appointed under the National Contingency Plan, if such actions do not rise to the level of participating in management under subparagraph (A) of this paragraph and paragraph (26)(A)(vi);

(39) "extension of credit" has the meaning provided in section 101(20)(G)(i) of the Comprehensive Environmental Response, Compensation and Liability Act of 1980 (42 U.S.C. 9601(20)(G)(i));

(40) "financial or administrative function" has the meaning provided in section 101(20)(G)(ii) of the Comprehensive Environmental Response, Compensation and Liability Act of 1980 (42 U.S.C. 9601(20)(G)(ii));

(41) "foreclosure" and "foreclose" each has the meaning provided in section 101(20)(G)(iii) of the Comprehensive Environmental Response, Compensation and Liability Act of 1980 (42 U.S.C. 9601(20)(G)(iii));

(42) "lender" has the meaning provided in section 101(20)(G)(iv) of the Comprehensive Environmental Response, Compensation and Liability Act of 1980 (42 U.S.C. 9601(20)(G)(iv));

(43) "operational function" has the meaning provided in section 101(20)(G)(v) of the Comprehensive Environmental Response, Compensation and Liability Act of 1980 (42 U.S.C. 9601(20)(G)(v)); and

(44) "security interest" has the meaning provided in section 101(20)(G)(vi) of the Comprehensive Environmental Response, Compensation and Liability Act of 1980 (42 U.S.C. 9601(20)(G)(vi)).

§2702. Elements of liability
[OPA §1002]

(a) In general — Notwithstanding any other provision or rule of law, and subject to the provisions of this Act, each responsible party for a vessel or a facility from which oil is discharged, or which poses the substantial threat of a discharge of oil, into or upon the navigable waters or adjoining shorelines or the exclusive economic zone is liable for the removal costs and damages specified in subsection (b) of this section that result from such incident.

(b) Covered removal costs and damages

(1) Removal costs — The removal costs referred to in subsection (a) of this section are —

(A) all removal costs incurred by the United States, a State, or an Indian tribe under subsection (c), (d), (e), or (l) of section 1321 of this title, under the Intervention on the High Seas Act (33 U.S.C. §§1471 et seq.), or under State law; and

(B) any removal costs incurred by any person for acts taken by the person which are consistent with the National Contingency Plan.

(2) Damages — The damages referred to in subsection (a) of this section are the following:

(A) Natural resources — Damages for injury to, destruction of, loss of, or loss of use of, natural resources, including the reasonable costs of assessing the damage, which shall be recoverable by a United States trustee, a State trustee, an Indian tribe trustee, or a foreign trustee.

(B) Real or personal property — Damages for injury to, or economic losses resulting from destruction of, real or personal property, which shall be recoverable by a claimant who owns or leases that property.

(C) Subsistence use — Damages for loss of subsistence use of natural resources, which shall be recoverable by any claimant who so uses natural resources which have been injured, destroyed, or lost, without regard to the ownership or management of the resources.

(D) Revenues — Damages equal to the net loss of taxes, royalties, rents, fees, or net profit shares due to the injury, destruction, or loss of real property, personal property, or natural resources, which shall be recoverable by the Government of the United States, a State, or a political subdivision thereof.

(E) Profits and earning capacity — Damages equal to the loss of profits or impairment of earning capacity due to the injury, destruction, or loss of real property, personal property, or natural resources, which shall be recoverable by any claimant.

(F) Public services — Damages for net costs of providing increased or additional public services during or after removal activities, including protection from fire, safety, or health hazards, caused by a discharge of oil, which shall be recoverable by a State, or a political subdivision of a State.

(c) **Excluded discharges** — This subchapter does not apply to any discharge —

(1) permitted by a permit issued under Federal, State, or local law;

(2) from a public vessel; or

(3) from an onshore facility which is subject to the Trans-Alaska Pipeline Authorization Act (43 U.S.C. §§1651 *et seq.*).

(d) **Liability of third parties**

(1) In general

(A) Third party treated as responsible party — Except as provided in subparagraph (B), in any case in which a responsible party establishes that a discharge or threat of a discharge and the resulting removal costs and damages were caused solely by an act or omission of one or more third parties described in section 2703(a)(3) of this title (or solely by such an act or omission in combination with an act of God or an act of war), the third party or parties shall be treated as the responsible party or parties for purposes of determining liability under this subchapter.

(B) Subrogation of responsible party — If the responsible party alleges that the discharge or threat of a discharge was caused solely by an act or omission of a third party, the responsible party —

(i) in accordance with section 2713 of this title, shall pay removal costs and damages to any claimant; and

(ii) shall be entitled by subrogation to all rights of the United States Government and the claimant to recover removal costs or damages from the third party or the Fund paid under this subsection.

(2) Limitation applied

(A) Owner or operator of vessel or facility — If the act or omission of a third party that causes an incident occurs in connection with a vessel or facility owned or operated by the third party, the liability of the third party shall be subject to the limits provided in section 2704 of this title as applied with respect to the vessel or facility.

(B) Other cases — In any other case, the liability of a third party or parties shall not exceed the limitation which would have been applicable to the responsible party of the vessel or facility from which the discharge actually occurred if the responsible party were liable.

§2703. Defenses to liability
[OPA §1003]

(a) **Complete defenses** — A responsible party is not liable for removal costs or damages under section 2702 of this title if the responsible party establishes, by a preponderance of the evidence, that the discharge or substantial threat of a discharge of oil and the resulting damages or removal costs were caused solely by —

(1) an act of God;

(2) an act of war;

(3) an act or omission of a third party, other than an employee or agent of the responsible party or a third party whose act or omission occurs in connection with any contractual relationship with the responsible party (except where the sole contractual arrangement arises in connection with carriage by a common carrier by rail), if the responsible party establishes, by a preponderance of the evidence, that the responsible party —

(A) exercised due care with respect to the oil concerned, taking into consideration the characteristics of the oil and in light of all relevant facts and circumstances; and

(B) took precautions against foreseeable acts or omissions of any such third party and the foreseeable consequences of those acts or omissions; or

(4) any combination of paragraphs (1), (2), and (3).

(b) **Defenses as to particular claimants** — A responsible party is not liable under section 2702 of this title to a claimant, to the extent that the incident is caused by the gross negligence or willful misconduct of the claimant.

(c) **Limitation on complete defense** — Subsection (a) of this section does not apply with respect to a responsible party who fails or refuses —

(1) to report the incident as required by law if the responsible party knows or has reason to know of the incident;

(2) to provide all reasonable cooperation and assistance requested by a responsible official in connection with removal activities; or

(3) without sufficient cause, to comply with an order issued under subsection (c) or (e) of section 1321 of this title or the Intervention on the High Seas Act (33 U.S.C. §§1471 *et seq.*).

(d) **Definition of contractual relationship**

(1) In general — For purposes of subsection (a)(3) of this section the term "contractual relationship" includes, but is not limited to, land contracts, deeds, easements, leases, or

other instruments transferring title or possession, unless —

(A) the real property on which the facility concerned is located was acquired by the responsible party after the placement of the oil on, in, or at the real property on which the facility concerned is located;

(B) one or more of the circumstances described in subparagraph (A), (B), or (C) of paragraph (2) is established by the responsible party by a preponderance of the evidence; and

(C) the responsible party complies with paragraph (3).

(2) Required circumstance — The circumstances referred to in paragraph (1)(B) are the following:

(A) At the time the responsible party acquired the real property on which the facility is located the responsible party did not know and had no reason to know that oil that is the subject of the discharge or substantial threat of discharge was located on, in, or at the facility.

(B) The responsible party is a government entity that acquired the facility —

(i) by escheat;

(ii) through any other involuntary transfer or acquisition; or

(iii) through the exercise of eminent domain authority by purchase or condemnation.

(C) The responsible party acquired the facility by inheritance or bequest.

(3) Additional requirements — For purposes of paragraph (1)(C), the responsible party must establish by a preponderance of the evidence that the responsible party —

(A) has satisfied the requirements of subsection (a)(3)(A) and (B) of this section;

(B) has provided full cooperation, assistance, and facility access to the persons that are authorized to conduct removal actions, including the cooperation and access necessary for the installation, integrity, operation, and maintenance of any complete or partial removal action;

(C) is in compliance with any land use restrictions established or relied on in connection with the removal action; and

(D) has not impeded the effectiveness or integrity of any institutional control employed in connection with the removal action.

(4) Reason to know

(A) Appropriate inquiries — To establish that the responsible party had no reason to know of the matter described in paragraph (2)(A), the responsible party must demonstrate to a court that —

(i) on or before the date on which the responsible party acquired the real property on which the facility is located, the responsible party carried out all appropriate inquiries, as provided in subparagraphs (B) and (D), into the previous ownership and uses of the real property on which the facility is located in accordance with generally accepted good commercial and customary standards and practices; and

(ii) the responsible party took reasonable steps to —

(I) stop any continuing discharge;

(II) prevent any substantial threat of discharge; and

(III) prevent or limit any human, environmental, or natural resource exposure to any previously discharged oil.

(B) Regulations establishing standards and practices

Not later than 2 years after August 9, 2004, the Secretary, in consultation with the Administrator of the Environmental Protection Agency, shall by regulation establish standards and practices for the purpose of satisfying the requirement to carry out all appropriate inquiries under subparagraph (A).

(C) Criteria — In promulgating regulations that establish the standards and practices referred to in subparagraph (B), the Secretary shall include in such standards and practices provisions regarding each of the following:

(i) The results of an inquiry by an environmental professional.

(ii) Interviews with past and present owners, operators, and occupants of the facility and the real property on which the facility is located for the purpose of gathering information regarding the potential for oil at the facility and on the real property on which the facility is located.

(iii) Reviews of historical sources, such as chain of title documents, aerial photographs, building department records, and land use records, to determine previous uses and occupancies of the real property on which the facility is located since the property was first developed.

(iv) Searches for recorded environmental cleanup liens against the facility and the real property on which the facility is located that are filed under Federal, State, or local law.

(v) Reviews of Federal, State, and local government records, waste disposal records, underground storage tank records, and waste handling, generation, treatment, disposal, and spill records, concerning oil at or near the facility and on the real property on which the facility is located.

(vi) Visual inspections of the facility, the real property on which the facility is located, and adjoining properties.

1069

(vii) Specialized knowledge or experience on the part of the responsible party.

(viii) The relationship of the purchase price to the value of the facility and the real property on which the facility is located, if oil was not at the facility or on the real property.

(ix) Commonly known or reasonably ascertainable information about the facility and the real property on which the facility is located.

(x) The degree of obviousness of the presence or likely presence of oil at the facility and on the real property on which the facility is located, and the ability to detect the oil by appropriate investigation.

(D) Interim standards and practices

(i) Real property purchased before May 31, 1997 —

With respect to real property purchased before May 31, 1997, in making a determination with respect to a responsible party described in subparagraph (A), a court shall take into account —

    (I) any specialized knowledge or experience on the part of the responsible party;

    (II) the relationship of the purchase price to the value of the facility and the real property on which the facility is located, if the oil was not at the facility or on the real property;

    (III) commonly known or reasonably ascertainable information about the facility and the real property on which the facility is located;

    (IV) the obviousness of the presence or likely presence of oil at the facility and on the real property on which the facility is located; and

    (V) the ability of the responsible party to detect oil by appropriate inspection.

(ii) Real property purchased on or after May 31, 1997 —

With respect to real property purchased on or after May 31, 1997, until the Secretary promulgates the regulations described in clause (ii), the procedures of the American Society for Testing and Materials, including the document known as "Standard E1527-97", entitled "Standard Practice for Environmental Site Assessment: Phase I Environmental Site Assessment Process", shall satisfy the requirements in subparagraph (A).

(E) Site inspection and title search — In the case of real property for residential use or other similar use purchased by a nongovernmental or noncommercial entity, inspection and title search of the facility and the real property on which the facility is located that reveal no basis for further investigation shall be considered to satisfy the requirements of this paragraph.

(5) Previous owner or operator — Nothing in this paragraph or in subsection (a)(3) of this section shall diminish the liability of any previous owner or operator of such facility who would otherwise be liable under this Act. Notwithstanding this paragraph, if a responsible party obtained actual knowledge of the discharge or substantial threat of discharge of oil at such facility when the responsible party owned the facility and then subsequently transferred ownership of the facility or the real property on which the facility is located to another person without disclosing such knowledge, the responsible party shall be treated as liable under section 2702(a) of this title and no defense under subsection (a) of this section shall be available to such responsible party.

(6) Limitation on defense — Nothing in this paragraph shall affect the liability under this Act of a responsible party who, by any act or omission, caused or contributed to the discharge or substantial threat of discharge of oil which is the subject of the action relating to the facility.

§2704. Limits on liability
[OPA §1004]

(a) General rule — Except as otherwise provided in this section, the total of the liability of a responsible party under section 2702 of this title and any removal costs incurred by, or on behalf of, the responsible party, with respect to each incident shall not exceed —

(1) for a tank vessel, the greater of —

    (A) with respect to a single-hull vessel, including a single-hull vessel fitted with double sides only or a double bottom only, $3,000 per gross ton;

    (B) with respect to a vessel other than a vessel referred to in subparagraph (A), $1,900 per gross ton; or

    (C)(i) with respect to a vessel greater than 3,000 gross tons that is —

        (I) a vessel described in subparagraph (A), $22,000,000; or

        (II) a vessel described in subparagraph (B), $16,000,000; or

    (ii) with respect to a vessel of 3,000 gross tons or less that is —

        (I) a vessel described in subparagraph (A), $6,000,000; or

        (II) a vessel described in subparagraph (B), $4,000,000;

(2) for any other vessel, $950 per gross ton or $800,000, whichever is greater;

(3) for an offshore facility except a deepwater port, the total of all removal costs plus $75,000,000; and

(4) for any onshore facility and a deepwater port, $350,000,000.

(b) Division of liability for mobile offshore drilling units

(1) Treated first as tank vessel — For purposes of determining the responsible party and applying this chapter and except as provided in paragraph (2), a mobile offshore drilling unit which is being used as an offshore facility is deemed to be a tank vessel with respect to the discharge, or the substantial threat of a discharge, of oil on or above the surface of the water.

(2) Treated as facility for excess liability — To the extent that removal costs and damages from any incident described in paragraph (1) exceed the amount for which a responsible party is liable (as that amount may be limited under subsection (a)(1) of this section), the mobile offshore drilling unit is deemed to be an offshore facility. For purposes of applying subsection (a)(3) of this section, the amount specified in that subsection shall be reduced by the amount for which the responsible party is liable under paragraph (1).

(c) Exceptions

(1) Acts of responsible party — Subsection (a) of this section does not apply if the incident was proximately caused by —

(A) gross negligence or willful misconduct of, or

(B) the violation of an applicable Federal safety, construction, or operating regulation by, the responsible party, an agent or employee of the responsible party, or a person acting pursuant to a contractual relationship with the responsible party (except where the sole contractual arrangement arises in connection with carriage by a common carrier by rail).

(2) Failure or refusal of responsible party — Subsection (a) of this section does not apply if the responsible party fails or refuses —

(A) to report the incident as required by law and the responsible party knows or has reason to know of the incident;

(B) to provide all reasonable cooperation and assistance requested by a responsible official in connection with removal activities; or

(C) without sufficient cause, to comply with an order issued under subsection (c) or (e) of section 1321 of this title or the Intervention on the High Seas Act (33 U.S.C. §1471 et seq.).

(3) OCS facility or vessel — Notwithstanding the limitations established under subsection (a) of this section and the defenses of section 2703 of this title, all removal costs incurred by the United States Government or any State or local official or agency in connection with a discharge or substantial threat of a discharge of oil from any Outer Continental Shelf facility or a vessel carrying oil as cargo from such a facility shall be borne by the owner or operator of such facility or vessel.

(4) Certain tank vessels

Subsection (a)(1) shall not apply to —

(A) a tank vessel on which the only oil carried as cargo is an animal fat or vegetable oil, as those terms are used in section 2720 of this title; and

(B) a tank vessel that is designated in its certificate of inspection as an oil spill response vessel (as that term is defined in section 2101 of Title 46), and that is used solely for removal.

(d) Adjusting limits of liability

(1) Onshore facilities — Subject to paragraph (2), the President may establish by regulation, with respect to any class or category of onshore facility, a limit of liability under this section of less than $350,000,000, but not less than $8,000,000, taking into account size, storage capacity, oil throughput, proximity to sensitive areas, type of oil handled, history of discharges, and other factors relevant to risks posed by the class or category of facility.

(2) Deepwater ports and associated vessels

(A) Study — The Secretary shall conduct a study of the relative operational and environmental risks posed by the transportation of oil by vessel to deepwater ports (as defined in section 1502 of this title) versus the transportation of oil by vessel to other ports. The study shall include a review and analysis of offshore lightering practices used in connection with that transportation, an analysis of the volume of oil transported by vessel using those practices, and an analysis of the frequency and volume of oil discharges which occur in connection with the use of those practices.

(B) Report — Not later than 1 year after August 18, 1990, the Secretary shall submit to the Congress a report on the results of the study conducted under subparagraph (A).

(C) Rulemaking proceeding — If the Secretary determines, based on the results of the study conducted under this subparagraph (A), that the use of deepwater ports in connection with the transportation of oil by vessel results in a lower operational or environmental risk than the use of other ports, the Secretary shall initiate, not later than the 180th day following the date of submission of the report to the Congress under subparagraph (B), a rulemaking proceeding to lower the limits of liability under this section for deepwater ports as the Secretary determines appropriate. The Secretary may establish a limit of liability of less than $350,000,000, but not less than $50,000,000, in accordance with paragraph (1).

(3) Periodic reports — The President shall, within 6 months after August 18, 1990, and from time to time thereafter, report to the Congress on the desirability of adjusting the limits of liability specified in subsection (a) of this section.

(4) Adjustment to reflect Consumer Price Index — The President, by regulations issued not

later than 3 years after July 11, 2006, and not less than every 3 years thereafter, shall adjust the limits on liability specified in subsection (a) of this section to reflect significant increases in the Consumer Price Index.

§2705. Interest; partial payment of claims
[OPA §1005]

(a) General rule — The responsible party or the responsible party's guarantor is liable to a claimant for interest on the amount paid in satisfaction of a claim under this chapter for the period described in subsection (b) of this section. The responsible party shall establish a procedure for the payment or settlement of claims for interim, short-term damages. Payment or settlement of a claim for interim, short-term damages representing less than the full amount of damages to which the claimant ultimately may be entitled shall not preclude recovery by the claimant for damages not reflected in the paid or settled partial claim.

(b) Period

　(1) In general — Except as provided in paragraph (2), the period for which interest shall be paid is the period beginning on the 30th day following the date on which the claim is presented to the responsible party or guarantor and ending on the date on which the claim is paid.

　(2) Exclusion of period due to offer by guarantor — If the guarantor offers to the claimant an amount equal to or greater than that finally paid in satisfaction of the claim, the period described in paragraph (1) does not include the period beginning on the date the offer is made and ending on the date the offer is accepted. If the offer is made within 60 days after the date on which the claim is presented under section 2713(a) of this title, the period described in paragraph (1) does not include any period before the offer is accepted.

　(3) Exclusion of periods in interests of justice — If in any period a claimant is not paid due to reasons beyond the control of the responsible party or because it would not serve the interests of justice, no interest shall accrue under this section during that period.

　(4) Calculation of interest — The interest paid under this section shall be calculated at the average of the highest rate for commercial and finance company paper of maturities of 180 days or less obtaining on each of the days included within the period for which interest must be paid to the claimant, as published in the Federal Reserve Bulletin.

　(5) Interest not subject to liability limits

　　(A) In general — Interest (including prejudgment interest) under this paragraph is in addition to damages and removal costs for which claims may be asserted under section 2702 of this title and shall be paid without regard to any limitation of liability under section 2704 of this title.

　(B) Payment by guarantor — The payment of interest under this subsection by a guarantor is subject to section 2716(g) of this title.

§2706. Natural resources
[OPA §1006]

(a) Liability — In the case of natural resource damages under section 2702(b)(2)(A) of this title, liability shall be —

　(1) to the United States Government for natural resources belonging to, managed by, controlled by, or appertaining to the United States;

　(2) to any State for natural resources belonging to, managed by, controlled by, or appertaining to such State or political subdivision thereof;

　(3) to any Indian tribe for natural resources belonging to, managed by, controlled by, or appertaining to such Indian tribe; and

　(4) in any case in which section 2707 of this title applies, to the government of a foreign country for natural resources belonging to, managed by, controlled by, or appertaining to such country.

(b) Designation of trustees

　(1) In general — The President, or the authorized representative of any State, Indian tribe, or foreign government, shall act on behalf of the public, Indian tribe, or foreign country as trustee of natural resources to present a claim for and to recover damages to the natural resources.

　(2) Federal trustees — The President shall designate the Federal officials who shall act on behalf of the public as trustees for natural resources under this Act.

　(3) State trustees — The Governor of each State shall designate State and local officials who may act on behalf of the public as trustee for natural resources under this chapter and shall notify the President of the designation.

　(4) Indian tribe trustees — The governing body of any Indian tribe shall designate tribal officials who may act on behalf of the tribe or its members as trustee for natural resources under this chapter and shall notify the President of the designation.

　(5) Foreign trustees — The head of any foreign government may designate the trustee who shall act on behalf of that government as trustee for natural resources under this Act.

(c) Functions of trustees

　(1) Federal trustees — The Federal officials designated under subsection (b)(2) of this section —

　　(A) shall assess natural resource damages under section 2702(b)(2)(A) of this title for the natural resources under their trusteeship;

　　(B) may, upon request of and reimbursement from a State or Indian tribe and at the Federal officials' discretion, assess damages for the natural resources under the State's or tribe's trusteeship; and

　　(C) shall develop and implement a plan for the restoration, rehabilitation, replacement, or acquisition of the equivalent, of the natural resources under their trusteeship.

(2) State trustees — The State and local officials designated under subsection (b)(3) of this section —

　(A) shall assess natural resource damages under section 2702(b)(2)(A) of this title for the purposes of this chapter for the natural resources under their trusteeship; and

　(B) shall develop and implement a plan for the restoration, rehabilitation, replacement, or acquisition of the equivalent, of the natural resources under their trusteeship.

(3) Indian tribe trustees — The tribal officials designated under subsection (b)(4) of this section —

　(A) shall assess natural resource damages under section 2702(b)(2)(A) of this title for the purposes of this chapter for the natural resources under their trusteeship; and

　(B) shall develop and implement a plan for the restoration, rehabilitation, replacement, or acquisition of the equivalent, of the natural resources under their trusteeship.

(4) Foreign trustees — The trustees designated under subsection (b)(5) of this section —

　(A) shall assess natural resource damages under section 2702(b)(2)(A) of this title for the purposes of this chapter for the natural resources under their trusteeship; and

　(B) shall develop and implement a plan for the restoration, rehabilitation, replacement, or acquisition of the equivalent, of the natural resources under their trusteeship.

(5) Notice and opportunity to be heard — Plans shall be developed and implemented under this section only after adequate public notice, opportunity for a hearing, and consideration of all public comment.

(d) Measure of damages

(1) In general — The measure of natural resource damages under section 2702(b)(2)(A) of this title is —

　(A) the cost of restoring, rehabilitating, replacing, or acquiring the equivalent of, the damaged natural resources;

　(B) the diminution in value of those natural resources pending restoration; plus

　(C) the reasonable cost of assessing those damages.

(2) Determine costs with respect to plans — Costs shall be determined under paragraph (1) with respect to plans adopted under subsection (c) of this section.

(3) No double recovery — There shall be no double recovery under this chapter for natural resource damages, including with respect to the costs of damage assessment or restoration, rehabilitation, replacement, or acquisition for the same incident and natural resource.

(e) Damage assessment regulations

(1) Regulations — The President, acting through the Under Secretary of Commerce for Oceans and Atmosphere and in consultation with the Administrator of the Environmental Protection Agency, the Director of the United States Fish and Wildlife Service, and the heads of other affected agencies, not later than 2 years after August 18, 1990, shall promulgate regulations for the assessment of natural resource damages under section 2702(b)(2)(A) of this title resulting from a discharge of oil for the purpose of this Act.

(2) Rebuttable presumption — Any determination or assessment of damages to natural resources for the purposes of this Act made under subsection (d) of this section by a Federal, State, or Indian trustee in accordance with the regulations promulgated under paragraph (1) shall have the force and effect of a rebuttable presumption on behalf of the trustee in any administrative or judicial proceeding under this Act.

(f) Use of recovered sums — Sums recovered under this Act by a Federal, State, Indian, or foreign trustee for natural resource damages under section 2702(b)(2)(A) of this title shall be retained by the trustee in a revolving trust account, without further appropriation, for use only to reimburse or pay costs incurred by the trustee under subsection (c) of this section with respect to the damaged natural resources. Any amounts in excess of those required for these reimbursements and costs shall be deposited in the Fund.

(g) Compliance — Review of actions by any Federal official where there is alleged to be a failure of that official to perform a duty under this section that is not discretionary with that official may be had by any person in the district court in which the person resides or in which the alleged damage to natural resources occurred. The court may award costs of litigation (including reasonable attorney and expert witness fees) to any prevailing or substantially prevailing party. Nothing in this subsection shall restrict any right which any person may have to seek relief under any other provision of law.

§2707. Recovery by foreign claimants
[OPA §1007]
(a) Required showing by foreign claimants

(1) In general — In addition to satisfying the other requirements of this Act, to recover removal costs or damages resulting from an incident a foreign claimant shall demonstrate that —

　(A) the claimant has not been otherwise compensated for the removal costs or damages; and

　(B) recovery is authorized by a treaty or executive agreement between the United States and the claimant's country, or the Secretary of State, in consultation with the Attorney General and other appropriate officials, has certified that the claimant's country provides a comparable remedy for United States claimants.

(2) Exceptions — Paragraph (1)(B) shall not apply with respect to recovery by a resident of Canada in the case of an incident described in subsection (b)(4) of this section.

(b) **Discharges in foreign countries** — A foreign claimant may make a claim for removal costs and damages resulting from a discharge, or substantial threat of a discharge, of oil in or on the territorial sea, internal waters, or adjacent shoreline of a foreign country, only if the discharge is from —

(1) an Outer Continental Shelf facility or a deepwater port;

(2) a vessel in the navigable waters;

(3) a vessel carrying oil as cargo between 2 places in the United States; or

(4) a tanker that received the oil at the terminal of the pipeline constructed under the Trans-Alaska Pipeline Authorization Act (43 U.S.C. §§1651 *et seq.*), for transportation to a place in the United States, and the discharge or threat occurs prior to delivery of the oil to that place.

(c) **"Foreign claimant" defined** — In this section, the term "foreign claimant" means —

(1) a person residing in a foreign country;

(2) the government of a foreign country; and

(3) an agency or political subdivision of a foreign country.

§2708. Recovery by responsible party
[OPA §1008]

(a) **In general** — The responsible party for a vessel or facility from which oil is discharged, or which poses the substantial threat of a discharge of oil, may assert a claim for removal costs and damages under section 2713 of this title only if the responsible party demonstrates that —

(1) the responsible party is entitled to a defense to liability under section 2703 of this title; or

(2) the responsible party is entitled to a limitation of liability under section 2704 of this title.

(b) **Extent of recovery** — A responsible party who is entitled to a limitation of liability may assert a claim under section 2713 of this title only to the extent that the sum of the removal costs and damages incurred by the responsible party plus the amounts paid by the responsible party, or by the guarantor on behalf of the responsible party, for claims asserted under section 2713 of this title exceeds the amount to which the total of the liability under section 2702 of this title and removal costs and damages incurred by, or on behalf of, the responsible party is limited under section 2704 of this title.

§2709. Contribution
[OPA §1009]

A person may bring a civil action for contribution against any other person who is liable or potentially liable under this Act or another law. The action shall be brought in accordance with section 2717 of this title.

§2710. Indemnification agreements
[OPA §1010]

(a) **Agreements not prohibited** — Nothing in this Act prohibits any agreement to insure, hold harmless, or indemnify a party to such agreement for any liability under this Act.

(b) **Liability not transferred** — No indemnification, hold harmless, or similar agreement or conveyance shall be effective to transfer liability imposed under this Act from a responsible party or from any person who may be liable for an incident under this Act to any other person.

(c) **Relationship to other causes of action** — Nothing in this Act, including the provisions of subsection (b) of this section, bars a cause of action that a responsible party subject to liability under this Act, or a guarantor, has or would have, by reason of subrogation or otherwise, against any person.

§2711. Consultation on removal actions
[OPA §1011]

The President shall consult with the affected trustees designated under section 2706 of this title on the appropriate removal action to be taken in connection with any discharge of oil. For the purposes of the National Contingency Plan, removal with respect to any discharge shall be considered completed when so determined by the President in consultation with the Governor or Governors of the affected States. However, this determination shall not preclude additional removal actions under applicable State law.

§2712. Uses of Fund
[OPA §1012]

(a) **Uses generally** — The Fund shall be available to the President for —

(1) the payment of removal costs, including the costs of monitoring removal actions, determined by the President to be consistent with the National Contingency Plan —

(A) by Federal authorities; or

(B) by a Governor or designated State official under subsection (d) of this section;

(2) the payment of costs incurred by Federal, State, or Indian tribe trustees in carrying out their functions under section 2706 of this title for assessing natural resource damages and for developing and implementing plans for the restoration, rehabilitation, replacement, or acquisition of the equivalent of damaged resources determined by the President to be consistent with the National Contingency Plan;

(3) the payment of removal costs determined by the President to be consistent with the National

Contingency Plan as a result of, and damages resulting from, a discharge, or a substantial threat of a discharge, of oil from a foreign offshore unit;

(4) the payment of claims in accordance with section 2713 of this title for uncompensated removal costs determined by the President to be consistent with the National Contingency Plan or uncompensated damages; and

(5) the payment of Federal administrative, operational, and personnel costs and expenses reasonably necessary for and incidental to the implementation, administration, and enforcement of this Act (including, but not limited to, sections 1004(d)(2), 1006(e), 4107, 4110, 4111, 4112, 4117, 5006, 8103, and title VII) and subsections (b), (c), (d), (j), and (l) of section 1321 of this title with respect to prevention, removal, and enforcement related to oil discharges, provided that —

    (A) not more than $25,000,000 in each fiscal year shall be available to the Secretary for operations and support incurred by the Coast Guard;

    (B) not more than $15,000,000 in each fiscal year shall be available to the Under Secretary of Commerce for Oceans and Atmosphere for expenses incurred by, and activities related to, response and damage assessment capabilities of the National Oceanic and Atmospheric Administration;

    (C) not more than $30,000,000 each year through the end of fiscal year 1992 shall be available to establish the National Response System under section 1321(j) of this title, including the purchase and prepositioning of oil spill removal equipment; and

    (D) not more than $27,250,000 in each fiscal year shall be available to carry out subchapter IV of this chapter.

(b) Defense to liability for Fund — The Fund shall not be available to pay any claim for removal costs or damages to a particular claimant, to the extent that the incident, removal costs, or damages are caused by the gross negligence or willful misconduct of that claimant.

(c) Obligation of Fund by Federal officials — The President may promulgate regulations designating one or more Federal officials who may obligate money in accordance with subsection (a) of this section.

(d) Access to Fund by State officials

(1) Immediate removal — In accordance with regulations promulgated under this section, the President, upon the request of the Governor of a State or pursuant to an agreement with a State under paragraph (2), may obligate the Fund for payment in an amount not to exceed $250,000 for removal costs consistent with the National Contingency Plan required for the immediate removal of a discharge, or the mitigation or prevention of a substantial threat of a discharge, of oil.

(2) Agreements

    (A) In general — The President shall enter into an agreement with the Governor of any interested State to establish procedures under which the Governor or a designated State official may receive payments from the Fund for removal costs pursuant to paragraph (1).

    (B) Terms — Agreements under this paragraph —

        (i) may include such terms and conditions as may be agreed upon by the President and the Governor of a State;

        (ii) shall provide for political subdivisions of the State to receive payments for reasonable removal costs; and

        (iii) may authorize advance payments from the Fund to facilitate removal efforts.

(e) Regulations — The President shall —

(1) not later than 6 months after August 18, 1990, publish proposed regulations detailing the manner in which the authority to obligate the Fund and to enter into agreements under this subsection shall be exercised; and

(2) not later than 3 months after the close of the comment period for such proposed regulations, promulgate final regulations for that purpose.

(f) Rights of subrogation — Payment of any claim or obligation by the Fund under this Act shall be subject to the United States Government acquiring by subrogation all rights of the claimant or State to recover from the responsible party.

(g) Repealed. Pub. L. 115-282

(h) Period of limitations for claims

(1) Removal costs — No claim may be presented under this subchapter for recovery of removal costs for an incident unless the claim is presented within 6 years after the date of completion of all removal actions for that incident.

(2) Damages — No claim may be presented under this section for recovery of damages unless the claim is presented within 3 years after the date on which the injury and its connection with the discharge in question were reasonably discoverable with the exercise of due care, or in the case of natural resource damages under section 2702(b)(2)(A) of this title, if later, the date of completion of the natural resources damage assessment under section 2706(e) of this title.

(3) Minors and incompetents — The time limitations contained in this subsection shall not begin to run —

    (A) against a minor until the earlier of the date when such minor reaches 18 years of age or the date on which a legal representative is duly appointed for the minor, or

(B) against an incompetent person until the earlier of the date on which such incompetent's incompetency ends or the date on which a legal representative is duly appointed for the incompetent.

(i) Limitation on payment for same costs — In any case in which the President has paid an amount from the Fund for any removal costs or damages specified under subsection (a) of this section, no other claim may be paid from the Fund for the same removal costs or damages.

(j) Obligation in accordance with plan

(1) In general — Except as provided in paragraph (2), amounts may be obligated from the Fund for the restoration, rehabilitation, replacement, or acquisition of natural resources only in accordance with a plan adopted under section 2706(c) of this title.

(2) Exception — Paragraph (1) shall not apply in a situation requiring action to avoid irreversible loss of natural resources or to prevent or reduce any continuing danger to natural resources or similar need for emergency action.

(k) Preference for private persons in area affected by discharge

(1) In general — In the expenditure of Federal funds for removal of oil, including for distribution of supplies, construction, and other reasonable and appropriate activities, under a contract or agreement with a private person, preference shall be given, to the extent feasible and practicable, to private persons residing or doing business primarily in the area affected by the discharge of oil.

(2) Limitation — This subsection shall not be considered to restrict the use of Department of Defense resources.

(l) Reports

(1) In general — Each year, on the date on which the President submits to Congress a budget under section 1105 of title 31, United States Code, the President, through the Secretary of the Department in which the Coast Guard is operating, shall —

(A) provide a report on disbursements for the preceding fiscal year from the Fund, regardless of whether those disbursements were subject to annual appropriations, to —

(i) the Senate Committee on Commerce, Science, and Transportation; and

(ii) the House of Representatives Committee on Transportation and Infrastructure; and

(B) make the report available to the public on the National Pollution Funds Center Internet website.

(2) Contents

The report shall include —

(A) a list of each incident that —

(i) occurred in the preceding fiscal year; and

(ii) resulted in disbursements from the Fund, for removal costs and damages, totaling $500,000 or more;

(B) a list of each incident that —

(i) occurred in the fiscal year preceding the preceding fiscal year; and

(ii) resulted in disbursements from the Fund, for removal costs and damages, totaling $500,000 or more; and

(C) an accounting of any amounts reimbursed to the Fund in the preceding fiscal year that resulted in disbursements from the Fund, for removal costs and damages, totaling $500,000 or more.

(3) Agency recordkeeping — Each Federal agency that receives amounts from the Fund shall maintain records describing the purposes for which such funds were obligated or expended in such detail as the Secretary may require for purposes of the report required under paragraph (1).

§2713. Claims procedure
[OPA §1013]

(a) Presentation — Except as provided in subsection (b) of this section, all claims for removal costs or damages shall be presented first to the responsible party or guarantor of the source designated under section 2714(a) of this title.

(b) Presentation to Fund

(1) In general — Claims for removal costs or damages may be presented first to the Fund —

(A) if the President has advertised or otherwise notified claimants in accordance with section 2714(c) of this title;

(B) by a responsible party who may assert a claim under section 2708 of this title;

(C) by the Governor of a State for removal costs incurred by that State; or

(D) by a United States claimant in a case where a foreign offshore unit has discharged oil causing damage for which the Fund is liable under section 2712(a) of this title.

(2) Limitation on presenting claim — No claim of a person against the Fund may be approved or certified during the pendency of an action by the person in court to recover costs which are the subject of the claim.

(c) Election — If a claim is presented in accordance with subsection (a) of this section and —

(1) each person to whom the claim is presented denies all liability for the claim, or

(2) the claim is not settled by any person by payment within 90 days after the date upon which (A) the claim was presented, or (B) advertising was begun pursuant to section 2714(b) of this title, whichever is later,

the claimant may elect to commence an action in court against the responsible party or guarantor or to present the claim to the Fund.

(d) Uncompensated damages — If a claim is presented in accordance with this section, including a claim for interim, short-term damages representing less than the full amount of damages to which the claimant ultimately may be entitled, and full and adequate compensation is unavailable, a claim for the uncompensated damages and removal costs may be presented to the Fund.

(e) Procedure for claims against Fund — The President shall promulgate, and may from time to time amend, regulations for the presentation, filing, processing, settlement, and adjudication of claims under this Act against the Fund.

§2714. Designation of source and advertisement
[OPA §1014]

(a) Designation of source and notification — When the President receives information of an incident, the President shall, where possible and appropriate, designate the source or sources of the discharge or threat. If a designated source is a vessel or a facility, the President shall immediately notify the responsible party and the guarantor, if known, of that designation.

(b) Advertisement by responsible party or guarantor

(1) If a responsible party or guarantor fails to inform the President, within 5 days after receiving notification of a designation under subsection (a) of this section, of the party's or the guarantor's denial of the designation, such party or guarantor shall advertise the designation and the procedures by which claims may be presented, in accordance with regulations promulgated by the President. Advertisement under the preceding sentence shall begin no later than 15 days after the date of the designation made under subsection (a) of this section. If advertisement is not otherwise made in accordance with this subsection, the President shall promptly and at the expense of the responsible party or the guarantor involved, advertise the designation and the procedures by which claims may be presented to the responsible party or guarantor. Advertisement under this subsection shall continue for a period of no less than 30 days.

(2) An advertisement under paragraph (1) shall state that a claimant may present a claim for interim, short-term damages representing less than the full amount of damages to which the claimant ultimately may be entitled and that payment of such a claim shall not preclude recovery for damages not reflected in the paid or settled partial claim.

(c) Advertisement by President — If

(1) the responsible party and the guarantor both deny a designation within 5 days after receiving notification of a designation under subsection (a) of this section,

(2) the source of the discharge or threat was a public vessel, or

(3) the President is unable to designate the source or sources of the discharge or threat under subsection (a) of this section,

the President shall advertise or otherwise notify potential claimants of the procedures by which claims may be presented to the Fund.

§2715. Subrogation
[OPA §1015]

(a) In general — Any person, including the Fund, who pays compensation pursuant to this Act to any claimant for removal costs or damages shall be subrogated to all rights, claims, and causes of action that the claimant has under any other law.

(b) Interim damages

(1) In general — If a responsible party, a guarantor, or the Fund has made payment to a claimant for interim, short-term damages representing less than the full amount of damages to which the claimant ultimately may be entitled, subrogation under subsection (a) of this section shall apply only with respect to the portion of the claim reflected in the paid interim claim.

(2) Final damages — Payment of such a claim shall not foreclose a claimant's right to recovery of all damages to which the claimant otherwise is entitled under this Act or under any other law.

(c) Actions on behalf of Fund — At the request of the Secretary, the Attorney General shall commence an action on behalf of the Fund to recover any compensation paid by the Fund to any claimant pursuant to this chapter, and all costs incurred by the Fund by reason of the claim, including interest (including prejudgment interest), administrative and adjudicative costs, and attorney's fees. Such an action may be commenced against any responsible party or (subject to section 2716 of this title) guarantor, or against any other person who is liable, pursuant to any law, to the compensated claimant or to the Fund, for the cost or damages for which the compensation was paid. Such an action shall be commenced against the responsible foreign government or other responsible party to recover any removal costs or damages paid from the Fund as the result of the discharge, or substantial threat of discharge, of oil from a foreign offshore unit or other facility located seaward of the exclusive economic zone.

(d) Authority to settle — The head of any department or agency responsible for recovering amounts for which a person is liable under this title may consider, compromise, and settle a claim for such amounts, including such costs paid from the Fund, if the claim has not been referred to the Attorney General. In any case in which the total amount to be recovered may exceed $500,000 (excluding interest), a claim may be compromised and settled under the preceding sentence only with the prior written approval of the Attorney General.

§2716. Financial responsibility
[OPA §1016]

(a) Requirement — The responsible party for —

(1) any vessel over 300 gross tons (except a non-self-propelled vessel that does not carry oil as cargo or fuel) using any place subject to the jurisdiction of the United States;

(2) any vessel using the waters of the exclusive economic zone to transship or lighter oil destined for a place subject to the jurisdiction of the United States; or

(3) any tank vessel over 100 gross tons using any place subject to the jurisdiction of the United States;

shall establish and maintain, in accordance with regulations promulgated by the Secretary, evidence of financial responsibility sufficient to meet the maximum amount of liability to which the responsible party could be subjected under section 2704(a) or (d) of this title, in a case where the responsible party would be entitled to limit liability under that section. If the responsible party owns or operates more than one vessel, evidence of financial responsibility need be established only to meet the amount of the maximum liability applicable to the vessel having the greatest maximum liability.

(b) Sanctions

(1) Withholding clearance —

The Secretary of the Treasury shall withhold or revoke the clearance required by section 60105 of Title 46 of any vessel subject to this section that does not have the evidence of financial responsibility required for the vessel under this section.

(2) Denying entry to or detaining vessels — The Secretary may —

(A) deny entry to any vessel to any place in the United States, or to the navigable waters, or

(B) detain at the place,

any vessel that, upon request, does not produce the evidence of financial responsibility required for the vessel under this section.

(3) Seizure of vessel — Any vessel subject to the requirements of this section which is found in the navigable waters without the necessary evidence of financial responsibility for the vessel shall be subject to seizure by and forfeiture to the United States.

(c) Offshore facilities

(1) In general

(A) Evidence of financial responsibility required — Except as provided in paragraph (2), a responsible party with respect to an offshore facility that —

(i)(I) is located seaward of the line of ordinary low water along that portion of the coast that is in direct contact with the open sea and the line marking the seaward limit of inland waters; or

(II) is located in coastal inland waters, such as bays or estuaries, seaward of the line of ordinary low water along that portion of the coast that is not in direct contact with the open sea;

(ii) is used for exploring for, drilling for, producing, or transporting oil from facilities engaged in oil exploration, drilling, or production; and

(iii) has a worst-case oil spill discharge potential of more than 1,000 barrels of oil (or a lesser amount if the President determines that the risks posed by such facility justify it),

shall establish and maintain evidence of financial responsibility in the amount required under subparagraph (B) or (C), as applicable.

(B) Amount required generally — Except as provided in subparagraph (C), the amount of financial responsibility for offshore facilities that meet the criteria of subparagraph (A) is —

(i) $35,000,000 for an offshore facility located seaward of the seaward boundary of a State; or

(ii) $10,000,000 for an offshore facility located landward of the seaward boundary of a State.

(C) Greater amount — If the President determines that an amount of financial responsibility for a responsible party greater than the amount required by subparagraph (B) is justified based on the relative operational, environmental, human health, and other risks posed by the quantity or quality of oil that is explored for, drilled for, produced, or transported by the responsible party, the evidence of financial responsibility required shall be for an amount determined by the President not exceeding $150,000,000.

(D) Multiple facilities — In a case in which a person is a responsible party for more than one facility subject to this subsection, evidence of financial responsibility need be established only to meet the amount applicable to the facility having the greatest financial responsibility requirement under this subsection.

(E) Definition — For the purpose of this paragraph, the seaward boundary of a State shall be determined in accordance with section 1301(b) of Title 43.

(2) Deepwater ports — Each responsible party with respect to a deepwater port shall establish and maintain evidence of financial responsibility sufficient to meet the maximum amount of

liability to which the responsible party could be subjected under section 2704(a) of this title in a case where the responsible party would be entitled to limit liability under that section. If the Secretary exercises the authority under section 2704(d)(2) of this title to lower the limit of liability for deepwater ports, the responsible party shall establish and maintain evidence of financial responsibility sufficient to meet the maximum amount of liability so established. In a case in which a person is the responsible party for more than one deepwater port, evidence of financial responsibility need be established only to meet the maximum liability applicable to the deepwater port having the greatest maximum liability.

(e) Methods of financial responsibility

Financial responsibility under this section may be established by any one, or by any combination, of the following methods which the Secretary (in the case of a vessel) or the President (in the case of a facility) determines to be acceptable: evidence of insurance, surety bond, guarantee, letter of credit, qualification as a self-insurer, or other evidence of financial responsibility. Any bond filed shall be issued by a bonding company authorized to do business in the United States. In promulgating requirements under this section, the Secretary or the President, as appropriate, may specify policy or other contractual terms, conditions, or defenses which are necessary, or which are unacceptable, in establishing evidence of financial responsibility to effectuate the purposes of this chapter.

(f) Claims against guarantor

(1) In general — Subject to paragraph (2), a claim for which liability may be established under section 2702 of this title may be asserted directly against any guarantor providing evidence of financial responsibility for a responsible party liable under that section for removal costs and damages to which the claim pertains. In defending against such a claim, the guarantor may invoke —

(A) all rights and defenses which would be available to the responsible party under this Act;

(B) any defense authorized under subsection (e) of this section; and

(C) the defense that the incident was caused by the willful misconduct of the responsible party.

The guarantor may not invoke any other defense that might be available in proceedings brought by the responsible party against the guarantor.

(2) Further requirement — A claim may be asserted pursuant to paragraph (1) directly against a guarantor providing evidence of financial responsibility under subsection (c)(1) of this section with respect to an offshore facility only if —

(A) the responsible party for whom evidence of financial responsibility has been provided has denied or failed to pay a claim under this chapter on the basis of being insolvent, as defined under section 101(32) of Title 11, and applying generally accepted accounting principles;

(B) the responsible party for whom evidence of financial responsibility has been provided has filed a petition for bankruptcy under Title 11; or

(C) the claim is asserted by the United States for removal costs and damages or for compensation paid by the Fund under this chapter, including costs incurred by the Fund for processing compensation claims.

(3) Rulemaking authority — Not later than 1 year after the October 19, 1996, the President shall promulgate regulations to establish a process for implementing paragraph (2) in a manner that will allow for the orderly and expeditious presentation and resolution of claims and effectuate the purposes of this Act.

(g) Limitation on guarantor's liability — Nothing in this chapter shall impose liability with respect to an incident on any guarantor for damages or removal costs which exceed, in the aggregate, the amount of financial responsibility which that guarantor has provided for a responsible party pursuant to this section. The total liability of the guarantor on direct action for claims brought under this chapter with respect to an incident shall be limited to that amount.

(h) Continuation of regulations — Any regulation relating to financial responsibility, which has been issued pursuant to any provision of law repealed or superseded by this chapter, and which is in effect on the date immediately preceding the effective date of this Act, is deemed and shall be construed to be a regulation issued pursuant to this section. Such a regulation shall remain in full force and effect unless and until superseded by a new regulation issued under this section.

(i) Unified certificate — The Secretary may issue a single unified certificate of financial responsibility for purposes of this Act and any other law.

§2716a. Financial responsibility civil penalties

[OPA §4303]

(a) Administrative — Any person who, after notice and an opportunity for a hearing, is found to have failed to comply with the requirements of section 2716 of this title or the regulations issued under that section, or with a denial or detention order issued under subsection (b)(2) of that section, shall be liable to the United States for a civil penalty, not to exceed $25,000 per day of violation. The amount of the civil penalty shall be assessed by the President by written notice. In determining the amount of the penalty, the President shall take into account the nature, circumstances, extent, and gravity of the violation, the degree of culpability, any history of prior violation, ability to pay, and such other matters as justice may require. The President may compromise, modify, or remit, with or without conditions, any civil penalty which is subject to imposition or which had been imposed under this paragraph. If any person fails to pay an assessed civil penalty after it has become final, the President may refer the matter to the Attorney General for collection.

(b) Judicial — In addition to, or in lieu of, assessing a penalty under subsection (a) of this section, the President may request the Attorney General to secure such relief as necessary to compel compliance with section 2716 of this title, including a judicial order terminating operations. The district courts of the United States shall have jurisdiction to grant any relief as the public interest and the equities of the case may require.

§2717. Litigation, jurisdiction, and venue
[OPA §1017]

(a) Review of regulations — Review of any regulation promulgated under this chapter may be had upon application by any interested person only in the Circuit Court of Appeals of the United States for the District of Columbia. Any such application shall be made within 90 days from the date of promulgation of such regulations. Any matter with respect to which review could have been obtained under this subsection shall not be subject to judicial review in any civil or criminal proceeding for enforcement or to obtain damages or recovery of response costs.

(b) Jurisdiction — Except as provided in subsections (a) and (c) of this section, the United States district courts shall have exclusive original jurisdiction over all controversies arising under this chapter, without regard to the citizenship of the parties or the amount in controversy. Venue shall lie in any district in which the discharge or injury or damages occurred, or in which the defendant resides, may be found, has its principal office, or has appointed an agent for service of process. For the purposes of this section, the Fund shall reside in the District of Columbia.

(c) State court jurisdiction — A State trial court of competent jurisdiction over claims for removal costs or damages, as defined under this Act, may consider claims under this Act or State law and any final judgment of such court (when no longer subject to ordinary forms of review) shall be recognized, valid, and enforceable for all purposes of this Act.

(d) Assessment and collection of tax — The provisions of subsections (a), (b), and (c) of this section shall not apply to any controversy or other matter resulting from the assessment or collection of any tax, or to the review of any regulation promulgated under Title 26.

(e) Savings provision — Nothing in this title shall apply to any cause of action or right of recovery arising from any incident which occurred prior to August 18, 1990. Such claims shall be adjudicated pursuant to the law applicable on the date of the incident.

(f) Period of limitations

(1) Damages — Except as provided in paragraphs (3) and (4), an action for damages under this Act shall be barred unless the action is brought within 3 years after —

(A) the date on which the loss and the connection of the loss with the discharge in question are reasonably discoverable with the exercise of due care, or

(B) in the case of natural resource damages under section 2702(b)(2)(A) of this title, the date of completion of the natural resources damage assessment under section 2706(c) of this title.

(2) Removal costs — An action for recovery of removal costs referred to in section 2702(b)(1) of this title must be commenced within 3 years after completion of the removal action. In any such action described in this subsection, the court shall enter a declaratory judgment on liability for removal costs or damages that will be binding on any subsequent action or actions to recover further removal costs or damages. Except as otherwise provided in this paragraph, an action may be commenced under this subchapter for recovery of removal costs at any time after such costs have been incurred.

(3) Contribution — No action for contribution for any removal costs or damages may be commenced more than 3 years after —

(A) the date of judgment in any action under this chapter for recovery of such costs or damages, or

(B) the date of entry of a judicially approved settlement with respect to such costs or damages.

(4) Subrogation — No action based on rights subrogated pursuant to this chapter by reason of payment of a claim may be commenced under this chapter more than 3 years after the date of payment of such claim.

(5) Commencement — The time limitations contained herein shall not begin to run —

(A) against a minor until the earlier of the date when such minor reaches 18 years of age or the date on which a legal representative is duly appointed for such minor, or

(B) against an incompetent person until the earlier of the date on which such incompetent's incompetency ends or the date on which a legal representative is duly appointed for such incompetent.

§2718. Relationship to other law
[OPA §1018]

(a) Preservation of State authorities; Solid Waste Disposal Act — Nothing in this Act or the Act of March 3, 1851 shall —

(1) affect, or be construed or interpreted as preempting, the authority of any State or political subdivision thereof from imposing any additional liability or requirements with respect to —

(A) the discharge of oil or other pollution by oil within such State; or

(B) any removal activities in connection with such a discharge; or

(2) affect, or be construed or interpreted to affect or modify in any way the obligations or liabilities of any person under the Solid Waste Disposal Act (42 U.S.C. §§6901 *et seq.*) or State law, including common law.

(b) Preservation of State funds — Nothing in this Act or in section 9509 of Title 26 shall in any way affect, or be construed to affect, the authority of any State —

(1) to establish, or to continue in effect, a fund any purpose of which is to pay for costs or damages arising out of, or directly resulting from, oil pollution or the substantial threat of oil pollution; or

(2) to require any person to contribute to such a fund.

(c) Additional requirements and liabilities; penalties — Nothing in this chapter, the Act of March 3, 1851 (46 U.S.C. §§183 *et seq.*), or section 9509 of Title 26, shall in any way affect, or be construed to affect, the authority of the United States or any State or political subdivision thereof —

(1) to impose additional liability or additional requirements; or

(2) to impose, or to determine the amount of, any fine or penalty (whether criminal or civil in nature) for any violation of law;

relating to the discharge, or substantial threat of a discharge, of oil.

(d) Federal employee liability — For purposes of section 2679(b)(2)(B) of Title 28, nothing in this Act shall be construed to authorize or create a cause of action against a Federal officer or employee in the officer's or employee's personal or individual capacity for any act or omission while acting within the scope of the officer's or employee's office or employment.

§2719. State financial responsibility
[OPA §1019]

A State may enforce, on the navigable waters of the State, the requirements for evidence of financial responsibility under section 2716 of this title.

§2720. Differentiation among fats, oils, and greases

(a) In general — Except as provided in subsection (c) of this section, in issuing or enforcing any regulation or establishing any interpretation or guideline relating to the transportation, storage, discharge, release, emission, or disposal of a fat, oil, or grease under any Federal law, the head of that Federal agency shall —

(1) differentiate between and establish separate classes for —

(A) animal fats and oils and greases, and fish and marine mammal oils, within the meaning of paragraph (2) of section 61(a) of Title 13, and oils of vegetable origin, including oils from the seeds, nuts, and kernels referred to in paragraph (1)(A) of that section; and

(B) other oils and greases, including petroleum; and

(2) apply standards to different classes of fats and oils based on considerations in subsection (b) of this section.

(b) Considerations — In differentiating between the class of fats, oils, and greases described in subsection (a)(1)(A) of this section and the class of oils and greases described in subsection (a)(1)(B) of this section, the head of the Federal agency shall consider differences in the physical, chemical, biological, and other properties, and in the environmental effects, of the classes.

(c) Exception — The requirements of this Act shall not apply to the Food and Drug Administration and the Food Safety and Inspection Service.

(d) Omitted.

SUBCHAPTER II — PRINCE WILLIAM SOUND PROVISIONS

§2731. Oil Spill Recovery Institute
[OPA §5001]

(a) Establishment of Institute — The Secretary of Commerce shall provide for the establishment of a Prince William Sound Oil Spill Recovery Institute (hereinafter in this section referred to as the "Institute") through the Prince William Sound Science and Technology Institute located in Cordova, Alaska.

(b) Functions — The Institute shall conduct research and carry out educational and demonstration projects designed to —

(1) identify and develop the best available techniques, equipment, and materials for dealing with oil spills in the arctic and subarctic marine environment; and

(2) complement Federal and State damage assessment efforts and determine, document, assess, and understand the long-range effects of Arctic or Subarctic oil spills on the natural resources of Prince William Sound and its adjacent waters (as generally depicted on the map entitled "EXXON

VALDEZ oil spill dated March 1990"), and the environment, the economy, and the lifestyle and well-being of the people who are dependent on them, except that the Institute shall not conduct studies or make recommendations on any matter which is not directly related to Arctic or Subarctic oil spills or the effects thereof.

(c) Advisory board

(1) In general — The policies of the Institute shall be determined by an advisory board, composed of 16 members appointed as follows:

(A) One representative appointed by each of the Commissioners of Fish and Game, Environmental Conservation, and Natural Resources of the State of Alaska, all of whom shall be State employees.

(B) One representative appointed by each of the Secretaries of Commerce and the Interior and the Commandant of the Coast Guard, who shall be Federal employees.

(C) Two representatives from the fishing industry appointed by the Governor of the State of Alaska from among residents of communities in Alaska that were affected by the EXXON VALDEZ oil spill, who shall serve terms of 2 years each. Interested organizations from within the fishing industry may submit the names of qualified individuals for consideration by the Governor.

(D) Two Alaska Natives who represent Native entities affected by the EXXON VALDEZ oil spill, at least one of whom represents an entity located in Prince William Sound, appointed by the Governor of Alaska from a list of 4 qualified individuals submitted by the Alaska Federation of Natives, who shall serve terms of 2 years each.

(E) Two representatives from the oil and gas industry to be appointed by the Governor of the State of Alaska who shall serve terms of 2 years each. Interested organizations from within the oil and gas industry may submit the names of qualified individuals for consideration by the Governor.

(F) Two at-large representatives from among residents of communities in Alaska that were affected by the EXXON VALDEZ oil spill who are knowledgeable about the marine environment and wildlife within Prince William Sound, and who shall serve terms of 2 years each, appointed by the remaining members of the Advisory Board. Interested parties may submit the names of qualified individuals for consideration by the Advisory Board.

(G) One nonvoting representative of the Institute of Marine Science.

(H) One nonvoting representative appointed by the Prince William Sound Science and Technology Institute.

(2) Chairman — The representative of the Secretary of Commerce shall serve as Chairman of the Advisory Board.

(3) Policies — Policies determined by the Advisory Board under this subsection shall include policies for the conduct and support, through contracts and grants awarded on a nationally competitive basis, of research, projects, and studies to be supported by the Institute in accordance with the purposes of this section.

(4) Scientific review — The Advisory Board may request a scientific review of the research program every five years by the National Academy of Sciences which shall perform the review, if requested, as part of its responsibilities under section 2761(b)(2) of this title.

(d) Scientific and technical committee

(1) In general — The Advisory Board shall establish a scientific and technical committee, composed of specialists in matters relating to oil spill containment and cleanup technology, arctic and subarctic marine ecology, and the living resources and socioeconomics of Prince William Sound and its adjacent waters, from the University of Alaska, the Institute of Marine Science, the Prince William Sound Science and Technology Institute, and elsewhere in the academic community.

(2) Functions — The Scientific and Technical Committee shall provide such advice to the Advisory Board as the Advisory Board shall request, including recommendations regarding the conduct and support of research, projects, and studies in accordance with the purposes of this section. The Advisory Board shall not request, and the Committee shall not provide, any advice which is not directly related to Arctic or Subarctic oil spills or the effects thereof.

(e) Director — The Institute shall be administered by a Director appointed by the Advisory Board. The Prince William Sound Science and Technology Institute and the Scientific and Technical Committee may each submit independent recommendations for the Advisory Board's consideration for appointment as Director. The Director may hire such staff and incur such expenses on behalf of the Institute as are authorized by the Advisory Board.

(f) Evaluation — The Secretary of Commerce may conduct an ongoing evaluation of the activities of the Institute to ensure that funds received by the Institute are used in a manner consistent with this section.

(g) Audit — The Comptroller General of the United States, and any of his or her duly authorized representatives, shall have access, for purposes of audit and examination, to any books, documents, papers, and records of the Institute and its administering agency that are pertinent to the funds received and expended by the Institute and its administering agency.

(h) Status of employees — Employees of the Institute shall not, by reason of such employment, be considered to be employees of the Federal Government for any purpose.

(i) Termination — The authorization in section 2736(b) of this title providing funding for the Institute shall terminate 1 year after the date on which the Secretary, in consulation with the Secretary of Interior, determines that oil and gas exploration, development, and production in the state of Alaska have ceased.

(j) Use of funds — No funds made available to carry out this section may be used to initiate litigation. No funds made available to carry out this section may be used for the acquisition of real property (including buildings) or construction of any building. No more than 20 percent of funds made available to carry out this section may be used to lease necessary facilities and to administer the Institute. The Advisory Board may compensate its Federal representatives for their reasonable travel costs. None of the funds authorized by this section shall be used for any purpose other than the functions specified in subsection (b) of this section.

(k) Research — The Institute shall publish and make available to any person upon request the results of all research, educational, and demonstration projects conducted by the Institute. The Administrator shall provide a copy of all research, educational, and demonstration projects conducted by the Institute to the National Oceanic and Atmospheric Administration.

(l) "Prince William Sound and its adjacent waters" defined — In this section, the term "Prince William Sound and its adjacent waters" means such sound and waters as generally depicted on the map entitled "EXXON VALDEZ oil spill dated March 1990".

§2732. Terminal and tanker oversight and monitoring

[OPA §5002]
(a) Short title and findings

(1) Short title — This section may be cited as the "Oil Terminal and Oil Tanker Environmental Oversight and Monitoring Act of 1990".

(2) Findings — The Congress finds that —

(A) the March 24, 1989, grounding and rupture of the fully loaded oil tanker, the EXXON VALDEZ, spilled 11 million gallons of crude oil in Prince William Sound, an environmentally sensitive area;

(B) many people believe that complacency on the part of the industry and government personnel responsible for monitoring the operation of the Valdez terminal and vessel traffic in Prince William Sound was one of the contributing factors to the EXXON VALDEZ oil spill;

(C) one way to combat this complacency is to involve local citizens in the process of preparing, adopting, and revising oil spill contingency plans;

(D) a mechanism should be established which fosters the long-term partnership of industry, government, and local communities in overseeing compliance with environmental concerns in the operation of crude oil terminals;

(E) such a mechanism presently exists at the Sullom Voe terminal in the Shetland Islands and this terminal should serve as a model for others;

(F) because of the effective partnership that has developed at Sullom Voe, Sullom Voe is considered the safest terminal in Europe;

(G) the present system of regulation and oversight of crude oil terminals in the United States has degenerated into a process of continual mistrust and confrontation.

(H) only when local citizens are involved in the process will the trust develop that is necessary to change the present system from confrontation to consensus;

(I) a pilot program patterned after Sullom Voe should be established in Alaska to further refine the concepts and relationships involved; and

(J) similar programs should eventually be established in other major crude oil terminals in the United States because the recent oil spills in Texas, Delaware, and Rhode Island indicate that the safe transportation of crude oil is a national problem.

(b) Demonstration programs

(1) Establishment — There are established 2 Oil Terminal and Oil Tanker Environmental Oversight and Monitoring Demonstration Programs (hereinafter referred to as "Programs") to be carried out in the State of Alaska.

(2) Advisory function — The function of these Programs shall be advisory only.

(3) Purpose — The Prince William Sound Program shall be responsible for environmental monitoring of the terminal facilities in Prince William Sound and the crude oil tankers operating in Prince William Sound. The Cook Inlet Program shall be responsible for environmental monitoring of the terminal facilities and crude oil tankers operating in Cook Inlet located South of the latitude at Point Possession and North of the latitude at Amatuli Island, including offshore facilities in Cook Inlet.

(4) Suits barred — No program, association, council, committee or other organization created by this section may sue any person or entity, public or private, concerning any matter arising under this section except for the performance of contracts.

(c) Oil Terminal Facilities and Oil Tanker Operations Association

(1) Establishment — There is established an Oil Terminal Facilities and Oil Tanker Operations Association (hereinafter in this section referred to as the "Association") for each of the Programs established under subsection (b) of this section.

(2) Membership — Each Association shall be comprised of 4 individuals as follows:

(A) One individual shall be designated by the owners and operators of the terminal facilities and shall represent those owners and operators.

(B) One individual shall be designated by the owners and operators of the crude oil tankers calling at the terminal facilities and shall represent those owners and operators.

(C) One individual shall be an employee of the State of Alaska, shall be designated by the Governor of the State of Alaska, and shall represent the State government.

(D) One individual shall be an employee of the Federal Government, shall be designated by the President, and shall represent the Federal Government.

(3) Responsibilities — Each Association shall be responsible for reviewing policies relating to the operation and maintenance of the oil terminal facilities and crude oil tankers which affect or may affect the environment in the vicinity of their respective terminals. Each Association shall provide a forum among the owners and operators of the terminal facilities, the owners and operators of crude oil tankers calling at those facilities, the United States, and the State of Alaska to discuss and to make recommendations concerning all permits, plans, and site-specific regulations governing the activities and actions of the terminal facilities which affect or may affect the environment in the vicinity of the terminal facilities and of crude oil tankers calling at those facilities.

(4) Designation of existing organization — The Secretary may designate an existing nonprofit organization as an Association under this subsection if the organization is organized to meet the purposes of this section and consists of at least the individuals listed in paragraph (2).

(d) Regional Citizens' Advisory Councils

(1) Membership — There is established a Regional Citizens' Advisory Council (hereinafter in this section referred to as the "Council") for each of the programs established by subsection (b) of this section.

(2) Membership — Each Council shall be composed of voting members and nonvoting members, as follows:

(A) Voting members — Voting members shall be Alaska residents and, except as provided in clause (vii) of this paragraph, shall

be appointed by the Governor of the State of Alaska from a list of nominees provided by each of the following interests, with one representative appointed to represent each of the following interests, taking into consideration the need for regional balance on the Council:

(i) Local commercial fishing industry organizations, the members of which depend on the fisheries resources of the waters in the vicinity of the terminal facilities.

(ii) Aquaculture associations in the vicinity of the terminal facilities.

(iii) Alaska Native Corporations and other Alaska Native organizations the members of which reside in the vicinity of the terminal facilities.

(iv) Environmental organizations the members of which reside in the vicinity of the terminal facilities.

(v) Recreational organizations the members of which reside in or use the vicinity of the terminal facilities.

(vi) The Alaska State Chamber of Commerce, to represent the locally based tourist industry.

(vii)(I) For the Prince William Sound Terminal Facilities Council, one representative selected by each of the following municipalities: Cordova, Whittier, Seward, Valdez, Kodiak, the Kodiak Island Borough, and the Kenai Peninsula Borough.

(II) For the Cook Inlet Terminal Facilities Council, one representative selected by each of the following municipalities: Homer, Seldovia, Anchorage, Kenai, Kodiak, the Kodiak Island Borough, and the Kenai Peninsula Borough.

(B) Nonvoting members — One ex-officio, nonvoting representative shall be designated by, and represent, each of the following:

(i) The Environmental Protection Agency.

(ii) The Coast Guard.

(iii) The National Oceanic and Atmospheric Administration.

(iv) The United States Forest Service.

(v) The Bureau of Land Management.

(vi) The Alaska Department of Environmental Conservation.

(vii) The Alaska Department of Fish and Game.

(viii) The Alaska Department of Natural Resources.

(ix) The Division of Emergency Services, Alaska Department of Military and Veterans Affairs.

(3) Terms

(A) Duration of Councils — The term of the Councils shall continue throughout the life of the operation of the Trans-Alaska Pipeline System and so long as oil is transported to or from Cook Inlet.

(B) Three years — The voting members of each Council shall be appointed for a term of 3 years except as provided for in subparagraph (C).

(C) Initial appointments — The terms of the first appointments shall be as follows:

(i) For the appointments by the Governor of the State of Alaska, one-third shall serve for 3 years, one-third shall serve for 2 years, and one-third shall serve for one year.

(ii) For the representatives of municipalities required by subsection (d)(2)(A)(vii) of this section, a drawing of lots among the appointees shall determine that one-third of that group serves for 3 years, one-third serves for 2 years, and the remainder serves for 1 year.

(4) Self-governing — Each Council shall elect its own chairperson, select its own staff, and make policies with regard to its internal operating procedures. After the initial organizational meeting called by the Secretary under subsection (i) of this section, each Council shall be self-governing.

(5) Dual membership and conflicts of interest prohibited

(A) No individual selected as a member of the Council shall serve on the Association.

(B) No individual selected as a voting member of the Council shall be engaged in any activity which might conflict with such individual carrying out his functions as a member thereof.

(6) Duties — Each Council shall —

(A) provide advice and recommendations to the Association on policies, permits, and site-specific regulations relating to the operation and maintenance of terminal facilities and crude oil tankers which affect or may affect the environment in the vicinity of the terminal facilities;

(B) monitor through the committee established under subsection (e) of this section, the environmental impacts of the operation of the terminal facilities and crude oil tankers;

(C) monitor those aspects of terminal facilities' and crude oil tankers' operations and maintenance which affect or may affect the environment in the vicinity of the terminal facilities;

(D) review through the committee established under subsection (f) of this section, the adequacy of oil spill prevention and contingency plans for the terminal facilities and the adequacy of oil spill prevention and contingency plans for crude oil tankers, operating in Prince William Sound or in Cook Inlet;

(E) provide advice and recommendations to the Association on port operations, policies and practices;

(F) recommend to the Association —

(i) standards and stipulations for permits and site-specific regulations intended to minimize the impact of the terminal facilities' and crude oil tankers' operations in the vicinity of the terminal facilities;

(ii) modifications of terminal facility operations and maintenance intended to minimize the risk and mitigate the impact of terminal facilities, operations in the vicinity of the terminal facilities and to minimize the risk of oil spills;

(iii) modifications of crude oil tanker operations and maintenance in Prince William Sound and Cook Inlet intended to minimize the risk and mitigate the impact of oil spills; and

(iv) modifications to the oil spill prevention and contingency plans for terminal facilities and for crude oil tankers in Prince William Sound and Cook Inlet intended to enhance the ability to prevent and respond to an oil spill; and

(G) create additional committees of the Council as necessary to carry out the above functions, including a scientific and technical advisory committee to the Prince William Sound Council.

(7) No estoppel — No Council shall be held liable under State or Federal law for costs or damages as a result of rendering advice under this section. Nor shall any advice given by a voting member of a Council, or program representative or agent, be grounds for estopping the interests represented by the voting Council members from seeking damages or other appropriate relief.

(8) Scientific work — In carrying out its research, development and monitoring functions, each Council is authorized to conduct its own scientific research and shall review the scientific work undertaken by or on behalf of the terminal operators or crude oil tanker operators as a result of a legal requirement to undertake that work. Each Council shall also review the relevant scientific work undertaken by or on behalf of any government entity relating to the terminal facilities or crude oil tankers. To the extent possible, to avoid unnecessary duplication, each Council shall coordinate its independent scientific work with the scientific work performed by or on behalf of the terminal operators and with the scientific work performed by or on behalf of the operators of the crude oil tankers.

(e) Committee for Terminal and Oil Tanker Operations and Environmental Monitoring

(1) Monitoring Committee — Each Council shall establish standing Terminal and Oil Tanker Operations and Environmental Monitoring Committee (hereinafter in this section referred to as the "Monitoring Committee") to devise and manage a comprehensive program of monitoring the environmental impacts of the operations of terminal facilities and of crude oil tankers while operating in Prince William Sound and Cook Inlet. The membership of the Monitoring Committee shall be made up of members of the Council, citizens, and recognized scientific experts selected by the Council.

(2) Duties — In fulfilling its responsibilities, the Monitoring Committee shall —

(A) advise the Council on a monitoring strategy that will permit early detection of environmental impacts of terminal facility operations and crude oil tanker operations while in Prince William Sound and Cook Inlet;

(B) develop monitoring programs and make recommendations to the Council on the implementation of those programs;

(C) at its discretion, select and contract with universities and other scientific institutions to carry out specific monitoring projects authorized by the Council pursuant to an approved monitoring strategy;

(D) complete any other tasks assigned by the Council; and

(E) provide written reports to the Council which interpret and assess the results of all monitoring programs.

(f) Committee for Oil Spill Prevention, Safety, and Emergency Response

(1) Technical Oil Spill Committee — Each Council shall establish a standing technical committee (hereinafter referred to as "Oil Spill Committee") to review and assess measures designed to prevent oil spills and the planning and preparedness for responding to, containing, cleaning up, and mitigating impacts of oil spills. The membership of the Oil Spill Committee shall be made up of members of the Council, citizens, and recognized technical experts selected by the Council.

(2) Duties — In fulfilling its responsibilities, the Oil Spill Committee shall —

(A) periodically review the respective oil spill prevention and contingency plans for the terminal facilities and for the crude oil tankers while in Prince William Sound or Cook Inlet, in light of new technological developments and changed circumstances;

(B) monitor periodic drills and testing of the oil spill contingency plans for the terminal facilities and for crude oil tankers while in Prince William Sound and Cook Inlet;

(C) study wind and water currents and other environmental factors in the vicinity of the terminal facilities which may affect the ability to prevent, respond to, contain, and clean up an oil spill;

(D) identify highly sensitive areas which may require specific protective measures in the event of a spill in Prince William Sound or Cook Inlet;

(E) monitor developments in oil spill prevention, containment, response, and cleanup technology;

(F) periodically review port organization, operations, incidents, and the adequacy and maintenance of vessel traffic service systems designed to assure safe transit of crude oil tankers pertinent to terminal operations;

(G) periodically review the standards for tankers bound for, loading at, exiting from, or otherwise using the terminal facilities;

(H) complete any other tasks assigned by the Council; and

(I) provide written reports to the Council outlining its findings and recommendations.

(g) Agency cooperation — On and after the expiration of the 180-day period following August 18, 1990, each Federal department, agency, or other instrumentality shall, with respect to all permits, site-specific regulations, and other matters governing the activities and actions of the terminal facilities which affect or may affect the vicinity of the terminal facilities, consult with the appropriate Council prior to taking substantive action with respect to the permit, site-specific regulation, or other matter. This consultation shall be carried out with a view to enabling the appropriate Association and Council to review the permit, site-specific regulation, or other matters and make appropriate recommendations regarding operations, policy or agency actions. Prior consultation shall not be required if an authorized Federal agency representative reasonably believes that an emergency exists requiring action without delay.

(h) Recommendations of Council — In the event that the Association does not adopt, or significantly modifies before adoption, any recommendation of the Council made pursuant to the authority granted to the Council in subsection (d) of this section, the Association shall provide to the Council, in writing, within 5 days of its decision, notice of its decision and a written statement of reasons for its rejection or significant modification of the recommendation.

(i) Administrative actions — Appointments, designations, and selections of individuals to serve as members of the Associations and Councils under this section shall be submitted to the Secretary prior to the expiration of the 120-day period following August 18, 1990. On or before the expiration of the 180-day period following August 18, 1990, the Secretary shall call an initial meeting of each Association and Council for organizational purposes.

(j) Location and compensation

(1) Location — Each Association and Council established by this section shall be located in the State of Alaska.

(2) Compensation — No member of an Association or Council shall be compensated for the member's services as a member of the Association or Council, but shall be allowed travel expenses, including per diem in lieu of subsistence, at a rate established by the Association or Council not to exceed the rates authorized for employees of agencies under sections 5702 and 5703 of Title 5. However, each Council may enter into contracts to provide compensation and expenses to members of the committees created under subsections (d), (e), and (f) of this section.

(k) Funding

(1) Requirement — Approval of the contingency plans required of owners and operators of the Cook Inlet and Prince William Sound terminal facilities and crude oil tankers while operating in Alaskan waters in commerce with those terminal facilities shall be effective only so long as the respective Association and Council for a facility are funded pursuant to paragraph (2).

(2) Prince William Sound program — The owners or operators of terminal facilities or crude oil tankers operating in Prince William Sound shall provide, on an annual basis, an aggregate amount of not more than $2,000,000, as determined by the Secretary. Such amount —

(A) shall provide for the establishment and operation on the environmental oversight and monitoring program in Prince William Sound;

(B) shall be adjusted annually by the Anchorage Consumer Price Index; and

(C) may be adjusted periodically upon the mutual consent of the owners or operators of terminal facilities or crude oil tankers operating in Prince William Sound and the Prince William Sound terminal facilities Council.

(3) Cook Inlet program — The owners or operators of terminal facilities, offshore facilities, or crude oil tankers operating in Cook Inlet shall provide, on an annual basis, an aggregate amount of not less than $1,400,000, as determined by the Secretary. Such amount —

(A) shall provide for the establishment and operation of the environmental oversight and monitoring program in Cook Inlet;

(B) shall be adjusted annually by the Anchorage Consumer Price Index; and

(C) may be adjusted periodically upon the mutual consent of the owners or operators of terminal facilities, offshore facilities, or crude oil tankers operating in Cook Inlet and the Cook Inlet Council.

(l) Reports

(1) Associations and Councils — Prior to the expiration of the 36-month period following August 18, 1990, each Association and Council established by this section shall report to the President and the Congress concerning its activities under this section, together with its recommendations.

(2) GAO — Prior to the expiration of the 36-month period following August 18, 1990, the Government Accountability Office shall report to the President and the Congress as to the handling of funds, including donated funds, by the entities carrying out the programs under this section, and the effectiveness of the demonstration programs carried out under this section, together with its recommendations.

(m) Definitions — As used in this section, the term —

(1) "terminal facilities" means —

(A) in the case of the Prince William Sound Program, the entire oil terminal complex located in Valdez, Alaska, consisting of approximately 1,000 acres including all buildings, docks (except docks owned by the City of Valdez if those docks are not used for loading of crude oil), pipes, piping, roads, ponds, tanks, crude oil tankers only while at the terminal dock, tanker escorts owned or operated by the operator of the terminal, vehicles, and other facilities associated with, and necessary for, assisting tanker movement of crude oil into and out of the oil terminal complex; and

(B) in the case of the Cook Inlet Program, the entire oil terminal complex including all buildings, docks, pipes, piping, roads, ponds, tanks, vessels, vehicles, crude oil tankers only while at the terminal dock, tanker escorts owned or operated by the operator of the terminal, emergency spill response vessels owned or operated by the operator of the terminal, and other facilities associated with, and necessary for, assisting tanker movement of crude oil into and out of the oil terminal complex;

(2) "crude oil tanker" means a tanker (as that term is defined under section 2101 of Title 46) —

(A) in the case of the Prince William Sound Program, calling at the terminal facilities for the purpose of receiving and transporting oil to refineries, operating north of Middleston Island and bound for or exiting from Prince William Sound; and

(B) in the case of the Cook Inlet Program, calling at the terminal facilities for the purpose of receiving and transporting oil to refineries and operating in Cook Inlet and the Gulf of Alaska north of Amatuli Island, including tankers transiting to Cook Inlet from Prince William Sound;

(3) "vicinity of the terminal facilities" means that geographical area surrounding the environment of terminal facilities which is directly affected or may be directly affected by the operation of the terminal facilities; and

(4) "Secretary" means the Secretary of the department in which the Coast Guard is operating.

(n) Savings clause

(1) Regulatory authority — Nothing in this section shall be construed as modifying, repealing, superseding, or preempting any municipal, State or Federal law or regulation, or in any way affecting litigation arising from oil spills or the rights and responsibilities of the United States or the State of Alaska, or municipalities thereof, to preserve and protect the environment through regulation of land, air, and water uses, of safety, and of related development. The monitoring provided for by this section shall be designed to help assure compliance with applicable laws and regulations and shall only extend to activities —

(A) that would affect or have the potential to affect the vicinity of the terminal facilities and the area of crude oil tanker operations included in the Programs; and

(B) are subject to the United States or State of Alaska, or municipality thereof, law, regulation, or other legal requirement.

(2) Recommendations — This subsection is not intended to prevent the Association or Council from recommending to appropriate authorities that existing legal requirements should be modified or that new legal requirements should be adopted.

(o) Alternative voluntary advisory group in lieu of Council — The requirements of subsections (c) through (*l*) of this section, as such subsections apply respectively to the Prince William Sound Program and the Cook Inlet Program, are deemed to have been satisfied so long as the following conditions are met:

(1) Prince William Sound — With respect to the Prince William Sound Program, the Alyeska Pipeline Service Company or any of its owner companies enters into a contract for the duration of the operation of the Trans-Alaska Pipeline System with the Alyeska Citizens Advisory Committee in existence on August 18, 1990, or a successor organization, to fund that Committee or organization on an annual basis in the amount provided for by subsection (k)(2)(A) of this section and the President annually certifies that the Committee or organization fosters the general goals and purposes of this section and is broadly representative of the communities and interests in the vicinity of the terminal facilities and Prince William Sound.

(2) Cook Inlet — With respect to the Cook Inlet Program, the terminal facilities, offshore facilities, or crude oil tanker owners and operators enter into a contract with a voluntary advisory organization to fund that organization on an annual basis and the President annually certifies that the organization fosters the general goals and purposes of this section and is broadly representative of the communities and interests in the vicinity of the terminal facilities and Cook Inlet.

§2733. Bligh Reef light
[OPA §5003]

The Secretary of Transportation shall within one year after August 18, 1990, install and ensure operation of an automated navigation light on or adjacent to Bligh Reef in Prince William Sound, Alaska, of sufficient power and height to provide long-range warning of the location of Bligh Reef.

§2734. Vessel traffic service system
[OPA §5004]

The Secretary of Transportation shall within one year after August 18, 1990 —

(1) acquire, install, and operate such additional equipment (which may consist of radar, closed circuit television, satellite tracking systems, or other shipboard dependent surveillance), train and locate such personnel, and issue such final regulations as are necessary to increase the range of the existing VTS system in the Port of Valdez, Alaska, sufficiently to track the locations and movements of tank vessels carrying oil from the Trans-Alaska Pipeline when such vessels are transiting Prince William Sound, Alaska, and to sound an audible alarm when such tankers depart from designated navigation routes; and

(2) submit to the Committee on Commerce, Science, and Transportation of the Senate and the Committee on Merchant Marine and Fisheries of the House of Representatives a report on the feasibility and desirability of instituting positive control of tank vessel movements in Prince William Sound by Coast Guard personnel using the Port of Valdez, Alaska, VTS system, as modified pursuant to paragraph (1).

§2735. Equipment and personnel requirements under tank vessel and facility response plans
[OPA §5005]

(a) In general — In addition to the requirements for response plans for vessels established by section 1321(j) of this title, a response plan for a tanker loading cargo at a facility permitted under the Trans-Alaska Pipeline Authorization Act (43 U.S.C. §§1651 *et seq.*), and a response plan for such a facility, shall provide for —

(1) prepositioned oil spill containment and removal equipment in communities and other strategic locations within the geographic

boundaries of Prince William Sound, including escort vessels with skimming capability; barges to receive recovered oil; heavy duty sea boom, pumping, transferring, and lightering equipment; and other appropriate removal equipment for the protection of the environment, including fish hatcheries;

(2) the establishment of an oil spill removal organization at appropriate locations in Prince William Sound, consisting of trained personnel in sufficient numbers to immediately remove, to the maximum extent practicable, a worst case discharge or a discharge of 200,000 barrels of oil, whichever is greater;

(3) training in oil removal techniques for local residents and individuals engaged in the cultivation or production of fish or fish products in Prince William Sound;

(4) practice exercises not less than 2 times per year which test the capacity of the equipment and personnel required under this paragraph; and

(5) periodic testing and certification of equipment required under this paragraph, as required by the Secretary.

(b) Definitions — In this section —

(1) the term "Prince William Sound" means all State and Federal waters within Prince William Sound, Alaska, including the approach to Hinchenbrook Entrance out to and encompassing Seal Rocks; and

(2) the term "worst case discharge" means —

(A) in the case of a vessel, a discharge in adverse weather conditions of its entire cargo; and

(B) in the case of a facility, the largest foreseeable discharge in adverse weather conditions.

§2736. Funding
[OPA §5006]

(a) Sections 2731, 2733, and 2734 — Amounts in the Fund shall be available, without further appropriations and without fiscal year limitation, to carry out section 2731 of this title in the amount as determined in subsection (b) of this section, and to carry out sections 2733 and 2734 of this title, in an amount not to exceed $5,000,000.

(b) Use of interest only — The amount of funding to be made available annually to carry out section 2731 of this title shall be the interest produced by the Fund's investment of the $22,500,000 remaining funding authorized for the Prince William Sound Oil Spill Recovery Institute and currently deposited in the Fund and invested by the Secretary of the Treasury in income producing securities along with other funds comprising the Fund. The National Pollution Funds Center shall transfer all such accrued interest, including the interest earned from the date funds in the Trans-Alaska Liability Pipeline Fund were transferred into the Oil Spill Liability Trust Fund pursuant to

section 8102(a)(2)(B)(ii), to the Prince William Sound Oil Spill Recovery Institute annually, beginning 60 days after October 19, 1996.

(c) Use for section 2712 — Beginning 1 year after the date on which the Secretary, in consultation with the Secretary of the Interior, determines that oil and gas exploration, development, and production in the State of Alaska have ceased, the funding authorized for the Prince William Sound Oil Spill Recovery Institute and deposited in the Fund shall thereafter be made available for purposes of section 2712 of this title in Alaska.

(d) Section 2738 — Amounts in the Fund shall be available, without further appropriation and without fiscal year limitation, to carry out section 2738(b) of this title, in an annual amount not to exceed $5,000,000 of which up to $3,000,000 may be used for the lease payment to the Alaska SeaLife Center under section 2738(b)(2) of this title: *Provided,* That the entire amount is designated by the Congress as an emergency requirement pursuant to section 901(b)(2)(A) of Title 2: *Provided further,* That the entire amount shall be available only to the extent an official budget request that includes designation of the entire amount of the request as an emergency requirement as defined in the Balanced Budget and Emergency Deficit Control Act of 1985, as amended, is transmitted by the President to the Congress.

§2737. Limitation
[OPA §5007]

Notwithstanding any other law, tank vessels that have spilled more than 1,000,000 gallons of oil into the marine environment after March 22, 1989, are prohibited from operating on the navigable waters of Prince William Sound, Alaska.

§2738. North Pacific Marine Research Institute
[OPA §5008]

(a) Institute established — The Secretary of Commerce shall establish a North Pacific Marine Research Institute (hereafter in this section referred to as the "Institute") to be administered at the Alaska SeaLife Center by the North Pacific Research Board.

(b) Functions — The Institute shall —

(1) conduct research and carry out education and demonstration projects on or relating to the North Pacific marine ecosystem with particular emphasis on marine mammal, sea bird, fish, and shellfish populations in the Bering Sea and Gulf of Alaska including populations located in or near Kenai Fjords National Park and the Alaska Maritime National Wildlife Refuge; and

(2) lease, maintain, operate, and upgrade the necessary research equipment and related facilities necessary to conduct such research at the Alaska SeaLife Center.

(c) Evaluation and audit — The Secretary of Commerce may periodically evaluate the activities of the Institute to ensure that funds received by the Institute are used in a manner consistent with this section. The Federal Advisory Committee Act (5 U.S.C. App. 2) shall not apply to the Institute.

(d) Status of employees — Employees of the Institute shall not, by reason of such employment, be considered to be employees of the Federal Government for any purpose.

(e) Use of funds — No funds made available to carry out this section may be used to initiate litigation, or for the acquisition of real property (other than facilities leased at the Alaska SeaLife Center). No more than 10 percent of the funds made available to carry out subsection (b)(1) may be used to administer the Institute. The administrative funds of the Institute and the administrative funds of the North Pacific Research Board created under Public Law 105-83 may be used to jointly administer such programs at the discretion of the North Pacific Research Board.

(f) Availability of research — The Institute shall publish and make available to any person on request the results of all research, educational, and demonstration projects conducted by the Institute. The Institute shall provide a copy of all research, educational, and demonstration projects conducted by the Institute to the National Park Service, the United States Fish and Wildlife Service, and the National Oceanic and Atmospheric Administration.

SUBCHAPTER III — MISCELLANEOUS

§2751. Savings provisions
[OPA §6001]

(a) Cross-references — A reference to a law replaced by this chapter, including a reference in a regulation, order, or other law, is deemed to refer to the corresponding provision of this Act.

(b) Continuation of regulations — An order, rule, or regulation in effect under a law replaced by this chapter continues in effect under the corresponding provision of this chapter until repealed, amended, or superseded.

(c) Rule of construction — An inference of legislative construction shall not be drawn by reason of the caption or catch line of a provision enacted by this Act.

(d) Actions and rights — Nothing in this chapter shall apply to any rights and duties that matured, penalties that were incurred, and proceedings that were begun before August 18, 1990, except as provided by this section, and shall be adjudicated pursuant to the law applicable on the date prior to August 18, 1990.

(e) Admiralty and maritime law — Except as otherwise provided in this Act, this Act does not affect —

(1) admiralty and maritime law; or

(2) the jurisdiction of the district courts of the United States with respect to civil actions under admiralty and maritime jurisdiction, saving to suitors in all cases all other remedies to which they are otherwise entitled.

§2752. Annual appropriations
[OPA §6002]

(a) Required — Except as provided in subsection (b) of this section, amounts in the Fund shall be available only as provided in annual appropriation Acts.

(b) Exceptions — Subsection (a) of this section shall not apply to sections 2706(f), 2712(a)(4), or 2736 of this title, and shall not apply to an amount not to exceed $50,000,000 in any fiscal year which the President may make available from the Fund to carry out section 1321(c) of this title and to initiate the assessment of natural resources damages required under section 2706 of this title. To the extent that such amount is not adequate, the Coast Guard (1) may obtain an advance from the Fund of such sums as may be necessary, up to a maximum of $100,000,000, and within 30 days shall notify Congress of the amount advanced and the facts and circumstances necessitating the advance and (2) in the case of the discharge of oil that began in 2010 in connection with the explosion on, and sinking of, the mobile offshore drilling unit Deepwater Horizon, may, without further appropriation, obtain 1 or more advances from the Fund as needed, up to a maximum of $100,000,000 for each advance, with the total amount of all advances not to exceed the amounts available under section 9509(c)(2) of the Internal Revenue Code of 1986, and within 7 days of each advance, shall notify Congress of the amount advanced and the facts and circumstances necessitating the advance. Amounts advanced shall be repaid to the Fund when, and to the extent that, removal costs are recovered by the Coast Guard from responsible parties for the discharge or substantial threat of discharge. Sums to which this subsection applies shall remain available until expended.

§2753. Repealed. Pub. L. 104-134, Title I, §101(c), Apr. 26, 1996, 110 Stat. 1321-177; renumbered Title I Pub. L. 104-410, §1(a), May 2, 1996, 110 Stat. 1327

SUBCHAPTER IV — OIL POLLUTION RESEARCH AND DEVELOPMENT PROGRAM

§2761. Oil pollution research and development program
(a) Definitions

In this section—

(1) the term "Chair" means the Chairperson of the Interagency Committee designated under subsection (c)(2);

(2) the term "Commandant" means the Commandant of the Coast Guard;

(3) the term "institution of higher education" means an institution of higher education, as defined in section 1001(a) of Title 20;

(4) the term "Interagency Committee" means the Interagency Coordinating Committee on Oil Pollution Research established under subsection (b);

(5) the term "Under Secretary" means the Under Secretary of Commerce for Oceans and Atmosphere; and

(6) the term "Vice Chair" means the Vice Chairperson of the Interagency Committee designated under subsection (c)(3).

(b) Establishment of Interagency Coordinating Committee on Oil Pollution Research

(1) Establishment

There is established an Interagency Coordinating Committee on Oil Pollution Research.

(2) Purpose

The Interagency Committee shall coordinate a comprehensive program of oil pollution research, technology development, and demonstration among the Federal agencies, in cooperation and coordination with industry, 4-year institutions of higher education and research institutions, State governments, and other nations, as appropriate, and shall foster cost-effective research mechanisms, including the joint funding of research.

(c) Membership

(1) Composition

The Interagency Committee shall be composed of—

(A) at least 1 representative of the Coast Guard;

(B) at least 1 representative of the National Oceanic and Atmospheric Administration;

(C) at least 1 representative of the Environmental Protection Agency;

(D) at least 1 representative of the Department of the Interior;

(E) at least 1 representative of the Bureau of Safety and Environmental Enforcement;

(F) at least 1 representative of the Bureau of Ocean Energy Management;

(G) at least 1 representative of the United States Fish and Wildlife Service;

(H) at least 1 representative of the Department of Energy;

(I) at least 1 representative of the Pipeline and Hazardous Materials Safety Administration;

(J) at least 1 representative of the Federal Emergency Management Agency;

(K) at least 1 representative of the Navy;

(L) at least 1 representative of the Corps of Engineers;

(M) at least 1 representative of the United States Arctic Research Commission; and

(N) at least 1 representative of each of such other Federal agencies as the President considers to be appropriate.

(2) Chairperson

The Commandant shall designate a Chairperson from among the members of the Interagency Committee selected under paragraph (1)(A).

(3) Vice Chairperson

The Under Secretary shall designate a Vice Chairperson from among the members of the Interagency Committee selected under paragraph (1)(B).

(4) Meetings

(A) Quarterly meetings

At a minimum, the members of the Interagency Committee shall meet once each quarter.

(B) Public summaries

After each meeting, a summary shall be made available by the Chair or Vice Chair, as appropriate.

(d) Duties of the Interagency Committee

(1) Research

The Interagency Committee shall—

(A) coordinate a comprehensive program of oil pollution research, technology development, and demonstration among the Federal agencies, in cooperation and coordination with industry, 4-year institutions of higher education and research institutions, States, Indian tribes, and other countries, as appropriate; and

(B) foster cost-effective research mechanisms, including the joint funding of research and the development of public-private partnerships for the purpose of expanding research.

(2) Oil pollution research and technology plan

(A) Implementation plan

Not later than 180 days after January 1, 2021, the Interagency Committee shall submit to Congress a research plan to report on the state of oil discharge prevention and response capabilities that—

(i) identifies current research programs conducted by Federal agencies, States, Indian tribes, 4-year institutions of higher education, and corporate entities;

(ii) assesses the current status of knowledge on oil pollution prevention, response, and mitigation technologies and effects of oil pollution on the environment;

(iii) identifies significant oil pollution research gaps, including an assessment of major technological deficiencies in responses to past oil discharges;

(iv) establishes national research priorities and goals for oil pollution technology development related to prevention, response, mitigation, and environmental effects;

(v) assesses the research on the applicability and effectiveness of the prevention, response, and mitigation technologies to each class of oil;

(vi) estimates the resources needed to conduct the oil pollution research and development program established pursuant to subsection (e), and timetables for completing research tasks;

(vii) summarizes research on response equipment in varying environmental conditions, such as in currents, ice cover, and ice floes; and

(viii) includes such other information or recommendations as the Interagency Committee determines to be appropriate.

(B) Advice and guidance

(i) National Academy of Sciences contract

The Chair, through the department in which the Coast Guard is operating, shall contract with the National Academy of Sciences to—

(I) provide advice and guidance in the preparation and development of the research plan;

(II) assess the adequacy of the plan as submitted, and submit a report to Congress on the conclusions of such assessment; and

(III) provide organization guidance regarding the implementation of the research plan, including delegation of topics and research among Federal agencies represented on the Interagency Committee.

(ii) NIST advice and guidance

The National Institute of Standards and Technology shall provide the Interagency Committee with advice and guidance on issues relating to quality assurance and standards measurements relating to its activities under this section.

(C) 10-year updates

Not later than 10 years after January 1, 2021, and every 10 years thereafter, the Interagency Committee shall submit to Congress a research plan that updates the information contained in the previous research plan submitted under this subsection.

(e) Oil pollution research and development program

(1) Establishment

The Interagency Committee shall coordinate the establishment, by the agencies represented on the Interagency Committee, of a program for conducting oil pollution research, technology,

and development, as provided in this subsection.

(2) Innovative oil pollution technology

The program established under paragraph (1) shall provide for research, development, and demonstration of new or improved technologies and methods that are effective in preventing, mitigating, or restoring damage from oil discharges and that protect the environment, including—

(A) development of improved designs for vessels and facilities, and improved operational practices;

(B) research, development, and demonstration of improved technologies to measure the ullage of a vessel tank, prevent discharges from tank vents, prevent discharges during lightering and bunkering operations, contain discharges on the deck of a vessel, prevent discharges through the use of vacuums in tanks, and otherwise contain discharges of oil from vessels and facilities;

(C) research, development, and demonstration of new or improved systems of mechanical, chemical, biological, and other methods (including the use of dispersants, solvents, and bioremediation) for the recovery, removal, and disposal of oil, including evaluation of the environmental effects of the use of such systems;

(D) research and training, in consultation with the National Response Team, to improve industry's and Government's ability to quickly and effectively remove an oil discharge, including the long-term use, as appropriate, of the National Spill Control School in Corpus Christi, Texas, and the Center for Marine Training and Safety in Galveston, Texas;

(E) research to improve information systems for decisionmaking, including the use of data from coastal mapping, baseline data, and other data related to the environmental effects of oil discharges, and cleanup technologies;

(F) development of technologies and methods to protect public health and safety from oil discharges, including the population directly exposed to an oil discharge;

(G) development of technologies, methods, and standards for protecting removal personnel, including training, adequate supervision, protective equipment, maximum exposure limits, and decontamination procedures;

(H) research and development of methods to restore and rehabilitate natural resources damaged by oil discharges;

(I) research to evaluate the relative effectiveness and environmental impacts of bioremediation technologies; and

(J) the demonstration of a satellite-based, dependent surveillance vessel traffic system in Narragansett Bay to evaluate the utility of such system in reducing the risk of oil discharges from vessel collisions and groundings in confined waters.

(3) Oil pollution technology evaluation

The program established under paragraph (1) shall provide for oil pollution prevention and mitigation technology evaluation including—

(A) the evaluation and testing of technologies developed independently of the research and development program established under paragraph (1);

(B) the establishment, where appropriate, of standards and testing protocols traceable to national standards to measure the performance of oil pollution prevention or mitigation technologies; and

(C) the use, where appropriate, of controlled field testing to evaluate real-world application of oil discharge prevention or mitigation technologies.

(4) Oil pollution effects research

(A) The Committee shall establish a research program to monitor and evaluate the environmental effects of acute and chronic oil discharges on coastal and marine resources (including impacts on protected areas such as sanctuaries) and protected species, and such program shall include the following elements:

(i) The development of improved models and capabilities for predicting the environmental fate, transport, and effects of oil discharges.

(ii) The development of methods, including economic methods, to assess damages to natural resources resulting from oil discharges.

(iii) Research to understand and quantify the effects of sublethal impacts of oil discharge on living natural marine resources, including impacts on pelagic fish species, marine mammals, and commercially and recreationally targeted fish and shellfish species.

(iv) The identification of types of ecologically sensitive areas at particular risk to oil discharges and the preparation of scientific monitoring and evaluation plans, one for each of several types of ecological conditions, to be implemented in the event of major oil discharges in such areas.

(v) The collection of environmental baseline data in ecologically sensitive areas at particular risk to oil discharges where such data are insufficient.

(vi) Research to understand the long-term effects of major oil discharges and the long-term effects of smaller endemic oil discharges.

(vii) The identification of potential impacts on ecosystems, habitat, and wildlife from the additional toxicity, heavy metal concentrations, and increased corrosiveness of mixed crude, such as diluted bitumen crude.

(viii) The development of methods to restore and rehabilitate natural resources and ecosystem functions damaged by oil discharges.

(B) The Department of Commerce in consultation with the Environmental Protection Agency shall monitor and scientifically evaluate the long-term environmental effects of oil discharges if—

(i) the amount of oil discharged exceeds 250,000 gallons;

(ii) the oil discharge has occurred on or after January 1, 1989; and

(iii) the Interagency Committee determines that a study of the long-term environmental effects of the discharge would be of significant scientific value, especially for preventing or responding to future oil discharges.

Areas for study may include the following sites where oil discharges have occurred: the New York/New Jersey Harbor area, where oil was discharged by an Exxon underwater pipeline, the T/B CIBRO SAVANNAH, and the M/V BT NAUTILUS; Narragansett Bay where oil was discharged by the WORLD PRODIGY; the Houston Ship Channel where oil was discharged by the RACHEL B; the Delaware River, where oil was discharged by the PRESIDENTE RIVERA and the T/V ATHOS I, and Huntington Beach, California, where oil was discharged by the AMERICAN TRADER.

(C) Research conducted under this paragraph by, or through, the United States Fish and Wildlife Service shall be directed and coordinated by the National Wetland Research Center.

(5) Marine simulation research

The program established under paragraph (1) shall include research on the greater use and application of geographic and vessel response simulation models, including the development of additional data bases and updating of existing data bases using, among others, the resources of the National Maritime Research Center. It shall include research and vessel simulations for—

(A) contingency plan evaluation and amendment;

(B) removal and strike team training;

(C) tank vessel personnel training; and

(D) those geographic areas where there is a significant likelihood of a major oil discharge.

(6) Demonstration projects

The United States Coast Guard, in conjunction with such agencies as the President may designate, shall conduct 4 port oil pollution minimization demonstration projects, one each with (A) the Port Authority of New York and New Jersey, (B) the Ports of Los Angeles and Long Beach, California, (C) the Port of New Orleans, Louisiana, and (D) ports on the Great Lakes, for the purpose of developing and demonstrating integrated port oil pollution prevention and cleanup systems which utilize the information and implement the improved practices and technologies developed from the research, development, and demonstration program established in this section. Such systems shall utilize improved technologies and management practices for reducing the risk of oil discharges, including, as appropriate, improved data access, computerized tracking of oil shipments, improved vessel tracking and navigation systems, advanced technology to monitor pipeline and tank conditions, improved oil spill response capability, improved capability to predict the flow and effects of oil discharges in both the inner and outer harbor areas for the purposes of making infrastructure decisions, and such other activities necessary to achieve the purposes of this section.

(7) Simulated environmental testing

(A) In general

Agencies represented on the Interagency Committee shall ensure the long-term use and operation of the Oil and Hazardous Materials Simulated Environmental Test Tank (OHMSETT) Research Center in New Jersey for oil pollution technology testing and evaluations.

(B) Other testing facilities

Nothing in subparagraph (A) shall be construed as limiting the ability of the Interagency Committee to contract or partner with a facility or facilities other than the Center described in subparagraph (A) for the purpose of oil pollution technology testing and evaluations, provided such a facility or facilities have testing and evaluation capabilities equal to or greater than those of such Center.

(C) In-kind contributions

(i) In general

The Secretary of the department in which the Coast Guard is operating and the Administrator of the Environmental Protection Agency may accept donations of crude oil and crude oil product samples in the form of in-kind contributions for use by the Federal Government for product testing, research and development, and for other purposes as the Secretary and the Administrator determine appropriate.

(ii) Use of donated oil

Oil accepted under clause (i) may be used directly by the Secretary and shall be provided to other Federal agencies or departments through interagency agreements to carry out the purposes of this Act.

(8) Regional research program

(A) Consistent with the research plan in subsection (d), the Interagency Committee shall coordinate a program of competitive grants to universities or other research institutions, or groups of universities or research institutions, for the purposes of conducting a coordinated research program related to the regional aspects of oil pollution, such as prevention, removal, mitigation, and the effects of discharged oil on regional environments. For the purposes of this paragraph, a region means a Coast Guard district as set out in part 3 of title 33, Code of Federal Regulations (2010).

(B) The Interagency Committee shall coordinate the publication by the agencies represented on the Interagency Committee of a solicitation for grants under this subsection. The application shall be in such form and contain such information as may be required in the published solicitation. The applications shall be reviewed by the Interagency Committee, which shall make recommendations to the appropriate granting agency represented on the Interagency Committee for awarding the grant. The granting agency shall award the grants recommended by the Interagency Committee unless the agency decides not to award the grant due to budgetary or other compelling considerations and publishes its reasons for such a determination in the Federal Register. No grants may be made by any agency from any funds authorized for this paragraph unless such grant award has first been recommended by the Interagency Committee.

(C) Any university or other research institution, or group of universities or research institutions, may apply for a grant for the regional research program established by this paragraph. The applicant must be located in the region, or in a State a part of which is in the region, for which the project is proposed as part of the regional research program. With respect to a group application, the entity or entities which will carry out the substantial portion of the proposed research must be located in the region, or in a State a part of which is in the region, for which the project is proposed as part of the regional research program.

(D) The Interagency Committee shall make recommendations on grants in such a manner as to ensure an appropriate balance within a region among the various aspects of oil pollution research, including prevention, removal, mitigation, and the effects of discharged oil on regional environments. In addition, the Interagency Committee shall make recommendations for grants based on the following criteria:

(i) There is available to the applicant for carrying out this paragraph demonstrated research resources.

(ii) The applicant demonstrates the capability of making a significant contribution to regional research needs.

(iii) The projects which the applicant proposes to carry out under the grant are consistent with the research plan under subsection (d) and would further the objectives of the research and development program established in this section.

(E) Grants provided under this paragraph shall be for a period up to 3 years, subject to annual review by the granting agency, and provide not more than 80 percent of the costs of the research activities carried out in connection with the grant.

(F) No funds made available to carry out this subsection may be used for the acquisition of real property (including buildings) or construction of any building.

(G) Nothing in this paragraph is intended to alter or abridge the authority under existing law of any Federal agency to make grants, or enter into contracts or cooperative agreements, using funds other than those authorized in this Act for the purposes of carrying out this paragraph.

(9) Funding

For each of the fiscal years 1991, 1992, 1993, 1994, and 1995, $6,000,000 of amounts in the Fund shall be available to carry out the regional research program in paragraph (8), such amounts to be available in equal amounts for the regional research program in each region; except that if the agencies represented on the Interagency Committee determine that regional research needs exist which cannot be addressed within such funding limits, such agencies may use their authority under paragraph (10) to make additional grants to meet such needs. For the purposes of this paragraph, the research program carried out by the Prince William Sound Oil Spill Recovery Institute established under section 2731 of this title, shall not be eligible to receive grants under this paragraph until the authorization for funding under section 2736(b) of this title expires.

(10) Grants

In carrying out the research and development program established under paragraph (1), the Under Secretary may enter into contracts and cooperative agreements and make grants to universities, research institutions, and other persons, and States and Indian tribes. Such contracts, cooperative agreements, and grants shall address research and technology priorities set forth in the oil pollution research plan under subsection (d).

(11) Utilization of resources

In carrying out research under this section, the Department of Transportation shall continue to utilize the resources of the Pipeline and Hazardous Materials Safety Administration of the Department of Transportation, to the maximum extent practicable.

(f) International cooperation

In accordance with the research plan submitted under subsection (d), the Interagency Committee shall coordinate and cooperate with other nations and foreign research entities in conducting oil pollution research, development, and demonstration activities, including controlled field tests of oil discharges.

(g) Biennial reports

The Chair shall submit to Congress every 2 years on October 30 a report on the activities carried out under this section in the preceding 2 fiscal years, and on activities proposed to be carried out under this section in the current 2 fiscal year period.

(h) Funding

Not to exceed $22,000,000 of amounts in the Fund shall be available annually to carry out this section except for subsection (e)(8). Of such sums—

(1) funds authorized to be appropriated to carry out the activities under subsection (c)(4) shall not exceed $5,000,000 for fiscal year 1991 or $3,500,000 for any subsequent fiscal year; and

2) not less than $3,000,000 shall be available for carrying out the activities in subsection (c)(6) for fiscal years 1992, 1993, 1994, and 1995.

All activities authorized in this section, including subsection (e)(8), are subject to appropriations.

§2762. Submerged oil program

[OPA §7002]

(a) Program.

(1) Establishment. The Under Secretary of Commerce for Oceans and Atmosphere, in conjunction with the Commandant of the Coast Guard, shall establish a program to detect, monitor, and evaluate the environmental effects of submerged oil in the Delaware River and Bay region. The program shall include the following elements:

(A) The development of methods to remove, disperse, or otherwise diminish the persistence of submerged oil.

(B) The development of improved models and capacities for predicting the environmental fate, transport, and effects of submerged oil.

(C) The development of techniques to detect and monitor submerged oil.

(2) Report. Not later than 3 years after the date of enactment of the Delaware River Protection Act of 2006 [enacted July 11, 2006], the Secretary of Commerce shall submit to the Committee on Commerce, Science, and Transportation of the

Senate and the Committee on Transportation and Infrastructure of the House of Representatives a report on the activities carried out under this subsection and activities proposed to be carried out under this subsection.

(b) Demonstration project.

(1) Removal of submerged oil. The Commandant of the Coast Guard, in conjunction with the Under Secretary of Commerce for Oceans and Atmosphere, shall conduct a demonstration project for the purpose of developing and demonstrating technologies and management practices to remove submerged oil from the Delaware River and other navigable waters.

(2) Funding. There is authorized to be appropriated to the Commandant of the Coast Guard $2,000,000 for each of fiscal years 2006 through 2010 to carry out this subsection.

TITLE 46. SHIPPING

SUBTITLE II — VESSELS AND SEAMEN

PART B — INSPECTION AND REGULATION OF VESSELS

CHAPTER 37 — CARRIAGE OF LIQUID BULK DANGEROUS CARGOES

[46 U.S.C.] §3703a. Tank vessel construction standards

[OPA §4115]

(a) Except as otherwise provided in this section, a vessel to which this chapter applies shall be equipped with a double hull —

(1) if it is constructed or adapted to carry, or carries, oil in bulk as cargo or cargo residue; and

(2) when operating on the waters subject to the jurisdiction of the United States, including the Exclusive Economic Zone.

(b) This section does not apply to —

(1) a vessel used only to respond to a discharge of oil or a hazardous substance;

(2) a vessel of less than 5,000 gross tons as measured under section 14502 of this title, or an alternate tonnage measured under section 14302 of this title as prescribed by the Secretary under section 14104 of this title equipped with a double containment system determined by the Secretary to be as effective as a double hull for the prevention of a discharge of oil;

(3) a vessel documented under chapter 121 of this title that was equipped with a double hull before August 12, 1992;

(4) a barge of less than 1,500 gross tons (as measured under chapter 145 of this title) carrying refined petroleum product in bulk as cargo in or adjacent to waters of the Bering Sea, Chukchi Sea, and Arctic Ocean and waters tributary thereto and

in the waters of the Aleutian Islands and the Alaskan Peninsula west of 155 degrees west longitude; or

(5) a vessel in the National Defense Reserve Fleet pursuant to section 11 of the Merchant Ship Sales Act of 1946 (50 App. U.S.C. §1744).

(c)(1) In this subsection, the age of a vessel is determined from the later of the date on which the vessel —

(A) is delivered after original construction;

(B) is delivered after completion of a major conversion; or

(C) had its appraised salvage value determined by the Coast Guard and is qualified for documentation as a wrecked vessel under section 12112.

(2) A vessel of less than 5,000 gross tons as measured under section 14502 of this title, or an alternate tonnage measured under section 14302 of this title as prescribed by the Secretary under section 14104 of this title for which a building contract or contract for major conversion was placed before June 30, 1990, and that was delivered under that contract before January 1, 1994, and a vessel of less than 5,000 gross tons as measured under section 14502 of this title, or an alternate tonnage measured under section 14302 of this title as prescribed by the Secretary under section 14104 of this title that had its appraised salvage value determined by the Coast Guard before June 30, 1990, and that qualified for documentation as a wrecked vessel under section 12112 before January 1, 1994, may not operate in the navigable waters or the Exclusive Economic Zone of the United States after January 1, 2015, unless the vessel is equipped with a double hull or with a double containment system determined by the Secretary to be as effective as a double hull for the prevention of a discharge of oil.

(3) A vessel for which a building contract or contract for major conversion was placed before June 30, 1990, and that was delivered under that contract before January 1, 1994, and a vessel that had its appraised salvage value determined by the Coast Guard before June 30, 1990, and that qualified for documentation as a wrecked vessel under section 12112 before January 1, 1994, may not operate in the navigable waters or Exclusive Economic Zone of the United States unless equipped with a double hull —

(A) in the case of a vessel of at least 5,000 gross tons but less than 15,000 gross tons as measured under section 14502 of this title, or an alternate tonnage measured under section 14302 of this title as prescribed by the Secretary under section 14104, if the vessel is 25 years old or older and has a single hull, or is 30 years old or older and has a double bottom or double sides;

(B) in the case of a vessel of at least 15,000 gross tons but less than 30,000 gross tons as measured under section 14502 of this title, or an alternate tonnage measured under section 14302 of this title as prescribed by the Secretary under section 14104, if the vessel is 25 years old or older and has a single hull, or is 30 years old or older and has a double bottom or double sides;

(C) in the case of a vessel of at least 30,000 gross tons as measured under section 14502 of this title, or an alternate tonnage measured under section 14302 of this title as prescribed by the Secretary under section 14104, if the vessel is 25 years old or older and has a single hull, or is 30 years old or older and has a double bottom or double sides;

(4) Except as provided in subsection (b) of this section —

(A) a vessel that has a single hull may not operate after January 1, 2010; and

(B) a vessel that has a double bottom or double sides may not operate after January 1, 2015.

(d) The operation of barges described in subsection (b)(5) outside waters described in that subsection shall be on any conditions as the Secretary may require.

(e)(1) For the purposes of this section, the gross tonnage of a vessel shall be the gross tonnage that would have been recognized by the Secretary on July 1, 1997, as the tonnage measured under section 14502 of this title, or as an alternate tonnage measured under section 14302 of this title as prescribed by the Secretary under section 14104 of this title.

(2) This subsection does not apply to a tank vessel that, before July 1, 1997, had undergone, or was the subject of a contract for, alterations that reduce the gross tonnage of the tank vessel, as shown by reliable evidence acceptable to the Secretary.

§3704. Coastwise trade vessels

A segregated ballast tank, a crude oil washing system, or an inert gas system, required by this chapter or a regulation prescribed under this chapter, on a vessel entitled to engage in the coastwise trade under chapter 551 of this title shall be installed in the United States (except the trust territories). A vessel failing to comply with this section may not engage in the coastwise trade.

§3705. Crude oil tanker minimum standards

(a) A new crude oil tanker of at least 20,000 deadweight tons shall be equipped with —

(1) protectively located segregated ballast tanks;

(2) a crude oil washing system; and

(3) a cargo tank protection system consisting of a fixed deck froth system and a fixed inert gas system.

(b) An existing crude oil tanker of at least 40,000 deadweight tons shall be equipped with —

(1) segregated ballast tanks; or

(2) a crude oil washing system.

(c) An existing crude oil tanker of at least 20,000 deadweight tons but less than 40,000 deadweight tons, and at least 15 years of age, shall be equipped with segregated ballast tanks or a crude oil washing system.

(d) An existing crude oil tanker of at least 20,000 deadweight tons shall be equipped with an inert gas system. However, for a crude oil tanker of less than 40,000 deadweight tons not fitted with high capacity tank washing machines, the Secretary may grant an exemption if the vessel's owner can show clearly that compliance would be unreasonable and impracticable due to the vessel's design characteristics.

(e) A crude oil tanker engaged in transferring oil from an offshore oil exploitation or production facility on the Outer Continental Shelf of the United States shall be equipped with segregated ballast tanks, or may operate with dedicated clean ballast tanks or special ballast arrangements. However, the tanker shall comply with other applicable minimum standards of this section.

§3706. Product carrier minimum standards

(a) A new product carrier of at least 30,000 deadweight tons shall be equipped with protectively located segregated ballast tanks.

(b) A new product carrier of at least 20,000 deadweight tons shall be equipped with a cargo tank protection system consisting of a fixed deck froth system and a fixed inert gas system or, if the product carrier carries dedicated products incompatible with the cargo tank protection system, an alternate protection system authorized by the Secretary.

(c) An existing product carrier of at least 40,000 deadweight tons shall be equipped with segregated ballast tanks or may operate with dedicated clean ballast tanks.

(d) An existing product carrier of at least 20,000 deadweight tons but less than 40,000 deadweight tons, and at least 15 years of age, shall be equipped with segregated ballast tanks or may operate with dedicated clean ballast tanks.

(e) An existing product carrier of at least 40,000 deadweight tons, or an existing product carrier of at least 20,000 deadweight tons but less than 40,000 deadweight tons that is fitted with high-capacity tank washing machines, shall be equipped with an inert gas system.

§3707. Tanker minimum standards

(a) A new tanker of at least 10,000 gross tons as measured under section 14502 of this title, or an alternate tonnage measured under section 14302 of this title as prescribed by the Secretary under section 14104 of this title shall be equipped with —

(1) 2 remote steering gear control systems operable separately from the navigating bridge;

(2) the main steering gear control in the steering gear compartment;

(3) means of communications and rudder angle indicators on the navigating bridge, a remote steering gear control station, and the steering gear compartment;

(4) at least 2 identical and adequate power units for the main steering gear;

(5) an alternative and adequate power supply, either from an emergency source of electrical power or from another independent source of power located in the steering gear compartment; and

(6) means of automatic starting and stopping of power units with attendant alarms at all steering stations.

(b) An existing tanker of at least 10,000 gross tons as measured under section 14502 of this title, or an alternate tonnage measured under section 14302 of this title as prescribed by the Secretary under section 14104 of this title shall be equipped with —

(1) 2 remote steering gear control systems operable separately from the navigating bridge;

(2) the main steering gear control in the steering gear compartment; and

(3) means of communications and rudder angle indicators on the navigating bridge, a remote steering gear control station, and the steering gear compartment.

§3708. Self-propelled tank vessel minimum standards

A self-propelled tank vessel of at least 10,000 gross tons as measured under section 14502 of this title, or an alternate tonnage measured under section 14302 of this title as prescribed by the Secretary under section 14104 of this title shall be equipped with —

(1) a dual radar system with short-range and long-range capabilities, each with true-north features;

(2) an electronic relative motion analyzer that is at least functionally equivalent to equipment complying with specifications established by the Secretary of Transportation;

(3) an electronic position-fixing device;

(4) adequate communications equipment;

(5) a sonic depth finder;

(6) a gyrocompass; and

(7) up-to-date charts.

§3709. Exemptions

The Secretary may exempt a vessel from the minimum requirements established by sections 3704-3706 of this title for segregated ballast, crude oil washing, and dedicated clean ballast if the Secretary decides that shore-based reception facilities are a preferred method of handling ballast and that adequate facilities are readily available.

§3710. Evidence of compliance by vessels of the United States

(a) A vessel of the United States to which this chapter applies that has on board oil or hazardous material in bulk as cargo or cargo residue must have a certificate of inspection issued under this part, endorsed to indicate that the vessel complies with regulations prescribed under this chapter.

(b) Each certificate endorsed under this section is valid for not more than 5 years and may be renewed as specified by the Secretary. In appropriate circumstances, the Secretary may issue a temporary certificate valid for not more than 30 days. A certificate shall be suspended or revoked if the Secretary finds that the vessel does not comply with the conditions under which the certificate was issued.

§3711. Evidence of compliance by foreign vessels

(a) A foreign vessel to which this chapter applies may operate on the navigable waters of the United States, or transfer oil or hazardous material in a port or place under the jurisdiction of the United States, only if the vessel has been issued a certificate of compliance by the Secretary. The Secretary may issue the certificate only after the vessel has been examined and found to be in compliance with this chapter and regulations prescribed under this chapter. The Secretary may accept any part of a certificate, endorsement, or document, issued by the government of a foreign country under a treaty, convention, or other international agreement to which the United States is a party, as a basis for issuing a certificate of compliance.

(b) A certificate issued under this section is valid for not more than 24 months and may be renewed as specified by the Secretary. In appropriate circumstances, the Secretary may issue a temporary certificate valid for not more than 30 days.

(c) A certificate shall be suspended or revoked if the Secretary finds that the vessel does not comply with the conditions under which the certificate was issued.

§3712. Notification of noncompliance

The Secretary shall notify the owner, charterer, managing operator, agent, master, or individual in charge of a vessel found not to be in compliance with a regulation prescribed under this part and state how compliance may be achieved.

§3713. Prohibited acts

(a) A person may not —

(1) violate this chapter or a regulation prescribed under this chapter;

(2) refuse to permit any official, authorized by the Secretary to enforce this chapter, to board a vessel or to enter a shore area, place, or premises, under a person's control to make an inspection under this chapter; or

(3) refuse to obey a lawful directive issued under this chapter.

(b) A vessel to which this chapter applies may not —

(1) operate on the navigable waters of the United States or use a port or place subject to the jurisdiction of the United States when not in compliance with this chapter or a regulation prescribed under this chapter;

(2) fail to comply with a lawful directive issued under this chapter; or

(3) carry a type or grade of oil or hazardous material in bulk as cargo or cargo residue unless its certificate is endorsed to allow that carriage.

§3714. Inspection and examination

(a)(1) The Secretary shall have each vessel to which this chapter applies inspected or examined at least once each year.

(2) Each of those vessels that is more than 10 years of age shall undergo a special and detailed inspection of structural strength and hull integrity as specified by the Secretary.

(3) The Secretary may make contracts for conducting inspections or examinations in the United States and in foreign countries. An inspector conducting an inspection or examination under contract may not issue a certificate of inspection or a certificate of compliance, but the inspector may issue a temporary certificate.

(4) The Secretary shall prescribe by regulation reasonable fees for an inspection or examination conducted under this section outside the United States, or which, when involving a foreign vessel, is conducted under a contract authorized by paragraph (3) of this subsection. The owner, charterer, or managing operator of a vessel inspected or examined by the Secretary is liable for the fees. Amounts received as fees shall be deposited in the Treasury.

(5) The Secretary may allow provisional entry of a vessel to conduct an inspection or examination under this chapter.

(b) Each vessel to which this chapter applies shall have on board those documents the Secretary considers necessary for inspection and enforcement, including documents listing —

(1) the type, grade, and approximate quantities of cargo on board;

(2) the shipper and consignee of the cargo;

(3) the places of origin and destination of the vessel; and

(4) the name of an agent in the United States authorized to accept service of legal process.

(c) Each vessel to which this chapter applies that operates in the United States shall have a person designated as authorized to accept service of legal process for the vessel.

§3715. Lightering

(a) A vessel may transfer oil or hazardous material in a port or place subject to the jurisdiction of the United States, when the cargo has been transferred from another vessel on the navigable waters of the United States or in the marine environment, only if —

(1) the transfer was conducted consistent with regulations prescribed by the Secretary;

(2) both the delivering and receiving vessels had on board, at the time of transfer, a certificate of inspection or a certificate of compliance, as would have been required under section 3710 or 3711 of this title, had the transfer taken place in a port or place subject to the jurisdiction of the United States;

(3) the delivering and the receiving vessel had on board at the time of transfer, a certificate of financial responsibility as would have been required under section 1016 of the Oil Pollution Act of 1990, had the transfer taken place in a place subject to the jurisdiction of the United States;

(4) the delivering and the receiving vessel had on board at the time of transfer, evidence that each vessel is operating in compliance with section 311(j) of the Federal Water Pollution Control Act (33 U.S.C. 1321(j)); and

(5) the delivering and the receiving vessel are operating in compliance with section 3703a of this title.

(b) The Secretary shall prescribe regulations to carry out subsection (a) of this section. The regulations shall include provisions on —

(1) minimum safe operating conditions, including sea state, wave height, weather, proximity to channels or shipping lanes, and other similar factors;

(2) the prevention of spills;

(3) equipment for responding to a spill;

(4) the prevention of any unreasonable interference with navigation or other reasonable uses of the high seas, as those uses are defined by treaty, convention, or customary international law;

(5) the establishment of lightering zones; and

(6) requirements for communication and prearrival messages.

§3716. Tank washings

(a) A vessel may not transfer cargo in a port or place subject to the jurisdiction of the United States if, before arriving, the vessel has discharged tank washings containing oil or hazardous material in preparation for loading at that port or place in violation of the laws of the United States or in a manner or quantities inconsistent with a treaty to which the United States is a party.

(b) The Secretary shall establish effective control and supervisory measures to carry out this section.

§3717. Marine safety information system

(a) The Secretary shall establish a marine safety information system that shall contain information about each vessel to which this chapter applies that operates on the navigable waters of the United States, or that transfers oil or hazardous material in a port or place under the jurisdiction of the United States. In acquiring this information, the Secretary shall make full use of publicly available information. The Secretary may by regulation require the vessel to provide information that the Secretary considers necessary to carry out this subsection, including —

(1) the name of each person with an ownership interest in the vessel;

(2) details of compliance with the financial responsibility requirements of applicable laws or regulations;

(3) registration information, including all changes in the name of the vessel;

(4) the history of marine casualties and serious repair problems of the vessel; and

(5) a record of all inspections and examinations of a vessel conducted under section 3714 of this title.

(b) On written request from the Secretary, the head of each department, agency, or instrumentality of the United States Government shall provide available information that the Secretary considers necessary to confirm the information received under subsection (a) of this section.

§3718. Penalties

(a)(1) A person violating this chapter or a regulation prescribed under this chapter is liable to the United States Government for a civil penalty of not more than $25,000. Each day of a continuing violation is a separate violation.

(2) Each vessel to which this chapter applies that is operated in violation of this chapter or a regulation prescribed under this chapter is liable in rem for a civil penalty under this subsection.

(b) A person willfully and knowingly violating this chapter or a regulation prescribed under this chapter commits a class D felony.

(c) Instead of the penalties provided by subsection (b) of this section, a person willfully and knowingly violating this chapter or a regulation prescribed under this chapter, and using a dangerous weapon, or engaging in conduct that causes bodily injury or fear of imminent bodily injury to an official authorized to enforce this chapter or a regulation prescribed under this chapter, commits a class C felony.

(d) The district courts of the United States have jurisdiction to restrain a violation of this chapter or a regulation prescribed under this chapter.

(e)(1) If any owner, operator, or individual in charge of a vessel is liable for any penalty or fine under this section, or if reasonable cause exists to believe that the owner, operator, or individual in charge may be subject to any penalty or fine under this section, the Secretary of Homeland Security, upon the request of the Secretary, shall with respect to such vessel refuse or revoke any clearance required by section 60105 of this title.

(2) Clearance or a permit refused or revoked under this subsection may be granted upon filing of a bond or other surety satisfactory to the Secretary.

§3719. Reduction of oil spills from single hull non-self-propelled tank vessels

The Secretary shall, in consultation with the National Towing Safety Advisory Committee and taking into consideration the characteristics, methods of operation, and the size and nature of service of single hull non-self-propelled tank vessels and towing vessels, prescribe regulations requiring a single hull non-self-propelled tank vessel that operates in the open ocean or coastal waters, or the vessel towing it, to have at least one of the following:

(1) A crew member and an operable anchor on board the tank vessel that together are capable of arresting the tank vessel without additional assistance under reasonably foreseeable sea conditions.

(2) An emergency system on the tank vessel or towing vessel that without additional assistance under reasonably foreseeable sea conditions will allow the tank vessel to be retrieved by the towing vessel if the tow line ruptures.

(3) Any other measure or combination of measures that the Secretary determines will provide protection against grounding of the tank vessel comparable to that provided by the measures described in paragraph (1) or (2).

Refuse Act of 1899

33 U.S.C. §§407 & 411

§407. Deposit of refuse in navigable waters generally

It shall not be lawful to throw, discharge, or deposit, or cause, suffer, or procure to be thrown, discharged, or deposited either from or out of any ship, barge, or other floating craft of any kind, or from the shore, wharf, manufacturing establishment, or mill of any kind, any refuse matter of any kind or description whatever other than that flowing from streets and sewers and passing therefrom in a liquid state, into any navigable water of the United States, or into any tributary of any navigable water from which the same shall float or be washed into such navigable water; and it shall not be lawful to deposit, or cause, suffer, or procure to be deposited material of any kind in any place on the bank of any navigable water, or on the bank of any tributary of any navigable water, where the same shall be liable to be washed into such navigable water, either by ordinary or high tides, or by storms or floods, or otherwise, whereby navigation shall or may be impeded or obstructed: *Provided*, That nothing herein contained shall extend to, apply to, or prohibit the operations in connection with the improvement of navigable waters or construction of public works, considered necessary and proper by the United States officers supervising such improvement or public work:

And provided further, That the Secretary of the Army, whenever in the judgment of the Chief of Engineers anchorage and navigation will not be injured thereby, may permit the deposit of any material above mentioned in navigable waters, within limits to be defined and under conditions to be prescribed by him, provided application is made to him prior to depositing such material; and whenever any permit is so granted the conditions thereof shall be strictly complied with, and any violation thereof shall be unlawful.

§411. Penalty for wrongful deposit of refuse; use of or injury to harbor improvements, and obstruction of navigable waters generally

Every person and every corporation that shall violate, or that shall knowingly aid, abet, authorize, or instigate a violation of the provisions of sections 407, 408, 409, 414, and 415 of this title shall be guilty of a misdemeanor, and on conviction thereof shall be punished by a fine of up to $25,000 per day, or by imprisonment (in the case of a natural person) for not less than thirty days nor more than one year, or by both such fine and imprisonment, in the discretion of the court, one-half of said fine to be paid to the person or persons giving information which shall lead to conviction.

Ocean Policy to Advance the Economic, Security, and Environmental Interests of the United States, Executive Order 13,840

83 Fed. Reg. 29431 (2018)

By the authority vested in me as President by the Constitution and the laws of the United States of America, it is hereby ordered as follows:

Section 1. *Purpose.* The ocean, coastal, and Great Lakes waters of the United States are foundational to the economy, security, global competitiveness, and well-being of the United States. Ocean industries employ millions of Americans and support a strong national economy. Domestic energy production from Federal waters strengthens the Nation's security and reduces reliance on imported energy. Our Armed Forces protect our national interests in the ocean and along the Nation's coasts. Goods and materials that support our economy and quality of life flow through maritime commerce. Our fisheries resources help feed the Nation and present tremendous export opportunities. Clean, healthy waters support fishing, boating, and other recreational opportunities for all Americans.

This order maintains and enhances these and other benefits to the Nation through improved public access to marine data and information, efficient interagency coordination on ocean-related matters, and engagement with marine industries, the science and technology community, and other ocean stakeholders. To advance these national interests, this order recognizes and supports Federal participation in regional ocean partnerships, to the extent appropriate and consistent with national security interests and statutory authorities.

Sec. 2. *Policy.* It shall be the policy of the United States to:

(a) coordinate the activities of executive departments and agencies (agencies) regarding ocean-related matters to ensure effective management of ocean, coastal, and Great Lakes waters and to provide economic, security, and environmental benefits for present and future generations of Americans;

(b) continue to promote the lawful use of the ocean by agencies, including United States Armed Forces;

(c) exercise rights and jurisdiction and perform duties in accordance with applicable domestic law and — if consistent with applicable domestic law — international law, including customary international law;

(d) facilitate the economic growth of coastal communities and promote ocean industries, which employ millions of Americans, advance ocean science and technology, feed the American people, transport American goods, expand recreational opportunities, and enhance America's energy security;

(e) ensure that Federal regulations and management decisions do not prevent productive and sustainable use of ocean, coastal, and Great Lakes waters;

(f) modernize the acquisition, distribution, and use of the best available ocean-related science and knowledge, in partnership with marine industries; the ocean science and technology community; State, tribal, and local governments; and other ocean stakeholders, to inform decisions and enhance entrepreneurial opportunity; and

(g) facilitate, as appropriate, coordination, consultation, and collaboration regarding ocean-related matters, consistent with applicable law, among Federal, State, tribal, and local governments, marine industries, the ocean science and technology community, other ocean stakeholders, and foreign governments and international organizations.

Sec. 3. *Definitions.* For the purposes of this order, the following definitions apply:

(a) "Ocean-related matters" means management, science, and technology matters involving the ocean, coastal, and Great Lakes waters of the United States (including its territories and possessions), and related seabed, subsoil, waters superadjacent to the seabed, and natural resources.

(b) "Regional ocean partnership" means a regional organization of coastal or Great Lakes States, territories, or possessions voluntarily convened by governors to address cross-jurisdictional ocean matters, or the functional equivalent of such a regional ocean organization designated by the governor or governors of a State or States.

Sec. 4. *Interagency Coordination.*

(a) To ensure appropriate coordination by Federal agencies on ocean-related matters, there is hereby established the interagency Ocean Policy Committee (Committee).

(i) The Committee shall consist of the following:

(1) The Chairman of the Council on Environmental Quality (CEQ) and the Director of the Office of Science and Technology Policy (OSTP), who shall serve as Co-Chairs;

(2) The Secretary of State, Secretary of Defense, Attorney General, Secretary of the

Interior, Secretary of Agriculture, Secretary of Commerce, Secretary of Transportation, Secretary of Energy, Secretary of Homeland Security, Administrator of the Environmental Protection Agency, Director of the Office of Management and Budget, Administrator of the National Aeronautics and Space Administration, Director of the National Science Foundation, Director of National Intelligence, Chairman of the Joint Chiefs of Staff, Under Secretary of Commerce for Oceans and Atmosphere, Assistant Secretary of the Army (Civil Works), and Commandant of the Coast Guard;

(3) The Assistants to the President for National Security Affairs, Homeland Security and Counterterrorism, Domestic Policy, and Economic Policy;

(4) A representative from the Office of the Vice President designated by the Vice President; and

(5) Such other officers or employees of the Federal Government as the Co-Chairs may from time to time designate.

(b) The Co-Chairs, in coordination with the Assistants to the President for National Security Affairs, Homeland Security and Counterterrorism, Domestic Policy, and Economic Policy, shall regularly convene and preside at meetings of the Committee, determine its agenda, and direct its work, and shall establish and direct subcommittees of the Committee as appropriate. The Committee shall, as appropriate, establish subcommittees with responsibility for advising the Committee on matters pertaining to ocean science and technology and ocean-resource management.

(i) Committee members may designate, to perform their Committee or subcommittee functions, any person who is within their department, agency, or office who is:

(1) a civilian official appointed by the President;

(2) a member of the Senior Executive Service or the Senior Intelligence Service;

(3) a general officer or flag officer; or

(4) an employee of the Office of the Vice President.

(ii) Consistent with applicable law and subject to the availability of appropriations, OSTP or CEQ shall provide the Committee with funding, including through the National Science and Technology Council pursuant to title VII, section 723 of the Consolidated Appropriations Act, 2018 (Public Law 115-141), or any successor provision, or through the Office of Environmental Quality pursuant to the Office of Environmental Quality Management Fund, 42 U.S.C. 4375. OSTP or CEQ shall, to the extent permitted by law and subject to the availability of appropriations, provide administrative support as needed to implement this order.

(iii) The Committee shall be administered by an Executive Director and such full-time staff as the Co-Chairs recommend.

Sec. 5. *Functions.* To implement the policy set forth in section 2 of this order, the Committee shall, to the extent permitted by law:

(a) provide advice regarding policies concerning ocean-related matters to:

(i) the President; and

(ii) the head of any agency who is a member of the Committee;

(b) engage and collaborate, under existing laws and regulations, with stakeholders, including regional ocean partnerships, to address ocean-related matters that may require interagency or intergovernmental solutions;

(c) coordinate the timely public release of unclassified data and other information related to the ocean, coasts, and Great Lakes that agencies collect, and support the common information management systems, such as the Marine Cadastre, that organize and disseminate this information;

(d) coordinate and inform the ocean policy-making process and identify priority ocean research and technology needs, to facilitate:

(i) the use of science in the establishment of policy; and

(ii) the collection, development, dissemination, and exchange of information between and among agencies on ocean-related matters;

(e) coordinate and ensure Federal participation in projects conducted under the National Oceanographic Partnership Program through the Committee's members, as appropriate, to maximize the effectiveness of agency investments in ocean research; and

(f) obtain information and advice concerning ocean-related matters from:

(i) State, tribal, and local governments; and

(ii) private-sector entities and individuals.

Sec. 6. *Cooperation.* To the extent permitted by law, agencies shall cooperate with the Committee and provide it such information as it, through the Co-Chairs, may request. The Committee shall base its decisions on the consensus of its members. With respect to those matters for which consensus cannot be reached, the Assistant to the President for National Security Affairs shall coordinate with the Co-Chairs to present the disputed issue or issues for decision by the President. Within 90 days of the date of this order, agencies shall review their regulations, guidance, and policies for consistency with this order, and shall consult with CEQ, OSTP, and the Office of Management and Budget (OMB) regarding any modifications, revisions, or rescissions of any regulations, guidance, or policies necessary to comply with this order.

Sec. 7. *Revocation.* Executive Order 13547 of July 19, 2010 (Stewardship of the Ocean, Our Coasts, and the Great Lakes), is hereby revoked.

Sec. 8. *General Provisions.*

(a) Nothing in this order shall be construed to impair or otherwise affect:

(i) the authority granted by law to an executive department, agency, or the head thereof;

(ii) the functions of the Director of OMB relating to budgetary, administrative, or legislative proposals; or

(iii) functions assigned by the President to the National Security Council or Homeland Security Council (including subordinate bodies) relating to matters affecting foreign affairs, national security, homeland security, or intelligence.

(b) This order shall be implemented consistent with applicable law and subject to the availability of appropriations.

(c) This order is not intended to, and does not, create any right or benefit, substantive or procedural, enforceable at law or in equity by any party against the United States, its departments, agencies, or entities, its officers, employees, or agents, or any other person.

DONALD J. TRUMP
THE WHITE HOUSE
June 19, 2018

7

LAND USE REGULATION

Few federal statutes seek directly to control land uses, whose regulation remains largely the province of state and local governments. Instead, the federal government has sought to influence land use patterns by encouraging better land use planning by lower levels of government. The Coastal Zone Management Act exemplifies this pattern because it does not impose federal land use controls, but rather provides financial assistance to states who adopt plans for managing development in coastal areas.

A GUIDE TO MATERIALS ON THE COASTAL ZONE MANAGEMENT ACT AVAILABLE ON THE INTERNET

The Coastal Zone Management Program established by the Coastal Zone Management Act is administered at the federal level by the Coastal Programs Division of the National Oceanic and Atmospheric Administration's Office of Ocean and Coastal Resource Management (OCRM). The OCRM has a website that provides information about the Coastal Zone Management Program at *https://coast.noaa.gov/*. Program guidance documents, contact information for federal officials involved in the program, and a list of the managers of state programs can be found at this website.

NOAA's Coastal Ocean Program (COP), part of the National Centers for Coastal Ocean Science (NCCOS), provides scientific information on management of coastal resources. Its website is located at *https://coastalscience.noaa.gov/*. The U.S. Geological Survey has been involved in projects to protect coastal resources in the San Francisco Bay area. Lessons learned from these projects are available online at *https://pubs.usgs.gov/fs/1995/0053/report.pdf*.

Several states participating in the Coastal Zone Management Program have websites with information concerning their activities. The Massachusetts Office of Coastal Zone Management's site is at *http://www.mass.gov/eea/agencies/czm*. Hawaii's Coastal Zone Management Program's site is at *http://planning.hawaii.gov/czm*. The website for Maryland's program is at *http://dnr.maryland.gov/ccs/Pages/coastalpolicies.aspx*.

COASTAL ZONE MANAGEMENT ACT LEGISLATIVE HISTORY TIMELINE

October 27, 1972: President Nixon signs into law the Coastal Zone Management Act, Pub. L. 92-583, 86 Stat. 1280, which authorizes federal grants to states who develop federally approved coastal management plans and which requires that federal activities that affect the coastal zone be implemented in a manner consistent with the state plans.

July 26, 1976: President Ford signs Pub. L. 94-370, 90 Stat. 1013, which reauthorizes the Coastal Zone Management Act (CZMA) and creates a coastal energy impact assistance program.

October 17, 1980: President Carter signs Pub. L. 96-464, 94 Stat. 2060, which reauthorizes the CZMA and adds new grant programs for states that seek to move beyond basic coastal management efforts.

November 5, 1990: President Bush signs Pub. L. 101-508, 104 Stat. 1388, which amends the CZMA to require state plans to control coastal nonpoint source pollution.

June 3, 1996: President Clinton signs the Coastal Zone Protection Act of 1996, Pub. L. 104-150, 110 Stat. 1380.

PRINCIPAL PROVISIONS OF THE COASTAL ZONE MANAGEMENT ACT

§§302 & 303 (16 U.S.C. §§1451 & 1452) Congressional Findings and Declaration of Policy: finds that because land uses in the coastal zone and adjacent lands that drain into it may significantly affect the quality of coastal waters and habitats, the federal government should assist the states in developing land and water use management programs for the coastal zone.

§306 (16 U.S.C. §1455) Administrative Grants: authorizes federal grants to coastal states for administering coastal zone management programs approved by the Secretary of Commerce after a determination that they include each of the elements required by law.

§306A (16 U.S.C. §1455a) Coastal Resource Improvement Program: authorizes federal grants to coastal states to preserve or restore coastal resources, to redevelop deteriorating and underutilized urban waterfronts and ports, and to provide public access to coastal areas.

§306B (16 U.S.C. §1455b) Coastal Nonpoint Pollution Control Programs: requires states with approved coastal zone management programs to prepare Coastal Nonpoint Pollution Control Programs for approval by the Secretary of Commerce pursuant to federal guidance specifying management measures for controlling sources of nonpoint pollution in coastal areas.

§307 (16 U.S.C. §1456) Federal Consistency: requires that the activities of federal agencies that affect the coastal zone be carried out in a manner consistent to the maximum extent practicable with the enforceable policies of approved state management programs.

Coastal Zone Management Act
16 U.S.C. §§1451 to 1466

§1451. Congressional findings
[CZMA §302]

The Congress finds that —

(a) There is a national interest in the effective management, beneficial use, protection, and development of the coastal zone.

(b) The coastal zone is rich in a variety of natural, commercial, recreational, ecological, industrial, and esthetic resources of immediate and potential value to the present and future well-being of the Nation.

(c) The increasing and competing demands upon the lands and waters of our coastal zone occasioned by population growth and economic development, including requirements for industry, commerce, residential development, recreation, extraction of mineral resources and fossil fuels, transportation and naviga-tion, waste disposal, and harvesting of fish, shellfish, and other living marine resources, have resulted in the loss of living marine resources, wildlife, nutrient-rich areas, permanent and adverse changes to ecological systems, decreasing open space for public use, and shoreline erosion.

(d) The habitat areas of the coastal zone, and the fish, shellfish, other living marine resources, and wildlife therein, are ecologically fragile and consequently extremely vulnerable to destruction by man's alterations.

(e) Important ecological, cultural, historic, and esthetic values in the coastal zone which are essential to the well-being of all citizens are being irretrievably damaged or lost.

(f) New and expanding demands for food, energy, minerals, defense needs, recreation, waste disposal, transportation, and industrial activities in the Great Lakes, territorial sea, exclusive economic zone, and Outer Continental Shelf are placing stress on these areas and are creating the need for resolution of serious conflicts among important and competing uses and values in coastal and ocean waters;

(g) Special natural and scenic characteristics are being damaged by ill-planned development that threatens these values.

(h) In light of competing demands and the urgent need to protect and to give high priority to natural systems in the coastal zone, present state and local institutional arrangements for planning and regulating land and water uses in such areas are inadequate.

(i) The key to more effective protection and use of the land and water resources of the coastal zone is to encourage the states to exercise their full authority over the lands and waters in the coastal zone by assisting the states, in cooperation with Federal and local governments and other vitally affected interests, in developing land and water use programs for the coastal zone, including unified policies, criteria, standards, methods, and processes for dealing with land and water use decisions of more than local significance.

(j) The national objective of attaining a greater degree of energy self-sufficiency would be advanced by providing Federal financial assistance to meet state and local needs resulting from new or expanded energy activity in or affecting the coastal zone.

(k) Land uses in the coastal zone, and the uses of adjacent lands which drain into the coastal zone, may significantly affect the quality of coastal waters and habitats, and efforts to control coastal water pollution from land use activities must be improved.

(*l*) Because global warming may result in a substantial sea level rise with serious adverse effects in the coastal zone, coastal states must anticipate and plan for such an occurrence.

(m) Because of their proximity to and reliance upon the ocean and its resources, the coastal states have substantial and significant interests in the protection, management, and development of the resources of the exclusive economic zone that can only be served by the active participation of coastal states in all Federal programs affecting such resources and, wherever appropriate, by the development of state ocean resource plans as part of their federally approved coastal zone management programs.

§1452. Congressional declaration of policy
[CZMA §303]

The Congress finds and declares that it is the national policy —

(1) to preserve, protect, develop, and where possible, to restore or enhance, the resources of the Nation's coastal zone for this and succeeding generations;

(2) to encourage and assist the states to exercise effectively their responsibilities in the coastal zone through the development and implementation of management programs to achieve wise use of the land and water resources of the coastal zone, giving full consideration to ecological, cultural, historic, and esthetic values as well as the needs for compatible economic development, which programs should at least provide for —

(A) the protection of natural resources, including wetlands, flood plains, estuaries, beaches, dunes, barrier islands, coral reefs, and fish and wildlife and their habitat, within the coastal zone,

(B) the management of coastal development to minimize the loss of life and property caused by improper development in flood-prone, storm surge, geological hazard, and erosion-prone areas and in areas likely to be affected by or vulnerable to sea level rise, land subsidence, and saltwater intrusion, and by the destruction of natural protective features such as beaches, dunes, wetlands, and barrier islands,

(C) the management of coastal development to improve, safeguard, and restore the quality of coastal waters, and to protect natural resources and existing uses of those waters,

(D) priority consideration being given to coastal-dependent uses and orderly processes for siting major facilities related to national defense, energy, fisheries development, recreation, ports and transportation, and the location, to the maximum extent practicable, of new commercial and industrial developments in or adjacent to areas where such development already exists,

(E) public access to the coasts for recreation purposes,

(F) assistance in the redevelopment of deteriorating urban waterfronts and ports, and sensitive preservation and restoration of historic, cultural, and esthetic coastal features,

(G) the coordination and simplification of procedures in order to ensure expedited governmental decisionmaking for the management of coastal resources,

(H) continued consultation and coordination with, and the giving of adequate consideration to the views of, affected Federal agencies,

(I) the giving of timely and effective notification of, and opportunities for public and local government participation in, coastal management decisionmaking,

(J) assistance to support comprehensive planning, conservation, and management for living marine resources, including planning for the siting of pollution control and aquaculture facilities within the coastal zone, and improved coordination between State and Federal coastal zone management agencies and State and wildlife agencies, and

(K) the study and development, in any case in which the Secretary considers it to be appropriate, of plans for addressing the adverse effects upon the coastal zone of land subsidence and of sea level rise; and

(3) to encourage the preparation of special area management plans which provide for increased specificity in protecting significant natural resources, reasonable coastal-dependent economic growth, improved protection of life and property in hazardous areas, including those areas likely to be affected by land subsidence, sea level rise, or fluctuating water levels of the Great Lakes, and improved predictability in governmental decisionmaking;

(4) to encourage the participation and cooperation of the public, state and local governments, and interstate and other regional agencies, as well as of the Federal agencies having programs affecting the coastal zone, in carrying out the purposes of this chapter;

(5) to encourage coordination and cooperation with and among the appropriate Federal, State, and local agencies, and international organizations where appropriate, in collection, analysis, synthesis, and dissemination of coastal management information, research results, and technical assistance, to support State and Federal regulation of land use practices affecting the coastal and ocean resources of the United States; and

(6) to respond to changing circumstances affecting the coastal environment and coastal resource management by encouraging States to consider such issues as ocean uses potentially affecting the coastal zone.

§1453. Definitions
[CZMA §304]

For purposes of this chapter —

(1) The term "coastal zone" means the coastal waters (including the lands therein and thereunder) and the adjacent shorelands (including the waters

therein and thereunder), strongly influenced by each other and in proximity to the shorelines of the several coastal states, and includes islands, transitional and intertidal areas, salt marshes, wetlands, and beaches. The zone extends, in Great Lakes waters, to the international boundary between the United States and Canada and, in other areas, seaward to the outer limit of State title and ownership under the Submerged Lands Act (43 U.S.C. 1301 *et seq.*), the Act of March 2, 1917 (48 U.S.C. 749) (48 U.S.C. 731 *et seq.*), the Covenant to Establish a Commonwealth of the Northern Mariana Islands in Political Union with the United States of America, as approved by the Act of March 24, 1976 (48 U.S.C. 1801 *et seq.*), or section 1 of the Act of November 20, 1963 (48 U.S.C. 1705), as applicable. The zone extends inland from the shorelines only to the extent necessary to control shorelands, the uses of which have a direct and significant impact on the coastal waters, and to control those geographical areas which are likely to be affected by or vulnerable to sea level rise. Excluded from the coastal zone are lands the use of which is by law subject solely to the discretion of or which is held in trust by the Federal Government, its officers or agents.

(2) The term "coastal resource of national significance" means any coastal wetland, beach, dune, barrier island, reef, estuary, or fish and wildlife habitat, if any such area is determined by a coastal state to be of substantial biological or natural storm protective value.

(3) The term "coastal waters" means (A) in the Great Lakes area, the waters within the territorial jurisdiction of the United States consisting of the Great Lakes, their connecting waters, harbors, roadsteads, and estuary-type areas such as bays, shallows, and marshes and (B) in other areas, those waters, adjacent to the shorelines, which contain a measurable quantity or percentage of sea water, including, but not limited to, sounds, bays, lagoons, bayous, ponds, and estuaries.

(4) The term "coastal state" means a state of the United States in, or bordering on, the Atlantic, Pacific, or Arctic Ocean, the Gulf of Mexico, Long Island Sound, or one or more of the Great Lakes. For the purposes of this chapter, the term also includes Puerto Rico, the Virgin Islands, Guam, the Commonwealth of the Northern Mariana Islands, and the Trust Territories of the Pacific Islands, and American Samoa.

(5) The term "coastal energy activity" means any of the following activities if, and to the extent that (A) the conduct, support, or facilitation of such activity requires and involves the siting, construction, expansion, or operation of any equipment or facility; and (B) any technical requirement exists which, in the determination of the Secretary, necessitates that the siting, construction, expansion, or operation of such equipment or facility be carried out in, or in close proximity to, the coastal zone of any coastal state;

(i) Any outer Continental Shelf energy activity.

(ii) Any transportation, conversion, treatment, transfer, or storage of liquefied natural gas.

(iii) Any transportation, transfer, or storage of oil, natural gas, or coal (including, but not limited to, by means of any deepwater port, as defined in section 1502(10) of title 33).

For purposes of this paragraph, the siting, construction, expansion, or operation of any equipment or facility shall be "in close proximity to" the coastal zone of any coastal state if such siting, construction, expansion, or operation has, or is likely to have, a significant effect on such coastal zone.

(6) The term "energy facilities" means any equipment or facility which is or will be used primarily

(A) in the exploration for, or the development, production, conversion, storage, transfer, processing, or transportation of, any energy resource; or

(B) for the manufacture, production, or assembly of equipment, machinery, products, or devices which are involved in any activity described in subparagraph (A).

The term includes, but is not limited to (i) electric generating plants; (ii) petroleum refineries and associated facilities; (iii) gasification plants; (iv) facilities used for the transportation, conversion, treatment, transfer, or storage of liquefied natural gas; (v) uranium enrichment or nuclear fuel processing facilities; (vi) oil and gas facilities, including platforms, assembly plants, storage depots, tank farms, crew and supply bases, and refining complexes; (vii) facilities including deepwater ports, for the transfer of petroleum; (viii) pipelines and transmission facilities; and (ix) terminals which are associated with any of the foregoing.

(6a) The term "enforceable policy" means State policies which are legally binding through constitutional provisions, laws, regulations, land use plans, ordinances, or judicial or administrative decisions, by which a State exerts control over private and public land and water uses and natural resources in the coastal zone.

(7) The term "estuary" means that part of a river or stream or other body of water having unimpaired connection with the open sea, where the sea water is measurably diluted with fresh water derived from land drainage. The term includes estuary-type areas of the Great Lakes.

(8) The term "estuarine sanctuary" means a research area which may include any part or all of an estuary and any island, transitional area, and upland in, adjoining, or adjacent to such estuary, and which constitutes to the extent feasible a natural unit, set aside to provide scientists and students the opportunity to examine over a period of time the ecological relationships within the area.

(9) The term "Fund" means the Coastal Zone Management Fund established under section 1456a(b) of this title.

(10) The term "land use" means activities which are conducted in, or on the shorelands within, the coastal zone, subject to the requirements outlined in section 1456(g) of this title.

(11) The term "local government" means any political subdivision of, or any special entity created by, any coastal state which (in whole or part) is located in, or has authority over, such state's coastal zone and which (A) has authority to levy taxes, or to establish and collect user fees, or (B) provides any public facility or public service which is financed in whole or part by taxes or user fees. The term includes, but is not limited to, any school district, fire district, transportation authority, and any other special purpose district or authority.

(12) The term "management program" includes, but is not limited to, a comprehensive statement in words, maps, illustrations, or other media of communication, prepared and adopted by the state in accordance with the provisions of this chapter, setting forth objectives, policies, and standards to guide public and private uses of lands and waters in the coastal zone.

(13) The term "outer Continental Shelf energy activity" means any exploration for, or any development or production of, oil or natural gas from the outer Continental Shelf (as defined in section 1331(a) of title 43) or the siting, construction, expansion, or operation of any new or expanded energy facilities directly required by such exploration, development, or production.

(14) The term "person" means any individual; any corporation, partnership, association, or other entity organized or existing under the laws of any state; the Federal Government; any state, regional, or local government; or any entity of any such Federal, state, regional, or local government.

(15) The term "public facilities and public services" means facilities or services which are financed, in whole or in part, by any state or political subdivision thereof, including, but not limited to, highways and secondary roads, parking, mass transit, docks, navigation aids, fire and police protection, water supply, waste collection and treatment (including drainage), schools and education, and hospitals and health care. Such term may also include any other facility or service so financed which the Secretary finds will support increased population.

(16) The term "Secretary" means the Secretary of Commerce.

(17) The term "special area management plan" means a comprehensive plan providing for natural resource protection and reasonable coastal-dependent economic growth containing a detailed and comprehensive statement of policies; standards and criteria to guide public and private uses of lands and waters; and mechanisms for timely implementation in specific geographic areas within the coastal zone.

(18) The term "water use" means a use, activity, or project conducted in or on waters within the coastal zone.

§1454. Management program development grants
[CZMA §305]

Any coastal state which has completed the development of its management program shall submit such program to the Secretary for review and approval pursuant to section 1455 of this title.

§1455. Administrative grants
[CZMA §306]

(a) Authorization; matching funds — The Secretary may make grants to any coastal state for the purpose of administering that State's management program, if the State matches any such grant according to the following ratios of Federal-to-State contributions for the applicable fiscal year:

(1) For those States for which programs were approved prior to November 5, 1990, 1 to 1 for any fiscal year.

(2) For programs approved after November 5, 1990, 4 to 1 for the first fiscal year, 2.3 to 1 for the second fiscal year, 1.5 to 1 for the third fiscal year, and 1 to 1 for each fiscal year thereafter.

(b) Grants to coastal states; requirements — The Secretary may make a grant to a coastal state under subsection (a) of this section only if the Secretary finds that the management program of the coastal state meets all applicable requirements of this chapter and has been approved in accordance with subsection (d) of this section.

(c) Allocation of grants to coastal states — Grants under this section shall be allocated to coastal states with approved programs based on rules and regulations promulgated by the Secretary which shall take into account the extent and nature of the shoreline and area covered by the program, population of the area, and other relevant factors. The Secretary shall establish, after consulting with the coastal states, maximum and minimum grants for any fiscal year to promote equity between coastal states and effective coastal management.

(d) Mandatory adoption of State management program for coastal zone — Before approving a management program submitted by a coastal state, the Secretary shall find the following:

(1) The State has developed and adopted a management program for its coastal zone in accordance with rules and regulations promulgated by the Secretary, after notice, and with the opportunity of full participation by relevant Federal agencies, State agencies, local governments, regional organizations, port authorities, and other interested parties and individuals, public and private, which is adequate to carry out the purposes of this chapter and is consistent with the policy declared in section 1452 of this title.

(2) The management program includes each of the following required program elements:

(A) An identification of the boundaries of the coastal zone subject to the management program.

(B) A definition of what shall constitute permissible land uses and water uses within the coastal zone which have a direct and significant impact on the coastal waters.

(C) An inventory and designation of areas of particular concern within the coastal zone.

(D) An identification of the means by which the State proposes to exert control over the land uses and water uses referred to in subparagraph (B), including a list of relevant State constitutional provisions, laws, regulations, and judicial decisions.

(E) Broad guidelines on priorities of uses in particular areas, including specifically those uses of lowest priority.

(F) A description of the organizational structure proposed to implement such management program, including the responsibilities and interrelationships of local, areawide, State, regional, and interstate agencies in the management process.

(G) A definition of the term "beach" and a planning process for the protection of, and access to, public beaches and other public coastal areas of environmental, recreational, historical, esthetic, ecological, or cultural value.

(H) A planning process for energy facilities likely to be located in, or which may significantly affect, the coastal zone, including a process for anticipating the management of the impacts resulting from such facilities.

(I) A planning process for assessing the effects of, and studying and evaluating ways to control, or lessen the impact of, shoreline erosion, and to restore areas adversely affected by such erosion.

(3) The State has —

(A) coordinated its program with local, areawide, and interstate plans applicable to areas within the coastal zone —

(i) existing on January 1 of the year in which the State's management program is submitted to the Secretary; and

(ii) which have been developed by a local government, an areawide agency, a regional agency, or an interstate agency; and

(B) established an effective mechanism for continuing consultation and coordination between the management agency designated pursuant to paragraph (6) and with local governments, interstate agencies, regional agencies, and areawide agencies within the coastal zone to assure the full participation of those local governments and agencies in carrying out the purposes of this chapter; except that the Secretary shall not find any mechanism to be effective for purposes of this subparagraph unless it requires that —

(i) the management agency, before implementing any management program decision which would conflict with any local zoning ordinance, decision, or other action, shall send a notice of the management program decision to any local government whose zoning authority is affected;

(ii) within the 30-day period commencing on the date of receipt of that notice, the local government may submit to the management agency written comments on the management program decision, and any recommendation for alternatives; and

(iii) the management agency, if any comments are submitted to it within the 30-day period by any local government —

(I) shall consider the comments;

(II) may, in its discretion, hold a public hearing on the comments; and

(III) may not take any action within the 30-day period to implement the management program decision.

(4) The State has held public hearings in the development of the management program.

(5) The management program and any changes thereto have been reviewed and approved by the Governor of the State.

(6) The Governor of the State has designated a single State agency to receive and administer grants for implementing the management program.

(7) The State is organized to implement the management program.

(8) The management program provides for adequate consideration of the national interest involved in planning for, and managing the coastal zone, including the siting of facilities such as energy facilities which are of greater than local significance. In the case of energy facilities, the Secretary shall find that the State has given consideration to any applicable national or interstate energy plan or program.

(9) The management program includes procedures whereby specific areas may be designated for the purpose of preserving or restoring them for their conservation, recreational, ecological, historical, or esthetic values.

(10) The State, acting through its chosen agency or agencies (including local governments, areawide agencies, regional agencies, or interstate agencies) has authority for the management of the coastal zone in accordance with the management program. Such authority shall include power —

(A) to administer land use and water use regulations to control development to ensure compliance with the management program, and to resolve conflicts among competing uses; and

(B) to acquire fee simple and less than fee simple interests in land, waters, and other property through condemnation or other means when necessary to achieve conformance with the management program.

(11) The management program provides for any one or a combination of the following general techniques for control of land uses and water uses within the coastal zone:

(A) State establishment of criteria and standards for local implementation, subject to administrative review and enforcement.

(B) Direct State land and water use planning and regulation.

(C) State administrative review for consistency with the management program of all development plans, projects, or land and water use regulations, including exceptions and variances thereto, proposed by any State or local authority or private developer, with power to approve or disapprove after public notice and an opportunity for hearings.

(12) The management program contains a method of assuring that local land use and water use regulations within the coastal zone do not unreasonably restrict or exclude land uses and water uses of regional benefit.

(13) The management program provides for —

(A) the inventory and designation of areas that contain one or more coastal resources of national significance; and

(B) specific and enforceable standards to protect such resources.

(14) The management program provides for public participation in permitting processes, consistency determinations, and other similar decisions.

(15) The management program provides a mechanism to ensure that all State agencies will adhere to the program.

(16) The management program contains enforceable policies and mechanisms to implement the applicable requirements of the Coastal Nonpoint Pollution Control Program of the State required by section 1455b of this title.

(e) Amendment or modification of State management program for coastal zone — A coastal state may amend or modify a management program which it has submitted and which has been approved by the Secretary under this section, subject to the following conditions:

(1) The State shall promptly notify the Secretary of any proposed amendment, modification, or other program change and submit it for the Secretary's approval. The Secretary may suspend all or part of any grant made under this section pending State submission of the proposed amendments, modification, or other program change.

(2) Within 30 days after the date the Secretary receives any proposed amendment, the Secretary shall notify the State whether the Secretary approves or disapproves the amendment, or whether the Secretary finds it is necessary to extend the review of the proposed amendment for a period not to exceed 120 days after the date the Secretary received the proposed amendment. The Secretary may extend this period only as necessary to meet the requirements of the National Environmental Policy Act of 1969 (42 U.S.C. 4321 *et seq.*). If the

Secretary does not notify the coastal state that the Secretary approves or disapproves the amendment within that period, then the amendment shall be conclusively presumed as approved.

(3)(A) Except as provided in subparagraph (B), a coastal state may not implement any amendment, modification, or other change as part of its approved management program unless the amendment, modification, or other change is approved by the Secretary under this subsection.

(B) The Secretary, after determining on a preliminary basis, that an amendment, modification, or other change which has been submitted for approval under this subsection is likely to meet the program approval standards in this section, may permit the State to expend funds awarded under this section to begin implementing the proposed amendment, modification, or change. This preliminary approval shall not extend for more than 6 months and may not be renewed. A proposed amendment, modification, or change which has been given preliminary approval and is not finally approved under this paragraph shall not be considered an enforceable policy for purposes of section 1456 of this title.

§1455a. Coastal resource improvement program [CZMA §306A]

(a) Definitions — For purposes of this section —

(1) The term "eligible coastal state" means a coastal state that for any fiscal year for which a grant is applied for under this section —

(A) has a management program approved under section 1455 of this title; and

(B) in the judgment of the Secretary, is making satisfactory progress in activities designed to result in significant improvement in achieving the coastal management objectives specified in section 1452(2)(A) through (K) of this title.

(2) The term "urban waterfront and port" means any developed area that is densely populated and is being used for, or has been used for, urban residential recreational, commercial, shipping or industrial purposes.

(b) Resource management improvement grants — The Secretary may make grants to any eligible coastal state to assist that state in meeting one or more of the following objectives:

(1) The preservation or restoration of specific areas of the state that (A) are designated under the management program procedures required by section 1455(d)(9) of this title because of their conservation recreational, ecological, or esthetic values, or (B) contain one or more coastal resources of national significance, or for the purpose of restoring and enhancing shellfish production by the purchase and distribution of clutch material on publicly owned reef tracts.

(2) The redevelopment of deteriorating and underutilized urban waterfronts and ports that are designated in the state's management program pursuant to section 1455(d)(2)(C) of this title as areas of particular concern.

(3) The provision of access to public beaches and other public coastal areas and to coastal waters in accordance with the planning process required under section 1455(d)(2)(G) of this title.

(4) The development of a coordinated process among State agencies to regulate and issue permits for aquaculture facilities in the coastal zone.

(c) Uses, terms and conditions of grants

(1) Each grant made by the Secretary under this section shall be subject to such terms and conditions as may be appropriate to ensure that the grant is used for purposes consistent with this section.

(2) Grants made under this section may be used for —

(A) the acquisition of fee simple and other interests in land;

(B) low-cost construction projects determined by the Secretary to be consistent with the purposes of this section, including but not limited to, paths, walkways, fences, parks, and the rehabilitation of historic buildings and structures; except that not more than 50 per centum of any grant made under this section may be used for such construction projects;

(C) in the case of grants made for objectives described in subsection (b)(2) of this section —

(i) the rehabilitation or acquisition of piers to provide increased public use, including compatible commercial activity.

(ii) the establishment of shoreline stabilization measures including the installation or rehabilitation of bulkheads for the purpose of public safety or increasing public access and use, and

(iii) the removal or replacement of pilings where such action will provide increased recreational use of urban waterfront areas, but activities provided for under this paragraph shall not be treated as construction projects subject to the limitations in paragraph (B);

(D) engineering designs, specifications, and other appropriate reports; and

(E) educational, interpretive, and management costs and such other related costs as the Secretary determines to be consistent with the purposes of this section.

(d) State matching contributions; ratio; maximum amount of grants

(1) The Secretary may make grants to any coastal state for the purpose of carrying out the project or purpose for which such grants are awarded, if the state matches any such grant according to the following ratios of Federal to state contributions for the applicable fiscal year: 4 to 1 for fiscal year 1986; 2.3 to 1 for fiscal year 1987; 1.5 to 1 for fiscal year 1988; and 1 to 1 for each fiscal year after fiscal year 1988.

(2) Grants provided under this section may be used to pay a coastal state's share of costs required under any other Federal program that is consistent with the purposes of this section.

(3) The total amount of grants made under this section to any eligible coastal state for any fiscal year may not exceed an amount equal to 10 per centum of the total amount appropriated to carry out this section for such fiscal year.

(e) Allocation of grants to local governments and other agencies

With the approval of the Secretary, an eligible coastal state may allocate to a local government, an areawide agency designated under section 3334 of Title 42, a regional agency, or an interstate agency, a portion of any grant made under this section for the purpose of carrying out this section; except that such an allocation shall not relieve that state of the responsibility for ensuring that any funds so allocated are applied in furtherance of the state's approved management program.

(f) Other technical and financial assistance

In addition to providing grants under this section, the Secretary shall assist eligible coastal states and their local governments in identifying and obtaining other sources of available Federal technical and financial assistance regarding the objectives of this section.

§1455b. Protecting coastal waters
[CZMA §306B]

(a) In general

(1) Program development — Not later than 30 months after the date of the publication of final guidance under subsection (g) of this section, each State for which a management program has been approved pursuant to section 306 of the Coastal Zone Management Act of 1972 (16 U.S.C. 1455) shall prepare and submit to the Secretary and the Administrator a Coastal Nonpoint Pollution Control Program for approval pursuant to this section. The purpose of the program shall be to develop and implement management measures for nonpoint source pollution to restore and protect coastal waters, working in close conjunction with other State and local authorities.

(2) Program coordination — A State program under this section shall be coordinated closely with State and local water quality plans and programs developed pursuant to sections 1288, 1313, 1329, and 1330 of title 33 and with State plans developed pursuant to the Coastal Zone Management Act of 1972, as amended by this Act (16 U.S.C. 1451 *et seq.*). The program shall serve as an update and expansion of the State nonpoint source management program developed under section 1329 of title 33, as the program under that section relates to land and water uses affecting coastal waters.

(b) Program contents — Each State program under this section shall provide for the implementation, at a minimum, of management measures in conformity with the guidance published under subsection (g) of this section, to protect coastal waters generally, and shall also contain the following:

(1) Identifying land uses — The identification of, and a continuing process for identifying, land uses which, individually or cumulatively, may cause or contribute significantly to a degradation of —

(A) those coastal waters where there is a failure to attain or maintain applicable water quality standards or protect designated uses, as determined by the State pursuant to its water quality planning processes; or

(B) those coastal waters that are threatened by reasonably foreseeable increases in pollution loadings from new or expanding sources.

(2) Identifying critical coastal areas —The identification of, and a continuing process for identifying, critical coastal areas adjacent to coastal waters referred to in paragraph (1)(A) and (B), within which any new land uses or substantial expansion of existing land uses shall be subject to management measures in addition to those provided for in subsection (g) of this section.

(3) Management measures — The implementation and continuing revision from time to time of additional management measures applicable to the land uses and areas identified pursuant to paragraphs (1) and (2) that are necessary to achieve and maintain applicable water quality standards under section 1313 of title 33 and protect designated uses.

(4) Technical assistance — The provision of technical and other assistance to local governments and the public for implementing the measures referred to in paragraph (3), which may include assistance in developing ordinances and regulations, technical guidance, and modeling to predict and assess the effectiveness of such measures, training, financial incentives, demonstration projects, and other innovations to protect coastal water quality and designated uses.

(5) Public participation — Opportunities for public participation in all aspects of the program, including the use of public notices and opportunities for comment, nomination procedures, public hearings, technical and financial assistance, public education, and other means.

(6) Administrative coordination — The establishment of mechanisms to improve coordination among State agencies and between State and local officials responsible for land use programs and permitting, water quality permitting and enforcement, habitat protection, and public health and safety, through the use of joint project review, memoranda of agreement, or other mechanisms.

(7) State coastal zone boundary modification — A proposal to modify the boundaries of the State coastal zone as the coastal management agency of

the State determines is necessary to implement the recommendations made pursuant to subsection (e) of this section. If the coastal management agency does not have the authority to modify such boundaries, the program shall include recommendations for such modifications to the appropriate State authority.

(c) Program submission, approval, and implementation

(1) Review and approval — Within 6 months after the date of submission by a State of a program pursuant to this section, the Secretary and the Administrator shall jointly review the program. The program shall be approved if —

(A) the Secretary determines that the portions of the program under the authority of the Secretary meet the requirements of this section and the Administrator concurs with that determination; and

(B) the Administrator determines that the portions of the program under the authority of the Administrator meet the requirements of this section and the Secretary concurs with that determination.

(2) Implementation of approved program — If the program of a State is approved in accordance with paragraph (1), the State shall implement the program, including the management measures included in the program pursuant to subsection (b) of this section, through —

(A) changes to the State plan for control of nonpoint source pollution approved under section 1329 of title 33; and

(B) changes to the State coastal zone management program developed under section 306 of the Coastal Zone Management Act of 1972, as amended by this Act (16 U.S.C. 1455).

(3) Withholding coastal management assistance — If the Secretary finds that a coastal State has failed to submit an approvable program as required by this section, the Secretary shall withhold for each fiscal year until such a program is submitted a portion of grants otherwise available to the State for the fiscal year under section 306 of the Coastal Zone Management Act of 1972 (16 U.S.C. 1455), as follows:

(A) 10 percent for fiscal year 1996.

(B) 15 percent for fiscal year 1997.

(C) 20 percent for fiscal year 1998.

(D) 30 percent for fiscal year 1999 and each fiscal year thereafter.

The Secretary shall make amounts withheld under this paragraph available to coastal States having programs approved under this section.

(4) Withholding water pollution control assistance — If the Administrator finds that a coastal State has failed to submit an approvable program as required by this section, the Administrator shall withhold from grants available to the State under section 1329 of title 33, for each fiscal year until such a program is submitted, an amount equal to

a percentage of the grants awarded to the State for the preceding fiscal year under that section, as follows:

(A) For fiscal year 1996, 10 percent of the amount awarded for fiscal year 1995.

(B) For fiscal year 1997, 15 percent of the amount awarded for fiscal year 1996.

(C) For fiscal year 1998, 20 percent of the amount awarded for fiscal year 1997.

(D) For fiscal year 1999 and each fiscal year thereafter, 30 percent of the amount awarded for fiscal year 1998 or other preceding fiscal year. The Administrator shall make amounts withheld under this paragraph available to States having programs approved pursuant to this subsection.

(d) Technical assistance — The Secretary and the Administrator shall provide technical assistance to coastal States and local governments in developing and implementing programs under this section. Such assistance shall include —

(1) methods for assessing water quality impacts associated with coastal and uses;

(2) methods for assessing the cumulative water quality effects of coastal development;

(3) maintaining and from time to time revising an inventory of model ordinances, and providing other assistance to coastal States and local governments in identifying, developing, and implementing pollution control measures; and

(4) methods to predict and assess the effects of coastal land use management measures on coastal water quality and designated uses.

(e) Inland coastal zone boundaries

(1) Review — The Secretary, in consultation with the Administrator of the Environmental Protection Agency, shall, within 18 months after November 5, 1990, review the inland coastal zone boundary of each coastal State program which has been approved or is proposed for approval under section 306 of the Coastal Zone Management Act of 1972 (16 U.S.C. 1455), and evaluate whether the State's coastal zone boundary extends inland to the extent necessary to control the land and water uses that have a significant impact on coastal waters of the State.

(2) Recommendation — If the Secretary, in consultation with the Administrator, finds that modifications to the inland boundaries of a State's coastal zone are necessary for that State to more effectively manage land and water uses to protect coastal waters, the Secretary, in consultation with the Administrator, shall recommend appropriate modifications in writing to the affected State.

(f) Financial assistance

(1) In general — Upon request of a State having a program approved under section 306 of the Coastal Zone Management Act of 1972 (16 U.S.C. 1455), the Secretary, in consultation with the Administrator, may provide grants to the State for use for developing a State program under this section.

(2) Amount — The total amount of grants to a State under this subsection shall not exceed 50 percent of the total cost to the State of developing a program under this section.

(3) State share — The State share of the cost of an activity carried out with a grant under this subsection shall be paid from amounts from non-Federal sources.

(4) Allocation — Amounts available for grants under this subsection shall be allocated among States in accordance with regulations issued pursuant to section 306(c) of the Coastal Zone Management Act of 1972 (16 U.S.C. 1455(c)), except that the Secretary may use not more than 25 percent of amounts available for such grants to assist States which the Secretary, in consultation with the Administrator, determines are making exemplary progress in preparing a State program under this section or have extreme needs with respect to coastal water quality.

(g) Guidance for coastal nonpoint source pollution control

(1) In general — The Administrator, in consultation with the Secretary and the Director of the United States Fish and Wildlife Service and other Federal agencies, shall publish (and periodically revise thereafter) guidance for specifying management measures for sources of nonpoint pollution in coastal waters.

(2) Content — Guidance under this subsection shall include, at a minimum

(A) a description of a range of methods, measures, or practices, including structural and nonstructural controls and operation and maintenance procedures, that constitute each measure;

(B) a description of the categories and subcategories of activities and locations for which each measure may be suitable;

(C) an identification of the individual pollutants or categories or classes of pollutants that may be controlled by the measures and the water quality effects of the measures;

(D) quantitative estimates of the pollution reduction effects and costs of the measures;

(E) a description of the factors which should be taken into account in adapting the measures to specific sites or locations; and

(F) any necessary monitoring techniques to accompany the easures to assess over time the success of the measures in reducing pollution loads and improving water quality.

(3) Publication — The Administrator, in consultation with the Secretary, shall publish —

(A) proposed guidance pursuant to this subsection not later than 6 months after November 5, 1990; and

(B) final guidance pursuant to this subsection not later than 18 months after November 5, 1990.

(4) Notice and comment — The Administrator shall provide to coastal States and other interested persons an opportunity to provide written comments on proposed guidance under this subsection.

(5) Management measures — For purposes of this subsection, the term "management measures" means economically achievable measures for the control of the addition of pollutants from existing and new categories and classes of nonpoint sources of pollution, which reflect the greatest degree of pollutant reduction achievable through the application of the best available nonpoint pollution control practices, technologies, processes, siting criteria, operating methods, or other alternatives.

(h) Authorization of appropriations

(1) Administrator — There is authorized to be appropriated to the Administrator for use for carrying out this section not more than $1,000,000 for each of fiscal years 1992, 1993, and 1994.

(2) Secretary

(A) Of amounts appropriated to the Secretary for a fiscal year under section 318(a)(4) of the Coastal Zone Management Act of 1972, as amended by this Act, not more than $1,000,000 shall be available for use by the Secretary for carrying out this section for that fiscal year, other than for providing in the form of grants under subsection (f) of this section.

(B) There is authorized to be appropriated to the Secretary for use for providing in the form of grants under subsection (f) of this section not more than —

(i) $6,000,000 for fiscal year 1992;

(ii) $12,000,000 for fiscal year 1993;

(iii) $12,000,000 for fiscal year 1994; and

(iv) $12,000,000 for fiscal year 1995.

(i) Definitions — In this section —

(1) the term "Administrator" means the Administrator of the Environmental Protection Agency;

(2) the term "coastal State" has the meaning given the term "coastal state" under section 304 of the Coastal Zone Management Act of 1972 (16 U.S.C. 1453);

(3) each of the terms "coastal waters" and "coastal zone" has the meaning that term has in the Coastal Zone Management Act of 1972 (16 U.S.C. 1451 *et seq.*);

(4) the term "coastal management agency" means a State agency designated pursuant to section 306(d)(6) of the Coastal Zone Management Act of 1972 (16 U.S.C. 1455(d)(6));

(5) the term "land use" includes a use of waters adjacent to coastal waters; and

(6) the term "Secretary" means the Secretary of Commerce.

§1456. Coordination and cooperation
[CZMA §307]

(a) Federal agencies — In carrying out his functions and responsibilities under this chapter, the Secretary shall consult with, cooperate with, and, to the maximum extent practicable, coordinate his activities with other interested Federal agencies.

(b) Adequate consideration of views of Federal agencies — The Secretary shall not approve the management program submitted by a state pursuant to section 1455 of this title unless the views of Federal agencies principally affected by such program have been adequately considered.

(c) Consistency of Federal activities with State management programs; Presidential exemption; certification —

(1)(A) Each Federal agency activity within or outside the coastal zone that affects any land or water use or natural resource of the coastal zone shall be carried out in a manner which is consistent to the maximum extent practicable with the enforceable policies of approved State management programs. A Federal agency activity shall be subject to this paragraph unless it is subject to paragraph (2) or (3).

(B) After any final judgment, decree, or order of any Federal court that is appealable under section 1291 or 1292 of title 28, or under any other applicable provision of Federal law, that a specific Federal agency activity is not in compliance with subparagraph (A), and certification by the Secretary that mediation under subsection (h) of this section is not likely to result in such compliance, the President may, upon written request from the Secretary, exempt from compliance those elements of the Federal agency activity that are found by the Federal court to be inconsistent with an approved State program, if the President determines that the activity is in the paramount interest of the United States. No such exemption shall be granted on the basis of a lack of appropriations unless the President has specifically requested such appropriations as part of the budgetary process, and the Congress has failed to make available the requested appropriations.

(C) Each Federal agency carrying out an activity subject to paragraph (1) shall provide a consistency determination to the relevant State agency designated under section 1455(d)(6) of this title at the earliest practicable time, but in no case later than 90 days before final approval of the Federal activity unless both the Federal agency and the State agency agree to a different schedule.

(2) Any Federal agency which shall undertake any development project in the coastal zone of a state shall insure that the project is, to the maximum extent practicable, consistent with the enforceable policies of approved state management programs.

(3)(A) After final approval by the Secretary of a state's management program, any applicant for a required Federal license or permit to conduct an activity, in or outside of the coastal zone, affecting any land or water use or natural resource of the coastal zone of that state shall provide in the application to the licensing or permitting agency a certification that the proposed activity complies with the enforceable policies of the state's approved program and that such activity will be conducted in a manner consistent with the program. At the same time, the applicant shall furnish to the state or its designated agency a copy of the certification, with all necessary information and data. Each coastal state shall establish procedures for public notice in the case of all such certifications and, to the extent it deems appropriate, procedures for public hearings in connection therewith. At the earliest practicable time, the state or its designated agency shall notify the Federal agency concerned that the state concurs with or objects to the applicant's certification. If the state or its designated agency fails to furnish the required notification within six months after receipt of its copy of the applicant's certification, the state's concurrence with the certification shall be conclusively presumed. No license or permit shall be granted by the Federal agency until the state or its designated agency has concurred with the applicant's certification or until, by the state's failure to act, the concurrence is conclusively presumed, unless the Secretary, on his own initiative or upon appeal by the applicant, finds after providing a reasonable opportunity for detailed comments from the Federal agency involved and from the state, that the activity is consistent with the objectives of this chapter or is otherwise necessary in the interest of national security.

(B) After the management program of any coastal state has been approved by the Secretary under section 1455 of this title, any person who submits to the Secretary of the Interior any plan for the exploration or development of, or production from, any area which has been leased under the Outer Continental Shelf Lands Act (43 U.S.C. 1331 *et seq.*) and regulations under such Act shall, with respect to any exploration, development, or production described in such plan and affecting any land or water use or natural resource of the coastal zone of such state, attach to such plan a certification that each activity which is described in detail in such plan complies with the enforceable policies of such state's approved management program and will be carried out in a manner consistent with such program. No Federal official or agency shall grant such person any license or permit for any activity described in detail in such plan until such state or its designated agency receives a copy of such certification and plan, together with any other necessary data and information, and until —

(i) such state or its designated agency, in accordance with the procedures required

to be established by such state pursuant to subparagraph (A), concurs with such person's certification and notifies the Secretary and the Secretary of the Interior of such concurrence;

(ii) concurrence by such state with such certification is conclusively presumed as provided for in subparagraph (A), except if such state fails to concur with or object to such certification within three months after receipt of its copy of such certification and supporting information, such state shall provide the Secretary, the appropriate federal agency, and such person with a written statement describing the status of review and the basis for further delay in issuing a final decision, and if such statement is not so provided, concurrence by such state with such certification shall be conclusively presumed; or

(iii) the Secretary finds, pursuant to subparagraph (A), that each activity which is described in detail in such plan is consistent with the objectives of this chapter or is otherwise necessary in the interest of national security.

If a state concurs or is conclusively presumed to concur, or if the Secretary makes such a finding, the provisions of subparagraph (A) are not applicable with respect to such person, such state, and any Federal license or permit which is required to conduct any activity affecting land uses or water uses in the coastal zone of such state which is described in detail in the plan to which such concurrence or finding applies. If such state objects to such certification and if the Secretary fails to make a finding under clause (iii) with respect to such certification, or if such person fails substantially to comply with such plan as submitted, such person shall submit an amendment to such plan, or a new plan, to the Secretary of the Interior. With respect to any amendment or new plan submitted to the Secretary of the Interior pursuant to the preceding sentence, the applicable time period for purposes of concurrence by conclusive presumption under subparagraph (A) is 3 months.

(d) Application of local governments for Federal assistance; relationship of activities with approved management programs — State and local governments submitting applications for Federal assistance under other Federal programs, in or outside of the coastal zone, affecting any land or water use of natural resource of the coastal zone shall indicate the views of the appropriate state or local agency as to the relationship of such activities to the approved management program for the coastal zone. Such applications shall be submitted and coordinated in accordance with the provisions of section 6506 of Title 31. Federal agencies shall not approve proposed projects that are inconsistent with the enforceable policies of a coastal state's management program, except upon a finding by the Secretary that such project is consistent with the purposes of this chapter or necessary in the interest of national security.

(e) Construction with other laws — Nothing in this chapter shall be construed —

(1) to diminish either Federal or state jurisdiction, responsibility, or rights in the field of planning, development, or control of water resources, submerged lands, or navigable waters; nor to displace, supersede, limit, or modify any interstate compact or the jurisdiction or responsibility of any legally established joint or common agency of two or more states or of two or more states and the Federal Government; nor to limit the authority of Congress to authorize and fund projects;

(2) as superseding, modifying, or repealing existing laws applicable to the various Federal agencies; nor to affect the jurisdiction, powers, or prerogatives of the International Joint Commission, United States and Canada, the Permanent Engineering Board, and the United States operating entity or entities established pursuant to the Columbia River Basin Treaty, signed at Washington, January 17, 1961, or the International Boundary and Water Commission, United States and Mexico.

(f) Construction with existing requirements of water and air pollution programs — Notwithstanding any other provision of this chapter, nothing in this chapter shall in any way affect any requirement (1) established by the Federal Water Pollution Control Act, as amended (33 U.S.C. 1251 *et seq.*), or the Clean Air Act, as amended (42 U.S.C. 7401 *et seq.*), or (2) established by the Federal Government or by any state or local government pursuant to such Acts. Such requirements shall be incorporated in any program developed pursuant to this chapter and shall be the water pollution control and air pollution control requirements applicable to such program.

(g) Concurrence with programs which affect inland areas — When any state's coastal zone management program, submitted for approval or proposed for modification pursuant to section 1455 of this title, includes requirements as to shorelands which also would be subject to any Federally supported national land use program which may be hereafter enacted, the Secretary, prior to approving such program, shall obtain the concurrence of the Secretary of the Interior, or such other Federal official as may be designated to administer the national land use program, with respect to that portion of the coastal zone management program affecting such inland areas.

(h) Mediation of disagreements — In case of serious disagreement between any Federal agency and a coastal state —

(1) in the development or the initial implementation of a management program under section 1454 of this title; or

(2) in the administration of a management program approved under section 1455 of this title; the Secretary, with the cooperation of the Executive Office of the President, shall seek to mediate the differences involved in such disagreement. The process of such mediation shall, with respect to any disagreement described in paragraph (2), include public hearings which shall be conducted in the local area concerned.

(i) Application fee for appeals — (1) With respect to appeals under subsections (c)(3) and (d) of this section which are submitted after November 5, 1990, the Secretary shall collect an application fee of not less than $200 for minor appeals and not less than $500 for major appeals, unless the Secretary, upon consideration of an applicant's request for a fee waiver, determines that the applicant is unable to pay the fee.

(2)(A) The Secretary shall collect such other fees as are necessary to recover the full costs of administering and processing such appeals under subsection (c) of this section.

(B) If the Secretary waives the application fee under paragraph (1) or an applicant, the Secretary shall waive all other fees under this subsection or the applicant.

(3) Fees collected under this subsection shall be deposited into the Coastal Zone Management Fund established under section 1456a of this title.

§1456a. Coastal Zone Management Fund [CZMA §308]

(a)(1) The obligations of any coastal state or unit of general purpose local government to repay loans made pursuant to this section as in effect before November 5, 1990, and any repayment schedule established pursuant to this chapter as in effect before November 5, 1990, are not altered by any provision of this chapter. Such loans shall be repaid under authority of this subsection and the Secretary may issue regulations governing such repayment. If the Secretary finds that any coastal state or unit of local government is unable to meet its obligations pursuant to this subsection because the actual increases in employment and related population resulting from coastal energy activity and the facilities associated with such activity do not provide adequate revenues to enable such State or unit to meet such obligations in accordance with the appropriate repayment schedule, the Secretary shall, after review of the information submitted by such State or unit, take any of the following actions:

(A) Modify the terms and conditions of such loan.

(B) Refinance the loan.

(C) Recommend to the Congress that legislation be enacted to forgive the loan.

(2) Loan repayments made pursuant to this subsection shall be retained by the Secretary as offsetting collections, and shall be deposited into the Coastal Zone Management Fund established under subsection (b) of this section.

(b)(1) The Secretary shall establish and maintain a fund, to be known as the "Coastal Zone Management Fund", which shall consist of amounts retained and deposited into the Fund under subsection (a) of this section and fees deposited into the Fund under section 1456(i)(3) of this title.

(2) Subject to amounts provided in appropriation Acts, amounts in the Fund shall be available to the Secretary for use for the following:

(A) Expenses incident to the administration of this chapter, in an amount not to exceed for each of fiscal years 1997, 1998, and 1999 the higher of —

(i) $4,000,000; or

(ii) 8 percent of the total amount appropriated under this chapter for the fiscal year.

(B) After use under subparagraph (A) —

(i) projects to address management issues which are regional in scope, including interstate projects;

(ii) demonstration projects which have high potential for improving coastal zone management, especially at the local level;

(iii) emergency grants to State coastal zone management agencies to address unforeseen or disaster-related circumstances;

(iv) appropriate awards recognizing excellence in coastal zone management as provided in section 1460 of this title;

(v) to provide financial support to coastal states for use for investigating and applying the public trust doctrine to implement State management programs approved under section 1455 of this title.

(vi) Redesignated (v).

(3) Omitted

§1456b. Coastal zone enhancement grants [CZMA §309]

(a) "Coastal zone enhancement objective" defined

For purposes of this section, the term "coastal zone enhancement objective" means any of the following objectives:

(1) Protection, restoration, or enhancement of the existing coastal wetlands base, or creation of new coastal wetlands.

(2) Preventing or significantly reducing threats to life and destruction of property by eliminating development and redevelopment in high-hazard areas, managing development in other hazard areas, and anticipating and managing the effects of potential sea level rise and Great Lakes level rise.

(3) Attaining increased opportunities for public access, taking into account current and future public access needs, to coastal areas of recreational, historical, aesthetic, ecological, or cultural value.

(4) Reducing marine debris entering the Nation's coastal and ocean environment by managing uses and activities that contribute to the entry of such debris.

(5) Development and adoption of procedures to assess, consider, and control cumulative and secondary impacts of coastal growth and development, including the collective effect on various individual uses or activities on coastal resources, such as coastal wetlands and fishery resources.

(6) Preparing and implementing special area management plans for important coastal areas.

(7) Planning for the use of ocean resources.

(8) Adoption of procedures and enforceable policies to help facilitate the siting of energy facilities and Government facilities and energy-related activities and Government activities which may be of greater than local significance.

(9) Adoption of procedures and policies to evaluate and facilitate the siting of public and private aquaculture facilities in the coastal zone, which will enable States to formulate, administer, and implement strategic plans for marine aquaculture.

(b) Limits on grants

(1) Subject to the limitations and goals established in this section, the Secretary may make grants to coastal states to provide funding for development and submission for Federal approval of program changes that support attainment of one or more coastal zone enhancement objectives.

(2)(A) In addition to any amounts provided under section 1455 of this title, and subject to the availability of appropriations, the Secretary may make grants under this subsection to States for implementing program changes approved by the Secretary in accordance with section 1455(e) of this title.

(B) Grants under this paragraph to implement a program change may not be made in any fiscal year after the second fiscal year that begins after the approval of that change by the Secretary.

(c) Evaluation of State proposals by Secretary

— The Secretary shall evaluate and rank State proposals for funding under this section, and make funding awards based on those proposals, taking into account the criteria established by the Secretary under subsection (d) of this section. The Secretary shall ensure that funding decisions under this section take into consideration the fiscal and technical needs of proposing States and the overall merit of each proposal in terms of benefits to the public.

(d) Promulgation of regulations by Secretary

— Within 12 months following November 5, 1990, and consistent with the notice and participation requirements established in section 1463 of this title, the Secretary shall promulgate regulations concerning coastal zone enhancement grants that establish —

(1) specific and detailed criteria that must be addressed by a coastal state (including the State's priority needs for improvement as identified by the Secretary after careful consultation with the State) as part of the State's development and implementation of coastal zone enhancement objectives;

(2) administrative or procedural rules or requirements as necessary to facilitate the development and implementation of such objectives by coastal states; and

(3) other funding award criteria as are necessary or appropriate to ensure that evaluations of proposals, and decisions to award funding, under this section are based on objective standards applied fairly and equitably to those proposals.

(e) No State contribution required — A State shall not be required to contribute any portion of the cost of any proposal for which funding is awarded under this section.

(f) Funding — Beginning in fiscal year 1991, not less than 10 percent and not more than 20 percent of the amounts appropriated to implement sections 1455 and 1455a of this title shall be retained by the Secretary for use in implementing this section, up to a maximum of $10,000,000 annually.

(g) Eligibility; suspension of State for non-compliance — If the Secretary finds that the State is not undertaking the actions committed to under the terms of the grant, the Secretary shall suspend the State's eligibility for further funding under this section for at least one year.

§1456c. Technical assistance
[CZMA §310]

(a) The Secretary shall conduct a program of technical assistance and management-oriented research necessary to support the development and implementation of State coastal management program amendments under section 1456b of this title, and appropriate to the furtherance of international cooperative efforts and technical assistance in coastal zone management. Each department, agency, and instrumentality of the executive branch of the Federal Government may assist the Secretary, on a reimbursable basis or otherwise, in carrying out the purposes of this section, including the furnishing of information to the extent permitted by law, the transfer of personnel with their consent and without prejudice to their position and rating, and the performance of any research, study, and technical assistance which does not interfere with the performance of the primary duties of such department, agency, or instrumentality. The Secretary may enter into contracts or other arrangements with any qualified person for the purposes of carrying out this subsection.

(b)(1) The Secretary shall provide for the coordination of technical assistance, studies, and research activities under this section with any other such activities that are conducted by or subject to the authority of the Secretary.

(2) The Secretary shall make the results of research and studies conducted pursuant to this section available to coastal states in the form of technical assistance publications, workshops, or other means appropriate.

(3) The Secretary shall consult with coastal states on a regular basis regarding the development and implementation of the program established by this section.

§1456d. Coastal and Estuarine Land Conservation Program

The Secretary shall establish a Coastal and Estuarine Land Conservation Program, for the purpose of protecting important coastal and estuarine areas that have significant conservation, recreation, ecological, historical, or aesthetic values, or that are threatened by conversion from their natural or recreational state to other uses: Provided further, That by September 30, 2002, the Secretary shall issue guidelines for this program delineating the criteria for grant awards: Provided further, That the Secretary shall distribute these funds in consultation with the States' Coastal Zone Managers' or Governors' designated representatives based on demonstrated need and ability to successfully leverage funds, and shall give priority to lands which can be effectively managed and protected and which have significant ecological value: Provided further, That grants funded under this program shall require a 100 percent match from other sources.

§1456-1. Authorization of the Coastal and Estuarine Land Conservation Program

(a) In General. The Secretary may conduct a Coastal and Estuarine Land Conservation Program, in cooperation with appropriate State, regional, and other units of government, for the purposes of protecting important coastal and estuarine areas that have significant conservation, recreation, ecological, historical, or aesthetic values, or that are threatened by conversion from their natural, undeveloped, or recreational state to other uses or could be managed or restored to effectively conserve, enhance, or restore ecological function. The program shall be administered by the National Ocean Service of the National Oceanic and Atmospheric Administration through the Office of Ocean and Coastal Resource Management.

(b) Property acquisition grants. The Secretary shall make grants under the program to coastal states with approved coastal zone management plans or National Estuarine Research Reserve units for the purpose of acquiring property or interests in property described in subsection (a) that will further the goals of—

(1) a Coastal Zone Management Plan or Program approved under this title;

(2) a National Estuarine Research Reserve management plan;

(3) a regional or State watershed protection or management plan involving coastal states with approved coastal zone management programs; or

(4) a State coastal land acquisition plan that is consistent with an approved coastal zone management program.

(c) Grant process. The Secretary shall allocate funds to coastal states or National Estuarine Research Reserves under this section through a competitive grant process in accordance with guidelines that meet the following requirements:

(1) The Secretary shall consult with the coastal state's coastal zone management program, any National Estuarine Research Reserve in that State, and the lead agency designated by the Governor for coordinating the implementation of this section (if different from the coastal zone management program).

(2) Each participating coastal state, after consultation with local governmental entities and other interested stakeholders, shall identify priority conservation needs within the State, the values to be protected by inclusion of lands in the program, and the threats to those values that should be avoided.

(3) Each participating coastal state shall to the extent practicable ensure that the acquisition of property or easements shall complement working waterfront needs.

(4) The applicant shall identify the values to be protected by inclusion of the lands in the program, management activities that are planned and the manner in which they may affect the values identified, and any other information from the landowner relevant to administration and management of the land.

(5) Awards shall be based on demonstrated need for protection and ability to successfully leverage funds among participating entities, including Federal programs, regional organizations, State and other governmental units, landowners, corporations, or private organizations.

(6) The governor, or the lead agency designated by the governor for coordinating the implementation of this section, where appropriate in consultation with the appropriate local government, shall determine that the application is consistent with the State's or territory's approved coastal zone plan, program, and policies prior to submittal to the Secretary.

(7)(A) Priority shall be given to lands described in subsection (a) that can be effectively managed and protected and that have significant ecological value.

(B) Of the projects that meet the standard in subparagraph (A), priority shall be given to lands that —

(i) are under an imminent threat of conversion to a use that will degrade or otherwise diminish their natural, undeveloped, or recreational state; and

(ii) serve to mitigate the adverse impacts caused by coastal population growth in the coastal environment.

(8) In developing guidelines under this section, the Secretary shall consult with coastal states, other Federal agencies, and other interested stakeholders with expertise in land acquisition and conservation procedures.

(9) Eligible coastal states or National Estuarine Research Reserves may allocate grants to local governments or agencies eligible for assistance under section 306A(e) [16 U.S.C.S. §1455a].

(10) The Secretary shall develop performance measures that the Secretary shall use to evaluate and report on the program's effectiveness in accomplishing its purposes, and shall submit such evaluations to Congress triennially.

(d) Limitations and private property protections.

(1) A grant awarded under this section may be used to purchase land or an interest in land, including an easement, only from a willing seller. Any such purchase shall not be the result of a forced taking under this section. Nothing in this section requires a private property owner to participate in the program under this section.

(2) Any interest in land, including any easement, acquired with a grant under this section shall not be considered to create any new liability, or have any effect on liability under any other law, of any private property owner with respect to any person injured on the private property.

(3) Nothing in this section requires a private property owner to provide access (including Federal, State, or local government access) to or use of private property unless such property or an interest in such property (including a conservation easement) has been purchased with funds made available under this section.

(e) Recognition of authority to control land use. Nothing in this title modifies the authority of Federal, State, or local governments to regulate land use.

(f) Matching requirements.

(1) In general. The Secretary may not make a grant under the program unless the Federal funds are matched by non-Federal funds in accordance with this subsection.

(2) Cost share requirement.

(A) In general. Grant funds under the program shall require a 100 percent match from other non-Federal sources.

(B) Waiver of requirement. The Secretary may grant a waiver of subparagraph (A) for underserved communities, communities that have an inability to draw on other sources of funding because of the small population or low income of the community, or for other reasons the Secretary deems appropriate and consistent with the purposes of the program.

(3) Other Federal funds. Where financial assistance awarded under this section represents only a portion of the total cost of a project, funding from other Federal sources may be applied to the cost of the project. Each portion shall be subject to match requirements under the applicable provision of law.

(4) Source of matching cost share. For purposes of paragraph (2)(A), the non-Federal cost share for a project may be determined by taking into account the following:

(A) The value of land or a conservation easement may be used by a project applicant as non-Federal match, if the Secretary determines that —

(i) the land meets the criteria set forth in section 2(b) and is acquired in the period beginning 3 years before the date of the submission of the grant application and ending 3 years after the date of the award of the grant;

(ii) the value of the land or easement is held by a non-governmental organization included in the grant application in perpetuity for conservation purposes of the program; and

(iii) the land or easement is connected either physically or through a conservation planning process to the land or easement that would be acquired.

(B) The appraised value of the land or conservation easement at the time of the grant closing will be considered and applied as the non-Federal cost share.

(C) Costs associated with land acquisition, land management planning, remediation, restoration, and enhancement may be used as non-Federal match if the activities are identified in the plan and expenses are incurred within the period of the grant award, or, for lands described in (A), within the same time limits described therein. These costs may include either cash or in-kind contributions.

(g) Reservation of funds for National Estuarine Research Reserve sites. No less than 15 percent of funds made available under this section shall be available for acquisitions benefitting National Estuarine Research Reserves.

(h) Limit on administrative costs. No more than 5 percent of the funds made available to the Secretary under this section shall be used by the Secretary for planning or administration of the program. The Secretary shall provide a report to Congress with an account of all expenditures under this section for fiscal year 2009 and triennially thereafter.

(i) Title and management of acquired property. If any property is acquired in whole or in part with funds made available through a grant under this section, the grant recipient shall provide —

(1) such assurances as the Secretary may require that —

(A) the title to the property will be held by the grant recipient or another appropriate public agency designated by the recipient in perpetuity;

(B) the property will be managed in a manner that is consistent with the purposes for which the land entered into the program and shall not convert such property to other uses; and

(C) if the property or interest in land is sold, exchanged, or divested, funds equal to the current value will be returned to the Secretary in accordance with applicable Federal law for redistribution in the grant process; and

(2) certification that the property (including any interest in land) will be acquired from a willing seller.

(j) Requirement for property used for non-Federal match. If the grant recipient elects to use any land or interest in land held by a nongovernmental organization as a non-Federal match under subsection (g), the grant recipient must to the Secretary's satisfaction demonstrate in the grant application that such land or interest will satisfy the same requirements as the lands or interests in lands acquired under the program.

(k) Definitions. In this section:

(1) Conservation easement. The term "conservation easement" includes an easement or restriction, recorded deed, or a reserve interest deed where the grantee acquires all rights, title, and interest in a property, that do not conflict with the goals of this section except those rights, title, and interests that may run with the land that are expressly reserved by a grantor and are agreed to at the time of purchase.

(2) Interest in property. The term "interest in property" includes a conservation easement.

(l) Authorization of appropriations. There are authorized to be appropriated to the Secretary to carry out this section $60,000,000 for each of fiscal years 2009 through 2013.

§1457. Public hearings
[CZMA §311]

All public hearings required under this chapter must be announced at least thirty days prior to the hearing date. At the time of the announcement, all agency materials pertinent to the hearings, including documents, studies, and other data, must be made available to the public for review and study. As similar materials are subsequently developed, they shall be made available to the public as they become available to the agency.

§1458. Review of performance
[CZMA §312]

(a) Evaluation of adherence with terms of grants — The Secretary shall conduct a continuing review of the performance of coastal states with respect to coastal management. Each review shall include a written evaluation with an assessment and detailed findings concerning the extent to which the state has implemented and enforced the program approved by the Secretary, addressed the coastal management needs identified in section 1452(2)(A) through (K) of this title, and adhered to the terms of any grant, loan, or cooperative agreement funded under this chapter.

(b) Public participation; notice of meetings; reports—In evaluating a coastal state's performance, the Secretary shall conduct the evaluation in an open and public manner, and provide full opportunity for public participation, including holding public meetings in the State being evaluated and providing opportunities for the submission of written and oral comments by the public. The Secretary shall provide the public with at least 45 days' notice of such public meetings by placing a notice in the Federal Register, by publication of timely notices in newspapers of general circulation within the State being evaluated, and by communications with persons and organizations known to be interested in the evaluation. Each evaluation shall be prepared in report form and shall include written responses to the written comments received during the evaluation process. The final report of the evaluation shall be completed within 120 days after the last public meeting held in the State being evaluated. Copies of the evaluation shall be immediately provided to all persons and organizations participating in the evaluation process.

(c) Suspension of financial assistance for noncompliance; notification of Governor; length of suspension

(1) The Secretary may suspend payment of any portion of financial assistance extended to any coastal state under this chapter, and may withdraw any unexpended portion of such assistance, if the Secretary determines that the coastal state is failing to adhere to

　　(A) the management program or a State plan developed to manage a national estuarine reserve established under section 1461 of this title, or a portion of the program or plan approved by the Secretary, or (B) the terms of any grant or cooperative agreement funded under this chapter.

(2) Financial assistance may not be suspended under paragraph (1) unless the Secretary provides the Governor of the coastal state with —

　　(A) written specifications and a schedule for the actions that should be taken by the State in order that such suspension of financial assistance may be withdrawn; and

　　(B) written specifications stating how those funds from the suspended financial assistance

shall be expended by the coastal state to take the actions referred to in subparagraph (A).

(3) The suspension of financial assistance may not last for less than 6 months or more than 36 months after the date of suspension.

(d) Withdrawal of approval of program — The Secretary shall withdraw approval of the management program of any coastal state and shall withdraw financial assistance available to that State under this chapter as well as any unexpended portion of such assistance, if the Secretary determines that the coastal state has failed to take the actions referred to in subsection (c)(2)(A) of this section.

(e) Notice and hearing — Management program approval and financial assistance may not be withdrawn under subsection (d) of this section, unless the Secretary gives the coastal state notice of the proposed withdrawal and an opportunity for a public hearing on the proposed action. Upon the withdrawal of management program approval under this subsection (d) of this section, the Secretary shall provide the coastal state with written specifications of the actions that should be taken, or not engaged in, by the state in order that such withdrawal may be canceled by the Secretary.

§1459. Records and audit
[CZMA §313]

(a) Maintenance of records by recipients of grants or financial assistance — Each recipient of a grant under this chapter or of financial assistance under section 1456a of this title, as in effect before November 5, 1990, shall keep such records as the Secretary shall prescribe, including records which fully disclose the amount and disposition of the funds received under the grant and of the proceeds of such assistance, the total cost of the project or undertaking supplied by other sources, and such other records as will facilitate an effective audit.

(b) Access by Secretary and Comptroller General to records, books, etc., of recipients of grants or financial assistance for audit and examination — The Secretary and the Comptroller General of the United States, or any of their duly authorized representatives, shall —

(1) after any grant is made under this chapter or any financial assistance is provided under section 1456a of this title, as in effect before November 5, 1990; and

(2) until the expiration of 3 years after —

　　(A) completion of the project, program, or other undertaking for which such grant was made or used, or

　　(B) repayment of the loan or guaranteed indebtedness for which such financial assistance was provided, have access for purposes of audit and examination to any record, book, document, and paper which belongs to or is used or controlled by, any recipient of the grant funds or any person who entered into any transaction relating to such financial assistance and which is pertinent for purposes of determining if the grant funds or the proceeds of such financial assistance are being, or were, used in accordance with the provisions of this chapter.

§1460. Walter B. Jones excellence in coastal zone management awards
[CZMA §314]

(a) Establishment — The Secretary shall, using sums in the Coastal Zone Management Fund established under section 1456a of this title and other amounts available to carry out this chapter (other than amounts appropriated to carry out sections 1454, 1455, 1455a, 1456b, 1456c, and 1461 of this title), implement a program to promote excellence in coastal zone management by identifying and acknowledging outstanding accomplishments in the field.

(b) Annual selection of recipients — The Secretary shall elect annually —

(1) one individual, other than an employee or officer of the Federal Government, whose contribution to the field of coastal zone management has been the most significant;

(2) 5 local governments which have made the most progress in developing and implementing the coastal zone management principles embodied in this chapter; and

(3) up to 10 graduate students whose academic study promises to contribute materially to development of new or improved approaches to coastal zone management.

(c) Solicitation of nominations for local government recipients — In making selections under subsection (b)(2) of this section the Secretary shall solicit nominations from the coastal states, and shall consult with experts in local government planning and land use.

(d) Solicitation of nominations for graduate student recipients — In making selections under subsection (b)(3) of this section the Secretary shall solicit nominations from coastal states and the National Sea Grant College Program.

(e) Funding; types of awards — Using sums in the Coastal Zone Management Fund established under section 1456a of this title and other amounts available to carry out this chapter (other than amounts appropriated to carry out sections 1454, 1455, 1455a, 1456b, 1456c, and 1461 of this title), the Secretary shall establish and execute appropriate awards, to be known as the "Walter B. Jones Awards", including —

(1) cash awards in an amount not to exceed $5,000 each;

(2) research grants; and

(3) public ceremonies to acknowledge such awards.

§1461. National Estuarine Research Reserve System
[CZMA §315]

(a) Establishment of System — There is established the National Estuarine Research Reserve System (hereinafter referred to in this section as the "System") that consists of —

(1) each estuarine sanctuary designated under this section as in effect before April 7, 1986; and

(2) each estuarine area designated as a national estuarine reserve under subsection (b) of this section.

Each estuarine sanctuary referred to in paragraph (1) is hereby designated as a national estuarine reserve.

(b) Designation of national estuarine reserves — After April 7, 1986, the Secretary may designate an estuarine area as a national estuarine reserve if —

(1) the Governor of the coastal state in which the area is located nominates the area for that designation; and

(2) the Secretary finds that —

(A) the area is a representative estuarine ecosystem that is suitable for long-term research and contributes to the biogeographical and typological balance of the System;

(B) the law of the coastal state provides long-term protection for reserve resources to ensure a stable environment for research;

(C) designation of the area as a reserve will serve to enhance public awareness and understanding of estuarine areas, and provide suitable opportunities for public education and interpretation; and

(D) the coastal state in which the area is located has complied with the requirements of any regulations issued by the Secretary to implement this section.

(c) Estuarine research guidelines — The Secretary shall develop guidelines for the conduct of research within the System that shall include —

(1) a mechanism for identifying, and establishing priorities among, the coastal management issues that should be addressed through coordinated research within the System;

(2) the establishment of common research principles and objectives to guide the development of research programs within the System;

(3) the identification of uniform research methodologies which will ensure comparability of data, the broadest application of research results, and the maximum use of the System for research purposes;

(4) the establishment of performance standards upon which the effectiveness of the research efforts and the value of reserves within the System in addressing the coastal management issues identified in paragraph (1) may be measured; and

(5) the consideration of additional sources of funds for estuarine research than the funds

authorized under this chapter, and strategies for encouraging the use of such funds within the System, with particular emphasis on mechanisms established under subsection (d) of this section. In developing the guidelines under this section, the Secretary shall consult with prominent members of the estuarine research community.

(d) Promotion and coordination of estuarine research — The Secretary shall take such action as is necessary to promote and coordinate the use of the System for research purposes including —

(1) requiring that the National Oceanic and Atmospheric Administration, in conducting or supporting estuarine research, give priority consideration to research that uses the System; and

(2) consulting with other Federal and State agencies to promote use of one or more reserves within the System by such agencies when conducting estuarine research.

(e) Financial assistance —

(1) The Secretary may, in accordance with such rules and regulations as the Secretary shall promulgate, make grants —

(A) to a coastal state —

(i) for purposes of acquiring such lands and waters, and any property interests therein, as are necessary to ensure the appropriate long-term management of an area as a national estuarine reserve,

(ii) for purposes of operating or managing a national estuarine reserve and constructing appropriate reserve facilities, or

(iii) for purposes of conducting educational or interpretive activities; and

(B) to any coastal state or public or private person for purposes of supporting research and monitoring within a national estuarine reserve that are consistent with the research guidelines developed under subsection (c) of this section.

(2) Financial assistance provided under paragraph (1) shall be subject to such terms and conditions as the Secretary considers necessary or appropriate to protect the interests of the United States, including requiring coastal states to execute suitable title documents setting forth the property interest or interests of the United States in any lands and waters acquired in whole or part with such financial assistance.

(3)(A) The amount of the financial assistance provided under paragraph (1)(A)(i) with respect to the acquisition of lands and waters, or interests therein, for any one national estuarine reserve may not exceed an amount equal to 50 percent of the costs of the lands, waters, and interests therein or $5,000,000, whichever amount is less.

(B) The amount of the financial assistance provided under paragraph (1)(A)(ii) and (iii) and paragraph (1)(B) may not exceed 70 percent of the costs incurred to achieve the purposes described in those paragraphs with respect to a

reserve; except that the amount of the financial assistance provided under paragraph (1)(A)(iii) may be up to 100 percent of any costs for activities that benefit the entire System.

(C) Notwithstanding subparagraphs (A) and (B), financial assistance under this subsection provided from amounts recovered as a result of damage to natural resources located in the coastal zone may be used to pay 100 percent of the costs of activities carried out with the assistance.

(f) Evaluation of System performance —

(1) The Secretary shall periodically evaluate the operation and management of each national estuarine reserve, including education and interpretive activities, and the research being conducted within the reserve.

(2) If evaluation under paragraph (1) reveals that the operation and management of the reserve is deficient, or that the research being conducted within the reserve is not consistent with the research guidelines developed under subsection (c) of this section, the Secretary may suspend the eligibility of that reserve for financial assistance under subsection (e) of this section until the deficiency or inconsistency is remedied.

(3) The Secretary may withdraw the designation of an estuarine area as a national estuarine reserve if evaluation under paragraph (1) reveals that —

(A) the basis for any one or more of the findings made under subsection (b)(2) of this section regarding that area no longer exists; or

(B) a substantial portion of the research conducted within the area, over a period of years, has not been consistent with the research guidelines developed under subsection (c) of this section.

(g) Report — The Secretary shall include in the report required under section 1462 of this title information regarding —

(1) new designations of national estuarine reserves;

(2) any expansion of existing national estuarine reserves;

(3) the status of the research program being conducted within the System; and

(4) a summary of the evaluations made under subsection (f) of this section.

§1462. Coastal zone management reports [CZMA §316]

(a) Biennial reports — The Secretary shall consult with the Congress on a regular basis concerning the administration of this chapter and shall prepare and submit to the President for transmittal to the Congress a report summarizing the administration of this chapter during each period of two consecutive fiscal years. Each report, which shall be transmitted to the Congress not later than April 1 of the year following the close of the biennial period to which it pertains, shall include, but not be restricted to

(1) an identification of the state programs approved pursuant to this chapter during the preceding Federal fiscal year and a description of those programs; (2) a listing of the states participating in the provisions of this chapter and a description of the status of each state's programs and its accomplishments during the preceding Federal fiscal year; (3) an itemization of the allocation of funds to the various coastal states and a breakdown of the major projects and areas on which these funds were expended; (4) an identification of any state programs which have been reviewed and disapproved, and a statement of the reasons for such actions; (5) a summary of evaluation findings prepared in accordance with subsection (a) of section 1458 of this title, and a description of any sanctions imposed under subsections (c) and (d) of section 1458 of this title; (6) a listing of all activities and projects which, pursuant to the provisions of subsection (c) or subsection (d) of section 1456 of this title, are not consistent with an applicable approved state management program; (7) a summary of the regulations issued by the Secretary or in effect during the preceding Federal fiscal year; (8) a summary of a coordinated national strategy and program for the Nation's coastal zone including identification and discussion of Federal, regional, state, and local responsibilities and functions therein; (9) a summary of outstanding problems arising in the administration of this chapter in order of priority; (10) a description of the economic, environmental, and social consequences of energy activity affecting the coastal zone and an evaluation of the effectiveness of financial assistance under section 1456a of this title in dealing with such consequences; (11) a description and evaluation of applicable interstate and regional planning and coordination mechanisms developed by the coastal states; (12) a summary and evaluation of the research, studies, and training conducted in support of coastal zone management; and (13) such other information as may be appropriate.

(b) Recommendations for legislation — The report required by subsection (a) of this section shall contain such recommendations for additional legislation as the Secretary deems necessary to achieve the objectives of this chapter and enhance its effective operation.

(c) Review of other Federal programs; report to Congress —

(1) The Secretary shall conduct a systematic review of Federal programs, other than this chapter, that affect coastal resources for purposes of identifying conflicts between the objectives and administration of such programs and the purposes and policies of this chapter. Not later than 1 year after October 17, 1980, the Secretary shall notify each Federal agency having appropriate jurisdiction of any conflict between its program and the purposes and policies of this chapter identified as a result of such review.

(2) The Secretary shall promptly submit a report to the Congress consisting of the information required under paragraph (1) of this subsection. Such report shall include recommendations for changes necessary to resolve existing conflicts among Federal laws and programs that affect the uses of coastal resources.

§1463. Rules and regulations
[CZMA §317]

The Secretary shall develop and promulgate, pursuant to section 553 of title 5, after notice and opportunity for full participation by relevant Federal agencies, state agencies, local governments, regional organizations, port authorities, and other interested parties, both public and private, such rules and regulations as may be necessary to carry out the provisions of this chapter.

§1463a. Omitted

§1463b. National Coastal Resources Research and Development Institute

(a) Establishment by Secretary; administration — The Secretary of Commerce shall provide for the establishment of a National Coastal Resources Research and Development Institute (hereinafter in this section referred to as the "Institute") to be administered by the Oregon State Marine Science Center.

(b) Purposes of Institute — The Institute shall conduct research and carry out educational and demonstration projects designed to promote the efficient and responsible development of ocean and coastal resources, including arctic resources. Such projects shall be based on biological, geological, genetic, economic and other scientific research applicable to the purposes of this section and shall include studies on the economic diversification and environmental protection of the Nation's coastal areas.

(c) Determination of Institute policies —

(1) The policies of the Institute shall be determined by a Board of Governors composed of —

(A) two representatives appointed by the Governor of Oregon;

(B) one representative appointed by the Governor of Alaska;

(C) one representative appointed by the Governor of Washington;

(D) one representative appointed by the Governor of California; and

(E) one representative appointed by the Governor of Hawaii.

(2) Such policies shall include the selection, on a nationally competitive basis, of the research, projects, and studies to be supported by the Institute in accordance with the purposes of this section.

(d) Establishment of Advisory Council; functions and composition —

(1) The Board of Governors shall establish an Advisory Council composed of specialists in ocean and coastal resources from the academic community.

(2) To the maximum extent practicable, the Advisory Council shall be composed of such specialists from every coastal region of the Nation.

(3) The Advisory Council shall provide such advice to the Board of Governors as such Board shall request, including recommendations regarding the support of research, projects, and studies in accordance with the purposes of this section.

(e) Administration of Institute — The Institute shall be administered by a Director who shall be appointed by the Chancellor of the Oregon Board of Higher Education in consultation with the Board of Governors.

(f) Evaluation of Institute by Secretary — The Secretary of Commerce shall conduct an ongoing evaluation of the activities of the Institute to ensure that funds received by the Institute under this section are used in a manner consistent with the provisions of this section.

(g) Report to Secretary — The Institute shall report to the Secretary of Commerce on its activities within 2 years after July 17, 1984.

(h) Access to Institute books, records, and documents — The Comptroller General of the United States, and any of his duly authorized representatives, shall have access, for the purpose of audit and examination, to any books, documents, papers and records of the Institute that are pertinent to the funds received under this section.

(i) Status of Institute employees — Employees of the Institute shall not, by reason of such employment, be considered to be employees of the Federal Government for any purpose.

(j) Authorization of appropriations — For the purposes of this section, there are authorized to be appropriated in each fiscal year $5,000,000, commencing with fiscal year 1985.

§1464. Authorization of appropriations
[CZMA §318]

(a) Sums appropriated to Secretary — There are authorized to be appropriated to the Secretary, to remain available until expended —

(1) for grants under sections 1455, 1455a, and 1456b of this title —

(A) $47,600,000 for fiscal year 1997;

(B) $49,000,000 for fiscal year 1998; and

(C) $50,500,000 for fiscal year 1999; and

(2) for grants under section 1461 of this title —

(A) $4,400,000 for fiscal year 1997;

(B) $4,500,000 for fiscal year 1998; and

(C) $4,600,000 for fiscal year 1999.

(b) Limitations — Federal funds received from other sources shall not be used to pay a coastal state's share of costs under section 1455 or 1456b of this title.

(c) Reversion to Secretary of unobligated State funds; availability of funds — The amount of any grant, or portion of a grant, made to a State under any section of this chapter which is not obligated by such State during the fiscal year, or during the second fiscal year after the fiscal year, for which

it was first authorized to be obligated by such State shall revert to the Secretary. The Secretary shall add such reverted amount to those funds available for grants under the section for such reverted amount was originally made available.

§1465. Appeals to Secretary
[CZMA §319]

(a) Notice — Not later than 30 days after the date of the filing of an appeal to the Secretary of a consistency determination under section 307 [16 U.S.C.S. §1456], the Secretary shall publish an initial notice in the Federal Register.

(b) Closure of record

(1) In general. Not later than the end of the 160-day period beginning on the date of publication of an initial notice under subsection (a), except as provided in paragraph (3), the Secretary shall immediately close the decision record and receive no more filings on the appeal.

(2) Notice. After closing the administrative record, the Secretary shall immediately publish a notice in the Federal Register that the administrative record has been closed.

(3) Exception.

(A) In general. Subject to subparagraph (B), during the 160-day period described in paragraph (1), the Secretary may stay the closing of the decision record —

(i) for a specific period mutually agreed to in writing by the appellant and the State agency; or

(ii) as the Secretary determines necessary to receive, on an expedited basis—

(I) any supplemental information specifically requested by the Secretary to complete a consistency review under this Act; or

(II) any clarifying information submitted by a party to the proceeding related to information in the consolidated record compiled by the lead Federal permitting agency.

(B) Applicability. The Secretary may only stay the 160-day period described in paragraph (1) for a period not to exceed 60 days.

(c) Deadline for decision

(1) In general. Not later than 60 days after the date of publication of a Federal Register notice stating when the decision record for an appeal has been closed, the Secretary shall issue a decision or publish a notice in the Federal Register explaining why a decision cannot be issued at that time.

(2) Subsequent decision. Not later than 15 days after the date of publication of a Federal Register notice explaining why a decision cannot be issued within the 60-day period, the Secretary shall issue a decision.

§1466. Appeals relating to offshore mineral development — For any Federal administrative agency proceeding that is an appeal or review under section 319 of the Coastal Zone Management Act of 1972 (16 U.S.C. 1465), as amended by this Act, related to any Federal authorization for the permitting, approval, or other authorization of an energy project, the lead Federal permitting agency for the project shall, with the cooperation of Federal and State administrative agencies, maintain a consolidated record of all decisions made or actions taken by the lead agency or by another Federal or State administrative agency or officer. Such record shall be the initial record for appeals or reviews under that Act, provided that the record may be supplemented as expressly provided pursuant to section 319 of that Act [16 U.S.C. §1465].

8

ENVIRONMENTAL IMPACT ASSESSMENT

Environmental impact assessment has become one of the most universal elements of environmental law throughout the world. The legal requirement that environmental assessment be conducted prior to making decisions likely to have a significant effect on the environment originated in the National Environmental Policy Act (NEPA) of 1969. This chapter contains the text of the NEPA and its implementing regulations issued by the Council on Environmental Quality (CEQ).

A GUIDE TO MATERIALS ON ENVIRONMENTAL IMPACT ASSESSMENT AVAILABLE ON THE INTERNET

The website of the Council on Environmental Quality (CEQ), the White House agency responsible for coordinating federal agency compliance with the National Environmental Policy Act (NEPA), is located at *https://www.whitehouse.gov/ceq/*.

EPA describes its NEPA responsibilities at *http://www.epa.gov/compliance/nepa/index.html*. It provides links to EPA's Environmental Impact Statement Database, instructions for federal agencies on how to submit an EIS, information on how to obtain copies of other agencies' EISs, and information on how EPA complies with NEPA for many of its own actions.

The National Association of Environmental Professionals (NAEP) has a NEPA Working Group that has a website located at *http://www.naep.org*. A report criticizing efforts to weaken NEPA has been written by former EPA attorney Robert Dreher. Called "NEPA Under Siege," it is available online at *https://www.sierraforestlegacy. org/Resources/Conservation/LawsPoliciesRegulation/ForestPlanningRegulations/NEPA/NEPA-UnderSiege.pdf*.

NEPA's EIS requirement is the most widely emulated feature of U.S. environmental law throughout the world. CEQ maintains a webpage with links to environmental impact assessment agencies in 37 countries *(https://ceq.doe.gov/get-involved/international_impact_assessment.html)*, and to the webpages of dozens of nongovernmental organizations and international entities involved in impact assessment. The International Association for Impact Assessment maintains a website *(http://www.iaia.org)* that provides information concerning how impact assessment is conducted around the world and what are considered to be best practices for it.

NEPA TIMELINE

January 1, 1970: On national television, President Richard Nixon signs the National Environmental Policy Act of 1969, Pub. L. 91-190, 83 Stat. 852. The Act mandates that federal agencies prepare and consider environmental impact statements before undertaking any major federal action likely to have a significant effect on the environment.

April 3, 1970: President Nixon signs the Environmental Quality Improvement Act of 1970, Pub. L. No. 91-224, 84 Stat. 114, which creates an Office of Environmental Quality in the Executive Office of the President to be chaired by the chairman of CEQ.

December 31, 1970: Section 309 is added to the Clean Air Act by Pub. L. 91-604, 84 Stat. 1676. It requires that the U.S. Environmental Protection Agency (EPA) comment on environmental impact statements (EISs) prepared by other federal agencies and that EPA's comments be made public and transmitted to CEQ for action if the agency finds the impacts to be "environmentally unsatisfactory."

August 9, 1975: President Ford signs Pub. L. 94-83, 89 Stat. 424, which adds Section 102(D) to NEPA providing that environmental impact statements can be prepared by state agencies or officials with statewide jurisdiction for programs funded by federal grants so long as the federal official responsible for the program participates in its preparation and evaluates it independently prior to its approval and adoption.

August 5, 2016: The Council on Environmental Quality (CEQ) issues its final guidance entitled "Final Guidance for Federal Departments and Agencies on Consideration of Greenhouse Gas Emissions and the Effects of Climate Change in National Environmental Policy Act Reviews," 81 Fed. Reg. 51866.

January 24, 2017: President Trump issues Executive Order 13,766 ("Expediting Environmental Reviews and Approvals for High Priority Infrastructure Projects"), 82 Fed. Reg. 8567. It requires decisions within 30 days on requests to designate projects as "high priority infrastructure projects" and it provides that such projects should receive expedited reviews.

March 28, 2017: President Trump issues Executive Order 13,783 ("Promoting Energy Independence and Economic Growth"), 82 Fed Reg. 16093, which rescinds the CEQ's August 5, 2016 guidance on how agencies should consider greenhouse gas emissions and the effects of climate change in NEPA reviews.

August 15, 2017: President Trump issues Executive Order 13,807 ("Establishing Discipline and Accountability in the Environmental Review and Permitting Process for Infrastructure"), 82 Fed. Reg. 40463. The executive order seeks to reduce significantly the average length of time for federal environmental reviews.

July 16, 2020: The Council on Environmental Quality promulgates new regulations, 85 Fed. Reg. 43304, comprehensively revising procedures for implementing NEPA for the first time since 1978.

PRINCIPAL PROVISIONS OF NEPA

§101 (42 U.S.C. §4331) Congressional Declaration of National Environmental Policy: declares it to be the continuing policy of the Federal Government to use all practicable means to create and to maintain conditions under which man and nature can exist in productive harmony.

§102 (42 U.S.C. §4332) Cooperation of agencies; reports; availability of information; recommendations; international and national coordination of effects: requires all federal agencies prior to taking major action significantly affecting the quality of the environment to prepare an environmental impact statement that includes a detailed statement of environmental impacts, alternatives to the proposed impact, and any irretrievable commitment of resources involved. Also requires all federal agencies to study and to develop alternatives to recommended actions involving unresolved resource conflicts.

§202 (42 U.S.C. §4342) Establishment; Membership; Chairman; Appointments: establishes a three-member Council on Environmental Quality (CEQ) in the Executive Office of the President.

§202 (42 U.S.C. §4342) Duties and Functions: outlines duties and functions of CEQ, including annual reporting on the state of the environment, information gathering and review and appraisal of federal programs and activities.

National Environmental Policy Act

42 U.S.C. §§4321 to 4347

§4321. Congressional declaration of purpose
[NEPA §2]

The purposes of this chapter are: To declare a national policy which will encourage productive and enjoyable harmony between man and his environment; to promote efforts which will prevent or eliminate damage to the environment and biosphere and stimulate the health and welfare of man; to enrich the understanding of the ecological systems and natural resources important to the Nation; and to establish a Council on Environmental Quality.

SUBCHAPTER I — POLICIES AND GOALS

§4331. Congressional declaration of national environmental policy
[NEPA §101]

(a) The Congress, recognizing the profound impact of man's activity on the interrelations of all components of the natural environment, particularly the profound influences of population growth, high-density urbanization, industrial expansion, resource exploitation, and new and expanding technological advances and recognizing further the critical importance of restoring and maintaining environmental quality to the overall welfare and development of man, declares that it is the continuing policy of the Federal Government, in cooperation with State and local governments, and other concerned public and private organizations, to use all practicable means and measures, including financial and technical assistance, in a manner calculated to foster and promote the general welfare, to create and maintain conditions under which man and nature can exist in productive harmony, and fulfill the social, economic, and other requirements of present and future generations of Americans.

(b) In order to carry out the policy set forth in this chapter, it is the continuing responsibility of the Federal Government to use all practicable means, consistent with other essential considerations of national policy, to improve and coordinate Federal plans, functions, programs, and resources to the end that the Nation may —

(1) fulfill the responsibilities of each generation as trustee of the environment for succeeding generations;

(2) assure for all Americans safe, healthful, productive, and aesthetically and culturally pleasing surroundings;

(3) attain the widest range of beneficial uses of the environment without degradation, risk to health or safety, or other undesirable and unintended consequences;

(4) preserve important historic, cultural, and natural aspects of our national heritage, and maintain, wherever possible, an environment which supports diversity, and variety of individual choice;

(5) achieve a balance between population and resource use which will permit high standards of living and a wide sharing of life's amenities; and

(6) enhance the quality of renewable resources and approach the maximum attainable recycling of depletable resources.

(c) The Congress recognizes that each person should enjoy a healthful environment and that each person has a responsibility to contribute to the preservation and enhancement of the environment.

§4332. Cooperation of agencies; reports; availability of information; recommendations; international and national coordination of efforts

[NEPA §102]

The Congress authorizes and directs that, to the fullest extent possible: (1) the policies, regulations, and public laws of the United States shall be interpreted and administered in accordance with the policies set forth in this chapter, and (2) all agencies of the Federal Government shall —

(A) utilize a systematic, interdisciplinary approach which will insure the integrated use of the natural and social sciences and the environmental design arts in planning and in decisionmaking which may have an impact on man's environment;

(B) identify and develop methods and procedures, in consultation with the Council on Environmental Quality established by subchapter II of this chapter, which will insure that presently unquantified environmental amenities and values may be given appropriate consideration in decisionmaking along with economic and technical considerations;

(C) include in every recommendation or report on proposals for legislation and other major Federal actions significantly affecting the quality of the human environment, a detailed statement by the responsible official on —

(i) the environmental impact of the proposed action,

(ii) any adverse environmental effects which cannot be avoided should the proposal be implemented,

(iii) alternatives to the proposed action,

(iv) the relationship between local short-term uses of man's environment and the maintenance and enhancement of long-term productivity, and

(v) any irreversible and irretrievable commitments of resources which would be involved in the proposed action should it be implemented.

Prior to making any detailed statement, the responsible Federal official shall consult with and obtain the comments of any Federal agency which has jurisdiction by law or special expertise with respect to any environmental impact involved. Copies of such statement and the comments and views of the appropriate Federal, State, and local agencies, which are authorized to develop and enforce environmental standards, shall be made available to the President, the Council on Environmental Quality and to the public as provided by section 552 of Title 5, and shall accompany the proposal through the existing agency review processes;

(D) Any detailed statement required under subparagraph (C) after January 1, 1970, for any major Federal action funded under a program of grants to States shall not be deemed to be legally insufficient solely by reason of having been prepared by a State agency or official, if:

(i) the State agency or official has statewide jurisdiction and has the responsibility for such action,

(ii) the responsible Federal official furnishes guidance and participates in such preparation,

(iii) the responsible Federal official independently evaluates such statement prior to its approval and adoption, and

(iv) after January 1, 1976, the responsible Federal official provides early notification to, and solicits the views of, any other State or any Federal land management entity of any action or any alternative thereto which may have significant impacts upon such State or affected Federal land management entity and, if there is any disagreement on such impacts, prepares a written assessment of such impacts and views for incorporation into such detailed statement.

The procedures in this subparagraph shall not relieve the Federal official of his responsibilities for the scope, objectivity, and content of the entire statement or of any other responsibility under this chapter; and further, this subparagraph does not affect the legal sufficiency of statements prepared by State agencies with less than statewide jurisdiction.

(E) study, develop, and describe appropriate alternatives to recommended courses of action in any proposal which involves unresolved conflicts concerning alternative uses of available resources;

(F) recognize the worldwide and long-range character of environmental problems and, where consistent with the foreign policy of the United States, lend appropriate support to initiatives, resolutions, and programs designed to maximize international cooperation in anticipating and preventing a decline in the quality of mankind's world environment;

(G) make available to States, counties, municipalities, institutions, and individuals, advice and information useful in restoring, maintaining, and enhancing the quality of the environment;

(H) initiate and utilize ecological information in the planning and development of resource-oriented projects; and

(I) assist the Council on Environmental Quality established by subchapter II of this chapter.

§4333. Conformity of administrative procedures to national environmental policy
[NEPA §103]

All agencies of the Federal Government shall review their present statutory authority, administrative regulations, and current policies and procedures for the purpose of determining whether there are any deficiencies or inconsistencies therein which prohibit full compliance with the purposes and provisions of this chapter and shall propose to the President not later than July 1, 1971, such measures as may be necessary to bring their authority and policies into conformity with the intent, purposes, and procedures set forth in this chapter.

§4334. Other statutory obligations of agencies
[NEPA §104]

Nothing in section 4332 or 4333 of this title shall in any way affect the specific statutory obligations of any Federal agency (1) to comply with criteria or standards of environmental quality, (2) to coordinate or consult with any other Federal or State agency, or (3) to act, or refrain from acting contingent upon the recommendations or certification of any other Federal or State agency.

§4335. Efforts supplemental to existing authorizations
[NEPA §105]

The policies and goals set forth in this chapter are supplementary to those set forth in existing authorizations of Federal agencies.

SUBCHAPTER II — COUNCIL ON ENVIRONMENTAL QUALITY

§4342. Establishment; membership; Chairman; appointments
[NEPA §202]

There is created in the Executive Office of the President a Council on Environmental Quality (hereinafter referred to as the "Council"). The Council shall be composed of three members who shall be appointed by the President to serve at his pleasure, by and with the advice and consent of the Senate. The President shall designate one of the members of the Council to serve as Chairman. Each member shall be a person who, as a result of his training, experience, and attainments, is exceptionally well qualified to analyze and interpret environmental trends and information of all kinds; to appraise programs and activities of the Federal Government in the light of the policy set forth in subchapter I of this chapter; to be conscious of and responsive to the scientific, economic, social, aesthetic, and cultural needs and interests of the Nation; and to formulate and recommend national policies to promote the improvement of the quality of the environment.

§4343. Employment of personnel, experts and consultants
[NEPA §203]

(a) **Authority** — The Council may employ such officers and employees as may be necessary to carry out its functions under this chapter. In addition, the Council may employ and fix the compensation of such experts and consultants as may be necessary for the carrying out of its functions under this chapter, in accordance with section 3109 of Title 5 (but without regard to the last sentence thereof).

(b) **Voluntary and uncompensated services** — Notwithstanding section 1342 of Title 31, the Council may accept and employ voluntary and uncompensated services in furtherance of the purposes of the Council.

§4344. Duties and functions
[NEPA §204]

It shall be the duty and function of the Council —

(1) to assist and advise the President in the preparation of the Environmental Quality Report required by section 4341 of this title;

(2) to gather timely and authoritative information concerning the conditions and trends in the quality of the environment both current and prospective, to analyze and interpret such information for the purpose of determining whether such conditions and trends are interfering, or are likely to interfere, with the achievement of the policy set forth in subchapter I of this chapter, and to compile and submit to the President studies relating to such conditions and trends;

(3) to review and appraise the various programs and activities of the Federal Government in the light of the policy set forth in subchapter I of this chapter for the purpose of determining the extent to which such programs and activities are contributing to the achievement of such policy, and to make recommendations to the President with respect thereto;

(4) to develop and recommend to the President national policies to foster and promote the improvement of environmental quality to meet

the conservation, social, economic, health, and other requirements and goals of the Nation;

(5) to conduct investigations, studies, surveys, research, and analyses relating to ecological systems and environmental quality;

(6) to document and define changes in the natural environment, including the plant and animal systems, and to accumulate necessary data and other information for a continuing analysis of these changes or trends and an interpretation of their underlying causes;

(7) to report at least once each year to the President on the state and condition of the environment; and

(8) to make and furnish such studies, reports thereon, and recommendations with respect to matters of policy and legislation as the President may request.

§4345. Consultation with Citizens' Advisory Committee on Environmental Quality and other representatives
[NEPA §205]

In exercising its powers, functions, and duties under this Act, the Council shall —

(1) consult with the Citizens' Advisory Committee on Environmental Quality established by Executive Order No. 11472, dated May 29, 1969, and with such representatives of science, industry, agriculture, labor, conservation organizations, State and local governments and other groups, as it deems advisable; and

(2) utilize, to the fullest extent possible, the services, facilities and information (including statistical information) of public and private agencies and organizations, and individuals, in order that duplication of effort and expense may be avoided, thus assuring that the Council's activities will not unnecessarily overlap or conflict with similar activities authorized by law and performed by established agencies.

§4346. Tenure and compensation of members
[NEPA §206]

Members of the Council shall serve full time and the Chairman of the Council shall be compensated at the rate provided for Level II of the Executive Schedule Pay Rates (5 U.S.C. §5313). The other members of the Council shall be compensated at the rate provided for Level IV of the Executive Schedule Pay Rates (5 U.S.C. §5315).

§4346a. Travel reimbursement by private organizations and Federal, State, and local governments
[NEPA §207]

The Council may accept reimbursements from any private nonprofit organization or from any department, agency, or instrumentality of the Federal Government, any State, or local government, for the reasonable travel expenses incurred by an officer or employee of the Council in connection with his attendance at any conference, seminar, or similar meeting conducted for the benefit of the Council.

§4346b. Expenditures in support of international activities
[NEPA §208]

The Council may make expenditures in support of its international activities, including expenditures for: (1) international travel; (2) activities in implementation of international agreements; and (3) the support of international exchange programs in the United States and in foreign countries.

§4347. Authorization of appropriations
[NEPA §209]

There are authorized to be appropriated to carry out the provisions of this chapter not to exceed $300,000 for fiscal year 1970, $700,000 for fiscal year 1971, and $1,000,000 for each fiscal year thereafter.

NEPA Regulations

40 C.F.R. §§1500 TO 1508

PART 1507—AGENCY COMPLIANCE

1507.1   Compliance.
1507.2   Agency capability to comply.
1507.3   Agency NEPA procedures.
1507.4   Agency NEPA program information.

PART 1508—DEFINITIONS

1508.1   Definitions.
1508.2   [Reserved]

§1500.1 Purpose and policy.

(a) The National Environmental Policy Act (NEPA) is a procedural statute intended to ensure Federal agencies consider the environmental impacts of their actions in the decision-making process. Section 101 of NEPA establishes the national environmental policy of the Federal Government to use all practicable means and measures to foster and promote the general welfare, create and maintain conditions under which man and nature can exist in productive harmony, and fulfill the social, economic, and other requirements of present and future generations of Americans. Section 102(2) of NEPA establishes the procedural requirements to carry out the policy stated in section 101 of NEPA. In particular, it requires Federal agencies to provide a detailed statement on proposals for major Federal actions significantly affecting the quality of the human environment. The purpose and function of NEPA is satisfied if Federal agencies have considered relevant environmental information, and the public has been informed regarding the decision-making process. NEPA does not mandate particular results or substantive outcomes. NEPA's purpose is not to generate paperwork or litigation, but to provide for informed decision making and foster excellent action.

(b) The regulations in this subchapter implement section 102(2) of NEPA. They provide direction to Federal agencies to determine what actions are subject to NEPA's procedural requirements and the level of NEPA review where applicable. The regulations in this subchapter are intended to ensure that relevant environmental information is identified and considered early in the process in order to ensure informed decision making by Federal agencies. The regulations in this subchapter are also intended to ensure that Federal agencies conduct environmental reviews in a coordinated, consistent, predictable and timely manner, and to reduce unnecessary burdens and delays. Finally, the regulations in this subchapter promote concurrent environmental reviews to ensure timely and efficient decision making.

§1500.2 [Reserved]

§1500.3 NEPA compliance.

(a) *Mandate.* This subchapter is applicable to and binding on all Federal agencies for implementing the procedural provisions of the National Environmental Policy Act of 1969, as amended (Pub. L. 91-190, 42 U.S.C. 4321 *et seq.*) (NEPA or the Act), except where compliance would be inconsistent with other statutory requirements. The regulations in this subchapter are issued pursuant to NEPA; the Environmental Quality Improvement Act of 1970, as amended (Pub. L. 91-224, 42 U.S.C. 4371 *et seq.*); section 309 of the Clean Air Act, as amended (42 U.S.C. 7609); Executive Order 11514, Protection and Enhancement of Environmental Quality (March 5, 1970), as amended by Executive Order 11991, Relating to the Protection and Enhancement of Environmental Quality (May 24, 1977); and Executive Order 13807,Establishing Discipline and Accountability in the Environmental Review and Permitting Process for Infrastructure Projects (August 15, 2017). The regulations in this subchapter apply to the whole of section 102(2) of NEPA. The provisions of the Act and the regulations in this subchapter must be read together as a whole to comply with the law.

(b) *Exhaustion.* (1) To ensure informed decision making and reduce delays, agencies shall include a request for comments on potential alternatives and impacts, and identification of any relevant information, studies, or analyses of any kind concerning impacts affecting the quality of the human environment in the notice of intent to prepare an environmental impact statement (§1501.9(d)(7) of this chapter).

(2) The draft and final environmental impact statements shall include a summary of all alternatives, information, and analyses submitted by State, Tribal, and local governments and other public commenters for consideration by the lead and cooperating agencies in developing the draft and final environmental impact statements (§1502.17 of this chapter).

(3) For consideration by the lead and cooperating agencies, State, Tribal, and local governments and other public commenters must submit comments within the comment periods provided, and comments shall be as specific as possible (§§1503.1 and 1503.3 of this chapter). Comments or objections of any kind not submitted, including those based on submitted alternatives, information, and analyses, shall be forfeited as unexhausted.

(4) Informed by the submitted alternatives, information, and analyses, including the summary in the final environmental impact statement (§1502.17 of this chapter) and the agency's response to comments in the final environmental impact statement (§1503.4 of this chapter), together with any other material in the record that he or she determines relevant, the decision maker shall certify in the record of decision that the agency considered all of the alternatives, information, and analyses, and

objections submitted by States, Tribal, and local governments and other public commenters for consideration by the lead and cooperating agencies in developing the environmental impact statement (§1505.2(b) of this chapter).

(c) *Review of NEPA compliance.* It is the Council's intention that judicial review of agency compliance with the regulations in this subchapter not occur before an agency has issued the record of decision or taken other final agency action. It is the Council's intention that any allegation of noncompliance with NEPA and the regulations in this subchapter should be resolved as expeditiously as possible. Consistent with their organic statutes, and as part of implementing the exhaustion provisions in paragraph (b) of this section, agencies may structure their procedures to include an appropriate bond or other security requirement.

(d) *Remedies.* Harm from the failure to comply with NEPA can be remedied by compliance with NEPA's procedural requirements as interpreted in the regulations in this subchapter. It is the Council's intention that the regulations in this subchapter create no presumption that violation of NEPA is a basis for injunctive relief or for a finding of irreparable harm. The regulations in this subchapter do not create a cause of action or right of action for violation of NEPA, which contains no such cause of action or right of action. It is the Council's intention that any actions to review, enjoin, stay, vacate, or otherwise alter an agency decision on the basis of an alleged NEPA violation be raised as soon as practicable after final agency action to avoid or minimize any costs to agencies, applicants, or any affected third parties. It is also the Council's intention that minor, nonsubstantive errors that have no effect on agency decision making shall be considered harmless and shall not invalidate an agency action.

(e) *Severability.* The sections of this subchapter are separate and severable from one another. If any section or portion therein is stayed or determined to be invalid, or the applicability of any section to any person or entity is held invalid, it is the Council's intention that the validity of the remainder of those parts shall not be affected, with the remaining sections to continue in effect.

§1500.4 Reducing paperwork.

Agencies shall reduce excessive paperwork by:

(a) Using categorical exclusions to define categories of actions that normally do not have a significant effect on the human environment and therefore do not require preparation of an environmental impact statement (§1501.4 of this chapter).

(b) Using a finding of no significant impact when an action not otherwise excluded will not have a significant effect on the human environment and therefore does not require preparation of an environmental impact statement (§1501.6 of this chapter).

(c) Reducing the length of environmental documents by means such as meeting appropriate page limits (§§1501.5(f) and 1502.7 of this chapter).

(d) Preparing analytic and concise environmental impact statements (§1502.2 of this chapter).

(e) Discussing only briefly issues other than significant ones (§1502.2(b) of this chapter).

(f) Writing environmental impact statements in plain language (§1502.8 of this chapter).

(g) Following a clear format for environmental impact statements (§1502.10 of this chapter).

(h) Emphasizing the portions of the environmental impact statement that are useful to decision makers and the public (*e.g.,* §§1502.14 and 1502.15 of this chapter) and reducing emphasis on background material (§1502.1 of this chapter).

(i) Using the scoping process, not only to identify significant environmental issues deserving of study, but also to deemphasize insignificant issues, narrowing the scope of the environmental impact statement process accordingly (§1501.9 of this chapter).

(j) Summarizing the environmental impact statement (§1502.12 of this chapter).

(k) Using programmatic, policy, or plan environmental impact statements and tiering from statements of broad scope to those of narrower scope, to eliminate repetitive discussions of the same issues (§§1501.11 and 1502.4 of this chapter).

(l) Incorporating by reference (§1501.12 of this chapter).

(m) Integrating NEPA requirements with other environmental review and consultation requirements (§1502.24 of this chapter).

(n) Requiring comments to be as specific as possible (§1503.3 of this chapter).

(o) Attaching and publishing only changes to the draft environmental impact statement, rather than rewriting and publishing the entire statement when changes are minor (§1503.4(c) of this chapter).

(p) Eliminating duplication with State, Tribal, and local procedures, by providing for joint preparation of environmental documents where practicable (§1506.2 of this chapter), and with other Federal procedures, by providing that an agency may adopt appropriate environmental documents prepared by another agency (§1506.3 of this chapter).

(q) Combining environmental documents with other documents (§1506.4 of this chapter).

§1500.5 Reducing delay.

Agencies shall reduce delay by:

(a) Using categorical exclusions to define categories of actions that normally do not have a significant effect on the human environment (§1501.4 of this chapter) and therefore do not require preparation of an environmental impact statement.

(b) Using a finding of no significant impact when an action not otherwise excluded will not have a significant effect on the human environment (§1501.6 of this chapter) and therefore does not require preparation of an environmental impact statement.

(c) Integrating the NEPA process into early planning (§1501.2 of this chapter).

(d) Engaging in interagency cooperation before or as the environmental assessment or environmental impact statement is prepared, rather than awaiting submission of comments on a completed document (§§1501.7 and 1501.8 of this chapter).

(e) Ensuring the swift and fair resolution of lead agency disputes (§1501.7 of this chapter).

(f) Using the scoping process for an early identification of what are and what are not the real issues (§1501.9 of this chapter).

(g) Meeting appropriate time limits for the environmental assessment and environmental impact statement processes (§1501.10 of this chapter).

(h) Preparing environmental impact statements early in the process (§1502.5 of this chapter).

(i) Integrating NEPA requirements with other environmental review and consultation requirements (§1502.24 of this chapter).

(j) Eliminating duplication with State, Tribal, and local procedures by providing for joint preparation of environmental documents where practicable (§1506.2 of this chapter) and with other Federal procedures by providing that agencies may jointly prepare or adopt appropriate environmental documents prepared by another agency (§1506.3 of this chapter).

(k) Combining environmental documents with other documents (§1506.4 of this chapter).

(l) Using accelerated procedures for proposals for legislation (§1506.8 of this chapter).

§1500.6 Agency authority.

Each agency shall interpret the provisions of the Act as a supplement to its existing authority and as a mandate to view policies and missions in the light of the Act's national environmental objectives, to the extent consistent with its existing authority. Agencies shall review their policies, procedures, and regulations accordingly and revise them as necessary to ensure full compliance with the purposes and provisions of the Act as interpreted by the regulations in this subchapter. The phrase "to the fullest extent possible" in section 102 of NEPA means that each agency of the Federal Government shall comply with that section, consistent with §1501.1 of this chapter. Nothing contained in the regulations in this subchapter is intended or should be construed to limit an agency's other authorities or legal responsibilities.

§1501.1 NEPA thresholds.

(a) In assessing whether NEPA applies or is otherwise fulfilled, Federal agencies should determine:

(1) Whether the proposed activity or decision is expressly exempt from NEPA under another statute;

(2) Whether compliance with NEPA would clearly and fundamentally conflict with the requirements of another statute;

(3) Whether compliance with NEPA would be inconsistent with Congressional intent expressed in another statute;

(4) Whether the proposed activity or decision is a major Federal action;

(5) Whether the proposed activity or decision, in whole or in part, is a non-discretionary action for which the agency lacks authority to consider environmental effects as part of its decision-making process; and

(6) Whether the proposed action is an action for which another statute's requirements serve the function of agency compliance with the Act.

(b) Federal agencies may make determinations under this section in their agency NEPA procedures (§1507.3(d) of this chapter) or on an individual basis, as appropriate.

(1) Federal agencies may seek the Council's assistance in making an individual determination under this section.

(2) An agency shall consult with other Federal agencies concerning their concurrence in statutory determinations made under this section where more than one Federal agency administers the statute.

§1501.2 Apply NEPA early in the process.

(a) Agencies should integrate the NEPA process with other planning and authorization processes at the earliest reasonable time to ensure that agencies consider environmental impacts in their planning and decisions, to avoid delays later in the process, and to head off potential conflicts.

(b) Each agency shall:

(1) Comply with the mandate of section 102(2)(A) of NEPA to utilize a systematic, interdisciplinary approach which will ensure the integrated use of the natural and social sciences and the environmental design arts in planning and in decision making which may have an impact on man's environment, as specified by §1507.2(a) of this chapter.

(2) Identify environmental effects and values in adequate detail so the decision maker can appropriately consider such effects and values alongside economic and technical analyses. Whenever practicable, agencies shall review and publish environmental documents and appropriate analyses at the same time as other planning documents.

(3) Study, develop, and describe appropriate alternatives to recommended courses of action in any proposal that involves unresolved conflicts concerning alternative uses of available resources as provided by section 102(2)(E) of NEPA.

(4) Provide for actions subject to NEPA that are planned by private applicants or other non-Federal entities before Federal involvement so that:

(i) Policies or designated staff are available to advise potential applicants of studies or other information foreseeably required for later Federal action.

(ii) The Federal agency consults early with appropriate State, Tribal, and local governments and with interested private persons and organizations when their involvement is reasonably foreseeable.

(iii) The Federal agency commences its NEPA process at the earliest reasonable time (§§1501.5(d) and 1502.5(b) of this chapter).

§1501.3 Determine the appropriate level of NEPA review.

(a) In assessing the appropriate level of NEPA review, Federal agencies should determine whether the proposed action:

(1) Normally does not have significant effects and is categorically excluded (§1501.4);

(2) Is not likely to have significant effects or the significance of the effects is unknown and is therefore appropriate for an environmental assessment (§1501.5); or

(3) Is likely to have significant effects and is therefore appropriate for an environmental impact statement (part 1502 of this chapter).

(b) In considering whether the effects of the proposed action are significant, agencies shall analyze the potentially affected environment and degree of the effects of the action. Agencies should consider connected actions consistent with §1501.9(e)(1).

(1) In considering the potentially affected environment, agencies should consider, as appropriate to the specific action, the affected area (national, regional, or local) and its resources, such as listed species and designated critical habitat under the Endangered Species Act. Significance varies with the setting of the proposed action. For instance, in the case of a site-specific action, significance would usually depend only upon the effects in the local area.

(2) In considering the degree of the effects, agencies should consider the following, as appropriate to the specific action:

(i) Both short- and long-term effects.

(ii) Both beneficial and adverse effects.

(iii) Effects on public health and safety.

(iv) Effects that would violate Federal, State, Tribal, or local law protecting the environment.

§1501.4 Categorical exclusions.

(a) For efficiency, agencies shall identify in their agency NEPA procedures (§1507.3(e)(2)(ii) of this chapter) categories of actions that normally do not have a significant effect on the human environment, and therefore do not require preparation of an environmental assessment or environmental impact statement.

(b) If an agency determines that a categorical exclusion identified in its agency NEPA procedures covers a proposed action, the agency shall evaluate the action for extraordinary circumstances in which a normally excluded action may have a significant effect.

(1) If an extraordinary circumstance is present, the agency nevertheless may categorically exclude the proposed action if the agency determines that there are circumstances that lessen the impacts or other conditions sufficient to avoid significant effects.

(2) If the agency cannot categorically exclude the proposed action, the agency shall prepare an environmental assessment or environmental impact statement, as appropriate.

§1501.5 Environmental assessments.

(a) An agency shall prepare an environmental assessment for a proposed action that is not likely to have significant effects or when the significance of the effects is unknown unless the agency finds that a categorical exclusion (§1501.4) is applicable or has decided to prepare an environmental impact statement.

(b) An agency may prepare an environmental assessment on any action in order to assist agency planning and decision making.

(c) An environmental assessment shall:

(1) Briefly provide sufficient evidence and analysis for determining whether to prepare an environmental impact statement or a finding of no significant impact; and

(2) Briefly discuss the purpose and need for the proposed action, alternatives as required by section 102(2)(E) of NEPA, and the environmental impacts of the proposed action and alternatives, and include a listing of agencies and persons consulted.

(d) For applications to the agency requiring an environmental assessment, the agency shall commence the environmental assessment as soon as practicable after receiving the application.

(e) Agencies shall involve the public, State, Tribal, and local governments, relevant agencies, and any applicants, to the extent practicable in preparing environmental assessments.

(f) The text of an environmental assessment shall be no more than 75 pages, not including appendices, unless a senior agency official approves in writing an assessment to exceed 75 pages and establishes a new page limit.

(g) Agencies may apply the following provisions to environmental assessments:

(1) Section 1502.21 of this chapter—Incomplete or unavailable information;

(2) Section 1502.23 of this chapter—Methodology and scientific accuracy; and

(3) Section 1502.24 of this chapter—Environmental review and consultation requirements.

§1501.6 Findings of no significant impact.

(a) An agency shall prepare a finding of no significant impact if the agency determines, based on the environmental assessment, not to prepare an environmental impact statement because the proposed action will not have significant effects.

(1) The agency shall make the finding of no significant impact available to the affected public as specified in §1506.6(b) of this chapter.

(2) In the following circumstances, the agency shall make the finding of no significant impact available for public review for 30 days before the agency makes its final determination whether to prepare an environmental impact statement and before the action may begin:

(i) The proposed action is or is closely similar to one that normally requires the preparation of an environmental impact statement under the procedures adopted by the agency pursuant to §1507.3 of this chapter; or

(ii) The nature of the proposed action is one without precedent.

(b) The finding of no significant impact shall include the environmental assessment or incorporate it by reference and shall note any other environmental documents related to it (§1501.9(f)(3)). If the assessment is included, the finding need not repeat any of the discussion in the assessment but may incorporate it by reference.

(c) The finding of no significant impact shall state the authority for any mitigation that the agency has adopted and any applicable monitoring or enforcement provisions. If the agency finds no significant impacts based on mitigation, the mitigated finding of no significant impact shall state any enforceable mitigation requirements or commitments that will be undertaken to avoid significant impacts.

§1501.7 Lead agencies.

(a) A lead agency shall supervise the preparation of an environmental impact statement or a complex environmental assessment if more than one Federal agency either:

(1) Proposes or is involved in the same action; or

(2) Is involved in a group of actions directly related to each other because of their functional interdependence or geographical proximity.

(b) Federal, State, Tribal, or local agencies, including at least one Federal agency, may act as joint lead agencies to prepare an environmental impact statement or environmental assessment (§1506.2 of this chapter).

(c) If an action falls within the provisions of paragraph (a) of this section, the potential lead agencies shall determine, by letter or memorandum, which agency will be the lead agency and which will be cooperating agencies. The agencies shall resolve the lead agency question so as not to cause delay. If there is disagreement among the agencies, the following factors (which are listed in order of descending importance) shall determine lead agency designation:

(1) Magnitude of agency's involvement.

(2) Project approval or disapproval authority.

(3) Expertise concerning the action's environmental effects.

(4) Duration of agency's involvement.

(5) Sequence of agency's involvement.

(d) Any Federal agency, or any State, Tribal, or local agency or private person substantially affected by the absence of lead agency designation, may make a written request to the senior agency officials of the potential lead agencies that a lead agency be designated.

(e) If Federal agencies are unable to agree on which agency will be the lead agency or if the procedure described in paragraph (c) of this section has not resulted in a lead agency designation within 45 days, any of the agencies or persons concerned may file a request with the Council asking it to determine which Federal agency shall be the lead agency. A copy of the request shall be transmitted to each potential lead agency. The request shall consist of:

(1) A precise description of the nature and extent of the proposed action; and

(2) A detailed statement of why each potential lead agency should or should not be the lead agency under the criteria specified in paragraph (c) of this section.

(f) Any potential lead agency may file a response within 20 days after a request is filed with the Council. As soon as possible, but not later than 20 days after receiving the request and all responses to it, the Council shall determine which Federal agency will be the lead agency and which other Federal agencies will be cooperating agencies.

(g) To the extent practicable, if a proposal will require action by more than one Federal agency and the lead agency determines that it requires preparation of an environmental impact statement, the lead and cooperating agencies shall evaluate the proposal in a single environmental impact statement and issue a joint record of decision. To the extent practicable, if a proposal will require action by more than one Federal agency and the lead agency determines that it requires preparation of an environmental assessment, the lead and cooperating agencies should evaluate the proposal in a single environmental assessment and, where appropriate, issue a joint finding of no significant impact.

(h) With respect to cooperating agencies, the lead agency shall:

(1) Request the participation of each cooperating agency in the NEPA process at the earliest practicable time.

(2) Use the environmental analysis and proposals of cooperating agencies with jurisdiction by law or special expertise, to the maximum extent practicable.

(3) Meet with a cooperating agency at the latter's request.

(4) Determine the purpose and need, and alternatives in consultation with any cooperating agency.

(i) The lead agency shall develop a schedule, setting milestones for all environmental reviews and authorizations required for implementation of the action, in consultation with any applicant and all joint lead, cooperating, and participating agencies, as soon as practicable.

(j) If the lead agency anticipates that a milestone will be missed, it shall notify appropriate officials at the responsible agencies. As soon as practicable, the responsible agencies shall elevate the issue to the appropriate officials of the responsible agencies for timely resolution.

§1501.8 Cooperating agencies.

(a) The purpose of this section is to emphasize agency cooperation early in the NEPA process. Upon request of the lead agency, any Federal agency with jurisdiction by law shall be a cooperating agency. In addition, upon request of the lead agency, any other Federal agency with special expertise with respect to any environmental issue may be a cooperating agency. A State, Tribal, or local agency of similar qualifications may become a cooperating agency by agreement with the lead agency. An agency may request that the lead agency designate it a cooperating agency, and a Federal agency may appeal a denial of its request to the Council, in accordance with §1501.7(e).

(b) Each cooperating agency shall:

(1) Participate in the NEPA process at the earliest practicable time.

(2) Participate in the scoping process (described in §1501.9).

(3) On request of the lead agency, assume responsibility for developing information and preparing environmental analyses, including portions of the environmental impact statement or environmental assessment concerning which the cooperating agency has special expertise.

(4) On request of the lead agency, make available staff support to enhance the lead agency's interdisciplinary capability.

(5) Normally use its own funds. To the extent available funds permit, the lead agency shall fund those major activities or analyses it requests from cooperating agencies. Potential lead agencies shall include such funding requirements in their budget requests.

(6) Consult with the lead agency in developing the schedule (§1501.7(i)), meet the schedule, and elevate, as soon as practicable, to the senior agency official of the lead agency any issues relating to purpose and need, alternatives, or other issues that may affect any agencies' ability to meet the schedule.

(7) Meet the lead agency's schedule for providing comments and limit its comments to those matters for which it has jurisdiction by law or special expertise with respect to any environmental issue consistent with §1503.2 of this chapter.

(8) To the maximum extent practicable, jointly issue environmental documents with the lead agency.

(c) In response to a lead agency's request for assistance in preparing the environmental documents (described in paragraph (b)(3), (4), or (5) of this section), a cooperating agency may reply that other program commitments preclude any involvement or the degree of involvement requested in the action that is the subject of the environmental impact statement or environmental assessment. The cooperating agency shall submit a copy of this reply to the Council and the senior agency official of the lead agency.

§1501.9 Scoping.

(a) *Generally.* Agencies shall use an early and open process to determine the scope of issues for analysis in an environmental impact statement, including identifying the significant issues and eliminating from further study non-significant issues. Scoping may begin as soon as practicable after the proposal for action is sufficiently developed for agency consideration. Scoping may include appropriate pre-application procedures or work conducted prior to publication of the notice of intent.

(b) *Invite cooperating and participating agencies.* As part of the scoping process, the lead agency shall invite the participation of likely affected Federal, State, Tribal, and local agencies and governments, the proponent of the action, and other likely affected or interested persons (including those who might not be in accord with the action), unless there is a limited exception under §1507.3(f)(1) of this chapter.

(c) *Scoping outreach.* As part of the scoping process the lead agency may hold a scoping meeting or meetings, publish scoping information, or use other means to communicate with those persons or agencies who may be interested or affected, which the agency may integrate with any other early planning meeting. Such a scoping meeting will often be appropriate when the impacts of a particular action are confined to specific sites.

(d) *Notice of intent.* As soon as practicable after determining that a proposal is sufficiently developed to allow for meaningful public comment and requires an environmental impact statement, the lead agency shall publish a notice of intent to prepare an environmental impact statement in the **Federal Register**, except as provided in §1507.3(f)(3) of this chapter. An agency also may publish notice in accordance with §1506.6 of this chapter. The notice shall include, as appropriate:

(1) The purpose and need for the proposed action;

(2) A preliminary description of the proposed action and alternatives the environmental impact statement will consider;

(3) A brief summary of expected impacts;

(4) Anticipated permits and other authorizations;

(5) A schedule for the decision-making process;

(6) A description of the public scoping process, including any scoping meeting(s);

(7) A request for identification of potential alternatives, information, and analyses relevant to the proposed action (*see* §1502.17 of this chapter); and

(8) Contact information for a person within the agency who can answer questions about the proposed action and the environmental impact statement.

(e) *Determination of scope.* As part of the scoping process, the lead agency shall determine the scope and the significant issues to be analyzed in depth in the environmental impact statement. To determine the scope of environmental impact statements, agencies shall consider:

(1) Actions (other than unconnected single actions) that may be connected actions, which means that they are closely related and therefore should be discussed in the same impact statement. Actions are connected if they:

(i) Automatically trigger other actions that may require environmental impact statements;

(ii) Cannot or will not proceed unless other actions are taken previously or simultaneously; or

(iii) Are interdependent parts of a larger action and depend on the larger action for their justification.

(2) Alternatives, which include the no action alternative; other reasonable courses of action; and mitigation measures (not in the proposed action).

(3) Impacts.

(f) *Additional scoping responsibilities.* As part of the scoping process, the lead agency shall:

(1) Identify and eliminate from detailed study the issues that are not significant or have been covered by prior environmental review(s) (§1506.3 of this chapter), narrowing the discussion of these issues in the statement to a brief presentation of why they will not

have a significant effect on the human environment or providing a reference to their coverage elsewhere.

(2) Allocate assignments for preparation of the environmental impact statement among the lead and cooperating agencies, with the lead agency retaining responsibility for the statement.

(3) Indicate any public environmental assessments and other environmental impact statements that are being or will be prepared and are related to but are not part of the scope of the impact statement under consideration.

(4) Identify other environmental review, authorization, and consultation requirements so the lead and cooperating agencies may prepare other required analyses and studies concurrently and integrated with the environmental impact statement, as provided in §1502.24 of this chapter.

(5) Indicate the relationship between the timing of the preparation of environmental analyses and the agencies' tentative planning and decision-making schedule.

(g) *Revisions.* An agency shall revise the determinations made under paragraphs (b), (c), (e), and (f) of this section if substantial changes are made later in the proposed action, or if significant new circumstances or information arise which bear on the proposal or its impacts.

§1501.10 Time limits.

(a) To ensure that agencies conduct NEPA reviews as efficiently and expeditiously as practicable, Federal agencies should set time limits appropriate to individual actions or types of actions (consistent with the time intervals required by §1506.11 of this chapter).

(b) To ensure timely decision making, agencies shall complete:

(1) Environmental assessments within 1 year unless a senior agency official of the lead agency approves a longer period in writing and establishes a new time limit. One year is measured from the date of agency decision to prepare an environmental assessment to the publication of an environmental assessment or a finding of no significant impact.

(2) Environmental impact statements within 2 years unless a senior agency official of the lead agency approves a longer period in writing and establishes a new time limit. Two years is measured from the date of the issuance of the notice of intent to the date a record of decision is signed.

(c) The senior agency official may consider the following factors in determining time limits:

(1) Potential for environmental harm.

(2) Size of the proposed action.

(3) State of the art of analytic techniques.

(4) Degree of public need for the proposed action, including the consequences of delay.

(5) Number of persons and agencies affected.

(6) Availability of relevant information.

(7) Other time limits imposed on the agency by law, regulations, or Executive order.

(d) The senior agency official may set overall time limits or limits for each constituent part of the NEPA process, which may include:

(1) Decision on whether to prepare an environmental impact statement (if not already decided).

(2) Determination of the scope of the environmental impact statement.

(3) Preparation of the draft environmental impact statement.

(4) Review of any comments on the draft environmental impact statement from the public and agencies.

(5) Preparation of the final environmental impact statement.

(6) Review of any comments on the final environmental impact statement.

(7) Decision on the action based in part on the environmental impact statement.

(e) The agency may designate a person (such as the project manager or a person in the agency's office with NEPA responsibilities) to expedite the NEPA process.

(f) State, Tribal, or local agencies or members of the public may request a Federal agency to set time limits.

§1501.11 Tiering.

(a) Agencies should tier their environmental impact statements and environmental assessments when it would eliminate repetitive discussions of the same issues, focus on the actual issues ripe for decision, and exclude from consideration issues already decided or not yet ripe at each level of environmental review. Tiering may also be appropriate for different stages of actions.

(b) When an agency has prepared an environmental impact statement or environmental assessment for a program or policy and then prepares a subsequent statement or assessment on an action included within the entire program or policy (such as a project- or site-specific action), the tiered document needs only to summarize and incorporate by reference the issues discussed in the broader document. The tiered document shall concentrate on the issues specific to the subsequent action. The tiered document shall state where the earlier document is available.

(c) Tiering is appropriate when the sequence from an environmental impact statement or environmental assessment is:

(1) From a programmatic, plan, or policy environmental impact statement or environmental assessment to a program, plan, or policy statement or assessment of lesser or narrower scope or to a site-specific statement or assessment.

(2) From an environmental impact statement or environmental assessment on a specific action at an early stage (such as need and site selection) to a supplement (which is preferred) or a subsequent statement or assessment at a later stage (such as environmental mitigation). Tiering in such cases is appropriate when it helps the lead agency to focus on the issues that are ripe for decision and exclude from consideration issues already decided or not yet ripe.

§1501.12 Incorporation by reference.

Agencies shall incorporate material, such as planning studies, analyses, or other relevant information, into environmental documents by reference when the effect will be to cut down on bulk without impeding agency and public review of the action. Agencies shall cite the incorporated material in the document and briefly describe its content. Agencies may not incorporate material by reference unless it is reasonably available for inspection by potentially interested persons within the time allowed for comment. Agencies shall not incorporate by reference material based on proprietary data that is not available for review and comment.

§1502.1 Purpose of environmental impact statement.

The primary purpose of an environmental impact statement prepared pursuant to section 102(2)(C) of NEPA is to ensure agencies consider the environmental impacts of their actions in decision making. It shall provide full and fair discussion of significant environmental impacts and shall inform decision makers and the public of reasonable alternatives that would avoid or minimize adverse impacts or enhance the quality of the human environment. Agencies shall focus on significant environmental issues and alternatives and shall reduce paperwork and the accumulation of extraneous background data. Statements shall be concise, clear, and to the point, and shall be supported by evidence that the agency has made the necessary environmental analyses. An environmental impact statement is a document that informs Federal agency decision making and the public.

§1502.2 Implementation.

(a) Environmental impact statements shall not be encyclopedic.

(b) Environmental impact statements shall discuss impacts in proportion to their significance. There shall be only brief discussion of other than significant issues. As in a finding of no significant impact, there should be only enough discussion to show why more study is not warranted.

(c) Environmental impact statements shall be analytic, concise, and no longer than necessary to comply with NEPA and with the regulations in this subchapter. Length should be proportional to potential environmental effects and project size.

(d) Environmental impact statements shall state how alternatives considered in it and decisions based on it will or will not achieve the requirements of sections 101 and 102(1) of NEPA as interpreted in the regulations in this subchapter and other environmental laws and policies.

(e) The range of alternatives discussed in environmental impact statements shall encompass those to be considered by the decision maker.

(f) Agencies shall not commit resources prejudicing selection of alternatives before making a final decision (*see also* §1506.1 of this chapter).

(g) Environmental impact statements shall serve as the means of assessing the environmental impact of proposed agency actions, rather than justifying decisions already made.

§1502.3 Statutory requirements for statements.

As required by section 102(2)(C) of NEPA, environmental impact statements are to be included in every Federal agency recommendation or report on proposals for legislation and other major Federal actions significantly affecting the quality of the human environment.

§1502.4 Major Federal actions requiring the preparation of environmental impact statements.

(a) Agencies shall define the proposal that is the subject of an environmental impact statement based on the statutory authorities for the proposed action. Agencies shall use the criteria for scope (§1501.9(e) of this chapter) to determine which proposal(s) shall be the subject of a particular statement. Agencies shall evaluate in a single environmental impact statement proposals or parts of proposals that are related to each other closely enough to be, in effect, a single course of action.

(b) Environmental impact statements may be prepared for programmatic Federal actions, such as the adoption of new agency programs. When agencies prepare such statements, they should be relevant to the program decision and timed to coincide with meaningful points in agency planning and decision making.

(1) When preparing statements on programmatic actions (including proposals by more than one agency), agencies may find it useful to evaluate the proposal(s) in one of the following ways:

(i) Geographically, including actions occurring in the same general location, such as body of water, region, or metropolitan area.

(ii) Generically, including actions that have relevant similarities, such as common timing, impacts, alternatives, methods of implementation, media, or subject matter.

(iii) By stage of technological development including Federal or federally assisted research, development or demonstration programs for new technologies that, if applied, could significantly affect the quality of the human environment. Statements on

such programs should be available before the program has reached a stage of investment or commitment to implementation likely to determine subsequent development or restrict later alternatives.

(2) Agencies shall as appropriate employ scoping (§1501.9 of this chapter), tiering (§1501.11 of this chapter), and other methods listed in §§1500.4 and 1500.5 of this chapter to relate programmatic and narrow actions and to avoid duplication and delay. Agencies may tier their environmental analyses to defer detailed analysis of environmental impacts of specific program elements until such program elements are ripe for final agency action.

§1502.5 Timing.

An agency should commence preparation of an environmental impact statement as close as practicable to the time the agency is developing or receives a proposal so that preparation can be completed in time for the final statement to be included in any recommendation or report on the proposal. The statement shall be prepared early enough so that it can serve as an important practical contribution to the decision-making process and will not be used to rationalize or justify decisions already made (§§1501.2 of this chapter and 1502.2). For instance:

(a) For projects directly undertaken by Federal agencies, the agency shall prepare the environmental impact statement at the feasibility analysis (go/no-go) stage and may supplement it at a later stage, if necessary.

(b) For applications to the agency requiring an environmental impact statement, the agency shall commence the statement as soon as practicable after receiving the application. Federal agencies should work with potential applicants and applicable State, Tribal, and local agencies and governments prior to receipt of the application.

(c) For adjudication, the final environmental impact statement shall normally precede the final staff recommendation and that portion of the public hearing related to the impact study. In appropriate circumstances, the statement may follow preliminary hearings designed to gather information for use in the statements.

(d) For informal rulemaking, the draft environmental impact statement shall normally accompany the proposed rule.

§1502.6 Interdisciplinary preparation.

Agencies shall prepare environmental impact statements using an interdisciplinary approach that will ensure the integrated use of the natural and social sciences and the environmental design arts (section 102(2)(A) of NEPA). The disciplines of the preparers shall be appropriate to the scope and issues identified in the scoping process (§1501.9 of this chapter).

§1502.7 Page limits.

The text of final environmental impact statements (paragraphs (a)(4) through (6) of §1502.10) shall be 150 pages or fewer and, for proposals of unusual scope or complexity, shall be 300 pages or fewer unless a senior agency official of the lead agency approves in writing a statement to exceed 300 pages and establishes a new page limit.

§1502.8 Writing.

Agencies shall write environmental impact statements in plain language and may use appropriate graphics so that decision makers and the public can readily understand such statements. Agencies should employ writers of clear prose or editors to write, review, or edit statements, which shall be based upon the analysis and supporting data from the natural and social sciences and the environmental design arts.

§1502.9 Draft, final, and supplemental statements.

(a) *Generally.* Except for proposals for legislation as provided in §1506.8 of this chapter, agencies shall prepare environmental impact statements in two stages and, where necessary, supplement them, as provided in paragraph (d)(1) of this section.

(b) *Draft environmental impact statements.* Agencies shall prepare draft environmental impact statements in accordance with the scope decided upon in the scoping process (§1501.9 of this chapter). The lead agency shall work with the cooperating agencies and shall obtain comments as required in part 1503 of this chapter. To the fullest extent practicable, the draft statement must meet the requirements established for final statements in section 102(2)(C) of NEPA as interpreted in the regulations in this subchapter. If a draft statement is so inadequate as to preclude meaningful analysis, the agency shall prepare and publish a supplemental draft of the appropriate portion. At appropriate points in the draft statement, the agency shall discuss all major points of view on the environmental impacts of the alternatives including the proposed action.

(c) *Final environmental impact statements.* Final environmental impact statements shall address comments as required in part 1503 of this chapter. At appropriate points in the final statement, the agency shall discuss any responsible opposing view that was not adequately discussed in the draft statement and shall indicate the agency's response to the issues raised.

(d) *Supplemental environmental impact statements.* Agencies:

(1) Shall prepare supplements to either draft or final environmental impact statements if a major Federal action remains to occur, and:

(i) The agency makes substantial changes to the proposed action that are relevant to environmental concerns; or

(ii) There are significant new circumstances or information relevant to environmental concerns and bearing on the proposed action or its impacts.

(2) May also prepare supplements when the agency determines that the purposes of the Act will be furthered by doing so.

(3) Shall prepare, publish, and file a supplement to a statement (exclusive of scoping (§1501.9 of this chapter)) as a draft and final statement, as is appropriate to the stage of the statement involved, unless the Council approves alternative procedures (§1506.12 of this chapter).

(4) May find that changes to the proposed action or new circumstances or information relevant to environmental concerns are not significant and therefore do not require a supplement. The agency should document the finding consistent with its agency NEPA procedures (§1507.3 of this chapter), or, if necessary, in a finding of no significant impact supported by an environmental assessment.

§1502.10 Recommended format.

(a) Agencies shall use a format for environmental impact statements that will encourage good analysis and clear presentation of the alternatives including the proposed action. Agencies should use the following standard format for environmental impact statements unless the agency determines that there is a more effective format for communication:

(1) Cover.

(2) Summary.

(3) Table of contents.

(4) Purpose of and need for action.

(5) Alternatives including the proposed action (sections 102(2)(C)(iii) and 102(2)(E) of NEPA).

(6) Affected environment and environmental consequences (especially sections 102(2)(C)(i), (ii), (iv), and (v) of NEPA).

(7) Submitted alternatives, information, and analyses.

(8) List of preparers.

(9) Appendices (if any).

(b) If an agency uses a different format, it shall include paragraphs (a)(1) through (8) of this section, as further described in §§1502.11 through 1502.19, in any appropriate format.

§1502.11 Cover.

The cover shall not exceed one page and include:

(a) A list of the responsible agencies, including the lead agency and any cooperating agencies.

(b) The title of the proposed action that is the subject of the statement (and, if appropriate, the titles of related cooperating agency actions), together with the State(s) and county(ies) (or other jurisdiction(s), if applicable) where the action is located.

(c) The name, address, and telephone number of the person at the agency who can supply further information.

(d) A designation of the statement as a draft, final, or draft or final supplement.

(e) A one-paragraph abstract of the statement.

(f) The date by which the agency must receive comments (computed in cooperation with EPA under §1506.11 of this chapter).

(g) For the final environmental impact statement, the estimated total cost to prepare both the draft and final environmental impact statement, including the costs of agency full-time equivalent (FTE) personnel hours, contractor costs, and other direct costs. If practicable and noted where not practicable, agencies also should include costs incurred by cooperating and participating agencies, applicants, and contractors.

§1502.12 Summary.

Each environmental impact statement shall contain a summary that adequately and accurately summarizes the statement. The summary shall stress the major conclusions, areas of disputed issues raised by agencies and the public, and the issues to be resolved (including the choice among alternatives). The summary normally will not exceed 15 pages.

§1502.13 Purpose and need.

The statement shall briefly specify the underlying purpose and need for the proposed action. When an agency's statutory duty is to review an application for authorization, the agency shall base the purpose and need on the goals of the applicant and the agency's authority.

§1502.14 Alternatives including the proposed action.

The alternatives section should present the environmental impacts of the proposed action and the alternatives in comparative form based on the information and analysis presented in the sections on the affected environment (§1502.15) and the environmental consequences (§1502.16). In this section, agencies shall:

(a) Evaluate reasonable alternatives to the proposed action, and, for alternatives that the agency eliminated from detailed study, briefly discuss the reasons for their elimination.

(b) Discuss each alternative considered in detail, including the proposed action, so that reviewers may evaluate their comparative merits.

(c) Include the no action alternative.

(d) Identify the agency's preferred alternative or alternatives, if one or more exists, in the draft statement and identify such alternative in the final statement unless another law prohibits the expression of such a preference.

(e) Include appropriate mitigation measures not already included in the proposed action or alternatives.

(f) Limit their consideration to a reasonable number of alternatives.

§1502.15 Affected environment.

The environmental impact statement shall succinctly describe the environment of the area(s) to be affected or created by the alternatives under consideration, including the reasonably foreseeable environmental trends and planned actions in the area(s). The environmental impact statement may combine the description with evaluation of the environmental consequences (§1502.16), and it shall be no longer than is necessary to understand the effects of the alternatives. Data and analyses in a statement shall be commensurate with the importance of the impact, with less important material summarized, consolidated, or simply referenced. Agencies shall avoid useless bulk in statements and shall concentrate effort and attention on important issues. Verbose descriptions of the affected environment are themselves no measure of the adequacy of an environmental impact statement.

§1502.16 Environmental consequences.

(a) The environmental consequences section forms the scientific and analytic basis for the comparisons under §1502.14. It shall consolidate the discussions of those elements required by sections 102(2)(C)(i), (ii), (iv), and (v) of NEPA that are within the scope of the statement and as much of section 102(2)(C) (iii) of NEPA as is necessary to support the comparisons. This section should not duplicate discussions in §1502.14. The discussion shall include:

(1) The environmental impacts of the proposed action and reasonable alternatives to the proposed action and the significance of those impacts. The comparison of the proposed action and reasonable alternatives shall be based on this discussion of the impacts.

(2) Any adverse environmental effects that cannot be avoided should the proposal be implemented.

(3) The relationship between short-term uses of man's environment and the maintenance and enhancement of long-term productivity.

(4) Any irreversible or irretrievable commitments of resources that would be involved in the proposal should it be implemented.

(5) Possible conflicts between the proposed action and the objectives of Federal, regional, State, Tribal, and local land use plans, policies and controls for the area concerned. (§1506.2(d) of this chapter)

(6) Energy requirements and conservation potential of various alternatives and mitigation measures.

(7) Natural or depletable resource requirements and conservation potential of various alternatives and mitigation measures.

(8) Urban quality, historic and cultural resources, and the design of the built environment, including the reuse and conservation potential of various alternatives and mitigation measures.

(9) Means to mitigate adverse environmental impacts (if not fully covered under §1502.14(e)).

(10) Where applicable, economic and technical considerations, including the economic benefits of the proposed action.

(b) Economic or social effects by themselves do not require preparation of an environmental impact statement. However, when the agency determines that economic or social and natural or physical environmental effects are interrelated, the environmental impact statement shall discuss and give appropriate consideration to these effects on the human environment.

§1502.17 Summary of submitted alternatives, information, and analyses.

(a) The draft environmental impact statement shall include a summary that identifies all alternatives, information, and analyses submitted by State, Tribal, and local governments and other public commenters during the scoping process for consideration by the lead and cooperating agencies in developing the environmental impact statement.

(1) The agency shall append to the draft environmental impact statement or otherwise publish all comments (or summaries thereof where the response has been exceptionally voluminous) received during the scoping process that identified alternatives, information, and analyses for the agency's consideration.

(2) Consistent with §1503.1(a)(3) of this chapter, the lead agency shall invite comment on the summary identifying all submitted alternatives, information, and analyses in the draft environmental impact statement.

(b) The final environmental impact statement shall include a summary that identifies all alternatives, information, and analyses submitted by State, Tribal, and local governments and other public commenters for consideration by the lead and cooperating agencies in developing the final environmental impact statement.

§1502.18 List of preparers.

The environmental impact statement shall list the names, together with their qualifications (expertise, experience, professional disciplines), of the persons who were primarily responsible for preparing the environmental impact statement or significant background papers, including basic components of the statement. Where possible, the environmental impact statement shall identify the persons who are responsible for a particular analysis, including analyses in background papers. Normally the list will not exceed two pages.

§1502.19 Appendix.

If an agency prepares an appendix, the agency shall publish it with the environmental impact statement, and it shall consist of:

(a) Material prepared in connection with an environmental impact statement (as distinct from material that is not so prepared and is incorporated by reference (§1501.12 of this chapter)).

(b) Material substantiating any analysis fundamental to the impact statement.

(c) Material relevant to the decision to be made.

(d) For draft environmental impact statements, all comments (or summaries thereof where the response has been exceptionally voluminous) received during the scoping process that identified alternatives, information, and analyses for the agency's consideration.

(e) For final environmental impact statements, the comment summaries and responses consistent with §1503.4 of this chapter.

§1502.20 Publication of the environmental impact statement.

Agencies shall publish the entire draft and final environmental impact statements and unchanged statements as provided in §1503.4(c) of this chapter. The agency shall transmit the entire statement electronically (or in paper copy, if so requested due to economic or other hardship) to:

(a) Any Federal agency that has jurisdiction by law or special expertise with respect to any environmental impact involved and any appropriate Federal, State, Tribal, or local agency authorized to develop and enforce environmental standards.

(b) The applicant, if any.

(c) Any person, organization, or agency requesting the entire environmental impact statement.

(d) In the case of a final environmental impact statement, any person, organization, or agency that submitted substantive comments on the draft.

§1502.21 Incomplete or unavailable information.

(a) When an agency is evaluating reasonably foreseeable significant adverse effects on the human environment in an environmental impact statement, and there is incomplete or unavailable information, the agency shall make clear that such information is lacking.

(b) If the incomplete but available information relevant to reasonably foreseeable significant adverse impacts is essential to a reasoned choice among alternatives, and the overall costs of obtaining it are not unreasonable, the agency shall include the information in the environmental impact statement.

(c) If the information relevant to reasonably foreseeable significant adverse impacts cannot be obtained because the overall costs of obtaining it are unreasonable or the means to obtain it are not known, the agency shall include within the environmental impact statement:

(1) A statement that such information is incomplete or unavailable;

(2) A statement of the relevance of the incomplete or unavailable information to evaluating reasonably foreseeable significant adverse impacts on the human environment;

(3) A summary of existing credible scientific evidence that is relevant to evaluating the reasonably foreseeable significant adverse impacts on the human environment; and

(4) The agency's evaluation of such impacts based upon theoretical approaches or research methods generally accepted in the scientific community.

(d) For the purposes of this section, "reasonably foreseeable" includes impacts that have catastrophic consequences, even if their probability of occurrence is low, provided that the analysis of the impacts is supported by credible scientific evidence, is not based on pure conjecture, and is within the rule of reason.

§1502.22 Cost-benefit analysis.

If the agency is considering a cost-benefit analysis for the proposed action relevant to the choice among alternatives with different environmental effects, the agency shall incorporate the cost-benefit analysis by reference or append it to the statement as an aid in evaluating the environmental consequences. In such cases, to assess the adequacy of compliance with section 102(2)(B) of NEPA (ensuring appropriate consideration of unquantified environmental amenities and values in decision making, along with economical and technical considerations), the statement shall discuss the relationship between that analysis and any analyses of unquantified environmental impacts, values, and amenities. For purposes of complying with the Act, agencies need not display the weighing of the merits and drawbacks of the various alternatives in a monetary cost-benefit analysis and should not do so when there are important qualitative considerations. However, an environmental impact statement should at least indicate those considerations, including factors not related to environmental quality, that are likely to be relevant and important to a decision.

§1502.23 Methodology and scientific accuracy.

Agencies shall ensure the professional integrity, including scientific integrity, of the discussions and analyses in environmental documents. Agencies shall make use of reliable existing data and resources. Agencies may make use of any reliable data sources, such as remotely gathered information or statistical models. They shall identify any methodologies used and shall make explicit reference to the scientific and other sources relied upon for conclusions in the statement. Agencies may place discussion of methodology in an appendix. Agencies are not required

to undertake new scientific and technical research to inform their analyses. Nothing in this section is intended to prohibit agencies from compliance with the requirements of other statutes pertaining to scientific and technical research.

§1502.24 Environmental review and consultation requirements.

(a) To the fullest extent possible, agencies shall prepare draft environmental impact statements concurrent and integrated with environmental impact analyses and related surveys and studies required by all other Federal environmental review laws and Executive orders applicable to the proposed action, including the Fish and Wildlife Coordination Act (16 U.S.C. 661 *et seq.*), the National Historic Preservation Act of 1966 (54 U.S.C. 300101 *et seq.*), and the Endangered Species Act of 1973 (16 U.S.C. 1531 *et seq.*).

(b) The draft environmental impact statement shall list all Federal permits, licenses, and other authorizations that must be obtained in implementing the proposal. If it is uncertain whether a Federal permit, license, or other authorization is necessary, the draft environmental impact statement shall so indicate.

§1503.1 Inviting comments and requesting information and analyses.

(a) After preparing a draft environmental impact statement and before preparing a final environmental impact statement the agency shall:

(1) Obtain the comments of any Federal agency that has jurisdiction by law or special expertise with respect to any environmental impact involved or is authorized to develop and enforce environmental standards.

(2) Request the comments of:

(i) Appropriate State, Tribal, and local agencies that are authorized to develop and enforce environmental standards;

(ii) State, Tribal, or local governments that may be affected by the proposed action;

(iii) Any agency that has requested it receive statements on actions of the kind proposed;

(iv) The applicant, if any; and

(v) The public, affirmatively soliciting comments in a manner designed to inform those persons or organizations who may be interested in or affected by the proposed action.

(3) Invite comment specifically on the submitted alternatives, information, and analyses and the summary thereof (§1502.17 of this chapter).

(b) An agency may request comments on a final environmental impact statement before the final decision and set a deadline for providing such comments. Other agencies or persons may make comments consistent with the time periods under §1506.11 of this chapter.

(c) An agency shall provide for electronic submission of public comments, with reasonable measures to ensure the comment process is accessible to affected persons.

§1503.2 Duty to comment.

Cooperating agencies and agencies that are authorized to develop and enforce environmental standards shall comment on statements within their jurisdiction, expertise, or authority within the time period specified for comment in §1506.11 of this chapter. A Federal agency may reply that it has no comment. If a cooperating agency is satisfied that the environmental impact statement adequately reflects its views, it should reply that it has no comment.

§1503.3 Specificity of comments and information.

(a) To promote informed decision making, comments on an environmental impact statement or on a proposed action shall be as specific as possible, may address either the adequacy of the statement or the merits of the alternatives discussed or both, and shall provide as much detail as necessary to meaningfully participate and fully inform the agency of the commenter's position. Comments should explain why the issues raised are important to the consideration of potential environmental impacts and alternatives to the proposed action, as well as economic and employment impacts, and other impacts affecting the quality of the human environment. Comments should reference the corresponding section or page number of the draft environmental impact statement, propose specific changes to those parts of the statement, where possible, and include or describe the data sources and methodologies supporting the proposed changes.

(b) Comments on the submitted alternatives, information, and analyses and summary thereof (§1502.17 of this chapter) should be as specific as possible. Comments and objections of any kind shall be raised within the comment period on the draft environmental impact statement provided by the agency, consistent with §1506.11 of this chapter. If the agency requests comments on the final environmental impact statement before the final decision, consistent with §1503.1(b), comments and objections of any kind shall be raised within the comment period provided by the agency. Comments and objections of any kind not provided within the comment period(s) shall be considered unexhausted and forfeited, consistent with §1500.3(b) of this chapter.

(c) When a participating agency criticizes a lead agency's predictive methodology, the participating agency should describe the alternative methodology that it prefers and why.

(d) A cooperating agency shall specify in its comments whether it needs additional information to fulfill other applicable environmental reviews or consultation requirements and what information it needs. In particular, it shall specify any additional information it needs to comment adequately on the draft statement's analysis of significant site-specific effects associated with the granting or approving by that cooperating agency of necessary Federal permits, licenses, or authorizations.

(e) When a cooperating agency with jurisdiction by law specifies mitigation measures it considers necessary to allow the agency to grant or approve applicable permit, license, or related requirements or concurrences, the cooperating agency shall cite to its applicable statutory authority.

§1503.4 Response to comments.

(a) An agency preparing a final environmental impact statement shall consider substantive comments timely submitted during the public comment period. The agency may respond to individual comments or groups of comments. In the final environmental impact statement, the agency may respond by:

(1) Modifying alternatives including the proposed action.

(2) Developing and evaluating alternatives not previously given serious consideration by the agency.

(3) Supplementing, improving, or modifying its analyses.

(4) Making factual corrections.

(5) Explaining why the comments do not warrant further agency response, recognizing that agencies are not required to respond to each comment.

(b) An agency shall append or otherwise publish all substantive comments received on the draft statement (or summaries thereof where the response has been exceptionally voluminous).

(c) If changes in response to comments are minor and are confined to the responses described in paragraphs (a)(4) and (5) of this section, an agency may write any changes on errata sheets and attach the responses to the statement instead of rewriting the draft statement. In such cases, only the comments, the responses, and the changes and not the final statement need be published (§1502.20 of this chapter). The agency shall file the entire document with a new cover sheet with the Environmental Protection Agency as the final statement (§1506.10 of this chapter).

§1504.1 Purpose.

(a) This part establishes procedures for referring to the Council Federal interagency disagreements concerning proposed major Federal actions that might cause unsatisfactory environmental effects. It provides means for early resolution of such disagreements.

(b) Section 309 of the Clean Air Act (42 U.S.C. 7609) directs the Administrator of the Environmental Protection Agency to review and comment publicly on the environmental impacts of Federal activities, including actions for which agencies prepare environmental impact statements. If, after this review, the Administrator determines that the matter is "unsatisfactory from the standpoint of public health or welfare or environmental quality," section 309 directs that the matter be referred to the Council (hereafter "environmental referrals").

(c) Under section 102(2)(C) of NEPA (42 U.S.C. 4332(2)(C)), other Federal agencies may prepare similar reviews of environmental impact statements, including judgments on the acceptability of anticipated environmental impacts. These reviews must be made available to the President, the Council, and the public.

§1504.2 Criteria for referral.

Environmental referrals should be made to the Council only after concerted, timely (as early as practicable in the process), but unsuccessful attempts to resolve differences with the lead agency. In determining what environmental objections to the matter are appropriate to refer to the Council, an agency should weigh potential adverse environmental impacts, considering:

(a) Possible violation of national environmental standards or policies;

(b) Severity;

(c) Geographical scope;

(d) Duration;

(e) Importance as precedents;

(f) Availability of environmentally preferable alternatives; and

(g) Economic and technical considerations, including the economic costs of delaying or impeding the decision making of the agencies involved in the action.

§1504.3 Procedure for referrals and response.

(a) A Federal agency making the referral to the Council shall:

(1) Notify the lead agency at the earliest possible time that it intends to refer a matter to the Council unless a satisfactory agreement is reached;

(2) Include such a notification whenever practicable in the referring agency's comments on the environmental assessment or draft environmental impact statement;

(3) Identify any essential information that is lacking and request that the lead agency make it available at the earliest possible time; and

(4) Send copies of the referring agency's views to the Council.

(b) The referring agency shall deliver its referral to the Council no later than 25 days after the lead agency has made the final environmental impact statement available to the Environmental Protection Agency, participating agencies, and the public, and in the case of an environmental assessment, no later than 25 days after the lead agency makes it available. Except when the lead agency grants an extension of this period, the Council will not accept a referral after that date.

(c) The referral shall consist of:

(1) A copy of the letter signed by the head of the referring agency and delivered to the lead agency informing the lead agency of the referral and the reasons for it; and

(2) A statement supported by factual evidence leading to the conclusion that the matter is unsatisfactory from the standpoint of public health or welfare or environmental quality. The statement shall:

(i) Identify any disputed material facts and incorporate (by reference if appropriate) agreed upon facts;

(ii) Identify any existing environmental requirements or policies that would be violated by the matter;

(iii) Present the reasons for the referral;

(iv) Contain a finding by the agency whether the issue raised is of national importance because of the threat to national environmental resources or policies or for some other reason;

(v) Review the steps taken by the referring agency to bring its concerns to the attention of the lead agency at the earliest possible time; and

(vi) Give the referring agency's recommendations as to what mitigation alternative, further study, or other course of action (including abandonment of the matter) are necessary to remedy the situation.

(d) No later than 25 days after the referral to the Council, the lead agency may deliver a response to the Council and the referring agency. If the lead agency requests more time and gives assurance that the matter will not go forward in the interim, the Council may grant an extension. The response shall:

(1) Address fully the issues raised in the referral;

(2) Be supported by evidence and explanations, as appropriate; and

(3) Give the lead agency's response to the referring agency's recommendations.

(e) Applicants may provide views in writing to the Council no later than the response.

(f) No later than 25 days after receipt of both the referral and any response or upon being informed that there will be no response (unless the lead agency agrees to a longer time), the Council may take one or more of the following actions:

(1) Conclude that the process of referral and response has successfully resolved the problem.

(2) Initiate discussions with the agencies with the objective of mediation with referring and lead agencies.

(3) Obtain additional views and information.

(4) Determine that the issue is not one of national importance and request the referring and lead agencies to pursue their decision process.

(5) Determine that the referring and lead agencies should further negotiate the issue, and the issue is not appropriate for Council consideration until one or more heads of agencies report to the Council that the agencies' disagreements are irreconcilable.

(6) Publish its findings and recommendations (including, where appropriate, a finding that the submitted evidence does not support the position of an agency).

(7) When appropriate, submit the referral and the response together with the Council's recommendation to the President for action.

(g) The Council shall take no longer than 60 days to complete the actions specified in paragraph (f)(2), (3), or (5) of this section.

(h) The referral process is not intended to create any private rights of action or to be judicially reviewable because any voluntary resolutions by the agency parties do not represent final agency action and instead are only provisional and dependent on later consistent action by the action agencies.

§1505.1 [Reserved]

§1505.2 Record of decision in cases requiring environmental impact statements.

(a) At the time of its decision (§1506.11 of this chapter) or, if appropriate, its recommendation to Congress, each agency shall prepare and timely publish a concise public record of decision or joint record of decision. The record, which each agency may integrate into any other record it prepares, shall:

(1) State the decision.

(2) Identify alternatives considered by the agency in reaching its decision, specifying the alternative or alternatives considered environmentally preferable. An agency may discuss preferences among alternatives based on relevant factors including economic and technical considerations and agency statutory missions. An agency shall identify and discuss all such factors, including any essential considerations of national policy, that the agency balanced in making its decision and state how those considerations entered into its decision.

(3) State whether the agency has adopted all practicable means to avoid or minimize environmental harm from the alternative selected, and if not, why the agency did not. The agency shall adopt and summarize, where applicable, a monitoring and enforcement program for any enforceable mitigation requirements or commitments.

(b) Informed by the summary of the submitted alternatives, information, and analyses in the final environmental impact statement (§1502.17(b) of

this chapter), together with any other material in the record that he or she determines to be relevant, the decision maker shall certify in the record of decision that the agency has considered all of the alternatives, information, analyses, and objections submitted by State, Tribal, and local governments and public commenters for consideration by the lead and cooperating agencies in developing the environmental impact statement. Agency environmental impact statements certified in accordance with this section are entitled to a presumption that the agency has considered the submitted alternatives, information, and analyses, including the summary thereof, in the final environmental impact statement (§1502.17(b)).

§1505.3 Implementing the decision.

Agencies may provide for monitoring to assure that their decisions are carried out and should do so in important cases. Mitigation (§1505.2(a)(3)) and other conditions established in the environmental impact statement or during its review and committed as part of the decision shall be implemented by the lead agency or other appropriate consenting agency. The lead agency shall:

(a) Include appropriate conditions in grants, permits, or other approvals.

(b) Condition funding of actions on mitigation.

(c) Upon request, inform cooperating or participating agencies on progress in carrying out mitigation measures that they have proposed and were adopted by the agency making the decision.

(d) Upon request, publish the results of relevant monitoring.

§1506.1 Limitations on actions during NEPA process.

(a) Except as provided in paragraphs (b) and (c) of this section, until an agency issues a finding of no significant impact, as provided in §1501.6 of this chapter, or record of decision, as provided in §1505.2 of this chapter, no action concerning the proposal may be taken that would:

(1) Have an adverse environmental impact; or

(2) Limit the choice of reasonable alternatives.

(b) If any agency is considering an application from a non-Federal entity and is aware that the applicant is about to take an action within the agency's jurisdiction that would meet either of the criteria in paragraph (a) of this section, then the agency shall promptly notify the applicant that the agency will take appropriate action to ensure that the objectives and procedures of NEPA are achieved. This section does not preclude development by applicants of plans or designs or performance of other activities necessary to support an application for Federal, State, Tribal, or local permits or assistance. An agency considering a proposed action for Federal funding may authorize such activities, including, but not limited to, acquisition of interests in land (*e.g.*, fee simple, rights-of-way, and conservation easements), purchase of long lead-time equipment, and purchase options made by applicants.

(c) While work on a required programmatic environmental review is in progress and the action is not covered by an existing programmatic review, agencies shall not undertake in the interim any major Federal action covered by the program that may significantly affect the quality of the human environment unless such action:

(1) Is justified independently of the program;

(2) Is itself accompanied by an adequate environmental review; and

(3) Will not prejudice the ultimate decision on the program. Interim action prejudices the ultimate decision on the program when it tends to determine subsequent development or limit alternatives.

§1506.2 Elimination of duplication with State, Tribal, and local procedures.

(a) Federal agencies are authorized to cooperate with State, Tribal, and local agencies that are responsible for preparing environmental documents, including those prepared pursuant to section 102(2)(D) of NEPA.

(b) To the fullest extent practicable unless specifically prohibited by law, agencies shall cooperate with State, Tribal, and local agencies to reduce duplication between NEPA and State, Tribal, and local requirements, including through use of studies, analysis, and decisions developed by State, Tribal, or local agencies. Except for cases covered by paragraph (a) of this section, such cooperation shall include, to the fullest extent practicable:

(1) Joint planning processes.

(2) Joint environmental research and studies.

(3) Joint public hearings (except where otherwise provided by statute).

(4) Joint environmental assessments.

(c) To the fullest extent practicable unless specifically prohibited by law, agencies shall cooperate with State, Tribal, and local agencies to reduce duplication between NEPA and comparable State, Tribal, and local requirements. Such cooperation shall include, to the fullest extent practicable, joint environmental impact statements. In such cases, one or more Federal agencies and one or more State, Tribal, or local agencies shall be joint lead agencies. Where State or Tribal laws or local ordinances have environmental impact statement or similar requirements in addition to but not in conflict with those in NEPA, Federal agencies may cooperate in fulfilling these requirements, as well as those of Federal laws, so that one document will comply with all applicable laws.

(d) To better integrate environmental impact statements into State, Tribal, or local planning processes, environmental impact statements shall discuss any inconsistency of a proposed action with any approved State, Tribal, or local plan or law (whether or not federally sanctioned). Where an inconsistency exists, the statement should describe the extent to which the agency would reconcile its proposed action with the plan or law. While the statement should discuss any inconsistencies, NEPA does not require reconciliation.

§1506.3 Adoption.

(a) *Generally.* An agency may adopt a Federal draft or final environmental impact statement, environmental assessment, or portion thereof, or categorical exclusion determination provided that the statement, assessment, portion thereof, or determination meets the standards for an adequate statement, assessment, or determination under the regulations in this subchapter.

(b) *Environmental impact statements.*

(1) If the actions covered by the original environmental impact statement and the proposed action are substantially the same, the adopting agency shall republish it as a final statement consistent with §1506.10. If the actions are not substantially the same, the adopting agency shall treat the statement as a draft and republish it, consistent with §1506.10.

(2) Notwithstanding paragraph (b)(1) of this section, a cooperating agency may adopt in its record of decision without republishing the environmental impact statement of a lead agency when, after an independent review of the statement, the cooperating agency concludes that its comments and suggestions have been satisfied.

(c) *Environmental assessments.* If the actions covered by the original environmental assessment and the proposed action are substantially the same, the adopting agency may adopt the environmental assessment in its finding of no significant impact and provide notice consistent with §1501.6 of this chapter.

(d) *Categorical exclusions.* An agency may adopt another agency's determination that a categorical exclusion applies to a proposed action if the action covered by the original categorical exclusion determination and the adopting agency's proposed action are substantially the same. The agency shall document the adoption.

(e) *Identification of certain circumstances.* The adopting agency shall specify if one of the following circumstances is present:

(1) The agency is adopting an assessment or statement that is not final within the agency that prepared it.

(2) The action assessed in the assessment or statement is the subject of a referral under part 1504 of this chapter.

(3) The assessment or statement's adequacy is the subject of a judicial action that is not final.

§1506.4 Combining documents.

Agencies should combine, to the fullest extent practicable, any environmental document with any other agency document to reduce duplication and paperwork.

§1506.5 Agency responsibility for environmental documents.

(a) *Responsibility.* The agency is responsible for the accuracy, scope (§1501.9(e) of this chapter), and content of environmental documents prepared by the agency or by an applicant or contractor under the supervision of the agency.

(b) *Information.* An agency may require an applicant to submit environmental information for possible use by the agency in preparing an environmental document. An agency also may direct an applicant or authorize a contractor to prepare an environmental document under the supervision of the agency.

(1) The agency should assist the applicant by outlining the types of information required or, for the preparation of environmental documents, shall provide guidance to the applicant or contractor and participate in their preparation.

(2) The agency shall independently evaluate the information submitted or the environmental document and shall be responsible for its accuracy, scope, and contents.

(3) The agency shall include in the environmental document the names and qualifications of the persons preparing environmental documents, and conducting the independent evaluation of any information submitted or environmental documents prepared by an applicant or contractor, such as in the list of preparers for environmental impact statements (§1502.18 of this chapter). It is the intent of this paragraph (b)(3) that acceptable work not be redone, but that it be verified by the agency.

(4) Contractors or applicants preparing environmental assessments or environmental impact statements shall submit a disclosure statement to the lead agency that specifies any financial or other interest in the outcome of the action. Such statement need not include privileged or confidential trade secrets or other confidential business information.

(5) Nothing in this section is intended to prohibit any agency from requesting any person, including the applicant, to submit information to it or to prohibit any person from submitting information to any agency for use in preparing environmental documents.

§1506.6 Public involvement.

Agencies shall:

(a) Make diligent efforts to involve the public in preparing and implementing their NEPA procedures (§1507.3 of this chapter).

(b) Provide public notice of NEPA-related hearings, public meetings, and other opportunities for public involvement, and the availability of environmental documents so as to inform those persons and agencies who may be interested or affected by their proposed actions. When selecting appropriate methods for providing public notice, agencies shall consider the ability of affected persons and agencies to access electronic media.

(1) In all cases, the agency shall notify those who have requested notice on an individual action.

(2) In the case of an action with effects of national concern, notice shall include publication in the **Federal Register**. An agency may notify organizations that have requested regular notice.

(3) In the case of an action with effects primarily of local concern, the notice may include:

(i) Notice to State, Tribal, and local agencies that may be interested or affected by the proposed action.

(ii) Notice to interested or affected State, Tribal, and local governments.

(iii) Following the affected State or Tribe's public notice procedures for comparable actions.

(iv) Publication in local newspapers (in papers of general circulation rather than legal papers).

(v) Notice through other local media.

(vi) Notice to potentially interested community organizations including small business associations.

(vii) Publication in newsletters that may be expected to reach potentially interested persons.

(viii) Direct mailing to owners and occupants of nearby or affected property.

(ix) Posting of notice on and off site in the area where the action is to be located.

(x) Notice through electronic media (*e.g.*, a project or agency website, email, or social media).

(c) Hold or sponsor public hearings, public meetings, or other opportunities for public involvement whenever appropriate or in accordance with statutory requirements applicable to the agency. Agencies may conduct public hearings and public meetings by means of electronic communication except where another format is required by law. When selecting appropriate methods for public involvement, agencies shall consider the ability of affected entities to access electronic media.

(d) Solicit appropriate information from the public.

(e) Explain in its procedures where interested persons can get information or status reports on environmental impact statements and other elements of the NEPA process.

(f) Make environmental impact statements, the comments received, and any underlying documents available to the public pursuant to the provisions of the Freedom of Information Act, as amended (5 U.S.C. 552).

§1506.7 Further guidance.

(a) The Council may provide further guidance concerning NEPA and its procedures consistent with Executive Order 13807, Establishing Discipline and Accountability in the Environmental Review and Permitting Process for Infrastructure Projects (August 5, 2017), Executive Order 13891, Promoting the Rule of Law Through Improved Agency Guidance Documents (October 9, 2019), and any other applicable Executive orders.

(b) To the extent that Council guidance issued prior to September 14, 2020 is in conflict with this subchapter, the provisions of this subchapter apply.

§1506.8 Proposals for legislation.

(a) When developing legislation, agencies shall integrate the NEPA process for proposals for legislation significantly affecting the quality of the human environment with the legislative process of the Congress. Technical drafting assistance does not by itself constitute a legislative proposal. Only the agency that has primary responsibility for the subject matter involved will prepare a legislative environmental impact statement.

(b) A legislative environmental impact statement is the detailed statement required by law to be included in an agency's recommendation or report on a legislative proposal to Congress. A legislative environmental impact statement shall be considered part of the formal transmittal of a legislative proposal to Congress; however, it may be transmitted to Congress up to 30 days later in order to allow time for completion of an accurate statement that can serve as the basis for public and Congressional debate. The statement must be available in time for Congressional hearings and deliberations.

(c) Preparation of a legislative environmental impact statement shall conform to the requirements of the regulations in this subchapter, except as follows:

(1) There need not be a scoping process.

(2) Agencies shall prepare the legislative statement in the same manner as a draft environmental impact statement and need not prepare a final statement unless any of the following conditions exist. In such cases, the agency shall prepare and publish the statements consistent with §§1503.1 of this chapter and 1506.11:

(i) A Congressional committee with jurisdiction over the proposal has a rule requiring both draft and final environmental impact statements.

(ii) The proposal results from a study process required by statute (such as those required

by the Wild and Scenic Rivers Act (16 U.S.C. 1271 *et seq.*)).

(iii) Legislative approval is sought for Federal or federally assisted construction or other projects that the agency recommends be located at specific geographic locations. For proposals requiring an environmental impact statement for the acquisition of space by the General Services Administration, a draft statement shall accompany the Prospectus or the 11(b) Report of Building Project Surveys to the Congress, and a final statement shall be completed before site acquisition.

(iv) The agency decides to prepare draft and final statements.

(d) Comments on the legislative statement shall be given to the lead agency, which shall forward them along with its own responses to the Congressional committees with jurisdiction.

§1506.9 Proposals for regulations.

Where the proposed action is the promulgation of a rule or regulation, procedures and documentation pursuant to other statutory or Executive order requirements may satisfy one or more requirements of this subchapter. When a procedure or document satisfies one or more requirements of this subchapter, the agency may substitute it for the corresponding requirements in this subchapter and need not carry out duplicative procedures or documentation. Agencies shall identify which corresponding requirements in this subchapter are satisfied and consult with the Council to confirm such determinations.

§1506.10 Filing requirements.

(a) Agencies shall file environmental impact statements together with comments and responses with the Environmental Protection Agency (EPA), Office of Federal Activities, consistent with EPA's procedures.

(b) Agencies shall file statements with the EPA no earlier than they are also transmitted to participating agencies and made available to the public. EPA may issue guidelines to agencies to implement its responsibilities under this section and §1506.11.

§1506.11 Timing of agency action.

(a) The Environmental Protection Agency shall publish a notice in the Federal Register each week of the environmental impact statements filed since its prior notice. The minimum time periods set forth in this section are calculated from the date of publication of this notice.

(b) Unless otherwise provided by law, including statutory provisions for combining a final environmental impact statement and record of decision, Federal agencies may not make or issue a record of decision under §1505.2 of this chapter for the proposed action until the later of the following dates:

(1) 90 days after publication of the notice described in paragraph (a) of this section for a draft environmental impact statement.

(2) 30 days after publication of the notice described in paragraph (a) of this section for a final environmental impact statement.

(c) An agency may make an exception to the rule on timing set forth in paragraph (b) of this section for a proposed action in the following circumstances:

(1) Some agencies have a formally established appeal process after publication of the final environmental impact statement that allows other agencies or the public to take appeals on a decision and make their views known. In such cases where a real opportunity exists to alter the decision, the agency may make and record the decision at the same time it publishes the environmental impact statement. This means that the period for appeal of the decision and the 30-day period set forth in paragraph (b)(2) of this section may run concurrently. In such cases, the environmental impact statement shall explain the timing and the public's right of appeal and provide notification consistent with §1506.10; or

(2) An agency engaged in rulemaking under the Administrative Procedure Act or other statute for the purpose of protecting the public health or safety may waive the time period in paragraph (b)(2) of this section, publish a decision on the final rule simultaneously with publication of the notice of the availability of the final environmental impact statement, and provide notification consistent with §1506.10, as described in paragraph (a) of this section.

(d) If an agency files the final environmental impact statement within 90 days of the filing of the draft environmental impact statement with the Environmental Protection Agency, the decision-making period and the 90-day period may run concurrently. However, subject to paragraph (e) of this section, agencies shall allow at least 45 days for comments on draft statements.

(e) The lead agency may extend the minimum periods in paragraph (b) of this section and provide notification consistent with §1506.10. Upon a showing by the lead agency of compelling reasons of national policy, the Environmental Protection Agency may reduce the minimum periods and, upon a showing by any other Federal agency of compelling reasons of national policy, also may extend the minimum periods, but only after consultation with the lead agency. The lead agency may modify the minimum periods when necessary to comply with other specific statutory requirements. (§1507.3(f)(2) of this chapter) Failure to file timely comments shall not be a sufficient reason for extending a period. If the lead agency does not concur with the extension of time, EPA may not extend it for more than 30 days. When the Environmental Protection Agency

reduces or extends any period of time it shall notify the Council.

§1506.12 Emergencies.

Where emergency circumstances make it necessary to take an action with significant environmental impact without observing the provisions of the regulations in this subchapter, the Federal agency taking the action should consult with the Council about alternative arrangements for compliance with section 102(2)(C) of NEPA. Agencies and the Council will limit such arrangements to actions necessary to control the immediate impacts of the emergency. Other actions remain subject to NEPA review.

§1506.13 Effective date.

The regulations in this subchapter apply to any NEPA process begun after September 14, 2020. An agency may apply the regulations in this subchapter to ongoing activities and environmental documents begun before September 14, 2020.

§1507.1 Compliance.

All agencies of the Federal Government shall comply with the regulations in this subchapter.

§1507.2 Agency capability to comply.

Each agency shall be capable (in terms of personnel and other resources) of complying with the requirements of NEPA and the regulations in this subchapter. Such compliance may include use of the resources of other agencies, applicants, and other participants in the NEPA process, but the agency using the resources shall itself have sufficient capability to evaluate what others do for it and account for the contributions of others. Agencies shall:

(a) Fulfill the requirements of section 102(2)(A) of NEPA to utilize a systematic, interdisciplinary approach that will ensure the integrated use of the natural and social sciences and the environmental design arts in planning and in decision making that may have an impact on the human environment. Agencies shall designate a senior agency official to be responsible for overall review of agency NEPA compliance, including resolving implementation issues.

(b) Identify methods and procedures required by section 102(2)(B) of NEPA to ensure that presently unquantified environmental amenities and values may be given appropriate consideration.

(c) Prepare adequate environmental impact statements pursuant to section 102(2)(C) of NEPA and cooperate on the development of statements in the areas where the agency has jurisdiction by law or special expertise or is authorized to develop and enforce environmental standards.

(d) Study, develop, and describe alternatives to recommended courses of action in any proposal that involves unresolved conflicts concerning alternative uses of available resources, consistent with section 102(2)(E) of NEPA.

(e) Comply with the requirements of section 102(2)(H) of NEPA that the agency initiate and utilize ecological information in the planning and development of resource-oriented projects.

(f) Fulfill the requirements of sections 102(2)(F), 102(2)(G), and 102(2)(I), of NEPA, Executive Order 11514, Protection and Enhancement of Environmental Quality, section 2, as amended by Executive Order 11991, Relating to Protection and Enhancement of Environmental Quality, and Executive Order 13807, Establishing Discipline and Accountability in the Environmental Review and Permitting for Infrastructure Projects.

§1507.3 Agency NEPA procedures.

(a) Where existing agency NEPA procedures are inconsistent with the regulations in this subchapter, the regulations in this subchapter shall apply, consistent with §1506.13 of this chapter, unless there is a clear and fundamental conflict with the requirements of another statute. The Council has determined that the categorical exclusions contained in agency NEPA procedures as of September 14, 2020 are consistent with this subchapter.

(b) No more than 12 months after September 14, 2020, or 9 months after the establishment of an agency, whichever comes later, each agency shall develop or revise, as necessary, proposed procedures to implement the regulations in this subchapter, including to eliminate any inconsistencies with the regulations in this subchapter. When the agency is a department, it may be efficient for major subunits (with the consent of the department) to adopt their own procedures. Except for agency efficiency (see paragraph (c) of this section) or as otherwise required by law, agency NEPA procedures shall not impose additional procedures or requirements beyond those set forth in the regulations in this subchapter.

(1) Each agency shall consult with the Council while developing or revising its proposed procedures and before publishing them in the **Federal Register** for comment. Agencies with similar programs should consult with each other and the Council to coordinate their procedures, especially for programs requesting similar information from applicants.

(2) Agencies shall provide an opportunity for public review and review by the Council for conformity with the Act and the regulations in this subchapter before adopting their final procedures. The Council shall complete its review within 30 days of the receipt of the proposed final procedures. Once in effect, the agency shall publish its NEPA procedures and ensure that they are readily available to the public.

(c) Agencies shall adopt, as necessary, agency NEPA procedures to improve agency efficiency and ensure

that agencies make decisions in accordance with the Act's procedural requirements. Such procedures shall include:

(1) Designating the major decision points for the agency's principal programs likely to have a significant effect on the human environment and assuring that the NEPA process begins at the earliest reasonable time, consistent with §1501.2 of this chapter, and aligns with the corresponding decision points.

(2) Requiring that relevant environmental documents, comments, and responses be part of the record in formal rulemaking or adjudicatory proceedings.

(3) Requiring that relevant environmental documents, comments, and responses accompany the proposal through existing agency review processes so that decision makers use the statement in making decisions.

(4) Requiring that the alternatives considered by the decision maker are encompassed by the range of alternatives discussed in the relevant environmental documents and that the decision maker consider the alternatives described in the environmental documents. If another decision document accompanies the relevant environmental documents to the decision maker, agencies are encouraged to make available to the public before the decision is made any part of that document that relates to the comparison of alternatives.

(5) Requiring the combination of environmental documents with other agency documents. Agencies may designate and rely on one or more procedures or documents under other statutes or Executive orders as satisfying some or all of the requirements in this subchapter, and substitute such procedures and documentation to reduce duplication. When an agency substitutes one or more procedures or documents for the requirements in this subchapter, the agency shall identify the respective requirements that are satisfied.

(d) Agency procedures should identify those activities or decisions that are not subject to NEPA, including:

(1) Activities or decisions expressly exempt from NEPA under another statute;

(2) Activities or decisions where compliance with NEPA would clearly and fundamentally conflict with the requirements of another statute;

(3) Activities or decisions where compliance with NEPA would be inconsistent with Congressional intent expressed in another statute;

(4) Activities or decisions that are non-major Federal actions;

(5) Activities or decisions that are non-discretionary actions, in whole or in part, for which the agency lacks authority to consider environmental effects as part of its decision-making process; and

(6) Actions where the agency has determined that another statute's requirements serve the function of agency compliance with the Act.

(e) Agency procedures shall comply with the regulations in this subchapter except where compliance would be inconsistent with statutory requirements and shall include:

(1) Those procedures required by §§1501.2(b)(4) (assistance to applicants) and 1506.6(e) of this chapter (status information).

(2) Specific criteria for and identification of those typical classes of action:

(i) Which normally do require environmental impact statements.

(ii) Which normally do not require either an environmental impact statement or an environmental assessment and do not have a significant effect on the human environment (categorical exclusions (§1501.4 of this chapter)). Any procedures under this section shall provide for extraordinary circumstances in which a normally excluded action may have a significant environmental effect. Agency NEPA procedures shall identify when documentation of a categorical exclusion determination is required.

(iii) Which normally require environmental assessments but not necessarily environmental impact statements.

(3) Procedures for introducing a supplement to an environmental assessment or environmental impact statement into its formal administrative record, if such a record exists.

(f) Agency procedures may:

(1) Include specific criteria for providing limited exceptions to the provisions of the regulations in this subchapter for classified proposals. These are proposed actions that are specifically authorized under criteria established by an Executive order or statute to be kept secret in the interest of national defense or foreign policy and are in fact properly classified pursuant to such Executive order or statute. Agencies may safeguard and restrict from public dissemination environmental assessments and environmental impact statements that address classified proposals in accordance with agencies' own regulations applicable to classified information. Agencies should organize these documents so that classified portions are included as annexes, so that the agencies can make the unclassified portions available to the public.

(2) Provide for periods of time other than those presented in §1506.11 of this chapter when necessary to comply with other specific statutory requirements, including requirements of lead or cooperating agencies.

(3) Provide that, where there is a lengthy period between the agency's decision to prepare an environmental impact statement and the time of actual preparation, the agency may publish the notice of intent required by §1501.9(d) of this chapter at a reasonable time in advance of preparation of the draft statement. Agency procedures shall provide for publication of supplemental notices to inform the public of a pause in its preparation of an environmental impact statement and for any agency decision to withdraw its notice of intent to prepare an environmental impact statement.

(4) Adopt procedures to combine its environmental assessment process with its scoping process.

(5) Establish a process that allows the agency to use a categorical exclusion listed in another agency's NEPA procedures after consulting with that agency to ensure the use of the categorical exclusion is appropriate. The process should ensure documentation of the consultation and identify to the public those categorical exclusions the agency may use for its proposed actions. Then, the agency may apply the categorical exclusion to its proposed actions.

§1507.4 Agency NEPA program information.

(a) To allow agencies and the public to efficiently and effectively access information about NEPA reviews, agencies shall provide for agency websites or other means to make available environmental documents, relevant notices, and other relevant information for use by agencies, applicants, and interested persons. Such means of publication may include:

(1) Agency planning and environmental documents that guide agency management and provide for public involvement in agency planning processes;

(2) A directory of pending and final environmental documents;

(3) Agency policy documents, orders, terminology, and explanatory materials regarding agency decision-making processes;

(4) Agency planning program information, plans, and planning tools; and

(5) A database searchable by geographic information, document status, document type, and project type.

(b) Agencies shall provide for efficient and effective interagency coordination of their environmental program websites, including use of shared databases or application programming interface, in their implementation of NEPA and related authorities.

§1508.1 Definitions.

The following definitions apply to the regulations in this subchapter. Federal agencies shall use these terms uniformly throughout the Federal Government.

(a) *Act* or *NEPA* means the National Environmental Policy Act, as amended (42 U.S.C. 4321, *et seq.*).

(b) *Affecting* means will or may have an effect on.

(c) *Authorization* means any license, permit, approval, finding, determination, or other administrative decision issued by an agency that is required or authorized under Federal law in order to implement a proposed action.

(d) *Categorical exclusion* means a category of actions that the agency has determined, in its agency NEPA procedures (§1507.3 of this chapter), normally do not have a significant effect on the human environment.

(e) *Cooperating agency* means any Federal agency (and a State, Tribal, or local agency with agreement of the lead agency) other than a lead agency that has jurisdiction by law or special expertise with respect to any environmental impact involved in a proposal (or a reasonable alternative) for legislation or other major Federal action that may significantly affect the quality of the human environment.

(f) *Council* means the Council on Environmental Quality established by title II of the Act.

(g) *Effects* or *impacts* means changes to the human environment from the proposed action or alternatives that are reasonably foreseeable and have a reasonably close causal relationship to the proposed action or alternatives, including those effects that occur at the same time and place as the proposed action or alternatives and may include effects that are later in time or farther removed in distance from the proposed action or alternatives.

(1) Effects include ecological (such as the effects on natural resources and on the components, structures, and functioning of affected ecosystems), aesthetic, historic, cultural, economic (such as the effects on employment), social, or health effects. Effects may also include those resulting from actions that may have both beneficial and detrimental effects, even if on balance the agency believes that the effect will be beneficial.

(2) A "but for" causal relationship is insufficient to make an agency responsible for a particular effect under NEPA. Effects should generally not be considered if they are remote in time, geographically remote, or the product of a lengthy causal chain. Effects do not include those effects that the agency has no ability to prevent due to its limited statutory authority or would occur regardless of the proposed action.

(3) An agency's analysis of effects shall be consistent with this paragraph (g). Cumulative impact, defined in 40 CFR 1508.7 (1978), is repealed.

(h) *Environmental assessment* means a concise public document prepared by a Federal agency to aid an agency's compliance with the Act and support its determination of whether to prepare an environmental impact statement or a finding of no significant impact, as provided in §1501.6 of this chapter.

(i) *Environmental document* means an environmental assessment, environmental impact statement, finding of no significant impact, or notice of intent.

(j) *Environmental impact statement* means a detailed written statement as required by section 102(2)(C) of NEPA.

(k) *Federal agency* means all agencies of the Federal Government. It does not mean the Congress, the Judiciary, or the President, including the performance of staff functions for the President in his Executive Office. For the purposes of the regulations in this subchapter, Federal agency also includes States, units of general local government, and Tribal governments assuming NEPA responsibilities from a Federal agency pursuant to statute.

(l) *Finding of no significant impact* means a document by a Federal agency briefly presenting the reasons why an action, not otherwise categorically excluded (§1501.4 of this chapter), will not have a significant effect on the human environment and for which an environmental impact statement therefore will not be prepared.

(m) *Human environment* means comprehensively the natural and physical environment and the relationship of present and future generations of Americans with that environment. (*See also* the definition of "effects" in paragraph (g) of this section.)

(n) *Jurisdiction by law* means agency authority to approve, veto, or finance all or part of the proposal.

(o) *Lead agency* means the agency or agencies, in the case of joint lead agencies, preparing or having taken primary responsibility for preparing the environmental impact statement.

(p) *Legislation* means a bill or legislative proposal to Congress developed by a Federal agency, but does not include requests for appropriations or legislation recommended by the President.

(q) *Major Federal action* or *action* means an activity or decision subject to Federal control and responsibility subject to the following:

(1) Major Federal action does not include the following activities or decisions:

(i) Extraterritorial activities or decisions, which means agency activities or decisions with effects located entirely outside of the jurisdiction of the United States;

(ii) Activities or decisions that are nondiscretionary and made in accordance with the agency's statutory authority;

(iii) Activities or decisions that do not result in final agency action under the Administrative Procedure Act or other statute that also includes a finality requirement;

(iv) Judicial or administrative civil or criminal enforcement actions;

(v) Funding assistance solely in the form of general revenue sharing funds with no Federal agency control over the subsequent use of such funds;

(vi) Non-Federal projects with minimal Federal funding or minimal Federal involvement where the agency does not exercise sufficient control and responsibility over the outcome of the project; and

(vii) Loans, loan guarantees, or other forms of financial assistance where the Federal agency does not exercise sufficient control and responsibility over the effects of such assistance (for example, action does not include farm ownership and operating loan guarantees by the Farm Service Agency pursuant to 7 U.S.C. 1925 and 1941 through 1949 and business loan guarantees by the Small Business Administration pursuant to 15 U.S.C. 636(a), 636(m), and 695 through 697g).

(2) Major Federal actions may include new and continuing activities, including projects and programs entirely or partly financed, assisted, conducted, regulated, or approved by Federal agencies; new or revised agency rules, regulations, plans, policies, or procedures; and legislative proposals (§1506.8 of this chapter).

(3) Major Federal actions tend to fall within one of the following categories:

(i) Adoption of official policy, such as rules, regulations, and interpretations adopted under the Administrative Procedure Act, 5 U.S.C. 551 *et seq.* or other statutes; implementation of treaties and international conventions or agreements, including those implemented pursuant to statute or regulation; formal documents establishing an agency's policies which will result in or substantially alter agency programs.

(ii) Adoption of formal plans, such as official documents prepared or approved by Federal agencies, which prescribe alternative uses of Federal resources, upon which future agency actions will be based.

(iii) Adoption of programs, such as a group of concerted actions to implement a specific policy or plan; systematic and connected agency decisions allocating agency resources to implement a specific statutory program or executive directive.

(iv) Approval of specific projects, such as construction or management activities located in a defined geographic area. Projects include actions approved by permit or other regulatory decision as well as Federal and federally assisted activities.

(r) *Matter* includes for purposes of part 1504 of this chapter:

(1) With respect to the Environmental Protection Agency, any proposed legislation, project, action or regulation as those terms are used in section 309(a) of the Clean Air Act (42 U.S.C. 7609).

(2) With respect to all other agencies, any proposed major Federal action to which section 102(2)(C) of NEPA applies.

(s) *Mitigation* means measures that avoid, minimize, or compensate for effects caused by a proposed action or alternatives as described in an environmental document or record of decision and that have a nexus to those effects. While NEPA requires consideration of mitigation, it does not mandate the form or adoption of any mitigation. Mitigation includes:

(1) Avoiding the impact altogether by not taking a certain action or parts of an action.

(2) Minimizing impacts by limiting the degree or magnitude of the action and its implementation.

(3) Rectifying the impact by repairing, rehabilitating, or restoring the affected environment.

(4) Reducing or eliminating the impact over time by preservation and maintenance operations during the life of the action.

(5) Compensating for the impact by replacing or providing substitute resources or environments.

(t) *NEPA process* means all measures necessary for compliance with the requirements of section 2 and title I of NEPA.

(u) *Notice of intent* means a public notice that an agency will prepare and consider an environmental impact statement.

(v) *Page* means 500 words and does not include explanatory maps, diagrams, graphs, tables, and other means of graphically displaying quantitative or geospatial information.

(w) *Participating agency* means a Federal, State, Tribal, or local agency participating in an environmental review or authorization of an action.

(x) *Proposal* means a proposed action at a stage when an agency has a goal, is actively preparing to make a decision on one or more alternative means of accomplishing that goal, and can meaningfully evaluate its effects. A proposal may exist in fact as well as by agency declaration that one exists.

(y) *Publish* and *publication* mean methods found by the agency to efficiently and effectively make environmental documents and information available for review by interested persons, including electronic publication, and adopted by agency NEPA procedures pursuant to §1507.3 of this chapter.

(z) *Reasonable alternatives* means a reasonable range of alternatives that are technically and economically feasible, meet the purpose and need for the proposed action, and, where applicable, meet the goals of the applicant.

(aa) *Reasonably foreseeable* means sufficiently likely to occur such that a person of ordinary prudence would take it into account in reaching a decision.

(bb) *Referring agency* means the Federal agency that has referred any matter to the Council after a determination that the matter is unsatisfactory from the standpoint of public health or welfare or environmental quality.

(cc) *Scope* consists of the range of actions, alternatives, and impacts to be considered in an environmental impact statement. The scope of an individual statement may depend on its relationships to other statements (§1501.11 of this chapter).

(dd) *Senior agency official* means an official of assistant secretary rank or higher (or equivalent) that is designated for overall agency NEPA compliance, including resolving implementation issues.

(ee) *Special expertise* means statutory responsibility, agency mission, or related program experience.

(ff) *Tiering* refers to the coverage of general matters in broader environmental impact statements or environmental assessments (such as national program or policy statements) with subsequent narrower statements or environmental analyses (such as regional or basin-wide program statements or ultimately site-specific statements) incorporating by reference the general discussions and concentrating solely on the issues specific to the statement subsequently prepared.

§1508.2 [Reserved]

9

BIODIVERSITY PROTECTION

Federal efforts to protect wildlife have a long history. In 1903 President Theodore Roosevelt created the first National Wildlife Refuge on Pelican Island, Florida in order to protect a species of bird that had become endangered due to the popularity of hats made with its feathers. In 1916 the United States entered into a treaty with Great Britain to protect many species of birds that migrate annually between Canada and the United States. To implement the Migratory Bird Treaty of 1916, Congress enacted legislation prohibiting the killing, capturing or selling of migratory birds except as permitted by regulations issued by the U.S. Secretary of Agriculture. This gave rise to the Supreme Court's decision in 1920 in *Missouri v. Holland*, which confirmed the supremacy of federal laws enacted to enforce treaties over state laws regulating wildlife.

Despite this long history of federal efforts to protect endangered species, it was only in the last few decades that these efforts have come to be seen in the larger context of protection of biological diversity. "Biodiversity" is defined by the 1992 International Convention on Biological Diversity as "the variability among living organisms from all sources, including terrestrial, marine, and other aquatic ecosystems and the ecological complexes of which they are a part." This definition "includes diversity within species, between species, and of ecosystems," thus embracing genetic diversity (variations among individuals of the same species) and the diversity of natural communities (ecosystems).

The federal Endangered Species Act (ESA) is the cornerstone of efforts to protect biological diversity in the United States. It encompasses protections not only for species themselves, but also for the natural systems upon which they depend. The ESA ultimately is the safety net when broader efforts to protect species fail.

A GUIDE TO MATERIALS ON PROTECTION OF BIODIVERSITY AVAILABLE ON THE INTERNET

The U.S Fish and Wildlife Service of the Department of Interior is responsible for administering the Endangered Species Act (ESA) for plants and wildlife. It maintains an endangered species webpage located at *http://www.fws.gov/endangered/*. The central webpage provides news updates concerning species protection efforts and it has extensive links to information about implementation of the ESA, including information on federal interagency consultations *(http://www.fws.gov/endangered/what-we-do/consultations-overview.html)*, the habitat conservation planning process *(http://www.fws.gov/endangered/what-we-do/hcp-overview.html)*, listing decisions *(http://www.fws.gov/endangered/what-we-do/listing-overview.html)*, and a summary of the history of the ESA and its implementation *(http://www.fws.gov/endangered/laws-policies/esa-history.html)*. The website has links to downloadable publications at *http://www.fws.gov/endangered/esa-library/index.html*.

The Endangered Species Bulletin is the primary means by which the U.S. Fish and Wildlife Service disseminates information on rulemakings (listings, reclassifications, and delistings), recovery plans and activities, regulatory changes, interagency consultations, changes in species' status, research developments, new ecological threats, and a variety of other issues. It is printed on a bimonthly schedule, with six editions per year and an annual index. Copies of the Bulletin dating back to 1976 are available online at *http://www.fws.gov/endangered/news/bulletin.html*.

The National Marine Fisheries Service (NMFS) of the U.S. Department of Commerce is the agency responsible for implementing provisions of the Endangered Species Act applicable to marine species. A source of online information about its activities is the NOAA Fisheries' Office of Protected Resources, which maintains a website located at *http://www.nmfs.noaa.gov/pr*. This website contains information concerning the agency's implementation of both the Endangered Species Act and the Marine Mammal Protection Act, including information on how to obtain permits under both statutes. It also provides information on how teachers can educate children on the importance of conserving endangered species.

The UN Environment Programme's World Conservation Monitoring Centre monitors global species protection efforts. Its website is at *http://www.unep-wcmc.org*. A variety of non-governmental organizations have webpages devoted to endangered species issues. The Endangered Species Coalition, a coalition of more than 400 conservation, scientific, business, and religious organizations that supports stronger species protection efforts, has a website at *http://www.endangered.org*. The World Wildlife Fund's webpage is at *http://www.worldwildlife.org/species/directory*. An industry lobbying group active on ESA issues, which calls itself the Endangered Species Act Reform Coalition, has a website at *http://www.nesarc.org*.

ENDANGERED SPECIES ACT LEGISLATIVE HISTORY TIMELINE

October 15, 1966: President Johnson signs the Endangered Species Preservation Act, Pub. L. 89-669, 80 Stat, 926, which provides limited protection for native animal species listed as endangered. The law directs the Departments of Interior, Agriculture, and Defense to make efforts to protect listed species and to preserve their habitats and it authorizes federal land acquisition for species preservation.

December 5, 1969: President Nixon signs the Endangered Species Conservation Act of 1969, Pub. L. 91-135, 83 Stat. 275, which seeks to provide additional protection to species in danger of "worldwide extinction" by prohibiting their importation and subsequent sale within the United States.

December 28, 1973: President Nixon signs into law the Endangered Species Act (ESA), Pub. L. 93-205, 87 Stat. 884. The law broadly prohibits actions that harm endangered animal species and it bars Federal agencies from authorizing, funding, or carrying out any action that would jeopardize a listed species or destroy or modify its critical habitat.

November 10, 1978: President Carter signs Pub. L. 95-632, 92 Stat. 3751, which amends the ESA to authorize a cabinet-level committee (known as the "God squad") in exceptional circumstances to grant exemptions from §7's ban on federal actions that would jeopardize listed species. The amendments also direct that critical habitat be designated when species are listed after considering economic and other impacts of the designation.

October 13, 1982: President Reagan signs Pub. L. 97-304, 96 Stat. 1411, which amends §4 of the ESA to strengthen provisions for listing species. The amendments require that listing determinations be made solely on the basis of biological information, without consideration of economic effects and they require that listing decisions be made within one year after their proposal. The amendments also provide for the designation of experimental populations of listed species that could be subject to different treatment under the Act to facilitate their recovery.

October 7, 1988: President Reagan signs Pub. L. 100-478, 102 Stat. 2306, which amends the ESA to facilitate species recovery and to strengthen protections for endangered plants. The amendments require more extensive monitoring of recovering species and they prohibit the destruction of endangered plants on Federal land and their taking when it violates State law.

PRINCIPAL PROVISIONS OF THE ENDANGERED SPECIES ACT

§3 (16 U.S.C. §1532) Definitions:

§3(6) defines "endangered species" as "any species which is in danger of extinction throughout all or a significant portion of its range."

§3(20) defines "threatened species" as "any species which is likely to become endangered within the foreseeable future throughout all or a significant portion of its range."

§4 (16 U.S.C. §1533) Species Listings:

§4(a) requires the Secretary of Commerce or the Secretary of the Interior to determine whether any species is endangered or threatened and to designate critical habitat for listed species.

§4(b) provides that listing determinations are to be based solely on the best scientific and commercial data and that critical habitat designations are to be based on the best scientific data available taking into consideration the economic impact of specifying any particular area as critical habitat. Provides that citizens may petition to force listing determinations.

§4(c) requires the Secretary to publish in the Federal Register a list of all endangered and threatened species and to review the list every five years to determine whether any species should be removed from the list or changed in status.

§4(d) requires the Secretary to issue "such regulations as he deems necessary and advisable to provide for the conservation" of species listed as threatened, including prohibiting any acts prohibited under §9 for endangered species of fish, wildlife, or plants.

§4(f) requires the Secretary to develop and implement recovery plans for endangered and threatened species unless they will not promote species conservation.

§7 (16 U.S.C. §1536) Review of Federal Actions:

§7(a) requires all federal agencies to carry out programs to conserve endangered and threatened species and provides that all federal agencies must insure, in consultation with the Secretary, that their actions are not likely to jeopardize the continued existence of any endangered species or threatened species or result in the destruction of, or adverse modification of, such species' critical habitat.

§7(c) requires federal agencies to conduct a biological assessment of any endangered or threatened species likely to be affected by an agency action if the Secretary advises the agency that such species may be present in the area of the proposed action.

§7(e)-(h) provides that if a "jeopardy" determination bars an action, its proponents may seek an exemption from a cabinet-level "Endangered Species Committee" (known as the "God squad").

§9 (16 U.S.C. §1538) Prohibitions:

§9(a) prohibits the sale, import, export, or transport of endangered species.

§9(a)(1)(B) & (C) make it unlawful to "take" (broadly defined by §3(19) to cover harassing, harming, killing, capturing, or collecting) any endangered animal species.

§9(a)(2)(B) prohibits removal or damage of endangered plants on federal land or anywhere else if in knowing violation of state law.

§10 (16 U.S.C. §1539) Habitat Conservation Plans:

§10(a) authorizes the issuance of permits allowing the incidental taking of endangered species by persons with an approved habitat conservation plan to minimize and mitigate the impacts of the taking so long as it will not appreciably reduce the likelihood of the survival and recovery of the species in the wild.

§11 (16 U.S.C. §1540) Enforcement:

§11(a) & (b) provides civil and criminal penalties for violations of the Act.

§11(g) authorizes citizen suits against violators of the Act and against the Secretaries for failure to perform any nondiscretionary duty.

Endangered Species Act

16 U.S.C. §§1531 to 1544

§1531. Congressional findings and declaration of purposes and policy
[ESA §2]

(a) Findings — The Congress finds and declares that —

(1) various species of fish, wildlife, and plants in the United States have been rendered extinct as a consequence of economic growth and development untempered by adequate concern and conservation;

(2) other species of fish, wildlife, and plants have been so depleted in numbers that they are in danger of or threatened with extinction;

(3) these species of fish, wildlife, and plants are of esthetic, ecological, educational, historical, recreational, and scientific value to the Nation and its people;

(4) the United States has pledged itself as a sovereign state in the international community to conserve to the extent practicable the various species of fish or wildlife and plants facing extinction, pursuant to —

(A) migratory bird treaties with Canada and Mexico;

(B) the Migratory and Endangered Bird Treaty with Japan;

(C) the Convention on Nature Protection and Wildlife Preservation in the Western Hemisphere;

(D) the International Convention for the Northwest Atlantic Fisheries;

(E) the International Convention for the High Seas Fisheries of the North Pacific Ocean;

(F) the Convention on International Trade in Endangered Species of Wild Fauna and Flora; and

(G) other international agreements; and

(5) encouraging the States and other interested parties, through Federal financial assistance and a system of incentives, to develop and maintain conservation programs which meet national and international standards is a key to meeting the Nation's international commitments and to better safeguarding, for the benefit of all citizens, the Nation's heritage in fish, wildlife, and plants.

(b) Purposes — The purposes of this chapter are to provide a means whereby the ecosystems upon which endangered species and threatened species depend may be conserved, to provide a program for the conservation of such endangered species and threatened species, and to take such steps as may be appropriate to achieve the purposes of the treaties and conventions set forth in subsection (a) of this section.

(c) Policy

(1) It is further declared to be the policy of Congress that all Federal departments and agencies shall seek to conserve endangered species and threatened species and shall utilize their authorities in furtherance of the purposes of this chapter.

(2) It is further declared to be the policy of Congress that Federal agencies shall cooperate with State and local agencies to resolve water resource issues in concert with conservation of endangered species.

§1532. Definitions
[ESA §3]

For the purpose of this chapter —

(1) The term "alternative courses of action" means all alternatives and thus is not limited to original project objectives and agency jurisdiction.

(2) The term "commercial activity" means all activities of industry and trade, including, but not limited to, the buying or selling of commodities and activities conducted for the purpose of facilitating such buying and selling: *Provided, however,* That it does not include exhibition of commodities by museums or similar cultural or historical organizations.

(3) The terms "conserve", "conserving", and "conservation" mean to use and the use of all methods and procedures which are necessary to

bring any endangered species or threatened species to the point at which the measures provided pursuant to this chapter are no longer necessary. Such method and procedures include, but are not limited to, all activities associated with scientific resources management such as research, census, law enforcement, habitat acquisition and maintenance, propagation, live trapping, and transplantation, and, in the extraordinary case where population pressures within a given ecosystem cannot be otherwise relieved, may include regulated taking.

(4) The term "Convention" means the Convention on International Trade in Endangered Species of Wild Fauna and Flora, signed on March 3, 1973, and the appendices thereto.

(5)(A) The term "critical habitat" for a threatened or endangered species means —

    (i) the specific areas within the geographical area occupied by the species, at the time it is listed in accordance with the provisions of section 1533 of this title, on which are found those physical or biological features (I) essential to the conservation of the species and (II) which may require special management considerations or protection; and

    (ii) specific areas outside the geographical area occupied by the species at the time it is listed in accordance with the provisions of section 1533 of this title, upon a determination by the Secretary that such areas are essential for the conservation of the species.

(B) Critical habitat may be established for those species now listed as threatened or endangered species for which no critical habitat has heretofore been established as set forth in subparagraph (A) of this paragraph.

(C) Except in those circumstances determined by the Secretary, critical habitat shall not include the entire geographical area which can be occupied by the threatened or endangered species.

(6) The term "endangered species" means any species which is in danger of extinction throughout all or a significant portion of its range other than a species of the Class Insecta determined by the Secretary to constitute a pest whose protection under the provisions of this chapter would present an overwhelming and overriding risk to man.

(7) The term "Federal agency" means any department, agency, or instrumentality of the United States.

(8) The term "fish or wildlife" means any member of the animal kingdom, including without limitation any mammal, fish, bird (including any migratory, nonmigratory, or endangered bird for which protection is also afforded by treaty or other international agreement), amphibian, reptile, mollusk, crustacean, arthropod or other invertebrate,

and includes any part, product, egg, or offspring thereof, or the dead body or parts thereof.

(9) The term "foreign commerce" includes, among other things, any transaction —

    (A) between persons within one foreign country;

    (B) between persons in two or more foreign countries;

    (C) between a person within the United States and a person in a foreign country; or

    (D) between persons within the United States, where the fish and wildlife in question are moving in any country or countries outside the United States.

(10) The term "import" means to land on, bring into, or introduce into, or attempt to land on, bring into, or introduce into, any place subject to the jurisdiction of the United States whether or not such landing, bringing, or introduction constitutes an importation within the meaning of the customs laws of the United States.

(11) Repealed. Pub. L. 97-304, Sec. 4(b), Oct. 13, 1982, 96 Stat. 1420.

(12) The term "permit or license applicant" means, when used with respect to an action of a Federal agency for which exemption is sought under section 1536 of this title, any person whose application to such agency for a permit or license has been denied primarily because of the application of section 1536(a) of this title to such agency action.

(13) The term "person" means an individual, corporation, partnership, trust, association, or any other private entity; or any officer, employee, agent, department, or instrumentality of the Federal Government, of any State, municipality, or political subdivision of a State, or of any foreign government; any State, municipality, or political subdivision of a State; or any other entity subject to the jurisdiction of the United States.

(14) The term "plant" means any member of the plant kingdom, including seeds, roots and other parts thereof.

(15) The term "Secretary" means, except as otherwise herein provided, the Secretary of the Interior or the Secretary of Commerce as program responsibilities are vested pursuant to the provisions of Reorganization Plan Numbered 4 of 1970; except that with respect to the enforcement of the provisions of this chapter and the Convention which pertain to the importation or exportation of terrestrial plants, the term also means the Secretary of Agriculture.

(16) The term "species" includes any subspecies of fish or wildlife or plants, and any distinct population segment of any species of vertebrate fish or wildlife which interbreeds when mature.

(17) The term "State" means any of the several States, the District of Columbia, the

Commonwealth of Puerto Rico, American Samoa, the Virgin Islands, Guam, and the Trust Territory of the Pacific Islands.

(18) The term "State agency" means any State agency, department, board, commission, or other governmental entity which is responsible for the management and conservation of fish, plant, or wildlife resources within a State.

(19) The term "take" means to harass, harm, pursue, hunt, shoot, wound, kill, trap, capture, or collect, or to attempt to engage in any such conduct.

(20) The term "threatened species" means any species which is likely to become an endangered species within the foreseeable future throughout all or a significant portion of its range.

(21) The term "United States", when used in a geographical context, includes all States.

§1533. Determination of endangered species and threatened species
[ESA §4]
(a) Generally

(1) The Secretary shall by regulation promulgated in accordance with subsection (b) determine whether any species is an endangered species or a threatened species because of any of the following factors:

(A) the present or threatened destruction, modification, or curtailment of its habitat or range;

(B) overutilization for commercial, recreational, scientific, or educational purposes;

(C) disease or predation;

(D) the inadequacy of existing regulatory mechanisms; or

(E) other natural or manmade factors affecting its continued existence.

(2) With respect to any species over which program responsibilities have been vested in the Secretary of Commerce pursuant to Reorganization Plan Numbered 4 of 1970 —

(A) in any case in which the Secretary of Commerce determines that such species should —

(i) be listed as an endangered species or a threatened species, or

(ii) be changed in status from a threatened species to an endangered species,

he shall so inform the Secretary of the Interior; who shall list such species in accordance with this section;

(B) in any case in which the Secretary of Commerce determines that such species should —

(i) be removed from any list published pursuant to subsection (c) of this section, or

(ii) be changed in status from an endangered species to a threatened species,

he shall recommend such action to the Secretary of the Interior and the Secretary of the Interior, if he concurs in the recommendation, shall implement such action; and

(C) the Secretary of the Interior may not list or remove from any list any such species, and may not change the status of any such species which are listed, without a prior favorable determination made pursuant to this section by the Secretary of Commerce.

(3)(A) The Secretary, by regulation promulgated in accordance with subsection (b) and to the maximum extent prudent and determinable —

(i) shall, concurrently with making a determination under paragraph (1) that a species is an endangered species or a threatened species, designate any habitat of such species which is then considered to be critical habitat; and

(ii) may, from time-to-time thereafter as appropriate, revise such designation.

(B)(i) The Secretary shall not designate as critical habitat any lands or other geographical areas owned or controlled by the Department of Defense, or designated for its use, that are subject to an integrated natural resources management plan prepared under section 670a of this title, if the Secretary determines in writing that such plan provides a benefit to the species for which critical habitat is proposed for designation.

(ii) Nothing in this paragraph affects the requirement to consult under section 1536(a)(2) of this title with respect to an agency action (as that term is defined in that section).

(iii) Nothing in this paragraph affects the obligation of the Department of Defense to comply with section 1538 of this title, including the prohibition preventing extinction and taking of endangered species and threatened species.

(b) Basis for determinations

(1)(A) The Secretary shall make determinations required by subsection (a)(1) solely on the basis of the best scientific and commercial data available to him after conducting a review of the status of the species and after taking into account those efforts, if any, being made by any State or foreign nation, or any political subdivision of a State or foreign nation, to protect such species, whether by predator control, protection of habitat and food supply, or other conservation practices, within any area under its jurisdiction; or on the high seas.

(B) In carrying out this section, the Secretary shall give consideration to species which have been —

(i) designated as requiring protection from unrestricted commerce by any foreign nation, or pursuant to any international agreement; or

(ii) identified as in danger of extinction, or likely to become so within the foreseeable future, by any State agency or by any agency of a foreign nation that is responsible for the conservation of fish or wildlife or plants.

(2) The Secretary shall designate critical habitat, and make revisions thereto, under subsection (a)(3) on the basis of the best scientific data available and after taking into consideration the economic impact, the impact on national security, and any other relevant impact, of specifying any particular area as critical habitat. The Secretary may exclude any area from critical habitat if he determines that the benefits of such exclusion outweigh the benefits of specifying such area as part of the critical habitat, unless he determines, based on the best scientific and commercial data available, that the failure to designate such area as critical habitat will result in the extinction of the species concerned.

(3)(A) To the maximum extent practicable, within 90 days after receiving the petition of an interested person under section 553(e) of Title 5, to add a species to, or to remove a species from, either of the lists published under subsection (c), the Secretary shall make a finding as to whether the petition presents substantial scientific or commercial information indicating that the petitioned action may be warranted. If such a petition is found to present such information, the Secretary shall promptly commence a review of the status of the species concerned. The Secretary shall promptly publish each finding made under this subparagraph in the Federal Register.

(B) Within 12 months after receiving a petition that is found under subparagraph (A) to present substantial information indicating that the petitioned action may be warranted, the Secretary shall make one of the following findings:

(i) The petitioned action is not warranted, in which case the Secretary shall promptly publish such finding in the Federal Register.

(ii) The petitioned action is warranted, in which case the Secretary shall promptly publish in the Federal Register a general notice and the complete text of a proposed regulation to implement such action in accordance with paragraph (5).

(iii) The petitioned action is warranted, but that —

(I) the immediate proposal and timely promulgation of a final regulation implementing the petitioned action in accordance with paragraphs (5) and (6) is precluded by pending proposals to determine whether any species is an endangered species or a threatened species, and

(II) expeditious progress is being made to add qualified species to either of the lists published under subsection (c) and to remove from such lists species for which the pro-tections of this chapter are no longer necessary,

in which case the Secretary shall promptly publish such finding in the Federal Register, together with a description and evaluation of the reasons and data on which the finding is based.

(C)(i) A petition with respect to which a finding is made under subparagraph (B)(iii) shall be treated as a petition that is resubmitted to the Secretary under subparagraph (A) on the date of such finding and that presents substantial scientific or commercial information that the petitioned action may be warranted.

(ii) Any negative finding described in subparagraph (A) and any finding described in subparagraph (B)(i) or (iii) shall be subject to judicial review.

(iii) The Secretary shall implement a system to monitor effectively the status of all species with respect to which a finding is made under subparagraph (B)(iii) and shall make prompt use of the authority under paragraph 7 to prevent a significant risk to the well being of any such species.

(D)(i) To the maximum extent practicable, within 90 days after receiving the petition of an interested person under section 553(e) of Title 5, to revise a critical habitat designation, the Secretary shall make a finding as to whether the petition presents substantial scientific information indicating that the revision may be warranted. The Secretary shall promptly publish such finding in the Federal Register.

(ii) Within 12 months after receiving a petition that is found under clause (i) to present substantial information indicating that the requested revision may be warranted, the Secretary shall determine how he intends to proceed with the requested revision, and shall promptly publish notice of such intention in the Federal Register.

(4) Except as provided in paragraphs (5) and (6) of this subsection, the provisions of section 553 of Title 5 (relating to rulemaking procedures), shall apply to any regulation promulgated to carry out the purposes of this chapter.

(5) With respect to any regulation proposed by the Secretary to implement a determination, designation, or revision referred to in subsection (a)(1) or (3), the Secretary shall —

(A) not less than 90 days before the effective date of the regulation —

　(i)　publish a general notice and the complete text of the proposed regulation in the Federal Register, and

　(ii)　give actual notice of the proposed regulation (including the complete text of the regulation) to the State agency in each State in which the species is believed to occur, and to each county or equivalent jurisdiction in which the species is believed to occur, and invite the comment of such agency, and each such jurisdiction, thereon;

(B) insofar as practical, and in cooperation with the Secretary of State, give notice of the proposed regulation to each foreign nation in which the species is believed to occur or whose citizens harvest the species on the high seas, and invite the comment of such nation thereon;

(C) give notice of the proposed regulation to such professional scientific organizations as he deems appropriate;

(D) publish a summary of the proposed regulation in a newspaper of general circulation in each area of the United States in which the species is believed to occur; and

(E) promptly hold one public hearing on the proposed regulation if any person files a request for such a hearing within 45 days after the date of publication of general notice.

(6)(A) Within the one-year period beginning on the date on which general notice is published in accordance with paragraph (5)(A)(i) regarding a proposed regulation, the Secretary shall publish in the Federal Register —

　(i)　if a determination as to whether a species is an endangered species or a threatened species, or a revision of critical habitat, is involved, either —

　　(I)　a final regulation to implement such determination,

　　(II)　a final regulation to implement such revision or a finding that such revision should not be made,

　　(III)　notice that such one-year period is being extended under subparagraph (B)(i), or

　　(IV)　notice that the proposed regulation is being withdrawn under subparagraph (B)(ii), together with the finding on which such withdrawal is based; or

　(ii)　subject to subparagraph (C), if a designation of critical habitat is involved, either —

　　(I)　a final regulation to implement such designation, or

　　(II)　notice that such one-year period is being extended under such subparagraph.

(B)(i) If the Secretary finds with respect to a proposed regulation referred to in subparagraph (A)(i) that there is substantial disagreement regarding the sufficiency or accuracy of the available data relevant to the determination or revision concerned, the Secretary may extend the one-year period specified in subparagraph (A) for not more than six months for purposes of soliciting additional data.

　(ii)　If a proposed regulation referred to in subparagraph (A)(i) is not promulgated as a final regulation within such one-year period (or longer period if extension under clause (i) applies) because the Secretary finds that there is not sufficient evidence to justify the action proposed by the regulation, the Secretary shall immediately withdraw the regulation. The finding on which a withdrawal is based shall be subject to judicial review. The Secretary may not propose a regulation that has previously been withdrawn under this clause unless he determines that sufficient new information is available to warrant such proposal.

　(iii)　If the one-year period specified in subparagraph (A) is extended under clause (i) with respect to a proposed regulation, then before the close of such extended period the Secretary shall publish in the Federal Register either a final regulation to implement the determination or revision concerned, a finding that the revision should not be made, or a notice of withdrawal of the regulation under clause (ii), together with the finding on which the withdrawal is based.

(C) A final regulation designating critical habitat of an endangered species or a threatened species shall be published concurrently with the final regulation implementing the determination that such species is endangered or threatened, unless the Secretary deems that —

　(i)　it is essential to the conservation of such species that the regulation implementing such determination be promptly published; or

　(ii)　critical habitat of such species is not then determinable, in which case the Secretary, with respect to the proposed regulation to designate such habitat, may extend the one-year period specified in subparagraph (A) by not more than one additional year, but not later than the close of such additional year the Secretary must publish a final regulation, based on such data as may be available at that time, designating, to the maximum extent prudent, such habitat.

(7) Neither paragraph (4), (5), or (6) of this subsection nor section 553 of Title 5 shall apply to any regulation issued by the Secretary in regard to any emergency posing a significant risk to the well-being of any species of fish or wildlife or plants, but only if —

　(A) at the time of publication of the regulation in the Federal Register the Secretary publishes therein detailed reasons why such regulation is necessary; and

　(B) in the case such regulation applies to resident species of fish or wildlife, or plants, the Secretary gives actual notice of such regulation to the State agency in each State in which such species is believed to occur.

Such regulation shall, at the discretion of the Secretary, take effect immediately upon the publication of the regulation in the Federal Register. Any regulation promulgated under the authority of this paragraph shall cease to have force and effect at the close of the 240-day period following the date of publication unless, during such 240-day period, the rulemaking procedures which would apply to such regulation without regard to this paragraph are complied with. If at any time after issuing an emergency regulation the Secretary determines, on the basis of the best appropriate data available to him, that substantial evidence does not exist to warrant such regulation, he shall withdraw it.

(8) The publication in the Federal Register of any proposed or final regulation which is necessary or appropriate to carry out the purposes of this chapter shall include a summary by the Secretary of the data on which such regulation is based and shall show the relationship of such data to such regulation; and if such regulation designates or revises critical habitat, such summary shall, to the maximum extent practicable, also include a brief description and evaluation of those activities (whether public or private) which, in the opinion of the Secretary, if undertaken may adversely modify such habitat, or may be affected by such designation.

(c) Lists

(1) The Secretary of the Interior shall publish in the Federal Register a list of all species determined by him or the Secretary of Commerce to be endangered species and a list of all species determined by him or the Secretary of Commerce to be threatened species. Each list shall refer to the species contained therein by scientific and common name or names, if any, specify with respect to each such species over what portion of its range it is endangered or threatened, and specify any critical habitat within such range. The Secretary shall from time to time revise each list published under the authority of this subsection to reflect recent determinations, designations, and revisions made in accordance with subsections (a) and (b).

(2) The Secretary shall —

　(A) conduct, at least once every five years, a review of all species included in a list which is published pursuant to paragraph (1) and which is in effect at the time of such review; and

　(B) determine on the basis of such review whether any such species should —

　　(i)　be removed from such list;

　　(ii)　be changed in status from an endangered species to a threatened species; or

　　(iii)　be changed in status from a threatened species to an endangered species.

Each determination under subparagraph (B) shall be made in accordance with the provisions of subsections (a) and (b).

(d) Protective regulations

(d) Protective regulations — Whenever any species is listed as a threatened species pursuant to subsection (c) of this section, the Secretary shall issue such regulations as he deems necessary and advisable to provide for the conservation of such species. The Secretary may by regulation prohibit with respect to any threatened species any act prohibited under section 1538(a)(1) of this title, in the case of fish or wildlife, or section 1538(a)(2) of this title, in the case of plants, with respect to endangered species; except that with respect to the taking of resident species of fish or wildlife, such regulations shall apply in any State which has entered into cooperative agreement pursuant to section 1535(c) of this title only to the extent that such regulations have also been adopted by such State.

(e) Similarity of appearance cases — The Secretary may, by regulation of commerce or taking, and to the extent he deems advisable, treat any species as an endangered species or threatened species even though it is not listed pursuant to this section if he finds that —

　(A) such species so closely resembles in appearance, at the point in question, a species which has been listed pursuant to such section that enforcement personnel would have substantial difficulty in attempting to differentiate between the listed and unlisted species;

　(B) the effect of this substantial difficulty is an additional threat to an endangered or threatened species; and

　(C) such treatment of an unlisted species will substantially facilitate the enforcement and further the policy of this chapter.

(f) Recovery plans

(1) The Secretary shall develop and implement plans (hereinafter in this subsection referred to as "recovery plans") for the conservation and survival of endangered species and threatened species listed pursuant to this section, unless he finds that such a plan will not promote the conservation of the species. The Secretary, in developing and implementing recovery plans, shall, to the maximum extent practicable —

(A) give priority to those endangered species or threatened species, without regard to taxonomic classification, that are most likely to benefit from such plans, particularly those species that are, or may be, in conflict with construction or other development projects or other forms of economic activity;

(B) incorporate in each plan —

(i) a description of such site-specific management actions as may be necessary to achieve the plan's goal for the conservation and survival of the species;

(ii) objective, measurable criteria which, when met, would result in a determination, in accordance with the provisions of this section, that the species be removed from the list; and

(iii) estimates of the time required and the cost to carry out those measures needed to achieve the plan's goal and to achieve intermediate steps toward that goal.

(2) The Secretary, in developing and implementing recovery plans, may procure the services of appropriate public and private agencies and institutions, and other qualified persons. Recovery teams appointed pursuant to this subsection shall not be subject to the Federal Advisory Committee Act.

(3) The Secretary shall report every two years to the Committee on Environment and Public Works of the Senate and the Committee on Merchant Marine and Fisheries of the House of Representatives on the status of efforts to develop and implement recovery plans for all species listed pursuant to this section and on the status of all species for which such plans have been developed.

(4) The Secretary shall, prior to final approval of a new or revised recovery plan, provide public notice and an opportunity for public review and comment on such plan. The Secretary shall consider all information presented during the public comment period prior to approval of the plan.

(5) Each Federal agency shall, prior to implementation of a new or revised recovery plan, consider all information presented during the public comment period under paragraph (4).

(g) Monitoring

(1) The Secretary shall implement a system in cooperation with the States to monitor effectively for not less than five years the status of all species which have recovered to the point at which the measures provided pursuant to this chapter are no longer necessary and which, in accordance with the provisions of this section, have been removed from either of the lists published under subsection (c).

(2) The Secretary shall make prompt use of the authority under paragraph 7 of subsection (b) of this section to prevent a significant risk to the well being of any such recovered species.

(h) Agency guidelines; publication in Federal Register; scope; proposals and amendments: notice and opportunity for comments — The Secretary shall establish, and publish in the Federal Register, agency guidelines to insure that the purposes of this section are achieved efficiently and effectively. Such guidelines shall include, but are not limited to —

(1) procedures for recording the receipt and the disposition of petitions submitted under subsection (b)(3) of this section;

(2) criteria for making the findings required under such subsection with respect to petitions;

(3) a ranking system to assist in the identification of species that should receive priority review under subsection (a)(1) of this section; and

(4) a system for developing and implementing, on a priority basis, recovery plans under subsection (f) of this section.

The Secretary shall provide to the public notice of, and opportunity to submit written comments on, any guideline (including any amendment thereto) proposed to be established under this subsection.

(i) Submission to State agency of justification for regulations inconsistent with State agency's comments or petition — If, in the case of any regulation proposed by the Secretary under the authority of this section, a State agency to which notice thereof was given in accordance with subsection (b)(5)(A)(ii) files comments disagreeing with all or part of the proposed regulation, and the Secretary issues a final regulation which is in conflict with such comments, or if the Secretary fails to adopt a regulation pursuant to an action petitioned by a State agency under subsection (b)(3), the Secretary shall submit to the State agency a written justification for his failure to adopt regulations consistent with the agency's comments or petition.

§1534. Land acquisition
[ESA §5]

(a) Implementation of conservation program; authorization of Secretary and Secretary of Agriculture — The Secretary, and the Secretary of Agriculture with respect to the National Forest System, shall establish and implement a program to conserve fish, wildlife, and plants, including those which are listed as endangered species or threatened species pursuant to section 1533 of this title. To carry out such a program, the appropriate Secretary —

(1) shall utilize the land acquisition and other authority under the Fish and Wildlife Act of 1956, as amended (16 U.S.C. §§742a *et seq.*), the Fish and Wildlife Coordination Act, as amended (16 U.S.C. §§661 *et seq.*), and the Migratory Bird Conservation Act (16 U.S.C. §§715 *et seq.*), as appropriate; and

(2) is authorized to acquire by purchase, donation, or otherwise, lands, waters, or interest therein,

and such authority shall be in addition to any other land acquisition authority vested in him.

(b) Availability of funds for acquisition of lands, waters, etc. — Funds made available pursuant to chapter 2003 of Title 54 may be used for the purpose of acquiring lands, waters, or interests therein under subsection (a) of this section.

§1535. Cooperation with States
[ESA §6]

(a) Generally — In carrying out the program authorized by this chapter, the Secretary shall cooperate to the maximum extent practicable with the States. Such cooperation shall include consultation with the States concerned before acquiring any land or water, or interest therein, for the purpose of conserving any endangered species or threatened species.

(b) Management agreements — The Secretary may enter into agreements with any State for the administration and management of any area established for the conservation of endangered species or threatened species. Any revenues derived from the administration of such areas under these agreements shall be subject to the provisions of section 715s of this title.

(c) Cooperative agreements

(1) In furtherance of the purposes of this chapter, the Secretary is authorized to enter into a cooperative agreement in accordance with this section with any State which establishes and maintains an adequate and active program for the conservation of endangered species and threatened species. Within one hundred and twenty days after the Secretary receives a certified copy of such a proposed State program, he shall make a determination whether such program is in accordance with this chapter. Unless he determines, pursuant to this paragraph, that the State program is not in accordance with this chapter, he shall enter into a cooperative agreement with the State for the purpose of assisting in implementation of the State program. In order for a State program to be deemed an adequate and active program for the conservation of endangered species and threatened species, the Secretary must find, and annually thereafter reconfirm such finding, that under the State program —

(A) authority resides in the State agency to conserve resident species of fish or wildlife determined by the State agency or the Secretary to be endangered or threatened;

(B) the State agency has established acceptable conservation programs, consistent with the purposes and policies of this chapter, for all resident species of fish or wildlife in the State which are deemed by the Secretary to be endangered or threatened, and has furnished a copy of such plan and program together with all pertinent details, information, and data requested to the Secretary;

(C) the State agency is authorized to conduct investigations to determine the status and requirements for survival of resident species of fish and wildlife;

(D) the State agency is authorized to establish programs, including the acquisition of land or aquatic habitat or interests therein, for the conservation of resident endangered or threatened species of fish or wildlife; and

(E) provision is made for public participation in designating resident species of fish or wildlife as endangered or threatened; or

that under the State program —

(i) the requirements set forth in subparagraphs (C), (D), and (E) of this paragraph are complied with, and

(ii) plans are included under which immediate attention will be given to those resident species of fish and wildlife which are determined by the Secretary or the State agency to be endangered or threatened and which the Secretary and the State agency agree are most urgently in need of conservation programs; except that a cooperative agreement entered into with a State whose program is deemed adequate and active pursuant to clause (i) and this clause shall not affect the applicability of prohibitions set forth in or authorized pursuant to section 1533(d) of this title or section 1538(a)(1) of this title with respect to the taking of any resident endangered or threatened species.

(2) In furtherance of the purposes of this chapter the Secretary is authorized to enter into a cooperative agreement in accordance with this section with any State which establishes and maintains an adequate and active program for the conservation of endangered species and threatened species of plants. Within one hundred and twenty days after the Secretary receives a certified copy of such a proposed State program, he shall make a determination whether such program is in accordance with this chapter. Unless he determines, pursuant to this paragraph, that the State program is not in accordance with this chapter, he shall enter into a cooperative agreement with the State for the purpose of assisting in implementation of the State program. In order for a State program to be deemed an adequate and active program for the conservation of endangered species of plants and threatened species of plants, the Secretary must find, and annually thereafter reconfirm such finding, that under the State program —

(A) authority resides in the State agency to conserve resident species of plants determined by the State agency or the Secretary to be endangered or threatened;

(B) the State agency has established acceptable conservation programs, consistent with the purposes and policies of this chapter, for all resident species of plants in the State which are deemed by the Secretary to be endangered or threatened, and has furnished a copy of such plan and program together with all pertinent details, information, and data requested to the Secretary;

(C) the State agency is authorized to conduct investigations to determine the status and requirements for survival of resident species of plants; and

(D) provision is made for public participation in designating resident species of plants as endangered or threatened; or that under the State program —

(i) the requirements set forth in subparagraphs (C) and (D) of this paragraph are complied with, and

(ii) plans are included under which immediate attention will be given to those resident species of plants which are determined by the Secretary or the State agency to be endangered or threatened and which the Secretary and the State agency agree are most urgently in need of conservation programs; except that a cooperative agreement entered into with a State whose program is deemed adequate and active pursuant to clause (i) and this clause shall not affect the applicability of prohibitions set forth in or authorized pursuant to section 1533(d) or section 1538(a)(1) of this title with respect to the taking of any resident endangered or threatened species.

(d) Allocation of funds

(1) The Secretary is authorized to provide financial assistance to any State, through its respective State agency, which has entered into a cooperative agreement pursuant to subsection (c) of this section to assist in development of programs for the conservation of endangered and threatened species or to assist in monitoring the status of candidate species pursuant to subparagraph (C) of section 1533(b)(3) of this title and recovered species pursuant to section 1533(g) of this title. The Secretary shall allocate each annual appropriation made in accordance with the provisions of subsection (i) of this section to such States based on consideration of—

(A) the international commitments of the United States to protect endangered species or threatened species;

(B) the readiness of a State to proceed with a conservation program consistent with the objectives and purposes of this chapter;

(C) the number of endangered species and threatened species within a State;

(D) the potential for restoring endangered species and threatened species within a State;

(E) the relative urgency to initiate a program to restore and protect an endangered species or threatened species in terms of survival of the species;

(F) the importance of monitoring the status of candidate species within a State to prevent a significant risk to the well being of any such species; and

(G) the importance of monitoring the status of recovered species within a State to assure that such species do not return to the point at which the measures provided pursuant to this chapter are again necessary.

So much of the annual appropriation made in accordance with provisions of subsection (i) of this section allocated for obligation to any State for any fiscal year as remains unobligated at the close thereof is authorized to be made available to that State until the close of the succeeding fiscal year. Any amount allocated to any State which is unobligated at the end of the period during which it is available for expenditure is authorized to be made available for expenditure by the Secretary in conducting programs under this section.

(2) Such cooperative agreements shall provide for (A) the actions to be taken by the Secretary and the States; (B) the benefits that are expected to be derived in connection with the conservation of endangered or threatened species; (C) the estimated cost of these actions; and (D) the share of such costs to be borne by the Federal Government and by the States; except that —

(i) the Federal share of such program costs shall not exceed 75 percent of the estimated program cost stated in the agreement; and

(ii) the Federal share may be increased to 90 percent whenever two or more States having a common interest in one or more endangered or threatened species, the conservation of which may be enhanced by cooperation of such States, enter jointly into an agreement with the Secretary.

The Secretary may, in his discretion, and under such rules and regulations as he may prescribe, advance funds to the State for financing the United States pro rata share agreed upon in the cooperative agreement. For the purposes of this section, the non-Federal share may, in the discretion of the Secretary, be in the form of money or real property, the value of which will be determined by the Secretary, whose decision shall be final.

(e) Review of State programs

— Any action taken by the Secretary under this section shall be subject to his periodic review at no greater than annual intervals.

(f) Conflicts between Federal and State laws

— Any State law or regulation which applies with respect to the importation or exportation of, or interstate or foreign commerce in, endangered species or threatened species is void to the extent that it may effectively (1) permit what is prohibited by this chapter or by any regulation which implements this chapter, or (2) prohibit what is authorized pursuant to an exemption or permit provided for in this chapter or in any regulation which implements this chapter. This chapter shall not otherwise be construed to void any State law or regulation which is intended to conserve migratory, resident, or introduced fish or wildlife, or to permit or prohibit sale of such fish or wildlife. Any State law or regulation respecting the taking of an endangered species or threatened species may be more restrictive than the exemptions or permits provided for in this chapter or in any regulation which implements this chapter but not less restrictive than the prohibitions so defined.

(g) Transition

(1) For purposes of this subsection, the term "establishment period" means, with respect to any State, the period beginning on December 28, 1973, and ending on whichever of the following dates first occurs: (A) the date of the close of the 120-day period following the adjournment of the first regular session of the legislature of such State which commences after December 28, 1973, or (B) the date of the close of the 15-month period following December 28, 1973.

(2) The prohibitions set forth in or authorized pursuant to sections 1533(d) and 1538(a)(1)(B) of this title shall not apply with respect to the taking of any resident endangered species or threatened species (other than species listed in Appendix I to the Convention or otherwise specifically covered by any other treaty or Federal law) within any State —

(A) which is then a party to a cooperative agreement with the Secretary pursuant to subsection (c) of this section (except to the extent that the taking of any such species is contrary to the law of such State); or

(B) except for any time within the establishment period when —

(i) the Secretary applies such prohibition to such species at the request of the State, or

(ii) the Secretary applies such prohibition after he finds, and publishes his finding, that an emergency exists posing a significant risk to the well-being of such species and that the prohibition must be applied to protect such species. The Secretary's finding and publication may be made without regard to the public hearing or comment provisions of section 553 of title 5 or any other provision of this chapter; but such prohibition shall expire 90 days after the date of its imposition unless the Secretary further extends such prohibition by publishing notice and a statement of justification of such extension.

(h) Regulations — The Secretary is authorized to promulgate such regulations as may be appropriate to carry out the provisions of this section relating to financial assistance to States.

(i) Appropriations

(1) To carry out the provisions of this section for fiscal years after September 30, 1988, there shall be deposited into a special fund known as the cooperative endangered species conservation fund, to be administered by the Secretary, an amount equal to 5 percent of the combined amounts covered each fiscal year into the Federal aid to wildlife restoration fund under section 669b of this title, and paid, transferred, or otherwise credited each fiscal year to the Sport Fishing Restoration Account established under 1016 of the Act of July 18, 1984.

(2) Amounts deposited into the special fund are authorized to be appropriated annually and allocated in accordance with subsection (d) of this section.

§1536. Interagency cooperation
[ESA §7]
(a) Federal agency actions and consultations

(1) The Secretary shall review other programs administered by him and utilize such programs in furtherance of the purposes of this chapter. All other Federal agencies shall, in consultation with and with the assistance of the Secretary, utilize their authorities in furtherance of the purposes of this chapter by carrying out programs for the conservation of endangered species and threatened species listed pursuant to section 1533 of this title.

(2) Each Federal agency shall, in consultation with and with the assistance of the Secretary, insure that any action authorized, funded, or carried out by such agency (hereinafter in this section referred to as an "agency action") is not likely to jeopardize the continued existence of any endangered species or threatened species or result in the destruction or adverse modification of habitat of such species which is determined by the Secretary, after consultation as appropriate with affected States, to be critical, unless such agency has been granted an exemption for such action by the Committee pursuant to subsection (h) of this section. In fulfilling the requirements of this paragraph each agency shall use the best scientific and commercial data available.

(3) Subject to such guidelines as the Secretary may establish, a Federal agency shall consult with the Secretary on any prospective agency action at the request of, and in cooperation with, the prospective permit or license applicant if the applicant has reason to believe that an endangered species or a threatened species may be present in the area affected by his project and that implementation of such action will likely affect such species.

(4) Each Federal agency shall confer with the Secretary on any agency action which is likely to jeopardize the continued existence of any species proposed to be listed under section 1533 of this

title or result in the destruction or adverse modification of critical habitat proposed to be designated for such species. This paragraph does not require a limitation on the commitment of resources as described in subsection (d) of this section.

(b) Opinion of Secretary

(1)(A) Consultation under subsection (a)(2) of this section with respect to any agency action shall be concluded within the 90-day period beginning on the date on which initiated or, subject to subparagraph (B), within such other period of time as is mutually agreeable to the Secretary and the Federal agency.

(B) In the case of an agency action involving a permit or license applicant, the Secretary and the Federal agency may not mutually agree to conclude consultation within a period exceeding 90 days unless the Secretary, before the close of the 90th day referred to in subparagraph (A) —

(i) if the consultation period proposed to be agreed to will end before the 150th day after the date on which consultation was initiated, submits to the applicant a written statement setting forth —

(I) the reasons why a longer period is required,

(II) the information that is required to complete the consultation, and

(III) the estimated date on which consultation will be completed; or

(ii) if the consultation period proposed to be agreed to will end 150 or more days after the date on which consultation was initiated, obtains the consent of the applicant to such period.

The Secretary and the Federal agency may mutually agree to extend a consultation period established under the preceding sentence if the Secretary, before the close of such period, obtains the consent of the applicant to the extension.

(2) Consultation under subsection (a)(3) of this section shall be concluded within such period as is agreeable to the Secretary, the Federal agency, and the applicant concerned.

(3)(A) Promptly after conclusion of consultation under paragraph (2) or (3) of subsection (a) of this section, the Secretary shall provide to the Federal agency and the applicant, if any, a written statement setting forth the Secretary's opinion, and a summary of the information on which the opinion is based, detailing how the agency action affects the species or its critical habitat. If jeopardy or adverse modification is found, the Secretary shall suggest those reasonable and prudent alternatives which he believes would not violate subsection (a)(2) of this section and can be taken by the Federal agency or applicant in implementing the agency action.

(B) Consultation under subsection (a)(3) of this section, and an opinion issued by the Secretary incident to such consultation, regarding an agency action shall be treated respectively as a consultation under subsection (a)(2) of this section, and as an opinion issued after consultation under such subsection, regarding that action if the Secretary reviews the action before it is commenced by the Federal agency and finds, and notifies such agency, that no significant changes have been made with respect to the action and that no significant change has occurred regarding the information used during the initial consultation.

(4) If after consultation under subsection (a)(2) of this section, the Secretary concludes that —

(A) the agency action will not violate such subsection, or offers reasonable and prudent alternatives which the Secretary believes would not violate such subsection;

(B) the taking of an endangered species or a threatened species incidental to the agency action will not violate such subsection; and

(C) if an endangered species or threatened species of a marine mammal is involved, the taking is authorized pursuant to section 1371(a)(5) of this title;

the Secretary shall provide the Federal agency and the applicant concerned, if any, with a written statement that —

(i) specifies the impact of such incidental taking on the species,

(ii) specifies those reasonable and prudent measures that the Secretary considers necessary or appropriate to minimize such impact,

(iii) in the case of marine mammals, specifies those measures that are necessary to comply with section 1371(a)(5) of this title with regard to such taking, and

(iv) sets forth the terms and conditions (including, but not limited to, reporting requirements) that must be complied with by the Federal agency or applicant (if any), or both, to implement the measures specified under clauses (ii) and (iii).

(c) Biological assessment

(1) To facilitate compliance with the requirements of subsection (a)(2) of this section, each Federal agency shall, with respect to any agency action of such agency for which no contract for construction has been entered into and for which no construction has begun on November 10, 1978, request of the Secretary information whether any species which is listed or proposed to be listed may be present in the area of such proposed action. If the Secretary advises, based on the best scientific and commercial data available, that such species may be present, such agency shall conduct a biological assessment for the purpose of identifying any

endangered species or threatened species which is likely to be affected by such action. Such assessment shall be completed within 180 days after the date on which initiated (or within such other period as is mutually agreed to by the Secretary and such agency, except that if a permit or license applicant is involved, the 180-day period may not be extended unless such agency provides the applicant, before the close of such period, with a written statement setting forth the estimated length of the proposed extension and the reasons therefor) and, before any contract for construction is entered into and before construction is begun with respect to such action. Such assessment may be undertaken as part of a Federal agency's compliance with the requirements of section 102 of the National Environmental Policy Act of 1969 (42 U.S.C. §4332).

(2) Any person who may wish to apply for an exemption under subsection (g) of this section for that action may conduct a biological assessment to identify any endangered species or threatened species which is likely to be affected by such action. Any such biological assessment must, however, be conducted in cooperation with the Secretary and under the supervision of the appropriate Federal agency.

(d) Limitation on commitment of resources — After initiation of consultation required under subsection (a)(2) of this section, the Federal agency and the permit or license applicant shall not make any irreversible or irretrievable commitment of resources with respect to the agency action which has the effect of foreclosing the formulation or implementation of any reasonable and prudent alternative measures which would not violate subsection (a)(2) of this section.

(e) Endangered Species Committee

(1) There is established a committee to be known as the Endangered Species Committee (hereinafter in this section referred to as the "Committee").

(2) The Committee shall review any application submitted to it pursuant to this section and determine in accordance with subsection (h) of this section whether or not to grant an exemption from the requirements of subsection (a)(2) of this section for the action set forth in such application.

(3) The Committee shall be composed of seven members as follows:

(A) The Secretary of Agriculture.

(B) The Secretary of the Army.

(C) The Chairman of the Council of Economic Advisors.

(D) The Administrator of the Environmental Protection Agency.

(E) The Secretary of the Interior.

(F) The Administrator of the National Oceanic and Atmospheric Administration.

(G) The President, after consideration of any recommendations received pursuant to subsection (g)(2)(B) of this section shall appoint one individual from each affected State, as determined by the Secretary, to be a member of the Committee for the consideration of the application for exemption for an agency action with respect to which such recommendations are made, not later than 30 days after an application is submitted pursuant to this section.

(4)(A) Members of the Committee shall receive no additional pay on account of their service on the Committee.

(B) While away from their homes or regular places of business in the performance of services for the Committee, members of the Committee shall be allowed travel expenses, including per diem in lieu of subsistence, in the same manner as persons employed intermittently in the Government service are allowed expenses under section 5703 of Title 5.

(5)(A) Five members of the Committee or their representatives shall constitute a quorum for the transaction of any function of the Committee, except that, in no case shall any representative be considered in determining the existence of a quorum for the transaction of any function of the Committee if that function involves a vote by the Committee on any matter before the Committee.

(B) The Secretary of the Interior shall be the Chairman of the Committee.

(C) The Committee shall meet at the call of the Chairman or five of its members.

(D) All meetings and records of the Committee shall be open to the public.

(6) Upon request of the Committee, the head of any Federal agency is authorized to detail, on a nonreimbursable basis, any of the personnel of such agency to the Committee to assist it in carrying out its duties under this section.

(7)(A) The Committee may for the purpose of carrying out its duties under this section hold such hearings, sit and act at such times and places, take such testimony, and receive such evidence, as the Committee deems advisable.

(B) When so authorized by the Committee, any member or agent of the Committee may take any action which the Committee is authorized to take by this paragraph.

(C) Subject to the Privacy Act (5 U.S.C. §552a), the Committee may secure directly from any Federal agency information necessary to enable it to carry out its duties under this section. Upon request of the Chairman of the Committee, the head of such Federal agency shall furnish such information to the Committee.

(D) The Committee may use the United States mails in the same manner and upon the same conditions as a Federal agency.

(E) The Administrator of General Services shall provide to the Committee on a reimbursable basis such administrative support services as the Committee may request.

(8) In carrying out its duties under this section, the Committee may promulgate and amend such rules, regulations, and procedures, and issue and amend such orders as it deems necessary.

(9) For the purpose of obtaining information necessary for the consideration of an application for an exemption under this section the Committee may issue subpoenas for the attendance and testimony of witnesses and the production of relevant papers, books, and documents.

(10) In no case shall any representative, including a representative of a member designated pursuant to paragraph (3)(G) of this subsection, be eligible to cast a vote on behalf of any member.

(f) Promulgation of regulations; form and contents of exemption application — Not later than 90 days after November 10, 1978, the Secretary shall promulgate regulations which set forth the form and manner in which applications for exemption shall be submitted to the Secretary and the information to be contained in such applications. Such regulations shall require that information submitted in an application by the head of any Federal agency with respect to any agency action include, but not be limited to —

(1) a description of the consultation process carried out pursuant to subsection (a)(2) of this section between the head of the Federal agency and the Secretary; and

(2) a statement describing why such action cannot be altered or modified to conform with the requirements of subsection (a)(2) of this section.

(g) Application for exemption; report to Committee

(1) A Federal agency, the Governor of the State in which an agency action will occur, if any, or a permit or license applicant may apply to the Secretary for an exemption for an agency action of such agency if, after consultation under subsection (a)(2) of this section, the Secretary's opinion under subsection (b) of this section indicates that the agency action would violate subsection (a)(2) of this section. An application for an exemption shall be considered initially by the Secretary in the manner provided for in this subsection, and shall be considered by the Committee for a final determination under subsection (h) of this section after a report is made pursuant to paragraph (5). The applicant for an exemption shall be referred to as the "exemption applicant" in this section.

(2)(A) An exemption applicant shall submit a written application to the Secretary, in a form prescribed under subsection (f) of this section, not later than 90 days after the completion of the consultation process; except that, in the case of any agency action involving a permit or license applicant, such application shall be submitted not later than 90 days after the date on which the Federal agency concerned takes final agency action with respect to the issuance of the permit or license. For

purposes of the preceding sentence, the term "final agency action" means (i) a disposition by an agency with respect to the issuance of a permit or license that is subject to administrative review, whether or not such disposition is subject to judicial review; or (ii) if administrative review is sought with respect to such disposition, the decision resulting after such review. Such application shall set forth the reasons why the exemption applicant considers that the agency action meets the requirements for an exemption under this subsection.

(B) Upon receipt of an application for exemption for an agency action under paragraph (1), the Secretary shall promptly (i) notify the Governor of each affected State, if any, as determined by the Secretary, and request the Governors so notified to recommend individuals to be appointed to the Endangered Species Committee for consideration of such application; and (ii) publish notice of receipt of the application in the Federal Register, including a summary of the information contained in the application and a description of the agency action with respect to which the application for exemption has been filed.

(3) The Secretary shall within 20 days after the receipt of an application for exemption, or within such other period of time as is mutually agreeable to the exemption applicant and the Secretary —

(A) determine that the Federal agency concerned and the exemption applicant have —

    (i) carried out the consultation responsibilities described in subsection (a) of this section in good faith and made a reasonable and responsible effort to develop and fairly consider modifications or reasonable and prudent alternatives to the proposed agency action which would not violate subsection (a)(2) of this section;

    (ii) conducted any biological assessment required by subsection (c) of this section; and

    (iii) to the extent determinable within the time provided herein, refrained from making any irreversible or irretrievable commitment of resources prohibited by subsection (d) of this section; or

(B) deny the application for exemption because the Federal agency concerned or the exemption applicant have not met the requirements set forth in subparagraph (A)(i), (ii), and (iii).

The denial of an application under subparagraph (B) shall be considered final agency action for purposes of chapter 7 of Title 5.

(4) If the Secretary determines that the Federal agency concerned and the exemption applicant have met the requirements set forth in paragraph (3)(A)(i), (ii), and (iii) he shall, in consultation with the Members of the Committee, hold a hearing on the application for exemption in accordance with sections 554, 555, and 556 (other than subsection (b)(1) and (2) thereof) of Title 5 and prepare the report to be submitted pursuant to paragraph (5).

(5) Within 140 days after making the determinations under paragraph (3) or within such other period of time as is mutually agreeable to the exemption applicant and the Secretary, the Secretary shall submit to the Committee a report discussing —

(A) the availability of reasonable and prudent alternatives to the agency action, and the nature and extent of the benefits of the agency action and of alternative courses of action consistent with conserving the species or the critical habitat;

(B) a summary of the evidence concerning whether or not the agency action is in the public interest and is of national or regional significance;

(C) appropriate reasonable mitigation and enhancement measures which should be considered by the Committee; and

(D) whether the Federal agency concerned and the exemption applicant refrained from making any irreversible or irretrievable commitment of resources prohibited by subsection (d) of this section.

(6) To the extent practicable within the time required for action under subsection (g) of this section, and except to the extent inconsistent with the requirements of this section, the consideration of any application for an exemption under this section and the conduct of any hearing under this subsection shall be in accordance with sections 554, 555, and 556 (other than subsection (b)(3) of section 556) of Title 5.

(7) Upon request of the Secretary, the head of any Federal agency is authorized to detail, on a nonreimbursable basis, any of the personnel of such agency to the Secretary to assist him in carrying out his duties under this section.

(8) All meetings and records resulting from activities pursuant to this subsection shall be open to the public.

(h) Grant of exemption

(1) The Committee shall make a final determination whether or not to grant an exemption within 30 days after receiving the report of the Secretary pursuant to subsection (g)(5) of this section. The Committee shall grant an exemption from the requirements of subsection (a)(2) of this section for an agency action if, by a vote of not less than five of its members voting in person —

(A) it determines on the record, based on the report of the Secretary, the record of the hearing held under subsection (g)(4) of this section and on such other testimony or evidence as it may receive, that —

(i) there are no reasonable and prudent alternatives to the agency action;

(ii) the benefits of such action clearly outweigh the benefits of alternative courses of action consistent with conserving the species or its critical habitat, and such action is in the public interest

(iii) the action is of regional or national significance; and

(iv) neither the Federal agency concerned nor the exemption applicant made any irreversible or irretrievable commitment of resources prohibited by subsection (d) of this section; and

(B) it establishes such reasonable mitigation and enhancement measures, including, but not limited to, live propagation, transplantation, and habitat acquisition and improvement, as are necessary and appropriate to minimize the adverse effects of the agency action upon the endangered species, threatened species, or critical habitat concerned.

Any final determination by the Committee under this subsection shall be considered final agency action for purposes of chapter 7 of Title 5.

(2)(A) Except as provided in subparagraph (B), an exemption for an agency action granted under paragraph (1) shall constitute a permanent exemption with respect to all endangered or threatened species for the purposes of completing such agency action —

(i) regardless whether the species was identified in the biological assessment; and

(ii) only if a biological assessment has been conducted under subsection (c) of this section with respect to such agency action.

(B) An exemption shall be permanent under subparagraph (A) unless —

(i) the Secretary finds, based on the best scientific and commercial data available, that such exemption would result in the extinction of a species that was not the subject of consultation under subsection (a)(2) of this section or was not identified in any biological assessment conducted under subsection (c) of this section, and

(ii) the Committee determines within 60 days after the date of the Secretary's finding that the exemption should not be permanent.

If the Secretary makes a finding described in clause (i), the Committee shall meet with respect to the matter within 30 days after the date of the finding.

(i) Review by Secretary of State; violation of international treaty or other international obligation of United States — Notwithstanding any other provision of this chapter, the Committee shall be prohibited from considering for exemption any application made to it, if the Secretary of State, after a review of the proposed agency action and its potential implications, and after hearing, certifies, in writing, to the Committee within 60 days of any application made under this section that the granting of any such exemption and the carrying out of such action would be in violation of an international treaty obligation or other international obligation of the United States. The Secretary of State shall, at the time of such certification, publish a copy thereof in the Federal Register.

(j) Exemption for national security reasons — Notwithstanding any other provision of this chapter, the Committee shall grant an exemption for any agency action if the Secretary of Defense finds that such exemption is necessary for reasons of national security.

(k) Exemption decision not considered major Federal action; environmental impact statement — An exemption decision by the Committee under this section shall not be a major Federal action for purposes of the National Environmental Policy Act of 1969 (42 U.S.C. §§4321 *et seq.*): *Provided*, That an environmental impact statement which discusses the impacts upon endangered species or threatened species or their critical habitats shall have been previously prepared with respect to any agency action exempted by such order.

(*l*) Committee order granting exemption; cost of mitigation and enhancement measures; report by applicant to Council on Environmental Quality

(1) If the Committee determines under subsection (h) of this section that an exemption should be granted with respect to any agency action, the Committee shall issue an order granting the exemption and specifying the mitigation and enhancement measures established pursuant to subsection (h) of this section which shall be carried out and paid for by the exemption applicant in implementing the agency action. All necessary mitigation and enhancement measures shall be authorized prior to the implementing of the agency action and funded concurrently with all other project features.

(2) The applicant receiving such exemption shall include the costs of such mitigation and enhancement measures within the overall costs of continuing the proposed action. Notwithstanding the preceding sentence the costs of such measures shall not be treated as project costs for the purpose of computing benefit-cost or other ratios for the proposed action. Any applicant may request the Secretary to carry out such mitigation and enhancement measures. The costs incurred by the Secretary in carrying out any such measures shall be paid by the applicant receiving the exemption. No later than one year after the granting of an exemption, the exemption applicant shall submit to the Council on Environmental Quality a report describing its compliance with the mitigation and enhancement measures prescribed by this section. Such a report shall be submitted annually until all such mitigation and enhancement measures have been completed.

Notice of the public availability of such reports shall be published in the Federal Register by the Council on Environmental Quality.

(m) Notice requirement for citizen suits not applicable — The 60-day notice requirement of section 1540(g) of this title shall not apply with respect to review of any final determination of the Committee under subsection (h) of this section granting an exemption from the requirements of subsection (a)(2) of this section.

(n) Judicial review — Any person, as defined by section 1532(13) of this title, may obtain judicial review, under chapter 7 of Title 5, of any decision of the Endangered Species Committee under subsection (h) of this section in the United States Court of Appeals for (1) any circuit wherein the agency action concerned will be, or is being, carried out, or (2) in any case in which the agency action will be, or is being, carried out outside of any circuit, the District of Columbia, by filing in such court within 90 days after the date of issuance of the decision, a written petition for review. A copy of such petition shall be transmitted by the clerk of the court to the Committee and the Committee shall file in the court the record in the proceeding, as provided in section 2112, of Title 28. Attorneys designated by the Endangered Species Committee may appear for, and represent the Committee in any action for review under this subsection.

(o) Exemption as providing exception on taking of endangered species — Notwithstanding sections 1533(d) and 1538(a)(1)(B) and (C) of this title, sections 1371 and 1372 of this title, or any regulation promulgated to implement any such section —

(1) any action for which an exemption is granted under subsection (h) of this section shall not be considered to be a taking of any endangered species or threatened species with respect to any activity which is necessary to carry out such action; and

(2) any taking that is in compliance with the terms and conditions specified in a written statement provided under subsection (b)(4)(iv) of this section shall not be considered to be a prohibited taking of the species concerned.

(p) Exemptions in Presidentially declared disaster areas — In any area which has been declared by the President to be a major disaster area under the Disaster Relief and Emergency Assistance Act (42 U.S.C. §§5121 *et seq.*), the President is authorized to make the determinations required by subsections (g) and (h) of this section for any project for the repair or replacement of a public facility substantially as it existed prior to the disaster under section 405 or 406 of the Disaster Relief and Emergency Assistance Act (42 U.S.C. §5171 or 5172), and which the President determines (1) is necessary to prevent the recurrence of such a natural disaster and to reduce the potential loss of human life, and (2) to involve an emergency situation which does not allow the ordinary procedures of this section to be followed. Notwithstanding any other provision of this section, the Committee shall accept the determinations of the President under this subsection.

§1537. International cooperation
[ESA §8]

(a) **Financial assistance** — As a demonstration of the commitment of the United States to the worldwide protection of endangered species and threatened species, the President may, subject to the provisions of section 1306 of Title 31, use foreign currencies accruing to the United States Government under the Food for Peace Act [7 U.S.C.A. §1691 *et seq.*] or any other law to provide to any foreign country (with its consent) assistance in the development and management of programs in that country which the Secretary determines to be necessary or useful for the conservation of any endangered species or threatened species listed by the Secretary pursuant to section 1533 of this title. The President shall provide assistance (which includes, but is not limited to, the acquisition, by lease or otherwise, of lands, waters, or interests therein) to foreign countries under this section under such terms and conditions as he deems appropriate. Whenever foreign currencies are available for the provision of assistance under this section, such currencies shall be used in preference to funds appropriated under the authority of section 1542 of this title.

(b) **Encouragement of foreign programs** — In order to carry out further the provisions of this chapter, the Secretary, through the Secretary of State, shall encourage —

(1) foreign countries to provide for the conservation of fish or wildlife and plants including endangered species and threatened species listed pursuant to section 1533 of this title;

(2) the entering into of bilateral or multilateral agreements with foreign countries to provide for such conservation; and

(3) foreign persons who directly or indirectly take fish or wildlife or plants in foreign countries or on the high seas for importation into the United States for commercial or other purposes to develop and carry out with such assistance as he may provide, conservation practices designed to enhance such fish or wildlife or plants and their habitat.

(c) **Personnel** — After consultation with the Secretary of State, the Secretary may —

(1) assign or otherwise make available any officer or employee of his department for the purpose of cooperating with foreign countries and international organizations in developing personnel resources and programs which promote the conservation of fish or wildlife or plants; and

(2) conduct or provide financial assistance for the educational training of foreign personnel, in this country or abroad, in fish, wildlife, or plant management, research and law enforcement and to render professional assistance abroad in such matters.

(d) **Investigations** — After consultation with the Secretary of State and the Secretary of the Treasury, as appropriate, the Secretary may conduct or cause to be conducted such law enforcement investigations and research abroad as he deems necessary to carry out the purposes of this chapter.

§1537a. Convention implementation
[ESA §8a]

(a) **Management Authority and Scientific Authority** — The Secretary of the Interior (hereinafter in this section referred to as the "Secretary") is designated as the Management Authority and the Scientific Authority for purposes of the Convention and the respective functions of each such Authority shall be carried out through the United States Fish and Wildlife Service.

(b) **Management Authority functions** — The Secretary shall do all things necessary and appropriate to carry out the functions of the Management Authority under the Convention.

(c) **Scientific Authority functions; determinations**

(1) The Secretary shall do all things necessary and appropriate to carry out the functions of the Scientific Authority under the Convention.

(2) The Secretary shall base the determinations and advice given by him under Article IV of the Convention with respect to wildlife upon the best available biological information derived from professionally accepted wildlife management practices; but is not required to make, or require any State to make, estimates of population size in making such determinations or giving such advice.

(d) **Reservations by the United States under Convention** — If the United States votes against including any species in Appendix I or II of the Convention and does not enter a reservation pursuant to paragraph (3) of Article XV of the Convention with respect to that species, the Secretary of State, before the 90th day after the last day on which such a reservation could be entered, shall submit to the Committee on Merchant Marine and Fisheries of the House of Representatives, and to the Committee on the Environment and Public Works of the Senate, a written report setting forth the reasons why such a reservation was not entered.

(e) **Wildlife preservation in Western Hemisphere**

(1) The Secretary of the Interior (hereinafter in this subsection referred to as the "Secretary"), in cooperation with the Secretary of State, shall act on behalf of, and represent, the United States in all regards as required by the Convention on Nature Protection and Wildlife Preservation in the Western Hemisphere (56 Stat. 1354, T.S. 982, hereinafter in this subsection referred to as the "Western Convention"). In the discharge of these responsibilities, the Secretary and the Secretary of

State shall consult with the Secretary of Agriculture, the Secretary of Commerce, and the heads of other agencies with respect to matters relating to or affecting their areas of responsibility.

(2) The Secretary and the Secretary of State shall, in cooperation with the contracting parties to the Western Convention and, to the extent feasible and appropriate, with the participation of State agencies, take such steps as are necessary to implement the Western Convention. Such steps shall include, but not be limited to —

(A) cooperation with contracting parties and international organizations for the purpose of developing personnel resources and programs that will facilitate implementation of the Western Convention;

(B) identification of those species of birds that migrate between the United States and other contracting parties, and the habitats upon which those species depend, and the implementation of cooperative measures to ensure that such species will not become endangered or threatened; and

(C) identification of measures that are necessary and appropriate to implement those provisions of the Western Convention which address the protection of wild plants.

(3) No later than September 30, 1985, the Secretary and the Secretary of State shall submit a report to Congress describing those steps taken in accordance with the requirements of this subsection and identifying the principal remaining actions yet necessary for comprehensive and effective implementation of the Western Convention.

(4) The provisions of this subsection shall not be construed as affecting the authority, jurisdiction, or responsibility of the several States to manage, control, or regulate resident fish or wildlife under State law or regulations.

§1538. Prohibited acts
[ESA §9]
(a) Generally

(1) Except as provided in sections 1535(g)(2) and 1539 of this title, with respect to any endangered species of fish or wildlife listed pursuant to section 1533 of this title it is unlawful for any person subject to the jurisdiction of the United States to —

(A) import any such species into, or export any such species from the United States;

(B) take any such species within the United States or the territorial sea of the United States;

(C) take any such species upon the high seas;

(D) possess, sell, deliver, carry, transport, or ship, by any means whatsoever, any such species taken in violation of subparagraphs (B) and (C);

(E) deliver, receive, carry, transport, or ship in interstate or foreign commerce, by any means whatsoever and in the course of commercial activity, any such species;

(F) sell or offer for sale in interstate or foreign commerce any such species; or

(G) violate any regulation pertaining to such species or to any threatened species of fish or wildlife listed pursuant to section 1533 of this title and promulgated by the Secretary pursuant to authority provided by this chapter.

(2) Except as provided in sections 1535(g)(2) and 1539 of this title, with respect to any endangered species of plants listed pursuant to section 1533 of this title, it is unlawful for any person subject to the jurisdiction of the United States to —

(A) import any such species into, or export any such species from, the United States;

(B) remove and reduce to possession any such species from areas under Federal jurisdiction; maliciously damage or destroy any such species on any such area; or remove, cut, dig up, or damage or destroy any such species on any other area in knowing violation of any law or regulation of any State or in the course of any violation of a State criminal trespass law;

(C) deliver, receive, carry, transport, or ship in interstate or foreign commerce, by any means whatsoever and in the course of a commercial activity, any such species;

(D) sell or offer for sale in interstate or foreign commerce any such species; or

(E) violate any regulation pertaining to such species or to any threatened species of plants listed pursuant to section 1533 of this title and promulgated by the Secretary pursuant to authority provided by this chapter.

(b) Species held in captivity or controlled environment

(1) The provisions of subsections (a)(1)(A) and (a)(1)(G) of this section shall not apply to any fish or wildlife which was held in captivity or in a controlled environment on (A) December 28, 1973, or (B) the date of the publication in the Federal Register of a final regulation adding such fish or wildlife species to any list published pursuant to subsection (c) of section 1533 of this title: *Provided,* That such holding and any subsequent holding or use of the fish or wildlife was not in the course of a commercial activity. With respect to any act prohibited by subsections (a)(1)(A) and (a)(1)(G) of this section which occurs after a period of 180 days from (i) December 28, 1973, or (ii) the date of publication in the Federal Register of a final regulation adding such fish or wildlife species to any list published pursuant to subsection (c) of section 1533 of this title, there shall be a rebuttable presumption that the fish or wildlife involved in such act is not entitled to the exemption contained in this subsection.

(2)(A) The provisions of subsection (a)(1) of this section shall not apply to —

    (i) any raptor legally held in captivity or in a controlled environment on November 10, 1978; or

    (ii) any progeny of any raptor described in clause (i);

until such time as any such raptor or progeny is intentionally returned to a wild state.

(B) Any person holding any raptor or progeny described in subparagraph (A) must be able to demonstrate that the raptor or progeny does, in fact, qualify under the provisions of this paragraph, and shall maintain and submit to the Secretary, on request, such inventories, documentation, and records as the Secretary may by regulation require as being reasonably appropriate to carry out the purposes of this paragraph. Such requirements shall not unnecessarily duplicate the requirements of other rules and regulations promulgated by the Secretary.

(c) Violation of Convention

(1) It is unlawful for any person subject to the jurisdiction of the United States to engage in any trade in any specimens contrary to the provisions of the Convention, or to possess any specimens traded contrary to the provisions of the Convention, including the definitions of terms in article I thereof.

(2) Any importation into the United States of fish or wildlife shall, if —

    (A) such fish or wildlife is not an endangered species listed pursuant to section 1533 of this title but is listed in Appendix II to the Convention,

    (B) the taking and exportation of such fish or wildlife is not contrary to the provisions of the Convention and all other applicable requirements of the Convention have been satisfied,

    (C) the applicable requirements of subsections (d), (e), and (f) of this section have been satisfied, and

    (D) such importation is not made in the course of a commercial activity,

be presumed to be an importation not in violation of any provision of this chapter or any regulation issued pursuant to this chapter.

(d) Imports and exports

(1) In general — It is unlawful for any person, without first having obtained permission from the Secretary, to engage in business —

    (A) as an importer or exporter of fish or wildlife (other than shellfish and fishery products which (i) are not listed pursuant to section 1533 of this title as endangered species or threatened species, and (ii) are imported for purposes of human or animal consumption or taken in waters under the jurisdiction of the United States or on the high seas for recreational purposes) or plants; or

    (B) as an importer or exporter of any amount of raw or worked African elephant ivory.

(2) Requirements — Any person required to obtain permission under paragraph (1) of this subsection shall —

    (A) keep such records as will fully and correctly disclose each importation or exportation of fish, wildlife, plants, or African elephant ivory made by him and the subsequent disposition made by him with respect to such fish, wildlife, plants, or ivory;

    (B) at all reasonable times upon notice by a duly authorized representative of the Secretary, afford such representative access to his place of business, an opportunity to examine his inventory of imported fish, wildlife, plants, or African elephant ivory and the records required to be kept under subparagraph (A) of this paragraph, and to copy such records; and

    (C) file such reports as the Secretary may require.

(3) Regulations — The Secretary shall prescribe such regulations as are necessary and appropriate to carry out the purposes of this subsection.

(4) Restriction on consideration of value or amount of African elephant ivory imported or exported — In granting permission under this subsection for importation or exportation of African elephant ivory, the Secretary shall not vary the requirements for obtaining such permission on the basis of the value or amount of ivory imported or exported under such permission.

(e) Reports — It is unlawful for any person importing or exporting fish or wildlife (other than shellfish and fishery products which (1) are not listed pursuant to section 1533 of this title as endangered or threatened species, and (2) are imported for purposes of human or animal consumption or taken in waters under the jurisdiction of the United States or on the high seas for recreational purposes) or plants to fail to file any declaration or report as the Secretary deems necessary to facilitate enforcement of this chapter or to meet the obligations of the Convention.

(f) Designation of ports

(1) It is unlawful for any person subject to the jurisdiction of the United States to import into or export from the United States any fish or wildlife (other than shellfish and fishery products which (A) are not listed pursuant to section 1533 of this title as endangered species or threatened species, and (B) are imported for purposes of human or animal consumption or taken in waters under the jurisdiction of the United States or on the high seas for recreational purposes) or plants, except at a port or ports designated by the Secretary of the Interior.

For the purpose of facilitating enforcement of this chapter and reducing the costs thereof, the Secretary of the Interior, with approval of the Secretary of the Treasury and after notice and opportunity for public hearing, may, by regulation, designate ports and change such designations. The Secretary of the Interior, under such terms and conditions as he may prescribe, may permit the importation or exportation at nondesignated ports in the interest of the health or safety of the fish or wildlife or plants, or for other reasons, if, in his discretion, he deems it appropriate and consistent with the purpose of this subsection.

(2) Any port designated by the Secretary of the Interior under the authority of section 668cc-4(d) of this title, shall, if such designation is in effect on December 27, 1973, be deemed to be a port designated by the Secretary under paragraph (1) of this subsection until such time as the Secretary otherwise provides.

(g) **Violations** — It is unlawful for any person subject to the jurisdiction of the United States to attempt to commit, solicit another to commit, or cause to be committed, any offense defined in his section.

§1539. Exceptions
[ESA §10]
(a) Permits

(1) The Secretary may permit, under such terms and conditions as he shall prescribe —

(A) any act otherwise prohibited by section 1538 of this title for scientific purposes or to enhance the propagation or survival of the affected species, including, but not limited to, acts necessary for the establishment and maintenance of experimental populations pursuant to subsection (j) of this section; or

(B) any taking otherwise prohibited by section 1538(a)(1)(B) of this title if such taking is incidental to, and not the purpose of, the carrying out of an otherwise lawful activity.

(2)(A) No permit may be issued by the Secretary authorizing any taking referred to in paragraph (1)(B) unless the applicant therefor submits to the Secretary a conservation plan that specifies —

(i) the impact which will likely result from such taking;

(ii) what steps the applicant will take to minimize and mitigate such impacts, and the funding that will be available to implement such steps;

(iii) what alternative actions to such taking the applicant considered and the reasons why such alternatives are not being utilized; and

(iv) such other measures that the Secretary may require as being necessary or appropriate for purposes of the plan.

(B) If the Secretary finds, after opportunity for public comment, with respect to a permit application and the related conservation plan that —

(i) the taking will be incidental;

(ii) the applicant will, to the maximum extent practicable, minimize and mitigate the impacts of such taking;

(iii) the applicant will ensure that adequate funding for the plan will be provided;

(iv) the taking will not appreciably reduce the likelihood of the survival and recovery of the species in the wild; and

(v) the measures, if any, required under subparagraph (A)(iv) will be met;

and he has received such other assurances as he may require that the plan willbe implemented, the Secretary shall issue the permit. The permit shall contain such terms and conditions as the Secretary deems necessary or appropriate to carry out the purposes of this paragraph, including, but not limited to, such reporting requirements as the Secretary deems necessary for determining whether such terms and conditions are being complied with.

(C) The Secretary shall revoke a permit issued under this paragraph if he finds that the permittee is not complying with the terms and conditions of the permit.

(b) Hardship exemptions

(1) If any person enters into a contract with respect to a species of fish or wildlife or plant before the date of the publication in the Federal Register of notice of consideration of that species as an endangered species and the subsequent listing of that species as an endangered species pursuant to section 1533 of this title will cause undue economic hardship to such person under the contract, the Secretary, in order to minimize such hardship, may exempt such person from the application of section 1538(a) of this title to the extent the Secretary deems appropriate if such person applies to him for such exemption and includes with such application such information as the Secretary may require to prove such hardship; except that (A) no such exemption shall be for a duration of more than one year from the date of publication in the Federal Register of notice of consideration of the species concerned, or shall apply to a quantity of fish or wildlife or plants in excess of that specified by the Secretary; (B) the one-year period for those species of fish or wildlife listed by the Secretary as endangered prior to December 28, 1973, shall expire in accordance with the terms of section 668cc-3 [1] of this title; and (C) no such exemption may be granted for the importation or exportation of a specimen listed in Appendix I of the Convention which is to be used in a commercial activity.

(2) As used in this subsection, the term "undue economic hardship" shall include, but not be limited to:

(A) substantial economic loss resulting from inability caused by this chapter to perform contracts with respect to species of fish and wildlife entered into prior to the date of publication in the Federal Register of a notice of consideration of such species as an endangered species;

(B) substantial economic loss to persons who, for the year prior to the notice of consideration of such species as an endangered species, derived a substantial portion of their income from the lawful taking of any listed species, which taking would be made unlawful under this chapter; or

(C) curtailment of subsistence taking made unlawful under this chapter by persons (i) not reasonably able to secure other sources of subsistence; and (ii) dependent to a substantial extent upon hunting and fishing for subsistence and (iii) who must engage in such curtailed taking for subsistence purposes.

(3) The Secretary may make further requirements for a showing of undue economic hardship as he deems fit. Exceptions granted under this section may be limited by the Secretary in his discretion as to time, area, or other factor of applicability.

(c) **Notice and review** — The Secretary shall publish notice in the Federal Register of each application for an exemption or permit which is made under this subsection. Each notice shall invite the submission from interested parties, within thirty days after the date of the notice, of written data, views, or arguments with respect to the application; except that such thirty-day period may be waived by the Secretary in an emergency situation where the health or life of an endangered animal is threatened and no reasonable alternative is available to the applicant, but notice of any such waiver shall be published by the Secretary in the Federal Register within ten days following the issuance of the exemption or permit. Information received by the Secretary as a part of any application shall be available to the public as a matter of public record at every stage of the proceeding.

(d) **Permit and exemption policy** — The Secretary may grant exceptions under subsections (a)(1)(A) and (b) of this section only if he finds and publishes his finding in the Federal Register that (1) such exceptions were applied for in good faith, (2) if granted and exercised will not operate to the disadvantage of such endangered species, and (3) will be consistent with the purposes and policy set forth in section 1531 of this title.

(e) **Alaska natives**

(1) Except as provided in paragraph (4) of this subsection the provisions of this chapter shall not apply with respect to the taking of any endangered species or threatened species, or the importation of any such species taken pursuant to this section, by —

(A) any Indian, Aleut, or Eskimo who is an Alaskan Native who resides in Alaska; or

(B) any non-native permanent resident of an Alaskan native village;

if such taking is primarily for subsistence purposes. Non-edible byproducts of species taken pursuant to this section may be sold in interstate commerce when made into authentic native articles of handicrafts and clothing; except that the provisions of this subsection shall not apply to any non-native resident of an Alaskan native village found by the Secretary to be not primarily dependent upon the taking of fish and wildlife for consumption or for the creation and sale of authentic native articles of handicrafts and clothing.

(2) Any taking under this subsection may not be accomplished in a wasteful manner.

(3) As used in this subsection —

(i) The term "subsistence" includes selling any edible portion of fish or wildlife in native villages and towns in Alaska for native consumption within native villages or towns; and

(ii) The term "authentic native articles of handicrafts and clothing" means items composed wholly or in some significant respect of natural materials, and which are produced, decorated, or fashioned in the exercise of traditional native handicrafts without the use of pantographs, multiple carvers, or other mass copying devices. Traditional native handicrafts include, but are not limited to, weaving, carving, stitching, sewing, lacing, beading, drawing, and painting.

(4) Notwithstanding the provisions of paragraph (1) of this subsection, whenever the Secretary determines that any species of fish or wildlife which is subject to taking under the provisions of this subsection is an endangered species or threatened species, and that such taking materially and negatively affects the threatened or endangered species, he may prescribe regulations upon the taking of such species by any such Indian, Aleut, Eskimo, or non-Native Alaskan resident of an Alaskan native village. Such regulations may be established with reference to species, geographical description of the area included, the season for taking, or any other factors related to the reason for establishing such regulations and consistent with the policy of this chapter. Such regulations shall be prescribed after a notice and hearings in the affected judicial districts of Alaska and as otherwise required by section 1373 of this title, and shall be removed as soon as the Secretary determines that the need for their impositions has disappeared.

(f) Pre-Act endangered species parts exemption; application and certification; regulation; validity of sales contract; separability; renewal of exemption; expiration of renewal certification

(1) As used in this subsection —

(A) The term "pre-Act endangered species part" means —

(i) any sperm whale oil, including derivatives thereof, which was lawfully held within the United States on December 28, 1973, in the course of a commercial activity; or

(ii) any finished scrimshaw product, if such product or the raw material for such product was lawfully held within the United States on December 28, 1973, in the course of a commercial activity.

(B) The term "scrimshaw product" means any art form which involves the substantial etching or engraving of designs upon, or the substantial carving of figures, patterns, or designs from, any bone or tooth of any marine mammal of the order Cetacea. For purposes of this subsection, polishing or the adding of minor superficial markings does not constitute substantial etching, engraving, or carving.

(2) The Secretary, pursuant to the provisions of this subsection, may exempt, if such exemption is not in violation of the Convention, any pre-Act endangered species part from one or more of the following prohibitions:

(A) The prohibition on exportation from the United States set forth in section 1538(a)(1)(A) of this title.

(B) Any prohibition set forth in section 1538(a)(1)(E) or (F) of this title.

(3) Any person seeking an exemption described in paragraph (2) of this subsection shall make application therefor to the Secretary in such form and manner as he shall prescribe, but no such application may be considered by the Secretary unless the application —

(A) is received by the Secretary before the close of the one-year period beginning on the date on which regulations promulgated by the Secretary to carry out this subsection first take effect;

(B) contains a complete and detailed inventory of all pre-Act endangered species parts for which the applicant seeks exemption;

(C) is accompanied by such documentation as the Secretary may require to prove that any endangered species part or product claimed by the applicant to be a pre-Act endangered species part is in fact such a part; and

(D) contains such other information as the Secretary deems necessary and appropriate to carry out the purposes of this subsection.

(4) If the Secretary approves any application for exemption made under this subsection, he shall issue to the applicant a certificate of exemption which shall specify —

(A) any prohibition in section 1538(a) of this title which is exempted;

(B) the pre-Act endangered species parts to which the exemption applies;

(C) the period of time during which the exemption is in effect, but no exemption made under this subsection shall have force and effect after the close of the three-year period beginning on the date of issuance of the certificate unless such exemption is renewed under paragraph (8); and

(D) any term or condition prescribed pursuant to paragraph (5)(A) or (B), or both, which the Secretary deems necessary or appropriate.

(5) The Secretary shall prescribe such regulations as he deems necessary and appropriate to carry out the purposes of this subsection. Such regulations may set forth —

(A) terms and conditions which may be imposed on applicants for exemptions under this subsection (including, but not limited to, requirements that applicants register inventories, keep complete sales records, permit duly authorized agents of the Secretary to inspect such inventories and records, and periodically file appropriate reports with the Secretary); and

(B) terms and conditions which may be imposed on any subsequent purchaser of any pre-Act endangered species part covered by an exemption granted under this subsection;

to insure that any such part so exempted is adequately accounted for and not disposed of contrary to the provisions of this chapter. No regulation prescribed by the Secretary to carry out the purposes of this subsection shall be subject to section 1533(f)(2)(A)(i) of this title.

(6)(A) Any contract for the sale of pre-Act endangered species parts which is entered into by the Administrator of General Services prior to the effective date of this subsection and pursuant to the notice published in the Federal Register on January 9, 1973, shall not be rendered invalid by virtue of the fact that fulfillment of such contract may be prohibited under section 1538(a)(1)(F) of this title.

(B) In the event that this paragraph is held invalid, the validity of the remainder of this chapter, including the remainder of this subsection, shall not be affected.

(7) Nothing in this subsection shall be construed to —

(A) exonerate any person from any act committed in violation of paragraphs (1)(A), (1)(E), or (1)(F) of section 1538(a) of this title prior to July 12, 1976; or

(B) immunize any person from prosecution for any such act.

(8)(A)(i) Any valid certificate of exemption which was renewed after October 13, 1982, and was in effect on March 31, 1988, shall be deemed to be renewed for a six-month period beginning on October 7, 1988. Any person holding such a certificate may apply to the Secretary for one additional renewal of such certificate for a period not to exceed 5 years beginning on October 7, 1988.

(B) If the Secretary approves any application for renewal of an exemption under this paragraph, he shall issue to the applicant a certificate of renewal of such exemption which shall provide that all terms, conditions, prohibitions, and other regulations made applicable by the previous certificate shall remain in effect during the period of the renewal.

(C) No exemption or renewal of such exemption made under this subsection shall have force and effect after the expiration date of the certificate of renewal of such exemption issued under this paragraph.

(D) No person may, after January 31, 1984, sell or offer for sale in interstate or foreign commerce, any pre-Act finished scrimshaw product unless such person holds a valid certificate of exemption issued by the Secretary under this subsection, and unless such product or the raw material for such product was held by such person on October 13, 1982.

(g) Burden of proof — In connection with any action alleging a violation of section 1538 of this title, any person claiming the benefit of any exemption or permit under this chapter shall have the burden of proving that the exemption or permit is applicable, has been granted, and was valid and in force at the time of the alleged violation.

(h) Certain antique articles; importation; port designation; application for return of articles

(1) Sections 1533(d) and 1538(a) and (c) of this title do not apply to any article which —

(A) is not less than 100 years of age;

(B) is composed in whole or in part of any endangered species or threatened species listed under section 1533 of this title;

(C) has not been repaired or modified with any part of any such species on or after December 28, 1973; and

(D) is entered at a port designated under paragraph (3).

(2) Any person who wishes to import an article under the exception provided by this subsection shall submit to the customs officer concerned at the time of entry of the article such documentation as the Secretary of the Treasury, after consultation with the Secretary of the Interior, shall by regulation require as being necessary to establish that the article meets the requirements set forth in paragraph (1)(A), (B), and (C).

(3) The Secretary of the Treasury, after consultation with the Secretary of the Interior, shall designate one port within each customs region at which articles described in paragraph (1)(A), (B), and (C) must be entered into the customs territory of the United States.

(4) Any person who imported, after December 27, 1973, and on or before November 10, 1978, any article described in paragraph (1) which —

(A) was not repaired or modified after the date of importation with any part of any endangered species or threatened species listed under section 1533 of this title;

(B) was forfeited to the United States before November 10, 1978, or is subject to forfeiture to the United States on such date of enactment, pursuant to the assessment of a civil penalty under section 1540 of this title; and

(C) is in the custody of the United States on November 10, 1978;

may, before the close of the one-year period beginning on November 10, 1978, make application to the Secretary for return of the article. Application shall be made in such form and manner, and contain such documentation, as the Secretary prescribes. If on the basis of any such application which is timely filed, the Secretary is satisfied that the requirements of this paragraph are met with respect to the article concerned, the Secretary shall return the article to the applicant and the importation of such article shall, on and after the date of return, be deemed to be a lawful importation under this chapter.

(i) Noncommercial transshipments — Any importation into the United States of fish or wildlife shall, if —

(1) such fish or wildlife was lawfully taken and exported from the country of origin and country of reexport, if any;

(2) such fish or wildlife is in transit or transshipment through any place subject to the jurisdiction of the United States en route to a country where such fish or wildlife may be lawfully imported and received;

(3) the exporter or owner of such fish or wildlife gave explicit instructions not to ship such fish or wildlife through any place subject to the jurisdiction of the United States, or did all that could have reasonably been done to prevent transshipment, and the circumstances leading to the transshipment were beyond the exporter's or owner's control;

(4) the applicable requirements of the Convention have been satisfied; and

(5) such importation is not made in the course of a commercial activity,

be an importation not in violation of any provision of this chapter or any regulation issued pursuant to this chapter while such fish or wildlife remains in the control of the United States Customs Service.

(j) Experimental populations

(1) For purposes of this subsection, the term "experimental population" means and population (including any offspring arising solely therefrom) authorized by the Secretary for release under paragraph (2), but only when, and at such times as, the population is wholly separate geographically from nonexperimental populations of the same species.

(2)(A) The Secretary may authorize the release (and the related transportation) of any population (including eggs, propagules, or individuals) of an endangered species or a threatened species outside the current range of such species if the Secretary determines that such release will further the conservation of such species.

(B) Before authorizing the release of any population under subparagraph (A), the Secretary shall by regulation identify the population and determine, on the basis of the best available information, whether or not such population is essential to the continued existence of an endangered species or a threatened species.

(C) For the purposes of this chapter, each member of an experimental population shall be treated as a threatened species; except that —

(i) solely for purposes of section 1536 of this title (other than subsection (a)(1) thereof), an experimental population determined under subparagraph (B) to be not essential to the continued existence of a species shall be treated, except when it occurs in an area within the National Wildlife Refuge System or the National Park System, as a species proposed to be listed under section 1533 of this title; and

(ii) critical habitat shall not be designated under this chapter for any experimental population determined under subparagraph (B) to be not essential to the continued existence of a species.

(3) The Secretary, with respect to populations of endangered species or threatened species that the Secretary authorized, before October 13, 1982, for release in geographical areas separate from the other populations of such species, shall determine by regulation which of such populations are an experimental population for the purposes of this subsection and whether or not each is essential to the continued existence of an endangered species or a threatened species.

§1540. Penalties and enforcement
[ESA §11]

(a) Civil penalties

(1) Any person who knowingly violates, and any person engaged in business as an importer or exporter of fish, wildlife, or plants who violates, any provision of this chapter, or any provision of any permit or certificate issued hereunder, or of any regulation issued in order to implement subsection (a)(1)(A), (B), (C), (D), (E), or (F), (a)(2)(A), (B), (C), or (D), (c), (d) (other than regulation relating to recordkeeping or filing of reports), (f) or (g) of section 1538 of this title, may be assessed a civil penalty by the Secretary of not more than $25,000 for each violation. Any person who knowingly violates, and any person engaged in business as an importer or exporter of fish, wildlife, or plants who violates, any provision of any other regulation issued under this chapter may be assessed a civil penalty by the Secretary of not more than $12,000 for each such violation. Any person who otherwise violates any provision of this chapter, or any regulation, permit, or certificate issued hereunder, may be assessed a civil penalty by the Secretary of not more than $500 for each such violation. No penalty may be assessed under this subsection unless such person is given notice and opportunity for a hearing with respect to such violation. Each violation shall be a separate offense. Any such civil penalty may be remitted or mitigated by the Secretary. Upon any failure to pay a penalty assessed under this subsection, the Secretary may request the Attorney General to institute a civil action in a district court of the United States for any district in which such person is found, resides, or transacts business to collect the penalty and such court shall have jurisdiction to hear and decide any such action. The court shall hear such action on the record made before the Secretary and shall sustain his action if it is supported by substantial evidence on the record considered as a whole.

(2) Hearings held during proceedings for the assessment of civil penalties authorized by paragraph (1) of this subsection shall be conducted in accordance with section 554 of title 5. The Secretary may issue subpenas for the attendance and testimony of witnesses and the production of relevant papers, books, and documents, and administer oaths. Witnesses summoned shall be paid the same fees and mileage that are paid to witnesses in the courts of the United States. In case of contumacy or refusal to obey a subpoena served upon any person pursuant to this paragraph, the district court of the United States for any district in which such person is found or resides or transacts business, upon application by the United States and after notice to such person, shall have jurisdiction to issue an order requiring such person to appear and give testimony before the Secretary or to appear and produce documents before the Secretary, or both, and any failure to obey such order of the court may be punished by such court as a contempt thereof.

(3) Notwithstanding any other provision of this chapter, no civil penalty shall be imposed if it

can be shown by a preponderance of the evidence that the defendant committed an act based on a good faith belief that he was acting to protect himself or herself, a member of his or her family, or any other individual from bodily harm, from any endangered or threatened species.

(b) Criminal violations

(1) Any person who knowingly violates any provision of this chapter, of any permit or certificate issued hereunder, or of any regulation issued in order to implement subsection (a)(1)(A), (B), (C), or (D), (E), or (F); (a)(2)(A), (B), (C), or (D), (c), (d) (other than a regulation relating to recordkeeping, or filing of reports), (f) or (g) of section 1538 of this title shall, upon conviction, be fined not more than $50,000 or imprisoned for not more than one year, or both. Any person who knowingly violates any provision of any other regulation issued under this chapter shall, upon conviction, be fined not more than $25,000 or imprisoned for not more than six months, or both.

(2) The head of any Federal agency which has issued a lease, license, permit, or other agreement authorizing a person to import or export fish, wildlife, or plants, or to operate a quarantine station for imported wildlife, or authorizing the use of Federal lands, including grazing of domestic livestock, to any person who is convicted of a criminal violation of this chapter or any regulation, permit, or certificate issued hereunder may immediately modify, suspend, or revokeeach lease, license, permit, or other agreement. The Secretary shall also suspend for a period of up to one year, or cancel, any Federal hunting or fishing permits or stamps issued to any person who is convicted of a criminal violation of any provision of this chapter or any regulation, permit, or certificate issued hereunder. The United States shall not be liable for the payments of any compensation, reimbursement, or damages in connection with the modification, suspension, or revocation of any leases, licenses, permits, stamps, or other agreements pursuant to this section.

(3) Notwithstanding any other provision of this chapter, it shall be a defense to prosecution under this subsection if the defendant committed the offense based on a good faith belief that he was acting to protect himself or herself, a member of his or her family, or any other individual, from bodily harm from any endangered or threatened species.

(c) District court jurisdiction — The several district courts of the United States, including the courts enumerated in section 460 of Title 28, shall have jurisdiction over any actions arising under this chapter. For the purpose of this chapter, American Samoa shall be included within the judicial district of the District Court of the United States for the District of Hawaii.

(d) Rewards and incidental expenses — The Secretary or the Secretary of the Treasury shall pay, from sums received as penalties, fines, or forfeitures of property for any violation of this chapter or any regulation issued hereunder (1) a reward to any person who furnishes information which leads to an arrest, a criminal conviction, civil penalty assessment, or forfeiture of property for any violation of this chapter or any regulation issued hereunder, and (2) the reasonable and necessary costs incurred by any person in providing temporary care for any fish, wildlife, or plant pending the disposition of any civil or criminal proceeding alleging a violation of this chapter with respect to that fish, wildlife, or plant. The amount of the reward, if any, is to be designated by the Secretary or the Secretary of the Treasury, as appropriate. Any officer or employee of the United States or any State or local government who furnishes information or renders service in the performance of his official duties is ineligible for payment under this subsection. Whenever the balance of sums received under this section and section 3375(d) of this title, as penalties or fines, or from forfeitures of property, exceed $500,000, the Secretary of the Treasury shall deposit an amount equal to such excess balance in the cooperative endangered species conservation fund established under section 1535(i) of this title.

(e) Enforcement

(1) The provisions of this chapter and any regulations or permits issued pursuant thereto shall be enforced by the Secretary, the Secretary of the Treasury, or the Secretary of the Department in which the Coast Guard is operating, or all such Secretaries. Each such Secretary may utilize by agreement, with or without reimbursement, the personnel, services, and facilities of any other Federal agency or any State agency for purposes of enforcing this chapter.

(2) The judges of the district courts of the United States and the United States magistrate judges may, within their respective jurisdictions, upon proper oath or affirmation showing probable cause, issue such warrants or other process as may be required for enforcement of this chapter and any regulation issued thereunder.

(3) Any person authorized by the Secretary, the Secretary of the Treasury, or the Secretary of the Department in which the Coast Guard is operating, to enforce this chapter may detain for inspection and inspect any package, crate, or other container, including its contents, and all accompanying documents, upon importation or exportation. Such person may make arrests without a warrant for any violation of this chapter if he has reasonable grounds to believe that the person to be arrested is committing the violation in his presence or view, and may execute and serve any arrest warrant, search warrant, or other warrant or civil or criminal process issued by any officer or court of competent jurisdiction for enforcement of this chapter. Such person so authorized may search and seize, with or without a warrant, as authorized by law. Any fish, wildlife, property, or item so seized shall be

held by any person authorized by the Secretary, the Secretary of the Treasury, or the Secretary of the Department in which the Coast Guard is operating pending disposition of civil or criminal proceedings, or the institution of an action in rem for forfeiture of such fish, wildlife, property, or item pursuant to paragraph (4) of this subsection; except that the Secretary may, in lieu of holding such fish, wildlife, property, or item, permit the owner or consignee to post a bond or other surety satisfactory to the Secretary, but upon forfeiture of any such property to the United States, or the abandonment or waiver of any claim to any such property, it shall be disposed of (other than by sale to the general public) by the Secretary in such a manner, consistent with the purposes of this chapter, as the Secretary shall by regulation prescribe.

(4)(A) All fish or wildlife or plants taken, possessed, sold, purchased, offered for sale or purchase, transported, delivered, received, carried, shipped, exported, or imported contrary to the provisions of this chapter, any regulation made pursuant thereto, or any permit or certificate issued hereunder shall be subject to forfeiture to the United States.

(B) All guns, traps, nets, and other equipment, vessels, vehicles, aircraft, and other means of transportation used to aid the taking, possessing, selling, purchasing, offering for sale or purchase, transporting, delivering, receiving, carrying, shipping, exporting, or importing of any fish or wildlife or plants in violation of this chapter, any regulation made pursuant thereto, or any permit or certificate issued thereunder shall be subject to forfeiture to the United States upon conviction of a criminal violation pursuant to subsection (b)(1) of this section.

(5) All provisions of law relating to the seizure, forfeiture, and condemnation of a vessel for violation of the customs laws, the disposition of such vessel or the proceeds from the sale thereof, and the remission or mitigation of such forfeiture, shall apply to the seizures and forfeitures incurred, or alleged to have been incurred, under the provisions of this chapter, insofar as such provisions of law are applicable and not inconsistent with the provisions of this chapter; except that all powers, rights, and duties conferred or imposed by the customs laws upon any officer or employee of the Treasury Department shall, for the purposes of this chapter, be exercised or performed by the Secretary or by such persons as he may designate.

(6) The Attorney General of the United States may seek to enjoin any person who is alleged to be in violation of any provision of this chapter or regulation issued under authority thereof.

(f) Regulations — The Secretary, the Secretary of the Treasury, and the Secretary of the Department in which the Coast Guard is operating, are authorized to promulgate such regulations as may be appropriate to enforce this chapter, and charge reasonable fees for expenses to the Government connected with permits or certificates authorized by this chapter including processing applications and reasonable inspections, and with the transfer, board, handling, or storage of fish or wildlife or plants and evidentiary items seized and forfeited under this chapter. All such fees collected pursuant to this subsection shall be deposited in the Treasury to the credit of the appropriation which is current and chargeable for the cost of furnishing the services. Appropriated funds may be expended pending reimbursement from parties in interest.

(g) Citizen suits

(1) Except as provided in paragraph (2) of this subsection any person may commence a civil suit on his own behalf —

(A) to enjoin any person, including the United States and any other governmental instrumentality or agency (to the extent permitted by the eleventh amendment to the Constitution), who is alleged to be in violation of any provision of this chapter or regulation issued under the authority thereof; or

(B) to compel the Secretary to apply, pursuant to section 1535(g)(2)(B)(ii) of this title, the prohibitions set forth in or authorized pursuant to section 1533(d) or 1538(a)(1)(B) of this title with respect to the taking of any resident endangered species or threatened species within any State; or

(C) against the Secretary where there is alleged a failure of the Secretary to perform any act or duty under section 1533 of this title which is not discretionary with the Secretary.

The district courts shall have jurisdiction, without regard to the amount in controversy or the citizenship of the parties, to enforce any such provision or regulation, or to order the Secretary to perform such act or duty, as the case may be. In any civil suit commenced under subparagraph (B) the district court shall compel the Secretary to apply the prohibition sought if the court finds that the allegation that an emergency exists is supported by substantial evidence.

(2)(A) No action may be commenced under subparagraph (1)(A) of this section —

(i) prior to sixty days after written notice of the violation has been given to the Secretary, and to any alleged violator of any such provision or regulation;

(ii) if the Secretary has commenced action to impose a penalty pursuant to subsection (a) of this section; or

(iii) if the United States has commenced and is diligently prosecuting a criminal action in a court of the United States or a State to redress a violation of any such provision or regulation.

(B) No action may be commenced under subparagraph (1)(B) of this section —

(i) prior to sixty days after written notice has been given to the Secretary setting forth the reasons why an emergency is thought to exist with respect to an endangered species or a threatened species in the State concerned; or

(ii) if the Secretary has commenced and is diligently prosecuting action under section 1535(g)(2)(B)(ii) of this title to determine whether any such emergency exists.

(C) No action may be commenced under subparagraph (1)(C) of this section prior to sixty days after written notice has been given to the Secretary; except that such action may be brought immediately after such notification in the case of an action under this section respecting an emergency posing a significant risk to the well-being of any species of fish or wildlife or plants.

(3)(A) Any suit under this subsection may be brought in the judicial district in which the violation occurs.

(B) In any such suit under this subsection in which the United States is not a party, the Attorney General, at the request of the Secretary, may intervene on behalf of the United States as a matter of right.

(4) The court, in issuing any final order in any suit brought pursuant to paragraph (1) of this subsection, may award costs of litigation (including reasonable attorney and expert witness fees) to any party, whenever the court determines such award is appropriate.

(5) The injunctive relief provided by this subsection shall not restrict any right which any person (or class of persons) may have under any statute or common law to seek enforcement of any standard or limitation or to seek any other relief (including relief against the Secretary or a State agency).

(h) Coordination with other laws — The Secretary of Agriculture and the Secretary shall provide for appropriate coordination of the administration of this chapter with the administration of the animal quarantine laws (as defined in section 136a(f) of Title 21) and section 306 of the Tariff Act of 1930 (19 U.S.C. §1306). Nothing in this chapter or any amendment made by this chapter shall be construed as superseding or limiting in any manner the functions of the Secretary of Agriculture under any other law relating to prohibited or restricted importations or possession of animals and other articles and no proceeding or determination under this chapter shall preclude any proceeding or be considered determinative of any issue of fact or law in any proceeding under any Act administered by the Secretary of Agriculture. Nothing in this chapter shall be construed as superseding or limiting in any manner the functions and responsibilities of the Secretary of the Treasury under the Tariff Act of 1930 (19 U.S.C. §§1202 *et seq.*), including, without limitation, section 527 of that Act (19 U.S.C. §1527), relating to the importation of wildlife taken, killed, possessed, or exported to the United States in violation of the laws or regulations of a foreign country.

§1541. Endangered plants
[ESA §12]

The Secretary of the Smithsonian Institution, in conjunction with other affected agencies, is authorized and directed to review (1) species of plants which are now or may become endangered or threatened and (2) methods of adequately conserving such species, and to report to Congress, within one year after December 28, 1973, the results of such review including recommendations for new legislation or the amendment of existing legislation.

§1542. Authorization of appropriations
[ESA §15]

(a) In general — Except as provided in subsections (b), (c), and (d) of this section, there are authorized to be appropriated —

(1) not to exceed $35,000,000 for fiscal year 1988, $36,500,000 for fiscal year 1989, $38,000,000 for fiscal year 1990, $39,500,000 for fiscal year 1991, and $41,500,000 for fiscal year 1992 to enable the Department of the Interior to carry out such functions and responsibilities as it may have been given under this chapter;

(2) not to exceed $5,750,000 for fiscal year 1988, $6,250,000 for each of fiscal years 1989 and 1990, and $6,750,000 for each of fiscal years 1991 and 1992 to enable the Department of Commerce to carry out such functions and responsibilities as it may have been given under this chapter; and

(3) not to exceed $2,200,000 for fiscal year 1988, $2,400,000 for each of fiscal years 1989 and 1990, and $2,600,000 for each of fiscal years 1991 and 1992, to enable the Department of Agriculture to carry out its functions and responsibilities with respect to the enforcement of this chapter and the Convention which pertain to the importation or exportation of plants.

(b) Exemptions — There are authorized to be appropriated to the Secretary to assist him and the Endangered Species Committee in carrying out their functions under sections 1536(e), (g), and (h) of this title not to exceed $600,000 for each of fiscal years 1988, 1989, 1990, 1991, and 1992.

(c) Convention implementation — There are authorized to be appropriated to the Department of the Interior for purposes of carrying out section 1537a(e) of this title not to exceed $400,000 for each of fiscal years 1988, 1989, and 1990, and $500,000 for each of fiscal years 1991 and 1992, and such sums shall remain available until expended.

§1543. Construction with Marine Mammal Protection Act of 1972
[ESA §17]

Except as otherwise provided in this chapter, no provision of this chapter shall take precedence over any more restrictive conflicting provision of the Marine Mammal Protection Act of 1972 (16 U.S.C. §§1361 *et seq.*).

§1544. Annual cost analysis by Fish and Wildlife Service
[ESA §18]

Notwithstanding section 3003 of Public Law 104-66 (31 U.S.C. 1113 note; 109 Stat. 734) on or before January 15, 1990, and each January 15 thereafter, the Secretary of the Interior, acting through the Fish and Wildlife Service, shall submit to the Congress an annual report covering the preceding fiscal year which shall contain —

(1) an accounting on a species by species basis of all reasonably identifiable Federal expenditures made primarily for the conservation of endangered or threatened species pursuant to this chapter; and

(2) an accounting on a species by species basis of all reasonably identifiable expenditures made primarily for the conservation of endangered or threatened species pursuant to this chapter by States receiving grants under section 1535 of this title.

10
PUBLIC LAND MANAGEMENT

One-third of the land area of the United States is owned by the federal government. How public lands should be managed has been a subject of persistent controversy. For the first century of our nation, the federal government sought to transfer public lands to private interests to encourage settlement and development. Today, most laws encouraging disposal of public lands have been repealed. Public lands are now managed in four systems: (1) general public lands, managed by the Bureau of Land Management (BLM); (2) national forests, managed by the U.S. Forest Service; (3) national wildlife refuges, managed by the U.S. Fish and Wildlife Service; and (4) national parks, managed by the National Park Service. Each of these agencies is part of the U.S. Department of the Interior, except for the Forest Service, which is housed in the Department of Agriculture.

Most public lands, including the 264 million acres managed by the BLM and the 191 million acres in the national forest system (except for wilderness areas), are to be managed for "multiple use" as defined in the Federal Land Policy and Management Act and the National Forest Management Act for the national forests. The Multiple Use, Sustained Yield Act defines "multiple use" as utilization "in the combination that will best meet the needs of the American people," a mandate ambiguous enough to ensure persistent controversy among competing interests. The Antiquities Act authorizes the President to create national monuments to protect "objects of historic or scientific interest" situated on public lands.

For national wildlife refuges, Congress has established conservation of wildlife as the dominant use with other uses, such as grazing or recreation, allowed only if compatible with the purposes for which a refuge was established. National parks, national monuments, and national wilderness areas enjoy even greater protection. National parks are to be managed "to conserve the scenery and the natural and historic objects and wildlife therein and to provide for the enjoyment of the same in such manner and by such means as will leave them unimpaired for the enjoyment of future generations." 16 U.S.C. §1. Wilderness areas must be managed under the Wilderness Act to preserve their "primeval character and influence" and "natural condition" with motorized equipment, permanent roads, and commercial enterprises generally prohibited. 16 U.S.C. §1131(c).

This chapter reproduces the text of the Antiquities Act, the Multiple Use Sustained Yield Act (MUSYA), the Forest and Rangeland Renewable Resources Act (FRRRPA) as amended by the National Forest Management Act (NFMA), and the Federal Land Policy and Management Act (FLPMA).

A GUIDE TO MATERIALS ON PUBLIC LANDS AVAILABLE ON THE INTERNET

The headquarters of the U.S. Forest Service maintains a website at *http://www.fs.fed.us*. Many individual national forests maintain their own websites, which can be located through links on the headquarters webpage at *https://hrm.gdcii.com/directory*. National forests can be searched by name, state, or region on an interactive map. The Forest Service's website provides information about land and resource management issues. Its website also includes information on appeals and litigation concerning management plans *(http://www.fs.fed.us/emc/applit/index.htm)* and Forest Service directives concerning the planning process *(http://www.fs.fed.us/im/directives)*.

The BLM's website is located at *http://www.blm.gov/*. It provides news updates about developments affecting the public lands and information about BLM's activities administering them. The National Park Service's "ParkNet" website is located at *http://www.nps.gov/*. It provides considerable information about visiting the national parks. For information about the history of the Park Service and its role in protecting the national parks see *http://www.nps.gov/aboutus/index.htm*.

In addition to the laws whose text is reproduced below, many other laws affect the management of public lands and forest areas.

The Public Lands Interpretive Association, a nonprofit educational organization, in partnership with the Bureau of Land Management and the USDA Forest Service Intermountain Region, operates a Public Lands Information Center website located at *http://www.publiclands.org*. The site is dedicated to providing information about recreational opportunities on western public lands.

For an industry perspective on forest issues, see the website of the American Forest and Paper Association located at *http://afandpa.org*. The Property and Environment Research Center (PERC) in Bozeman, Montana, which promotes "free market environmentalism," has been active on public lands issues. Its website is located at *http://www.perc.org*.

The early history of the national debate over use of the public lands is well documented in an extraordinary online exhibition maintained by the Library of Congress. Entitled "The Evolution of the Conservation Movement: 1850-1920," the exhibition can be located online at *http://memory.loc.gov/ammem/amrvhtml/*. It contains a very rich collection of photographs and documents pertaining to the history of the conservation movement that can be viewed and downloaded. Another source of information is the Forest History Society's website at *http://foresthistory.org*.

HISTORICAL TIMELINE OF LEGISLATION AFFECTING THE MANAGEMENT OF THE PUBLIC LANDS

March 1, 1872: President Grant signs the Yellowstone National Park Act, 17 Stat. 32, establishing Yellowstone as the first national park.

May 10, 1872: President Grant signs the General Mining Law of 1872, , providing that private parties may patent and develop hardrock mineral deposits on public lands that have not been expressly withdrawn from mineral entry.

March 3, 1891: President Benjamin Harrison signs the Forest Reserve Act, 26 Stat. 1095, which authorizes him to withdraw forest lands from development under the Homestead Act. Harrison used this legislation, which was repealed in 1976, to set aside 13 million acres of forest reserve, the precursor to creation of the National Forest System.

June 4, 1897: The Forest Service Organic Administration Act of 1897 is enacted into law. This legislation, which served for decades as the primary legislation governing the administration of national forest lands, requires that such lands be managed to protect the forest, to preserve water flows, and to furnish a continued supply of timber.

March 14, 1903: President Theodore Roosevelt issues Executive Order 1,014, creating the first National Wildlife Refuge at Pelican Island, Florida.

June 8, 1906: The Antiquities Act of 1906, Pub. L. No. 209, 34 Stat. 225, is signed into law by President Theodore Roosevelt. The Act gives the president the authority to issue proclamations designating federal lands as national monuments to preserve objects of "historic or scientific interest." Reservations of land are to be limited to the smallest area compatible with the proper care and management of the objects to be protected. Roosevelt used the Act to create the first national monument, Devils Tower National Monument, in September 1906. The Act authorizes the President to declare federal lands as national monuments for the purpose of protecting sites and objects of antiquity.

August 25, 1916: The National Park Service (NPS) is created by act of Congress, 39 Stat. 535. Located in the Department of the Interior, the NPS is charged with administration of the national parks, monuments and reservations.

February 25, 1920: The Mineral Leasing Act, 41 Stat. 437, is enacted, authorizing the leasing of public lands for mineral development, including the extraction of coal, oil and gas.

March 16, 1934: The Migratory Bird Hunting and Conservation Stamp Act of 1934, 48 Stat. 452, known as the "Duck Stamp Act," becomes law. By imposing a federal licensing fee on hunters, this legislation creates a new funding mechanism for acquisition of wildlife refuges to protect migratory waterfowl as required by the 1916 migratory bird treaty between the U.S. and Canada.

June 28, 1934: The Taylor Grazing Act, 48 Stat. 1269, regulating grazing on federal lands, becomes law. It directs the Secretary of the Interior to establish grazing districts and to implement a permit system to manage livestock grazing in the districts.

August 7, 1953: The Outer Continental Shelf Lands Act of 1953 (OCSLA), 67 Stat. 462, becomes law, authorizing the Secretary of the Interior to issue leases for mineral exploration and development on the Outer Continental Shelf through a competitive bidding process.

June 12, 1960: President Eisenhower signs the Multiple Use Sustained Yield Act of 1960, Pub. L. 86-517, 74 Stat. 215. The Act declares that public lands and national forests should be managed for multiple uses, including outdoor recreation, grazing, provision of timber, and protection of watersheds and fish and wildlife.

September 3, 1964: President Johnson signs into law the Wilderness Act, Pub. L. 88-577, 78 Stat. 890, establishing the National Wilderness Preservation System. The Act designates certain lands as wilderness areas and directs the Secretary of the Interior and the Secretary of Agriculture to review other areas for possible inclusion in the System. The Act defines wilderness as an area where the earth and its community of life are untrammeled by man, where man himself is a visitor who does not remain; an area of underdeveloped federal land retaining its primeval character and influence, without permanent improvements or human habitation and which is protected and managed so as to preserve its natural conditions.

On the same day, President Johnson also signs into law the Land and Water Conservation Fund Act, Pub. L. 88-578, 78 Stat. 897. This legislation authorizes creation of the Land and Water Conservation Fund to be funded at a level of $900 million per year from user fees charged at federal recreation areas and from the proceeds of leases on federal property. The fund is to be used to acquire public lands and waters for purposes of conservation and recreation.

October 15, 1966: President Johnson signs the National Wildlife Refuge System Administration Act, Pub. L. 89-669, 80 Stat. 927, which directs the Secretary of the Interior, through the U.S. Fish and Wildlife Service, to manage and administer national wildlife refuges for the protection and conservation of fish and wildlife.

October 2, 1968: The Wild and Scenic Rivers Act, Pub. L. 90-542, 82 Stat. 906, is signed into law. The Act withdraws federal lands that include rivers designated as wild and scenic rivers from entry, sale or disposition and it prohibits federal agencies from licensing or funding construction of waterworks affecting rivers so designated.

August 17, 1974: The Forest and Rangeland Renewable Resource Planning Act of 1974 (FRRRPA), Pub. L. 93-378, 88 Stat. 476, is signed into law. The Act directs the Secretary of Agriculture, through the U.S. Forest Service to improve the management of renewable resources on national forest lands.

October 21, 1976: President Ford signs into law the Federal Land Policy Management Act (FLPMA) of 1976, Pub. L. 94-579, 90 Stat. 2762, which provides a unified framework for BLM's management of the millions of acres of land under its jurisdiction. FLPMA directs the BLM to pursue multiple use management of public lands "so that they are utilized in the combination that will best meet the present and future needs of the American people."

October 22, 1976: President Ford signs the National Forest Management Act (NFMA) of 1976, Pub. L. 94-588, 90 Stat. 2949, which amends and expands the FRRRPA governing management of federal forest lands. The NFMA requires the Secretary of Agriculture to perform comprehensive assessments of forest lands and, based on the results of such assessment, to develop and to implement a management plan for each unit of the National Forest System. These plans, which are to be based on multiple-use, sustained-yield principles, must be revised and updated whenever significant changes occur in a unit and at least once every 15 years.

December 2, 1980: President Carter signs the Alaska National Interest Lands Conservation Act (ANILCA), Pub. L. 96-487, 94 Stat. 2371. The Act vastly expands the size of protected federal lands in Alaska, creating or expanding sixteen wildlife refuges covering 77 million acres of land. It also adds several new units to the National Park System, the National Wild and Scenic Rivers System, the National Wilderness Preservation System, and the National Forest System while providing a comprehensive scheme for management of all federal lands in Alaska.

December 7, 2003: President Bush signs the Healthy Forest Restoration Act of 2003, Pub. L. 108-148, to facilitate federal projects to clear fire hazards on federal land and to encourage the use of community wildfire protection plans to protect at-risk communities.

March 12, 2019: President Trump signs the John D. Dingell Jr. Conservation, Management and Recreation Act, Pub. L. 116-9, which permanently reauthorizes the Land and Water Conservation Fund and comprehensively updates and reforms management of public lands. The legislation was passed by overwhelming bipartisan majorities in both houses of Congress.

Antiquities Act
54 U.S.C. § 320301

§320301. National monuments

(a) Presidential Declaration.—The President may, in the President's discretion, declare by public proclamation historic landmarks, historic and prehistoric structures, and other objects of historic or scientific interest that are situated on land owned or controlled by the Federal Government to be national monuments.

(b) Reservation of Land.—The President may reserve parcels of land as a part of the national monuments. The limits of the parcels shall be confined to the smallest area compatible with the proper care and management of the objects to be protected.

(c) Relinquishment to Federal Government.—When an object is situated on a parcel covered by a bona fide unperfected claim or held in private ownership, the parcel, or so much of the parcel as may be necessary for the proper care and management of the object, may be relinquished to the Federal Government and the Secretary may accept the relinquishment of the parcel on behalf of the Federal Government.

(d) Limitation on Extension or Establishment of National Monuments in Wyoming.—No extension or establishment of national monuments in Wyoming may be undertaken except by express authorization of Congress.

Multiple Use Sustained Yield Act

16 U.S.C. §§528 to 531

SUBCHAPTER I—ESTABLISHMENT AND ADMINISTRATION

§528. Development and administration of renewable surface resources for multiple use and sustained yield of products and services; Congressional declaration of policy and purpose
[MUSYA §1]

It is the policy of the Congress that the national forests are established and shall be administered for outdoor recreation, range, timber, watershed, and wildlife and fish purposes. The purposes of sections 528 to 531 of this title are declared to be supplemental to, but not in derogation of, the purposes for which the national forests were established as set forth in section 475 of this title. Nothing herein shall be construed as affecting the jurisdiction or responsibilities of the several States with respect to wildlife and fish on the national forests. Nothing herein shall be construed so as to affect the use or administration of the mineral resources of national forest lands or to affect the use or administration of Federal lands not within national forests.

§529. Authorization of development and administration; consideration to relative values of resources; areas of wilderness
[MUSYA §2]

The Secretary of Agriculture is authorized and directed to develop and administer the renewable surface resources of the national forests for multiple use and sustained yield of the several products and services obtained therefrom. In the administration of the national forests due consideration shall be given to the relative values of the various resources in particular areas. The establishment and maintenance of areas of wilderness are consistent with the purposes and provisions of sections 528 to 531 of this title.

§530. Cooperation for purposes of development and administration with State and local governmental agencies and others
[MUSYA §3]

In the effectuation of sections 528 to 531 of this title the Secretary of Agriculture is authorized to cooperate with interested State and local governmental agencies and others in the development and management of the national forests.

§531. Definitions
[MUSYA §4]

As used in sections 528 to 531 of this title the following terms shall have the following meanings:

(a) "Multiple use" means: The management of all the various renewable surface resources of the national forests so that they are utilized in the combination that will best meet the needs of the American people; making the most judicious use of the land for some or all of these resources or related services over areas large enough to provide sufficient latitude for periodic adjustments in use to conform to changing needs and conditions; that some land will be used for less than all of the resources; and harmonious and coordinated management of the various resources, each with the other, without impairment of the productivity of the land, with consideration being given to the relative values of the various resources, and not necessarily the combination of uses that will give the greatest dollar return or the greatest unit output.

(b) "Sustained yield of the several products and services" means the achievement and maintenance in perpetuity of a high-level annual or regular periodic output of the various renewable resources of the national forests without impairment of the productivity of the land.

Forest and Rangeland Renewable Resources Planning Act

16 U.S.C. §§1600 to 1614

CHAPTER 36—FOREST AND RANGELAND RENEWABLE RESOURCES PLANNING

SUBCHAPTER I—PLANNING

SUBCHAPTER I—PLANNING

§1600. Congressional findings
[FRRRPA §2]

The Congress finds that —

(1) the management of the Nation's renewable resources is highly complex and the uses, demand for, and supply of the various resources are subject to change over time;

(2) the public interest is served by the Forest Service, Department of Agriculture, in cooperation with other agencies, assessing the Nation's renewable resources, and developing and preparing a national renewable resource program, which is periodically reviewed and updated;

(3) to serve the national interest, the renewable resource program must be based on a comprehensive assessment of present and anticipated uses, demand for, and supply of renewable resources from the Nation's public and private forests and rangelands, through analysis of environmental and economic impacts, coordination of multiple use and sustained yield opportunities as provided in the Multiple-Use Sustained-Yield Act of 1960 (74 Stat. 215; 16 U.S.C. §§528-531), and public participation in the development of the program;

(4) the new knowledge derived from coordinated public and private research programs will promote a sound technical and ecological base for effective management, use, and protection of the Nation's renewable resources;

(5) inasmuch as the majority of the Nation's forests and rangeland is under private, State, and local governmental management and the Nation's major capacity to produce goods and services is based on these nonfederally managed renewable resources, the Federal Government should be a catalyst to encourage and assist these owners in the efficient long-term use and improvement of these lands and their renewable resources consistent with the principles of sustained yield and multiple use;

(6) the Forest Service, by virtue of its statutory authority for management of the National Forest System, research and cooperative programs, and its role as an agency in the Department of Agriculture, has both a responsibility and an opportunity to be a leader in assuring that the Nation maintains a natural resource conservation posture that will meet the requirements of our people in perpetuity; and

(7) recycled timber product materials are as much a part of our renewable forest resources as are the trees from which they originally came, and in order to extend our timber and timber fiber resources and reduce pressures for timber production

from Federal lands, the Forest Service should expand its research in the use of recycled and waste timber product materials, develop techniques for the substitution of these secondary materials for primary materials, and promote and encourage the use of recycled timber product materials.

§1601. Renewable Resource Assessment [FRRRPA §3(A)]

(a) Preparation by Secretary of Agriculture; time of preparation, updating and contents — In recognition of the vital importance of America's renewable resources of the forest, range, and other associated lands to the Nation's social and economic well-being, and of the necessity for a long term perspective in planning and undertaking related national renewable resource programs administered by the Forest Service, the Secretary of Agriculture (referred to in this subchapter as "the Secretary") shall prepare a Renewable Resource Assessment (hereinafter called the "Assessment"). The Assessment shall be prepared not later than December 31, 1975, and shall be updated during 1979 and each tenth year thereafter, and shall include but not be limited to —

(1) an analysis of present and anticipated uses, demand for, and supply of the renewable resources, with consideration of the international resource situation, and an emphasis of pertinent supply and demand and price relationship trends;

(2) an inventory, based on information developed by the Forest Service and other Federal agencies, of present and potential renewable resources, and an evaluation of opportunities for improving their yield of tangible and intangible goods and services, together with estimates of investment costs and direct and indirect returns to the Federal Government;

(3) a description of Forest Service programs and responsibilities in research, cooperative programs and management of the National Forest System, their interrelationships, and the relationship of these programs and responsibilities to public and private activities;

(4) a discussion of important policy considerations, laws, regulations, and other factors expected to influence and affect significantly the use, ownership, and management of forest, range, and other associated lands;

(5) an analysis of the potential effects of global climate change on the condition of renewable resources on the forests and rangelands of the United States; and

(6) an analysis of the rural and urban forestry opportunities to mitigate the buildup of atmospheric carbon dioxide and reduce the risk of global climate change.

(b) Omitted

(c) Contents of Assessments — The Secretary shall report in the 1979 and subsequent Assessments on:

(1) the additional fiber potential in the National Forest System including, but not restricted to, forest mortality, growth, salvage potential, potential increased forest products sales, economic constraints, alternate markets, contract considerations, and other multiple use considerations;

(2) the potential for increased utilization of forest and wood product wastes in the National Forest System and on other lands, and of urban wood wastes and wood product recycling, including recommendations to the Congress for actions which would lead to increased utilization of material now being wasted both in the forests and in manufactured products; and

(3) the milling and other wood fiber product fabrication facilities and their location in the United States, noting the public and private forested areas that supply such facilities, assessing the degree of utilization into product form of harvested trees by such facilities, and setting forth the technology appropriate to the facilities to improve utilization either individually or in aggregate units of harvested trees and to reduce wasted wood fibers. The Secretary shall set forth a program to encourage the adoption by these facilities of these technologies for improving wood fiber utilization.

(d) * Public involvement; consultation with governmental departments and agencies — In developing the reports required under subsection (c) of this section, the Secretary shall provide opportunity for public involvement and shall consult with other interested governmental departments and agencies.

(d) * Congressional policy of multiple use sustained yield management; examination and certification of lands; estimate of appropriations necessary for reforestation and other treatment; budget requirements; authorization of appropriations [NB* *two subsection (d)s were enacted.*]

(1) It is the policy of the Congress that all forested lands in the National Forest System shall be maintained in appropriate forest cover with species of trees, degree of stocking, rate of growth, and conditions of stand designed to secure the maximum benefits of multiple use sustained yield management in accordance with land management plans. Accordingly, the Secretary is directed to identify and report to the Congress annually at the time of submission of the President's budget together with the annual report provided for under section 1606(c) of this title, beginning with submission of the President's budget for fiscal year 1978, the amount and location by forests and States and by productivity class, where practicable, of all lands in the National Forest System where objectives of land management plans indicate the need to reforest areas that have been cut-over or otherwise denuded or deforested, and all lands with stands of trees that are not growing at their best potential rate of

growth. All national forest lands treated from year to year shall be examined after the first and third growing seasons and certified by the Secretary in the report provided for under this subsection as to stocking rate, growth rate in relation to potential and other pertinent measures. Any lands not certified as satisfactory shall be returned to the backlog and scheduled for prompt treatment. The level and types of treatment shall be those which secure the most effective mix of multiple use benefits.

(2) Notwithstanding the provisions of section 1607 of this title, the Secretary shall annually for eight years following October 22, 1976, transmit to the Congress in the manner provided in this subsection an estimate of the sums necessary to be appropriated, in addition to the funds available from other sources, to replant and otherwise treat an acreage equal to the acreage to be cut over that year, plus a sufficient portion of the backlog of lands found to be in need of treatment to eliminate the backlog within the eight-year period. After such eight-year period, the Secretary shall transmit annually to the Congress an estimate of the sums necessary to replant and otherwise treat all lands being cut over and maintain planned timber production on all other forested lands in the National Forest System so as to prevent the development of a backlog of needed work larger than the needed work at the beginning of the fiscal year. The Secretary's estimate of sums necessary, in addition to the sums available under other authorities, for accomplishment of the reforestation and other treatment of National Forest System lands under this section shall be provided annually for inclusion in the President's budget and shall also be transmitted to the Speaker of the House and the President of the Senate together with the annual report provided for under section 1606(c) of this title at the time of submission of the President's budget to the Congress beginning with the budget for fiscal year 1978. The sums estimated as necessary for reforestation and other treatment shall include moneys needed to secure seed, grow seedlings, prepare sites, plant trees, thin, remove deleterious growth and underbrush, build fence to exclude livestock and adverse wildlife from regeneration areas and otherwise establish and improve growing forests to secure planned production of trees and other multiple use values.

(3) Effective for the fiscal year beginning October 1, 1977, and each fiscal year thereafter, there is hereby authorized to be appropriated for the purpose of reforesting and treating lands in the National Forest System $200,000,000 annually to meet requirements of this subsection (d). All sums appropriated for the purposes of this subsection shall be available until expended.

(e) Report on herbicides and pesticides — The Secretary shall submit an annual report to the Congress on the amounts, types, and uses of herbicides and pesticides used in the National Forest System, including the beneficial or adverse effects of such uses.

§1602. Renewable Resource Program; preparation by Secretary of Agriculture and transmittal to President; purpose and development of program; time of preparation, updating and contents

[FRRRPA §4]

In order to provide for periodic review of programs for management and administration of the National Forest System, for research, for cooperative State and private Forest Service programs, and for conduct of other Forest Service activities in relation to the findings of the Assessment, the Secretary, utilizing information available to the Forest Service and other agencies within the Department of Agriculture, including data prepared pursuant to section 1010a of Title 7, shall prepare and transmit to the President a recommended Renewable Resource Program (hereinafter called the "Program"). The Program transmitted to the President may include alternatives, and shall provide in appropriate detail for protection, management, and development of the National Forest System, including forest development roads and trails; for cooperative Forest Service programs; and for research. The Programs shall be developed in accordance with principles set forth in the Multiple-Use Sustained-Yield Act of June 12, 1960 (74 Stat. 215; 16 U.S.C. §§528-531), and the National Environmental Policy Act of 1969 (83 Stat. 852) [42 U.S.C. §§4321 et seq.]. The Program shall be prepared not later than December 31, 1975, to cover the four-year period beginning October 1, 1976, and at least each of the four fiscal decades next following such period, and shall be updated no later than during the first half of the fiscal year ending September 30, 1980, and the first half of each fifth fiscal year thereafter to cover at least each of the four fiscal decades beginning next after such updating. The Program shall include, but not be limited to —

(1) an inventory of specific needs and opportunities for both public and private program investments. The inventory shall differentiate between activities which are of a capital nature and those which are of an operational nature;

(2) specific identification of Program outputs, results anticipated, and benefits associated with investments in such a manner that the anticipated costs can be directly compared with the total related benefits and direct and indirect returns to the Federal Government;

(3) a discussion of priorities for accomplishment of inventoried Program opportunities, with specified costs, outputs, results, and benefits;

(4) a detailed study of personnel requirements as needed to implement and monitor existing and ongoing programs; and

(5) Program recommendations which —

(A) evaluate objectives for the major Forest Service programs in order that multiple-use and sustained-yield relationships among and within the renewable resources can be determined;

(B) explain the opportunities for owners of forests and rangeland to participate in programs to improve and enhance the condition of the land and the renewable resource products therefrom;

(C) recognize the fundamental need to protect and, where appropriate, improve the quality of soil, water, and air resources;

(D) state national goals that recognize the interrelationships between and interdependence within the renewable resources;

(E) evaluate the impact of the export and import of raw logs upon domestic timber supplies and prices; and

(F) account for the effects of global climate change on forest and rangeland conditions, including potential effects on the geographic ranges of species, and on forest and rangeland products.

§1603. National Forest System resources inventories; development, maintenance, and updating by Secretary as part of Assessment
[FRRRPA §5]

As a part of the Assessment, the Secretary shall develop and maintain on a continuing basis a comprehensive and appropriately detailed inventory of all National Forest System lands and renewable resources. This inventory shall be kept current so as to reflect changes in conditions and identify new and emerging resources and values.

§1604. National Forest System land and resource management plans
[FRRRPA §6]

(a) Development, maintenance, and revision by Secretary as part of program; coordination — As a part of the Program provided for by section 1602 of this title, the Secretary shall develop, maintain, and, as appropriate, revise land and resource management plans for units of the National Forest System, coordinated with the land and resource management planning processes of State and local governments and other Federal agencies.

(b) Criteria — In the development and maintenance of land management plans for use on units of the National Forest System, the Secretary shall use a systematic interdisciplinary approach to achieve integrated consideration of physical, biological, economic, and other sciences.

(c) Incorporation of standards and guidelines by Secretary; time of completion; progress reports; existing management plans — The Secretary shall begin to incorporate the standards and guidelines required by this section in plans for units of the National Forest System as soon as practicable after October 22, 1976 and shall attempt to complete such incorporation for all such units by no later than September 30, 1985. The Secretary shall report to the Congress on the progress of such incorporation in the annual report required by section 1606(c) of this title. Until such time as a unit of the National Forest System is managed under plans developed in accordance with this subchapter, the management of such unit may continue under existing land and resource management plans.

(d) Public participation and consultation

(1) In general — The Secretary shall provide for public participation in the development, review, and revision of land management plans including, but not limited to, making the plans or revisions available to the public at convenient locations in the vicinity of the affected unit for a period of at least three months before final adoption, during which period the Secretary shall publicize and hold public meetings or comparable processes at locations that foster public participation in the review of such plans or revisions.

(2) No additional consultation required after approval of land management plans

(A) In general — Except as provided in subparagraph (B), notwithstanding any other provision of law, the Secretary shall not be required to engage in consultation under this section or any other provision of law (including section 7 of Public Law 93-205 (16 U.S.C. 1536) and section 402.16 of title 50, Code of Federal Regulations (or a successor regulation)) with respect to —

(i) the listing of a species as threatened or endangered, or a designation of critical habitat pursuant to Public Law 93-205 (16 U.S.C. 1531 et seq.), if a land management plan has been adopted by the Secretary as of the date of listing or designation; and

(ii) any provision of a land management plan adopted as described in clause (i).

(B) Exception — Subparagraph (A) shall not apply if —

(i) 15 years have passed since the date on which the Secretary adopted the land management plan described in clause (i) of that subparagraph; and

(ii) 5 years have passed since the date of enactment of this section, or the date of the listing of a species as threatened or endangered for a species known to occur on the unit or the designation of critical habitat within the unit as described in clause (i) of that subparagraph, whichever is later.

(C) Effect of paragraph — Nothing in this paragraph affects any applicable requirement of the Secretary to consult with the head of any other Federal department or agency —

(i) regarding any project carried out, or proposed to be carried out, to implement a land management plan pursuant to Public Law 93-205 (16 U.S.C. 1531 et seq.), including any requirement to consult regarding the consideration of cumulative impacts of completed, ongoing, and planned projects; or

(ii) with respect to —

(I) the development of a modification to a land management plan; or

(II) an amendment or revision to a land management plan in accordance with paragraph (4) or (5) of subsection (f).

(e) Required assurances — In developing, maintaining, and revising plans for units of the National Forest System pursuant to this section, the Secretary shall assure that such plans —

(1) provide for multiple use and sustained yield of the products and services obtained therefrom in accordance with the Multiple-Use Sustained-Yield Act of 1960 [16 U.S.C. §§528-531], and, in particular, include coordination of outdoor recreation, range, timber, watershed, wildlife and fish, and wilderness; and

(2) determine forest management systems, harvesting levels, and procedures in the light of all of the uses set forth in subsection (c)(1) of this section, the definition of the terms "multiple use" and "sustained yield" as provided in the Multiple-Use Sustained-Yield Act of 1960, and the availability of lands and their suitability for resource management.

(f) Required provisions — Plans developed in accordance with this section shall —

(1) form one integrated plan for each unit of the National Forest System, incorporating in one document or one set of documents, available to the public at convenient locations, all of the features required by this section;

(2) be embodied in appropriate written material, including maps and other descriptive documents, reflecting proposed and possible actions, including the planned timber sale program and the proportion of probable methods of timber harvest within the unit necessary to fulfill the plan;

(3) be prepared by an interdisciplinary team. Each team shall prepare its plan based on inventories of the applicable resources of the forest;

(4) be amended in any manner whatsoever after final adoption after public notice, and, if such amendment would result in a significant change in such plan, in accordance with the provisions

of subsections (e) and (f) of this section and public involvement comparable to that required by subsection (d) of this section; and

(5) be revised (A) from time to time when the Secretary finds conditions in a unit have significantly changed, but at least every fifteen years, and (B) in accordance with the provisions of subsections (e) and (f) of this section and public involvement comparable to that required by subsection (d) of this section.

(g) Promulgation of regulations for development and revision of plans; environmental considerations; resource management guidelines; guidelines for land management plans — As soon as practicable, but not later than two years after October 22, 1976, the Secretary shall in accordance with the procedures set forth in section 553 of Title 5 promulgate regulations, under the principles of the Multiple-Use Sustained-Yield Act of 1960 [16 U.S.C. §§528 to 531], that set out the process for the development and revision of the land management plans, and the guidelines and standards prescribed by this subsection. The regulations shall include, but not be limited to —

(1) specifying procedures to insure that land management plans are prepared in accordance with the National Environmental Policy Act of 1969 [42 U.S.C. §4321 *et seq.*], including, but not limited to, direction on when and for what plans an environmental impact statement required under section 102(2)(C) of that Act [42 U.S.C. §4332(2)(C)] shall be prepared;

(2) specifying guidelines which —

(A) require the identification of the suitability of lands for resource management;

(B) provide for obtaining inventory data on the various renewable resources, and soil and water, including pertinent maps, graphic material, and explanatory aids; and

(C) provide for methods to identify special conditions or situations involving hazards to the various resources and their relationship to alternative activities;

(3) specifying guidelines for land management plans developed to achieve the goals of the Program which —

(A) insure consideration of the economic and environmental aspects of various systems of renewable resource management, including the related systems of silviculture and protection of forest resources, to provide for outdoor recreation (including wilderness), range, timber, watershed, wildlife, and fish;

(B) provide for diversity of plant and animal communities based on the suitability and capability of the specific land area in order to meet overall multiple-use objectives, and within the multiple-use objectives of a land management plan adopted pursuant to this section, provide, where appropriate, to the degree practicable, for steps to be taken to preserve the diversity of tree species similar to that existing in the region controlled by the plan;

(C) insure research on and (based on continuous monitoring and assessment in the field) evaluation of the effects of each management system to the end that it will not produce substantial and permanent impairment of the productivity of the land;

(D) permit increases in harvest levels based on intensified management practices, such as reforestation, thinning, and tree improvement if (i) such practices justify increasing the harvests in accordance with the Multiple-Use Sustained-Yield Act of 1960, and (ii) such harvest levels are decreased at the end of each planning period if such practices cannot be successfully implemented or funds are not received to permit such practices to continue substantially as planned;

(E) insure that timber will be harvested from National Forest System lands only where —

(i) soil, slope, or other watershed conditions will not be irreversibly damaged;

(ii) there is assurance that such lands can be adequately restocked within five years after harvest;

(iii) protection is provided for streams, streambanks, shorelines, lakes, wetlands, and other bodies of water from detrimental changes in water temperatures, blockages of water courses, and deposits of sediment, where harvests are likely to seriously and adversely affect water conditions or fish habitat; and

(iv) the harvesting system to be used is not selected primarily because it will give the greatest dollar return or the greatest unit output of timber; and

(F) insure that clearcutting, seed tree cutting, shelterwood cutting, and other cuts designed to regenerate an even-aged stand of timber will be used as a cutting method on National Forest System lands only where —

(i) for clearcutting, it is determined to be the optimum method, and for other such cuts it is determined to be appropriate, to meet the objectives and requirements of the relevant land management plan;

(ii) the interdisciplinary review as determined by the Secretary has been completed and the potential environmental, biological, esthetic, engineering, and economic impacts on each advertised sale area have been assessed, as well as the consistency of the sale with the multiple use of the general area;

(iii) cut blocks, patches, or strips are shaped and blended to the extent practicable with the natural terrain;

(iv) there are established according to geographic areas, forest types, or other suitable classifications the maximum size limits for areas to be cut in one harvest operation, including provision to exceed the established limits after appropriate public notice and review by the responsible Forest Service officer one level above the Forest Service officer who normally would approve the harvest proposal: *Provided*, That such limits shall not apply to the size of areas harvested as a result of natural catastrophic conditions such as fire, insect and disease attack, or windstorm; and

(v) such cuts are carried out in a manner consistent with the protection of soil, watershed, fish, wildlife, recreation, and esthetic resources, and the regeneration of the timber resource.

(h) Scientific committee to aid in promulgation of regulations; termination; revision committees; clerical and technical assistance; compensation of committee members

(1) In carrying out the purposes of subsection (g) of this section, the Secretary of Agriculture shall appoint a committee of scientists who are not officers or employees of the Forest Service. The committee shall provide scientific and technical advice and counsel on proposed guidelines and procedures to assure that an effective interdisciplinary approach is proposed and adopted. The committee shall terminate upon promulgation of the regulations, but the Secretary may, from time to time, appoint similar committees when considering revisions of the regulations. The views of the committees shall be included in the public information supplied when the regulations are proposed for adoption.

(2) Clerical and technical assistance, as may be necessary to discharge the duties of the committee, shall be provided from the personnel of the Department of Agriculture.

(3) While attending meetings of the committee, the members shall be entitled to receive compensation at a rate of $100 per diem, including traveltime, and while away from their homes or regular places of business they may be allowed travel expenses, including per diem in lieu of subsistence, as authorized by section 5703 of Title 5 for persons in the Government service employed intermittently.

(i) Consistency of resource plans, permits, contracts, and other instruments with land management plans; revision — Resource plans and permits, contracts, and other instruments for the use and occupancy of National Forest System lands shall be consistent with the land management plans. Those resource plans and permits, contracts, and other such instruments currently in existence shall be revised as soon as practicable to be made consistent with such plans. When land management plans are revised, resource plans and permits, contracts, and other instruments, when necessary, shall be revised as soon as practicable. Any revision in present or future permits, contracts, and other instruments made pursuant to this section shall be subject to valid existing rights.

(j) Effective date of land management plans and revisions — Land management plans and revisions shall become effective thirty days after completion of public participation and publication of notification by the Secretary as required under subsection (d) of this section.

(k) Development of land management plans — In developing land management plans pursuant to this subchapter, the Secretary shall identify lands within the management area which are not suited for timber production, considering physical, economic, and other pertinent factors to the extent feasible, as determined by the Secretary, and shall assure that, except for salvage sales or sales necessitated to protect other multiple-use values, no timber harvesting shall occur on such lands for a period of 10 years. Lands once identified as unsuitable for timber production shall continue to be treated for reforestation purposes, particularly with regard to the protection of other multiple-use values. The Secretary shall review his decision to classify these lands as not suited for timber production at least every 10 years and shall return these lands to timber production whenever he determines that conditions have changed so that they have become suitable for timber production.

(*l*) Program evaluation; process for estimating long-term costs and benefits; summary of data included in annual report — The Secretary shall —

(1) formulate and implement, as soon as practicable, a process for estimating long-terms costs and benefits to support the program evaluation requirements of this subchapter. This process shall include requirements to provide information on a representative sample basis of estimated expenditures associated with the reforestation, timber stand improvement, and sale of timber from the National Forest System, and shall provide a comparison of these expenditures to the return to the Government resulting from the sale of timber; and

(2) include a summary of data and findings resulting from these estimates as a part of the annual report required pursuant to section 1606(c) of this title, including an identification on a representative sample basis of those advertised timber sales made below the estimated expenditures for such timber as determined by the above cost process; and

(m) Establishment of standards to ensure culmination of mean annual increment of growth; silvicultural practices; salvage harvesting; exceptions — The Secretary shall establish —

(1) standards to insure that, prior to harvest, stands of trees throughout the National Forest System shall generally have reached the culmination of mean annual increment of growth (calculated on the basis of cubic measurement or other methods of calculation at the discretion of the Secretary): *Provided,* That these standards shall not preclude the use of sound silvicultural practices, such as thinning or other stand improvement measures: *Provided further,* That these standards shall not preclude the Secretary from salvage or sanitation harvesting of timber stands which are substantially damaged by fire, windthrow or other catastrophe, or which are in imminent danger from insect or disease attack; and

(2) exceptions to these standards for the harvest of particular species of trees in management units after consideration has been given to the multiple uses of the forest including, but not limited to, recreation, wildlife habitat, and range and after completion of public participation processes utilizing the procedures of subsection (d) of this section.

§1605. Protection, use and management of renewable resources on non-Federal lands; utilization of Assessment, surveys and Program by Secretary to assist States, etc.
[FRRRPA §7]

The Secretary may utilize the Assessment, resource surveys, and Program prepared pursuant to this subchapter to assist States and other organizations in proposing the planning for the protection, use, and management of renewable resources on non-Federal land.

§1606. Budget requests by President for Forest Service activities
[FRRRPA §8]

(a) Transmittal to Speaker of House and President of Senate of Assessment, Program and Statement of Policy used in framing requests; time for transmittal; implementation by President of programs established under Statement of Policy unless Statement subsequently disapproved by Congress; time for disapproval — On the date Congress first convenes in 1976 and thereafter following each updating of the Assessment and the Program, the President shall transmit to the Speaker of the House of Representatives and the President of the Senate, when Congress convenes, the Assessment as set forth in section 1601 of this title and the Program as set forth in section 1602 of this title, together with a detailed Statement of Policy intended to be used in framing budget requests by that Administration for Forest Service activities for the five- or ten-year program period beginning during the term of such Congress for such further action deemed appropriate by the Congress. Following the transmission of such Assessment, Program, and Statement of Policy, the

President shall, subject to other actions of the Congress, carry out programs already established by law in accordance with such Statement of Policy or any subsequent amendment or modification thereof approved by the Congress, unless, before the end of the first period of ninety calendar days of continuous session of Congress after the date on which the President of the Senate and the Speaker of the House are recipients of the transmission of such Assessment, Program, and Statement of Policy, either House adopts a resolution reported by the appropriate committee of jurisdiction disapproving the Statement of Policy. For the purpose of this subsection, the continuity of a session shall be deemed to be broken only by an adjournment sine die, and the days on which either House is not in session because of an adjournment of more than three days to a day certain shall be excluded in the computation of the ninety-day period. Notwithstanding any other provision of this subchapter, Congress may revise or modify the Statement of Policy transmitted by the President, and the revised or modified Statement of Policy shall be used in framing budget requests.

(b) Contents of requests to show extent of compliance of projected programs and policies with policies approved by Congress; requests not conforming to approved policies; expenditure of appropriations — Commencing with the fiscal budget for the year ending September 30, 1977, requests presented by the President to the Congress governing Forest Service activities shall express in qualitative and quantitative terms the extent to which the programs and policies projected under the budget meet the policies approved by the Congress in accordance with subsection (a) of this section. In any case in which such budget so presented recommends a course which fails to meet the policies so established, the President shall specifically set forth the reason or reasons for requesting the Congress to approve the lesser programs or policies presented. Amounts appropriated to carry out the policies approved in accordance with subsection (a) of this section shall be expended in accordance with the Congressional Budget and Impoundment Control Act of 1974.

(c) Annual evaluation report to Congress of Program components; time of submission; status of major research programs; application of findings; status, etc., of cooperative forestry assistance programs and activities — For the purpose of providing information that will aid Congress in its oversight responsibilities and improve the accountability of agency expenditures and activities, the Secretary shall prepare an annual report which evaluates the component elements of the Program required to be prepared by section 1602 of this title which shall be furnished to the Congress at the time of submission of the annual fiscal budget commencing with the third fiscal year after August 17, 1974. With regard to the research component of the program, the report shall include, but not be limited to, a description

of the status of major research programs, significant findings, and how these findings will be applied in National Forest System management and in cooperative State and private Forest Service programs. With regard to the cooperative forestry assistance part of the Program, the report shall include, but not be limited to, a description of the status, accomplishments, needs, and work backlogs for the programs and activities conducted under the Cooperative Forestry Assistance Act of 1978 [16 U.S.C. §2101 *et seq.*].

(d) Required contents of annual evaluation report — These annual evaluation reports shall set forth progress in implementing the Program required to be prepared by section 1602 of this title, together with accomplishments of the Program as they relate to the objectives of the Assessment. Objectives should be set forth in qualitative and quantitative terms and accomplishments should be reported accordingly. The report shall contain appropriate measurements of pertinent costs and benefits. The evaluation shall assess the balance between economic factors and environmental quality factors. Program benefits shall include, but not be limited to, environmental quality factors such as esthetics, public access, wildlife habitat, recreational and wilderness use, and economic factors such as the excess of cost savings over the value of foregone benefits and the rate of return on renewable resources.

(e) Additional required contents of annual evaluation report — The reports shall indicate plans for implementing corrective action and recommendations for new legislation where warranted.

(f) Form of annual evaluation report — The reports shall be structured for Congress in concise summary form with necessary detailed data in appendices.

§1606a. Reforestation Trust Fund

(a) Establishment; source of funds — There is established in the Treasury of the United States a trust fund, to be known as the Reforestation Trust Fund (hereinafter in this section referred to as the "Trust Fund"), consisting of such amounts as are transferred to the Trust Fund under subsection (b)(1) of this section and any interest earned on investment of amounts in the Trust Fund under subsection (c)(2) of this section.

(b) Transfer of certain tariff receipts to Trust Fund; fiscal year limitation; quarterly transfers; adjustment of estimates

(1) Subject to the limitation in paragraph (2), the Secretary of the Treasury shall transfer to the Trust Fund an amount equal to the sum of the tariffs received in the Treasury after January 1, 1989, under headings 4401 through 4412 and subheadings 4418.50.00, 4418.90.20, 4420.10.00, 4420.90.80, 4421.90.10 through 4421.90.20, and 4421.90.70 of chapter 44, subheadings 6808.00.00 and 6809.11.00 of chapter 68 and subheading 9614.10.00 of chapter 96 of the Harmonized Tariff Schedule of the United States.

(2) The Secretary shall not transfer more than $30,000,000 to the Trust Fund for any fiscal year.

(3) The amounts required to be transferred to the Trust Fund under paragraph (1) shall be transferred at least quarterly from the general fund of the Treasury to the Trust Fund on the basis of estimates made by the Secretary of the Treasury. Proper adjustment shall be made in the amounts subsequently transferred to the extent prior estimates were in excess of or less than the amounts required to be transferred.

(c) Report to Congress; printing as House and Senate document; investments; sale and redemption of obligations; credits for Trust Fund

(1) It shall be the duty of the Secretary of the Treasury to hold the Trust Fund, and (after consultation with the Secretary of Agriculture) to report to the Congress each year on the financial condition and the results of the operations of the Trust Fund during the preceding fiscal year and on its expected condition and operations during the next fiscal year. Such report shall be printed as both a House and Senate document of the session of the Congress to which the report is made.

(2)(A) It shall be the duty of the Secretary of the Treasury to invest such portion of the Trust Fund as is not, in his judgment, required to meet current withdrawals. Such investments may be made only in interest-bearing obligations of the United States or in obligations guaranteed as to both principal and interest by the United States. For such purpose, such obligations may be acquire (i) on original issue at the issue price, or (ii) by purchase of outstanding obligations at the market price. The purposes for which obligations of the United States may be issued under chapter 31 of Title 31 are hereby extended to authorize the issuance at par of special obligations exclusively to the Trust Fund. Such special obligations shall bear interest at a rate equal to the average rate of interest, computed as to the end of the calendar month next preceding the date of such issue, borne by all marketable interest-bearing obligations of the United States then forming a part of the Public Debt; except that where such average rate is not a multiple of one-eighth of 1 percent, the rate of interest of such special obligations shall be the multiple of one-eighth of 1 percent next lower than such average rate. Such special obligations shall be issued only if the Secretary of the Treasury determines that the purchase of other interest-bearing obligations of the United States, or of obligations guaranteed as to both principal and interest by the United States on original issue or at the market price, is not in the public interest.

(B) Any obligation acquired by the Trust Fund (except special obligations issued exclusively to the Trust Fund) may be sold by the Secretary of the Treasury at the market price,

and such special obligations may be redeemed at par plus accrued interest.

(C) The interest on, and the proceeds from the sale or redemption of, any obligations held in the Trust Fund shall be credited to and form a part of the Trust Fund.

(d) Obligations from Trust Fund — The Secretary of Agriculture is hereafter authorized to obligate such sums as are available in the Trust Fund (including any amounts not obligated in previous fiscal years) for —

(1) reforestation and timber stand improvement as specified in section 1601(d) of this title and other forest stand improvement activities to enhance forest health and reduce hazardous fuel loads of forest stands in the National Forest System; and

(2) properly allocable administrative costs of the Federal Government for the activities specified above.

§1607. National Forest System renewable resources; development and administration by Secretary in accordance with multiple use and sustained yield concepts for products and services; target year for operational posture of resources; budget requests
[FRRRPA §9]

The Secretary shall take such action as will assure that the development and administration of the renewable resources of the National Forest System are in full accord with the concepts for multiple use and sustained yield of products and services as set forth in the Multiple-Use Sustained-Yield Act of 1960 [16 U.S.C. §§528-531]. To further these concepts, the Congress hereby sets the year 2000 as the target year when the renewable resources of the National Forest System shall be in an operating posture whereby all backlogs of needed treatment for their restoration shall be reduced to a current basis and the major portion of planned intensive multiple-use sustained-yield management procedures shall be installed and operating on an environmentally-sound basis. The annual budget shall contain requests for funds for an orderly program to eliminate such backlogs: *Provided,* That when the Secretary finds that (1) the backlog of areas that will benefit by such treatment has been eliminated, (2) the cost of treating the remainder of such area exceeds the economic and environmental benefits to be secured from their treatment, or (3) the total supplies of the renewable resources of the United States are adequate to meet the future needs of the American people, the budget request for these elements of restoration may be adjusted accordingly.

§1608. National Forest Transportation System
[FRRRPA §10]

(a) Congressional declaration of policy; time for development; method of financing; financing of forest development roads — The Congress declares that the installation of a proper system of transportation to service the National Forest System, as is provided for in sections 532 to 538 of this title, shall be carried forward in time to meet anticipated needs on an economical and environmentally sound basis, and the method chosen for financing the construction and maintenance of the transportation system should be such as to enhance local, regional, and national benefits: *Provided*, That limitations on the level of obligations for construction of forest roads by timber purchasers shall be established in annual appropriation Acts.

(b) Construction of temporary roadways in connection with timber contracts, and other permits or leases — Unless the necessity for a permanent road is set forth in the forest development road system plan, any road constructed on land of the National Forest System in connection with a timber contract or other permit or lease shall be designed with the goal of reestablishing vegetative cover on the roadway and areas where the vegetative cover has been disturbed by the construction of the road, within ten years after the termination of the contract, permit, or lease either through artificial or natural means. Such action shall be taken unless it is later determined that the road is needed for use as a part of the National Forest Transportation System.

(c) Standards of roadway construction — Roads constructed on National Forest System lands shall be designed to standards appropriate for the intended uses, considering safety, cost of transportation, and impacts on land and resources.

§1609. National Forest System
[FRRRPA §11]

(a) Congressional declaration of constituent elements and purposes; lands etc., included within; return of lands to public domain — Congress declares that the National Forest System consists of units of federally owned forest, range, and related lands throughout the United States and its territories, united into a nationally significant system dedicated to the long-term benefit for present and future generations, and that it is the purpose of this section to include all such areas into one integral system. The "National Forest System" shall include all national forest lands reserved or withdrawn from the public domain of the United States, all national forest lands acquired through purchase, exchange, donation, or other means, the national grasslands and land utilization projects administered under Title III of the Bankhead-Jones Farm Tenant Act [7 U.S.C. §§1010 *et seq.*], and other lands, waters, or interests therein which are administered by the Forest Service or are designated for administration through the Forest Service as a part of the system. Notwithstanding the provisions of section 473 of this title, no land now or hereafter reserved or withdrawn from the public domain as national forests pursuant to section 471 of this title, or any act supplementary to and amendatory thereof, shall be returned to the public domain except by an act of Congress.

(b) Location of Forest Service offices — The on-the-ground field offices, field supervisory offices, and regional offices of the Forest Service shall be so situated as to provide the optimum level of convenient, useful services to the public, giving priority to the maintenance and location of facilities in rural areas and towns near the national forest and Forest Service program locations in accordance with the standards in section 2204b-1(b) of Title 7.

§1610. Implementation of provisions by Secretary; utilization of information and data of other organizations; avoidance of duplication of planning, etc.; "renewable resources" defined
[FRRRPA §12]

In carrying out this subchapter, the Secretary shall utilize information and data available from other Federal, State, and private organizations and shall avoid duplication and overlap of resource assessment and program planning efforts of other Federal agencies. The term "renewable resources" shall be construed to involve those matters within the scope of responsibilities and authorities of the Forest Service on August 17, 1974 and on the date of enactment of any legislation amendatory or supplementary thereto.

§1611. Timber
[FRRRPA §13]

(a) Limitations on removal; variations in allowable sale quantity; public participation — The Secretary shall limit the sale of timber from each national forest to a quantity equal to or less than a quantity which can be removed from such forest annually in perpetuity on a sustained-yield basis: *Provided*, That, in order to meet overall multiple-use objectives, the Secretary may establish an allowable sale quantity for any decade which departs from the projected long-term average sale quantity that would otherwise be established: *Provided further*, That any such planned departure must be consistent with the multiple-use management objectives of the land management plan. Plans for variations in the allowable sale quantity must be made with public participation as required by section 1604(d) of this title. In addition, within any decade, the Secretary may sell a quantity in excess of the annual allowable sale quantity established pursuant to this section in the case of any national forest so long as the average sale quantities of timber from such national forest over the decade covered by the plan do not exceed such quantity limitation. In those cases where a forest has less than two hundred thousand acres of commercial forest land, the Secretary may use two or more forests for purposes of determining the sustained yield.

(b) Salvage harvesting — Nothing in subsection (a) of this section shall prohibit the Secretary from salvage or sanitation harvesting of timber stands which are substantially damaged by fire, windthrow, or other catastrophe, or which are in imminent danger from insect or disease attack. The Secretary may either substitute such timber for timber that would otherwise be sold under the plan or, if not feasible, sell such timber over and above the plan volume.

§1612. Public participation
[FRRRPA §14]

(a) Adequate notice and opportunity to comment — In exercising his authorities under this subchapter and other laws applicable to the Forest Service, the Secretary, by regulation, shall establish procedures, including public hearings where appropriate, to give the Federal, State, and local governments and the public adequate notice and an opportunity to comment upon the formulation of standards, criteria, and guidelines applicable to Forest Service programs.

(b) Advisory boards — In providing for public participation in the planning for and management of the National Forest System, the Secretary, pursuant to the Federal Advisory Committee Act (86 Stat. 770) and other applicable law, shall establish and consult such advisory boards as he deems necessary to secure full information and advice on the execution of his responsibilities. The membership of such boards shall be representative of a cross section of groups interested in the planning for and management of the National Forest System and the various types of use and enjoyment of the lands thereof.

§1613. Promulgation of regulations
[FRRRPA §15]

The Secretary of Agriculture shall prescribe such regulations as he determines necessary and desirable to carry out the provisions of this subchapter.

§1614. Severability
[FRRRPA §16]

If any provision of this subchapter or the application thereof to any person or circumstances is held invalid, the validity of the remainder of this subchapter and of the application of such provision to other persons and circumstances shall not be affected thereby.

Federal Land Policy and Management Act

43 U.S.C. §§1701 to 1787

SUBCHAPTER VI—DESIGNATED MANAGEMENT AREAS

SUBCHAPTER I—GENERAL PROVISIONS

§1701. Congressional declaration of policy
[FLPMA §102]

(a) The Congress declares that it is the policy of the United States that —

(1) the public lands be retained in Federal ownership, unless as a result of the land use planning procedure provided for in this Act, it is determined that disposal of a particular parcel will serve the national interest;

(2) the national interest will be best realized if the public lands and their resources are periodically and systematically inventoried and their present and future use is projected through a land use planning process coordinated with other Federal and State planning efforts;

(3) public lands not previously designated for any specific use and all existing classifications of public lands that were effected by executive action or statute before October 21, 1976, be reviewed in accordance with the provisions of this Act;

(4) the Congress exercise its constitutional authority to withdraw or otherwise designate or dedicate Federal lands for specified purposes and that Congress delineate the extent to which the Executive may withdraw lands without legislative action;

(5) in administering public land statutes and exercising discretionary authority granted by them, the Secretary be required to establish comprehensive rules and regulations after considering the views of the general public; and to structure adjudication procedures to assure adequate third party participation, objective administrative review of initial decisions, and expeditious decision-making;

(6) judicial review of public land adjudication decisions be provided by law;

(7) goals and objectives be established by law as guidelines for public land use planning, and that management be on the basis of multiple use and sustained yield unless otherwise specified by law;

(8) the public lands be managed in a manner that will protect the quality of scientific, scenic, historical, ecological, environmental, air and atmospheric, water resource, and archeological values; that, where appropriate, will preserve and protect certain public lands in their natural condition; that will provide food and habitat for fish and wildlife and domestic animals; and that will provide for outdoor recreation and human occupancy and use;

(9) the United States receive fair market value of the use of the public lands and their resources unless otherwise provided for by statute;

(10) uniform procedures for any disposal of public land, acquisition of non-Federal land for public purposes, and the exchange of such lands be established by statute, requiring each disposal, acquisition, and exchange to be consistent with the prescribed mission of the department or agency involved, and reserving to the Congress review of disposals in excess of a specified acreage;

(11) regulations and plans for the protection of public land areas of critical environmental concern be promptly developed;

(12) the public lands be managed in a manner which recognizes the Nation's need for domestic sources of minerals, food, timber, and fiber from the public lands including implementation of the Mining and Minerals Policy Act of 1970 (84 Stat. 1876, 30 U.S.C. §21a) as it pertains to the public lands; and

(13) the Federal Government should, on a basis equitable to both the Federal and local taxpayer, provide for payments to compensate States and local governments for burdens created as a result of the immunity of Federal lands from State and local taxation.

(b) The policies of this Act shall become effective only as specific statutory authority for their implementation is enacted by this Act or by subsequent legislation and shall then be construed as supplemental to and not in derogation of the purposes for which public lands are administered under other provisions of law.

§1702. Definitions
[FLPMA §103]

Without altering in any way the meaning of the following terms as used in any other statute, whether or not such statute is referred to in, or amended by, this Act, as used in this Act —

(a) The term "areas of critical environmental concern" means areas within the public lands where special management attention is required (when such areas are developed or used or where no development is required) to protect and prevent irreparable damage to important historic, cultural, or scenic values, fish and wildlife resources or other natural systems or processes, or to protect life and safety from natural hazards.

(b) The term "holder" means any State or local governmental entity, individual, partnership, corporation, association, or other business entity receiving or using a right-of-way under subchapter V of this chapter.

(c) The term "multiple use" means the management of the public lands and their various resource values so that they are utilized in the combination that will best meet the present and future needs of the American people; making the most judicious use of the land for some or all of these resources or related services over areas large enough to provide sufficient latitude for periodic adjustments in use to conform to changing needs and conditions; the use of some land for less than all of the resources; a combination of balanced and diverse resource uses that takes into account the long-term needs of future generations for renewable and nonrenewable resources, including, but not limited to, recreation, range, timber, minerals, watershed, wildlife and fish, and natural scenic, scientific and historical values; and harmonious and coordinated management of the various resources without permanent impairment of the productivity of the land and the quality of the environment with consideration being given to the relative values of the resources and not necessarily to the combination of uses that will give the greatest economic return or the greatest unit output.

(d) The term "public involvement" means the opportunity for participation by affected citizens in rulemaking, decisionmaking, and planning with respect to the public lands, including public meetings or hearings held at locations near the affected lands, or advisory mechanisms, or such other procedures as may be necessary to provide public comment in a particular instance.

(e) The term "public lands" means any land and interest in land owned by the United States within the several States and administered by the Secretary of the Interior through the Bureau of Land Management, without regard to how the United States acquired ownership, except —

(1) lands located on the Outer Continental Shelf; and

(2) lands held for the benefit of Indians, Aleuts, and Eskimos.

(f) The term "right-of-way" includes an easement, lease, permit, or license to occupy, use, or traverse public lands granted for the purpose listed in subchapter V of this chapter.

(g) The term "Secretary", unless specifically designated otherwise, means the Secretary of the Interior.

(h) The term "sustained yield" means the achievement and maintenance in perpetuity of a high-level annual or regular periodic output of the various renewable resources of the public lands consistent with multiple use.

(i) The term "wilderness" as used in section 1782 of this title shall have the same meaning as it does in section 1131(c) of Title 16.

(j) The term "withdrawal" means withholding an area of Federal land from settlement, sale, location, or entry, under some or all of the general land laws, for the purpose of limiting activities under those laws in order to maintain other public values in the area or reserving the area for a particular public purpose or program; or transferring jurisdiction over an area of Federal land, other than "property" governed by the Federal Property and Administrative Services Act, as amended (40 U.S.C. §472) from one department, bureau or agency to another department, bureau or agency.

(k) An "allotment management plan" means a document prepared in consultation with the lessees or permittees involved, which applies to livestock operations on the public lands or on lands within National Forests in the eleven contiguous Western States and which:

(1) prescribes the manner in, and extent to, which livestock operations will be conducted in order to meet the multiple-use, sustained-yield, economic and other needs and objectives as determined for the lands by the Secretary concerned; and

(2) describes the type, location, ownership, and general specifications for the range improvements to be installed and maintained on the lands to meet the livestock grazing and other objectives of land management; and

(3) contains such other provisions relating to livestock grazing and other objectives found by the Secretary concerned to be consistent with the provisions of this Act and other applicable law.

(*l*) The term "principal or major uses" includes, and is limited to, domestic livestock grazing, fish and wildlife development and utilization, mineral exploration and production, rights-of-way, outdoor recreation, and timber production.

(m) The term "department" means a unit of the executive branch of the Federal Government which is headed by a member of the President's Cabinet and the term "agency" means a unit of the executive branch of the Federal Government which is not under the jurisdiction of a head of a department.

(n) The term "Bureau" means the Bureau of Land Management.

(o) The term "eleven contiguous Western States" means the States of Arizona, California, Colorado, Idaho, Montana, Nevada, New Mexico, Oregon, Utah, Washington, and Wyoming.

(p) The term "grazing permit and lease" means any document authorizing use of public lands or lands in National Forests in the eleven contiguous western States for the purpose of grazing domestic livestock.

§1703. Cooperative action and sharing of resources

In fiscal year 2012 and each fiscal year thereafter, the Secretaries of the Interior and Agriculture, subject to annual review of Congress, may establish programs involving the land management agencies referred to in this section to conduct projects, planning, permitting, leasing, contracting and other activities, either jointly or on behalf of one another; may co-locate in Federal offices and facilities leased by an agency of either Department; and promulgate special rules as needed to test the feasibility of issuing unified permits, applications, and leases. The Secretaries of the Interior and Agriculture may make reciprocal delegations of their respective authorities, duties and responsibilities in support of the 'Service First' initiative agency-wide to promote customer service and efficiency. Nothing herein shall alter, expand or limit the applicability of any public law or regulation to lands administered by the Bureau of Land Management, National Park Service, Fish and Wildlife Service, or the Forest Service. To facilitate the sharing of resources under the Service First initiative, the Secretaries of the Interior and Agriculture may make transfers of funds and reimbursement of funds on an annual basis, including transfers and reimbursements for multi-year projects, except that this authority may not be used to circumvent requirements and limitations imposed on the use of funds.

SUBCHAPTER II—LAND USE PLANNING AND LAND ACQUISITION AND DISPOSITION

§1711. Continuing inventory and identification of public lands; preparation and maintenance

[FLPMA §201]

(a) The Secretary shall prepare and maintain on a continuing basis an inventory of all public lands and their resource and other values (including, but not limited to, outdoor recreation and scenic values), giving priority to areas of critical environmental concern. This inventory shall be kept current so as to reflect changes in conditions and to identify new and emerging resource and other values. The preparation and maintenance of such inventory or the identification of such areas shall not, of itself, change or prevent change of the management or use of public lands.

(b) As funds and manpower are made available, the Secretary shall ascertain the boundaries of the public lands; provide means of public identification thereof including, where appropriate, signs and maps; and provide State and local governments with data from the inventory for the purpose of planning and regulating the uses of non-Federal lands in proximity of such public lands.

§1712. Land use plans
[FLPMA §202]

(a) **Development, maintenance, and revision by Secretary** — The Secretary shall, with public involvement and consistent with the terms and conditions of this Act, develop, maintain, and, when appropriate, revise land use plans which provide by tracts or areas for the use of the public lands. Land use plans shall be developed for the public lands regardless of whether such lands previously have been classified, withdrawn, set aside, or otherwise designated for one or more uses.

(b) **Coordination of plans for National Forest System lands with Indian land use planning and management programs for purposes of development and revision** — In the development and revision of land use plans, the Secretary of Agriculture shall coordinate land use plans for lands in the National Forest System with the land use planning and management programs of and for Indian tribes by, among other things, considering the policies of approved tribal land resource management programs.

(c) **Criteria for development and revision**—In the development and revision of land use plans, the Secretary shall —

(1) use and observe the principles of multiple use and sustained yield set forth in this and other applicable law;

(2) use a systematic interdisciplinary approach to achieve integrated consideration of physical, biological, economic, and other sciences;

(3) give priority to the designation and protection of areas of critical environmental concern;

(4) rely, to the extent it is available, on the inventory of the public lands, their resources, and other values;

(5) consider present and potential uses of the public lands;

(6) consider the relative scarcity of the values involved and the availability of alternative means (including recycling) and sites for realization of those values;

(7) weigh long-term benefits to the public against short-term benefits;

(8) provide for compliance with applicable pollution control laws, including State and Federal air, water, noise, or other pollution standards or implementation plans; and

(9) to the extent consistent with the laws governing the administration of the public lands, coordinate the land use inventory, planning, and management activities of or for such lands with the land use planning and management programs of other Federal departments and agencies and of the States and local governments within which the lands are located, including, but not limited to, the statewide outdoor recreation plans developed under the Act of September 3, 1964 (78 Stat. 897), as amended [16 U.S.C. §§460l-4 *et seq.*], and of or

for Indian tribes by, among other things, considering the policies of approved State and tribal land resource management programs. In implementing this directive, the Secretary shall, to the extent he finds practical, keep apprised of State, local, and tribal land use plans; assure that consideration is given to those State, local, and tribal plans that are germane in the development of land use plans for public lands; assist in resolving, to the extent practical, inconsistencies between Federal and non-Federal Government plans, and shall provide for meaningful public involvement of State and local government officials, both elected and appointed, in the development of land use programs, land use regulations, and land use decisions for public lands, including early public notice of proposed decisions which may have a significant impact on non-Federal lands. Such officials in each State are authorized to furnish advice to the Secretary with respect to the development and revision of land use plans, land use guidelines, land use rules, and land use regulations for the public lands within such State and with respect to such other land use matters as may be referred to them by him. Land use plans of the Secretary under this section shall be consistent with State and local plans to the maximum extent he finds consistent with Federal law and the purposes of this Act.

(d) Review and inclusion of classified public lands; review of existing land use plans; modification and termination of classifications — Any classification of public lands or any land use plan in effect on October 21, 1976, is subject to review in the land use planning process conducted under this section, and all public lands, regardless of classification, are subject to inclusion in any land use plan developed pursuant to this section. The Secretary may modify or terminate any such classification consistent with such land use plans.

(e) Management decisions for implementation of developed or revised plans — The Secretary may issue management decisions to implement land use plans developed or revised under this section in accordance with the following:

(1) Such decisions, including but not limited to exclusions (that is, total elimination) of one or more of the principal or major uses made by a management decision shall remain subject to reconsideration, modification, and termination through revision by the Secretary or his delegate, under the provisions of this section, of the land use plan involved.

(2) Any management decision or action pursuant to a management decision that excludes (that is, totally eliminates) one or more of the principal or major uses for two or more years with respect to a tract of land of one hundred thousand acres or more shall be reported by the Secretary to the House of Representatives and the Senate. If within ninety days from the giving of such notice (exclusive of days on which either House has adjourned for more than three consecutive days), the Congress adopts a concurrent resolution of nonapproval of the management decision or action, then the management decision or action shall be promptly terminated by the Secretary. If the committee to which a resolution has been referred during the said ninety day period, has not reported it at the end of thirty calendar days after its referral, it shall be in order to either discharge the committee from further consideration of such resolution or to discharge the committee from consideration of any other resolution with respect to the management decision or action. A motion to discharge may be made only by an individual favoring the resolution, shall be highly privileged (except that it may not be made after the committee has reported such a resolution), and debate thereon shall be limited to not more than one hour, to be divided equally between those favoring and those opposing the resolution. An amendment to the motion shall not be in order, and it shall not be in order to move to reconsider the vote by which the motion was agreed to or disagreed to. If the motion to discharge is agreed to or disagreed to, the motion may not be made with respect to any other resolution with respect to the same management decision or action. When the committee has reprinted, or has been discharged from further consideration of a resolution, it shall at any time thereafter be in order (even though a previous motion to the same effect has been disagreed to) to move to proceed to the consideration of the resolution. The motion shall be highly privileged and shall not be debatable. An amendment to the motion shall not be in order, and it shall not be in order to move to reconsider the vote by which the motion was agreed to or disagreed to.

(3) Withdrawals made pursuant to section 1714 of this title may be used in carrying out management decisions, but public lands shall be removed from or restored to the operation of the Mining Law of 1872, as amended (R.S. 2318-2352; 30 U.S.C. §§21 *et seq.*) or transferred to another department, bureau, or agency only by withdrawal action pursuant to section 1714 of this title or other action pursuant to applicable law: *Provided*, That nothing in this section shall prevent a wholly owned Government corporation from acquiring and holding rights as a citizen under the Mining Law of 1872.

(f) Procedures applicable to formulation of plans and programs for public land management — The Secretary shall allow an opportunity for public involvement and by regulation shall establish procedures, including public hearings where appropriate, to give Federal, State, and local governments and the public, adequate notice and opportunity to comment upon and participate in the formulation of plans and programs relating to the management of the public lands.

§1713. Sales of public land tracts
[FLPMA §203]

(a) Criteria for disposal; excepted lands — A tract of the public lands (except land in units of the National Wilderness Preservation System, National Wild and Scenic Rivers Systems, and National System of Trails) may be sold under this Act where, as a result of land use planning required under section 1712 of this title, the Secretary determines that the sale of such tract meets the following disposal criteria:

(1) such tract because of its location or other characteristics is difficult and uneconomic to manage as part of the public lands, and is not suitable for management by another Federal department or agency; or

(2) such tract was acquired for a specific purpose and the tract is no longer required for that or any other Federal purpose; or

(3) disposal of such tract will serve important public objectives, including but not limited to, expansion of communities and economic development, which cannot be achieved prudently or feasibly on land other than public land and which outweigh other public objectives and values, including, but not limited to, recreation and scenic values, which would be served by maintaining such tract in Federal ownership.

(b) Conveyance of land of agricultural value and desert in character — Where the Secretary determines that land to be conveyed under clause (3) of subsection (a) of this section is of agricultural value and is desert in character, such land shall be conveyed either under the sale authority of this section or in accordance with other existing law.

(c) Congressional approval procedures applicable to tracts in excess of two thousand five hundred acres — Where a tract of the public lands in excess of two thousand five hundred acres has been designated for sale, such sale may be made only after the end of the ninety days (not counting days on which the House of Representatives or the Senate has adjourned for more than three consecutive days) beginning on the day the Secretary has submitted notice of such designation to the Senate and the House of Representatives, and then only if the Congress has not adopted a concurrent resolution stating that such House does not approve of such designation. If the committee to which a resolution has been referred during the said ninety day period, has not reported it at the end of thirty calendar days after its referral, it shall be in order to either discharge the committee from further consideration of such resolution or to discharge the committee from consideration of any other resolution with respect to the designation. A motion to discharge may be made only by an individual favoring the resolution, shall be highly privileged (except that it may not be made after the committee has reported such a resolution), and debate thereon shall be limited to not more than one hour, to be divided equally between those favoring and those opposing the resolution. An amendment to the motion shall not be in order, and it shall not be in order to move to reconsider the vote by which the motion was agreed to or disagreed to. If the motion to discharge is agreed to or disagreed to, the motion may not be made with respect to any other resolution with respect to the same designation. When the committee has reprinted, or has been discharged from further consideration of a resolution, it shall at any time thereafter be in order (even though a previous motion to the same effect has been disagreed to) to move to proceed to the consideration of the resolution. The motion shall be highly privileged and shall not be debatable. An amendment to the motion shall not be in order, and it shall not be in order to move to reconsider the vote by which the motion was agreed to or disagreed to.

(d) Sale price — Sales of public lands shall be made at a price not less than their fair market value as determined by the Secretary.

(e) Maximum size of tracts — The Secretary shall determine and establish the size of tracts of public lands to be sold on the basis of the land use capabilities and development requirements of the lands; and, where any such tract which is judged by the Secretary to be chiefly valuable for agriculture is sold, its size shall be no larger than necessary to support a family-sized farm.

(f) Competitive bidding requirements — Sales of public lands under this section shall be conducted under competitive bidding procedures to be established by the Secretary. However, where the Secretary determines it necessary and proper in order (1) to assure equitable distribution among purchasers of lands, or (2) to recognize equitable considerations or public policies, including but not limited to, a preference to users, he may sell those lands with modified competitive bidding or without competitive bidding. In recognizing public policies, the Secretary shall give consideration to the following potential purchasers:

(1) the State in which the land is located;

(2) the local government entities in such State which are in the vicinity of the land;

(3) adjoining landowners;

(4) individuals; and

(5) any other person.

(g) Acceptance or rejection of offers to purchase — The Secretary shall accept or reject, in writing, any offer to purchase made through competitive bidding at his invitation no later than thirty days after the receipt of such offer or, in the case of a tract in excess of two thousand five hundred acres, at the end of thirty days after the end of the ninety-day period provided in subsection (c) of this section, whichever is later, unless the offeror waives his right to a decision within such thirty-day period. Prior to the expiration of such periods the Secretary may refuse to accept any offer or may withdraw any land or interest in land from sale under this section when he determines that consummation of the sale would not be consistent with this Act or other applicable law.

§1714. Withdrawals of lands
[FLPMA §204]

(a) Authorization and limitation; delegation of authority — On and after the effective date of this Act the Secretary is authorized to make, modify, extend, or revoke withdrawals but only in accordance with the provisions and limitations of this section. The Secretary may delegate this withdrawal authority only to individuals in the Office of the Secretary who have been appointed by the President, by and with the advice and consent of the Senate.

(b) Application and procedures applicable subsequent to submission of application

(1) Within thirty days of receipt of an application for withdrawal, and whenever he proposes a withdrawal on his own motion, the Secretary shall publish a notice in the Federal Register stating that the application has been submitted for filing or the proposal has been made and the extent to which the land is to be segregated while the application is being considered by the Secretary. Upon publication of such notice the land shall be segregated from the operation of the public land laws to the extent specified in the notice. The segregative effect of the application shall terminate upon (a) rejection of the application by the Secretary, (b) withdrawal of lands by the Secretary, or (c) the expiration of two years from the date of the notice.

(2) The publication provisions of this subsection are not applicable to withdrawals under subsection (e) hereof.

(c) Congressional approval procedures applicable to withdrawals aggregating five thousand acres or more

(1) On and after October 21, 1976, a withdrawal aggregating five thousand acres or more may be made (or such a withdrawal or any other withdrawal involving in the aggregate five thousand acres or more which terminates after such date of approval may be extended) only for a period of not more than twenty years by the Secretary on his own motion or upon request by a department or agency head. The Secretary shall notify both Houses of Congress of such a withdrawal no later than its effective date and the withdrawal shall terminate and become ineffective at the end of ninety days (not counting days on which the Senate or the House of Representatives has adjourned for more than three consecutive days) beginning on the day notice of such withdrawal has been submitted to the Senate and the House of Representatives, if the Congress has adopted a concurrent resolution stating that such House does not approve the withdrawal. If the committee to which a resolution has been referred during the said ninety day period, has not reported it at the end of thirty calendar days after its referral, it shall be in order to either discharge the committee from further consideration of such resolution or to discharge the committee from consideration of any other resolution with respect to the Presidential recommendation. A motion to discharge may be made only by an individual favoring the resolution, shall be highly privileged (except that it may not be made after the committee has reported such a resolution), and debate thereon shall be limited to not more than one hour, to be divided equally between those favoring and those opposing the resolution. An amendment to the motion shall not be in order, and it shall not be in order to move to reconsider the vote by which the motion was agreed to or disagreed to. If the motion to discharge is agreed to or disagreed to, the motion may not be made with respect to any other resolution with respect to the same Presidential recommendation. When the committee has reprinted, or has been discharged from further consideration of a resolution, it shall at any time thereafter be in order (even though a previous motion to the same effect has been disagreed to) to move to proceed to the consideration of the resolution. The motion shall be highly privileged and shall not be debatable. An amendment to the motion shall not be in order, and it shall not be in order to move to reconsider the vote by which the motion was agreed to or disagreed to.

(2) With the notices required by subsection (c)(1) of this section and within three months after filing the notice under subsection (e) of this section, the Secretary shall furnish to the committees —

(1) a clear explanation of the proposed use of the land involved which led to the withdrawal;

(2) an inventory and evaluation of the current natural resource uses and values of the site and adjacent public and nonpublic land and how it appears they will be affected by the proposed use, including particularly aspects of use that might cause degradation of the environment, and also the economic impact of the change in use on individuals, local communities, and the Nation;

(3) an identification of present users of the land involved, and how they will be affected by the proposed use;

(4) an analysis of the manner in which existing and potential resource uses are incompatible with or in conflict with the proposed use, together with a statement of the provisions to be made for continuation or termination of existing uses, including an economic analysis of such continuation or termination;

(5) an analysis of the manner in which such lands will be used in relation to the specific requirements for the proposed use;

(6) a statement as to whether any suitable alternative sites are available (including cost estimates) for the proposed use or for uses such a withdrawal would displace;

(7) a statement of the consultation which has been or will be had with other Federal departments and agencies, with regional, State, and local government bodies, and with other appropriate individuals and groups;

(8) a statement indicating the effect of the proposed uses, if any, on State and local government interests and the regional economy;

(9) a statement of the expected length of time needed for the withdrawal;

(10) the time and place of hearings and of other public involvement concerning such withdrawal;

(11) the place where the records on the withdrawal can be examined by interested parties; and

(12) a report prepared by a qualified mining engineer, engineering geologist, or geologist which shall include but not be limited to information on: general geology, known mineral deposits, past and present mineral production, mining claims, mineral leases, evaluation of future mineral potential, present and potential market demands.

(d) Withdrawals aggregating less than five thousand acres; procedure applicable — A withdrawal aggregating less than five thousand acres may be made under this subsection by the Secretary on his own motion or upon request by a department or an agency head —

(1) for such period of time as he deems desirable for a resource use; or

(2) for a period of not more than twenty years for any other use, including but not limited to use for administrative sites, location of facilities, and other proprietary purposes; or

(3) for a period of not more than five years to preserve such tract for a specific use then under consideration by the Congress.

(e) Emergency withdrawals; procedure applicable; duration — When the Secretary determines, or when the Committee on Natural Resources of the House of Representatives or the Committee on Energy and Natural Resources of the Senate notifies the Secretary, that an emergency situation exists and that extraordinary measures must be taken to preserve values that would otherwise be lost, the Secretary notwithstanding the provisions of subsections (c)(1) and (d) of this section, shall immediately make a withdrawal and file notice of such emergency withdrawal with both of those Committees. Such emergency withdrawal shall be effective when made but shall last only for a period not to exceed three years and may not be extended except under the provisions of subsection (c)(1) or (d), whichever is applicable, and (b)(1) of this section. The information required in subsection (c)(2) of this subsection shall be furnished the committees within three months after filing such notice.

(f) Review of existing withdrawals and extensions; procedure applicable to extensions;

duration — All withdrawals and extensions thereof, whether made prior to or after October 21, 1976, having a specific period shall be reviewed by the Secretary toward the end of the withdrawal period and may be extended or further extended only upon compliance with the provisions of subsection (c)(1) or (d) of this section, whichever is applicable, and only if the Secretary determines that the purpose for which the withdrawal was first made requires the extension, and then only for a period no longer than the length of the original withdrawal period. The Secretary shall report on such review and extensions to the Committee on Natural Resources of the House of Representatives and the Committee on Energy and Natural Resources of the Senate.

(g) Processing and adjudication of existing applications — All applications for withdrawal pending on October 21, 1976 shall be processed and adjudicated to conclusion within fifteen years of October 21, 1976, in accordance with the provisions of this section. The segregative effect of any application not so processed shall terminate on that date.

(h) Public hearing required for new withdrawals — All new withdrawals made by the Secretary under this section (except an emergency withdrawal made under subsection (e) of this section) shall be promulgated after an opportunity for a public hearing.

(i) Consent for withdrawal of lands under administration of department or agency other than Department of the Interior — In the case of lands under the administration of any department or agency other than the Department of the Interior, the Secretary shall make, modify, and revoke withdrawals only with the consent of the head of the department or agency concerned, except when the provisions of subsection (e) of this section apply.

(j) Applicability of other Federal laws withdrawing lands as limiting authority — The Secretary shall not make, modify, or revoke any withdrawal created by Act of Congress; make a withdrawal which can be made only by Act of Congress; modify or revoke any withdrawal creating national monuments under the Act of June 8, 1906 (34 Stat. 225; 16 U.S.C. §§431-433); or modify, or revoke any withdrawal which added lands to the National Wildlife Refuge System prior to October 21, 1976, or which thereafter adds lands to that System under the terms of this Act. Nothing in this Act is intended to modify or change any provision of the Act of February 27, 1976 (90 Stat. 199; 16 U.S.C. §668dd(a)).

(k) Authorization of appropriations for processing applications — There is hereby authorized to be appropriated the sum of $10,000,000 for the purpose of processing withdrawal applications pending on the effective date of this Act, to be available until expended.

(*l*) Review of existing withdrawals in certain States; procedure applicable for determination of future status of lands; authorization of appropriations

(1) The Secretary shall, within fifteen years of October 21, 1976, review withdrawals existing on

October 21, 1976, in the States of Arizona, California, Colorado, Idaho, Montana, Nevada, New Mexico, Oregon, Utah, Washington, and Wyoming of (1) all Federal lands other than withdrawals of the public lands administered by the Bureau of Land Management and of lands which, on October 21, 1976, were part of Indian reservations and other Indian holdings, the National Forest System, the National Park System, the National Wildlife Refuge System, other lands administered by the Fish and Wildlife Service or the Secretary through the Fish and Wildlife Service, the National Wild and Scenic Rivers System, and the National System of Trails; and (2) all public lands administered by the Bureau of Land Management and of lands in the National Forest System (except those in wilderness areas, and those areas formally identified as primitive or natural areas or designated as national recreation areas) which closed the lands to appropriation under the Mining Law of 1872 (17 Stat. 91, as amended; 30 U.S.C. §§22 *et seq.*) or to leasing under the Mineral Leasing Act of 1920 (41 Stat. 437, as amended; 30 U.S.C. §§181 *et seq.*).

(2) In the review required by paragraph (1) of this subsection, the Secretary shall determine whether, and for how long, the continuation of the existing withdrawal of the lands would be, in his judgment, consistent with the statutory objectives of the programs for which the lands were dedicated and of the other relevant programs. The Secretary shall report his recommendations to the President, together with statements of concurrence or nonconcurrence submitted by the heads of the departments or agencies which administer the lands. The President shall transmit this report to the President of the Senate and the Speaker of the House of Representatives, together with his recommendations for action by the Secretary, or for legislation. The Secretary may act to terminate withdrawals other than those made by Act of the Congress in accordance with the recommendations of the President unless before the end of ninety days (not counting days on which the Senate and the House of Representatives has adjourned for more than three consecutive days) beginning on the day the report of the President has been submitted to the Senate and the House of Representatives the Congress has adopted a concurrent resolution indicating otherwise. If the committee to which a resolution has been referred during the said ninety day period, has not reported it at the end of thirty calendar days after its referral, it shall be in order to either discharge the committee from further consideration of such resolution or to discharge the committee from consideration of any other resolution with respect to the Presidential recommendation. A motion to discharge may be made only by an individual favoring the resolution, shall be highly privileged (except that it may not be made after the committee has reported such a resolution), and debate thereon shall be limited to not more

than one hour, to be divided equally between those favoring and those opposing the resolution. An amendment to the motion shall not be in order, and it shall not be in order to move to reconsider the vote by which the motion was agreed to or disagreed to. If the motion to discharge is agreed to or disagreed to, the motion may not be made with respect to any other resolution with respect to the same Presidential recommendation. When the committee has reprinted, or has been discharged from further consideration of a resolution, it shall at any time thereafter be in order (even though a previous motion to the same effect has been disagreed to) to move to proceed to the consideration of the resolution. The motion shall be highly privileged and shall not be debatable. An amendment to the motion shall not be in order, and it shall not be in order to move to reconsider the vote by which the motion was agreed to or disagreed to.

(3) There are hereby authorized to be appropriated not more than $10,000,000 for the purpose of paragraph (1) of this subsection to be available until expended to the Secretary and to the heads of other departments and agencies which will be involved.

§1715. Acquisitions of public lands and access over non-Federal lands to National Forest System units

[FLPMA §205]

(a) Authorization and limitations on authority of Secretary of the Interior and Secretary of Agriculture — Notwithstanding any other provisions of law, the Secretary, with respect to the public lands and the Secretary of Agriculture, with respect to the acquisition of access over non-Federal lands to units of the National Forest System, are authorized to acquire pursuant to this Act by purchase, exchange, donation, or eminent domain, lands or interests therein: *Provided,* That with respect to the public lands, the Secretary may exercise the power of eminent domain only if necessary to secure access to public lands, and then only if the lands so acquired are confined to as narrow a corridor as is necessary to serve such purpose. Nothing in this subsection shall be construed as expanding or limiting the authority of the Secretary of Agriculture to acquire land by eminent domain within the boundaries of units of the National Forest System.

(b) Conformity to departmental policies and land-use plan of acquisitions — Acquisitions pursuant to this section shall be consistent with the mission of the department involved and with applicable departmental land-use plans.

(c) Status of lands and interests in lands upon acquisition by Secretary of the Interior; transfers to Secretary of Agriculture of lands and interests in lands acquired within National Forest System boundaries — Except as provided in subsection (e) of this section, lands and interests in lands acquired by the Secretary pursuant to this section or section 1716 of this title shall, upon acceptance of title, become public lands, and, for the administration of public land laws not repealed by this Act, shall remain public lands. If such acquired lands or interests in lands are located within the exterior boundaries of a grazing district established pursuant to section 315 of this title, they shall become a part of that district. Lands and interests in lands acquired pursuant to this section which are within boundaries of the National Forest System may be transferred to the Secretary of Agriculture and shall then become National Forest System lands and subject to all the laws, rules, and regulations applicable thereto.

(d) Status of lands and interests in lands upon acquisition by Secretary of Agriculture — Lands and interests in lands acquired by the Secretary of Agriculture pursuant to this section shall, upon acceptance of title, become National Forest System lands subject to all the laws, rules, and regulations applicable thereto.

(e) Status and administration of lands acquired in exchange for lands revested in or reconveyed to United States — Lands acquired by the Secretary pursuant to this section or section 1716 of this title in exchange for lands which were revested in the United States pursuant to the provisions of the Act of June 9, 1916 (39 Stat. 218) or reconveyed to the United States pursuant to the provisions of the Act of February 26, 1919 (40 Stat. 1179), shall be considered for all purposes to have the same status as, and shall be administered in accordance with the same provisions of law applicable to, the revested or reconveyed lands exchanged for the lands acquired by the Secretary.

§1716. Exchanges of public lands or interests therein within the National Forest System [FLPMA §206]

(a) Authorization and limitations on authority of Secretary of the Interior and Secretary of Agriculture — A tract of public land or interests therein may be disposed of by exchange by the Secretary under this Act and a tract of land or interests therein within the National Forest System may be disposed of by exchange by the Secretary of Agriculture under applicable law where the Secretary concerned determines that the public interest will be well served by making that exchange: *Provided*, That when considering public interest the Secretary concerned shall give full consideration to better Federal land management and the needs of State and local people, including needs for lands for the economy, community expansion, recreation areas, food, fiber, minerals, and fish and wildlife and the Secretary concerned finds that the values and the objectives which Federal lands or interests to be conveyed may serve if retained in Federal ownership are not more than the values of the non-Federal lands or interests and the public objectives they could serve if acquired.

(b) Implementation requirements; cash equalization waiver — In exercising the exchange authority granted by subsection (a) of this section or by section 1715(a) of this title, the Secretary concerned may accept title to any non-Federal land or interests therein in exchange for such land, or interests therein which he finds proper for transfer out of Federal ownership and which are located in the same State as the non-Federal land or interest to be acquired. For the purposes of this subsection, unsurveyed school sections which, upon survey by the Secretary, would become State lands, shall be considered as "non-Federal lands". The values of the lands exchanged by the Secretary under this Act and by the Secretary of Agriculture under applicable law relating to lands within the National Forest System either shall be equal, or if they are not equal, the values shall be equalized by the payment of money to the grantor or to the Secretary concerned as the circumstances require so long as payment does not exceed 25 per centum of the total value of the lands or interests transferred out of Federal ownership. The Secretary concerned and the other party or parties involved in the exchange may mutually agree to waive the requirement for the payment of money to equalize values where the Secretary concerned determines that the exchange will be expedited thereby and that the public interest will be better served by such a waiver of cash equalization payments and where the amount to be waived is no more than 3 per centum of the value of the lands being transferred out of Federal ownership or $15,000, whichever is less, except that the Secretary of Agriculture shall not agree to waive any such requirement for payment of money to the United States. The Secretary concerned shall try to reduce the amount of the payment of money to as small an amount as possible.

(c) Status of lands acquired upon exchange by Secretary of the Interior — Lands acquired by the Secretary by exchange under this section which are within the boundaries of any unit of the National Forest System, National Park System, National Wildlife Refuge System, National Wild and Scenic Rivers System, National Trails System, National Wilderness Preservation System, or any other system established by Act of Congress, or the boundaries of the California Desert Conservation Area, or the boundaries of any national conservation area or national recreation area established by Act of Congress, upon acceptance of title by the United States shall immediately be reserved for and become a part of the unit or area within which they are located, without further action by the Secretary, and shall thereafter be managed in accordance with all laws, rules, and regulations applicable to such unit or area.

(d) Appraisal of land; submission to arbitrator; determination to proceed or withdraw from exchange; use of other valuation process; suspension of deadlines

(1) No later than ninety days after entering into an agreement to initiate an exchange of land or interests therein pursuant to this Act or other applicable law, the Secretary concerned and other party or parties involved in the exchange shall

arrange for appraisal (to be completed within a time frame and under such terms as are negotiated by the parties) of the lands or interests therein involved in the exchange in accordance with subsection (f) of this section.

(2) If within one hundred and eighty days after the submission of an appraisal or appraisals for review and approval by the Secretary concerned, the Secretary concerned and the other party or parties involved cannot agree to accept the findings of an appraisal or appraisals, the appraisal or appraisals shall be submitted to an arbitrator appointed by the Secretary from a list of arbitrators submitted to him by the American Arbitration Association for arbitration to be conducted in accordance with the real estate valuation arbitration rules of the American Arbitration Association. Such arbitration shall be binding for a period of not to exceed two years on the Secretary concerned and the other party or parties involved in the exchange insofar as concerns the value of the lands which were the subject of the appraisal or appraisals.

(3) Within thirty days after the completion of the arbitration, the Secretary concerned and the other party or parties involved in the exchange shall determine whether to proceed with the exchange, modify the exchange to reflect the findings of the arbitration or any other factors, or to withdraw from the exchange. A decision to withdraw from the exchange may be made by either the Secretary concerned or the other party or parties involved.

(4) Instead of submitting the appraisal to an arbitrator, as provided in paragraph (2) of this section, the Secretary concerned and the other party or parties involved in an exchange may mutually agree to employ a process of bargaining or some other process to determine the values of the properties involved in the exchange.

(5) The Secretary concerned and the other party or parties involved in an exchange may mutually agree to suspend or modify any of the deadlines contained in this subsection.

(e) Simultaneous issue of patents or titles — Unless mutually agreed otherwise by the Secretary concerned and the other party or parties involved in an exchange pursuant to this Act or other applicable law, all patents or titles to be issued for land or interests therein to be acquired by the Federal Government and lands or interest therein to be transferred out of Federal ownership shall be issued simultaneously after the Secretary concerned has taken any necessary steps to assure that the United States will receive acceptable title.

(f) New rules and regulations; appraisal rules and regulations; "costs and other responsibilities or requirements" defined

(1) Within one year after August 20, 1988, the Secretaries of the Interior and Agriculture shall promulgate new and comprehensive rules and regulations governing exchanges of land and interests therein pursuant to this Act and other applicable law. Such rules and regulations shall fully reflect the changes in law made by subsections (d) through (i) of this section and shall include provisions pertaining to appraisals of lands and interests therein involved in such exchanges.

(2) The provisions of the rules and regulations issued pursuant to paragraph (1) of this subsection governing appraisals shall reflect nationally recognized appraisal standards, including, to the extent appropriate, the Uniform Appraisal Standards for Federal Land Acquisitions: *Provided, however,* That the provisions of such rules and regulations shall —

(A) ensure that the same nationally approved appraisal standards are used in appraising lands or interest therein being acquired by the Federal Government and appraising lands or interests therein being transferred out of Federal ownership; and

(B) with respect to costs or other responsibilities or requirements associated with land exchanges —

(i) recognize that the parties involved in an exchange may mutually agree that one party (or parties) will assume, without compensation, all or part of certain costs or other responsibilities or requirements ordinarily borne by the other party or parties; and

(ii) also permit the Secretary concerned, where such Secretary determines it is in the public interest and it is in the best interest of consummating an exchange pursuant to this Act or other applicable law, and upon mutual agreement of the parties, to make adjustments to the relative values involved in an exchange transaction in order to compensate a party or parties to the exchange for assuming costs or other responsibilities or requirements which would ordinarily be borne by the other party or parties.

As used in this subparagraph, the term "costs or other responsibilities or requirements" shall include, but not be limited to, costs or other requirements associated with land surveys and appraisals, mineral examinations, title searches, archeological surveys and salvage, removal of encumbrances, arbitration pursuant to subsection (d) of this section, curing deficiencies preventing highest and best use, and other costs to comply with laws, regulations and policies applicable to exchange transactions, or which are necessary to bring the Federal or non-Federal lands or interests involved in the exchange to their highest and best use for the appraisal and exchange purposes. Prior to making any adjustments pursuant to this subparagraph, the Secretary concerned shall be satisfied that the amount of such adjustment is reasonable and accurately reflects the approximate value of any costs or services provided or any responsibilities or requirements assumed.

(g) Exchanges to proceed under existing laws and regulations pending new rules and regulations — Until such time as new and comprehensive rules and regulations governing exchange of land and interests therein are promulgated pursuant to subsection (f) of this section, land exchanges may proceed in accordance with existing laws and regulations, and nothing in the Act shall be construed to require any delay in, or otherwise hinder, the processing and consummation of land exchanges pending the promulgation of such new and comprehensive rules and regulations. Where the Secretary concerned and the party or parties involved in an exchange have agreed to initiate an exchange of land or interests therein prior to the day of enactment of such subsections, subsections (d) through (i) of this section shall not apply to such exchanges unless the Secretary concerned and the party or parties involved in the exchange mutually agree otherwise.

(h) Exchange of lands or interests of approximately equal value; conditions; "approximately equal value" defined

(1) Notwithstanding the provisions of this Act and other applicable laws which require that exchanges of land or interests therein be for equal value, where the Secretary concerned determines it is in the public interest and that the consummation of a particular exchange will be expedited thereby, the Secretary concerned may exchange lands or interests therein which are of approximately equal value in cases where —

(A) the combined value of the lands or interests therein to be transferred from Federal ownership by the Secretary concerned in such exchange is not more than $150,000; and

(B) the Secretary concerned finds in accordance with the regulations to be promulgated pursuant to subsection (f) of this section that a determination of approximately equal value can be made without formal appraisals, as based on a statement of value made by a qualified appraiser and approved by an authorized officer; and

(C) the definition of and procedure for determining "approximately equal value" has been set forth in regulations by the Secretary concerned and the Secretary concerned documents how such determination was made in the case of the particular exchange involved.

(2) As used in this subsection, the term "approximately equal value" shall have the same meaning with respect to lands managed by the Secretary of Agriculture as it does in the Act of January 22, 1983 (commonly known as the "Small Tracts Act").

(i) Segregation from appropriation under mining and public land laws

(1) Upon receipt of an offer to exchange lands or interests in lands pursuant to this Act or other applicable laws, at the request of the head of the department or agency having jurisdiction over the lands involved, the Secretary of the Interior may temporarily segregate the Federal lands under consideration for exchange from appropriation under the mining laws. Such temporary segregation may only be made for a period of not to exceed five years. Upon a decision not to proceed with the exchange or upon deletion of any particular parcel from the exchange offer, the Federal lands involved or deleted shall be promptly restored to their former status under the mining laws. Any segregation pursuant to this paragraph shall be subject to valid existing rights as of the date of such segregation.

(2) All non-Federal lands which are acquired by the United States through exchange pursuant to this Act or pursuant to other law applicable to lands managed by the Secretary of Agriculture shall be automatically segregated from appropriation under the public land law, including the mining laws, for ninety days after acceptance of title by the United States. Such segregation shall be subject to valid existing rights as of the date of such acceptance of title. At the end of such ninety day period, such segregation shall end and such lands shall be open to operation of the public land laws and to entry, location, and patent under the mining laws except to the extent otherwise provided by this Act or other applicable law, or appropriate actions pursuant thereto.

§1717. Qualifications of conveyees
[FLPMA §207]

No tract of land may be disposed of under this Act, whether by sale, exchange, or donation, to any person who is not a citizen of the United States, or in the case of a corporation, is not subject to the laws of any State or of the United States.

§1718. Documents of conveyance; terms, covenants, etc.
[FLPMA §208]

The Secretary shall issue all patents or other documents of conveyance after any disposal authorized by this Act. The Secretary shall insert in any such patent or other document of conveyance he issues, except in the case of land exchanges, for which the provisions of subsection 1716(b) of this title shall apply, such terms, covenants, conditions, and reservations as he deems necessary to insure proper land use and protection of the public interest: *Provided*, That a conveyance of lands by the Secretary, subject to such terms, covenants, conditions, and reservations, shall not exempt the grantee from compliance with applicable

Federal or State law or State land use plans: *Provided further*, That the Secretary shall not make conveyances of public lands containing terms and conditions which would, at the time of the conveyance, constitute a violation of any law or regulation pursuant to State and local land use plans, or programs.

§1719. Mineral interests; reservation and conveyance requirements and procedures
[FLPMA §209]

(a) All conveyances of title issued by the Secretary, except those involving land exchanges provided for in section 1716 of this title, shall reserve to the United States all minerals in the lands, together with the right to prospect for, mine, and remove the minerals under applicable law and such regulations as the Secretary may prescribe, except that if the Secretary makes the findings specified in subsection (b) of this section, the minerals may then be conveyed together with the surface to the prospective surface owner as provided in subsection (b) of this section.

(b)(1) The Secretary, after consultation with the appropriate department or agency head, may convey mineral interests owned by the United States where the surface is or will be in non-Federal ownership, regardless of which Federal entity may have administered the surface, if he finds (1) that there are no known mineral values in the land, or (2) that the reservation of the mineral rights in the United States is interfering with or precluding appropriate nonmineral development of the land and that such development is a more beneficial use of the land than mineral development.

(2) Conveyance of mineral interests pursuant to this section shall be made only to the existing or proposed record owner of the surface, upon payment of administrative costs and the fair market value of the interests being conveyed.

(3) Before considering an application for conveyance of mineral interests pursuant to this section —

(i) the Secretary shall require the deposit by the applicant of a sum of money which he deems sufficient to cover administrative costs including, but not limited to, costs of conducting an exploratory program to determine the character of the mineral deposits in the land, evaluating the data obtained under the exploratory program to determine the fair market value of the mineral interests to be conveyed, and preparing and issuing the documents of conveyance: *Provided*, That, if the administrative costs exceed the deposit, the applicant shall pay the outstanding amount; and, if the deposit exceeds the administrative costs, the applicant shall be given a credit for or refund of the excess; or

(ii) the applicant, with the consent of the Secretary, shall have conducted, and submitted to the Secretary the results of, such an exploratory program, in accordance with standards promulgated by the Secretary.

(4) Moneys paid to the Secretary for administrative costs pursuant to this subsection shall be paid to the agency which rendered the service and deposited to the appropriation then current.

§1720. Coordination by Secretary of the Interior with State and local governments
[FLPMA §210]

At least sixty days prior to offering for sale or otherwise conveying public lands under this Act, the Secretary shall notify the Governor of the State within which such lands are located and the head of the governing body of any political subdivision of the State having zoning or other land use regulatory jurisdiction in the geographical area within which such lands are located, in order to afford the appropriate body the opportunity to zone or otherwise regulate, or change or amend existing zoning or other regulations concerning the use of such lands prior to such conveyance. The Secretary shall also promptly notify such public officials of the issuance of the patent or other document of conveyance for such lands.

§1721. Conveyances of public lands to States, local governments, etc.
[FLPMA §211]

(a) **Unsurveyed islands; authorization and limitations on authority** — The Secretary is authorized to convey to States or their political subdivisions under the Recreation and Public Purposes Act (44 Stat. 741 as amended; 43 U.S.C. §§869 *et seq.*), as amended, but without regard to the acreage limitations contained therein, unsurveyed islands determined by the Secretary to be public lands of the United States. The conveyance of any such island may be made without survey: *Provided, however*, That such island may be surveyed at the request of the applicant State or its political subdivision if such State or subdivision donates money or services to the Secretary for such survey, the Secretary accepts such money or services, and such services are conducted pursuant to criteria established by the Director of the Bureau of Land Management. Any such island so surveyed shall not be conveyed without approval of such survey by the Secretary prior to the conveyance.

(b) **Omitted lands; authorization and limitations on authority**

(1) The Secretary is authorized to convey to States and their political subdivisions under the Recreation and Public Purposes Act [43 U.S.C. §§869 to 869-4], but without regard to the acreage limitations contained therein, lands other than islands determined by him after survey to be public lands of the United States erroneously or fraudulently omitted from the original surveys (hereinafter referred to as "omitted lands"). Any such conveyance shall not be made without a survey: *Provided*, That the prospective recipient may donate money or services to the Secretary for the surveying necessary prior to conveyance

if the Secretary accepts such money or services, such services are conducted pursuant to criteria established by the Director of the Bureau of Land Management, and such survey is approved by the Secretary prior to the conveyance.

(2) The Secretary is authorized to convey to the occupant of any omitted lands which, after survey, are found to have been occupied and developed for a five-year period prior to January 1, 1975, if the Secretary determines that such conveyance is in the public interest and will serve objectives which outweigh all public objectives and values which would be served by retaining such lands in Federal ownership. Conveyance under this subparagraph shall be made at not less than the fair market value of the land, as determined by the Secretary, and upon payment in addition of administrative costs, including the cost of making the survey, the cost of appraisal, and the cost of making the conveyance.

(c) Conformity with land use plans and programs and coordination with State and local governments of conveyances

(1) No conveyance shall be made pursuant to this section until the relevant State government, local government, and areawide planning agency designated pursuant to section 204 of the Demonstration Cities and Metropolitan Development Act of 1966 (80 Stat. 1255, 1262) [42 U.S.C. §3334] and/or section 6506 of Title 31 have notified the Secretary as to the consistency of such conveyance with applicable State and local government land use plans and programs.

(2) The provisions of section 1720 of this title shall be applicable to all conveyances under this section.

(d) Applicability of other statutory requirements for authorized use of conveyed lands — The final sentence of section 1(c) of the Recreation and Public Purposes Act [43 U.S.C. §869(c)] shall not be applicable to conveyances under this section.

(e) Limitations on uses of conveyed lands — No conveyance pursuant to this section shall be used as the basis for determining the baseline between Federal and State ownership, the boundary of any State for purposes of determining the extent of a State's submerged lands or the line of demarcation of Federal jurisdiction, or any similar or related purpose.

(f) Applicability to lands within National Forest System, National Park System, National Wildlife Refuge System, and National Wild and Scenic Rivers System — The provisions of this section shall not apply to any lands within the National Forest System, defined in the Act of August 17, 1974 (88 Stat. 476; 16 U.S.C. §1601), the National Park System, the National Wildlife Refuge System, and the National Wild and Scenic Rivers System.

(g) Applicability to other statutory provisions authorizing sale of specific omitted lands — Nothing in this section shall supersede the provisions of the Act of December 22, 1928 (45 Stat. 1069; 43 U.S.C. §1068), as amended, and the Act of May 31, 1962 (76 Stat. 89), or any other Act authorizing the sale of specific omitted lands.

§1722. Sale of public lands subject to unintentional trespass
[FLPMA §214]

(a) Preference right of contiguous landowners; offering price — Notwithstanding the provisions of the Act of September 26, 1968 (82 Stat. 870; 43 U.S.C. §§1431-1435), hereinafter called the "1968 Act", with respect to applications under the 1968 Act which were pending before the Secretary as of the effective date of this subsection and which he approves for sale under the criteria prescribed by the 1968 Act, he shall give the right of first refusal to those having a preference right under section 2 of the 1968 Act [43 U.S.C. §1432]. The Secretary shall offer such lands to such preference right holders at their fair market value (exclusive of any values added to the land by such holders and their predecessors in interest) as determined by the Secretary as of September 26, 1973.

(b) Procedures applicable — Within three years after October 21, 1976, the Secretary shall notify the filers of applications subject to paragraph (a) of this section whether he will offer them the lands applied for and at what price; that is, their fair market value as of September 26, 1973, excluding any value added to the lands by the applicants or their predecessors in interest. He will also notify the President of the Senate and the Speaker of the House of Representatives of the lands which he has determined not to sell pursuant to paragraph (a) of this section and the reasons therefor. With respect to such lands which the Secretary determined not to sell, he shall take no other action to convey those lands or interests in them before the end of ninety days (not counting days on which the House of Representatives or the Senate has adjourned for more than three consecutive days) beginning on the date the Secretary has submitted such notice to the Senate and House of Representatives. If, during that ninety-day period, the Congress adopts a concurrent resolution stating the length of time such suspension of action should continue, he shall continue such suspension for the specified time period. If the committee to which a resolution has been referred during the said ninety-day period, has not reported it at the end of thirty calendar days after its referral, it shall be in order to either discharge the committee from further consideration of such resolution or to discharge the committee from consideration of any other resolution with respect to the suspension of action. A motion to discharge may be made only by an individual favoring the resolution, shall be highly privileged (except that it may not be made after the committee has reported such a resolution), and debate thereon shall be limited to not more than one hour, to be divided equally between those favoring and those opposing the resolution. An amendment to the motion shall not be in order, and it shall not be in order to move to reconsider the vote by which the motion was agreed to or disagreed to. If the motion to discharge is agreed to or disagreed to, the motion may not be made with respect to any other resolution with respect to the same suspension of action. When the committee has reprinted, or has been discharged from further consideration of a resolution, it shall at any time thereafter be in order (even though a previous motion to the same effect has been disagreed to) to move to proceed to the consideration of the resolution. The motion shall be highly privileged and shall not be debatable. An amendment to the motion shall not be in order, and it shall not be in order to move to reconsider the vote by which the motion was agreed to or disagreed to.

(c) Time for processing of applications and sales — Within five years after October 21, 1976, the Secretary shall complete the processing of all applications filed under the 1968 Act and hold sales covering all lands which he has determined to sell thereunder.

§1723. Temporary revocation authority [FLPMA §215]

(a) Exchange involved — When the sole impediment to consummation of an exchange of lands or interests therein (hereinafter referred to as an exchange) determined to be in the public interest, is the inability of the Secretary of the Interior to revoke, modify, or terminate part or all of a withdrawal or classification because of the order (or subsequent modification or continuance thereof) of the United States District Court for the District of Columbia dated February 10, 1986, in Civil Action No. 85-2238 (National Wildlife Federation v. Robert E. Burford, et al.), the Secretary of the Interior is hereby authorized, notwithstanding such order (or subsequent modification or continuance thereof), to use the authority contained herein, in lieu of other authority provided in this Act including section 1714 of this title, to revoke, modify, or terminate in whole or in part, withdrawals or classifications to the extent deemed necessary by the Secretary to enable the United States to transfer land or interests therein out of Federal ownership pursuant to an exchange.

(b) Requirements — The authority specified in subsection (a) of this section may be exercised only in cases where —

(1) a particular exchange is proposed to be carried out pursuant to this Act, as amended, or other applicable law authorizing such an exchange;

(2) the proposed exchange has been prepared in compliance with all laws applicable to such exchange;

(3) the head of each Federal agency managing the lands proposed for such transfer has submitted to the Secretary of the Interior a statement of concurrence with the proposed revocation, modification, or termination;

(4) at least sixty days have elapsed since the Secretary of the Interior has published in the Federal Register a notice of the proposed revocation, modification, or termination; and

(5) at least sixty days have elapsed since the Secretary of the Interior has transmitted to the Committee on Natural Resources of the House of Representatives and the Committee on Energy and Natural Resources of the United States Senate a report which includes —

(A) a justification for the necessity of exercising such authority in order to complete an exchange;

(B) an explanation of the reasons why the continuation of the withdrawal or a classification or portion thereof proposed for revocation, modification, or termination is no longer necessary for the purposes of the statutory or other program or programs for which the withdrawal or classification was made or other relevant programs;

(C) assurances that all relevant documents concerning the proposed exchange or purchase for which such authority is proposed to be exercised (including documents related to compliance with the National Environmental Policy Act of 1969 [42 U.S.C. §§4321 et seq.] and all other applicable provisions of law) are available for public inspection in the office of the Secretary concerned located nearest to the lands proposed for transfer out of Federal ownership in furtherance of such exchange and that the relevant portions of such documents are also available in the offices of the Secretary concerned in Washington, District of Columbia; and

(D) an explanation of the effect of the revocation, modification, or termination of a withdrawal or classification or portion thereof and the transfer of lands out of Federal ownership pursuant to the particular proposed exchange, on the objectives of the land management plan which is applicable at the time of such transfer to the land to be transferred out of Federal ownership.

(c) Limitations

(1) Nothing in this section shall be construed as affirming or denying any of the allegations made by any party in the civil action specified in subsection (a) of this section, or as constituting an expression of congressional opinion with respect to the merits of any allegation, contention, or argument made or issue raised by any party in such action, or as expanding or diminishing the jurisdiction of the United States District Court for the District of Columbia.

(2) Except as specifically provided in this section, nothing in this section shall be construed as modifying, terminating, revoking, or otherwise affecting any provision of law applicable to land exchanges, withdrawals, or classifications.

(3) The availability or exercise of the authority granted in subsection (a) of this section may

not be considered by the Secretary of the Interior in making a determination pursuant to this Act or other applicable law as to whether or not any proposed exchange is in the public interest.

(d) Termination — The authority specified in subsection (a) of this section shall expire either (1) on December 31, 1990, or (2) when the Court order (or subsequent modification or continuation thereof) specified in subsection (a) of this section is no longer in effect, whichever occurs first.

SUBCHAPTER III—ADMINISTRATION

§1731. Bureau of Land Management
[FLPMA §301]

(a) Director; appointment, qualifications, functions, and duties — The Bureau of Land Management established by Reorganization Plan Numbered 3, of 1946 shall have as its head a Director. Appointments to the position of Director shall hereafter be made by the President, by and with the advice and consent of the Senate. The Director of the Bureau shall have a broad background and substantial experience in public land and natural resource management. He shall carry out such functions and shall perform such duties as the Secretary may prescribe with respect to the management of lands and resources under his jurisdiction according to the applicable provisions of this Act and any other applicable law.

(b) Statutory transfer of functions, powers and duties relating to administration of laws — Subject to the discretion granted to him by Reorganization Plan Numbered 3 of 1950, the Secretary shall carry out through the Bureau all functions, powers, and duties vested in him and relating to the administration of laws which, on October 21, 1976, were carried out by him through the Bureau of Land Management established by section 403 of Reorganization Plan Numbered 3 of 1946. The Bureau shall administer such laws according to the provisions thereof existing as of October 21, 1976, as modified by the provisions of this Act or by subsequent law.

(c) Associate Director, Assistant Directors, and other employees; appointment and compensation — In addition to the Director, there shall be an Associate Director of the Bureau and so many Assistant Directors, and other employees, as may be necessary, who shall be appointed by the Secretary subject to the provisions of title 5 governing appointments in the competitive service, and shall be paid in accordance with the provisions of chapter 51 and subchapter 3 of chapter 53 of such title relating to classification and General Schedule pay rates.

(d) Existing regulations relating to administration of laws — Nothing in this section shall affect any regulation of the Secretary with respect to the administration of laws administered by him through the Bureau on October 21, 1976.

§1732. Management of use, occupancy, and development of public lands
[FLPMA §302]

(a) Multiple use and sustained yield requirements applicable; exception — The Secretary shall manage the public lands under principles of multiple use and sustained yield, in accordance with the land use plans developed by him under section 1712 of this title when they are available, except that where a tract of such public land has been dedicated to specific uses according to any other provisions of law it shall be managed in accordance with such law.

(b) Easements, permits, etc., for utilization through habitation, cultivation, and development of small trade or manufacturing concerns; applicable statutory requirements — In managing the public lands, the Secretary shall, subject to this Act and other applicable law and under such terms and conditions as are consistent with such law, regulate, through easements, permits, leases, licenses, published rules, or other instruments as the Secretary deems appropriate, the use, occupancy, and development of the public lands, including, but not limited to, long-term leases to permit individuals to utilize public lands for habitation, cultivation, and the development of small trade or manufacturing concerns: *Provided,* That unless otherwise provided for by law, the Secretary may permit Federal departments and agencies to use, occupy, and develop public lands only through rights-of-way under section 1767 of this title, withdrawals under section 1714 of this title, and, where the proposed use and development are similar or closely related to the programs of the Secretary for the public lands involved, cooperative agreements under section 1737(b) of this title: *Provided further,* That nothing in this Act shall be construed as authorizing the Secretary concerned to require Federal permits to hunt and fish on public lands or on lands in the National Forest System and adjacent waters or as enlarging or diminishing the responsibility and authority of the States for management of fish and resident wildlife. However, the Secretary concerned may designate areas of public land and of lands in the National Forest System where, and establish periods when, no hunting or fishing will be permitted for reasons of public safety, administration, or compliance with provisions of applicable law. Except in emergencies, any regulations of the Secretary concerned relating to hunting and fishing pursuant to this section shall be put into effect only after consultation with the appropriate State fish and game department. Nothing in this Act shall modify or change any provision of Federal law relating to migratory birds or to endangered or threatened species. Except as provided in section 1744, section 1782, and subsection (f) of section 1781 of this title and in the last sentence of this paragraph, no provision of this section or any other section of this Act shall in any way amend the Mining Law of 1872 or impair the rights of any locators or claims under that Act, including, but not limited to, rights of ingress and egress. In managing the public lands the Secretary shall, by regulation or otherwise, take any action necessary to prevent unnecessary or undue degradation of the lands.

(c) Revocation or suspension provision in instrument authorizing use, occupancy or development; violation of provision; procedure applicable — The Secretary shall insert in any instrument providing for the use, occupancy, or development of the public lands a provision authorizing revocation or suspension, after notice and hearing, of such instrument upon a final administrative finding of a violation of any term or condition of the instrument, including, but not limited to, terms and conditions requiring compliance with regulations under Acts applicable to the public lands and compliance with applicable State or Federal air or water quality standard or implementation plan: *Provided*, That such violation occurred on public lands covered by such instrument and occurred in connection with the exercise of rights and privileges granted by it: *Provided further*, That the Secretary shall terminate any such suspension no later than the date upon which he determines the cause of said violation has been rectified: *Provided further*, That the Secretary may order an immediate temporary suspension prior to a hearing or final administrative finding if he determines that such a suspension is necessary to protect health or safety or the environment: *Provided further*, That, where other applicable law contains specific provisions for suspension, revocation, or cancellation of a permit, license, or other authorization to use, occupy, or develop the public lands, the specific provisions of such law shall prevail.

(d) Authorization to utilize certain public lands in Alaska for military purposes

(1) The Secretary of the Interior, after consultation with the Governor of Alaska, may issue to the Secretary of Defense or to the Secretary of a military department within the Department of Defense or to the Commandant of the Coast Guard a nonrenewable general authorization to utilize public lands in Alaska (other than within a conservation system unit or the Steese National Conservation Area or the White Mountains National Recreation Area) for purposes of military maneuvering, military training, or equipment testing not involving artillery firing, aerial or other gunnery, or other use of live ammunition or ordnance.

(2) Use of public lands pursuant to a general authorization under this subsection shall be limited to areas where such use would not be inconsistent with the plans prepared pursuant to section 1712 of this title. Each such use shall be subject to a requirement that the using department shall be responsible for any necessary cleanup and decontamination of the lands used, and to such other terms and conditions (including but not limited to restrictions on use of off-road or all-terrain vehicles) as the Secretary of the Interior may require to —

(A) minimize adverse impacts on the natural, environmental, scientific, cultural, and other resources and values (including fish and wildlife habitat) of the public lands involved; and

(B) minimize the period and method of such use and the interference with or restrictions on other uses of the public lands involved.

(3)(A) A general authorization issued pursuant to this subsection shall not be for a term of more than three years and shall be revoked in whole or in part, as the Secretary of the Interior finds necessary, prior to the end of such term upon a determination by the Secretary of the Interior that there has been a failure to comply with its terms and conditions or that activities pursuant to such an authorization have had or might have a significant adverse impact on the resources or values of the affected lands.

(B) Each specific use of a particular area of public lands pursuant to a general authorization under this subsection shall be subject to specific authorization by the Secretary and to appropriate terms and conditions, including such as are described in paragraph (2) of this subsection.

(4) Issuance of a general authorization pursuant to this subsection shall be subject to the provisions of section 1712(f) of this title, section 3120 of Title 16, and all other applicable provisions of law. The Secretary of a military department (or the Commandant of the Coast Guard) requesting such authorization shall reimburse the Secretary of the Interior for the costs of implementing this paragraph. An authorization pursuant to this subsection shall not authorize the construction of permanent structures or facilities on the public lands.

(5) To the extent that public safety may require closure to public use of any portion of the public lands covered by an authorization issued pursuant to this subsection, the Secretary of the military Department concerned or the Commandant of the Coast Guard shall take appropriate steps to notify the public concerning such closure and to provide appropriate warnings of risks to public safety.

(6) For purposes of this subsection, the term "conservation system unit" has the same meaning as specified in section 3102 of Title 16.

§1733. Enforcement authority
[FLPMA §303]
(a) Regulations for implementation of management, use, and protection requirements; violations; criminal penalties — The Secretary shall issue regulations necessary to implement the provisions of this Act with respect to the management, use, and protection of the public lands, including the property located thereon. Any person who knowingly and willfully violates any such regulation which is lawfully

issued pursuant to this Act shall be fined no more than $1,000 or imprisoned no more than twelve months, or both. Any person charged with a violation of such regulation may be tried and sentenced by any United States magistrate judge designated for that purpose by the court by which he was appointed, in the same manner and subject to the same conditions and limitations as provided for in section 3401 of Title 18.

(b) Civil actions by Attorney General for violations of regulations; nature of relief; jurisdiction — At the request of the Secretary, the Attorney General may institute a civil action in any United States district court for an injunction or other appropriate order to prevent any person from utilizing public lands in violation of regulations issued by the Secretary under this Act.

(c) Contracts for enforcement of Federal laws and regulations by local law enforcement officials; procedure applicable; contract requirements and implementation

(1) When the Secretary determines that assistance is necessary in enforcing Federal laws and regulations relating to the public lands or their resources he shall offer a contract to appropriate local officials having law enforcement authority within their respective jurisdictions with the view of achieving maximum feasible reliance upon local law enforcement officials in enforcing such laws and regulations. The Secretary shall negotiate on reasonable terms with such officials who have authority to enter into such contracts to enforce such Federal laws and regulations. In the performance of their duties under such contracts such officials and their agents are authorized to carry firearms; execute and serve any warrant or other process issued by a court or officer of competent jurisdiction; make arrests without warrant or process for a misdemeanor he has reasonable grounds to believe is being committed in his presence or view, or for a felony if he has reasonable grounds to believe that the person to be arrested has committed or is committing such felony; search without warrant or process any person, place, or conveyance according to any Federal law or rule of law; and seize without warrant or process any evidentiary item as provided by Federal law. The Secretary shall provide such law enforcement training as he deems necessary in order to carry out the contracted for responsibilities. While exercising the powers and authorities provided by such contract pursuant to this section, such law enforcement officials and their agents shall have all the immunities of Federal law enforcement officials.

(2) The Secretary may authorize Federal personnel or appropriate local officials to carry out his law enforcement responsibilities with respect to the public lands and their resources. Such designated personnel shall receive the training and have the responsibilities and authority provided for in paragraph (1) of this subsection.

(d) Cooperation with regulatory and law enforcement officials of any State or political subdivision in enforcement of laws or ordinances — In connection with the administration and regulation of the use and occupancy of the public lands, the Secretary is authorized to cooperate with the regulatory and law enforcement officials of any State or political subdivision thereof in the enforcement of the laws or ordinances of such State or subdivision. Such cooperation may include reimbursement to a State or its subdivision for expenditures incurred by it in connection with activities which assist in the administration and regulation of use and occupancy of the public lands.

(e) Uniformed desert ranger force in California Desert Conservation Area; establishment; enforcement of Federal laws and regulations — Nothing in this section shall prevent the Secretary from promptly establishing a uniformed desert ranger force in the California Desert Conservation Area established pursuant to section 1781 of this title for the purpose of enforcing Federal laws and regulations relating to the public lands and resources managed by him in such area. The officers and members of such ranger force shall have the same responsibilities and authority as provided for in paragraph (1) of subsection (c) of this section.

(f) Applicability of other Federal enforcement provisions — Nothing in this Act shall be construed as reducing or limiting the enforcement authority vested in the Secretary by any other statute.

(g) Unlawful activities — The use, occupancy, or development of any portion of the public lands contrary to any regulation of the Secretary or other responsible authority, or contrary to any order issued pursuant to any such regulation, is unlawful and prohibited.

§1734. Fees, charges, and commissions [FLPMA §304]

(a) Authority to establish and modify — Notwithstanding any other provision of law, the Secretary may establish reasonable filing and service fees and reasonable charges, and commissions with respect to applications and other documents relating to the public lands and may change and abolish such fees, charges, and commissions.

(b) Deposits for payments to reimburse reasonable costs of United States — The Secretary is authorized to require a deposit of any payments intended to reimburse the United States for reasonable costs with respect to applications and other documents relating to such lands. The moneys received for reasonable costs under this subsection shall be deposited with the Treasury in a special account and are hereby authorized to be appropriated and made available until expended. As used in this section "reasonable costs" include, but are not limited to, the costs of special studies; environmental impact statements; monitoring construction, operation, maintenance, and termination of any authorized facility; or other special activities. In determining whether costs are reasonable under this section, the Secretary may take into consideration actual costs (exclusive of management overhead), the monetary value of the rights or privileges sought by the applicant, the efficiency to the government processing involved, that portion of the cost incurred for the benefit of the general public interest rather than for the exclusive benefit of the applicant, the public service provided, and other factors relevant to determining the reasonableness of the costs.

(c) Refunds — In any case where it shall appear to the satisfaction of the Secretary that any person has made a payment under any statute relating to the sale, lease, use, or other disposition of public lands which is not required or is in excess of the amount required by applicable law and the regulations issued by the Secretary, the Secretary, upon application or otherwise, may cause a refund to be made from applicable funds.

§1734a. Availability of excess fees

In fiscal year 1997 and thereafter, all fees, excluding mining claim fees, in excess of the fiscal year 1996 collections established by the Secretary of the Interior under the authority of section 1734 of this title for processing, recording, or documenting authorizations to use public lands or public land natural resources (including cultural, historical, and mineral) and for providing specific services to public land users, and which are not presently being covered into any Bureau of Land Management appropriation accounts, and not otherwise dedicated by law for a specific distribution, shall be made immediately available for program operations in this account and remain available until expended.

§1735. Forfeitures and deposits
[FLPMA §305]

(a) Credit to separate account in Treasury; appropriation and availability — Any moneys received by the United States as a result of the forfeiture of a bond or other security by a resource developer or purchaser or permittee who does not fulfill the requirements of his contract or permit or does not comply with the regulations of the Secretary; or as a result of a compromise or settlement of any claim whether sounding in tort or in contract involving present or potential damage to the public lands shall be credited to a separate account in the Treasury and are hereby authorized to be appropriated and made available, until expended as the Secretary may direct, to cover the cost to the United States of any improvement, protection, or rehabilitation work on those public lands which has been rendered necessary by the action which has led to the forfeiture, compromise, or settlement.

(b) Expenditure of moneys collected administering Oregon and California Railroad and Coos Bay Wagon Road Grant lands — Any moneys collected under this Act in connection with lands administered under the Act of August 28, 1937 (50 Stat. 874; 43 U.S.C. §§1181a-1181j), shall be expended for the benefit of such land only.

(c) Refunds — If any portion of a deposit or amount forfeited under this Act is found by the Secretary to be in excess of the cost of doing the work authorized under this Act, the Secretary, upon application or otherwise, may cause a refund of the amount in excess to be made from applicable funds.

§1736. Working capital fund
[FLPMA §306]

(a) Establishment; availability of fund — There is hereby established a working capital fund for the management of the public lands. This fund shall be available without fiscal year limitation for expenses necessary for furnishing, in accordance with the Federal Property and Administrative Services Act of 1949 (63 Stat. 377, as amended), and regulations promulgated thereunder, supplies and equipment services in support of Bureau programs, including but not limited to, the purchase or construction of storage facilities, equipment yards, and related improvements and the purchase, lease, or rent of motor vehicles, aircraft, heavy equipment, and fire control and other resource management equipment within the limitations set forth in appropriations made to the Secretary for the Bureau.

(b) Initial funding; subsequent transfers — The initial capital of the fund shall consist of appropriations made for that purpose together with the fair and reasonable value at the fund's inception of the inventories, equipment, receivables, and other assets, less the liabilities, transferred to the fund. The Secretary is authorized to make such subsequent transfers to the fund as he deems appropriate in connection with the functions to be carried on through the fund.

(c) Payments credited to fund; amount; advancement or reimbursement — The fund shall be credited with payments from appropriations, and funds of the Bureau, other agencies of the Department of the Interior, other Federal agencies, and other sources, as authorized by law, at rates approximately equal to the cost of furnishing the facilities, supplies, equipment, and services (including depreciation and accrued annual leave). Such payments may be made in advance in connection with firm orders, or by way of reimbursement.

(d) Authorization of appropriations — There is hereby authorized to be appropriated a sum not to exceed $3,000,000 as initial capital of the working capital fund.

§1736a. Revolving fund derived from disposal of salvage timber

There is hereby established in the Treasury of the United States a special fund to be derived on and after

October 5, 1992, from the Federal share of moneys received from the disposal of salvage timber prepared for sale from the lands under the jurisdiction of the Bureau of Land Management, Department of the Interior. The money in this fund shall be immediately available to the Bureau of Land Management without further appropriation, for the purposes of planning and preparing salvage timber for disposal, the administration of salvage timber sales, and subsequent site preparation and reforestation.

§1737. Implementation provisions
[FLPMA §307]

(a) **Investigations, studies, and experiments** — The Secretary may conduct investigations, studies, and experiments, on his own initiative or in cooperation with others, involving the management, protection, development, acquisition, and conveying of the public lands.

(b) **Contracts and cooperative agreements** — Subject to the provisions of applicable law, the Secretary may enter into contracts and cooperative agreements involving the management, protection, development, and sale of public lands.

(c) **Contributions and donations of money, services, and property** — The Secretary may accept contributions or donations of money, services, and property, real, personal, or mixed, for the management, protection, development, acquisition, and conveying of the public lands, including the acquisition of rights-of-way for such purposes. He may accept contributions for cadastral surveying performed on federally controlled or intermingled lands. Moneys received hereunder shall be credited to a separate account in the Treasury and are hereby authorized to be appropriated and made available until expended, as the Secretary may direct, for payment of expenses incident to the function toward the administration of which the contributions were made and for refunds to depositors of amounts contributed by them in specific instances where contributions are in excess of their share of the cost.

(d) **Recruitment of volunteers** — The Secretary may recruit, without regard to the civil service classification laws, rules, or regulations, the services of individuals contributed without compensation as volunteers for aiding in or facilitating the activities administered by the Secretary through the Bureau of Land Management.

(e) **Restrictions on activities of volunteers** — In accepting such services of individuals as volunteers, the Secretary —

(1) shall not permit the use of volunteers in hazardous duty or law enforcement work, or in policymaking processes or to displace any employee; and

(2) may provide for services or costs incidental to the utilization of volunteers, including transportation, supplies, lodging, subsistence, recruiting, training, and supervision.

(f) **Federal employment status of volunteers** — Volunteers shall not be deemed employees of the United States except for the purposes of —

(1) the tort claims provisions of Title 28;

(2) subchapter 1 of chapter 81 of Title 5; and

(3) claims relating to damage to, or loss of, personal property of a volunteer incident to volunteer service, in which case the provisions of section 3721 of Title 31 shall apply.

(g) **Authorization of appropriations** — Effective with fiscal years beginning after September 30, 1984, there are authorized to be appropriated such sums as may be necessary to carry out the provisions of subsection (d) of this section, but not more than $250,000 may be appropriated for any one fiscal year.

§1738. Contracts for surveys and resource protection; renewals; funding requirements
[FLPMA §308]

(a) The Secretary is authorized to enter into contracts for the use of aircraft, and for supplies and services, prior to the passage of an appropriation therefor, for airborne cadastral survey and resource protection operations of the Bureau. He may renew such contracts annually, not more than twice, without additional competition. Such contracts shall obligate funds for the fiscal years in which the costs are incurred.

(b) Each such contract shall provide that the obligation of the United States for the ensuing fiscal years is contingent upon the passage of an applicable appropriation, and that no payment shall be made under the contract for the ensuing fiscal years until such appropriation becomes available for expenditure.

§1739. Advisory councils
[FLPMA §309]

(a) **Establishment; membership; operation** — The Secretary shall establish advisory councils of not less than ten and not more than fifteen members appointed by him from among persons who are representative of the various major citizens' interests concerning the problems relating to land use planning or the management of the public lands located within the area for which an advisory council is established. At least one member of each council shall be an elected official of general purpose government serving the people of such area. To the extent practicable there shall be no overlap or duplication of such councils. Appointments shall be made in accordance with rules prescribed by the Secretary. The establishment and operation of an advisory council established under this section shall conform to the requirements of the Federal Advisory Committee Act (86 Stat. 770).

(b) **Meetings** — Notwithstanding the provisions of subsection (a) of this section, each advisory council established by the Secretary under this section shall meet at least once a year with such meetings being called by the Secretary.

(c) Travel and per diem payments — Members of advisory councils shall serve without pay, except travel and per diem will be paid each member for meetings called by the Secretary.

(d) Functions — An advisory council may furnish advice to the Secretary with respect to the land use planning, classification, retention, management, and disposal of the public lands within the area for which the advisory council is established and such other matters as may be referred to it by the Secretary.

(e) Public participation; procedures applicable — In exercising his authorities under this Act, the Secretary, by regulation, shall establish procedures, including public hearings where appropriate, to give the Federal, State, and local governments and the public adequate notice and an opportunity to comment upon the formulation of standards and criteria for, and to participate in, the preparation and execution of plans and programs for, and the management of, the public lands.

§1740. Rules and regulations
[FLPMA §310]

The Secretary, with respect to the public lands, shall promulgate rules and regulations to carry out the purposes of this Act and of other laws applicable to the public lands, and the Secretary of Agriculture, with respect to lands within the National Forest System, shall promulgate rules and regulations to carry out the purposes of this Act. The promulgation of such rules and regulations shall be governed by the provisions of chapter 5 of Title 5, without regard to section 553(a)(2). Prior to the promulgation of such rules and regulations, such lands shall be administered under existing rules and regulations concerning such lands to the extent practical.

§1741. Annual reports
[FLPMA §311]

(a) Purpose; time for submission — For the purpose of providing information that will aid Congress in carrying out its oversight responsibilities for public lands programs and for other purposes, the Secretary shall prepare a report in accordance with subsections (b) and (c) of this section and submit it to the Congress no later than one hundred and twenty days after the end of each fiscal year beginning with the report for fiscal year 1979.

(b) Format — A list of programs and specific information to be included in the report as well as the format of the report shall be developed by the Secretary after consulting with the Committee on Natural Resources of the House of Representatives and the Committee on Energy and Natural Resources of the Senate and shall be provided to the committees prior to the end of the second quarter of each fiscal year.

(c) Contents — The report shall include, but not be limited to, program identification information, program evaluation information, and program budgetary information for the preceding current and succeeding fiscal years.

§1742. Search, rescue, and protection forces; emergency situations authorizing hiring
[FLPMA §312]

Where in his judgment sufficient search, rescue, and protection forces are not otherwise available, the Secretary is authorized in cases of emergency to incur such expenses as may be necessary (a) in searching for and rescuing, or in cooperating in the search for and rescue of, persons lost on the public lands, (b) in protecting or rescuing, or in cooperating in the protection and rescue of, persons or animals endangered by an act of God, and (c) in transporting deceased persons or persons seriously ill or injured to the nearest place where interested parties or local authorities are located.

§1742a. Good Samaritan Search and Recovery Act

(a) Definitions

In this section:

(1) Eligible

The term "eligible", with respect to an organization or individual, means that the organization or individual, respectively, is—

(A) acting in a not-for-profit capacity; and

(B) composed entirely of members who, at the time of the good Samaritan search-and-recovery mission, have attained theage of majority under the law of the State where the mission takes place.

(2) Good Samaritan search-and-recovery mission

The term "good Samaritan search-and-recovery mission" means a search conducted by an eligible organization or individual for 1 or more missing individuals believed to be deceased at the time that the search is initiated.

(3) Secretary

The term "Secretary" means the Secretary or the Secretary of Agriculture, as applicable.

(b) Process

(1) In general

Each Secretary shall develop and implement a process to expedite access to Federal land under the administrative jurisdiction of the Secretary for eligible organizations and individuals to request access to Federal land to conduct good Samaritan search-and-recovery missions.

(2) Inclusions

The process developed and implemented under this subsection shall include provisions to clarify that—

(A) an eligible organization or individual granted access under this section—

(i) shall be acting for private purposes; and

(ii) shall not be considered to be a Federal volunteer;

(B) an eligible organization or individual conducting a good Samaritan search-and-recovery mission under this section shall not be considered to be a volunteer under section 102301(c) of Title 54;

(C) chapter 171 of title 28, (commonly known as the "Federal Tort Claims Act"), shall not apply to an eligible organization or individual carrying out a privately requested good Samaritan search-and-recovery mission under this section; and

(D) chapter 81 of title 5, (commonly known as the "Federal Employees Compensation Act"), shall not apply to an eligible organization or individual conducting a good Samaritan search-and-recovery mission under this section, and the conduct of the good Samaritan search-and-recovery mission shall not constitute civilian employment.

(c) Release of Federal Government from liability

The Secretary shall not require an eligible organization or individual to have liability insurance as a condition of accessing Federal land under this section, if the eligible organization or individual—

(1) acknowledges and consents, in writing, to the provisions described in subparagraphs (A) through (D) of subsection (b)

(2); and

(2) signs a waiver releasing the Federal Government from all liability relating to the access granted under this section and agrees to indemnify and hold harmless the United States from any claims or lawsuits arising from any conduct by the eligible organization or individual on Federal land.

(d) Approval and denial of requests

(1) In general

The Secretary shall notify an eligible organization or individual of the approval or denial of a request by the eligible organization or individual to carry out a good Samaritan search-and-recovery mission under this section by not later than 48 hours after the request is made.

(2) Denials

If the Secretary denies a request from an eligible organization or individual to carry out a good Samaritan search-and-recovery mission under this section, the Secretary shall notify the eligible organization or individual of—

(A) the reason for the denial of the request; and

(B) any actions that the eligible organization or individual can take to meet the requirements for the request to be approved.

(e) Partnerships

Each Secretary shall develop search-and-recovery-focused partnerships with search-and-recovery organizations—

(1) to coordinate good Samaritan search-and-recovery missions on Federal land under the administrative jurisdiction of the Secretary; and

(2) to expedite and accelerate good Samaritan

search-and-recovery mission efforts for missing individuals on Federal land under the administrative jurisdiction of the Secretary.

(f) Report

Not later than 180 days after March 12, 2019, the Secretaries shall submit to Congress a joint report describing—

(1) plans to develop partnerships described in subsection (e)(1); and

(2) efforts carried out to expedite and accelerate good Samaritan search-and-recovery mission efforts for missing individuals on Federal land under the administrative jurisdiction of each Secretary pursuant to subsection (e)(2).

§1743. Disclosure of financial interests by officers or employees
[FLPMA §313]

(a) Annual written statement; availability to public — Each officer or employee of the Secretary and the Bureau who —

(1) performs any function or duty under this Act; and

(2) has any known financial interest in any person who (A) applies for or receives any permit, lease, or right-of-way under, or (B) applies for or acquires any land or interests therein under, or (C) is otherwise subject to the provisions of, this Act,

shall, beginning on February 1, 1977, annually file with the Secretary a written statement concerning all such interests held by such officer or employee during the preceding calendar year. Such statement shall be available to the public.

(b) Implementation of requirements — The Secretary shall —

(1) act within ninety days after October 21, 1976 —

(A) to define the term "known financial interests" for the purposes of subsection (a) of this section; and

(B) to establish the methods by which the requirement to file written statements specified in subsection (a) of this section will be monitored and enforced, including appropriate provisions for the filing by such officers and employees of such statements and the review by the Secretary of such statements; and

(2) report to the Congress on June 1 of each calendar year with respect to such disclosures and the actions taken in regard thereto during the preceding calendar year.

(c) Exempted personnel — In the rules prescribed in subsection (b) of this section, the Secretary may identify specific positions within the Department of the Interior which are of a nonregulatory or nonpolicymaking nature and provide that officers or employees occupying such positions shall be exempt from the requirements of this section.

(d) Violations; criminal penalties — Any officer or employee who is subject to, and knowingly violates, this section, shall be fined not more than $2,500 or imprisoned not more than one year, or both.

§1744. Recordation of mining claims
[FLPMA §314]

(a) Filing requirements — The owner of an unpatented lode or placer mining claim located prior to October 21, 1976, shall, within the three-year period following October 21, 1976 and prior to December 31 of each year thereafter, file the instruments required by paragraphs (1) and (2) of this subsection. The owner of an unpatented lode or placer mining claim located after October 21, 1976 shall, prior to December 31 of each year following the calendar year in which the said claim was located, file the instruments required by paragraphs (1) and (2) of this subsection:

(1) File for record in the office where the location notice or certificate is recorded either a notice of intention to hold the mining claim (including but not limited to such notices as are provided by law to be filed when there has been a suspension or deferment of annual assessment work), an affidavit of assessment work performed thereon, on a detailed report provided by section 28-1 of title 30, relating thereto.

(2) File in the office of the Bureau designated by the Secretary a copy of the official record of the instrument filed or recorded pursuant to paragraph (1) of this subsection, including a description of the location of the mining claim sufficient to locate the claimed lands on the ground.

(b) Additional filing requirements — The owner of an unpatented lode or placer mining claim or mill or tunnel site located prior to October 21, 1976 shall, within the three-year period following October 21, 1976, file in the office of the Bureau designated by the Secretary a copy of the official record of the notice of location or certificate of location, including a description of the location of the mining claim or mill or tunnel site sufficient to locate the claimed lands on the ground. The owner of an unpatented lode or placer mining claim or mill or tunnel site located after October 21, 1976 shall, within ninety days after the date of location of such claim, file in the office of the Bureau designated by the Secretary a copy of the official record of the notice of location or certificate of location, including a description of the location of the mining claim or mill or tunnel site sufficient to locate the claimed lands on the ground.

(c) Failure to file as constituting abandonment; defective or untimely filing — The failure to file such instruments as required by subsections (a) and (b) of this section shall be deemed conclusively to constitute an abandonment of the mining claim or mill or tunnel site by the owner; but it shall not be considered a failure to file if the instrument is defective or not timely filed for record under other Federal laws permitting filing or recording thereof, or if the instrument is filed for record by or on behalf of some but not all of the owners of the mining claim or mill or tunnel site.

(d) Validity of claims, waiver of assessment, etc., as unaffected — Such recordation or application by itself shall not render valid any claim which would not be otherwise valid under applicable law. Nothing in this section shall be construed as a waiver of the assessment and other requirements of such law.

§1745. Disclaimer of interest in lands
[FLPMA §315]

(a) Issuance of recordable document; criteria — After consulting with any affected Federal agency, the Secretary is authorized to issue a document of disclaimer of interest or interests in any lands in any form suitable for recordation, where the disclaimer will help remove a cloud on the title of such lands and where he determines (1) a record interest of the United States in lands has terminated by operation of law or is otherwise invalid; or (2) the lands lying between the meander line shown on a plat of survey approved by the Bureau or its predecessors and the actual shoreline of a body of water are not lands of the United States; or (3) accreted, relicted, or avulsed lands are not lands of the United States.

(b) Procedures applicable — No document or disclaimer shall be issued pursuant to this section unless the applicant therefor has filed with the Secretary an application in writing and notice of such application setting forth the grounds supporting such application has been published in the Federal Register at least ninety days preceding the issuance of such disclaimer and until the applicant therefor has paid to the Secretary the administrative costs of issuing the disclaimer as determined by the Secretary. All receipts shall be deposited to the then-current appropriation from which expended.

(c) Construction as quit-claim deed from United States — Issuance of a document of disclaimer by the Secretary pursuant to the provisions of this section and regulations promulgated hereunder shall have the same effect as a quit-claim deed from the United States.

§1746. Correction of conveyance documents
[FLPMA §316]

The Secretary may correct patents or documents of conveyance issued pursuant to section 1718 of this title or to other Acts relating to the disposal of public lands where necessary in order to eliminate errors. In addition, the Secretary may make corrections of errors in any documents of conveyance which have heretofore been issued by the Federal Government to dispose of public lands. Any corrections authorized by this section which affect the boundaries of, or jurisdiction over, land administered by another Federal agency shall be made only after consultation with, and the approval of, the head of such other agency.

§1747. Loans to States and political subdivisions; purposes; amounts; allocation; terms and conditions; interest rate; security; limitations; forebearance for benefit of borrowers; recordkeeping requirements; discrimination prohibited; deposit of receipts
[FLPMA §317]

(1) The Secretary is authorized to make loans to States and their political subdivisions in order to relieve social or economic impacts occasioned by the development of minerals leased in such States pursuant to the Act of February 25, 1920, as amended [30 U.S.C. §§181 *et seq.*]. Such loans shall be confined to the uses specified for the 50 per centum of mineral leasing revenues to be received by such States and subdivisions pursuant to section 35 of such Act [30 U.S.C. §191].

(2) The total amount of loans outstanding pursuant to this section for any State and political subdivisions thereof in any year shall be not more than the anticipated mineral leasing revenues to be received by that State pursuant to section 35 of the Act of February 25, 1920, as amended [30 U.S.C. §191], for the ten years following.

(3) The Secretary, after consultation with the Governors of the affected States, shall allocate such loans among the States and their political subdivisions in a fair and equitable manner, giving priority to those States and subdivisions suffering the most severe impacts.

(4) Loans made pursuant to this section shall be subject to such terms and conditions as the Secretary determines necessary to assure the achievement of the purpose of this section. The Secretary shall promulgate such regulations as may be necessary to carry out the provisions of this section no later than three months after August 20, 1978.

(5) Loans made pursuant to this section shall bear interest equivalent to the lowest interest rate paid on an issue of at least $1,000,000 of tax exempt bonds of such State or any agency thereof within the preceding calendar year.

(6) Any loan made pursuant to this section shall be secured only by a pledge of the revenues received by the State or the political subdivision thereof pursuant to section 35 of the Act of February 25, 1920, as amended [30 U.S.C. §191], and shall not constitute an obligation upon the general property or taxing authority of such unit of government.

(7) Notwithstanding any other provision of law, loans made pursuant to this section may be used for the non-Federal share of the aggregate cost of any project or program otherwise funded by the Federal Government which requires a non-Federal share for such project or program and which provides planning or public facilities otherwise eligible for assistance under this section.

(8) Nothing in this section shall be construed to preclude any forebearance for the benefit of the borrower including loan restructuring, which may be determined by the Secretary as justified by the failure of anticipated mineral development or related revenues to materialize as expected when the loan was made pursuant to this section.

(9) Recipients of loans made pursuant to this section shall keep such records as the Secretary shall prescribe by regulation, including records which fully disclose the disposition of the proceeds of such assistance and such other records as the Secretary may require to facilitate an effective audit. The Secretary and the Comptroller General of the United States or their duly authorized representatives shall have access, for the purpose of audit, to such records.

(10) No person in the United States shall, on the grounds of race, color, religion, national origin, or sex be excluded from participation in, be denied the benefits of, or be subjected to discrimination under, any program or activity funded in whole or part with funds made available under this section.

(11) All amounts collected in connection with loans made pursuant to this section, including interest payments or repayments of principal on loans, fees, and other moneys, derived in connection with this section, shall be deposited in the Treasury as miscellaneous receipts.

§1748. Funding requirements
[FLPMA §318]

(a) **Authorization of appropriations** — There are authorized to be appropriated such sums as are necessary to carry out the purposes and provisions of this Act, but no amounts shall be appropriated to carry out after October 1, 2002, any program, function, or activity of the Bureau under this or any other Act unless such sums are specifically authorized to be appropriated as of October 21, 1976 or are authorized to be appropriated in accordance with the provisions of subsection (b) of this section.

(b) **Procedure applicable for authorization of appropriations** — Consistent with section 1110 of Title 31, beginning May 15, 1977, and not later than May 15 of each second even numbered year thereafter, the Secretary shall submit to the Speaker of the House of Representatives and the President of the Senate a request for the authorization of appropriations for all programs, functions, and activities of the Bureau to be carried out during the four-fiscal-year period beginning on October 1 of the calendar year following the calendar year in which such request is submitted. The Secretary shall include in his request, in addition to the information contained in his budget request and justification statement to the Office of Management and Budget, the funding levels which he determines can be efficiently and effectively utilized in the execution of his responsibilities for each such program, function, or activity, notwithstanding any budget guidelines or limitations imposed by any official or agency of the executive branch.

(c) Distribution of receipts from Bureau from disposal of lands, etc. — Nothing in this section shall apply to the distribution of receipts of the Bureau from the disposal of lands, natural resources, and interests in lands in accordance with applicable law, nor to the use of contributed funds, private deposits for public survey work, and townsite trusteeships, nor to fund allocations from other Federal agencies, reimbursements from both Federal and non-Federal sources, and funds expended for emergency firefighting and rehabilitation.

(d) Purchase of certain public lands from Land and Water Conservation — In exercising the authority to acquire by purchase granted by section 1715(a) of this title, the Secretary may use the Land and Water Conservation Fund to purchase lands which are necessary for proper management of public lands which are primarily of value for outdoor recreation purposes.

§1748a. FLAME Wildfire Suppression Reserve Funds

(a) Definitions — In this section:

(1) Federal land — The term "Federal land" means —

(A) public land, as defined in section 1702 of this title;

(B) units of the National Park System;

(C) refuges of the National Wildlife Refuge System;

(D) land held in trust by the United States for the benefit of Indian tribes or members of an Indian tribe; and

(E) land in the National Forest System, as defined in section 1609(a) of Title 16.

(2) FLAME Fund — The term "FLAME Fund" means a FLAME Wildfire Suppression Reserve Fund established by subsection (b).

(3) Relevant congressional committees — The term "relevant congressional committees" means the Committee on Appropriations, the Committee on Natural Resources, and the Committee on Agriculture of the House of Representatives and the Committee on Appropriations, the Committee on Energy and Natural Resources, and the Committee on Indian Affairs of the Senate.

(4) Secretary concerned — The term "Secretary concerned" means —

(A) the Secretary of the Interior, with respect to —

(i) Federal land described in subparagraphs (A), (B), (C), and (D) of paragraph (1); and

(ii) the FLAME Fund established for the Department of the Interior; and

(B) the Secretary of Agriculture, with respect to —

(i) National Forest System land; and

(ii) the FLAME Fund established for the Department of the Agriculture.

(b) Establishment of FLAME Funds — There is established in the Treasury of the United States the following accounts:

(1) The FLAME Wildfire Suppression Reserve Fund for the Department of the Interior.

(2) The FLAME Wildfire Suppression Reserve Fund for the Department of Agriculture.

(c) Purpose of FLAME Funds — The FLAME Funds shall be available to cover the costs of large or complex wildfire events and as a reserve when amounts provided for wildfire suppression and Federal emergency response in the Wildland Fire Management appropriation accounts are exhausted.

(d) Funding

(1) Credits to Funds — A FLAME Fund shall consist of the following:

(A) Such amounts as are appropriated to that FLAME Fund.

(B) Such amounts as are transferred to that FLAME Fund under paragraph (5).

(2) Authorization of appropriations

(A) Authorization of appropriations

There are authorized to be appropriated to the FLAME Funds such amounts as are necessary to carry out this section.

(B) Congressional intent—It is the intent of Congress that, for fiscal year 2011 and each fiscal year thereafter, the amounts requested by the President for a FLAME Fund should be not less than the amount estimated by the Secretary concerned as the amount necessary for that fiscal year for wildfire suppression activities of the Secretary that meet the criteria specified in subsection (e)(2)(B)(i).

(C) Sense of Congress on designation of FLAME Fund appropriations, supplemental funding request, and supplement to other suppression funding

It is the sense of Congress that for fiscal year 2011 and each fiscal year thereafter--

(i) amounts appropriated to a FLAME Fund in excess of the amount estimated by the Secretary concerned as the amount necessary for that fiscal year for wildfire suppression activities of the Secretary that meet the criteria specified in subsection (e)(2)(B)(i) should be designated as amounts necessary to meet emergency needs;

(ii) the Secretary concerned should promptly make a supplemental request for additional funds to replenish the FLAME Fund if the Secretary determines that the FLAME Fund will be exhausted within 30 days; and

(iii) funding made available through the FLAME Fund should be used to supplement the funding otherwise appropriated to the Secretary concerned for wildfire suppression and Federal emergency response in the Wildland Fire Management appropriation accounts.

(3) Availability — Amounts in a FLAME Fund shall remain available to the Secretary concerned until expended.

(4) Notice of insufficient funds — The Secretary concerned shall notify the relevant congressional

committees if the Secretary estimates that only 60 days worth of funds remain in the FLAME Fund administered by that Secretary.

(5) Transfer authority — If a FLAME Fund has insufficient funds, the Secretary concerned administering the other FLAME Fund may transfer amounts to the FLAME Fund with insufficient funds. Not more than $100,000,000 may be transferred from a FLAME Fund during any fiscal year under this authority.

(e) Use of FLAME Fund

(1) In general — Subject to paragraphs (2) and (3), amounts in a FLAME Fund shall be available to the Secretary concerned to transfer to the Wildland Fire Management appropriation account of that Secretary to pay the costs of wildfire suppression activities of that Secretary that are separate from amounts for wildfire suppression activities annually appropriated to that Secretary under the Wildland Fire Management appropriation account of that Secretary.

(2) Declaration required

(A) In general — Amounts in a FLAME Fund shall be available for transfer under paragraph (1) only after that Secretary concerned issues a declaration that a wildfire suppression event is eligible for funding from the FLAME Fund.

(B) Declaration criteria — A declaration by the Secretary concerned under subparagraph (A) may be issued only if —

(i) in the case of an individual wildfire incident —

(I) the fire covers 300 or more acres; or

(II) the Secretary concerned determines that the fire has required an emergency Federal response based on the significant complexity, severity, or threat posed by the fire to human life, property, or resources; or

(ii) the cumulative costs of wildfire suppression and Federal emergency response activities for the Secretary concerned will exceed, within 30 days, all of the amounts previously appropriated (including amounts appropriated under an emergency designation, but excluding amounts appropriated to the FLAME Fund) to the Secretary concerned for wildfire suppression and Federal emergency response.

(3) State, private, and tribal land—Use of a FLAME Fund for emergency wildfire suppression activities on State land, private land, and tribal land shall be consistent with any existing agreements in which the Secretary concerned has agreed to assume responsibility for wildfire suppression activities on the land.

(f) Treatment of anticipated and predicted activities

— For fiscal year 2011 and subsequent fiscal years, the Secretary concerned shall request funds within the Wildland Fire Management appropriation account of that Secretary for regular wildfire suppression activities that do not meet the criteria specified in subsection (e)(2)(B)(i).

(g) Prohibition on other transfers

— The Secretary concerned may not transfer funds from non-fire accounts to the Wildland Fire Management appropriation account of that Secretary unless amounts in the FLAME Fund of that Secretary and any amounts appropriated to that Secretary for the purpose of wildfire suppression will be exhausted within 30 days.

(h) Accounting and reports

(1) Accounting and reporting requirements — The Secretary concerned shall account and report on amounts transferred from the respective FLAME Fund in a manner that is consistent with existing National Fire Plan reporting procedures.

(2) Annual report — The Secretary concerned shall submit to the relevant congressional committees and make available to the public an annual report that —

(A) describes the obligation and expenditure of amounts transferred from the FLAME Fund; and

(B) includes any recommendations that the Secretary concerned may have to improve the administrative control and oversight of the FLAME Fund.

(3) Estimates of wildfire suppression costs to improve budgeting and funding

(A) In general — Consistent with the schedule provided in subparagraph (C), the Secretary concerned shall submit to the relevant congressional committees an estimate of anticipated wildfire suppression costs for the applicable fiscal year.

(B) Independent review — The methodology for developing the estimates under subparagraph (A) shall be subject to periodic independent review to ensure compliance with subparagraph (D).

(C) Schedule — The Secretary concerned shall submit an estimate under subparagraph (A) during —

(i) the first week of March of each year;

(ii) the first week of May of each year;

(iii) the first week of July of each year; and

(iv) if a bill making appropriations for the Department of the Interior and the Forest Service for the following fiscal year has not been enacted by September 1, the first week of September of each year.

(D) Requirements—An estimate of anticipated wildfire suppression costs shall be developed using the best available-

(i) climate, weather, and other relevant data; and

(ii) models and other analytic tools.

(i) Termination of authority — The authority of the Secretary concerned to use the FLAME Fund established for that Secretary shall terminate at the end of the third fiscal year in which no appropriations to, or withdrawals from, that FLAME Fund have been made for a period of three consecutive fiscal years. Upon termination of such authority, any amounts remaining in the affected FLAME Fund shall be transferred to, and made a part of, the Wildland Fire Management appropriation account of the Secretary concerned for wildland suppression activities.

§1748a-1. Request for additional wildfire suppression funds

If the amount provided for wildfire suppression operations for that fiscal year will be exhausted within 30 calendar days, the Secretary of the Interior or the Secretary of Agriculture (as applicable), in consultation with the Director of the Office of Management and Budget, shall promptly submit a request to Congress for supplemental appropriations.

§1748a-2. Reporting requirements

(a) In general

Not later than 90 days after the end of the fiscal year for which additional new budget authority is used, pursuant to section 901(b)(2)(F)(i) of Title 2, as added by section 102 of this division, the Secretary of the Interior or the Secretary of Agriculture (as applicable), in consultation with the Director of the Office of Management and Budget, shall—

(1) prepare an annual report with respect to the additional new budget authority;

(2) submit to the Committees on Appropriations, the Budget, and Natural Resources of the House of Representatives and the Committees on Appropriations, the Budget, and Energy and Natural Resources of the Senate the annual report prepared under paragraph (1); and

(3) make the report prepared under paragraph (1) available to the public.

(b) Components

The annual report prepared under subsection (a) (1) shall—

(1) document obligations and outlays of the additional new budget authority for wildfire suppression operations;

(2) identify risk-based factors that influenced management decisions with respect to wildfire suppression operations;

(3) analyze a statistically significant sample of large fires, including an analysis for each fire of—

(A) cost drivers;

(B) the effectiveness of risk management techniques and whether fire operations strategy tracked the risk assessment;

(C) any resulting ecological or other benefits to the landscape;

(D) the impact of investments in wildfire suppression operations preparedness;

(E) effectiveness of wildfire suppression operations, including an analysis of resources lost versus dollars invested;

(F) effectiveness of any fuel treatments on fire behavior and suppression expenditures;

(G) levels of exposure experienced by firefighters;

(H) suggested corrective actions; and

(I) any other factors the Secretary of the Interior or Secretary of Agriculture (as applicable) determines to be appropriate;

(4) include an accounting of overall fire management and spending by the Department of the Interior or the Department of Agriculture, which shall be analyzed by fire size, cost, regional location, and other factors;

(5) describe any lessons learned in the conduct of wildfire suppression operations; and

(6) include any other elements that the Secretary of the Interior or the Secretary of Agriculture (as applicable) determines to be necessary.

§1748b. Cohesive wildfire management strategy

(a) Strategy required — Not later than one year after October 30, 2009, the Secretary of the Interior and the Secretary of Agriculture, acting jointly, shall submit to Congress a report that contains a cohesive wildfire management strategy, consistent with the recommendations described in recent reports of the Government Accountability Office regarding management strategies.

(b) Elements of strategy — The strategy required by subsection (a) shall provide for—

(1) the identification of the most cost-effective means for allocating fire management budget resources;

(2) the reinvestment in non-fire programs by the Secretary of the Interior and the Secretary of Agriculture;

(3) employing the appropriate management response to wildfires;

(4) assessing the level of risk to communities;

(5) the allocation of hazardous fuels reduction funds based on the priority of hazardous fuels reduction projects;

(6) assessing the impacts of climate change on the frequency and severity of wildfire; and

(7) studying the effects of invasive species on wildfire risk.

(c) Revision — At least once during each five-year period beginning on the date of the submission of the cohesive wildfire management strategy under subsection (a), the Secretary of the Interior and the Secretary of Agriculture shall revise the strategy to address any changes affecting the strategy, including changes with respect to landscape, vegetation, climate, and weather.

§1748b-1. Wildfire Technology Modernization

(a) Purpose

The purpose of this section is to promote the use of the best available technology to enhance the effective and cost-efficient

response to wildfires—

(1) to meet applicable protection objectives; and

(2) to increase the safety of—

(A) firefighters; and

(B) the public.

(b) Definitions

In this section:

(1) Secretaries

The term "Secretaries" means—

(A) the Secretary of Agriculture; and

(B) the Secretary.

(2) Secretary concerned

The term "Secretary concerned" means—

(A) the Secretary of Agriculture, with respect to activities under the Department of Agriculture; and

(B) the Secretary, with respect to activities under the Department of the Interior.

(c) Unmanned aircraft systems

(1) Definitions

In this subsection, the terms "unmanned aircraft" and "unmanned aircraft system" have the meanings given those terms in section 44801 of Title 49.

(2) Establishment of program

Not later than 180 days after March 12, 2019, the Secretary, in consultation with the Secretary of Agriculture, shall establish a research, development, and testing program, or expand an applicable existing program, to assess unmanned aircraft system technologies, including optionally piloted aircraft, across the full range of wildland fire management operations in order to accelerate the deployment and integration of those technologies into the operations of the Secretaries.

(3) Expanding use of unmanned aircraft systems on wildfires

In carrying out the program established under paragraph (2), the Secretaries, in coordination with the Federal Aviation Administration, State wildland firefighting agencies, and other relevant Federal agencies, shall enter into an agreement under which the Secretaries shall develop consistent protocols and plans for the use on wildland fires of unmanned aircraft system technologies, including for the development of real-time maps of the location of wildland fires.

(d) Location systems for wildland firefighters

(1) In general

Not later than 2 years after March 12, 2019, subject to the availability of appropriations, the Secretaries, in coordination with State wildland firefighting agencies, shall jointly develop and operate a tracking system (referred to in this subsection as the "system") to remotely locate the positions of fire resources for use by wildland firefighters, including, at a minimum, any fire resources assigned to Federal type 1 wildland fire incident management teams.

(2) Requirements

The system shall—

(A) use the most practical and effective technology available to the Secretaries to remotely track the location of an active resource, such as a Global Positioning System;

(B) depict the location of each fire resource on the applicable maps developed under subsection (c)(3);

(C) operate continuously during the period for which any firefighting personnel are assigned to the applicable Federal wildland fire; and

(D) be subject to such terms and conditions as the Secretary concerned determines necessary for the effective implementation of the system.

(3) Operation

The Secretary concerned shall—

(A) before commencing operation of the system—

(i) conduct not fewer than 2 pilot projects relating to the operation, management, and effectiveness of the system; and

(ii) review the results of those pilot projects;

(B) conduct training, and maintain a culture, such that an employee, officer, or contractor shall not rely on the system for safety; and

(C) establish procedures for the collection, storage, and transfer of data collected under this subsection to ensure—

(i) data security; and

(ii) the privacy of wildland fire personnel.

(e) Wildland fire decision support

(1) Protocol

To the maximum extent practicable, the Secretaries shall ensure that wildland fire management activities conducted by the Secretaries, or conducted jointly by the Secretaries and State wildland firefighting agencies, achieve compliance with applicable incident management objectives in a manner that—

(A) minimizes firefighter exposure to the lowest level necessary; and

(B) reduces overall costs of wildfire incidents.

(2) Wildfire decision support system

(A) In general

The Secretaries, in coordination with State wildland firefighting agencies, shall establish a system or expand an existing system to track and monitor decisions made by the Secretaries or State wildland firefighting agencies in managing wildfires.

(B) Components

The system established or expanded under subparagraph (A) shall be able to alert the Secretaries if—

(i) unusual costs are incurred;

(ii) an action to be carried out would likely—

(I) endanger the safety of a firefighter; or

(II) be ineffective in meeting an applicable suppression or protection goal; or

(iii) a decision regarding the management of a wildfire deviates from—

(I) an applicable protocol established by the Secretaries, including the requirement under paragraph (1); or

(II) an applicable spatial fire management plan or fire management plan of the Secretary concerned.

(f) Smoke projections from active wildland fires

The Secretaries shall establish a program, to be known as the "Interagency Wildland Fire Air Quality Response Program", under which the Secretary concerned—

(1) to the maximum extent practicable, shall assign 1 or more air resource advisors to a type 1 incident management team managing a Federal wildland fire; and

(2) may assign 1 or more air resource advisors to a type 2 incident management team managing a wildland fire.

(g) Omitted

(h) Rapid Response Erosion Database

(1) In general

The Secretaries, in consultation with the Administrator of the National Aeronautics and Space Administration and the Secretary of Commerce, shall establish and maintain a database, to be known as the "Rapid Response Erosion Database" (referred to in this subsection as the "Database").

(2) Open-source Database

(A) Availability

The Secretaries shall make the Database (including the original source code)—

(i) web-based; and

(ii) available without charge.

(B) Components

To the maximum extent practicable, the Database shall provide for—

(i) the automatic incorporation of spatial data relating to vegetation, soils, and elevation into an applicable map created by the Secretary concerned that depicts the changes in land-cover and soil properties caused by a wildland fire; and

(ii) the generation of a composite map that can be used by the Secretary concerned to model the effectiveness of treatments in the burned area to prevent flooding, erosion, and landslides under a range of weather scenarios.

(3) Use

The Secretary concerned shall use the Database, as applicable, in developing recommendations for emergency stabilization treatments or modifications to drainage structures to protect values-at-risk following a wildland fire.

(4) Coordination

The Secretaries may share the Database, and any results generated in using the Database, with any State or unit of local government.

(i) Predicting where wildfires will start

(1) In general

The Secretaries, in consultation with the Administrator of the National Aeronautics and Space Administration, the Secretary of Energy, and the Secretary of Commerce, through the capabilities and assets located at the National Laboratories, shall establish and maintain a system to predict the locations of future wildfires for fire-prone areas of the United States.

(2) Cooperation; components

The system established under paragraph (1) shall be based on, and seek to enhance, similar systems in existence on March 12, 2019, including the Fire Danger Assessment System.

(3) Use in forecasts

Not later than 1 year after March 12, 2019, the Secretaries shall use the system established under paragraph (1), to the maximum extent practicable, for purposes of developing any wildland fire potential forecasts.

(4) Coordination

The Secretaries may share the system established under paragraph (1), and any results generated in using the system, with any State or unit of local government.

(j) Termination of authority

The authority provided by this section terminates on the date that is 10 years after March 12, 2019.

(k) Savings clause

Nothing in this section—

(1) requires the Secretary concerned to establish a new program, system, or database to replace an existing program, system, or database that meets the objectives of this section; or

(2) precludes the Secretary concerned from using existing or future technology that—

(A) is more efficient, safer, or better meets the needs of firefighters, other personnel, or the public; and

(B) meets the objectives of this section.

§1748c. Bureau of Land Management Foundation

(a) Definitions — In this section:

(1) Board — The term "Board" means the Board of Directors of the Foundation established under subsection (c).

(2) Foundation — The term "Foundation" means the Bureau of Land Management Foundation established by subsection (b)(1)(A).

(3) Public land — The term "public land" has the meaning given the term "public lands" in section 103 of the Federal Land Policy and Management Act of 1976 (43 U.S.C. 1702).

(4) Secretary — The term "Secretary" means the Secretary of the Interior.

(5) Wild free-roaming horses and burros — The term "wild free-roaming horses and burros" has the meaning given the term in section 2 of Public Law 92-195 (commonly known as the "Wild Free-Roaming Horses and Burros Act") (16 U.S.C. 1332).

(b) Establishment and purposes —

(1) Establishment —

(A) In general — There is established a foundation, to be known as the "Bureau of Land Management Foundation".

(B) Limitation — The Foundation shall not be considered to be an agency or establishment of the United States.

(C) Tax exemption — The Foundation shall be considered to be a charitable and nonprofit corporation under section 501(c)(3) of the Internal Revenue Code of 1986.

(2) Purposes — The purposes of the Foundation are —

(A) to encourage, accept, and administer private gifts of money and real and personal property for the benefit of, or in connection with the activities and services of, the Bureau of Land Management;

(B) to carry out activities that advance the purposes for which public land is administered;

(C) to carry out and encourage educational, technical, scientific, and other assistance or activities that support the mission of the Bureau of Land Management; and

(D) to assist the Bureau of Land Management with challenges that could be better addressed with the support of a foundation, including —

(i) reclamation and conservation activities;

(ii) activities relating to wild free-roaming horses and burros; and

(iii) the stewardship of cultural and archeological treasures on public land.

(c) Board of Directors —

(1) Establishment —

(A) In general — The Foundation shall be governed by a Board of Directors.

(B) Composition —

(i) In general — The Board shall consist of not more than 9 members.

(ii) Ex-officio member — The Director of the Bureau of Land Management shall be an ex-officio, nonvoting member of the Board.

(C) Requirements —

(i) Citizenship — A member appointed to the Board shall be a citizen of the United States.

(ii) Expertise — A majority of members appointed to the Board shall have education or experience relating to natural, cultural, conservation, or other resource management, law, or research.

(iii) Diverse points of view — To the maximum extent practicable, the members of the Board shall represent diverse points of view.

(2) Date of initial appointment — Not later than 1 year after May 5, 2017, the Secretary shall appoint the initial members of the Board.

(3) Terms —

(A) In general — Except as provided in subparagraph (B), a member of the Board shall be appointed for a term of 6 years.

(B) Initial appointments — The Secretary shall stagger the initial appointments to the Board, as the Secretary determines to be appropriate, in a manner that ensures that —

(i) 1/3 of the members shall serve for a term of 2 years;

(ii) 1/3 of the members shall serve for a term of 4 years; and

(iii) 1/3 of the members shall serve for a term of 6 years.

(C) Vacancies — A vacancy on the Board shall be filled —

(i) not later than 60 days after the date of the vacancy;

(ii) in the manner in which the original appointment was made; and

(iii) for the remainder of the term of the member vacating the Board.

(D) Removal for failure to attend meetings —

(i) In general — A member of the Board may be removed from the Board by a majority vote of the Board, if the individual fails to attend 3 consecutive regularly scheduled meetings of the Board.

(ii) Requirements — A vacancy as the result of a removal under clause (i) shall be filled in accordance with subparagraph (C).

(E) Limitation — A member of the Board shall not serve more than 12 consecutive years on the Board.

(4) Chairperson —

(A) In general — The Board shall elect a Chairperson from among the members of the Board.

(B) Term — The Chairperson of the Board —

(i) shall serve as Chairperson for a 2-year term; and

(ii) may be reelected as Chairperson while serving as a member of the Board.

(5) Quorum — A majority of the voting members of the Board shall constitute a quorum for the transaction of business of the Board.

(6) Meetings — The Board shall meet —

(A) at the call of the Chairperson; but

(B) not less than once each calendar year.

(7) Reimbursement of expenses —

(A) In general — Serving as a member of the Board shall not constitute employment by the Federal Government for any purpose.

(B) Reimbursement — A member of the Board shall serve without pay, other than reimbursement for the actual and necessary traveling and subsistence expenses incurred in the performance of the duties of the member for the Foundation, in accordance with section 5703 of title 5, United States Code.

(8) General powers — The Board may —

(A) appoint officers and employees in accordance with paragraph (9);

(B) adopt a constitution and bylaws consistent with the purposes of the Foundation and this section; and

(C) carry out any other activities that may be necessary to function and to carry out this section.

(9) Officers and employees —

(A) In general — No officer or employee may be appointed to the Foundation until the date on which the Board determines that the Foundation has sufficient funds to pay for the service of the officer or employee.

(B) Limitation — Appointment as an officer or employee of the Foundation shall not constitute employment by the Federal Government.

(10) Limitation and conflicts of interest —

(A) Prohibition on political activity — The Foundation shall not participate or intervene in a political campaign on behalf of any candidate for public office.

(B) Limitation on participation — No member of the Board or officer or employee of the Foundation shall participate, directly or indirectly, in the consideration or determination of any question before the Foundation that affects —

(i) the financial interests of the member of the Board, officer, or employee; or

(ii) the interests of any corporation partnership, entity, or organization in which the member of the Board, officer, or employee —

(I) is an officer, director, or trustee; or

(II) has any direct or indirect financial interest.

(d) Powers and obligations —

(1) In general — The Foundation —

(A) shall have perpetual succession; and

(B) may conduct business throughout the several States, territories, and possessions of the United States.

(2) Notice; service of process —

(A) Designated agent — The Foundation shall at all times maintain a designated agent in the District of Columbia authorized to accept service of process for the Foundation.

(B) Service of process — The serving of notice to, or service of process on, the agent required under this paragraph, or mailed to the business address of the agent, shall be deemed to be notice to, or the service of process on, the Foundation.

(3) Seal — The Foundation shall have an official seal, to be selected by the Board, which shall be judicially noticed.

(4) Powers — To carry out the purposes of the Foundation, the Foundation shall have, in addition to powers otherwise authorized by this section, the usual powers of a not-for-profit corporation in the District of Columbia, including the power —

(A) to accept, receive, solicit, hold, administer, and use any gift, devise, or bequest, absolutely or in trust, of real or personal property, or any income from, or other interest in, the property;

(B) to acquire by donation, gift, devise, purchase, or exchange, and to dispose of, any real or personal property or interest in the property;

(C) to sell, donate, lease, invest, reinvest, retain, or otherwise dispose of any property or income from property, unless limited by the instrument of transfer;

(D) to borrow money and issue bonds, debentures, or other debt instruments;

(E) to sue and be sued, and complain and defend itself in any court of competent jurisdiction, except that the members of the

Board shall not be held personally liable, except in a case of gross negligence;

(F) (i) to enter into contracts or other agreements with public agencies, private organizations, and persons; and

(ii) to make such payments as may be necessary to carry out the purposes of the contracts or agreements; and

(G) to carry out any activity necessary and proper to advance the purposes of the Foundation.

(5) Real property —

(A) In general — For purposes of this section, an interest in real property shall include mineral and water rights, rights-of-way, and easements, appurtenant or in gross.

(B) Acceptance — A gift, devise, or bequest of real property may be accepted by the Foundation, regardless of whether the property is encumbered, restricted, or subject to beneficial interests of a private person, if any current or future interest in the property is for the benefit of the Foundation.

(C) Declining gifts — The Foundation may, at the discretion of the Foundation, decline any gift, devise, or bequest of real property.

(D) Prohibition on condemnation — No land, water, or interest in land or water, that is owned by the Foundation shall be subject to condemnation by any State, political subdivision of a State, or agent or instrumentality of a State or political subdivision of a State.

(e) Administrative services and support —

(1) Funding —

(A) In general — For the purposes of assisting the Foundation in establishing an office and meeting initial administrative, project, and other expenses, the Secretary may provide to the Foundation, from funds appropriated under subsection (j), such sums as are necessary for fiscal years 2017 and 2018.

(B) Availability of funds — Funds made available under subparagraph (A) shall remain available to the Foundation until expended for authorized purposes.

(2) Administrative expenses —

(A) In general — The Secretary may provide to the Foundation personnel, facilities, equipment, and other administrative services, subject to such limitations, terms, and conditions as the Secretary may establish.

(B) Reimbursement — The Foundation may reimburse the Secretary for any support provided under subparagraph (A), in whole or in part, and any reimbursement received by the Secretary under this subparagraph shall be deposited in the Treasury to the credit of the appropriations then current

and chargeable for the cost of providing the services.

(f) Volunteers — The Secretary may accept, without regard to the civil service classification laws (including regulations), the services of the Foundation, the Board, and the officers, employees, and agents of the Foundation, without compensation from the Department of the Interior, as volunteers for the performance of the functions under section 307(d) of the Federal Land Policy and Management Act of 1976 (43 U.S.C. 1737(d)).

(g) Audits and report requirements —

(1) Audits — For purposes of section 10101 of title 36, the Foundation shall be considered to be a private corporation established under Federal law.

(2) Annual reports — At the end of each fiscal year, the Board shall submit to Congress a report that describes the proceedings and activities of the Foundation during that fiscal year, including a full and complete statement of the receipts, expenditures, and investments.

(h) United States release from liability —

(1) In general — The United States shall not be liable for any debt, default, act, or omission of the Foundation.

(2) Full faith and credit — The full faith and credit of the United States shall not extend to any obligation of the Foundation.

(i) Limitation on authority — Nothing in this section authorizes the Foundation to perform any function the authority for which is provided to the Bureau of Land Management under any other provision of law.

(j) Authorization of appropriations — There are authorized to be appropriated such sums as are necessary to carry out this section.

§1748d. Report on wildfire, insect infestation, and disease prevention on Federal land

Not later than 180 days after December 20, 2018, and every year thereafter, the Secretary and the Secretary of Interior shall submit to the Committee on Agriculture of the House of Representatives, the Committee on Natural Resources of the House of Representatives, the Committee on Agriculture, Nutrition, and Forestry of the Senate, and the Committee on Energy and Natural Resources of the Senate a jointly written report on—

(1) the number of acres of Federal land treated by the Secretary or the Secretary of the Interior for wildfire, insect infestation, or disease prevention;

(2) the number of acres of Federal land categorized as a high or extreme fire risk;

(3) the total timber production from Federal land;

(4) the number of acres and average fire intensity of wildfires affecting Federal land treated for wildfire, insect infestation, or disease prevention;

(5) the number of acres and average fire intensity of wildfires affecting Federal land not treated for wildfire, insect infestation, or disease prevention;

(6) the Federal response time for each fire on greater than 25,000 acres;

(7) the number of miles of roads and trails on Federal land in need of maintenance;

(8) the number of miles of roads on Federal land in need of decommissioning;

(9) the maintenance backlog, as of the date of the report, for roads, trails, and recreational facilities on Federal land;

(10) other measures needed to maintain, improve, or restore water quality on Federal land; and

(11) other measures needed to improve ecosystem function or resiliency on Federal land.

SUBCHAPTER IV—RANGE MANAGEMENT

§1751. Grazing fees; feasibility study; contents; submission of report; annual distribution and use of range betterment funds; nature of distributions
[FLPMA §401]

(a) The Secretary of Agriculture and the Secretary of the Interior shall jointly cause to be conducted a study to determine the value of grazing on the lands under their jurisdiction in the eleven Western States with a view to establishing a fee to be charged for domestic livestock grazing on such lands which is equitable to the United States and to the holders of grazing permits and leases on such lands. In making such study, the Secretaries shall take into consideration the costs of production normally associated with domestic livestock grazing in the eleven Western States, differences in forage values, and such other factors as may relate to the reasonableness of such fees. The Secretaries shall report the result of such study to the Congress not later than one year from and after October 21, 1976, together with recommendations to implement a reasonable grazing fee schedule based upon such study. If the report required herein has not been submitted to the Congress within one year after October 21, 1976, the grazing fee charge then in effect shall not be altered and shall remain the same until such report has been submitted to the Congress. Neither Secretary shall increase the grazing fee in the 1977 grazing year.

(b)(1) Congress finds that a substantial amount of the Federal range lands is deteriorating in quality, and that installation of additional range improvements could arrest much of the continuing deterioration and could lead to substantial betterment of forage conditions with resulting benefits to wildlife, watershed protection, and livestock production. Congress therefore directs that 50 per centum or $10,000,000 per annum, whichever is greater of all moneys received by the United States as fees for grazing domestic livestock on public lands (other than from ceded Indian lands) under the Taylor Grazing Act (48 Stat. 1269; 43 U.S.C. §§315 *et seq.*) and the Act of August 28, 1937 (50 Stat. 874; 43 U.S.C. §1181d), and on lands in National Forests in the sixteen contiguous Western States under the provisions of this section shall be credited to a separate account in the Treasury, one-half of which is authorized to be appropriated and made available for use in the district, region, or national forest from which such moneys were derived, as the respective Secretary may direct after consultation with district, regional, or national forest user representatives, for the purpose of on-the-ground range rehabilitation, protection, and improvements on such lands, and the remaining one-half shall be used for on-the-ground range rehabilitation, protection, and improvements as the Secretary concerned directs. Any funds so appropriated shall be in addition to any other appropriations made to the respective Secretary for planning and administration of the range betterment program and for other range management. Such rehabilitation, protection, and improvements shall include all forms of range land betterment including, but not limited to, seeding and reseeding, fence construction, weed control, water development, and fish and wildlife habitat enhancement as the respective Secretary may direct after consultation with user representatives. The annual distribution and use of range betterment funds authorized by this paragraph shall not be considered a major Federal action requiring a detailed statement pursuant to section 4332(c) of Title 42.

(2) All distributions of moneys made under subsection (b)(1) of this section shall be in addition to distributions made under section 10 of the Taylor Grazing Act (43 U.S.C. §315i) and shall not apply to distribution of moneys made under section 11 of that Act (43 U.S.C. §315j). The remaining moneys received by the United States as fees for grazing domestic livestock on the public lands shall be deposited in the Treasury as miscellaneous receipts.

§1752. Grazing leases and permits
[FLPMA §402]

(a) **Terms and conditions** — Except as provided in subsection (b) of this section, permits and leases for domestic livestock grazing on public lands issued by the Secretary under the Act of June 28, 1934 (48 Stat. 1269, as amended; 43 U.S.C. §§315 *et seq.*) or the Act of August 28, 1937 (50 Stat. 874, as amended; 43 U.S.C. §§1181a-1181j), or by the Secretary of Agriculture, with respect to lands within National Forests in the sixteen contiguous Western States, shall be for a term of ten years subject to such terms and conditions the Secretary concerned deems appropriate and consistent with the governing law, including, but not limited to, the authority of the

Secretary concerned to cancel, suspend, or modify a grazing permit or lease, in whole or in part, pursuant to the terms and conditions thereof, or to cancel or suspend a grazing permit or lease for any violation of a grazing regulation or of any term or condition of such grazing permit or lease.

(b) Terms of lesser duration — Permits or leases may be issued by the Secretary concerned for a period shorter than ten years where the Secretary concerned determines that —

(1) the land is pending disposal; or

(2) the land will be devoted to a public purpose prior to the end of ten years; or

(3) it will be in the best interest of sound land management to specify a shorter term: *Provided*, That the absence from an allotment management plan of details the Secretary concerned would like to include but which are undeveloped shall not be the basis for establishing a term shorter than ten years: *Provided further*, That the absence of completed land use plans or court ordered environmental statements shall not be the sole basis for establishing a term shorter than ten years unless the Secretary determines on a case-by-case basis that the information to be contained in such land use plan or court ordered environmental impact statement is necessary to determine whether a shorter term should be established for any of the reasons set forth in items (1) through (3) of this subsection.

(c) First priority for renewal of expiring permit or lease — So long as (1) the lands for which the permit or lease is issued remain available for domestic livestock grazing in accordance with land use plans prepared pursuant to section 1712 of this title or section 1604 of title 16, (2) the permittee or lessee is in compliance with the rules and regulations issued and the terms and conditions in the permit or lease specified by the Secretary concerned, and (3) the permittee or lessee accepts the terms and conditions to be included by the Secretary concerned in the new permit or lease, the holder of the expiring permit or lease shall be given first priority for receipt of the new permit or lease.

(d) Allotment management plan requirements — All permits and leases for domestic livestock grazing issued pursuant to this section may incorporate an allotment management plan developed by the Secretary concerned. However, nothing in this subsection shall be construed to supersede any requirement for completion of court ordered environmental impact statements prior to development and incorporation of allotment management plans. If the Secretary concerned elects to develop an allotment management plan for a given area, he shall do so in careful and considered consultation, cooperation and coordination with the lessees, permittees, and landowners involved, the district grazing advisory boards established pursu-

ant to section 1753 of this title, and any State or States having lands within the area to be covered by such allotment management plan. Allotment management plans shall be tailored to the specific range condition of the area to be covered by such plan, and shall be reviewed on a periodic basis to determine whether they have been effective in improving the range condition of the lands involved or whether such lands can be better managed under the provisions of subsection (e) of this section. The Secretary concerned may revise or terminate such plans or develop new plans from time to time after such review and careful and considered consultation, cooperation and coordination with the parties involved. As used in this subsection, the terms "court ordered environmental impact statement" and "range condition" shall be defined as in the "Public Rangelands Improvement Act of 1978 [43 U.S.C. §§1901 *et seq.*]".

(e) Omission of allotment management plan requirements and incorporation of appropriate terms and conditions; reexamination of range conditions — In all cases where the Secretary concerned has not completed an allotment management plan or determines that an allotment management plan is not necessary for management of livestock operations and will not be prepared, the Secretary concerned shall incorporate in grazing permits and leases such terms and conditions as he deems appropriate for management of the permitted or leased lands pursuant to applicable law. The Secretary concerned shall also specify therein the numbers of animals to be grazed and the seasons of use and that he may reexamine the condition of the range at any time and, if he finds on reexamination that the condition of the range requires adjustment in the amount or other aspect of grazing use, that the permittee or lessee shall adjust his use to the extent the Secretary concerned deems necessary. Such readjustment shall be put into full force and effect on the date specified by the Secretary concerned.

(f) Allotment management plan applicability to non-Federal lands; appeal rights — Allotment management plans shall not refer to livestock operations or range improvements on non-Federal lands except where the non-Federal lands are intermingled with, or, with the consent of the permittee or lessee involved, associated with, the Federal lands subject to the plan. The Secretary concerned under appropriate regulations shall grant to lessees and permittees the right of appeal from decisions which specify the terms and conditions of allotment management plans. The preceding sentence of this subsection shall not be construed as limiting any other right of appeal from decisions of such officials.

(g) Cancellation of permit or lease; determination of reasonable compensation; notice — Whenever a permit or lease for grazing domestic livestock is canceled in whole or in part, in order to devote the lands covered by the permit or lease to another public purpose, including disposal, the permittee or lessee shall receive from the United States a reasonable compensation for the adjusted value, to be determined by the Secretary concerned, of his interest in authorized permanent improvements placed or constructed by the permittee or lessee on lands covered by such permit or lease, but not to exceed the fair market value of the terminated portion of the permittee's or lessee's interest therein. Except in cases of emergency, no permit or lease shall be canceled under this subsection without two years' prior notification.

(h) Applicability of provisions to rights, etc., in or to public lands or lands in National Forests — Nothing in this Act shall be construed as modifying in any way law existing on October 21, 1976, with respect to the creation of right, title, interest or estate in or to public lands or lands in National Forests by issuance of grazing permits and leases.

§1753. Omitted

SUBCHAPTER V—RIGHTS-OF-WAY

§1761. Grant, issue, or renewal of rights-of-way

[FLPMA §501]

(a) Authorized purposes — The Secretary, with respect to the public lands (including public lands, as defined in section 1702(e) of this title, which are reserved from entry pursuant to section 24 of the Federal Power Act (16 U.S.C. §818)) and, the Secretary of Agriculture, with respect to lands within the National Forest System (except in each case land designated as wilderness), are authorized to grant, issue, or renew rights-of-way over, upon, under, or through such lands for —

(1) reservoirs, canals, ditches, flumes, laterals, pipes, pipelines, tunnels, and other facilities and systems for the impoundment, storage, transportation, or distribution of water;

(2) pipelines and other systems for the transportation or distribution of liquids and gases, other than water and other than oil, natural gas, synthetic liquid or gaseous fuels, or any refined product produced therefrom, and for storage and terminal facilities in connection therewith;

(3) pipelines, slurry and emulsion systems, and conveyor belts for transportation and distribution of solid materials, and facilities for the storage of such materials in connection therewith;

(4) systems for generation, transmission, and distribution of electric energy, except that the applicant shall also comply with all applicable requirements of the Federal Energy Regulatory Commission under the Federal Power Act, in-

cluding part 1 thereof (41 Stat. 1063, 16 U.S.C. §§791a-825r);

(5) systems for transmission or reception of radio, television, telephone, telegraph, and other electronic signals, and other means of communication;

(6) roads, trails, highways, railroads, canals, tunnels, tramways, airways, livestock driveways, or other means of transportation except where such facilities are constructed and maintained in connection with commercial recreation facilities on lands in the National Forest System; or

(7) such other necessary transportation or other systems or facilities which are in the public interest and which require rights-of-way over, upon, under, or through such lands.

(b) Procedures applicable; administration

(1) The Secretary concerned shall require, prior to granting, issuing, or renewing a right-of-way, that the applicant submit and disclose those plans, contracts, agreements, or other information reasonably related to the use, or intended use, of the right-of-way, including its effect on competition, which he deems necessary to a determination, in accordance with the provisions of this Act, as to whether a right-of-way shall be granted, issued, or renewed and the terms and conditions which should be included in the right-of-way.

(2) If the applicant is a partnership, corporation, association, or other business entity, the Secretary concerned, prior to granting a right-to-way pursuant to this subchapter, shall require the applicant to disclose the identity of the participants in the entity, when he deems it necessary to a determination, in accordance with the provisions of this subchapter, as to whether a right-of-way shall be granted, issued, or renewed and the terms and conditions which should be included in the right-of-way. Such disclosures shall include, where applicable: (A) the name and address of each partner; (B) the name and address of each shareholder owning 3 per centum or more of the shares, together with the number and percentage of any class of voting shares of the entity which such shareholder is authorized to vote; and (C) the name and address of each affiliate of the entity together with, in the case of an affiliate controlled by the entity, the number of shares and the percentage of any class of voting stock of that affiliate owned, directly or indirectly, by that entity, and, in the case of an affiliate which controls that entity, the number of shares and the percentage of any class of voting stock of that entity owned, directly or indirectly, by the affiliate.

(3) The Secretary of Agriculture shall have the authority to administer all rights-of-way granted or issued under authority of previous Acts with respect to lands under the jurisdiction of the

Secretary of Agriculture, including rights-of-way granted or issued pursuant to authority given to the Secretary of the Interior by such previous Acts.

(c) Permanent easement for water systems; issuance, preconditions, etc.

(1) Upon receipt of a written application pursuant to paragraph (2) of this subsection from an applicant meeting the requirements of this subsection, the Secretary of Agriculture shall issue a permanent easement, without a requirement for reimbursement, for a water system as described in subsection (a)(1) of this section, traversing Federal lands within the National Forest System ("National Forest Lands"), constructed and in operation or placed into operation prior to October 21, 1976, if —

(A) the traversed National Forest lands are in a State where the appropriation doctrine governs the ownership of water rights;

(B) at the time of submission of the application the water system is used solely for agricultural irrigation or livestock watering purposes;

(C) the use served by the water system is not located solely on Federal lands;

(D) the originally constructed facilities comprising such system have been in substantially continuous operation without abandonment;

(E) the applicant has a valid existing right, established under applicable State law, for water to be conveyed by the water system;

(F) a recordable survey and other information concerning the location and characteristics of the system as necessary for proper management of National Forest lands is provided to the Secretary of Agriculture by the applicant for the easement; and

(G) the applicant submits such application on or before December 31, 1996.

(2)(A) Nothing in this subsection shall be construed as affecting any grants made by any previous Act. To the extent any such previous grant of right-of-way is a valid existing right, it shall remain in full force and effect unless an owner thereof notifies the Secretary of Agriculture that such owner elects to have a water system on such right-of-way governed by the provisions of this subsection and submits a written application for issuance of an easement pursuant to this subsection, in which case upon the issuance of an easement pursuant to this subsection such previous grant shall be deemed to have been relinquished and shall terminate.

(B) Easements issued under the authority of this subsection shall be fully transferable with all existing conditions and without the imposition of fees or new conditions or stipulations at the time of transfer. The holder shall notify the Secretary of Agriculture within sixty days of any address change of the holder or change in ownership of the facilities.

(C) Easements issued under the authority of this subsection shall include all changes or modifications to the original facilities in existence as of October 21, 1976, the date of enactment of this Act.

(D) Any future extension or enlargement of facilities after October 21, 1976, shall require the issuance of a separate authorization, not authorized under this subsection.

(3)(A) Except as otherwise provided in this subsection, the Secretary of Agriculture may terminate or suspend an easement issued pursuant to this subsection in accordance with the procedural and other provisions of section 1766 of this title. An easement issued pursuant to this subsection shall terminate if the water system for which such easement was issued is used for any purpose other than agricultural irrigation or livestock watering use. For purposes of subparagraph (D) of paragraph (1) of this subsection, non-use of a water system for agricultural irrigation or livestock watering purposes for any continuous five-year period shall constitute a rebuttable presumption of abandonment of the facilities comprising such system.

(B) Nothing in this subsection shall be deemed to be an assertion by the United States of any right or claim with regard to the reservation, acquisition, or use of water. Nothing in this subsection shall be deemed to confer on the Secretary of Agriculture any power or authority to regulate or control in any manner the appropriation, diversion, or use of water for any purpose (nor to diminish any such power or authority of such Secretary under applicable law) or to require the conveyance or transfer to the United States of any right or claim to the appropriation, diversion, or use of water.

(C) Except as otherwise provided in this subsection, all rights-of-way issued pursuant to this subsection are subject to all conditions and requirements of this Act.

(D) In the event a right-of-way issued pursuant to this subsection is allowed to deteriorate to the point of threatening persons or property and the holder of the right-of-way, after consultation with the Secretary of Agriculture, refuses to perform the repair and maintenance necessary to remove the threat to persons or property, the Secretary shall have the right to undertake such repair and maintenance on the right-of-way and to assess the holder for the costs of such repair and maintenance, regardless of whether the Secretary had required the holder to furnish a bond or other security pursuant to subsection (i) of this section.

(d) Rights-of-way on certain Federal lands — With respect to any project or portion thereof that was licensed pursuant to, or granted an exemption from, part I of the Federal Power Act [16 U.S.C. §§791a *et seq.*] which is located on lands subject to a reservation under section 24 of the Federal Power Act (16 U.S.C. §818) and which did not receive a permit, right-of-way or other approval under this section prior to October 24, 1992, no such permit, right-of-way, or other approval shall be required for continued operation, including continued operation pursuant to section 15 of the Federal Power Act [16 U.S.C. §808], of such project unless the Commission determines that such project involves the use of any additional public lands or National Forest lands not subject to such reservation.

§1761a. Streamlining the Forest Service process for consideration of communications facility location applications

(a) Definitions

In this section:

(1) Communications facility

The term "communications facility" includes—

(A) any infrastructure, including any transmitting device, tower, or support structure, and any equipment, switches, wiring, cabling, power sources, shelters, or cabinets, associated with the licensed or permitted unlicensed wireless or wireline transmission of writings, signs, signals, data, images, pictures, and sounds of all kinds; and

(B) any antenna or apparatus that—

(i) is designed for the purpose of emitting radio frequency;

(ii) is designed to be operated, or is operating, from a fixed location pursuant to authorization by the Federal Communications Commission or is using duly authorized devices that do not require individual licenses; and

(iii) is added to a tower, building, or other structure.

(2) Communications site

The term "communications site" means an area of covered land designated for communications uses.

(3) Communications use

The term "communications use" means the placement and operation of a communications facility.

(4) Communications use authorization

The term "communications use authorization" means an easement, right-of-way, lease, license, or other authorization to locate or modify a communications facility on covered land by the Forest Service for the primary purpose of authorizing the occupancy and use of the covered land for communications use.

(5) Covered land

The term "covered land" means National Forest System land.

(6) Forest Service

The term "Forest Service" means the United States Forest Service of the Department of Agriculture.

(7) Organizational unit

The term "organizational unit" means, within the Forest Service—

(A) a regional office;

(B) the headquarters;

(C) a management unit; or

(D) a ranger district office.

(b) Regulations

Notwithstanding section 1455 of Title 47 or section 606 of the Repack Airwaves Yielding Better Access for Users of Modern Services Act of 2018 (Public Law 115-141), not later than 1 year after December 20, 2018, the Secretary shall issue regulations—

(1) to streamline the process for considering applications to locate or modify communications facilities on covered land;

(2) to ensure, to the maximum extent practicable, that the process is uniform and standardized across the organizational units of the Forest Service; and

(3) to require that the applications described in paragraph (1) be considered and granted on a competitively neutral, technology neutral, and non-discriminatory basis.

(c) Requirements

The regulations issued under subsection (b) shall include the following:

(1) Procedures for the tracking of applications described in subsection (b)(1), including—

(A) identifying the number of applications—

(i) received;

(ii) approved; and

(iii) denied;

(B) in the case of an application that is denied, describing the reasons for the denial; and

(C) describing the amount of time between the receipt of an application and the issuance of a final decision on an application.

(2) Provision for minimum lease terms of not less than 15 years for leases with respect to the location of communications facilities on covered land.

(3) A structure of fees for—

(A) submitting an application described in subsection (b)(1), based on the cost to the   Forest Service of considering such an application; and

(B) issuing communications use authorizations, based on the cost to the Forest Service of any maintenance or other activities required to be performed by the Forest Service as a result of the location or modification of the communications facility.

(4) Provision for prioritization or streamlining of the consideration of applications to locate or modify communications facilities on covered land in a previously disturbed right-of-way.

(d) Additional considerations

In issuing regulations under subsection (b), the Secretary shall consider—

(1) how discrete reviews in considering an application described in subsection (b)(1) can be conducted simultaneously, rather than sequentially, by any organizational units of the Forest Service that must approve the location or modification; and

(2) how to eliminate overlapping requirements among the organizational units of the Forest Service with respect to the location or modification of a communications facility on covered land administered by those organizational units.

(e) Communication of streamlined process to organizational units

The Secretary shall, with respect to the regulations issued under subsection (b)—

(1) communicate the regulations to the organizational units of the Forest Service; and

(2) ensure that the organizational units of the Forest Service follow the regulations.

(f) Deposit and availability of fees

(1) Special account

The Secretary of the Treasury shall establish a special account in the Treasury for the Forest Service for the deposit of fees collected by the Forest Service under subsection (c)(3) for communications use authorizations on covered land granted, issued, or executed by the Forest Service.

(2) Requirements for fees collected

Fees collected by the Forest Service under subsection (c)(3) shall be—

(A) collected only to the extent provided in advance in appropriations Acts;

(B) based on the costs described in subsection (c)(3); and

(C) competitively neutral, technology neutral, and nondiscriminatory with respect to other users of the communications site.

(3) Deposit of fees

Fees collected by the Forest Service under subsection (c)(3) shall be deposited in the special account established for the Forest Service under paragraph (1).

(4) Availability of fees

Amounts deposited in the special account for the Forest Service shall be available, to the extent and in such amounts as are provided in advance in appropriation Acts, to the Secretary to cover costs incurred by the Forest Service described in subsection (c)(3), including the following:

(A) Preparing needs assessments or other programmatic analyses necessary to designate

communications sites and issue communications use authorizations.

(B) Developing management plans for communications sites.

(C) Training for management of communications sites.

(D) Obtaining or improving access to communications sites.

(5) No additional appropriations authorized

Except as provided in paragraph (4), no other amounts are authorized to be appropriated to carry out this section.

(g) Savings provisions

(1) Real property authorities

Nothing in this section, or the amendments made by this section, shall be construed as providing any executive agency with any new leasing or other real property authorities not existing prior to December 20, 2018.

(2) Effect on other laws

Nothing in this section, or the amendments made by this section, and no actions taken pursuant to this section, or the amendments made by this section, shall impact a decision or determination by any executive agency to sell, dispose of, declare excess or surplus, lease, reuse, or redevelop any Federal real property pursuant to Title 40, the Federal Assets Sale and Transfer Act of 2016 (40 U.S.C. 1303 note; Public Law 114-287), or any other law governing real property activities of the Federal Government. No agreement entered into pursuant to this section, or the amendments made by this section, may obligate the Federal Government to hold, control, or otherwise retain or use real property that may otherwise be deemed as excess, surplus, or that could otherwise be sold, leased, or redeveloped.

§1762. Roads
[FLPMA §502]

(a) **Authority to acquire, construct, and maintain; financing arrangements** — The Secretary, with respect to the public lands, is authorized to provide for the acquisition, construction, and maintenance of roads within and near the public lands in locations and according to specifications which will permit maximum economy in harvesting timber from such lands tributary to such roads and at the same time meet the requirements for protection, development, and management of such lands for utilization of the other resources thereof. Financing of such roads may be accomplished (1) by the Secretary utilizing appropriated funds, (2) by requirements on purchasers of timber and other products from the public lands, including provisions for amortization of road costs in contracts, (3) by cooperative financing with other public agencies and with private agencies or persons, or (4) by a combination of these methods: *Provided,*

That, where roads of a higher standard than that needed in the harvesting and removal of the timber and other products covered by the particular sale are to be constructed, the purchaser of timber and other products from public lands shall not, except when the provisions of the second proviso of this subsection apply, be required to bear that part of the costs necessary to meet such higher standard, and the Secretary is authorized to make such arrangements to this end as may be appropriate: *Provided further*, That when timber is offered with the condition that the purchaser thereof will build a road or roads in accordance with standards specified in the offer, the purchaser of the timber will be responsible for paying the full costs of construction of such roads.

(b) Recordation of copies of affected instruments — Copies of all instruments affecting permanent interests in land executed pursuant to this section shall be recorded in each county where the lands are located.

(c) Maintenance or reconstruction of facilities by users — The Secretary may require the user or users of a road, trail, land, or other facility administered by him through the Bureau, including purchasers of Government timber and other products, to maintain such facilities in a satisfactory condition commensurate with the particular use requirements of each. Such maintenance to be borne by each user shall be proportionate to total use. The Secretary may also require the user or users of such a facility to reconstruct the same when such reconstruction is determined to be necessary to accommodate such use. If such maintenance or reconstruction cannot be so provided or if the Secretary determines that maintenance or reconstruction by a user would not be practical, then the Secretary may require that sufficient funds be deposited by the user to provide his portion of such total maintenance or reconstruction. Deposits made to cover the maintenance or reconstruction of roads are hereby made available until expended to cover the cost to the United States of accomplishing the purposes for which deposited: *Provided*, That deposits received for work on adjacent and overlapping areas may be combined when it is the most practicable and efficient manner of performing the work, and cost thereof may be determined by estimates: *And provided further*, That unexpended balances upon accomplishment of the purpose for which deposited shall be transferred to miscellaneous receipts or refunded.

(d) Fund for user fees for delayed payment to grantor — Whenever the agreement under which the United States has obtained for the use of, or in connection with, the public lands a right-of-way or easement for a road or an existing road or the right to use an existing road provides for delayed payments to the Government's grantor, any fees or other collections received by the Secretary for the use of the road

may be placed in a fund to be available for making payments to the grantor.

§1763. Right-of-way corridors; criteria and procedures applicable for designation
[FLPMA §503]

In order to minimize adverse environmental impacts and the proliferation of separate rights-of-way, the utilization of rights-of-way in common shall be required to the extent practical, and each right-of-way or permit shall reserve to the Secretary concerned the right to grant additional rights-of-way or permits for compatible uses on or adjacent to rights-of-way granted pursuant to this Act. In designating right-of-way corridors and in determining whether to require that rights-of-way be confined to them, the Secretary concerned shall take into consideration national and State land use policies, environmental quality, economic efficiency, national security, safety, and good engineering and technological practices. The Secretary concerned shall issue regulations containing the criteria and procedures he will use in designating such corridors. Any existing transportation and utility corridors may be designated as transportation and utility corridors pursuant to this subsection without further review.

§1764. General requirements
[FLPMA §504]

(a) Boundary specifications; criteria; temporary use of additional lands — The Secretary concerned shall specify the boundaries of each right-of-way as precisely as is practical. Each right-of-way shall be limited to the ground which the Secretary concerned determines (1) will be occupied by facilities which constitute the project for which the right-of-way is granted, issued, or renewed, (2) to be necessary for the operation or maintenance of the project, (3) to be necessary to protect the public safety, and (4) will do no unnecessary damage to the environment. The Secretary concerned may authorize the temporary use of such additional lands as he determines to be reasonably necessary for the construction, operation, maintenance, or termination of the project or a portion thereof, or for access thereto.

(b) Terms and conditions of right-of-way or permit — Each right-of-way or permit granted, issued, or renewed pursuant to this section shall be limited to a reasonable term in light of all circumstances concerning the project. In determining the duration of a right-of-way the Secretary concerned shall, among other things, take into consideration the cost of the facility, its useful life, and any public purpose it serves. The right-of-way shall specify whether it is or is not renewable and the terms and conditions applicable to the renewal.

(c) Applicability of regulations or stipulations — Rights-of-way shall be granted, issued, or renewed pursuant to this subchapter under such regulations or stipulations, consistent with the provisions of this subchapter or any other applicable law, and shall also be subject to such terms and conditions as the Secretary concerned may prescribe regarding extent, duration, survey, location, construction, maintenance, transfer or assignment, and termination.

(d) Submission of plan of construction, operation, and rehabilitation by new project applicants; plan requirements — The Secretary concerned prior to granting or issuing a right-of-way pursuant to this subchapter for a new project which may have a significant impact on the environment, shall require the applicant to submit a plan of construction, operation, and rehabilitation for such right-of-way which shall comply with stipulations or with regulations issued by that Secretary, including the terms and conditions required under section 1765 of this title.

(e) Regulatory requirements for terms and conditions; revision and applicability of regulations — The Secretary concerned shall issue regulations with respect to the terms and conditions that will be included in rights-of-way pursuant to section 1765 of this title. Such regulations shall be regularly revised as needed. Such regulations shall be applicable to every right-of-way granted or issued pursuant to this subchapter and to any subsequent renewal thereof, and may be applicable to rights-of-way not granted or issued, but renewed pursuant to this subchapter.

(f) Removal or use of mineral and vegetative materials — Mineral and vegetative materials, including timber, within or without a right-of-way, may be used or disposed of in connection with construction or other purposes only if authorization to remove or use such materials has been obtained pursuant to applicable laws or for emergency repair work necessary for those rights-of-way authorized under section 1761(c) of this title.

(g) Rental payments; amount, waiver, etc. — The holder of a right-of-way shall pay in advance the fair market value thereof, as determined by the Secretary granting, issuing, or renewing such right-of-way. The Secretary concerned may require either annual payment or a payment covering more than one year at a time except that private individuals may make at their option either annual payments or payments covering more than one year if the annual fee is greater than one hundred dollars. The Secretary concerned may waive rentals where a right-of-way is granted, issued or renewed in consideration of a right-of-way conveyed to the United States in connection with a cooperative cost share program between the United States and the holder. The Secretary concerned may, by regulation or prior to promulgation of such regulations, as a condition of a right-of-way, require an applicant for or holder of a right-of-way to reimburse the United States for all reasonable administrative and other costs incurred in processing an application for such right-of-way

and in inspection and monitoring of construction, operation, and termination of the facility pursuant to such right-of-way: *Provided, however,* That the Secretary concerned need not secure reimbursement in any situation where there is in existence a cooperative cost share right-of-way program between the United States and the holder of a right-of-way. Rights-of-way may be granted, issued, or renewed to a Federal, State, or local government or any agency or instrumentality thereof, to nonprofit associations or nonprofit corporations which are not themselves controlled or owned by profitmaking corporations or business enterprises, or to a holder where he provides without or at reduced charges a valuable benefit to the public or to the programs of the Secretary concerned, or to a holder in connection with the authorized use or occupancy of Federal land for which the United States is already receiving compensation for such lesser charge, including free use as the Secretary concerned finds equitable and in the public interest. Such rights-of-way issued at less than fair market value are not assignable except with the approval of the Secretary issuing the right-of-way. The moneys received for reimbursement of reasonable costs shall be deposited with the Treasury in a special account and are hereby authorized to be appropriated and made available until expended. Rights-of-way shall be granted, issued, or renewed, without rental fees, for electric or telephone facilities eligible for financing pursuant to the Rural Electrification Act of 1936, as amended [7 U.S.C. §§901 *et seq.*], determined without regard to any application requirement under that Act, or any extensions from such facilities: *Provided,* That nothing in this sentence shall be construed to affect the authority of the Secretary granting, issuing, or renewing the right-of-way to require reimbursement of reasonable administrative and other costs pursuant to the second sentence of this subsection.

(h) Liability for damage or injury incurred by United States for use and occupancy of rights-of-way; indemnification of United States; no-fault liability; amount of damages

(1) The Secretary concerned shall promulgate regulations specifying the extent to which holders of rights-of-way under this subchapter shall be liable to the United States for damage or injury incurred by the United States caused by the use and occupancy of the rights-of-way. The regulations shall also specify the extent to which such holders shall indemnify or hold harmless the United States for liabilities, damages, or claims caused by their use and occupancy of the rights-of-way.

(2) Any regulation or stipulation imposing liability without fault shall include a maximum limitation on damages commensurate with the foreseeable risks or hazards presented. Any liability for damage or injury in excess of this amount shall be determined by ordinary rules of negligence.

(i) Bond or security requirements — Where he deems it appropriate, the Secretary concerned may require a holder of a right-of-way to furnish a bond, or other security, satisfactory to him to secure all or any of the obligations imposed by the terms and conditions of the right-of-way or by any rule or regulation of the Secretary concerned.

(j) Criteria for grant, issue, or renewal of right-of-way — The Secretary concerned shall grant, issue, or renew a right-of-way under this subchapter only when he is satisfied that the applicant has the technical and financial capability to construct the project for which the right-of-way is requested, and in accord with the requirements of this subchapter.

§1765. Terms and conditions
[FLPMA §505]

Each right-of-way shall contain —

(a) terms and conditions which will (i) carry out the purposes of this Act and rules and regulations issued thereunder; (ii) minimize damage to scenic and esthetic values and fish and wildlife habitat and otherwise protect the environment; (iii) require compliance with applicable air and water quality standards established by or pursuant to applicable Federal or State law; and (iv) require compliance with State standards for public health and safety, environmental protection, and siting, construction, operation, and maintenance of or for rights-of-way for similar purposes if those standards are more stringent than applicable Federal standards; and

(b) such terms and conditions as the Secretary concerned deems necessary to (i) protect Federal property and economic interests; (ii) manage efficiently the lands which are subject to the right-of-way or adjacent thereto and protect the other lawful users of the lands adjacent to or traversed by such right-of-way; (iii) protect lives and property; (iv) protect the interests of individuals living in the general area traversed by the right-of-way who rely on the fish, wildlife, and other biotic resources of the area for subsistence purposes; (v) require location of the right-of-way along a route that will cause least damage to the environment, taking into consideration feasibility and other relevant factors; and (vi) otherwise protect the public interest in the lands traversed by the right-of-way or adjacent thereto.

§1766. Suspension or termination; grounds; procedures applicable
[FLPMA §506]

Abandonment of a right-of-way or noncompliance with any provision of this subchapter condition of the right-of-way, or applicable rule or regulation of the Secretary concerned may be grounds for suspension or termination of the right-of-way if, after due notice to the holder of the right-of-way and, and with respect to easements, an appropriate administrative proceeding pursuant to section 554 of Title 5, the Secretary

concerned determines that any such ground exists and that suspension or termination is justified. No administrative proceeding shall be required where the right-of-way by its terms provides that it terminates on the occurrence of a fixed or agreed-upon condition, event, or time. If the Secretary concerned determines that an immediate temporary suspension of activities within a right-of-way for violation of its terms and conditions is necessary to protect public health or safety or the environment, he may abate such activities prior to an administrative proceeding. Prior to commencing any proceeding to suspend or terminate a right-of-way the Secretary concerned shall give written notice to the holder of the grounds for such action and shall give the holder a reasonable time to resume use of the right-of-way or to comply with this subchapter condition, rule, or regulation as the case may be. Failure of the holder of the right-of-way to use the right-of-way for the purpose for which it was granted, issued, or renewed, for any continuous five-year period, shall constitute a rebuttable presumption of abandonment of the right-of-way except that where the failure of the holder to use the right-of-way for the purpose for which it was granted, issued, or renewed for any continuous five-year period is due to circumstances not within the holder's control, the Secretary concerned is not required to commence proceedings to suspend or terminate the right-of-way.

§1767. Rights-of-way for Federal departments and agencies
[FLPMA §507]

(a) The Secretary concerned may provide under applicable provisions of this subchapter for the use of any department or agency of the United States a right-of-way over, upon, under or through the land administered by him, subject to such terms and conditions as he may impose.

(b) Where a right-of-way has been reserved for the use of any department or agency of the United States, the Secretary shall take no action to terminate, or otherwise limit, that use without the consent of the head of such department or agency.

§1768. Conveyance of lands covered by right-of-way; terms and conditions
[FLPMA §508]

If under applicable law the Secretary concerned decides to transfer out of Federal ownership any lands covered in whole or in part by a right-of-way, including a right-of-way granted under the Act of November 16, 1973 (87 Stat. 576; 30 U.S.C. §185), the lands may be conveyed subject to the right-of-way; however, if the Secretary concerned determines that retention of Federal control over the right-of-way is necessary to assure that the purposes of this subchapter will be carried out, the terms and conditions of the right-of-way complied with, or the lands protected, he shall (a) reserve to the United States that portion of the lands which lies within the boundaries of the right-of-way, or (b) convey the lands, including that portion within the boundaries of the right-of-way, subject to the right-of-way and reserving to the United States the right to enforce all or any of the terms and conditions of the right-of-way, including the right to renew it or extend it upon its termination and to collect rents.

§1769. Existing right-of-way or right-of-use unaffected; exceptions; rights-of-way for railroad and appurtenant communication facilities; applicability of existing terms and conditions
[FLPMA §509]

(a) Nothing in this subchapter shall have the effect of terminating any right-of-way or right-of-use heretofore issued, granted, or permitted. However, with the consent of the holder thereof, the Secretary concerned may cancel such a right-of-way or right-of-use and in its stead issue a right-of-way pursuant to the provisions of this subchapter.

(b) When the Secretary concerned issues a right-of-way under this subchapter for a railroad and appurtenant communication facilities in connection with a realinement of a railroad on lands under his jurisdiction by virtue of a right-of-way granted by the United States, he may, when he considers it to be in the public interest and the lands involved are not within an incorporated community and are of approximately equal value, notwithstanding the provisions of this subchapter, provide in the new right-of-way the same terms and conditions as applied to the portion of the existing right-of-way relinquished to the United States with respect to the payment of annual rental, duration of the right-of-way, and the nature of the interest in lands granted. The Secretary concerned or his delegate shall take final action upon all applications for the grant, issue, or renewal of rights-of-way under subsection (b) of this section no later than six months after receipt from the applicant of all information required from the applicant by this subchapter.

§1770. Applicability of provisions to other Federal laws
[FLPMA §510]

(a) **Right-of-way** — Effective on and after October 21, 1976, no right-of-way for the purposes listed in this subchapter shall be granted, issued, or renewed over, upon, under, or through such lands except under and subject to the provisions, limitations, and conditions of this subchapter: *Provided,* That nothing in this subchapter shall be construed as affecting or modifying the provisions of sections 532 to 538 of Title 16 and in the event of conflict with, or inconsistency between, this subchapter and sections 532 to 538 of Title 16, the latter shall prevail: *Provided further,* That nothing in this Act should be construed as making it mandatory that, with respect to forest roads, the Secretary of Agriculture limit rights-of-way grants or their term of years or

require disclosure pursuant to section 1761(b) of this title or impose any other condition contemplated by this Act that is contrary to present practices of that Secretary under sections 532 to 538 of Title 16. Any pending application for a right-of-way under any other law on the effective date of this section shall be considered as an application under this subchapter. The Secretary concerned may require the applicant to submit any additional information he deems necessary to comply with the requirements of this subchapter.

(b) **Highway use** — Nothing in this subchapter shall be construed to preclude the use of lands covered by this subchapter for highway purposes pursuant to sections 107 and 317 of Title 23.

(c) **Application of antitrust laws**

(1) Nothing in this subchapter shall be construed as exempting any holder of a right-of-way issued under this subchapter from any provision of the antitrust laws of the United States.

(2) For the purposes of this subsection, the term "antitrust laws" includes the Act of July 2, 1890 (26 Stat. 15 U.S.C. §§1 *et seq.*); the Act of October 15, 1914 (38 Stat. 730, 15 U.S.C. §§12 *et seq.*); the Federal Trade Commission Act (38 Stat. 717; 15 U.S.C. §§41 *et seq.*); and sections 73 and 74 of the Act of August 27, 1894 [15 U.S.C. §§8, 9].

§1771. Coordination of applications
[FLPMA §511]

Applicants before Federal departments and agencies other than the Department of the Interior or Agriculture seeking a license, certificate, or other authority for a project which involve a right-of-way over, upon, under, or through public land or National Forest System lands must simultaneously apply to the Secretary concerned for the appropriate authority to use public lands or National Forest System lands and submit to the Secretary concerned all information furnished to the other Federal department or agency.

§1772. Vegetation management, facility inspection, and operation and maintenance relating to electric transmission and distribution facility rights of way

(a) Definitions

In this section:

(1) Hazard tree

The term "hazard tree" means any tree or part thereof (whether located inside or outside a right-of-way) that has been designated, prior to tree failure, by a certified or licensed arborist or forester under the supervision of the Secretary concerned or the owner or operator of a transmission or distribution facility to be—

(A) dead, likely to die within the routine vegetation management cycle, or likely to fail within the routine vegetation management cycle; and

(B) if the tree or part of the tree failed, likely to—

(i) cause substantial damage or disruption to a transmission or distribution facility; or

(ii) come within 10 feet of an electric power line.

(2) Owner; operator

The terms "owner" and "operator" include contractors or other agents engaged by the owner or operator of an electric transmission or distribution facility.

(3) Plan

The term "plan" means a vegetation management, facility inspection, and operation and maintenance plan that—

(A) is prepared by the owner or operator of 1 or more electric transmission or distribution facilities to cover 1 or more electric transmission and distribution rights-of-way; and

(B) provides for the long-term, cost-effective, efficient, and timely management of facilities and vegetation within the width of the right-of-way and abutting Federal land, including hazard trees, to enhance electric reliability, promote public safety, and avoid fire hazards.

(4) Secretary concerned

The term "Secretary concerned" means—

(A) the Secretary, with respect to public lands; and

(B) the Secretary of Agriculture, with respect to National Forest System land.

(b) Guidanc e

(1) In general

To enhance the reliability of the electric grid and reduce the threat of wildfire damage to, and wildfire caused by vegetation related conditions within, electric transmission and distribution rights-of-way and abutting Federal land, including hazard trees, the Secretary concerned shall issue and periodically update guidance to ensure that provisions are appropriately developed and implemented for utility vegetation management, facility inspection, and operation and maintenance of rights-of-way, regardless of the means by which the rights-of-way are established (including by grant, special use authorization, and easement).

(2) Limitation

The guidance issued under paragraph (1) shall be compatible with mandatory reliability standards established by the Electric Reliability Organization.

(3) Considerations

The guidance issued under paragraph (1) shall take into account—

(A) all applicable law, including fire safety and electric system reliability requirements (including reliability standards established by the Electric Reliability Organization under section 824o of Title 16); and

(B) the Memorandum of Understanding on Vegetation Management for Powerline Rights-of-Way between the Edison Electric Institute, Utility Arborist Association, the Department of the Interior, the Department of Agriculture, and the Environmental Protection Agency signed in 2016.

(4) Requirements

The guidance issued under paragraph (1) shall—

(A) be developed in consultation with the owners of transmission and distribution facilities that hold rights-of-way;

(B) seek to minimize the need for case-by-case approvals for—

(i) routine vegetation management, facility inspection, and operation and maintenance activities; and

(ii) utility vegetation management activities that are necessary to control hazard trees; and

(C) provide for prompt and timely review of requests to conduct vegetation management activities that require approval of the Secretary concerned, especially activities requiring expedited or immediate action.

(c) Vegetation management, facility inspection, and operation and maintenance plans

(1) Development and submission

Consistent with subsection (b), the Secretary concerned shall provide owners and operators of electric transmission or distribution facilities located on public lands and National Forest System land, as applicable, with the option to develop and submit a plan.

(2) ERO standards

Owners and operators subject to mandatory reliability standards established by the Electric Reliability Organization (or superseding standards) may use those standards as part of the plan.

(3) Plan requirements

A plan developed under paragraph (1) shall—

(A) identify the applicable transmission or distribution facilities to be maintained;

(B) take into account operations and maintenance plans for the applicable transmission or distribution line;

(C) describe the vegetation management, inspection, and operation and maintenance methods that may be used to comply with all applicable law, including fire safety requirements and reliability standards established by the Electric Reliability Organization;

(D) include schedules for—

(i) the applicable owner or operator to notify the Secretary concerned about routine and major maintenance;

(ii) the applicable owner or operator to request approval from the Secretary concerned about undertaking routine and major maintenance; and

(iii) the Secretary concerned to respond to a request by an owner or operator under clause (ii); and

(E) describe processes for—

(i) identifying changes in conditions; and

(ii) modifying the approved plan, if necessary.

(4) Review and approval process

(A) In general

The Secretary concerned shall jointly develop a consolidated and coordinated process for the review and approval of plans submitted under paragraph (1) that—

(i) includes timelines and benchmarks for—

(I) the submission of agency comments on the plans and schedules for final decision; and

(II) the timely review of modifications of the plans in cases in which modifications are necessary;

(ii) is consistent with applicable law; and

(iii) includes a process for modifications to a plan in a prompt manner if changed conditions necessitate a modification to a plan; and

(iv) ensures, to the maximum extent practicable, a prompt review and approval process not to exceed 120 days.

(B) Plan modification

Upon reasonable advance notice to an owner or operator of an electric transmission or distribution facility of any changed conditions that warrant a modification to a plan, the Secretary concerned shall—

(i) provide an opportunity for the owner or operator to submit a proposed plan modification, consistent with the process described under subparagraph (A)(iii), to address the changed condition identified by the Secretary concerned;

(ii) consider the proposed plan modification consistent with the process described under paragraph (4)(A); and

(iii) allow the owner or operator to continue to implement any element of the approved plan that does not directly and adversely affect the condition precipitating the need for modification.

(5) Categories of actions not requiring environmental analysis

With respect to the development and approval of plans submitted under paragraph (1), as well as with respect to actions carried out under such plans, the Secretary concerned shall identify categories of actions for which neither an environmental impact statement nor an environmental assessment shall be required under section 1508.4

of title 40, Code of Federal Regulations (or a successor regulation).

(d) Certain owners and operators

(1) In general

The owner or operator of an electric transmission or distribution facility that is not subject to the mandatory reliability standards established by the Electric Reliability Organization or that sold less than or equal to 1,000,000 megawatt hours of electric energy for purposes other than resale during each of the 3 calendar years immediately preceding March 23, 2018, may enter into an agreement with the Secretary concerned in lieu of a plan under subsection (c).

(2) Minimum requirements

The Secretary concerned shall ensure that the minimum requirements for an agreement under paragraph (1)—

(A) reflect the relative financial resources of the applicable owner or operator compared to other owners or operators of an electric transmission or distribution facility;

(B) include schedules as described in subsection (c)(3)(D);

(C) are subject to modification requirements as described in subsection (c)(4)(B); and

(D) comply with applicable law.

(e) Emergency conditions

If vegetation or hazard trees have contacted or present an imminent danger of contacting an electric transmission or distribution line from within or adjacent to an electric transmission or distribution right-of-way, the owner or operator of the electric transmission or distribution lines—

(1) may prune or remove the vegetation or hazard tree—

(A) to avoid the disruption of electric service; and

(B) to eliminate immediate fire and safety hazards; and

(2) shall notify the appropriate local agent of the Secretary concerned not later than 1 day after the date of the response to emergency conditions.

(f) Activities that require approval

(1) In general

Except as provided under paragraph (3), the owner or operator of an electric transmission or distribution facility may conduct vegetation management activities that require approval of the Secretary concerned in accordance with a plan approved under subsection (c) or an agreement entered into under subsection (d) only with the approval of the Secretary concerned.

(2) Requirement to respond

The Secretary concerned shall respond to a request for approval to conduct vegetation management activities in accordance with the applicable schedules in a plan approved under subsection (c) or an agreement entered into under subsection (d).

(3) Authorized activities

The owner or operator of an electric transmission or distribution facility may conduct vegetation management activities that require approval of the Secretary concerned in accordance with a plan approved under subsection (c) or an agreement entered into under subsection (d) without the approval of the Secretary concerned if—

(A) the owner or operator submitted a request to the Secretary concerned in accordance with the applicable schedule in a plan approved under subsection (c) or an agreement entered into under subsection (d);

(B) the vegetation management activities, including the removal of hazard trees, proposed in the request under subparagraph (A) are in accordance with a plan approved under subsection (c) or an agreement entered into under subsection (d); and

(C) the Secretary concerned fails to respond to the request under subparagraph (A) in accordance with the applicable schedule in a plan approved under subsection (c) or an agreement entered into under subsection (d).

(g) Liability

(1) In general

The Secretary concerned shall not impose strict liability for damages or injury resulting from—

(A) the Secretary concerned unreasonably withholding or delaying—

(i) approval of a plan under subsection (c); or

(ii) entrance into an agreement under subsection (d); or

(B) the Secretary concerned unreasonably failing to adhere to an applicable schedule in a plan approved under subsection (c) or an agreement entered into under subsection (d).

(2) Damages

For the period ending 10 years after March 23, 2018, the Secretary concerned shall not impose strict liability in an amount greater than $500,000 per incident for damages or injury resulting from activities conducted by an owner or operator in accordance with an approved agreement under subsection (d).

(3) Rule of construction

Nothing in paragraph (2) shall be construed to effect any liability imposed by the Secretary concerned under section 251.56(d) of title 36, Code of Federal Regulations (as in effect on March 23, 2018) and section 2807.12 of title 43, Code of Federal Regulations (as in effect on March 23, 2018), for activities conducted by an owner or operator in accordance with an approved plan under subsection (c).

(h) Reporting requirement

(1) Activities that require approval

The Secretary concerned shall report requests and actions made under subsection (f) annually on the website of the Secretary concerned.

(2) Liability

Not later than four years after March 23, 2018, the Secretary concerned shall prepare and submit a report to the Committee on Natural Resources of the House of Representatives and the Committee on Energy and Natural Resources of the Senate that describes the effect on the Treasury of the strict liability limitation established by subsection (g)(2).

(i) Training and guidance

In consultation with the electric utility industry, the Secretary concerned is encouraged to develop a program to train personnel of the Department of the Interior and the Forest Service involved in vegetation management decisions relating to electric transmission and distribution facilities to ensure that the personnel—

(1) understand electric system reliability requirements as the requirements relate to vegetation management of transmission and distribution rights-of-way on Federal land, including reliability standards established by the Electric Reliability Organization and fire safety requirements;

(2) assist owners and operators of electric transmission and distribution facilities in complying with applicable electric reliability and fire safety requirements;

(3) encourage and assist willing owners and operators of electric transmission and distribution facilities to incorporate on a voluntary basis vegetation management practices to enhance habitats and forage for pollinators and for other wildlife if the practices are compatible with the integrated vegetation management practices necessary for reliability and safety; and

(4) understand how existing and emerging unmanned technologies can help electric utilities, the Federal Government, State and local governments, and private landowners—

(A) to more efficiently identify vegetation management needs;

(B) to reduce the risk of wildfires; and

(C) to lower ratepayer energy costs.

(j) Implementation

The Secretary concerned shall—

(1) not later than 1 year after March 23, 2018, propose regulations, or amend existing regulations, to implement this section; and

(2) not later than 2 years after March 23, 2018, finalize regulations, or amend existing regulations, to implement this section.

(k) Existing vegetation management, facility inspection, and operation and maintenance plans

Nothing in this section requires an owner or operator to develop and submit a new plan under this section if a plan consistent with this section has already been approved by the Secretary concerned before March 23, 2018.

SUBCHAPTER VI—DESIGNATED MANAGEMENT AREAS

§1781. California Desert Conservation Area [FLPMA §601]

(a) Congressional findings — The Congress finds that —

(1) the California desert contains historical, scenic, archeological, environmental, biological, cultural, scientific, educational, recreational, and economic resources that are uniquely located adjacent to an area of large population;

(2) the California desert environment is a total ecosystem that is extremely fragile, easily scarred, and slowly healed;

(3) the California desert environment and its resources, including certain rare and endangered species of wildlife, plants, and fishes, and numerous archeological and historic sites, are seriously threatened by air pollution, inadequate Federal management authority, and pressures of increased use, particularly recreational use, which are certain to intensify because of the rapidly growing population of southern California;

(4) the use of all California desert resources can and should be provided for in a multiple use and sustained yield management plant to conserve these resources for future generations, and to provide present and future use and enjoyment, particularly outdoor recreation uses, including the use, where appropriate, of off-road recreational vehicles;

(5) the Secretary has initiated a comprehensive planning process and established an interim management program for the public lands in the California desert; and

(6) to insure further study of the relationship of man and the California desert environment, preserve the unique and irreplaceable resources, including archeological values, and conserve the use of the economic resources of the California desert, the public must be provided more opportunity to participate in such planning and management, and additional management authority must be provided to the Secretary to facilitate effective implementation of such planning and management.

(b) Statement of purpose — It is the purpose of this section to provide for the immediate and future protection and administration of the public lands in the California desert within the framework of a program of multiple use and sustained yield, and the maintenance of environmental quality.

(c) Description of Area

(1) For the purpose of this section, the term "California desert" means the area generally depicted on a map entitled "California Desert Conservation Area—Proposed" dated April 1974, and described as provided in subsection (c)(2) of this section.

(2) As soon as practicable after October 21, 1976, the Secretary shall file a revised map and a legal description of the California Desert Conservation Area with the Committees on Interior and Insular Affairs of the United States Senate and the House of Representatives, and such map and description shall have the same force and effect as if included in this Act. Correction of clerical and typographical errors in such legal description and a map may be made by the Secretary. To the extent practicable, the Secretary shall make such legal description and map available to the public promptly upon request.

(d) Preparation and implementation of comprehensive long-range plan for management, use, etc. — The Secretary, in accordance with section 1712 of this title, shall prepare and implement a comprehensive, long-range plan for the management, use, development, and protection of the public lands within the California Desert Conservation Area. Such plan shall take into account the principles of multiple use and sustained yield in providing for resource use and development, including, but not limited to, maintenance of environmental quality, rights-of-way, and mineral development. Such plan shall be completed and implementation thereof initiated on or before September 30, 1980.

(e) Interim program for management, use, etc. — During the period beginning on October 21, 1976, and ending on the effective date of implementation of the comprehensive, long-range plan, the Secretary shall execute an interim program to manage, use, and protect the public lands, and their resources now in danger of destruction, in the California Desert Conservation Area, to provide for the public use of such lands in an orderly and reasonable manner such as through the development of campgrounds and visitor centers, and to provide for a uniformed desert ranger force.

(f) Applicability of mining laws — Subject to valid existing rights, nothing in this Act shall affect the applicability of the United States mining laws on the public lands within the California Desert Conservation Area, except that all mining claims located on public lands within the California Desert Conservation Area shall be subject to such reasonable regulations as the Secretary may prescribe to effectuate the purposes of this section. Any patent issued on any such mining claim shall recite this limitation and continue to be subject to such regulations. Such regulations shall provide for such measures as may be reasonable to protect the scenic, scientific, and environmental values of the public lands of the California Desert Conservation Area against undue impairment, and to assure against pollution of the streams and waters within the California Desert Conservation Area.

(g) Advisory Committee; establishment; functions

(1) The Secretary, within sixty days after October 21, 1976, shall establish a California

Desert Conservation Area Advisory Committee (hereinafter referred to as "advisory committee") in accordance with the provisions of section 1739 of this title.

(2) It shall be the function of the advisory committee to advise the Secretary with respect to the preparation and implementation of the comprehensive, long-range plan required under subsection (d) of this section.

(h) Management of lands under jurisdiction of Secretary of Agriculture and Secretary of Defense — The Secretary of Agriculture and the Secretary of Defense shall manage lands within their respective jurisdictions located in or adjacent to the California Desert Conservation Area, in accordance with the laws relating to such lands and wherever practicable, in a manner consonant with the purpose of this section. The Secretary, the Secretary of Agriculture, and the Secretary of Defense are authorized and directed to consult among themselves and take cooperative actions to carry out the provisions of this subsection, including a program of law enforcement in accordance with applicable authorities to protect the archeological and other values of the California Desert Conservation Area and adjacent lands.

(i) Omitted

(j) Authorization of appropriations — There are authorized to be appropriated for fiscal years 1977 through 1981 not to exceed $40,000,000 for the purpose of this section, such amount to remain available until expended.

§1781a. Acceptance of donation of certain existing permits or leases

(1) During fiscal year 2012 and thereafter, the Secretary of the Interior shall accept the donation of any valid existing permits or leases authorizing grazing on public lands within the California Desert Conservation Area. With respect to each permit or lease donated under this paragraph, the Secretary shall terminate the grazing permit or lease, ensure a permanent end (except as provided in paragraph (2)), to grazing on the land covered by the permit or lease, and make the land available for mitigation by allocating the forage to wildlife use consistent with any applicable Habitat Conservation Plan, section 10(a)(1)(B) permit, or section 7 consultation under the Endangered Species Act of 1973 (16 U.S.C. 1531 *et seq.*).

(2) If the land covered by a permit or lease donated under paragraph (1) is also covered by another valid existing permit or lease that is not donated under such paragraph, the Secretary of the Interior shall reduce the authorized grazing level on the land covered by the permit or lease to reflect the donation of the permit or lease under paragraph (1). To ensure that there is a permanent reduction in the level of grazing on the land covered by a permit or lease donated under paragraph

(1), the Secretary shall not allow grazing use to exceed the authorized level under the remaining valid existing permit or lease that is not donated.

§1782. Bureau of Land Management Wilderness Study

[FLPMA §603]

(a) Lands subject to review and designation as wilderness — Within fifteen years after October 21, 1976, the Secretary shall review those roadless areas of five thousand acres or more and roadless islands of the public lands, identified during the inventory required by section 1711(a) of this title as having wilderness characteristics described in the Wilderness Act of September 3, 1964 (78 Stat. 890; 16 U.S.C. §§1131 *et seq.*) and shall from time to time report to the President his recommendation as to the suitability or nonsuitability of each such area or island for preservation as wilderness: *Provided*, That prior to any recommendations for the designation of an area as wilderness the Secretary shall cause mineral surveys to be conducted by the United States Geological Survey and the United States Bureau of Mines to determine the mineral values, if any, that may be present in such areas: *Provided further*, That the Secretary shall report to the President by July 1, 1980, his recommendations on those areas which the Secretary has prior to November 1, 1975, formally identified as natural or primitive areas. The review required by this subsection shall be conducted in accordance with the procedure specified in section 3(d) of the Wilderness Act [16 U.S.C. §1132(d)].

(b) Presidential recommendation for designation as wilderness — The President shall advise the President of the Senate and the Speaker of the House of Representatives of his recommendations with respect to designation as wilderness of each such area, together with a map thereof and a definition of its boundaries. Such advice by the President shall be given within two years of the receipt of each report from the Secretary. A recommendation of the President for designation as wilderness shall become effective only if so provided by an Act of Congress.

(c) Status of lands during period of review and determination — During the period of review of such areas and until Congress has determined otherwise, the Secretary shall continue to manage such lands according to his authority under this Act and other applicable law in a manner so as not to impair the suitability of such areas for preservation as wilderness, subject, however, to the continuation of existing mining and grazing uses and mineral leasing in the manner and degree in which the same was being conducted on October 21, 1976: *Provided*, That, in managing the public lands the Secretary shall by regulation or otherwise take any action required to prevent unnecessary or undue degradation of the lands and their resources or to afford environmental protection.

Unless previously withdrawn from appropriation under the mining laws, such lands shall continue to be subject to such appropriation during the period of review unless withdrawn by the Secretary under the procedures of section 1714 of this title for reasons other than preservation of their wilderness character. Once an area has been designated for preservation as wilderness, the provisions of the Wilderness Act [16 U.S.C. §§1131 *et seq.*] which apply to national forest wilderness areas shall apply with respect to the administration and use of such designated area, including mineral surveys required by section 4(d)(2) of the Wilderness Act [16 U.S.C. §1133(d)(2)], and mineral development, access, exchange of lands, and ingress and egress for mining claimants and occupants.

§1783. Yaquina Head Outstanding Natural Area

(a) Establishment — In order to protect the unique scenic, scientific, educational, and recreational values of certain lands in and around Yaquina Head, in Lincoln County, Oregon, there is hereby established, subject to valid existing rights, the Yaquina Head Outstanding Natural Area (hereinafter referred to as the "area"). The boundaries of the area are those shown on the map entitled "Yaquina Head Area", dated July 1979, which shall be on file and available for public inspection in the Office of the Director, Bureau of Land Management, United States Department of the Interior, and the State Office of the Bureau of Land Management in the State of Oregon.

(b) Administration by Secretary of the Interior; management plan; quarrying permits

(1) The Secretary of the Interior (hereinafter referred to as the "Secretary") shall administer the Yaquina Head Outstanding Natural Area in accordance with the laws and regulations applicable to the public lands as defined in section 103(e) of the Federal Land Policy and Management Act of 1976, as amended (43 U.S.C. §1702) [43 U.S.C. §1702(e)], in such a manner as will best provide for —

(A) the conservation and development of the scenic, natural, and historic values of the area;

(B) the continued use of the area for purposes of education, scientific study, and public recreation which do not substantially impair the purposes for which the area is established; and

(C) protection of the wildlife habitat of the area.

(2) The Secretary shall develop a management plan for the area which accomplishes the purposes and is consistent with the provisions of this section. This plan shall be developed in accordance with the provisions of section 202 of the Federal Land Policy and Management Act of 1976, as amended (43 U.S.C. §1712).

(3) Notwithstanding any other provision of this section, the Secretary is authorized to issue permits or to contract for the quarrying of materials from the area in accordance with the management plan for the area on condition that the lands be reclaimed and restored to the satisfaction of the Secretary. Such authorization to quarry shall require payment of fair market value for the materials to be quarried, as established by the Secretary, and shall also include any terms and conditions which the Secretary determines necessary to protect the values of such quarry lands for purposes of this section.

(c) Revocation of 1866 reservation of lands for lighthouse purposes; restoration to public lands status — The reservation of lands for lighthouse purposes made by Executive order of June 8, 1866, of certain lands totaling approximately 18.1 acres, as depicted on the map referred to in subsection (a) of this section, is hereby revoked. The lands referred to in subsection (a) of this section are hereby restored to the status of public lands as defined in section 103(e) of the Federal Land Policy and Management Act of 1976, as amended (43 U.S.C. §1702) [43 U.S.C. §1702(e)], and shall be administered in accordance with the management plan for the area developed pursuant to subsection (b) of this section, except that such lands are hereby withdrawn from settlement, sale, location, or entry, under the public land laws, including the mining laws (30 U.S.C., ch. 2), leasing under the mineral leasing laws (30 U.S.C. §§181 *et seq.*), and disposals under the Materials Act of July 31, 1947, as amended (30 U.S.C. §601, 602) [43 U.S.C. §§601 *et seq.*].

(d) Acquisition of lands not already in Federal ownership — The Secretary shall, as soon as possible but in no event later than twenty-four months following March 5, 1980, acquire by purchase, exchange, donation, or condemnation all or any part of the lands and waters and interests in lands and waters within the area referred to in subsection (a) of this section which are not in Federal ownership except that State land shall not be acquired by purchase or condemnation. Any lands or interests acquired by the Secretary pursuant to this section shall become public lands as defined in the Federal Land Policy and Management Act of 1976, as amended [43 U.S.C. §§1701 *et seq.*]. Upon acquisition by the United States, such lands are automatically withdrawn under the provisions of subsection (c) of this section except that lands affected by quarrying operations in the area shall be subject to disposals under the Materials Act of July 31, 1947, as amended (30 U.S.C. §601, 602) [30 U.S.C. §§601 *et seq.*]. Any lands acquired pursuant to this subsection shall be administered in accordance with the management plan for the area developed pursuant to subsection (b) of this section.

(e) Wind energy research — The Secretary is authorized to conduct a study relating to the use of lands in the area for purposes of wind energy research. If the Secretary determines after such study that the conduct of wind energy research activity will not substantially impair the values of the lands in the area for purposes of this section, the Secretary is further authorized to issue permits for the use of such lands as a site for installation and field testing of an experimental wind turbine generating system. Any permit issued pursuant to this subsection shall contain such terms and conditions as the Secretary determines necessary to protect the values of such lands for purposes of this section.

(f) Reclamation and restoration of lands affected by quarrying operations — The Secretary shall develop and administer, in addition to any requirements imposed pursuant to subsection (b)(3) of this section, a program for the reclamation and restoration of all lands affected by quarrying operations in the area acquired pursuant to subsection (d) of this section. All revenues received by the United States in connection with quarrying operations authorized by subsection (b)(3) of this section shall be deposited in a separate fund account which shall be established by the Secretary of the Treasury. Such revenues are hereby authorized to be appropriated to the Secretary as needed for reclamation and restoration of any lands acquired pursuant to subsection (d) of this section. After completion of such reclamation and restoration to the satisfaction of the Secretary, any unexpended revenues in such fund shall be returned to the general fund of the United States Treasury.

(g) Authorization of appropriations — There are hereby authorized to be appropriated in addition to that authorized by subsection (f) of this section, such sums as may be necessary to carry out the provisions of this section.

§1784. Lands in Alaska; designation as wilderness; management by Bureau of Land Management pending Congressional action

Notwithstanding any other provision of law, section 1782 of this title shall not apply to any lands in Alaska. However, in carrying out his duties under sections 1711 and 1712 of this title and other applicable laws, the Secretary may identify areas in Alaska which he determines are suitable as wilderness and may, from time to time, make recommendations to the Congress for inclusion of any such areas in the National Wilderness Preservation System, pursuant to the provisions of the Wilderness Act [16 U.S.C. §§1131 et seq.]. In the absence of congressional action relating to any such recommendation of the Secretary, the Bureau of Land Management shall manage all such areas which are within its jurisdiction in accordance with the applicable land use plans and applicable provisions of law.

§1785. Fossil Forest Research Natural Area

(a) Establishment — To conserve and protect natural values and to provide scientific knowledge, education, and interpretation for the benefit of future generations, there is established the Fossil Forest Research Natural Area (referred to in this section as the "Area"), consisting of the approximately 2,770 acres in the Farmington District of the Bureau of Land Management, New Mexico, as generally depicted on a map entitled "Fossil Forest", dated June 1983.

(b) Map and legal description

(1) In general — As soon as practicable after November 12, 1996, the Secretary of the Interior shall file a map and legal description of the Area with the Committee on Energy and Natural Resources of the Senate and the Committee on Resources of the House of Representatives.

(2) Force and effect — The map and legal description described in paragraph (1) shall have the same force and effect as if included in this Act.

(3) Technical corrections — The Secretary of the Interior may correct clerical, typographical, and cartographical errors in the map and legal description subsequent to filing the map pursuant to paragraph (1).

(4) Public inspection — The map and legal description shall be on file and available for public inspection in the Office of the Director of the Bureau of Land Management, Department of the Interior.

(c) Management

(1) In general — The Secretary of the Interior, acting through the Director of the Bureau of Land Management, shall manage the Area —

(A) to protect the resources within the Area; and

(B) in accordance with this Act, the Federal Land Policy and Management Act of 1976 (43 U.S.C. §§1701 et seq.), and other applicable provisions of law.

(2) Mining

(A) Withdrawal — Subject to valid existing rights, the lands within the Area are withdrawn from all forms of appropriation under the mining laws and from disposition under all laws pertaining to mineral leasing, geothermal leasing, and mineral material sales.

(B) Coal preference rights — The Secretary of the Interior is authorized to issue coal leases in New Mexico in exchange for any preference right coal lease application within the Area. Such exchanges shall be made in accordance with applicable existing laws and regulations relating to coal leases after a determination has been made by the Secretary that the applicant is entitled to a preference right lease and that the exchange is in the public interest.

(C) Oil and gas leases — Operations on oil and gas leases issued prior to November 12, 1996, shall be subject to the applicable provisions of Group 3100 of title 43, Code of Federal Regulations (including section 3162.5-1), and such other terms, stipulations, and conditions as the Secretary of the Interior considers necessary to avoid significant disturbance of the land surface or impairment of the natural, educational, and scientific research values of the Area in existence on November 12, 1996.

(3) Grazing — Livestock grazing on lands within the Area may not be permitted.

(d) Inventory — Not later than 3 full fiscal years after November 12, 1996, the Secretary of the Interior, acting through the Director of the Bureau of Land Management, shall develop a baseline inventory of all categories of fossil resources within the Area. After the inventory is developed, the Secretary shall conduct monitoring surveys at intervals specified in the management plan developed for the Area in accordance with subsection (e) of this section.

(e) Management plan

(1) In general — Not later than 5 years after November 12, 1996, the Secretary of the Interior shall develop and submit to the Committee on Energy and Natural Resources of the Senate and the Committee on Resources of the House of Representatives a management plan that describes the appropriate use of the Area consistent with this subsection.

(2) Contents — The management plan shall include —

(A) a plan for the implementation of a continuing cooperative program with other agencies and groups for —

(i) laboratory and field interpretation; and

(ii) public education about the resources and values of the Area (including vertebrate fossils);

(B) provisions for vehicle management that are consistent with the purpose of the Area and that provide for the use of vehicles to the minimum extent necessary to accomplish an individual scientific project;

(C) procedures for the excavation and collection of fossil remains, including botanical fossils, and the use of motorized and mechanical equipment to the minimum extent necessary to accomplish an individual scientific project; and

(D) mitigation and reclamation standards for activities that disturb the surface to the detriment of scenic and environmental values.

§1786. Piedras Blancas Historic Light Station
(a) Definitions

In this section:

(1) Light Station

The term "Light Station" means Piedras Blancas Light Station.

(2) Outstanding Natural Area

The term "Outstanding Natural Area" means the Piedras Blancas Historic Light Station Outstanding Natural Area established pursuant to subsection (c).

(3) Public lands

The term "public lands" has the meaning stated in section 103(e) of the Federal Land Policy and Management Act of 1976 (43 U.S.C. 1703(e)).

(4) Secretary

The term "Secretary" means the Secretary of the Interior.

(b) Findings

Congress finds as follows:

(1) The publicly owned Piedras Blancas Light Station has nationally recognized historical structures that should be preserved for present and future generations.

(2) The coastline adjacent to the Light Station is internationally recognized as having significant wildlife and marine habitat that provides critical information to research institutions throughout the world.

(3) The Light Station tells an important story about California's coastal prehistory and history in the context of the surrounding region and communities.

(4) The coastal area surrounding the Light Station was traditionally used by Indian people, including the Chumash and Salinan Indian tribes.

(5) The Light Station is historically associated with the nearby world-famous Hearst Castle (Hearst San Simeon State Historical Monument), now administered by the State of California.

(6) The Light Station represents a model partnership where future management can be successfully accomplished among the Federal Government, the State of California, San Luis Obispo County, local communities, and private groups.

(7) Piedras Blancas Historic Light Station Outstanding Natural Area would make a significant addition to the National Landscape Conservation System administered by the Department of the Interior's Bureau of Land Management.

(8) Statutory protection is needed for the Light Station and its surrounding Federal lands to ensure that it remains a part of our historic, cultural, and natural heritage and to be a source of inspiration for the people of the United States.

(c) Designation of the Piedras Blancas Historic Light Station Outstanding Natural Area

(1) In general

In order to protect, conserve, and enhance for the benefit and enjoyment of present and future generations the unique and nationally important historical, natural, cultural, scientific, educational, scenic, and recreational values of certain lands in and around the Piedras Blancas Light Station, in San Luis Obispo County, California, while allowing certain recreational and research activities to continue, there is established, subject to valid existing rights, the Piedras Blancas Historic Light Station Outstanding Natural Area.

(2) Maps and legal descriptions

The boundaries of the Outstanding Natural Area as those shown on the map entitled "Piedras Blancas Historic Light Station: Outstanding Natural Area", dated May 5, 2004, which shall be on file and available for public inspection in the Office of the Director, Bureau of Land Management, United States Department of the Interior, and the State office of the Bureau of Land Management in the State of California.

(3) Basis of management

The Secretary shall manage the Outstanding Natural Area as part of the National Landscape Conservation System to protect the resources of the area, and shall allow only those uses that further the purposes for the establishment of the Outstanding Natural Area, the Federal Land Policy and Management Act of 1976 (43 U.S.C. 1701 *et seq.*), and other applicable laws.

(4) Withdrawal

Subject to valid existing rights, and in accordance with the existing withdrawal as set forth in Public Land Order 7501 (Oct. 12, 2001, Vol. 66, No. 198, Federal Register 52149), the Federal lands and interests in lands included within the Outstanding Natural Area are hereby withdrawn from —

(A) all forms of entry, appropriation, or disposal under the public land laws;

(B) location, entry, and patent under the public land mining laws; and

(C) operation of the mineral leasing and geothermal leasing laws and the mineral materials laws.

(d) Management of the Piedras Blancas Historic Light Station Outstanding Natural Area

(1) In general

The Secretary shall manage the Outstanding Natural Area in a manner that conserves, protects, and enhances the unique and nationally important historical, natural, cultural, scientific, educational, scenic, and recreational values of that area, including an emphasis on preserving and restoring the Light Station facilities, consistent with the requirements of subsection (c)(3).

(2) Uses

Subject to valid existing rights, the Secretary shall only allow such uses of the Outstanding Natural Area as the Secretary finds are likely to further the purposes for which the Outstanding Natural Area is established as set forth in subsection (c)(1).

(3) Management plan

Not later than 3 years after of May 8, 2008, the Secretary shall complete a comprehensive management plan consistent with the requirements of section 202 of the Federal Land Policy and Management Act of 1976 (43 U.S.C. 1712) to provide long-term management guidance for the public lands within the Outstanding Natural Area and fulfill the purposes for which it is established, as set forth in subsection (c)(1). The management plan shall be developed in consultation with appropriate Federal, State, and local government agencies, with full public participation, and the contents shall include —

(A) provisions designed to ensure the protection of the resources and values described in subsection (c)(1);

(B) objectives to restore the historic Light Station and ancillary buildings;

(C) an implementation plan for a continuing program of interpretation and public education about the Light Station and its importance to the surrounding community;

(D) a proposal for minimal administrative and public facilities to be developed or improved at a level compatible with achieving the resources objectives for the Outstanding Natural Area as described in paragraph (1) and with other proposed management activities to accommodate visitors and researchers to the Outstanding Natural Area; and

(E) cultural resources management strategies for the Outstanding Natural Area, prepared in consultation with appropriate departments of the State of California, with emphasis on the preservation of the resources of the Outstanding Natural Area and the interpretive, education, and long-term scientific uses of the resources, giving priority to the enforcement of the Archaeological Resources Protection Act of 1979 (16 U.S.C. 470aa *et seq.*) and the National Historic Preservation Act (16 U.S.C. 470 *et seq.*) within the Outstanding Natural Area.

(4) Cooperative agreements

In order to better implement the management plan and to continue the successful partnerships with the local communities and the Hearst San Simeon State Historical Monument, administered by the California Department of Parks and Recreation, the Secretary may enter into cooperative agreements with the appropriate Federal, State, and local agencies pursuant to section 307(b) of the Federal Land Management Policy and Management Act of 1976 (43 U.S.C. 1737(b)).

(5) Research activities

In order to continue the successful partnership with research organizations and agencies and to assist in the development and implementation of the management plan, the Secretary may authorize within the Outstanding Natural Area appropriate research activities for the purposes identified in subsection (c)(1) and pursuant to section 307(a) of the Federal Land Policy and Management Act of 1976 (43 U.S.C. 1737(a)).

(6) Acquisition

State and privately held lands or interests in lands adjacent to the Outstanding Natural Area and identified as appropriate for acquisition in the management plan may be acquired by the Secretary as part of the Outstanding Natural Area only by —

(A) donation;

(B) exchange with a willing party; or

(C) purchase from a willing seller.

(7) Additions to the Outstanding Natural Area

Any lands or interest in lands adjacent to the Outstanding Natural Area acquired by the United States after May 8, 2008 shall be added to and administered as part of the Outstanding Natural Area.

(8) Overflights

Nothing in this section or the management plan shall be construed to —

(A) restrict or preclude overflights, including low level overflights, military, commercial, and general aviation overflights that can be seen or heard within the Outstanding Natural Area;

(B) restrict or preclude the designation or creation of new units of special use airspace or the establishment of military flight training routes over the Outstanding Natural Area; or

(C) modify regulations governing low-level overflights above the adjacent Monterey Bay National Marine Sanctuary.

(9) Law enforcement activities

Nothing in this section shall be construed to preclude or otherwise affect coastal border security operations or other law enforcement activities by the Coast Guard or other agencies within the Department of Homeland Security, the Department of Justice, or any other Federal, State, and local law enforcement agencies within the Outstanding Natural Area.

(10) Native American uses and interests

In recognition of the past use of the Outstanding Natural Area by Indians and Indian tribes for traditional cultural and religious purposes, the Secretary shall ensure access to the Outstanding Natural Area by Indians and Indian tribes for such traditional cultural and religious purposes. In implementing this subsection, the Secretary, upon the request of an Indian tribe or Indian religious community, shall temporarily close to the general public use of one or more specific portions of the Outstanding Natural Area in order to protect the privacy of traditional cultural and religious activities in such areas by the Indian tribe or Indian religious community. Any such closure shall be made to affect the smallest practicable area for the minimum period necessary for such purposes. Such access shall be consistent with the purpose and intent of Public Law 95-341 (42 U.S.C. 1996 *et seq.*; commonly referred to as the "American Indian Religious Freedom Act").

(11) No buffer zones

The designation of the Outstanding Natural Area is not intended to lead to the creation of protective perimeters or buffer zones around area. The fact that activities outside the Outstanding Natural Area and not consistent with the purposes of this section can be seen or heard within the Outstanding Natural Area shall not, of itself, preclude such activities or uses up to the boundary of the Outstanding Natural Area.

(e) Authorization of appropriations

There are authorized to be appropriated such sums as are necessary to carry out this section.

§1787. Jupiter Inlet Lighthouse Outstanding Natural Area

(a) Definitions

In this section:

(1) Commandant

The term "Commandant" means the Commandant of the Coast Guard.

(2) Lighthouse

The term "Lighthouse" means the Jupiter Inlet Lighthouse located in Palm Beach County, Florida.

(3) Local Partners

The term "Local Partners" includes —

(A) Palm Beach County, Florida;

(B) the Town of Jupiter, Florida;

(C) the Village of Tequesta, Florida; and

(D) the Loxahatchee River Historical Society.

(4) Management plan

The term "management plan" means the management plan developed under subsection (c)(1).

(5) Map

The term "map" means the map entitled "Jupiter Inlet Lighthouse Outstanding Natural Area" and dated October 29, 2007.

(6) Outstanding Natural Area

The term "Outstanding Natural Area" means the Jupiter Inlet Lighthouse Outstanding Natural Area established by subsection (b)(1).

(7) Public land

The term "public land" has the meaning given the term "public lands" in section 103(e) of the Federal Land Policy and Management Act of 1976 (43 U.S.C. 1702(e)).

(8) Secretary

The term "Secretary" means the Secretary of the Interior.

(9) State

The term "State" means the State of Florida.

(b) Establishment of the Jupiter Inlet Light-

house Outstanding Natural Area

(1) Establishment

Subject to valid existing rights, there is established for the purposes described in paragraph (2) the Jupiter Inlet Lighthouse Outstanding Natural Area, the boundaries of which are depicted on the map.

(2) Purposes

The purposes of the Outstanding Natural Area are to protect, conserve, and enhance the unique and nationally important historic, natural, cultural, scientific, educational, scenic, and recreational values of the Federal land surrounding the Lighthouse for the benefit of present generations and future generations of people in the United States, while —

(A) allowing certain recreational and research activities to continue in the Outstanding Natural Area; and

(B) ensuring that Coast Guard operations and activities are unimpeded within the boundaries of the Outstanding Natural Area.

(3) Availability of map

The map shall be on file and available for public inspection in appropriate offices of the Bureau of Land Management.

(4) Withdrawal

(A) In general

Subject to valid existing rights, subsection (e), and any existing withdrawals under the Executive orders and public land order described in subparagraph (B), the Federal land and any interests in the Federal land included in the Outstanding Natural Area are withdrawn from —

(i) all forms of entry, appropriation, or disposal under the public land laws;

(ii) location, entry, and patent under the mining laws; and

(iii) operation of the mineral leasing and geothermal leasing laws and the mineral materials laws.

(B) Description of Executive orders

The Executive orders and public land order described in subparagraph (A) are —

(i) the Executive Order dated October 22, 1854;

(ii) Executive Order No. 4254 (June 12, 1925); and

(iii) Public Land Order No. 7202 (61 Fed. Reg. 29758).

(c) Management plan

(1) In general

Not later than 3 years after May 8, 2008, the Secretary, in consultation with the Commandant, shall develop a comprehensive management plan in accordance with section 202 of the Federal Land Policy and Management Act of 1976 (43 U.S.C. 1712) to —

(A) provide long-term management guid-
ance for the public land in the Outstanding Natural Area; and

(B) ensure that the Outstanding Natural Area fulfills the purposes for which the Outstanding Natural Area is established.

(2) Consultation; public participation

The management plan shall be developed —

(A) in consultation with appropriate Federal, State, county, and local government agencies, the Commandant, the Local Partners, and other partners; and

(B) in a manner that ensures full public participation.

(3) Existing plans

The management plan shall, to the maximum extent practicable, be consistent with existing resource plans, policies, and programs.

(4) Inclusions

The management plan shall include —

(A) objectives and provisions to ensure—

(i) the protection and conservation of the resource values of the Outstanding Natural Area; and

(ii) the restoration of native plant communities and estuaries in the Outstanding Natural Area, with an emphasis on the conservation and enhancement of healthy, functioning ecological systems in perpetuity;

(B) objectives and provisions to maintain or recreate historic structures;

(C) an implementation plan for a program of interpretation and public education about the natural and cultural resources of the Lighthouse, the public land surrounding the Lighthouse, and associated structures;

(D) a proposal for administrative and public facilities to be developed or improved that —

(i) are compatible with achieving the resource objectives for the Outstanding Natural Area described in subsection (d) (1)(A)(ii); and

(ii) would accommodate visitors to the Outstanding Natural Area;

(E) natural and cultural resource management strategies for the Outstanding Natural Area, to be developed in consultation with appropriate departments of the State, the Local Partners, and the Commandant, with an emphasis on resource conservation in the Outstanding Natural Area and the interpretive, educational, and long-term scientific uses of the resources; and

(F) recreational use strategies for the Outstanding Natural Area, to be prepared in consultation with the Local Partners, appropriate departments of the State, and the Coast Guard, with an emphasis on passive recreation.

(5) Interim plan

Until a management plan is adopted for the Outstanding Natural Area, the Jupiter Inlet Coordinated Resource Management Plan (including any updates or amendments to the Jupiter Inlet Coordinated Resource Management Plan) shall be in effect.

(d) Management of the Jupiter Inlet Lighthouse Outstanding Natural Area

    (1) Management

        (A) In general

The Secretary, in consultation with the Local Partners and the Commandant, shall manage the Outstanding Natural Area —

           (i) as part of the National Landscape Conservation System;

           (ii) in a manner that conserves, protects, and enhances the unique and nationally important historical, natural, cultural, scientific, educational, scenic, and recreational values of the Outstanding Natural Area, including an emphasis on the restoration of native ecological systems; and

           (iii) in accordance with the Federal Land Policy and Management Act of 1976 (43 U.S.C. 1701 *et seq.*) and other applicable laws.

        (B) Limitation

In managing the Outstanding Natural Area, the Secretary shall not take any action that precludes, prohibits, or otherwise affects the conduct of ongoing or future Coast Guard operations or activities on lots 16 and 18, as depicted on the map.

    (2) Uses

Subject to valid existing rights and subsection (e), the Secretary shall only allow uses of the Outstanding Natural Area that the Secretary, in consultation with the Commandant and Local Partners, determines would likely further the purposes for which the Outstanding Natural Area is established.

    (3) Cooperative agreements

To facilitate implementation of the management plan and to continue the successful partnerships with local communities and other partners, the Secretary may, in accordance with section 307(b) of the Federal Land Management Policy and Management Act of 1976 (43 U.S.C. 1737(b)), enter into cooperative agreements with the appropriate Federal, State, county, other local government agencies, and other partners (including the Loxahatchee River Historical Society) for the long-term management of the Outstanding Natural Area.

    (4) Research activities

To continue successful research partnerships, pursue future research partnerships, and assist in the development and implementation of the management plan, the Secretary may, in accordance

with section 307(a) of the Federal Land Policy and Management Act of 1976 (43 U.S.C. 1737(a)), authorize the conduct of appropriate research activities in the Outstanding Natural Area for the purposes described in subsection (b)(2).

    (5) Acquisition of land

        (A) In general

Subject to subparagraph (B), the Secretary may acquire for inclusion in the Outstanding Natural Area any State or private land or any interest in State or private land that is —

           (i) adjacent to the Outstanding Natural Area; and

           (ii) identified in the management plan as appropriate for acquisition.

        (B) Means of acquisition

Land or an interest in land may be acquired under subparagraph (A) only by donation, exchange, or purchase from a willing seller with donated or appropriated funds.

        (C) Additions to the Outstanding Natural Area

Any land or interest in land adjacent to the Outstanding Natural Area acquired by the United States after May 8, 2008, under subparagraph (A) shall be added to, and administered as part of, the Outstanding Natural Area.

    (6) Law enforcement activities

Nothing in this section, the management plan, or the Jupiter Inlet Coordinated Resource Management Plan (including any updates or amendments to the Jupiter Inlet Coordinated Resource Management Plan) precludes, prohibits, or otherwise affects —

        (A) any maritime security, maritime safety, or environmental protection mission or activity of the Coast Guard;

        (B) any border security operation or law enforcement activity by the Department of Homeland Security or the Department of Justice; or

        (C) any law enforcement activity of any Federal, State, or local law enforcement agency in the Outstanding Natural Area.

    (7) Future disposition of Coast Guard facilities

If the Commandant determines, after May 8, 2008, that Coast Guard facilities within the Outstanding Natural Area exceed the needs of the Coast Guard, the Commandant may relinquish the facilities to the Secretary without removal, subject only to any environmental remediation that may be required by law.

(e) Effect on ongoing and future Coast Guard operations

Nothing in this section, the management plan, or the Jupiter Inlet Coordinated Resource Management Plan (including updates or amendments to the Jupiter Inlet Coordinated Resource Management Plan) precludes, prohibits, or otherwise affects ongoing or future Coast Guard operations or activities in the Outstanding Natural Area, including —

(1) the continued and future operation of, access to, maintenance of, and, as may be necessitated for Coast Guard missions, the expansion, enhancement, or replacement of, the Coast Guard High Frequency antenna site on lot 16;

(2) the continued and future operation of, access to, maintenance of, and, as may be necessitated for Coast Guard missions, the expansion, enhancement, or replacement of, the military family housing area on lot 18;

(3) the continued and future use of, access to, maintenance of, and, as may be necessitated for Coast Guard missions, the expansion, enhancement, or replacement of, the pier on lot 18;

(4) the existing lease of the Jupiter Inlet Lighthouse on lot 18 from the Coast Guard to the Loxahatchee River Historical Society; or

(5) any easements or other less-than-fee interests in property appurtenant to existing Coast Guard facilities on lots 16 and 18.

(f) Authorization of appropriations

There are authorized to be appropriated such sums as are necessary to carry out this section.

Promoting Active Management of America's Forests, Rangelands, and Other Federal Lands to Improve Conditions and Reduce Wildfire Risk, Executive Order 13,855

84 Fed. Reg. 65 (2019)

By the authority vested in me as President by the Constitution and the laws of the United States of America, it is hereby ordered as follows:

Section 1. *Policy.* It is the policy of the United States to protect people, communities, and watersheds, and to promote healthy and resilient forests, rangelands, and other Federal lands by actively managing them through partnerships with States, tribes, communities, non-profit organizations, and the private sector. For decades, dense trees and undergrowth have amassed in these lands, fueling catastrophic wildfires. These conditions, along with insect infestation, invasive species, disease, and drought, have weakened our forests, rangelands, and other Federal lands, and have placed communities and homes at risk of damage from catastrophic wildfires.

Active management of vegetation is needed to treat these dangerous conditions on Federal lands but is often delayed due to challenges associated with regulatory analysis and current consultation requirements. In addition, land designations and policies can reduce emergency responder access to Federal land and restrict management practices that can promote wildfire-resistant landscapes. With the same vigor and commitment that characterizes our efforts to fight wildfires, we must actively manage our forests, rangelands, and other Federal lands to improve conditions and reduce wildfire risk.

In recognition of these regulatory, policy, and coordinating challenges, the Secretary of the Interior and the Secretary of Agriculture (the Secretaries) each shall implement the following policies in their respective departments:

(a) Shared Management Priorities. The goal of Federal fire management policy for forests, rangelands, and other Federal lands shall be to agree on a set of shared priorities with Federal land managers, States, tribes, and other landowners to manage fire risk across landscapes.

(b) Coordinating Federal, State, Tribal, and Local Assets. Wildfire prevention and suppression and post-wildfire restoration require a variety of assets and skills across landscapes. Federal, State, tribal, and local governments should coordinate the deployment of appropriate assets and skills to restore our landscapes and communities after damage caused by fires and to help reduce hazardous fuels through active forest management in order to protect communities, critical infrastructure, and natural and cultural resources.

(c) Removing Hazardous Fuels, Increasing Active Management, and Supporting Rural Economies. Post-fire assessments show that reducing vegetation through hazardous fuel management and strategic forest health treatments is effective in reducing wildfire severity and loss. Actions must be taken across landscapes to prioritize treatments in order to enhance fuel reduction and forest-restoration projects that protect life and property, and to benefit rural economies through encouraging utilization of the by-products of forest restoration.

Sec. 2. *Goals.*

(a) To protect communities and watersheds, to better prevent catastrophic wildfires, and to improve the health of America's forests, rangelands, and other Federal lands, the Secretaries shall each develop goals and implementation plans for wildfire prevention activities and programs in their respective departments. In the development of such goals and plans:

(i) The Secretary of the Interior shall review the Secretary's 2019 budget justifications and give all due consideration to establishing the following objectives for 2019, as feasible and appropriate in light of those budget justifications, and consistent with applicable law and available appropriations:

(A) Treating 750,000 acres of Department of the Interior (DOI)-administered lands to reduce fuel loads;

(B) Treating 500,000 acres of DOI-administered lands to protect water quality and mitigate severe flooding and erosion risks arising from forest fires;

(C) Treating 750,000 acres of DOI-administered lands for native and invasive species;

(D) Reducing vegetation giving rise to wildfire conditions through forest health treatments by increasing health treatments as part of DOI's offering for sale 600 million board feet of timber from DOI-administered lands; and

(E) Performing maintenance on public roads needed to provide access for emergency services and restoration work; and

(ii) The Secretary of Agriculture shall review the Secretary's 2019 budget justifications and give all due consideration to establishing the following objectives for 2019, as feasible and appropriate in light of those budget justifications, and consistent with applicable law and available appropriations:

(A) Treating 3.5 million acres of Department of Agriculture (USDA) Forest Service (FS) lands to reduce fuel load;

(B) Treating 2.2 million acres of USDA FS lands to protect water quality and mitigate severe flooding and erosion risks arising from forest fires;

(C) Treating 750,000 acres of USDA FS lands for native and invasive species;

(D) Reducing vegetation giving rise to wildfire conditions through forest health treatments by increasing health treatments as part of USDA's offering for sale at least 3.8 billion board feet of timber from USDA FS lands; and

(E) Performing maintenance on roads needed to provide access on USDA FS lands for emergency services and restoration work.

(b) For the years following establishment of the objectives in subsection (a) of this section, the Secretaries shall consider annual treatment objectives that meet or exceed those established in subsection (a) of this section, using the full range of available and appropriate management tools, including prescribed burns and mechanical thinning. The Secretaries shall also refine and develop performance metrics to better capture the risk reduction benefits achieved through application of these management tools.

(c) In conjunction with establishment of goals, and by no later than March 31, 2019, the Secretaries shall identify salvage and log recovery options from lands damaged by fire during the 2017 and 2018 fire seasons, insects, or disease.

Sec. 3. *Coordination and Efficient Processes.* Effective Federal agency coordination and efficient administrative actions and decisions are essential to improving the condition of America's forests, rangelands, and other Federal lands. To advance the policies set forth in this order and the goals set by the Secretaries, the Secretaries shall:

(a) Coordinate with the heads of all relevant Federal agencies to prioritize and promptly implement post-wildfire rehabilitation, salvage, and forest restoration;

(b) Streamline agency administrative and regulatory processes and policies relating to fuel reduction in forests, rangelands, and other Federal lands and forest restoration when appropriate by:

(i) Adhering to minimum statutory and regulatory time periods, to the maximum extent practicable, for comment, consultation, and administrative review processes related to active management of forests, rangelands, and other Federal lands, including management of wildfire risks;

(ii) Using all applicable categorical exclusions set forth in law or regulation for fire management, restoration, and other management projects in forests, rangelands, and other Federal lands when implementing the requirements of the National Environmental Policy Act (42 U.S.C. 4321 et seq.);

(iii) Consistent with applicable law, developing and using new categorical exclusions to implement active management of forests, rangelands, and other Federal lands; and

(iv) Immediately prioritizing efforts to reduce the time required to comply with consultation obligations under the Endangered Species Act of 1973 (16 U.S.C. 1531 et seq.).

Sec. 4. *Unmanned Aerial Systems.* To reduce fire and forest health risks as described in section 1 of this order, the Secretaries shall, in coordination with the Administrator of the Federal Aviation Administration, maximize appropriate use of unmanned aerial systems to accelerate forest management and support firefighting and post-fire rehabilitation in forests, rangelands, and other Federal lands.

Sec. 5. *Wildfire Strategy.*

(a) In collaboration with Federal, State, tribal, and local partners, the Secretaries shall jointly develop, by December 31, 2020, a strategy to support local Federal land managers in project decision-making and inform local fire management decisions related to forests, rangelands, and other Federal lands, thereby protecting habitats and communities, and reducing risks to physical infrastructure.

(b) In developing the strategy described in subsection (a) of this section, the Secretaries shall:

(i) Identify DOI- and USDA FS-administered lands with the highest probability of catastrophic wildfires, as well as areas on those lands where there is a high probability that wildfires would threaten people, structures, or other high-value assets, in order to direct and prioritize actions to meet land management goals and to protect communities;

(ii) Examine the costs and challenges relating to management of DOI- and USDA FS-administered lands, including costs associated with wildfire suppression, implementation of applicable statutory requirements, and litigation;

(iii) Review land designations and policies that may limit active forest management and increase the risk of catastrophic wildfires;

(iv) Consider market conditions as appropriate when preparing timber sales, including biomass and biochar opportunities, and encourage export of these or similar forest-treatment products to the maximum extent permitted by law, in order to promote active forest management, mitigate wildfire risk, and encourage post-fire forest restoration;

(v) Develop recommended actions and incentives to expand uses, markets, and utilization of forest products resulting from restoration and fuel reduction projects in forests, rangelands, and other Federal lands, including biomass and small-diameter materials;

(vi) Assess how effectively Federal programs and investments support forest-product infrastructure and market access;

(vii) Identify and assess methods, including methods undertaken pursuant to section 3(b)(iv) of this order, to more effectively and efficiently streamline consultation under the Endangered Species Act;

(viii) In conjunction with the Administrator of the Environmental Protection Agency, identify methods to reduce interagency regulatory barriers, improve alignment of Federal, State, and tribal policy, and identify redundant policies and procedures to promote efficiencies in implementing the Clean Water Act of 1972 (33 U.S.C. 1251 et seq.), Clean Air Act (42 U.S.C. 7401 et seq.), and other applicable Federal environmental laws; and

(ix) Develop procedures and guidance to facilitate timely compliance with the National Environmental Policy Act.

Sec. 6. *Collaborative Partnerships.* To reduce fuel loads, restore watersheds, and improve forest, rangeland, and other Federal land conditions, and to utilize available expertise and efficiently deploy resources,

the Secretaries shall expand collaboration with States, tribes, communities, non-profit organizations, and the private sector. Such expanded collaboration by the Secretaries shall, at a minimum, address:

(a) Supporting road activities needed to maintain forest, rangeland, and other Federal land health and to mitigate wildfire risk by expanding existing or entering into new Good Neighbor Authority agreements, consistent with applicable law; and

(b) Achieving the land management restoration goals set forth in section 2 of this order and reducing fuel loads by pursuing long-term stewardship contracts, including 20-year contracts, with States, tribes, non-profit organizations, communities, and the private sector, consistent with applicable law.

Sec. 7. *General Provisions.*

(a) Nothing in this order shall be construed to impair or otherwise affect:

(i) the authority granted by law to an executive department or agency, or the head thereof; or

(ii) the functions of the Director of the Office of Management and Budget relating to budgetary, administrative, or legislative proposals.

(b) This order shall be implemented consistent with applicable law and subject to the availability of appropriations.

(c) This order is not intended to, and does not, create any right or benefit, substantive or procedural, enforceable at law or in equity by any party against the United States, its departments, agencies, or entities, its officers, employees, or agents, or any other person.

DONALD J. TRUMP
THE WHITE HOUSE
December 21, 2018

11

CASE SUPPLEMENT

This chapter contains lightly-edited copies of recent judicial decisions addressing important issues of environmental law. These include the Ninth Circuit's decision in *Juliana v. United States* dismissing a major climate change lawsuit, and ten decisions by the U.S. Supreme Court. The Supreme Court decisions cover the gamut of environmental law—the Superfund law (CERCLA), the Clean Water Act, the Endangered Species Act, and issues of preemption, regulatory takings, and removal of state climate litigation to federal courts.

CLIMATE LITIGATION: THE *JULIANA* CASE

In November 2016 a federal district court in Oregon rejected a motion to dismiss a "future generations" climate change lawsuit against the President and top U.S. officials. Juliana v. United States, 217 F. Supp. 3d 1224 (D. Ore. 2016). The plaintiffs, who include 21 people then between the ages of eight and nineteen, allege that the federal government knew about the dangers of climate change for more than 50 years, but failed to take action to protect them. The children argue that this violated their substantive due process rights to life, liberty and property as well as the government's public trust obligations to hold natural resources in trust for future generations. The plaintiffs seek a declaration that their rights have been violated and an order requiring federal officials to develop a plan to control emissions of greenhouse gases.

The court rejected the government's arguments that the case raises a non-justiciable political question and that the plaintiffs lack standing. Federal district Judge Ann Aiken distinguished Washington Environmental Council v. Bellon, 732 F.3d 1131 (9th Cir. 2013), a case where an environmental group was held not to have standing to challenge a permit for a refinery for contributing to climate change. She noted that on a motion for summary judgment the court must accept the plaintiffs' allegations of injury and causation as true and that the lawsuit seeks to redress much more significant sources of GHG emissions than the refineries whose permitting was challenged in *Bellon*. The court also held that plaintiffs had adequately pleaded substantive due process and public trust violations by the federal government.

The Justice Department then petitioned the Ninth Circuit for a writ of mandamus to halt discovery and any trial, arguing that the federal government should not be subject to burdensome discovery when the plaintiffs have failed to state a justiciable claim. On March 7, 2018, a panel of Ninth Circuit judges denied without prejudice the federal government's motion for a writ of mandamus. In re United States, 884 F.3d 830 (9th Cir. 2018). The court held that the federal government had not met the "high bar for mandamus relief" at this stage of the litigation. It observed that it was "mindful that some of the plaintiffs' claims as currently pleaded are quite broad, and some of the remedies plaintiffs seek may not be available as redress." But the court left it for the district court to develop the record and to consider the claims raised by the plaintiffs. On July 30, 2018, the U.S. Supreme Court refused the federal government's request to stay discovery and the upcoming trial. United States v. U.S. District Court for Oregon, 139 S. Ct. 1 (2018). Like the Ninth Circuit, the Court cautioned that the "breadth of respondents' claims is striking, and it opined that "the justiciability of those claims presents substantial grounds for difference of opinion." The Court's order denying a writ of mandamus advised the federal district court hearing the case to "take these concerns into account in assessing the burdens of discovery and trial, as well as the desirability of a prompt ruling on the Government's pending dispositive motions."

On October 15, 2018, the district court again largely denied the government's dispositive notions and confirmed that an anticipated 50-day trial would commence on October 29. Many observers anticipated that this would be the "trial of the century" on climate change. The federal government then sought from both the Ninth Circuit and the Supreme Court a writ of mandamus ordering the district court to dismiss the case.

On October 19, 2018, Chief Justice John Roberts granted an administrative stay of discovery and trial pending the Court's disposition of the government's mandamus motion. In re United States, 139 S. Ct. 16 (2018). On November 2, the Court vacated the stay, but pointedly placed pressure on the Ninth Circuit to intervene. In Re United States, 139 S. Ct. 452 (2018). The Court noted that the government's mandamus petition also was before the Ninth Circuit. Although the Ninth Circuit previously had denied two mandamus motions by the government, the Ninth Circuit's "basis for denying relief rested, in large part, on the early stage of the litigation, the likelihood that plaintiffs' claims would narrow as the case progressed, and the possibility of attaining relief through ordinary dispositive motions." The Supreme Court stated that these reasons were, "to a large extent, no longer pertinent" since the trial had been held in abeyance only because of the Chief Justice's stay. Justices Thomas and Gorsuch stated that they would have granted the stay.

In response, the Ninth Circuit on November 8 issued its own stay of the district court proceedings and it directed Judge Aiken promptly to resolve the government's motion for reconsideration of the denial of a request to certify the case for interlocutory review. Judge Aiken then reluctantly agreed on November 21, 2018 to certify the case for interlocutory review. Juliana v. United States, 2018 WL 6303774. On January 7, 2019, the Ninth Circuit agreed to hear the government's appeal of the denial of its motion to dismiss. Judge Friedland dissented from the decision to grant interlocutory review because he believed that the district judge did not truly believe that interlocutory review was warranted, but rather had responded to pressure from the higher courts. On June 4, 2019 a three-judge panel of the 9th Circuit heard oral argument. On January 17, 2020 it split 2-1 in rendering the following opinion

JULIANA v. UNITED STATES
947 F.3d 1159 (9th Cir. 2020)

HURWITZ, Circuit Judge:

In the mid-1960s, a popular song warned that we were "on the eve of destruction." The plaintiffs in this case have presented compelling evidence that climate change has brought that eve nearer. A substantial evidentiary record documents that the federal government has long promoted fossil fuel use despite knowing that it can cause catastrophic climate change, and that failure to change existing policy may hasten an environmental apocalypse.

The plaintiffs claim that the government has violated their constitutional rights, including a claimed right under the Due Process Clause of the Fifth Amendment to a "climate system capable of sustaining human life." The central issue before us is whether, even assuming such a broad constitutional right exists, an Article III court can provide the plaintiffs the redress they seek — an order requiring the government to develop a plan to "phase out fossil fuel emissions and draw down excess atmospheric CO2." Reluctantly, we conclude that such relief is beyond our constitutional power. Rather, the plaintiffs' impressive case for redress must be presented to the political branches of government.

I

The plaintiffs are twenty-one young citizens, an environmental organization, and a "representative of future generations." Their original complaint named as defendants the President, the United States, and federal agencies (collectively, "the government"). The operative complaint accuses the government of continuing to "permit, authorize, and subsidize" fossil fuel use despite long being aware of its risks, thereby causing various climate-change related injuries to the plaintiffs. Some plaintiffs claim psychological harm, others impairment to recreational interests, others exacerbated medical conditions, and others damage to property. The complaint asserts violations of: (1) the plaintiffs' substantive rights under the Due Process Clause of the Fifth Amendment; (2) the plaintiffs' rights under the Fifth Amendment to equal protection of the law; (3) the plaintiffs' rights under the Ninth Amendment; and (4) the public trust doctrine. The plaintiffs seek declaratory relief and an injunction ordering the government to implement a plan to "phase out fossil fuel emissions and draw down excess atmospheric [carbon dioxide]."

The district court denied the government's motion to dismiss, concluding that the plaintiffs had standing to sue, raised justiciable questions, and stated a claim for infringement of a Fifth Amendment due process right to a "climate system capable of sustaining human life." The court defined that right as one to be free from catastrophic climate change that "will cause human deaths, shorten human lifespans, result in widespread damage to property, threaten human food sources, and dramatically alter the planet's ecosystem." The court also concluded that the plaintiffs had stated a viable "danger-creation due process claim" arising from the government's failure to regulate third-party emissions. Finally, the court held that the plaintiffs had stated a public trust claim grounded in the Fifth and the Ninth Amendments. . . .

The government then moved for summary judgment and judgment on the pleadings. The district court granted summary judgment on the Ninth Amendment claim, dismissed the President as a defendant, and dismissed the equal protection claim in part. But the court otherwise denied the government's motions, again holding that the plaintiffs had standing to sue and finding that they had presented sufficient evidence to survive summary judgment. . . .

The district court initially declined the government's request to certify those orders for interlocutory appeal. But, while considering a second mandamus petition from the government, we invited the district court to revisit certification, noting the Supreme Court's justiciability concerns. The district court then reluctantly certified the orders denying the motions for interlocutory appeal . . . and stayed the proceedings, while "stand[ing] by its prior rulings . . . as well as its belief that this case would be better served by further factual development at trial." We granted the government's petition for permission to appeal.

II

The plaintiffs have compiled an extensive record, which at this stage in the litigation we take in the light most favorable to their claims. The record leaves little basis for denying that climate change is occurring at an increasingly rapid pace. It documents that since the dawn of the Industrial Age, atmospheric carbon dioxide has skyrocketed to levels not seen for almost three million years. For hundreds of thousands of years, average carbon concentration fluctuated between 180 and 280 parts per million. Today, it is over 410 parts per million and climbing. Although carbon levels rose gradually after the last Ice Age, the most recent surge has occurred more than 100 times faster; half of that increase has come in the last forty years.

Copious expert evidence establishes that this unprecedented rise stems from fossil fuel combustion and will wreak havoc on the Earth's climate if unchecked. Temperatures have already risen 0.9 degrees Celsius above pre-industrial levels and may rise more than 6 degrees Celsius by the end of the century. The hottest years on record all fall within this decade, and each year since 1997 has been hotter than the previous average. This extreme heat is melting polar ice caps and may cause sea levels to rise 15 to 30 feet by 2100. The problem is approaching "the point of no return." Absent some action, the destabilizing climate will bury cities, spawn life-threatening natural disasters, and jeopardize critical food and water supplies.

The record also conclusively establishes that the federal government has long understood the risks of fossil fuel use and increasing carbon dioxide emissions. As early as 1965, the Johnson Administration cautioned that fossil fuel emissions threatened significant changes to climate, global temperatures, sea levels, and other stratospheric properties. In 1983, an Environmental Protection Agency ("EPA") report projected an increase of 2 degrees Celsius by 2040, warning that a "wait and see" carbon emissions policy was extremely risky. And, in the 1990s, the EPA implored the government to act before it was too late. Nonetheless, by 2014, U.S. fossil fuel emissions had climbed to 5.4 billion metric tons, up substantially from 1965. This growth shows no signs of abating. From 2008 to 2017, domestic petroleum and natural gas production increased by nearly 60%, and the country is now expanding oil and gas extraction four times faster than any other nation.

The record also establishes that the government's contribution to climate change is not simply a result of inaction. The government affirmatively promotes fossil fuel use in a host of ways, including beneficial tax provisions, permits for imports and exports, subsidies for domestic and overseas projects, and leases for fuel extraction on federal land.

A

The government by and large has not disputed the factual premises of the plaintiffs' claims. [The court then rejects the government's argument that because the plaintiffs' claims are based on agency actions, they must be brought only under the Administrative Procedure Act.]

B

The government also argues that the plaintiffs lack Article III standing to pursue their constitutional claims. To have standing under Article III, a plaintiff must have (1) a concrete and particularized injury that (2) is caused by the challenged conduct and (3) is likely redressable by a favorable judicial decision. A plaintiff need only establish a genuine dispute as to these requirements to survive summary judgment.

1

The district court correctly found the injury requirement met. At least some plaintiffs claim concrete and particularized injuries. Jaime B., for example, claims that she was forced to leave her home because of water scarcity, separating her from relatives on the Navajo Reservation. Levi D. had to evacuate his coastal home multiple times because of flooding. These injuries are not simply "'conjectural' or 'hypothetical;'" at least some of the plaintiffs have presented evidence that climate change is affecting them now in concrete ways and will continue to do so unless checked.

The government argues that the plaintiffs' alleged injuries are not particularized because climate change affects everyone. But, "it does not matter how many persons have been injured" if the plaintiffs' injuries are "concrete and personal." And, the Article III injury requirement is met if only one plaintiff has suffered concrete harm.

2

The district court also correctly found the Article III causation requirement satisfied for purposes of summary judgment. Causation can be established "even if there are multiple links in the chain," as long as the chain is not "hypothetical or tenuous." The causal chain here is sufficiently established. The plaintiffs' alleged injuries are caused by carbon emissions from fossil fuel production, extraction, and transportation. A significant portion of those emissions occur in this country; the United States accounted for over 25% of worldwide emissions from 1850 to 2012, and currently accounts for about 15%. See *Massachusetts*, 549 U.S. at 524-25 (finding that emissions amounting to about 6% of the worldwide total showed cause of alleged injury "by any standard"). And, the plaintiffs' evidence shows that federal subsidies and leases have increased those emissions. About 25% of fossil fuels extracted in the United States come from federal waters and lands, an activity that requires authorization from the federal government.

Relying on *Washington Environmental Council v. Bellon*, 732 F.3d 1131, 1141-46 (9th Cir. 2013), the government argues that the causal chain is too attenuated because it depends in part on the independent actions of third parties. *Bellon* held that the causal chain between local agencies' failure to regulate five oil refineries and the plaintiffs' climate-change related injuries was "too tenuous to support standing" because the refineries had a "scientifically indiscernible" impact on climate change. But the plaintiffs here do not contend that their injuries were caused by a few isolated agency decisions. Rather, they blame a host of federal policies, from subsidies to drilling permits, spanning "over 50 years," and direct actions by the government. There is at least a genuine factual dispute as to whether those policies were a "substantial factor" in causing the plaintiffs' injuries.

3

The more difficult question is whether the plaintiffs' claimed injuries are redressable by an Article III court. In analyzing that question, we start by stressing what the plaintiffs do and do not assert. They do not claim that the government has violated a statute or a regulation. They do not assert the denial of a procedural right. Nor do they seek damages under the Federal Tort Claims Act. Rather, their sole claim is that the government has deprived them of a substantive constitutional right to a "climate system capable of sustaining human life," and they seek remedial declaratory and injunctive relief.

Reasonable jurists can disagree about whether the asserted constitutional right exists. In analyzing redressability, however, we assume its existence. But that merely begins our analysis, because "not all meritorious legal claims are redressable in federal court." To establish Article III redressability, the plaintiffs must show that the relief they seek is both (1) substantially likely to redress their injuries; and (2) within the district court's power to award. Redress need not be guaranteed, but it must be more than "merely speculative."

The plaintiffs first seek a declaration that the government is violating the Constitution. But that relief alone is not substantially likely to mitigate the plaintiffs' asserted concrete injuries. A declaration, although undoubtedly likely to benefit the plaintiffs psychologically, is unlikely by itself to remediate their alleged injuries absent further court action.

The crux of the plaintiffs' requested remedy is an injunction requiring the government not only to cease permitting, authorizing, and subsidizing fossil fuel use, but also to prepare a plan subject to judicial approval to draw down harmful emissions. The plaintiffs thus seek not only to enjoin the Executive from exercising discretionary authority expressly granted by Congress, see, e.g., 30 U.S.C. § 201 (authorizing the Secretary of the Interior to lease land for coal mining), but also to enjoin Congress from exercising power expressly granted by the Constitution over public lands, see U.S. Const. art. IV, § 3, cl. 2 ("The Congress shall have Power to dispose of and make all needful Rules and Regulations respecting the Territory or other Property belonging to the United States.").

As an initial matter, we note that although the plaintiffs contended at oral argument that they challenge only affirmative activities by the government, an order simply enjoining those activities will not, according to their own experts' opinions, suffice to stop catastrophic climate change or even ameliorate their injuries. The plaintiffs' experts opine that the federal government's leases and subsidies have contributed to global carbon emissions. But they do not show that even the total elimination of the challenged programs would halt the growth of carbon dioxide levels in the atmosphere, let alone decrease that growth. Nor does any expert contend that elimination of the challenged pro-carbon fuels programs would by itself prevent further injury to the plaintiffs. Rather, the record shows that many of the emissions causing climate change happened decades ago or come from foreign and non-governmental sources.

Indeed, the plaintiffs' experts make plain that reducing the global consequences of climate change demands much more than cessation of the government's promotion of fossil fuels. Rather, these experts opine that such a result calls for no less than a fundamental transformation of this country's energy system, if not that of the industrialized world. One expert opines that atmospheric carbon reductions must come "largely via reforestation," and include rapid and immediate decreases in emissions from many sources. "[L]eisurely reductions of one of two percent per year," he explains, "will not suffice." Another expert has opined that although the required emissions reductions are "technically feasible," they can be achieved only through a comprehensive plan for "nearly complete decarbonization" that includes both an "unprecedently rapid build out" of renewable energy and a "sustained commitment to infrastructure transformation over decades." And, that commitment, another expert emphasizes, must include everything from energy efficient lighting to improved public transportation to hydrogen-powered aircraft.

The plaintiffs concede that their requested relief will not alone solve global climate change, but they assert that their "injuries would be to some extent ameliorated." Relying on *Massachusetts v. EPA*, the district court apparently found the redressability requirement satisfied because the requested relief would likely slow or reduce emissions. That case, however, involved a procedural right that the State of Massachusetts was allowed to assert "without meeting all the normal standards for redressability;" in that context, the Court found redressability because "there [was] some possibility that the requested relief [would] prompt the injury-causing party to reconsider the decision that allegedly harmed the litigant." The plaintiffs here do not assert a procedural right, but rather a substantive due process claim.[7]

We are therefore skeptical that the first redressability prong is satisfied. But even assuming that it is, the plaintiffs do not surmount the remaining hurdle — establishing that the specific relief they seek is within the power of an Article III court. There is much to recommend the adoption of a comprehensive scheme to decrease fossil fuel emissions and combat climate change, both as a policy matter in general and a matter of national survival in particular. But it is beyond the power of an Article III court to order, design, supervise, or implement the plaintiffs' requested remedial plan. As the opinions of their experts make plain, any effective plan would necessarily require a host of complex policy decisions entrusted, for better or worse, to the wisdom and discretion of the executive and legislative branches. These decisions range, for example, from determining how much to invest in public transit to how quickly to transition to renewable energy, and plainly require consideration of "competing social, political, and economic forces," which must be made by the People's "elected representatives, rather than by federal judges interpreting the basic charter of Government for the entire country."

The plaintiffs argue that the district court need not itself make policy decisions, because if their general request for a remedial plan is granted, the political branches can decide what policies will best "phase out fossil fuel emissions and draw down excess atmospheric CO2." To be sure, in some circumstances, courts may order broad injunctive relief while leaving the "details of implementation" to the government's discretion. But, even under such a scenario, the plaintiffs' request for a remedial plan would subsequently require the judiciary to pass judgment on the sufficiency of the government's response to the order, which necessarily would entail a broad range of policymaking. And inevitably, this kind of plan will demand action not only by the Executive, but also by Congress. Absent court intervention, the political branches might conclude — however inappropriately in the plaintiffs' view — that economic or defense considerations called for continuation of the very programs challenged in this suit, or a less robust approach to addressing climate change than the plaintiffs believe is necessary. "But we cannot substitute our own assessment for the Executive's [or Legislature's] predictive judgments on such matters, all of which 'are delicate, complex, and involve large

---

[7] The dissent reads *Massachusetts* to hold that "a perceptible reduction in the advance of climate change is sufficient to redress a plaintiff's climate change-induced harms." But *Massachusetts* "permitted a State to challenge EPA's refusal to regulate greenhouse gas emissions," that as a sovereign it was "entitled to special solicitude in [the] standing analysis." Here, in contrast, the plaintiffs are not sovereigns, and a substantive right, not a procedural one, is at issue.

elements of prophecy.'" And, given the complexity and long-lasting nature of global climate change, the court would be required to supervise the government's compliance with any suggested plan for many decades.[8]

As the Supreme Court recently explained, "a constitutional directive or legal standards" must guide the courts' exercise of equitable power. *Rucho v. Common Cause*, 139 S. Ct. 2484, 2508 (2019). *Rucho* found partisan gerrymandering claims presented political questions beyond the reach of Article III courts. The Court did not deny extreme partisan gerrymandering can violate the Constitution. But, it concluded that there was no "limited and precise" standard discernible in the Constitution for redressing the asserted violation. The Court rejected the plaintiffs' proposed standard because unlike the one-person, one-vote rule in vote dilution cases, it was not "relatively easy to administer as a matter of math."

Rucho reaffirmed that redressability questions implicate the separation of powers, noting that federal courts "have no commission to allocate political power and influence" without standards to guide in the exercise of such authority. Absent those standards, federal judicial power could be "unlimited in scope and duration," and would inject "the unelected and politically unaccountable branch of the Federal Government [into] assuming such an extraordinary and unprecedented role." Because "it is axiomatic that 'the Constitution contemplates that democracy is the appropriate process for change,'" some questions — even those existential in nature — are the province of the political branches. The Court found in *Rucho* that a proposed standard involving a mathematical comparison to a baseline election map is too difficult for the judiciary to manage. It is impossible to reach a different conclusion here.

The plaintiffs' experts opine that atmospheric carbon levels of 350 parts per million are necessary to stabilize the global climate. But, even accepting those opinions as valid, they do not suggest how an order from this Court can achieve that level, other than by ordering the government to develop a plan. Although the plaintiffs' invitation to get the ball rolling by simply ordering the promulgation of a plan is beguiling, it ignores that an Article III court will thereafter be required to determine whether the plan is sufficient to remediate the claimed constitutional violation of the plaintiffs' right to a "climate system capable of sustaining human life." We doubt that any such plan can be supervised or enforced by an Article III court. And, in the end, any plan is only as good as the court's power to enforce it.

C

Our dissenting colleague quite correctly notes the gravity of the plaintiffs' evidence; we differ only as to whether an Article III court can provide their requested redress. In suggesting that we can, the dissent reframes the plaintiffs' claimed constitutional right variously as an entitlement to "the country's perpetuity," or as one to freedom from "the amount of fossil-fuel emissions that will irreparably devastate our Nation." But if such broad constitutional rights exist, we doubt that the plaintiffs would have Article III standing to enforce them. Their alleged individual injuries do not flow from a violation of these claimed rights. Indeed, any injury from the dissolution of the Republic would be felt by all citizens equally, and thus would not constitute the kind of discrete and particularized injury necessary for Article III standing. A suit for a violation of these reframed rights, like one for a violation of the Guarantee Clause, would also plainly be nonjusticiable.

More importantly, the dissent offers no metrics for judicial determination of the level of climate change that would cause "the willful dissolution of the Republic," nor for measuring a constitutionally acceptable "perceptible reduction in the advance of climate change." Contrary to the dissent, we cannot find Article III redressability requirements satisfied simply because a court order might "postpone[ ] the day when remedial measures become insufficiently effective." Indeed, as the dissent recognizes, a guarantee against government conduct that might threaten the Union — whether from political gerrymandering, nuclear proliferation, Executive misconduct, or climate change — has traditionally been viewed by Article III courts as "not separately enforceable." Nor has the Supreme Court recognized "the perpetuity principle" as a basis for interjecting the judicial branch into the policy-making purview of the political branches.

Contrary to the dissent, we do not "throw up [our] hands" by concluding that the plaintiffs' claims are nonjusticiable. Rather, we recognize that "Article III protects liberty not only through its role in implementing the separation of powers, but also by specifying the defining characteristics of Article III judges." Not every problem posing a threat — even a clear and present danger — to the American Experiment can be solved by federal judges. As Judge Cardozo once aptly warned, a judicial commission does not confer the power of "a knight-errant, roaming at will in pursuit of his own ideal of beauty or of goodness;" rather, we

---

[8] However belatedly, the political branches are currently debating such action. Many resolutions and plans have been introduced in Congress, ranging from discrete measures to encourage clean energy innovation to the "Green New Deal" and comprehensive proposals for taxing carbon and transitioning all sectors of the economy away from fossil fuels. The proposed legislation, consistent with the opinions of the plaintiffs' experts, envisions that tackling this global problem involves the exercise of discretion, trade-offs, international cooperation, private-sector partnerships, and other value judgments ill-suited for an Article III court.

are bound "to exercise a discretion informed by tradition, methodized by analogy, disciplined by system.'" Benjamin N. Cardozo, The Nature of the Judicial Process 141 (1921).

The dissent correctly notes that the political branches of government have to date been largely deaf to the pleas of the plaintiffs and other similarly situated individuals. But, although inaction by the Executive and Congress may affect the form of judicial relief ordered when there is Article III standing, it cannot bring otherwise nonjusticiable claims within the province of federal courts.

The plaintiffs have made a compelling case that action is needed; it will be increasingly difficult in light of that record for the political branches to deny that climate change is occurring, that the government has had a role in causing it, and that our elected officials have a moral responsibility to seek solutions. We do not dispute that the broad judicial relief the plaintiffs seek could well goad the political branches into action. We reluctantly conclude, however, that the plaintiffs' case must be made to the political branches or to the electorate at large, the latter of which can change the composition of the political branches through the ballot box. That the other branches may have abdicated their responsibility to remediate the problem does not confer on Article III courts, no matter how well-intentioned, the ability to step into their shoes.

III

For the reasons above, we reverse the certified orders of the district court and remand this case to the district court with instructions to dismiss for lack of Article III standing.

REVERSED.

STATON, District Judge, dissenting:

In these proceedings, the government accepts as fact that the United States has reached a tipping point crying out for a concerted response — yet presses ahead toward calamity. It is as if an asteroid were barreling toward Earth and the government decided to shut down our only defenses. Seeking to quash this suit, the government bluntly insists that it has the absolute and unreviewable power to destroy the Nation.

My colleagues throw up their hands, concluding that this case presents nothing fit for the Judiciary. On a fundamental point, we agree: No case can singlehandedly prevent the catastrophic effects of climate change predicted by the government and scientists. But a federal court need not manage all of the delicate foreign relations and regulatory minutiae implicated by climate change to offer real relief, and the mere fact that this suit cannot alone halt climate change does not mean that it presents no claim suitable for judicial resolution.

Plaintiffs bring suit to enforce the most basic structural principle embedded in our system of ordered liberty: that the Constitution does not condone the Nation's willful destruction. So viewed, plaintiffs' claims adhere to a judicially administrable standard. And considering plaintiffs seek no less than to forestall the Nation's demise, even a partial and temporary reprieve would constitute meaningful redress. Such relief, much like the desegregation orders and statewide prison injunctions the Supreme Court has sanctioned, would vindicate plaintiffs' constitutional rights without exceeding the Judiciary's province. For these reasons, I respectfully dissent.

I

As the majority recognizes, and the government does not contest, carbon dioxide ("CO2") and other greenhouse gas ("GHG") emissions created by burning fossil fuels are devastating the planet. According to one of plaintiffs' experts, the inevitable result, absent immediate action, is "an inhospitable future . . . marked by rising seas, coastal city functionality loss, mass migrations, resource wars, food shortages, heat waves, mega-storms, soil depletion and desiccation, freshwater shortage, public health system collapse, and the extinction of increasing numbers of species." Even government scientists project that, given current warming trends, sea levels will rise two feet by 2050, nearly four feet by 2070, over eight feet by 2100, 18 feet by 2150, and over 31 feet by 2200. To put that in perspective, a three-foot sea level rise will make two million American homes uninhabitable; a rise of approximately 20 feet will result in the total loss of Miami, New Orleans, and other coastal cities. So, as described by plaintiffs' experts, the injuries experienced by plaintiffs are the first small wave in an oncoming tsunami — now visible on the horizon of the not-so-distant future — that will destroy the United States as we currently know it.

What sets this harm apart from all others is not just its magnitude, but its irreversibility. The devastation might look and feel somewhat different if future generations could simply pick up the pieces and restore the Nation. But plaintiffs' experts speak of a certain level of global warming as "locking in" this catastrophic damage. Put more starkly by plaintiffs' expert, Dr. Harold R. Wanless, "[a]tmospheric warming will continue for some 30 years after we stop putting more greenhouse gasses into the atmosphere. But that warmed atmosphere will continue warming the ocean for centuries, and the accumulating heat in the oceans will persist for millennia" (emphasis added). Indeed, another of plaintiffs' experts echoes, "[t]he fact that GHGs dissipate very slowly from the atmosphere . . . and that the costs of taking CO2 out of the atmosphere through non-biological carbon capture and storage are very high means that the consequences of GHG emissions should be viewed as effectively irreversible" (emphasis added). In other words, "[g]iven the self-reinforcing nature of climate change," the tipping point may well have arrived, and we may be rapidly approaching the point of no return.

Despite countless studies over the last half century warning of the catastrophic consequences of anthropogenic greenhouse gas emissions, many of which the government conducted, the government not only failed to act but also "affirmatively promote[d] fossil fuel use in a host of ways." According to plaintiffs' evidence, our nation is crumbling — at our government's own hand — into a wasteland. In short, the government has directly facilitated an existential crisis to the country's perpetuity.[3]

II

In tossing this suit for want of standing, the majority concedes that the children and young adults who brought suit have presented enough to proceed to trial on the first two aspects of the inquiry (injury in fact and traceability). But the majority provides two-and-a-half reasons for concluding that plaintiffs' injuries are not redressable. After detailing its "skeptic[ism]" that the relief sought could "suffice to stop catastrophic climate change or even ameliorate [plaintiffs'] injuries[,]" the majority concludes that, at any rate, a court would lack any power to award it. In the majority's view, the relief sought is too great and unsusceptible to a judicially administrable standard.

To explain why I disagree, I first step back to define the interest at issue. While standing operates as a threshold issue distinct from the merits of the claim, "it often turns on the nature and source of the claim asserted." And, unlike the majority, I believe the government has more than just a nebulous "moral responsibility" to preserve the Nation.

A

The Constitution protects the right to "life, liberty, and property, to free speech, a free press, [and] freedom of worship and assembly." Through "reasoned judgment," the Supreme Court has recognized that the Due Process Clause, enshrined in the Fifth and Fourteenth Amendments, also safeguards certain "interests of the person so fundamental that the [government] must accord them its respect." These include the right to marry, to maintain a family and rear children, and to pursue an occupation of one's choosing, As fundamental rights, these "may not be submitted to vote; they depend on the outcome of no elections."

Some rights serve as the necessary predicate for others; their fundamentality therefore derives, at least in part, from the necessity to preserve other fundamental constitutional protections. For example, the right to vote "is of the essence of a democratic society, and any restrictions on that right strike at the heart of representative government." Because it is "preservative of all rights," the Supreme Court has long regarded suffrage "as a fundamental political right." This holds true even though the right to vote receives imperfect express protection in the Constitution itself: While several amendments proscribe the denial or abridgement of suffrage based on certain characteristics, the Constitution does not guarantee the right to vote ab initio.

Much like the right to vote, the perpetuity of the Republic occupies a central role in our constitutional structure as a "guardian of all other rights," And, of course, in our system, that organized society consists of the Union. Without it, all the liberties protected by the Constitution to live the good life are meaningless. . .

Less than a century after the country's founding, the perpetuity principle undergirding the Constitution met its greatest challenge. Faced with the South's secession, President Lincoln reaffirmed that the Constitution did not countenance its own destruction. "[T]he Union of these States is perpetual[,]" he reasoned in his First Inaugural Address, because "[p]erpetuity is implied, if not expressed, in the fundamental law of all national governments. It is safe to assert that no government proper ever had a provision in its organic law for its own termination." President Abraham Lincoln, First Inaugural Address (Mar. 4, 1861). In justifying this constitutional principle, Lincoln drew from history, observing that "[t]he Union is much older than the

---

[3] My asteroid analogy would therefore be more accurate if I posited a scenario in which the government itself accelerated the asteroid towards the earth before shutting down our defenses.

Constitution." Id. He reminded his fellow citizens, "one of the declared objects for ordaining and establishing the Constitution was 'to form a more perfect Union.'" Id. (emphasis added) (quoting U.S. Const. pmbl.). While secession manifested the existential threat most apparently contemplated by the Founders — political dissolution of the Union — the underlying principle applies equally to its physical destruction.

This perpetuity principle does not amount to "a right to live in a contaminant-free, healthy environment." To be sure, the stakes can be quite high in environmental disputes, as pollution causes tens of thousands of premature deaths each year, not to mention disability and diminished quality of life. Many abhor living in a polluted environment, and some pay with their lives. But mine-run environmental concerns "involve a host of policy choices that must be made by . . . elected representatives, rather than by federal judges interpreting the basic charter of government[.]" The perpetuity principle is not an environmental right at all, and it does not task the courts with determining the optimal level of environmental regulation; rather, it prohibits only the willful dissolution of the Republic.[6]

That the principle is structural and implicit in our constitutional system does not render it any less enforceable. To the contrary, our Supreme Court has recognized that "[t]here are many [ ] constitutional doctrines that are not spelled out in the Constitution" but are nonetheless enforceable as "historically rooted principle[s] embedded in the text and structure of the Constitution." For instance, the Constitution does not in express terms provide for judicial review, sovereign immunity (outside of the Eleventh Amendment's explicit restriction), the anticommandeering doctrine, or the regimented tiers of scrutiny applicable to many constitutional rights. Yet these doctrines, as well as many other implicit principles, have become firmly entrenched in our constitutional landscape. And, in an otherwise justiciable case, a private litigant may seek to vindicate such structural principles, for they "protect the individual as well" as the Nation.

In [*Franchise Tax Board of California v.*] *Hyatt*, for instance, the Supreme Court held that a state could not be sued in another state's courts without its consent. Although nothing in the text of the Constitution expressly forbids such suits, the Court concluded that they contravened "the 'implicit ordering of relationships within the federal system necessary to make the Constitution a workable governing charter and to give each provision within that document the full effect intended by the Framers.'" So too here.

Nor can the perpetuity principle be rejected simply because the Court has not yet had occasion to enforce it as a limitation on government conduct. Only over time, as the Nation confronts new challenges, are constitutional principles tested. For instance, courts did not recognize the anticommandeering doctrine until the 1970s because "[f]ederal commandeering of state governments [was] such a novel phenomenon." And the Court did not recognize that cell-site data fell within the Fourth Amendment until 2018. In so holding, the Court rejected "a 'mechanical interpretation' of the Fourth Amendment" because "technology has enhanced the Government's capacity to encroach upon areas normally guarded from inquisitive eyes[.]" Thus, it should come as no surprise that the Constitution's commitment to perpetuity only now faces judicial scrutiny, for never before has the United States confronted an existential threat that has not only gone unremedied but is actively backed by the government.

The mere fact that we have alternative means to enforce a principle, such as voting, does not diminish its constitutional stature. Americans can vindicate federalism, separation of powers, equal protection, and voting rights through the ballot box as well, but that does not mean these constitutional guarantees are not independently enforceable. By its very nature, the Constitution "withdraw[s] certain subjects from the vicissitudes of political controversy, to place them beyond the reach of majorities and officials and to establish them as legal principles to be applied by the courts." When fundamental rights are at stake, individuals "need not await legislative action."

Indeed, in this *sui generis* circumstance, waiting is not an option. Those alive today are at perhaps the singular point in history where society (1) is scientifically aware of the impending climate crisis, and (2) can avoid the point of no return. And while democracy affords citizens the right "to debate so they can learn and decide and then, through the political process, act in concert to try to shape the course of their own times[,]" that process cannot override the laws of nature. Or, more colloquially, we can't shut the stable door after the horse has bolted.

As the last fifty years have made clear, telling plaintiffs that they must vindicate their right to a habitable United States through the political branches will rightfully be perceived as telling them they have no recourse. The political branches must often realize constitutional principles, but in a justiciable case or controversy, courts serve as the ultimate backstop. To this issue, I turn next.

---

[6] Unwilling to acknowledge that the very nature of the climate crisis places this case in a category of one, the government argues that "the Constitution does not provide judicial remedies for every social and economic ill." . . . The perpetuity principle, however, cabins the right and avoids any slippery slope. While the principle's goal is to preserve the most fundamental individual rights to life, liberty, and property, it is not triggered absent an existential threat to the country arising from a "point of no return" that is, at least in part, of the government's own making.

B

Of course, "it is not the role of courts, but that of the political branches, to shape the institutions of government in such fashion as to comply with the laws and the Constitution." So federal courts are not free to address every grievance. "Whether a party has a sufficient stake in an otherwise justiciable controversy to obtain judicial resolution of that controversy is what has traditionally been referred to as the question of standing to sue." Standing is "a doctrine rooted in the traditional understanding of a case or controversy," developed to "ensure that federal courts do not exceed their authority as it has been traditionally understood."

A case is fit for judicial determination only if the plaintiff has: "(1) suffered an injury in fact, (2) that is fairly traceable to the challenged conduct of the defendant, and (3) that is likely to be redressed by a favorable judicial decision." As to the first two elements, my colleagues and I agree: Plaintiffs present adequate evidence at this pre-trial stage to show particularized, concrete injuries to legally-protected interests, and they present further evidence to raise genuine disputes as to whether those injuries — at least in substantial part — are fairly traceable to the government's conduct at issue. Because I find that plaintiffs have also established the third prong for standing, redressability, I conclude that plaintiffs' legal stake in this action suffices to invoke the adjudicative powers of the federal bench.

1

"Redressability" concerns whether a federal court is capable of vindicating a plaintiff's legal rights. I agree with the majority that our ability to provide redress is animated by two inquiries, one of efficacy and one of power. First, as a causal matter, is a court order likely to actually remediate the plaintiffs' injury? If so, does the judiciary have the constitutional authority to levy such an order?

Addressing the first question, my colleagues are skeptical that curtailing the government's facilitation of fossil-fuel extraction and combustion will ameliorate the plaintiffs' harms. I am not, as the nature of the injury at stake informs the effectiveness of the remedy.

As described above, the right at issue is not to be entirely free from any climate change. Rather, plaintiffs have a constitutional right to be free from *irreversible and catastrophic climate change*. Plaintiffs have begun to feel certain concrete manifestations of this violation, ripening their case for litigation, but such prefatory harms are just the first barbs of an *ongoing* injury flowing from an *ongoing* violation of plaintiffs' rights. The bulk of the injury is yet to come. Therefore, practical redressability is not measured by our ability to stop climate change in its tracks and immediately undo the injuries that plaintiffs suffer today — an admittedly tall order; it is instead measured by our ability to curb by some meaningful degree what the record shows to be an otherwise inevitable march to the point of no return. Hence, the injury at issue is not climate change writ large; it is climate change beyond the threshold point of no return. As we approach that threshold, the significance of every emissions reduction is magnified.

The majority portrays any relief we can offer as just a drop in the bucket. In a previous generation, perhaps that characterization would carry the day and we would hold ourselves impotent to address plaintiffs' injuries. But we are perilously close to an overflowing bucket. These final drops matter. *A lot.* Properly framed, a court order — even one that merely postpones the day when remedial measures become insufficiently effective — would likely have a real impact on preventing the impending cataclysm. Accordingly, I conclude that the court could do something to help the plaintiffs before us.

And "something" is all that standing requires. In *Massachusetts v. EPA* the Supreme Court explicitly held that a non-negligible reduction in emissions — there, by regulating vehicles emissions — satisfied the redressability requirement of Article III standing:

> While it may be true that regulating motor-vehicle emissions will not by itself *reverse* global warming, it by no means follows that we lack jurisdiction to decide whether EPA has a duty to take steps to *slow* or *reduce* it. Because of the enormity of the potential consequences associated with manmade climate change, the fact that the effectiveness of a remedy might be delayed during the (relatively short) time it takes for a new motor-vehicle fleet to replace an older one is essentially irrelevant. Nor is it dispositive that developing countries such as China and India are poised to increase greenhouse gas emissions substantially over the next century: A reduction in domestic emissions would slow the pace of global emissions increases, no matter what happens elsewhere.
>
> . . .
> . . . The risk of catastrophic harm, though remote, is nevertheless real.

In other words, under Article III, a perceptible reduction in the advance of climate change is sufficient to redress a plaintiff's climate change-induced harms. Full stop. The majority dismisses this precedent because *Massachusetts v. EPA* involved a procedural harm, whereas plaintiffs here assert a purely substantive right. But this difference in posture does not affect the outcome.

While the redressability requirement is relaxed in the procedural context, that does not mean (1) we must engage in a similarly relaxed analysis whenever we invoke *Massachusetts v.EPA* or (2) we cannot rely on *Massachusetts v. EPA*'s substantive examination of the relationship between government action and the course of climate change. Accordingly, here, we do not consider the likelihood that plaintiffs will prevail in any newly-awarded agency procedure, nor whether granting access to that procedure will redress plaintiffs' injury. Rather, we assume plaintiffs *will* prevail — removing the procedural link from the causal chain — and we resume our traditional analysis to determine whether the desired outcome would in fact redress plaintiffs' harms. In Massachusetts v. EPA, the remaining substantive inquiry was whether reducing emissions from fossil-fuel combustion would likely ameliorate climate change-induced injuries despite the global nature of climate change (regardless of whether renewed procedures were themselves likely to mandate such lessening). The Supreme Court unambiguously answered that question in the affirmative. That holding squarely applies to the instant facts,[8] rendering the absence of a procedural right here irrelevant.[9]

2

The majority laments that it cannot step into the shoes of the political branches, but appears ready to yield even if those branches walk the Nation over a cliff. This deference-to-a-fault promotes separation of powers to the detriment of our countervailing constitutional mandate to intervene where the political branches run afoul of our foundational principles. Our tripartite system of government is often and aptly described as one of "checks and balances." The doctrine of standing preserves *balance* among the branches by keeping separate questions of general governance and those of specific legal entitlement. But the doctrine of judicial review compels federal courts to fashion and effectuate relief to right legal wrongs, even when — as frequently happens — it requires that we instruct the other branches as to the constitutional limitations on their power. Indeed, sometimes "the [judicial and governance] roles briefly and partially coincide when a court, in granting relief against actual harm that has been suffered, . . . orders the alteration of an institutional organization or procedure that causes the harm." In my view, this Court must confront and reconcile this tension before deciding that thorny questions of standing preclude review in this case. And faithful application of our history and precedents reveals that a failure to do so leads to the wrong result.

Taking the long (but essential) way around, I begin first by acknowledging explicitly what the majority does not mention: our history plainly establishes an ambient presumption of judicial review to which separation-of-powers concerns provide a rebuttal under limited circumstances. Few would contest that "[i]t is emphatically the province and duty of the judicial department" to curb acts of the political branches that contravene those fundamental tenets of American life so dear as to be constitutionalized and thus removed from political whims. This presumptive authority entails commensurate power to grant appropriate redress, as recognized in *Marbury*, "which effectively place[s] upon those who would deny the existence of an effective legal remedy the burden of showing why their case was special." That is, "there must be something 'peculiar' (i.e., special) about a case that warrants 'excluding the injured party from legal redress and placing it within that class of cases which come under the description of *damnum absque injuria* — a loss without an injury.'" In sum, although it is the plaintiffs' burden to establish injury in fact, causation, and redressability, it is the government's burden to establish why this otherwise-justiciable controversy implicates grander separation-of-powers concerns not already captured by those requirements. We do not otherwise abdicate our duty to enforce constitutional rights.

Without explicitly laying this groundwork, the majority nonetheless suggests that this case is "special" — and beyond our redress — because plaintiffs' requested relief requires (1) the messy business of evaluating

---

[8] Indeed, the majority has already acknowledged as much in finding plaintiffs' injuries traceable to the government's misconduct because the traceability and redressability inquiries are largely coextensive. Here, where the requested relief is simply to stop the ongoing misconduct, the inquiries are nearly identical.

[9] Nor am I persuaded that *Massachusetts v. EPA* is distinguishable because of the relaxed standing requirements and "special solicitude" in cases brought by a state against the United States. When *Massachusetts v. EPA* was decided, more than a decade ago, there was uncertainty and skepticism as to whether an individual could state a sufficiently definite climate change-induced harm based on gradually warming air temperatures and rising seas. But the Supreme Court sidestepped such questions of the *concreteness* of the plaintiffs' injuries by finding that "[Massachusetts's] stake in the outcome of this case is sufficiently concrete to warrant the exercise of federal judicial power." Here and now, the plaintiffs submit *undisputed scientific evidence* that their distinct and discrete injuries are caused by climate change brought about by emissions from fossil-fuel combustion. They need not rely on the "special solicitude," of a state to be heard. Regardless, any distinction would go to the concreteness or particularity of plaintiffs' injuries and not to the issue of redressability.

competing policy considerations to steer the government away from fossil fuels and (2) the intimidating task of supervising implementation over many years, if not decades. . I admit these are daunting tasks, but we are constitutionally empowered to undertake them. There is no justiciability exception for cases of great complexity and magnitude.

3

I readily concede that courts must on occasion refrain from answering those questions that are truly reserved for the political branches, even where core constitutional precepts are implicated. This deference is known as the "political question doctrine," and its applicability is governed by a well-worn multifactor test that counsels judicial deference where there is:

> [1] a textually demonstrable constitutional commitment of the issue to a coordinate political department; or [2] a lack of judicially discoverable and manageable standards for resolving it; or [3] the impossibility of deciding without an initial policy determination of a kind clearly for nonjudicial discretion; or [4] the impossibility of a court's undertaking independent resolution without expressing lack of the respect due coordinate branches of government; or [5] an unusual need for unquestioning adherence to a political decision already made; or [6] the potentiality of embarrassment from multifarious pronouncements by various departments on one question.

Baker v. Carr, 369 U.S. 186, 217 (1962). In some sense, these factors are frontloaded in significance. "We have characterized the first three factors as 'constitutional limitations of a court's jurisdiction' and the other three factors as 'prudential considerations.'" Moreover, "we have recognized that the first two are likely the most important." Yet, we have also recognized that the inquiry is highly case-specific, the factors "often collaps[e] into one another[,]" and any one factor of sufficient weight is enough to render a case unfit for judicial determination. Regardless of any intra-factor flexibility and flow, however, there is a clear mandate to apply the political question doctrine both shrewdly and sparingly.

> Unless one of these formulations is inextricable from the case at bar, there should be no dismissal for non-justiciability on the ground of a political question's presence. The doctrine of which we treat is one of "political questions," not one of "political cases." The courts cannot reject as "no law suit" a bona fide controversy as to whether some action denominated "political" exceeds constitutional authority.

Baker, 369 U.S. at 217. Rather, when detecting the presence of a "political question," courts must make a "discriminating inquiry into the precise facts and posture of the particular case" and refrain from "resolution by any semantic cataloguing."

Here, confronted by difficult questions on the constitutionality of *policy*, the majority creates a minefield of *politics* en route to concluding that we cannot adjudicate this suit. And the majority's map for navigating that minefield is *Rucho v. Common Cause*, 139 S. Ct. 2484 (2019), an inapposite case about gerrymandering. My colleagues conclude that climate change is too political for the judiciary to touch by likening it to the process of political representatives drawing political maps to elect other political representatives. I vehemently disagree.

The government does not address on appeal the district judge's reasoning that the first, third, fourth, fifth and sixth *Baker* factors do not apply here. Neither does the majority rely on any of these factors in its analysis. In relevant part, I find the opinion below both thorough and well-reasoned, and I adopt its conclusions. I note, however, that the absence of the first *Baker* factor — whether the Constitution textually delegates the relevant subject matter to another branch — is especially conspicuous. As the district judge described, courts invoke this factor only where the Constitution makes an unambiguous commitment of responsibility to one branch of government. Very few cases turn on this factor, and almost all that do pertain to two areas of constitutional authority: foreign policy and legislative proceedings.

Since this matter has been under submission, the Supreme Court cordoned off an additional area from judicial review based in part on a textual commitment to another branch: partisan gerrymandering. Obviously, the Constitution does not explicitly address climate change. But neither does climate change *implicitly* fall within a recognized political-question area. As the district judge described, the questions of energy policy at stake here may have rippling effects on foreign policy considerations, but that is not enough to wholly exempt the subject matter from our review.

Without endorsement from the constitutional text, the majority's theory is grounded exclusively in the second *Baker* factor: a (supposed) lack of clear judicial standards for shaping relief. Relying heavily on *Rucho*, the majority contends that we cannot formulate standards (1) to determine what relief "is sufficient to remediate the claimed constitutional violation" or (2) to "supervise[ ] or enforce[ ]" such relief.

The first point is a red herring. Plaintiffs submit ample evidence that there is a discernable "tipping point" at which the government's conduct turns from facilitating mere pollution to inducing an unstoppable cataclysm in violation of plaintiffs' rights. Indeed, the majority itself cites plaintiffs' evidence that "atmospheric carbon levels of 350 parts per million are necessary to stabilize the climate." This clear line stands in stark contrast to *Rucho*, which held that — even assuming an excessively partisan gerrymander was unconstitutional — no standards exist by which to determine *when a rights violation has even occurred*. There, "[t]he central problem [wa]s not determining whether a jurisdiction has engaged in partisan gerrymandering. It [wa]s determining when political gerrymandering has gone too far."

Here, the right at issue is fundamentally one of a discernable standard: the amount of fossil-fuel emissions that will irreparably devastate our Nation. That amount can be established by scientific evidence like that proffered by the plaintiffs. Moreover, we need not *definitively* determine that standard today. Rather, we need conclude only that plaintiffs have submitted sufficient evidence to create a genuine dispute as to whether such an amount can possibly be determined as a matter of scientific fact. Plaintiffs easily clear this bar. Of course, plaintiffs will have to carry their burden of proof to establish this fact in order to prevail at trial, but that issue is not before us. We must not get ahead of ourselves.

The procedural posture of this case also informs the question of oversight and enforcement. It appears the majority's real concerns lie not in the judiciary's ability to draw a line between lawful and unlawful conduct, but in our ability to equitably walk the government back from that line without wholly subverting the authority of our coequal branches. My colleagues take great issue with plaintiffs' request for a "plan" to reduce fossil-fuel emissions. I am not so concerned. At this stage, we need not promise plaintiffs the moon (or, more apropos, the earth in a habitable state). For purposes of standing, we need hold only that the trial court could fashion some sort of meaningful relief should plaintiffs prevail on the merits.[13]

Nor would any such remedial "plan" necessarily require the courts to muck around in policymaking to an impermissible degree; the scope and number of policies a court would have to reform to provide relief is irrelevant to the second *Baker* factor, which asks only if there are judicially discernable standards to guide that reformation. Indeed, our history is no stranger to widespread, programmatic changes in government functions ushered in by the judiciary's commitment to requiring adherence to the Constitution. Upholding the Constitution's prohibition on cruel and unusual punishment, for example, the Court ordered the overhaul of prisons in the Nation's most populous state. And in its finest hour, the Court mandated the racial integration of every public school — state and federal — in the Nation, vindicating the Constitution's guarantee of equal protection under the law. In the school desegregation cases, the Supreme Court was explicitly unconcerned with the fact that crafting relief would require individualized review of thousands of state and local policies that facilitated segregation. Rather, a unanimous Court held that the judiciary could work to dissemble segregation over time while remaining cognizant of the many public interests at stake:

> To effectuate [the plaintiffs'] interest[s] may call for elimination of a variety of obstacles in making the transition to school systems operated in accordance with the constitutional principles set forth in [Brown I]. Courts of equity may properly take into account the public interest in the elimination of such obstacles in a systematic and effective manner. But it should go without saying that the vitality of these constitutional principles cannot be allowed to yield simply because of disagreement with them.
>
> . . . [T]he courts may find that additional time is necessary to carry out the ruling in an effective manner. The burden rests upon the defendants to establish that such time is necessary in the public interest and is consistent with good faith compliance at the earliest practicable date. To that end, the courts may consider problems related to administration, arising from the physical condition of the school plant, the school transportation system, personnel, revision of school districts and attendance areas into compact units to achieve a system of determining admission to the public schools on a nonracial basis, and revision of local laws and regulations which may be necessary in solving the foregoing problems.

Brown v. Bd. Of Educ. (Brown II), 349 U.S. 294, 300-01 (1955).

As we are all too aware, it took decades to even partially realize *Brown*'s promise, but the slow churn of constitutional vindication did not dissuade the *Brown* Court, and it should not dissuade us here. Plaintiffs' request for a "plan" is neither novel nor judicially incognizable. Rather, consistent with our historical practices,

---

[13] It is possible, of course, that the district court ultimately concludes that it is unable to provide meaningful redress based on the facts proved at trial, but trial has not yet occurred. Our present occasion is to decide only whether plaintiffs have raised a genuine dispute as to the judiciary's ability to provide meaningful redress under *any* subset of the facts at issue today.

their request is a recognition that remedying decades of institutionalized violations may take some time. Here, too, decelerating from our path toward cataclysm will undoubtedly require "elimination of a variety of obstacles." Those obstacles may be great in number, novelty, and magnitude, but there is no indication that they are devoid of discernable standards. Busing mandates, facilities allocation, and district-drawing were all "complex policy decisions" faced by post-*Brown* trial courts, and I have no doubt that disentangling the government from promotion of fossil fuels will take an equally deft judicial hand. Mere complexity, however, does not put the issue out of the courts' reach. Neither the government nor the majority has articulated why the courts could not weigh scientific and prudential considerations — as we often do — to put the government on a path to constitutional compliance.

The majority also expresses concern that any remedial plan would require us to compel "the adoption of a comprehensive scheme to decrease fossil fuel emissions and combat climate change[.]" Even if the operative complaint is fairly read as requesting an affirmative scheme to address all drivers of climate change, however caused, such an overbroad request does not doom our ability to redress those drivers implicated by the conduct at issue here. Courts routinely grant plaintiffs less than the full gamut of requested relief, and our inability to compel legislation that addresses emissions beyond the scope of this case — such as those purely in the private sphere or within the control of foreign governments — speaks nothing to our ability to enjoin the government from exercising its discretion in violation of plaintiffs' constitutional rights.

4

In sum, resolution of this action requires answers only to scientific questions, not political ones. And plaintiffs have put forth sufficient evidence demonstrating their entitlement to have those questions addressed at trial in a court of law.

As discussed above, the majority reaches the opposite conclusion not by marching purposefully through the *Baker* factors, which carve out a narrow set of nonjusticiable political cases, but instead by broadly invoking *Rucho* in a manner that would cull from our dockets any case that presents administrative issues "too difficult for the judiciary to manage." That simply is not the test. Difficult questions are not necessarily political questions and, beyond reaching the wrong conclusion in this case, the majority's application of *Rucho* threatens to eviscerate judicial review in a swath of complicated but plainly apolitical contexts.

Rucho's limitations should be apparent on the face of that opinion. *Rucho* addresses the political process itself, namely whether the metastasis of partisan politics has unconstitutionally invaded the drawing of political districts within states. Indeed, the *Rucho* opinion characterizes the issue before it as a request for the Court to reallocate political power between the major parties. *Baker* factors aside, *Rucho* surely confronts fundamentally "political" questions in the common sense of the term. Nothing about climate change, however, is inherently political. The majority is correct that redressing climate change will require consideration of scientific, economic, energy, and other policy factors. But that endeavor does not implicate the way we elect representatives, assign governmental powers, or otherwise structure our polity.

Regardless, we do not limit our jurisdiction based on common parlance. Instead, legal and constitutional principles define the ambit of our authority. In the present case, the *Baker* factors provide the relevant guide and further distinguish *Rucho*. As noted above, *Rucho*'s holding that policing partisan gerrymandering is beyond the courts' competence rests heavily on the first *Baker* factor, i.e., the textual and historical delegation of electoral-district drawing to state legislatures. The *Rucho* Court decided it could not discern mathematical standards to navigate a way out of that particular political thicket. It did not, however, hold that mathematical (or scientific) difficulties in creating appropriate standards divest jurisdiction in any context. Such an expansive reading of *Rucho* would permit the "political question" exception to swallow the rule.

Global warming is certainly an imposing conundrum, but so are diversity in higher education, the intersection between prenatal life and maternal health, the role of religion in civic society, and many other social concerns. These issues may not have been considered within the purview of the judicial branch had the Court imported wholesale *Rucho*'s "manageable standards" analysis even in the absence of *Rucho*'s inherently political underpinnings. Beyond the outcome of the instant case, I fear that the majority's holding strikes a powerful blow to our ability to hear important cases of widespread concern.

III

To be sure, unless there is a constitutional violation, courts should allow the democratic and political processes to perform their functions. And while all would now readily agree that the 91 years between the

Emancipation Proclamation and the decision in *Brown v. Board* was too long, determining when a court must step in to protect fundamental rights is not an exact science. In this case, my colleagues say that time is "never"; I say it is now.

Were we addressing a matter of social injustice, one might sincerely lament any delay, but take solace that "the arc of the moral universe is long, but it bends towards justice." The denial of an individual, constitutional right — though grievous and harmful — can be corrected in the future, even if it takes 91 years. And that possibility provides hope for future generations.

Where is the hope in today's decision? Plaintiffs' claims are based on science, specifically, an impending point of no return. If plaintiffs' fears, backed by the government's own studies, prove true, history will not judge us kindly. When the seas envelop our coastal cities, fires and droughts haunt our interiors, and storms ravage everything between, those remaining will ask: Why did so many do so little?

I would hold that plaintiffs have standing to challenge the government's conduct, have articulated claims under the Constitution, and have presented sufficient evidence to press those claims at trial. I would therefore affirm the district court.

With respect, I dissent.

REVIEWABILITY OF REMAND ORDERS IN STATE CLIMATE LITIGATION

This case involves one of the many state tort suits state and local governments have filed against the oil industry seeking to recover damages for the costs of adapting to climate change. The city of Baltimore sued 21 domestic and foreign companies that extract, produce and sell fossil fuels. Baltimore argued that the companies' actions created a public nuisance under state common law by contributing to climate change while deliberately misleading the public about the effects of their products. After the suit was filed in Maryland state court, the fossil fuel companies removed it to federal court, arguing that the allegations in the complaint pertain to actions taken at the direction of federal officers and that the claims necessarily arise under federal common law and should be preempted by the Clean Air Act.

The federal district court for Maryland rejected each of their asserted grounds for removal, a decision that the companies appealed to the U.S. Court of Appeals for the Fourth Circuit. Noting that 28 U.S.C. §1447(d) prohibits appellate review of a lower court's remand order except for cases removed on federal-officer (28 U.S.C. §1442) and civil rights grounds, the court then reviewed and rejected the companies' claim that contracts they had to supply oil to the Department of Defense justified federal-officer removal. The Court then concluded that the removal statute did not permit it to review any of the other grounds for removal rejected in the district court's remand order. Mayor and City Council of Baltimore v. BP P.L.C., 952 F.3d 452 (4th Cir. 2020). The latter conclusion was consistent with prior holdings by the other circuits in reviewing remand orders, see City of San Mateo v. Chevron Corp., 960 F.3d 586 (9th Cir. 2020).

Arguing that these holdings conflict with a decision by the Seventh Circuit in Lu Junhong v. Boeing, 792 F.3d 805 (7th Cir. 2015), BP and the other defendants then sought Supreme Court review. The Court granted review to consider whether 28 USC 1447(d) allows other issues encompassed in a district court's remand order to be reviewed by a US Court of Appeals when the removing defendants premised removal in part on the federal-officer removal statute, 28 U.S.C. §1442.

In their merits briefs the oil companies maintained that the word "order" in 28 U.S.C. §1447(d) should be interpreted as in *Lu Junhong*. They also invited the Court to rule that all state climate litigation, because it involves a global problem, arises exclusively under federal common law and thus should be heard in federal court where it would be displaced by the Clean Air Act under American Electric Power v. Connecticut, 564 U.S. 410 (2011). The Trump administration's Solicitor General supported petitioners on the statutory argument and said petitioners may be correct about the cases arising under federal common law, even though the complaints plead exclusively state claims. Respondents argued that when Congress last amended the removal statute all circuits agreed with their interpretation of the removal act and that their lawsuits do not arise under federal common law, an issue that was not properly before the Court.

BP PLC v. MAYOR AND CITY COUNCIL OF BALTIMORE
141 S.Ct. 1332 (2021)

Justice GORSUCH delivered the opinion of the Court.

This case began when Baltimore's mayor and city council sued various energy companies for promoting fossil fuels while allegedly concealing their environmental impacts. But the merits of that claim have nothing to do with this appeal. The only question before us is one of civil procedure: Does 28 U.S.C. §1447(d) permit a court of appeals to review any issue in a district court order remanding a case to state court where the defendant premised removal in part on the federal officer removal statute, §1442, or the civil rights removal statute, §1443?

I

Three years ago, Baltimore's mayor and city council (we refer to them collectively as the City) filed suit in Maryland state court. The City's complaint included a number of state-law causes of action, but most centered on the defendants' alleged failure to warn about the dangers of their products—and the injuries the City says it suffered as a result.

Soon after the City filed suit, the defendants removed the case to federal court. In support of their action, the defendants invoked a variety of federal statutes. Most relevant for our purposes, they pointed to a provision that promises a federal forum for any action against an "officer (or any person acting under that officer) of the United States or of any agency thereof, in an official or individual capacity, for or relating to any act under color of such office." 28 U.S.C. §1442(a)(1).

This statute authorized the removal of the City's suit, the defendants said, because some of their challenged exploration, drilling, and production operations took place at the federal government's behest. The companies also identified a number of other statutes that they believed independently supported removal: the federal-question statute, 28 U.S.C. §1331; the Outer Continental Shelf Lands Act, 43 U.S.C. §1349(b); the admiralty jurisdiction statute, 28 U.S.C. §1333; and the bankruptcy removal statute, 28 U.S.C. §1452.

Once the case arrived in federal court, the City filed a motion seeking to have it remanded back to state court. The City argued that none of the companies' grounds for removal justified retaining federal jurisdiction. In an extensive order, the district court reviewed each of the defendants' cited bases for removal before ultimately agreeing with the City and remanding the case to state court.

Normally that would have ended the matter. Since at least 1949, federal appellate courts have generally lacked the power to review a district court order remanding a case to state court. See Act of May 24, 1949, §84, 63 Stat. 102. But like most rules, this one has accrued exceptions with time. In the Civil Rights Act of 1964, Congress created an exception allowing appellate review for cases " 'removed pursuant to' " 28 U.S.C. §1443, a provision that guarantees a federal forum for certain federal civil rights claims. See §901, 78 Stat. 266. So before a civil rights case is returned to state court, a federal court of appeals usually *can* intervene to test the soundness of the district court's remand order.

In 2011, Congress added a similar exception for suits against federal officers or agencies removed pursuant to 28 U.S.C. §1442. See Removal Clarification Act, §2, 125 Stat. 545–546. Here, too, Congress has deemed it appropriate to allow appellate review before a district court may remand a case to state court. All told, then, the law as it stands today provides that "[a]n order remanding a case to the State court from which it was removed is not reviewable on appeal or otherwise, except that an order remanding a case to the State court from which it was removed pursuant to section 1442 or 1443 of this title shall be reviewable by appeal or otherwise." 28 U.S.C. §1447(d).

After the district court ordered the City's case remanded to state court, the defendants sought to appeal—and this much everyone seemed to agree they were free to do. After all, the defendants had relied on the federal officer removal statute found in §1442 when they removed the case to federal court—and the current version of §1447(d) permits an appeal in just these circumstances. The real trouble began only when it came to the scope of the defendants' appeal. The Fourth Circuit read §1447(d) as authorizing it to review only the *part* of the district court's remand order discussing §1442. As a result, the court of appeals refused to consider whether the district court may have erred when it rejected the defendants' other grounds for removal. Finding (only) the district court's §1442 analysis sound, the Fourth Circuit proceeded to affirm.

This ruling highlighted a circuit split. The Seventh Circuit, for example, has reasoned that §1447(d) extends appellate review to the *whole* of an " 'order remanding a case to the State court from which it was removed pursuant to section 1442 or 1443.' " See *Lu Junhong v. Boeing Co.*, 792 F.3d 805, 811 (2015). On that reading of the statute, appellate review is not confined to a defendant's removal arguments under the federal officer and civil rights removal statutes. Instead, a court of appeals may review the merits of all theories for removal that a district court has rejected. Because the courts of appeals disagree over the scope of their appellate authority under §1447(d), we agreed to take this case to resolve the question.

II

A

When called on to interpret a statute, this Court generally seeks to discern and apply the ordinary meaning of its terms at the time of their adoption. Here, the relevant portion of §1447(d) provides that "an order remanding a case to the State court from which it was removed pursuant to section 1442 or 1443 of this title shall be reviewable by appeal."

To our minds, the first telling clue lies in the statute's use of the term "order." Whether we look to the time of §1447(d)'s adoption or amendment, a judicial "order" meant then what it means today: a "written direction or command delivered by ... a court or judge." So an "order remanding a case" was (and is) a formal command from a district court returning the case to state court. In this case, the district court's remand order rejected *all* of the defendants' grounds for removal. For good reason too. Normally, federal jurisdiction is not optional; subject to exceptions not relevant here, "courts are obliged to decide cases within the scope of federal jurisdiction" assigned to them. So the district court wasn't at liberty to remove the City's case from its docket until it determined that it lacked any authority to entertain the suit. From this it would seem to follow that, when a district court's removal order rejects all of the defendants' grounds for removal, §1447(d) authorizes a court of appeals to review each and every one of them. After all, the statute allows courts of appeals to examine the whole of a district court's "order," not just some of its parts or pieces.

Of course, §1447(d) extends appellate review only to *some* orders—those remanding a "case ... removed pursuant to section 1442 or 1443." But it's hard to see how that qualification changes the calculus. To remove a case, a defendant must comply with 28 U.S.C. §1446. Essentially, that statute requires the defendant to provide affected parties and courts with a notice stating its grounds for removal. §§1446(a), (d). The combination of these actions "effect[s] the removal." §1446(d). To remove a case "pursuant to" §1442 or §1443, then, just means that a defendant's notice of removal must assert the case is removable "in accordance with or by reason of " one of those provisions.2 Here, everyone admits the defendants' notice of removal did just that by citing §1442 as one of its grounds for removal. Once that happened and the district court ordered the case remanded to state court, the whole of its order became reviewable on appeal.

Nor does it matter if (as here) a defendant removes a case "pursuant to" *multiple* federal statutes. Often enough, parties act pursuant to a variety of legal authorities. A criminal defendant may suggest he is eligible for sentencing relief pursuant to multiple provisions. A civil litigant might file a complaint pursuant to more than one statute. Likewise, a party may assert multiple grounds for removing a case to federal court—as the defendants did here. Indeed, the general removal statute contemplates just this possibility when, in contrast, it speaks of actions "removed *solely* under" the diversity jurisdiction statute. §1446(b)(2)(A) (emphasis added). Yet, the particular provision at issue before us does not contain any comparable language like that limiting appellate review *solely* to issues under §1442 or §1443. Instead and again, §1447(d) permits appellate review of the district court's remand order—without any further qualification.

B

How does the City reply? It suggests that exceptions to statutory rules should be construed narrowly—and that our reading of §1447(d)'s exception to its general rule against appellate review is too permissive.

We disagree. As a preliminary matter, the factual premise underlying the City's argument is surely contestable. One might just as easily conceive of §1447(d)'s usual rule barring appellate review as *itself* an exception to the even more general rule that final district court orders are appealable under 28 U.S.C. §1291. More fundamentally, the City's legal premise is also in error. This Court has " 'no license to give statutory exemptions anything but a fair reading.' " Exceptions and exemptions are no less part of Congress's work than its rules and standards—and all are worthy of a court's respect. That a law might temper its pursuit of one goal by accommodating others can come as no surprise. Often legislation becomes possible only because of such compromises. Often lawmakers tread in areas fraught with competing social demands where everyone agrees trade-offs are required. Whatever the reason for a legislative compromise, we have no right to place our thumbs on one side of the scale or the other.

Alternatively, the City suggests that, if Congress had wanted appellate courts to review every issue in a remand order, it would have said as much. Sometimes, the City observes, Congress does exactly that, expressly directing courts to resolve "all" legal issues in certain cases. But the defendants remind us that Congress also knows how to limit appellate review to particular "questions" rather than the whole of a district court's "order"; sometimes it does just that too. In the end, all of the parties' fencing about language Congress *didn't* use persuades us of only one thing—that we are best served by focusing on the language it *did* employ.

All of which leaves the City to offer a different argument from a new direction. Now, the City contends, the defendants never really removed this case pursuant to §1442. On this account, a case is not "removed pursuant to section 1442 or 1443" until a federal court (district or appellate) holds that one of these statutes authorizes removal. Because that never happened here, the City reasons, the defendants were not entitled to *any* appellate review. But this argument isn't only novel—the City didn't pursue it below and no court of appeals has adopted it. It is also mistaken. As we've seen, it is generally a defendant's actions under §1446 that "effect the removal." Once a defendant complies with §1446, a state court may not proceed "further unless and until the case is remanded." 28 U.S.C. §1446(d). That's why normally it's the plaintiff who must seek judicial intervention if it wishes to have the matter remanded to state court—just as the City did here.

III

A

To the extent any doubt remains about how best to read §1447(d), we believe our most analogous precedent resolves it. In *Yamaha Motor Corp., U. S. A. v. Calhoun*, 516 U.S. 199, 204 (1996), this Court faced a dispute about the meaning of 28 U.S.C. §1292(b). That statute allows a district court to certify "an order" to the court of appeals if it "involves a controlling question of law as to which there is substantial ground for difference of opinion," and if "an immediate appeal from the order may materially advance the ultimate termination of the litigation." In *Yamaha* the Court asked the parties to address whether §1292(b) authorizes appellate courts to review any question contained in the district court's order—or whether it allows those courts to address only the "controlling question of law" the district court certified for further review.

The answer there is telling here. The Court held that, "[a]s the text of §1292(b) indicates, appellate jurisdiction applies to the *order* certified to the court of appeals, and is not tied to the particular question formulated by the district court." Although appellate courts "may not reach beyond the certified order to address other orders made in the case," they "may address any issue fairly included within the certified order because it is the *order* that is appealable, and not the controlling question identified by the district court." Exactly the same might be said of our case: "[B]ecause it is the [district court's removal] *order* that is appealable," a court of appeals "may address any issue fairly included within" it.

The City seeks to distinguish *Yamaha* but we don't see how we fairly might. The City observes that §1292(b) allows an appeal from an order that "involves" a controlling question of law. By using the word "involves," the City submits, Congress sought to make plain that the reviewable issues on appeal can be broader than the certified controlling question of law. And, the City stresses, the word "involves" does not appear in §1447(d). But that is beside the point. Nothing in *Yamaha* turned on the presence of the word "involves" in §1292(b). Instead, the Court's reasoning centered on the statute's use of the word "order." By allowing appellate courts to review a district court's "order," the Court explained, Congress had allowed review of any issue fairly encompassed within it. That reasoning applies with no less force here.

B

If *Yamaha* does much to undermine its argument, the City seeks to draw support from other of this Court's cases. Principally, it points to *Murdock v. Memphis*, 20 Wall. 590, 22 L.Ed. 429 (1875), and *United States v. Keitel*, 211 U.S. 370 (1908). But both decisions were driven by concerns unique to their statutory contexts; their reasoning is not easily generalizable to other jurisdictional statutes; and neither comes nearly as close to the mark as *Yamaha*.

Start with *Murdock*. That case involved 28 U.S.C. §1257, a statute permitting this Court to review certain state court "judgments or decrees." Concerned with the constitutional implications of allowing federal courts to review questions of state law, the Court in *Murdock* construed the statute as authorizing this Court to examine only issues of federal law contained within state court judgments and decrees. Along the way, the Court took pains to reserve the question whether Congress could ever authorize this Court to review matters of state law already definitively resolved by state courts. By contrast, no comparable concern with the Constitution's federal structure exists here. At some level, of course, removal practices implicate questions of comity between federal and state authorities. But today we are asked to decide only whether a federal court of appeals may review one or many federal law rulings issued by an inferior federal court. That comparatively humble question lies nowhere near *Murdock's* bounds.

Keitel involved the now-repealed Criminal Appeals Act. That law authorized the government to appeal adverse criminal "decision[s] or judgment[s]" based on certain enumerated grounds, such as the invalidity of a federal statute. For its part, the Court held that this language allowed the government to appeal only the statutorily enumerated questions. Like *Murdock* the Court in *Keitel* rested heavily on the statute's context in reaching its conclusion. A new entitlement allowing the government to appeal an adverse criminal judgment was, in the Court's view, "exceptional." Meanwhile, here again, nothing in our case implicates that concern.

Closer to home, the City directs our attention to *Carlsbad Technology, Inc. v. HIF Bio, Inc.*, 556 U.S. 635, 638 (2009), and *Thermtron Products, Inc. v. Hermansdorfer*, 423 U.S. 336, 345–346 (1976). Those cases addressed the first clause of §1447(d), which generally bars appellate review of remand orders. *Carlsbad* and *Thermtron* held this bar applies only to remand orders premised on a lack of subject matter jurisdiction or a defect in removal procedure; other remand orders remain appealable. The Court said this conclusion was necessary to make sense of §1447(d)'s interaction with §1447(c).

None of this, however, helps the City's cause. Some have questioned *Carlsbad* and *Thermtron*. But even taken on their own terms, both decisions *permitted* rather than foreclosed appellate review of certain remand orders. And the fact that this Court deemed certain orders appealable under the statute's first clause simply does not settle, one way or another, the scope of appellate review under the statute's second clause.

Having exhausted our cases, the City seeks support in lower court decisions. It draws our attention to 2011 when Congress amended §1447(d) to authorize appellate review of remand orders in cases removed under the federal officer statute. By that time, the City says, a number of courts of appeals had already interpreted the prior version of §1447(d) that allowed appeals from remand orders in cases removed under the Civil Rights Act. And many of those courts had read §1447(d) as permitting them to review only the part of a remand order addressing the civil rights removal ground. From this fact, the City reasons, it follows that Congress implicitly ratified and endorsed parallel limits on appellate review when it adopted its 2011 amendments.

Again, we do not see it. It seems most unlikely to us that a smattering of lower court opinions could ever represent the sort of "judicial consensus so broad and unquestioned that we must presume Congress knew of and endorsed it." And it certainly cannot do so where, as here, "the text and structure of the statute are to the contrary." This Court bears no "warrant to ignore clear statutory language on the ground that other courts have done so." Our duty is to follow the law as we find it, not to follow rotely whatever lower courts once might have said about it.

Separately, the City worries that our interpretation might upset lower court decisions on a *different* question. The City points out that, when a district court remands a case, it may require the defendant to pay certain of the plaintiff's fees and costs. See 28 U.S.C. §1447(c). While §1447(d) generally precludes appellate review of remand orders, many lower courts have suggested that these §1447(c) fee and cost awards are nonetheless reviewable on appeal. The City contends that our reading of §1447(d) could put an end to all that. It could, the City reasons, because if an "order remanding a case" really means the whole order, then the statute may bar appellate review of fee and cost awards contained within those orders. That much, however, does not necessarily follow. Often enough fee and cost awards are treated as collateral to the merits and independently appealable. In any event, the question is not presented in this case and we do not purport to resolve it.

IV

The City concludes by asking us to consider the policy consequences that follow from giving the text its ordinary meaning. Barring appellate review of remand orders, the City says, serves the worthy goal of allowing the parties to get on with litigating the merits of their cases in state court. Meanwhile, the City submits, allowing exceptions to this rule promises only to impair that efficiency interest.

The difficulties with this argument are by now familiar. As this Court has explained, "even the most formidable" policy arguments cannot "overcome" a clear statutory directive. Besides, everyone agrees that the statute tempers its obvious concern with efficiency when it comes to cases removed pursuant to §1442 or §1443. For that subset of cases, Congress has expressed a heightened concern for accuracy, authorized appellate review, and accepted the delay it can entail. The fact that the law as written allows appellate courts to examine *all* (and not just *come*) removal grounds in these cases perhaps just demonstrates, as Judge Easterbrook has suggested, a congressional judgment that the "marginal delay from adding ... extra issue[s] to a case where the time for briefing, argument, and decision has already been accepted is likely to be small." See *Lu Junhong*, 792 F.3d at 813.

In fact, allowing a fuller form of appellate review may actually help expedite some appeals. Suppose a court of appeals finds the §1442 or §1443 issue a difficult and close one, but believes removal is clearly and easily warranted on another basis. Allowing the court to address that easier question and avoid harder ones may facilitate a prompter resolution of the proceeding for all involved. At the least, a rational Congress could have thought that considerations like these warranted allowing a court of appeals the power to review the whole of a district court's remand order rather than just certain select aspects of it.

That leaves the City to argue about different consequences. It warns that our interpretation will invite gamesmanship: Defendants may frivolously add §1442 or §1443 to their other grounds for removal, all with an eye to ensuring appellate review down the line if the case is remanded. But the answers here too are familiar. Once more, this Court's task is to discern and apply the law's plain meaning as faithfully as we can, not "to assess the consequences of each approach and adopt the one that produces the least mischief."

Nor is it as if Congress has been blind to the City's concerns. As the City itself acknowledges, thanks to §1447(c) a district court may order a defendant to pay the plaintiff's costs and expenses (including attorney's fees) if it frivolously removes a case from state court. Additionally, the Federal Rules of Civil Procedure allow courts to sanction frivolous arguments made in virtually any context. Rules 11(b)–(c). Congress, thus, has already addressed the City's concerns in *other* statutes and rules—just not in §1447(d). To the extent that experience may prove these other measures insufficient, Congress is of course free to revise its work anytime. But that forum, not this one, is the proper place for such lawmaking.

* * *

The Fourth Circuit erred in holding that it was powerless to consider all of the defendants' grounds for removal under §1447(d). In light of that error, the defendants ask us to consider some of those additional grounds ourselves. That task, however, does not implicate the circuit split that we took this case to resolve and we believe the wiser course is to leave these matters for the Fourth Circuit to resolve in the first instance. The judgment of the Fourth Circuit is vacated, and the case is remanded for further proceedings consistent with this opinion.

So ordered.

Justice ALITO took no part in the consideration or decision of this case.

Justice SOTOMAYOR, dissenting.

Civil defendants in state court may remove a case to federal district court by asserting one or more bases for federal jurisdiction. If the district court concludes that the case was improperly removed, it issues an order remanding the case back to state court. For more than a century, the rule has been that such remand orders are generally not subject to appellate review. This rule, codified at 28 U.S.C. §1447(d), "reflects Congress's longstanding policy of not permitting interruption of the litigation of the merits of a removed case by prolonged litigation of questions of jurisdiction of the district court to which the cause is removed."

Originally, there were no exceptions to §1447(d)'s bar on appellate review. See §1447(d) (1946 ed., Supp. III). Then, as part of the Civil Rights Act of 1964, Congress created appellate jurisdiction over " 'order[s] remanding a case to the State court from which it was removed pursuant to section 1443,' " the civil rights removal statute. §901, 78 Stat. 266, 28 U.S.C. §1447(d) (1964 ed.). In 2011, Congress extended this exception to cases removed pursuant to §1442, the federal officer removal statute. See §1447(d) (2012 ed.).

The Court today holds that a defendant who invokes either §1442 or §1443 when removing a case to federal court is entitled to appellate review of not just those grounds, but also any other grounds for removal the defendant asserts. I disagree. That interpretation lets defendants sidestep §1447(d)'s bar on appellate review by shoehorning a §1442 or §1443 argument into their case for removal. In other words, it lets the exception swallow the rule. Furthermore, when Congress amended §1447(d) to permit appellate review of decisions under §1442, every Court of Appeals to have addressed the question interpreted §1447(d) to permit appellate review of arguments under §1443 only, not of other arguments for removal addressed in the same order. If Congress wanted to disturb that consensus, it would have said so. I respectfully dissent.

I

Section 1447(d) permits appellate review of "an order remanding a case to the State court from which it was removed pursuant to section 1442 or 1443." Everyone agrees how this provision operates in two scenarios. First, if a defendant removes a suit to federal court without invoking either §1442 or §1443, appellate courts may not review the district court's remand order. Second, if a defendant removes a suit solely under §1442 or §1443, appellate review is available for the remand order addressing that single ground for removal.

But what if a defendant removes a case to federal court on multiple grounds, only one of which is §1442 or §1443? Section 1447(d) does not speak clearly to that scenario. In some statutes, Congress takes care to specify when it means "this and only this ground." See, §1446(b)(2)(A) (addressing civil actions "removed solely under section 1441(a)"). Other times, Congress makes clear that reliance on a certain ground even "in part" will suffice. See, *e.g.*, §1295(a)(2) (providing for jurisdiction in the Court of Appeals for the Federal Circuit over certain district court decisions "if the jurisdiction of that court was based, in whole or in part, on section 1346 of this title"). Section 1447(d) contains neither kind of clarifying language, leaving uncertain how the provision applies to cases that are not removed under §1442 or §1443 alone.

There are three possible ways forward. The first possibility is that §1447(d) permits appellate review of any asserted basis for removal so long as the suit was removed in part pursuant to §1442 or §1443. That is the interpretation urged by petitioners and adopted by the Court today. The problem with this interpretation is that it stretches the exception in §1447(d) too far. It allows defendants to bootstrap their entire case for removal into the court of appeals simply by tacking on an argument under §1442 or §1443. Indeed, under this interpretation, a defendant could formally abandon its argument under §1442 or §1443and seek an appeal exclusively of other grounds for removal. That bizarre outcome, inexplicable in light of the manifest objective of limiting the exceptions in §1447(d), cautions heavily against this interpretation.

Another possibility is that a suit removed pursuant to multiple grounds is not a suit removed pursuant to §1442 or §1443 at all, meaning no appellate review whatsoever is available under §1447(d). For good reason, no one advocates this interpretation. Such a rule would certainly avoid prolonged disputes about whether a case belongs in state or federal court, but only by denying appellate review for claims of jurisdiction under the federal-officer and civil-rights removal statutes. That result is hard to square with Congress' express directive that such claims get a second look.

The third possibility is that §1447(d) allows appellate review of a defendant's assertion of removal jurisdiction under the federal-officer or civil-rights removal statute alone. Any other grounds for removal would remain subject to §1447(d)'s bar on appellate review. This interpretation best accords with "Congress's longstanding policy of not permitting interruption of the litigation of the merits of a removed case" with lengthy jurisdictional disputes, while still allowing review of the two grounds Congress carved out for special treatment. It also follows this Court's usual policy of construing both statutory exceptions and procedures for removal narrowly.

Over the course of several decades, eight Courts of Appeals (every one to consider the question) adopted this third view of §1447(d). See, *e.g.*, *Patel v. Del Taco, Inc.*, 446 F.3d 996, 998 (C.A.9 2006); *Alabama v. Conley*, 245 F.3d 1292, 1293, n. 1 (C.A.11 2001) (per curiam); *Thornton v. Holloway*, 70 F.3d 522, 524 (C.A.8 1995); *State Farm Mut. Auto Ins. Co. v. Baasch*, 644 F.2d 94, 96–97 (C.A.2 1981) (per curiam); *Detroit Police Lieutenants and Sergeants Assn. v. Detroit*, 597 F.2d 566, 567–568 (C.A.6 1979) (per curiam); *Noel v. McCain*, 538 F.2d 633, 635 (C.A.4 1976); *Robertson v. Ball*, 534 F.2d 63, 65–66 (C.A.5 1976) (per curiam); *Pennsylvania ex rel. Gittman v. Gittman*, 451 F.2d 155, 156–157 (C.A.3 1971) (per curiam).

Congress legislated against the backdrop of this consensus when, in 2011, it amended §1447(d) to extend its appellate-review exception, which previously applied to §1443 alone, to cover §1442 as well. Critically, Congress did not amend the remainder of the provision. Instead, it simply added the words "1442 or." See Removal Clarification Act, 125 Stat. 546. Had Congress disagreed with the settled interpretation of §1447(d), it presumably would have done something about it.

The Court dismisses the possibility of congressional ratification by characterizing an unbroken line of decisions from two-thirds of the Courts of Appeals spanning nearly half a century as "a smattering of lower court opinions." *Ante* at 1541. I would not assume that so many decisions reaching the same conclusion over such a long period were beneath Congress' notice. " 'If a word or phrase has been given a uniform interpretation by inferior courts, a later version of that act perpetuating the wording is presumed to carry forward that interpretation.' " That Congress did not disturb the prevailing interpretation of §1447(d) is a compelling reason this Court should not either.

II

The Court sees things differently. In its view, it "does [not] matter" whether "a defendant removes a case 'pursuant to' multiple federal statutes" or just one. Either way, §1447(d) grants the court of appeals jurisdiction over the "order" remanding the case back to state court. According to the Court, once the court of appeals takes jurisdiction over an order, it necessarily takes jurisdiction over all grounds for removal encompassed within it.

In support of this theory, the Court looks to *Yamaha Motor Corp., U. S. A. v. Calhoun*, 516 U.S. 199 (1996). That case concerned 28 U.S.C. §1292(b), a distinct statute that permits appellate review of an interlocutory "order not otherwise appealable" if the district court certifies that the order "involves a controlling question of law as to which there is substantial ground for difference of opinion." §1292(b). Looking to "the text of §1292(b)," the *Yamaha* Court determined that, having taken jurisdiction over a §1292(b) order, a court of appeals may reach any issue fairly encompassed within it. 516 U.S. at 205, 116 S.Ct. 619. In the Court's view today, *Yamaha* means that appellate review of a remand order under §1447(d) must likewise be plenary.

Yamaha does not do the work the Court says it does. Section 1292(b) provides that an interlocutory order is appealable if it merely "involves" a certified issue. There was thus no question in *Yamaha* that §1292(b) accounts for certified orders that address multiple issues, some of which are not "controlling question[s] of law as to which there is substantial ground for difference of opinion." §1292(b). Section 1447(d) lacks comparable language about what happens when a party removes a case on multiple grounds. That is precisely what makes it ambiguous.

The Court is left with the premise that appellate jurisdiction over an order (as with a judgment, decree, or sentence) usually means jurisdiction over all legal issues addressed within it. *Ante,* at 1537 – 1539. I agree that this premise will often hold true. But not always, as the Court itself recognizes. Context matters. To recap, in 1964, Congress created a limited exception for claims of removal under §1443 to what had long been an absolute prohibition on appellate review of remand orders. After nearly half a century of courts interpreting that exception narrowly, Congress extended the exception to §1442 without otherwise amending §1447(d). Section 1447(d) only unambiguously permits appellate review over remand orders that are based solely on one of those two grounds. Granting defendants appellate review of other grounds of removal whenever they tack on an argument under §1442 or §1443 would allow the exception to trump the rule. In these circumstances, the Court should seek an interpretation of §1447(d) that not only respects its carveout for arguments under §1442 and §1443 but also preserves its general bar on appellate review.

III

Unfortunately, I fear today's decision will reward defendants for raising strained theories of removal under §1442 or §1443 by allowing them to circumvent the bar on appellate review entirely. Look no further than this case. In 2018, the Mayor and City Council of Baltimore sued petitioners for allegedly concealing the connection between fossil fuels and climate change. Petitioners listed eight grounds for removal to federal court, including §1442. But petitioners now ask only for a ruling that removal was proper under §1441(a) (federal-question jurisdiction). Had petitioners relied solely on §1441(a) before the District Court, as they do now, no one disputes their argument would be unreviewable on appeal.

Not to worry, petitioners assure us: The threat of sanctions will sufficiently deter gamesmanship. While sanctions help ward off egregious misconduct, they are no failsafe. See, e.g., *Martin v. Franklin Capital Corp.,* 546 U.S. 132, 141 (2005) ("Absent unusual circumstances, courts may award attorney's fees under §1447(c) only where the removing party lacked an objectively reasonable basis for seeking removal"). A federal-officer claim can be so weak it is not worth pursuing on appeal, but not so meritless as to warrant sanctions. Again, look to this case. Petitioners no longer advance their argument under calling it only "substantial." Brief for Petitioners 35. Yet that argument somehow opens a back door to appellate review that would otherwise be closed to them. Meanwhile, Baltimore, which has already waited nearly three years to begin litigation on the merits, is consigned to waiting once more.

* * *

Section 1447(d) places "broad restrictions on the power of federal appellate courts to review district court orders remanding removed cases to state court." After today's decision, defendants can sidestep these restrictions by making near-frivolous arguments for removal under §1442 or §1443. Congress, of course, can amend §1447(d) to make even clearer that appellate review of a district court remand order extends to only §1442 or §1443. Because I believe §1447 already bears that meaning, I respectfully dissent.

PREEMPTION UNDER THE ATOMIC ENERGY ACT

In the case below the owner of a large uranium deposit in southwestern Virginia argued that the Atomic Energy Act preempted a state law imposing a moratorium on uranium mining.

VIRGINIA URANIUM, INC. v. WARREN
139 S.Ct. 1894 (2019)

GORSUCH, J., announced the judgment of the Court and delivered an opinion, in which THOMAS and KAVANAUGH, JJ., joined. GINSBURG, J., filed an opinion concurring in the judgment, in which SOTOMAYOR and KAGAN, JJ., joined. ROBERTS, C.J., filed a dissenting opinion, in which BREYER and ALITO, JJ., joined.

JUSTICE GORSUCH announced the judgment of the Court and delivered an opinion, in which JUSTICE THOMAS and JUSTICE KAVANAUGH join.

Virginia Uranium insists that the federal Atomic Energy Act (AEA) preempts a state law banning uranium mining, but we do not see it. True, the AEA gives the Nuclear Regulatory Commission significant authority over the milling, transfer, use, and disposal of uranium, as well as the construction and operation of nuclear power plants. But Congress conspicuously chose to leave untouched the States' historic authority over the regulation of mining activities on private lands within their borders. Nor do we see anything to suggest that the enforcement of Virginia's law would frustrate the AEA's purposes and objectives. And we are hardly free to extend a federal statute to a sphere Congress was well aware of but chose to leave alone. In this, as in any field of statutory interpretation, it is our duty to respect not only what Congress wrote but, as importantly, what it didn't write.

I

Virginia Uranium thought its plan was pretty straightforward. First, the company wanted to use conventional mining techniques to extract raw uranium ore from a site near Coles Hill, Virginia. Next, it intended to mill that ore into a usable form. Typically performed at the mine site, milling involves grinding the ore into sand-sized grains and then exposing it to a chemical solution that leaches out pure uranium. Once dried, the resulting mixture forms a solid "yellowcake," which the company planned to sell to enrichment facilities that produce fuel for nuclear reactors. Finally, because the leaching process does not remove all of the uranium from the ore, the company expected to store the leftover "tailings" near the mine to reduce the chances of contaminating the air or water.

But putting the plan into action didn't prove so simple. Pursuant to the AEA, the NRC regulates milling and tailing storage activities nationwide, and it has issued an array of rules on these subjects. None of those, though, proved the real problem for Virginia Uranium. The company hit a roadblock even before it could get to the point where the NRC's rules kick in: State law flatly prohibits uranium mining in Virginia.

To overcome that obstacle, Virginia Uranium filed this lawsuit. The company alleged that, under the Constitution's Supremacy Clause, the AEA preempts state uranium mining laws like Virginia's and ensconces the NRC as the lone regulator in the field. And because the NRC's regulations say nothing about uranium mining, the company continued, it remains free to mine as it will in Virginia or elsewhere.

Both the district court and a divided panel of the Fourth Circuit rejected the company's argument. The courts acknowledged that the AEA affords the NRC considerable authority over the nuclear fuel life cycle. But both courts found missing from the AEA any hint that Congress sought to strip States of their traditional power to regulate mining on private lands within their borders. Given the significance of the question presented, we granted review.

II

The Supremacy Clause supplies a rule of priority. It provides that the "Constitution, and the Laws of the United States which shall be made in Pursuance thereof," are "the supreme Law of the Land . . . any Thing in the Constitution or Laws of any state to the Contrary notwithstanding." Art. VI, cl. 2. This Court has sometimes used different labels to describe the different ways in which federal statutes may displace state laws — speaking, for example, of express, field, and conflict preemption. But these categories "are not rigidly distinct." And at least one feature unites them: Invoking some brooding federal interest or appealing to a judicial policy preference should never be enough to win preemption of a state law; a litigant must point specifically to "a constitutional text or a federal statute" that does the displacing or conflicts with state law.

Before us, Virginia Uranium contends that the AEA (and only the AEA) unseats state uranium mining regulations and that it does so under the doctrines of both field and conflict preemption. We examine these arguments about the AEA's preemptive effect much as we would any other about statutory meaning, looking to the text and context of the law in question and guided by the traditional tools of statutory interpretation. Here, no more than in any statutory interpretation dispute, is it enough for any party or court to rest on a supposition (or wish) that "it must be in there somewhere."

A

We begin with the company's claim that the text and structure of the AEA reserve the regulation of uranium mining for the purpose of addressing nuclear safety concerns to the NRC alone — and almost immediately problems emerge. Unlike many federal statutes, the AEA contains no provision preempting state law in so many words. Even more pointedly, the statute grants the NRC extensive and sometimes exclusive authority to regulate nearly every aspect of the nuclear fuel life cycle *except* mining. Companies like Virginia Uranium must abide the NRC's rules and regulations if they wish to handle enriched uranium, to mill uranium ore or store tailings, or to build or run a nuclear power plant. But when it comes to mining, the statute speaks very differently, expressly stating that the NRC's regulatory powers arise only "*after* [uranium's] removal from its place of deposit in nature." 42 U.S.C. §2092 (emphasis added). As the government itself has conceded, this means that "uranium mining" lies "outside the NRC's jurisdiction," and the agency's grip takes hold only "at the mill, rather than at the mine."

What the text states, context confirms. After announcing a general rule that mining regulation lies outside the NRC's jurisdiction, the AEA carves out a notably narrow exception. On *federal* lands, the statute says, the NRC may regulate uranium mining. And if the federal government wants to control mining of uranium on *private* land, the AEA tells the NRC exactly what to do: It may purchase or seize the land by eminent domain and *make* it federal land. Congress thus has spoken directly to the question of uranium mining on private land, and every bit of what it's said indicates that state authority remains untouched.

Later amendments to the AEA point to the same conclusion. Some years after the statute's passage, Congress added a provision, currently codified in §2021, allowing the NRC to devolve certain of its regulatory powers to the States. Unsurprisingly, Congress indicated that the NRC must maintain regulatory control over especially sensitive activities like the construction of nuclear power plants. §2021(c). But under §2021(b) the NRC may now, by agreement, pass to the States some of its preexisting authorities to regulate various nuclear materials "for the protection of the public health and safety from radiation hazards." Out of apparent concern that courts might (mis)read these new provisions as prohibiting States from regulating any activity even tangentially related to nuclear power without first reaching an agreement with the NRC, Congress added subsection (k):

> "Nothing in this section [that is, §2021] shall be construed to affect the authority of any State or local agency to regulate activities for purposes other than protection against radiation hazards."

Section 2021, thus, did nothing to extend the NRC's power to activities, like mining, historically beyond its reach. Instead, it served only to allow the NRC to share with the States some of the powers previously reserved to the federal government. Even then, the statute explained in subsection (k) that States remain free to regulate the activities discussed in §2021 for purposes *other than* nuclear safety without the NRC's consent. Indeed, if anything, subsection (k) might be described as a *non-preemption* clause.

Virginia Uranium's case hinges on a very different construction of subsection (k). The company suggests that, properly read, the provision greatly expands the preemptive effect of the AEA and demands the displacement of *any* state law (touching on mining or any other subject) if that law was enacted for the purpose of protecting the public against "radiation hazards." And, the company adds, Virginia's law bears just such an impermissible purpose.

In our view, this reading nearly turns the provision on its head. Subsection (k) does not displace traditional state regulation over mining or otherwise extend the NRC's grasp to matters previously beyond its control. It does not expose every state law on every subject to a searching judicial inquiry into its latent purposes. Instead and much more modestly, it clarifies that "nothing in this [new] section [2021]" — a section allowing for the devolution-by-agreement of federal regulatory authority — should be construed to curtail the States' ability to regulate the activities discussed in that *same section* for purposes other than protecting against radiation hazards. So only state laws that seek to regulate the activities discussed in §2021 without an NRC agreement — activities like the construction of nuclear power plants — may be scrutinized to ensure their purposes aim at something other than regulating nuclear safety. Really, to accomplish all it wants, Virginia Uranium would have to persuade us to read 13 words out of the statute and add 2 more:

> ~~Nothing in this section shall be construed to affect the authority of~~ any State or local agency ~~to~~ **may** regulate activities **only** for purposes other than protection against radiation hazards.

That may be a statute some would prefer, but it is not the statute we have.

Just consider what would follow from Virginia Uranium's interpretation. Not only would States be prohibited from regulating uranium mining to protect against radiation hazards; the federal government likely would be barred from doing so as well. After all, the NRC has long believed, and still maintains, that the AEA affords it no authority to regulate uranium mining on private land. Nor does Virginia Uranium dispute the federal government's understanding. Admittedly, if Virginia Uranium were to prevail here, the NRC might respond by changing course and seeking to regulate uranium mining for the first time. But given the statute's terms, the prospects that it might do so successfully in the face of a legal challenge appear gloomy. Admittedly, as well, federal air and water and other regulations might apply at a uranium mine much as at any other workplace. But the possibility that both state and federal authorities would be left unable to regulate the unique risks posed by an activity as potentially hazardous as uranium mining seems more than a little unlikely, and quite a lot to find buried deep in subsection (k). Talk about squeezing elephants into mouseholes.

B

If the best reading of the AEA doesn't require us to hold the state law before us preempted, Virginia Uranium takes another swing in the same direction. Only this time, the company submits, our precedents have adopted a different, even if maybe doubtful, reading of the AEA that we must follow. Most prominently, Virginia Uranium points to this Court's decision in *Pacific Gas & Elec. Co. v. State Energy Resources Conservation and Development Comm'n*, 461 U.S. 190 (1983).

But here, too, problems quickly appear. *Pacific Gas rejected* a preemption challenge to a state law prohibiting the construction of new nuclear power plants. Along the way, the Court expressly dismissed the notion that §2021 establishes the federal government as "the sole regulator of all matters nuclear." The Court observed that subsection (k) addresses itself only to "the preemptive effect of 'this section,' that is [§2021]." And the Court acknowledged that subsection (k) does not "cut back on pre-existing state authority outside the NRC's jurisdiction," a field that surely includes uranium mining. None of this remotely helps Virginia Uranium's cause.

Still, Virginia Uranium seeks to make the best of a bad situation. The company points out that *Pacific Gas* upheld the state law at issue there only after observing that it was enacted out of concern with economic development, not for the purpose of addressing radiation safety hazards. From this, the company reasons, we should infer that *any* state law enacted with the purpose of addressing nuclear hazards must fall thanks to our precedent.

But even that much does not follow. Since the passage of the AEA, the NRC has always played a significant role in regulating the construction of nuclear power plants. Indeed, under §2021(c) this remains one area where the NRC generally cannot devolve its responsibilities to the States. And because §2021 classifies the construction of nuclear power plants as one of the core remaining areas of special federal concern, any state law regulating that activity risks being subjected to an inquiry into its purposes under subsection (k). But the activity Virginia's law regulates — mining on private land — isn't one the AEA has ever addressed, and it isn't one §2021 discusses, so subsection (k) does not authorize any judicial inquiry into state legislative purpose in this case.

Admittedly, there is a wrinkle here. *Pacific Gas* seemed to accept California's argument that its law addressed *whether* new power plants may be built, while the NRC's regulatory power under §2021(c) extends only to the question *how* such plants are constructed and operated. And accepting (without granting) these premises, it would appear that California's law did *not* implicate an activity addressed by §2021, so an inquiry into state legislative purpose under subsection (k) was not statutorily authorized. Yet *Pacific Gas* inquired anyway, perhaps on the unstated belief that the state law just came "too close" to a core power §2021(c) reserves to the federal government. Does that mean we must do the same? Certainly Virginia Uranium sees it that way.

We do not. Just because *Pacific Gas* may have made more of state legislative purposes than the terms of the AEA allow does not mean we must make more of them yet. It is one thing to do as *Pacific Gas* did and inquire exactingly into state legislative purposes when state law prohibits a regulated activity like the construction of a nuclear plant, and thus comes close to trenching on core federal powers reserved to the federal government by the AEA. It is another thing to do as Virginia Uranium wishes and impose the same exacting scrutiny on state laws prohibiting an activity like mining far removed from the NRC's historic powers. And without some clearer congressional mandate suggesting an inquiry like that would be appropriate, we decline to undertake it on our own authority. The preemption of state laws represents "a serious intrusion into state sovereignty." And to order preemption based not on the strength of a clear congressional command, or even on the strength of a judicial gloss requiring that much of us, but based only on a doubtful *extension* of a questionable judicial gloss would represent not only a significant federal intrusion into state sovereignty. It would also represent a significant judicial intrusion into Congress's authority to delimit the preemptive effect of its laws. Being in for a dime doesn't mean we have to be in for a dollar.

This Court's later cases confirm the propriety of restraint in this area. In a decision issued just a year after *Pacific Gas* (and by the same author), this Court considered whether the AEA preempted state tort remedies for radiation injuries after a nuclear plant accident. *Silkwood v. Kerr-McGee Corp.*, 464 U.S. 238 (1984). In doing so, the Court did not inquire into state legislative purposes, apparently because it thought state tort law (unlike a law prohibiting the construction of a nuclear power plant) fell beyond any fair understanding of the NRC's reach under the AEA. Exactly the same, as we have seen, can be said of Virginia's mining law. In fact, if the *Silkwood* Court *had* inquired into state legislative purposes, the law there might well have been harder to sustain than the one now before us. State tort laws, after all, plainly intend to regulate public safety. And as applied in *Silkwood*, state tort law sought to regulate the safety of a nuclear plant's operations, an area of special federal interest under §2021(c). Nothing comparable, of course, can be said of the mining regulations before us. Some years later, this Court in *English v. General Elec. Co.*, 496 U.S. 72 (1990), went further still, casting doubt on whether an inquiry into state legislative purposes had been either necessary or appropriate in *Pacific Gas* itself.

If *Pacific Gas* and its progeny alone marked our path, this case might be a close one, as our dissenting colleagues suggest. But for us any lingering doubt dissipates when we consult other cases in this area and this Court's traditional tools of statutory interpretation.

Start with the fact that this Court has generally treated field preemption inquiries like this one as depending on *what* the State did, not *why* it did it. Indeed, this Court has analyzed most every other modern field preemption doctrine dispute in this way — from immigration, to arbitration, to foreign affairs, to railroads, to energy, to civil procedure. It is unclear why we would proceed differently here without some clear congressional instruction requiring it.

Our field preemption cases proceed as they do, moreover, for good reasons. Consider just some of the costs to cooperative federalism and individual liberty we would invite by inquiring into state legislative purpose too precipitately. The natural tendency of regular federal judicial inquiries into state legislative intentions would be to stifle deliberation in state legislatures and encourage resort to secrecy and subterfuge. That would inhibit the sort of open and vigorous legislative debate that our Constitution recognizes as vital to testing ideas and improving laws. In Virginia Uranium's vision as well, federal courts would have to allow depositions of state legislators and governors, and perhaps hale them into court for cross-examination at trial about their subjective motivations in passing a mining statute. And at the end of it all, federal courts would risk subjecting similarly situated persons to radically different legal rules as judges uphold and strike down materially identical state regulations based only on the happenstance of judicial assessments of the "true" intentions lurking behind them. In light of all this, it can surprise no one that our precedents have long warned against undertaking potential misadventures into hidden state legislative intentions without a clear statutory mandate for the project.

To be sure, Virginia Uranium insists that we don't need to worry about concerns like these in this case. We don't, the company says, because Virginia has admitted that it enacted its law with the (impermissible) purpose of protecting the public from nuclear safety hazards. But the Commonwealth denies making any such admission. Instead, it says it has merely accepted as true the allegations in the company's complaint about the intentions animating state law for purposes of the Commonwealth's own motion to dismiss this suit under Federal Rule of Civil Procedure 12(b)(6). If the case were to proceed beyond the pleadings stage, Virginia insists, a more searching judicial inquiry into the law's motivation would be inevitable. Whoever may be right about the status of Virginia's admissions in this case, though, the point remains that following Virginia Uranium's lead would require serious intrusions into state legislative processes in future cases.

Beyond these concerns, as well, lie well-known conceptual and practical ones this Court has also advised against inviting unnecessarily. State legislatures are composed of individuals who often pursue legislation for multiple and unexpressed purposes, so what legal rules should determine when and how to ascribe a particular intention to a particular legislator? What if an impermissible intention existed but wasn't necessary to her vote? And what percentage of the legislature must harbor the impermissible intention before we can impute it to the collective institution? Putting all that aside, how are courts supposed to conduct a reasonable inquiry into these questions when recorded state legislative history materials are often not as readily available or complete as their federal counterparts? And if trying to peer inside legislators' skulls is too fraught an enterprise, shouldn't we limit ourselves to trying to glean legislative purposes from the statutory text where we began? Even *Pacific Gas* warned future courts against too hastily accepting a litigant's invitation to "become embroiled in attempting to ascertain" state legislative "motive[s]," acknowledging that such inquiries "often" prove "unsatisfactory venture[s]. What motivates one legislator to vote for a statute is not necessarily what motivates scores of others to enact it." We think these warnings wise, and we heed them today.

C

If the AEA doesn't occupy the field of radiation safety in uranium mining, Virginia Uranium suggests the statute still displaces state law through what's sometimes called conflict preemption. In particular, the company suggests, Virginia's mining law stands as an impermissible "obstacle to the accomplishment and execution of the full purposes and objectives of Congress." On Virginia Uranium's account, Congress sought to capture the benefits of developing nuclear power while mitigating its safety and environmental costs. And, the company contends, Virginia's moratorium disrupts the delicate "balance" Congress sought to achieve between these benefits and costs. Maybe the text of the AEA doesn't touch on mining in so many words, but its authority to regulate later stages of the nuclear fuel life cycle would be effectively undermined if mining laws like Virginia's were allowed.

A sound preemption analysis cannot be as simplistic as that. No more than in field preemption can the Supremacy Clause be deployed here to elevate abstract and unenacted legislative desires above state law; only federal laws "made in pursuance of" the Constitution, through its prescribed processes of bicameralism and presentment, are entitled to preemptive effect. So any "[e]vidence of pre-emptive purpose," whether express or implied, must therefore be "sought in the text and structure of the statute at issue."

Sound and well-documented reasons underlie this rule too. Efforts to ascribe unenacted purposes and objectives to a federal statute face many of the same challenges as inquiries into state legislative intent. Trying to discern what motivates legislators individually and collectively invites speculation and risks overlooking the reality that individual Members of Congress often pursue multiple and competing purposes, many of which are compromised to secure a law's passage and few of which are fully realized in the final product. Hefty inferences may be required, as well, when trying to estimate whether Congress would have wanted to prohibit States from pursuing regulations that may happen to touch, in various degrees and different ways, on unenacted federal purposes and objectives. Worse yet, in piling inference upon inference about hidden legislative wishes we risk displacing the legislative compromises actually reflected in the statutory text — compromises that sometimes may seem irrational to an outsider coming to the statute cold, but whose genius lies in having won the broad support our Constitution demands of any new law. In disregarding these legislative compromises, we may only wind up displacing perfectly legitimate state laws on the strength of "purposes" that only we can see, that may seem perfectly logical to us, but that lack the democratic provenance the Constitution demands before a federal law may be declared supreme.

So it may be that Congress meant the AEA to promote the development of nuclear power. It may be that Congress meant the AEA to balance that goal against various safety concerns. But it also may be that Members of Congress held many other disparate or conflicting goals in mind when they voted to enact and amend the AEA, and many different views on exactly how to manage the competing costs and benefits. If polled, they might have reached very different assessments, as well, about the consistency of Virginia's law with their own purposes and objectives. The only thing a court can be sure of is what can be found in the law itself. And every indication in the law before us suggests that Congress elected to leave mining regulation on private land to the States and grant the NRC regulatory authority only *after* uranium is removed from the earth. That compromise may not be the only permissible or even the most rationally attractive one, but it is surely both permissible and rational to think that Congress might have chosen to regulate the more novel aspects of nuclear power while leaving to States their traditional function of regulating mining activities on private lands within their boundaries.

As an alternative to proceeding down the purposes-and-objectives branch of conflict preemption, Virginia Uranium might have pursued another. Our cases have held that we can sometimes infer a congressional intent to displace a state law that makes compliance with a federal statute impossible. But Virginia Uranium hasn't pursued an argument along any of these lines, and understandably so. Not only *can* Virginia Uranium comply with both state and federal laws; it is also unclear whether laws like Virginia's might have a meaningful impact on the development of nuclear power in this country. Some estimate that the United States currently imports over 90 percent of the uranium used in this country. Domestic uranium mines currently exist on federal lands as well and are thus beyond the reach of state authorities. And if the federal government concludes that development of the Coles Hill deposit or any other like it is crucial, it may always purchase the site (or seize it through eminent domain) under the powers Congress has supplied. All this may be done without even amending the AEA, itself another course which Congress is always free to pursue — but which this Court should never be tempted into pursuing on its own.

The judgment of the court of appeals is

Affirmed.

JUSTICE GINSBURG, with whom JUSTICE SOTOMAYOR and JUSTICE KAGAN join, concurring in the judgment.

Soon after discovery of a large deposit of uranium ore in Virginia in the late 1970s, the Commonwealth banned uranium mining. Petitioners (collectively, Virginia Uranium) now seek to mine that deposit. They challenge the Commonwealth's uranium mining ban as preempted by the Atomic Energy Act (AEA or Act), 42 U.S.C. §2011 *et seq.*, either because the ban intrudes on the federally occupied field of nuclear safety, or because it obstructs realization of federal purposes and objectives.

I reach the same bottom-line judgment as does Justice Gorsuch: The Commonwealth's mining ban is not preempted. And I agree with much contained in Justice Gorsuch's opinion. his discussion of the perils of inquiring into legislative motive sweeps well beyond the confines of this case, and therefore seems to me inappropriate in an opinion speaking for the Court, rather than for individual members of the Court. Further, Virginia Uranium's obstacle preemption arguments fail under existing doctrine, so there is little reason to question, as Justice Gorsuch does, whether that doctrine should be retained. For these reasons, I join the Court's judgment, and separately state how I would resolve the instant controversy.

I

. . .

B

In the late 1970s, uranium ore was discovered under Coles Hill, an unincorporated community in Pittsylvania County, Virginia. Totaling 119 million pounds of uranium ore, the deposit is the Nation's largest. After a private company began leasing mineral rights to the deposit, the Virginia General Assembly directed the state Coal and Energy Commission to study the effects on the environment and public health of uranium exploration, mining, and milling.

The next year, the General Assembly authorized uranium exploration but imposed a one-year moratorium on uranium mining. The Assembly's stated purpose was "to encourage and promote the safe and efficient exploration for uranium resources within the Commonwealth, and to assure . . . that uranium mining and milling will be subject to statutes and regulations which protect the environment and the health and safety of the public." The Assembly soon extended the ban "until a program for permitting uranium mining is established by statute." The Commonwealth has not established a permitting program, so the ban remains in force.

A slowdown in construction of new nuclear powerplants in the 1980s contributed to a "precipitous decline in the price of uranium ore." Rising prices in the first decade of the new millennium prompted renewed interest in mining the deposit, and Virginia Uranium lobbied to have the ban repealed.

When efforts to persuade the state legislature proved unsuccessful, Virginia Uranium brought this suit seeking a declaration that the ban is preempted by federal law and an injunction requiring the Commonwealth to issue uranium mining permits. Respondents, Virginia Department of Mines, Minerals, and Energy officials (together, the Commonwealth Defendants), moved to dismiss the complaint for failure to state a claim, and the District Court granted the motion. The Court of Appeals for the Fourth Circuit affirmed, holding in principal part that because the Commonwealth's mining ban did not regulate an activity overseen by the NRC, there was no need to consider the purposes for which the ban was imposed. Given the importance of the issue, and to resolve a division of authority among the Courts of Appeals, we granted Virginia Uranium's petition for a writ of certiorari.

II

Under the Supremacy Clause, the "Constitution, and the Laws of the United States which shall be made in Pursuance thereof," are "the supreme Law of the Land." Art. VI, cl. 2. "Put simply, federal law preempts contrary state law."

This Court has delineated three circumstances in which state law must yield to federal law. First, and most obvious, federal law operates exclusively when Congress expressly preempts state law. Second, state law can play no part when "Congress has legislated comprehensively to occupy an entire field of regulation, leaving no room for the States to supplement federal law." Third, state law is rendered inoperative when it "actually conflicts with federal law," as when a private party cannot "comply with both state and federal requirements," or when state law "creates an unacceptable 'obstacle to the accomplishment and execution of the full purposes and objectives of Congress.'" Whatever the category of preemption asserted, "the purpose of Congress is the ultimate touchstone" in determining whether federal law preempts state law. Virginia Uranium invokes both field and obstacle preemption; I address each in turn.

A

Virginia Uranium's primary contention is that Congress has occupied the field of nuclear safety regulation, preempting state laws enacted because of concerns about the radiation safety of federally regulated activities. Defining the preempted field by reference to the purpose for which state laws were enacted finds "some support in the text of the [AEA]," and, in particular, §2021(k). Again, this provision states that "[n]othing in [§2021] shall be construed to affect the authority of any State . . . to regulate activities *for purposes other than protection against radiation hazards*." (Emphasis added.) Section 2021(k) presupposes federal preemption of at least some state laws enacted to guard "against radiation hazards." Virginia Uranium and the dissent read this subsection to include within the preempted sphere *all* state laws motivated by concerns about the radiation hazards of NRC-regulated activities. The Commonwealth Defendants would exclude from federal foreclosure state laws directed to activities not regulated by the NRC. The Commonwealth Defendants have the better reading of the statute.

1

The Commonwealth has forbidden only conventional uranium mining on private land, an activity all agree is not federally regulated. The controlling AEA provision, §2092, triggers federal regulation only when source material is "remov[ed] from its place of deposit in nature." Federal authorities have long read that provision to preclude federal regulation of conventional uranium mining. In contrast to the AEA's express provisions for uranium mining on public lands, the Act is nearly silent about conventional uranium mining on private lands. Indeed, insofar as the Act addresses private conventional mining, it does so to bar federal regulators from obtaining reports about ore "prior to removal from its place of deposit in nature." Every indication, then, is that Congress left private conventional mining unregulated. And if Congress did not provide for regulation of private conventional mining, it is hard to see how or why state law on the subject would be preempted, whatever the reason for the law's enactment.

2

Virginia Uranium's argument to the contrary rests on §2021(k), but that provision, correctly read, lends no support for Virginia Uranium's cause. By its terms, §2021(k) addresses only state authority to regulate "activities" for nonradiological purposes. Read in context of §2021 as a whole, "activities" means activities *regulated by the NRC*.

The AEA's context and history are corroborative. Prior to enactment of §2021(k), the Federal Government and States shared responsibility for most steps of the nuclear fuel cycle, with the former regulating primarily for public health and safety, and the latter regulating for economic and other nonradiological purposes. Section 2021 was designed "to heighten the States' role," by enabling federal regulators to cede their previously exclusive authority over the nuclear safety of several lower risk activities, §2021(b). Given this aim, §2021(k) is most sensibly read to clarify that the door newly opened for state regulation left in place pre-existing state authority "to regulate activities for purposes other than protection against radiation hazards." The House and Senate Reports are explicit on this point: Section §2021(k) was "intended to make it clear that the bill does not impair the State[s'] authority to regulate activities of [federal] licensees for the manifold health, safety, and economic purposes other than radiation protection"; the bill simply provides a means for States to obtain heretofore exclusively federal authority to regulate these activities for "protection against radiation hazards." Nothing suggests that Congress "intended to cut back on pre-existing state authority outside the NRC's jurisdiction." That authority encompassed state laws regulating conventional uranium mining, even if enacted because of concerns about the radiological safety of postextraction, NRC-regulated steps in the nuclear fuel cycle.

3

Virginia Uranium leans most heavily on a statement in the Court's *PG&E* opinion: "[T]he Federal Government has occupied the entire field of nuclear safety concerns." But in neither *PG&E* nor in later decisions in its wake, *Silkwood v. Kerr-McGee Corp.*, 464 U.S. 238 (1984), and *English*, 496 U.S. 72, did the Court rest preemption on the purposes for which state laws were enacted. Indeed, in all three, the Court held that the state laws at issue were not preempted.

Moreover, without gainsaying that it may sometimes be appropriate to inquire into the purpose for which a state law was enacted, *PG&E* calls for no such inquiry here. *PG&E* considered whether the AEA preempted a California law conditioning approval to build new nuclear plants on a finding that an adequate method existed for disposing of spent nuclear fuel. The Court upheld the law because it was enacted out of concern for economic development, not because of radiation safety hazards.

It is unsurprising that the *PG&E* Court asked why the California law had been enacted. The State's law addressed construction of a nuclear powerplant, an activity closely regulated by the Federal Government for nuclear safety purposes. Court therefore inquired whether the state law was enacted, in §2021(k)'s words, "for purposes other than protection against radiation hazards." Here, in contrast, the Commonwealth's mining ban targets an exclusively state-regulated activity.

4

I am not persuaded by the Solicitor General's argument that the Commonwealth's mining ban is preempted because it is a pretext for regulating the radiological safety hazards of milling and tailings storage. To the degree the AEA preempts state laws enacted for certain purposes, §2021(k) stakes out the boundaries of the preempted field, *i.e.*, state laws that apply to federally licensed activities and are driven by concerns about the radiological safety of those activities. We have no license to expand those boundaries.

The case on which the Solicitor General primarily relies, *National Meat Assn. v. Harris*, 565 U.S. 452 (2012), does not counsel otherwise. *National Meat* concerned a set of California laws that "dictat[ed] what slaughterhouses must do with pigs that cannot walk, known in the trade as nonambulatory pigs." The question presented: Did California's prescriptions conflict with the Federal Meat Inspection Act's express preemption of state law that imposed requirements "in addition to, or different than those made under" the Act? 21 U.S.C. §678. One of the California provisions, a ban on the sale of meat or products from nonambulatory pigs, regulated a subject outside the scope of the Federal Meat Inspection Act. *National Meat*, 565 U.S., at 463. The Court nevertheless concluded that the sale ban fell within the scope of the Act's express preemption clause because it was intended to work together with other California provisions to impose additional requirements on slaughterhouse operations.

National Meat is not controlling here. No express preemption provision is involved. The mining ban sets no safety standards for federally supervised milling or tailings storage activities. True enough, the ban makes it far less likely, though not impossible, that such activities will take place in the Commonwealth. In that regard, the Commonwealth's mining ban is more aptly analogized to state bans on slaughtering horses, upheld by courts of appeals and distinguished in *National Meat* from California's nonambulatory pig laws. Horse slaughtering bans, *National Meat* explained, "work[ed] at a remove from the sites and activities that the FMIA most directly governs" by ensuring that "no horses will be delivered to, inspected at, or handled by a slaughterhouse, because no horses will be ordered for purchase in the first instance." The distinction drawn in *National Meat* thus supports this conclusion: A state law regulating an upstream activity within the State's authority is not preempted simply because a downstream activity falls within a federally occupied field.

B

Nor is the Commonwealth's mining ban preempted as an "unacceptable obstacle to the accomplishment and execution of the full purposes and objectives of Congress." Together, Virginia Uranium and the United States identify four ways in which the mining ban supposedly conflicts with federal purposes and objectives. None carry the day.

First, Virginia Uranium contends that the mining ban conflicts with the "delicate balance" federal law has struck between promoting nuclear power and ensuring public safety. But the Federal Government does not regulate the radiological safety of conventional uranium mining on private land, so federal law struck *no* balance in this area.

Second, Virginia Uranium contends that the mining ban "*prohibit[s]* the achievement of one of Congress[']' 'primary purpose[s]': 'the promotion of nuclear power.'" *PG&E*, however, dismissed the suggestion that Congress had a policy of promoting nuclear power "at all costs." Given the absence of federal regulation in point, it is improbable that the Federal Government has a purpose or objective of promoting conventional uranium mining on private land.

Virginia Uranium warns of dire consequences if all 50 States enact bans similar to the Commonwealth's. But, as the Court of Appeals explained, numerous domestic uranium recovery facilities are federally regulated (either because they sit on federal land or use unconventional mining techniques) and are "thus beyond the reach of any state bans"; and the AEA authorizes the Federal Government to develop uranium deposits on public lands and to acquire private deposits. Federal purposes and objectives do not require judicial supplementation of the AEA's express provisions for maintaining the uranium supply.

The dissent suggests that national security may require further domestic uranium production. If the Executive Branch — which presumably knows more about "the critical role of uranium to the country's energy industry and national defense," — agrees, it can arrange for acquisition of the site by the United States, and then for commencement of mining notwithstanding the Commonwealth's ban. Yet the site remains in private hands.

Third, Virginia Uranium argues that §2021 provides the sole means for States to regulate radiological safety hazards resulting from milling and tailings storage, and that Virginia has effectively regulated milling and tailings storage without obtaining authority to do so through an adequate §2021 agreement. As explained, Virginia has not regulated the radiological safety of tailings storage; it has prohibited only an antecedent activity subject to exclusive state authority.

Finally, the United States contends that Virginia's mining ban frustrates federal purposes and objectives by "prevent[ing] the occurrence of" activities that Congress intended the Federal Government to regulate. But federal regulation of certain activities does not mean that States must authorize activities antecedent to those federally regulated. For example, federal regulation of nuclear powerplants does not demand that States allow the construction of such powerplants in the first place.

* * *

For the reasons stated, I concur in the Court's judgment affirming the judgment of the Court of Appeals.

CHIEF JUSTICE ROBERTS, with whom JUSTICE BREYER and JUSTICE ALITO join, dissenting.

Although one party will be happy with the result of today's decision, both will be puzzled by its reasoning. That's because the lead opinion sets out to defeat an argument that no one made, reaching a conclusion with which no one disagrees. Specifically, the opinion devotes its analysis to whether the field of uranium mining safety is preempted under the Atomic Energy Act, ultimately concluding that it is not. But no party disputes that. Rather, the question we agreed to address is whether a State can purport to regulate a field that is *not* preempted (uranium mining safety) as an indirect means of regulating other fields that *are* preempted (safety concerns about uranium milling and tailings). And on that question, our precedent is clear: The AEA prohibits state laws that have the purpose and effect of regulating preempted fields.

As relevant here, processing uranium ore involves three steps: mining, milling, and storing "tailings." *Mining* is the extracting of uranium ore from the ground; *milling* is the process of turning the substance into a usable form; and *tailings* are the leftover radioactive waste that must be safely stored.

There is no dispute over which of these fields the AEA reserves to the exclusive jurisdiction of the Nuclear Regulatory Commission. The parties agree that the field of uranium *mining* safety is not preempted. And it is undisputed that radiological safety concerns about *milling* and *tailings* are preempted fields. Indeed, that shared understanding was the basis of the question presented.[1]

Despite all this, the lead opinion insists that petitioners (hereafter the company) press an entirely different argument. "Before us, Virginia Uranium contends that the AEA (and only the AEA) unseats state uranium mining regulations," but "almost immediately problems emerge." Problems do immediately emerge in the opinion, but they are of its own making. The company does not argue that the AEA reserves the field of uranium *mining* safety. After attributing this failing argument to the company, the lead opinion then proceeds to explain why the argument must, in fact, fail.

Turning to the question presented, however, the company's theory of the case is fairly straightforward. The property at issue here contains the largest known uranium deposit in the country and one of the largest in the world. Shortly after its discovery, Virginia enacted a complete ban on uranium mining. According to the company, the ban was not motivated by concerns about mining safety. Instead, it was motivated by Virginia's desire to ban the more hazardous steps that come after mining — uranium milling and the storage of radioactive tailings — due to the Commonwealth's disagreement with the NRC over how to safely regulate those activities. And, crucially, Virginia has yet to put forward any other rationale to support the ban. Thus, the question before us is whether, consistent with the AEA and our precedents, the Commonwealth may purport to regulate a non-preempted field (mining safety) with the purpose and effect of indirectly regulating a preempted field (milling and tailings). That should have made for an easy case.

Under our AEA precedents, a state law is preempted not only when it "conflicts with federal law," but also when its *purpose* is to regulate within a preempted field. Because "the Federal Government has occupied the entire field of nuclear safety concerns," a state law that is "grounded in [such] safety concerns falls squarely within the prohibited field." For example, even though a State may generally regulate its roads, it may not shut down all of the roads to a nuclear power plant simply because it disagrees with the NRC's nuclear safety

---

[1] "Does the AEA preempt a state law that on its face regulates an activity within its jurisdiction (here uranium mining), but has the purpose and effect of regulating the radiological safety hazards of activities entrusted to the NRC (here, the milling of uranium and the management of the resulting tailings)?"

regulations. Here, because Virginia has not even disputed that its uranium mining ban was "grounded in" its "nuclear safety concerns" about uranium milling and tailings, the company's preemption claim should not have been dismissed.

The lead opinion and the concurrence miss that simple analysis because they shrink from our AEA precedents, particularly *Pacific Gas*. In *Pacific Gas*, California had banned the construction of nuclear power plants until the State could ensure that new plants would have a viable method for permanently disposing of nuclear waste. On its face, the ban did not purport to regulate a preempted field; it did not regulate the *manner* in which nuclear power plants may be constructed or operated, which is a field preempted by the AEA. If it had, the Court noted, the ban "would clearly be impermissible." The California statute instead purported to address the antecedent question *whether* new plants should be constructed at all — an area within the State's traditional authority over the generation and cost of electricity.

But the Court did not stop its preemption analysis there. Instead, it was "necessary" to look beyond the face of the statute to determine California's "rationale" for the ban. California had argued that it could exercise its traditional authority over power generation to "completely prohibit new construction until its safety concerns [we]re satisfied by the Federal Government." The Court flatly "reject[ed]" this line of reasoning. Because the AEA reserves the "field of nuclear safety concerns" to the Federal Government, a state law that was "grounded in" those concerns would fall "squarely within the prohibited field." In other words, if the purpose of California's ban on nuclear plant construction was to regulate radiological safety, it would be preempted. California's statute ultimately avoided that outcome, however, because the State had put forward an independent "nonsafety rationale" — namely, its concern that new nuclear plants would not be economically viable if they were unable to permanently dispose of nuclear waste. On that basis, the Court determined that the ban was not preempted.

Pacific Gas should control the outcome here. Like California's ban in that case, Virginia's ban on its face regulates a non-preempted field — uranium mining safety. Like the plaintiffs challenging the California ban, the mining company argues that the statute's purpose is really to regulate a preempted field — safety concerns about uranium milling and tailings. But unlike California in *Pacific Gas*, Virginia in this case has not put forward a "nonsafety rationale." That should have been the end of the story, at least at this stage of the litigation.

Neither the lead opinion nor the concurrence explain why this Court inquired into purpose in *Pacific Gas* but can dispense with that "necessary" step here; they just say the Court can. At one point, the lead opinion suggests that the AEA "authorize[s]" a purpose inquiry only when a state law "comes close to trenching on core federal powers." But the opinion does not say where that rule comes from. Certainly not the statute or our precedents. And the lead opinion never explains why the safety concerns about nuclear plants in *Pacific Gas* are more "core" to the AEA than the safety concerns about uranium milling and tailings storage at issue here.

The central argument from my colleagues appears to be that the AEA authorizes a purpose inquiry only when a State "targets" or "seek[s] to regulate" an activity that is also regulated by the federal statute. And because the Virginia statute *seeks* to regulate mining, the AEA "does not authorize any judicial inquiry into state legislative purpose in this case." But it is conceded that the mining ban was adopted because of radiological safety concerns about milling and tailings. That is why Virginia argues, as it must, that its mining ban would not be preempted even if it expressly stated that it was enacted due to the Commonwealth's disagreement with the NRC's nuclear safety regulations. If such a statute does not "target" or "seek to regulate" a preempted field, what would?

States may try to regulate one activity by exercising their authority over another. That is the whole point of the purpose inquiry mandated by *Pacific Gas*. Indeed, *Pacific Gas* specifically "emphasize[d]" that the California law did *not* expressly seek to regulate "the construction or operation of a nuclear powerplant," that is, the statute on its face was not directed at a preempted field.

The AEA's purpose inquiry is most useful precisely when the challenged state law does *not* purport to regulate a preempted field. If a State disagrees with the AEA's nuclear safety regulations, and thus wants to block nuclear development within its borders, it has myriad ways to do so through its broad police powers. Under the rule adopted by the lead opinion and the concurrence, so long as the State is not boneheaded enough to express its real purpose in the statute, the State will have free rein to subvert Congress's judgment on nuclear safety.

A State could, for instance, restrict the ability of a county to provide a nuclear facility with municipal services like law enforcement, fire protection, and garbage collection. If it wanted to target investors, a State could eliminate limited liability for the stockholders of companies that operate nuclear facilities. Although these examples may seem farfetched, they have already happened. See *Skull Valley Band of Goshute Indians v. Nielson*, 376 F. 3d 1223, 1247–1248, 1250–1252 (CA10 2004). In *Skull Valley*, however, the Tenth Circuit correctly applied our precedent and concluded that the "state cannot use its authority to regulate law enforcement and other similar matters as a means of regulating radiological hazards." Neither the lead opinion nor the concurrence hazards an answer for cases like *Skull Valley*.

As these examples show, AEA preemption cannot turn on the label a State affixes to its regulations. That approach would simply invite evasion, which is why we have rejected it in our preemption cases more generally. For example, in *National Meat Assn. v. Harris*, 565 U.S. 452 (2012), we addressed a preemption challenge involving slaughterhouses in California. A federal statute preempted state regulation of slaughterhouses' front-end procedures for inspecting, handling, and slaughtering livestock. California, however, had regulated the back-end operations of slaughterhouses by prohibiting the *sale* of meat from livestock that had not been inspected, handled, and slaughtered according to the State's regulations.

Although the federal statute's preemption clause did "not usually foreclose state regulation of the commercial sales activities of slaughterhouses," we unanimously held that California's sales regulation was preempted because it was a transparent attempt to circumvent federal law. Concluding otherwise, we noted, would allow a State to "impose any regulation on slaughterhouses just by framing it as a ban on the sale of meat produced in whatever way the State disapproved." *Id.*, at 464. And that "would make a mockery of the [federal statute's] preemption provision."

The concurrence argues that *National Meat* is distinguishable because there the State regulated a downstream, non-preempted activity (sale of meat) in an effort to regulate an upstream, preempted activity (processing of livestock). Here, however, Virginia's regulation is upstream (mining) and the preempted activity is downstream (milling and tailings). That's true but beside the point. Regardless whether the state regulation is downstream like *National Meat*, upstream like here and *Pacific Gas*, or entirely out of the stream like *Skull Valley*, States may not legislate with the purpose and effect of regulating a federally preempted field.

That common sense approach is consistent with the text of the AEA, which recognizes that States continue to have authority "to regulate activities for *purposes* other than protection against radiation hazards." 42 U.S.C. §2021(k) (emphasis added). The lead opinion finds this purpose-based approach discomfiting, citing the "well-known conceptual and practical" difficulties about inquiring into legislative motive. The statute and our precedent plainly require such an approach here, however, and the difficulty of the task does not permit us to choose an easier way. I respectfully dissent.

CAN A NON-CERCLA SETTLEMENT TRIGGER A CERCLA CONTRIBUTION CLAIM?

In this case the government of the U.S Territory of Guam challenged the dismissal of a CERCLA action it filed against the U.S. Navy over the cleanup of the Ordot Dump, the largest dumpsite in Guam. The Ordot Dump was created by the U.S. Navy when it ruled the island after World War II and later used for decades as a municipal dumpsite prior to its closing in 2011. In 2002, EPA sued Guam for violating the Clean Water Act due to discharges from the Ordot Dump leaching into the Lonfit River that flows into the ocean. This litigation was settled by consent decree between the Navy and Guam in 2004.

In 2017, Guam sued the Navy seeking to recover for part of its costs of cleaning up the dump under §107 of CERCLA or as a contribution action under §113(f)(3)(B) of CERCLA. In February 2020, the U.S. Court of Appeals for the D.C. Circuit ruled that the 2004 settlement between the Navy and Guam meant that the territory could only recover from the Navy through a contribution action under §113(f)(3)(B) of CERCLA. Because Guam's action had been filed after expiration of the three-year statute of limitations for CERCLA contribution claims, the court dismissed the action.

The Supreme Court granted review to decide whether a settlement that is not under CERCLA can trigger a contribution claim under CERCLA §113(f)(3)(B). Justice Thomas wrote the following opinion for a unanimous Court.

TERRITORY OF GUAM v. UNITED STATES
141 S.Ct. 1608 (2021)

Justice Thomas delivered the opinion of the Court.

The Comprehensive Environmental Response, Compensation, and Liability Act of 1980, commonly known as CERCLA, establishes a complex statutory scheme for responding to certain environmental hazards. Several of its provisions address what is often the crucial question in a remedial action: Who pays?

Today's case involves §113(f)(3)(B) of the Act, which allows "[a] person who has resolved its liability to the United States or a State" in a settlement to seek "contribution"—that is, money from another responsible individual. The question is whether a party must resolve a CERCLA-specific liability in order to trigger this right, or whether a broader array of settlements involving environmental liability will do. We hold that CERCLA contribution requires resolution of a CERCLA-specific liability.

I

Guam and the United States are engaged in a long-running dispute over the Ordot Dump, a " '280-foot mountain of trash' " near the center of the island. The Navy constructed the dump in the 1940s, and then allegedly deposited toxic military waste there for several decades. The United States later ceded control of the site to Guam, which itself used the dump as a public landfill. But that did not end the Federal Government's involvement. In the late 20th century, the Environmental Protection Agency (EPA) determined that the dump posed an ecological hazard. After Guam allegedly failed to comply with agency directives to remediate the site, the EPA sued under the Clean Water Act, asserting that Guam was " 'discharging pollutants ... into waters of the United States without obtaining a permit.' "

That litigation ended in 2004, when Guam and the EPA entered into a consent decree. The decree required Guam, among other things, to pay a civil penalty and to close and cover the dump. Guam's compliance would, in turn, be "in full settlement and satisfaction of the civil judicial claims of the United States . . . as alleged in the Complaint"—that is, claims under the Clean Water Act. But Guam was not completely free. As the agreement explained, "the United States d[id] not waive any rights or remedies available to it for any violation by the Government of Guam of federal and territorial laws and regulations," "[e]xcept as specifically provided [i]n [the decree]."

Thirteen years later, it was Guam's turn to sue—this time under CERCLA. According to Guam's complaint, the United States' earlier use of the dump exposed it to liability on two fronts. The first was a cost-recovery action under §107(a), which allows a State (or here, a Territory), to recover "all costs of [a] removal or remedial action" from "any person who at the time of disposal of any hazardous substance owned or operated any facility at which such hazardous substances were disposed of." See also §101(27). The second was a §113(f) "contribution" action. Under that provision, a "person who has resolved its liability to the United States . . . for some or all of a response action or for some or all of the costs of such action in [a] settlement may seek contribution from any person who is not [already] party to a [qualifying] settlement." §113(f)(3)(B).

Rather than increase Guam's odds of recovery, however, the second legal theory led to the dismissal of its complaint. According to the D. C. Circuit, if a party *can* assert a contribution claim under §113(f), it *cannot* assert a cost-recovery claim under §107(a). The court then determined that Guam possessed a contribution claim—at least at one point—because the remedial measures and conditional release in the Clean Water Act decree sufficiently " 'resolved Guam's liability' " for the dump. But because the 2004 decree had triggered the since-expired 3-year statute of limitations for contribution actions, Guam had no remedy at all. We granted certiorari.

II

Guam now attacks two links in this chain of reasoning: First, Guam retreats from its complaint and argues that it *never* had a viable contribution claim under §113(f), leaving it free to pursue a cost-recovery action under §107(a). The reason, argues Guam, is that a contribution claim arises only if a settlement resolves liability under CERCLA, and not under some other law such as the Clean Water Act. Second, Guam contends that even if resolution of a non-CERCLA liability is enough, the decree did not adequately "resolve" *any* sort of liability because Guam did not formally admit responsibility and because the agreement left Guam open to future enforcement action.

We need only address the first point to decide this case. A settlement must resolve a CERCLA liability to trigger a contribution action under §113(f)(3)(B).

Our analysis focuses on the totality of subsection 113(f), which governs the scope of a "contribution" claim under CERCLA. This subsection begins with an anchor provision—entitled "contribution"—that allows "[a]ny person [to] seek contribution from any other person who is liable or potentially liable under section [1]07(a) of [CERCLA], during or following any civil action under section [1]06 of [CERCLA] or under section [1]07(a) of [CERCLA]." §113(f)(1). It next describes how parties can insulate themselves from contribution, explaining that "[a] person who has resolved its liability to the United States or a State in an administrative or judicially approved settlement shall not be liable for claims for contribution regarding matters addressed in the settlement." §113(f)(2). And finally, it discusses the treatment of "[p]ersons not party to [a] settlement." §113(f)(3). Most relevant here, "[a] person who has resolved its liability to the United States . . . for some or all of a response action or for some or all of the costs of such action in an administrative or judicially approved settlement may seek contribution from any person who is not party to a settlement referred to in [§113(f)(2)]." §113(f)(3)(B).

That this subsection centers on and is entitled "contribution" is the first clue that it is concerned only with the distribution of CERCLA liability. A contribution suit does not exist in a vacuum, but rather is a tool for apportioning the burdens of a predicate "common liability" among the responsible parties. The most obvious place to look for that threshold liability is CERCLA's reticulated statutory matrix of environmental duties and liabilities. Cf. *Burlington N. & S. F. R. Co. v. United States*, 556 U.S. 599, 610, (2009) ("[Section 107(a) (3)] liability may not extend beyond the limits of the statute itself "). After all, "[s]tatutes must 'be read as a whole,' " —an especially salient approach in this case given that CERCLA's very title reinforces that it is a "Comprehensive" Act.

Remaining within the bounds of CERCLA is also consistent with the familiar principle that a federal contribution action is virtually always a creature of a specific statutory regime. In fact, there is no "general federal right to contribution" whatsoever. That modest understanding is difficult to reconcile with the United States' invitation to treat §113(f)(3)(B) as a free-roving contribution right for a host of environmental liabilities arising under other laws.

The interlocking language and structure of the relevant text confirm this understanding. The provision at issue here—§113(f)(3)(B)—recognizes a statutory right to contribution in the specific circumstance where a person "has resolved its liability" via "settlement." But as explained above, this entitlement to postsettlement contribution does not stand alone. On the contrary, §113(f)(3)(B) exists within " 'the specific context' " of subsection (f), which outlines the broader workings of CERCLA contribution.

This §113(f) family of contribution provisions anticipates a predicate CERCLA liability, especially when properly read in "sequenc[e]" as " 'integral parts of a whole.' " The §113(f)(1) anchor provision is especially clear on this point, allowing contribution "during or following any civil action under §[1]06 of this title or under §[1]07 of this title." And though §§113(f)(2) and 113(f)(3) are not quite as explicit, their phrasing and context still presume that a CERCLA liability is necessary to trigger contribution.

Section 113(f)(2), for example, explains that a settlement by one party "does not discharge any of the other *potentially liable persons* unless its terms so provide." (Emphasis added.) The highlighted phrase is a "natural referent" to the text of the anchor provision, which creates a CERCLA-specific contribution right against "any other person who is liable or *potentially liable* under §[1]07 of [CERCLA]," §113(f)(1) (emphasis added).

Section 113(f)(3)(B)—the provision at issue here—also has language that is best "understood only with reference" to the CERCLA regime. The provision's final clause explains that contribution is available "from any person who is not party to a settlement referred to in [§113(f)(2)]." As discussed above, §113(f)(2) in turn mirrors the §113(f)(1) anchor provision that requires a predicate CERCLA liability. Section 113(f)(3) (B)'s opening clause separately ties itself to the CERCLA regime by permitting contribution after a party "has resolved its liability . . . for some or all of a *response action* or for some or all of the costs of *such action*." (Emphasis added.) Not only does the anchor provision also discuss allocation of "response costs," §113(f) (1), but the phrase "response action" is a familiar CERCLA phrase that appears dozens of times throughout the Act. *E.g.*, §101 (12 appearances); §107 (17 appearances).

To be sure, as the Government points out, remedial measures that a party takes under another environmental statute might resemble steps taken in a formal CERCLA "response action." But relying on that functional overlap to reinterpret the phrase "resolved its liability ... for some or all of a response action" to mean "settled an environmental liability that might have been actionable under CERCLA" would stretch the statute beyond Congress' actual language.

Perhaps more important, the Government's interpretation would place undue stress on the word "resolve." This term conveys certainty and finality. See Webster's Third New International Dictionary 1933 (1986) ("make clear or certain"); American Heritage Dictionary 1107 (1981) ("remove or dispel (doubts); . . . bring to a conclusion"). It would be rather odd to say that a party has "resolved its liability" if that party remains vulnerable to a CERCLA suit. All the more so given that it will not always be clear whether the substance of a prior environmental settlement was sufficiently similar to a quasi-CERCLA "response action." As even the Government admits, " 'response action' is, indeed, a broad term, [but] it is not an unlimited term [that covers] everything under the sun." Rather than requiring parties and courts to estimate whether a prior settlement was close enough to CERCLA, the far simpler approach is to ask whether a settlement expressly discharged a CERCLA liability.

No more persuasive are the United States' efforts to emphasize the differences among §113(f)'s provisions. The Government observes that §113(f)(3)(B)—unlike the §113(f)(1) anchor provision—does not expressly demand a predicate CERCLA action. That distinction, so the argument goes, implies that a broader range of environmental liabilities can trigger §113(f)(3)(B). But this effort to tear §113(f)(3)(B) away from its companions based on a negative implication falters in light of the other strong textual links among them. Section 113(f)(3)(B)'s use of the familiar phrase "response action," express cross-reference to another CERCLA provision, and placement in the statutory scheme prevent us from so easily severing it from the larger Act.

Similarly unavailing is the Government's theory that a tightly unified interpretation of these provisions would create surplusage problems. The United States argues, for example, that a reading of §113(f)(3)(B) that does nothing more than allow a party to seek contribution after settling a CERCLA liability would be redundant with §113(f)(1), which already permits contribution "during or following any civil action under [§§106 and 107]." But there is legitimate reason for separate provisions, even if both allow contribution only for a CERCLA liability. For example, §113(f)(3)(B) specifies the consequences of a particular type of resolution (*i.e.*, settlement), explaining that an "administrative or judicially approved settlement" is sufficient and reinforcing that a contribution claim will not extend to parties who have already settled. This sort of belt-and-suspenders approach hardly compels an all-encompassing reading of §113(f)(3)(B). Rather than try "to avoid surplusage at all costs," we interpret §113(f)(3)(B) in light of its text and place within a comprehensive statutory scheme.

* * *

The most natural reading of §113(f)(3)(B) is that a party may seek contribution under CERCLA only after settling a CERCLA-specific liability. We thus reverse the judgment of the Court of Appeals and remand the case for further proceedings consistent with this opinion.

It is so ordered.

THE IMPACT OF CERCLA ON STATE COMMON LAW REMEDIES

Nearly a century of pollution from the Anaconda Copper Smelter in Butte, Montana eventually rendered a vast swath of surrounding land a Superfund site to be cleaned up pursuant to the Comprehensive Environmental Response, Compensation, and Liability Act (CERCLA). Landowners near the site brought a state common law action against Atlantic Richfield Company (ARCO), the current site owner, for restoration damages and other claims. After a Montana state trial court granted the landowners' motion for summary judgment, ARCO sought review from the Supreme Court of Montana. The court held (1) landowners claim for restoration damages arose solely under state common law and did not challenge the CERCLA cleanup, and (2) that the landowners were not "potentially responsible parties" under CERCLA. ARCO then obtained review from the US Supreme Court where it argued that the landowners' common-law claim for restoration damages was a jurisdictionally barred "challenge" to the EPA's cleanup under 42 U.S.C. §9613 of CERCLA. ARCO argued that the landowners were "potentially responsible parties" who must seek EPA approval under 42 U.S.C. §9622(e)(6) of CERCLA before engaging in remedial action, even though the EPA has never ordered the landowners to pay for a cleanup, and that CERCLA preempts state common-law claims for restoration that seek cleanup remedies that may conflict with EPA-ordered remedies.

ATLANTIC RICHFIELD COMPANY v. CHRISTIAN
140 S.Ct. 1335 (2020)

CHIEF JUSTICE ROBERTS delivered the opinion of the Court.

For nearly a century, the Anaconda Copper Smelter in Butte, Montana contaminated an area of over 300 square miles with arsenic and lead. Over the past 35 years, the Environmental Protection Agency has worked with the current owner of the smelter, Atlantic Richfield Company, to implement a cleanup plan under the Comprehensive Environmental Response, Compensation, and Liability Act of 1980. EPA projects that the cleanup will continue through 2025.

A group of 98 landowners sued Atlantic Richfield in Montana state court for common law nuisance, trespass, and strict liability. Among other remedies, the landowners sought restoration damages, which under Montana law must be spent on rehabilitation of the property. The landowners' proposed restoration plan includes measures beyond those the agency found necessary to protect human health and the environment.

We consider whether the Act strips the Montana courts of jurisdiction over the landowners' claim for restoration damages and, if not, whether the Act requires the landowners to seek EPA approval for their restoration plan.

I

A

In 1980, Congress enacted the Comprehensive Environmental Response, Compensation, and Liability Act, U.S.C. §9601 *et seq.*, also known as the Superfund statute, to address "the serious environmental and health risks posed by industrial pollution." The Act seeks "to promote the timely cleanup of hazardous waste sites and to ensure that the costs of such cleanup efforts [are] borne by those responsible for the contamination."

The Act directs EPA to compile and annually revise a prioritized list of contaminated sites for cleanup, commonly known as Superfund sites. 42 U.S.C. §9605. EPA may clean those sites itself or compel responsible parties to perform the cleanup. §§9604, 9606, 9615. If the Government performs the cleanup, it may recover its costs from responsible parties. §9607(a)(4)(A). Responsible parties are jointly and severally liable for the full cost of the cleanup, but may seek contribution from other responsible parties. §9613(f)(1).

Prior to selecting a cleanup plan, EPA conducts (or orders a private party to conduct) a remedial investigation and feasibility study to assess the contamination and evaluate cleanup options. Section 122(e)(6) of the Act provides that, once the study begins, "no potentially responsible party may undertake any remedial action" at the site without EPA approval. 42 U.S.C. §9622(e)(6).

The Act prescribes extensive public consultation while a cleanup plan is being developed. It requires an opportunity for public notice and comment on proposed cleanup plans. §§9613(k), 9617. It requires "substantial and meaningful involvement by each State in initiation, development, and selection" of cleanup actions in that State. §9621(f)(1). And, in most instances, it requires that remedial action comply with "legally applicable or relevant and appropriate" requirements of state environmental law. §9621(d)(2)(A).

But once a plan is selected, the time for debate ends and the time for action begins. To insulate cleanup plans from collateral attack, §113(b) of the Act provides federal district courts with "exclusive original jurisdiction over all controversies arising under" the Act, and §113(h) then strips such courts of jurisdiction "to review any challenges to removal or remedial action," except in five limited circumstances. §§9613(b), (h).

B

Between 1884 and 1902, the Anaconda Copper Mining Company built three copper smelters 26 miles west of the mining town of Butte, Montana. The largest one, the Washoe Smelter, featured a 585-foot smoke stack, taller than the Washington Monument. The structure still towers over the area today, as part of the Anaconda Smoke Stack State Park. Together, the three smelters refined tens of millions of pounds of copper ore mined in Butte, the "Richest Hill on Earth," to feed burgeoning demand for telephone wires and power lines. "It was hot. It was dirty. It was dangerous. But it was a job for thousands." Dunlap, A Dangerous Job That Gave Life to a Town: A Look Back at the Anaconda Smelter, Montana Standard (Aug. 8, 2018). From 1912 to 1973, Anaconda Company payrolls totaled over $2.5 billion, compensating around three-quarters of Montana's work force.

Bust followed boom. By the 1970s, the falling price of copper, an ongoing energy crisis, and the nationalization of Anaconda's copper mines in Chile and Mexico squeezed Anaconda. But what others saw as an ailing relic, Atlantic Richfield saw as a turnaround opportunity, purchasing the Anaconda Company for the discount price of $700 million. Unfortunately, Atlantic Richfield was unable to revive Anaconda's fortunes. By 1980 Atlantic Richfield had closed the facility for good, and by 1984 Fortune had dubbed the purchase one of the "Decade's Worst Mergers."

Atlantic Richfield's troubles were just beginning. After Congress passed the Superfund statute in 1980, Atlantic Richfield faced strict and retroactive liability for the many tons of arsenic and lead that Anaconda had spewed across the area over the previous century. In 1983, EPA designated an area of more than 300 square miles around the smelters as one of the inaugural Superfund sites. In the 35 years since, EPA has managed an extensive cleanup at the site, working with Atlantic Richfield to remediate more than 800 residential and commercial properties; remove 10 million cubic yards of tailings, mine waste, and contaminated soil; cap in place 500 million cubic yards of waste over 5,000 acres; and reclaim 12,500 acres of land. To date, Atlantic Richfield estimates that it has spent roughly $450 million implementing EPA's orders. More work remains. As of 2015, EPA's plan anticipated cleanup of more than 1,000 additional residential yards, revegetation of 7,000 acres of uplands, removal of several waste areas, and closure of contaminated stream banks and railroad beds. EPA projects that remedial work will continue through 2025.

C

In 2008, a group of 98 owners of property within the Superfund site filed this lawsuit against Atlantic Richfield in Montana state court, asserting trespass, nuisance, and strict liability claims under state common law. The landowners sought restoration damages, among other forms of relief.

Under Montana law, property damages are generally measured by the "difference between the value of the property before and after the injury, or the diminution in value." But "when the damaged property serves as a private residence and the plaintiff has an interest in having the property restored, diminution in value will not return the plaintiff to the same position as before the tort." In that circumstance, the plaintiff may seek restoration damages, even if they exceed the property's diminution in value.

To collect restoration damages, a plaintiff must demonstrate that he has "reasons personal" for restoring the property and that his injury is temporary and abatable, meaning "[t]he ability to repair [the] injury must be more than a theoretical possibility." The injured party must "establish that the award actually will be used for restoration."

The landowners here propose a restoration plan that goes beyond EPA's own cleanup plan, which the agency had found "protective of human health and the environment." For example, the landowners propose a maximum soil contamination level of 15 parts per million of arsenic, rather than the 250 parts per million level set by EPA. And the landowners seek to excavate offending soil within residential yards to a depth of two feet rather than EPA's chosen depth of one. The landowners also seek to capture and treat shallow groundwater through an 8,000-foot long, 15-foot deep, and 3-foot wide underground permeable barrier, a plan the agency rejected as costly and unnecessary to secure safe drinking water.

The landowners estimate that their cleanup would cost Atlantic Richfield $50 to $58 million. Atlantic Richfield would place that amount in a trust and the trustee would release funds only for restoration work.

In the trial court, Atlantic Richfield and the landowners filed competing motions for summary judgment on whether the Act precluded the landowners' claim for restoration damages.[6] The court granted judgment for the landowners on that issue and allowed the lawsuit to continue. After granting a writ of supervisory control, the Montana Supreme Court affirmed.

The Montana Supreme Court rejected Atlantic Richfield's argument that §113 stripped the Montana courts of jurisdiction over the landowners' claim for restoration damages. The court recognized that §113 strips federal courts (and, it was willing to assume, state courts) of jurisdiction to review challenges to EPA cleanup plans. But the Montana Supreme Court reasoned that the landowners' plan was not such a challenge because it would not "stop, delay, or change the work EPA is doing." The landowners were "simply asking to be allowed to present their own plan to restore their own private property to a jury of twelve Montanans who will then assess the merits of that plan."

The Montana Supreme Court also rejected Atlantic Richfield's argument that the landowners were potentially responsible parties (sometimes called PRPs) prohibited from taking remedial action without EPA approval under §122(e)(6) of the Act. The Court observed that the landowners had "never been treated as PRPs for any purpose — by either EPA or [Atlantic Richfield] — during the entire thirty-plus years" since the designation of the Superfund site, and that the statute of limitations for a claim against the landowners had run. "Put simply, the PRP horse left the barn decades ago."

Justice Baker concurred, stressing that on remand Atlantic Richfield could potentially defeat the request for restoration damages on the merits by proving that the restoration plan conflicted with EPA's cleanup plan. Justice McKinnon dissented. She argued that the landowners' restoration plan did conflict with the Superfund cleanup and thus constituted a challenge under §113(h) of the Act, over which Montana courts lacked jurisdiction.

We granted certiorari. 587 U. S. ___ (2019).

---

[6] Atlantic Richfield concedes that the Act preserves the landowners' claims for other types of compensatory damages under Montana law, including loss of use and enjoyment of property, diminution of value, incidental and consequential damages, and annoyance and discomfort. We therefore consider only the landowners' claim for restoration damages.

II

We begin with two threshold questions: whether this Court has jurisdiction to review the decision of the Montana Supreme Court and, if so, whether the Montana courts have jurisdiction over the landowners' claim for restoration damages.

A

Congress has authorized this Court to review "[f]inal judgments or decrees rendered by the highest court of a State." 28 U.S.C. §1257(a). To qualify as final, a state court judgment must be "an effective determination of the litigation and not of merely interlocutory or intermediate steps therein." The landowners contend that, because the Montana Supreme Court allowed the case to proceed to trial, its judgment was not final and we lack jurisdiction.

But the Montana Supreme Court exercised review in this case through a writ of supervisory control. Under Montana law, a supervisory writ proceeding is a self-contained case, not an interlocutory appeal. Thus we have held that a "writ of supervisory control issued by the Montana Supreme Court is a final judgment within our jurisdiction."

The landowners protest that our precedents only support reviewing supervisory writ proceedings that are limited to jurisdictional questions. But the scope of our jurisdiction to review supervisory writ proceedings is not so restricted. When the Montana Supreme Court issues a writ of supervisory control, it initiates a separate lawsuit. It is the nature of the Montana proceeding, not the issues the state court reviewed, that establishes our jurisdiction.

B

We likewise find that the Act does not strip the Montana courts of jurisdiction over this lawsuit. It deprives state courts of jurisdiction over claims brought under the Act. But it does not displace state court jurisdiction over claims brought under other sources of law.

Section 113(b) of the Act provides that "the United States district courts shall have exclusive original jurisdiction over all controversies arising under this chapter," so state courts lack jurisdiction over such actions. This case, however, does not "arise under" the Act. The use of "arising under" in §113(b) echoes Congress's more familiar use of that phrase in granting federal courts jurisdiction over "all civil actions arising under the Constitution, laws, or treaties of the United States." 28 U.S.C. §1331. In the mine run of cases, "[a] suit arises under the law that creates the cause of action." The landowners' common law claims for nuisance, trespass, and strict liability therefore arise under Montana law and not under the Act. As a result, the Montana courts retain jurisdiction over this lawsuit, notwithstanding the channeling of Superfund claims to federal courts in §113(b). . . .

Atlantic Richfield takes a different view, arguing that §113(h) implicitly broadens the scope of actions precluded from state court jurisdiction under §113(b). Section 113(h) states that "[n]o Federal court shall have jurisdiction under Federal law other than under section 1332 of title 28 (relating to diversity of citizenship jurisdiction) . . . to review any challenges to removal or remedial action" selected under the Act. 42 U.S.C. §9613(h).

The company's argument proceeds in five steps. Step one: Section 113(h) removes federal court jurisdiction over all cleanup challenges, regardless of whether they originate in federal or state law (except for when the court is sitting in diversity). Step two: Section 113(h) can only remove jurisdiction that §113(b) provides in the first place. Step three: Section 113(b) thus provides federal courts jurisdiction over all cleanup challenges, whether brought under federal or state law. Step four: The grant of jurisdiction to federal courts in §113(b) is exclusive to federal courts. Step five: State courts thus do not have jurisdiction over cleanup challenges.

This interpretation faces several insurmountable obstacles. First, by its own terms, §113(h) speaks of "Federal court[s]," not state courts. There is no textual basis for Atlantic Richfield's argument that Congress precluded *state* courts from hearing a category of cases in §113(b) by stripping *federal* courts of jurisdiction over those cases in §113(h). And if that were Congress's goal, it would be hard to imagine a more oblique way of achieving it. Often the simplest explanation is the best: Section 113(b) deprives state courts of jurisdiction over cases "arising under" the Act — just as it says — while §113(h) deprives federal courts of jurisdiction over certain "challenges" to Superfund remedial actions — just as it says.

Second, the company's argument does not account for the exception in §113(h) for federal courts sitting in diversity. Section 113(h) permits federal courts in diversity cases to entertain state law claims regardless of whether they are challenges to cleanup plans. Atlantic Richfield does not even try to explain why the

Act would permit such state law claims to proceed in federal court, but not in state court. The Act permits federal courts and state courts alike to entertain state law claims, including challenges to cleanups.

That leads us to the third difficulty with Atlantic Richfield's argument. We have recognized a "deeply rooted presumption in favor of concurrent state court jurisdiction" over federal claims. Only an "explicit statutory directive," an "unmistakable implication from legislative history," or "a clear incompatibility between state-court jurisdiction and federal interests" can displace this presumption. Explicit, unmistakable, and clear are not words that describe Atlantic Richfield's knotty interpretation of §§113(b) and (h).

It would be one thing for Atlantic Richfield to try to surmount the clear statement rule that applies to the uncommon, but not unprecedented, step of stripping state courts of jurisdiction over *federal* claims. But Atlantic Richfield's position requires a more ambitious step: Congress stripping state courts of jurisdiction to hear their own *state* claims. We would not expect Congress to take such an extraordinary step by implication. Yet the only provision Atlantic Richfield invokes addresses "[f]ederal court[s]" without even mentioning state courts, let alone stripping those courts of jurisdiction to hear state law claims. 42 U.S.C. §9613(h).

Finally, the Government, supporting Atlantic Richfield, emphasizes that the opening clause of §113(b) excepts §113(h) from its application. See 42 U.S.C. §9613(b) ("Except as provided in subsections (a) and (h) of this section . . . ."). According to the Government, because "exceptions must by definition be narrower than the corresponding rule," all challenges to remedial plans under §113(h) — whether based in federal or state law — must "arise under" the Act for purposes of §113(b).

We reject the premise and with it the conclusion. "Thousands of statutory provisions use the phrase 'except as provided in . . . ' followed by a cross-reference in order to indicate that one rule should prevail over another in any circumstance in which the two conflict." Such clauses explain what happens in the case of a clash, but they do not otherwise expand or contract the scope of either provision by implication.

The actions referred to in §113(h) do not fall entirely within §113(b). Challenges to remedial actions under federal statutes other than the Act, for example, are precluded by §113(h) but do not fall within §113(b). To cite another example, §113(h) addresses state law challenges to cleanup plans in federal court, although those actions also do not fall within §113(b). At the same time, §113(b) is not subsumed by §113(h). Many claims brought under the Act, such as those to recover cleanup costs under §107, are not challenges to cleanup plans.

Sections 113(b) and 113(h) thus each do work independent of one another. The two provisions overlap in a particular type of case: challenges to cleanup plans in federal court that arise under the Act. In such cases, the exceptions clause in §113(b) instructs that the limitation of §113(h) prevails. It does nothing more.

III

Although the Montana Supreme Court answered the jurisdictional question correctly, the Court erred by holding that the landowners were not potentially responsible parties under the Act and therefore did not need EPA approval to take remedial action. Section 122(e)(6), titled "Inconsistent response action," provides that "[w]hen either the President, or a potentially responsible party . . . has initiated a remedial investigation and feasibility study for a particular facility under this chapter, no potentially responsible party may undertake any remedial action at the facility unless such remedial action has been authorized by the President." 42 U.S.C. §9622(e)(6). Both parties agree that this provision would require the landowners to obtain EPA approval for their restoration plan if the landowners qualify as potentially responsible parties.

To determine who is a potentially responsible party, we look to the list of "covered persons" in §107, the liability section of the Act. §9607(a). "Section 107(a) lists four classes of potentially responsible persons (PRPs) and provides that they 'shall be liable' for, among other things, 'all costs of removal or remedial action incurred by the United States Government.'" The first category under §107(a) includes any "owner" of "a facility." §9607(a)(1). "Facility" is defined to include "any site or area where a hazardous substance has been deposited, stored, disposed of, or placed, or otherwise come to be located." §9601(9)(B). Arsenic and lead are hazardous substances. Because those pollutants have "come to be located" on the landowners' properties, the landowners are potentially responsible parties.

The landowners and JUSTICE GORSUCH argue that even if the landowners were once potentially responsible parties, they are no longer because the Act's six-year limitations period for recovery of remedial costs has run, and thus they could not be held liable in a hypothetical lawsuit. 42 U.S.C. §9613(g)(2)(B).

This argument collapses status as a potentially responsible party with liability for the payment of response costs. A property owner can be a potentially responsible party even if he is no longer subject to suit in court. As we have said, "[E]ven parties not responsible for contamination may fall within the broad definitions of PRPs in §§107(a)(1)–(4)." That includes " 'innocent' . . . landowner[s] whose land has been contaminated by another," who would be shielded from liability by the Act's so-called "innocent landowner" or "third party" defense in §107(b)(3). The same principle holds true for parties that face no liability because of the Act's limitations period.

Interpreting "potentially responsible parties" to include owners of polluted property reflects the Act's objective to develop, as its name suggests, a "Comprehensive Environmental Response" to hazardous waste pollution. Section 122(e)(6) is one of several tools in the Act that ensure the careful development of a single EPA-led cleanup effort rather than tens of thousands of competing individual ones.

Yet under the landowners' interpretation, property owners would be free to dig up arsenic-infected soil and build trenches to redirect lead-contaminated groundwater without even notifying EPA, so long as they have not been sued within six years of commencement of the cleanup.[7] We doubt Congress provided such a fragile remedy for such a serious problem. And we suspect most other landowners would not be too pleased if Congress required EPA to sue each and every one of them just to ensure an orderly cleanup of toxic waste in their neighborhood. A straightforward reading of the text avoids such anomalies.

JUSTICE GORSUCH argues that equating "potentially responsible parties" with "covered persons" overlooks the fact that the terms "use different language, appear in different statutory sections, and address different matters." He contends that "potentially responsible party" as used in §122(e)(6) should be read as limited to the settlement context, and that if Congress intended the phrase to have broader reach — to refer more generally to those potentially liable under §107(a) — then Congress would have used the term "covered person."

But there is no reason to think Congress used these phrases to refer to two distinct groups of persons. Neither phrase appears among the Act's list of over 50 defined terms. 42 U.S.C. §9601. "Covered persons," in fact, appears in the caption to §107(a) and nowhere else. Meanwhile, "potentially responsible parties" are referenced not just in the section on settlements, but also in the Act's sections regarding EPA response authority, cleanup standards and procedures, cleanup contractors, Superfund moneys, Federal Government cleanup sites, and civil proceedings. §§9604, 9605, 9611, 9613, 9619, 9620, 9622. Across the statute "potentially responsible parties" refers to what it says: parties that may be held accountable for hazardous waste in particular circumstances. The only place in the Act that identifies such persons is the list of "Covered persons" in §107(a). Congress therefore must have intended "potentially responsible party" in §122(e)(6) (as elsewhere in the Act) to refer to "Covered persons" in §107(a).

Turning from text to consequences, the landowners warn that our interpretation of §122(e)(6) creates a permanent easement on their land, forever requiring them "to get permission from EPA in Washington if they want to dig out part of their backyard to put in a sandbox for their grandchildren." Tr. of Oral Arg. 62. The grandchildren of Montana can rest easy: The Act does nothing of the sort.

Section 122(e)(6) refers only to "remedial action," a defined term in the Act encompassing technical actions like "storage, confinement, perimeter protection using dikes, trenches, or ditches, clay cover, neutralization, cleanup of released hazardous substances and associated contaminated materials," and so forth. 42 U.S.C. §9601(24). While broad, the Act's definition of remedial action does not reach so far as to cover planting a garden, installing a lawn sprinkler, or digging a sandbox. In addition, §122(e)(6) applies only to sites on the Superfund list. The Act requires EPA to annually review and reissue that list. §9605(a)(8)(B). EPA delists Superfund sites once responsible parties have taken all appropriate remedial action and the pollutant no longer poses a significant threat to public health or the environment.

The landowners and JUSTICE GORSUCH alternatively argue that the landowners are not potentially responsible parties because they did not receive the notice of settlement negotiations required by §122(e)(1). Under a policy dating back to 1991, EPA does not seek to recover costs from residential landowners who are not responsible for contamination and do not interfere with the agency's remedy. EPA, Policy Towards Owners of Residential Property at Superfund Sites, OSWER Directive #9834.6 (July 3, 1991), https://www.epa.gov/sites/production/files/documents/policy-owner-rpt.pdf. EPA views this policy as an exercise of its "enforcement discretion in pursuing potentially responsible parties." Because EPA has a policy of not suing innocent homeowners for pollution they did not cause, it did not include the landowners in settlement negotiations.

But EPA's nonenforcement policy does not alter the landowners' status as potentially responsible parties. Section 107(a) unambiguously defines potentially responsible parties and EPA does not have authority to alter that definition. Section 122(e)(1) requires notification of settlement negotiations to all potentially responsible parties. To say that provision determines who is a potentially responsible party in the first instance would render the Act circular. Even the Government does not claim that its decisions whether to send notices of settlement negotiations carry such authority.

---

[7] EPA does have other tools to address serious environmental harm. Under §106, for example, EPA can initiate an injunctive abatement action if it finds an "imminent and substantial endangerment to the public health or welfare or the environment." 42 U.S.C. §9606(a). But EPA may have good reasons to preserve the status quo of a cleanup site even absent an imminent threat. More importantly, the landowners' interpretation would require EPA to monitor tens of thousands of properties across 1,335 Superfund sites nationwide to ensure landowners do not derail an EPA cleanup. EPA, Superfund: National Priorities List (NPL) (Apr. 13, 2020), https://www.epa.gov/superfund/superfund-national-priorities-list-npl. Congress provided a far more effective and efficient solution in §122(e) (6): Landowners at Superfund sites containing hazardous waste must seek EPA approval before initiating their own bespoke cleanups.

In short, even if EPA ran afoul of §122(e)(1) by not providing the landowners notice of settlement negotiations, that does not change the landowners' status as potentially responsible parties.

The landowners relatedly argue that the limitation in §122(e)(6) on remedial action by potentially responsible parties cannot carry the weight we assign to it because it is located in the Act's section on settlement negotiations. Congress, we are reminded, does not "hide elephants in mouseholes."

We take no issue with characterizing §122(e)(6) as an elephant. It is, after all, one of the Act's crucial tools for ensuring an orderly cleanup of toxic waste. But §122 of the Act is, at the risk of the tired metaphor spinning out of control, less a mousehole and more a watering hole — exactly the sort of place we would expect to find this elephant.

Settlements are the heart of the Superfund statute. EPA's efforts to negotiate settlement agreements and issue orders for cleanups account for approximately 69% of all cleanup work currently underway. The Act commands EPA to proceed by settlement "[w]henever practicable and in the public interest . . . in order to expedite effective remedial actions and minimize litigation." 42 U.S.C. §9622(a). EPA, for its part, "prefers to reach an agreement with a potentially responsible party (PRP) to clean up a Superfund site instead of issuing an order or paying for it and recovering the cleanup costs later." The Act encourages potentially responsible parties to enter into such agreements by authorizing EPA to include a "covenant not to sue," which caps the parties' liability to the Government. §9622(c)(1). The Act also protects settling parties from contribution claims by other potentially responsible parties. §9613(f)(2). Once finalized, the terms of a settlement become legally binding administrative orders, subject to civil penalties of up to $25,000 a day. §§9609(a)(1)(E), 9622(*l*). Moreover, subsection (e) is an important component of §122. It establishes a reticulated scheme of notices, proposals, and counterproposals for the settlement negotiation process. §9622(e). And the subsection places a moratorium on EPA remedial actions while negotiations are under way. §9622(e)(2)(A). It is far from surprising to find an analogous provision restricting potentially responsible parties from taking remedial actions in the same subsection.

JUSTICE GORSUCH also contends that our interpretation violates the Act's "saving clauses," which provide that the Act does not preempt liability or requirements under state law. But we have long rejected interpretations of sweeping saving clauses that prove "absolutely inconsistent with the provisions of the act" in which they are found. Interpreting the Act's saving clauses to erase the clear mandate of §122(e)(6) would allow the Act "to destroy itself."

What is more, Atlantic Richfield remains potentially liable under state law for compensatory damages, including loss of use and enjoyment of property, diminution of value, incidental and consequential damages, and annoyance and discomfort. The damages issue before the Court is whether Atlantic Richfield is also liable for the landowners' own remediation beyond that required under the Act. Even then, the answer is yes — so long as the landowners first obtain EPA approval for the remedial work they seek to carry out.

We likewise resist JUSTICE GORSUCH's evocative claim that our reading of the Act endorses "paternalistic central planning" and turns a cold shoulder to "state law efforts to restore state lands." Such a charge fails to appreciate that cleanup plans generally must comply with "legally applicable or relevant and appropriate" standards of state environmental law. 42 U.S.C. §9621(d)(2)(A)(ii). Or that States must be afforded opportunities for "substantial and meaningful involvement" in initiating, developing, and selecting cleanup plans. §9621(f)(1). Or that EPA usually must defer initiating a cleanup at a contaminated site that a State is already remediating. §9605(h). It is not "paternalistic central planning" but instead the "spirit of cooperative federalism [that] run[s] throughout CERCLA and its regulations."

As a last ditch effort, the landowners contend that, even if §107(a) defines potentially responsible parties, they qualify as contiguous property owners under §107(q), which would pull them outside the scope of §107(a). The landowners are correct that contiguous property owners are not potentially responsible parties. Section 107(q)(1)(A) provides that "[a] person that owns real property that is contiguous to or otherwise similarly situated with respect to, and that is or may be contaminated by a release or threatened release of a hazardous substance from, real property that is not owned by that person shall not be considered" an owner of a facility under §107(a). §9607(q)(1)(A). The problem for the landowners is that there are eight further requirements to qualify as a contiguous property owner. §§9607(q)(1)(A)(i)– (viii). Each landowner individually must "establish by a preponderance of the evidence" that he satisfies the criteria. §9607(q)(1)(B).

The landowners cannot clear this high bar. One of the eight requirements is that, at the time the person acquired the property, the person "did not know or have reason to know that the property was or could be contaminated by a release or threatened release of one or more hazardous substances." §9607(q)(1)(A)(viii)(II). All of the landowners here purchased their property after the Anaconda Company built the Washington Monument sized smelter. Indeed "evidence of public knowledge" of contamination was "almost overwhelming." In the early 1900s, the Anaconda Company actually obtained smoke and tailing easements authorizing the disposition of smelter waste onto many properties now owned by the landowners. The landowners had reason to know their property "could be contaminated by a release or threatened release" of a hazardous substance. 42 U.S.C. §9607(q)(1)(A)(viii)(II).

At any rate, contiguous landowners must provide "full cooperation, assistance, and access" to EPA and those carrying out Superfund cleanups in order to maintain that status. §9607(q)(1)(A)(iv). But the Government has represented that the landowners' restoration plan, if implemented, would interfere with its cleanup by, for example, digging up contaminated soil that has been deliberately capped in place. If that is true, the landowners' plan would soon trigger a lack of cooperation between EPA and the landowners. At that point, the landowners would no longer qualify as contiguous landowners and we would be back to square one.

* * *

The Montana Supreme Court erred in holding that the landowners were not potentially responsible parties under §122(e)(6) and therefore did not need to seek EPA approval. Montana law requires that "an award of restoration damages actually . . . be used to repair the damaged property." But such action cannot be taken in the absence of EPA approval. That approval process, if pursued, could ameliorate any conflict between the landowners' restoration plan and EPA's Superfund cleanup, just as Congress envisioned. In the absence of EPA approval of the current restoration plan, we have no occasion to entertain Atlantic Richfield's claim that the Act otherwise preempts the plan.

The judgment of the Montana Supreme Court is affirmed in part and vacated in part. The case is remanded for further proceedings not inconsistent with this opinion.

It is so ordered.

JUSTICE ALITO, concurring in part and dissenting in part.

I agree with the Court that the judgment below must be reversed, and I join all of the Court's opinion except Part II–B. I thus agree with the Court that we possess jurisdiction to decide this case. I also agree that the landowners are potentially responsible parties under §122(e)(6) of the Comprehensive Environmental Response, Compensation, and Liability Act of 1980 (CERCLA) and, as a result, cannot bring their Montana restoration damages claim without the consent of the Environmental Protection Agency (EPA). At this point, however, I am not willing to endorse the Court's holding in Part II–B that state courts have jurisdiction to entertain "challenges" to EPA-approved CERCLA plans.

I

I would not decide that question because it is neither necessary nor prudent for us to do so. As I understand the Court's opinion, the Montana Supreme Court has two options on remand: (1) enter a stay to allow the landowners to seek EPA approval or (2) enter judgment against the landowners on their restoration damages claim without prejudice to their ability to refile if they obtain EPA approval. Either way, the case cannot proceed without the EPA's blessing. And because the EPA has submitted multiple filings indicating that it believes that the landowners' plan presents serious environmental risks, it is likely that the EPA will not approve that plan, and the case will then die. If that happens, the question of the state courts' jurisdiction will be academic.

Alternatively, if the EPA approves the landowners' plan, either in full or to a degree that they find satisfactory, they may not wish to press this litigation. And if they do choose to go forward, the question of state-court jurisdiction can be decided at that time.

For these reasons, there is no need to reach out and decide the question now,[1] and there are good reasons not to do so. While the question of state-court jurisdiction may turn out not to matter in this case, that question may have important implications in other cases. Specifically, if the fears expressed by the Government materialize, state courts and juries, eager to serve local interests, may disregard the EPA's expert judgment regarding the best plan for a CERCLA site and may mandate relief that exacerbates environmental problems. Thus, much is potentially at stake, and the question whether CERCLA allows state courts to entertain suits like the one in this case depends on the interpretation of devilishly difficult statutory provisions, CERCLA §§113(b) and (h), 42 U.S.C. §§9613(b) and (h).

With much at stake, we should be confident that our answer is correct, and we have no basis for such confidence here. The question of state-court jurisdiction is only one of many in this case, and the briefing and argument on that issue left important questions without fully satisfactory answers. The Court tries to clear up what §113 means, but as I will attempt to show, the Court's interpretation presents serious problems. Under these circumstances, the better course is not to decide this perplexing question at this juncture.

II

A

CERCLA §113 is like a puzzle with pieces that are exceedingly difficult, if not impossible, to fit together. Here is what these provisions say, with language that is not pertinent for present purposes omitted:

> "(b) Jurisdiction; venue
> "Except as provided in subsectio [n] . . . (h) of this section [and another provision not relevant for present purposes], the United States district courts shall have exclusive original jurisdiction over all controversies arising under this chapter, without regard to the citizenship of the parties or the amount in controversy. . . .
>
> . . .
> "(h) Timing of review
> "No Federal court shall have jurisdiction under Federal law other than under section 1332 of title 28 (relating to diversity of citizenship jurisdiction) or under State law which is applicable or relevant and appropriate under section 9621 of this title [CERCLA §121, 42 U.S.C. §9621] (relating to cleanup standards) to review any challenges to removal or remedial action selected under section 9604 of this title, or to review any order issued under section 9606(a) of this title [concerning emergency measures ordered by the President], in any action except one of [a list of specific CERCLA provisions]." 42 U.S.C. §9613.

For present purposes, the pertinent parts are as follows:

- First, §113(b) sets out a general rule conferring on the federal district courts exclusive jurisdiction over claims "arising under" CERCLA. And it does so "without regard to the citizenship of the parties or the amount in controversy."
- Second, §§113(b) and (h), taken together, reduce this grant of jurisdiction by taking away jurisdiction over *most* claims that "challeng[e]" a "removal or remedial action."
- Third, this reduction does not apply to a challenge to removal or remedial action if it is brought under the diversity jurisdiction statute, 28 U.S.C. §1332.
- Fourth, this reduction also does not apply to a challenge to removal or remedial action if it is brought in federal court "under State law which is applicable or relevant and appropriate under [§121] (relating to cleanup standards)." Under §121, cleanup standards must comply with certain state-law requirements, and thus the thrust of this last provision seems to be that a removal or remedial action may be challenged in federal court for noncompliance with such requirements.

With these pieces laid out, we may consider how the Court and respondents, on the one hand, and the Government and petitioner, on the other, try to fit them together.

B

The logical first step in any effort to understand how §§113(b) and (h) apply to the landowners' state-law restoration damages claim is to determine whether the claim falls within the scope of the exclusive jurisdiction that §113(b) confers on the federal district courts — in other words, whether such a claim is one that "aris[es] under" CERCLA. If it does not, then that ends the inquiry. And that is what the Court holds. *Ante*, at 8–9.

The Court interprets the phrase "arising under" in §113(b) to mean the same thing as that phrase means in the federal-question jurisdiction statute, 28 U.S.C. §1331. Under that provision, as the Court puts it, "[i]n the mine run of cases, '[a] suit arises under the law that creates the cause of action.'" *Ante*, at 9 (quoting *American Well Works Co.* v. *Layne & Bowler Co.*, 241 U. S. 257, 260 (1916)). Thus, the Court concludes, a claim arises under CERCLA only if it is based on CERCLA, and since the landowners' restoration damages claim is based on Montana law, it is obviously not based on CERCLA and does not fall within the exclusive jurisdiction conferred on the district courts by §113(b). This makes short work of the question of state-court jurisdiction, but it presents serious problems.

First, it cannot explain why §113(b) says that the jurisdiction it confers is "without regard to the citizenship of the parties or the amount in controversy." If that jurisdiction is limited to claims that are based on CERCLA, district courts have jurisdiction to entertain all those claims under 28 U.S.C. §1331, which does not require either diversity or any minimum amount in controversy. So why go out of the way to say that §113(b) jurisdiction does not require diversity or any minimum amount in controversy? The only logical reason is to ensure that the provision covers suits that *could not be brought under 28 U.S.C. §1331.* Thus, §113(b) jurisdiction must be broader than general federal-question jurisdiction. By denying this, the Court's interpretation turns the phrase "without regard to the citizenship of the parties or the amount in controversy" into a meaningless and useless appendage.

Second, under the Court's interpretation, there is no reason why §113(h) should specify that its reduction of the scope of the jurisdiction conferred by §113(b) does not affect a district court's jurisdiction in diversity cases. If the jurisdiction granted by §113(b) is limited to claims based on CERCLA, why would anyone think that it had any impact on state-law claims?

Third, if the jurisdiction conferred by §113(b) is limited to claims based on CERCLA, it is unclear how a district court could entertain a claim "under State law which is applicable or relevant and appropriate under [§121] (relating to cleanup standards)." Yet §113(h) exempts such a claim from its general withdrawal of jurisdiction over challenges to removal or remedial action. It seems clear that Congress did not regard these claims as claims under CERCLA itself, since it describes them as "under State law" and did not include them on the list of claims under CERCLA that it likewise exempted from §113(h)'s general withdrawal of jurisdiction over challenges to removal or remedial action. §§113(h)(1)–(5). These three problems raise serious doubt about the correctness of the Court's interpretation.

C

The Government and petitioner advance a different interpretation of §§113(b) and (h), and although this interpretation solves the problems noted above, it has problems of its own. The Court, as noted, runs into trouble by interpreting the phrase "arising under" CERCLA in §113(b) to mean what "arising under" means in 28 U.S.C. §1331. The Government obviates this difficulty by arguing that "arising under" in §113(b) has a broader meaning, such as the meaning of the same phrase in Article III of the Constitution. Government suggests that "arising under" in §113(b) may reach " 'any case or controversy that might call for the application of federal law.'" If §113(b) uses the phrase in something like this sense, the jurisdiction it confers can reach some claims under state law, and that would explain §113(b)'s specification that this jurisdiction is not dependent on either diversity or amount in controversy. In other words, this language makes clear that federal district courts have jurisdiction to hear these state-law claims without the restrictions that usually apply when federal courts entertain such claims.

Up to this point, the interpretation favored by the Government and petitioner proceeds smoothly, but it stumbles when it moves from §113(b) to §113(h). That provision reduces the grant of jurisdiction in §113(b) by taking away jurisdiction over challenges to removal and remedial action unless, among other things, those claims are brought in a diversity action. The upshot is that federal district courts are left with jurisdiction over most state-law claims that challenge removal and remedial action only where the parties are diverse. If it turns out that diversity is lacking, the district courts cannot entertain the same claims. And not only that. Because §113(b)'s grant of jurisdiction to the federal district courts is exclusive, the state courts cannot entertain those claims either.

It is hard to fathom why Congress might have wanted such a scheme. Congress might have wanted all the state-law claims covered by §113(b) to be heard exclusively in federal court in order to prevent state courts and juries from unduly favoring home-state interests. But having granted the federal district courts jurisdiction to hear these claims in §113(b), why would Congress take away that jurisdiction in cases where the parties happen not to be diverse? And why would Congress go further and prevent the state courts from hearing these claims? The Government and petitioner provide no answer, and none is apparent. . . .

* * *

Section 113 may simply be a piece of very bad draftsmanship, with pieces that cannot be made to fit together. Or it may be a puzzle with a solution that neither the parties, the Court, nor I have been able to solve. In a later case, briefing and argument may provide answers that have thus far eluded us. Since we are not required to attempt an answer in this case, the prudent course is to hold back.

JUSTICE GORSUCH, with whom JUSTICE THOMAS joins, concurring in part and dissenting in part.
For nearly a century, Atlantic Richfield's predecessor operated a smelter near the town of Opportunity, Montana. At one time, the smelter produced much of the Nation's copper supply and served as the State's

largest employer. Eventually, though, it became apparent the smelter was producing more than just copper and jobs. Studies showed that the plant emitted up to 62 tons of arsenic and 10 tons of lead each day. Thanks to what was once the world's tallest brick smokestack, these heavy metals blanketed the town and the whole of the Deer Lodge Valley — contaminating hundreds of square miles. Today, the smokestack is all that is left of the once massive operation. It stands alone in a state park, much of which remains dangerously contaminated and closed to the public. Visitors may view the stack, but only from a distance, through fences and between huge slag piles.

This case involves nearly 100 nearby residents. Some have lived in their homes for decades, some long before the environmental consequences of the smelter were fully appreciated. They say they have thought about moving, but for many their property values aren't what they once were. Besides, as one homeowner put it, "I couldn't find a kitchen door that's got all my kids' heights on it."

The federal government has tried to help in its own way. In 1983, the government designated the 300-square-mile area surrounding the smelter a Superfund site under the Comprehensive Environmental Response, Compensation, and Liability Act of 1980 (CERCLA). After years of study and negotiation, the government ordered Atlantic Richfield to remove up to 18 inches of soil in residential yards with arsenic levels exceeding 250 parts per million (ppm). For so-called "pasture land" — that is, nearly everything else — the government set the threshold for soil removal at 1,000 ppm. By way of reference, even 100 ppm is sometimes considered too toxic for local landfills, and the federal government itself has elsewhere set a threshold of 25 ppm. Some States set residential cleanup levels as low as 0.04 ppm.

The cleanup work that followed left much to be desired. By 2016, Atlantic Richfield claimed that it had virtually finished work on the landowners' properties. Yet, only 24 of their 77 properties had been remediated, and only about 5 percent of the total acreage had been touched. Soil near Tammy Peters's daycare playground, for example, still shows an arsenic level of 292 ppm. But because the "weighted average" for her yard is below 250 ppm, Atlantic Richfield performed no cleanup of the playground at all.

So the landowners here proceeded as landowners historically have: They sought remedies for the pollution on their lands in state court under state law. Their choice can come as no surprise. The federal government enjoys no general power to regulate private lands; it may intervene only consistent with the Commerce Clause or some other constitutionally enumerated power. Nor does the federal government always intervene as fully as it might even when it can. Meanwhile, the regulation of real property and the protection of natural resources is a traditional and central responsibility of state governments. And States have long allowed landowners to seek redress for the pollution of their lands through ancient common law causes of action like nuisance and trespass. The landowners employed exactly these theories when they brought suit in state court seeking restoration damages from Atlantic Richfield — money that could be used only to remove arsenic, lead, and other toxins from their properties. The Montana Supreme Court has held that the landowners' case states a viable claim for relief and warrants trial.

Now, however, Atlantic Richfield wants us to call a halt to the proceedings. The company insists that CERCLA preempts and prohibits common law tort suits like this one. On Atlantic Richfield's telling, CERCLA even prevents private landowners from voluntarily remediating their own properties at their own expense. No one may do anything in 300 square miles of Montana, the company insists, without first securing the federal government's permission.

But what in the law commands that result? Everything in CERCLA suggests that it seeks to supplement, not supplant, traditional state law remedies and promote, not prohibit, efforts to restore contaminated land. Congress hardly could have been clearer. It stated that, "[n]othing in this [Act] shall be construed or interpreted as preempting any State from imposing any additional liability or requirements with respect to the release of hazardous substances within such State." 42 U.S.C. §9614(a). It added that "[n]othing in this [Act] shall affect or modify in any way the obligations or liabilities of any person under other Federal or State law, including common law, with respect to releases of hazardous substances or other pollutants or contaminants." §9652(d). And it said again that "[t]his [Act] does not affect or otherwise impair the rights of any person under Federal, State, or common law, except with respect to the timing of review as provided" elsewhere in provisions that even the Court today does not invoke as limits on recovery here. §9659(h). Three times Congress made its point as plainly as anyone might.

So how does Atlantic Richfield seek to transform CERCLA from a tool to aid cleanups into a ban on them? The company has to point to *something* in the statutory text that trumps these many provisions and preempts the landowners' right to use state law to restore their lands. After all, merely "[i]nvoking some brooding federal interest or appealing to a judicial policy preference should never be enough to win preemption of a state law"; instead, a party like Atlantic Richfield seeking to displace state law must identify " 'a constitutional text or a federal statute' that does the displacing."

In answer, Atlantic Richfield directs our attention to §122(e)(6). It's a provision buried in a section captioned "Settlements." The section outlines the process private parties must follow to negotiate a settlement and release of CERCLA liability with the federal government. Subsection (e)(6) bears the title "Inconsistent response action" and states that, "[w]hen either the President, or a potentially responsible party pursuant to an administrative order or consent decree under this chapter, has initiated a remedial investigation and feasibility study for a particular facility under this chapter, no potentially responsible party may undertake any remedial action at the facility unless such remedial action has been authorized by the President." 42 U.S.C. §9622(e)(6). So even read for all its worth, this provision only bars those "potentially responsible" to the federal government from initiating cleanup efforts without prior approval. To get where it needs to go, Atlantic Richfield must find some way to label the innocent landowners here "potentially responsible part[ies]" on the hook for cleanup duties with the federal government.

They are hardly that. When interpreting a statute, this Court applies the law's ordinary public meaning at the time of the statute's adoption, here 1980. To be "potentially responsible" for something meant then, as it does today, that a person could *possibly* be held accountable for it; the outcome is *capable of* happening. American Heritage Dictionary 1025 (1981); Webster's New Collegiate Dictionary 893 (1980). And there is simply no way the landowners here are potentially, possibly, or capable of being held liable by the federal government for anything. In the first place, the federal government never notified the landowners that they might be responsible parties, as it must under §122(e)(1). Additionally, everyone admits that the period allowed for bringing a CERLCA claim against them has long since passed under §113(g)(2)(B). On any reasonable account, the landowners are potentially responsible to the government for exactly nothing.

Statutory context is of a piece with the narrow text. Nothing in §122 affects the rights of strangers to the federal government's settlement process. Everything in the section speaks to the details of that process. The section requires the government to provide all potentially responsible parties with notice that they might be held responsible for remedial measures. §9622(e)(1). It instructs the government to give a potentially responsible party a list of everyone else so designated. *Ibid.* It specifies procedures for sharing proposals and counterproposals among this group. §§9622(e)(2)(3). It allows the government to release from federal liability those who agree to settle and clean up hazardous sites. See §§9622(a)–(c). And because parties who settle with the federal government may seek cleanup costs they incurred prior to settlement from other potentially responsible parties, subsection (e)(6) bars a potentially responsible party from taking unauthorized remedial measures. See §§922(e)(1)–(3), (h). This ensures the government can control the shape of any final settlement and no private party can unilaterally incur costs that it might then foist on others. At the end of it all, the section does just what its title suggests. It governs the *settlement* process among those who have *something to settle*. It says nothing about the rights and duties of individuals who, like the landowners here, have nothing to settle because they face no potential liability.

Then there's what the rest of the statute tells us. As we've seen, CERCLA says again and again that it does not impair the rights of individuals under state law. That instruction makes perfect sense and does plenty of work if §122 only requires those potentially liable to the federal government to secure permission before engaging in cleanup efforts. By contrast, reading §122 to bar nearly everyone from undertaking remedial efforts without federal permission renders CERCLA's many and emphatic promises about protecting existing state law rights practically dead letters. Sure, the federal government would still have to "involv[e]" state officials and comply with state laws — or at least those laws federal agency employees deem "relevant and appropriate." §§9621(f)(1), (d)(2)(A)(ii). But CERCLA would promise nothing more than observer status for state law and those who wish to rely on it. States and private landowners alike who lack any potential federal liability could be barred even from undertaking remedial efforts on their own lands at their own expense, required instead to host toxic wastes involuntarily and indefinitely. Rather than supplementing state remedial efforts, CERCLA would rule them all.

Reading CERCLA this way would raise uneasy constitutional questions too. If CERCLA really did allow the federal government to order innocent landowners to house another party's pollutants involuntarily, it would invite weighty takings arguments under the Fifth Amendment. And if the statute really did grant the federal government the power to regulate virtually each shovelful of dirt homeowners may dig on their own properties, it would sorely test the reaches of Congress's power under the Commerce Clause.

Atlantic Richfield's replies do nothing to address these problems. Instead of making some helpful textual or contextual rejoinder about §122, the company asks us look somewhere else entirely. Now, Atlantic Richfield says, we should direct our attention to §107, a provision that lists four classes of "[c]overed persons" the federal government is authorized to sue under CERCLA. One of these classes encompasses any person who owns a "facility" where hazardous waste has "come to be located." §§9607, 9601(9). Because the landowners' properties qualify as "facilit[ies]" where Atlantic Richfield's waste has come to be located, everyone admits the landowners themselves are "[c]overed persons." And, according to Atlantic Richfield, this necessarily means they are *also* "potentially responsible part[ies]" subject to §122(e)(6)'s requirement that they seek federal permission before proceeding with any cleanup.

But notice the linguistic contortion and logical leap. Linguistically, §107 identifies the "[c]overed persons" the government is authorized to sue. Section 122 requires a "potentially responsible party" seeking settlement with and discharge of liability from the federal government to obtain its permission before engaging in a cleanup. The terms use different language, appear in different statutory sections, and address different matters. Nor are these two sections the only ones like them. CERCLA differentiates between covered persons and potentially responsible parties in many places: Some sections apply to all persons covered by §107 (see, *e.g.*, 42 U.S.C. §§9619(d), 9624(b)), while others extend their mandates only to potentially responsible parties (see, *e.g.*, §§9604, 9605, 9611). Logically, too, the concepts are distinct. Yes, a potentially responsible party must be a covered person the government is authorized to sue. But the inverse does not follow. It is possible to be a person the government is authorized to sue without also being a person the government has chosen to single out for potential responsibility. Atlantic Richfield's argument, thus, essentially proceeds like this: Disregard the differences in language; then assume Congress chose its terms randomly throughout the law; and, finally, conflate logically distinct concepts.

Our case illustrates the significance of the distinction Congress drew and Atlantic Richfield would have us ignore. Maybe the federal government was once authorized by §107 to include the innocent landowners here in a CERCLA suit. But few statutes pursue their purpose single-mindedly or require their full enforcement. And as we've seen, at least two things happened that preclude these landowners from being held responsible for anything: The government chose not to notify them of potential liability under §122(e)(3), and it declined to bring suit within the period prescribed by §113(g)(2)(B). Under the plain and ordinary meaning of the statutory terms before us, these landowners are not potentially responsible parties and CERCLA doesn't require them to seek permission from federal officials before cleaning their own lands. If Congress had wished to extend its ask-before-cleaning rule to every covered person — including those the government chooses not to pursue for potential liability — all it had to do was say so. Congress displayed no trouble using the term "[c]overed persons" elsewhere in the statute. See, *e.g.*, §§9619(d), 9624(b)(2). Conspicuously, it made a different choice here.

Without any plausible foundation in the statute to support its position, Atlantic Richfield resorts to this odd argument. Maybe the terms "[c]overed persons" and "potentially responsible party" are different and the statute uses them in different places to do different things. But, the company insists, we must conflate them now because this Court has conflated them before. In particular, Atlantic Richfield points to language in *United States* v. *Atlantic Research Corp.*, 551 U. S. 128 (2007), where the Court spoke of "Section 107(a) [as] defin[ing] four categories of PRPs [potentially responsible parties]." *Id.*, at 131–132.

That may be so but it does not make it so. The relationship between the terms "[c]overed persons" under §107 and "potentially responsible part[ies]" under §122 is of critical importance in this case, but it was not briefed, argued, or decided in *Atlantic Research*. Instead, the only question there concerned the meaning of the term "[c]overed persons" under §107. Though the Court employed the term "PRP" to describe "[c]overed persons," nothing turned on the use or meaning of the acronym: Replace every reference to "PRP" with "[c]overed person" and the Court's holding and reasoning remains the same. This Court has long warned that matters "'lurk[ing] in the record, neither brought to the attention of the court nor ruled upon,'" should not be read as having decided anything. We have warned, too, against reading our judicial opinions as if they were some sort of legislative code because, otherwise, innocent and inconsequential judicial remarks might mistakenly come to trump democratically adopted laws. Atlantic Richfield would have us ignore these teachings and confuse a stray remark with a rule of law.

In the end, the company's case cannot help but be seen for what it really is: an appeal to policy. On its view, things would be so much more orderly if the federal government ran everything. And, let's be honest, the implication here is that property owners cannot be trusted to clean up their lands without causing trouble (especially for Atlantic Richfield). Nor, we are told, should Montanans worry so much: The restrictions Atlantic Richfield proposes aren't really *that* draconian because homeowners would still be free to do things like build sandboxes for their grandchildren (provided, of course, they don't scoop out too much arsenic in the process).

But, as in so many cases that come before this Court, the policy arguments here cut both ways. Maybe paternalistic central planning cannot tolerate parallel state law efforts to restore state lands. But maybe, too, good government and environmental protection would be better served if state law remedies proceeded alongside federal efforts. State and federal law enforcement usually work in just this way, complementing rather than displacing one another. And, anyway, how long would Atlantic Richfield have us enforce what amounts to a federal easement requiring landowners to house toxic waste on their lands? The government has been on site since 1983; work supposedly finished around the landowners' homes in 2016; the completion of "primary" cleanup efforts is "estimated" to happen by 2025. So, yes, once a Superfund site is "delisted," the restrictions on potentially responsible parties fade away. But this project is well on its way to the half-century mark and still only a "preliminary" deadline lies on the horizon. No one before us will even hazard a guess when the work will finish and a "delisting" might come. On Atlantic Richfield's view, generations have come and gone and more may follow before the plaintiffs can clean their land.

The real problem, of course, is that Congress, not this Court, is supposed to make judgments between competing policy arguments like these. And, as we've seen, Congress has offered its judgment repeatedly and clearly. CERCLA sought to add to, not detract from, state law remedial efforts. It endorsed a federalized, not a centralized, approach to environmental protection. What if private or state cleanup efforts really do somehow interfere with federal interests? Congress didn't neglect the possibility. But instead of requiring state officials and local landowners to beg Washington for permission, Congress authorized the federal government to seek injunctive relief in court. See §9606(a). Atlantic Richfield would have us turn this system upside down, recasting the statute's presumption in favor of cooperative federalism into a presumption of federal absolutism.

While I agree with the Court's assessment in Parts I and II of its opinion that we have jurisdiction to hear this case, I cannot agree with its ruling on the merits in Part III. Departing from CERCLA's terms in this way transforms it from a law that supplements state environmental restoration efforts into one that prohibits them. Along the way, it strips away ancient common law rights from innocent landowners and forces them to suffer toxic waste in their backyards, playgrounds, and farms. Respectfully, that is not what the law was written to do; that is what it was written to prevent.

DO POLLUTANT DISCHARGES THAT FLOW THROUGH GROUNDWATER REQUIRE A PERMIT UNDER §402 OF THE CLEAN WATER ACT?

A wastewater treatment plant in Hawaii disposes of its partially treated sewage by injecting it underground into groundwater through which it eventually flows to the Pacific Ocean. Under §402 of the Clean Water Act (CWA) a permit is required for pollutant discharges to "the waters of the United States, including the territorial seas." The County of Maui, owner of the treatment plant, maintained that it did not need to obtain a §402 permit because its discharges pass through groundwater. The US Court of Appeals for the 9th Circuit ruled in favor of a citizens' group that sued the County for an unpermitted discharge, holding that any pollutant discharge to the ocean was "fairly traceable" to the County's discharge to groundwater. Although EPA supported the group before the 9th Circuit, during the Trump administration it changed sides and argued before the US Supreme Court that any pollutant discharge that passed through groundwater was exempt from the §402 permit requirement. A majority of the Supreme Court disagreed in the following case.

COUNTY OF MAUI v. HAWAII WILDLIFE FUND
140 S.Ct. 1462 (2020)

JUSTICE BREYER delivered the opinion of the Court.

The Clean Water Act forbids the "addition" of any pollutant from a "point source" to "navigable waters" without the appropriate permit from the Environmental Protection Agency (EPA). Federal Water Pollution Control Act, §§301(a), 502(12)(A), as amended by the Federal Water Pollution Control Act Amendments of 1972 (Clean Water Act), 33 U.S.C. §§1311(a), 1362(12)(A). The question presented here is whether the Act "requires a permit when pollutants originate from a point source but are conveyed to navigable waters by a nonpoint source," here, "groundwater." Suppose, for example, that a sewage treatment plant discharges polluted water into the ground where it mixes with groundwater, which, in turn, flows into a navigable river, or perhaps the ocean. Must the plant's owner seek an EPA permit before emitting the pollutant? We conclude that the statutory provisions at issue require a permit if the addition of the pollutants through groundwater is the functional equivalent of a direct discharge from the point source into navigable waters.

I

A

Congress' purpose as reflected in the language of the Clean Water Act is to "'restore and maintain the . . . integrity of the Nation's waters,'" §101(a). Prior to the Act, Federal and State Governments regulated water pollution in large part by setting water quality standards. The Act restructures federal regulation by insisting that a person wishing to discharge *any* pollution into navigable waters first obtain EPA's permission to do so.

The Act's provisions use specific definitional language to achieve this result. First, the Act defines "pollutant" broadly, including in its definition, for example, any solid waste, incinerator residue, "'heat,'" "'discarded equipment,'" or sand (among many other things). §502(6), 86 Stat. 886. Second, the Act defines a "point source" as "'any discernible, confined and discrete conveyance . . . from which pollutants are or may be discharged,'" including, for example, any "'container,'" "'pipe, ditch, channel, tunnel, conduit,'" or "'well.'" §502(14). Third, it defines the term "discharge of a pollutant" as "'any addition of any pollutant to navigable waters [including navigable streams, rivers, the ocean, or coastal waters] from any point source.'" §502(12).

The Act then sets forth a statutory provision that, using these terms, broadly states that (with certain exceptions) "'the discharge of any pollutant by any person'" without an appropriate permit "'shall be unlawful.'" §301. The question here, as we have said, is whether, or how, this statutory language applies to a pollutant that reaches navigable waters only after it leaves a "point source" and then travels through groundwater before reaching navigable waters. In such an instance, has there been a "discharge of a pollutant," that is, has there been "any addition of any pollutant to navigable waters from any point source?"

B

The petitioner, the County of Maui, operates a wastewater reclamation facility on the island of Maui, Hawaii. The facility collects sewage from the surrounding area, partially treats it, and pumps the treated water through four wells hundreds of feet underground. This effluent, amounting to about 4 million gallons each day, then travels a further half mile or so, through groundwater, to the ocean.

In 2012, several environmental groups, the respondents here, brought this citizens' Clean Water Act lawsuit against Maui. They claimed that Maui was "discharg[ing]" a "pollutant" to "navigable waters," namely, the Pacific Ocean, without the permit required by the Clean Water Act. The District Court, relying in part upon a detailed study of the discharges, found that a considerable amount of effluent from the wells ended up in the ocean (a navigable water). It wrote that, because the "path to the ocean is clearly ascertainable," the discharge from Maui's wells into the nearby groundwater was "functionally one into navigable water." 24 F. Supp. 3d 980, 998 (Haw. 2014). And it granted summary judgment in favor of the environmental groups.

The Ninth Circuit affirmed the District Court, but it described the relevant statutory standard somewhat differently. The appeals court wrote that a permit is required when "the pollutants are *fairly traceable* from the point source to a navigable water such that the discharge is the functional equivalent of a discharge into the navigable water." 886 F. 3d 737, 749 (2018) (emphasis added). The court left "for another day the task of determining when, if ever, the connection between a point source and a navigable water is too tenuous to support liability . . . ."

Maui petitioned for certiorari. In light of the differences in the standards adopted by the different Courts of Appeals, we granted the petition. Compare, *e.g.,* 886 F. 3d, at 749 ("fairly traceable"), with *Upstate Forever* v. *Kinder Morgan Energy Partners, L. P.,* 887 F. 3d 637, 651 (CA4 2018) ("direct hydrological connection"), and *Kentucky Waterways Alliance* v. *Kentucky Util. Co.,* 905 F. 3d 925, 932–938 (CA6 2018) (discharges through groundwater are excluded from the Act's permitting requirements).

II

The linguistic question here concerns the statutory word "from." Is pollution that reaches navigable waters only through groundwater pollution that is "from" a point source, as the statute uses the word? The word "from" is broad in scope, but context often imposes limitations. "Finland," for example, is often not the right kind of answer to the question, "Where have you come from?" even if long ago you were born there.

The parties here disagree dramatically about the scope of the word "from" in the present context. The environmental groups, the respondents, basically adopt the Ninth Circuit's view — that the permitting requirement applies so long as the pollutant is "fairly traceable" to a point source even if it traveled long and far (through groundwater) before it reached navigable waters. They add that the release from the point source must be "a proximate cause of the addition of pollutants to navigable waters."

Maui, on the other hand, argues that the statute creates a "bright-line test." point source or series of point sources must be "the *means of delivering* pollutants to navigable waters." They add that, if "at least one nonpoint source (*e.g.,* unconfined rainwater runoff or groundwater)" lies "between the point source and the navigable water," then the permit requirement "does not apply." A pollutant is "from" a point source only if a point source is the last "conveyance" that conducted the pollutant to navigable waters.

The Solicitor General, as *amicus curiae*, supports Maui, at least in respect to groundwater. Reiterating the position taken in a recent EPA "Interpretive Statement," he argues that, given the Act's structure and history, "a release of pollutants to groundwater is not subject to" the Act's permitting requirement "even if the pollutants subsequently migrate to jurisdictional surface waters," such as the ocean.

We agree that statutory context limits the reach of the statutory phrase "from any point source" to a range of circumstances narrower than that which the Ninth Circuit's interpretation suggests. At the same time, it is significantly broader than the total exclusion of all discharges through groundwater described by Maui and the Solicitor General.

III

Virtually all water, polluted or not, eventually makes its way to navigable water. This is just as true for groundwater. Given the power of modern science, the Ninth Circuit's limitation, "fairly traceable," may well allow EPA to assert permitting authority over the release of pollutants that reach navigable waters many years after their release (say, from a well or pipe or compost heap) and in highly diluted forms.

The respondents suggest that the standard can be narrowed by adding a "proximate cause" requirement. That is, to fall within the permitting provision, the discharge from a point source must "proximately cause" the pollutants' eventual addition to navigable waters. But the term "proximate cause" derives from general tort law, and it takes on its specific content based primarily on "policy" considerations. In the context of water pollution, we do not see how it significantly narrows the statute beyond the words "fairly traceable" themselves.

Our view is that Congress did not intend the point source-permitting requirement to provide EPA with such broad authority as the Ninth Circuit's narrow focus on traceability would allow. First, to interpret the word "from" in this literal way would require a permit in surprising, even bizarre, circumstances, such as for pollutants carried to navigable waters on a bird's feathers, or, to mention more mundane instances, the 100-year migration of pollutants through 250 miles of groundwater to a river.

Second, and perhaps most important, the structure of the statute indicates that, as to groundwater pollution and nonpoint source pollution, Congress intended to leave substantial responsibility and autonomy to the States. Much water pollution does not come from a readily identifiable source. Rainwater, for example, can carry pollutants (say, as might otherwise collect on a roadway); it can pollute groundwater, and pollution collected by unchanneled rainwater runoff is not ordinarily considered point source pollution. Over many decades, and with federal encouragement, the States have developed methods of regulating nonpoint source pollution through water quality standards, and otherwise.

The Act envisions EPA's role in managing nonpoint source pollution and groundwater pollution as limited to studying the issue, sharing information with and collecting information from the States, and issuing monetary grants. Although the Act grants EPA specific authority to regulate certain point source pollution (it can also delegate some of this authority to the States acting under EPA supervision, see §402(b)), these permitting provisions refer to "point sources" and "navigable waters," and say nothing at all about non-point source regulation or groundwater regulation. We must doubt that Congress intended to give EPA the authority to apply the word "from" in a way that could interfere as seriously with States' traditional regulatory authority — authority the Act preserves and promotes — as the Ninth Circuit's "fairly traceable" test would.

Third, those who look to legislative history to help interpret a statute will find that this Act's history strongly supports our conclusion that the permitting provision does not extend so far. Fifty years ago, when Congress was considering the bills that became the Clean Water Act, William Ruckelshaus, the first EPA Administrator, asked Congress to grant EPA authority over "ground waters" to "assure that we have control over the water table . . . so we can . . . maintai[n] a control over all the sources of pollution, be they discharged directly into any stream or through the ground water table." Representative Les Aspin similarly pointed out that there were "conspicuou[s]" references to groundwater in all sections of the bill *except* the permitting section at issue here. The Senate Committee on Public Works "recognize[d] the essential link between ground and surface waters."

But Congress did not accept these requests for general EPA authority over groundwater. It rejected Representative Aspin's amendment that would have extended the permitting provision to groundwater. Instead, Congress provided a set of more specific groundwater-related measures such as those requiring *States* to maintain "affirmative controls over the injection or placement in wells" of "any pollutants that may affect ground water." These *specific* state-related programs were, in the words of the Senate Public Works Committee, "designed to protect ground waters and eliminate the use of deep well disposal as an uncontrolled alternative to toxic and pollution control." The upshot is that Congress was fully aware of the need to address groundwater pollution, but it satisfied that need through a variety of state-specific controls. Congress left general groundwater regulatory authority to the States; its failure to include groundwater in the general EPA permitting provision was deliberate.

Finally, longstanding regulatory practice undermines the Ninth Circuit's broad interpretation of the statute. EPA itself for many years has applied the permitting provision to pollution discharges from point sources that reached navigable waters only after traveling through groundwater. But, in doing so, EPA followed a narrower interpretation than that of the Ninth Circuit. EPA has opposed applying the Act's permitting requirements to discharges that reach groundwater only after lengthy periods. Indeed, in this very case (prior to its recent Interpretive Statement), EPA asked the Ninth Circuit to apply a more limited "direct hydrological connection" test. The Ninth Circuit did not accept this suggestion.

We do not defer here to EPA's interpretation of the statute embodied in this practice. Indeed, EPA itself has changed its mind about the meaning of the statutory provision. But this history, by showing that a comparatively narrow view of the statute is administratively workable, offers some additional support for the view that Congress did not intend as broad a delegation of regulatory authority as the Ninth Circuit test would allow.

As we have said, the specific meaning of the word "from" necessarily draws its meaning from context. The apparent breadth of the Ninth Circuit's "fairly traceable" approach is inconsistent with the context we have just described.

IV

A

Maui and the Solicitor General argue that the statute's permitting requirement does not apply if a pollutant, having emerged from a "point source," must travel through any amount of groundwater before reaching navigable waters. That interpretation is too narrow, for it would risk serious interference with EPA's ability to regulate ordinary point source discharges.

Consider a pipe that spews pollution directly into coastal waters. There is an "addition of" a "pollutant to navigable waters from [a] point source." Hence, a permit is required. But Maui and the Government read the permitting requirement *not* to apply if there is *any* amount of groundwater between the end of the pipe and the edge of the navigable water. If that is the correct interpretation of the statute, then why could not the pipe's owner, seeking to avoid the permit requirement, simply move the pipe back, perhaps only a few yards, so that the pollution must travel through at least some groundwater before reaching the sea? We do not see how Congress could have intended to create such a large and obvious loophole in one of the key regulatory innovations of the Clean Water Act.

B

Maui argues that the statute's language requires its reading. That language requires a permit for a "discharge." A "discharge" is "any addition" of a pollutant to navigable waters *"from any point source."* And a "point source" is "any discernible, confined and discrete *conveyance*" (such as a pipe, ditch, well, etc.). Reading "from" and "conveyance" together, Maui argues that the statutory meaning of "from any point source" is not about *where* the pollution originated, but about *how* it got there. Under what Maui calls the means-of-delivery test, a permit is required only if a point source itself ultimately delivers the pollutant to navigable waters. Under this view, if the pollutant must travel through groundwater to reach navigable waters, then it is the groundwater, not the pipe, that is the conveyance.

Congress sometimes adopts less common meanings of common words, but this esoteric definition of "from," as connoting a means, does not remotely fit in this context. The statute couples the word "from" with the word "to" — strong evidence that Congress was referring to a destination ("navigable waters") and an origin ("any point source"). Further underscoring that Congress intended this every day meaning is that the object of "from" is a "point *source*" — a source, again, connoting an origin. That Maui's proffered interpretation would also create a serious loophole in the permitting regime also indicates it is an unreasonable one.

C

The Solicitor General agrees that, as a general matter, the permitting requirement applies to at least some additions of pollutants to navigable waters that come indirectly from point sources. But the Solicitor General argues that the proper interpretation of the statute is the one reflected in EPA's recent Interpretive

Statement. After receiving more than 50,000 comments from the public, and after the Ninth Circuit released its opinion in this case, EPA wrote that "the best, if not the only, reading" of the statutory provisions is that "*all* releases of pollutants to groundwater" are excluded from the scope of the permitting program, "even where pollutants are conveyed to jurisdictional surface waters via groundwater."

Neither the Solicitor General nor any party has asked us to give what the Court has referred to as *Chevron* deference to EPA's interpretation of the statute. Even so, we often pay particular attention to an agency's views in light of the agency's expertise in a given area, its knowledge gained through practical experience, and its familiarity with the interpretive demands of administrative need. But here, as we have explained, to follow EPA's reading would open a loophole allowing easy evasion of the statutory provision's basic purposes. Such an interpretation is neither persuasive nor reasonable.

EPA correctly points out that Congress did not require a permit for *all* discharges to groundwater; rather, Congress authorized study and funding related to groundwater pollution. But there is quite a gap between "not all" and "none." The statutory text itself alludes to no exception for discharges through groundwater. These separate provisions for study and funding that EPA points to would be a "surprisingly indirect route" to convey "an important and easily expressed message" — that the permit requirement simply does not apply if the pollutants travel through groundwater. In truth, the most these provisions show is that Congress thought that the problem of groundwater pollution, as distinct from navigable water pollution, would primarily be addressed by the States or perhaps by other federal statutes.

EPA's new interpretation is also difficult to reconcile with the statute's reference to "*any* addition" of a pollutant to navigable waters. It is difficult to reconcile EPA's interpretation with the statute's inclusion of "wells" in the definition of "point source," for wells most ordinarily would discharge pollutants through groundwater. And it is difficult to reconcile EPA's interpretation with the statutory provisions that allow EPA to delegate its permitting authority to a State *only if* the State (among other things) provides " 'adequate authority' " to " 'control the disposal of pollutants into wells.'" §402(b). What need would there be for such a proviso if the federal permitting program the State replaces did not include such discharges (from wells through groundwater) in the first place?

In short, EPA's oblique argument about the statute's references to groundwater cannot overcome the statute's structure, its purposes, or the text of the provisions that actually govern.

D

Perhaps, as the two dissents suggest, the language could be narrowed to similar effect by reading the statute to refer only to the pollutant's immediate origin. But there is no linguistic basis here to so limit the statute in that way. Again, whether that is the correct reading turns on context. JUSTICE THOMAS insists that in the case of a discharge through groundwater, the pollutants are added "from the groundwater." Indeed, but that does not mean they are not also "from the point source." When John comes to the hotel, John might have come from the train station, from Baltimore, from Europe, from any two of those three places, or from all three. A sign that asks all persons who arrive *from* Baltimore to speak to the desk clerk includes those who took a taxi *from* the train station. There is nothing unnatural about such a construction. As the plurality correctly noted in *Rapanos* v. *United States*, the statute here does not say "directly" from or "immediately" from. Indeed, the expansive language of the provision — *any* addition from *any* point source — strongly suggests its scope is not so limited.

JUSTICE ALITO appears to believe that there are only two possible ways to read "from": as referring either to the *immediate* source, or else to the *original* source. Because he agrees that the statute cannot reasonably be read always to reach the original source, he concludes the statute must refer only to the immediate origin. But as the foregoing example illustrates, context may indicate that "from" includes an intermediate stop — Baltimore, not Europe or the train station.

JUSTICE THOMAS relies on the word "addition," but we fail to see how that word limits the statute to discharges directly to navigable waters. Ordinary language abounds in counter examples: A recipe might instruct to "add the drippings from the meat to the gravy"; that instruction does not become incomprehensible, or even peculiar, simply because the drippings will have first collected in a pan or on a cutting board. And while it would be an unusual phrasing (as statutory phrasings often are), we do not see how the recipe's meaning would transform if it instead said to "add the drippings to the gravy from the meat." To take another example: If Timmy is told to "add water to the bath from the well" he will know just what it means — even though he will have to use a bucket to complete the task.

And although JUSTICE THOMAS resists the inevitable implications of his reading of the statute that reading would create the same loopholes as those offered by the petitioner and the Government, and more. It would necessarily exclude a pipe that drains onto the beach next to navigable waters, even if the pollutants then flow to those waters. It also seems to exclude a pipe that hangs out over the water and adds pollutants to the air, through which the pollutants fall to navigable waters. The absurdity of such an interpretation is obvious enough.

We therefore reject this reading as well: Like Maui's and the Government's, it is inconsistent with the statutory text and simultaneously creates a massive loophole in the permitting scheme that Congress established.

E

For the reasons set forth in Part III and in this Part, we conclude that, in light of the statute's language, structure, and purposes, the interpretations offered by the parties, the Government, and the dissents are too extreme.

V

Over the years, courts and EPA have tried to find general language that will reflect a middle ground between these extremes. The statute's words reflect Congress' basic aim to provide federal regulation of identifiable sources of pollutants entering navigable waters without undermining the States' longstanding regulatory authority over land and groundwater. We hold that the statute requires a permit when there is a direct discharge from a point source into navigable waters or when there is the *functional equivalent of a direct discharge*. We think this phrase best captures, in broad terms, those circumstances in which Congress intended to require a federal permit. That is, an addition falls within the statutory requirement that it be "from any point source" when a point source directly deposits pollutants into navigable waters, or when the discharge reaches the same result through roughly similar means.

Time and distance are obviously important. Where a pipe ends a few feet from navigable waters and the pipe emits pollutants that travel those few feet through groundwater (or over the beach), the permitting requirement clearly applies. If the pipe ends 50 miles from navigable waters and the pipe emits pollutants that travel with groundwater, mix with much other material, and end up in navigable waters only many years later, the permitting requirements likely do not apply.

The object in a given scenario will be to advance, in a manner consistent with the statute's language, the statutory purposes that Congress sought to achieve. As we have said (repeatedly), the word "from" seeks a "point source" origin, and context imposes natural limits as to when a point source can properly be considered the origin of pollution that travels through groundwater. That context includes the need, reflected in the statute, to preserve state regulation of groundwater and other nonpoint sources of pollution. Whether pollutants that arrive at navigable waters after traveling through groundwater are "from" a point source depends upon how similar to (or different from) the particular discharge is to a direct discharge.

The difficulty with this approach, we recognize, is that it does not, on its own, clearly explain how to deal with middle instances. But there are too many potentially relevant factors applicable to factually different cases for this Court now to use more specific language. Consider, for example, just some of the factors that may prove relevant (depending upon the circumstances of a particular case): (1) transit time, (2) distance traveled, (3) the nature of the material through which the pollutant travels, (4) the extent to which the pollutant is diluted or chemically changed as it travels, (5) the amount of pollutant entering the navigable waters relative to the amount of the pollutant that leaves the point source, (6) the manner by or area in which the pollutant enters the navigable waters, (7) the degree to which the pollution (at that point) has maintained its specific identity. Time and distance will be the most important factors in most cases, but not necessarily every case.

At the same time, courts can provide guidance through decisions in individual cases. The Circuits have tried to do so, often using general language somewhat similar to the language we have used. And the traditional common-law method, making decisions that provide examples that in turn lead to ever more refined principles, is sometimes useful, even in an era of statutes.

The underlying statutory objectives also provide guidance. Decisions should not create serious risks either of undermining state regulation of groundwater or of creating loopholes that undermine the statute's basic federal regulatory objectives.

EPA, too, can provide administrative guidance (within statutory boundaries) in numerous ways, including through, for example, grants of individual permits, promulgation of general permits, or the development of general rules. Indeed, over the years, EPA and the States have often considered the Act's application to discharges through groundwater.

Both Maui and the Government object that to subject discharges to navigable waters through groundwater to the statute's permitting requirements, as our interpretation will sometimes do, would vastly expand the scope of the statute, perhaps requiring permits for each of the 650,000 wells like petitioner's or for each of the over 20 million septic systems used in many Americans' homes.

But EPA has applied the permitting provision to some (but not to all) discharges through groundwater for over 30 years. In that time we have seen no evidence of unmanageable expansion. EPA and the States also have tools to mitigate those harms, should they arise, by (for example) developing general permits for recurring situations or by issuing permits based on best practices where appropriate. Judges, too, can mitigate any hardship or injustice when they apply the statute's penalty provision. That provision vests courts with broad discretion to set a penalty that takes account of many factors, including "any good-faith efforts to comply" with the Act, the "seriousness of the violation," the "economic impact of the penalty on the violator," and "such other matters as justice may require." See 33 U.S.C. §1319(d). We expect that district judges will exercise their discretion mindful, as we are, of the complexities inherent to the context of indirect discharges through groundwater, so as to calibrate the Act's penalties when, for example, a party could reasonably have thought that a permit was not required.

In sum, we recognize that a more absolute position, such as the means-of-delivery test or that of the Government or that of the Ninth Circuit, may be easier to administer. But, as we have said, those positions have consequences that are inconsistent with major congressional objectives, as revealed by the statute's language, structure, and purposes. We consequently understand the permitting requirement, §301, as applicable to a discharge (from a point source) of pollutants that reach navigable waters after traveling through groundwater if that discharge is the functional equivalent of a direct discharge from the point source into navigable waters.

VI

Because the Ninth Circuit applied a different standard, we vacate its judgment and remand the case for further proceedings consistent with this opinion.

It is so ordered.

JUSTICE KAVANAUGH, concurring.

I join the Court's opinion in full. I write separately to emphasize three points.

First, the Court's interpretation of the Clean Water Act regarding pollution "from" point sources adheres to the interpretation set forth in Justice Scalia's plurality opinion in *Rapanos* v. *United States*, 547 U. S. 715 (2006). The Clean Water Act requires a permit for "any addition of any pollutant to navigable waters from any point source." 33 U.S.C. §1362(12)(A); see §§1311(a), 1342(a). The key word is "from." The question in this case is whether the County of Maui needs a permit for its Lahaina Wastewater Reclamation Facility. No one disputes that pollutants originated at Maui's wastewater facility (a point source), and no one disputes that the pollutants ended up in the Pacific Ocean (a navigable water). Maui contends, however, that it does not need a permit. Maui says that the pollutants did not come "from" the Lahaina facility because the pollutants traveled through groundwater before reaching the ocean.

Justice Scalia's plurality opinion in *Rapanos* explained why Maui's interpretation of the Clean Water Act is incorrect. In that case, Justice Scalia stated that polluters could not "evade the permitting requirement of §1342(a) simply by discharging their pollutants into noncovered intermittent watercourses that lie upstream of covered waters." Justice Scalia reasoned that the Clean Water Act does not merely "forbid the 'addition of any pollutant *directly* to navigable waters from any point source,' but rather the 'addition of any pollutant *to* navigable waters.' Thus, from the time of the CWA's enactment, lower courts have held that the discharge into intermittent channels of any pollutant *that naturally washes downstream* likely violates §1311(a), even if the pollutants discharged from a point source do not emit 'directly into' covered waters, but pass 'through conveyances' in between."

In other words, under Justice Scalia's interpretation in *Rapanos*, the fact that the pollutants from Maui's wastewater facility reach the ocean via an indirect route does not itself exempt Maui's facility from the Clean Water Act's permitting requirement for point sources. The Court today adheres to Justice Scalia's analysis in *Rapanos* on that issue.

Second, as Justice Scalia's opinion in *Rapanos* pointed out and as the Court's opinion today explains, the statute does not establish a bright-line test regarding when a pollutant may be considered to have come "from" a point source. The source of the vagueness is Congress' statutory text, not the Court's opinion. The Court's opinion seeks to translate the vague statutory text into more concrete guidance.

Third, JUSTICE THOMAS' dissent states that "the Court does not commit" to "which factors are the most important" in determining whether pollutants that enter navigable waters come "from" a point source. That critique is not accurate, as I read the Court's opinion. The Court identifies relevant factors to consider and emphasizes that "[t]ime and distance are obviously important." And the Court expressly adds that "[t]ime and distance will be the most important factors in most cases, but not necessarily every case." Although the statutory text does not supply a bright-line test, the Court's emphasis on time and distance will help guide application of the statutory standard going forward.

With those additional comments, I join the Court's opinion in full.

JUSTICE THOMAS, with whom JUSTICE GORSUCH joins, dissenting.

The Clean Water Act (CWA) requires a federal permit for "the discharge of any pollutant by any person." 33 U.S.C. §1311(a); see §1342. The CWA defines a "discharge" as "any addition of any pollutant to navigable waters from any point source." §1362(12). Based on the statutory text and structure, I would hold that a permit is required only when a point source discharges pollutants directly into navigable waters. The Court adopts this interpretation in part, concluding that a permit is required for "a direct discharge." But the Court then departs from the statutory text by requiring a permit for "the *functional equivalent of a direct discharge,*" which it defines through an open-ended inquiry into congressional intent and practical considerations. Because I would adhere to the text, I respectfully dissent.

I

A

In interpreting the statutory definition of "discharge," the Court focuses on the word "from," but the most helpful word is "addition." That word, together with "to" and "from," limits the meaning of "discharge" to the augmentation of navigable waters.

Dictionary definitions of "addition" denote an augmentation or increase. Webster's Third New International Dictionary defines "addition" as "the act or process of adding: the joining or uniting of one thing to another." Webster's Third New International Dictionary 24 (1961); see also *ibid.* (listing "increase" and "augmentation" as synonyms for "addition"). Other dictionary definitions from around the time of the statute's enactment are in accord. See, *e.g.,* American Heritage Dictionary 14, 15 (1981) (defining "addition" as "[t]he act or process of adding" and defining "add" as "[t]o join or unite so as to increase in size, quantity, or scope"); see also Webster's New International Dictionary 29, 30 (2d ed. 1957) (defining "addition" as the "[a]ct, process, or instance of adding," and defining "add" as to "join or unite, as one thing to another, or as several particulars, so as to increase the number, augment the quantity, enlarge the magnitude, or so as to form into one aggregate").

The inclusion of the term "addition" in the CWA indicates that the statute excludes anything other than a direct discharge. When a point source releases pollutants to groundwater, one would naturally say that the groundwater has been augmented with pollutants from the point source. If the pollutants eventually reach navigable waters, one would not naturally say that the navigable waters have been augmented with pollutants from the point source. The augmentation instead occurs with pollutants from the groundwater.

The prepositions "from" and "to" reinforce this reading. When pollutants are released from a point source to another point source or groundwater, they are added *to* the second *from* the first. If the pollutants are later released to navigable waters, they are added *to* the navigable waters *from* the second point source or the groundwater. One would not naturally say that the pollutants are added to the navigable waters from the original point source.

Interpreting "discharge" to mean a direct discharge makes sense of other parts of the definition as well. It respects the statutory definition of a point source as a "conveyance," see §1362(14), because a point source that releases pollutants directly into navigable waters is a means of conveyance. And it makes sense of the word "any" before "point source," because that term clarifies that any kind of point source may require a permit.

The structure of the CWA confirms this interpretation. It authorizes the Environmental Protection Agency (EPA) to regulate discharges from point sources, including through the permitting process, but it reserves to the States the primary responsibility for regulating other sources of pollution, including groundwater. With respect to these sources, the EPA merely collects information, coordinates with the States, and provides funding. In the CWA, Congress expressly stated its "policy . . . to recognize, preserve, and protect the primary responsibilities and rights of States to prevent, reduce, and eliminate pollution." §1251(b). Thus, construing the EPA's power to regulate point sources to allow the agency to regulate nonpoint sources and groundwater is in serious tension with Congress' design.

My reading is also consistent with our decision in *South Fla. Water Management Dist.* v. *Miccosukee Tribe,* 541 U. S. 95 (2004). The petitioner in that case argued that no permit was required when a point source was not the original source of the pollutant but instead conveyed the pollutant from further up a chain of sources. We rejected that argument because "a point source need not be the original source of the pollutant; it need only convey the pollutant to 'navigable waters.'" Although that case did not involve the exact question presented here, the direct-discharge interpretation comports well with that previous decision.

B

The Court's main textual argument reads the word "from" in isolation. But as the Court recognizes, "the word 'from' necessarily draws its meaning from context." The Court's example using "arrive" instead of "addition" is thus unpersuasive, because "from" takes different meanings with different verbs. The Court's culinary example also misses the mark, *ante*, at 14, because if the drippings from the meat collect in the pan before the chef adds them to the gravy, the drippings are added to the gravy from the pan, not from the meat. This point becomes clear if we reorder the majority's recipe to match the statute; the chef has not added the drippings to the gravy from the meat. The Court's bathwater example, *ante*, at 14, suffers from the same problem; if the well water is put in a bucket before it is put in the bathtub, it is added to the bathtub from the bucket. Only by reading the phrase in its entirety can we interpret the definition of "discharge."

The Court also asserts that a narrower reading than the one it adopts would create a "massive loophole" in the statute. Far from creating a loophole, my reading is the most logical because it is consonant with the scope of Congress' power. The CWA presumably was passed as an exercise of Congress' authority "to regulate Commerce with foreign Nations, and among the several States, and with the Indian Tribes." U. S. Const., Art. I, §8, cl. 3. My interpretation ties the statute more closely to navigable waters, on the theory that they are at least a channel of these kinds of commerce. . . .

Further, the Court's interpretation creates practical problems of its own. As the Court acknowledges, its opinion gives almost no guidance, save for a list of seven factors. But the Court does not commit to whether those factors are the only relevant ones, whether those factors are always relevant, or which factors are the most important. It ultimately does little to explain how functionally equivalent an indirect discharge must be to require a permit. . . .

Finally, the Court speculates as to "those circumstances in which Congress intended to require a federal permit." But we are not a superlegislature (or super-EPA) tasked with making good policy — assuming that is even what the Court accomplishes today. "Our job is to follow the text even if doing so will supposedly undercut a basic objective of the statute."

II

I do agree with the Court on several points. First, the interpretation adopted by respondents and the Ninth Circuit is unsupportable. That interpretation — which would require permits for discharges that are "'fairly traceable'" to, and proximately caused by, a point source — is atextual and unsettles the CWA's careful balance between federal regulation of point-source pollution and state regulation of nonpoint-source pollution.

Second, I agree that the interpretation adopted by petitioner and JUSTICE ALITO reads the word "any" unnaturally, although the majority appears to deploy that argument itself in another part of the opinion. Petitioner's and JUSTICE ALITO's interpretation also gives insufficient weight to the meaning of "addition."

Finally, I agree with the Court's implicit conclusion that *Rapanos v. United States*, 547 U. S. 715 (2006), does not resolve this case. That plurality opinion, which I joined, observed that lower courts have required a permit when pollutants pass through a chain of point sources. But we expressly said in *Rapanos* that "we [did] not decide this issue." We are not bound by dictum in a plurality opinion or by the lower court opinions it cited.

III

The best reading of the statute is that a "discharge" is the release of pollutants directly from a point source to navigable waters. The application of this interpretation to the undisputed facts of this case makes a remand unnecessary. Petitioner operates a wastewater treatment facility and injects treated wastewater into four underground injection control wells. All parties agree that the wastewater enters groundwater from the wells and does not directly enter navigable waters. Based on these undisputed facts, there is no "discharge," so I would reverse the judgment of the Ninth Circuit. I respectfully dissent.

JUSTICE ALITO, dissenting.

If the Court is going to devise its own legal rules, instead of interpreting those enacted by Congress, it might at least adopt rules that can be applied with a modicum of consistency. Here, however, the Court makes up a rule that provides no clear guidance and invites arbitrary and inconsistent application.

The text of the Clean Water Act generally requires a permit when a discharge "from" a "point source" (such as a pipe) "add[s]" a pollutant "to" navigable waters (such as the Pacific Ocean). There are two ways to read this text. A pollutant that reaches the ocean could be understood to have been added "from" a pipe if the pipe originally discharged the pollutant and the pollutant eventually made its way to the ocean by flowing over or under the surface of the ground. Or a pollutant that reaches the ocean could be understood to have come "from" a pipe if the pollutant is discharged from the pipe directly into the ocean.

There is no comprehensible alternative to these two interpretations, but the Court refuses to accept either. Both alternatives, it believes, lead to unacceptable results, and it therefore tries to find a middle way. It holds that a permit is required "when there is a direct discharge from a point source into navigable waters or when there is the *functional equivalent of a direct discharge.*" *Ante,* at 15. This is not a plausible interpretation of the statutory text and, to make matters worse, the Court's test has no clear meaning.

Just what is the "functional equivalent" of a "direct discharge"? The Court provides no real answer. All it will say is that the distance a pollutant travels and the time this trip entails are the most important factors, but *at least five other factors* may have a bearing on the question, and even this list is not exhaustive. Entities like water treatment authorities that need to know whether they must get a permit are left to guess how this nebulous standard will be applied. Regulators are given the discretion, at least in the first instance, to make of this standard what they will. And the lower courts? The Court's advice, in essence, is: "That's your problem. Muddle through as best you can." . . .

II

The Clean Water Act generally makes it unlawful to "discharge" a "pollutant"3 without a permit. 33 U.S.C. §1311(a). The Act defines the "discharge of a pollutant" as "any addition of any pollutant to navigable waters[4] from any point source." §1362(12). And a "point source" is broadly defined as "any discernible, confined and discrete conveyance . . . from which pollutants are or may be discharged." §1362(14). The Act includes a non-exhaustive list of conveyances that fall within this definition, and included on that list are such things as "pipe[s]," "ditch[es]," "channel[s]," and "well[s]." *Ibid.*

Putting all these statutory terms together, the rule can be stated as follows: A permit is required when a pollutant is "add[ed]" to navigable waters "from" a "point source." In this case, the parties and the EPA agree that *most* of the elements of this rule are met. Specifically, they agree that: The effluent emitted by the wells is a "pollutant"; this effluent reaches navigable waters (the Pacific Ocean); and the wells are "point source[s]." The disputed question is whether the emission of effluent from those wells qualifies as a "discharge," that is, the addition of a pollutant *"from" a point source.* §1362(12) (emphasis added).

There are two possible interpretations of this phrase. The first is that pollutants are added to navigable waters from a point source whenever they originally came from the point source. The second is that pollutants are added to navigable waters only if they were discharged from a point source directly into navigable waters.

Dissatisfied with those options, the Court tries to find a third, but its interpretation is very hard to fit into the statutory text. Under the Court's interpretation, it appears that a pollutant that leaves a point source and heads toward navigable waters via some non-point source (such as by flowing over the ground or by means of groundwater) is "from" the point source for some portion of its journey, but once it has travelled a certain distance or once a certain amount of time has elapsed, it is no longer "from" the point source and is instead "from" a nonpoint source.

This is an implausible reading of the statute. The Court has many inventive examples of the different meanings that can be conveyed by the simple statement that A comes from B, but one of the Court's examples — the traveler who flies from Europe to Baltimore — illustrates the problem. If we apply the Court's interpretation of §1362 to this traveler's journey, he would be "from" Europe for the first part of the flight, but at some point he might cease to be "from" Europe and would then be from someplace else, maybe Greenland or geographical coordinates in the middle of the Atlantic. This is a very strange notion, and therefore, I think the statutory text compels us to choose between the two alternatives set out above.

The Court rejects both of these because it thinks they lead to unacceptably extreme results. "Originally from" would impose liability even if pollutants discharged into ground water had to travel 250 miles over the course of 100 years before reaching navigable waters. And "'immediately'" or "'directly' from," the Court thinks, would mean that a polluter could evade the permit requirement by discharging pollutants from a pipe located just a few feet from navigable waters.

To escape these possibilities, the Court devises its own test: A permit is required, the Court holds, "when there is a direct discharge from a point source into navigable waters or when there is the *functional equivalent of a direct discharge.*" *Ante,* at 15 (emphasis in original). The Clean Water Act, however, says nothing about "the functional equivalent" of a direct discharge. That is the Court's own concoction, and the Court provides no clear explanation of its meaning.

The term "functional equivalent" may have a quasi-technical ring, but what does it mean? "Equivalent" means "equal" in some respect, and "functional" signifies a relationship to a function. The function of a direct discharge from a point source into navigable waters is to convey the entirety of the discharge into navigable waters without any delay. Therefore, the "functional equivalent" of a direct discharge of a pollutant into navigable waters would seem to be a discharge that is equal to a direct discharge in these respects. If that is what the Court meant by "the functional equivalent of a direct discharge," the test would apply at best to only a small set of situations not involving a direct discharge. The Court's example of a pipe that emits pollutants a few feet from the ocean would presumably qualify on *de minimis* grounds, but if the pipe were moved back any significant distance, the discharge would not be exactly equal to a direct discharge. There would be some lag from the time of the discharge to the time when the pollutant reaches navigable waters; some of the pollutant might not reach that destination; and the pollutant might have changed somewhat in composition by the time it reached the navigable waters.

For these reasons, the Court's reference to "the functional equivalent of a direct discharge," if taken literally, would be of little importance, but the Court's understanding of this concept is very different from the literal meaning of the phrase. As used by the Court, "the functional equivalent of a direct discharge" means a discharge that is sufficiently similar to a direct discharge to warrant a permit in light of the Clean Water Act's "language, structure, and purposes." But what, in concrete terms, does this mean? How similar is sufficiently similar?

The Court provides this guidance. It explains that time and distance are the most important factors, but it does not set any time or distance limits except to observe that a permit is needed where the discharge is a few feet away from navigable waters and that a permit is not required where the discharge is far away and it takes "many years" for the pollutants to complete the journey. Beyond this, the Court provides a list (and a non-exhaustive one at that!) of five other factors that *may* be relevant: "the nature of the material through which the pollutant travels," "the extent to which the pollutant is diluted or chemically changed as it travels," "the amount of pollutant entering the navigable waters relative to the amount of the pollutant that leaves the point source," "the manner by or area in which the pollutant enters the navigable waters," and "the degree to which the pollution (at that point) has maintained its specific identity."

The Court admits that its rule "does not, on its own, clearly explain how to deal with middle instances," but that admission does not go far enough. How the rule applies to "middle instances" is anybody's guess. Except in extreme cases, dischargers will be able to argue that the Court's multifactor test does not require a permit. Opponents will be able to make the opposite argument. Regulators will be able to justify whatever result they prefer in a particular case. And judges will be left at sea.

III

A

Instead of concocting our own rule, I would interpret the words of the statute, and in my view, the better of the two possible interpretations is that a permit is required when a pollutant is discharged directly from a point source to navigable waters. This interpretation is consistent with the statutory language and better fits the overall scheme of the Clean Water Act. And properly understood, it does not have the sort of extreme consequences that the Court finds unacceptable.

Take the Court's example of a pipe that discharges pollutants a short distance from the ocean. This pipe qualifies as a point source. 33 U.S.C. §1362(14). If its discharge goes directly into another point source and that point source discharges directly into navigable waters, there is a direct discharge into navigable waters, and a permit is needed.

That a permit is required in this situation is important because the Clean Water Act's definition of a "point source" is very broad, and as a result, many discharges onto the surface of land are likely to be covered. As noted, "point source[s]" include "ditch[es]" and "channel[s]," as well as "any discernible, confined and discrete conveyance . . . from which pollutants . . . may be discharged." §1362(14). Therefore if water discharged on the surface of the land finds or creates a passage leading to navigable waters, a permit may be required if the course that the discharge takes is (1) a "conveyance" that is (2) "discernible" and (3) "confined."

Those three requirements are rather easily satisfied. When a liquid flows over the surface of land to navigable waters, the surface is a conveyance, *i.e.*, a "means of carrying or transporting something" from one place to another. This conveyance would be "discernible," *i.e.*, capable of being seen. And it would be "confined," *i.e.*, held within bounds, if the topography of the land in question imposes some boundaries on its flow.

If the term "point source" is read in this way, it would have a broad reach and would cover many of the cases that trouble the Court. Moreover — and I find this point particularly important — even if this interpretation fails to capture every case that seems to call out for regulation, that would not mean that these cases would necessarily remain unchecked. The States have the authority to regulate the discharge of pollutants by nonpoint sources. They are entrusted with a vital role under the Clean Water Act, and there is no reason to believe that they would tolerate cases of abuse. . . .

* * *

The Court adopts a nebulous standard, enumerates a non-exhaustive list of potentially relevant factors, and washes its hands of the problem. We should not require regulated parties to "feel their way on a case-by-case basis" where the costs of uncertainty are so great. The Court's decision invites "arbitrary and inconsistent decisionmaking." And "[t]hat is not what the Clean [Water] Act contemplates."

I would reverse the judgment below and instruct the lower courts to apply the test set out above. I therefore respectfully dissent.

PREREQUISITES FOR BRINGING TAKINGS CLAIMS AGAINST GOVERNMENT ENTITIES IN FEDERAL COURT

In the case below the Supreme Court overturned a precedent requiring property owners first to seek compensation in state court before pursuing federal litigation claiming that a state or local regulation has taken their property. By a 5-4 majority the Court overruled Williamson County Regional Planning Commission v. Hamilton Bank of Johnson City, 473 U.S. 172 (1985), which had been viewed as a significant barrier to takings litigation in federal court.

KNICK v. TOWNSHIP OF SCOTT
139 S.Ct. 2162 (2019)

Roberts, C.J., delivered the opinion of the Court, in which Thomas, Alito, Gorsuch, and Kavanaugh, JJ., joined. Thomas, J., filed a concurring opinion. Kagan, J., filed a dissenting opinion, in which Ginsburg, Breyer, and Sotomayor, JJ., joined.

Chief Justice Roberts delivered the opinion of the Court.
The Takings Clause of the Fifth Amendment states that "private property [shall not] be taken for public use, without just compensation." In *Williamson County Regional Planning Comm'n v. Hamilton Bank of Johnson City*, 473 U.S. 172 (1985), we held that a property owner whose property has been taken by a local government has not suffered a violation of his Fifth Amendment rights — and thus cannot bring a federal takings claim in federal court — until a state court has denied his claim for just compensation under state law.

The *Williamson County* Court anticipated that if the property owner failed to secure just compensation under state law in state court, he would be able to bring a "ripe" federal takings claim in federal court. See *id.*, at 194. But as we later held in *San Remo Hotel, L.P. v. City and County of San Francisco*, 545 U.S. 323 (2005), a state court's resolution of a claim for just compensation under state law generally has preclusive effect in any subsequent federal suit. The takings plaintiff thus finds himself in a Catch-22: He cannot go to federal court without going to state court first; but if he goes to state court and loses, his claim will be barred in federal court. The federal claim dies aborning.

The *San Remo* preclusion trap should tip us off that the state-litigation requirement rests on a mistaken view of the Fifth Amendment. The Civil Rights Act of 1871, after all, guarantees "a federal forum for claims of unconstitutional treatment at the hands of state officials," and the settled rule is that "exhaustion of state remedies 'is *not* a prerequisite to an action under [42 U.S.C.] §1983.' " But the guarantee of a federal forum rings hollow for takings plaintiffs, who are forced to litigate their claims in state court.

We now conclude that the state-litigation requirement imposes an unjustifiable burden on takings plaintiffs, conflicts with the rest of our takings jurisprudence, and must be overruled. A property owner has an actionable Fifth Amendment takings claim when the government takes his property without paying for it. That does not mean that the government must provide compensation in advance of a taking or risk having its action invalidated: So long as the property owner has some way to obtain compensation after the fact, governments need not fear that courts will enjoin their activities. But it does mean that the property owner has suffered a violation of his Fifth Amendment rights when the government takes his property without just compensation, and therefore may bring his claim in federal court under §1983 at that time.

I

Petitioner Rose Mary Knick owns 90 acres of land in Scott Township, Pennsylvania, a small community just north of Scranton. Knick lives in a single-family home on the property and uses the rest of the land as a grazing area for horses and other farm animals. The property includes a small graveyard where the ancestors of Knick's neighbors are allegedly buried. Such family cemeteries are fairly common in Pennsylvania, where "backyard burials" have long been permitted.

In December 2012, the Township passed an ordinance requiring that "[a]ll cemeteries . . . be kept open and accessible to the general public during daylight hours." The ordinance defined a "cemetery" as "[a] place or area of ground, whether contained on private or public property, which has been set apart for or otherwise utilized as a burial place for deceased human beings." The ordinance also authorized Township "code enforcement" officers to "enter upon any property" to determine the existence and location of a cemetery.

In 2013, a Township officer found several grave markers on Knick's property and notified her that she was violating the ordinance by failing to open the cemetery to the public during the day. Knick responded by seeking declaratory and injunctive relief in state court on the ground that the ordinance effected a taking of her property. Knick did not seek compensation for the taking by bringing an "inverse condemnation" action under state law. Inverse condemnation is "a cause of action against a governmental defendant to recover the value of property which has been taken in fact by the governmental defendant." Inverse condemnation stands in contrast to direct condemnation, in which the government initiates proceedings to acquire title under its eminent domain authority. Pennsylvania, like every other State besides Ohio, provides a state inverse condemnation action. In response to Knick's suit, the Township withdrew the violation notice and agreed to stay enforcement of the ordinance during the state court proceedings. The court, however, declined to rule on Knick's request for declaratory and injunctive relief because, without an ongoing enforcement action, she could not demonstrate the irreparable harm necessary for equitable relief.

Knick then filed an action in Federal District Court under 42 U.S.C. §1983, alleging that the ordinance violated the Takings Clause of the Fifth Amendment. The District Court dismissed Knick's takings claim under *Williamson County* because she had not pursued an inverse condemnation action in state court. On appeal, the Third Circuit noted that the ordinance was "extraordinary and constitutionally suspect," but affirmed the District Court in light of *Williamson County*.

We granted certiorari to reconsider the holding of *Williamson County* that property owners must seek just compensation under state law in state court before bringing a federal takings claim under §1983.

II

In *Williamson County*, a property developer brought a takings claim under §1983 against a zoning board that had rejected the developer's proposal for a new subdivision. *Williamson County* held that the developer's Fifth Amendment claim was not "ripe" for two reasons. First, the developer still had an opportunity to seek a variance from the appeals board, so any taking was therefore not yet final. Knick does not question the validity of this finality requirement, which is not at issue here.

The second holding of *Williamson County* is that the developer had no federal takings claim because he had not sought compensation "through the procedures the State ha[d] provided for doing so." That is the holding Knick asks us to overrule. According to the Court, "if a State provides an adequate procedure for seeking just compensation, the property owner cannot claim a violation of the [Takings] Clause until it has used the procedure and been denied just compensation." The Court concluded that the developer's federal takings claim was "premature" because he had not sought compensation through the State's inverse condemnation procedure.

The unanticipated consequences of this ruling were not clear until 20 years later, when this Court decided *San Remo*. In that case, the takings plaintiffs complied with *Williamson County* and brought a claim for compensation in state court. The complaint made clear that the plaintiffs sought relief only under the takings clause of the State Constitution, intending to reserve their Fifth Amendment claim for a later federal suit if the state suit proved unsuccessful. When that happened, however, and the plaintiffs proceeded to federal court, they found that their federal claim was barred. This Court held that the full faith and credit statute, 28 U.S.C. §1738, required the federal court to give preclusive effect to the state court's decision, blocking any subsequent consideration of whether the plaintiff had suffered a taking within the meaning of the Fifth Amendment. The adverse state court decision that, according to *Williamson County*, gave rise to a ripe federal takings claim simultaneously barred that claim, preventing the federal court from ever considering it.

The state-litigation requirement relegates the Takings Clause "to the status of a poor relation" among the provisions of the Bill of Rights. Plaintiffs asserting any other constitutional claim are guaranteed a federal forum under §1983, but the state-litigation requirement "hand[s] authority over federal takings claims to state courts." Fidelity to the Takings Clause and our cases construing it requires overruling *Williamson County* and restoring takings claims to the full-fledged constitutional status the Framers envisioned when they included the Clause among the other protections in the Bill of Rights.

III

A

Contrary to *Williamson County*, a property owner has a claim for a violation of the Takings Clause as soon as a government takes his property for public use without paying for it. The Clause provides: "[N]or shall private property be taken for public use, without just compensation." It does not say: "Nor shall private property be taken for public use, without an available procedure that will result in compensation." If a local government takes private property without paying for it, that government has violated the Fifth Amendment — just as the Takings Clause says — without regard to subsequent state court proceedings. And the property owner may sue the government at that time in federal court for the "deprivation" of a right "secured by the Constitution." 42 U.S.C. §1983.

We have long recognized that property owners may bring Fifth Amendment claims against the Federal Government as soon as their property has been taken. The Tucker Act, which provides the standard procedure for bringing such claims, gives the Court of Federal Claims jurisdiction to "render judgment upon any claim against the United States founded either upon the Constitution" or any federal law or contract for damages "in cases not sounding in tort." We have held that "[i]f there is a taking, the claim is 'founded upon the Constitution' and within the jurisdiction of the Court of Claims to hear and determine." And we have explained that "the act of taking" is the "event which gives rise to the claim for compensation."

The Fifth Amendment right to full compensation arises at the time of the taking, regardless of post-taking remedies that may be available to the property owner. That principle was confirmed in *Jacobs v. United States*, 290 U.S. 13 (1933), where we held that a property owner found to have a valid takings claim is entitled to compensation as if it had been "paid contemporaneously with the taking" — that is, the compensation must generally consist of the total value of the property when taken, plus interest from that time. We rejected the view of the lower court that a property owner is entitled to interest only when the government provides a particular remedy — direct condemnation proceedings — and not when the owner brings a takings suit under the Tucker Act. "The form of the remedy d[oes] not qualify the right. It rest[s] upon the Fifth Amendment."

Jacobs made clear that, no matter what sort of procedures the government puts in place to remedy a taking, a property owner has a Fifth Amendment entitlement to compensation as soon as the government takes his property without paying for it. Whether the government does nothing, forcing the owner to bring a takings suit under the Tucker Act, or whether it provides the owner with a statutory compensation remedy by initiating direct condemnation proceedings, the owner's claim for compensation "rest[s] upon the Fifth Amendment."

Although *Jacobs* concerned a taking by the Federal Government, the same reasoning applies to takings by the States. The availability of any particular compensation remedy, such as an inverse condemnation claim under state law, cannot infringe or restrict the property owner's federal constitutional claim — just as the existence of a state action for battery does not bar a Fourth Amendment claim of excessive force. The fact that the State has provided a property owner with a procedure that may subsequently result in just compensation cannot deprive the owner of his Fifth Amendment right to compensation under the Constitution, leaving only the state law right. And that is key because it is the existence of the Fifth Amendment right that allows the owner to proceed directly to federal court under §1983.

Williamson County had a different view of how the Takings Clause works. According to *Williamson County*, a taking does not give rise to a federal constitutional right to just compensation at that time, but instead gives a right to a state law procedure that will eventually result in just compensation. As the Court put it, "if a State provides an adequate procedure for seeking just compensation, the property owner cannot claim a violation of the [Takings] Clause until it has used the procedure and been denied just compensation." In the absence of a state remedy, the Fifth Amendment right to compensation would attach immediately. But, under *Williamson County*, the presence of a state remedy qualifies the right, preventing it from vesting until exhaustion of the state procedure. That is what *Jacobs* confirmed could not be done.

Just two years after *Williamson County*, in *First English Evangelical Lutheran Church of Glendale v. County of Los Angeles*, 482 U.S. 304 (1987), the Court returned to the understanding that the Fifth Amendment right to compensation automatically arises at the time the government takes property without paying for it.

Relying heavily on *Jacobs* and other Fifth Amendment precedents neglected by *Williamson County, First English* held that a property owner is entitled to compensation for the temporary loss of his property. We explained that "government action that works a taking of property rights necessarily implicates the 'constitutional obligation to pay just compensation.'" Because of "the self-executing character" of the Takings Clause "with respect to compensation," a property owner has a constitutional claim for just compensation at the time of the taking. The government's post-taking actions (there, repeal of the challenged ordinance) cannot nullify the property owner's existing Fifth Amendment right: "[W]here the government's activities have already worked a taking of all use of property, no subsequent action by the government can relieve it of the duty to provide compensation."

In holding that a property owner acquires an irrevocable right to just compensation immediately upon a taking, *First English* adopted a position Justice Brennan had taken in an earlier dissent. In that opinion, Justice Brennan explained that "once there is a 'taking,' compensation *must* be awarded" because "[a]s soon as private property has been taken, whether through formal condemnation proceedings, occupancy, physical invasion, or regulation, the landowner has *already* suffered a constitutional violation."

First English embraced that view, reaffirming that "in the event of a taking, the compensation remedy is required by the Constitution." Compensation under the Takings Clause is a remedy for the "constitutional violation" that "the landowner has *already* suffered" at the time of the uncompensated taking.

A later payment of compensation may remedy the constitutional violation that occurred at the time of the taking, but that does not mean the violation never took place. The violation is the only reason compensation was owed in the first place. A bank robber might give the loot back, but he still robbed the bank. The availability of a subsequent compensation remedy for a taking without compensation no more means there never was a constitutional violation in the first place than the availability of a damages action renders negligent conduct compliant with the duty of care.

In sum, because a taking without compensation violates the self-executing Fifth Amendment at the time of the taking, the property owner can bring a federal suit at that time. Just as someone whose property has been taken by the Federal Government has a claim "founded . . . upon the Constitution" that he may bring under the Tucker Act, someone whose property has been taken by a local government has a claim under §1983 for a "deprivation of [a] right[] . . . secured by the Constitution" that he may bring upon the taking in federal court. The "general rule" is that plaintiffs may bring constitutional claims under §1983 "without first bringing any sort of state lawsuit, even when state court actions addressing the underlying behavior are available." This is as true for takings claims as for any other claim grounded in the Bill of Rights.

B

Williamson County effectively established an exhaustion requirement for §1983 takings claims when it held that a property owner must pursue state procedures for obtaining compensation before bringing a federal suit. But the Court did not phrase its holding in those terms; if it had, its error would have been clear. Instead, *Williamson County* broke with the Court's longstanding position that a property owner has a constitutional claim to compensation at the time the government deprives him of his property, and held that there can be no uncompensated taking, and thus no Fifth Amendment claim actionable under §1983, until the property owner has tried and failed to obtain compensation through the available state procedure. "[U]ntil it has used the procedure and been denied just compensation," the property owner "'has no claim against the Government' for a taking."

Williamson County drew that understanding of the Clause from *Ruckelshaus v. Monsanto Co.*, a decision from the prior Term. *Monsanto* did not involve a takings claim for just compensation. The plaintiff there sought to enjoin a federal statute because it effected a taking, even though the statute set up a special arbitration procedure for obtaining compensation, and the plaintiff could bring a takings claim pursuant to the Tucker Act if arbitration did not yield sufficient compensation. The Court rejected the plaintiff's claim because "[e]quitable relief is not available to enjoin an alleged taking of private property for a public use, duly authorized by law, when a suit for compensation can be brought against the sovereign subsequent to the taking." That much is consistent with our precedent: Equitable relief was not available because monetary relief was under the Tucker Act.

That was enough to decide the case. But *Monsanto* went on to say that if the plaintiff obtained compensation in arbitration, then "no taking has occurred and the [plaintiff] has no claim against the Government." Certainly it is correct that a fully compensated plaintiff has no further claim, but that is because the taking has been *remedied* by compensation, not because there was *no taking* in the first place. The statute in *Monsanto* simply required the plaintiff to attempt to vindicate its claim to compensation through arbitration before proceeding under the Tucker Act. The case offers no support to *Williamson County* in this regard, because Congress — unlike the States — is free to require plaintiffs to exhaust administrative remedies before bringing constitutional claims.

Williamson County also relied on *Monsanto* when it analogized its new state-litigation requirement to federal takings practice, stating that "taking[s] claims against the Federal Government are premature until the property owner has availed itself of the process provided by the Tucker Act." But the Court was simply confused. A claim for just compensation brought under the Tucker Act is not a prerequisite to a Fifth Amendment takings claim — it *is* a Fifth Amendment takings claim. A party who loses a Tucker Act suit has nowhere else to go to seek compensation for an alleged taking. . . .

The dissent, doing what respondents do not even dare to attempt, defends the original rationale of *Williamson County* — that there is no Fifth Amendment violation, and thus no Fifth Amendment claim, until the government denies the property owner compensation in a subsequent proceeding. But although the dissent makes a more thoughtful and considered argument than *Williamson County*, it cannot reconcile its view with our repeated holdings that a property owner acquires a constitutional right to compensation at the time of the taking. The only reason that a taking would automatically entitle a property owner to the remedy of compensation is that, as Justice Brennan explained, with the uncompensated taking "the landowner has *already* suffered a constitutional violation." The dissent here provides no more reason to resist that conclusion than did *Williamson County.*

C

The Court in *Williamson County* relied on statements in our prior opinions that the Clause "does not provide or require that compensation shall be actually paid in advance of the occupancy of the land to be taken. But the owner is entitled to reasonable, certain and adequate provision for obtaining compensation" after a taking. Respondents rely on the same cases in contending that uncompensated takings for which compensation is subsequently available do not violate the Fifth Amendment at the time of the taking. But respondents read those statements too broadly. They concerned requests for injunctive relief, and the availability of subsequent compensation meant that such an equitable remedy was not available. Simply because the property owner was not entitled to injunctive relief at the time of the taking does not mean there was no violation of the Takings Clause at that time.

The history of takings litigation provides valuable context. At the time of the founding there usually was no compensation remedy available to property owners. On occasion, when a legislature authorized a particular government action that took private property, it might also create a special owner-initiated procedure for obtaining compensation. But there were no general causes of action through which plaintiffs could obtain compensation for property taken for public use.

Until the 1870s, the typical recourse of a property owner who had suffered an uncompensated taking was to bring a common law trespass action against the responsible corporation or government official. The official would then raise the defense that his trespass was lawful because authorized by statute or ordinance, and the plaintiff would respond that the law was unconstitutional because it provided for a taking without just compensation. If the plaintiff prevailed, he nonetheless had no way at common law to obtain money damages for a permanent taking — that is, just compensation for the total value of his property. He could obtain only retrospective damages, as well as an injunction ejecting the government from his property going forward.

As Chancellor Kent explained when granting a property owner equitable relief, the Takings Clause and its analogs in state constitutions required that "a fair compensation must, in all cases, be *previously* made to the individuals affected." If a government took property without payment, a court would set aside the taking because it violated the Constitution and order the property restored to its owner. The Framers meant to prohibit the Federal Government from *taking* property without paying for it. Allowing the government to *keep* the property pending subsequent compensation to the owner, in proceedings that hardly existed in 1787, was not what they envisioned.

Antebellum courts, which had no means of compensating a property owner for his loss, had no way to redress the violation of an owner's Fifth Amendment rights other than ordering the government to give him back his property. But in the 1870s, as state courts began to recognize implied rights of action for damages under the state equivalents of the Takings Clause, they declined to grant injunctions because property owners had an adequate remedy at law. On the federal level, Congress enabled property owners to obtain compensation for takings in federal court when it passed the Tucker Act in 1887, and we subsequently joined the state courts in holding that the compensation remedy is required by the Takings Clause itself.

Today, because the federal and nearly all state governments provide just compensation remedies to property owners who have suffered a taking, equitable relief is generally unavailable. As long as an adequate provision for obtaining just compensation exists, there is no basis to enjoin the government's action effecting a taking. But that is because, as the Court explained in *First English*, such a procedure is a remedy for a taking that violated the Constitution, not because the availability of the procedure somehow prevented the violation from occurring in the first place.

The dissent contends that our characterization of *Cherokee Nation* effectively overrules "a hundred-plus years of legal rulings." But under today's decision every one of the cases cited by the dissent would come out the same way — the plaintiffs would not be entitled to the relief they requested because they could instead pursue a suit for compensation. The premise of such a suit for compensation is that the property owner has already suffered a violation of the Fifth Amendment that may be remedied by money damages.

* * *

We conclude that a government violates the Takings Clause when it takes property without compensation, and that a property owner may bring a Fifth Amendment claim under §1983 at that time. That does not as a practical matter mean that government action or regulation may not proceed in the absence of contemporaneous compensation. Given the availability of post-taking compensation, barring the government from acting will ordinarily not be appropriate. But because the violation is complete at the time of the taking, pursuit of a remedy in federal court need not await any subsequent state action. Takings claims against local governments should be handled the same as other claims under the Bill of Rights. *Williamson County* erred in holding otherwise.

IV

The next question is whether we should overrule *Williamson County*, or whether *stare decisis* counsels in favor of adhering to the decision, despite its error. The doctrine of *stare decisis* reflects a judgment "that 'in most matters it is more important that the applicable rule of law be settled than that it be settled right.'" The doctrine "is at its weakest when we interpret the Constitution," as we did in *Williamson County*, because only this Court or a constitutional amendment can alter our holdings.

We have identified several factors to consider in deciding whether to overrule a past decision, including "the quality of [its] reasoning, the workability of the rule it established, its consistency with other related decisions, . . . and reliance on the decision." All of these factors counsel in favor of overruling *Williamson County*.

Williamson County was not just wrong. Its reasoning was exceptionally ill founded and conflicted with much of our takings jurisprudence. Its key conclusion, which it drew from unnecessary language in *Monsanto* — that a property owner does not have a ripe federal takings claim until he has unsuccessfully pursued an initial state law claim for just compensation — ignored *Jacobs* and many subsequent decisions holding that a property owner acquires a Fifth Amendment right to compensation at the time of a taking. This contradiction was on stark display just two years later in *First English*.

The decision has come in for repeated criticism over the years from Justices of this Court and many respected commentators. Even the academic defenders of the state-litigation requirement base it on federalism concerns (although they do not reconcile those concerns with the settled construction of §1983) rather than the reasoning of the opinion itself. See Echeverria, *Horne v. Department of Agriculture*: An Invitation to Reexamine "Ripeness" Doctrine in Takings Litigation, 43 Env. L. Rep. 10735, 10744 (2013); Sterk, The Demise of Federal Takings Litigation, 48 Wm. & Mary L. Rev. 251, 288 (2006).

Because of its shaky foundations, the state-litigation requirement has been a rule in search of a justification for over 30 years. We eventually abandoned the view that the requirement is an element of a takings claim and recast it as a "prudential" ripeness rule. No party defends that approach here. Respondents have taken a new tack, adopting a §1983-specific theory at which *Williamson County* did not even hint. The fact that the justification for the state-litigation requirement continues to evolve is another factor undermining the force of *stare decisis*.

The state-litigation requirement has also proved to be unworkable in practice. *Williamson County* envisioned that takings plaintiffs would ripen their federal claims in state court and then, if necessary, bring a federal suit under §1983. But, as we held in *San Remo*, the state court's resolution of the plaintiff's inverse condemnation claim has preclusive effect in any subsequent federal suit. The upshot is that many takings plaintiffs never have the opportunity to litigate in a federal forum that §1983 by its terms seems to provide. That significant consequence was not considered by the Court in *Williamson County*.

The dissent argues that our constitutional holding in *Williamson County* should enjoy the "enhanced" form of *stare decisis* we usually reserve for statutory decisions, because Congress could have eliminated the *San Remo* preclusion trap by amending the full faith and credit statute. But takings plaintiffs, unlike plaintiffs bringing any other constitutional claim, would still have been forced to pursue relief under state law before they could bring suit in federal court. Congress could not have lifted that unjustified exhaustion requirement because, under *Williamson County*, a property owner had no federal claim until a state court denied him compensation.

Finally, there are no reliance interests on the state-litigation requirement. We have recognized that the force of *stare decisis* is "reduced" when rules that do not "serve as a guide to lawful behavior" are at issue. Our holding that uncompensated takings violate the Fifth Amendment will not expose governments to new liability; it will simply allow into federal court takings claims that otherwise would have been brought as inverse condemnation suits in state court.

Governments need not fear that our holding will lead federal courts to invalidate their regulations as unconstitutional. As long as just compensation remedies are available — as they have been for nearly 150 years — injunctive relief will be foreclosed. For the same reason, the Federal Government need not worry that courts will set aside agency actions as unconstitutional under the Administrative Procedure Act. 5 U.S.C. §706(2)(B). Federal courts will not invalidate an otherwise lawful uncompensated taking when the property owner can receive complete relief through a Fifth Amendment claim brought under the Tucker Act.

In light of all the foregoing, the dissent cannot, with respect, fairly maintain its extreme assertions regarding our application of the principle of *stare decisis*.

* * *

The state-litigation requirement of *Williamson County* is overruled. A property owner may bring a takings claim under §1983 upon the taking of his property without just compensation by a local government. The judgment of the United States Court of Appeals for the Third Circuit is vacated, and the case is remanded for further proceedings consistent with this opinion.

It is so ordered.

JUSTICE THOMAS, concurring.

The Fifth Amendment's Takings Clause prohibits the government from "tak[ing]" private property "without just compensation." The Court correctly interprets this text by holding that a violation of this Clause occurs as soon as the government takes property without paying for it.

The United States, by contrast, urges us not to enforce the Takings Clause as written. It worries that requiring payment to accompany a taking would allow courts to enjoin or invalidate broad regulatory programs "merely" because the program takes property without paying for it. According to the United States, "there is a 'nearly infinite variety of ways in which government actions or regulations can affect property interests,'" and it ought to be good enough that the government "implicitly promises to pay compensation for any taking" if a property owner successfully sues the government in court. Government officials, the United States contends, should be able to implement regulatory programs "without fear" of injunction or invalidation under the Takings Clause, "even when" the program is so far reaching that the officials "cannot determine whether a taking will occur."

This "sue me" approach to the Takings Clause is untenable. The Fifth Amendment does not merely provide a damages remedy to a property owner willing to "shoulder the burden of securing compensation" after the government takes property without paying for it. Instead, it makes just compensation a "prerequisite" to the government's authority to "tak[e] property for public use." A "purported exercise of the eminent-domain power" is therefore "invalid" unless the government "pays just compensation before or at the time of its taking." If this requirement makes some regulatory programs "unworkable in practice," so be it — our role is to enforce the Takings Clause as written.

Of course, as the Court correctly explains, the United States' concerns about injunctions may be misplaced. Injunctive relief is not available when an adequate remedy exists at law. And even when relief is appropriate for a particular plaintiff, it does not follow that a court may enjoin or invalidate an entire regulatory "program," by granting relief "beyond the parties to the case."

Still, "[w]hen the government repudiates [its] duty" to pay just compensation, its actions "are not only unconstitutional" but may be "tortious as well." I do not understand the Court's opinion to foreclose the application of ordinary remedial principles to takings claims and related common-law tort claims, such as trespass. I therefore join it in full.

JUSTICE KAGAN, with whom JUSTICE GINSBURG, JUSTICE BREYER, and JUSTICE SOTOMAYOR join, dissenting.

Today, the Court formally overrules *Williamson County Regional Planning Comm'n v. Hamilton Bank of Johnson City*, 473 U.S. 172 (1985). But its decision rejects far more than that single case. *Williamson County* was rooted in an understanding of the Fifth Amendment's Takings Clause stretching back to the late 1800s. On that view, a government could take property so long as it provided a reliable mechanism to pay just compensation, even if the payment came after the fact. No longer. The majority today holds, in conflict with precedent after precedent, that a government violates the Constitution whenever it takes property without advance compensation — no matter how good its commitment to pay. That conclusion has no basis in the Takings Clause. Its consequence is to channel a mass of quintessentially local cases involving complex state-law issues into federal courts. And it transgresses all usual principles of *stare decisis*. I respectfully dissent.

I

Begin with the basics — the meaning of the Takings Clause. The right that Clause confers is not to be free from government takings of property for public purposes. Instead, the right is to be free from those takings when the government fails to provide "just compensation." In other words, the government *can* take private property for public purposes, so long as it fairly pays the property owner. That precept, which the majority does not contest, comes straight out of the constitutional text: "[P]rivate property [shall not] be taken for public use, without just compensation." Amdt. 5. "As its language indicates, [the Takings Clause] does not prohibit the taking of private property, but instead places a condition on the exercise of that power." And that constitutional choice accords with ancient principles about what governments do. The eminent domain power — the capacity to "take private property for public uses" — is an integral "attribute of sovereignty." Small surprise, then, that the Constitution does not prohibit takings for public purposes, but only requires the government to pay fair value.

In that way, the Takings Clause is unique among the Bill of Rights' guarantees. It is, for example, unlike the Fourth Amendment's protection against excessive force — which the majority mistakenly proposes as an analogy. See *ante*, at 8. Suppose a law enforcement officer uses excessive force and the victim recovers damages for his injuries. Did a constitutional violation occur? Of course. The Constitution prohibits what the officer did; the payment of damages merely remedied the constitutional wrong. But the Takings Clause is different because it does not prohibit takings; to the contrary, it permits them provided the government gives just compensation. So when the government "takes and pays," it is not violating the Constitution at all. Put another way, a Takings Clause violation has two necessary elements. First, the government must take the property. Second, it must deny the property owner just compensation. If the government has not done both, no constitutional violation has happened. All this is well-trod ground. Even the majority (despite its faulty analogy) does not contest it.

Similarly well-settled — until the majority's opinion today — was the answer to a follow-on question: At what point has the government denied a property owner just compensation, so as to complete a Fifth Amendment violation? For over a hundred years, this Court held that advance or contemporaneous payment was not required, so long as the government had established reliable procedures for an owner to later obtain just compensation (including interest for any time elapsed). The rule got its start in *Cherokee Nation v. Southern Kansas R. Co.*, 135 U.S. 641 (1890), where the Tribe argued that a federal statute authorizing condemnation of its property violated the Fifth Amendment because the law did not require advance payment. The Court disagreed. It held that the Takings Clause "does not provide or require that compensation shall be actually paid in advance of the occupancy of the land to be taken" so long as the government made available to the owner "reasonable, certain and adequate provision for obtaining compensation" afterward. Decade after decade, the Court repeated that principle. As another case put the point: The Takings Clause does not demand "that compensation should be made previous to the taking" so long as "adequate means [are] provided for a reasonably just and prompt ascertainment and payment of the compensation." And the Court also made clear that a statute creating a right of action against the responsible government entity generally qualified as a constitutionally adequate compensatory mechanism.

Williamson County followed from those decisions as night the day. The case began when a local planning commission rejected a property owner's development proposal. The owner chose not to seek compensation through the procedure the State had created — an "inverse condemnation" action against the commission. Instead, the owner sued in federal court alleging a Takings Clause violation under 42 U.S.C. §1983. Consistent with the century's worth of precedent I have recounted above, the Court found that no Fifth Amendment violation had yet occurred. The Court first recognized that "[t]he Fifth Amendment does not proscribe the taking of property; it proscribes taking without just compensation." Next, the Court stated (citing no fewer than five precedents) that the Amendment does not demand that "compensation be paid in advance of, or contemporaneously with, the taking." "[A]ll that is required," the Court continued, is that the State have provided "a 'reasonable, certain and adequate provision for obtaining compensation.'" Here, the State had done so: Nothing suggested that the inverse condemnation procedure was inadequate. So the property owner's claim was "not yet ripe": The owner could not "claim a violation of the [Takings] Clause until it [had] used the procedure and been denied."

So contrary to the majority's portrayal, *Williamson County* did not result from some inexplicable confusion about "how the Takings Clause works." Far from it. *Williamson County* built on a long line of decisions addressing the elements of a Takings Clause violation. The Court there said only two things remotely new.

First, the Court found that the State's inverse condemnation procedure qualified as a "reasonable, certain and adequate" procedure. But no one in this case disputes anything to do with that conclusion — including that the equivalent Pennsylvania procedure here is similarly adequate. Second, the Court held that a §1983 suit could not be brought until a property owner had unsuccessfully invoked the State's procedure for obtaining payment. But that was a direct function of the Court's prior holdings. Everyone agrees that a §1983 suit cannot be brought before a constitutional violation has occurred. And according to the Court's repeated decisions, a Takings Clause violation does not occur until an owner has used the government's procedures and failed to obtain just compensation. All *Williamson County* did was to put the period on an already-completed sentence about when a takings claim arises.

Today's decision thus overthrows the Court's long-settled view of the Takings Clause. The majority declares, as against a mountain of precedent, that a government taking private property for public purposes must pay compensation at that moment or in advance. If the government fails to do so, a constitutional violation has occurred, regardless of whether "reasonable, certain and adequate" compensatory mechanisms exist. And regardless of how many times this Court has said the opposite before. Under cover of overruling "only" a single decision, today's opinion smashes a hundred-plus years of legal rulings to smithereens.

II

So how does the majority defend taking down *Williamson County* and its many precursors? Its decision rests on four ideas: a comparison between takings claims and other constitutional claims, a resort to the Takings Clause's text, and theories about two lines of this Court's precedent. All are misguided. The majority uses the term "shaky foundations." It knows whereof it speaks.

The first crack comes from the repeated assertion (already encountered in the majority's Fourth Amendment analogy) that *Williamson County* treats takings claims worse than other claims founded in the Bill of Rights. That is not so. The distinctive aspects of litigating a takings claim merely reflect the distinctive aspects of the constitutional right. Once again, a Fourth Amendment claim arises at the moment a police officer uses excessive force, because the Constitution prohibits that thing and that thing only. (Similarly, for the majority's other analogies, a bank robber commits his offense when he robs a bank and a tortfeasor when he acts negligently — because that conduct, and it alone, is what the law forbids.) Or to make the same point a bit differently, even if a government could compensate the victim in advance — as the majority requires here — the victim would still suffer constitutional injury when the force is used. But none of that is true of Takings Clause violations. That kind of infringement, as explained, is complete only after *two* things occur: (1) the government takes property, and (2) it fails to pay just compensation. All *Williamson County* and its precursors do is recognize that fact, by saying that a constitutional claim (and thus a §1983 suit) arises only after the second condition is met — when the property owner comes away from the government's compensatory procedure empty-handed. That is to treat the Takings Clause exactly as its dual elements require — and because that is so, neither worse nor better than any other right.

Second, the majority contends that its rule follows from the constitutional text, because the Takings Clause does not say "[n]or shall private property be taken for public use, without an available procedure that will result in compensation." There is a reason the majority devotes only a few sentences to that argument. Because here's another thing the text does not say: "Nor shall private property be taken for public use, without advance or contemporaneous payment of just compensation, notwithstanding ordinary procedures." In other words, the text no more states the majority's rule than it does *Williamson County*'s (and its precursors'). As constitutional text often is, the Takings Clause is spare. It says that a government taking property must pay just compensation — but does not say through exactly what mechanism or at exactly what time. That was left to be worked out, consistent with the Clause's (minimal) text and purpose. And from 1890 until today, this Court worked it out *Williamson County*'s way, rather than the majority's. Under our caselaw, a government could use reliable post-taking compensatory mechanisms (with payment calculated from the taking) without violating the Takings Clause.

Third, the majority tries to explain away that mass of precedent, with a theory so, well, inventive that it appears in neither the petitioner's nor her 15-plus *amici*'s briefs. Don't read the decisions "too broadly," the majority says. Yes, the Court in each rejected a takings claim, instructing the property owner to avail herself instead of a government-created compensatory mechanism. But all the Court meant (the majority says) was that the plaintiffs had sought the wrong kind of relief: They could not get injunctions because the available compensatory procedures gave an adequate remedy at law. The Court still believed (so says the majority) that the cases involved constitutional violations. Or said otherwise (again, according to the majority), the Court still understood the Takings Clause to prohibit delayed payment.

Points for creativity, but that is just not what the decisions say. Most of the cases involved requests for injunctions, but the equity/law distinction played little or no role in our analyses. Instead, the decisions addressed directly what the Takings Clause requires (or not). And as already shown, they held that the Clause does not demand advance payment. Beginning again at the beginning, *Cherokee Nation* decided that the Takings Clause "does not provide or require that compensation shall be actually paid in advance." In *Backus v. Fort Street Union Depot Co.*, 169 U.S. 557, 567–568 (1898), the Court declared that a property owner had no "constitutional right to have the amount of his compensation finally determined and paid before yielding possession." By the time of *Williams v. Parker*, 188 U.S., at 502, the Court could state that "it is settled by repeated decisions" that the Constitution allows the taking of property "prior to any payment." Similarly, in *Joslin Mfg. Co. v. Providence*, 262 U.S. 668, 677 (1923), the Court noted that "[i]t has long been settled that the taking of property . . . need not be accompanied or preceded by payment, but that the requirement of just compensation is satisfied when" there is a pledge of "reasonably prompt ascertainment and payment." In *Hurley v. Kincaid*, 285 U.S. 95, 104 (1932), the Court repeated that the "Fifth Amendment does not entitle [a property owner] to be paid in advance of the taking." I could go on — there are eighty more years to cover, and more decisions in the early years too — but by now you probably get the idea.

Well, just one more especially good demonstration. In *Yearsley v. W. A. Ross Constr. Co.*, 309 U.S. 18 (1940), the plaintiffs sought money damages for an alleged Takings Clause violation. For that reason, the Court's theory about suits seeking injunctions has no possible application. Still, the Court rejected the claim: The different remedy requested made no difference in the result. And yet more important: In refusing to find a Takings Clause violation, the Court used the exact same reasoning as it had in all the cases requesting injunctions. Once again, the Court did not focus on the nature of the relief sought. It simply explained that the government had provided a procedure for obtaining post-taking compensation — and that was enough. "The Fifth Amendment does not entitle him [the owner] to be paid in advance of the taking," held the Court, quoting the last injunction case described above. Because the government had set up an adequate compensatory mechanism, the taking was "within [the government's] constitutional power." Once again, the opposite of what the majority pronounces today.[4]

Fourth and finally, the majority lays claim to another line of decisions — involving the Tucker Act — but with no greater success. The Tucker Act waives the Federal Government's sovereign immunity and grants the Court of Federal Claims jurisdiction over suits seeking compensation for takings. According to the majority, this Court's cases establish that such an action "*is* a claim for a violation of the Fifth Amendment" — that is, for a constitutional offense that has al- ready happened because of the absence of advance payment (emphasis in original). But again, the precedents say the opposite. The Tucker Act is the Federal Government's equivalent of a State's inverse condemnation procedure, by which a property owner can obtain just compensation. The former, no less than the latter, *forestalls* any constitutional violation by ensuring that an owner gets full and fair payment for a taking. The Court, for example, stated in *United States v. Riverside Bayview Homes, Inc.*, 474 U.S. 121, 128 (1985), that "so long as [post-taking Tucker Act] compensation is available for those whose property is in fact taken, the governmental action is not unconstitutional." Similarly, we held in *Preseault v. ICC*, 494 U.S. 1, 4–5 (1990) that when "compensation is available to [property owners] under the Tucker Act[,] the requirements of the Fifth Amendment are satisfied." And again, in *Ruckelshaus v. Monsanto Co.*, 467 U.S. 986, 1016 (1984) we rejected a takings claim because the plaintiff could "seek just compensation under the Tucker Act" and "[t]he Fifth Amendment does not require that compensation precede the taking." All those decisions (and there are others) rested on the premise, merely reiterated in *Williamson County*, that the "availability of a suit for compensation against the sovereign will defeat a contention that the action is unconstitutional as a violation of the Fifth Amendment."

To the extent it deals with these cases (mostly, it just ignores them), the majority says only that they (like *Williamson County*) were "confused" or wrong. But maybe the majority should take the hint: When a theory requires declaring precedent after precedent after precedent wrong, that's a sign the theory itself may be wrong. The majority's theory is just that.

---

[4] The majority's supposed best case to the contrary, *First English Evangelical Lutheran Church of Glendale v. County of Los Angeles*, 482 U.S. 304 (1987), is not so good, as is apparent from its express statement that it accords with *Williamson County*. See 482 U.S., at 320, n.10. In *First English*, the Court held that a property owner was entitled to compensation for the temporary loss of his property, occurring while a (later-repealed) regulation was in effect. The Court made clear that a government's duty to compensate for a taking — including a temporary taking — arises from the Fifth Amendment, as of course it does. But the Court nowhere suggested that a Fifth Amendment violation happens even before a government denies the required compensation. (You will scan the majority's description of *First English* in vain for a quote to that effect — because no such quote exists.) To the contrary, the Court went out of its way to recognize the *Williamson County* principle that "no constitutional violation occurs until just compensation has been denied."

III

And not only wrong on prior law. The majority's overruling of *Williamson County* will have two damaging consequences. It will inevitably turn even well-meaning government officials into lawbreakers. And it will subvert important principles of judicial federalism.

To begin with, today's decision means that government regulators will often have no way to avoid violating the Constitution. There are a "nearly infinite variety of ways" for regulations to "affect property interests." And under modern takings law, there is "no magic formula" to determine "whether a given government interference with property is a taking." For that reason, a government actor usually cannot know in advance whether implementing a regulatory program will effect a taking, much less of whose property. Until today, such an official could do his work without fear of wrongdoing, in any jurisdiction that had set up a reliable means for property owners to obtain compensation. Even if some regulatory action turned out to take someone's property, the official would not have violated the Constitution. But no longer. Now, when a government undertakes land-use regulation (and what government doesn't?), the responsible employees will almost inescapably become constitutional malefactors. That is not a fair position in which to place persons carrying out their governmental duties.

Still more important, the majority's ruling channels to federal courts a (potentially massive) set of cases that more properly belongs, at least in the first instance, in state courts — where *Williamson County* put them. The regulation of land use, this Court has stated, is "perhaps the quintessential state activity." And a claim that a land- use regulation violates the Takings Clause usually turns on state-law issues. In that respect, takings claims have little in common with other constitutional challenges. The question in takings cases is not merely whether a given state action meets federal constitutional standards. Before those standards can come into play, a court must typically decide whether, under state law, the plaintiff has a property interest in the thing regulated. See *Phillips v. Washington Legal Foundation*, 524 U.S. 156, 164 (1998); see also Sterk, The Demise of Federal Takings Litigation, 48 Wm. & Mary L. Rev. 251, 288 (2006) ("[I]f background state law did not recognize or create property in the first instance, then a subsequent state action cannot take property"). Often those questions — how does pre-existing state law define the property right?; what interests does that law grant?; and conversely what interests does it deny? — are nuanced and complicated. And not a one of them is familiar to federal courts.

This case highlights the difficulty. The ultimate constitutional question here is: Did Scott Township's cemetery ordinance "go[] too far" (in Justice Holmes's phrase), so as to effect a taking of Rose Mary Knick's property? But to answer that question, it is first necessary to address an issue about background state law. In the Township's view, the ordinance did little more than codify Pennsylvania common law, which (the Township says) has long required property owners to make land containing human remains open to the public. If the Township is right on that state-law question, Knick's constitutional claim will fail: The ordinance, on that account, didn't go far at all. But Knick contends that no common law rule of that kind exists in Pennsylvania. And if she is right, her takings claim may yet have legs. But is she? Or is the Township? I confess: I don't know. Nor, I would venture, do my colleagues on the federal bench. But under today's decision, it will be the Federal District Court for the Middle District of Pennsylvania that will have to resolve this question of local cemetery law.

And if the majority thinks this case is an outlier, it's dead wrong; indeed, this case will be easier than many. Take *Lucas v. South Carolina Coastal Council*, 505 U.S. 1003 (1992). There, this Court held that a South Carolina ban on development of beachfront property worked a taking of the plaintiff's land — unless the State's nuisance law already prohibited such development. The Court then — quite sensibly — remanded the case to the South Carolina Supreme Court to resolve that question. (And while spotting the nuisance issue, the Court may have overlooked other state-law constraints on development. In some States, for example, the public trust doctrine or public prescriptive easements limit the development of beachfront land. Or consider *Stop the Beach Renourishment, Inc. v. Florida Dept. of Environmental Protection*, 560 U.S. 702 (2010). The federal constitutional issue there was whether a decision of the Florida Supreme Court relating to beachfront property constituted a taking. To resolve that issue, though, the Court first had to address whether, under pre-existing Florida property law, "littoral-property owners had rights to future accretions and contact with the water superior to the State's right to fill in its submerged land." The Court bit the bullet and decided that issue itself, as it sometimes has to (though thankfully with the benefit of a state high court's reasoning). But there is no such necessity here — and no excuse for making complex state-law issues part of the daily diet of federal district courts.

State courts are — or at any rate, are supposed to be — the "ultimate expositors of state law." The corollary is that federal courts should refrain whenever possible from deciding novel or difficult state-law questions. That stance, as this Court has long understood, respects the "rightful independence of the state governments," "avoid[s] needless friction with state policies," and promotes "harmonious relation[s] between state and federal authority." For that reason, this Court has promoted practices of certification and abstention to put difficult state-law issues in state judges' hands. We may as well not have bothered. Today's decision sends a flood of complex state-law issues to federal courts. It makes federal courts a principal player in local and state land-use disputes. It betrays judicial federalism.

IV

Everything said above aside, *Williamson County* should stay on the books because of *stare decisis*. Adherence to precedent is "a foundation stone of the rule of law." "[I]t promotes the evenhanded, predictable, and consistent development of legal principles, fosters reliance on judicial decisions, and contributes to the actual and perceived integrity of the judicial process." *Stare decisis*, of course, is "not an inexorable command." But it is not enough that five Justices believe a precedent wrong. Reversing course demands a "special justification — over and above the belief that the precedent was wrongly decided." The majority offers no reason that qualifies.

In its only real stab at a special justification, the majority focuses on what it calls the "*San Remo* preclusion trap." As the majority notes, this Court held in a post-*Williamson County* decision interpreting the full faith and credit statute, 28 U.S.C. §1738, that a state court's resolution of an inverse condemnation proceeding has preclusive effect in a later federal suit. The interaction between *San Remo* and *Williamson County* means that "many takings plaintiffs never have the opportunity to litigate in a federal forum." According to the majority, that unanticipated result makes *Williamson County* itself "unworkable."

But in highlighting the preclusion concern, the majority only adds to the case for respecting *stare decisis* — because that issue can always be addressed by Congress. When "correction can be had by legislation," Justice Brandeis once stated, the Court should let stand even "error[s on] matter[s] of serious concern." Or otherwise said, *stare decisis* then "carries enhanced force." Here, Congress can reverse the *San Remo* preclusion rule any time it wants, and thus give property owners an opportunity — *after* a state-court proceeding — to litigate in federal court. The *San Remo* decision, as noted above, interpreted the federal full faith and credit statute; Congress need only add a provision to that law to flip the Court's result. In fact, Congress has already considered proposals responding to *San Remo* — though so far to no avail. Following this Court's normal rules of practice means leaving the *San Remo* "ball[in] Congress's court," so that branch can decide whether to pick it up.

And the majority has no other special justification. It says *Williamson County* did not create "reliance interests." But even if so, those interests are a *plus-factor* in the doctrine; when they exist, *stare decisis* becomes "superpowered." The absence of reliance is not itself a reason for overruling a decision. Next, the majority says that the "justification for [*Williamson County's*] state-litigation requirement" has "evolve[d]." But to start with, it has not. The original rationale — in the majority's words, that the requirement "is an element of a takings claim," — has held strong for 35 years (including in the cases the majority cites), and is the same one I rely on today. And anyway, "evolution" in the way a decision is described has never been a ground for abandoning *stare decisis*. Here, the majority's only citation is to last Term's decision overruling a 40-year-old precedent (citing *Janus v. State, County, and Municipal Employees*, 585 U.S. ___, ___ (2018)). If that is the way the majority means to proceed — relying on one subversion of *stare decisis* to support another — we may as well not have principles about precedents at all.

What is left is simply the majority's view that *Williamson County* was wrong. The majority repurposes all its merits arguments — all its claims that *Williamson County* was "ill founded" — to justify its overruling. But the entire idea of *stare decisis* is that judges do not get to reverse a decision just because they never liked it in the first instance. Once again, they need a reason *other than* the idea "that the precedent was wrongly decided." For it is hard to overstate the value, in a country like ours, of stability in the law.

Just last month, when the Court overturned another longstanding precedent, Justice Breyer penned a dissent. See *Franchise Tax Bd. of Cal. v. Hyatt*, 587 U.S. ___, ___ (2019). He wrote of the dangers of reversing legal course "only because five Members of a later Court" decide that an earlier ruling was incorrect. He concluded: "Today's decision can only cause one to wonder which cases the Court will overrule next." Well, that didn't take long. Now one may wonder yet again.

IS A REGULATION GIVING UNION ORGANIZERS ACCESS TO PRIVATE PROPERTY A *PER SE* PHYSICAL TAKING?

In the case below a California labor regulation required growers to give union organizers access to their property to speak with farmworkers. Seeking to block the organizers from coming onto their property, owners of the orchards sued, claiming that the regulation constituted a *per se* physical taking because it deprived them of their right to exclude others from their property. By a 6-3 vote the U.S. Supreme Court agreed with the growers. The decision is included in this Supplement because it has considerable relevance for how the current Supreme Court will approach takings claims by property owners subject to regulation, including challenges to regulations designed to facilitate inspections to assess environmental compliance.

CEDAR POINT NURSERY v. HASSID
141 S.Ct. 2063 (2021)

CHIEF JUSTICE ROBERTS delivered the opinion of the Court.

A California regulation grants labor organizations a "right to take access" to an agricultural employer's property in order to solicit support for unionization. Agricultural employers must allow union organizers onto their property for up to three hours per day, 120 days per year. The question presented is whether the access regulation constitutes a *per se* physical taking under the Fifth and Fourteenth Amendments.

I

The California Agricultural Labor Relations Act of 1975 gives agricultural employees a right to self-organization and makes it an unfair labor practice for employers to interfere with that right. The state Agricultural Labor Relations Board has promulgated a regulation providing, in its current form, that the self-organization rights of employees include "the right of access by union organizers to the premises of an agricultural employer for the purpose of meeting and talking with employees and soliciting their support." Under the regulation, a labor organization may "take access" to an agricultural employer's property for up to four 30-day periods in one calendar year. In order to take access, a labor organization must file a written notice with the Board and serve a copy on the employer. Two organizers per work crew (plus one additional organizer for every 15 workers over 30 workers in a crew) may enter the employer's property for up to one hour before work, one hour during the lunch break, and one hour after work. Organizers may not engage in disruptive conduct, but are otherwise free to meet and talk with employees as they wish. Interference with organizers' right of access may constitute an unfair labor practice, which can result in sanctions against the employer.

Cedar Point Nursery is a strawberry grower in northern California. It employs over 400 seasonal workers and around 100 full-time workers, none of whom live on the property. According to the complaint, in October 2015, at five o'clock one morning, members of the United Farm Workers entered Cedar Point's property without prior notice. The organizers moved to the nursery's trim shed, where hundreds of workers were preparing strawberry plants. Calling through bullhorns, the organizers disturbed operations, causing some workers to join the organizers in a protest and others to leave the worksite altogether. Cedar Point filed a charge against the union for taking access without giving notice. The union responded with a charge of its own, alleging that Cedar Point had committed an unfair labor practice.

Fowler Packing Company is a Fresno-based grower and shipper of table grapes and citrus. It has 1,800 to 2,500 employees in its field operations and around 500 in its packing facility. As with Cedar Point, none of Fowler's workers live on the premises. In July 2015, organizers from the United Farm Workers attempted to take access to Fowler's property, but the company blocked them from entering. The union filed an unfair labor practice charge against Fowler, which it later withdrew.

Believing that the union would likely attempt to enter their property again in the near future, the growers filed suit in Federal District Court against several Board members in their official capacity. The growers argued that the access regulation effected an unconstitutional *per se* physical taking under the Fifth and Fourteenth Amendments by appropriating without compensation an easement for union organizers to enter their property. They requested declaratory and injunctive relief prohibiting the Board from enforcing the regulation against them.

The District Court denied the growers' motion for a preliminary injunction and granted the Board's motion to dismiss. The court rejected the growers' argument that the access regulation constituted a *per se* physical taking, reasoning that it did not "allow the public to access their property in a permanent and continuous manner for whatever reason." In the court's view, the regulation was instead subject to evaluation under the multifactor balancing test of *Penn Central Transportation Co. v. New York City*, 438 U.S.104 (1978), which the growers had made no attempt to satisfy.

A divided panel of the Court of Appeals for the Ninth Circuit affirmed. The court identified three categories of regulatory actions in takings jurisprudence: regulations that impose permanent physical invasions, regulations that deprive an owner of all economically beneficial use of his property, and the remainder of regulatory actions. On the court's understanding, while regulations in the first two categories constitute *per se* takings, those in the third must be evaluated under *Penn Central*. The court agreed with the District Court that the access regulation did not fall into the first category because it did not "allow random members of the public to unpredictably traverse [the growers'] property 24 hours a day, 365 days a year." And given that the growers did not contend that the regulation deprived them of all economically beneficial use of their property, *per se* treatment was inappropriate.

Judge Leavy dissented. He observed that this Court had never allowed labor organizers to enter an employer's property for substantial periods of time when its employees lived off premises. *See NLRB v. Babcock & Wilcox Co.*, 351 U.S. 105, 113 (1956). As he saw it, the regulation constituted a physical occupation and therefore effected a *per se* taking.

The Ninth Circuit denied rehearing en banc. Judge Ikuta dissented, joined by seven other judges. She reasoned that the access regulation appropriated from the growers a traditional form of private property—an easement in gross—and transferred that property to union organizers. The appropriation of such an easement, she concluded, constituted a *per se* physical taking under the precedents of this Court. *Id.*, at 1168.

II

A

The Takings Clause of the Fifth Amendment, applicable to the States through the Fourteenth Amendment, provides: "[N]or shall private property be taken for public use, without just compensation." The Founders recognized that the protection of private property is indispensable to the promotion of individual freedom. As John Adams tersely put it, "[p]roperty must be secured, or liberty cannot exist." Discourses on Davila, in 6 Works of John Adams 280 (C. Adams ed. 1851). This Court agrees, having noted that protection of property rights is "necessary to preserve freedom" and "empowers persons to shape and to plan their own destiny in a world where governments are always eager to do so for them." *Murr v. Wisconsin*, 582 U.S. ___, ___ (2017).

When the government physically acquires private property for a public use, the Takings Clause imposes a clear and categorical obligation to provide the owner with just compensation. *Tahoe-Sierra Preservation Council, Inc. v. Tahoe Regional Planning Agency*, 535 U.S. 302, 321 (2002). The Court's physical takings jurisprudence is "as old as the Republic." *Id.*, at 322. The government commits a physical taking when it uses its power of eminent domain to formally condemn property. The same is true when the government physically takes possession of property without acquiring title to it. And the government likewise effects a physical taking when it occupies property—say, by recurring flooding as a result of building a dam. These sorts of physical appropriations constitute the "clearest sort of taking," and we assess them using a simple, *per se* rule: The government must pay for what it takes.

When the government, rather than appropriating private property for itself or a third party, instead imposes regulations that restrict an owner's ability to use his own property, a different standard applies. *Id.*, at 321–322. jurisprudence governing such use restrictions has developed more recently. Before the 20th century, the Takings Clause was understood to be limited to physical appropriations of property. In *Pennsylvania Coal Co. v. Mahon*, 260 U.S. 393 (1922), however, the Court established the proposition that "while property may be regulated to a certain extent, if regulation goes too far it will be recognized as a taking." This framework now applies to use restrictions as varied as zoning ordinances, *Village of Euclid v. Ambler Realty Co.*, 272 U.S. 365, 387–388 (1926), orders barring the mining of gold, *United States v. Central Eureka Mining Co.*, 357 U.S. 155, 168 (1958), and regulations prohibiting the sale of eagle feathers, *Andrus v. Allard*, 444 U.S. 51, 65–66 (1979). To determine whether a use restriction effects a taking, this Court has generally applied the flexible test developed in *Penn Central*, balancing factors such as the economic impact of the regulation, its interference with reasonable investment-backed expectations, and the character of the government action.

Our cases have often described use restrictions that go "too far" as "regulatory takings." But that label can mislead. Government action that physically appropriates property is no less a physical taking because it arises from a regulation. That explains why we held that an administrative reserve requirement compelling raisin growers to physically set aside a percentage of their crop for the government constituted a physical rather than a regulatory taking. *Horne*, 576 U.S., at 361. The essential question is not, as the Ninth Circuit seemed to think, whether the government action at issue comes garbed as a regulation (or statute, or ordinance, or miscellaneous decree). It is whether the government has physically taken property for itself or someone else—by whatever means—or has instead restricted a property owner's ability to use his own property. Whenever a regulation results in a physical appropriation of property, a *per se* taking has occurred, and *Penn Central* has no place.

B

The access regulation appropriates a right to invade the growers' property and therefore constitutes a *per se* physical taking. The regulation grants union organizers a right to physically enter and occupy the growers' land for three hours per day, 120 days per year. Rather than restraining the growers' use of their own property, the regulation appropriates for the enjoyment of third parties the owners' right to exclude.

The right to exclude is "one of the most treasured" rights of property ownership. According to Blackstone, the very idea of property entails "that sole and despotic dominion which one man claims and exercises over the external things of the world, in total exclusion of the right of any other individual in the universe." 2 W. Blackstone, Commentaries on the Laws of England 2 (1766). In less exuberant terms, we have stated that the right to exclude is "universally held to be a fundamental element of the property right," and is "one of the most essential sticks in the bundle of rights that are commonly characterized as property."

Given the central importance to property ownership of the right to exclude, it comes as little surprise that the Court has long treated government-authorized physical invasions as takings requiring just compensation. The Court has often described the property interest taken as a servitude or an easement.

For example, in *United States v. Causby* we held that the invasion of private property by overflights effected a taking. 328 U.S. 256 (1946). The government frequently flew military aircraft low over the Causby farm, grazing the treetops and terrorizing the poultry. *Id.*, at 259. The Court observed that ownership of the land extended to airspace that low, and that "invasions of it are in the same category as invasions of the surface." *Id.*, at 265. Because the dam- ages suffered by the Causbys "were the product of a direct invasion of [their] domain," we held that "a servitude has been imposed upon the land."

We similarly held that the appropriation of an easement effected a taking in *Kaiser Aetna v. United States*. A real-estate developer dredged a pond, converted it into a marina, and connected it to a nearby bay and the ocean. 444 U.S., at 167. The government asserted that the developer could not exclude the public from the marina because the pond had become a navigable water. We held that the right to exclude "falls within [the] category of interests that the Government cannot take without compensation." After noting that "the imposition of the navigational servitude" would "result in an actual physical invasion of the privately owned marina" by members of the public, we cited *Causby* and *Portsmouth* for the proposition that "even if the Government physically invades only an easement in property, it must nonetheless pay just compensation."

In *Loretto v. Teleprompter Manhattan CATV Corp.*, we made clear that a permanent physical occupation constitutes a *per se* taking regardless whether it results in only a trivial economic loss. New York adopted a law requiring landlords to allow cable companies to install equipment on their properties. Loretto alleged that the installation of a 1/2-inch diameter cable and two 11/2-cubic-foot boxes on her roof caused a taking. We agreed, stating that where government action results in a "permanent physical occupation of property, our cases uniformly have found a taking to the extent of the occupation, without regard to whether the action achieves an important public benefit or has only minimal economic impact on the owner."

We reiterated that the appropriation of an easement constitutes a physical taking in *Nollan* v. *California Coastal Commission*. The Nollans sought a permit to build a larger home on their beachfront lot. 483 U.S., at 828. The California Coastal Commission issued the permit subject to the condition that the Nollans grant the public an easement to pass through their property along the beach. *Ibid.* As a starting point to our analysis, we explained that, had the Commission simply required the Nollans to grant the public an easement across their property, "we have no doubt there would have been a taking." *Id.*, at 831; see also *Dolan*, 512 U.S., at 384 (holding that compelled dedication of an easement for public use would constitute a taking).

More recently, in *Horne v. Department of Agriculture*, we observed that "people still do not expect their property, real or personal, to be actually occupied or taken away." 576 U.S., at 361. The physical appropriation by the government of the raisins in that case was a *per se* taking, even if a regulatory limit with the same economic impact would not have been. "The Constitution," we explained, "is concerned with means as well as ends."

The upshot of this line of precedent is that government-authorized invasions of property—whether by plane, boat, cable, or beachcomber—are physical takings requiring just compensation. As in those cases, the government here has appropriated a right of access to the growers' property, allowing union organizers to traverse it at will for three hours a day, 120 days a year. The regulation appropriates a right to physically invade the growers' property—to literally "take access," as the regulation provides. It is therefore a *per se* physical taking under our precedents. Accordingly, the growers' complaint states a claim for an uncompensated taking in violation of the Fifth and Fourteenth Amendments.

C

The Ninth Circuit saw matters differently, as do the Board and the dissent. In the decision below, the Ninth Circuit took the view that the access regulation did not qualify as a *per se* taking because, although it grants a right to physically invade the growers' property, it does not allow for permanent and continuous access "24 hours a day, 365 days a year." The dissent likewise concludes that the regulation cannot amount to a *per se* taking because it allows "access short of 365 days a year." That position is insupportable as a matter of precedent and common sense. There is no reason the law should analyze an abrogation of the right to exclude in one manner if it extends for 365 days, but in an entirely different manner if it lasts for 364.

To begin with, we have held that a physical appropriation is a taking whether it is permanent or temporary. Our cases establish that "compensation is mandated when a leasehold is taken and the government occupies property for its own purposes, even though that use is temporary." *Tahoe-Sierra*, 535 U.S., at 322. The duration of an appropriation—just like the size of an appropriation, see *Loretto*, 458 U.S., at 436–437—bears only on the amount of compensation. For example, after finding a taking by physical invasion, the Court in *Causby* remanded the case to the lower court to determine "whether the easement taken was temporary or permanent," in order to fix the compensation due.

To be sure, *Loretto* emphasized the heightened concerns associated with "[t]he permanence and absolute exclusivity of a physical occupation" in contrast to "temporary limitations on the right to exclude," and stated that "[n]ot every physical *invasion* is a taking." The latter point is well taken, as we will explain. But *Nollan* clarified that appropriation of a right to physically invade property may constitute a taking "even though no particular individual is permitted to station himself permanently upon the premises."

Next, we have recognized that physical invasions constitute takings even if they are intermittent as opposed to continuous. *Causby* held that overflights of private property effected a taking, even though they occurred on only 4% of takeoffs and 7% of landings at the nearby airport. And while *Nollan* happened to involve a legally continuous right of access, we have no doubt that the Court would have reached the same conclusion if the easement demanded by the Commission had lasted for only 364 days per year. After all, the easement was hardly continuous as a practical matter. As Justice Brennan observed in dissent, given the shifting tides, "public passage for a portion of the year would either be impossible or would not occur on [the Nollans'] property." What matters is not that the easement notionally ran round the clock, but that the government had taken a right to physically invade the Nollans' land. And when the government physically takes an interest in property, it must pay for the right to do so. The fact that a right to take access is exercised only from time to time does not make it any less a physical taking.

Even the Board declines to defend the Ninth Circuit's absolutist stance. It prudently concedes that "a requirement that landowners grant an easement otherwise identical to the one in *Nollan* but limited to daylight hours, might very well qualify as 'a taking without regard to other factors that a court might ordinarily examine.'" But the access regulation, it contends, nevertheless fails to qualify as a *per se* taking because it "authorizes only limited and intermittent access for a narrow purpose." That position is little more defensible than the Ninth Circuit's. The fact that the regulation grants access only to union organizers and only for a limited time does not trans- form it from a physical taking into a use restriction. Saying that appropriation of a three hour per day, 120 day per year right to invade the growers' premises "does not constitute a taking of a property interest but rather . . . a mere restriction on its use, is to use words in a manner that deprives them of all their ordinary meaning."

The Board also takes issue with the growers' premise that the access regulation appropriates an easement. In the Board's estimation, the regulation does not exact a true easement in gross under California law because the access right may not be transferred, does not burden any particular parcel of property, and may not be recorded. This, the Board says, reinforces its conclusion that the regulation does not take a constitutionally protected property interest from the growers. The dissent agrees, suggesting that the access right cannot effect a *per se* taking because it does not require the growers to grant the union organizers an easement as defined by state property law.

These arguments misconstrue our physical takings doctrine. As a general matter, it is true that the property rights protected by the Takings Clause are creatures of state law. But no one disputes that, without the access regulation, the growers would have had the right under California law to exclude union organizers from their property. And no one disputes that the access regulation took that right from them. The Board cannot absolve itself of takings liability by appropriating the growers' right to exclude in a form that is a slight mismatch from state easement law. Under the Constitution, property rights "cannot be so easily manipulated."

Our decisions consistently reflect this intuitive approach. We have recognized that the government can commit a physical taking either by appropriating property through a condemnation proceeding or by simply "enter[ing] into physical possession of property without authority of a court order." In the latter situation, the government's intrusion does not vest it with a property interest recognized by state law, such as a fee simple or a leasehold. Yet we recognize a physical taking all the same. Any other result would allow the government to appropriate private property without just compensation so long as it avoids formal condemnation. We have never tolerated that outcome. For much the same reason, in *Portsmouth, Causby,* and *Loretto* we never paused to consider whether the physical invasions at issue vested the intruders with formal easements according to the nuances of state property law (nor do we see how they could have). Instead, we followed our traditional rule: Because the government appropriated a right to invade, compensation was due. That same test governs here.

The Board and the dissent further contend that our decision in *PruneYard Shopping Center* v. *Robins,* 447 U.S. 74 (1980), establishes that the access regulation cannot qualify as a *per se* taking. There the California Supreme Court held that the State Constitution protected the right to engage in leafleting at the PruneYard, a privately owned shopping center. The shopping center argued that the decision had taken without just compensation its right to exclude. Applying the *Penn Central* factors, we held that no compensable taking had occurred.

The Board and the dissent argue that *PruneYard* shows that limited rights of access to private property should be evaluated as regulatory rather than *per se* takings. We disagree. Unlike the growers' properties, the PruneYard was open to the public, welcoming some 25,000 patrons a day. Limitations on how a business generally open to the public may treat individuals on the premises are readily distinguishable from regulations granting a right to invade property closed to the public.

The Board also relies on our decision in *NLRB* v. *Babcock & Wilcox Co.* But that reliance is misplaced. In *Babcock,* the National Labor Relations Board found that several employers had committed unfair labor practices under the National Labor Relations Act by preventing union organizers from distributing literature on company property. 351 U.S., at 109. We held that the statute did not require employers to allow organizers onto their property, at least outside the unusual circumstance where their employees were otherwise "beyond the reach of reasonable union efforts to communicate with them." The Board contends that *Babcock's* approach of balancing property and organizational rights should guide our analysis here. But *Babcock* did not involve a takings claim. Whatever specific takings issues may be presented by the highly contingent access right we recognized under the NLRA, California's access regulation effects a *per se* physical taking under our precedents.

D

In its thoughtful opinion, the dissent advances a distinctive view of property rights. The dissent encourages readers to consider the issue "through the lens of ordinary English," and contends that, so viewed, the "regulation does not *appropriate* anything." Rather, the access regulation merely "*regulates* . . . the owners' right to exclude," so it must be assessed "under *Penn Central's* fact-intensive test." "A right to enter my woods only on certain occasions," the dissent elaborates, "is a taking only if the regulation allowing it goes 'too far.'" The dissent contends that our decisions in *Causby, Portsmouth,* and *Kaiser Aetna* applied just such a flexible approach, under which the Court "balanced several factors" to determine whether the physical invasions at issue effected a taking. According to the dissent, this kind of latitude toward temporary invasions is a practical necessity for governing in our complex modern world.

With respect, our own understanding of the role of property rights in our constitutional order is markedly different. In "ordinary English" "appropriation" means "*taking* as one's own," 1 Oxford English Dictionary 587 (2d ed. 1989) (emphasis added), and the regulation expressly grants to labor organizers the "right to *take* access," Cal. Code Regs., tit. 8, §20900(e)(1)(C) (emphasis added). We cannot agree that the right to exclude is an empty formality, subject to modification at the government's pleasure. On the contrary, it is a "fundamental element of the property right" that cannot be balanced away. Our cases establish that appropriations of a right to invade are *per se* physical takings, not use re- strictions subject to *Penn Central*: "[W]hen [government] planes use private airspace to approach a government airport, [the government] is required to pay for that share no matter how small." And while *Kaiser Aetna* may have referred to the test from *Penn Central*, the Court concluded categorically that the government must pay just compensation for physical invasions. With regard to the complexities of modern society, we think they only reinforce the importance of safeguarding the basic property rights that help preserve individual liberty, as the Founders explained.

In the end, the dissent's permissive approach to property rights hearkens back to views expressed (in dissent) for decades. See, *e.g., Nollan,* 483 U.S., at 864 (Brennan, J., dissenting) ("[The Court's] reasoning is hardly suited to the complex reality of natural resource protection in the 20th century."); *Loretto,* 458 U.S., at 455 (Blackmun, J., dissenting) ("[T]oday's decision . . . represents an archaic judicial response to a modern social problem."); *Causby,* 328 U.S., at 275 (Black, J., dissenting) ("Today's opinion is, I fear, an opening wedge for an unwarranted judicial interference with the power of Congress to develop solutions for new and vital national problems."). As for today's considered dissent, it concludes with "Better the devil we know . . . ," but its objections, to borrow from then-Justice Rehnquist's invocation of Wordsworth, "bear[] the sound of 'Old, unhappy, far-off things, and battles long ago,' " *Kaiser Aetna*, 444 U.S., at 177.

III

The Board, seconded by the dissent, warns that treating the access regulation as a *per se* physical taking will endanger a host of state and federal government activities involving entry onto private property. That fear is unfounded.

First, our holding does nothing to efface the distinction between trespass and takings. Isolated physical invasions, not undertaken pursuant to a granted right of access, are properly assessed as individual torts rather than appropriations of a property right. This basic distinction is firmly grounded in our precedent. And lower courts have had little trouble applying it.

The distinction between trespass and takings accounts for our treatment of temporary government-induced flooding in *Arkansas Game and Fish Commission v. United States*, 568 U.S. 23 (2012). There we held, "simply and only," that such flooding "gains no automatic exemption from Takings Clause inspection." Because this type of flooding can present complex questions of causation, we instructed lower courts evaluating takings claims based on temporary flooding to consider a range of factors including the duration of the invasion, the degree to which it was intended or foreseeable, and the character of the land at issue. Applying those factors on remand, the Federal Circuit concluded that the government had effected a taking in the form of a temporary flowage easement. *Arkansas Game and Fish Comm'n v. United States*, 736 F. 3d 1364, 1372 (2013). Our approach in *Arkansas Game and Fish Commission* reflects nothing more than an application of the traditional trespass-versus-takings distinction to the unique considerations that accompany temporary flooding.

Second, many government-authorized physical invasions will not amount to takings because they are consistent with longstanding background restrictions on property rights. As we explained in *Lucas v. South Carolina Coastal Council*, the government does not take a property interest when it merely asserts a "pre-existing limitation upon the land owner's title." For example, the government owes a landowner no compensation for requiring him to abate a nuisance on his property, because he never had a right to engage in the nuisance in the first place.

These background limitations also encompass traditional common law privileges to access private property. One such privilege allowed individuals to enter property in the event of public or private necessity. The common law also recognized a privilege to enter property to effect an arrest or enforce the criminal law under certain circumstances. Because a property owner traditionally had no right to exclude an official engaged in a reasonable search, government searches that are consistent with the Fourth Amendment and state law cannot be said to take any property right from landowners.

Third, the government may require property owners to cede a right of access as a condition of receiving certain benefits, without causing a taking. In *Nollan*, we held that "a permit condition that serves the same legitimate police- power purpose as a refusal to issue the permit should not be found to be a taking if the refusal to issue the permit would not constitute a taking." The inquiry, we later explained, is whether the permit condition bears an "essential nexus" and "rough proportionality" to the impact of the proposed use of the property.

Under this framework, government health and safety inspection regimes will generally not constitute takings. When the government conditions the grant of a benefit such as a permit, license, or registration on allowing access for reasonable health and safety inspections, both the nexus and rough proportionality requirements of the constitutional conditions framework should not be difficult to satisfy. See, *e.g.*, 7 U.S.C. §136g(a)(1)(A) (pesticide inspections); 16 U.S.C. §823b(a) (hydroelectric project investigations); 21 U.S.C. §374(a)(1) (pharmaceutical inspections); 42 U.S.C. §2201(*o*) (nuclear material inspections).

None of these considerations undermine our determination that the access regulation here gives rise to a *per se* physical taking. Unlike a mere trespass, the regulation grants a formal entitlement to physically invade the growers' land. Unlike a law enforcement search, no traditional background principle of property law requires the growers to admit union organizers onto their premises. And unlike standard health and safety inspections, the access regulation is not germane to any benefit provided to agricultural employers or any risk posed to the public. The access regulation amounts to simple appropriation of private property.

* * *

The access regulation grants labor organizations a right to invade the growers' property. It therefore constitutes a *per se* physical taking.

The judgment of the United States Court of Appeals for the Ninth Circuit is reversed, and the case is remanded for further proceedings consistent with this opinion.

It is so ordered.

JUSTICE KAVANAUGH, concurring.

I join the Court's opinion, which carefully adheres to constitutional text, history, and precedent. I write separately to explain that, in my view, the Court's precedent in *NLRB v. Babcock & Wilcox Co.*, 351 U.S. 105 (1956), also strongly supports today's decision.

In *Babcock*, the National Labor Relations Board argued that the National Labor Relations Act afforded union organizers a right to enter company property to communicate with employees. Several employers responded that the Board's reading of the Act would infringe their Fifth Amendment property rights. The employers contended that Congress, "even if it could constitutionally do so, has at no time shown any intention of destroying property rights secured by the *Fifth Amendment*, in protecting employees' rights of collective bargaining under the Act. Until Congress should evidence such intention by specific legislative language, our courts should not construe the Act on such dangerous constitutional grounds."

This Court agreed with the employers' argument that the Act should be interpreted to avoid unconstitutionality. The Court reasoned that "the National Government" via the Constitution "preserves property rights," including "the right to exclude from property." *Babcock*, 351 U.S., at 112. Against the backdrop of the Constitution's strong protection of property rights, the Court interpreted the Act to afford access to union organizers only when "needed,"—that is, when the employees live on company property and union organizers have no other reasonable means of communicating with the employees. As I read it, *Babcock* recognized that employers have a basic Fifth Amendment right to exclude from their private property, subject to a "necessity" exception similar to that noted by the Court today.

Babcock strongly supports the growers' position in today's case because the California union access regulation intrudes on the growers' property rights far more than *Babcock* allows. When this same California union access regulation was challenged on constitutional grounds before the California Supreme Court in 1976, that court upheld the regulation by a 4-to-3 vote. *Agricultural Labor Rel. Bd. v. Superior Ct. of Tulare Cty.*, 16 Cal. 3d 392. Justice William Clark wrote the dissent. Justice Clark stressed that "property rights are fundamental." And he concluded that the California union access regulation "violates the rule" of *Babcock* and thus "violates the constitutional provisions protecting private property." In my view, Justice Clark had it exactly right.

With those comments, I join the Court's opinion in full.

JUSTICE BREYER, with whom JUSTICE SOTOMAYOR and JUSTICE KAGAN join, dissenting.

A California regulation provides that representatives of a labor organization may enter an agricultural employer's property for purposes of union organizing. They may do so during four months of the year, one hour before the start of work, one hour during an employee lunch break, and one hour after work. The question before us is how to characterize this regulation for purposes of the Constitution's Takings Clause.

Does the regulation *physically appropriate* the employers' property? If so, there is no need to look further; the Government must pay the employers "just compensation." Or does the regulation simply *regulate* the employers' property rights? If so, then there is every need to look further; the government need pay the employers "just compensation" only if the regulation "goes too far." *Pennsylvania Coal Co. v. Mahon*, 260 U.S. 393, 415 (1922) (Holmes, J., for the Court); see also *Penn Central Transp. Co. v. New York City*, 438 U.S. 104, 124 (1978) (determining whether a regulation is a taking by examining the regulation's "economic impact," the extent of interference with "investment-backed expectations," and the "character of the governmental action").

The Court holds that the provision's "access to organizers" requirement amounts to a physical appropriation of property. In its view, virtually every government-authorized invasion is an "appropriation." But this regulation does not "appropriate" anything; it regulates the employers' right to exclude others. At the same time, our prior cases make clear that the regulation before us allows only a *temporary* invasion of a landowner's property and that this kind of temporary invasion amounts to a taking only if it goes "too far." See, *e.g.*, *Loretto v. Teleprompter Manhattan CATV Corp.*, 458 U.S. 419, 434 (1982). In my view, the majority's conclusion threatens to make many ordinary forms of regulation unusually complex or impractical. And though the majority attempts to create exceptions to narrow its rule, the law's need for feasibility suggests that the majority's framework is wrong. With respect, I dissent from the majority's conclusion that the regulation is a *per se* taking.

I

"In view of the nearly infinite variety of ways in which government actions or regulations can affect property interests, the Court has recognized few invariable rules in this area." Instead, most government action affecting property rights is analyzed case by case under *Penn Central's* fact-intensive test. Petitioners do not argue that the provision at issue is a "regulatory taking" under that test.

Instead, the question before us is whether the access regulation falls within one of two narrow categories of government conduct that are *per se* takings. The first is when " 'the government directly appropriates private property for its own use.' " The second is when the government causes a permanent physical occupation of private property. It does not.

A

Initially it may help to look at the legal problem—a problem of characterization—through the lens of ordinary English. The word "regulation" rather than "appropriation" fits this provision in both label and substance. It is contained in Title 8 of the California Code of Regulations. It was adopted by a state regulatory board, namely, the California Agricultural Labor Relations Board, in 1975. It is embedded in a set of related detailed regulations that describe and limit the access at issue. In addition to the hours of access just mentioned, it provides that union representatives can enter the property only "for the purpose of meeting and talking with employees and soliciting their support"; they have access only to "areas in which employees congregate before and after working" or "at such location or locations as the employees eat their lunch"; and they cannot engage in "conduct disruptive of the employer's property or agricultural operations, including injury to crops or machinery or interference with the process of boarding buses." From the employers' perspective, it restricts when and where they can exclude others from their property.

At the same time, the provision only awkwardly fits the terms "physical taking" and "physical appropriation." The "access" that it grants union organizers does not amount to any traditional property interest in land. It does not, for example, take from the employers, or provide to the organizers, any freehold estate (*e.g.*, a fee simple, fee tail, or life estate); any concurrent estate (*e.g.*, a joint tenancy, tenancy in common, or tenancy by the entirety); or any leasehold estate (*e.g.*, a term of years, periodic tenancy, or tenancy at will). Nor (as all now agree) does it provide the organizers with a formal easement or access resembling an easement, as the employers once argued, since it does not burden any particular parcel of property.

The majority concludes that the regulation nonetheless amounts to a physical taking of property because, the majority says, it "appropriates" a "right to invade" or a "right to exclude" others. It thereby likens this case to cases in which we have held that appropriation of property rights amounts to a physical *per se* taking. See *ante,* at 5–6 (citing *United States v. Pewee Coal Co.*, 341 U.S. 114, 115 (1951) (plurality opinion) (seizure and operation of a coal mine by the United States); *United States v. General Motors Corp.*, 323 U.S. 373, 375 (1945) (condemnation of a warehouse building by the United States); *Horne*, 576 U.S., at 361 (transfer of "[a]ctual raisins," and title to the raisins, from growers to the Government)).

It is important to understand, however, that, technically speaking, the majority is wrong. The regulation does not *appropriate* anything. It does not take from the owners a right to invade (whatever that might mean). It does not give the union organizations the right to exclude anyone. It does not give the government the right to exclude anyone. What does it do? It gives union organizers the right temporarily to invade a portion of the property owners' land. It thereby limits the landowners' right to exclude certain others. The regulation *regulates* (but does not *appropriate*) the owners' right to exclude.

Why is it important to understand this technical point? Because only then can we understand the issue before us. That issue is whether a regulation that *temporarily* limits an owner's right to exclude others from property *automatically* amounts to a Fifth Amendment taking. Under our cases, it does not.

B

Our cases draw a distinction between regulations that provide permanent rights of access and regulations that provide nonpermanent rights of access. They either state or hold that the first type of regulation is a taking *per se,* but the second kind is a taking only if it goes "too far." And they make this distinction for good reason.

Consider the Court's reasoning in an important case in which the Court found a *per se* taking. In *Loretto*, the Court considered the status of a New York law that required landlords to permit cable television companies to install cable facilities on their property. We held that the installation amounted to a permanent physical occupation of the property and hence to a *per se* taking. In reaching this holding we specifically said that "[n]ot every physical invasion is a taking." We explained that the "permanence and absolute exclusivity of a physical occupation distinguish it from temporary limitations on the right to exclude." And we provided an example of a federal statute that did *not* effect a *per se* taking—an example almost identical to the regulation before us. That statute provided " 'access . . . limited to (i) union organizers; (ii) prescribed non-working areas of the employer's premises; and (iii) the duration of the organization activity.' "

We also explained why permanent physical occupations are distinct from temporary limitations on the right to exclude. We said that, when the government permanently occupies property, it "does not simply take a single 'strand' from the 'bundle' of property rights: it chops through the bundle, taking a slice of every strand," "effectively destroy[ing]" "the rights 'to possess, use and dispose of it.'" We added that the property owner "ha[d] no right to possess the occupied space himself, and also ha[d] no power to exclude the occupier from pos- session and use of the space." *Ibid.* The requirement "forever denie[d] the owner any power to control the use of the property" or make any "nonpossessory use" of it. It would "ordinarily empty the right" to sell or transfer the occupied space "of any value, since the purchaser w[ould] also be unable to make any use of the property." *Ibid.* The owner could not "exercise control" over the equipment's installation, and so could not "minimize [its] physical, esthetic, and other effects." Thus, we concluded, a permanent physical occupation "is perhaps the most serious form of invasion of an owner's property interests."

Now consider *PruneYard Shopping Center v. Robins*, 447 U.S. 74 (1980). We there considered the status of a state constitutional requirement that a privately owned shopping center permit other individuals to enter upon, and to use, the property to exercise their rights to free speech and petition. We held that this require- ment was not a *per se* taking in part because (even though the individuals may have "'physically invaded'" the owner's property) "[t]here [wa]s nothing to suggest that preventing [the owner] from prohibiting this sort of activity w[ould] unreasonably impair the value or use of th[e] property as a shop- ping center," and the owner could "adop[t] time, place, and manner regulations that w[ould] minimize any interference with its commercial functions."

In *Nollan v. California Coastal Comm'n*, 483 U.S. 825 (1987), we held that the State's taking of an easement across a landowner's property did constitute a *per se* taking. But consider the Court's reason: "[I]ndividuals are given a *permanent and continuous* right to pass to and fro." *Id.*, at 832 (emphasis added). We clarified that by "permanent" and "continuous" we meant that the "real property may continuously be traversed, even though no particular individual is permitted to station himself permanently upon the premises."

In *Arkansas Game and Fish Comm'n*, 568 U.S. 23, we again said that permanent physical occupations are *per se* takings, but temporary invasions are not. Rather, they " 'are subject to a more complex balancing process to determine whether they are a taking.' " *Id.*, at 36; see also *id.*, at 38–39 (courts should consider the length of the invasion, the "degree to which the invasion is intended or is the foreseeable result of authorized government action," "the character of the land at issue," "the owner's 'reasonable investment- backed expectations' regarding the land's use," and the "[s]everity of the interference" (citing, *inter alia*, *Penn Central*, 438 U.S., at 130–131)).

As these cases have used the terms, the regulation here at issue provides access that is "temporary," not "permanent." Unlike the regulation in *Loretto*, it does not place a "fixed structure on land or real property." The employers are not "forever denie[d]" "any power to control the use" of any particular portion of their property. And it does not totally reduce the value of any section of the property. Unlike in *Nollan*, the pub- lic cannot walk over the land whenever it wishes; rather a subset of the public may enter a portion of the land three hours per day for four months per year (about 4% of the time). At bottom, the regulation here, unlike the regulations in *Loretto* and *Nollan*, is not "functionally equivalent to the classic taking in which government directly appropriates private property or ousts the owner from his domain."

At the same time, *PruneYard*'s holding that the taking was "temporary" (and hence not a *per se* taking) fits this case almost perfectly. There the regulation gave non-owners the right to enter privately owned property for the purpose of speaking generally to others, about matters of their choice, subject to reasonable time, place, and manner restrictions. The regulation before us grants a far smaller group of people the right to enter landowners' property for far more limited times in order to speak about a specific subject. Employers have more power to control entry by setting work hours, lunch hours, and places of gathering. On the other hand, as the majority notes, the shopping center in *PruneYard* was open to the public generally. All these factors, however, are the stuff of which regulatory-balancing, not absolute *per se*, rules are made.

Our cases have recognized, as the majority says, that the right to exclude is a " 'fundamental element of the property right.' " For that reason, "[a] 'taking' may *more readily* be found when the interference with property can be characterized as a physical invasion by government." But a taking is not inevitably found just because the interference with property can be characterized as a physical invasion by the government, or, in other words, when it affects the right to exclude.

The majority refers to other cases. But those cases do not help its cause. That is because the Court in those cases (some of which preceded *Penn Central* and others of which I have discussed above) did not apply a *"per se* takings" approach. In *United States v. Causby*, 328 U.S. 256, 259 (1946), for example, the question was whether government flights over a piece of land constituted a taking. The flights amounted to 4% of the takeoffs, and 7% of the landings, at a nearby airport. But the planes flew "in considerable numbers and rather close together." And the flights were "so low and so frequent as to be a direct and immediate interference with the enjoyment and use of the land." Taken together, those flights "destr[oyed] the use of the property as a commercial chicken farm." Based in part on that economic damage, the Court found that the rule allowing these overflights went "too far."

In *Portsmouth Harbor Land & Hotel Co. v. United States*, 260 U.S. 327, 329 (1922), the Court held that the Government's firing of guns across private property would be a taking only if the shots were sufficiently frequent to establish an "intent to fire across the claimants' land at will." The frequency of the projectiles itself mattered less than whether the Government acted "'with the purpose and effect of subordinating the strip of land . . . to the right and privilege of the Government to fire projectiles directly across it for the purpose of practice or otherwise, *whenever it saw fit*, in time of peace, with the result of depriving the owner of its profitable use.'" Again, the Court balanced several factors—permanence, severity, and economic impact—rather than treating the mere fact of entry as dispositive.

In *Kaiser Aetna v. United States*, 444 U.S. 164, the Court considered whether the Government had taken property by converting a formerly "private pond" (with a private access fee) into a "public aquatic park" (with free navigation-related access for the public). *Id.*, at 176, 180. The Court held there was a taking. But in doing so, it applied a *Penn Central,* not a *per se,* analysis. The Court wrote that "[m]ore than one factor contribute[d] to" the conclusion that the Government had gone "far beyond ordinary regulation or improvement." And it found there was a taking.

If there is ambiguity in these cases, it concerns whether the Court considered the occupation at issue to be *temporary* (requiring *Penn Central's* "too far" analysis) or *permanent* (automatically requiring compensation). Nothing in them suggests the majority's view, namely, that compensation is automatically required for a *temporary* right of access. Nor does anything in them support the distinction that the majority gleans between "trespass" and "takings."

The majority also refers to *Nollan* as support for its claim that the "fact that a right to take access is exercised only from time to time does not make it any less a physical taking." True. Here, however, unlike in *Nollan,* the right taken is not a right to have access to the property at any time (which access different persons "exercis[e] . . . from time to time"). Rather here we have a right that does not allow access at any time. It allows access only from "time to time." And that makes all the difference. A right to enter my woods whenever you wish is a right to use that property permanently, even if you exercise that right only on occasion. A right to enter my woods only on certain occasions is not a right to use the woods permanently. In the first case one might reasonably use the term *per se* taking. It is as if my woods are yours. In the second case it is a taking only if the regulation allowing it goes "too far," considering the factors we have laid out in *Penn Central*. That is what our cases say.

Finally, the majority says that *Nollan* would have come out the same way had it involved, similar to the regulation here, access short of 365 days a year. Perhaps so. But, if so, that likely would be because the Court would have viewed the access as an "easement," and therefore an appropriation. Or, perhaps, the Court would have viewed the regulation as going "too far." I can assume, purely for argument's sake, that that is so. But the law is clear: A regulation that provides *temporary,* not *permanent,* access to a landowner's property, and that does not amount to a taking of a traditional property interest, is not a *per se* taking. That is, it does not automatically require compensation. Rather, a court must consider whether it goes "too far."

C

The persistence of the permanent/temporary distinction that I have described is not surprising. That distinction serves an important purpose. We live together in communities. (Approximately 80% of Americans live in urban areas. U.S. Census Bureau, Urban Area Facts (Mar. 30, 2021), https://www.census.gov/programs-surveys/ geography/guidance/geo-areas/urban-rural/ua-facts.html.) Modern life in these communities requires different kinds of regulation. Some, perhaps many, forms of regulation re- quire access to private property (for government officials or others) for different reasons and for varying periods of time. Most such temporary-entry regulations do not go "too far." And it is impractical to compensate every property owner for any brief use of their land. As we have frequently said, "[g]overnment hardly could go on if to some extent values incident to property could not be diminished without paying for every such change in the general law." Thus, the law has not, and should not, convert all temporary-access-permitting regulations into *per se* takings automatically requiring compensation.

Consider the large numbers of ordinary regulations in a host of different fields that, for a variety of purposes, permit temporary entry onto (or an "invasion of") a property owner's land. They include activities ranging from examination of food products to inspections for compliance with preschool licensing requirements. See, *e.g.*, 29 U.S.C. §657(a) (authorizing inspections and investigations of "any . . . workplace or environment where work is performed" during "regular working hours and at other reasonable times"); 21 U.S.C. §606(a) (authorizing "examination and inspection of all meat food products . . . at all times, by day or night"); 42 U.S.C. §5413(b) (authorizing inspections anywhere "manufactured homes are manufactured, stored, or held for sale" at "reasonable times and without advance notice"); Miss. Code Ann. §49–27–63 (2012) (authorizing inspections of "coastal wetlands" "from time to time"); Mich. Comp. Laws §208.1435(5) (2010) (authorizing inspections of any "historic resource" "at any time during the rehabilitation process"); Mont. Code Ann. §81–22–304 (2019) (granting a "right of entry . . . [into] any premises where dairy products . . . are produced, manufactured, [or] sold" "during normal business hours"); Neb. Rev. Stat. §43–1303(5) (2016) (authorizing visitation of "foster care facilities in order to ascertain whether the individual physical, psychological, and sociological needs of each foster child are being met"); Va. Code Ann. §22.1–289.032(C)(8) (Cum. Supp. 2020) (authorizing "annual inspection" of "preschool programs of accredited private schools"); Cincinnati, Ohio, Municipal Code §603–1 (2021) (authorizing entry "at any time" for any place in which "animals are slaughtered"); Dallas, Tex., Code of Ordinance §33–5(a) (2021) (authorizing inspection of "assisted living facilit[ies]" "at reasonable times"); 6 N. Y. Rules & Regs. §360.7 (Supp. 2020) (authorizing inspection of solid waste management facilities "at all reasonable times, locations, whether announced or unannounced"); see also *Boise Cascade Corp. v. United States*, 296 F. 3d 1339, 1352 (CA Fed. 2002) (affirming an injunction requiring property owner to allow Government agents to enter its property to conduct owl surveys). The majority tries to deal with the adverse impact of treating these, and other, temporary invasions as if they were *per se* physical takings by creating a series of exceptions from its *per se* rule. It says: (1) "Isolated physical invasions, not undertaken pursuant to a granted right of access, are properly assessed as individual torts rather than appropriations of a property right." It also would except from its *per se* rule (2) government access that is "consistent with longstanding background restrictions on property rights," including "traditional common law privileges to access private property." And it adds that (3) "the government may require property owners to cede a right of access as a condition of receiving certain benefits, without causing a taking." How well will this new system work? I suspect that the majority has substituted a new, complex legal scheme for a comparatively simpler old one. As to the first exception, what will count as "isolated"?

How is an "isolated physical invasion" different from a "temporary" invasion, sufficient under present law to invoke *Penn Central*? And where should one draw the line between trespass and takings? Imagine a school bus that stops to allow public school children to picnic on private land. Do three stops a year place the stops outside the exception? One stop every week? Buses from one school? From every school? Under current law a court would know what question to ask. The stops are temporary; no one assumes a permanent right to stop; thus the court will ask whether the school district has gone "too far." Under the majority's approach, the court must answer a new question (apparently about what counts as "isolated").

As to the second exception, a court must focus on "traditional common law privileges to access private property." Just what are they? We have said before that the government can, without paying compensation, impose a limitation on land that "inhere[s] in the title itself, in the restrictions that background principles of the State's law of property and nuisance already place upon land ownership." But we defined a very narrow set of such background principles. To these the majority adds "public or private necessity," the enforcement of criminal law "under certain circumstances," and reasonable searches. Do only those exceptions that existed in, say, 1789 count? Should courts apply those privileges as they existed at that time, when there were no union organizers? Or do we bring some exceptions (but not others) up to date, *e.g.*, a necessity exception for preserving animal habitats?

As to the third, what is the scope of the phrase "certain benefits"? Does it include the benefit of being able to sell meat labeled "inspected" in interstate commerce? What about the benefit of having electricity? Of sewage collection? Of internet accessibility? Myriad regulatory schemes based on just these sorts of benefits depend upon intermittent, temporary government entry onto private property.

Labor peace (brought about through union organizing) is one such benefit, at least in the view of elected representatives. They wrote laws that led to rules governing the organizing of agricultural workers. Many of them may well have believed that union organizing brings with it "benefits," including community health and educational benefits, higher standards of living, and (as I just said) labor peace. See, *e.g.*, 1975 Cal. Stats. ch. 1, §1 (stating that the purpose of the Agricultural Labor Relations Act was to "ensure peace in the agricultural fields by guaranteeing justice for all agricultural workers and stability in labor relations"). A landowner, of course, may deny the existence of these benefits, but a landowner might do the same were a regulatory statute to permit brief access to verify proper preservation of wetlands or the habitat enjoyed by an endangered species or, for that matter, the safety of inspected meat. So, if a regulation authorizing temporary access for purposes of organizing agricultural workers falls outside of the Court's exceptions and is a *per se* taking, then to what other forms of regulation does the Court's *per se* conclusion also apply?

II

Finally, I touch briefly on remedies, which the majority does not address. The Takings Clause prohibits the Government from taking private property for public use without "just compensation." But the employers do not seek compensation. They seek only injunctive and declaratory relief. Indeed, they did not allege any damages. On remand, California should have the choice of foreclosing injunctive relief by providing compensation. See, *e.g.*, *Knick v. Township of Scott*, 588 U.S. __, __ (2019) (slip op., at 23) ("As long as just compensation remedies are available—as they have been for nearly 150 years—injunctive relief will be foreclosed").

* * *

I recognize that the Court's prior cases in this area are not easy to apply. Moreover, words such as "temporary," "permanent," or "too far" do not define themselves. But I do not believe that the Court has made matters clearer or better. Rather than adopt a new broad rule and indeterminate exceptions, I would stick with the approach that I believe the Court's case law sets forth. "Better the devil we know . . . ." A right of access such as the right at issue here, a nonpermanent right, is not automatically a "taking." It is a regulation that falls within the scope of *Penn Central*. Because the Court takes a different view, I respectfully dissent.

DESIGNATION OF CRITICAL HABITAT UNDER THE ENDANGERED SPECIES ACT

In the case below a timber company argued that the U.S. Fish & Wildlife Service had erred when it listed part of its property as critical habitat for the endangered dusky gopher frog even though the frog did not currently occupy the property.

WEYERHAEUSER COMPANY v. U.S. FISH & WILDLIFE SERVICE
139 S.Ct. 361 (2018)

CHIEF JUSTICE ROBERTS delivered the opinion of the Court.

The Endangered Species Act directs the Secretary of the Interior, upon listing a species as endangered, to also designate the "critical habitat" of the species. A group of landowners whose property was designated as critical habitat for an endangered frog challenged the designation. The landowners urge that their land cannot be *critical* habitat because it is not *habitat*, which they contend refers only to areas where the frog could currently survive. The court below ruled that the Act imposed no such limitation on the scope of critical habitat.

The Act also authorizes the Secretary to exclude an area that would otherwise be included as critical habitat, if the benefits of exclusion outweigh the benefits of designation. The landowners challenged the decision of the Secretary not to exclude their property, but the court below held that the Secretary's action was not subject to judicial review.

We granted certiorari to review both rulings.

I

A

The amphibian *Rana sevosa* is popularly known as the "dusky gopher frog" — "dusky" because of its dark coloring and "gopher" because it lives underground. The dusky gopher frog is about three inches long, with a large head, plump body, and short legs. Warts dot its back, and dark spots cover its entire body. It is noted for covering its eyes with its front legs when it feels threatened, peeking out periodically until danger passes. Less endearingly, it also secretes a bitter, milky substance to deter would-be diners.

The frog spends most of its time in burrows and stump holes located in upland longleaf pine forests. In such forests, frequent fires help maintain an open canopy, which in turn allows vegetation to grow on the forest floor. The vegetation supports the small insects that the frog eats and provides a place for the frog's eggs to attach when it breeds. The frog breeds in "ephemeral" ponds that are dry for part of the year. Such ponds are safe for tadpoles because predatory fish cannot live in them.

The dusky gopher frog once lived throughout coastal Alabama, Louisiana, and Mississippi, in the longleaf pine forests that used to cover the southeast. But more than 98% of those forests have been removed to make way for urban development, agriculture, and timber plantations. The timber plantations consist of fast-growing loblolly pines planted as close together as possible, resulting in a closed-canopy forest inhospitable to the frog. The near eradication of the frog's habitat sent the species into severe decline. By 2001, the known wild population of the dusky gopher frog had dwindled to a group of 100 at a single pond in southern Mississippi. That year, the Fish and Wildlife Service, which administers the Endangered Species Act of 1973 on behalf of the Secretary of the Interior, listed the dusky gopher frog as an endangered species.

B

When the Secretary lists a species as endangered, he must also designate the critical habitat of that species. The ESA defines "critical habitat" as:

> "(i) the specific areas within the geographical area occupied by the species . . . on which are found those physical or biological features (I) essential to the conservation of the species and (II) which may require special management considerations or protection; and
> "(ii) specific areas outside the geographical area occupied by the species . . . upon a determination by the Secretary that such areas are essential for the conservation of the species." §1532(5)(A).

Before the Secretary may designate an area as critical habitat, the ESA requires him to "tak[e] into consideration the economic impact" and other relevant impacts of the designation. §1533(b)(2). The statute goes on to authorize him to "exclude any area from critical habitat if he determines that the benefits of such exclusion outweigh the benefits of [designation]," unless exclusion would result in extinction of the species.

A critical-habitat designation does not directly limit the rights of private landowners. It instead places conditions on the Federal Government's authority to effect any physical changes to the designated area, whether through activities of its own or by facilitating private development. Section 7 of the ESA requires all federal agencies to consult with the Secretary to "[e]nsure that any action authorized, funded, or carried out by such agency" is not likely to adversely affect a listed species' critical habitat. If the Secretary determines that an agency action, such as issuing a permit, would harm critical habitat, then the agency must terminate the action, implement an alternative proposed by the Secretary, or seek an exemption from the Cabinet-level Endangered Species Committee.

Due to resource constraints, the Service did not designate the frog's critical habitat in 2001, when it listed the frog as endangered. In the following years, the Service discovered two additional naturally occurring populations and established another population through translocation. The first population nonetheless remains the only stable one and by far the largest.

In 2010, in response to litigation by the Center for Biological Diversity, the Service published a proposed critical-habitat designation. The Service proposed to designate as occupied critical habitat all four areas with existing dusky gopher frog populations. The Service found that each of those areas possessed the three features that the Service considered "essential to the conservation" of the frog and that required special protection: ephemeral ponds; upland open-canopy forest containing the holes and burrows in which the frog could live; and open-canopy forest connecting the two. But the Service also determined that designating only those four sites would not adequately ensure the frog's conservation. Because the existing dusky gopher frog populations were all located in two adjacent counties on the Gulf Coast of Mississippi, local events such as extreme weather or an outbreak of an infectious disease could jeopardize the entire species.

To protect against that risk, the Service proposed to designate as *unoccupied* critical habitat a 1,544-acre site in St. Tammany Parish, Louisiana. The site, dubbed "Unit 1" by the Service, had been home to the last known population of dusky gopher frogs outside of Mississippi. The frog had not been seen in Unit 1 since 1965, and a closed-canopy timber plantation occupied much of the site. But the Service found that the site retained five ephemeral ponds "of remarkable quality," and determined that an open-canopy forest could be restored on the surrounding uplands "with reasonable effort." Although the uplands in Unit 1 lacked the open-canopy forests (and, of course, the frogs) necessary for designation as occupied critical habitat, the Service concluded that the site met the statutory definition of unoccupied critical habitat because its rare, high-quality breeding ponds and its distance from existing frog populations made it essential for the conservation of the species.

After issuing its proposal, the Service commissioned a report on the probable economic impact of designating each area, including Unit 1, as critical habitat for the dusky gopher frog. Petitioner Weyerhaeuser Company, a timber company, owns part of Unit 1 and leases the remainder from a group of family landowners. While the critical-habitat designation has no direct effect on the timber operations, St. Tammany Parish is a fast-growing part of the New Orleans metropolitan area, and the landowners have already invested in plans to more profitably develop the site. App. 80–83. The report recognized that anyone developing the area may need to obtain Clean Water Act permits from the Army Corps of Engineers before filling any wetlands on Unit 1. Because Unit 1 is designated as critical habitat, Section 7 of the ESA would require the Corps to consult with the Service before issuing any permits.

According to the report, that consultation process could result in one of three outcomes. First, it could turn out that the wetlands in Unit 1 are not subject to the Clean Water Act permitting requirements, in which case the landowners could proceed with their plans unimpeded. Second, the Service could ask the Corps not to issue permits to the landowners to fill some of the wetlands on the site, in effect prohibiting development on 60% of Unit 1. The report estimated that this would deprive the owners of $20.4 million in development value. Third, by asking the Corps to deny even more of the permit requests, the Service could bar all development of Unit 1, costing the owners $33.9 million. The Service concluded that those potential costs were not "disproportionate" to the conservation benefits of designation. "Consequently," the Service announced, it would not "exercis[e] [its] discretion to exclude" Unit 1 from the dusky gopher frog's critical habitat.

C

Weyerhaeuser and the family landowners sought to vacate the designation in Federal District Court. They contended that Unit 1 could not be critical habitat for the dusky gopher frog because the frog could not survive there: Survival would require replacing the closed-canopy timber plantation encircling the ponds with an open-canopy longleaf pine forest. The District Court nonetheless upheld the designation. The court determined that Unit 1 satisfied the statutory definition of unoccupied critical habitat, which requires only that the Service deem the land "essential for the conservation [of] the species."

Weyerhaeuser also challenged the Service's decision not to exclude Unit 1 from the dusky gopher frog's critical habitat, arguing that the Service had failed to adequately weigh the benefits of designating Unit 1 against the economic impact. In addition, Weyerhaeuser argued that the Service had used an unreasonable methodology for estimating economic impact and, regardless of methodology, had failed to consider several categories of costs. The court approved the Service's methodology and declined to consider Weyerhaeuser's challenge to the decision not to exclude.

The Fifth Circuit affirmed. The Court of Appeals rejected the suggestion that the definition of critical habitat contains any "habitability requirement." The court also concluded that the Service's decision not to exclude Unit 1 was committed to agency discretion by law and was therefore unreviewable. Judge Owen dissented. She wrote that Unit 1 could not be "essential for the conservation of the species" because it lacked the open-canopy forest that the Service itself had determined was "essential to the conservation" of the frog.

The Fifth Circuit denied rehearing en banc. Judge Jones dissented, joined by Judges Jolly, Smith, Clement, Owen, and Elrod. They reasoned that critical habitat must first be habitat, and Unit 1 in its present state could not be habitat for the dusky gopher frog. The dissenting judges also concluded that the Service's decision not to exclude Unit 1 was reviewable for abuse of discretion.

We granted certiorari to consider two questions: (1) whether "critical habitat" under the ESA must also be habitat; and (2) whether a federal court may review an agency decision not to exclude a certain area from critical habitat because of the economic impact of such a designation.

II

A

Our analysis starts with the phrase "critical habitat." According to the ordinary understanding of how adjectives work, "critical habitat" must also be "habitat." Adjectives modify nouns—they pick out a subset of a category that possesses a certain quality. It follows that "critical habitat" is the subset of "habitat" that is "critical" to the conservation of an endangered species.

Of course, "[s]tatutory language cannot be construed in a vacuum," and so we must also consider "critical habitat" in its statutory context. Section 4(a)(3)(A)(i), which the lower courts did not analyze, is the sole source of authority for critical-habitat designations. That provision states that when the Secretary lists a species as endangered he must also "designate any *habitat of such species* which is then considered to be critical habitat." (emphasis added). Only the "habitat" of the endangered species is eligible for designation as critical habitat. Even if an area otherwise meets the statutory definition of unoccupied critical habitat because the Secretary finds the area essential for the conservation of the species, Section 4(a)(3)(A)(i) does not authorize the Secretary to designate the area as *critical* habitat unless it is also *habitat* for the species.

The Center for Biological Diversity contends that the statutory definition of critical habitat is complete in itself and does not require any independent inquiry into the meaning of the term "habitat," which the statute leaves undefined. But the statutory definition of "critical habitat" tells us what makes habitat "critical," not what makes it "habitat." Under the statutory definition, critical habitat comprises areas occupied by the species "on which are found those physical or biological features (I) essential to the conservation of the species and (II) which may require special management considerations or protection," as well as unoccupied areas that the Secretary determines to be "essential for the conservation of the species." That is no baseline definition of habitat—it identifies only certain areas that are indispensable to the conservation of the endangered species. The definition allows the Secretary to identify the subset of habitat that is critical, but leaves the larger category of habitat undefined.

The Service does not now dispute that critical habitat must be habitat, although it made no such concession below. Instead, the Service argues that habitat includes areas that, like Unit 1, would require some degree of modification to support a sustainable population of a given species. Weyerhaeuser, for its part, urges that habitat cannot include areas where the species could not currently survive. (Habitat can, of course, include areas where the species does not currently *live*, given that the statute defines critical habitat to include unoccupied areas.) The Service in turn disputes Weyerhaeuser's premise that the administrative record shows that the frog could not survive in Unit 1.

The Court of Appeals concluded that "critical habitat" designations under the statute were not limited to areas that qualified as habitat. The court therefore had no occasion to interpret the term "habitat" in Section 4(a)(3)(A)(i) or to assess the Service's administrative findings regarding Unit 1. Accordingly, we vacate the judgment below and remand to the Court of Appeals to consider these questions in the first instance.

B

Weyerhaeuser also contends that, even if Unit 1 could be properly classified as critical habitat for the dusky gopher frog, the Service should have excluded it from designation under Section 4(b)(2) of the ESA. That provision requires the Secretary to "tak[e] into consideration the economic impact . . . of specifying any particular area as critical habitat" and authorizes him to "exclude any area from critical habitat if he determines that the benefits of such exclusion outweigh the benefits of specifying such area as part of the critical habitat." To satisfy its obligation to consider economic impact, the Service commissioned a report estimating the costs of its proposed critical-habitat designation. The Service concluded that the costs of designating the proposed areas, including Unit 1, were not "disproportionate" to the conservation benefits and, "[c]onsequently," declined to make any exclusions.

Weyerhaeuser claims that the Service's conclusion rested on a faulty assessment of the costs and benefits of designation and that the resulting decision not to exclude should be set aside. Specifically, Weyerhaeuser contends that the Service improperly weighed the costs of designating Unit 1 against the benefits of designating *all* proposed critical habitat, rather than the benefits of designating Unit 1 in particular. Weyerhaeuser also argues that the Service did not fully account for the economic impact of designating Unit 1 because it ignored, among other things, the costs of replacing timber trees with longleaf pines, maintaining an open canopy through controlled burning, and the tax revenue that St.

Tammany Parish would lose if Unit 1 were never developed. The Court of Appeals did not consider Weyerhaeuser's claim because it concluded that a decision not to exclude a certain area from critical habitat is unreviewable.

The Administrative Procedure Act creates a "basic presumption of judicial review [for] one 'suffering legal wrong because of agency action.' " As we explained recently, "legal lapses and violations occur, and especially so when they have no consequence. That is why this Court has so long applied a strong presumption favoring judicial review of administrative action." The presumption may be rebutted only if the relevant statute precludes review, 5 U.S.C. §701(a)(1), or if the action is "committed to agency discretion by law," §701(a)(2). The Service contends, and the lower courts agreed, that Section 4(b)(2) of the ESA commits to the Secretary's discretion decisions not to exclude an area from critical habitat.

This Court has noted the "tension" between the prohibition of judicial review for actions "committed to agency discretion" and the command in §706(2)(A) that courts set aside any agency action that is "arbitrary, capricious, an abuse of discretion, or otherwise not in accordance with law." A court could never determine that an agency abused its discretion if all matters committed to agency discretion were unreviewable. To give effect to §706(2)(A) and to honor the presumption of review, we have read the exception in §701(a)(2) quite narrowly, restricting it to "those rare circumstances where the relevant statute is drawn so that a court would have no meaningful standard against which to judge the agency's exercise of discretion." The Service contends that Section 4(b)(2) of the ESA is one of those rare statutory provisions.

There is, at the outset, reason to be skeptical of the Service's position. The few cases in which we have applied the §701(a)(2) exception involved agency decisions that courts have traditionally regarded as unreviewable, such as the allocation of funds from a lump-sum appropriation. By contrast, this case involves the sort of routine dispute that federal courts regularly review: An agency issues an order affecting the rights of a private party, and the private party objects that the agency did not properly justify its determination under a standard set forth in the statute.

Section 4(b)(2) states that the Secretary

> "shall designate critical habitat . . . after taking into consideration the economic impact, the impact on national security, and any other relevant impact, of specifying any particular area as critical habitat. The Secretary may exclude any area from critical habitat if he determines that the benefits of such exclusion outweigh the benefits of specifying such area . . . unless he determines . . . that the failure to designate such area as critical habitat will result in the extinction of the species concerned." 16 U.S.C. §1533(b)(2).

Although the text meanders a bit, we recognized in *Bennett v. Spear*, 520 U.S. 154 (1997), that the provision describes a unified process for weighing the impact of designating an area as critical habitat. The first sentence of Section 4(b)(2) imposes a "categorical requirement" that the Secretary "tak[e] into consideration" economic and other impacts before such a designation. *Id.*, at 172, 117 S. Ct. 1154 (emphasis deleted). The second sentence authorizes the Secretary to act on his consideration by providing that he may exclude an area from critical habitat if he determines that the benefits of exclusion outweigh the benefits of designation. The Service followed that procedure here (albeit in a flawed manner, according to Weyerhaeuser). It commissioned a report to estimate the costs of designating the proposed critical habitat, concluded that those costs were not "disproportionate" to the benefits of designation, and "[c]onsequently" declined to "exercis[e] [its] discretion to exclude any areas from [the] designation of critical habitat."

Bennett explained that the Secretary's "ultimate decision" to designate or exclude, which he "arriv[es] at" after considering economic and other impacts, is reviewable "for abuse of discretion." The Service dismisses that language as a "passing reference . . . not necessarily inconsistent with the Service's understanding," which is that the Secretary's decision not to exclude an area is wholly discretionary and therefore unreviewable. Brief for Federal Respondents 50. The Service bases its understanding on the second sentence of Section 4(b)(2), which states that the Secretary "*may* exclude [an] area from critical habitat if he determines that the benefits of such exclusion outweigh the benefits of [designation]."

The use of the word "may" certainly confers discretion on the Secretary. That does not, however, segregate his discretionary decision not to exclude from the procedure mandated by Section 4(b)(2), which directs the Secretary to consider the economic and other impacts of designation when making his exclusion decisions. Weyerhaeuser's claim is the familiar one in administrative law that the agency did not appropriately consider all of the relevant factors that the statute sets forth to guide the agency in the exercise of its discretion. Specifically, Weyerhaeuser contends that the Service ignored some costs and conflated the benefits of designating Unit 1 with the benefits of designating all of the proposed critical habitat. This is the sort of claim that federal courts routinely assess when determining whether to set aside an agency decision as an abuse of discretion under §706(2)(A).

Section 4(b)(2) requires the Secretary to consider economic impact and relative benefits before deciding whether to exclude an area from critical habitat or to proceed with designation. The statute is, therefore, not "drawn so that a court would have no meaningful standard against which to judge the [Secretary's] exercise of [his] discretion" not to exclude.

Because it determined that the Service's decisions not to exclude were committed to agency discretion and therefore unreviewable, the Court of Appeals did not consider whether the Service's assessment of the costs and benefits of designation was flawed in a way that rendered the resulting decision not to exclude Unit 1 arbitrary, capricious, or an abuse of discretion. Accordingly, we remand to the Court of Appeals to consider that question, if necessary, in the first instance.

* * *

The judgment of the Court of Appeals for the Fifth Circuit is vacated, and the case is remanded for further proceedings consistent with this opinion.

It is so ordered.

Justice Kavanaugh took no part in the consideration or decision of this case.

ARE DRAFT BIOLOGICAL OPINIONS DISCOVERABLE UNDER THE FREEDOM OF INFORMATION ACT?

Section 7 of the Endangered Species Act, 16 U.S.C. §1536, requires the U.S. Fish & Wildlife Service (FWS) and/or the National Marine Fisheries Service (NMFS) to consult with any federal agency before taking any action likely to jeopardize the continued existence of an endangered species or to adversely modify the critical habitat of such a species. For nearly two years the U.S. Environmental Protection Agency (EPA) consulted with both the FWS and the NMFS while developing a regulation for cooling water intake structures under the Clean Water Act. Preliminary drafts of a biological opinion prepared by the Services concluded that EPA's rule would jeopardize endangered species, but the final opinion provided to EPA instead supported a "no jeopardy" determination. The Sierra Club ultimately filed suit to obtain a wide range of documents under the Freedom of Information Act (FOIA), including documents that the government argued were exempt from disclosure by the deliberative process privilege. After reviewing the documents in camera, the district court and later the U.S. Court of Appeals for the Ninth Circuit ordered the Services to release 11 of the documents in full and another with a single sentence redated. The court concluded that some of the documents were not pre-decisional because they involved a different rule than the one ultimately adopted by EPA and that others were not deliberative because no further deliberation occurred over the jeopardy determination after the documents were prepared.

The Services sought and obtained review in the Supreme Court. In the decision below the Court addressed the question whether Exemption 5 of the Freedom of Information Act, 5 U.S.C. §552(b)(5), which incorporates the deliberative process privilege, protects against disclosure of pre-decisional drafts of a biological opinion.

U.S. FISH & WILDLIFE SERVICE v. SIERRA CLUB, INC.
141 S.Ct. 777 (2021)

Justice Barrett delivered the opinion of the Court.

The Freedom of Information Act (FOIA) requires that federal agencies make records available to the public upon request, unless those records fall within one of nine exemptions. Exemption 5 incorporates the privileges available to Government agencies in civil litigation, such as the deliberative process privilege, attorney-client privilege, and attorney work-product privilege. This case concerns the deliberative process privilege, which protects from disclosure documents generated during an agency's deliberations about a policy, as opposed to documents that embody or explain a policy that the agency adopts. We must decide whether the privilege protects in-house drafts that proved to be the agencies' last word about a proposal's potential threat to endangered species. We hold that it does.

I

A

In April 2011, the Environmental Protection Agency (EPA) proposed a rule on the design and operation of "cooling water intake structures," which withdraw large volumes of water from various sources to cool industrial equipment. EPA's stated goal was to require industrial facilities to use "the best technology available" for "minimizing adverse environmental impact." 76 Fed. Reg. 22174 (2011). But it was unclear whether the proposed rule would achieve that goal, at least when it came to aquatic wildlife. The water withdrawn by these structures typically contains fish and other organisms that can become trapped in the intake system and die. If the EPA's rule did not adequately guard against this risk, it would jeopardize species protected under the Endangered Species Act of 1973, 16 U.S.C. §1531 *et seq.*

When an agency plans to undertake action that might "adversely affect" a protected species, the agency must consult with the U.S. Fish and Wildlife Service (FWS) and National Marine Fisheries Service (NMFS) (together, "Services") before proceeding. See 16 U.S.C. §1536(a)(2); 50 CFR §§402.01-402.17 (2019).1The goal of the consultation is to assist the Services in preparing an official "biological opinion" on whether the agency's proposal will jeopardize the continued existence of threatened or endangered species. §402.14(g)(4). These opinions are known as " 'jeopardy' " or " 'no jeopardy' " biological opinions. §402.14(h)(1)(iv), as amended, 84 Fed. Reg. 45017 (2019). If the Services conclude that the action will cause "jeopardy," they must propose "reasonable and prudent alternatives" to the action that would avoid harming the threatened species. 16 U.S.C. §1536(b)(3)(A); 50 CFR §402.14(h)(2). And if a "jeopardy" biological opinion is issued, the agency must either implement the reasonable and prudent alternatives, terminate the action altogether, or seek an exemption from the Endangered Species Committee. 16 U.S.C. §§1536(b)(4), (g), 1538(a).

The EPA began informally consulting with the Services about its proposed regulations on cooling water intake structures in 2012, see 50 CFR §402.13, and it requested a formal consultation in 2013, see §402.14. Throughout this period, the Services and the EPA conducted meetings, held conference calls, and exchanged emails and draft documents on the proposed rule and its potential effect on endangered species.

As a result of the consultation, the EPA made changes to its proposed rule, and the Services received the revised version in November 2013. Soon after, the Services tentatively agreed to provide the EPA with draft biological opinions by December 6, 2013, and final opinions by December 20, 2013. See §402.14(g)(5) (requiring the Services to provide a "draft biological opinion" to action agency upon request).

Staff members at NMFS completed a draft biological opinion on December 6, and staff members at FWS completed a draft on December 9. Both drafts concluded that the proposed rule was likely to jeopardize certain species and identified possible reasonable and prudent alternatives that the EPA could pursue. Staff members sent the drafts to the relevant decisionmakers within each Service and prepared to circulate them to the EPA.

But decisionmakers at the Services neither approved the drafts nor sent them to the EPA. Instead, concluding that "more work needed to be done," the decisionmakers decided to continue discussions with the EPA. App. 37, 58-59. The EPA was still engaged in an internal debate about key elements of the rule, and the Services wanted a better grasp of what the EPA proposed to do. So the Services shelved the draft opinions and agreed with the EPA to extend the period of consultation.

Over the next several months, the Services and the EPA continued to discuss the rule, and in March 2014, the EPA sent the Services a proposed rule that differed significantly from the 2013 version. Satisfied that the revised rule was unlikely to harm any protected species, the Services issued a joint final "no jeopardy" biological opinion, thereby terminating the formal consultation. See 50 CFR §402.14(m)(1), as amended, 84 Fed. Reg. 45016. The EPA issued its final rule that same day.

B

Sierra Club, an environmental organization, later submitted FOIA requests for records related to the Services' consultations with the EPA. The Services turned over thousands of documents, but they invoked the deliberative process privilege for others—including the draft biological opinions analyzing the EPA's 2013 proposed rule. The deliberative process privilege shields documents that reflect an agency's preliminary thinking about a problem, as opposed to its final decision about it. The Services asserted that as drafts, the withheld documents were necessarily nonfinal and therefore protected.

Sierra Club sued the Services in the Northern District of California, alleging that the withheld documents were subject to disclosure under FOIA. The District Court agreed with Sierra Club, and the Ninth Circuit affirmed in part. 925 F.3d 1000 (CA9 2019). As relevant here, it held that the draft biological opinions were not privileged because even though they were labeled as drafts, they represented the Services' final opinion that the EPA's 2013 proposed rule was likely to have an adverse effect on certain endangered species.2 Judge Wallace dissented in part on the ground that the drafts were part of the ongoing consultation process rather than summaries of the Services' final views.

We granted certiorari.

II

A

FOIA mandates the disclosure of documents held by a federal agency unless the documents fall within one of nine enumerated exemptions. See 5 U.S.C. §552(b). The fifth of those exemptions protects "inter-agency or intra-agency memorandums or letters that would not be available by law to a party other than an agency in litigation with the agency." §552(b)(5). As the text indicates—albeit in a less-than-straightforward way—this exemption incorporates the privileges available to Government agencies in civil litigation. That list includes the deliberative process privilege, attorney-client privilege, and attorney work-product privilege.

This case concerns the deliberative process privilege, which is a form of executive privilege. To protect agencies from being "forced to operate in a fishbowl," the deliberative process privilege shields from disclosure "documents reflecting advisory opinions, recommendations and deliberations comprising part of a process by which governmental decisions and policies are formulated." The privilege is rooted in "the obvious realization that officials will not communicate candidly among themselves if each remark is a potential item of discovery and front page news." To encourage candor, which improves agency decisionmaking, the privilege blunts the chilling effect that accompanies the prospect of disclosure.

This rationale does not apply, of course, to documents that embody a final decision, because once a decision has been made, the deliberations are done. The privilege therefore distinguishes between predecisional, deliberative documents, which are exempt from disclosure, and documents reflecting a final agency decision and the reasons supporting it, which are not. Documents are "predecisional" if they were generated before the agency's final decision on the matter, and they are "deliberative" if they were prepared to help the agency formulate its position. There is considerable overlap between these two prongs because a document cannot be deliberative unless it is predecisional.

It is not always self-evident whether a document represents an agency's final decision, but one thing is clear: A document is not final solely because nothing else follows it. Sometimes a proposal dies on the vine. That happens in deliberations—some ideas are discarded or simply languish. Yet documents discussing such dead-end ideas can hardly be described as reflecting the agency's chosen course. What matters, then, is not whether a document is last in line, but whether it communicates a policy on which the agency has settled.

To decide whether a document communicates the agency's settled position, courts must consider whether the agency treats the document as its final view on the matter. When it does so, the deliberative "process by which governmental decisions and policies are formulated" will have concluded, and the document will have "real operative effect." In other words, once cited as the agency's final view, the document reflects "the 'consummation' of the agency's decisionmaking process" and not a "merely tentative" position. By contrast, a document that leaves agency decisionmakers "free to change their minds" does not reflect the agency's final decision.

B

The deliberative process privilege protects the draft biological opinions at issue here because they reflect a preliminary view—not a final decision—about the likely effect of the EPA's proposed rule on endangered species.

We start with the obvious point that the Services identified these documents as "drafts." A draft is, by definition, a preliminary version of a piece of writing subject to feedback and change. That is not to say that the label "draft" is determinative. As we have explained before, a court must evaluate the documents "in the context of the administrative process which generated them." Here, though, the administrative context confirms that the drafts are what they sound like: opinions that were subject to change.

Consider the regulatory process that generates a draft biological opinion. The governing regulation distinguishes between draft and final biological opinions by separating the steps at which each is produced. If the Services prepare a biological opinion, they must "make available" to the action agency—in this case, the EPA—a "draft" of that opinion and generally may not issue the final opinion "while the draft is under review" by the action agency. 50 CFR §402.14(g)(5). This provision thus specifically contemplates further review by the agency after receipt of the draft, and with it, the possibility of changes to the biological opinion *after* the Services send the agency the draft.

Consistent with this understanding, the agreement between the Services and the EPA allowed for the possibility of postcirculation changes. The Services were scheduled to provide the EPA with draft copies of the biological opinions on December 6 and final versions by December 20. If the drafts were to be final and immune from change, there would have been little reason to include a two-week period between the Services' circulation of the drafts and their submission of the final product. The logical inference is that the Services expected the EPA to provide comments that they might incorporate into the final opinion.

Sierra Club contends, though, that while these documents may have been called "drafts," they were actually intended to give the EPA a sneak peek at a conclusion that the Services had already reached and were unwilling to change. And Sierra Club says that the EPA responded accordingly: Once the EPA knew that a jeopardy opinion was coming, it revised its proposed rule. Sierra Club insists that the draft opinions thus had an "operative effect" on the EPA and must be treated as final under our precedent.

Sierra Club misunderstands our precedent. While we have identified a decision's "real operative effect" as an indication of its finality, that reference is to the legal, not practical, consequences that flow from an agency's action. In this regulatory scheme, a final biological opinion leads to "direct and appreciable legal consequences" because it alters "the legal regime to which the action agency is subject, authorizing it" to take action affecting an endangered species "if (but only if) it complies with the prescribed conditions." That is not true of a draft biological opinion.

To be sure, a draft biological opinion might carry a practical consequence if it prompts the action agency to change its proposed rule. For example, the agency might adopt an alternative approach that avoids jeopardizing an endangered species. But many documents short of a draft biological opinion could prompt an agency to alter its rule. An agency might make changes in response to the Services' views—or, for that matter, the views of the agency's own officials—at any stage of the consultation process. And even Sierra Club does not contend that any email or memorandum that has the effect of changing an agency's course constitutes a final administrative decision. That approach would gut the deliberative process privilege.

Sierra Club's proposed effects-based test is therefore not the right one. To determine whether the privilege applies, we must evaluate not whether the drafts provoked a response from the EPA but whether the Services treated them as final.

They did not. The drafts were prepared by lower-level staff and sent to the Services' decisionmakers for approval. Sierra Club characterizes the drafts as polished documents lacking only an autopen signature. But the determinative fact is not their level of polish—it is that the decisionmakers at the Services neither approved the drafts nor sent them to the EPA. Instead, the decisionmakers concluded that "more work needed to be done" and extended the time for consultation with the EPA. These documents, then, are best described not as draft biological opinions but as drafts of draft biological opinions. Sierra Club's argument thus fails on its own terms: Even assuming that a draft biological opinion would have expressed the Services' settled conclusion, a draft of a draft is a far cry from an "agency decision already made."

It is true, as Sierra Club emphasizes, that the staff recommendations proved to be the last word within the Services about the 2013 version of the EPA's proposed rule. But that does not change our analysis. The recommendations were not last because they were final; they were last because they died on the vine. Further consultation with the Services prompted the EPA to alter key features of its 2013 proposal, so there was never a need for the Services to render a definitive judgment about it. The opinion that came to fruition was the Services' joint "no jeopardy" opinion about the 2014 version of the EPA's proposed rule. The staff recommendations were thus part of a deliberative process that worked as it should have: The Services and the EPA consulted about how the rule would affect aquatic wildlife until the EPA settled on an approach that would not jeopardize any protected species.

Sierra Club warns that ruling against it here would permit the Services to stamp every document "draft," thereby protecting even final agency decisions and creating " 'secret [agency] law.' " It is true that a draft document will typically be predecisional because, as we said earlier, calling something a draft communicates that it is not yet final. But determining whether an agency's position is final for purposes of the deliberative process privilege is a functional rather than formal inquiry. If the evidence establishes that an agency has hidden a functionally final decision in draft form, the deliberative process privilege will not apply. The Services, however, did not engage in such a charade here.

* * *

The deliberative process privilege protects the draft biological opinions from disclosure because they are both predecisional and deliberative. We reverse the contrary judgment of the Court of Appeals and remand the case for further proceedings consistent with this opinion.

It is so ordered.

Justice Breyer, with whom Justice Sotomayor joins, dissenting.

Because the word "draft" may here prove misleading, it should help the reader understand my argument if he or she keeps in mind three different but related kinds of documents: "Final Biological Opinions," "Draft Biological Opinions," and "Drafts of Draft Biological Opinions." A Final Biological Opinion, as its name suggests, embodies a final agency decision, for example, a decision by the Services that a proposed Environmental Protection Agency (EPA) action will jeopardize an endangered species. We all agree, I believe, that a Final Biological Opinion is not deliberative and that Exemption 5 of the Freedom of Information Act (FOIA) does not protect it from disclosure. I also agree with the Court about the third kind of document, a Draft of a Draft Biological Opinion. That kind of document normally is not final. It normally is deliberative. And Exemption 5 normally protects it from disclosure.

But what about the second kind of document, a Draft Biological Opinion? Does it normally set forth a "final" Services view, or is it normally a "deliberative" document? I agree with the Court that whether a document is "final" or "deliberative" primarily depends upon its "function[ ]" within an agency's decision-making process. I believe that, in the context before us, the Services' Draft Biological Opinions reflect "final" decisions regarding the "jeopardy" the EPA's then-proposed actions would have caused. Hence, they would normally fall outside, not within, Exemption 5.

Five features of the Draft Biological Opinion lead me to this conclusion. First, literally speaking, a Draft Biological Opinion is a "final" document with respect to its content. That is in fact the key difference between a Draft Biological Opinion and a Draft of a Draft Biological Opinion. If further deliberation about the draft's content is likely, the document is not a Draft Biological Opinion. It is a Draft of a Draft. I recognize that in principle a Service might change its mind about the content of even the most final of Draft Biological Opinions. It might then prepare a new Draft Biological Opinion. But, in principle, a Service could also change its mind about a Final Biological Opinion, withdrawing a Final Biological Opinion already issued and substituting a new one in its place. The mere possibility of a future change does not alter the finality, or the final effect, of the original document.

Second, a Final Biological Opinion and a Draft Biological Opinion finding jeopardy serve the same functions within the formal administrative process. Both explain the Services' findings. Both set forth "reasonable and prudent" modifications or alternatives. 16 U.S.C. §1536(b)(3)(A). And both have substantially the same effect on the EPA (the action agency in this case). In response to both documents, the EPA has essentially four options: It can drop the proposed action; it can accept the proposed modifications; it can take the proposed action and potentially expose itself to considerable penalties, or it can seek a Cabinet-level exemption. The EPA could also, of course, propose a new course of action embodying modifications not proposed by the Services—possibly generating a new consultation—but that is just as true of a Final Biological Opinion.

A Draft Biological Opinion differs from a Final Biological Opinion in only one way that matters. The Services must make the Draft Biological Opinion available to the EPA before it issues a Final Biological Opinion. 50 CFR §402.14(g)(5). It then continues its consultation with the EPA but *not* with an eye toward changing the Services' environmental analysis or conclusions. Rather, the negotiations are designed to find less damaging alternatives to the original EPA-proposed action. See *ibid.*(allowing the action agency to request the Draft Biological Opinion "for the purpose of analyzing the reasonable and prudent alternatives"). If the agencies find suitable alternatives, the EPA will then publicly adopt those alternatives, and the process will culminate in a Final Biological Opinion finding no jeopardy.

The function of a Draft Biological Opinion finding jeopardy then is much the same as that of a Final Biological Opinion finding jeopardy. Transmitting the Draft Biological Opinion to the EPA simply allows the EPA to make its choice before a Final Biological Opinion issues.

Third, agency practice shows that the Draft Biological Opinion, not the Final Biological Opinion, is the document that informs the EPA of the Services' conclusions about jeopardy and alternatives and triggers within the EPA the process of deciding what to do about those conclusions.

Amici tell us without contradiction that "out of 6,829 formal consultations" between 2008 and 2015, the Fish and Wildlife Service "issued a [Final Biological Opinion finding] jeopardy" "only *twice*." Brief for Center for Biological Diversity et al. as *Amici Curiae* 22-23. If a Final Biological Opinion is discoverable under FOIA, as all seem to agree it is, why would a Draft Biological Opinion, embodying the same Service conclusions (and leaving the EPA with the same four choices), not be?

Fourth, permitting discovery of Draft Biological Opinions under FOIA is unlikely to chill frank discussion within a Service because the Services' staff are already aware that these Drafts may well be made public. And for good reason. When a private party prompts the agency action under review, say, by seeking an EPA permit, regulations require the Service to make the Draft Biological Opinion available to the private applicant, removing the Draft Biological Opinion from Exemption 5's protection. See 50 CFR §402.14(g)(5) (requiring disclosure of Draft Biological Opinions to private applicants if requested); see also *Department of Interior v. Klamath Water Users Protective Assn.*, 532 U.S. 1, 4-5 (2001) (documents exchanged between agency and third party not covered by Exemption 5 because they are no longer inter-agency or intra-agency communications). To hold that Draft Biological Opinions are discoverable when a private party seeks an EPA permit but not when, as here, the EPA seeks to write a generally applicable rule that governs private party conduct seems highly anomalous.

Even where there is no private applicant, the evaluating agencies have a long history of disclosing Draft Biological Opinions to the public. The EPA too may well release a Service's Draft Biological Opinion.

Fifth, legal consequences flow from the Services' completion of a Draft Biological Opinion. The Services' regulations state that "[i]f requested, the Service shall make available to the Federal agency [*i.e.*, the EPA] the draft biological opinion for the purpose of analyzing the reasonable and prudent alternatives." 50 CFR §402.14(g)(5). Once the Draft Biological Opinion is under review at the EPA, the Services may not issue a Final Biological Opinion prior to the specified deadline. Moreover, as explained, Draft Biological Opinions, like Final Biological Opinions, limit the EPA's set of available options. Cf. *Bennett v. Spear*, 520 U.S. 154, 178 (1997) (holding that a Final Biological Opinion has "legal consequences," even though the action agency is not legally obligated to accept the opinion's recommendations or conclusions, because the opinion "alter[s] the legal regime to which the action agency is subject"). Why, then, would these same consequences (together with the other factors mentioned above) not also place Draft Biological Opinions outside Exemption 5's protection?

In sum, the likely finality of a Draft Biological Opinion, its similarity to a Final Biological Opinion, the similar purposes it serves, the agency's actual practice, the anomaly that would otherwise exist depending upon the presence or absence of a private party, and the presence of at least some regulation-based legal constraints—convince me that a Draft Biological Opinion would not normally enjoy a deliberative privilege from FOIA disclosure.

The question remains whether the particular documents at issue here are Draft Biological Opinions or Drafts of Draft Biological Opinions. As the majority points out, there are reasons to believe some of them may be the latter. The National Marine Fisheries Service's documents contain highlighting and editing marks reflective of a work-in-progress. But the Fish and Wildlife Service documents do not, and the record indicates they may have been complete but for a final signature. See App. 105. Given the fact-intensive nature of this question, I would remand to allow the Court of Appeals to determine just how much work was left to be done. If the court determines that the documents are merely Drafts of Draft Biological Opinions, I agree with the majority that a segregability analysis would be appropriate.

For these reasons, with respect, I dissent.

WHICH AGENCY HAS AUTHORITY TO PERMIT A PIPELINE TO CROSS UNDER THE APPALACHIAN TRAIL—THE FOREST SERVICE OR THE NATIONAL PARK SERVICE?

In the decision below the U.S. Supreme Court reviewed a decision that voided the Forest Service's issuance of a permit to allow a pipeline to cross underneath the Appalachian Trail because the trail is administered by the National Park Service.

U.S. FOREST SERVICE v. COWPASTURE RIVER PRESERVATION ASSOCIATION
2020 140 S.Ct. 1837 (2020)

THOMAS, J., delivered the opinion of the Court, in which ROBERTS, C.J., and BREYER, ALITO, GORSUCH, and KAVANAUGH, JJ., joined, and in which GINSBURG, J., joined except as to Part III-B-2. SOTOMAYOR, J., filed a dissenting opinion, in which KAGAN, J., joined.

JUSTICE THOMAS delivered the opinion of the Court.

We granted certiorari in these consolidated cases to decide whether the United States Forest Service has authority under the Mineral Leasing Act to grant rights-of-way through lands within national forests traversed by the Appalachian Trail. We hold that the Mineral Leasing Act does grant the Forest Service that authority and therefore reverse the judgment of the Court of Appeals for the Fourth Circuit.

I

A

In 2015, petitioner Atlantic Coast Pipeline, LLC (Atlantic) filed an application with the Federal Energy Regulatory Commission to construct and operate an approximately 604-mile natural gas pipeline extending from West Virginia to North Carolina. The pipeline's proposed route traverses 16 miles of land within the George Washington National Forest. The Appalachian National Scenic Trail (Appalachian Trail or Trail) also crosses parts of the George Washington National Forest.

To construct the pipeline, Atlantic needed to obtain special use permits from the United States Forest Service for the portions of the pipeline that would pass through lands under the Forest Service's jurisdiction. In 2018, the Forest Service issued these permits and granted a right-of-way that would allow Atlantic to place a 0.1-mile segment of pipe approximately 600 feet below the Appalachian Trail in the George Washington National Forest.

B

Respondents Cowpasture River Preservation Association, Highlanders for Responsible Development, Shenandoah Valley Battlefields Foundation, Shenandoah Valley Network, Sierra Club, Virginia Wilderness Committee, and Wild Virginia filed a petition for review in the Fourth Circuit. They contended that the issuance of the special use permit for the right-of-way under the Trail, as well as numerous other aspects of the Forest Service's regulatory process, violated the Mineral Leasing Act (Leasing Act), the National Environmental Policy Act, the National Forest Management Act. and the Administrative Procedure Act. Atlantic intervened in the suit.

The Fourth Circuit vacated the Forest Service's special use permit after holding that the Leasing Act did not empower the Forest Service to grant the pipeline right-of-way beneath the Trail. As relevant here, the court concluded that the Appalachian Trail had become part of the National Park System because, though originally charged with the Trail's administration, the Secretary of the Interior delegated that duty to the National Park Service. In the Fourth Circuit's view, this delegation made the Trail part of the National Park System because the Trail was now an "area of land . . . administered by the Secretary [of the Interior] acting through the Director [of the National Park Service]." Because it concluded the Trail was now within the National Park System, the court held that the Trail was beyond the authority of "the Secretary of the Interior or appropriate agency head" to grant pipeline rights-of-way under the Leasing Act.

II

These cases involve the interaction of multiple federal laws. We therefore begin by summarizing the relevant statutory and regulatory background.

A

Congress enacted the Weeks Act in 1911 which provided for the acquisition of lands for inclusion in the National Forest System. The Weeks Act also directed that lands acquired for the National Forest System "shall be permanently reserved, held, and administered as national forest lands." Though Congress initially granted the Secretary of Agriculture the authority to administer national forest lands, the Secretary has delegated that authority to the Forest Service.

What is now known as the George Washington National Forest was established as a national forest in 1918, and renamed the George Washington National Forest in 1932. No party here disputes that the George Washington National Forest was acquired for inclusion in the National Forest System and that it is under the jurisdiction of the Forest Service.

B

Enacted in 1968, the National Trails System Act (Trails Act), among other things, establishes national scenic and national historic trails. The Appalachian Trail was one of the first two trails created under the Act.

Under the statute, the Appalachian Trail "shall be ad- ministered primarily as a footpath by the Secretary of the Interior, in consultation with the Secretary of Agriculture." The statute empowers the Secretary of the

Interior to establish the location and width of the Appalachian Trail by entering into "rights-of-way" agreements with other federal agencies as well as States, local governments, and private landowners. However, the Trails Act also contains a proviso stating that "[n]othing contained in this chapter shall be deemed to transfer among Federal agencies any management responsibilities established under any other law for federally administered lands which are components of the National Trails System."

The Trails Act currently establishes 30 national historic and national scenic trails. It assigns responsibility for most of those trails to the Secretary of the Interior. Though the Act is silent on the issue of delegation, the Department of the Interior has delegated the administrative responsibility over each of those trails to either the National Park Service or the Bureau of Land Management, both of which are housed within the Department of the Interior. Currently, the National Park Service administers 21 trails, the Bureau of Land Management administers 1 trail, and the two agencies co-administer 2 trails. The Secretary of Interior delegated his authority over the Appalachian Trail to the National Park Service in 1969.

C

In 1920, Congress passed the Leasing Act, which enabled the Secretary of the Interior to grant pipeline rights-of-way through "public lands, including the forest reserves." Congress amended the Leasing Act in 1973 to provide that not only the Secretary of the Interior but also any "appropriate agency head" may grant "[r]ights-of-way through any Federal lands . . . for pipeline purposes." Notably, the 1973 amendment also defined "Federal lands" to include "all lands owned by the United States, except lands in the National Park System, lands held in trust for an Indian or Indian tribe, and lands on the Outer Continental Shelf." In 1970, Congress defined the National Park System as "any area of land and water now and hereafter administered by the Secretary of the Interior, through the National Park Service for park, monument, historic, parkway, recreational, or other purposes."

III

We are tasked with determining whether the Leasing Act enables the Forest Service to grant a subterranean pipeline right-of-way some 600 feet under the Appalachian Trail. To do this, we first focus on the distinction between the *lands* that the Trail traverses and the Trail itself, because the lands (not the Trail) are the object of the relevant statutes.

Under the Leasing Act, the "Secretary of the Interior or appropriate agency head" may grant pipeline rights-of-way across "Federal *lands*." 30 U.S.C. §185(a) (emphasis added). The Forest Service is an "appropriate agency head" for "Federal lands" over "which [it] has jurisdiction." As stated above, it is undisputed that the Forest Service has jurisdiction over the "Federal lands" within the George Washington National Forest. The question before us, then, becomes whether these *lands* within the forest have been removed from the Forest Service's jurisdiction and placed under the Park Service's control because the Trail crosses them. If no transfer of jurisdiction has occurred, then the lands remain National Forest lands, *i.e.*, "Federal lands" subject to the grant of a pipeline right-of-way. If, on the other hand, jurisdiction over the lands has been transferred to the Park Service, then the lands fall under the Leasing Act's carve-out for "*lands* in the National Park System," thus precluding the grant of the right-of-way.

We conclude that the lands that the Trail crosses remain under the Forest Service's jurisdiction and, thus, continue to be "Federal lands" under the Leasing Act.

A

We begin our analysis by examining the interests and authority granted under the Trails Act. Pursuant to the Trails Act, the Forest Service entered into "right-of-way" agreements with the National Park Service "for [the] approximately 780 miles of Appalachian Trail route within national forests," including the George Washington National Forest. These "right-of-way" agreements did not convert "Federal lands" into "lands" within the "National Park System."

1

A right-of-way is a type of easement. In 1968, as now, principles of property law defined a right-of-way easement as granting a nonowner a limited privilege to "use the lands of another." Specifically, a right-of-way grants the limited "right to pass . . . through the estate of another." Courts at the time of the Trails Act's enactment acknowledged that easements grant only nonpossessory rights of use limited to the purposes specified in the easement agreement. And because an easement does not dispossess the original owner, "a possessor and an easement holder can simultaneously utilize the same parcel of land," Thus, it was, and is, elementary that the grantor of the easement retains ownership over *"the land itself."* Stated more plainly, easements are not land, they merely burden land that continues to be owned by another.

If analyzed as a right-of-way between two private landowners, determining whether any land had been transferred would be simple. If a rancher granted a neighbor an easement across his land for a horse trail, no one would think that the rancher had conveyed ownership over that land. Nor would anyone think that the rancher had ceded his own right to use his land in other ways, including by running a water line underneath the trail that connects to his house. He could, however, make the easement grantee responsible for administering the easement apart from the land. Likewise, when a company obtains a right-of-way to lay a segment of pipeline through a private owner's land, no one would think that the company had obtained ownership over the land through which the pipeline passes.

Although the Federal Government owns all lands involved here, the same general principles apply. We must ascertain whether one federal agency has transferred jurisdiction over lands—meaning "jurisdiction to exercise the incidents of ownership"—to another federal agency. The Trails Act refers to the granted interests as "rights-of-way," both when describing agreements with the Federal Government and with private and state property owners. When applied to a private or state property owner, "right-of-way" would carry its ordinary meaning of a limited right to enjoy another's land. Nothing in the statute suggests that the term adopts a more expansive meaning when the right is granted to a federal agency, and we do "not lightly assume that Congress silently attaches different meanings to the same term in the same . . . statute," Accordingly, as would be the case with private or state property owners, a right-of-way between two agencies grants only an easement across the land, not jurisdiction over the land itself.

The dissent notes that the Federal Government has referred to the Trail as an "area" and a "unit" and has described the Trail in terms of "acres." In the dissent's view, this indicates that the Trail and the land are the same. This is not so. Like other right-of-way easements, the Trail burdens "a particular parcel of land." It is thus not surprising that the Government might refer to the Trail as an "area," much as one might mark out on his property the "area" of land burdened by a sewage easement. The fact remains that the land and the easement are still separate.

The dissent also cites provisions of the Trails Act that discuss "lands" to be included in the Trail. But this, too, is consistent with our conclusion that the Trail is an easement. Like all easements, the parcel of land burdened by the easement has particular metes and bounds. In fact, without such descriptions, parties to an easement agreement would be unable to understand their rights or enforce another party's obligations under the easement agreement. Thus, there is nothing noteworthy about the fact that the Trails Act discusses whether particular lands should be included within the metes and bounds of the tracts of land burdened by the easement. In short, none of the characterizations identified by the dissent changes the fact that the burden on the land and the land itself remain separate.

In sum, read in light of basic property law principles, the plain language of the Trails Act and the agreement between the two agencies did not divest the Forest Service of jurisdiction over the lands that the Trail crosses. It gave the Department of the Interior (and by delegation the National Park Service) an easement for the specified and limited purpose of establishing and administering a Trail, but the land itself remained under the jurisdiction of the Forest Service. To restate this conclusion in the parlance of the Leasing Act, the lands that the Trail crosses are still "Federal lands," and the Forest Service may grant a pipeline right-of-way through them—just as it granted a right-of-way for the Trail. Sometimes a complicated regulatory scheme may cause us to miss the forest for the trees, but at bottom, these cases boil down to a simple proposition: A trail is a trail, and land is land.

2

The various duties described in the Trails Act reinforce that the agency responsible for the Trail has a limited role of administering a trail easement, but that the underlying land remains within the jurisdiction of the Forest Service. The Trails Act states that the Secretary of the Interior (and by delegation the National Park Service) shall "administe[r]" the Trail "primarily as a footpath." The Secretary is charged with designating Trail uses, providing Trail markers, and establishing interpretative and informational sites "to present information to the public about the [T]rail." He also has the authority to pass regulations governing Trail protection and good conduct and can regulate the "protection, management, development, and administration" of the Trail. Though the Trails Act states that the responsible agency shall *"provide* for" the maintenance of the Trail, it is the Forest Service that *performs* the necessary physical work. As the Government explained at oral argument (and as respondents did not dispute), "[i]f a tree falls on forest lands over the trail, it's the Forest Service that's responsible for it. You don't call the nine [National] Park Service employees at Harpers Ferry [in West Virginia] and ask them to come out and fix the tree." These statutory duties refer to the Trail easement, not the lands over which the easement passes.

The dissent resists this conclusion by asserting that the National Park Service "administers" the Trail, and that so long as that is true, the Trail is land within the National Park System. But the National Park Service does not administer the "land" crossed by the Trail. It administers the *Trail* as an easement—an easement that is separate from the underlying land.

3

Finally, Congress has used unequivocal and direct language in multiple statutes when it wished to transfer land from one agency to another, just as one would expect if a property owner conveyed land in fee simple to another private property owner. In the Wild and Scenic Rivers Act, for instance, which was enacted the same day as the Trails Act, Congress specified that "[a]ny component of the national wild and scenic rivers system that is administered by the Secretary of the Interior through the National Park Service *shall become a part of the [N]ational [P]ark [S]ystem.*"). That statute also explicitly permits the head of an agency "to transfer to the appropriate secretary *jurisdiction over such lands.*" Congress has also authorized the Department of the Interior "to transfer to the jurisdiction of the Secretary of Agriculture for national forest purposes *lands* or *interests in lands* acquired for or in connection with the Blue Ridge Parkway" and specifies that "[l]ands transferred under this Act shall become national forest lands." Similar language appears in a host of other statutes. The fact that Congress chose to speak in terms of rights-of-way in the Trails Act, rather than in terms of land transfers, reinforces the conclusion that the Park Service has a limited role over only the Trail, not the lands that the Trail crosses.

For these reasons, we hold that the Trails Act did not transfer jurisdiction of the lands crossed by the Trail from the Forest Service to the Department of the Interior. It created a trail easement and gave the Department of the Interior the administrative responsibilities concomitant with administering the Trail as a trail. Accordingly, because the Department of the Interior had no jurisdiction over any lands, its delegation to the National Park Service did not convert the Trail into *"lands* in the National Park System," — *i.e.,* an *"area of land . . .* administered by the Secretary [of the Interior] acting through the Director [of the National Park Service]." The Forest Service therefore retained the authority to grant Atlantic a pipeline right-of-way.

B

1

Respondents take a markedly different view, which is shared by the dissent. According to respondents, the Trail cannot be separated from the underlying land. In their view, if the National Park Service administers the Trail, then it also administers the lands that the Trail crosses, and no pipeline rights-of-way may be granted.

Respondents' argument that the National Park Service administers the Trail (and therefore the lands that the Trail crosses) proceeds in four steps. First, the Trails Act granted the Department of the Interior the authority to ad- minister the Trail. Second, the Department of the Interior delegated those responsibilities to the National Park Service in 1969. Third, in 1970, Congress defined the National Park System to include "any area of land and water administered by the Secretary [of the Interior] acting through the Director [of the National Park Service]." Under respondents' view, the 1970 National Park System definition made the Trail part of the National Park System. But one more step was still required to place the Trail outside the Forest Service's Leasing Act pipeline authority. That final step occurred in 1973, when the amendment to the Leasing Act carved out lands in the National Park System from the definition of the "Federal lands" through which pipeline rights-of-way could be granted. Because the Trail had become part of the National Park Service in 1970, respondents conclude that the 1973 carve-out applied to the Trail. Therefore, in their view, the Forest Service cannot grant pipeline rights-of-way under the parcels on which there is a right-of-way for the Appalachian Trail.

This circuitous path misses the mark. As described above, under the plain language of the Trails Act and basic property principles, responsibility for the Trail and jurisdiction over the lands that the Trail crosses can and must be separated for purposes of determining whether the Forest Service can grant a right-of-way.

Even accepting respondents' argument on its own terms, however, we remain unpersuaded. Respondents' entire theory depends on an administrative action about which the statutes at issue are completely silent: the Department of the Interior's voluntary decision to assign responsibility over a given trail to the National Park Service rather than to the Bureau of Land Management. To reiterate, respondents contend that the Department of the Interior's decision to delegate responsibility over a trail to the National Park Service renders that trail an "area of land . . . administered by the Secretary [of the Interior], acting through the [Park Service.]" Respondents' theory requires us to accept that, without a word from Congress, the Department of the Interior has the power to vastly expand the scope of the National Park Service's jurisdiction through its delegation choices. After all, respondents' view would not just apply to the approximately 2,000-mile-long Appalachian Trail. It would apply equally to all 21 national historic and national scenic trails currently administered by the National Park Service. Under our precedents, when Congress wishes to "'alter the fundamental details of a regulatory scheme,'" as respondents contend it did here through delegation, we would expect it to speak with the requisite clarity to place that intent beyond dispute. We will not presume that the act of delegation, rather than clear congressional command, worked this vast expansion of the Park Service's jurisdiction and significant curtailment of the Forest Service's express authority to grant pipeline rights-of-way on "lands owned by the United States."

Respondents' theory also has striking implications for federalism and private property rights. Respondents do not contest that, in addition to federal lands, these 21 trails cross lands owned by States, local governments, and private landowners. Under respondents' view, these privately owned and state-owned lands would also become lands in the National Park System. Our precedents re- quire Congress to enact exceedingly clear language if it wishes to significantly alter the balance between federal and state power and the power of the Government over private property.

Finally, reliance on the Department of the Interior's delegation of its Trails Act authority is especially questionable here, given that Congress has used express language in other statutes when it wished to transfer lands between agencies. Congress not only failed to enact similar language in the Trails Act, but it clearly expressed the opposite view. The entire Trails Act must be read against the backdrop of the Weeks Act, which states that lands acquired for the National Forest System—including the George Washington National Forest—"shall be permanently reserved, held, and administered as national forest lands." The Trails Act further provides that "[n]othing contained in this chapter shall be deemed to transfer among Federal agencies any management responsibilities established under any other law for federally administered lands which are components of the National Trails System." These two provisions, when combined with the Trails Act's use of the term "rights-of-way" and the administrative duties set out in the Trails Act, provide much clearer — and more textual—guides to Congress' intent than an agency's silent decision to delegate responsibilities to the National Park Service.

In sum, we conclude that the Department of the Interior's unexplained decision to assign responsibility over certain trails to the National Parks System and the Leasing Act's definition of federal lands simply cannot bear the weight of respondents' interpretation.

IV

We hold that the Department of the Interior's decision to assign responsibility over the Appalachian Trail to the National Park Service did not transform the land over which the Trail passes into land within the National Park System. Accordingly, the Forest Service had the authority to issue the permit here.

For the foregoing reasons, we reverse the judgment of the Court of Appeals and remand the cases for further proceedings consistent with this opinion.

It is so ordered.

JUSTICE SOTOMAYOR, with whom JUSTICE KAGAN joins, dissenting.

The majority's complicated discussion of private-law easements, footpath maintenance, differently worded statutes, and policy masks the simple (and only) dispute here. Is the Appalachian National Scenic Trail "lan[d] in the National Park System"? If it is, then the Forest Service may not grant a natural-gas pipeline right-of-way that crosses the Trail on federally owned land. So says the Mineral Leasing Act, and the parties do not disagree.

By definition, lands in the National Park System include "any area of land" "administered" by the Park Service for "park, monument, historic, parkway, recreational, or other purposes." So says the National Park Service Organic Act, and the parties agree.

The Appalachian Trail, in turn, is "administered" by the Park Service to ensure "outdoor recreation" and to conserve "nationally significant scenic, historic, natural, or cultural qualities." So say the National Trails System Act and relevant regulations, and again the parties agree.

Thus, as the Government puts it, the only question here is whether parts of the Appalachian Trail are "'lands'" within the meaning of those statutes. Those laws, a half century of agency understanding, and common sense confirm that the Trail is land, land on which generations of people have walked. Indeed, for 50 years the "Federal Government has referred to the Trail" as a "'unit'" of the National Park System. A "unit" of the Park System is by definition either "land" or "water" in the Park System. Federal law does not distinguish "land" from the Trail any more than it distinguishes "land" from the many monuments, historic buildings, parkways, and recreational areas that are also units of the Park System. Because the Trail is land in the Park System, "no federal agency" has "authority under the Mineral Leasing Act to grant a pipeline right-of-way across such lands."

By contrast, today's Court suggests that the Trail is not "land" in the Park System at all. The Court strives to separate "the *lands* that the Trail traverses" from "the Trail itself," reasoning that the Trail is simply an "easement," "not land." In doing so, however, the Court relies on anything except the provisions that actually answer the question presented. Because today's Court condones the placement of a pipeline that subverts the plain text of the statutes governing the Appalachian Trail, I respectfully dissent. . . .